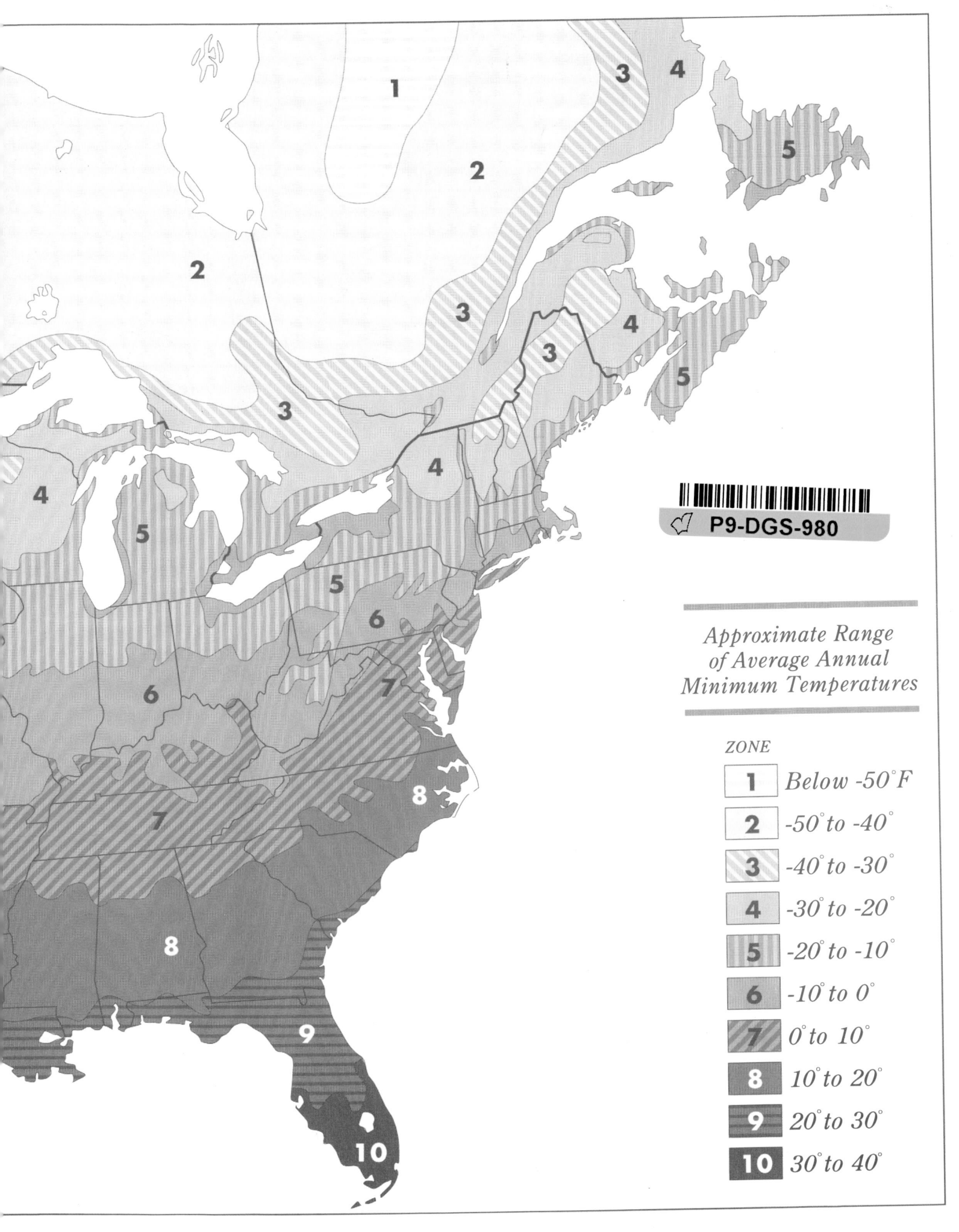

P9-DGS-980

Approximate Range
of Average Annual
Minimum Temperatures

ZONE

1	Below -50°F
2	-50° to -40°
3	-40° to -30°
4	-30° to -20°
5	-20° to -10°
6	-10° to 0°
7	0° to 10°
8	10° to 20°
9	20° to 30°
10	30° to 40°

ENCYCLOPEDIA
of GARDEN
PLANTS

DATE DUE			

THE AMERICAN HORTICULTURAL SOCIETY

ENCYCLOPEDIA *of* GARDEN PLANTS

Editor-in-Chief

CHRISTOPHER BRICKELL

Horticultural Consultant

JOHN ELSLEY

MACMILLAN PUBLISHING COMPANY
NEW YORK

A Dorling Kindersley Book

Senior Editor Jane Aspden

Editors Liza Bruml, Joanna Chisholm, Roger Smoothy, Jo Weeks

Additional editorial assistance from Jane Birdsell, Lynn Bresler,
Jenny Engelmann, Kate Grant, Shona Grimbly, Susanna Longley,
Andrew Mikolajski, Diana Miller, Celia Van Oss,
Anthony Whitehorn

Senior Art Editor Ina Stradins
Designer Amanda Lunn
Additional design assistance from Arthur Brown, Peter Luff

Editorial Director Jackie Douglas
Art Director Roger Bristow
Managing Art Editor Alex Arthur

Photographers Eric Crichton, John Glover, Jerry Harpur,
Andrew Lawson, Andrew de Lory, with Neil Holmes, Jacqui Hurst
Illustrators Vanessa Luff, Amanda Lunn, Eric Thomas
Page make-up and typesetting Arthur Brown, Peter Cooling,
Monika Cunnington

Advisors and consultants In addition to the contributors listed
on the Contents page, Dorling Kindersley would like to thank
Barry Ambrose, John Bond, Tony Clements, Sheila Ecklin,
the late Thomas Everett, Jim Gardiner, Ralph Gould,
David Kerly, and the staff of the Royal Horticultural
Society at Vincent Square and Wisley Garden

Copyright © 1989 Dorling Kindersley Limited, London

First published in Great Britain in 1989 by Dorling Kindersley Publishers Limited,
9 Henrietta Street, London WC2 8PS

Reprinted and updated 1992

Macmillan Publishing Company
866 Third Avenue, New York, N.Y. 10022

Library of Congress Cataloging-in-Publication Data

The American Horticultural Society encyclopedia of garden plants /
editor-in-chief, Christopher Brickell; horticultural consultant,
John Elsley.
    p. cm.
    Includes index.
    ISBN 0–02–557920–7
    1. Plants, Ornamental—Dictionaries. I. Brickell, Christopher.
II. American Horticultural Society III. Title: Encyclopedia of
garden plants.
SB403.2.A46 1989   89–32155
635.9'03—dc20   CIP

Macmillan books are available at special discounts for bulk purchases for sales
promotions, premiums, fund-raising, or educational use. For details, contact:

Special Sales Director
Macmillan Publishing Company
866 Third Avenue
New York, N.Y. 10022

10 9 8 7

Text film output by The Setting Studio, Newcastle-upon-Tyne, England
Color reproduction by Colourscan, Singapore
Printed and bound in Italy by A. Mondadori Editore, Verona

Foreword

THE AMERICAN HORTICULTURAL SOCIETY *is delighted to be associated with this fine compendium of garden plants. We are especially honored to work once again with our good friends at the Royal Horticultural Society. In particular, we take pleasure in working with Christopher Brickell of the RHS, certainly no stranger to our country. He is well respected for his leadership throughout the horticultural world, has lectured widely, and has generously hosted groups from the American Horticultural Society. Such international cooperation in the field of horticulture is of particular benefit to all gardeners, and this volume is testimony to that spirit.*

The 8,000 plants described in the encyclopedia provide more than enough gardening possibilities for even the advanced gardener, and there are plants for all zones of the continental United States. Notes on culture and propagation are additionally useful. Gardeners will delight in the exquisite photography and the helpful organization of the color prints by plant type, size, color, and season of interest.

This is a book which will serve many purposes and will be a reference for life. We hope you will find much pleasure and challenge within its covers.

American Horticultural Society
Carolyn Marsh Lindsay
President

If one was to single out the greatest need in American gardening today, reliable information would top the list. *The American Horticultural Society Encyclopedia of Garden Plants* offers both amateur and professional horticulturists a wealth of theoretical and practical information on the potential garden value of a very extensive and varied range of plants—over 8,000, half of which are accompanied by excellent color photographs. The book's value as a reliable reference source is further enhanced by its dual organization of material—the systematic arrangement of the plants within botanical groupings in the dictionary section, and their organization by size, color, and season of interest in the extensive color section. Each entry provides the reader with basic practical data pertaining to any given plant's cultural requirements and growth characteristics. Readers armed with such sound information can then study the various offerings at local nurseries or in the wealth of nursery catalogs available in the United States, and make well-informed plant selections for inclusion in their home landscapes.

The horticultural and botanical accuracy of *The American Horticultural Society Encyclopedia of Garden Plants* is assured by the overall editorship of Christopher Brickell, Director General of the Royal Horticultural Society and an acknowledged world authority on horticultural nomenclature, and the research work of a team of British horticultural experts. Though the publication's origin inevitably poses some limitations on its absolute practical use to the North American audience, the addition of North American hardiness zones (some of which by necessity are estimated) and American common names increase the book's value considerably on this side of the Atlantic. Certain groups, however, like roses and dahlias, are represented to a large extent by European cultivars or selections, many of which, due to their genetic constitutions, may not be successfully cultivated in our North American climate. However, commensurate or superior alternative American selections, closely resembling those described and better adapted to growing in local environments, may usually be found in the extensive offerings of American nurserymen. In several noteworthy groups—including hemerocallis (daylilies), hostas, and peonies—American hybridizers have made such tremendous advances compared with those of our overseas counterparts that our choices within such groups are frequently the envy of gardeners throughout the world! Factors like this can only assist in creating distinctive American gardens in the future.

Although overseas influence in horticulture is certain to continue in the years to come, American gardeners should never overlook the fact that inspiration and admiration can be found in our own country's rich gardening heritage—a heritage that today is being enriched and expanded upon to an extent exceeded nowhere in the gardening world. From the early inspirational works of Thomas Jefferson to such modern classic publications as Father John L. Fiala's monograph on lilacs, American botanical and horticultural publications rank in scholarship and enlightenment with the most impressive imports.

Ernest Henry Wilson, Alfred Rehder, Liberty Hyde Bailey, Dr. Arlow B. Stout, Louise Beebe Wilder, John C. Wister, and Elizabeth Lawrence are but a sampling of the authors whose works have not only stood the test of time but will continue to influence the evolutionary path of American gardening.

A direct consequence of America's widely diverse climates, along with the rich ethnic history of its population, is the establishment of gardens that regionally depict these unique characteristics. The European influence is exemplified in the splendid estate gardens of Long Island and the Delaware Valley, while in the warmer, more humid climate of the South, similar influences result in more relaxed southern landscapes. Northwestern gardens and climates conjure thoughts of Britain more than elsewhere in North America, while further south, Californians utilize a unique palette of plants to employ color to perfection. Throughout the country, the Far Eastern influence is increasingly evident in both garden design and the culture of native Asiatic plants.

Present day American landscape architects also have a proud tradition to uphold—Frederick Law Olmsted, Beatrix Farrand, and Thomas Church each achieved distinction in their particular fields of expertise. Highly respected garden designers from overseas have found North America an appreciative and fertile environment for their talents—Englishman Russell Page is a recent example.

Throughout the continent botanical gardens and arboreta continue to proliferate, catering to the needs and interests of amateur and professional gardeners and landscapers alike. They play an important role in plant introductions from overseas and the ongoing studies of our own immensely rich native flora, and today's enthusiasm for new information is reaching new heights.

Not to be forgotten is the proud history of the American nursery industry; today's nurserymen are the world's finest in both knowledge and technology of product. Nowhere else are professional and amateur plant breeders exceeding the achievements of their American counterparts; as already mentioned, ongoing work in such plant groups as hemerocallis, hostas, and peonies, as well as viburnums, hollies, rhododendrons, and irises, is resulting in the availability of greatly improved selections for the enrichment of ornamental landscapes not only in North America but worldwide.

I am confident that as a direct result of the fascinating range of plants included in *The American Horticultural Society Encyclopedia of Garden Plants*, the curiosity of readers will be stimulated, ultimately creating a demand for an increasingly interesting range of garden-worthy plants with which to enhance and beautify North American gardens.

John Elsley
Greenwood, South Carolina
February, 1989

Contents

CONTRIBUTORS

Susyn Andrews *Hollies*
Larry Barlow *Chrysanthemums*
Kenneth A. Beckett *The Planter's Guide, Shrubs, Climbers, Bromeliads*
John Brookes *Creating a Garden*
Eric Catterall *Begonias*
Allen J. Coombes *Plant Origins and Names, Trees, Shrubs, Glossary of Terms*
Philip Damp *Dahlias*
Kate Donald *Peonies, Daffodils*
Kath Dryden *Rock plants*
Raymond Evison *Clematis*
Diana Grenfell *Hostas*
Peter Harkness *Roses*
David Hitchcock *Carnations and Pinks*
Terry Hewitt *Cacti and other Succulents*
Hazel Key *Pelargoniums*
Sidney Linnegar *Irises*
Brian Mathew *Irises, Bulbs*
Victoria Matthews *Climbers, Lilies, Tulips*
David McClintock *Grasses, Bamboos, Rushes, and Sedges*
Diana Miller *Perennials, African violets*
John Paton *Perennials*
Charles Puddle *Camellias*
Wilma Rittershausen (*with* **Sabina Knees**) *Orchids*
Peter Q. Rose *Ivies*
Keith Rushforth *Conifers*
A.D. Schilling *Rhododendrons and Azaleas*
Arthur Smith *Gladioli*
Philip Swindells *Ferns, Primulas* (*with* **Kath Dryden** *and* **Jack Wemyss-Cooke**), *Water plants, Water lilies*
John Thirkell *Delphiniums*
Alan Toogood *Annuals and Biennials*
Major General Patrick Turpin *Heathers*
Michael Upward *Perennials*
John Wright *Fuchsias*

How to Use this Book

The American Horticultural Society Encyclopedia of Garden Plants is the ideal reference when planning a garden, selecting plants, or identifying specimens; it provides a wealth of information on the appearance and cultivation of thousands of individual plants.

How to plan your garden
In Creating a Garden you will find advice on garden styles, how to position and group plants, and the use of color and texture—all the background information you need before selecting individual specimens. The Planter's Guide recommends plants for particular sites or uses. Cross-references to The Plant Catalog and Plant Dictionary lead you to the photograph and description of any plant you choose.

How to identify and select plants
If you know a plant but cannot recall its name, have a specimen that you want to identify, or simply wish to choose plants for your garden, The Plant Catalog will provide the answer. First turn to the appropriate chapter, e.g., Shrubs, Perennials, or Bulbs. Then decide on the size and season of interest you want. In each section you will find plants grouped by color from which to make your choice. By comparing a specimen with the photograph and its description, a plant may easily be identified. Zone numbers or hardiness ratings (for annuals and biennials) are given with each caption and show at a glance which plants are suitable for growing in your particular area. The U.S.D.A. zone map is printed inside the front and back of the book.

How to find a particular plant
The Plant Dictionary lists all plants in the encyclopedia alphabetically by genus, with clear and detailed descriptions of plants not

The Plant Catalog

Size categories (based on plant heights)

	LARGE	MEDIUM	SMALL
TREES	over 50ft (15m)	30–50ft (10–15m)	up to 30ft (10m)
CONIFERS	over 50ft (15m)	30–50ft (10–15m)	up to 30ft (10m)
SHRUBS	over 10ft (3m)	5–10ft (1.5–3m)	up to 5ft (1.5m)
PERENNIALS	over 4ft (1.2m)	2–4ft (60cm–1.2m)	up to 2ft (60cm)
ROCK PLANTS	over 6in (15cm)	—	up to 6in (15cm)
BULBS (including CORMS and TUBERS)	over 2ft (60cm)	9in–2ft (23–60cm)	up to 9in (23cm)
CACTI and other SUCCULENTS	over 3ft (1m)	9in–3ft (23cm–1m)	up to 9in (23cm)

The color wheel
Within each section the plants are grouped by the color of their main feature. They are always arranged in the same order: from white through reds and blues to yellows and oranges. Variegated plants are categorized by the color of their variegation (i.e., white or yellow), succulents by the color of their flowers, if produced.

The symbols

- ☼ Prefers sun
- ☼ Prefers partial shade
- ☼ Tolerates full shade
- pH Needs acid soil

- ◌ Prefers well-drained soil
- ◐ Prefers moist soil
- ● Prefers wet soil

❋ In Europe will withstand 32°F (0°C)	
❋❋ In Europe will withstand 23°F (-5°C)	These hardiness symbols do not apply to North America.
❋❋❋ In Europe will withstand 5°F (-15°C)	

CHAPTER HEADINGS
Where appropriate each chapter is subdivided into sections, according to the approximate size of the plants (see chart, left) and their main season of interest or type.

COLOR BOXES
Color boxes at the top of the page show the color range of plants featured beneath, e.g.,

PLANT PORTRAITS
Color photographs assist the identification and selection of plants.

CAPTIONS
Captions describe the plants in detail and draw attention to any special uses they may have.

SIZE AND SHAPE
For Trees, Conifers, and Shrubs a scale drawing shows the size and shape of each plant at maturity. For other plants their approximate height (H) and spread (S) are given at the end of each caption. (The "height" of a trailing plant is the length of its stems, either hanging or spreading.)

PLANT NAMES
The full botanical name is given for each plant. Synonyms (syn.) and common names are included where appropriate.

FROST TENDER PLANTS
For frost tender plants the minimum temperature required for its cultivation is given.

CULTIVATION AND HARDINESS
Symbols and zone numbers show a plant's preferred growing conditions and hardiness. However the climatic and soil conditions of your particular site should also be taken into account as they may affect a plant's growth.

Shrubs/medium WINTER INT
□ WHITE–PINK

Dombeya burgessiae, syn. *D. mastersii* (Rosemound)
Evergreen shrub with rounded, 3-lobed, downy leaves and dense clusters of fragrant white flowers, with pink to red veins, in autumn-winter.
Min. 41°F (5°C).
☼ ◌ 10

*Chamelaucium u[ ]form] (Geraldton
Evergreen, wiry-ste[ ]
Each needlelike lea[ ]
tip. Flowers rangin[ ]
purple to pink, lave[ ]
white appear in late
or spring. Min. 41°F
☼ ◌ 9–10

Acokanthera oblongifolia, syn. *A. spectabilis, Carissa spectabilis* (Wintersweet)
Evergreen, rounded shrub. Has fragrant white or pinkish flowers in late winter and spring and poisonous, black fruits in autumn.
Min. 50°F (10°C).
☼ ◌ 10

Viburnum x bodn[ ]
Deciduous, upright s[ ]
bronze, young leaves
dark green. Racemes
open to fragrant pink[ ]
mild periods from lat[ ]
autumn to early sprin[ ]
☼ ◌ ❋❋❋ 7–[ ]

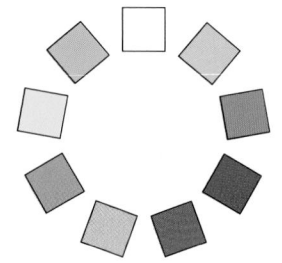

Euphorbia pulcherrima
(Christmas star, Poinsettia)
Evergreen, sparingly branched shrub. Has small, greenish red flowers surrounded by bright red, pink, yellow, or white bracts from late autumn to spring.
Min. 59°F (15°C).
☼ ◌ 9–10

illustrated and cross-references to the photographs, as well as advice on cultivation and planting sites for the whole genus. Synonyms are also listed. If only the common name is known, then turn to the *Index of Common Names*, which will give you the correct botanical name and lead you either to an illustration or to *The Plant Dictionary*.

Plant names

How plants were introduced and a clear explanation of botanical nomenclature is given in *Plant Origins and Names*. The plant names in this book are those considered to be correct as the book goes to press, but as taxonomic work is continually in progress names may be superseded. Many synonyms have been included, with cross-references in *The Plant Dictionary*, so that plants may also be found using alternative or older names.

The Feature Boxes

Plant groups or genera of special interest to the gardener are presented in separate feature boxes within the appropriate chapters.

GROUP CHARACTERISTICS
The introduction outlines the merits of each group of plants and gives guidance on cultivation and planting positions.

FLOWER FORMS
Detailed descriptions of the flower forms and horticultural classifications within a genus are given where appropriate.

LINE DRAWINGS
Clear line drawings show the different flower forms.

PLANT PORTRAITS
Close-up photographs of individual flowers or plants allow quick identification or selection.

PLANT NAMES
Full botanical name is given and the group or classification where appropriate. Plant descriptions appear in *The Plant Dictionary*.

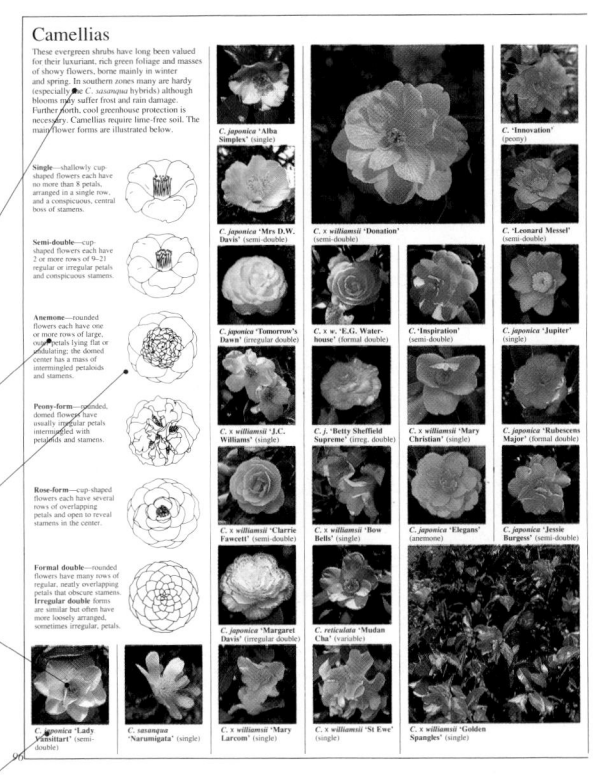

Camellias
These evergreen shrubs have long been valued for their luxuriant, rich green foliage and masses of showy flowers, borne mainly in winter and spring. In southern zones many are hardy (especially the *C. sasanqua* hybrids) although blooms may suffer frost and rain damage. Further north, cool greenhouse protection is necessary. Camellias require lime-free soil. The many flower forms are illustrated below.

Stachyurus praecox
Deciduous, spreading, open shrub with purplish red shoots. Drooping spikes of pale greenish yellow flowers open in late winter and early spring, before pointed, deep green leaves appear.

Duranta repens, syn. *D. plumieri*
Fast-growing, usually evergreen, bushy shrub, upright when young. Has simple or branched spikes of lilac-blue flowers, mainly in summer, followed by yellow fruits.
Min. 50°F (10°C).

The Plant Dictionary

The Plant Dictionary contains entries for every genus in the encyclopedia of over 4,000 recommended plants not in *The Plant Catalog*. It also functions as the index to *The Plant Catalog*.

GENUS NAMES
The genus name is followed by the family name and, where appropriate, common names for the whole genus.

GENUS ENTRIES
Each genus entry covers its distinctive characteristics, hardiness range, and advice on siting plants, their cultivation, propagation, and, if relevant, pruning and pests and diseases.

SYNONYMS
Synonyms cross-refer to the correct botanical name.

PLANT DESCRIPTIONS
Entries on species and cultivars give full botanical names, synonyms, common names, and zone numbers. Cultivation needs are included if they are specific to the plant. For cultivars, characteristics at variance with the species are given. Technical terms are explained in the *Glossary of Terms*.

SAGITTARIA (Alismataceae)
Genus of deciduous, perennial, submerged and marginal water plants, grown for their foliage and flowers. Fully hardy to frost tender, min. 41°F (5°C). Some species are suitable for pools, others for aquariums. All require full sun. Remove fading foliage as necessary. Propagate by division in spring or summer or by breaking off turions (scaly, young shoots) in spring.
S. japonica. See *S. sagittifolia* 'Flore Pleno'.
S. latifolia illus. p.372.
S. sagittifolia (Arrowhead). Deciduous, perennial, marginal water plant. H 18in (45cm), S 12in (30cm). Fully hardy, zones 5–10. Upright, green leaves are acutely arrow-shaped. In summer produces 3-petaled, white flowers with dark purple centers. May be grown in up to 9in (23cm) depth of water. **'Flore Pleno'** (syn. *S. japonica*; Japanese arrowhead) has double flowers.

Plant Origins and Names

Common names

Although many have familiar common names, plants are usually listed under their botanical names. Why should this be? There are a number of reasons. Many plants either do not have a common name, or they share a common name with others. More confusingly, the same common name may be used in different regions to describe different plants: in Scotland "plane" refers to *Acer pseudoplatanus* (sycamore), in England to the London plane (*Platanus* x *acerifolia*), while in North America the native plane (*Platanus occidentalis*) may be called plane or sycamore. Unlike botanical names, which bring related plants together by grouping them in separate genera (all true hollies belong to the genus *Ilex*), the same word is often used in common names for quite unrelated plants, as in sea holly (*Eryngium*), hollyhock (*Alcea*), and summer holly (*Comarostaphylis diversifolia*), none of which is related to the true holly. Conversely, one plant may have several common names: "heartsease," "love-in-idleness" and "Johnny-jump-up" are all charming titles for *Viola tricolor*. Even greater confusion arises when a vernacular common name is in Malay, Chinese, or Arabic. In botany, as in other scientific disciplines, the use of Latin has been found to be a convenient and precise basis of a universal language for naming plants.

The binomial system

Greek and Roman scholars laid the foundations of our method of naming plants, and their practice of observing and describing nature in detail was continued in the monasteries and universities of Europe, where Latin remained the common language. The binomial system in use today, however, was largely due to the influence of the famous eighteenth-century Swedish botanist, Carl Linnaeus (1707–78). In his definitive works *Genera plantarum* and *Species plantarum*, Linnaeus classified each plant by using two words in Latin form, instead of adopting the descriptive phrases that had been in common usage among the botanists and herbalists of his day. The first word was the name of the genus (e.g., *Ilex*) and the second the specific epithet (e.g., *opaca*). Together they provided a name by which a particular plant (species) could be universally known (*Ilex opaca*, American holly). Other species in the same genus were then given different epithets (*Ilex crenata*, *Ilex pernyi*, *Ilex serrata*, and so on).

The meaning of plant names

A greater appreciation of botanical names may be gained by knowing something of their meaning. A name may be commemorative: The *Fuchsia* is a tribute to Leonhart Fuchs, a German physician and herbalist. It may tell us where a plant comes from, as with *Parrotia persica* (of Persia, now Iran). A plant may bear the name of the collector who introduced it: *Primula forrestii* was brought into cultivation by George Forrest. Or the name may tell us something about physical character: *Pelargonium* derives from the Greek *pelargos* (a stork), an appropriate description of the fruits of these plants which resemble storks' bills; *quinquefolia*, the epithet of *Parthenocissus quinquefolia*, means with foliage made up of five leaflets, from the Latin *quinque* ("five") and *folium* ("leaf").

Generic names, like all Latin nouns, are either male, female, or neuter and the specific epithets, usually adjectives, therefore agree in gender with the genus.

Plant introductions

Just as the origins of plant names may be traced to Classical civilization, so can the first plant introductions. At its peak, the Roman Empire covered a vast area, from western Europe to Asia, and as the Romans traveled

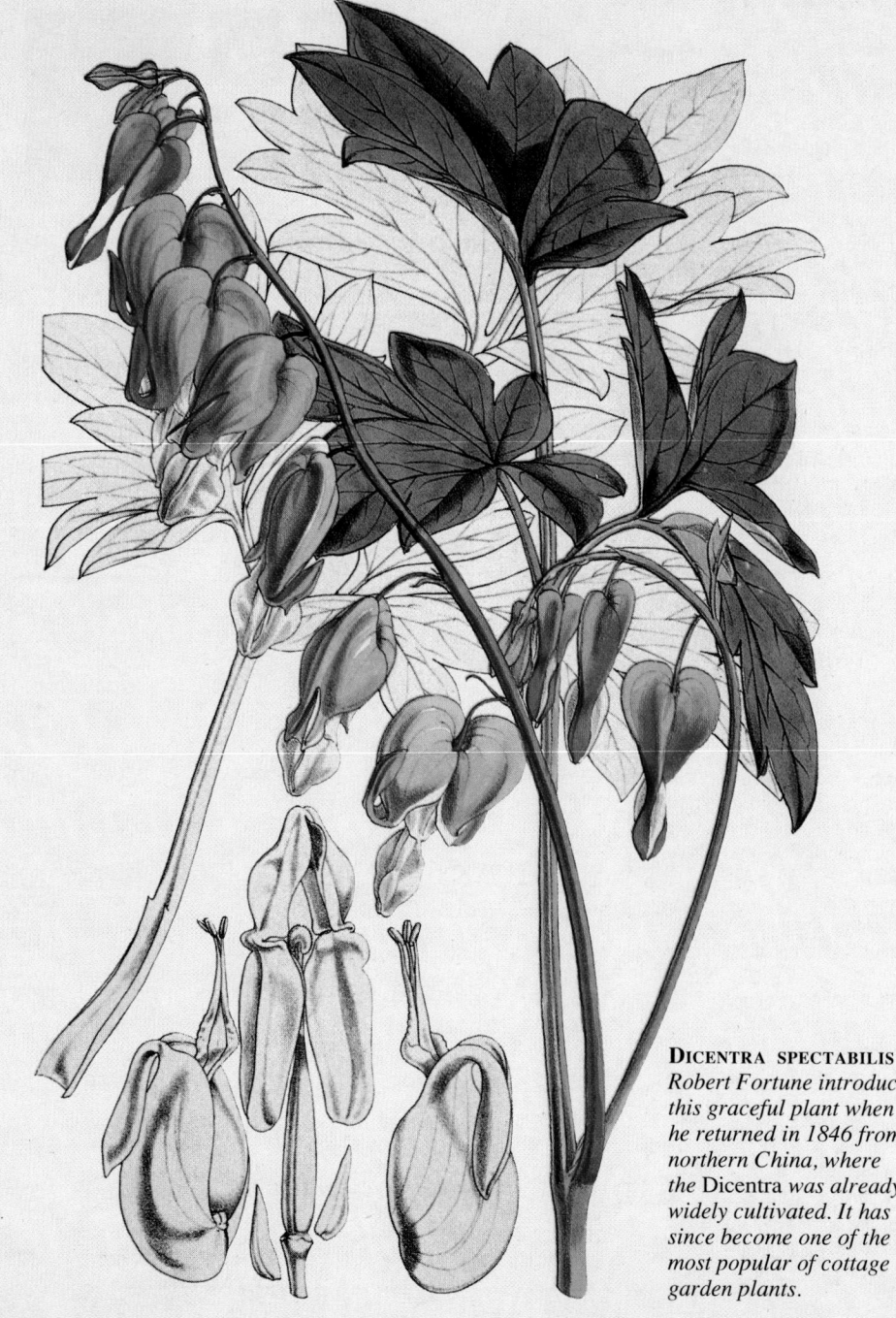

DICENTRA SPECTABILIS
Robert Fortune introduced this graceful plant when he returned in 1846 from northern China, where the Dicentra *was already widely cultivated. It has since become one of the most popular of cottage garden plants.*

they brought with them plants used for food or ornament, such as the Spanish chestnut, peach, fig, and many herbs. Later, North America proved to be a major source of new plants; by the end of the sixteenth century some of these could be found growing in British gardens and in the seventeenth century many more were introduced by private collectors such as the two John Tradescants (father and son), who were at one time gardeners to Charles I and others of the nobility. In 1824 the Royal Horticultural Society employed David Douglas, a Scot, to travel to America's West Coast and gather vast quantities of seed from hitherto unknown species including the Douglas fir and Sitka spruce.

The greatest rewards for the plant collector, however, were to be found in the rich and diverse flora of the East. Access to China was restricted until the Treaty of Nanking in 1842, but in the following year Robert Fortune began an expedition, under the aegis of the Royal Horticultural Society, that was to yield many ornamental garden plants. In his wake went the French botanist-missionaries, including Armand David who discovered the lovely *Davidia* tree.

The Golden Age of plant hunting was the early part of this century, when thousands of species were introduced to cultivation. Ernest Henry Wilson, one of the most famous plant hunters, who collected in the East for the Royal Botanic Gardens at Kew, England,

The family tree

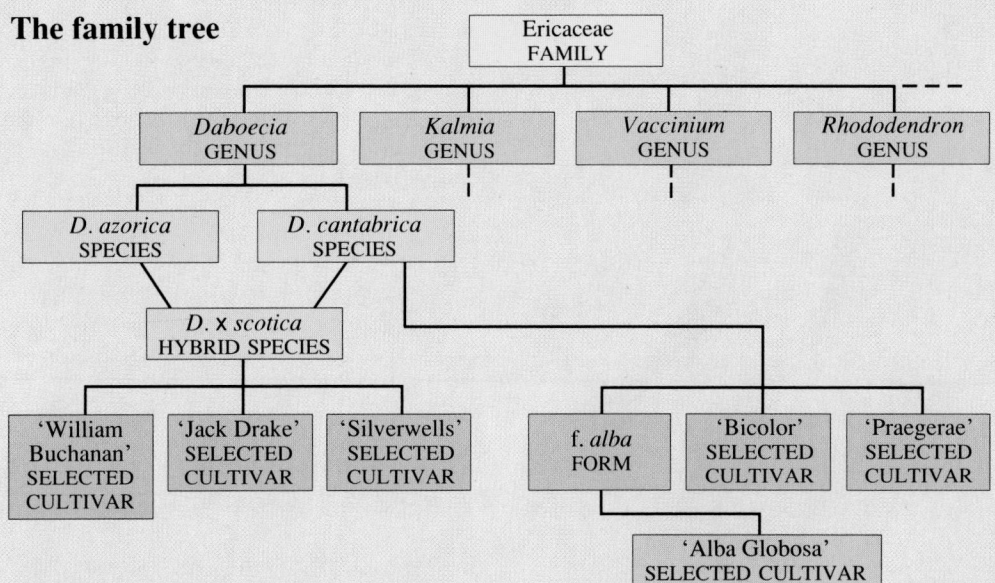

and the Arnold Arboretum in Boston, Mass., discovered over 3,000 species. In the same period, George Forrest introduced many rhododendrons and other plants from China and Tibet. Frank Kingdon Ward, who had traveled widely in the Himalayas, published several very readable accounts of his experiences in the 1920s, collecting unusual primulas, lilies, rhododendrons, and gentians.

Plant-hunting expeditions to areas of the Sino-Himalayan region, closed for many years to westerners, continue to be sponsored today, and new plants are still being introduced, if in less dramatic quantities than at the turn of the century.

International codes
Over the years the Linnean system of plant classification has been developed by scientists so that the entire plant kingdom is divided and subdivided into a multi-branched "family tree," according to each plant's botanical characteristics. International cooperation has been essential in order that the system be reliable for scientific, commercial, and horticultural use. To this end, there are now rules laid down in the *International Code of Nomenclature for Cultivated Plants* (1980) and the *International Code of Botanical Nomenclature* (1988).

The plant kingdom
The plant kingdom may be broadly divided into vascular and non-vascular plants. Vascular plants are of most interest to the gardener and have specialized conducting tissue that enables them to grow in a wider range of habitats and reach a larger size than the nonvascular plants such as algae, fungi, mosses, and liverworts. Vascular plants are classified into many groups, mainly according to the way they bear their seeds. For example conifers, part of the Gymnosperm group, are distinct as they bear their naked seeds in conelike fruits. The basic division with these groups is the family.

The family
The botanical division of the family may contain clearly related and specialized plants such as the orchids (Orchidaceae) and the bromeliads (Bromeliaceae), or, like the Rosaceae, embrace plants as diverse in terms of what they offer the gardener as *Alchemilla*, *Cotoneaster*, *Crataegus*, *Geum*, *Malus*, *Prunus*, *Pyracantha*, *Sorbus*, and *Spiraea*.

CARL LINNAEUS
Linnaeus in Lapp costume: Engraving from a portrait by M. Hoffman of about 1737

MAGNOLIA WILSONII
One of the finest summer-flowering shrubs, Magnolia wilsonii *was discovered in 1904 by Ernest Henry Wilson, who was collecting for Messrs. Veitch (nurserymen) in Sichuan, China. Wilson later brought back many thousands of species for the Arnold Arboretum in Boston.*

DAVID DOUGLAS
Crayon drawing by Sir Daniel Macnee, 1828

Plants are grouped in particular families according to the structure of their flowers, fruits, and other organs.

The genus and its species

A family may contain one genus (*Eucryphia* is the only genus in Eucryphiaceae) or many (the daisy family Compositae has over 1,000 genera). Each genus comprises related plants, such as oaks (*Quercus*), maples (*Acer*), and lilies (*Lilium*), with several features in common. A genus may contain one or many species. Thus a reference to a member of the genus *Lilium* could be to any of the lilies, but one to *Lilium candidum* would denote a particular lily (in this case the Madonna lily). Just as some families form closely related groups, so certain genera form separate horticultural groups within families. An example of this would be the heaths or heathers (including *Erica* and *Calluna*) within the family Ericaceae, which also includes *Rhododendron*, *Kalmia*, and *Vaccinium*.

Subspecies, varieties, and forms

Species are usually variable in the wild and may be split into three botanically recognized but occasionally overlapping subdivisions. The subspecies (subsp.) is a distinct variant, usually because of its geographical distribution; the variety (botanical *varietas*, abbreviated to "var.") differs slightly in its botanical structure; and the form (*forma*, f.) has only minor variations, such as of habit or color of leaf, flower, or fruit.

Cultivars

Many plants grown in gardens may be adequately described by their botanical names, but numerous variants exist in cultivation which differ slightly from the normal form of the species. These forms may be of considerable horticultural interest, for their variegated leaves or variously colored flowers,

and so on. They may be found as individuals in the wild and introduced to cultivation, be selected from a batch of seedlings, or occur as a mutation; they are known as cultivars—a contraction of "cultivated varieties." To come true to type many cultivars need to be propagated vegetatively (by cuttings, grafting, or division) or grown annually from specially selected seed.

The naming of cultivars is governed by the *International Code of Nomenclature for Cultivated Plants*. Cultivars named since 1959 must be given vernacular names, which are printed in roman type within quotes (*Phygelius aequalis* 'Yellow Trumpet'), to distinguish them clearly from wild varieties in Latin form, appearing in italic.

Hybrids

Sexual crosses between botanically distinct species or genera are known as hybrids and are indicated by a multiplication sign. If the cross is between species in different genera, the result is called an intergeneric hybrid and, when two (occasionally three) genera are concerned, the name given is a condensed form of the names of the genera involved: x *Cupressocyparis* covers hybrids between all species of *Chamaecyparis* and *Cupressus*. If more than three genera are involved, then the hybrids are called after a person and given the ending *-ara*. Thus x *Potinara*, covering hybrids of *Brassavola*, *Cattleya*, *Laelia*, and *Sophronitis*, commemorates M. Potin of the French orchid society. Most common, however, are hybrids between species in the same genus (interspecific hybrids), which are given a collective name similar to a species name but preceded by a multiplication sign; for example *Epimedium* x *rubrum* covers hybrids between *E. alpinum* and *E. grandiflorum*.

When one plant is grafted onto another, a new plant may occasionally arise at the point of grafting which contains the tissues of both parents. For naming purposes, these graft chimeras or graft hybrids are treated in the same way as sexual hybrids, but instead of placing a multiplication sign before the name, they are denoted by a plus sign, as in + *Laburnocytisus adamii*, a graft hybrid between species of *Laburnum* and *Cytisus*.

GENTIANA SINO-ORNATA
George Forrest had a special interest in gentians, collecting hundreds of specimens during his trips to China. He first discovered this plant in 1904, during a hazardous expedition high in the mountain ranges of northwestern Yunnan. It is one of his finest introductions, and is admired for its exquisite beauty and late and prolonged flowering during autumn, when few other plants bring color into the garden.

Cultivars of hybrids should be listed under a botanical name if one is available (*Viburnum* x *bodnantense* 'Dawn') or, if the parentage is complex or obscure, by giving just the generic name followed by the cultivar name (*Rosa* 'Buff Beauty').

Group names

Botanical names of hybrids can provide a convenient way of gathering together cultivars of like parentage, as with the cultivated forms of *Camellia* x *williamsii*. But occasionally, especially with some orchids and many annuals, such names have not been allocated for groups with hybrid parents. For these, group names in modern language and roman type without quotation marks are used. Thus the orchid group *Paphiopedilum* Freckles covers hybrid cultivars with similar parentage, as does the group of annuals *Dahlia*, Disco Series. Distinct members within a group may be recognized as cultivars, for example *Miltoniopsis* Anjou 'St Patrick' or *Viola*, Imperial Series 'Orange Prince'.

Name changes

It is often confusing and frustrating to encounter name changes in new publications. Long-established and often well-known names disappear, only to be replaced by new, unfamiliar ones. But there are good reasons for such changes. A plant may originally have been incorrectly identified; research may discover that a plant earlier had a different name (the *International Code of Botanical Nomenclature* states that the valid name for a plant is the earliest correctly published one); a name may be found to apply to two different plants; or new scientific knowledge may mean that a plant's classification, such as the genus to which it belongs, has to be changed. In this Encyclopedia, numerous synonyms have been given in order to minimize the problems of identifying or purchasing plants.

CREATING
a GARDEN

How to group plants effectively, plan and
structure your garden, and use color, light,
and texture to enhance its natural beauty.

Style

Gardens, like homes, may have many different atmospheres or styles. Some are instantly familiar, such as the haphazard abundance of an English cottage garden or the sparse elegance of a Japanese garden, while others, such as a *jardin sauvage*, may prove harder to define.

Design influences

Styles may have particular historical associations, showing for example the influence of the formal, stepped stone terraces of Renaissance Italy, the elegant grandeur of classical French gardens, such as Versailles, or the showy, colorful, and exotic plantings of Edwardian and Victorian England.

Different styles have also developed as a result of varying regional cultures. This is particularly true of the United States where the Northeastern cottage-type gardens contrast with the chaparral gardens of the Southwest or Southern California, or the sleepy gardens of the South with their magnolias and oaks shading the veranda.

These examples may seem too ambitious for the average gardener, but they can provide the source of his or her inspiration and be adapted to a particular site. It may be impossible to reproduce a classical French layout or an elegant Italian hillside landscape in a small city garden, but a sense of classical formality is within everyone's reach with the use of just a few stone steps, a small fountain, and a handsome stone pot filled with annuals, or perhaps an architectural, evergreen shrub or clipped tree. When choosing a style, bear in mind the prevailing climate, space, and soil type.

Proportion

To create a style in your own garden, be sensitive to the scale and mood of the surrounding landscape and buildings. A classical-style house, for instance, may well require a garden constructed to a formal layout; the proportions between the windows and doors could suggest the pattern made in the garden by paths, pools, terraces, borders, and lawn areas. Care should be taken with the relationships of these elements, to each other and the garden as well as to the house. Whereas broad sweeps of color and grand paths lend elegance to a large garden with open views, narrow borders of diminutive flowers and little winding paths would be lost in so large a space, although ideally suited to a small, informal cottage garden.

Perspective

You can alter the apparent shape of your garden by creating false perspective in your design, using the edges of different areas (paths, beds,

or terraces) as "lines." Horizontal lines will make the site seem wider while vertical lines will increase its length. To accentuate length even more, make vertical lines converge as they approach the bottom of the garden. Skillful placement of upright or prostrate trees and shrubs will enhance this effect.

Attention may be drawn to a particular spot, within or beyond the garden, by creating a dynamic, or moving, line such as a curving path that leads to a focal point—a pond, arbor, specimen tree, or magnificent view. Formal or enclosed gardens with no dominant point of interest are, however, best served by static patterns, like those created by box hedges bordering geometric beds.

Materials

Paths, paved areas, fencing, and garden buildings should harmonize with the house and its surroundings in materials as well as in form.

You may have difficulty in deciding what will be appropriate; try determining instead what will not be suitable and continue by a process of elimination. For example, crazy paving will not enhance an eighteenth-century town house.

Try to make the garden a continuation of the interior in terms of color and style. This concept may be taken further, so that the view from within blends harmoniously with the interior décor and does not jolt the senses, whether you are viewing the interior from the garden, or the garden from the interior. Plants are, of course, the most important "materials" used to create a garden's style. Your choice will be limited by the location, soil type, and climate of the area. Bright Mediterranean flowers such as rock roses will not thrive in a shady woodland, nor will heathers and camellias flourish in highly calcareous soils. Take advantage of the assets at your disposal and do not try to fight nature. Not only will inappropriate plants never

ITALIAN-STYLE TERRACE
Above: This elegant terrace has been created on a modest scale using terracotta pots and a small, wall-mounted fountain. The strong, horizontal lines of the pergola are softened by climbing roses, honeysuckle, and the decorative leaves of Vitis coignetiae.

EXOTIC GARDEN
Left: A Japanese mood has been conjured here by combining a clear stream, cascading down stepped rocks, with a carefully placed, distinctive, dwarf Japanese maple (Acer palmatum 'Dissectum Atropurpureum').

SEMI-FORMAL GARDEN
Right: The classical pavilion sets the formal tone of this country garden. Shrubs and hedges are clipped into strong, carefully related, architectural shapes and lead the eye towards the austere building and to the bonsai tree, on a plinth in front of it, which provides the focal point. The path has been designed to harmonize with the pavilion, in materials as well as design.

thrive, but very often when they are grown away from their natural habitat they appear to be irritatingly out of place.

Making a style your own

Most important of all, do not forget your own relationship with the garden—let it reflect your personality. If you are a relaxed person who likes pottering, you might allow herbaceous perennials to overspill their formal boundaries, or leave a few self-sown seedlings to interrupt a well-groomed gravel path. On the other hand, if you like everything around you to be ordered and tidy, you will probably be happier with a neat, symmetrical layout, perhaps blocks of annuals or Hybrid Tea (modern) roses rather than old-fashioned (old garden) varieties.

Do not overlook more practical requirements, either. If you have a young family, there is little point in siting an attractive lily pond in the middle of the garden as you will have to cover it with ugly safety mesh. Instead lay large areas to lawn and plant robust trees and shrubs. If a person using a wheelchair will be spending time in the garden, some stepped levels should be removed. Should you want to introduce a variety of levels, use gently sloping ramps or undulating banks. You might also build some raised beds; these would make gardening easier for the handicapped or for elderly gardeners.

Consider realistically how much time you are willing to spend on maintenance, since some gardens are much more time-consuming than others. If time is limited, concentrate on trees, shrubs, and ground cover; perennials and bulbs provide variety of color, form, and texture, but usually demand rather more gardening time. For maximum commitment, grow more specialized plants, for example, rock plants that may have demanding cultivation requirements, or plant or sow annuals and biennials.

Keeping the planting simple

A common mistake made by gardeners is to include too many varieties of plants in a small area. There is something to be learned from a specialist's garden—the rose grower's, for example, or that of the enthusiast who cultivates only conifers and heathers. Their gardens look good because the choice of plants is restricted, giving rise to a comparatively simple design.

If you do not want to be quite so limited, you can prevent a mixed planting from becoming too complex and unfocused by designing

COTTAGE-STYLE GARDEN
Below left: A haphazard mixture of mainly perennial plants is here combined with the shrub Piptanthus nepalensis, *which scrambles up an old stone wall, while beneath it* Corydalis ochroleuca, Hypericum 'Hidcote' *and lady's-mantle* (Alchemilla mollis) *grow happily through each other. Note the limited color range of the planting, making it informal rather than chaotic.*

JAPANESE-STYLE GARDEN
Below right: Bamboo, stepping stones and, in the distance, complementary foliage plants evoke a tranquil atmosphere in this Japanese-style garden. Such a style may be adapted to suit sunny or shaded sites and requires very little maintenance.

within a particular color range and by taking special care when grouping different varieties of plants together. This applies to foliage as well as to flowers, as is demonstrated so effectively in the famous white garden at Sissinghurst in Kent, England.

Remembering the detail

Once the overall style and layout of your garden have been decided upon and the range of plants within it chosen, make sure that the furnishings do not ruin the effect. A wrought-iron bench, for instance, might be too sophisticated for many gardens, whereas a simple wooden one would rarely jar. An elaborate Italianate urn would probably be too grand for an informal, suburban garden, even if planted with humble daisies. A period garden may be difficult to furnish economically, but on the whole, plain pots and ornaments are successful, especially in small, confined areas, and have the additional advantage of suiting a variety of plantings. Once you have decided on the style of furniture for your garden, do not stray from your original concept, as slight deviations will soon create a sense of clutter and all your planning will have been in vain.

ROMANTIC GARDEN
Left: A circular seat is placed in the leafy shade of a country garden made romantic by rough grass and a beautiful, sprawling shrub rose.

INFORMAL GARDEN
Below: Even in this deceptively simple planting of herbaceous perennials, bulbs, annuals, and shrubs, each plant has been carefully selected to balance the others in form, color, and texture. The barberry (Berberis) *and elegant, arching sprays of Solomon's seal* (Polygonatum) *provide continuity and cohesiveness to the planting scheme.*

Structure

"Structuring" a garden does not mean physically shifting earth or laying paving slabs, but developing it from the basic ground plan by using elements of the planting together with man-made features, such as paths and gravel areas, to relate a garden to its setting.

Introducing different levels

Once you have decided on the style of garden you wish to create and have sketched a layout, you can start to turn your plan into three-dimensional reality. Consider the differences in height that occur, or could be introduced to the site, and then decide on the plant masses, their relationship to the landscape beyond the garden and to the other elements in the garden, including each other.

Changes in ground level may already exist and can be accentuated by building steps at these points or to a pool, vantage point, or summerhouse. Fences and walls or structures such as pergolas, dovecotes, and arbors all give vertical emphasis or become useful screens, as can hedges, trees, or certain shrubs. Raised beds are invaluable for adding interest to a small, flat plot, and much variety can be introduced by arranging plants of different heights.

USING STRUCTURAL PLANTS
An upright tree such as a juniper may dominate too small a group of plants (A), but may help relate that group to the scale of a wall behind it (B). The same tree may block a view (C) or sited to one side of it act as a counterbalance (D). By incorporating another similar group within the field of vision, a more sophisticated, repetitive effect may be created. Movement and progression will result from placing one juniper forward of the other (E), but sited equidistant from the viewpoint the two plantings provide an elegant frame (F).

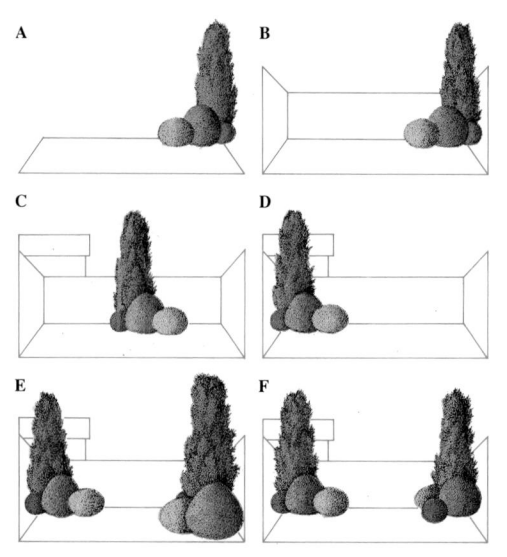

VISUALLY RESHAPING A FLAT SITE
Above: The forms of trees and shrubs may be used to introduce a variety of levels to a site. Prostrate and dwarf conifers contrast with the light, horizontal branches of golden-leaved Abies, *the open-branched locust tree* (Robinia pseudoacacia) *and, in the background, the dark, upright form of* Picea.

CHANGES IN LEVEL
Left: Steps and a low wall serve to emphasize a change in level. The domed forms of the topiary yews (Taxus), *flanking a flowering crab apple* (Malus), *highlight the sobriety of the former and the fresh abandon of the latter.*

CREATING HARMONY
Purple-leaved elder helps relate the background trees to the foreground perennials, including Salvia officinalis 'Purpurascens'.

Proportionate plantings

When planning your design, avoid crowding the basic pattern with a totally random sprinkling of plants. Think instead in terms of proportionate masses and build up the structure by adding key plants judiciously. There is much more to the look of a garden than the sum total of the individual plants that are growing within it; no matter how special a plant might be, to create a harmonious whole, it must relate to its neighbor. Moreover, each group of plants must then be in proportion to the bed in which it is situated, which in turn should relate to the whole garden.

The three-dimensional shape of the garden is largely determined by the plant masses and their siting. When you next come across a satisfying group of shrubs or perennials, analyze how the individual shapes of the plant masses are working structurally and how together they combine to form a unified whole. You will find that it is the proportionate relationship they create with each other that makes the color masses work so well together.

Using structural plants

No selection of plants is seen in isolation—there is always the backdrop of a garage, wall, neighbor's house, or view. The style and planting of a garden should blend rather than jar with this background. By introducing structural, or architectural, plants (those with strong forms), you can provide the bridge between the garden and what lies beyond it, help to relate the garden to the house or bind together scattered plants. Whether spiky and aggressive like a yucca or soft and romantic like a weeping willow, the distinctive outline will add a focal point to the design. Structural plants help to contribute solidity and scale and, by using key plants of diminishing size, create an illusion of space through false perspective.

SENSITIVE USE OF PROPORTION
This satisfyingly mixed border is well proportioned. The strong forms of two Cupressus, *neatly linked to the house by a Chinese wisteria* (Wisteria sinensis) *growing along the wall, encourage an easy transition from the starkly outlined mass of the house to the softer groupings of the plants. The* Cupressus *are in turn counterbalanced by a whitebeam* (Sorbus aria 'Lutescens'). *Shrubs and herbaceous perennials have been arranged so that the smallest are at the front of the border—yet these are all planted in sufficient quantity to make each group solid and balanced. An alternative planting (below left) has been devised for a hotter climate, using a ti tree* (Cordyline fruticosa) *as the dominant feature: Considerably fewer plants are included in the underplanting, but the proportions of the two schemes are similar.*

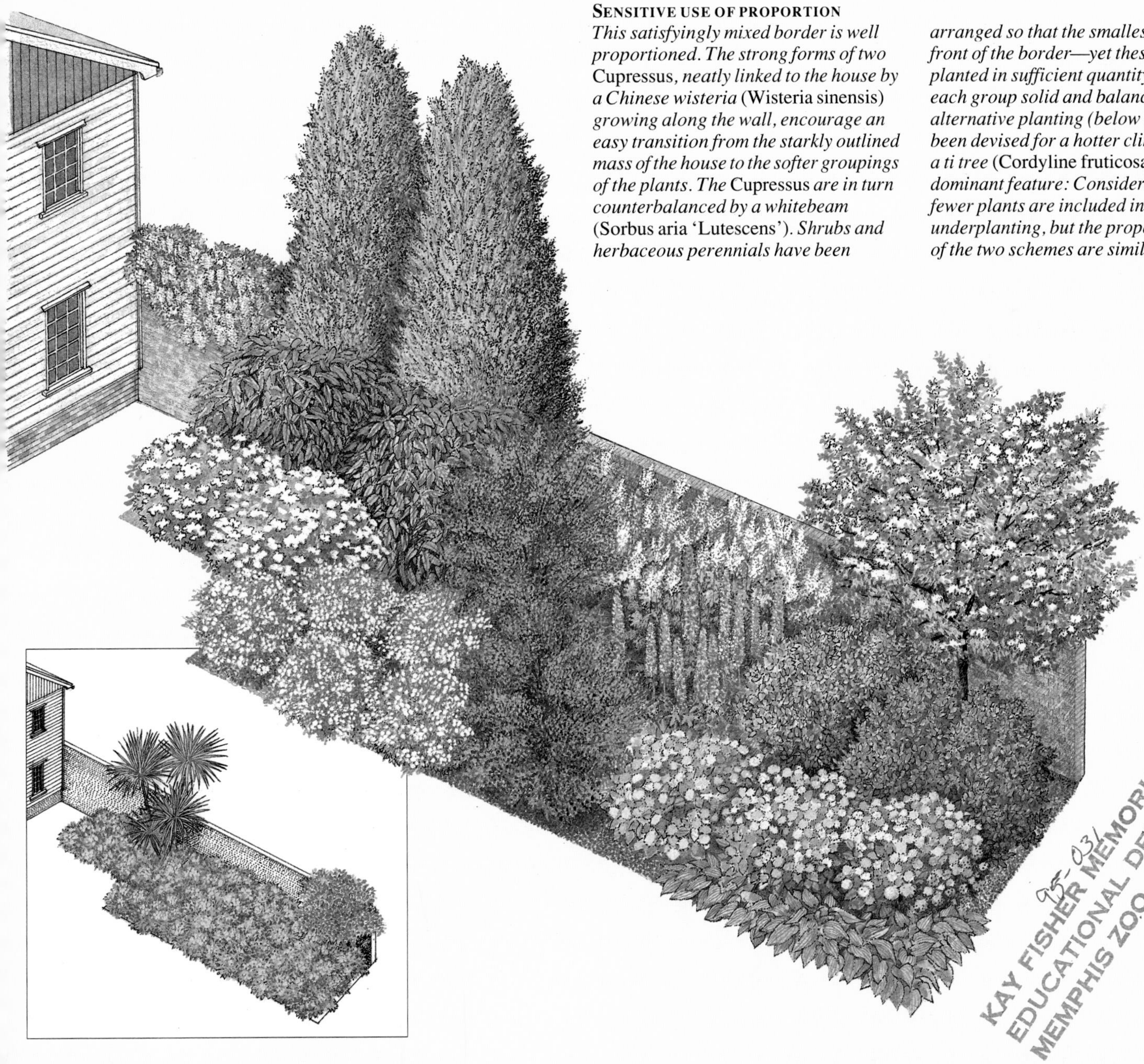

Gardening through the Year

The most successful gardens are those that provide interest throughout the year. Since few plants are at their peak for all twelve months, their impact in a group will alter as the year progresses. For example, a tree that is spectacular in spring, when it is covered in blossom, may fade into the background during the rest of the year. The appearance of the group as a whole will therefore change with the seasons.

When selecting plants, remember to take into account seasonal variations in their appearance and thus ensure that each grouping sustains year-round interest. A planting of summer-flowering perennials alone may look dull in spring, autumn, and winter. Consider all the merits of each plant—its size, habit, leaf form, color, bark, and texture—and not merely the flower color. These are the long-term qualities of a plant, which will be on display after its main season of interest has passed.

Ideally, you should provide a succession of "feature" plants against a relatively unchanging background of shrubs and trees. In this way, when the eye-catching flowers of one plant in the bed are over, another begins to blossom. Alternatively, you might like to plan a succession of feature plants in the garden as a whole, rather than just one border. In this way, the focal point will move from one area of the garden to another.

SPRING
In the rock garden, Narcissus cyclamineus *nod cheerfully above* Euphorbia myrsinites.

MID-SUMMER
Above: In this cottage garden—suggestive of a wild meadow—red poppies, perhaps garish in a more dense planting, look delightful sprinkled among the cooler tones of white bellflowers (Campanula) *and a few pale blue delphiniums.*

LATE AUTUMN
Right: Evergreen and berried trees and shrubs may now be fully appreciated. Upright, dark green conifers contrast attractively with the dazzling, silvery white leaves of Elaeagnus umbellata, *while the red berries of* Cotoneaster horizontalis *provide a colorful foreground.*

Winter to spring

During winter, flower interest in the garden is likely to be minimal, and it is then that the bold shapes and foliage color provided by evergreens, such as conifers, holly, and ivy, come into their own. Less obviously, the colors and textures of twigs, branches, bark, and berries of deciduous trees and shrubs also have roles to play in providing visual interest during the winter months. The branches of the elegant willow, for instance, can look quite brilliant in winter sunlight; silver birches are especially attractive, graceful, open trees with lovely, white bark that glistens on even the grayest day. The shapes of deciduous as well as evergreen plants play an important part at this time, whether silhouetted against a clear, winter sky or bearing a cloak of snow.

With the arrival of spring, the garden is soon awash with color. Some is provided by spring-flowering trees and shrubs, such as flowering cherries and magnolias, and by myriad rock plants, but most of the color comes from an abundance of flowering bulbs and corms. As these die down, they are followed by camellias, forsythias, rhododendrons, and azaleas and the fresh green of young leaves, with scented viburnum and lilac flowers appearing in succession through late spring.

Summer to autumn

In early summer, more color is added by a profusion of perennials and biennials, often lasting until autumn. Shrub interest diminishes as the season progresses, which is when the annuals make their contribution, brightening up the heavy green face of summer. Annual flowers, although often extremely bright, last for only short periods, so it is necessary to sow seeds and transplant seedlings successively to maintain the display. Self-seeding annuals will emerge year after year in a random way, often providing short explosions of color in unexpected places. The wealth of interesting plants that bloom in late summer, including clematis, remontant (repeat-flowering) roses, as well as annuals and herbaceous perennials, creates a pitfall of its own: You will have to be selective, otherwise the effect in the garden as a whole will be overwhelming.

As summer fades, the greenery starts to flare into the fiery colors of autumn, the intensity of the colors and their duration depending on the weather. In your planting include trees or shrubs with spectacular autumn leaves, such as acers; they can make the garden as handsome in this season as in any other. Late-flowering perennials, such as Michaelmas daisies and chrysanthemums, brighten up the garden until the arrival of the first frosts, when the flowers rot and the browned leaves fall, returning us to the winter landscape.

SEASONAL PLANTING
In this small plot (9 square yards), the interplay between a group of shrubs, perennials, and bulbs can be followed throughout the seasons. Although plants will have changing roles to play at different times of year, each has been chosen to relate successfully within the whole as well as to its neighbor.

WINTER
Evergreen rosemary contrasts with fleshy, purple Bergenia *leaves, variegated* Iris foetidissima *foliage and feathery twigs of* Acer palmatum 'Senkaki'. *Snowdrops and winter aconites (Eranthis hyemalis) will stud the ground by early spring.*

SPRING
Bergenia *now bears its tight, red flower clusters and the scented blooms of* Viburnum opulus *open. Fresh green is provided by young* Acer *leaves and delphinium shoots.*

SUMMER
Blue spikes of delphinium dominate early on. Foreground interest moves from the fernlike, gray leaves of the Achillea *to its long-lasting, platelike, yellow flower heads.*

AUTUMN
Yellowish Acer *and bronze-red* Viburnum *foliage command most attention, although later the* Viburnum *berries will also become noteworthy.* Iris *seed pods open to reveal their orange fruits and late-flowering chrysanthemums brighten the foreground.*

Planning

A visually satisfying composition of plants comprises several elements. Look at the characteristics of the individual plants, and consider the effects those characteristics have on each other. The shapes and forms of their leaves and flowers, their color and texture are all important. Think also about the changing size of plants: A small shrub planted now may dominate the garden in five years' time.

Any combination of plants should not be seen in isolation but should be considered in relation to the overall garden plan, the house, and its surroundings. For example, a small tree or large shrub backing a small group of iris, ballota, and meadow rue would work well, but replace the single tree or shrub with a bank of trees and more of the smaller plants would be needed to prevent them from being "swamped." Similarly, two irises, three ballotas, and a meadow rue would probably be too few plants when sited against a two-story house.

Restricting your choice of plants

Most people tend to be shy of buying more than one or two of a particular kind of plant, or, with such a wide range of suitable subjects available, cannot resist the temptation of including yet another species. It is just this collecting instinct that makes overall planting schemes look fractured and detracts from the strong, simple lines of the basic concept. The plant collector and the garden designer are very often a difficult pair to reconcile!

Aim for simple, bold plant masses to begin with; later, if the effect seems too stark, widen the range of plants slightly to add a little light relief. Keep your choice of suitable plants narrow and try to see them growing, by visiting well-established gardens, before you make your final selection.

The magnificent, large-scale plantings within grand borders in the gardens of historic houses that can be admired by the general public are made up of groups of perhaps twelve of this plant and eight of that; to simulate them on a domestic scale calls for an iron discipline. The same applies to planting bulbs—two's and three's tend to look messy; try groups or drifts instead. Remember, your planting is garden furnishing, and you would not cover individual chairs in the same room with contrasting fabrics if you wished to create a calm, comfortable atmosphere to relax in and enjoy.

SHAPE AND SCALE
Above left: Huge-leaved Gunnera manicata, *tall giant lily* (Cardiocrinum giganteum), *bushy ferns, and yellow flag irises* (Iris pseudacorus), *although very varied in shape and scale, still form a cohesive planting for a damp site.*

COLOR RANGES
Above: The transition in color tone from the golden fronds of Juniperus x media 'Pfitzeriana' *through the orange-yellow clump of coneflowers* (Rudbeckia) *to the reddish orange montbretia* (Crocosmia) *is smooth and pleasing. More varieties in smaller quantities might be difficult for the eye to absorb within this strong color range.*

SIMPLE, BOLD PLANT MASSES
Far left: Erect, silvery blue Arizona cypress (Cupressus glabra) *is balanced by the horizontal, golden foliage of* Acer japonicum 'Aureum'; *both trees seem stabilized by the solid-looking plants at their feet.*

STRUCTURED INFORMALITY
Left: Old stone slabs and exposed gravel punctuate the planting of lady's-mantle (Alchemilla mollis), *variegated* Cornus, *roses, and sweet Williams, which might otherwise appear unruly.*

23

Siting your plants

A useful discipline when selecting and siting plants is to start with the largest and work towards the smallest. First decide on the background planting, or "chorus line." This could be either trees or shrubs, depending on the scale of the location. Forest trees may provide a link with a wood beyond, but they can become too large for the average town garden, whereas medium-sized trees will provide privacy, shelter, and a "backdrop" for your garden. Climbers may be grown around the trees or trained along garden walls or fencing. Against this background, site the occasional feature plant—a more decorative small tree or a large shrub.

Think in the same way about shrubs. Use a backing group to cover a fence, to provide a screen between your garden and your neighbor's, or to camouflage unsightly buildings. Evergreens are obviously more suitable for this than deciduous shrubs. I find many conifers too demanding in both their shape and color for inclusion in the chorus line: They make better specimen plants. Plant a group of shrubs—two or three in a small town garden, maybe seven or eight in a larger country one.

In front of these shrubs, plant the flowering specimens and among the perennials and biennials introduce the smallest shrubs, including many herbs such as thyme, sage, or lavender. At this stage consider carefully the position of any feature plants.

Allowing for growth

It is essential, when planning where to site your plants, to envisage your scaled associations of plant masses not only as they appear now but

CREATING A BACKDROP
Above: Climbing plants such as Clematis 'Nelly Moser', *here grown through* Rosa 'American Pillar', *may be used to soften or screen buildings as well as to act as a foil for other plants.*

VERDANT CHORUS LINE
Left: The large shrubs Chimonanthus praecox *and* Corokia cotoneaster *form a verdant "chorus line" for smaller, more decorative flowering plants, in this case purple sage, lady's-mantle (Alchemilla mollis), and* Campanula persicifolia. *The stone wall also makes a handsome, contrasting backdrop.*

also as they will have developed in five years' time. Site the plants to allow enough room for them to expand and merge together over that time span. Beware of selecting trees that will ultimately become far too large for the scale of your garden as a whole, even if they look delightful at the garden center.

If the planting seems too far apart initially, fill in the gaps between your groupings with bulbs, annuals, or short-lived perennials that may be moved easily later. These will then bulk out the planting scheme, providing a temporary source of interest and color, until the larger plants have reached maturity.

CLASSIC BORDER PLANTING
The striking foliage of Elaeagnus pungens 'Maculata', *the rich red rose, and the golden yellow flowers of* Potentilla fruticosa *provide a classic background for a mass of low-growing perennials and violas.*

PLANTING FOR THE FUTURE
*It is easy to forget how quickly trees and shrubs grow, so they should be well spaced. It may help to mark out one yard sections with string. This bed has been planted for winter interest. Rosebud cherry (*Prunus subhirtella 'Autumnalis'*) dominates the bed, while two evergreen Mexican orange bushes (*Choisya ternata*) are contrasted with darker* Sarcococca humilis, *which bears fragrant flowers in late winter. Against these, the variegated* Iris foetidissima *stands out well. White-flowered* Bergenia 'Silberlicht' *is placed under the cherry and beyond the Mexican orange bushes are grouped three* Helleborus corsicus.

YEAR 1

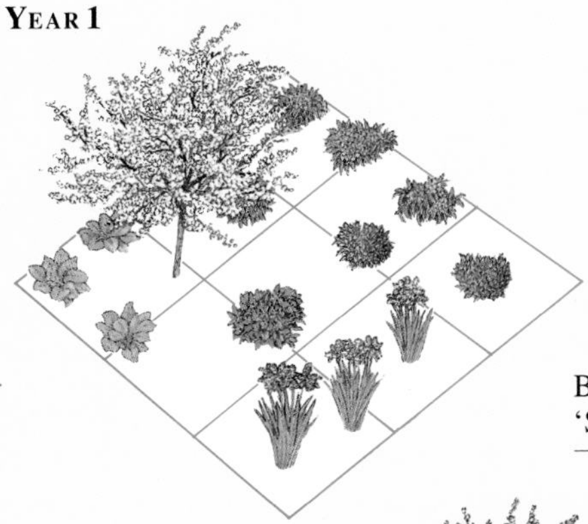

YEAR 3

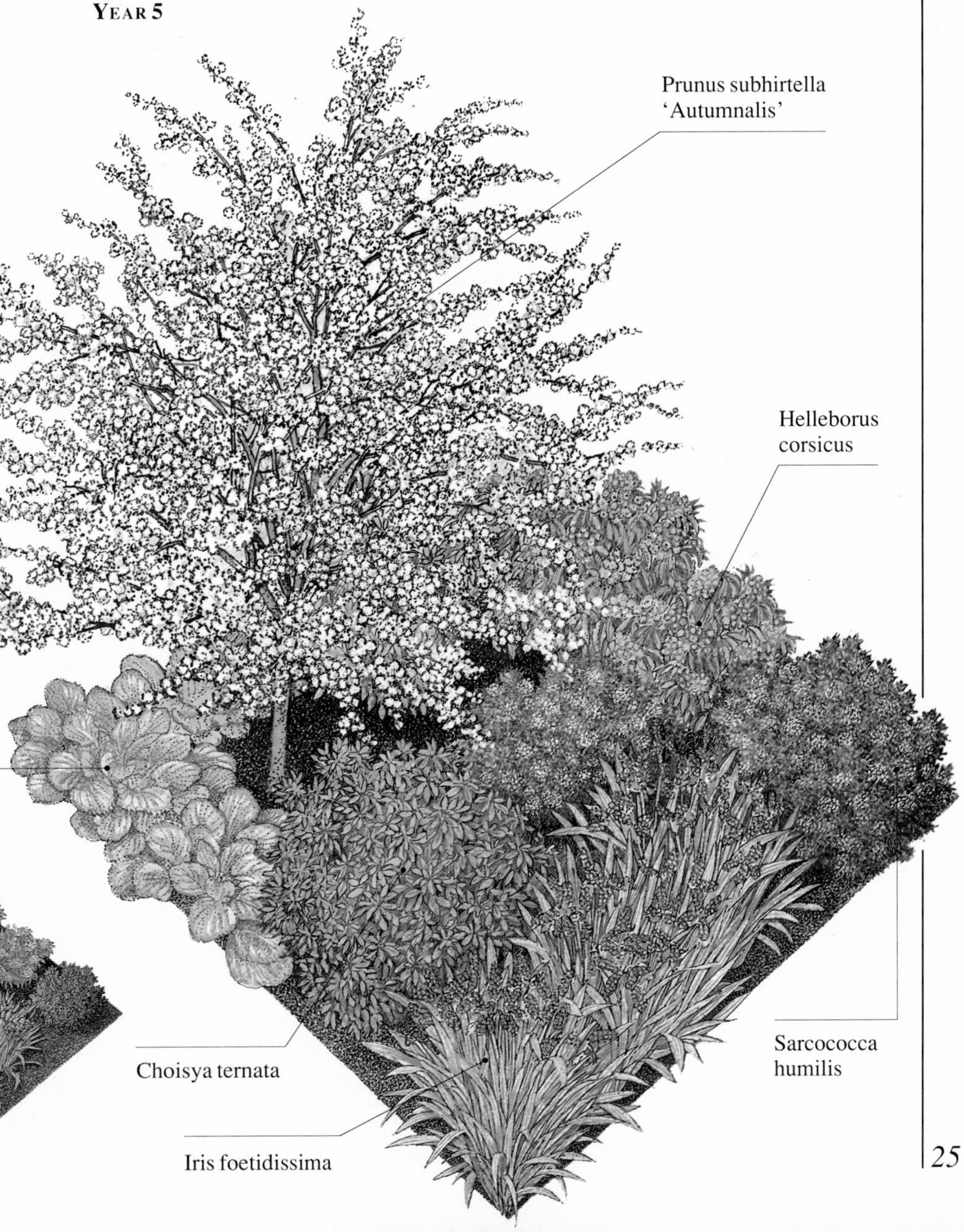

CONTINUING CARE AND MAINTENANCE
This bed should reach its peak of glory after about five years. Trimming may be necessary 6–10 years after planting.

YEAR 5

Prunus subhirtella 'Autumnalis'

Helleborus corsicus

Bergenia 'Silberlicht'

Choisya ternata

Iris foetidissima

Sarcococca humilis

25

Using Color

Everyone interprets the moods that colors create in different ways, and many people change their minds according to the weather, the time of day, or their emotional state. Individuals with perfectly normal color vision perceive colors differently, and color blindness is a surprisingly common phenomenon.

Color choice is first and foremost about personal preferences. Although there are some fundamental design rules on how to use color, including the avoidance of such obvious clashes as hot orange with delicate pink, they really constitute only a broad guide for the use of flat planes of basic color. Often they have little to do with the realities of a garden—the textures of living plants, the changing light, the varying hues of a color range, the season of the year, and the location.

The intricacies of color perception

The key to perceiving color is light. Soft colors look wonderful in the early morning, in the evening and in dull or damp weather. In the Mediterranean sunshine, these colors would look blanched, and strong colors, which may be overpowering in a soft light, come into their

own. Happily, nature has ensured that plants with strong-colored flowers are usually native to sunny regions.

The damp light of a temperate climate is quite unlike humid, tropical light or clear, desert light; sharp, winter light is quite distinct from the hazy light of a summer noon, and both differ from misty, autumnal and dusky, evening lights. All have different effects on colors, altering our perception of them and transforming the mood of the garden. If you are only going to be using your garden at one time of day, for example the evening, bear this in mind when choosing your plants: White flowers can take on a luminous quality in fading light but dark blue ones will be invisible.

Apart from climatic conditions, other factors determine how we notice color. The sea, for example, can alter color perception, reflecting light for some distance inland. A background building or fence will also influence color tones by reflecting or absorbing light: Whether shiny or matt, made of glass, stone, brick, or wood, it will influence our view of the colors of plants grown in front of it. Colors themselves affect each other too. The many shades of green modify any colors placed in front of them, as do the mousy brown colors of a wintery landscape. The individual color

GLOWING PINKS
Right: The pinks and purple-blues of this late summer bed set off each other excellently. The key to this success is the positioning of Artemisia ludoviciana 'Silver Queen' *and agapanthus between the strong pinks of* Aster novae-angliae 'Alma Potschke' *and ice-plant* (Sedum spectabile 'Brilliant').

AUTUMNAL HUES
Far right: Rich bronze-red Japanese maple (Acer palmatum) *and golden yellow* Fothergilla major—*in classic colors associated with a temperate autumn—glow even in misty light.*

SUBTLE COLORS
Far left: The pastel colors of catmint (Nepeta x faassenii) *and* Campanula lactiflora 'Loddon Anna' *are used here to provide a subtle backdrop for the vivid carmine red of the phlox.*

COLOR AND TEXTURE
Left: This planting deliberately juxtaposes extremes of color and texture, producing an almost layered effect. The sword-shaped leaves and reddish orange flowers of monbretia (Crocosmia) *contrast strongly with the yellow of feathery dill and erect, spiky* Verbascum; *the yellow creates a link between the foreground and the background.*

STRONG COMPOSITIONS
Below: This interesting contrast of a deep yellow daylily (Hemerocallis) *set against the intense purple-blues of* Hydrangea *and* Agapanthus *makes a striking statement.*

masses in a group influence each other, as well as affecting the whole planting. A largely white planting with a touch of purple will create one mood; but what about the reverse—a largely purple planting with a touch of white? The mood of one will be bright and sharp, the other somber and tranquil.

Considering the character of the site

In the days before the introduction of foreign species and mass hybridization, there was an indigenous range of colors in every area. To help design a harmonious garden you might keep to this spirit of planting by analyzing the location of the garden; the particular flavor of a place is dictated by its climate and the shapes and colors of its natural plant forms.

The background color may be a dark, coniferous green with the gray of granite or it may be deciduous green with mellower sandstone or limestone. In chalky areas, indigenous vegetation might include a proportion of gray foliage with the darker greens of yew or box. Although there are some bright-colored flowers in the temperate zones, the really brilliantly colored flowers originate in hotter climates, where the

intensity of the sun accentuates them. Thus the nearer the equator you go, the brighter the indigenous flowers.

Seasonal color associations

As well as geographical factors, there is a natural progression of dominant colors through the seasons. Pale spring colors transmute into the blues of early summer; hotter pinks of mid-summer are transformed into yellows and bronzes as autumn approaches, before turning into the browns of winter. When choosing plants for individual plant groups it is wise to avoid the use of certain colors against these seasonal backdrops, lest they introduce a jarring note. For example, refrain from setting soft pink against spring green, using purple in mid-summer or planting bright blue in autumn.

Even within the walls of a town garden with a backdrop of bricks and mortar, the seasons should still influence your color choices. In temperate zones, for a natural look, try whites and pale lemon in spring; pinks, blues, and grays in mid-summer; in late summer a little red but mainly yellows; and in autumn some bronze and purple.

Color preferences

There remain, of course, more personal preferences for certain color combinations. Strong colors are often more appreciated by the young than by the elderly, as they are invigorating. It follows that, in the garden, strong colors may be more appropriate when associated with various kinds of activity—near a tennis court, for instance, or around a pool. Softer colors, including shades of gray and pink, are calm and peaceful. Change pink to salmon, add a touch of purple and terracotta, and a broadly soft range becomes quite solid.

Making your personal mark

Your individual style and feelings about the moods that different colors create will be the final factors conditioning the colors in your garden, just as they are in the decoration of your home. If the garden is small, the result of linking the colors with those in the room adjacent to it will have a dramatic effect on both room and garden. Where room and garden meet, avoid clashes such as pink roses against orange-red brick or curtains. Conversely where the garden is larger, gradually change the colors in it so that, although those of the flowers nearest the house still link with the interior, those at the bottom of the garden work with the backdrop of the fence, hedge, or countryside beyond.

Color may be used to enhance perspective, too: Hotter ranges of color (reds, oranges, and pinks) look better closer to the house, while cool colors (blues and whites) introduced at a distance from it will increase the sense of space. Once you begin thinking in color ranges, you will start to eliminate many of the plant options and this will help further to simplify your plan.

A SENSE OF CALM
Above: Soft colors and forms intermingle harmoniously in this shady site, where the pinkish mauve of the lacecap hydrangea is echoed in the foreground by the purple Ajuga *leaves and the tiny, pink flowers of* Lamium maculatum. *The delicate tracery of the ferns blends comfortably with the bolder, bluish leaves of* Hosta sieboldiana var. elegans.

SYMPATHETIC PLANTING
Right: This damp corner in a cottage garden contains a deliberately limited color scheme, yet with invigorating results. When set against the ferns and grasses, the yellow heads of Tibetan primrose (Primula florindae) *and* Ligularia przewalskii *seem natural, because they have an affinity with the character and location of the site.*

Texture

When considering different plant groupings, avoid thinking only in terms of color combinations. A really successful design is a blend not only of color—foliage as well as flowers—but of texture also.

Texture is the soft, fluffy quality of fennel foliage and the dense, furry surface of gray stachys leaves, the spiky nature of many cacti and the smooth surface of evergreen leaves. It is an important aspect of the garden, contributed more by leaves than flowers (whose main role is to provide color).

Try to set plants with very different textures next to one another. Group the rough with the smooth, the hairy with the spiky, and so on. It is the proportionate, yet contrasting relationship of purple fennel and gray stachys that we find so appealing. Varying foliage textures influence the quality of light reflected or diffused by the plant and so the effect of a mass of flat, dull leaves will be notably different from a mass of bright, shiny leaves. For a damp spot, ornamental grasses will contrast well with feathery ferns and the leathery leaves of hostas.

Arrange your plants so that you maintain an interesting balance of texture and shape in all seasons. Think, also, about the texture of objects in your garden. A large, smooth stone placed by a composition of plants of bold shapes can create a most pleasing scene.

PLAY ON TEXTURES
Above: Spiky branches of Scotch thistle (Onopordum acanthium) *provide a dramatic foil for glossy-leaved ivy, soft-leaved* Nicotiana, *and fine-leaved lilies and marguerites. The paving slabs, the smooth terracotta pot (planted with marguerites), and the carved stone pot (with* Helichrysum petiolare 'Aureum') *add further variety to the scene.*

DISTINCTIVE TEXTURES
Far left: The creamy plumes of pampas grass (Cortaderia selloana) *will help to add a textural dimension to any garden, but they must be in proportion to the surrounding trees and shrubs if they are not to look out of place.*

SUCCESSFUL COMBINATIONS
Left: This blend of flower and leaves skillfully exploits the changing textures and colors between Bowles' golden sedge (Carex elata 'Aurea') *in the foreground, the feathery plumes of a deep red* Astilbe *and pink* Candelabra primulas *through to the enormous, prickly-edged leaves of* Gunnera manicata.

The Planter's Guide

The following lists suggest plants that are suitable for growing in particular situations, or that have special uses or characteristics. For each category the list is broadly subdivided into groups, following the arrangement of the Plant Catalog, pp.38–400. Individual plants that appear in the Plant Catalog are followed by page numbers. Refer to the Plant Dictionary if a whole genus or a plant not followed by a page number is recommended.

Plants are not always consistent in their growing habits and much of their success depends on climate, available nutrients in the soil, planting site, and weather. If a plant is listed for a particular purpose (coastal sites, shade, etc.), it should thrive there happily in normal growing conditions, even if the situation is not the plant's naturally preferred location.

○ – evergreen or semi-evergreen plants, including those with overwintering rosettes of leaves.

Plants for hedges and windbreaks

△ – moderately to fast growing.

Trees
Alnus cordata, p.41△
Arbutus andrachne ○
Arbutus unedo, p.66 ○
Carpinus betulus
Carpinus betulus 'Fastigiata', p.72
Crataegus monogyna
Fagus sylvatica, p.43
Ilex aquifolium ○
Ilex aquifolium 'Argentea Marginata', p.70 ○
Laurus nobilis ○
Melaleuca quinquenervia ○ △
Metrosideros excelsa, p.56 ○ △
Nothofagus dombeyi, p.47 ○ △
Nothofagus obliqua, p.42△
Olea europaea ○
Populus x *canadensis* 'Robusta', p.40△
Prunus lusitanica ○
Syzygium paniculatum, p.54 ○
Umbellularia californica, p.48 ○
Zelkova serrata, p.45

Conifers
Abies grandis, p.76 ○ △
Cedrus deodara
Cephalotaxus harringtonia ○
Chamaecyparis lawsoniana ○ △
x *Cupressocyparis leylandii*, p.73 ○ △
Cupressus macrocarpa ○ △
Juniperus communis ○
Larix decidua △
Picea omorika, p.75 ○ △

Pinus nigra ○
Pinus radiata, p.76 ○ △
Pseudotsuga menziesii var. *glauca*, p.74 ○ △
Taxus baccata ○
Thuja plicata ○ △
Tsuga canadensis, p.79 ○ △

Shrubs
Berberis darwinii, p.86 ○
Buxus sempervirens 'Suffruticosa', p.145 ○
Choisya ternata, p.95 ○
Codiaeum variegatum, p.145 ○
Cotoneaster simonsii, p.116△
Dodonaea viscosa 'Purpurea', p.119 ○ △
Duranta repens, p.118 ○ △
Elaeagnus x *ebbingei* ○ △
Escallonia 'Langleyensis', p.110 ○
Euonymus japonicus 'Macrophyllus' ○
Griselinia littoralis ○
Hibiscus rosa-sinensis ○
Lavandula cvs ○
Leptospermum scoparium cvs ○ △
Ligustrum ovalifolium, p.94 ○ △
Lonicera nitida ○
Photinia x *fraseri* 'Birmingham', p.85 ○ △
Pittosporum tenuifolium, p.95 ○ △
Prunus laurocerasus ○
Prunus lusitanica ○
Pyracantha x *watereri*, p.104 ○ △
Rosmarinus officinalis and cvs ○
Tamarix ramosissima, p.88△

Roses
Rosa californica△
Rosa 'Céleste', p.149△
Rosa 'Felicia', p.149△
Rosa 'Frühlingsmorgen' △
Rosa gallica var. *officinalis*△
Rosa gallica 'Versicolor', p.151△
Rosa glauca, p.150△
Rosa 'Great Maiden's Blush', p.149△
Rosa 'Marguerite Hilling', p.150△
Rosa moyesii 'Geranium', p.151△
Rosa 'Nevada', p.149△
Rosa 'Penelope', p.148△
Rosa 'Président de Sèze' △
Rosa rugosa, p.15△
Rosa 'Tuscany Superb' △

Grasses (including Bamboos)
Arundo donax△
Cortaderia selloana 'Sunningdale Silver', p.180 ○
Miscanthus sacchariflorus△
Phyllostachys bambusoides, p.182 ○ △
Semiarundinaria fastuosa, p.182 ○
Sinarundinaria nitida ○
Stipa gigantea, p.181 ○

Perennials
Echinops bannaticus, p.190△
Eupatorium fistulosum, p.193△
Filipendula camtschatica△
Helianthus atrorubens 'Monarch'
Macleaya microcarpa 'Coral Plume', p.189△
Phormium tenax ○
Rudbeckia laciniata 'Goldquelle', p.191△
Silphium laciniatum△
Veronica virginica f. *alba*, p.202

Plants for coastal and exposed sites

Trees
Acer pseudoplatanus and cvs
Agonis flexuosa, p.63 ○
Alnus incana, p.40
Arbutus unedo, p.66 ○
Eucalyptus coccifera, p.46 ○
Eucalyptus globulus ○
Eucalpytus gunnii, p.46 ○
Ficus macrophylla ○
Fraxinus excelsior
Ilex aquifolium cvs, pp.70–71 ○
Laurus nobilis ○
Melaleuca quinquenervia ○
Salix alba
Schefflera actinophylla, p.57 ○
Schinus molle ○
Sorbus aria 'Lutescens', p.51 ○
Tabebuia chrysotricha, p.69
Thevetia peruviana, p.66 ○
Tipuana tipu

Conifers
x *Cupressocyparis leylandii*, p.73 ○
Cupressus macrocarpa ○
Cupressus sempervirens, p.77 ○
Pinus nigra subsp. *nigra*, p.76 ○

Shrubs
Acacia verticillata ○
Bupleurum fruticosum, p.114 ○
Cytisus x *spachianus* ○
Duranta repens, p.118 ○
Elaeagnus pungens 'Maculata', p.95 ○
Erica cinerea 'Eden Valley', p.147 ○
Escallonia rubra var. *macrantha* 'Crimson Spire' ○
Euonymus japonicus ○
Euphorbia characias subspp., p.124 ○
Felicia amelloides 'Santa Anita', p.136 ○
Genista hispanica, p.138
Halimium lasianthum subsp. *formosum*, p.137 ○
Hibiscus rosa-sinensis ○
Hippophäe rhamnoides, p.92
Lavandula angustifolia 'Hidcote', p.135 ○
Malvaviscus arboreus, p.89 ○
Pittosporum crassifolium ○
Pyracantha coccinea 'Lalandei' ○
Rosmarinus officinalis, p.135 ○
Senecio 'Sunshine', p.138 ○
Viburnum tinus, p.117 ○

Climbers
Antigonon leptopus, p.167 ○
Bougainvillea glabra, p.172 ○
Eccremocarpus scaber, p.175 ○
Ercilla volubilis ○
Euonymus fortunei 'Coloratus' ○
Ficus pumila ○
Hedera canariensis ○
Muehlenbeckia complexa
Pandorea jasminoides, p.166 ○
Pyrostegia venusta, p.176 ○
Schisandra rubriflora, p.169
Solandra maxima, p.164 ○
Tripterygium regelii
Tropaeolum tuberosum 'Ken Aslet', p.174
Wisteria sinensis, p.173

Perennials
Anaphalis margaritacea, p.200
Anchusa azurea 'Loddon Royalist', p.213
Anthurium andraeanum, p.223 ○
Artemisia absinthium 'Lambrook Silver' ○
Centaurea hypoleuca 'John Coutts', p.236
Echinacea purpurea
Erigeron 'Charity', p.235
Eryngium variifolium, p.243 ○
Euphorbia griffithii 'Fireglow', p.216
Geranium sanguineum, p.294
IRISES, pp.196–7, some ○
Kniphofia caulescens, p.221 ○
Lupinus 'Thundercloud'
Peperomia obtusifolia 'Variegata', p.261 ○
Phormium tenax ○
Pilea cadierei, p.256 ○
Romneya coulteri, p.188
Salvia argentea, p.201
Senecio x *hybridus* Series ○
Senecio maritima 'Silver Dust', p.278 ○
Tradescantia fluminensis ○

Annuals and Biennials
Antirrhinum majus and cvs
Calendula officinalis, Series and cvs
Clarkia amoena and Series
Coreopsis tinctoria, p.280
Cynoglossum amabile 'Firmament', p.278
Dahlia, Coltness Hybrids, p.273
Eschscholzia californica, p.282
Gilia capitata, p.277
Helichrysum bracteatum cvs
Helipterum roseum, p.265
Impatiens, Novette Series ○
Kochia scoparia f. *trichophylla*, p.279
Limnanthes douglasii, p.280
Matthiola
Portulaca grandiflora, Series and cvs
Tagetes

Rock plants
Achillea clavennae, p.313 ○
Aethionema grandiflorum, p.292 ○
Dianthus deltoides ○
Draba aizoides ○
Epilobium glabellum, p.291 ○
Iberis sempervirens, p.286 ○
Origanum laevigatum, p.294
Oxalis enneaphylla
Phlox subulata 'Marjory', p.318 ○
Pulsatilla vulgaris, p.288
Saxifraga paniculata ○
Sedum spathulifolium 'Cape Blanco', p.331 ○
Sempervivum arachnoideum, p.329 ○
Thlaspi rotundifolium, p.305
Viola cornuta, p.289

Bulbs, Corms, and Tubers
Amaryllis belladonna, p.342
Canna x *generalis* cvs
Crinum
Crocus
DAFFODILS, pp.348–9
Eucharis grandiflora, p.355 ○
Freesia
Galtonia candicans, p.332
Hippeastrum

Hyacinthus orientalis cvs
Hymenocallis
Nerine
Scilla
Sprekelia formosissima, p.343
TULIPS, pp.344–5
Veltheimia bracteata, p.355
Zantedeschia aethiopica ○

Shrubs preferring wall protection

Abutilon megapotamicum ○
Acacia pravissima, p.69 ○
Artemisia arborescens, p.143 ○
Buddleia crispa, p.111
Ceanothus impressus, p.113 ○
Chaenomeles speciosa 'Moerloosii', p.98
Chimonanthus praecox
Cytisus × *spachianus* ○
Daphne odora 'Aureomarginata', p.142 ○
Elsholtzia stauntonii, p.141
Escallonia 'Iveyi', p.86 ○
Fabiana imbricata 'Violacea', p.113 ○
Feijoa sellowiana, p.111 ○
Fremontodendron 'California Glory', p.91 ○
Garrya elliptica, p.93 ○
Jasminum mesnyi, p.165 ○
Lagerstroemia indica, p.64
Leptospermum scoparium 'Red Damask', p.99 ○
Lonicera fragrantissima
Melianthus major ○
Olearia × *scilloniensis* ○
Pyracantha atalantioides 'Aurea', p.92 ○
Robinia hispida, p.109
Rosa banksiae 'Lutea', p.162 ○
Rosa 'Mermaid', p.162
Rosmarinus officinalis, p.135 ○
Salvia involucrata 'Bethellii', p.193
Solanum crispum 'Glasnevin', p.172 ○
Tibouchina urvilleana, p.90
Viburnum foetens, p.117

Plants to provide quick cover

Shrubs
Ceanothus thyrsiflorus var. *repens*, p.136 ○
Hypericum calycinum, p.138 ○
Lantana camara ○

Climbers
Hedera helix (small cvs) ○
Hydrangea anomala subsp. *petiolaris*, p.166
Lonicera japonica cvs ○
Pueraria lobata
Trachelospermum asiaticum ○
Trachelospermum jasminoides, p.165 ○

Ferns
Dryopteris dilatata
Polystichum aculeatum ○
Polystichum setiferum cvs, pp.185,187 ○

Perennials
Alchemilla mollis, p.245
Anthemis punctata subsp. *cupaniana*, p.233 ○
Duchesnea indica ○
Euphorbia amygdaloides subsp. *robbiae*, p.228 ○

Galeobdolon argentatum ○
Geranium macrorrhizum, p.236 ○
Heterocentron elegans, p.241 ○
Lamium maculatum and cvs ○
Osteospermum jucundum, p.236 ○
Pulmonaria (most), some ○
Stachys byzantina, p.260 ○
Symphytum × *uplandicum* 'Variegatum', p.199

Annuals and Biennials
Lathyrus odoratus 'Bijou', p.268
Portulaca grandiflora, Series and cvs
Sanvitalia procumbens, p.280
Tropaeolum majus, Series and cvs

Rock plants
Acaena anserinifolia ○
Arabis caucasica and cvs ○
Aubrieta ○
Campanula poscharskyana, p.321
Helianthemum ○
Phlox douglasii cvs ○
Phlox subulata ○
Phuopsis stylosa, p.292
Polygonum affine and cvs
Polygonum vacciniifolium, p.327 ○
Saxifraga stolonifera ○
Tiarella cordifolia, p.287 ○
Waldsteinia ○

Ground-cover plants for shaded areas

Shrubs
Daphne laureola var. *philippi*, p.124 ○
Epigaea asiatica ○
Euonymus fortunei 'Kewensis' ○
Gaultheria shallon, p.130 ○
Leucothoë fontanesiana ○
Mahonia repens ○
Pachysandra terminalis, p.328 ○
Ruscus hypoglossum, p.144 ○
Sarcococca humilis, p.142 ○
Vinca minor, p.144 ○

Climbers
Berberidopsis corallina, p.169 ○
Epipremnum aureum 'Marble Queen', p.177 ○
Ficus pumila ○
Hedera colchica 'Dentata', p.179 ○
Hedera helix cvs, p.179 ○
Hydrangea anomala subsp. *petiolaris*, p.166
Rhoicissus capensis ○
Rhoicissus rhomboidea ○
Schizophragma hydrangeoides

Ferns
Adiantum venustum, p.187
Blechnum penna-marina ○
Polypodium vulgare, p.187 ○
Polystichum setiferum cvs, pp.185,187 ○

Perennials
Alchemilla mollis, p.245
Asarum caudatum ○
Aspidistra elatior ○
Bergenia cordifolia 'Purpurea', p.226 ○
Brunnera macrophylla
Duchesnea indica ○
Epimedium perralderianum ○
Euphorbia amygdaloides subsp. *robbiae*, p.228 ○
Galeobdolon argentatum ○
Geranium macrorrhizum, p.236 ○
Hosta fortunei 'Albopicta', p.244
Luzula sylvatica 'Marginata' ○

Pellionia daveauana, p.259 ○
Plectranthus oertendahlii ○
Pulmonaria saccharata, p.228 ○
Symphytum grandiflorum
Tellima grandiflora 'Purpurea', p.258 ○
Tolmiea menziesii
Tradescantia fluminensis 'Variegata', p.256 ○
Waldsteinia ternata, p.325 ○

Rock plants
Asarina procumbens, p.324
Cardamine trifolia, p.302
Homogyne alpina ○
Mitchella repens ○
Prunella grandiflora, p.321 ○
Saxifraga stolonifera ○
Saxifraga × *urbium* ○
Tiarella cordifolia, p.287 ○

Ground-cover plants for sunny areas

Conifers
Juniperus communis 'Prostrata' ○
Juniperus conferta ○
Juniperus sabina var. *tamariscifolia*, p.82 ○
Juniperus squamata 'Blue Carpet' ○
Microbiota decussata, p.82 ○
Picea abies 'Inversa' ○

Shrubs
Arctostaphylos uva-ursi, p.328 ○
Calluna vulgaris 'White Lawn' ○
Ceanothus thyrsiflorus var. *repens*, p.136 ○
Cotoneaster microphyllus var. *cochleatus* ○
Cotoneaster 'Skogholm' ○
Erica carnea 'Springwood White', p.146 ○
Hebe pinguifolia 'Pagei', p.291 ○
Hypericum calycinum, p.138 ○
Lantana montevidensis, p.135 ○
Leiophyllum buxifolium ○
Pernettya prostrata ○
Rosmarinus officinalis 'Prostratus' ○
Salix repens, p.124
Stephanandra incisa 'Crispa'

Climbers
Anredera cordifolia ○
Campsis radicans
Clematis armandii, p.170 ○
Clematis rehderiana, p.171
Clematis tangutica, p.171
Decumaria sinensis ○
Hardenbergia comptoniana, p.164 ○
Hibbertia scandens ○
Kennedia rubicunda, p.163 ○
Lathyrus latifolius, p.169
Lonicera japonica 'Halliana', p.173 ○
Parthenocissus tricuspidata, p.176
Pueraria lobata
Pyrostegia venusta, p.176 ○
Trachelospermum asiaticum ○
Vitis coignetiae, p.176
Vitis davidii

Perennials
Anthemis punctata subsp. *cupaniana*, p.233 ○
Centaurea montana, p.241
Euphorbia polychroma, p.232
Geranium sanguineum, p.294
Heterocentron elegans, p.241 ○
Lamium maculatum, p.226 ○
Lysimachia punctata, p.214
Nepeta × *faassenii*, p.242

Osteospermum jucundum, p.236 ○
Peltiphyllum peltatum, p.197
Phlomis russeliana, p.214
Rheum palmatum 'Atrosanguineum', p.189
Stachys byzantina, p.260 ○

Annuals and Biennials
Any of spreading habit.

Rock plants
Acaena microphylla, p.329 ○
Arabis caucasica 'Variegata', p.302 ○
Armeria maritima 'Vindictive', p.320 ○
Aubrieta cvs ○
Aurinia saxatilis, p.290 ○
Campanula poscharskyana, p.321
Dianthus gratianopolitanus, p.317 ○
Dryas octopetala, p.315 ○
Helianthemum 'Ben More', p.294 ○
Hypericum olympicum
Iberis sempervirens, p.286 ○
Lithodora diffusa 'Heavenly Blue', p.297 ○
Nierembergia repens, p.314
Phlox douglasii 'Crackerjack', p.319 ○
Phuopsis stylosa, p.292
Polygonum affine and cvs
Thymus praecox ○
Veronica prostrata 'Kapitan', p.297

Plants for paving and wall crevices

Annuals and Biennials (not walls)
Ageratum houstonianum (small cvs)
Ionopsidium acaule
Limnanthes douglasii, p.280
Lobelia erinus cvs
Lobularia maritima
Malcolmia maritima, p.267
Nemophila maculata, p.263
Nemophila menziesii, p.277
Portulaca grandiflora, Series and cvs

Rock plants
Acaena microphylla, p.329 ○
Aethionema 'Warley Rose', p.316 ○
Alyssum montanum ○
Aubrieta ○
Campanula poscharskyana, p.321
Dianthus deltoides ○
Erinus alpinus, p.306 ○
Gypsophila repens and cvs ○
Helianthemum ○
Hypericum olympicum
Lithodora diffusa 'Heavenly Blue', p.297 ○
Parahebe lyallii ○
Phlox douglasii cvs ○
Ramonda myconi (wall only), p.322 ○
Saxifraga cotyledon, p.292 ○
Sedum spathulifolium 'Cape Blanco', p.331 ○
Sempervivum montanum, p.330 ○
Thymus praecox and cvs ○

Plants for dry shade

Conifers
Taxus baccata 'Adpressa' ○

Shrubs
Buxus sempervirens ○
Daphne laureola ○
Elaeagnus × *ebbingei* ○
Gaultheria shallon, p.130 ○

Hypericum x *inodorum* 'Elstead', p.138
Ilex aquifolium, p.70 ○
Lonicera pileata, p.144 ○
Mahonia aquifolium, p.125 ○
Osmanthus decorus ○
Ruscus aculeatus ○
Viburnum rhytidophyllum, p.86 ○
Vinca major ○
Vinca minor, p.144 ○

Climbers
Berberidopsis corallina, p.169 ○
Cissus striata ○
Epipremnum aureum 'Marble Queen', p.177 ○
Hedera canariensis ○
Lapageria rosea, p.168 ○
Lonicera japonica 'Halliana', p.173 ○
Philodendron scandens, p.178 ○

Ferns
Ceterach officinarum, p.185 ○
Cyrtomium falcatum, p.185 ○
Davallia canariensis ○
Microlepia strigosa, p.184 ○
Nephrolepis exaltata, p.186 ○
Phyllitis scolopendrium, p.187 ○
Polypodium vulgare, p.187 ○
Pteris cretica, p.185 ○

Perennials
Achimenes
Alchemilla mollis, p.245
Chirita lavandulacea, p.250 ○
Chirita sinensis ○
Epimedium pinnatum subsp. *colchicum* ○
Galeobdolon argentatum ○
Iris foetidissima ○
Kohleria digitaliflora, p.204
Luzula sylvatica 'Marginata' ○
Streptocarpus saxorum, p.241 ○
Symphytum grandiflorum
Tellima grandiflora ○
Tolmiea menziesii ○
Tradescantia zebrina 'Quadricolor' ○

Bulbs, Corms, and Tubers
Clivia miniata, p.350 ○
Haemanthus albiflos ○
Hyacinthoides hispanica, p.346
Hyacinthoides non-scriptus, p.346

Plants for moist shade

Shrubs
Clethra arborea ○
Crataegus laevigata 'Punicea'
Kalmia latifolia, p.109 ○
Lindera benzoin, p.99
Neillia thibetica, p.108
Paeonia lutea var. *ludlowii*, p.199
Paeonia suffruticosa 'Rock's Variety', p.198
Pieris formosa var. *forrestii* 'Wakehurst', p.110 ○
Pittosporum eugenioides ○
Prunus laurocerasus ○
RHODODENDRONS, pp.100–102, most ○
Salix magnifica
Sarcococca ruscifolia ○
Skimmia japonica, p.143 ○
Viburnum 'Pragense', p.107 ○

Climbers
Akebia quinata, p.164, sometimes ○
Decumaria sinensis ○
Dioscorea discolor, p.177 ○
Humulus lupulus 'Aureus', p.164

Hydrangea anomala subsp. *petiolaris*, p.166
Lonicera tragophylla
Macleania insignis ○
Mikania scandens ○
Passiflora coccinea, p.163 ○
Pileostegia viburnoides, p.166 ○
Schizophragma integrifolium, p.166
Smilax china
Thunbergia mysorensis, p.165 ○
Trachelospermum jasminoides, p.165 ○

Ferns
Athyrium nipponicum, p.187
Blechnum tabulare ○
Cyathea australis, p.72 ○
Cyathea medullaris ○
Dicksonia antarctica, p.184 ○
Dryopteris goldiana
Lunathyrium japonicum ○
Lygodium japonicum ○
Matteuccia struthiopteris, p.186
Onoclea sensibilis, p.186
Osmunda claytoniana
Polystichum munitum, p.184 ○
Selaginella martensii, p.185 ○
Woodwardia radicans ○

Perennials
Actaea pachypoda, p.217
Anemone x *hybrida* cvs
Anthurium scherzerianum, p.258 ○
Aruncus dioicus, p.188
Begonia rex and hybrids ○
Bergenia ○
Calathea zebrina, p.223 ○
Cardamine pentaphyllos, p.227
Convallaria majalis, p.225
Deinanthe caerulea
Dichorisandra reginae, p.211 ○
Digitalis x *mertonensis* ○
Helleborus orientalis, pp.256, 257, 258 ○
HOSTAS, p.244
Kirengeshoma palmata, p.221
Maranta leuconeura 'Erythroneura', p.259 ○
Polygonatum x *hybridum*, p.197
PRIMULAS (many), pp.230–31
Ruellia devosiana, p.234 ○
Trillium grandiflorum, p.225
Uvularia grandiflora, p.229
Vancouveria hexandra, p.287

Bulbs, Corms, and Tubers
Arisaema
Arisarum proboscideum
Arum italicum 'Pictum', p.363
Camassia leichtlinii, p.332
Galanthus elwesii, p.369
Galanthus nivalis and cvs
Galanthus plicatus
Leucojum aestivum, p.332
Leucojum vernum, p.356
Narcissus cyclamineus, p.349

Plants for sandy soil

Trees
Acacia dealbata, p.56 ○
Acer negundo
Agonis flexuosa, p.63 ○
Banksia serrata ○
Betula pendula 'Dalecarlica', p.47
Castanea sativa
Celtis australis, p.41
Cercis siliquastrum, p.61
Eucalyptus ficifolia ○
Gleditsia triacanthos
Melia azedarach, p.49

Nothofagus obliqua, p.42
Phoenix canariensis ○
Quercus ilex ○
Schinus molle ○

Conifers
Abies grandis, p.76 ○
x *Cupressocyparis leylandii* and cvs ○
Cupressus glabra ○
Juniperus ○
Larix decidua
Pinus pinaster, p.75 ○
Pinus radiata, p.76 ○
Pseudotsuga menziesii var. *glauca*, p.74 ○
Thuja occidentalis and cvs ○

Shrubs
Berberis empetrifolia, p.125 ○
Calluna vulgaris and cvs ○
Ceanothus thyrsiflorus and forms ○
Cistus ○
Cytisus scoparius forms
Erica arborea var. *alpina*, p.146 ○
Erica cinerea and cvs ○
Erica pageana ○
Genista tinctoria, p.125
Hakea lissosperma ○
Lavandula ○
Pernettya mucronata and cvs ○
Physocarpus opulifolius
Rosa pimpinellifolia, p.148
Rosmarinus officinalis and cvs ○
Spartium junceum, p.115
Ulex europaeus, p.125
Yucca gloriosa, p.105 ○

Climbers
Adlumia fungosa
Anredera cordifolia ○
Bomarea andimarcana ○
Clianthus puniceus, p.163 ○
Kennedia rubicunda, p.163 ○
Merremia tuberosa ○
Mutisia oligodon ○
Periploca graeca
Petrea volubilis, p.164 ○
Semele androgyna ○
Streptosolen jamesonii, p.178 ○
Solanum wendlandii, p.172 ○
Tropaeolum tricolorum, p.163
Vitis vinifera 'Purpurea', p.176

Perennials
Acanthus spinosus, p.210
Aphelandra squarrosa 'Louisae', p.215 ○
Artemisia ludoviciana var. *albula*, p.223
Asphodeline lutea, p.199
Billbergia nutans, p.222 ○
Centranthus ruber, p.207
Cryptanthus zonatus ○
Echinops sphaerocephalus, p.188
Eryngium tripartitum, p.212
Foeniculum vulgare 'Purpureum'
Gaillardia x *grandiflora* cvs
Limonium latifolium 'Blue Cloud', p.242
Nepeta x *faassenii*, p.242
Origanum vulgare 'Aureum', p.245
Papaver orientale
PELARGONIUMS, pp.206–7 ○
Romneya coulteri, p.188
Ruellia devosiana, p.234 ○
Sansevieria trifasciata 'Laurentii', p.224 ○
Strelitzia reginae, p.224 ○

Annuals and Biennials
Anchusa capensis cvs
Antirrhinum majus and cvs
Brachycome iberidifolia, p.278

Chrysanthemum segetum, p.281
Cleome hassleriana
Coreopsis tinctoria, p.280
Exacum affine, p.275 ○
Helichrysum bracteatum, Monstrosum Series, p.284
Impatiens, Novette Series ○
Limnanthes douglasii, p.280
Limonium sinuatum, p.266
Linaria maroccana 'Fairy Lights', p.274
Lobularia maritima
Mentzelia lindleyi, p.280
Papaver rhoeas, Shirley Series, pp.266, 272
Portulaca grandiflora, Series and cvs
Schizanthus
Tagetes
Verbena x *hybrida*, Series and cvs

Rock plants
Acaena caesiiglauca, p.330 ○
Achillea x *kellereri*, p.315 ○
Aethionema 'Warley Rose', p.316 ○
Arabis ferdinandi-coburgii 'Variegata', p.328 ○
Arenaria montana, p.314
Armeria juniperifolia, p.305 ○
Cytisus x *beanii*, p.289
Dianthus deltoides ○
Gypsophila repens ○
Helianthemum ○
Iberis saxatilis, p.314 ○
Linum suffruticosum subsp. *salsoloides*
Phlox bifida, p.321 ○
Saponaria ocymoides, p.318
Sedum ○
Sempervivum ○

Bulbs, Corms, and Tubers
Babiana rubro-cyanea, p.360
Brodiaea coronaria
Crocus
Freesia
IRISES (bulbous species), pp.196–7
Ixia
Muscari
Narcissus tazetta and Div.8 hybrids
Ornithogalum
Scilla
Tigridia pavonia, p.353
Zephyranthes

Cacti and other Succulents (all)

Plants for clay soils

□ – tolerates slow-draining soil; others require reasonable drainage.

Trees
Alnus glutinosa □
Castanospermum australe ○
Drimys winteri, p.51 ○
Fraxinus
Juglans nigra, p.42
Melaleuca quinquenervia ○ □
Oxydendrum arboreum, p.50 □
Populus □
Pterocarya fraxinifolia □
Quercus palustris, p.43
Quercus robur
Salix 'Chrysocoma', p.48 □
Salix matsudana 'Tortuosa', p.58 □

Conifers
Cryptomeria ○ □
Metasequoia □
Taxodium distichum □

Shrubs
Aronia arbutifolia, p.97 □
Calycanthus floridus □
Clethra alnifolia
Cornus alba 'Sibirica', p.118 □
Kalmia latifolia, p.109 ○
Ledum groenlandicum, p.122 ○ □
Magnolia virginiana ○
Salix caprea □
Salix purpurea □
Sambucus racemosa
Tetrapanax papyriferus, p.94 ○
Viburnum lentago
Viburnum opulus

Climbers
Celastrus scandens
Humulus lupulus 'Aureus', p.164 ○
Rosa filipes 'Kiftsgate', p.160 ○
Vitis coignetiae, p.176

Ferns
Matteuccia struthiopteris, p.186 □
Onoclea sensibilis, p.186 □
Osmunda regalis, p.186 □
Polystichum setiferum cvs, pp.185,187 ○
Thelypteris palustris, p.186 □
Woodwardia radicans ○ □
Woodwardia virginica □

Perennials
Aruncus dioicus, p.188 □
Cyperus papyrus, p.181 ○ □
Filipendula ulmaria 'Aurea', p.245 □
Gunnera manicata, p.190 □
Helonias bullata ○ □
Houttuynia cordata 'Chamaeleon', p.373 □
Iris laevigata, p.197 □
Lythrum □
Mimulus guttatus □
Peltiphyllum peltatum, p.197 □
Primula florindae, p.231 □
Primula japonica □
Scrophularia auriculata 'Variegata' □
Trollius □

Water plants
Butomus umbellatus, p.374 □
Caltha palustris, p.377 □
Lysichiton americanus, p.377 □
Pontederia cordata, p.374 □
Ranunculus lingua, p.377 □
Sagittaria latifolia, p.372 □
Thalia dealbata □

Plants for chalk and limestone

Trees
Acer negundo 'Variegatum', p.52
Cercis siliquastrum, p.61
Crataegus
Fagus sylvatica, p.43
Fraxinus ornus, p.49
Ilex aquifolium cvs, pp.70–71 ○
Malus
Morus nigra
Phillyrea latifolia ○
Prunus avium 'Plena', p.49
Robinia pseudoacacia 'Frisia', p.54
Sorbus aria and cvs
Tilia tomentosa

Conifers
Calocedrus decurrens, p.78 ○
Cedrus libani, p.75 ○
Chamaecyparis lawsoniana and cvs ○
x *Cupressocyparis leylandii* and cvs ○
Cupressus glabra ○

Juniperus ○
Picea omorika, p.75 ○
Pinus nigra ○
Taxus baccata and cvs ○
Thuja orientalis and cvs ○
Thuja plicata and cvs ○

Shrubs
Berberis darwinii, p.86 ○
Buddleia davidii and cvs
Ceanothus impressus, p.113 ○
Choisya ternata, p.95 ○
Cistus ○
Cotoneaster, some ○
Deutzia
Malus sargentii, p.84
Malus sieboldii, p.97
Nerium oleander, p.88 ○
Philadelphus
Phlomis fruticosa, p.138 ○
Potentilla (all shrubby species)
Rosa rugosa, p.151
Syringa
Viburnum tinus, p.117 ○
Vitex agnus-castus
Yucca aloifolia, p.121 ○

Climbers
Campsis x *tagliabuana* 'Mme Galen', p.175
Celastrus orbiculatus
CLEMATIS, pp.170–71, some ○
Eccremocarpus scaber, p.175 ○
IVIES, p.179 ○
Lonicera, some ○
Passiflora caerulea, p.172 ○
Rosa 'Albéric Barbier', p.160 ○
Rosa 'Albertine', p.161 ○
Rosa banksiae 'Lutea', p.162 ○
Trachelospermum jasminoides, p.165 ○
Wisteria sinensis, p.173

Ferns
Asplenium trichomanes, p.185 ○
Dryopteris filix-mas, p.184
Phyllitis scolopendrium, p.187 ○
Polypodium vulgare 'Cornubiense', p.186 ○

Perennials
Acanthus spinosus, p.210
Achillea filipendulina 'Gold Plate', p.215
Bergenia ○
Doronicum
Eryngium, some ○
Gypsophila paniculata cvs
Helenium
IRISES (most), pp.196–7, some ○
Salvia nemorosa
Scabiosa caucasica 'Clive Greaves', p.242
Sidalcea
Verbascum ○
Veronica spicata

Annuals and Biennials
Ageratum houstonianum and cvs
Calendula officinalis and Series and cvs
Callistephus chinensis, Series and cvs
Cheiranthus cheiri and Series and cvs ○
Gomphrena globosa, p.275
Humea elegans, p.274
Lavatera trimestris 'Silver Cup', p.268
Limonium sinuatum, p.266
Lobularia maritima
Matthiola
Salvia horminum, p.275
Tagetes
Ursinia anthemoides, p.282
Xeranthemum annuum
Zinnia

Rock plants
Aethionema ○
Alyssum ○
Campanula (most rock garden species), some ○
Chrysanthemum hosmariense, p.286 ○
Dianthus (most rock garden species) ○
Draba ○
Erysimum helveticum, p.313 ○
Gypsophila repens ○
Helianthemum ○
Leontopodium alpinum, p.286
Origanum dictamnus
Papaver burseri (*P. alpinum* group)
Saponaria ocymoides, p.318
Saxifraga (most) ○
Thymus caespititius, p.315 ○
Veronica (all rock garden species), some ○

Bulbs, Corms, and Tubers
Babiana
Chionodoxa
Colchicum
Crinum x *powellii*, p.333
Crocus
Cyclamen hederifolium, p.367
DAFFODILS, pp.348–9
GLADIOLI, p.334
Leucocoryne ixioides, p.346
Lilium regale, p.338
Muscari
Pancratium illyricum, p.350
Scilla
TULIPS, pp.344–5
Zephyranthes

Plants requiring neutral to acid soil

Trees
Arbutus menziesii ○
CAMELLIAS, pp.96–7 ○
Embothrium coccineum, p.66 ○
Rhodoleia championii ○
Stewartia
Styrax japonica, p.50

Conifers
Abies ○
Picea (most) ○
Pinus densiflora ○
Pinus pumila ○
Pseudolarix amabilis, p.79
Pseudotsuga ○
Sciadopitys verticillata, p.78 ○
Tsuga heterophylla ○

Shrubs
Arctostaphylos (some) ○
CAMELLIAS, pp.96–7 ○
Desfontainia spinosa, p.111 ○
Epacris impressa, p.123 ○
Gaultheria ○
HEATHERS (most), pp.146–7 ○
Leucothöe ○
Pernettya ○
Philesia magellanica ○
Pieris ○
RHODODENDRONS, pp.100–102, most ○
Styrax officinalis, p.86 ○
Telopea speciosissima, p.110 ○
Vaccinium, most ○
Zenobia pulverulenta, p.106

Climbers
Agapetes (several) ○
Berberidopsis corallina, p.169 ○
Mitraria coccinea, p.164 ○

Perennials
Cypripedium reginae, p.252
Drosera ○
Nepenthes ○
Sarracenia flava, p.245
Trillium
Uvularia

Rock plants
Arctostaphylos ○
Cassiope ○
Corydalis cashmeriana
Cyananthus
Epigaea ○
Galax urceolata, p.291 ○
Gentiana sino-ornata, p.327
Leucothöe keiskei ○
Lithodora diffusa ○
Mitchella repens ○
Ourisia ○
Pernettya ○
Phyllodoce ○
Pieris nana ○
Shortia ○
Vaccinium, most ○

Plants with decorative fruits or seed heads

Trees
Annona reticulata
Arbutus ○
Cornus kousa
Cotoneaster frigidus
Crataegus (most)
HOLLIES (most), pp.70–71, most ○
Koelreuteria paniculata, p.65
Magnolia, some ○
Malus (most)
Schinus molle ○
Sorbus (most)

Conifers
Abies (some) ○
Cedrus (some) ○
Picea (some) ○
Pinus (some) ○

Shrubs
Aucuba japonica, p.120 ○
Berberis (most), some ○
Callicarpa bodinieri
Cotoneaster (most), some ○
Decaisnea fargesii, p.90
Euonymus (many), some ○
Hippophäe rhamnoides, p.92
Hypericum x *inodorum* 'Elstead', p.138
Pernettya mucronata and cvs ○
Pyracantha ○
ROSES (most), pp.148–62, some ○
Sambucus racemosa
Skimmia (some) ○
Symphoricarpos
Viburnum (several), some ○

Climbers
Actinidia chinensis
Akebia, sometimes ○
Cardiospermum halicacabum
Celastrus orbiculatus
Clematis orientalis
Holboellia coriacea ○
ROSES (several), pp.148–62, some ○
Trichosanthes anguina
Tropaeolum speciosum, p.168

Perennials
Actaea
Clintonia borealis
Disporum hookeri

Duchesnea indica ○
Irisfoetidissima ○
Ophiopogon ○
Physalis alkekengi
Phytolacca
Podophyllum

Annuals and Biennials
Briza maxima
Capsicum annuum cvs
Coix lacryma-jobi, p.182
Lagurus ovatus, p.180
Lunaria annua, p.269
Martynia annua, p.264
Nicandra physalodes
Nigella damascena and cvs
Zea mays

Rock plants
Acaena microphylla, p.329 ○
Cornus canadensis, p.314
Dryas octopetala, p.315 ○
Gaultheria (most) ○
Maianthemum
Mitchella repens ○
Nertera granadensis, p.327 ○
Pulsatilla (most)

Bulbs, Corms, and Tubers
Allium christophii, p.352 ○
Arisaema triphyllum, p.352 ○
Arum italicum 'Pictum', p.363 ○
Cardiocrinum giganteum, p.333

Water plants
Nelumbo
Nuphar lutea, p.377
Thalia dealbata

Plants with aromatic foliage

Trees
Agonis flexuosa, p.63 ○
Eucalyptus ○
Laurus nobilis ○
Populus balsamifera
Populus trichocarpa
Sassafras albidum, p.42
Umbellularia californica, p.48 ○

Conifers
Calocedrus decurrens, p.78 ○
Chamaecyparis ○
Cupressus ○
Juniperus ○
Pseudotsuga menziesii ○
Thuja (most) ○

Shrubs
Aloysia triphylla, p.111
Artemisia abrotanum, p.144
Choisya ternata, p.95 ○
Elsholtzia stauntonii, p.141
Helichrysum italicum ○
Hyssopus officinalis, p.136
Lavandula (most) ○
Lindera
Myrtus communis, p.97 ○
PELARGONIUMS (scented-leaved forms), pp.206–7 ○
Prostanthera ○
Rhododendron rubiginosum ○
Rosmarinus officinalis, p.135 ○
Salvia officinalis cvs ○

Perennials
Artemisia absinthium 'Lambrook Silver' ○
Chamaemelum nobile ○

Chrysanthemum parthenium, p.263
Geranium macrorrhizum, p.236 ○
Houttuynia cordata 'Chamaeleon', p.373
Mentha, some ○
Monarda didyma
Myrrhis odorata, p.201
Origanum vulgare
Perovskia atriplicifolia

Rock plants
Mentha requienii ○
Origanum laevigatum, p.294
Satureja montana
Thymus ○

Plants with fragrant flowers

Trees
Bauhinia variegata, p.69
Clethra arborea ○
Drimys winteri, p.51 ○
Magnolia grandiflora ○
Magnolia kobus, p.48
Malus hupehensis, p.48
Pittosporum tenuifolium, p.95 ○
Pittosporum undulatum ○
Robinia pseudoacacia
Styrax japonica, p.50
Tilia x *euchlora*
Virgilia capensis ○

Shrubs
Buddleia davidii and cvs
Chimonanthus praecox
Choisya ternata, p.95 ○
Cytisus battandieri, p.91 ○
Daphne (many), most ○
Hamamelis mollis
Lonicera fragrantissima
Magnolia stellata, p.97
Osmanthus ○
Philadelphus (many)
Pittosporum tobira ○
ROSES (many), pp.148–60, some ○
Sarcococca ○
Syringa (many)
Viburnum (many), some ○

Climbers
Clematis montana 'Elizabeth'
Hoya carnosa, p.166 ○
Jasminum (many), most ○
Lathyrus odoratus
Lonicera (many), some ○
Mandevilla laxa
ROSES (many), pp.160–62, some ○
Stephanotis floribunda, p.163 ○
Trachelospermum ○
Wattakaka sinensis
Wisteria

Perennials
CARNATIONS and PINKS (most), pp.238–9 ○
Convallaria majalis, p.225
Cosmos atrosanguineus, p.208
Crambe cordifolia, p.188
Hedychium gardnerianum, p.194
Hosta plantaginea, p.244
Iris graminea
Iris unguicularis ○
Meehania urticifolia
Nicotiana sylvestris, p.188
Petasites fragrans ○
Primula elatior, p.231
Primula veris, p.231
Tulbaghia natalensis
Verbena x *hybrida* 'Defiance', p.272 ○

Annuals and Biennials
Centaurea moschata, p.279
Cheiranthus cheiri, Series and cvs ○
Exacum affine, p.275 ○
Lathyrus odoratus and cvs
Lobularia maritima
Matthiola incana
Nicotiana alata, p.200
Primula Series
Reseda odorata, p.263
Scabiosa atropurpurea

Rock plants
Alyssum montanum ○
Dianthus (most) ○
Erysimum helveticum, p.313 ○
Papaver nudicaule
Primula auricula
Viola odorata ○

Bulbs, Corms, and Tubers
Arisaema candidissimum, p.364
Chlidanthus fragrans, p.365
Crinum bulbispermum
Crocus angustifolius
Crocus longiflorus
Cyclamen persicum, p.370
Cyclamen repandum
Eucharis grandiflora, p.355 ○
Hymenocallis
LILIES (several), p.338
Narcissus jonquilla and Div.7 hybrids
Narcissus tazetta and Div.8 hybrids
Ornithogalum arabicum, p.351
Polianthes tuberosa

Flowers for cutting

Shrubs
Calluna vulgaris (tall cvs) ○
Camellia japonica cvs ○
Erica ○
Forsythia
Hamamelis mollis
Lonicera fragrantissima
Philadelphus
ROSES (some), pp.148–62, some ○
Salix caprea
Syringa cvs
Turraea obtusifolia, p.140 ○

Perennials
Anaphalis
Anchusa azurea
Anemone x *hybrida* cvs
Astrantia major, p.234
CARNATIONS and PINKS, pp.238–9 ○
Cattleya (most)
CHRYSANTHEMUMS, pp.218–19
Cymbidium (most) ○
DELPHINIUMS (most), p.192
Helleborus niger, p.257
Phalaenopsis (most) ○
Phlox paniculata cvs
Rudbeckia (most)
Strelitzia reginae, p.224 ○

Annuals and Biennials
Amaranthus caudatus, p.270
Callistephus chinensis, Series and cvs
Centaurea cyanus and cvs
Centaurea moschata, p.279
Cosmos, Bright Lights Series
Gaillardia pulchella 'Lollipops', p.282
Gypsophila elegans, p.262
Helipterum roseum, p.265
Lathyrus odoratus and cvs
Limonium sinuatum, p.266
Matthiola cvs

Moluccella laevis, p.279
Xeranthemum annuum
Zinnia elegans group (tall hybrids)

Bulbs, Corms, and Tubers
Allium (tall species)
Alstroemeria (tall species and cvs)
DAFFODILS (tall species and cvs), pp.348–9
DAHLIAS, pp.340–41
GLADIOLI (most), p.334
LILIES (some), p.338
Nerine bowdenii, p.354
Ornithogalum thyrsoides, p.351
Polianthes tuberosa
TULIPS (tall cvs), pp.344–5
Zantedeschia aethiopica ○

Flowers for drying

Trees
Acacia dealbata, p.56 ○
Acacia longifolia ○
Acacia verticillata ○
Syringa cvs

Shrubs
Acacia (most) ○
Calluna vulgaris and cvs ○
Cassinia ○
Fothergilla major, p.95
Garrya elliptica, p.93 ○
Helichrysum (most) ○
Holodiscus discolor, p.87
Lavandula ○
Rosmarinus officinalis and cvs ○

Perennials
Achillea, some ○
Artemisia (several), some ○
Astilbe (most)
Catananche caerulea 'Major', p.242
Echinops
Eryngium, some ○
Eupatorium (some)
Gypsophila paniculata 'Bristol Fairy', p.200
Limonium (most)
Lythrum
Rodgersia
Solidago (most)
Typha

Annuals and Biennials
Amaranthus caudatus, p.270
Centaurea cyanus
Gilia capitata, p.277
Gomphrena globosa, p.275
Gypsophila elegans, p.262
Helichrysum bracteatum, Monstrosum Series, p.284
Helipterum
Limonium sinuatum, p.266
Moluccella laevis, p.279
Onopordum acanthium, p.266
Salvia horminum and Series
Scabiosa atropurpurea
Tagetes, Erecta group hybrids
Xeranthemum annuum

Trailing plants for walls or baskets

Conifers
Juniperus conferta ○
Juniperus horizontalis and cvs ○
Juniperus squamata 'Blue Carpet' ○
Microbiota decussata, p.82 ○

Shrubs
Ceanothus thyrsiflorus var. *repens*, p.136 ○
Cotoneaster microphyllus ○
Hebe pinguifolia 'Pagei', p.291 ○
Helichrysum petiolare, p.143 ○
Leptospermum humifusum, p.128 ○
Salix lindleyana
Salix repens, p.124

Perennials
Alloplectus nummularia ○
Campanula isophylla ○
Columnea (most) ○
Cyanotis kewensis ○
Episcia cupreata, p.257 ○
Lotus berthelotii, p.240 ○
Pelargonium peltatum and cvs ○
Pellionia daveauana, p.259 ○
Peperomia scandens ○
Ruellia devosiana, p.234 ○
Tradescantia fluminensis and cvs ○
Tradescantia zebrina, p.257 ○
Verbena peruviana ○

Annuals and Biennials
Limnanthes douglasii, p.280
Lobelia erinus cvs
Nemophila maculata, p.263
Nolana paradoxa
Petunia, Cascade Series
Petunia, Jamboree Series
Portulaca grandiflora, Series and cvs
Sanvitalia procumbens, p.280
Tropaeolum majus, Series and cvs

Rock plants
Acaena 'Blue Haze' ○
Arabis caucasica ○
Cymbalaria muralis ○
Cytisus x *beanii*, p.289
Euphorbia myrsinites, p.311 ○
Gypsophila repens ○
Lithodora diffusa cvs ○
Lysimachia nummularia 'Aurea', p.326 ○
Oenothera missouriensis, p.325
Othonnopsis cheirifolia, p.298 ○
Parahebe catarractae, p.296 ○
Parochetus communis, p.324 ○
Phlox subulata ○
Polygonum vacciniifolium, p.327 ○
Pterocephalus perennis subsp. *perennis*, p.320 ○
Saxifraga stolonifera ○

Plants for containers

Trees
Acer negundo
Cordyline australis and cvs ○
Crataegus laevigata and cvs
Eucalyptus (when young) ○
Ficus (most) ○
Ilex aquifolium and cvs ○
Jacaranda mimosifolia, p.52
Laurus nobilis ○
Malus (small species and cvs)
Melia azederach, p.49
Olea europaea ○
Phoenix canariensis ○
Prunus (small species and cvs)
Sorbus (small species and cvs)
Washingtonia ○

Conifers
All the small species and cvs of the following:
Abies ○
Chamaecyparis ○

Juniperus ○
Picea ○
Pinus ○
Thuja ○
Thujopsis dolabrata ○

Shrubs
Buxus sempervirens and cvs ○
Catharanthus roseus, p.128
Erica ○
FUCHSIAS, pp.132–3
Hebe ○
Hydrangea macrophylla and cvs
Lavandula ○
Myrtus communis, p.97 ○
Pittosporum ○
RHODODENDRONS (most), pp.100–102, most ○
ROSES (most), pp.148–62, some ○
Santolina ○
Senecio (shrubby species) ○
Spiraea
Viburnum tinus, p.117 ○

Climbers
Cissus antarctica, p.178 ○
CLEMATIS (small cvs), pp.170–71, some ○
Cobaea scandens, p.172 ○
Eccremocarpus scaber, p.175 ○
Hedera helix and cvs ○
Ipomoea, some ○
Jasminum (climbing species), some ○
Lathyrus (climbing species)
Lonicera (climbing species), some ○
Mandevilla ○
Passiflora ○
Stephanotis floribunda, p.163 ○
Tropaeolum (climbing species)

Ferns
Adiantum (most)
Athyrium nipponicum, p.187
Phyllitis scolopendrium 'Marginatum', p.187 ○
Polypodium vulgare 'Cornubiense', p.186 ○
Polystichum setiferum 'Divisilobum', p.185 ○

Perennials
Agapanthus
Bergenia ○
Geranium, some ○
Geum
Hemerocallis
Heuchera x *brizoides* cvs ○
HOSTAS, p.244
Phormium ○
PRIMULAS (tall species and cvs), pp.230–31
Pulmonaria, some ○
Rudbeckia fulgida 'Goldsturm', p.215
Salvia (many)
Stachys, some ○
Verbena, some ○
Veronica spicata

Annuals and Biennials
Ageratum
Browallia speciosa, p.223
Calendula officinalis, Series and cvs
Callistephus chinensis, Series and cvs
Coleus blumei, Series and cvs
Impatiens, Novette Series ○
Kochia scoparia f. *trichophylla*, p.279
Lobelia erinus cvs
Nemesia strumosa and Series
Petunia
Salpiglossis sinuata, Series and cvs
Tagetes
Viola x *wittrockiana* hybrids

Rock plants
All rock plants are suitable, the following being recommended:
Campanula (many), some ○
Dianthus (many) ○
Geranium (several), some ○
Hebe ○
Helianthemum ○
Iberis sempervirens, p.286 ○
Penstemon (many), some ○
Phlox (several) ○
Polygonum affine ○
Primula auricula and hybrids
Saponaria ocymoides, p.318
Saxifraga (many) ○
Silene schafta, p.319

Bulbs, Corms, and Tubers
All bulbous plants are suitable, the following being recommended:
Begonia x *tuberhybrida* hybrids
Crinum
Crocus
DAFFODILS, pp.348–9
Hyacinthus orientalis cvs
LILIES (most), p.338
TULIPS, pp.344–5
Zantedeschia aethiopica 'Crowborough', p.332 ○

Water plants
Watertight containers are ideal for growing the following:
Aponogeton distachyos, p.373
Eichhornia crassipes, p.374 ○
Menyanthes trifoliata, p.372
Nelumbo nucifera and cvs
Pontederia cordata, p.374
Thalia dealbata
WATER LILIES (small cvs), p.376

Architectural plants

Trees
Cordyline ○
Dracaena draco, p.72 ○
Eucalyptus (many) ○
Jacaranda mimosifolia, p.52
Kalopanax pictus, p.53
Magnolia (several), some ○
Paulownia tomentosa, p.49
Phoenix canariensis ○
Salix (several)
Trachycarpus fortunei, p.57 ○
Trochodendron aralioides, p.57 ○
Washingtonia ○

Conifers
Abies ○
Araucaria ○
Calocedrus decurrens, p.78 ○
Cedrus ○
Juniperus x *media* 'Pfitzeriana', p.83 ○
Metasequoia glyptostroboides, p.74
Picea ○
Pseudolarix amabilis, p.79
Sciadopitys verticillata, p.78 ○
Sequoia sempervirens ○
Sequoiadendron giganteum, p.74 ○
Taxodium distichum, p.76
Tsuga heterophylla ○

Shrubs
Aesculus parviflora, p.88
Brachyglottis repanda, p.95 ○
Cycas revoluta, p.120 ○
Daphniphyllum macropodum, p.86 ○
Eriobotrya japonica ○
Fatsia japonica and *F.j.* 'Variegata', p.119 ○

Mahonia (most) ○
Parkinsonia aculeata ○
Protea ○
Rhus typhina and *R.t.* 'Laciniata', p.92
Yucca ○

Climbers
Epipremnum aureum 'Marble Queen', p.177 ○
Hedera colchica 'Dentata', p.179 ○
Monstera deliciosa, p.178 ○
Schizophragma hydrangeoides
Schizophragma integrifolium, p.166
Vitis coignetiae, p.176

Ferns
Blechnum tabulare ○
Cyathea australis, p.72 ○
Dicksonia antarctica, p.184 ○
Matteuccia struthiopteris, p.186
Phyllitis scolopendrium 'Marginatum', p.187 ○
Platycerium bifurcatum, p.184 ○
Polystichum munitum, p.184 ○
Woodwardia radicans ○
Woodwardia virginica

Perennials
Acanthus spinosus, p.210
Angelica archangelica, p.190
Berkheya macrocephala, p.215
Crambe cordifolia, p.188
Cynara cardunculus, p.190
Echinops bannaticus, p.190
Ensete ventricosum, p.195 ○
Gunnera manicata, p.190
Heliconia ○
Ligularia (most)
Macleaya
Meconopsis (most), several ○
Peltiphyllum peltatum, p.197
Phormium tenax and cvs ○
Rodgersia

Annuals and Biennials
Amaranthus tricolor cvs
Helianthus annuus and cvs
Humea elegans, p.274
Onopordum acanthium, p.266
Silybum marianum, p.266
Verbascum densiflorum ○

Bulbs, Corms, and Tubers
Arisaema (most)
Arum creticum, p.347
Begonia rex and hybrids ○
Begonia x *tuberhybrida* hybrids
Canna x *generalis* cvs
Dracunculus vulgaris, p.336
GLADIOLI (most), p.334
Sauromatum venosum, p.343
Zantedeschia aethiopica ○

Water plants
Colocasia esculenta and cvs ○
Eichhornia crassipes, p.374 ○
Lysichiton americanus, p.377
Nelumbo nucifera and cvs
Orontium aquaticum, p.377
Sagittaria
Thalia dealbata

Cacti and other Succulents
Most of the larger species, especially the following:
Aeonium tabuliforme, p.398 ○
Aloe (most) ○
Carnegiea gigantea, p.378 ○
Cereus (most) ○
Cyphostemma juttae, p.380
Euphorbia candelabrum ○
Opuntia (most) ○

The PLANT CATALOG

A photographic and descriptive guide to over
4,000 garden plants, arranged by plant type,
size, season of interest, and color.

☐ PINK

Aesculus hippocastanum
(European horse chestnut)
Vigorous, deciduous, spreading tree.
Has large leaves with 5 or 7 leaflets and
spires of white flowers, flushed pink and
yellow in centers, in spring.
Spiny fruits contain glossy,
brown nuts in autumn.

☀ ◊ ❄❄❄ 4–7

Magnolia campbellii var.
mollicomata
Deciduous tree similar to *M. campbellii*
(below) but producing lilac-pink
flowers slightly earlier in the year and
on trees about 10 years old
or more.

☀ ◊ ❄❄ 7–9

Magnolia x veitchii 'Peter Veitch'
Fast-growing, deciduous, spreading tree
with large, fragrant, pale pink and white
flowers borne in mid-spring, before dark
green leaves emerge. Usually flowers
within 10 years of planting.

☀ ◊ ❄❄ 7–9

Magnolia campbellii
Deciduous tree, upright when young,
later spreading. Large, slightly
fragrant, pale to deep pink flowers are
borne on leafless branches from late
winter to mid-spring on
trees 15–20 years old
or more.

☀ ◊ ❄❄ 7–9

Magnolia sprengeri 'Wakehurst'
Deciduous, spreading tree. Large,
fragrant flowers, rich pink inside, deep
purplish pink outside, appear on the
leafless branches during mid-spring.

☀ ◊ ❄❄ 7–9

Magnolia campbellii 'Darjeeling'
Deciduous tree similar to *M. campbellii*
(left) but bearing large, very deep pink
flowers from late winter to mid-spring
on trees 15–20 years old or more.

☀ ◊ ❄❄ 7–9

☐ RED–YELLOW

Aesculus x carnea 'Briotii'
(Ruby horse chestnut)
Deciduous, round-headed tree. Leaves, consisting of 5 or 7 leaflets, are glossy, dark green. Panicles of red flowers are borne in late spring.

☀ ◊ ❄❄❄ 5–8

Acer macrophyllum
(Bigleaf maple, Oregon maple)
Deciduous, round-headed tree with large, deeply lobed, dark green leaves that turn yellow and orange in autumn. Yellowish green flowers in spring are followed by pale green fruits.

☀ ◊ ❄❄❄ 6–9

☐ WHITE

Aesculus chinensis
Slow-growing, deciduous, spreading tree. Leaves are glossy, dark green with 7 leaflets. Slender spires of white flowers are produced in mid-summer.

☀ ◊ ❄❄❄ 5–8

Populus alba (Silver-leaved poplar, White poplar)
Deciduous, spreading tree with wavy-margined or lobed leaves, dark green above, white beneath, turning yellow in autumn.

☀ ◊ ❄❄❄ 4–9

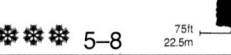

Magnolia hypoleuca,
syn. *M. obovata*
(Whiteleaf Japanese magnolia)
Vigorous, deciduous, upright tree. Large, fragrant, pink-flushed, white or pale cream flowers with crimson stamens appear in early summer.

☀ ◊ ❄❄❄ 5–9

☐ [colour key]

Populus maximowiczii
Fast-growing, deciduous, conical tree. Oval, heart-shaped, bright green leaves have green-veined, white undersides and turn yellow in autumn. Bears long, pendent seed heads surrounded by silky, white hairs in late summer.

☀ ◖ ❄❄❄ 4–7

Liriodendron tulipifera (Tulip tree)
Vigorous, deciduous, spreading tree. Deep green leaves, with a cut-off or notched tip and lobed sides, turn yellow in autumn. Tulip-shaped, orange-marked, greenish white flowers appear in mid-summer.

☀ ◊ ❄❄❄ 4–9

Castanea sativa 'Albomarginata'
Deciduous, spreading tree. Has glossy, white-edged, dark green leaves that turn yellow in autumn. Spikes of creamy yellow flowers in summer are followed by edible fruits in autumn.

☀ ◊ ❄❄❄ 5–8

☐ RED–PURPLE

Prunus serotina
(Black cherry, Rum cherry)
Deciduous, spreading tree. Spikes of fragrant white flowers appear in early summer followed by red fruits that turn black in autumn. Glossy, dark green leaves become yellow in autumn.

☀ ◊ ❄❄❄ 4–8

Brachychiton acerifolius,
syn. *Sterculia acerifolia*
(Flame bottle tree, Flame tree)
Deciduous tree with clusters of bright scarlet flowers in late winter, spring or summer before 3–7-lobed, lustrous leaves develop.
Min. 45–50°F (7–10°C).

☀ ◊ 9–10

Fagus sylvatica f. **purpurea**
(European purple beech)
Deciduous, round-headed tree with oval, wavy-margined, purple leaves. In autumn, leaves turn a rich coppery color.

☀ ◊ ❄❄❄ 4–7

◼◼ PURPLE–GREEN   ◻ GREEN

***Acer platanoides* 'Crimson King'**
(Crimson King Norway maple)
Vigorous, deciduous, spreading tree.
Leaves are large, lobed, and deep
reddish purple, turning orange in
autumn. Tiny, red-tinged,
deep yellow flowers are
carried in mid-spring.

☼ ◊ ❄❄❄ 4–7

Populus canescens
(Gray poplar)
Vigorous, deciduous, spreading tree
with slightly lobed leaves, gray when
young, glossy, dark green in summer
and yellow in autumn.
Usually bears grayish
red catkins in spring.

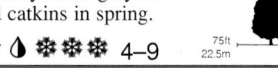

☼ ◊ ❄❄❄ 4–9

***Populus* x *canadensis* 'Serotina
de Selys'**, syn. *P.* x *c.* 'Serotina
Erecta'
Fast-growing, deciduous, upright tree.
Has broadly oval, gray-green leaves,
pale green when young,
and red catkins in spring.

☼ ◊ ❄❄❄ 4–9

Quercus macranthera
Handsome, deciduous, spreading,
stout-branched tree with large, deeply
lobed, dark green leaves.

☼ ◊ ❄❄❄ 6–8

Alnus incana (White alder)
Deciduous, conical tree useful for cold,
wet areas and poor soils. Yellow-brown
catkins are carried in late winter and
early spring, followed by oval, dark
green leaves.

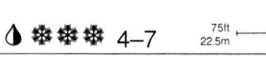

☼ ◊ ❄❄❄ 4–7

Fagus sylvatica* f. *pendula
(Weeping European beech)
Deciduous, weeping tree with oval,
wavy-edged leaves that in autumn
take on rich hues of yellow and
orange-brown.

☼ ◊ ❄❄❄ 4–7

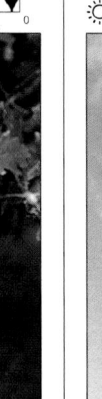

Quercus robur* f. *fastigiata
(Pyramidal English oak)
Deciduous, upright, columnar tree
of dense habit carrying lobed, dark
green leaves.

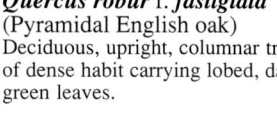
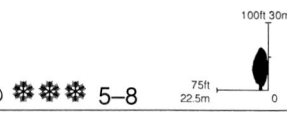

☼ ◊ ❄❄❄ 5–8

***Populus* x *canadensis* 'Robusta'**
Fast-growing, deciduous, conical tree
with upright branches. Broadly oval,
bronze, young leaves mature to glossy,
dark green. Bears long, red catkins
in spring.

☼ ◊ ❄❄❄ 4–9

Alnus cordata (Italian alder)
Fast-growing, deciduous, conical tree.
Yellow, male catkins appear in late
winter and early spring, followed by
heart-shaped, glossy, deep green
leaves. Has persistent,
round, woody fruits
in autumn.

☼ ◊ ❄❄❄ 5–7   75ft 22.5m / 100ft 30m

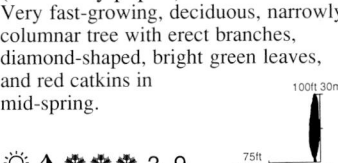

***Populus nigra* 'Italica'**
(Lombardy poplar)
Very fast-growing, deciduous, narrowly
columnar tree with erect branches,
diamond-shaped, bright green leaves,
and red catkins in
mid-spring.

☼ ◊ ❄❄❄ 3–9   75ft 22.5m / 100ft 30m

Quercus canariensis
Deciduous or semi-evergreen tree,
narrow when young, broadening with
age. Large, shallowly lobed, rich green
leaves become yellowish brown in
autumn, often persisting
into late winter.

☼ ◊ ❄❄❄ 7–9   75ft 22.5m / 100ft 30m

Acer lobelii (Lobel maple)
Deciduous, upright tree of narrow
width, well suited for growing in
restricted space. Has wavy-edged,
lobed leaves that turn yellow
in autumn.

☼ ◊ ❄❄❄ 7–9   75ft 22.5m / 100ft 30m

Juglans regia (English walnut,
Persian walnut)
Deciduous tree with a spreading head.
Leaves, usually with 5 or 7 leaflets, are
aromatic, bronze-purple when young,
glossy, green when
mature. Produces
edible nuts.

☼ ◊ ❄❄❄ 5–8   75ft 22.5m / 100ft 30m

Tilia oliveri
Deciduous, spreading, open tree with
pointed, heart-shaped leaves, bright
green above and silvery white beneath.
Produces small, fragrant, greenish
yellow flowers in summer,
followed by winged fruits.

☼ ◊ ❄❄❄ 5–8   75ft 22.5m / 100ft 30m

Quercus muehlenbergii
(Chinquapin oak, Yellow
chestnut oak)
Deciduous, round-headed tree with
sharply toothed, bright green leaves.

☼ ◊ ❄❄❄ 4–8   75ft 22.5m / 100ft 30m

Celtis australis
(European hackberry)
Deciduous, spreading tree. Has oval,
pointed, sharply toothed, dark green
leaves and small, purple-black fruits.

☼ ◊ ❄❄❄ 6–9   75ft 22.5m / 100ft 30m

Trees/large SUMMER INTEREST

■ GREEN

Platanus × acerifolia
(London plane tree)
Vigorous, deciduous, spreading tree
with ornamental, flaking bark. Has
large, sharply lobed, bright green
leaves. Spherical fruit
clusters hang from
shoots in autumn.

☼ ◊ ❄❄❄ 5–8

Nothofagus procera
Fast-growing, deciduous, conical tree.
Leaves, with many impressed veins,
are dark green, turning orange and red
in autumn.

☼ ◊ ❄❄❄ 8–9

Juglans nigra
(Eastern black walnut)
Handsome, fast-growing, deciduous,
spreading tree with large, aromatic
leaves of many pointed, glossy, dark
green leaflets. Produces
edible nuts in autumn.

☼ ◊ ❄❄❄ 5–9

Sassafras albidum (Sassafras)
Deciduous, upright, later spreading
tree. Aromatic, glossy, dark green
leaves vary from oval to deeply lobed
and turn yellow or red in autumn. Has
insignificant, yellowish
green flowers in spring.

☼ ◊ ❄❄❄ 5–8

Juglans ailantifolia var.
cordiformis (Heartnut)
Deciduous, spreading tree with large,
aromatic leaves consisting of many
glossy, bright green leaflets. Long,
yellow-green, male catkins
are borne in early summer.
In autumn has edible nuts.

☼ ◊ ❄❄❄ 5–8

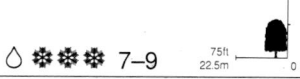

Quercus nigra
(Possum oak, Water oak)
Deciduous, spreading tree with glossy,
bright green foliage retained until well
into winter.

◊ ❄❄❄ 7–9

Nothofagus obliqua
Elegant, fast-growing, deciduous tree
with slender, arching branches. Has
deep green leaves that turn orange and
red in autumn.

☼ ◊ ❄❄❄ 8–9

Firmiana simplex, syn. *F.
platanifolia, Sterculia platanifolia*
(Chinese parasol tree)
Robust, deciduous tree with large,
lobed leaves, small, showy, lemon
yellow flowers, and
papery, leaflike fruits.
Min. 36°F (2°C).

☼ ◊ 8–10

Tilia 'Petiolaris'
(Pendent silver linden)
Deciduous, spreading tree with pendent
branches. Pointed, heart-shaped leaves,
dark green above, silver beneath,
shimmer in the breeze. Has
fragrant, creamy yellow
flowers in late summer.

☼ ◊ ❄❄❄ 5–9

Quercus petraea 'Columna'
Deciduous, upright, slender tree
with large, wavy-edged, leathery,
dark green leaves, tinged bronze
when young.

☀ ◊ ❅❅❅❅ 5–8   100ft 30m / 75ft 22.5m / 0

Quercus frainetto
Fast-growing, deciduous, spreading
tree with a large, domed head and
handsome, large, deeply lobed, dark
green leaves.

☀ ◊ ❅❅❅ 6–8   100ft 30m / 75ft 22.5m / 0

Quercus palustris
(Pin oak, Swamp oak)
Fast-growing, deciduous, spreading
tree with slender branches, pendulous
at the tips. Deeply lobed, glossy, bright
green leaves turn scarlet
or red-brown in autumn.

☀ ◊ ❅❅❅ 5–8   100ft 30m / 75ft 22.5m / 0

Carya ovata (Shagbark hickory)
Deciduous tree with flaking, gray
bark. Has dark green leaves, usually
consisting of 5 slender leaflets, that
turn golden yellow in autumn.

☀ ◊ ❅❅❅❅ 5–8   100ft 30m / 75ft 22.5m / 0

Quercus castaneifolia
Deciduous, spreading tree with sharply
toothed leaves, glossy, dark green
above, gray beneath.

☀ ◊ ❅❅❅❅ 7–9   100ft 30m / 75ft 22.5m / 0

Fagus sylvatica (European beech)
Deciduous, spreading tree with wavy-
edged, oval leaves. These are pale
green when young, mid- to dark green
when mature, and turn rich yellow and
orange-brown in autumn,
when nuts are produced.

☀ ◊ ❅❅❅ 4–7   100ft 30m / 75ft 22.5m / 0

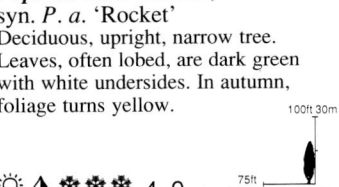

Populus alba 'Raket',
syn. *P. a.* 'Rocket'
Deciduous, upright, narrow tree.
Leaves, often lobed, are dark green
with white undersides. In autumn,
foliage turns yellow.

☀ ◐ ❅❅❅ 4–9   100ft 30m / 75ft 22.5m / 0

Quercus laurifolia (Laurel oak)
Deciduous, round-headed tree with
narrow, glossy, bright green leaves,
bronze-tinged when young, that are
retained until late in the year.

☀ ◊ ❅❅❅ 7–9   100ft 30m / 75ft 22.5m / 0

🟩🟨 GREEN–YELLOW

Quercus rubra (Red oak)
Fast-growing, deciduous, spreading tree. Attractively lobed leaves, often large, are deep green and become reddish or yellowish brown in autumn.

☀ ◊ ❄❄❄ 4–8

***Liriodendron tulipifera* 'Aureomarginatum'**
Vigorous, deciduous tree. Deep green leaves have yellow margins, cut-off or notched tips, and lobed sides. Bears cup-shaped, greenish white flowers, splashed orange, in summer on mature trees.

☀ ◊ ❄❄❄ 4–9

Pterocarya* x *rehderiana
Very fast-growing, deciduous, spreading tree. Has glossy, bright green leaves consisting of narrow, paired leaflets that turn yellow in autumn and long catkins of winged fruits in late summer and autumn.

☀ ◊ ❄❄❄ 5–9

Trees/large AUTUMN INTEREST

🟪🟥 PINK–RED

Chorisia speciosa (Floss-silk tree)
Fast-growing, deciduous tree, the trunk and branches studded with thick, conical thorns. Pink to burgundy flowers appear as indented, light green leaves fall.
Min. 59°F (15°C).

☀ ◊ 9–10

***Acer rubrum* 'Scanlon'**
Deciduous, upright tree. Has lobed, dark green foliage that in autumn becomes bright red, particularly in acid or neutral soil. Clusters of small, red flowers decorate bare branches in spring.

☀ ◊ ❄❄❄ 4–9

Liquidambar styraciflua
(American sweet gum)
Deciduous, conical to spreading tree. Shoots develop corky ridges. Lobed, glossy, dark green leaves turn brilliant orange, red, and purple in autumn.

☀ ◊ ❄❄❄ 6–9

Quercus ellipsoidalis
Deciduous, spreading tree with deep-lobed, glossy, dark green leaves that turn dark purplish red, then red in autumn.

☀ ◊ ❄❄❄ 4–7

Quercus coccinea (Scarlet oak)
Deciduous, round-headed tree. Glossy, dark green leaves have deeply cut lobes ending in slender teeth. In autumn, they turn bright red, usually persisting for several weeks on the tree.

☀ ◊ ❄❄❄ 5–9

Acer pseudoplatanus* f. *erythrocarpum
Vigorous, deciduous, spreading tree with lobed, deep green leaves. Wings of young autumn fruits are bright red.

☀ ◊ ❄❄❄ 5–8

***Acer rubrum* 'Schlesingeri'**
Deciduous, round-headed tree. In early autumn, dark green leaves turn deep red. Tiny, red flowers appear on bare wood in spring.

☀ ◊ ❄❄❄ 4–9

Acer rubrum (Red maple, Scarlet maple, Swamp maple)
Deciduous, round-headed tree. Dark green leaves turn bright red in autumn, producing best color in acid or neutral soil. In spring, bare branches are covered with tiny, red flowers.

☀ ◊ ❄❄❄ 4–9

Cercidiphyllum japonicum
(Katsura tree)
Fast-growing, deciduous, spreading
tree. Leaves, bronze when young, turn
rich green, then yellow to purple in
autumn, especially on acid
soil. Fallen leaves smell
of burnt toffee.

 5–9

Nyssa sylvatica (Black gum,
Black tupelo, Sour gum)
Deciduous, broadly conical tree with
oval, glossy, dark to mid-green leaves
that turn brilliant yellow, orange, and
red in autumn.

5–9

Quercus alba
(White oak)
Deciduous, spreading tree. Deeply
lobed, glossy, dark green leaves turn
reddish purple in autumn.

 5–9

Spathodea campanulata (African
tulip tree, Flame-of-the-forest)
Evergreen, showy tree. Leaves have
9–19 deep green leaflets. Clusters
of tulip-shaped, scarlet or orange-
red flowers appear
intermittently. Min.
61–4°F (16–18°C).

10

Prunus avium
(Mazzard cherry, Sweet cherry)
Deciduous, spreading tree with red-
banded bark. Has sprays of white
flowers in spring, deep red fruits, and
dark green leaves that turn
red and yellow in autumn.

 4–8

***Acer platanoides* 'Lorbergii'**
Vigorous, deciduous, spreading tree.
Deeply divided, pale green leaves with
slender lobes turn yellow or reddish
orange in autumn. Tiny, yellow
flowers appear in
mid-spring.

 4–7

Quercus phellos (Willow oak)
Elegant, deciduous, spreading tree.
Narrow, willowlike, pale green leaves
turn yellow then brown
in autumn.

 6–9

Zelkova serrata (Japanese zelkova)
Deciduous, spreading tree with sharp-
toothed, finely pointed, dark green
leaves that turn yellow or orange
in autumn.

 6–8

***Sophora japonica* 'Violacea'**
Fast-growing, deciduous, round-
headed tree. Large sprays of pealike,
white flowers, tinged with lilac-pink,
appear in late summer and
early autumn.

 5–9

■□ WHITE–GREEN   ■ GREEN

Betula ermanii (Erman birch)
Elegant, deciduous, open-branched tree that has peeling, pinkish white bark, distinctively marked with large lenticels. Oval, glossy, green leaves give excellent autumn color.

☀ ◊ ❄❄❄ 5–8   100ft 30m / 75ft 22.5m / 0

Ficus benghalensis (Banyan tree)
Evergreen, wide-spreading tree with trunklike prop roots. Has oval, leathery leaves, rich green with pale veins, to 8in (20cm) long, and small, figlike, brown fruits. Min. 59–64°F (15–18°C).

☀ ◊ 9–10   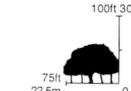 100ft 30m / 75ft 22.5m / 0

Eucalyptus coccifera
(Tasmanian snow gum)
Evergreen tree with peeling, blue-gray and white bark and aromatic, pointed, gray-green leaves. Bears clusters of white flowers, with numerous stamens, in summer.

☀ ◊ ❄❄ 9–10   100ft 30m / 75ft 22.5m / 0

Eucalyptus dalrympleana
(Mountain gum)
Vigorous, evergreen tree. Creamy white, young bark becomes pinkish gray, then peels. Leaves are long, narrow, and pendent. Clusters of white flowers appear in late summer and autumn.

☀ ◊ ❄❄ 9–10   100ft 30m / 75ft 22.5m / 0

Eucalyptus gunnii (Cider gum)
Evergreen, conical tree with peeling, cream, pinkish, and brown bark. Leaves are silver-blue when young, blue-green when mature. Clusters of white flowers, with numerous stamens, appear in mid-summer.

☀ ◊ ❄❄ 8–10   100ft 30m / 75ft 22.5m / 0

Betula papyrifera
(Canoe birch, Paper birch)
Vigorous, deciduous, open-branched, round-headed tree with peeling, shiny, white bark, yellowish catkins in spring, and oval, coarsely serrated leaves that turn clear yellow in autumn.

☀ ◊ ❄❄❄ 2–8   100ft 30m / 75ft 22.5m / 0

Ficus elastica 'Doescheri'
Vigorous, evergreen, upright then spreading tree with oblong to oval, leathery, lustrous, deep green leaves, patterned with gray-green, yellow, and white. Min. 50°F (10°C).

☀ ◊ 10    100ft 30m / 75ft 22.5m / 0

Archontophoenix alexandrae
(Alexandra palm)
Evergreen palm with feather-shaped, arching leaves. Mature trees bear sprays of small, white or cream flowers. Min. 59°F (15°C).

☀ ◊ 10   100ft 30m / 75ft 22.5m / 0

Quercus* x *turneri
Semi-evergreen, rounded, dense tree.
Lobed, leathery, dark green leaves
fall just before new foliage appears
in spring.

☼ ◊ ❋❋❋ 6–9

Nothofagus dombeyi
Elegant, evergreen, loosely conical
tree with shoots that droop at the tips.
Leaves are sharply toothed, glossy,
and dark green.

☼ ◖ ❋❋ 8–9

Quercus suber (Cork oak)
Evergreen, round-headed tree with
thick, corky bark. Oval, leathery leaves
are glossy, dark green above and
grayish beneath.

☼ ◊ ❋❋ 7–9

***Betula pendula* 'Dalecarlica'**
(Cutleaf European birch)
Elegant, deciduous, slender tree with
white bark and lightly pendulous
branchlets. Deeply cut leaves have
serrated lobes and provide
excellent golden color
in autumn.

☼ ◊ ❋❋❋ 3–8

Washingtonia robusta
(Washington palm)
Fast-growing, evergreen palm with
large, fan-shaped leaves and, in summer,
tiny, creamy white flowers in large,
long-stalked sprays. Black
berries appear in winter-
spring. Min. 50°F (10°C).

☼ ◊ 9–10

Macadamia integrifolia
(Queensland nut)
Evergreen, spreading tree with edible,
brown nuts in autumn. Has whorls of
leathery, semi-glossy leaves and
panicles of small, creamy
yellow flowers in spring.
Min. 50–55°F (10–13°C).

☼ ◊ 10

Arecastrum romanzoffianum
(Queen palm)
Majestic, evergreen palm. Has arching
or pendent, feather-shaped leaves with
lustrous, green leaflets. Mature trees
carry huge clusters of small,
yellow flowers in summer.
Min. 64°F (18°C).

☼ ◊ 10

Quercus* x *hispanica
'Lucombeana'
Semi-evergreen, spreading tree with
toothed leaves, glossy, dark green
above, gray beneath.

☼ ◊ ❋❋❋ 7–9

■ GREEN

□ YELLOW

Betula albo-sinensis
(Chinese paper birch)
Elegant, deciduous, open-branched
tree with serrated, oval to lance-
shaped, pale green leaves. Peeling bark
is honey-colored or
reddish maroon with
a gray bloom.

☼ ◊ ❀❀❀ 6–8   100ft 30m / 75ft 22.5m / 0

Umbellularia californica
(California laurel)
Evergreen, spreading tree with
aromatic, leathery, glossy, dark green
leaves and creamy yellow flowers in
late spring. Pungent leaves
may cause nausea and
headache when crushed.

☼ ◖ ❀❀ 8–10   100ft 30m / 75ft 22.5m / 0

Salix alba var. **vitellina**
(Golden willow)
Deciduous, spreading tree, usually cut
back hard to promote growth of strong,
young shoots that are bright orange-
yellow in winter. Lance-
shaped, green leaves
appear in spring.

☼ ◖ ❀❀❀ 4–9   100ft 30m / 75ft 22.5m / 0

Nothofagus betuloides
Evergreen, columnar tree with dense
growth of oval, glossy, dark green
leaves on bronze-red shoots.

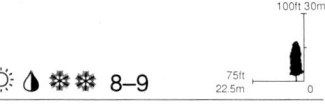

☼ ◖ ❀❀ 8–9   100ft 30m / 75ft 22.5m / 0

Salix 'Chrysocoma', syn. *S. alba*
'Tristis' (Golden weeping willow)
Deciduous, wide-spreading tree with
slender, pendulous, yellow shoots
falling to the ground as a curtain.
Yellow-green, young
leaves mature to
darker green.

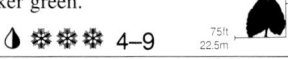

☼ ◖ ❀❀❀ 4–9   100ft 30m / 75ft 22.5m / 0

□ WHITE

Malus hupehensis (Tea crab apple)
Vigorous, deciduous, spreading tree.
Has deep green leaves, large, fragrant
white flowers, pink in bud, from mid-
to late spring, followed by small, red-
tinged, yellow crab apples
in late summer and
autumn.

☼ ◊ ❀❀❀ 5–8   50ft 15m / 0

Malus baccata var. **mandschurica**
Vigorous, deciduous, spreading tree
with dark green leaves and a profusion
of white flowers in clusters in mid-
spring, followed by long-lasting, small,
red or yellow crab apples.

☼ ◊ ❀❀❀ 3–7   50ft 15m / 0

Salix daphnoides
Fast-growing, deciduous, spreading
tree. Has lance-shaped, glossy, dark
green leaves, silver, male catkins in
spring, and purple shoots with bluish
white bloom in winter.

☼ ◖ ❀❀❀ 5–9   50ft 15m / 0

Pyrus calleryana 'Chanticleer'
(Chanticleer pear)
Deciduous, conical tree with glossy
leaves that turn purplish in autumn.
Sprays of small, white flowers appear
in spring. Resists
fire blight.

☼ ◊ ❀❀❀ 5–8   50ft 15m / 0

Magnolia kobus
Deciduous, broadly conical tree.
Bears a profusion of fragrant, pure
white flowers in mid-spring before
small, slightly aromatic, dark green
leaves appear.

☼ ◊ ❀❀❀ 5–9   50ft 15m / 0

Magnolia 'Charles Coates'
Deciduous, rounded, open, spreading
tree. Very fragrant, creamy white
flowers with red stamens appear in late
spring and early summer amid large,
light green leaves.

☼ ◊ ❀❀❀ 6–9   50ft 15m / 0

Prunus avium 'Plena'
(Double mazzard cherry)
Deciduous, spreading tree with reddish brown bark and masses of double, pure white flowers in spring. Dark green foliage turns red in autumn.

☼ ◊ ❄❄❄ 4–8

Paulownia tomentosa,
syn. *P. imperialis* (Empress tree, Princess tree, Royal paulownia)
Deciduous, spreading tree. Has large, lobed leaves and terminal sprays of fragrant, foxglovelike, pinkish lilac flowers in spring.

☼ ◊ ❄❄ 6–9

Cornus nuttallii
(Pacific dogwood)
Deciduous, conical tree. Large, white bracts, surrounding tiny flowers, appear in late spring. Has oval, dark green leaves.

☼ ◊ ❄❄❄ 7–8

Fraxinus ornus (Flowering ash)
Deciduous, round-headed tree. Has deep green leaves with 5–9 leaflets. Panicles of scented, creamy white flowers appear in late spring and early summer.

☼ ◊ ❄❄❄ 6–9

Melia azedarach (Chinaberry)
Deciduous, spreading tree. Has dark green leaves with many leaflets and fragrant, star-shaped, pinkish lilac flowers in spring, followed by pale orange-yellow fruits in autumn.

☼ ◊ ❄❄ 7–10

Prunus mahaleb
(Mahaleb cherry)
Deciduous, round-headed, bushy tree that bears a profusion of fragrant, cup-shaped, white flowers from mid- to late spring. Rounded, glossy, dark green leaves turn yellow in autumn.

☼ ◊ ❄❄❄ 6–8

Halesia monticola
(Mountain silver-bell)
Fast-growing, deciduous, conical or spreading tree. Masses of pendent, bell-shaped, white flowers appear in late spring before leaves, followed by 4-winged fruits in autumn.

☼ ◊ ❄❄❄ 6–9

Prunus padus
Deciduous, spreading tree, conical when young. Bears fragrant white flowers in pendent spikes during late spring, followed by small, black fruits in late summer. Dark green leaves turn yellow in autumn.

☼ ◊ ❄❄❄ 4–8

Prunus serrulata var. **spontanea**
Deciduous, spreading tree bearing cup-shaped, white or pink flowers from mid- to late spring. Oval leaves, bronze when young, mature to deep green.

☼ ◊ ❄❄❄ 6–9

▢▢ PINK–YELLOW

▢ WHITE

Prunus 'Kanzan'
Deciduous, vase-shaped tree. Large, double, pink to purple flowers are borne profusely from mid- to late spring amid bronze, young leaves that mature to dark green.

☼ ◊ ❋❋❋ 6–8

Malus 'Profusion'
Deciduous, spreading tree. Dark green foliage is purple when young. Cup-shaped, deep purplish pink flowers are freely borne in late spring, followed by small, reddish purple crab apples in late summer and autumn.

☼ ◊ ❋❋❋ 5–8

Gleditsia triacanthos 'Sunburst'
(Sunburst honey lotus)
Deciduous, spreading tree with fernlike, glossy foliage that is golden yellow when young, deep green in summer.

☼ ◊ ❋❋❋ 5–9

Styrax japonica
(Japanese snowbell)
Deciduous, spreading tree bearing in early summer a profusion of pendent, fragrant, bell-shaped, white flowers amid glossy, dark green foliage.

☼ ◊ pH ❋❋❋ 5–9

Ostrya virginiana (American hop hornbeam, Ironwood)
Deciduous, conical tree with dark brown bark and deep green leaves, yellow in autumn. Has yellowish catkins in spring, followed by greenish white fruit clusters.

☼ ◊ ❋❋❋ 5–9

Oxydendrum arboreum
(Sorrel tree, Sourwood)
Deciduous, spreading tree with glossy, dark green foliage that turns bright red in autumn. Sprays of white flowers appear in late summer and autumn.

☼ ◊ pH ❋❋❋ 5–9

Davidia involucrata
(Dove tree, Handkerchief tree)
Deciduous, conical tree with heart-shaped, vivid green leaves, felted beneath. Large, white bracts appear on mature trees from late spring.

☼ ◊ ❋❋❋ 7–9

Magnolia fraseri
(Fraser magnolia)
Deciduous, spreading, open tree. Fragrant white or pale yellow flowers open in late spring and early summer amid large, pale green leaves.

☼ ◊ ❋❋❋ 6–9

Sorbus cuspidata
Deciduous, broadly conical tree. Has very large, veined, gray-green leaves, white-haired when young. Heads of pink-stamened, white flowers in late spring or early summer are followed by russet or yellowish red fruits.

☼ ◊ ❋❋❋ 6–8

Catalpa bignonioides
(Southern catalpa)
Deciduous, spreading tree. Large, light green leaves are purplish when young. White flowers marked with yellow and purple appear in summer, followed by long, cylindrical, pendent pods.

☼ ◊ ❄❄❄ 5–9

Cornus macrophylla
(Bigleaf dogwood)
Deciduous, spreading tree. Clusters of small, creamy white flowers appear in summer. Glossy, bright green leaves are large, pointed, and oval.

☼ ◊ ❄❄❄ 7–8

Catalpa speciosa (Northern catalpa)
Deciduous, spreading tree. Heads of large, white flowers marked with yellow and purple are borne in mid-summer among glossy, green leaves.

☼ ◊ ❄❄❄ 5–9

Magnolia tripetala
Deciduous, spreading, open tree, conical when young. Has large, dark green leaves, clustered at shoot tips, and rather unpleasantly scented, creamy white flowers with narrow petals in late spring and early summer.

☼ ◊ ❄❄❄ 5–9

***Sorbus aria* 'Lutescens'**
Deciduous, spreading tree, upright when young. Young foliage is silvery, maturing to gray-green. White flowers in late spring and early summer are followed by orange-red fruits in autumn.

☼ ◊ ❄❄❄ 6–8

Stewartia pseudocamellia
(Japanese stewartia)
Deciduous, spreading tree with ornamental, peeling bark. Bears white flowers in mid-summer. Foliage turns orange and red in autumn.

☼ ◊ pH ❄❄❄ 7–9

Drimys winteri (Winter's bark)
Evergreen, conical, sometimes shrubby tree with long, glossy, pale or dark green leaves, usually bluish white beneath. Bears clusters of fragrant, star-shaped, white flowers in early summer.

☼ ◊ ❄❄ 9–10

***Magnolia grandiflora* 'Exmouth'**
Evergreen, broadly conical or rounded, dense-foliaged tree. Large, very fragrant, creamy white flowers appear intermittently from mid-summer to early autumn. Leaves are narrow, leathery, and dark green.

☼ ◊ ❄❄ 7–9

***Quercus cerris* 'Variegata'**
(Variegated turkey oak)
Deciduous, spreading tree. Strongly toothed or lobed, glossy, dark green leaves are edged with creamy white.

☼ ◊ ❄❄❄ 7–9

Acer pseudoplatanus 'Simon Louis Frères'
Deciduous, spreading tree. Young leaves are marked with creamy white and pink; older foliage is pale green with white markings.

☀ ◊ ❄❄❄ 5–8

Acer negundo 'Variegatum' (Variegated box elder)
Fast-growing, deciduous, spreading tree. Has pinkish- then white-margined, bright green leaves with 3 or 5 leaflets. Inconspicuous, greenish yellow flowers appear in late spring.

☀ ◊ ❄❄❄ 3–9

Jacaranda mimosifolia, syn. *J. ovalifolia* (Jacaranda)
Fast-growing, deciduous, rounded tree with fernlike leaves of many tiny, bright green leaflets. Has trusses of vivid blue to blue-purple flowers in spring and early summer. Min. 45°F (7°C).

☀ ◊ 10

Broussonetia papyrifera (Common paper-mulberry)
Deciduous, round-headed tree. Dull green leaves are large, broadly oval, toothed and sometimes lobed. In early summer, small globes of purple flowers appear on female plants.

☀ ◊ ❄❄ 7–9

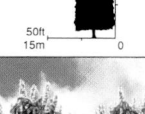

Aesculus indica 'Sydney Pearce'
Deciduous, spreading tree with glossy, dark green leaves, bronze when young and orange or yellow in autumn. Pinkish white flowers, marked red and yellow, appear from early to mid-summer.

☀ ◊ ❄❄❄ 4–8

Sorbus thibetica 'John Mitchell', syn. *S.* 'Mitchellii'
Strong-growing, deciduous, conical tree with dark green leaves, silvery beneath. Has white flowers in spring and brown fruits in late summer.

☀ ◊ ❄❄❄ 5–7

Hovenia dulcis (Japanese raisin-tree)
Deciduous, spreading tree with large, glossy, dark green leaves. In summer it may bear small, greenish yellow flowers, the stalks of which become red, fleshy, and edible.

☀ ◊ ❄❄❄ 6–8

Cedrela sinensis, syn. *Toona sinensis* (Chinese toon)
Deciduous, spreading tree with shaggy bark when old. Dark green leaves with many leaflets turn yellow in autumn. Bears fragrant white flowers in mid-summer. Shoots are onion-scented.

☀ ◊ ❄❄❄ 6–9

Populus tremula 'Pendula'
Vigorous, deciduous, weeping tree. Leaves, reddish when young, gray-green in summer, and yellow in autumn, tremble in the wind. Has purplish catkins in late winter and spring.

☀ ◊ ❄❄❄ 4–9

Quercus marilandica
(Blackjack oak)
Deciduous, spreading tree. Large leaves, 3-lobed at the apex, are glossy, dark green above, paler beneath, and turn yellow, red, or brown in autumn.

☼ ◌ ❋❋❋ 6–9

Fraxinus velutina (Velvet ash)
Deciduous, spreading tree. Leaves vary but usually consist of 3 or 5 narrow, velvety, gray-green leaflets.

☼ ◌ ❋❋❋ 6–8

Quercus garryana
(Oregon oak, Oregon white oak)
Slow-growing, deciduous, spreading tree with deeply lobed, glossy, bright green leaves.

☼ ◌ ❋❋❋ 7–9

Tilia cordata 'Rancho'
Deciduous, conical, dense tree, spreading when young. Has small, oval, glossy, dark green leaves and clusters of small, fragrant, cup-shaped, yellowish flowers are borne in mid-summer.

☼ ◌ ❋❋❋ 4–8

Meliosma veitchiorum
Deciduous, spreading tree with stout, gray shoots and large, dark green, red-stalked leaves with 9 or 11 leaflets. Small, fragrant white flowers in late spring are followed by violet fruits in autumn.

☼ ◌ ❋❋ 7–9

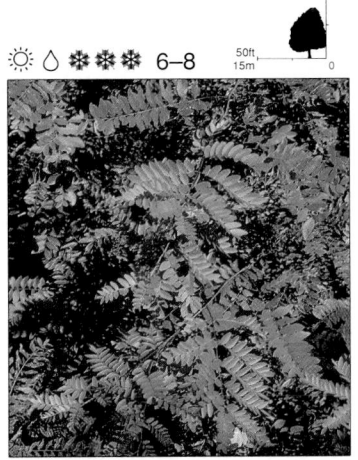

Gleditsia japonica
Deciduous, conical tree with a trunk armed with spines. Shoots are purplish when young. Fernlike leaves consist of many small, green leaflets.

☼ ◌ ❋❋❋ 8–10

Emmenopterys henryi
Deciduous, spreading tree. Large, pointed, dark green leaves are bronze-purple when young. Clusters of white flowers (some bearing a large, white bract) are rarely produced except in hot summers.

☼ ◌ ❋❋ 8–10

Idesia polycarpa
Deciduous, spreading tree with large, heart-shaped, glossy, dark green leaves on long stalks. Small, fragrant yellow-green flowers in mid-summer are followed in autumn, on female plants, by red fruits hanging in clusters.

☼ ◌ ❋❋❋ 7–9

Kalopanax pictus, syn. *K. ricinifolius, Acanthopanax ricinifolium*
Deciduous, spreading tree with spiny stems, large, 5–7-lobed, glossy, dark green leaves, and umbels of small, white flowers, followed by black fruits in autumn.

☼ ◌ ❋❋❋ 5–9

Quercus macrocarpa
(Bur oak, Mossy-cup oak)
Slow-growing, deciduous, spreading tree. Large, oblong-oval, lobed, glossy, dark green leaves turn yellow or brown in autumn.

☼ ◌ ❋❋❋ 3–9

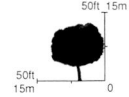

Quercus macrolepis
Deciduous or semi-evergreen, spreading tree. Has gray-green leaves with angular lobes.

☼ ◌ ❋❋❋ 8–9

Quercus rubra 'Aurea'
Slow-growing, deciduous, spreading tree. Large, lobed leaves are clear yellow when young, becoming green by mid-summer. Produces best color in an open but sheltered position.

☼ ◌ ❋❋❋ 4–8

53

GREEN–YELLOW

WHITE–RED

Phellodendron chinense
Deciduous, spreading tree. Aromatic leaves, with 7–13 oblong leaflets, are dark green, turning yellow in autumn. Pendent racemes of greenish flowers in early summer are followed on female trees by berrylike, black fruits.

☼ ◊ ❄❄❄ 6–9

Eucryphia × nymansensis
Evergreen, columnar tree. Some of the leathery, glossy, dark green leaves are simple, others consist of 3 (rarely 5) leaflets. Clusters of large, white flowers open in late summer or early autumn.

☼◐ ◊ ❄❄ 8–9

Acer davidii 'Madeline Spitta'
Deciduous tree with upright branches that are striped green and white. Glossy, dark green foliage turns orange in autumn after the appearance of winged, green fruits that ripen reddish brown.

☼ ◊ ❄❄❄ 6–8

Sorbus aucuparia
(European mountain ash, Rowan)
Deciduous, spreading tree. Leaves have leaflets that turn red or yellow in autumn. Bears white flowers in spring and red fruits in autumn.

☼ ◊ ❄❄❄ 4–7

Robinia pseudoacacia 'Frisia'
Deciduous, spreading tree with luxuriant leaves divided into oval leaflets, golden yellow when young, greenish yellow in summer, and orange-yellow in autumn.

☼ ◊ ❄❄❄ 4–9

Sorbus hupehensis 'Rosea'
Deciduous, spreading tree with leaves of 4–8 pairs of blue-green leaflets turning orange-red in late autumn. White flowers in spring are followed by long-lasting, pink fruits.

☼ ◊ ❄❄❄ 6–8

Ulmus 'Dicksonii', syn.
U. carpinifolia 'Sarniensis Aurea',
U. 'Wheatleyi Aurea'
Slow-growing, deciduous, conical tree of dense growth. Carries small, broadly oval, bright golden yellow leaves.

☼ ◊ ❄❄❄ 6–8

Syzygium paniculatum, syn.
Eugenia australis, E. paniculata
(Brush cherry eugenia)
Evergreen tree with glossy leaves, coppery when young. Has creamy white flowers, with reddish sepals, and fragrant rose-purple fruits. Min. 50°F (10°C).

☼ ◊ 9–10

Sorbus commixta, syn. *S. discolor*
of gardens (Japanese mountain ash)
Vigorous, deciduous, spreading tree. Leaves have 6–8 pairs of glossy, deep green leaflets that turn orange and red in autumn. White flowers in spring are followed by bright red fruits.

☼ ◊ ❄❄❄ 6–8

Acer rubrum 'Columnare'
Deciduous, slender, upright tree with lobed, dark green foliage that becomes a fiery column of red and yellow in autumn.

☼ ◊ ❄❄❄ 4–9

Acer rufinerve
Deciduous tree with arching branches striped green and white. In autumn, lobed, dark green leaves turn brilliant red and orange.

☼ ◊ ❄❄❄ 6–9

Stewartia monadelpha
Deciduous, spreading tree with peeling bark and glossy, dark green leaves that turn orange and red in autumn. Small, violet-anthered, white flowers appear in mid-summer, followed by small fruits.

☼ ◊ pH ❄❄❄ 7–9

Acer saccharum 'Temple's Upright'
Deciduous, columnar tree. In autumn, large, lobed leaves turn brilliant orange and red.

☼ ◊ ❄❄❄ 4–8

Aesculus flava, syn. *A. octandra* (Yellow buckeye)
Deciduous, spreading tree. Glossy, dark green leaves, with 5 or 7 oval leaflets, redden in autumn. Has yellow flowers in late spring and early summer followed by round fruits (chestnuts).

☼ ◊ ❄❄❄ 6–9

Acer henryi
Deciduous, spreading tree. Dark green leaves with 3 oval, toothed leaflets turn bright orange and red in autumn.

☼ ◊ ❄❄❄ 6–8

Parrotia persica (Persian parrotia)
Deciduous, spreading, short-trunked tree with flaking, gray and fawn bark. Rich green leaves turn yellow, orange, and red-purple in autumn. Small, red flowers are borne on bare wood in early spring.

☼ ◊ ❄❄❄ 6–9

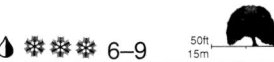

Nyssa sinensis
(Chinese sow gum)
Deciduous, spreading tree. Has long, narrow, pointed leaves that are purplish when young, dark green when mature, and brilliant scarlet in autumn.

☼ ◊ ❄❄❄ 7–9

Acer capillipes
Deciduous, spreading tree. Has lobed, bright green leaves that turn brilliant red and orange in autumn. Older branches are striped green and white.

☼ ◊ ❄❄❄ 6–9

Quercus × heterophylla
Deciduous, spreading tree with toothed, glossy, bright green leaves that turn orange-red and yellow in autumn.

☼ ◊ ❄❄❄ 6–9

Sorbus 'Joseph Rock'
Deciduous, upright tree. Bright green leaves composed of many leaflets turn orange, red, and purple in autumn. White flowers in late spring are followed by large clusters of small, yellow berries in late summer and autumn.

☼ ◊ ❄❄❄ 7–8

Cladrastis lutea (Yellowwood)
Deciduous, round-headed tree. Leaves of 7 or 9 rounded-oval leaflets are dark green, turning yellow in autumn. Clusters of fragrant, pealike, yellow-marked, white flowers appear in early summer.

☼ ◊ ❄❄❄ 4–9

Betula utilis var. jacquemontii
Elegant, deciduous, open-branched tree with bright white bark. Oval, serrated, green leaves turn clear yellow in autumn.

☀ ◊ ❄❄❄ 6–8

Arbutus × andrachnoides
Evergreen, bushy, spreading tree with peeling, reddish brown bark and glossy, dark green foliage. Clusters of small, white flowers in autumn to spring are followed by small, strawberrylike, orange or red fruits.

☀ ◊ ❄❄ 8–9

Michelia doltsopa
Evergreen, rounded tree with oval, glossy, dark green leaves, paler beneath. Strongly scented, magnolia-like flowers, with white to pale yellow petals, appear in winter-spring.

☀ ◊ pH ❄ 8–9

Acacia dealbata (Silver wattle)
Fast-growing, evergreen, spreading tree. Has feathery, blue-green leaves with many leaflets. Racemes of globular, fragrant, bright yellow flower heads are borne in winter-spring.

☀ ◊ ❄❄ 9–10

Metrosideros excelsa (Christmas tree, New Zealand Christmas tree)
Robust, evergreen, wide-spreading tree. Oval leaves are gray-green above, white felted beneath. Showy tufts of crimson stamens appear in large, terminal clusters in winter. Min. 41˚F (5˚C).

☀ ◊ 10

WHITE–GREEN

Ficus benjamina 'Variegata'
Evergreen, dense, round-headed, weeping tree, often with aerial roots. Has slender, pointed, lustrous leaves that are rich green with white variegation. Min. 59–64°F (15–18°C).

☀ ◊ 10

Trochodendron aralioides
(Wheel tree)
Evergreen, broadly conical tree with glossy, dark green foliage. In late spring and early summer bears clusters of unusual, petal-less, wheel-like, green flowers.

☀ ◑ ❄❄ 8–10

Schefflera actinophylla
(Australian umbrella tree)
Evergreen, upright tree with large, spreading leaves of 5–16 leaflets. Has large sprays of small, dull red flowers in summer or autumn. Min. 61°F (16°C).

☀ ◊ 10

Acer pensylvanicum
(Moosewood, Striped maple)
Deciduous, upright tree. Shoots are boldly striped green and white. Large, lobed leaves turn bright yellow in autumn.

☀ ◊ ❄❄❄❄ 4–8

Eucalyptus pauciflora
(Cabbage gum, Ghost gum)
Evergreen, spreading tree with peeling, white, young bark and red, young shoots. In summer, white flower clusters appear amid glossy, bright gray-green foliage.

☀ ◊ ❄❄ 9–10

Trachycarpus fortunei
(Windmill palm)
Evergreen palm with unbranched stem and a head of large, deeply divided, fanlike, green leaves. Sprays of fragrant, creamy yellow flowers appear in early summer.

☀ ◊ ❄❄ 8–10

Eucalyptus niphophila
(Snow gum)
Evergreen, spreading tree. Has patchworklike, flaking bark, red-rimmed, gray-green leaves, and white flowers in summer.

☀ ◊ ❄❄ 8–10

Quercus myrsinifolia
(Chinese evergreen oak)
Evergreen, rounded tree with narrow, pointed, glossy, dark green leaves, reddish purple when young.

☀ ◊ ❄❄ 7–9

Prunus maackii (Amur chokeberry)
Deciduous, spreading tree with peeling, yellowish brown bark. Produces spikes of small, white flowers in mid-spring and pointed, dark green leaves that turn yellow in autumn.

☀ ◊ ❄❄❄ 3–7

GREEN–ORANGE

Jubaea chilensis, syn. *J. spectabilis*
(Chile wine palm)
Slow-growing, evergreen palm with a
massive trunk and large, silvery green
leaves. Has small, maroon and yellow
flowers in spring and
woody, yellow fruits in
autumn. Min. 50°F (10°C).

☼ ◊ 9–10

Livistona chinensis
(Chinese fan palm)
Slow-growing, evergreen palm with a
stout trunk. Has fan-shaped, glossy
leaves, 3–10ft (1–3m) across. Mature
trees bear loose clusters of
berrylike, black fruits in
autumn. Min. 45°F (7°C).

☼ ◊ 9–10

Quercus agrifolia (California live
oak, Coast live oak)
Evergreen, spreading tree bearing
rigid, spiny-toothed, glossy, dark
green leaves.

☼ ◊ ❄❄❄❄ 9–10

Salix matsudana 'Tortuosa'
(Contorted willow, Corkscrew
willow)
Fast-growing, deciduous, spreading
tree with curiously twisted shoots and
contorted, narrow,
tapering, bright
green leaves.

☼ ◗ ❄❄❄❄ 5–9

Corynocarpus laevigata
(New Zealand laurel)
Evergreen, upright tree that spreads with
age. Has leathery leaves and clusters of
small, greenish flowers in spring-
summer. Plumlike, orange
fruits appear in winter.
Min. 45–50°F (7–10°C).

☼ ◊ 10

☐ WHITE

Mespilus germanica
Deciduous, spreading tree or shrub.
Has dark green leaves that turn
orange-brown in autumn, white
flowers in spring-summer, and
brown fruits in autumn,
edible when half rotten.

☼ ◊ ❄❄❄ 6–9

Crataegus laciniata,
syn. *C. orientalis*
Deciduous, spreading tree with deeply
lobed, hairy, dark green leaves. A
profusion of white flowers in late
spring or early summer is
followed by red fruits
tinged with yellow.

☼ ◊ ❄❄❄ 6–8

Amelanchier laevis (Allegheny
serviceberry)
Deciduous, spreading tree or large
shrub. Oval, bronze, young leaves turn
dark green in summer, red and orange
in autumn. Sprays of
white flowers in spring are
followed by fleshy, red fruits.

☼ ◗ ❄❄❄❄ 5–7

Cornus florida 'White Cloud'
Deciduous, spreading tree. Massed
flower heads, comprising large, white
bracts around tiny flowers, appear in
spring. Oval, pointed, dark green
leaves turn red and purple
in autumn.

☼ ◊ ❄❄❄❄ 5–8

Aesculus californica
(California buckeye)
Deciduous, spreading, sometimes
shrubby tree. Dense heads of fragrant,
sometimes pink-tinged, white flowers
appear in spring and early
summer. Small, dark green
leaves have 5–7 leaflets.

☼ ◊ ❄❄ 9–10

Magnolia salicifolia
(Anise magnolia)
Deciduous, conical tree with aromatic, oval leaves, green above, gray-white beneath. Fragrant, pure white flowers open in mid-spring before foliage appears.

☼ ◊ ❀❀❀ 6–9 30ft 10m / 30ft 10m / 0

Magnolia cylindrica
Deciduous, spreading tree or large shrub. Fragrant, upright, creamy white flowers are produced in mid-spring before young leaves turn dark green.

☼ ◊ ❀❀❀ 6–9 30ft 10m / 30ft 10m / 0

Magnolia 'Wada's Memory'
Deciduous, densely conical tree with aromatic, dark green foliage and a profusion of large, fragrant white flowers borne from mid- to late spring before oval leaves appear.

☼ ◊ ❀❀❀ 6–8 30ft 10m / 30ft 10m / 0

Prunus 'Mount Fuji', syn.
P. 'Shirotae' (Mount Fuji cherry)
Deciduous, spreading tree with slightly arching branches. Large, fragrant, single or semi-double, pure white flowers appear in mid-spring. Foliage turns orange-red in autumn.

☼ ◊ ❀❀❀ 6–8 30ft 10m / 30ft 10m / 0

Prunus 'Tai Haku'
(Great white cherry)
Vigorous, deciduous, spreading tree. Very large, single, pure white flowers are borne in mid-spring among bronzed-red, young leaves that mature to dark green.

☼ ◊ ❀❀❀ 6–8 30ft 10m / 30ft 10m / 0

Prunus incisa
(Fuji cherry)
Deciduous, spreading tree. White or pale pink flowers appear in early spring. Sharply toothed, dark green leaves are reddish when young, orange-red in autumn.

☼ ◊ ❀❀❀ 6–8 30ft 10m / 30ft 10m / 0

Prunus 'Ukon'
Vigorous, deciduous, spreading tree. Semi-double, pale greenish white flowers open from pink buds in mid-spring amid pale bronze, young foliage that later turns dark green.

☼ ◊ ❀❀❀ 6–8 30ft 10m / 30ft 10m / 0

Deciduous, spreading tree. Creamy white bracts around tiny flowers turn to deep pink in summer. These are often followed by heavy crops of strawberrylike fruits in autumn.

☼ ◊ ❀❀❀ 5–9 30ft 10m / 30ft 10m / 0

Cornus 'Norman Hadden'

Prunus 'Shogetsu',
syn. *P.* 'Shimidsu'
Deciduous, round-topped tree. In late spring, pink buds open to large, double, white flowers that hang in clusters from long stalks. Oval, green leaves turn orange and red in autumn.

☼ ◊ ❀❀❀ 6–8 30ft 10m / 30ft 10m / 0

Prunus* x *yedoensis
(Yoshino cherry)
Deciduous, round-headed tree with
spreading, arching branches and dark
green foliage. Sprays of pink buds
open to white or pale pink
flowers in early spring.

☼ ◊ ❆❆❆ 6–8

***Prunus* 'Spire'**,
syn. *P*. x *hillieri* 'Spire'
Deciduous, vase-shaped tree, conical
when young. Soft pink flowers appear
profusely from early to mid-spring.
Dark green leaves, bronze
when young, turn brilliant
orange-red in autumn.

☼ ◊ ❆❆❆ 6–8

***Prunus* 'Hokusai'**
Deciduous, spreading tree. Oval,
bronze, young leaves mature to dark
green, then turn orange and red in
autumn. Semi-double, pale pink
flowers are borne in
mid-spring.

☼ ◊ ❆❆❆ 6–8

***Prunus subhirtella* 'Stellata'**,
syn. *P*. 'Pink Star'
Deciduous, spreading tree. Pink
flowers with narrow, pointed petals,
red in bud, open from early to mid-
spring. Dark green leaves
turn yellow in autumn.

☼ ◊ ❆❆❆ 6–8

***Prunus* 'Pandora'**
Deciduous tree, upright when young,
later spreading. Massed, pale pink
flowers appear in early spring. Leaves
are bronze when young, dark green in
summer, and often orange
and red in autumn.

☼ ◊ ❆❆❆ 6–8

Malus* x *arnoldiana
Deciduous, low, spreading tree with
arching branches. In mid- to late spring
red buds open to fragrant pink flowers
that fade to white. Bears small, red-
flushed, yellow crab
apples in autumn.
Leaves are oval.

☼ ◊ ❆❆❆ 5–8

Prunus sargentii (Sargent cherry)
Deciduous, spreading tree. Oval, dark
green leaves are red when young,
turning brilliant orange-red in early
autumn. Clusters of blush pink
flowers appear in
mid-spring.

☼ ◊ ❆❆❆ 5–9

***Prunus* 'Shirofugen'**
Deciduous, spreading tree with bronze-
red leaves turning orange-red in autumn.
Pale pink buds open to fragrant, double,
white blooms that turn pink before they
fade in late spring.

☼ ◊ ❆❆❆ 6–8

***Prunus* 'Pink Perfection'**
Deciduous, upright tree that bears
double, pale pink flowers in late
spring. Oval leaves are bronze when
young, dark green in summer.

☼ ◊ ❆❆❆ 6–8

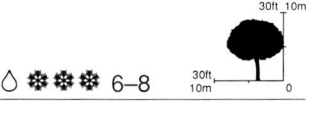

Prunus 'Accolade'
Deciduous, spreading tree with clusters of deep pink buds opening to semi-double, pale pink flowers in early spring. Toothed, green leaves turn orange-red in autumn.

☀ ◊ ❄ ❄ ❄ 6–8

Prunus subhirtella 'Pendula Rubra'
Deciduous, weeping tree that bears deep pink flowers in spring before oval, dark green leaves appear; these turn yellow in autumn.

☀ ◊ ❄ ❄ ❄ 6–8

Cercis siliquastrum (Judas tree)
Deciduous, spreading, bushy tree. Clusters of pealike, bright pink flowers appear in mid-spring, before or with heart-shaped leaves, followed by long, purplish red pods in late summer.

☀ ◊ ❄ ❄ ❄ 8–9

Prunus persica 'Prince Charming'
Deciduous, upright, bushy-headed tree with narrow, bright green leaves. Double, deep rose-pink flowers are produced in mid-spring.

☀ ◊ ❄ ❄ ❄ 6–9

Malus 'Magdeburgensis'
Deciduous, spreading tree with dark green foliage. Dense clusters of large, semi-double, deep pink flowers appear in late spring, occasionally followed by small, yellow crab apples in autumn.

☀ ◊ ❄ ❄ ❄ 5–8

Prunus 'Cheal's Weeping',
syn. *P.* 'Kiku-shidare' of gardens
Deciduous, weeping tree. Has double, bright pink flowers that cover pendent branches from mid- to late spring.

☀ ◊ ❄ ❄ ❄ 6–8

Malus floribunda
(Japanese flowering crab apple)
Deciduous, spreading, dense-headed tree with pale pink flowers, red in bud, appearing from mid- to late spring, followed by tiny, pea-shaped, yellow crab apples in autumn.

☀ ◊ ❄ ❄ ❄ 5–8

Dombeya x cayeuxii
(Pink ball dombeya)
Evergreen, bushy tree with rounded, toothed, hairy leaves to 8in (20cm) long. Pink flowers appear in pendent, ball-like clusters in winter or spring. Min. 50–55°F (10–13°C).

☀ ◊ 10

Prunus 'Yae-murasaki'
Deciduous, spreading tree with bright green leaves, bronze when young, orange-red in autumn. Semi-double, deep pink flowers are produced in mid-spring.

☀ ◊ ❄ ❄ ❄ 6–8

■□ RED–YELLOW

Malus 'Royalty'
Deciduous, spreading tree with glossy, purple foliage. Crimson-purple flowers appear from mid- to late spring, followed by dark red crab apples in autumn.

☼ ◊ ❋❋❋ 5–8

Acer pseudoplatanus 'Brilliantissimum'
Slow-growing, deciduous, spreading tree. Lobed leaves are salmon pink when young, then turn yellow and finally dark green in summer.

☼ ◊ ❋❋❋ 5–8

Malus 'Lemoinei'
Deciduous, spreading tree. Oval leaves are deep reddish purple when young, later becoming tinged with bronze. Wine red flowers in late spring are followed by dark reddish purple crab apples in autumn.

☼ ◊ ❋❋❋ 5–8

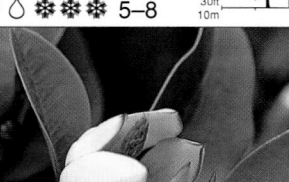

Michelia figo (Banana shrub)
Evergreen tree or rounded shrub. Has oval, glossy, rich green leaves and banana-scented, creamy yellow flowers, edged maroon, in spring-summer. Min. 41°F (5°C).

☼ ◊ 8–9

Aesculus × neglecta 'Erythroblastos'
Deciduous, spreading tree. Leaves with 5 leaflets emerge bright pink, turn yellow, then dark green, and finally orange and yellow in autumn. May bear panicles of flowers in summer.

☼ ◗ ◊ ❋❋❋ 7–8

Sophora tetraptera
(New Zealand sophora)
Semi-evergreen, spreading tree or large shrub with dark green leaves composed of many tiny leaflets. Clusters of golden yellow flowers appear in late spring.

☼ ◊ ❋ 9–10

□ WHITE

Cornus alternifolia 'Argentea'
Deciduous, spreading tree grown for its attractive, narrowly oval, white-variegated leaves. Has small heads of white flowers in spring.

☼ ◊ ❋❋❋ 4–8

Acer crataegifolium 'Veitchii'
Deciduous, bushy tree with green-and-white-streaked branches. Small, pointed, dark green leaves, blotched with white and paler green, turn deep pink and reddish purple in autumn.

☼ ◊ ❋❋❋ 6–8

Cornus controversa 'Variegata'
Deciduous tree with layered branches. Clusters of small, white flowers appear in summer. Leaves are bright green with broad, creamy white margins and turn yellow in autumn.

☼ ◊ ❋❋❋ 6–9

Magnolia x _wieseneri_, syn. _M._ x _watsonii_ (Watson magnolia)
Deciduous, spreading, open tree or shrub. Rounded, white buds open in late spring and early summer to fragrant, creamy white flowers, flushed pink outside and with crimson stamens.

☼ ◊ ✿✿✿ 5–9

Crataegus flava
Deciduous, spreading tree. Has small, dark green leaves and white flowers in late spring and early summer, followed by greenish yellow fruits.

☼ ◊ ✿✿✿ 7–9

Hoheria angustifolia
Evergreen, columnar tree with narrow, dark green leaves. Shallowly cup-shaped, white flowers are borne from mid- to late summer.

☼ ◊ ✿✿ 9

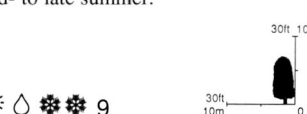

Eucryphia glutinosa
Deciduous, upright or spreading tree. Glossy, dark green leaves, consisting of 3–5 leaflets, turn orange-red in autumn. Large, fragrant white flowers appear from mid- to late summer.

☽ ◊ pH ✿✿✿ 8–10

Magnolia wilsonii
(Wilson magnolia)
Deciduous, spreading tree or shrub. In late spring and early summer, fragrant, cup-shaped, white flowers with crimson stamens hang from arching branches amid narrow, dark green leaves.

☼ ◊ ✿✿ 7–9

Hoheria lyallii
Deciduous, spreading tree with deeply toothed, gray-green leaves. Clusters of white flowers are borne in mid-summer.

☼ ◊ ✿✿ 9

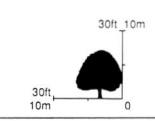

Agonis flexuosa (Peppermint tree)
Evergreen, weeping tree. Aromatic, lance-shaped, leathery leaves are bronze-red when young. In spring-summer, mature trees carry an abundance of small, white flowers.
Min. 50°F (10°C).

☼ ◊ 10

Eucryphia lucida
Evergreen, upright, bushy tree with narrow, glossy, dark green leaves and fragrant white flowers in early or mid-summer.

☽ ◊ pH ✿✿ 9

Maackia amurensis
(Amur maackia)
Deciduous, spreading tree with deep green leaves consisting of 7–11 leaflets. Upright, dense spikes of white flowers appear from mid- to late summer.

☼ ◊ ✿✿✿ 5–7

Albizia julibrissin
(Mimosa, Silk tree)
Deciduous, spreading tree. Large leaves are light to mid-green and divided into many leaflets. Clusters of brushlike, clear pink flowers appear in late summer or autumn.

☼ ◊ ✿ 7–10

Cornus florida 'Spring Song'
Deciduous, spreading tree. Pink bracts, surrounding tiny flowers, appear in spring-summer. Leaves are oval, pointed, and dark green, turning red and purple in autumn.

☼ ◊ ✿✿✿ 5–8

PINK–PURPLE

Lagerstroemia indica
(Crape myrtle)
Deciduous, rounded tree or large
shrub. Has trusses of flowers with
strongly waved, pink, white, or purple
petals in summer and
early autumn.

☼ ◊ ❄ 7–10

Malus yunnanensis var. *veitchii*
Deciduous, upright tree with lobed,
heart-shaped leaves, covered with gray
down beneath. Bears white, sometimes
pink-tinged, flowers in late spring
and a mass of small, red-
flushed, brown crab apples
in late summer and autumn.

☼ ◊ ❄❄❄ 6–8

Aesculus pavia 'Atrosanguinea'
Deciduous, round-headed, sometimes
shrubby tree. In summer, panicles of
deep red flowers appear among glossy,
dark green leaves, which have 5
narrow leaflets.

☼ ◊ ❄❄❄ 6–9

**Crataegus laevigata 'Paul's
Scarlet'** (Paul's scarlet hawthorn)
Deciduous, spreading tree. Has toothed,
glossy, dark green leaves and a
profusion of double, red flowers
in late spring and
early summer.

☼ ◊ ❄❄❄ 5–8

Cercis canadensis 'Forest Pansy'
Deciduous, spreading tree or shrub. In
mid-spring has flowers that are magenta
in bud, opening to pale pink, before
heart-shaped, reddish purple
leaves appear.

☼ ◊ ❄❄❄ 5–9

PURPLE–GREEN

Prunus cerasifera 'Nigra'
(Black Myrobalan plum)
Deciduous, round-headed tree with
deep purple leaves, red when young.
Pink flowers are borne in profusion
from early to mid-spring.

☼ ◊ ❄❄❄ 5–9

Ehretia dicksonii
Deciduous, spreading tree with stout,
ridged branches and large, dark green
leaves. Large, flattish heads of small,
fragrant white flowers are borne in
mid-summer.

☼ ◊ ❄❄ 9–10

Pyrus salicifolia 'Pendula'
(Weeping willowleaf pear)
Deciduous, weeping, mound-shaped
tree with white flowers in mid-spring
and narrow, gray leaves.

☼ ◊ ❄❄❄ 5–9

Pseudopanax ferox
Evergreen, upright tree with long, narrow, rigid, sharply toothed leaves that are dark bronze-green overlaid white or gray.

☼ ◊ ❄❄ 10

Ulmus 'Camperdownii'
Deciduous, strongly weeping tree with sinuous branches. Leaves are very large, rough, and dull green.

☼ ◊ ❄❄❄ 5–8

Juglans microcarpa,
syn. *J. rupestris*
(Little walnut, Texan walnut)
Deciduous, bushy-headed tree with large, aromatic leaves of many narrow, pointed leaflets that turn yellow in autumn.

☼ ◊ ❄❄❄ 6–9

Cydonia oblonga 'Vranja'
Deciduous, spreading tree. Pale green leaves, gray-felted beneath, mature to dark green and set off large, white or pale pink flowers in late spring and, later, very fragrant, golden yellow fruits.

☼ ◊ ❄❄❄ 5–9

Betula pendula 'Youngii'
(Young's weeping birch)
Deciduous, weeping tree that forms a mushroom-shaped dome of threadlike branchlets. Has triangular, serrated leaves and smooth, white bark that is fissured black at maturity.

☼ ◊ ❄❄❄ 3–8

Acer carpinifolium
(Hornbeam maple)
Elegant, deciduous tree, often with several main stems. Prominent-veined, hornbeamlike leaves turn golden brown in autumn.

☼ ◊ ❄❄ 6–8

Acer japonicum 'Aureum'
Deciduous, bushy tree or large shrub. Has rounded, many-lobed, pale yellow leaves.

☼ ◊ ❄❄❄ 6–8

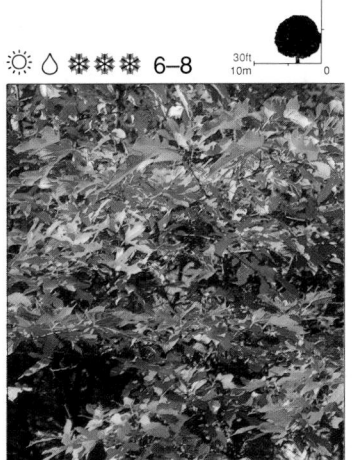

Morus alba 'Laciniata'
Deciduous, spreading tree. Has rounded, deeply lobed, glossy leaves that turn yellow in autumn and bears edible, pink, red, or purple fruits in summer.

☼ ◊ ❄❄❄ 5–9

Koelreuteria paniculata
(Golden-rain tree, Varnish tree)
Deciduous, spreading tree with green leaves, turning yellow in autumn. Bears sprays of yellow flowers in summer, followed by inflated, bronze-pink fruits.

☼ ◊ ❄❄ 6–9

Laburnum × watereri 'Vossii'
Deciduous, spreading tree. Leaves, consisting of 3 leaflets, are glossy, deep green. Pendent chains of large, yellow flowers are borne in late spring and early summer.

☼ ◊ ❄❄❄ 6–8

Genista aetnensis
(Mount Etna broom)
Almost leafless, rounded tree with
many slender, bright green branches
and a profusion of fragrant, pealike,
golden yellow flowers
in mid-summer.

☀ ◊ ❀❀ 9–10

Albizia distachya,
syn. *A. lophantha* (Plume albizia)
Fast-growing, deciduous, spreading
tree. Has fernlike, dark green leaves
comprising many leaflets. Creamy
yellow flower spikes
appear in spring-summer.

☀ ◊ ❀ 7–10

Thevetia peruviana,
syn. *T. neriifolia* (Yellow oleander)
Evergreen, erect tree with narrow,
lance-shaped, rich green leaves and
funnel-shaped, yellow or orange-
yellow flowers from
winter to summer. Min.
61–4°F (16–18°C).

☀ ◊ ❀ 10

Laburnum alpinum
(Scotch laburnum)
Deciduous, spreading tree. Leaves
consist of 3 leaflets and are glossy,
dark green. Long, slender chains of
bright yellow flowers
appear in late spring
or early summer.

☀ ◊ ❀❀❀ 5–8

Embothrium coccineum
(Chilean fire brush, Chilean fire tree)
Evergreen or semi-evergreen, upright,
suckering tree with lance-shaped,
glossy, deep green leaves. Clusters of
brilliant orange-red flowers
are borne in late spring
and early summer.

☀ ◊ pH ❀❀ 9–10

Sorbus cashmiriana
(Kashmir mountain ash)
Deciduous, spreading tree with leaves
consisting of 6–9 pairs of rich green
leaflets. Pink-flushed, white flowers in
early summer are followed
by large, white fruits
in autumn.

☀ ◊ ❀❀❀ 5–7

Sorbus vilmorinii
Elegant, deciduous, spreading, arching
tree. Leaves of 9–14 pairs of dark
green leaflets become orange- or
bronze-red in autumn. Has white
blooms in late spring and
small, deep pink fruits
in autumn.

☀ ◊ ❀❀❀❀ 6–8

Arbutus unedo (Strawberry tree)
Evergreen, spreading tree or shrub
with rough, brown bark and glossy,
deep green leaves. Pendent, urn-
shaped, white flowers appear in
autumn-winter as previous
season's strawberrylike,
red fruits ripen.

☀ ◊ ❀❀ 8–9

Cornus florida 'Welchii'
Deciduous, spreading tree. Bears white
bracts, surrounding tiny flowers, in
spring. Dark green leaves, edged with
white and pink, turn red and purple
in autumn.

☀ ◊ ❀❀❀ 5–8

Malus 'Veitch's Scarlet'
Deciduous, spreading tree with dark
green foliage. Carries white flowers in
late spring and crimson-flushed, scarlet
crab apples in autumn.

☀ ◊ ❀❀❀ 6–8

Crataegus macrosperma var. **acutiloba**
Deciduous, spreading tree with broad, sharply toothed, dark green leaves. White flowers with red anthers in late spring are followed by bright red fruits in autumn.

 4–8

Stranvaesia davidiana
Evergreen, spreading tree or large shrub with narrow, glossy, dark green leaves, older ones turning red in autumn. Sprays of white flowers in early summer are followed by clusters of bright red fruits in autumn.

 7–9

Malus 'Cowichan'
Deciduous, spreading tree. Has dark green foliage, reddish purple when young. Pink flowers appear in mid-spring, followed by reddish purple crab apples.

 5–8

Crataegus pedicellata
Deciduous, spreading tree with sharply toothed, lobed, dark green leaves that turn orange and red in autumn. White flowers with red anthers in late spring are followed by bright red fruits in autumn.

 6–8

Malus 'John Downie'
Deciduous tree, narrow and upright when young, conical when mature. White flowers, borne amid bright green foliage in late spring, are followed by large, edible, red-flushed, orange crab apples in autumn.

 5–8

Acer palmatum var. **coreanum**
Deciduous, bushy-headed tree or large shrub. Leaves are deeply lobed and green, turning brilliant red in autumn. Small, reddish purple flowers are borne in spring.

 5–8

Acer japonicum 'Aconitifolium'
Deciduous, bushy tree or large shrub. Deeply divided, green leaves turn red in autumn. Reddish purple flowers appear in mid-spring.

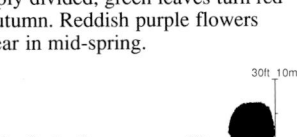 6–8

Malus prunifolia
(Plum-leaved crab apple)
Deciduous, spreading tree. Has dark green leaves and fragrant white flowers in mid-spring. In autumn bears long-lasting, small, red or occasionally yellowish crab apples.

4–8

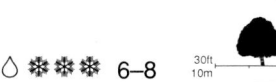

Acer japonicum 'Vitifolium'
Vigorous, deciduous, bushy tree or large shrub with large, rounded, lobed, green leaves that turn brilliant red, orange, and purple in autumn.

6–8

■ RED

Rhus trichocarpa
Deciduous, spreading tree. Large, ash-like leaves with 13–17 leaflets are pinkish when young, dark green in summer, and purple-red to orange in autumn. Bears pendent, bristly, yellow fruits.

☀ ◊ ❄❄❄ 7–9

Acer ginnala (Amur maple)
Deciduous, spreading tree or large shrub. Clusters of fragrant, creamy white flowers are borne in early summer amid dainty, bright green leaves that turn red in autumn.

☀ ◊ ❄❄❄ 6–8

Cornus 'Eddie's White Wonder'
Deciduous, spreading tree or shrub. Large, white bracts, surrounding insignificant flowers, appear in late spring. Oval leaves are green, turning red and purple in autumn.

☀ ◊ ❄❄❄ 6–9

Malus 'Professor Sprenger'
Deciduous, rounded, dense tree. Dark green leaves turn yellow in late autumn. White flowers, pink in bud, open from mid- to late spring and are followed by orange-red crab apples in autumn.

☀ ◊ ❄❄❄ 5–8

Malus x zumi 'Calocarpa'
(Redbud crab apple)
Deciduous, spreading tree. Dark green leaves are sometimes deeply lobed. White flowers in late spring are followed by dense clusters of long-lasting, cherrylike, red crab apples in autumn.

☀ ◊ ❄❄❄ 5–8

Plumeria rubra
(Frangipani, Nosegay)
Deciduous, spreading tree or large shrub, sparingly branched. Has fragrant flowers, in shades of yellow, orange, pink, red, and white, in summer-autumn. Min. 55°F (13°C).

☀ ◊ 10

Acer triflorum
Slow-growing, deciduous, spreading tree with peeling, gray-brown bark. Leaves, composed of 3 leaflets, are dark green and turn brilliant orange-red in autumn. Clusters of tiny, yellow-green flowers appear in late spring.

☀ ◊ ❄❄❄ 5–8

Malus 'Marshall Oyama'
Deciduous, upright tree with dark green leaves. Pink-flushed, white flowers borne in late spring are followed by a profusion of large, rounded, crimson and yellow crab apples in autumn.

☀ ◊ ❄❄❄ 5–8

Tecoma stans, syn. *Bignonia stans*, *Stenolobium stans* (Yellow-bells)
Evergreen, rounded, upright tree or large shrub. Leaves have 5–13 leaflets. Has funnel-shaped, yellow flowers from spring to autumn. Min. 55°F (13°C).

☀ ◊ 9–10

☐ YELLOW

Picrasma quassioides
Deciduous, spreading tree with glossy, bright green leaves, composed of 9–13 leaflets, that turn brilliant yellow, orange, and red in autumn.

☼ ◊ ✽✽✽ 6–9

Malus 'Golden Hornet'
Deciduous, spreading tree with dark green foliage and open cup-shaped, white flowers in late spring. In autumn, branches are weighed down by a profusion of golden yellow crab apples.

☼ ◊ ✽✽✽ 5–8

☐◼ WHITE–PINK

Bauhinia variegata 'Candida'
Deciduous tree, rounded when young, spreading with age. Has broadly oval, deeply notched leaves and fragrant, pure white flowers, 4in (10cm) across, in winter-spring or sometimes later. Min. 59–64°F (15–18°C).

☼ ◊ 10

Bauhinia variegata
Deciduous, rounded tree with broadly oval, deeply notched leaves. Fragrant magenta to lavender flowers, to 4in (10cm) across, appear in winter-spring or sometimes later. Min. 59–64°F (15–18°C).

☼ ◊ 10

☐ YELLOW

Acacia pravissima
(Ovens acacia, Ovens wattle)
Evergreen, spreading, arching tree or shrub. Has triangular, spine-tipped, silver-gray phyllodes (flat, leaflike stalks) and small heads of bright yellow flowers in late winter or early spring.

☼ ◊ ❄ 10

Acacia baileyana (Cootamundra wattle, Golden mimosa)
Evergreen, spreading, graceful tree with arching branches and finely divided, blue-gray leaves. Clusters of small, golden yellow flower heads appear in winter-spring.

☼ ◊ ❄ 10

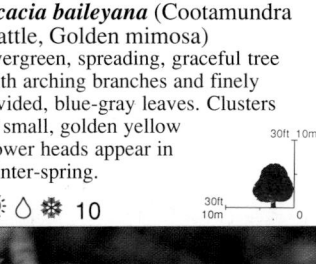

Tabebuia chrysotricha
(Golden trumpet tree)
Deciduous, round-headed tree with dark green leaves, divided into 3–5 oval leaflets, and rich yellow flowers, 3in (7cm) long, borne in late winter or early spring. Min. 61–4°F (16–18°C).

☼ ◊ 10

Hollies

The American holly, *Ilex opaca*, is one of the best-known evergreen trees, but there are many other hollies, including lesser-known *Ilex* cultivars, that make attractive garden plants. In size they range from tall, specimen trees to small shrubs useful in the rock garden or for growing in pots. Hollies respond well to pruning and many may be clipped to form good hedges. Leaves of different species and cultivars may be smooth-edged or spiny and vary considerably in color, several having gold, yellow, cream, white, or gray variegation. Small, often white, male and female flowers, borne on separate plants during summer, are followed by attractive, red, yellow, or black berries. In almost all cases hollies are unisexual, that is, the berries are borne only on female plants, so to obtain fruits it is usually necessary to grow plants of both sexes. Most plants are fully hardy.

I. fargesii var. *brevifolia*

I. aquifolium 'Pyramidalis'

I. aquifolium 'Argentea Marginata Pendula'

I. × altaclerensis 'Camelliifolia'

I. aquifolium 'Argentea Marginata'

I. ciliospinosa

I. pernyi

I. crenata var. *paludosa*

I. fargesii

I. aquifolium 'Scotica'

I. × altaclerensis 'Lawsoniana'

I. macrocarpa

I. × koehneana

I. crenata 'Helleri'

I. × altaclerensis 'Balearica'

I. crenata 'Latifolia'

I. cornuta 'Burfordii'

I. × altaclerensis 'N.F. Barnes'

I. verticillata

I. aquifolium

I. opaca

I. × aquipernyi

I. crenata 'Convexa'

I. × altaclerensis 'Belgica'

I. × meserveae 'Blue Princess'

I. aquifolium 'Silver Milkmaid'

I. aquifolium 'Silver Queen'

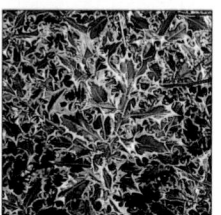

I. aquifolium 'Elegantissima'

I. aquifolium 'Mme. Briot'

I. x altaclerensis 'Belgica Aurea'

I. aquifolium 'Crispa Aurea Picta'

I. aquifolium 'Ovata Aurea'

I. aquifolium 'Aurifodina'

I. aquifolium 'Watereriana'

I. serrata f. leucocarpa

I. aquifolium 'Pyramidalis Aurea Marginata'

I. x altaclerensis 'Camelliifolia Variegata'

I. chinensis

I. crenata 'Variegata'

I. pedunculosa

Pittosporum crassifolium
'Variegatum' (Variegated karo)
Evergreen, bushy-headed, dense tree
or shrub with gray-green leaves edged
with white. Clusters of small, fragrant,
deep reddish purple
flowers appear
in spring.

☼ ◊ ❀ 9–10

Pittosporum eugenioides
'Variegatum'
(Variegated tarata pittosporum)
Evergreen, columnar tree. Wavy-edged,
glossy, dark green leaves have white
margins. Honey-scented,
pale yellow flowers are
borne in spring.

☼ ◊ ❀ 9–10

Acer laxiflorum
Deciduous, spreading tree with white-
bloomed shoots and arching branches
streaked white and green. In late
summer has pale red, winged fruits.
Pointed, red-stalked, dark
green leaves turn orange
in autumn.

☼ ◊ ❀❀❀ 7–9

Grevillea banksii
Evergreen, loosely branched tree or
tall shrub. Has leaves divided into
5–11 slender leaflets, silky-downy
beneath. Spiderlike, red flowers
appear in dense heads
intermittently throughout
the year. Min. 50°F (10°C).

☼ ◊ 10

***Dracaena marginata* 'Tricolor'**
Slow-growing, evergreen, upright tree
or shrub with narrow, strap-shaped,
cream-striped, rich green leaves,
prominently edged with red.
Min. 55°F (13°C).

☼ ◊ 10

Cordyline australis
'Atropurpurea' (Bronze dracaena)
Slow-growing, evergreen tree with
purple to purplish green leaves. Has
terminal sprays of white flowers
in summer and small,
globular, white fruits in
autumn. Min. 41°F (5°C).

☼ ◊ 10

GRAY–GREEN

Leucadendron argenteum
(Silver leucadendron, Silver tree)
Evergreen, conical to columnar tree,
spreading with age. Leaves are covered
with long, silky, white hairs. Has
insignificant flowers set in
silvery bracts in autumn-
winter. Min. 45°F (7°C).

☼ ◊ 10

Butia capitata,
syn. *Cocos capitata* (Jelly palm)
Slow-growing, evergreen palm.
Feather-shaped leaves, composed of
many leathery leaflets, are strongly
arching to recurved, 6ft
(2m) or more long. Min.
41°F (5°C).

☼ ◊ 9–10

***Carpinus betulus* 'Fastigiata'**
Deciduous, erect tree, with a very
distinctive, flamelike outline, that
becomes more open with age. Oval,
prominently veined, dark green leaves
turn yellow and orange
in autumn.

☼ ◊ ❊❊❊ 5–9

Cyathea australis
(Australian tree fern)
Evergreen, upright tree fern with a
robust, almost black trunk. Finely
divided leaves, 6–12ft (2–4m) long,
are light green, bluish beneath.
Min. 55°F (13°C).

☼ ◊ 10

Eucalyptus perriniana
(Round-leaved snowgum)
Fast-growing, evergreen, spreading
tree with rounded, gray-blue, young
leaves joined around stems. Leaves on
mature trees are long and
pendulous. White flowers
appear in late summer.

☼ ◊ ❊❊ 9–10

Meryta sinclairii (Puka)
Evergreen, round-headed tree with
large, glossy, deep green leaves.
Greenish flowers appear sporadically
in spring to autumn, followed by
berrylike, black fruits.
Min. 41°F (5°C).

☼ ◗ 10

Pittosporum dallii
Evergreen, rounded, dense tree or
shrub. Has purplish stems and sharply
toothed, deep green leaves. Clusters of
small, fragrant, shallowly cup-shaped,
white flowers are borne
in summer.

☼ ◗ ❊❊ 9–10

Beaucarnea recurvata, syn.
Nolina recurvata, N. tuberculata
(Elephant-foot tree, Pony-tail)
Slow-growing, evergreen tree or shrub
with a sparsely branched stem.
Recurving leaves, 3ft (1m)
long, persist after turning
brown. Min. 45°F (7°C).

☼ ◊ 9–10

Dracaena draco (Dragon tree)
Slow-growing, evergreen tree,
eventually with a wide-branched head.
Has stiff, lance-shaped, gray- or blue-
green leaves. Mature trees bear clusters
of orange berries, usually
from mid- to late summer.
Min. 55°F (13°C).

☼ ◊ 10

Lithocarpus henryi
Slow-growing, evergreen, broadly
conical tree with glossy, pale
green leaves that are long,
narrow, and pointed.

☼ ◗ ❊❊ 8–10

Chrysalidocarpus lutescens,
syn. *Areca lutescens*
(Yellow butterfly palm)
Evergreen, suckering palm, forming
clumps of robust, canelike stems. Has
long, arching leaves of
slender, yellowish green
leaflets. Min. 61°F (16°C).

☼ ◊ 10

Acer griseum (Paperbark maple)
Deciduous, spreading tree with
striking, peeling, orange-brown bark.
Dark green leaves have 3 leaflets and
turn red and orange in autumn.

☼ ◊ ❊❊❊ 6–8

CONIFERS/large

***Abies concolor* 'Candicans'**
Conical conifer with silvery foliage
that contrasts well with dark gray bark.
Oblong to ovoid, pale blue or green
cones are 3–5in (8–12cm) long.

☼◑ ⬤ ❄❄❄ 4–7

Pinus* x *holfordiana
Broadly conical, open conifer with
large cones, brown when ripe. Pendent, glaucous blue-green leaves are
held in 5s.

☼ ⬤ ❄❄❄ 6–7

Cupressus cashmeriana
Handsome, broadly conical conifer that
spreads with age. Has aromatic foliage
borne in pendent, flat, glaucous blue
sprays. Bears small, globose, dark
brown, mature cones.

☼ ⬤ ❄❄ 9–10

x *Cupressocyparis leylandii*
(Leyland cypress)
Vigorous, upright, columnar conifer,
tapering at the apex. Will grow 3ft
(1m) a year, so is a popular screening
plant. Dark green or gray-
green foliage is held in
flat sprays.

☼ ◑⬤ ❄❄❄ 6–9

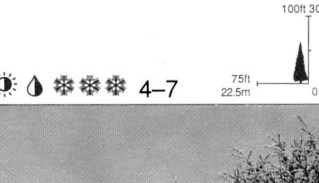

Cedrus atlantica* f. *glauca
(Blue Atlas cedar)
Conical conifer with silvery blue
foliage that is very bright, especially
in spring. Erect, cylindrical cones are
produced in autumn.
Is widely planted
as a specimen tree.

☼ ⬤ ❄❄❄ 7–9

Pinus peuce (Macedonian pine)
Upright conifer, forming a slender
pyramid. Has dense, gray-green
foliage and cylindrical, green cones
with white resin that ripen brown in
autumn. Is an attractive tree
that grows consistently
well in all sites.

☼ ⬤ ❄❄❄ 5–9

Conifers/large

Pinus coulteri
(Big-cone pine, Coulter pine)
Fast-growing conifer with large, broadly ovoid, prickly cones, each 2–4¹/₂lb (1–2kg). Gray-green leaves in crowded clusters are sparsely set on branches. Grows in all soils, even heavy clays.

☼ ◗ ✳✳✳ 7–9   100ft 30m / 75ft 22.5m / 0

Abies veitchii (Veitch fir)
Upright conifer with dark green leaves, silvery beneath, and cylindrical, violet-blue cones.

Chamaecyparis lawsoniana 'Intertexta'
Elegant, weeping conifer with aromatic, gray-green foliage carried in lax, pendulous sprays. Old trees become columnar with some splayed branches.

☼◑ ◗ ✳✳✳ 6–9   100ft 30m / 75ft 22.5m / 0

☼ ◗ ✳✳✳ 4–7   100ft 30m / 75ft 22.5m / 0

Pseudotsuga menziesii var. **glauca**
(Rocky Mountain Douglas fir)
Fast-growing, conical conifer with thick, grooved, corky, gray-brown bark, aromatic, glaucous blue-green leaves, and sharply pointed buds. Cones have projecting, 3-pronged bracts.

☼◑ ◗ ✳✳✳ 5–7   100ft 30m / 75ft 22.5m / 0

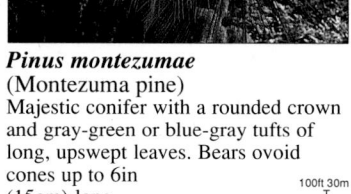
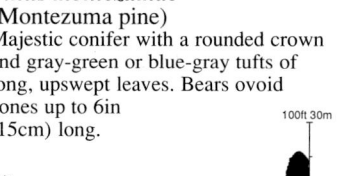

Pinus strobus (Eastern white pine)
Conifer with an open, sparse, whorled crown. Has gray-green foliage and cylindrical cones. Smooth, gray bark becomes fissured with age. Does not tolerate pollution.

☼ ◗ ✳✳✳ 4–9   100ft 30m / 75ft 22.5m / 0

Metasequoia glyptostroboides
(Dawn redwood)
Fast-growing, deciduous, upright conifer with fibrous, reddish bark. Soft, blue-green leaves turn yellow, pink, and red in autumn. Cones are globose to ovoid, ³/₄in (2 cm) long.

☼◑ ◗ ✳✳✳ 5–10   100ft 30m / 75ft 22.5m / 0

Pinus montezumae
(Montezuma pine)
Majestic conifer with a rounded crown and gray-green or blue-gray tufts of long, upswept leaves. Bears ovoid cones up to 6in (15cm) long.

☼ ◗ ✳✳ 6–8   100ft 30m / 75ft 22.5m / 0

Sequoiadendron giganteum
(Giant redwood, Giant sequoia)
Very fast-growing, conical conifer. Has thick, fibrous, red-brown bark and sharp, bluish green leaves. Is one of the world's largest trees when mature.

☼ ◗ ✳✳✳ 6–9   100ft 30m / 75ft 22.5m / 0

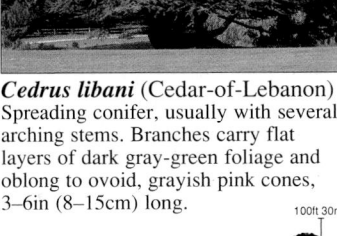

Cedrus libani (Cedar-of-Lebanon)
Spreading conifer, usually with several arching stems. Branches carry flat layers of dark gray-green foliage and oblong to ovoid, grayish pink cones, 3–6in (8–15cm) long.

☼ ◊ ❅❅❅ 7–9

Pinus muricata (Bishop pine)
Fast-growing, often flat-topped conifer. Leaves are blue- or gray-green and held in pairs. Ovoid cones, 3–3½in (7–9cm) long, rarely open. Does particularly well in poor, sandy soil.

☼ ◊ ❅❅❅ 7–9

Picea omorika (Serbian spruce)
Narrow, conical conifer, resembling a church spire, with dark green leaves that are white below. Branches are pendulous and arch out at tips. Violet-purple cones age to glossy brown. Grows steadily in all soils.

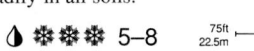 ☼◐ ◊ ❅❅❅ 5–8

Araucaria araucana (Monkey-puzzle-tree)
Open, spreading conifer with gray bark, wrinkled like elephant hide. Has flattened, sharp, glossy, dark green leaves and 6in (15cm) long cones. Makes a fine specimen tree.

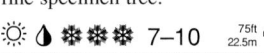 ☼ ◊ ❅❅❅ 7–10

Pinus ponderosa (Ponderosa pine, Western yellow pine)
Conical or upright conifer, grown for its distinctive, deeply fissured bark, with smooth, brown plates, and bold grayish green foliage. Bears ovoid, purplish brown cones.

☼ ◊ ❅❅❅ 5–8

Pinus jeffreyi (Jeffrey pine)
Upright, narrow-crowned conifer with stout, gray-green leaves, 5–10in (12–26cm) long. Bark is black with fine, deep fissures and shoots have an attractive, grayish bloom.

☼ ◊ ❅❅❅ 6–8

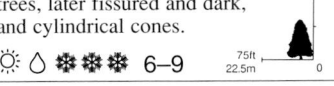

Pinus wallichiana, syn. *P. chylla, P. excelsa, P. griffithii* (Bhutan pine, Himalayan pine)
Conical conifer with long, drooping, blue-green leaves in 5s. Has smooth bark, gray-green on young trees, later fissured and dark, and cylindrical cones.

☼ ◊ ❅❅❅ 6–9

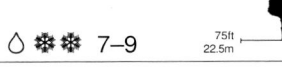

Pinus pinaster (Cluster pine)
Vigorous, domed conifer with a long, branchless trunk. Has gray-green leaves and whorls of rich brown cones. Purple-brown bark is deeply fissured. Is well suited to dry, sandy soil.

☼ ◊ ❅❅ 7–9

Ginkgo biloba (Maidenhair tree)
Long-lived, deciduous conifer, upright when young, spreading with age. Has fan-shaped, 5in (12cm) long, bright green leaves. Bears fruits, with edible kernels, in late summer and autumn, if male and female plants are grown together.

 ☼◐ ◊ ❅❅❅ 5–9

Conifers/large

Pinus nigra subsp. ***nigra***
(Austrian pine)
Broadly crowned conifer, with well-spaced branches, often with several stems. Paired, dark green leaves are densely tufted. Tolerates an exposed site.

☼ ◊ ❄❄❄❄ 5–8

Pinus radiata, syn. *P. insignis*
(Monterey pine)
Very fast-growing conifer, conical when young, domed when mature. Black bark contrasts well with soft, bright green leaves. Makes an excellent windbreak.

☼ ◊ ❄❄❄ 7–9

Abies grandis (Grand fir)
Very vigorous, narrow, conical conifer, with a neat habit. Green leaves have an orange aroma when crushed. Cones, 3in (7–8cm) long, ripen red-brown. Makes a useful specimen tree.

☼◑ ◊ ❄❄❄❄ 7–9

Pinus leucodermis, syn.
P. heldreichii var. *leucodermis*
Conical, dense conifer with paired dark green leaves. Ovoid cones, 2–4in (5–10cm) long, are cobalt blue in their second summer, brown when ripe.

☼ ◊ ❄❄❄ 6–8

Picea abies (Norway spruce)
Fast-growing, pyramidal conifer with dark green leaves. Narrow, pendulous, glossy, brown cones are 4–8in (10–20cm) long. Is much used as a Christmas tree but less useful as an ornamental.

☼◑ ◊ ❄❄❄❄ 3–8

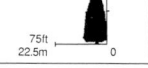

x ***Cupressocyparis leylandii***
'Harlequin'
Fast-growing, columnar conifer with a conical tip. Gray-green foliage, with patches of clear ivory white, is held in plumelike sprays.

☼ ◊ ❄❄❄❄ 6–9

x ***Cupressocyparis leylandii***
'Castlewellan'
Vigorous, upright conifer, slightly slower-growing than the species, grown for its bronze-yellow foliage.

☼ ◊ ❄❄❄ 6–9

Picea orientalis 'Skylands'
Graceful, dense, upright conifer that retains the gold coloration of short, glossy leaves throughout the year. Narrowly oblong cones are dark purple, males turning brick red in spring.

☼◑ ◊ ❄❄❄❄ 5–8

Taxodium distichum
(Bald cypress)
Deciduous, broadly conical conifer with small, globose to ovoid cones. Soft, yewlike, fresh green leaves turn rich brown in late autumn. Grows in a very wet site, producing special breathing roots.

☼ ◊ ❄❄❄ 5–10

Conifers/medium

Abies procera 'Glauca'
Upright conifer with smooth, silvery
bark and blue foliage. In drought
conditions unsightly cracks will appear
in bark and wood. Purplish brown
cones are cylindrical,
6–10in (15–25cm) long.

☼◐ ◊ ❋❋❋❋ 6–8

Picea glauca 'Coerulea'
Upright, dense, conical conifer with
needlelike, blue-green to silver leaves
and ovoid, light brown cones.

☼ ◊ ❋❋❋ 3–6

Juniperus chinensis 'Keteleeri'
(Keteleer juniper)
Regular, slender, columnar, dense
conifer with scalelike, aromatic,
grayish green leaves and peeling,
brown bark. Makes a
reliable, free-fruiting
form for formal use.

☼ ◊ ❋❋❋ 5–9

Picea breweriana (Brewer's
spruce, Brewer's weeping spruce)
Upright conifer with level branches
and completely pendulous branchlets,
to 6ft (2m) long. Leaves are stout and
blue-green. Bears oblong,
purplish cones, 2¹/₂–3in
(6–8cm) long.

☼◐ ◊ ❋❋❋❋ 6–8

Picea pungens 'Koster'
Upright conifer with whorled branches.
Has scaly, gray bark and attractive,
needlelike, silvery blue leaves that
fade to green with age. Tends to suffer
from aphid attack.

☼ ◊ ❋❋❋❋ 3–8

**Chamaecyparis lawsoniana
'Pembury Blue'**
Magnificent, conical conifer with
aromatic, bright blue-gray foliage
held in pendulous sprays.

☼ ◊ ❋❋❋ 6–9

Picea engelmannii
(Engelmann spruce)
Broadly conical conifer. Leaves
encircle shoots and are prickly or soft,
lush, glaucous or bluish green. Bears
small, cylindrical cones.
Is good for a very
poor site.

☼◐ ◊ ❋❋❋❋ 3–8

Cupressus sempervirens
(Italian cypress)
Very narrow, upright conifer that
grows fast when young. Aromatic,
gray-green foliage is held in erect
sprays. Glossy, gray-
brown cones are
globose or ovoid.

☼ ◊ ❋❋ 8–10

Pinus parviflora
(Japanese white pine)
Slow-growing, conical or spreading
conifer with fine, bluish foliage and
purplish brown bark. Leaves are held
in 5s. Bears ovoid cones,
2–4in (5–10cm) long.

☼ ◊ ❋❋❋ 6–9

Conifers/medium

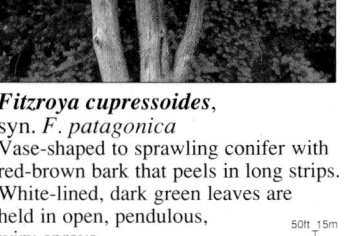

Fitzroya cupressoides,
syn. *F. patagonica*
Vase-shaped to sprawling conifer with red-brown bark that peels in long strips. White-lined, dark green leaves are held in open, pendulous, wiry sprays.

☀◐ ◊ ❄❄❄ 7–9

Podocarpus salignus
Upright conifer. Leaves are willowlike, 2–4in (5–11cm) long, and glossy above. Attractive, fibrous, red-brown bark peels in strips.

☀◐ ◊ ❄❄ 10

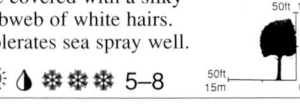

Pinus thunbergii
(Japanese black pine)
Rounded conifer, conical when young, with dark green leaves and gray-brown cones, 1½–2½in (4–6cm) long. Buds are covered with a silky cobweb of white hairs. Tolerates sea spray well.

☀ ◊ ❄❄❄ 5–8

Pinus rigida (Pitch pine)
Conical conifer, often with sucker shoots from trunk. Twisted, dark green leaves are borne in 3s. Ovoid to globose, red-brown cones, 1¼–3in (3–8cm) long, persist, open, on the tree.

☀ ◊ ❄❄❄ 5–7

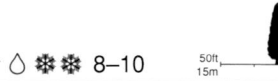

Austrocedrus chilensis,
syn. *Libocedrus chilensis*
(Chilean incense cedar)
Conical conifer with flattened, feathery sprays of 4-ranked, small, dark green leaves, white beneath.

☀ ◊ ❄❄ 8–10

Cunninghamia lanceolata
(Common China fir)
Upright conifer, mop-headed on a dry site, with distinctive, thick and deeply furrowed, red-brown bark. Glossy, green leaves are sharply pointed and lance-shaped.

☀◐ ◊ ❄❄❄ 7–9

Phyllocladus trichomanoides
Slow-growing conifer, conical when young, that develops a more rounded top with age. Leaflike, deep green, modified shoots, 4–6in (10–15cm) long, have 5–10 lobed segments.

☀◐ ◊ ❄❄ 10

Sciadopitys verticillata
(Japanese umbrella pine)
Conical conifer with reddish brown bark. Deep green leaves, yellowish beneath, are whorled at the ends of shoots, like umbrella spokes. Ovoid cones ripen over 2 years.

☀◐ ◊ ❄❄❄ 5–9

Calocedrus decurrens,
syn. *Libocedrus decurrens*
(California incense cedar)
Upright conifer with short, horizontal branches and flaky, gray bark, brown beneath. Has flat sprays of aromatic, dark green leaves. Resists honey fungus.

☀◐ ◊ ❄❄❄ 6–9

Pinus cembra
(Arolla pine, Swiss stone pine)
Dense, conical conifer with dark green or bluish green leaves grouped in 5s. Ovoid, bluish or purplish cones, 2½– 3in (6–8cm) long, ripen brown.

☀ ◊ ❄❄❄ 3–7

Pinus contorta var. **latifolia**
(Lodgepole pine)
Conical conifer with bright green leaves, 2½–4in (6–9cm) long. Small, oval cones remain closed on the tree. Is suitable for a wet site.

☀ ◊ ❄❄❄ 6–8

Pseudolarix amabilis,
syn. *P. kaempferi* (Golden larch)
Deciduous, open-crowned conifer,
slow-growing when young. Has clusters
of linear, fresh green leaves, 1–2¹/₂in
(2.5–6cm) long, which
gradually turn bright
orange-gold in autumn.

☼ ◊ ❄❄❄ 5–9

Pinus banksiana
(Gray pine, Jack pine)
Slender, conical, scrubby-looking
conifer with fresh green leaves in
twisted, divergent pairs. Curved
cones, 1¹/₄–2¹/₂in (3–6cm)
long, point forward
along shoots.

☼ ◊ ❄❄❄ 3–8

Picea morrisonicola
Upright, conical conifer that becomes
columnar with age. Needlelike, deep
green leaves are pressed down on
slender, pale brown shoots. Cones are
cylindrical and 2–3in
(5–7cm) long.

☼◗ ◊ ❄❄ 7–9

Torreya californica
(California nutmeg)
Upright conifer with very prickly,
glossy, dark green leaves, yellowish
green beneath, similar to those of yew.
Fruits are olivelike.

☼◗ ◊ ❄❄ 7–10

Chamaecyparis lawsoniana
'**Green Pillar**'
Conical conifer with upright branches.
Aromatic foliage is bright green and
becomes tinged with gold in spring. Is
suitable for hedging as
requires little clipping.

☼◗ ◊ ❄❄❄ 6–9

Chamaecyparis thyoides
(White cedar)
Upright conifer with aromatic, green or
blue-gray leaves in rather erratic, fan-
shaped sprays on very fine shoots.
Cones are small, round,
and glaucous blue-gray.

☼◗ ◊ ❄❄❄ 4–9

Tsuga canadensis
(Eastern hemlock)
Broadly conical conifer, often with
several stems. Gray shoots have
2-ranked, dark green leaves, often
inverted to show silver
lines beneath. Cones are
ovoid and light brown.

☼◗ ◊ ❄❄❄ 4–8

Chamaecyparis lawsoniana
'**Lanei**'
Upright conifer that forms a neat
column of aromatic, golden yellow-
tipped foliage.

☼◗ ◊ ❄❄❄ 6–9

Pinus contorta
(Beach pine, Shore pine)
Dense, conical or domed conifer. Has
paired, bright green leaves and conical
to ovoid cones, 1¹/₄–3in (3–8cm) long.
Is well suited to a windy,
barren site and tolerates
waterlogged ground.

☼ ◊ ❄❄❄ 6–8

Pinus halepensis (Aleppo pine)
Conical, open-crowned conifer with an
open growth of bright green leaves,
2¹/₂–4¹/₂in (6–11cm) long, and ovoid,
glossy, brown cones. Young trees
retain glaucous, juvenile
needles for several years.

☼ ◊ ❄❄❄ 9–10

Pinus virginiana (Jersey pine,
Spruce pine, Virginia scrub pine)
Conifer of untidy habit. Gray- to yellow-
green leaves are 1¹/₂–3in (4–7cm) long.
Young shoots have a pinkish white
bloom. Bears oblong to
conical, red-brown cones,
2¹/₂in (6cm) long.

☼ ◊ ❄❄❄ 5–9

Conifers/small

Picea mariana 'Doumetii'
(Doumet spruce)
Densely branched, globose or broadly
conical conifer with short, needlelike,
silvered, dark green leaves and
pendulous, ovoid,
purplish cones.

☼ ◐ ❀❀❀ 3–6

Pinus aristata (Bristle-cone pine)
Slow-growing, bushy conifer. Leaves
are in bundles of 5, very dense and blue-
white to gray-green, flecked with white
resin. Ovoid cones, 1½–4in (4–10cm)
long, have bristly prickles.
Is the oldest-known living
plant (over 4000 years old).

☼ ◐ ❀❀❀ 4–8

Juniperus virginiana 'Burkii'
Slow-growing, upright, dense conifer.
Aromatic, blue-grayish green foliage
develops a purplish tinge in winter.
Scale- and needlelike leaves occur on
same shoot. Has small fruits
with a pronounced bloom.

☼ ◐ ❀❀❀ 3–9

**Juniperus virginiana 'Robusta
Green'**, syn. *J. chinensis*
'Robusta Green'
Slow-growing, columnlike, conical
conifer, making only 3in (7–8cm) a
year, with aromatic, green
foliage and small, gray-
green juniper berries.

☼ ◐ ❀❀❀ 3–9

**Chamaecyparis lawsoniana
'Columnaris'**
Narrow, upright conifer that forms a
neat column of aromatic, blue-gray
foliage. Will tolerate poor soil and
some clipping. Is an
effective, small,
specimen tree.

☼ ◐ ❀❀❀ 6–9

Pinus sylvestris f. *fastigiata*
(Pyramidal Scotch pine)
Upright conifer with erect branches
forming a narrow, obelisk shape. Has
flaky, red-brown bark, blue-green
foliage, and conical cones.
Suffers wind damage in an
exposed site.

☼ ◐ ❀❀❀ 3–7

Pinus bungeana (Lace-bark pine)
Slow-growing, bushy conifer with dark
green foliage, planted for its exquisite,
gray-green bark that flakes to reveal
creamy yellow patches, darkening to
red or purple.

☼ ◐ ❀❀❀ 5–9

Juniperus chinensis 'Obelisk'
Slender, irregularly columnar conifer.
Has ascending branches and long,
prickly, needlelike, aromatic, dark
green leaves. Tolerates a wide range of
soils and conditions but
is particularly suited
to a hot, dry site.

☼ ◐ ❀❀❀ 5–9

Pinus cembroides (Mexican nut
pine, Mexican pinyon pine, Pinyon)
Slow-growing, bushy conifer, rarely
more than 20–22ft (6–7m) high. Scaly
bark is a striking silver-gray or grayish
brown. Leaves, in 2s and
3s, are sparse and dark
green to gray-green.

☼ ◊ ❄❄ 7–10

Abies koreana (Korean fir)
Broadly conical conifer. Produces
cylindrical, violet-blue cones when
less than 3ft (1m) tall. Leaves are
dark green above, silver beneath.

◐ ◊ ❄❄❄ 6–8

Cryptomeria japonica 'Cristata'
Conical conifer with twisted, curved
shoots and soft, fibrous bark. Foliage
is bright green, ageing brown.

◐ ◊ ❄❄❄ 6–9

Thujopsis dolabrata 'Variegata'
Slow-growing, broadly conical, bushy
conifer. Stout, hatchet-shaped leaves
have irregular, creamy patches above,
and are silvery beneath.

◐ ◖ ❄❄❄ 6–9

Cryptomeria japonica
'Pyramidata'
Narrowly columnar or obelisk-shaped
conifer. Foliage is blue-green when
young, maturing to dark green.

◐ ◊ ❄❄❄ 6–9

Pinus pinea
(Italian stone pine, Umbrella pine)
Conifer with a rounded crown on a
short trunk. Leaves are dark green, but
blue-green, juvenile foliage is retained
on young trees. Broadly
ovoid cones ripen shiny
brown; seeds are edible.

☼ ◊ ❄❄❄ 9–10

Taxus cuspidata (Japanese yew)
Evergreen, spreading conifer. Leaves
are dark green above, yellowish green
beneath, sometimes becoming tinged
red-brown in cold weather. Tolerates
very dry and shady
conditions.

☼ ◊ ❄❄❄ 5–7

Cedrus deodara 'Aurea'
Slow-growing, upright conifer with
pendent branch tips and golden yellow
leaves when young in spring-summer.
Foliage matures to yellowish green.
Makes a dramatic, small-
garden evergreen.

◐ ◊ ❄❄❄ 7–9

Chamaecyparis obtusa 'Crippsii'
Attractive, conical conifer, grown for
its flattened sprays of aromatic, bright
golden foliage. Bark is stringy and red-
brown. Cones are round, 1/2in (1cm)
across, and brown.

◐ ◖ ❄❄❄❄ 4–8

Cupressus macrocarpa
'Goldcrest'
Fast-growing, conical conifer with
aromatic, golden yellow foliage held
in plumelike sprays that are useful
in flower arrangements.
Dislikes being clipped.

☼ ◊ ❄❄ 7–10

Dwarf conifers

Dwarf conifers are valuable plants, especially for the small garden, requiring very little attention and providing year-round interest. They can be planted as features in their own right, displaying to advantage their varied shapes, habits, and often striking colors, or, in the rock garden for example, to provide scale or act as a foil for other plants such as bulbs. Several species and cultivars are spreading and good for ground cover.

Almost all conifers are suitable for a wide range of growing conditions, although *Cedrus* and *Juniperus* do not tolerate shade and *Juniperus* and *Pinus* are best for dry, freely drained, sandy soils. Most *Abies*, *Taxus*, *Thuja*, and *Tsuga* are particularly shade tolerant. Some species may be clipped to form a low hedge but new growth will seldom be made if plants are cut back into wood more than 3 or 4 years old.

Picea pungens 'Montgomery'

Abies lasiocarpa var. *arizonica* 'Compacta'

Picea omorika 'Gnom'

Juniperus squamata 'Holger'

Picea omorika 'Gnom'

Pinus sylvestris 'Doone Valley'

Juniperus scopulorum 'Springbank'

Juniperus squamata 'Blue Star'

Juniperus horizontalis 'Douglasii'

Juniperus squamata 'Chinese Silver'

Abies concolor 'Glauca Compacta'

Juniperus virginiana 'Grey Owl'

Juniperus × *media* 'Pfitzeriana Glauca'

Juniperus sabina 'Mas'

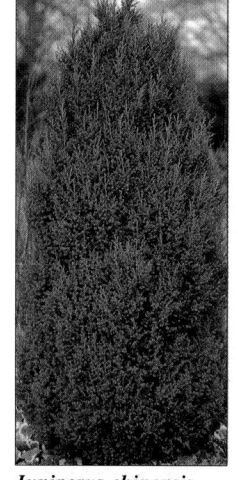

Juniperus chinensis 'Stricta'

Thuja occidentalis 'Caespitosa'

Microbiota decussata

Juniperus procumbens

Juniperus scopulorum 'Skyrocket'

Juniperus procumbens 'Nana'

Juniperus horizontalis 'Turquoise Spreader'

Abies balsamea 'Nana'

Abies cephalonica 'Meyer's Dwarf'

Pseudotsuga menziesii 'Fretsii'

Abies lasiocarpa 'Roger Watson'

Picea mariana 'Nana'

Podocarpus nivalis

Juniperus sabina 'Cupressifolia'

Juniperus recurva 'Densa'

Juniperus sabina var. *tamariscifolia*

Picea abies 'Ohlendorffii'

Picea abies 'Reflexa'

Pinus sylvestris 'Nana'

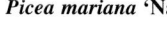

Pseudotsuga menziesii 'Oudemansii'

Chamaecyparis lawsoniana 'Gnome'

Chamaecyparis lawsoniana 'Minima'

Picea abies 'Gregoryana'

Chamaecyparis obtusa 'Intermedia'

Juniperus × *media* 'Pfitzeriana'

Pinus leucodermis 'Schmidtii'

Chamaecyparis obtusa 'Nana Pyramidalis'

Juniperus communis 'Hibernica'

Picea glauca var. *albertiana* 'Conica'

Cedrus libani 'Sargentii'

Pinus leucodermis 'Compact Gem'

Thuja orientalis 'Aurea Nana'

Thuja orientalis 'Semperaurea'

Thuja occidentalis 'Filiformis'

Thuja plicata 'Hillieri'

Juniperus davurica 'Expansa Variegata'

Juniperus × *media* 'Pfitzeriana Aurea'

Juniperus × *media* 'Plumosa Aurea'

Cryptomeria japonica 'Spiralis'

Juniperus × *media* 'Blue Gold'

Cryptomeria japonica 'Sekkan-sugi'

Taxus baccata 'Dovastonii Aurea'

Chamaecyparis obtusa 'Nana Aurea'

Chamaecyparis pisifera 'Filifera Aurea'

Thuja plicata 'Collyer's Gold'

Taxus baccata 'Aurea'

Tsuga canadensis 'Aurea'

Pinus sylvestris 'Aurea'

Pinus sylvestris 'Gold Coin'

Abies nordmanniana 'Golden Spreader'

Thuja plicata 'Stoneham Gold'

Cryptomeria japonica 'Elegans Compacta'

☐ WHITE

Osmanthus delavayi,
syn. *Siphonosmanthus delavayi*
Evergreen, rounded, bushy shrub with
arching branches. Has small, glossy,
dark green leaves and a profusion of
very fragrant, tubular,
white flowers from
mid- to late spring.

☼ ◊ ❄❄ 7–9

Pieris japonica
(Lily-of-the-valley bush)
Evergreen, rounded, bushy, dense
shrub with glossy, dark green foliage
that is bronze when young. Produces
drooping racemes of white
flowers during spring.

☼ ◑ pH ❄❄❄❄ 6–8

Amelanchier lamarckii
Deciduous, spreading shrub. Young
leaves unfold bronze as abundant
sprays of star-shaped, white flowers
open from mid- to late spring. Foliage
matures to dark green,
then turns brilliant red
and orange in autumn.

☼ ◑ ❄❄❄❄ 4–8

Osmanthus × burkwoodii,
syn. × *Osmarea burkwoodii*
Evergreen, rounded, dense shrub.
Glossy foliage is dark green and sets
off a profusion of small, very fragrant
white flowers from
mid- to late spring.

☼ ◊ ❄❄ 7–9

Malus sargentii
(Sargent crab apple)
Deciduous, spreading shrub or small
tree. A profusion of white flowers in
late spring is followed by long-lasting,
deep red fruits. Oval, dark
green leaves are
sometimes lobed.

☼ ◊ ❄❄❄ 4–8

Anopterus glandulosus
(Tasmanian laurel)
Evergreen, bushy shrub or,
occasionally, small tree. Has narrow,
glossy, dark green leaves. Clusters of
cup-shaped, white or pink
flowers appear from mid-
to late spring.

☼ ◑ pH ❄ 10

Viburnum plicatum 'Mariesii'
Deciduous, bushy, spreading shrub
with tiered branches clothed in dark
green leaves, which turn reddish
purple in autumn. Large, rounded
heads of flowers with
white bracts appear in late
spring and early summer.

☼ ◊ ❄❄❄❄ 5–8

Dipelta yunnanensis
Deciduous, arching shrub with peeling
bark and glossy leaves. In late spring
produces tubular, creamy white
flowers, marked orange inside.

☼ ◊ ❄❄❄ 7–9

Staphylea pinnata
(European bladdernut)
Deciduous, upright shrub that in late
spring carries clusters of white flowers,
tinted pink with age, followed by
bladderlike, green fruits.
Foliage is divided and
bright green.

☼ ◑ ❄❄❄ 5–8

Dipelta floribunda
Vigorous, deciduous, upright, treelike shrub with peeling, pale brown bark. Fragrant, pale pink flowers, marked yellow inside, open in late spring and early summer. Has pointed, green leaves.

☼ ◊ ❄❄❄ 6–9   20ft 6m

Staphylea holocarpa 'Rosea'
Deciduous, upright shrub or spreading, small tree. From mid- to late spring, before leaves emerge, bears pink flowers, followed by bladderlike, pale green fruits. Bronze, young leaves mature to blue-green.

☼ ◗ ❄❄❄❄ 6–8   20ft 6m

Magnolia x *soulangeana* 'Rustica Rubra', syn. *M.* x *s.* 'Rubra'
Deciduous, rounded, spreading shrub. Large, goblet-shaped, purplish red blooms, suffused pink, appear from mid-spring to early summer, before and after leaves emerge.

☼ ◊ ❄❄❄ 5–9   20ft 6m

Photinia x *fraseri* 'Birmingham'
Evergreen, upright, bushy, dense shrub with glossy, dark green leaves that are bright purple-red when young. Broad heads of small, white flowers are carried in late spring.

☼ ◊ ❄❄ 7–10   20ft 6m

Enkianthus campanulatus
(Redvein enkianthus)
Deciduous, bushy, spreading shrub with red shoots and tufts of dull green leaves that turn bright red in autumn. Small, bell-shaped, red-veined, creamy yellow flowers appear in late spring.

☼ ◊ pH ❄❄❄ 5–9   20ft 6m

Magnolia x *loebneri* 'Leonard Messel'
Deciduous, upright shrub or small tree. In mid-spring, fragrant flowers with many pale lilac-pink petals appear before and after oval, deep green leaves emerge.

☼ ◊ ❄❄❄ 5–9   25ft 8m

Viburnum x *carlcephalum*
(Fragrant snowball viburnum)
Deciduous, rounded, bushy shrub. In late spring large, rounded heads of pink buds open to fragrant white flowers. These are borne amid dark green foliage that often turns red in autumn.

☼ ◊ ❄❄❄ 5–9   20ft 6m

Magnolia x *soulangeana*
(Saucer magnolia)
Deciduous, rounded, spreading shrub or small tree. Bears large, fragrant, tuliplike, purple-flushed, white blooms from mid-spring to early summer, the first before leaves emerge.

☼ ◊ ❄❄❄ 5–9   20ft 6m

Magnolia liliiflora 'Nigra'
Deciduous, upright, compact shrub that bears large, deep purple flowers, pale pink or white inside, amid dark green leaves from mid-spring to mid-summer.

☼ ◊ ❄❄❄ 6–9   20ft 6m

◼◼◻◻ PURPLE–ORANGE

◻ WHITE

Daphniphyllum macropodum
Evergreen, bushy, dense shrub with
stout shoots and dark green leaves.
Small flowers, green on female
plants, purplish on male plants,
appear in late spring.

☼ ◐ ❋❋ 8–10

Syringa 'Mme. Lemoine'
Deciduous, bushy shrub, upright when
young, later spreading. In late spring
and early summer bears compact
panicles of large, fragrant, double,
white flowers above
heart-shaped leaves.

☼ ◌ ❋❋❋ 3–8

Buddleia davidii 'Peace'
Vigorous, deciduous, arching shrub.
Long, pointed, dark green leaves,
white-felted beneath, set off long
plumes of fragrant white flowers from
mid-summer to autumn.

☼ ◌ ❋❋❋ 5–9

Olearia virgata
Evergreen, arching, graceful shrub with
very narrow, dark gray-green leaves.
Produces an abundance of small, star-
shaped, white flower heads in early
summer, arranged in small
clusters along stems.

☼ ◌ ❋❋ 9–10

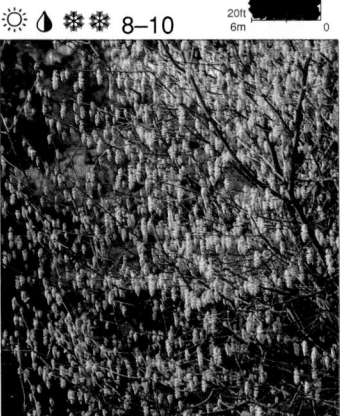

Corylopsis glabrescens
Deciduous, open shrub. Oval leaves,
with bristlelike teeth along margins,
are dark green above, blue-green
beneath. Drooping spikes of fragrant,
bell-shaped, pale yellow
flowers appear in mid-
spring on bare branches.

☼ ◐ pH ❋❋❋ 6–9

Ligustrum sinense
Deciduous or semi-evergreen, upright,
bushy shrub with oval, pale green
leaves. Large panicles of fragrant,
tubular, white flowers are borne
in mid-summer, followed
by small, purplish
black fruits.

☼ ◌ ❋❋❋ 7–9

Escallonia 'Iveyi'
Evergreen, upright shrub. Glossy, dark
green foliage sets off large racemes of
fragrant, tubular, pure white flowers,
with short lobes, borne from mid-
to late summer.

☼ ◌ ❋❋❋ 7–9

Styrax officinalis
(Californian storax)
Deciduous, loose to dense shrub or
small tree. Fragrant, bell-shaped, white
flowers appear in early summer among
oval, dark green leaves
with grayish white
undersides.

☼ ◐ pH ❋❋ 8–10

Berberis darwinii
(Darwin barberry)
Vigorous, evergreen, arching shrub.
Has small, glossy, dark green leaves
and a profusion of rounded, deep
orange-yellow flowers
from mid- to late spring
followed by bluish berries.

☼ ◐ ❋❋❋ 7–9

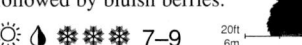

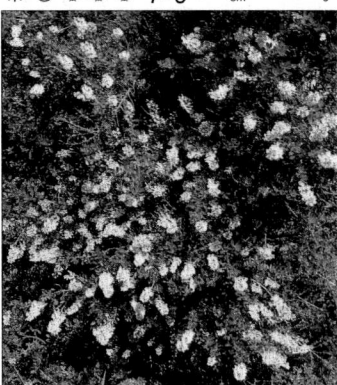

Escallonia leucantha
Evergreen, upright shrub. Narrow,
oval, glossy, dark green leaves set off
large racemes of small, shallowly cup-
shaped, white flowers in mid-summer.

☼ ◌ ❋❋ 8–9

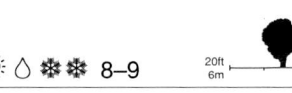

Hydrangea paniculata 'Floribunda'
Deciduous, open shrub. Bears dense,
conical heads of small, fertile, central
flowers surrounded by large, white ray
flowers in late summer.
Leaves are large, pointed,
and dark green.

☼ ◐ ❋❋ 4–9

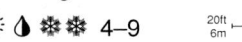

Viburnum rhytidophyllum
(Leatherleaf viburnum)
Vigorous, evergreen, open shrub with
long, narrow, deep green leaves. Has
dense heads of small, creamy white
flowers in late spring and
early summer, then red
fruits that mature to black.

☼ ◐ ❋❋❋ 5–9

Sparmannia africana
(African hemp)
Evergreen, erect shrub or small tree.
Has large, shallowly lobed leaves and
clusters of white flowers, with yellow
and red-purple stamens, in
late spring and summer.
Min. 45°F (7°C).

☼ ◊ 9–10

Chionanthus virginicus (Old-
man's beard, White fringe tree)
Deciduous, bushy shrub or small tree.
Has large, glossy, dark green leaves
that turn yellow in autumn. Drooping
sprays of fragrant white
flowers appear in
early summer.

☼ ◉ ❄❄❄ 5–9

Myrtus luma, syn. *M. apiculata*,
Myrceugenia apiculata
Strong-growing, evergreen, upright
shrub with peeling, golden brown and
gray-white bark. Has cup-shaped, white
flowers amid aromatic, dark
green leaves from mid-
summer to mid-autumn.

☼ ◊ ❄❄ 9–10

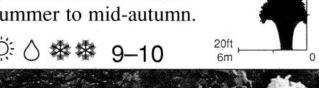

Abutilon vitifolium **'Album'**
Fast-growing, deciduous, upright
shrub. Large, bowl-shaped, white
blooms, pink-tinged when young, are
freely borne in late spring and early
summer amid deeply
lobed, sharply toothed,
gray-green leaves.

☼ ◊ ❄❄ 7–9

Xanthoceras sorbifolium
Deciduous, upright shrub or small tree
with bright green leaves divided into
many slender leaflets. In late spring
and early summer produces spikes of
white flowers with red
patches inside at the
base of the petals.

☼ ◊ ❄❄❄ 5–9

Hydrangea heteromalla
'Bretschneideri'
Deciduous, slightly arching shrub.
Broad heads of small, greenish white
flowers, the outer ones ageing to deep
pink, appear from mid- to
late summer. Has narrow,
dark green leaves.

☼ ◉ ❄❄❄ 7–9

Datura x ***candida***, syn. *Brugmansia*
x *candida* (Angel's trumpet)
Semi-evergreen, rounded shrub or
small tree. Has downy, oval leaves and
strongly scented, pendulous, white
flowers, sometimes cream
or pinkish, in summer-
autumn. Min. 50°F (10°C).

☼ ◊ 10

Cornus mas **'Variegata'**
(Variegated Cornelian cherry)
Deciduous, bushy, dense shrub or
small tree. Small, star-shaped, yellow
flowers appear on bare branches in
early spring before white-
edged, dark green
leaves develop.

☼ ◊ ❄❄❄ 5–8

Holodiscus discolor
(Ocean-spray)
Fast-growing, deciduous, arching shrub.
Has lobed, toothed, dark green leaves
and large, pendent sprays of small,
creamy white flowers in
mid-summer.

☼ ◊ ❄❄❄ 6–9

☐ WHITE

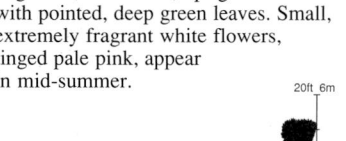

Abelia triflora
Vigorous, deciduous, upright shrub
with pointed, deep green leaves. Small,
extremely fragrant white flowers,
tinged pale pink, appear
in mid-summer.

☼ ◊ ❄❄ 7–9

Clethra delavayi
Deciduous, open shrub with lance-
shaped, toothed, rich green leaves.
Dense, spreading clusters of pink buds
opening to scented, white flowers
appear in mid-summer.

☼ ◊ pH ❄❄ 5–8

☐ PINK

Kolkwitzia amabilis 'Pink Cloud'
(Pink cloud beauty bush)
Deciduous, arching shrub that bears a
mass of bell-shaped, pink flowers amid
small, oval, green leaves in late spring
and early summer.

☼ ◊ ❄❄❄ 5–9

Abelia × grandiflora
(Glossy abelia)
Vigorous, semi-evergreen, arching
shrub. Has glossy, dark green foliage
and an abundance of fragrant pink-
tinged, white flowers
from mid-summer to
mid-autumn.

☼ ◊ ❄❄ 6–9

Tamarix ramosissima, syn.
T. pentandra (Five-stamen tamarisk)
Graceful, deciduous, arching shrub or
small tree with tiny, narrow, blue-
green leaves. In late summer and
early autumn bears large,
upright plumes of
small, pink flowers.

☼ ◊ ❄❄❄ 5–9

Syringa yunnanensis
Deciduous, upright shrub. In early
summer, large, oval, pointed, dark
green leaves set off slender panicles
of 4-petaled, pale pink or
white flowers.

☼ ◊ ❄❄❄ 5–8

Nerium oleander
Evergreen, upright, bushy shrub with
leathery, deep green leaves. Clusters of
salver-form, pink, white, red, apricot,
or yellow flowers appear from spring
to autumn, often on dark red
stalks. Min. 50°F (10°C).

☼ ◊ 8–10

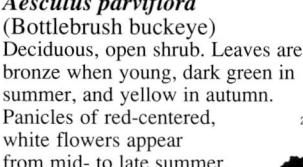

Aesculus parviflora
(Bottlebrush buckeye)
Deciduous, open shrub. Leaves are
bronze when young, dark green in
summer, and yellow in autumn.
Panicles of red-centered,
white flowers appear
from mid- to late summer.

☼ ◊ ❄❄❄ 5–9

Syringa 'Maréchal Foch'
Deciduous, bushy shrub, upright when young, later spreading. Broad, open panicles of large, fragrant, single, carmine pink flowers appear in late spring to early summer. Leaves are heart-shaped and green.

☼ ◊ ❋❋❋ 3–8   20ft 6m

Malvaviscus arboreus
(Wax mallow)
Vigorous, evergreen, rounded shrub. Serrated, bright green leaves are soft-haired. Has bright red flowers with protruding stamens in summer-autumn. Min. 55–61°F (13–16°C).

☼ ◊ 10   20ft 6m

Cotinus coggygria 'Notcutt's Variety'
Deciduous, bushy shrub with deep reddish purple foliage. Long-lasting, purplish pink plumes of massed, small flowers are produced in late summer.

☼ ◊ ❋❋❋ 5–9   20ft 6m

Corylus maxima 'Purpurea'
(Purple giant filbert)
Vigorous, deciduous, open shrub or small tree with deep purple leaves. Purplish catkins, with yellow anthers, hang from bare branches in late winter. Edible nuts mature in autumn.

☼ ◊ ❋❋❋ 4–9   20ft 6m

Buddleia davidii 'Royal Red'
Vigorous, deciduous, arching shrub. Has long, pointed, dark green leaves with white-felted undersides and plumes of fragrant, rich purple-red flowers from mid-summer to autumn.

☼ ◊ ❋❋❋ 5–9   20ft 6m

Acer palmatum 'Atropurpureum'
Deciduous, bushy-headed shrub or small tree with lobed, reddish purple foliage that turns brilliant red in autumn. Small, reddish purple flowers are borne in mid-spring.

☼ ◊ ❋❋❋ 5–8   20ft 6m

Acer palmatum var. heptalobum 'Rubrum'
Deciduous, bushy-headed shrub or small tree. Large leaves are red when young, bronze in summer, and brilliant red, orange, or yellow in autumn. Has small, reddish purple flowers in mid-spring.

☼ ◊ ❋❋❋ 5–8   20ft 6m

Buddleia alternifolia
Deciduous, arching shrub that can be trained as a weeping tree. Has slender, pendent shoots and narrow, gray-green leaves. Neat clusters of fragrant lilac-purple flowers appear in early summer.

☼ ◊ ❋❋❋ 6–9   20ft 6m

Buddleia davidii 'Harlequin'
Vigorous, deciduous, arching shrub. Leaves are long, pointed, and dark green with creamy white margins. Plumes of fragrant red-purple flowers appear from mid-summer to autumn.

☼ ◊ ❋❋❋ 5–9   20ft 6m

Buddleia colvilei (Colvil buddleia)
Deciduous, arching shrub, often treelike with age. Large, white-centered, deep pink to purplish red flowers are borne in drooping racemes amid dark green foliage during early summer.

☼ ◊ ❋❋ 8–9   20ft 6m

Prunus spinosa 'Purpurea'
Deciduous, dense, spiny shrub or small tree. Bright red, young leaves become deep reddish purple. Bears saucer-shaped, pale pink flowers from early to mid-spring, followed by blue-bloomed, black fruits.

☼ ◊ ❋❋❋ 5–9   20ft 6m

Syringa 'Esther Staley'
Deciduous, bushy shrub, upright when young, later spreading. Broadly conical panicles of red buds open to fragrant lilac-pink flowers from mid-spring to early summer. Leaves are broad, heart-shaped, and green.

☼ ◊ ❋❋❋ 3–8   20ft 6m

■■ PURPLE–GREEN

☐ YELLOW

Syringa 'Blue Hyacinth'
Deciduous, bushy shrub, upright when young, later spreading. Bears large, loose panicles of fragrant, pale lilac-blue flowers from mid-spring to early summer and has broadly heart-shaped, green leaves.

☼ ◊ ❉❉❉ 3–8

Elaeagnus angustifolia
Deciduous, bushy shrub or spreading, small tree. Has narrow, silvery gray leaves and small, fragrant, creamy yellow flowers, with spreading lobes, in early summer, followed by small, oval, yellow fruits.

☼ ◊ ❉❉❉ 2–9

Syringa 'Mme. Antoine Buchner'
Deciduous, bushy shrub, upright when young, later spreading. In late spring and early summer long, narrow panicles of deep purple-red buds open to fragrant, double, pinkish mauve flowers, fading with age. Has heart-shaped leaves.

☼ ◊ ❉❉❉ 3–8

Acer palmatum var. **heptalobum 'Lutescens'**
Deciduous, bushy-headed shrub or small tree. Large, lobed leaves become clear yellow in autumn. In mid-spring produces small, reddish purple flowers, followed by winged fruits.

☼ ◊ ❉❉❉ 5–8

Syringa 'Primrose'
Deciduous, bushy shrub, upright when young, later spreading. Small, dense panicles of faintly fragrant, pale yellow flowers are borne in late spring and early summer. Has heart-shaped, green leaves.

☼ ◊ ❉❉❉ 3–8

Syringa 'Charles Joly'
Deciduous, bushy shrub, upright when young, later spreading. From mid-spring to early summer carries dense panicles of large, fragrant, double, deep purple-red flowers above heart-shaped, dark green leaves.

☼ ◊ ❉❉❉ 3–8

Tibouchina urvilleana,
syn. *T. semidecandra* (Glory bush)
Evergreen, slender-branched shrub. Velvet-haired leaves are prominently veined. Has satiny, blue-purple flowers in clusters from summer to early winter. Min. 45°F (7°C).

☼ ◊ pH 9–10

Decaisnea fargesii
Deciduous, upright, semi-arching, open shrub with stout, blue-bloomed shoots and large, deep green leaves of paired leaflets. Racemes of greenish flowers in early summer are followed by pendent, sausage-shaped, bluish fruits.

☼ ◊ ❉❉ 7–9

Paliurus spina-christi
(Christ thorn)
Deciduous, bushy shrub with slender, thorny shoots. Has oval, glossy, bright green leaves, tiny, yellow flowers in summer, and curious, woody, winged fruits in autumn.

☼ ◊ ❉❉ 7–9

Datura 'Grand Marnier'
Robust, evergreen shrub with large, oval to elliptic leaves. Pendent, flared, trumpet-shaped, peach-colored flowers open from an inflated calyx in summer. Min. 45–50°F (7–10°C).

☼ ◊ 10

Datura sanguinea,
syn. *Brugmansia sanguinea*
Semi-evergreen, erect to rounded shrub or small tree with lobed, young leaves. Has large, trumpet-shaped, yellow and orange-red flowers from late summer to winter. Min. 50°F (10°C).

☼ ◊ 10

Caesalpinia gilliesii
(Bird-of-paradise shrub)
Deciduous, open shrub or small tree. Has finely divided, dark green leaves and bears short racemes of yellow flowers with long, red stamens from mid- to late summer.

☼ ◊ ❊ ❊ 10

Crotalaria agatiflora
(Canary-bird bush)
Evergreen, somewhat spreading, loose shrub with gray-green leaves. Racemes of greenish yellow flowers appear in summer and also intermittently during the year. Min. 59°F (15°C).

☼ ◊ 10

Genista cinerea
(Ashy woadwaxen)
Deciduous, arching shrub that produces an abundance of fragrant, pealike, yellow blooms from early to mid-summer. Has silky, young shoots and narrow, gray-green leaves.

☼ ◊ ❊ ❊ 7–9

Cytisus battandieri
(Morocco broom)
Semi-evergreen, open shrub. Leaves have 3 silver-gray leaflets. Large, dense racemes of pineapple-scented, yellow flowers appear from early to mid-summer.

☼ ◊ ❊ ❊ 7–9

Buddleia globosa
(Globe butterfly bush)
Deciduous or semi-evergreen, open shrub with dark green foliage. Dense, rounded clusters of orange-yellow flowers are carried in early summer.

☼ ◊ ❊ ❊ 7–9

Fremontodendron 'California Glory'
Very vigorous, evergreen or semi-evergreen, upright shrub. Has rounded, lobed, dark green leaves and large, bright yellow flowers from late spring to mid-autumn.

☼ ◊ ❊ ❊ 8–10

■■□ RED–YELLOW

Cotoneaster 'Cornubia'
Vigorous, semi-evergreen, arching
shrub. Clusters of white flowers,
produced in early summer amid dark
green foliage, are followed by large,
pendent clusters of
decorative, bright
red fruits.

☀ ◊ ❄❄ 7–8

Rhus typhina 'Laciniata',
syn. *R.t.* 'Dissecta'
Deciduous, spreading, open shrub or
small tree with velvety shoots. Fernlike,
dark green leaves turn brilliant orange-
red in autumn, when deep
red fruit clusters are
also borne.

☀ ◊ ❄❄❄ 3–8

Cotinus coggygria 'Flame'
Deciduous, bushy, treelike shrub with
dark green leaves that turn brilliant
orange-red in autumn. From late
summer, showy, plumelike, purplish
pink flower heads appear
above the foliage.

☀ ◊ ❄❄❄ 5–9

Hippophäe rhamnoides
(Common sea buckthorn)
Deciduous, bushy, arching shrub or
small tree with narrow, silvery leaves.
Tiny, yellow flowers borne in mid-
spring are followed in
autumn on female plants
by bright orange berries.

☀ ◊ ❄❄❄ 3–8

Acer palmatum var. heptalobum
Deciduous, bushy-headed shrub or
small tree with large, lobed, green
leaves that turn brilliant red, orange, or
yellow in autumn. Bears small, reddish
purple flowers
in mid-spring.

☀ ◊ ❄❄❄ 5–8

Hamamelis vernalis 'Sandra'
Deciduous, upright, open shrub. Bears
small, fragrant, spidery, deep yellow
blooms in late winter and early spring.
Oval leaves are purple when young,
green in summer, purple,
red, orange, and yellow
in autumn.

☀ ◊ pH ❄❄❄ 5–9

Acer palmatum 'Senkaki', syn. *A.p.*
'Sango Kaku' (Coralbark maple)
Deciduous, bushy-headed shrub or
small tree. Has bright coral pink, young
shoots in winter. Palmate leaves are
orange-yellow in spring,
green in summer, and pink
then yellow in autumn.

☀ ◊ ❄❄❄ 5–8

Euonymus myrianthus
Evergreen, bushy shrub with pointed,
leathery, green leaves. Dense clusters
of small, greenish yellow flowers in
summer are followed by yellow fruits
that open to show orange-
red seeds.

☀ ◊ ❄❄ 7–9

Pyracantha atalantioides 'Aurea'
Vigorous, evergreen, upright, spiny
shrub, arching with age. Has narrowly
oval, glossy, dark green leaves. White
flowers appear in early summer,
followed by large clusters
of small, yellow berries
in early autumn.

☀ ◊ ❄❄ 6–9

Shrubs/large

Mahonia* x *media* 'Charity'
Evergreen, upright, dense shrub with
large leaves composed of many spiny,
dark green leaflets. Slender, upright,
later spreading spikes of fragrant
yellow flowers are borne
from early autumn to
early spring.

☽ ◊ ✽✽ 7–9

Mahonia* x *media* 'Buckland'
Evergreen, upright, dense shrub. Has
large leaves with many spiny, dark
green leaflets. Clustered, upright then
spreading, long, branched spikes of
fragrant yellow flowers
appear from late autumn
to early spring.

☽ ◊ ✽✽ 7–9

Hamamelis virginiana
(Common witch-hazel)
Deciduous, upright, open shrub. Small,
fragrant, spidery, yellow flowers with
4 narrow petals open in autumn as
leaves fall. Broadly oval
leaves turn yellow
in autumn.

☼ ◊ pH ✽✽✽ 4–9

Cotoneaster lacteus
Evergreen, arching shrub suitable for
hedging. Oval, dark green leaves set
off shallowly cup-shaped, white
flowers from early to mid-summer.
Long-lasting, red fruits are
carried in large clusters
in autumn-winter.

☼ ◊ ✽✽✽ 7–9

Hamamelis* x *intermedia* 'Diane'
Deciduous, open, spreading shrub that
produces fragrant, spidery, deep red
flowers on bare branches from mid- to
late winter. Broadly oval, green leaves
turn yellow and red
in autumn.

☼ ◊ pH ✽✽✽✽ 5–9

Cyphomandra betacea
(Tomato tree)
Evergreen, sparingly branched shrub or
small tree, upright when young, with
large, heart-shaped, rich green leaves.
Has edible, tomatolike,
red fruits from summer to
winter. Min. 50°F (10°C).

☼ ◊ 9–10

Garrya elliptica (Silk-tassel bush)
Evergreen, bushy, dense shrub with
leathery, wavy-edged, dark green
leaves. Gray-green catkins, longer on
male than female plants, are borne
from mid-winter to
early spring.

☼ ◊ ✽✽ 8–10

Azara microphylla (Boxleaf azara)
Elegant, evergreen shrub or small tree.
Has tiny, glossy, dark green leaves and
small clusters of vanilla-scented, deep
yellow flowers in late winter and
early spring.

☼ ◊ ✽✽ 8–10

Corylus avellana* 'Contorta'
(Harry Lauder's walking stick)
Deciduous, bushy shrub with curiously
twisted shoots and broad, sharply
toothed, green leaves. In late winter,
bare branches are covered
with pendent, pale
yellow catkins.

☼ ◊ ✽✽✽ 3–9

□ YELLOW

Shrubs/large ALL YEAR INTEREST

□ WHITE–GREEN

Hamamelis × *intermedia* 'Arnold Promise'
Deciduous, spreading, open shrub. Large, fragrant, spidery, yellow flowers with 4 narrow, crimped petals appear from mid- to late winter. Broadly oval, green leaves turn yellow in autumn.

☼ ◊ pH ❄❄❄ 5–9

Hamamelis japonica 'Sulphurea'
Deciduous, upright, open shrub. In mid-winter, fragrant, spidery, pale yellow flowers with 4 narrow, crimped petals are borne on leafless branches. Broadly oval, dark green leaves turn yellow in autumn.

☼ ◊ pH ❄❄❄ 5–9

Hamamelis mollis 'Coombe Wood'
Deciduous, spreading, open shrub. From mid- to late winter bears very fragrant, spidery, golden yellow flowers with 4 narrow petals. Broadly oval, green leaves turn yellow in autumn.

☼ ◊ pH ❄❄❄ 5–9

Dracaena deremensis 'Warneckii'
Slow-growing, evergreen, upright, sparsely branched shrub, later spreading. Erect to arching, lance-shaped leaves are banded gray-green and cream. Min. 59–64°F (15–18°C).

☼ ◊ 10

Ligustrum ovalifolium
Vigorous, evergreen or semi-evergreen, upright, dense shrub with glossy leaves. Dense racemes of small, tubular, white, rather unpleasantly scented, flowers appear in mid-summer, followed by black fruits.

☼ ◊ ❄❄❄ 6–10

Prunus lusitanica 'Variegata'
Slow-growing, evergreen, bushy shrub with reddish purple shoots. Has oval, glossy, dark green, white-edged leaves. Fragrant, shallowly cup-shaped, creamy white flowers in summer are followed by purple fruits.

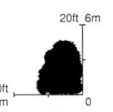

☼ ◊ ❄❄ 7–9

Prunus lusitanica subsp. *azorica* (Azores laurel)
Evergreen, bushy shrub with reddish purple shoots and bright green leaves, red when young. Bears spikes of small, fragrant white flowers in summer, followed by purple fruits.

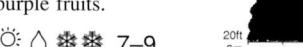

☼ ◊ ❄❄ 7–9

Tetrapanax papyriferus, syn. *Fatsia papyrifera* (Rice-paper plant)
Evergreen, upright, suckering shrub. Long-stalked, circular leaves are deeply lobed. Has bold sprays of small, creamy white flowers in summer and black berries in autumn-winter.

☼ ◊ ❄ 10

Griselinia littoralis 'Variegata'
Evergreen, upright shrub of bushy, dense habit. Leathery leaves are gray-green, marked with bright green and creamy white. Bears inconspicuous, yellow-green flowers in late spring.

☼ ◊ ❄❄ 9–10

Pittosporum 'Garnettii'
Evergreen, columnar or conical shrub of bushy, dense habit. Rounded, gray-green leaves, irregularly edged with creamy white, become tinged with deep pink in cold areas. May bear small, greenish purple flowers in spring-summer.

☼ ◊ ❄❄ 9–10

Polyscias guilfoylei 'Victoriae'
Slow-growing, evergreen, rounded shrub or small tree with leaves that are divided into several oval to rounded, serrated, white-margined, deep green leaflets. Min. 59–64°F (15–18°C).

☼ ◊ 9–10

Dizygotheca elegantissima,
syn. *Aralia elegantissima*
Evergreen, upright, open shrub. Large
leaves have 7–10 coarsely toothed, lustrous, sometimes bronze-tinted, gray-green, leaflets.
Min. 55°F (13°C).

☼ ◑ 10   20ft/6m 0

Ligustrum lucidum 'Excelsum Superbum'
Evergreen, upright shrub or small tree.
Large, glossy, bright green leaves are
marked with pale green and yellow-edged. Small, tubular,
white flowers open in late
summer and early autumn.

☼ ◑ ❋❋ 6–10   20ft/6m 0

Pieris floribunda
(Mountain pieris)
Evergreen, bushy, dense, leafy shrub
with oval, glossy, dark green leaves.
Greenish white flower buds appear
in winter, opening to urn-shaped, white blooms
from early to mid-spring.

☼ ◑ pH ❋❋❋ 5–8   10ft/3m 0

Enkianthus perulatus
(White enkianthus)
Deciduous, bushy, dense shrub. Dark
green leaves turn bright red in autumn.
A profusion of small, pendent, urn-shaped, white flowers is
borne in mid-spring.

☼ ◑ pH ❋❋❋ 6–9   10ft/3m 0

Brachyglottis repanda
Evergreen, bushy shrub or tree, upright
when young, with robust, downy, white
stems. Has veined leaves, white
beneath, and fragrant white flower
heads in summer.
Min. 37°F (3°C).

☼ ◑ 9–10   20ft/6m 0

Osmanthus heterophyllus 'Aureomarginatus'
Evergreen, upright shrub. Sharply
toothed, hollylike, glossy, bright
green leaves have yellow margins.
Small, fragrant white
flowers are produced
in autumn.

☼ ◑ ❋❋ 7–9   20ft/6m 0

Fothergilla major, syn.
F. monticola (Large fothergilla)
Deciduous, upright shrub with glossy,
dark green leaves, slightly bluish white
beneath, that turn red, orange, and
yellow in autum.Tufts of
fragrant white flowers
appear in late spring.

☼ ◑ pH ❋❋❋ 5–9   10ft/3m 0

Pieris japonica 'Scarlett O'Hara'
Evergreen, rounded, bushy, dense
shrub. Young foliage and shoots are
bronze-red, leaves becoming glossy,
dark green. Produces sprays of white
flowers in spring.

☼ ◑ pH ❋❋❋ 6–8   10ft/3m 0

Pittosporum tenuifolium
(Kohuhu)
Evergreen, columnar, later rounded
shrub or small tree with purple shoots
and wavy-edged, oval, glossy, green
leaves. Bears honey-scented,
purple flowers in
late spring.

☼ ◑ ❋❋ 9–10   20ft/6m 0

Elaeagnus pungens 'Maculata'
Evergreen, bushy, slightly spiny shrub.
Glossy, dark green leaves are marked
with a large, central, deep yellow
patch. Very fragrant, urn-shaped,
creamy white flowers
open from mid- to
late autumn.

☼ ◑ ❋❋ 7–9   20ft/6m 0

Choisya ternata
(Mexican orange bush)
Evergreen, rounded, dense shrub with
aromatic, glossy, bright green leaves
composed of 3 leaflets. Clusters of
fragrant white blooms open
in late spring and often
occur again in autumn.

☼ ◑ ❋❋ 8–10   10ft/3m 0

95

Camellias

These evergreen shrubs have long been valued for their luxuriant, rich green foliage and masses of showy flowers, borne mainly in winter and spring. In southern zones many are hardy (especially the *C. sasanqua* hybrids) although blooms may suffer frost and rain damage. Further north, cool greenhouse protection is necessary. Camellias require lime-free soil. The main flower forms are illustrated below.

Single—shallowly cup-shaped flowers each have no more than 8 petals, arranged in a single row, and a conspicuous, central boss of stamens.

Semi-double—cup-shaped flowers each have 2 or more rows of 9–21 regular or irregular petals and conspicuous stamens.

Anemone—rounded flowers each have one or more rows of large, outer petals lying flat or undulating; the domed center has a mass of intermingled petaloids and stamens.

Peony-form—rounded, domed flowers have usually irregular petals intermingled with petaloids and stamens.

Rose-form—cup-shaped flowers each have several rows of overlapping petals and open to reveal stamens in the center.

Formal double—rounded flowers have many rows of regular, neatly overlapping petals that obscure stamens. **Irregular double** forms are similar but often have more loosely arranged, sometimes irregular, petals.

C. japonica 'Alba Simplex' (single)

C. japonica 'Mrs D.W. Davis' (semi-double)

C. x *williamsii* 'Donation' (semi-double)

C. 'Innovation' (peony)

C. 'Leonard Messel' (semi-double)

C. japonica 'Tomorrow's Dawn' (irregular double)

C. x *w.* 'E.G. Water-house' (formal double)

C. 'Inspiration' (semi-double)

C. japonica 'Jupiter' (single)

C. x *williamsii* 'J.C. Williams' (single)

C. j. 'Betty Sheffield Supreme' (irreg. double)

C. x *williamsii* 'Mary Christian' (single)

C. japonica 'Rubescens Major' (formal double)

C. x *williamsii* 'Clarrie Fawcett' (semi-double)

C. x *williamsii* 'Bow Bells' (single)

C. japonica 'Elegans' (anemone)

C. japonica 'Jessie Burgess' (semi-double)

C. japonica 'Margaret Davis' (irregular double)

C. reticulata 'Mudan Cha' (variable)

C. japonica 'Lady Vansittart' (semi-double)

C. sasanqua 'Narumigata' (single)

C. x *williamsii* 'Mary Larcom' (single)

C. x *williamsii* 'St Ewe' (single)

C. x *williamsii* 'Golden Spangles' (single)

C. japonica 'Gloire de Nantes' (semi-double)

C. japonica 'Julia Drayton' (variable)

C. japonica 'Guilio Nuccio' (semi-double)

C. 'William Hertrich' (semi-double)

C. reticulata 'Houye Diechi' (semi-double)

C. japonica 'R.L. Wheeler' (variable)

C. japonica 'Adolphe Audusson' (semi-double)

C. 'Anticipation' (peony)

C. japonica 'Alexander Hunter' (single)

C. reticulata 'Zaotaohung' (variable)

C. 'Dr. Clifford Parks' (variable)

C. japonica 'Althaeiflora' (peony)

C. reticulata 'Zaomu-dan' (irregular double)

C. x williamsii 'Caerhays' (variable)

C. japonica 'Mathotiana' (formal double)

Shrubs/medium SPRING INTEREST

WHITE–PINK

Aronia arbutifolia
(Red chokeberry)
Deciduous shrub, upright when young, later arching. Clusters of small, white flowers with red anthers appear in late spring, followed by red berries. Dark green foliage turns red in autumn.

☀ ◊ ❄❄❄ 4–8

Magnolia stellata (Star magnolia)
Deciduous, bushy, dense shrub. Fragrant, star-shaped, white flowers with many narrow petals open from silky buds during early to mid-spring. Leaves are narrow and deep green.

☀ ◊ ❄❄❄ 5–9

Myrtus communis
(Common myrtle)
Evergreen, bushy shrub with aromatic, glossy, dark green foliage. Fragrant white flowers are borne from mid-spring to early summer, followed by purple-black berries.

☀ ◊ ❄❄ 9–10

Malus sieboldii (Toringo crab apple)
Deciduous, spreading shrub with arching branches. Bears white or pale to deep pink flowers in mid-spring followed by small, red or yellow fruits. Dark green leaves turn red or yellow in autumn.

☀ ◊ ❄❄❄ 5–9

Prunus mume 'Omoi-no-mama'
Deciduous, spreading shrub with fragrant, semi-double, occasionally single, pink-flushed, white flowers wreathing young growths in early spring before oval, toothed leaves appear.

☀ ◊ ❄❄❄ 7–9

Viburnum plicatum 'Pink Beauty'
Deciduous, bushy shrub. Dark green leaves become reddish purple in autumn. In late spring and early summer bears white, later pink, blooms, followed by red, then black, fruits.

☀ ◊ ❄❄❄ 5–8

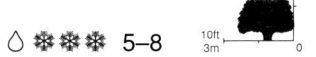

97

Chaenomeles speciosa 'Moerloosii'
Vigorous, deciduous, bushy shrub. Has glossy, dark green leaves and pink-flushed, white flowers in early spring, followed by greenish yellow fruits.

☼ ◊ ❄❄❄ 5–9

Prunus mume 'Beni-shidare', syn. *P.m.* 'Beni-shidon'
Deciduous, spreading shrub with fragrant, single, carmine flowers in early spring before pointed, dark green leaves appear.

☼ ◊ ❄❄❄ 7–9

Enkianthus cernuus var. **rubens**
Deciduous, bushy shrub with dense clusters of dull green leaves that turn deep reddish purple in autumn. Small, bell-shaped, deep red flowers appear in late spring.

☼ ◑ pH ❄❄❄ 6–9

Greyia sutherlandii
Deciduous or semi-evergreen, rounded shrub. Coarsely serrated, leathery leaves turn red in autumn. Spikes of small, bright red flowers appear in spring with new foliage.
Min. 45–50°F
(7–10°C).

☼ ◊ 10

Cotoneaster divaricatus
Deciduous, spreading, bushy shrub. Leaves are glossy, dark green, turning red in autumn. Shallowly cup-shaped, pink-flushed, white flowers in late spring and early summer are followed by deep red fruits.

☼ ◊ ❄❄❄ 6–8

Leucospermum reflexum
Evergreen, erect shrub with ascending branchlets. Has small, blue-gray or gray-green leaves. Slender, tubular, crimson flowers with long styles are carried in tight, rounded heads in spring-summer.
Min. 50°F (10°C).

☼ ◊ 10

Ribes sanguineum 'Pulborough Scarlet'
Deciduous, upright shrub that bears pendent, tubular, deep red flowers in spring amid aromatic, dark green leaves, with 3–5 lobes, sometimes followed by black fruits with a white bloom.

☼ ◊ ❄❄❄ 6–8

Acer palmatum 'Corallinum'
Very slow-growing, deciduous, bushy-headed shrub or small tree. Lobed, bright reddish pink, young foliage becomes green, then brilliant red, orange, or yellow in autumn. Reddish purple flowers appear in mid-spring.

☼ ◊ ❄❄❄ 5–8

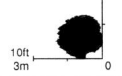

Telopea truncata (Tasmanian waratah)
Evergreen, upright shrub, bushy with age. Has deep green leaves and dense, rounded heads of small, tubular, crimson flowers in late spring and summer.

☼ ◊ pH ❄ 10

Banksia coccinea
Evergreen, dense shrub with toothed, dark green leaves, gray-green beneath. Flower heads comprising clusters of bright red flowers with prominent styles and stigmas are borne in late winter and spring. Min. 50°F (10°C).

☼ ◊ 10

Leptospermum scoparium 'Red Damask'

Evergreen, upright, bushy shrub. Narrow, aromatic, dark green leaves set off sprays of double, dark red flowers in late spring and summer.

 ☼ ◊ ❋❋ 9–10

Berberis thunbergii f. *atropurpurea*

Deciduous, arching, dense shrub. Reddish purple foliage turns bright red in autumn. Globose to cup-shaped, red-tinged, pale yellow flowers in mid-spring are followed by red fruits.

☼ ◊ ❋❋❋ 5–9

Corylopsis pauciflora
(Buttercup winter-hazel)

Deciduous, bushy, dense shrub. Oval, bright green leaves, bronze when young, have bristlelike teeth. Bears fragrant, tubular to bell-shaped, pale yellow flowers from early to mid-spring.

◑ ◊ pH ❋❋❋ 6–9

Syringa x *persica* (Persian lilac)

Deciduous, bushy, dense shrub that produces small, dense panicles of fragrant purple flowers in late spring. Leaves are narrow, pointed, and dark green.

☼ ◊ ❋❋❋ 5–9

Berberis gagnepainii

Evergreen, bushy, dense shrub. Massed, globose to cup-shaped, yellow flowers appear among long, narrow, pointed, dark green leaves in late spring followed in autumn by blue-bloomed, black berries.

☼ ◊ ❋❋❋ 7–9

Lindera benzoin (Spicebush)

Deciduous, bushy shrub with aromatic, bright green leaves that turn yellow in autumn. Tiny, greenish yellow flowers in mid-spring are followed by red berries on female plants.

☼ ◑ pH ❋❋❋ 5–9

Kerria japonica (Japanese kerria)

Graceful, deciduous, arching shrub. Buttercuplike, golden yellow flowers are borne along green shoots from mid- to late spring. Foliage is bright green.

☼ ◊ ❋❋❋ 5–9

Forsythia suspensa
(Weeping forsythia)

Graceful, deciduous, arching shrub with slender shoots. Nodding, narrowly trumpet-shaped, bright yellow flowers open from early to mid-spring, before leaves appear.

☼ ◊ ❋❋❋ 6–8

Rhododendrons and Azaleas

Rhododendrons and azaleas both belong to the huge genus *Rhododendron*, one of the largest in the plant kingdom. "Azalea" is the common name used for all the deciduous species and hybrids of the dwarf, small-leaved evergreens. In stature the genus ranges from alpine shrubs of only a few inches high to tall, spreading trees, in the wild reaching 80ft (24m). Many specimens will grow well in pots where it is often easier to provide suitable growing conditions.

Like most of the related heathers (also Ericaceae), rhododendrons should be grown in an acid soil rich in organic matter but with excellent drainage. Most prefer cool, woodland conditions although many dwarf forms will thrive in more open sites. Once established, they require very little attention apart from an annual mulch and occasional feeding, and provide a colorful display for many years.

R. auriculatum
(rhododendron)

R. fictolacteum
(rhododendron)

R. 'Silver Moon'
(azalea)

R. 'Beauty of Littleworth'
(rhododendron)

R. 'Palestrina' (azalea)

R. occidentale (azalea)

R. yakushimanum
(rhododendron)

R. fulvum
(rhododendron)

R. calophytum
(rhododendron)

R. racemosum
(rhododendron)

R. schlippenbachii
(azalea)

R. 'Seven Stars'
(rhododendron)

R. souliei
(rhododendron)

R. argyrophyllum
(rhododendron)

R. sutchuenense
(rhododendron)

R. 'Nobleanum'
(rhododendron)

R. williamsianum
(rhododendron)

R. orbiculare
(rhododendron)

R. 'Mrs. G.W. Leak'
(rhododendron)

R. yunnanense
(rhododendron)

R. 'Seta'
(rhododendron)

R. 'Corneille' (azalea)

R. 'Azuma-kagami'
(azalea)

R. 'Strawberry Ice'
(azalea)

R. 'Kirin' (azalea)

R. 'Percy Wiseman'
(rhododendron)

R. 'Pink Pearl'
(rhododendron)

R. 'Elizabeth'
(rhododendron)

R. davidsonianum
(rhododendron)

R. 'Queen Elizabeth II'
(rhododendron)

R. 'Rosalind'
(rhododendron)

R. 'Hinodegiri'
(azalea)

R. 'May Day'
(rhododendron)

R. kaempferi (azalea)

R. oreotrephes
(rhododendron)

R. 'Blue Peter'
(rhododendron)

R. wardii
(rhododendron)

R. calostrotum
(rhododendron)

R. 'Hinomayo' (azalea)

R. thomsonii
(rhododendron)

R. cinnabarinum
(rhododendron)

R. hippophaeoides
(rhododendron)

R. lutescens
(rhododendron)

R. 'President Roosevelt'
(rhododendron)

R. 'John Cairns'
(azalea)

R. 'Iro-hayama'
(azalea)

R. augustinii
(rhododendron)

R. xanthocodon
(rhododendron)

R. 'Hatsugiri' (azalea)

R. arboreum
(rhododendron)

R. 'Cynthia'
(rhododendron)

R. 'Vuyk's Scarlet'
(azalea)

R. 'Homebush'
(azalea)

R. 'Susan'
(rhododendron)

Rhododendrons and Azaleas continued

R. 'Narcissiflorum'
(azalea)

R. 'Hawk Crest'
(rhododendron)

R. luteum (azalea)

R. 'Curlew'
(rhododendron)

R. 'George Reynolds'
(azalea)

R. 'Yellowhammer'
(rhododendron)

**R. 'Moonshine
Crescent'** (rhododendron)

R. macabeanum
(rhododendron)

R. 'Freya' (azalea)

R. 'Medway' (azalea)

R. 'Fabia'
(rhododendron)

**R. 'Glory of Little-
worth'** (azalea x rhodo.)

R. 'Frome' (azalea)

R. 'Gloria Mundi'
(azalea)

Shrubs/medium SPRING INTEREST
☐ YELLOW

Berberis verruculosa
Slow-growing, evergreen, bushy
shrub. Has glossy, dark green leaves
with blue-white undersides. Clusters
of small, cup-shaped, bright yellow
flowers in late spring and
early summer are followed
by blue-black fruits.

☀ ◌ ❄❄❄ 6–9

Berberis julianae
(Winter barberry)
Evergreen, bushy, dense shrub. Has
glossy, dark green leaves, yellow
flowers in late spring and early
summer, and egg-shaped,
blue-black fruits
in autumn.

☀ ◌ ❄❄❄ 6–9

Forsythia x intermedia
'Spectabilis'
Vigorous, deciduous, spreading shrub
with stout growths. A profusion of
large, deep yellow flowers is borne
from early to mid-spring
before sharply toothed,
dark green leaves appear.

☀ ◌ ❄❄❄ 5–9

☐ WHITE

Azara serrata
Evergreen, upright shrub with glossy, bright green foliage and rounded bunches of fragrant yellow flowers in late spring or early summer.

☼ ◊ ❋❋ 8–9

Berberis x *stenophylla*
Evergreen, arching shrub with slender shoots and narrow, spine-tipped, deep green leaves, blue-gray beneath. Massed, golden yellow flowers appear from mid- to late spring followed by small, blue-black fruits.

☼ ◊ ❋❋❋ 6–9

Carissa grandiflora 'Tuttlei'
Evergreen, spreading, compact shrub with thorny stems and leathery, glossy, rich green leaves. Has fragrant white flowers in spring-summer and edible, plumlike, red fruits in autumn. Min. 55°F (13°C).

☼ ◊ 9–10

Philadelphus 'Beauclerk'
Deciduous, slightly arching shrub. Large, fragrant flowers, white with a small, central, pale purple blotch, are produced from early to mid-summer. Leaves are dark green.

☼ ◊ ❋❋❋ 5–8

Forsythia x *intermedia* 'Beatrix Farrand'
Vigorous, deciduous, bushy, arching shrub with stout shoots. A profusion of large, deep yellow flowers appears from early to mid-spring before oval, coarsely toothed, green leaves emerge.

☼ ◊ ❋❋❋ 5–9

Berberis x *lologensis* 'Stapehill'
Vigorous, evergreen, arching shrub. Glossy, dark green foliage sets off profuse racemes of globose to cup-shaped, orange flowers from mid- to late spring.

☼ ◊ ❋❋❋ 6–9

Acacia cultriformis (Knife acacia)
Evergreen, arching shrub that produces small, round heads of bright yellow flowers in early spring. Has triangular, silver-gray phyllodes (flattened, leaflike stalks).

☼ ◊ ❋ 10

Berberis linearifolia 'Orange King'
Evergreen, upright, stiff-branched shrub with narrow, rigid, dark green leaves. Bears large, globose to cup-shaped, deep orange flowers in late spring.

☼ ◊ ❋❋❋ 6–9

Exochorda x *macrantha* 'The Bride'
Deciduous, arching, dense shrub that forms a mound of pendent branches. Large, white flowers are produced in abundance amid dark green foliage in late spring and early summer.

☼ ◊ ❋❋❋ 5–9

☐ WHITE

Deutzia scabra (Fuzzy deutzia)
Deciduous, upright shrub with
narrowly oval, dark green leaves
that from early to mid-summer set off
dense, upright clusters of 5-petaled,
white blooms.

☼ ◊ ❄❄❄ 5–9

Philadelphus 'Belle Etoile'
Deciduous, arching shrub. Very
fragrant white flowers each with a
pale purple mark at the base are borne
profusely among green foliage in late
spring and early summer.

☼ ◊ ❄❄❄ 5–8

Pyracantha x _watereri_
Evergreen, upright, dense, spiny shrub
with glossy, dark green foliage.
Shallowly cup-shaped, white flowers
in early summer are succeeded by
bright red berries
in autumn.

☼ ◊ ❄❄❄ 6–8

Spiraea canescens (Hoary spiraea)
Deciduous shrub with upright shoots
arching at the top. Small heads of
white flowers are borne in profusion
amid narrowly oval, gray-green
leaves from early to
mid-summer.

☼ ◊ ❄❄❄❄ 7–9

**_Deutzia_ x _magnifica_
'Staphyleoides'**
Vigorous, deciduous, upright shrub.
Large, 5-petaled, pure white blooms,
borne in dense clusters in early
summer, have recurved
petals. Leaves are
bright green.

☼ ◊ ❄❄❄ 5–9

Fallugia paradoxa (Apache plume)
Deciduous, bushy shrub that bears
white flowers in mid-summer, followed
by silky, pink- and red-tinged, green
fruits. Dark green leaves are finely
cut and feathery.

☼ ◊ ❄❄ 6–9

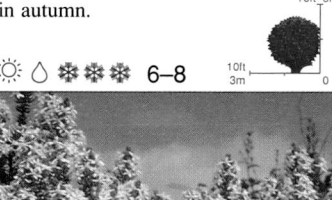

Aronia melanocarpa
(Black chokeberry)
Deciduous, bushy shrub. White flowers
appear in late spring and early summer,
followed by black fruits. Has glossy,
dark green leaves that
turn red in autumn.

☼ ◊ ❄❄❄❄ 4–9

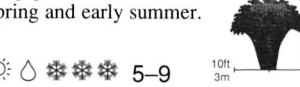

Rubus 'Benenden',
syn. _R._ 'Tridel'
Deciduous, arching, thornless shrub
with peeling bark. Large, roselike, pure
white flowers are borne among lobed,
deep green leaves in late
spring and early summer.

☼ ◊ ❄❄❄ 5–9

Olearia nummulariifolia
Evergreen, rounded shrub with stiff,
upright shoots densely covered with
small, very thick, mid- to dark green
leaves. Small, fragrant white flowers
appear in mid-summer.

☼ ◊ ❄❄ 9–10

Sorbaria sorbifolia, syn. *Spiraea sorbifolia* (Ural false spiraea)
Deciduous, upright shrub that forms thickets by suckering. Green leaves consist of many sharply toothed leaflets. Large panicles of small, white flowers appear in summer.

☀ ◊ ❄❄❄ 2–9

Yucca gloriosa (Spanish-dagger)
Evergreen shrub with a stout stem crowned with a tuft of long, pointed, deep green leaves, blue-green when young. Bears very long panicles of bell-shaped, white flowers in summer-autumn.

☀ ◊ ❄❄❄ 7–10

Prinsepia uniflora
Deciduous, arching, spiny shrub. From late spring to summer bears small, fragrant white flowers amid narrow, glossy, dark green leaves followed by cherrylike, deep red fruits. Grows best in hot sun.

☀ ◊ ❄❄❄ 4–8

Philadelphus 'Boule d'Argent'
Deciduous, bushy, arching shrub with dark green foliage that sets off clusters of slightly fragrant, semi-double to double, pure white flowers from early to mid-summer.

☀ ◊ ❄❄❄ 5–9

Hydrangea arborescens 'Grandiflora'
Deciduous, upright, bushy shrub that produces large, rounded heads of white flowers from mid-summer to early autumn. Has broad, oval, pointed, bright green leaves.

☀ ◊ ❄❄❄ 4–9

Philadelphus 'Dame Blanche'
Deciduous, bushy, compact shrub with dark, peeling bark. Dark green foliage sets off slightly fragrant, semi-double to loosely double, pure white flowers borne in profusion from early to mid-summer.

☀ ◊ ❄❄❄ 5–9

Escallonia virgata
(Twiggy escallonia)
Graceful, deciduous, spreading shrub with arching shoots and small, glossy, dark green leaves. Bears racemes of small, open cup-shaped, white flowers from early to mid-summer.

☀ ◊ ❄❄ 7–9

Eucryphia milliganii
Evergreen, upright, narrow shrub. Has tiny, dark green leaves, bluish white beneath, and small, white flowers, borne in mid-summer.

☀ ◊ pH ❄❄ 8–9

☐ WHITE

Osteomeles schweriniae
Evergreen, arching shrub with long, slender shoots. Leaves, consisting of many small leaflets, are dark green. Clusters of small, white flowers in early summer are followed by red, later blue-black, fruits.

☼ ◊ ❀❀ 7–10

Carpenteria californica
(Evergreen mock-orange)
Evergreen, bushy shrub. Glossy, dark green foliage sets off fragrant yellow-centered, white flowers borne during summer.

☼ ◊ ❀❀ 7–9

Zenobia pulverulenta
Deciduous or semi-evergreen, slightly arching shrub, often with bluish white-bloomed shoots. Glossy leaves have a bluish white reverse when young. Bears fragrant, bell-shaped, white flowers from early to mid-summer.

◐ ◊ pH ❀❀❀ 6–9

Hydrangea quercifolia
(Oak-leaf hydrangea)
Deciduous, mound-forming, bushy shrub with deeply lobed, dark green leaves that turn red and purple in autumn. White flower heads are borne from mid-summer to mid-autumn.

◐ ◊ ❀❀ 5–9

Styrax wilsonii (Wilson snowbell)
Deciduous, bushy shrub with slender shoots that produce an abundance of yellow-centered, white flowers in early summer. Leaves are small and deep green.

☼ ◊ pH ❀❀ 7–10

Symplocos paniculata
(Asiatic sweetleaf, Sapphire berry)
Deciduous, bushy shrub or small tree. Panicles of small, fragrant white flowers in late spring and early summer are followed by small, metallic blue berries. Has dark green leaves.

☼ ◊ ❀❀❀ 6–9

Ceanothus incanus
(Coast whitethorn)
Evergreen, bushy shrub. Has spreading, spiny shoots, broad, gray-green leaves, and large racemes of white flowers in late spring and early summer.

☼ ◊ ❀❀ 8–9

Ozothamnus rosmarinifolius, syn. **Helichrysum rosmarinifolium**
Evergreen, upright, dense shrub with woolly, white shoots and narrow, dark green leaves. Clusters of fragrant white flower heads open in early summer.

☼ ◊ ❀❀ 8–9

Philadelphus 'Lemoinei'
Deciduous, upright, slightly arching shrub that produces profuse racemes of small, extremely fragrant white flowers from early to mid-summer.

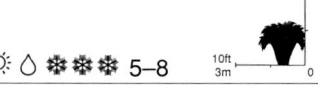

☼ ◊ ❀❀ 5–8

Cornus alba 'Elegantissima'
Vigorous, deciduous shrub. Young shoots are bright red in winter. Has white-edged, gray-green leaves and small, creamy white flowers in late spring and early summer followed by white fruits.

☼ ◊ ❀❀❀ 2–8

Clethra barbinervis
Deciduous, upright shrub with peeling bark. Has oval, toothed, dark green leaves that turn red and yellow in autumn. Racemes of fragrant white flowers are borne in late summer and early autumn.

☼ ◊ pH ❀❀❀ 5–8

Hydrangea paniculata 'Brussels Lace'
Deciduous, open shrub with large, pointed, dark green leaves. Bears delicate, open panicles of white flowers in late summer and early autumn.

☼ ◊ ❀❀❀ 4–8

Viburnum dilatatum 'Catskill'
Deciduous, low, spreading shrub with sharply toothed, dark green leaves that turn yellow, orange, and red in autumn. Flat heads of creamy white flowers in late spring and early summer are followed by bright red fruits.

☼ ◊ ❄❄❄ 5–9

Olearia x haastii
(New Zealand daisy-bush)
Evergreen, bushy, dense shrub. Has small, oval, glossy, dark green leaves and is covered with heads of fragrant, daisylike, white flowers from mid- to late summer. Good for hedging.

☼ ◊ ❄❄ 8–10

Philadelphus coronarius 'Variegatus'
Deciduous, bushy shrub with racemes of very fragrant, creamy white flowers in late spring and early summer and leaves broadly edged with white.

☼ ◊ ❄❄❄ 5–9

Spiraea nipponica 'Snowmound',
syn. *S.n.* var. *tosaensis* of gardens
Deciduous, spreading shrub with stout, arching, reddish branches. Small, narrow, dark green leaves set off profuse, dense clusters of small, white flowers in early summer.

☼ ◊ ❄❄❄ 4–9

Eriogonum giganteum
(St. Catherine's lace)
Evergreen, rounded shrub with oblong to oval, woolly, white leaves. Small, white flowers are carried in branching clusters to 12in (30cm) or more wide in summer.
Min. 41°F (5°C).

☼ ◊ 9–10

Viburnum 'Pragense',
syn. *V.* x *pragense*
Evergreen, rounded, bushy shrub that has dark green foliage and domed heads of white flowers opening from pink buds in late spring and early summer.

☼ ◊ ❄❄❄ 5–8

Leptospermum flavescens
Graceful, evergreen, arching shrub with small, glossy, bright green leaves. Bears an abundance of small, pink-tinged, white flowers in mid-summer.

☼ ◊ ❄❄ 9–10

Philadelphus delavayi
f. **melanocalyx**
Deciduous, upright shrub, grown for its extremely fragrant flowers, with pure white petals and deep purple sepals, opening from early to mid-summer. Leaves are dark green.

☼ ◊ ❄❄❄ 6–9

Hibiscus syriacus 'Red Heart'
Deciduous, upright shrub that bears large, white flowers with conspicuous red centers from late summer to mid-autumn. Oval leaves are lobed and deep green.

☼ ◊ ❄❄❄ 6–9

◻◻ WHITE–PINK

◻ PINK

Stephanandra tanakae
Deciduous, arching shrub with orange-brown shoots and sharply toothed, green leaves that turn orange and yellow in autumn. Small, yellow-green buds open to white flowers from early to mid-summer.

☼ ◊ ❄❄❄ 5–8

Lonicera tatarica
(Tatarian honeysuckle)
Deciduous, bushy shrub. Tubular to trumpet-shaped, 5-lobed, white, pink, or red flowers cover dark green foliage in late spring and early summer and are succeeded by red berries.

☼ ◊ ❄❄❄ 3–9

Syringa microphylla 'Superba'
Deciduous, bushy shrub that produces abundant, small, open panicles of very fragrant pink flowers from late spring to early autumn. Has oval, pointed leaves.

☼ ◊ ❄❄❄ 5–8

Protea neriifolia
Evergreen, bushy, upright shrub with narrow leaves. Flower heads, about 5in (13cm) long, are red, pink, or white, the bracts tipped with tufts of black hair, and appear in spring-summer. Min. 41–5°F (5–7°C).

☼ ◊ pH 10

Lonicera xylosteum
(European fly honeysuckle)
Deciduous, upright, bushy, dense shrub. Creamy white flowers are produced amid gray-green leaves in late spring and early summer and are followed by red berries.

☼ ◊ ❄❄❄❄ 4–9

Escallonia 'Donard Seedling'
Vigorous, evergreen, arching shrub with small, glossy, dark green leaves. Masses of pink flower buds open to white blooms, flushed with pale pink, from early to mid-summer.

☼ ◊ ❄❄ 8–9

Acer palmatum 'Butterfly'
Slow-growing, deciduous, mounded shrub or small tree with lobed, gray-green leaves edged with cream and pink. In mid-spring bears small, reddish purple flowers.

☼ ◊ ❄❄❄❄ 5–8

Deutzia longifolia 'Veitchii'
Deciduous, arching shrub with narrow, pointed leaves and large clusters of 5-petaled, deep pink flowers from early to mid-summer.

☼ ◊ ❄❄❄ 7–9

Neillia thibetica
Deciduous, arching shrub. Slender spikes of rose-pink flowers are borne profusely in late spring and early summer. Leaves are sharply toothed.

☼ ◊ ❄❄❄ 6–9

Escallonia 'Apple Blossom'
Evergreen, bushy, dense shrub. From early to mid-summer apple-blossom pink flowers are borne in profusion amid glossy, dark green leaves.

☼ ◊ ❄❄ 8–9

Robinia hispida (Rose acacia)
Deciduous shrub of loose habit with brittle, bristly stems that carry dark green leaves composed of 7–13 leaflets. Pendent racemes of deep rose-pink blooms open in late spring and early summer.

☼ ◊ ❄❄❄ 6–10

Indigofera heterantha,
syn. *I. gerardiana*
Deciduous, slightly arching shrub. Has grayish green leaves consisting of many small leaflets and spikes of small, purplish pink flowers from early summer to early autumn.

☼ ◊ ❄❄ 6–9

Lavatera olbia 'Rosea'
Semi-evergreen, erect shrub that produces abundant clusters of hollyhocklike, deep pink flowers throughout summer. Has lobed, sage green leaves.

☼ ◊ ❄❄ 8–10

Medinilla magnifica
Evergreen, upright shrub, with sparingly produced, 4-angled, robust stems and boldly veined leaves. Pink to coral red flowers hang in long trusses beneath large, pink bracts in spring-summer. Min. 61–4°F (16–18°C).

☼ ◊ 10

Hibiscus syriacus 'Woodbridge'
Deciduous, upright shrub. From late summer to mid-autumn large, reddish pink flowers, with deeper-colored centers, appear amid lobed, dark green leaves.

☼ ◊ ❄❄❄ 6–9

Kalmia latifolia (Mountain laurel)
Evergreen, bushy, dense shrub. In early summer large clusters of pink flowers open from distinctively crimped buds amid glossy, rich green foliage.

☼ ◊ pH ❄❄❄ 5–9

Hibiscus rosa-sinensis 'The President'
Evergreen, bushy shrub with toothed, oval, glossy, dark green leaves. In summer bears large, magenta-centered, bright pink flowers with prominent, yellow anthers. Min. 59°F (15°C).

☼ ◊ 9–10

Lavatera assurgentiflora
Semi-evergreen shrub with twisted, gray stems. Clusters of hollyhocklike, darkly veined, deep cerise blooms open in mid-summer. Palmate, green leaves are white-haired beneath.

☼ ◊ ❄❄ 9–10

■ PINK–RED

Melaleuca elliptica
Evergreen, rounded shrub with long, leathery, usually grayish green leaves. Flowers, consisting of a brush of red stamens, are borne in dense, terminal spikes in spring-summer.

☼ ◊ ❄ 10

Cestrum elegans (Red cestrum)
Vigorous, evergreen, arching shrub. Nodding shoots carry downy, deep green foliage. Dense racemes of tubular, purplish red flowers in late spring and summer are followed by deep red fruits.

☼ ◊ ❄❄ 10

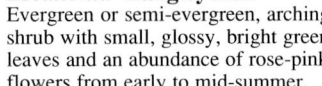

 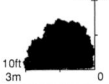

Escallonia 'Langleyensis'
Evergreen or semi-evergreen, arching shrub with small, glossy, bright green leaves and an abundance of rose-pink flowers from early to mid-summer.

☼ ◊ ❄❄ 8–9

■ RED

Pieris formosa var. **forrestii 'Wakehurst'**
Evergreen, bushy, dense shrub. Young leaves are brilliant red in early summer, becoming pink, creamy yellow, and finally dark green. Bears urn-shaped, white flowers in spring-summer.

☼ ◊ pH ❄❄❄ 7–9

Calycanthus occidentalis (California sweet shrub)
Deciduous, bushy shrub. Leaves are large, aromatic, and dark green. Fragrant, purplish red flowers with many strap-shaped petals appear during summer.

☼ ◊ ❄❄❄ 6–9

Crinodendron hookerianum, syn. **Tricuspidaria lanceolata**
Evergreen, stiff-branched shrub. In late spring and early summer, lanternlike, red flowers hang from shoots clothed with narrow, dark green leaves.

☼ ◊ pH ❄❄ 9–10

Lonicera ledebourii
Deciduous, bushy shrub. Red-tinged, orange-yellow flowers are borne amid dark green foliage in late spring and early summer and are followed by black berries. As these ripen, deep red bracts enlarge around them.

☼ ◊ ❄❄❄ 5–9

Bauhinia punctata, syn. **B. galpinii** (Red bauhinia)
Semi-evergreen or evergreen, spreading shrub, occasionally semi-climbing. Has 2-lobed leaves and, in summer, fragrant, bright brick red flowers. Min. 41°F (5°C).

☼ ◊ 10

Telopea speciosissima (Waratah)
Evergreen, erect, fairly bushy shrub with coarsely serrated leaves. Has tubular, red flowers in dense, globose heads, surrounded by bright red bracts, in spring-summer.

☼ ◊ pH ❄ 10

Erythrina crista-galli
(Cockspur coral-tree)
Deciduous, mainly upright shrub or
small tree. Leaves have 3 oval leaflets.
Has leafy racemes of crimson flowers
in summer-autumn. Dies
back to ground level in
winter in cold areas.

☼ ◊ ❄ 9–10

Erythrina × bidwillii
Deciduous, upright shrub with pale
to mid-green leaves divided into 3
leaflets, up to 4in (10cm) long. Bright
red flowers are carried in racemes in
late summer or autumn.

☼ ◊ ❄ 9–10

Feijoa sellowiana
(Pineapple guava)
Evergreen, bushy shrub or tree. Dark
green leaves have white undersides. In
mid-summer bears large, dark red
flowers with white-edged
petals, followed by edible,
red-tinged, green fruits.

☼ ◊ ❄❄ 9–10

Acalypha wilkesiana
(Painted copperleaf)
Evergreen, bushy shrub. Oval, serrated
leaves are 4in (10cm) or more long,
rich copper green, variably splashed
with shades of red. Min.
61°F (16°C).

☼◐ ◊ 10

Desfontainia spinosa
Evergreen, bushy, dense shrub with
spiny, hollylike, glossy, dark green
leaves. Long, tubular, drooping, red
flowers tipped with yellow are borne
from mid-summer to
late autumn.

☼◐ ◊ pH ❄❄ 9–10

***Callistemon citrinus* 'Splendens'**
Evergreen, arching shrub with broad,
lemon-scented, gray-green leaves that
are bronze-red when young. In early
summer, bright red flowers are borne
in bottlebrushlike spikes.

☼ ◊ ❄ 9–10

***Acer palmatum* 'Bloodgood'**
Deciduous, bushy-headed shrub or
small tree with deep reddish purple
leaves that turn brilliant red in autumn.
Small, reddish purple flowers in mid-
spring are often followed
by decorative, winged,
red fruits.

☼ ◊ ❄❄❄ 5–8

Aloysia triphylla, syn. *Lippia
citriodora* (Lemon verbena)
Deciduous, bushy shrub. Leaves
are pale green and lemon-scented.
Racemes of tiny, lilac-tinged, white
flowers appear in
early summer.

☼◐ ◊ ❄❄ 8–10

Callistemon rigidus
(Stiff bottlebrush)
Evergreen, slightly arching, bushy
shrub with long, narrow, sharply
pointed, dark green leaves and dense
spikes of deep red flowers
in late spring and
early summer.

☼ ◊ ❄❄ 9–10

Rhus glabra (Smooth sumac)
Deciduous, bushy shrub with bluish
white-bloomed, reddish purple stems.
Deep blue-green leaves turn red in
autumn. Bears panicles of greenish red
flower heads in summer
followed by red fruits on
female plants.

☼ ◊ ❄❄❄ 2–9

Buddleia crispa
Deciduous, upright, bushy shrub that
from mid- to late summer bears
racemes of small, fragrant lilac
flowers with white eyes. Has woolly,
white shoots and oval,
grayish green leaves.

☼ ◊ ❄❄ 9

■ PURPLE

Hibiscus sinosyriacus 'Lilac Queen'
Deciduous, spreading, open shrub. From late summer to mid-autumn produces large, pale lilac flowers with red centers. Broad, lobed leaves are dark green.

☼ ◊ ❆ ❆ ❆ 6–9

Hydrangea macrophylla 'Lilacina'
Deciduous, bushy shrub. In late summer bears flat, open heads of tiny, deep lilac, central flowers and larger, sterile, pinkish purple, outer flowers. Has oval, toothed, glossy leaves.

☼ ◊ ❆ ❆ 6–10

Hydrangea aspera subsp. **aspera**, syn. *H. villosa*
Deciduous, upright shrub with peeling bark and from late summer to mid-autumn heads of small, blue or purple, central flowers and larger, white, sometimes flushed purplish pink, outer ones.

☼ ◊ ❆ ❆ ❆ 7–9

Prostanthera ovalifolia
Evergreen, rounded, bushy shrub with tiny, sweetly aromatic, oval, thick-textured leaves. Cup-shaped, 2-lipped, purple flowers appear in short, leafy racemes in spring-summer. Min. 41°F (5°C).

☼ ◊ 9–10

Melaleuca nesophylla (Western tea-myrtle)
Evergreen, bushy shrub or small tree with oval, gray-green leaves. Flowers, consisting of a brush of lavender to rose-pink stamens, are borne in rounded, terminal heads in summer.

☼ ◊ ❆ 10

Abutilon x suntense 'Violetta'
Fast-growing, deciduous, upright, arching shrub that carries an abundance of large, bowl-shaped, deep violet flowers in late spring and early summer. Vinelike leaves are sharply toothed and dark green.

☼ ◊ ❆ ❆ 9–10

Prostanthera rotundifolia
(Roundleaf mintbush)
Evergreen, rounded, bushy shrub with
tiny, sweetly aromatic, deep green
leaves and short, leafy racemes of bell-
shaped, lavender to purple-
blue flowers in late
spring or summer.

☼ ◊ ❄ 9–10

***Solanum rantonnetii* 'Royal
Robe'**
Evergreen, loosely rounded shrub
with smooth, bright green leaves. In
summer has clusters of rich purple-
blue flowers that open
almost flat. Min.
45°F (7°C).

☼ ◊ 9–10

***Hydrangea macrophylla* 'Veitchii'**
Deciduous, bushy shrub. Oval, toothed,
glossy leaves set off large, white, later
pink, bracts surrounding lilac-blue
flowers borne in flat, open heads
from mid- to
late summer.

☀ ◐ ❄❄ 6–10

Sophora davidii, syn. *S. viciifolia*
(Vetch sophora)
Deciduous, bushy shrub with arching
shoots. Produces short racemes of small,
pealike, purple and white flowers in late
spring and early summer.
Gray-green leaves have
many leaflets.

☼ ◊ ❄❄❄ 6–9

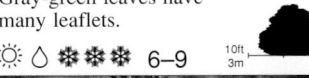

***Fabiana imbricata* 'Violacea'**
Evergreen, upright shrub with shoots
that are densely covered with tiny,
heathlike, deep green leaves. Tubular,
lilac flowers are borne profusely in
early summer.

☼ ◊ ❄❄ 9–10

***Hydrangea macrophylla*
'Blue Wave'**
Deciduous, bushy shrub with flat, open
heads of rich blue or lilac to pink
flowers from mid- to late summer.
Light green leaves are
oval, toothed, and glossy.

☼ ◊ ❄❄ 6–10

***Hibiscus syriacus* 'Blue Bird'**
Deciduous, upright shrub that carries
large, red-centered, lilac-blue flowers
from late summer to mid-autumn. Has
lobed, deep green leaves.

☼ ◊ ❄❄❄ 6–9

Ceanothus impressus
(Santa Barbara ceanothus)
Evergreen, bushy shrub. Spreading
growth is covered with small, crinkled,
dark green leaves. Deep blue flowers
appear in small clusters
from mid-spring to
early summer.

☼ ◊ ❄❄ 8–10

***Hydrangea macrophylla*
'Blue Bonnet'**
Deciduous, bushy shrub that produces
dense, domed heads of rich blue or pink
flowers from mid- to late summer.
Leaves are oval, pointed,
and dark green.

☼ ◊ ❄❄ 6–10

Eleutherococcus sieboldianus,
syn. *Acanthopanax sieboldianus*
Elegant, deciduous, bushy shrub. Has
glossy, bright green leaves, divided
into 5 leaflets, and is armed with
spines. Clusters of small,
greenish flowers appear
in early summer.

☼ ◊ ❄❄❄ 5–9

Zanthoxylum piperitum
(Japan pepper)
Deciduous, bushy, spiny shrub or small
tree with aromatic, glossy, dark green
leaves composed of many leaflets.
Small, red fruits follow
tiny, greenish yellow,
spring flowers.

☼ ◊ ❄❄❄ 6–10

***Ptelea trifoliata* 'Aurea'**
Deciduous, bushy, dense shrub or low
tree. Leaves, consisting of 3 leaflets,
are bright yellow when young,
maturing to pale green. Bears racemes
of greenish flowers in
summer, followed by
winged, green fruits.

☼ ◊ ❄❄❄ 5–9

■ GREEN–YELLOW

Itea ilicifolia
(Hollyleaf sweetspire)
Evergreen, bushy shrub with arching
shoots and oval, sharply toothed, dark
green leaves. Long, catkinlike
racemes of small, greenish
flowers appear in late
summer and early autumn.

 7–9

Callistemon pallidus
Evergreen, arching shrub. Gray-green
foliage is pink-tinged when young and
in early summer is covered with dense
spikes of creamy yellow flowers that
resemble bottlebrushes.

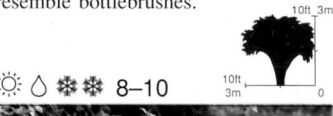 8–10

**Physocarpus opulifolius 'Dart's
Gold'**
Deciduous, compact shrub with peeling
bark and oval, lobed, golden yellow
leaves. Produces clusters of shallowly
cup-shaped, white or pale
pink flowers in
late spring.

 2–8

Cornus alba 'Spaethii'
Vigorous, deciduous shrub with bright
red, young shoots in winter. Bright
green leaves are yellow-edged. Bears
small, creamy white flowers in late
spring and early summer,
followed by rounded,
white fruits.

 2–8

Bupleurum fruticosum
Evergreen, bushy shrub with slender
shoots. From mid-summer to early
autumn rounded heads of small,
yellow flowers are borne amid glossy,
dark bluish green foliage.

 7–10

Colutea arborescens (Bladder
senna, Common bladder senna)
Fast-growing, deciduous, open shrub.
Has pale green leaves with many
leaflets, pealike, yellow flowers
throughout summer, and
bladderlike seed pods in
late summer and autumn.

  6–9

Piptanthus nepalensis,
syn. *P. laburnifolius*
Deciduous or semi-evergreen, open
shrub with leaves consisting of 3 large,
dark blue-green leaflets. Racemes of
pealike, bright yellow
flowers appear in
spring-summer.

 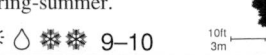 9–10

Jasminum humile
(Italian jasmine)
Evergreen, bushy shrub that bears
bright yellow flowers on long, slender,
green shoots from early spring to late
autumn. Leaves, with 5 or
7 leaflets, are bright green.

 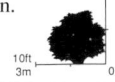 7–9

Hibbertia cuneiformis,
syn. *Candollea cuneiformis*
Evergreen, upright, bushy shrub with
small, oval leaves, serrated at tips. Has
small clusters of bright yellow flowers,
with spreading petals, in
spring-summer. Min.
41–5°F (5–7°C).

 10

YELLOW–ORANGE

WHITE–RED

Colutea × media
Vigorous, deciduous, open shrub. Gray-green leaves have many leaflets. Racemes of yellow flowers, tinged with copper orange, appear in summer, followed by bladderlike, papery, red-tinged seed pods.

☀ ◊ ❄❄❄ 6–9

Dendromecon rigida
(Bush poppy)
Vigorous, evergreen, upright shrub. Large, fragrant, golden yellow flowers appear amid gray-green foliage from spring to autumn. Best grown against a wall.

☀ ◊ ❄❄❄ 9–10

Colletia armata
Almost leafless, arching, stoutly branched shrub armed with rigid, gray-green spines. Pink flower buds open in late summer to fragrant, tubular, white blooms that last into autumn.

☀ ◊ ❄❄❄ 7–10

Calliandra haematocephala
[pink form]
Evergreen, spreading shrub. Leaves have 16–24 narrowly oval leaflets. Flower heads consist of many pink-stamened florets from late autumn to spring. Min. 45°F (7°C).

☀ ◊ 10

Cassia corymbosa
(Flowery senna)
Vigorous, evergreen or semi-evergreen shrub. Leaves have 4–6 oval, bright green leaflets; sprays of bowl-shaped, rich yellow flowers appear in late summer. Min. 45°F (7°C).

☀ ◊ 9–10

Cassia didymobotrya
Evergreen, rounded, sometimes spreading shrub with leaves of several leaflets; spikes of rich yellow flowers open from glossy, blackish brown buds throughout the year. Min. 55°F (13°C).

☀ ◊ 10

Clerodendrum trichotomum
Deciduous, upright, bushy-headed, treelike shrub. Clusters of deep pink and greenish white buds open to fragrant white flowers above large leaves from late summer to mid-autumn, followed by decorative, blue berries.

☀ ◊ ❄❄❄ 7–9

Euonymus hamiltonianus var. sieboldianus 'Red Elf'
Deciduous, upright shrub with mid- to dark green foliage. Decorative, deep pink fruits, borne in profusion after tiny, green flowers in early summer, open in autumn to reveal red seeds.

☀ ◊ ❄❄❄ 5–8

Spartium junceum
(Spanish broom)
Deciduous, upright, almost leafless shrub that arches with age. Fragrant, pealike, golden yellow flowers appear from early summer to early autumn on dark green shoots.

☀ ◊ ❄❄ 7–10

Abutilon pictum 'Thompsonii'
Robust, evergreen, upright shrub with 3–5-lobed, serrated, rich green, heavily yellow-mottled leaves. Yellow-orange flowers with crimson veins are borne from summer to autumn. Min. 41–5°F (5–7°C).

☀ ◊ 8–10

Viburnum farreri, syn. V. fragrans (Fragrant viburnum)
Deciduous, upright shrub. In late autumn and during mild periods in winter and early spring bears fragrant white or pale pink flowers. Dark green foliage is bronze when young.

☀ ◊ ❄❄❄ 6–9

Euonymus europaeus 'Red Cascade'
Deciduous, bushy shrub or small tree with narrowly oval, green leaves that redden in autumn as red fruits open to show orange seeds. Has inconspicuous, greenish flowers in early summer.

☀ ◊ ❄❄❄ 4–8

Shrubs/medium

■ RED ■■ PURPLE–BLUE ■ ORANGE

Viburnum betulifolium
Deciduous, upright, arching shrub.
Bright green leaves are slightly glossy
beneath. Heads of small, white flowers
in early summer are succeeded by
profuse nodding clusters
of decorative, bright red
fruits in autumn-winter.

☼ ◊ ❄❄❄ 6–9

Euonymus alatus (Burning bush)
Deciduous, bushy, dense shrub with
shoots that develop corky wings. Dark
green leaves turn brilliant red in
autumn. Inconspicuous, greenish
flowers in summer are
followed by small, purple
and red fruits.

☼ ◊ ❄❄❄ 4–9

Callicarpa bodinieri var. **giraldii**
Deciduous, bushy shrub. Leaves are
pale green, often bronze-tinged when
young. Tiny, lilac flowers in mid-
summer are followed by
small, violet berries.

☼ ◊ ❄❄❄ 6–8

Berberis 'Barbarossa'
Semi-evergreen, arching shrub. Has
narrowly oval, dark green leaves and
racemes of rounded, yellow flowers in
late spring and early summer, followed
by globose, orange-
scarlet fruits.

☼ ◊ ❄❄❄ 7–9

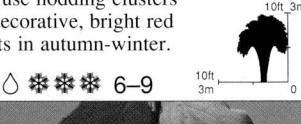

Nymania capensis
Evergreen, more or less rounded,
rigidly branched shrub or small tree. In
spring has flowers with upright, pink
to rose-purple petals. Bears papery,
inflated, red fruits in
autumn. Min. 45–50°F
(7–10°C).

☼ ◊ 10

Clerodendrum bungei
Evergreen or deciduous, upright,
suckering shrub or sub-shrub with
coarsely serrated, heart-shaped leaves.
Has domed clusters of small, fragrant
red-purple to deep pink
flowers in late summer
and early autumn.

☼ ◊ ❄❄ 9–10

Zanthoxylum simulans
Deciduous, bushy shrub or small tree
with stout spines. Aromatic, glossy,
bright green leaves consist of 5
leaflets. Tiny, yellowish green flowers
in late spring and early
summer are followed
by orange-red fruits.

☼ ◊ ❄❄❄ 7–10

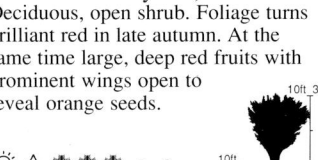

Euonymus latifolius
(Broadleaf euonymus)
Deciduous, open shrub. Foliage turns
brilliant red in late autumn. At the
same time large, deep red fruits with
prominent wings open to
reveal orange seeds.

☼ ◊ ❄❄❄ 6–9

Cornus alba 'Kesselringii'
Vigorous, deciduous shrub with deep
purplish stems. Dark green leaves
become flushed reddish purple in
autumn. Creamy white flowers in late
spring and early summer
are followed by
white fruits.

☼ ◊ ❄❄❄ 2–8

Ceanothus 'Autumnal Blue'
Fast-growing, evergreen, bushy shrub.
Has glossy, bright green foliage and
large panicles of pale to mid-blue
flowers from late spring to autumn.

☼ ◊ ❄❄ 8–9

Cotoneaster simonsii
Deciduous or semi-evergreen, upright
shrub. Has oval, glossy, dark green
leaves, shallowly cup-shaped, white
flowers in early summer, and long-
lasting, orange-red fruits
in autumn. Is suitable
for hedging.

☼ ◊ ❄❄❄ 6–9

□□ ORANGE–YELLOW

Colquhounia coccinea
Evergreen or semi-evergreen, open shrub. Has aromatic, sage green leaves and whorls of scarlet or orange flowers in late summer and autumn.

☀ ◌ ❄❄ 8–9

Leonotis leonurus (Lion's-ear)
Semi-evergreen, sparingly branched, erect shrub. Has lance-shaped leaves and whorls of tubular, bright orange flowers in late autumn and early winter.

☀ ◌ ❄ 9–10

Pyracantha 'Golden Charmer'
Evergreen, arching, bushy, spiny shrub with glossy, bright green leaves. Flattish clusters of white flowers in early summer are succeeded by large, bright orange berries in early autumn.

☀ ◌ ❄❄❄ 6–9

Cotoneaster franchetii var. *sternianus*
Evergreen or semi-evergreen, arching shrub. Leaves are gray-green, white beneath. Pink-tinged, white flowers in early summer are followed by orange-red fruits.

☀ ◌ ❄❄❄ 7–9

Pyracantha 'Golden Dome'
Evergreen, rounded, very dense, spiny shrub. Dark green foliage sets off white flowers borne in early summer. These are followed by orange-yellow berries in early autumn.

☀ ◌ ❄❄❄ 6–9

□ WHITE

Rubus biflorus
Deciduous, upright shrub with chalky white, young shoots in winter. Leaves, consisting of 5–7 oval leaflets, are dark green above, white beneath. White flowers in late spring and early summer are followed by edible, yellow fruits.

☀ ◌ ❄❄❄ 6–9

Rubus thibetanus
Deciduous, arching shrub with white-bloomed, brownish purple, young shoots in winter and fernlike, glossy, dark green foliage, white beneath. Small, pink flowers from mid- to late summer are followed by black fruits.

☀ ◌ ❄❄❄ 7–9

Viburnum foetens
Deciduous, bushy shrub that has aromatic, dark green leaves. Dense clusters of pink buds open to very fragrant white flowers from mid-winter to early spring.

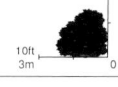

☀ ◌ ❄❄❄ 6–9

Viburnum tinus (Laurustinus)
Evergreen, bushy, dense shrub with oval, dark green leaves. Freely produced flat heads of small, white blooms open from pink buds during late winter and spring.

☀ ◌ ❄❄ 7–9

Chamelaucium uncinatum [white form] (Geraldton wax plant)
Evergreen, wiry-stemmed, bushy shrub. Each needlelike leaf has a tiny, hooked tip. Flowers ranging from deep rose-purple to pink, lavender, or white appear in late winter or spring. Min. 41°F (5°C).

☀ ◌ pH 9–10

Calliandra haematocephala [white form]
Evergreen, spreading shrub. Leaves have 16–24 leaflets. Flower heads comprising many white-stamened florets appear from late autumn to spring. Min. 45°F (7°C).

☀ ◌ 10

■□ WHITE–PINK   ■■ RED–PURPLE   □ YELLOW

Dombeya burgessiae,
syn. *D. mastersii* (Rosemound)
Evergreen shrub with rounded,
3-lobed, downy leaves and dense
clusters of fragrant white flowers,
with pink to red veins,
in autumn-winter.
Min. 41°F (5°C).

☀ ◊ 10

Chamelaucium uncinatum [pink
form] (Geraldton wax plant)
Evergreen, wiry-stemmed, bushy shrub.
Each needlelike leaf has a tiny, hooked
tip. Flowers ranging from deep rose-
purple to pink, lavender, or
white appear in late winter
or spring. Min. 41°F (5°C).

☀ ◊ pH 9–10

Cornus alba 'Sibirica'
(Siberian dogwood)
Deciduous, upright shrub with scarlet,
young shoots in winter. Has dark green
foliage and heads of creamy white
flowers in late spring and
early summer, succeeded
by rounded, white fruits.

☀ ◊ ❄❄❄ 2–8

Stachyurus praecox
Deciduous, spreading, open shrub with
purplish red shoots. Drooping spikes
of pale greenish yellow flowers open
in late winter and early spring, before
pointed, deep green
leaves appear.

☀ ◊ ❄❄❄ 7–9

Acokanthera oblongifolia, syn.
A. spectabilis, *Carissa spectabilis*
(Wintersweet)
Evergreen, rounded shrub. Has fragrant
white or pinkish flowers in late winter
and spring and poisonous,
black fruits in autumn.
Min. 50°F (10°C).

☀ ◊ 10

Viburnum × bodnantense 'Dawn'
Deciduous, upright shrub with oval,
bronze, young leaves that mature to
dark green. Racemes of deep pink buds
open to fragrant pink flowers during
mild periods from late
autumn to early spring.

☀ ◊ ❄❄❄ 7–9

Ardisia crenata, syn. *A. crenulata*
(Coral ardisia, Coralberry,
Spiceberry)
Evergreen, upright, open shrub. Has
fragrant, star-shaped, white flowers in
early summer, followed by
long-lasting, bright red
fruits. Min. 50°F (10°C).

☀◑ ◊ 9–10

Daphne bholua
Evergreen, occasionally deciduous,
upright shrub with leathery, dark green
foliage. Terminal clusters of richly
fragrant, purplish pink and white
flowers are borne
in winter.

☀ ◊ ❄❄ 8–9

Euphorbia pulcherrima
(Christmas star, Poinsettia)
Evergreen, sparingly branched shrub.
Has small, greenish red flowers
surrounded by bright red, pink, yellow,
or white bracts from
late autumn to spring.
Min. 59°F (15°C).

☀ ◊ 9–10

Iochroma cyaneum,
syn. *I. tubulosum*
Evergreen, semi-upright, slender-
branched shrub. Tubular, deep purple-
blue flowers, with flared mouths, appear
in dense clusters from late
autumn to early summer.
Min. 45–50°F (7–10°C).

☀ ◊ 10

Duranta repens, syn. *D. plumieri*
(Golden-dewdrop)
Fast-growing, usually evergreen,
bushy shrub, upright when young. Has
simple or branched spikes of lilac-blue
flowers, mainly in summer,
followed by yellow fruits.
Min. 50°F (10°C).

☀ ◊ 10

□ YELLOW

■■□ WHITE–PURPLE

Mahonia japonica
Evergreen, upright shrub with deep green leaves consisting of many spiny leaflets. Long, spreading sprays of fragrant yellow flowers appear from late autumn to spring, followed by purple-blue fruits.

 7–9

Jasminum nudiflorum
(Winter jasmine)
Deciduous, arching shrub with oval, dark green leaves. Bright yellow flowers appear on slender, leafless, green shoots in winter and early spring.

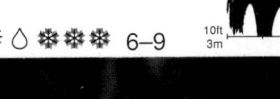 6–9

x *Citrofortunella mitis*, syn. *Citrus mitis* (Calamondin, Panama orange)
Evergreen, bushy shrub with leathery, glossy leaves. Intermittently during the year has tiny, fragrant white flowers followed by orange-yellow fruits. Min. 41–50°F (5–10°C).

9–10

Euonymus japonicus '*Macrophyllus Albus*'
Evergreen, upright, bushy and dense shrub with oval, dark green leaves broadly edged with white. Produces clusters of insignificant, greenish white flowers in late spring.

 7–10

Euonymus fortunei '**Silver Queen**'
Evergreen, bushy, sometimes scandent shrub with a dense growth of dark green leaves, broadly edged with white. Produces insignificant, greenish white flowers in spring.

 6–9

Dracaena sanderiana
(Belgian evergreen)
Evergreen, upright shrub with seldom branching, canelike stems. Lance-shaped leaves, 6–10in (15–25cm) long, are pale to gray-green, with bold, creamy white edges. Min. 55°F (13°C).

 10

Fatsia japonica '**Variegata**'
(Variegated Japanese fatsia)
Evergreen, rounded, bushy, and dense shrub with palmate, glossy, dark green leaves, variegated marginally with creamy white, and large sprays of small, white flowers in autumn.

8–10

Nandina domestica '**Firepower**'
Elegant, evergreen or semi-evergreen, bamboolike, dwarf shrub. Leaves have dark green leaflets, purplish red when young and in autumn-winter. Bears small, white flowers in summer followed in warm areas by orange-red fruits.

7–10

Dodonaea viscosa '**Purpurea**'
Evergreen, bushy shrub or tree. Firm-textured leaves are flushed copper purple. Has clusters of small, reddish or purplish seed capsules in late summer or autumn. Makes a good hedging plant for windy sites. Min. 41°F (5°C).

9–10

119

■ GREEN

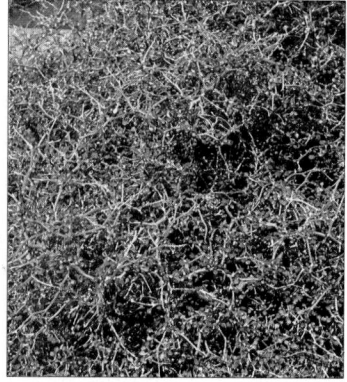

Corokia cotoneaster
Evergreen, bushy, open shrub with interlacing shoots. Has small, spoon-shaped, dark green leaves, fragrant yellow flowers in late spring, and red fruits in autumn.

 9–10

Encephalartos ferox
Slow-growing, evergreen, palmlike plant, almost trunkless for many years. Feather-shaped leaves, 2–6ft (60–180cm) long, have many serrated and spine-tipped, leathery, grayish leaflets. Min. 50–55°F (10–13°C).

 10

Cycas revoluta (Japanese fern palm, Japanese sago palm)
Slow-growing, evergreen, palmlike plant; may produce several trunks. Leaves have spine-tipped leaflets with rolled margins. Bears tight clusters of reddish fruits in autumn. Min. 55°F (13°C).

9–10

Aucuba japonica (Japanese aucuba)
Evergreen, dense, bushy shrub with stout, green shoots and glossy, dark green leaves. Small, purplish flowers in mid-spring are followed on female plants by rounded to egg-shaped, bright red berries.

7–10

Arctostaphylos patula
(Green-leaf manzanita)
Evergreen, rounded shrub with reddish brown bark and bright gray-green foliage. Urn-shaped, white or pale pink flowers appear from mid- to late spring, followed by brown fruits.

 7–10

Rhapis excelsa (Bamboo palm, Slender lady palm)
Evergreen fan palm, eventually forming clumps. Leaves are 8–12in (20–30cm) long, composed of 20 or more narrow, glossy, deep green lobes in fan formation. Min. 59°F (15°C).

9–10

Buxus sempervirens 'Handsworthensis'
Vigorous, evergreen, upright, bushy shrub or small tree. Has broad, very dark green leaves. Ideal for hedging or screening.

6–9

X Fatshedera lizei (Fatshedera)
Evergreen, loose-branched shrub that forms a mound of deeply lobed, glossy, deep green leaves. Sprays of small, white flowers appear in autumn. May also be trained as a climber.

7–10

Ficus deltoidea,
syn. F. diversifolia (Mistletoe fig)
Slow-growing, evergreen, bushy shrub with bright green leaves, red-brown-tinted beneath. Bears small, greenish white fruits that mature to dull yellow. Min. 59–64°F (15–18°C).

 10

Philodendron selloum
Evergreen, unbranched shrub with a robust, erect stem. Glossy, deep green leaves, to 2ft (60cm) or more long, are divided into many fingerlike lobes. Occasionally produces greenish white spathes. Min. 59–64°F (15–18°C).

 10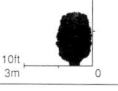

Polyscias filicifolia
(Fern-leaf aralia)
Evergreen, erect, sparingly branched shrub. Leaves are 12in (30cm) long and are divided into many small, serrated, bright green leaflets. Min. 59–64°F (15–18°C).

10

Chamaedorea elegans, syn.
Neanthe bella (Good-luck palm, Parlor palm)
Evergreen, slender palm, suckering with age. Feather-shaped leaves of many glossy leaflets are 2–3ft (60–100cm) long. Min. 64°F (18°C).

8–10

☐ WHITE

Portulacaria afra (Elephant bush)
Semi-evergreen, upright shrub with horizontal branches and tiny, fleshy, bright green leaves. Clusters of pale pink flowers appear in late spring and summer. Min. 45–50°F (7–10°C).

☼ ◊ 9–10

Elaeagnus x ebbingei 'Limelight'
Evergreen, bushy, dense shrub with glossy, dark green leaves, silver beneath, centrally marked yellow and pale green. Bears small, fragrant white flowers in autumn.

☼ ◊ ❄❄❄ 7–9

Salix hastata 'Wehrhahnii'
Deciduous, upright-branched shrub with deep purple stems that contrast with silver-gray catkins borne in early spring before foliage appears. Stems later turn yellow. Has oval, bright green leaves.

☼ ◊ ❄❄❄ 6–9

Buxus balearica
Evergreen, treelike shrub suitable for hedging in mild areas. Has broadly oval, bright green leaves.

☼ ◊ ❄❄ 8–10

Ligustrum 'Vicaryi' (Golden Vicaryi privet, Golden privet)
Semi-evergreen, bushy, dense shrub with broad, oval, golden yellow leaves. Dense racemes of small, white flowers appear in mid-summer.

☼ ◊ ❄❄❄ 5–9

Yucca aloifolia (Spanish-bayonet)
Slow-growing, evergreen shrub or small tree with few branches. Has sword-shaped, deep green leaves, 20–30in (50–75cm) long, and large panicles of purple-tinted, white flowers in summer-autumn. Min. 45°F (7°C).

☼ ◊ 8–10

Aucuba japonica 'Crotonifolia'
Evergreen, bushy, dense shrub with stout, green shoots. Large, glossy, dark green leaves are heavily mottled yellow. Small, purplish flowers in mid-spring are followed by bright red berries.

☼ ◊ ❄❄ 7–10

Deutzia gracilis (Slender deutzia)
Deciduous, upright or spreading shrub. Massed, 5-petaled, pure white flowers are borne in upright clusters amid bright green foliage in late spring and early summer.

☼ ◊ ❄❄❄ 5–9

Prunus glandulosa 'Alba Plena' (White dwarf double-flowering almond)
Deciduous, open shrub, with narrowly oval, green leaves, bearing racemes of double, white flowers in late spring.

☼ ◊ ❄❄❄ 5–8

☐ WHITE

Ledum groenlandicum
(Labrador tea)
Evergreen, bushy shrub. Foliage is dark green and aromatic. Rounded heads of small, white flowers are carried from mid-spring to early summer.

☀ ◊ pH ✳✳✳ 2–6

Spiraea × vanhouttei
(Vanhoutte spiraea)
Deciduous, compact shrub with slender, arching shoots. In late spring and early summer, abundant, small, dense clusters of white flowers appear amid diamond-shaped, dark green leaves.

☀ ◊ ✳✳✳ 4–8

Azorina vidalii,
syn. *Campanula vidalii*
Evergreen sub-shrub with erect stems. Has coarsely serrated, glossy, dark green leaves and racemes of bell-shaped, white or pink flowers in spring and summer. Min. 41°F (5°C).

☀ ◊ 8–9

Prunus laurocerasus 'Zabeliana'
Evergreen, wide-spreading, open shrub. Leaves are very narrow and glossy, dark green. Spikes of white flowers in late spring are followed by cherrylike, red, then black, fruits.

☀ ◊ ✳✳✳ 7–9

Prunus laurocerasus 'Otto Luyken'
Evergreen, very dense shrub. Has upright, narrow, glossy, dark green leaves, spikes of white flowers in late spring, followed by cherrylike, red, then black, fruits.

☀ ◊ ✳✳✳ 7–9

× Gaulnettya 'Wisley Pearl'
Evergreen, bushy, dense shrub with oval, deeply veined, dark green leaves. Small, white flowers in late spring and early summer are followed by decorative, purplish red fruits.

☀ ◊ pH ✳✳✳ 7–9

Deutzia × rosea
Deciduous, bushy, dense shrub. In late spring and early summer produces massed, broad clusters of 5-petaled, pale pink flowers. Leaves are oval and dark green.

☀ ◊ ✳✳✳ 6–9

Prunus × cistena
(Purpleleaf sand cherry)
Slow-growing, deciduous, upright shrub with deep reddish purple leaves, red when young. Small, pinkish white flowers from mid- to late spring may be followed by purple fruits.

☀ ◊ ✳✳✳ 4–8

Viburnum × juddii
(Judd viburnum)
Deciduous, rounded, bushy shrub with dark green foliage. Rounded heads of very fragrant pink-tinged, white flowers open from pink buds from mid- to late spring.

☀ ◊ ✳✳✳ 5–9

Viburnum carlesii
Deciduous, bushy, dense shrub with dark green leaves that redden in autumn. Rounded heads of very fragrant white-and-pink flowers, pink in bud, appear from mid- to late spring, followed by decorative, black fruits.

☀ ◊ ✳✳✳ 6–9

Daphne × burkwoodii 'Somerset'
Semi-evergreen, upright shrub that bears dense clusters of very fragrant white-and-pink flowers in late spring and sometimes again in autumn. Leaves are lance-shaped and pale to mid-green.

☀ ◊ ✳✳✳ 5–9

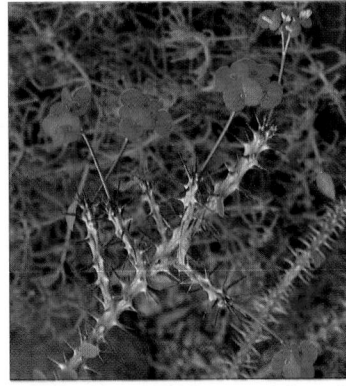

Daphne retusa
Evergreen, rounded, densely branched shrub clothed with leathery, glossy leaves notched at the tips. In late spring and early summer, deep purple buds open to very fragrant pink-flushed, white flowers borne in terminal clusters.

☼ ◊ ✽✽✽ 8–9

Menziesia ciliicalyx var. *purpurea*
Deciduous, bushy shrub with bright green foliage and racemes of nodding, purplish pink blooms in late spring and early summer.

☼◑ ◊ pH ✽✽✽ 6–9

Euphorbia milii (Crown-of-thorns)
Fairly slow-growing, mainly evergreen, spiny, semi-succulent shrub. Clusters of tiny, yellowish flowers, enclosed by 2 bright red bracts, open intermittently during the year.
Min. 46°F (8°C).

☼ ◊ 9–10

Chaenomeles × *superba* 'Rowallane'
Deciduous, spreading, low shrub. Has glossy, dark green foliage and bears a profusion of large, red flowers during spring.

☼ ◊ ✽✽✽✽ 5–8

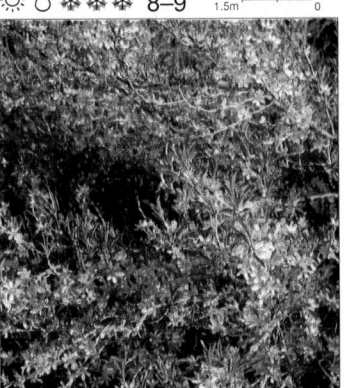

Prunus tenella
(Dwarf Russian almond)
Deciduous, bushy shrub with upright shoots and narrowly oval, glossy leaves. Shallowly cup-shaped, bright pink flowers appear from mid- to late spring.

☼ ◊ ✽✽✽ 2–8

Ribes sanguineum 'Brocklebankii'
Deciduous, spreading shrub. Has aromatic, pale yellow leaves and pendent clusters of small, pale pink flowers in spring, followed by white-bloomed, black fruits.

☼ ◊ ✽✽✽ 6–8

Epacris impressa
Evergreen, usually erect, fairly open, heathlike shrub with short, red-tipped leaves. Tubular, pink or red flowers appear in late winter and spring.
Min. 41°F (5°C).

☼ ◊ pH 8–9

Cantua buxifolia,
syn. *C. dependens* (Magic flower, Sacred-flower-of-Peru)
Evergreen, arching, bushy shrub. Has gray-green foliage and drooping clusters of bright red and magenta flowers from mid- to late spring.

☼ ◊ ✽ 10

■■ RED–GREEN

■■ GREEN–YELLOW

Chaenomeles × *superba* 'Nicoline'
Deciduous, bushy, dense shrub. Has glossy, dark green leaves and a profusion of large, scarlet flowers in spring, followed by yellow fruits.

☼ ◊ ❋❋❋ 5–8

Salix lanata (Woolly willow)
Deciduous, bushy, dense shrub with stout, woolly, gray shoots and broad, silver-gray leaves. Large, yellowish green catkins appear in late spring with foliage.

☼ ◊ ❋❋❋ 1–5

Boronia megastigma
Evergreen, well branched, wiry-stemmed shrub. Small leaves have 3–5 narrow leaflets. Fragrant, bowl-shaped, brownish purple-and-yellow flowers hang from leaf axils in late winter and spring. Min. 45–50°F (7–10°C).

☼ ◊ pH 9–10

Euphorbia characias subsp. *characias*
Evergreen, upright shrub with clusters of narrow, gray-green leaves. During spring and early summer bears dense spikes of pale yellowish green flowers with deep purple centers.

☼ ◊ ❋❋ 7–10

Euphorbia characias subsp. *wulfenii*
Evergreen, upright shrub. Stems are biennial, producing clustered, gray-green leaves one year and spikes of yellow-green blooms the following spring.

☼ ◊ ❋❋ 7–10

Arctostaphylos 'Emerald Carpet'
Evergreen shrub that, with a low, dense growth of oval, bright green leaves and purple stems, makes excellent ground cover. Bears small, urn-shaped, white flowers in spring.

☼ ◊ pH ❋❋ 2–7

Daphne laureola var. *philippi*
Evergreen, dwarf shrub with oval, dark green leaves. Slightly fragrant, tubular, pale green flowers with short, spreading lobes appear in late winter and early spring, followed by black fruits.

☼ ◊ ❋❋❋ 7–9

Salix repens (Creeping willow)
Deciduous, prostrate or semi-upright and bushy shrub. Silky, gray catkins become yellow from mid- to late spring, before small, narrowly oval leaves, which are gray-green above, silvery beneath, appear.

☼ ◊ ❋❋❋ 4–9

Cytisus × *praecox* (Warminster broom)
Deciduous, densely branched shrub. From mid- to late spring, pealike, creamy yellow flowers appear in profusion amid tiny, silky, gray-green leaves with 3 leaflets.

☼ ◊ ❋❋❋ 6–9

Mahonia aquifolium (Mountain grape holly, Oregon grape)
Evergreen, open shrub. Leaves, with glossy, bright green leaflets, often turn red or purple in winter. Bunches of small, yellow flowers in spring are followed by blue-black berries.

☽ ◊ ❄ ❄ ❄ 6–9

Berberis empetrifolia
Evergreen, arching, prickly shrub with narrow, gray-green leaves, globose, golden yellow flowers in late spring, and black fruits in autumn.

☼ ◊ ❄ ❄ ❄ 7–9

Genista tinctoria (Common woodwaxen, Dyers' greenweed)
Deciduous, spreading, dwarf shrub that bears dense spires of pealike, golden yellow flowers in spring and summer. Leaves are narrow and dark green.

☼ ◊ ❄ ❄ ❄ 2–8

***Caragana arborescens* 'Nana'**
Deciduous, bushy, dwarf shrub with green leaves consisting of many oval leaflets. Pealike, yellow flowers are borne in late spring.

☼ ◊ ❄ ❄ ❄ 2–8

***Cytisus* × *praecox* 'Allgold'**
Deciduous, densely branched shrub with silky, gray-green leaves, divided into 3 leaflets, and a profusion of pealike, yellow flowers from mid- to late spring.

☼ ◊ ❄ ❄ ❄ 6–9

Coronilla valentina* subsp. *glauca
Evergreen, bushy, dense shrub. Has blue-gray leaves with 5 or 7 leaflets. Fragrant, pealike, yellow flowers are borne from mid-spring to early summer.

☼ ◊ ❄ ❄ 7–9

Chorizema ilicifolium
(Holly flame pea)
Evergreen, sprawling or upright shrub with spiny-toothed, leathery leaves. Has spikes of bicolored, orange and pinkish red flowers in spring-summer.
Min. 45°F (7°C).

☼ ◊ pH 9–10

Pachystachys lutea
(Golden candle)
Evergreen, more or less rounded, loose shrub often grown annually from cuttings. Has tubular, white flowers in tight, golden-bracted spikes in spring-summer.
Min. 55–9°F (13–15°C).

☽ ◊ 10

Ulex europaeus (Common gorse)
Leafless or almost leafless, bushy shrub with year-round, dark green shoots and spines that make it appear evergreen. Bears massed, fragrant, pealike, yellow flowers in spring.

☼ ◊ ❄ ❄ ❄ 7–9

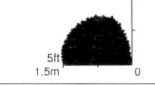

Acacia pulchella
Semi-evergreen or deciduous shrub with spiny twigs and rich green foliage. Tiny, deep yellow flowers appear in dense, globular heads in spring.
Min. 41–5°F (5–7°C).

☼ ◊ 9–10

Nematanthus gregarius, syn.
N. radicans, *Hypocyrta radicans*
Evergreen, prostrate or slightly ascending shrub with fleshy, glossy leaves. Inflated, tubular, orange and yellow flowers appear mainly from spring to autumn.
Min. 55–9°F (13–15°C).

☽ ◊ 10

☐ WHITE

Deutzia monbeigii
Elegant, deciduous, arching shrub. Clusters of small, 5-petaled, white flowers appear in profusion among small, dark green leaves from early to mid-summer.

☀ ◊ ✻✻✻✻ 7–9

Olearia phlogopappa var. **subrepanda**
Evergreen, upright, compact shrub. Heads of daisylike, white flowers are borne profusely from mid-spring to early summer amid narrow, toothed, gray-green leaves.

☀ ◊ ✻✻✻ 9–10

Westringia fruticosa, syn. *W. rosmariniformis*
Evergreen, compact, rounded shrub. Crowded leaves, in whorls of 4, are white-felted beneath. White to palest blue flowers open in spring-summer. Min. 41–5°F (5–7°C).

☀ ◊ 9–10

Potentilla 'Abbotswood'
Deciduous, bushy shrub. Large, pure white flowers are borne amid dark blue-green leaves, divided into 5 narrowly oval leaflets, throughout summer-autumn.

☀ ◊ ✻✻✻✻ 3–7

Hebe brachysiphon 'White Gem'
Evergreen, rounded shrub that produces a dense mound of small, glossy leaves covered in early summer with tight racemes of small, white flowers.

☀ ◊ ✻✻✻✻ 9–10

Gardenia jasminoides 'Fortuniana'
Fairly slow-growing, evergreen, leafy shrub with oval, glossy leaves up to 4in (10cm) long and fragrant, double, white flowers from summer to winter. Min. 59°F (15°C).

☀ ◊ pH ⌣ 8–10

Potentilla 'Manchu', syn. *P. davurica* var. *mandschurica* of gardens
Deciduous, mound-forming shrub with reddish pink, prostrate shoots. Pure white flowers are borne amid divided, silvery gray leaves from late spring to early autumn.

☀ ◊ ✻✻✻✻ 3–7

Rhodotypos scandens, syn. *R. kerrioides* (Jetbead)
Deciduous, upright or slightly arching shrub. In late spring and early summer, amid sharply toothed leaves, bears shallowly cupped, white flowers, followed by small, pea-shaped, black fruits.

☀ ◊ ✻✻✻✻ 5–8

Cuphea hyssopifolia
(Elfin herb, False heather)
Evergreen, rounded, dense shrub with tiny, narrowly lance-shaped, deep green leaves. Rose-purple to lilac or white flowers appear in summer-autumn.

☀ ◊ ✻ 10

Philadelphus 'Manteau d'Hermine'
Deciduous, compact, bushy shrub. Clusters of fragrant, double, creamy white flowers appear amid small, pale to mid-green leaves from early to mid-summer.

☀ ◊ ✻✻✻✻ 5–8

Convolvulus cneorum (Silverbush)
Evergreen, rounded, bushy, dense shrub. Pink-tinged buds that open to white flowers with yellow centers are borne from late spring to late summer among narrow, silky, silvery green leaves.

☀ ◊ ✻✻✻ 8–10

Halimium umbellatum
Evergreen, upright shrub. Narrow, glossy, dark green leaves are white beneath. White flowers, centrally blotched with yellow, are produced in early summer from reddish buds.

☼ ◊ ❋❋ 8–10

Cistus salviifolius
(Sageleaf rock rose)
Evergreen, bushy, dense shrub with slightly wrinkled, gray-green foliage. White flowers, with central, yellow blotches, appear in profusion during early summer.

☼ ◊ ❋❋ 8–10

Potentilla 'Farrer's White'
Deciduous, bushy shrub with divided, gray-green leaves. Bears an abundance of white flowers during summer-autumn.

☼ ◊ ❋❋❋❋ 3–8

Cistus monspeliensis
Evergreen, bushy shrub with narrow, wrinkled, dark green leaves and small, white flowers freely borne from early to mid-summer.

☼ ◊ ❋❋ 8–10

Cistus × cyprius
Evergreen, bushy shrub with sticky shoots and narrow, glossy, dark green leaves. In early summer bears large, white flowers, with a red blotch at each petal base, that appear in succession for some weeks but last only a day.

☼ ◊ ❋❋ 7–10

× Halimiocistus sahucii
Evergreen, bushy, dense shrub with narrow, dark green leaves that set off an abundance of pure white flowers in late spring and early summer.

☼ ◊ ❋❋ 7–9

Cistus × corbariensis
(White rock rose)
Evergreen, bushy, dense shrub. Has wrinkled, wavy-edged, dark green leaves and massed white flowers, with central, yellow blotches, in late spring and early summer.

☼ ◊ ❋❋ 7–9

Cistus × aguilari 'Maculatus'
Evergreen, bushy shrub with narrow, wavy-edged, slightly sticky, rich green leaves. Large, white flowers, with a central, deep red-and-yellow pattern, appear from early to mid-summer.

☼ ◊ ❋❋ 9–10

Cistus ladanifer
Evergreen, upright, open shrub. Leaves are narrow, dark green, and sticky. Large, white flowers, with red markings around the central tuft of stamens, are borne in profusion during early summer.

☼ ◊ ❋❋ 8–10

☐ WHITE

Leptospermum humifusum
Evergreen, widely arching, semi-prostrate shrub with reddish shoots and small, dark green leaves that turn bronze-purple in winter. Small, open cup-shaped, white flowers, red-flushed in bud, appear in early summer.

☼ ◊ ❈❈❈ 8–10

Catharanthus roseus, syn. *Vinca rosea* (Madagascar periwinkle)
Evergreen, spreading shrub that becomes untidy with age. Has white to rose-pink flowers in spring to autumn, also in winter in warm areas. Min. 41–5°F (5–7°C).

☼ ◊ 10

Rhaphiolepis umbellata
(Indian thorn, Yeddo rhaphiolepis)
Evergreen, bushy shrub with rounded, leathery, dark green leaves and clusters of fragrant white flowers in early summer.

☼ ◊ ❈❈❈ 8–10

Yucca whipplei
Evergreen, virtually stemless shrub that forms a dense tuft of slender, pointed, blue-green leaves. Very long panicles of fragrant, greenish white flowers are produced in late spring and early summer.

☼ ◊ ❈❈ 7–9

Weigela florida 'Variegata'
Deciduous, bushy, dense shrub. Carries a profusion of funnel-shaped, pink flowers in late spring and early summer and has green leaves broadly edged with creamy white.

☼ ◊ ❈❈❈ 5–9

Vaccinium corymbosum
(Highbush blueberry)
Deciduous, upright, slightly arching shrub. Small, white or pinkish flowers in late spring and early summer are followed by sweet, edible, blue-black berries. Foliage turns red in autumn.

☼ ◊ pH ❈❈❈ 4–8

Yucca flaccida 'Ivory'
Evergreen, very short-stemmed shrub that produces tufts of narrow, dark green leaves and long panicles of bell-shaped, white flowers from mid- to late summer.

☼ ◊ ❈❈❈ 5–9

Ozothamnus ledifolius,
syn. *Helichrysum ledifolium*
Evergreen, dense shrub. Yellow shoots are covered with small, aromatic leaves, glossy, dark green above, yellow beneath. Small, white flower heads are borne in early summer.

☼ ◊ ❈❈ 9–10

Lomatia silaifolia
Evergreen, bushy shrub. Spikes of creamy white flowers, each with 4 narrow, twisted petals, are borne amid deeply divided, dark green leaves from mid- to late summer.

☼ ◊ pH ❄❄ 10

Cassinia vauvilliersii
Evergreen, upright shrub. Whitish shoots are covered with tiny, dark green leaves and heads of small, white flowers from mid- to late summer.

☼ ◊ ❄❄ 10

Viburnum acerifolium
Deciduous, upright-branched shrub with bright green leaves that turn orange, red, and purple in autumn. Decorative, red fruits, which turn purple-black, follow heads of creamy white flowers in early summer.

☼ ◊ ❄❄❄ 4–8

Eriogonum arborescens
Evergreen, sparingly branched shrub. Small leaves have recurved edges and woolly, white undersides. Leafy umbels of small, white or pink flowers appear from spring to autumn.
Min. 41°F (5°C).

☼ ◊ 9–10

Hebe recurva
Evergreen, spreading, open shrub. Leaves are narrow, curved, and blue-gray. Small spikes of white flowers appear from mid- to late summer.

☼ ◊ ❄❄ 9–10

Hebe albicans
Evergreen shrub that forms a dense mound of blue-gray foliage covered with small, tight clusters of white flowers from early to mid-summer.

☼ ◊ ❄❄ 9–10

Deutzia 'Mont Rose'
Deciduous, bushy shrub that produces clusters of pink or pinkish purple flowers, in early summer, with yellow anthers and occasionally white markings. Leaves are sharply toothed and dark green.

☼ ◊ ❄❄❄ 5–9

Hydrangea involucrata 'Hortensis'
Deciduous, open shrub. Has broad, heart-shaped, bristly leaves and clusters of cream, pink, and green flowers during late summer and autumn.

☼◑ ◊ ❄❄ 7–9

Potentilla 'Daydawn'
Deciduous, rather arching, bushy shrub. Creamy yellow flowers, flushed with orange-pink, appear among divided, green leaves from early summer to mid-autumn.

☼ ◊ ❄❄❄ 3–8

Protea cynaroides (King protea)
Evergreen, rounded, bushy shrub. Has water lily-shaped flower heads, 5–8in (13–20cm) wide, with silky-haired, petal-like, pink to red bracts, in spring-summer. Leaves are oval and mid- to dark green.
Min. 5–7°C (41–5°F).

☼ ◊ pH 10

Abelia 'Edward Goucher'
(Goucher abelia)
Deciduous or semi-evergreen, arching shrub. Oval, bright green leaves are bronze when young. Bears a profusion of lilac-pink flowers from mid-summer to autumn.

☼ ◊ ❄❄ 7–9

■ PINK

Abelia schumannii
Deciduous, arching shrub. Pointed leaves are bronze when young. Yellow-blotched, rose-purple-and-white flowers appear from mid-summer to mid-autumn.

☀ ◊ ❄❄ 7–9

Myoporum parvifolium
Evergreen, spreading to prostrate shrub with semi-succulent leaves. In summer has clusters of small, honey-scented, white or pink flowers, with purple spots, and tiny, purple fruits in autumn. Min. 36–41°F (2–5°C).

☀ ◊ 9–10

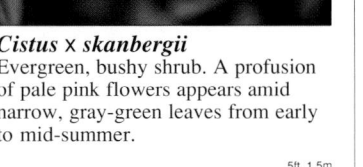

Cistus × skanbergii
Evergreen, bushy shrub. A profusion of pale pink flowers appears amid narrow, gray-green leaves from early to mid-summer.

☀ ◊ ❄❄ 8–9

Pimelea ferruginea
Evergreen, rounded, dense shrub with tiny, recurved, deep green leaves. Small, tubular, rich pink flowers appear in dense heads in spring or early summer. Min. 45°F (7°C).

☀ ◊ pH 7–9

Gaultheria shallon (Salal, Shallon)
Evergreen, bushy shrub. Red shoots carry broad, sharply pointed, dark green leaves. Racemes of urn-shaped, pink flowers in late spring and early summer are followed by purple berries.

☀ ◊ pH ❄❄❄ 6–8

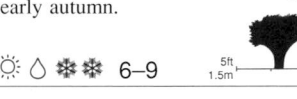

Indigofera dielsiana
Deciduous, upright, open shrub. Dark green leaves consist of 7–11 oval leaflets. Slender, erect spikes of pale pink flowers are borne from early summer to early autumn.

☀ ◊ ❄❄ 6–9

Hydrangea macrophylla '***Générale Vicomtesse de Vibraye***'
Deciduous, bushy shrub that produces rounded, dense heads of pale blue or pink flowers from mid- to late summer. Foliage is light green.

☀ ◊ ❄❄ 6–9

Phlomis italica (Italian sage)
Evergreen, upright shrub. In mid-summer, whorls of lilac-pink flowers are borne at the ends of shoots amid narrow, woolly, gray-green leaves.

☀ ◊ ❄❄ 8–9

Deutzia × elegantissima '***Rosealind***'
Deciduous, rounded, bushy, dense shrub that produces clusters of 5-petaled, deep pink flowers from late spring to early summer.

☀ ◊ ❄❄❄ 5–8

Weigela florida 'Foliis Purpureis'
Deciduous, low, bushy shrub that bears funnel-shaped flowers, deep pink outside, pale pink to white inside, in late spring and early summer. Leaves are dull purple or purplish green.

☼ ◊ ❄❄❄❄ 5–9

Ceanothus 'Perle Rose'
Deciduous, bushy shrub that, from mid-summer to early autumn, bears dense racemes of bright carmine pink flowers amid broadly oval, green leaves.

☼ ◊ ❄❄ 7–10

Spiraea japonica 'Little Princess'
Slow-growing, deciduous, mound-forming shrub that produces copious small heads of rose-pink blooms from mid- to late summer. Small, dark green leaves are bronze when young.

☼ ◊ ❄❄❄❄ 4–9

Hebe 'Great Orme'
Evergreen, rounded, open shrub. Has deep purplish shoots and glossy, dark green foliage. Slender spikes of deep pink flowers that fade to white are produced from mid-summer to mid-autumn.

☼ ◊ ❄❄ 9–10

Penstemon isophyllus
Slightly untidy, deciduous shrub or sub-shrub that, from mid- to late summer, carries long sprays of large, white-and-red-throated, deep pink flowers above spear-shaped, glossy, green leaves.

☼ ◊ ❄❄ 8–9

Spiraea japonica 'Goldflame'
Deciduous, upright, slightly arching shrub with orange-red, young leaves that turn to bright yellow and finally pale green. Bears heads of deep rose-pink flowers from mid- to late summer.

☼ ◊ ❄❄❄❄ 4–9

Justicia carnea, syn. *Jacobinia carnea, J. pohliana*
Evergreen, sparingly branched shrub with velvety-haired leaves. Has spikes of pink to rose-purple flowers in summer-autumn. Min. 50–59°F (10–15°C).

☼ ◊ 9–10

Pentas lanceolata, syn. *P. carnea* (Egyptian star-cluster, Star-cluster)
Mainly evergreen, loosely rounded shrub with hairy, bright green leaves. In summer-autumn produces dense clusters of pink, lilac, red, or white flowers. Min. 50–59°F (10–15°C).

☼ ◊ 10

Spiraea japonica 'Anthony Waterer'
Deciduous, upright, compact shrub. Red, young foliage matures to dark green. Heads of crimson-pink blooms appear from mid- to late summer.

☼ ◊ ❄❄❄❄ 4–9

Fuchsias

With their vividly colored blooms and long flowering season (usually throughout summer and well into autumn), fuchsias make outstanding shrubs for the greenhouse and for the garden. Single to double flowers often have flared or elegantly recurved sepals. In mild areas a few may be grown outside all year; in cool climates most are best grown in a greenhouse, in a hanging basket, or as summer bedding.

Fuchsias raised from cuttings are sparingly branched and often become straggly unless pruned from an early stage by pinching out the growing tips. To produce standard plants, the leader shoot is left, supported, but emerging side-shoots are pinched back to one pair of leaves. When the stem has reached the required height and has produced 2 or 3 pairs of leaves above this, it is then pinched out and the plant is left to develop naturally.

F. 'Jack Shahan'

F. arborescens

F. 'Lady Thumb'

F. 'Peppermint Stick'

F. 'Autumnale'

F. 'Harry Gray'

F. 'Pink Galore'

F. 'Swingtime'

F. 'White Ann'

F. 'Rufus'

F. 'Riccartonii'

F. 'Annabel'

F. 'Leonora'

F. 'Nellie Nuttall'

F. 'Red Spider'

F. 'Dollar Princess'

F. 'Golden Dawn'

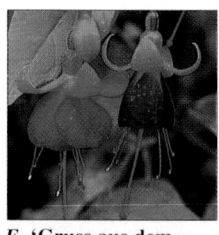
F. 'Gruss aus dem Bodenthal'

F. 'Ann Howard Tripp'

F. 'Tom Thumb'

F. 'Other Fellow'

F. magellanica

F. 'White Spider'

F. 'Jack Acland'

F. 'Kwintet'

F. **'Mrs. Popple'**

F. **'Cascade'**

F. **'La Campanella'**

F. **'Golden Marinka'**

F. **'Mary Poppins'**

F. **'Rose of Castile'**

F. **'Celia Smedley'**

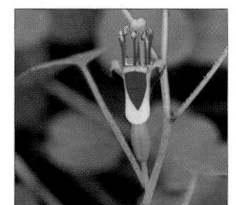

F. × *bacillaris*

F. **'Estelle Marie'**

F. boliviana **'Alba'**

F. **'Thalia'**

F. procumbens

F. **'Lye's Unique'**

F. fulgens

F. **'Koralle'**

Shrubs/small SUMMER INTEREST

Cistus creticus
Evergreen, bushy shrub. Pink or purplish pink flowers, each with a central, yellow blotch, appear amid gray-green leaves from early to mid-summer.

☀️ ◌ ❋❋ 9–10

***Escallonia rubra* 'Woodside'**
Evergreen, bushy, dense shrub. Has small, glossy, dark green leaves and short racemes of small, tubular, crimson flowers in summer-autumn.

☀️ ◌ ❋❋ 8–9

Kalmia angustifolia* f. *rubra
(Lambkill kalmia, Purple sheep laurel)
Evergreen, bushy, mound-forming shrub with oval, dark green leaves and clusters of small, deep red flowers in early summer.

☀️ ◌ pH ❋❋❋❋ 7–8

Sutherlandia frutescens
Evergreen, upright shrub. Has leaves of 13–21 gray-haired, deep green leaflets; bright red flowers in late spring and summer are followed by pale green, later red-flushed, inflated seed pods. Min. 50°F (10°C).

☀️ ◌ 10

Crossandra nilotica
Evergreen, upright to spreading, leafy shrub with oval, pointed, rich green leaves. Small, tubular, apricot to pale brick red flowers with spreading petals are carried in short spikes from spring to autumn.
Min. 59°F (15°C).

☀️ ◌ 10

Ixora coccinea
Evergreen, rounded shrub with glossy, dark green leaves to 4in (10cm) long. Small, tubular, red, pink, orange, or yellow flowers appear in dense heads in summer. Min. 55–61°F (13–16°C).

☀️ ◌ 10

Potentilla 'Red Ace'
Deciduous, spreading, bushy, dense shrub. Bright vermilion flowers, pale yellow on the backs of petals, are produced from late spring to mid-autumn but fade quickly in full sun.

☀ ◊ ❄❄❄❄ 3–8

Phygelius aequalis
Evergreen or semi-evergreen, upright sub-shrub. Clusters of tubular, pale red flowers with yellow throats appear from mid-summer to early autumn. Leaves are oval and dark green.

☀ ◊ ❄❄ 7–9

Salvia fulgens
Evergreen, upright sub-shrub. Oval leaves are white and woolly beneath, hairy above. Racemes of tubular, 2-lipped, scarlet flowers appear in late summer.

☀ ◊ ❄ 9–10

Salvia microphylla var. **neurepia**
Evergreen, upright, well-branched shrub with pale to mid-green leaves. Has tubular, bright red flowers from purple-tinted, green calyces in late summer and autumn.

☀ ◊ ❄ 10

Grevillea 'Robyn Gordon'
Evergreen, sprawling shrub with leathery, dark green leaves. At intervals from early spring to late summer, arching stems bear racemes of crimson flowers with protruding, recurved styles. Min. 41–50°F (5–10°C).

☀ ◊ 10

Acer palmatum 'Dissectum Atropurpureum'
Deciduous shrub that forms a mound of deeply divided, bronze-red or purple foliage that turns brilliant red, orange, or yellow in autumn. Has small, reddish purple flowers in mid-spring.

☀ ◊ ❄❄❄ 5–8

Justicia brandegeana, syn. *Beloperone guttata, Drejerella guttata* (Shrimp plant)
Evergreen, rounded shrub intermittently, but mainly in summer, producing white flowers surrounded by shrimp pink bracts. Min. 50–59°F (10–15°C).

☀ ◊ 9–10

Acer palmatum 'Chitoseyama'
Deciduous, arching, mound-forming shrub or small tree with lobed, green foliage that gradually turns brilliant red from late summer to autumn. Produces small, reddish purple flowers in mid-spring.

☀ ◊ ❄❄❄ 5–8

134

Hebe hulkeana 'Lilac Hint'
Evergreen, upright, open-branched
shrub with toothed, glossy, pale green
leaves. A profusion of small, pale lilac
flowers appears in large racemes in
late spring and
early summer.

☼ ◊ ❋❋ 9–10

Hebe 'E.A. Bowles'
Evergreen, rounded, bushy shrub with
narrow, glossy, pale green leaves and
slender spikes of lilac flowers produced
from mid-summer to late autumn.

☼ ◊ ❋❋ 9–10

Heliotropium arborescens, syn. *H.
peruvianum* (Common heliotrope)
Evergreen, bushy shrub. Semi-glossy,
dark green leaves are finely wrinkled.
Purple to lavender flowers are borne in
dense, flat clusters from
late spring to winter.
Min. 45°F (7°C).

☼ ◊ 10

Lavandula stoechas
(Spanish lavender)
Evergreen, bushy, dense shrub. Heads
of tiny, fragrant, deep purple flowers,
topped by rose-purple bracts, appear in
late spring and summer.
Mature leaves are silver-
gray and aromatic.

☼ ◊ ❋❋ 7–9

Rosmarinus officinalis (Rosemary)
Evergreen, bushy, dense shrub with
aromatic, narrow leaves. Small,
purplish blue to blue flowers appear
from mid-spring to early summer and
sometimes in autumn.
Used as a culinary herb.

☼ ◊ ❋❋ 7–9

Hydrangea macrophylla subsp.
serrata
Deciduous, bushy, dense shrub with
slender stems and light green leaves.
From mid- to late summer bears flat
heads of pink, lilac, or
white inner and pink or
blue outer flowers.

☼◐ ◊◗ ❋❋ 6–9

Polygala myrtifolia 'Grandiflora'
Evergreen, erect shrub with small,
grayish green leaves. White-veined,
rich purple flowers appear from late
spring to autumn. Min. 45°F (7°C).

☼ ◊ 10

Hebe 'Autumn Glory'
Evergreen shrub that forms a mound
of purplish red shoots and rounded,
deep green leaves, over which dense
racemes of deep purple-blue flowers
appear from mid-summer
to early winter.

☼ ◊ ❋❋ 9–10

Desmodium tiliifolium
(Beggarweed)
Deciduous, upright sub-shrub. Leaves
consist of 3 large leaflets. Large
racemes of pale lilac to deep pink
flowers appear from late
summer to mid-autumn.

☼ ◊ ❋❋ 9–10

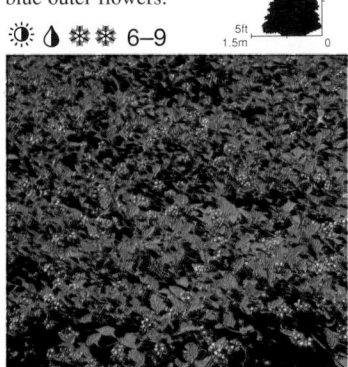

Lantana montevidensis, syn.
L. delicatissima, L. sellowiana
Evergreen, trailing, or mat-forming
shrub with serrated leaves. Has heads of
rose-purple flowers, each with a yellow
eye, intermittently all year
but mainly in summer.
Min. 50–55°F (10–13°C).

☼ ◊ 10

**Brunfelsia pauciflora
'Macrantha'**
Evergreen, spreading shrub with
leathery leaves. Blue-purple flowers,
which age to white in about 3 days,
appear from winter to
summer. Min. 50–55°F
(10–13°C).

☼◐ ◊ 10

Lavandula angustifolia 'Hidcote'
(Hidcote lavender)
Evergreen, bushy shrub with dense
spikes of fragrant, deep purple flowers
from mid- to late summer and narrow,
aromatic, silver-
gray leaves.

☼ ◊ ❋❋❋ 6–9

■■ PURPLE–BLUE

□ GREEN–YELLOW

Hebe 'Purple Queen'
Evergreen, compact, bushy shrub with glossy, deep green leaves that are purple-tinged when young. Dense racemes of deep purple flowers appear from early summer to mid-autumn.

☼ ◊ ❄❄❄ 9–10

Felicia amelloides 'Santa Anita'
Evergreen, bushy, spreading shrub. Blue flower heads with bright yellow centers are borne on long stalks from late spring to autumn among round to oval, bright green leaves.

☼ ◊ ❄ 10

Symphoricarpos orbiculatus 'Foliis Variegatis',
syn. S.o. 'Variegatus'
Deciduous, bushy, dense shrub with yellow-edged, bright green leaves. Occasionally bears white or pink flowers in summer-autumn.

☼ ◊ ❄❄❄ 3–9

Hyssopus officinalis (Hyssop)
Semi-evergreen or deciduous, bushy shrub with aromatic, narrowly oval, deep green leaves. Small, blue flowers appear from mid-summer to early autumn. Sometimes used as a culinary herb.

☼ ◊ ❄❄❄ 6–9

Caryopteris × clandonensis 'Arthur Simmonds'
Deciduous, bushy sub-shrub. Masses of blue to purplish blue flowers appear amid narrowly oval, irregularly toothed, gray-green leaves from late summer to autumn.

☼ ◊ ❄❄ 7–9

Ceanothus 'Gloire de Versailles'
Vigorous, deciduous, bushy shrub. Has broadly oval, green leaves and large racemes of pale blue flowers from mid-summer to early autumn.

☼ ◊ ❄❄ 7–9

Justicia brandegeana 'Chartreuse'
Evergreen, arching shrub producing white flowers surrounded by pale yellow-green bracts mainly in summer but also intermittently during the year. Min. 50–59°F (10–15°C).

☼ ◊ 9–10

Ceanothus thyrsiflorus var. repens
Evergreen, dense shrub that forms a mound of broad, glossy, dark green leaves. Racemes of blue flowers are borne in late spring and early summer.

☼ ◊ ❄❄ 8–9

Hydrangea macrophylla subsp. serrata 'Bluebird'
Deciduous, bushy shrub with flat, open heads of pale pink, pale purple, or blue flowers from mid- to late summer. Light green foliage turns red in autumn.

◑ ◊ ❄❄ 6–9

Perovskia atriplicifolia 'Blue Spire'
Deciduous, upright sub-shrub with gray-white stems. Profuse spikes of violet-blue flowers appear from late summer to mid-autumn above aromatic, deeply cut, gray-green leaves.

☼ ◊ ❄❄❄ 6–9

Weigela middendorffiana (Middendorff weigela)
Deciduous, arching, bushy shrub. From mid-spring to early summer funnel-shaped, sulfur yellow flowers, spotted with orange inside, are borne amid bright green foliage.

☼ ◊ ❄❄ 5–9

Potentilla 'Vilmoriniana'
Deciduous, upright shrub that bears
pale yellow or creamy white flowers
from late spring to mid-autumn.
Leaves are silver-gray and divided
into narrow leaflets.

☼ ◊ ❋❋❋ 3–8

Phygelius aequalis
'Yellow Trumpet'
Evergreen or semi-evergreen, upright
sub-shrub. Bears clusters of pendent,
tubular, pale creamy yellow flowers
from mid-summer to
early autumn.

☼ ◊ ❋❋ 7–9

Potentilla 'Elizabeth'
Deciduous, bushy, dense shrub with
small, deeply divided leaves and large,
bright yellow flowers that appear from
late spring to mid-autumn.

☼ ◊ ❋❋❋ 3–8

***Potentilla* 'Friedrichsenii'**
Vigorous, deciduous, upright shrub.
From late spring to mid-autumn pale
yellow flowers are produced amid
gray-green leaves.

☼ ◊ ❋❋❋ 3–8

***Halimium ocymoides* 'Susan'**
Evergreen, spreading shrub with
narrow, oval, gray-green leaves.
Numerous single or semi-double,
bright yellow flowers with central,
deep purple-red markings
are borne in small clusters
in summer.

☼ ◊ ❋❋ 9–10

***Santolina pinnata* subsp.**
***neapolitana* 'Sulphurea'**
Evergreen, rounded, bushy shrub with
aromatic, deeply cut, feathery, gray-
green foliage. Produces heads of pale
primrose yellow flowers
in mid-summer.

☼ ◊ ❋❋ 9–10

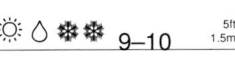

Lupinus arboreus (Tree lupine)
Fast-growing, semi-evergreen,
sprawling shrub that in early summer
usually bears short spikes of fragrant,
clear yellow flowers above hairy, pale
green leaves composed of
6–9 leaflets.

☼ ◊ ❋❋ 8–10

***Grevillea juniperina* f. sulphurea,**
syn. *G. sulphurea*
Evergreen, rounded, bushy shrub with
almost needlelike leaves, recurved and
dark green above, silky-haired beneath.
Has clusters of small,
spidery, pale yellow
flowers in spring-summer.

☼ ◊ ❋ 9–10

***Halimium lasianthum* subsp.**
formosum
Evergreen, spreading, bushy shrub. Has
gray-green foliage and golden yellow
flowers with central, deep red blotches,
borne in late spring and
early summer.

☼ ◊ ❋❋ 9–10

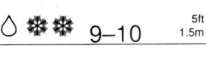

☐ YELLOW

Phlomis fruticosa
(Jerusalem sage)
Evergreen, spreading shrub with
upright shoots. Whorls of deep golden
yellow flowers are produced amid
sagelike, gray-green
foliage from early to
mid-summer.

☼ ◊ ❋❋ 8–10

Hypericum calycinum
(Aaron's beard, St. John's-wort)
Evergreen or semi-evergreen dwarf
shrub that makes good ground cover.
Has large, bright yellow flowers from
mid-summer to mid-
autumn and dark
green leaves.

☼ ◊ ❋❋❋ 7–9

Hypericum kouytchense
Deciduous or semi-evergreen, arching
shrub. Golden yellow flowers with
conspicuous stamens are borne among
foliage from mid-summer to early
autumn, followed by
decorative, bronze-red
fruit capsules.

☼ ◊ ❋❋❋ 8–9

Berberis thunbergii 'Aurea'
Deciduous, bushy, spiny shrub with
small, golden yellow leaves. Racemes
of small, red-tinged, pale yellow
flowers in mid-spring are followed by
red berries in autumn.

☼ ◊ ❋❋❋ 5–9

Genista hispanica
(Spanish gorse)
Deciduous, bushy, very spiny shrub
with few leaves but dense clusters of
golden yellow flowers borne profusely
in late spring and
early summer.

☼ ◊ ❋❋ 7–9

Hypericum 'Hidcote'
(Hidcote hypericum)
Evergreen or semi-evergreen, bushy,
dense shrub. Bears an abundance of
large, golden yellow flowers from mid-
summer to early autumn
amid narrowly oval, dark
green leaves.

☼ ◊ ❋❋❋ 6–9

Reinwardtia indica,
syn. *R. trigyna* (Yellow flax)
Evergreen, upright sub-shrub,
branching from the base. Has grayish
green leaves and small clusters of
yellow flowers mainly in
summer but also during
the year. Min. 50°F (10°C).

☼ ◊ 10

Cytisus nigricans (Spike broom)
Deciduous, upright shrub with dark
green leaves composed of 3 leaflets.
Has a long-lasting display of tall,
slender spires of yellow flowers
during summer.

☼ ◊ ❋❋❋ 6–9

Senecio 'Sunshine'
Evergreen, bushy shrub that forms a
mound of silvery gray, young leaves,
later becoming dark green. Large
clusters of bright yellow flower heads
are produced on felted
shoots from early to
mid-summer.

☼ ◊ ❋❋ 9–10

Hypericum × inodorum 'Elstead'
Deciduous or semi-evergreen, upright
shrub. Abundant, small, yellow flowers
borne from mid-summer to early
autumn are followed by ornamental,
orange-red fruits. Dark
green leaves are aromatic
when crushed.

☼ ◊ ❋❋❋ 6–9

Euryops pectinatus
Evergreen, upright shrub. Deep-cut,
gray-green leaves set off large heads of
daisylike, bright yellow flowers, borne
in late spring and early summer and
often again in winter.
Min. 41–5°F (5–7°C).

☼ ◊ 9–10

Senecio monroi
Evergreen, bushy, dense shrub that makes an excellent windbreak in mild, coastal areas. Has small, wavy-edged, dark green leaves with white undersides. Bears heads of bright yellow flowers in mid-summer.

☼ ◊ ❄❄ 9–10

Abutilon 'Kentish Belle'
Semi-evergreen, arching shrub with purple shoots and deeply lobed, purple-veined, dark green leaves. Bears large, pendent, bell-shaped, orange-yellow and red flowers in summer-autumn.

☼ ◊ ❄ 9–10

Isoplexis canariensis,
syn. *Digitalis canariensis*
Evergreen, rounded, sparingly branched shrub. Bears foxglovelike, yellow to red- or brownish orange flowers in dense, upright spikes, to 12in (30cm) tall, in summer. Min. 45°F (7°C).

☼ ◊ 9–10

Potentilla 'Sunset'
Deciduous shrub, bushy at first, later arching. Deep orange flowers that fade in hot sun appear from early summer to mid-autumn. Green leaves are divided into narrowly oval leaflets.

◑ ◊ ❄❄❄ 3–8

Grindelia chiloensis,
syn. *G. speciosa*
Mainly evergreen, bushy shrub with sticky stems. Sticky, lance-shaped, serrated leaves are up to 5in (12cm) long. Has large, daisylike, yellow flower heads in summer.

☼ ◊ ❄❄ 10

Juanulloa aurantiaca
Evergreen, upright, sparingly branched shrub, best supported. Leaves are felted beneath. Tubular, orange flowers, each with an urn-shaped, ribbed calyx, are borne in short, nodding clusters in summer. Min. 55–9°F (13–15°C).

☼ ◊ 9–10

Cytisus scoparius f. **andreanus**
Deciduous, arching shrub with narrow, dark green leaves that are divided into 3 leaflets. Bears a profusion of bright yellow-and-red flowers along elegant, green branchlets in late spring and early summer.

☼ ◊ ❄❄❄ 7–9

Mimulus aurantiacus, syn.
M. glutinosus, Diplacus glutinosus
Evergreen, domed to rounded shrub with sticky, lance-shaped, glossy, rich green leaves. Has tubular, orange, yellow, or red-purple flowers from late spring to autumn.

☼ ◊ ❄ 7–10

Lantana 'Spreading Sunset'
Evergreen, rounded to spreading shrub with finely wrinkled, deep green leaves. Has tiny, tubular flowers in a range of colors, carried in rounded, dense heads from spring to autumn. Min. 50–55°F (10–13°C).

☼ ◊ 9–10

☐ ORANGE

Cuphea ignea (Cigar plant)
Evergreen, spreading, bushy sub-shrub
with bright green leaves. From spring
to autumn has tubular, dark orange-red
flowers, each with a dark band and a
white ring at the mouth.
Min. 36°F (2°C).

☼ ◊ 10

Cuphea cyanea
Evergreen, rounded sub-shrub with
narrowly oval, sticky-haired leaves.
Tubular flowers, orange-red, yellow,
and violet-blue, are carried in summer.

☼ ◊ ❋ 10

Justicia spicigera,
syn. *J. ghiesbreghtiana* of gardens,
Jacobinia spicigera
Evergreen, well-branched shrub with
spikes of tubular, orange or red flowers
in summer and occasionally
other seasons. Min.
50–59°F (10–15°C).

☼ ◊
9–10

Shrubs/small AUTUMN INTEREST

☐☐▨ WHITE–RED

Turraea obtusifolia
Evergreen, rounded, arching, bushy
shrub with oval to lance-shaped leaves.
Bears fragrant white flowers from
autumn to spring, followed by orange-
yellow fruits like tiny,
peeled tangerines.
Min. 55°F (13°C).

☼ ◊ 10

Calliandra eriophylla
(Fairy duster, False mesquite)
Evergreen, stiff, dense shrub. Leaves
have numerous tiny leaflets. From late
spring to autumn has pompons of tiny,
pink-anthered, white florets,
followed by brown seed
pods. Min. 55°F (13°C).

☼ ◊ 10

***Berberis* 'Rubrostilla'**
Deciduous, arching shrub. Globose
to cup-shaped, pale yellow flowers
appear in early summer, followed by a
profusion of large, coral red fruits.
Gray-green leaves turn
brilliant red in
late autumn.

☼ ◊ ❋❋❋
7–9

Cotoneaster horizontalis
(Rock spray cotoneaster)
Deciduous, stiff-branched, spreading
shrub. Glossy, dark green leaves redden
in late autumn. Bears pinkish white
flowers from late spring to
early summer, followed by
red fruits.

☼ ◊ ❋❋❋ 5–9

***Vaccinium angustifolium* var.
*laevifolium*** (Lowbush blueberry)
Deciduous, bushy shrub with bright
green leaves that redden in autumn.
Edible, blue fruits follow white,
sometimes pinkish,
spring flowers.

☼ ◊ pH ❋❋❋ 3–7

***Viburnum opulus* 'Compactum'**
(Compact European cranberry bush)
Deciduous, dense shrub. Has deep
green leaves, red in autumn, and
profuse white flowers in spring and
early summer followed by
bunches of bright
red berries.

☼ ◊ ❋❋❋ 4–8

■ RED

■ PURPLE–YELLOW

□ WHITE

Bouvardia ternifolia,
syn. *B. triphylla*
Mainly evergreen, upright, bushy shrub with leaves in whorls of 3. Has tubular, bright scarlet flowers from summer to early winter. Min. 45–50°F (7–10°C).

☀ ◊ 9–10

Elsholtzia stauntonii
(Mint shrub, Staunton elsholtzia)
Deciduous, open sub-shrub. Sharply toothed, mint-scented, dark green leaves turn red in autumn. Slender spires of pale purplish flowers appear during late summer and autumn.

☀ ◊ ❋❋ 5–7

Skimmia japonica 'Fructu-albo'
Evergreen, bushy, dense, dwarf shrub. Has aromatic, dark green leaves and dense clusters of small, white flowers from mid- to late spring, succeeded by white berries.

Vaccinium corymbosum 'Pioneer'
Deciduous, upright, slightly arching shrub. Dark green leaves turn bright red in autumn. Small, white or pinkish flowers in late spring are followed by sweet, edible, blue-black berries.

☀ ◊ pH ❋❋ 4–8

Ceratostigma willmottianum
(Chinese plumbago, Wilmott blue leadwort)
Deciduous, open shrub. Has leaves that turn red in late autumn and bright, rich blue flowers from late summer until well into autumn.

☀ ◊ ❋❋ 7–10

☀ ◊ ❋❋❋ 7–9

Vaccinium parvifolium
Deciduous, upright shrub. Has small, dark green leaves that become bright red in autumn. Edible, bright red fruits are produced after small, pinkish white flowers borne in late spring and early summer.

☀ ◊ pH ❋❋❋❋ 6–8

Coriaria terminalis var. **xanthocarpa**
Deciduous, arching sub-shrub. Leaves have oval leaflets and turn red in autumn. Greenish flowers in late spring are followed by decorative, succulent, yellow fruits in late summer and autumn.

☀ ◊ ❋❋ 9–10

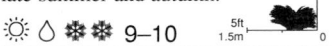

Pernettya mucronata 'Wintertime'
Evergreen, bushy, dense shrub. Has prickly, glossy, dark green leaves and white flowers in late spring and early summer, followed by large, long-lasting, white berries.

☀ ◊ pH ❋❋❋❋ 8–9

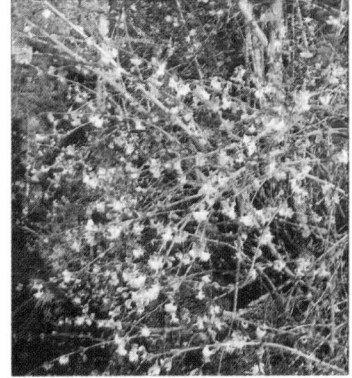

Lonicera x purpusii
Semi-evergreen, bushy, dense shrub with oval, dark green leaves. Small clusters of fragrant, short-tubed, white flowers, with spreading petal lobes and yellow anthers, appear in winter and early spring.

☀ ◊ ❋❋❋ 7–9

141

◻◼ WHITE–PINK

◼ RED

Sarcococca humilis
Evergreen, low, clump-forming shrub that spreads by underground stems. Tiny, fragrant white flowers with pink anthers appear amid glossy, dark green foliage in late winter and are followed by spherical, black fruits.

☀ ◊ ❄❄ 6–9

Sarcococca hookeriana var. *digyna*
Evergreen, clump-forming, suckering, dense shrub with narrow, bright green leaves. Tiny, fragrant white flowers, with pink anthers, open in winter and are followed by spherical, black fruits.

☀ ◊ ❄❄ 6–9

Pernettya mucronata 'Mulberry Wine'
Evergreen, bushy, dense shrub with large, globose, magenta berries that mature to deep purple. These follow white flowers borne in spring-summer. Leaves are glossy, dark green.

☀ ◊ pH ❄❄❄ 8–9

Skimmia japonica 'Rubella'
Evergreen, upright, dense shrub with aromatic, red-rimmed, bright green foliage. Deep red flower buds in autumn and winter open to dense clusters of small, white flowers in spring.

☀ ◊ ❄❄❄ 7–9

Daphne odora 'Aureomarginata'
Evergreen, bushy shrub with glossy, dark green leaves narrowly edged with yellow. Clusters of very fragrant, deep purplish pink and white flowers appear from mid-winter to early spring.

☀ ◊ ❄❄ 7–9

Daphne mezereum
(February daphne, Mezereon)
Deciduous, upright shrub. Very fragrant purple or pink blooms clothe the bare stems in late winter and early spring, followed by red fruits. Mature leaves are narrowly oval and dull gray-green.

☀ ◊ ❄❄❄ 5–8

Correa pulchella
Evergreen, fairly bushy, slender-stemmed shrub with oval leaves. Small, pendent, tubular, rose-red flowers appear from summer to winter, sometimes at other seasons.

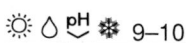

☀ ◊ pH ❄ 9–10

Skimmia japonica subsp. *reevesiana*, syn. *S. reevesiana*
Evergreen, bushy, rather weak-growing shrub with pointed, aromatic, dark green leaves. Clusters of small, white flowers in spring are followed by deep crimson berries.

☀ ◊ ❄❄❄ 7–9

Shrubs/small ALL YEAR INTEREST

▨ RED–GREEN

▨ WHITE–GREEN

Viburnum davidii
Evergreen shrub that forms a dome of
dark green foliage, over which rounded
heads of small, white flowers appear in
late spring. If plants of both sexes are
grown, female plants bear
decorative, metallic
blue fruits.

☼ ◊ ❅❅❅ 7–9

Vinca major 'Variegata'
Evergreen, spreading, arching,
prostrate sub-shrub. Has bright green
leaves broadly edged with creamy
white and large, bright blue flowers
borne from late spring to
early autumn.

◑ ◊ ❅❅❅ 7–9

Helichrysum petiolare,
syn. *H. petiolatum*
Evergreen shrub that forms mounds of
trailing, silver-green shoots and gray-
felted leaves. Has creamy yellow
flowers in summer. Usually
grown as an annual for
ground cover and edging.

☼ ◊ ❅ 10

Skimmia japonica
Evergreen, bushy, dense shrub. Has
aromatic, mid- to dark green leaves and
dense clusters of small, white flowers
from mid- to late spring, followed on
female plants by bright
red fruits if plants of both
sexes are grown.

☼◑ ◊ ❅❅❅ 7–9

Breynia disticha, syn. *B. nivosa*,
Phyllanthus nivosus (Snowbush)
Evergreen, well-branched shrub with
slender stems. Leaves are green with
white marbling; tiny, greenish flowers,
borne intermittently,
have no petals.
Min. 55°F (13°C).

☼◑ ◊ 10

Pandanus veitchii, syn. *P. tectorius*
'Veitchii' (Veitch screw pine)
Evergreen, upright, arching shrub with
rosettes of long, light green leaves that
have spiny, white to cream margins.
Min. 55–61°F (13–16°C).

☼ ◊ 10

Calocephalus brownii
Evergreen, intricately branched shrub
with velvety, gray branches and tiny,
scalelike leaves. Clusters of flower
heads, silver in bud, yellowish when
expanded, appear in
summer. Min. 45–50°F
(7–10°C).

☼ ◊ 10

Ribes laurifolium
Evergreen, spreading shrub. Has
leathery, deep green leaves and pendent
racemes of greenish yellow flowers in
late winter and early spring. Produces
edible, black berries on
female plants if plants of
both sexes are grown.

☼ ◊ ❅❅ 7–9

Coprosma x kirkii 'Variegata'
Evergreen, densely branched shrub,
prostrate when young, later semi-erect.
White-margined leaves are borne singly
or in small clusters. Tiny, translucent,
white fruits appear in
autumn on female plants
if both sexes are grown.

☼ ◊ ❅ 8–10

Artemisia arborescens
Evergreen, upright shrub, grown for its
finely cut, silvery white foliage. Heads
of small, bright yellow flowers are
borne in summer and early autumn.

☼ ◊ ❅ 9–10

☐ GREEN

Ballota acetabulosa
Evergreen sub-shrub that forms a mound of rounded, gray-green leaves, felted beneath. Whorls of small, pink flowers open from mid- to late summer.

☀ ◊ ❄❄ 8–9

Vaccinium glauco-album
Evergreen shrub with deep green leaves that when young are pale green above, bluish white beneath. Pink-tinged, white flowers in late spring and early summer are followed by white-bloomed, blue-black fruits.

☀ ◊ pH ❄❄ 7–9

Hebe cupressoides
Evergreen, upright, dense shrub with cypresslike, gray-green foliage. Tiny, pale lilac flowers are borne on mature plants from early to mid-summer.

☀ ◊ ❄❄ 8–9

Ruscus hypoglossum
Evergreen, clump-forming shrub with arching shoots. Pointed, glossy, bright green "leaves" are actually flattened shoots that bear tiny, yellow flowers in spring, followed by large, bright red berries.

☀ ◊ ❄❄ 7–9

Vinca minor (Dwarf periwinkle, Myrtle)
Evergreen, spreading, prostrate sub-shrub that forms extensive mats of small, glossy, dark green leaves. Bears small, purple, blue, or white flowers, mainly from mid-spring to early summer.

☀ ◊ ❄❄❄ 4–8

Mimosa pudica (Sensitive plant, Touch-me-not)
Short-lived, evergreen shrub with prickly stems; needs support. Fernlike leaves fold when touched. Has minute, pale mauve-pink flowers in summer-autumn. Min. 55–61°F (13–16°C).

☀ ◊ 10

Eurya emarginata
Slow-growing, evergreen, rounded, densely branched shrub with small, leathery, deep green leaves. Small, greenish white flowers in late spring or summer are followed by tiny, purple-black berries.

☀ ◊ ❄ 8–10

Lonicera pileata (Privet honeysuckle)
Evergreen, spreading, low, dense shrub with narrow, dark green leaves and tiny, short-tubed, creamy white flowers in late spring, followed by violet-purple berries. Makes good ground cover.

☀ ◊ ❄❄❄ 5–9

Chamaerops humilis (Dwarf fan palm, European fan palm)
Slow-growing, evergreen palm, suckering with age. Fan-shaped leaves, 2–3ft (60–90cm) across, have green to gray-green lobes. Has tiny, yellow flowers in summer.

☀ ◊ ❄ 9–10

Artemisia abrotanum (Old-man, Southernwood)
Deciduous or semi-evergreen, moderately bushy shrub. Aromatic, gray-green leaves have many very slender lobes. Has clusters of small, yellowish flower heads in late summer.

☀ ◊ ❄❄❄ 6–9

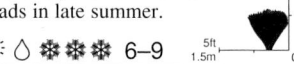

Buxus microphylla 'Green Pillow'
Evergreen, compact, dwarf shrub, forming a dense, rounded mass of small, oval, dark green leaves. Bears insignificant flowers in late spring or early summer.

☀ ◊ ❄❄❄ 5–9

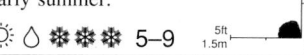

Sabal minor (Dwarf palmetto)
Evergreen, suckering fan palm with stems mainly underground. Has leaves of 20–30 green or gray-green lobes. Erect sprays of small, white flowers are followed by shiny, black berries. Min. 41°F (5°C).

☀ ◊ 8–10

Buxus sempervirens 'Suffruticosa'
Evergreen, dwarf shrub that forms a tight, dense mass of oval, bright green leaves. Bears insignificant flowers in late spring or early summer. Trimmed to about 6in (15cm) is used for edging.

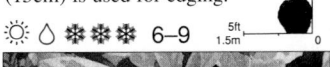 6–9

Ruta graveolens 'Jackman's Blue'
Evergreen, compact, bushy sub-shrub. Has aromatic, finely divided, blue foliage. In summer, clusters of small, mustard yellow flowers are borne.

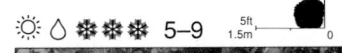 5–9

Leucothöe fontanesiana 'Rainbow' (Rainbow fetterbush)
Evergreen, arching shrub with sharply toothed, leathery, dark green leaves that age from pink- to cream-variegated. Racemes of white flowers open below shoots in spring.
5–9

Lonicera nitida 'Baggesen's Gold'
Evergreen, bushy shrub with long, arching shoots covered with tiny, bright yellow leaves. Insignificant, yellowish green flowers in mid-spring are occasionally followed by mauve fruits.
7–9

Salvia officinalis 'Icterina'
Evergreen or semi-evergreen, bushy shrub used as a culinary herb. Has aromatic, gray-green leaves variegated with pale green and yellow. Occasionally bears small spikes of tubular, 2-lipped, purplish flowers.

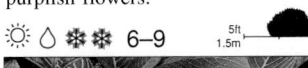 6–9

Codiaeum variegatum (Croton)
Evergreen, erect, sparingly branched shrub. Leathery, glossy leaves vary greatly in size and shape, and are variegated with red, pink, orange, or yellow. Min. 50–55°F (10–13°C).
10

Sanchezia speciosa,
syn. *S. nobilis* of gardens
Evergreen, erect, soft-stemmed shrub. Glossy leaves have yellow- or white-banded main veins. Tubular, yellow flowers appear in axils of red bracts, in summer. Min. 59–64°F (15–18°C).

 10

Euonymus fortunei 'Emerald and Gold'
(Emerald and gold winter creeper)
Evergreen, bushy shrub with bright green leaves edged with bright yellow and tinged with pink in winter.

 5–9

Pittosporum tenuifolium 'Tom Thumb'
Evergreen, rounded, dense shrub with pale green, young leaves that contrast with deep reddish brown, older foliage. Bears cup-shaped, purplish flowers in summer.

 9–10

145

Heathers

As a group of plants, heathers (or heaths) are remarkable in that there are species and cultivars available to provide interest at all times of the year. Several are grown for their golden foliage, which often turns a deep burnt orange in winter, while others flower for a long period during summer, autumn, or winter. Flowers come in a variety of colors, and are occasionally bicolored; those with double flowers may be dried for winter decoration. This group of plants is not as well adapted to the climatic extremes of the United States as they are to the more moderate oceanic climates of Europe.

There are three genera: *Calluna*, *Daboecia*, and *Erica*. All *Calluna* and *Daboecia* cultivars and most *Erica* species must be grown in acid soil but otherwise heathers require little attention. Main seasons of interest are given for each plant.

E. vagans 'Lyonesse' (sum.-aut.)

E. arborea var. *alpina* (win.-spr.)

E. ciliaris 'David McClintock' (sum.)

C. vulgaris 'Silver Queen' (sum.-aut.)

E. × *darleyensis* 'Darley Dale' (win.-spr.)

C. vulgaris 'Elsie Purnell' (sum.-aut.)

E. × *williamsii* 'P.D. Williams' (sum.)

C. vulgaris 'Kinlochruel' (sum.-aut.)

E. cinerea 'Hookstone White' (sum.)

E. canaliculata (win.-spr.)

C. vulgaris 'My Dream' (sum.-aut.)

C. vulgaris 'J.H. Hamilton' (sum.-aut.)

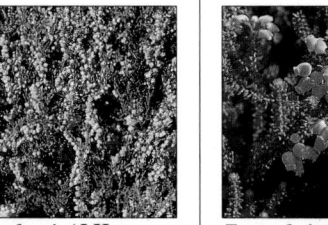
E. mackaiana 'Plena' (sum.)

C. vulgaris 'Spring Cream' (spr.-aut.)

E. mackaiana 'Dr. Ronald Gray' (sum.)

E. × *darleyensis* 'White Perfection' (win.-spr.)

D. cantabrica 'Snowdrift' (spr.-aut.)

E. tetralix 'Alba Mollis' (sum.-aut.)

E. × *darleyensis* 'White Glow' (win.-spr.)

C. vulgaris 'Anthony Davis' (sum.-aut.)

E. × *darleyensis* 'Ghost Hills' (win.-spr.)

E. × *veitchii* 'Pink Joy' (win.-spr.)

E. carnea 'Springwood White' (win.-spr.)

E. × *darleyensis* 'Archie Graham' (win.-spr.)

D. cantabrica 'Bicolor' (spr.-aut.)

E. × *veitchii* 'Exeter' (win.-spr.)

E. ciliaris 'White Wings' (sum.)

C. vulgaris 'County Wicklow' (sum.-aut.)

E. × *watsonii* 'Dawn' (sum.)

D. × *scotica* 'William Buchanan' (spr.-aut.)

146

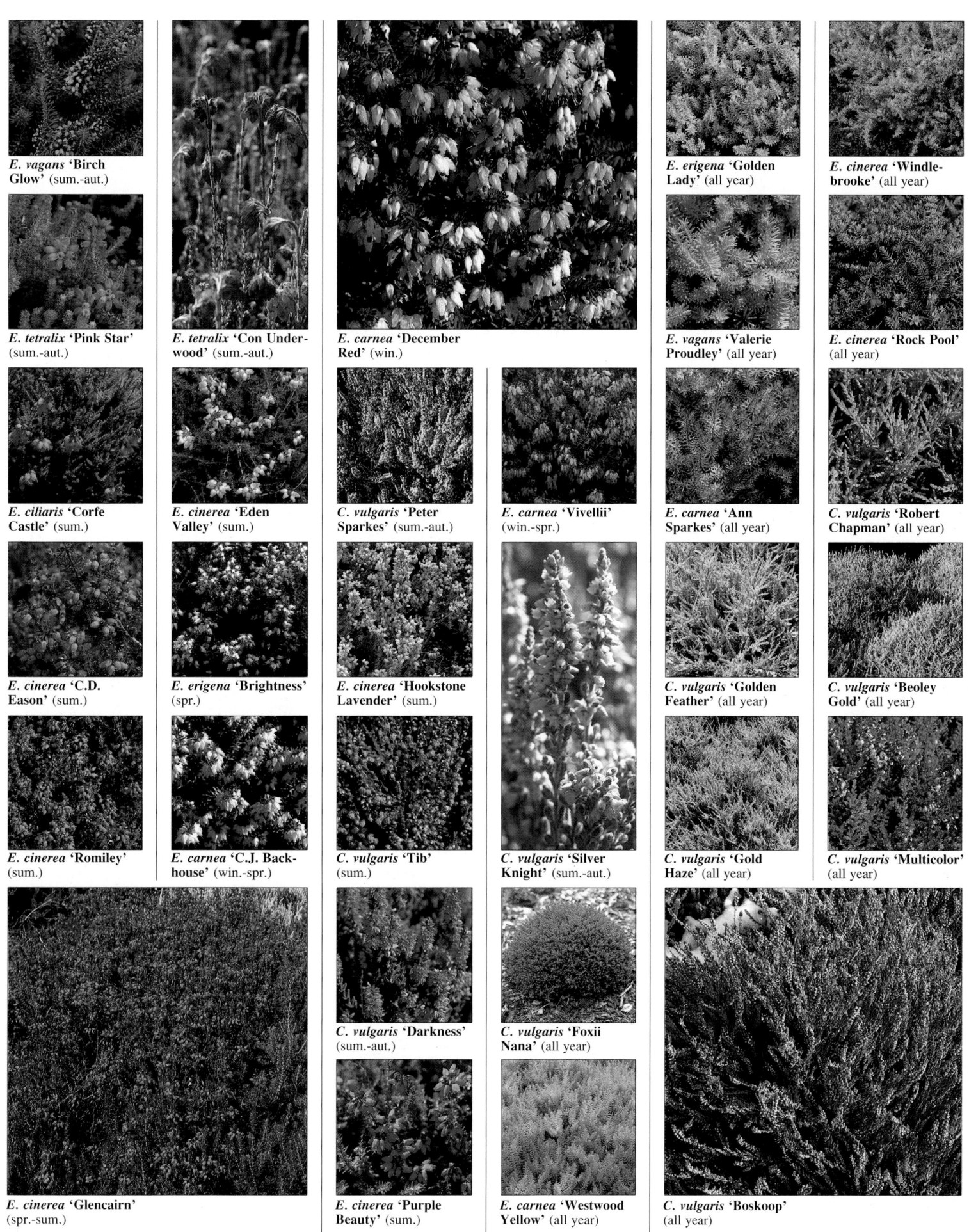

E. vagans 'Birch Glow' (sum.-aut.)

E. tetralix 'Pink Star' (sum.-aut.)

E. tetralix 'Con Underwood' (sum.-aut.)

E. carnea 'December Red' (win.)

E. erigena 'Golden Lady' (all year)

E. cinerea 'Windlebrooke' (all year)

E. ciliaris 'Corfe Castle' (sum.)

E. cinerea 'Eden Valley' (sum.)

C. vulgaris 'Peter Sparkes' (sum.-aut.)

E. carnea 'Vivellii' (win.-spr.)

E. vagans 'Valerie Proudley' (all year)

E. cinerea 'Rock Pool' (all year)

E. cinerea 'C.D. Eason' (sum.)

E. erigena 'Brightness' (spr.)

E. cinerea 'Hookstone Lavender' (sum.)

E. carnea 'Ann Sparkes' (all year)

C. vulgaris 'Robert Chapman' (all year)

E. cinerea 'Romiley' (sum.)

E. carnea 'C.J. Backhouse' (win.-spr.)

C. vulgaris 'Tib' (sum.)

C. vulgaris 'Silver Knight' (sum.-aut.)

C. vulgaris 'Golden Feather' (all year)

C. vulgaris 'Beoley Gold' (all year)

C. vulgaris 'Gold Haze' (all year)

C. vulgaris 'Multicolor' (all year)

E. cinerea 'Glencairn' (spr.-sum.)

C. vulgaris 'Darkness' (sum.-aut.)

C. vulgaris 'Foxii Nana' (all year)

E. cinerea 'Purple Beauty' (sum.)

E. carnea 'Westwood Yellow' (all year)

C. vulgaris 'Boskoop' (all year)

147

ROSES/shrub and old garden

☐ WHITE

R. 'Mme. Hardy'
Vigorous, upright Damask rose with plentiful, leathery, matt leaves. Richly fragrant, quartered-rosette, fully double flowers, 4in (10cm) across, white with green eyes, are borne in summer. H 5ft (1.5m), S 4ft (1.2m).

☼ ◊ ✸✸✸ 4–9

R. 'Boule de Neige'
Upright Bourbon rose with arching stems and very fragrant, cupped to rosette, fully double flowers. White flowers, sometimes tinged with pink, 3in (8cm) across, appear in summer-autumn. Leaves are glossy and dark green. H 5ft (1.5m), S 4ft (1.2m).

☼ ◊ ✸✸✸ 4–9

R. pimpinellifolia 'Plena'
Dense, spreading, prickly species rose with cupped, double, creamy-white flowers, 1½in (4cm) across, in early summer. Has small, fernlike, dark green leaves and blackish hips. H 3ft (1m), S 4ft (1.2m).

☼ ◊ ✸✸✸ 4–9

R. 'Penelope'
Dense, bushy shrub rose, with plentiful, dark green foliage, that bears many scented, cupped, double, pink-cream flowers, 3in (8cm) across, in clusters in summer-autumn. H and S 3ft (1m), more if lightly pruned.

☼ ◊ ✸✸✸ 4–9

Categories of Rose

Grown for the extraordinary beauty of their flowers, roses have been in cultivation for some hundreds of years. They have been widely hybridized, producing a vast number of shrubs suitable for growing as specimen plants, in the border, as hedges, and as climbers for training on walls, pergolas, and pillars. Roses are classified in three main groups:

Species

Species, or wild, roses and **species hybrids**, which share most of the characteristics of the parent species, bear flowers generally in one flush in summer and hips in autumn.

Old Garden Roses

Alba—large, freely branching roses with clusters of flowers in mid-summer and abundant, grayish green foliage.
Bourbon—open, remontant shrub roses that may be trained to climb. Flowers are borne, often 3 to a cluster, in summer-autumn.
China—remontant shrubs with flowers borne singly or in clusters in summer-autumn; provide shelter.
Damask—open shrubs bearing loose clusters of usually very fragrant flowers mainly in summer.
Gallica—fairly dense shrubs producing richly colored flowers, often 3 to a cluster, in the summer months.
Hybrid Perpetual—vigorous, remontant shrubs with flowers borne singly or in 3s in summer-autumn.
Moss—often lax shrubs with a furry, mosslike growth on stems and calyx and flowers in summer.
Noisette—remontant climbing roses that bear large clusters of flowers, with a slight spicy fragrance, in summer-autumn; provide shelter.
Portland—upright, rather dense, remontant shrubs, bearing loose clusters of flowers in summer-autumn.
Provence (Centifolia)—lax, thorny shrubs bearing scented flowers in summer.
Sempervirens—semi-evergreen climbing roses that bear numerous flowers in late summer.
Tea—remontant shrubs and climbers with elegant, pointed buds that open to loose flowers with a spicy fragrance; provide shelter.

Modern Garden roses

Shrub—a diverse group, illustrated here with the Old Garden Roses because of their similar characteristics. Most are remontant and are larger than bush roses, with flowers borne singly or in sprays in summer and/or autumn.

Flower shapes

With the mass hybridization that has occurred in recent years, roses have been developed to produce plants with a wide variety of characteristics, in particular different forms of flower, often with a strong fragrance. These flower types, illustrated below, give a general indication of the shape of the flower at its perfect state (which in some cases may be before it has opened fully). Growing conditions may affect the form of the flower. Flowers may be single (4–7 petals), semi-double (8–14 petals), double (15–30 petals), or fully double (over 30 petals).

Flat—open, usually single or semi-double flowers have petals that are almost flat.

Cupped—open, single to fully double flowers have petals curving outwards gently from the center.

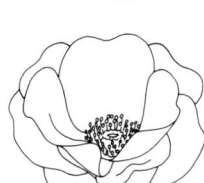

Pointed—elegant, Hybrid Tea shape, semi-double to fully double flowers have high, tight centers.

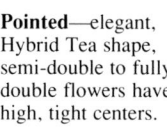

Urn-shaped—classic, curved, flat-topped, semi-double to fully double flowers are of Hybrid Tea type.

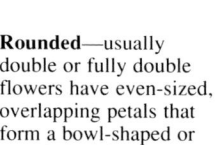

Rounded—usually double or fully double flowers have even-sized, overlapping petals that form a bowl-shaped or rounded outline.

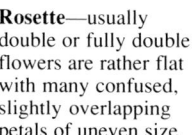

Rosette—usually double or fully double flowers are rather flat with many confused, slightly overlapping petals of uneven size.

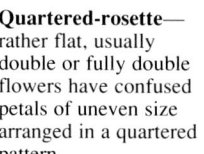

Quartered-rosette—rather flat, usually double or fully double flowers have confused petals of uneven size arranged in a quartered pattern.

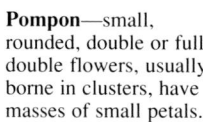

Pompon—small, rounded, double or fully double flowers, usually borne in clusters, have masses of small petals.

Large-flowered bush (Hybrid Tea)—remontant shrubs with large flowers borne in summer-autumn.
Cluster-flowered bush (Floribunda)—remontant shrubs with usually large sprays of flowers in summer-autumn.
Dwarf clustered-flowered bush (Patio)—neat, remontant shrubs with sprays of flowers borne in summer-autumn.
Miniature bush—very small, remontant shrubs with sprays of tiny flowers in summer-autumn.

Polyantha—tough, compact, remontant shrubs with many small flowers in summer-autumn.
Ground cover—trailing and spreading roses, some flowering in summer only, others remontant, flowering in summer-autumn.
Climbing—vigorous climbing roses, diverse in growth and flower, some flowering in summer only, others remontant, flowering in summer-autumn.
Rambler—vigorous climbing roses with flexible stems that bear clusters of flowers mostly in summer.

R. 'Dupontii'
Upright, bushy shrub rose with
abundant, grayish foliage. Bears many
clusters of fragrant, flat, single, white
flowers, tinged with blush pink, 2¹/₂in
(6cm) across, in mid-summer. H and
S 7ft (2.2m).

☀ ◊ ❄❄❄ 4–9

R. 'Nevada'
Dense, arching shrub rose with
abundant, light green leaves. Scented,
flat, semi-double, creamy white
flowers, 4in (10cm) across, are borne
freely in summer and more sparsely in
autumn. H and S 7ft (2.2m).

☀ ◊ ❄❄❄ 4–9

R. 'Pearl Drift', syn. R. 'Leggab'
Bushy, spreading shrub rose that
produces clusters of lightly scented,
cupped, double, blush pink flowers,
4in (10cm) across, in summer-
autumn. Leaves are plentiful and
glossy. H 3ft (1m), S 4ft (1.2m).

☀ ◊ ❄❄❄ 4–9

R. 'Fantin-Latour'
Vigorous, shrubby Provence rose.
Flowers appear in summer and are
fragrant, cupped to flat, fully double,
blush pink, with neat, green button
eyes, and 4in (10cm) across. Has
broad, dark green leaves. H 5ft (1.5m),
S 4ft (1.2m).

☀ ◊ ❄❄❄ 4–9

R. 'Great Maiden's Blush',
syn. R. 'Cuisse de Nymphe'
Vigorous, upright Alba rose. Very
fragrant, rosette, fully double, pinkish
white flowers, 3in (8cm) across,
appear in mid-summer. H 6ft (2m),
S 4¹/₂ft (1.3m).

☀ ◊ ❄❄❄ 4–9

R. 'Felicia'
Vigorous shrub rose with abundant
grayish green foliage. Scented, cupped,
double flowers, 3in (8cm) across, are
light pink, tinged with apricot, and are
borne in summer-autumn. H 5ft
(1.5m), S 7ft (2.2m).

☀ ◊ ❄❄❄❄ 4–9

R. 'Conrad Ferdinand Meyer'
Vigorous, arching shrub rose with
cupped, fully double, pink flowers,
3in (7cm) across, that are richly
fragrant and borne in large numbers
in summer, fewer in autumn. Foliage
is leathery and prone to rust. H 8ft
(2.5m), S 4ft (1.2m).

☀ ◊ ❄❄❄ 4–9

R. 'Céleste', syn. R. 'Celestial'
Vigorous, spreading, bushy Alba rose.
Fragrant, cupped, double, light pink
flowers, 3in (8cm) across, appear in
summer. Makes a good hedge. H 5ft
(1.5m), S 4ft (1.2m).

☀ ◊ ❄❄❄ 4–9

R. eglanteria, syn. R. rubiginosa
(Sweetbrier)
Vigorous, arching, thorny species rose
that has distinctive, apple-scented
foliage. Bears cupped, single, pink
flowers, 2.5cm (1in) across, in mid-
summer and red hips in autumn.
H and S 8ft (2.4m).

☀ ◊ ❄❄❄ 5–9

Roses/shrub and old garden

R. 'Rosy Cushion',
syn. *R.* 'Interall'
Dense, spreading shrub rose with
plentiful, glossy, dark green leaves.
Bears clusters of scented, cupped, semi-
double flowers, 2½in (6cm) across, that
are pink with ivory centers, in summer-
autumn. H 3ft (1m), S 4ft (1.2m).

☼ ◊ ❄❄❄ 4–9

R. glauca, syn. *R. rubrifolia*
Vigorous, arching species rose, grown
for its fine, grayish purple leaves and
red stems. Flat, single, cerise-pink
flowers, 1½in (4cm) across, with pale
centers and gold stamens, appear in
early summer, followed by red hips in
autumn. H 6ft (2m), S 5ft (1.5m).

☼ ◊ ❄❄❄❄ 5–9

R. 'Marguerite Hilling',
syn. *R.* 'Pink Nevada'
Dense, arching shrub rose. Many
scented, flat, semi-double, rose-pink
flowers, 4in (10cm) across, are borne
in summer and a few in autumn. Has
plentiful, light green foliage. H and
S 7ft (2.2m).

☼ ◊ ❄❄❄ 4–9

R. ' Reine Victoria'
Lax Bourbon rose with slender stems
and light green leaves. Sweetly
scented, rosette, double flowers, 3in
(8cm) across, in shades of pink, are
borne in summer-autumn. Grows well
on a pillar. H 6ft (2m),
S 4ft (1.2m).

☼ ◊ ❄❄❄ 4–9

R. 'Complicata'
Very vigorous Gallica rose, with
thorny, arching growth. Slightly
fragrant, cupped, single flowers, 4½in
(11cm) across, are pink with pale
centers and appear in mid-summer.
H 7ft (2.2m), S 8ft (2.5m). Useful as
a large hedge.

☼ ◊ ❄❄❄ 4–9

R. 'Königin von Dänemark',
syn. *R.* 'Belle Courtisanne'
Vigorous, rather open Alba rose.
Heavily scented, quartered-rosette,
fully double, warm pink flowers, 3in
(8cm) across and with green button
eyes, appear in mid-summer. H 5ft
(1.5m), S 4ft (1.2m).

☼ ◊ ❄❄❄ 4–9

R. 'Bonica',
syn. *R.* 'Meidonomac'
Vigorous, spreading shrub rose bearing
large sprays of slightly fragrant, cup-
shaped, fully double, rose-pink flowers,
3in (7cm) across, in summer-autumn.
Foliage is glossy and plentiful. H 3ft
(90cm), S 3½ft (1.1m).

☼ ◊ ❄❄❄ 4–9

R. 'Pink Grootendorst'
Upright, bushy shrub rose with
plentiful, small leaves. Rosette, double
flowers, 2in (5cm) across, have
serrated, clear pink petals. Blooms
are carried in sprays in summer-
autumn. H 6ft (2m), S 5ft (1.5m).

☼ ◊ ❄❄❄ 4–9

R. 'Constance Spry'
Shrub rose of arching habit that will
climb if supported. Cupped, fully
double, pink flowers, 5in (12cm)
across, with a spicy scent, are borne
freely on nodding stems in summer.
Leaves are large and plentiful. H 6ft
(2m), S 5ft (1.5m).

☼ ◊ ❄❄❄ 4–9

R. 'Mrs. John Laing'
Bushy Hybrid Perpetual rose with plentiful, light green foliage. Produces many richly fragrant, rounded, fully double, pink flowers, 5in (12cm) across, in summer and a few in autumn. H 3ft (1m), S 2¹/₂ft (80cm).

 ☼ ◊ ❉❉❉ 4–9

R. chinensis 'Mutabilis'
Open species rose with coppery, young foliage. Shallowly cup-shaped, single, buff-yellow flowers, 2¹/₂in (6cm) across, that age to coppery pink or crimson, appear freely in summer-autumn. Prefers a sunny, sheltered wall. H and S 3ft (1m), to 6ft (2m) against a wall.

☼ ◊ ❉❉ 6–9

R. rugosa
(Hedgehog rose, Rugosa rose)
Vigorous, dense species rose with wrinkled leaves and large, red hips. Cupped, single, white or purplish red flowers, 3¹/₂in (9cm) across, appear in good succession in summer-autumn. H and S 3–6ft (1–2m).

☼ ◊ ❉❉❉ 4–9

R. 'Roseraie de l'Haÿ'
Vigorous, dense shrub rose. Bears many strongly scented, cupped to flat, double, reddish purple flowers, 4¹/₂in (11cm) across, in summer-autumn. Leaves are abundant and disease-resistant. H 7ft (2.2m), S 6ft (2m).

☼ ◊ ❉❉❉ 4–9

R. 'Old Blush China',
syn. *R.* 'Parson's Pink China'
Bushy China rose that may be trained as a climber on a sheltered wall. Cupped, double, pink flowers, 2¹/₂in (6cm) across, are produced freely from summer to late autumn. H 3ft (1m), S 2¹/₂ft (80cm) or more.

☼ ◊ ❉❉❉ 6–9

R. moyesii 'Geranium'
Vigorous, arching species rose. Flat, single flowers, 2in (5cm) across, are dusky scarlet with yellow stamens and are borne close to branches in summer. Has small, dark green leaves and in autumn large, red hips. H 10ft (3m), S 8ft (2.5m).

☼ ◊ ❉❉❉ 5–9

R. gallica 'Versicolor'
(Rosa mundi)
Neat, bushy Gallica rose. In summer produces striking, slightly scented, flat, semi-double flowers, 2in (5cm) across, very pale blush pink with crimson stripes. H 2¹/₂ft (75cm), S 3ft (1m).

☼ ◊ ❉❉❉ 5–9

R. 'Mme. Isaac Pereire'
Vigorous, arching Bourbon rose. Fragrant, cupped to quartered-rosette, fully double flowers, 6in (15cm) across, are deep purplish pink and are produced freely in summer- autumn. H 7ft (2.2m), S 6ft (2m).

☼ ◊ ❉❉❉ 4–9

R. 'Henri Martin',
syn. *R.* 'Red Moss'
Vigorous, upright Moss rose. Rosette, double, purplish crimson flowers, 3¹/₂in (9cm) across, appear in summer and have a light scent and some furry, green "mossing" of the calyces under-neath. H 5ft (1.5m), S 3ft (1m).

☼ ◊ ❉❉❉ 4–9

Roses/shrub and old garden

R. 'Empereur du Maroc'
Compact, shrubby Hybrid Perpetual
rose. Fragrant, quartered-rosette, fully
double flowers, 3in (8cm) across, are
rich purplish crimson and are borne
freely in summer and more sparsely in
autumn. H 4ft (1.2 m), S 3ft (1m).

☼ ◊ ❀❀❀ 4–9

R. 'Belle de Crécy'
Gallica rose of rather lax growth and
few thorns. Rosette, fully double
flowers, 3in (8cm) across, are pink,
tinged grayish purple with green eyes,
have a rich, spicy fragrance, and are
produced in summer. H 4ft (1.2 m),
S 3ft (1m).

☼ ◊ ❀❀❀ 4–9

R. 'Cardinal Hume',
syn. *R.* 'Harregale'
Bushy, spreading shrub rose. Cupped,
fully double, reddish purple flowers,
3in (7.5cm) across, are borne in dense
clusters in summer-autumn and have a
musky scent. H 3ft (90cm), S 3ft (1m).

☼ ◊ ❀❀❀ 4–9

R. 'William Lobb',
syn. *R.* 'Duchesse d'Istrie'
Moss rose with strong, arching, prickly
stems that will climb if supported. In
summer bears rosette, double, deep
purplish crimson flowers, 3½in (9cm)
across, that fade to lilac-gray. H and
S 6ft (2m).

☼ ◊ ❀❀❀ 4–9

R. primula
(Primrose rose, Primula rose)
Lax, arching species rose that bears
scented, cupped, single, primrose
yellow flowers, 1½in (4cm) across, in
late spring. Foliage is plentiful,
aromatic, and fernlike. May die back
in hard winters. H and S 6ft (2m).

☼ ◊ ❀❀❀ 5–8

R. 'Cardinal de Richelieu'
Vigorous, compact Gallica rose that
bears plentiful, dark green foliage and
fragrant, rounded, fully double, deep
burgundy purple flowers, 3in (8cm)
across, in summer. H 4ft (1.2m),
S 3ft (1m).

☼ ◊ ❀❀❀ 4–9

R. 'Tour de Malakoff'
Provence rose of open growth.
Scented, rosette, double flowers, 5in
(12cm) across, are magenta with violet
veins, fading to grayish purple, and
appear in summer. H 6ft (2m),
S 5ft (1.5m).

☼ ◊ ❀❀❀ 4–9

R. foetida 'Persiana',
syn. *R.* 'Persian Yellow'
Upright, arching, species rose with
cupped, double, yellow flowers, 1in
(2.5cm) across, in early summer.
Glossy leaves are prone to blackspot.
Prune spent branches only and shelter
from cold winds. H and S 5ft (1.5m).

☼ ◊ ❀❀❀ 4–9

R. ecae
Erect, wiry species rose. Cupped,
single, bright yellow flowers, ¾in
(2cm) across, with a musky scent, are
borne close to reddish stems in late
spring. Foliage is fernlike and
graceful. Needs shelter. H 5ft (1.5m),
S 4ft (1.2m).

☼ ◊ ❀❀❀ 6–9

Roses/modern

☐ YELLOW ☐☐ WHITE–PINK

R. 'Iceberg',
syn. *R*. 'Schneewittchen'
Cluster-flowered bush rose. Produces
many sprays of cupped, fully double,
white flowers, 3in (7cm) across, in
summer-autumn. Has abundant, glossy
leaves. H 30in (75cm), S 26in (65cm),
more if not pruned hard.

☼ ◊ ❀❀❀ 4–9

R. 'Canary Bird'
Vigorous, dense, arching species
hybrid with small, fernlike leaves.
Cupped, single, yellow flowers, 2in
(5cm) across, with a musky scent,
appear in late spring and sparsely in
autumn. May die back in hard winters.
H and S 7ft (2.1m).

☼ ◊ ❀❀❀ 4–9

R. 'Margaret Merril'
Upright, cluster-flowered bush rose.
Very fragrant, double, blush white or
white flowers, are well-formed, urn-
shaped, and 4in (10cm) across, and are
borne singly or in clusters in summer-
autumn. H 3ft (1m), S 2ft (60cm).

☼ ◊ ❀❀❀ 4–9

R. 'Elizabeth Harkness'
Neat, upright, large-flowered bush rose
with abundant, dark green foliage.
Fragrant, pointed, fully double flowers,
5in (12cm) across, are pale creamy
pink, tinted buff, and are borne in
summer-autumn. H 2½ft (80cm),
S 2ft (60cm).

☼ ◊ ❀❀❀ 4–9

R. 'Graham Thomas',
syn. *R*. 'Ausmas'
Vigorous, arching shrub rose of lax
growth, with glossy, bright green
leaves. In summer-autumn bears
cupped, fully double, yellow flowers,
4½in (11cm) across, with some scent.
H 4ft (1.2m), S 5ft (1.5m).

☼ ◊ ❀❀❀❀ 4–9

R. 'Grouse', syn. *R*. 'Korimro'
Trailing, ground cover rose with very
abundant, glossy foliage and flat,
single, blush pink flowers, 1½in (4cm)
across, borne close to stems in summer-
autumn. Has a pleasant fragrance.
H 18in (45cm), S 10ft (3m).

☼ ◊ ❀❀❀ 4–9

R. 'The Fairy'
Dense, cushion-forming, dwarf cluster-
flowered bush rose with abundant,
small, glossy leaves. Rosette, double,
pink flowers, 1in (2.5cm) across, are
borne freely in late summer and
autumn. H and S 2ft (60cm).

☼ ◊ ❀❀❀ 4–9

R. 'Nozomi',
syn. *R*. 'Heideröslein'
Creeping, ground cover rose bearing
flat, single, blush pink and white
flowers, 1in (2.5cm) across, close to
stems in summer. Has small, dark green
leaves. May be used for a container.
H 18in (45cm), S 4ft (1.2m).

☼ ◊ ❀❀❀ 4–9

Roses/modern

R. 'Pink Bells',
syn. *R*. 'Poulbells'
Very dense, spreading, ground cover
rose with abundant, small, dark green
leaves and many pompon, fully
double, pink flowers, 1in (2.5cm)
across, borne in clusters in summer.
H 2¹/₂ft (75cm), S 4ft (1.2m).

☼ ◊ ❀❀❀ 4–9

R. 'Queen Elizabeth'
Upright, cluster-flowered bush rose
that bears long-stemmed, rounded,
fully double, pink flowers, 4in (10cm)
across, singly or in clusters, in summer-
autumn. Leaves are large and leathery.
H 5ft (1.5m), S 2¹/₂ft (75cm), more if
not pruned hard.

☼ ◊ ❀❀❀ 4–9

R. 'Iced Ginger'
Upright, cluster-flowered bush rose
with sparse, reddish foliage. Pointed,
fully double, buff to copper pink
flowers, 4¹/₂in (11cm) across, are
borne singly or in clusters in summer-
autumn. H 3ft (1m), S 28in (70cm).

☼ ◊ ❀❀❀ 4–9

R. 'Alpine Sunset'
Compact, large-flowered bush rose
with fragrant, rounded, fully double,
peach yellow flowers, 8in (20cm)
across, appearing on short stems in
summer-autumn. Has large, semi-
glossy leaves. May die back in hard
winters. H and S 2ft (60cm).

☼ ◊ ❀❀❀ 4–9

R. 'Sexy Rexy', syn. *R*. 'Macrexy'
Compact, bushy, cluster-flowered bush
rose. Bears clusters of slightly fragrant,
cupped, camellialike, fully double,
pink flowers, 3in (8cm) across, in
summer-autumn. Leaves are dark
green. H and S 2ft (60cm).

☼ ◊ ❀❀❀ 4–9

R. 'Peek-a-boo', syn. *R*. 'Brass
Ring', *R*. 'Dicgrow'
Dense, cushion-forming, dwarf cluster-
flowered bush rose with many sprays of
urn-shaped, double, apricot pink flowers,
1¹/₂in (4cm) across, from summer to
early winter. Leaves are narrow and
dark green. H and S 18in (45cm).

☼ ◊ ❀❀❀ 4–9

R. 'Lovely Lady',
syn. *R*. 'Dicjubell'
Dense, rounded, large-flowered bush
rose. Slightly scented, pointed, fully
double, rose-pink flowers, 4in (10cm)
across, are produced freely in summer-
autumn. H 30in (80cm), S 28in (70cm).

☼ ◊ ❀❀❀ 4–9

R. 'Rosemary Harkness',
syn. *R*. 'Harrowbond'
Vigorous, large-flowered bush rose with
abundant, glossy leaves. Bears fragrant,
pointed, double flowers, 4in (10cm)
across, in shades of salmon pink and
orange, singly or in clusters in summer-
autumn. H 3ft (1m), S 2¹/₂ft (75cm).

☼ ◊ ❀❀❀ 4–9

R. 'Blessings'
Upright, large-flowered bush rose with
slightly fragrant, salmon pink flowers
that are urn-shaped and fully double,
4in (10cm) across, and are borne
singly or in clusters in summer-
autumn. Has large, dark green leaves.
H 3ft (1m), S 2¹/₂ft (75cm).

☼ ◊ ❀❀❀ 4–9

R. 'Silver Jubilee'
Dense, upright, large-flowered bush
rose. Bears slightly scented, pointed,
fully double, soft salmon pink flowers,
5in (12cm) across, very freely in
summer-autumn. Foliage is
abundant and glossy. H 3¹/₂ft (1.1m),
S 2¹/₂ft (75cm).

☼ ◊ ❋❋❋ 4–9

R. 'Escapade'
Dense, cluster-flowered bush rose.
Fragrant, cupped, semi-double, rose-
violet flowers, 3in (8cm) across, with
white eyes, are borne in sprays in
summer-autumn. Foliage is light green
and glossy. H 2¹/₂ft (75cm),
S 2ft (60cm).

☼ ◊ ❋❋❋ 4–9

R. 'Anisley Dickson',
syn. *R*. 'Dickimono', *R*. 'Dicky',
R. 'Münchner Kindl',
Vigorous, cluster-flowered bush rose.
Carries large clusters of slightly
fragrant, pointed, double, salmon pink
flowers, 3in (8cm) across, in summer -
autumn. H 3ft (1m), S 2¹/₂ft (75cm).

☼ ◊ ❋❋❋ 4–9

R. 'Keepsake',
syn. *R*. 'Kormalda'
Neat, bushy, large-flowered bush rose
with plentiful, glossy leaves. Slightly
scented, rounded, fully double, pink
flowers, 5in (12cm) across, are freely
produced in summer-autumn. H 2¹/₂ft
(75cm), S 2ft (60cm).

☼ ◊ ❋❋❋ 4–9

R. 'Paul Shirville', syn.
R. 'Harqueterwife', *R*. 'Heartthrob'
Spreading, large-flowered bush rose.
Bears fragrant, pointed, fully double,
rosy salmon pink flowers, 3¹/₂in (9cm)
across, in summer-autumn. Leaves are
glossy, reddish, and abundant.
H and S 2¹/₂ft (75cm).

☼ ◊ ❋❋❋ 4–9

R. 'Double Delight'
Large-flowered bush rose of upright,
uneven growth. Fragrant, rounded,
fully double flowers, 5in (12cm)
across, are creamy white, edged with
red, and are borne in summer-
autumn. H 3ft (1m), S 2ft (60cm).

☼ ◊ ❋❋ 4–9

R. 'Anna Ford',
syn. *R*. 'Harpiccolo'
Dwarf cluster-flowered bush rose.
Has urn-shaped (opening flat), double,
orange-red flowers, 1¹/₂in (4cm)
across, borne in summer-autumn, and
many small, dark green leaves. H 18in
(45cm), S 15in (38cm).

☼ ◊ ❋❋❋ 4–9

R. 'Trumpeter', syn. *R*. 'Mactru'
Neat, bushy, cluster-flowered bush
rose with many cupped, fully double,
bright red flowers, 2¹/₂in (6cm) across,
in summer-autumn. Leaves are deep
green and semi-glossy. H 24in (60cm),
S 20in (50cm).

☼ ◊ ❋❋❋ 4–9

155

Roses/modern

□ YELLOW

***R.* 'Royal William'**, syn.
R. 'Duftzauber '84', *R.* 'Korzaun'
Vigorous, large-flowered bush rose
with large, dark green leaves. Slightly
scented, pointed, fully double, deep
crimson flowers, 5in (12cm) across,
are carried on long stems in summer-
autumn. H 3ft (1m), S 2½ft (75cm).

☼ ◊ ❋❋❋ 4–9

***R.* 'Precious Platinum'**,
syn. *R.* 'Opa Potschke'
Vigorous, large-flowered bush rose
with abundant, glossy leaves. Bears
slightly scented, rounded, fully double,
deep crimson-scarlet flowers, 4in
(10cm) across, in summer-autumn.
H 3ft (1m), S 2ft (60cm).

☼ ◊ ❋❋❋ 4–9

***R.* 'Wee Jock'**, syn. *R.* 'Cocabest'
Dense, bushy, dwarf cluster-flowered
bush rose. Bears rosette, fully double,
crimson flowers, 1½in (4cm) across, in
summer-autumn. Plentiful leaves are
small and dark green. H and
S 18in (45cm).

☼ ◊ ❋❋❋ 4–9

***R.* 'Champagne Cocktail'**,
syn. *R.* 'Horflash'
Upright, cluster-flowered bush rose.
Fragrant, cupped, double, yellow-pink
flowers, 3½in (9cm) across, opening
wide, are borne in summer-autumn.
H 3ft (1m), S 2ft (60cm).

☼ ◊ ❋❋❋ 4–9

***R.* 'Alexander'**,
syn. *R.* 'Alexandra'
Vigorous, upright, large-flowered bush
rose with abundant, dark green foliage.
Slightly scented, pointed, double,
bright red flowers, 5in (12cm) across,
are borne on long stems in summer-
autumn. H 5ft (1.5m), S 2½ft (75cm).

☼ ◊ ❋❋❋ 4–9

***R.* 'The Times'**,
syn. *R.* 'Korpeahn'
Spreading, cluster-flowered bush rose.
Slightly scented, cupped, double, deep
crimson flowers, 3in (8cm) across, are
borne in wide clusters in summer-
autumn. Foliage is dark green and
plentiful. H 2ft (60cm), S 2½ft (75cm).

☼ ◊ ❋❋❋ 4–9

***R.* 'Alec's Red'**
Vigorous, large-flowered bush rose
bearing strongly fragrant, deep cherry
red flowers that are pointed and fully
double, 6in (15cm) across, in summer-
autumn. H 3ft (1m), S 2ft (60cm).

☼ ◊ ❋❋❋ 4–9

***R.* 'Peace'**, syn. *R.* 'Gioia', *R.*
'Gloria Dei', *R.* 'Mme. A. Meilland'
Vigorous, shrubby, large-flowered bush
rose with scented, pointed to rounded,
fully double flowers, 6in (15cm) across,
borne freely in clusters in summer-
autumn. Has abundant, large, glossy
foliage. H 4ft (1.2m), S 3ft (1m).

☼ ◊ ❋❋❋ 4–9

***R.* 'Rugul'**, syn. *R.* 'Guletta',
R. 'Tapis Jaune'
Compact, dense, dwarf cluster-
flowered bush rose with cupped to flat,
double, yellow flowers, 2in (5cm)
across, that are borne in summer-
autumn, and rich green leaves.
H 12in (30cm), S 16in (40cm).

☼ ◊ ❋❋❋ 4–9

R. 'Grandpa Dickson',
syn. *R*. 'Irish Gold'
Neat, upright, large-flowered bush rose
with sparse, pale, glossy foliage. Bears
many slightly scented, pointed, fully
double, light yellow flowers, 7in
(18cm) across, in summer-autumn.
H 2¹/₂ft (80cm), S 2ft (60cm).

☼ ◊ ❀❀❀ 4–9

R. 'Simba', syn. *R*. 'Goldsmith',
R. 'Korbelma'
Upright, large-flowered bush rose
with lightly fragrant, urn-shaped, fully
double, yellow flowers, 3¹/₂in (9cm)
across, borne freely in summer-autumn.
Leaves are large and dark green.
H 2¹/₂ft (75cm), S 2ft (60cm).

☼ ◊ ❀❀❀ 4–9

R. 'Mountbatten',
syn. *R*. 'Harmantelle'
Shrubby, cluster-flowered bush rose
with disease-resistant foliage. Bears
scented, rounded, fully double, yellow
flowers, 4in (10cm) across, singly or in
clusters, in summer-autumn.
H 4ft (1.2m), S 2¹/₂ft (75cm).

☼ ◊ ❀❀❀ 4–9

R. 'Korresia', syn. *R*. 'Friesia'
Bushy, upright, cluster-flowered bush
rose. Bears open sprays of strongly
scented, urn-shaped, double flowers,
3in (8cm) across, with waved, yellow
petals, in summer-autumn. H 2¹/₂ft
(75cm), S 2ft (60cm).

☼ ◊ ❀❀❀ 4–9

R. 'Bright Smile',
syn. *R*. 'Dicdance'
Low, bushy, cluster-flowered bush
rose with bright, glossy leaves. Bears
clusters of slightly scented, flat, semi-
double, yellow flowers, 3in (8cm)
across, in summer-autumn.
H and S 18in (45cm).

☼ ◊ ❀❀❀ 4–9

R. 'Freedom', syn. *R*. 'Dicjem'
Neat, large-flowered bush rose, with
many shoots and abundant, glossy
foliage. Bears many lightly scented,
rounded, double, bright yellow
flowers, 3¹/₂in (9cm) across, in
summer-autumn. H 2¹/₂ft (75cm),
S 2ft (60cm).

☼ ◊ ❀❀❀ 4–9

R. 'Glenfiddich'
Upright, cluster-flowered bush rose.
Slightly fragrant, urn-shaped, double,
amber yellow flowers, 4in (10cm)
across, are borne singly or in clusters in
summer-autumn. H 2¹/₂ft (75cm),
S 2ft (60cm).

☼ ◊ ❀❀❀ 4–9

R. 'Amber Queen',
syn. *R*. 'Harroony'
Spreading, cluster-flowered bush rose.
Amber flowers are fragrant, rounded
and fully double, 3in (8cm) across, and
are borne in summer-autumn. Has
abundant, reddish foliage. H and
S 20in (50cm).

☼ ◊ ❀❀❀ 4–9

Roses/modern

R. 'Pot o' Gold',
syn. *R*. 'Dicdivine'
Large-flowered bush rose of neat, even
growth. Fragrant, rounded, fully double,
golden yellow flowers, 3¹/₂in (9cm)
across, are carried singly or in wide
sprays in summer-autumn. H 2¹/₂ft
(75cm), S 2ft (60cm).

☼ ◊ ✿✿✿ 4–9

R. 'Sweet Magic',
syn. *R*. 'Dicmagic'
Bushy, dwarf cluster-flowered bush
rose. Bears sprays of lightly fragrant,
urn-shaped, double, pink-flushed,
golden orange flowers, 1¹/₂in (4cm)
across, in summer-autumn. H 15in
(38cm), S 12in (30cm).

☼ ◊ ✿✿✿ 4–9

R. 'Troika', syn. *R*. 'Royal Dane'
Vigorous, dense, large-flowered bush
rose with plentiful, semi-glossy leaves.
Fragrant, pointed, double flowers, 6in
(15cm) across, are orange-red, tinged
with pink, and are borne in summer-
autumn. H 3ft (1m), S 2¹/₂ft (75cm).

☼ ◊ ✿✿✿ 4–9

R. 'Piccadilly'
Vigorous, bushy, large-flowered bush
rose with pointed, double, red and
yellow flowers, 5in (12cm) across,
produced freely singly or in clusters
in summer-autumn. Abundant foliage
is reddish and glossy. H 3ft (1m),
S 2ft (60cm).

☼ ◊ ✿✿✿ 4–9

R. 'Southampton',
syn. *R*. 'Susan Ann'
Upright, cluster-flowered bush rose.
Bears fragrant, pointed, double, apricot
flowers, 3in (8cm) across, singly or in
clusters in summer-autumn. Foliage is
glossy and disease-resistant. H 3ft
(1m), S 2ft (60cm).

☼ ◊ ✿✿✿ 4–9

R. 'Doris Tysterman'
Vigorous, upright, large-flowered bush
rose with lightly scented, pointed, fully
double, orange-red flowers, 4in (10cm)
across, borne in summer-autumn.
Leaves are large, glossy, and dark
green. H 4ft (1.2m), S 2¹/₂ft (75cm).

☼ ◊ ✿✿✿ 4–9

R. 'Anne Harkness',
syn. *R*. 'Harkaramel'
Upright, cluster-flowered bush rose.
Urn-shaped, double, amber flowers,
3in (8cm) across, are borne in sprays
of many blooms in late summer and
autumn. H 4ft (1.2m), S 2ft (60cm).

☼ ◊ ✿✿✿ 4–9

R. 'Remember Me',
syn. *R*. 'Cocdestin'
Vigorous, dense, large-flowered
bush rose with pointed, fully double,
copper orange flowers, 3¹/₂in (9cm)
across, freely borne in summer-
autumn. Leaves are abundant and
glossy. H 3ft (1m), S 2¹/₂ft (75cm).

☼ ◊ ✿✿✿ 4–9

R. 'Just Joey'
Open, branching, large-flowered bush
rose with leathery, dark green foliage.
Bears rounded, fully double flowers,
5in (12cm) across, with waved,
copper pink petals and some scent,
in summer-autumn. H 2¹/₂ft (75cm),
S 2ft (60cm).

☼ ◊ ✿✿✿ 4–9

Roses/miniature

■ RED

R. 'Snowball', syn. *R.* 'Angelita',
R. 'Macangel'
Compact, creeping, miniature bush
rose with pompon, fully double, white
flowers, 1in (2.5cm) across, that are
borne in summer-autumn. Leaves are
small, glossy, and plentiful. H 8in
(20cm), S 12in (30cm).

☼ ◊ ✽✽✽ 4–9

R. 'Baby Masquerade',
syn. *R.* 'Baby Carnival'
Dense, miniature bush rose with
plentiful, leathery foliage and clusters
of rosette, double, yellow-pink
flowers, 1in (2.5cm) across, in summer-
autumn. H and S 16in (40cm), more if
not pruned.

☼ ◊ ✽✽✽ 4–9

R. 'Sheri Anne'
Upright, miniature bush rose with
glossy, leathery foliage. Slightly
scented, rosette, double, light red
flowers, 1in (2.5cm) across, are borne
in summer-autumn. H 18in (45cm),
S 12in (30cm).

☼ ◊ ✽✽✽ 4–9

R. 'Angela Rippon',
syn. *R.* 'Ocarina', *R.* 'Ocaru'
Miniature bush rose with slightly
fragrant, urn-shaped, fully double,
salmon pink flowers, 1½in (4cm)
across, in summer-autumn, and many
small, dark green leaves. H 18in
(45cm), S 12in (30cm).

☼ ◊ ✽✽✽ 4–9

R. 'Stacey Sue'
Spreading, miniature bush rose with
plentiful, dark green foliage and
rosette, fully double, pink flowers,
1in (2.5cm) across, that are borne
freely in summer-autumn. H and
S 15in (38cm).

☼ ◊ ✽✽✽ 4–9

R. 'Hula Girl'
Wide, bushy, miniature bush rose with
glossy, dark green foliage. Slightly
scented, urn-shaped, fully double,
salmon orange flowers, 1in (2.5cm)
across, are produced freely in summer-
autumn. H 18in (45cm), S 16in (40cm).

☼ ◊ ✽✽✽ 4–9

R. 'Fire Princess'
Upright, miniature bush rose with
small, glossy leaves. Bears sprays of
rosette, fully double, scarlet flowers,
1½in (4cm) across, in summer-autumn.
H 18in (45cm), S 12in (30cm).

☼ ◊ ✽✽✽ 4–9

R. 'Red Ace', syn. *R.* 'Amruda'
Compact, miniature bush rose with
rosette, double, dark red flowers, 1½in
(4cm) across, borne in summer-
autumn. H 14in (35cm), S 12in (30cm).

☼ ◊ ✽✽✽ 4–9

Roses/climbing

☐ WHITE

R. 'Orange Sunblaze',
syn. *R.* 'Meijikitar', *R.* 'Sunblaze'
Compact, miniature bush rose. Rosette,
fully double, bright orange-red
flowers, 1½in (4cm) across, are freely
produced in summer-autumn. Has
plentiful, dark green leaves. H and
S 12in (30cm).

☼ ◊ ❋❋❋ 4–9

R. 'Albéric Barbier'
Vigorous, semi-evergreen rambler
rose. Slightly fragrant, rosette, fully
double, creamy white flowers, 3in
(8cm) across, appear in clusters in
summer. Leaves are small and bright
green. Tolerates a north-facing wall.
H to 15ft (5m), S 10ft (3m).

☼ ◊ ❋❋❋ 4–9

R. 'Rise 'n Shine',
syn. *R.* 'Golden Sunblaze'
Bushy, upright, miniature bush rose
with dark green leaves that bears
rosette, fully double, yellow flowers,
1in (2.5cm) across, in summer-autumn.
H 16in (40cm), S 10in (25cm).

☼ ◊ ❋❋❋ 4–9

R. 'Paul's Lemon Pillar'
Stiff, upright climbing rose with large
leaves and scented, pointed to rounded,
fully double, lemon white flowers,
6in (15cm) across, that appear in
summer. Prefers a sunny, sheltered
wall. H 15ft (5m), S 10ft (3m).

☼ ◊ ❋❋❋ 4–9

R. 'Félicité Perpétue'
Sempervirens climbing rose with long,
slender stems. Clusters of rosette, fully
double, blush pink to white flowers,
1½in (4cm) across, appear in mid-
summer. Small leaves are semi-
evergreen. Prune spent wood only.
H 15ft (5m), S 12ft (4m).

☼ ◊ ❋❋❋ 4–9

R. 'Colibri',
syn. *R.* 'Meidanover'
Upright, rather open, miniature bush
rose. Urn-shaped, double, red-veined,
orange flowers, 1½in (4cm) across, are
borne in summer-autumn. H 15in
(38cm), S 10in (25cm).

☼ ◊ ❋❋❋ 4–9

R. filipes 'Kiftsgate'
Rampant climbing rose with abundant,
glossy, light green foliage. Cupped to
flat, single, creamy white flowers,
1in (2.5cm) across, appear in late
summer in spectacular clusters. Use to
grow up a tree or in a wild garden.
H and S 30ft (10m) or more.

☼ ◊ ❋❋❋ 5–9

R. 'Mme. Alfred Carrière'
Noisette climbing rose with slender,
smooth stems. Very fragrant, rounded,
double flowers are creamy white,
tinged pink, 1½in (4cm) across, and are
borne in summer-autumn. H to 18ft
(5.5m), S 10ft (3m).

☼ ◊ ❋❋❋ 5–9

R. 'Gloire de Dijon'
Stiffly branched Noisette or climbing
Tea rose. Fragrant, quartered-rosette,
fully double, creamy buff flowers,
4in (10cm) across, are borne in
summer-autumn. H 12ft (4m),
S 8ft (2.5m).

☼ ◊ ❋❋❋ 5–9

R. 'New Dawn', syn.
R. 'Everblooming Dr. W. van Fleet'
Vigorous, very hardy climbing rose.
Fragrant, cupped, double, pale pearl
pink flowers, 3in (8cm) across, are
borne in clusters in summer-autumn.
Tolerates a north-facing wall. H and
S 15ft (5m).

☼ ◊ ❀❀❀ 4–9

R. 'Breath of Life',
syn. *R.* 'Harquanne'
Stiff, upright climbing rose with large,
lightly scented, rounded, fully double,
pinkish apricot flowers, 4in (10cm)
across, borne in summer-autumn.
Leaves are semi-glossy. H 9ft (2.8m),
S 7ft (2.2m).

☼ ◊ ❀❀❀ 4–9

R. 'Albertine'
Vigorous rambler rose with arching,
thorny, reddish stems. Scented, cup-
shaped, fully double, salmon pink
flowers, 3in (8cm) across, are borne in
abundant clusters in summer. Is prone
to mildew in a dry site. H to 15ft (5m),
S 10ft (3m).

☼ ◊ ❀❀❀ 4–9

R. 'Handel'
Stiff, upright climbing rose. Slightly
scented, urn-shaped, double flowers,
3in (8cm) across, are cream, edged
with pinkish red, and produced in
clusters in summer-autumn. Has
glossy, dark green foliage. H 10ft
(3m), S 7ft (2.2m).

☼ ◊ ❀❀❀ 4–9

R. 'Mme. Grégoire Staechelin',
syn. *R.* 'Spanish Beauty'
Vigorous, arching climbing rose with
large clusters of blooms in summer.
Bears rounded to cupped, fully double
flowers, 5in (13cm) across, with ruffled,
clear pink petals, shaded carmine. H to
20ft (6m), S to 12ft (4m).

☼ ◊ ❀❀❀ 4–9

R. 'Chaplin's Pink Companion'
Vigorous climbing rose with glossy,
dark green foliage and slightly scented,
rounded, double, light pink flowers,
2in (5cm) across, borne freely in large
clusters in summer. H and S 10ft (3m).

☼ ◊ ❀❀❀ 4–9

R. 'Pink Perpétue'
Stiffly branched climbing rose that
may be pruned to grow as a shrub.
Bears clusters of cupped to rosette,
double, deep pink flowers, 3in (8cm)
across, in summer-autumn. Leathery
foliage is plentiful. H 9ft (2.8m),
S 8ft (2.5m).

☼ ◊ ❀❀❀ 4–9

R. 'Zéphirine Drouhin'
Lax, arching Bourbon rose that will
climb if supported. Bears fragrant,
cupped, double, deep pink flowers,
3in (8cm) across, in summer-autumn.
Is prone to mildew. May be grown as
a hedge. H to 8ft (2.5m), S to 6ft (2m).

☼ ◊ ❀❀❀ 4–9

R. 'Rosy Mantle'
Stiff, open-branched climbing rose.
Very fragrant, pointed, fully double,
rose-pink flowers, 4in (10cm) across,
are borne in summer-autumn. Dark
green foliage is rather sparse. H 8ft
(2.5m), S 6ft (2m).

☼ ◊ ❀❀❀ 4–9

Roses/climbing

R. 'Dortmund'
Upright climbing rose that may be pruned to make a shrub. Flat, single, red flowers, 4in (10cm) across, with white eyes and a slight scent, are borne freely in clusters in summer-autumn. Has healthy, dark green foliage. H 10ft (3m), S 6ft (1.8m).

☼ ◊ ✽✽✽ 4–9

R. 'Guinée'
Vigorous, stiffly branched climbing rose. Fragrant, cupped, fully double, blackish red to maroon flowers, 4¹/₂in (11cm) across, are borne in summer. Leaves are large and leathery. H 15ft (5m), S 7ft (2.2m).

☼ ◊ ✽✽✽ 4–9

R. 'Golden Showers'
Stiff, upright climbing rose that may be pruned to grow as a shrub. In summer-autumn produces many fragrant, pointed, double, yellow flowers, 4in (10cm) across, that open flat. H 6ft (2m), S 7ft (2.2m) or more.

☼ ◊ ✽✽✽ 4–9

R. banksiae 'Lutea'
(Yellow Lady Bank's rose)
Vigorous climbing rose bearing clusters of many scentless, rosette, fully double, yellow flowers, ³/₄in (2cm) across, in late spring. Needs a sunny, sheltered wall and pruning of spent wood only. H and S to 30ft (10m).

☼ ◊ ✽✽✽ 7–9

R. 'Danse du Feu',
syn. **R.** 'Spectacular'
Vigorous, stiffly branched climbing rose with abundant, glossy foliage. Bears rounded, double, scarlet flowers, 3in (8cm) across, in summer-autumn. H and S 8ft (2.5m).

☼ ◊ ✽✽✽ 4–9

R. 'Veilchenblau',
syn. **R.** 'Blue Rambler'
Vigorous rambler rose. Rosette, double, violet flowers, streaked white, 1in (2.5cm) across, have a fruity scent and appear in clusters in summer. H 12ft (4m), S 7ft (2.2m).

☼ ◊ ✽✽✽ 4–9

R. 'Dublin Bay'
Dense, shrubby climbing rose that may be pruned to grow as a shrub. Bears clusters of cupped, double, bright crimson flowers, 4in (10cm) across, in summer-autumn. Foliage is glossy, dark green, and plentiful. H and S 7ft (2.2m).

☼ ◊ ✽✽✽ 4–9

R. 'Mermaid'
Slow-growing climbing rose that produces flat, single, primrose yellow flowers, 5in (12cm) across, in summer-autumn. Has stiff, reddish stems, large, hooked thorns, and glossy, dark green leaves. Prefers a sunny, sheltered wall. H and S to 20ft (6m).

☼ ◊ ✽✽ 4–9

R. 'Maigold'
Vigorous climbing rose with prickly, arching stems that may be pruned to grow as a shrub. Fragrant, cupped, semi-double, bronze-yellow flowers, 4in (10cm) across, are borne freely in early summer and sparsely in autumn. H and S 8ft (2.5m).

☼ ◊ ✽✽✽ 4–9

☐ WHITE   ◼☐ PINK–RED

Beaumontia grandiflora
(Easter-lily vine, Herald's trumpet)
Vigorous, evergreen, woody-stemmed,
twining climber with rich green leaves
that are hairy beneath. Has large,
fragrant white flowers from late spring
to summer. H 25ft (8m). Min. 45–50°F
(7–10°C).

☼ ◊ 10

Mandevilla splendens,
Evergreen, woody-stemmed, twining
climber. Has lustrous leaves and
trumpet-shaped, rose-pink flowers,
with yellow centers, appearing in late
spring or early summer. H 10ft (3m).
Min. 45–50°F (7–10°C).

☼ ◊ 10

Clianthus puniceus (Parrot beak)
Evergreen or semi-evergreen, woody-
stemmed, scrambling climber with
leaves composed of many leaflets.
In spring and early summer bears
drooping clusters of unusual, clawlike,
brilliant red flowers. H 12ft (4m).

☼ ◊ ❄ 10

Kennedia rubicunda
Fast-growing, evergreen, woody-
stemmed, twining climber with leaves
divided into 3 leaflets. Coral red
flowers are borne in small trusses in
spring-summer. H to 10ft (3m). Min.
41–5°F (5–7°C).

☼ ◊ 10

Stephanotis floribunda
(Madagascar jasmine)
Moderately vigorous, evergreen,
woody-stemmed, twining climber with
leathery, glossy leaves. Scented, waxy,
white flowers appear in small clusters
from spring to autumn. H 15ft (5m) or
more. Min. 55–61°F (13–16°C).

☼ ◊ 10

Passiflora coccinea
(Red passion flower)
Vigorous, evergreen, woody-stemmed,
tendril climber with rounded, oblong
leaves. Has bright deep scarlet flowers,
with red, pink, and white crowns, from
spring to autumn. H 10–12ft (3–4m).
Min. 59°F (15°C).

☼ ◊ 10

Clianthus puniceus f. ***albus***
(White parrot beak)
Evergreen or semi-evergreen, woody-
stemmed, scrambling climber. Has
drooping clusters of clawlike, creamy
white flowers in spring and early
summer. Leaves consist of many small
leaflets. H 12ft (4m).

☼ ◊ ❄ 10

Distictis buccinatoria, syn.
Phaedranthus buccinatorius
(Blood-red trumpet vine)
Vigorous, evergreen, woody-stemmed,
tendril climber. Has trumpet-shaped,
rose-crimson flowers, orange-yellow
within, from early spring to summer. H
to 15ft (5m) or more. Min. 41°F (5°C).

☼ ◊ 10

Tropaeolum tricolorum
Herbaceous climber with delicate
stems, small tubers, and 5–7-lobed
leaves. Small, orange or yellow
flowers with black-tipped, reddish
orange calyces are borne from
early spring to early summer.
H to 3ft (1m). Min. 41°F (5°C).

☼ ◊ 10

Climbers SPRING INTEREST

Agapetes serpens
Evergreen, arching to pendulous, scandent shrub, best grown with support as a perennial climber. Has small, lance-shaped, lustrous leaves and pendent flowers, rose-red with darker veins, in spring. H 6–10ft (2–3m). Min. 41°F (5°C).

☀ ◊ pH 10

Hardenbergia comptoniana
Evergreen, woody-stemmed, twining climber with leaves of 3 or 5 lance-shaped leaflets. Has racemes of pealike, deep purple-blue flowers in spring. H to 8ft (2.5m).

☀ ◊ ❄ 10

Strongylodon macrobotrys
(Jade vine)
Fast-growing, evergreen, woody-stemmed, twining climber with claw-like, luminous, blue-green flowers in long, pendent spikes in winter-spring. Leaves have 3 oval, glossy leaflets. H to 70ft (20m). Min. 64°F (18°C).

☀ ◊ 10

Mitraria coccinea
Evergreen, woody-stemmed, scrambling climber with oval, toothed leaves. Small, tubular, orange-red flowers are borne singly in leaf axils during late spring to summer. H to 6ft (2m).

☀ ◊ pH ❄ 10

Akebia quinata (Five-leaf akebia)
Woody-stemmed, twining climber, semi-evergreen in mild winters or warm areas, with leaves of 5 leaflets. Vanilla-scented, brownish purple flowers appear in late spring, followed by sausage-shaped, purplish fruits. H 30ft (10m) or more.

☀ ◊ ❄❄❄ 4–9

Petrea volubilis (Queen's-wreath)
Strong-growing, evergreen, woody-stemmed, twining climber with elliptic, rough-textured leaves and deep violet and lilac-blue flowers carried in simple or branched spikes from late winter to late summer. H 20ft (6m) or more. Min. 55–9°F (13–15°C).

☀ ◊ 10

Humulus lupulus 'Aureus'
(Yellow-leaved hop)
Herbaceous, twining climber with rough, hairy stems and toothed, yellowish leaves divided into 3 or 5 lobes. Greenish, female flower spikes are borne in pendent clusters in autumn. H to 20ft (6m).

☀ ◊ ❄❄❄ 6–9

Manettia inflata, syn. *M. bicolor*
(Brazilian-firecracker, Twining firecracker)
Fast-growing, evergreen, semi-woody-stemmed, twining climber with glossy leaves. Has small, funnel-shaped, red flowers, with yellow tips, in spring-summer. H 6ft (2m). Min. 41°F (5°C).

☀ ◊ 10

Clytostoma callistegioides
Fast-growing, evergreen, woody-stemmed, tendril climber. Each leaf has 2 oval leaflets and a tendril. Small, nodding clusters of purple-veined lavender flowers, fading to pale pink, are bourne in spring-summer. H to 15ft (5m). Min. 50–55°F (10–13°C).

☀ ◊ 10

Sollya heterophylla
(Australian bluebell creeper)
Evergreen, woody-based, twining climber with narrowly lance-shaped to oval leaves, ³/₄–2¹/₂in (2–6cm) long. Nodding clusters of 4–9 broadly bell-shaped, sky blue flowers are carried from spring to autumn. H to 10ft (3m).

☀ ◊ ❄ 9–10

Solandra maxima
(Cup-of-gold vine)
Strong-growing, evergreen, woody-stemmed, scrambling climber with glossy leaves. In spring-summer bears fragrant, pale yellow, later golden flowers. H 23–30ft (7–10m) or more. Min. 55-61°F (13-16°C).

☀ ◊ 10

☐ YELLOW

☐ WHITE

Thunbergia mysorensis
Evergreen, woody-stemmed, twining climber. Has narrow leaves and pendent spikes of flowers with yellow tubes and recurved, reddish brown lobes from spring to autumn. H 20ft (6m). Min. 59°F (15°C).

☀ ◊ 10

Bougainvillea glabra **'Snow White'**
Vigorous, evergreen or semi-evergreen, woody-stemmed, scrambling climber with rounded-oval leaves. In summer has clusters of white floral bracts with green veins. H to 15ft (5m). Min. 45–50°F (7–10°C).

☀ ◊ 9–10

***Wisteria sinensis* 'Alba'**
(White Chinese wisteria)
Vigorous, deciduous, woody-stemmed, twining climber. Leaves are 10–12in (25–30cm) long with 11 leaflets. Has strongly scented, pealike, white flowers in racemes, 8–12in (20–30cm) long, in early summer. H to 100ft (30m).

☀ ◊ ❋❋❋ 5–9

Araujia sericofera, syn. *A. sericifera* (White bladder flower)
Evergreen, woody-stemmed, twining climber with leaves that are white-downy beneath. Has scented, white flowers, often striped pale maroon inside, from late summer to autumn. H to 23ft (7m).

☀ ◊ ❋ 10

Jasminum mesnyi, syn. *J. primulinum* (Primrose jasmine)
Evergreen or semi-evergreen, woody-stemmed, scrambling climber. Leaves are divided into 3 leaflets; semi-double, pale yellow flowers appear in spring. H to 10ft (3m).

☀ ◊ ❋ 8–10

***Solanum jasminoides* 'Album'**
(White potato vine)
Semi-evergreen, woody-stemmed, scrambling climber. Oval to lance-shaped leaves are sometimes lobed or divided into leaflets. Has star-shaped, white flowers, ³/₄–1in (2–2.5cm) across, in summer-autumn. H to 20ft (6m).

☀ ◊ ❋ 8–10

Trachelospermum jasminoides
(Confederate jasmine, Star jasmine)
Evergreen, woody-stemmed, twining climber with oval leaves up to 4in (10cm) long. Very fragrant white flowers are carried in summer, followed by pairs of pods, up to 6in (15cm) long, containing tufted seeds. H to 28ft (9m).

☀ ◊ ❋❋ 8–10

***Wisteria floribunda* 'Alba'**
(White Japanese wisteria)
Deciduous, woody-stemmed, twining climber with leaves of 11–19 oval leaflets. Scented, pealike, white flowers are carried in drooping racemes, up to 2ft (60cm) long, in early summer. H to 28ft (9m).

☀ ◊ ❋❋❋ 5–9

Climbers

WHITE

WHITE–PINK

Hydrangea anomala subsp. **petiolaris**, syn. *H. petiolaris* (Climbing hydrangea)
Deciduous, woody-stemmed, root climber. Has toothed leaves and lacy heads of small, white flowers in summer, only sparingly borne on young plants. H to 50ft (15m).

☼ ◊ ❀❀❀❀ 4–9

Clerodendrum thomsoniae (Bleeding heart, Glory bower)
Vigorous, evergreen, woody-stemmed, scandent shrub with oval, rich green leaves. Flowers with crimson petals and bell-shaped, pure white calyces appear in clusters in summer. H 10ft (3m) or more. Min. 61°F (16°C).

☼ ◊ 10

Hoya bella (Miniature wax plant)
Evergreen, woody-stemmed, trailing shrub with long, pendulous stems and narrowly oval, pointed, bright green leaves. In summer bears tiny, star-shaped, white flowers, with red centers, in pendulous, flattened clusters. H 18in (45cm). Min. 50–54°F (10–12°C).

☼ ◊ 10

Hoya australis
Moderately vigorous, evergreen, woody-stemmed, twining, root climber with fleshy, rich green leaves. Has trusses of 20–50 fragrant, star-shaped flowers, white with red-purple markings, in summer. H to 15ft (5m). Min. 59°F (15°C).

☼ ◊ 10

Pandorea jasminoides, syn. *Bignonia jasminoides* (Bower vine)
Evergreen, woody-stemmed, twining climber with leaves of 5–9 leaflets. Has clusters of funnel-shaped, white flowers, with pink-flushed throats, from late winter to summer. H 15ft (5m). Min. 41°F (5°C).

☼ ◊ 10

Hoya carnosa (Wax plant)
Fairly vigorous, evergreen, woody-stemmed, twining, root climber. Scented, star-shaped flowers, white, fading to pink, with deep pink centers, are borne in dense trusses in summer-autumn. H to 15ft (5m) or more. Min. 41–5°F (5–7°C).

☼ ◊ 10

Pileostegia viburnoides, syn. *Schizophragma viburnoides*
Slow-growing, evergreen, woody-stemmed, root climber. Tiny, white or cream flowers, with many prominent stamens, are borne in heads from late summer to autumn. H to 20ft (6m).

☼ ◊ ❀❀ 7–10

Schizophragma integrifolium
Deciduous, woody-stemmed, root climber with oval or heart-shaped leaves. In summer, white flowers are borne in flat heads up to 12in (30cm) across, marginal sterile flowers each having a large, white bract. H to 40ft (12m).

☼ ◊ ❀❀ 5–9

Jasminum officinale (Common white jasmine, Poet's jessamine)
Semi-evergreen or deciduous, woody-stemmed, twining climber with leaves comprising 7 or 9 leaflets. Clusters of fragrant, 4- or 5-lobed, white flowers are borne in summer-autumn. H to 40ft (12m).

☼ ◊ ❀❀ 9–10

Lathyrus odoratus 'Selana'
Vigorous, annual, tendril climber with oval, green leaves and large, fragrant pink-flushed, white flowers from summer to early autumn. H 6ft (2m).

☼ ◊ ❀❀❀ HH

Actinidia kolomikta
(Kolomikta actinidia)
Deciduous, woody-stemmed, twining
climber with 3–6in (8–16cm) long
leaves, the upper sections often creamy
white and pink. Has small, cup-shaped,
white flowers in summer, male and
female on separate plants. H 12ft (4m).

☼ ◊ ❄❄❄ 4–9

**Mandevilla x amabilis 'Alice du
Pont'**
Vigorous, evergreen, woody-stemmed,
twining climber with oval, impressed
leaves. Has large clusters of trumpet-
shaped, glowing pink flowers in summer.
H 10ft (3m). Min. 45–50°F (7–10°C).

☼ ◊ 10

Lathyrus grandiflorus (Everlasting
pea, Two-flowered pea)
Herbaceous, tendril climber with
unwinged stems and neat racemes of
pink-purple and red flowers in summer.
H to 5ft (1.5m).

☼ ◊ ❄❄❄ 6–9

Lonicera x heckrottii,
syn. *L.* 'Gold Flame'
Deciduous, woody-stemmed, twining
climber that needs support. Leaves are
oblong or oval, bluish beneath, upper
ones joined into shallow cups. Scented,
orange-throated, pink flowers appear in
clusters in summer. H to 15ft (5m).

☼ ◊ ❄❄ 4–9

Lathyrus odoratus 'Xenia Field'
Moderately fast-growing, annual,
slender, tendril climber with oval,
green leaves. Large, fragrant pink-and-
cream flowers appear from summer to
early autumn. H 6ft (2m).

☼ ◊ ❄❄❄ HH

Antigonon leptopus (Coral vine)
Fast-growing, evergreen, woody-
stemmed, tendril climber with crinkly,
pale green leaves. Has dense trusses of
bright pink, sometimes red or white,
flowers mainly in summer but all year
in tropical conditions. H 20ft (6m).
Min. 59°F (15°C).

☼ ◊ 8–10

Asarina erubescens
Evergreen, soft-stemmed, scandent,
perennial climber, sometimes woody-
stemmed, often grown as an annual.
Stems and leaves are downy. Rose-pink
flowers, 2¾in (7cm) long, are borne
in summer-autumn. H to 10ft (3m)
or more. Min. 41°F (5°C).

☼ ◊ 10

Ipomoea horsfalliae
Strong-growing, evergreen, woody-
stemmed, twining climber. Leaves have
5–7 radiating lobes or leaflets; stalked
clusters of deep rose-pink or rose-purple
flowers, 2½in (6cm) long, appear from
summer to winter. H 6–10ft (2–3m).
Min. 45–50°F (7–10°C).

☼ ◊ 10

Climbers SUMMER INTEREST

PINK–RED

Lonicera sempervirens (Coral honeysuckle, Trumpet honeysuckle)
Evergreen or deciduous, woody-stemmed, twining climber with oval leaves, bluish beneath, upper ones united and saucerlike. Has salmon red to orange flowers, yellow inside, in whorls on shoot tips in summer. H to 12ft (4m).

4–9

Lapageria rosea
(Chilean bellflower, Chile-bells)
Evergreen, woody-stemmed, twining climber with oblong to oval, leathery leaves. Has pendent, fleshy, pink to red flowers, 2¾–3½in (7–9cm) long, with paler flecks, from summer to late autumn. H to 15ft (5m).

10

***Lathyrus odoratus* 'Red Ensign'**
Vigorous, annual, tendril climber with oval, green leaves and large, sweetly scented, rich scarlet flowers from summer to early autumn. H 6ft (2m).

HH

***Lonicera* x *brownii* 'Dropmore Scarlet'**
Deciduous, woody-stemmed, twining climber with oval, blue-green leaves. Small, fragrant red flowers with orange throats are borne throughout summer. H to 12ft (4m).

4–9

***Bougainvillea* 'Miss Manila'**
Vigorous, mainly evergreen, woody-stemmed, scrambling climber with rounded-oval leaves. Bears clusters of pink floral bracts in summer. H to 15ft (5m). Min. 45–50°F (7–10°C).

10

Mina lobata, syn. *Ipomoea versicolor*, *Quamoclit lobata*
Deciduous or semi-evergreen, twining climber with 3-lobed leaves, usually grown as an annual. One-sided racemes of small, tubular, dark red flowers fade to orange, then creamy yellow, in summer. H to 15ft (5m).

T

***Bougainvillea* 'Dania'**
Vigorous, mainly evergreen, woody-stemmed, scrambling climber. Has rounded-oval leaves and bears clusters of deep pink floral bracts in summer. H to 15ft (5m). Min. 45–50°F (7–10°C).

10

Ipomoea quamoclit,
syn. *Quamoclit pinnata*
(Cardinal climber, Cypress vine)
Twining, annual climber with oval, bright green leaves cut into many threadlike segments. Slender, tubular, orange or scarlet flowers are carried in summer-autumn. H 6–12ft (2–4m).

T

Tropaeolum speciosum
(Vermilion nasturtium)
Herbaceous, twining climber with a creeping rhizome and lobed, blue-green leaves. Bears scarlet flowers in summer, followed by bright blue fruits surrounded by deep red calyces. Roots should be in shade. H to 10ft (3m).

7–9

Quisqualis indica
(Rangoon creeper)
Fairly fast-growing, deciduous or semi-evergreen, scandent shrub, often grown as an annual. From late spring to late summer has fragrant flowers, varying from orange to red, sometimes pink.
H 10–15ft (3–5m). Min. 50°F (10°C).

☼ ◊ 10

Rhodochiton atrosanguineum,
syn. *R. volubile*
Evergreen, leaf-stalk climber, usually grown as an annual, with toothed leaves. Has tubular, blackish purple flowers, with bell-shaped, red-purple calyces, from late spring to late autumn.
H to 10ft (3m). Min. 41°F (5°C).

☼ ◊ 10

Aristolochia elegans
(Calico flower)
Fast-growing, evergreen, woody-stemmed, twining climber with heart-to kidney-shaped leaves. Heart-shaped, 5in (12cm) wide flowers, maroon with white marbling, are carried in summer.
H to 23ft (7m). Min. 55°F (13°C).

☼ ◊ 10

Lathyrus latifolius (Everlasting pea, Perennial sweet pea)
Herbaceous, tendril climber with winged stems. Leaves have broad stipules and a pair of leaflets. Has small racemes of pink-purple flowers in summer and early autumn. H 6ft (2m) or more.

☼ ◊ ❀❀❀ 5–9

Schisandra rubriflora
Deciduous, woody-stemmed, twining climber with leathery, toothed leaves, paler beneath. Has small, crimson flowers in spring or early summer and drooping, red fruits in late summer.
H to 20ft (6m).

☼ ◊ ❀❀❀ 8–10

Berberidopsis corallina
(Chile vine, Coral vine)
Evergreen, woody-stemmed, twining climber with oval to heart-shaped, leathery leaves edged with small spines. Pendent clusters of globular, deep red flowers are produced in summer to early autumn. H 14ft (4.5m).

☼ ◊ ❀❀ 8–9

Lablab purpureus, syn. *Dolichos lablab*, *D. lignosus* (Hyacinth bean)
Deciduous, woody-stemmed, twining climber, often grown as an annual. Purple, pinkish, or white flowers in summer are followed by long pods with edible seeds.
H 30ft (10m). Min. 41°F (5°C).

☼ ◊ 10/T

Bougainvillea glabra 'Variegata'
Vigorous, mainly evergreen, woody-stemmed, scrambling climber. Rounded-oval, dark green leaves are edged with creamy white. Has an abundance of bright purple floral bracts in summer. H to 15ft (5m). Min. 45–50°F (7–10°C).

☼ ◊ 10

Clematis

Among the climbers, clematis are unsurpassed in their long period of flowering (with species flowering in almost every month of the year), variety of flower shapes and colors, and tolerance of almost any aspect and climate. Some spring-flowering species and cultivars are vigorous and excellent for rapidly covering buildings, old trees, and pergolas. Other, less rampant cultivars display often large, exquisite blooms from early summer to autumn in almost every color. Clematis look attractive when trained on walls or trellises and when grown in association with other climbers, trees, or shrubs, treating them as hosts. Less vigorous cultivars may also be left unsupported to scramble at ground level, where their flowers will be clearly visible.

The various types of clematis (see the Plant Dictionary) may be divided into 3 groups, each of which has different pruning requirements. Incorrect pruning may result in cutting out the stems that will produce flowers in the current season, so the following guidelines should be followed closely.

Group 1
Early-flowering species, Alpina, Macropetala, and Montana types
Flower stems are produced direct from the previous season's ripened stems. Prune after flowering to allow new growth to be produced and ripened for the next season. Remove dead or damaged stems and cut back other shoots that have outgrown their allotted space.

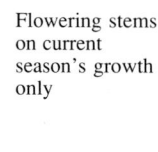

Flower stem direct from the previous season's ripened stems

Group 2
Early, large-flowered cultivars
Flowers are produced on short, current season's stems, so prune before new growth starts, in early spring. Remove dead or damaged stems and cut back all others to where strong, leaf-axil buds are visible. (These buds will produce the first crop of flowers.)

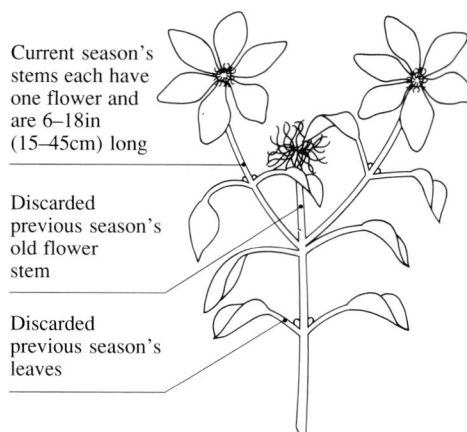

Current season's stems each have one flower and are 6–18in (15–45cm) long

Discarded previous season's old flower stem

Discarded previous season's leaves

Group 3
Late, large-flowered cultivars, Late-flowering species, Small-flowered cultivars, and Herbaceous types
Flowers are produced on the current season's growth only, so prune before new growth commences, in early spring. Remove all of the previous season's stems down to a pair of strong, leaf-axil buds, 6–12in (15–30cm) above the soil.

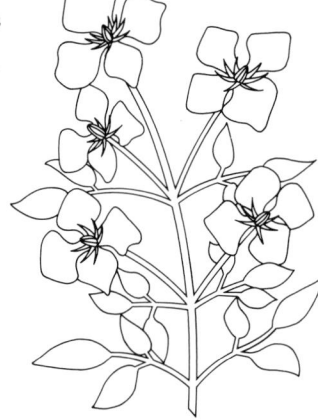

Flowering stems on current season's growth only

C. florida 'Sieboldii' (3, small-fl.)

C. recta (3, herbaceous)

C. montana var. *rubens* (1, Montana)

C. 'Huldine' (3, late large-fl.)

C. montana 'Tetrarose' (1, Montana)

C. macropetala 'Markham's Pink' (1, Macrop.)

C. 'Hagley Hybrid' (3, late large-fl.)

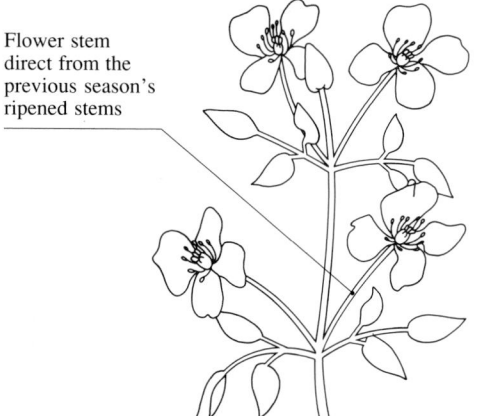

C. montana (1, Montana)

C. 'Henryi' (2, early large-fl.)

C. 'Mrs. George Jackman' (2, early large-fl.)

C. armandii (1, early-fl.)

C. flammula (3, late-fl.)

C. 'Nelly Moser' (2, early large-fl.)

C. 'Lincoln Star'
(2, early large-fl.)

C. 'Ascotiensis'
(3, late large-fl.)

C. 'Perle d'Azur'
(3, late large-fl.)

C. 'Duchess of Albany'
(3, small-fl.)

C. viticella 'Mme. Julia Correvon' (3, late-fl.)

C. 'Star of India'
(3, late large-fl.)

C. 'Jackmanii'
(3, late large-fl.)

C. macropetala
(1, Macropetala)

C. viticella 'Purpurea Plena Elegans' (3, late-fl.)

C. 'Gravetye Beauty'
(3, small-fl.)

C. 'The President'
(2, early large-fl.)

C. 'Beauty of Worcester'
(2, early large-fl.)

C. integrifolia
(3, herbaceous)

C. 'Proteus'
(2, early large-fl.)

C. 'Richard Pennell'
(2, early large-fl.)

C. viticella 'Etoile Violette' (3, late-fl.)

C. heracleifolia 'Wyevale' (3, herbaceous)

C. rehderiana
(3, late-fl.)

C. 'Elsa Spath'
(2, early large-fl.)

C. 'Lasurstern'
(2, early large-fl.)

C. 'William Kennett'
(2, early large-fl.)

C. cirrhosa (1, early-fl.)

C. viticella 'Abundance'
(3, late-fl.)

C. 'Ernest Markham'
(3, late large-fl.)

C. 'Vyvyan Pennell'
(2, early large-fl.)

C. tangutica (3, late-fl.)

C. 'Ville de Lyon'
(3, late large-fl.)

C. 'Countess of Lovelace' (2, early large-fl.)

C. 'H.F. Young'
(2, early large-fl.)

C. alpina 'Frances Rivis' (1, Alpina)

C. orientalis 'Bill MacKenzie' (3, late-fl.)

Bougainvillea glabra
(Paper flower)
Vigorous, evergreen or semi-evergreen, woody-stemmed, scrambling climber with rounded-oval leaves. Clusters of floral bracts, in shades of cyclamen purple, appear in summer. H to 15ft (5m). Min. 45–50°F (7–10°C).

☼ ◊ 10

***Lathyrus odoratus* 'Lady Diana'**
Moderately fast-growing, annual, slender, tendril climber with oval, green leaves. Fragrant, pale violet-blue flowers are borne from summer to early autumn. H 6ft (2m).

☼ ◊ ❋❋❋ T

***Solanum crispum* 'Glasnevin'**
Vigorous, evergreen or semi-evergreen, woody-stemmed, scrambling climber with oval leaves. Has clusters of lilac to purple flowers, 1in (2.5cm) across, in summer. H to 20ft (6m).

☼ ◊ ❋❋ 8–9

***Passiflora* x *caponii* 'John Innes'**
Strong-growing, evergreen, woody-stemmed, tendril climber with 3-lobed leaves. Has bowl-shaped, nodding, white flowers, flushed claret purple, with purple-banded, white crowns, in summer-autumn. H 25ft (8m). Min. 45–50°F (7–10°C).

☼ ◊ 10

Ipomoea hederacea
(Ivy-leaved morning-glory)
Annual, twining climber with heart-shaped or 3-lobed, mid- to bright green leaves. Has funnel-shaped, red, purple, pink, or blue flowers in summer to early autumn. H 10–12ft (3–4m).

☼ ◊ ❋ T

***Codonopsis convolvulacea*,**
syn. *C. vinciflora*
Herbaceous, twining climber with 2in (5cm) long, oval or lance-shaped leaves. Widely bell- to saucer-shaped, bluish violet flowers, 1–2in (2.5–5cm) across, are borne in summer. H to 6ft (2m).

☼ ◊ ❋❋❋ 7–9

Cobaea scandens (Cup-and-saucer vine, Mexican ivy, Monastery bells)
Evergreen or deciduous, woody-stemmed, tendril climber, grown as an annual. From late summer to first frosts has flowers that open yellow-green and age to purple. H 12–15ft (4–5m). Min. 39°F (4°C).

☼ ◊ 9–10

Solanum wendlandii (Costa Rican nightshade, Giant potato creeper)
Robust, mainly evergreen, prickly-stemmed, scrambling climber with oblong, variably lobed leaves. Lavender flowers appear in late summer and autumn. H 10–20ft (3–6m). Min. 50°F (10°C).

☼ ◊ 10

Passiflora caerulea
(Blue crown passion flower)
Fast-growing, evergreen or semi-evergreen, woody-stemmed, tendril climber. Has white flowers, sometimes pink-flushed, with blue- or purple-banded crowns, in summer-autumn. H 30ft (10m).

☼ ◊ ❋ 8–10

Passiflora quadrangularis
(Granadilla)
Strong-growing, evergreen, woody-
stemmed climber with angled, winged
stems. White, pink, red, or pale violet
flowers, the crowns banded white and
deep purple, appear mainly in summer.
H 15–25ft (5–8m). Min. 50°F (10°C).

☼ ◊ 10

***Convolvulus tricolor* 'Heavenly
Blue'**, syn. *Ipomoea
rubrocaerulea* 'Heavenly Blue'
Fast-growing, annual, twining climber
with heart-shaped leaves and large,
funnel-shaped, sky blue flowers borne
from summer to early autumn. H to
10ft (3m).

☼ ◊ ❊ T

Lonicera* × *americana
Very free-flowering, deciduous, woody-
stemmed, twining climber. Leaves are
oval, upper ones united and saucerlike.
Clusters of strongly fragrant yellow
flowers, flushed with red-purple, appear
in summer. H to 23ft (7m).

◑ ◊ ❊❊❊ 6–9

***Lonicera japonica* 'Halliana'**
Evergreen or semi-evergreen, woody-
stemmed, twining climber with soft-
haired stems and oval, sometimes
lobed, bright green leaves. Very
fragrant white flowers, ageing to pale
yellow, are borne in summer and
autumn. H to 30ft (10m).

☼ ◊ ❊❊❊ 4–10

Wisteria* × *formosa
Deciduous, woody-stemmed, twining
climber with leaves of 9–15 narrowly
oval leaflets. Scented, pealike, mauve
and pale lilac flowers are carried in
early summer in drooping racemes,
10in (25cm) long, followed by velvety
pods. H to 80ft (25m) or more.

☼ ◊ ❊❊❊ 6–9

***Plumbago auriculata*,**
syn. *P. capensis*
(Cape leadwort, Cape plumbago)
Fast-growing, evergreen, woody-
stemmed, scrambling climber. Trusses
of sky blue flowers are carried from
summer to early winter. H 10–20ft
(3–6m). Min. 45°F (7°C).

☼ ◊ 9–10

***Lonicera periclymenum* 'Graham
Thomas'**
Deciduous, woody-stemmed, twining
climber. Oval or oblong leaves are
bluish beneath; fragrant white flowers,
ageing to yellow, are borne in summer.
H to 23ft (7m).

☼ ◊ ❊❊❊ 5–9

***Wisteria sinensis*,** syn.
W. chinensis (Chinese wisteria)
Vigorous, deciduous, woody-stemmed,
twining climber. Has leaves of 11
leaflets and fragrant lilac or pale violet
flowers, in racemes 8–12in (20–30cm)
long, in early summer, followed by
velvety pods. H to 100ft (30m).

☼ ◊ ❊❊❊ 5–9

***Oxypetalum caeruleum*,**
syn. *Tweedia caerulea*
Herbaceous, twining climber with
white-haired stems. Small, fleshy, pale
blue flowers, maturing purple, appear
in summer and early autumn; has green
fruits to 6in (15cm) long. H to 3ft (1m).
Min. 41°F (5°C).

☼ ◊ 10

YELLOW–ORANGE

**Allemanda cathartica
'Hendersonii'**
Fast-growing, evergreen, woody-
stemmed, scrambling climber. Has
lance-shaped leaves in whorls and
trumpet-shaped, rich bright yellow
flowers in summer-autumn. H to 15ft
(5m). Min. 55–9°F (13–15°C).

☀ ◊ 10

Thunbergia alata (Black-eyed
Susan vine, Clock vine)
Moderately fast-growing, annual,
twining climber. Has toothed, oval to
heart-shaped leaves and rounded, rather
flat, small flowers, orange-yellow with
very dark brown centers, from early
summer to early autumn. H 10ft (3m).

☀ ◊ ✽ T

Thladiantha dubia
Fast-growing, herbaceous or
deciduous, tendril climber. Oval to
heart-shaped leaves, 4in (10cm) long,
are hairy beneath; bell-shaped, yellow
flowers are carried in summer.
H 10ft (3m).

☀ ◊ ✽✽ 8–10

Stigmaphyllon ciliatum
Fast-growing, evergreen, woody-
stemmed, twining climber with heart-
shaped, pale green leaves fringed with
hairs. Bright yellow flowers with
ruffled petals appear in spring-summer.
H 15ft (5m) or more. Min. 59–64°F
(15–18°C).

☀ ◊ 10

Macfadyena unguis-cati
(Cat's-claw)
Fast-growing, evergreen, woody-
stemmed, tendril climber. Leaves have
2 leaflets and a tendril. Has yellow
flowers, 10cm (4in) long, in late spring
or early summer. H 25–30ft (8–10m).
Min. 41°F (5°C).

☀ ◊ 9–10

**Tropaeolum tuberosum
'Ken Aslet'**
Herbaceous climber with yellowish,
red-streaked tubers and blue-green
leaves. From mid-summer to autumn
has flowers with red sepals and orange
petals. In cool areas, lift and store
tubers in winter. H to 8ft (2.5m).

☀ ◊ ✽ 8–10

■ ORANGE

□■■ WHITE–RED

Bomarea caldasii,
syn. *B. kalbreyeri* of gardens
Herbaceous, twining climber with
rounded clusters of 5–40 tubular to
funnel-shaped, orange-red flowers,
spotted crimson within, in summer.
H 10–12ft (3–4m).

☼ ◊ ❄ 10

Lonicera × tellmanniana
Deciduous, woody-stemmed, twining
climber with oval leaves; upper ones
are joined and resemble saucers.
Bright yellowish orange flowers are
carried in clusters at the ends of
shoots in late spring and summer.
H to 15ft (5m).

☼ ◊ ❄❄ 7–9

Eccremocarpus scaber
(Chilean glory flower)
Evergreen, sub-shrubby, tendril
climber, often grown as an annual. In
summer has racemes of small, orange-
red flowers, followed by inflated fruit
pods containing many winged seeds.
H 6–10ft (2–3m).

☼ ◊ ❄ 9–10

Thunbergia gregorii
(Orange clock vine)
Evergreen, woody-stemmed, twining
climber, usually grown as an annual.
Triangular-oval leaves have winged
stalks. Glowing orange flowers are
carried in summer. H to 10ft (3m).
Min. 50°F (10°C).

☼ ◊ 10

Polygonum baldschuanicum,
syn. *Bilderdykia baldschuanica*,
Fallopia baldschuanica
(Bokhara fleece flower)
Vigorous, deciduous, woody-stemmed,
twining climber with drooping panicles
of pink or white flowers in summer-
autumn. H 40ft (12m) or more.

☼ ◊ ❄❄❄ 5–9

Senecio confusus
(Mexican flame vine)
Evergreen, woody-stemmed, twining
climber bearing clusters of daisylike,
orange-yellow flower heads, ageing to
orange-red, mainly in summer. H to
10ft (3m) or more. Min. 45–50°F
(7–10°C).

☼ ◊ 10

Mutisia decurrens
Evergreen, tendril climber with
narrowly oblong leaves, 2¾–5in
(7–13cm) long. Flower heads, 4–5in
(10–13cm) across with red or orange
ray flowers, are produced in summer.
Proves difficult to establish, but is
worthwhile. H to 10ft (3m).

☼ ◊ ❄❄ 9–10

**Campsis × tagliabuana 'Mme.
Galen'** (Mme. Galen trumpet vine)
Deciduous, woody-stemmed, root
climber with leaves of 7 or more
narrowly oval, toothed leaflets.
Trumpet-shaped, orange-pink flowers
are borne in pendent clusters from late
summer to autumn. H to 30ft (10m).

☼ ◊ ❄❄ 4–10

Passiflora manicata
Fast-growing, evergreen, woody-
stemmed, tendril climber with slender,
angular stems and 3-lobed leaves. Red
flowers, with deep purple and white
crowns, appear in summer-autumn.
H 10–15ft (3–5m). Min. 45°F (7°C).

☼ ◊ 10

■■ RED–PURPLE

Parthenocissus tricuspidata,
syn. *Ampelopsis veitchii*
(Boston ivy, Japanese ivy)
Vigorous, deciduous, woody-stemmed,
tendril climber. Has spectacular,
crimson, autumn leaf color and dull
blue berries. Will cover large expanses
of wall. H to 70ft (20m).

☀ ◊ ❈ ❈ ❈ 5–9

Parthenocissus tricuspidata
'Lowii' (Low's Japanese creeper)
Vigorous, deciduous, woody-stemmed,
tendril climber with deeply cut and
crinkled, 3–7-lobed leaves that turn
crimson in autumn. Has insignificant
flowers, followed by dull blue berries.
H to 70ft (20m).

☀ ◊ ❈ ❈ ❈ 5–9

Vitis coignetiae
(Crimson glory vine)
Vigorous, deciduous, woody-stemmed,
tendril climber. Large leaves, brown-
haired beneath, are brightly colored in
autumn. Has tiny, pale green flowers in
summer, followed by purplish-bloomed,
black berries. H to 50ft (15m).

☀ ◊ ❈ ❈ ❈ 5–9

Parthenocissus thompsonii,
syn. *Vitis thompsonii*
Deciduous, woody-stemmed, tendril
climber. Has glossy, green leaves with
5 leaflets that turn red-purple in autumn,
and black berries. Provide some shade
for best autumn color. H to 30ft (10m).

☀ ◊ ❈ ❈ 7–9

Vitis vinifera 'Purpurea'
(Purpleleaf grape)
Deciduous, woody-stemmed, tendril
climber with toothed, 3- or 5-lobed,
purplish leaves, white-haired when
young. Has tiny, pale green flowers
in summer and tiny, green or purple
berries. H to 23ft (7m).

☀ ◊ ❈ ❈ ❈ 6–9

Parthenocissus tricuspidata
'Veitchii' (Veitch's Japanese
creeper)
Vigorous, deciduous, woody-stemmed,
tendril climber. Has spectacular, red-
purple, autumn leaf color and dull blue
berries. Greenish flowers are
insignificant. H to 70ft (20m).

☀ ◊ ❈ ❈ ❈ 5–9

■■ PURPLE–ORANGE

Billardiera longiflora
Evergreen, woody-stemmed, twining
climber with narrow leaves. Small,
bell-shaped, sometimes purple-tinged,
green-yellow flowers are produced
singly in leaf axils in summer, followed
by purple-blue fruits in autumn.
H to 6ft (2m).

☀ ◊ ❈ 8–10

Tropaeolum tuberosum
Herbaceous, tuberous-rooted, leaf-stalk
climber. Grayish green leaves have
3–5 lobes; has cup-shaped flowers with
orange-yellow petals, orange-red sepals,
and a long spur from mid-summer to
late autumn. H 6–10ft (2–3m).

☀ ◊ ❈ 8–10

Pyrostegia venusta (Flame vine)
Fast-growing, evergreen, woody-
stemmed, tendril climber with clusters
of dense, tubular, glowing golden
orange flowers borne from autumn to
spring. H 30ft (10m) or more. Min.
55–9°F (13–15°C).

☀ ◊ 10

☐☐☐ WHITE–ORANGE

☐☐ WHITE–GREEN

Asparagus scandens
(Basket asparagus)
Evergreen, scrambling climber with lax
stems and short, curved, leaflike shoots
in whorls of 3. Tiny, nodding, white
flowers appear in clusters of 2–3 in
summer, followed by red berries. H
3ft (1m) or more. Min. 50°F (10°C).

☼ ◊ 10

Epipremnum pictum 'Argyraeus',
syn. *Scindapsus pictus* 'Argyraeus'
Slow-growing, evergreen, woody-
stemmed, root climber. Heart-shaped
leaves are dark green with silver
markings. H 6–10ft (2–3m) or more.
Min. 59–64°F (15–18°C).

☼ ◐ 10

Jasminum polyanthum
Evergreen, woody-stemmed, twining
climber. Dark green leaves have 5 or
7 leaflets. Large clusters of 5-lobed,
fragrant white flowers, sometimes
reddish on the outside, are carried
from late summer to winter. H 10ft
(3m) or more.

☼ ◊ ❄ 9–10

Senecio macroglossus
'Variegatus'
Evergreen, woody-stemmed, twining
climber with triangular, fleshy leaves,
bordered in white to cream, and,
mainly in winter, daisylike, cream
flower heads. H 10ft (3m). Min. 45°F
(7°C), but best at 50°F (10°C).

☼ ◊ 10

Syngonium podophyllum
'Trileaf Wonder'
Evergreen, woody-stemmed, root
climber with tufted stems and arrow-
head-shaped leaves when young.
Mature leaves have 3 glossy leaflets
with pale green or silvery gray veins.
H 6ft (2m) or more. Min. 64°F (18°C).

☼ ◊ 10

Agapetes macrantha
Evergreen or semi-evergreen, loose,
scandent shrub that may be trained
against supports. Has lance-shaped
leaves and narrowly urn-shaped, white
or pinkish white flowers, patterned in
red, in winter. H 3–6ft (1–2m). Min.
59–64°F (15–18°C).

☼ ◊ pH 10

Canarina canariensis,
syn. *C. campanula*
Herbaceous, tuberous, scrambling
climber with triangular, serrated leaves.
Has waxy, orange flowers with red veins
from late autumn to spring. H 6–10ft
(2–3m). Min. 45°F (7°C).

☼ ◊ 10

**Epipremnum aureum 'Marble
Queen'**, syn. *Scindapsus aureus*
'Marble Queen'
Fairly fast-growing, evergreen, woody-
stemmed, root climber. Leaves are
streaked and marbled with white. Is
less robust than the species. H 10–30ft
(3–10m). Min. 59–64°F (15–18°C).

☼ ◐ 10

Dioscorea discolor
Evergreen, woody-stemmed, twining
climber. Heart-shaped, olive green
leaves are 5–6in (12–15cm) long,
marbled silver, paler green, and brown,
and are red beneath. H to 6ft (2m).
Min. 41°F (5°C).

☼ ◊ 10

Syngonium podophyllum, syn.
Nephthytis triphylla of gardens
Evergreen, woody-stemmed, root
climber with tufted stems and arrow-
head-shaped leaves when young.
Mature plants have leaves of 7–9
glossy leaflets up to 12in (30cm) long.
H 6ft (2m). Min. 61–4°F (16–18°C).

☀ ◊ 10

Tetrastigma voinierianum, syn.
Cissus voinieriana (Chestnut vine)
Strong-growing, evergreen, woody-
stemmed, tendril climber. Young
stems and leaves are rust-colored and
hairy; mature leaves turn lustrous,
deep green above. H 30ft (10m) or
more. Min. 59–64°F (15–18°C).

☀ ◊ 10

Philodendron melanochrysum
Robust, fairly slow-growing,
evergreen, woody-based, root climber.
Heart-shaped leaves, to 30in (75cm)
long, are lustrous, deep olive green
with a coppery sheen and have pale
veins. H 10ft (3m) or more. Min.
59–64°F (15–18°C).

☀ ◊ 10

Cissus antarctica (Kangaroo
treebine, Kangaroo vine)
Moderately vigorous, evergreen,
woody-stemmed, tendril climber.
Oval, pointed, coarsely serrated leaves
are lustrous, rich green. H to 15ft (5m).
Min. 45°F (7°C).

☀ ◊ 10

Philodendron scandens
Fairly fast-growing, evergreen, woody-
based, root climber. Rich green leaves
are 4–6in (10–15cm) long when
young, to 12in (30cm) long on mature
plants. H 12ft (4m) or more. Min.
59–64°F (15–18°C).

☀ ◊ 10

Gynura aurantiaca (Velvet plant)
Evergreen, woody-based, soft-
stemmed, semi-scrambling climber or
lax shrub with purple-haired stems and
leaves. Clusters of daisylike, orange-
yellow flower heads are borne in
winter. H 6–10ft (2–3m), less as a
shrub. Min. 61°F (16°C).

☀ ◊ 10

Monstera deliciosa (Ceriman,
Swiss-cheese plant)
Robust, evergreen, woody-stemmed,
root climber with large-lobed, holed
leaves, 16–36in (40–90cm) long.
Mature plants bear cream spathes,
followed by scented, edible fruits. H to
20ft (6m). Min. 59–64°F (15–18°C).

☀ ◊ 10

Cissus rhombifolia (Grape ivy,
Venezuela treebine)
Moderately vigorous, evergreen,
woody-stemmed, tendril climber with
lustrous leaves divided into 3 coarsely
toothed leaflets. H 10ft (3m) or more.
Min. 45°F (7°C).

☀ ◊ 9–10

Streptosolen jamesonii
(Marmalade bush)
Evergreen or semi-evergreen, loosely
scrambling shrub. Has oval, finely
corrugated leaves and, mainly in
spring-summer, many bright orange
flowers. H 6–10ft (2–3m).
Min. 45°F (7°C).

☀ ◊ 9–10

Ivies

Ivies (*Hedera*) are evergreen, climbing, and trailing plants suitable for growing up walls and fences or as ground cover. Plants take a year or so to establish but thereafter growth is rapid. There is a large number of cultivars available, of which the non-variegated forms are shade tolerant. With height and access to light, the typical, ivy-shaped leaves may become less lobed. Not all ivies are fully hardy.

H. helix 'Gracilis'

H. helix 'Digitata'

H. helix 'Adam'

H. helix 'Erecta'

H. helix 'Merion Beauty'

H. helix 'Nigra'

H. helix 'Heise'

H. helix 'Eva'

H. helix 'Ivalace'

H. helix 'Woerner'

H. helix 'Glacier'

H. helix 'Angularis Aurea'

H. colchica 'Dentata'

H. helix 'Telecurl'

H. helix 'Lobata Major'

H. helix 'Glymii'

H. helix 'Anna Marie'

H. helix 'Goldheart'

H. helix 'Pedata'

H. helix 'Deltoidea'

H. helix var. *hibernica* 'Sulphurea'

H. helix 'Manda's Crested'

H. helix 'Buttercup'

H. helix 'Green Ripple'

H. helix var. *hibernica*

H. canariensis 'Ravensholst'

H. helix 'Pittsburgh'

H. helix 'Parsley Crested'

H. helix 'Atropurpurea'

H. colchica 'Sulphur Heart'

GRASSES, BAMBOOS, RUSHES, AND SEDGES

***Cortaderia selloana*
'Silver Comet'**
Evergreen, clump-forming, perennial
grass with very narrow, sharp-edged,
recurved leaves, 3ft (1m) long, that
have silver margins. Carries plumelike
panicles of spikelets from late summer.
H 4–5ft (1.2–1.5m), S 3ft (1m).

☀ ◊ ❀❀❀ 7–10

Phalaris arundinacea* var. *picta
(Gardener's-garters, Ribbon grass)
Evergreen, spreading, perennial grass
with broad, white-striped leaves.
Produces narrow panicles of spikelets
in summer. Can be invasive. H 3ft
(1m), S indefinite.

◑ ◉ ❀❀❀ 4–9

***Holcus mollis* 'Variegatus'**
(Variegated velvet grass)
Evergreen, spreading, perennial grass
with white-striped leaves and hairy
nodes. In summer carries purplish
white flower spikes. H 12–18in
(30–45cm), S indefinite.

◑ ◊ ❀❀❀ 5–9

***Pleioblastus variegatus*, syn.
Arundinaria fortunei, *A. variegata***
(Dwarf white-stripe bamboo)
Evergreen, slow-spreading bamboo
with narrow, slightly downy, white-
striped leaves. Stems are branched near
the base. H 30in (80cm), S indefinite.

☀ ◊ ❀❀❀ 7–9

***Arundo donax* 'Versicolor', syn.
A.d. 'Variegata'** (Striped giant reed)
Herbaceous, rhizomatous, perennial
grass with strong stems bearing broad,
creamy white-striped leaves. May bear
dense, erect panicles of whitish yellow
spikelets in late summer. H 8–10ft
(2.5–3m), S 2ft (60cm).

☀ ◉ ❀ 7–10

***Sasa veitchii*, syn.
*S. albomarginata*** (Kuma bamboo)
Evergreen, slow-spreading bamboo.
Leaves, 10in (25cm) long, soon
develop white edges. Stems, often
purple, produce a single branch at each
node. White powder appears beneath
nodes. H to 5ft (1.5m), S indefinite.

☀ ◊ ❀❀❀ 6–10

Lagurus ovatus (Hare's-tail grass)
Tuft-forming, annual grass that in
early summer bears dense, egg-shaped,
soft panicles of white flower spikes,
with golden stamens, that last well into
autumn. Leaves are long, narrow, and
flat. Self seeds readily. H 18in (45cm),
S 6in (15cm).

☀ ◊ ❀❀❀ HH

***Cortaderia selloana* 'Sunningdale
Silver'**
Evergreen, clump-forming, perennial
grass with narrow, sharp-edged,
recurved leaves, 5ft (1.5m) long. Bears
long-lasting, feathery panicles of
creamy white spikelets in late summer.
H 7ft (2.1m), S 4ft (1.2m).

☀ ◊ ❀❀ 7–10

***Glyceria maxima* 'Variegata',**
syn. *G. aquatica* 'Variegata'
(Manna grass, Sweet grass)
Herbaceous, spreading, perennial grass
with cream-striped leaves, often tinged
pink at the base. Bears open panicles
of greenish spikelets in summer.
H 30in (80cm), S indefinite.

◑ ◉ ❀❀❀ 5–9

***Miscanthus sinensis* 'Zebrinus'**
(Zebra grass)
Herbaceous, clump-forming, perennial
grass. Leaves, hairy beneath, have
transverse, yellowish white ring
markings. May carry awned, hairy,
white spikelets in fan-shaped panicles
in autumn. H 4ft (1.2m), S 18in (45cm).

☀ ◊ ❀❀ 5–10

***Scirpus lacustris* subsp.
tabernaemontani 'Zebrinus',**
syn. *S. tabernaemontani* 'Zebrinus'
Evergreen, spreading, perennial sedge
with leafless stems, striped horizontally
with white, and brown spikelets in
summer. Withstands brackish water.
H 5ft (1.5m), S indefinite.

☀ ◉ ❀❀❀ 6–9

Luzula nivea (Snowy wood rush)
Evergreen, slow-spreading, perennial rush with fairly dense clusters of shining, white flower spikes in early summer. Leaves are edged with white hairs. H 24in (60cm), S 18–24in (45–60cm).

◑ ◊ ❀❀❀ 4–9

Hordeum jubatum
(Squirreltail barley, Squirreltail grass)
Tufted, short-lived perennial or annual grass. In summer to early autumn has flat, arching, feathery, plumelike flower spikes with silky awns.
H 1–2ft (30–60cm), S 1ft (30cm).

☼ ◊ ❀❀❀ 4–8

Pennisetum villosum,
syn. *P. longistylum* (Feathertop)
Herbaceous, tuft-forming, perennial grass with long-haired stems. In autumn has panicles of creamy pink spikelets, fading to pale brown, with very long, bearded bristles.
H to 3ft (1m), S 20in (50cm).

☼ ◊ ❀❀ 8–10

Stipa gigantea (Feather grass)
Evergreen, tuft-forming, perennial grass with narrow leaves, 18in (45cm) or more long. In summer carries elegant, open panicles of silvery spikelets, with long awns and dangling, golden anthers, which persist well into winter. H 8ft (2.5m), S 3ft (1m).

☼ ◊ ❀❀ 5–9

Cyperus papyrus
(Paper plant, Papyrus)
Evergreen, clump-forming, perennial sedge with stout, triangular, leafless stems, each carrying huge umbels of spikelets with up to 100 rays in summer. Grows in water. H to 10–15ft (3–5m), S 3ft (1m). Min. 45–50°F (7–10°C).

☼ ● 9–10

Helictotrichon sempervirens, syn.
Avena candida, A. sempervirens
(Avena grass, Blue oat grass)
Evergreen, tufted, perennial grass with stiff, silvery blue leaves up to 12in (30cm) or more long. Produces erect panicles of straw-colored flower spikes in summer. H 3ft (1m), S 2ft (60cm).

☼ ◊ ❀❀❀ 4–9

Bambusa multiplex, syn.
B. glaucescens (Hedge bamboo)
Evergreen, clump-forming bamboo with narrow leaves, 4–6in (10–15cm) long. Useful for hedges and wind-breaks. H to 50ft (15m), S indefinite.

☼ ◊ ❀ 8–10

Bouteloua gracilis,
syn. *B. oligostachya*
(Blue grama, Mosquito grass)
Semi-evergreen, tuft-forming, narrow-leaved, perennial grass. In summer bears comblike flower spikes, 1½in (4cm) long, held at right-angles to stems. H 20in (50cm), S 8in (20cm).

☼ ◊ ❀❀❀ 5–9

Melica altissima 'Atropurpurea'
Evergreen, tuft-forming, perennial grass with broad leaves, short-haired beneath. Purple spikelets in narrow panicles, 4in (10cm) long, hang from the tops of stems during summer.
H and S 2ft (60cm).

☼ ◊ ❀❀❀ 6–9

Grasses, bamboos, rushes, and sedges

◻ GREEN

Arundinaria anceps, syn.
*A. jaunsarensis, Sinarundinaria
jaunsarensis*
Evergreen, spreading bamboo with
erect, later arching, stems bearing
several branches at each node.
H 6–10ft (2–3m), S indefinite.

☼ ◊ ❄ 7–10

Semiarundinaria fastuosa,
syn. *Arundinaria fastuosa*
(Narihira bamboo)
Evergreen, clump-forming bamboo with
6in (15cm) long leaves and short, tufted
branches at each node. Culm sheaths
open to reveal polished, purplish
interiors. H 20ft (6m), S indefinite.

☼ ◊ ❄❄❄ 7–10

Shibataea kumasasa
(Ruscus-leaved bamboo)
Evergreen, clump-forming bamboo
with stubby, side branches on greenish
brown stems. Leaves are broad, 2–4in
(5–10cm) long. H 3–5ft (1–1.5m),
S 1ft (30cm).

☼ ◊ ❄❄❄ 6–10

Panicum capillare
(Old-witch grass, Witchgrass)
Tuft-forming, annual grass with broad
leaves and hairy stems. Top half of
each stem carries a dense panicle of
numerous, minute, greenish brown
spikelets on delicate stalks in summer.
H 2–3ft (60cm–1m), S 1ft (30cm).

☼ ◊ ❄❄❄ 5–9

Phyllostachys nigra var. ***henonis***,
syn. *P.* 'Henonis' (Henon bamboo)
Evergreen, clump-forming bamboo
with bristled auricles on culm sheaths
and a profusion of leaves. H 30ft
(10m), S 6–10ft (2–3m).

☼ ◊ ❄❄❄ 7–10

Juncus effusus f. ***spiralis***
(Corkscrew rush)
Evergreen, tuft-forming, perennial rush
with leafless stems that twist and curl
and are often prostrate. Fairly dense,
greenish brown flower panicles form
in summer. H 3ft (1m), S 2ft (60cm).

☼ ◊ ❄❄❄ 5–9

Chusquea culeou
Slow-growing, evergreen, clump-
forming bamboo. Bears long-lasting
culm sheaths, shining white when
young, at the swollen nodes of stout,
solid stems. H to 15ft (5m), S 8ft
(2.5m) or more.

☼ ◊ ❄❄❄ 6–9

Cyperus involucratus,
syn. *C. alternifolius* of gardens,
C. flabelliformis (Umbrella plant)
Evergreen, tuft-forming, perennial
sedge with leaflike bracts forming a
whorl beneath the clustered flower
spikes in summer. H to 3ft (1m),
S 1ft (30cm). Min. 39–45°F (4–7°C).

☼ ◊ 9–10

Pseudosasa japonica,
syn. *Arundinaria japonica*
(Arrow bamboo, Metake)
Evergreen, clump-forming bamboo
with long-persistent, roughly
pubescent, brown sheaths and broad
leaves, 14in (35cm) long. H 15ft (5m),
S indefinite.

☼ ◊ ❄❄❄ 7–10

Phyllostachys bambusoides
(Timber bamboo)
Evergreen, clump-forming bamboo
with stout, erect, green stems. Bears
leaf sheaths with prominent bristles,
and large, broad leaves. H 20–25ft
(6–8m), S indefinite.

☼ ◊ ❄❄❄ 7–10

Coix lacryma-jobi (Job's-tears)
Tuft-forming, annual grass with broad
leaves and insignificant spikelets
followed by hard, beadlike, green
fruits turning shiny, grayish mauve in
autumn. H 1½–3ft (45cm–1m),
S 4–6in (10–15cm).

☼ ◊ ❄ 5–10

Phyllostachys flexuosa
Evergreen, clump-forming bamboo
with slender, markedly zigzag stems
that turn black with age. Leaf sheaths
have no bristles. Leaves stay green all
winter. H 20–25ft (6–8m), S indefinite.

☼ ◊ ❄❄❄ 8–10

Miscanthus sinensis 'Gracillimus'
(Maiden grass)
Herbaceous, clump-forming, perennial
grass with very narrow leaves, hairy
beneath, often turning bronze. May bear
fan-shaped panicles of awned, hairy,
white spikelets in early autumn. H 4ft
(1.2m), S 18in (45cm).

 ☼ ◊ ❀❀ 5–10

Carex pendula (Drooping sedge)
Evergreen, tuft-forming, graceful,
perennial sedge with narrow, green
leaves, 18in (45cm) long. Solid,
triangular stems freely produce
pendent, greenish brown flower spikes
in summer. H 3ft (1m), S 1ft (30cm).

☼ ◊ ❀❀❀ 5–9

Phyllostachys viridiglaucescens
Evergreen, clump-forming bamboo
with greenish brown stems that arch at
the base. Has white powder beneath
nodes. H 20–25ft (6–8m), S indefinite.

☼ ◊ ❀❀ 7–10

**Spartina pectinata 'Aureo Margi-
nata'**, syn. *S.p.* 'Aureo-variegata'
(Variegated prairie cord grass)
Herbaceous, spreading, rhizomatous
grass with long, arching, yellow-striped
leaves, that turn orange-brown in late
autumn to winter. H to 6ft (2m),
S indefinite.

☼ ◑ ❀❀❀ 5–9

Carex oshimensis 'Evergold'
Evergreen, tuft-forming, perennial
sedge with narrow, yellow-striped
leaves, 8in (20cm) long. Solid,
triangular stems may carry insignificant
flower spikes in summer. H 8in (20cm),
S 6–8in (15–20cm).

☼ ◊ ❀❀❀ 7–9

Carex elata 'Aurea',
syn. *C. stricta* 'Aurea'
(Bowles' golden sedge)
Evergreen, tuft-forming, perennial
sedge with golden yellow leaves.
Solid, triangular stems bear blackish
brown flower spikes in summer.
H to 16in (40cm), S 6in (15cm).

☼ ● ❀❀❀ 5–9

Pleioblastus viridistriatus,
syn. *Arundinaria auricoma*,
A. viridistriata (Running bamboo)
Evergreen, slow-spreading bamboo with
purple stems and broad, softly downy,
bright yellow leaves with green stripes.
H 5ft (1.5m), S indefinite.

☼ ◊ ❀❀❀ 8–10

**Alopecurus pratensis 'Aureo-
marginatus'**, syn. *A.p.* 'Aureo-
variegatus', *A.p.* 'Aureus'
Herbaceous, tuft-forming, perennial
grass with yellow or yellowish green-
streaked leaves and dense flower spikes
in summer. H and S 9–12in (23–30cm).

☼ ◊ ❀❀❀ 5–8

Hakonechloa macra 'Aureola'
Slow-growing, herbaceous, shortly
rhizomatous grass with purple stems and
green-striped, yellow leaves that age to
reddish brown. Open panicles of reddish
brown flower spikes may appear in early
autumn and last into winter. H 16in
(40cm), S 18–24in (45–60cm).

☼ ◊ ❀❀❀ 5–9

FERNS

Phlebodium aureum
'Mandaianum'
Evergreen fern with creeping rhizomes.
Has arching, deeply lobed, glaucous
fronds with attractive, orange-yellow
sporangia on reverses; pinnae are deeply
cut and wavy. H 3–5ft (1–1.5m),
S 2ft (60cm). Min. 41°F (5°C).

☼ ◊ 10

Dryopteris filix-mas (Male fern)
Deciduous or semi-evergreen fern with
'shuttlecocks' of elegantly arching,
upright, broadly lance-shaped, green
fronds that arise from crowns of large,
upright, brown-scaled rhizomes.
H 4ft (1.2m), S 3ft (1m).

☼ ◊ ✴✴✴ 4–8

Platycerium bifurcatum
(Common staghorn fern)
Evergreen, epiphytic fern with broad,
platelike sterile fronds and long,
arching or pendent, forked, gray-green
fertile fronds bearing velvety,
brownish spore patches beneath. H and
S 3ft (1m). Min. 41°F (5°C).

☼ ◊ 10

Dicksonia antarctica
(Tasmanian tree fern)
Evergreen, treelike fern. Stout trunks
are covered with brown fibers and
crowned by spreading, somewhat
arching, broadly lance-shaped, much-
divided, palmlike fronds. H 30ft (10m)
or more, S 12ft (4m).

☼ ◊ ✴ 10

Polystichum aculeatum
'Pulcherrimum'
Evergreen or semi-evergreen fern with
broadly lance-shaped, daintily cut,
sharp-edged fronds that are yellowish
green in spring and mature to a glossy,
rich dark green. H 24in (60cm),
S 30in (75cm).

☼ ◊ ✴✴✴ 4–8

Blechnum capense
Evergreen fern with lance-shaped,
spreading, dark green fronds arising
from a creeping, almost black rhizome.
Extreme ends of blade divisions are
narrowed and spore-bearing. H 18in
(45cm), S 24in (60cm).

☼ ◊ ✴✴✴ 2–8

Polystichum munitum
(Western sword fern)
Evergreen fern with erect, leathery,
lance-shaped, dark green fronds that
consist of small, spiny-margined
pinnae. H 4ft (1.2m), S 1ft (30cm).

☼ ◊ ✴✴✴ 5–8

Polypodium glycyrrhiza
(Licorice fern)
Deciduous fern. Has oblong-triangular
to narrowly oval, divided, green fronds,
with lance-shaped to oblong pinnae,
that arise from a licorice-scented
rootstock. H and S 18in (45cm).

☼ ◊ ✴✴✴ 3–8

Microlepia strigosa (Lace fern)
Evergreen fern. Broad, irregularly
lance-shaped, deeply cut and divided,
pale green fronds arise from a creeping
rootstock. H 3ft (90cm), S 2ft (60cm).
Min. 41°F (5°C).

☼ ◊ 10

Polypodium scouleri
(Leathery polypody)
Evergreen, creeping fern with triangular to oval, leathery, divided fronds that arise from a spreading rootstock. H and S 12–16in (30–40cm).

☀ ◐ ❄❄ 6–8

Pteris cretica (Stove fern)
Evergreen or semi-evergreen fern with triangular to broadly oval, divided, pale green fronds that have fingerlike pinnae. H 18in (45cm), S 12in (30cm). Min. 41°F (5°C).

☀ ◐ 10

Adiantum pedatum var. **aleuticum**
Semi-evergreen fern with a short rootstock. Has glossy, dark brown or blackish stems and dainty, divided, fingerlike fronds, with blue-green pinnae, that are more crowded than those of *A. pedatum*. Grows well in alkaline soils. H and S to 18in (45cm).

☀ ◐ ❄❄ 3–8

Phlebodium aureum,
syn. *Polypodium aureum*
Evergreen fern with creeping, golden-scaled rhizomes. Has arching, deeply lobed, green or glaucous fronds with attractive, orange-yellow sporangia on reverses. H 3–5ft (90cm–1.5m), S 2ft (60cm). Min. 41°F (5°C).

☀ ◐ 10

Selaginella martensii
Evergreen, mosslike perennial with dense, much-branched, frondlike sprays of glossy, rich green foliage. H and S 9in (23cm). Min. 41°F (5°C).

☀ ◐ 10

Ceterach officinarum
(Rusty-back fern)
Semi-evergreen fern with lance-shaped, leathery, dark green fronds divided into alternate, bluntly rounded lobes. Backs of young fronds are covered with silvery scales that mature to reddish brown. H and S 6in (15cm).

☀ ◐ ❄❄❄ 5–8

Cyrtomium falcatum
(Holly fern, Japanese holly fern)
Evergreen fern. Fronds are lance-shaped and have hollylike, glossy, dark green pinnae; young fronds are often covered with whitish or brown scales. H 12–24in (30–60cm), S 12–18in (30–45cm).

☀ ◐ ❄ 7–9

Asplenium trichomanes
(Maidenhair spleenwort)
Semi-evergreen fern that has long, slender, tapering fronds with glossy, black, later brown midribs bearing many rounded-oblong, bright green pinnae. Is suitable for limestone soils. H 6in (15cm), S 6–12in (15–30cm).

☀ ◐ ❄❄❄ 3–8

Polystichum setiferum
'Divisilobum'
Evergreen or semi-evergreen fern. Broadly lance-shaped or oval, soft-textured, much-divided, spreading fronds are clothed with white scales as they unfurl. H 24in (60cm), S 18in (45cm).

☀ ◐ ❄❄❄ 5–8

Ferns

Thelypteris palustris (Marsh fern)
Deciduous fern. Has strong, erect,
lance-shaped, pale green fronds, with
widely separated, deeply cut pinnae,
produced from wiry, creeping, blackish
rhizomes. Grows well beside a pool or
stream. H 30in (75cm), S 12in (30cm).

☀ ◑ ❄❄❄ 5–8

Nephrolepis exaltata (Sword fern)
Evergreen fern. Has erect, sometimes
spreading, lance-shaped, divided, pale
green fronds borne on wiry stems.
H and S 3ft (90cm) or more.
Min. 41°F (5°C).

☀ ◑ 10

Osmunda regalis (Royal fern)
Deciduous fern with elegant, broadly
oval to oblong, divided, bright green
fronds, pinkish when young. Mature
plants bear tassel-like, rust brown
fertile flower spikes at ends of taller
fronds. H 6ft (2m), S 3ft (1m).

☀ ◑ ❄❄❄❄ 3–9

Selaginella kraussiana
Evergreen, trailing, more or less
prostrate, mosslike perennial with
bright green foliage. H ¹/₂in (1cm),
S indefinite. Min. 41°F (5°C).

☀ ◑ 10

Polypodium vulgare
'Cornubiense'
Evergreen fern with narrow, lance-
shaped, divided, fresh green fronds;
segments are further sub-divided to
give an overall lacy effect. H and
S 10–12in (25–30cm).

☀ ◑ ❄❄❄ 5–8

Onoclea sensibilis
(Bead fern, Sensitive fern)
Deciduous, creeping fern with
handsome, arching, almost triangular,
divided, fresh pale green fronds, often
suffused pinkish brown in spring. In
autumn, fronds turn an attractive
yellowish brown. H and S 18in (45cm).

☀ ◑ ❄❄❄ 4–8

Adiantum pedatum
(Common maidenhair fern)
Semi-evergreen fern with a stout,
creeping rootstock. Dainty, divided,
fingerlike, green fronds are produced
on glossy, dark brown or blackish
stems. H and S to 18in (45cm).

☀ ◑ pH ❄❄ 3–8

Matteuccia struthiopteris
(Ostrich fern)
Deciduous, rhizomatous fern. Lance-
shaped, erect, divided fronds are
arranged like a shuttlecock; outermost,
fresh green sterile fronds surround
denser, dark brown fertile fronds.
H 3ft (1m), S 1¹/₂ft (45cm).

☀ ◑ ❄❄❄ 2–8

***Polystichum setiferum* 'Proliferum'**
Evergreen or semi-evergreen fern. Broadly lance-shaped or oval, finely divided, soft and mosslike, spreading fronds are clothed with white scales as they unfurl. Largest fronds bear plantlets on upper sides of their mid-ribs. H 24in (60cm), S 18in (45cm).

☀ ◑ ❀❀❀ 5–8

Asplenium nidus (Bird's-nest fern)
Evergreen fern. Produces broadly lance-shaped, glossy, bright green fronds in a shuttlecocklike arrangement. H 2–4ft (60cm–1.2m), S 1–2ft (30–60cm). Min. 41°F (5°C).

☀ ◑ 10

***Athyrium nipponicum*,**
syn. *A. goeringianum*
(Japanese painted fern)
Deciduous fern. Broad, triangular, divided, purple-tinged, grayish green fronds arise from a scaly, creeping, brownish or reddish rootstock. H and S 12in (30cm).

☀ ◑ ❀❀ 3–8

Cryptogramma crispa
(Parsley fern)
Deciduous fern with broadly oval to triangular, finely divided, bright pale green fronds that resemble parsley. In autumn, fronds turn bright rusty brown and persist throughout winter. H 6–9in (15–23cm), S 6–12in (15–30cm).

☀ ◑ pH ❀❀❀ 5–8

Polypodium vulgare
(Common polypody, Wall fern)
Evergreen fern with narrow, lance-shaped, divided, herringbonelike, green fronds, arising from creeping rhizomes covered with copper brown scales. Suits a rock garden. H and S 10–12in (25–30cm).

☀ ◑ ❀❀❀ 5–8

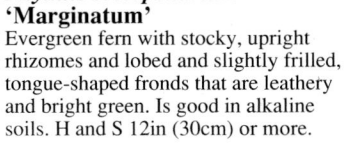

***Phyllitis scolopendrium*,**
syn. *Asplenium scolopendrium,*
Scolopendrium vulgare
(Hart's-tongue fern)
Evergreen fern with stocky rhizomes and tongue-shaped, leathery, bright green fronds. Is good in alkaline soils. H 18–30in (45–75cm), S to 18in (45cm).

☀ ◑ ❀❀❀ 4–8

Phyllitis scolopendrium
'Marginatum'
Evergreen fern with stocky, upright rhizomes and lobed and slightly frilled, tongue-shaped fronds that are leathery and bright green. Is good in alkaline soils. H and S 12in (30cm) or more.

☀ ◑ ❀❀❀ 4–8

Adiantum venustum
Deciduous fern. Bears delicate, pale green fronds, tinged brown when young, consisting of many small, triangular pinnae, on glossy stems. H 9in (23cm), S 12in (30cm).

☀ ◑ pH ❀❀ 3–8

☐ WHITE

Epilobium angustifolium f. album
(White-flowered fireweed)
Vigorous, upright perennial bearing
sprays of pure white flowers along
wandlike stems in late summer. Leaves
are small and lance-shaped. May spread
rapidly. H 4–5ft (1.2–1.5m), S 20in
(50cm) or more.

☼ ◊ ❀❀❀ 3–7

Crambe cordifolia
(Heartleaf crambe)
Robust perennial with clouds of small,
fragrant white flowers borne in
branching sprays in summer above
mounds of large, crinkled, and lobed,
dark green leaves. H to 6ft (2m),
S 4ft (1.2m).

☼ ◊ ❀❀❀ 6–9

Eremurus himalaicus
Upright perennial with strap-shaped,
basal leaves. In early summer has huge,
dense racemes of open cup-shaped, pure
white blooms with long stamens. Cover
crowns in winter with compost or
bracken. Needs staking. H 6–8ft
(2–2.5m), S 3ft (1m).

☼ ◊ ❀❀ 5–8

Sanguisorba canadensis
(American burnet, Giant burnet)
Clump-forming perennial. In late
summer bears slightly pendent spikes
of bottlebrushlike, white flowers on
stems that arise from toothed, divided
leaves. H 4–6ft (1.2–2m), S 2ft (60cm).

☼ ◊ ❀❀❀ 3–8

Nicotiana sylvestris
Branching perennial, often grown as
an annual, carrying panicles of
fragrant, tubular, white flowers at the
ends of stems in late summer. Has
long, rough, green leaves. H 5ft
(1.5m), S 2½ft (75cm).

☼ ◊ ❀❀ 9–10

Eryngium eburneum
Evergreen, arching perennial bearing
heads of thistlelike, green flowers with
white stamens on branched stems in
late summer. Has arching, spiny,
grasslike leaves. H 5–6ft (1.5–2m),
S 2ft (60cm).

☼ ◊ ❀ 9–10

Romneya coulteri
Vigorous, bushy, sub-shrubby
perennial, grown for its large, fragrant
white flowers, with prominent centers
of golden stamens, that appear in late
summer. Has deeply divided, gray
leaves. H and S 6ft (2m).

☼ ◊ ❀❀ 8–10

Echinops sphaerocephalus
(Great globe thistle)
Massive, bushy perennial with deeply
cut leaves, pale gray beneath, and gray
stems bearing round, grayish white
flower heads in late summer. H 6ft
(2m), S 3ft (1m).

☼ ◊ ❀❀❀ 3–9

Aruncus dioicus, syn. A. sylvester,
Spiraea aruncus (Goat's beard)
Hummock-forming perennial carrying
large leaves with lance-shaped leaflets
on tall stems and above them, in mid-
summer, branching plumes of tiny,
creamy white flowers. H 6ft (2m),
S 4ft (1.2m).

☼ ◊ ❀❀❀ 3–9

Artemisia lactiflora
(Ghost plant, White mugwort)
Vigorous, erect perennial. Many sprays of creamy white buds open to off-white flower heads in summer. Dark green leaves are jagged-toothed. Needs staking and is best as a foil to stronger colors. H 4–5ft (1.2–1.5m), S 20in (50cm).

 ☼ ◊ ❄❄❄ 4–9

Lavatera cachemiriana,
syn. *L. cachemirica*
Semi-evergreen, woody-based perennial or sub-shrub with wiry stems bearing panicles of trumpet-shaped, silky, clear pink flowers in summer. Has ivy-shaped, downy, green leaves. H 5–6ft (1.5–2m), S 3ft (1m).

☼ ◊ ❄❄ 6–8

Filipendula rubra
(Queen-of-the-prairie)
Vigorous, upright perennial with large, jagged leaves and feathery plumes of tiny, soft pink flowers on tall, branching stems in mid-summer. Will rapidly colonize a boggy site. H 6–8ft (2–2.5m), S 4ft (1.2m).

◐ ● ❄❄❄ 3–8

Meconopsis napaulensis
Clump-forming, short-lived perennial or biennial bearing pale to deep blue, pink, or red flowers in late spring and early summer. Deeply cut foliage is covered with bronze hairs. H 6ft (2m), S 3ft (1m).

☼ ◊ pH ❄❄❄ 6–8

Alpinia zerumbet,
syn. *A. nutans, A. speciosa*
(Shellflower, Shell ginger)
Evergreen, clump-forming perennial. Has racemes of white flowers, with yellow lips and pink- or red-marked throats, mainly in summer. H 10ft (3m), S 3ft (1m). Min. 64°F (18°C).

◐ ◊ 9–10

***Macleaya microcarpa* 'Coral Plume'** (Plume poppy)
Clump-forming perennial that in summer produces branching spikes of rich pink-buff flowers. Large, rounded, lobed leaves are gray-green above, gray-white beneath. H 6–8ft (2–2.5m), S 3–4ft (1–1.2m).

☼ ◊ ❄❄❄ 4–9

Eremurus robustus
Upright perennial with straplike leaves that die back during summer as huge racemes of cup-shaped, pink blooms appear. Cover crowns in winter with compost or bracken. Needs staking. H 7ft (2.2m), S 3ft (1m).

☼ ◊ ❄❄ 5–8

***Rheum palmatum* 'Atrosanguineum'**
Clump-forming perennial with very large, lobed, deeply cut leaves that are deep red-purple when young. Bears large, fluffy panicles of crimson flowers in early summer. H and S 6ft (2m).

☼ ◊ ❄❄❄ 5–9

Perennials/large

■□ PURPLE–BLUE   □□ GREEN–YELLOW

Veratrum nigrum
Erect, stately perennial that from late
summer onwards bears long spikes of
chocolate purple flowers at the ends of
stout, upright stems. Stems are clothed
with ribbed, oval to narrowly oval
leaves. H 6ft (2m), S 2ft (60cm).

☀◐ ◊ ❄❄❄ 7–9

Verbena patagonica,
syn. *V. bonariensis*
Perennial with a basal clump of dark
green leaves. Upright, wiry stems carry
tufts of tiny, purplish blue flowers in
summer-autumn. H 5ft (1.5m),
S 20in (50cm).

☀ ◊ ❄ 7–10

Cynara cardunculus (Cardoon)
Stately perennial with large clumps of
arching, pointed, divided, silver-gray
leaves, above which rise large,
thistlelike, blue-purple flower heads
borne singly on stout, gray stems in
summer. Flower heads dry well. H 6ft
(2m), S 3ft (1m).

☀ ◊ ❄❄ 9–10

***Campanula lactiflora* 'Prichard's
Variety'**
Upright perennial with slender stems
carrying branching heads of large,
nodding, bell-shaped, violet-blue
flowers from early summer to late
autumn. May need staking. H 4–5ft
(1.2–1.5m), S 2ft (60cm).

☀ ◊ ❄❄❄ 4–8

Echinops bannaticus
Upright perennial with narrow, deeply
cut leaves and globose, pale to mid-
blue heads of flowers, borne on
branching stems in late summer.
Flower heads dry well. H 4–5ft
(1.2–1.5m), S 2¹/₂ft (75cm).

☀ ◊ ❄❄❄ 8–10

***Galega* x *hartlandii* 'Lady Wilson'**
Vigorous, upright perennial with spikes
of small, pealike, blue and pinkish
white flowers in summer above bold
leaves divided into oval leaflets. Needs
staking. H to 5ft (1.5m), S 3ft (1m).

☀ ◊ ❄❄❄ 5–10

Gunnera manicata
Architectural perennial with rounded,
prickly-edged leaves, to 5ft (1.5m)
across. Has conical, light green flower
spikes in early summer, followed by
orange-brown seed pods. Needs mulch
cover for crowns in winter and a
sheltered site. H 6ft (2m), S 7ft (2.2m).

☀ ◊ ❄❄❄ 7–10

Angelica archangelica
Upright perennial, usually grown as a
biennial, with deeply divided, bright
green leaves and umbels of white or
green flowers in late summer. Stems
have culinary usage and when crystal-
lized may be used for confectionery
decoration. H 6ft (2m), S 3ft (1m).

☀ ◊ ❄❄❄ 4–9

Ferula communis (Giant fennel)
Upright perennial. Large, cow
parsleylike umbels of yellow flowers
are borne from late spring to summer
on the tops of stems that arise from a
mound of finely cut, green foliage. H
6–7ft (2–2.3m), S 3–4ft (1–1.2m).

☀ ◊ ❄❄ 7–10

Verbascum olympicum
Semi-evergreen, rosette-forming
biennial or short-lived perennial.
Branching stems, arising from feltlike,
gray foliage at the plant base, bear
sprays of 5-lobed, bright golden
flowers from mid-summer onwards.
H 6ft (2m), S 3ft (1m).

☼ ◊ ❄❄❄ 7–9

Ligularia przewalskii
Loosely clump-forming perennial with
stems clothed in deeply cut, round, dark
green leaves. Narrow spires of small,
daisylike, yellow flower heads appear
from mid- to late summer.
H 4–6ft (1.2–2m), S 3ft (1m).

☼ ◐ ❄❄❄ 4–8

Heliopsis 'Light of Loddon'
Upright perennial bearing dahlialike,
double, bright orange flower heads on
strong stems in late summer. Dark
green leaves are coarse and serrated.
H 4–5ft (1.2–1.5m), S 2ft (60cm).

☼ ◊ ❄❄❄ 4–8

Hedychium densiflorum
Clump-forming, rhizomatous perennial
bearing a profusion of short-lived,
fragrant orange or yellow flowers in
dense spikes during late summer.
Broadly lance-shaped leaves are glossy
green. H 4–6ft (1.2–2m), S 2ft (60cm).

☼ ◐ ❄❄ 7–10

Rudbeckia laciniata 'Goldquelle'
Erect perennial. In late summer and
autumn, daisylike, double, bright
yellow flower heads with green centers
are borne singly on stout stems. Has
deeply divided, green foliage. H 5–6ft
(1.5–2m), S 2–2¹/₂ft (60–75 cm).

☼ ◊ ❄❄❄ 3–9

Inula magnifica
Robust, clump-forming, upright
perennial with a mass of lance-shaped
to elliptic, rough leaves. Leafy stems
bear terminal heads of large, daisylike,
yellow flower heads in late summer.
Needs staking. H 6ft (1.8m), S 3ft
(1m).

☼ ◊ ❄❄❄ 5–8

Ligularia stenocephala
Loosely clump-forming perennial with
jagged-edged, round, green leaves.
Large heads of daisylike, yellow-orange
flowers open on purplish stems from
mid- to late summer. H 4ft (1.2m) or
more, S 2ft (60cm).

☼ ◐ ❄❄❄ 4–8

Heliconia psittacorum
(Parakeet flower, Parrot's-flower)
Tufted perennial with long-stalked,
lance-shaped leaves. In summer,
mature plants carry green-tipped,
orange flowers with narrow, glossy,
orange-red bracts. H to 6ft (2m),
S 3ft (1m). Min. 64°F (18°C).

☼ ◊ 10

Delphiniums

Delphiniums are one of the most attractive of the tall perennials with their showy spires of flowers in summer. They are best suited to areas of the United States that experience extended, cooler springs. In addition to the classic blues, hybrids are available in a broad range of colors from white through the pastel shades of dusky pink and lilac to the richer mauves and violet-purples. Plants should be securely staked .

D. 'Butterball'

D. 'Sandpiper'

D. 'Olive Poppleton'

D. 'Emily Hawkins'

D. 'Fanfare'

D. 'Mighty Atom'

D. 'Strawberry Fair'

D. 'Langdon's Royal Flush'

D. 'Bruce'

D. 'Gillian Dallas'

D. belladonna 'Blue Bees'

D. 'Lord Butler'

D. 'Spindrift'

D. 'Blue Dawn'

D. 'Loch Leven'

D. 'Blue Nile'

D. grandiflorum 'Blue Butterfly'

D. 'Chelsea Star'

D. 'Sungleam'

WHITE–PINK

PINK–PURPLE

Cimicifuga simplex
(Kamchatka bugbane)
Upright perennial with arching spikes
of tiny, slightly fragrant, star-shaped,
white flowers in autumn. Leaves are
glossy and divided. Needs staking.
H 4–5ft (1.2–1.5m), S 2ft (60cm).

☼ ◐ ❄❄❄ 4–8

Eupatorium fistulosum
(Joe-Pye weed)
Stately, upright perennial with terminal
heads of tubular, pinkish purple flowers
borne in late summer and early autumn.
Coarse, oval leaves are arranged in
whorls along purplish stems. H to 7ft
(2.2m), S to 3ft (1m).

☼ ◐ ❄❄❄ 3–8

**Anemone x hybrida 'Honorine
Jobert'**
Vigorous, branching perennial. Slightly
cupped, white flowers with contrasting
yellow stamens are carried on wiry
stems in late summer and early autumn
above deeply divided, dark green
leaves. H 5ft (1.5m), S 2ft (60cm).

◐ ◊ ❄❄❄ 6–8

**Aster novae-angliae 'Harrington's
Pink'**
Upright perennial that in autumn bears
clusters of daisylike, clear pink flower
heads with yellow centers. Has lance-
shaped, dull green leaves. May need
some staking. H 4–5ft (1.2–1.5m),
S to 2ft (60cm).

☼ ◊ ❄❄❄ 5–8

Salvia involucrata 'Bethellii'
Sub-shrubby perennial that produces
long racemes of large, cerise-crimson
blooms, with pink bracts, in late
summer and autumn. Leaves are oval
to heart-shaped. H 4–5ft (1.2–1.5m),
S 3ft (1m).

☼ ◊ ❄ 7–9

**Anemone x hybrida
'Bressingham Glow'**
Vigorous, branching perennial with
slightly cupped, rose-purple flowers
borne on wiry stems in late summer
and early autumn over clumps of
deeply divided, dark green leaves.
H 4–5ft (1.2–1.5m), S 2ft (60cm).

◐ ◊ ❄❄❄ 6–8

GREEN–YELLOW

Asclepias physocarpa,
syn. *Gomphocarpus physocarpus*
Deciduous, erect, hairy sub-shrub with
lance-shaped leaves, 4in (10cm) long.
Has umbels of 5-horned, creamy white
flowers in summer, followed by large,
inflated, globose seed pods with soft
bristles. H to 6ft (2m), S to 2ft (60cm).

☼ ◊ ❀ 9–10

Helianthus 'Loddon Gold'
Upright perennial bearing showy,
large, vivid deep yellow flower heads
with rounded, double centers in late
summer and early autumn. Needs
staking and may spread quickly.
H 5ft (1.5m), S 2ft (60cm).

☼ ◊ ❀❀❀ 5–8

Hedychium gardnerianum
Upright, rhizomatous perennial. In late
summer and early autumn has many
spikes of short-lived, fragrant, lemon
yellow and red flowers. Lance-shaped
leaves are grayish green, most markedly
when young. H 5–6ft (1.5–2m), S 2½ft
(75cm). Min. 41°F (5°C).

☼ ◑ 9–10

Rudbeckia 'Herbstsonne'
Erect perennial bearing daisylike,
yellow flower heads, with conical,
green centers, that are carried singly on
tall stems in late summer and autumn.
Leaves are shallowly lobed. H 5–7ft
(1.5–2.3m), S 2–2½ft (60–75cm).

☼ ◊ ❀❀❀ 3–9

Helianthus x multiflorus
Upright perennial. Has large, yellow
flower heads, with double centers
surrounded by larger, rayed segments,
that are borne in late summer and early
autumn. Needs staking and may spread
rapidly. H 5ft (1.5m), S 2ft (60cm).

☼ ◊ ❀❀❀ 5–9

PINK–PURPLE

Strelitzia nicolai
Evergreen, palmlike perennial with a
stout trunk. Has leaves, 5ft (1.5m) or
more long, on very long stalks and
intermittently bears beaklike, white
and pale blue flowers in boat-shaped,
dark purple bracts. H 25ft (8m), S 15ft
(5m). Min. 41–50°F (5–10°C).

◑ ◊ 10

Musa ornata
Evergreen, palmlike, suckering
perennial with oblong, waxy, bluish
green leaves to 6ft (2m) long. In
summer has erect, yellow-orange
flowers with pinkish bracts and
greenish yellow fruits. H to 10ft (3m),
S 7ft (2.2m). Min. 64°F (18°C).

☼ ◊ 10

Calathea ornata 'Sanderiana'
Evergreen, clump-forming perennial.
Broadly oval, leathery, glossy leaves,
to 2ft (60cm) long, are dark green with
pink to white lines above, and purple
beneath. Has short spikes of white to
mauve flowers. H 4–5ft (1.2–1.5m),
S 3ft (1m). Min. 59°F (15°C).

☀ ◊ 10

Doryanthes palmeri (Spear lily)
Evergreen perennial with a rosette of
arching, ribbed leaves, to 6ft (2m)
long. Intermittently bears panicles of
small, red-bracted, orange-red flowers,
white within. Flowers are often
replaced by bulbils. H 6–8ft (2–2.5m),
S 8ft (2.5m). Min. 50°F (10°C).

☼ ◊ 10

Phormium tenax 'Purpureum'
Evergreen, upright perennial with bold,
stiff, pointed leaves that are rich
reddish purple to dark copper. In
summer, panicles of reddish flowers
appear on purplish blue stems.
H 6–8ft (2–2.5m), S 3ft (1m).

☼ ◊ ❀❀ 9–10

□ BLUE–GREEN

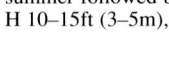

Pycnostachys dawei
Strong-growing, bushy perennial with toothed, oblong leaves, 5–12in (12–30cm) long, that are reddish below. Has compact spikes of tubular, 2-lipped, bright blue flowers in winter-spring. H 4–5ft (1.2–1.5m), S 1–3ft (30–90cm). Min. 59°F (15°C).

☀ ◊ 9–10

Musa basjoo, syn. M. japonica
Evergreen, palmlike, suckering perennial with arching leaves to 3ft (1m) long. Has drooping, pale yellow flowers with brownish bracts in summer followed by green fruits. H 10–15ft (3–5m), S 6–8ft (2–2.5m).

☀ ◊ ❄ 9–10

Ranunculus aconitifolius 'Flore Pleno'
Clump-forming perennial with deeply divided, dark green leaves. Double, pure white flowers are borne on strong, branched stems in spring-summer. H 24–30in (60–75cm), S 20in (50cm).

☀ ◊ ❄❄❄ 5–9

Ranunculus aconitifolius
Vigorous, clump-forming perennial with deeply divided, dark green leaves. Single, white flowers about 1in (3cm) across are borne in spring and early summer. H and S 3ft (1m).

☀ ◊ ❄❄❄ 5–9

Ensete ventricosum,
syn. Musa arnoldiana, M. ensete
Evergreen, palmlike perennial with small, bananalike fruits. Has 20ft (6m) long leaves with reddish midribs and, intermittently, reddish green flowers with dark red bracts. H 20ft (6m), S 10ft (3m) or more. Min. 50°F (10°C).

☀ ◊ 10

Smilacina racemosa
(False Solomon's-seal)
Arching perennial. Has oval, light green leaves terminating in feathery sprays of white flowers that appear from spring to mid-summer and are followed by fleshy, reddish fruits. H 2½–3ft (75–90cm), S 1½ft (45cm).

☀◑ ◊ pH ❄❄❄ 4–9

Irises

These beautiful flowers were originally named after Iris, the Greek goddess of the rainbow, as the shades of their coloring and markings are reminiscent of those of the rainbow. Their distinctive flowers often have "beards" (short hairs) or crests along the centers of the falls.

The genus is classified into many divisions, some of which are used horticulturally for irises with similar characteristics or cultural requirements. Of these, the easiest to grow are the bearded, crested, Xiphium, and dwarf Reticulata groups. Siberian and Japanese types are excellent in bog gardens or by water, but also tolerate drier conditions. Others, such as Juno, Oncocyclus, and Regelia irises, may be less easy to cultivate, though their flowers are among the most beautiful. Full details of all groups and guidance on their cultivation are given in the Plant Dictionary.

I. 'Bold Print'
(bearded)

I. chrysographes
(Siberian)

I. 'Sapphire Star'
(Japanese)

I. 'Matinata' (bearded)

I. hoogiana (Regelia)

I. 'Dreaming Yellow'
(Siberian)

I. 'Geisha Gown'
(Japanese)

I. pallida **'Aurea Variegata'** (bearded)

I. versicolor (beardless)

I. latifolia (Xiphium)

I. xiphium **'Wedgewood'**
(Xiphium)

I. bucharica (Juno)

I. 'Annabel Jane'
(bearded)

I. tectorum (Evansia)

I. 'Mary Frances'
(bearded)

I. reticulata **'Cantab'**
(Reticulata)

I. 'Paradise Bird'
(bearded)

I. rosenbachiana
(Juno)

I. douglasiana (Pacific Coast)

I. 'Mountain Lake'
(Siberian)

I. magnifica (Juno)

I. missouriensis
(Pacific Coast)

I. 'Rippling Rose'
(bearded)

I. 'Krasnia' (bearded)

I. 'Joyce' (Reticulata)

I. iberica (Oncocyclus)

I. cristata (Evansia)

I. tenax (Pacific Coast)

I. 'Fulvala' (beardless)

I. laevigata (Japanese)

I. setosa (beardless)

I. 'Harmony'
(Reticulata)

I. histrioides 'Major'
(Reticulata)

I. 'Early Light'
(bearded)

I. variegata (bearded)

I. forrestii (Siberian)

I. innominata (Pacific Coast)

I. danfordiae
(Reticulata)

I. pseudacorus
(beardless)

I. 'Sun Miracle'
(bearded)

I. 'Eye Bright'
(bearded)

I. 'Shepherd's Delight'
(bearded)

I. 'Peach Frost'
(bearded)

I. 'Carnaby' (bearded)

I. fulva (beardless)

I. 'Blue-eyed
Brunette' (bearded)

I. 'Flamenco'
(bearded)

Perennials/medium SPRING INTEREST

Polygonatum* x *hybridum
Arching, leafy perennial with fleshy rhizomes. In late spring, clusters of small, pendent, tubular, greenish white flowers are produced in axils of neat, oval leaves. H 4ft (1.2m), S 3ft (1m).

☀ ◊ ❄❄❄ 4–9

Peltiphyllum peltatum
Spreading perennial with large, rounded leaves. Has clusters of white or pale pink flowers in spring on white-haired stems before foliage appears. H 3–4ft (1–1.2m), S 2ft (60cm).

☀ ◊ ❄❄❄ 5–9

Geranium phaeum
(Mourning widow)
Clump-forming perennial with lobed, soft green leaves and maroon-purple flowers, with reflexed petals, borne on rather lax stems in late spring. H 30in (75cm), S 18in (45cm).

☀ ◊ ❄❄❄ 4–9

Symphytum caucasicum
(Comfrey)
Clump-forming perennial carrying clusters of pendent, azure blue flowers in spring above rough, hairy foliage. Is best suited to a wild garden. H and S 2–3ft (60–90cm).

☀ ◊ ❄❄❄ 4–9

***Tanacetum coccineum* 'Brenda',**
syn. *Pyrethrum* 'Brenda'
Erect perennial with somewhat aromatic, feathery leaves. Daisylike, single, magenta-pink flower heads are borne in late spring and early summer. H 24in (60cm), S 18in (45cm) or more.

☀ ◊ ❄❄❄ 5–9

Peonies

Peonies have long been valued for their bold foliage and showy blooms, filling the border with subtle shades of mainly pinks and reds in late spring and early to mid-summer. As well as a wide variety of border hybrids, there are several tree peonies—open shrubs often over 6ft (2m) high. Peony flowers vary from single to double or anemone-form (with broad, outer petals and a mass of petaloids in the center).

P. emodi (single)

P. suffruticosa 'Rock's Variety' (semi-double)

P. 'White Wings' (single)

P. 'Krinkled White' (single)

P. 'Whitleyi Major' (single)

P. 'Duchesse de Nemours' (double)

P. 'Cornelia Shaylor' (double)

P. 'Shirley Temple' (double)

P. 'Mother of Pearl' (single)

P. 'Kelway's Supreme' (double)

P. 'Avant Garde' (single)

P. suffruticosa 'Reine Elizabeth' (double)

P. 'Sarah Bernhardt' (double)

P. 'Ballerina' (double)

P. 'Bowl of Beauty' (anemone)

P. 'Globe of Light' (anemone)

P. mascula (single)

P. veitchii (single)

P. 'Kelway's Gorgeous' (single)

P. 'Magic Orb' (double)

P. officinalis 'China Rose' (single)

P. 'Silver Flare' (single)

P. 'Auguste Dessert' (semi-double)

P. 'Instituteur Doriat'
(anemone)

P. peregrina 'Sunshine'
(single)

P. 'Knighthood'
(double)

P. tenuifolia (single)

P. 'Sir Edward Elgar'
(single)

P. delavayi (single)

P. lutea var. **ludlowii**
(single)

P. wittmanniana
(single)

P. 'Laura Dessert'
(double)

P. 'Souvenir de Maxime Cornu' (double)

P. 'Mme. Louis Henri'
(semi-double)

P. 'Argosy' (single)

P. officinalis 'Rubra Plena' (double)   **P. mlokosewitschii**
(single)

Perennials/medium SPRING INTEREST

▦ BLUE–YELLOW

Symphytum × uplandicum 'Variegatum'
Perennial with large, hairy, gray-green leaves that have broad, cream margins. In late spring and early summer, pink or blue buds open to tubular, blue or purplish blue flowers. H 3ft (1m), S 2ft (60cm).

☼ ◓ ❀❀❀ 4–9

Aciphylla aurea (Golden Spaniard)
Evergreen, rosette-forming perennial with long, bayonetlike, yellow-green leaves. Bears spikes of golden flowers up to 6ft (2m) tall from late spring to early summer. H and S in leaf 2–2¹⁄₂ft (60–75cm).

☼ ◊ ❀❀ 8–10

Doronicum pardalianches, syn. **D. cordatum** (Leopard's bane)
Clump-forming perennial with heart-shaped, bright green leaves and, in spring, small, daisylike, clear yellow flower heads on slender, branching stems. Spreads freely. H 2¹⁄₂ft (75cm), S 2ft (60cm).

☼ ◊ ❀❀❀ 4–8

Chelidonium majus 'Flore Pleno'
Upright perennial with divided, bright green leaves and many cup-shaped, double, yellow flowers borne on branching sprays in late spring and early summer. Seeds freely and is best in a wild garden. H 24–30in (60–90cm), S 12in (30cm).

☼ ◊ ❀❀❀ 5–8

Asphodeline lutea (King's spear)
Neat, clump-forming perennial that bears dense spikes of star-shaped, yellow flowers amid narrow, gray-green leaves in late spring. H 3–4ft (1–1.2m), S 2–3ft (60cm–1m).

☼ ◊ ❀❀ 6–9

199

☐ WHITE

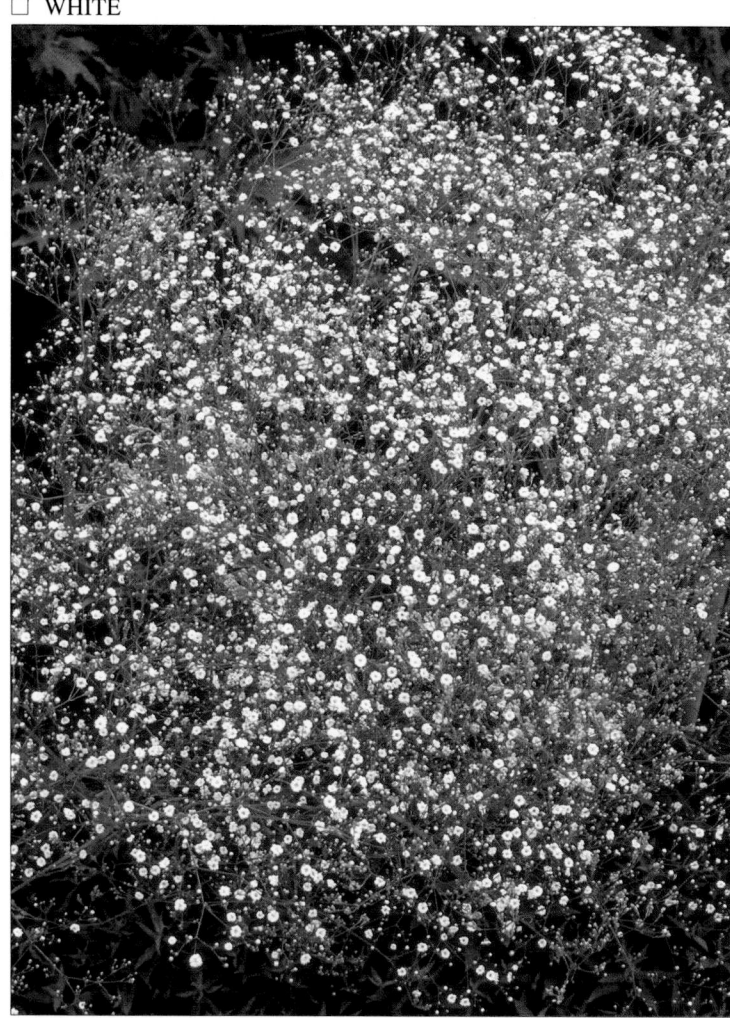

Gypsophila paniculata 'Bristol Fairy'
Perennial with small, dark green leaves and wiry, branching stems bearing panicles of tiny, double, white flowers in summer. H 2–2½ft (60–75cm), S 3ft (1m).

☼ ◊ ❀ ❀ ❀ 4–9

Achillea ptarmica 'The Pearl'
(Sneezewort)
Upright perennial with large heads of small, pomponlike, white flowers in summer and tapering, glossy, dark green leaves. May spread rapidly. H and S 2½ft (75cm).

☼ ◊ ❀ ❀ ❀ 4–9

Nicotiana alata, syn. *N. affinis*
Rosette-forming perennial, normally grown as an annual, that in late summer bears clusters of tubular, creamy white flowers, pale brownish violet externally, which are fragrant at night. Has oval, green leaves. H 30in (75cm), S 12in (30cm).

☼ ◊ ❀ ❀ 10

Libertia grandiflora
Loosely clump-forming, rhizomatous perennial that in early summer produces spikes of white flowers above grasslike, dark green leaves, which turn brown at the tips. Has decorative seed pods in autumn. H 30in (75cm), S 24in (60cm).

☼ ◊ ❀ ❀ 9–10

Hesperis matronalis
(Sweet rocket)
Upright perennial with long spikes of many 4-petaled, white or violet flowers borne in summer. Flowers have a strong fragrance in the evening. Leaves are smooth and narrowly oval. H 2½ft (75cm), S 2ft (60cm).

☼ ◊ ❀ ❀ ❀ 4–9

Asphodelus albus
Upright perennial with clusters of star-shaped, white flowers borne in late spring and early summer. Has narrow, basal tufts of green leaves. H 3ft (1m), S 18in (45cm).

☼ ◊ ❀ ❀ ❀ 8–10

Anaphalis margaritacea, syn.
A. yedoensis (Pearly everlasting)
Bushy perennial that has lance-shaped, gray-green or silvery gray leaves with white margins and many heads of small, white flowers borne on erect stems in late summer. Flower heads dry well. H 2–2½ft (60–75cm), S 2ft (60cm).

☼ ◊ ❀ ❀ ❀ 4–8

Dicentra spectabilis f. **alba**
(White bleeding heart)
Leafy perennial forming a hummock of fernlike, deeply cut, light green foliage with arching sprays of pendent, heart-shaped, pure white flowers in late spring and summer. H 2–2½ft (60–75cm), S 2ft (60cm).

◑ ◊ ❀ ❀ ❀ 4–8

Salvia argentea (Silver sage)
Rosette-forming perennial, usually
grown as an annual or biennial. Has
woolly, silver foliage. In summer,
branching clusters of sagelike, white
flowers are produced on strong, upright
stems. H 2–3ft (60cm–1m),
S 18in (45cm).

☼ ◊ ❀❀ 5–8

Thalictrum aquilegiifolium
'White Cloud'
Perennial with divided, grayish green
leaves. In summer produces terminal
sprays of delicate, fluffy, white flowers.
H 3–4ft (1–1.2m), S 1ft (30cm).

☼ ◊ ❀❀❀ 5–9

Chrysanthemum* x *superbum
'Elizabeth'
Robust perennial with large, daisylike,
single, pure white flower heads borne
singly in summer. Divide and replant
every 2 years. H 3ft (1m), S 2ft (60cm).

☼ ◊ ❀❀❀ 4–8

Rodgersia podophylla
Clump-forming, rhizomatous perennial
with large, many-veined leaves that are
bronze when young and later become
green, then copper-tinted. Panicles of
creamy white flowers are borne well
above foliage in summer. H 4ft (1.2m),
S 3ft (1m).

☼ ◊ ❀❀❀ 5–8

Dictamnus albus (Gas plant)
Upright perennial bearing, in early
summer, spikes of fragrant, star-
shaped, white flowers with long
stamens. Light green leaves are
divided into oval leaflets. Dislikes
disturbance. H 3ft (1m), S 2ft (60cm).

☼ ◊ ❀❀❀ 3–8

Rodgersia sambucifolia
Clump-forming, rhizomatous perennial
with emerald green, sometimes
bronze-tinged leaves composed of
large leaflets. Sprays of creamy white
flowers appear above foliage in
summer. H 3–4ft (1–1.2m), S 3ft (1m).

☼ ◊ ❀❀❀ 5–8

Myrrhis odorata (Sweet Cicely)
Graceful perennial that resembles cow
parsley. Has aromatic, fernlike, green
foliage and fragrant, bright creamy
white flowers in early summer. H
2–3ft (60cm–1m), S 2ft (60cm).

☼ ◊ ❀❀❀ 4–8

Chrysanthemum frutescens,
syn. *Argyranthemum frutescens*
(Marguerite daisy)
Evergreen, woody-based, bushy
perennial that bears many daisylike,
white, yellow, or pink flower heads
throughout summer. Attractive leaves
are fresh green. H and S 3ft (1m).

☼ ◊ ❀ 9–10

***Aruncus dioicus* 'Kneiffii'**
Hummock-forming perennial that has
deeply cut, feathery leaves with lance-
shaped leaflets on elegant stems and
bears branching plumes of tiny, star-
shaped, creamy white flowers in mid-
summer. H 3ft (1m), S 20in (50cm).

☼ ◊ ❀❀❀ 4–9

☐ WHITE

Rodgersia aesculifolia
Clump-forming, rhizomatous perennial
that is excellent for a bog garden or
pool side. In mid-summer, plumes of
fragrant, pinkish white flowers rise
from crinkled, bronze foliage like that
of a horse chestnut tree. H and
S 3ft (1m).

☼ ◊ ❀❀❀ 5–8

Lysimachia clethroides
(Gooseneck loosestrife)
Vigorous, clump-forming, spreading
perennial carrying spikes of small,
white flowers above green foliage in
late summer. H 3ft (1m), S 2–3ft
(60cm–1m).

☼ ◊ ❀❀❀ 4–9

Morina longifolia
Evergreen perennial that produces
rosettes of large, spiny, thistlelike, rich
green leaves. Whorls of hooded,
tubular, white flowers, flushed pink
within, are borne well above foliage in
mid-summer. H 2–2½ft (60–75cm),
S 1ft (30cm).

☼ ◊ ❀❀❀ 5–8

Veronica virginica f. **alba**
Upright perennial. In late summer,
spires of small, white flowers, with
pink-flushed bases and pink anthers,
crown stems clothed with whorls of
narrow, dark green leaves. H 4ft
(1.2m), S 18in (45cm).

☼ ◊ ❀❀❀ 4–8

Papaver orientale 'Perry's White'
Hairy-leaved perennial with deep,
fleshy roots. Satiny, white flowers with
purple centers appear on strong stems
in early summer. May need support.
H 2½ft (75cm), S 2ft (60cm).

☼ ◊ ❀❀❀ 4–9

Phlox maculata 'Omega'
Erect perennial. Tall, broad, cylindrical
heads of white flowers, each with a
lilac eye, are freely borne in summer
above well-clothed, stout, leafy stems.
H 3ft (1m), S 18in (45cm).

☼ ◊ ❀❀❀ 5–8

Gillenia trifoliata (Bowman's-root)
Upright perennial with many wiry,
branching stems carrying clusters of
dainty, white flowers with reddish
brown calyces in summer. Leaves are
dark green and lance-shaped. Needs
staking. Thrives in most situations.
H 3–4ft (1–1.2m), S 2ft (60cm).

☼ ◊ ❀❀❀ 5–9

Digitalis ferruginea
Perennial, best treated as a biennial,
with long, slender spikes bearing many
funnel-shaped, pale orange-brown and
white flowers in mid-summer above
basal rosettes of oval, rough leaves.
Propagate from seed. H 3–4ft
(1–1.2m), S 1ft (30cm).

☼ ◊ ❀❀❀ 4–8

Valeriana officinalis
(Common valerian)
Clump-forming, fleshy perennial that
bears spikes of white to deep pink
flowers in summer. Leaves are deeply
toothed. Has disadvantage of attracting
cats. H 3–4ft (1–1.2m), S 3ft (1m).

☼ ◊ ❀❀❀ 4–9

Linaria purpurea 'Canon Went'
Upright perennial bearing spikes of snapdragonlike, pink blooms with orange-tinged throats from mid- to late summer. Has narrow, gray-green leaves. H 2–3ft (60cm–1m), S 2ft (60cm).

☼ ◊ ❋❋❋ 5–8

Dictamnus albus var. **purpureus**
Upright perennial. In early summer bears stiff spikes of fragrant, star-shaped, purplish pink, sometimes paler, flowers with long stamens. Has light green leaves divided into oval leaflets. Dislikes disturbance. H 3ft (1m), S 2ft (60cm).

☼ ◊ ❋❋❋ 3–8

Monarda didyma 'Croftway Pink'
Clump-forming perennial carrying whorls of hooded, soft pink blooms throughout summer above neat mounds of aromatic foliage. H 3ft (1m), S 18in (45cm).

☼ ◑ ❋❋❋ 4–8

Chrysanthemum frutescens 'Mary Wootton'
Evergreen, woody-based, bushy perennial bearing daisylike, pink flower heads throughout summer. Has attractive, fernlike, divided, pale green foliage. H and S to 3ft (1m).

☼ ◊ ❋ 9–10

Geranium x **oxonianum 'Winscombe'**
Semi-evergreen, carpeting perennial with dense, dainty, lobed leaves and cup-shaped, deep pink flowers, which fade to pale pink, borne throughout summer. H 24–30in (60–75cm), S 18in (45cm).

☼ ◊ ❋❋❋ 5–8

Malva moschata
(Musk mallow, Musk rose)
Bushy, branching perennial producing successive spikes of saucer-shaped, rose-pink flowers during early summer. Narrow, lobed, divided leaves are slightly scented. H 2–3ft (60cm–1m), S 2ft (60cm).

☼ ◊ ❋❋❋ 4–8

Polygonum bistorta 'Superbum'
Vigorous, clump-forming perennial that from early to late summer produces spikes of soft pink flowers above oval leaves. H 2–2¹⁄₂ft (60–75cm), S 2ft (60cm).

☼ ◑ ❋❋❋ 4–8

Sidalcea 'Jimmy Whittet',
syn. S. 'Jimmy Whitelet'
Perennial with basal clumps of bright green leaves. In summer bears delicate, single, purplish pink flowers up erect stems. H 3–4ft (1–1.2m), S 3ft (1m).

☼ ◊ ❋❋❋ 5–8

Astilbe 'Venus'
Leafy perennial bearing feathery, tapering plumes of tiny, pale pink flowers in summer. Foliage is broad and divided into leaflets; flowers remain on the plant, dried and brown, well into winter. Prefers humus-rich soil. H and S to 3ft (1m).

☼ ◊ ❊❊❊ 4–8

Astilbe 'Ostrich Plume'
Leafy perennial with handsome, divided foliage and arching, feathery, tapering plumes of tiny, coral pink flowers in summer. Dry, brown flowers remain on the plant well into winter. Prefers humus-rich soil. H and S to 3ft (1m).

☼ ◊ ❊❊❊ 5–8

Echinacea purpurea 'Robert Bloom'
Upright perennial. Has lance-shaped, dark green leaves and large, daisylike, deep crimson-pink flower heads, with conical, brown centers, borne singly on strong stems in summer. Needs humus-rich soil. H 4ft (1.2m), S 20in (50cm).

☼ ◊ ❊❊❊ 4–9

Lupinus 'The Chatelaine'
Clump-forming perennial carrying spikes of pink-and-white flowers above divided, green foliage in early summer. H 4ft (1.2m), S 18in (45cm).

☼ ◊ ❊❊❊ 5–8

Centaurea pulcherrima
Upright perennial with deeply cut, silvery leaves. Rose-pink flower heads, with thistlelike centers paler than surrounding star-shaped ray petals, are borne singly on slender stems in summer. H 2½ft (75cm), S 2ft (60cm).

☼ ◊ ❊❊❊ 4–8

Phlox paniculata 'Eva Cullum'
Upright perennial that in mid-summer bears conical heads of clear pink flowers with magenta eyes. H 2½ft (75cm), S 2ft (60cm).

☼ ◊ ❊❊❊ 4–8

Physostegia virginiana 'Variegata'
Erect perennial. In late summer produces spikes of tubular, purplish pink blooms that can be placed into position. Toothed, green leaves are white-variegated. H 3–4ft (1–1.2m), S 2ft (60cm).

☼ ◖ ❊❊❊ 4–8

Rehmannia elata
Straggling perennial bearing foxglovelike, yellow-throated, rose-purple flowers in leaf axils of notched, stem-clasping, soft leaves from early to mid-summer. H 3ft (1m), S 18in (45cm). Min. 34°F (1°C).

☼ ◊ 9–10

Kohleria digitaliflora
Erect, bushy, rhizomatous perennial with white-haired stems. Has scalloped, hairy leaves and stalked clusters of tubular, very hairy, pink-and-white flowers, with purple-spotted, green lobes, in summer-autumn. H 24in (60cm) or more, S 18in (45cm). Min. 59°F (15°C).

☼ ◊ 10

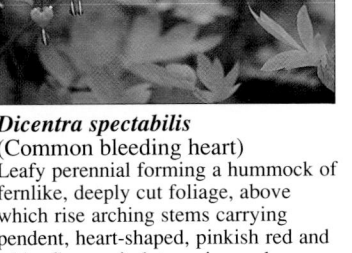

Dicentra spectabilis
(Common bleeding heart)
Leafy perennial forming a hummock of
fernlike, deeply cut foliage, above
which rise arching stems carrying
pendent, heart-shaped, pinkish red and
white flowers in late spring and
summer. H 30in (75cm), S 20in (50cm).

☼ ◐ ❋❋❋ 4–8

Phlox paniculata 'Harlequin'
Upright perennial that produces
conical heads of reddish purple flowers
in late summer. Foliage is variegated
ivory white. H 3–4ft (1–1.2m),
S 1½ft (45cm).

☼ ◑ ❋❋❋ 4–8

Lythrum salicaria 'Firecandle'
Clump-forming perennial for a
waterside or bog garden. Bears slender
spikes of intense rose-red blooms from
mid- to late summer. Small, lance-
shaped leaves are borne on flower
stems. H 3ft (1m), S 18in (45cm).

☼ ◐ ❋❋❋ 4–9

Mirabilis jalapa (Marvel-of-Peru)
Bushy, tuberous perennial. Fragrant,
trumpet-shaped, crimson, pink, white,
or yellow flowers, opening in evening,
cover green foliage in summer. H 2–4ft
(60cm–1.2m), S 2–2½ft (60–75cm).

☼ ◊ ❋ 10

Phlox paniculata 'Brigadier'
Upright perennial that in late summer
carries conical heads of deep reddish
pink flowers, suffused orange, above
lance-shaped, dark green leaves.
H 4ft (1.2m), S 2ft (60cm).

☼ ◐ ❋❋❋ 4–8

Lythrum virgatum 'The Rocket'
Clump-forming perennial that carries
slender spikes of rose-red flowers
above green foliage during summer.
Good for a waterside or bog garden.
H 3ft (1m), S 1½ft (45cm).

☼ ◐ ❋❋❋ 4–9

Geranium psilostemon,
syn. *G. armenum*
(Armenian cranesbill)
Clump-forming perennial that has
broad, deeply cut leaves with good
autumn color and many cup-shaped,
single, black-centered, magenta flowers
in mid-summer. H and S 4ft (1.2m).

☼ ◊ ❋❋❋ 4–9

Lupinus 'Inverewe Red'
Upright perennial with divided, bright
green leaves. In early summer bears
tall, upright racemes of red flowers.
Cut back after flowering. May be
shortlived. H 3–4ft (1–1.2m),
S 2ft (60cm).

☼ ◊ ❋❋❋ 5–8

Pelargoniums

Pelargoniums are among the most popular and widely cultivated plants, grown throughout the world for their colorful flowers. They are mostly tolerant and adaptable, growing happily in pots or beds and flowering almost continuously in warm climates or under glass. To flower well, they need warmth, sunshine (without too much humidity), and well-drained soil.

Zonal—the common geranium: plants with rounded leaves, distinctively marked with a darker "zone," and single to double flowers.
Regal—shrubby plants with deeply serrated leaves and exotic, broadly trumpet-shaped flowers that are prone to weather damage in the open.
Ivy-leaved—trailing plants, ideal for hanging baskets, with lobed, somewhat fleshy leaves and single to double flowers.
Scented-leaved and **species**—plants with small, often irregularly star-shaped flowers; scented-leaved forms are grown for their fragrant leaves.

P. 'Alberta' (zonal)

P. 'Lesley Judd' (regal)

P. 'Ivalo' (zonal)

P. peltatum 'Lachs-königin' (ivy-leaved)

P. 'Mini Cascade' (ivy-leaved)

P. x *fragrans* (scented-leaved)

P. 'Mauritania' (zonal)

P. 'Dale Queen' (zonal)

P. 'Purple Emperor' (regal)

P. 'Irene' (zonal)

P. 'Fraicher Beauty' (zonal)

P. 'Timothy Clifford' (zonal)

P. 'Schöne Helena' (zonal)

P. 'Francis Parrett' (zonal)

P. 'Tip Top Duet' (regal)

P. peltatum 'Tavira' (ivy-leaved)

P. 'Rollinson's Unique' (unclassified)

P. 'Mr. Henry Cox' (zonal)

P. frutetorum 'The Boar' (zonal)

P. 'Autumn Festival' (regal)

P. peltatum 'Amethyst' (ivy-leaved)

P. 'Manx Maid' (regal)

P. 'Rouletta' (ivy-leaved)

P. 'Friesdorf' (zonal)

P. 'Paul Humphris' (zonal)

P. 'Bredon' (regal)

P. 'Mme. Fournier'
(zonal)

P. 'Caligula'
(zonal)

P. 'Dolly Varden'
(zonal)

P. 'Flower of Spring'
(zonal)

P. 'Mrs. Pollock'
(zonal)

P. 'Orange Ricard'
(zonal)

P. 'Royal Oak'
(scented-leaved)

P. capitatum
(scented-leaved)

P. 'Purple Unique'
(unclassified)

P. 'Mabel Grey'
(scented-leaved)

P. 'Mrs. Quilter'
(zonal)

P. 'Elégante'
(ivy-leaved)

P. tomentosum
(scented-leaved)

P. crispum 'Variega-tum' (scented-leaved)

Perennials/medium SUMMER INTEREST

◻ RED

Penstemon 'Garnet'
Vigorous, semi-evergreen, bushy
perennial bearing sprays of tubular,
deep wine red flowers from mid-
summer to autumn. Has narrow, fresh
green leaves. H 2–2¹/₂ft (60–75cm),
S 2ft (60cm).

☼ ◊ ❀❀ 4–9

Filipendula purpurea
Upright perennial with deeply divided
leaves. Produces large, terminal heads
of masses of tiny, rich reddish purple
flowers in summer. Makes a good
waterside plant. H 4ft (1.2m),
S 2ft (60cm).

◑ ◉ ❀❀❀ 4–9

Centranthus ruber (Red valerian)
Perennial forming loose clumps of
fleshy leaves. Branching heads of small,
star-shaped, deep reddish pink or white
flowers are borne above foliage from
late spring to autumn. Thrives in poor,
exposed conditions. H 2–3ft (60cm–1m),
S 1¹/₂–2ft (45–60cm) or more.

☼ ◊ ❀❀❀ 5–9

■ RED

Aquilegia vulgaris 'Nora Barlow'
Leafy perennial that in summer has several short-spurred, funnel-shaped, double, red flowers, pale green at the tips, on long stems. Leaves are gray-green, rounded, and deeply divided. H 24–30in (60–75cm), S 20in (50cm).

☼ ◊ ✻✻✻ 5–9

Polygonum amplexicaule 'Firetail'
Clump-forming perennial that carries slender spikes of bright red flowers above heart-shaped leaves in summer-autumn. H and S 3–4ft (1–1.2m).

☼ ◐ ✻✻✻ 5–9

Astilbe 'Montgomery'
Leafy perennial bearing feathery, tapering plumes of tiny, deep salmon red flowers in summer. Foliage is broad and divided into leaflets; flowers, brown when dried, remain on the plant well into winter. Prefers humus-rich soil. H 2¹/₂ft (75cm), S to 3ft (1m).

◐ ◐ ✻✻✻ 5–8

Knautia macedonica,
syn. *Scabiosa rumelica*
Upright perennial with deeply divided leaves and many rather lax, branching stems bearing double, almost globular, bright crimson flower heads in summer. Needs staking. H 2¹/₂ft (75cm), S 2ft (60cm).

☼ ◊ ✻✻✻ 5–9

Cosmos atrosanguineus,
syn. *Bidens atrosanguinea*
Upright, tuberous perennial with chocolate-scented, maroon-crimson flower heads in late summer. In warm sites tubers may overwinter if protected. H 24in (60cm) or more, S 18in (45cm).

☼ ◊ ✻ 7–9

Polygonum milletii
Compact perennial that produces slender spikes of rich crimson flowers above narrow leaves from mid-summer to early autumn. H and S 2ft (60cm) or more.

☼ ◐ ✻✻✻ 5–9

Lobelia 'Cherry Ripe'
Clump-forming perennial bearing spikes of cerise-scarlet flowers from mid- to late summer. Leaves, usually fresh green, are often tinged red-bronze. H 3ft (1m), S 9in (23cm).

☼ ◊ ✻ 3–8

Hemerocallis 'Stafford'
Vigorous, clump-forming perennial that from mid- to late summer bears trumpet-shaped, bright red flowers, with maroon and yellow throats and a narrow, yellow midrib on each petal, that last only a day. Leaves are strap-shaped. H 2¹/₂ft (75cm), S 2ft (60cm).

☼ ◊ ✻✻✻ 3–9

Lobelia 'Queen Victoria'
Clump-forming perennial. From late summer to mid-autumn spikes of blazing red flowers on branching stems arise from basal, deep red-purple foliage. H 3ft (1m), S 1ft (30cm).

☼ ◊ ✻ 3–8

Ruellia graecizans, syn. *R. amoena*
Evergreen, bushy sub-shrub with wide-spreading stems. Oval, pointed leaves are 4in (10cm) long. Intermittently bears clusters of small, tubular, scarlet flowers on stalks to 4in (10cm) long. H and S 2ft (60cm) or more. Min. 59°F (15°C).

◐ ◊ 9–10

Hedysarum coronarium
(French honeysuckle)
Spreading, shrubby perennial or
biennial. Spikes of pealike, bright red
flowers are produced in summer above
divided, green leaves. H and
S 3ft (1m).

☼ ◊ ❋❋❋ 4–9

Russelia equisetiformis,
syn. *R. juncea* (Coral plant)
Evergreen, branching, bushy sub-shrub
with rushlike stems and tiny leaves.
Showy, pendent clusters of tubular,
scarlet flowers appear in summer-
autumn. H to 3ft (1m) or more, S 2ft
(60cm). Min. 59°F (15°C).

☼ ◊ 5–9

Anigozanthos manglesii
Vigorous, bushy perennial that bears
racemes of large, tubular, woolly, red-
and-green flowers in spring and early
summer. Has long, narrow, gray-green
leaves. May suffer from ink disease.
H 3ft (1m), S 18in (45cm).

☼ ◊ pH ❋ 10

Kohleria eriantha
Robust, bushy, rhizomatous perennial
with reddish-haired stems. Oval
leaves, to 5in (13cm) long, are edged
with red hairs. Has tubular, red
flowers, with yellow-spotted lobes, in
nodding clusters in summer. H and S
3ft (1m) or more. Min. 59°F (15°C).

☼◖ ◊ 9–10

**Monarda didyma 'Cambridge
Scarlet'**
Clump-forming perennial that
throughout summer bears whorls of
hooded, rich red flowers above neat
mounds of aromatic, hairy foliage.
H 3ft (1m), S 18in (45cm).

☼ ◊ ❋❋❋ 4–8

Papaver orientale 'Allegro Viva'
Hairy-leaved perennial with very deep,
fleshy roots. Papery, bright scarlet
flowers are borne in summer on strong
stems. H 24–30in (60–75cm),
S 18in (45cm).

Glycyrrhiza glabra (Licorice)
Upright perennial that has pealike,
purple-blue and white flowers, borne
in short spikes on erect stems in late
summer, and large leaves divided into
oval leaflets. Is grown commercially
for production of licorice. H 4ft
(1.2m), S 3ft (1m).

☼ ◊ ❋❋❋ 9–10

Columnea × banksii
Evergreen, trailing perennial with oval,
fleshy leaves, glossy above, purplish
red below. Tubular, hooded, brilliant
red flowers, to 3in (8cm) long, appear
from spring to winter. Makes a useful
plant for a hanging basket. H 3ft
(90cm), S indefinite. Min. 59°F (15°C).

☼ ◊ 10

☼ ◊ ❋❋❋ 4–9

Acanthus hungaricus,
syn. *A. longifolius*
Perennial with long, deeply cut, basal,
dark green leaves. Spikes of white or
pink-flushed flowers, set in spiny, red-
purple bracts, are carried in summer.
H 2–3ft (60cm–1m), S 3ft (1m).

☼ ◊ ❋❋❋ 7–9

Perennials/medium SUMMER INTEREST

■ PURPLE

Acanthus spinosus
(Spiny bear's breech)
Stately perennial that has very large, arching, deeply cut and spiny-pointed, glossy, dark green leaves. Spires of funnel-shaped, soft mauve and white flowers are borne freely in summer. H 4ft (1.2m), S 2ft (60cm) or more.

☼ ○ ❄❄❄ 5–9

***Phlox paniculata* 'Norah Leigh'**
Upright perennial with ivory-variegated, green leaves, above which conical heads of pale lilac flowers are borne in summer. H 3ft (1m), S 2ft (60cm).

☼ ● ❄❄❄ 4–8

Linaria triornithophora
(Three-birds-flying)
Upright perennial that from early to late summer produces spikes of snapdragonlike, purple and yellow flowers above narrow, gray-green leaves. H 3ft (1m), S 2ft (60cm).

☼ ○ ❄❄ 6–9

Monarda fistulosa
(Wild bergamot)
Clump-forming perennial that produces small heads of lilac-purple flowers from mid- to late summer. H 4ft (1.2m), S 18in (45cm).

☼ ● ❄❄❄ 4–8

***Geranium sylvaticum* 'Mayflower'**
(Forest-loving geranium)
Upright perennial with a basal clump of deeply lobed leaves, above which rise branching stems of cup-shaped, violet-blue flowers in early summer. H 3ft (1m), S 2ft (60cm).

◑ ○ ❄❄❄ 4–8

Thalictrum aquilegiifolium
(Columbine, Meadow rue)
Clump-forming perennial with a mass of finely divided, gray-green leaves, resembling those of maidenhair fern. Bunched heads of fluffy, lilac-purple flowers are borne in summer. H 3–4ft (1–1.2m), S 18in (45cm).

☼ ○ ❄❄❄ 5–9

***Campanula glomerata* 'Superba'**
Vigorous, clump-forming perennial with dense, rounded heads of large, bell-shaped, purple flowers borne in summer. Bears oval leaves in basal rosettes and on flower stems. Must be divided and replanted regularly. H 2½ft (75cm), S 3ft (1m) or more.

☼ ○ ❄❄❄ 3–8

***Veronica longifolia* 'Romiley Purple'**
Clump-forming perennial that in summer freely produces large spikes of purple flowers above whorled, green leaves. H 3–4ft (1–1.2m), S 1–2ft (30–60cm).

☼ ○ ❄❄❄ 4–8

Campanula trachelium
(Nettle-leaved bluebell)
Upright perennial with rough, serrated, oval, pointed, basal leaves. Wide, bell-shaped, blue or purple-blue flowers are spaced along erect stems in summer. H 2–3ft (60cm–1m), S 1ft (30cm).

 ☼ ◊ ❋❋❋ 5–8

Dichorisandra reginae
Evergreen, erect, clump-forming perennial. Glossy, often silver-banded and flecked leaves are purple-red beneath. Has small spikes of densely set, purple-blue flowers in summer-autumn. H 2–2½ft (60–75cm), S to 1ft (30cm). Min. 68°F (20°C).

 ◐ ◊ 10

Echinops ritro 'Veitch's Blue'
Upright perennial with round, thistlelike, purplish blue heads of flowers carried in late summer on silvery stems. Sharply divided leaves have pale down beneath. H 4ft (1.2m), S 2½ft (75cm).

 ☼ ◊ ❋❋❋ 4–9

Galega orientalis (Goat's rue)
Vigorous, upright but compact perennial that in summer bears spikes of pealike, blue-tinged, violet flowers above delicate leaves divided into oval leaflets. Needs staking. Spreads freely. H 4ft (1.2m), S 2ft (60cm).

☼ ◊ ❋❋❋ 5–8

Campanula trachelium 'Bernice'
Upright perennial that has wide, bell-shaped, double, purple-violet flowers carried along erect stems in summer. Leaves are mostly basal and are rough, serrated, oval, and pointed. H 2½ft (75cm), S 1ft (30cm).

☼ ◊ ❋❋❋ 5–8

Salvia nemorosa 'May Night',
syn. *S.* x *superba* 'May Night'
Neat, clump-forming perennial with narrow, wrinkled leaves. In late spring and summer bears stiff racemes of violet-blue flowers. H 3ft (1m), S 18in (45cm).

 ☼ ◊ ❋❋❋ 5–9

Aconitum x **bicolor**
Compact, tuberous perennial with hooded, violet-blue and white flowers borne in summer along upright, sometimes branching stems. Has deeply cut, divided, glossy, dark green leaves and poisonous roots. H 4ft (1.2m), S 20in (50cm).

 ☼ ◊ ❋❋❋ 5–8

Baptisia australis
(Blue false indigo)
Upright perennial bearing spikes of pealike, violet-blue flowers in summer. Bright green leaves are divided into oval leaflets. Dark gray seed pods may be used for winter decoration. H 2½ft (75cm), S 2ft (60cm).

☼ ◊ ❋❋❋ 4–9

■■ PURPLE–BLUE

Dianella tasmanica
Upright perennial with nodding, star-shaped, bright blue or purple-blue flowers carried in branching sprays in summer, followed by deep blue berries in autumn. Has untidy, evergreen, strap-shaped leaves. H 4ft (1.2m), S 20in (50cm).

☀ ◊ ❀❀ 9–10

Eryngium alpinum
Upright perennial with basal rosettes of heart-shaped, deeply toothed, glossy foliage, above which rise stout stems bearing, in summer, heads of conical, purplish blue flowers, surrounded by blue bracts and soft spines. H 2¹/₂–3ft (75cm–1m), S 2ft (60cm).

☀ ◊ ❀❀❀ 5–8

Eryngium tripartitum
Perennial with wiry stems above a basal rosette of coarsely toothed, gray-green leaves. Conical, metallic blue flower heads on blue stems are borne in summer-autumn and may be dried for winter decoration. H 3–4ft (1–1.2m), S 20in (50cm).

☀ ◊ ❀❀❀ 5–8

Meconopsis grandis 'Branklyn'
Erect perennial that carries large, pendent, poppylike, blue flowers on stout stems in early summer. Erect, oblong, slightly toothed, and hairy leaves are produced at the base of the plant. H 3–4ft (1–1.2m), S 1–1¹/₂ft (30–45cm).

☀ ◊ ᵖᴴ ❀❀❀ 8

Eryngium x oliverianum
Upright perennial that produces large, rounded heads of thistlelike, blue to lavender blue flowers in late summer. Has heart-shaped, jagged-edged, basal, green leaves. H 2–3ft (60cm–1m), S 1¹/₂–2ft (45–60cm).

☀ ◊ ❀❀❀ 5–8

Campanula persicifolia 'Telham Beauty'
Perennial with basal rosettes of narrow, bright green leaves. In summer, large, nodding, cup-shaped, light blue flowers are borne on slender spikes. H 3ft (1m), S 1ft (30cm).

☀ ◊ ❀❀❀ 4–8

Cichorium intybus
(Chicory, Escarole)
Clump-forming perennial with basal rosettes of light green leaves and daisy-like, bright blue flower heads borne along upper parts of willowy stems in summer. Flowers are at their best before noon. H 4ft (1.2m), S 18in (45cm).

☀ ◊ ❀❀❀ 4–8

Meconopsis betonicifolia
(Himalayan blue poppy)
Clump-forming perennial that bears blue flowers in late spring and early summer. Oblong, green leaves are produced in basal rosettes and in decreasing size up flowering stems. H 3–4ft (1–1.2m), S 1¹/₂ft (45cm).

☀ ◊ ᵖᴴ ❀❀❀ 8

Agapanthus 'Dorothy Palmer'
Clump-forming perennial bearing rounded heads of rich blue flowers, fading to reddish mauve, on erect stems in late summer. Leaves are narrow and grayish green. Protect crowns in winter with mulch. H 3ft (1m), S 20in (50cm).

☀ ◊ ❀❀ 8–10

Agapanthus praecox subsp. **orientalis**, syn. *A. orientalis*
Perennial with large, dense umbels of sky blue flowers borne on strong stems in late summer over clumps of broad, almost evergreen, dark green leaves. Makes a good plant for pots. H 3ft (1m), S 2ft (60cm).

☼ ◊ ✤ 9–10

Cynoglossum nervosum
(Great hound's tongue)
Clump-forming perennial with bright blue flowers, similar to forget-me-nots, carried in small clusters on branching stems in summer over narrow, green leaves. H 30in (75cm), S 20in (50cm).

☼ ◊ ✤✤✤ 5–8

Anchusa azurea 'Loddon Royalist'
Upright perennial that bears flat, single, deep blue flowers on branching spikes in early summer. Most of the lance-shaped, coarse, hairy leaves are at the base of plant. Needs staking. H 4ft (1.2m), S 2ft (60cm).

☼ ◊ ✤✤✤ 4–8

Rheum alexandrae
Clump-forming perennial with panicles of cream flowers, opening in early summer, that are hidden by large, greenish white to cream bracts, which turn to red. Leaves are glossy and dark green. H 3ft (1m), S 2ft (60cm).

☼ ◊ ✤✤✤ 6–8

Anigozanthos flavidus
Bushy perennial with racemes of large, woolly, tubular, sometimes red-tinged, yellowish green flowers, with reddish anthers, borne in spring-summer. Narrow leaves, to 2ft (60cm) long, are green. H 4ft (1.2m), S 18 in (45cm).

☼ ◊ pH ✤ 10

Nepeta govaniana
Upright, well-branched perennial. During summer, sprays of long, tubular, pale yellow flowers are borne above a mass of pointed, gray-green leaves. H 3ft (1m), S 2ft (60cm).

☼ ◊ ✤✤✤ 5–9

Verbascum 'Gainsborough'
Semi-evergreen, rosette-forming, short-lived perennial bearing branched racemes of 5-lobed, pale sulfur yellow flowers throughout summer above oval, green leaves borne on flower stems. H 2–4ft (60cm–1.2m), S 1–2ft (30–60cm).

☼ ◊ ✤✤✤ 5–9

Thalictrum lucidum
Perennial with glossy leaves composed of numerous leaflets. Strong stems bear loose panicles of fluffy, greenish yellow flowers in summer. H 3–4ft (1–1.2m), S 20in (50cm).

☼ ◊ ✤✤✤ 6–9

☐ YELLOW

Chrysanthemum frutescens 'Jamaica Primrose'
Evergreen, woody-based, bushy perennial with divided, fernlike, pale green leaves and many daisylike, single, soft yellow flower heads borne throughout summer. Treat as an annual in cold climates. H and S to 3ft (1m).

☼ ◊ ✿ 9–10

Aconitum vulparia, syn. *A. lycoctonum*
Upright, fibrous perennial with hooded, straw yellow flowers borne on wiry, branching stems in summer. Leaves are dark green and deeply divided. Needs staking. H 3–4ft (1–1.2m), S 1–2ft (30–60cm).

☼ ◊ ✿✿✿ 5–8

Hemerocallis 'Marion Vaughn'
Clump-forming perennial that in mid-summer bears fragrant, trumpet-shaped, green-throated, pale lemon yellow flowers, lasting only a day. Each petal has a raised, near-white midrib. Leaves are strap-shaped. H 3ft (1m), S 2ft (60cm).

☼ ◑ ◊ ✿✿✿ 3–9

Lysimachia punctata
Clump-forming perennial that in summer produces spikes of bright yellow flowers above green leaves. H 2–2¹/₂ft (60–75cm), S 2ft (60cm).

☼ ◊ ✿✿✿ 5–8

Anthemis tinctoria 'E.C. Buxton'
Clump-forming perennial with a mass of daisylike, lemon yellow flower heads borne singly in summer on slim stems. Cut back hard after flowering to promote a good rosette of crinkled leaves for winter. H and S 3ft (1m).

☼ ◊ ✿✿✿ 4–8

Gentiana lutea
Erect, unbranched perennial with oval, stalkless leaves to 30cm (1ft) long. In summer has dense whorls of tubular, yellow flowers in axils of greenish bracts. H 3–4ft (1–1.2m), S 2ft (60cm).

☼ ◊ ✿✿✿ 7–8

Phlomis russeliana
(Sticky Jerusalem sage)
Evergreen perennial, forming excellent ground cover, with large, rough, heart-shaped leaves. Stout flower stems bear whorls of hooded, butter yellow flowers in summer. H 3ft (1m), S 2ft (60cm) or more.

☼ ◊ ✿✿✿ 5–9

Hemerocallis lilio-asphodelus, syn. *H. flava* (Lemon daylily)
Robust, clump-forming, spreading perennial. Very fragrant, delicate, lemon to chrome yellow flowers last only 1 or 2 days in late spring and early summer. Leaves are strap-shaped. H and S 2ft (60cm) or more.

☼ ◊ ✿✿✿ 3–9

Solidago 'Laurin'
Compact perennial bearing spikes of deep yellow flowers in late summer. H 24–30in (60–75cm), S 18in (45 cm).

☼ ◊ ✿✿✿ 4–9

Inula hookeri
Clump-forming perennial with lance-shaped to elliptic, hairy leaves and a mass of slightly scented, daisylike, greenish yellow flower heads borne in summer. H 30in (75cm), S 18in (45cm).

☼ ◊ ✿✿✿ 4–8

Solidago 'Goldenmosa'
Clump-forming perennial. Sprays of tufted, mimosalike, yellow flower heads are carried in late summer and autumn above lance-shaped, toothed, hairy, yellowish green leaves. H 3ft (1m), S 2ft (60cm).

☼ ◊ ✿✿✿ 4–9

Hemerocallis citrina
Vigorous, coarse-growing, clump-forming perennial. Many large, very fragrant, trumpet-shaped, rich lemon yellow flowers, lasting only a day, open at night in mid-summer. Strap-shaped leaves are dark green. H and S 2¹/₂ft (75cm).

☼ ◊ ✿✿✿ 3–9

Thermopsis montana
Upright perennial bearing spikes of bright yellow flowers above divided, green leaves in summer. H 2–3ft (60cm–1m), S 2ft (60cm).

☼ ◊ ✿✿✿ 3–8

Achillea 'Coronation Gold'
Upright perennial with feathery, silvery leaves. Bears large, flat heads of small, golden flower heads in summer that dry well for winter decoration. Should be divided and replanted every third year. H 3ft (1m), S 2ft (60cm).

☼ ◊ ✿✿✿ 4–8

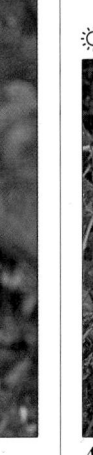

Verbascum nigrum
Semi-evergreen, clump-forming perennial bearing narrow spikes of small, 5-lobed, purple-centered, yellow flowers during summer and autumn. Oblong, green leaves are downy beneath. H 2–3ft (60cm–1m), S 2ft (60cm).

☼ ◊ ✿✿✿ 6–8

Berkheya macrocephala
Upright perennial bearing large, daisylike, yellow flower heads on branched, spiny-leaved stems. Prefers rich soil and a warm, sheltered position. H and S 3ft (1m).

☼ ◊ ✿✿ 9–10

Rudbeckia fulgida 'Goldsturm'
Erect perennial. In late summer and autumn, daisylike, golden flower heads with conical, black centers are borne at the ends of strong stems. Has narrow, rough, green leaves. H 30in (75cm), S 12in (30cm) or more.

☼ ◖ ✿✿✿ 4–9

Aphelandra squarrosa 'Louisae'
Evergreen, erect perennial. Long, oval, glossy, slightly wrinkled, dark green leaves have white veins and midribs. Bears dense spikes of golden yellow flowers from axils of yellow bracts in late summer to autumn. H to 3ft (1m), S 2ft (60cm). Min. 55°F (13°C).

☼ ◖ 10

Achillea filipendulina 'Gold Plate'
Upright perennial with stout, leafy stems carrying broad, flat, terminal heads of yellow flowers in summer, above filigree foliage. Flower heads retain color if dried. Divide plants regularly. H 4ft (1.2m) or more, S 2ft (60cm).

☼ ◊ ✿✿✿ 4–8

☐ YELLOW

Heliopsis 'Ballet Dancer'
Upright perennial flowering freely in
late summer and bearing double, yellow
flower heads with frilled petals. Dark
green leaves are coarse and serrated.
H 3–4ft (1–1.2m), S 2ft (60cm).

☼ ◊ ❋❋❋ 4–9

Hemerocallis 'Golden Chimes'
Graceful, clump-forming perennial
producing small, delicate, trumpet-
shaped, golden yellow flowers with a
brown reverse, lasting only a day, from
early to mid-summer. Has narrow,
strap-shaped, green leaves. H 2½ft
(75cm), S 2ft (60cm).

☼ ◕ ❋❋❋ 4–9

Kniphofia 'Royal Standard'
Upright perennial with grasslike, basal
tufts of leaves and terminal spikes of
scarlet buds, opening to lemon yellow
flowers, borne on erect stems in late
summer. Protect crowns with winter
mulch. H 3–4ft (1–1.2m), S 2ft (60cm).

☼ ◊ ❋❋ 5–9

☐ ORANGE

Sphaeralcea ambigua
Branching, shrubby perennial. Broadly
funnel-shaped, orange-coral blooms are
produced singly in leaf axils from
summer until the onset of cold weather.
Leaves are soft and hairy. H and
S 2½–3ft (75cm–1m).

☼ ◊ ❋ 9–10

Kniphofia thomsonii var.
snowdenii
Upright perennial, with grasslike, basal
foliage. In summer bears coral pink
flowers, with yellowish interiors,
spaced widely along terminal spikes.
Protect crowns with winter mulch.
H 3ft (1m), S 20in (50cm).

☼ ◊ ❋❋ 5–9

Hemerocallis fulva 'Kwanso
Flore Plena'
Vigorous, clump-forming perennial
that from mid- to late summer carries
trumpet-shaped, double, tawny-orange
blooms, which last only a day. Strap-
shaped leaves are light green. H 3ft
(1m), S 2½ft (75cm).

☼ ◕ ❋❋❋ 3–9

Asclepias tuberosa
(Butterfly weed)
Erect, tuberous perennial with long,
lance-shaped leaves. Small, 5-horned,
bright orange-red flowers are borne
in summer and followed by narrow,
pointed pods, to 6in (15cm) long.
H to 30in (75cm), S 18in (45cm).

☼ ◊ ❋❋❋ 4–9

Euphorbia griffithii 'Fireglow'
Bushy perennial that bears orange-red
flowers in terminal umbels in early
summer. Leaves are lance-shaped,
green and have pale red midribs. H to
3ft (1m), S 20in (50cm).

☼ ◊ ❋❋❋ 4–9

Lychnis chalcedonica
(Maltese-cross)
Neat, clump-forming perennial that
bears flat heads of small, vermilion
flowers at the tips of stout stems in
early summer. H 3–4ft (1–1.2m),
S 12–18in (30–45cm).

☼ ◊ ❋❋❋ 4–8

☐ WHITE–PINK

☐ PINK

Aster vimineus 'Delight'
Spreading perennial bearing clusters of small, daisylike, white flower heads in autumn. Leaves are narrow and lance-shaped. Needs staking. H 4ft (1.2m), S 3ft (1m) or more.

☼ ◊ ✤✤✤ 5–8

Actaea pachypoda, syn. A. alba
(White baneberry, White cohosh)
Compact, clump-forming perennial with spikes of small, fluffy, white flowers in summer and clusters of white berries, borne on stiff, fleshy, scarlet stalks, in autumn. H 3ft (1m), S 20in (50cm).

☀ ◐ ✤✤✤ 4–9

Aster ericoides 'White Heather'
Bushy perennial providing long-lasting sprays of neat, daisylike, white flower heads in late autumn. Has small, lance-shaped, fresh green leaves and wiry, branching stems, which may need support. H 30in (75cm), S 20in (50cm).

☼ ◊ ✤✤✤ 5–8

Polygonum campanulatum
Compact, mat-forming perennial bearing elegant, branching heads of bell-shaped, pink or white flowers from mid-summer to early autumn. Has oval leaves, brown-felted beneath. H and S 3ft (1m).

☀ ◐ ✤✤✤ 5–9

Chrysanthemum rubellum
'Clara Curtis'
Bushy perennial producing many clusters of flat, daisylike, clear pink flower heads throughout summer and autumn. Divide plants every other spring. H 30in (75cm), S 18in (45cm).

☼ ◊ ✤✤✤ 5–9

Aster novae-angliae
'Herbstschnee'
Compact, upright perennial producing clusters of daisylike, white flower heads with yellow centers in autumn. Leaves are lance-shaped and dull green. May need some staking. H 2¹/₂–3¹/₂ft (75cm–1.1m), S to 2ft (60cm).

☼ ◊ ✤✤✤ 5–8

Aster cordifolius 'Silver Spray'
Bushy perennial with dense, arching stems producing graceful sprays of small, pink-tinged, white flower heads in autumn. Green leaves are lance-shaped with cordate bases. Needs staking. H 4ft (1.2m), S 3ft (1m).

☼ ◊ ✤✤✤ 5–8

Anemone hupehensis
Branching perennial that bears soft pink flowers, with rounded petals, in late summer and early autumn. Leaves are dark green and deeply divided, with toothed leaflets. H 2–2¹/₂ft (60–75cm), S 18in (45cm).

◑ ◊ ✤✤ 5–9

Chelone obliqua (Red turtlehead)
Upright perennial that bears terminal spikes of hooded, lilac-pink flowers in late summer and autumn. Leaves are dark green and lance-shaped. H 3ft (1m), S 20in (50cm).

◑ ◐ ✤✤✤ 5–9

Chrysanthemums

Florists' chrysanthemum hybrids are excellent for garden decoration, cutting, and for exhibition. They are grouped according to their differing flower forms, approximate flowering season (early, mid-, or late autumn), and habit (see the Plant Dictionary for more information). The best groups for garden decoration are the sprays, pompons, and early reflexed chrysanthemums. The dwarf charms, forming a dense, dome-shaped mass of flowers, look most attractive displayed in pots. Most groups have only one large flower per stem, although the sprays, charms, and pompons have several. The various flower forms are described below.

Incurved—fully double, dense, spherical flowers have incurved petals arising from the base of the flower and closing tightly over the crown.

Fully reflexed—fully double flowers have curved, pointed petals reflexing outwards and downwards from the crown, back to touch the stem.

Reflexed—fully double flowers are similar to those of fully reflexed forms except that the petals are less strongly reflexed and form an umbrellalike or spiky outline.

Intermediate—fully double, roughly spherical flowers have loosely incurving petals, which may close at the crown or may reflex for the bottom half of each flower.

Anemone-centered—single flowers each have a central, dome-shaped disc, up to half the bloom width, and up to 5 rows of flat or occasionally spoon-type ray petals at right angles to the stem.

Single—flowers each have about 5 rows of flat petals borne at right angles to the stem, that may incurve or reflex at the tips; the prominent, central disc is golden throughout or has a small, green center.

Pompon—fully double, dense, spherical, or occasionally hemispherical, flowers have tubular petals with flat, rounded tips, growing outwards from the crown.

Spoon-type—flowers are similar to those of single forms except that the ray petals are tubular and open out at their tips to form a spoon shape.

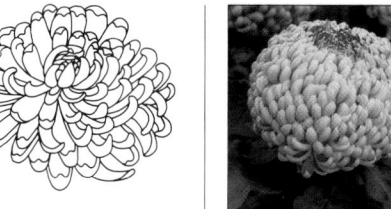
C. **'Salmon Fairweather'** (incurved)

C. **'Madeleine'** (spray, reflexed)

C. **'Roblush'** (spray, reflexed)

C. **'Brietner'** (reflexed)

C. **'Dorridge Dream'** (incurved)

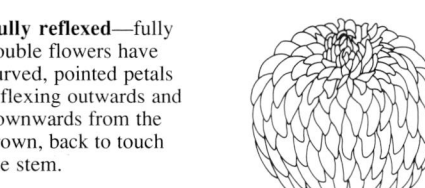
C. **'Pavilion'** (intermediate)

C. **'Dawn Mist'** (spray, single)

C. **'Alison Kirk'** (incurved)

C. **'Duke of Kent'** (reflexed)

C. **'Marian Gosling'** (reflexed)

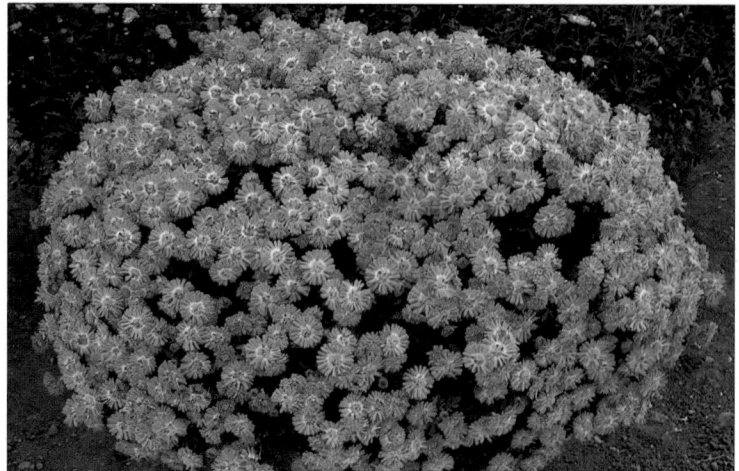
C. **'Pennine Flute'** (spray, spoon-type)

C. **'Cloudbank'** (spray, anemone)

C. **'Michael Fish'** (intermediate)

C. **'Pennine Oriel'** (spray, anemone)

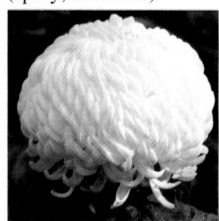

C. **'Ringdove'** (charm)

C. **'Talbot Jo'**
(spray, single)

C. **'Chippendale'**
(reflexed)

C. **'Rose Yvonne Arnaud'** (reflexed)

C. **'Yellow John Hughes'** (incurved)

C. **'Wendy'**
(spray, reflexed)

C. **'Bronze Hedgerow'**
(single)

C. **'Skater's Waltz'**
(intermediate)

C. **'Sentry'**
(reflexed)

C. **'Discovery'**
(intermediate)

C. **'Edwin Painter'**
(single)

C. **'Sally Ball'**
(spray, anemone)

C. **'Peach Margaret'**
(spray, reflexed)

C. **'Yvonne Arnaud'**
(reflexed)

C. **'George Griffiths'**
(reflexed)

C. **'Marlene Jones'**
(intermediate)

C. **'Yellow Brietner'**
(reflexed)

C. **'Peach Brietner'**
(reflexed)

C. **'Purple Pennine Wine'** (spray, reflexed)

C. **'Redwing'**
(spray, single)

C. **'Primrose West Bromwich'** (reflexed)

C. **'Pennine Alfie'**
(spray, spoon-type)

C. **'Golden Woolman's Glory'** (single)

C. **'Bronze Fairie'**
(pompon)

C. **'Bronze Yvonne Arnaud'** (reflexed)

C. **'Salmon Margaret'**
(spray, reflexed)

C. **'Autumn Days'**
(intermediate)

C. **'Maria'**
(pompon)

C. **'Green Satin'**
(intermediate)

C. **'Pennine Jewel'**
(spray, spoon-type)

C. **'Salmon Fairie'**
(pompon)

C. **'Oracle'**
(intermediate)

C. **'Cherry Chintz'**
(reflexed)

C. **'Marion'**
(spray, reflexed)

C. **'Rytorch'**
(spray, single)

C. **'Buff Margaret'**
(spray, reflexed)

Perennials/medium

Aster novi-belgii 'Orlando'
Upright perennial that in autumn carries panicles of large, daisylike, bright pink flower heads with golden centers. Small, lance-shaped, dark green leaves are borne on flower stems. Spray regularly as prone to mildew. May need staking. H 3ft (1m), S to 18in (45cm).

☼ ◊ ❋❋❋ 4–8

Strobilanthes atropurpureus
Upright, branching perennial with oval, toothed leaves. Spikes of numerous, violet-blue to purple flowers appear in summer-autumn. H to 4ft (1.2m), S to 2ft (60cm).

☼◗ ◊ ❋❋ 7–9

Aster novi-belgii 'Marie Ballard'
Upright perennial carrying panicles of large, daisylike, double, blue flower heads in autumn. Spray regularly as is prone to mildew. May need staking. H 3ft (1m), S to 18in (45cm).

☼ ◊ ❋❋❋ 4–8

Gentiana asclepiadea
(Willow gentian)
Arching perennial with narrow, oval leaves to 3in (8cm) long. In late summer to autumn has arching sprays of trumpet-shaped, deep blue flowers, spotted and striped inside. H to 3ft (90cm), S to 2ft (60cm).

☼◗ ◗ ❋❋❋ 6–9

Aster novi-belgii 'Carnival'
Upright perennial bearing panicles of large, daisylike, double, cerise-red flower heads with yellow centers in autumn. Small, lance-shaped, dark green leaves are borne on flower stems. Is prone to mildew. May need staking. H 30in (75cm), S to 18in (45cm).

☼ ◊ ❋❋❋ 4–8

Aster x frikartii 'Mönch'
Bushy perennial that bears daisylike, soft lavender blue flower heads with yellowish green centers continuously from mid-summer to late autumn. Leaves are rough and oval. May need staking. H 30in (75cm), S 18in (45cm).

☼ ◊ ❋❋❋ 5–9

Tricyrtis formosana,
syn. *T. stolonifera*
Upright, rhizomatous perennial. In early autumn bears spurred flowers, heavily spotted with purplish pink and with yellow-tinged throats. Glossy, dark green leaves clasp stems.
H 2–3ft (60cm–1m), S 18in (45cm).

☼◗ ◗ ❋❋❋ 6–9

Aster turbinellus
Upright perennial with small, daisylike, violet flower heads borne in autumn in airy sprays on wiry stems. Leaves are narrow and lance-shaped. Is easy to grow and disease-resistant. H 4ft (1.2m), S 2ft (60cm).

☼ ◊ ❋❋❋ 4–8

Kniphofia 'Percy's Pride'
Upright perennial with large, terminal spikes of creamy flowers, tinged green and yellow, borne on erect stems in autumn. Protect crowns with winter mulch. H 3ft (1m), S 20in (50cm).

☼ ◊ ❋❋ 5–9

Kirengeshoma palmata
Upright perennial with rounded, lobed, bright green leaves, above which strong stems bearing clusters of narrowly funnel-shaped, creamy yellow flowers appear in late summer to autumn. H 3ft (1m), S 2ft (60cm).

☀ ◗ ❈❈❈ 5–8

Helenium 'Wyndley'
Bushy perennial with branching stems bearing sprays of daisylike, orange-yellow flower heads for a long period in late summer and autumn. Foliage is dark green. Needs regular division in spring or autumn. H 30in (75cm), S 20in (50cm).

☀ ◗ ❈❈❈ 4–8

Kniphofia caulescens
Stately, evergreen, upright perennial with basal tufts of narrow, blue-green leaves and smooth, stout stems bearing terminal spikes of reddish salmon flowers in autumn. H 4ft (1.2m), S 2ft (60cm).

☀ ◗ ❈❈ 6–9

Kniphofia triangularis,
syn. *K. galpinii*
Upright perennial with fine, grasslike, basal leaves and erect, wiry stems bearing small, terminal spikes of flame red flowers in autumn. Protect crowns with winter mulch. H to 3ft (1m), S 20in (50cm).

☀ ◗ ❈❈ 6–9

Helenium 'Moerheim Beauty'
Upright perennial with strong, branching stems bearing sprays of daisylike, rich reddish orange flower heads in early autumn above dark green foliage. Needs regular division in spring or autumn. H 3ft (1m), S 2ft (60cm).

☀ ◗ ❈❈❈ 4–8

Ctenanthe oppenheimiana 'Tricolor'
Robust, evergreen, bushy perennial. Has leathery, lance-shaped leaves, to over 12in (30cm) long, splashed with large, cream blotches, and, intermittently, spikes of 3-petaled, white flowers. H and S 3ft (1m). Min. 59°F (15°C).

☀ ◗ 10

Plectranthus coleoides 'Variegatus'
Evergreen, bushy perennial. Oval leaves, to 2½in (6cm) long, are grayish green with scalloped, white margins. Irregularly has tubular, white to pale mauve flowers. H and S 2ft (60cm) or more. Min. 50°F (10°C).

☀ ◗ 10

Dieffenbachia 'Exotica',
syn. *D. seguine* 'Exotica'
Evergreen, tufted perennial, sometimes woody at base. Broadly lance-shaped leaves, to 18in (45cm) long, have extensive, creamy white blotches. H and S 3ft (1m) or more. Min. 59°F (15°C).

☀ ◗ 10

Anthurium crystallinum
(Strap flower)
Evergreen, erect, tufted perennial. Long, velvety, dark green leaves are distinctively pale green- to white-veined. Has long-lasting, red-tinged, green spathes. H to 2½ft (75cm), S to 2ft (60cm). Min 59°F (15°C).

☀ ◗ 10

Hypoestes phyllostachya,
syn. *H. sanguinolenta* of gardens
(Freckle-face, Pink polka-dot plant)
Evergreen, bushy perennial or sub-shrub. Dark green leaves are covered with irregular, pink spots. Bears small, tubular, lavender flowers intermittently. H and S 30in (75cm). Min. 50°F (10°C).

☀ ◗ 9–10

Caladium x hortulanum 'Pink Beauty'
Tuberous perennial. Has long-stalked, triangular, pink-mottled, green leaves, to 18in (45cm) long, with darker pink veins. White spathes appear in summer. H and S 3ft (90cm). Min. 66°F (19°C).

☀ ◗ 10

Bromeliads

Bromeliads, or plants that belong to the family Bromeliaceae, are distinguished by their bold, usually rosetted foliage and showy flowers. Although many are epiphytes, or air plants (absorbing their food through moisture in the atmosphere and not from the host on which they grow), and are suitable for growing outdoors only in tropical regions, they will grow happily indoors in cooler climates.

Aechmea fasciata

Billbergia nutans

Bromelia balansae

Tillandsia lindenii

Cryptanthus zonatus 'Zebrinus'

Puya alpestris

Tillandsia caput-medusae

Ananas bracteatus 'Tricolor'

Aechmea distichantha

Neoregelia carolinae f. **tricolor**

Guzmania monostachia

Dyckia remotiflora

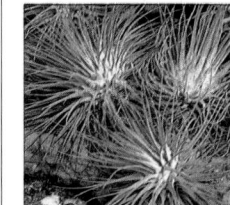

Tillandsia argentea

Aechmea 'Foster's Favorite'

Guzmania lingulata var. **minor**

Cryptanthus 'Pink Starlight'

Aechmea recurvata

Guzmania lingulata

Tillandsia fasciculata

Cryptanthus bivittatus

Tillandsia usneoides

Tillandsia stricta

Vriesea splendens

Neoregelia concentrica

Tillandsia cyanea

Puya chilensis

Perennials/medium

■ RED
■■■ PURPLE–GREEN

Anthurium andraeanum
(Flamingo lily)
Evergreen, erect perennial. Long-stalked, oval leaves, with a heart-shaped base, are 8in (20cm) long. Has long-lasting, bright red spathes with yellow spadices. H 24–30in (60–75cm), S 20in (50cm). Min. 59°F (15°C).

☼ ◊ 10

Phormium tenax 'Dazzler'
Evergreen, upright perennial with tufts of bold, stiff, pointed leaves in tones of yellow, salmon pink, orange-red, and bronze. Bluish purple stems carry panicles of reddish flowers in summer. H 6–8ft (2–2.5m) in flower, S 3ft (1m).

☼ ◊ ❋❋ 9–10

Nepenthes hookeriana
Evergreen, epiphytic, insectivorous perennial with oval, leathery leaves to 12in (30cm) long and pendent, pale green pitchers, each with reddish purple markings and a spurred lid, to 5in (13cm) long. H 2–2½ft (60–75cm). Min. 64°F (18°C).

☼ ◊ 10

Browallia speciosa
Bushy perennial, usually grown as an annual, propagated by seed each year. Has oval leaves to 4in (10cm) long and showy, violet-blue flowers with white eyes, the season depending when sown. H 24–30in (60–75cm), S 18in (45cm). Min. 50–59°F (10–15°C).

☼ ◊ 10

Alocasia cuprea (Giant caladium)
Evergreen, tufted perennial. Oval leaves are 12in (30cm) long, with a metallic sheen and darker, impressed veins above, purple below; leaf stalks arise from the lower surface. Purplish spathes appear intermittently. H and S to 3ft (1m). Min. 59°F (15°C).

☼ ◊ 10

Xanthosoma sagittifolium
Wide-spreading, tufted perennial with thick stems. Broadly arrow-shaped leaves, 2ft (60cm) or more on long leaf stalks, are green with a grayish bloom. Has green spathes intermittently during the year. H to 6ft (2m) in flower, S 6ft (2m) or more. Min. 59°F (15°C).

☼ ◊ 10

Artemisia ludoviciana var. **albula**
Bushy perennial, grown for its aromatic, lance-shaped leaves which are silvery white and woolly on both surfaces and have jagged margins. Bears slender plumes of tiny, grayish white flower heads in summer. H 4ft (1.2m), S 2ft (60cm).

☼ ◊ ❋❋❋ 5–8

Columnea microphylla
'Variegata'
Evergreen, trailing perennial. Has rounded leaves narrowly bordered with cream and tubular, hooded, scarlet flowers, with yellow throats, in winter-spring. H 3ft (1m) or more, S indefinite. Min. 59°F (15°C).

☼ ◊ 10

Aciphylla squarrosa
Evergreen, clump-forming perennial with tufts of pointed, divided leaves. In summer bears spiky, yellow flowers in compound umbels with male and female flowers often mixed. H and S 3–4ft (1–1.2m).

☼ ◊ ❋❋ 10

Asparagus densiflorus, syn.
A. sprengeri (Sprenger asparagus)
Evergreen, trailing perennial with clusters of narrow, leaflike, bright green stems. In summer has pink-tinged, white flowers, followed by red berries. Suits a hanging basket. H to 3ft (1m), S 20in (50cm). Min. 50°F (10°C).

☼ ◊ 9–10

Calathea zebrina (Zebra plant)
Robust, evergreen, clump-forming perennial with long-stalked, velvety, dark green leaves, to 2ft (60cm) long (less if pot-grown), with paler veins, margins, and midribs. Has short spikes of white to pale purple flowers. H and S to 3ft (90cm). Min. 59°F (15°C).

☼ ◊ 10

Asparagus densiflorus 'Myersii', syn. *A. meyeri*, *A. myersii* (Meyer's asparagus fern)
Evergreen, erect perennial with spikes of tight, feathery clusters of leaflike stems and pinkish white flowers in summer, then red berries. H to 3ft (1m), S 20in (50cm). Min. 50°F (10°C).

☼◐ ○ 9–10

Globba winitii
Evergreen, clump-forming perennial with lance-shaped leaves to 8in (20cm) long. Intermittently has pendent racemes of tubular, yellow flowers with large, reflexed, reddish purple bracts. H 3ft (1m), S 1ft (30cm). Min. 64°F (18°C).

☼ ○ 10

Epimedium x youngianum 'Niveum'
Compact, ground-cover perennial with heart-shaped, serrated, bronze-tinted leaflets that turn green in late spring, when small, cup-shaped, snow white flowers are borne. H 6–12in (15–30cm), S 12in (30cm).

☼◐ ○ ❄❄❄ 5–9

Pachyphragma macrophyllum, syn. *Thlaspi macrophyllum*
Creeping, mat-forming perennial with rosettes of rounded, long-stalked, glossy, bright green leaves, each to 4in (10cm) long. Bears many racemes of tiny, white flowers in spring. H to 12in (30cm), S indefinite.

☼◐ ◐ ❄❄❄ 5–9

Dieffenbachia seguine 'Rudolph Roehrs', syn. *D. s.* 'Roehrsii'
Evergreen, tufted perennial, sometimes woody at the base. Broadly lance-shaped leaves, to 18in (45cm) long, are yellowish green or white with green midribs and margins. H and S 3ft (1m) or more. Min. 59°F (15°C).

☼◐ ○ 10

Peristrophe hyssopifolia 'Aureo-variegata'
Evergreen, bushy perennial. Small leaves are broadly lance-shaped with long, pointed tips and central, creamy yellow blotches. Has tubular, rose-pink flowers in winter. H to 2ft (60cm) or more, S 4ft (1.2m). Min. 59°F (15°C).

☼ ○ 10

Lamium maculatum 'White Nancy'
Semi-evergreen, mat-forming perennial with white-variegated, green foliage and spikes of hooded, white flowers in late spring and summer. H 6in (15cm), S 3ft (1m).

☼ ◐ ❄❄❄ 4–8

Trillium cernuum f. album
Clump-forming perennial with nodding, maroon-centered, white flowers borne in spring beneath luxuriant, 3-parted, green leaves. H 12–18in (30–45cm), S 12in (30cm).

☀ ◐ ❄❄❄ 5–9

Sansevieria trifasciata 'Laurentii'
Evergreen, stemless perennial with a rosette of about 5 stiff, erect, lance-shaped and pointed leaves with yellow margins. Occasionally has pale green flowers. Propagate by division to avoid reversion. H 1½–4ft (45cm–1.2m), S 4in (10cm). Min. 50–59°F (10–15°C).

☼ ○ 9–10

Strelitzia reginae
Evergreen, clump-forming perennial with long-stalked, bluish green leaves. Has beaklike, orange-and-blue flowers in boat-shaped, red-edged bracts mainly in spring. H over 3ft (1m), S 2½ft (75cm). Min. 41–50°F (5–10°C).

☼◐ ○ 9–10

Pulmonaria 'Sissinghurst White'
Semi-evergreen, clump-forming perennial that bears funnel-shaped, white flowers in spring above long, elliptic, green, paler spotted leaves. H 12in (30cm), S 18–24in (45–60cm).

◑ ○ ❄❄❄ 4–9

Lamium maculatum 'Album'
Semi-evergreen, mat-forming perennial that has dark green leaves with central, white stripes. Bears clusters of hooded, white flowers in spring-summer. H 8in (20cm), S 3ft (1m).

☼◐ ◐ ❄❄❄ 4–8

Convallaria majalis
(Lily-of-the-valley)
Low-growing, rhizomatous perennial
with narrowly oval, mid- to dark green
leaves and, in spring, sprays of small,
very fragrant, pendulous, bell-shaped,
white flowers. Likes humus-rich soil.
H 6in (15cm), S indefinite.

☀ ◊ ❀❀❀ 4–9

Trillium ovatum (Coast trillium)
Clump-forming perennial with white
flowers, later turning pink, that are
carried singly in spring just above red-
stalked, 3-parted, dark green foliage.
H 10–15in (25–38cm), S 8in (20cm).

☀ ◊ ❀❀❀❀ 5–9

Adonis brevistyla
Clump-forming perennial. Buttercuplike flowers, borne singly at tips of
stems in early spring, are white, tinged
blue outside. Has finely cut, green
leaves. H and S 6–9in (15–23cm).

☀ ◊ ❀❀❀ 4–8

Trillium chloropetalum
Clump-forming perennial with reddish
green stems carrying 3-parted, gray-
marbled, dark green leaves. Flowers
vary from purplish pink to white and
appear above foliage in spring. H and
S 12–18in (30–45cm).

☀ ◊ ❀❀❀ 4–9

Trillium grandiflorum
(Wake-robin)
Clump-forming perennial. Large, pure
white flowers that turn pink with age
are borne singly in spring just above
large, 3-parted, dark green leaves.
H 15in (38cm), S 12in (30cm).

☀ ◊ ❀❀❀ 5–9

Podophyllum emodi,
syn. *P. hexandrum*
(Himalayan May apple)
Perennial with pairs of 3-lobed, brown-
mottled leaves followed by white or
pink flowers in spring and fleshy, red
fruits in summer. H 12–18in
(30–45cm), S 12in (30cm).

☀ ◊ ❀❀❀ 5–8

Anemone sylvestris
(Snowdrop windflower)
Carpeting perennial that may be
invasive. Fragrant, semi-pendent, white
flowers with yellow centers are borne
in spring and early summer. Has
divided, green leaves. H and S
12in (30cm).

☀ ◊ ❀❀❀ 4–9

Epimedium pubigerum
Evergreen, carpeting perennial, grown
for its dense, smooth, heart-shaped,
divided foliage and clusters of cup-
shaped, creamy white or pink flowers
in spring. H and S 18in (45cm).

☀ ◊ ❀❀❀ 5–9

Bergenia 'Silberlicht',
syn. *B.* 'Silver Light'
Evergreen, clump-forming perennial
that has flat, oval, green leaves with
toothed margins. Clusters of white
flowers, sometimes suffused with pink,
are borne on erect stems in spring.
H 12in (30cm), S 20in (50cm).

☀ ◊ ❀❀❀ 3–8

□ PINK

□ RED

Bergenia cordifolia 'Purpurea'
Evergreen, clump-forming perennial, useful for ground cover, with large, rounded, purple-tinged, deep green leaves. Clusters of bell-shaped, rose-pink flowers are carried on red stems from late winter to early spring.
H and S 20in (50cm).

☀ ◊ ❄❄❄ 3–8

Epimedium x rubrum
(Red barrenwort)
Carpeting perennial with dense, heart-shaped, divided leaves that are dark brownish red in spring when clusters of cup-shaped, crimson flowers with yellow spurs appear. H 12in (30cm), S 8in (20cm).

☀ ◊ ❄❄❄ 5–9

Epimedium grandiflorum 'Rose Queen'
Carpeting perennial with dense, heart-shaped, divided leaves, tinged with copper, and wiry stems bearing clusters of cup-shaped, spurred, deep pink flowers in spring. H and S 12in (30cm).

☀ ◊ ❄❄❄ 5–9

Trillium erectum
Clump-forming perennial with 3-lobed, green leaves and bright maroon-purple flowers in spring. H 12–18in (30–45cm), S 12in (30cm).

☀ ◊ ❄❄❄ 5–9

Bergenia ciliata
Evergreen, clump-forming perennial with attractive, large, rounded, hairy leaves. In spring bears clusters of white flowers that age to pink. Leaves are often damaged by frost, although fresh ones will appear in spring. H 12in (30cm), S 20in (50cm).

☀ ◊ ❄❄ 5–8

Geranium macrorrhizum 'Ingwersen's Variety'
Compact, carpeting perennial, useful as weed-suppressing ground cover. Small, soft rose-pink flowers appear in late spring and early summer. Aromatic leaves turn bronze- and scarlet-tinted in autumn. H 1ft (30cm), S 2ft (60cm).

☀ ◊ ❄❄❄ 4–8

Heloniopsis orientalis
Clump-forming perennial with basal rosettes of narrowly lance-shaped leaves, above which rise nodding, rose-pink flowers in spring.
H and S 12in (30cm).

☀ ◊ ❄❄❄ 4–8

Lamium maculatum
Semi-evergreen, mat-forming perennial with mauve-tinged, often pink-flushed leaves that have central, silvery stripes. Clusters of hooded, mauve-pink flowers are borne in mid-spring. H 6in (15cm), S 3ft (1m).

☀ ◊ ❄❄❄ 4–8

Trillium sessile (Toadshade)
Clump-forming perennial that in spring bears red-brown flowers, nestling in a collar of 3-lobed leaves, marked white, pale green, or bronze. H 12–15in (30–38cm), S 12–18in (30–45cm).

☀ ◊ ❄❄❄ 5–9

Anemone nemorosa 'Allenii'
Carpeting perennial with many large, cup-shaped, single, rich lavender blue flowers appearing in spring over deeply divided leaves. H 6in (15cm), S 12in (30cm) or more.

☀◗ ❀❀❀ 4–8

Glaucidium palmatum
Leafy perennial that has large, lobed leaves and, in spring, large, delicate, cup-shaped, lavender flowers. A woodland plant, it requires humus-rich soil and a sheltered position. H and S 20in (50cm).

☀◗ ❀❀❀ 6–9

Geranium nodosum
Clump-forming perennial with lobed, glossy leaves and delicate, cup-shaped, lilac or lilac-pink flowers borne in spring-summer. Thrives in deep shade. H and S 18in (45cm).

☀◗ ❀❀❀ 5–8

Lathyrus vernus
Clump-forming perennial bearing in spring small, pealike, bright purple and blue flowers veined with red, several on each slender stem. Leaves are soft and fernlike. Proves difficult to transplant successfully. H and S 12in (30cm).

☀◗ ❀❀❀ 5–9

Anemone nemorosa 'Robinsoniana'
Carpeting perennial with flat, star-shaped, lavender blue flowers, pale creamy gray beneath, borne singly on maroon stems. Leaves are deeply divided into lance-shaped segments. H 6in (15cm), S 12in (30cm).

☀◗ ❀❀❀ 4–8

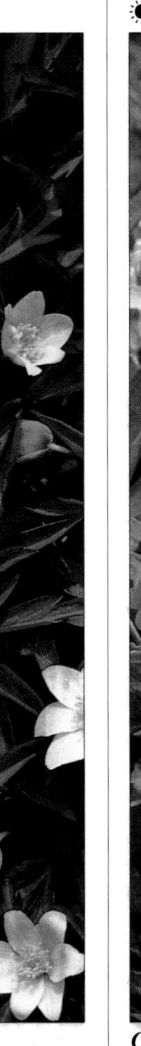

Cardamine pentaphyllos,
syn. *Dentaria pentaphylla*
Upright perennial spreading by fleshy, horizontal rootstocks. Produces clusters of large, white or pale purple flowers in spring. H 12–24in (30–60cm), S 18–24in (45–60cm).

☀◗ ❀❀❀ 5–9

■■ PURPLE–BLUE

■■□ BLUE–YELLOW

Pulmonaria saccharata
(Bethlehem sage)
Semi-evergreen, clump-forming
perennial. In spring bears funnel-
shaped flowers, opening pink and
turning to blue. Long, elliptic leaves
are variably spotted with creamy
white. H 12in (30cm), S 24in (60cm).

☼ ◐ ❋❋❋ 4–8

Lathraea clandestina
Spreading perennial that grows as a
parasite on willow or poplar roots.
Fleshy, underground stems have
colorless scales instead of leaves.
Bears bunches of hooded, purple
flowers from late winter to early
spring. H 4in (10cm), S indefinite.

☼ ◐ ❋❋❋ 5–9

Brunnera macrophylla 'Dawson's
White', syn. B. m. 'Variegata'
Ground-cover perennial with heart-
shaped leaves, marked creamy white.
In spring bears delicate sprays of
small, bright blue flowers. Shelter
from wind to prevent leaf damage.
H 18in (45cm), S 24in (60cm).

☼ ◐ ❋❋❋ 4–8

Euphorbia seguieriana
Bushy perennial with large, terminal
clusters of yellowish green flowers in
late spring and narrowly lance-shaped,
glaucous leaves on slender stems.
H and S 18in (45cm).

☼ ◐ ❋❋ 6–9

Lamium orvala
Clump-forming perennial that forms a
mound of green leaves, sometimes
with central, white stripes. Clusters of
pink or purple-pink flowers open in
late spring to early summer. H and
S 12in (30cm).

☼ ◐ ❋❋❋ 4–8

Pulmonaria angustifolia
'Mawson's Variety'
Clump-forming perennial that in early
spring bears clusters of funnel-shaped,
blue flowers, tinged red with age, above
narrow leaves. H and S 9in (23cm).

☼ ◐ ❋❋❋ 4–8

Meconopsis quintuplinervia
Mat-forming perennial. Lavender blue
flowers, deepening to purple at the
bases, are carried singly on hairy stems
in late spring and early summer above
a dense mat of large, green leaves. H
12–18in (30–45cm), S 12in (30cm).

☼ ◐ pH ❋❋❋ 7–8

Scopolia carniolica
Clump-forming perennial that carries
spikes of nodding, purple-brown
flowers, yellow inside, in early spring.
H and S 24in (60cm).

☼ ◐ ❋❋❋ 5–8

Mertensia virginica
Elegant perennial that in spring carries
funnel-shaped, rich blue flowers,
hanging in clusters from tops of stems.
Oval leaves are soft blue-green. Dies
down in summer. Crowns are prone to
slug damage. H 12–24in (30–60cm),
S 12–18in (30–45cm).

☼ ◐ ❋❋❋ 4–9

Euphorbia amygdaloides subsp.
robbiae
Evergreen, spreading perennial with
rosettes of dark green leaves, useful as
ground cover even in poor, dry soil
and semi-shade. Bears open, rounded
heads of lime green flowers in spring.
H 18–24in (45–60cm), S 24in (60cm).

☼ ◐ ❋❋❋ 7–9

Euphorbia cyparissias
(Cypress spurge)
Rounded, leafy perennial with a mass
of slender, gray-green leaves and
umbels of small, bright lime green
flowers in late spring. May be
invasive. H and S 12in (30cm).

☼ ◐ ❋❋❋ 4–9

Valeriana phu 'Aurea'
Perennial with rosettes of lemon to
butter yellow, young foliage that turns
green by summer, when heads of
insignificant, white flowers appear.
H 15in (38cm), S 12–15in (30–38cm).

☼ ◊ ❄❄❄ 5–8

Petasites japonicus
Spreading, invasive perennial that in
early spring produces dense cones of
small, daisylike, yellowish white
flowers before large, light green leaves
appear. H 2ft (60cm), S 5ft (1.5m).

☼ ◊ ❄❄❄ 5–9

Cardamine enneaphyllos,
syn. *Dentaria enneaphylla*
Lax perennial spreading by fleshy,
horizontal rootstocks. In spring,
nodding, pale yellow or white flowers
open at the ends of shoots arising from
deeply divided leaves. H 12–24in
(30–60cm), S 18–24in (45–60cm).

◑ ◊ ❄❄❄ 5–8

**Epimedium × versicolor
'Neo-sulphureum'**
Carpeting perennial with dense, heart-
shaped, divided leaves, tinted reddish
purple in spring when cup-shaped,
pale yellow flowers are borne in small,
pendent clusters on wiry stems. H and
S 12in (30cm).

◑ ◊ ❄❄❄ 5–9

Trollius 'Alabaster'
Clump-forming perennial producing
rounded, yellowish white flowers in
spring. These emerge from a basal
mass of rounded, deeply divided, green
leaves. H 24in (60cm), S 18in (45cm).

☼ ◊ ❄❄❄ 5–8

Anemone × lipsiensis,
syn. *A. × seemannii*
Prostrate, carpeting perennial that in
spring has many single, pale yellow
flowers with bright yellow stamens.
Leaves are deeply cut with long
leaflets. H 6in (15cm), S 12in (30cm).

☼ ◊ ❄❄❄ 5–8

Uvularia grandiflora
(Big merrybells)
Clump-forming perennial. Clusters of
long, bell-shaped, yellow flowers hang
gracefully from slender stems in
spring. H 18–24in (45–60cm),
S 12in (30cm).

☼ ◊ ❄❄❄ 5–9

Anemone ranunculoides
Spreading perennial for damp
woodland, bearing buttercuplike,
single, deep yellow flowers in spring.
Divided leaves have short stalks.
H and S 8in (20cm).

☼ ◊ ❄❄❄ 4–8

Primulas

There are primulas to suit almost every kind of garden situation, ranging from the pool side to the scree, but most have particular needs and care should be taken with their cultivation. Among the various botanical groups, Candelabra and Auricula primulas are the most widely known, and have a distinctive arrangement of their flowers. (For fuller details see the Plant Dictionary.)

P. allionii

P. vulgaris 'Gigha White'

P. sieboldii 'Wine Lady'

P. polyneura

P. pulverulenta (Candelabra)

P. sonchifolia

P. frondosa

P. 'Craddock White'

P. malacoides [single]

P. warshenewskiana

P. secundiflora

P. petiolaris

P. denticulata f. *alba*

P. farinosa

P. malacoides [double]

P. melanops

P. japonica 'Miller's Crimson' (Candelabra)

P. modesta var. *fauriei*

P. japonica 'Postford White' (Candelabra)

P. vulgaris subsp. *sibthorpii*

P. × *scapeosa*

P. clusiana

P. vialii

P. gracilipes

P. pulverulenta 'Bartley' (Candelabra)

P. clarkei

P. hirsuta

P. 'Mrs. J.H. Wilson' (Auricula)

P. rosea

P. sieboldii

P. edgeworthii

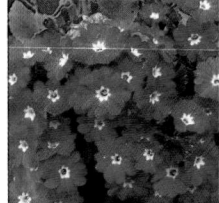
P. × *pubescens* 'Janet'

P. 'Mark'
(Auricula)

P. 'Linda Pope'

P. aureata

P. florindae

P. bulleyana
(Candelabra)

P. 'Adrian'
(Auricula)

P. reidii var. **williamsii**

P. alpicola var. **luna**

P. denticulata

P. vulgaris

P. sikkimensis

P. forrestii

P. 'Janie Hill'
(Auricula)

P. 'Moonstone'
(Auricula)

P. elatior

P. veris

P. 'Blossom'
(Auricula)

P. marginata
'Prichard's Variety'

P. bhutanica

P. 'Blairside Yellow'
(Auricula)

P. chungensis
(Candelabra)

P. 'Inverewe'
(Candelabra)

P. flaccida

P. 'Margaret Martin'
(Auricula)

P. helodoxa
(Candelabra)

P. x kewensis

P. marginata

P. 'Chloë'
(Auricula)

P. palinuri

P. verticillata

P. Gold Lace Group

■□ YELLOW–ORANGE

Trollius europaeus
(Common globeflower)
Clump-forming perennial that in spring
bears rounded, lemon yellow flowers
above deeply divided, green leaves.
H 24in (60cm), S 18in (45cm).

☼ ◐ ❀❀❀ 5–8

Adonis amurensis (Amur adonis)
Clump-forming perennial that in late
winter and early spring bears
buttercuplike, golden blooms singly at
the tips of stems. Green foliage is
finely cut. H 12in (30cm), S 9–12in
(23–30cm).

☼ ◐ ❀❀❀ 4–8

Euphorbia polychroma, syn.
E. epithymoides (Cushion spurge)
Rounded, bushy perennial with green
leaves and heads of bright yellow
flowers carried for several weeks in
spring. H and S 20in (50cm).

☼ ◐ ❀❀❀ 5–9

Meconopsis cambrica
(Welsh poppy)
Spreading perennial that in late spring
carries lemon yellow or rich orange
blooms. Double forms are available.
Has deeply divided, fernlike foliage.
H 12–18in (30–45cm), S 12in (30cm).

☼ ◐ ❀❀❀ 6–8

Adonis vernalis
Clump-forming perennial that in early
spring produces buttercuplike, greenish
yellow blooms singly at the tips of
stems. Green leaves are delicately
dissected. H and S 9–12in (23–30cm).

☼ ◐ ❀❀❀ 5–8

Epimedium × warleyense
(Warley epimedium)
Carpeting perennial with heart-shaped,
divided, light green leaves, tinged
purple-red, and cup-shaped, rich orange
flowers borne in clusters on wiry stems
in spring. H and S 12in (30cm).

☼ ◐ ❀❀❀ 5–9

□ WHITE

Campanula alliariifolia
Mound-forming perennial with heart-
shaped leaves, above which rise
nodding, bell-shaped, creamy white
flowers borne along arching, wiry
stems throughout summer. H 24in
(60cm), S 20in (50cm).

☼ ◐ ❀❀❀ 4–8

Galium odoratum, syn. *Asperula
odorata* (Sweet woodruff)
Carpeting perennial that bears whorls
of star-shaped, white flowers above
neat, whorled leaves in summer. All
parts of plant are aromatic. H 6in
(15cm), S 12in (30cm) or more.

☼ ◐ ❀❀❀ 5–8

Anemone rivularis
Perennial with stiff, free-branching
stems bearing delicate, cup-shaped,
white flowers in summer above deeply
divided, dark green leaves. H 24in
(60cm), S 12in (30cm).

☼ ◐ ❀❀❀ 6–8

Anemone narcissiflora
Leafy perennial that in late spring and
early summer produces cup-shaped,
single, white flowers with a blue or
purplish pink stain on reverse of
petals. Leaves are dark green and
deeply divided. H to 24in (60cm),
S 20in (50cm).

☼ ◐ ❀❀❀ 5–8

**Chrysanthemum × superbum
'Esther Read'**
Robust perennial with large, daisylike,
double, white flower heads borne
singly on strong stems in summer.
Divide and replant every two years.
H and S 18in (45cm).

☼ ◐ ❀❀❀ 4–8

Anthemis punctata subsp.
cupaniana
Evergreen, carpeting perennial with
dense, finely cut, silvery foliage that
turns green in winter. Small, daisylike,
white flower heads with yellow centers
are borne singly on short stems in early
summer. H and S 12in (30cm).

☼ ◊ ❋❋ 6–9

Anaphalis triplinervis var.
intermedia, syn. *A. nubigena*
Dwarf, leafy perennial that has woolly,
silvery stems and lance-shaped leaves.
Carries dense, terminal clusters of
white flower heads in late summer.
H 8–12in (20–30cm), S 6in (15cm).

☼ ◊ ❋❋❋ 4–9

Aegopodium podagraria
'Variegata'
(Variegated Bishop's weed)
Vigorous, spreading perennial, excellent
for ground cover, with lobed, creamy
white-variegated leaves. Insignificant,
white flowers borne in summer are best
removed. H 4in (10cm), S indefinite.

☼ ◊ ❋❋❋ 4–9

Tradescantia 'Osprey'
Clump-forming perennial with
narrowly lance-shaped leaves, 6–12in
(15–30cm) long. Has clusters of white
flowers with purple-blue stamens,
surrounded by 2 leaflike bracts, in
summer. H to 24in (60cm),
S 18in (45cm).

☼ ◊ ❋❋❋ 5–9

Anthericum liliago
Upright perennial that in early summer
bears tall racemes of trumpet-shaped,
white flowers above clumps of long,
narrow, gray-green leaves. H 18–24in
(45–60cm), S 12in (30cm).

☼ ◊ ❋❋❋ 5–9

Mentha suaveolens 'Variegata'
(Variegated apple mint, Variegated
pineapple mint)
Spreading perennial with soft, woolly
leaves, splashed with white and cream,
that smell of apples. Seldom produces
flowers. H 12–18in (30–45cm),
S 24in (60cm).

☼ ◊ ❋❋❋ 5–9

Crambe maritima (Sea kale)
Robust perennial with a mound of
wide, curved, lobed, silvery green
leaves. Bears large heads of small,
fragrant white flowers, opening into
branching sprays in summer. H and
S 24in (60cm).

☼ ◊ ❋❋❋ 6–9

Astilbe 'Irrlicht'
Leafy perennial bearing tapering,
feathery plumes of tiny, white flowers
in summer. Foliage is dark green and
flowers remain on the plant, dried and
brown, well into winter. Prefers humus-
rich soil. H 1½–2ft (45–60cm),
S to 3ft (1m).

☼ ◖ ❋❋❋ 5–9

Heuchera cylindrica 'Greenfinch'
Evergreen, clump-forming perennial
with rosettes of heart-shaped, lobed
leaves and, in summer, graceful spikes
of small, bell-shaped, pale green or
greenish white flowers. H 18–24in
(45–60cm), S 20in (50cm).

☼ ◊ ❋❋❋ 4–8

Geranium clarkei 'Kashmir
White', syn. *G. pratense* 'Kashmir
White'
Carpeting, rhizomatous perennial with
divided leaves and loose clusters of cup-
shaped flowers, white with pale lilac-
pink veins, borne for a long period in
summer. H and S 18–24in (45–60cm).

☼ ◊ ❋❋❋ 4–8

Streptocarpus caulescens
Erect perennial with small, narrow to
oval, fleshy, dark green leaves. Stalked
clusters of small, tubular, violet-striped,
white or violet flowers are carried in
leaf axils intermittently. H and S to
18in (45cm) or more. Min. 50–59°F
(10–15°C).

☽ ◖ 9–10

☐ WHITE

Geranium renardii
Compact, clump-forming perennial
with circular, lobed, sage green leaves
and purple-veined, white flowers, borne
in early summer. H and S 12in (30cm).

☼ ◊ ❈❈❈ 6–8

Diplarrhena moraea
Clump-forming perennial with fans of
long, strap-shaped leaves and clusters
of irislike, white flowers, with centers
of yellow and purple, borne on wiry
stems in early summer. H 18in (45cm),
S 9in (23cm).

☼ ◊ ❈ 9–10

Osteospermum 'Whirligig'
Lax, evergreen, clump-forming, semi-
woody perennial that bears bluish
white flower heads singly, but in great
profusion, during summer. Leaves are
gray-green. H 24in (60cm), S 12–18in
(30–45cm).

☼ ◊ ❈ 9–10

☐☒ WHITE–PINK

Ruellia devosiana
Evergreen, bushy sub-shrub with
spreading, purplish branches. Leaves
are broadly lance-shaped, dark green
with paler veins above and purple
below. Has mauve-tinged, white
flowers in spring-summer. H and S to
18in (45cm) or more. Min. 59°F (15°C).

☼ ◊ 10

Heuchera 'Palace Purple'
Clump-forming perennial with
persistent, heart-shaped, deep purple
leaves and sprays of small, white
flowers in summer. Cut leaves last
well in water. H and S 18in (45cm).

☼ ◊ ❈❈❈ 4–8

Melittis melissophyllum
Erect perennial that in early summer
bears white flowers with purple lower
lips in axils of oval, rough, green
leaves. H and S 12in (30cm).

☼ ◊ ❈❈❈ 6–9

Astrantia major var. **involucrata**
Clump-forming perennial very similar
to *A. major* (below) but with longer
bracts surrounding centers of flower
heads. H 24in (60cm), S 18in (45cm).

☼ ◊ ❈❈❈ 5–8

Astrantia major
Clump-forming perennial producing
greenish white, sometimes pink-tinged
flower heads throughout summer-
autumn above a dense mass of divided,
green leaves. H 24in (60cm),
S 18in (45cm).

☼ ◊ ❈❈❈ 5–8

Astrantia maxima
Clump-forming perennial that bears
rose-pink flower heads during
summer-autumn. H 24in (60cm),
S 12in (30cm).

☼ ◊ ❈❈❈ 5–8

Mimulus 'Andean Nymph'
Spreading perennial, with hairy leaves, that in summer bears snapdragonlike, rose-pink flowers tipped with creamy yellow and spotted deep pink. H 9in (23cm), S 10in (25cm).

☼ ◐ ❄ 9–10

Dicentra eximia 'Spring Morning'
Neat, leafy perennial with small, heart-shaped, pink flowers hanging in arching sprays in late spring and summer. Attractive, fernlike foliage is gray-green and finely cut. H and S 12in (30cm).

☼◐ ◊ ❄❄❄ 4–8

Penstemon 'Pennington Gem'
Vigorous, semi-evergreen perennial that produces sprays of tubular, pink flowers from mid-summer to autumn. Leaves are narrow and fresh green. H 18–24in (45–60cm), S 18in (45cm).

☼ ◊ ❄❄ 5–8

Penstemon 'Apple Blossom'
Semi-evergreen, bushy perennial that carries sprays of small, tubular, pale pink flowers from mid-summer onwards above narrow, fresh green foliage. H and S 18in (45cm).

☼ ◊ ❄❄ 5–8

x Heucherella tiarelloides
Evergreen, ground-cover perennial that has dense clusters of leaves and feathery sprays of tiny, bell-shaped, pink flowers in early summer. H and S 18in (45cm).

☼◐ ◊ ❄❄❄ 4–8

x Heucherella 'Bridget Bloom'
Evergreen, clump-forming perennial with dense, bright green leaves and, in early summer, many feathery sprays of tiny, bell-shaped, rose-pink flowers, which continue intermittently until autumn. H 18in (45cm), S 12in (30cm).

☼◐ ◊ ❄❄❄ 4–8

Erigeron 'Charity'
Clump-forming perennial with a mass of daisylike, light pink flower heads with greenish yellow centers borne for a long period in summer. May need some support. H and S to 2ft (60cm).

☼ ◊ ❄❄❄ 5–9

Geranium endressii
(Pyrenean cranesbill)
Semi-evergreen, compact, carpeting perennial with small, lobed leaves and cup-shaped, rose-pink flowers borne throughout summer. H 18in (45cm), S 24in (60cm).

☼ ◊ ❄❄❄ 4–8

■ PINK

Geranium endressii 'Wargrave Pink'
Semi-evergreen, carpeting perennial with dense, dainty, lobed, basal leaves acting as weed-suppressing ground cover. Cup-shaped, bright salmon pink flowers are borne throughout summer. H 18in (45cm), S 24in (60cm).

 ☼ ◊ ❈❈❈ 4–8

Lychnis flos-jovis
Clump-forming perennial with rounded clusters of deep rose-pink flowers, opening in mid-summer, that are set off by gray foliage. H and S 18in (45cm).

 ☼ ◊ ❈❈❈ 5–9

Geranium macrorrhizum
(Bigroot cranesbill)
Semi-evergreen, carpeting perennial bearing magenta flowers in early summer. Rounded, divided leaves make good, weed-proof ground cover and assume bright tints in autumn. H 12–15in (30–38cm), S 24in (60cm).

◐ ◊ ❈❈❈ 4–8

Osteospermum jucundum,
syn. *O. barberiae, Dimorphotheca barberiae*
Evergreen, neat, clump-forming perennial with aromatic, green leaves. In late summer, soft pink flower heads, mostly dark-eyed, are borne singly but in abundance. H and S 12in (30cm).

☼ ◊ ❈❈ 9–10

Penstemon 'Pink Endurance'
Semi-evergreen, dwarf perennial that produces short sprays of rose-pink flowers above narrow, green leaves in summer. H and S 12–15in (30–38cm).

☼ ◊ ❈❈ 5–8

Centaurea hypoleuca 'John Coutts'
Upright perennial. Deep rose-red flower heads, with thistlelike centers encircled by star-shaped ray petals, are borne singly on slender stems in summer. Deeply divided leaves are white-gray beneath. H 24in (60cm), S 18in (45cm).

☼ ◊ ❈❈❈ 4–8

Polygonum sphaerostachyum
Compact perennial carrying neat spikes of rich rose-pink blooms above narrowly lance-shaped, glaucous leaves in late summer. H 18–24in (45–60cm), S 12in (30cm).

 ☼ ◐ ❈❈❈ 4–9

Physostegia virginiana 'Vivid'
Erect, compact perennial that in late summer and early autumn bears spikes of tubular, dark lilac-pink flowers that can be placed in position. Has toothed, green leaves. H and S 12–24in (30–60cm).

☼ ◐ ❈❈❈ 4–8

Erodium manescavii
Mound-forming perennial with divided, fernlike, blue-green leaves. Produces loose clusters of single, deep pink, darker blotched flowers throughout summer. H 18in (45cm), S 24in (60cm).

☼ ◊ ❈❈ 5–8

Incarvillea mairei
Compact, clump-forming perennial
that has short stems bearing several
trumpet-shaped, purplish pink flowers
in early summer. Leaves are divided
into oval leaflets. Protect crowns with
winter mulch. H and S 12in (30cm).

☼ ◊ ❋❋❋ 7–8

Liatris spicata, syn. _L. callilepis_
(Gayfeather)
Clump-forming perennial. In late
summer bears spikes of crowded, rose-
purple flower heads on stiff stems that
arise from basal tufts of grasslike,
green foliage. H 24in (60cm),
S 12in (30cm).

☼ ◊ ❋❋❋ 4–9

Achimenes 'Little Beauty'
Bushy perennial with oval, toothed
leaves. Large, funnel-shaped, deep pink
flowers with yellow eyes are carried in
summer. H 10in (25cm), S 12in (30cm).
Min. 50°F (10°C).

☼ ◊ 9–10

Incarvillea delavayi
(Hardy gloxinia)
Clump-forming perennial with deeply
divided leaves and erect stems bearing
several trumpet-shaped, pinkish red
flowers in early summer. Has attractive
seed pods. H 18–24in (45–60cm),
S 12in (30cm).

☼ ◊ ❋❋❋ 6–8

Sinningia 'Red Flicker'
Short-stemmed, tuberous perennial with
rosettes of oval, velvety leaves, to 8in
(20cm) long. In summer has fleshy,
nodding, funnel-shaped, pinkish red
flowers, pouched on lower sides. H to
12in (30cm), S 18in (45cm). Min.
59°F (15°C).

☼◑ ◔ 10

**_Potentilla nepalensis_ 'Miss
Willmott'**
Clump-forming perennial with
palmate, strawberrylike, bright green
leaves. Numerous slender, branching
stems carry warm cherry red-centered,
pink flowers throughout summer.
H 20in (50cm), S 24in (60cm).

☼ ◊ ❋❋❋ 5–8

Mimulus lewisii
Upright perennial with downy, sticky,
gray leaves that provide an excellent
foil for snapdragonlike, deep rose-pink
flowers borne singly in summer.
Tolerates dry soil. H 24in (60cm),
S 18in (45cm).

☼ ◔ ❋❋ 9

Verbena 'Sissinghurst'
Mat-forming perennial that throughout
summer bears heads of brilliant pink
flowers above green foliage. Is excellent
for edging a path or growing in a tub.
H 6–8in (15–20cm), S 18in (45cm).

☼ ◊ ❋ 5–9

Carnations and Pinks

Although perhaps best known for providing excellent cut flowers, carnations and pinks are also renowned in the garden for their usually fragrant, attractive blooms, produced mainly in summer, and for their distinctive, evergreen foliage. All except the perpetual-flowering and several of the species carnations are frost hardy.

Border carnations—plants are of upright habit and flower prolifically once in mid-summer; each stem bears 5 or more flowers.

Perpetual-flowering carnations—similar in habit to border carnations, they are usually grown for cut flowers and bloom year-round in the greenhouse. Plants are normally disbudded, leaving one flower per stem, but spray forms have up to 5 flowers per stem.

Old-fashioned pinks—these have a low, spreading habit and form neat cushions of foliage; masses of fragrant flowers are produced in mid-summer.

Modern pinks—usually more vigorous than old-fashioned pinks, they are repeat-flowering with 2 or 3 main flushes of flowers in summer.

D. '**Gran's Favourite**'
(old-fashioned pink)

D. '**Pink Jewel**'
(modern pink)

D. '**Mrs. Sinkins**'
(old-fashioned pink)

D. '**Fair Folly**'
(modern pink)

D. '**Forest Treasure**'
(border carnation)

D. '**Joy**' (modern pink)

D. '**Valda Wyatt**'
(modern pink)

D. '**Haytor**'
(modern pink)

D. '**Nives**' (perpetual-flowering carnation)

D. '**Alice**'
(modern pink)

D. '**Pierrot**' (perpetual-flowering carnation)

D. '**Prudence**'
(old-fashioned pink)

D. '**Emile Paré**'
(old-fashioned pink)

D. '**Houndspool Ruby**'
(modern pink)

D. '**Musgrave's Pink**'
(old-fashioned pink)

D. '**Doris**'
(modern pink)

D. '**White Ladies**'
(old-fashioned pink)

D. '**Eva Humphries**'
(border carnation)

D. '**Truly Yours**'
(perpetual-flowering carnation)

D. '**Christopher**'
(modern pink)

■ RED

D. 'Bookham Perfume' (border carnation)

D. 'Borello' (perpetual-flowering carnation)

D. 'Astor' (perpetual-flowering carnation)

D. 'Happiness' (border carnation)

D. 'Aldridge Yellow' (border carnation)

D. 'Nina' (perpetual-flowering carnation)

D. 'Valencia' (perpetual-flowering carnation)

D. 'Raggio di Sole' (perpetual-fl. carnation)

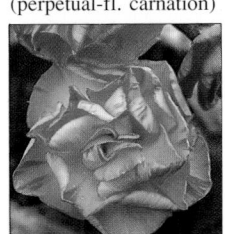

D. 'Christine Hough' (border carnation)

D. 'Clara' (perpetual-flowering carnation)

D. 'Albisola' (perpetual-flowering carnation)

Lychnis viscaria 'Splendens Plena'
Clump-forming perennial bearing spikes of double, magenta flowers in early summer. Stems and large, oval to lance-shaped, basal leaves are covered in sticky hairs. H 12–18in (30–45cm), S 9in (23cm) or more.

☼ ◊ ❋❋❋ 4–8

Lychnis coronaria
Clump-forming perennial, often grown as a biennial. From mid- to late summer, brilliant rose-crimson flowers are borne in panicles on branched, gray stems that rise from neat, gray leaves. H 18–24in (45–60cm), S 18in (45cm).

☼ ◊ ❋❋❋ 4–8

Sinningia 'Switzerland'
Short-stemmed, tuberous perennial with rosettes of oval, velvety leaves, to 8in (20cm) long. In summer has large, fleshy, trumpet-shaped, bright scarlet flowers with ruffled, white borders. H to 12in (30cm), S 18in (45cm). Min. 59°F (15°C).

☼ ◑ ◗ 9–10

Astilbe 'Fanal'
Leafy perennial with strong stems. In summer bears neat, tapering, feathery panicles of tiny, crimson-red flowers that turn brown and keep their shape in winter. Broad leaves are divided into leaflets. Prefers humus-rich soil. H 2ft (60cm), S to 3ft (1m).

◑ ● ❋❋❋ 5–9

Heuchera 'Red Spangles'
Evergreen perennial forming clumps of heart-shaped, purplish green leaves. Bears spikes of small, bell-shaped, crimson-scarlet flowers in summer. H and S 12in (30cm).

☼ ◊ ❋❋❋ 4–8

■ RED

Lotus berthelotii
(Coral gem, Parrot's-beak)
Straggling perennial suitable for a
hanging basket or large pan in an alpine
house. Has hairy, silvery branches and
leaves, and clusters of pealike, scarlet
flowers in summer. H 12in (30cm),
S indefinite. Min. 41°F (5°C).

 8–9

Columnea crassifolia
Evergreen, shrubby perennial with
fleshy, lance-shaped leaves. Erect,
tubular, hairy, scarlet flowers, about
3in (8cm) long, each with a yellow
throat, are carried from spring to
autumn. H and S to 18in (45cm).
Min. 59°F (15°C).

 10

Potentilla atrosanguinea
(Ruby cinquefoil)
Clump-forming perennial with hairy,
palmate, strawberrylike leaves. Loose
clusters of dark red flowers are borne
throughout summer. H 20in (50cm),
S 24in (60cm).

☼ ◊ ❋❋❋ 5–8

■ PURPLE

Polemonium carneum
Clump-forming perennial that carries
clusters of cup-shaped, pink or lilac-
pink flowers in early summer. Foliage
is finely divided. H and S 18in (45cm).

☼ ◊ ❋❋❋ 4–9

***Gaillardia* x *grandiflora* 'Dazzler'**
Upright, rather open perennial bearing
large, terminal, daisylike, yellow-
tipped, red flower heads for a long
period in summer. Leaves are soft and
divided. Needs staking and may be
short-lived. H 24in (60cm),
S 20in (50cm).

☼ ◊ ❋❋❋ 4–8

Kaempferia pulchra
Tufted, aromatic perennial with
horizontal, dark green leaves,
variegated with paler green above.
Short spikes of lilac-pink flowers
appear from the center of tufts in
summer. H 6in (15cm), S 12in (30cm).
Min. 64°F (18°C).

◐ ◗ 9–10

***Mimulus* 'Royal Velvet'**
Compact perennial, often grown as an
annual, producing in summer many
large, snapdragonlike, mahogany red
flowers with mahogany-speckled, gold
throats. H 12in (30cm), S 9in (23cm).

 ☼ ◗ ❋ 9–10

Tulbaghia violacea
(Society garlic)
Vigorous, semi-evergreen, clump-
forming perennial that in summer-
autumn carries umbels of lilac-purple
or lilac-pink flowers above a mass of
narrow, glaucous, blue-gray leaves.
H 18–24in (45–60cm), S 12in (30cm).

☼ ◊ ❋ 8–10

***Smithiantha* 'Orange King'**
Strong-growing, erect, rhizomatous
perennial. Large, scalloped, velvety
leaves are emerald green with dark red-
marked veins. In summer-autumn has
tubular, orange-red flowers, red-spotted
within and with yellow lips. H and S to
24in (60cm). Min. 59°F (15°C).

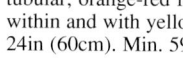 ◐ ◊ 9–10

Streptocarpus saxorum
Evergreen, rounded, woody-based
perennial with small, oval, hairy leaves
in whorls. Lilac flowers with white
tubes arise from leaf axils in summer-
autumn. H and S 12in (30cm) or more.
Min. 50–59°F (10–15°C).

☼◐ ◊ 10

Polemonium pulcherrimum
Vigorous perennial with bright green
leaves divided into leaflets. Tubular,
purple-blue flowers with throats of
yellow or white are borne in summer.
H 20in (50cm), S 12in (30cm).

☼ ◊ ✿✿✿ 4–8

Verbena rigida, syn. *V. venosa*
(Vervain)
Neat, compact perennial bearing heads
of pale violet flowers from mid-
summer onwards. Has lance-shaped,
rough, green leaves borne on flower
stems. H 18–24in (45–60cm), S 12in
(30cm).

☼ ◊ ✿ 4–9

Heterocentron elegans
(Spanish-shawl)
Evergreen, mat-forming perennial with
dense, creeping, green foliage. Massed,
bright deep purple flowers open in
summer-autumn and, under glass, in
winter. H 2in (5cm), S indefinite.
Min. 41°F (5°C).

☼ ◊ 10

Tradescantia 'Purple Dome'
Clump-forming perennial with narrow,
lance-shaped leaves, 6–12in (15–30cm)
long. Has clusters of rich purple
flowers, surrounded by 2 leaflike
bracts, in summer. H to 24in (60cm),
S 18in (45cm).

☼ ◊ ✿✿✿ 5–8

Erigeron 'Serenity'
Clump-forming perennial bearing
many daisylike, violet flower heads,
with yellow centers, borne singly for
many weeks in summer. Needs some
support. H and S to 2ft (60cm).

☼ ◊ ✿✿✿ 5–8

Stachys macrantha 'Superba'
Clump-forming perennial with heart-
shaped, soft, wrinkled, green leaves,
from which arise stout stems
producing whorls of hooded, purple-
violet flowers in summer. H 12–18in
(30–45cm), S 12–24in (30–60cm).

☼ ◊ ✿✿✿ 4–8

Centaurea montana
(Mountain bluet)
Spreading perennial with many rather
lax stems carrying, in early summer,
one or more large, purple, blue, white,
or pink flower heads with thistlelike
centers encircled by star-shaped ray
petals. H 20in (50cm), S 24in (60cm).

☼ ◊ ✿✿✿ 3–8

Platycodon grandiflorus
(Balloon flower)
Neat, clump-forming perennial that in
summer bears clusters of large,
balloonlike buds opening to bell-shaped,
blue or purplish flowers. Has bluish
green leaves. H 18–24in (45–60cm),
S 12–18in (30–45cm).

☼ ◊ ✿✿✿ 4–9

■ PURPLE

Geranium × magnificum
Clump-forming perennial with hairy, deeply lobed leaves and cup-shaped, prominently veined, violet-blue flowers borne in small clusters in summer. H 18in (45cm), S 24in (60cm).

☀ ◊ ❋❋❋ 4–8

Geranium himalayense, syn. *G. grandiflorum* (Lilac cranesbill)
Clump-forming perennial with large, cup-shaped, violet-blue flowers borne on long stalks in summer over dense tufts of neatly cut leaves. H 12in (30cm), S 24in (60cm).

☀ ◊ ❋❋❋ 4–8

Catananche caerulea 'Major'
Perennial forming clumps of grassy, gray-green leaves, above which rise wiry, branching stems each carrying a daisylike, lavender blue flower head in summer. Propagate regularly by root cuttings. H 18–24in (45–60cm), S 24in (30cm).

☀ ◊ ❋❋❋ 5–8

Nepeta × faassenii (Catmint)
Bushy, clump-forming perennial, useful for edging. Forms mounds of small, grayish green leaves, from which loose spikes of tubular, soft lavender blue flowers appear in early summer. H and S 18in (45cm).

☀ ◊ ❋❋❋ 4–8

Stokesia laevis (Stokes aster)
Perennial with overwintering, evergreen rosettes. In summer, cornflowerlike, lavender- or purple-blue flower heads are borne freely. Leaves are narrow. H and S 12–18in (30–45cm).

☀ ◊ ❋❋❋ 5–8

Scabiosa caucasica 'Clive Greaves'
Clump-forming perennial that throughout summer has violet-blue flower heads with pincushionlike centers. Basal leaves are lance-shaped and slightly lobed on the stems. H and S 18–24in (45–60cm).

☀ ◊ ❋❋❋ 4–9

Limonium latifolium 'Blue Cloud'
Clump-forming perennial. In late summer carries diffuse clusters of bluish mauve flowers that can be dried for indoor decoration. Has large, leathery, dark green leaves. H 12in (30cm), S 18in (45cm).

☀ ◊ ❋❋❋ 4–9

Anemonopsis macrophylla
Clump-forming perennial with waxy, nodding, purplish blue flowers, borne on slender, branching stems in summer, above fernlike leaves. H 18–24in (45–60cm), S 20in (50cm).

◐ ◊ ❋❋❋ 5–8

Geranium 'Johnson's Blue'
Vigorous, clump-forming perennial with many divided leaves and cup-shaped, deep lavender blue flowers borne throughout summer. H 12in (30cm), S 24in (60cm).

☀ ◊ ❋❋❋ 4–8

Polemonium caeruleum (Jacob's ladder)
Clump-forming perennial. Clusters of cup-shaped, lavender blue flowers with orange-yellow stamens open in summer amid finely divided foliage. H and S 18–24in (45–60cm).

☀ ◊ ❋❋❋ 4–8

Eryngium bourgatii
Clump-forming perennial that from mid- to late summer carries heads of thistlelike, blue-green, then lilac-blue, flowers on branched, wiry stems well above deeply cut, basal, gray-green leaves. H 18–24in (45–60cm), S 12in (30cm).

☀ ◊ ❋❋❋ 5–9

Campanula × burghaltii
Mound-forming perennial with long, pendent, funnel-shaped, pale lavender flowers displayed on erect, wiry stems in summer. Leaves are oval, soft, and leathery. May need staking. H 24in (60cm), S 12in (30cm).

☀ ◊ ❋❋❋ 4–8

Rhazya orientalis
Neat, clump-forming perennial. In summer, heads of small, star-shaped, gray-blue flowers open on tops of wiry stems clothed with green, sometimes grayish, leaves. H 18–24in (45–60cm), S 12–18in (30–45 cm).

☼ ◊ ❀❀❀ 5–8

Veronica perfoliata,
syn. *Parahebe perfoliata*
Evergreen sub-shrub with willowy stems clasped by leathery, glaucous leaves. Elegant, long, branching sprays of blue flowers are borne in summer. H 18–24in (45–60cm), S 18in (45cm).

☼ ◊ ❀❀ 7–9

Eryngium variifolium
Evergreen, rosette-forming perennial with stiff stems that in late summer bear heads of thistlelike, gray-blue flowers, each with a collar of white bracts. Jagged-edged leaves are green, marbled with white. H 18in (45cm), S 10in (25cm).

☼ ◊ ❀❀❀ 5–9

Veronica gentianoides
Mat-forming perennial with spikes of very pale blue flowers opening in early summer on tops of stems that arise from glossy, basal leaves. H and S 18in (45cm).

☼ ◊ ❀❀❀ 5–8

Amsonia tabernaemontana,
syn. *A. salicifolia* (Blue star)
Clump-forming perennial with willowy stems bearing drooping clusters of small, tubular, pale blue flowers in summer. Leaves are small and narrow. H 18–24in (45–60cm), S 12in (30cm).

☼ ◊ ❀❀❀ 4–8

Myosotidium hortensia
(Chatham Island forget-me-not)
Evergreen, clump-forming perennial bearing large clusters of forget-me-notlike, blue flowers in summer above a basal mound of large, ribbed, glossy leaves. H 18–24in (45–60cm), S 24in (60cm).

☼ ◖ ❀ 9

Linum narbonense
Clump-forming, short-lived perennial, best renewed frequently from seed. Has lance-shaped, grayish green leaves and heads of somewhat cup-shaped, pale to deep blue flowers in spring-summer. H 12–24in (30–60cm), S 12in (30cm).

☼ ◊ ❀❀❀ 5–8

Geranium wallichianum
'Buxton's Blue'
Spreading perennial with clumps of luxuriant, white-flecked, light green leaves and large, white-centered, blue or blue-purple flowers borne from mid-summer to autumn. H 12–18in (30–45cm), S 3ft (1m).

☼ ◊ ❀❀❀ 4–8

Salvia patens (Gentian sage)
Erect, branching perennial that in late summer and autumn produces whorls of pale or deep blue flowers on stems clothed with oval, green leaves. H 18–24in (45–60cm), S 18in (45cm).

☼ ◊ ❀ 7–9

Hostas

The luxuriance of their foliage and attractive habit have made hostas, or plantain lilies, increasingly sought after as plants for every garden, large or small. Native to the East, they also add an exotic touch to any waterside or damp, shady corner.

Hosta species vary in size from plants a few inches high to vigorous forms that will make a clump of up to 5ft (1.5m) across in a few years. Their elegant leaves are diverse in shape, texture, and coloration, with subtle variegations and shadings. Many hostas also produce decorative spikes of flowers, which rise graciously above the foliage in mid-summer.

Suitable for a range of situations, from pots to borders and pool sides, hostas are essentially shade- and moisture-loving plants, preferring rich, well-drained soils. Leaves must be protected from slugs to avoid damage.

H. sieboldiana

H. sieboldiana 'Frances Williams'

H. undulata var. *univittata*

H. tokudama 'Aureo-nebulosa'

H. plantaginea

H. ventricosa 'Aureo-maculata'

H. 'Gold Standard'

H. 'Halcyon'

H. ventricosa

H. decorata f. *decorata*

H. sieboldiana var. *elegans*

H. tardiflora

H. 'Royal Standard'

H. fortunei 'Aurea Marginata'

H. lancifolia

H. 'August Moon'

H. crispula

H. montana 'Aurea Marginata'

H. fortunei 'Albopicta'

Perennials/small SUMMER INTEREST

GREEN–YELLOW

Artemisia pontica
(Roman wormwood)
Vigorous, upright perennial with aromatic, feathery, silver-green foliage and tall spikes of small, grayish flower heads in summer. May spread.
H 24in (60cm), S 8in (20cm).

☀ ◊ ❋❋❋ 4–8

Alchemilla conjuncta
Clump-forming perennial that has neat, wavy, star-shaped leaves with pale margins. Loose clusters of tiny, greenish yellow flowers, with conspicuous, outer calyces, appearing in mid-summer may be dried for winter decoration. H and S 12in (30cm).

☀ ◑ ❋❋❋ 4–8

Tovara virginiana 'Painter's Palette'
Mounded perennial grown for its attractive leaves, which are green with central, brown zones, ivory yellow splashes and stripes, and an overall deep pink tinge. Seldom flowers in cultivation. H and S 2ft (60cm).

☀ ◑ ❋❋❋ 3–9

Alchemilla mollis (Lady's-mantle)
Clump-forming, ground-cover perennial that has rounded, pale green leaves with crinkled edges. Bears small sprays of tiny, bright greenish yellow flowers with conspicuous, outer calyces, in mid-summer that may be dried. H and S 20in (50cm).

☀ ◊ ❋❋❋ 4–8

Sarracenia flava
Erect perennial with red-marked, yellow-green pitchers (modified leaves) that have hooded tops. From late spring to early summer bears nodding, yellow or greenish yellow flowers. H and S 18in (45cm). Min. 41°F (5°C).

☀ ● 7–9

Origanum vulgare 'Aureum'
(Golden oregano)
Woody-based perennial forming a dense mat of aromatic, golden yellow, young leaves that turn pale yellow-green in mid-summer. Occasionally bears tiny, mauve flowers in summer.
H in leaf 3in (8cm), S indefinite.

☀ ◊ ❋❋❋ 4–8

YELLOW

Sisyrinchium striatum
(Argentine blue-eyed grass)
Semi-evergreen perennial that forms tufts of long, narrow, gray-green leaves. Bears slender spikes of purple-striped, straw yellow flowers in summer. Self seeds freely. H 18–24in (45–60cm), S 12in (30cm).

☀ ◊ ❋❋❋ 7–8

Filipendula ulmaria 'Aurea'
Leafy perennial, grown for its divided, bright golden yellow foliage in spring which turns pale green in summer. Clusters of creamy white flowers are carried in branching heads in mid-summer. H and S 12in (30cm).

☀ ◑ ❋❋❋ 4–8

Kniphofia 'Little Maid'
Upright perennial with grasslike leaves and short, erect stems bearing terminal spikes of pale creamy yellow flowers in summer. Protect crowns with winter mulch. H 24in (60cm), S 18in (45cm).

☀ ◊ ❋❋❋ 5–9

Osteospermum 'Buttermilk'
Evergreen, upright, semi-woody perennial. Daisylike, pale yellow flower heads with dark eyes are borne singly amid gray-green foliage from mid-summer to autumn. H 24in (60cm), S 12in (30cm).

☀ ◊ ❋ 9–10

☐ YELLOW

Achillea taygetea
Perennial with erect stems bearing flat
heads of lemon yellow flowers
throughout summer above clumps of
feathery, gray leaves. Divide and
replant every third year. H 24in (60cm),
S 20in (50cm).

☼ ◊ ❄❄❄ 5–8

Potentilla recta 'Warrenii',
syn. *P. r.* 'Macrantha'
Clump-forming perennial with lobed,
green leaves. Rich golden yellow
flowers are borne on open, branched
stems throughout summer. H 20in
(50cm), S 24in (60cm).

☼ ◊ ❄❄❄ 4–8

Gaillardia aristata
Upright, rather open perennial that has
large, terminal, daisylike, single flower
heads, rich yellow with red centers, for
a long period in summer and soft,
aromatic, divided leaves. Needs staking
and may be short-lived. H 24in (60cm),
S 20in (50cm).

☼ ◊ ❄❄❄ 3–9

Calceolaria biflora
Evergreen perennial with a basal
rosette of soft-haired, oval, toothed
leaves about 6in (15cm) long. Clusters
of small, pouched, yellow flowers
appear in summer. H 12in (30cm),
S 6in (15cm).

◑ ◊ ❄❄❄ 9–10

x **Solidaster luteus**,
syn. x *S. hybridus*
Clump-forming perennial. From mid-
summer onwards, slender stems carry
dense heads of bright creamy yellow
flowers above narrow, green leaves.
H 24in (60cm), S 30in (75cm).

☼ ◊ ❄❄❄ 5–9

Helichrysum 'Sulphur Light'
Clump-forming perennial that bears
silver-gray leaves and a mass of everlasting, fluffy, sulfur yellow flower
heads from mid- to late summer. H
16–24in (40–60cm), S 12in (30cm).

☼ ◊ ❄❄ 5–9

Achillea 'Moonshine'
(Moonshine yarrow)
Upright perennial that bears flat heads
of bright yellow flowers throughout
summer above a mass of small,
feathery, gray-green leaves. Divide
plants regularly in spring. H 24in
(60cm), S 20in (50cm).

☼ ◊ ❄❄❄ 4–8

Barbarea vulgaris 'Variegata'
Perennial with rosettes of long,
toothed, glossy leaves, blotched with
cream, above which rise branching
heads of small, silvery yellow flowers
in early summer. H 10–18in
(25–45cm), S to 9in (23cm).

☼ ◊ ❄❄❄ 4–9

Oenothera tetragona 'Fireworks'
Clump-forming perennial that from
mid- to late summer bears spikes of
fragrant, cup-shaped, bright yellow
flowers. Has reddish stems and glossy,
green foliage. H and S 12–15in
(30–38cm).

☼ ◊ ❄❄❄ 5–9

Ranunculus speciosus 'Plenus',
syn. *R. gouanii* 'Plenus'
Clump-forming perennial with divided, toothed leaves sometimes spotted gray and white. Neat, pomponlike, double, yellow flowers appear in early summer. H 20in (50cm), S 12in (30cm).

☼ ◊ ❄❄❄ 4–8

Mimulus luteus
Spreading perennial. Throughout summer, snapdragonlike, occasionally red-spotted, yellow flowers are freely produced above hairy, green foliage. H and S 12in (30cm).

☼ ◊ ❄❄ 9–10

Meconopsis integrifolia
Rosette-forming biennial or short-lived perennial carrying spikes of large, pale yellow flowers in late spring and early summer. Has large, pale green leaves. H 18–24in (45–60cm), S 24in (60cm).

☼ ◊ ᴾᴴ ❄❄ 7–9

Geum 'Lady Stratheden'
Clump-forming perennial with lobed leaves and cup-shaped, double, bright yellow flowers with prominent, green stamens borne on slender, branching stems for a long period in summer. H 18–24in (45–60cm), S 18in (45cm).

☼ ◊ ❄❄❄ 5–9

Potentilla megalantha
Clump-forming perennial with large, palmate, hairy, soft green leaves. Large, rich yellow flowers are produced in summer. H 8in (20cm), S 6in (15cm).

☼ ◊ ❄❄❄ 5–9

Buphthalmum salicifolium
Spreading perennial that carries daisylike, deep yellow flower heads singly on willowy stems throughout summer. May need staking. Divide regularly; spreads on rich soil. H 2ft (60cm), S 3ft (1m).

☼ ◊ ❄❄❄ 4–9

Gazania uniflora
Mat-forming perennial, grown as an annual in all except mildest areas. Yellow or orange-yellow flower heads, sometimes with central white spots, are borne singly in early summer above rosettes of narrow, silver-backed leaves. H 9in (23cm), S 8–12in (20–30cm).

☼ ◊ ❄ 8–10

Potentilla 'Yellow Queen'
Clump-forming perennial with strawberrylike, dark green leaves and bright yellow flowers in mid-summer. H to 24in (60cm) or more, S 18in (45cm).

☼ ◊ ❄❄❄ 5–8

Ranunculus acris 'Flore Pleno'
Clump-forming perennial. Wiry stems with lobed and cut leaves act as a foil for rosetted, double, golden yellow flowers in late spring and early summer. H and S 18–24in (45–60cm).

☼ ◊ ❄❄❄ 4–8

☐ YELLOW

Sedum aizoon 'Aurantiacum'
Erect perennial with red stems carrying
fleshy, toothed, dark green leaves. In
summer produces gently rounded heads
of dark yellow flowers followed by red
seed capsules. H and S 18in (45cm).

☼ ◊ ❊❊❊ 4–9

Hieracium lanatum
Clump-forming perennial that produces
mounds of broad, downy, gray leaves,
above which dandelionlike, yellow
flower heads appear on wiry stems in
summer. H 12–18in (30–45cm),
S 12in (30cm).

☼ ◊ ❊❊❊ 5–8

Hemerocallis 'Corky'
Clump-forming perennial. Trumpet-
shaped, lemon yellow flowers, brown
on outsides, open in late spring and
early summer above slender, strap-
shaped, green leaves. Flowers, borne
prolifically, last only a day. H and
S 18in (45cm).

☼ ◊ ❊❊❊ 3–9

Eriophyllum lanatum
Perennial forming low cushions of
divided, silvery leaves. Daisylike,
yellow flower heads are produced
freely in summer, usually singly, on
gray stems. H and S 12in (30cm).

☼ ◊ ❊❊ 5–8

Tropaeolum polyphyllum
Prostrate perennial with spurred, short,
trumpet-shaped, rich yellow flowers,
borne singly in summer above trailing,
gray-green leaves and stems. May
spread widely once established but is
good on a bank. H 2–3in (5–8cm),
S 12in (30cm) or more.

☼ ◊ ❊❊❊ 7–9

Coreopsis verticillata
(Threadleaf coreopsis)
Bushy perennial with finely divided,
dark green foliage and many tiny, star-
shaped, golden flower heads borne
throughout summer. Divide and replant
in spring. H 16–24in (40–60cm),
S 12in (30cm).

☼ ◊ ❊❊❊ 4–9

Inula ensifolia (Swordleaf inula)
Clump-forming perennial with small,
lance-shaped to elliptic leaves, bearing
many daisylike, yellow flower heads,
singly on wiry stalks, in late summer.
H and S 12in (30cm).

☼ ◊ ❊❊❊ 4–9

Coreopsis lanceolata
(Lance coreopsis)
Bushy perennial that in summer freely
produces daisylike, bright yellow
flower heads on branching stems.
Lance-shaped leaves are borne on
flower stems. Propagate by seed or
division. H 18in (45cm), S 12in (30cm).

☼ ◊ ❊❊❊ 4–9

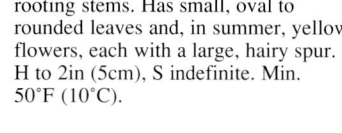

Impatiens repens
Evergreen, creeping perennial with
rooting stems. Has small, oval to
rounded leaves and, in summer, yellow
flowers, each with a large, hairy spur.
H to 2in (5cm), S indefinite. Min.
50°F (10°C).

☼ ◊ 8–10

Calceolaria 'John Innes'
Vigorous, evergreen, clump-forming
perennial that in spring-summer
produces large, pouchlike, reddish
brown-spotted, deep yellow flowers,
several to each stem. Has broadly
oval, basal, green leaves. H 6–8in
(15–20cm), S 10–12in (25–30 cm).

☼ ◊ ❊❊ 7–8

ORANGE

Aeschynanthus speciosus, syn. *A. splendens*

Evergreen, trailing perennial with waxy, narrowly oval leaves usually carried in whorls. Erect, tubular, bright orange-red flowers are borne in large clusters in summer. H and S 12–24in (30–60cm). Min. 64°F (18°C).

☼ ◗ 10

Sedum rosea var. *heterodontum*

Clump-forming perennial with dense, flattish heads of yellow or red, sometimes greenish flowers borne from spring to early summer. Thick, unbranched stems are clothed with oval, toothed, blue-green leaves. H 18in (45cm), S 10in (25cm).

☼ ◊ ❄❄❄ 2–8

Tricyrtis hirta var. *alba*

Upright, rhizomatous perennial that bears clusters of large, bell-shaped, spurred, white flowers, occasionally purple-spotted, in upper leaf axils of hairy, stem-clasping, dark green leaves during late summer and early autumn. H 18–24in (45–60cm), S 18in (45cm).

☼ ◗ ❄❄❄ 4–9

Aster lateriflorus ‘Horizontalis’

Branching, twiggy perennial with unusual, tiny, daisylike, white, sometimes pink-tinged flower heads, with darker pink centers, appearing in autumn. Foliage may become coppery purple in autumn. H 24in (60cm), S 18in (45cm).

☼ ◊ ❄❄❄ 4–8

Geum × *borisii*

Clump-forming perennial with irregularly lobed leaves, above which in summer rise slender, branching, hairy stems bearing single, orange flowers with prominent, yellow stamens. H and S 12in (30cm).

☼ ◊ ❄❄❄ 5–8

Schizostylis coccinea ‘Sunrise’

Clump-forming, rhizomatous perennial that in early autumn produces spikes of large, shallowly cup-shaped, pink flowers above grasslike, green foliage. H 24in (60cm), S 9–12in (23–30cm).

☼ ◗ ❄❄ 6–9

Sedum spectabile 'Brilliant'
Clump-forming perennial that from late summer to autumn produces flat heads of bright rose-pink flowers. These are borne profusely over a mass of fleshy, gray-green leaves and attract butterflies. H and S 12–18in (30–45cm).

☀ ◊ ❄❄❄ 4–9

Aster novi-belgii 'Royal Ruby'
Compact, bushy perennial bearing panicles of large, daisylike, rich red flower heads, with yellow centers, in autumn. Spray regularly as liable to mildew. H and S to 18in (45cm).

☀ ◊ ❄❄❄ 4–8

Schizostylis coccinea 'Grandiflora'
Rhizomatous perennial with long, narrow, grasslike leaves. Gladioluslike spikes of cup-shaped, bright crimson flowers appear in autumn. H 2ft (60cm) or more, S 1ft (30cm) or more.

☀ ◊ ❄❄ 6–9

Cautleya spicata
Upright perennial that in summer and early autumn bears spikes of light orange or soft yellow flowers in maroon-red bracts. Has handsome, long, green leaves. Needs a sheltered site and rich, deep soil. H 24in (60cm), S 20in (50cm).

☀ ◊ ❄❄ 7–9

Senecio pulcher
Perennial with leathery, hairy, dark green leaves. In summer-autumn produces handsome, daisylike, yellow-centered, bright purplish pink flower heads. H 18–24in (45–60cm), S 20in (50cm).

☀ ◊ ❄ 8–10

Aster amellus 'King George'
Bushy perennial that in autumn carries many large, terminal, daisylike, deep blue-violet flower heads with yellow centers. Leaves are oval and rough. H and S 20in (50cm).

☀ ◊ ❄❄❄ 5–8

Liriope muscari (Blue lilyturf)
Evergreen, spreading perennial that in autumn carries spikes of thickly clustered, rounded-bell-shaped, lavender or purple-blue flowers among narrow, glossy, dark green leaves. H 12in (30cm), S 18in (45cm).

☀ ◊ ❄❄❄ 6–10

Chirita lavandulacea
Evergreen, erect perennial with downy, pale green leaves to 8in (20cm) long. In leaf axils has clusters of lavender blue flowers with white tubes. Can be sown in succession to flower from spring to autumn. H and S 2ft (60cm). Min. 59°F (15°C).

☀ ◊ 10

Aster thomsonii 'Nanus'
Compact perennial that produces its long-petaled, daisylike, lilac-blue flower heads for a very long period in summer-autumn. Leaves are slightly heart-shaped. H 18in (45cm), S 9in (23cm).

☀ ◊ ❄❄❄ 5–8

Aster 'Professor A. Kippenburg'
Compact, bushy perennial that carries large clusters of daisylike, yellow-centered, clear blue flower heads in autumn. H 12in (30cm), S to 18in (45cm).

☀ ◊ ❄❄❄ 4–8

Arctotheca calendula (Capeweed)
Carpeting perennial. Leaves are woolly below, rough-haired above. Heads of daisylike, bright yellow flower heads, with darker yellow centers, appear from late spring to autumn. H 12in (30cm), S indefinite. Min. 41°F (5°C).

☀ ◊ 9–10

Begonias

The genus *Begonia* is one of the most versatile. Semperflorens begonias are excellent for summer bedding, while the Rex group has distinctive and handsome foliage. Other groups, such as the x *tuberhybrida* cultivars with their large and showy blooms, are grown mainly for their flowers. Many also make attractive plants for hanging baskets. (See the Plant Dictionary for additional information.)

B. x *tuberhybrida* 'Billie Langdon'

B. scharffii

B. rex 'Merry Christmas'

B. masoniana

B. prismatocarpa

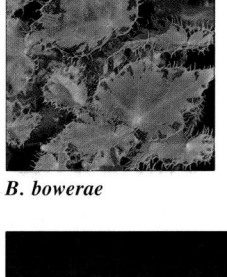

B. bowerae

B. albo-picta

B. x *weltoniensis*

B. 'Orpha C. Fox'

B. x *tuberhybrida* 'Flamboyant'

B. x *tuberhybrida* 'Apricot Cascade'

B. foliosa

B. 'Ingramii'

B. x *tuberhybrida* 'Roy Hartley'

B. rex 'Helen Lewis'

B. x *tuberhybrida* 'Can-Can'

B. olsoniae

B. metallica

B. 'Lucerna'

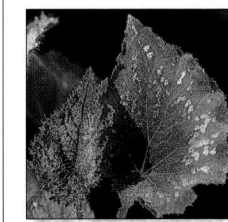

B. rex 'Duartei'

B. manicata 'Crispa'

B. 'Orange Rubra'

B. manicata

B. serratipetala

B. semperflorens 'Red Ascot'

B. semperflorens 'Organdy'

B. 'Thurstonii'

B. pustulata 'Argentea'

B. 'Norah Bedson'

B. 'Oliver Twist'

B. sutherlandii

251

Orchids

Flamboyant, exotic, even seductive, the orchid is prized for its unusual flowers. Its aura of mystique and many popular misconceptions may have discouraged gardeners from growing these beautiful plants, but their cultivation is not always difficult and some will thrive happily indoors as house plants.

There are two main groups. Terrestrials grow in a wide range of habitats in the wild; many are at least frost hardy. Epiphytes, the more showy of the two and mostly native to the tropics, cling to tree branches or rocks, obtaining nourishment through their leaves and aerial roots. They need special composts and in cool climates must be grown in greenhouses (see "Orchids" in the Plant Dictionary).

(Key: x *Brass.* – x *Brassolaeliocattleya*; x *Soph.* – x *Sophrolaeliocattleya*; x *Oda.* – x *Odontioda*; *Odm.* – *Odontoglossum*; e – epiphyte; t – terrestrial)

Coelogyne cristata [e]

Masdevallia infracta [e]

Odm. rossii [e]

Cypripedium acaule [t]

Masdevallia tovarensis [e]

Dendrobium infundibulum [e]

Coelogyne flaccida [e]

Calanthe vestita [t]

Odm. cervantesii [e]

Dendrobium aphyllum [e]

Phalaenopsis Allegria [e]

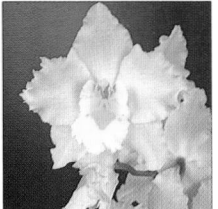

Odm. Royal Occasion [e]

Paphiopedilum Freckles [t]

Brassavola nodosa [e]

Paphiopedilum fairrieanum [t]

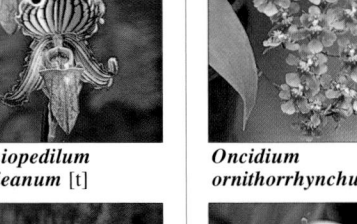

Oncidium ornithorrhynchum [e]

Paphiopedilum niveum [t]

Coelogyne nitida [e]

Cymbidium Portlett Bay [e]

Paphiopedilum callosum [t]

Cypripedium reginae [t]

Spiranthes cernua [t]

Odm. crispum [e]

Miltoniopsis Robert Strauss 'Ardingly' [e]

Cymbidium Strathbraan [e]

Paphiopedilum bellatulum [t]

Angraecum sesquipedale [e]

Paphiopedilum appletonianum [t]

Odm. bictoniense [e]

Dendrobium nobile [e]

Calypso bulbosa [t]

x *Laeliocattleya* Rojo 'Mont Millais' [e]

Odm. cordatum [e]

Ophrys tenthredini-fera [t]

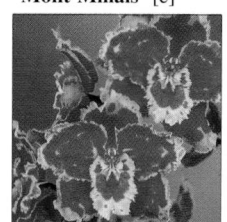

x *Oda.* Mount Bingham [e]

Cymbidium Strath Kanaid [e]

x *Wilsonara* Hambuh-ren Stern 'Cheam' [e]

x *Brass.* Hetherington 'Coronation' [e]

Pleione bulbocodi-oides [t]

Cattleya J.A. Carbone [e]

x *Vuylstekeara* Cambria 'Lensing's Favorite' [e]

Cymbidium Pontac 'Mont Millais' [e]

x *Oda.* Pacific Gold x *Odm. cordatum* [e]

Laelia anceps [e]

Bletilla striata [t]

x *Soph.* Trizac 'Purple Emperor' [e]

Odm. grande [e]

x *Brassocattleya* Mount Adams [e]

x *Brass.* St. Helier [e]

Miltoniopsis Anjou 'St. Patrick' [e]

Epidendrum ibaguense [e]

Cattleya bowringiana [e]

Odm. Le Nez Point [e]

Cymbidium Strathdon 'Cooksbridge Noel' [e]

Paphiopedilum x *maudiae* [t]

x *Odontocidium* Artur Elle 'Colombian' [e]

Phalaenopsis Lady Jersey x Lippeglut [e]

Masdevallia coccinea [e]

x *Oda.* Petit Port [e]

Phaius tankervilleae [t]

Paphiopedilum Lyric 'Glendora' [t]

x *Odontocidium* Tiger Butter x *Wilsonara* Wigg's 'Kay' [e]

253

Orchids continued

Phalaenopsis cornu-cervi [e]

Cymbidium devonianum [e]

Paphiopedilum sukhakulii [t]

Gomesa planifolia [e]

Paphiopedilum Buckhurst 'Mont Millais' [t]

Miltonia candida var. *grandiflora* [e]

Zygopetalum mackayi [e]

Paphiopedilum haynaldianum [t]

Odm. Eric Young [e]

x *Aliceara* Dark Warrior [e]

Zygopetalum Perrenoudii [e]

Coelogyne speciosa [e]

Masdevallia wagneriana [e]

x *Odontocidium* Tigersun 'Orbec' [e]

Gongora quinquenervis [e]

Cymbidium King's Lock 'Cooksbridge' [e]

Ophrys fusca [t]

Phalaenopsis Lundy [e]

Oncidium tigrinum [e]

Bulbophyllum careyanum [e]

Orchis morio [t]

Cymbidium grandiflorum [e]

Cymbidium Caithness Ice 'Trinity' [e]

Cymbidium elegans [e]

Miltonia clowesii [e]

Cymbidium tracyanum [e]

Ophrys lutea var. *lutea* [t]

Vanda Rothschildiana [e]

Cypripedium calceolus [t]

Cypripedium macranthon [t]

Epidendrum difforme [e]

Maxillaria
porphyrostele [e]

x *Potinara* **Cherub**
'Spring Daffodil' [e]

Laelia cinnabarina [e]

Dendrobium
chrysotoxum [e]

Lycaste cruenta [e]

Oncidium papilio [e]

x *Odontocidium* **Tiger**
Hambuhren [e]

Oncidium flexuosum [e]

Ada aurantiaca [e]

Cypripedium calceolus
var. *pubescens* [t]

x *Soph.* **Hazel Boyd**
'Apricot Glow' [e]

Cymbidium **Christmas**
Angel 'Cooksbridge
Sunburst' [e]

Paphiopedilum
venustum [t]

x *Oda.* (**Chantos**
x **Marzorka**) x *Odm.*
Buttercrisp [e]

☐ WHITE

***Spathiphyllum* 'Mauna Loa'**
Robust, evergreen, tufted perennial
with rhizomes. Has long, lance-shaped,
glossy leaves. Irregularly bears fleshy,
white spadices of fragrant flowers,
enclosed in large, oval, white spathes.
H and S 18–24in (45–60cm).
Min. 59°F (15°C).

☀ ◐ 10

Episcia dianthiflora (Lace flower)
Evergreen perennial with creeping,
prostrate stems. Has thick, velvety
leaves with brownish midribs and,
intermittently, pure white flowers with
fringed petals. H 4in (10cm),
S indefinite. Min. 59°F (15°C).

☀ ◐ 10

Hemigraphis repanda
Evergreen, prostrate perennial with
spreading, rooting stems. Lance-
shaped, toothed, purple-tinged leaves,
2in (5cm) long, are darker purple
below. Has tiny, tubular, white flowers
intermittently. H to 6in (15cm),
S indefinite. Min. 59°F (15°C).

☀ ◐ 10

☐ WHITE

Spathiphyllum wallisii
Evergreen, tufted, rhizomatous
perennial. Has clusters of long, lance-
shaped leaves. Fleshy, white spadices
of fragrant flowers in white spathes are
irregularly produced. H and S 12in
(30cm) or more. Min. 59°F (15°C).

☼◑ ◊ 10

Pilea cadierei (Aluminum plant)
Evergreen, bushy perennial with
broadly oval leaves, each with a sharply
pointed tip and raised, silvery patches
that appear quilted. Has insignificant,
greenish flowers. H and S 12in (30cm).
Min. 50°F (10°C).

☼◑ ◊ 9–10

**Tradescantia fluminensis
'Variegata'**, syn. *T. albiflora*
'Variegata'
Evergreen, trailing perennial with
rooting stems and leaves, irregularly
striped creamy white. Intermittently
has clusters of white flowers. H 12in
(30cm), S indefinite. Min 59°F (15°C).

☼ ◊ 8–10

Fittonia verschaffeltii var.
argyroneura, syn. *F. argyroneura*
(Fittonia)
Evergreen, creeping perennial with
small, oval, white-veined, olive green
leaves. Remove flowers if they form.
H to 6in (15cm), S indefinite. Min.
59°F (15°C).

☀ ◊ 9–10

**Tradescantia fluminensis
'Albovittata'**, syn. *T. albiflora*
'Albovittata'
Strong-growing, evergreen perennial
with trailing, rooting stems. Bluish
green leaves have broad, white stripes.
Bears small, white flowers. H 12in
(30cm), S indefinite. Min. 59°F (15°C).

☼ ◊ 8–10

**Aglaonema commutatum
'Treubii'**
Evergreen, erect, tufted perennial.
Lance-shaped leaves, to 12in (30cm)
long, are marked with pale green or
silver. Occasionally has greenish white
spathes. H and S to 18in (45cm).
Min. 59°F (15°C).

☼ ◊ 10

Glechoma hederacea 'Variegata'
(Variegated ground ivy)
Evergreen, carpeting perennial that has
small, heart-shaped leaves, with white
marbling, on trailing stems. Bears
insignificant flowers in summer.
Spreads rapidly but is useful for a
container. H 6in (15cm), S indefinite.

☼ ◊ ❀❀❀ 5–9

Helleborus orientalis [white form]
(Lenten rose)
Evergreen, clump-forming perennial
with dense, divided foliage, above
which rise nodding, cup-shaped, white,
pink, or purple flowers, sometimes
darker spotted, in winter or early spring.
H and S 18in (45cm).

☼ ◊◑ ❀❀❀ 5–9

Peperomia caperata
(Emerald-ripple)
Evergreen, bushy perennial with
pinkish leaf stalks. Has oval, fleshy,
wrinkled, dark green leaves, to 2in
(5cm) long, with sunken veins; spikes
of white flowers appear irregularly. H
and S to 6in (15cm). Min. 50°F (10°C).

☼ ◊ 10

***Chlorophytum comosum*
'Vittatum'** (Spider plant)
Evergreen, tufted, rosette-forming
perennial. Long, narrow, lance-shaped,
creamy white leaves have green stripes
and margins. Irregularly has small, star-
shaped, white flowers on thin stems.
H and S 12in (30cm). Min. 41°F (5°C).

☀ ◊ 9–10

***Aspidistra elatior* 'Variegata'**
Evergreen, rhizomatous perennial with
upright, narrow, glossy, dark green
leaves which are longitudinally cream-
striped. Occasionally has inconspicuous,
cream to purple flowers near soil level.
H 24in (60cm), S 18in (45cm). Min.
41–50°F (5–10°C).

☀ ◊ 7–10

***Oplismenus hirtellus* 'Variegatus'**
Evergreen, creeping, perennial grass
with wiry, rooting stems. Lance-
shaped, long-pointed, white-striped
leaves, with wavy margins, are often
tinged pink. Bears inconspicuous
flowers intermittently. H 8in (20cm) or
more, S indefinite. Min. 54°F (12°C).

☀ ◊ 9–10

***Streptocarpus* 'Nicola'**
Evergreen, stemless perennial with
a rosette of strap-shaped, wrinkled
leaves. Funnel-shaped, rose-pink
flowers are produced intermittently in
small clusters. H 10in (25cm), S 20in
(50cm). Min. 50–59°F (10–15°C).

☀ ◊ 10

Tradescantia zebrina, syn.
Zebrina pendula (Wandering Jew)
Evergreen, trailing or mat-forming
perennial. Bluish green leaves, purple-
tinged beneath, have 2 broad, silver
bands. Has pink or violet-blue flowers
intermittently during the year. H 6in
(15cm), S indefinite. Min. 59°F (15°C).

☀ ◊ 9–10

Helleborus niger (Christmas rose)
Evergreen, clump-forming perennial
with divided, deep green leaves and
cup-shaped, nodding, white flowers
with golden stamens borne in winter
or early spring. H and S 12in (30cm).

☀ ◊ ❄❄❄ 4–8

Helleborus* x *sternii
Evergreen, clump-forming perennial
with divided leaves and cup-shaped,
often pink-tinged, pale green flowers
borne in terminal clusters in winter and
early spring. H and S 18in (45cm).

☀ ◊ ❄❄ 6–9

Helleborus orientalis [pink form]
(Lenten rose)
Evergreen, clump-forming perennial
with dense, divided foliage, above
which rise nodding, cup-shaped, white,
pink, or purple flowers, sometimes
darker spotted, in winter or early
spring. H and S 18in (45cm).

☀ ◊ ❄❄❄ 5–9

Episcia cupreata (Flame violet)
Evergreen, creeping perennial. Has
small, downy, wrinkled leaves, usually
silver-veined or -banded, and,
intermittently, scarlet flowers marked
yellow within. H 4in (10cm),
S indefinite. Min. 59°F (15°C).

☀ ◊ 9–10

African violets

African violet is the common name for the genus *Saintpaulia*, although frequently used for the many hybrids of *S. ionantha*. These small, rosetted perennials may be grown as summer bedding in warm, humid climates but also make attractive, indoor pot plants, flowering freely if kept in a draught-free, light, and humid position. The selection below shows the range of flower colors and forms available.

S. 'Miss Pretty'

S. 'Garden News'

S. 'Fancy Pants'

S. 'Pip Squeak'

S. 'Colorado'

S. 'Rococo Pink'

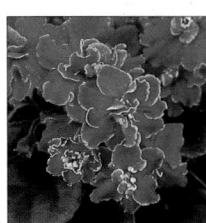
S. 'Kristi Marie'

S. 'Porcelain'

S. 'Bright Eyes'

S. 'Delft'

Perennials/small WINTER/ALL YEAR

Anthurium scherzerianum
(Flamingo flower)
Evergreen, tufted perennial with erect, leathery, dark green leaves to 8in (20cm) long. Has large, long-lasting, bright red spathes and fleshy, orange to yellow spadices. H and S 12–24in (30–60cm). Min 59°F (15°C).

☼ ◊ 10

Helleborus orientalis [purple form]
(Lenten rose)
Evergreen, clump-forming perennial with dense, divided foliage, above which rise nodding, cup-shaped, white, pink, or purple flowers, sometimes darker spotted, in winter or early spring. H and S 18in (45cm).

☼ ◊ ❋❋❋ 5–9

Gerbera jamesonii
(Transvaal daisy)
Evergreen, upright perennial with daisy-like, variably colored flower heads, borne intermittently on long stems, and basal rosettes of large, jagged leaves. Flowers are excellent for cutting. H 24in (60cm), S 18in (45cm).

☼ ◊ ❋ 8–10

***Phormium tenax* 'Bronze Baby'**
Evergreen, upright perennial with tufts of bold, stiff, pointed, wine red leaves. Panicles of reddish flowers are occasionally produced on purplish stems during summer. H and S 18–24in (45–60cm).

☼ ◊ ❋❋ 9–10

***Tellima grandiflora* 'Purpurea'**
(Alaska fringecup)
Semi-evergreen, clump-forming perennial with a mass of hairy, basal, reddish purple leaves, underlaid dark green. In late spring, erect stems bear spikes of bell-shaped, pinkish cream flowers. H and S 24in (60cm).

☼ ◊ ❋❋❋ 4–8

Fittonia verschaffeltii
(Fittonia, Nerve net)
Evergreen, creeping perennial with small, oval, red-veined, olive green leaves. Flowers are best removed if they form. H to 6in (15cm), S indefinite. Min 59°F (15°C).

☼ ◊ 9–10

Ophiopogon planiscapus 'Nigrescens'
Evergreen, spreading, clump-forming perennial, grown for its distinctive, grasslike, black leaves. Racemes of lilac flowers in summer are followed by black fruits. H 9in (23cm), S 12in (30cm).

☀ ◊ ❀❀❀ 6–10

Tradescantia pallida 'Purple Heart'
Evergreen, creeping perennial with dark purple stems and slightly fleshy leaves. Has pink or pink-and-white flowers in summer. H 12–16in (30–40cm), S 12in (30cm) or more. Min. 59°F (15°C).

☀ ◊ 9–10

Ajuga reptans 'Atropurpurea'
Evergreen, ground-cover perennial, spreading freely by runners, with small rosettes of glossy, deep bronze-purple leaves. Short spikes of blue flowers appear in spring. H 6in (15cm), S 3ft (1m).

☀ ◊ ❀❀❀ 3–8

Pellionia daveauana, syn. *P. repens* (Trailing watermelon begonia)
Evergreen, creeping perennial with rooting stems. Broadly oval, olive green leaves have purplish brown edges and paler green centers. Flowers are insignificant. H 4in (10cm), S indefinite. Min. 59°F (15°C).

☀ ◊ 10

Tradescantia sillamontana, syn. *T. pexata*, *T. velutina*
Evergreen, erect perennial. Oval, stem-clasping leaves are densely covered with white, woolly hairs. Has clusters of small, bright purplish pink flowers in summer. H and S to 12in (30cm). Min. 50–59°F (10–15°C).

☀ ◊ 9–10

Tetranema roseum, syn. *T. mexicanum* (Mexican foxglove)
Short-stemmed perennial with crowded, stalkless leaves, bluish green beneath. Intermittently, has nodding, purple flowers with paler throats. H to 8in (20cm), S 12in (30cm). Min. 55°F (13°C).

☀ ◊ 10

Ajuga reptans 'Multicolor', syn. *A.r.* 'Rainbow'
Evergreen, mat-forming perennial. Dark green leaves, marked with cream and pink, make good ground cover. Spikes of small, blue flowers appear in spring. H 5in (12cm), S 18in (45cm).

☀ ◊ ❀❀❀ 3–8

Streptocarpus 'Constant Nymph'
Evergreen, stemless perennial with a rosette of strap-shaped, wrinkled leaves. Funnel-shaped, purplish blue flowers, darker veined and yellow-throated, are intermittently produced in small clusters. H 10in (25cm), S 20in (50cm). Min. 50–59°F (10–15°C).

☀ ◊ 10

Cyanotis somaliensis (Fuzzy-ears)
Evergreen, creeping perennial. Small, narrow, glossy, dark green leaves with white hairs surround stems. Has purplish blue flowers in leaf axils in winter-spring. H 2in (5cm), S indefinite. Min. 50–59°F (10–15°C).

☀ ◊ 9–10

Maranta leuconeura 'Erythroneura', syn. *M. l.* 'Erythrophylla'
Evergreen perennial. Oblong leaves have veins marked red, with paler yellowish green midribs, and are upright at night, flat by day. H and S to 12in (30cm). Min. 59°F (15°C).

☀ ◊ 10

Sansevieria trifasciata 'Hahnii'
Evergreen, stemless perennial with a rosette of about 5 stiff, erect, broadly lance-shaped and pointed leaves, banded horizontally with pale green or white. Occasionally has small, pale green flowers. H 6–12in (15–30cm), S 4in (10cm). Min. 59°F (15°C).

☀ ◊ 9–10

■ GREEN

Calathea makoyana
Evergreen, clump-forming perennial.
Horizontal leaves, 12in (30cm) long,
are dark and light green above, reddish
purple below. Intermittently has short
spikes of white flowers. H to 2ft (60cm),
S to 4ft (1.2m). Min. 59°F (15°C).

☀ ◊ 10

Aglaonema pictum
Evergreen, erect, tufted perennial.
Oval leaves, to 6in (15cm) long, are
irregularly marked with grayish white
or gray-green. Has creamy white
spathes in summer. H and S to 2ft
(60cm). Min. 59°F (15°C).

☀ ◊ 10

Aglaonema commutatum 'Silver King'
Evergreen, erect, tufted perennial.
Broadly lance-shaped leaves, to 12in
(30cm) long, are marked with dark and
light green. Has greenish white spathes
in summer. H and S to 18in (45cm).
Min. 59°F (15°C).

☀ ◊ 10

Maranta leuconeura var. **kerchoviana** (Rabbit's-foot)
Evergreen perennial that intermittently
bears white to mauve flowers. Oblong
leaves with dark brown blotches
become greener with age and are
upright at night, flat by day. H and
S to 12in (30cm). Min. 59°F (15°C).

☀ ◊ 10

Welwitschia mirabilis, syn. *W. bainesii*
Evergreen perennial with short, woody
trunk. Has 2 strap-shaped leaves, to 8ft
(2.5m) long, with tips splitting to form
many tendril-like strips. Bears small,
reddish brown cones. H to 12in (30cm),
S indefinite. Min. 50°F (10°C).

☀ ◊ 10

Peperomia marmorata
Evergreen, bushy perennial with
insignificant flowers. Has oval, long-
pointed, fleshy, dull green leaves,
marked with grayish white and quilted
above, reddish below. H and S to 8in
(20cm). Min. 50°F (10°C).

☀ ◊ 10

Stachys byzantina, syn. *S. lanata*, *S. olympica* (Lamb's-ears)
Evergreen, mat-forming perennial with
woolly, gray foliage excellent for a
border front or as ground cover. Bears
mauve-pink flowers in summer. H
12–15in (30–38cm), S 24in (60cm).

☀ ◊ ❄❄❄ 4–9

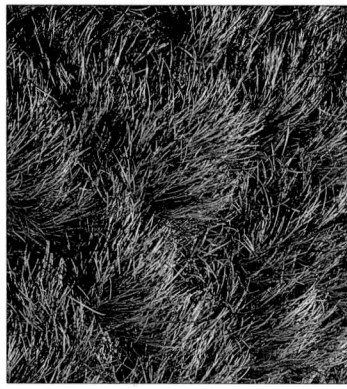

Ophiopogon japonicus (Mondo grass)
Evergreen, clump- or mat-forming
perennial with grasslike, glossy, dark
green foliage. Spikes of lilac flowers in
late summer are followed by blue-
black berries. H 12in (30cm),
S indefinite.

☀ ◊ ❄❄❄ 7–10

Helleborus lividus subsp. **corsicus**
Clump-forming perennial with
evergreen, divided, spiny, dark green
leaves and cup-shaped, pale green
flowers borne in large clusters in
winter-spring. H 24in (60cm),
S 18in (45cm).

☀ ◊ ❄❄ 7–9

Soleirolia soleirolii, syn. *Helxine soleirolii*
(Angel's tears, Baby's tears)
Usually evergreen, invasive, prostrate
perennial with small, round, vivid green
leaves that form a carpet. May choke
other plants if not controlled. H 2in
(5cm), S indefinite.

☀ ◊ ❄❄ 10

Callisia repens (Little jewel)
Evergreen, creeping perennial with
rooting stems and densely packed
leaves, sometimes white-banded and
often purplish beneath. Rarely, has
inconspicuous, white flowers in winter.
H 4in (10cm), S indefinite. Min.
59°F (15°C).

☀ ◊ 10

Drosera spathulata
Evergreen, insectivorous perennial with rosettes of spoon-shaped leaves that have sensitive, red, glandular hairs. Has many small, pink or white flowers on leafless stems in summer. H and S to 3in (8cm). Min. 41–50°F (5–10°C).

☼ ◗ 9–10

Peperomia glabella
Evergreen perennial with wide-spreading, red stems. Has broadly oval, fleshy, glossy, bright green leaves, to 2in (5cm) long, and insignificant flowers. H to 6in (15cm), S 12in (30cm). Min. 50°F (10°C).

☼ ◊ 10

Helleborus viridis
Clump-forming perennial with deciduous, divided, dark green leaves. Bears cup-shaped, green flowers in late winter or early spring. H and S 12in (30cm).

☼ ◊ ❄❄❄ 6–8

Drosera capensis
Evergreen, insectivorous perennial. Rosettes of narrow leaves have sensitive, red, glandular hairs. Many small, purple flowers are borne on leafless stems in summer. H and S to 6in (15cm). Min. 41–50°F (5–10°C).

☼ ◗ 10

Peperomia obtusifolia 'Variegata'
Evergreen, bushy perennial with spade-shaped, fleshy leaves, to 8in (20cm) long, that have irregular, yellowish green to creamy white margins and usually grayish centers. Flowers are insignificant. H and S to 6in (15cm). Min. 50°F (10°C).

☼◐ ◊ 10

Pilea nummulariifolia
(Creeping Charlie)
Evergreen, mat-forming perennial with creeping, rooting, reddish stems. Rounded, pale green leaves, about ³/₄in (2cm) wide, have a corrugated surface. Flowers are insignificant. H to 2in (5cm), S 12in (30cm). Min. 50°F (10°C).

☼ ◊ 10

Iresine herbstii 'Aureo-reticulata'
Evergreen, bushy perennial with red stems and inconspicuous flowers. Rounded, green leaves, 4in (10cm) long, have yellow or red veins and notched tips. H to 24in (60cm), S 18in (45cm). Min. 50–59°F (10–15°C).

☼ ◊ 10

Dionaea muscipula
(Venus's flytrap)
Evergreen, insectivorous perennial with rosettes of 6 or more spreading, hinged leaves, pink-flushed inside, edged with stiff bristles. Clusters of tiny, white flowers are carried in summer. H 4in (10cm), S 12in (30cm). Min. 41°F (5°C).

☼ ◗ 8–9

Helleborus foetidus
(Stinking hellebore)
Evergreen, clump-forming perennial with deeply divided, dark green leaves and, in late winter and early spring, panicles of cup-shaped, red-margined, pale green flowers. H and S 18in (45cm).

◑ ◊ ❄❄❄ 7–9

Sansevieria trifasciata 'Golden Hahnii'
Evergreen, stemless perennial with a rosette of about 5 stiff, erect, broadly lance-shaped leaves with wide, yellow borders. Sometimes bears small, pale green flowers. H 6–12in (15–30cm), S 4in (10cm). Min. 59°F (15°C).

☼ ◊ 9–10

Nautilocalyx lynchii
Robust, evergreen, erect, bushy perennial. Broadly lance-shaped, slightly wrinkled leaves are glossy, greenish red above, reddish beneath. In summer has tubular, red-haired, pale yellow flowers with red calyces. H and S to 24in (60cm). Min. 59°F (15°C).

◑ ◊ 10

☐ WHITE

Gypsophila elegans
(Baby's-breath)
Fast-growing, erect, bushy annual.
Has lance-shaped, grayish green leaves
and clouds of tiny, white flowers in
branching heads from summer to
early autumn. H 24in (60cm), S 12in
(30cm) or more.

☼ ◊ ❋❋❋ H

Digitalis purpurea f. **alba**
(White foxglove)
Slow-growing, short-lived perennial,
grown as a biennial. Has a rosette of
large, pointed-oval leaves and erect
stems carrying tubular, white flowers
in summer. H 3–5ft (1–1.5m),
S 1–1½ft (30–45cm).

◐ ◊ ❋❋❋ 4–8

Omphalodes linifolia
Fairly fast-growing, slender, erect
annual with lance-shaped, gray-green
leaves. Tiny, slightly scented, rounded,
white flowers, rarely tinged blue, are
carried in summer. H 6–12in
(15–30cm), S 6in (15cm).

☼ ◊ ❋ H

Lavatera trimestris 'Mont Blanc'
Moderately fast-growing, erect,
branching annual with oval, lobed
leaves. Shallowly trumpet-shaped,
brilliant white flowers appear from
summer to early autumn. H to 24in
(60cm), S 18in (45cm).

☼ ◊ ❋❋❋ H

Iberis amara (Rocket candytuft)
Fast-growing, erect, bushy annual
with lance-shaped, green leaves.
Has flattish heads of small, scented,
4-petaled, white flowers in summer.
H 12in (30cm), S 6in (15cm).

☼ ◊ ❋❋❋ H

**Lobularia maritima 'Little
Dorrit'**, syn. *Alyssum maritimum*
'Little Dorrit'
Fast-growing, compact annual with
lance-shaped, grayish green leaves and
heads of scented, 4-petaled, white
flowers in summer and early autumn.
H 3–6in (8–15cm), S 8–12in (20–30cm).

☼ ◊ ❋❋❋ H

Matthiola 'Giant Imperial'
Fast-growing, erect, bushy biennial,
grown as an annual. Has lance-shaped,
grayish green leaves and long spikes of
highly scented, white to creamy yellow
flowers in summer. Produces excellent
flowers for cutting. H to 24in (60cm),
S 12in (30cm).

☼ ◊ ❋❋❋ H

Petunia, Recoverer Series
[white]
Moderately fast-growing, branching,
bushy perennial, grown as an annual.
Has oval, mid- to deep green leaves
and large, flared, trumpet-shaped,
white flowers in summer-autumn. H
6–12in (15–30cm), S 12in (30cm).

☼ ◊ ❋ HH

Dimorphotheca pluvialis, syn. *D. annua*
Branching annual with oval, hairy, deep green leaves. In summer has small, daisylike flower heads, the rays purple beneath and white above, with brownish purple centers. H 8–12in (20–30cm), S 6in (15cm).

 ☼ ◊ ❋ HH

Chrysanthemum parthenium (Feverfew)
Moderately fast-growing, short-lived, bushy perennial, grown as an annual. Lobed, green leaves are aromatic; small, daisylike, white flower heads are carried in summer and early autumn. H and S 8–18in (20–45cm).

☼ ◊ ❋❋❋ H

Reseda odorata
Moderately fast-growing, erect, branching annual with oval leaves. Cone-shaped heads of small, very fragrant, somewhat star-shaped, white flowers with orange-brown stamens appear in summer and early autumn. H 12–24in (30–60cm), S 12in (30cm).

☼ ◊ ❋❋❋ H

Euphorbia marginata (Snow-on-the-mountain, Summer icicle)
Moderately fast-growing, upright, bushy annual. Has pointed-oval, bright green leaves; upper leaves are white-margined. Broad, petal-like, white bracts surround insignificant flowers in summer. H 24in (60cm), S 12in (30cm).

☼ ◊ ❋ HH

Nemophila maculata (Five-spot nemophila)
Fast-growing, spreading annual with lobed leaves. Small, bowl-shaped, white flowers with purple-tipped petals are carried in summer. H and S 6in (15cm).

 ☼ ◊ ❋❋❋ H

Viola, Floral Dance Series [white]
Bushy perennial, grown as an annual or biennial. Has oval, green leaves and rounded, 5-petaled, white flowers in winter. H 6–8in (15–20cm), S 8in (20cm).

☼ ◊ ❋❋❋ H

Salvia splendens, **Carabiniere Series** [white]
Slow-growing, bushy perennial, grown as an annual. Has oval, serrated, fresh green leaves and dense racemes of tubular, white flowers in summer and early autumn. H to 12in (30cm), S 8–12in (20–30cm).

☼ ◊ ❋ T

Nicotiana, Domino Series
Fairly slow-growing, bushy annual with pointed-oval leaves. Somewhat trumpet-shaped flowers, to 3in (8cm) long, appear in a wide range of colors in summer and early autumn. H and S 12in (30cm).

☼ ◊ ❋ T

Eustoma grandiflorum, syn. *Lisianthus russellianus*
Slow-growing, upright annual with lance-shaped, deep green leaves. Poppylike, pink, purple, blue, or white flowers, 2in (5cm) wide, are carried in summer. H 24in (60cm), S 12in (30cm). Min. 39–45° (4–7°C).

☼ ◊ HH

Annuals and Biennials

Hibiscus trionum (Flower-of-an-hour, Goodnight-at-noon)
Fairly fast-growing, upright annual with oval, serrated leaves. Trumpet-shaped, creamy white or pale yellow flowers, with purplish brown centers, are borne from late summer to early autumn. H 24in (60cm), S 12in (30cm).

☼ ◊ ❋ HH

Zea mays 'Gracillima Variegata'
Fairly fast-growing, erect annual with lance-shaped leaves, striped green and creamy white. Has tassel-like, silvery flower heads, followed by large, bright yellow seed heads (cobs). H 3ft (90cm), S 1–1¹/₂ft (30–45cm).

☼ ◊ ❋ HH

Impatiens balsamina (Balsam)
Fairly fast-growing, erect, compact, bushy annual with lance-shaped leaves. Small, spurred, pink or white flowers are borne in summer and early autumn. H to 30in (75cm), S 18in (45cm).

☼ ◊ ❋ T

Martynia annua, syn. *M. louisiana*
Fairly fast-growing, upright annual with long-stalked leaves. Has foxglovelike, lobed, creamy white flowers marked red, pink, and yellow in summer, followed by horned, green, then brown, fruits. H 24in (60cm), S 12in (30cm).

☼ ◊ ❋ T

Chrysanthemum carinatum 'Monarch Court Jesters'
Fast-growing, erect, branching annual. Has feathery, gray-green leaves and, in summer, daisylike, zoned flower heads, to 3in (8cm) wide, in various color combinations. H 24in (60cm), S 12in (30cm).

☼ ◊ ❋❋❋ H

Lathyrus odoratus 'Knee Hi'
Fast-growing annual with oval, divided, green leaves and large, fragrant flowers, in shades of pink, red, blue, or white, that are borne in summer or early autumn. H and S 3ft (90cm).

☼ ◊ ❋❋❋ H

Crepis rubra (Hawk's beard)
Fairly fast-growing, rosette-forming annual with lance-shaped, serrated leaves. In summer bears dandelionlike, pink, occasionally red or white flower heads. H 12in (30cm), S 6in (15cm).

☼ ◊ ❋❋❋ H

Silene coeli-rosa, syn. *Agrostemma coeli-rosa, Lychnis coeli-rosa, Viscaria elegans* (Rose-of-heaven)
Moderately fast-growing, erect annual with lance-shaped, grayish green leaves. Has 5-petaled, pinkish purple flowers, with white centers, in summer. H 18in (45cm), S 6in (15cm).

☼ ◊ ❋❋❋ HH

Helipterum roseum,
syn. *Acroclinium roseum*
Moderately fast-growing, erect annual.
Lance-shaped leaves are grayish green;
small, daisylike, papery, semi-double,
pink flower heads appear in summer.
Flowers dry well. H 12in (30cm),
S 6in (15cm).

☼ ◊ ❋ T

***Primula*, Posy Series**
Rosette-forming perennial, normally
grown as a biennial, with lance-shaped
leaves. Fragrant, flat, almost stemless
flowers, in shades of pink, red, yellow,
purple, or white, with contrasting
centers, appear in spring. H 3in (8cm),
S 4in (10cm).

☼ ◊ ❋❋❋ H

***Matthiola*, Brompton Series**
Fast-growing, erect, bushy biennial,
grown as an annual. Lance-shaped
leaves are grayish green; long spikes
of highly scented flowers in shades of
pink, red, purple, yellow, or white are
borne in summer. H 18in (45cm),
S 12in (30cm).

☼ ◊ ❋❋❋ H

Alcea rosea,
syn. *Althaea rosea* (Hollyhock)
Biennial with tall, erect stems and
lobed, rough-textured leaves. Spikes
of single flowers, in a range of colors
including pink, yellow, and cream,
appear in summer and early autumn.
H 5–6ft (1.5–2m), S to 2ft (60cm).

☼ ◊ ❋❋❋ H

***Matthiola* 'Giant Excelsior'**
Fast-growing, erect, bushy biennial,
grown as an annual. Lance-shaped
leaves are grayish green; long spikes
of highly scented flowers in shades of
pink, red, pale blue, or white appear in
summer. H to 30in (75cm),
S 12in (30cm).

☼ ◊ ❋❋❋ H

Helipterum manglesii,
syn. *Rhodanthe manglesii*
Moderately fast-growing, erect annual.
Has pointed-oval, grayish green leaves
and daisylike, papery, red, pink, or
white flower heads, in summer and
early autumn. Flowers dry well.
H 12in (30cm), S 6in (15cm).

☼ ◊ ❋ T

***Papaver somniferum*, Peony-
flowered Series**
Fast-growing, erect annual with lobed,
pale grayish green leaves. Has large,
rounded, often cup-shaped, double
flowers in a mixture of colors—red,
pink, purple, or white—in summer.
H 30in (75cm), S 12in (30cm).

☼ ◊ ❋❋❋ H

***Pelargonium*, Orbit Series**
[salmon]
Slow-growing, evergreen, branching,
bushy perennial, grown as an annual,
with lobed leaves, zoned with bronze or
red. Has large, rounded heads of salmon
pink flowers in summer-autumn. H and
S 12–24in (30–60cm).

☼ ◊ ❋ T

***Antirrhinum majus*, Madame
Butterfly Series**
Erect perennial, grown as an annual.
Leaves are lance-shaped; spikes of
tubular, 2-lipped, double flowers
are carried from spring to autumn.
Is available in a mixture of colors.
H 24–30in (60–75cm), S 18in (45cm).

☼ ◊ ❋ HH

***Salvia splendens*, Cleopatra
Series** [salmon]
Slow-growing, bushy perennial, grown
as an annual. Oval, serrated leaves are
fresh green; dense racemes of tubular,
salmon pink flowers are carried in
summer and early autumn. H to 12in
(30cm), S 8–12in (20–30cm).

☼ ◊ ❋ T

***Impatiens*, Novette Series**
[salmon]
Fast-growing, evergreen, bushy
perennial, grown as an annual, with
pointed-oval, fresh green leaves. Small,
flat, spurred, salmon pink flowers are
carried from spring to autumn. H and
S 6in (15cm).

☼ ◊ ❋ T

Annuals and Biennials

***Zinnia*, Thumbelina Series**
[Erecta group]
Moderately fast-growing, sturdy, erect
annual with oval to lance-shaped leaves.
In summer and early autumn has large,
daisylike, double and semi-double
flower heads in a range of colors.
H 6in (15cm), S 12in (30cm).

☼ ◊ ❄ T

***Eschscholzia californica*,**
Ballerina Series
Fast-growing, slender, erect annual.
Has feathery, bluish green leaves and
cup-shaped, 4-petaled, frilled, double
flowers, in shades of red, yellow, pink,
or orange, in summer-autumn.
H 12in (30cm), S 6in (15cm).

☼ ◊ ❄❄❄ H

***Petunia*, Victorious Series**
Moderately fast-growing, branching,
bushy perennial, grown as an annual.
Has oval leaves and ruffled, flared,
trumpet-shaped, double flowers in a
mixture of colors in summer-autumn.
H 6–12in (15–30cm), S 12in (30cm).

☼ ◊ ❄ T

***Papaver rhoeas*, Shirley Series**
[double] (Shirley poppy)
Fast-growing, slender, erect annual
with lobed, light green leaves. Rounded,
often cup-shaped, double flowers, in
shades of red, pink, or white, including
bicolors, are borne in summer. H 24in
(60cm), S 12in (30cm).

☼ ◊ ❄❄❄ H

***Schizanthus* 'Hit Parade'**
Moderately fast-growing, erect, bushy
annual with deeply divided leaves.
Tubular flowers, in a mixture of rich
colors including pink, red, purple, or
white, often with contrasting markings
inside, appear in summer-autumn.
H and S 12in (30cm). Min. 41°F (5°C).

☼ ◊ T

Onopordum acanthium
(Cotton thistle, Scotch thistle)
Slow-growing, erect, branching biennial.
Large, lobed, spiny leaves are hairy and
bright silvery gray; winged, branching
flower stems bear deep purplish pink
flower heads in summer. H 6ft (1.8m),
S 3ft (90cm).

☼ ◊ ❄❄❄ H

***Cleome hassleriana* 'Colour
Fountain'**
Fast-growing, bushy annual with hairy
stems and divided leaves. In summer
has heads of narrow-petaled flowers,
with long protruding stamens, in shades
of pink, mauve, purple, or white. H
3–4ft (1–1.2m), S 1½–2ft (45–60cm).

☼ ◊ ❄ HH

***Centaurea cyanus* [tall, rose]**
(Bachelor's button, Cornflower)
Fast-growing, erect, branching annual
with lance-shaped, gray-green leaves.
Branching heads of daisylike, rose-pink
flower heads are carried in summer and
early autumn. H to 3ft (90cm),
S 1ft (30cm).

☼ ◊ ❄❄❄ H

Silybum marianum
Biennial with a basal rosette of deeply
lobed, very spiny, heavily white-
marbled, deep green leaves. Has
thistlelike, dark purplish pink flower
heads on erect stems in summer and
early autumn. H 4ft (1.2m),
S 2ft (60cm).

☼ ◊ ❄❄❄ H

***Lobularia maritima* 'Wonder-
land'**, syn. *Alyssum maritimum*
'Wonderland'
Fast-growing, compact annual with
lance-shaped leaves. Bears heads of
tiny, scented, deep purplish pink
flowers in summer and early autumn.
H to 6in (15cm), S to 12in (30cm).

☼ ◊ ❄❄❄ H

Limonium sinuatum
Fairly slow-growing, bushy, upright
perennial, grown as an annual. Has
lance-shaped, lobed, deep green leaves
and, in summer and early autumn, tiny,
blue, pink, or white flowers borne in
clusters on winged stems. H 18in
(45cm), S 12in (30cm).

☼ ◊ ❄ T

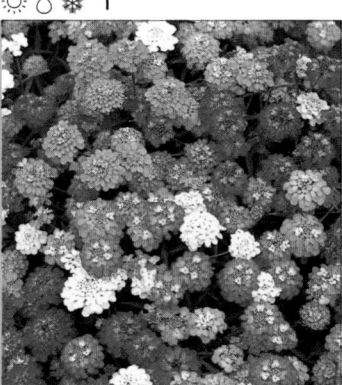

***Iberis umbellata*, Fairy Series**
Fast-growing, upright, bushy annual
with lance-shaped, green leaves. Heads
of small, 4-petaled flowers, in shades of
pink, red, purple, or white, are carried
in summer and early autumn.
H and S 8in (20cm).

☼ ◊ ❄❄❄ T

Petunia, Bonanza Series
Moderately fast-growing, branching, bushy perennial, grown as an annual. Has oval leaves and frilled, flared, trumpet-shaped, double flowers in a mixture of colors in summer-autumn. H 6–12in (15–30cm), S 12in (30cm).

☼ ◊ ❄ T

Agrostemma githago 'Milas'
Fast-growing, slender, upright, thin-stemmed annual. Has lance-shaped leaves and 5-petaled, purplish pink flowers, 3in (8cm) wide, in summer. H 2–3ft (60–90cm), S 1ft (30cm).

☼ ◊ ❄❄❄ HH

Malcolmia maritima
(Virginia stock)
Fast-growing, slim, erect annual with oval, grayish green leaves. Carries tiny, fragrant, 4-petaled, pink, red, or white flowers from spring to autumn. Sow seeds in succession for a long flowering season. H 8in (20cm), S 2–3in (5–8cm).

☼ ◊ ❄❄❄ H

Matthiola, Brompton Series [pink]
Fast-growing, erect, bushy biennial, grown as an annual, with lance-shaped, grayish green leaves. Long spikes of highly scented, pink flowers are carried in summer. H 18in (45cm), S 12in (30cm).

☼ ◊ ❄❄❄ H

Lunaria annua 'Variegata'
Fast-growing, erect biennial with pointed-oval, serrated, white-variegated leaves. Heads of small, scented, 4-petaled, deep purplish pink flowers are borne in spring and early summer, followed by rounded, silvery seed pods. H 30in (75cm), S 12in (30cm).

◑ ◊ ❄❄❄ H

Silene armeria 'Electra'
Moderately fast-growing, erect annual with oval, grayish green leaves. Heads of 5-petaled, bright rose-pink flowers are carried in summer and early autumn. H 12in (30cm), S 6in (15cm).

☼ ◊ ❄❄❄ H

Annuals and Biennials

Lavatera trimestris 'Silver Cup'
Moderately fast-growing, erect,
branching annual with oval, lobed
leaves. Shallowly trumpet-shaped,
rose-pink flowers are carried in
summer and early autumn. H 24in
(60cm), S 18in (45cm).

☼ ◊ ❀❀❀ H

**Dianthus chinensis, Baby Doll
Series**
Neat, bushy annual or biennial, grown
as an annual. Light or mid-green
leaves are lance-shaped; small, single,
zoned flowers in various colors are
carried in summer and early autumn.
H 6in (15cm), S 6–12in (15–30cm).

☼ ◊ ❀❀❀ HH

Lathyrus odoratus 'Bijou'
Fast-growing annual with oval, divided,
green leaves and large, fragrant flowers,
in shades of pink, red, or blue, that are
carried in summer or early autumn.
H and S 18in (45cm).

☼ ◊ ❀❀❀ H

Clarkia 'Brilliant'
(Rocky Mountain garland)
Fast-growing, erect, bushy annual
with oval leaves. Large, rosettelike,
double, bright reddish pink flowers are
carried in long spikes in summer and
early autumn. H to 24in (60cm),
S 12in (30cm).

☼ ◊ ❀❀❀ HH

**Callistephus chinensis, Milady
Series** [rose]
Moderately fast-growing, erect, bushy
annual with oval, toothed leaves. Has
large, daisylike, double, rose-pink
flower heads in summer and early
autumn. H 10–12in (25–30cm),
S 12–18in (30–45cm).

☼ ◊ ❀ T

Brassica oleracea forms
(Kale, Ornamental cabbage)
Moderately fast-growing, evergreen,
rounded biennial, grown as an annual.
Has heads of large, often crinkled
leaves, in combinations of red/green,
white/pink, pink/green. Do not allow to
flower. H and S 12–18in (30–45cm).

☼ ◊ ❀❀❀ H

Coleus blumei (Common coleus)
Fast-growing, bushy perennial, grown
as an annual. Pointed-oval, serrated
leaves are a bright mixture of colors,
including shades of pink, red, green,
or yellow. Flower spikes should be
removed. H to 18in (45cm), S 12in
(30cm) or more. Min. 50°F (10°C).

☼ ◊ T

Malope trifida (Mallowwort)
Moderately fast-growing, erect,
branching annual with rounded, lobed
leaves. Flared, trumpet-shaped, reddish
purple flowers, to 3in (8cm) wide and
with deep pink veins, are carried in
summer and early autumn. H 3ft
(90cm), S 1ft (30cm).

☼ ◊ ❀❀❀ H

Matthiola, Ten-week Series
[dwarf]
Fast-growing, erect, bushy biennial,
grown as an annual. Lance-shaped
leaves are grayish green; long spikes of
highly scented, single to double flowers,
in shades of pink, red, or white, appear
in summer. H and S 12in (30cm).

☼ ◊ ❀❀❀ H

***Petunia*, Resisto Series**
[rose-pink]
Moderately fast-growing, branching, bushy perennial, grown as an annual. Has oval leaves and rain-resistant, flared, trumpet-shaped, rose-pink flowers in summer-autumn. H 6–12in (15–30cm), S 12in (30cm).

☼ ◊ ❀ HH

***Antirrhinum majus*, Princess Series** [white, with purple eye]
Erect perennial, grown as an annual, branching from the base. Has lance-shaped leaves and spikes of tubular, 2-lipped, white and pinkish purple flowers borne from spring to autumn. H and S 18in (45cm).

☼ ◊ ❀ HH

Lunaria annua*, syn. *L. biennis
(Honesty, Money plant)
Fast-growing, erect biennial with pointed-oval, serrated leaves. Heads of scented, 4-petaled, white to deep purple flowers, in spring and early summer, are followed by rounded, silvery seed pods. H 30in (75cm), S 12in (30cm).

◑ ◊ ❀❀❀ H

***Silene coeli-rosa* 'Rose Angel'**
Moderately fast-growing, slim, erect annual. Has lance-shaped, grayish green leaves and 5-petaled, deep rose-pink flowers in summer. H 12in (30cm), S 6in (15cm).

☼ ◊ ❀❀❀ H

***Xeranthemum annuum* [double]**
(Common immortelle)
Erect annual with lance-shaped, silvery leaves and branching heads of daisylike, papery, double flower heads in shades of pink, mauve, purple, or white, in summer. Produces good dried flowers. H 24in (60cm), S 18in (45cm).

☼ ◊ ❀ H

***Clarkia* 'Arianna'**
Fast-growing annual with slender, erect, branching stems. Has lance-shaped leaves and spikes of frilled, waved, rosettelike, semi-double, deep rose-pink flowers in summer and early autumn. H 18in (45cm), S 12in (30cm).

☼ ◊ ❀❀❀ H

***Dorotheanthus bellidiformis*, Magic Carpet Series**
Carpeting annual with succulent, lance-shaped, pale green leaves. Daisylike flower heads, in bright shades of red, pink, yellow, or white, open only in summer sunshine. H 6in (15cm), S 12in (30cm).

☼ ◊ ❀ T

***Cosmos* 'Sensation'**
Moderately fast-growing, bushy, erect annual. Has feathery, green leaves and daisylike flower heads, to 4in (10cm) wide, in shades of red, pink, or white, from early summer to early autumn. H 3ft (90cm), S 2ft (60cm).

☼ ◊ ❀❀❀ T

***Impatiens*, Rosette Series**
Fast-growing, evergreen, bushy perennial, grown as an annual. Has small, flat, spurred, double or semi-double flowers, in shades of red, pink, orange, or white, from spring to autumn. H and S 12in (30cm).

◑ ◊ ❀ T

Annuals and Biennials

***Impatiens*, Super Elfin Series
'Lipstick'**
Fast-growing, evergreen, bushy
perennial, grown as an annual. Has
pointed-oval, fresh green leaves and
small, flat, spurred, rose-red flowers
from spring to autumn. H and
S 8in (20cm).

☀◐❄ T

***Phlox drummondii*, Cecily Series**
Moderately fast-growing, slim, erect
annual with lance-shaped, pale green
leaves. Has heads of large, flat flowers,
in red, pink, blue, purple, or white, all
with contrasting centers, in summer
and early autumn. H 6in (15cm),
S 4in (10cm).

☀◊❄ H

***Nicotiana alata*, Sensation Series**
Fairly slow-growing, erect, branching
annual with pointed-oval leaves.
Scented, trumpet-shaped flowers, 3in
(8cm) long, appear in a wide range of
colors in summer and early autumn.
H 2¹/₂–3ft (75–90cm), S 1ft (30cm).

☀◊❄ T

***Verbena* × *hybrida* 'Showtime'**
Fairly slow-growing, bushy perennial,
grown as an annual. Has lance-shaped,
serrated, mid- to deep green leaves and
clusters of small, tubular flowers, in a
range of colors, in summer-autumn.
H 8in (20cm), S 12in (30cm).

☀◊❄ T

***Portulaca grandiflora*, Sundance
Series**
Slow-growing, semi-trailing annual
with lance-shaped, succulent, bright
green leaves. Cup-shaped flowers,
with conspicuous stamens, appear in a
mixture of colors in summer and early
autumn. H to 8in (20cm), S 6in (15cm).

☀◊❄ T

***Petunia* 'Mirage Velvet'**
Branching, bushy perennial, grown as
an annual, with oval, dark green
leaves. Large, flared, trumpet-shaped,
rich red flowers, with almost black
centers, appear in summer-autumn.
H 10in (25cm), S 12in (30cm).

☀◊❄ HH

Amaranthus caudatus
(Love-lies-bleeding)
Bushy annual with oval, pale green
leaves. Pendulous panicles of tassel-
like, red flowers, 18in (45cm) long, are
carried in summer-autumn. H to 4ft
(1.2m), S 1¹/₂ft (45cm).

☀◊❄ T

***Dianthus barbatus*, Roundabout
Series** [dwarf]
Slow-growing, upright, bushy
biennial with lance-shaped leaves. In
early summer has flat heads of zoned
and eyed flowers in shades of pink,
red, or white. H 6in (15cm), S 8–12in
(20–30cm).

☀◊❄❄❄ H

***Petunia*, Star Series** [crimson]
Moderately fast-growing, branching,
bushy perennial, grown as an annual.
Has oval, mid- to deep green leaves
and large, flared, trumpet-shaped,
white-striped, deep red flowers in
summer-autumn. H 6–12in (15–30cm),
S 12in (30cm).

☀◊❄ HH

***Phlox drummondii*, Twinkle
Series**
Moderately fast-growing, slim, erect
annual. Lance-shaped leaves are pale
green; heads of star-shaped flowers in
a bright mixture of colors, some with
contrasting centers, are carried in
summer. H 6in (15cm), S 4in (10cm).

☀◊❄ H

***Alcea rosea* 'Chater's Double'**
Erect biennial with lobed, rough-
textured leaves. Spikes of rosettelike,
double flowers in several different
colors are carried on upright stems in
summer and early autumn. H 6–8ft
(1.8–2.4m), S to 2ft (60cm).

☀◊❄❄❄ H

Viola 'Roggli Giants'
Fairly fast-growing, bushy perennial, grown as an annual or biennial, with oval, serrated leaves. In summer-autumn has rounded, 5-petaled flowers, 4in (10cm) across, in a wide range of colors. H and S to 8in (20cm).

☼ ◊ ❄❄❄ H

Impatiens, Novette Series 'Red Star'
Fast-growing, evergreen, bushy perennial, grown as an annual. Has pointed-oval, fresh green leaves and from spring to autumn small, flat, spurred, red flowers with star-shaped, white markings. H and S 6in (15cm).

☼ ◊ ❄ T

Impatiens, Confection Series
Fast-growing, evergreen, bushy perennial, grown as an annual. Has fresh green leaves and small, flat, spurred, double or semi-double flowers, in shades of red or pink, from spring to autumn. H and S 8–12in (20–30cm).

☼ ◊ ❄ T

Dianthus chinensis 'Fire Carpet'
Slow-growing, bushy annual or biennial, grown as an annual. Lance-shaped leaves are light or mid-green. Small, rounded, single, bright red flowers are carried in summer and early autumn. H 8in (20cm), S 6–12in (15–30cm).

☼ ◊ ❄❄❄ HH

Linum grandiflorum 'Rubrum' (Scarlet flax)
Fairly fast-growing, slim, erect annual. Lance-shaped leaves are gray-green; small, rounded, flattish, deep red flowers are carried in summer. H 18in (45cm), S 6in (15cm).

☼ ◊ ❄❄❄ H

Dianthus barbatus, Monarch Series [auricula-eyed]
Slow-growing, upright, bushy biennial with lance-shaped leaves. Bicolored flowers are carried in flat heads, to 5in (12cm) wide, in early summer. H 18in (45cm), S 8–12 in (20–30cm).

☼ ◊ ❄❄❄ H

Bellis perennis 'Pomponette'
Slow-growing, carpeting perennial, grown as a biennial. Has oval leaves and small, daisylike, double flower heads, in red, pink, or white, in spring. H and S 4–6in (10–15cm).

☼ ◊ ❄❄❄ T

Impatiens, Novette Series [red]
Fast-growing, evergreen, bushy perennial, grown as an annual. Pointed-oval leaves are fresh green; small, flat, spurred, red flowers are carried from spring to autumn. H and S 6in (15cm).

☼ ◑ ◊ ❄ T

Phlox drummondii, Twinkle Series
Moderately fast-growing, slim, erect annual with lance-shaped, pale green leaves. Heads of star-shaped flowers, some with contrasting centers, appear in summer in a bright mixture of colors. H 6in (15cm), S 4in (10cm).

☼ ◊ ❄ H

Annuals and Biennials

***Verbena × hybrida* 'Defiance'**
Fairly slow-growing, bushy perennial, grown as an annual. Has lance-shaped, serrated, mid- to deep green leaves and clusters of small, fragrant, tubular, white-eyed, deep red flowers in summer-autumn. H 8in (20cm), S 12in (30cm).

☼ ◊ ❄ T

***Salvia splendens* 'Flare Path'**
Slow-growing, bushy perennial, grown as an annual. Has oval, serrated, fresh green leaves and dense racemes of tubular, pure scarlet flowers in summer and early autumn. H to 12in (30cm), S 8–12in (20–30cm).

☼ ◊ ❄ T

***Nemesia strumosa*, Carnival Series**
Fairly fast-growing, bushy annual with serrated, pale green leaves. In summer has small, somewhat trumpet-shaped flowers in a range of colors, including yellow, red, orange, purple, and white. H 8–12in (20–30cm), S 6in (15cm).

☼ ◊ ❄ T

***Petunia*, Picotee Series** [red]
Fairly fast-growing, branching, bushy perennial, grown as an annual, with oval leaves. Has flared, somewhat trumpet-shaped, red flowers, edged with white, in summer-autumn. H 6–12in (15–30cm), S 12in (30cm).

☼ ◊ ❄ HH

***Pelargonium*, Diamond Series** [scarlet]
Slow-growing, evergreen, branching, compact perennial, grown as an annual, with rounded, lobed leaves. Large, rounded heads of weather-resistant, red flowers are carried in summer-autumn. H and S 12–24in (30–60cm).

☼ ◊ ❄ T

***Petunia*, Resisto Series**
Fairly fast-growing, bushy perennial, grown as an annual, with oval leaves. Has rain-resistant, flared, somewhat trumpet-shaped flowers in a range of bright colors in summer-autumn. H 6–12in (15–30cm), S 12in (30cm).

☼ ◊ ❄ HH

***Zinnia*, Ruffles Series** [Erecta group; scarlet]
Moderately fast-growing, sturdy, upright annual with oval to lance-shaped leaves. Ruffled, daisylike, double, scarlet flower heads are carried in summer and early autumn. H 24in (60cm), S 12in (30cm).

☼ ◊ ❄ T

***Papaver rhoeas*, Shirley Series** [single] (Shirley poppy)
Fast-growing, slender, erect annual with lobed, light green leaves. Rounded, often cup-shaped, single flowers, in shades of red, pink, salmon, or white, appear in summer. H 24in (60cm), S 12in (30cm).

☼ ◊ ❄❄❄ H

***Primula*, Pacific Series** [dwarf]
Rosette-forming perennial, normally grown as a biennial, with lance-shaped leaves. Has heads of large, fragrant, flat flowers in shades of blue, yellow, red, pink, or white in spring. H 4–6in (10–15cm), S 8in (20cm).

☼ ◊ ❄❄❄ H

Alonsoa warscewiczii
(Heartleaf maskflower)
Perennial, grown as an annual, with
slender, branching, red stems carrying
oval, toothed, deep green leaves.
Spurred, bright scarlet flowers are
produced during summer-autumn.
H 12–24in (30–60cm), S 12in (30cm).

☼ ◊ ❄ T

Zinnia, Ruffles Series [Erecta
group]
Moderately fast-growing, sturdy,
upright annual with pale or mid-green
leaves. Ruffled, pompon, double flower
heads in a mixture of colors are carried
in summer and early autumn. H 24in
(60cm), S 12in (30cm).

☼ ◊ ❄ T

**_Capsicum annuum_ 'Holiday
Time'**
Moderately fast-growing, evergreen,
bushy perennial, grown as an annual,
with oval leaves. In autumn-winter,
cone-shaped fruits turn from yellow
to red. H and S 8–12in (20–30cm).
Min. 39°F (4°C).

☼ ◊ T

Viola, Floral Dance Series [mixed]
Fairly fast-growing, bushy perennial,
grown as an annual or biennial. Has
oval leaves and rounded, 5-petaled
flowers in a wide range of colors in
winter. H 6–8in (15–20cm),
S 8in (20cm).

☼ ◊ ❄ ❄ ❄ H

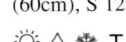

Salpiglossis sinuata 'Splash'
Moderately fast-growing, erect,
branching annual. Has lance-shaped,
pale green leaves and widely flared,
trumpet-shaped, multicolored flowers
in summer and early autumn. H 24in
(60cm), S 12in (30cm).

☼ ◊ ❄ T

Tagetes patula 'Cinnabar'
Fast-growing, bushy annual with
aromatic, very feathery, deep green
leaves. Heads of rounded, daisylike,
single, rich rust red flowers, yellow-
red beneath, are carried in summer and
early autumn. H and S 12in (30cm).

☼ ◊ ❄ HH

**_Chrysanthemum carinatum_
'Monarch Court Jesters'**
Fast-growing, erect, branching annual.
In summer has feathery, gray-green
leaves and daisylike, zoned flower
heads, to 3in (8cm) wide, in various
color combinations. H 24in (60cm),
S 12in (30cm).

☼ ◊ ❄ ❄ ❄ H

Coleus blumei 'Brightness'
Fast-growing, bushy perennial, grown
as an annual. Has pointed-oval, serrated,
rust red leaves, edged with green.
Flower spikes should be removed.
H to 18in (45cm), S 12in (30cm) or
more. Min 50°F (10°C).

☼ ◊ T

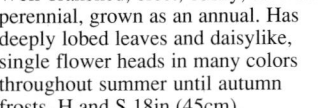

Dahlia, Coltness Hybrids
Well-branched, erect, bushy, tuberous
perennial, grown as an annual. Has
deeply lobed leaves and daisylike,
single flower heads in many colors
throughout summer until autumn
frosts. H and S 18in (45cm).

☼ ◊ ❄ T

Annuals and Biennials

■ RED

■ PURPLE

Amaranthus hybridus var. ***erythro-stachys***, syn. *A. hypochondriacus* (Prince's feather)
Bushy annual with upright, sometimes flattened panicles, 6in (15cm) or more long, of dark red flowers in summer-autumn. Leaves are heavily suffused purple. H to 4ft (1.2m), S 1¹/₂ft (45cm).

☼ ◊ ❄ T

***Ricinus communis* 'Impala'**
Fast-growing, evergreen, erect, shrub, usually grown as an annual. Has deeply lobed, bronze leaves to 12in (30cm) wide and clusters of small, red flowers in summer, followed by globular, prickly, red seed heads. H 5ft (1.5m), S 3ft (90cm).

☼ ◊ ❄ T

Humea elegans (Incense plant)
Erect, branching biennial with a strong fragrance of incense. Has lance-shaped leaves and heads of tiny, pink, brownish red, or crimson flowers in summer-autumn. H to 6ft (1.8m), S 3ft (90cm). Min. 39°F (4°C).

☼ ◊ T

Trachelium caeruleum (Throatwort)
Moderately fast-growing, erect perennial, grown as an annual. Has oval, serrated leaves and clustered heads of small, tubular, lilac-blue or white flowers in summer. H 2–3ft (60–90cm), S 1ft (30cm).

☼ ◊ ❄ H

Psylliostachys suworowii, syn. *Statice suworowii*
Fairly slow-growing, erect, branching annual with lance-shaped leaves. Bears branching spikes of small, tubular, pink to purple flowers in summer and early autumn. Flowers are good for drying. H 18in (45cm), S 12in (30cm).

☼ ◊ ❄ T

Salvia sclarea var. ***turkestanica*** (Clary sage)
Moderately fast-growing, erect biennial, grown as an annual. Has aromatic, oval, hairy leaves and panicles of tubular, white and lavender purple flowers with prominent, lavender purple bracts in summer. H 30in (75cm), S 12in (30cm).

☼ ◊ ❄❄❄ HH

***Linaria maroccana* 'Fairy Lights'**
Fast-growing, erect, bushy annual with lance-shaped, pale green leaves. Tiny, snapdragonlike flowers, in shades of red, pink, purple, yellow, or white, are borne in summer. H 8in (20cm), S 6in (15cm).

☼ ◊ ❄❄❄ H

Schizanthus pinnatus
Moderately fast-growing, upright, bushy annual with feathery, light green leaves. In summer-autumn has rounded, lobed, multicolored flowers in shades of pink, purple, white, or yellow. H 1–4ft (30cm–1.2m), S 1ft (30cm). Min. 41°F (5°C).

☼ ◊ T

Exacum affine (German violet)
Evergreen, bushy biennial, usually
grown as an annual. Has oval, glossy
leaves and masses of tiny, scented,
saucer-shaped, purple flowers, with
yellow stamens, in summer and early
autumn. H and S 8–12in (20–30cm).
Min. 45–50°F (7–10°C).

 ☀ ◊ T

Collinsia grandiflora (Bluelips)
Moderately fast-growing, slender-
stemmed annual. Upper leaves are
lance-shaped; lower are oval. Whorls
of pale purple flowers, with purplish
blue lips, are carried in spring-summer.
H and S 6–12in (15–30cm).

☼ ◊ ✽✽✽ HH

***Scabiosa atropurpurea*, Cockade
Series**
Moderately fast-growing, erect, bushy
annual with lobed leaves and large,
rounded, double flower heads, in shades
of red, pink, purple, or blue, on slender
stems in summer and early autumn.
H 3ft (90cm), S 8–12in (20–30cm).

☀ ◊ ✽✽✽ HH

***Campanula medium* 'Bells of
Holland'**
Slow-growing, evergreen, clump-
forming, erect biennial with lance-
shaped, toothed leaves. In spring and
early summer has bell-shaped flowers
in a mixture of blue, lilac, pink, or white.
H to 24in (60cm), S 12in (30cm).

☀ ◊ ✽✽✽ H

Echium vulgare [dwarf]
(Viper's bugloss)
Moderately fast-growing, erect, bushy
annual or biennial with lance-shaped,
dark green leaves. Spikes of tubular
flowers, in shades of white, pink, blue,
or purple, appear in summer. H 12in
(30cm), S 8in (20cm).

☀ ◊ ✽✽✽ H

Nierembergia hippomanica var.
***violacea* 'Purple Robe'**
Moderately fast-growing, rounded,
branching perennial, grown as an
annual, with narrow, lance-shaped
leaves. Has cup-shaped, dark bluish
purple flowers in summer and early
autumn. H and S 6–8in (15–20cm).

☀ ◊ ✽ HH

Salvia horminum (Annual sage)
Moderately fast-growing, upright,
branching annual with oval leaves.
Tubular, lipped flowers, enclosed by
purple, pink, or white bracts, are carried
in spikes at tops of stems in summer
and early autumn. H 18in (45cm),
S 8in (20cm).

☀ ◊ ✽✽✽ HH

Orychophragmus violaceus
Moderately fast-growing, upright
annual or biennial with branching
flower stems and pointed-oval, pale
green leaves. Heads of 4-petaled,
purple-blue flowers are carried in
spring. H 12–24in (30–60cm),
S 12in (30cm).

☀ ◊ ✽ HH

***Callistephus chinensis*, Thousand
Wonders Series**
Moderately fast-growing, erect, bushy
annual with oval, toothed leaves. In
summer and early autumn has daisylike,
double flower heads in pink, blue,
purple, red, or white. H to 8in (20cm),
S 12in (30cm).

☀ ◊ ✽ T

Gomphrena globosa
(Globe amaranth)
Moderately fast-growing, upright,
bushy annual with oval, hairy leaves.
Has oval, cloverlike flower heads in
pink, yellow, orange, purple, or white
in summer and early autumn. H 12in
(30cm), S 8in (20cm).

☀ ◊ ✽ T

***Petunia* 'Blue Frost'**
Fairly fast-growing, branching, bushy
perennial, grown as an annual. Has
oval leaves and in summer-autumn
produces flared, somewhat trumpet-
shaped, violet-blue flowers, edged
with white. H 6–12in (15–30cm),
S 12in (30cm).

☀ ◊ ✽ HH

***Salvia splendens*, Cleopatra
Series** [violet]
Slow-growing, bushy perennial, grown
as an annual. Oval, serrated leaves are
dark green; dense racemes of tubular,
deep violet-purple flowers are carried
in summer and early autumn. H to 12in
(30cm), S 8–12in (20–30cm).

☀ ◊ ✽ T

275

Annuals and Biennials

Senecio 'Spring Glory'
Slow-growing, evergreen, mound- or dome-shaped perennial, grown as a biennial, with large, oval, serrated, mid- to deep green leaves. Heads of large, daisylike flowers in a mixture of colors are carried in spring. H 8in (20cm), S 12in (30cm). Min. 41°F (5°C).

☼ ◊ T

Callistephus chinensis, Milady Series [blue]
Moderately fast-growing, erect, bushy annual with oval, toothed leaves. Has large, daisylike, double, purplish blue flower heads in summer and early autumn. H 10–12in (25–30cm), S 12–18in (30–45cm).

☼ ◊ ❋ T

Petunia, Resisto Series [blue]
Moderately fast-growing, branching, bushy perennial, grown as an annual. Has oval leaves and rain-resistant, flared, trumpet-shaped, intense blue flowers in summer-autumn. H 6–12in (15–30cm), S 12in (30cm).

☼ ◊ ❋ HH

Convolvulus tricolor 'Blue Flash'
Moderately fast-growing, upright, bushy annual with oval to lance-shaped leaves. Has small, saucer-shaped, intense blue flowers with cream and yellow centers in summer. H 8–12in (20–30cm), S 8in (20cm).

☼ ◊ ❋❋❋ T

Salvia farinacea 'Victoria'
Moderately fast-growing perennial, grown as an annual, with many erect stems. Has oval or lance-shaped leaves and spikes of tubular, violet-blue flowers in summer. H 18in (45cm), S 12in (30cm).

☼ ◊ ❋ HH

Lobelia erinus 'Sapphire'
Slow-growing, pendulous, spreading annual or occasionally perennial. Oval to lance-shaped leaves are pale green; small, sapphire blue flowers with white centers are produced continuously in summer and early autumn. H 8in (20cm), S 6in (15cm).

☼ ◊ ❋ H

Viola 'Joker'
Bushy, spreading perennial, usually grown as an annual or biennial. Large, rounded, 5-petaled, purplish blue flowers, with black and white 'faces' and yellow eyes, appear in summer. H and S 6in (15cm).

☼ ◊ ❋❋❋ H

Primula, Super Giants Series [blue]
Rosette-forming perennial, usually grown as a biennial, with lance-shaped leaves. Heads of large, fragrant, flat, blue flowers appear in spring. H and S to 12in (30cm).

☼ ◊ ❋❋❋ H

Consolida ambigua, Imperial Series
Fast-growing, upright, branching annual with feathery leaves. Long spikes of rounded, spurred, double flowers, pink, blue, or white, are carried in summer. H 4ft (1.2 m), S 1ft (30cm).

☼ ◊ ❋❋❋ H

Torenia fournieri
(Bluewings, Wishbone flower)
Moderately fast-growing, erect,
branching annual with serrated, light
green leaves. Dark blue-purple flowers,
paler and yellow within, are carried in
summer and early autumn. H 12in
(30cm), S 8in (20cm). Min. 41°F (5°C).

☀ ◊ T

Gilia capitata (Blue thimble
flower)
Erect, branching annual. Has very
feathery, green leaves and tiny, dense,
rounded heads of soft lavender blue
flowers in summer and early autumn.
Is good for cut flowers. H 18in (45cm),
S 8in (20cm).

☀ ◊ ❄❄❄ H

***Ageratum houstonianum* 'Blue
Mink'**
Moderately fast-growing, hummock-
forming annual. Has pointed-oval
leaves and clusters of feathery,
brushlike, pastel blue flower heads in
summer-autumn. Makes a useful edging
plant. H and S 8–12in (20–30cm).

☀ ◊ ❄ T

***Nigella damascena* 'Miss Jekyll'**
Fast-growing, slender, erect annual.
Feathery leaves are bright green; small,
rounded, many-petaled, semi-double,
blue flowers are carried in summer,
followed by inflated seed pods which
can be cut and dried. H 18in (45cm),
S 8in (20cm).

☀ ◊ ❄❄❄ H

***Nigella damascena* 'Persian Jewels'**
Fast-growing, slender, erect annual with
feathery, bright green leaves. Small,
semi-double flowers, in shades of blue,
pink, or white, appear in summer,
followed by inflated seed pods which
can be cut and dried. H 18in (45cm),
S 8in (20cm).

☀ ◊ ❄❄❄ H

***Ageratum houstonianum* 'Blue
Danube'**
Moderately fast-growing, hummock-
forming annual with pointed-oval
leaves. Has clusters of feathery,
brushlike, lavender blue flower heads
in summer-autumn. Makes a useful
edging plant. H and S 6in (15cm).

☀ ◊ ❄ T

Sedum caeruleum
(Blue stonecrop)
Moderately fast-growing annual with
branching flower stems. Oval, light
green leaves become red-tinged when
clusters of small, star-shaped, light blue
flowers with white centers are borne in
summer. H and S 4–6in (10–15cm).

☀ ◊ ❄❄❄ H

***Nemophila menziesii*,**
syn. *N. insignis* (Baby-blue-eyes)
Fast-growing, spreading annual with
serrated, gray-green leaves. Small,
bowl-shaped, blue flowers with white
centers are carried in summer.
H 8in (20cm), S 6in (15cm).

☀ ◊ ❄❄❄ T

***Viola* 'Azure Blue'**
Bushy perennial, grown as an annual
or biennial. Has oval, green leaves and
rounded, 5-petaled, azure blue flowers
in spring. H 6–8in (15–20cm),
S 8in (20cm).

☀ ◊ ❄❄❄ H

Annuals and Biennials

Centaurea cyanus [tall, blue]
(Bachelor's button, Cornflower)
Fast-growing, erect, branching annual.
Has lance-shaped, gray-green leaves
and branching heads of daisylike, blue
flowers in summer and early autumn.
H to 3ft (90cm), S 1ft (30cm).

☼ ◊ ❋❋❋ H

Myosotis 'Blue Ball'
(Woodland forget-me-not)
Slow-growing, bushy, compact
perennial, often grown as a biennial.
Has lance-shaped leaves and, in spring
and early summer, spikes of tiny,
5-lobed, deep blue flowers. H to 8in
(20cm), S 6in (15cm).

◑ ◊ ❋❋❋ H

Phacelia campanularia
(California bluebell)
Moderately fast-growing, branching,
bushy annual with oval, serrated, deep
green leaves. Bell-shaped, pure blue
flowers, 1in (2.5cm) wide, are carried
in summer and early autumn. H 8in
(20cm), S 6in (15cm).

☼ ◊ ❋❋❋ H

Lobelia erinus 'Crystal Palace'
Slow-growing, spreading, compact,
bushy annual or occasionally
perennial. Bronzed leaves are oval to
lance-shaped; small, deep blue flowers
are produced continuously in summer
and early autumn. H 4–8in (10–20cm),
S 4–6in (10–15cm).

☼ ◊ ❋ H

Brachycome iberidifolia
(Swan River daisy)
Moderately fast-growing, thin-stemmed,
bushy annual with deeply cut leaves.
Has small, fragrant, daisylike flower
heads, usually blue but also pink,
mauve, purple, or white, in summer and
early autumn. H and S to 18in (45cm).

☼ ◊ ❋❋❋ HH

**Cynoglossum amabile
'Firmament'**
Slow-growing, upright, bushy annual or
biennial with lance-shaped, hairy, gray-
green leaves. Pendulous, tubular, pure
sky blue flowers are carried in summer.
H 18in (45cm), S 12in (30cm).

☼ ◊ ❋❋❋ H

Anchusa capensis 'Blue Angel'
Bushy biennial, grown as an annual.
Has lance-shaped, bristly leaves.
Heads of shallowly bowl-shaped,
brilliant blue flowers are borne in
summer. H and S 8in (20cm).

☼ ◊ ❋❋ T

Senecio maritima 'Silver Dust'
Moderately fast-growing, evergreen,
bushy sub-shrub, usually grown as an
annual, with deeply lobed, silver leaves.
Small, daisylike, yellow flower heads
appear in summer but are best removed.
H and S 12in (30cm).

☼ ◊ ❋ HH

Felicia bergeriana
(Kingfisher daisy)
Fairly fast-growing, mat-forming
annual. Has lance-shaped, hairy, gray-
green leaves. Small, daisylike, blue
flower heads with yellow centers open
only in sunshine in summer and early
autumn. H and S 6in (15cm).

☼ ◊ ❋❋❋ HH

Commelina coelestis (Blue
spiderwort, Mexican dayflower)
Fairly fast-growing, upright perennial,
usually grown as an annual, with lance-
shaped leaves. Small, 3-petaled, pure
blue flowers, each lasting only a day,
are produced in succession in summer.
H to 18in (45cm), S 12in (30cm).

☼ ◊ ❋ HH

Borago officinalis (Borage)
Spreading, clump-forming, annual herb.
Has oval, crinkled, rough-haired leaves
and sprays of star-shaped, blue flowers
in summer and early autumn. Young
leaves are sometimes used as a coolant
in drinks. Self seeds prolifically.
H 3ft (90cm), S 1ft (30cm).

☼ ◊ ❋❋❋ H

Nicotiana langsdorfii
Fairly slow-growing, erect, branching
perennial, grown as an annual, with
oval to lance-shaped leaves. Slightly
pendent, bell-shaped, pale green to
yellow-green flowers appear in
summer. H 3–5ft (1–1.5m),
S 1ft (30cm).

☼ ◊ ❋ T

278

Moluccella laevis (Bells-of-Ireland,
Molucca balm, Shellflower)
Fairly fast-growing, erect, branching
annual. Rounded leaves are pale green;
spikes of small, tubular, white flowers,
each surrounded by a conspicuous,
pale green calyx, appear in summer.
H 24in (60cm), S 8in (20cm).

☼ ◊ ❄ H

Zinnia 'Envy' [Elegans group]
Moderately fast-growing, sturdy,
erect annual. Has oval to lance-
shaped leaves and large, daisylike,
double, green flower heads in summer
and early autumn. H 24in (60cm),
S 12in (30cm).

☼ ◊ ❄ T

Kochia scoparia f. ***trichophylla***
(Burning bush, Firebush, Summer
cypress)
Moderately fast-growing, erect, very
bushy annual. Narrow, lance-shaped,
light green leaves, 2–3in (5–8cm) long,
turn red in autumn. Has insignificant
flowers. H 3ft (90cm), S 2ft (60cm).

☼ ◊ ❄ HH

Ricinus communis
(Castor bean, Castor-oil-plant)
Fast-growing, evergreen, erect, shrub,
usually grown as an annual. Has large,
deeply lobed, green leaves and heads
of green and red flowers in summer,
followed by globular, prickly seed
pods. H 5ft (1.5m), S 3ft (90cm).

☼ ◊ ❄ T

Centaurea moschata (Sweet sultan)
Fast-growing, upright, slender-stemmed
annual with lance-shaped, grayish green
leaves. Large, fragrant, cornflowerlike
flower heads, to 3in (8cm) across, in a
wide range of colors, are carried in
summer and early autumn. H 18in
(45cm), S 8in (20cm).

☼ ◊ ❄❄❄ HH

Platystemon californicus
Moderately fast-growing, upright,
compact annual with lance-shaped,
grayish green leaves. Saucer-shaped,
cream or pale yellow flowers, about
1in (2.5cm) across, appear in summer.
H 12in (30cm), S 4in (10cm).

☼ ◊ ❄❄❄ H

Smyrnium perfoliatum
Slow-growing, upright biennial. Upper
leaves, rounded and yellow-green,
encircle stems which bear heads of
yellowish green flowers in summer.
H 2–3ft (60cm–1m), S 2ft (60cm).

☼ ◊ ❄❄❄ H

Argemone mexicana
(Mexican prickly-poppy)
Spreading perennial, grown as an
annual, with leaves divided into white-
marked, grayish green leaflets. In
summer has fragrant, poppylike,
yellow or orange flowers, 3in (8cm)
wide. H to 24in (60cm), S 12in (30cm).

☼ ◊ ❄ HH

Glaucium flavum
(Yellow-horned poppy)
Slow-growing, erect biennial with
oval, lobed, light grayish green leaves.
Poppylike, vivid yellow flowers, 3in
(8cm) wide, appear in summer and
early autumn. H 12–24in (30–60cm),
S 18in (45cm).

☼ ◊ ❄❄❄ H

Annuals and Biennials

***Calendula officinalis* 'Kablouna'**
Fast-growing, bushy annual with strongly aromatic, lance-shaped leaves. From spring to autumn has crested, daisylike, orange, gold, or yellow flower heads. H 24in (60cm), S 12–24in (30–60cm).

☼ ◊ ❀❀❀ H

***Mentzelia lindleyi*,**
syn. *Bartonia aurea* (Blazing star)
Fairly fast-growing, bushy annual with fleshy stems and lance-shaped, serrated leaves. Has fragrant, cup-shaped, deep yellow flowers, with conspicuous stamens, in summer. H 18in (45cm), S 8in (20cm).

☼ ◊ ❀❀❀ H

***Viola* 'Super Chalon Giants'**
Fairly fast-growing, bushy perennial, grown as an annual or biennial. Has oval, serrated leaves and, in summer-autumn, 5-petaled, ruffled and waved, bicolored flowers. H 6–8in (15–20cm), S 8in (20cm).

☼ ◊ ❀❀❀ H

Limnanthes douglasii (Meadow foam, Poached-egg plant)
Fast-growing, slender, erect annual. Feathery leaves are glossy, light green; slightly fragrant, cup-shaped, white flowers with yellow centers are carried from early to late summer. H 6in (15cm), S 4in (10cm).

☼ ◊ ❀❀❀ H

Eschscholzia caespitosa
Fast-growing, slender, erect annual with feathery, bluish green leaves. Cup-shaped, 4-petaled, yellow flowers, 1in (2.5cm) wide, appear in summer and early autumn. H and S 6in (15cm).

☼ ◊ ❀❀❀ H

***Antirrhinum majus*, Wedding Bells Series**
Erect perennial, branching from the base, grown as an annual. Has lance-shaped leaves and, from late spring to autumn, spikes of small, trumpet-shaped flowers in a range of colors. H 30in (75cm), S 18in (45cm).

☼ ◊ ❀ HH

Sanvitalia procumbens (Creeping zinnia, Trailing sanvitalia)
Moderately fast-growing, prostrate annual with pointed-oval leaves. Daisylike, yellow flower heads, 1in (2.5cm) wide, with black centers, are borne in summer. H 6in (15cm), S 12in (30cm).

☼ ◊ ❀❀❀ T

Lindheimera texana
(Texas star daisy)
Moderately fast-growing, erect, branching annual with hairy stems and oval, serrated, hairy leaves. Daisylike, yellow flower heads appear in late summer and early autumn. H 12–24in (30–60cm), S 12in (30cm).

☼ ◊ ❀❀❀ H

***Tagetes* 'Gold Coins'**
[Erecta group]
Fast-growing, erect, bushy annual. Has aromatic, feathery, glossy, deep green leaves and large, daisylike, double flower heads in shades of yellow and orange in summer and early autumn. H 3ft (90cm), S 1–1½ft (30–45cm).

☼ ◊ ❀ HH

***Helianthus annuus* 'Taiyo'**
[intermediate]
Fast-growing, erect annual with large, rounded-oval, serrated leaves. Large, daisylike, yellow flower heads with black centers appear in summer. H to 4ft (1.2m), S 1–1½ft (30–45cm).

☼ ◊ ❀❀❀ H

Coreopsis tinctoria (Calliopsis)
Fast-growing, erect, bushy annual with lance-shaped leaves. Large, daisylike, bright yellow flower heads with red centers are carried in summer and early autumn. H 2–3ft (60–90cm), S 8in (20cm).

☼ ◊ ❀❀❀ H

Viola, Clear Crystals Series
[yellow]
Bushy perennial, grown as an annual
or biennial. Has oval leaves and
rounded, 5-petaled, yellow flowers
in summer. H 6–8in (15–20cm),
S 8in (20cm).

 ☼ ◊ ❄❄❄ H

Viola, Icequeen Series [yellow]
Bushy, spreading perennial, grown as
an annual or biennial. Has oval leaves
and large, rounded, 5-petaled, yellow
flowers with dark central blotches in
winter and early spring. H 4–5in
(10–12cm), S 5–6in (12–15cm).

☼ ◊ ❄❄❄ H

Viola, Crystal Bowl Series
[yellow]
Bushy, spreading perennial, usually
grown as an annual or biennial, with
oval leaves. Large, rounded, 5-petaled,
yellow flowers are carried in summer.
H and S 6in (15cm).

☼ ◊ ❄❄❄ H

Chrysanthemum segetum (Corn
chrysanthemum, Corn marigold)
Moderately fast-growing, erect annual
with lance-shaped, gray-green leaves.
Daisylike, single flower heads, to 3in
(8cm) wide, in shades of yellow, are
carried in summer and early autumn.
H 18in (45cm), S 12in (30cm).

☼ ◊ ❄❄❄ H

Cladanthus arabicus (Cladanthus)
Moderately fast-growing, hummock-
forming annual with aromatic, feathery,
light green leaves. Has fragrant,
daisylike, single, deep yellow flower
heads, 2in (5cm) wide, in summer and
early autumn. H 24in (60cm),
S 12in (30cm).

☼ ◊ ❄❄❄ HH

Antirrhinum majus 'Coronette'
Erect, bushy, compact perennial,
grown as an annual, with lance-shaped
leaves. Spikes of tubular, 2-lipped
flowers in a wide range of colors
appear from spring to autumn. H 24in
(60cm), S 12in (30cm).

☼ ◊ ❄ HH

Coreopsis 'Sunray'
Spreading, clump-forming perennial,
grown as an annual by sowing under
glass in early spring. Has lance-
shaped, serrated leaves and daisylike,
double, bright yellow flower heads in
summer. H 18in (45cm), S 12–18in
(30–45cm).

☼ ◊ ❄❄❄ H

Helianthus annuus
(Common sunflower)
Fast-growing, erect annual with oval,
serrated, green leaves. Daisylike,
yellow flower heads to 12in (30cm)
or more wide, with brown or purplish
centers, appear in summer. H 3–10ft
(1–3m), S 1–1½ft (30–45cm).

☼ ◊ ❄❄❄ H

**Helianthus, Chrysanthemum-
flowered Series**
Fast-growing, erect annual with large,
oval, serrated, green leaves. Globose,
daisylike, double, deep yellow flower
heads, 6in (15cm) wide, are carried in
summer. H 5ft (1.5m), S 1–1½ft
(30–45cm).

☼ ◊ ❄❄❄ H

281

Annuals and Biennials

***Zinnia* 'Belvedere Dwarfs'**
[Elegans group]
Moderately fast-growing, sturdy, erect
annual with oval to lance-shaped leaves.
Large, daisylike, double flower heads
in a mixture of colors appear in
summer and early autumn. H and
S 12in (30cm).

☼ ◊ ❄ T

Ursinia anthemoides
(Dill-leaf ursinia)
Moderately fast-growing, bushy annual
with feathery, pale green leaves. Small,
daisylike, purple-centered flower heads
with orange-yellow rays, purple beneath,
appear in summer and early autumn.
H 12in (30cm), S 8in (20cm).

☼ ◊ ❄ HH

***Gaillardia pulchella* 'Lollipops'**
Moderately fast-growing, upright
annual with lance-shaped, hairy,
grayish green leaves. Daisylike, double,
red-and-yellow flower heads, 2in (5cm)
wide, are carried in summer. H and
S 12in (30cm).

☼ ◊ ❄❄❄ H

***Calceolaria*, Bikini Series**
Compact, bushy annual or biennial.
Has oval, slightly hairy, green leaves,
and heads of small, rounded, pouched
flowers in shades of yellow, orange, or
red in summer. H and S 8in (20cm).
Min. 41°F (5°C).

☼ ◊ HH

***Tagetes* 'Crackerjack'**
[Erecta group]
Fast-growing, erect, bushy annual
with aromatic, deeply cut, glossy, deep
green leaves. Has large, double flower
heads, in yellow and orange shades, in
summer and early autumn. H 24in
(60cm), S 12–18in (30–45cm).

☼ ◊ ❄ HH

***Tagetes patula* 'Naughty Marietta'**
Fast-growing, bushy annual with
aromatic, deeply cut, deep green leaves.
Heads of daisylike, bicolored flowers,
deep yellow and maroon, are carried in
summer and early autumn. H and
S 12in (30cm).

☼ ◊ ❄ HH

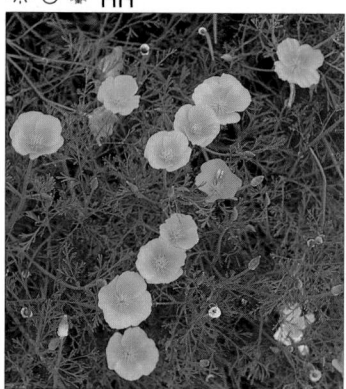

Eschscholzia californica
(California poppy)
Fast-growing, slender, erect annual
with feathery, bluish green leaves.
Cup-shaped, 4-petaled, vivid orange-
yellow flowers are borne in summer-
autumn. H 12in (30cm), S 6in (15cm).

☼ ◊ ❄❄❄ H

***Viola* 'Redwing'**
Bushy, spreading perennial, usually
grown as an annual or biennial. Large,
rounded, 5-petaled, reddish brown and
yellow flowers appear in summer.
H and S 6–8in (15–20cm).

☼ ◊ ❄❄❄ H

***Eschscholzia californica* [mixed]**
(California poppy)
Fast-growing, slender, erect annual.
Feathery leaves are bluish green; cup-
shaped, 4-petaled, single flowers, in
shades of red, orange, yellow, or
cream, are borne in summer-autumn.
H 12in (30cm), S 6in (15cm).

☼ ◊ ❄❄❄ H

Calceolaria 'Sunshine'
Evergreen, compact, bushy perennial, grown as an annual. Has oval leaves and heads of small, rounded, pouched, bright golden yellow flowers in late spring and summer. H and S 8in (20cm).

☀ ◊ ❉ HH

Tropaeolum majus 'Alaska'
Fast-growing, bushy annual with rounded, variegated leaves. Spurred, trumpet-shaped flowers, in shades of red or yellow, appear in summer and early autumn. H and S 12in (30cm).

☀ ◊ ❉❉❉ T

Primula, Pacific Series
Rosette-forming perennial, normally grown as a biennial, with lance-shaped leaves. Has heads of large, fragrant, flat flowers in shades of blue, yellow, red, pink, or white in spring. H and S 8–9in (20–22cm).

☀ ◊ ❉❉❉ H

Nemesia strumosa, Triumph Series
Fairly fast-growing, bushy, compact annual with lance-shaped, serrated, pale green leaves. Small, somewhat trumpet-shaped flowers, in a range of bright colors, are borne in summer. H 8in (20cm), S 6in (15cm).

☀ ◊ ❉ T

Viola, Universal Series [apricot]
Bushy, spreading perennial, usually grown as a biennial. Large, rounded, 5-petaled, deep apricot flowers are borne in winter-spring. H and S 6–8in (15–20cm).

☀ ◊ ❉❉❉ H

Antirrhinum majus 'Trumpet Serenade'
Erect perennial, branching from the base, grown as an annual. Has lance-shaped leaves and, from spring to autumn, spikes of open trumpet-shaped, bicolored flowers in a mixture of pastel shades. H and S 12in (30cm).

☀ ◊ ❉ HH

Viola 'Scarlet Clan'
Slow- to fairly fast-growing, bushy perennial, grown as an annual or biennial. Has oval leaves and rounded, 5-petaled, orange-yellow flowers, each with a scarlet blotch, in summer. H 6–8in (15–20cm), S 8in (20cm).

☀ ◊ ❉❉❉ H

Calendula officinalis (Fiesta Series) 'Gitana'
Fast-growing, bushy annual with strongly aromatic, lance-shaped, pale green leaves. Daisylike, double flower heads, ranging from cream to orange in color, are carried from spring to autumn. H and S 12in (30cm).

☀ ◊ ❉❉❉ H

Annuals and Biennials

***Rudbeckia hirta* 'Marmalade'**
Moderately fast-growing, erect, branching perennial, grown as an annual, with lance-shaped leaves. In summer-autumn bears daisylike, deep golden orange flower heads, 3in (8cm) wide, with black centers. H 18in (45cm), S 12in (30cm).

☼ ◊ ❋❋❋ HH

***Rudbeckia hirta* 'Goldilocks'**
Moderately fast-growing, erect, branching perennial, grown as an annual. Has lance-shaped leaves and daisylike, double or semi-double, golden orange flower heads, 3in (8cm) across, in summer-autumn. H 24in (60cm), S 12in (30cm).

☼ ◊ ❋❋❋ HH

***Tagetes patula* 'Orange Winner'**
Fast-growing, bushy annual with aromatic, feathery, deep green leaves. Crested, daisylike, double, bright orange flower heads are carried in summer and early autumn. H 6in (15cm), S to 12in (30cm).

☼ ◊ ❋ HH

***Tagetes* 'Tangerine Gem'**
Fast-growing, bushy annual with aromatic, feathery leaves. Small, single, deep orange flower heads appear in summer and early autumn. H 8in (20cm), S 12in (30cm).

☼ ◊ ❋ HH

***Tagetes* 'Paprika'**
Fast-growing, bushy annual with aromatic, feathery leaves. In summer and early autumn has daisylike, single, red flower heads edged with gold. H 6in (15cm), S 12in (30cm).

☼ ◊ ❋ HH

***Erysimum hieraciifolium* 'Orange Bedder'**
Slow-growing, short-lived, evergreen, bushy perennial, grown as a biennial. Has lance-shaped, green leaves. Heads of scented, 4-petaled, brilliant orange flowers appear in spring. H and S 12in (30cm).

☼ ◊ ❋❋❋ H

***Rudbeckia hirta* 'Rustic Dwarfs'**
Moderately fast-growing, erect, branching perennial, grown as an annual, with lance-shaped, green leaves. Bears daisylike, yellow, mahogany, or bronze flower heads, 3in (8cm) wide, in summer-autumn. H 24in (60cm), S 12in (30cm).

☼ ◊ ❋❋❋ HH

***Tithonia rotundifolia* 'Torch'**
Slow-growing, erect annual with rounded, lobed leaves. Has daisylike, bright orange or scarlet flower heads, 2–3in (5–8 cm) wide, in summer and early autumn. H 3ft (90cm), S 1ft (30cm).

☼ ◊ ❋ T

***Helichrysum bracteatum*, Monstrosum Series**
Moderately fast-growing, erect, branching annual. Has daisylike, papery, double flower heads, in pink, red, orange, yellow, or white, in summer and early autumn. Flowers dry well. H 3ft (90cm), S 1ft (30cm).

☼ ◊ ❋ HH

Calendula officinalis 'Geisha Girl'
Fast-growing, bushy annual with strongly aromatic, lance-shaped, pale green leaves. Heads of double, orange flowers with incurved petals are borne from late spring to autumn. H 24in (60cm), S 12–24in (30–60cm).

 ☼ ◊ ❋❋❋ H

Tropaeolum majus, Jewel Series
Fast-growing, bushy annual with rounded leaves. Spurred, trumpet-shaped flowers, in shades of red, yellow, or orange, are held well above leaves from early summer to early autumn. H and S 12in (30cm).

☼ ◊ ❋❋❋ T

Emilia javanica, syn. *E. flammea* (Flora's paintbrush, Tassel flower)
Moderately fast-growing, upright annual with lance-shaped, grayish green leaves. Has branching sprays of rounded, double, red or yellow flower heads in summer. H 12–24in (30–60cm), S 12in (30cm) or more.

☼ ◊ ❋ HH

Zinnia, Burpee Hybrids
[Elegans group]
Moderately fast-growing, sturdy, erect annual with oval to lance-shaped leaves. Has large, cactus-dahlialike, double flower heads in a range of colors in summer and early autumn. H 24in (60cm), S 12in (30cm).

☼ ◊ ❋ T

Cheiranthus cheiri 'Fire King'
Moderately fast-growing, evergreen, bushy perennial, grown as a biennial, with lance-shaped leaves. Heads of 4-petaled, reddish orange flowers are carried in spring. H 15in (38cm), S 12–15in (30–38cm).

☼ ◊ ❋❋❋ HH

Mimulus, Malibu Series [orange]
Fast-growing, branching perennial, grown as an annual, with pointed-oval, pale green leaves. In summer has flared, tubular, vibrant deep orange flowers. H 6in (15cm), S to 12in (30cm).

☽ ◊ ❋ T

Solanum pseudocapsicum 'Balloon'
Evergreen, bushy shrub, grown as an annual. Has lance-shaped leaves and, in summer, small, star-shaped, white flowers. Large, cream fruits turn orange in winter. H 12in (30cm), S 12–18in (30–45cm). Min. 41°F (5°C).

☼ ◊ T

Solanum pseudocapsicum 'Red Giant'
Fairly slow-growing, evergreen, bushy shrub, usually grown as an annual. Has lance-shaped, deep green leaves, small, white flowers in summer and large, round, orange-red fruits in winter. H and S 12in (30cm). Min. 41°F (5°C).

☼ ◊ T

Clarkia amoena, Princess Series [salmon]
Fast-growing annual with slender upright stems and lance-shaped leaves. Spikes of frilled, salmon pink flowers are carried in summer. H and S 12in (30cm).

☼ ◊ ❋❋❋ H

Sanvitalia procumbens 'Mandarin Orange'
Moderately fast-growing, prostrate annual. Has pointed-oval leaves and daisylike, orange flower heads, 1in (2.5cm) wide, in summer. H 6in (15cm), S 12in (30cm).

☼ ◊ ❋❋❋ T

Dahlia 'Dandy'
Well-branched, erect, bushy, tuberous perennial, grown as an annual. Has pointed-oval, serrated leaves and heads of daisylike flowers, with contrasting central collars of quilled petals, in shades of red, yellow, or orange in summer. H and S 2ft (60cm).

☼ ◊ ❋ T

Celosia cristata 'Fairy Fountains'
Moderately fast-growing, erect, bushy perennial, grown as an annual. Has pointed-oval leaves and conical, feathery flower heads, to 6in (15cm) tall, in a wide range of colors in summer-autumn. H and S 12in (30cm).

☼ ◊ ❋ T

☐ WHITE

Leontopodium alpinum (Edelweiss)
Short-lived perennial with tufts of lance-shaped, woolly leaves. Clusters of small, silvery white flower heads, borne in spring or early summer, are surrounded by petal-like, thick, felted bracts that form a star shape. Dislikes winter and summer wet. H and S 6–8in (15–20cm).

☼ ◊ ✽✽✽✽ 4–6

Lithophragma parviflorum
Clump-forming, tuberous perennial that has small, open clusters of campionlike, white or pink flowers in spring above a basal cluster of kidney-shaped, deeply toothed leaves. Lies dormant in summer. H 6–8in (15–20cm), S to 8in (20cm).

◐ ◊ ✽✽✽✽ 4–6

Iberis sempervirens (Candytuft)
Evergreen, spreading sub-shrub, with narrowly oblong, dark green leaves. Bears dense, rounded heads of white flowers in late spring and early summer. Trim after flowering. H 6–12in (15–30cm), S 18–24in (45–60cm).

☼ ◊ ✽✽✽ 5–9

Pulsatilla alpina (Alpine anemone)
Tufted perennial with feathery leaves. Produces upright, or somewhat nodding, cup-shaped, white, sometimes blue- or pink-flushed flowers singly in spring and early summer, followed by feathery seed heads. H 6–12in (15–30cm), S to 4in (10cm).

☼ ◊ ✽✽✽ 3–5

Saxifraga granulata (Fair-maids-of-France, Meadow saxifrage)
Clump-forming perennial that loses its kidney-shaped, crumpled, glossy leaves in summer. Sticky stems carry loose panicles of rounded, white flowers in late spring. H 9–15in (23–38cm), S to 6in (15cm) or more.

◐ ◑ ✽✽✽ 3–6

Chrysanthemum hosmariense
Evergreen, shrubby perennial with finely cut, bright silvery green leaves that clothe lax, woody stems. From late spring to early autumn, daisylike, white flower heads are borne singly above foliage. H 6in (15cm) or more, S 12in (30cm).

☼ ◊ ✽✽✽ 8–9

Andromeda polifolia 'Alba'
(White-flowered bog rosemary)
Evergreen, open, twiggy shrub bearing terminal clusters of pitcher-shaped, white flowers in spring and early summer. Glossy, dark green leaves are leathery and lance-shaped. H 18in (45cm), S 24in (60cm).

☼ ◑ pH ✽✽✽✽ 2–6

Cassiope 'Muirhead'
Evergreen, loose, bushy shrub with scalelike, dark green leaves on upright branches. In spring, these bear tiny, virtually stemless, bell-shaped, white flowers along their length. H and S 8in (20cm).

☼ ◑ pH ✽✽✽ 2–6

Cassiope 'Edinburgh'
Evergreen, dwarf shrub with tiny, dark green leaves tightly pressed to upright stems. In spring, many small, bell-shaped, white flowers are borne singly in leaf axils. H and S 8in (20cm).

◐ ◑ pH ✽✽✽ 2–6

Saxifraga hirsuta
Evergreen, mound-forming perennial with rosettes of round, hairy leaves and, in late spring and early summer, loose panicles of tiny, star-shaped, white flowers, often yellow-spotted at the base of petals. H 6–8in (15–20cm), S 8in (20cm).

☀ ◑ ✿✿✿ 3–6

Jeffersonia diphylla
(American twinleaf)
Slow-growing, tufted perennial with distinctive, 2-lobed, light to mid-green leaves. Bears solitary cup-shaped, white flowers with prominent, yellow stamens in late spring. Do not disturb roots. H 6–9in (15–23cm), S to 9in (23cm).

☀ ◑ ✿✿✿ 5–7

Daphne blagayana
Evergreen, prostrate shrub with trailing branches each bearing a terminal cluster of oval, leathery leaves and, in early spring, dense clusters of fragrant, tubular, white flowers. Likes humus-rich soil. H 12–16in (30–40cm), S 24–32in (60–80cm) or more.

☀ ◑ ✿✿✿ 7–9

Tiarella cordifolia (False mitrewort)
Vigorous, evergreen, spreading perennial. Lobed, pale green leaves sometimes have darker marks; veins turn bronze-red in winter. Bears many spikes of profuse white flowers in late spring and early summer. H 6–8in (15–20cm), S to 12in (30cm) or more.

☀◑ ◑ ✿✿✿ 5–9

Saxifraga 'Tumbling Waters'
Slow-growing, evergreen, mat-forming perennial with a tight rosette of narrow, lime-encrusted leaves. After several years produces arching sprays of white flowers in conical heads; main rosette then dies but small offsets survive. H to 24in (60cm), S to 8in (20cm).

☀ ◑ ✿✿✿ 5–7

Vancouveria hexandra
(American barrenwort)
Vigorous, spreading perennial with sprays of tiny, white flowers in late spring and early summer. Has leathery leaves divided into almost hexagonal leaflets. Makes good woodland ground cover. H 8in (20cm), S indefinite.

☀◑ ◑ ✿✿✿ 5–7

Dodecatheon meadia f. **alba**
(White-flowered shooting star)
Clump-forming perennial with basal rosettes of oval, pale green leaves. In spring, strong stems bear several white flowers with dark centers and reflexed petals. Lies dormant in summer. H 8in (20cm), S 6in (15cm).

☀◑ ◑ ✿✿✿ 5–7

Saxifraga × geum
Evergreen, mat-forming perennial with shallow-rooted rosettes of spoon-shaped, hairy leaves. In summer, star-shaped, pink-spotted, white flowers, deep pink in bud, are borne in loose panicles on slender stems. H 6–8in (15–20cm), S 12in (30cm).

☀◑ ◑ ✿✿✿ 5–7

Andromeda polifolia
(Bog rosemary)
Evergreen, open, twiggy shrub with narrow, leathery, glossy, green leaves. Bears terminal clusters of pitcher-shaped, pink flowers in spring and early summer. H 12–18in (30–45cm), S 24in (60cm).

☀ ◑ pH ⌣ ✿✿✿ 2–6

Andromeda polifolia 'Compacta'
Evergreen, compact, twiggy shrub that bears delicate, terminal clusters of pitcher-shaped, coral pink flowers, with white undertones, in spring and early summer. Leaves are lance-shaped and glossy, dark green. H 6–9in (15–23cm), S 12in (30cm).

☀ ◑ pH ✿✿✿ 2–6

Dodecatheon hendersonii
Clump-forming perennial with a flat rosette of kidney-shaped leaves, above which deep pink flowers with reflexed petals appear in late spring. Needs a dry, dormant summer period. H 12in (30cm), S 3in (8cm).

☀ ◑ ✿✿✿ 5–7

Phyllodoce × intermedia
'Drummondii'
Evergreen, bushy, dwarf shrub with narrow, heathlike, glossy leaves. From late spring to early summer bears terminal clusters of pitcher-shaped, rich pink flowers on slender, red stalks. H and S 9in (23cm).

☀◑ ◑ pH ✿✿✿ 2–5

Rock plants/large SPRING INTEREST

Daphne cneorum (Garland daphne)
Evergreen, low-growing shrub with
trailing branches clothed in small, oval,
leathery, dark green leaves. Fragrant,
deep rose-pink flowers are borne in
terminal clusters in late spring. Prefers
humus-rich soil. H 9in (23cm),
S to 6ft (2m).

☼ ◊ ❅❅❅ 5–8

Dodecatheon 'Red Wings'
Clump-forming perennial with a basal
cluster of oblong, soft, pale green
leaves. In late spring and early summer
bears small, loose clusters of deep
magenta flowers, with reflexed petals,
on strong stems. Lies dormant in
summer. H 8in (20cm), S 4in (10cm).

☼ ◊ ❅❅❅ 5–7

Phyllodoce empetriformis
(Mountain heather)
Evergreen, mat-forming shrub with
fine, narrow, heathlike leaves and
terminal clusters of bell-shaped,
purplish pink flowers in late spring
and early summer. H 6–9in (15–23cm),
S 8in (20cm).

☼◗ ◊ ᵖᴴ ❅❅❅ 2–5

Phyllodoce caerulea,
syn. *P. taxifolia*
Evergreen, dwarf shrub with fine,
narrow, heathlike leaves. Bears bell-
shaped, purple to purplish pink flowers,
singly or in clusters, in late spring and
summer. H and S to 12in (30cm).

☼◗ ◊ ᵖᴴ ❅❅❅ 4–6

Pulsatilla vulgaris (Pasque flower)
Tufted perennial with feathery, light
green leaves. In spring bears nodding,
cup-shaped flowers, in shades of purple,
red, pink, or white, with bright yellow
centers. Flower stems rapidly elongate
as feathery seeds mature. H and
S 6–9in (15–23cm).

☼ ◊ ❅❅❅ 5–7

Erinacea anthyllis,
syn. *E. pungens*
Slow-growing, evergreen sub-shrub
with hard, blue-green spines. Pealike,
soft lavender flowers appear in axils of
spines in late spring or early summer.
H and S 6–10in (15–25cm).

☼ ◊ ❅❅ 7–8

Pulsatilla halleri
Tufted perennial, intensely hairy in all
parts, that in spring bears nodding,
later erect, cup-shaped flowers in
shades of purple. Has feathery leaves
and seed heads. H 6–15in (15–38cm),
S 6–8in (15–20cm).

☼ ◊ ❅❅❅ 5–7

Aquilegia alpina
(Alpine columbine)
Short-lived, upright perennial with
spurred, clear blue or violet-blue
flowers on slender stems in spring and
early summer. Has basal rosettes of
rounded, finely divided leaves. Needs
rich soil. H 18in (45cm), S 6in (15cm).

☼ ◊ ❅❅❅ 4–7

Viola cornuta (Horned violet,
Tufted violet)
Rhizomatous perennial with oval,
toothed leaves and flat-faced, rather
angular, spurred, pale to deep purplish
blue, occasionally white flowers in
spring and much of summer. H 5–8in
(12–20cm), S to 8in (20cm) or more.

☼ ◊ ❅ ❅ ❅ 5–8

Omphalodes verna (Blue-eyed
Mary, Creeping forget-me-not)
Semi-evergreen, clump-forming
perennial that in spring bears long,
loose sprays of flat, bright blue flowers
with white eyes. Leaves are oval.
H and S 8in (20cm) or more.

◑ ◊ ❅ ❅ ❅ 5–8

Omphalodes cappadocica
Spreading perennial with creeping
underground stems and many loose
sprays of flat, bright blue flowers in
spring-summer above tufts of oval,
hairy, basal leaves. H 6–8in
(15–20cm), S 10in (25cm) or more.

◑ ◊ ❅ ❅ ❅ 5–8

Salix helvetica
Deciduous, spreading, much-branched,
dwarf shrub that has small, oval, glossy
leaves, white-haired beneath. In spring
bears short-stalked, silky, gray, then
yellow catkins. H 24in (60cm),
S 12in (30cm).

☼ ◊ ❅ ❅ ❅ 5–7

Betula nana (Dwarf arctic birch)
Deciduous, bushy, dwarf shrub with
small, toothed leaves that turn bright
yellow in autumn. Has tiny, yellowish
brown catkins in spring. H 12in
(30cm), S 18in (45cm).

☼ ◊ pH ❅ ❅ ❅ 2–5

Corydalis cheilanthifolia
Evergreen perennial with fleshy roots.
Produces spreading rosettes of fernlike,
near-prostrate, sometimes bronze-tinted,
green leaves. In late spring and early
summer bears dense spikes of short-
spurred, yellow flowers. H 8–12in
(20–30cm), S 6–8in (15–20cm).

☼ ◊ ❅ ❅ 5–7

Corydalis wilsonii
Evergreen perennial with a fleshy
rootstock. Forms rosettes of near-
prostrate, divided, bluish green leaves.
Loose racemes of spurred, green-
tipped, yellow flowers are produced in
spring. H and S 4–10in (10–25cm).

☼ ◊ ❅ ❅ 6–7

***Aurinia saxatilis* 'Citrina'**,
syn. *Alyssum saxatile* 'Citrinum'
Evergreen, clump-forming perennial
with oval, hairy, gray-green leaves.
Bears racemes of many small, pale
lemon yellow flowers in late spring
and early summer. H 9in (23cm),
S 12in (30cm).

☼ ◊ ❅ ❅ ❅ 4–7

Chiastophyllum oppositifolium,
syn. *Cotyledon simplicifolia*
Evergreen, trailing perennial with
large, oblong, serrated, succulent
leaves. In late spring and early summer
bears many tiny, yellow flowers in
arching sprays. H 6–8in (15–20cm),
S 6in (15cm).

◑ ◊ ❅ ❅ ❅ 6–9

Cytisus* x *beanii
Deciduous, low-growing shrub with
arching sprays of pealike, golden
yellow flowers that appear in late spring
and early summer on previous year's
wood. Leaves, divided into 3 leaflets,
are small, linear, and hairy. H 6–16in
(15–40cm), S 12–30in (30–75cm).

☼ ◊ ❅ ❅ ❅ 7–8

***Aurinia saxatilis* 'Variegata'**,
syn. *Alyssum saxatile* 'Variegatum'
Evergreen perennial that bears racemes
of many small, yellow flowers in
spring above a mat of large, oval, soft
gray-green leaves with cream margins.
H 9in (23cm), S 12in (30cm).

☼ ◊ ❅ ❅ ❅ 4–7

Rock plants/large SPRING INTEREST

 YELLOW–ORANGE

Hylomecon japonicum
Vigorous, spreading perennial with large, cup-shaped, bright yellow flowers that are borne singly on slender stems in spring. Soft, dark green leaves are divided into 4 unequal lobes. H to 12in (30cm), S 8in (20cm).

☀◐ ❁❁❁ 5–8

Stylophorum diphyllum
(Celandine poppy)
Perennial with basal rosettes of large, lobed, hairy leaves. Bears open cup-shaped, golden yellow flowers in spring on upright, branched stems. Prefers rich, woodland conditions. H and S to 12in (30cm) or more.

☀◐ ❁❁❁❁ 6–8

Aurinia saxatilis, syn. *Alyssum saxatile* (Basket-of-gold))
Evergreen perennial forming low clumps of oval, hairy, gray-green leaves. Has substantial spikes of small, chrome yellow flowers in spring. H 9in (23cm), S 12in (30cm).

☀ ◌ ❁❁❁ 4–7

Cheiranthus 'Bredon'
Semi-evergreen, rounded, woody perennial clothed in oval, dark green leaves. In late spring bears dense spikes of flat, bright mustard yellow flowers. H 12–18in (30–45cm), S 18in (45cm).

☀ ◌ ❁❁❁ 8–9

Cheiranthus 'Harpur Crewe'
Evergreen, shrubby perennial with stiff stems and narrow leaves. Fragrant, double, deep yellow flowers, in tight, terminal clusters, open in succession from late spring to mid-summer. Grows best in poor soil and in a sheltered site. H and S 12in (30cm).

☀ ◌ ❁❁❁ 8–9

Berberis x **stenophylla 'Corallina Compacta'**
Evergreen, neat, dwarf shrub with spiny stems clothed in small, narrowly oval leaves. In late spring bears many tiny, bright orange flowers. Is slow-growing and difficult to propagate. H and S to 10in (25cm).

☀ ◌ ❁❁❁ 6–9

Rock plants/large SUMMER INTEREST

☐ WHITE

Parnassia palustris
Perennial with low, basal tufts of heart-shaped, pale to mid-green leaves. Bears saucer-shaped, white flowers, with dark green or purplish green veins, on erect stems in late spring and early summer. H 8in (20cm), S 2½in (6cm) or more.

☀ ● ❁❁❁ 3–6

Armeria pseudarmeria,
syn. *A. latifolia*
Evergreen, clump-forming perennial with large, spherical heads of white flowers occasionally suffused pink; these are borne in summer on stiff stems above long, narrow, glaucous leaves. H and S 12in (30cm).

☀ ◌ ❁❁❁ 6–7

Celmisia walkeri
Evergreen, loose, spreading perennial with long, oval or lance-shaped leaves, glossy, green above and hairy, white beneath. Has large, daisylike, white flower heads in summer. H 9in (23cm), S to 6ft (2m).

☀ ● ᴾᴴ ❁❁ 9

Helianthemum apenninum
Evergreen, spreading, much-branched shrub that bears saucer-shaped, pure white flowers in mid-summer. Stems and small, linear leaves are covered in white down. H and S 18in (45cm).

☼ ◊ ❄❄❄ 6–8

Saxifraga cuneifolia
Evergreen, carpeting perennial with neat rosettes of rounded leaves. In late spring and early summer bears panicles of tiny, white flowers, frequently with yellow, pink, or red spots, on slender stems. H 6–8in (15–20cm), S 12in (30cm) or more.

◑ ◊ ❄❄❄ 4–6

Cytisus purpureus f. **albus**
Deciduous, low-growing shrub with semi-erect stems clothed in leaves, divided into 3 leaflets. A profusion of pealike, white flowers appear in early summer on previous year's wood. H 18in (45cm), S 24in (60cm).

☼ ◊ ❄❄❄ 6–9

Helianthemum 'Wisley White'
Evergreen, spreading shrub, with oblong, gray-green leaves, bearing saucer-shaped, white flowers for a long period in summer. H 9in (23cm), S 12in (30cm) or more.

☼ ◊ ❄❄❄ 6–8

Galax urceolata, syn. *G. aphylla*
Evergreen, clump-forming perennial. Large, round, leathery, green leaves on slender stems turn bronze in autumn-winter. Has dense spikes of small, white flowers in late spring and early summer. H 6–8in (15–20cm), S to 12in (30cm).

☼ ◊ pH ❄❄❄ 5–8

Epilobium glabellum
Semi-evergreen, clump-forming perennial. Bears outward-facing, cup-shaped, white flowers singly on slender stems in summer above oval, green leaves. Makes useful ground cover. H to 8in (20cm), S 6in (15cm).

◑ ◊ ❄❄❄ 5–8

Hebe pinguifolia 'Pagei'
Evergreen, semi-prostrate shrub with small, oblong, slightly cupped, intensely glaucous leaves. Bears short spikes of small, pure white flowers in late spring or early summer. Is excellent for ground or rock cover. H 6–12in (15–30cm), S 2–3ft (60cm–1m).

☼ ◊ ❄❄ 8–9

Corydalis ochroleuca
Evergreen, clump-forming perennial with fleshy, fibrous roots and much divided, semi-erect, basal, gray-green leaves. Bears fairly dense spikes of slender, yellow-tipped, creamy white flowers in late spring and summer. H and S 8–12in (20–30cm).

☼ ◊ ❄❄❄ 6–8

Hebe canterburiensis
Evergreen, low-growing, spreading shrub with small, oval, glossy, dark green leaves densely packed on stems. In early summer, short racemes of small, white flowers are freely produced in leaf axils. H and S 1–3ft (30–90cm).

☼ ◊ ❄❄ 8–9

■ WHITE–PINK

Saxifraga cotyledon
Evergreen perennial with large, pale green rosettes of leaves, dying after flowering. In late spring and early summer produces arching, conical panicles of cup-shaped, white flowers sometimes strongly marked red internally. H and S to 12in (30cm).

☼ ◊ ✽✽✽ 4–6

Aethionema grandiflorum, syn. *A. pulchellum*
Short-lived, evergreen or semi-evergreen, lax shrub. Bears tiny, pale to deep rose-pink flowers in loose sprays in spring-summer. Blue-green leaves are narrow and lance-shaped. H 12in (30cm), S 9in (23cm).

☼ ◊ ✽✽✽ 6–8

Onosma albo-roseum
Semi-evergreen, clump-forming perennial covered in fine hairs, which may irritate skin. Clusters of long, pendent, tubular flowers, borne for a long period in summer, open white and then turn pink. H 6–12in (15–30cm), S 8in (20cm).

☼ ◊ ✽✽✽ 7–9

Saxifraga 'Southside Seedling'
Evergreen, mat-forming perennial, with large, pale green rosettes of leaves, dying after flowering. In late spring and early summer bears arching panicles of open cup-shaped, white flowers, strongly red-banded within. H and S to 12in (30cm).

☼ ◊ ✽✽✽ 4–6

Rhodothamnus chamaecistus
Evergreen, low-growing, dwarf shrub with narrowly oval leaves, edged with bristles. In late spring and early summer bears cup-shaped, rose- to lilac-pink flowers, with dark stamens, in leaf axils. H 6–8in (15–20cm), S to 10in (25cm).

☼ ◊ pH ✽✽✽ 7

■ PINK

Anthyllis montana
Rounded, bushy or somewhat spreading perennial with loose branches and finely cut foliage. Heads of cloverlike, pale pink flowers with red markings are borne in late spring and early summer. H and S 12in (30cm).

☼ ◊ ✽✽ 6–8

Phuopsis stylosa, syn. *Crucianella stylosa*
Low-growing perennial with whorls of pungent, pale green leaves and rounded heads of small, tubular, pink flowers in summer. Is good grown over a bank or large rock. H 12in (30cm), S 12in (30cm) or more.

☼ ◊ ✽✽✽ 5–8

Lewisia 'George Henley'
Evergreen, clump-forming perennial with rosettes of narrow, fleshy, dark green leaves. Bears dense sprays of open cup-shaped, deep pink flowers, with magenta veins, from late spring to late summer. H 6in (15cm) or more, S 4in (10cm).

☼ ◊ pH ✽✽✽ 6–7

Origanum 'Kent Beauty'
Prostrate perennial with trailing stems clothed in aromatic, rounded-oval leaves. In summer bears short spikes of tubular, pale pink flowers with darker bracts. Is suitable for a wall or ledge. H 6–8in (15–20cm), S 12in (30cm).

☼ ◊ ❋❋ 5–8

Astilbe 'Perkeo'
Erect, compact perennial bearing small plumes of tiny, salmon pink flowers from mid- to late summer on fine stems. Has stiff, deeply cut, crinkled leaves. H 6–8in (15–20cm), S 4in (10cm).

☼◗ ◊ ❋❋❋ 5–8

Crassula sarcocaulis
Evergreen or, in severe climates, semi-evergreen, bushy sub-shrub with tiny, oval, succulent leaves. Bears terminal clusters of tiny, red buds opening to pale pink flowers in summer. H and S 12in (30cm).

☼ ◊ ❋❋ 5–9

Diascia cordata
Prostrate perennial with stems clothed in heart-shaped, pale green leaves. Bears terminal clusters of spurred, flat-faced, bright pink flowers in summer and early autumn. H 6–8in (15–20cm), S 8in (20cm).

☼ ◊ ❋❋ 7–9

Ononis fruticosa
Deciduous shrub that in summer bears pendent clusters of large, pealike, purplish pink blooms with darker streaks. Leaves are divided into 3 serrated leaflets, which are hairy when young. H and S 12–24in (30–60cm).

☼ ◊ ❋❋❋ 6–8

Helianthemum 'Wisley Pink'
Evergreen, lax shrub with saucer-shaped, soft, pale pink flowers with orange centers borne for a long period in summer. Has oblong, gray-green leaves. H and S 12in (30cm) or more.

☼ ◊ ❋❋❋ 6–8

Oxalis deppei, syn. *O. tetraphylla*
Tuft-forming, tuberous perennial with brown-marked, basal leaves, usually divided into 4 leaflets. Produces loose sprays of widely funnel-shaped, deep pink flowers in late spring and summer. Needs a sheltered site. H 6–10in (15–30cm), S 4–6in (10–15cm).

☼ ◊ ❋❋ 7–9

Diascia rigescens
Trailing perennial with semi-erect stems covered in heart-shaped, green leaves. Spurred, flat-faced, salmon pink flowers are borne along stem length in summer and early autumn. H 9in (23cm), S to 12in (30cm).

☼ ◊ ❋❋ 7–9

Geranium orientalitibeticum
Spreading perennial with tuberous, underground runners. Has cup-shaped, pink flowers, with white centers, in summer. Leaves are deeply cut and marbled in shades of green. May be invasive. H in flower 6–10in (15–25cm), S indefinite.

☼ ◊ ❋❋❋ 6–8

Rock plants/large SUMMER INTEREST

■ PINK

Cortusa matthioli
Clump-forming perennial with a basal
rosette of rounded, dull green leaves
and, in late spring and early summer,
one-sided racemes of small, pendent,
bell-shaped, reddish or pinkish purple
flowers. H 6–10in (15–20cm),
S 4in (10cm).

 5–8

Origanum laevigatum
Deciduous, mat-forming sub-shrub
with small, aromatic, dark green
leaves, branching, red stems, and a
profusion of tiny, tubular, cerise-pink
flowers, surrounded by red-purple
bracts, in summer. H 9–12in
(23–30cm), S 8in (20cm) or more.

☼ ◊ ❄❄ 5–9

Geranium sanguineum
(Blood-red cranesbill)
Hummock-forming, spreading perennial
with many cup-shaped, deep magenta-
pink flowers borne in summer above
round, deeply divided, dark green
leaves. Makes good ground cover. H to
10in (25cm), S 12in (30cm) or more.

☼ ◊ ❄❄❄ 4–8

***Lewisia,* Cotyledon Hybrids**
Evergreen, clump-forming perennials
with rosettes of large, thick, toothed
leaves. In early summer bear clusters
of flowers, in various shades of pink to
purple, on erect stems. Is good for a
rock crevice or an alpine house. H to
12in (30cm), S 6in (15cm) or more.

☼ ◊ pH ❄❄❄ 6–7

Dianthus carthusianorum
Evergreen perennial carrying rounded,
upward-facing, cherry red or deep pink
flowers on slender stems in summer
above small tufts of grasslike leaves.
H 8in (20cm), S 2¹/₂in (6cm).

☼ ◊ ❄❄❄ 5–7

■ RED

Penstemon newberryi* f. *humilior
Evergreen, mat-forming shrub with
arching branches clothed in small,
leathery, dark green leaves. Bears short
sprays of tubular, lipped, cherry red to
deep pink flowers in early summer.
H 6–8in (15–20cm), S 12in (30cm).

☼ ◊ ❄❄ 7–9

***Helianthemum* 'Raspberry
Ripple'**
Evergreen, spreading shrub with saucer-
shaped, red-centered, white flowers that
are borne in mid-summer. Has small,
linear, gray-green leaves. H 6–9in
(15–23cm), S 9–12in (23–30cm).

☼ ◊ ❄❄❄ 6–8

***Helianthemum* 'Ben More'**
Evergreen, spreading, twiggy shrub
that bears a succession of saucer-
shaped, reddish orange flowers in
loose, terminal clusters in late spring
and summer. Has small, glossy, dark
green leaves. H 9–12in (23–30cm),
S 12in (30cm).

☼ ◊ ❄❄❄ 6–8

Penstemon pinifolius
Evergreen, bushy shrub with branched
stems clothed in fine, dark green
leaves. In summer, very narrow,
tubular, orange-red flowers are borne
in loose, terminal spikes. H 4–8in
(10–20cm), S 6in (15cm).

☼ ◊ ❄❄❄ 8–9

***Helianthemum* 'Fire Dragon'**
Evergreen, spreading shrub with
saucer-shaped, orange-scarlet flowers
in late spring and summer. Leaves are
linear and gray-green. H 9–12in
(23–30cm), S 18in (45cm).

☼ ◊ ❄❄❄ 6–8

Zauschneria californica 'Glasnevin'
Clump-forming, woody-based perennial with lance-shaped, gray-green leaves. From late summer to early autumn bears terminal clusters of tubular, deep orange-scarlet flowers. H 12in (30cm), S 18in (45cm).

☼ ◊ ❀❀ 8–10

Punica granatum var. nana
(Dwarf pomegranate)
Slow-growing, deciduous, rounded shrub that, in summer, bears funnel-shaped, red flowers with somewhat crumpled petals, followed by small, rounded, orange-red fruits. H and S 1–3ft (30–90cm).

☼ ◊ ❀ 8–10

Delphinium nudicaule
(Scarlet larkspur)
Short-lived, upright perennial with erect stems bearing deeply divided, basal leaves and, in summer, spikes of hooded, red or occasionally yellow flowers, with contrasting stamens. H 8in (20cm), S 2–4in (5–10cm).

☼ ◊ ❀❀❀ 5–7

Calceolaria arachnoidea
Evergreen, clump-forming perennial with a basal rosette of wrinkled leaves, covered in white down. Upright stems carry spikes of many pouch-shaped, dull purple flowers in summer. Is best treated as a biennial. H 10in (25cm), S 5in (12cm).

☼ ◐ ❀ 8–9

Erodium petraeum subsp. **crispum**
Compact, mound-forming perennial with flat-faced, pink flowers, veined and marked with purple-red, borne on stiff stems in late spring and summer. Grayish green leaves are crinkled and deeply cut. H 6–8in (15–20cm), S 8in (20cm) or more.

☼ ◊ ❀❀ 5–8

Scabiosa lucida
Clump-forming perennial with tufts of oval leaves and rounded heads of pale lilac to deep mauve flowers, borne on erect stems in summer. H 8in (20cm), S 6in (15cm).

☼ ◊ ❀❀❀ 4–7

Penstemon serrulatus,
syn. *P. diffusus*
Semi-evergreen sub-shrub, deciduous in severe climates, that has small, elliptic, dark green leaves and tubular, blue to purple flowers borne in loose spikes in summer. Soil should not be too dry. H 24in (60cm), S 12in (30cm).

☼ ◊ ❀❀❀ 6–8

Erigeron alpinus
Clump-forming perennial of variable size that bears daisylike, lilac-pink flower heads on erect stems in summer. Leaves are long, oval, and hairy. Suits a sunny border, bank, or large rock garden. H 10in (25cm), S 8in (20cm).

☼ ◊ ❀❀❀ 5–8

Semiaquilegia ecalcarata
Short-lived, upright perennial with narrow, lobed leaves. In summer each slender stem bears several pendent, open bell-shaped, dusky pink to purple flowers, with no spurs. H 8in (20cm), S 2½in (6cm).

☼ ◊ ❀❀❀ 5–7

■ PURPLE–BLUE

Parahebe catarractae
Evergreen sub-shrub with oval,
toothed, green leaves and, in summer,
loose sprays of small, open funnel-
shaped, white flowers, heavily zoned
and veined pinkish purple. H and
S 12in (30cm).

☀ ◊ ❄❄❄ 8–9

Wulfenia amherstiana
Evergreen perennial with rosettes of
narrowly spoon-shaped, toothed
leaves. Erect stems bear loose clusters
of small, tubular, purple or pinkish
purple flowers in summer. H 6–12in
(15–30cm), S to 12in (30cm).

☀ ◊ ❄❄❄ 7–9

Phlox 'Chatahoochee'
Short-lived, clump-forming perennial
that has saucer-shaped, red-eyed, bright
lavender flowers throughout summer-
autumn. Narrow, pointed leaves are
dark reddish purple when young.
H 6–8in (15–20cm), S 12in (30cm).

☀ ◊ ❄❄ 5–9

Campanula barbata
Evergreen perennial with a basal rosette
of oval, hairy, gray-green leaves. In
summer bears one-sided racemes of
bell-shaped, white to lavender blue
flowers. Is short-lived but sets seed
freely. H 8in (20cm), S 5in (12cm).

☀ ◊ ❄❄❄ 5–8

Phlox divaricata subsp. **laphamii**
Semi-evergreen, creeping perennial
with oval leaves and upright stems
bearing loose clusters of saucer-
shaped, pale to deep violet-blue
flowers in summer. H 12in (30cm)
or more, S 8in (20cm).

◑ ◊ ❄❄❄ 4–8

Convolvulus sabatius, syn. *C.*
mauritanicus
Trailing perennial with slender stems
clothed in small, oval leaves and open
trumpet-shaped, vibrant blue-purple
flowers in summer and early autumn.
Shelter in a rock crevice in a cold site.
H 6–8in (15–20cm), S 12in (30cm).

☀ ◊ ❄ 8–9

Sisyrinchium graminoides, syn.
S. angustifolium, S. bermudiana
Semi-evergreen, erect perennial with
tufts of grasslike leaves. Small, irislike,
pale to dark purplish blue flowers with
yellow bases are borne in terminal
clusters in late spring and early summer.
H to 12in (30cm), S 3in (8cm).

☀ ◊ ❄❄❄ 7–9

Lithodora oleifolia,
syn. *Lithospermum oleifolium*
Evergreen shrub with oval, pointed,
silky, green leaves. Curving stems
carry loose sprays of several small,
funnel-shaped, light blue flowers in
early summer. H 6–8in (15–20cm),
S to 3ft (1m).

☀ ◊ ❄❄ 7–8

Linum perenne (Perennial flax)
Upright perennial with slender stems,
clothed in grasslike leaves, that bear
terminal clusters of open funnel-
shaped, clear blue flowers in
succession throughout summer.
H 12in (30cm), S to 6in (15cm).

☀ ◊ ❄❄❄ 5–8

Moltkia suffruticosa
Deciduous, upright sub-shrub. In summer bears clusters of funnel-shaped, bright blue flowers, pink in bud, on hairy stems. Leaves are long, pointed, and hairy. H 6–16in (15–40cm), S 12in (30cm).

☼ ◊ ❀❀❀ 7–8

Veronica prostrata 'Trehane'
Dense, mat-forming perennial bearing upright spikes of small, saucer-shaped, deep violet-blue flowers in early summer above narrow, toothed, yellow or yellowish green leaves. H in flower 6–8in (15–20cm), S indefinite.

☼ ◊ ❀❀❀ 4–7

Veronica prostrata
(Prostrate speedwell)
Dense, mat-forming perennial that has upright spikes of small, saucer-shaped, brilliant blue flowers in early summer. Foliage is narrowly oval and toothed. H to 12in (30cm), S indefinite.

☼ ◊ ❀❀❀ 4–7

Veronica prostrata 'Kapitan'
Dense, mat-forming perennial bearing erect spikes of small, saucer-shaped, bright deep blue flowers in early summer. Foliage is narrowly oval and toothed. H to 12in (30cm), S indefinite.

☼ ◊ ❀❀❀ 4–7

Mertensia echioides
Clump-forming perennial with basal rosettes of long, oval, hairy, blue-green leaves. Slender stems carry many open funnel-shaped, dark blue flowers in summer. H 6–9in (15–23cm), S 6in (15cm).

☼ ◊ ❀❀❀ 6–8

Phyteuma scheuchzeri
Tufted perennial with narrow, dark green leaves and terminal heads of spiky, blue flowers that are borne in summer. Seeds freely; dislikes winter wet. H 6–8in (15–20cm), S 4in (10cm).

☼ ◊ ❀❀❀ 5–7

Symphyandra wanneri
Clump-forming perennial with branching stems and oval, hairy leaves. In summer bears pendent, bell-shaped, blue to violet-blue flowers in loose, terminal spikes. H 6–9in (15–23cm), S 10in (25cm).

☼ ◊ ❀❀❀ 6–8

Lithodora diffusa 'Heavenly Blue'
Evergreen, prostrate shrub with trailing stems bearing oblong, pointed, hairy leaves and, in summer, a profusion of open funnel-shaped, deep blue flowers in leaf axils. Trim stems hard after flowering. H 6–12in (15–30cm), S to 18in (45cm).

☼ ◊ pH ❀❀ 6–8

***Veronica austriaca* subsp. *teucrium*,** syn. *V. teucrium*
Spreading perennial with narrow spikes of small, flat, outward-facing, bright blue flowers in summer. Leaves are small, divided, hairy, and grayish green. H and S 10–24in (25–60cm).

☀ ◊ ✿✿✿ 5–8

Verbascum 'Letitia'
Evergreen, stiff-branched shrub with toothed, gray leaves. Produces outward-facing, 5-lobed, bright yellow flowers, with reddish orange centers, continuously from late spring to mid-autumn. Hates winter wet; is good in an alpine house. H and S to 10in (25cm).

☀ ◊ ✿✿ 8–9

Helianthemum 'Wisley Primrose'
Fast-growing, evergreen, compact shrub with saucer-shaped, soft pale yellow flowers in summer. Has oblong, gray-green leaves. H 9in (23cm), S 12in (30cm) or more.

☀ ◊ ✿✿✿ 6–8

Othonnopsis cheirifolia
Evergreen shrub with narrow, somewhat fleshy, gray leaves. In early summer bears daisylike, yellow flower heads singly on upright stems. Needs a warm, sheltered site. H 8–12in (20–30cm), S 12in (30cm) or more.

☀ ◊ ✿ 6–8

Erodium chrysanthum
Mound-forming perennial, grown for its dense, silvery stems and finely cut, fernlike leaves. Has small sprays of cup-shaped, sulfur or creamy yellow flowers in late spring and summer. H and S 9in (23cm).

☀ ◊ ✿✿✿ 7–8

Euryops acraeus, syn. *E. evansii* of gardens
Evergreen, dome-shaped shrub with stems clothed in toothed, silvery blue leaves. Bears solitary daisylike, bright yellow flower heads in late spring and early summer. H and S 12in (30cm).

☀ ◐ ✿✿✿ 9–10

Hypericum olympicum 'Citrinum'
Deciduous, dense, rounded sub-shrub with tufts of upright stems, clothed in small, oval, gray-green leaves. Bears terminal clusters of lemon yellow flowers throughout summer. H and S 6–12in (15–30cm).

☀ ◊ ✿✿✿ 6–8

Linum arboreum
Evergreen, compact shrub with blue-green leaves. In summer has a succession of funnel-shaped, bright yellow flowers opening in sunny weather and borne in terminal clusters. H and S to 12in (30cm).

☀ ◊ ✿✿ 6–9

Eriogonum umbellatum
(Sulfur flower)
Evergreen, prostrate to upright perennial with mats of green leaves, white and woolly beneath. In summer bears heads of tiny, yellow flowers that later turn copper. Dwarf forms are available. H 3–12in (8–30cm), S 6–12in (15–30cm).

☀ ◊ ✿✿ 7–9

Corydalis lutea (Yellow corydalis)
Evergreen, clump-forming perennial
with fleshy, fibrous roots and much
divided, semi-erect, basal, gray-green
leaves. Bears slender, yellow flowers,
with short spurs, in dense racemes in
late spring and summer. H and
S 8–12in (20–30cm).

☼ ◊ ❀❀❀ 5–8

Verbascum dumulosum
Evergreen, mat-forming, shrubby
perennial with hairy, gray or gray-green
leaves. In late spring and early summer
bears a succession of 5-lobed, bright
yellow flowers in short racemes.
Dislikes winter wet. H 6in (15cm) or
more, S 9–12in (23–30cm) or more.

☼ ◊ ❀❀ 6–8

Chrysogonum virginianum
Mat-forming perennial with daisylike,
yellow flower heads borne on short
stems in summer-autumn and oval,
toothed leaves. Although plant spreads
by underground runners, it is not
invasive. H 6–8in (15–20cm),
S 4–6in (10–15cm) or more.

◑ ◊ ❀❀❀ 5–8

Sedum reflexum
(Yellow stonecrop)
Evergreen perennial with loose mats of
rooting stems bearing narrow, fleshy
leaves. Carries flat, terminal heads of
tiny, bright yellow flowers in summer.
Makes good ground cover. H 6–8in
(15–20cm), S indefinite.

☼ ◊ ❀❀❀ 5–9

Ranunculus gramineus
Erect, slender perennial with grasslike,
blue-green leaves. Bears several cup-
shaped, bright yellow flowers in late
spring and early summer. Prefers rich
soil. Seedlings will vary in height and
flower size. H 16–20in (40–50cm),
S 3–4in (8–10cm).

☼ ◊ ❀❀❀ 6–8

Ononis natrix
Deciduous, compact, erect shrub with
pealike, red-streaked, yellow flowers
in pendent clusters in summer. Hairy
leaves are divided into 3 leaflets.
H and S 12in (30cm) or more.

☼ ◊ ❀❀❀ 7–8

Genista lydia
Deciduous, domed shrub with slender,
arching branches and blue-green leaves.
Massed terminal clusters of pealike,
bright yellow flowers appear in late
spring and early summer. Will trail
over a large rock or wall. H 18–24in
(45–60cm), S 24in (60cm) or more.

☼ ◊ ❀❀❀ 6–9

Crepis aurea
Clump-forming perennial with a basal
cluster of oblong, light green leaves.
In summer produces dandelionlike,
orange flower heads, singly, on stems
covered with black and white hairs.
H 4–12in (10–30cm), S 6in (15cm).

☼ ◊ ❀❀❀ 5–7

WHITE–BLUE

Gaultheria cuneata
Evergreen, compact shrub with stiff
stems clothed in leathery, oval leaves.
In summer bears nodding, urn-shaped,
white flowers, in leaf axils, followed
by white berries in autumn. H and
S 12in (30cm).

☼ ◐ ◊ pH ❋❋❋ 4–7

Ceratostigma plumbaginoides
(Dwarf plumbago, Leadwort)
Bushy perennial that bears small,
terminal clusters of single, brilliant
blue flowers on reddish, branched
stems in late summer and autumn.
Oval leaves turn rich red in autumn.
H 18in (45cm), S 8in (20cm).

☼ ◊ ❋❋❋❋ 5–8

Sorbus reducta
Deciduous shrub forming a low thicket
of upright branches. Small, gray-green
leaves, divided into leaflets, turn
bronze-red in late autumn. In early
summer bears loose clusters of flat,
white flowers, followed by pink berries.
H and S to 12in (30cm) or more.

☼ ◊ ❋❋❋ 5–7

Gentiana septemfida
Evergreen perennial with many upright,
then arching stems clothed with oval
leaves. Bears heads of trumpet-shaped,
blue flowers in summer-autumn. Likes
humus-rich soil but tolerates reasonably
drained, heavy clay. H 6–8in
(15–20cm), S 12in (30cm).

☼ ◊ ❋❋❋ 6–8

WHITE–GRAY

Ranunculus calandrinioides
Clump-forming perennial that loses its
long, oval, blue-green leaves in
summer; in a reasonable winter will
bear a succession of cup-shaped, pink-
flushed, white flowers for many
weeks. Needs very sharp drainage.
H and S to 8in (20cm).

☼ ◊ ❋❋❋❋ 7–8

Celmisia coriacea
Evergreen perennial with swordlike,
silver leaves in large clumps and, in
summer, daisylike, white flower
heads borne singly on hairy stems.
H and S 12in (30cm).

☼ ◊ pH ❋❋ 9–10

Cyathodes colensoi
Evergreen, low-growing shrub with
stiff stems clothed in tiny, gray-green
leaves. Bears clusters of small, tubular,
white flowers in spring at the ends of
new growth. Red or white berries in
late summer are rare in cultivation.
H and S 12in (30cm).

☀ ◐ ◊ ❋❋ 8–9

Tanacetum argenteum,
syn. **Achillea argentea**
Mat-forming perennial, usually
evergreen, grown for its finely cut,
bright silver leaves. Has a profusion of
small, daisylike, white flower heads in
summer. H in flower 6–9in (15–23cm),
S 8in (20cm).

☼ ◊ ❋❋❋ 5–7

■■ GRAY–GREEN

Tanacetum densum subsp. ***amani***
Clump-forming perennial retaining
fernlike, hairy, gray leaves in winter in
mild climates. Bears daisylike, yellow
flower heads with woolly bracts in
summer. Dislikes winter wet. H and
S 8in (20cm).

 ☼ ◊ ❀❀❀ 6–8

Helichrysum coralloides
Evergreen, upright shrub with gray
stems clothed in neatly packed, small,
dark green leaves, marked silver.
Occasionally bears terminal clusters of
fluffy, yellow flower heads. Suits a cold
frame or an alpine house. Hates winter
wet. H 6–9in (15–23cm), S 6in (15cm).

☼ ◊ ❀❀ 9–10

Salix* x *boydii
Very slow-growing, deciduous, upright
shrub forming a gnarled, branched
bush. Has oval, rough-textured leaves;
catkins are rarely produced. Will
tolerate light shade. H to 6–9in
(15–23cm), S to 12in (30cm).

☼ ◕ ❀❀❀ 4–7

***Hebe cupressoides* 'Boughton
Dome'**
Slow-growing, evergreen, dome-
shaped shrub with scalelike, stem-
clasping, dark gray-green leaves. Has
terminal clusters of small, 4-lobed,
blue-tinged, white flowers in summer.
H 12in (30cm), S to 24in (60cm).

☼ ◊ ❀❀ 8–9

Helichrysum selago
Evergreen, upright shrub with stiff
stems covered in scalelike leaves.
Fluffy, creamy white flower heads,
produced intermittently, are borne in
terminal clusters. Makes a good foil
for spring bulbs. H and S 6–9in
(15–23cm).

☼ ◊ ❀❀❀ 9–10

Ballota pseudodictamnus
Evergreen, mound-forming sub-shrub
with rounded, gray-green leaves and
stems covered with woolly, white
hairs. In summer bears whorls of
small, pink flowers with conspicuous,
enlarged, pale green calyces. H 2ft
(60cm), S 3ft (90cm).

☼ ◊ ❀❀ 7–9

Cerastium tomentosum
(Snow-in-summer)
Very vigorous, ground-cover perennial,
only suitable for a hot, dry bank, with
prostrate stems covered by tiny, gray
leaves. In late spring and summer bears
star-shaped, white flowers above
foliage. H 3in (8cm), S indefinite.

☼ ◊ ❀❀❀ 4–7

Androsace pyrenaica
Evergreen perennial with small
rosettes of tiny, hairy leaves, tightly
packed to form hard cushions. Minute,
stemless, single, white flowers appear
in spring. H 1½in (4cm), S to
4in (10cm).

☼ ◊ ❀❀❀ 4–5

Arenaria tetraquetra
Evergreen perennial that forms a hard,
gray-green cushion of small leaves.
Stemless, star-shaped, white flowers
appear in late spring. Is well-suited for
a trough or an alpine house. H 1in
(2.5cm), S 6in (15cm) or more.

☼ ◊ ❀❀❀ 3–5

☐ WHITE

Arabis caucasica 'Variegata'
(Variegated wall rock-cress)
Evergreen, mat-forming perennial
with rosettes of oval, cream-splashed,
green leaves. Bears bunches of single,
sometimes pink-flushed, white flowers
from early spring to summer. H and
S 6in (15cm).

☼ ◑ ❀❀❀❀ 4–8

Cardamine trifolia
Ground-cover perennial with creeping
stems clothed in rounded, toothed,
3-parted leaves. In late spring and early
summer bears loose heads of open cup-
shaped, white flowers on bare stems.
H 4–6in (10–15cm), S 12in (30cm).

☼ ◑ ❀❀❀❀ 5–7

Saxifraga scardica
Slow-growing, evergreen perennial
with hard cushions composed of blue-
green rosettes of leaves. In spring
bears small clusters of upward-facing,
cup-shaped, white flowers. Does best
in an alpine house or sheltered scree.
H 1in (2.5cm), S 3in (8cm).

☼◑ ◑ ❀❀❀❀ 4–6

Arenaria balearica
(Corsican sandwort)
Prostrate perennial that is evergreen in
all but the most severe winters. Forms a
green film over a wet, porous rock face.
Minute, white flowers stud mats of
foliage in late spring and early summer.
H less than $^{1}/_{2}$in (1cm), S indefinite.

☼◑ ◑ ❀❀❀ 4–7

Androsace vandellii,
syn. *A. imbricata*
Evergreen, dense, cushion-forming
perennial with narrow, gray leaves and
a profusion of stemless, white flowers
in spring. Needs careful cultivation with
a deep collar of grit under the cushion.
H 1in (2.5cm), S to 4in (10cm).

☼ ◑ pH ❀❀❀❀ 4–7

Weldenia candida
Perennial with rosettes of strap-shaped,
wavy-margined leaves, growing from
tuberous roots. Bears a succession of
upright, cup-shaped, pure white
flowers in late spring and early
summer. H and S 3–6in (8–15cm).

☼ ◑ ❀ 4–8

Dicentra cucullaria
(Dutchman's breeches)
Compact perennial with fernlike
foliage and arching stems each bearing
a few small, yellow-tipped, white
flowers, like tiny, inflated trousers, in
spring. Lies dormant in summer.
H 6in (15cm), S to 12in (30cm).

◑ ◑ ❀❀❀❀ 4–8

Maianthemum canadense
Vigorous, ground-cover, rhizomatous perennial with large, upright, oval, wavy-edged, glossy leaves. Slender stems bear sprays of small, white flowers in late spring and early summer followed by red berries. H 4in (10cm), S indefinite.

 ☼ ◊ pH ❀❀❀❀ 4–8

Sanguinaria canadensis
(Bloodroot)
Rhizomatous, perennial with fleshy, underground stems that exude red sap when cut. In spring bears white flowers, sometimes pink-flushed or slate-blue on reverses, as blue-gray leaves unfurl. H 4–6in (10–15cm), S 12in (30cm).

◑ ◊ ❀❀❀❀ 3–9

Ranunculus alpestris
Short-lived, evergreen, clump-forming perennial that bears cup-shaped, white flowers on erect stems from late spring to mid-summer. Glossy, dark green leaves are rounded and serrated. H 1–5in (2.5–12cm), S 4in (10cm).

☼ ◊ ❀❀❀❀ 7–8

Cassiope lycopodioides
Evergreen, prostrate, mat-forming shrub with slender stems densely set with minute, scalelike, dark green leaves. In spring, short, reddish stems carry tiny, bell-shaped, white flowers, in red calyces, singly in leaf axils. H 3in (8cm), S 12in (30cm).

◑ ◊ pH ❀❀❀❀ 4–7

Saxifraga burseriana
Slow-growing, evergreen perennial with hard cushions of spiky, gray-green leaves. In spring bears open cup-shaped, white flowers on short stems. H 1–2in (2.5–5cm), S to 4in (10cm).

☼ ◊ ❀❀❀❀ 4–6

Pulsatilla vernalis
Tufted perennial with rosettes of feathery leaves. Densely hairy, brown flower buds appear in late winter and open in early spring to somewhat nodding, open cup-shaped, pearl white flowers. Buds dislike winter wet. H 2–4in (5–10cm), S 4in (10cm).

☼ ◊ ❀❀❀❀ 5–8

Androsace villosa
Evergreen, mat-forming perennial with very hairy rosettes of tiny leaves. Bears umbels of small, white flowers, with yellow centers that turn red, in spring. H 1in (2.5cm), S 8in (20cm).

☼ ◊ ❀❀❀❀ 4–7

Salix apoda
Slow-growing, deciduous, prostrate shrub. In early spring, male forms bear fat, silky, silver catkins with orange to pale yellow stamens and bracts. Oval, leathery leaves are hairy when young, becoming dark green later. H to 6in (15cm), S 12–24in (30–60cm).

☼ ◊ ❀❀❀❀ 4–8

Ranunculus ficaria 'Albus'
Mat-forming perennial bearing in early spring cup-shaped, single, creamy white flowers with glossy petals. Leaves are heart-shaped and dark green. Can spread rapidly; is good for a wild garden. H 2in (5cm), S 8in (20cm).

☼ ◊ ❀❀❀ 4–8

■ WHITE–PINK

Cassiope mertensiana
Evergreen, dwarf shrub with scalelike, dark green leaves tightly pressed to stems. In early spring carries bell-shaped, creamy white flowers, with green or red calyces, in leaf axils. H 6in (15cm), S 8in (20cm).

☼ ◊ pH ❊❊❊ 2–6

Scoliopus bigelovii
Compact perennial with basal pairs of veined, dull green leaves, sometimes marked brown. In early spring bears clusters of upward-facing flowers with purple inner petals and greenish white outer petals with deep purple lines. H 3–4in (8–10cm), S 4–6in (10–15cm).

☼ ◊ ❊❊ 6–8

Gypsophila cerastioides
Prostrate perennial with a profusion of small, saucer-shaped, purple-veined, white flowers borne in late spring and early summer above mats of rounded, velvety foliage. H ³⁄₄in (2cm), S to 4in (10cm) or more.

☼ ◊ ❊❊❊ 5–8

Paraquilegia grandiflora
Tufted perennial with fernlike, blue-green leaves. In spring, pale lavender blue buds open to pendent, cup-shaped, almost white flowers borne singly on arching stems. May be difficult to establish. H and S 4–6in (10–15cm).

☼ ◊ ❊❊❊ 5–8

Corydalis popovii
Tuberous perennial with leaves divided into 3–6 bluish green leaflets. In spring bears loose racemes of deep red-purple and white flowers, each with a long spur. Keep dry when dormant. H and S 4–6in (10–15cm).

☼ ◊ ❊❊ 7–8

Cotula atrata var. luteola
Evergreen, mat-forming perennial that in late spring and early summer bears blackish red flower heads with creamy yellow stamens. Leaves are small, finely cut, and dark green. Needs adequate moisture; best in an alpine house. H 1in (2.5cm), S to 10in (25cm).

☼ ◊ ❊❊❊ 5–6

Anemonella thalictroides
Perennial with delicate, fernlike leaves growing from a cluster of small tubers. From spring to early summer bears small, cup-shaped, white or pink flowers, singly on finely branched stems. Needs humus-rich soil. H 4in (10cm), S 1¹⁄₂in (4cm) or more.

◐ ◊ ❊❊❊ 4–9

Lewisia tweedyi
Evergreen, rosetted perennial with large, fleshy leaves and stout, branched stems that bear open cup-shaped, many-petaled, white to pink flowers in spring. Best grown in an alpine house. H 6in (15cm), S 5–6in (12–15cm).

☼ ◊ pH ❊❊❊ 6–7

Shortia galacifolia (Oconee-bells)
Evergreen, clump-forming, dwarf perennial with round, toothed, leathery, glossy leaves. In late spring bears cup- to trumpet-shaped, often pink-flushed, white flowers with deeply serrated petals. H to 6in (15cm), S 6–9in (15–23cm).

◐ ◊ pH ❊❊❊ 5–9

Daphne jasminea
Evergreen, compact shrub. Bears small, white flowers, pink-flushed externally, in late spring and early summer and again in autumn. Brittle stems are clothed in gray-green leaves. Suits an alpine house or a dry wall. H 3–4in (8–10cm), S to 12in (30cm).

☼ ◊ ❊❊❊ 7–9

Epigaea gaultherioides,
syn. Orphanidesia gaultherioides
Evergreen, prostrate sub-shrub with cup-shaped, shell pink flowers borne in terminal clusters in spring. Hairy stems carry heart-shaped, dark green leaves. Is difficult to grow and propagate. H to 4in (10cm), S 10in (25cm) or more.

● ◊ pH ❊❊ 8–9

Trillium rivale
Perennial with oval leaves, divided into 3 leaflets. In spring bears open cup-shaped, white or pale pink flowers with dark-spotted, heart-shaped petals, singly on upright, later arching stems. H to 6in (15cm), S 4in (10cm).

☼ ◐ ❁❁❁ 5–8

Saxifraga 'Jenkinsiae'
Slow-growing perennial with very tight, gray-green cushions of foliage. Carries a profusion of open cup-shaped, lilac-pink flowers on slender stems in early spring. H 3–4in (8–10cm), S to 6in (15cm).

☼ ◐ ❁❁❁ 4–6

Androsace carnea
Evergreen, cushion-forming perennial that has small rosettes of pointed leaves with hairy margins. In spring, 2 or more stems rise above each rosette, bearing tiny, single, pink flowers. Suits a trough. H and S 2in (5cm).

☼ ◐ ❁❁❁ 4–7

Thlaspi rotundifolium
Clump-forming perennial with dense tufts of round leaves and tight, flat heads of small, open cup-shaped, pale to deep purplish or lilac-pink flowers in spring. Needs ample moisture and cool conditions. May be short-lived. H 2–3in (5–8cm), S 4in (10cm).

☼ ◐ ❁❁❁ 5–7

Oxalis acetosella f. **rosea**
Creeping, rhizomatous perennial forming mats of 3-lobed leaves. Cup-shaped, soft pink flowers, each ¹/₂in (1cm) across, with 5 darker-veined petals, are produced in spring. H 2in (5cm), S indefinite.

☼ ◐ ❁❁❁ 5–8

Armeria juniperifolia,
syn. *A. caespitosa, A. cespitosa*
Evergreen, cushion-forming perennial composed of loose rosettes of sharp-pointed, mid- to gray-green leaves. Pale pink flowers are borne in spherical umbels in late spring and early summer. H 2–3in (5–8cm), S 6in (15cm).

☼ ◐ ❁❁❁ 5–7

Arenaria purpurascens
Evergreen, mat-forming perennial with sharp-pointed, glossy leaves, above which rise many small clusters of star-shaped, pale to deep purplish pink flowers in early spring. H ¹/₂in (1cm), S to 6in (15cm).

☼ ◐ ❁❁❁ 4–7

Silene acaulis (Moss campion)
Evergreen, cushion-forming perennial with minute, bright green leaves studded with tiny, stemless, 5-petaled, pink flowers in spring. May be difficult to bring into flower; prefers a cool climate. H to 1in (2.5cm), S 6in (15cm).

☼ ◐ ❁❁❁ 3–5

Arabis caucasica 'Rosabella'
Evergreen, mat-forming perennial with a profusion of single, deep pink flowers in spring and early summer and large rosettes of small, oval, soft green leaves. H 6in (15cm), S 12in (30cm).

☼ ◐ ❁❁❁ 4–8

■ PINK

Oxalis adenophylla
Mat-forming, fibrous-rooted, tuberous perennial with gray-green leaves divided into narrow, fingerlike, wavy lobes. In spring bears rounded, purplish pink flowers, each 1–1½in (2.5–4cm) across, with darker purple eyes. H to 2in (5cm), S 3–4in (8–10cm).

☼ ◊ ✻✻✻ 7–10

Shortia soldanelloides
(Fringe-bells)
Evergreen, mat-forming perennial with rounded, toothed leaves and small, pendent, bell-shaped and fringed, deep pink flowers in late spring. H 2–4in (5–10cm), S 4–6in (10–15cm).

☀ ◊ pH ✻✻✻ 6–8

Saxifraga oppositifolia
(Purple mountain saxifrage)
Evergreen, prostrate perennial with clusters of tiny, white-flecked leaves. Has open cup-shaped, dark purple, purplish pink or, rarely, white flowers in early spring. Likes an open position. H 1–2in (2.5–5cm), S 6in (15cm).

☼ ◑ ✻✻✻ 2–6

Erinus alpinus
Semi-evergreen, short-lived perennial with rosettes of soft, green leaves covered, in late spring and summer, with small, purple, pink, or white flowers. Self seeds freely. H and S 2–3in (5–8cm).

☼ ◊ ✻✻✻ 4–7

***Daphne petraea* 'Grandiflora'**
Slow-growing, evergreen, compact shrub that bears terminal clusters of fragrant, rich pink flowers in late spring and tiny, glossy leaves. Suits an alpine house, a sheltered, humus-rich rock garden, or a trough. H to 6in (15cm), S to 10in (25cm).

☼ ◊ ✻✻✻ 5–7

Claytonia megarhiza* subsp. *nivalis
Evergreen perennial with a rosette of spoon-shaped, succulent leaves. Bears small heads of tiny, deep pink flowers in spring. Grows best in a deep pot of gritty compost in an alpine house. H ½in (1cm), S 3in (8cm).

☼ ◊ ✻✻✻ 5–7

***Antennaria dioica* 'Rosea'**
Semi-evergreen perennial forming a spreading mat of tiny, oval, woolly leaves. Bears fluffy, rose-pink flower heads in small, terminal clusters in late spring and early summer. Is good as ground cover with small bulbs. H 1in (2.5cm), S to 16in (40cm).

☼ ◊ ✻✻✻ 4–7

Daphne arbuscula
Evergreen, prostrate shrub. In late spring bears many very fragrant, tubular, deep pink flowers in terminal clusters. Narrow, leathery, dark green leaves are crowded at the ends of branches. Likes humus-rich soil. H 4–6in (10–15cm), S 20in (50cm).

☼ ◊ ✻✻✻ 5–7

***Vaccinium vitis-idaea* 'Minus'**
(Lingonberry, Mountain cranberry)
Evergreen, mat-forming sub-shrub with tiny, oval, leathery leaves. In late spring bears small, erect racemes of many tiny, bell-shaped, deep pink or deep pink-and-white flowers. H in flower 2–3in (5–8cm), S 4–6in (10–15cm).

☼ ◑ pH ✻✻✻ 2–5

Anagallis tenella 'Studland'
Short-lived perennial that forms
prostrate mats of tiny, bright green
leaves studded in spring with honey-
scented, star-shaped, bright pink
flowers. H ½in (1cm), S 6in (15cm)
or more.

☼ ◑ ❀❀❀❀ 5–7

Androsace carnea subsp. **laggeri**
Evergreen, cushion-forming perennial
composed of small, tight rosettes of
pointed leaves. Cup-shaped, deep pink
flowers are borne in small clusters
above cushions in spring. H and
S 2in (5cm).

☼ ◊ ❀❀❀❀ 4–7

Corydalis solida 'George Baker',
syn. *C.s.* 'G.P. Baker'
Tuberous perennial with fernlike,
divided leaves and dense racemes of
spurred, rich deep rose-red flowers in
spring. H and S 4–6in (10–15cm).

☼ ◊ ❀❀❀❀ 5–7

**Saxifraga grisebachii 'Wisley
Variety'**
Evergreen perennial with mounded
rosettes of leaves edged with lime crust.
Crosier-shaped stems, covered in pale
pink to bright red hairs, bear dense
racemes of dark red flowers in spring.
H 4in (10cm), S 6in (15cm).

☼ ◊ ❀❀❀ 4–6

Saxifraga sempervivum
Evergreen, hummock-forming
perennial with tight rosettes of tufted,
silvery green leaves. Crosier-shaped
flower stems, covered in silvery hairs
and emerging from rosettes, bear
racemes of dark red flowers in early
spring. H and S 4–6in (10–15cm).

☼ ◊ ❀❀❀❀ 4–6

Cotula atrata
Evergreen, mat-forming perennial with
small, finely cut, grayish green leaves
and blackish red flower heads in late
spring and early summer. Is uncommon
and not easy to grow successfully.
H 1in (2.5cm), S to 10in (25cm).

☼ ◊ ❀❀❀❀ 5–6

Corydalis diphylla
Tuberous perennial with semi-erect,
basal leaves, divided into narrow
leaflets, and loose racemes of purple-
lipped flowers with white spurs in
spring. Protect tubers from excess
moisture in summer. H 4–6in
(10–15cm), S 3–4in (8–10cm).

☼ ◑ ❀❀ 5–8

Polygonatum hookeri
Slow-growing, dense, rhizomatous
perennial that bears loose spikes of
several small, bell-shaped, lilac-pink
flowers in late spring and early
summer. Leaves are tiny and lance-
shaped. Suits a peat bed. H to 2in
(5cm), S to 12in (30cm).

☼ ◑ ❀❀❀❀ 5–9

Aubrieta 'Joy'
Vigorous, evergreen, trailing perennial
that forms mounds of soft green
leaves. In spring bears double, pale
mauve flowers on short stems.
H 4in (10cm), S 8in (20cm).

☼ ◊ ❀❀❀❀ 5–7

■ PURPLE

Aubrieta deltoidea 'Argenteo-variegata'
Evergreen, compact perennial, grown for its trailing, green leaves which are heavily splashed with creamy white. Produces pinkish lavender flowers in spring. H 2in (5cm), S 6in (15cm).

☼ ◊ ❀❀❀❀ 5–7

Mazus reptans
Prostrate perennial that has tubular, purple or purplish pink flowers, with protruding, white lips, spotted red and yellow, borne singly on short stems in spring. Narrow, toothed leaves are in pairs along stem. H to 2in (5cm), S 12in (30cm) or more.

☼ ◗ ❀❀❀ 5–8

Soldanella villosa
Evergreen, clump-forming perennial with round, leathery, hairy-stalked leaves and nodding, bell-shaped, fringed, purplish lavender flowers borne on erect stems in early spring. Dislikes winter wet. H 4in (10cm), S 4–6in (10–15cm).

◑ ◊ ❀❀❀❀ 4–7

Aubrieta 'Carnival'
Vigorous, evergreen, mound-forming perennial that carries many short spikes of large, single, violet-purple flowers in spring above small, soft green leaves. H 4in (10cm), S 12in (30cm).

☼ ◊ ❀❀❀ 5–7

Saxifraga stribrnyi
Evergreen, mound-forming perennial with small, lime-encrusted rosettes of leaves. Crosier-shaped stems, covered in pinkish buff hairs, bear racemes of deep maroon-red flowers above leaves in late spring and early summer. H 3in (8cm), S 4–5in (10–12cm).

☼ ◊ ❀❀❀ 4–6

Polygala chamaebuxus var. **grandi-flora**, syn. *P.c.* var. *rhodoptera*
Evergreen, woody-based perennial that bears terminal clusters of pealike, reddish purple and yellow flowers in late spring and early summer. Leaves are small, oval, leathery, and dark green. H 6in (15cm), S to 12in (30cm).

☼ ◊ ❀❀❀ 4–7

Soldanella alpina
Evergreen, clump-forming perennial with tufts of leaves and short, bell-shaped, fringed, pinkish lavender or purplish pink flowers in early spring. Is difficult to flower well. H to 3in (8cm), S 3–4in (8–10cm).

◑ ◊ ❀❀❀ 4–7

Aubrieta 'J.S. Baker'
Evergreen perennial with single, purple flowers in spring borne above mounds of small, soft green leaves. H 4in (10cm), S 8in (20cm).

☼ ◊ ❀❀❀ 5–7

Viola calcarata
Clump-forming perennial, with oval leaves, that bears flat, outward-facing, single, white, lavender, or purple flowers for a long period from late spring to summer. Prefers rich soil. H 4–6in (10–15cm), S to 8in (20cm).

☼ ◗ ❀❀❀ 5–7

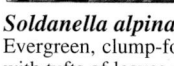

Aubrieta 'Cobalt Violet'
Evergreen, mound-forming perennial
with single, blue-violet flowers carried
in short, terminal spikes in spring
above a mat of small, soft green
leaves. H 4in (10cm), S 8in (20cm).

☼ ◊ ❋❋❋ 5–7

Viola tricolor
(Johnny-jump-up, Wild pansy)
Short-lived perennial or annual with
neat, flat-faced flowers in combinations
of white, yellow, and shades of purple
from spring to autumn. Self seeds
profusely. H 2–6in (5–15cm),
S 2–6in (5–15cm) or more.

☼ ◊ ❋❋❋ 3–8

Hepatica nobilis var. **japonica**
Slow-growing perennial with leathery,
lobed leaves, semi-evergreen in all but
very cold or arid climates. Bears
slightly cupped, lilac-mauve, pink,
or white flowers in spring. H to 3in
(8cm), S to 5in (12cm).

◑ ◊ ❋❋❋ 4–8

Viola labradorica 'Purpurea'
Clump-forming perennial with tiny,
flat-faced, purple flowers in spring-
summer. Leaves are kidney-shaped and
dark purple-green. Is invasive but suits
a bank, woodland, or wild garden.
H 1–2in (2.5–5cm), S indefinite.

◑ ◊ ❋❋❋ 4–8

Jeffersonia dubia,
syn. *Plagiorhegma dubia*
Tufted perennial with 2-lobed, blue-
green leaves, sometimes flushed pink
when unfolding. Bears cup-shaped,
pale lilac to purplish blue flowers
singly in spring. H 4–6in (10–15cm),
S to 9in (23cm).

◑ ◊ ❋❋❋ 5–8

Jancaea heldreichii
Perennial with rosettes of thick, hairy,
silver-green leaves, above which rise
slender stems bearing clusters of tiny,
lavender blue flowers in late spring. Is
rare and difficult to grow and is best in
an alpine house. H and S to 3in (8cm).

◑ ◊ ❋❋ 5–7

Viola pedata (Bird's-foot violet)
Clump-forming perennial with finely
divided foliage and yellow-centered,
pale violet, rarely white flowers borne
singly on slender stems in late spring
and early summer. Needs sharp
drainage; grow in an alpine house.
H 2in (5cm), S 3in (8cm).

☼ ◊ pH ❋❋❋ 3–8

Mertensia maritima
Prostrate perennial with oval, fleshy,
bright silver-blue or silver-gray leaves.
Stout stems carry clusters of pendent,
funnel-shaped, sky blue flowers in
spring. Is prone to slug damage. Needs
very sharp drainage. H 4–6in
(10–15cm), S 5in (12cm).

☼ ◊ ❋❋❋ 3–7

Synthyris stellata
Evergreen, mounded, rhizomatous
perennial that bears dense spikes of
small, violet-blue flowers in spring
above rounded, deeply toothed leaves.
Tolerates sun if soil remains moist.
H 4–6in (10–15cm), S 6in (15cm).

◑ ◊ ❋❋❋ 5–7

◼ BLUE

Myosotis alpestris
Short-lived, clump-forming perennial producing dense clusters of tiny, bright blue flowers with creamy yellow eyes in late spring and early summer, just above tufts of hairy leaves. Prefers gritty soil. H and S 4–6in (10–15cm).

☼ ◊ ❋❋❋ 5–7

Anchusa caespitosa
Evergreen, mound-forming perennial with rosettes of lance-shaped, dark green leaves. In spring, stemless, white-centered, blue flowers appear in centers of rosettes. Old plants do not flower well; take early summer cuttings. H 1–2in (2.5–5cm), S to 9in (23cm).

☼ ◊ ❋❋❋ 5–7

◼◼ BLUE–GREEN

Gentiana acaulis, syn. *G. excisa*, *G. kochiana*
Evergreen, clump-forming perennial with narrowly oval, glossy leaves. Bears trumpet-shaped, deep blue flowers, with green-spotted throats, on short stems in spring and often in autumn. H in leaf ³/₄in (2cm), S to 4in (10cm) or more.

☼ ◊ ❋❋❋ 4–7

Viola tricolor 'Bowles' Black'
Clump-forming perennial with flat-faced, very dark violet, almost black, flowers, borne continuously from spring to autumn. Oval leaves are sometimes lobed and toothed. Is short-lived; treat as biennial. H 2–6in (5–15cm), S 2–3in (5–8cm).

☼ ◊ ❋❋❋ 3–8

Gentiana verna
Evergreen perennial, often short-lived, with small rosettes of oval, dark green leaves. In early spring, tubular, bright blue flowers with white throats are held upright on short stems. H and S to 2in (5cm).

☼ ◊ ❋❋❋ 4–7

Salix reticulata
Deciduous, spreading, mat-forming shrub. Carries plump, reddish brown, then yellow catkins on male plants in spring and rounded, slightly crinkled leaves. Likes cool, peaty soil. H 2–3in (5–8cm), S 8in (20cm) or more.

☼ ◖ ❋❋❋ 2–5

Mandragora officinarum
Rosetted, fleshy-rooted perennial with
coarse, wavy-edged leaves. Bears
funnel-shaped, yellowish or purplish
white flowers in spring, followed by
large, tomatolike, shiny, yellow fruits.
H 2in (5cm), S 12in (30cm).

☼ ◊ ❈❈❈ 6–8

Hacquetia epipactis
Clump-forming perennial spreading by
short rhizomes. In late winter and early
spring bears yellow or yellow-green
flower heads, encircled by apple green
bracts, before rounded, 3-parted leaves
appear. H 2¹/₂in (6cm), S 6–9in
(15–23cm).

◑ ◑ ❈❈❈ 5–7

Euphorbia myrsinites
(Myrtle euphorbia)
Evergreen, prostrate perennial with
terminal clusters of bright yellow-green
flowers in spring. Woody stems are
clothed in small, fleshy, gray leaves.
Is good on a wall or ledge. H 2–3in
(5–8cm), S to 8in (20cm) or more.

☼ ◊ ❈❈ 5–8

Saxifraga 'Hindhead Seedling'
Evergreen perennial that forms a hard
dome of small, tufted, spiny, blue-
green leaves. In spring bears upward-
facing, open cup-shaped, pale yellow
flowers, 2 or 3 to each short stem.
H 1in (2.5cm), S 3in (8cm).

◑ ◊ ❈❈❈❈ 4–6

Saxifraga × apiculata
Evergreen perennial with a tight
cushion of bright green foliage.
Bears clusters of open cup-shaped,
pale yellow flowers in early spring.
H 4–6in (10–15cm), S 6in (15cm)
or more.

◑ ◊ ❈❈❈❈ 4–6

Saxifraga 'Elizabethae'
Evergreen, cushion-forming perennial,
composed of densely packed, tiny
rosettes of spiny leaves. In spring, tight
clusters of small, upward-facing,
bright yellow flowers are carried on
tops of red-based stems. H 1in
(2.5cm), S 4–6in (10–15cm).

◑ ◊ ❈❈❈❈ 4–6

Viola aetolica
Clump-forming perennial with oval
leaves. Flat-faced, yellow flowers are
borne singly on upright stems in late
spring and early summer. H 2–3in
(5–8cm), S 6in (15cm).

☼ ◊ ❈❈❈ 5–7

Draba rigida
Evergreen perennial with tight
hummocks of minute, dark green
leaves. Tiny clusters of bright yellow
flowers on fine stems cover hummocks
in spring. Suits a trough, scree garden,
or alpine house. Dislikes winter wet.
H 1¹/₂in (4cm), S 2¹/₂in (6cm).

☼ ◊ ❈❈❈ 4–6

Dionysia aretioides
Evergreen perennial forming cushions
of soft, hairy, grayish green leaves that
are covered in early spring by scented,
stemless, round, bright yellow flowers.
H 2–4in (5–10cm), S 6–12in (15–30cm).

☼ ◊ ❈❈❈ 5–7

Draba longisiliqua
Semi-evergreen, cushion-forming
perennial composed of firm rosettes of
tiny, silver leaves. Bears sprays of
small, yellow flowers on long stalks in
spring. Needs plenty of water in
growth; is best grown in an alpine
house. H 2–3in (5–8cm), S 6in (15cm).

☼ ◊ ❈❈❈ 4–6

Saxifraga sancta
Evergreen, mat-forming perennial with
tufts of bright green leaves. Bears short
racemes of upward-facing, open cup-
shaped, bright yellow flowers in
spring. H 2in (5cm), S 6in (15cm).

◑ ◊ ❈❈❈❈ 4–6

☐ YELLOW

Draba mollissima
Semi-evergreen, cushion-forming
perennial covered in spring with clusters
of tiny, yellow flowers on slender stems.
Minute leaves form a soft, green dome,
which should be packed beneath with
small stones. Grow in an alpine house.
H 1¹/₂in (4cm), S 6in (15cm) or more.

☼ ◊ ❄❄ 4–6

Dionysia tapetodes
Evergreen, prostrate perennial
producing a tight mat of tiny, gray-
green leaves. Bears small, upward-
facing, yellow flowers in early spring.
H ¹/₂in (1cm), S to 6in (15cm).

☼ ◊ ❄❄❄ 5–7

Morisia monanthos,
syn. *M. hypogaea*
Prostrate perennial with flat rosettes
of divided, leathery, dark green leaves.
Bears stemless, flat, bright yellow
flowers in late spring and early
summer. Needs very sharp drainage.
H 1in (2.5cm), S to 3in (8cm).

☼ ◊ ❄❄❄ 5–7

Ranunculus ficaria 'Flore Pleno'
Mat-forming perennial with heart-
shaped, dark green leaves and, in early
spring, double, bright yellow flowers
with glossy petals. May spread rapidly.
Is good for a wild garden. H 1–2in
(2.5–5cm), S 8in (20cm).

☼ ◊ ❄❄❄ 4–8

Vitaliana primuliflora,
syn. *Douglasia vitaliana*
Evergreen, prostrate perennial forming
a mat of rosetted leaves that are
covered in spring with many small
clusters of stemless, tubular, bright
yellow flowers. H 1in (2.5cm),
S 8in (20cm).

☼ ◊ ❄❄❄❄ 5–7

Viola 'Jackanapes'
Clump-forming perennial with oval,
toothed leaves. Produces flat-faced
flowers with reddish brown, upper petals
and yellow, lower ones throughout late
spring and summer. H 3–5in (8–12cm),
S to 8in (20cm) or more.

☼ ◊ ❄❄❄ 5–7

□ YELLOW

□ WHITE

Trollius pumilus
Tufted perennial with leaves divided into 5 segments, each further lobed. Carries solitary cup-shaped, bright yellow flowers in late spring and early summer. H 6in (15cm), S 6in (15cm) or more.

☼ ◊ ❀❀❀ 5–7

Silene alpestris,
syn. *Heliosperma alpestris*
Perennial with branching stems and narrow leaves. Bears small, rounded, fringed, white, occasionally pink-flushed flowers in late spring and early summer. Self seeds freely. H 4–6in (10–15cm), S 8in (20cm).

☼ ◊ ❀❀❀ 4–7

Haberlea rhodopensis
'Virginalis'
Evergreen perennial with small, arching sprays of funnel-shaped, pure white flowers borne in late spring and early summer above neat rosettes of oval, toothed, dark green leaves. H and S in flower 4–6in (10–15cm).

◐ ◊ ❀❀❀ 5–7

Cyananthus lobatus f. **albus**
Prostrate perennial with branched stems clothed in small, wedge-shaped, dull green leaves. Bears funnel-shaped, single, white flowers with spreading lobes in late summer. H 3in (8cm), S 12in (30cm).

◐ ◊ ❀❀❀ 6–7

Erysimum helveticum,
syn. *E. pumilum*
Semi-evergreen, clump-forming perennial with closely packed tufts of long, narrow leaves and many fragrant, bright yellow flowers borne in flat heads in late spring and early summer. H 4in (10cm), S 6in (15cm).

☼ ◊ ❀❀❀ 5–7

Phlox stolonifera 'Bruce's White'
Evergreen, low-growing perennial with flowering side shoots that bear heads of open saucer-shaped, white blooms in early summer. Has oval, pale green leaves. Cut back flowered shoots by half after flowering. H to 6in (15cm), S 12in (30cm).

◐ ◊ pH ❀❀❀ 4–8

Potentilla alba
Vigorous, mat-forming perennial bearing loose sprays of flat, single, white flowers in summer. Leaves are divided into oval leaflets and are silvery beneath. H 2–3in (5–8cm), S 3in (8cm).

☼ ◊ ❀❀❀ 4–7

Campanula carpatica
'Bressingham White'
Clump-forming perennial bearing open cup-shaped, white flowers, singly on unbranched stems, in summer. Has abundant, rounded, bright green leaves. H 4–6in (10–15cm), S 6in (15cm).

☼ ◊ ❀❀❀ 4–7

Ranunculus ficaria
'Aurantiacus'
Mat-forming perennial bearing in early spring cup-shaped, single, orange flowers with glossy petals. Leaves are heart-shaped. May spread rapidly and is good for a wild garden. H 2in (5cm), S 8in (20cm).

☼ ◊ ❀❀❀ 4–8

Achillea clavennae
Semi-evergreen, carpeting perennial that bears loose clusters of white flower heads with gold centers from summer to mid-autumn. Leaves are narrowly oval, many-lobed, and covered with fine, white hairs. Dislikes winter wet. H 6in (15cm), S 9in (23cm) or more.

☼ ◊ ❀❀❀ 5–8

Lewisia rediviva [white form]
(Bitter root)
Tufted, rosetted perennial with clusters of fine, narrow leaves that are summer-deciduous. Bears large, white flowers that open in bright weather in late spring and early summer. H ½–1½in (1–4cm), S to 2in (5cm).

☼ ◊ pH ❀❀❀ 6–7

Arenaria montana
Prostrate perennial that forms loose
mats of small, narrowly oval leaves
and bears large, round, white flowers
in summer. Suits a wall or rock
crevice. Must have adequate moisture.
H 2in (5cm), S 5in (12cm).

☀️◐ ◊ ❅❅❅ 3–5

Epilobium chlorifolium var. kaikourense
Clump-forming, woody-based
perennial with deciduous but persistent,
oval, hairy, bronze and dark green
leaves. In summer has short spikes of
funnel-shaped, white to pink flowers.
H 4in (10cm), S 6in (15cm).

☀️ ◊ ❅❅❅❅ 4–6

Gentiana saxosa
Evergreen, hummock-forming
perennial clothed in small, spoon-
shaped, fleshy, dark green leaves.
Produces small, upturned, bell-shaped,
white flowers in early summer. Is a
short-lived scree plant. H 2in (5cm),
S 6in (15cm).

☀️ ◊ ❅❅❅ 5–7

Iberis saxatilis
Evergreen, dwarf sub-shrub that in late
spring and early summer produces large
heads of numerous small, white flowers,
which become tinged violet with age.
Glossy, dark green leaves are linear and
cylindrical. Trim after flowering.
H 3–5in (8–12cm), S 12in (30cm).

☀️ ◊ ❅❅❅❅ 4–8

Cornus canadensis (Bunchberry)
Ground-cover perennial with whorls of
oval leaves. In late spring and early
summer bears green, sometimes purple-
tinged flowers, within white bracts,
followed by red berries. H 4–6in
(10–15cm), S 12in (30cm) or more.

☀️◐ ◊ pH ❅❅❅❅ 2–7

Celmisia ramulosa
Evergreen, shrubby perennial with
small, hairy, gray-green leaves.
Daisylike, white flower heads are
borne singly on short stems in late
spring and early summer. H and
S 4in (10cm).

☀️ ◊ pH ❅❅ 7–8

Ourisia caespitosa
Evergreen, prostrate perennial with
creeping rootstocks and stems bearing
tiny, oval leaves and many outward-
facing, open cup-shaped, white flowers
in late spring and early summer. H 1in
(2.5cm), S 4in (10cm).

☀️ ◊ ❅❅❅❅ 5–7

Nierembergia repens (White cup)
Mat-forming perennial with upright,
open bell-shaped, yellow-centered, white
flowers, occasionally flushed pink with
age, borne for a long period in summer.
Leaves are small, oval, and light green.
Is useful for cracks in paving. H 2in
(5cm), S 8in (20cm) or more.

☀️ ◊ ❅❅ 4–8

Anacyclus depressus
Short-lived, prostrate perennial that has
clusters of white flower heads, with red
reverses to ray petals, in summer.
Flowers close in dull light. Stems
clothed in fine leaves radiate from
central root. Dislikes wet. H 1–2in
(2.5–5cm) or more, S 4in (10cm).

☀️ ◊ ❅❅ 6–8

Petrocosmea kerrii
Evergreen perennial with compact
rosettes of oval, pointed, hairy, rich
green leaves. In summer bears clusters
of short, outward-facing, tubular, open-
mouthed, white flowers. Suits an alpine
house. H to 3in (8cm), S 5–6in
(12–15cm). Min. 36–41°F (2–5°C).

☀️ ◊ 4–5

Dryas octopetala (Mountain avens)
Evergreen, prostrate perennial forming
mats of oval, lobed, leathery, dark green
leaves on stout stems. In late spring and
early summer, cup-shaped, creamy
white flowers are borne just above
foliage, followed by attractive, feathery
seeds. H 2¹/₂in (6cm), S indefinite.

 ☼ ◊ ❈❈❈ 3–6

Achillea × kellereri
Semi-evergreen perennial that bears
daisylike, white flower heads in loose
clusters in summer. Leaves are
feathery and gray-green. Is good for a
wall or bank. Dislikes winter wet and
must have perfect drainage. H 6in
(15cm), S 9in (23cm) or more.

 ☼ ◊ ❈❈❈ 5–7

Carlina acaulis
Clump-forming perennial that in
summer-autumn bears large, stemless,
thistlelike, single, off-white or pale
brown flower heads, with papery bracts,
on rosettes of long, spiny-margined,
deeply cut leaves. H 3–4in (8–10cm),
S 6–9in (15–23cm).

☼ ◊ ❈❈❈ 5–7

Linnaea borealis (Twinflower)
Evergreen, mat-forming, sub-shrubby
perennial with rooting stems bearing
small, oval leaves, above which in
summer rise threadlike stems bearing
pairs of small, fragrant, tubular, pale
pink and white flowers. H ³/₄in (2cm),
S 12in (30cm) or more.

☼◑ ◊ pH❤ ❈❈❈ 3–6

Dianthus pavonius,
syn. *D. neglectus* (Rock pink)
Evergreen, prostrate perennial with
comparatively large, rounded, pale to
deep pink flowers, buff on reverses,
borne on short stems in summer above
low mats of spiky leaves. H 2in (5cm),
S 3in (8cm).

☼ ◊ pH❤ ❈❈❈ 4–6

***Gypsophila repens* 'Dorothy
Teacher'**
Semi-evergreen, prostrate perennial.
Sprays of small, rounded, white flowers,
which age to deep pink, cover mats of
narrow, bluish green leaves in summer.
Trim stems after flowering. H 1–2in
(2.5–5cm), S 12in (30cm) or more.

☼ ◊ ❈❈❈ 4–7

Petrorhagia saxifraga,
syn. *Tunica saxifraga*
Mat-forming perennial with tufts of
grasslike leaves. In summer bears a
profusion of small, pale pink flowers,
veined deeper pink, on slender stems.
Grows best on poor soil and self seeds
easily. H 4in (10cm), S 6in (15cm).

☼ ◊ ❈❈❈ 5–7

Thymus caespititius
Evergreen, mat-forming, aromatic sub-
shrub with slender, woody stems
covered in minute, hairy leaves. Bears
tiny, pale lilac or lilac-pink flowers in
small clusters in summer. H 1in
(2.5cm), S 8in (20cm).

☼ ◊ ❈❈ 4–7

Convolvulus althaeoides
Vigorous perennial with long, trailing
stems clothed in heart-shaped, cut,
green leaves, overlaid silver. Bears
large, open trumpet-shaped, pink
flowers in summer. May be invasive
in a mild climate. H 2in (5cm),
S indefinite.

☼ ◊ ❈ 6–8

Geranium sanguineum var. ***striatum***, syn. *G.s.* var. *lancastriense*
Hummock-forming, spreading perennial that has cup-shaped, pink flowers, with darker veins, borne singly in summer above round, deeply divided, dark green leaves. H 4–6in (10–15cm), S 12in (30cm) or more.

☼ ◊ ❋❋❋ 4–8

Ourisia microphylla
Semi-evergreen, mat-forming perennial, with neat, scalelike, pale green leaves, bearing a profusion of small, pink flowers in late spring and early summer. Is difficult to grow in an arid climate. H 2–4in (5–10cm), S 6in (15cm).

☼ ◐ ❋❋❋ 5–7

Asperula suberosa
Clump-forming perennial with a mound of loose stems bearing tiny, hairy, gray leaves and, in early summer, many tubular, pale pink flowers. Dislikes winter wet but needs moist soil in summer. Is best in an alpine house. H 3in (8cm), S to 12in (30cm).

☼ ◐ ❋❋❋ 5–6

Erodium corsicum
Compact, clump-forming perennial that has soft, gray-green leaves with wavy margins. Bears flat-faced, pink flowers, with darker veins, on stiff, slender stems in late spring and summer. Grows best in an alpine house as dislikes winter wet. H 3in (8cm), S 6in (15cm).

☼ ◊ ❋❋❋ 4–7

***Rhodohypoxis baurii* 'Margaret Rose'**
Perennial with a tuberlike rootstock and an erect, basal tuft of narrowly lance-shaped, hairy leaves. Bears a succession of upright, flattish, pale pink flowers on slender stems in spring and early summer. H 2–4in (5–10cm), S 1–2in (2.5–5cm).

☼ ◊ ❋❋ 9

Saponaria* x *olivana
Compact perennial with a firm cushion of narrow leaves. Flowering stems, produced around edges of the cushion, bear flat, single, pale pink flowers in summer. Needs very sharp drainage. H 3in (8cm), S 4in (10cm).

☼ ◊ ❋❋❋ 4–7

***Aethionema* 'Warley Rose'**
Short-lived, evergreen or semi-evergreen, compact sub-shrub with tiny, linear, bluish green leaves. Bears racemes of small, pink flowers on short stems in profusion in spring-summer. H and S 6in (15cm).

☼ ◊ ❋❋❋ 4–8

***Phlox adsurgens* 'Wagon Wheel'**
Evergreen, prostrate perennial forming wide mats of woody stems, clothed in oval leaves. Bears heads of wheel-shaped, pink flowers with narrow petals in summer. Needs humus-rich soil. H 4in (10cm), S 12in (30cm).

☼◑ ◊ pH ❋❋❋ 4–8

***Polygonum affine* 'Donald Lowndes'**
Evergreen, mat-forming perennial that has stout, branching, spreading stems clothed with pointed leaves. In summer bears dense spikes of small, red flowers, which become paler with age. H 3–6in (8–15cm), S to 6in (15cm).

☼ ◐ ❋❋❋ 4–8

Geranium dalmaticum
Prostrate, spreading perennial with outward-facing, almost flat, shell pink flowers borne in summer above divided, dark green leaves. Will grow taller in partial shade and is evergreen in all but severest winters. H 3–4in (8–10cm) or more, S 5–8in (12–20cm).

 ☼ ◊ ❀❀❀ 5–8

Erigeron karvinskianus,
syn. *E. mucronatus*
Spreading perennial with lax stems bearing narrowly lance-shaped, hairy leaves and, in summer-autumn, daisylike flower heads that open white, turn pink, and fade to purple. H 4–6in (10–15cm), S indefinite.

☼ ◊ ❀❀ 5–7

Aethionema armenum
Short-lived, evergreen or semi-evergreen, dense sub-shrub with narrow, blue-green leaves. Carries loose sprays of tiny, pale to deep pink flowers in summer. H and S 6in (15cm).

☼ ◊ ❀❀❀ 5–7

Androsace lanuginosa
Evergreen, trailing perennial with loose stems, covered in silky hairs, carrying deep green leaves and, in summer, clusters of small, flat, lilac-pink or pale pink flowers with dark pink or yellow eyes. H 1½in (4cm), S to 7in (18cm).

☼ ◊ ❀❀❀ 4–5

Dianthus 'Little Jock'
Evergreen, compact, clump-forming perennial with spiky, silvery green foliage. In summer produces strongly fragrant, rounded, semi-double, pink flowers, with darker eyes, above foliage. H and S 4in (10cm).

☼ ◊ ❀❀❀ 4–8

Dianthus gratianopolitanus,
syn. *D. caesius* (Cheddar pink)
Evergreen perennial with loose mats of narrow, gray-green leaves. In summer produces very fragrant, flat, pale pink flowers on slender stems. H to 6in (15cm), S to 12in (30cm).

☼ ◊ ❀❀❀ 5–8

Loiseleuria procumbens
(Alpine azalea)
Evergreen, prostrate shrub with small, oval leaves, hairy and beige beneath. Has terminal clusters of open funnel-shaped, rose-pink to white flowers in early summer. H to 3in (8cm), S 4–6in (10–15cm).

☼ ◊ pH ❀❀❀ 2–5

Acantholimon glumaceum
Evergreen, cushion-forming perennial with hard, spiny, dark green leaves and short spikes of small, star-shaped, pink flowers in summer. H 4in (10cm), S 8in (20cm).

☼ ◊ ❀❀❀ 7–9

317

■ PINK

Dianthus 'Pike's Pink'
Evergreen, compact, cushion-forming
perennial, with spiky, gray-green
foliage, that bears fragrant, rounded,
double, pink flowers in summer. H and
S 4in (10cm).

☀ ◊ ❄❄❄ 5–8

Saponaria caespitosa
Mat-forming perennial with small,
lance-shaped leaves. Tiny, flat, single,
pink to purple flowers are borne in
small heads in summer. Needs very
sharp drainage. H 3in (8cm),
S 4in (10cm).

☀ ◊ ❄❄❄ 4–7

Oxalis depressa, syn. *O. inops*
Tuberous perennial with 3-lobed leaves
and short-stemmed, widely funnel-
shaped, bright rose-pink flowers, $^3/_4$in
(2cm) across, in summer. Needs a
sheltered site or cool greenhouse.
H 2in (5cm), S 3–4in (8–10cm).

☀ ◊ ❄❄ 8–9

Androsace villosa var.
jacquemontii
Evergreen, mat-forming perennial with
small rosettes of hairy, gray-green
leaves. Bears tiny, pinkish purple
flowers on red stems in late spring and
early summer. Suits an alpine house.
H $^1/_2$–$1^1/_2$in (1–4cm), S 8in (20cm).

☀ ◊ ❄❄❄ 4–7

Dianthus microlepis
Evergreen perennial with tiny tufts of
minute, fine, grasslike leaves, above
which rise numerous small, rounded,
pink flowers in early summer. Is best
suited to a trough. H 2in (5cm),
S 8in (20cm).

☀ ◊ ❄❄❄ 5–7

Saponaria ocymoides
(Rock soapwort)
Perennial with compact or loose,
sprawling mats of hairy, oval leaves,
above which a profusion of tiny, flat,
pale pink to crimson flowers is carried
in summer. Is excellent on a dry bank.
H 1–3in (2.5–8cm), S 16in (40cm).

☀ ◊ ❄❄❄ 4–8

Dianthus myrtinervius
Evergreen, spreading perennial with
numerous small, rounded, pink flowers
that appear in summer above tiny,
grasslike leaves. H 2in (5cm),
S 8in (20cm).

☀ ◊ ❄❄❄ 5–8

Dianthus 'La Bourboule',
syn. *D.* 'La Bourbille'
Evergreen perennial with small clumps
of tufted, spiky foliage. Bears a
profusion of strongly fragrant, small,
single, pink flowers in summer. H 2in
(5cm), S 3in (8cm).

☀ ◊ ❄❄❄ 5–8

Dianthus alpinus
Evergreen, compact perennial that bears
comparatively large, rounded, rose-pink
to crimson flowers, singly in summer,
above mats of narrow, dark green
foliage. Likes humus-rich soil.
H 2in (5cm), S 3in (8cm).

☀ ◊ ❄❄❄ 5–8

Phlox subulata 'Marjory'
Evergreen, mound-forming perennial
with fine leaves and a profusion of flat,
star-shaped, bright rose-pink flowers in
early summer. Trim after flowering.
H 4in (10cm), S 8in (20cm).

☀ ◊ ❄❄❄ 4–9

Dianthus 'Annabelle'
Evergreen, compact, clump-forming
perennial with spiky, gray-green
foliage. In summer bears fragrant,
rounded, semi-double, cerise-pink
flowers, singly on slender stems.
H and S 4in (10cm).

 ☼ ◊ ✿✿✿ 5–8

Phlox 'Camla'
Evergreen, mound-forming perennial
with wiry, arching stems and fine
leaves. Has a profusion of open saucer-
shaped, rich pink flowers in early
summer. Trim after flowering. Needs
humus-rich soil. H 5in (12cm),
S 12in (30cm).

☼ ◊ ✿✿✿ 5–8

Geranium cinereum 'Ballerina'
Spreading, rosetted perennial that
bears cup-shaped, purplish pink
flowers, with deep purple veins, on lax
stems in late spring and summer. Basal
leaves are round, deeply divided, and
soft. H 4in (10cm), S 12in (30cm).

☼ ◊ ✿✿✿ 4–9

Teucrium polium
Deciduous, dome-shaped sub-shrub
that has much-branched, woolly, white
or yellowish stems and leaves with
scalloped margins. Bears yellowish
white or pinkish purple flowers in flat
heads in summer. Requires very sharp
drainage. H and S 6in (15cm).

☼ ◊ ✿✿✿ 5–8

Lewisia rediviva [pink form]
(Bitter root)
Tufted, rosetted perennial. Clusters of
narrow leaves are summer-deciduous.
Large, many-petaled, pink flowers
open in bright weather in late spring and
early summer. Suits an alpine house.
H ¹/₂–1¹/₂in (1–4cm), S to 2in (5cm).

☼ ◊ pH ✿✿✿ 6–7

Phlox douglasii 'Crackerjack'
Evergreen, compact, mound-forming
perennial. Has a profusion of saucer-
shaped, bright crimson or magenta
flowers in early summer. Leaves are
lance-shaped. Cut back after flowering.
H to 3in (8cm), S 8in (20cm).

☼ ◊ ✿✿✿ 5–7

Silene schafta
Spreading perennial with tufts of
narrow, oval leaves. Bears sprays of
5-petaled, rose-magenta flowers from
late spring to late autumn. H 4–6in
(10–15cm), S 3–4in (8–10cm).

☼ ◊ ✿✿✿ 5–6

Geranium cinereum var.
subcaulescens
Spreading perennial with round, deeply
divided, soft leaves. In summer bears
brilliant purple-magenta flowers, with
striking, black eyes and stamens, on lax
stems. Is a good foil for silver-leaved
plants. H 4in (10cm), S 12in (30cm).

☼ ◊ ✿✿✿ 4–9

☐ PINK

Rhodohypoxis baurii 'Albrighton'
Perennial with a tuberlike rootstock
and an erect, basal tuft of narrowly
lance-shaped, hairy leaves. Bears a
succession of erect, deep pink flowers
singly on slender stems in spring and
early summer. H 2–4in (5–10cm),
S 1–2in (2.5–5cm).

☼ ◊ ❀❀❀ 9

Armeria maritima 'Vindictive'
Evergreen, clump-forming perennial
with grasslike, dark blue-green leaves,
above which rise stiff stems bearing
spherical heads of small, deep rose-
pink flowers for a long period in
summer. H 4in (10cm), S 6in (15cm).

☼ ◊ ❀❀❀❀ 4–7

**_Dianthus deltoides_ 'Flashing
Light'**
Evergreen, mat-forming perennial.
Many small, flat, upward-facing,
brilliant cerise flowers are borne singly
above tiny, oblong, pointed leaves.
H 4–6in (10–15cm), S 8in (20cm).

☼ ◊ ❀❀❀❀ 5–8

☐☐ RED–PURPLE

Rhodohypoxis baurii 'Douglas'
Perennial with a tuberlike rootstock
and an erect, basal tuft of narrowly
lance-shaped, hairy leaves. Bears a
succession of upright, flattish, rich
deep red flowers singly on slender
stems in spring and early summer.
H 2–4in (5–10cm), S 1–2in (2.5–5cm).

☼ ◊ ❀❀ 9

Penstemon hirsutus 'Pygmaeus'
Short-lived, evergreen, compact sub-
shrub that bears tubular, lipped, hairy,
purple- or blue-flushed, white flowers
in summer. Has tightly packed, dark
green leaves and is suitable for a
trough. H and S 3in (8cm).

☼ ◊ ❀❀❀❀ 5–8

**_Pterocephalus perennis_ subsp.
perennis**, syn. _P. p._ var. _parnassi_
Semi-evergreen, mat-forming perennial
with crinkled, hairy leaves. Bears tight,
rounded heads of tubular, pinkish
lavender flowers, singly on short stems
in summer, followed by feathery seed
heads. H 2in (5cm), S 4in (10cm).

☼ ◊ ❀❀❀❀ 5–7

☐ PURPLE

**_Phlox douglasii_ 'Boothman's
Variety'**
Evergreen, mound-forming perennial
with lance-shaped leaves and masses of
pale lavender blue flowers, with violet-
blue markings around eyes, in early
summer. Cut back after flowering.
H to 2in (5cm), S 8in (20cm).

☼ ◊ ❀❀❀❀ 5–7

Physoplexis comosa,
syn. _Phyteuma comosum_
Tufted perennial with deeply cut leaves
and round heads of bottle-shaped,
violet-blue, rarely white, flowers in
summer. Suits crevices but dislikes
winter wet. H 3in (8cm), S 4in (10cm).

☼ ◊ ❀❀❀❀ 5–7

Globularia meridionalis, syn.
G. cordifolia subsp. _bellidifolia_
Evergreen, dome-shaped sub-shrub. In
summer, globular, fluffy, lavender to
lavender purple flower heads are borne
singly just above glossy leaves. H to
4in (10cm), S to 8in (20cm).

☼ ◊ ❀❀❀❀ 5–7

Thymus leucotrichus
Evergreen, aromatic, mound-forming sub-shrub with fine, twiggy stems and narrow leaves fringed with white hairs. Bears dense heads of small, pinkish purple flowers with purple bracts in summer. H 4–5in (10–12cm), S 6in (15cm).

☼ ◊ ❊❊❊ 4–7

***Phlox* 'Emerald Cushion'**
Evergreen perennial with emerald green mounds of fine leaves, studded in late spring and early summer with large, saucer-shaped, bright violet-blue flowers. Trim after flowering. H 3in (8cm), S 6in (15cm).

☼ ◊ ❊❊❊❊ 4–8

Phlox bifida (Cleft phlox)
Evergreen, mound-forming perennial with lance-shaped leaves. Bears a profusion of small heads of star-shaped, lilac or white flowers with deeply cleft petals in summer. Cut back stems by half after flowering. H 4–6in (10–15cm), S 6in (15cm).

☼ ◊ ❊❊❊❊ 4–8

***Viola* 'Haslemere'**
Clump-forming perennial with small, oval, toothed leaves and flat-faced, lavender pink flowers borne from late spring to late summer. Soil should not be too dry. H 3–6in (8–15cm), S to 8in (20cm).

☼ ◊ ❊❊❊ 5–7

Campanula poscharskyana
Rampant, spreading perennial with bell-shaped, violet flowers borne on leafy stems in summer. Leaves are round with serrated edges. Vigorous runners make it suitable for a bank or a wild garden. H 4–6in (10–15cm), S indefinite.

☼ ◊ ❊❊❊❊ 4–7

Prunella grandiflora (Self-heal)
Semi-evergreen, basal-rosetted, ground-cover perennial with whorls of purple flowers borne in terminal spikes on leafy stems in summer. May be invasive; cut old flower stems before they seed. H 4–6in (10–15cm), S 12in (30cm).

☼ ◐ ❊❊❊❊ 5–8

Aster alpinus
Clump-forming, spreading perennial with lance-shaped, dark green leaves. Bears daisylike, purplish blue or pinkish purple flower heads, with yellow centers, from mid- to late summer. H 6in (15cm), S 12–18in (30–45cm).

☼ ◊ ❊❊❊ 5–7

Thymus herba-barona
(Caraway-scented thyme)
Evergreen sub-shrub with a loose mat of tiny, caraway-scented, dark green leaves. In summer, small, lilac flowers are borne in terminal clusters. H in flower 2–4in (5–10cm), S to 8in (20cm).

☼ ◊ ❊❊ 4–7

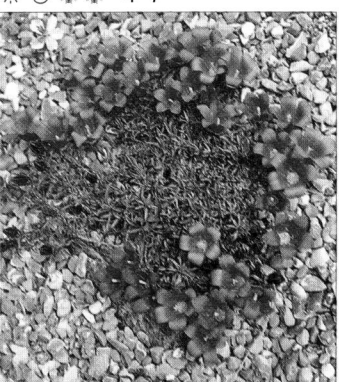

Edraianthus serpyllifolius
Evergreen, prostrate perennial with tight mats of tiny leaves and small, bell-shaped, deep violet flowers, borne on short stems in early summer. Is uncommon and seldom sets seed in gardens. H ½in (1cm), S to 2in (5cm).

☼ ◊ ❊❊❊ 4–7

Prunella webbiana
Semi-evergreen, spreading, mat-forming perennial with basal rosettes of leaves. In mid-summer bears short spikes of funnel-shaped, purple flowers in whorls. H 4–6in (10–15cm), S 12in (30cm).

☼ ◑ ❋❋❋ 5–8

Campanula 'Birch Hybrid'
Vigorous, evergreen perennial with tough, arching, prostrate stems and ivy-shaped, bright green leaves. Bears many open bell-shaped, deep violet flowers in summer. H 4in (10cm), S 12in (30cm) or more.

☼ ◊ ❋❋❋ 4–7

Campanula portenschlagiana (Dalmatian bellflower)
Vigorous, evergreen, prostrate perennial with dense mats of small, ivy-shaped leaves and large clusters of erect, open bell-shaped, violet flowers in summer. H 6in (15cm), S indefinite.

☼ ◊ ❋❋❋ 4–7

Ramonda myconi, syn. *R. pyrenaica* (Rosette-mullein)
Evergreen, rosette-forming perennial with hairy, crinkled leaves and, in late spring and early summer, flat, blue-mauve, pink, or white flowers, borne on branched stems. H 3in (8cm), S to 4in (10cm).

◉ ◑ ❋❋❋ 5–7

Viola 'Huntercombe Purple'
Perennial forming wide clumps of neat, oval, toothed leaves. Has a profusion of flat-faced, rich violet flowers from spring to late summer. Divide clumps every 3 years. H 4–6in (10–15cm), S 6–12in (15–30cm) or more.

☼ ◊ ❋❋❋ 5–7

Pinguicula grandiflora
Clump-forming perennial with a basal rosette of sticky, oval, pale green leaves. In summer bears spurred, open funnel-shaped, violet-blue to purple flowers singly on upright, slender stems. H 5–6in (12–15cm), S 2in (5cm).

☼ ● ❋❋❋ 3–5

Campanula 'G.F. Wilson'
Neat, mound-forming perennial with large, upturned, bell-shaped, violet flowers in summer. Has rounded, pale yellow-green leaves. H 3–4in (8–10cm), S 5–6in (12–15cm).

☼ ◊ ❋❋❋ 4–7

Edraianthus pumilio
Short-lived perennial with low tufts of fine, grasslike leaves. In early summer, upturned, bell-shaped, pale to deep lavender flowers, on very short stems, appear amid foliage. H 1in (2.5cm), S 3in (8cm).

☼ ◊ ❋❋❋ 4–7

Cyananthus microphyllus
Mat-forming perennial with very fine, red stems clothed in tiny leaves. Bears funnel-shaped, violet-blue flowers at the end of each stem in late summer. Likes humus-rich soil. H ³/₄in (2cm), S 8in (20cm).

☼ ◐ ❀❀❀ 5–7

Townsendia grandiflora
Short-lived, evergreen perennial with basal rosettes of small, spoon-shaped leaves. Upright stems carry solitary daisylike, violet or violet-blue flower heads in late spring and early summer. H to 6in (15cm), S 4in (10cm).

☼ ◐ ❀❀❀ 4–7

Sisyrinchium bellum
Semi-evergreen, upright, clump-forming perennial that for a long period in summer and early autumn has many flowering stems carrying tiny tufts of irislike, blue to violet-blue flowers. Foliage is grasslike. Self seeds readily. H to 5in (12cm), S 4in (10cm).

☼ ◊ ❀❀ 7–8

Aquilegia jonesii
Compact perennial that bears short-spurred, violet-blue flowers in summer, a few to each slender stem. Has small rosettes of finely divided, blue-gray or gray-green leaves. Is uncommon, suitable for an alpine house only. H 1in (2.5cm), S to 2in (5cm).

☼ ◊ ❀❀❀

Pratia pedunculata
Vigorous, evergreen, creeping perennial with small leaves and a profusion of star-shaped, blue or occasionally purplish blue flowers borne in summer. Makes good ground cover in a moist site. H ¹/₂in (1cm), S indefinite.

☀ ◐ ❀❀ 5–7

Hedyotis michauxii, syn.
Houstonia serpyllifolia
Vigorous perennial with rooting stems. Produces mats of green foliage studded with star-shaped, violet-blue flowers in late spring and early summer. H 3in (8cm), S 12in (30cm).

☀ ◐ ❀❀❀ 5–8

Globularia cordifolia
Evergreen, mat-forming, dwarf shrub with creeping, woody stems clothed in tiny, oval leaves. Bears stemless, round, fluffy, blue to pale lavender blue flower heads in summer. H 1–2in (2.5–5cm), S to 8in (20cm).

☼ ◊ ❀❀❀ 5–7

Campanula cochleariifolia,
syn. *C. pusilla*
Spreading perennial. Runners produce mats of rosetted, tiny, round leaves. Bears small clusters of white, lavender, or pale blue flowers in summer on many thin stems above foliage. H 3in (8cm), S indefinite.

☼ ◊ ❀❀❀ 5–7

Trachelium asperuloides, syn.
Diosphaera asperuloides
Mat-forming perennial with threadlike stems clothed in minute leaves, above which rise many tiny, upright, tubular, pale blue flowers in summer. Do not remove old stems in winter. H 3in (8cm), S to 6in (15cm).

☼ ◊ ❀❀ 5–7

Eritrichium nanum
Clump-forming perennial with tufts of hairy, gray-green leaves. Bears small, stemless, flat, pale blue flowers in late spring and early summer. Requires sharp drainage. Is only suitable for an alpine house. H ³/₄in (2cm), S 1in (2.5cm).

☼ ◊ ❀❀❀ 5–7

■ BLUE   ▢ GREEN–YELLOW   ▢ YELLOW

Parochetus communis
Evergreen, prostrate perennial with cloverlike leaves and pealike, brilliant blue flowers that are borne almost continuously. Grows best in an alpine house. H 1–2in (2.5–5cm), S indefinite.

☼ ◐ ◊ ❄ 8–9

Gunnera magellanica
Mat-forming perennial, grown for its rounded, toothed leaves, often bronze-tinged when young, on short, creeping stems. Small, green, unisexual flowers, with reddish-bracts, are borne on male and female plants. Likes peaty soil. H 1in (2.5cm), S to 12in (30cm).

☼ ◐ ◊ ❄❄❄ 8–9

Mitella breweri
Neat, clump-forming, rhizomatous perennial with slender, hairy stems bearing small, pendent, tubular, greenish white flowers, with flared mouths, in summer. Has lobed, kidney-shaped, basal leaves. H and S 6in (15cm).

☼ ◊ ❄❄❄❄ 5–7

Asarina procumbens,
syn. *Antirrhinum asarina*
Semi-evergreen perennial with trailing stems bearing soft, hairy leaves and tubular, pale cream flowers, with yellow palates, throughout summer. Dislikes winter wet. Self seeds freely. H ½–1in (1–2.5cm), S 9–12in (23–30cm).

☼ ◊ ❄❄ 6–8

Polygala calcarea 'Bulley's Variety'
Evergreen, prostrate perennial with rosettes of small, narrowly oval leaves and loose heads of deep blue flowers in late spring and early summer. Likes humus-rich soil. Suits a trough. H 1in (2.5cm), S 3–4in (8–10cm).

☼ ◊ ❄❄❄ 5–7

Polygala calcarea (Lime polygala)
Evergreen, prostrate, occasionally upright, perennial. Has small, narrowly oval leaves and pale to dark blue flowers in loose heads in late spring and early summer. Likes humus-rich soil. Suits a trough. May be difficult to establish. H 1in (2.5cm), S to 6in (15cm).

☼ ◊ ❄❄❄ 5–7

Sedum acre (Gold-moss sedum)
Evergreen, mat-forming perennial with dense, spreading shoots, clothed in tiny, fleshy, pale green leaves, each bearing a flat, terminal head of tiny, yellow flowers in summer. Is invasive but easily controlled. H 1–2in (2.5–5cm), S indefinite.

☼ ◊ ❄❄❄ 4–9

Papaver miyabeanum
Short-lived, clump-forming perennial with basal rosettes of finely cut, hairy, soft gray leaves. Bears pendent, open cup-shaped, pale yellow flowers in summer. Dislikes winter wet. H and S 2–4in (5–10cm).

☼ ◊ ❄❄❄ 5–7

Polygala chamaebuxus
Evergreen, woody-based perennial
with tiny, hard, dark green leaves. In
late spring and early summer bears
many racemes of small, pealike, white-
and-yellow flowers, sometimes
marked brown. Needs humus-rich soil.
H 2in (5cm), S 8in (20cm).

☼ ◊ ❋❋❋ 4–7

Sedum acre 'Aureum'
Evergreen, dense, mat-forming perennial
with spreading shoots, yellow-tipped in
spring and early summer, and clothed in
tiny, fleshy, yellow leaves. Bears flat
heads of tiny, bright yellow flowers in
summer. Is invasive but easy to control.
H 1–2in (2.5–5cm), S indefinite.

☼ ◊ ❋❋❋ 4–9

Scutellaria orientalis
Rhizomatous perennial with hairy, gray,
rooting stems. Has terminal spikes of
tubular, yellow flowers, with brownish
purple lips, in summer. Leaves are
toothed and oval. May be invasive in a
small space. H 2–4in (5–10cm), S to 9in
(23cm).

☼ ◊ ❋❋❋ 5–8

Waldsteinia ternata, syn.
W. trifolia (Barren-strawberry)
Semi-evergreen perennial with loose,
spreading mats of toothed, 3-parted
leaves. Bears saucer-shaped, yellow
flowers in late spring and early
summer. Is good on a bank. H 4in
(10cm), S 8–12in (20–30cm).

☼ ◊ ❋❋❋ 4–8

Oenothera missouriensis
(Missouri primrose sundrops)
Spreading perennial with stout stems
and oval leaves. Throughout summer
bears a succession of wide, bell-shaped,
yellow flowers, sometimes spotted red,
that open at sundown. H to 4in (10cm),
S to 16in (40cm) or more.

☼ ◊ ❋❋❋ 5–8

Linum flavum 'Compactum'
Shrubby perennial with narrow leaves
and terminal clusters of many upward-
facing, open funnel-shaped, single,
bright yellow flowers in summer.
Provide a sunny, sheltered position
and protection from winter wet. H and
S 6in (15cm).

☼ ◊ ❋❋❋ 5–7

Potentilla eriocarpa
Clump-forming perennial with tufts of
oval, dark green leaves divided into
leaflets. Flat, single, pale yellow
flowers are borne throughout summer
just above leaves. H 2–3in (5–8cm),
S 4–6in (10–15cm).

☼ ◊ ❋❋❋ 5–7

Calceolaria tenella
Vigorous, evergreen, prostrate
perennial with creeping, reddish stems
and oval, green leaves, above which
rise small spikes of pouch-shaped, red-
spotted, yellow flowers in summer.
H 4in (10cm), S indefinite.

☼ ◐ ❋ 7–8

325

☐ YELLOW

☐☐ YELLOW–ORANGE

***Genista sagittalis*,**
syn. *Chamaespartium sagittale*
Deciduous, semi-prostrate shrub with
winged stems bearing a few oval, dark
green leaves. Pealike, yellow flowers
appear in dense, terminal clusters in early
summer, followed by hairy seed pods.
H 3in (8cm), S 12in (30cm) or more.

☼ ◊ ❄❄❄ 5–8

***Lysimachia nummularia* 'Aurea'**
Prostrate perennial. Creeping, rooting
stems bear pairs of round, soft yellow
leaves, which later turn greenish yellow
or green in dense shade. Has bright
yellow flowers in leaf axils in summer.
H 1–2in (2.5–5cm), S indefinite.

☼ ◊ ❄❄❄ 4–8

***Hypericum empetrifolium*
'Prostratum'**
Evergreen, prostrate shrub with angled
branches and bright green leaves that
have curled margins. Bears flat heads
of small, bright yellow flowers in
summer. Needs winter protection.
H ¾in (2cm), S 12in (30cm).

☼ ◊ ❄❄❄ 4–7

Hippocrepis comosa
Vigorous perennial with prostrate,
rooting stems bearing small, open
spikes of pealike, yellow flowers in
summer and leaves divided into
leaflets. Self seeds freely and may
spread rapidly. H 2–3in (5–8cm),
S indefinite.

☼ ◊ ❄❄❄ 5–7

***Calceolaria* 'Walter Shrimpton'**
Evergreen, mound-forming perennial
with glossy, dark green leaves. In early
summer bears short spikes of many
pouch-shaped, bronze-yellow flowers,
spotted rich brown, with white bands
across centers. H 4in (10cm),
S 9in (23cm).

☼ ◊ ❄❄❄ 7–8

Cytisus ardoinii
Deciduous, hummock-forming,
dwarf shrub with arching stems. In late
spring and early summer, pealike,
bright yellow flowers are produced in
pairs in leaf axils. Leaves are divided
into 3 leaflets. H 4in (10cm),
S 6in (15cm).

☼ ◊ ❄❄❄ 6–8

Potentilla aurea
Rounded perennial, with a woody
base, that in late summer bears loose
sprays of flat, single, yellow flowers
with slightly darker eyes. Leaves are
divided into oval, slightly silvered
leaflets. H 4in (10cm), S 8in (20cm).

☼ ◊ ❄❄❄ 5–8

Alstroemeria hookeri
Tuberous perennial with narrow leaves
and loose heads of widely flared,
orange-suffused, pink flowers in
summer; upper petals are spotted and
blotched red and yellow. H 4–6in
(10–15cm), S 18–24in (45–60cm).

☼ ◊ ❄❄ 7–9

■□ PINK–BLUE   ■□ BLUE–ORANGE

Polygonum vacciniifolium
Evergreen, prostrate perennial with many-branched, woody, red stems clothed in oval leaves, tinged red in autumn. Bears long, narrow, dense spikes of small, deep pink or rose-red flowers in late summer and autumn. H 4–6in (10–15cm), S to 12in (30cm).

☼ ◑ ❋❋❋ 4–8

Gentiana sino-ornata
Evergreen, prostrate, spreading perennial that, in autumn, bears trumpet-shaped, rich blue flowers singly at the ends of stems. Leaves are narrow. Lift and divide every 3 years. Needs moist soil. H in flower 2in (5cm), S to 12in (30cm).

☼ ◑ pH ❋❋❋ 5–7

Gaultheria procumbens
Vigorous, evergreen sub-shrub with prostrate stems carrying clusters of oval, leathery leaves that turn red in winter. In summer, solitary bell-shaped, pink-flushed, white flowers appear in leaf axils, followed by scarlet berries. H 2–6in (5–15cm), S indefinite.

☼ ◑ pH ❋❋❋ 3–8

Gentiana x macaulayi 'Wellsii'
Evergreen, prostrate perennial with trumpet-shaped, blue flowers in late summer and autumn. Spreading stems are clothed in narrow leaves. Soil should be quite moist. H in flower 2in (5cm), S 8in (20cm).

☼ ◑ pH ❋❋❋ 5–7

Oxalis lobata
Clump-forming perennial with woolly-coated tubers and leaves with up to 5 rounded lobes. Produces racemes of widely funnel-shaped, bright yellow flowers, 1/2–3/4in (1–2cm) across, in late summer and autumn. H 2in (5cm), S 3–4in (8–10cm).

☼ ◑ ❋ 7–9

Nertera granadensis,
syn. N. depressa (Bead plant)
Prostrate perennial with dense mats of tiny, bright green leaves. In early summer bears minute, greenish white flowers, followed by many shiny, orange berries. Needs ample moisture in summer. H to 1/2in (1cm), S 4in (10cm).

☼ ◑ ❋ 5–7

Arabis ferdinandi-coburgii 'Variegata'

Evergreen, mat-forming perennial with small, oval, green leaves, splashed with cream. Bears small, white flowers in spring and early summer. May revert to type with plain green leaves. H ³⁄₄in (2cm), S 12in (30cm).

☼ ◊ ❄❄❄ 5–7

Arctostaphylos uva-ursi 'Point Reyes'

Evergreen, prostrate shrub with long shoots and glossy leaves. In late spring and early summer bears terminal clusters of urn-shaped, pale pink to white flowers, followed by red berries. H 4in (10cm), S 20in (50cm).

☼ ◊ pH❄❄❄ 2–8

Jovibarba hirta,
syn. *Sempervivum hirtum*

Evergreen, mat-forming perennial with rosettes of hairy, green leaves, often suffused red, and terminal clusters of star-shaped, pale yellow flowers in summer. Dislikes winter wet. H 3–6in (8–15cm), S 4in (10cm).

☼ ◊ ❄❄❄ 6–9

Pachysandra terminalis

Evergreen, creeping perennial that has smooth leaves clustered at the ends of short stems. Bears spikes of tiny, white flowers, sometimes flushed purple, in early summer. Makes excellent ground cover in a moist or dry site. H 4in (10cm), S 8in (20cm).

☀ ◊ ❄❄❄ 4–8

Sedum lydium

Evergreen, mat-forming perennial with reddish stems and narrow, fleshy, often red-flushed leaves. Bears flat-topped, terminal clusters of tiny, white flowers in summer. H 2in (5cm), S to 6in (15cm).

☼ ◊ ❄❄❄ 5–8

Arctostaphylos uva-ursi
(Bearberry, Kinnikinnick)

Evergreen, low-growing shrub with arching, intertwining stems clothed in small, oval, bright green leaves. Bears urn-shaped, pinkish white flowers in summer followed by scarlet berries. H 4in (10cm), S 20in (50cm).

☼ ◊ pH❄❄❄ 2–8

Sedum obtusatum

Evergreen, prostrate perennial with small, fat, succulent leaves that turn bronze-red in summer. Loose, flat sprays of tiny, bright yellow flowers are borne in summer. Dislikes summer wet. H 2in (5cm), S 4–6in (10–15cm).

☼ ◊ ❄❄❄ 5–9

Trifolium repens 'Purpurascens'

Vigorous, semi-evergreen, ground-cover perennial, grown for its divided, bronze-green foliage, variably edged bright green. Produces heads of small, pealike, white blooms throughout summer. Suits a wild bank. H in flower 3–5in (8–12cm), S 8–12in (20–30cm) or more.

☼ ◊ ❄❄❄ 4–7

Acaena microphylla
Compact, mat-forming perennial,
usually evergreen, with leaves divided
into tiny leaflets, bronze-tinged when
young. Heads of small flowers with
spiny, dull red bracts are borne in
summer and develop into decorative
burs. H 2in (5cm), S 6in (15cm).

☼ ◊ ❄❄❄ 5–8

Sempervivum tectorum
Vigorous, evergreen perennial with
rosettes of purple-tipped leaves,
sometimes suffused deep red. In
summer has clusters of star-shaped,
reddish purple flowers on stems 12in
(30cm) tall. H 4–6in (10–15cm), S to
8in (20cm).

☼ ◊ ❄❄❄ 5–9

Sedum spathulifolium
Evergreen, mat-forming perennial with
rosettes of fleshy, green or silver leaves,
usually strongly suffused bronze-red,
and small clusters of tiny, yellow
flowers borne just above foliage in
summer. Tolerates shade. H 2in (5cm),
S indefinite.

☼ ◊ ❄❄❄ 5–9

Sempervivum arachnoideum
(Cobweb houseleek)
Evergreen, mat-forming perennial.
Rosettes of oval, fleshy leaves with red
tips are covered in a web of white hairs.
Bears loose clusters of star-shaped,
rose-red flowers in summer. H 2–5in
(5–12cm), S to 4in (10cm) or more.

☼ ◊ ❄❄❄ 5–9

Leucogenes grandiceps
Evergreen, dense, woody-based
perennial with neat rosettes of downy,
silver leaves. Yellow flower heads,
within woolly, white bracts, are borne
singly in spring or early summer. H and
S 4–6in (10–15cm).

☼ ◊ ❄❄ 7–8

Raoulia hookeri var. **albo-sericea**
Evergreen, prostrate perennial with
tiny rosettes of silver leaves. Flower
heads appear briefly in summer as
fragrant yellow fluff. Is best in poor,
gritty humus in an alpine house.
Dislikes winter wet. H to ½in (1cm),
S 10in (25cm).

☼ ◊ ❄❄❄ 8–9

Artemisia schmidtiana 'Nana'
(Silvermound artemisia)
Prostrate perennial with fernlike, silver
foliage. Has insignificant sprays of
daisylike, yellow flowers in summer.
Is suitable for a wall or bank. H 3in
(8cm), S 8in (20cm).

☼ ◊ ❄❄❄ 5–8

Sempervivum ciliosum
Evergreen, mat-forming perennial with
rosettes of hairy, gray-green leaves and,
in summer, heads of small, star-shaped,
yellow flowers. Dislikes winter wet; is
best grown in an alpine house. H 3–4in
(8–10cm), S 4in (10cm).

☼ ◊ ❄❄❄ 7–10

329

■ GREEN

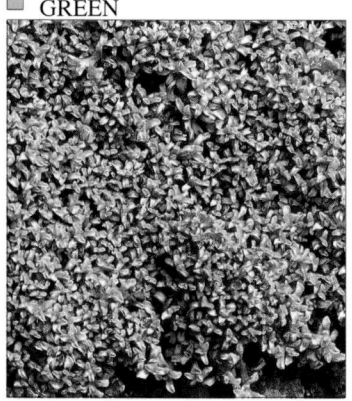

Raoulia australis
(Silvermat raoulia)
Evergreen, carpeting perennial
forming a hard mat of gray-green
leaves. Bears tiny, fluffy, sulfur yellow
flower heads in summer. H to 1/2in
(1cm), S 10in (25cm).

 8–9

Acaena caesiiglauca
Vigorous, ground-cover perennial,
usually evergreen. Has hairy ,glaucous
blue leaves divided into leaflets. Heads
of small flowers with spiny, brownish
green bracts, borne in summer, develop
into brownish red burs. H 2in (5cm),
S 30in (75cm) or more.

 5–8

Sempervivum montanum
Evergreen, mat-forming perennial with
dark green rosettes of fleshy, hairy
leaves. Star-shaped, wine red flowers
are borne in terminal clusters in
summer. Is a variable plant that
hybridizes freely. H 3–6in (8–15cm),
S 4in (10cm).

 5–9

Azorella trifurcata,
syn. *Bolax glebaria* of gardens
Evergreen perennial forming tight,
hard cushions of tiny, leathery, oval
leaves in rosettes. Bears many small,
stalkless umbels of yellow flowers in
summer. H to 4in (10cm), S 6in (15cm).

 6–7

Asarum europaeum
(European wild ginger)
Vigorous, evergreen, prostrate,
rhizomatous perennial with large,
kidney-shaped, leathery, glossy
leaves that hide tiny, brown flowers
appearing in spring. H 6in (15cm),
S indefinite.

 4–8

Sagina boydii
Evergreen perennial with hard cushions
of minute, stiff, bottle green leaves
in small rosettes. Bears insignificant
flowers in summer. Is difficult and
slow-growing. H 1/2in (1cm), S to
8in (20cm).

 5–7

Sempervivum giuseppii
Vigorous, evergreen perennial making prostrate mats of pea green leaf rosettes. Leaves are hairy, especially in spring, and have dark spots at tips. Bears terminal clusters of star-shaped, deep pink or red flowers in summer. H in flower 3–4in (8–10cm), S 4in (10cm).

☼ ◊ ❀❀❀ 5–9

Bolax gummifera
Very slow-growing, evergreen perennial with neat rosettes of small, blue-green leaves forming extremely hard cushions. Insignificant, yellow flowers are rarely produced. Grows well on tufa. H 1in (2.5cm), S 4in (10cm).

☼ ◊ ❀❀❀ 5–6

Plantago nivalis
Evergreen perennial with neat rosettes of thick, silver-haired, green leaves. Bears spikes of insignificant, dull gray flowers in summer. Dislikes winter wet. H in leaf 1in (2.5cm), S 2in (5cm).

☼ ◊ ❀❀❀ 6–7

Raoulia haastii
Evergreen perennial forming low, irregular hummocks of minute leaves that are apple green in spring, dark green in autumn, and chocolate brown in winter. Occasionally has small, fluffy, sulfur yellow flower heads in summer. H to ½in (1cm), S 10in (25cm).

☼ ◊ ❀❀❀ 7

Paronychia kapela subsp. **serpyllifolia**
Evergreen, very compact, mat-forming perennial with minute, silver leaves. Inconspicuous flowers, borne in summer, are surrounded by papery, silver bracts. Is good for covering tufa. H to ½in (1cm), S 8in (20cm).

☼ ◊ ❀❀❀ 5–7

Sedum kamtschaticum 'Variegatum'
Semi-evergreen, prostrate perennial with fleshy leaves, edged with cream. Has tracery of fleshy stems and leaf buds in winter and loose, terminal clusters of orange-flushed, yellow flowers in early autumn. H 2–3in (5–8cm), S 8in (20cm).

☼ ◊ ❀❀❀ 4–9

Sedum spathulifolium 'Cape Blanco', syn. *S.s.* 'Cappa Blanca'
Evergreen perennial that has flat rosettes of fleshy, silvery green leaves, frequently suffused purple. Carries small clusters of tiny, yellow flowers above foliage in summer. Tolerates shade. H 2in (5cm), S indefinite.

☼ ◊ ❀❀❀ 5–9

Saxifraga moschata 'Cloth of Gold'
Evergreen, hummock-forming perennial, grown for its small, soft rosettes of bright golden foliage; produces best color in shade. Has star-shaped, white flowers on slender stems in summer. H 4–6in (10–15cm), S 12in (15cm).

☼ ◊ ❀❀❀ 5–6

Leucojum aestivum (Meadow snowflake, Summer snowflake)
Spring-flowering bulb with long, strap-shaped, semi-erect, basal leaves. Bears heads of pendent, long-stalked, bell-shaped, green-tipped, white flowers on leafless stems. H 1½–3ft (50cm–1m), S 4–5in (10–12cm).

☼ ◊ ❀❀❀ 4–9

Fritillaria verticillata
Spring-flowering bulb with slender leaves in whorls up stem, which bears a loose spike of 1–15 bell-shaped, white flowers, ¾–1½in (2–4cm) long and checkered green or brown. H to 3ft (1m), S 3–4in (8–10cm).

☼ ◊ ❀❀ 7–9

Fritillaria raddeana
Robust, spring-flowering bulb with lance-shaped leaves in whorls on lower half of stem. Has a head of up to 20 widely conical, pale yellow or greenish yellow flowers, 1¼–1½in (3–4cm) long, topped by a "crown" of small leaves. H to 3ft (1m), S 6–9in (15–23cm).

☼ ◊ ❀❀❀ 6–9

Fritillaria persica
Spring-flowering bulb with narrow, lance-shaped, gray-green leaves along stem. Produces a spike of 10–20 or more narrow, bell-shaped, blackish or brownish purple flowers, ⅝–¾in (1.5–2cm) long. H to 5ft (1.5m), S 4in (10cm).

☼ ◊ ❀❀ 7–8

Fritillaria recurva (Red bell)
Spring-flowering bulb with whorls of narrow, lance-shaped, gray-green leaves. Bears a spike of up to 10 narrow, yellow-checkered, orange or red flowers with flared tips. H to 3ft (1m), S 3–4in (8–10cm).

☼ ◊ ❀❀ 6–9

Fritillaria imperialis (Crown imperial)
Spring-flowering bulb with glossy, pale green leaves carried in whorls on leafy stems. Has up to 5 widely bell-shaped, orange flowers crowned by small, leaflike bracts. H to 5ft (1.5m), S 9–12in (23–30cm).

☼ ◊ ❀❀❀ 5–9

Crinum × powellii 'Album'
Late summer- or autumn-flowering bulb, with a long neck, producing a group of semi-erect, strap-shaped leaves. Leafless flower stems carry heads of fragrant, widely funnel-shaped, white flowers. H to 3ft (1m), S 2ft (60cm).

☼ ◊ ❀❀ 7–10

Galtonia candicans (Summer hyacinth)
Late summer- or autumn-flowering bulb with widely strap-shaped, fleshy, semi-erect, basal, gray-green leaves. Leafless stem has a spike of up to 30 pendent, short-tubed, white flowers. H 3–4ft (1–1.2m), S 7–9in (18–23cm).

☼ ◊ ❀❀ 7–10

Zantedeschia aethiopica 'Crowborough'
Early to mid-summer-flowering tuber with arrow-shaped, semi-erect, basal, deep green leaves. Produces a succession of arumlike, white spathes, each with a yellow spadix. H 1½–3ft (45cm–1m), S 14–18in (35–45cm).

☼ ◊ ❀❀ 8–10

Camassia leichtlinii
Tuft-forming bulb with long, narrow, erect, basal leaves. Each leafless stem bears a dense spike of 6-petaled, star-shaped, bluish violet or white flowers, 1½–3in (4–8cm) across, in summer. H 3–5ft (1–1.5m), S 8–12in (20–30cm).

☼ ◊ ❀❀❀ 3–10

Hymenocallis × macrostephana
Evergreen, spring- or summer-flowering bulb with strap-shaped, semi-erect, basal leaves. Bears fragrant white or cream to greenish yellow flowers, 6–8in (15–20cm) wide. H 32in (80cm), S 12–18in (30–45cm). Min. 59°F (15°C).

☼ ◊ 7–10

***Zantedeschia aethiopica* 'Green Goddess'**
Very robust, summer-flowering tuber with arrow-shaped, semi-erect, basal, deep green leaves. Bears a succession of green spathes each with a large, central, green-splashed, white area. H 1½–3ft (45cm–1m), S 1½–2ft (45–60cm).

☼ ◊ ❄❄ 8–10

Camassia leichtlinii 'Semiplena'
Tuft-forming bulb with long, narrow, erect, basal leaves. Each leafless stem carries a dense spike of narrow-petaled, double, creamy white flowers, 1½–3in (4–8cm) across, in summer. H 3–5ft (1–1.5m), S 8–12in (20–30cm).

☼ ◊ ❄❄ 3–10

Cardiocrinum giganteum
Stout, leafy-stemmed bulb with bold, dark green leaves. In summer, long spikes carry fragrant, slightly pendent, cream flowers, 6in (15cm) long, with purple-red streaks inside, then brown seed pods. H to 10ft (3m), S 2½–3½ft (75cm–1.1m).

☼◐ ◊ ❄❄ 7–9

Nectaroscordum siculum subsp. **bulgaricum**, syn. *N. dioscoridis*
Late spring- to early summer-flowering bulb with pendent, bell-shaped, white flowers, flushed purple-red and green. In seed, stalks bend upwards, holding dry seed pods erect. H to 4ft (1.2m), S 1–1½ft (30–45cm).

☼◐ ◊ ❄❄ 7–10

Eucomis pallidiflora
Summer-flowering bulb with sword-shaped, crinkly edged, semi-erect, basal leaves. Bears a dense spike of star-shaped, greenish white flowers, crowned with a cluster of leaflike bracts. H to 30in (75cm), S 12–24in (30–60cm).

☼ ◊ ❄❄ 8–10

Eucomis comosa
Clump-forming bulb with strap-shaped, wavy-margined leaves, spotted purple beneath. Purple-spotted stem bears a spike of white or greenish white, sometimes pink-tinted flowers, with purple ovaries, crowned by a tuft of bracts. H to 28in (70cm), S 12–24in (30–60cm).

☼ ◊ ❄❄ 8–10

Nomocharis pardanthina, syn. *N. mairei*
Summer-flowering bulb with stems bearing whorls of lance-shaped leaves and up to 15 outward-facing, white or pale pink flowers, each with purple blotches and a dark purple eye. H to 3ft (1m), S 5–6in (12–15cm).

☼◐ ◊ ❄❄❄ 7–9

Crinum × powellii
Late summer- or autumn-flowering bulb with a long neck producing a group of strap-shaped, semi-erect leaves. Leafless flower stems bear heads of fragrant, widely funnel-shaped, pink flowers. H to 3ft (1m), S 2ft (60cm).

☼ ◊ ❄❄ 7–10

Gladioli

Gladiolus hybrids produce excellent flowers for garden decoration, flower arrangements, and exhibition. They are divided into the Grandiflorus group, with long, densely packed spikes of flowers, categorized as small, medium-sized, large, or giant according to the width of their lowest flowers, and the Primulinus group, with fairly loose spikes of small flowers. (See the Plant Dictionary for more information.)

G. 'Ice Cap'
(large)

G. 'Inca Queen'
(large)

G. 'Robin'
(Primulinus group)

G. 'Moon Mirage'
(giant)

G. 'Peter Pears'
(large)

G. 'Dancing Queen'
(large)

G. 'Miss America'
(medium)

G. 'Pink Lady'
(large)

G. 'Black Lash'
(small)

G. 'Tesoro'
(medium)

G. 'Café au Lait'
(Primulinus group)

G. x *colvillei* 'The Bride' (small)

G. 'Gigi'
(small)

G. 'Mexicali Rose'
(large)

G. 'Rutherford'
(Primulinus group)

G. 'Green Woodpecker'
(medium)

G. 'Rose Supreme'
(giant)

G. 'Deliverance'
(giant)

G. 'Drama'
(large)

G. 'Renegade'
(large)

G. 'Victor Borge'
(large)

G. 'Melodie'
(small)

G. 'Carioca'
(medium)

Crinum moorei
Summer-flowering bulb with a long
neck, up to 3ft (1m) tall, and strap-
shaped, semi-erect, gray-green leaves
grouped at neck top. Leafless flower
stems bear heads of long-tubed, funnel-
shaped, pink flowers. H 20–28in
(50–70cm), S 24in (60cm).

☼ ◊ ❄ 8–10

Notholirion campanulatum
Early summer-flowering bulb with
long, narrow leaves in a basal tuft.
Leafy stem bears a spike of 10–40
pendent, funnel-shaped flowers, each
1½–2in (4–5cm) long, with green-
tipped, deep rose-purple petals. H
to 3ft (1m), S 3–4in (8–10cm).

◑ ◊ ❄❄❄ 7–10

Watsonia pyramidata
Very robust, summer-flowering corm
with narrowly sword-shaped leaves
both at base and on stem. Produces a
loose, branched spike of rich pink
flowers, with 6 spreading, pointed,
rose-red lobes. H 3–5ft (1–1.5m),
S 1½–2ft (45–60cm).

☼ ◊ ❄ 8–10

Dierama pulcherrimum
(Fairy wand)
Evergreen, upright, summer-flowering
corm with long, narrow, straplike
leaves, above which rise elegant,
arching, wiry stems bearing funnel-
shaped, deep pink flowers. Prefers deep,
rich soil. H 5ft (1.5m), S1ft (30cm).

☼ ◐ ❄❄ 8–10

Gladiolus italicus, syn. *G. segetum*
Early summer-flowering corm with
a fan of erect, sword-shaped leaves
from the basal part of stem. Carries a
loose spike of up to 20 pinkish purple
flowers, 1½–2in (4–5cm) long. H to 3ft
(1m), S 4–6in (10–15cm).

☼ ◊ ❄❄ 8–10

Gladiolus communis subsp.
byzantinus
Early summer-flowering corm with a
dense spike of up to 20 deep purplish
red or purplish pink flowers, 1½–2½in
(4–6cm) long. Produces a fan of sword-
shaped, erect, basal leaves. H to 28in
(70cm), S 4–6in (10–15cm).

☼ ◊ ❄❄ 5–10

Phaedranassa carmioli
Spring- and summer-flowering bulb
with upright, elliptic or lance-shaped,
basal leaves. Bears a head of 6–10
pendent, pinkish red flowers, with
green bases and yellow-edged, green
lobes at each apex. H 20–28in
(50–70cm), S 12–18in (30–45cm).

☼ ◊ ❄ 8–10

Watsonia beatricis
Summer-flowering corm with long,
sword-shaped, erect leaves, some basal
and some on stem. Stem carries a dense,
branched spike of tubular, orange-red
flowers, each 2½–3in (6–8cm) long,
with 6 short lobes. H to 3ft (1m),
S 1–1½ft (30–45cm).

☼ ◊ ❄ 8–10

Alstroemeria 'Margaret'
Mid- to late summer-flowering tuber
with narrowly lance-shaped, twisted,
bright green leaves. Stout, leafy stems
bear widely flared, funnel-shaped,
deep red flowers. H 3ft (1m), S 2–3ft
(60cm–1m).

☼ ◊ ❄❄ 6–10

■ RED

Dracunculus vulgaris,
syn. *Arum dracunculus*
Spring- and summer-flowering tuber
with deeply divided leaves at apex of
thick, blotched stem. A blackish maroon
spadix protrudes from a deep maroon-
purple spathe, 14in (35cm) long. H to
3ft (1m), S 1½–2ft (45–60cm).

☼ ◊ ❋❋ 8–10

***Gloriosa superba* 'Rothschildiana'**
Deciduous, summer-flowering,
tuberous, tendril climber. Upper leaf
axils each bear a large flower that has
6 reflexed, red petals with scalloped,
yellow edges. H to 6ft (2m), S 1–1½ft
(30–45cm). Min. 46°F (8°C).

☼ ◊ 10

***Crocosmia* 'Bressingham Blaze'**
Clump-forming, late summer-
flowering corm with sword-shaped,
pleated, basal, erect leaves. Branched
stem bears widely funnel-shaped, fiery
red flowers. H 30in (75cm), S 6–8in
(15–20cm).

☼ ◊ ❋❋ 5–9

***Scadoxus multiflorus* subsp.
katherinae, syn. *Haemanthus
katherinae* (Blood lily)**
Very robust, clump-forming bulb with
lance-shaped, wavy-edged leaves. Bears
an umbel of up to 200 red flowers in
summer. H to 4ft (1.2m), S 1–1½ft
(30–45cm). Min. 50°F (10°C).

◐ ◊ 10

***Crocosmia* 'Lucifer'**
Robust, clump-forming corm with
sword-shaped, erect, basal, bright green
leaves. Bears funnel-shaped, deep rich
red flowers in dense, branching spikes
in mid-summer. H to 3ft (1m),
S 8–10in (20–25cm).

☼ ◊ ❋❋ 5–9

***Canna* x *generalis* 'Assault'**
Summer-flowering, rhizomatous
perennial with stout, leafy stems
bearing wide, purple-green leaves. Has
a spike of scarlet flowers surrounded
by purple bracts. H to 4ft (1.2m),
S 1½–2ft (45–60cm). Min. 59°F (15°C).

☼ ◐ 7–10

Crocosmia masonorum
Robust, clump-forming corm with
erect, basal, deep green leaves, pleated
lengthways. Erect, branched stem has
a horizontal, upper part which carries
upright, reddish orange flowers in
summer-autumn. H to 5ft (1.5m),
S 1–1½ft (30–45cm).

☼ ◊ ❋❋ 7–9

Allium rosenbachianum
Summer-flowering bulb with stout
stems and straplike, semi-erect, basal
leaves. Carries 50 or more star-shaped,
purplish pink flowers in a spherical
umbel, 3–5in (8–12cm) across. H to
3ft (1m), S 6–8in (15–20cm).

☼ ◊ ❋❋❋ 4–10

Dierama pendulum (Angel's
fishing-rods, Grassy-bell)
Clump-forming, late summer-flowering
corm with arching, basal leaves. Bears
pendulous, loose racemes of bell-
shaped, pinkish purple flowers,
1in (2.5cm) long. H to 5ft (1.5m),
S 6–8in (15–20cm).

☼ ◊ ❋❋ 7–9

Allium giganteum
Robust, summer-flowering bulb with long, wide, semi-erect, basal leaves. Produces a stout stem with a dense, spherical umbel, 5in (12cm) across, of 50 or more star-shaped, purple flowers. H to 6ft (2m), S 12–14in (30–35cm).

☼ ◊ ❄❄ 6–10

Allium aflatunense
Summer-flowering bulb with semi-erect, basal leaves dying away by flowering time. Carries 50 or more star-shaped, purple flowers in a large, tight, spherical umbel, 4in (10cm) across. H to 30in (75cm), S 6–8in (15–20cm).

☼ ◊ ❄❄ 4–10

Dichelostemma congestum, syn. *Brodiaea congesta*
Early summer-flowering bulb with semi-erect, basal leaves dying away when a dense head of funnel-shaped, purple flowers, each ⅝–¾in (1.5–2cm) long, appears. H to 3ft (1m), S 3–4in (8–10cm).

☼ ◊ ❄❄ 6–10

Neomarica caerulea
Summer-flowering rhizome with sword-shaped, semi-erect leaves in basal fans. Stems each bear a leaflike bract and a succession of irislike, blue flowers, with white, yellow, and brown central marks. H to 3ft (1m), S 3–5ft (1–1.5m). Min. 50°F (10°C).

☼ ◊ 10

Aristea major, syn. *A. thyrsiflora*
Robust, evergreen, clump-forming rhizome with sword-shaped, erect leaves, to 1in (2.5cm) across, and dense spikes of purple-blue flowers on short stalks in summer. H to 3ft (1m), S 1½–2ft (45–60cm).

☼ ◊ ❄ 9–10

Arisaema consanguineum
Summer-flowering tuber with robust, spotted stems and erect, umbrellalike leaves with narrow leaflets. Produces purplish white- or white-striped, green spathes, 6–8in (15–20cm) long, and bright red berries. H to 3ft (1m), S 1–1½ft (30–45cm).

◐ ◊ ❄❄ 8–9

Galtonia viridiflora
Clump-forming, summer-flowering bulb with widely strap-shaped, fleshy, semi-erect, basal, gray-green leaves. Leafless stem bears a spike of up to 30 pendent, short-tubed, funnel-shaped, pale green flowers. H 3–4ft (1–1.2m), S 7–9in (18–23cm).

☼ ◊ ❄❄ 7–9

Dietes bicolor
Evergreen, tuft-forming, summer-flowering rhizome with tough, long and narrow, erect, basal leaves. Branching stems each bear a succession of flattish, irislike, pale to mid-yellow flowers; each large petal has a brown patch. H to 3ft (1m), S 1–2ft (30–60cm).

☼ ◊ ❄ 9–10

Lilies

Lilies are graceful plants and bring elegance to the summer border. Their attractive, flamboyant flowers come in various shapes, some nodding, some upright, others in the distinctive turkscap form (with recurving petals), and are borne usually several per stem. Most widely grown are the numerous hybrids, available in a dazzling range of colors, but among the species are many that have been undeservedly neglected.

L. rubellum

L. 'Karen North'

L. Golden Clarion Hybrids

L. 'Apollo'

L. candidum

L. auratum var. *platyphyllum*

L. mackliniae

L. chalcedonicum

L. 'Destiny'

L. lancifolium var. *splendens*

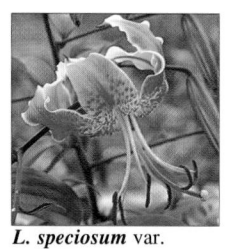
L. 'Sterling Star'

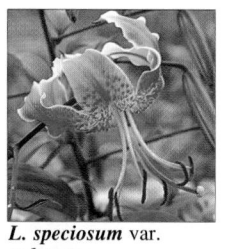
L. speciosum var. *rubrum*

L. pardalinum

L. 'Amber Gold'

L. 'Brushmarks'

L. longiflorum

L. 'Bright Star'

L. 'Connecticut King'

L. 'Enchantment'

L. regale

L. Imperial Gold Group

L. 'Journey's End'

L. hansonii

L. 'Harmony'

L. Olympic Hybrids

L. 'Corsage'

L. 'Black Beauty'

L. nepalense

L. bulbiferum var. *croceum*

L. 'Black Magic'

L. martagon

L. 'Lady Bowes Lyon'

L. monadelphum

☐ YELLOW

Crocosmia 'Citronella'
Clump-forming, late summer-
flowering corm with sword-shaped,
erect, basal, gray-green leaves.
Flowers are funnel-shaped and clear
golden yellow. H 24–30in (60–75cm),
S 6–8in (15–20cm).

☼ ◊ ❄❄ 6–9

Moraea huttonii
Summer-flowering corm with long,
narrow, semi-erect, basal leaves.
Tough stem bears a succession of
irislike, yellow flowers, 2–3in (5–7cm)
across, with brown marks near the
center. H 2½–3ft (75cm–1m),
S 6–10in (15–25cm).

☼ ◊ ❄❄ 9–10

Zantedeschia elliottiana
(Golden calla)
Summer-flowering tuber with heart-
shaped, semi-erect, basal leaves with
transparent marks. Bears a 6in (15cm)
long, yellow spathe surrounding a
yellow spadix. H 2–3ft (60cm–1m),
S 1½–2ft (45–60cm). Min. 50°F (10°C).

☼ ◊ 10

☐ ORANGE

Alstroemeria aurea, syn.
A. aurantiaca (Peruvian lily)
Summer-flowering, tuberous perennial
with narrow, lance-shaped, twisted
leaves and loose heads of orange
flowers, tipped with green and
streaked dark red. H to 3ft (1m),
S 2–3ft (60cm–1m).

☼ ◊ ❄❄ 6–10

Littonia modesta
Deciduous, summer-flowering,
tuberous, scandent climber with slender
stems bearing lance-shaped leaves with
tendrils at apex. Leaf axils bear pendent,
bell-shaped, orange flowers, 1½–2in
(4–5cm) across. H 3–6ft (1–2m), S
4–6in (10–15cm). Min. 61°F (16°C).

☼ ◊ 10

Canna iridiflora
Very robust, spring- or summer-
flowering, rhizomatous perennial with
broad, oblong leaves and spikes of
pendent, long-tubed, reddish pink or
orange flowers, each 4–6in (10–15cm)
long, with reflexed petals. H 10ft (3m),
S 1½–2ft (45–60cm). Min. 59°F (15°C).

☼ ◊ 8–10

Dahlias

The variety of border hybrids now available offers a dazzling display of color and form to every gardener, and no special skills are required to cultivate or propagate them. In color the flowers range from vibrant pinks and crimsons, through rich hues of mauves and purples, to the pastel shades of lilacs, pinks, and creams, and in size from the tiny pompons to huge exhibition blooms up to 1ft (30cm) or more across.

Dahlias are excellent for providing cut flowers and will bloom vigorously throughout summer until the first frosts—under the right conditions a single plant may produce up to 100 blooms. Their various flower types (shown below) form the basis of the recognized groups.

Single—each flower usually has 8–10 broad petals surrounding an open, central disc.

Anemone—fully double flowers each have one or more rings of flattened ray petals surrounding a dense group of shorter, tubular petals, usually longer than disc petals found in single dahlias.

Collerette—single flowers each have broad, outer petals, usually 8–10, and an inner "collar" of smaller petals surrounding an open, central disc.

Water-lily—fully double flowers have large, generally sparse ray petals, which are flat or with slightly incurved or recurved margins, giving the flower a flat appearance.

Decorative—fully double flowers have broad, flat petals that incurve slightly at their margins and usually reflex to the stem.

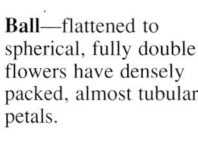

Ball—flattened to spherical, fully double flowers have densely packed, almost tubular petals.

Pompon—flattened to spherical, fully double flowers that are no more than 2in (5cm) across— a miniature form of ball flowers.

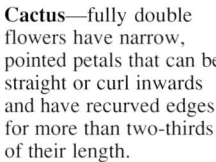

Cactus—fully double flowers have narrow, pointed petals that can be straight or curl inwards and have recurved edges for more than two-thirds of their length.

Semi-cactus—fully double flowers are similar to cactus flowers but have broader-based petals, the edges of which are generally recurved towards their tips.

Miscellaneous—flowers are in a wide range of unclassified types, including orchidlike (shown right), single, and double forms.

D. **'Majestic Kerkrade'** (cactus)

D. **'Pink Symbol'** (semi-cactus)

D. **'Rhonda'** (pompon)

D. **'Candy Keene'** (semi-cactus)

D. **'Athalie'** (cactus)

D. **'Vicky Crutchfield'** (water-lily)

D. **'Gilt Edge'** (decorative)

D. **'Angora'** (decorative)

D. **'Nina Chester'** (decorative)

D. **'Easter Sunday'** (collerette)

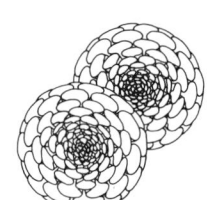

D. **'White Klankstad'** (cactus)

D. **'Small World'** (pompon)

D. **'Monk Marc'** (cactus)

D. **'Noreen'** (pompon)

D. **'Gay Princess'** (decorative)

D. **'By the Cringe'** (cactus)

D. 'Wootton Cupid' (ball)

D. 'Flutterby' (decorative)

D. 'Butterball' (decorative)

D. 'Shandy' (cactus)

D. 'Chinese Lantern' (decorative)

D. 'Chimborazo' (collerette)

D. 'Early Bird' (decorative)

D. 'Pontiac' (cactus)

D. 'Comet' (anemone)

D. 'Bassingbourne Beauty' (decorative)

D. 'Cortez Sovereign' (semi-cactus)

D. 'Corton Olympic' (decorative)

D. 'Fascination' (miscellaneous)

D. 'Brunton' (decorative)

D. 'Hamari Katrina' (semi-cactus)

D. 'Davenport Sunlight' (semi-cactus)

D. 'Frank Hornsey' (decorative)

D. 'Biddenham Sunset' (decorative)

D. 'Jocondo' (decorative)

D. 'Bishop of Llandaff' (miscellaneous)

D. 'East Anglian' (decorative)

D. 'Paul Chester' (cactus)

D. 'Quel Diable' (semi-cactus)

D. 'Betty Bowen' (decorative)

D. 'Corona' (semi-cactus)

D. 'Gay Mini' (decorative)

D. 'Whale's Rhonda' (pompon)

D. 'Scarlet Beauty' (water-lily)

D. 'Yellow Hammer' (single)

D. 'Clair de Lune' (collerette)

D. 'So Dainty' (semi-cactus)

D. 'Highgate Torch' (semi-cactus)

341

Bulbs/large AUTUMN INTEREST

Amaryllis belladonna 'Hathor'
Autumn-flowering bulb with a stout, purple stem bearing fragrant, pure white flowers, 4in (10cm) long, with yellow throats. Strap-shaped, semi-erect, basal leaves appear in late winter or spring. H 20–32in (50–80cm), S 12–18in (30–45cm).

☼ ◊ ❄❄ 7–10

x Amarcrinum memoria-corsii,
syn. x *A. howardii*, x *Crinodonna corsii*
Evergreen, clump-forming bulb with wide, semi-erect, basal leaves. Stout stems carry fragrant rose-pink flowers in loose heads in late summer and autumn. H and S to 3ft (1m).

☼ ◊ ❄❄ 8–10

Amaryllis belladonna
(Belladonna lily, Naked lady)
Autumn-flowering bulb with a stout, purple stem bearing fragrant, funnel-shaped, pink flowers, 4in (10cm) long. Forms strap-shaped, semi-erect, basal leaves after flowering. H 20–32in (50–80cm), S 12–18in (30–45cm).

☼ ◊ ❄❄ 7–10

x Amarygia parkeri,
syn. x *Brunsdonna parkeri*
Early autumn-flowering bulb. Stout stem carries a large head of funnel-shaped, deep rose flowers with yellow and white throats. Produces strap-shaped, semi-erect, basal leaves after flowering. H to 3ft (1m), S 2–3ft (60cm–1m).

☼ ◊ ❄❄ 9–10

Gladiolus papilio,
syn. *G. purpureo-auratus*
Clump-forming, summer- or autumn-flowering corm with stolons. Bears up to 10 yellow or white flowers, suffused violet, with hooded, upper petals and darker yellow patches on lower petals. H to 3ft (1m), S 6in (15cm).

☼ ◊ ❄❄ 9–10

Bulbs/medium SPRING INTEREST

Allium neapolitanum, syn. *A. cowanii* (Daffodil garlic, Naples onion)
Spring-flowering bulb with narrow, semi-erect leaves on the lower quarter of flower stems. Stems each develop an umbel, 2–4in (5–10cm) across, of up to 40 white flowers. H 8–20in (20–50cm), S 4–5in (10–12cm).

☼ ◊ ❄❄ 6–10

Calochortus venustus
Late spring-flowering bulb with 1 or 2 narrow, erect leaves near the base of the branched stem. Bears 1–4 white, yellow, purple, or red flowers, with a dark red, yellow-margined blotch on each large petal. H 8–24in (20–60cm), S 2–4in (5–10cm).

☼ ◊ ❄❄ 6–10

Calochortus albus
(Fairy lantern, White globe lily)
Spring-flowering bulb with long, narrow, erect, gray-green leaves near the base of the loosely branched stem. Each branch carries a pendent, globose, white or pink flower. H 8–20in (20–50cm), S 2–4in (5–10cm).

☼ ◊ ❄❄ 4–10

Erythronium oregonum
Clump-forming, spring-flowering tuber with 2 semi-erect, mottled, basal leaves. Has up to 3 pendent, white flowers, with yellow eyes and often brown rings near center; petals reflex as flowers open. Increases rapidly by offsets. H to 14in (35cm), S 5in (12cm).

◐ ◊ ❄❄ 3–9

Pamianthe peruviana
Evergreen, spring-flowering bulb with a stemlike neck and strap-shaped, semi-erect leaves with drooping tips. Stem has a head of 2–4 fragrant white flowers, each with a bell-shaped cup and 6 spreading petals. H 20in (50cm), S 18–24in (45–60cm). Min. 54°F (12°C).

◐ ◊ 10

Erythronium 'White Beauty'
Vigorous, clump-forming tuber with 2 semi-erect, basal, mottled leaves. In spring has a loose spike of 1–10 pendent, reflexed, white flowers, each with a brown ring near the center. Increases rapidly by offsets. H 8–12in (20–30cm), S 4–5in (10–12cm).

◐ ◊ ❄❄❄ 3–9

Erythronium hendersonii
Spring-flowering tuber with 2 semi-erect, basal, brown- and green-mottled leaves. Flower stem carries up to 10 lavender or lavender pink flowers, with reflexed petals and deep purple, central eyes. H 8–12in (20–30cm), S 4–5in (10–12cm).

☼ ◊ ❄❄ 3–9

Sprekelia formosissima
(Aztec-lily, Jacobean-lily)
Clump-forming, spring-flowering bulb with strap-shaped, semi-erect, basal leaves. Stem bears a deep red flower, 5in (12cm) wide, that has 6 narrow petals with green-striped bases. H 6–14in (15–35cm), S 5–6in (12–15cm).

☼ ◊ ❄ 8–10

Sauromatum venosum,
syn. *S. guttatum* (Voodoo lily)
Early spring-flowering tuber. Bears a large, acrid, purple-spotted spathe, then a lobed leaf on a long, spotted stalk. H 12–18in (30–45cm), S 12–14in (30–35cm). Min. 41-5°F (5–7°C).

◐ ◊ 10

Fritillaria meleagris (Checkered lily, Snake's-head fritillary)
Spring-flowering bulb with slender stems producing scattered, narrow, gray-green leaves. Has solitary bell-shaped, prominently checkered flowers, in shades of pinkish purple or white. H to 12in (30cm), S 2–3in (5–8cm).

☼ ◊ ❄❄❄ 3–8

Fritillaria camschatcensis
(Black lily)
Spring-flowering bulb. Stout stems carry lance-shaped, glossy leaves, mostly in whorls. Bears up to 8 bell-shaped, deep blackish purple or brown flowers. Needs humus-rich soil. H 6–24in (15–60cm), S 3–4in (8–10cm).

◐ ◊ ❄❄❄ 3–8

Allium unifolium
Late spring-flowering bulb with one semi-erect, basal, gray-green leaf. Each flower stem carries a domed umbel, 2in (5cm) across, of up to 30 purplish pink flowers. H to 12in (30cm), S 3–4in (8–10cm).

☼ ◊ ❄❄ 4–10

Anemone pavonina
Leafy tuber with cup-shaped, single, dark-centered, scarlet, purple, or blue flowers rising above divided, frilly leaves in early spring. H 16in (40cm), S 8in (20cm).

☼ ◊ ❄❄ 8–10

Fritillaria pyrenaica
Spring-flowering bulb with scattered, lance-shaped leaves, often rather narrow. Develops 1, or rarely 2, broadly bell-shaped flowers with flared-tipped, checkered, deep brownish or blackish purple petals. H 6–12in (15–30cm), S 2–3in (5–8cm).

☼ ◊ ❄❄❄ 6–8

Tulips

Tulips suit a wide range of planting schemes and are excellent in the rock garden, in formal bedding, as elegant cut flowers, and for pots. Their bold flowers are generally simple in outline and held upright, with colors that are often bright and strong. Many of the species deserve to be more widely grown, alongside the large variety of hybrids now available. *Tulipa* is classified in 12 divisions, described below.

Div.1 Single early—cup-shaped, single flowers, often opening wide in the sun, are borne from early to mid-spring.

Div.2 Double early—long-lasting, double flowers open wide in early and mid-spring.

Div.3 Triumph—sturdy stems bear rather conical, single flowers, becoming more rounded, in mid- and late spring.

Div.4 Darwin hybrids—large, single flowers are borne on strong stems from mid- to late spring.

Div.5 Single late—single flowers, variable but usually with pointed petals, are borne in late spring and very early summer.

Div.6 Lily-flowered—strong stems bear narrow-waisted, single flowers, with long, pointed, often reflexed petals, in late spring.

Div.7 Fringed—flowers are similar to those in Div.6, but have fringed petals.

Div.8 Viridiflora—variable, single flowers, with partly greenish petals, are borne in late spring.

Div.9 Rembrandt—flowers are similar to those in Div.6, but have striped or feathered patterns caused by virus, and appear in late spring.

Div.10 Parrot—has large, variable, single flowers, with frilled or fringed and usually twisted petals, in late spring.

Div.11 Double late (peony-flowered)—usually bowl-shaped, double flowers appear in late spring.

Div.12 Kaufmanniana hybrids—single flowers are usually bicolored, open flat in the sun, and appear in early spring. Leaves are usually mottled or striped.

Div.13 Fosteriana hybrids—large, single flowers open wide in the sun from early to mid-spring. Leaves are often mottled or striped.

Div.14 Greigii hybrids—large, single flowers appear in mid- and late spring. Mottled or striped leaves are often wavy-edged.

Div.15 Miscellaneous—a diverse category of other species and their cultivars and hybrids. Flowers appear in spring and early summer.

T. **'Diana'** (Div.1)

T. **'Peach Blossom'** (Div.2)

T. **'Purissima'** (Div.13)

T. **'Clara Butt'** (Div.5)

T. **'China Pink'** (Div.6)

T. **'Spring Green'** (Div.8)

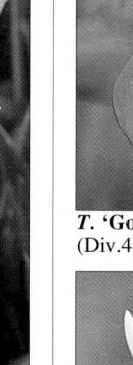

T. **'Gordon Cooper'** (Div.4)

T. **'Red Parrot'** (Div.10)

T. clusiana (Div.15)

T. **'Mme. Lefèbre'** (Div.13)

T. saxatilis (Div.15)

T. **'Palestrina'** (Div.5)

T. **'Estella Rijnveld'** (Div.10)

T. sprengeri (Div.15)

T. **'White Triumphator'** (Div.6)

T. **'White Dream'** (Div.3)

T. biflora (Div.15)

T. turkestanica (Div.15)

T. **'Angélique'** (Div.11)

T. **'Union Jack'** (Div.5)

T. **'Garden Party'** (Div.3)

T. linifolia (Div.15)

T. hageri (Div.15)

T. 'Oranje Nassau' (Div.2)

T. 'Glück' (Div.12)

T. 'Blue Parrot' (Div.10)

T. 'Maja' (Div.7)

T. 'Dreamboat' (Div.14)

T. 'Balalaika' (Div.5)

T. marjolettii (Div.15)

T. 'Queen of Night' (Div.5)

T. 'Bellona' (Div.1)

T. undulatifolia (Div.15)

T. 'Dreaming Maid' (Div.3)

T. batalinii (Div.15)

T. 'West Point' (Div.6)

T. 'Artist' (Div.8)

T. 'Shakespeare' (Div.12)

T. 'Plaisir' (Div.14)

T. sylvestris (Div.15)

T. 'Dillenburg' (Div.5)

T. orphanidea (Div.15)

T. 'Margot Fonteyn' (Div.3)

T. 'Greuze' (Div.5)

T. urumiensis (Div.15)

T. 'Prinses Irene' (Div.1)

T. praestans 'Van Tubergen's Variety' (Div.15)

T. 'Keizerskroon' (Div.1)

T. violacea (Div.15)

T. kaufmanniana (Div.15)

T. clusiana var. *chrysantha* (Div.15)

T. acuminata (Div.15)

T. humilis (Div.15)

T. tarda (Div.15)

T. 'Cape Cod' (Div.14)

T. whittallii (Div.15)

■ BLUE

Muscari latifolium
Spring-flowering bulb with one strap-shaped, semi-erect, basal, gray-green leaf. Has a dense spike of tiny, bell-shaped, blackish violet to blue flowers with constricted mouths; upper ones are paler and smaller. H to 10in (25cm), S 2–3in (5–8cm).

☼ ◊ ❄❄ 2–10

Leucocoryne ixioides
(Glory-of-the-sun)
Spring-flowering bulb with long, narrow, semi-erect, basal leaves that are withered by flowering time. Wiry, slender flower stem has a loose head of up to 10 soft blue flowers. H 12–16in (30–40cm), S 3–4in (8–10cm).

☼ ◊ ❄ 9–10

Hyacinthoides hispanica,
syn. *Scilla campanulata*,
S. hispanica (Spanish bluebell)
Clump-forming, spring-flowering bulb with strap-shaped, glossy leaves and a loose spike of pendent, bell-shaped, blue, white, or pink flowers. H to 12in (30cm), S 4–6in (10–15cm).

◐ ◊ ❄❄❄ 4–9

■■ BLUE–GREEN

Ixiolirion tataricum,
syn. *I. montanum* (Siberian lily)
Spring- to early summer-flowering bulb with long, narrow, semi-erect leaves on the lower part of stem. Has a loose cluster of blue flowers with a darker, central line along each petal. H to 16in (40cm), S 3–4in (8–10cm).

☼ ◊ ❄❄❄ 7–10

Hyacinthoides non-scriptus,
syn. *Scilla non-scripta* (Wild hyacinth)
Tuft-forming, spring-flowering bulb with strap-shaped leaves. An erect stem, arching at the apex, bears fragrant blue, pink, or white flowers. H 8–16in (20–40cm), S 3–4in (8–10cm).

☼ ◐ ❄❄❄ 6–9

Hermodactylus tuberosus, syn.
Iris tuberosa (Snake's-head iris)
Spring-flowering perennial with finger-like tubers. Very long, narrow, gray-green leaves are square in cross-section. Has a fragrant, yellowish green flower with large, blackish brown-tipped petals. H 8–16in (20–40cm), S 2–3in (5–8cm).

☼ ◊ ❄❄❄ 7–9

Fritillaria pontica
Spring-flowering bulb with stems carrying lance-shaped, gray-green leaves, the topmost in a whorl of 3. Has solitary broadly bell-shaped, green flowers, 1¼–1¾in (3–4.5cm) long, often suffused brown. H 6–18in (15–45cm), S 2–3in (5–8cm).

◐ ◊ ❄❄❄ 7–8

Ixia viridiflora
Spring- to early summer-flowering corm with very narrow, erect leaves mostly at stem base. Carries a spike of flattish, jade green flowers, 1–2in (2.5–5cm) across, with purple-black eyes. H 12–24in (30–60cm), S 1–2in (2.5–5cm).

☼ ◊ ❄ 9–10

Fritillaria cirrhosa
Spring-flowering bulb with slender stems and narrow, whorled leaves; upper leaves have tendril-like tips. Produces up to 4 widely bell-shaped flowers, purple or yellowish green with dark purple checkered patterns. H to 24in (60cm), S 2–3in (5–8cm).

☼ ◊ ❄❄❄ 6–8

Fritillaria pallidiflora
Robust, spring-flowering bulb with
broadly lance-shaped, gray-green
leaves, scattered or in pairs on stem.
Has 1–5 widely bell-shaped, yellow
to greenish yellow flowers, usually
faintly checkered brownish red within.
H 6–28in (15–70cm), S 3–4in (8–10cm).

☼ ◊ ❉❉❉ 5–8

Arum creticum
Spring-flowering tuber that bears white
or yellow spathes, each bottle-shaped at
the base, slightly reflexed at the apex
and with a protruding, yellow spadix.
Has arrow-shaped, semi-erect, deep
green leaves in autumn. H 12–20in
(30–50cm), S 6–12in (20–30cm).

☼ ◊ ❉❉ 8–10

Ferraria crispa, syn. *F. undulata*
Spring-flowering corm with leafy stem
bearing a succession of upward-facing,
brown or yellowish brown flowers,
1¹/₂–2in (4–5cm) across, with 6 wavy-
edged, spreading petals that are
conspicuously lined and blotched.
H 8–16in (20–40cm), S 3–4in (8–10cm).

☼ ◊ ❉ 9–10

Gladiolus 'Christabel'
Spring-flowering corm with a wiry
stem producing a loose spike of
fragrant, widely funnel-shaped,
primrose yellow flowers, 2¹/₂–3in
(6–8cm) across, with purple-brown-
veined, upper petals. H to 18in (45cm),
S 3–4in (8–10cm).

☼ ◊ ❉ 8–10

Erythronium 'Pagoda'
Robust, spring-flowering tuber with
2 semi-erect, basal, faintly mottled,
glossy leaves. Flower stem produces
up to 10 pendent, pale yellow flowers
with reflexed petals. H 10–14in
(25–35cm), S 6–8in (15–20cm).

☼ ◊ ❉❉❉ 4–9

Calochortus luteus
(Yellow mariposa)
Late spring-flowering bulb with long,
narrow, erect leaves near the base of the
loosely branched stem. Each branch
bears a 3-petaled, yellow flower with
central, brown blotches. H 8–18in
(20–45cm), S 2–4in (5–10cm).

☼ ◊ ❉❉ 5–10

Daffodils

The charm and beauty of the daffodil (botanically known as *Narcissus*) grace the garden early in the year. The diversity of its flowers provides infinite variation, from the tiny Cyclamineus daffodil, with its swept back petals, to the stately trumpet daffodil. Many may be naturalized, forming a golden carpet in grass or a wild garden, but dwarf forms are best in rock gardens, brightening the landscape before most other plants emerge.

The genus is classified in 12 divisions. Their flower forms are illustrated below, with the exception of Div.10, the wild species, and Div.12, the miscellaneous category. Both have varying flowers, including hoop-petticoat forms, produced between autumn and early summer.

Div.1 Trumpet— usually solitary flowers, each has a trumpet that is as long as, or longer, than the petals. Early to late spring-flowering.

Div.2 Large-cupped— solitary flowers, each has a cup at least one-third the length of, but shorter than, the petals. Spring-flowering.

Div.3 Small-cupped— flowers are often borne singly; each has a cup not more than one-third the length of the petals. Spring- or early summer-flowering.

Div.4 Double— most have solitary large, fully, or semi-double flowers with the cup and petals, or just the cup, replaced by petaloid structures. Some have smaller flowers in clusters of 4 or more. Spring- or early summer-flowering.

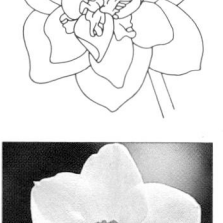

Div.5 Triandrus— nodding flowers, with short, sometimes straight-sided cups and narrow, reflexed petals, are borne 2–6 per stem. Spring-flowering.

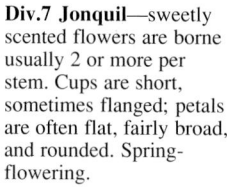

Div.6 Cyclamineus— flowers are borne usually 1 or 2 per stem with cups that are sometimes flanged and often longer than those of Div.5. Petals are narrow, pointed, and reflexed. Early to mid-spring flowering.

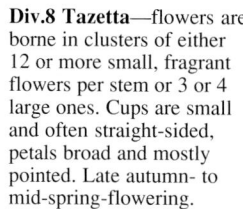

Div.7 Jonquil— sweetly scented flowers are borne usually 2 or more per stem. Cups are short, sometimes flanged; petals are often flat, fairly broad, and rounded. Spring-flowering.

Div.8 Tazetta— flowers are borne in clusters of either 12 or more small, fragrant flowers per stem or 3 or 4 large ones. Cups are small and often straight-sided, petals broad and mostly pointed. Late autumn- to mid-spring-flowering.

Div.9 Poeticus— flowers each have a small, colored cup and glistening white petals. They are borne usually 1 but sometimes 2 per stem and may be sweetly fragrant. Late spring- or early summer-flowering.

Div.11 Split-cupped— usually solitary flowers have cups that are typically split for more than half of their length. Cup segments lie back on the petals and may be ruffled. Spring-flowering.

N. 'Passionale' (Div.2)

N. 'Dove Wings' (Div.6)

N. 'Trousseau' (Div.1)

N. 'February Silver' (Div.6)

N. 'Portrush' (Div.3)

N. 'Jack Snipe' (Div.6)

N. 'Thalia' (Div.5)

N. watieri (Div.10)

N. 'Merlin' (Div.3)

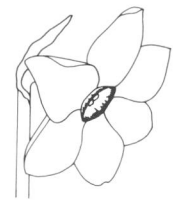

N. 'Kilworth' (Div.2)

N. 'Satin Pink' (Div.2)

N. 'Ice Follies' (Div.3)

N. canaliculatus (Div.8)

N. 'Actaea' (Div.9)

N. 'Pride of Cornwall' (Div.8)

N. 'Bridal Crown' (Div.4)

N. 'Irene Copeland' (Div.4)

N. 'Cheerfulness' (Div.4)

N. 'Little Beauty' (Div.1)

N. romieuxii (Div.10)

N. 'Charity May' (Div.6)

N. minor (Div.10)

N. bulbocodium subsp. *bulbocodium* (Div.10)

N. jonquilla (Div.10)

N. 'Pencrebar' (Div.4)

N. 'St. Keverne' (Div.2)

N. 'Ambergate' (Div.2)

N. triandrus (Div.10)

N. 'Binkie' (Div.2)

N. 'Fortune' (Div.2)

N. 'Tête-à-Tête' (Div.6)

N. 'Tahiti' (Div.4)

N. 'Lemon Glow' (Div.1)

N. 'Liberty Bells' (Div.5)

N. x *odorus* 'Rugulosus' (Div.10)

N. 'Jumblie' (Div.6)

N. 'Cassata' (Div.11)

N. 'Hawera' (Div.5)

N. 'Rip van Winkle' (Div.4)

N. 'Sweetness' (Div.7)

N. 'Golden Ducat' (Div.4)

N. 'Suzy' (Div.7)

N. rupicola (Div.10)

N. 'Bob Minor' (Div.1)

N. 'Bartley' (Div.6)

N. 'Sealing Wax' (Div.2)

N. 'Spellbinder' (Div.1)

N. cyclamineus (Div.10)

N. 'February Gold' (Div.6)

N. 'Kingscourt' (Div.1)

N. 'Home Fires' (Div.2)

349

Bulbs/medium SPRING INTEREST

■ ORANGE

Stenomesson variegatum,
syn. *S. coccineum*, *S. incarnatum*,
S. viridiflorum
Clump-forming bulb. Bears reddish
yellow, pink, or white flowers, with 6
green lobes at the apex, in winter or
spring. H 12–24in (30–60cm), S 12in
(30cm). Min. 50°F (10°C).

☼ ◊ 10

Urceolina peruviana
Late spring-flowering bulb with strap-
shaped, semi-erect, basal leaves. Flower
stem bears a head of pendent, urn-
shaped, red or orange flowers, ¾–1½in
(2–4cm) long, with protruding, yellow
anthers. H 8–12in (20–30cm), S 4–6in
(10–15cm). Min. 41°F (5°C).

☼ ◊ 10

Clivia miniata (Kaffir lily)
Evergreen, tuft-forming rhizome with
strap-shaped, semi-erect, basal, dark
green leaves, 16–24in (40–60cm) long.
Stems each produce a head of 10–20
orange or red flowers in spring or
summer. H 16in (40cm), S 12–24in
(30–60cm). Min. 50°F (10°C).

☼ ◊ 10

Bulbs/medium SUMMER INTEREST

□ WHITE

Crinum asiaticum
Clump-forming bulb with strap-shaped,
semi-erect, basal, dark green leaves,
3ft (1m) long. Leafless flower stems
produce heads of long-tubed, white
flowers, with narrow petals, in spring
or summer. H 1½–2ft (45–60cm),
S 2–3ft (60cm–1m). Min. 61°F (16°C).

☼ ◊ 10

Ornithogalum narbonense
Clump-forming, late spring- to
summer-flowering bulb with long,
narrow, semi-erect, basal, gray-green
leaves. Leafless stem produces a spike
of star-shaped, white flowers, ¾in
(2cm) wide. H 12–16in (30–40cm),
S 4–6in (10–15cm).

☼ ◊ ❀❀ 7–10

Pancratium illyricum
Summer-flowering bulb with strap-
shaped, semi-erect, basal, grayish green
leaves. Leafless stem has a head of
5–12 fragrant, 6-petaled, white flowers,
3in (8cm) across. H to 18in (45cm),
S 10–12in (25–30cm).

☼ ◊ ❀❀ 8–10

Triteleia hyacinthina,
syn. *Brodiaea hyacinthina*
Late spring- to early summer-flowering
corm with long, narrow, semi-erect or
spreading, basal leaves. Heads of white,
sometimes purple-tinged flowers are
borne on wiry stems. H 12–20in
(30–50cm), S 3–4in (8–10cm).

☼ ◊ ❀❀ 6–10

Arisaema sikokianum
Early summer-flowering tuber with
erect leaves divided into 3–5 leaflets.
Produces deep brownish purple and
white spathes, 6in (15cm) long, with
clublike, white spadices protruding
from the mouths. H 12–20in
(30–50cm), S 12–18in (30–45cm).

☼ ◊ ❀❀ 5–9

Ornithogalum thyrsoides (African wonder flower, Chincherinchee)
Summer-flowering bulb with strap-shaped, semi-erect, basal leaves. Bears a dense, conical spike of cup-shaped, white flowers, 3/4–1 1/4in (2–3cm) across. H 12–18in (30–45cm), S 4–6in (10–15cm).

☼ ◊ ❄ 7–10

Ornithogalum arabicum
Early summer-flowering bulb with strap-shaped, semi-erect leaves in a basal cluster. Has a flattish head of up to 15 scented, white or creamy white flowers, 1 1/2–2in (4–5cm) across, with black ovaries in centers. H 12–18in (30–45cm), S 4–6in (10–15cm).

☼ ◊ ❄ 7–10

Tritonia rubrolucens,
syn. *T. rosea, Crocosmia rosea*
Late summer-flowering corm with narrowly sword-shaped, erect leaves in a flattish, basal fan. Has 5–10 funnel-shaped, pink flowers in a loose, one-sided spike. H 12–20in (30–50cm), S 3–4in (8–10cm).

☼ ◊ ❄❄ 7–10

Lycoris radiata (Spider lily)
Late summer-flowering bulb with a head of 5 or 6 bright rose-red flowers with narrow, wavy-margined, reflexed petals and conspicuous anthers. Has strap-shaped, semi-erect, basal leaves after flowering time. H 12–16in (30–40cm), S 4–6in (10–15cm).

☼ ◊ ❄❄ 8–10

Zigadenus fremontii
Clump-forming, early summer-flowering bulb with long, strap-shaped, semi-erect, basal leaves. Stem produces a spike of star-shaped, pale creamy green flowers with darker green nectaries on petal bases. H 12–20in (30–50cm), S 4–6in (10–15cm).

☼ ◊ ❄❄ 8–9

Allium cernuum (Allegheny onion)
Clump-forming, summer-flowering bulb with narrow, semi-erect, basal leaves. Each stem produces up to 30 cup-shaped, pink or white flowers in a loose, nodding umbel, 3/4–1 1/2in (2–4cm) across. H 12–28in (30–70cm), S 3–5in (8–12cm).

☼ ◊ ❄❄❄ 4–10

Hymenocallis narcissiflora,
syn. *Ismene calathina*
(Basket flower, Peruvian daffodil)
Spring- or summer-flowering bulb with semi-erect, basal leaves, dying down in winter. Bears a loose head of 2–5 fragrant white flowers. H to 24in (60cm), S 12–18in (30–45cm).

☼ ◊ ❄ 8–10

Alstroemeria pelegrina,
syn. *A. gayana*
Summer-flowering tuber with narrow, lance-shaped leaves. Each leafy stem has 1–3 white flowers, stained pinkish mauve and spotted yellow and brownish purple. H 1–2ft (30–60cm), S 2–3ft (60cm–1m).

☼ ◊ ❄❄ 8–10

Hippeastrum advenum
Clump-forming, spring- to summer-flowering bulb with narrowly strap-shaped, semi-erect, basal, gray-green leaves. Leafless stem carries a head of 2–8 narrowly funnel-shaped, red flowers, 2in (5cm) long. H to 16in (40cm), S 6–8in (15–20cm).

☼ ◊ ❄❄ 9–10

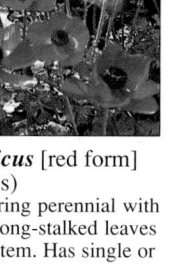

Ranunculus asiaticus [red form]
(Persian ranunculus)
Early summer-flowering perennial with
clawlike tubers and long-stalked leaves
both at base and on stem. Has single or
double flowers in red, white, pink,
yellow, or orange. H 18–22in
(45–55cm), S 4in (10cm).

☼ ◊ ✳ 8–10

Allium schubertii
Early summer-flowering bulb with
widely strap-shaped, semi-erect, basal
leaves. Bears large umbels of 40 or
more star-shaped, pink or purple flowers
on very unequal stalks, followed by
brown seed capsules. H 12–24in
(30–60cm), S 6–8in (15–20cm).

☼ ◊ ✳✳ 4–10

Patersonia umbrosa
Evergreen, clump-forming, spring- and
early summer-flowering rhizome with
erect, basal leaves. Tough flower stems
each carry a succession of irislike,
purple-blue flowers, 1¼–1½in (3–4cm)
across. H 12–18in (30–45cm),
S 12–24in (30–60cm).

☼ ◊ ✳ 9–10

Allium caeruleum, syn. *A. azureum*
(Blue garlic)
Summer-flowering bulb with narrow,
erect leaves on the lower third of slender
flower stems, which bear 30–50 star-
shaped, blue flowers in a dense umbel,
1¼–1½in (3–4cm) across. H 8–32in
(20–80cm), S 4–6in (10–15cm).

☼ ◊ ✳✳ 4–10

Allium christophii, syn.
A. albopilosum (Giant allium)
Summer-flowering bulb with semi-
erect, hairy, gray leaves that droop at
tips. Has a large, spherical umbel of
50 or more star-shaped, purplish violet
flowers, which dry well. H 6–16in
(15–40cm), S 6–8in (15–20cm).

☼ ◊ ✳✳ 4–10

Gloxinia perennis
Late summer- to autumn-flowering
rhizome with heart-shaped, toothed,
hairy leaves on spotted stems. Has bell-
shaped, lavender blue flowers, with
rounded lobes and purple-blotched
throats. H to 24in (60cm), S 12–14in
(30–35cm). Min. 50°F (10°C).

☼ ◊ 10

Triteleia laxa, syn. *Brodiaea laxa*
Early summer-flowering corm with
narrow, semi-erect, basal leaves. Stem
carries a large, loose umbel of funnel-
shaped, deep to pale purple-blue
flowers, ¾–2in (2–5cm) long, mostly
held upright. H 4–20in (10–50cm),
S 3–4in (8–10cm).

☼ ◊ ✳✳ 6–10

Arisaema griffithii
Summer-flowering tuber with large,
erect leaves above a green or purple
spathe, 8–10in (20–25cm) long,
strongly netted with paler veins and
expanded like a cobra's hood. Protect in
winter or lift for frost-free storage. H to
24in (60cm), S 18–24in (45–60cm).

☼ ◊ ✳ 7–9

Arisaema triphyllum, syn.
A. atrorubens (Jack-in-the-pulpit)
Summer-flowering tuber with 3-lobed,
erect leaves. Produces green or purple
spathes, hooded at tips, followed by
bright red berries. H 16–20in
(40–50cm), S 12–18in (30–45cm).

☼ ◊ ✳✳✳ 4–9

Arisaema jacquemontii
Summer-flowering tuber with 1 or 2 erect leaves, divided into wavy-edged leaflets. Produces slender, white-lined, green spathes that are hooded at tips and drawn out into long points. H 12–20in (30–50cm), S 12–15in (30–38cm).

☼ ◊ ❄ 7–9

Eucomis bicolor
Summer-flowering bulb with wavy-margined, semi-erect, basal leaves. Stem, often spotted purple, bears a spike of green or greenish white flowers, with 6 purple-edged petals, topped by a cluster of leaflike bracts. H 12–20in (30–50cm), S 12–24in (30–60cm).

☼ ◊ ❄❄ 8–10

Cyrtanthus mackenii var. cooperi
Clump-forming, summer-flowering bulb with long, narrow, semi-erect, basal leaves. Leafless stems each carry a head of up to 10 fragrant, tubular, cream or yellow flowers, 2in (5cm) long and slightly curved. H 12–16in (30–40cm), S 3–4in (8–10cm).

☼ ◊ ❄ 9–10

Calochortus barbatus,
syn. *Cyclobothra lutea*
Summer-flowering bulb with narrow, erect leaves near the base of the loosely branched stem. Each branch bears a pendent, yellow or greenish yellow flower that is hairy inside. H 12–24in (30–60cm), S 2–4in (5–10cm).

☼ ◊ ❄❄ 6–10

Ranunculus asiaticus
[yellow form] (Persian ranunculus)
Early summer-flowering perennial with clawlike tubers and long-stalked, palmate leaves at base and on stem. Has single or double flowers in yellow, white, pink, red, or orange. H 18–22in (45–55cm), S 3–4in (8–10cm).

☼ ◊ ❄ 8–10

Cypella herbertii
Summer-flowering bulb with a fan of narrow, sword-shaped, erect, basal leaves. Branched flower stem carries a succession of short-lived, irislike, orange-yellow flowers, each spotted purple in the center. H 12–20in (30–50cm), S 3–4in (8–10cm).

☼ ◊ ❄ 9–10

Polianthes geminiflora,
syn. *Bravoa geminiflora*
Summer-flowering tuber with narrowly strap-shaped, semi-erect leaves in a basal tuft. Stems each carry long spikes of downward-curving, tubular, red or orange flowers in pairs. H 8–16in (20–40cm), S 4–6in (10–15cm).

☼ ◊ ❄ 9–10

Sandersonia aurantiaca
(Chinese-lantern lily)
Deciduous, summer-flowering, tuberous climber with a slender stem bearing scattered, lance-shaped leaves, some tendril-tipped. Orange flowers are produced in axils of upper leaves. H 24in (60cm), S 10–12in (25–30cm).

☼ ◊ ❄ 9–10

Alstroemeria, Ligtu Hybrids
Summer-flowering tuber with narrow, twisted leaves and heads of widely flared flowers in shades of pink, yellow, or orange, often spotted or streaked with contrasting colors. H 1½–2ft (45–60cm), S 2–3ft (60cm–1m).

☼ ◊ ❄❄ 6–10

Crocosmia 'Jackanapes'
Clump-forming, late summer-flowering corm with sword-shaped, erect, basal leaves. Produces striking bicolored, yellow and orange-red flowers. H 16–24in (40–60cm), S 6–8in (15–20cm).

☼ ◊ ❄❄ 6–9

Tigridia pavonia (Mexican shell-flower, Tiger flower)
Summer-flowering bulb with sword-shaped, pleated, erect leaves near stem base. A succession of short-lived flowers vary from white to orange, red, or yellow, often with contrasting spots. H to 18in (45cm), S 4–6in (12–15cm).

☼ ◊ ❄ 8–10

WHITE–PINK

PINK–ORANGE

Nerine bowdenii f. **alba**
Autumn-flowering bulb with a stout
stem and strap-shaped, semi-erect,
basal leaves. Produces a head of 5–10
white, often pink-flushed flowers;
petals widen slightly towards wavy-
margined, recurved tips. H 18–24in
(45–60cm), S 5–6in (12–15cm).

☼ ◊ ❊❊ 8–10

Nerine undulata
Autumn-flowering bulb with narrowly
strap-shaped, semi-erect, basal leaves.
Flower stem carries a head of pink
flowers with very narrow petals
crinkled for their whole length.
H 12–18in (30–45cm), S 4–5in
(10–12cm).

☼ ◊ ❊ 9–10

Zephyranthes grandiflora,
syn. *Z. carinata*, *Z. rosea*
Late summer- to early autumn-
flowering bulb with narrowly strap-
shaped, semi-erect, basal leaves. Each
stem bears a funnel-shaped, pink
flower, held almost erect. H 8–12in
(20–30cm), S 3–4in (8–10cm).

☼ ◊ ❊ 7–10

Nerine 'Orion'
Autumn-flowering bulb with strap-
shaped, semi-erect, basal leaves. Stout,
leafless stem bears a head of pale pink
flowers with very wavy-margined
petals that have recurved tips.
H 12–20in (30–50cm), S 8–10in
(20–25cm).

☼ ◊ ❊ 9–10

Nerine bowdenii
Autumn-flowering bulb with a stout
stem and strap-shaped, semi-erect,
basal leaves. Carries a head of 5–10
glistening, pink flowers with petals that
widen slightly towards wavy-margined,
recurved tips. H 18–24in (45–60cm),
S 5–6in (12–15cm).

☼ ◊ ❊❊ 8–10

Scilla scilloides, syn. *S. chinensis*
(Chinese autumn squill)
Late summer- and autumn-flowering
bulb with 2–4 narrowly strap-shaped,
semi-erect, basal leaves. Stem bears a
slender, dense spike of up to 30 flattish,
pink flowers, 1/4–1/2in (0.5–1cm) across.
H to 12in (30cm), S 2in (5cm).

☼ ◊ ❊❊ 5–10

Nerine 'Brian Doe'
Autumn-flowering bulb with strap-
shaped, semi-erect, basal leaves. Stout,
leafless stem bears a head of salmon
flowers with 6 reflexed, wavy-
margined petals. H 12–20in
(30–50cm), S 8–10in (20–25cm).

☼ ◊ ❊ 9–10

Nerine sarniensis (Guernsey lily)
Autumn-flowering bulb with strap-
shaped, semi-erect, basal leaves.
Leafless stem carries a spherical head
of up to 20 deep orange-pink flowers,
2 1/2–3in (6–8cm) across, with wavy-
margined petals. H 18–24in
(45–60cm), S 5–6in (12–15cm).

☼ ◊ ❊ 9–10

Bulbs/medium

***Eucharis grandiflora*,**
syn. *E. amazonica* (Amazon lily)
Evergreen, clump-forming bulb with
strap-shaped, semi-erect, basal leaves.
Bears a head of up to 6 fragrant, slightly
pendent, white flowers at almost any
season. H 16–24in (40–60cm), S 2–3ft
(60cm–1m). Min. 59°F (15°C).

☼ ◐ ○ 10

***Hippeastrum* 'Apple Blossom'**
Winter- to spring-flowering bulb with
strap-shaped, semi-erect, basal leaves
produced as, or just after, flowers
form. Stout stem has a head of 2–6
white flowers, becoming pink at petal
tips. H 12–20in (30–50cm), S 12in
(30cm). Min. 55°F (13°C).

☼ ○ 10

***Hippeastrum* 'Striped'**
Winter- to spring-flowering bulb with
strap-shaped, semi-erect, basal leaves
produced with, or just after, flowers.
Stout stem has a head of 2–6 widely
funnel-shaped flowers, striped white
and red. H 20in (50cm), S 12in
(30cm). Min. 55°F (13°C).

☼ ○ 10

***Veltheimia bracteata*,**
syn. *V. undulata*, *V. viridifolia*
Clump-forming, winter-flowering bulb
with semi-erect, strap-shaped, basal,
glossy leaves and dense spikes of
pendent, tubular, pink, red, or yellowish
red flowers. H 12–18in (30–45cm), S
10–15in (25–38cm). Min. 50°F (10°C).

☼ ○ 10

***Freesia* 'Everett'**
Winter- and spring-flowering corm
with narrow, erect, bright green leaves
in basal fans and a spike of large,
fragrant, pinkish red flowers. H to 12in
(30cm), S ⅝–1in (1.5–2.5cm).

☼ ○ ❄ 9–10

***Hippeastrum* 'Red Lion'**
Tuft-forming, winter- and spring-
flowering bulb with a stout stem
bearing a head of 2–6 dark red flowers
with yellow anthers. Strap-shaped
leaves appear with, or just after,
flowers. H 12–20in (30–50cm),
S 12in (30cm). Min. 55°F (13°C).

☼ ◐ ○ 10

***Hippeastrum* 'Orange Sovereign'**
Winter- to spring-flowering bulb with
strap-shaped, semi-erect, basal, gray-
green leaves produced as, or just after,
flowers form. Stout stem carries a
head of 2–6 rich orange-red flowers.
H 12–20in (30–50cm), S 12in (30cm).
Min. 55°F (13°C).

◐ ○ 10

Lachenalia glaucina
Late winter- and early spring-
flowering bulb with 2 strap-shaped,
semi-erect, basal leaves, usually
spotted purple. Has a spike of fragrant,
bell-shaped, whitish blue or pale lilac
flowers, wavy-margined at tips. H to
12in (30cm), S 2–3in (5–8cm).

☼ ○ ❄ 9–10

***Freesia* 'Yellow River'**
Winter- and spring-flowering corm
with narrow, erect, bright green leaves
in basal fans and a spike of large,
fragrant, bright yellow flowers. H to
12in (30cm), S ⅝–1in (1.5–2.5cm).

☼ ○ ❄ 9–10

☐ WHITE

Leucojum vernum
(Spring snowflake)
Spring-flowering bulb with strap-shaped, semi-erect, basal leaves. Leafless stem carries 1 or 2 pendent, bell-shaped flowers, ⅝–¾in (1.5–2cm) long, with 6 green-tipped, white petals. H 4–6in (10–15cm), S 3–4in (8–10cm).

☼ ◑ ❀❀❀ 4–8

Ornithogalum balansae,
syn. *O. oligophyllum*
Spring-flowering bulb with 2 narrow, green or slightly grayish green leaves, becoming wider towards tips. Has a broad head of 2–5 white flowers, green outside, that open wide. H 2–6in (5–15cm), S 2–3in (5–8cm).

☼ ◊ ❀❀❀ 7–10

Anemone blanda 'White Splendour'
Knobbly tuber with semi-erect leaves that have 3 deeply toothed lobes. Bears upright, flattish, white flowers, 1½–2in (4–5cm) across, with 9–14 narrow petals, in early spring. H 2–4in (5–10cm), S 4–6in (10–15cm).

☼ ◊ ❀❀❀ 6–9

Crocus vernus subsp. ***albiflorus***
Spring-flowering corm. Has very narrow, semi-erect, basal leaves each with a central, white line. Bears white, sometimes purple, flowers, 1½–2½in (4–6cm) long. Stigmas are small, frilly and orange or yellow. H to 4in (10cm), S 1–3in (2.5–8cm).

☼ ◊ ❀❀❀ 3–8

Puschkinia scilloides 'Alba'
(White-striped squill)
Spring-flowering bulb with usually 2 strap-shaped, semi-erect, basal leaves. Produces a dense spike of star-shaped, white flowers, ⅝–¾in (1.5–2cm) across. H 6in (15cm), S 1–2in (2.5–5cm).

☼ ◊ ❀❀❀ 3–9

Crocus sieberi 'Bowles' White'
Spring-flowering corm. Bears very narrow, semi-erect, basal leaves, with white lines along centers, and fragrant, long-tubed, funnel-shaped, pure white flowers with large, deep yellow areas in throats. H to 4in (10cm), S 1–3in (2.5–8cm).

☼ ◊ ❀❀❀ 3–8

Crocus malyi
Spring-flowering corm with 1 or 2 funnel-shaped, white flowers that have yellow throats, brown or purple tubes, and showy, bright orange stigmas. Leaves are very narrow, semi-erect, and basal with central, white lines. H to 4in (10cm), S 1–3in (2.5–8cm).

☼ ◊ ❄❄❄ 3–8

Crocus 'Snow Bunting'
Spring-flowering corm. Fragrant, long-tubed, funnel-shaped, white flowers have mustard yellow centers and orange stigmas. Very narrow, semi-erect, basal leaves are dark green with white lines along centers. H to 4in (10cm), S 1–3in (2.5–8cm).

☼ ◊ ❄❄❄ 3–8

Ornithogalum lanceolatum
Spring-flowering, dwarf bulb with a flattish rosette of prostrate, lance-shaped, basal leaves. Carries a head of flattish, star-shaped, white flowers, 1¼–1½in (3–4cm) across, broadly striped green outside. H 2–4in (5–10cm), S 4–6in (10–15cm).

☼ ◊ ❄❄ 5–10

Ornithogalum montanum
Clump-forming, spring-flowering bulb with strap-shaped, semi-erect, basal, gray-green leaves. Leafless stem produces a head of star-shaped, white flowers, 1¼–1½in (3–4cm) across, striped green outside. H and S 4–6in (10–15cm).

☼ ◊ ❄❄❄ 5–10

Sternbergia candida
Spring-flowering bulb. Strap-shaped, semi-erect, basal, grayish green leaves appear together with a fragrant, funnel-shaped, white flower, 1½–2in (4–5cm) long, borne on a leafless stem. H 4–8in (10–20cm), S 3–4in (8–10cm).

☼ ◊ ❄❄ 6–9

Crocus 'Cream Beauty'
Spring-flowering corm. Scented, rich cream flowers, with deep yellow throats, are stained purplish brown outside at base. Bears very narrow, semi-erect, basal, dark green leaves, each with a white line along the center. H to 4in (10cm), S 1–3in (2.5–8cm).

☼ ◊ ❄❄❄ 3–8

Erythronium californicum
Clump-forming, spring-flowering tuber. Bears 2 semi-erect, basal, mottled leaves. Up to 3 white or creamy white flowers, sometimes red-brown externally, have reflexed petals, yellow eyes and often brown rings near centers. H 6–14in (15–35cm), S 4–5in (10–12cm).

◐ ◊ ❄❄ 3–9

Allium akaka
Spring-flowering bulb with 1–3 broad, prostrate and basal, gray-green leaves and an almost stemless, spherical umbel, 2–3in (5–7cm) across, of 30–40 star-shaped, white to pinkish white flowers with red centers. H 6–8in (15–20cm), S 5–6in (12–15cm).

☼ ◊ ❄❄ 4–9

Allium karataviense
Late spring-flowering bulb with narrowly elliptic to elliptic, prostrate, basal, grayish purple leaves. Stem bears 50 or more star-shaped, pale purplish pink flowers in a spherical umbel, 6in (15cm) or more across. H to 8in (20cm), S 10–12in (25–30cm).

☼ ◊ ❄❄ 4–9

■ PINK

Erythronium dens-canis
(European dog's-tooth violet)
Spring-flowering tuber with 2 basal,
mottled leaves. Stem has a pendent,
pink, purple, or white flower, with
bands of brown, purple, and yellow
near the center and reflexed petals. H
6–10in (15–25cm), S 3–4in (8–10cm).

☼◑ ◊ ❀❀❀ 3–9

Chionodoxa forbesii 'Pink Giant'
Early spring-flowering bulb with 2
narrow, semi-erect, basal leaves. Leafless
stem produces a spike of 5–10 flattish,
white-eyed, pink flowers, ³/₄–1in
(2–2.5cm) across, that face outwards
or slightly downwards. H 4–10in
(10–25cm), S 1–2in (2.5–5cm).

☼ ◊ ❀❀❀❀ 3–9

Allium acuminatum, syn.
A. murrayanum (Pink wild onion)
Spring-flowering bulb with 2–4 long,
narrow, semi-erect, basal leaves. Stem
bears an umbel, 2in (5cm) across, of
up to 30 small, purplish pink flowers.
H 4–12in (10–30cm), S 2–3in (5–8cm).

☼ ◊ ❀❀ 4–9

Anemone blanda 'Radar'
Knobbly tuber with semi-erect, deep
green leaves with 3 deeply toothed
lobes. In early spring, stems each bear
an upright, flattish, white-centered,
deep reddish carmine flower with 9–14
narrow petals. H 2–4in (5–10cm),
S 4–6in (10–15cm).

☼◑ ◊ ❀❀❀❀ 6–9

Cyclamen libanoticum
Spring-flowering tuber with ivy-
shaped, dull green leaves with lighter
patterns and purplish green undersides.
Has musty-scented, clear pink flowers,
each with deep carmine marks at the
mouth. Grows best in an alpine house.
H to 4in (10cm), S 4–6in (10–15cm).

☼◑ ◊ ❀ 9

Anemone biflora
Spring-flowering tuber with deeply
lobed, toothed, semi-erect leaves.
Bears 5-petaled, saucer-shaped, bright
red, coppery pink, or yellowish red
flowers, 1¹/₄–1¹/₂in (3–4cm) across.
Needs warm, dry, summer dormancy.
H 2–4in (5–10cm), S 2–3in (5–8cm).

☼ ◊ ❀❀ 6–9

Allium oreophilum,
syn. *A. ostrowskianum*
Spring- and summer-flowering, dwarf
bulb with 2 narrow, semi-erect, basal
leaves. Has loose, domed umbels of
up to 10 widely bell-shaped, deep rose-
pink flowers, ⁵/₈–³/₄in (1.5–2cm) across.
H 2–4in (5–10cm), S 3–4in (8–10cm).

☼ ◊ ❀❀❀❀ 4–9

Hyacinthus orientalis 'Pink Pearl'
Clump-forming, winter- or spring-
flowering bulb with strap-shaped, semi-
erect, basal, glossy leaves, developing
fully only after flowering. Has a dense
spike of fragrant, tubular, carmine
pink flowers. H 4–8in (10–20cm),
S 2¹/₂–4in (6–10cm).

☼ ◊ ❀❀ 6–9

Hyacinthus orientalis 'Jan Bos'
Clump-forming, winter- or spring-flowering bulb with strap-shaped, semi-erect, basal, glossy leaves, developing fully only after flowering. Has a compact spike of fragrant, tubular, crimson flowers. H 4–8in (10–20cm), S 2¹/₂–4in (6–10cm).

 ☼ ◊ ❄❄ 6–9

Anemone x fulgens
Spring- or early summer-flowering tuber with deeply divided, semi-erect, basal leaves. Stout stems each carry an upright, bright red flower, 2–3in (5–7cm) across, with 10–15 petals. H 4–12in (10–30cm), S 3–4in (8–10cm).

☼ ◊ ❄❄ 7–9

Sparaxis tricolor (Harlequin flower)
Spring-flowering corm with erect, lance-shaped leaves in a basal fan. Stem produces a loose spike of up to 5 flattish, orange, red, purple, pink, or white flowers, 2–2¹/₂in (5–6cm) across, with black or red centers. H 4–12in (10–30cm), S 3–5in (8–12cm).

☼ ◊ ❄ 9–10

Crocus vernus (Dutch crocus)
Spring-flowering corm. Flowers are either striped or in shades of white, purple, or violet. Stigmas are large, frilly, and orange or yellow. Is good as a forced, indoor pot plant or for naturalizing. H to 4in (10cm), S 1–3in (2.5–8cm).

☼ ◊ ❄❄❄ 3–8

Crocus dalmaticus
Spring-flowering corm. Very narrow, semi-erect leaves have central, white lines. Bears 1–3 purple-veined, pale violet flowers, with yellow centers, overlaid with silver or yellow wash outside. H to 4in (10cm), S 1–3in (2.5–8cm).

☼ ◊ ❄❄❄ 3–8

Crocus minimus
Late spring-flowering corm with very narrow, semi-erect, basal, dark green leaves that have central, white lines. Bears 1 or 2 flowers, purple inside and stained darker violet or sometimes darker striped on outside. H 2¹/₂–3in (6–7cm), S 1–3in (2.5–8cm).

☼ ◊ ❄❄ 3–8

Bulbocodium vernum
Spring-flowering corm with stemless, widely funnel-shaped, reddish purple flowers. Narrow, semi-erect, basal leaves appear with flowers but do not elongate until later. Dies down in summer. H 1¹/₄–1¹/₂in (3–4cm), S 1¹/₄–2in (3–5cm).

☼ ◊ ❄❄❄ 3–9

Crocus vernus 'Princess Juliana'
Spring-flowering corm with 4–5in (10–12cm) long, purple flowers with darker purple veins; stigmas are large, frilly, and orange or yellow. Bears very narrow, semi-erect, basal leaves each with a central, white line. H to 4in (10cm), S 1–3in (2.5–8cm).

☼ ◊ ❄❄❄ 3–8

Crocus tommasinianus
Spring-flowering corm with slender, long-tubed, funnel-shaped flowers, very variable in color: lilac, purple, or violet, sometimes with darker tips to petals and sometimes silver outside. Naturalizes well. H to 4in (10cm), S 1–3in (2.5–8cm).

☼ ◊ ❄❄❄ 3–8

■ PURPLE

Babiana rubro-cyanea
Spring-flowering corm with lance-shaped, erect, folded leaves in a basal fan. Carries short spikes of 5–10 flowers, each with 6 petals, purple-blue at the top and red at the base. H 6–8in (15–20cm), S 2–3in (5–8cm). Min. 50°F (10°C).

☼ ◊ 9–10

Crocus etruscus (Italian crocus)
Spring-flowering corm with very narrow, semi-erect, basal, dark green leaves that have central, white lines. Bears long-tubed, funnel-shaped, pale purple-blue flowers, washed silver outside, with violet veining. H to 4in (10cm), S 1–3in (2.5–8cm).

☼ ◊ ❄❄ 5–8

***Crocus vernus* ‘Pickwick’**
Spring-flowering corm. Narrow leaves have central, white lines. Pale lilac flowers, 4–5in (10–12cm) long, have dark stripes and purplish bases. Is good as a forced, indoor pot plant, for garden use, or for naturalizing in grass. H to 4in (10cm), S 1–3in (2.5–8cm).

☼ ◊ ❄❄❄ 3–8

***Crocus* ‘Blue Pearl’**
Early spring-flowering corm. Produces narrow, semi-erect, basal leaves, with white lines along the centers. Fragrant, long-tubed, funnel-shaped, soft lavender blue flowers, bluish white within, have golden yellow throats. H to 4in (10cm), S 1–3in (2.5–8cm).

☼ ◊ ❄❄❄ 3–8

***Ipheion uniflorum* ‘Froyle Mill’**
Spring-flowering bulb with narrow, semi-erect, basal, pale green leaves that smell of onions if crushed. Each leafless stem carries a star-shaped, violet-blue flower, 1¼–1½in (3–4cm) across. H 4–6in (10–15cm), S 2–3in (5–8cm).

☼ ◊ ❄❄ 6–9

Crocus biflorus (Scotch crocus)
Early spring-flowering corm. Has narrow, semi-erect, basal leaves, each with a white line along the center. Bears fragrant white or purplish white flowers, with yellow throats, vertically striped purple outside. H to 4in (10cm), S 1–3in (2.5–8cm).

☼ ◊ ❄❄❄ 3–8

Gynandriris sisyrinchium
Spring-flowering corm with 1 or 2 semi-erect, narrow, basal leaves. Wiry stems each carry a succession of lavender- to violet-blue flowers, 1¼–1½in (3–4cm) across, with white or orange patches on the 3 larger petals. H 4–8in (10–20cm), S 3–4in (8–10cm).

☼ ◊ ❄❄ 9–10

***Muscari comosum* ‘Plumosum’**, syn. *M.c.* ‘Monstrosum’ (Feathered grape hyacinth)
Spring-flowering bulb with up to 5 strap-shaped, semi-erect, basal, gray-green leaves. Sterile flowers are replaced by a fluffy mass of purple threads. H to 10in (25cm), S 4–5in (10–12cm).

☼ ◊ ❄❄ 2–9

Romulea bulbocodium
Spring-flowering corm with long, semi-erect, threadlike leaves in a basal tuft. Slender flower stems each carry 1–6 upward-facing flowers, usually pale lilac-purple with yellow or white centers. H 2–4in (5–10cm), S 1–2in (2.5–5cm).

☼ ◊ ❄❄ 9

Puschkinia scilloides,
syn. *P. libanotica* (Striped squill)
Spring-flowering bulb with usually
2 strap-shaped, semi-erect, basal
leaves. Carries a dense spike of star-
shaped, pale blue flowers with a darker
blue stripe down each petal center.
H 6in (15cm), S 1–2in (2.5–5cm).

☼ ◊ ❀❀❀ 3–9

Hyacinthella leucophaea
Spring-flowering bulb with 2 narrowly
strap-shaped, semi-erect, basal leaves
and a thin, wiry, leafless flower stem.
Carries a short spike of tiny, bell-
shaped, very pale blue, almost white
flowers. H 4in (10cm), S 1–2in
(2.5–5cm).

☼ ◊ ❀❀ 6–9

Bellevalia hyacinthoides,
syn. *Strangweia spicata*
Spring-flowering bulb with prostrate,
narrow leaves in a basal cluster. Bears
a dense spike of up to 20 bell-shaped,
pale lavender blue, almost white
flowers with darker, central veins.
H 2–6in (5–15cm), S 2in (5cm).

☼ ◊ ❀❀ 7–9

Tecophilaea cyanocrocus var.
leichtlinii
Spring-flowering corm with 1 or 2
narrowly lance-shaped, semi-erect,
basal leaves and solitary upward-
facing, widely funnel-shaped, pale
blue flowers with large, white centers.
H 3–4in (8–10cm), S 2–3in (5–8cm).

☼ ◊ ❀❀❀ 7–9

Scilla mischtschenkoana,
syn. *S. tubergeniana*
Early spring-flowering bulb with 2 or
3 strap-shaped, semi-erect, basal
leaves. Stems elongate as cup-shaped
or flattish, pale blue flowers, with
darker blue veins, open. H 2–4in
(5–10cm), S 2in (5cm).

☼ ◊ ❀❀❀ 1–8

Scilla siberica 'Atrocoerulea'
Early spring-flowering bulb with
2–4 strap-shaped, semi-erect, basal,
glossy leaves, widening towards tips.
Bell-shaped, deep rich blue flowers,
$1/2$–$5/8$in (1–1.5cm) long, are borne in
a short spike. H 4–6in (10–15cm),
S 2in (5cm).

☼ ◊ ❀❀❀ 1–8

Brimeura amethystina,
syn. *Hyacinthus amethystinus*
Late spring-flowering bulb with very
narrow, semi-erect, basal leaves. Each
leafless stem bears a spike of up to
15 pendent, tubular, blue flowers.
H 4–10in (10–25cm), S 1–2in
(2.5–5cm).

☼ ◊ ❀❀ 5–9

Muscari aucheri,
syn. *M. tubergenianum*
Spring-flowering bulb with 2 strap-
shaped, grayish green leaves. Bears
small, almost spherical, bright blue
flowers with white-rimmed mouths;
upper flowers are often paler. H 2–6in
(5–15cm), S 2–3in (5–8cm).

☼ ◊ ❀❀❀ 2–9

Chionodoxa luciliae,
syn. *C. gigantea*
Early spring-flowering bulb with
2 somewhat curved, semi-erect, basal
leaves. Leafless stem bears 1–3 upward-
facing, blue flowers with white eyes.
H 2–4in (5–10cm), S 1–2in (2.5–5cm).

☼ ◊ ❄❄❄ 3–9

Chionodoxa forbesii, syn.
C. luciliae of gardens, *C. siehei,*
C. tmolusii
Early spring-flowering bulb with 2
semi-erect, narrow, basal leaves. Bears
a spike of 5–10 outward-facing, rich
blue-lilac flowers with white eyes. H
4–10in (10–25cm), S 1–2in (2.5–5cm).

☼ ◊ ❄❄❄ 3–9

Hyacinthus orientalis 'Delft Blue'
Clump-forming, winter- or spring-
flowering bulb with strap-shaped, semi-
erect, basal, glossy leaves, developing
fully only after flowering. Has a dense
spike of fragrant, tubular, violet-flushed,
soft blue flowers. H 4–8in (10–20cm),
S 2½–4in (6–10cm).

☼ ◊ ❄❄ 6–9

Tecophilaea cyanocrocus
(Chilean crocus)
Spring-flowering corm with 1 or 2
lance-shaped, semi-erect, basal leaves.
Carries upward-facing, funnel-shaped,
deep gentian blue flowers, 1½–2in
(4–5cm) across, with white throats.
H 3–4in (8–10cm), S 2–3in (5–8cm).

☼ ◊ ❄❄❄ 7–9

Muscari armeniacum
Spring-flowering bulb with 3–6 long,
narrow, semi-erect, basal leaves. Carries
a dense spike of small, fragrant, bell-
shaped, deep blue flowers with
constricted mouths that have a rim
of small, paler blue or white "teeth".
H 6–8in (15–20cm), S 3–4in (8–10cm).

☼ ◊ ❄❄❄ 2–9

Muscari neglectum, syn.
M. racemosum (Starch hyacinth)
Spring-flowering bulb. Bears 4–6 often
prostrate leaves from autumn to early
summer. Has small, ovoid, deep blue
or blackish blue flowers with white-
rimmed mouths. Increases rapidly.
H 4–8in (10–20cm), S 3–4in (8–10cm).

☼ ◊ ❄❄❄ 2–9

Anemone blanda 'Atrocaerulea'
Knobbly tuber with semi-erect, dark
green leaves that have 3 deeply
toothed lobes. In early spring, stems
each bear an upright, flattish, deep
blue flower, 1½–2in (4–5cm) across,
with 9–14 narrow petals. H 2–4in
(5–10cm), S 4–6in (10–15cm).

◐ ◊ ❄❄❄ 6–9

x Chionoscilla allenii
Early spring-flowering bulb with
2 narrow, semi-erect, basal, dark
green leaves and flattish, star-shaped,
deep blue flowers, ½–¾in (1–2cm)
across, in a loose spike. H 4–6in
(10–15cm), S 1–2in (2.5–5cm).

☼ ◊ ❄❄❄ 3–9

Hyacinthus orientalis 'Ostara'
Clump-forming, winter- or spring-
flowering bulb with semi-erect, basal,
glossy leaves, developing fully only
after flowering. Has a large spike of
fragrant blue flowers, with a dark stripe
along each petal center. H 4–8in
(10–20cm), S 2½–4in (6–10cm).

☼ ◊ ❄❄ 6–9

Ledebouria socialis,
syn. *Scilla violacea*
Evergreen, spring-flowering bulb with
lance-shaped, semi-erect, basal, dark-
spotted, gray or green leaves. Produces
a short spike of bell-shaped, purplish
green flowers. H 2–4in (5–10cm),
S 3–4in (8–10cm).

☼ ◊ ❄ 9–10

Calochortus amabilis (Golden
fairy lantern, Golden lantern)
Spring-flowering bulb with one long,
narrow, erect leaf, near the base of the
loosely branched stem. A fringed,
deep yellow, sometimes green-tinged
flower hangs from each branch. H
4–12in (10–30cm), S 2–4in (5–10cm).

☼ ◊ ❄❄ 6–10

***Crocus* 'E.A. Bowles'**
Early spring-flowering corm with
scented, funnel-shaped, deep yellow
flowers, stained bronze near base on
outside. Leaves are narrow, semi-erect,
and basal, each with a central, white
line. Increases well by offsets. H to 4in
(10cm), S 1–3in (2.5–8cm).

☼ ◊ ❄❄❄ 3–8

Crocus cvijicii
Spring-flowering corm with usually
one funnel-shaped, yellow flower.
Produces very narrow, semi-erect,
basal leaves, each with a white line
along the center, which scarcely show
at flowering time. H 1½–2in (4–5cm),
S 1–2in (2.5–5cm).

☼ ◊ ❄❄❄ 3–8

***Arum italicum* 'Pictum'**
Late spring-flowering tuber. Produces
semi-erect leaves, with cream or white
veins, in autumn, followed by pale
green or creamy white spathes, then red
berries in autumn. Is good for flower
arrangements. H 6–10in (15–25cm),
S 8–12in (20–30cm).

☼ ◊ ❄❄ 7–9

Erythronium americanum
Spring-flowering tuber with 2 semi-
erect, basal leaves, mottled green and
brown, and a pendent, yellow flower,
often bronze outside, with petals
reflexing in sunlight. Forms clumps by
stolons. H 2–10in (5–25cm), S 2–3in
(5–8cm).

◐ ◊ ❄❄❄ 3–9

Colchicum luteum
Spring-flowering corm with wineglass-
shaped, yellow flowers – the only
known yellow *Colchicum*. Semi-erect,
basal leaves are short at flowering time
but later expand. H 2–4in (5–10cm),
S 2–3in (5–8cm).

☼ ◊ ❄❄❄ 7–9

Fritillaria pudica (Indian rice,
Rice root, Yellow bell)
Spring-flowering bulb with stems
bearing scattered, narrowly lance-
shaped, gray-green leaves. Has 1 or
2 deep yellow, sometimes red-tinged
flowers, ½–1in (1–2.5cm) long.
H 2–8in (5–20cm), S 2in (5cm).

☼ ◊ ❄❄❄ 2–9

Muscari macrocarpum
Spring-flowering bulb with 3–5 semi-
erect, basal, grayish green leaves.
Carries a dense spike of fragrant
brown-rimmed, bright yellow flowers.
Upper flowers may initially be
brownish purple. H 4–8in (10–20cm),
S 4–6in (10–15cm).

☼ ◊ ❄❄ 2–9

***Hyacinthus orientalis* 'City of
Haarlem'**
Clump-forming, winter- or spring-
flowering bulb with strap-shaped, semi-
erect, basal, glossy leaves, developing
fully only after flowering. Has a dense
spike of fragrant, pale yellow flowers.
H 4–8in (10–20cm), S 2½–4in (6–10cm).

☼ ◊ ❄❄ 6–9

Dipcadi serotinum
Spring-flowering bulb with 2–5 very
narrow, semi-erect, basal leaves.
Leafless stem has a loose spike of
nodding, tubular, brown or dull orange
flowers, ½–⅝in (1–1.5cm) long.
H 4–12in (10–30cm), S 2–3in (5–8cm).

☼ ◊ ❄❄ 8–10

363

◧ WHITE–PINK   ■ RED

Lloydia serotina
Early summer-flowering bulb with
wiry stems bearing scattered,
threadlike, semi-erect leaves near stem
base. Carries 1 or 2 bell-shaped, white
flowers, ½–⅝in (1–1.5cm) long, with
purple or purple-red veins. H 2–6in
(5–15cm), S 1–2in (2.5–5cm).

☼ ◊ ❀❀❀ 6–9

Albuca humilis
Summer-flowering, dwarf bulb with
very narrow, basal, dark green leaves.
Carries a loose head of 1–3 cup-shaped,
white flowers, ½in (1cm) long, striped
green, later reddish, outside. H 2–4in
(5–10cm), S 2–3in (5–8cm).

☼ ◊ ❀ 9–10

Hippeastrum rutilum,
syn. *H. striatum*
Spring- and summer-flowering bulb
with strap-shaped, semi-erect, basal,
bright green leaves. Funnel-shaped
flowers have pointed, scarlet petals with
central, green stripes. H 12in (30cm),
S 8–10in (20–25cm). Min. 59°F (15°C).

☼ ◊ 10

Cyrtanthus brachyscyphus,
syn. *C. parviflorus*
Clump-forming, summer-flowering bulb
with strap-shaped, semi-erect, basal,
bright green leaves. Leafless stem bears
a head of 6–12 tubular, orange- or
brilliant red flowers with 6 lobes. H
8–12in (20–30cm), S 4–6in (10–15cm).

☼ ◊ ❀ 9–10

Calochortus subalpinus
Summer-flowering bulb with one long,
narrow, semi-erect, basal leaf. Has 1–3
erect, saucer-shaped, creamy white
flowers with yellow hairs and usually a
small, purple mark at the base of the
3 smaller petals. H 6–8in (15–20cm),
S 2–3in (5–7cm).

☼ ◊ ❀❀ 5–10

Arisaema candidissimum
Early summer-flowering tuber with
large, cowl-like, pink-striped, white
spathes, enclosing tiny, fragrant
flowers on spadices, followed by
broad, 3-parted, semi-erect leaves,
12in (30cm) long. H 4–6in (10–15cm),
S 12–18in (30–45cm).

☼ ◊ ❀❀ 7–9

Haemanthus coccineus (Blood lily)
Summer-flowering bulb with 2 elliptic
leaves, hairy beneath, that lie flat on the
ground. Spotted stem, forming before
leaves, bears a cluster of tiny, red flowers
with prominent stamens, within fleshy,
red or pink bracts. H to 12in (30cm),
S 8–12in (20–30cm). Min. 50°F (10°C).

☼ ◊ 10

Cyclamen purpurascens,
syn. *C. europaeum, C. fatrense*
Summer- and autumn-flowering tuber
with rounded, silver-patterned leaves.
Bears very fragrant lilac-pink to reddish
purple flowers. H to 4in (10cm),
S 4–6in (10–15cm).

☼ ◊ ❀❀ 5–9

Allium schoenoprasum (Chives)
Clump-forming, summer-flowering
bulb with narrow, hollow, erect, dark
green leaves at base. Stems each carry
up to 20 tiny, bell-shaped, pale purple
or pink flowers in a dense umbel up to
2in (5cm) across. H 5–10in (12–25cm),
S 2–4in (5–10cm).

☼ ◊ ❀❀❀ 3–9

Allium narcissiflorum,
syn. *A. pedemontanum*
Clump-forming, summer-flowering
bulb with very narrow, erect, gray-
green leaves on the lower part of the
flower stem. Has an umbel of up to 15
bell-shaped, pinkish purple flowers.
H 6–12in (15–30cm), S 3–4in (8–10cm).

☼ ◊ ❀❀❀ 4–9

Allium cyathophorum var. *farreri*
Clump-forming, summer-flowering bulb
with tufts of narrow, erect, basal leaves.
Each stem bears a small, loose umbel,
⅝–1½in (1.5–4cm) wide, of up to 30
bell-shaped, dark reddish purple flowers
with sharply pointed petals. H 6–12in
(15–30cm), S 4–6in (10–15cm).

☼ ◊ ❀❀❀ 4–9

Chlidanthus fragrans
(Delicate lily)
Summer-flowering bulb with narrow,
semi-erect leaves in a basal tuft.
Leafless stem carries a head of 3–5
fragrant, funnel-shaped, yellow flowers,
1½–2¼in (4–7cm) long. H 4–12in
(10–30cm), S 3–4in (8–10cm).

☼ ◊ ❀ 8–10

Roscoea humeana
Summer-flowering tuber. Erect, broadly
lance-shaped, rich green leaves form a
stemlike sheath at base. Carries up to
10 long-tubed, purple flowers, each with
a hooded, upper petal, a wide, pendent
lip, and 2 narrower petals. H 6–10in
(15–25cm), S 6–8in (15–20cm).

☼ ◊ ❀❀ 7–9

Scilla peruviana (Cuban lily)
Early summer-flowering bulb with a
basal cluster of up to 10 lance-shaped,
semi-erect leaves. Stem bears a broadly
conical head of up to 50 flattish, violet-
blue flowers, ⅝–1¼in (1.5–3cm)
across. H 4–10in (10–25cm),
S 6–8in (15–20cm).

☼ ◊ ❀❀ 8–10

Allium moly (Lily leek)
Clump-forming, summer-flowering
bulb with 1–3 broad, semi-erect, basal,
gray-green leaves. Stems each bear up
to 40 star-shaped, yellow flowers in a
fairly dense umbel, 1½–3in (4–8cm)
across. H 4–14in (10–35cm), S 4–5in
(10–12cm).

☼ ◊ ❀❀❀ 3–9

Roscoea cautleoides
Summer-flowering tuber. Erect, lance-
shaped leaves form a stemlike sheath at
base. Has up to 5 long-tubed, yellow
flowers, each with a hooded, upper
petal, a broad, 2-lobed, lower lip, and 2
narrower petals. H 6–10in (15–25cm),
S 4–6in (10–15cm).

☼ ◊ ❀❀ 7–9

Hypoxis angustifolia
Summer-flowering corm with slender,
hairy, semi-erect, basal leaves. Stems
each carry 3–7 star-shaped, yellow
flowers, ⅝–¾in (1.5–2cm) across.
H 4–8in (10–20cm), S 2–3in (5–8cm).

☼ ◊ ❀ 5–9

□ WHITE

Cyclamen hederifolium var. **album**
(White-flowered ivy-leaved cyclamen)
Autumn-flowering tuber. Pure white
flowers, with reflexed petals, appear
before or with leaves, which vary but
are often ivy-shaped with silvery
green patterns. H to 4in (10cm),
S 4–6in (10–15cm).

☼◑ ◊ ❋❋ 5–9

Colchicum speciosum 'Album'
Vigorous, autumn-flowering corm with
large, semi-erect, basal leaves in late
winter or spring. Cup-shaped, white
flowers successfully withstand bad
weather. H and S 6–8in (15–20cm).

☼ ◊ ❋❋❋ 4–9

Leucojum autumnale
(Autumn snowflake)
Autumn-flowering bulb with threadlike,
erect, basal leaves appearing with, or
just after, flowers. Slender stems each
produce a head of 1–4 bell-shaped,
white flowers, tinged pink at bases.
H 4–6in (10–15cm), S 1–2in (2.5–5cm).

☼ ◊ ❋❋❋ 5–9

■□ WHITE–PINK

Zephyranthes candida
Autumn-flowering bulb with narrow,
erect, basal leaves forming rushlike
tufts. Each leafless stem carries
crocuslike, white flowers, to 2$\frac{1}{2}$in
(6cm) across. H 6–10in (15–25cm),
S 2–3in (5–8cm).

☼ ◊ ❋❋ 7–10

Cyclamen africanum
Autumn-flowering tuber with ivy-
shaped, deep green leaves with lighter
patterns. Bears pendent, white or pink
flowers, with reflexed petals and
darker stains around mouths, as or just
before leaves appear. H to 4in (10cm),
S 4–6in (10–15cm).

☼◑ ◊ ❋ 8–9

Cyclamen mirabile
Autumn-flowering tuber with pale
pink flowers with toothed petals and
dark purple-stained mouths. Heart-
shaped, patterned leaves, purplish
green beneath, are minutely toothed
on margins. H to 4in (10cm),
S 2–3in (5–8cm).

◑ ◊ ❋❋ 8–9

Habranthus robustus
Late summer- to early autumn-
flowering bulb with narrowly strap-
shaped, semi-erect, basal leaves.
Leafless flower stems each bear a
funnel-shaped, pink flower inclined at
an angle. H 8–12in (20–30cm),
S 8–10cm (3–4in).

☼ ◊ ❋ 9–10

Colchicum autumnale
(Autumn crocus)
Autumn-flowering corm with up to 8
long-tubed, wineglass-shaped, purple,
pink, or white flowers, followed by
3–5 large, strap-shaped, semi-erect,
basal, glossy leaves in spring. H and
S 4–6in (10–15cm).

☼ ◊ ❋❋❋ 4–9

Colchicum byzantinum
Robust, autumn-flowering corm with up to 20 large, funnel-shaped, pale purplish pink flowers, 4–6in (10–15cm) long. In spring produces very broad, semi-erect, basal leaves, ribbed lengthways. H and S 6–8in (15–20cm).

 ☼ ◊ ❄❄❄ 4–9

Cyclamen graecum
Autumn-flowering tuber with heart-shaped, toothed, velvety, dark green leaves, patterned silver or light green. Flowers are pink or white, with purple stains around mouths. Grows best in an alpine house. H to 4in (10cm), S 4–6in (10–15cm).

☼ ◊ ❄❄ 8–9

Crocus kotschyanus, syn. *C. zonatus*
Autumn-flowering corm. Pinkish lilac or purplish blue flowers have yellow centers and white anthers. Narrow, semi-erect, basal leaves, with white lines along centers, appear in winter-spring. H to 4in (10cm), S 1¼–3in (3–8cm).

☼ ◊ ❄❄❄ 3–8

Crocus goulimyi
Autumn-flowering corm with usually one long-tubed, pale lilac to pinkish lilac flower, with a white throat and 3 inner petals usually paler than the 3 outer ones. Leaves and flowers appear together. Needs a warm site. H to 4in (10cm), S 1¼–3in (3–8cm).

☼ ◊ ❄❄ 3–8

Cyclamen hederifolium, syn. *C. neapolitanum*
Autumn-flowering tuber. Pale to deep pink flowers, stained darker at mouths, appear before or with foliage. Leaves vary but are often ivy-shaped with silvery green patterns. H to 4in (10cm), S 4–6in (10–15cm).

☼ ◊ ❄❄ 5–9

Cyclamen rohlfsianum
Autumn-flowering tuber with coarsely toothed leaves, zoned with light and dark green patterns, and pale pink-lilac flowers, stained darker at mouths. H to 4in (10cm), S 4–6in (10–15cm).

☼ ◊ ❄❄ 8–9

Cyclamen cilicium
Autumn-flowering tuber with broadly heart-shaped leaves that have light and dark green zones. Has white or pink flowers, each with a dark purple stain at the mouth, just before or with leaves. H to 4in (10cm), S 2–4in (5–10cm).

 ☼ ◊ ❄❄ 5–9

Colchicum bivonae, syn. *C. bowlesianum*, *C. sibthorpii*
Autumn-flowering corm with large, funnel-shaped, pinkish purple flowers, strongly checkered darker purple and with purple anthers. Produces 8–10 erect leaves in spring. H 4–6in (10–15cm), S 6–8in (15–20cm).

☼ ◊ ❄❄ 4–9

■ PINK–PURPLE

Colchicum cilicicum
Autumn-flowering corm with large, cup-shaped, pale pink to deep rose-purple flowers, sometimes slightly checkered. Very broad, semi-erect, basal leaves, ribbed lengthways, appear soon after flowers have faded. H and S 6–8in (15–20cm).

☼ ◊ ❅❅ 4–9

Merendera montana,
syn. M. *bulbocodium*
Autumn-flowering corm with narrowly strap-shaped, semi-erect, basal leaves, produced just after upright, broad-petaled, funnel-shaped, rose- or purple-lilac flowers appear. H to 2in (5cm), S 2–3in (5–8cm).

☼ ◊ ❅❅❅❅ 6–9

Crocus medius
Autumn-flowering corm with 1 or 2 funnel-shaped, uniform rich purple flowers, with contrasting, yellow anthers and red stigmas cut into many threadlike branches. Linear, basal leaves appear in winter-spring, after flowering. H to 4in (10cm), S 1–3in (2.5–8cm).

☼ ◊ ❅❅ 3–8

Biarum tenuifolium
Late summer- or autumn-flowering tuber producing clusters of acrid, narrow, erect, basal leaves after stemless, upright, and often twisted, blackish purple spathes appear. H to 8in (20cm), S 3–4in (8–10cm).

☼ ◊ ❅❅ 7–9

Colchicum agrippinum
Early autumn-flowering corm. Narrow, slightly waved, semi-erect, basal leaves develop in spring. Bears erect, funnel-shaped, bright purplish pink flowers with a darker checkered pattern and pointed petals. H 4–6in (10–15cm), S 3–4in (8–10cm).

☼ ◊ ❅❅❅ 4–9

Crocus banaticus
Autumn-flowering corm with usually one long-tubed, pale violet flower; outer 3 petals are much larger than inner 3. Very narrow, semi-erect, basal leaves, each with a paler line along the center, appear in spring. H to 4in (10cm), S 1–3in (2.5–8cm).

☼ ◐ ◊ ❅❅❅ 3–8

Colchicum 'Waterlily'
Autumn-flowering corm with rather broad, semi-erect, basal leaves in winter or spring. Tightly double flowers have 20–40 pinkish lilac petals. H 4–6in (10–15cm), S 6–8in (15–20cm).

☼ ◊ ❅❅❅ 4–9

Crocus nudiflorus (Autumn crocus)
Autumn-flowering corm with linear, basal leaves in winter-spring. Usually bears one slender, long-tubed, rich purple flower, with a frilly, bright orange or yellow stigma. Naturalizes in grass. H to 4in (10cm), S 1–3in (2.5–8cm).

☼ ◊ ❅❅❅ 3–8

Crocus pulchellus
Autumn-flowering corm. Bears long-tubed, pale lilac-blue flowers with darker veins, conspicuous, yellow throats, and white anthers. Leaves are very narrow, semi-erect, and basal, with white lines along centers. H to 4in (10cm), S 1–3in (2.5–8cm).

☼ ◊ ❅❅❅ 3–8

■□□ PURPLE–YELLOW

□ WHITE

Crocus speciosus 'Oxonian'
Autumn-flowering corm with dark
violet-blue flowers, each with a
network of darker veins and a much-
divided, orange stigma. Narrow, basal
leaves, each with a central, white line,
appear in winter-spring. H to 4in
(10cm), S 1–3in (2.5–8cm).

☀ ◊ ❄❄❄ 3–8

Arum pictum
Autumn-flowering tuber. Arrow-shaped,
semi-erect, glossy leaves, with cream
veins, appear at the same time as a cowl-
like, deep purple-brown spathe and dark
purple spadix. H 6–10in (15–25cm),
S 6–8in (15–20cm).

☀ ◊ ❄ 7–9

Sternbergia lutea (Mount Etna
lily, Winter daffodil)
Autumn-flowering bulb with strap-
shaped, semi-erect, basal, deep green
leaves appearing together with a funnel-
shaped, bright yellow flower, 1–2¹/₂in
(2.5–6cm) long, on a leafless stem.
H 1–6in (2.5–15cm), S 3–4in (8–10cm).

☀ ◊ ❄ 6–9

Galanthus nivalis 'Flore Pleno'
Late winter- and early spring-flowering
bulb with semi-erect, basal, gray-green
leaves. Bears rosetted, many-petaled,
double, white flowers, some inner
petals having a green mark at the apex.
H 4–6in (10–15cm), S 2–3in (5–8cm).

☼ ◊ ❄❄❄ 3–9

**Galanthus nivalis 'Pusey Green
Tips'**
Late winter- and early spring-flowering
bulb with narrowly strap-shaped, semi-
erect, basal, gray-green leaves. Each
stem bears a white flower with many
mostly green-tipped petals. H 4–6in
(10–15cm), S 2–3in (5–8cm).

☀ ◊ ❄❄❄ 3–9

Galanthus gracilis, syn. *G. graecus*
Late winter- and early spring-flowering
bulb with slightly twisted, strap-shaped,
semi-erect, basal, gray-green leaves.
Bears white flowers with 3 inner petals,
each marked with a green blotch at the
apex and base. H 4–6in (10–15cm),
S 2–3in (5–8cm).

☼ ◊ ❄❄❄ 3–9

Galanthus rizehensis
Late winter- and early spring-flowering
bulb with very narrow, strap-shaped,
semi-erect, basal, dark green leaves.
Produces white flowers, ⁵/₈–³/₄in
(1.5–2cm) long, with a green patch at
the apex of each inner petal. H 4–8in
(10–20cm), S 2in (5cm).

☼ ◊ ❄❄❄ 3–9

Galanthus elwesii
Late winter- and early spring-flowering
bulb with semi-erect, basal, gray-green
leaves that widen gradually towards tips.
Each inner petal of the white flowers
bears green marks at the apex and base,
which may merge. H 4–12in (10–30cm),
S 2–3in (5–8cm).

☀ ◊ ❄❄❄ 3–9

Galanthus 'Atkinsii'
Vigorous, late winter- and early
spring-flowering bulb with strap-
shaped, semi-erect, basal, gray-green
leaves. Each stem carries a slender,
white flower with a green mark at the
apex of each inner petal. H 4–10in
(10–25cm), S 2–3¹/₂in (5–9cm).

☼ ◊ ❄❄❄ 3–9

☐ WHITE

Galanthus nivalis 'Lutescens'
Late winter- and early spring-
flowering bulb with narrowly strap-
shaped, semi-erect, basal, gray-green
leaves. Flowers are ⅝–¾in (1.5–2cm)
long and white with yellow patches
at the apex of each inner petal. H 4in
(10cm), S 1–2in (2.5–5cm).

☼◑ ◊ ❋❋❋ 3–9

Galanthus ikariae, syn. *G. latifolius*
Late winter- and early spring-flowering
bulb with strap-shaped, semi-erect,
basal, glossy, bright green leaves.
Produces one white flower, ⅝–1in
(1.5–2.5cm) long, marked with a green
patch at the apex of each inner petal.
H 4–10in (10–25cm), S 2–3in (5–8cm).

☼ ◊ ❋❋❋ 3–9

Galanthus nivalis 'Scharlockii'
Vigorous, late winter- and early spring-
flowering bulb with semi-erect, basal,
gray-green leaves. Has white flowers,
with green marks at the apex of inner
petals, overtopped by 2 narrow spathes
that resemble donkey's ears. H 4–6in
(10–15cm), S 2–3in (5–8cm).

☼◑ ◊ ❋❋❋ 3–9

Galanthus plicatus subsp.
byzantinus
Late winter- and early spring-flowering
bulb. Semi-erect, basal, deep green
leaves have a gray bloom and reflexed
margins. White flowers have green
marks at bases and tips of inner petals.
H 4–8in (10–20cm), S 2–3in (5–8cm).

☼◑ ◊ ❋❋❋ 3–9

Cyclamen coum subsp. **coum**
'Album'
Winter-flowering tuber with rounded,
deep green leaves, sometimes silver-
patterned. Carries white flowers, each
with a maroon mark at the mouth.
H to 4in (10cm), S 2–4in (5–10cm).

☼◑ ◊ ❋❋ 5–9

☐ PINK

Cyclamen persicum
Winter- or spring-flowering tuber with
heart-shaped leaves, marked light and
dark green and silver. Fragrant, slender,
white or pink flowers, 1¼–1½in
(3–4cm) long, are stained carmine at
mouths. H 4–8in (10–20cm), S 4–6in
(10–15cm). Min. 41–5°F (5–7°C).

☼ ◊ 9–10

Cyclamen persicum 'Pearl Wave'
Winter- and spring-flowering tuber
with heart-shaped leaves, marked light
and dark green and silver. Produces
fragrant, slender, deep pink flowers,
with 2–2½in (5–6cm) long, frilly-edged
petals. H 4–8in (10–20cm), S 4–6in
(10–15cm). Min. 41–5°F (5–7°C).

☼ ◊ 9–10

Cyclamen coum subsp. **coum**
Winter-flowering tuber with rounded
leaves, plain deep green or silver-
patterned. Produces bright carmine
flowers with dark stains at mouths.
H to 4in (10cm), S 2–4in (5–10cm).

☼ ◊ ❋❋ 5–9

***Cyclamen persicum* 'Esmeralda'**
Winter-flowering tuber with heart-shaped, silver-patterned leaves and broad-petaled, carmine red flowers. H 4–8in (10–20cm), S 6–8in (15–20cm). Min. 41–5°F (5–7°C).

☀ ◊ 9–10

***Cyclamen persicum* 'Renown'**
Winter- and spring-flowering tuber with heart-shaped, bright silver-green leaves, each with a central, dark green mark. Carries fragrant, slender, scarlet flowers, 2–2¹⁄₂in (5–6cm) long. H 4–8in (10–20cm), S 4–6in (10–15cm). Min. 41–5°F (5–7°C).

☀ ◊ 9–10

***Lachenalia* 'Quadricolor'**
Winter- to spring-flowering bulb with 2 strap-shaped, semi-erect, basal leaves. Has a spike of 10–20 purplish red buds opening to greenish yellow or orange flowers. H 6–10in (15–25cm), S 2–3in (5–8cm).

☀ ◊ ❄ 9–10

***Lachenalia* 'Nelsonii'**
Winter- to spring-flowering bulb with 2 strap-shaped, purple-spotted, semi-erect, basal leaves. Has a spike of 10–20 pendent, tubular, green-tinged, bright yellow flowers, 1¹⁄₄in (3cm) long. H 6–10in (15–25cm), S 2–3in (5–8cm).

☀ ◊ ❄ 9–10

***Cyclamen persicum*, Kaori Series**
Winter-flowering tuber with neat, heart-shaped, silver-marbled leaves. Produces fragrant flowers, 1¹⁄₂in (4cm) long, in a wide range of colors. H 4–8in (10–20cm), S 4–6in (10–15cm). Min. 41–5°F (5–7°C).

☀ ◊ 9–10

***Eranthis hyemalis*,**
syn. *E. cilicicus* (Winter aconite)
Clump-forming tuber. Bears stalkless, cup-shaped, yellow flowers, ³⁄₄–1in (2–2.5cm) across, from late winter to early spring. A dissected, leaflike bract forms a ruff beneath each bloom. H 2–4in (5–10cm), S 3–4in (8–10cm).

☀ ◊ ❄ ❄ ❄ 4–9

WATER PLANTS

Menyanthes trifoliata (Bog bean)
Deciduous, perennial, marginal water
plant that has 3-parted leaves and
fringed, white flowers borne in spring.
H 9in (23cm), S 12in (30cm).

☼ 💧 ❅❅❅ 5–8

Alisma plantago-aquatica
(Water plantain)
Deciduous, perennial, marginal water
plant with upright, oval, bright green
leaves that emerge well above water.
Loose, conical panicles of small, pinkish
to white flowers appear in summer.
H 30in (75cm), S 18in (45cm).

☼ 💧 ❅❅❅ 5–8

Lysichiton camtschatcensis
Vigorous, deciduous, perennial,
marginal water or bog plant. Pure white
spathes, surrounding spikes of small,
insignificant flowers, are borne in
spring, before oblong to oval, bright
green leaves emerge. H 30in (75cm),
S 24in (60cm).

☼ 💧 ❅❅❅ 7–9

Hydrocharis morsus-ranae
(Frog's-bit)
Deciduous, perennial, floating water
plant with rosettes of kidney-shaped,
olive green leaves and small, white
flowers during summer. S 4in (10cm),
but young plantlets remain attached to
form a mass up to 3ft (1m) across.

☼ 💧 ❅❅❅ 7–10

Calla palustris (Water arum)
Deciduous or semi-evergreen, perennial,
spreading, marginal water plant with
heart-shaped, glossy, mid- to dark
green leaves. In spring produces large,
white spathes usually followed by red
or orange fruits. H 10in (25cm),
S 12in (30cm).

☼ 💧 ❅❅❅ 3–8

Sagittaria latifolia (Arrowhead)
Deciduous, perennial, marginal water
plant with curved, soft green leaves
and sprays of white flowers in summer.
H 5ft (1.5m), S 2ft (60cm).

☼ 💧 ❅❅❅ 5–10

Saururus cernuus (Lizard's tail, Swamp lily, Water-dragon)
Deciduous, perennial, marginal water or bog plant. Has clumps of heart-shaped leaves and racemes of creamy flowers in summer. H 9in (23cm), S 12in (30cm).

☼ ◊ ❄❄❄ 5–9

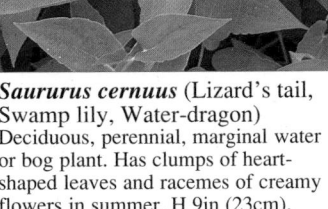

Aponogeton distachyos
(Cape pondweed, Water hawthorn)
Deciduous, perennial, deep-water plant with floating, oblong, mid- to dark green leaves, often splashed with purple. Very fragrant, "forked", white flowers with black stamens are produced throughout summer. S 4ft (1.2m).

☼ ◊ ❄❄ 9–10

Caltha leptosepala
Deciduous, perennial, marginal water plant with heart-shaped, dark green leaves and buttercuplike, white flowers produced in spring. H and S 12in (30cm).

☼ ◊ ❄❄❄ 5–9

Hottonia palustris (Water violet)
Deciduous, perennial, submerged water plant. Dense whorls of much-divided, light green leaves form a spreading mass of foliage. Lilac or whitish flowers appear above water surface in summer. S indefinite.

☼ ◊ ❄❄❄ 5–9

Acorus calamus '**Variegatus**'
(Variegated sweet flag)
Semi-evergreen, perennial, marginal water plant. Swordlike, tangerine-scented leaves have cream variegation and are flushed rose-pink in spring. H 30in (75cm), S 24in (60cm).

☼ ◊ ❄❄❄ 4–10

Acorus gramineus '**Variegatus**'
(Variegated grassy-leaved sweet flag)
Semi-evergreen, perennial, marginal or submerged water plant. Narrow, stiff, grasslike leaves are dark green with cream variegation. H 10in (25cm), S 6in (15cm).

☼ ◊ ❄❄ 6–10

Stratiotes aloides (Water soldier)
Semi-evergreen, perennial, submerged, free-floating water plant. Spiny, olive green leaves are arranged in rosettes. Produces cup-shaped, white, sometimes pink-tinged flowers in summer. Increases by producing small water buds. S 12in (30cm).

☼ ◊ ❄❄❄ 6–9

Houttuynia cordata '**Chamaeleon**', syn. *H.c.* 'Variegata'
Vigorous, deciduous, perennial, ground-cover, marginal water plant. Aromatic, leathery leaves are splashed yellow and red. Has small sprays of white flowers in summer. Needs some sun to enhance variegation. H 4in (10cm), S indefinite.

☼ ◊ ❄❄❄ 5–9

Nelumbo nucifera (Sacred lotus)
Vigorous, deciduous, perennial, marginal water plant. Sturdy stems carry very large, platelike, blue-green leaves and, in summer, large, vivid rose-pink flowers, maturing to flesh pink. H 3–5ft (1–1.5m) above water surface, S 4ft (1.2m). Min. 45°F (7°C).

☼ ◊ 5–10

Water plants

Butomus umbellatus
(Flowering rush)
Deciduous, perennial, rushlike,
marginal water plant with narrow,
twisted leaves and umbels of pink to
rose-red flowers in summer. H 3ft
(1m), S 1¹/2ft (45cm).

☼ ● ❈❈❈❈ 6–10

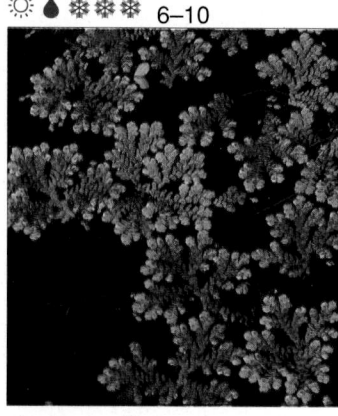

Azolla caroliniana
(Mosquito plant, Water fern)
Deciduous, perennial, floating water
fern with divided fronds that vary from
red to purple in full sun and from pale
green to blue-green in shade. Helps
reduce algae by lessening light in
water. S indefinite.

☼ ● ❈ 7–10

Pontederia cordata
(Pickerel weed)
Deciduous, perennial, marginal water
plant. In late summer, dense spikes of
blue flowers emerge between lance-
shaped, glossy, dark green leaves.
H 30in (75cm), S 18in (45cm).

☼ ● ❈❈❈ 4–9

Myosotis scorpioides 'Mermaid'
Deciduous, perennial, marginal water
plant for mud or very shallow water.
Narrow leaves form sprawling mounds.
Bears small, blue, forget-me-not
flowers throughout summer. H 6in
(15cm), S 12in (30cm).

☼ ● ❈❈❈❈ 4–10

Eichhornia crassipes
(Water hyacinth)
Evergreen or semi-evergreen, perennial
water plant, with glossy leaves, floating
on air-filled leaf stalks. Bears spikes of
blue-and-lilac flowers in summer. May
be invasive in warm conditions. S 9in
(23cm). Min. 34°F (1°C).

☼ ● 8–10

Colocasia esculenta (Taro root)
Deciduous, perennial, marginal water
plant with large, bold, mid- to dark
green leaves, often with prominent,
white veins. Bears insignificant
spathes in summer. May be grown in
wet soil in a pot. H 3¹/2ft (1.1m), S 2ft
(60cm). Min. 34°F (1°C).

☼ ● 9–10

Typha latifolia (Common cattail)
Deciduous, perennial, marginal water
plant with large clumps of foliage.
Produces spikes of beige flowers in late
summer, followed by decorative,
cylindrical, dark brown seed heads. Is
invasive. H to 8ft (2.5m), S 2ft (60cm).

☼ ● ❈❈❈ 3–10

Myriophyllum aquaticum,
syn. *M. proserpinacoides*
(Parrot's-feather, Water-feather)
Deciduous, perennial, partially or
completely submerged water plant.
Spreading, finely divided, blue-green
foliage turns reddish in autumn if it
surfaces. S indefinite.

☼ ● ❈ 7–10

Potamogeton crispus
Deciduous, perennial, submerged
water plant that produces spreading
colonies of seaweedlike, bronze- or
mid-green foliage. Insignificant,
reddish flowers are borne in summer.
Prefers cool water. S indefinite.

☼ ● ❈❈❈ 7–10

Pistia stratiotes (Water lettuce)
Deciduous, perennial, floating water
plant for a pool or aquarium, evergreen
in tropical conditions. Hairy, soft green
foliage is lettucelike in arrangement.
Produces tiny, greenish flowers at
varying times. H and S 4in (10cm).
Min. 50–59°F (10–15°C).

☼ ● 8–10

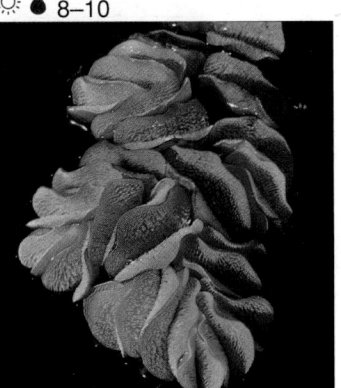

Salvinia auriculata
Deciduous, perennial, floating water
plant, evergreen in tropical conditions,
that forms spreading colonies. Has
rounded, pale to mid-green leaves,
sometimes suffused purplish brown, in
pairs on branching stems. S indefinite.
Min. 50–59°F (10–15°C).

☼ ● 10

Trapa natans
(Jesuit nut, Water chestnut)
Annual, floating water plant with
diamond-shaped leaves, often marked
purple, arranged in neat rosettes. Bears
white flowers in summer. S 9in (23cm).

☼ ● ❋❋ 6–10

Lagarosiphon major,
syn. *Elodea crispa* of gardens
Semi-evergreen, perennial, spreading,
submerged water plant that forms dense,
underwater swards of foliage. Ascending
stems are covered in narrow, reflexed,
dark green leaves. Bears insignificant
flowers in summer. S indefinite.

☼ ● ❋❋❋ 4–9

Typha minima (Dwarf cattail)
Deciduous, perennial, marginal water
plant with grasslike leaves. Spikes of
rust brown flowers in late summer are
succeeded by decorative, cylindrical
seed heads. H 18–24in (45–60cm),
S 12in (30cm).

☼ ● ❋❋❋ 6–9

Euryale ferox (Gorgon)
Annual, deep-water plant. Has
floating, rounded, spiny, olive green
leaves with rich purple undersides and
bears small, violet-purple flowers in
summer. Is suitable only for a tropical
pool. S 5ft (1.5m). Min. 41°F (5°C).

☼ ● 7–10

Sparganium erectum,
syn. *S. ramosum*
Vigorous, deciduous or semi-
evergreen, perennial, marginal water
plant with narrow leaves. Bears small,
greenish brown burs in summer. H 3ft
(1m), S 2ft (60cm).

☼ ● ❋❋❋ 5–9

Myriophyllum verticillatum
(Myriad leaf)
Deciduous, perennial, spreading,
submerged water plant, overwintering
by club-shaped winter buds. Slender
stems are covered with whorls of finely
divided, olive green leaves. S indefinite.

☼ ● ❋❋❋ 4–10

Hydrocleys nymphoides
(Water poppy)
Deciduous, perennial, deep-water
plant, evergreen in tropical conditions,
with floating, oval leaves. Poppylike,
yellow flowers are held above foliage
during summer. S to 2ft (60cm).
Min. 34°F (1°C).

☼ ● 9–10

Water lilies

The serene and classic beauty of a water lily will add a focal point and color to any water garden. Neat, small-leaved plants will grow in only 3in (8cm) of water, but more vigorous plants may need up to 3ft (1m). Their large, platelike leaves provide shelter for fish and also help to reduce the spread of algae. Usually hardy, water lilies make few demands, although they prefer an open, sunny site and still water.

N. caroliniana 'Nivea'

N. 'Gladstoniana'

N. marliacea 'Carnea'

N. 'Escarboucle'

N. 'Virginia'

N. 'American Star'

N. 'James Brydon'

N. × *laydekeri* 'Fulgens'

N. 'Blue Beauty'

N. marliacea 'Albida'

N. 'Rose Arey'

N. 'Fire Crest'

N. pygmaea 'Helvola'

N. pygmaea 'Alba'

N. alba

N. 'Attraction'

N. 'Sunrise'

N. marliacea 'Chromatella'

Water plants

YELLOW

Lysichiton americanus
(Western skunk cabbage, Yellow skunk cabbage)
Vigorous, deciduous, perennial, marginal water or bog plant. In spring, before large, fresh green leaves appear, produces showy, bright yellow spathes. H 3ft (1m), S 2¹/₂ft (75cm).

 7–9

Caltha palustris 'Flore Plena'
(Double marsh marigold)
Deciduous, perennial, marginal water plant with rounded, dark green leaves. Bears clusters of double, bright golden yellow flowers in spring. H and S 10in (25cm).

 4–9

Nymphoides peltata (Water-fringe, Yellow floating-heart)
Deciduous, perennial, deep-water plant with floating, small, round leaves, often spotted and splashed with brown. Produces small, fringed, yellow flowers throughout summer. S 24in (60cm).

7–10

Caltha palustris (Marsh marigold)
Deciduous, perennial, marginal water plant that has rounded, dark green leaves and bears clusters of cup-shaped, bright golden yellow flowers in spring. H 24in (60cm), S 18in (45cm).

4–9

Ranunculus lingua
(Greater spearwort)
Deciduous, perennial, marginal water plant with stout stems and lance-shaped, glaucous leaves. Clusters of yellow flowers are borne in late spring. H 3ft (90cm), S 1¹/₂ft (45cm).

 4–8

Nuphar lutea
(Spatterdock, Yellow pond lily)
Vigorous, deciduous, perennial, deep-water plant for a large pool. Leaves are leathery. Small, sickly-smelling, bottle-shaped, yellow flowers open in summer and are followed by decorative seed heads. S 5ft (1.5m).

5–10

Orontium aquaticum
(Golden-club)
Deciduous, perennial, deep-water plant or, less suitably, marginal water plant. In spring, pencil-like, gold-and-white flower spikes emerge from floating, oblong, blue-gray or blue-green leaves. S 24in (60cm).

7–10

☐ WHITE

Trichocereus bridgesii
Columnar, perennial cactus with
4–8-ribbed, blue-green stems branching
at base. Areoles each produce up to 6
spines. Jasmine-scented, funnel-shaped,
white flowers open at night in summer.
H to 15ft (5m), S 3ft (1m).
Min. 50°F (10°C).

☀ ◊ 10

Cereus forbesii
Columnar, perennial cactus with a
branching, blue-green stem bearing
dark spines on 4–7 prominent ribs.
Has 10in (25cm) long, cup-shaped,
white flowers at night in summer,
followed by red fruits. H 22ft (7m),
S 10ft (3m). Min. 45°F (7°C).

☀ ◊ 10

Selenicereus grandiflorus
(Queen-of-the-night)
Climbing, perennial cactus. Has
7-ribbed, ¹/₂–³/₄in (1–2cm) wide, green
stems with yellow spines. White
flowers, 7–12in (18–30cm) across,
open at night in summer. H 10ft (3m),
S indefinite. Min. 41°F (5°C).

◑ ◊ 10

Myrtillocactus geometrizans
(Blue-flame)
Columnar, perennial cactus with a
much-branched, 5- or 6-ribbed, blue-
green stem. Bears short, black spines,
on plants over 1ft (30cm) tall, and white
flowers at night in summer. H to 12ft
(4m), S 6ft (2m). Min. 54°F (12°C).

☀ ◊ 10

Cereus peruvianus
Columnar, perennial cactus. Has a
branching, silvery blue stem with
golden spines on 4–8 sharply indented
ribs. Carries cup-shaped, white flowers,
4in (10cm) across, at night in summer,
followed by pear-shaped, red fruits. H
15ft (5m), S 12ft (4m). Min. 45°F (7°C).

☀ ◊ 10

Azureocereus hertlingianus,
syn. *Browningia hertlingianus*
Slow-growing, columnar, perennial
cactus with a silvery blue stem, golden
spines and tufted areoles. Nocturnal,
white flowers appear in summer, only
on plants over 3ft (1m) high. H 25ft
(8m), S 12ft (4m). Min. 45°F (7°C).

☀ ◊ 10

Pachypodium lameri
Treelike, perennial succulent with a
spiny, pale green stem crowned by
linear leaves. Has fragrant, trumpet-
shaped, creamy white flowers in
summer, on plants over 5ft (1.5m) tall.
Stems branch after each flowering. H
20ft (6m), S 6ft (2m). Min. 52°F (11°C).

☀ ◊ 10

Carnegiea gigantea (Saguaro)
Very slow-growing, perennial cactus
with a thick, 12–24-ribbed, spiny, green
stem. Tends to branch and bears short,
funnel-shaped, fleshy, white flowers at
stem tips in summer, only when over
12ft (4m) high. H to 40ft (12m), S 10ft
(3m). Min. 45°F (7°C).

☀ ◊ 10

Lemaireocereus marginatus,
syn. *Marginatocereus marginatus*
(Organ-pipe cactus)
Columnar, perennial cactus with a 5- or
6-ribbed, branching, shiny stem. Areoles
bear minute spines. Produces funnel-
shaped, white flowers in summer. H 22ft
(7m), S 10ft (3m). Min. 52°F (11°C).

 ◌ 10

Agave parviflora
Basal-rosetted, perennial succulent.
Has narrow, white-marked, dark green
leaves with white fibers peeling from
edges. Produces white flowers in
summer. H 5ft (1.5m), S 20in (50cm).
Min. 41°F (5°C).

 ◌ 10

Stetsonia coryne (Toothpick cactus)
Treelike, perennial cactus with a short,
swollen trunk bearing 8- or 9-ribbed,
blue-green stems. Black spines fade
with age to white with black tips.
Funnel-shaped, white flowers appear at
night in summer. H 25ft (8m), S 12ft
(4m). Min. 50°F (10°C).

 ◌ 10

Crassula ovata, syn. *C. argentea*,
C. portulacea (Chinese rubber
plant, Jade plant)
Perennial succulent with a swollen
stem crowned by glossy, green leaves,
at times red-edged. Bears 5-petaled,
white flowers in autumn-winter. H 12ft
(4m), S 6ft (2m). Min. 41°F (5°C).

☀ ◌ 10

Trichocereus spachianus
(White torch cactus)
Clump-forming, perennial cactus with
glossy, green stems bearing 10–15 ribs
and pale golden spines. Fragrant,
funnel-shaped, white flowers open at
night in summer. H and S 6ft (2m).
Min. 46°F (8°C).

☀ ◌ 10

Espostoa lanata (Peruvian old-
man cactus, Snowball cactus)
Very slow-growing, columnar,
perennial cactus with a branching,
woolly, green stem. Foul-smelling,
white flowers appear in summer, only
on plants over 3ft (1m) high. H to 12ft
(4m), S 6ft (2m). Min. 50°F (10°C).

 ◌ 10

Pereskia aculeata (Barbados
gooseberry, Lemon vine)
Fast-growing, deciduous, climbing
cactus with broad, glossy leaves.
Orange-centered, creamy white
flowers appear in autumn, only on
plants over 3ft (1m) high. H to 30ft
(10m), S 15ft (5m). Min. 41°F (5°C).

☀ ◌ 9–10

Agave americana 'Variegata'
(Variegated century plant)
Basal-rosetted, perennial succulent.
Has sharply pointed, sword-shaped,
blue-green leaves with yellow edges.
Stem carries white flowers, each 3½in
(9cm) long, in spring-summer. Offsets
freely. H and S 6ft (2m).

 ◌ ❋ 9–10

Cacti and other Succulents/large

Haageocereus versicolor
Columnar, perennial cactus. Dense,
radial spines, golden, red, or brown, at
times form colored bands around a
longer, central spine up the green stem.
Long-tubed, white flowers appear near
crown of plant in summer. H to 6ft
(2m), S 3ft (1m). Min. 52°F (11°C).

☼ ◊ 10

Crassula arborescens
(Silver-dollar plant)
Perennial succulent with a thick,
robust stem crowned by branches
bearing rounded, silvery blue leaves,
often with red edges. Has 5-petaled,
pink flowers in autumn-winter. H 12ft
(4m), S 6ft (2m). Min. 45°F (7°C).

☼ ◊ 10

Pereskia grandifolia,
syn. *Rhodocactus grandifolius*
(Rose cactus)
Deciduous, bushy, perennial cactus
with black spines. Single roselike, pink
flowers form in summer-autumn only
on plants over 1ft (30cm) high. H 15ft
(5m), S 10ft (3m). Min. 50°F (10°C).

☼ ◊ 10

Adenium obesum (Desert rose)
Treelike, perennial succulent with a
fleshy, tapering, green trunk and stems
crowned by oval, glossy, green leaves,
dull green beneath. Carries funnel-
shaped, pink to pinkish red flowers,
white inside, in summer. H 6ft (2m),
S 20in (50cm). Min. 59°F (15°C).

☼◑ ◊ 10

Lophocereus schottii
Columnar, perennial cactus, branching
with age. Olive to dark green stem,
covered with small, white spines, bears
4–15 ribs. Funnel-shaped, pink flowers,
1¼in (3cm) across, are produced at
night in summer. H 22ft (7m), S 6ft
(2m). Min. 50°F (10°C).

☼ ◊ 10

Pilosocereus palmeri
Columnar, perennial cactus with a
10–12-ribbed, blue-green stem. Crown
has long, white hairs. Bears tubular,
pink flowers, with cream anthers, at
night in summer, on plants over 5ft
(1.5m) tall. H to 20ft (6m), S 3ft (1m).
Min. 52°F (11°C).

☼ ◊ 10

Aloe arborescens 'Variegata'
Evergreen, bushy, succulent-leaved
shrub. Each stem is crowned by
rosettes of long, slender, blue-green
leaves with toothed edges and cream
stripes. Produces numerous spikes of
red flowers in late winter and spring.
H and S 6ft (2m). Min. 45°F (7°C).

☼ ◊ 10

Aloe ferox
Evergreen, succulent tree with a woody
stem crowned by a dense rosette of
sword-shaped, blue-green leaves that
have spined margins. Carries an erect
spike of bell-shaped, orange-scarlet
flowers in spring. H to 10ft (3m),
S 5–6ft (1.5–2m). Min. 45°F (7°C).

☼ ◊ 10

Aloe ciliaris (Climbing aloe)
Climbing, perennial succulent with a
slender stem crowned by a rosette of
narrow, green leaves. Has white teeth
where leaf base joins stem. Bears bell-
shaped, scarlet flowers, with yellow
and green mouths, in spring. H 15ft
(5m), S 1ft (30cm). Min. 45°F (7°C).

☼◑ ◊ 10

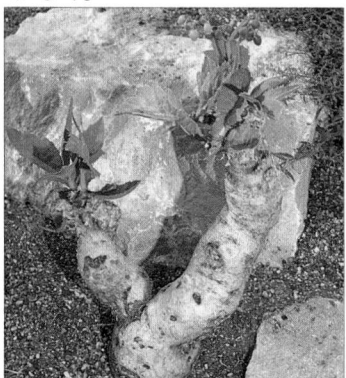

Cyphostemma juttae,
syn. *Cissus juttae*
Perennial succulent. Swollen stem has
peeling bark and deciduous, scandent
branches with broad leaves. Bears
inconspicuous, yellow-green flowers in
summer. Green fruits turn yellow or red.
H and S 6ft (2m). Min. 50°F (10°C).

☼ ◊ 10

Lemaireocereus euphorbioides,
syn. *Rooksbya euphorbioides*
Columnar, perennial cactus. Has gray-
green to dark green stems, 4in (10cm)
across, with 8–10 ribs and 1 or 2 black
spines per areole. Funnel-shaped, wine
red flowers appear in summer. H to 10ft
(3m), S 3ft (1m). Min. 52°F (11°C).

☼ ◊ 10

Pedilanthus tithymaloides 'Variegata'
Bushy, perennial succulent with stems angled at each node. Leaves have white or pink marks. Stem tips carry small, greenish flowers in red to yellowish green bracts in summer. H to 10ft (3m), S 1ft (30cm). Min. 50°F (10°C).

☀ ◊ 10

Cephalocereus senilis (Old-man cactus)
Very slow-growing, columnar, perennial cactus with a green stem covered in long, white hairs, masking short, white spines. Is unlikely to flower in cultivation. H 50ft (15m), S 6in (15cm). Min. 41°F (5°C).

☀ ◊ 10

Furcraea foetida 'Mediopicta', syn. *F. gigantea* 'Mediopicta'
Basal-rosetted, perennial succulent with broad, sword-shaped, green leaves, striped with creamy white, to 8ft (2.5m) long. Has bell-shaped, green flowers, with white interiors, in summer. H 10ft (3m), S 15ft (5m). Min. 43°F (6°C).

☀ ◊ 10

Kalanchoe beharensis (Velvetleaf)
Bushy, perennial succulent with triangular to lance-shaped, olive green leaves, covered with fine, brown hairs. Bell-shaped, yellow flowers appear in late winter, only on plants over 6ft (2m) high. H and S to 12ft (4m). Min. 50°F (10°C).

☀ ◊ 10

Bowiea volubilis (Climbing onion)
Bulbous succulent with climbing, much-branched, slender stems and no proper leaves. Produces small, star-shaped, green flowers at tips of stems in summer. Provide support. H 3–6ft (1–2m), S 1½–2ft (45–60cm). Min. 50°F (10°C).

☀ ◊ 10

Ferocactus acanthodes
Slow-growing, columnar, perennial cactus, spherical when young. Green, 10–20-ribbed stem is covered with large, hooked, red or yellow spines. Funnel-shaped, yellow flowers form in summer on plants over 10in (25cm) wide. H 10ft (3m), S 32in (80cm). Min. 41°F (5°C).

☀ ◊ 10

Cleistocactus strausii (Silver torch)
Fast-growing, columnar, perennial cactus with 3in (8cm) wide stems carrying short, dense, white spines. Masses of long, tubular, red flowers appear in spring, only on plants over 2ft (60cm) high. H 10ft (3m), S 3–6ft (1–2m). Min. 41°F (5°C).

☀ ◊ 10

Pachycereus pringlei
Slow-growing, columnar, perennial cactus with a branched, bluish green stem that has 10–15 ribs. Large areoles each have 15–25 black-tipped, white spines. Is unlikely to flower in cultivation. H 35ft (11m), S 10ft (3m). Min. 50°F (10°C).

☀ ◊ 10

Echinocactus grusonii (Golden barrel cactus)
Slow-growing, hemispherical, perennial cactus. Spined, green stem has 30 ribs. Woolly crown bears a ring of straw-colored flowers in summer, only on stems over 15in (38cm) wide. H and S to 6ft (2m). Min. 52°F (11°C).

☀ ◊ 10

Opuntia robusta
Bushy, perennial cactus. Silvery blue stem has flattened, oval segments with either no spines or 8–12 white ones, to 2in (5cm) long, per areole. Saucer-shaped, yellow flowers, 3in (7cm) across, appear in spring-summer. H and S 15ft (5m). Min. 41°F (5°C).

☀ ◊ 10

Cacti and other Succulents/medium

Gymnocalycium gibbosum
Spherical to columnar, perennial
cactus that has a dark green stem with
12–19 rounded ribs, pale yellow
spines, darkening with age, and white
flowers, to 3in (7cm) long, in summer.
H 12in (30cm), S 8in (20cm).
Min. 41°F (5°C).

☼ ◌ 10

Trichocereus candicans
Clump-forming, perennial cactus.
Grass green stems, with up to 11 ribs,
branch freely from base. Areoles each
have 10–15 radial spines and 4 central
ones. Fragrant, funnel-shaped, white
flowers open at night in summer. H 3ft
(1m), S indefinite. Min. 46°F (8°C).

☼ ◌ 10

Echinopsis multiplex
Spherical to columnar, perennial
cactus with a 13–15-ribbed, green stem
and ³/₄–1¹/₂in (2–4cm) long spines. Has
4in (10cm) wide, tubular, white to
lavender flowers, to 8in (20cm) long,
in spring-summer. Offsets freely.
H and S 12in (30cm). Min. 41°F (5°C).

☼ ◌ 10

Agave victoriae-reginae
(Queen Victoria century plant)
Slow-growing, domed, perennial
succulent with a basal rosette of spine-
less, white-striped and -edged leaves.
Has cream flowers on a 12ft (4m) tall
stem in spring-summer after 20–30 years.
H and S 2ft (60cm). Min. 41°F (5°C).

☼ ◌ 10

Rhipsalis cereuscula (Coral cactus)
Pendent, perennial cactus with 4- or
5-angled or cylindrical, green stems
and branches, to 1¹/₄in (3cm) long, in
whorls. Stem tips each bear bell-
shaped, white flowers in winter-spring.
H 24in (60cm), S 20in (50cm).
Min. 50°F (10°C).

☼ ◌ 10

Epiphyllum lauii
Bushy, perennial cactus, usually with
strap-shaped, red-tinged, glossy stems
which may also be spiny, cylindrical,
or 4-angled. Has fragrant white flowers,
with brown sepals, in spring-summer.
H 12in (30cm), S 20in (50cm).
Min. 50°F (10°C).

☼ ◌ 10

Epiphyllum anguliger
(Fishbone cactus)
Erect, then pendent, perennial cactus.
Has strap-shaped, flattened, green
stems with indented margins. Produces
tubular, 4in (10cm) wide, white
flowers in summer. H 3ft (1m),
S 16in (40cm). Min. 52°F (11°C).

☼ ◌ 10

Rhipsalis warmingiana
Erect, then pendent, perennial cactus
with slender, notched, cylindrical,
green branches, sometimes tinged
red or brown, with 2–4 angles. Has
green-white flowers in winter-spring,
followed by violet berries. H 3ft (1m),
S 20in (50cm). Min. 52°F (11°C).

☼ ◌ 10

Rhipsalis tucumanensis
Pendent, perennial cactus with
cylindrical, green stems, to ¹/₂in (1cm)
across, branching less than many other
Rhipsalis species. Has masses of very
pale pink flowers in early summer,
then pinkish white berries. H 3ft (1m),
S 20in (50cm). Min. 50°F (10°C).

☼ ◌ 10

Senecio rowleyanus
(String-of-beads)
Pendent, perennial succulent. Very
slender, green stems bear cylindrical,
green leaves. Has heads of fragrant,
tubular, white flowers from spring to
autumn. Suits a hanging pot. H 3ft (1m),
S indefinite. Min. 41°F (5°C).

☼ ◊ 10

Ceropegia woodii
(Heart vine, Rosary vine)
Semi-evergreen, trailing, succulent
sub-shrub with tuberous roots. Has
silvery green leaves, reddening in sun,
and hairy, pinkish green flowers, from
spring to autumn. H 3ft (1m),
S indefinite. Min. 45°F (7°C).

◐ ◊ 10

Senecio articulatus 'Variegatus'
Deciduous, spreading, perennial
succulent. Has gray-marked, silvery
blue stems with weak joints. Bears
cream- and pink-marked, blue-green
leaves in summer and yellow flower
heads from spring to autumn. H 2ft
(60cm), S indefinite. Min. 50°F (10°C).

☼ ◊ 10

Nopalxochia phyllanthoides, syn.
Epiphyllum 'Deutsche Kaiserin'
Pendent, epiphytic, perennial cactus
with flattened, toothed, glossy, green
stems, each 2in (5cm) across. Stem
margins each bear pink flowers, to 4in
(10cm) across, in spring. H 2ft (60cm),
S 3ft (1m). Min. 50°F (10°C).

◐ ◊ 10

Hesperaloe parviflora,
syn. *Yucca parviflora*
Basal-rosetted, perennial succulent,
often with peeling, white fibers at leaf
edges. Flower stems each bear a raceme
of bell-shaped, pink to red flowers in
summer-autumn. H 3ft (1m) or more,
S 6ft (2m). Min. 37°F (3°C).

☼ ◊ 10

Borzicactus celsianus,
syn. *Oreocereus celsianus*
(Old-man-of-the-mountains)
Slow-growing, perennial cactus. Green
stem has heavy, golden spines and
wispy, white spines. Mature plants
bear pink flowers in summer. H 3ft
(1m), S 1ft (30cm). Min. 50°F (10°C).

☼ ◊ 10

**Kalanchoe fedtschenkoi
'Variegata'**
(Variegated rainbow kalanchoe)
Bushy, perennial succulent. Blue-green
and cream leaves also color red. Bears
a new plantlet in each leaf notch. Has
brownish pink flowers in late winter.
H and S to 3ft (1m). Min. 50°F (10°C).

☼ ◊ 10

Echinocereus schmollii,
syn. *Wilcoxia schmollii*
(Lamb's-tail cactus)
Erect to prostrate, tuberous cactus
with 8–10-ribbed, purplish green stems
and mostly white spines. Has pinkish
purple flowers in spring-summer.
H and S 12in (30cm). Min. 46°F (8°C).

☼ ◊ 10

Kalanchoe daigremontiana
(Devil's-backbone)
Erect, perennial succulent with a stem
bearing fleshy, boat-shaped, toothed
leaves. Produces a plantlet in each leaf
notch. Umbels of pink flowers appear
at stem tops in winter. H to 3ft (1m),
S 1ft (30cm). Min. 45°F (7°C).

☼ ◊ 10

Echinocereus reichenbachii var.
baileyi, syn. *E. baileyi*
Columnar, perennial cactus with a
slightly branched stem bearing 12–23
ribs and yellowish white, 1¼in (3cm)
long spines. Produces pink flowers
with darker bases in spring. H 12in
(30cm), S 8in (20cm). Min. 45°F (7°C).

☼ ◊ 10

Cacti and other Succulents/medium

Kalanchoe 'Wendy'
Semi-erect, perennial succulent with
narrowly oval, glossy, green leaves,
3in (7cm) long. In late winter bears
bell-shaped, pinkish red flowers, ³/₄in
(2cm) long, with yellow tips. Is ideal
for a hanging basket. H and S 12in
(30cm). Min. 50°F (10°C).

☀◐ ◊ 10

Aporocactus flagelliformis
(Rattail cactus)
Pendent, perennial cactus with pencil-
thick, green stems bearing short,
golden spines. Has double, cerise
flowers along stems in spring. Keep
dry in winter. Is good for a hanging
basket. H 3ft (1m), S indefinite.

☀◐ ◊ ❄ 10

Epiphyllum 'Gloria'
Erect, then pendent, perennial cactus.
Strap-shaped, flattened, green stems
have toothed edges. Produces pinkish
red flowers, 4in (10cm) across, in
spring. H 1ft (30cm), S 3ft (1m).
Min. 41°F (5°C).

☀◐ ◊ 10

Epiphyllum 'M.A. Jeans'
Erect, then pendent, perennial cactus.
Strap-shaped, flattened, green stems
have shallowly toothed edges. In spring
has deep pink flowers, 3in (8cm) across,
with white anthers. H 12in (30cm),
S 20in (50cm). Min. 41°F (5°C).

☀◐ ◊ 10

Echinocereus pentalophus
Clump-forming, perennial cactus with
spined, green stems, 1¹/₄–1¹/₂in (3–4cm)
wide, that have 4–8 ribs, later rounded.
Has trumpet-shaped, bright pink
flowers, paler at base, to 5in (12cm)
across, in spring. H 2ft (60cm),
S 3ft (1m). Min. 41°F (5°C).

☀ ◊ 10

Lampranthus spectabilis
Spreading, perennial succulent with
erect stems and narrow, cylindrical,
gray-green leaves. In summer produces
daisylike flowers, cerise with yellow
centers or golden yellow throughout.
H 1ft (30cm), S indefinite.
Min. 41°F (5°C).

☀ ◊ 10

Kalanchoe blossfeldiana Hybrids
Bushy, perennial succulent with oval to
oblong, toothed, glossy, green leaves.
Produces clusters of yellow, orange,
pink, red, or purple flowers, year round.
Makes an excellent house plant. H and
S 1ft (30cm). Min. 50°F (10°C).

☼ ◊ 10

**Gymnocalycium mihanovichii
'Red Head'**, syn. *G.m.* var. *hibotan*
Perennial cactus with a red stem, 8
angular ribs, and curved spines. Must be
grafted on to any fast-growing stock as
it contains no chlorophyll. Has pink
flowers in spring-summer. H and S as
per graft stock. Min. 50°F (10°C).

☼ ◊ 10

Aloe variegata
(Kanniedood aloe, Tiger aloe)
Humped, perennial succulent. Has
triangular, white-marked, dark green
leaves with pronounced keels beneath.
Bears a spike of pinkish red flowers in
spring. Is a good house plant. H 12in
(30cm), S 4in (10cm). Min. 45°F (7°C).

☼ ◊ 10

Echeveria pulvinata (Plush plant)
Bushy, perennial succulent with
brown-haired stems each crowned by a
rosette of thick, rounded, green leaves
that become red-edged in autumn.
Leaves have short, white hairs. Bears
red flowers in spring. H 12in (30cm),
S 20in (50cm). Min. 41°F (5°C).

☼ ◊ 10

Oroya neoperuviana
Spherical, perennial cactus with a
much-ribbed, dark green stem covered
in yellow spines, ⁵/₈in (1.5cm) long,
with darker bases. Orange-red buds
develop into pink flowers, with yellow
bases, in spring-summer. H 10in
(25cm), S 8in (20cm). Min. 50°F(10°C).

☼ ◊ 10

Dudleya pulverulenta
(Chalk lettuce)
Basal-rosetted, perennial succulent
with strap-shaped, pointed, silvery
gray leaves. Bears masses of star-
shaped, red flowers in spring-summer.
H 2ft (60cm), S 1ft (30cm).
Min. 45°F (7°C).

☼ ◊ 10

Kalanchoe 'Tessa'
Prostrate to pendent, perennial
succulent with narrowly oval, green
leaves, 1¼in (3cm) long. Bears tubular,
orange-red flowers, ³/₄in (2cm) long, in
late winter. H 1ft (30cm), S 2ft (60cm).
Min. 50°F (10°C).

☼ ◊ 10

Ferocactus hamatacanthus,
syn. *Hamatocactus hamatacanthus*
Slow-growing, spherical to columnar,
perennial cactus with a 13-ribbed
stem that bears hooked, red spines, to
5in (12cm) long. Has yellow blooms in
summer, then spherical, red fruits.
H and S 2ft (60cm). Min. 41°F (5°C).

☼ ◊ 10

Crassula falcata (Propeller plant,
Scarlet paintbrush)
Bushy, perennial succulent that
branches freely. Produces long, fleshy,
gray leaves, each twisted like a
propeller, and large clusters of fragrant
red flowers in late summer. H and
S 3ft (1m). Min. 45°F (7°C).

☼ ◊ 10

Cacti and other Succulents/medium

Mammillaria hahniana (Old-lady cactus, Old-woman cactus)
Spherical to columnar, perennial cactus with a green stem bearing long, woolly, white hairs. Carries cerise flowers in spring and spherical, red fruits in autumn. H 16in (40cm), S 6in (15cm). Min. 41°F (5°C).

☼ ◊ 10

Opuntia erinacea (Grizzly bear)
Bushy, perennial cactus with a green stem consisting of 6in (15cm) long, flattened segments. Areoles bear 6–15 flattened, 8in (20cm) long, hairlike spines. Has masses of saucer-shaped, red or yellow flowers in summer. H 20in (50cm), S 6ft (2m). Min. 41°F (5°C).

☼ ◊ 10

Beschorneria yuccoides
Clump-forming, perennial succulent with a basal rosette of up to 20 rough, grayish green leaves, to 3ft (1m) long and 2in (5cm) across. Produces pendent, tubular, bright red flowers in summer in spikes over 6ft (2m) tall. H 3ft (1m), S 10ft (3m).

☼ ◊ ❄ 9–10

Aloe barbadensis, syn. *A. vera*
Clump-forming, perennial succulent with basal rosettes of tapering, thick leaves, mottled green, later gray-green. Flower stems carry bell-shaped, yellow flowers in summer. Propagate by offsets as plant is sterile. H 2ft (60cm), S indefinite. Min. 50°F (10°C).

☼ ◊ 10

Tylecodon reticulata, syn. *Cotyledon reticulata*
Deciduous, bushy, succulent shrub. Swollen branches bear cylindrical leaves in winter. Has tubular, green-yellow flowers on a woody stem in autumn. H and S 1ft (30cm). Min. 45°F (7°C).

☼ ◊ 10

Astrophytum myriostigma (Bishop's cap, Monk's hood)
Slow-growing, spherical to slightly elongated, perennial cactus. Fleshy stem has 4–6 ribs and is flecked with tiny tufts of white spines. Bears yellow flowers in summer. H 12in (30cm), S 8in (20cm). Min. 41°F (5°C).

☼ ◊ 10

Mammillaria geminispina
Clump-forming, perennial cactus. Has a spherical, green stem densely covered with short, white, radial spines and very long, white, central spines. Has red flowers, ½–¾in (1–2cm) across, in spring. H 10in (25cm), S 20in (50cm). Min. 41°F (5°C).

☼ ◊ 10

Agave filifera (Thread agave)
Basal-rosetted, perennial succulent with narrow, green leaves, each spined at the tip. White leaf margins gradually break away, leaving long, white fibers. Carries yellow-green flowers on an 8ft (2.5m) tall stem in summer. Offsets freely. H 3ft (1m), S 6ft (2m).

☼ ◊ ❄ 10

x *Pachyveria glauca*
Clump-forming, perennial succulent with a dense, basal rosette of fleshy, incurved, oval, silvery blue leaves, to 2½in (6cm) long, with darker marks. Bears star-shaped, yellow flowers, each with a red tip, in spring. H and S 12in (30cm). Min. 41°F (5°C).

☼ ◊ 10

Agave parryi
Basal-rosetted, perennial succulent with stiff, broad, gray-green leaves, each to 12in (30cm) long with a solitary dark spine at its pointed tip. Flower stem, to 12ft (4m) long, bears creamy yellow flowers in summer. H 20in (50cm), S 3ft (1m). Min. 41°F (5°C).

☀ ◊ 10

Aeonium haworthii (Pinwheel)
Bushy, perennial succulent. Freely branching stems bear rosettes, 5in (12cm) across, of blue-green leaves, often with red margins. Has a terminal spike of star-shaped, pink-tinged, pale yellow flowers in spring. H 2ft (60cm), S 3ft (1m). Min. 41°F (5°C).

◑ ◊ 10

Leuchtenbergia principis
Basal-rosetted, perennial cactus with narrow, angular, dull gray-green tubercles, each 4in (10cm) long and crowned by papery spines to 4in (10cm) long. Crown bears yellow flowers, to 3in (7cm) across, in summer. H and S 12in (30cm). Min. 43°F (6°C).

☀ ◊ 10

Copiapoa cinerea
Very slow-growing, clump-forming, perennial cactus. Blue-green stem bears up to 25 ribs and black spines. Has a woolly, white-gray crown and, on plants over 4in (10cm) across, yellow flowers in spring-summer. H 20in (50cm), S 6ft (2m). Min. 50°F (10°C).

◑ ◊ 10

Kalanchoe tomentosa (Panda-bear plant, Plush plant, Pussy-ears)
Bushy, perennial succulent with thick, oval, gray leaves, covered with velvety bristles and often edged with brown at tips. Has yellowish purple flowers in winter. H 20in (50cm), S 12in (30cm). Min. 50°F (10°C).

☀ ◊ 10

Opuntia microdasys var. **alba**
Bushy, perennial cactus with green, flattened, oval segments. Spineless areoles, with slender, barbed, white hairs, are set in diagonal rows. Funnel-shaped, yellow flowers appear in summer. H 2ft (60cm), S 1ft (30cm). Min. 50°F (10°C).

☀ ◊ 10

Ferocactus setispinus,
syn. **Hamatocactus setispinus**
Slow-growing, perennial cactus with a 13-ribbed stem and yellow or white spines. Fragrant yellow flowers with red throats appear in summer, only on plants over 2in (5cm) across. H and S 12in (30cm). Min. 41°F (5°C).

☀ ◊ 10

Lobivia haageana
Columnar, perennial cactus with a 20–25-ribbed, bluish to dark green stem that has yellow, radial spines with longer, darker, central ones. In summer produces yellow flowers, 3in (7cm) across, with red throats. H 12in (30cm), S 6in (15cm). Min. 41°F (5°C).

☀ ◊ 10

Agave attenuata
Perennial succulent with a thick stem crowned by a rosette of sword-shaped, spineless, pale green leaves. Arching flower stem, to 5ft (1.5m) long, is densely covered with yellow flowers in spring-summer. H 3ft (1m), S 6ft (2m). Min. 41°F (5°C).

☀ ◊ 10

Dioscorea elephantipes,
syn. **Testudinaria elephantipes**
(Elephant's foot)
Very slow-growing, deciduous, perennial succulent with a domed, woody trunk, annual, climbing stems, and yellow flowers in autumn. H 20in (50cm), S 3ft (1m). Min. 50°F (10°C).

☀ ◊ 10

Epiphyllum 'Jennifer Ann'
Erect, then pendent, perennial cactus. Has strap-shaped, flattened, green stems with toothed margins. Bears yellow flowers, 6in (15cm) across, in spring. H 12in (30cm), S 20in (50cm). Min. 41°F (5°C).

◑ ◊ 10

Cacti and other Succulents/medium

Aeonium arboreum 'Schwarzkopf'
Bushy, perennial succulent with stems each crowned by a rosette, to 6in (15cm) across, of narrow, purple leaves. Bears golden pyramids of flowers in spring on 2–3-year-old stems, which then die. H to 2ft (60cm), S 3ft (1m). Min. 41°F (5°C).

☀ ◌ 9–10

Aloe striata (Coral aloe)
Basal-rosetted, perennial succulent. Has broad, blue-green leaves, with white margins and marks, that become suffused red in full sun. Has a panicle of reddish orange flowers in spring. Makes a good house plant. H and S 3ft (1m). Min. 45°F (7°C).

☀ ◌ 10

Parodia chrysacanthion
Spherical, perennial cactus with a much-ribbed, green stem densely covered with bristlelike, golden spines, each ¹/₂–³/₄in (1–2cm) long. Crown bears yellow flowers in spring and, often, pale yellow wool. H and S 1ft (30cm). Min. 50°F (10°C).

☀ ◌ 10

Hatiora salicornioides (Dancing bones, Drunkard's dream)
Bushy, perennial, epiphytic cactus with freely branching, 1¹/₄in (3cm) long stems. Has joints with expanded tips and terminal, bell-shaped, golden yellow flowers in spring. H and S 1ft (30cm). Min. 52°F (11°C).

☀ ◌ 10

Cotyledon undulata (Silver crown)
Evergreen, upright, succulent sub-shrub with a swollen stem bearing oval, green leaves, densely coated in white wax, with flat, wavy tips. Each 28in (70cm) long flower stem bears a bell-shaped, orange flower in autumn. H and S 20in (50cm). Min. 45°F (7°C).

☀ ◌ 10

Notocactus leninghausii (Golden ball cactus)
Clump-forming, perennial cactus with a much-ribbed, golden-spined stem. Woolly crown slopes towards sun. In summer, on plants over 4in (10cm) tall, yellow blooms open flat. H 3ft (1m), S 1ft (30cm). Min. 50°F (10°C).

☀ ◌ 10

Opuntia tunicata
Mounded, perennial cactus. Has cylindrical, green stem segments densely covered with 2in (5cm) long, golden spines that are enclosed in a papery sheath. Bears shallowly saucer-shaped, yellow flowers in spring-summer. H 2ft (60cm), S 3ft (1m). Min. 50°F (10°C).

☀ ◌ 10

Kalanchoe tubiflora
Erect, perennial succulent with long, almost cylindrical, gray-green leaves with reddish brown mottling and flattened, notched tips that form plantlets. Bears an umbel of pale orange-yellow flowers in late winter. H to 3ft (1m), S 1ft (30cm). Min. 46°F (8°C).

☀ ◌ 10

Lampranthus aurantiacus
Erect, then prostrate, sparse-branching perennial succulent with short, cylindrical, tapering, gray-green leaves. Masses of daisylike, bright orange flowers, 2in (5cm) wide, open in summer sun. H 20in (50cm), S 28in (70cm). Min. 41°F (5°C).

☀ ◌ 10

Cacti and other Succulents/small

Mammillaria plumosa
Clump-forming, perennial cactus. Has a spherical, green stem completely covered with feathery, white spines. Carries cream flowers in mid-winter. Is difficult to grow. Add calcium to soil. H 5in (12cm), S 16in (40cm). Min. 50°F (10°C).

☼ ◊ 10

Gibbaeum velutinum
Clump-forming, perennial succulent with paired, fingerlike, velvety, bluish gray-green leaves, to 2¹/₂in (6cm) long. Produces daisylike, pink, lilac, or white flowers, 2in (5cm) across, in spring. H 3in (8cm), S 12in (30cm). Min. 41°F (5°C).

☼ ◊ 10

Haworthia truncata
Clump-forming, perennial succulent with a basal fan of broad, erect, rough, blue-gray leaves with pale gray lines and flat ends. Produces small, tubular, white flowers, with spreading petals, from spring to autumn. H ³/₄in (2cm), S 4in (10cm). Min. 50°F (10°C).

☼ ◊ 10

Lithops marmorata
Egg-shaped, perennial succulent, divided into 2 unequal-sized, swollen, pale gray leaves with dark gray marks on convex, upper surfaces. Bears a white flower in late summer or early autumn. H ³/₄–1¹/₄in (2–3cm), S 2in (5cm). Min. 41°F (5°C).

☼ ◊ 10

Lithops karasmontana
Egg-shaped, perennial succulent, divided into 2 unequal-sized, gray leaves, that have pink, upper surfaces with sunken, darker pink marks. Bears a white flower in late summer or early autumn. H to 1¹/₂in (4cm), S 2in (5cm). Min. 41°F (5°C).

☼ ◊ 10

Adromischus maculatus
Clump-forming, perennial succulent with rounded, glossy, green leaves with purple marks. Leaf tips are often wavy. Carries tubular, purplish white flowers, on a 12in (30cm) tall stem, in summer. H 2¹/₂in (6cm), S 4–6in (10–15cm). Min. 45°F (7°C).

☼ ◊ 10

Echinocereus leucanthus, syn. *Wilcoxia albiflora*
Clump-forming, tuberous cactus with spined, 6- or 7-ribbed, prostrate stems. In spring bears often terminal, dark-throated, white flowers, softly streaked purple, with green stigmas. H 8in (20cm), S 12in (30cm). Min. 46°F (8°C).

☼ ◊ 10

Trichodiadema mirabile
Bushy to prostrate, perennial succulent with cylindrical, dark green leaves tipped with dark brown bristles and covered in papillae. Stem tip bears white flowers, 1¹/₂in (4cm) across, from spring to autumn. H 6in (15cm), S 12in (30cm). Min. 41°F (5°C).

☼ ◊ 10

Haworthia attenuata var. **clariperla**
Clump-forming, perennial succulent with a basal rosette of triangular, 1¹/₄in (3cm) long, dark green leaves, that have pronounced, white dots. Has tubular, white flowers, with spreading petals, from spring to autumn. H 3in (7cm), S 10in (25cm). Min. 41°F (5°C).

☼ ◊ 10

Cacti and other Succulents/small

☐ WHITE

Crassula socialis
Spreading, perennial succulent with short, dense rosettes, to ¹/₂in (1cm) across, of fleshy, triangular, green leaves. Produces clusters of star-shaped, white flowers on 1¹/₄in (3cm) tall stems in spring. H 2in (5cm), S indefinite. Min. 41°F (5°C).

☀ ◊ 10

Strombocactus disciformis
Very slow-growing, hemispherical, perennial cactus with a gray-green to brown stem set with a spiral of blunt tubercles. Woolly crown has bristlelike spines, which soon fall off, and cream flowers in summer. H 1¹/₄in (3cm), S 4in (10cm). Min. 41°F (5°C).

☀ ◊ 10

Mammillaria schiedeana
Clump-forming, perennial cactus. Green stem is covered with short, feathery, yellow spines that turn white. Produces cream flowers and narrow, red seed pods in late summer. H 4in (10cm), S 12in (30cm). Min. 50°F (10°C).

☀ ◊ 10

Neoporteria villosa
Clump-forming, perennial cactus with a branched, green to dark gray-green stem. Has dense, sometimes curved, gray spines, 1¹/₄in (3cm) long. Produces tubular, pink or white flowers in spring or autumn. H 6in (15cm), S 4in (10cm). Min. 46°F (8°C).

☀ ◊ 10

Oophytum nanum
Clump-forming, perennial succulent with 2 united, very fleshy, bright green leaves. Has daisylike, white flowers, ¹/₂in (1cm) across, in autumn. Is covered in a dry, paperlike sheath, except in spring. H ³/₄in (2cm), S ¹/₂in (1cm). Min. 41°F (5°C).

☀ ◊ 10

Lithops lesliei var. ***albinica***
Egg-shaped, perennial succulent, divided into 2 unequal-sized leaves; convex, pale green, upper surfaces have dark green and yellow marks. Bears a white flower in late summer or early autumn. H ³/₄–1¹/₄in (2–3cm), S 2in (5cm). Min. 41°F (5°C).

☀ ◊ 10

Haworthia arachnoidea,
syn. *H. setata* (Lace haworthia)
Slow-growing, clump-forming, perennial succulent with a basal rosette of triangular leaves. Bears soft, white teeth along leaf margins. Has white flowers from spring to autumn. H 2in (5cm), S 4in (10cm). Min. 43°F (6°C).

☀ ◊ 10

Conophytum truncatum
Slow-growing, clump-forming, perennial succulent with pea-shaped, dark spotted, blue-green leaves, each with a sunken fissure at the tip. Produces cream flowers, ⁵/₈in (1.5cm) across, in autumn. H ⁵/₈in (1.5cm), S 6in (15cm). Min. 39°F (4°C).

☀ ◊ 10

Mammillaria elongata
(Golden star cactus, Lace cactus)
Clump-forming, perennial cactus. Has a columnar, green stem, 1¹/₄in (3cm) across, densely covered with yellow, golden, or brown spines. Bears cream flowers in summer. Offsets freely. H 6in (15cm), S 12in (30cm). Min. 41°F (5°C).

☀ ◊ 10

Mammillaria bocasana (Powder-puff cactus, Snowball cactus)
Clump-forming, perennial cactus. Long, white hairs cover a hemispherical stem. Has cream or rose-pink flowers in summer and red seed pods the following spring-summer. H 4in (10cm), S 12in (30cm). Min. 41°F (5°C).

☼ ◊ 10

Crassula multicava
Bushy, perennial succulent with oval, gray-green leaves, 3in (8cm) across. Carries numerous clusters of small, star-shaped, pink flowers on elongated stems in spring, followed by small plantlets. H 6in (15cm), S 3ft (1m). Min. 45°F (7°C).

◐ ◊ 10

Notocactus rutilans
Columnar, perennial cactus with a 20-ribbed stem, often spiralled. Areoles each have about 15 radial spines and 2 upward- or downward-pointing, central spines. Has cream-centered, pink flowers in summer. H 4in (10cm), S 2in (5cm). Min. 50°F (10°C).

◐ ◊ 10

Neoporteria napina var. ***mitis***
Flattened spherical, perennial cactus with very short, gray spines pressed flat against a greenish brown stem. Produces white, pink, carmine, or brown flowers, 2in (5cm) across, from crown in summer. H ³⁄₄in (2cm), S 1¹⁄₂in (3.5cm). Min. 46°F (8°C).

☼ ◊ 10

Oscularia deltoides
Spreading, perennial succulent. Has chunky, triangular, blue-green leaves, to ¹⁄₂in (1cm) long, with small-toothed, often reddened leaf margins. Fragrant pink flowers, ¹⁄₂–³⁄₄in (1–2cm) wide, appear in early summer. H 6in (15cm), S 3ft (1m). Min. 37°F (3°C).

☼ ◊ 10

Lophophora williamsii (Dumpling cactus, Mescal button, Peyote)
Very slow-growing, clump-forming, perennial cactus with an 8-ribbed, blue-green stem. Masses of pink flowers appear in summer on plants over 1¹⁄₄in (3cm) high. H 2in (5cm), S 3in (8cm). Min. 50°F (10°C).

☼ ◊ 10

Epithelantha micromeris
Slow-growing, spherical, perennial cactus with a green stem completely obscured by close-set areoles bearing tiny, white spines. Bears funnel-shaped, pale pinkish red flowers, ¹⁄₄in (0.5cm) across, on a woolly crown in summer. H and S 1¹⁄₂in (4cm). Min. 50°F (10°C).

☼ ◊ 10

Echeveria elegans
Clump-forming, perennial succulent with a basal rosette of broad, fleshy, pale silvery blue leaves, edged with red, and yellow-tipped, pink flowers in summer. Keep dry in winter. Makes a good bedding plant. H 2in (5cm), S 20in (50cm). Min. 41°F (5°C).

☼ ◊ 10

Coryphantha vivipara
Spherical, perennial cactus with a green stem densely covered with gray spines. Bears funnel-shaped, pink flowers, 1¹⁄₂in (3.5cm) across, in summer. Is much more difficult to grow than many other species in this genus. H and S 2in (5cm). Min. 41°F (5°C).

☼ ◊ 10

Cacti and other Succulents/small

□ PINK

Schlumbergera 'Gold Charm'
Erect, then pendent, perennial cactus.
Has flattened, oblong, green stem
segments with toothed margins.
Yellow flowers in early autumn turn
pinkish orange in winter. H 6in (15cm),
S 12in (30cm). Min. 50°F (10°C).

☼ ◊ 10

Mammillaria sempervivi
Slow-growing, spherical, perennial
cactus. Has a dark green stem with
short, white spines. Has white wool
between short, angular tubercles on
plants over 1¹/₂in (4cm) high. Bears
cerise flowers in spring. H and S 3in
(7cm). Min. 41°F (5°C).

☼ ◊ 10

Melocactus communis
Flattened spherical, perennial cactus.
Has an 18–20-ribbed stem with yellow-
brown spines. Crown matures to a white
column with fine, brown spines. Bears
pink flowers in summer. H 8in (20cm),
S 10in (25cm). Min. 59°F (15°C).

☼ ◊ 10

Ariocarpus fissuratus
Very slow-growing, flattened
spherical, perennial cactus. Gray stem
is covered with rough, triangular
tubercles each producing a tuft of
wool. Has 1¹/₂in (4cm) wide, pink-red
flowers in autumn. H 4in (10cm),
S 6in (15cm). Min. 41°F (5°C).

☼ ◊ 10

Echinofossulocactus violaciflorus
Spherical, perennial cactus with a green
stem carrying about 35 wavy ribs.
Areoles each have a flat, upper, radial
spine and rounded, lower ones. Bears
pink to violet flowers, sometimes
bicolored with white, in spring. H and
S 4in (10cm). Min. 41°F (5°C).

☼ ◊ 10

Aptenia cordifolia (Baby sun rose)
Fast-growing, prostrate, perennial
succulent with oval, glossy, green
leaves and, in summer, daisylike,
bright pink flowers. Is ideal for ground
cover. H 2in (5cm), S indefinite. Min.
45°F (7°C).

☼ ◊ 10

Rhipsalidopsis rosea
Bushy, perennial cactus with slender,
3- or 4-angled, bristly, green stem
segments, usually tinged purple, to 2in
(5cm) long. Has masses of bell-shaped,
pink flowers, to 1¹/₂in (4cm) across, in
spring. H and S 4in (10cm). Min.
50°F (10°C).

☽ ◊ 10

Ophthalmophyllum villetii
Clump-forming, perennial succulent
with 2 fleshy, gray-green leaves that
are broad, erect and united for most of
their length but have distinctly divided,
upper lobes. Pale pink flowers appear
in late summer. H 1in (2.5cm), S ¹/₂in
(1cm). Min. 41°F (5°C).

☼ ◊ 10

Thelocactus bicolor (Texas pride)
Spherical to columnar, perennial
cactus with an 8–13-ribbed stem.
Areoles each have 4 usually flattened,
yellow, central spines, or bicolored
yellow and red, and numerous shorter,
radial spines. Flowers are purple-pink.
H and S 8in (20cm). Min. 45°F (7°C).

☼ ◊ 10

Rebutia violaciflora
Clump-forming, perennial cactus with
a tuberculate, dark green stem. Areoles
each produce 15–20 brown spines, to
¹/₄in (0.5cm) long. Has trumpet-shaped,
deep pink to violet flowers, to ³/₄in
(2cm) across, in spring. H 2in (5cm),
S 6in (15cm). Min. 41°F (5°C).

☼ ◊ 10

Mammillaria zeilmanniana
(Rose-pincushion)
Clump-forming, perennial cactus with
a spherical, green stem that has hooked
spines and bears a ring of deep pink
to purple flowers in spring. H 6in
(15cm), S 12in (30cm).
Min. 50°F (10°C).

☼ ◊ 10

Lobivia backebergii
Clump-forming, almost spherical,
perennial cactus with a 10–15-ribbed,
spined, dark green stem. Has short-
lived, funnel-shaped, pink, red, or
purple flowers, with lighter-colored
throats, in summer. H 4in (10cm),
S 6in (15cm). Min. 41°F (5°C).

☼ ◊ 10

Lobivia pentlandii
Clump-forming or solitary, variable,
perennial cactus with a 10–20-ribbed,
green stem. Areoles each have 6–20
spines. Has white, pink, purple, or
orange flowers, with lighter-colored
throats, in summer. H 3in (8cm),
S 4in (10cm). Min. 41°F (5°C).

☼ ◊ 10

Frithia pulchra
Basal-rosetted, perennial succulent
with erect, rough, gray leaves,
cylindrical with flattened tips. Produces
masses of stemless, daisylike, bright
pink flowers, with paler centers, in
summer. H 1¼in (3cm), S 2½in (6cm).
Min. 50°F (10°C).

☼ ◊ 10

Crassula schmidtii
Carpeting, perennial succulent with
dense rosettes of linear, dark green
leaves, pitted and marked, each
1¼–1½in (3–4cm) long. Bears masses
of star-shaped, bright pinkish red
flowers in clusters in winter. H 4in
(10cm), S 12in (30cm). Min. 45°F (7°C).

◐ ◊ 10

Echeveria secunda
Clump-forming, perennial succulent
with short stems each crowned by a
rosette of broad, fleshy, light green to
gray leaves, reddened towards tips.
Bears cup-shaped, red-and-yellow
flowers in spring-summer. H 1½in
(4cm), S 12in (30cm). Min. 41°F (5°C).

☼ ◊ 10

Graptopetalum bellum,
syn. *Tacitus bellus*
Basal-rosetted, perennial succulent
with triangular to oval, gray leaves, 2in
(5cm) long. Has clusters of deep pink
to red flowers, ¾in (2cm) across, in
spring-summer. H 1¼in (3cm),
S 6in (15cm). Min. 50°F (10°C).

◐ ◊ 10

Argyroderma pearsonii,
syn. *A. schlechteri*
Prostrate, egg-shaped, perennial
succulent. A united pair of very fleshy,
silvery gray leaves has a deep fissure in
which a red flower, 1¼in (3cm) across,
appears in summer. H 1¼in (3cm),
S 2in (5cm). Min. 41°F (5°C).

☼ ◊ 10

Schlumbergera truncata,
syn. *Zygocactus truncatus*
(Crab cactus, Thanksgiving cactus)
Erect, then pendent, perennial cactus.
Oblong stem segments have toothed
margins. Bears purple-red flowers in
early autumn and winter. H 6in (15cm),
S 12in (30cm). Min. 50°F (10°C).

◐ ◊ 10

Cacti and other Succulents/small

Cephalophyllum alstonii
Prostrate, perennial succulent with cylindrical, gray-green leaves, to 3in (7cm) long. Carries daisylike, dark red flowers, 3in (8cm) across, in summer. H 4in (10cm), S 3ft (1m). Min. 41°F (5°C).

☀ ◊ 10

Parodia sanguiniflora
Clump-forming, perennial cactus. Has a much-ribbed, green stem densely covered with brown, radial spines and red, central spines, some of which are hooked. Bears blood red, occasionally yellow flowers in spring. H 3in (8cm), S 12in (30cm). Min. 50°F (10°C).

☀ ◊ 10

Rebutia krainziana
Clump-forming, perennial cactus with a tuberculate, dark green stem. Bears prominent, white areoles with very short, white spines. Trumpet-shaped, bright red flowers, to 2in (5cm) across, appear at stem base in spring. H 2in (5cm), S 8in (20cm). Min. 41°C (5°C).

☀ ◊ 10

Parodia nivosa
Ovoid, perennial cactus that has a much-ribbed, green stem with stiff, white spines, each ¹⁄₂–³⁄₄in (1–2cm) long. Has a white, woolly crown and bright red flowers, to 2in (5cm) across, in summer. H to 6in (15cm), S 4in (10cm). Min. 50°F (10°C).

☀ ◊ 10

Sulcorebutia tiraquensis
Variable, flattened spherical, perennial cactus with a green stem. Elongated areoles bear spines of gold, dark brown, red-brown, or bicolored red and white. Has dark pink- or orange-red flowers in spring. H 6in (15cm), S 4in (10cm). Min. 50°F (10°C).

☀ ◊ 10

Argyroderma fissum,
syn. *A. brevipes*
Clump-forming, perennial succulent with finger-shaped, fleshy leaves, 2–4in (5–10cm) long and often reddish at the tip. Has light red flowers between leaves in summer. H 6in (15cm), S 4in (10cm). Min. 41°F (5°C).

☀ ◊ 10

Cotyledon ladysmithensis
Evergreen, freely branching, later prostrate, succulent sub-shrub with fleshy, green leaves, swollen and blunt at tips and covered with short, golden brown hairs. Clusters of tubular, brownish red flowers appear in autumn. H and S 8in (20cm). Min. 41°F (5°C).

☀ ◊ 10

Opuntia verschaffeltii
Clump-forming, perennial cactus with cylindrical, usually spineless stems, to 10in (25cm) long. Stem tips each bear short-lived, cylindrical leaves from spring to autumn. Has orange-red flowers in spring. H 6in (15cm), S 3–6ft (1–2m). Min. 41°F (5°C).

☀ ◊ 10

Echeveria agavoides
(Moulded-wax, Wax agave)
Basal-rosetted, perennial succulent with tapering, light green leaves, often red-margined. Carries cup-shaped, red flowers, ¹⁄₂in (1cm) long, in summer. H 6in (15cm), S 12in (30cm). Min. 41°F (5°C).

☀ ◊ 10

Rebutia spegazziniana
Clump-forming, perennial cactus with
a spherical, spined, green stem, to 1¹/₂in
(4cm) across, becoming columnar with
age. Bears masses of slender-tubed,
orange-red flowers at base in late
spring. H 4in (10cm), S 8in (20cm).
Min. 41°F (5°C).

 ○ 10

Notocactus haselbergii
(Scarlet ball cactus)
Slow-growing, flattened spherical,
perennial cactus with a stem covered
in white spines. Slightly sunken crown
bears red flowers, with yellow stigmas,
in spring. H 4in (10cm), S 10in
(25cm). Min. 50°F (10°C).

 ○ 10

Echinocereus triglochidiatus var.
paucispinus (Claret cup hedgehog)
Clump-forming, perennial cactus with
a 4in (10cm) wide, dark green stem
that has 6 or 7 ribs and 4–6 spines,
1¹/₄–1¹/₂in (3–4cm) long, per areole. Has
orange-red flowers in spring. H 8in
(20cm), S 20in (50cm). Min. 41°C (5°C).

 ○ 10

Schlumbergera 'Bristol Beauty'
Erect, then pendent, perennial cactus
with flattened, green stem segments
with toothed margins. Bears reddish
purple flowers, with silvery white
tubes, in early autumn and winter.
H 6in (15cm), S 12in (30cm).
Min. 50°F (10°C).

 ○ 10

Chamaecereus silvestri
(Peanut cactus)
Clump-forming, perennial cactus with
finger-shaped, spined, green stems,
initially erect, then prostrate. Produces
funnel-shaped, orange-red flowers in
late spring. H 4in (10cm), S indefinite.
Min. 37°F (3°C).

○ 10

Neolloydia conoidea
Clump-forming, perennial cactus. Has
a columnar, blue-green stem densely
covered with white, radial spines and
longer, black, central spines. Bears
funnel-shaped, purple-violet flowers in
summer. H 4in (10cm), S 6in (15cm).
Min. 50°F (10°C).

○ 10

Rhipsalidopsis gaertneri
(Easter cactus)
Bushy, perennial cactus with flat,
oblong, glossy, green stem segments,
each to 2in (5cm) long, often tinged
red at edges. Segment ends each bear
orange-red flowers in spring. H 6in
(15cm), S 8in (20cm). Min. 43°F (6°C).

○ 10

Pachyphytum oviferum (Pearly
moonstones, Sugared almonds)
Clump-forming, perennial succulent with
a basal rosette of oval, pinkish blue
leaves. Stem bears 10–15 bell-shaped
flowers, with powder blue calyces and
orange-red petals, in spring. H 4in
(10cm), S 12in (30cm). Min. 50°F (10°C).

○ 10

Caralluma joannis
Clump-forming, perennial succulent
with blue-gray stems and rudimentary
leaves on stem angles. Bears clusters
of star-shaped, purple flowers, with
short, fine hairs on petal tips, in late
summer near stem tips. H 8in (20cm),
S 3ft (1m). Min. 52°F (11°C).

○ 10

Cacti and other Succulents/small

■ PURPLE　　　　　　　　　　　　　□□ GREEN–YELLOW

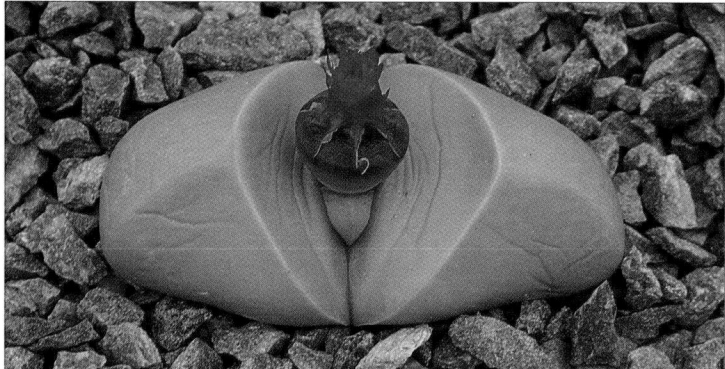

Argyroderma delaetii,
syn. *A. blandum*
Prostrate, egg-shaped, perennial
succulent with 2 very fleshy, silvery
green leaves between which daisylike,
pink-purple flowers, 2in (5cm) across,
appear in late summer. H 1¼in (3cm),
S 2in (5cm). Min. 41°F (5°C).

☼ ◊ 10

Duvalia corderoyi
Clump-forming, perennial succulent.
Has a prostrate, leafless stem with 6
often purple, indistinct ribs. Bears star-
shaped, dull green flowers, ½in (1cm)
across and covered in purple hairs, in
summer-autumn. H 2in (5cm), S 24in
(60cm). Min. 50°F (10°C).

◐ ◊ 10

Crassula deceptrix
Slow-growing, clump-forming,
perennial succulent with branching
stems surrounded by fleshy, gray leaves
set in 4 rows. Each leaf has minute lines
around raised dots. Bears insignificant
flowers in spring. H and S 4in (10cm).
Min. 41°F (5°C).

☼ ◊ 10

Echinofossulocactus pentacanthus
Spherical, perennial cactus with a green
stem bearing 25–50 narrow, wavy ribs.
Areoles each have a flat, upper, radial
spine and more rounded, lower ones that
form a cross. Bears a funnel-shaped,
white-edged, violet flower in spring.
H and S 3in (8cm). Min. 41°F (5°C).

☼ ◊ 10

Stapelia variegata
Clump-forming, perennial succulent
with 4-angled, indented, dark green
stems, branching freely from base.
Flowers, variable in color and blotched
yellow, purple- or red-brown, appear in
summer-autumn. H to 4in (10cm),
S indefinite. Min. 52°F (11°C).

◐ ◊ 10

Huernia macrocarpa var. ***arabica***
Clump-forming, perennial succulent
with finger-shaped, 4- or 5-sided,
green stems. Produces short-lived,
deciduous leaves and, in autumn, bell-
shaped, white-haired, dark purple
flowers with recurved petal tips. H and
S 4in (10cm). Min. 46°F (8°C).

☼ ◊ 10

Stapelia flavirostris
Clump-forming, perennial succulent
with 4-angled, hairy, toothed, green
stems. In summer-autumn carries star-
shaped, purple-brown flowers, to 4in
(10cm) across, ridged with white or
purple hairs. H to 8in (20cm),
S indefinite. Min. 52°F (11°C).

◐ ◊ 10

Stapelia gigantea (Zulu giant)
Clump-forming, perennial succulent
with 4-angled, velvety, green stems.
In summer-autumn bears star-shaped,
red-marked, yellow-brown flowers,
12in (30cm) across, with white-haired,
recurved edges. H to 8in (20cm),
S indefinite. Min. 52°F (11°C).

◐ ◊ 10

Ancistrocactus scheeri, syn.
A. megarhizus (Fishhook cactus)
Globose to columnar, perennial cactus.
Stem bears spines and, in spring,
funnel-shaped, straw-colored flowers.
Lowest and longest spines are darker
and hooked. H 4in (10cm), S 2¹/₂in
(6cm). Min. 36°F (2°C).

☀ ◊ 10

Frailea pulcherrima
Columnar, perennial cactus with a
much-ribbed, dark green stem bearing
white to light brown spines. Buds,
which rarely open to flattish, yellow
flowers in summer, become tufts of
spherical, spiny seed pods. H to 2in
(5cm), S ³/₄in (2cm). Min. 41°F (5°C).

◐ ◊ 10

Maihuenia poeppigii
Slow-growing, clump-forming, perennial
cactus. Has a cylindrical, branched,
spiny, green-brown stem. Most branches
produce a spike of cylindrical, green
leaves at the tip, crowned by a funnel-
shaped, yellow flower in summer.
H 2¹/₂in (6cm), S 12in (30cm).

☀ ◊ ❊ ❊ ❊ 10

Aloinopsis schooneesii
Dwarf, mounded, perennial succulent
with tuberous roots and fleshy, almost
spherical, blue-green leaves arranged
tightly in tufts. Produces flattish,
yellow flowers in winter-spring.
H 1¹/₄in (3cm), S to 3in (7cm).
Min. 45°F (7°C).

☀ ◊ 10

Astrophytum ornatum
Elongated, spherical, perennial cactus
with a very fleshy, 8-ribbed stem.
Crown of each rib bears 2–4¹/₂in
(5–11cm) long spines on each raised
areole. Has yellow flowers, 3in (8cm)
across, in summer. H 6in (15cm),
S 5in (12cm). Min. 41°F (5°C).

☀ ◊ 10

Aichryson x domesticum
'Variegatum'
Prostrate, perennial succulent with
stems crowned by rosettes of hairy,
cream-marked, green leaves, sometimes
pure cream. Has star-shaped, yellow
flowers in spring. H 6in (15cm),
S 16in (40cm). Min. 41°F (5°C).

☀ ◊ 10

Notocactus mammulosus
Spherical, perennial cactus. Green stem
has about 20 ribs and straight, stiff,
yellow-brown to white spines, to ¹/₂in
(1cm) long. Woolly crown produces
masses of golden flowers in summer.
H and S 4in (10cm). Min. 41°F (5°C).

☀ ◊ 10

Gymnocalycium andreae
Clump-forming, spherical, perennial
cactus with a glossy, dark green stem
bearing 8 rounded ribs and up to 8 pale
yellow-white spines per areole. Has
2in (5cm) wide, yellow flowers in
spring-summer. H 2¹/₂in (6cm),
S 4in (10cm). Min. 50°F (10°C).

☀ ◊ 10

Euphorbia obesa (Basketball
euphorbia, Living baseball)
Spherical, perennial succulent.
Spineless, dark green stem, often
checkered light green, has 8 low ribs.
Crown bears rounded heads of cupped,
yellow flowers in summer. H 5in
(12cm), S 6in (15cm). Min. 50°F (10°C).

☀ ◊ 10

Cacti and other Succulents/small

Rhombophyllum rhomboideum
Clump-forming, perennial succulent.
Linear, glossy, gray-green leaves have
expanded middles and white margins.
Stems, 3/4–2in (2–5cm) long, bear 3–7
yellow flowers, to 1 1/2in (4cm) across,
in summer. H 2in (5cm), S 6in (15cm).
Min. 41°F (5°C).

☼ ◊ 10

Schwantesia ruedebuschii
Mat-forming, perennial succulent with
cylindrical, bluish green leaves, 1–2in
(3–5cm) long, with expanded tips.
Leaf edges each produce 3–7 minute,
blue teeth with brown tips. Has yellow
flowers in summer. H 2in (5cm),
S 8in (20cm). Min. 41°F (5°C).

☼ ◊ 10

Pleiospilos simulans
Clump-forming, perennial succulent
with 1 or 2 pairs of thick, gray leaves,
to 3in (8cm) long and slightly less
wide, thickening towards tips. Bears
coconut-scented, yellow flowers in
early autumn. H 4in (10cm), S 12in
(30cm). Min. 41°F (5°C).

☼ ◊ 10

Lithops pseudotruncatella var.
pulmonuncula
Egg-shaped, perennial succulent,
divided into 2 unequal-sized, gray
leaves with dark green and red marks o
upper surfaces. Bears a yellow flower i
summer or autumn. H 3/4–1 1/4in (2–3cm
S 1 1/2in (4cm). Min. 41°F (5°C).

☼ ◊ 10

Aeonium tabuliforme
Prostrate, almost stemless, short-lived,
perennial succulent with a basal rosette,
to 12in (30cm) across, like a flat, bright
green plate. Has star-shaped, yellow
flowers in spring, then dies. Propagate
from seed. H 2in (5cm), S 12in (30cm).
Min. 41°F (5°C).

◐ ◊ 10

Lithops schwantesii var.
kuibisensis
Egg-shaped, perennial succulent,
divided into 2 unequal-sized, silvery
blue leaves with blue or red marks on
upper surface. Has a yellow flower in
late summer or autumn. H 3/4–1 1/4in (2–
3cm), S 1 1/4in (3cm). Min. 41°F (5°C).

☼ ◊ 10

Lithops dorotheae
Egg-shaped, perennial succulent,
divided into 2 unequal-sized leaves, pale
pink-yellow to green with darker marks
and red dots and lines on upper surfaces.
Produces a daisylike, yellow flower in
summer or autumn. H 3/4–1 1/4in (2–3cm),
S 2in (5cm). Min. 41°F (5°C).

☼ ◊ 10

Mammillaria microhelia
Columnar, perennial cactus with a 2in
(5cm) wide, green stem bearing cream
or brown spines, discoloring with age.
Has 5/8in (1.5cm) wide, yellow or pink
flowers in spring. Offsets slowly with
age. H 8in (20cm), S 16in (40cm).
Min. 41°F (5°C).

☼ ◊ 10

Opuntia humifusa
Prostrate, perennial cactus. Each areole
bears up to 3 spines, 1 1/4in (3cm) long.
Has flat, rounded to oval, purple-tinged,
dark green stem segments, 3–7in
(7–18cm) long. Bears 3in (8cm) wide,
yellow flowers in spring-summer. Keep
dry in winter. H 6in (15cm), S 3ft (1m).

☼ ◊ ❋❋❋ 10

Agave utahensis
Basal-rosetted, perennial succulent
with rigid, blue-gray leaves, each with
spines up margins and a long, dark
spine at tip. Flower stem, to 5ft (1.5m)
long, carries yellow flowers in
summer. H 9in (23cm) or more,
S 6ft (2m).

☼ ◊ ❋ 7–10

Graptopetalum paraguayense
(Mother-of-pearl plant)
Clump-forming, perennial succulent
with a basal rosette, 6in (15cm) across,
of gray-green leaves, often tinged pink.
Bears star-shaped, yellow-and-red
flowers in summer. H 4in (10cm),
S 3ft (1m). Min. 41°F (5°C).

◐ ◊ 10

Coryphantha cornifera,
syn. *C. radians*
Spherical to columnar, perennial cactus
with angular tubercles, each bearing a
curved, dark, central spine and shorter,
radial spines. Has funnel-shaped,
yellow flowers in summer. H 6in
(15cm), S 4in (10cm). Min. 41°F (5°C).

☼ ◊ 10

Conophytum bilobum
Slow-growing, clump-forming,
perennial succulent with 2-lobed,
fleshy, green leaves, each 1¹/₂in (4cm)
long and ³/₄in (2cm) wide. Has a flared,
yellow flower, 1¹/₄in (3cm) across, in
autumn. H 1¹/₂in (4cm), S 6in (15cm).
Min. 39°F (4°C).

☼ ◊ 10

Faucaria tigrina (Tiger's jaw)
Clump-forming, stemless, perennial
succulent. Fleshy, green leaves, 2in
(5cm) long, have 9 or 10 teeth along
each margin. Bears daisylike, yellow
flowers, 2in (5cm) across, in autumn.
H 4in (10cm), S 20in (50cm).
Min. 43°F (6°C).

☼ ◊ 10

Wigginsia vorwerkiana
Slow-growing, flattened spherical,
perennial cactus with a glossy stem, up
to 20 wartlike ribs, bearing yellow-
white spines, and yellow blooms in
summer. H 3in (8cm), S 3¹/₂in (9cm).
Min. 41°F (5°C).

☼ ◊ 10

Glottiphyllum nelii
Clump-forming, perennial succulent
with semi-cylindrical, fleshy, green
leaves, to 2in (5cm) long. Carries
daisylike, golden yellow flowers,
1¹/₂in (4cm) across, in spring-summer.
H 2in (5cm), S 12in (30cm).
Min. 41°F (5°C).

☼ ◊ 10

Lobivia shaferi
Columnar, perennial cactus. Has
narrow, much-ribbed, green stems
covered with pale, radial spines often
surrounded by 1–3 very stout, central
spines, to 1in (2.5cm) long. Produces
yellow flowers in summer. H and
S 4in (10cm). Min. 41°F (5°C).

☼ ◊ 10

Fenestraria aurantiaca var.
rhopalophylla
Clump-forming, perennial succulent
with a basal rosette of cylindrical,
erect, glossy leaves, each with a
flattened tip. Has yellow flowers in
late summer and autumn. H 2in (5cm),
S 12in (30cm). Min. 43°F (6°C).

☼ ◊ 10

Titanopsis calcarea (Jewel plant)
Clump-forming, perennial succulent
with a basal rosette of very fleshy,
triangular, blue-gray leaves covered
in wartlike, gray-white and beige
tubercles. Has yellow flowers from
autumn to spring. H 1¹/₄in (3cm),
S 4in (10cm). Min. 46°F (8°C).

☼ ◊ 10

Pleiospilos bolusii (Living rock
cactus, Mimicry plant)
Clump-forming, perennial succulent
with 1 or 2 pairs of gray leaves, often
wider than long and narrowing at
incurved tips. Has golden yellow
flowers in early autumn. H 4in (10cm),
S 8in (20cm). Min. 41°F (5°C).

☼ ◊ 10

Cacti and other Succulents/small

Sulcorebutia arenacea
Spherical, perennial cactus. Has a
brown-green stem densely covered
with white spines on spirally arranged
tubercles. Golden yellow blooms, to
1¹⁄₄in (3cm) across, appear in spring.
Is slow to offset. H 2in (5cm), S 2¹⁄₂in
(6cm). Min. 50°F (10°C).

☼ ◊ 10

Gasteria liliputana
Clump-forming, perennial succulent
with a basal rosette of strap-shaped,
glossy, dark green leaves blotched with
white. Flower stems, to 6in (15cm)
long, bears spikes of bell-shaped,
orange-green flowers in spring. H 3in
(7cm), S 4in (10cm). Min. 41°F (5°C).

☼ ◊ 10

Pachyphytum compactum
Clump-forming, perennial succulent
with a basal rosette of green leaves, each
narrowing to a blunt point, with angular,
paler edges. Stems each bear 3–10
flowers with green to pink calyces and
orange petals in spring. H 6in (15cm),
S indefinite. Min. 41°F (5°C).

☼ ◊ 10

Conophytum notabile
Slow-growing, spherical, perennial
succulent forming clumps of 2-lobed,
very fleshy, gray-green leaves, often
with a red spot on edge of fissure
between the lobes. Carries copper
orange flowers in autumn. H 1¹⁄₄in
(3cm), S indefinite. Min. 39°F (4°C).

☼ ◊ 10

Malephora crocea
Erect or spreading, perennial succulent
with semi-cylindrical, blue-green
leaves on short shoots. Carries solitary
daisylike, orange-yellow flowers,
reddened on outsides, in spring-
summer. H 8in (20cm), S 3ft (1m).
Min. 41°F (5°C).

☼ ◊ 10

Borzicactus aurantiacus,
syn. *Submatucana aurantiaca*
Spherical, perennial cactus with a
15–17-ribbed, green stem. Elongated
areoles each bear up to 30 golden
brown spines. Carries orange-yellow
flowers in summer. H 5in (12cm),
S 16in (40cm). Min. 50°F (10°C).

☼ ◊ 10

Aloe aristata (Lace aloe)
Clump-forming, perennial succulent
that has a basal rosette of pointed, dark
green leaves with white spots and soft-
toothed edges. Has orange flowers in
spring. Offsets freely. H 4in (10cm),
S 12in (30cm). Min. 45°F (7°C).

☼ ◊ 10

Rebutia aureiflora
Clump-forming, perennial cactus with
a dark green stem, often tinged violet-
red, that has stiff, radial spines and
longer, soft, central spines. Has masses
of yellow, violet, or red flowers in late
spring. H 4in (10cm), S 8in (20cm).
Min. 41°F (5°C).

☼ ◊ 10

Gasteria verrucosa (Warty aloe)
Clump-forming, perennial succulent
with a fan of stiff, strap-shaped, dark
green leaves, to 15cm (6in) long, with
raised, white dots and incurved edges.
Has spikes of bell-shaped, orange-
green flowers in spring. H 4in (10cm),
S 12in (30cm). Min. 41°F (5°C).

☼ ◊ 10

Rebutia muscula
Clump-forming, perennial cactus. Has
a dark green stem densely covered
with soft, white spines, to 0.5cm (¹⁄₄in)
long. Bears bright orange flowers,
³⁄₄–1¹⁄₄in (2–3cm) across, in late
spring. H 4in (10cm), S 6in (15cm).
Min. 41°F (5°C).

☼ ◊ 10

The PLANT DICTIONARY

A complete guide to the characteristics
and cultivation of over 8,000 plants.

A

ABELIA (Caprifoliaceae)
Genus of deciduous, semi-evergreen or evergreen shrubs, grown for their foliage and freely borne flowers. Fully to half hardy, but in cold areas does best against a south- or west-facing wall. Requires a sheltered, sunny position and fertile, well-drained soil. Remove dead wood in late spring and prune out older branches after flowering to restrict growth, if required. Propagate by softwood cuttings in summer.
A. **'Edward Goucher'** illus. p.129.
A. floribunda. Evergreen, arching shrub. H 10ft (3m), S 12ft (4m). Half hardy, zones 8–10. Has oval, glossy, dark green leaves and, in early summer, drooping, tubular, bright red flowers.
A. × *grandiflora* illus. p.88. **'Francis Mason'** is a vigorous, semi-evergreen, arching shrub. H 6ft (2m), S 10ft (3m). Frost hardy, zones 6–9. Has coppery yellow, young shoots and oval, yellowish green leaves, darker in centers. Bears a profusion of fragrant, bell-shaped, white flowers, tinged with pink, from mid-summer to mid-autumn.
A. schumannii illus. p.130.
A. triflora illus. p.88.

ABELIOPHYLLUM (Oleaceae)
Genus of one species of deciduous shrub, grown for its winter flowers. Fully hardy, but in cold areas grow against a south- or west-facing wall. Requires plenty of sun and fertile, well-drained soil. Thin out excess older shoots after flowering each year to encourage vigorous, young growth. Propagate by softwood cuttings in summer.
A. distichum. Deciduous, open shrub. H and S 4ft (1.2m). Zones 5–9. In late winter has fragrant, star-shaped, white flowers, tinged with pink, on bare stems; flowers may be damaged by hard frosts. Leaves are oval and dark green.

ABIES (Pinaceae)
Genus of tall conifers with whorled branches. Spirally arranged leaves are needlelike, flattened, usually soft, and often have silvery bands beneath. Bears erect cones that ripen in their first autumn to release seeds and scales. See also CONIFERS.
A. alba (Silver fir). Fast-growing, conical conifer. H 50–80ft (15–25m), S 15–25ft (5–8m). Fully hardy, zones 5–8. Has silvery gray bark and dull green leaves with silvery undersides. Cylindrical cones, 4–6in (10–15cm) long, ripen to red-brown.
A. amabilis (Pacific fir). Conical conifer. H 50ft (15m), S 12–15ft (4–5m). Fully hardy, zones 6–8. Dense, notched, square-tipped, glossy, dark green leaves, banded with white beneath, are borne on hairy, gray shoots. Has oblong, violet-blue cones, 3^1/$_2$–6in (9–15cm) long. **'Spreading Star'**, H 20in (50cm), S 12–15ft

(4–5m), is a procumbent form suitable for ground cover.
A. balsamea (Balsam fir). f. *hudsonia* is a dense, dwarf conifer of flattened to globose habit. H and S 2–3ft (60cm–1m). Fully hardy, zones 4–7. Has smooth, gray bark and gray-green leaves that are semi-spirally arranged. **'Nana'** (illus. p.82) is another dwarf form that makes a dense, globose mound with spirally arranged leaves.
A. cephalonica (Greek fir). Upright conifer with a conical crown; old trees have massive, spreading, erect branches. H 70–100ft (20–30m), S 15–30ft (5–10m). Fully hardy, zones 6–8. Sharp, stiff, glossy, deep green leaves are whitish green beneath. Cylindrical, tapered cones, 4–6in (10–15cm) long, are brown when ripe. **'Meyer's Dwarf'** (syn. *A.c.* 'Nana'; illus. p.82), H 20in (50cm), S 5ft (1.5m), has short leaves and forms a spreading, flat-topped mound.
A. concolor (White fir). Upright conifer. H 50–100ft (15–30m), S 15–25ft (5–8m). Fully hardy, zones 4–7. Has widely spreading, blue-green or gray leaves and cylindrical, green or pale blue cones, 3–5in (8–12cm) long. **'Candicans'** illus. p.73. **'Glauca Compacta'** (syn. *A.c.* 'Compacta'; illus. p.82), H to 6ft (2m), S 6–10ft (2–3m), is a cultivar with steel blue foliage.
A. delavayi (Delavay fir). Upright conifer with tiered, spreading branches. H 30–50ft (10–15m), S 12–20ft (4–6m). Fully hardy, zones 6–8. Has maroon shoots and curved, bright deep green leaves, spirally arranged, with vivid silver bands beneath and rolled margins. Narrowly cylindrical cones, 2^1/$_2$–6in (6–15cm) long, are violet-blue.
A. grandis illus. p.76.
A. homolepis (Nikko fir). Conifer that is conical when young, later columnar. H 50ft (15m), S 20ft (6m). Fully hardy, zones 5–7. Pink-gray bark peels in fine flakes. Has pale green leaves, silver beneath, and cylindrical, violet-blue cones, 3–5in (8–12cm) long. Tolerates urban conditions.
A. koreana illus. p.81.
A. lasiocarpa (Subalpine fir). Narrowly conical conifer. H 30–50ft (10–15m), S 10–12ft (3–4m). Fully hardy, zones 4–7. Has gray or blue-green leaves and cylindrical, violet-blue cones, 2^1/$_2$–4in (6–10cm) long. var. *arizonica* **'Compacta'** (illus. p.82), H 12–15ft (4–5m), S 5–6ft (1.5–2m), is a slow-growing, ovoid to conical tree with corky bark and blue foliage. **'Roger Watson'** (illus. p.82), H and S 2^1/$_2$ft (75cm), is dwarf and conical, with silvery gray leaves.
A. nordmanniana (Caucasian fir). Columnar, dense conifer. H 50–80ft (15–25m), S 15ft (5m). Fully hardy, zones 5–7. Luxuriant foliage is rich green. Cylindrical cones, 4–6in (10–15cm) long, are green-brown,

ripening to brown. **'Golden Spreader'** (illus. p.83), H and S 3ft (1m), is a dwarf form with a spreading habit and bright golden yellow leaves.
A. procera (Noble fir). Narrowly conical conifer. H 50ft (15m), S 15ft (5m). Fully hardy, zones 6–8. Has attractive, smooth, silvery gray bark and gray-green or bright blue-gray leaves. Produces stoutly cylindrical, green cones, 6–10in (15–25cm) long, that ripen to brown. **'Glauca'** illus. p.77.
A. veitchii illus. p.74.

ABUTILON (Malvaceae)
Genus of evergreen, semi-evergreen, or deciduous shrubs, perennials, and annuals, grown for their flowers and foliage. Frost hardy to frost tender, min. 41–5°F (5–7°C). Needs full sun or partial shade and fertile, well-drained soil. Water potted specimens freely when in full growth, less at other times. In the growing season, young plants may need tip pruning to promote bushy growth. Mature specimens may have previous season's stems cut back hard annually in early spring. Stake lax-growing species if necessary. Propagate by seed in spring or by softwood, greenwood, or semi-ripe cuttings in summer. Whitefly and red spider mite may be troublesome.
A. globosum of gardens. See *A.* × *hybridum.*
A. × *hybridum,* syn. *A. globosum* of gardens. **'Ashford Red'** is a strong-growing, evergreen, rounded shrub. H and S 6–10ft (2–3m). Half hardy, zones 9–10. Has maple- to heart-shaped, serrated, rich green leaves. Pendent, bell-shaped, crimson flowers are carried from spring to autumn. **'Golden Fleece'** has yellow flowers.
A. **'Kentish Belle'** illus. p.139.
A. megapotamicum. Evergreen shrub with long, slender branches normally trained against a wall. H and S to 10ft (3m). Half hardy, zones 8–10. Pendent, bell-shaped, yellow-and-red flowers appear from late spring to autumn. Leaves are oval, with heart-shaped bases, and dark green.
A. pictum, syn. *A. striatum* of gardens. **'Thompsonii'** illus. p.115.
A. striatum of gardens. See *A. pictum.*
A. × *suntense.* Fast-growing, deciduous, upright, arching shrub. H 15ft (5m), S 10ft (3m). Half hardy, zones 9–10. Produces oval, lobed, toothed, dark green leaves and has an abundance of large, bowl-shaped, pale to deep purple, occasionally white, flowers from late spring to early summer. **'Violetta'** illus. p.112.
A. vitifolium. Fast-growing, deciduous, upright shrub. H 12ft (4m), S 8ft (2.5m). Frost hardy, zones 7–9. Produces masses of large, bowl-shaped, purplish blue flowers in late spring and early summer. Has oval, lobed, sharply toothed, gray-green leaves. **'Album'** illus. p.87.

ACACIA (Leguminosae)
Mimosa
Genus of evergreen, semi-evergreen, or deciduous trees and shrubs, grown for their tiny flowers, composed of massed stamens, and for their foliage. Many species have phyllodes instead of true leaves. Frost hardy to frost tender, min. 41–5°F (5–7°C). Needs full sun and well-drained soil. Propagate by seed in spring. Red spider mite and mealy bug may be problematic.
A. baileyana illus. p.69.
A. cultriformis illus. p.103.
A. dealbata illus. p.56.
A. juniperina. Evergreen, bushy shrub. H 3ft (1m), S 5ft (1.5m). Frost hardy, zones 8–10. Has very narrow, cylindrical, spinelike, rich green phyllodes and, in mid-spring, globular clusters of pale yellow flowers.
A. longifolia (Sydney golden wattle). Evergreen, spreading tree. H and S 20ft (6m). Frost hardy, zones 8–10. Has narrowly oblong, dark green phyllodes. Cylindrical clusters of golden yellow flowers open in early spring.
A. neriifolia. Evergreen, bushy shrub or tree. H and S 10ft (3m). Half hardy, zone 10. Has narrowly lance-shaped, usually gray-green phyllodes. Produces dense, globular heads of bright yellow flowers in spring.
A. podalyriifolia. Evergreen, bushy shrub. H and S 10ft (3m). Half hardy, zone 10. Has rounded, sharply pointed, silver-blue phyllodes. Long racemes of fragrant yellow flowers open in winter or early spring.
A. pravissima illus. p.69.
A. pulchella illus. p.125.
A. verticillata (Prickly Moses). Evergreen, spreading tree or bushy shrub. H and S 28ft (9m). Half hardy, zones 9–10. Produces needlelike, dark green phyllodes and, in spring, dense, bottlebrushlike spikes of bright yellow flowers.

ACAENA (Rosaceae)
Genus of mainly summer-flowering sub-shrubs and perennials, evergreen in all but the severest winters, grown for their leaves and colored burs, and as ground cover. Has tight, rounded heads of small flowers. Is good for a rock garden but some species may be invasive. Fully to frost hardy. Needs sun or partial shade and well-drained soil. Propagate by division in early spring or by seed in autumn.
A. anserinifolia. Vigorous, evergreen, prostrate sub-shrub. H 4in (10cm), S 30in (75cm) or more. Fully hardy, zones 7–9. Has brown-green leaves, divided into 9–13 oval, toothed leaflets. In summer, red-spined, brownish burs develop from spherical heads of greenish brown flowers.
A. **'Blue Haze'.** Vigorous, evergreen, prostrate perennial. H 4in (10cm), S 30in (75cm) or more. Fully hardy, zones 7–9. Leaves are divided into 9–15 oval, toothed, steel blue leaflets.

Produces spherical, brownish red flower heads that develop in autumn to dark red burs with pinkish red spines.
A. buchananii. Vigorous, evergreen, prostrate perennial. H ³/₄in (2cm), S 30in (75cm) or more. Fully hardy, zones 6–9. Bears glaucous leaves, composed of 11–17 oval, toothed leaflets. Globose, green flower heads, borne in summer, develop into spiny, yellow-green burs.
A. caesiiglauca illus. p.330.
A. microphylla illus. p.329.

ACALYPHA (Euphorbiaceae)
Genus of evergreen shrubs and perennials, grown for their flowers and foliage. Frost tender, min. 50–55°F (10–13°C), but best at min. 61°F (16°C). Needs partial shade and humus-rich, well-drained soil. Water potted plants freely when in full growth, much less at other times and in low temperatures. Stem tips may be removed in growing season to promote branching of young plants. Propagate by softwood, greenwood, or semi-ripe cuttings in summer. Red spider mite, whitefly, and mealy bug may be troublesome.
A. hispida (Red-hot cattail). Evergreen, upright, soft-stemmed shrub. H 6ft (2m) or more, S 3–6ft (1–2m). Zone 10. Has oval, toothed, lustrous, deep green leaves. Tiny, crimson flowers hang in long, dense, catkinlike spikes intermittently year-round.
A. wilkesiana illus. p.111.

ACANTHOLIMON (Plumbaginaceae)
Genus of evergreen perennials, grown for their flowers and tight cushions of spiny leaves. Is suitable for rock gardens and walls. Fully hardy. Prefers sun and well-drained soil. Dislikes damp winters. Seed is rarely set in cultivation. Propagate by softwood cuttings in late spring.
A. glumaceum illus. p.317.
A. venustum. Evergreen, cushion-forming perennial. H and S 4in (10cm). Zones 7–9. Small spikes of star-shaped, pink flowers, on 1¹/₄in (3cm) stems, appear from late spring to early summer amid rosetted, spear-shaped, spiny, blue-green leaves that are edged with silver. Needs a very hot, well-drained site. Makes an excellent alpine house plant.

ACANTHOPANAX. See ELEUTHEROCOCCUS.
A. ricinifolium. See *Kalopanax pictus.*

ACANTHUS (Acanthaceae)
Bear's breech
Genus of perennials, some of which are semi-evergreen, grown for their large, deeply cut leaves and their spikes of flowers. Fully hardy. Prefers full sun, warm conditions, and well-drained soil, but will tolerate shade. Protect crowns in first winter after planting. Long, thonglike roots make plants difficult to eradicate if wrongly placed. Propagate by seed or division in early autumn or spring or by root cuttings in winter.
A. dioscoridis. Upright, architectural perennial. H to 3ft (1m), S 18in

(45cm). Zones 8–10. Has oval, deeply cut, rigid, basal leaves and hairy stems. Bears dense spikes of small, funnel-shaped, purple-and-white flowers in summer.
A. hungaricus, syn. *A. longifolius,* illus. p.209.
A. longifolius. See *A. hungaricus.*
A. mollis. Semi-evergreen, stately, upright perennial. H 4ft (1.2m), S 18in (45cm). Zones 8–10. Has long, oval, deeply cut, bright green leaves and, in summer, produces many spikes of funnel-shaped, mauve-and-white flowers.
A. spinosus illus. p.210.

ACER (Aceraceae)
Maple
Genus of deciduous or evergreen trees and shrubs, grown for their foliage, which often colors brilliantly in autumn and, in some cases, for their ornamental bark or stems. Small but often attractive flowers are followed by 2-winged fruits. Fully to frost hardy. Requires sun or semi-shade and fertile, well-drained soil. Many maples produce their best autumn color on neutral to acid soil. Propagate species by seed as soon as ripe or in autumn; cultivars by various grafting methods in late winter or early spring, or by budding in summer. Leaf-eating caterpillars or aphids sometimes infest plants, and maple tar spot may affect *A. platanoides* and *A. pseudoplatanus.*
A. buergerianum (Trident maple). Deciduous, spreading tree. H 30ft (10m) or more, S 25ft (8m). Fully hardy, zones 5–9. Has 3-lobed, glossy, dark green leaves, usually providing a long-lasting display of red, orange, and purple in autumn.
A. campestre (Common maple, Field maple). Deciduous, round-headed tree. H and S 30ft (10m). Fully hardy, zones 5–8. Small, palmate, deeply lobed, green leaves turn red or yellow in autumn. Is suitable for hedging and does well on chalky soil.
A. capillipes illus. p.55.
A. cappadocicum (Cappadocian maple). Deciduous, spreading tree. H 70ft (20m), S 50ft (15m). Fully hardy, zones 6–9. Has 5-lobed, bright green leaves that turn yellow in autumn. '**Aureum**' has bright yellow, young leaves that turn light green in summer and later assume yellow autumn tints.
A. carpinifolium illus. p.65.
A. circinatum (Vine maple). Deciduous, spreading, bushy tree or shrub. H 15ft (5m) or more, S 20ft (6m). Fully hardy, zones 6–9. Rounded, 7–9-lobed, green leaves turn brilliant orange and red in autumn. Bears clusters of small, purple-and-white flowers in spring.
A. cissifolium. Deciduous, spreading tree. H 25ft (8m), S 40ft (12m). Fully hardy, zones 5–9. Leaves consist of 3 oval, toothed leaflets, bronze-tinged when young, dark green in summer, turning red and yellow in autumn. Does best in semi-shade and on neutral to acid soil.
A. crataegifolium (Hawthorn maple). Deciduous, arching tree. H and S 30ft (10m). Fully hardy, zones 6–8. Branches are streaked green and white.

Small, oval, green leaves turn orange in autumn. '**Veitchii**' illus. p.62.
A. davidii (Père David's maple, Snakebark maple). Deciduous tree with upright branches. Fully hardy, zones 6–8. H and S 50ft (15m). Branches are striped green and white. Has oval, glossy, dark green leaves that often turn yellow or orange in autumn. '**Madeline Spitta**' illus. p.54.
A. ginnala illus. p.68.
A. giraldii. Deciduous, spreading tree. H and S 30ft (10m). Frost hardy, zones 7–9. Shoots have a blue-gray bloom. Large, sycamorelike, shallowly lobed leaves, with long, pink stalks, are dark green above, blue-white beneath.
A. grandidentatum. Deciduous, spreading tree. H and S 25ft (8m) or more. Fully hardy, zones 6–8. Has broad, 3- or 5-lobed, bright green leaves that turn bright orange-red in early autumn.
A. griseum illus. p.72.
A. grosseri var. **hersii** (Hers's maple, Snakebark maple). Deciduous, upright and spreading tree. H and S 30ft (10m). Fully hardy, zones 6–8. Has white-striped trunk and branches. Broadly oval, deeply lobed, bright green leaves turn red in autumn.
A. henryi illus. p.55.
A. japonicum (Full-moon maple, Japanese maple). Deciduous, bushy tree or shrub. H and S 30ft (10m). Fully hardy, zones 6–8. Rounded, lobed leaves are green, turning red in autumn. Clusters of small, reddish purple flowers open in mid-spring. Shelter from strong winds. '**Aconitifolium**' and '**Vitifolium**' illus. p.67. '**Aureum**' illus. p.65.
A. laxiflorum illus. p.71.
A. lobelii illus. p.41.
A. macrophyllum illus. p.39.
A. monspessulanum (Montpelier maple). Deciduous, usually compact, round-headed tree or shrub. H and S 40ft (12m). Fully hardy, zones 6–9. Small, 3-lobed, glossy, dark green leaves remain on the tree until late autumn.
A. negundo (Ash-leaved maple, Box elder). Fast-growing, deciduous, spreading tree. H 50ft (15m), S 25ft (8m). Fully hardy, zones 3–9. Bright green leaves have 3–5 oval leaflets. Clusters of inconspicuous, greenish yellow flowers are borne in late spring. '**Variegatum**' illus. p.52. var. **violaceum** has purplish branchlets covered in a glaucous bloom and bears prominent clusters of tassel-like, purplish pink flowers.
A. nikoense (Nikko maple). Slow-growing, deciduous, round-headed tree. H and S 40ft (12m). Fully hardy, zones 5–8. Leaves have 3 oval, bluish green leaflets that turn brilliant red and yellow in autumn.
A. opalus (Italian maple). Deciduous, round-headed tree. H and S 50ft (15m). Fully hardy, zones 6–9. Clusters of small, yellow flowers emerge from early to mid-spring before foliage. Leaves are broad, 5-lobed, and dark green, turning yellow in autumn.
A. palmatum (Japanese maple). Deciduous, bushy-headed shrub or tree. H and S 20ft (6m) or more. Fully

hardy, zones 5–8. Palmate, deeply lobed, green leaves turn brilliant orange, red, or yellow in autumn. Clusters of small, reddish purple flowers are borne in mid-spring. '**Atropurpureum**' illus. p.89. '**Bloodgood**' illus. p.111. '**Butterfly**' illus. p.108. '**Chitoseyama**' illus. p.134. '**Corallinum**' illus. p.98. var. **coreanum** illus. p.67. '**Dissectum Atropurpureum**' illus. p.134. var. **heptalobum** illus. p.92. var. **heptalobum** '**Lutescens**' illus. p.90. var. **heptalobum** '**Rubrum**' illus. p.89. '**Osakazuki**' has larger leaves, with 7 lobes, that turn brilliant scarlet in autumn. '**Senkaki**' (syn. *A.p.* 'Sango Kaku') illus. p.92.
A. pensylvanicum illus. p.57. '**Erythrocladum**' is a deciduous, upright tree. H 30ft (10m), S 20ft (6m). Fully hardy, zones 4–8. Has brilliant candy pink, young shoots in winter and large, boldly lobed, green leaves that turn bright yellow in autumn.
A. platanoides (Norway maple). Vigorous, deciduous, spreading tree. H 80ft (25m), S 50ft (15m). Fully hardy, zones 4–7. Has large, broad, sharply lobed, bright green leaves that turn yellow or orange in autumn and clusters of yellow flowers borne in mid-spring before the leaves appear. '**Columnare**', H 40ft (12m), S 25ft (8m), is dense and columnar. '**Crimson King**' illus. p.40. '**Deborah**' (Deborah Norway maple), H 45ft (14m), S 40ft (12m), has reddish purple leaves in spring that turn dark bronze green in summer and tolerates urban pollution. '**Drummondii**' has leaves broadly edged with creamy white. '**Emerald Queen**' is upright when young. '**Globosum**', H 25ft (8m), S 30ft (10m), has a dense, round crown. '**Lorbergii**' illus. p.45. '**Royal Red**' has deep reddish purple leaves. Those of '**Schwedleri**' are bright red when young, mature to purplish green in summer, and turn orange-red in autumn. '**Summershade**' has dark green leaves.
A. pseudoplatanus (Sycamore). Fast-growing, deciduous, spreading tree. H 100ft (30m), S 50ft (15m). Fully hardy, zones 5–8. Has broadly 5-lobed, dark green leaves. Makes a fine specimen tree and is good for an exposed position. '**Brilliantissimum**' illus. p.62. f. **erythrocarpum** illus. p.44. '**Simon Louis Frères**' illus. p.52.
A. rubrum illus. p.44. '**Columnare**' illus. p.54. '**Morgan**' (Morgan red maple), is a deciduous, spreading tree. H 45ft (14m), S 40ft (12m). Fully hardy, zones 4–9. Produces 3- or 5-lobed, glossy, dark green leaves that turn orange-red to red in autumn, particularly on neutral to acid soil. In spring, bare branches are covered with clusters of tiny, red flowers. Is tolerant of pollution. Leaves of '**October Glory**', H 70ft (20m), become intense red in autumn. '**Red Sunset**' has dense growth that also turns brilliant red in autumn. '**Scanlon**' and '**Schlesingeri**' illus. p.44.
A. rufinerve illus. p.55. f. **albolimbatum** is a deciduous, arching tree. H 30ft (10m), S 25ft (8m). Fully hardy, zones 6–9.

Branches are striped green and white. Has 3-lobed, green leaves, mottled and edged with white, that turn brilliant orange and red in autumn.

A. saccharinum (Silver maple). Fast-growing, deciduous, spreading tree. H 80ft (25m), S 50ft (15m). Fully hardy, zones 4–9. Deeply lobed, green leaves, with silver undersides, turn yellow in autumn. **'Wieri'** has pendent, lower branches and very deeply lobed leaves.

A. saccharum (Sugar maple). **'Green Mountain'** is a deciduous, spreading tree with an oval crown. H 70ft (20m), S 40ft (12m). Fully hardy, zones 4–8. Large, 5-lobed, bright green leaves turn brilliant scarlet in autumn. **'Temple's Upright'** illus. p.55.

A. triflorum illus. p.68.

A. velutinum. Deciduous, spreading tree. H 70ft (20m), S 50ft (15m). Fully hardy, zones 7–9. Produces large, sycamorelike, lobed, dark green leaves, with undersides covered with pale brown down. var. **vanvolxemii** (Van Volxem's maple) has even larger leaves, slightly glaucous and smooth beneath.

ACHILLEA (Compositae)

Genus of mainly upright perennials, some of which are semi-evergreen, suitable for borders and rock gardens. Has fernlike foliage and large, usually platelike, flower heads mainly in summer. Flower heads may be dried for winter decoration. Fully hardy. Tolerates most soils but does best in a sunny, well-drained site. Tall species and cultivars need staking. Propagate by division in early spring or autumn or by softwood cuttings in early summer.

A. argentea. See Tanacetum argenteum.

A. clavennae illus. p.313.

A. clypeolata. Semi-evergreen, upright perennial. H 18in (45cm), S 12in (30cm). Zones 4–8. Has divided, hairy, silver leaves and dense, flat heads of small, yellow flowers in summer. Divide plants regularly in spring.

A. 'Coronation Gold' illus. p.215.

A. filipendulina 'Gold Plate' illus. p.215.

A. x kellereri illus. p.315.

A. x lewisii 'King Edward'. Semi-evergreen, rounded, compact, woody-based perennial. H 4in (10cm), S 9in (23cm) or more. Zones 4–8. Has feathery, soft, gray-green leaves. Compact heads of minute, buff-yellow flower heads open in summer. Is suitable for a rock garden, wall, or bank.

A. millefolium (Yarrow). **'Fire King'** is a vigorous, upright perennial. H and S 24in (60cm). Zones 3–8. Has a mass of feathery, dark green leaves and flat heads of rich red flowers in summer.

A. 'Moonshine' illus. p.246.

A. ptarmica 'The Pearl' illus. p.200.

A. taygetea illus. p.246.

ACHIMENES (Gesneriaceae)

Genus of erect or trailing perennials with small rhizomes and showy flowers, often grown as annuals or house plants. Frost tender, min. 50°F (10°C). Prefers bright light, but not direct sun, and well-drained soil. Use

tepid water for watering pot-grown plants. Allow to dry out after flowering and store rhizomes in a frost-free place over winter. Propagate by division of rhizomes or by seed, if available, in spring or by stem cuttings in summer.

A. antirrhina. Erect perennial. H and S 14in (35cm) or more. Zone 10. Has oval, toothed leaves, to 2in (5cm) or more long and of unequal size in each opposite pair. In summer bears funnel-shaped, red-orange flowers, to 1½in (4cm) long, with yellow throats.

A. 'Brilliant'. Erect, compact perennial. H and S 1ft (30cm). Zone 10. Has oval, toothed leaves and, in summer, large, funnel-shaped, scarlet flowers.

A. coccinea. See A. erecta.

A. erecta, syn. A. coccinea, A. pulchella. Erect, bushy, branching perennial. H and S 18in (45cm). Zone 10. Has narrowly oval, toothed leaves, often in whorls of 3. Tubular, scarlet flowers with yellow eyes appear in summer.

A. grandiflora. Erect perennial. H and S to 2ft (60cm). Zone 10. Oval, toothed leaves are often reddish below. In summer has tubular, dark pink to purple flowers with white eyes.

A. 'Little Beauty' illus. p.237.

A. 'Paul Arnold'. Erect, compact, free-flowering perennial. H and S 1ft (30cm). Zone 10. Has oval, toothed leaves. Large, funnel-shaped, purple flowers are produced in summer.

A. 'Peach Blossom'. Trailing perennial. H and S to 10in (25cm). Zone 10. Has oval, toothed leaves. Large, funnel-shaped, peach-colored flowers appear in summer.

A. pulchella. See A. erecta.

ACHNATHERUM (Gramineae). See GRASSES, BAMBOOS, RUSHES, and SEDGES.

A. calamagrostis, syn. Stipa calamagrostis. Evergreen, tuft-forming, perennial grass. H 3ft (1m), S 1½ft (45cm). Fully hardy, zones 6–10. Leaves are bluish green and inrolled. In summer bears decorative, large, loose panicles of sand brown spikelets that dry and last well into winter.

Acidanthera bicolor var. **murieliae.** See Gladiolus callianthus.

ACIPHYLLA (Umbelliferae)

Genus of evergreen perennials, grown mainly for the architectural value of their spiky foliage but also for their flowers, which are produced more freely on male plants. Frost hardy. Requires sun and well-drained soil. Protect neck of plant from winter wet with a deep layer of stone chippings. Propagate by seed when fresh, in late summer, or in early spring.

A. aurea illus. p.199.

A. scott-thomsonii (Giant Spaniard). Evergreen, rosette-forming perennial. H to 14ft (4.5m), S 2–3ft (60cm–1m). Zones 8–10. Much-dissected, spiny foliage is bronze when young, maturing to silver-gray. Prickly spikes of tiny, creamy yellow flowers are rarely produced. Prefers a moist but well-drained site.

A. squarrosa illus. p.223.

ACOKANTHERA (Apocynaceae)

Genus of evergreen shrubs and trees, grown for their flowers and overall appearance. Frost tender, min. 50°F (10°C). Requires full light and well-drained soil. Water potted plants moderately, less when not in full growth. Propagate by seed in spring or autumn or by semi-ripe cuttings in summer.

A. oblongifolia, syn. A. spectabilis, Carissa spectabilis, illus. p.118.

A. spectabilis. See A. oblongifolia.

ACONITUM (Ranunculaceae)

Monkshood, Wolf's bane

Genus of perennials with poisonous, tuberous or fibrous roots and upright, sometimes scandent, stems, bearing hooded flowers in summer. Leaves are mostly rounded in outline. Is good for rock gardens and borders. Fully hardy. Prefers sun, but tolerates some shade and this may enhance flower color. Requires fertile, well-drained soil. Propagate by division in autumn, every 2–3 years, or by seed in autumn.

A. anthora. Compact, tuberous perennial. H 24in (60cm), S 20in (50cm). Zones 5–8. Has erect, leafy stems that bear several hooded, yellow flowers in summer. Leaves are divided and dark green.

A. x bicolor illus. p.211. **'Newry Blue'** is an upright, tuberous perennial. H 4ft (1.2m), S 20in (50cm). Zones 5–8. Bears hooded, dark blue flowers on erect stems in summer and has deeply divided, glossy, dark green leaves. **'Sparks Variety'** bears violet-blue flowers on branching stems.

A. 'Bressingham Spire'. Compact, upright, tuberous perennial. H 3ft (1m), S 20in (50cm). Zones 5–8. Hooded, violet-blue flowers are borne in very erect spikes in summer. Leaves are deeply divided, glossy, and dark green.

A. carmichaelii 'Arendsii'. Erect, tuberous perennial. H 5ft (1.5m), S 1ft (30cm). Zones 3–8. Has divided, rich green leaves and, in autumn, spikes of hooded, rich deep blue flowers. Upright stems may need staking, particularly if in a shady site.

A. 'Ivorine'. Upright, tuberous perennial. H 5ft (1.5m), S 20in (50cm). Zones 5–8. Bears hooded, creamy white flowers in erect spikes in early summer. Strong stems bear deeply divided, glossy, green leaves.

A. lycoctonum. See A. vulparia.

A. napellus (Helmet flower, Monkshood). Upright, tuberous perennial. H 5ft (1.5m), S 1ft (30cm). Zones 5–8. Has tall, slender spires of hooded, light indigo blue flowers in late summer and deeply cut, green leaves. f. **album** has white flowers.

A. volubile. Wiry, scandent, fibrous perennial. H 6–8ft (2–2.5m), S 3–4ft (1–1.2m). Zones 6–8. Hooded, lilac flowers are borne in drooping clusters in late summer. Leaves are divided and green. Is best grown where it can be supported or scramble through a shrub.

A. vulparia, syn. A. lycoctonum, illus. p.214.

ACORUS (Araceae)

Genus of semi-evergreen, perennial, marginal and submerged water plants,

grown for their often aromatic foliage. Fully to frost hardy. Needs an open, sunny position. A. calamus requires up to 10in (25cm) depth of water. Tidy up fading foliage in autumn and lift and divide every 3 or 4 years, in spring, as clumps become congested.

A. calamus (Sweet flag). **'Variegatus'** illus. p.373.

A. gramineus (Grassy-leaved sweet flag). **'Pusillus'** is a semi-evergreen, perennial, marginal water plant or submerged aquarium plant. Frost hardy, zones 6–10. H and S 4in (10cm). Has narrow, grasslike, stiff leaves. Rarely, insignificant, greenish flower spikes are produced in summer. **'Variegatus'** illus. p.373.

Acroclinium roseum. See Helipterum roseum.

ACTAEA (Ranunculaceae)

Baneberry

Genus of clump-forming perennials, grown for their colorful, poisonous berries. Fully hardy. Likes woodland conditions—moist, peaty soil and shade. Propagate by division in spring or by seed in autumn.

A. alba. See A. pachypoda.

A. pachypoda, syn. A. alba, illus. p.217.

A. rubra (Red baneberry). Clump-forming perennial. H 20in (50cm), S 12in (30cm). Zones 4–8. Small, fluffy, white flowers are followed in autumn by clusters of poisonous, rounded, scarlet berries, borne above oval, divided, bright green leaves.

ACTINIDIA (Actinidiaceae)

Genus of mainly deciduous, woody-stemmed, twining climbers. Fully hardy to frost tender, min. 50°F (10°C). Prefers partial shade (A. kolomikta will withstand full sun). Grow in any well-drained soil that does not dry out. Prune in winter if necessary. Propagate by seed in spring or autumn, by semi-ripe cuttings in mid-summer, or by layering in winter.

A. chinensis, syn. A. deliciosa (Chinese gooseberry, Kiwi fruit). Vigorous, mainly deciduous, woody-stemmed, twining climber. H 28–30ft (9–10m). Frost hardy, zones 7–9. Heart-shaped leaves are 5–8in (13–20cm) long. In summer bears clusters of cup-shaped, white, later yellowish flowers, followed by edible, hairy, brown fruits. To obtain fruits, male and female plants must be grown.

A. deliciosa. See A. chinensis.

A. kolomikta illus. p.167.

A. polygama (Silver vine). Mainly deciduous, woody-stemmed, twining climber. H 12–20ft (4–6m). Frost hardy, zones 4–9. Heart-shaped leaves, 3–5in (7–13cm) long, are bronze when young and sometimes have creamy, upper sections. In summer has scented, cup-shaped, white flowers, usually in groups of 3 male, female, or bisexual, followed by edible but not very tasty, egg-shaped, bright yellow fruits.

ADA. See ORCHIDS.

A. aurantiaca (illus. p.255). Evergreen, epiphytic orchid for a cool greenhouse. H 9in (23cm). Zone 10.

Bears sprays of tubular, orange flowers, 1in (2.5cm) long, in early spring. Has narrowly oval leaves, 4in (10cm) long. Needs shade in summer.

ADANSONIA (Bombacaceae)
Baobab
Genus of deciduous or semi-evergreen, mainly spring-flowering trees, grown for their characteristically swollen trunks, their foliage, and for shade. Has flowers only on large, mature specimens. Frost tender, min. 55–61°F (13–16°C). Requires full light and sharply drained soil. Allow soil of potted specimens almost to dry out between waterings. Propagate by seed in spring. Pot specimens under glass are prone to red spider mite.
A. digitata. Slow-growing, semi-evergreen, rounded tree. H and S 50ft (15m) or more. Zone 10. Has palmate leaves of 5–7 lustrous, green leaflets. Produces fragrant, pendent, long-stalked, white flowers, with 5 reflexed petals, in spring, followed by edible, sausage-shaped, brown fruits.

ADENIUM (Apocynaceae)
Desert rose
Genus of perennial succulents with fleshy, swollen trunks. Frost tender, min. 59°F (15°C). Needs sun or partial shade and well-drained soil; plants are very prone to rotting. Propagate by seed in spring or summer.
A. obesum illus. p.380.

ADENOCARPUS (Leguminosae)
Genus of deciduous or semi-evergreen shrubs, grown for their profuse, broomlike, yellow flowers in spring or early summer. Frost to half hardy. Requires full sun and well-drained soil. Does best grown against a south- or west-facing wall. Propagate by seed in autumn.
A. viscosus. Semi-evergreen, arching shrub. H and S 3ft (1m). Frost hardy, zones 9–10. Gray-green leaves with 3 narrowly lance-shaped leaflets densely cover shoots. Produces dense, terminal racemes of orange-yellow flowers in late spring.

ADENOPHORA (Campanulaceae)
Gland bellflower
Genus of summer-flowering, fleshy-rooted perennials. Fully hardy. Requires full sun and rich, well-drained but not over-dry soil. May become invasive but resents disturbance. Propagate by basal cuttings in early spring or by seed in autumn.
A. potaninii. Rosette-forming perennial. H 18in (45cm) or more, S 24in (60cm). Zones 4–8. Bears arching sprays of bell-shaped, pale bluish lavender flowers in late summer. Has oval to lance-shaped, basal, green leaves.

Adhatoda duvernoia. See *Duvernoia adhatodoides.*
Adhatoda vasica. See *Justicia adhatoda.*

ADIANTUM (Polypodiaceae)
Genus of deciduous, semi-evergreen, or evergreen ferns. Fully hardy to frost tender, min. 45–55°F (7–13°C). Prefers

semi-shade and moist, neutral to acid soil (*A. pedatum* var. *aleuticum* prefers alkaline soil). Remove fading fronds regularly. Propagate by spores in summer.
A. capillus-veneris (Maidenhair fern). Semi-evergreen or evergreen fern. H and S 12in (30cm). Half hardy, zones 9–10. Has dainty, triangular to oval, segmented, arching, light green fronds on black stems.
A. pedatum illus. p.186.
var. *aleuticum* illus. p.185.
A. raddianum (Delta maidenhair). Semi-evergreen or evergreen fern. H and S 12in (30cm). Frost tender, min. 45°F (7°C), zone 10. Triangular, divided, pale green segments are borne on finely dissected fronds with purplish black stems. **'Fritz-Luthii'** has bright green fronds. **'Grandiceps'** (Tassel maidenhair) has elegant, tasselled fronds.
A. tenerum. Semi-evergreen or evergreen fern. H 1–3ft (30cm–1m), S 2–3ft (60cm–1m). Frost tender, min. 55°F (13°C), zone 10. Broadly lance-shaped, much-divided, spreading, green fronds consist of rounded or diamond-shaped pinnae. **'Glory of Moordrecht'** has more erect fronds and will withstand temperatures down to 50°F (10°C).
A. venustum illus. p.187.

ADLUMIA (Fumariaceae)
Genus of one species of herbaceous, biennial, leaf-stalk climber, grown for its leaves and flowers. Frost hardy. Grow in any soil, in semi-shade. Propagate by seed in spring.
A. fungosa (Allegheny vine, Climbing fumitory). Herbaceous, biennial, leaf-stalk climber. H 10–12ft (3–4m). Zones 4–8. Delicate leaves have numerous leaflets. Tiny, tubular, spurred, white or purplish flowers are carried in drooping panicles in summer.

ADONIS (Ranunculaceae)
Genus of spring-flowering perennials, grown for their foliage and flowers. Fully hardy. Does best in semi-shade and in moist but well-drained soil. Propagate by seed when fresh, in late summer, or by division after flowering.
A. amurensis illus. p.232.
A. brevistyla illus. p.225.
A. vernalis illus. p.232.

ADROMISCHUS (Crassulaceae)
Genus of perennial succulents and evergreen sub-shrubs with rounded, thin or fat leaves. Frost tender, min. 45°F (7°C). Needs partial shade and very well-drained soil. Propagate by leaf or stem cuttings in spring or summer.
A. festivus (Plovers' eggs). Slow-growing, clump-forming, perennial succulent. H 4in (10cm), S 6in (15cm). Zone 10. Has egg-shaped, purple-blotched, gray-green leaves, each with a wavy-edged, compressed tip. Flower stem, to 12in (30cm) long, bears small, tubular, pink flowers in summer.
A. maculatus illus. p.389.

AECHMEA (Bromeliaceae)
Genus of evergreen, rosette-forming, epiphytic perennials, grown for their

foliage, flowers, and fruits. Frost tender, min. 50–59°F (10–15°C). May be grown in full light or semi-shade. Provide a rooting medium of equal parts humus-rich soil and either sphagnum moss or bark or plastic chips used for orchid culture. Using soft water, water moderately in summer, sparingly at other times, and keep cuplike, rosette centers filled with water from spring to autumn. Propagate by offsets in late spring.
A. distichantha (illus. p.222). Evergreen, basal-rosetted, epiphytic perennial. H and S to 3ft (1m). Zone 10. Forms dense rosettes of narrowly oblong, round-tipped, arching leaves that are dull green above, gray and scaly beneath. Bears panicles of small, tubular, purple or blue flowers among white-felted, pink bracts, usually in summer.
A. fasciata, syn. *Billbergia rhodocyanea* (Urn plant; illus. p.222). Evergreen, tubular-rosetted, epiphytic perennial. H 16–24in (40–60cm), S 12–20in (30–50cm). Zone 10. Produces loose rosettes of broadly oblong, round-tipped, incurved, arching leaves with dense, gray scales and silver cross-banding. From spring to autumn bears dense, pyramidal panicles of tubular, blue-purple flowers among pink bracts, just above foliage.
A. **'Foster's Favorite'** illus. p.222. Evergreen, basal-rosetted, epiphytic perennial. H and S 12–24in (30–60cm). Zone 10. Has loose rosettes of strap-shaped, arching, lustrous, wine red leaves. Drooping spikes of small, tubular, deep purple-blue flowers, in summer, are followed by pear-shaped, red fruits.
A. fulgens (Coralberry). Evergreen, basal-rosetted, epiphytic perennial. H and S 16–30in (40–75cm). Zone 10. Forms loose rosettes of broadly oblong, arching, glossy, green leaves with gray scales beneath and rounded or pointed tips. In summer produces, above foliage, erect panicles of small, tubular, violet-purple flowers that turn red with age. These are succeeded by small, rounded to ovoid, red fruits on red stalks.
A. nudicaulis. Evergreen, basal-rosetted, epiphytic perennial. H and S 16–30in (40–75cm). Zone 10. Produces loose rosettes of a few broadly strap-shaped, arching, olive green leaves with spiny edges and usually banded with gray scales beneath. Spikes of small, tubular, yellow flowers open above large, red bracts in summer.
A. recurvata (illus. p.222). Evergreen, basal-rosetted, epiphytic perennial. H and S 6–8in (15–20cm). Zone 10. Narrowly triangular, tapered, spiny-edged, arching, red-flushed, green leaves are produced in dense rosettes. In summer bears a short, dense spike of tubular, red-and-white flowers, with red bracts, just above leaves.

AEGOPODIUM (Umbelliferae)
Bishop's weed, Gout weed, Ground elder
Genus of invasive, rhizomatous perennials, most of which are weeds although *A. podagraria* 'Variegata' provides excellent ground cover.

Fully hardy. Tolerates sun or shade and any well-drained soil. Propagate by division of rhizomes in spring or autumn.
A. podagraria **'Variegata'** illus. p.233.

AEONIUM (Crassulaceae)
Genus of perennial succulents, some of which are short-lived, and evergreen, succulent shrubs, grown for their rosettes of bright green or blue-green, occasionally purple, leaves. Frost tender, min. 41°F (5°C). Prefers partial shade and very well-drained soil. Most species grow from autumn to spring and are semi-dormant in mid-summer. Propagate by seed in summer or, for branching species, by stem cuttings in spring or summer.
A. arboreum. Bushy, perennial succulent. H to 2ft (60cm), S 3ft (1m). Zones 9–10. Branched stems are each crowned by a rosette, up to 6in (15cm) across, of broadly lance-shaped, glossy, bright green leaves. In spring produces cones of small, star-shaped, golden flowers on 2–3-year-old stems, which then die back. **'Schwarzkopf'** illus. p.388.
A. haworthii illus. p.387.
A. tabuliforme illus. p.398.

AESCHYNANTHUS (Gesneriaceae)
Genus of evergreen, climbing, trailing, or creeping perennials, useful for growing in hanging baskets. Frost tender, min. 64°F (18°C). Needs a fairly humid atmosphere and a position out of direct sun. Water sparingly in low temperatures. Propagate by tip cuttings in spring or summer.
A. marmoratus, syn. *A. zebrinus.* Evergreen, trailing perennial. H and S to 2ft (60cm). Zone 10. Oval, waxy leaves are dark green, veined yellowish green above, purplish below. Has tubular, greenish flowers, marked dark brown, in terminal clusters in summer.
A. pulcher (Lipstick plant, Royal red bugler). Evergreen, climbing, or trailing perennial. H and S indefinite. Zone 10. Has thick, oval leaves and small, tubular, hooded, bright red flowers, with yellow throats, borne in terminal clusters from summer to winter.
A. speciosus, syn. *A. splendens,* illus. p.249.
A. splendens. See *A. speciosus.*
A. x *splendidus.* Vigorous, evergreen, trailing perennial. H and S 3ft (1m) or more. Zone 10. Leaves are thick, narrowly oval, to 5in (13cm) long. Has clusters of erect, tubular, bright orange-red flowers, marked with brown-red, in summer-autumn.
A. zebrinus. See *A. marmoratus.*

AESCULUS (Hippocastanaceae)
Buckeye, Horse chestnut
Genus of deciduous trees and shrubs, grown for their bold, divided leaves and conspicuous, upright panicles or clusters of flowers, followed by fruits (horse chestnuts) sometimes with spiny outer casings. Fully to frost hardy. Requires sun or semi-shade and fertile, well-drained soil. Propagate species by seed in autumn, cultivars by budding in late summer, or by grafting in late

winter. Leaf spot may affect young foliage, and coral spot fungus may attack damaged wood.

A. californica illus. p.58.
A. × *carnea* (Red horse chestnut). **'Briotii'** illus. p.39.
A. chinensis illus. p.39.
A. flava, syn. *A. octandra*, illus. p.55.
A. glabra (Ohio buckeye). Deciduous, round-headed, sometimes shrubby tree. H and S 30ft (10m). Fully hardy, zones 4–8. Leaves, usually composed of 5 narrowly oval leaflets, are dark green. Bears 4-petaled, greenish yellow flowers in upright clusters in late spring and early summer.
A. hippocastanum illus. p.38.
'Baumannii' is a vigorous, deciduous, spreading tree. H 100ft (30m), S 50ft (15m). Fully hardy, zones 4–7. Large, dark green leaves, consisting of 5 or 7 narrowly oval leaflets, turn yellow in autumn. Has large panicles of long-lasting, double, yellow- or red-marked, white flowers from mid- to late spring.
A. indica (Indian horse chestnut). Deciduous, spreading, elegant tree. H 70ft (20m), S 40ft (12m). Frost hardy, zones 4–8. Glossy, dark green leaves with usually 7 narrowly oval leaflets are bronze when young, orange or yellow in autumn. Upright panicles of 4-petaled, pink-tinged, white flowers, marked with red or yellow, appear in mid-summer. **'Sydney Pearce'** illus. p.52.
A. × *neglecta* (Sunrise horse chestnut). **'Erythroblastos'** illus. p.62.
A. octandra. See *A. flava*.
A. parviflora illus. p.88.
A. pavia (Red buckeye). Deciduous, round-headed, sometimes shrubby tree. H 15ft (5m), S 10ft (3m). Fully hardy, zones 6–9. Glossy, dark green leaves consist of 5 narrowly oval leaflets. Has panicles of 4-petaled, red flowers in early summer. **'Atrosanguinea'** illus. p.64.
A. turbinata (Japanese horse chestnut). Deciduous, spreading, stout-branched tree. H 70ft (20m), S 40ft (12m). Fully hardy, zones 6–8. Large, dark green leaves consist of 5 or 7 narrowly oval leaflets. Panicles of creamy white flowers appear in late spring and early summer.

AETHIONEMA (Cruciferae)
Genus of short-lived, evergreen or semi-evergreen shrubs, sub-shrubs, and perennials, grown for their prolific flowers. Fully hardy. Requires sun and well-drained soil. Propagate by softwood cuttings in spring or by seed in autumn. Most species self seed readily.
A. armenum illus. p.317.
A. grandiflorum, syn. *A. pulchellum*, illus. p.292.
A. iberideum. Evergreen or semi-evergreen, rounded, compact shrub. H and S 6in (15cm). Zones 7–9. Bears small, lance-shaped, gray-green leaves and, in summer, ³/₄in (2cm) stems each bear a raceme of small, saucer-shaped, white flowers.
A. pulchellum. See *A. grandiflorum*.
A. **'Warley Rose'** illus. p.316.
A. **'Warley Ruber'**. Evergreen or semi-evergreen, rounded, compact sub-shrub. H and S 6in (15cm). Zones

4–8. Has tiny, linear, bluish green leaves. Racemes of small, deep rose-pink flowers appear on ³/₄–1¹/₄in (2–3cm) stems in spring-summer.

AGAPANTHUS (Liliaceae)
Genus of clump-forming perennials, some of which are evergreen, with erect stems that carry large umbels of bell- to tubular-bell-shaped or trumpet-shaped flowers, usually blue and often fading to purple with age. Leaves are strap-shaped. Narrow-leaved forms are frost hardy, broad-leaved ones half hardy. Grow in full sun and in moist but well-drained soil. Protect crowns in winter with ash or mulch. Plants increase slowly but may be propagated by division in spring; may also be raised from seed in autumn or spring. Named cultivars will not come true from seed.
A. africanus (African lily). Evergreen, clump-forming perennial. H 3ft (1m), S 20in (50cm). Half hardy, zones 9–10. In late summer produces rounded umbels of deep blue flowers on upright stems, above broad, dark green leaves.
A. **'Alice Gloucester'**. Clump-forming perennial. H 3ft (1m), S 20in (50cm). Frost hardy, zones 7–10. Bears large, dense, rounded umbels of white flowers in summer, above narrow, green leaves.
A. **'Ben Hope'**. Clump-forming perennial. H 3–4ft (1–1.2m), S 20in (50cm). Frost hardy, zones 7–10. Erect stems support dense, rounded umbels of deep blue flowers in late summer and early autumn, over narrow, grayish green leaves.
A. campanulatus. Clump-forming perennial. H 2–4ft (60cm–1.2m), S 20in (50cm). Frost hardy, zones 8–10. Produces rounded umbels of blue flowers that are borne on strong stems in summer, above narrow, grayish green leaves.
A. **'Cherry Holley'**. Clump-forming perennial. H 3ft (1m), S 20in (50cm). Frost hardy, zones 7–10. In summer produces rounded umbels of dark blue flowers that are carried above narrow leaves. Flowers do not fade to purple with age.
A. **'Dorothy Palmer'** illus. p.212.
A. inapertus. Clump-forming perennial. H 5ft (1.5m), S 2ft (60cm). Frost hardy, zones 9–10. Pendent, narrowly tubular, blue flowers are borne on very erect stems, above narrow, bluish green leaves, in late summer and autumn.
A. **'Lilliput'**. Compact, clump-forming perennial. H 32in (80cm), S 20in (50cm). Frost hardy, zones 7–10. Produces small, rounded umbels of dark blue flowers in summer. Leaves are narrow and green.
A. **'Loch Hope'**. Clump-forming perennial. H 3–4ft (1–1.2m), S 20in (50cm). Frost hardy, zones 7–10. Bears large, rounded umbels of deep blue flowers in late summer and early autumn, above narrow, grayish green leaves.
A. orientalis. See *A. praecox* subsp. *orientalis*.
A. praecox subsp. *orientalis*, syn. *A. orientalis*, illus. p.213.

AGAPETES, syn. PENTAPTERYGIUM (Ericaceae)
Genus of evergreen or deciduous, scandent shrubs and semi-scrambling climbers, grown for their flowers. Frost tender, min. 41–64°F (5–18°C). Provide a humus-rich, well-drained but not dry, neutral to acid soil and full light or partial shade. Water potted specimens freely in full growth, moderately at other times. Overlong stems may be cut back to promote branching, but are best tied to supports. Propagate by seed in spring or by semi-ripe cuttings in late summer.
A. **'Ludgvan Cross'**, syn. *A. rugosa* × *serpens*. Evergreen, scandent shrub with arching or pendulous stems. H and S 6–10ft (2–3m). Min. 41°F (5°C), zone 10. Lance-shaped leaves are dark green. Urn-shaped, red flowers with darker patterns are produced in spring.
A. macrantha illus. p.177.
A. rugosa. Evergreen, loose shrub with arching or spreading stems. H and S to 10ft (3m). Min. 41°F (5°C), zone 10. Leaves are lance-shaped, wrinkled, and bright green. In spring, clusters of pendent, urn-shaped, white flowers, patterned with purple-red, are produced from leaf axils.
A. rugosa × *serpens*. See *A.* **'Ludgvan Cross'**.
A. serpens illus. p.164.

AGASTACHE (Labiatae)
Mexican giant hyssop
Genus of summer-flowering perennials with aromatic leaves. Half hardy. Needs fertile, well-drained soil and full sun. Plants are short-lived and should be propagated each year by softwood or semi-ripe cuttings in late summer.
A. mexicana, syn. *Brittonastrum mexicanum*, *Cedronella mexicana*. Upright perennial with aromatic leaves. H to 3ft (1m), S to 1ft (30cm). Zone 10. In summer bears whorls of small, tubular flowers in shades of pink to crimson. Leaves are oval, pointed, toothed, and green.

Agathaea coelestis. See *Felicia amelloides*.

AGATHOSMA (Rutaceae)
Genus of evergreen shrubs, grown for their flowers and overall appearance. Frost tender, min. 41–5°F (5–7°C). Needs full light and well-drained, acid soil. Water potted specimens moderately, less when not in full growth. Propagate by semi-ripe cuttings in late summer.
A. pulchella, syn. *Barosma pulchella*. Evergreen, rounded, wiry, aromatic shrub. H and S to 3ft (1m). Zone 10. Has a dense mass of small, oval, leathery leaves. Small, 5-petaled, purple flowers are freely produced in terminal clusters in spring-summer.

AGAVE (Agavaceae)
Genus of rosetted, perennial succulents with sword-shaped, sharp-toothed leaves. Small species, to 1ft (30cm) high, flower only after 5–10 years; tall species, to 15ft (5m) high, may take 20–40 years to flower. Most species with hard, blue-gray leaves are half hardy; gray-green- or green-leaved

species are usually frost tender, min. 41°F (5°C). Needs full sun and well-drained soil. Propagate by seed or offsets in spring or summer.
A. americana (Century plant). Basal-rosetted, perennial succulent. H 3–6ft (1–2m), S 6–10ft (2–3m) or more. Half hardy, zones 9–10. Has sharply pointed, toothed leaves, to 5–6ft (1.5–2m) long. Branched flower stem, to 25ft (8m) long, produces dense, tapering spikes of bell-shaped, white to pale creamy yellow flowers, each 3¹/₂in (9cm) long, in spring-summer. Offsets freely. **'Medio-picta'**, H and S 6ft (2m), has central, yellow stripes along leaves. **'Variegata'** illus. p.379.
A. attenuata illus. p.387.
A. filifera illus. p.386.
A. parryi illus. p.387.
A. parviflora illus. p.379.
A. utahensis illus. p.398.
A. victoriae-reginae illus. p.382.

AGERATUM (Compositae)
Flossflower
Genus of annuals and biennials. Half hardy to frost tender, min. 36–9°F (2–4°C). Grow in sun and in fertile, well-drained soil, which should not be allowed to dry out otherwise growth and flowering will be poor. Dead-head plants regularly to ensure continuous flowering. Propagate by seed sown outdoors in late spring.
A. houstonianum. Moderately fast-growing, hummock-forming annual. Tall cultivars, H and S 12in (30cm); medium, H and S 8in (20cm); dwarf, H and S 6in (15cm). Frost tender. All have oval, green leaves and clusters of feathery, brushlike flower heads throughout summer and into autumn. Is useful for edging. **'Bengali'** (medium) has light pink flowers, deepening with age. **'Blue Danube'** (dwarf) and **'Blue Mink'** (tall) illus. p.277. **'Pinkie'** (tall) is a warm shade of pink; and **'White Cushion'** (medium) has white flowers.

AGLAONEMA (Araceae)
Chinese evergreen
Genus of evergreen, erect, tufted perennials, grown mainly for their foliage. Frost tender, most species requiring min. 59°F (15°C). Tolerates shade, although variegated forms need more light, and prefers moist but well-drained soil. Water moderately when in full growth, less in winter. Propagate by division or stem cuttings in summer. Mealy bug may be a problem.
A. commutatum. Evergreen, erect, tufted perennial. H and S to 18in (45cm) or more. Zone 10. Broadly lance-shaped leaves are 1ft (30cm) long and dark green with irregular, grayish white patches along lateral veins. Has greenish white spathes in summer. **'Silver King'** illus. p.260; **'Treubii'** illus. p.256.
A. **'Malay Beauty'**, syn. *A.* 'Pewter'. Evergreen, erect, tufted perennial. H and S 1ft (30cm) or more. Zone 10. Oval leaves, to 1ft (30cm) long, are very dark green, mottled greenish white and cream. Has greenish white spathes in summer.

A. **'Pewter'.** See *A.* 'Malay Beauty'.
A. pictum illus. p.260.

AGONIS (Myrtaceae)
Willow myrtle
Genus of evergreen, mainly spring-flowering shrubs and trees, grown for their foliage, flowers, and graceful appearance. Frost tender, min. 50°F (10°C). Needs full light and well-drained but moisture-retentive soil. Water potted specimens moderately, scarcely at all in winter. Pruning is tolerated when necessary. Propagate by seed in spring or by semi-ripe cuttings in summer.
A. flexuosa illus. p.63.

AGROSTEMMA (Caryophyllaceae)
Corn cockle
Genus of summer-flowering annuals. Fully to half hardy. Grow in sun; flowers best in very well-drained soil that is not very fertile. Support with stakes and dead-head to prolong flowering. Propagate by seed sown *in situ* in spring or early autumn.
A. coeli-rosa. See *Silene coeli-rosa.*
A. githago. Fast-growing, erect annual with thin stems. H 2–3ft (60cm–1m), S 1ft (30cm). Half hardy. Has lance-shaped, green leaves and, in summer, 5-petaled, open trumpet-shaped, pink flowers, 3in (8cm) wide. Seeds are tiny, rounded, dark brown, and poisonous. **'Milas'** illus. p.267.

AICHRYSON (Crassulaceae)
Genus of annual and perennial succulents, often shrublike, grown for their fleshy, spoon-shaped to rounded, hairy leaves. Most species are short-lived, dying after flowering. Frost tender, min. 41°F (5°C). Needs full sun or partial shade and very well-drained soil. Propagate by seed or stem cuttings in spring or summer.
A. x *domesticum* **'Variegatum'** illus. p.397.

AILANTHUS (Simaroubaceae)
Genus of deciduous trees, grown for their foliage and 3–5-winged fruits; is extremely tolerant of urban pollution. Fully hardy. Needs sun or semi-shade and deep, fertile, well-drained soil. To grow as shrubs, cut back hard in spring, after which vigorous shoots bearing very large leaves are produced. Propagate by seed in autumn or by suckers or root cuttings in winter.
A. altissima (Tree-of-Heaven). Fast-growing, deciduous, spreading tree. H 80ft (25m), S 50ft (15m). Zones 5–8. Has large, dark green leaves consisting of 15–30 paired, oval leaflets. Large clusters of small, green flowers in mid-summer are followed by attractive, winged, green, then reddish brown fruits.

AJUGA (Labiatae)
Genus of annuals and perennials, some of which are semi-evergreen or evergreen and excellent as ground cover. Fully hardy. Tolerates sun or shade and any soil, but grows more vigorously in moist conditions. Propagate by division in spring.
A. pyramidalis (Pyramidal bugle). Semi-evergreen, mat-forming perennial. H 6in (15cm), S 18in

(45cm). Zones 3–8. Forms a creeping carpet of oblong to spoon-shaped, deep green leaves, above which appear spikes of whorled, 2-lipped, blue flowers in spring. **'Metallica Crispa'** has crisp, curled leaves, with a metallic bronze lustre, and dark blue flowers.
A. reptans (Carpet bugle).
'Atropurpurea' illus. p.259. **'Jungle Beauty'** is a semi-evergreen, mat-forming perennial. H 15in (38cm), S 24in (60cm). Zones 3–8. Has large, oval, toothed or slightly lobed, dark green leaves, sometimes suffused purple, and, in spring, spikes of whorled, 2-lipped, blue flowers. **'Multicolor'** (syn. *A.r.* 'Rainbow') illus. p.259.

AKEBIA (Lardizabalaceae)
Genus of deciduous or semi-evergreen, woody-stemmed, twining climbers, grown for their leaves and flowers. Individual plants seldom produce fruits; cross-pollination between 2 individuals is required for fruit formation. Frost hardy. Prefers full sun and any good, well-drained soil. Tolerates an east- or north-facing position. Dislikes disturbance. Propagate by seed in autumn or spring, by semi-ripe cuttings in summer, or by layering in winter.
A. x *pentaphylla.* Mainly deciduous, woody-stemmed, twining climber. H to 30ft (10m). Zones 5–8. Green leaves, bronze-tinted when young, have 3 or 5 oval leaflets. Drooping racemes of small, 3-petaled, purple flowers (larger, female at base of plant, smaller, male at apex) are borne in spring.
A. quinata illus. p.164.
A. trifoliata. Deciduous, woody-stemmed, twining climber. H to 30ft (10m) or more. Zones 5–8. Green leaves, bronze-tinted when young, have 3 oval leaflets; drooping racemes of 3-petaled, purple flowers appear in spring, followed by sausage-shaped, purplish fruits.

ALANGIUM (Alangiaceae)
Genus of deciduous or evergreen trees and shrubs, grown for their foliage and flowers. Frost hardy. Needs full sun and any fertile, well-drained soil. Propagate by seed in spring or by softwood cuttings in summer.
A. platanifolium. Deciduous, upright, treelike shrub. H 10ft (3m), S 6ft (2m). Zones 7–9. Has maplelike, 3-lobed, green leaves. Fragrant, tubular, white flowers are borne from early to mid-summer.

ALBIZIA (Leguminosae)
Genus of deciduous or semi-evergreen trees, grown for their feathery foliage and unusual flower heads, composed of numerous stamens and resembling bottlebrushes. Half hardy: grow against a south- or west-facing wall; in cold areas do not plant out until late spring. Requires full sun and well-drained soil. *A. julibrissin* may be grown as a summer bedding plant for its foliage. Propagate by seed in autumn.
A. distachya, syn. *A. lophantha*, illus. p.66.
A. julibrissin illus. p.63.
A. lophantha. See *A. distachya.*

ALBUCA (Liliaceae)
Genus of spring- or summer-flowering bulbs. Half hardy to frost tender, min. 50°F (10°C). Needs an open, sunny position and well-drained soil. Dies down in spring or late summer after flowering. Propagate by seed in spring or by offsets when dormant.
A. canadensis. Spring-flowering bulb. H 6in (15cm), S 3–4in (8–10cm). Half hardy, zones 9–10. Has 3–6 narrowly lance-shaped, erect, basal leaves. Produces a loose spike of tubular, yellow flowers, $5/8$–$3/4$in (1.5–2cm) long, with a green stripe on each petal.
A. humilis illus. p.364.
A. major. Early spring-flowering bulb. H 20in–3ft (50cm–1m), S 5–6in (12–15cm). Frost tender, zone 10. Has long, lance-shaped, erect, basal leaves and robust stems, each with a loose spike of up to 12 tubular, yellow flowers, $5/8$–$3/4$in (1.5–2cm) long, with green or brown stripes outside.

ALCEA (Malvaceae)
Hollyhock
Genus of biennials and short-lived perennials, grown for their tall spikes of flowers. Fully hardy. Needs full sun and well-drained soil. Propagate by seed in late summer or spring. Rust may be a problem.
A. rosea, syn. *Althaea rosea* (biennial), illus. p.265. **'Chater's Double'** (biennial) illus. p.270. **'Majorette'** is an erect biennial, grown as an annual. H 2ft (60cm), S to 1ft (30cm). Rounded, lobed, pale green leaves are rough-textured. Spikes of rosettelike, double flowers in several different colors are produced in summer and early autumn. **'Summer Carnival'** (annual or biennial), H 6–8ft (1.8–2.4m), S to 2ft (60cm), has double flowers in mixed colors.

ALCHEMILLA (Rosaceae)
Lady's-mantle
Genus of perennials that bear sprays of tiny, greenish yellow flowers, with conspicuous, outer calyces, in summer. Some are good for ground cover. Fully hardy. Grows in all but boggy soils, in sun or partial shade. Propagate by seed or division in spring or autumn.
A. alpina (Alpine lady's-mantle). Mound-forming perennial. H 6in (15cm), S 24in (60cm) or more. Zones 3–7. Rounded, lobed, pale green leaves are covered in silky hairs. Bears upright spikes of tiny, greenish yellow flowers, with conspicuous, green, outer calyces, in summer. Is suitable for ground cover and a dry bank.
A. conjuncta illus. p.245.
A. mollis illus. p.245.

---

x ALICEARA. See ORCHIDS.
x *A.* **Dark Warrior** (illus. p.254). Evergreen, epiphytic orchid for a cool greenhouse. H 10in (25cm). Zone 10. Has sprays of wispy, mauve-brown, cream yellow, or green flowers, $1^1/2$in (4cm) across; flowering season varies. Leaves, 4in (10cm) long, are narrowly oval. Grow in semi-shade in summer.

ALISMA (Alismataceae)
Genus of deciduous, perennial, marginal water plants, grown for

their foliage and for their flowers. Fully to frost hardy. Requires an open, sunny position in mud or up to 10in (25cm) depth of water. Tidy up fading foliage in autumn and remove dying flower spikes before ripening seeds are dispersed. Propagate by division in spring or by seed in late summer.
A. natans. See *Luronium natans.*
A. plantago-aquatica illus. p.372.
A. ranunculoides. See *Baldellia ranunculoides.*

ALLEMANDA (Apocynaceae)
Genus of evergreen, woody-stemmed, scrambling climbers, grown for their trumpet-shaped flowers. Frost tender, min. 55–9°F (13–15°C). Prefers partial shade in summer and humus-rich, well-drained, neutral to acid soil. Water regularly, less when not in full growth. Stems must be staked. Prune previous season's growth back to 1 or 2 nodes in spring. Propagate by softwood cuttings in spring or summer. Whitefly and red spider mite may be troublesome.
A. cathartica (Golden trumpet). **'Hendersonii'** illus. p.174.

ALLIUM (Liliaceae)
Onion
Genus of perennials, some of which are edible, with bulbs, rhizomes, or fibrous rootstocks. Nearly all have narrow, basal leaves smelling of onions when crushed, and most have small flowers packed together in a dense, spherical or shuttlecock-shaped umbel. Dried umbels of tall border species are good for winter decoration. Fully to frost hardy. Requires an open, sunny situation and well-drained soil; is best left undisturbed to form clumps. Plant in autumn. Propagate by seed in autumn or by division of clumps—spring-flowering varieties in late summer and summer-flowering ones in spring.
A. acuminatum, syn. *A. murrayanum*, illus. p.358.
A. aflatunense illus. p.337.
A. akaka illus. p.357.
A. albopilosum. See *A. christophii.*
A. azureum. See *A. caeruleum.*
A. beesianum. Clump-forming, late summer-flowering bulb. H 8–12in (20–30cm), S 2–4in (5–10cm). Fully hardy, zones 6–10. Has linear, gray-green leaves and, in late summer, pendent heads of bell-shaped, blue flowers.
A. caeruleum, syn. *A. azureum*, illus. p.352.
A. campanulatum. Clump-forming, summer-flowering bulb. H 4–12in (10–30cm), S 2–4in (5–10cm). Frost hardy, zones 9–10. Linear, semi-erect, basal leaves die away before flowering time. Bears a domed umbel, 1–3in (2.5–7cm) wide, of up to 30 small, star-shaped, pale pink or white flowers.
A. carinatum subsp. *pulchellum*, syn. *A. pulchellum.* Clump-forming, summer-flowering bulb. H 1–2ft (30–60cm), S 3–4in (8–10cm). Fully hardy, zones 6–9. Has linear, semi-erect leaves sheathing stem in lower two-thirds. Bears an umbel of pendent, cup-shaped, purple flowers.

A. cernuum illus. p.351.
A. christophii, syn. *A. albopilosum*, illus. p.352.
A. cowanii. See *A. neapolitanum*.
A. cyaneum. Tuft-forming, summer-flowering bulb. H 4–12in (10–30cm), S 2–3in (5–8cm). Fully hardy, zones 5–9. Leaves are threadlike and erect. Stems each bear a small, dense umbel of 5 or more pendent, cup-shaped, blue or violet-blue flowers, 1/4in (0.5cm) long.
A. cyathophorum var. *farreri* illus. p.365.
A. flavum. Clump-forming, summer-flowering bulb. H 4–12in (10–30cm), S 3–4in (8–10cm). Fully hardy, zones 4–10. Leaves are linear and semi-erect on lower half of slender flower stem. Produces a loose umbel of up to 30 bell-shaped, yellow flowers, each 1/4in (0.5cm) long, on thin, arching stalks.
A. giganteum illus. p.337.
A. kansuense. See *A. sikkimense*.
A. karataviense illus. p.357.
A. macranthum. Tuft-forming, summer-flowering bulb. H 8–12in (20–30cm), S 4–5in (10–12cm). Fully hardy, zones 4–10. Has linear leaves on lower part of flower stem, which bears a loose umbel of up to 20 bell-shaped, deep purple flowers, each 1/2in (1cm) long, on slender stalks.
A. mairei. Clump-forming, late summer- to autumn-flowering bulb. H 4–8in (10–20cm), S 4–5in (10–12cm). Fully hardy, zones 4–10. Leaves are erect, threadlike, and basal. Wiry stems each carry a small, shuttlecock-shaped umbel of up to 20 upright, bell-shaped, pink flowers, each 1/2in (1cm) long.
A. moly illus. p.365.
A. murrayanum. See *A. acuminatum*.
A. narcissiflorum, syn. *A. pedemontanum*, illus. p.365.
A. neapolitanum, syn. *A. cowanii*, illus. p.342.
A. oreophilum, syn. *A. ostrowskianum*, illus. p.358.
A. ostrowskianum. See *A. oreophilum*.
A. pedemontanum. See *A. narcissiflorum*.
A. pulchellum. See *A. carinatum* subsp. *pulchellum*.
A. rosenbachianum illus. p.336.
A. schoenoprasum illus. p.365.
A. schubertii illus. p.352.
A. sikkimense, syn. *A. kansuense*. Tuft-forming, summer-flowering bulb. H 4–10in (10–25cm), S 2–4in (5–10cm). Fully hardy, zones 6–10. Leaves are linear, erect, and basal. Up to 15 bell-shaped, blue flowers, 1/4–1/2in (0.5–1cm) long, are borne in a small, pendent umbel.
A. sphaerocephalon. Clump-forming, summer-flowering bulb. H to 24in (60cm), S 3–4in (8–10cm). Fully hardy, zones 6–10. Has linear, semi-erect leaves on basal third of slender, wiry stems and a very dense umbel, 3/4–11/2in (2–4cm) across, of up to 40 small, bell-shaped, pinkish purple flowers.
A. unifolium illus. p.343.

ALLOPLECTUS (Gesneriaceae)
Genus of evergreen, usually summer-flowering perennials and sub-shrubs, grown mainly for their flowers and leaves. Lax, prostrate species are best in hanging baskets. Frost tender, min. 61–4°F (16–18°C). Needs partial shade and humus-rich, well-drained soil. Water potted plants moderately, much less in low temperatures. Propagate by seed in spring or by softwood cuttings of stem tips in summer. Red spider mite and mealy bug may be troublesome.
A. nummularia, syn. *Hypocyrta nummularia* (Clog plant). Evergreen perennial with slender, trailing stems rooting at swollen nodes. H 3in (8cm), S 18in (45cm) or more. Zone 10. Broad, oval to rounded, hairy leaves have toothed, reddish margins. At any time of year may produce solitary tubular, bright red flowers, each with a pouch to 1/2in (1cm) deep on lower side, a violet ring at the neck, and 5 very small, yellow lobes.

ALNUS (Betulaceae)
Alder
Genus of deciduous trees and shrubs, grown mainly for their ability to thrive in wet situations. Flowers are borne in catkins in late winter or early spring, males conspicuous and attractive, females forming persistent, woody, conelike fruits. Fully hardy. Most do best in sun and any moist or even waterlogged soil, but *A. cordata* also grows well on poor, dry soils. Propagate species by seed in autumn, cultivars by budding in late summer or by hardwood cuttings in early winter.
A. cordata illus. p.41.
A. glutinosa (Black alder, Common alder). 'Aurea' is a slow-growing, deciduous, conical tree. H to 80ft (25m), S 30ft (10m). Zones 4–7. Has rounded leaves, bright yellow until mid-summer, later becoming pale green. Bears yellow-brown catkins in early spring. Is useful in a boggy area. 'Imperialis', H 30ft (10m), S 12ft (4m), is slow-growing and has deeply cut, lobed leaves.
A. incana illus. p.40. 'Aurea' is a deciduous, conical tree. H 70ft (20m), S 25ft (8m). Zones 4–7. Has reddish yellow or orange shoots in winter and broadly oval, yellow leaves. Reddish yellow or orange catkins are borne in late winter and early spring. Is useful for cold, wet areas and poor soils. 'Ramulis Coccineis' has red, winter shoots and buds, and orange catkins.

ALOCASIA (Araceae)
Genus of evergreen perennials with underground rhizomes, grown for their attractive foliage. Produces tiny flowers on a spadix enclosed in a leaflike spathe. Frost tender, min. 59°F (15°C). Needs high humidity, partial shade, and well-drained soil. Propagate by seed, stem cuttings, or division of rhizomes in spring.
A. cuprea illus. p.223.
A. lowii var. *veitchii.* See *A. veitchii*.
A. macrorrhiza (Giant elephant's-ear, Taro). Evergreen, tufted perennial with a thick, trunklike stem. H to 10ft (3m) or more, S 6ft (2m). Zone 10. Broad, arrow-shaped, glossy, green leaves, to 3ft (1m) long, are carried on stalks 3ft (1m) long. Has yellowish green spathes to 8in (20cm) high.

A. picta. See *A. veitchii*.
A. veitchii, syn. *A. lowii* var. *veitchii*, *A. picta*. Evergreen, tufted perennial. H 3ft (1m) or more, S 30in (75cm). Zone 10. Narrow leaves, triangular with arrow-shaped bases, are 18in (45cm) long and green with grayish midribs, veins, and margins, purple beneath. Spathes are greenish.

ALOE (Liliaceae)
Genus of evergreen, rosetted trees, shrubs, perennials, and scandent climbers with succulent foliage and tubular to bell-shaped flowers. Frost tender, min. 45–50°F (7–10°C). Tree aloes and shrubs with a spread over 1ft (30cm) prefer full sun; most smaller species prefer partial shade. Needs very well-drained soil. Propagate by seed, stem cuttings, or offsets in spring or summer.
A. arborescens. Evergreen, bushy, succulent-leaved shrub. H and S 6ft (2m). Zone 10. Stems are each crowned by rosettes of widely spreading, long, slender, curved, dull blue-green leaves with toothed margins. Long flower stems produce masses of tubular to bell-shaped, red flowers in late winter and spring. 'Variegata' illus. p.380.
A. aristata illus. p.400.
A. barbadensis, syn. *A. vera*, illus. p.386.
A. brevifolia. Basal-rosetted, perennial succulent, producing many offsets. H 6in (15cm), S 12in (30cm). Zone 10. Has broadly sword-shaped, fleshy, blue-green leaves with a few teeth along edges. In spring, flower stems, 20in (50cm) long, carry narrowly bell-shaped, bright red flowers.
A. ciliaris illus. p.380.
A. ferox illus. p.380.
A. humilis. Rosetted, perennial succulent. H 4in (10cm), S 12in (30cm). Zone 10. Has a dense, basal rosette of narrowly sword-shaped, spine-edged, fleshy, blue-green leaves, often erect, with incurving tips. Flower stems are 12in (30cm) long and each bears a spike of bell-shaped, orange flowers in spring. Offsets freely.
A. striata illus. p.388.
A. variegata illus. p.385.
A. vera. See *A. barbadensis*.

ALOINOPSIS (Aizoaceae)
Genus of dwarf, tuberous, perennial succulents with daisylike flowers from late summer to early spring. Frost tender, min. 45°F (7°C). Requires a sunny site and very well-drained soil. Is very susceptible to overwatering. Propagate by seed in summer.
A. schooneesii illus. p.397.

ALONSOA (Scrophulariaceae)
Genus of perennials, grown as annuals. May be used for cut flowers. Half hardy to frost tender, min. 36–9°F (2–4°C). Grow in sun and in rich, well-drained soil. Flowering may be poor outdoors in a wet summer. Young plants should have growing shoots pinched out to encourage bushy growth. Propagate by seed sown outdoors in late spring. Aphids may be troublesome, particularly on plants grown in greenhouses.
A. warscewiczii illus. p.273.

ALOPECURUS (Gramineae). See GRASSES, BAMBOOS, RUSHES, and SEDGES.
A. pratensis 'Aureomarginatus', syn. *A.p.* 'Aureo-variegatus', *A.p.* 'Aureus', illus. p.183.

ALOYSIA (Verbenaceae)
Genus of deciduous or evergreen, summer-flowering shrubs, grown for their aromatic foliage and sprays of tiny flowers. Frost to half hardy; in cold areas plant against a south- or west-facing wall or raise afresh each year. Needs full sun and well-drained soil. Cut out any dead wood in early summer. Propagate by softwood cuttings in summer.
A. triphylla, syn. *Lippia citriodora*, illus. p.111.

ALPINIA (Zingiberaceae)
Genus of mainly evergreen perennials with fleshy rhizomes, grown for their flowers. Frost tender, min. 64°F (18°C). Needs humus-rich, well-drained soil, partial shade, and a moist atmosphere. Is not easy to grow successfully in pots. Propagate by division in late spring or early summer. Red spider mite may be a problem.
A. calcarata (Indian ginger). Evergreen, upright, clump-forming perennial. H and S to 3ft (1m). Zone 10. Has stalkless, aromatic, lance-shaped leaves, to 1ft (30cm) long. At any time of year may bear horizontal spikes of whitish flowers, with 1in (2.5cm) long, yellow lips marked reddish purple.
A. nutans. See *A. zerumbet*.
A. speciosa. See *A. zerumbet*.
A. zerumbet, syn. *A. nutans*, *A. speciosa*, illus. p.189.

ALSOPHILA. See CYATHEA.

ALSTROEMERIA (Alstroemeriaceae)
Genus of mostly summer-flowering, tuberous perennials with showy, multicolored flowers. Flowers are good for cutting as they last well. Frost hardy, but in very cold winters protect by covering dormant tubers with dry bracken or loose peat. Needs well-drained soil and a sunny, sheltered site. Propagate by seed or division in early spring.
A. aurantiaca. See *A. aurea*.
A. aurea, syn. *A. aurantiaca*, illus. p.339.
A. gayana. See *A. pelegrina*.
A. hookeri illus. p.326.
A., Ligtu Hybrids illus. p.353.
A. 'Margaret' illus. p.335.
A. pelegrina, syn. *A. gayana*, illus. p.351.
A. 'Walter Fleming'. Summer-flowering, tuberous perennial. H to 3ft (1m), S 2–3ft (60cm–1m). Zones 8–10. Each leafy stem bears narrowly lance-shaped, twisted leaves and widely funnel-shaped, deep yellow flowers, 2–21/2in (5–6cm) across, flushed purple with reddish purple spots.

ALTERNANTHERA (Amaranthaceae)
Genus of bushy perennials, grown for their attractive, colored foliage.

Is useful for carpeting or bedding. Frost tender, min. 59–64°F (15–18°C). Needs sun or partial shade and moist but well-drained soil. Propagate by tip cuttings or division in spring.

A. amoena. See *A. ficoidea* 'Amoena'.

A. ficoidea (Parrot leaf). **'Amoena'** (syn. *A. amoena*) is a mat-forming perennial. H 2in (5cm), S indefinite. Zone 10. Has narrowly oval, green leaves, marked red, yellow, and orange, with wavy margins. **'Versicolor'** (syn. *A. versicolor*) is an erect form, H and S to 1ft (30cm), with rounded to spoon-shaped leaves shaded brown, red, and yellow.

A. versicolor. See *A. ficoidea* 'Versicolor'.

Althaea rosea. See *Alcea rosea.*

ALYSSUM (Cruciferae)
Genus of perennials, some of which are evergreen, and annuals, grown for their flowers. Fully hardy. Needs sun and well-drained soil. Cut back lightly after flowering. Propagate by softwood cuttings in late spring or by seed in autumn.

A. maritimum. See *Lobularia maritima.*

A. montanum. Evergreen, prostrate perennial. H and S 6in (15cm). Zones 4–9. Leaves are small, oval, hairy, and gray. Flower stems, 6in (15cm) long, each bear an open, spherical raceme of small, very fragrant, soft yellow flowers in summer. Is good in a rock garden.

A. saxatile. See *Aurinia saxatilis.*

A. wulfenianum. Prostrate perennial. H ³/₄in (2cm), S 8in (20cm). Zones 7–9. Loose heads of small, bright yellow flowers appear in summer above small, oval, gray leaves.

AMARANTHUS (Amaranthaceae)
Genus of annuals, grown for their dense panicles of tiny flowers or for their colorful foliage. Half hardy to frost tender, min. 36–9°F (2–4°C). Grow in sun and in rich or fertile, well-drained soil. Propagate from seed sown outdoors in late spring. Aphids may sometimes be troublesome.

A. caudatus illus. p.270.

A. hybridus var. **erythrostachys,** syn. *A. hypochondriacus,* illus. p.274.

A. hypochondriacus. See *A. hybridus* var. *erythrostachys.*

A. tricolor **'Joseph's Coat'.** Bushy annual. H to 3ft (1m), S 1¹/₂ft (45cm) or more. Frost tender. Has oval, scarlet, green, and yellow leaves, to 8in (20cm) long, and small panicles of tiny, red flowers in summer. Leaves of **'Molten Fire'** are crimson, bronze, and purple.

---

x AMARCRINUM (Amaryllidaceae)
Hybrid genus (*Amaryllis* x *Crinum*) of one robust, evergreen bulb, grown for its large, funnel-shaped flowers. Frost hardy. Needs sun and well-drained soil. Plant with neck just covered by soil. Propagate by division in spring.

x A. howardii. See x *A. memoria-corsii.*

x A. memoria-corsii, syn. x *A. howardii,* x *Crinodonna corsii,* illus. p.342.

---

x AMARYGIA (Amaryllidaceae)
Hybrid genus (*Amaryllis* x *Brunsvigia*) of stout, autumn-flowering bulbs, cultivated for their large, showy flowers. Frost hardy. Needs full sun and, preferably, shelter of a wall. Plant bulbs just beneath surface of well-drained soil. Propagate by division in spring.

x A. parkeri, syn. x *Brunsdonna parkeri,* illus. p.342.

AMARYLLIS (Amaryllidaceae)
Genus of autumn-flowering bulbs, grown for their funnel-shaped flowers. Frost hardy, but in cool areas should be grown against a south-facing wall for protection. Requires well-drained soil and a sheltered, sunny situation. Plant bulbs under at least 3in (8cm) of soil. Propagate by division in late spring, as leaves die down, or in late summer, before growth recommences.

A. belladonna and **'Hathor'** illus. p.342.

AMELANCHIER (Rosaceae)
Juneberry, Serviceberry, Shadbush
Genus of deciduous, spring-flowering trees and shrubs, grown for their profuse flowers and their foliage, which is frequently brightly colored in autumn. Fully hardy. Requires sun or semi-shade and well-drained but not too dry, preferably neutral to acid soil. Propagate in autumn by seed, in late autumn to early spring by layering or, in the case of suckering species, by division. Fireblight is sometimes a problem.

A. alnifolia (Saskatoon serviceberry). Deciduous, upright, suckering shrub. H 12ft (4m) or more, S 10ft (3m) or more. Zones 5–9. Leaves are oval to rounded and dark green. Erect spikes of star-shaped, creamy white flowers are borne in late spring, followed by small, edible, juicy, rounded, purple-black fruits.

A. arborea (Shadbush Juneberry). Deciduous, spreading, sometimes shrubby, tree. H 30ft (10m), S 40ft (12m). Zones 5–9. Clusters of star-shaped, white flowers appear in mid-spring as oval, white-haired, young leaves unfold. Foliage matures to dark green, turning to red or yellow in autumn. Rounded fruits are small, dry, and reddish purple.

A. asiatica (Asian serviceberry). Deciduous, spreading tree or shrub of elegant habit. H 25ft (8m), S 30ft (10m). Zones 5–8. Leaves are oval and dark green, usually woolly when young and turning yellow or red in autumn. Star-shaped, white flowers are borne profusely in late spring, followed by edible, juicy, rounded, blackcurrantlike fruits.

A. canadensis (Shadblow serviceberry). Deciduous, upright, dense shrub. H 20ft (6m), S 10ft (3m). Zones 4–8. Star-shaped, white flowers are borne from mid- to late spring amid unfolding, oval, white-haired leaves that mature to dark green and turn orange-red in autumn. Fruits are edible, rounded, blackish purple, sweet, and juicy.

A. laevis illus. p.58.

A. lamarckii illus. p.84.

A. stolonifera (Running serviceberry). Deciduous, upright, thicket-forming shrub. H and S 6ft (2m). Zones 4–7. Star-shaped, white flowers appear from mid- to late spring, followed by edible, juicy, rounded, blue-black fruits. Has oval, dark green leaves that color orange-yellow in autumn.

AMORPHA (Leguminosae)
Genus of deciduous shrubs and sub-shrubs, grown for their flowers and foliage. Is useful for cold, dry, exposed positions. Fully hardy. Requires full sun and well-drained soil. Propagate by softwood cuttings in summer or by seed in autumn.

A. canescens (Lead plant). Deciduous, open sub-shrub. H 3ft (1m), S 5ft (1.5m). Zones 2–7. Dense spikes of tiny, pealike, purple flowers, with orange anthers, are produced in late summer and early autumn, amid oval, gray-haired leaves divided into 21–41 narrowly oval leaflets.

AMORPHOPHALLUS (Araceae)
Genus of tuberous perennials, cultivated for their huge and dramatic, but foul-smelling, spathes, which surround tiny flowers on stout spadices. Frost tender, min. 50°F (10°C). Requires partial shade and humus-rich soil kept continuously moist during growing season. Keep tubers dry in winter. Propagate by seed in spring or by offsets in spring or summer.

A. rivieri. Summer-flowering, tuberous perennial. H to 16in (40cm), S 2–3ft (60cm–1m). Zone 10. Has a flattish, wavy-edged, dark reddish brown spathe, to 16in (40cm) long, from which protrudes an erect, dark brown spadix. Brownish green-mottled, pale green stem, 3ft (1m) long, bears one large, deeply lobed leaf after flowering.

AMPELOPSIS (Vitaceae)
Genus of deciduous, woody-stemmed, tendril climbers, some of which are twining, grown for their leaves. Frost hardy. Grow in any soil in a sheltered position, in sun or partial shade. Needs plenty of room as grows quickly and can cover a large area. Propagate by greenwood or semi-ripe cuttings in mid-summer.

A. aconitifolia, syn. *Vitis aconitifolia* (Monk's hood vine). Fast-growing, deciduous, woody-stemmed, twining, tendril climber. H to 40ft (12m). Zones 4–8. Rounded leaves have 3 or 5 toothed, lobed, dark green leaflets; inconspicuous, greenish flowers appear in late summer, followed by orange berries.

A. brevipedunculata var. **maximowiczii,** syn. *A. heterophylla, Vitis heterophylla* (Porcelain ampelopsis). Vigorous, deciduous, woody-stemmed, twining, tendril climber with hairy, young stems. H to 15ft (5m) or more. Zones 4–8. Has dark green leaves that vary in size and shape and are almost hairless beneath. Inconspicuous, greenish flowers are produced in summer, followed by bright blue berries.

A. heterophylla. See *A. brevipedunculata* var. *maximowiczii.*

A. sempervirens. See *Cissus striata.*

A. tricuspidata. See *Parthenocissus tricuspidata.*

A. veitchii. See *Parthenocissus tricuspidata.*

AMSONIA (Apocynaceae)
Blue star
Genus of slow-growing, clump-forming, summer-flowering perennials. Fully hardy. Grow in well-drained soil and in semi-shade. Is best left undisturbed for some years. Propagate by division in spring, by softwood cuttings in summer, or by seed in autumn.

A. salicifolia. See *A. tabernaemontana.*

A. tabernaemontana, syn. *A. salicifolia,* illus. p.243.

Anacharis densa. See *Egeria densa.*

ANACYCLUS (Compositae)
Genus of summer-flowering, prostrate perennials with stems radiating from a central rootstock. Frost hardy. Needs full sun and well-drained soil. Propagate by softwood cuttings in spring or by seed in autumn.

A. depressus illus. p.314.

ANAGALLIS (Primulaceae)
Genus of annuals and creeping perennials, grown for their flowers. Fully to frost hardy. Plant in an open, sunny site in fertile, moist soil. Propagate by seed or division in spring. Raise *A. tenella* by soft tip cuttings in spring or early summer.

A. tenella (Bog pimpernel). **'Studland'** illus. p.307.

ANANAS (Bromeliaceae)
Genus of evergreen, rosette-forming perennials, grown for their foliage and edible fruits (pineapples). Frost tender, min. 55–9°F (13–15°C). Prefers full light, but tolerates some shade. Needs fertile, well-drained soil. Water moderately during growing season, sparingly at other times. Propagate by suckers or cuttings of "leafy" fruit tops in spring or summer.

A. bracteatus (Red pineapple, Wild pineapple). **'Tricolor'** (syn. *A.b.* 'Striatus'; illus. p.222) is an evergreen, basal-rosetted perennial. H and S 3ft (1m). Zone 10. Forms dense rosettes of strap-shaped, spiny-edged, arching, deep green leaves, longitudinally yellow-striped and often with marginal, red spines. Dense spikes of small, tubular, lavender violet flowers, with prominent, reddish pink bracts, appear usually in summer, followed by brownish orange-red fruits, 6in (15cm) or more long.

A. comosus **'Variegatus'.** Evergreen, basal-rosetted perennial. H and S 24in (60cm) or more. Zone 10. Produces very narrowly strap-shaped, channeled, rigid, gray-green leaves that are suffused pink, have cream margins, are gray-scaled beneath, and sometimes have spiny edges. Has tubular, purple-blue flowers with inconspicuous, green bracts. Fruits are the edible pineapples but those produced on pot-grown plants are much smaller than those grown commercially.

ANAPHALIS (Compositae)
Pearly everlasting
Genus of perennials with heads of small, papery flowers, used dried for winter decoration. Fully hardy. Prefers sun but will grow in semi-shade. Soil should be well-drained but not too dry. Propagate by seed in autumn or by division in winter or spring.

A. margaritacea, syn. *A. yedoensis*, illus. p.200.

A. nubigena. See *A. triplinervis* var. *intermedia*.

A. triplinervis var. *intermedia*, syn. *A. nubigena*, illus. p.233.

A. yedoensis. See *A. margaritacea*.

ANCHUSA (Boraginaceae)
Genus of annuals, biennials, and perennials, some of which are evergreen, with usually blue flowers. Fully hardy to frost tender, min 36–9°F (2–4°C). Needs sun and well-drained soil; resents too much winter wet. Tall, perennial species may need to be staked and allowed room to spread. Propagate perennials by root cuttings in winter, annuals and biennials by seed in autumn or spring.

A. azurea, syn. *A. italica*. **'Little John'** is a coarse-growing, basal-rosetted perennial. H 20in (50cm), S 24in (60cm). Fully hardy, zones 4–8. Has branching racemes of large, open cup-shaped, dark blue flowers in early summer. Leaves are narrowly oval and hairy. **'Loddon Royalist'** illus. p.213. **'Opal'**, H 4ft (1.2m), has paler blue flowers.

A. caespitosa illus. p.310.

A. capensis (Cape forget-me-not, Summer forget-me-not). **'Blue Angel'** illus. p.278. **'Blue Bird'** is a bushy biennial, grown as an annual. H to 18in (45cm), S 8in (20cm). Frost tender. Has lance-shaped, bristly, green leaves and, in summer, heads of shallowly bowl-shaped, sky blue flowers.

A. italica. See *A. azurea*.

ANCISTROCACTUS (Cactaceae)
Genus of perennial cacti, grown for their spherical to short, globose to columnar stems, each with 10–20 tuberculate ribs. Flowers are sometimes prevented from opening by density of spines. Frost tender, min. 36°F (2°C) if completely dry. Needs sun and very well-drained soil. May rot if overwatered. Propagate by seed in spring.

A. megarhizus. See *A. scheeri*.

A. scheeri, syn. *A. megarhizus*, illus. p.397.

A. uncinatus. Globose to columnar, perennial cactus. H 8in (20cm), S 4in (10cm). Zones 9–10. Stem is blue-green. Areoles each produce a very long, hooked, reddish spine and 15–18 straight ones. Has cup-shaped, brown-green or reddish flowers, ^{3}/$_4$in (2cm) across, in spring.

ANDROMEDA (Ericaceae)
Genus of evergreen shrubs with an open, twiggy habit. Fully hardy. Needs full light and humus-rich, moist, acid soil. Propagate by semi-ripe cuttings in late summer or by seed in spring.

A. polifolia illus. p.287. **'Alba'** illus. p.286. **'Compacta'** illus. p.287.

ANDROSACE (Primulaceae)
Genus of annuals and evergreen perennials, usually compact cushion-forming and often with soft, hairy leaves. Many species are suitable for cold greenhouses and troughs with winter cover. Fully to frost hardy. Needs sun and very well-drained soil; some species prefer acid soil. Resents wet foliage in winter. Propagate by tip cuttings in summer or by seed in autumn. Is prone to botrytis and attack by aphids.

A. carnea illus. p.305. subsp. *laggeri* illus. p.307.

A. chamaejasme. Evergreen, basal-rosetted, variable perennial with easily rooted stolons. H 1^1/$_4$–2^1/$_2$in (3–6cm), S to 6in (15cm). Fully hardy, zones 4–7. Has open, hairy rosettes of oval leaves. In spring bears clusters of 2–8 flattish, white flowers, each with a yellow eye that sometimes turns red with age.

A. cylindrica. Evergreen, basal-rosetted perennial. H ^{1}/$_2$–^{3}/$_4$in (1–2cm), S 4in (10cm). Fully hardy, zones 4–7. Leaves are linear and glossy. Flower stems each carry up to 10 small, flattish, white flowers, each with a yellow-green eye, in early spring. Is suitable for a cold greenhouse.

A. hedraeantha. Evergreen, tight cushion-forming perennial. H ^{1}/$_2$–^{3}/$_4$in (1–2cm), S to 4in (10cm). Fully hardy, zones 4–7. Bears loose rosettes of narrowly oval, glossy leaves. Umbels of 5–10 flattish, yellow-throated, pink flowers are borne in spring. Is best in a cold greenhouse.

A. hirtella. Evergreen, tight cushion-forming perennial. H ^{1}/$_2$in (1cm), S to 4in (10cm). Fully hardy, zones 4–7. Produces rosettes of small, thick, linear to oblong, hairy leaves. Almond-scented, flattish, white flowers appear in spring on very short stems, 1 or 2 per rosette.

A. imbricata. See *A. vandellii*.

A. lanuginosa illus. p.317.

A. pyrenaica illus. p.301.

A. sarmentosa. Evergreen, mat-forming perennial, spreading by runners. H 1^1/$_2$–4in (4–10cm), S 12in (30cm). Fully hardy, zones 4–7. Has open rosettes of small, narrowly elliptic, hairy leaves. Large clusters of flattish, yellow-eyed, bright pink flowers open in spring. Is a good rock plant in all but very wet areas.

A. sempervivoides. Evergreen, mat-forming, tufted perennial with stolons. H ^{1}/$_2$–3in (1–7cm), S 12in (30cm). Fully hardy, zones 4–7. Has leathery, oblong or spoon-shaped leaves. In spring produces small heads of 4–10 flattish, pink flowers, with yellow, then red, eyes. Is a good rock plant.

A. vandellii, syn. *A. imbricata*, illus. p.302.

A. villosa illus. p.303. var. *jacquemontii* illus. p.318.

ANEMONE (Ranunculaceae)
Windflower
Genus of spring-, summer- and autumn-flowering perennials, sometimes tuberous or rhizomatous, with mainly rounded, shallowly cup-shaped flowers. Leaves are rounded to oval, often divided into 3–15 leaflets. Fully to frost hardy. Most species thrive in humus-rich, well-drained soil in full light or semi-shade. Propagate by division in spring, by seed sown in late summer, when fresh, or by root cuttings in winter.

A. apennina (Apennine anemone). Spreading, spring-flowering, rhizomatous perennial. H and S 6–8in (15–20cm). Fully hardy, zones 6–9. Fernlike leaves have 3 deeply toothed lobes. Each stem carries a large, upright, flattish, blue, white, or pink flower, with 10–20 narrow petals.

A. biflora illus. p.358.

A. blanda. Spreading, early spring-flowering perennial with a knobbly tuber. H 2–4in (5–10cm), S 4–6in (10–15cm). Fully hardy, zones 6–9. Broadly oval, semi-erect leaves have 3 deeply toothed lobes. Each stem bears an upright, flattish, blue, white, or pink flower, 1^1/$_2$–2in (4–5cm) across, with 9–14 narrow petals. **'Atrocaerulea'** illus. p.362. **'Radar'** illus. p.358. **'White Splendour'** illus. p.356.

A. coronaria. Spring-flowering perennial with a misshapen tuber. H 2–10in (5–25cm), S 4–6in (10–15cm). Frost hardy, zones 8–10. Produces parsleylike, divided, semi-erect leaves. Each stiff stem carries a large, 5–8-petaled, shallowly cup-shaped flower in shades of red, pink, blue, or purple. Garden groups include **De Caen Series** and **St. Brigid Series**, which have larger flowers varying in color from white through red to blue.

A. × *fulgens* illus. p.359.

A. hepatica. See *Hepatica nobilis*.

A. hupehensis illus. p.217. **'September Charm'** is a branching perennial. H 30in (75cm), S 20in (50cm). Fully hardy, zones 5–9. Has shallowly cup-shaped, rose-pink flowers in late summer and early autumn and deeply divided, dark green leaves.

A. × *hybrida*, syn. *A. japonica* of gardens. Group of vigorous, branching, perennials. H 5ft (1.5m), S 2ft (60cm). Fully hardy, zones 6–8. Bears shallowly cup-shaped, single, semi-double, or double flowers in late summer and early autumn. Leaves are deeply divided and dark green. **'Bressingham Glow'** (semi-double) and **'Honorine Jobert'** (single) illus. p.193. **'Max Vogel'** has semi-double, pinkish mauve flowers on wiry stems. **'Prince Henry'** has single, deep pink flowers on slender stems.

A. japonica of gardens. See *A.* × *hybrida*.

A. × *lipsiensis*, syn. *A.* × *seemannii*, illus. p.229.

A. narcissiflora illus. p.232.

A. nemorosa (Wood anemone). Vigorous, carpeting, rhizomatous perennial. H 6in (15cm), S 12in (30cm). Fully hardy, zones 4–8. Produces masses of star-shaped, single, white flowers, with prominent, yellow stamens, in spring and early summer, above deeply cut, green leaves. Likes woodland conditions. **'Allenii'** and **'Robinsoniana'** illus. p.227. **'Vestal'** has anemone-centered, double, white flowers. **'Wilk's Giant'** has larger, single, white flowers.

A. pavonina (Giant French anemone, Poppy-flowered anemone) illus. p.343. **De Caen Series** is a group of early spring-flowering tubers. H 12–18in (30–45cm), S 10–12in (25–30cm). Frost hardy, zones 8–10. Bears cup-shaped, single, scarlet, pink, purple, or white flowers above deeply lobed, frilly leaves.

A. ranunculoides illus. p.229. **'Flore Pleno'** is a spreading, rhizomatous perennial. H and S 8in (20cm). Fully hardy, zones 4–8. Bears buttercuplike, double, yellow flowers in spring. Leaves are divided. Likes damp, woodland conditions.

A. rivularis illus. p.232.

A. × *seemannii*. See *A.* × *lipsiensis*.

A. sylvestris illus. p.225. **'Macrantha'** is a carpeting perennial that can be invasive. H and S 12in (30cm). Fully hardy, zones 4–9. Produces large, fragrant, semi-pendent, shallowly cup-shaped, white flowers in spring and early summer. Leaves are divided and green.

A. vitifolia. Branching, clump-forming perennial. H 4ft (1.2m), S 20in (50cm). Fully hardy, zones 5–9. In summer bears open cup-shaped, occasionally pink-flushed, white flowers with yellow stamens. Vinelike leaves are woolly beneath.

ANEMONELLA (Ranunculaceae)
Genus of one species of tuberous perennial, grown for its flowers. Fully hardy. Needs shade and humus-rich, moist soil. Propagate by seed when fresh or by division every 3–5 years in autumn.

A. thalictroides illus. p.304. **'Oscar Schoaf'** (syn. *A.t.* 'Schoaf's Double') is a slow-growing, tuberous perennial. H 4in (10cm), S 1^1/$_2$in (4cm) or more. Zones 4–9. Has delicate, fernlike leaves. From spring to early summer bears small, cup-shaped, double, strawberry pink flowers, singly on finely branched, slender stems.

ANEMONOPSIS (Ranunculaceae)
False anemone
Genus of one species of perennial, related to *Anemone*. Fully hardy. Likes a sheltered, semi-shaded position and humus-rich, moist but well-drained soil. Propagate by division in spring or by seed sown in late summer, when fresh.

A. macrophylla illus. p.242.

ANEMOPAEGMA (Bignoniaceae)
Genus of evergreen, tendril climbers, grown for their flowers. Frost tender, min. 55–9°F (13–15°C). Needs humus-rich, well-drained soil and partial shade in summer. Water regularly and freely when in full growth, less at other times. Provide support and in summer thin out stems at intervals; shorten all growths by half in spring. Propagate by softwood or semi-ripe cuttings in spring or summer.

A. chamberlaynii. Fast-growing, evergreen, tendril climber. H to 20ft (6m). Zone 10. Leaves have 2 pointed, oval leaflets and a 3-hooked tendril. Foxglovelike, primrose yellow flowers are carried in pairs from upper leaf axils in summer.

ANGELICA (Umbelliferae)
Genus of summer-flowering, often short-lived perennials, some of which have culinary and medicinal uses. Fully hardy. Grows in sun or shade and in any well-drained soil. Remove seed heads when produced, otherwise plants may die. Propagate by seed when ripe.
A. archangelica illus. p.190.

ANGRAECUM. See ORCHIDS.
A. sesquipedale, syn. *Macroplectrum sesquipedale* (illus. p.252). Evergreen, epiphytic orchid for an intermediate greenhouse. H 12in (30cm) or more. Zone 10. Waxy, apple white flowers, 3in (8cm) across, each with a 12in (30cm) long spur, are borne, usually 2 to a stem, in winter. Has narrowly oval, semi-rigid, horizontal leaves, 6in (15cm) long. Needs shade in summer.

ANGULOA. See ORCHIDS.
A. clowesii (Cradle orchid). Deciduous, epiphytic orchid for a cool greenhouse. H 24in (60cm). Zone 10. Fragrant, erect, cup-shaped, lemon yellow flowers, 4in (10cm) long, each with a loosely hinged, yellow lip, are borne singly in early summer. Broadly oval, ribbed leaves are 18in (45cm) long. Grow in semi-shade in summer.

ANIGOZANTHOS (Haemodoraceae)
Kangaroo paw
Genus of perennials, with thick rootstocks and fans of sword-shaped leaves, grown for their curious flowers. Half hardy. Needs an open, sunny position and does best in well-drained, peaty or leafy, acid soil. Propagate by division in spring or by seed when fresh, in late summer.
A. flavidus illus. p.213.
A. manglesii illus. p.209.
A. rufa. Tufted perennial. H 3ft (1m), S 2ft (60cm). Zones 9–10. Panicles of 2-lipped, rich burgundy flowers, covered with purple hairs, appear in spring. Has long, sword-shaped, stiff, green leaves.

ANISODONTEA (Malvaceae)
Genus of evergreen shrubs and perennials, grown for their flowers. Frost tender, min. 37–41°F (3–5°C). Needs full light and well-drained soil. Water potted plants freely when in full growth, very little at other times. In growing season, young plants may need tip pruning to promote a bushy habit. Propagate by seed in spring or by greenwood or semi-ripe cuttings in late summer.
A. capensis, syn. *A. hypomadarum* of gardens, *Malvastrum capensis*, *M. hypomadarum* of gardens. Evergreen, erect, bushy shrub. H to 3ft (1m), S 2ft (60cm) or more. Zone 10. Each oval leaf has 3–5 deep lobes. Bowl-shaped, 5-petaled, rose-magenta flowers, with darker veins, appear from spring to autumn.
A. hypomadarum of gardens. See *A. capensis*.

ANNONA (Annonaceae)
Cherimoya, Custard apple, Sweet sop
Genus of deciduous or evergreen shrubs and trees, grown for their edible fruits and ornamental appearance.

Frost tender, min. 59°F (15°C), preferably higher. Needs full light or partial shade and fertile, moisture-retentive but well-drained soil. Water potted specimens moderately when in full growth, sparingly in winter. Propagate by seed in spring or by semi-ripe cuttings in late summer. Red spider mite may be a nuisance.
A. reticulata (Bullock's heart, Custard apple). Mainly deciduous, rounded tree. H 20ft (6m) or more, S 10–15ft (3–5m). Zone 10. Has oblong to lance-shaped, 5–10in (13–25cm) long leaves. Cup-shaped, olive green flowers, often flushed purple, appear in summer, followed by edible, heart-shaped, red-flushed, greenish brown fruits, each 5in (13cm) long.

Anoiganthus breviflorus. See *Cyrtanthus breviflorus.*

ANOMATHECA (Iridaceae)
Genus of upright, summer-flowering corms, grown for their red flowers, followed by egg-shaped seed pods that split to reveal red seeds. Frost hardy. Plant 2in (5cm) deep in an open, sunny situation and in well-drained soil. In cold areas, lift corms and store dry for winter. Propagate by seed in spring.
A. laxa, syn. *Lapeirousia cruenta*, *L. laxa*. Upright, summer-flowering corm. H 4–12in (10–30cm), S 2–3in (5–8cm). Zones 8–10. Narrowly sword-shaped, erect, basal leaves form a flat fan. Each stem bears a loose spike of long-tubed, red flowers, 1in (2.5cm) across. Lower petals have basal, darker red spots.

ANOPTERUS (Grossulariaceae, Saxifragaceae)
Genus of evergreen shrubs or small trees, grown for their foliage and flowers. Half hardy. Needs shade or semi-shade and moist but well-drained soil. Propagate by semi-ripe cuttings in summer.
A. glandulosus illus. p.84.

ANREDERA (Basellaceae)
Madeira vine, Mignonette vine
Genus of evergreen, tuberous, twining climbers, grown for their luxuriant foliage and small, scented flowers. Frost tender, min. 45°F (7°C). If grown in cool areas will die down in winter. Provide well-drained soil and full light. Water moderately in growing season, sparingly at other times. Provide support. Cut back previous season's growth by half or to just above ground level in spring. Propagate by tubers, produced at stem bases, in spring or by softwood cuttings in summer.
A. cordifolia, syn. *Boussingaultia baselloides*. Fast-growing, evergreen, tuberous, twining climber. H to 20ft (6m). Zone 10. Has oval to lance-shaped, fleshy leaves and tiny, fragrant, white flowers borne in clusters from upper leaf axils in summer.

ANTENNARIA (Compositae)
Cat's ears
Genus of evergreen or semi-evergreen perennials, grown for their almost stemless flower heads and mats of often woolly leaves. Makes good

ground cover. Fully hardy. Needs sun and well-drained soil. Propagate by seed or division in spring.
A. dioica. Semi-evergreen, mat-forming, dense perennial. H 1in (2.5cm), S 10in (25cm). Zones 4–7. Leaves are tiny, oval, usually woolly, and greenish white. Short stems carry fluffy, white or pale pink flower heads in late spring and early summer. Is good for a rock garden. Compact 'Nyewoods' has very deep rose-pink flowers. 'Rosea' illus. p.306.

ANTHEMIS (Compositae)
Camomile, Dog fennel
Genus of carpeting and clump-forming perennials, some of which are evergreen, grown for their daisylike flower heads and fernlike foliage. Fully to frost hardy. Prefers sun and well-drained soil. May need staking. Cut to ground level after flowering for good leaf rosettes in winter. Propagate by division in spring or, for some species, by basal cuttings in late summer, autumn, or spring.
A. nobile 'Treneague'. See *Chamaemelum nobile* 'Treneague'.
A. punctata subsp. *cupaniana* illus. p.233.
A. sancti-johannis (St. John's camomile). Evergreen, spreading, bushy perennial. H and S 2ft (60cm). Frost hardy, zones 4–9. In summer bears many daisylike, bright orange flower heads among fernlike, shaggy, green leaves.
A. tinctoria (Golden Marguerite, Yellow camomile). Evergreen, clump-forming perennial. H and S 3ft (1m). Fully hardy, zones 4–8. Has a mass of daisylike, yellow flower heads in mid-summer, borne singly above a basal clump of fernlike, crinkled, green leaves. Propagate by basal cuttings in spring or late summer. 'E.C. Buxton' illus. p.214.

ANTHERICUM (Liliaceae)
Spider plant
Genus of upright perennials with saucer- or trumpet-shaped flowers rising in spikelike racemes from clumps of leaves. Fully hardy. Likes a sunny site and fertile, well-drained soil that does not dry out in summer. Propagate by division in spring or by seed in autumn.
A. liliago illus. p.233.
A. ramosum. Upright perennial. H 3ft (1m), S 1ft (30cm). Zones 5–8. Erect racemes of small, saucer-shaped, white flowers are borne in summer above a clump of grasslike, grayish green leaves.

Antholyza paniculata. See *Crocosmia paniculata.*

ANTHURIUM (Araceae)
Genus of evergreen, erect, climbing or trailing perennials, some grown for their foliage and others for their brightly colored flower spathes. Frost tender, min. 59°F (15°C). Prefers bright light in winter and indirect sun in summer; needs a fairly moist atmosphere and moist, but not waterlogged, peaty soil. Propagate by division in spring.

A. andraeanum illus. p.223.
A. crystallinum illus. p.221.
A. 'Rothschildianum', syn. *A.* x *rothschildianum*. Evergreen, erect, short-stemmed perennial. H and S 12in (30cm). Zone 10. Produces upright, oblong leaves, to 8in (20cm) long. Intermittently bears a long-lasting, red spathe, spotted with white, that surrounds a yellow spadix.
A. x *rothschildianum.* See *A.* 'Rothschildianum'.
A. scherzerianum illus. p.258.
A. veitchii (King anthurium). Evergreen, erect, short-stemmed perennial. H 3ft (1m) or more, S to 3ft (1m). Zone 10. Glossy, corrugated leaves, to 3ft (1m) long, are oval, with heart-shaped bases on 2–3ft (60cm–1m) long leaf stalks. Intermittently bears a long-lasting, leathery, green to white spathe that surrounds a cream spadix.

ANTHYLLIS (Leguminosae)
Genus of rounded, bushy perennials, grown for their flowers and finely divided leaves. Frost hardy. Needs sun and well-drained soil. Propagate by softwood cuttings in summer or by seed in autumn.
A. hermanniae. Rounded, bushy perennial. H and S to 2ft (60cm). Zones 6–8. Spiny, tangled stems bear simple or 3-parted, bright green leaves. Has small, pealike, yellow flowers in summer. Is good for a rock garden.
A. montana illus. p.292. 'Rubra' is a rounded or spreading, woody-based perennial. H and S 12in (30cm). Zones 6–8. Divided leaves consist of 17–41 narrowly oval leaflets. Heads of cloverlike, bright pink flowers are borne in late spring and early summer. Is good for a rock garden.

ANTIGONON (Polygonaceae)
Genus of evergreen, woody-stemmed, tendril climbers, grown for their foliage and profuse clusters of small flowers. Frost tender, min. 59°F (15°C). Grow in any fertile, well-drained soil with full light. Water freely in growing season, sparingly at other times. Needs tropical conditions to flower well. Provide support. Thin out congested growth in early spring. Propagate by seed in spring or by softwood cuttings in summer.
A. leptopus illus. p.167.

ANTIRRHINUM (Scrophulariaceae)
Snapdragon
Genus of perennials and semi-evergreen sub-shrubs, usually grown as annuals, flowering from spring to autumn. Fully to half hardy. Needs sun and rich, well-drained soil. Dead-head to prolong flowering season. Propagate by seed sown outdoors in late spring or by stem cuttings in early autumn or spring. Rust disease may be a problem with *A. majus*, but rust-resistant cultivars are available.
A. asarina. See *Asarina procumbens*.
A. majus. Erect perennial, branching from the base. Cultivars are grown as annuals and are grouped according to size and flower type: tall, H 2–3ft (60cm–1m), S 12–18in (30–45cm); intermediate, H and S 18in (45cm); dwarf, H 8–12in (20–30cm), S 12in

(30cm); peloric, regular tubular-shaped flowers; penstemon, trumpet-shaped flowers; double; and irregular tubular-shaped flowers. Half hardy. All have lance-shaped leaves and, from spring to autumn, carry spikes of usually 2-lipped, sometimes double, flowers in a variety of colors, including white, pink, red, purple, yellow, and orange. **'Coronette'** (tall, peloric) illus. p.281. **'His Excellency'** (intermediate, irregular tubular-shaped) has scarlet flowers. **Hyacinth-flowered Series** (intermediate, penstemon) has dense spikes of large, wide flowers. **'Little Darling'** (dwarf, penstemon) has trumpet-shaped flowers. **Madame Butterfly Series** (tall, peloric) illus. p.265. **Princess Series** (intermediate, peloric) has flowers in a mixture of colors (white with purple eye, illus. p.269). **Royal Carpet Series** (dwarf, irregular tubular-shaped) is a compact form. **Supreme Series** (tall, peloric) has double, ruffled flowers. **'Trumpet Serenade'** (dwarf, penstemon) illus. p.283. **Wedding Bells Series** (tall, penstemon) illus. p.280.

APHELANDRA (Acanthaceae)
Genus of evergreen shrubs and perennials with showy flowers. Frost tender, min. 55°F (13°C). Grows best in bright light but out of direct sun in summer. Use soft water and keep soil moist but not waterlogged. Benefits from feeding when flower spikes are forming. Propagate by seed or tip cuttings from young stems in spring.
A. squarrosa (Zebra plant). **'Dania'** is an evergreen, compact perennial. H 3ft (1m), S slightly less. Zone 10. Oval, glossy, dark green leaves, with white veins and midribs, are nearly 1ft (30cm) long. Has dense, 4-sided spikes, to 6in (15cm) long, of 2-lipped, bright yellow flowers in axils of yellow bracts in autumn. **'Louisae'** illus. p.215.

APONOGETON (Aponogetonaceae)
Genus of deciduous, perennial, deep-water plants, grown for their floating foliage and often heavily scented flowers. Frost hardy to frost tender, min. 61°F (16°C). Requires an open, sunny position. Fading foliage needs tidying up in autumn. Propagate by division in spring or by seed when fresh.
A. distachyos illus. p.373.

APOROCACTUS (Cactaceae)
Genus of perennial cacti, grown for their pendent, slender, fleshy stems and bright flowers. Is suitable for hanging baskets. Half hardy to frost tender, min. 41°F (5°C). Needs partial shade and very well-drained soil. Propagate by stem cuttings in spring or summer.
A. flagelliformis illus. p.384.

APTENIA (Aizoaceae)
Genus of fast-growing, perennial succulents, with trailing, freely branching stems, that make good ground cover. Frost tender, min. 45°F (7°C). Requires full sun and very well-drained soil. Keep dry in winter. Propagate by seed or stem cuttings in spring or summer.

A. cordifolia illus. p.392. **'Variegata'** is a fast-growing, prostrate, perennial succulent. H 2in (5cm), S indefinite. Zone 10. Has oval, glossy, bright green leaves, with creamy white margins, and small, daisylike, bright pink flowers in summer.

AQUILEGIA (Ranunculaceae)
Columbine
Genus of graceful, clump-forming, short-lived perennials, grown for their mainly bell-shaped, spurred flowers in spring and summer. Is suitable for rock gardens. Fully to frost hardy. Prefers well-drained soil in an open, sunny site. Propagate species by seed in autumn or spring. Selected forms only occasionally come true from seed (e.g., *A. vulgaris* 'Nora Barlow') as they cross freely; they should be widely segregated. Is prone to aphid attack.
A. alpina illus. p.288.
A. canadensis (Common columbine). Clump-forming, leafy perennial. H 24in (60cm), S 12in (30cm). Fully hardy, zones 4–9. In early summer bears semi-pendent, bell-shaped flowers, with yellow sepals and red spurs, several per slender stem, above fernlike, dark green foliage.
A. chrysantha. Vigorous, clump-forming perennial. H 4ft (1.2m), S 2ft (60cm). Fully hardy, zones 4–9. Bears semi-pendent, bell-shaped, soft yellow flowers, with long spurs, several per stem, in early summer. Has fernlike, divided, green leaves.
A. flabellata. Clump-forming perennial. H 10in (25cm), S 4in (10cm). Fully hardy, zones 4–9. Bell-shaped, soft blue flowers, each with fluted petals and a short spur, are produced in summer. Rounded, finely divided leaves form an open, basal rosette. Needs semi-shade and moist soil. **'Nana Alba'** has white flowers.
A. jonesii illus. p.323.
A. longissima. Clump-forming, leafy perennial. H 24in (60cm), S 20in (50cm). Fully hardy, zones 4–9. Bell-shaped, pale yellow flowers, with very long, bright yellow spurs, are produced, several per stem, in early summer, above fernlike, divided, green leaves.
A. **'Mrs. Scott Elliott'.** Clump-forming, leafy perennial. H 3ft (1m), S 20in (50cm). Fully hardy, zones 5–9. Bell-shaped flowers of various colors, often bicolored, have long spurs and appear in early summer on branching, wiry stems. Has fernlike, divided, bluish green leaves.
A. scopulorum. Clump-forming perennial. H 2¹/₂in (6cm), S 3¹/₂in (9cm). Frost hardy, zones 5–9. In summer produces bell-shaped, fluted, pale blue, or rarely pink, flowers, each with a cream center and very long spurs. Leaves are divided into 9 oval, glaucous leaflets.
A. vulgaris. Clump-forming, leafy perennial. H 3ft (1m), S 20in (50cm). Fully hardy, zones 5–9. Many funnel-shaped, short-spurred flowers, in shades of pink, crimson, purple and white, are borne, several per long stem, in early summer. Leaves are gray-green, rounded, and divided into leaflets. **'Nora Barlow'** illus. p.208.

ARABIS (Cruciferae)
Genus of robust, evergreen perennials. Makes excellent ground cover in a rock garden. Fully to frost hardy. Needs sun and well-drained soil. Propagate by softwood cuttings in summer or by seed in autumn.
A. albida. See *A. caucasica.*
A. blepharophylla. Short-lived, evergreen, mat-forming perennial. H 5in (12cm), S 6in (15cm). Fully hardy, zones 5–8. Bears loose rosettes of oval, toothed, dark green leaves with hairy, gray edges. In spring has fragrant, 4-petaled, bright pink to white flowers.
A. caucasica, syn. *A. albida* (Wall rock-cress). Evergreen, mat-forming perennial. H 6in (15cm), S 10in (25cm). Fully hardy, zones 4–8. Bears loose rosettes of oval, toothed, green leaves and, in late spring and summer, fragrant, 4-petaled, white, occasionally pink, flowers. Is excellent on a dry bank. Trim back after flowering. **'Plena'** has double, white flowers. **'Rosabella'** illus. p.305. **'Variegata'** illus. p.302.
A. ferdinandi-coburgii **'Variegata'** illus. p.328.

ARALIA (Araliaceae)
Genus of deciduous trees, shrubs, and perennials, grown for their bold leaves and small, but profusely borne flowers. Fully hardy. Requires sun or semi-shade, some shelter, and fertile, well-drained soil. Propagate those listed below by seed in autumn or by suckers or root cuttings in late winter.
A. elata (Japanese angelica tree). Deciduous tree or suckering shrub with sparse, stout, prickly stems. H and S 30ft (10m), zones 4–9. Has large, dark green leaves with numerous oval, paired leaflets. Billowing heads of tiny, white flowers, forming a large panicle, 1–2ft (30–60cm) long, are borne in late summer and autumn. **'Aureo-variegata'** has leaflets broadly edged with yellow. Leaflets of **'Variegata'** have creamy white margins.
A. elegantissima. See *Dizygotheca elegantissima.*
A. japonica. See *Fatsia japonica.*
A. sieboldii. See *Fatsia japonica.*

ARAUCARIA (Araucariaceae). See CONIFERS.
A. araucana illus. p.75.
A. heterophylla (Norfolk Island pine). Upright conifer. H 100ft (30m), S 15–25ft (5–8m). Half hardy, zones 9–10. Has spirally set, needlelike, incurved leaves. Cones are seldom produced in cultivation. Is often grown as a shade-tolerant house plant.

ARAUJIA (Asclepiadaceae)
Genus of evergreen, woody-stemmed, twining climbers with stems that exude milky juice when cut. Half hardy. Grow in sun and fertile, well-drained soil. Propagate by seed in spring or by stem cuttings in late summer or early autumn.
A. sericifera. See *A. sericofera.*
A. sericofera, syn. *A. sericifera*, illus. p.165.

ARBUTUS (Ericaceae)
Genus of evergreen trees and shrubs, grown for their leaves, clusters of

small, urn-shaped flowers, ornamental bark, and strawberrylike fruits, which are edible but tasteless. Frost hardy, but protect from strong, cold winds when young. Prefers full sun and needs fertile, well-drained soil; *A. menziesii* requires acid soil. Propagate by semi-ripe cuttings in late summer or by seed in autumn.
A. andrachne (Grecian strawberry tree). Evergreen, spreading tree or shrub. H and S 20ft (6m), zones 7–9. Has oval, glossy, dark green leaves and peeling, reddish brown bark. Panicles of urn-shaped, white flowers in late spring are followed by orange-red fruits. Prefers a sheltered position.
A. × *andrachnoides* illus. p.56.
A. menziesii (Madroña, Madroñe). Evergreen, spreading tree. H and S 50ft (15m), zones 7–9. Has smooth, peeling, reddish bark and oval, dark green leaves. Large, upright, terminal panicles of urn-shaped, white flowers in early summer are followed by orange or red fruits.
A. unedo illus. p.66.

ARCHONTOPHOENIX (Palmae)
King palm
Genus of evergreen palms, grown for their majestic appearance. Frost tender, min. 59°F (15°C). Needs full light or partial shade and humus-rich, well-drained soil. Water potted specimens moderately, much less when temperatures are low. Propagate by seed in spring at not less than 75°F (24°C). Red spider mite may be troublesome.
A. alexandrae illus. p.46.
A. cunninghamiana (Illawarra palm, Piccabeen palm). Evergreen palm. H 50–70ft (15–20m), S 6–15ft (2–5m). Zone 10. Has long, arching, feather-shaped leaves. Mature trees produce large clusters of small, lavender or lilac flowers in summer, followed by large, egg-shaped, red fruits.

Arcterica nana. See *Pieris nana.*

ARCTOSTAPHYLOS (Ericaceae)
Manzanita
Genus of evergreen trees and shrubs, grown for their foliage, flowers and fruits. Some species are also grown for their bark, others for ground cover. Fully hardy to frost tender, min. 45°F (7°C). Provide shelter from strong winds. Does best in full sun and well-drained, acid soil. Propagate by semi-ripe cuttings in summer or by seed in autumn.
A. alpina. See *Arctous alpinus.*
A. diversifolia. See *Comarostaphylis diversifolia.*
A. **'Emerald Carpet'** illus. p.124.
A. manzanita. Evergreen, upright shrub. H and S 6ft (2m) or more. Frost hardy, zones 7–8. Has peeling, reddish brown bark and oval, leathery, gray-green leaves. From early to mid-spring produces small, urn-shaped, deep pink flowers followed by globose, red fruits.
A. nevadensis (Pine-mat manzanita). Evergreen, prostrate shrub. H 4in (10cm), S 3ft (1m). Frost hardy, zones 7–8. Has small, oval leaves. In summer, pendent, urn-shaped, white flowers are

borne in clusters in leaf axils, followed by globose, brownish red fruits. Is useful as ground cover.

A. nummularia. Evergreen, erect to prostrate shrub. H 1ft (30cm) or more, S 3ft (1m). Frost hardy, zones 7–8. Leaves are small, rounded, leathery, and toothed. Pendent, urn-shaped, white flowers are borne in clusters from leaf axils in summer, followed by globose, green fruits. Makes good ground cover.

A. patula illus. p.120.

A. pumila. Evergreen, prostrate shrub. H 2in (5cm), S 12in (30cm). Frost tender, zones 7–8. Has hairy branches with small, oval, dull green leaves, hairy beneath. Clusters of urn-shaped, white flowers are produced from leaf axils in summer, followed by globose, brown fruits.

A. stanfordiana (Stanford manzanita). Evergreen, erect shrub. H and S 5ft (1.5m). Half hardy, zone 8. Bark is smooth and reddish brown. Has narrowly oval, glossy, bright green leaves. Drooping clusters of urn-shaped, pink flowers are borne from early to mid-spring, followed by globose, bright red fruits.

A. uva-ursi illus. p.328. **'Point Reyes'** illus. p.328. **'Vancouver Jade'** is an evergreen, trailing, sometimes arching shrub. H 4in (10cm), S 20in (50cm). Fully hardy, zones 2–8. Has small, oval, bright green leaves and bears urn-shaped, white flowers in summer. subsp. **hookeri 'Monterey Carpet'** is an open, half hardy shrub, H 4–6in (10–15cm), S 16in (40cm) or more. Zone 8. Has hairy branchlets bearing glossy, pale green leaves and, in early summer, urn-shaped, white flowers, sometimes flushed pink, followed by globose, red fruits.

ARCTOTHECA (Compositae)
Genus of creeping perennials. Frost tender, min. 41°F (5°C). Grow in bright light and in fertile, well-drained soil; avoid humid conditions. Propagate by seed or division in spring.

A. calendula illus. p.250.

ARCTOTIS (Compositae)
Genus of annuals and perennials, grown for their flower heads and foliage. Frost tender, min. 34–41°F (1–5°C). Requires full sun and leafy loam with sharp sand added. Propagate by seed in autumn or spring or by stem cuttings year-round.

A. stoechadifolia (African daisy). Compact perennial, often grown as an annual. H 20in (50cm) or more, S 16in (40cm). Zone 10. Daisylike, creamy white flower heads with blue centers are borne singly throughout summer and into autumn. Chrysanthemumlike leaves are dark green above, gray beneath. var. **grandis** is larger and has longer leaves.

ARCTOUS (Ericaceae)
Genus of one species of deciduous shrub, similar to *Arctostaphylos*, grown for its attractive habit and foliage. Fully hardy. Needs partial shade and moist, peaty, acid soil. Propagate by softwood cuttings or seed in spring.

A. alpinus, syn. *Arctostaphylos alpina*. Deciduous, creeping shrub. H 2in (5cm), S to 5in (12cm). Zones 2–7. Has drooping, terminal clusters of tiny, urn-shaped, pink-flushed, white flowers in late spring, followed by rounded, purple-black berries. Leaves are oval, toothed, glossy, and bright green.

ARDISIA (Myrsinaceae)
Genus of evergreen shrubs and trees, grown for their fruits and foliage. Half hardy to frost tender, min. 50°F (10°C). Needs partial shade and humus-rich, well-drained but not dry soil. Water potted plants freely when in full growth, moderately at other times. Cut back old plants in early spring if required. Propagate by seed in spring or by semi-ripe cuttings in summer.

A. crenata, syn. *A. crenulata*, illus. p.118.

A. crenulata. See *A. crenata*.

Areca lutescens. See *Chrysalidocarpus lutescens.*

ARECASTRUM (Palmae)
Queen palm
Genus of one species of evergreen palm, grown for its majestic appearance. Frost tender, min. 64°F (18°C). Requires full light or partial shade and humus-rich, well-drained soil. Water potted specimens moderately, less when temperatures are low. Propagate by seed in spring at not less than 75°F (24°C). Red spider mite may be a nuisance.

A. romanzoffianum illus. p.47.

Aregelia carolinae. See *Neoregelia carolinae.*

ARENARIA (Carophyllaceae)
Sandwort
Genus of spring- and summer-flowering annuals and perennials, some of which are evergreen. Fully to frost hardy. Most need sun and well-drained, sandy soil. Propagate by division or softwood cuttings in early summer or by seed in autumn or spring.

A. balearica illus. p.302.

A. montana illus. p.314.

A. purpurascens illus. p.305.

A. tetraquetra illus. p.301.

ARGEMONE (Papaveraceae)
Genus of robust perennials, most of which are best treated as annuals. Fully to half hardy. Grow in sun and in very well-drained soil. Do not provide supports as they may damage the rather fleshy stems. Dead-head plants to prolong flowering. Propagate by seed sown outdoors in late spring.

A. mexicana illus. p.279.

Argyranthemum frutescens. See *Chrysanthemum frutescens.*

ARGYRODERMA (Aizoaceae)
Genus of perennial succulents, grown for their very fleshy, gray-green leaves united in a prostrate, egg shape. In summer, daisylike flowers appear in central split between leaves. Frost tender, min. 41°F (5°C). Needs full sun and very well-drained soil. Overwatering will cause leaves to

split or plant to rot. Propagate by seed in summer.

A. blandum. See *A. delaetii*.

A. brevipes. See *A. fissum*.

A. delaetii, syn. *A. blandum*, illus. p.396.

A. fissum, syn. *A. brevipes*, illus. p.394.

A. pearsonii, syn. *A. schlechteri*, illus. p.393.

A. schlechteri. See *A. pearsonii*.

ARIOCARPUS (Cactaceae)
Living rock
Genus of extremely slow-growing, perennial cacti with large, swollen roots. Produces flattened, spherical, green stems with angular tubercles and tufts of wool. Frost tender, min. 41°F (5°C). Prefers full sun and extremely well-drained, lime-rich soil. Is very prone to rotting. Propagate by seed in spring or summer.

A. fissuratus illus. p.392.

ARISAEMA (Araceae)
Genus of tuberous perennials, grown for their large, curious, hooded spathes, each enclosing a pencil-shaped spadix. Forms spikes of fleshy, red fruits in autumn, before plant dies down. Fully to half hardy. Needs sun or partial shade and humus-rich soil. Plant tubers 6in (15cm) deep in spring. Propagate by seed in autumn or spring or by offsets in spring.

A. atrorubens. See *A. triphyllum*.

A. candidissimum illus. p.364.

A. consanguineum illus. p.337.

A. griffithii illus. p.352.

A. jacquemontii illus. p.353.

A. ringens. Early spring-flowering, tuberous perennial. H 10–12in (25–30cm), S 12–18in (30–45cm). Half hardy, zones 7–9. Bears 2 erect leaves, each with 3 long-pointed lobes, and a widely hooded, green spathe, enclosing the spadix, that has paler green stripes and is edged with dark brown-purple.

A. sikokianum illus. p.350.

A. tortuosum. Summer-flowering, tuberous perennial. H 1–3ft (30cm–1m), S 1–1¹/₂ft (30–45cm). Half hardy, zones 8–9. Each dark green-mottled, pale green stem bears 2–3 erect leaves, divided into several oval leaflets. A hooded, green or purple spathe, with a protruding, S-shaped spadix, overtops leaves. Produces spikes of attractive, fleshy, red fruits in autumn.

A. triphyllum, syn. *A. atrorubens*, illus. p.352.

ARISARUM (Araceae)
Genus of tuberous perennials, grown mainly for their curious, hooded spathes enclosing spadices with minute flowers. Frost hardy. Needs partial shade and humus-rich, well-drained soil. Propagate in autumn by division of an established clump of tubers, which produce offsets freely.

A. proboscideum (Mouse plant). Clump-forming, spring-flowering, tuberous perennial. H to 4in (10cm), S 8–12in (20–30cm). Zones 5–7. Leaves are arrow-shaped and prostrate. Produces a spadix of minute flowers concealed in a hooded, dark brown

spathe that is drawn out into a tail up to 6in (15cm) long—a mouselike effect.

ARISTEA (Iridaceae)
Genus of evergreen, clump-forming, rhizomatous perennials, grown for their spikes of blue flowers in spring or summer. Half hardy. Prefers sun and well-drained soil. Established plants cannot be moved satisfactorily. Propagate by seed in autumn or spring.

A. ecklonii. Evergreen, clump-forming, rhizomatous perennial. H 12–24in (30–60cm), S 8–16in (20–40cm). Zones 9–10. Has long, sword-shaped, tough leaves, overtopped in summer by loosely branched spikes of saucer-shaped, blue flowers, produced in long succession.

A. major, syn. *A. thyrsiflora*, illus. p.337.

A. thyrsiflora. See *A. major*.

ARISTOLOCHIA (Aristolochiaceae)
Birthwort
Genus of evergreen or deciduous, woody-stemmed, twining and scrambling climbers, grown for their foliage and flowers. Frost hardy to frost tender, min. 50–55°F (10–13°C). Needs well-drained soil and partial shade in summer. Water regularly, less when not in full growth. Needs support. Cut back previous season's growth to 2 or 3 nodes in spring. Propagate by seed in spring or by semi-ripe cuttings in summer. Red spider mite and whitefly may be a nuisance.

A. elegans illus. p.169.

A. gigas. See *A. grandiflora*.

A. grandiflora, syn. *A. gigas* (Pelican flower, Swan flower). Fast-growing, evergreen, woody-stemmed, twining climber. H 22ft (7m) or more. Frost tender, zone 10. Leaves are broadly oval, 6–10in (15–25cm) long. In summer bears large, unpleasant-smelling, tubular, purple-veined, white flowers, each with a long tail and expanding at the mouth into a heart-shaped lip.

A. griffithii, syn. *Isotrema griffithii*. Moderately vigorous, evergreen, woody-stemmed, twining climber. H 15–20ft (5–6m). Half hardy, zones 9–10; deciduous in cold winters. Has heart-shaped leaves and tubular, dark red flowers, each with an expanded, spreading lip, in summer.

ARMERIA (Plumbaginaceae)
Genus of evergreen perennials and, occasionally, sub-shrubs, grown for their tuftlike clumps or rosettes of leaves and their flower heads. Fully to frost hardy. Requires sun and well-drained soil. Propagate by semi-ripe cuttings in summer or by seed in autumn.

A. caespitosa. See *A. juniperifolia*.

A. cespitosa. See *A. juniperifolia*.

A. juniperifolia, syn. *A. caespitosa, A. cespitosa*, illus. p.305. **'Bevans Variety'** is an evergreen, densely cushioned sub-shrub. H 2–3in (5–8cm), S 6in (15cm). Fully hardy, zones 5–7. Has narrow, pointed, mid- to gray-green leaves in loose rosettes. Round heads of small, deep pink flowers are borne in late spring and early summer.

A. latifolia. See *A. pseudarmeria.*
A. maritima (Sea pink, Thrift).
Evergreen, clump-forming perennial
or dwarf sub-shrub. H 4in (10cm), S
6in (15cm). Fully hardy, zones 4–7.
Leaves are narrow, grasslike, and dark
green. Stiff stems carry round heads of
many small, white to pink flowers in
summer. Makes a good edging plant.
'Vindictive' illus. p.320.
A. pseudarmeria, syn. *A. latifolia,* illus.
p.290. **'Bees Ruby'** is an evergreen,
clump-forming, dwarf sub-shrub. H
and S 12in (30cm). Fully hardy, zones
6–7. Round heads of many small, ruby
red flowers are produced in summer
on stiff stems above narrow, grasslike,
dark green leaves.

ARNEBIA (Boraginaceae)
Genus of perennials with hairy leaves,
suitable for rock gardens and banks.
Fully hardy. Needs sun and gritty,
well-drained soil. Propagate by seed
in autumn, by root cuttings in winter,
or by division in spring.
A. echioides. See *A. pulchra.*
A. pulchra, syn. *A. echioides,*
Echioides longiflorum, Macrotomia
echioides (Prophet flower). Clump-
forming perennial. H 9–12in (23–30cm),
S 10in (25cm). Zones 6–8. Leaves are
lance-shaped to narrowly oval, hairy,
and light green. In summer bears loose
racemes of tubular, bright yellow
flowers, each with 5 spreading lobes
and fading, dark spots at petal bases.

ARNICA (Compositae)
Genus of rhizomatous perennials,
grown for their large, daisylike flower
heads. Is suitable for large rock
gardens. Fully hardy. Prefers sun
and humus-rich, well-drained soil.
Propagate by division or seed in spring.
A. montana. Tufted, rhizomatous
perennial. H 12in (30cm), S 6in
(15cm). Zones 5–8. Bears narrowly
oval to oval, hairy, gray-green leaves
and, in summer, solitary daisylike,
golden flower heads, 2in (5cm) wide.
Prefers acid soil.

ARONIA (Rosaceae)
Chokeberry
Genus of deciduous shrubs, grown
for their flowers, fruits, and colorful
autumn foliage. Fully hardy. Needs
sun (to produce its best autumn color)
or semi-shade and fertile, well-drained
soil. Propagate by softwood or semi-
ripe cuttings in summer, by seed in
autumn, or by division from early
autumn to spring.
A. arbutifolia illus. p.97.
A. melanocarpa illus. p.104.
A. prunifolia (Purple-fruited
chokeberry). Deciduous, upright shrub.
H 10ft (3m), S 8ft (2.5m). Zones 5–9.
Oval, glossy, dark green leaves redden
in autumn. Has star-shaped, white
flowers in late spring and early
summer, followed by spherical,
purplish black fruits.

ARRHENATHERUM (Gramineae).
See GRASSES, BAMBOOS,
RUSHES, and SEDGES.
A. elatius (False oat grass).
'Variegatum' is a loosely tuft-
forming, herbaceous, perennial grass.

H 20in (50cm), S 8in (20cm). Fully
hardy, zones 5–8. Has a basal stem
swelling, hairless, gray-green leaves,
with white margins, and open panicles
of brownish spikelets in summer.

ARTEMISIA (Compositae)
Wormwood
Genus of perennials and spreading,
dwarf sub-shrubs and shrubs, some
of which are evergreen or semi-
evergreen, grown mainly for their
fernlike, silvery foliage that is
sometimes aromatic. Fully to half
hardy. Prefers an open, sunny, well-
drained site; dwarf types benefit from
a winter protection of sharp grit or
gravel. Trim lightly in spring.
Propagate by division in spring or
autumn or by softwood or semi-ripe
cuttings in summer.
A. abrotanum illus. p.144.
A. absinthium 'Lambrook Silver'.
Evergreen, bushy perennial, woody at
base. H 32in (80cm), S 20in (50cm).
Frost hardy, zones 4–8. Has a mass of
finely divided, aromatic, silvery gray
leaves. Tiny, insignificant, gray flower
heads are borne in long panicles in
summer. Needs protection in an
exposed site.
A. arborescens illus. p.143. **'Faith**
Raven' is an evergreen, upright shrub.
H 4ft (1.2m), S 3ft (1m). Zones 9–10.
Differs from the species only in that it
is frost hardy. Has finely cut, aromatic,
silvery white foliage and, in summer
and early autumn, rounded heads of
small, bright yellow flowers.
A. assoana. See *A. pedemontana.*
A. canescens. Semi-evergreen, bushy
perennial. H 20in (50cm), S 12in
(30cm). Fully hardy, zones 4–8. Has
delicate, finely cut, curling, silvery
gray leaves. In summer, insignificant,
yellow flower heads are borne on
erect, silver stems. Makes good
ground cover.
A. frigida. Semi-evergreen, mat-
forming perennial with a woody base.
H 12in (30cm) in flower, S 12in (30cm)
or more. Fully hardy, zones 5–8. Has
small, fernlike, aromatic, silky, gray-
white leaves, divided into many linear
lobes. In summer produces narrow
panicles of small, rounded, yellow
flower heads.
A. lactiflora illus. p.189.
A. lanata. See *A. pedemontana.*
A. ludoviciana var. **albula** illus. p.223.
A. pedemontana, syn. *A. assoana,*
A. lanata. Evergreen or semi-
evergreen, prostrate perennial. H and S
12in (30cm). Fully hardy, zones 5–8.
Fernlike foliage is densely covered
with silvery white hairs. Small clusters
of small, rounded, yellow flower heads
are borne in summer. Suits a rock
garden or wall.
A. pontica illus. p.245.
A. 'Powis Castle'. Vigorous,
evergreen sub-shrub. H 3ft (1m), S 4ft
(1.2m). Frost hardy, zones 5–8. Has
abundant, finely cut, aromatic, silvery
gray foliage and sprays of insignificant,
yellowish gray flower heads in summer.
A. schmidtiana. Semi-evergreen,
hummock-forming perennial with
creeping stems. H 3–12in (8–30cm), S
24in (60cm). Frost hardy, zones 5–8.
Has fernlike, very finely and deeply

cut, silver leaves and, in summer,
bears short racemes of small, rounded,
pale yellow flower heads. Is suitable
for a large rock garden, wall, or bank.
Needs sandy, peaty soil. **'Nana'** illus.
p.329.
A. stelleriana. Evergreen, rounded,
rhizomatous perennial with a woody
base. H 1–2ft (30–60cm), S 2–3ft
(60cm–1m). Fully hardy, zones 3–8.
White-haired, silver leaves are deeply
lobed or toothed. Bears slender sprays
of small, yellow flower heads in
summer. Needs light soil. **'Boughton**
Silver', S 3ft (1m), is vigorous and
arching in habit.
A. tridentata (Sagebrush). Evergreen,
spreading sub-shrub. H 4ft (1.2m),
S 6ft (2m). Frost hardy, zones 6–9.
Bears peeling bark and wedge-shaped,
terminally toothed, aromatic, silvery
gray leaves. Arching panicles of small,
spherical, yellow flower heads appear
in mid-autumn.

ARUM (Araceae)
Cuckoo pint, Lords and ladies
Genus of tuberous perennials, grown
for their ornamental leaves and
attractive spathes, each enclosing a
pencil-shaped spadix of tiny flowers.
Fully to half hardy. Prefers sun or
partial shade and moist but well-
drained soil. Propagate by seed in
autumn or by division in early autumn.
A. creticum illus. p.347.
A. dioscoridis. Spring-flowering,
tuberous perennial. H 8–14in
(20–35cm), S 12–18in (30–45cm).
Frost hardy, zones 7–9. Has a sail-like,
green or purple spathe, blotched dark
purple, surrounding a blackish purple
spadix. Arrow-shaped, semi-erect
leaves appear in autumn. Needs a
sheltered, sunny site.
A. dracunculus. See *Dracunculus*
vulgaris.
A. italicum 'Pictum' illus. p.363.
A. pictum illus. p.369.

ARUNCUS (Rosaceae)
Genus of perennials, grown for their
hummocks of broad, fernlike leaves
and their plumes of white flowers in
summer. Fully hardy. Thrives in any
well-drained soil and in full light.
Propagate by seed in autumn or by
division in spring or autumn.
A. dioicus, syn. *A. sylvester, Spiraea*
aruncus, illus. p.188. **'Kneiffii'** illus.
p.201.
A. sylvester. See *A. dioicus.*

ARUNDINARIA (Bambusoideae).
See GRASSES, BAMBOOS,
RUSHES, and SEDGES.
A. anceps, syn. *A. jaunsarensis,*
Sinarundinaria jaunsarensis, illus.
p.182.
A. auricoma. See *Pleioblastus*
viridistriatus.
A. falconeri. See *Thamnocalamus*
falconeri.
A. fastuosa. See *Semiarundinaria*
fastuosa.
A. fortunei. See *Pleioblastus*
variegatus.
A. japonica. See *Pseudosasa japonica.*
A. jaunsarensis. See *A. anceps.*
A. murielae. See *Thamnocalamus*
spathaceus.

A. nitida. See *Sinarundinaria nitida.*
A. variegata. See *Pleioblastus*
variegatus.
A. viridistriata. See *Pleioblastus*
viridistriatus.

ARUNDO (Gramineae). See
GRASSES, BAMBOOS, RUSHES,
and SEDGES.
A. donax (Giant reed). Herbaceous,
rhizomatous, perennial grass. H to 20ft
(6m), S 3ft (1m). Half hardy, zones
7–10. Thick stems bear broad, floppy,
blue-green leaves. Produces dense,
erect panicles of whitish yellow
spikelets in summer. May also be
grown in moist soil. **'Versicolor'**
(syn. *A.d.* 'Variegata') illus. p.180.

ASARINA, syn. MAURANDIA
(Scrophulariaceae)
Genus of evergreen climbers and
perennials, often with scandent stems,
grown for their flowers. Is herbaceous
in cold climates. Frost hardy to frost
tender, min. 41°F (5°C). Grow in full
light and in any well-drained soil.
Propagate by seed in spring.
A. barclaiana. Evergreen, soft-
stemmed, scandent climber, herbaceous
in cold climates. H to 6ft (2m). Frost
tender, zone 10. Has angular, heart-
shaped, hairless leaves. Trumpet-
shaped, purple flowers, each with a
whitish throat, 2½–3in (6–7cm) long,
are produced in summer-autumn.
A. erubescens illus. p.167.
A. procumbens, syn. *Antirrhinum*
asarina, illus. p.324.

ASARUM, syn. HEXASTYLIS
(Aristolochiaceae)
Wild ginger
Genus of rhizomatous perennials,
some of which are evergreen, with
pitcher-shaped flowers carried under
kidney- or heart-shaped leaves. Makes
good ground cover, although leaves
may become damaged in severe
weather. Fully hardy. Prefers shade
and humus-rich, moist but well-
drained soil. Propagate by division
in spring. Self seeds readily.
A. caudatum (British Columbia
wild ginger). Evergreen, prostrate,
rhizomatous perennial. H 3in (8cm),
S 10in (25cm) or more. Zones 6–8.
Bears heart-shaped, leathery, glossy,
dark green leaves, 2–4in (5–10cm)
across, which in early summer conceal
small, pitcher-shaped, reddish brown
or brownish purple flowers with tail-
like lobes.
A. europaeum illus. p.330.
A. hartwegii. Evergreen, prostrate,
rhizomatous perennial. H 3in (8cm),
S 10in (25cm) or more. Zones 6–8.
Pitcher-shaped, very dark brown,
almost black, flowers, with tail-like
lobes, appear in early summer beneath
heart-shaped, silver-marked, green
leaves, 2–4in (5–10cm) wide.
A. shuttleworthii (Southern wild
ginger). Evergreen, prostrate,
rhizomatous perennial. H 3in (8cm),
S 10in (25cm) or more. Zones 6–9.
Has broadly heart-shaped, usually
silver-marked, green leaves, 3in (8cm)
across. Bears pitcher-shaped, dark
brown flowers, mottled violet inside,
in early summer.

ASCLEPIAS (Asclepiadaceae)
Milkweed, Silkweed
Genus of tuberous perennials or sub-shrubs, some of which are evergreen, grown for their flowers. Stems exude milky, white latex when cut. Fully hardy to frost tender, min. 41–50°F (5–10°C). Fully to half hardy species prefer sun and a humus-rich, well-drained soil. Propagate by division or seed in spring. Frost tender species need sun and a moist atmosphere; cut back during periods of growth to keep bushy. Water very sparingly in low temperatures. Propagate by tip cuttings or seed in spring.
A. curassavica (Bloodflower). Evergreen, bushy, tuberous sub-shrub. H and S 3ft (1m). Frost tender, zone 10. Has narrowly oval leaves to 6in (15cm) long. Umbels of small, but showy, 5-horned, orange-red flowers with yellow centers are produced in summer-autumn; narrowly ovoid, pointed fruits, with silky seeds, are 3in (8cm) long.
A. hallii. Upright, tuberous perennial. H to 3ft (1m), S 2ft (60cm). Fully hardy, zones 5–9. Has oblong leaves, to 5in (13cm) long. Umbels of small, 5-horned, dark pink flowers are carried in summer; tightly packed silky seeds are enclosed in narrowly ovoid fruits, to 6in (15cm) long.
A. physocarpa, syn. *Gomphocarpus physocarpus*, illus. p.194.
A. syriaca. Upright, tuberous perennial. H and S 3ft (1m) or more. Fully hardy, zones 4–9. Bears oval leaves to 8in (20cm) long. Umbels of small, 5-horned, purplish pink flowers are carried on drooping flower stalks in summer, followed by narrowly ovoid fruits, to 6in (15cm) long and filled with silky seeds.
A. tuberosa illus. p.216.

ASIMINA (Annonaceae)
Genus of deciduous or evergreen shrubs and trees, grown for their foliage and flowers. Fully hardy. Prefers full sun and fertile, deep, moist but well-drained soil. Propagate by seed in autumn or by layering or root cuttings in winter.
A. triloba (Pawpaw). Deciduous, open shrub. H and S 12ft (4m). Zones 6–8. Large, oval, green leaves emerge in late spring or early summer, just after, or at same time as, 6-petaled, purplish brown flowers. Later has small, globular, brownish fruits.

ASPARAGUS (Liliaceae)
Genus of perennials and scrambling climbers and shrubs, some of which are evergreen, grown for their foliage. Fully hardy to frost tender, min. 50°F (10°C). Grow in partial shade or bright light, but not direct sun, in any fertile, well-drained soil. Propagate by seed or division in spring.
A. densiflorus, syn. *A. sprengeri*, illus. p.223. **'Myersii'** (syn. *A. meyeri*, *A. myersii*) illus. p.224.
A. meyeri. See *A. densiflorus* 'Myersii'.
A. myersii. See *A. densiflorus* 'Myersii'.
A. scandens illus. p.177.
A. sprengeri. See *A. densiflorus*.

ASPERULA (Rubiaceae)
Genus of annuals and perennials; some species make good alpine house plants. Fully to frost hardy. Most species need sun and well-drained soil with moisture at roots. Dislikes winter wet on crown. Propagate by softwood cuttings or seed in early summer.
A. odorata. See *Galium odoratum*.
A. suberosa illus. p.316.

ASPHODELINE (Liliaceae)
Genus of perennials with thick, fleshy roots. Frost to half hardy. Requires sun and not over-rich soil. Propagate by division in early spring, taking care not to damage roots, or by seed in autumn or spring.
A. liburnica. Neat, clump-forming perennial. H 10–24in (25–60cm), S 12in (30cm). Frost hardy, zones 6–9. In spring produces racemes of shallowly cup-shaped, yellow flowers on slender stems above linear, gray-green leaves.
A. lutea illus. p.199.

ASPHODELUS (Liliaceae)
Genus of spring- or summer-flowering annuals and perennials. Frost to half hardy. Requires sun; most prefer fertile, well-drained soil. *A. albus* prefers light, well-drained soil. Propagate by division in spring or by seed in autumn.
A. acaulis. Prostrate perennial. H 2in (5cm), S 9in (23cm). Half hardy, zones 9–10. In spring or early summer, stemless, funnel-shaped, flesh pink flowers appear in the center of each cluster of grasslike, green leaves. Is suitable for an alpine house.
A. aestivus, syn. *A. microcarpus* (Asphodel). Upright perennial. H 3ft (1m), S 1ft (30cm). Frost hardy, zones 7–10. Dense panicles of star-shaped, white flowers are borne in late spring. Has basal rosettes of upright, then spreading, grasslike, channeled, leathery, green leaves.
A. albus illus. p.200.
A. microcarpus. See *A. aestivus*.

ASPIDISTRA (Liliaceae)
Genus of evergreen, rhizomatous perennials that spread slowly, grown mainly for their glossy foliage. Frost tender, min. 41–50°F (5–10°C). Very tolerant, but is best grown in a cool, shady position away from direct sunlight and in well-drained soil. Water frequently when in full growth, less at other times. Propagate by division of rhizomes in spring.
A. elatior (Cast-iron plant). Evergreen, rhizomatous perennial. H 2ft (60cm), S 18in (45cm). Zones 7–10. Has upright, narrow, pointed-oval leaves, to 2ft (60cm) long; occasionally, inconspicuous, cream to purple flowers are produced on short stalks near soil level. **'Variegata'** illus. p.257.

ASPLENIUM (Polypodiaceae)
Genus of evergreen or semi-evergreen ferns. Fully hardy to frost tender, min. 41°F (5°C). Plants described prefer partial shade, but *A. trichomanes* tolerates full sun. Grow in any moist soil, although potted plants should be grown in a compost including chopped sphagnum moss or coarse peat. Remove fading fronds regularly. Propagate by spores or bulbils, if produced, in late summer.
A. bulbiferum (Hen-and-chickens fern, Mother spleenwort). Semi-evergreen or evergreen fern. H 6–12in (15–30cm), S 12in (30cm). Frost tender, zone 10. Lance-shaped, finely divided, dark green fronds produce bulbils from which young plants develop.
A. nidus illus. p.187.
A. scolopendrium. See *Phyllitis scolopendrium*.
A. trichomanes illus. p.185.

ASTER (Compositae)
Michaelmas daisy
Genus of perennials and deciduous or evergreen sub-shrubs with daisylike flower heads borne in summer-autumn. Fully to half hardy. Prefers sun or partial shade and fertile, well-drained soil, with adequate moisture throughout summer. Tall species and cultivars require staking. Propagate by softwood cuttings in spring or by division in spring or autumn. Modern forms of *A. novi-belgii* require rigorous spraying against mildew and insect attack. Other species may also suffer.
A. acris. See *A. sedifolius*.
A. albescens, syn. *Microglossa albescens*. Deciduous, upright, slender-stemmed sub-shrub. H 3ft (1m), S 5ft (1.5m). Frost hardy, zones 7–9. Has narrowly lance-shaped, gray-green leaves. Produces flattish sprays of lavender blue flower heads, with yellow centers, in mid-summer.
A. alpinus illus. p.321. **'Beechwood'** is a clump-forming perennial. H 6in (15cm), S 12–18in (30–45cm). Fully hardy, zones 5–7. Leaves are lance-shaped and dark green. Purple flower heads with yellow centers are borne from mid- to late summer. Is suitable for a rock garden.
A. amellus 'King George' illus. p.250. **'Mauve Beauty'** is a clump-forming perennial. H and S 20in (50cm). Fully hardy, zones 5–8. Bears clusters of large, violet flower heads, with yellow centers, in autumn. Leaves are lance-shaped, coarse, and green. **'Rudolph Goethe'** with large, violet-blue flower heads and **'Violet Queen'** with deep violet flower heads are other good cultivars. **'Sonia'** has pink flower heads.
A. capensis. See *Felicia amelloides*.
A. cordifolius 'Silver Spray' illus. p.217.
A. ericoides 'White Heather' illus. p.217.
A. frikartii 'Mönch' illus. p.220.
A. lateriflorus. Branching perennial. H 24in (60cm), S 20in (50cm). Fully hardy, zones 4–8. Bears sprays of tiny, mauve flower heads, with pinkish brown centers, in autumn. Lance-shaped leaves are small and dark green. **'Horizontalis'** illus. p.249.
A. novae-angliae 'Alma Potschke'. Vigorous, upright perennial. H 30in (75cm), S to 24in (60cm). Fully hardy, zones 5–8. In autumn produces clusters of pink flower heads on stiff stems. Has lance-shaped, rough leaves. **'Harrington's Pink'** illus. p.193. **'Herbstschnee'** illus. p.217.

A. novi-belgii. **'Fellowship'** is a vigorous, upright perennial. H 4ft (1.2m), S 20in (50cm). Fully hardy, zones 4–8. Has pyramid-shaped panicles of large, clear pink flower heads in autumn and oval, green leaves. **'Little Pink Beauty'**, H 18in (45cm), is a good pink, dwarf cultivar. **'Carnival'** (illus. p.220), **'Orlando'** (illus. p.220) and **'Royal Ruby'** (illus. p.250) have deep red flowers. Good violet or blue cultivars are **'Climax'**, H 5ft (1.5m), which is light blue and mildew-resistant, **'Marie Ballard'** (illus. p.220), also blue, **'Raspberry Ripple'**, H 30in (75cm), with reddish violet flowers and **'Royal Velvet'**, H 4ft (1.2m), with deep violet flowers.
A. paniculatus. See *A. tradescantii*.
A. 'Professor A. Kippenburg' illus. p.250.
A. sedifolius, syn. *A. acris*. Bushy perennial. H 3ft (1m), S 2ft (60cm). Fully hardy, zones 5–8. Produces clusters of almost star-shaped, lavender blue flower heads, with yellow centers, in autumn. Has small, narrowly oval, bright green leaves. **'Nanus'**, H and S 20in (50cm), makes a compact dome of blooms.
A. thomsonii. Upright perennial. H 3ft (1m), S 20in (50cm). Fully hardy, zones 5–8. Produces long-petaled, pale lilac flower heads, freely in autumn. Leaves are slightly heart-shaped. **'Nanus'** illus. p.250.
A. tongolensis. Mat-forming perennial. H 20in (50cm), S 12in (30cm). Fully hardy, zones 6–8. Large, lavender blue flower heads, with orange centers, are borne singly in early summer. Has lance-shaped, hairy, dark green leaves.
A. tradescantii, syn. *A. paniculatus*. Erect perennial. H 4ft (1.2m), S 20in (50cm). Fully hardy, zones 5–8. Has lance-shaped, green leaves. In autumn, clusters of small, white flower heads, borne on wiry, leafy stems, provide a good foil to bright, autumn colors.
A. turbinellus illus. p.220.
A. vimineus 'Delight' illus. p.217.

ASTILBE (Saxifragaceae)
Genus of summer-flowering perennials, grown for their panicles of flowers that remain handsome even when dried brown in winter. Is suitable for borders and rock gardens. Fully hardy. Needs rich, moist soil and, in most species, partial shade. Leave undisturbed if possible, and give an annual spring mulch of well-rotted compost. Propagate species by seed in autumn, others by division in spring or autumn.
A. 'Bressingham Beauty'. Leafy, clump-forming perennial. H and S to 3ft (1m). Zones 5–8. In summer bears feathery, tapering panicles of small, star-shaped, rich pink flowers on strong stems. Broad leaves are divided into oblong to oval, toothed leaflets.
A. chinensis 'Pumila'. Clump-forming perennial. H 12in (30cm), S 8in (20cm). Zones 5–8. Lower two-thirds of flower stem bears deeply dissected, coarse, toothed, hairy, dark green leaves. Dense, fluffy spikes of tiny, star-shaped, deep raspberry red flowers appear in summer. Is good for a shaded, moist rock garden.

A. **'Fanal'** illus. p.239.
A. **'Granat'**. Clump-forming, leafy perennial. H 2ft (60cm), S to 3ft (1m). Zones 5–8. Produces pyramidal trusses of tiny, star-shaped, deep red flowers in summer above broad, bronze-flushed, rich green leaves, which are divided into oblong to oval, toothed leaflets.
A. **'Irrlicht'** illus. p.233.
A. **'Montgomery'** illus. p.208.
A. **'Ostrich Plume'** illus. p.204.
A. **'Perkeo'** illus. p.293.
A. simplicifolia **'Gnome'**. Arching, clump-forming, slender-stemmed perennial. H 6in (15cm), S 4in (10cm). Zones 5–8. Has oval, deeply lobed or cut, crimped, reddish green leaves in a basal rosette. Produces dense racemes of tiny, star-shaped, pink flowers in summer. Is good for a shaded, moist rock garden or peat bed. Self seeds in damp places but will not come true.
A. **'Sprite'**. Clump-forming, dwarf, leafy perennial. H 20in (50cm), S to 3ft (1m). Zones 5–8. Has feathery, tapering panicles of tiny, star-shaped, shell pink flowers in summer, borne above broad leaves divided into narrowly oval, toothed leaflets.
A. **'Venus'** illus. p.204.

ASTRANTIA (Umbelliferae)
Masterwort
Genus of perennials, widely used in flower arrangements. Fully hardy. Needs sun or semi-shade and well-drained soil. Propagate by division in spring or by seed when fresh, in late summer.
A. major and var. *involucrata* illus. p.234. **'Sunningdale Variegated'** is a clump-forming perennial. H 24in (60cm), S 18in (45cm). Zones 5–8. Produces rounded, sometimes pink-tinged, greenish white flower heads on wiry, branched stems throughout summer-autumn. Palmate, deeply 3–5-lobed, green leaves are variegated with yellow and cream.
A. maxima illus. p.234.

ASTROPHYTUM (Cactaceae)
Genus of slow-growing, perennial cacti, grown for their freely produced, flattish, yellow flowers, some with red centers. Frost tender, min. 41°F (5°C). Prefers sun and very well-drained, lime-rich soil. Dry completely in winter. Is prone to rot if wet. Propagate by seed in spring or summer.
A. asterias (Sea urchin, Silver dollar cactus). Slow-growing, slightly domed, perennial cactus. H 3–4in (8–10cm), S 4in (10cm). Zone 10. Spineless stem has about 8 low ribs bearing small, tufted areoles. Produces bright yellow flowers, to 2¹⁄₂in (6cm) across, in summer.
A. myriostigma illus. p.386.
A. ornatum illus. p.397.

Asystasia bella. See *Mackaya bella.*

ATHEROSPERMA (Monimiaceae, syn. Atherospermataceae)
Genus of evergreen trees, grown for

their foliage and flowers in summer. Frost tender, min. 37–41°F (3–5°C). Needs full light or partial shade and well-drained soil. Water potted specimens moderately, less in winter. Pruning is tolerated if necessary. Propagate by seed in spring or by semi-ripe cuttings in summer.
A. moschatum (Australian sassafras, Tasmanian sassafras). Evergreen, spreading tree, conical when young. H 50–80ft (15–25m), S 15–30ft (5–10m). Zone 10. Has lance-shaped, nutmeg-scented, glossy leaves, slightly toothed and covered with white down beneath. Produces small, saucer-shaped, creamy white flowers in summer.

ATHROTAXIS (Taxodiaceae)
Genus of conifers with awl-shaped leaves that clasp stems. See also CONIFERS.
A. selaginoides (King William pine). Irregularly conical conifer. H 50ft (15m) or more, S 15ft (5m). Half hardy, zones 8–9. Has tiny, thick-textured, loosely overlapping, dark green leaves and insignificant, globular cones.

ATHYRIUM (Polypodiaceae)
Genus of deciduous or, occasionally, semi-evergreen ferns. Fully hardy to frost tender, min. 41°F (5°C). Needs shade and humus-rich, moist soil. Remove fading fronds regularly. Propagate by spores in late summer or by division in autumn or winter.
A. filix-femina (Lady fern). Deciduous fern. H 2–4ft (60cm–1.2m), S 1–3ft (30cm–1m). Fully hardy, zones 4–9. Dainty, lance-shaped, much-divided, arching fronds are pale green. Has very variable frond dissection.
A. goeringianum. See *A. nipponicum.*
A. nipponicum, syn. *A. goeringianum*, illus. p.187.

ATRIPLEX (Chenopodiaceae)
Genus of annuals, perennials, and evergreen or semi-evergreen shrubs, grown for their foliage. Grows well beside the coast. Fully to half hardy. Needs full sun and well-drained soil. Propagate by softwood cuttings in summer or by seed in autumn.
A. halimus (Tree purslane). Semi-evergreen, bushy shrub. H 6ft (2m), S 10ft (3m). Frost hardy, zones 7–9. Oval leaves are silvery gray. Produces flowers very rarely.
A. hortensis **'Rubra'** (Red mountain spinach, Red orach). Fast-growing, erect annual. H 4ft (1.2m), S 1ft (30cm). Half hardy. Triangular, deep red leaves, to 6in (15cm) long, are edible. Produces insignificant flowers in summer.

AUBRIETA (Cruciferae)
Genus of evergreen, trailing and mound-forming perennials. Is useful on dry banks, walls, and in rock gardens. Fully hardy. Thrives in sun and in any well-drained soil. To maintain a compact shape, cut back hard after flowering. Propagate by

greenwood cuttings in summer or by semi-ripe cuttings in late summer or autumn.
A. **'Carnival'** illus. p.308.
A. **'Church Knowle'**. Evergreen, trailing, very compact perennial. H 3in (8cm), S 6–9in (15–23cm). Zones 5–7. Has small, stemless, 4-petaled, lavender blue flowers in spring. Leaves are rounded and toothed.
A. **'Cobalt Violet'** illus. p.309.
A. deltoidea **'Argenteo-variegata'** illus. p.308.
A. **'Dr. Mule's'**. Vigorous, evergreen, mound-forming perennial. H 2–3in (5–8cm), S 12in (30cm). Zones 5–7. Has rounded, toothed, soft green leaves and, in spring, large, double, rich purple flowers on short spikes.
A. **'Gurgedyke'**. Evergreen, mound-forming perennial. H 4in (10cm), S 8in (20cm). Zones 5–7. Bears rounded, toothed, soft green leaves. Produces 4-petaled, deep purple flowers in spring.
A. **'Joy'** illus. p.307.
A. **'J.S. Baker'** illus. p.308.

AUCUBA (Cornaceae)
Genus of evergreen shrubs, grown for their foliage and fruits. In order to obtain fruits, grow both male and female plants. Makes good house plants when kept in a cool, shaded position. Fully to frost hardy. Tolerates full sun to dense shade. Grow in any but waterlogged soil. To restrict growth, cut old shoots back hard in spring. Propagate by semi-ripe cuttings in summer.
A. japonica illus. p.120. **'Crotonifolia'** (male) illus. p.121. **'Gold Dust'** is an evergreen, bushy, dense, female shrub. H and S 8ft (2.5m). Frost hardy, zones 7–10. Has stout, green shoots and oval, glossy, gold-speckled, dark green leaves. Small, star-shaped, purple flowers in mid-spring are followed by egg-shaped, bright red fruits. Bright green leaves of **'Picturata'** (male) each have a central, golden blotch. Some plants of 'Crotonifolia' and 'Picturata' are known to be female and have produced fruits.

AURINIA (Cruciferae)
Genus of evergreen perennials, grown for their gray-green foliage and showy flower sprays. Is suitable for rock gardens, walls, and banks. Fully hardy. Needs sun and well-drained soil. Propagate by softwood or greenwood cuttings in early summer or by seed in autumn.
A. saxatilis, syn. *Alyssum saxatile*, illus. p.290. **'Citrina'** and **'Variegata'** illus. p.289. **'Dudley Neville'** is an evergreen, clump-forming perennial. H 9in (23cm), S 12in (30cm). Zones 4–7. Has oval, hairy, gray-green leaves and, in late spring and early summer, bears racemes of many small, 4-petaled, buff-yellow flowers.

AUSTROCEDRUS (Cupressaceae)
Genus of conifers with flattish sprays of scalelike leaves. See also CONIFERS.

A. chilensis, syn. *Libocedrus chilensis*, illus. p.78.

Avena candida. See *Helictotrichon sempervirens.*
Avena sempervirens. See *Helictotrichon sempervirens.*

AZARA (Flacourtiaceae)
Genus of evergreen shrubs and trees, grown for their foliage and yellow flowers that are composed of a mass of stamens. Frost to half hardy; in cold areas plant against a south- or west-facing wall for protection. Grows in sun or shade and in fertile, well-drained soil. Propagate by semi-ripe cuttings in summer.
A. lanceolata. Evergreen, bushy shrub or spreading tree. H and S 20ft (6m). Frost hardy, zones 8–10. Has narrowly oval, sharply toothed, bright green leaves. Small, rounded clusters of pale yellow flowers are carried in late spring or early summer.
A. microphylla illus. p.93.
A. serrata illus. p.103.

AZOLLA (Salviniaceae)
Genus of deciduous, perennial, floating water ferns, grown for their decorative foliage and to control algae by reducing light beneath water. Frost to half hardy. Grows in sun or shade. If not kept in check, may be invasive; reduce spread by removing portions with a net. Propagate by redistributing clusters of plantlets when they appear.
A. caroliniana illus. p.374.

AZORELLA (Hydrocotylaceae)
Genus of evergreen, tufted or spreading perennials, grown for their neat, rosetted foliage and their flowers. Is useful as alpine house plants. Fully hardy. Thrives in full light and well-drained soil. Propagate by division in spring.
A. trifurcata, syn. *Bolax glebaria* of gardens, illus. p.330.

AZORINA (Campanulaceae)
Genus of one species of evergreen sub-shrub, grown for its flowers in spring-summer. Frost tender, min. 41°F (5°C). Requires full sun or partial shade and well-drained soil. Water potted plants moderately, less when not in full growth. Cut out spent racemes after flowering. Propagate by seed or softwood or greenwood cuttings of non-flowering shoots in spring or summer.
A. vidalii, syn. *Campanula vidalii*, illus. p.122.

AZUREOCEREUS (Cactaceae)
Genus of slow-growing, eventually treelike, perennial cacti. Spiny, silvery-or green-blue stems, with up to 20 or more ribs, are crowned by stiff, erect, green-blue branches. Frost tender, min. 45°F (7°C). Requires sun and very well-drained soil. Propagate by seed in spring or summer.
A. hertlingianus, syn. *Browningia hertlingianus*, illus. p.378.

B

BABIANA (Iridaceae)
Genus of spring- and early summer-flowering corms, valued for their brightly colored flowers, somewhat like freesias. Frost tender, min. 50°F (10°C). Needs sun and well-drained soil. Propagate in autumn by seed or natural division of corms.
B. plicata. Spring-flowering corm. H 4–8in (10–20cm), S 2–3in (5–8cm). Zones 9–10. Has a fan of lance-shaped, erect, basal leaves and short spikes of funnel-shaped, violet-blue flowers, 1½–2in (4–5cm) long, with yellow-patched petals.
B. rubro-cyanea illus. p.360.
B. stricta. Spring-flowering corm. H 4–8in (10–20cm), S 2–3in (5–8cm). Zones 9–10. Has a fan of narrowly lance-shaped, erect, basal leaves and bears short spikes of up to 10 funnel-shaped, purple, blue, cream, or pale yellow flowers, 1–1½in (2.5–4cm) long and sometimes red-centered.

BACCHARIS (Compositae)
Genus of evergreen or deciduous, mainly autumn-flowering shrubs, grown for their foliage and fruits. Is useful for exposed, coastal gardens and dry soil. Fully hardy. Needs full sun and well-drained soil. Propagate by softwood cuttings in summer.
B. halimifolia (Groundsel bush). Vigorous, deciduous, bushy shrub. H and S 12ft (4m). Zones 5–10. Oval leaves are gray-green and sharply toothed. Has large clusters of minute, white flower heads in mid-autumn, then fluffy heads of tiny, white fruits.

BALDELLIA (Alismataceae)
Genus of deciduous or evergreen, perennial, bog plants and submerged water plants, grown for their foliage. Frost hardy. Prefers sun, but tolerates shade. Remove fading foliage regularly and excess growth as required. Propagate by division in spring or summer.
B. ranunculoides, syn. *Alisma ranunculoides, Echinodorus ranunculoides.* Deciduous, perennial, bog plant or submerged water plant. H 9in (23cm), S 6in (15cm). Zones 5–10. Has lance-shaped, green leaves and, in summer, umbels of small, 3-parted, pink or white flowers with basal, yellow marks.

BALLOTA (Labiatae)
Genus of perennials and evergreen or deciduous sub-shrubs, grown for their foliage and flowers. Frost hardy. Requires very well-drained soil and full sun. Cut back in spring before growth commences. Propagate by semi-ripe cuttings in summer.
B. acetabulosa illus. p.144.
B. pseudodictamnus illus. p.301.

BAMBUSA (Bambusoideae). See GRASSES, BAMBOOS, RUSHES, and SEDGES.

B. glaucescens. See *B. multiplex.*
B. multiplex, syn. *B. glaucescens,* illus. p.181.

BANKSIA (Proteaceae)
Genus of evergreen shrubs and trees, grown for their flowers, foliage, and overall appearance. Frost tender, min. 45–50°F (7–10°C). Requires full light and sharply drained, sandy soil that contains little phosphates or nitrates. Water potted plants moderately when in full growth, sparingly at other times. Plants grown under glass must be freely ventilated. Propagate by seed in spring.
B. baxteri. Evergreen, spreading, open shrub. H and S 6–10ft (2–3m). Zone 10. Leathery green leaves are strap-shaped, cut from the midrib into triangular, sharply pointed lobes. Produces dense, spherical heads of small, tubular, yellow flowers in summer.
B. coccinea illus. p.98.
B. ericifolia (Heath banksia). Evergreen, irregularly rounded, wiry, freely branching shrub. H and S to 10ft (3m). Zone 10. Has small, needlelike leaves and dense, upright, bottlebrushlike spikes, each 4–6in (10–15cm) long, of small, tubular, bronze-red or occasionally yellow flowers in late winter and spring.
B. serrata. Evergreen, bushy, upright shrub or tree. H 10–30ft (3–10m), S 5–10ft (1.5–3m). Zone 10. Oblong to lance-shaped, saw-toothed, leathery leaves are mid- to deep green. Small, tubular, cream flowers, reddish in bud, are produced in dense, upright, bottlebrushlike spikes, each 4–6in (10–15cm) long, from spring to late summer.

BAPTISIA (Leguminosae)
Genus of summer-flowering perennials, grown for their flowers. Fully hardy. Requires full sun and deep, well-drained, preferably neutral to acid soil. Is best not disturbed once planted. May be propagated by division in early spring or by seed in autumn.
B. australis illus. p.211.

Barbacenia elegans. See *Vellozia elegans.*

BARBAREA (Cruciferae)
Genus of summer-flowering perennials, biennials, and annuals. Most species are weeds or winter salad plants, but the variegated form of *B. vulgaris* is grown for decorative purposes. Fully hardy. Grows in sun or shade and in any well-drained but not very dry soil. Propagate by seed or division in spring.
B. vulgaris (Winter cress, Yellow rocket). **'Variegata'** illus. p.246.

BARLERIA (Acanthaceae)
Genus of evergreen shrubs and perennials, grown for their flowers.

Frost tender, min. 45–64°F (7–18°C). Needs full light or partial shade and fertile soil. Water potted plants well when in full growth, moderately at other times. In the growing season, prune tips of young plants to encourage branching. For a more compact habit, shorten long stems after flowering. Propagate by seed in spring or by greenwood or semi-ripe cuttings in summer.
B. cristata (Philippine violet). Evergreen, semi-erect shrub. H and S 2–4ft (60cm–1.2m). Min. 59–64°F (15–18°C), zone 10. Has elliptic, coarsely haired leaves. Tubular, light violet flowers, sometimes pale pink or white, are produced from upper leaf axils in summer.
B. obtusa. Evergreen, erect, spreading shrub. H and S to 3ft (1m). Min. 45–50°F (7–10°C), zone 10. Leaves are elliptic. Tubular, mauve flowers are borne from upper leaf axils in winter-spring.

Barosma pulchella. See *Agathosma pulchella.*

Bartonia aurea. See *Mentzelia lindleyi.*

BAUERA (Cunoniaceae, syn. Baueraceae)
Genus of evergreen shrubs, grown mainly for their flowers. Frost tender, min. 37–41°F (3–5°C). Needs full sun and humus-rich, well-drained, neutral to acid soil. Water potted specimens moderately, less when not in full growth. Remove straggly stems after plants have flowered. Propagate by seed in spring or by semi-ripe cuttings in late summer.
B. rubioides. Evergreen, bushy, wiry-stemmed shrub, usually of spreading habit. H and S 1–2ft (30–60cm). Zone 10. Leaves each have 3 oval to lance-shaped, glossy leaflets. Bowl-shaped, pink or white flowers appear in early spring and summer.

BAUHINIA (Leguminosae)
Genus of evergreen, semi-evergreen, or deciduous trees, shrubs, and scandent climbers, grown for their flowers. Frost tender, min. 41–64°F (5–18°C). Needs full light and fertile, well-drained soil. Water potted plants freely when in full growth, less in winter. Congested growth may be thinned out after flowering. Propagate by seed in spring.
B. galpinii. See *B. punctata.*
B. punctata, syn. *B. galpinii,* illus. p.110.
B. purpurea (Butterfly tree, Orchid tree). Mainly evergreen, spreading tree. H and S to 30ft (10m). Min. 41–5°F (5–7°C), zone 10. Has broadly oval, 2-lobed leaves and, in late autumn and winter, short, terminal sprays of fragrant, flattish, rose-purple to magenta flowers.

B. variegata (Buddhist bauhinia, Purple orchid tree) and **'Candida'** (White orchid tree) illus. p.69.

BEAUCARNEA (Agavaceae)
Genus of evergreen shrubs and trees, grown mainly for their intriguing, overall appearance. Frost tender, min. 45°F (7°C). Needs full light and sharply drained, fertile soil; drought conditions are tolerated. Water potted specimens moderately and allow compost almost to dry out between waterings. Propagate by seed or suckers in spring or by stem-tip cuttings in summer.
B. recurvata, syn. *Nolina recurvata, N. tuberculata,* illus. p.72.

BEAUMONTIA (Apocynaceae)
Genus of evergreen, woody-stemmed, twining climbers, grown for their large, fragrant flowers and handsome leaves. Frost tender, min. 45–50°F (7–10°C). Requires fertile, well-drained soil and full light. Water freely in the growing season, sparingly at other times. Provide support. Thin out previous season's growth after flowering. Propagate by semi-ripe cuttings in late summer.
B. grandiflora illus. p.163.

BEGONIA (Begoniaceae)
Genus of evergreen or deciduous shrubs and small, treelike plants, perennials, and annuals, grown for their colorful flowers and/or ornamental leaves. Prefers slightly acidic soil. Is susceptible to powdery mildew and botrytis from late spring to early autumn. Commonly cultivated begonias are divided into the following groups, each with varying cultivation requirements.

Cane-stemmed group
Evergreen, woody perennials, many known as "Angelwings," with usually erect, canelike stems bearing regularly spaced, swollen nodes and flowers in large, pendulous panicles. Encourage branching by pinching out growing tips. New growth develops from base of plant. Frost tender, min. 50°F (10°C). Grow under glass in good light but not direct sun (poor light reduces quantity of flowers) and in free-draining, loam-based compost. Stake tall plants. Propagate in spring by seed or tip cuttings.

Rex and rhizomatous group
Most of the Rex group are evergreen, rhizomatous begonias, though some have a tuberous character. Rex begonias are grown for their attractive foliage, while within the rhizomatous group flowers are also important. From horizontal (creeping) or erect rhizomes arise plain or crested, green or brown leaves, 1–12in (2.5–30cm) long, that are sometimes spirally twisted. Creeping rhizomatous types are more freely branched than erect ones and are

useful for hanging baskets. Unless otherwise stated, frost tender, min. 55–9°F (13–15°C), but preferably 64°F (18°C), with 40–75% relative humidity. Grow under glass in cool climates, in partial shade and in well-drained soil; water only sparingly. Do not allow water to remain on the leaves, otherwise they become susceptible to botrytis. Propagate in spring by seed, leaf cuttings, or division of rhizomes.

Semperflorens group
Evergreen, bushy perennials, often grown as half-hardy bedding annuals. Stems are soft, succulent, and branch freely, bearing generally rounded, green, bronze, or variegated leaves, 2in (5cm) long. Flowers are single or double. Pinch out growing tips to produce bushy plants. Frost tender, min. 55°F (13°C). Requires sun or partial shade and well-drained soil. Propagate in spring by seed or stem cuttings.

Shrublike group
Evergreen, multi-stemmed, bushy perennials, usually freely branched with flexible, erect, or pendent stems, often hairy. Leaves may be hairy or glabrous and up to 6in (15cm) across, 4–12in (10–30cm) long. Single flowers are pink, cream, or white. Frost tender, min. 45°F (7°C) with 55% relative humidity. Grow under glass in good light and moist but well-drained soil. Propagate in spring by seed or stem cuttings.

Tuberous group
Tuberous and semi-tuberous perennials, grown as annuals for their single flowers produced mainly in summer. Large-flowered, double types are known as *B.* x *tuberhybrida*. Most form bushy plants with leaves to 10in (25cm) long. Frost tender, min. 55°F (13°C). Outdoors, grow in dappled shade and moist conditions; under glass, plant in cool shade with 65–70% relative humidity. Tubers are dormant in winter. Start into growth in spring for mid-summer to early autumn flowering. Remove all buds until stems show at least 3 pairs of leaves; with large-flowered types allow only central male bud to flower, so remove flanking buds. Plants require staking. Propagate in spring by seed, stem or basal cuttings, or by division of tubers.

Winter-flowering group
Evergreen, low-growing, very compact perennials, with succulent, thin stems, that are often included in the tuberous group. Hiemalis types have single, semi-double, or double flowers in a wide color range; Cheimantha types differ in that flowers are single and white or pink; Rieger cultivars are improved Hiemalis types. Leaves are green or bronze, 2in (5cm) long. Flowers are borne mainly from late autumn to mid-spring. Frost tender, min. 64°F (18°C) with 40% relative humidity. Indirect sun and moist soil are preferred. Cut back old stems to 4in (10cm) after flowering. Propagate in spring by seed or stem cuttings.

B. albo-picta (illus. p.251). Fast-growing, evergreen, cane-stemmed begonia. H to 3ft (1m), S 1ft (30cm). Zone 10. Freely branched, green stems turn brown-green when mature. Narrowly oval to lance-shaped, wavy-edged, green leaves are silver-spotted. Has clusters of single, green-white flowers in summer-autumn.
B. angularis. See *B. stipulacea.*
B. 'Apricot Cascade'. See *B.* x *tuberhybrida.*
B. 'Beatrice Hadrell'. Evergreen, creeping, rhizomatous begonia. H 8–12in (20–30cm), S 10–12in (25–30cm). Zone 10. Oval leaves are deeply cleft, 3–6in (8–15cm) long, and dark green with paler veins. Produces single, pale pink flowers, above foliage, in early spring.
B. 'Bethlehem Star'. Evergreen, creeping, rhizomatous begonia. H 8–12in (20–30cm), S 10–12in (25–30cm). Zone 10. Oval, slightly indented, almost black leaves, less than 3in (8cm) long, each have a central, creamy green star. Bears masses of single, pale pink flowers, with darker pink spots, from late winter to early spring.
B. 'Billie Langdon'. See *B.* x *tuber-hybrida.*
B. 'Bokit'. See *B.* 'Bowkit'.
B. bowerae (Eyelash begonia; illus. p.251). Evergreen, creeping, rhizomatous begonia. H 10–12in (25–30cm), S 8–10in (20–25cm). Zone 10. Has 1in (2.5cm) long, oval, bright green leaves with chocolate brown marks and bristles around edges. Flowers, produced freely in winter, are single and white, tinted pink. 'Major' has larger leaves.
B. 'Bowkit', syn. *B.* 'Bokit'. Evergreen, erect, rhizomatous begonia. H 8–12in (20–30cm), S 10–14in (25–35cm). Zone 10. Has oval, spirally twisted, yellow-green leaves with brown tiger stripes. Bears masses of single, white flowers, flecked with pink, in winter.
B. 'Bridal Cascade'. See *B.* x *tuber-hybrida.*
B. 'Can-Can'. See *B.* x *tuberhybrida.*
B. x *cheimantha* 'Gloire de Lorraine' (Christmas begonia, Lorraine begonia). Evergreen, Cheimantha-type, winter-flowering begonia. H 12in (30cm), S 12–14in (30–35cm). Zone 10. Is well-branched with rounded, bright green leaves and single, white to pale pink flowers. Male flowers are sterile, female, highly infertile.
B. 'City of Ballarat'. See *B.* x *tuber-hybrida.*
B. coccinea (Angelwing begonia). Evergreen, cane-stemmed begonia. H 4ft (1.2m), S 1ft (30cm). Zone 10. Produces narrowly oval, glossy, green leaves, buff-colored beneath, and, in spring, profuse, single, pink or coral red flowers.
B. 'Cocktail'. See *B. semperflorens.*
B. 'Corallina de Lucerna'. See *B.* 'Lucerna'.
B. 'Crimson Cascade'. See *B.* x *tuber-hybrida.*
B. 'Curly Merry Christmas'. See *B. rex.*
B. dichroa. Evergreen, cane-stemmed begonia. H 14in (35cm), S 10in

(25cm). Zone 10. Oval leaves are green, 5in (12cm) long; occasionally new leaves bear silver spots. Produces small, single, orange flowers, each with a white ovary, in summer.
B. dregei (Mapleleaf begonia). Semi-tuberous begonia. H 30in (75cm), S 14in (35cm). Zone 10. Has small, maplelike, lobed, purple-veined, bronze leaves, with red beneath and occasionally silver-speckled when young. Profuse, pendent, single, white flowers are borne in summer. Needs winter resting period (not full dormancy).
B. 'Duartei'. See *B. rex.*
B. 'Erythrophylla', syn. *B.* 'Feastii'. Evergreen, creeping, rhizomatous begonia. H 8in (20cm), S 9–12in (23–30cm). Zone 10. Thick, green leaves, 3–6in (8–15cm) long, are almost rounded, with leaf stalks attached to center of red undersides; slightly wavy margins have white hairs. Produces single, light pink flowers well above foliage in early spring.
B. 'Feastii'. See *B.* 'Erythrophylla'.
B. 'Flamboyant'. See *B.* x *tuber-hybrida.*
B. foliosa (illus. p.251). Evergreen, shrublike begonia. H 12–20in (30–50cm), S 12–14in (30–35cm). Zone 10. Bears erect, then arching stems and oval, toothed, dark green leaves, 2in (1cm) long. Has very small, single, white flowers in spring and autumn. Is susceptible to whitefly.
var. *miniata* see *B. fuchsioides.*
B. fuchsioides, syn. *B. foliosa* var. *miniata* (Fuchsia begonia). Evergreen, shrublike begonia. H to 4ft (1.2m), S 1ft (30cm). Zone 10. Oval, toothed leaves are numerous and dark green, 1in (4cm) long. Pendent, single, bright red flowers are borne in winter.
B. 'Gold Cascade'. See *B.* x *tuber-hybrida.*
B. gracilis var. *martiana*, syn. *B. martiana.* Tuberous begonia. H 24–30in (60–75cm), S 16in (40cm). Zone 10. Small, oval to lance-shaped, lobed, pale green or brown-green leaves have tapering tips. Produces large, fragrant, single, pink flowers, 1in (2.5cm) across, in summer.
B. haageana. See *B. scharffii.*
B. 'Helen Lewis'. See *B. rex.*
B. 'Helene Harms'. See *B.* x *tuber-hybrida.*
B. x *hiemalis* 'Krefeld'. Evergreen, Rieger-type, winter-flowering begonia. H 10in (25cm), S 12in (30cm). Zone 10. Is semi-tuberous with succulent stems, oval, green leaves, and masses of single, vivid orange or bright crimson flowers. Is very susceptible to botrytis and mildew at base of stems, so water by pot immersion.
B. 'Ingramii' (illus. p.251). Evergreen, shrublike begonia. H 28in (70cm), S 18in (45cm). Zone 10. Produces elliptic, toothed, bright green leaves, 3in (8cm) long, and, intermittently from spring to autumn, masses of single, pink flowers on spreading branches.
B. 'Iron Cross'. See *B. masoniana.*
B. 'Lucerna', syn. *B.* 'Corallina de Lucerna' (illus. p.251). Vigorous, evergreen, cane-stemmed begonia. H

6–7ft (2–2.2m), S 1½–2ft (45–60cm). Zone 10. Has oval, silver-spotted, bronze-green leaves, 10–14in (25–35cm) long, with tapered tips and, year-round, large panicles of single, deep pink flowers; male flowers remain almost closed.
B. 'Mac's Gold'. Evergreen, creeping, rhizomatous begonia. H and S 8–10in (20–25cm). Zone 10. Star-shaped, lobed, yellow leaves, 3–6in (8–15cm) long, have chocolate brown marks. Has single, pink flowers intermittently during spring-summer but in moderate quantity.
B. 'Mme. Richard Galle'. See *B.* x *tuberhybrida.*
B. manicata (illus. p.251). Evergreen, erect, rhizomatous begonia. H 24in (60cm), S 12–16in (30–40cm). Zone 10. Bears large, oval, brown-mottled, green leaves and, below each leaf base, a collar of stiff, red hairs around leaf stalk. Produces single, pale pink flowers in very early spring. Propagate by plantlets during growing season. 'Crispa' (illus. p.251) has deeper pink flowers and light green leaves with crested margins.
B. martiana. See *B. gracilis* var. *martiana.*
B. masoniana, syn. *B.* 'Iron Cross' (Iron cross begonia; illus. p.251). Evergreen, creeping, rhizomatous begonia. H 18–24in (45–60cm), S 12–18in (30–45cm). Zone 10. Bears oval, toothed, rough, bright green leaves, 6in (15cm) long, with tapering tips and cross-shaped, black or dark brown centers. Has single, pink-flushed, white flowers during summer.
B. 'Masquerade'. See *B.* x *tuber-hybrida.*
B. mazae. Evergreen, trailing, rhizomatous begonia. H to 9in (23cm), S indefinite. Zone 10. Rounded leaves are bronze-green with red-brown veins. Has fragrant, single, pink flowers, with red spots, in early spring. Is good for a hanging basket.
B. 'Merry Christmas'. See *B. rex.*
B. metallica (Metal-leaf begonia; illus. p.251). Evergreen, shrublike begonia. H 20in–4ft (50cm–1.2m), S 18in (45cm). Zone 10. Bears white-haired stems and oval, toothed, silver-haired, bronze-green leaves, 7in (18cm) long, with dark green veins, red beneath. Has single, pink flowers, with red bristles, in summer-autumn.
B. 'Midas'. See *B.* x *tuberhybrida.*
B. 'Norah Bedson' (illus. p.251). Evergreen, creeping, rhizomatous begonia. H to 9in (23cm), S 10–12in (25–30cm). Zone 10. Produces rounded, bright green leaves, to 6in (15cm) long, with dark brown splashes, and single, pink flowers in early spring.
B. 'Oliver Twist' (illus. p.251). Evergreen, creeping, rhizomatous begonia. H 18–24in (45–60cm), S 10–18in (25–45cm). Zone 10. Oval leaves are pale to mid-green, to 12in (30cm) long, with heavily crested edges. Carries single, pink flowers in early spring.
B. olsoniae (illus. p.251). Evergreen, compact, shrublike begonia. H 9–12in (23–30cm), S 12in (30cm). Zone 10. Rounded, satiny, bronze-green leaves

have cream veins. Bears single, very pale pink flowers, year-round, on arching, 12in (30cm) long stems. Is suitable for a hanging basket.

B. 'Orange Cascade'. See *B. x tuberhybrida*.

B. 'Orange Rubra' (illus. p.251). Slow-growing, evergreen, cane-stemmed begonia. H 20in (50cm), S 18in (45cm). Zone 10. Oval leaves are light green. Produces abundant clusters of single, orange flowers throughout the year.

B. 'Organdy'. See *B. semperflorens*.

B. 'Orpha C. Fox' (illus. p.251). Evergreen, cane-stemmed begonia. H 3ft (1m), S 1ft (30cm). Zone 10. Oval, silver-spotted, olive green leaves, 6in (15cm) long, are maroon beneath. Produces large clusters of single, bright pink flowers year-round.

B. paulensis. Evergreen, creeping, rhizomatous begonia. H and S 10–12in (25–30cm). Zone 10. Erect stems bear rounded, green leaves, 6in (15cm) long, with "seersucker" surfaces criss-crossed with a spider's web of veins. Produces single, cream white flowers, with wine-colored hairs, in late spring.

B. 'Président Carnot'. Vigorous, evergreen, cane-stemmed begonia. H to 7ft (2.2m), S 1 1/2ft (45cm). Zone 10. Erect stems bear 11in (28cm) long, "angelwing," green leaves, with lighter spots. Produces large panicles of single, pink flowers, each 1 1/2in (4cm) across, year-round. Is less vigorous than *B.* 'Lucerna'.

B. 'Princess of Hanover'. See *B. rex*.

B. prismatocarpa (illus. p.251). Evergreen, creeping, rhizomatous begonia. H 6–8in (15–20cm), S 8–10in (20–25cm). Zone 10. Leaves are oval, lobed, light green, and less than 3in (8cm) long. Produces single, bright yellow flowers year-round. Needs 60–65% relative humidity.

B. pustulata. Evergreen, creeping, rhizomatous begonia. H 6–8in (15–20cm), S 8–10in (20–25cm). Zone 10. Bears oval, fine-haired, dark green leaves, with small blisters or pustules, and single, rose-pink flowers in summer. Prefers min. 72–5°F (22–4°C) and 70–75% relative humidity.

'Argentea' (syn. *B.* 'Silver'; illus. p.251) has silver-splashed leaves and creamy white flowers.

B. 'Red Ascot'. See *B. semperflorens*.

B. rex. Evergreen, creeping, rhizomatous begonia. H 12–16in (30–40cm), S 14in (35cm). Zone 10. Has 8–10in (20–25cm) long, heart-shaped, deep green leaves, with a lustrous, metallic sheen and purple-tinged edges, arising vertically from rhizome. Produces sparse, pale rose flowers in late winter and early spring. Is the parent of the following hybrids.

'Curly Merry Christmas' is a sport of *B.* 'Merry Christmas', but has spirally twisted leaves.

'Duartei' (illus. p.251), H and S 18–24in (45–60cm), has spirally twisted, red-haired, very dark green leaves, over 6in (15cm) long, with silver-gray streaks and almost black edges. Is difficult to grow to maturity.

'Helen Lewis' (illus. p.251), H and S 18–24in (45–60cm), has an erect rhizome and silky, deep royal purple

leaves, 6–8in (15–20cm) long, with silver bands. Slightly hairy, single, cream flowers are produced in early summer.

'Merry Christmas' (syn. *B. ruhrtal*; illus. p.251), H and S 10–12in (25–30cm), has satiny, red leaves, 6–8in (15–20cm) long, each with an outer, broad band of emerald green and a deep velvet red center, sometimes edged with gray.

'Princess of Hanover', H and S 10–12in (25–30cm), has spirally twisted, emerald leaves, 8in (20cm) long, with bands of silver edged with ruby red; entire leaf surfaces are covered with fine, pink hairs.

'Silver Helen Teupel', H and S 12–14in (30–35cm), has long, deeply cut, silver leaves, each with a glowing pink center, giving a feathered effect.

B. 'Roy Hartley'. See *B. x tuber-hybrida*.

B. ruhrtal. See *B.* 'Merry Christmas' (under *B. rex*).

B. scharffii, syn. *B. haageana* (illus. p.251). Evergreen, shrublike begonia. H 2–4ft (60cm–1.2m), S 2ft (60cm). Zone 10. Stems are often covered with white hairs. Has oval, fine-haired, dark metallic green leaves, 11in (28cm) long, with very tapered tips and reddish green undersides. Produces single, pinkish white flowers, each with a pink beard, from autumn to summer.

B. 'Scherzo'. Evergreen, creeping, rhizomatous begonia. H 10–12in (25–30cm), S 12–14in (30–35cm). Zone 10. Oval leaves are small, highly serrated, and yellow with black marks. Bears single, white flowers in early spring.

B. semperflorens. Slow-growing, evergreen begonia. H 12in (30cm), S 10in (25cm). Zone 10. Has fleshy, freely branched, green stems and rounded, fleshy, dark green leaves, 3in (8cm) long, with light green undersides. Leaf axils each bear a small, single, pink flower, sometimes with a white center, year-round, but especially in summer. Is the parent of the following hybrids.

'Cocktail', H and S 8–12in (20–30cm), has rounded, waxy, bronze leaves and pink, red, or white flowers from summer until autumn frosts.

'Organdy' (illus. p.251), H and S 6in (15cm), has rounded, waxy, green-bronze leaves and pink, red, or white flowers throughout summer until autumn frosts.

'Red Ascot' (illus. p.251), H and S 6in (15cm), has rounded, emerald green leaves and masses of crimson-red flowers in summer.

B. serratipetala (illus. p.251). Evergreen, trailing, shrublike begonia. H and S 18in (45cm). Zone 10. Has obliquely oval leaves that are highly serrated and bronze-green, with raised, deep pink spots. Produces mostly female, single, deep pink flowers intermittently throughout the year. Prefers 60% relative humidity, but with fairly dry roots.

B. 'Silver'. See *B. pustulata*.

B. 'Silver Helen Teupel'. See *B. rex*.

B. stipulacea, syn. *B. angularis*, *B. zebrina*. Evergreen, cane-stemmed

begonia. H 2–4ft (60cm–1.2m), S 1ft (30cm). Zone 10. Bears well-branched, angular stems and oval, wavy-edged, 8in (20cm) long, gray-green leaves, with silver-gray veins, pale green beneath. Carries single, white flowers in winter-spring.

B. sutherlandii (illus. p.251). Trailing, tuberous begonia. H 3ft (1m), S indefinite. Zone 10. Slender stems carry small, lance-shaped, lobed, bright green leaves, with red veins, and, in summer, loose clusters of single, orange flowers in profusion. Makes an excellent hanging-basket plant. Is particularly susceptible to mildew.

B. 'Thurstonii' (illus. p.251). Evergreen, shrublike begonia. H to 4ft (1.2m), S 1 1/2ft (45cm). Zone 10. Has rounded to oval, smooth, glossy, bronze-green leaves, with dark red veins, and, in summer, single, pink flowers.

B. x tuberhybrida. Group of large-flowered, double, tuberous begonias. H and S 30in (75cm). Zone 10. Bears male flowers, each of more than 4in (10cm) diameter, singly on stiff, succulent flower stems, from early summer to mid-autumn. Each flower resembles a double camellia flower or has a rose-bud center. Oval leaves are green, 8in (20cm) long. Multiflora cultivars, H and S 12in (30cm), are more bushy and have 3in (8cm) long leaves and single, semi-double, or double, male flowers, each 1 1/2–2in (4–5cm) across, in summer; tolerates full sun. Pendula cultivars, H to 3ft (1m), have long, thin, trailing stems; leaves are 2 1/2–3in (6–8cm) long. Masses of single or double flowers are borne in summer.

'Apricot Cascade' (Pendula group; illus. p.251) bears emerald green leaves and double, orange-apricot flowers. Other cascades are 'Bridal Cascade' (pink-edged petals), 'Crimson Cascade', 'Gold Cascade', and 'Orange Cascade'.

'Billie Langdon' (illus. p.251) has masses of heavily veined, double, white flowers, each 7in (18cm) across, with a perfect rose-bud center.

'Can-Can' (illus. p.251), H 3ft (1m), has double, yellow flowers, each 8in (20cm) wide, with rough-edged, red petals. Produces few side shoots.

'City of Ballarat' carries double, glowing orange flowers, each 7in (18cm) across, with broad petals and a formal center. Leaves are rich dark green.

'Flamboyant' (Multiflora group; illus. p.251) produces single, scarlet flowers in profusion. Leaves are slender and bright green.

'Helene Harms' (Multiflora group) has numerous semi-double, canary yellow flowers. Is excellent in a hanging basket.

'Mme. Richard Galle' (Multiflora group), H 12–18in (30–45cm), produces masses of small, double, soft apricot flowers.

'Masquerade', S to 3ft (1m), has double, white flowers, each 6in (15cm) across, with crinkled, red edges to broad petals. Makes an excellent pot plant, being prolific with side shoots.

'Midas' bears double, pale golden yellow flowers, each 6in (15cm) across, with broad petals. Is particularly susceptible to mildew. Early flowers sometimes develop leaflike petals.

'Roy Hartley' (illus. p.251) produces double, salmon-colored flowers, tinged with soft pink. Depth of color is very dependent on light intensity. Has few side-shoots. Is one of the best cultivars.

B. versicolor. Evergreen, creeping, rhizomatous begonia. H to 12in (30cm), S 6in (15cm). Zone 10. Produces broadly oval or oblong, velvety leaves, 3in (8cm) long, in shades of mahogany, apple green, and maroon, and, in spring-summer, single, salmon pink flowers. Provide min. 61–6°F (16–19°C) with 65–70% relative humidity.

B. x weltoniensis (Mapleleaf begonia; illus. p.251). Semi-tuberous begonia with a shrublike habit. H 12–20in (30–50cm), S 12in (30cm). Zone 10. Has small, oval, long-pointed, toothed, dark green leaves. Heads of 5–8 single, pink or white flowers appear from leaf axils in summer.

B. xanthina. Evergreen, bushy, creeping, rhizomatous begonia. H 10–12in (25–30cm), S 12–14in (30–35cm). Zone 10. Bears oval, dark green leaves, 6–9in (15–23cm) long, with yellow veins, purple and hairy beneath. Pendent, single, orange-yellow flowers are borne in summer. Provide min. 70–75°F (21–4°C) with 75% relative humidity. var. *pictifolia* has pale yellow flowers and silver-zoned leaves.

B. zebrina. See *B. stipulacea*.

BELAMCANDA (Iridaceae)
Genus of summer-flowering bulbs, grown for their irislike flowers. Frost hardy, but protect in cold winters. Needs sun and well-drained soil with added humus. Propagate by seed in spring.

B. chinensis. Summer-flowering bulb. H 1 1/2–3ft (45cm–1m), S 6–10in (15–25cm). Zones 5–10. Carries a fan of sword-shaped, semi-erect leaves. A loosely branched stem bears a succession of flattish, orange-red flowers, 1 1/2–2in (4–5cm) across, with darker blotches. Seeds are shiny and black.

BELLEVALIA (Liliaceae)
Genus of spring-flowering bulbs, similar to *Muscari*, but with longer, more tubular flowers. Some species have ornamental value, but most are uninteresting horticulturally. Frost hardy. Needs an open, sunny position and well-drained soil that dries out in summer. Propagate by seed, preferably in autumn.

B. hyacinthoides, syn. *Strangweia spicata*, illus. p.361.

B. pycnantha, syn. *Muscari paradoxum, M. pycnantha*. Spring-flowering bulb. H to 16in (40cm), S 2–3in (5–8cm). Zones 7–9. Has strap-shaped, semi-erect, basal, grayish green leaves. Tubular, deep dusky blue flowers, 1/4in (0.5cm) long and with yellow tips, are produced in a dense, conical spike.

BELLIS (Compositae)
Daisy
Genus of perennials, some grown as
biennials. Fully hardy to frost tender,
min. 36–9°F (2–4°C). Grow in sun or
semi-shade and in fertile, very well-
drained soil. Dead-head regularly.
Propagate by seed in early summer
or by division after flowering.
B. perennis (English daisy). Slow-
growing, carpeting perennial. Cultivars
are grown as biennials. H and S 6–8in
(15–20cm). Frost tender. All have
oval, green leaves and fully double
flower heads in spring. Large-flowered
(flower heads to 3in (8cm) wide) and
miniature-flowered (flower heads to
1in (2.5cm) wide) cultivars are
available. **Carpet Series** (large-
flowered), H and S 6in (15cm), which
is compact, and **'Goliath'** (large-
flowered), H 8in (20cm), are both
available in a mixture of red, pink,
and white. **'Pomponette'** (miniature-
flowered) illus. p.271. **'White Carpet'**
(large-flowered), H and S 6in (15cm),
is a compact, white-flowered cultivar.

Beloperone guttata. See *Justicia
brandegeana.*

BERBERIDOPSIS (Flacourtiaceae)
Genus of one species of evergreen,
woody-stemmed, twining climber.
Frost hardy. Dislikes strong winds and
strong sun and is best grown in a north
or west aspect. Soil, preferably lime-
free, should be well-drained. Cut out
dead growth in spring; train to required
shape. Propagate by seed in spring or
by stem cuttings or layering in late
summer or autumn.
B. corallina illus. p.169.

BERBERIS (Berberidaceae)
Barberry
Genus of deciduous, semi-evergreen,
or evergreen, spiny shrubs, grown
mainly for their rounded to cup-shaped
flowers, with usually yellow sepals
and petals, and for their fruits. The
evergreens are also cultivated for their
leaves, the deciduous shrubs for their
colorful autumn foliage. Fully to frost
hardy. Requires sun or semi-shade and
any but waterlogged soil. Propagate
species by seed in autumn, deciduous
hybrids and cultivars by softwood
or semi-ripe cuttings in summer,
evergreen hybrids and cultivars by
semi-ripe cuttings in summer.
B. aggregata. Deciduous, bushy shrub.
H and S 5ft (1.5m). Fully hardy, zones
6–9. Oblong to oval, green leaves
redden in autumn. Has dense clusters
of pale yellow flowers in late spring or
early summer, followed by egg-shaped,
white-bloomed, red fruits.
B. **'Barbarossa'** illus. p.116.
B. buxifolia (Magellan barberry).
Semi-evergreen or deciduous, arching
shrub. H 8ft (2.5m), S 10ft (3m). Fully
hardy, zones 6–9. Has oblong to oval,
spine-tipped, leathery, dark green
leaves. Deep orange-yellow flowers
appear from early to mid-spring and
are followed by spherical, black fruits
with a white bloom.
B. calliantha. Evergreen, bushy shrub.
H and S 3–5ft (1–1.5m). Fully hardy,
zones 7–9. Has oblong, sharply spiny,

glossy, green leaves, white beneath,
and large, pale yellow flowers in late
spring, followed by egg-shaped, black
fruits with a white bloom.
B. candidula (Paleleaf barberry).
Evergreen, bushy, compact shrub.
H and S 3ft (1m). Fully hardy, zones
6–9. Leaves are narrowly oblong,
glossy, dark green, white beneath.
Bright yellow flowers in late spring
are followed by egg-shaped, blue-
purple fruits.
B. x *carminea* **'Pirate King'.**
Deciduous, arching shrub. H 6ft (2m),
S 10ft (3m). Fully hardy, zones 6–9.
Produces oblong, dark green leaves
and, in late spring and early summer,
clusters of yellow flowers. Bears a
profusion of spherical, pale red fruits.
B. **'Chenaultii'** (Chenault barberry).
Evergreen, bushy shrub. H 5ft (1.5m),
S 6ft (2m). Fully hardy, zones 5–8.
Narrowly oblong, wavy-edged, glossy,
dark green leaves set off golden yellow
flowers in late spring and early
summer. Bears egg-shaped, blue-
black fruits.
B. coxii. Evergreen, bushy, dense
shrub. H 6ft (2m), S 10ft (3m). Fully
hardy, zones 7–9. Produces narrowly
oval, glossy, dark green leaves with
white undersides and, in late spring,
bears yellow flowers that are followed
by egg-shaped, blue-black fruits with
a gray-blue bloom.
B. darwinii illus. p.86.
B. empetrifolia illus. p.125.
B. gagnepainii illus. p.99.
B. jamesiana. Vigorous, deciduous,
arching shrub. H and S 12ft (4m).
Fully hardy, zones 7–9. Yellow
flowers in late spring are followed
by pendent racemes of spherical, red
berries. Oval, dark green leaves redden
in autumn.
B. julianae illus. p.102.
B. linearifolia **'Orange King'** illus.
p.103.
B. x *lologensis.* Vigorous, evergreen,
arching shrub. H 10ft (3m), S 15ft
(5m). Fully hardy, zones 6–9. Has
broadly oblong, glossy, dark green
leaves. Profuse clusters of orange
flowers are borne from mid- to late
spring. **'Stapehill'** illus. p.103.
B. x *ottawensis* **'Superba'**, syn.
B. x *o.* 'Purpurea'. Deciduous, arching
shrub. H and S 8ft (2.5m). Fully hardy,
zones 5–9. Produces rounded to oval,
deep reddish purple leaves. Bears
small, red-tinged, yellow flowers in
late spring, then egg-shaped, red fruits
in autumn.
B. **'Parkjuwel'.** Semi-evergreen,
bushy, rounded shrub. H and S 3ft
(1m). Fully hardy, zones 6–9. Leaves
are oval, glossy, and bright green;
some become red in autumn. Flowers
are of little value.
B. prattii. Deciduous, bushy shrub. H
and S 10ft (3m). Fully hardy, zones
6–9. Has oblong, glossy, dark green
leaves. Large clusters of small, yellow
flowers in late summer are followed
by a profusion of long-lasting, egg-
shaped, coral pink fruits.
B. **'Rubrostilla'** illus. p.140.
B. sargentiana. Evergreen, bushy
shrub. H and S 6ft (2m). Fully hardy,
zones 7–9. Leaves are oblong, glossy,
bright green. Yellow flowers in late

spring and early summer are succeeded
by egg-shaped, blue-black fruits.
B. x *stenophylla* illus. p.103.
'Corallina Compacta' illus. p.290.
B. thunbergii. Deciduous, arching,
dense shrub. H 6ft (2m), S 10ft (3m).
Fully hardy, zones 5–9. Broadly oval,
pale to mid-green leaves turn brilliant
orange-red in autumn. Small, red-
tinged, pale yellow flowers appear in
mid-spring, followed by egg-shaped,
bright red fruits. f. *atropurpurea* illus.
p.99. **'Atropurpurea Nana'** (syn.
B.t. 'Crimson Pygmy'), H and S 24in
(60cm), bears reddish purple foliage.
'Aurea' illus. p.138. Upright branches
of **'Erecta'** spread with age. **'Rose
Glow'** has reddish purple leaves
marbled with pink and white.
B. verruculosa illus. p.102.
B. wilsoniae. Deciduous or semi-
evergreen, bushy shrub. H 3ft (1m),
S 5ft (1.5m). Fully hardy, zones 6–9.
Narrowly oblong, gray-green leaves
become bright orange-red in autumn.
Produces yellow flowers in late spring
and early summer, then masses of
showy, spherical, coral red fruits.

BERCHEMIA (Rhamnaceae)
Genus of deciduous, twining climbers,
grown for their leaves and fruit. Is
useful for covering walls, fences, and
tree stumps. Fully hardy. Grow in sun
or shade, in any well-drained soil.
Propagate by seed in autumn or spring,
by semi-ripe cuttings in summer, or by
layering or root cuttings in winter.
B. racemosa **'Variegata'.** Deciduous,
twining climber. H 15ft (5m) or more.
Zones 6–9. Has heart-shaped, green
leaves, 1¼–3in (3–8cm) long and paler
beneath, that are variegated creamy
white, especially towards ends of
shoots. Clusters of small, bell-shaped,
greenish white flowers in summer are
followed by rounded, green fruits that
turn red, then black in autumn.

BERGENIA, syn. MEGASEA
(Saxifragaceae)
Genus of evergreen perennials with
thick, usually large, rounded to oval
or spoon-shaped, leathery leaves, with
indented veins, that make ideal ground
cover. Fully to frost hardy. Tolerates
sun or shade and any well-drained soil,
but leaf color is best on poor soil and
in full sun. Propagate by division in
spring after flowering.
B. **'Abendglut'**, syn. *B.* 'Evening
Glow'. Evergreen, clump-forming
perennial. H 9in (23cm), S 12in
(30cm). Fully hardy, zones 3–8.
Produces rosettes of oval, crinkled,
short-stemmed, maroon leaves, from
which arise racemes of open cup-
shaped, semi-double, deep magenta
flowers in spring.
B. **'Ballawley'.** Evergreen, clump-
forming perennial. H and S 24in
(60cm). Fully hardy, zones 3–8. Large,
rounded to oval, flat, deep green leaves
turn deep red in winter. Racemes of
cup-shaped, bright crimson flowers
are produced on red stems in spring.
Needs shelter from cold winds.
B. ciliata illus. p.226.
B. cordifolia. Evergreen, clump-
forming perennial. H 18in (45cm), S
24in (60cm). Fully hardy, zones 3–8.

Leaves are rounded, puckered, and
crinkle-edged. Produces racemes of
open cup-shaped, light pink flowers
in spring. **'Purpurea'** illus. p.226.
B. crassifolia. Evergreen, clump-
forming perennial. H 12in (30cm), S
18in (45cm). Fully hardy, zones 3–8.
Has oval or spoon-shaped, fleshy, flat
leaves that turn mahogany in winter.
Bears spikes of open, cup-shaped,
lavender pink flowers in spring.
B. **'Evening Glow'.** See
B. 'Abendglut'.
B. **'Morgenröte'.** Evergreen, clump-
forming perennial. H 18in (45cm), S
12in (30cm). Fully hardy, zones 3–8.
Leaves are rounded, crinkled, and deep
green. Spikes of open cup-shaped,
deep carmine flowers in spring are
often followed by a second crop in
summer.
B. purpurascens. Evergreen, clump-
forming perennial. H 18in (45cm), S
12in (30cm). Fully hardy, zones 3–8.
Oval to spoon-shaped, flat, dark green
leaves turn beetroot red in late autumn.
In spring bears racemes of open cup-
shaped, rich red flowers.
B. x *schmidtii.* Evergreen, clump-
forming perennial. H 12in (30cm), S
24in (60cm). Fully hardy, zones 4–8.
Oval, flat leaves have toothed margins.
Sprays of open cup-shaped, soft pink
flowers are borne in early spring on
short stems.
B. **'Silberlicht'**, syn. *B.* 'Silver Light',
illus. p.225.
B. **'Silver Light'.** See *B.* 'Silberlicht'.
B. stracheyi. Evergreen, clump-
forming perennial. H 9in (23cm), S
12in (30cm). Fully hardy, zones 4–8.
Small, rounded, flat leaves form neat
rosettes, among which nestle branched
heads of open cup-shaped, white or
pink flowers in spring.
B. **'Sunningdale'.** Evergreen, clump-
forming perennial. H 24in (60cm),
S 12in (30cm). Fully hardy, zones
3–8. Rounded, slightly crinkled, deep
green leaves are mahogany beneath.
Bears racemes of open cup-shaped,
lilac-carmine flowers on red stalks
in spring.

BERKHEYA (Compositae)
Genus of summer-flowering
perennials. Frost to half hardy, but,
except in mild areas, grow most
species against a south- or west-facing
wall. Requires full sun and fertile,
well-drained soil. Propagate by
division in spring or by seed in
autumn.
B. macrocephala illus. p.215.

BERTOLONIA (Melastomataceae)
Genus of evergreen perennials, grown
mainly for their foliage. Frost tender,
min. 59°F (15°C) but preferably
warmer. Requires a fairly shaded
position and high humidity, although
soil should not be waterlogged.
Propagate by tip or leaf cuttings in
spring or summer.
B. marmorata. Evergreen, rosette-
forming perennial. H 6in (15cm) or
more in flower, S 18in (45cm). Zone
10. Broadly oval, slightly fleshy leaves
have heart-shaped bases, silvery
midribs, and puckered surfaces, and are
reddish purple below, velvety green

above. Intermittently bears spikes of saucer-shaped, pinkish purple flowers.

BERZELIA (Bruniaceae)
Genus of evergreen, heatherlike, summer-flowering shrubs, grown for their flowers. Frost tender, min. 45°F (7°C). Requires full sun and well-drained, neutral to acid soil. Water potted plants moderately, less when not in full growth. Plants may be cut back lightly after flowering. Propagate by seed in spring or by semi-ripe cuttings in late summer.
B. lanuginosa. Evergreen, erect shrub with soft-haired, young shoots. H and S to 3ft (1m). Zone 10. Has small, heatherlike leaves. Compact, spherical heads of tiny, creamy white flowers are carried in dense, terminal clusters in summer.

BESCHORNERIA (Agavaceae)
Genus of perennial succulents with narrowly lance-shaped leaves forming erect, almost stemless, basal rosettes. Half hardy. Needs full sun and very well-drained soil. Propagate by seed or division in spring or summer.
B. yuccoides illus. p.386.

BESSERA (Liliaceae)
Genus of summer-flowering bulbs, grown for their striking, brightly colored flowers. Half hardy. Needs an open, sunny situation and well-drained soil. Propagate by seed in spring.
B. elegans (Coral-drops). Summer-flowering bulb. H to 24in (60cm), S 3–4in (8–10cm). Zones 9–10. Bears long, narrow, erect, basal leaves and slender, leafless stems, each producing a loose head of pendent, widely bell-shaped, bright red flowers on long, slender stalks.

Betonica officinalis. See *Stachys officinalis.*

BETULA (Betulaceae)
Birch
Genus of deciduous trees and shrubs, grown for their bark and autumn color. Fully hardy. Plant in a sunny position and in any moist but well-drained soil; some species prefer acid soil. Young trees should be transplanted in autumn. Propagate by grafting in late winter or by softwood cuttings in early summer.
B. albo-sinensis illus. p.48.
B. alleghaniensis, syn. *B. lutea* (Yellow birch). Deciduous, upright, open tree, often multi-stemmed. H 40ft (12m) or more, S 10ft (3m). Zones 4–7. Smooth, glossy, amber or golden brown bark peels in thin shreds. Oval, mid- to pale green leaves rapidly turn gold in autumn. Bears yellow-green catkins in spring.
B. ermanii illus. p.46.
B. 'Jermyns'. Deciduous, upright, open tree. H 50ft (15m), S 30ft (10m). Zones 4–7. Has peeling, bright white bark, which is particularly striking in winter, and long, elegant, yellow, male catkins in spring. Oval, green leaves have serrated edges.
B. lutea. See *B. alleghaniensis.*
B. maximowicziana (Monarch birch). Fast-growing, deciduous, broad-headed tree. H 60ft (18m), S 10ft (3m).

Zones 6–8. Has orange-brown or pink bark that does not peel and racemes of pendulous, yellowish catkins in spring. Large, oval, green leaves turn bright butter yellow in autumn.
B. nana illus. p.289.
B. papyrifera illus. p.46.
B. pendula (Silver birch). Deciduous, broadly columnar or conical, graceful tree. H 70ft (20m) or more, S 30ft (10m). Zones 3–8. Has slender, drooping shoots and silver-white bark that becomes black and rugged at base of trunk with age. Yellow-green catkins appear in spring. Oval, bright green leaves turn yellow in autumn. **'Dalecarlica'** illus. p.47. **'Tristis'** has a narrow crown. **'Youngii'** illus. p.65.
B. szechuanica (Szechuan birch). Vigorous, deciduous, open tree with stiff branches. H 46ft (14m), S 8ft (2.5m). Zones 6–8. Bark is strikingly chalky white when mature. Has triangular to oval, serrated, leathery, deep green leaves that turn brilliant gold in autumn. Bears yellow-green catkins in spring.
B. utilis (Himalayan birch). Deciduous, upright, open tree. H 60ft (18m), S 8ft (2.5m). Zones 6–8. Paper-thin, peeling bark is creamy white or dark copper brown. Yellow-brown catkins are borne in spring. Oval, green leaves, hairy beneath when young, turn golden yellow in autumn. var. *jacquemontii* illus. p.56.

BIARUM (Araceae)
Genus of mainly autumn-flowering, tuberous perennials with tiny flowers carried on a pencil-shaped spadix, enclosed within a tubular spathe. Upper part of spathe is hooded or flattened out and showy. Frost hardy, but during cold, wet winters protect in a cold frame or greenhouse. Needs a sunny position and well-drained soil. Dry out tubers when dormant in summer. Propagate in autumn by seed or offsets.
B. eximium. Early autumn-flowering, tuberous perennial. H and S 3–4in (8–10cm). Zones 7–9. Lance-shaped, semi-erect, basal leaves follow stemless, tubular, velvety, blackish maroon spathe, up to 6in (15cm) long and often lying flat on ground. Upper part is flattened out. Spadix is upright and black.
B. tenuifolium illus. p.368.

Bidens atrosanguinea. See *Cosmos atrosanguineus.*

BIFRENARIA. See ORCHIDS.
B. harrisoniae. Evergreen, epiphytic orchid for a cool greenhouse. H 4in (10cm). Zone 10. Fragrant, rounded, creamy white flowers, 3in (8cm) across, each with a hairy, reddish purple lip, are borne in spring-summer, 1 or 2 to a stem. Leaves are broadly oval, semi-rigid, and 6in (15cm) long. Provide semi-shade in summer.

BIGNONIA (Bignoniaceae)
Genus of one species of evergreen, tendril climber. Frost hardy; in cool areas may lose its leaves in winter. Needs sun and fertile soil to flower well. If necessary, prune in spring.

Propagate by stem cuttings in summer or autumn or by layering in winter.
B. capensis. See *Tecomaria capensis.*
B. capreolata, syn. *Doxantha capreolata* (Cross vine, Trumpet flower). Evergreen, tendril climber. H 30ft (10m) or more. Zones 6–10. Each leaf has 2 narrowly oblong leaflets and a branched tendril. In summer, funnel-shaped, reddish orange flowers appear in clusters in leaf axils. Pea-pod-shaped fruits, to 6in (15cm) long, are produced in autumn.
B. grandiflora. See *Campsis grandiflora.*
B. jasminoides. See *Pandorea jasminoides.*
B. pandorana. See *Pandorea pandorana.*
B. radicans. See *Campsis radicans.*
B. stans. See *Tecoma stans.*

Bilderdykia aubertii. See *Polygonum aubertii.*
Bilderdykia baldschuanica. See *Polygonum baldschuanicum.*

BILLARDIERA (Pittosporaceae)
Genus of evergreen, woody-stemmed, twining climbers, grown mainly for their fruits. Half hardy. Grow in any well-drained soil, in a sheltered position and partial shade. Propagate by seed in spring or stem cuttings in summer or autumn.
B. longiflora illus. p.176.

BILLBERGIA (Bromeliaceae)
Genus of evergreen, rosette-forming perennials, grown for their flowers and foliage. Frost tender, min. 41–5°F (5–7°C). Requires semi-shade and well-drained soil, ideally with the addition of sphagnum moss or plastic chips used for orchid culture. Water moderately when in full growth, sparingly at other times. Propagate by division or offsets after flowering or in late spring.
B. nutans (Queen's tears; illus. p.222). Evergreen, clump-forming, tubular-rosetted perennial. H and S to 16in (40cm). Zone 10. Strap-shaped leaves are usually dark green. In spring bears pendent clusters of tubular, purple-blue-edged, lime green flowers that emerge from pink bracts.
B. rhodocyanea. See *Aechmea fasciata.*
B. x windii (Angel's tears). Evergreen, clump-forming, tubular-rosetted perennial. H and S to 16in (40cm). Zone 10. Is similar to *B. nutans,* but has broader, spreading, gray-green leaves and larger bracts. Flowers intermittently from spring to autumn.

Biota orientalis. See *Thuja orientalis.*

BLECHNUM (Polypodiaceae)
Genus of evergreen or semi-evergreen ferns. Fully hardy to frost tender, min. 41°F (5°C). Most species prefer semi-shade. Requires moist, neutral to acid soil. Remove fading fronds regularly. Propagate *B. penna-marina* by division in spring, other species by spores in late summer.
B. capense illus. p.184.
B. magellanicum. See *B. tabulare.*
B. penna-marina. Fast-growing,

evergreen or semi-evergreen, carpeting fern. H 6–12in (15–30cm), S 12–18in (30–45cm). Frost hardy, zones 6–9. Has linear, dark green fronds, the outermost sterile, narrow, indented, and spreading, those at center fertile, short, and upright. Is suitable for a rock or peat garden.
B. spicant (Hard fern). Evergreen fern. H 12–30in (30–75cm), S 12–18in (30–45cm). Fully hardy, zones 4–8. Has narrowly lance-shaped, indented, leathery, spreading, dark green fronds. Prefers shade and peaty or leafy soil.
B. tabulare, syn. *B. magellanicum.* Evergreen or semi-evergreen fern. H 1–3ft (30cm–1m), S 1–2ft (30–60cm). Half hardy, zones 8–9. Outer, green sterile fronds are broadly lance-shaped, heavily indented, and arranged symmetrically. Inner fertile fronds are brown and fringed.

BLETILLA. See ORCHIDS.
B. striata (illus. p.253). Deciduous, terrestrial orchid. H to 24in (60cm). Half hardy, zones 5–8. In late spring or early summer produces loose spikes of magenta or white flowers, 1¼in (3cm) long. Has broadly lance-shaped leaves, 20in (50cm) long. Needs shade in summer.

BLOOMERIA (Liliaceae)
Genus of onionlike, spring-flowering bulbs, with spherical flower heads on leafless stems, which die down in summer. Frost hardy. Needs a sheltered, sunny situation and well-drained soil. Propagate by seed in autumn or by division in late summer or autumn.
B. crocea. Late spring-flowering bulb. H to 12in (30cm), S to 4in (10cm). Zones 8–9. Long, narrow, semi-erect, basal leaves die away at flowering time. Each leafless stem carries a loose, spherical head, 4–6in (10–15cm) across, of star-shaped, yellow flowers with dark stripes.

Bocconia cordata. See *Macleaya cordata.*

BOENNINGHAUSENIA (Rutaceae)
Genus of one species of deciduous sub-shrub, usually with soft, herbaceous stems and grown for its foliage and flowers. Frost hardy, although cut to ground level in winter. Requires full sun and fertile, well-drained but not too dry soil. Propagate by softwood cuttings in summer or by seed in autumn.
B. albiflora. Deciduous, bushy sub-shrub. H and S 3ft (1m). Zones 7–10. Has pungent, green leaves, divided into oval leaflets, and loose panicles of small, cup-shaped, white flowers from mid-summer to early autumn.

BOLAX (Hydrocotylaceae)
Genus of evergreen, hummock- and cushion-forming perennials, often included in *Azorella.* Is grown for its small, thick, tough leaves in symmetrical rosettes. Flowers are produced only rarely in cultivation. Is suitable for gritty screes, troughs, and alpine houses. Fully hardy. Needs sun and humus-rich, well-drained soil.

Propagate by rooting leaf rosettes in summer.
B. glebaria of gardens. See *Azorella trifurcata*.
B. gummifera illus. p.331.

BOMAREA (Alstroemeriaceae)
Genus of herbaceous or evergreen, tuberous-rooted, scrambling and twining climbers, grown for their tubular or bell-shaped flowers. Half hardy to frost tender, min. 41°F (5°C). Grow in any well-drained soil and in full light. Water regularly in growing season, sparingly when dormant. Provide support. Cut out old flowering stems at ground level when leaves turn yellow. Propagate by seed or division in early spring.
B. andimarcana, syn. *B. pubigera*. Evergreen, scrambling climber with straight, slender stems. H 6–10ft (2–3m). Frost tender, zones 9–10. Has lance-shaped leaves, white and hairy beneath. Produces nodding, tubular, green-tipped, pale yellow flowers, suffused pink, from early summer to autumn.
B. caldasii, syn. *B. kalbreyeri* of gardens, illus. p.175.
B. kalbreyeri of gardens. See *B. caldasii*.
B. pubigera. See *B. andimarcana*.

BORAGO (Boraginaceae)
Borage
Genus of annuals and perennials, grown for culinary use as well as for their flowers. Fully hardy. Requires sun and fertile, well-drained soil. For culinary use gather only young leaves. Propagate by seed sown outdoors in spring. Some species will self seed prolifically and may become a nuisance.
B. officinalis illus. p.278.

BORONIA (Rutaceae)
Genus of evergreen shrubs, grown primarily for their flowers. Frost tender, min. 45–50°F (7–10°C). Requires full light and sandy, neutral to acid soil. Water potted specimens moderately, less when not in full growth. To maintain a compact habit, long stems may be shortened after flowering. Propagate by seed in spring or by semi-ripe cuttings in late summer. Red spider mite may be a problem.
B. elatior. Evergreen, bushy, slender-stemmed shrub. H and S 3–5ft (1–1.5m). Zones 9–10. Leaves are divided into 5–13 linear leaflets. In spring, upper leaf axils produce almost spherical, 4-petaled, carmine red or yellow flowers.
B. megastigma illus. p.124.

BORZICACTUS (Cactaceae)
Genus of perennial cacti, grown for their lop-sided flowers and dry, splitting seed pods. Frost tender, min. 50°F (10°C); stem produces orange spots if kept below this temperature. Needs full sun and very well-drained soil. Propagate by seed in spring or summer.
B. aurantiacus, syn. *Submatucana aurantiaca*, illus. p.400.
B. celsianus, syn. *Oreocereus celsianus*, illus. p.383.

B. haynei, syn. *Matucana haynei*. Slow-growing, spherical to columnar, perennial cactus. H 24in (60cm), S 4in (10cm). Zone 10. Has a cylindrical, much-ribbed, green stem densely covered with short, white spines. Tubular, pinkish or orange-red flowers appear in summer from stem crown, only on plants over 6in (15cm) high.
B. trollii, syn. *Oreocereus trollii* (Old-man-of-the-Andes). Slow-growing, columnar, perennial cactus. H 28in (70cm), S 4in (10cm). Zone 10. Cylindrical, green stem, 3–4in (7–10cm), with thick, golden spines is almost hidden by long, wispy, hairlike, white spines. Tubular, pink flowers, recurved at tips and 4in (10cm) long, appear in summer on fully mature plants.

BOUGAINVILLEA (Nyctaginaceae)
Genus of deciduous or evergreen, woody-stemmed, scrambling climbers, grown for their showy floral bracts. Frost tender, min. 45–50°F (7–10°C). Grow in fertile, well-drained soil and in full light. Water moderately in the growing season; keep potted plants almost dry when dormant. Needs tying to a support. Cut back previous season's lateral growths in spring, leaving 3/4–1 1/4in (2–3cm) long spurs. Propagate by semi-ripe cuttings in summer or by hardwood cuttings when dormant. Whitefly and mealy bug may cause problems.
B. x buttiana 'Mrs. Butt'. Vigorous, evergreen, woody-stemmed, scrambling climber. H to 15ft (5m). Zone 10. Has elliptic leaves, 1 1/2–3in (4–8cm) long, and clusters of crimson-magenta floral bracts in summer. Floral bracts of **'Golden Glow'** are orange-yellow; those of **'Scarlet Queen'** are scarlet.
B. 'Dania' illus. p.168.
B. glabra illus. p.172. **'Snow White'** illus. p.165. **'Variegata'** illus. p.169.
B. 'Miss Manila' illus. p.168.
B. spectabilis. Strong-growing, mainly evergreen, woody-stemmed, scrambling climber; stems usually have a few spines. H to 22ft (7m). Zone 10. Has elliptic to oval leaves and, in summer, large trusses of red-purple floral bracts.

Boussingaultia baselloides. See *Anredera cordifolia*.

BOUTELOUA (Gramineae). See GRASSES, BAMBOOS, RUSHES, and SEDGES.
B. gracilis, syn. *B. oligostachya*, illus. p.181.
B. oligostachya. See *B. gracilis*.

BOUVARDIA (Rubiaceae)
Genus of deciduous, semi-evergreen, or evergreen, shrubs and perennials, grown for their flowers. Frost tender, min. 45–50°F (7–10°C), but 55–9°F (13–15°C) for winter-flowering species. Prefers full light and fertile, well-drained soil. Water freely when in full growth, moderately at other times. Cut back stems by half to three-quarters after flowering to maintain a neat habit. Propagate by softwood cuttings in spring or by greenwood or

semi-ripe cuttings in summer. Whitefly and mealy bug may be troublesome.
B. humboldtii. See *B. longiflora*.
B. longiflora, syn. *B. humboldtii*. Semi-evergreen, spreading shrub. H and S 3ft (1m) or more. Min. 55–9°F (13–15°C) until flowering ceases, then 45°F (7°C). Zones 9–10. Has small, lance-shaped leaves. Fragrant white flowers, each with a slender tube and 4 spreading petal lobes, are borne in terminal clusters from summer to early winter.
B. ternifolia, syn. *B. triphylla*, illus. p.141.
B. triphylla. See *B. ternifolia*.

BOWIEA (Liliaceae)
Genus of summer-flowering, bulbous succulents with scrambling, branched, green stems that produce no proper leaves; is grown mainly for botanical interest. Frost tender, min. 50°F (10°C). Needs sun and well-drained soil; plant with half of bulb above soil level. Support with sticks or canes. Propagate by seed, sown under glass in winter or spring. May produce offsets.
B. volubilis illus. p.381.

BOYKINIA (Saxifragaceae)
Genus of mound-forming perennials. Fully hardy. Most species require shade and humus-rich, moist but well-drained, acid soil. Propagate by division in spring or by seed in autumn.
B. aconitifolia. Mound-forming perennial. H 3ft (1m), S 6in (15cm). Zones 5–9. Has rounded to kidney-shaped, lobed leaves. In summer, flower stems carry very small, bell-shaped, white flowers.
B. jamesii. See *Telesonix jamesii*.

BRACHYCHILUM (Zingiberaceae)
Genus of aromatic perennials, grown for their flowers and ornamental fruits. Frost tender, min. 64°F (18°C). Prefers a humid atmosphere, humus-rich, moist but well-drained soil, and partial shade. May be grown in pots if roots are not too restricted. Propagate by division in spring or summer.
B. horsfieldii. Clump-forming, tufted perennial. H and S to 3ft (1m). Zone 10. Has short-stalked, lance-shaped, leathery leaves, to 1ft (30cm) long. Showy, tubular, yellow-and-white flowers, to 3in (8cm) across, appear in summer, followed by orange fruits that open to reveal red seeds.

BRACHYCHITON (Sterculiaceae)
Genus of evergreen or deciduous, mainly spring- and summer-flowering trees, grown for their flowers and overall appearance. Frost tender, min. 45–50°F (7–10°C). Needs full light and humus-rich, well-drained, preferably acid soil. Water potted specimens moderately, much less in winter. Pruning is tolerated if needed. Propagate by seed in spring. Red spider mite may be a nuisance.
B. acerifolius, syn. *Sterculia acerifolia*, illus. p.39.
B. populneus, syn. *Sterculia diversifolia* (Kurrajong). Evergreen, conical tree, pyramidal when young. H and S 50–70ft (15–20m). Zone 10.

Oval, pointed or 3–5-lobed, glossy, deep green leaves are chartreuse when young. In spring-summer has panicles of saucer-shaped, cream or greenish white flowers with red, purple, or yellow throats.

BRACHYCOME (Compositae)
Genus of annuals and perennials with daisylike flower heads. Fully to half hardy. Requires sun, a sheltered position, and rich, well-drained soil. Pinch out growing shoots of young plants to encourage a bushy habit. Propagate by seed sown under glass in spring or outdoors in late spring.
B. iberidifolia illus. p.278.

BRACHYGLOTTIS (Compositae)
Genus of evergreen shrubs and trees, grown for their bold foliage and overall effect. Some shrubby species were previously included in *Senecio*. Frost tender, min. 37°F (3°C). Needs full light or partial shade and well-drained soil. Water potted plants freely in summer, moderately at other times. Propagate by semi-ripe cuttings in late summer.
B. repanda illus. p.95.

BRASSAIA. See SCHEFFLERA.

BRASSAVOLA. See ORCHIDS.
B. nodosa (Lady-of-the-night; illus. p.252). Evergreen, epiphytic orchid for an intermediate greenhouse. H 9in (23cm). Zone 10. Narrow-petaled, pale green flowers, 2in (5cm) across and each with a white lip, are borne, 1–3 to a stem, in spring; they are fragrant at night. Leaves, 3–4in (8–10cm) long, are thick and cylindrical. Is best grown on a bark slab. Provide good light in summer.

BRASSICA (Cruciferae)
Genus of annuals and evergreen biennials, and perennials. Most are edible vegetables, e.g. cabbages and kales, but forms of *B. oleracea* are grown for their ornamental foliage. Fully hardy. Grow in sun and in fertile, well-drained soil. Lime-rich soil is recommended, though not essential. Propagate by seed sown outdoors in spring or under glass in early spring. Is susceptible to club root.
B. oleracea forms illus. p.268.

x BRASSOCATTLEYA. See ORCHIDS.
x B. Mount Adams (illus. p.253). Evergreen, epiphytic orchid for an intermediate greenhouse. H 18in (45cm). Zone 10. Intermittently produces lavender pink flowers, to 6in (15cm) across and each with a darker lip marked yellow and red, up to 4 per stem. Has oval, stiff leaves, 4–6in (10–15cm) long. Needs good light in summer.

x BRASSOLAELIOCATTLEYA. See ORCHIDS.
x B. St. Helier (illus. p.253). Evergreen, epiphytic orchid for an intermediate greenhouse. H 18in (45cm). Zone 10. Pinkish purple flowers, to 4in (10cm) across, each with a yellow-marked, rich red lip,

are produced 1–4 to a stem, mainly in spring. Bears oval, stiff leaves, 4–6in (10–15cm) long. Grow in good light in summer.

x *B. Hetherington* 'Coronation' (illus. p.253). Evergreen, epiphytic orchid for an intermediate greenhouse. H 18in (45cm). Zone 10. Produces fragrant, light pink flowers, 4in (10cm) across and each with a deep pink and yellow lip, up to 4 to a stem, mainly in spring. Leaves, 4–6in (10–15cm) long, are stiff and oval. Provide good light in summer.

Bravoa geminiflora. See *Polianthes geminiflora.*

BREYNIA (Euphorbiaceae)
Genus of evergreen shrubs and trees, grown for their foliage. Frost tender, min. 55°F (13°C). Needs full light or partial shade and fertile, well-drained soil. Water potted plants freely when in full growth, moderately at other times. Large bushes should be cut back hard after flowering. Propagate by greenwood or semi-ripe cuttings in summer. Whitefly, red spider mite, and mealy bug may be troublesome.
B. disticha, syn. *B. nivosa*, *Phyllanthus nivosus*, illus. p.143. **'Roseo-picta'** is an evergreen, rounded, well-branched shrub with slender stems. H and S to 3ft (1m). Zone 10. Has broadly oval, pink-flushed, green leaves that are variably bordered and splashed with white. Insignificant, petalless flowers are borne in spring-summer.
B. nivosa. See *B. disticha.*

BRIGGSIA (Gesneriaceae)
Genus of evergreen perennials, grown for their rosettes of hairy leaves. Frost tender, min. 36–41°F (2–5°C). Needs shade and peaty soil with plenty of moisture in summer and good air circulation in winter. Protect against damp in winter. Propagate by seed in spring.
B. muscicola. Evergreen, basal-rosetted perennial. H 3–4in (8–10cm), S 9in (23cm). Zones 9–10. Leaves are oval, silver-haired, and pale green. Arching flower stems bear loose clusters of tubular, pale yellow flowers, with protruding tips, in early summer. Is best grown in an alpine house.

BRIMEURA (Liliaceae)
Genus of spring-flowering bulbs, similar to miniature bluebells, grown for their flowers. Is good in rock gardens and shrub borders. Frost hardy. Requires partial shade. Prefers humus-rich, well-drained soil. Propagate by seed in autumn or by division in late summer.
B. amethystina, syn. *Hyacinthus amethystinus*, illus. p.361.

Brittonastrum mexicanum. See *Agastache mexicana.*

BRIZA (Gramineae), Quaking grass. See GRASSES, BAMBOOS, RUSHES, and SEDGES.
B. maxima (Greater quaking grass). Robust, tuft-forming, annual grass. H to 20in (50cm), S 3–4in (8–10cm).

Fully hardy. Green leaves are mainly basal. Has loose panicles of up to 10 pendent, purplish green spikelets, in early summer, that dry well for winter decoration. Self seeds readily.
B. media (Common quaking grass). Evergreen, tuft-forming, rhizomatous, perennial grass. H 12–24in (30–60cm), S 3–4in (8–10cm). Fully hardy, zones 5–9. Green leaves are mainly basal. In summer bears open panicles of up to 30 pendent, purplish brown spikelets that dry well for winter decoration.

BRODIAEA (Liliaceae)
Genus of mainly spring-flowering bulbs with colorful flowers produced in loose heads on leafless stems. Frost hardy. Needs a sheltered, sunny situation and light, well-drained soil. Dies down in summer. Propagate in autumn by seed or in late summer and autumn by offsets, which are produced freely.
B. congesta. See *Dichelostemma congestum.*
B. coronaria. Late spring- to early summer-flowering bulb. H 4–10in (10–25cm), S 3–4in (8–10cm). Zones 8–10. Long, narrow, semi-erect, basal leaves die down by flowering time. Leafless stems each carry a loose head of erect, funnel-shaped, violet-blue flowers on long, slender stalks.
B. hyacinthina. See *Triteleia hyacinthina.*
B. ida-maia. See *Dichelostemma ida-maia.*
B. ixioides. See *Triteleia ixioides.*
B. laxa. See *Triteleia laxa.*
B. peduncularis. See *Triteleia peduncularis.*
B. pulchella. See *Dichelostemma pulchellum.*

BROMELIA (Bromeliaceae)
Genus of evergreen, rosette-forming perennials, grown for their overall appearance. Frost tender, min. 41–5°F (5–7°C). Needs full light and well-drained soil. Water moderately in summer, sparingly at other times. Propagate by suckers in spring.
B. balansae (Heart-of-flame; illus. p.222). Evergreen, clump-forming, basal-rosetted perennial. H 3ft (1m), S 5ft (1.5m). Zone 10. Has narrowly strap-shaped, arching, mid- to gray-green leaves with large, hooked spines. Club-shaped panicles of tubular, red- or violet-purple flowers, with long, bright red bracts, are borne in spring-summer or sometimes later.

BROMUS (Gramineae). See GRASSES, BAMBOOS, RUSHES, and SEDGES.
B. ramosus (Hairy brome grass). Evergreen, tuft-forming, perennial grass. H to 6ft (2m), S 1ft (30cm). Fully hardy, zones 6–9. Green leaves are lax and hairy. Produces long, arching panicles of nodding, gray-green spikelets in summer. Prefers shade.

BROUSSONETIA (Moraceae)
Genus of deciduous trees and shrubs, grown for their foliage and unusual flowers. Male and female flowers are

produced on different plants. Frost hardy. Needs full sun and well-drained soil. Propagate by softwood cuttings in summer or by seed in autumn.
B. papyrifera illus. p.52.

BROWALLIA (Solanaceae)
Genus of shrubby perennials, usually grown as annuals, with showy flowers. Frost tender, min. 39–59°F (4–15°C). Grows best in sun or partial shade and in fertile, well-drained soil that should not dry out completely. Feed when flowering if pot-grown and pinch out young shoots to encourage bushiness. Propagate by seed in spring; for winter flowers, sow in late summer.
B. elata. Moderately fast-growing, bushy perennial, usually grown as an annual. H 12in (30cm), S 6in (15cm). Min. 39°F (4°C). Has oval, green leaves and, in summer, trumpet-shaped, blue flowers, 1½in (4cm) wide.
B. speciosa illus. p.223.

Browningia hertlingianus. See *Azureocereus hertlingianus.*

BRUCKENTHALIA (Ericaceae)
Genus of one species of evergreen shrub, grown for its bell-shaped flowers. Is related to *Calluna* and *Erica* and is suitable for rock gardens and peat beds. Fully hardy. Needs sun and well-drained, peaty, acid soil. Propagate in late summer by semi-ripe cuttings or in spring by seed.
B. spiculifolia (Spike heath). Evergreen, heathlike shrub. H and S 6in (15cm). Zones 6–8. Tiny, needlelike, glossy, dark green leaves clothe stiff stems. Terminal clusters of tiny, pink flowers are borne in summer.

Brugmansia arborea. See *Datura arborea.*
Brugmansia aurea. See *Datura aurea.*
Brugmansia bicolor. See *Datura rosei.*
Brugmansia x candida. See *Datura x candida.*
Brugmansia rosei. See *Datura rosei.*
Brugmansia sanguinea. See *Datura sanguinea.*

BRUNFELSIA (Solanaceae)
Genus of evergreen shrubs, grown for their flowers. Frost tender, min. 50–55°F (10–13°C), but 59–64°F (15–18°C) for good winter flowering. Needs semi-shade and humus-rich, well-drained soil. Water potted plants moderately, much less in low temperatures. Remove stem tips to promote branching in growing season. Propagate by semi-ripe cuttings in summer. Mealy bug and whitefly may cause problems.
B. calycina. See *B. pauciflora.*
B. pauciflora, syn. *B. calycina* (Yesterday-today-and-tomorrow). Evergreen, spreading shrub. H and S 2ft (60cm) or more. Zone 10. Bears oblong to lance-shaped, leathery, glossy leaves. Blue-purple flowers, each with a tubular base and 5 overlapping, wavy-edged petals, are carried from winter to summer.
'Macrantha' illus. p.135.

BRUNNERA (Boraginaceae)
Genus of spring-flowering perennials. Fully hardy. Prefers light shade and moist soil. Propagate by division in spring or autumn or by seed in autumn.
B. macrophylla (Siberian bugloss). Clump-forming perennial. H 18in (45cm), S 24in (60cm). Zones 4–8. Delicate sprays of small, star-shaped, forget-me-notlike, bright blue flowers in early spring are followed by heart-shaped, rough, long-stalked leaves. Makes good ground cover. **'Dawson's White'** (syn. *B.m.* 'Variegata') illus. p.228.

x *Brunsdonna parkeri.* See **x *Amarygia parkeri.***

BRUNSVIGIA (Amaryllidaceae)
Genus of autumn-flowering bulbs with heads of showy flowers. Half hardy. Needs sun and well-drained soil. Water in autumn to bring bulbs into growth and continue watering until summer, when leaves will die away and dormant bulbs should be kept fairly dry and warm. Propagate by seed in autumn or by offsets in late summer.
B. josephinae (Josephine's lily). Autumn-flowering bulb. H to 18in (45cm), S 18–24in (45–60cm). Zones 9–10. Bears a stout, leafless stem with a spherical head of 20–30 funnel-shaped, red flowers, 3–3½in (7–9cm) long, with recurved petal tips. Semi-erect, oblong leaves appear after flowering.

BUDDLEIA (Loganiaceae)
Genus of deciduous, semi-evergreen, or evergreen shrubs and trees, grown for their clusters of small, often fragrant flowers. Fully to half hardy. Requires full sun and fertile, well-drained soil. *B. crispa*, *B. davidii*, *B. fallowiana*, *B.* 'Lochinch', and *B.* x *weyeriana* should be cut back hard in spring. Prune *B. alternifolia* by removing shoots that have flowered. Other species may be cut back lightly after flowering. Propagate by semi-ripe cuttings in summer.
B. alternifolia (Fountain buddleia) illus. p.89.
B. asiatica. Evergreen, arching shrub. H and S 10ft (3m). Half hardy, zones 8–9. Long plumes of very fragrant, tubular, white flowers appear amid long, narrow, dark green leaves in late winter and early spring. Grow against a south- or west-facing wall.
B. colvilei illus. p.89. **'Kewensis'** is a deciduous, arching shrub, often treelike with age. H and S 15ft (5m). Frost hardy, zones 8–9. Has lance-shaped, dark green leaves. Large, tubular, white-throated, deep red flowers hang in drooping clusters in early summer.
B. crispa illus. p.111.
B. davidii (Butterfly bush). **'Black Knight'** is a vigorous, deciduous, arching shrub. H and S 15ft (5m). Fully hardy, zones 5–9. Leaves are long, lance-shaped, and dark green with white-felted undersides. Bears dense clusters of fragrant, tubular, dark violet-purple flowers from mid-summer to autumn. Flowers of **'Empire Blue'** are rich violet-blue. **'Harlequin'** illus. p.89. **'Peace'** illus. p.86. **'Pink Pearl'**

produces pale lilac-pink flowers. **'Royal Red'** illus. p.89.

B. fallowiana. Deciduous, arching shrub. H 6ft (2m), S 10ft (3m). Frost hardy, zones 8–9. Shoots and lance-shaped leaves, when young, are covered with white hairs; foliage then becomes dark gray-green. Fragrant, tubular, lavender purple flowers appear in late summer and early autumn. Is often damaged in very severe winters; grow against a wall in cold areas. var. **alba** has white flowers.

B. globosa illus. p.91.

B. 'Lochinch'. Deciduous, arching shrub. H and S 10ft (3m). Frost hardy, zones 5–9. Long plumes of fragrant, tubular, lilac-blue flowers are borne above lance-shaped, gray-green leaves in late summer and autumn.

B. madagascariensis. Evergreen, arching shrub. H and S 12ft (4m) or more. Half hardy, zone 9. Has narrowly lance-shaped, dark green leaves, white beneath, and, in late winter and spring, long clusters of tubular, orange-yellow flowers. Grow against a south- or west-facing wall.

B. x weyeriana. Deciduous, arching shrub. H and S 12ft (4m). Fully hardy, zones 6–8. Leaves are lance-shaped and dark green. Bears loose, rounded clusters of tubular, orange-yellow

flowers, often tinged purple, from mid-summer to autumn.

BULBOCODIUM (Liliaceae)
Genus of spring-flowering corms, related to *Colchicum* and suitable for rock gardens and cool greenhouses. Fully hardy. Needs an open, sunny site and well-drained soil. Propagate by seed in autumn or by division in late summer and early autumn.
B. vernum illus. p.359.

BULBOPHYLLUM. See ORCHIDS.
B. careyanum (illus. p.254). Evergreen, epiphytic orchid for an intermediate greenhouse. H 3in (8cm). Zone 10. In spring produces tight sprays of many slightly fragrant brown flowers, $1/4$in (0.5cm) across. Oval leaves are 3–4in (8–10cm) long. Is best grown in a hanging basket. Requires semi-shade in summer.

BUPHTHALMUM (Compositae)
Genus of summer-flowering perennials. Fully hardy. Requires full sun; grows well in any but rich soil. Propagate by seed in spring or autumn or by division in autumn. Needs frequent division to curb invasiveness.
B. salicifolium illus. p.247.
B. speciosum. See *Telekia speciosa.*

BUPLEURUM (Umbelliferae)
Genus of perennials and evergreen shrubs, grown for their foliage and flowers. Grows well in coastal gardens. Frost hardy. Needs full sun and well-drained soil. Propagate by semi-ripe cuttings in summer.
B. fruticosum illus. p.114.

BUTIA (Palmae)
Yatay palm
Genus of evergreen palms, grown for their overall appearance. Frost hardy to frost tender, min. 41°F (5°C). Grow in any fertile, well-drained soil and in full light or partial shade. Water regularly, less in winter. Propagate by seed in spring at not less than 75°F (24°C). Red spider mite may be a problem.
B. capitata, syn. *Cocos capitata,* illus. p.72.

BUTOMUS (Butomaceae)
Genus of one species of deciduous, perennial, rushlike, marginal water plant, grown for its flowers. Fully hardy. Requires an open, sunny situation in up to 10in (25cm) depth of water. Propagate by division in spring or by seed in spring or late summer.
B. umbellatus illus. p.374.

BUXUS (Buxaceae)
Box
Genus of evergreen shrubs and trees, grown for their foliage and habit. Is excellent for edging, hedging, and topiary work. Flowers are insignificant. Fully to frost hardy. Requires sun or semi-shade and any but waterlogged soil. Trim hedges during summer. Promote new growth by cutting back stems to 12in (30cm) or less in late spring. Propagate by semi-ripe cuttings in summer.
B. balearica illus. p.121.
B. microphylla (Small-leaved box). Evergreen, bushy shrub. H 3ft (1m), S 5ft (1.5m). Fully hardy, zones 5–9. Forms a dense, rounded mass of small, oblong, dark green leaves. **'Green Pillow'** illus. p.144.
B. sempervirens (Common box). Evergreen, bushy shrub or tree. H and S 15ft (5m). Fully hardy, zones 6–9. Leaves are oblong, glossy and dark green. Is good for growing as a hedge and for screening. **'Handsworthensis'** illus. p.120. **'Suffruticosa'** illus. p.145.
B. wallichiana (Himalayan box). Slow-growing, evergreen, bushy, open shrub. H and S 6ft (2m). Frost hardy, zones 7–9. Produces long, narrow, glossy, bright green leaves.

C

CABOMBA (Cabombaceae)
Genus of deciduous or semi-evergreen, perennial, submerged water plants with finely divided foliage. Is suitable for aquariums. Frost tender, min. 41°F (5°C). Prefers partial shade. Propagate by stem cuttings in spring or summer.
C. caroliniana (Fanwort, Fish grass, Washington grass). Deciduous or semi-evergreen, perennial, submerged water plant. S indefinite. Zones 9–10. Forms dense, spreading hummocks of fan-shaped, coarsely cut, bright green leaves. Is used as an oxygenating plant.

CAESALPINIA (Leguminosae)
Genus of deciduous or evergreen shrubs, trees, and scrambling climbers, grown for their foliage and flowers. Frost hardy to frost tender, min. 41–50°F (5–10°C). Requires full sun and fertile, well-drained soil. Propagate by softwood cuttings in summer or by seed in autumn or spring.
C. gilliesii illus. p.91.
C. pulcherrima, syn. *Poinciana pulcherrima* (Barbados pride). Evergreen shrub or tree of erect to spreading habit. H and S 10–20ft (3–6m). Frost tender, min. 41°F (5°C), zone 10. Has fernlike leaves composed of many small, green leaflets. In summer bears cup-shaped, yellow flowers, 1¼in (3cm) wide, with very long, red anthers, in short, dense, erect racemes.

CALADIUM (Araceae)
Genus of perennials grown mainly as annuals, with tubers from which arise long-stalked, ornamental leaves. Frost tender, min. 64–6°F (18–19°C). Needs partial shade and moist, humus-rich soil. After leaves die down, store tubers in a frost-free, dark place. Propagate by separating small tubers when replanting in spring.
C. x *hortulanum* (Angels' wings). **'Candidum'** is a tufted perennial. H and S to 3ft (90cm). Zone 10. Triangular, green-veined, white leaves, to 18in (45cm) long, have arrow-shaped bases and long leaf stalks. Intermittently bears white spathes; small flowers clustered on spadix sometimes produce whitish berries. **'John Peed'** has purple stems and waxy, green leaves with metallic orange-red centers and scarlet veins. **'Pink Beauty'** illus. p.221. **'Pink Cloud'** has large, dark green leaves with central areas mottled pink, and pink to white areas along the veins.

CALANTHE. See ORCHIDS.
C. vestita (illus. p.252). Deciduous, terrestrial orchid. H 24in (60cm). Frost tender, min. 64°F (18°C), zone 10. In winter bears sprays of many white flowers, 1½in (4cm) across, each with a large, red-marked lip. Has broadly oval, ribbed, soft leaves, 12in (30cm) long. In summer requires semi-shade and regular feeding.

CALATHEA (Marantaceae)
Genus of evergreen perennials with brightly colored and patterned leaves. Frost tender, min. 59°F (15°C). Prefers a shaded, humid position, without fluctuations of temperature, in humus-rich, well-drained soil. Water with soft water, sparingly in low temperatures, but do not allow to dry out completely. Propagate by division in spring.
C. lindeniana. Evergreen, clump-forming perennial. H 3ft (1m), S 2ft (60cm). Zone 10. Lance-shaped, long-stalked, more or less upright leaves, over 1ft (30cm) long, are dark green, with paler green, feathered midribs above and marked with reddish purple below. Intermittently bears short, erect spikes of 3-petaled, pale yellow flowers.
C. makoyana illus. p.260.
C. ornata **'Roseo-lineata'.** Evergreen, clump-forming, stemless perennial. H to 6ft (2m), S to 5ft (1.5m). Zone 10. Narrowly oval, leathery leaves, to 2ft (60cm) long, are dark green, with close-set, fine, pink stripes along the lateral veins and reddish purple below. Intermittently bears short, erect spikes of 3-petaled, white to mauve flowers. **'Sanderiana'** illus. p.194.
C. zebrina illus. p.223.

CALCEOLARIA (Scrophulariaceae)
Genus of annuals, biennials, and evergreen perennials, sub-shrubs, and scandent climbers, some of which are grown as annuals. Fully hardy to frost tender, min. 41–5°F (5–7°C). Most prefer sun but some like a shady, cool site and moist but well-drained soil, incorporating sharp sand and compost, and dislike wet conditions in winter. Propagate by softwood cuttings in late spring or summer or by seed in autumn.
C. **'Anytime'.** Compact, bushy annual or biennial. H 8in (20cm), S 6in (15cm). Half hardy. Has oval, slightly hairy, green leaves. In spring-summer bears heads of 2in (5cm) long, rounded, pouched flowers in shades of red and yellow, including bicolors.
C. arachnoidea illus. p.295.
C. biflora illus. p.246.
C., **Bikini Series** illus. p.282.
C. darwinii. Evergreen, clump-forming, short-lived perennial. H 3in (8cm), S 4in (10cm). Fully hardy, zones 7–10. Bears rounded, wrinkled, glossy, dark green leaves. In late spring, flower stems carry pendent, pouch-shaped, yellow flowers with dark brown spots on lower lips and central, white bands. Is difficult to grow. Needs a sheltered, sunny site in moist, gritty, peaty soil. Requires frequent spraying against aphids.
C. fothergillii. Evergreen, clump-forming, short-lived perennial. H and S 5in (12cm). Frost hardy, zones 6–8. Has a rosette of rounded, light green leaves with hairy edges. In summer bears solitary pouch-shaped, sulfur yellow flowers with crimson spots.

Is good for a sheltered rock ledge or in an alpine house. Needs gritty, peaty soil. Is prone to aphid attack.
C. integrifolia. Evergreen, upright sub-shrub, sometimes grown as an annual. H to 4ft (1.2m), S 2ft (60cm). Half hardy, zones 9–10. In summer bears crowded clusters of pouch-shaped, yellow to red-brown flowers above oblong to elliptic, green leaves, sometimes rust-colored beneath.
C. **'John Innes'** illus. p.248.
C., **Monarch Series.** Group of bushy annuals or biennials. H and S 12in (30cm). Half hardy. Has oval, lightly hairy, green leaves and, in spring-summer, bears heads of large, rounded, pouched flowers, 2in (5cm) long, in a wide range of colors.
C. pavonii. Robust, evergreen, scandent climber. H 6ft (2m) or more. Frost tender, min. 45°F (7°C), zone 10. Has oval, serrated, soft-haired leaves with winged stalks. Pouched, yellow flowers with brown marks appear in large trusses from late summer to winter.
C. polyrrhiza. Evergreen, prostrate perennial. H 1in (2.5cm), S 6in (15cm). Frost hardy, zones 6–8. Has rounded, hairy, green leaves along flower stem, which bears pouch-shaped, purple-spotted, yellow flowers in summer. Is good for a shady rock garden. May also be propagated by division in autumn or spring.
C. **'Sunshine'** illus. p.283.
C. tenella illus. p.325.
C. **'Walter Shrimpton'** illus. p.326.

CALENDULA (Compositae)
Marigold
Genus of annuals and evergreen shrubs. Annuals are fully hardy; shrubs are frost tender, min. 39°F (4°C). Grow in sun and in any well-drained soil. Dead-head to prolong flowering. Propagate annuals by seed sown outdoors in spring or autumn, shrubs by stem cuttings in summer. Annuals may self seed. Cucumber mosaic virus and powdery mildew may cause problems.
C. officinalis (Pot marigold). Fast-growing, bushy annual. Tall cultivars, H and S 2ft (60cm); dwarf forms, H and S 1ft (30cm). All have lance-shaped, strongly aromatic, pale green leaves. Daisylike, single or double flower heads are produced from spring to autumn. **'Art Shades'** (tall) has double, apricot, orange, or cream flowers. **Fiesta Series** (dwarf) has double flowers in colors ranging from cream to orange (see **'Gitana'** illus. p.283). **'Geisha Girl'** (tall) illus. p.285. **'Kablouna'** (tall) illus. p.280.

CALLA (Araceae)
Genus of one species of deciduous or semi-evergreen, perennial, spreading, marginal water plant, grown for its foliage and showy spathes that surround insignificant flower clusters. Fully hardy. Requires a sunny position,

in mud or up to 10in (25cm) depth of water. Propagate by division in spring or by seed in late summer.
C. palustris illus. p.372.

CALLIANDRA (Leguminosae)
Genus of evergreen trees, shrubs, and scandent semi-climbers, grown for their flowers and overall appearance. Frost tender, min. 45–64°F (7–18°C). Needs full light or partial shade and well-drained soil. Water potted plants freely when in full growth, much less when temperatures are low. To restrict growth, cut back stems by one-half to two-thirds after flowering. Propagate by seed in spring. Whitefly and mealy bug may be troublesome.
C. eriophylla illus. p.140.
C. haematocephala [pink form] illus. p.115, [white form] illus. p.117.

CALLICARPA (Verbenaceae)
Genus of deciduous, summer-flowering shrubs, grown for their small but striking, clustered fruits. Fully hardy. Does best in full sun and fertile, well-drained soil. Propagate by softwood cuttings in summer.
C. bodinieri (Bodinier beauty berry). Deciduous, bushy shrub. H 10ft (3m), S 8ft (2.5m). Zones 6–8. Has oval, dark green leaves. Tiny, star-shaped, lilac flowers in mid-summer are followed by dense clusters of spherical, violet fruits. var. *giraldii* illus. p.116.

CALLISIA (Commelinaceae)
Genus of evergreen, prostrate perennials, grown for their ornamental foliage and trailing habit. Frost tender, min. 50–59°F (10–15°C). Grow in full light, but out of direct sunlight, in fertile, well-drained soil. Propagate by tip cuttings in spring, either annually or when plants become straggly.
C. navicularis, syn. *Tradescantia navicularis.* Evergreen, low-growing perennial with creeping, rooting shoots, 20in (50cm) or more long. H 2–3in (5–8cm). Zones 9–10. Has 2 rows of oval, keeled leaves, 1in (2.5cm) long, sheathing the stem, and stalkless clusters of small, 3-petaled, pinkish purple flowers in leaf axils in summer-autumn.
C. repens illus. p.260.

CALLISTEMON (Myrtaceae)
Bottlebrush
Genus of evergreen shrubs, usually with narrow, pointed leaves, grown for their clustered flowers, which, with their profusion of long stamens, resemble bottlebrushes. Frost to half hardy, but in cool areas all except *C. sieberi* need protection of a south- or west-facing wall. Requires full sun and fertile, well-drained soil. Propagate by semi-ripe cuttings in summer or by seed in autumn or spring.
C. citrinus **'Splendens'** illus. p.111.
C. pallidus illus. p.114.
C. rigidus illus. p.111.

C. sieberi. Evergreen, bushy, dense shrub. H 5ft (1.5m). S 3ft (1m). Frost hardy, zones 8–10. Has short, narrowly lance-shaped, rigid, green leaves and, from mid- to late summer, small clusters of pale yellow flowers.

C. speciosus (Albany bottlebrush). Evergreen, bushy shrub. H and S 10ft (3m). Half hardy, zones 9–10. Produces long, narrow, gray-green leaves. Cylindrical clusters of bright red flowers appear in late spring and early summer.

C. subulatus. Evergreen, arching shrub. H and S 5ft (1.5m). Frost hardy, zones 8–10. Leaves are narrowly oblong and bright green. Dense spikes of crimson flowers are produced in summer.

C. viminalis. Evergreen, arching shrub. H and S 15ft (5m). Half hardy, zone 10. Narrowly oblong, bronze, young leaves mature to dark green. Bears clusters of bright red flowers in summer.

CALLISTEPHUS (Compositae)
China aster
Genus of one species of annual. Frost tender, min. 36–9°F (2–4°C). Requires sun, a sheltered position, and fertile, well-drained soil. Tall cultivars need support; all should be dead-headed. Propagate by seed sown under glass in spring; seed may also be sown outdoors in mid-spring. Wilt disease, virus diseases, foot rot, root rot, and aphids may all be troublesome.

C. chinensis. Moderately fast-growing, erect, bushy annual. Tall cultivars, H 24in (60cm), S 18in (45cm); intermediate, H 18in (45cm), S 12in (30cm); dwarf, H 10–12in (25–30cm), S 12–18in (30–45cm); very dwarf, H 8in (20cm), S 12in (30cm). All have oval, toothed, green leaves and flower in summer and early autumn. Different forms are available in a wide color range, including pink, red, blue, and white. **Andrella Series** (tall) has single, daisylike flower heads; those of **Duchess Series** (tall) are incurved and chrysanthemumlike. **Milady Series** (dwarf) has incurved, fully double flower heads available either in mixed or single colors (blue, illus. p.276; rose, illus. p.268). **Ostrich Plume Series** (tall) bears feathery, reflexed, fully double flower heads. **Pompon Series** (tall) has small, double flower heads; those of **'Powderpuffs'** (tall) are large and double. **Princess Series** (tall) has double flower heads with quilled petals. **Thousand Wonders Series** (very dwarf) illus. p.275.

CALLUNA (Ericaceae). See HEATHERS.

C. vulgaris (Ling, Scotch heather). Evergreen, bushy shrub. H to 24in (60cm), S 18in (45cm). Fully hardy, zones 5–7. Slightly fleshy, linear leaves, in opposite and overlapping pairs, may range in color from bright green to many shades of gray, yellow, orange, and red. Spikes of bell- to urn-shaped, single or double flowers are produced from mid-summer to late autumn. Unlike *Erica*, most of the flower color derives from the sepals. The following cultivars are H 18in

(45cm), have green leaves and bear single flowers in late summer and early autumn, unless otherwise stated. **'Alba Plena'**, H 12–18in (30–45cm), bears double, white flowers. **'Allegro'**, H 24in (60cm), is compact in habit and produces purple-red flowers. **'Alportii'**, H 24–36in (60–90cm), has purple-red flowers. **'Anthony Davis'** (illus. p.146) has gray leaves and white flowers. **'August Beauty'** bears long, pendulous stems and white flowers. **'Beechwood Crimson'** is bushy with crimson-purple flowers. **'Beoley Gold'** (illus. p.147), S 20in (50cm), has golden foliage and white flowers. **'Beoley Silver'**, H 16in (40cm), has silver foliage and white flowers. **'Bonfire Brilliance'**, H 12in (30cm), has bright, flame-colored foliage and mauve-pink flowers. **'Boskoop'** (illus. p.147), H 12in (30cm), is compact with golden foliage that turns deep orange in winter and lilac-pink flowers. **'County Wicklow'** (illus. p.146), H 12in (30cm), S 14in (35cm), is compact with double, shell pink flowers. **'Darkness'** (illus. p.147), H 16in (40cm), S 14in (35cm), is compact with crimson flowers. **'Drum-Ra'** is a typical form of the Scotch white heather. **'Elsie Purnell'** (illus. p.146) is a spreading cultivar with grayish green leaves and double, pale pink flowers. **'Finale'** bears dark pink flowers from late autumn to early winter. **'Foxii Nana'** (illus. p.147), H 6in (15cm), forms low mounds of bright green foliage and produces a few mauve-pink flowers. **'Fred J. Chapple'** has bright pink- and coral-tipped foliage in spring; mauve-pink flowers are borne on long stems. **'Gold Haze'** (illus. p.147) has bright golden foliage and white flowers. **'Golden Feather'** (illus. p.147) has bright yellow foliage, turning orange in winter, and mauve-pink flowers. **'H.E. Beale'**, H 20in (50cm), is one of the best double-flowered heathers, with pale pink flowers on long stems. **'Highland Rose'** has golden bronze foliage and deep pink flowers. **'Humpty-Dumpty'**, H 6in (15cm), is a hummock-forming cultivar that has emerald green foliage and a few white flowers. **'J.H. Hamilton'** (illus. p.146), H 8in (20cm), S 16in (40cm), is compact with double, salmon pink flowers. **'Kinlochruel'** (illus. p.146), H 12in (30cm), S 14in (35cm), bears an abundance of large, double, white flowers. **'Loch Turret'**, H 12in (30cm), has emerald green foliage and produces white flowers in early summer. **'Mair's Variety'**, an old cultivar, has white flowers on long spikes. **'Marleen'** is unusual in that its long-lasting, dark mauve flower buds, borne from early to late autumn, do not open fully. **'Mullion'**, H 10in (25cm), S 20in (50cm), is a spreading cultivar with rich mauve-pink flowers. **'Multicolor'** (illus. p.147), H 8in (20cm), is compact with foliage in shades of yellow, orange, red, and green year-round; flowers are mauve-pink. **'My Dream'** (illus. p.146), H 20in (50cm), produces double, white flowers that are borne on long, tapering stems. **'Orange Queen'** has yellow

and golden foliage and mauve flowers. **'Peter Sparkes'** (illus. p.147), H 20in (50cm), S 22in (55cm), bears double, deep pink flowers. **'Robert Chapman'** (illus. p.147) is a spreading cultivar and grown mainly for its foliage, which is golden yellow in summer, turning orange and brilliant red in winter; flowers are mauve-pink. **'Silver Knight'** (illus. p.147), H 12in (30cm), is of upright habit with gray leaves and mauve-pink flowers. **'Silver Queen'** (illus. p.146), H 16in (40cm), S 22in (55cm), is a spreading cultivar with dark mauve-pink flowers. **'Sister Anne'**, H 6in (15cm), has gray leaves and pale mauve-pink flowers. **'Spring Cream'** (illus. p.146) has bright green leaves, which have cream tips in spring, and white flowers. **'Sunset'**, H 10in (25cm), has brightly colored foliage, changing from golden yellow in spring to orange in summer and fiery red in winter; flowers are mauve-pink. **'Tib'** (illus. p.147), H 12in (30cm), S 16in (40cm), is the earliest-flowering double cultivar, producing small, double, deep pink flowers in early summer. **'White Lawn'**, H 4in (10cm), is a creeping cultivar with bright green foliage and white flowers on long stems; is suitable for a rock garden.

CALOCEDRUS (Cupressaceae). See CONIFERS.
C. decurrens, syn. *Libocedrus decurrens*, illus. p.78.

CALOCEPHALUS (Compositae)
Genus of annuals and evergreen shrubs and perennials, often grown annually from cuttings and used as summer bedding. Frost tender, min. 45–50°F (7–10°C). Requires full light and well-drained soil. Water potted plants moderately when in full growth, sparingly at other times. Remove stem tips of young plants to promote a bushy habit. Propagate by semi-ripe cuttings in late summer. Botrytis may be troublesome if plants are kept too cool and damp in winter.
C. brownii illus. p.143.

CALOCHONE (Rubiaceae)
Genus of evergreen, scrambling climbers, grown for their showy flowers. Frost tender, min. 64°F (18°C). Requires humus-rich, well-drained soil and full light. Water regularly, less in cold weather. Needs tying to a support. Thin out crowded stems after flowering. Propagate by semi-ripe cuttings in summer.
C. redingii. Moderately vigorous, evergreen, scrambling climber. H 10–15ft (3–5m). Zone 10. Has oval, pointed, hairy leaves, 3–5in (7–12cm) long. Trusses of primrose-shaped, red to orange-pink flowers appear in winter.

CALOCHORTUS (Liliaceae)
Cat's ears, Fairy lantern, Mariposa tulip
Genus of bulbs, grown for their spring and summer flowers. Frost hardy. Needs a sheltered, sunny position and well-drained soil. In cold, damp climates, cover or lift spring-flowering

species when dormant (in summer), or grow in cold frames or unheated greenhouses. After flowering, remove bulbils formed in leaf axils for propagation. Propagate by seed or bulbils—spring-flowering species in autumn, summer-flowering species in spring.
C. albus illus. p.342.
C. amabilis illus. p.363.
C. barbatus, syn. *Cyclobothra lutea*, illus. p.353.
C. luteus illus. p.347.
C. splendens. Late spring-flowering bulb. H 8–24in (20–60cm), S 2–4in (5–10cm). Zones 5–10. Bears 1 or 2 linear, erect leaves near base of branched stem and 1–4 upward-facing, saucer-shaped, pale purple flowers, 2–3in (5–7cm) across, with a darker blotch at the base of each of the 3 large petals.
C. subalpinus illus. p.364.
C. superbus. Late spring-flowering bulb. H 8–24in (20–60cm), S 2–4in (5–10cm). Zones 5–10. Is similar to *C. splendens*, but flowers are white, cream, or pale lilac, with a brown mark near the base of each of the 3 large petals.
C. venustus illus. p.342.
C. vestae. Late spring-flowering bulb. H 8–24in (20–60cm), S 2–4in (5–10cm). Zones 5–10. Is similar to *C. splendens*, but flowers are white or purple, with a rust brown mark near the base of each of the 3 large petals.
C. weedii. Summer-flowering bulb. H 1–2ft (30–60cm), S 2–4in (5–10cm). Zones 5–10. Has a linear, erect leaf near base of stem. Carries usually 2 upright, saucer-shaped flowers, 1¹/₂–2in (4–5cm) across, that are orange-yellow with brown lines and flecks and are hairy inside.

Calonyction aculeatum. See *Ipomoea alba.*

CALOSCORDUM (Liliaceae)
Genus of one species of summer-flowering bulb, related and similar to *Allium*. Is suitable for a rock garden. Frost hardy. Needs an open, sunny situation and well-drained soil. Lies dormant in winter. Propagate in early spring by seed or division before growth starts.
C. neriniflorum. Clump-forming bulb. H 4–10in (10–25cm), S 3–4in (8–10cm). Zones 5–10. Threadlike, semi-erect, basal leaves die down at flowering time. Each leafless stem produces a loose head of 10–20 small, funnel-shaped, pinkish red flowers in late summer.

CALOTHAMNUS (Myrtaceae)
Genus of evergreen, summer-flowering shrubs, grown for their flowers and overall appearance. Thrives in a dryish, airy environment. Frost tender, min. 50–59°F (10–15°C). Requires full sun and well-drained, sandy soil. Water potted plants moderately when in full growth, less at other times. Propagate by seed or semi-ripe cuttings in summer.
C. villosus (Woolly netbush). Evergreen, bushy shrub. H and S 2–4ft (60cm–1.2m). Zone 10. Has small,

dense, needlelike leaves covered with thick, gray down. Flowers appear in summer in dense, lateral clusters, each composed of bundles of branched, deep red stamens.

CALTHA (Ranunculaceae)
Genus of deciduous, perennial, marginal water plants, bog plants, or rock garden plants, grown for their attractive flowers. Fully hardy. Smaller growing species are suitable for rock gardens, troughs, and alpine houses and require moist but well-drained soil; larger species are best in marginal conditions. Most prefer an open, sunny position. Propagate species by seed in autumn or by division in autumn or early spring, selected forms by division in autumn or early spring.
C. introloba. Tuft-forming perennial. H and S 2in (5cm). Zones 5–7. Bears oval, lobed, glossy, dark green leaves. Erect, goblet-shaped, white flowers, flushed purple outside, open in late winter. Is good for a trough or alpine house. Prefers shade and humus-rich soil. Is difficult to grow in hot, dry climates.
C. leptosepala illus. p.373.
C. palustris and **'Flore Plena'** illus. p.377.

CALYCANTHUS (Calycanthaceae)
Genus of deciduous, summer-flowering shrubs, grown for their purplish or brownish red flowers with strap-shaped petals. Fully hardy. Requires sun or light shade and fertile, deep, moist but well-drained soil. Propagate by softwood cuttings in summer or by seed in autumn.
C. floridus (Carolina allspice). Deciduous, bushy shrub. H and S 6ft (2m). Zones 5–9. Has oval, aromatic, dark green leaves and, from early to mid-summer, fragrant, brownish red flowers with masses of spreading petals.
C. occidentalis illus. p.110.

CALYPSO. See ORCHIDS.
C. bulbosa (illus. p.253). Deciduous, terrestrial orchid. H 2–8in (5–20cm). Fully hardy, zones 8–10. Cormlike stem produces a single, oval, pleated leaf, 1¼–4in (3–10cm) long. Purplish pink flowers, ⅝–¾in (1.5–2cm) long, with hairy, purple-blotched, white or pale pink lips, are borne singly in late spring or early summer. Requires a damp, semi-shaded position with a mulch of leaf mold.

CAMASSIA (Liliaceae)
Genus of summer-flowering bulbs, suitable for borders and pond margins. Frost hardy. Requires sun or partial shade and deep, moist soil. Plant bulbs in autumn, 4in (10cm) deep. Lies dormant in autumn-winter. Propagate by seed in autumn or by division in late summer. If seed is not required, cut off stems after flowering.
C. leichtlinii illus. p.332. **'Semiplena'** illus. p.333.
C. quamash (Common camassia, Quamash). Clump-forming, summer-flowering bulb. H 8–32in (20–80cm), S 8–12in (20–30cm). Zones 4–10. Produces long, narrow, erect, basal

leaves. Each leafless stem bears a dense spike of star-shaped, blue, violet, or white flowers, to 3in (7cm) across.

CAMELLIA (Theaceae)
Genus of evergreen shrubs and trees, grown for their flowers and foliage. Flowers are classified according to the following types: single, semi-double, anemone-form, peony-form, rose-form, formal double, and irregular double (see p.96 for illustrations and descriptions). Grows well against walls and in pots. Fully hardy to frost tender, min. 45–50°F (7–10°C). Most forms prefer a sheltered position and semi-shade. Well-drained, neutral to acid soil is essential. Prune to shape after flowering. Propagate by semi-ripe or hardwood cuttings from mid-summer to early winter or by grafting in late winter or early spring. Aphids, thrips, and scale insects may cause problems under glass.
C. **'Anticipation'** (illus. p.97). Robust, evergreen, upright shrub. H 10ft (3m), S 5ft (1.5m). Frost hardy, zones 7–9. Has lance-shaped, dark green leaves. Large, peony-form, deep rose-pink blooms are freely produced in spring.
C. chrysantha. Fast-growing, evergreen, open shrub or tree. H 20ft (6m) or more, S 10ft (3m). Half hardy, zones 7–9. Has large, oval, leathery, veined leaves. Small, stalked, cup-shaped, single, clear yellow flowers are produced from leaf axils in spring.
C. **'Cornish Snow'.** Fast-growing, evergreen, upright, bushy shrub. H 10ft (3m), S 5ft (1.5m). Frost hardy, zones 7–9. Has lance-shaped leaves, bronze when young, maturing to dark green. In early spring bears a profusion of small, cup-shaped, single, white flowers.
C. cuspidata. Evergreen, upright shrub becoming bushy with age. H 10ft (3m), S 5ft (1.5m). Frost hardy, zones 7–9. Has small, lance-shaped leaves, bronze when young, maturing to purplish green. Small, cup-shaped, single, pure white flowers are freely produced from leaf axils in early spring.
C. **'Dr. Clifford Parks'** (illus. p.97). Evergreen, spreading shrub. H 12ft (4m), S 8ft (2.5m). Frost hardy, zones 7–9. In mid-spring has large, flame red flowers, often semi-double, peony- and anemone-form on the same plant. Leaves are large, oval, and dark green.
C. granthamiana. Evergreen, open shrub. H to 10ft (3m), S 6ft (2m). Half hardy, zones 8–9. Oval, leathery leaves are crinkly and glossy, deep green. In late autumn bears large, saucer-shaped, single, white flowers, to 7in (18cm) across, with up to 8 broad petals.
C. hiemalis. Evergreen, upright, bushy shrub. H 6–10ft (2–3m), S 5ft (1.5m). Frost hardy, zones 7–9. Has small, lance-shaped leaves and fragrant, single, cup-shaped, semi- or irregular double, white, pink, or red flowers borne in late autumn and winter. Is good for hedging.
C. hongkongensis. Evergreen, bushy shrub or tree. H to 10ft (3m), S 6ft (2m). Half hardy, zones 9–10. Lance-shaped leaves, 4in (10cm) long, are dark red when young, maturing to dark green. Cup-shaped, single, deep

crimson flowers, velvety on reverse of petals, are borne in late spring.
C. **'Innovation'** (illus. p.96). Evergreen, open, spreading shrub. H 15ft (5m), S 10ft (3m). Frost hardy, zones 7–9. Has large, oval, leathery leaves and, in spring, large, peony-form, lavender-shaded, claret red flowers with twisted petals.
C. **'Inspiration'** (illus. p.96). Evergreen, upright shrub. H 12ft (4m), S 6ft (2m). Frost hardy, zones 7–9. Leaves are oval and leathery. Saucer-shaped, semi-double, phlox pink flowers are freely produced in spring.
C. japonica (Common camellia). Evergreen shrub that is very variable in habit, foliage, and floral form. H 30ft (10m), S 25ft (8m). Frost hardy, zones 7–9. Numerous cultivars are available; they are spring-flowering unless otherwise stated. **'Adolphe Audusson'** (illus. p.97) is a very reliable, old cultivar that is suitable for all areas and will withstand lower temperatures than most other variants. Produces large, saucer-shaped, semi-double, dark red flowers with prominent, yellow stamens. Leaves are broadly lance-shaped and dark green. **'Alba Simplex'** (illus. p.96) is bushy in habit with broadly lance-shaped, mid- to yellow-green leaves and cup-shaped, single, white flowers in early spring. **'Alexander Hunter'** (illus. p.97), an upright, compact shrub, has flattish, single, deep crimson flowers, with some petaloids, and lance-shaped, dark green leaves. **'Althaeiflora'** (illus. p.97) has a vigorous, bushy habit, large, peony-form, dark red flowers, and broadly oval, very dark green leaves. **'Betty Sheffield Supreme'** (illus. p.96) is upright in habit with lance-shaped, green leaves and has irregular double flowers, basically white, but with each petal bordered with several shades of rose-pink. **'Donckelaeri'** is slow-growing, bushy, and pendulous with saucer-shaped, semi-double, red flowers, often white-marbled. Has lance-shaped, dark green leaves. **'Elegans'** (illus. p.96) has a spreading habit and anemone-form, deep rose-pink flowers with central petaloids often variegated white. Leaves are broadly lance-shaped and dark green. **'Fleur de Pêche'** (syn. *C.j.* 'Peachblossom') is bushy, with narrowly lance-shaped, dark green leaves and cup-shaped, semi-double, delicate pink flowers with deeper pink centers. **'Gloire de Nantes'** (illus. p.97) is an upright shrub, becoming bushy with age, that bears flattish to cup-shaped, semi-double, bright rose-pink flowers over a long period. Has oval to lance-shaped, glossy, dark green leaves. **'Grand Sultan'** see *C.j.* 'Mathotiana'. **'Guilio Nuccio'** (illus. p.97) is an upright, free-flowering cultivar that spreads with age. Produces large, cup-shaped, semi-double, rose-red flowers that each have wavy petals and often a confused center of petaloids and golden stamens. Dark green leaves are lance-shaped and occasionally have "fish tail" tips. **'Hagoromo'** see *C.j.* 'Magnoliiflora'. **'Jessie Burgess'** (illus. p.96) has a very strong, upright

growth and lance-shaped, green leaves. Bears large, cup-shaped, semi-double, rose-red flowers with a silver tint.
'Julia Drayton' (illus. p.97) has an upright habit and large, crimson flowers varying from formal double to rose-form. Dark green leaves are oval to lance-shaped and slightly twisted.
'Jupiter' (illus. p.96) is an upright shrub that bears lance-shaped, dark green leaves and large, saucer-shaped, single, pinkish red flowers with golden stamens. **'Kumasaka'** has an upright habit with narrowly lance-shaped, green leaves and produces formal double, or occasionally peony-form, deep rose-pink flowers. **'Lady Vansittart'** (illus. p.96) is upright, with unusual, hollylike, twisted, green foliage. Saucer-shaped, semi-double, white flowers are flushed rose-pink; flower color is variable and often self-colored mutations appear. **'Magnoliiflora'** (syn. *C.j.* 'Hagoromo') has a bushy habit and flattish to cup-shaped, semi-double, blush pink flowers. Twisted, light green leaves point downwards. **'Margaret Davis'** (illus. p.96) is a spreading cultivar, with oval to lance-shaped, dark green leaves. Has irregular double blooms with ruffled, creamy white petals, often lined with pink. Edges of each petal are bright rose-red. **'Mathotiana'** (syn. *C.j.* 'Grand Sultan', *C.j.* 'Te Deum'; illus. p.97) is of spreading habit; very large, formal double, velvety, dark crimson flowers become purplish with age and in warm climates often have rose-form centers. Leaves are lance-shaped to oval, slightly twisted, and dark green. **'Mrs. D.W. Davis'** (illus. p.96) is a dense, spreading cultivar that bears very large, pendulous, cup-shaped, semi-double, delicate pink flowers that are backed by oval to lance-shaped, dark green leaves. **'Peachblossom'** see *C.j.* 'Fleur de Pêche'. **'Pink Dawn'** has an upright habit, lance-shaped, green leaves, and formal double, deep pink flowers. **'R.L. Wheeler'** (illus. p.97) has a robust, upright growth, large, broadly oval, leathery, very dark green leaves, and very large, flattish, anemone-form to semi-double, rose-pink flowers, with distinctive rings of golden stamens, often including some petaloids. **'Rubescens Major'** (illus. p.96) is an upright cultivar, becoming bushy with age, with oval to lance-shaped, dark green leaves and bears formal double, crimson-veined, rose-red flowers. **'Te Deum'** see *C.j.* 'Mathotiana'. **'Tomorrow Park Hill'**, one of the best of many mutations of 'Tomorrow', is of vigorous, upright habit. Has lance-shaped, green leaves and bears irregular double flowers with deep pink, outer petals gradually fading to soft pink centers that are often variegated with white. **'Tomorrow's Dawn'** (illus. p.96) is similar, but with pale pink flowers, each with a white border and often red-streaked. **'Yamato-nishiki'** has a low, spreading habit and has thick petals forming flattish, single flowers with large, central bosses of many golden stamens; petals are white, streaked and blotched

pink and red. Small, lance-shaped leaves are dark green.

C. 'Leonard Messel' (illus. p.96). Evergreen, open shrub. H 12ft (4m), S 8ft (2.5m). Frost hardy, zones 7–9. Has large, oval, leathery, dark green leaves. In spring bears a profusion of large, flattish to cup-shaped, semi-double, rose-pink flowers.

C. maliflora. Evergreen, upright, bushy shrub. H 6ft (2m), S 3ft (1m). Frost hardy, zones 7–9. Has small, lance-shaped, thin-textured, light green leaves and, in spring, produces flattish to cup-shaped, semi-double, pale pink- or white-centered flowers with rose-pink margins.

C. oleifera. Evergreen, bushy shrub. H 6ft (2m), S 5ft (1.5m). Frost hardy, zones 7–9. Leaves are oval and dull green. Has cup-shaped, single, sometimes pinkish, white flowers in early spring.

C. reticulata. Evergreen, open, treelike shrub. H 30ft (10m) or more, S 15ft (5m). Half hardy, zones 9–10. Has large, oval, leathery leaves; large, saucer-shaped, single, rose-pink and salmon red flowers are borne in spring. Needs shelter. **'Butterfly Wings'** see *C.r.* 'Houye Diechi'. **'Captain Rawes'** has a profusion of large, semi-double, carmine rose blooms. **'Early Crimson'** see *C.r.* 'Zaotaohung'. **'Early Peony'** see *C.r.* 'Zaomudan'. **'Houye Diechi'** (syn. *C.r.* 'Butterfly Wings'; illus. p.97) produces very large, flattish to cup-shaped, semi-double, rose-pink flowers with wavy, central petals. **'Mudan Cha'** (syn. *C.r.* 'Moutancha', *C.r.* 'Peony Camellia'; illus. p.96) has very large, cup-shaped, semi- to irregular double, deep pink flowers that have curled petals. **'Robert Fortune'** (syn. *C.r.* 'Songzilin') is upright in habit and has large, formal double, deep red flowers. **'Zaomudan'** (syn. *C.r.* 'Early Peony'; illus. p.97) has large, irregular double, rose-pink flowers, each with inner petals forming a peony center. Flowers of **'Zaotaohung'** (syn. *C.r.* 'Early Crimson'; illus. p.97) are large, cup-shaped, semi- to formal double and crimson.

C. rosiflora. Evergreen, spreading shrub. H and S 3ft (1m). Frost hardy, zones 8–9. Leaves are oval and dark green. In spring produces small, saucer-shaped, single, rose-pink flowers.

C. saluenensis. Fast-growing, evergreen, bushy shrub. H to 12ft (4m), S to 8ft (2.5m). Half hardy, zones 9–10. Has lance-shaped, stiff, dull green leaves. Cup-shaped, single, white to rose-red flowers are freely produced in early spring. Some forms may withstand lower temperatures.

C. sasanqua. Fast-growing, evergreen, dense, upright shrub. H 10ft (3m), S 5ft (1.5m). Frost hardy, zones 7–9. Has lance-shaped, glossy, bright green leaves. In autumn bears a profusion of fragrant, flattish to cup-shaped, single, rarely semi-double, white flowers that may occasionally be pink or red. Does best in a hot, sunny site. **'Narumigata'** (illus. p.96) has large, cup-shaped, single, white flowers, sometimes pink-flushed. **'Onigoromo'** has cup-shaped,

single, pink-edged, white flowers and is useful for hedging.

C. tsaii. Evergreen, bushy shrub. H 12ft (4m), S 10ft (3m). Half hardy, zone 9. Small, lance-shaped, light green leaves turn bronze with age. Small, cup-shaped, single, white flowers are freely produced in spring.

C. vernalis. Fast-growing, evergreen, upright shrub. H to 10ft (3m), S 5ft (1.5m). Frost hardy, zones 7–9. Has lance-shaped, bright green leaves and, in late winter, fragrant, flattish to cup-shaped, single, white, pink, or red flowers. Some forms produce irregular double flowers.

C. 'William Hertrich' (illus. p.97). Strong-growing, evergreen, open shrub. H 15ft (5m), S 10ft (3m). Half hardy, zones 8–9. Is free-flowering with large, flattish to cup-shaped, semi-double blooms of a bright cherry red in spring. Petal formation is very irregular, and petals often form a confused center with only a few golden stamens. Leaves are large, oval, and deep green.

C. x williamsii 'Bow Bells' (illus. p.96). Evergreen, upright, spreading shrub. H 12ft (4m), S 8ft (2.5m). Fully hardy, zones 7–9. Has small, lance-shaped, green leaves and, in early spring, masses of cup-shaped, single, rose-pink flowers with deeper pink centers and veins. **'Caerhays'** (illus. p.97) is arching in habit with large, glossy leaves and large, anemone- to peony-form, crimson-pink flowers that become purplish with age. **'Clarrie Fawcett'** (illus. p.96) has an upright habit and cup-shaped, semi-double, rose-pink flowers; foliage is glossy. **'Donation'** (illus. p.96) is a compact, upright plant, very floriferous, with large, cup-shaped, semi-double, pink flowers. **'E.G. Waterhouse'** (illus. p.96) is an upright, free-flowering cultivar bearing formal double, pink flowers among pale green foliage. **'Elizabeth de Rothschild'** is vigorous and upright; cup-shaped, semi-double, rose-pink flowers appear among glossy foliage. **'Golden Spangles'** (illus. p.96) is a cup-shaped, single, deep pink cultivar with unusual, variegated foliage, yellowish in centers of leaves with dark green margins. **'J.C. Williams'** (illus. p.96) is of pendulous habit when mature and bears cup-shaped, single, pink flowers from early winter to late spring. **'Mary Christian'** (illus. p.96) is vigorous and free-flowering; has dark green foliage and cup-shaped, single, phlox pink flowers with deeper pink veins. Vigorous, upright **'Mary Larcom'** (illus. p.96) produces cup-shaped, single, cerise-pink flowers from mid-winter to late spring. Free-flowering **'St. Ewe'** (illus. p.96) has glossy, light green foliage and funnel-shaped, single, deep pink flowers.

CAMPANULA (Campanulaceae)
Bellflower
Genus of spring- and summer-flowering annuals, biennials, and perennials, some of which are evergreen. Fully to half hardy. Grows in sun or shade, but delicate flower colors are preserved best in shade.

Most forms prefer moist but well-drained soil. Propagate by softwood or basal cuttings in summer or by seed or division in autumn or spring. Is prone to slug attack, and rust may be a problem in autumn.

C. alliariifolia illus. p.232.
C. barbata illus. p.296.
C. betulifolia. Prostrate, slender-stemmed perennial. H 3/4in (2cm), S 12in (30cm). Fully hardy, zones 5–8. In summer, long, branching flower stems each carry a cluster of open bell-shaped, single, white to pink flowers, deep pink outside. Leaves are wedge-shaped.
C. 'Birch Hybrid' illus. p.322.
C. x burghaltii illus. p.242.
C. carpatica. Clump-forming perennial. H 3–4in (8–10cm), S to 12in (30cm). Fully hardy, zones 4–7. Leafy, branching stems bear rounded to oval, toothed leaves and, in summer, broadly bell-shaped, blue or white flowers. **'Bressingham White'** illus. p.313. **'Jewel'** has deep violet flowers. Flowers of **'Turbinata'** are pale lavender.
C. cochleariifolia, syn. *C. pusilla*, illus. p.323.
C. garganica. Spreading perennial. H 2in (5cm), S 12in (30cm). Fully hardy, zones 4–7. Has small, ivy-shaped leaves along stems. Clusters of star-shaped, single, pale lavender flowers are produced from leaf axils in summer. Makes an excellent wall or bank plant. **'W.H. Paine'** has bright lavender blue flowers, each with a white eye.
C. 'G.F. Wilson' illus. p.322.
C. glomerata 'Superba' illus. p.210.
C. x haylodgensis. Spreading perennial. H 2in (5cm), S 8in (20cm). Fully hardy, zones 5–8. Has small, heart-shaped leaves and, in summer, bears pomponlike, double, deep lavender blue flowers. Is suitable for a rock garden or wall.
C. isophylla. Evergreen, dwarf, trailing perennial, usually grown as an annual. H 4in (10cm), S 12in (30cm). Half hardy. In summer, star-shaped, blue or white flowers are borne above small, heart-shaped, toothed leaves. Is ideal for a hanging basket.
C. 'Joe Elliott'. Mound-forming perennial. H 3in (8cm), S 5in (12cm). Fully hardy, zones 5–8. In summer, large, funnel-shaped, lavender blue flowers almost obscure small, heart-shaped, downy, gray-green leaves. Is good for an alpine house, trough, or rock garden. Needs well-drained, alkaline soil. Protect from winter wet. Is prone to slug attack.
C. lactiflora. Upright, branching perennial. H 4ft (1.2m), S 2ft (60cm). Fully hardy, zones 4–8. In summer, slender stems bear racemes of large, nodding, bell-shaped, blue, occasionally pink, or white flowers. Leaves are narrowly oval. Needs staking on a windy site. **'Loddon Anna'** has soft dusty pink flowers. **'Prichard's Variety'** illus. p.190.
C. latifolia 'Brantwood'. Clump-forming, spreading perennial. H 4ft (1.2m), S 2ft (60cm). Fully hardy, zones 4–8. Strong stems are clothed with many bell-shaped, rich violet-

purple flowers in summer. Oval leaves are rough-textured.
C. latiloba. Rosette-forming perennial. H 3ft (1m), S 1 1/2ft (45cm). Fully hardy, zones 4–8. Leaves are oval. Widely cup-shaped flowers, in shades of blue, occasionally white, are borne in summer. **'Percy Piper'** has lavender flowers.
C. medium (Canterbury bells). Slow-growing, evergreen, erect, clump-forming biennial. Tall cultivars, H 3ft (1m), S 1ft (30cm); dwarf, H 2ft (60cm), S 1ft (30cm). Fully hardy. All have lance-shaped, toothed, fresh green leaves. Bell-shaped, single or double flowers, white or in shades of blue and pink, are produced in spring and early summer. **'Bells of Holland'** illus. p.275.
C. morettiana. Tuft-forming perennial. H 1in (2.5cm), S 3in (7cm). Frost hardy, zones 4–7. Leaves are ivy-shaped with fine hairs. Arching flower stems each carry a solitary erect, bell-shaped, violet-blue flower in late spring and early summer. Needs gritty, alkaline soil and a dry but not arid winter climate. Red spider mite may be troublesome.
C. persicifolia. Rosette-forming, spreading perennial. H 3ft (1m), S 1ft (30cm). Fully hardy, zones 4–8. In summer, nodding, bell-shaped, papery, white or blue flowers are borne above narrowly lance-shaped, bright green leaves. **'Fleur de Neige'** has double, white flowers. **'Pride of Exmouth'** bears double, powder blue flowers. **'Telham Beauty'** illus. p.212.
C. portenschlagiana illus. p.322.
C. poscharskyana illus. p.321.
C. pulla. Often short-lived perennial that spreads by underground runners. H 1in (2.5cm), S 4in (10cm). Fully hardy, zones 4–7. Tiny, rounded leaves form 1/2in (1cm) wide rosettes, each bearing a flower stem with a solitary pendent, bell-shaped, deep violet flower from late spring to early summer. Is good for a scree or rock garden. Needs gritty, alkaline soil that is not too dry. Slugs may prove troublesome.
C. pusilla. See *C. cochleariifolia*.
C. pyramidalis (Chimney bellflower). Erect, branching biennial. H 6ft (2m), S 2ft (60cm). Half hardy. Produces long racemes of star-shaped, blue or white flowers in summer. Leaves are heart-shaped. Needs staking.
C. raineri. Perennial that spreads by underground runners. H 1 1/2in (4cm), S 3in (8cm). Frost hardy, zones 5–7. Leaves are oval, toothed, and gray-green. Flower stems each carry a large, upturned, bell-shaped, pale lavender flower in summer. Is suitable for an alpine house or trough that is protected from winter wet. Requires semi-shade.
C. trachelium and **'Bernice'** illus. p.211.
C. vidalii. See *Azorina vidalii*.
C. zoysii. Tuft-forming perennial. H 2in (5cm), S 4in (10cm). Frost hardy, zones 5–7. Has tiny, rounded, glossy green leaves. In summer, flower stems each bear a bottle-shaped, lavender flower held horizontally. Needs gritty, alkaline soil. Is difficult to grow and flower well, dislikes winter wet, and is prone to slug attack.

CAMPSIS (Bignoniaceae)
Genus of deciduous, woody-stemmed, root climbers, grown for their flowers. Frost hardy; in cooler areas needs protection of a sunny wall. Grow in sun and fertile, well-drained soil and water regularly in summer. Prune in spring. Propagate by semi-ripe cuttings in summer or by layering in winter.
C. chinensis. See *C. grandiflora.*
C. grandiflora, syn. *Bignonia grandiflora*, *Campsis chinensis*, *Tecoma grandiflora* (Chinese trumpet creeper, Chinese trumpet vine). Deciduous, woody-stemmed, root climber. H 22–30ft (7–10m). Zones 7–9. Leaves have 7 or 9 oval, toothed leaflets, hairless beneath. Drooping clusters of trumpet-shaped, deep orange or red flowers, 2–3in (5–8cm) long, are produced in late summer and autumn, abundantly in warm areas.
C. radicans, syn. *Bignonia radicans*, *Tecoma radicans* (Trumpet creeper, Trumpet honeysuckle, Trumpet vine). Deciduous, woody-stemmed, root climber. H to 40ft (12m). Zones 5–9. Leaves of 7–11 oval, toothed leaflets are downy beneath. Small clusters of trumpet-shaped, orange, scarlet, or yellow flowers, 2$^1/_2$–3in (6–8cm) long, are carried in late summer and early autumn.
C. x *tagliabuana* '**Mme. Galen**' illus. p.175.

CAMPTOSORUS (Polypodiaceae)
Genus of semi-evergreen or deciduous ferns, grown for their curiosity value. Frost hardy. Needs shade and moist but well-drained soil, preferably lime-rich. Is not easy to cultivate. Propagate by division in spring or by spores in late summer.
C. rhizophyllus (Walking fern). Semi-evergreen or deciduous fern. H 6–9in (15–23cm), S 6–12in (15–30cm). Zones 5–8. Heart-shaped, green fronds are borne at ends of naked, reddish green stems. Is suitable for a rock garden.

CANARINA (Campanulaceae)
Genus of herbaceous, tuberous, scrambling climbers, grown for their flowers. Frost tender, min. 45°F (7°C). Grow in any fertile, well-drained soil and in full light. Water moderately from early autumn to late spring, then keep dry. Needs staking. Remove dead stems when dormant. Propagate by basal cuttings or seed sown in spring or autumn.
C. campanula. See *C. canariensis.*
C. canariensis, syn. *C. campanula*, illus. p.177.

Candollea cuneiformis. See *Hibbertia cuneiformis.*

CANNA (Cannaceae)
Genus of robust, showy, rhizomatous perennials, grown for their striking flowers and ornamental foliage. Is generally used for summer-bedding displays and container growing. Frost tender, min. 50–59°F (10–15°C). Requires a warm, sunny position and humus-rich, moist soil. If grown under glass or for summer bedding, encourage into growth in spring at

61°F (16°C) and store rhizomes in slightly damp soil or peat in winter. Propagate in spring by division or in winter by seed sown at 68°F (20°C) or more.
C. x *generalis* '**Assault**' illus. p.336. '**Dazzler**' is a rhizomatous perennial. H to 4ft (1.2m), S 1$^1/_2$–2ft (45–60cm). Min. 59°F (15°C), zones 7–10. Stout stems bear bold, broadly lance-shaped, bronze-green leaves, to 12in (30cm) wide. In summer produces a spike of large, orchidlike, brilliant cardinal red flowers, each with 3 large petals and a lower lip. '**Lucifer**', H 3ft (1m), has purple leaves and yellow-edged, red petals. '**Orange Perfection**', H 24–32in (60–80cm), has orange flowers.
C. iridiflora illus. p.339.

CANTUA (Polemoniaceae)
Genus of evergreen shrubs, grown for their showy flowers in spring. Only one species, however, is in general cultivation. Half hardy; is best grown against a south- or west-facing wall. Requires full sun and fertile, well-drained soil. Propagate by semi-ripe cuttings in summer.
C. buxifolia, syn. *C. dependens*, illus. p.123.
C. dependens. See *C. buxifolia.*

CAPSICUM (Solanaceae)
Genus of evergreen shrubs, sub-shrubs, and short-lived perennials, usually grown as annuals. Some species produce edible fruits (e.g. sweet peppers), others small, ornamental ones. Frost tender, min. 39°F (4°C). Grow in sun and in fertile, well-drained soil. Spray flowers with water to encourage fruit to set. Propagate by seed sown under glass in spring. Red spider mite may be troublesome.
C. annuum (Ornamental pepper). '**Holiday Cheer**' is a moderately fast-growing, evergreen, bushy perennial, grown as an annual. H and S 8–12in (20–30cm). Has oval, green leaves. Produces small, star-shaped, white flowers in summer and, in autumn-winter, spherical fruits that change from green to red. '**Holiday Time**' illus. p.273.

CARAGANA (Leguminosae)
Genus of deciduous shrubs, grown for their foliage and flowers. Fully hardy. Needs full sun and fertile but not over-rich, well-drained soil. Propagate species by softwood cuttings in summer or by seed in autumn, cultivars by softwood or semi-ripe cuttings or budding in summer or by grafting in winter.
C. arborescens. Fast-growing, deciduous, upright shrub. H 20ft (6m), S 12ft (4m). Zones 2–8. Has spine-tipped, dark green leaves, each composed of 8–12 oblong leaflets. Produces clusters of pealike, yellow flowers in late spring. Arching '**Lorbergii**', H 10ft (3m), S 8ft (2.5m), has very narrow leaflets and smaller flowers and is often grown as a tree by top-grafting; '**Nana**' illus. p.125. '**Walker**', H 1ft (30cm), S 6–10ft (2–3m), is prostrate but is usually top-grafted to form a weeping tree 6ft (2m) high and 2$^1/_2$ft (75cm) across.

C. frutex '**Globosa**' (Russian peashrub). Slow-growing, deciduous, upright shrub. H and S 1ft (30cm). Zones 2–8. Each green leaf has 4 oblong leaflets. Pealike, bright yellow flowers are borne only rarely in late spring.

CARALLUMA (Asclepiadaceae)
Genus of perennial succulents with 4–6-ribbed, fingerlike, blue-gray or -green to purple stems. Frost tender, min. 52°F (11°C). Needs sun and extremely well-drained soil. Water sparingly, only in the growing season. May be difficult to grow. Propagate by seed or stem cuttings in summer.
C. europaea. Clump-forming, perennial succulent. H 8in (20cm), S 3ft (1m). Zones 9–10. Rough, 4-angled, erect to procumbent, gray stems often arch over and root. Has clusters of small, star-shaped, yellow and brownish purple flowers near stem crown from mid- to late summer, followed by twin-horned, gray seed pods. Flowers smell faintly of rotten meat. Is one of the easier species to grow.
C. joannis illus. p.395.

CARDAMINE (Cruciferae)
Bitter cress
Genus of spring-flowering annuals and perennials. Some are weeds, but others are suitable for informal and woodland gardens. Fully hardy. Requires sun or semi-shade and moist soil. Propagate by seed or division in autumn.
C. enneaphyllos, syn. *Dentaria enneaphylla*, illus. p.229.
C. pentaphyllos, syn. *Dentaria pentaphylla*, illus. p.227.
C. pratensis (Cuckoo flower, Lady's smock). '**Flore Pleno**' is a neat, clump-forming perennial. H 18in (45cm), S 12in (30cm). Zones 5–8. Bears dense sheaves of double, lilac flowers in spring. Green leaves are divided into rounded leaflets. May also be propagated by leaf-tip cuttings in mid-summer. Prefers moist or wet conditions.
C. trifolia illus. p.302.

CARDIOCRINUM (Liliaceae)
Genus of summer-flowering, lilylike bulbs, grown for their spectacular flowers. Frost hardy. Needs partial shade and deep, humus-rich, moist soil. Plant bulbs just below soil surface, in autumn. Water well in summer and mulch with humus. After flowering, main bulb dies, but produces offsets. Propagate by offsets in autumn, to produce flowers within 5 years, or by seed in autumn or winter, for flowers in 7 years.
C. giganteum illus. p.333. var. *yunnanense* is a stout, leafy-stemmed bulb. H 5–6ft (1.5–2m), S 2$^1/_2$–3ft (75cm–1m). Zones 7–9. Has bold, heart-shaped, bronze-green leaves. Fragrant, pendent, trumpet-shaped, cream flowers, 6in (15cm) long, with purple-red streaks inside, are borne in long spikes in summer and are followed by decorative seed heads.

CARDIOSPERMUM (Sapindaceae)
Genus of herbaceous or deciduous, shrubby climbers, grown mainly for

their attractive fruits. Is useful for covering bushes or trellises. Frost tender, min. 41°F (5°C). Grow in full light and any soil. Propagate by seed in spring.
C. halicacabum (Balloon vine, Heart pea, Heart seed, Winter cherry). Deciduous, shrubby, scandent, perennial climber, usually grown as an annual or biennial. H to 10ft (3m). Zones 9–10. Has toothed leaves composed of 2 oblong leaflets. Produces inconspicuous, whitish flowers that appear in summer, followed by downy, spherical, inflated, 3-angled, straw-colored fruits containing black seeds, each with a heart-shaped, white spot.

CAREX (Cyperaceae). See GRASSES, BAMBOOS, RUSHES, and SEDGES.
C. buchananii (Leatherleaf sedge). Evergreen, tuft-forming, perennial sedge. H to 24in (60cm), S 8in (20cm). Fully hardy, zones 6–9. Very narrow, copper-colored leaves turn red towards base. Solid, triangular stems bear insignificant, brown spikelets in summer.
C. elata, syn. *C. stricta* (Tufted sedge). Evergreen, tuft-forming, perennial sedge. H to 3ft (1m), S 6in (15cm). Fully hardy, zones 5–9. Leaves are somewhat glaucous. Produces solid, triangular stems that bear blackish brown spikelets in summer. '**Aurea**' illus. p.183.
C. grayi (Mace sedge). Evergreen, tuft-forming, perennial sedge. H to 24in (60cm), S 8in (20cm). Fully hardy, zones 3–8. Has bright green leaves. Large, female spikelets, borne in summer, mature to pointed, knobbly, greenish brown fruits.
C. morrowii of gardens. See *C. oshimensis.*
C. oshimensis, syn. *C. morrowii* of gardens. Evergreen, tuft-forming, perennial sedge. H 8–20in (20–50cm), S 8–10in (20–25cm). Fully hardy, zones 7–9. Has narrow, green leaves. Solid, triangular stems bear insignificant spikelets in summer. '**Evergold**' illus. p.183.
C. pendula illus. p.183.
C. riparia (Greater pond sedge). '**Variegata**' is a vigorous, evergreen, perennial sedge. H 2–3ft (60cm–1m), S indefinite. Fully hardy, zones 4–8. Has broad, white-striped, green leaves and solid, triangular stems that bear narrow, bristle-tipped, dark brown spikelets in summer.
C. stricta. See *C. elata.*

CARISSA (Apocynaceae)
Genus of evergreen, spring- to summer-flowering shrubs, grown for their flowers and overall appearance. Frost tender, min. 50–55°F (10–13°C). Needs partial shade and well-drained soil. Water potted specimens moderately, less when temperatures are low. Propagate by seed when ripe or in spring or by semi-ripe cuttings in summer.
C. grandiflora (Natal plum). '**Tuttlei**' illus. p.103.
C. spectabilis. See *Acokanthera oblongifolia.*

CARLINA (Compositae)
Thistle
Genus of annuals, biennials, and perennials, grown for their ornamental flower heads. Fully hardy. Needs sun and well-drained soil. Propagate by seed: annuals in spring, perennials in autumn.
C. acaulis illus. p.315.

CARMICHAELIA (Leguminosae)
Genus of deciduous, usually leafless shrubs, grown for their profusion of tiny flowers in summer. Flattened, green shoots assume function of leaves. Frost to half hardy. Needs full sun and well-drained soil. Cut out dead wood in spring. Propagate by semi-ripe cuttings in summer or by seed in autumn or spring.
C. australis. Deciduous, upright shrub. H 6ft (2m), S 5ft (1.5m). Frost hardy, zones 9–10. Small clusters of pealike, pale lilac flowers appear from early to mid-summer. May need staking when mature.
C. enysii. Deciduous, mound-forming, dense shrub. H and S 1ft (30cm). Frost hardy, zones 9–10. Shoots are rigid. Pealike, violet flowers are borne in mid-summer. Is best grown in a rock garden.

CARNEGIEA (Cactaceae)
Genus of one species of very slow-growing, perennial cactus with thick, 12–24-ribbed, spiny stems. Is unlikely to flower or branch at less than 12ft (4m) high. Frost tender, min. 45°F (7°C). Requires full sun and very well-drained soil. Propagate by seed in spring or summer.
C. gigantea illus. p.378.

CARPENTERIA (Hydrangaceae)
Genus of one species of evergreen, summer-flowering shrub, cultivated for its flowers and foliage. Frost hardy. Grows well against a south- or west-facing wall. Prefers full sun and a fairly moist but well-drained soil. Propagate by greenwood cuttings in summer or by seed in autumn.
C. californica illus. p.106.

CARPINUS (Carpinaceae)
Hornbeam
Genus of deciduous trees, grown for their foliage, autumn color, and clusters of small, winged nuts. Fully hardy. Needs sun or semi-shade and fertile, well-drained soil. Propagate species by seed in autumn, cultivars by budding in late summer.
C. betulus (Common hornbeam). Deciduous, round-headed tree. H 80ft (25m), S 70ft (20m). Zones 5–9. Has a fluted trunk and oval, prominently veined, dark green leaves that turn yellow and orange in autumn. Bears green catkins from late spring to autumn, when clusters of winged nuts appear. **'Fastigiata'** illus. p.72.
C. caroliniana (American hornbeam). Deciduous, spreading tree with branches that droop at tips. H and S 30ft (10m). Zones 3–9. Has a fluted, gray trunk, green catkins in spring, and oval, bright green leaves that turn orange and red in autumn, when clusters of winged nuts appear.

C. tschonoskii. Deciduous, rounded tree of elegant habit, with branches drooping at tips. H and S 40ft (12m). Zones 6–9. Has oval, sharply toothed, glossy, dark green leaves, green catkins in spring, and clusters of small, winged nuts in autumn.
C. turczaninowii. Deciduous, spreading tree of graceful habit. H 40ft (12m), S 30ft (10m). Zones 6–9. Green catkins are borne in spring. Produces clusters of small, winged nuts in autumn, when small, oval, glossy, deep green leaves turn orange.

CARPOBROTUS (Aizoaceae)
Genus of mat-forming, perennial succulents with triangular, fleshy, dark green leaves and daisylike flowers. Is excellent for binding sandy soils. Half hardy to frost tender, min. 41°F (5°C). Needs full sun and well-drained soil. Propagate by seed or stem cuttings in spring or summer.
C. edulis (Hottentot fig). Carpeting, perennial succulent. H 6in (15cm), S indefinite. Frost tender, zones 9–10. Prostrate, rooting branches bear leaves $5/8$in (1.5cm) thick and 5in (12cm) long. Yellow, purple, or pink flowers, 5in (12cm) across, open in spring-summer from about noon in sun. Bears edible, figlike, brownish fruits in late summer and autumn.

CARRIEREA (Flacourtiaceae)
Genus of deciduous trees. Only *C. calycina*, grown for its flowers, is in general cultivation. Frost hardy. Needs full sun and fertile, well-drained soil. Propagate by softwood cuttings in summer.
C. calycina. Deciduous, spreading tree. H 25ft (8m), S 30ft (10m). Zones 7–9. Oval, glossy, green leaves set off upright clusters of cup-shaped, creamy white or greenish white flowers in early summer.

CARYA (Juglandaceae)
Hickory
Genus of deciduous trees, grown for their stately habit, divided leaves, autumn color and, in some cases, edible nuts. Has insignificant flowers in spring. Fully hardy. Requires sun or semi-shade and deep, fertile soil. Plant young seedlings in a permanent position during their first year as older plants resent transplanting. Propagate by seed in autumn.
C. cordiformis (Bitternut, Bitternut hickory). Vigorous, deciduous, spreading tree. H 80ft (25m), S 50ft (15m). Zones 5–8. Bark is smooth at first, later fissured. Bright yellow, winter leaf buds develop into large, dark green leaves, with usually 7 oval to oblong leaflets; these turn yellow in autumn. Nuts are pear-shaped or rounded, $3/4$–$1^1/2$in (2–4cm) long, each with a bitter kernel.
C. glabra (Pignut, Pignut hickory). Deciduous, spreading tree. H 80ft (25m), S 70ft (20m). Zones 5–8. Dark green leaves, with usually 5 narrowly oval leaflets, turn bright yellow and orange in autumn. Pear-shaped or rounded nuts, $3/4$–$1^1/2$in (2–4cm) long, each have a bitter kernel.
C. ovata illus. p.43.

CARYOPTERIS (Verbenaceae)
Genus of deciduous sub-shrubs, grown for their foliage and small, but freely produced, blue flowers. Frost hardy. Prefers full sun and light, well-drained soil. Cut back hard in spring. Propagate species by greenwood or semi-ripe cuttings in summer or by seed in autumn, cultivars by cuttings only in summer.
C. x *clandonensis* **'Arthur Simmonds'** illus. p.136. **'Heavenly Blue'** is a deciduous, bushy sub-shrub. H and S 3ft (1m). Zones 7–9. Forms an upright, compact mass of lance-shaped, gray-green leaves. Dense clusters of tubular, blue to purplish blue flowers, with prominent stamens, are borne from late summer to autumn.
C. incana (Common bluebeard). Deciduous, bushy sub-shrub. H and S 4ft (1.2m). Zones 7–9. Tubular, violet-blue flowers, with prominent stamens, are produced amid lance-shaped, gray-green leaves from late summer to early autumn.

CASSIA (Leguminosae)
Genus of annuals, perennials, and evergreen or deciduous trees and shrubs, grown for their flowers mainly produced from winter to summer. Fully hardy to frost tender, min. 45–64°F (7–18°C). Needs full light and fertile, well-drained soil. Water potted specimens freely when in full growth, moderately to sparingly in winter. Pruning is tolerated, severe if need be, but trees are best left to grow naturally. Propagate by seed in spring.
C. artemisioides (Silver cassia, Wormwood cassia). Evergreen, erect to spreading, wiry shrub. H and S 3–6ft (1–2m). Frost tender, min. 50–55°F (10–13°C), zone 10. Leaves each have 6–14 linear leaflets covered with silky, white down. Axillary spikes of cup-shaped, yellow flowers appear from winter to early summer.
C. corymbosa illus. p.115.
var. *plurijuga* (syn. *C. floribunda* of gardens) is a vigorous, evergreen or deciduous, rounded shrub with robust stems. H and S 5–6ft (1.5–2m). Frost tender, min. 45°F (7°C), zones 9–10. Bright green leaves consist of 4–6 oval leaflets. Carries very large clusters of bowl-shaped, rich yellow flowers in late summer.
C. didymobotrya illus. p.115.
C. fistula (Golden shower, Indian laburnum, Pudding pipe tree). Fast-growing, almost deciduous, ovoid tree. H 25–30ft (8–10m), S 12–20ft (4–6m). Frost tender, min. 61°F (16°C), zone 10. Has 12–18in (30–45cm) long leaves, each with 4–8 pairs of oval leaflets, coppery when young. In spring produces racemes of small, fragrant, 5-petaled, cup-shaped, bright yellow flowers. Cylindrical, dark brown pods, to 2ft (60cm) long, yield cassia pulp.
C. floribunda of gardens. See *C. corymbosa* var. *plurijuga*.
C. siamea. Fast-growing, evergreen, rounded tree. H and S 25–30ft (8–10m) or more. Frost tender, min. 61–4°F (16–18°C), zones 9–10. Leaves, 6–12in (15–30cm) long, have 7–12 pairs of elliptic leaflets. Large, terminal

panicles of small, cup-shaped, bright yellow flowers are borne in spring, followed by flat, dark brown pods, to 9in (23cm) long.

CASSINIA (Compositae)
Genus of evergreen shrubs, grown for their foliage and flowers. Frost hardy, but avoid cold, exposed positions. Needs full sun and fertile, well-drained soil. Propagate by softwood cuttings in summer.
C. fulvida. Evergreen, bushy shrub. H and S 6ft (2m). Zones 8–9. Has yellow shoots, small, oblong, dark green leaves and, in mid-summer, clustered heads of minute, white flowers. Is useful as a coastal hedging plant.
C. vauvilliersii illus. p.129.

CASSIOPE (Ericaceae)
Genus of evergreen, spring-flowering shrubs, suitable for peat beds and walls and for rock gardens. Fully hardy. Needs a sheltered, shaded or semi-shaded site and moist, peaty, acid soil. Propagate by semi-ripe or greenwood cuttings in summer or by seed in autumn or spring.
C. **'Edinburgh'** illus. p.286.
C. fastigiata. Evergreen, upright, loose shrub. H 12in (30cm), S 6–8in (15–20cm). Zones 7–8. In spring, bell-shaped, creamy white flowers, resting in green or red calyces, are borne on short stalks in leaf axils. Leaves are tiny and scalelike. Needs a semi-shaded situation.
C. lycopodioides illus. p.303.
C. mertensiana illus. p.304.
C. **'Muirhead'** illus. p.286.
C. selaginoides. Evergreen, spreading shrub. H 10in (25cm), S 6in (15cm). Zones 7–8. Stem is hidden by dense, scalelike, green leaves. Bears solitary relatively large, pendent, bell-shaped, white flowers in spring. Needs a shaded site.
C. tetragona. Evergreen, upright shrub. H 4–10in (10–25cm), S 4–6in (10–15cm). Zones 2–7. Dense, scalelike, dark green leaves conceal branched stems. In spring, leaf axils bear solitary pendent, bell-shaped, white flowers in red calyces. Needs a semi-shaded site.
C. wardii. Evergreen, upright to spreading, loose shrub. H 6in (15cm), S 8in (20cm). Zones 4–7. Semi-upright stems are densely clothed with scalelike, dark green leaves that give them a squared appearance. Bell-shaped, white flowers, set close to stem, open in spring. Needs shade in all but cool areas. May also be propagated by division of runners in spring.

CASTANEA (Fagaceae)
Chestnut
Genus of deciduous, summer-flowering trees and shrubs, grown for their foliage, stately habit, flowers, and edible fruits (chestnuts). Fully hardy. Requires sun or semi-shade; does particularly well in hot, dry areas. Needs fertile, well-drained soil; grows poorly on shallow, chalky soil. Propagate species by seed in autumn, cultivars by budding in summer or by grafting in late winter.

C. dentata (American chestnut). Deciduous, spreading tree with rough bark. H 100ft (30m), S 50ft (15m). Zones 5–8. Oblong, toothed, dull green leaves turn orange-yellow in autumn. Has catkins of greenish white flowers in summer, followed by typical spiny "chestnut" fruits.
C. sativa (Spanish chestnut, Sweet chestnut). Deciduous, spreading tree. H 100ft (30m), S 50ft (15m). Zones 5–8. Bark becomes spirally ridged with age. Oblong, glossy, dark green leaves turn yellow in autumn. Spikes of small, creamy yellow flowers in summer are followed by edible fruits in rounded, spiny husks.
'Albomarginata' illus. p.39.

CASTANOPSIS (Fagaceae)
Genus of evergreen shrubs and trees, grown for their habit and foliage. Flowers are insignificant. Frost hardy. Needs a sheltered position in sun or semi-shade and fertile, well-drained but not too dry, acid soil. Propagate by seed when ripe, in autumn.
C. cuspidata. Evergreen, bushy, spreading shrub or tree with drooping shoots. H and S 25ft (8m) or more. Zones 9–10. Bears long, oval, slender-tipped, leathery leaves, glossy, dark green above, bronze beneath.

CASTANOSPERMUM
(Leguminosae)
Black bean tree, Moreton Bay chestnut
Genus of one species of evergreen tree, grown for its overall ornamental appearance and for shade. Frost tender, min. 50–59°F (10–15°C). Requires full light and fertile, moisture-retentive but well-drained soil. Water potted specimens freely when in full growth, moderately at other times. Propagate by seed in spring.
C. australe. Strong-growing, evergreen, rounded tree. H 50ft (15m) or more, S 25ft (8m) or more. Zone 10. Has 18in (45cm) long leaves of 8–17 oval leaflets. Racemes of large, pealike, yellow flowers, borne in autumn on mature trees, age to orange and red. Cylindrical, reddish brown pods, each 10in (25cm) long, contain large, chestnutlike seeds.

CATALPA (Bignoniaceae)
Genus of deciduous, summer-flowering trees and shrubs, extremely resistant to urban pollution, grown for their foliage and bell- or trumpet-shaped flowers with frilly lobes. Trees are best grown as isolated specimens. Fully hardy. Prefers full sun and does best in hot summers. Needs deep, fertile, well-drained but not too dry soil. Propagate species by seed in autumn, cultivars by softwood cuttings in summer or by budding in late summer.
C. bignonioides illus. p.51. 'Aurea' is a deciduous, spreading tree. H and S 30ft (10m). Zones 5–9. Has broadly oval, bright yellow leaves, bronze when young. Bell-shaped, white flowers, marked with yellow and purple, appear in summer, followed by long, pendent, cylindrical pods, often persisting after leaf fall.
C. × *erubescens* 'Purpurea'. Deciduous, spreading tree. H and S

50ft (15m). Zones 5–9. Broadly oval or 3-lobed, very dark purple, young leaves mature to dark green. Fragrant, bell-shaped, white flowers, marked with yellow and purple, are borne from mid- to late summer.
C. ovata. Deciduous, spreading tree. H and S 30ft (10m). Zones 5–9. Has 3-lobed, purplish leaves when young, maturing to pale green. Large clusters of bell-shaped, white flowers, spotted with red and yellow, are borne from mid- to late summer.
C. speciosa illus. p.51.

CATANANCHE (Compositae)
Blue cupidone
Genus of perennials with daisylike flower heads that may be dried for winter flower arrangements. Fully hardy. Needs sun and light, well-drained soil. Propagate by seed in spring or by root cuttings in winter.
C. caerulea 'Major' illus. p.242.

CATHARANTHUS (Apocynaceae)
Genus of evergreen shrubs, grown for their flowers. *C. roseus* is often grown annually from seed or cuttings and used as a summer bedding plant in cool climates. Frost tender, min. 41–5°F (5–7°C). Needs full light and well-drained soil. Water potted specimens moderately, less when temperatures are low. Prune long or straggly stems in early spring to promote a more bushy habit. Propagate by seed in spring or by greenwood or semi-ripe cuttings in summer.
C. roseus, syn. *Vinca rosea*, illus. p.128.

CATTLEYA. See ORCHIDS.
C. bowringiana (illus. p.253). Evergreen, epiphytic orchid for a cool greenhouse. H 18in (45cm). Zone 10. In autumn bears large heads of rose-purple-lipped, magenta flowers, 3in (8cm) across. Has oval, stiff leaves, 3–4in (8–10cm) long. Grow in semi-shade during summer and do not spray from overhead.
C. J.A. Carbone (illus. p.253). Evergreen, epiphytic orchid for an intermediate greenhouse. H 18in (45cm). Zone 10. Large heads of fragrant, pinkish mauve flowers, 4in (10cm) across and each with a yellow-marked, deep pink lip, open in early summer. Has oval, stiff leaves, 4–6in (10–15cm) long. Avoid spraying from overhead.

CAUTLEYA (Zingiberaceae)
Genus of summer- and autumn-flowering perennials. Frost hardy. Grow in a sunny, wind-free position and in deep, rich, moist but well-drained soil. Propagate by seed or division in spring.
C. spicata illus. p.250.

CEANOTHUS (Rhamnaceae)
Genus of evergreen or deciduous shrubs and small trees, grown for their small but densely clustered, mainly blue flowers. Frost to half hardy; in cold areas plant against a south- or west-facing wall. Needs a sheltered site in full sun and light, well-drained soil. Cut dead wood from evergreens

in spring and trim their side-shoots after flowering. Cut back shoots of deciduous species to basal framework in early spring. Propagate by semi-ripe cuttings in summer.
C. arboreus 'Trewithen Blue'. Vigorous, evergreen, bushy, spreading shrub. H 20ft (6m), S 25ft (8m) or more. Frost hardy, zone 9. In spring and early summer, large, pyramidal clusters of rich blue flowers are borne amid broadly oval to rounded, dark green leaves.
C. 'Autumnal Blue' illus. p.116.
C. 'Blue Mound'. Evergreen, bushy, dense shrub. H 5ft (1.5m), S 6ft (2m). Frost hardy, zone 9. Forms a mound of oblong, glossy, dark green leaves, covered, in late spring, with rounded clusters of deep blue flowers.
C. 'Burkwoodii'. Evergreen, bushy, dense shrub. H 5ft (1.5m), S 6ft (2m). Frost hardy, zone 9. Has oval, glossy, dark green leaves, downy and gray beneath. Produces dense panicles of bright blue flowers from mid-summer to mid-autumn.
C. 'Burtonensis'. Evergreen, bushy, spreading shrub. H 6ft (2m) or more, S 12ft (4m). Frost hardy, zones 8–9. Has small, rounded, almost spherical, crinkled leaves that are lustrous and dark green. Small, deep blue flowers appear in clusters, $^{3}/_{4}$in (2cm) wide, from mid-spring to early summer.
C. 'Cascade'. Vigorous, evergreen, arching shrub. H and S 12ft (4m). Frost hardy, zone 9. Leaves are narrowly oblong, glossy, and dark green. Large panicles of powder blue flowers open in late spring and early summer.
C. 'Delight'. Fast-growing, evergreen, bushy shrub. H 10ft (3m), S 15ft (5m). Frost hardy, zone 9. Bears oblong, glossy, deep green leaves. Long clusters of rich blue flowers appear in late spring.
C. dentatus. Evergreen, bushy, dense shrub. H 5ft (1.5m), S 6ft (2m). Frost hardy, zone 9. Produces small, oblong, glossy, dark green leaves and is covered, in late spring, with rounded clusters of bright blue flowers.
C. 'Gloire de Versailles' illus. p.136.
C. gloriosus. Evergreen, prostrate shrub. H 1ft (30cm), S 6ft (2m). Frost hardy, zones 7–9. Leaves are oval and dark green. Rounded clusters of deep blue or purplish blue flowers appear from mid- to late spring. May suffer from chlorosis on chalky soils.
C. impressus illus. p.113.
C. incanus illus. p.106.
C. 'Italian Skies'. Evergreen, bushy, spreading shrub. H 5ft (1.5m), S 10ft (3m). Frost hardy, zone 9. Has small, oval, glossy, dark green leaves. Produces dense, conical clusters of bright blue flowers during late spring.
C. × *lobbianus*. Evergreen, bushy, dense shrub. H and S 6ft (2m). Frost hardy, zone 9. Rounded clusters of bright deep blue flowers are borne in late spring and early summer amid oval, dark green leaves.
C. 'Marie Simon'. Deciduous, bushy shrub. H and S 5ft (1.5m). Frost hardy, zone 9. Has broadly oval, green leaves. Conical clusters of soft pink flowers are carried in profusion from mid-summer to early autumn.

C. papillosus. Evergreen, arching shrub. H 10ft (3m), S 15ft (5m). Frost hardy, zone 9. Leaves are narrowly oblong, glossy, dark green, and sticky. Produces dense racemes of blue or purplish blue flowers during late spring.
C. 'Perle Rose' illus. p.131.
C. rigidus (Monterey ceanothus). Evergreen, bushy shrub of dense, spreading habit. H 4ft (1.2m), S 8ft (2.5m). Frost hardy, zone 9. Bears oblong to rounded, glossy, dark green leaves and, from mid-spring to early summer, rounded clusters of deep purplish blue flowers.
C. 'Southmead'. Evergreen, bushy, dense shrub. H and S 5ft (1.5m). Frost hardy, zone 9. Has small, oblong, glossy, dark green leaves. Deep blue flowers are produced in rounded clusters in late spring and early summer.
C. thyrsiflorus. Evergreen, bushy shrub or spreading tree. H and S 20ft (6m). Frost hardy, zones 8–9. Has broadly oval, glossy, green leaves and, in late spring and early summer, bears rounded clusters of pale blue flowers. var. *repens* illus. p.136.
C. × *veitchianus.* Vigorous, evergreen, bushy shrub. H and S 10ft (3m). Frost hardy, zone 9. Dense, oblong clusters of deep blue flowers are borne in late spring and early summer amid oblong, glossy, dark green leaves.

CEDRELA (Meliaceae)
Genus of deciduous trees, grown for their foliage, autumn color, and flowers. Fully hardy. Prefers full sun and requires fertile, well-drained soil. Propagate by seed in autumn or by root cuttings in winter.
C. sinensis, syn. *Toona sinensis*, illus. p.52.

Cedronella mexicana. See *Agastache mexicana.*

CEDRUS (Pinaceae), Cedar. See CONIFERS.
C. atlantica (Atlas cedar). Conifer that is conical when young, broadening with age. H 50–80ft (15–25m), S 15–30ft (5–10m). Fully hardy, zones 7–9. Leaves are spirally arranged, needlelike, dull green or bright blue-gray. Has ovoid cones, males pale brown, females pale green, ripening to brown. f. *fastigiata*, S 12–15ft (4–5m), has a narrower, more upright habit. f. *glauca* illus. p.73.
C. deodara (Deodar). Fast-growing conifer, densely conical with weeping tips when young, broader when mature. H 50–80ft (15–25m), S 15–30ft (5–10m). Fully hardy, zones 7–9. Has spirally arranged, needlelike, gray-green leaves and barrel-shaped, glaucous cones, 3–5in (8–12cm) long, ripening to brown. 'Aurea' illus. p.81.
C. libani illus. p.75. Open conifer with tiered, arching branches. H 80ft (25m), S 50ft (15m). Fully hardy, zones 7–9. Spirally arranged, needlelike, gray-green foliage is produced in dense, flat layers. Has grayish pink cones. 'Comte de Dijon', H 3–6ft (1–2m), S 2–4ft (60cm–1.2m), is a dwarf form that grows only 2in (5cm) a year.

'Sargentii' (illus. p.83), H and S 3–5ft (1–1.5m), has horizontal, then weeping branches and makes a rounded bush.

CEIBA (Bombacaceae)
Genus of evergreen, semi-evergreen, or deciduous trees, grown for their overall appearance and for shade. Frost tender, min. 59°F (15°C). Requires full light or light shade and fertile, moisture-retentive but well-drained soil. Water potted specimens freely while in full growth, less at other times. Pruning is tolerated if necessary. Propagate by seed in spring or by semi-ripe cuttings in summer.
C. pentandra (Kapok, Silk cotton tree). Fast-growing, semi-evergreen tree with a spine-covered trunk. H and S 80ft (25m) or more. Zone 10. Hand-shaped leaves have 5–9 elliptic leaflets, red when young, becoming green. Bears clusters of 5-petaled, white, yellow, or pink flowers in summer, followed by woody, brownish seed pods containing silky kapok fiber.

CELASTRUS (Celastraceae)
Genus of deciduous shrubs and twining climbers, grown for their attractive fruits. Species described bear male and female flowers on separate plants, so both sexes must be grown to obtain fruits. Fully to frost hardy. Grow in any soil and in full or partial shade. Likes regular feeding. Prune in spring to cut out old wood and maintain shape. Propagate by seed in autumn or spring or by semi-ripe cuttings in summer.
C. articulatus. See *C. orbiculatus.*
C. orbiculatus, syn. *C. articulatus* (Oriental bittersweet, Staff vine). Vigorous, deciduous, twining climber. H to 46ft (14m). Frost hardy, zones 5–8. Has small, rounded, toothed leaves. Clusters of 2–4 small, green flowers are produced in summer; tiny, long-lasting, spherical fruits begin green, turn black in autumn, then split and show yellow insides and red seeds.
C. scandens (American bittersweet, Staff tree). Deciduous, twining climber. H to 30ft (10m). Frost hardy, zones 4–8. Oval leaves are 2–4in (5–10cm) long; tiny, greenish flowers are borne in small clusters in leaf axils in summer; long-lasting, spherical fruits are produced in bunches, 2–3in (5–8cm) long; each splits to show an orange interior and scarlet seeds.

CELMISIA (Compositae)
Genus of evergreen, late spring- and summer-flowering perennials, grown for their foliage and daisylike flower heads. Is suitable for rock gardens and peat beds, but may be difficult to grow in hot, dry climates. Frost hardy. Needs a sheltered, sunny site and humus-rich, moist but well-drained, sandy, acid soil. Propagate by division in early summer or by seed when fresh.
C. bellidioides. Evergreen, mat-forming perennial. H 3/4in (2cm), S to 6in (15cm). Zones 8–9. Dark green leaves are rounded and leathery. Bears almost stemless, 1/2in (1cm) wide, daisylike, white flower heads in early summer.
C. coriacea illus. p.300.
C. ramulosa illus. p.314.

C. traversii. Slow-growing, evergreen, clump-forming perennial. H 6in (15cm), S 8in (20cm). Zones 8–9. Sword-shaped, dark green leaves have reddish brown margins and cream undersides. In summer carries 2 1/2–3in (6–7cm) wide, daisylike, white flower heads. Is difficult to establish.
C. walkeri illus. p.290.

CELOSIA (Amaranthaceae)
Genus of erect perennials, grown as annuals. Half hardy to frost tender, min. 36–9°F (2–4°C). Grows best in a sunny, sheltered position and in fertile, well-drained soil. Propagate by seed sown under glass in spring.
C. cristata (Cockscomb). Moderately fast-growing, erect, bushy perennial, grown as an annual. H 1–2ft (30–60cm), S 1ft (30cm). Frost tender. Has oval, green leaves and, in summer-autumn, pyramid-shaped, feathery flower heads, to 6in (15cm) tall, in red, yellow, pink, or apricot. Dwarf cultivars, H 1ft (30cm), include **'Fairy Fountains'**, illus. p.285, and **Geisha Series**, which is available in a wide color range.

CELTIS (Ulmaceae)
Hackberry, Nettle tree
Genus of deciduous trees, with inconspicuous flowers in spring, grown for their foliage and small fruits. Fully hardy. Needs full sun (doing best in hot summers) and fertile, well-drained soil. Propagate by seed in autumn.
C. australis illus. p.41.
C. occidentalis (Common hackberry). Deciduous, spreading tree. H and S 70ft (20m). Zones 2–9. Oval, sharply toothed, glossy, bright green leaves turn yellow in autumn, when they are accompanied by globose, yellowish red, then red-purple fruits.
C. sinensis (Chinese hackberry). Deciduous, rounded tree. H and S 30ft (10m). Zones 7–9. Has oval, glossy, dark green leaves, with fine teeth, and small, globose, orange fruits.

CENTAUREA (Compositae)
Knapweed
Genus of annuals and perennials, grown for their flower heads that each have a thistlelike center surrounded by a ring of slender ray petals. Fully to half hardy. Requires sun; grows in any well-drained soil, even poor soil. Propagate by seed or division in autumn or spring.
C. cyanus (Bachelor's button, Cornflower). Fast-growing, upright, branching annual. H 1–3ft (30cm–1m), S 1ft (30cm). Half hardy. Has lance-shaped, gray-green leaves and, in summer and early autumn, branching stems with usually double, daisylike flower heads in shades of blue, pink, red, purple, or white. Flowers are excellent for cutting. Tall (blue, illus. p.278; rose, illus. p.266) and dwarf cultivars are available. **'Jubilee Gem'** (dwarf) has large, double, deep blue flower heads.
C. dealbata. Erect perennial. H 3ft (1m), S 2ft (60cm). Fully hardy, zones 4–8. Lilac-purple flower heads are borne freely in summer, one or more to each stem. Has narrowly oval, finely

cut, light green leaves. **'Steenbergii'**, H 2ft (60cm), has carmine lilac flowers.
C. hypoleuca **'John Coutts'** illus. p.236.
C. macrocephala. Robust, clump-forming perennial. H 3ft (1m), S 2ft (60cm). Fully hardy, zones 3–8. In summer, stout stems bear large, yellow flower heads, enclosed in papery, silvery brown bracts. Green leaves are narrowly oval and deeply cut.
C. montana illus. p.241.
C. moschata illus. p.279.
C. pulcherrima illus. p.204.

CENTRADENIA (Melastomataceae)
Genus of evergreen perennials and shrubs, grown for their flowers and foliage. Frost tender, min. 55°F (13°C). Needs light shade and fertile, well-drained soil. Water potted plants freely when in full growth, moderately at other times. Tip prune young plants to promote a bushy habit; old plants become straggly unless they are trimmed each spring. Propagate from early spring to early summer by seed or softwood or greenwood cuttings. If grown as pot plants, propagate annually.
C. floribunda. Evergreen, loosely rounded, soft-stemmed shrub. H and S to 24in (60cm). Zone 10. Lance-shaped leaves are prominently veined, glossy, green above, bluish green beneath. Large, terminal clusters of 4-petaled, pink or white flowers develop from pink buds in late winter and spring.

CENTRANTHUS (Valerianaceae)
Genus of late spring- to autumn-flowering perennials. Fully hardy. Requires sun. Thrives in an exposed position and in poor, especially alkaline, soil. Propagate by seed in autumn or spring.
C. ruber illus. p.207.

CEPHALARIA (Dipsacaceae)
Genus of coarse, summer-flowering perennials, best suited to large borders and wild gardens. Fully hardy. Prefers sun and well-drained soil. Propagate by division in spring or by seed in autumn.
C. gigantea, syn. *C. tatarica* (Giant scabious, Yellow scabious). Robust, branching perennial. H 6ft (2m), S 4ft (1.2m). Zones 3–8. In early summer, wiry stems bear pincushionlike heads of primrose yellow flowers well above lance-shaped, deeply cut, dark green leaves.
C. tatarica. See *C. gigantea.*

CEPHALOCEREUS, syn. PILOSOCEREUS (Cactaceae)
Genus of slow-growing, columnar, perennial cacti with 20–30-ribbed, green stems. Frost tender, min. 41°F (5°C). Prefers full sun and extremely well-drained, lime-rich soil. Is prone to rot if overwatered. Propagate by seed in spring or summer.
C. senilis illus. p.381.

CEPHALOPHYLLUM (Aizoaceae)
Genus of clump-forming, bushy, perennial succulents with semi-cylindrical to cylindrical, green leaves.

Flowers are borne after 1 or 2 years. Frost tender, min. 41°F (5°C). Requires sun and well-drained soil. Propagate by seed in spring or summer.
C. alstonii illus. p.394.
C. pillansii. Clump-forming, perennial succulent. H 3in (8cm), S 24in (60cm). Zones 9–10. Leaves are cylindrical, 2 1/2in (6cm) long, dark green, and covered in darker dots. Short flower stems produce daisylike, red-centered, yellow flowers, 2 1/2in (6cm) across, from spring to autumn.

CEPHALOTAXUS
(Cephalotaxaceae). See CONIFERS.
C. harringtonia (Japanese plum yew). Bushy, spreading conifer. H 15ft (5m), S 10ft (3m). Frost hardy, zones 6–9. Needlelike, flattened leaves are glossy, dark green, grayish beneath, radiating around erect shoots. Bears ovoid, fleshy, green fruits that ripen to brown.

CERASTIUM (Caryophyllaceae)
Genus of annuals and perennials with star-shaped flowers. Some species are useful as ground cover. Fully hardy. Needs sun and well-drained soil. Propagate by division in spring.
C. alpinum (Alpine mouse-ear). Prostrate perennial. H 3in (8cm), S 16in (40cm). Zones 3–8. Tiny, oval, gray leaves cover stems. Flower stems carry solitary 1/2in (1cm) wide, star-shaped, white flowers throughout summer.
C. tomentosum illus. p.301.

CERATOPHYLLUM
(Ceratophyllaceae)
Genus of deciduous, perennial, submerged water plants, grown for their foliage. Is suitable for pools and cold-water aquariums. Fully to half hardy. Prefers an open, sunny position, but tolerates shade better than most submerged plants. Propagation occurs naturally when scaly, young shoots or winter buds separate from main plants. Alternatively, take stem cuttings in the growing season.
C. demersum (Hornwort). Deciduous, perennial, spreading, submerged water plant that sometimes floats. S indefinite. Fully hardy, zones 8–10. Has small, dark green leaves with 3 linear lobes. Is best suited to a cool-water pool.

CERATOPTERIS (Parkeriaceae)
Genus of deciduous or semi-evergreen, perennial, floating water ferns, grown for their attractive foliage. Is suitable for aquariums. Frost tender, min. 50°F (10°C). Prefers a sunny position. Remove fading fronds regularly. Propagate in summer by division or by buds that develop on the leaves.
C. thalictroides (Water fern). Semi-evergreen, perennial, spreading, floating water fern that sometimes roots and becomes submerged. S indefinite. Zones 9–10. Lance- or heart-shaped, soft green fronds are wavy-edged.

CERATOSTIGMA
(Plumbaginaceae)
Genus of deciduous, semi-evergreen, or evergreen shrubs and perennials, grown for their blue flowers and autumn color. Fully hardy to frost

tender, min. 50°F (10°C). Requires sun and well-drained soil. Cut out dead wood from shrubs in spring. Propagate shrubs by softwood cuttings in summer, perennials by division in spring.
C. griffithii. Evergreen or semi-evergreen, bushy, dense shrub. H 3ft (1m), S 5ft (1.5m). Half hardy, zones 9–10. Spoon-shaped, bristly, purple-edged, dull green leaves redden in autumn. Clusters of tubular, bright blue flowers, with spreading petal lobes, appear in late summer and autumn.
C. plumbaginoides illus. p.300.
C. willmottianum illus. p.141.

CERCIDIPHYLLUM
(Cercidiphyllaceae)
Genus of deciduous trees, grown for their foliage and often spectacular autumn color. Fully hardy. Late frosts may damage young foliage, but do not usually cause lasting harm. Needs sun or semi-shade and fertile, moist but well-drained soil. Propagate by seed in autumn.
C. japonicum illus. p.45.

CERCIS (Leguminosae)
Judas tree, Redbud
Genus of deciduous shrubs and trees with sometimes shrubby growth, cultivated for their foliage and profuse, small, pealike flowers. Fully hardy. Requires full sun and deep, fertile, well-drained soil. Plant out as young specimens. Resents transplanting. Propagate species by seed in autumn, cultivars by budding in late summer.
C. canadensis (Eastern redbud). Deciduous, spreading tree or shrub. H and S 30ft (10m). Zones 5–9. Heart-shaped, dark green leaves turn yellow in autumn. Pealike flowers are magenta in bud, opening to pale pink in mid-spring before leaves emerge. **'Forest Pansy'** illus. p.64.
C. siliquastrum illus. p.61.

CEREUS (Cactaceae)
Genus of columnar, perennial cacti with spiny stems, most having 4–10 pronounced ribs. Cup-shaped flowers usually open at night. Frost tender, min. 45°F (7°C). Needs full sun and very well-drained soil. Propagate in spring by seed or, for branching species, by stem cuttings.
C. forbesii illus. p.378.
C. peruvianus illus. p.378.
'Monstrosus' is a columnar, perennial cactus. H 15ft (5m), S 12ft (4m). Zone 10. Swollen, occasionally fan-shaped, silvery blue stems bear golden spines on 4–8 (or more) uneven ribs. Is unlikely to flower in cultivation.

CEROPEGIA (Asclepiadaceae)
Genus of semi-evergreen, succulent shrubs and sub-shrubs, most with slender, climbing or pendent stems, grown for their unusual flowers. Frost tender, min. 45–52°F (7–11°C). Needs partial shade and very well-drained soil. Propagate by seed or stem cuttings in spring or summer.
C. woodii is often used as grafting stock for difficult asclepiads.
C. haygarthii. Semi-evergreen, climbing, succulent sub-shrub. H 6ft (2m) or more, S indefinite. Min. 52°F

(11°C), zone 10. Bears oval or rounded, dark green leaves, ½–¾in (1–2cm) long, and, in summer, masses of small, white or pinkish white flowers, each with a pitcher-shaped tube, widening towards the top and then united at the tip by purplish spotted petals that form a short stem ending in 5 "knobs" edged with fine hairs. The whole resembles an insect hovering over a flower.
C. sandersonii (Fountain flower, Parachute plant). Semi-evergreen, scrambling, succulent sub-shrub. H 6ft (2m), S indefinite. Min. 52°F (11°C), zone 10. Leaves are triangular to oval, fleshy and ¾in (2cm) long. In summer-autumn has tubular, green flowers, 2in (5cm) long, with paler green to white marks; the petals are flared widely at tips to form "parachutes."
C. woodii illus. p.383.

CESTRUM (Solanaceae)
Genus of deciduous or evergreen shrubs and semi-scrambling climbers, grown for their showy flowers. Foliage has an unpleasant scent. Frost hardy to frost tender, min. 45–50°F (7–10°C); in cold areas grow frost hardy species against a south- or west-facing wall or in a greenhouse. Requires a sheltered, sunny site and fertile, well-drained soil. Water potted specimens freely when in full growth, moderately at other times. Scrambling species need support. Propagate frost hardy species by softwood cuttings in summer, tender species by seed in spring or by semi-ripe cuttings in summer.
C. aurantiacum. Mainly evergreen semi-scrambler that remains a rounded shrub if cut back annually. H and S to 6ft (2m). Frost tender, min. 45–50°F (7–10°C), zones 9–10; is deciduous at low temperatures. Bears oval, bright green leaves. Tubular, bright orange flowers are carried in large, terminal trusses in summer and may be followed by spherical, white fruits. Prune annually, cutting out old stems to near base after flowering.
C. elegans illus. p.110.
C. 'Newellii'. Evergreen, arching shrub. H and S 10ft (3m). Frost hardy, zones 9–10. Bears clusters of tubular, crimson flowers in late spring and summer. Leaves are large, broadly lance-shaped, and dark green.
C. parqui (Willow-leaved jessamine). Deciduous, open shrub. H and S 6ft (2m). Frost hardy, zones 7–10. Large clusters of tubular, yellowish green flowers, fragrant at night, are borne in profusion in summer amid narrowly lance-shaped, green leaves.

CETERACH (Polypodiaceae)
Genus of evergreen or semi-evergreen ferns, useful for planting in crevices. Fully hardy. Needs dappled shade and moist but well-drained, chalky soil. Remove fading fronds regularly. Propagate by division in spring or by spores in late summer.
C. officinarum illus. p.185.

CHAENOMELES (Rosaceae)
Flowering quince, Japonica
Genus of deciduous, usually thorny, spring-flowering shrubs, grown for

their showy flowers and fragrant fruits, used for preserves. Fully hardy. Prefers sun and well-drained soil. On wall-trained shrubs cut back side-shoots after flowering to 2 or 3 buds and shorten shoots growing away from wall during growing season. Propagate species by softwood or greenwood cuttings in summer or by seed in autumn, cultivars by cuttings only in summer. Fireblight and, on chalk soils, chlorosis are common problems.
C. cathayensis. Deciduous, spreading, open shrub with thorns. H and S 10ft (3m) or more. Zones 7–9. Produces long, narrow, pointed, green leaves. Small, 5-petaled, pink-flushed, white flowers appear from early to mid-spring, followed by large, egg-shaped, yellow-green fruits.
C. japonica (Japanese quince, Japonica). Deciduous, bushy, spreading shrub with thorns. H 3ft (1m), S 6ft (2m). Zones 5–9. Has oval, green leaves and, in spring, a profusion of 5-petaled, red or orange-red flowers, then spherical, yellow fruits.
C. speciosa. Vigorous, deciduous, bushy shrub with thorns. H 8ft (2.5m), S 15ft (5m). Zones 5–9. Leaves are oval, glossy, and dark green. Clustered, 5-petaled, red flowers are borne from early to mid-spring, followed by spherical, greenish yellow fruits. **'Moerloosii'** illus. p.98. Flowers of **'Nivalis'** are pure white. **'Simonii'**, H 3ft (1m), S 6ft (2m), bears masses of semi-double, deep red flowers.
C. × superba 'Crimson and Gold'. Deciduous, bushy, dense shrub with thorns. H 3ft (1m), S 6ft (2m). Zones 5–8. Has oval, glossy, dark green leaves. Bears masses of 5-petaled, deep red flowers, with conspicuous, golden yellow anthers, in spring, followed by spherical, yellow fruits. Flowers of **'Etna'**, H 5ft (1.5m), S 10ft (3m), are scarlet. **'Knap Hill Scarlet'**, H 5ft (1.5m), S 10ft (3m), produces large, brilliant red flowers. **'Nicoline'** illus. p.124. **'Rowallane'** illus. p.123.

CHAMAEBATIARIA (Rosaceae)
Genus of one species of deciduous shrub, grown for its foliage and summer flowers. Frost hardy. Needs a sheltered, sunny position and well-drained soil. Propagate by semi-ripe cuttings in summer.
C. millefolium. Deciduous, upright, open shrub. H and S 3ft (1m). Zones 6–9. Has finely divided, aromatic, gray-green leaves. Shallowly cup-shaped, white flowers, with yellow stamens, are borne in terminal, branching panicles from mid- to late summer.

CHAMAECEREUS (Cactaceae)
Genus of one species of clump forming, perennial cactus with a fingerlike, spiny, green stem. Frost tender, min. 37°F (3°C) if dry. Requires sun and well-drained soil. Propagate by stem cuttings in spring or summer.
C. silvestri illus. p.395.

CHAMAECYPARIS (Cupressaceae),
False cypress. See CONIFERS.
C. lawsoniana (Lawson false cypress). Upright, columnar conifer with

branches drooping at tips. H 50–80ft (15–25m), S 10–12ft (3–4m). Fully hardy, zones 6–9. Bears flattened sprays of scalelike, aromatic, dark green leaves and globular cones, the males brick red, the females insignificant and green. **'Columnaris'** illus. p.80. **'Ellwoodii'**, H 10ft (3m), S 5ft (1.5m), is erect with incurved, blue-gray leaves. **'Fletcheri'**, H 15–40ft (5–12m), S 6–10ft (2–3m), has incurved, gray leaves. **'Gnome'** (illus. p.83), H and S 20in (50cm), is a dwarf, bun-shaped form with blue foliage. **'Green Pillar'** illus. p.79. **'Intertexta'** illus. p.74. **'Kilmacurragh'**, H 30–50ft (10–15m), S 3ft (1m), has very bright green foliage. **'Lanei'** illus. p.79. **'Minima'** (illus. p.83), H and S 3ft (1m), is dwarf and globular, with light green foliage. **'Pembury Blue'** illus. p.77. **'Tamariscifolia'**, H 10ft (3m), S 12ft (4m), is a dwarf, spreading form. **'Triomf van Boskoop'**, H 70ft (20m), is broadly columnar, with gray-blue foliage. **'Wisselii'**, H 50ft (15m), S 6–10ft (2–3m), is fast-growing, with erect branches and blue-green leaves.
C. nootkatensis (Nootka false cypress). Almost geometrically conical conifer. H 50ft (15m), S 20ft (6m). Fully hardy, zones 5–8. Bears long, pendent sprays of scalelike, aromatic, gray-green leaves and globular, hooked, dark blue and green cones that ripen to brown. **'Pendula'** has a gaunt crown of arching, weeping foliage.
C. obtusa (Hinoki false cypress). Conical conifer. H 50–70ft (15–20m), S 15ft (5m). Fully hardy, zones 4–8. Has stringy, red-brown bark and scalelike, aromatic, dark green leaves with bright silver lines at sides and incurving tips. Small, rounded cones ripen to yellow-brown. **'Coralliformis'**, H to 20in (50cm), S 3ft (1m), is dwarf, with threadlike shoots. **'Crippsii'** illus. p.81. **'Intermedia'** (illus. p.83), H to 12in (30cm), S 16in (40cm), is a globular, open, dwarf shrub with downward-spreading, light green foliage. **'Kosteri'**, H 3–6ft (1–2m), S 6–10ft (2–3m), forms a sprawling bush with twisted, lustrous foliage. Extremely slow-growing **'Nana'**, eventual H 3ft (1m), S 5–6ft (1.5–2m), makes a flat-topped bush. **'Nana Aurea'** (illus. p.83), H and S 6ft (2m), is a form with golden yellow leaves. **'Nana Gracilis'**, H 6ft (2m), S 5–6ft (1.5–2m), is a form with glossy foliage. **'Nana Pyramidalis'** (illus. p.83), H and S to 24in (60cm), is a slow-growing, dense, conical, dwarf cultivar with horizontal, cup-shaped leaves. **'Tetragona Aurea'**, H 30ft (10m), S 6–10ft (2–3m), has golden- or bronze-yellow leaves.
C. pisifera (Sawara false cypress). Conical conifer with horizontal branches. H 50ft (15m), S 15ft (5m). Fully hardy, zones 5–8. Has ridged, peeling, red-brown bark, scalelike, aromatic, fresh green leaves, white at sides and beneath, and angular, yellow-brown cones. **'Boulevard'** has silver-blue foliage. **'Filifera'** has whiplike, hanging shoots and dark green foliage. **'Filifera Aurea'** (illus. p.83), H 40ft (12m), S 10–15ft (3–5m), also has whiplike shoots, but with golden

433

yellow leaves. **'Filifera Nana'**, H 2ft (60cm), S 3ft (1m), is a dwarf form with whiplike branches. **'Nana'**, H and S 20in (50cm), is also dwarf, with dark bluish green foliage. **'Plumosa'** is broadly conical to columnar, with yellowish gray-green leaves. **'Plumosa Rogersii'**, H 6ft (2m), S 3ft (1m), has yellow foliage. Slow-growing **'Squarrosa'**, H to 70ft (20m), has a broad crown and soft, blue-gray foliage.
C. thyoides illus. p.79. **'Andelyensis'** is a slow-growing, conical, dwarf conifer. H 10ft (3m), S 3ft (1m). Fully hardy, zones 4–9. Has wedge-shaped tufts of scalelike, aromatic, blue-green leaves. Globular cones are glaucous blue-gray.

CHAMAEDAPHNE (Ericaceae)
Genus of one species of evergreen shrub, grown for its white flowers. Fully hardy. Needs sun or semi-shade and moist, peaty, acid soil. Propagate by semi-ripe cuttings in summer.
C. calyculata (Leatherleaf). Evergreen, arching, open shrub. H 2¹/₂ft (75cm), S 3ft (1m). Zones 2–9. Leaves are small, oblong, leathery, and dark green. Produces leafy racemes of small, urn-shaped flowers that are borne on slender branches from mid- to late spring.

CHAMAEDOREA (Palmae)
Genus of evergreen palms, grown for their overall appearance. Frost tender, min. 64°F (18°C). Needs shade or semi-shade and humus-rich, well-drained soil. Water potted plants moderately, less when temperatures are low. Propagate by seed in spring at not less than 77°F (25°C). Red spider mite may be troublesome.
C. elegans, syn. *Neanthe bella*, illus. p.120.

CHAMAEMELUM (Compositae)
Genus of evergreen perennials, suitable as ground cover or to make a lawn. Flowers may be used to make tea. Fully hardy. Needs sun and well-drained soil. Propagate by division in spring or by seed in autumn.
C. nobile (Camomile). Evergreen, mat-forming, invasive perennial. H 4in (10cm), S 18in (45cm). Zones 6–9. Has finely divided, aromatic leaves and daisylike heads of white flowers, with yellow centers, borne in late spring or summer. **'Treneague'** (syn. *Anthemis nobile* 'Treneague') is a non-flowering, less invasive cultivar that, requiring less mowing and lacking flower heads, is better for a lawn.

CHAMAENERION. See EPILOBIUM.

CHAMAEROPS (Palmae)
Genus of evergreen palms, cultivated for their overall appearance. Half hardy to frost tender, min. 45°F (7°C). Needs full light and fertile, well-drained soil. Water potted plants moderately, less when not in full growth. Propagate by seed in spring at not less than 72°F (22°C) or by suckers in late spring. Red spider mite may be a nuisance.
C. humilis illus. p.144.

Chamaespartium sagittale. See *Genista sagittalis.*

CHAMELAUCIUM (Myrtaceae)
Genus of evergreen shrubs, grown for their flowers and overall appearance. Frost tender, min. 41°F (5°C), but best at 45–50°F (7–10°C). Requires full sun and well-drained, sandy, neutral to acid soil. Water potted specimens moderately, sparingly when not in full growth. To maintain a more compact habit, cut back flowered stems by half when the last bloom falls. Propagate by seed in spring or by semi-ripe cuttings in summer.
C. uncinatum [pink form] illus. p.118, [white form] illus. p.117.

CHASMANTHE (Iridaceae)
Genus of corms, grown for their showy flowers. Frost to half hardy. Needs full sun or partial shade and well-drained soil with plenty of water in growing season (late winter and early spring). Reduce watering in summer-autumn. Propagate by division in autumn.
C. aethiopica. Spring- and early summer-flowering corm. H to 32in (80cm), S 5–7in (12–18cm). Frost hardy, zones 8–10. Has narrowly sword-shaped, erect, basal leaves in a flat fan. Produces a spike of scarlet flowers, all facing one way, with yellow tubes, 2–2¹/₂in (5–6cm) long, and hooded, upper lips.
C. floribunda. Summer-flowering corm. H to 32in (80cm), S 5–7in (12–18cm). Half hardy, zones 9–10. Is similar to *C. aethiopica*, but the leaves are much wider, and the longer, orange or scarlet flowers do not all face in the same direction.

CHEILANTHES (Polypodiaceae)
Genus of evergreen ferns. Fully to half hardy. Needs full light and humus-rich, well-drained soil. Do not overwater potted plants or splash water on fronds. Remove fading foliage regularly. Propagate by spores in summer.
C. fragrans. Evergreen fern. H 3–9in (8–23cm), S 6–9in (15–23cm). Frost hardy, zones 8–10. Lance-shaped, dark green fronds, with many rounded pinnae, are slightly hairy beneath and have the fragrance of fresh violets.
C. lanosa (Hairy lip fern). Evergreen fern. H and S 6–9in (15–23cm). Fully hardy, zones 5–8. Leaves are triangular or lance-shaped and have much divided, soft green fronds on hairy, black stems.

CHEIRANTHUS (Cruciferae)
Wallflower
Genus of perennials and sub-shrubs, some of which are evergreen or semi-evergreen, grown for their flowers; some are suitable for rock gardens. Short-lived species are best treated as biennials. Fully to half hardy. Grow in any fertile soil in an open position. Propagate by seed in spring or by softwood or greenwood cuttings in summer.
C. x *allionii.* See *Erysimum hieraciifolium.*
C. **'Bowles Mauve'.** Bushy perennial. H to 30in (75cm), S 18in (45cm). Half hardy, zones 7–10. Narrowly lance-

shaped, dark green leaves are 2in (5cm) long. Many clusters of small, rich mauve flowers, each with 4 spreading petals, are borne in spring-summer.
C. **'Bredon'** illus. p.290.
C. cheiri (English wallflower). Moderately fast-growing, evergreen, bushy perennial, grown as an annual. Tall cultivars, H to 24in (60cm), S 15in (38cm); intermediate, H 12–18in (30–45cm), S 12in (30cm); dwarf, H and S 8in (20cm). Half hardy. All have lance-shaped, mid- to deep green leaves. Heads of fragrant, 4-petaled flowers in many colors, including red, yellow, bronze, white, and orange, are produced in spring. **Fair Lady Series** (intermediate) has flowers in a mixture of pale colors; **'Fire King'** (intermediate) illus. p.285; **'Rose Queen'** (tall) bears rose and pink flowers; flowers of **Tom Thumb Series** (dwarf) are in a mixture of colors.
C. **'Harpur Crewe'** illus. p.290.
C. **'Moonlight'.** Evergreen, mat-forming perennial. H 2in (5cm), S 8in (20cm) or more. Fully hardy, zones 8–10. Leaves are small and narrowly oval. Leafy stems each carry clusters of 4-petaled, pale yellow flowers, opening in succession during summer. Makes a good rock garden plant. Needs a sheltered, sunny site and poor, gritty soil.

CHEIRIDOPSIS (Aizoaceae)
Genus of clump-forming, perennial succulents with semi-cylindrical, green, glaucous green, or blue-gray leaves in pairs. Frost tender, min. 41°F (5°C). Needs sun and well-drained soil. Water in autumn to encourage flowers. Propagate by seed or stem cuttings in spring or summer.
C. candidissima. Clump-forming, perennial succulent. H 4in (10cm), S 8in (20cm). Zones 9–10. Has semi-cylindrical, slender, fleshy, blue-gray leaves, each 4in (10cm) long with a flat top, joined in pairs for almost half their length. Carries daisylike, shiny, white flowers, to 2¹/₂in (6cm) across, in spring.
C. purpurata. Carpeting, perennial succulent. H 4in (10cm), S 12in (30cm). Zones 9–10. Has semi-cylindrical, thick, short, glaucous green leaves, each with a flat top. In early spring produces daisylike, purple-pink flowers, 1¹/₂in (4cm) across.

CHELIDONIUM (Papaveraceae)
Celandine, Greater celandine
Genus of one species of perennial that rapidly forms ground cover. Fully hardy. Grows in sun or shade and in any but very wet soil. Propagate by seed or division in autumn.
C. majus **'Flore Pleno'** illus. p.199.

CHELONE (Scrophulariaceae)
Turtlehead
Genus of summer- and autumn-flowering perennials. Fully hardy. Requires semi-shade and moist soil. Propagate by soft-tip cuttings in summer or by division or seed in autumn or spring.
C. barbata. See *Penstemon barbatus.*
C. obliqua illus. p.217.

CHIASTOPHYLLUM (Crassulaceae)
Genus of one species of evergreen perennial, grown for its succulent leaves and attractive sprays of small, yellow flowers. Thrives in rock crevices. Fully hardy. Needs shade and well-drained soil that is not too dry. Propagate by side-shoot cuttings in early summer or by seed in autumn.
C. oppositifolium, syn. *Cotyledon simplicifolia*, illus. p.289.

CHIMONANTHUS (Calycanthaceae)
Genus of deciduous or evergreen, winter-flowering shrubs, grown for their flowers. Frost hardy, but in cold areas reduce susceptibility of flowers to frost by training plants against a south- or west-facing wall. Needs full sun and fertile, well-drained soil. Propagate species by seed when ripe, in late spring and early summer, cultivars by softwood cuttings in summer.
C. praecox (Wintersweet). Deciduous, bushy shrub. H 8ft (2.5m) or more, S 10ft (3m). Zones 7–9. Has oval, rough, glossy, dark green leaves. Bears very fragrant, many-petaled, cup-shaped, yellow flowers, with purple centers, on bare branches in mild periods during winter. **'Luteus'** has pure yellow flowers.

CHIONANTHUS (Oleaceae)
Genus of deciduous shrubs, grown for their profuse, white flowers. Flowers more freely in areas with hot summers. Fully hardy. Prefers full sun and fertile, well-drained but not too dry soil. Propagate by seed in autumn.
C. retusus (Chinese fringe tree). Deciduous, often treelike, arching shrub. H and S 10ft (3m). Zones 6–8. From early to mid-summer, star-shaped, pure white flowers appear in large clusters amid oval, bright green leaves.
C. virginicus illus. p.87.

CHIONOCHLOA (Gramineae). See GRASSES, BAMBOOS, RUSHES, and SEDGES.
C. conspicua (Hunangemoho grass). Evergreen, tussock-forming, perennial grass. H 4–5ft (1.2–1.5m), S 3ft (1m). Fully hardy, zones 7–10. Very long, green leaves are tinged reddish brown. Has stout, arching stems with long, loose, open panicles of cream spikelets in summer.

CHIONODOXA (Liliaceae)
Glory-of-the-snow
Genus of spring-flowering bulbs, related to *Scilla*. Is suitable for rock gardens and for naturalizing under shrubs, in sun or partial shade. Fully hardy. Requires well-drained soil, top dressed with leaf mold or mature garden compost in autumn. Propagate by seed in autumn or by division in late summer or autumn.
C. forbesii, syn. *C. luciliae* of gardens, *C. siehei*, *C. tmolusii*, illus. p.362.
'Pink Giant' illus. p.358.
C. gigantea. See *C. luciliae.*
C. luciliae, syn. *C. gigantea*, illus. p.362.
C. luciliae of gardens. See *C. forbesii.*

C. sardensis. Early spring-flowering bulb. H 4–8in (10–20cm), S 1–2in (2.5–5cm). Zones 5–9. Has 2 narrowly lance-shaped, semi-erect, basal leaves. Leafless stem has 5–10 flattish, slightly pendent or outward-facing, deep rich blue flowers, ⁵⁄₈–³⁄₄in (1.5–2cm) across and without white eyes.
C. siehei. See *C. forbesii.*
C. tmoiusii. See *C. forbesii.*

---

x CHIONOSCILLA (Liliaceae)
Hybrid genus (*Chionodoxa* x *Scilla*) of spring-flowering bulbs, suitable for rock gardens. Fully hardy. Needs full sun or partial shade and humus-rich, well-drained soil. Propagate by division in late summer or autumn.
x *C. allenii* illus. p.362.

CHIRITA (Gesneriaceae)
Genus of evergreen perennials or sub-shrubs, grown for their flowers. Frost tender, min. 59°F (15°C). Requires well-drained soil, a fairly humid atmosphere, and a light position out of direct sunlight. Propagate by tip cuttings in summer or, if available, seed in late winter or spring.
C. lavandulacea illus. p.250.
C. sinensis. Evergreen, stemless, rosetted perennial. H to 6in (15cm), S 10in (25cm) or more. Zones 9–10. Has oval, almost fleshy leaves, the corrugated, hairy surfaces usually patterned with silver marks. In spring-summer, clusters of tubular, lavender flowers are held above leaves.

CHLIDANTHUS (Amaryllidaceae)
Genus of one species of summer-flowering bulb, grown for its showy, funnel-shaped flowers. Half hardy. Needs a sunny site and well-drained soil. Plant in the open in spring and after flowering, if necessary, lift and dry off for winter. Propagate by offsets in spring.
C. fragrans illus. p.365.

CHLOROGALUM (Liliaceae)
Genus of summer-flowering bulbs, grown more for botanical interest than for floral display. Frost hardy, but in cold areas plant in a sheltered site. Requires sun and well-drained soil. Propagate by seed in autumn or spring.
C. pomeridianum. Summer-flowering bulb. H to 8ft (2.5m), S 6–8in (15–20cm). Zones 9–10. Semi-erect, basal leaves are long, narrow, and gray-green, with wavy margins. Carries a large, loosely branched head of small, saucer-shaped, white flowers, with a central, green or purple stripe on each petal, that open after midday.

CHLOROPHYTUM (Liliaceae)
Genus of evergreen, stemless perennials with short rhizomes, grown for their foliage. Frost tender, min. 41°F (5°C). Grow in a light position, away from direct sun, in fertile, well-drained soil. Water freely in the growing season but sparingly at other times if pot-grown. Propagate by seed, division, or plantlets (produced on flower stems of some species) at any time except winter.
C. capense of gardens. See *C. comosum.*

C. comosum, syn. *C. capense* of gardens (Spider plant). Evergreen, tufted perennial. H 12in (30cm), S indefinite. Zones 9–10. Very narrow leaves, to 18in (45cm) long, spread from a rosette. Racemes of many small, star-shaped, white flowers are carried on thin stems, to 2ft (60cm) or more long, at any time. Small rosettes of leaves may appear on flower stems, forming plantlets. **'Vittatum'** illus. p.257.

CHOISYA (Rutaceae)
Genus of evergreen shrubs, grown for their foliage and flowers. Frost to half hardy; in most areas needs some shelter. Requires full sun and fertile, well-drained soil. Propagate by semi-ripe cuttings in late summer.
C. ternata illus. p.95. **'Sundance'** is an evergreen, rounded, dense shrub. H and S 8ft (2.5m). Frost hardy, zones 8–10. Aromatic, glossy, bright yellow leaves each consist of 3 oblong leaflets. Fragrant, star-shaped, white flowers are produced in clusters in late spring and often again in autumn.

CHORDOSPARTIUM (Leguminosae)
Genus of one species of deciduous, almost leafless shrub, grown for its habit and flowers. Slender, green shoots assume function of leaves. Frost hardy. Requires a sheltered, sunny position and fertile, well-drained soil. Propagate by seed in autumn.
C. stevensonii. Deciduous, almost leafless, arching shrub. H 10ft (3m), S 6ft (2m). Zones 9–10. Produces small, pealike, purplish pink flowers in cylindrical racemes in mid-summer.

CHORISIA (Bombacaceae)
Genus of deciduous trees, usually with spine-covered trunks, grown mainly for their flowers in autumn and winter and their overall appearance. Frost tender, min. 59°F (15°C). Needs full light and well-drained soil. Water potted specimens freely when in full growth, very little when leafless. Pruning is tolerated if necessary. Propagate by seed in spring. Red spider mite may be troublesome.
C. speciosa illus. p.44.

CHORIZEMA (Leguminosae)
Genus of evergreen sub-shrubs, shrubs, and scandent climbers, grown mainly for their flowers. Frost tender, min. 45°F (7°C). Requires full light and humus-rich, well-drained, sandy soil, preferably neutral to acid. Water potted plants moderately, less when not in full growth. Tie climbers to supports, or grow in hanging baskets. Propagate by seed in spring or by semi-ripe cuttings in summer.
C. ilicifolium illus. p.125.

CHRYSALIDOCARPUS (Palmae)
Genus of evergreen palms, grown for their elegant appearance. Frost tender, min. 61°F (16°C). Needs full light or partial shade and fertile, well-drained soil. Water potted specimens moderately, much less when temperatures are low. Propagate by seed in spring at not less than 79°F

(26°C). Red spider mite may sometimes be a nuisance.
C. lutescens, syn. *Areca lutescens*, illus. p.72.

CHRYSANTHEMUM (Compositae)
Genus of annuals, perennials, some of which are evergreen, and evergreen sub-shrubs, grown for their flowers. Each flower head is referred to horticulturally as a flower, even though it does in fact comprise a large number of individual flowers or florets; this horticultural usage has been followed in the descriptions below. Leaves are usually deeply lobed or cut, often feathery, oval to lance-shaped. Florists' chrysanthemums (hybrids of *C. morifolium*) comprise the vast majority of chrysanthemums now cultivated and are perennials grown for garden decoration, cutting, and exhibition. Annuals are fully to half hardy. Florists' chrysanthemums are half hardy and should be lifted and stored in a frost-free place over winter. Other perennials are fully to half hardy. Provide a sunny site and reasonably fertile, well-drained soil. If grown for exhibition will require regular feeding. Pinch out growing tips to encourage lateral growths on which flowers will be borne, and stake tall plants with canes. Propagate annuals by seed sown in position in spring; thin out, but do not transplant. Propagate hardy perennials by division in autumn, after flowering, or in early spring. Florists' chrysanthemums should be propagated from basal softwood cuttings in spring. Spray regularly to control aphids, capsids, froghoppers, earwigs, mildew, and white rust.

Florists' chrysanthemums
Florists' chrysanthemums are grouped according to their widely varying flower forms, approximate flowering season (early, mid-, or late autumn), and habit. They are divided into disbudded and non-disbudded types.

Disbudded types—single, anemone-centered, incurved, intermediate, and reflexed—are so called as all buds, except the one that is to flower, are removed from each stem. To produce exhibition flowers, incurved, intermediate, and reflexed chrysanthemums may be restricted to only 2 blooms per plant by removing all except the 2 most vigorous laterals. In gardens, allow 4 or 5 blooms per plant to develop. Single and anemone-centered flowers should be reduced to 4–8 blooms per plant for exhibition, according to their vigor, and 10 or more for garden decoration or cutting. For descriptions and illustrations of flower forms see p.218.

Non-disbudded types—charm, pompon, and spray chrysanthemums—have several flowers per stem.
Charm chrysanthemums are dwarf plants that produce hundreds of star-shaped, single flowers, 1in (2.5cm) across, densely covering each plant to form a hemispherical to almost spherical head. For exhibition, finish growing in at least 12in (30cm) pots.

Plants for indoor decoration are grown in smaller pots and have correspondingly smaller, though equally dense, heads of blooms.
Pompon chrysanthemums are also dwarf. Each plant has 50 or more dense, spherical or occasionally hemispherical, fully double flowers that have tubular petals (for illustration see p.218). They are excellent for growing in borders.
Spray chrysanthemums have a variety of flower forms: single, anemone-centered, intermediate, reflexed, pompon, and spoon-type (in which each straight, tubular floret opens out like a spoon at its tip). Each plant should be allowed to develop 4 or 5 stems with at least 5 flowers per stem. Grow late-flowering sprays on up to 3 stems per plant. With controlled day length, to regulate flowering dates for exhibition purposes, late sprays should be allowed to develop at least 12 flowers per stem; without day length control, 6 or 7 flowers per stem.

Those most suitable for garden decoration are sprays, pompons, and early reflexed chrysanthemums. All are suitable for cutting, except for charms. Late-flowering chrysanthemums are only suitable for growing under glass as flowers need protection from poor weather; they should be grown in pots and placed in a greenhouse in early autumn, when the flower buds have developed. Intermediate cultivars are also less suitable for garden decoration as florets may collect and retain rain and thus become damaged. Those cultivars suitable for exhibition are noted below. Measurements of flowers given are the greatest normally achieved and may vary considerably depending on growing conditions.

C. **'Alison Kirk'** (illus. p.218). Incurved florists' chrysanthemum. H 4ft (1.2m), S 1–2ft (30–60cm). Produces white flowers, to 5–6in (12–15cm) across, in early autumn. Is more suitable for exhibition than for garden use.
C. alpinum. Tuft-forming, short-lived perennial. H 3in (7cm), S 5in (12cm). Fully hardy, zones 5–9. Small tufts of deeply cut leaves are produced from short, rhizomatous stems. Has large, daisylike, white flower heads, with yellow centers, in summer. Is good for a rock garden or scree. Propagate by division of underground stems in autumn or early spring.
C. **'Amber Yvonne Arnaud'.** Reflexed florists' chrysanthemum. H 4ft (1.2m), S 2–2¹⁄₂ft (60–75cm). Is a sport of *C.* 'Yvonne Arnaud' with fully reflexed, amber flowers in early autumn.
C. **'Autumn Days'** (illus. p.219). Intermediate florists' chrysanthemum. H 3¹⁄₂–4ft (1.1–1.2m), S to 2¹⁄₂ft (75cm). Bears loosely incurving, bronze flowers, 5in (12cm) across, in early autumn.
C. **'Bill Wade'.** Intermediate florists' chrysanthemum. H 4¹⁄₂ft (1.35m), S 2ft (60cm). Has loosely incurving, white flowers, 7–8in (18–20cm) across, in

early autumn. Is more suitable for exhibition than for garden use.

C. **'Brietner'** (illus. p.218). Reflexed florists' chrysanthemum. H 3¹/2–4ft (1.1–1.2m), S 2¹/2ft (75cm). Fully reflexed, pink flowers, to 5in (12cm) wide, appear in early autumn.

C. **'Bronze Fairie'** (illus. p.219). Pompon florists' chrysanthemum. H 1–2ft (30–60cm), S 2ft (60cm). Has bronze flowers, 1in (4cm) across, in early autumn.

C. **'Bronze Hedgerow'** (illus. p.219). Single florists' chrysanthemum. H 5ft (1.5m), S 2¹/2–3ft (75cm–1m). Produces bronze flowers, 5in (12cm) across, in late autumn.

C. **'Bronze Yvonne Arnaud'** (illus. p.219). Reflexed florists' chrysanthemum. H 4ft (1.2m), S 2–2¹/2ft (60–75cm). Is a sport of C. 'Yvonne Arnaud' with fully reflexed, bronze flowers in early autumn.

C. **'Buff Margaret'** (illus. p.219). Spray florists' chrysanthemum. H 4ft (1.2m), S to 2¹/2ft (75cm). Is similar to C. 'Peach Margaret', but has pale bronze flowers.

C. **carinatum**, syn. C. tricolor. **'Monarch Court Jesters'** (red with yellow centers) illus. p.273, (white with red centers) illus. p.264. **Tricolor Series** is a group of fast-growing, upright, branching annuals. H 12–24in (30–60cm), S 12in (30cm). Half hardy. Has feathery, light green leaves and, in summer, daisylike, single or double flower heads, to 3in (8cm) wide, in many color combinations. Tall cultivars, H 24in (60cm), S 12in (30cm), and dwarf, H and S 12in (30cm), are available.

C. **'Cherry Chintz'** (illus. p.219). Reflexed florists' chrysanthemum. H 4ft (1.2m), S 1¹/2ft (45cm). Has fully reflexed, red flowers, to 15cm (6in) across, in early autumn. Is excellent for exhibition.

C. **'Chessington'**. Intermediate florists' chrysanthemum. H 6–7ft (2–2.2m), S 2¹/2ft (75cm). Produces fairly tightly incurving, white flowers, 7–8in (18–20cm) across, in early autumn. Is more suitable for exhibition than for garden use.

C. **'Chippendale'** (illus. p.219). Reflexed florists' chrysanthemum. H 4ft (1.2m), S 1¹/2ft (45cm). Fully reflexed, pink flowers, 7in (18cm) or more wide, appear in mid-autumn. Is more suitable for exhibition than for garden use.

C. **'Christina'**. Intermediate florists' chrysanthemum. H 4¹/2–5ft (1.35–1.5m), S 2–2¹/2ft (60–75cm). Bears loosely incurving, white flowers, to 5¹/2in (14cm) wide, in early autumn. Is suitable for exhibition.

C. **'Claire Louise'**. Reflexed florists' chrysanthemum. H 4–4¹/2ft (1.2–1.35m), S 2¹/2ft (75cm). Produces fully reflexed, bronze flowers, to 6in (15cm) across, in early autumn. Is ideal for exhibition.

C. **'Cloudbank'** (illus. p.218). Spray florists' chrysanthemum. H 4ft (1.2m), S 2¹/2ft (75cm). Has anemone-centered, white flowers, 3–3¹/2in (8–9cm) wide, in late autumn. Is good for exhibition.

C. **coccineum**. See Tanacetum coccineum.

C. **coronarium** (Crown daisy). Fast-growing, upright, branching annual. H 1–3ft (30cm–1m), S 15in (38cm). Fully hardy. Has feathery, divided, light green leaves. In summer bears single or semi-double, daisylike, yellow or yellow-and-white flower heads, to 2in (5cm) across.

C. **'Dawn Mist'** (illus. p.218). Spray florists' chrysanthemum. H 4ft (1.2m), S 2¹/2–3ft (75cm–1m). Single, very pale pink flowers, to 3in (8cm) across, appear in early autumn.

C. **'Discovery'** (illus. p.219). Intermediate florists' chrysanthemum. H 4ft (1.2m), S 2¹/2ft (75cm). Produces loosely incurving, light yellow flowers, 4–5in (10–12cm) across, in early autumn.

C. **'Dorridge Dream'** (illus. p.218). Incurved florists' chrysanthemum. H 4ft (1.2m), S 2ft (60cm). Has rose-pink flowers, 5in (12cm) wide, in early autumn. Is excellent for exhibition.

C. **'Duke of Kent'** (illus. p.218). Reflexed florists' chrysanthemum. H 5ft (1.5m), S 1ft (30cm). Bears almost fully reflexed, white flowers, 10in (25cm) or more across, in late autumn. Use only for exhibition.

C. **'Edwin Painter'** (illus. p.219). Single florists' chrysanthemum. H 4¹/2–5ft (1.35–1.5m), S 2¹/2–3ft (75cm–1m). Produces yellow flowers, 5¹/2in (14cm) across, in late autumn. Is good for exhibition.

C. **'Fiona Lynn'**. Reflexed florists' chrysanthemum. H 5ft (1.5m), S 2¹/2ft (75cm). Fully reflexed, pink flowers, to 7–8in (18–20cm) across, are produced in early autumn. Is ideal for exhibition.

C. **frutescens**, syn. Argyranthemum frutescens (Marguerite), illus. p.201. **'Jamaica Primrose'** illus. p.214. **'Mary Wootton'** illus. p.203.

C. **'George Griffiths'** (illus. p.219). Reflexed florists' chrysanthemum. H 4–4¹/2ft (1.2–1.35m), S 2¹/2ft (75cm). Produces fully reflexed, deep red flowers, to 5¹/2in (14cm) wide, in early autumn. Is excellent for exhibition.

C. **'Ginger Nut'**. Intermediate florists' chrysanthemum. H 4ft (1.2m), S 2–2¹/2ft (60–75cm). Bears tightly incurving, light bronze flowers, to 5¹/2in (14cm) across, occasionally closing at top to form a true incurved flower, in early autumn. Is good for exhibition.

C. **'Golden Woolman's Glory'** (illus. p.219). Single florists' chrysanthemum. H 5ft (1.5m), S 3ft (1m). Golden flowers, to 7in (18cm) across, appear in late autumn. Is excellent for exhibition.

C. **'Green Satin'** (illus. p.219). Intermediate florists' chrysanthemum. H 4ft (1.2m), S 2ft (60cm). Produces loosely incurving, green flowers, to 5in (12cm) wide, in late autumn.

C. **haradjanii**. See Tanacetum haradjanii.

C. **hosmariense** illus. p.286.

C. **'Madeleine'** (illus. p.218). Spray florists' chrysanthemum. H 4ft (1.2m), S 2¹/2ft (75cm). Has reflexed, pink flowers, to 3in (8cm) across, in early autumn. Is good for exhibition.

C. **'Maria'** (illus. p.219). Pompon florists' chrysanthemum. H 1¹/2ft (45cm), S 1–2ft (30–60cm). Bears masses of pink flowers, to 1¹/2in (4cm) across, in early autumn.

C. **'Marian Gosling'** (illus. p.218). Reflexed florists' chrysanthemum. H 4–4¹/2ft (1.2–1.35m), S 2ft (60cm). Fully reflexed, pale pink flowers, to 5¹/2in (14cm) wide, appear in early autumn. Is good for exhibition.

C. **'Marion'** (illus. p.219). Spray florists' chrysanthemum. H 4ft (1.2m), S 2¹/2ft (75cm). Produces reflexed, pale yellow flowers, to 3in (8cm) wide, from late summer.

C. **'Marlene Jones'** (illus. p.219). Intermediate florists' chrysanthemum. H 3ft (1m), S to 2ft (60cm). Has loosely incurving, pale yellow flowers, 5–5¹/2in (12–14cm) wide, in early autumn. Is good for exhibition.

C. **'Mason's Bronze'**. Single florists' chrysanthemum. H 4¹/2–5ft (1.35–1.5m), S to 3ft (1m). Has bronze flowers, to 5in (12cm) wide, in late autumn. Is excellent for exhibition.

C. **maximum** of gardens. See C. × superbum.

C. **'Michael Fish'** (illus. p.218). Intermediate florists' chrysanthemum. H 4ft (1.2m), S 2–2¹/2ft (60–75cm). Bears fairly tightly incurving, white flowers, to 6in (15cm) wide, in early autumn. Is suitable for exhibition.

C. **'Oracle'** (illus. p.219). Intermediate florists' chrysanthemum. H 4ft (1.2m), S 2–2¹/2ft (60–75cm). Produces loosely incurving, pale bronze flowers, to 5in (12cm) wide, in early autumn. Is useful for exhibition.

C. **parthenium** illus. p.263. **'Aureum'** is a moderately fast-growing, short-lived, bushy perennial, grown as an annual. H and S 8–18in (20–45cm). Fully hardy, zones 4–9. Has oval, lobed, aromatic, green-gold leaves and, in summer and early autumn, daisylike, white flower heads.

C. **'Pavilion'** (illus. p.218). Intermediate florists' chrysanthemum. H 4¹/2ft (1.35m), S 2–2¹/2ft (60–75cm). Loosely incurving, white flowers, 7in (18cm) wide, appear in early autumn. Is more suitable for exhibition than for garden use.

C. **'Peach Brietner'** (illus. p.219). Reflexed florists' chrysanthemum. H 3¹/2–4ft (1.1–1.2m), S 2¹/2ft (75cm). Is a sport of C. 'Brietner' with fully reflexed, peach-colored flowers.

C. **'Peach Margaret'** (illus. p.219). Spray florists' chrysanthemum. H 4ft (1.2m), S to 2¹/2ft (75cm). Bears reflexed, pale salmon flowers, 3–3¹/2in (8–9cm) wide, in early autumn. Is excellent for exhibition.

C. **'Pennine Alfie'** (illus. p.219). Spray florists' chrysanthemum. H 4ft (1.2m), S 2–2¹/2ft (60–75cm). Spoon-type, pale bronze flowers, to 2¹/2–3in (6–8cm) wide, appear in early autumn. Is suitable for exhibition.

C. **'Pennine Flute'** (illus. p.218). Spray florists' chrysanthemum. H 4ft (1.2m), S 2–2¹/2ft (60–75cm). Is similar to C. 'Pennine Alfie', but has pink flowers.

C. **'Pennine Jewel'** (illus. p.219). Spray florists' chrysanthemum. H 4ft (1.2m), S 2–2¹/2ft (60–75cm). Spoon-

type, pale bronze flowers, 2¹/2–3in (6–8cm) wide, appear in early autumn. Is suitable for exhibition.

C. **'Pennine Oriel'** (illus. p.218). Spray florists' chrysanthemum. H 4ft (1.2m), S 2–2¹/2ft (60–75cm). Has anemone-centered, white flowers, to 3¹/2in (9cm) across, in early autumn. Is very good for exhibition.

C. **'Peter Rowe'**. Incurved florists' chrysanthemum. H 4¹/2ft (1.35m), S 2–2¹/2ft (60–75cm). Produces yellow flowers, to 5¹/2in (14cm) across, in early autumn. Is ideal for exhibition.

C. **'Primrose Fairweather'**. Incurved florists' chrysanthemum. H 3–3¹/2ft (1–1.1m), S to 2¹/2ft (75cm). Produces pale yellow flowers, to 5¹/2–6in (14–15cm) wide, in late autumn. Is good for exhibition.

C. **'Primrose West Bromwich'** (illus. p.219). Reflexed florists' chrysanthemum. H 7ft (2.2m), S 1¹/2–2ft (45–60cm). Fully reflexed, pale yellow flowers, to 7in (18cm) or more wide, appear in mid-autumn. Use only for exhibition.

C. **'Purple Pennine Wine'** (illus. p.219). Spray florists' chrysanthemum. H 4ft (1.2m), S 2–2¹/2ft (60–75cm). Bears reflexed, purplish red flowers, to 3in (8cm) wide, in early autumn. Is very good for exhibition.

C. **'Redwing'** (illus. p.219). Spray florists' chrysanthemum. H 4–4¹/2ft (1.2–1.35m), S 2ft (60cm). Bears single, red flowers, to 3in (8cm) wide, in early autumn. Is suitable for exhibition.

C. **'Ringdove'** (illus. p.218). Charm florists' chrysanthemum. H and S 3ft (1m). Has masses of pink flowers, 1in (2.5cm) across, in late autumn. Is excellent for exhibition.

C. **'Roblush'** (illus. p.218). Spray florists' chrysanthemum. H 5ft (1.5m), S 2¹/2–3ft (75cm–1m). Has reflexed, pale pink flowers, to 3in (8cm) wide, in late autumn. Is good for exhibition.

C. **'Rose Yvonne Arnaud'** (illus. p.219). Reflexed florists' chrysanthemum. H 4ft (1.2m), S 2–2¹/2ft (60–75cm). Is a sport of C. 'Yvonne Arnaud' with fully reflexed, red flowers in early autumn.

C. **rubellum**, syn. C. zawadskii var. latilobum. **'Clara Curtis'** illus. p.217.

C. **'Rytorch'** (illus. p.219). Spray florists' chrysanthemum. H 5ft (1.5m), S 2¹/2–3ft (75cm–1m). In late autumn produces single, pale bronze flowers, to 3in (8cm) wide with a yellow ring surrounding the central disc. Is good for exhibition.

C. **'Sally Ball'** (illus. p.219). Spray florists' chrysanthemum. H 4ft (1.2m), S 2¹/2ft (75cm). Anemone-centered, bronze flowers, to 3in (8cm) wide with a central, yellow-bronze disc, appear in early autumn. Is suitable for exhibition.

C. **'Salmon Fairie'** (illus. p.219). Pompon florists' chrysanthemum. H 1–2ft (30–60cm), S 2ft (60cm). Is similar to C. 'Bronze Fairie', but has salmon flowers.

C. **'Salmon Fairweather'** (illus. p.218). Incurved florists' chrysanthemum. H 3–3¹/2ft (1–1.1m), S to 2¹/2ft (75cm). Is similar to

C. 'Primrose Fairweather', but has pale salmon flowers.
C. **'Salmon Margaret'** (illus. p.219). Spray florists' chrysanthemum. H 4ft (1.2m), S to 2¹/₂ft (75cm). Is similar to *C.* 'Peach Margaret', but has salmon flowers.
C. segetum illus. p.281.
C. **'Sentry'** (illus. p.219). Reflexed florists' chrysanthemum. H 4–4¹/₂ft (1.2–1.35m), S 2–2¹/₂ft (60–75cm). Bears fully reflexed, deep red flowers, to 5in (12cm) wide, in early autumn. Is excellent for exhibition.
C. **'Skater's Waltz'** (illus. p.219). Intermediate florists' chrysanthemum. H 5ft (1.5m), S 2–2¹/₂ft (60–75cm). Produces loosely incurving, pink flowers, to 6–7in (15–18cm) wide, in late autumn.
C. x *superbum*, syn. *C. maximum* of gardens (Shasta daisy). **'Aglaia'** is a robust perennial. H 3ft (1m), S 2ft (60cm). Fully hardy, zones 4–8. Large, daisylike, semi-double, white flower heads are borne singly in summer. Has spoon-shaped, coarse, lobed, toothed leaves. Divide and replant every 2 years. **'Elizabeth'** illus. p.201. **'Esther Read'** illus. p.232. **'Wirral Supreme'** is double with short, central florets.
C. **'Talbot Jo'** (illus. p.219). Spray florists' chrysanthemum. H 4¹/₂ft (1.35m), S 2–2¹/₂ft (60–75cm). Bears single, pink flowers, to 3in (8cm) wide, in early autumn. Is suitable for exhibition.
C. tricolor. See *C. carinatum.*
C. uliginosum (sometimes included in *Leucanthemella* as *L. serotina*). Erect perennial. H 7ft (2.2m), S 2ft (60cm). Fully hardy, zones 4–9. Lance-shaped leaves are lobed and dark green. Leafy stems carry sprays of large, daisylike, green-centered, white flower heads in late autumn.
C. **'Venice'.** Reflexed florists' chrysanthemum. H 4ft (1.2m), S 2–2¹/₂ft (60–75cm). Has fully reflexed, pink flowers, to 6in (15cm) wide, in early autumn. Is good for exhibition.
C. **'Wendy'** (illus. p.219). Spray florists' chrysanthemum. H 4ft (1.2m), S 2–2¹/₂ft (60–75cm). Produces reflexed, pale bronze flowers, to 3in (8cm) wide, in early autumn. Is excellent for exhibition.
C. **'Yellow Brietner'** (illus. p.219). Reflexed florists' chrysanthemum. H 3¹/₂–4ft (1.1–1.2m), S 2¹/₂ft (75cm). Is a sport of *C.* 'Brietner' with fully reflexed, yellow flowers in early autumn.
C. **'Yellow John Hughes'** (illus. p.219). Incurved florists' chrysanthemum. H 4ft (1.2m), S 2–2¹/₂ft (60–75cm). Yellow flowers, to 5–5¹/₂in (12–14cm) wide, appear in late autumn. Is excellent for exhibition.
C. **'Yvonne Arnaud'** (illus. p.219). Reflexed florists' chrysanthemum. H 4ft (1.2m), S 2–2¹/₂ft (60–75cm). Bears fully reflexed, purple flowers, to 5in (12cm) wide, in early autumn.
C. zawadskii var. *latilobum.* See *C. rubellum.*

CHRYSOGONUM (Compositae)
Genus of one species of summer- to autumn-flowering perennial. Is good in rock gardens. Fully hardy. Needs

semi-shade and moist but well-drained, peaty, sandy soil. Propagate by seed when fresh or by division in spring.
C. virginianum illus. p.299.

CHUSQUEA (Bambusoideae). See GRASSES, BAMBOOS, RUSHES, and SEDGES.
C. culeou illus. p.182.

CICERBITA, syn. MULGEDIUM (Compositae)
Genus of perennials, grown for their attractive flower heads. Fully hardy. Requires shade and damp but well-drained soil. Propagate by division in spring or by seed in autumn. Some species may be invasive.
C. alpina, syn. *Lactuca alpina* (Mountain sow thistle). Branching, upright perennial. H to 6ft (2m), S 2ft (60cm). Zones 5–9. Green leaves are lobed with a large, terminal lobe. Elongated panicles of thistlelike, pale blue flower heads appear in summer.
C. bourgaei, syn. *Lactuca bourgaei.* Rampant, erect perennial. H to 6ft (2m), S 2ft (60cm). Zones 5–9. Leaves are oblong to lance-shaped, toothed, and light green. Bears many-branched panicles of thistlelike, mauve-blue or purplish blue flower heads in summer.

CICHORIUM (Compositae)
Chicory
Genus of annuals, biennials, and perennials, grown mainly as ornamental plants (*C. intybus* has edible leaves). Fully hardy. Needs full sun and well-drained soil. Propagate by seed in autumn or spring.
C. intybus illus. p.212.

CIMICIFUGA (Ranunculaceae)
Bugbane
Genus of perennials, grown for their flowers, which have an unusual, slightly unpleasant smell. Fully hardy. Grow in light shade and moist soil. Needs staking. Propagate by seed when fresh or by division in spring.
C. cordifolia. Erect perennial. H 5ft (1.5m), S 2ft (60cm). Zones 4–8. Stiff, tapering racemes of brown buds open in summer to produce feathery plumes of star-shaped, creamy white flowers. Broadly oval to lance-shaped, dissected leaves are light green.
C. racemosa. Clump-forming perennial. H 5ft (1.5m), S 2ft (60cm). Zones 3–8. Spikes of bottlebrushlike, pure white flowers are borne in mid-summer above broadly oval to lance-shaped, divided, fresh green leaves.
C. simplex illus. p.193. **'Elstead'** is an upright perennial. H 4ft (1.2m), S 2ft (60cm). Zones 4–8. Purple stems produce arching racemes of fragrant, bottlebrushlike, white flowers in autumn. Has broadly oval to lance-shaped, divided, glossy leaves. var. *ramosa*, H 7ft (2.2m), has large, much-divided leaves and white flowers on arching panicles.

Cineraria x *hybrida.* See *Senecio* x *hybridus.*

CINNAMOMUM (Lauraceae)
Genus of evergreen trees, grown for their attractive foliage and to provide

shade. Frost tender, min. 50°F (10°C). Requires full light or partial shade and fertile, moisture-retentive but well-drained soil. Water potted specimens freely when in full growth, less at other times. May be pruned if necessary. Propagate by seed in spring or by semi-ripe cuttings in summer.
C. camphora. Moderately fast-growing, evergreen, rounded tree. H and S 40ft (12m) or more. Zone 10. Oval, lustrous, rich green leaves, blue-gray-tinted beneath, reddish or coppery when young, are camphor-scented when bruised. Has insignificant flowers in spring.

CIONURA (Asclepiadaceae)
Genus of one species of deciduous, annual, twining climber, grown for its flowers. Half hardy. Grow in any soil and in full sun. Cut stems exude milky sap that may cause blisters. Prune after flowering. Propagate by seed in spring or by stem cuttings in late summer or early autumn.
C. erecta, syn. *Marsdenia erecta.* Deciduous, annual, twining climber. H 10ft (3m) or more. Half hardy. Heart-shaped, grayish green leaves are 1¹/₄–2¹/₂in (3–6cm) long. In summer, clusters of fragrant white flowers, with 5 spreading petals, are borne in leaf axils, followed by 3in (7cm) long fruits, containing many silky seeds, in autumn.

CIRSIUM (Compositae)
Genus of annuals, biennials, and perennials. Most species are not cultivated – indeed some are pernicious weeds – but *C. rivulare* has decorative flower heads. Fully hardy. Tolerates sun or shade and any but wet soil. Propagate by division in spring or by seed in autumn.
C. rivulare **'Atropurpureum'.** Erect perennial. H 4ft (1.2m), S 2ft (60cm). Zones 4–8. Heads of pincushionlike, deep crimson flowers are borne on erect stems in summer. Leaves are narrowly oval to oblong or lance-shaped and deeply cut, with weakly spiny margins.

CISSUS (Vitaceae)
Genus of evergreen, woody-stemmed, mainly tendril climbers, grown for their attractive foliage. Bears insignificant, greenish flowers, mainly in summer. Half hardy to frost tender, min. 45–64°F (7–18°C). Provide fertile, well-drained soil, with semi-shade in summer. Water regularly, less in cold weather. Needs staking. Thin out crowded stems in spring. Propagate by semi-ripe cuttings in summer.
C. antarctica illus. p.178.
C. bainesii. See *Cyphostemma bainesii.*
C. discolor (Rex begonia vine). Moderately vigorous, evergreen, tendril climber with slender, woody stems. H to 10ft (3m). Frost tender, min. 64°F (18°C), zone 10. Has oval, pointed leaves, 4–6in (10–15cm) long, deep green with silver bands above, maroon beneath.
C. hypoglauca. Evergreen, woody-stemmed, scrambling climber. H

6–10ft (2–3m). Frost tender, min. 45°F (7°C), zones 9–10. Leaves are divided into 4 or 5 oval leaflets, pale green above and blue-gray beneath.
C. juttae. See *Cyphostemma juttae.*
C. rhombifolia illus. p.178.
C. striata, syn. *Ampelopsis sempervirens*, *Vitis striata* (Ivy-of-Uruguay, Miniature grape ivy). Fast-growing, evergreen, woody-stemmed, tendril climber. H 30ft (10m) or more. Half hardy, zone 10. Has leaves of 3–5 oval, serrated, lustrous, green leaflets. Mature plants may produce glossy, black berries in autumn.
C. voinieriana. See *Tetrastigma voinierianum.*

CISTUS (Cistaceae)
Rock rose
Genus of evergreen shrubs, grown for their succession of freely borne, short-lived, showy flowers. Is good in coastal areas, withstanding sea winds well. Frost to half hardy; in cold areas needs shelter. Does best in full sun and light, well-drained soil. Resents being transplanted. Cut out any dead wood in spring, but do not prune hard. Propagate species by softwood or greenwood cuttings in summer or by seed in autumn, hybrids and cultivars by cuttings only in summer.
C. x *aguilari* **'Maculatus'** illus. p.127.
C. albidus (Whiteleaf rock rose). Evergreen, bushy shrub. H and S 3ft (1m). Half hardy, zones 7–9. Leaves are oblong and white-felted. Saucer-shaped, pale rose-pink flowers, each with a central, yellow blotch, open in early summer.
C. x *corbariensis* illus. p.127.
C. creticus illus. p.133.
C. x *cyprius* illus. p.127.
C. ladanifer (Crimson spot rock rose) illus. p.127.
C. laurifolius (Laurel rock rose). Evergreen, bushy, dense shrub. H and S 6ft (2m). Frost hardy, zones 7–9. Has oval, aromatic, dark green leaves and, in summer, saucer-shaped, white flowers, each with a central, yellow blotch.
C. x *lusitanicus.* Evergreen, bushy, compact shrub. H and S 3ft (1m). Frost hardy, zones 7–9. Leaves are narrowly oblong and dark green. Saucer-shaped, white flowers, each with a central, deep red blotch, appear from early to mid-summer.
C. monspeliensis illus. p.127.
C. parviflorus. Evergreen, bushy, dense shrub. H and S 3ft (1m). Frost hardy, zones 7–9. Small, saucer-shaped, pale pink flowers appear among oval, gray-green leaves in early summer.
C. **'Peggy Sammons'.** Evergreen, bushy shrub. H and S 3ft (1m). Frost hardy, zones 7–9. Has oval, gray-green leaves. Saucer-shaped, pale pink flowers are produced freely in early summer.
C. x *purpureus* (Purple rock rose). Evergreen, bushy, rounded shrub. H and S 3ft (1m). Frost hardy, zones 7–9. Produces saucer-shaped, deep purplish pink flowers, each blotched with deep red, from early to mid-summer. Leaves are narrowly lance-shaped and gray-green.

C. salviifolius illus. p.127.
C. 'Silver Pink'. Evergreen, bushy shrub. H 2ft (60cm), S 3ft (1m). Frost hardy, zones 7–9. Oval, dark green leaves set off large, saucer-shaped, clear pink flowers, each with conspicuous, yellow stamens, from early to mid-summer.
C. × skanbergii illus. p.130.

× CITROFORTUNELLA (Rutaceae)

Hybrid genus (*Citrus × Fortunella*) of evergreen shrubs and trees, grown for their flowers, fruits, and overall appearance. Frost tender, min. 41–50°F (5–10°C). Requires full light and fertile, well-drained but not dry soil. Water potted specimens freely when in full growth, moderately at other times. Propagate by seed when ripe or by greenwood or semi-ripe cuttings in summer. Whitefly, red spider mite, mealy bug, lime-induced and magnesium-deficiency chlorosis may be troublesome.
× *C. mitis*, syn. *Citrus mitis*, illus. p.119.

Citrus mitis. See × *Citrofortunella mitis.*

CLADANTHUS (Compositae)

Genus of one species of annual, grown for its fragrant foliage and daisylike flower heads. Fully hardy. Grow in sun and in reasonably fertile, very well-drained soil. Dead-head to prolong flowering. Propagate by seed sown outdoors in mid-spring.
C. arabicus illus. p.281.

CLADRASTIS (Leguminosae)

Genus of deciduous, summer-flowering trees, grown for their pendent, wisterialike flower clusters and autumn foliage. Fully hardy. Requires full sun and fertile, well-drained soil. Propagate by seed in autumn or by root cuttings in late winter. The wood is brittle: old trees are prone to damage by strong winds.
C. lutea illus. p.55.

CLARKIA, syn. GODETIA (Onagraceae)

Genus of annuals, grown for their flowers, which are good for cutting. Fully to half hardy. Grow in sun and in reasonably fertile, well-drained soil. Avoid rich soil as this encourages vegetative growth at the expense of flowers. Propagate by seed sown outdoors in spring, or in early autumn in mild areas. Botrytis may be troublesome.
C. amoena (Farewell-to-spring). Fast-growing annual with upright, thin stems. H to 2ft (60cm), S 1ft (30cm). Fully hardy. Has lance-shaped, green leaves. Spikes of 5-petaled, single or double flowers, in shades of pink, are produced in summer. Tall forms, H 2ft (60cm), have double flowers in shades of pink or red. **Azalea-flowered Series**, intermediate, H 15in (38cm), has semi-double flowers in shades of pink. **Princess Series**, dwarf, H 12in (30cm), has frilled flowers in shades of pink, including salmon (illus. p.285).
C. 'Arianna' illus. p.269.
C. 'Brilliant' illus. p.268.

CLAYTONIA (Portulacaceae)

Genus of mainly evergreen perennials with succulent leaves; is related to *Lewisia*. Grows best in alpine houses. Fully hardy. Prefers well-drained soil and tolerates sun or shade. Propagate by seed or division in autumn. May be difficult to grow.
C. megarhiza. Evergreen, basal-rosetted perennial with a long tap root. H 1/2in (1cm), S 3in (8cm). Zones 5–7. Leaves are spoon-shaped and fleshy. Bears small heads of tiny, bowl-shaped, white flowers in spring. Prefers sun and gritty soil. Is prone to aphid attack. subsp. *nivalis* illus. p.306.
C. virginica (Spring beauty). Clump-forming perennial with flat, black tubers. H 4in (10cm), S 8in (20cm) or more. Zones 5–8. Narrowly spoon-shaped leaves, reddish when young, later turn green and glossy. Branched stems bear cup-shaped, white or pink flowers, striped deep pink, in early spring. Needs shade.

CLEISTOCACTUS (Cactaceae)

Genus of columnar, perennial cacti with branched, cylindrical, much-ribbed stems with spines. Is one of the faster-growing cacti, some reaching 6ft (2m) in 5 years or less. Tubular flowers contain plenty of nectar and are pollinated by hummingbirds. Frost tender, min. 41°F (5°C). Needs full sun and very well-drained soil. Propagate by seed or stem cuttings in spring or summer.
C. baumannii. Erect, then prostrate, perennial cactus. H 3ft (1m) or more, S 15ft (5m). Zone 10. Has thick stems that produce long, uneven, variably colored spines. Bears S-shaped, tubular, bright orange-red flowers in spring-summer.
C. smaragdiflorus. Erect, then prostrate, perennial cactus. H 5ft (1.5m), S 20ft (6m). Zone 10. Is similar to *C. baumannii*, but has straight, tubular flowers with green-tipped petals.
C. straussii illus. p.381.

CLEMATIS (Ranunculaceae)

Genus of evergreen or deciduous, mainly twining climbers and herbaceous perennials, cultivated for their mass of flowers, often followed by decorative seed heads, and grown on walls and trellises and together with trees, shrubs, and other host plants. Only early-flowering species are evergreen, although some later-flowering species are semi-evergreen. Most species have nodding, bell-shaped flowers, with 4 petals (botanically known as perianth segments), or flattish flowers, each usually with 4–6 generally pointed petals. Large-flowered cultivars also bear flattish flowers, but with 4–10 petals. Flower color may vary according to climatic conditions: in general, the warmer the climate, the darker the flower color. Fully to half hardy. May be grown in shade or full sun, but prefers rich, well-drained soil with roots shaded. Propagate cultivars in early summer by softwood or semi-ripe cuttings or layering, species from seed sown in autumn. Aphids, mildew, and clematis wilt may cause problems.

Clematis may be divided into groups according to their approximate flowering seasons, habit, and pruning needs.

Group 1

Early-flowering species prefer a south- or south-west-facing wall. Small, single flowers, either bell-shaped, 1 1/4in (3cm) long, or flattish, 1 1/2–2in (4–5cm) wide, are borne on the previous season's ripened shoots in spring or, occasionally, in late winter. Leaves are evergreen, glossy, and divided into 3 lance-shaped, 5in (12cm) long leaflets or into 3 fernlike, 2in (5cm) long leaflets. Frost hardy.
Alpina and **macropetala** types tolerate exposed, north- or north-east-facing positions. Small, bell-shaped, single, semi-double, or double flowers, 3in (8cm) or less across, are borne on the previous season's ripened shoots in spring, occasionally also on the current season's shoots in summer. Pale to mid-green leaves are divided into 3–5 lance-shaped to broadly oval leaflets, 1 1/4in (3cm) long with serrated margins. Fully hardy.
Montana types are vigorous climbers, suitable for growing over large buildings and trees. Small, flattish, mainly single flowers, 1 1/2–3in (4–7cm) across, are borne on the previous season's ripened shoots in late spring. Leaves are mid- to purplish green and divided into 3 lance-shaped to broadly oval, serrated leaflets, 3in (8cm) long with pointed tips. Frost hardy.

Prune after flowering to allow new growth to be produced and ripened for the following season. Remove dead or damaged stems and cut back other shoots that have outgrown their allotted space.

Group 2

Early, large-flowered cultivars bear flattish, single, semi-double, or double flowers, 3–8in (8–20cm) across, that are borne on the previous season's ripened shoots and on new shoots, from early to late summer. Generally the second flush of flowers on semi-double and double forms produces single flowers. Usually pale to mid-green leaves are simple and oval, to 4in (10cm) long, or are divided into 3 oval or lance-shaped leaflets, 6–7in (15–18cm) long. Fully to frost hardy.

Prune before new growth starts, in early spring. Remove dead or damaged stems and cut back all remaining shoots to where strong, leaf-axil buds are visible. (These buds will produce first crop of flowers.)

Group 3

Late, large-flowered cultivars produce outward-facing, flattish, single flowers, 2 1/2–6in (6–15cm) across, borne on new shoots in summer or early autumn. Leaves are similar to those of early cultivars (group 2), described above. Frost hardy.
Late-flowering species and **small-flowered cultivars** have small, single or double flowers borne on the current season's shoots in summer-autumn.

Flowers vary in shape and may be star-shaped, tubular, bell-shaped, flattish, or resembling nodding lanterns; they vary in size from 1/2in (1cm) to 4in (10cm) across. Have pale to dark green or gray-green leaves divided into 3 lance-shaped to broadly oval leaflets, each 1/2in (1cm) long, or hairy and/or toothed leaves divided into 5 or more lance-shaped to broadly oval leaflets, each 1/2–4in (1–10cm) long. Fully to half hardy.
Herbaceous types produce single flowers that are either flattish, 1/2–3/4in (1–2cm) wide, or bell-shaped or tubular, 1/2–1 1/2in (1–4cm) long, and are produced on the current season's shoots in summer. Mid- to dark green or gray-green leaves are simple and lance-shaped to elliptic, 1–6in (2.5–15cm) long, or are divided into 3–5 rounded, serrated leaflets, each 4–6in (10–15cm) long with a pointed tip. Fully to frost hardy.

Prune before new growth begins in early spring. Remove all of the previous season's stems down to a pair of strong, leaf-axil buds, 6–12in (15–30cm) above soil level.

C. alpina. Alpina clematis (group 1). H 6–10ft (2–3m), S 5ft (1.5m). Fully hardy, zones 6–9. Has lantern-shaped, single, blue flowers, 1 1/2–3in (4–7cm) long, in spring and, occasionally, summer. Forms attractive, fluffy, silvery seed heads in summer. Is ideal for a north-facing or very exposed site. **'Columbine'** has 2in (5cm) long, pale blue petals. **'Frances Rivis'** (illus. p.171) is free-flowering, with slightly twisted, 3in (7cm) long, blue petals. **'Ruby'** has purplish pink flowers.
C. armandii (illus. p.170). Strong-growing, evergreen, early-flowering clematis (group 1). H 10–15ft (3–5m), S 6–10ft (2–3m). Frost hardy, zones 7–9. Bears scented, flattish, single, white flowers, 1 1/2in (4cm) across, in early spring. Needs a sheltered, south- or south-west-facing site.
C. 'Ascotiensis' (illus. p.171). Vigorous, late, large-flowered clematis (group 3). H 10–12ft (3–4m), S 3ft (1m). Frost hardy, zones 4–9. In summer produces single, bright violet-blue flowers, 3 1/2–5in (9–12cm) across, with pointed petals and brownish green anthers.
C. 'Barbara Jackman'. Compact, early, large-flowered clematis (group 2). H 8–10ft (2.5–3m), S 3ft (1m). Frost hardy, zones 4–9. In summer bears single, blue flowers, 4in (10cm) across, with magenta stripes and creamy yellow anthers. Prefers partial shade.
C. 'Beauty of Worcester' (illus. p.171). Early, large-flowered clematis (group 2). H 8–10ft (2.5–3m), S 3ft (1m). Frost hardy, zones 4–9. Has double, rich deep violet-blue flowers, 4in (10cm) across with cream anthers, in early summer and then single flowers in late summer.
C. 'Bees Jubilee'. Compact, early, large-flowered clematis (group 2). H 8ft (2.5m), S 3ft (1m). Frost hardy, zones 4–9. In early summer bears a profusion of single, deep pink flowers, 4–5in (10–12cm) across with brown

anthers and a central, rose-madder stripe on each petal. Prefers partial shade.

C. 'Carnaby'. Compact, early, large-flowered clematis (group 2). H 8ft (2.5m), S 3ft (1m). Frost hardy, zones 4–9. In early summer has a profusion of single, deep pink flowers, 3–4in (8–10cm) across, with a darker stripe on each petal and red anthers. Prefers partial shade.

C. cirrhosa (illus. p.171). Evergreen, early-flowering clematis (group 1). H 6–10ft (2–3m), S 3–6ft (1–2m). Frost hardy, zones 7–9. Produces bell-shaped, cream flowers, 1¼in (3cm) across and spotted red inside, in late winter and early spring during frost-free weather.

C. 'Comtesse de Bouchaud'. Strong-growing, late, large-flowered clematis (group 3). H 6–10ft (2–3m), S 3ft (1m). Frost hardy, zones 4–9. In summer has masses of single, bright mauve-pink flowers, 3–4in (8–10cm) across, with yellow anthers.

C. 'Countess of Lovelace' (illus. p.171). Early, large-flowered clematis (group 2). H 8ft (2.5m), S 3ft (1m). Frost hardy, zones 4–9. Has double, bluish lilac flowers, 4in (10cm) across, with pointed petals and cream anthers, in early summer, then single flowers in late summer.

C. 'Crimson King'. Late, large-flowered clematis (group 3). H 8–10ft (2.5–3m), S 3ft (1m). Frost hardy, zones 4–9. Is shy-flowering, bearing single, crimson flowers, 4in (10cm) across with red anthers, in summer.

C. 'Daniel Deronda'. Vigorous, early, large-flowered clematis (group 2). H 10ft (3m), S 3ft (1m). Frost hardy, zones 4–9. Has double and semi-double, deep purple-blue flowers, 4–5½in (10–14cm) across, with cream anthers, then single flowers in late summer.

C. 'Duchess of Albany' (illus. p.171). Vigorous, small-flowered clematis (group 3). H 8ft (2.5m), S 3ft (1m). Frost hardy, zones 4–9. In summer and early autumn has masses of small, tuliplike, single, soft pink flowers, 2½in (6cm) long, with brown anthers and a deeper pink stripe inside each petal.

C. 'Duchess of Edinburgh'. Early, large-flowered clematis (group 2). H 6–10ft (2–3m), S 3ft (1m). Frost hardy, zones 4–9. In summer produces double, white flowers, 3–4in (8–10cm) across, with yellow anthers and green, outer petals. May sometimes be weak-growing.

C. x durandii. Semi-herbaceous, late-flowering clematis (group 3). H 3–6ft (1–2m), S 1½–5ft (45cm–1.5m). Frost hardy, zones 6–9. In summer produces flattish, single, deep blue flowers, 2½–3in (6–8cm) across, with 4 petals and yellow anthers. Leaves are elliptic.

C. 'Edith'. Compact, early, large-flowered clematis (group 2). H 8ft (2.5m), S 3ft (1m). Frost hardy, zones 4–9. Single, 4in (10cm) wide flowers, with white petals and red anthers, are borne in summer. Is good for a patio garden.

C. 'Elsa Spath' (illus. p.171). Early, large-flowered clematis (group 2). H

6–10ft (2–3m), S 3ft (1m). Frost hardy, zones 4–9. Bears masses of single, 5in (12cm) wide flowers, with overlapping, rich mauve-blue petals and red anthers, throughout summer.

C. 'Ernest Markham' (illus. p.171). Vigorous, late, large-flowered clematis (group 3). H 10–12ft (3–4m), S 3ft (1m). Frost hardy, zones 4–9. In summer bears 4in (10cm) wide, single flowers with blunt-tipped, vivid magenta petals and chocolate anthers. Thrives in full sun.

C. flammula (illus. p.170). Vigorous, late-flowering clematis; may be semi-evergreen (group 3). H 10–15ft (3–5m), S 6ft (2m). Frost hardy, zones 7–9. Produces masses of almond-scented, flattish, single, white flowers, ¾in (2cm) across, in summer and early autumn.

C. florida 'Sieboldii' (illus. p.170). Weak-growing, small-flowered clematis (group 3). H 6–10ft (2–3m), S 3ft (1m). Frost hardy, zones 6–9. In summer has passion-flowerlike, single blooms, each 3in (8cm) wide with creamy white petals and a domed boss of petal-like, rich purple stamens. Needs a sheltered aspect.

C. 'General Sikorski'. Early, large-flowered clematis (group 2). H 10ft (3m), S 3ft (1m). Frost hardy, zones 4–9. Has a profusion of 4in (10cm) wide, single flowers, with large, overlapping, blue petals and cream anthers, in summer.

C. 'Gipsy Queen'. Vigorous, late, large-flowered clematis (group 3). H 10ft (3m), S 3ft (1m). Frost hardy, zones 4–9. Bears single, 4in (10cm) wide flowers, with velvety, violet-purple petals and red anthers, in summer.

C. 'Gravetye Beauty' (illus. p.171). Vigorous, small-flowered clematis (group 3). H 8ft (2.5m), S 3ft (1m). Frost hardy, zones 4–9. In summer and early autumn has masses of small, tuliplike, single, bright red flowers, 2½in (6cm) long, with brown anthers. Is similar to *C.* 'Duchess of Albany', but flowers are more open.

C. 'Hagley Hybrid' (illus. p.170). Vigorous, late, large-flowered clematis (group 3). H 8ft (2.5m), S 3ft (1m). Frost hardy, zones 4–9. Produces 3–4in (8–10cm) wide, single flowers with boat-shaped, rose-mauve petals and red anthers, in summer. Prefers partial shade.

C. 'Henryi' (illus. p.170). Vigorous, early, large-flowered clematis (group 2). H 10ft (3m), S 3ft (1m). Frost hardy, zones 4–9. Has 5in (12cm) wide, single flowers, with white petals and dark chocolate anthers, in summer.

C. heracleifolia var. *davidiana*. Herbaceous clematis (group 3). H 3ft (1m), S 2½ft (75cm). Fully hardy, zones 4–9. In summer, thick stems each bear axillary clusters of scented, tubular, single, pale blue flowers, ¾–1¼in (2–3cm) long, with reflexed petal tips. 'Wyevale' (illus. p.171) has strongly scented, dark blue flowers.

C. 'H.F. Young' (illus. p.171). Compact, early, large-flowered clematis (group 2). H 8ft (2.5m), S 3ft (1m). Frost hardy, zones 4–9. Bears 4in (10cm) wide, single flowers, with

violet-tinged, blue petals and cream anthers, in summer. Is ideal for a container or patio garden.

C. 'Horn of Plenty'. Vigorous, compact, early, large-flowered clematis (group 2). H 8ft (2.5m), S 3ft (1m). Frost hardy, zones 4–9. In early summer produces 5in (12cm) wide, single flowers, with rose-mauve petals, fading to mauve-blue, and dark red anthers. Is good for a patio garden.

C. 'Huldine' (illus. p.170). Very vigorous, late, large-flowered clematis (group 3). H 10–12ft (3–4m), S 6ft (2m). Frost hardy, zones 4–9. Has 2½in (6cm) wide, single, white flowers, mauve beneath and with cream anthers, in summer. Is ideal for an archway or pergola.

C. integrifolia (illus. p.171). Herbaceous clematis (group 3). H and S 30in (75cm). Fully hardy, zones 3–9. Leaves are narrowly lance-shaped. In summer bears bell-shaped, single, deep blue flowers, 1¼in (3cm) long with cream anthers, followed by attractive, gray-brown seed heads.

C. 'Jackmanii' (illus. p.171). Vigorous, late, large-flowered clematis (group 3). H 10ft (3m), S 3ft (1m). Frost hardy, zones 3–9. Masses of velvety, single, dark purple flowers, fading to violet, 3–4in (8–10cm) across, with light brown anthers, are borne in mid-summer.

C. 'Jackmanii Superba'. Vigorous, late, large-flowered clematis (group 3). Zones 3–9. Is similar to *C.* 'Jackmanii', but has more rounded, darker flowers.

C. 'John Huxtable'. Late, large-flowered clematis (group 3). H 6–10ft (2–3m), S 3ft (1m). Frost hardy, zones 4–9. Bears masses of 3in (8cm) wide, single, white flowers, with cream anthers, in mid-summer.

C. 'John Warren'. Early, large-flowered clematis (group 2). H 8–10ft (2.5–3m), S 3ft (1m). Frost hardy, zones 4–9. Produces 5–5½in (12–14cm) wide, single, French gray flowers, with overlapping, pointed, carmine-edged petals and red anthers, in early summer.

C. x jouiniana. Sprawling, sub-shrubby, late-flowering clematis (group 3). H 3ft (1m), S 10ft (3m). Frost hardy, zones 5–9. Has coarse foliage and, in summer, masses of tubular, single, soft lavender or off-white flowers, ¾in (2cm) wide with reflexed petal tips. Is non-clinging. 'Praecox' has slightly darker flowers, 2 weeks earlier.

C. 'Kathleen Wheeler'. Early, large-flowered clematis (group 2). H 8–10ft (2.5–3m), S 3ft (1m). Frost hardy, zones 4–9. Has single, plum mauve flowers, 5–5½in (12–14cm) across with yellow anthers, in early summer.

C. 'Lady Betty Balfour'. Vigorous, late, large-flowered clematis (group 3). H 10ft (3m), S 6ft (2m). Frost hardy, zones 4–9. Has 5in (12cm) wide, single flowers with rich purple petals, fading to purple-blue, and yellow anthers, in late summer and early autumn. Prefers a south- or south-west-facing aspect.

C. 'Lasurstern' (illus. p.171). Vigorous, early, large-flowered clematis (group 2). H 6–10ft (2–3m),

S 3ft (1m). Frost hardy, zones 4–9. In summer bears single, blue flowers, 4–5in (10–12cm) across, with overlapping, wavy-edged petals and cream anthers.

C. 'Lincoln Star' (illus. p.171). Early, large-flowered clematis (group 2). H 6–10ft (2–3m), S 3ft (1m). Frost hardy, zones 4–9. Has 4–5in (10–12cm) wide, single, raspberry pink flowers, with red anthers, in early summer. Early flowers are darker than late ones, which have very pale pink petal edges. Prefers partial shade.

C. macropetala (illus. p.171). Macropetala clematis (group 1). H 10ft (3m), S 5ft (1.5m). Fully hardy, zones 6–9. During late spring and summer has masses of semi-double, mauve-blue flowers, 2in (5cm) long and lightening in color towards the center, followed by fluffy, silvery seed heads. 'Markham's Pink' (illus. p.170) has pink flowers.

C. 'Mme. Le Coultre'. See *C.* 'Marie Boisselot'.

C. 'Marie Boisselot', syn. *C.* 'Mme. Le Coultre'. Vigorous, early, large-flowered clematis (group 2). H 10ft (3m), S 3ft (1m). Frost hardy, zones 4–9. Bears single flowers, 5in (12cm) across, with overlapping, white petals and cream anthers, in summer.

C. 'Miss Bateman'. Compact, early, large-flowered clematis (group 2). H 8ft (2.5m), S 3ft (1m). Frost hardy, zones 4–9. Masses of single, white flowers, 3–4in (8–10cm) across with red anthers, are produced in summer. Is good for a container or patio garden.

C. montana (illus. p.170). Vigorous, Montana clematis (group 1). H 22–40ft (7–12m), S 6–10ft (2–3m). Fully hardy, zones 6–9. In late spring bears masses of single, white flowers, 1½–2in (4–5cm) across, with yellow anthers. 'Elizabeth', H 30–40ft (10–12m), has scented, soft pink flowers with widely spaced petals. Flowers of var. *rubens* (illus. p.170) are pale pink. 'Tetrarose' (illus. p.170), H 22–25ft (7–8m), has coarse, 3in (8cm) long leaflets and 2½–3in (6–7cm) wide, deep satin-pink flowers.

C. 'Mrs. Cholmondeley'. Early, large-flowered clematis (group 2). H 6–10ft (2–3m), S 3ft (1m). Frost hardy, zones 4–9. In summer has single, light bluish lavender flowers, 4–5in (10–12cm) across with widely spaced petals and light chocolate anthers.

C. 'Mrs. George Jackman' (illus. p.170). Early, large-flowered clematis (group 2). H 6–10ft (2–3m), S 3ft (1m). Frost hardy, zones 4–9. Bears 4in (10cm) wide, semi-double flowers, with creamy white petals and light brown anthers, in early summer.

C. 'Mrs. N. Thompson'. Compact, early, large-flowered clematis (group 2). H 8ft (2.5m), S 3ft (1m). Frost hardy, zones 4–9. Produces masses of 3–4in (8–10cm) wide, single, magenta flowers, with a central, slightly darker stripe on each bluish purple-edged petal and red anthers, in summer. Is good for a container or patio garden.

C. 'Nelly Moser' (illus. p.170). Early, large-flowered clematis (group 2). H 11ft (3.5m), S 3ft (1m). Frost hardy, zones 4–9. In early summer has 5–6¹/₂in (12–16cm) wide, single, rose-mauve flowers, with reddish purple anthers and, on each petal, a carmine stripe that fades in strong sun. Prefers a shaded, east-, west-, or north-facing situation.

C. '**Niobe**'. Early, large-flowered clematis (group 2). H 6–10ft (2–3m), S 3ft (1m). Frost hardy, zones 4–9. Throughout summer bears masses of single, rich deep red flowers, 4–5¹/₂in (10–14cm) across with yellow anthers.

C. orientalis. Late-flowering clematis (group 3). H 10–12ft (3–4m), S 5ft (1.5m). Fully hardy, zones 6–9. Leaves are gray- to dark green. In summer has lantern-shaped, single, greenish yellow flowers, 1¹/₄in (3cm) wide with recurved petal tips followed by feathery seed heads. '**Bill MacKenzie**' (illus. p.171) is very vigorous, H 22ft (7m), S 10–12ft (3–4m), with 2¹/₂–3in (6–7cm) wide, yellow flowers. Is best pruned with shears.

C. '**Perle d'Azur**' (illus. p.171). Late, large-flowered clematis (group 3). H 10ft (3m), S 3ft (1m). Frost hardy, zones 4–9. Single, azure blue flowers, 3in (8cm) across with recurved petal tips and creamy green anthers, open in summer.

C. '**Proteus**' (illus. p.171). Early, large-flowered clematis (group 2). H 8–10ft (2.5–3m), S 3ft (1m). Frost hardy, zones 4–9. In early summer bears 4–5in (10–12cm) wide, double, mauve-pink flowers, becoming pinker towards centers and with cream anthers, then single flowers in late summer. Double flowers sometimes have green, outer petals.

C. '**Ramona**'. Early, large-flowered clematis (group 2). H 10ft (3m), S 3ft (1m). Frost hardy, zones 4–9. Has coarse, dark green leaves offset, in summer, by single, pale blue flowers, 4–5in (10–12cm) across with red anthers. Prefers a south- or south-west-facing position.

C. recta (illus. p.170). Clump-forming, herbaceous clematis (group 3). H 3–6ft (1–2m), S 20in (50cm). Fully hardy, zones 3–9. Leaves are dark or gray-green. Bears masses of sweetly scented, flattish, single, white flowers, ³/₄in (2cm) across, in mid-summer.

C. rehderiana (illus. p.171). Vigorous, late-flowering clematis (group 3). H 20–22ft (6–7m), S 6–10ft (2–3m). Frost hardy, zones 6–9. Bears loose clusters of fragrant, tubular, single, yellow flowers, ¹/₂–³/₄in (1–2cm) long, in late summer and early autumn. Leaves are coarse-textured.

C. '**Richard Pennell**' (illus. p.171). Early, large-flowered clematis (group 2). H 6–10ft (2–3m), S 3ft (1m). Frost hardy, zones 4–9. Produces 4–5in (10–12cm) wide, single flowers, with rich purple-blue petals and golden yellow anthers, in summer.

C. '**Rouge Cardinal**'. Early, large-flowered clematis (group 2). H 6–10ft (2–3m), S 3ft (1m). Frost hardy, zones 4–9. In summer has single, velvety, crimson flowers 3–4in (8–10cm) across with red anthers.

C. '**Serenata**'. Early, large-flowered clematis (group 2). H 6–10ft (2–3m), S 3ft (1m). Frost hardy, zones 4–9.

Produces 4in (10cm) wide, single flowers, with yellow anthers, in summer. Dusky purple petals each have a central stripe, slightly darker.

C. '**Souvenir de Capitaine Thuilleaux**'. Compact, early, large-flowered clematis (group 2). H 8ft (2.5m), S 3ft (1m). Frost hardy, zones 4–9. In early summer bears 3–4in (8–10cm) wide, single flowers, with red anthers and deep pink-striped, cream pink petals. Is ideal for a container or patio garden.

C. '**Star of India**' (illus. p.171). Vigorous, late, large-flowered clematis (group 3). H 10ft (3m), S 3ft (1m). Frost hardy, zones 4–9. Bears masses of 3–4in (8–10cm) wide, single, deep purple-blue flowers, with light brown anthers, in mid-summer; each petal has a deep carmine red stripe.

C. tangutica (illus. p.171). Vigorous, late-flowering clematis (group 3). H 15–20ft (5–6m), S 6–10ft (2–3m). Fully hardy, zones 6–9. Has lantern-shaped, single, yellow flowers, 1¹/₂in (4cm) long, throughout summer and early autumn, followed by fluffy, silvery seed heads.

C. '**The President**' (illus. p.171). Early, large-flowered clematis (group 2). H 6–10ft (2–3m), S 3ft (1m). Frost hardy, zones 4–9. In early summer bears masses of single, rich purple flowers, silver beneath, 4in (10cm) wide with red anthers.

C. '**Ville de Lyon**' (illus. p.171). Late, large-flowered clematis (group 3). H 6–10ft (2–3m), S 3ft (1m). Frost hardy, zones 4–9. In mid-summer has single, bright carmine red flowers, 3–4in (8–10cm) across, with darker petal edges and yellow anthers. Lower foliage tends to become scorched by late summer.

C. viticella. Late-flowering clematis (group 3). H 6–10ft (2–3m), S 3ft (1m). Fully hardy, zones 5–9. Produces nodding, open bell-shaped, single, purple-mauve flowers, 1¹/₂in (3.5cm) long, in summer. The following are hybrids of *C. viticella* with other species, but are placed here as they are of similar growth and flower character to this species. '**Abundance**' (illus. p.171) has flattish, rose-pink flowers, 2in (5cm) across with yellow anthers. '**Etoile Violette**' (illus. p.171), H 10–12ft (3–4m), S 5ft (1.5m), is vigorous, with masses of flattish, 1¹/₂–2¹/₂in (4–6cm) wide, violet-purple flowers. '**Mme. Julia Correvon**' (illus. p.171), H 8–11ft (2.5–3.5m), S 3ft (1m), has flattish, 2–3in (5–7cm) wide, wine red flowers with twisted petals. '**Purpurea Plena Elegans**' (illus. p.171), H 10–12ft (3–4m), S 5ft (1.5m), has double, 1¹/₂–2¹/₂in (4–6cm) wide, rose-purple flowers with petals formed in tight rosettes and, occasionally, green, outer petals.

C. '**Vyvyan Pennell**' (illus. p.171). Early, large-flowered clematis (group 2). H 6–10ft (2–3m), S 3ft (1m). Frost hardy, zones 4–9. Has double, lilac flowers, each 4–5in (10–12cm) wide with a central, lavender blue rosette of petals and golden yellow anthers, in early summer, then single, blue-mauve flowers.

C. '**W.E. Gladstone**'. Vigorous, early, large-flowered clematis (group 2). H 10–12ft (3–4m), S1m (3ft). Frost hardy, zones 4–9. Produces single, lavender flowers, 6in (15cm) wide with red anthers, in summer.

C. '**William Kennett**' (illus. p.171). Early, large-flowered clematis (group 2). H 6–10ft (2–3m), S 3ft (1m). Frost hardy, zones 4–9. In summer has masses of single flowers, 4–5in (10–12cm) across, with red anthers and tough, lavender blue petals each bearing a central, darker stripe that fades as the flower matures.

CLEOME (Capparidaceae)
Spider flower
Genus of annuals and a few evergreen shrubs, grown for their unusual, spidery flowers. Half hardy to frost tender, min. 39°F (4°C). Grow in sun and in fertile, well-drained soil. Remove dead flowers. Propagate by seed sown outdoors in late spring. Aphids may be a problem.

C. hassleriana, syn. *C. spinosa.* Fast-growing, bushy annual. H to 4ft (1.2m), S 18in (45cm). Half hardy. Has hairy, spiny stems and green leaves divided into lance-shaped leaflets. Large, rounded heads of narrow-petaled, pink-flushed, white flowers, with long, protruding stamens, appear in summer. '**Colour Fountain**' illus. p.266. '**Rose Queen**' has rose-pink flowers.

C. spinosa. See *C. hassleriana.*

CLERODENDRUM (Verbenaceae)
Genus of evergreen or deciduous, small trees, shrubs, sub-shrubs, and woody-stemmed, twining climbers, grown for their showy flowers. Fully hardy to frost tender, min. 50–61°F (10–16°C). Needs humus-rich, well-drained soil and full sun, with partial shade in summer. Water freely in growing season, less at other times. Stems require support. Thin out crowded growth in spring. Propagate by seed in spring, by softwood cuttings in late spring, or by semi-ripe cuttings in summer. Whitefly, red spider mite, and mealy bug may be a problem.

C. bungei illus. p.116.

C. fallax. See *C. speciosissimum.*

C. fragrans. See *C. philippinum.*

C. philippinum, syn. *C. fragrans*, *C.f.* var. *pleniflorum.* Evergreen or deciduous, bushy shrub. H and S to 8ft (2.5m). Frost tender, min. 50°F (10°C), zone 10. Leaves are broadly oval, coarsely and shallowly toothed, and downy. Fragrant, double, pink or white flowers are borne in domed, terminal clusters in summer.

C. speciosissimum, syn. *C. fallax.* Evergreen, erect to spreading, sparingly branched shrub. H and S to 10ft (3m). Frost tender, min. 59°F (15°C), zone 10. Bears broadly heart-shaped, wavy-edged leaves, each to 1ft (30cm) across, on long stalks and, from late spring to autumn, tubular, scarlet flowers, with spreading petal lobes, in 1ft (30cm) long, terminal clusters. Makes a good pot plant.

C. splendens. Vigorous, evergreen, woody-stemmed, twining climber. H 10ft (3m) or more. Frost tender, min.

59°F (15°C), zone 10. Has oval to elliptic, rich green leaves. Clusters of 5-petaled, tubular, scarlet flowers, 1in (2.5cm) wide, are produced in summer.

C. thomsoniae illus. p.166.

C. trichotomum illus. p.115.

CLETHRA (Clethraceae)
Genus of deciduous or evergreen shrubs and trees, grown for their fragrant white flowers. Fully to half hardy. Needs semi-shade and moist, peaty, acid soil. Propagate by softwood cuttings in summer or by seed in autumn.

C. alnifolia (Summersweet). Deciduous, bushy shrub. H and S 8ft (2.5m). Fully hardy, zones 4–9. Has oval, toothed, green leaves and, in late summer and early autumn, slender spires of small, bell-shaped flowers.

C. arborea (Lily-of-the-valley tree). Evergreen, bushy, dense shrub or tree. H 25ft (8m), S 20ft (6m). Half hardy, zone 9. Long, nodding clusters of small, strongly fragrant, bell-shaped flowers are produced among oval, toothed, rich green leaves from late summer to mid-autumn.

C. barbinervis (Japanese clethra) illus. p.106.

C. delavayi illus. p.88.

CLEYERA (Theaceae)
Genus of evergreen, summer-flowering shrubs and trees, grown for their foliage and flowers. Frost to half hardy. Requires a sheltered position in sun or semi-shade and moist, acid soil. Propagate by semi-ripe cuttings in summer.

C. fortunei. See *C. japonica* 'Tricolor'.

C. japonica. Evergreen, bushy shrub. H and S 10ft (3m). Frost hardy, zones 7–10. Small, fragrant, saucer-shaped, white flowers are borne from early to mid-summer amid narrowly oval, glossy, dark green leaves. Has small, spherical, black fruits. '**Tricolor**' (syn. *C. fortunei*), H and S 6ft (2m), is half hardy and produces pink-flushed, young leaves, later dark green edged with creamy white. Is sometimes confused in cultivation with *Eurya japonica* 'Variegata'.

CLIANTHUS (Leguminosae)
Genus of evergreen or semi-evergreen, woody-stemmed, scrambling climbers, grown for their attractive flowers. Half hardy to frost tender, min. 45°F (7°C). Grow outdoors in warm areas in well-drained soil and full sun. In cooler areas needs to be under glass. In spring prune out growing tips to give a bushier habit and cut out any dead wood. Propagate by seed in spring or stem cuttings in late summer.

C. puniceus and f. *albus* illus. p.163.

CLINTONIA (Liliaceae)
Genus of late spring- or summer-flowering, rhizomatous perennials. Fully hardy. Prefers shade and moist but well-drained, peaty, neutral to acid soil. Propagate by division in spring or by seed in autumn.

C. andrewsiana. Clump-forming, rhizomatous perennial. H 24in (60cm), S 12in (30cm). Zones 4–8. In early summer produces clusters of small,

bell-shaped, pinkish purple flowers at tops of stems, above sparse, broadly oval, glossy, rich green leaves. Bears globose, blue fruits in autumn.
C. borealis. Clump-forming, rhizomatous perennial. H and S 12in (30cm). Zones 4–8. Is similar to *C. andrewsiana*, but has nodding, yellowish green flowers followed by small, blackish fruits.
C. uniflora (Queencup). Spreading, rhizomatous perennial. H 6in (15cm), S 12in (30cm). Zones 4–8. Has oval, glossy, green leaves. Slender stems bear solitary star-shaped, white flowers in late spring, then large, globose, blue-black fruits.

CLITORIA (Leguminosae)
Genus of perennials and evergreen shrubs and twining climbers, grown for their large, pealike flowers. Frost tender, min. 59°F (15°C). Grow in any fertile, well-drained soil and in full light. Water moderately, less when not in full growth. Provide support for stems. Thin out crowded stems in spring. Propagate by seed in spring or by softwood cuttings in summer. Whitefly and red spider mite may be a problem.
C. ternatea. Evergreen, twining climber with slender stems. H 10–15ft (3–5m). Zone 10. Leaves are divided into 3 or 5 oval leaflets. Clear bright blue flowers, 3–5in (7–12cm) wide, are carried in summer.

CLIVIA (Amaryllidaceae)
Genus of robust, evergreen, rhizomatous perennials, cultivated for their funnel-shaped flowers. Suits borders and large containers. Frost tender, min. 50°F (10°C). Needs partial shade and well-drained soil. Water well in summer, less in winter. Propagate by seed in winter or spring or by division in spring or summer after flowering. Mealy bugs may cause problems.
C. miniata illus. p.350.
C. nobilis. Evergreen, spring- or summer-flowering, rhizomatous perennial. H 12–16in (30–40cm), S 12–24in (30–60cm). Zone 10. Has strap-shaped, semi-erect, basal leaves, 16–24in (40–60cm) long. Each leafless stem bears a dense, semi-pendent head of over 20 narrowly funnel-shaped, red flowers, with green tips and yellow margins to petals.

CLUSIA (Guttiferae)
Genus of evergreen, mainly summer-flowering climbers, shrubs, and trees, grown for their foliage and flowers. Frost tender, min. 61–4°F (16–18°C). Needs partial shade and well-drained soil. Water potted specimens moderately, very little when temperatures are low. Pruning is tolerated if necessary. Propagate by layering in spring or by semi-ripe cuttings in summer. Whitefly and red spider mite may be a problem.
C. rosea (Autograph tree, Copey, Fat pork tree, Pitch apple). Slow-growing, evergreen, rounded tree or shrub. H and S to 50ft (15m). Zone 10. Bears oval, lustrous, deep green leaves. Has cup-shaped, pink flowers, 2in (5cm)

wide, in summer, followed by globose, greenish fruits that yield a sticky resin.

CLYTOSTOMA (Bignoniaceae)
Genus of evergreen, woody-stemmed, tendril climbers, grown for their flowers. Frost tender, min. 50–55°F (10–13°C). Grow in well-drained soil, with partial shade in summer. Water freely in summer, less at other times. Provide support for stems. Thin out congested growth after flowering or in spring. Propagate by semi-ripe cuttings in summer.
C. callistegioides illus. p.164.

COBAEA (Cobaeaceae)
Genus of evergreen or deciduous, woody-stemmed, tendril climbers. Only one species is generally cultivated. Frost tender, min. 39°F (4°C). Grow outdoors in warm areas in any well-drained soil and in full light. In cool regions may be grown under glass or treated as an annual. Propagate by seed in spring.
C. scandens illus. p.172. f. *alba* is an evergreen, woody-stemmed, tendril climber. H 12–15ft (4–5m). Zones 9–10. Has long-stalked, bell-shaped, green, then white flowers from late summer until first frosts. Leaves have 4 or 6 oval leaflets.

Cocos capitata. See *Butia capitata.*

CODIAEUM (Euphorbiaceae)
Genus of evergreen shrubs, grown for their foliage. Frost tender, min. 50–55°F (10–13°C). Prefers partial shade and fertile, moist but well-drained soil. Remove tips from young plants to promote a branched habit. Propagate by greenwood cuttings from firm stem tips in spring or summer. Mealy bug and soft scale may be a nuisance.
C. variegatum illus. p.145.

CODONOPSIS (Campanulaceae)
Genus of perennials and mostly herbaceous, twining climbers, grown for their bell- or saucer-shaped flowers. Fully to frost hardy. Grow in semi-shade and in light, well-drained soil. Train over supports or leave to scramble through other, larger plants. Propagate by seed in autumn or spring.
C. clematidea. Herbaceous, twining climber. H to 5ft (1.5m). Frost hardy, zones 7–9. Has small, oval, green leaves. In summer produces nodding, bell-shaped flowers, 1in (2.5cm) long; they are white, tinged with blue, and marked inside with darker veining and 2 purple rings.
C. convolvulacea, syn. *C. vinciflora,* illus. p.172.
C. ovata. Upright perennial with scarcely twining stems. H to 12in (30cm). Frost hardy, zones 7–9. Has small, oval leaves and, in summer, small, bell-shaped, pale blue flowers, often with darker veins.
C. vinciflora. See *C. convolvulacea.*

COELOGYNE. See ORCHIDS.
C. cristata (illus. p.252). Evergreen, epiphytic orchid for a cool greenhouse. H 6in (15cm). Zone 10. In winter produces sprays of crisp, white

flowers, 2in (5cm) across and marked orange on each lip. Narrowly oval leaves are 3–4in (8–10cm) long. Needs good light in summer.
C. flaccida (illus. p.252). Evergreen, epiphytic orchid for a cool greenhouse. H 6in (15cm). Zone 10. During spring bears drooping spikes of fragrant, star-shaped, light buff flowers, 1¹⁄₂in (4cm) across, with yellow and brown marks on each lip. Has narrowly oval, semi-rigid leaves, 3–4in (8–10cm) long. Grow in semi-shade in summer.
C. nitida, syn. *C. ochracea* (illus. p.252). Evergreen, epiphytic orchid for a cool greenhouse. H 5in (12cm). Zone 10. In spring produces sprays of very fragrant white flowers, 1in (2.5cm) across and with a yellow mark on each lip. Narrowly oval, semi-rigid leaves are 3–4in (8–10cm) long. Requires semi-shade in summer.
C. ochracea. See *C. nitida.*
C. speciosa (illus. p.254). Vigorous, evergreen, epiphytic orchid for an intermediate greenhouse. H 10in (25cm). Zone 10. In summer, pendent, light green flowers, 2¹⁄₂in (6cm) across, with brown- and white-marked lips, open in succession along stems. Has broadly oval leaves, 9–10in (23–5cm) long. Grow in good light in summer.

COIX (Gramineae). See GRASSES, BAMBOOS, RUSHES, and SEDGES.
C. lacryma-jobi illus. p.182.

COLCHICUM (Liliaceae)
Genus of spring- and autumn-flowering corms, grown for their mainly goblet-shaped blooms, up to 8in (20cm) long, most of which emerge before leaves. Each corm bears 2–7 narrowly strap-shaped to broadly elliptic, basal leaves. Fully to frost hardy. Needs an open, sunny situation and well-drained soil. Propagate by seed or division in autumn.
C. agrippinum illus. p.368.
C. autumnale illus. p.366.
'Alboplenum' is an autumn-flowering corm. H and S 4–6in (10–15cm). Fully hardy, zones 4–9. In spring has 3–5 large, semi-erect, basal, glossy, green leaves. Produces a bunch of up to 8 long-tubed, rounded, double, white flowers with 15–30 narrow petals.
C. 'Beaconsfield'. Robust, autumn-flowering corm. H and S 6–8in (15–20cm). Fully hardy, zones 4–9. Has large, goblet-shaped, rich pinkish purple flowers, faintly checkered and white in centers. Large, semi-erect, basal leaves appear in spring.
C. bivonae, syn. *C. bowlesianum, C. sibthorpii,* illus. p.367.
C. bowlesianum. See *C. bivonae.*
C. byzantinum illus. p.367.
C. cilicicum illus. p.368.
C. 'Lilac Wonder'. Vigorous, autumn-flowering corm. H and S 6–8in (15–20cm). Fully hardy, zones 4–9. Produces goblet-shaped, deep lilac-pink flowers, 6–8in (15–20cm) long. Broad, semi-erect, basal leaves appear in spring.
C. luteum illus. p.363.
C. sibthorpii. See *C. bivonae.*
C. speciosum. Vigorous, autumn-flowering corm. H and S 6–8in

(15–20cm). Fully hardy, zones 4–9. Bears goblet-shaped, pale to deep pinkish purple flowers, 6–8in (15–20cm) long, often with white throats. Large, semi-erect, basal leaves develop in winter or spring. **'Album'** illus. p.366.
C. 'The Giant'. Robust, autumn-flowering corm. H and S 6–8in (15–20cm). Fully hardy, zones 4–9. Produces up to 5 funnel-shaped, deep mauve-pink flowers, each 6–8in (15–20cm) long and fading to white in the center. Broad, semi-erect, basal leaves form in winter or spring.
C. variegatum. Autumn-flowering corm. H 4–6in (10–15cm), S 3–4in (8–10cm). Frost hardy, zones 7–9. Bears widely funnel-shaped, reddish purple flowers with strong checkered patterns. More or less horizontal, basal leaves with wavy margins appear in spring. Needs a hot, sunny site.
C. 'Waterlily' illus. p.368.

COLEONEMA (Rutaceae)
Genus of evergreen, heathlike shrubs, grown for their flowers and overall appearance. Frost tender, min. 37–41°F (3–5°C). Needs full sun and well-drained, neutral to acid soil. Water potted plants moderately when in full growth, sparingly at other times. For a more compact habit, clip after flowering. Propagate by seed in spring or by semi-ripe cuttings in late summer.
C. pulchrum. Evergreen, spreading to domed shrub with wiry stems. H 2–4ft (60cm–1.2m), S 3–5ft (1–1.5m). Zones 9–10. Has soft, needlelike, bright green leaves. Carries 5-petaled, pale pink to red flowers in spring-summer.

COLEUS (Labiatae)
Genus of perennials, annuals, and evergreen sub-shrubs, grown for their colorful leaves and flowers. Makes excellent pot plants. Frost tender, min. 39–50°F (4–10°C). Grow in sun or partial shade and in fertile, well-drained soil, choosing a sheltered position. Water freely in summer, much less at other times. Pinch out growing shoots of young plants to encourage a bushy habit. Propagate by seed sown under glass in late winter or by softwood cuttings in spring or summer. Mealy bug and whitefly may cause problems.
C. blumei illus. p.268. **'Brightness'** illus. p.273. **'Fashion Parade'** is a fast-growing, bushy perennial, grown as an annual. H to 18in (45cm), S 12in (30cm) or more. Min. 50°F (10°C). Has multicolored, serrated leaves of various shapes, from oval and unlobed to deeply lobed. Spikes of tiny, blue flowers are produced in summer and should be removed. **'Scarlet Poncho'**, with a pendulous habit and oval, serrated, bright red leaves, and **Wizard Series**, also with oval, serrated leaves, but in a very wide range of leaf colors, are both dwarf forms, H 12in (30cm).
C. thyrsoideus. Fast-growing, bushy perennial, grown as an annual. H to 3ft (1m), S 2ft (60cm). Min. 39°F (4°C). Has oval, serrated, green leaves. Bears panicles of tubular, bright blue flowers in winter.

COLLETIA (Rhamnaceae)
Genus of deciduous, usually leafless shrubs, grown for their curious, spiny shoots and profuse, small flowers. Shoots assume function of leaves. Frost hardy. Requires a sheltered, sunny site and well-drained soil. Propagate by semi-ripe cuttings in late summer.
C. armata illus. p.115. **'Rosea'** is a deciduous, stoutly branched shrub. H 8ft (2.5m), S 15ft (5m). Zones 7–10. Shoots have rigid, gray-green spines. Bears fragrant, tubular, pink flowers in late summer and early autumn.
C. cruciata. See *C. paradoxa.*
C. paradoxa, syn. *C. cruciata.* Deciduous, arching shrub with stiff branches. H 10ft (3m), S 15ft (5m). Zones 7–10. Bears stout, flattened, blue-green spines. Fragrant, tubular, white flowers are produced in late summer and early autumn.

COLLINSIA (Scrophulariaceae)
Genus of spring- to summer-flowering annuals. Fully hardy. Grow in partial shade and in fertile, well-drained soil. Support with thin sticks. Propagate by seed sown outdoors in spring or early autumn.
C. grandiflora illus. p.275.

COLOCASIA (Araceae)
Genus of deciduous or evergreen, perennial, marginal water plants, grown for their foliage. Has edible tubers, known as 'taros', for which it is widely cultivated. Is suitable for the edges of frost-free pools; may also be grown in wet soil in pots. Frost tender, min. 34°F (1°C); with min. 77°F (25°C) is evergreen. Grows in sun or light shade and in mud or shallow water. Propagate by division in spring.
C. esculenta illus. p.374. **'Fontanesii'** is a deciduous, perennial, marginal water plant. H 3½ft (1.1m), S 2ft (60cm). Zones 9–10. Has large, bold, oval, green leaves with dark green veins and margins and blackish violet leaf stalks and spathe tubes. **'Illustris'** has brownish purple leaf stalks and dark green leaf blades with purple spots.

COLQUHOUNIA (Labiatae)
Genus of evergreen or semi-evergreen shrubs, grown for their flowers in late summer and autumn. Frost hardy, but is cut to ground level in cold winters. Needs a sheltered, sunny position and well-drained soil. Propagate by softwood cuttings in summer.
C. coccinea illus. p.117.

COLUMNEA (Gesneriaceae)
Genus of evergreen, creeping or trailing perennials or sub-shrubs, grown for their showy flowers. Trailing species are useful for hanging baskets. Frost tender, min. 59°F (15°C). Needs bright but indirect light, a fairly humid atmosphere, and moist soil, except in winter. Propagate by tip cuttings after flowering.
C. x banksii illus. p.209.
C. crassifolia illus. p.240.
C. gloriosa (Goldfish plant). Evergreen, trailing perennial with more or less unbranched stems. H or

S to 3ft (90cm). Zone 10. Oval leaves have reddish hairs. Has tubular, hooded, scarlet flowers, to 3in (8cm) long with yellow throats, in winter-spring.
C. microphylla. Evergreen perennial, sparsely branched on each trailing stem. H or S 3ft (1m) or more. Zone 10. Has small, rounded leaves with brown hairs; hooded, tubular, scarlet flowers, to 3in (8cm) long with yellow throats, are produced in winter-spring. **'Variegata'** illus. p.223.

COLUTEA (Leguminosae)
Genus of deciduous, summer-flowering shrubs, grown for their foliage, pealike flowers, and bladder-shaped seed pods. Fully hardy. Requires full sun and any but waterlogged soil. Propagate by softwood cuttings in summer or by seed in autumn.
C. arborescens illus. p.114.
C. x media illus. p.115.
C. orientalis. Deciduous, bushy shrub. H and S 6ft (2m). Zones 6–9. Has blue-gray leaves consisting of 7 or 9 oval leaflets. Clusters of yellow-marked, coppery red flowers in summer are followed by inflated, green, then pale brown seed pods.

COMAROSTAPHYLIS (Ericaceae)
Genus of evergreen shrubs and trees, often included in *Arctostaphylos*, grown for their foliage, flowers, and fruits. Frost to half hardy; in cold areas requires shelter. Needs full sun and well-drained, acid soil. Propagate by semi-ripe cuttings in summer or by seed in autumn.
C. diversifolia, syn. *Arctostaphylos diversifolia* (Summer holly). Evergreen, upright shrub or tree. H 15ft (5m), S 10ft (3m). Half hardy, zones 7–9. Leaves are oblong, glossy, and dark green. Terminal racemes of fragrant, urn-shaped, white flowers appear from early to mid-spring, followed by spherical, red fruits.

COMBRETUM (Combretaceae)
Genus of evergreen trees, shrubs, and scandent to twining climbers, grown for their small, showy flowers. Frost tender, min. 61°F (16°C). Provide humus-rich, well-drained soil, with partial shade in summer. Water freely in summer, less at other times. Support for stems is necessary. Thin out and spur back congested growth after flowering. Propagate by semi-ripe cuttings in summer. Red spider mite may be a problem.
C. grandiflorum. Moderately vigorous, evergreen, scandent to twining climber. H to 20ft (6m). Zone 10. Has oblong to elliptic, pointed leaves, 4–8in (10–20cm) long. Tubular, bright red flowers with long stamens are produced in summer in one-sided spikes, 4–5in (10–13cm) long.

COMMELINA (Commelinaceae)
Genus of perennials, usually grown as annuals. Half hardy. Grow in a sunny, sheltered position and in fertile, well-drained soil. Crowns should be lifted before the frosts and overwintered in slightly moist, frost-free conditions.

Propagate by seed sown under glass or by division in spring.
C. coelestis illus. p.278.

CONANDRON (Gesneriaceae)
Genus of one species of tuberous perennial, grown for its fleshy leaves and drooping flower clusters. Grow in alpine houses. Frost hardy. Needs shade and humus-rich, well-drained soil. Potted plants need moist soil in summer, dry when dormant in winter. Propagate by division or seed in spring.
C. ramondioides. Hummock-forming, tuberous perennial. H 12in (30cm), S 8in (20cm). Zones 7–8. Bears broadly oval, fleshy, wrinkled, green leaves with toothed edges. In mid-summer, each flower stem carries 5–25 tubular flowers, usually lilac, but white, purple, or pink forms also occur.

CONIFERS
Group of trees and shrubs distinguished botanically from others by producing seeds exposed or uncovered on the scales of fruits. Most conifers are evergreen, have needlelike leaves, and bear woody fruits (cones). All genera in the Cupressaceae family, however, have needlelike juvenile leaves and, excepting many junipers and some other selected forms, scalelike adult leaves. Conifers described in this book are evergreen unless otherwise stated.
   Conifers make excellent garden plants. Most provide year-round foliage, which may be green, blue, gray, bronze, gold, or silver. They range in height from trees 100ft (30m) or more to dwarf shrubs that grow less than 2in (5cm) every 10 years. Tall conifers may be planted as specimen trees or to provide shelter, screening, or hedging. Dwarf conifers make good features in their own right as well as in groups; they also associate well with heathers, add variety to rock gardens, and provide excellent ground cover. They may also be grown in containers.

Hardiness
Nearly all conifers described in this book are fully hardy. Some, such as *Picea sitchensis*, *P. omorika*, and *Pinus contorta*, are extremely tough and thrive in the coldest, most windswept positions. *Araucaria*, *Cupressus*, and *Pinus* are good for coastal conditions. *Athrotaxis*, *Austrocedrus*, *Cephalotaxus*, *Podocarpus*, and certain species noted in other genera are frost to half hardy and flourish only in mild localities. Elsewhere they need a very sheltered position or may be grown indoors as dwarf plants.
   Frost may damage new growth of several genera, especially *Abies*, *Larix*, *Picea*, and *Pseudotsuga*, and severe cold, dry spells in winter may temporarily harm mature foliage.

Position and soil
x *Cupressocyparis*, *Cupressus*, *Larix*, and *Pinus* need full sun. *Cedrus*, *Juniperus*, and *Pseudolarix* do not tolerate shade. All other conifers will thrive in sun or shade, and most *Abies* and all *Cephalotaxus*, *Podocarpus*,

Taxus, *Thuja*, *Torreya*, and *Tsuga* will grow in deep shade once established.
   In general, conifers grow well on most types of soil. However, certain genera and species will not do well on soils overlying chalk or limestone. In this book such conifers are: *Abies*, *Pseudolarix*, *Pseudotsuga*, and *Tsuga*; also *Picea*, except *P. likiangesis*, *P. omorika*, and *P. pungens*; and *Pinus*, except *P. aristata*, *P. armandii*, *P. cembroides*, *P. halepensis*, *P. leucodermis*, *P. nigra*, *P. peuce*, and *P. wallichiana*.
   Certain conifers tolerate extreme conditions. *Abies alba*, *A. homolepis*, *A. nordmanniana*, *Cryptomeria*, *Cunninghamia*, *Metasequoia*, *Pinus coulteri*, *P. peuce*, *P. ponderosa*, *Sciadopitys*, *Sequoia*, *Sequoiadendron*, and *Taxodium* will grow on heavy clay soils. *Picea omorika*, *P. sitchensis*, *Pinus contorta*, *Sciadopitys verticillata*, and *Thuja plicata* are all happy on wet soil, and *Metasequoia* and *Taxodium* thrive in waterlogged conditions. *Cupressus*, *Juniperus*, and *Pinus* grow well on dry, sandy soil.

Pruning
If a conifer produces more than one leader, remove all but one. Bear in mind when trimming hedges that most conifers will not make new growth when cut back into old wood or from branches that have turned brown. This does not, however, apply to *Cephalotaxus*, *Cryptomeria*, *Cunninghamia*, *Sequoia*, *Taxus*, and *Torreya*, and these conifers may be kept to a reasonable size in the garden by cutting back the main stem, which will later coppice (make new growth). Young specimens of *Araucaria*, *Ginkgo*, *Metasequoia*, and *Taxodium* will sometimes do the same.

Propagation
Seed is the easiest method of propagation, but forms selected for leaf color (other than blue in some species) do not come true. Sow in autumn or spring. All genera apart from *Abies*, *Cedrus*, *Picea* (except young plants or dwarf forms), *Pinus*, *Pseudolarix*, *Pseudotsuga*, and *Tsuga* (except young plants or dwarf forms) may be raised fairly easily from cuttings: current growth from autumn to spring for evergreens, softwood cuttings in summer for deciduous conifers. Tall-growing forms of Pinaceae (*Abies*, *Cedrus*, *Picea*, *Pinus*, *Pseudolarix*, *Pseudotsuga*, and *Tsuga*) are usually propagated by grafting in late summer, winter, or early spring. Layering may be possible for some dwarf conifers.

Pests and diseases
Honey fungus attacks many conifers, especially young plants. Most resistant to the disease are *Abies*, *Calocedrus*, *Larix*, *Pseudotsuga*, and *Taxus*. Green spruce aphid may be a problem on *Picea*, and conifer spinning mite may defoliate *Abies*, *Picea*, and some *Pinus*.

Tall-growing conifers are illustrated on pp.73–81, dwarf forms on pp.82–3. See also *Abies*, *Araucaria*, *Athrotaxis*,

Austrocedrus, Calocedrus, Cedrus, Cephalotaxus, Chamaecyparis, Cryptomeria, Cunninghamia, x *Cupressocyparis, Cupressus, Fitzroya, Ginkgo, Juniperus, Larix, Metasequoia, Microbiota, Phyllocladus, Picea, Pinus, Podocarpus, Pseudolarix, Pseudotsuga, Saxegothaea, Sciadopitys, Sequoia, Sequoiadendron, Taxodium, Taxus, Thuja, Thujopsis, Torreya,* and *Tsuga.*

CONOPHYTUM (Aizoaceae)

Genus of slow-growing, clump-forming, perennial succulents with spherical or 2-eared leaves that grow for only 2 months each year, after flowering. In early summer, old leaves gradually shrivel to papery sheaths from which new leaves and flowers emerge in late summer. Frost tender, min. 39°F (4°C) if dry. Requires full sun and well-drained soil. Keep dry in winter. Propagate by seed from spring to autumn or by division in late summer.

C. bilobum illus. p.399.
C. meyeri. Slow-growing, clump-forming, perennial succulent. H $^3/_4$–1$^1/_4$in (2–3cm), S 4in (10cm). Zones 9–10. Egg-shaped, gray-green leaves each have a 2-eared, fissured tip. Carries $^5/_8$–$^3/_4$in (1.5–2cm) wide, daisylike, yellow flowers in autumn.
C. notabile illus. p.400.
C. truncatum illus. p.390.

CONSOLIDA (Ranunculaceae)

Larkspur
Genus of annuals, providing excellent cut flowers. Fully hardy. Grow in sun and in fertile, well-drained soil. Stake stems of tall-growing plants. Propagate by seed sown outdoors in spring, or in early autumn in mild areas. Protect young plants from slugs and snails.

C. ajacis. See *C. ambigua.*
C. ambigua, syn. *C. ajacis, Delphinium consolida* (Annual delphinium, Rocket larkspur). Fast-growing, upright, branching annual. Giant forms, H to 4ft (1.2m), S 1ft (30cm); dwarf, H and S 1ft (30cm). All have feathery, green leaves and, throughout summer, spikes of rounded, spurred flowers. **Hyacinth-flowered Series** (dwarf) produces spikes of tubular flowers in shades of pink, mauve, blue, or white. **Imperial Series** illus. p.276.

CONVALLARIA (Liliaceae)

Lily-of-the-valley
Genus of spring-flowering, rhizomatous perennials. Fully hardy. Prefers partial shade and will grow in any soil but does best in humus-rich, moist soil. Propagate by division after flowering or in autumn.

C. majalis illus. p.225. **'Flore Pleno'** is a low-growing, rhizomatous perennial. H 9–12in (23–30cm), S indefinite. Zones 4–9. Sprays of small, very fragrant, pendent, bell-shaped flowers that are double and white open in spring. Narrowly oval leaves are mid- to dark green. **'Fortin's Giant'**, H 18in (45cm), has larger flowers and leaves that appear a little earlier.

CONVOLVULUS (Convolvulaceae)

Genus of dwarf, bushy, and climbing annuals, perennials, and evergreen shrubs and sub-shrubs. Fully hardy to frost tender, min 36°F (2°C). Grow in sun and in poor to fertile, well-drained soil. Dead-head to prolong flowering. Propagate by seed sown outdoors in mid-spring for hardy plants or under glass in spring for tender plants, perennials and sub-shrubs by softwood cuttings in late spring or summer.

C. althaeoides illus. p.315.
C. cneorum illus. p.126.
C. mauritanicus. See *C. sabatius.*
C. minor. See *C. tricolor.*
C. purpureus. See *Ipomoea purpurea.*
C. sabatius, syn. *C. mauritanicus,* illus. p.296.
C. tricolor, syn. *C. minor* (Dwarf morning-glory). Moderately fast-growing, upright, bushy, or climbing annual. H 8–12in (20–30cm), S 8in (20cm). Fully hardy to frost tender. Has oval to lance-shaped, green leaves. In summer bears saucer-shaped, blue or white flowers, 1in (2.5cm) wide, with yellowish white throats. Tall, climbing forms, H to 10ft (3m), are half hardy and have flowers to 4in (10cm) wide. **'Blue Flash'** (bushy) illus. p.276. **'Flying Saucers'** (climber) has blue-and-white-striped flowers. **'Heavenly Blue'** (syn. *Ipomoea rubrocaerulea* 'Heavenly Blue'; climber) illus. p.173. **'Major'** (climber) and **'Minor'** (bushy) have flowers in shades of blue, red, or white.

COPIAPOA (Cactaceae)

Genus of slow-growing, perennial cacti with funnel-shaped, yellow flowers. Many species have large tap roots. Frost tender, min. 46–50°F (8–10°C). Needs partial shade and very well-drained soil. Propagate by seed or grafting in spring or summer.

C. cinerea illus. p.387.
C. coquimbana. Clump-forming, spherical, then columnar, perennial cactus. H to 1ft (30cm), S 3ft (1m). Min. 46°F (8°C), zone 10. Dark gray-green stem has 10–17 ribs. Areoles bear 8–10 dark brown radial spines and 1 or 2 stouter central spines. Yellow flowers, 1$^1/_4$in (3cm) across, appear in summer. Is slow to form clumps.
C. echinoides. Flattened spherical, perennial cactus, ribbed like a sea-urchin. H 6in (15cm), S 4in (10cm). Min. 50°F (10°C), zone 10. Solitary gray-green stem bears dark brown spines, 1$^1/_4$in (3cm) long, which soon fade to gray. In summer produces pale yellow flowers, 1$^1/_2$in (4cm) across.
C. marginata. Clump-forming, perennial cactus. H 2ft (60cm), S 1ft (30cm). Min. 50°F (10°C), zone 10. Gray-green stem bears very close-set areoles with dark-tipped, pale brown spines, to 1$^1/_4$in (3cm) long. Has yellow flowers, $^3/_4$–2in (2–5cm) across, in spring-summer.

COPROSMA (Rubiaceae)

Genus of evergreen shrubs and trees, grown for their foliage and fruits. Separate male and female plants are needed to obtain fruits. Half hardy to frost tender, min. 36–41°F (2–5°C). Prefers full light and well-drained

soil. Water potted specimens freely in summer, moderately at other times. Propagate by seed in spring or by semi-ripe cuttings in late summer.
C. x kirkii. Evergreen, prostrate, then semi-erect, densely branched shrub. H to 3ft (1m), S 4–6ft (1.2–2m). Half hardy, zones 8–10. Narrowly oblong to lance-shaped, leathery, glossy leaves are borne singly or in small clusters. In late spring has insignificant flowers, followed on female plants by tiny, egg-shaped, translucent, white fruits with red speckles. **'Variegata'** illus. p.143.
C. repens. Evergreen, spreading, then erect shrub. H and S to 6ft (2m). Frost tender, min. 36°F (2°C), zones 8–10. Has broadly oval, leathery, lustrous, rich green leaves. Carries insignificant flowers in late spring, followed on female plants by egg-shaped, orange-red fruits from late summer to autumn. Leaves of **'Picturata'** each have a central, cream blotch.

CORDYLINE (Agavaceae)

Genus of evergreen shrubs and trees, grown primarily for their foliage, although some also have decorative flowers. Half hardy to frost tender, min. 41–61°F (5–16°C). Provide fertile, well-drained soil and full light or partial shade. Water potted plants moderately, less in winter. Propagate by seed or suckers in spring or by stem cuttings in summer. Red spider mite may be a nuisance.

C. australis (New Zealand cabbage palm). Slow-growing, evergreen, sparsely branched tree. H 50ft (15m) or more, S 15ft (5m) or more. Half hardy, zone 10. Each stem is crowned by a rosette of strap-shaped, 1–3ft (30cm–1m) long leaves. Has small, scented, white flowers in large, open panicles in summer and, in autumn, globose, white fruits. **'Atropurpurea'** illus. p.71. Long, sword-shaped leaves of **'Veitchii'** have red bases and midribs.
C. fruticosa, syn. *C. terminalis* (Good-luck plant, Ti tree). Slow-growing, evergreen, upright shrub, sparingly branched and suckering. H 6–12ft (2–4m), S 3–6ft (1–2m). Frost tender, min. 55°F (13°C), zone 10. Broadly lance-shaped, glossy, deep green leaves are 1–2ft (30–60cm) long. Produces branched panicles of small, white, purplish, or reddish flowers in summer. Foliage of **'Baptisii'** is deep green with pink and yellow stripes and spots. **'Imperialis'** has red- or pink-marked, deep green leaves.
C. indivisa, syn. *Dracaena indivisa.* Slow-growing, evergreen, erect tree or shrub. H 10ft (3m) or more, S 6ft (2m). Half hardy, zones 9–10. Bears lance-shaped, 2–6ft (60cm–2m) long, green leaves, orange-brown veined above, blue-gray tinted beneath. In summer has tiny, star-shaped, white flowers in dense clusters, 2ft (60cm) or more long, followed by tiny, spherical, blue-purple fruits.
C. terminalis. See *C. fruticosa.*

COREOPSIS (Compositae)

Tickseed
Genus of annuals and perennials, grown for their daisylike flower heads.

Fully to frost hardy. Needs full sun and fertile, well-drained soil. Propagate annuals by seed in spring; *C. lanceolata* by seed or division in spring; *C. auriculata* 'Superba', *C.* 'Goldfink', and *C. grandiflora* 'Badengold' by softwood cuttings or division in spring or summer; and *C. verticillata* by division in spring.
C. auriculata **'Superba'**. Bushy perennial. H and S 18in (45cm). Fully hardy, zones 4–9. Daisylike, rich yellow flower heads, with central, purple blotches, are produced thoughout summer. Oval to lance-shaped leaves are lobed and light green. Some plants grown as *C. auriculata* are the closely related annual, *C. basalis.*
C. **'Goldfink'**. Short-lived, dwarf, bushy perennial. H and S 12in (30cm). Fully hardy, zones 4–9. Sprays of daisylike, deep yellow flower heads appear in summer above narrowly oval, deep green leaves.
C. grandiflora **'Badengold'**. Short-lived, erect perennial with lax stems. H 30in (75cm), S 24in (60cm). Fully hardy, zones 4–9. Produces large, daisylike, rich buttercup yellow flower heads in summer and broadly lance-shaped, divided, bright green leaves.
C. lanceolata illus. p.248.
C. **'Sunray'** illus. p.281.
C. tinctoria illus. p.280. **'Golden Crown'** is a fast-growing, upright, bushy annual. H 24in (60cm), S 8in (20cm). Fully hardy. Has lance-shaped, deep green leaves and, in summer and early autumn, large, daisylike, deep yellow flower heads with brown centers.
C. verticillata illus. p.248.

CORIARIA (Coriariaceae)

Genus of deciduous, spring- or summer-flowering shrubs and sub-shrubs, grown for their habit, foliage, and fruits. Frost to half hardy. Needs full sun and fertile, well-drained soil. Propagate by softwood cuttings in summer or by seed in autumn.
C. terminalis. Deciduous, arching sub-shrub. H 3ft (1m), S 6ft (2m). Frost hardy, zones 9–10. Broadly lance-shaped, fernlike, green leaves turn red in autumn. Minute, green flowers in late spring are succeeded by small, spherical, black fruits. var. *xanthocarpa* illus. p.141.

CORNUS (Cornaceae)

Dogwood
Genus of deciduous shrubs and deciduous or evergreen trees, grown for their flowers, foliage, or brightly colored winter stems. Fully to half hardy. Needs sun or semi-shade and fertile, well-drained soil. Those grown for winter stem color do best in full sun. *C. florida, C. kousa,* and *C. nuttallii* dislike shallow, chalky soil. *C. canadensis* prefers acid soil. Plants grown for their stems should be cut back almost to ground level each year in early spring. Propagate *C. alba* and *C. stolonifera* 'Flaviramea' by softwood cuttings in summer or by hardwood cuttings in autumn or winter; variegated forms of *C. alternifolia* and *C. controversa*

by grafting in winter; *C. canadensis* by division in spring or autumn; *C. capitata*, *C. florida*, and *C. kousa* by seed in autumn or by softwood cuttings in summer; *C. nuttallii* by seed in autumn; all others described here by softwood cuttings in summer.
C. alba (Red-barked dogwood). Vigorous, deciduous, upright, then spreading shrub. H and S 10ft (3m). Fully hardy, zones 2–8. Young shoots are bright red in winter. Has oval, dark green leaves, often becoming red or orange in autumn. Flattened heads of star-shaped, creamy white flowers in late spring and early summer are succeeded by spherical, sometimes blue-tinted, white fruits.
'Elegantissima' illus. p.106.
'Gouchaultii' has pink-flushed leaves broadly edged with yellow.
'Kesselringii' illus. p.116. **'Sibirica'** illus. p.118. **'Spaethii'** illus. p.114.
C. alternifolia (Pagoda dogwood). Deciduous, spreading tree or bushy shrub, with tiered branches. H and S 20ft (6m). Fully hardy, zones 4–8. Oval, bright green leaves, which each taper to a point, often turn red in autumn. Clusters of tiny, star-shaped, creamy white flowers in early summer are followed by small, rounded, blue-black fruits. **'Argentea'** illus. p.62.
C. canadensis illus. p.314.
C. capitata, syn. *Dendrobenthamia capitata* (Evergreen dogwood). Evergreen or semi-evergreen, spreading tree. H and S up to 40ft (12m). Frost to half hardy, zones 8–9. Pale yellow bracts, surrounding insignificant flowers, appear in early summer, followed by large, strawberrylike, red fruits. Has oval, gray-green leaves. Is good for mild coastal areas.
C. controversa (Giant dogwood). Deciduous tree with layered branches. H and S 50ft (15m). Fully hardy, zones 6–9. Clusters of small, star-shaped, white flowers appear in summer. Leaves are oval, pointed, and bright green, turning purple in autumn. **'Variegata'** illus. p.62.
C. 'Eddie's White Wonder' illus. p.68.
C. florida (Flowering dogwood). Deciduous, spreading tree. H 20ft (6m), S 25ft (8m). Fully hardy, zones 5–8. Flower heads are borne in late spring, consisting of white or pinkish white bracts around tiny, insignificant flowers. Oval, pointed, dark green leaves turn red and purple in autumn.
'Apple Blossom' has pale pink bracts.
f. *rubra* bears pink or red bracts.
'Spring Song' illus. p.63. **'Welchii'** illus. p.66. **'White Cloud'** illus. p.58.
C. kousa. Deciduous, vase-shaped tree or shrub. H 22ft (7m), S 15ft (5m). Fully hardy, zones 5–8. Flower heads of large, white bracts, surrounding insignificant flowers, appear in early summer, followed, after a hot summer, by strawberrylike fruits. Oval, glossy, dark green leaves turn bright red-purple in autumn. var. *chinensis* has larger flower heads and more narrowly pointed bracts.
C. macrophylla illus. p.51.
C. mas (Cornelian cherry). Deciduous, spreading, open shrub or tree. H and S 15ft (5m). Fully hardy, zones 5–8.

Oval, dark green leaves change to reddish purple in autumn. Produces small, star-shaped, yellow flowers on bare shoots in late winter and early spring, then edible, oblong, bright red fruits. **'Aurea Elegantissima'**, H 6ft (2m), S 10ft (3m), has pink-tinged leaves edged with yellow. **'Variegata'** illus. p.87.
C. 'Norman Hadden' illus. p.59.
C. nuttallii illus. p.49.
C. stolonifera 'Flaviramea' (Yellowtwig dogwood). Vigorous, deciduous, spreading shrub with creeping, underground stems. H 6ft (2m), S 12ft (4m). Fully hardy, zones 2–8. Has bright greenish yellow, young shoots in winter and oval, dark green leaves. Small, star-shaped, white flowers appear in late spring and early summer, followed by spherical, white fruits.

COROKIA (Cornaceae)
Genus of evergreen shrubs, grown for their habit, foliage, flowers, and fruits. Is good in mild, coastal areas, where it is very wind-tolerant. Frost to half hardy; in cold areas protect from strong winds. Needs full sun and fertile, well-drained soil. Propagate by softwood cuttings in summer.
C. buddleioides. Evergreen, upright shrub. H 10ft (3m), S 6ft (2m). Half hardy, zones 9–10. Has slender, gray shoots and narrowly oblong, glossy, dark green leaves. Produces panicles of star-shaped, yellow flowers in late spring, followed by spherical, blackish red fruits.
C. cotoneaster illus. p.120.
C. × virgata. Evergreen, upright, dense shrub. H and S 10ft (3m). Frost hardy, zones 8–10. Leaves are oblong and glossy, dark green above, white beneath. Produces star-shaped, yellow flowers in mid-spring, followed by egg-shaped, bright orange fruits. Makes a good hedge, especially in coastal areas.

CORONILLA (Leguminosae)
Genus of deciduous or evergreen shrubs and perennials, grown for their foliage and flowers. Fully to half hardy; in cold areas grow half hardy species against a south- or west-facing wall. Requires full sun and light, well-drained soil. Propagate by softwood cuttings in summer.
C. valentina subsp. *glauca* illus. p.125.

CORREA (Rutaceae)
Genus of evergreen shrubs, grown for their flowers. Half hardy to frost tender, min. 37–41°F (3–5°C). Prefers full light or partial shade and fertile, well-drained, neutral to acid soil. Water potted specimens moderately, less when not in flower. Propagate by seed in spring or by semi-ripe cuttings in late summer.
C. backhousiana. Evergreen, rounded, well-branched shrub. H and S 6ft (2m). Half hardy, zone 10. Leaves are oval to elliptic and dark green, with dense, pale buff down beneath. Tubular, pale yellow-green to white flowers appear in spring and intermittently until autumn.

C. × harrisii. Evergreen, bushy, slender-stemmed shrub. H and S 6ft (2m). Frost tender, zones 9–10. Has narrowly oval leaves with short hairs beneath. Tubular, scarlet flowers are carried in summer-autumn, sometimes in other seasons.
C. pulchella illus. p.142.
C. reflexa, syn. *C. speciosa.* Evergreen, bushy, slender-stemmed shrub. H and S 6ft (2m). Frost tender, zones 9–10. Oval leaves have thick down beneath. Bears tubular, greenish yellow to crimson or rose flowers, with greenish white petal tips, in summer-autumn, sometimes in other seasons.
C. speciosa. See *C. reflexa.*

CORTADERIA (Gramineae). See GRASSES, BAMBOOS, RUSHES, and SEDGES.
C. selloana (Pampas grass). Evergreen, clump-forming, stately, perennial grass. H to 8ft (2.5m), S 4ft (1.2m). Frost hardy, zones 7–10. Has narrow, very sharp-edged, outward-curving leaves, 5ft (1.5m) long. In late summer, erect, plumelike, silvery panicles, up to 2ft (60cm) long, are borne above green leaves. Sexes are produced on separate plants; female flowers, with long, silky hairs, are more decorative. **'Silver Comet'** and **'Sunningdale Silver'** illus. p.180.

CORTUSA (Primulaceae)
Genus of clump-forming, spring- and summer-flowering perennials, related to *Primula*, with one-sided racemes of bell-shaped flowers. Fully hardy. Is not suited to hot, dry climates as needs shade and humus-rich, moist soil. Propagate by seed when fresh or by division in autumn.
C. matthioli illus. p.294.

CORYDALIS (Papaveraceae)
Genus of spring- and summer-flowering annuals and tuberous or fibrous-rooted perennials, some of which are evergreen, grown for their tubular, spurred, 2-lipped flowers or for their divided, fernlike leaves. Fully to frost hardy. Needs full sun or partial shade and well-drained soil; some species require humus-rich soil and cool growing conditions. Propagate by seed in autumn or by division when dormant: autumn for spring-flowering species, spring for summer-flowering species.
C. ambigua. Spring-flowering, tuberous perennial. H 4–6in (10–15cm), S 2–3in (5–8cm). Frost hardy, zones 7–8. Stem bears divided, semi-erect leaves and a short spike of 2-lipped, short-spurred, bright blue or purplish blue flowers. Dies down in summer.
C. bulbosa, syn. *C. cava.* Spring-flowering, tuberous perennial. H 4–8in (10–20cm), S 3–4in (8–10cm). Fully hardy, zones 6–8. Leaves are semi-erect, basal, and much divided. Carries dense spikes of tubular, dull purple flowers. Dies down in summer.
C. cashmeriana. Tuft-forming, fibrous-rooted perennial. H 4–10in (10–25cm), S 3–4in (8–10cm). Fully hardy, zones 6–8. Has divided, semi-erect, basal leaves and, in summer, dense spikes of 2-lipped, brilliant blue

flowers. Needs cool, partially shaded, humus-rich, neutral to acid soil. Is good for a rock garden. Dies down in winter.
C. cava. See *C. bulbosa.*
C. cheilanthifolia illus. p.289.
C. diphylla illus. p.307.
C. lutea illus. p.299.
C. nobilis. Perennial with long, fleshy, fibrous roots. H and S 8–14in (20–35cm). Fully hardy, zones 5–8. Bears much divided leaves on lower part of flower stems, each of which carries a dense spike of long-spurred, pale yellow flowers, with lips tipped green or brown, in early summer.
C. ochroleuca illus. p.291.
C. popovii illus. p.304.
C. solida. Tuft-forming, tuberous perennial. H 4–8in (10–20cm), S 3–5in (8–12cm). Fully hardy, zones 5–7. Leaves alternate on flower stem, which carries a dense spike of dull purplish red flowers in spring. Dies down in summer. **'George Baker'** (syn. *C.s.* 'G.P. Baker') illus. p.307.
C. wilsonii illus. p.289.

CORYLOPSIS (Hamamelidaceae)
Winter-hazel
Genus of deciduous shrubs and trees, grown for their fragrant yellow flowers, which are produced before hazel-like leaves emerge. Fully hardy, but late frosts may damage flowers. Prefers semi-shade and fertile, moist but well-drained, acid soil. Propagate by softwood cuttings in summer or by seed in autumn.
C. glabrescens illus. p.86.
C. pauciflora illus. p.99.
C. sinensis, syn. *C. willmottiae* (Willmott winter-hazel). Vigorous, deciduous, spreading, open shrub. H and S 12ft (4m). Zones 6–9. Leaves are bright green above, blue-green beneath. Clusters of bell-shaped, pale yellow flowers open from early to mid-spring. **'Spring Purple'** has deep plum purple, young leaves.
C. spicata (Spike winter-hazel) Deciduous, spreading, open shrub. H 6ft (2m), S 10ft (3m). Zones 5–8. Bristle-toothed leaves are dull, pale green above, blue-green beneath. Drooping clusters of bell-shaped, pale yellow flowers are borne in mid-spring.
C. willmottiae. See *C. sinensis.*

CORYLUS (Corylaceae)
Hazel
Genus of deciduous trees and shrubs, grown for their habit, catkins, and often edible fruits (nuts). Fully hardy. Prefers sun or semi-shade and fertile, well-drained soil. Cut out suckers as they arise. Propagate species by seed in autumn, cultivars by grafting in late summer or by suckers or layering in late autumn to early spring. Mildew may cause defoliation; other fungi and insects may spoil nuts.
C. avellana (Cobnut). **'Contorta'** illus. p.93.
C. colurna (Turkish hazel). Deciduous, conical tree. H 70ft (20m), S 22ft (7m). Zones 5–7. Has broadly oval, strongly toothed, almost lobed, dark green leaves. Long, yellow catkins are borne in late winter. Produces clusters of nuts set in fringed husks.

C. maxima (Giant filbert). Vigorous, deciduous, bushy, open shrub or tree. H 20ft (6m), S 15ft (5m). Zones 4–9. Bears oval, toothed, green leaves, long, yellow catkins in late winter, and edible, egg-shaped, brown nuts. **'Purpurea'** illus. p.89.

CORYNOCARPUS
(Corynocarpaceae)
Genus of evergreen trees, grown for their foliage and overall appearance. Frost tender, min. 45–50°F (7–10°C). Needs full light or partial shade and fertile, moisture-retentive but well-drained soil. Water potted specimens moderately, less when temperatures are low. Pruning is tolerated if necessary. Propagate by seed when ripe or by semi-ripe cuttings in summer.
C. laevigata illus. p.58.

CORYPHANTHA (Cactaceae)
Genus of perennial cacti with roughly spherical, spiny, green stems. Stems have elongated areoles in grooves running along upper sides of tubercles; many species only show this groove on very old plants. Has funnel-shaped flowers in summer, then cylindrical, green seed pods. Frost tender, min. 41°F (5°C). Needs full sun and very well-drained soil. Propagate by seed in spring or summer.
C. cornifera, syn. *C. radians*, illus. p.399.
C. radians. See *C. cornifera.*
C. vivipara illus. p.391.

COSMOS (Compositae)
Genus of summer- and early autumn-flowering annuals and tuberous perennials. Fully hardy to frost tender, min. 36–9°F (2–4°C). Needs sun and does best in moist but well-drained soil. In mild areas, tubers of half hardy *C. atrosanguineus* may be overwintered in ground if protected with a deep mulch. Propagate half-hardy species by basal cuttings in spring, annuals by seed in autumn or spring.
C. atrosanguineus, syn. *Bidens atrosanguinea*, illus. p.208.
C., **Bright Lights Series** (Yellow cosmos). Group of moderately fast-growing, upright, bushy annuals. H 2ft (60cm), S 1 1/2ft (45cm). Half hardy. Has feathery, deep green leaves and, in summer and early autumn, large, daisylike, single or semi-double, yellow, orange, or red flower heads.
C. **'Sensation'** illus. p.269.
C. **'Sunny Gold'.** Moderately fast-growing, upright, bushy annual. H and S 18in (45cm). Half hardy. Has feathery, deep green leaves; large, daisylike, golden yellow flower heads appear in summer and early autumn.
C. **'Sunny Red'.** Moderately fast-growing, upright, bushy annual. H 12in (30cm), S 18in (45cm). Half hardy. Feathery leaves are deep green; large, daisylike, orange-vermilion flower heads appear in summer and early autumn.

COSTUS (Zingiberaceae)
Spiral flag, Spiral ginger
Genus of mostly clump-forming, rhizomatous perennials with showy flowers. Frost tender, min. 64°F (18°C). Grow in a humid atmosphere, out of direct sunlight, in humus-rich soil. Propagate by division in spring. Pot-grown plants may be attacked by red spider mite.
C. speciosus (Malay ginger). Clump-forming, rhizomatous perennial. H 6ft (2m) or more, S 3ft (1m). Zone 10. Has narrowly oval, downy leaves, to 10in (25cm) long. Reddish bracts are spine-tipped, each surrounding one white or pink-flushed flower, to 4in (10cm) wide with a broad, yellow-centered lip; flowers are produced intermittently throughout the year.

COTINUS (Anacardiaceae)
Genus of deciduous shrubs and trees, grown for their foliage, flower heads, and autumn color. Individual flowers are inconspicuous. Fully hardy. Requires full sun or semi-shade and fertile but not over-rich soil. Purple-leaved forms need full sun to bring out their best colors. Propagate species by softwood or greenwood cuttings in summer or by seed in autumn, cultivars by cuttings only in summer.
C. coggygria, syn. *Rhus cotinus* (Smoke tree, Venetian sumac). Deciduous, bushy shrub. H and S 15ft (5m). Zones 5–9. Leaves are rounded or oval and light green, becoming yellow or red in autumn. From late summer, as insignificant fruits develop, masses of tiny flower stalks form showy, pale fawn, later gray, plumelike clusters. **'Flame'** illus. p.92. **'Notcutt's Variety'** illus. p.89. **'Royal Purple'** has deep pink plumes and deep purplish red leaves.
C. obovatus (American smoke tree). Vigorous, deciduous, bushy shrub or tree. H 30ft (10m), S 25ft (8m). Zones 4–8. Has large, oval leaves that are bronze-pink when young, maturing to green and turning orange, red, and purple in autumn.

COTONEASTER (Rosaceae)
Genus of deciduous, semi-evergreen, or evergreen shrubs and trees, grown for their foliage, flowers, and fruits. Some species make fine specimen plants; others may be used for hedging or ground cover. Fully to frost hardy. Deciduous species and cultivars prefer full sun, but evergreens do well in either sun or semi-shade. All resent waterlogged soil and are particularly useful for dry sites. Propagate species by cuttings in summer or by seed in autumn, hybrids and cultivars by cuttings only, in summer. Take semi-ripe cuttings for evergreens and semi-evergreens, softwood cuttings for deciduous plants. Fireblight is a common problem.
C. adpressus (Creeping cotoneaster). Deciduous, arching shrub. H 1ft (30cm), S 6ft (2m). Fully hardy, zones 5–8. Rounded, wavy-edged, dark green leaves redden in autumn. Produces small, 5-petaled, pink flowers in early summer, then spherical, red fruits.
C. **'Autumn Fire'**, syn. *C.* 'Herbst-feuer'. Evergreen, prostrate or arching shrub. H 1ft (30cm), S 6ft (2m). Fully hardy, zones 5–8. Has lance-shaped, bright green leaves. Small, 5-petaled, white flowers in early summer are followed by spherical, bright red fruits. May be grown as ground cover or a weeping standard.
C. bullatus var. *macrophyllus.* Deciduous, bushy, open shrub. H 15ft (5m), S 10ft (3m). Fully hardy, zones 6–8. Very large, oval, deeply veined, dark green leaves change to red in autumn. Clusters of small, 5-petaled, pink flowers appear in late spring and early summer, then spherical, bright red fruits.
C. congestus (Pyrenees cotoneaster). Evergreen, prostrate shrub. H 8in (20cm), S 6ft (2m). Fully hardy, zones 7–8. Forms dense mounds of oval, dull green leaves. Produces small, 5-petaled, pinkish white flowers in early summer and spherical, bright red fruits. Is good for a rock garden.
C. conspicuus, syn. *C.c.* var. *decorus* (Wintergreen cotoneaster). Evergreen, prostrate, arching shrub. H 1ft (30cm), S 6–10ft (2–3m). Fully hardy, zones 7–8. Leaves are oblong, glossy, very dark green. Small, 5-petaled, white flowers in late spring are succeeded by large, spherical, scarlet or orange-red fruits.
C. **'Coral Beauty'.** Evergreen, arching, dense shrub. H 3ft (1m), S 6ft (2m). Fully hardy, zones 6–8. Has small, oval, glossy, dark green leaves and, in early summer, small, 5-petaled, white flowers. Fruits are spherical and bright orange-red.
C. **'Cornubia'** illus. p.92.
C. dielsianus. Deciduous, arching shrub. H and S 8ft (2.5m). Fully hardy, zones 6–8. Slender shoots are clothed in oval, dark green leaves. Produces small, 5-petaled, pink flowers in early summer, then spherical, glossy, red fruits.
C. divaricatus illus. p.98.
C. **'Exburiensis'.** Evergreen or semi-evergreen, arching shrub. H and S 15ft (5m). Frost hardy, zones 6–8. Has narrowly lance-shaped, bright green leaves, small, 5-petaled, white flowers, in early summer, and spherical, yellow fruits, sometimes tinged pink later.
C. **'Firebird'.** Deciduous, bushy, open shrub. H and S 10ft (3m). Fully hardy, zones 6–8. Large, oval, deeply veined, dark green leaves redden in autumn. Small, 5-petaled, white flowers in early summer are followed by masses of spherical, bright red fruits.
C. franchetii. Evergreen or semi-evergreen, arching shrub. H and S 10ft (3m). Fully hardy, zones 7–9. Oval, gray-green leaves are white beneath. Bears small, 5-petaled, pink-tinged, white flowers in early summer, then a profusion of oblong, bright orange-red fruits. var. *sternianus* illus. p.117.
C. frigidus. Vigorous, deciduous tree, upright when young, arching when mature. H and S 30ft (10m). Fully hardy, zones 7–8. Has large, broadly oval, wavy-edged, dull green leaves and broad heads of small, 5-petaled, white flowers borne in early summer, followed by large clusters of long-lasting, small, spherical, bright red fruits.
C. glaucophyllus (Brightbead cotoneaster). Evergreen, arching, open shrub. H and S 10ft (3m). Fully hardy, zones 7–8. Leaves are oval, dark green, bluish white beneath. Produces small, 5-petaled, white flowers in mid-summer, followed by small, spherical, deep red fruits in autumn. var. *serotinus*, H and S 20ft (6m), flowers from mid- to late summer and its fruits last until spring.
C. **'Gnom'**, syn. *C.* 'Gnome'. Evergreen, prostrate shrub. H 8in (20cm), S 6ft (2m). Fully hardy, zones 7–8. Bears narrowly lance-shaped, dark green leaves, small, 5-petaled, white flowers, in early summer, and clusters of small, spherical, red fruits. Makes good ground cover.
C. **'Gnome'.** See *C.* 'Gnom'.
C. **'Herbstfeuer'.** See *C.* 'Autumn Fire'.
C. horizontalis illus. p.140.
C. hupehensis. Deciduous, arching shrub. H 6ft (2m), S 10ft (3m). Fully hardy, zones 5–8. Oval, bright green leaves become yellow in autumn. Has masses of small, 5-petaled, white flowers, in late spring, that are succeeded by large, spherical, bright red fruits.
C. **'Hybridus Pendulus'.** Evergreen, prostrate shrub, almost always grown as a weeping standard. H 6ft (2m), S 5ft (1.5m). Frost hardy, zones 6–8. Has oblong, dark green leaves. Small, 5-petaled, white flowers in early summer are followed by spherical, deep red fruits.
C. lacteus illus. p.93.
C. microphyllus (Littleleaf cotoneaster). Evergreen, spreading, dense shrub. H 3ft (1m), S 6ft (2m). Fully hardy, zones 6–8. Rigid shoots are clothed in small, oval, dark green leaves. Small, 5-petaled, white flowers in late spring are followed by spherical, red fruits. var. *cochleatus* is prostrate with notched leaves. var. *thymifolius*, H 2ft (60cm), is prostrate, with rigid branches and tiny, much narrower, blunt-ended, glossy leaves.
C. prostratus, syn. *C. rotundifolius* (Redbox cotoneaster). Evergreen, arching shrub. H 5ft (1.5m), S 8ft (2.5m). Fully hardy, zones 7–8. Has small, oval, glossy, dark green leaves. Produces small, 5-petaled, white flowers in early summer, followed by spherical, deep red fruits.
C. **'Rothschildianus'.** Evergreen or semi-evergreen, arching shrub. H and S 15ft (5m). Frost hardy, zones 6–8. Has narrowly oval, bright green leaves, small, 5-petaled, white flowers, in early summer, and large clusters of spherical, golden yellow fruits.
C. rotundifolius. See *C. prostratus.*
C. salicifolius (Willowleaf cotoneaster). Vigorous, evergreen, arching shrub. H and S 15ft (5m). Fully hardy, zones 7–8. Has narrowly lance-shaped, dark green leaves. Small, 5-petaled, white flowers, in early summer, are followed by clusters of small, spherical, red fruits.
C. simonsii illus. p.116.
C. **'Skogholm'**, syn. *C.* 'Skogsholmen'. Evergreen, arching, wide-spreading shrub. H 2ft (60cm), S 10ft (3m). Fully hardy, zones 6–8. Leaves are small, oval, and glossy, dark green. Bears small, 5-petaled, white flowers during early summer,

then rather sparse, spherical, red fruits. Makes good ground cover.
C. **'Skogsholmen'**. See *C.* **'Skogholm'**.
C. x *watereri* **'John Waterer'**. Vigorous, evergreen or semi-evergreen, arching shrub. H and S 15ft (5m). Frost hardy, zones 6–8. Has lance-shaped, dark green leaves, small, 5-petaled, white flowers, in early summer, and a profusion of spherical, red fruits in large clusters.

COTULA (Compositae)
Genus of perennials and a few marginal water plants, most of which are evergreen, grown for their neat foliage and buttonlike flower heads. Many species are useful for cracks in paving stones, but may be invasive. Fully to frost hardy. Most need sun and well-drained soil that is not too dry. Propagate by division in spring.
C. atrata illus. p.307. var. *luteola* illus. p.304.
C. coronopifolia (Brass buttons). Short-lived, deciduous, perennial, marginal water plant. H 6in (15cm), S 12in (30cm). Frost hardy, zones 7–9. Has fleshy stems, small, lance-shaped, green leaves and, in summer, buttonlike, yellow flower heads.

COTYLEDON (Crassulaceae)
Genus of evergreen, succulent shrubs and sub-shrubs, grown for their diverse foliage that ranges from large, oval, gray leaves to small, cylindrical, green leaves. Frost tender, min. 41–5°F (5–7°C). Likes a sunny or partially shaded site and very well-drained soil. Propagate by seed or stem cuttings in spring or summer.
C. ladysmithensis illus. p.394.
C. orbiculata. Evergreen, upright, succulent shrub. H and S 20in (50cm) or more. Min. 45°F (7°C), zone 10. Swollen stem bears thin, oval, green leaves, densely coated in white wax and sometimes red-edged. Flower stems, to 28in (70cm) long, have pendent, tubular, orange flowers in autumn.
C. paniculata. See *Tylecodon paniculata*.
C. reticulata. See *Tylecodon reticulata*.
C. simplicifolia. See *Chiastophyllum oppositifolium*.
C. undulata illus. p.388.
C. wallichii. See *Tylecodon wallichii*.

CRAMBE (Cruciferae)
Genus of annuals and perennials, grown for their bold leaves and large sprays of white flowers in summer. Leaf shoots of *C. maritima* (Sea kale) are eaten as a spring vegetable. Fully hardy. Will grow in any well-drained soil; prefers an open position in full sun but tolerates some shade. Propagate by division in spring or by seed in autumn or spring.
C. cordifolia illus. p.188.
C. maritima illus. p.233.

CRASPEDIA (Compositae)
Genus of basal-rosetted, summer-flowering perennials, some of which are best treated as annuals. Half hardy to frost tender, min. 41°F (5°C). Requires sun and well-drained soil.

Propagate by seed when very fresh in summer.
C. incana. Basal-rosetted perennial. H 8–12in (20–30cm), S 4in (10cm). Frost tender, zones 9–10. Has narrowly oval, basal leaves, with dense, woolly, white hairs beneath, and smaller leaves on flower stem. In summer bears many domed heads of 3–10 tiny, tubular, yellow flowers in large, terminal clusters.

CRASSULA (Crassulaceae)
Genus of perennial succulents and evergreen, succulent shrubs and sub-shrubs, ranging from $^3/_4$in (2cm) high, very succulent-leaved species to 15ft (5m), shrubby ones. Most are easy to grow. Frost hardy to frost tender, min. 41–5°F (5–7°C). Most prefer full sun; others like partial shade. Needs very well-drained soil and a little water in winter. Propagate by seed or stem cuttings in spring or autumn.
C. arborescens illus. p.380.
C. argentea. See *C. ovata*.
C. coccinea. See *Rochea coccinea*.
C. cooperi. Carpeting, perennial succulent. H $^3/_4$in (2cm), S 12in (30cm). Frost tender, min. 45°F (7°C), zones 9–10. Has small, spoon- to lance-shaped, light green leaves, pitted with darker green or blackish green marks. Bears clusters of minute, 5-petaled, white to pale pink flowers in winter. Prefers full sun.
C. deceptrix illus. p.396.
C. falcata illus. p.385.
C. lactea. Prostrate to semi-erect, perennial succulent. H 8in (20cm), S 3ft (1m). Frost tender, min. 41°F (5°C), zones 9–10. Leaves are triangular-oval, glossy, and dark green. In winter produces masses of small, 5-petaled, white flowers in terminal clusters. Likes partial shade.
C. lycopodioides. Dense, bushy, woody-based, perennial succulent. H 6in (15cm), S 12in (30cm). Frost tender, min. 41°F (5°C), zones 9–10. Bears small, scalelike, neatly overlapping, green leaves arranged in 4 rows around erect stems and, in spring, tiny, 5-petaled, greenish yellow flowers. Likes partial shade.
C. multicava illus. p.391.
C. ovata, syn. *C. argentea*, *C. portulacea*, illus. p.379.
C. portulacea. See *C. ovata*.
C. sarcocaulis illus. p.293.
C. schmidtii illus. p.393.
C. socialis illus. p.390.

+ CRATAEGOMESPILUS (Rosaceae)
Group of grafted, hybrid, deciduous trees (*Crataegus* and *Mespilus*), grown for their flowers, foliage, and fruits. Fully hardy. Requires sun or semi-shade and fertile, well-drained soil. Propagate by grafting in late summer.
+ *C. dardarii* (Bronvaux medlar). **'Jules d'Asnières'** is a deciduous, spreading tree. H and S 20ft (6m). Zones 6–9. Has drooping branches and spiny shoots. Variable, oval or deeply lobed, dark green leaves, gray when young, turn orange and yellow in autumn. Clusters of saucer-shaped, white, sometimes rose-tinted, flowers, produced in late spring or early summer,

are followed by small, rounded, red-brown fruits.

CRATAEGUS (Rosaceae)
Hawthorn, Thorn
Genus of deciduous, or more rarely semi-evergreen, spiny, often spreading trees and shrubs, grown for their clustered, 5-petaled, occasionally double flowers in spring-summer, ornamental fruits and, in some cases, autumn color. Fully hardy. Prefers full sun but is suitable for almost all situations and may be grown in any but very wet soil. Is particularly useful for growing in polluted urban areas, exposed sites, and coastal gardens. Propagate species by seed in autumn, cultivars by budding in late summer. Fireblight is sometimes a problem.
C. crus-galli (Cockspur thorn). Deciduous, flat-topped tree. H 25ft (8m), S 30ft (10m). Zones 4–7. Has shoots armed with long, curved thorns and oval, glossy, dark green leaves that turn bright crimson in autumn. Clusters of white flowers, with pink anthers, in late spring are followed by long-lasting, rounded, bright red fruits.
C. ellwangeriana. Deciduous, spreading tree. H and S 20ft (6m). Zones 5–7. Broadly oval, dark green leaves are shallowly toothed and lobed. Bears clusters of white flowers, with pink anthers, in late spring, followed by rounded, glossy, crimson fruits.
C. flava illus. p.63.
C. laciniata, syn. *C. orientalis*, illus. p.58.
C. laevigata, syn. *C. oxyacantha* (English hawthorn, May tree). **'Paul's Scarlet'** illus. p.64. **'Punicea'** is a deciduous, spreading tree. H and S 20ft (6m). Zones 5–8. In late spring and early summer, oval, lobed, toothed, glossy, dark green leaves set off clusters of crimson flowers, which are followed by rounded, red fruits.
C. x *lavallei* (Lavelle hawthorn). **'Carrierei'** is a vigorous, deciduous, spreading tree. H 22ft (7m), S 30ft (10m). Zones 5–7. Oval, glossy, dark green leaves turn red in late autumn. Has clusters of white flowers in late spring, followed by long-lasting, rounded, orange-red fruits.
C. macrosperma var. *acutiloba* illus. p.67.
C. mollis (Downy hawthorn). Deciduous, spreading tree. H 30ft (10m), S 40ft (12m). Zones 4–7. Large, broadly oval, lobed, dark green leaves have white-haired undersides when young. Bears heads of large, white flowers in late spring, followed by short-lived, rounded, red fruits.
C. monogyna (Single seed hawthorn). Deciduous, round-headed tree. H 30ft (10m), S 25ft (8m). Zones 5–7. Has broadly oval, deeply lobed, glossy, dark green leaves. Clusters of fragrant white flowers are borne from late spring to early summer, followed by rounded, red fruits. Makes a dense hedge. **'Biflora'** (Glastonbury thorn) has flowers and leaves in mild winters as well as in spring.
C. x *mordenensis* **'Snowbird'** (Snowbird hawthorn). Deciduous, rounded, spreading shrub. H 18–20ft

(5.5–6m), S 15–20ft (5–6m). Zones 4–8. Broadly oval, very glossy, dark green leaves have 2–4 lobes. Produces small, double, white flowers in late spring, followed by round, bright crimson fruits. Tolerates pollution and is resistant to rust. **'Toba'** (Toba hawthorn), H and S 12–15ft (4–5m), produces large, fragrant flowers that fade to pink. Is less hardy than 'Snowbird'.
C. orientalis. See *C. laciniata*.
C. oxyacantha. See *C. laevigata*.
C. pedicellata illus. p.67.
C. phaenopyrum (Washington hawthorn). Deciduous, round-headed tree. H and S 30ft (10m). Zones 4–8. Broadly oval leaves are sharply lobed, glossy, and dark green. Has clusters of white flowers, with pink anthers, from early to mid-summer, followed by rounded, glossy, red fruits that last through winter.
C. prunifolia. Deciduous, spreading, thorny tree. H 25ft (8m), S 30ft (10m). Zones 6–7. Oval, glossy, dark green leaves turn red or orange in autumn. Clusters of white flowers, with pink anthers, in early summer are followed by rounded, dark red fruits.
C. tanacetifolia (Tansy-leaved thorn). Deciduous, upright, usually thornless tree. H 30ft (10m), S 25ft (8m). Zones 6–7. Has oval to diamond-shaped, deeply cut, gray-green leaves. Clusters of fragrant white flowers, with red anthers, are produced in mid-summer and are followed by small, apple-shaped, yellow fruits.

CREMANTHODIUM (Compositae)
Genus of basal-rosetted perennials, grown for their pendent, half-closed, daisylike flower heads. Is often very difficult to grow in all but very cool areas with snow cover. Dislikes winter wet. Fully to frost hardy. Needs shade and humus-rich, moist but well-drained soil. Propagate by seed when fresh.
C. reniforme. Basal-rosetted perennial. H and S 8in (20cm). Fully hardy, zones 3–5. Leaves are large and kidney-shaped. Stout stems each carry a large, daisylike, yellow flower head in summer.

CREPIS (Compositae)
Dandelion
Genus of summer-flowering annuals, biennials, and perennials, some of which are evergreen, with long tap roots and leaves in flat rosettes. Many species are persistent weeds, but some are grown for their many-petaled, dandelionlike flower heads. Fully hardy. Tolerates sun or shade and prefers well-drained soil. Propagate annuals and biennials by seed in autumn, perennials by root cuttings (not from tap root) in late winter, although most species self seed freely.
C. aurea illus. p.299.
C. incana (Pink dandelion). Basal-rosetted perennial. H 8in (20cm), S 4in (10cm). Zones 5–7. Bears oblong, divided, hairy, grayish green leaves and, in summer, uneven discs of ragged, pink flower heads on stiff stems. Is good for a sunny rock garden or border.
C. rubra illus. p.264.

CRINODENDRON (Elaeocarpaceae)
Genus of evergreen shrubs and trees, grown for their flowers and foliage. Frost to half hardy. Requires shade or semi-shade, with plant base in cool shade. Soil should be fertile, moist but well-drained, and acid. Propagate by softwood cuttings in summer or by seed in autumn.
C. hookerianum, syn. *Tricuspidaria lanceolata*, illus. p.110.

x *Crinodonna corsii*. See
x *Amarcrinum memoria-corsii*.

CRINUM (Amaryllidaceae)
Genus of robust bulbs, grown for their often fragrant, funnel-shaped flowers. Frost hardy to frost tender, min. 61°F (16°C). Needs full sun, shelter, and rich, well-drained soil. Propagate by offsets in spring or by seed when fresh or in spring.
C. americanum. Tuft-forming, spring- and summer-flowering bulb. H 16–30in (40–75cm), S 24in (60cm). Half hardy, zones 9–10. Has 6–10 strap-shaped, semi-erect, basal leaves. Leafless stem bears a head of up to 6 fragrant, long-tubed, white flowers with narrow petals.
C. asiaticum illus. p.350.
C. bulbispermum, syn. *C. longifolium*. Summer-flowering bulb. H to 3ft (1m), S 2ft (60cm). Half hardy, zones 9–10. Leafless flower stem has a head of fragrant, long-tubed, white or pinkish red flowers with darker red stripes. Bears long, strap-shaped, semi-erect leaves grouped in a tuft on a short stalk.
C. longifolium. See *C. bulbispermum*.
C. macowanii. Autumn-flowering bulb. H and S 2ft (60cm) or more. Half hardy, zone 10. Is similar to *C. bulbispermum*, but leaves are wavy-edged.
C. moorei illus. p.335.
C. x powellii illus. p.333. **'Album'** illus. p.332.

CROCOSMIA (Iridaceae)
Montbretia
Genus of corms, grown for their brightly colored flowers produced mainly in summer. Forms dense clumps of sword-shaped, erect leaves. Frost hardy. Requires well-drained soil and an open, sunny site. In very cold areas, plant in a sheltered position or lift and store for winter. Propagate by division as growth commences in spring.
C. aurea. Tuft-forming, summer-flowering corm. H 20–30in (50–75cm), S 6–8in (15–20cm). Zones 6–9. Erect, basal leaves are long, narrow, and sword-shaped. Carries a loosely branched spike of tubular, orange or yellow flowers, each 1–2in (3–5cm) long and with 6 spreading petals.
C. **'Bressingham Blaze'** illus. p.336.
C. **'Citronella'** illus. p.339.
C. **'Emily McKenzie'**. Compact, late summer-flowering corm. H to 24in (60cm), S 6–8in (15–20cm). Zones 6–9. Leaves are erect, basal, and sword-shaped. Bears a dense spike of widely funnel-shaped, deep orange flowers, each with a dark mahogany throat.
C. **'Jackanapes'** illus. p.353.
C. **'Lucifer'** illus. p.336.

C. masonorum illus. p.336.
C. paniculata, syn. *Antholyza paniculata*. Summer-flowering corm. H to 5ft (1.5m), S 12–18in (30–45cm). Zones 6–9. Has sword-shaped, erect, basal leaves, pleated lengthways. Carries long-tubed, orange flowers on branched stems, which are strongly zigzag in shape.
C. rosea. See *Tritonia rubrolucens*.

CROCUS (Iridaceae)
Genus of mainly spring- or autumn-flowering corms with funnel-shaped to rounded, long-tubed flowers. Has long, very narrow, semi-erect, basal leaves, each with a white line along center, usually 1–5 per corm. Some autumn-flowering species have no leaves at flowering time, these appearing in winter or early spring. Most species are less than 4in (10cm) tall when in flower and have a spread of 1–3in (2.5–8cm). Is ideal for rock gardens and for slight forcing in bowls for an early indoor display. Fully to frost hardy. Most require well-drained soil and a sunny situation; *C. banaticus* prefers moist soil and semi-shade. Plant 2–2½in (5–6cm) deep, in late summer or early autumn. Propagate in early autumn by seed or division if clumps of corms have formed.
C. aerius of gardens. See *C. biflorus* subsp. *pulchricolor*.
C. ancyrensis. Spring-flowering corm. Frost hardy, zones 5–8. Produces up to 7 fragrant, bright orange-yellow flowers, 2–2½in (5–6cm) long.
C. angustifolius, syn. *C. susianus* (Cloth-of-gold crocus). Spring-flowering corm. Fully hardy, zones 3–8. Fragrant flowers are bright golden yellow, striped or stained bronze outside.
C. aureus. See *C. flavus*.
C. banaticus illus. p.368.
C. biflorus illus. p.360.
subsp. *alexandri* is an early spring-flowering corm. Fully hardy, zones 3–8. Carries fragrant, deep violet flowers, with white insides.
subsp. *pulchricolor* (syn. *C. aerius* of gardens) has rich deep blue flowers with golden yellow centers.
C. **'Blue Pearl'** illus. p.360.
C. cancellatus. Autumn-flowering corm. Frost hardy, zones 5–8. Slender flowers are pale blue, slightly striped outside. Leaves form after flowering, in spring.
C. cartwrightianus. Autumn-flowering corm. Frost hardy, zones 6–8. Produces leaves at same time as strongly veined, violet or white flowers, each 1½–2½in (4–6cm) across and with 3 long, bright red stigmas, similar to those of *C. sativus*.
C. chrysanthus. Spring-flowering corm. Fully hardy, zones 3–8. Scented flowers are orange-yellow throughout with deeper orange-red stigmas.
C. **'Cream Beauty'** illus. p.357.
C. cvijicii illus. p.363.
C. dalmaticus illus. p.359.
C. **'Dutch Yellow'**. Very vigorous, clump-forming, spring-flowering corm. Fully hardy, zones 3–8. Bears yellow flowers, 3–4in (8–10cm) long and faintly striped outside at bases. Naturalizes well in grass.

C. **'E.A. Bowles'** illus. p.363.
C. etruscus illus. p.360.
'Zwanenburg' is a spring-flowering corm. Frost hardy, zones 5–8. Bears pale purple-blue flowers, washed with biscuit brown and flecked violet outside.
C. flavus, syn. *C. aureus*. Spring-flowering corm. Fully hardy, zones 5–8. Fragrant flowers are bright yellow or orange-yellow throughout; often several flowers are produced together or in quick succession.
C. gargaricus. Spring-flowering corm. Frost hardy, zones 5–8. Bears yellow flowers, 1½–2in (4–5cm) long. Increases by stolons. Tolerates slightly damper conditions than most crocuses.
C. goulimyi illus. p.367.
C. imperati. Strikingly bicolored, spring-flowering corm. Frost hardy, zones 5–8. Develops 1 or 2 scented, purple flowers, 2½–3in (6–8cm) long, fawn with purple striping outside and with yellow throats.
C. korolkowii (Celandine crocus). Spring-flowering corm. Fully hardy, zones 3–8. Produces up to 20 narrow leaves. Carries fragrant yellow flowers, speckled or stained brown or purple outside. When open in sun, petals have glossy surfaces.
C. kotschyanus, syn. *C. zonatus*, illus. p.367. var. *leucopharynx* is a vigorous, autumn-flowering corm. Fully hardy, zones 3–8. Flowers are pale lilac-blue with white centers and white anthers. Leaves appear in winter-spring.
C. laevigatus. Very variable corm, flowering intermittently for a month or more in autumn or winter depending on the form. Frost hardy, zones 5–8. Fragrant flowers appear with leaves and are usually lilac-purple with bold stripes on outside; inside each has a yellow eye and cream white anthers.
C. longiflorus. Autumn-flowering corm. Frost hardy, zones 5–8. Produces fragrant, slender, purple flowers, with yellow centers and striped darker purple outside, at same time as leaves. Has yellow anthers and red stigmas.
C. malyi illus. p.357.
C. medius illus. p.368.
C. minimus illus. p.359.
C. niveus. Autumn-flowering corm. Frost hardy, zones 5–8. Produces 1 or 2 white or pale lavender flowers, 4–6in (10–15cm) long, with conspicuous, yellow throats. Leaves appear with flowers or just afterwards. Needs a warm, sunny site.
C. nudiflorus illus. p.368.
C. olivieri. Spring-flowering corm. Frost hardy, zones 5–8. Bears rounded, bright orange flowers. Flowers of subsp. *balansae* are stained or striped bronze-brown outside.
C. pulchellus illus. p.368.
C. salzmannii. See *C. serotinus* subsp. *salzmannii*.
C. sativus, syn. *C.s.* var. *cashmirianus* (Saffron crocus). Autumn-flowering corm. Frost hardy, zones 5–8. Leaves appear at the same time as saucer-shaped, purple flowers, 2–3in (5–7cm) across, that each have darker veining and 3 long, bright red stigmas that yield saffron.

C. serotinus subsp. *salzmannii*, syn. *C. salzmannii*. Autumn-flowering corm. Frost hardy, zones 5–8. Carries lilac-blue flowers, to 4in (10cm) long, sometimes with yellow throats. Leaves appear with flowers.
C. sieberi subsp. *sieberi*. Spring-flowering corm. Fully hardy, zones 3–8. Scented, white flowers have yellow throats and purple staining outside, either in horizontal bands or vertical stripes. subsp. *atticus* has fragrant, violet-blue flowers with frilly, orange stigmas. **'Bowles' White'** illus. p.356.
C. **'Snow Bunting'** illus. p.357.
C. speciosus. Autumn-flowering corm. Fully hardy, zones 3–8. Bears pale purple-blue flowers, each with a network of darker veins and a much-divided, orange stigma. Leaves appear in winter-spring. **'Oxonian'** illus. p.369.
C. susianus. See *C. angustifolius*.
C. tommasinianus illus. p.359.
C. tournefortii. Autumn-flowering corm. Frost hardy, zones 5–8. Leaves appear at same time as 1 or 2 pale lilac-blue flowers that open flattish to reveal a much-divided, orange stigma and white anthers. Requires a warm, sunny situation.
C. vernus illus. p.359. subsp. *albiflorus* illus. p.356. **'Joan of Arc'** is a spring-flowering corm. H to 4in (10cm), S 1–3in (2.5–8cm). Fully hardy, zones 3–8. Produces 4–5in (10–12cm) long, white flowers, with large, frilly, orange stigmas. Is good as an indoor pot plant, for general garden use, or for naturalizing in grass. **'Pickwick'** illus. p.360. **'Princess Juliana'** illus. p.359. **'Purpureus Grandiflorus'** has shiny, purple-blue flowers. **'Vanguard'** has silvery bluish lilac flowers, paler outside. Is a very early variety.
C. **'Zephyr'**. Autumn-flowering corm. Fully hardy, zones 3–8. Bears very pale silver-blue flowers, veined darker, each with a conspicuous, yellow throat and white anthers.
C. zonatus. See *C. kotschyanus*.
C. **'Zwanenburg Bronze'**. Spring-flowering corm. H to 4in (10cm), S 1–3in (2.5–8cm). Fully hardy, zones 3–8. Has bicolored flowers, rich yellow inside, stained bronze outside.

CROSSANDRA (Acanthaceae)
Genus of evergreen perennials, sub-shrubs, and shrubs, grown mainly for their flowers. Frost tender, min. 59°F (15°C). Needs partial shade or full light and humus-rich, well-drained soil. Water potted plants freely when in full growth, moderately at other times. For a strong branch system, cut back flowered growth by at least half in late winter. Propagate by seed in spring or by greenwood cuttings in late spring or summer. Whitefly may be troublesome.
C. infundibuliformis, syn. *C. undulifolia*. Evergreen, erect to spreading, soft-stemmed shrub or sub-shrub. H to 3ft (1m), S 2ft (60cm). Zone 10. Has oval to lance-shaped, glossy, deep green leaves and, in summer-autumn or earlier, fan-shaped, salmon red flowers in conical spikes, each 4in (10cm) long.

C. nilotica illus. p.133.
C. undulifolia. See *C. infundibuliformis.*

CROTALARIA (Leguminosae)
Genus of evergreen shrubs, perennials, and annuals, grown mainly for their flowers. Frost tender, min. 50–59°F (10–15°C). Requires full light and well-drained soil. Water potted specimens freely when in full growth, moderately at other times. For a more compact habit, cut back old stems by half after flowering. Propagate by seed in spring or by semi-ripe cuttings in summer. Red spider mite may be troublesome.
C. agatiflora illus. p.91.

Crucianella stylosa. See *Phuopsis stylosa.*

CRYPTANTHUS (Bromeliaceae)
Genus of evergreen, rosette-forming perennials, grown for their attractive foliage. Frost tender, min. 50–55°F (10–13°C). Needs semi-shade and well-drained soil, preferably mixed with sphagnum moss. Water moderately during the growing season, sparingly at other times. Propagate by offsets or suckers in late spring.
C. acaulis (Green earth star). Evergreen, clump-forming, basal-rosetted perennial. H to 4in (10cm), S 6–12in (15–30cm). Zone 10. Loose, flat rosettes of lance-shaped to narrowly triangular, wavy, green leaves have serrated edges. A cluster of fragrant, tubular, white flowers appears from the heart of each rosette, usually in summer. var. *ruber* has red-flushed foliage.
C. bivittatus (illus. p.222). Evergreen, clump-forming, basal-rosetted perennial. H to 6in (15cm), S 10–15in (25–38cm). Zone 10. Loose, flat rosettes of broadly lance-shaped, wavy, mid- to yellowish green leaves have finely toothed margins and are striped lengthways with 2 coppery fawn to buff bands. Small clusters of tubular, white flowers appear from center of each rosette, usually in summer.
C. bromelioides (Rainbow star). Evergreen, spreading, basal-rosetted perennial. H 8in (20cm) or more, S 14in (35cm) or more. Zone 10. Strap-shaped, wavy, finely toothed, arching, mid- to bright green leaves are produced in dense rosettes. Occasionally bears clusters of tubular, white flowers in center of each rosette, usually in summer. var. *tricolor* has carmine-suffused, white-striped foliage.
C. 'Pink Starlight' (illus. p.222). Vigorous, evergreen, spreading, basal-rosetted perennial. H 8in (20cm) or more, S 14in (35cm) or more. Zone 10. Strap-shaped, wavy, finely toothed, arching, green leaves are striped yellowish green, and heavily suffused deep pink. Clusters of tubular, white flowers occasionally appear from each rosette center in summer.
C. zonatus. Evergreen, basal-rosetted perennial. H 4–6in (10–15cm), S 12–16in (30–40cm). Zone 10. Forms loose, flat rosettes of strap-shaped, wavy, finely toothed, sepia-green leaves, cross-banded with gray-buff

and with grayish white scales beneath. A cluster of tubular, white flowers opens at center of each rosette, usually in summer. 'Zebrinus' (illus. p.222) has silver-banded foliage.

CRYPTOGRAMMA
(Polypodiaceae)
Genus of deciduous or semi-evergreen ferns. Fully hardy. Needs partial shade and moist but well-drained, neutral or acid soil. Remove fading fronds. Propagate by spores in late summer.
C. crispa illus. p.187.

CRYPTOMERIA (Taxodiaceae). See CONIFERS.
C. japonica (Japanese cedar). Fast-growing, columnar to conical, open conifer. H 50–70ft (15–20m), S 15–25ft (5–8m). Fully hardy, zones 6–9. Has soft, fibrous, red-brown bark, needlelike, incurved, mid- to dark green leaves, spirally arranged, and globular, brown cones. 'Bandai-sugi', H and S 6ft (2m), makes an irregularly rounded shrub with foliage that turns bronze in winter. 'Cristata' illus. p.81. 'Elegans Compacta' (syn. *C.j.* 'Elegans Nana'; illus. p.83), H 6–15ft (2–5m), S 6ft (2m), is a dwarf form. 'Pyramidata' illus. p.81. 'Sekkan-sugi' (illus. p.83), H 30ft (10m), S 10–12ft (3–4m), has semi-pendulous branches and light golden cream foliage. 'Spiralis' (illus. p.83), H and S 6–10ft (2–3m), forms a tree or dense shrub with spirally twisted foliage and is very slow-growing. 'Vilmoriniana', H and S 3ft (1m), forms a globular mound of yellow-green foliage that becomes bronze in winter.

CTENANTHE (Marantaceae)
Genus of evergreen, bushy perennials, grown for their ornamental foliage. Frost tender, min. 59°F (15°C). Requires a humid atmosphere, even temperature, and partial shade. Prefers moist but well-drained soil and soft water; do not allow to dry completely. Propagate by division in spring.
C. lubbersiana. Evergreen, clump-forming, bushy perennial. H and S to 30in (75cm) or more. Zone 10. Long-stalked, lance-shaped, sharply pointed leaves are 10in (25cm) long, green above, irregularly marked and striped with pale yellowish green, and pale greenish yellow below. Intermittently bears dense, one-sided spikes of many small, 3-petaled, white flowers.
C. oppenheimiana. Robust, evergreen, bushy perennial. H and S 3ft (1m) or more. Zone 10. Lance-shaped, leathery leaves are over 1ft (30cm) long, red below, dark green above with pale green or white bands along veins on either side of midribs. Dense, one-sided spikes of many small, 3-petaled, white flowers are produced intermittently. 'Tricolor' illus. p.221.

CUNNINGHAMIA (Taxodiaceae). See CONIFERS.
C. lanceolata illus. p.78.

CUPHEA (Lythraceae)
Genus of annuals, perennials, and evergreen shrubs and sub-shrubs,

grown for their flowers. Half hardy to frost tender, min. 36–45°F (2–7°C). Prefers full sun and fertile, well-drained soil. Water freely when in full growth, moderately at other times. Remove flowered shoots after flowering to maintain a bushy habit. Propagate by seed in spring or by greenwood cuttings in spring or summer. Red spider mite may be troublesome.
C. cyanea illus. p.140.
C. hyssopifolia illus. p.126.
C. ignea illus. p.140.

x CUPRESSOCYPARIS
(Cupressaceae). See CONIFERS.
x *C. leylandii* illus. p.73. 'Castlewellan' and 'Harlequin' illus. p.76. 'Leighton Green' is a very fast-growing, columnar conifer with a conical tip. H 80–120ft (25–35m), S 12–15ft (4–5m). Fully hardy, zones 6–9. Bears flattened sprays of paired, scalelike, rich green leaves and globular, glossy, dark brown cones. 'Robinson's Gold', H 50–70ft (15–20m), has bright golden leaves.

CUPRESSUS (Cupressaceae),
Cypress. See CONIFERS.
C. arizonica var. *glabra.* See *C. glabra.*
C. cashmeriana illus. p.73.
C. glabra, syn. *C. arizonica* var. *glabra* (Arizona cypress, Smooth cypress). Conical conifer. H 30–50ft (10–15m), S 10–15ft (3–5m). Fully hardy, zones 7–9. Has smooth, flaking, reddish purple bark and upright, spirally arranged sprays of scalelike, aromatic, glaucous blue-gray leaves flecked with white resin. Globular cones are chocolate brown.
C. lusitanica (Cedar-of-Goa, Mexican cypress). Conical conifer. H 70ft (20m), S 15–25ft (5–8m). Fully hardy, zones 9–10. Has fissured bark, spreading, spirally arranged sprays of scalelike, aromatic, gray-green leaves, and small, globular cones, glaucous blue when young, ripening to glossy brown.
C. macrocarpa (Monterey cypress). Fast-growing, evergreen conifer, columnar when young, often wide-spreading with age. H 70ft (20m), S 20–80ft (6–25m). Fully hardy, zones 7–10. Bark is shallowly fissured. Scalelike, aromatic, bright to dark green leaves are borne in plumelike sprays. Globular cones are glossy and brown. 'Goldcrest' illus. p.81.
C. sempervirens illus. p.77.

CYANANTHUS (Campanulaceae)
Genus of late summer-flowering perennials, suitable for rock gardens, walls, and troughs. Fully hardy. Needs partial shade and humus-rich, moist but well-drained soil. Propagate by softwood cuttings in spring or by seed in autumn.
C. lobatus. Prostrate perennial. H ³/₄in (2cm), S 8in (20cm). Zones 6–7. Branched stems are clothed in small, wedge-shaped, dull green leaves. In late summer, each stem carries a funnel-shaped, blue flower. f. *albus* illus. p.313.
C. microphyllus illus. p.323.

CYANOTIS (Commelinaceae)
Genus of evergreen, creeping perennials, grown for their foliage. Frost tender, min. 50–59°F (10–15°C). Prefers humus-rich, well-drained soil and sun or partial shade. Propagate by tip cuttings from spring to autumn.
C. kewensis (Teddy-bear vine). Evergreen perennial forming rosettes with trailing stems. H 2in (5cm), S 12in (30cm). Zone 10. Clasping the stem are 2 rows of overlapping, oval leaves, to 2in (5cm) long, dark green above, purple with velvety, brown hairs below. Carries stalkless clusters of 3-petaled, purplish pink flowers in axils of leaflike bracts almost all year round.
C. somaliensis illus. p.259.

CYATHEA, syn. ALSOPHILA,
SPHAEROPTERIS (Cyatheaceae)
Genus of evergreen tree ferns, grown for their foliage and overall appearance. Frost tender, min. 50–55°F (10–13°C). Needs a humid atmosphere, sun or partial shade, and humus-rich, moisture-retentive but well-drained soil. Water potted plants freely in summer, moderately at other times. Propagate by spores in spring.
C. arborea (West Indian tree fern). Evergreen, upright tree fern with a slender trunk. H 22–30ft (7–10m), S 6–10ft (2–3m). Zone 10. Produces 6–10ft (2–3m) long, arching, bright yellow-green fronds, delicately divided into small, oblong, serrated leaflets.
C. australis illus. p.72.
C. medullaris (Black tree fern, Mamaku). Evergreen, upright tree fern with a slender, black trunk. H 22–52ft (7–16m), S 20–40ft (6–12m). Zone 10. Arching fronds, each to 22ft (7m) long, are divided into small, oblong, glossy, dark green leaflets, paler beneath.

CYATHODES (Epacridaceae)
Genus of evergreen, heathlike shrubs, suitable for rock gardens and peat beds. Frost hardy to frost tender, min. 45°F (7°C). Needs a sheltered, shaded site and gritty, moist, peaty soil. Propagate in summer by seed or semi-ripe cuttings.
C. colensoi illus. p.300.

CYBISTAX (Bignoniaceae)
Genus of deciduous trees, grown for their spring flowers and for shade. Frost tender, min. 61–4°F (16–18°C). Needs full light and fertile, moisture-retentive but well-drained soil. Will not bloom when confined to a container. Young plants may be pruned to shape when leafless; otherwise pruning is not required. Propagate by seed or air-layering in spring or by semi-ripe cuttings in summer.
C. donnell-smithii, syn. *Tabebuia donnell-smithii.* Fairly fast-growing, deciduous, rounded tree. H and S 30ft (10m) or more. Zone 10. Leaves have 5–7 oval, 2–8in (5–20cm) long leaflets. Bell-shaped, 5-lobed, bright yellow flowers appear in spring before the leaves, often in great profusion.

CYCAS (Cycadaceae)
Genus of slow-growing, evergreen, woody-stemmed perennials, grown

for their palmlike appearance. Frost tender, min. 50–55°F (10–13°C). Prefers full light and humus-rich, well-drained soil. Water potted specimens moderately, less when not in full growth. Propagate in spring by seed or suckers taken from mature plants.
C. revoluta illus. p.120.

CYCLAMEN (Primulaceae)
Genus of tuberous perennials, some of which are occasionally evergreen, grown for their pendent flowers, each with 5 reflexed petals and a mouth often stained with a darker color. Fully hardy to frost tender, min. 41–5°F (5–7°C). Requires humus-rich, well-drained soil and sun or partial shade. If pot-grown, in summer dry off tubers of all except *C. purpurascens* (which is evergreen and flowers in summer); repot in autumn and water to restart growth. Propagate by seed in late summer or autumn. *C. persicum* and its cultivars are susceptible to black root rot.
C. africanum illus. p.366.
C. alpinum. See *C. trochopteranthum*.
C. cilicium illus. p.367.
C. coum subsp. *coum* and 'Album' illus. p.370. subsp. *caucasicum* is a winter-flowering, tuberous perennial. H to 4in (10cm), S 2–4in (5–10cm). Frost hardy, zones 5–9. Has heart-shaped, silver-patterned leaves and produces a succession of bright carmine flowers, each with a dark stain at the mouth.
C. creticum. Spring-flowering, tuberous perennial. H to 4in (10cm), S 2–4in (5–10cm). Frost hardy, zones 7–9. Produces heart-shaped, dark green leaves, sometimes silver-patterned, and fragrant white flowers.
C. cyprium. Autumn-flowering, tuberous perennial. H to 4in (10cm), S 2–4in (5–10cm). Frost hardy, zones 7–9. Heart-shaped, toothed, dark green leaves, with lighter patterns, appear with or just after fragrant white flowers, each with carmine marks around the mouth.
C. europaeum. See *C. purpurascens*.
C. fatrense. See *C. purpurascens*.
C. graecum illus. p.367.
C. hederifolium, syn. *C. neapolitanum* (Ivy-leaved cyclamen) illus. p.367. var. *album* illus. p.366.
C. libanoticum illus. p.358.
C. mirabile illus. p.366.
C. neapolitanum. See *C. hederifolium*.
C. persicum illus. p.370. 'Cardinal' is a winter- or spring-flowering, tuberous perennial. H 4–8in (10–20cm), S 6–8in (15–20cm). Frost tender, zones 9–10. Leaves are heart-shaped, marked light and dark green and silver. Produces usually fragrant, slender, bright pinkish scarlet flowers, each 2–2¹/₂in (5–6cm) long and stained carmine at the mouth. Needs plenty of light in winter. **Dwarf Scented Series** (syn. *C.p.*, Dwarf Fragrant Series), S 4–6in (10–15cm), has white, pink, or red flowers, 1¹/₂in (4cm) long. 'Esmeralda', **Kaori Series**, and 'Renown' illus. p.371. 'Pearl Wave' illus. p.370.
C. pseudibericum. Spring-flowering, tuberous perennial. H to 4in (10cm), S 4–6in (10–15cm). Frost hardy, zones

8–9. Has heart-shaped, toothed leaves patterned with silvery- and dark green zones. Flowers are deep carmine purple with darker, basal stains and white-rimmed mouths.
C. purpurascens, syn. *C. europaeum*, *C. fatrense*, illus. p.364.
C. repandum. Spring-flowering, tuberous perennial. H to 4in (10cm), S 4–6in (10–15cm). Frost hardy, zones 7–9. Has heart-shaped, jagged-toothed, dark green leaves with lighter patterns. Bears fragrant, slender, reddish purple flowers.
C. rohlfsianum illus. p.367.
C. trochopteranthum, syn. *C. alpinum*. Spring-flowering, tuberous perennial. H 4in (10cm), S 2–4in (5–10cm). Fully hardy, zones 5–9. Bears rounded or heart-shaped leaves, zoned with silver. Produces musty-scented, pale carmine or white flowers, stained dark carmine at mouths; petals are twisted and propeller-shaped.

Cyclobothra lutea. See *Calochortus barbatus*.

CYDONIA (Rosaceae)
Genus of one species of deciduous, spring-flowering tree, grown for its flowers and fruits, which are used as a flavoring and for preserves. Fully hardy, but grow against a south- or west-facing wall in cold areas. Requires sun and fertile, well-drained soil. Propagate species by seed in autumn, cultivars by softwood cuttings in summer. Mildew, brown rot, and fireblight may sometimes cause problems.
C. oblonga (Quince). 'Lusitanica' is a deciduous, spreading tree. H and S 15ft (5m). Zones 5–9. Broadly oval, dark green leaves are gray-felted beneath. Has a profusion of large, 5-petaled, pale pink flowers in late spring, followed by fragrant, pear-shaped, deep yellow fruits. 'Vranja' illus. p.65.
C. sinensis. See *Pseudocydonia sinensis*.

CYMBALARIA (Scrophulariaceae)
Genus of annuals, biennials, and short-lived perennials, related to *Linaria*, grown for their tiny flowers on slender stems. Is good for rock gardens, walls, and banks, but may be invasive. Fully hardy. Needs shade and moist soil. Propagate by seed in autumn. Self seeds readily.
C. muralis (Ivy-leaved toadflax, Kenilworth ivy). Spreading perennial. H 2in (5cm), S 5in (12cm). Zones 5–8. Bears small, ivy-shaped, pale green leaves and, in summer, masses of tiny, tubular, spurred, sometimes purple-tinted, white flowers.

CYMBIDIUM. See ORCHIDS.
C. Caithness Ice 'Trinity' (illus. p.254). Evergreen, epiphytic orchid for a cool greenhouse. H 30in (75cm). Zone 10. Sprays of green flowers, 4in (10cm) across, each with a red-marked, white lip, are borne in early spring. Has narrowly oval leaves, to 24in (60cm) long. Grow in semi-shade in summer.

C. Christmas Angel 'Cooksbridge Sunburst' (illus. p.255). Evergreen, epiphytic orchid for a cool greenhouse. H 30in (75cm). Zone 10. In winter produces sprays of yellow flowers, 4in (10cm) across and with red-spotted lips. Narrowly oval leaves are up to 24in (60cm) long. Grow in semi-shade in summer.
C. devonianum (illus. p.254). Evergreen, epiphytic orchid for a cool greenhouse. H 24in (60cm). Zone 10. In early summer bears pendent spikes of 1in (2.5cm) wide, olive green flowers overlaid with purple and with purple lips. Has broadly oval, semi-rigid leaves, to 12in (30cm) long. Needs semi-shade in summer.
C. elegans, syn. *Cyperorchis elegans* (illus. p.254). Evergreen, epiphytic orchid for a cool greenhouse. H 30in (75cm). Zone 10. Dense, pendent sprays of fragrant, tubular, yellow flowers, 1¹/₂in (4cm) across, appear in early summer. Has narrowly oval leaves, to 24in (60cm) long. Requires semi-shade in summer.
C. grandiflorum (illus. p.254). Evergreen, epiphytic orchid for a cool greenhouse. H 30in (75cm). Zone 10. In winter produces sprays of deep green flowers, 3in (8cm) across, each with a hairy, brown-spotted, creamy white lip. Narrowly oval leaves are up to 24in (60cm) long. Grow in semi-shade in summer.
C. King's Lock 'Cooksbridge' (illus. p.254). Evergreen, epiphytic orchid for a cool greenhouse. H 24in (60cm). Zone 10. Sprays of green flowers, 2in (5cm) across and each with a purple-marked, white lip, open in spring. Leaves are narrowly oval and up to 24in (60cm) long. Provide semi-shade in summer.
C. Pontac 'Mont Millais' (illus. p.253). Evergreen, epiphytic orchid for a cool greenhouse. H 30in (75cm). Zone 10. Bears sprays of 3in (8cm) wide, rich deep red flowers, edged and marked with white, in spring. Has narrowly oval leaves, to 24in (60cm) long. Grow in semi-shade in summer.
C. Portlett Bay (illus. p.252). Evergreen, epiphytic orchid for a cool greenhouse. H 30in (75cm). Zone 10. Red-lipped, white flowers, 4in (10cm) across, are borne in sprays in spring. Has narrowly oval leaves, to 24in (60cm) long. Provide semi-shade in summer.
C. Strath Kanaid (illus. p.253). Evergreen, epiphytic orchid for a cool greenhouse. H 24in (60cm). Zone 10. In spring bears arching spikes of deep red flowers, 2in (5cm) across. Lips are white, marked deep red. Narrowly oval leaves are up to 24in (60cm) long. Requires semi-shade in summer.
C. Strathbraan (illus. p.252). Evergreen, epiphytic orchid for a cool greenhouse. H 24in (60cm). Zone 10. In spring produces slightly arching spikes of off-white flowers, 2in (5cm) across, with red marks on each lip. Leaves are narrowly oval, to 24in (60cm) long. Requires semi-shade in summer.
C. Strathdon 'Cooksbridge Noel' (illus. p.253). Evergreen, epiphytic orchid for a cool greenhouse. H 3ft

(1m). Zone 10. Sprays of rich pink flowers, 2in (5cm) across, with red-spotted, yellow-tinged lips, appear in winter. Has narrowly oval leaves, up to 24in (60cm) long. Needs semi-shade in summer.
C. tracyanum (illus. p.254). Evergreen, epiphytic orchid for a cool greenhouse. H 30in (75cm). Zone 10. In autumn produces long spikes of fragrant, olive green flowers, 3in (8cm) across, overlaid with reddish dots and dashes. Has narrowly oval leaves, to 24in (60cm) long. Grow in semi-shade in summer.

CYNARA (Compositae)
Genus of architectural perennials, grown for their large heads of flowers. The plant described is grown both as a vegetable and as a decorative border plant. Frost hardy. Requires sun and fertile, well-drained soil. Propagate by seed or division in spring.
C. cardunculus illus. p.190.

CYNOGLOSSUM (Boraginaceae)
Hound's tongue
Genus of annuals, biennials and perennials, grown for their long flowering period from late spring to early autumn. Fully hardy. Needs sun and fertile but not over-rich soil. Propagate by division in spring or by seed in autumn or spring.
C. amabile (Chinese forget-me-not). 'Firmament' illus. p.278.
C. nervosum illus. p.213.

CYPELLA (Iridaceae)
Genus of summer-flowering bulbs, grown for their short-lived, irislike flowers that have 3 large, spreading outer petals and 3 small, incurved inner ones. Half hardy; may survive outdoors in cool areas if planted near a sunny wall. Needs well-drained soil and full sun. Lift bulbs when dormant; partially dry off in winter. Propagate by seed in spring.
C. herbertii illus. p.353.

Cyperorchis elegans. See *Cymbidium elegans*.

CYPERUS (Cyperaceae).
See GRASSES, BAMBOOS, RUSHES, and SEDGES.
C. albostriatus, syn. *C. diffusus* of gardens, *C. elegans* of gardens. Evergreen, perennial sedge. H 2ft (60cm), S indefinite. Frost tender, min. 45°F (7°C), zones 9–10. Stem has prominently veined, green leaves and up to 8 leaflike, green bracts surrounding a well-branched umbel of brown spikelets in summer. 'Variegatus' has white-striped leaves and bracts.
C. alternifolius of gardens. See *C. involucratus*.
C. diffusus of gardens. See *C. albostriatus*.
C. elegans of gardens. See *C. albostriatus*.
C. flabelliformis. See *C. involucratus*.
C. involucratus, syn. *C. alternifolius* of gardens, *C. flabelliformis*, illus. p.182.
C. isocladus of gardens. See *C. papyrus* 'Nanus'.

C. longus (Galingale). Evergreen, spreading, perennial sedge. H 5ft (1.5m), S indefinite. Fully hardy, zones 7–10. Bears rough-edged, glossy, dark green leaves and, in summer, attractive umbels of narrow, flattened, milk-chocolate-colored spikelets that keep their color well. Tolerates its roots in water.

C. papyrus illus. p.181. **'Nanus'** (syn. *C. isocladus* of gardens) is an evergreen, spreading, perennial sedge with a red rhizome; it is a dwarf variant of the species, sometimes considered distinct, and is often grown under misapplied names. H 32in (80cm), S indefinite. Frost tender, min. 45–50°F (7–10°C), zones 9–10. Triangular, leafless stems bear umbels of brown spikelets on 3–4in (8–10cm) stalks in summer.

CYPHOMANDRA (Solanaceae)
Genus of evergreen shrubs and trees, grown for their fruits and foliage. Frost tender, min. 50°F (10°C). Grow in full light or partial shade and in well-drained soil. Water potted specimens freely when in growth, sparingly at other times, when some leaves may fall. Tip prune at intervals while young to promote branching. Propagate by seed in spring. Whitefly and red spider mite may cause problems.

C. betacea illus. p.93.

CYPHOSTEMMA (Vitaceae)
Genus of deciduous, perennial succulents with very thick, fleshy, almost woody caudices and branches. Leaf undersides often exude small droplets of resin. Frost tender, min. 50°F (10°C). Needs full sun and very well-drained soil. Keep dry in winter. Is difficult to grow. Propagate by seed in spring.

C. bainesii, syn. *Cissus bainesii.* Deciduous, perennial succulent. H and S 2ft (60cm). Zone 10. Has a thick, swollen, bottle-shaped trunk, often unbranched, covered in peeling, papery, yellow bark. Fleshy, silvery green leaves, with deeply serrated edges, are divided into 3 oval leaflets and are silver-haired when young. Bears tiny, cup-shaped, yellow-green flowers in summer, then grapelike, red fruits.

C. juttae, syn. *Cissus juttae,* illus. p.380.

CYPRIPEDIUM (Slipper orchid).
See ORCHIDS.

C. acaule (Pink lady's slipper, Pink moccasin flower; illus. p.252). Deciduous, terrestrial orchid. H to 16in (40cm). Fully hardy, zones 5–8. Yellowish green or purple flowers, 1½–2½in (4–6cm) long, each with a pouched, pink or white lip, are borne singly in spring-summer. Leaves are broadly lance-shaped, pleated, and 4–12in (10–30cm) long. Does best in partial shade.

C. calceolus (Lady's slipper; illus. p.254). Deciduous, terrestrial orchid. H 30in (75cm). Fully hardy, zones 5–8. In spring-summer bears paired or solitary yellow-pouched, purple flowers, 1¼–3in (3–7cm) long. Broadly lance-shaped leaves, 2–8in

(5–20cm) long, are arranged in a spiral up stem. Stems and leaves are slightly hairy. Prefers partial shade. var. **pubescens** (Yellow lady's slipper; illus. p.255) has larger, purple-marked, greenish yellow flowers, larger leaves and is more hairy.

C. macranthon (illus. p.254). Deciduous, terrestrial orchid. H 20in (50cm). Fully hardy, zones 5–8. Pouched, violet or purplish red flowers, 1½–2½in (4–6cm) long, usually borne singly, open in spring-summer. Stems and oval leaves, 1½–3in (4–7cm) long, are slightly hairy. Prefers partial shade.

C. reginae (Showy lady's slipper; illus. p.252). Deciduous, terrestrial orchid. H to 3ft (1m). Fully hardy, zones 5–8. In spring-summer, white flowers, ¾–2in (2–5cm) long, each with a pouched, white-streaked, pink lip, are borne singly or in groups of 2 or 3. Stem and oval leaves, 4–10in (10–25cm) long, are hairy. Does best in partial shade.

CYRILLA (Cyrillaceae)
Genus of one very variable species of deciduous or evergreen shrub, grown for its flowers in late summer and autumn. Fully to half hardy. Prefers full sun and needs peaty, acid soil. Propagate by semi-ripe cuttings in summer.

C. racemiflora (Leatherwood). Deciduous or evergreen, bushy shrub. H and S 4ft (1.2m). Zones 6–9. Oblong, glossy, dark green leaves redden in autumn. Slender spires of small, 5-petaled, white flowers are borne in late summer and autumn.

CYRTANTHUS (Amaryllidaceae)
Genus of bulbs with brightly colored flowers, usually in summer. Frost hardy to frost tender, min. 59°F (15°C). Requires free-draining, light soil and full sun. In frost-free areas may flower for much of the year. Plant in spring. Water freely in the growing season. Propagate by seed or offsets in spring.

C. brachyscyphus, syn. *C. parviflorus,* illus. p.364.

C. breviflorus, syn. *Anoiganthus breviflorus.* Clump-forming summer-flowering bulb. H 8–12in (20–30cm), S 3–4in (8–10cm). Frost hardy, zone 10. Has narrowly strap-shaped, semi-erect, basal leaves. Leafless flower stem bears up to 6 funnel-shaped, yellow flowers, ¾–1¼in (2–3cm) long. Prefers a warm, sheltered situation.

C. mackenii. Clump-forming, summer-flowering bulb. H 12–16in (30–40cm), S 3–4in (8–10cm). Half hardy, zones 9–10. Bears strap-shaped, semi-erect, basal leaves. Leafless stems each carry an umbel of up to 10 fragrant, tubular, white flowers, 2in (5cm) long and slightly curved. var. **cooperi** illus. p.353.

C. obliquus. Clump-forming, summer-flowering bulb. H 8–24in (20–60cm), S 5–6in (12–15cm). Half hardy, zone 10. Bears widely strap-shaped, semi-erect, basal, grayish green leaves, twisted lengthways. Carries a head of up to 12 pendent, tubular, red-and-yellow flowers, each 3in (7cm) long.

C. parviflorus. See *C. brachyscyphus.*

C. purpureus, syn. *Vallota speciosa.* Clump-forming, summer-flowering bulb. H 12–20in (30–50cm), S 5–6in (12–15cm). Half hardy, zone 10. Bears widely strap-shaped, semi-erect, basal, bright green leaves. Stout stem produces a head of up to 5 widely funnel-shaped, scarlet flowers, 3–4in (8–10cm) long. Makes an excellent house plant.

C. sanguineus. Clump-forming, summer-flowering bulb. H 12–20in (30–50cm), S 5–6in (12–15cm). Half hardy, zone 10. Has strap-shaped, semi-erect, basal, bright green leaves. Stout stem bears 1 or 2 long-tubed, scarlet flowers, 3–4in (8–10cm) long.

CYRTOMIUM (Polypodiaceae)
Genus of evergreen ferns. Half hardy. Does best in semi-shade and humus-rich, moist soil. Remove fading fronds regularly. Propagate by division in spring or summer or by spores in summer.

C. falcatum illus. p.185.

CYSTOPTERIS (Polypodiaceae)
Genus of deciduous ferns, suitable for rock gardens. Fully hardy. Does best in semi-shade and in soil that is never allowed to dry out. Remove fronds as they fade. Propagate by division in spring, by spores in summer, or by bulbils when available.

C. bulbifera (Berry bladder fern). Deciduous fern. H 6in (15cm), S 9in (23cm). Zones 3–7. Broadly lance-shaped, much divided, dainty, pale green fronds produce tiny bulbils along their length. Propagate by bulbils as soon as mature.

C. dickeana. Deciduous fern. H 6in (15cm), S 9in (23cm). Zones 2–7. Has broadly lance-shaped, divided, delicate, pale green fronds, with oblong, blunt, indented pinnae, that arch downwards.

C. fragilis (Brittle bladder fern). Deciduous fern. H 6in (15cm), S 9in (23cm). Zones 2–7. Broadly lance-shaped, pale green fronds are delicate and much-divided into oblong, pointed, indented pinnae.

CYTISUS (Leguminosae)
Broom
Genus of deciduous or evergreen shrubs, grown for their abundant, pealike flowers. Fully to half hardy. Prefers full sun and fertile, but not over-rich, well-drained soil. Resents being transplanted. Propagate species by semi-ripe cuttings in summer or by seed in autumn, hybrids and cultivars by semi-ripe cuttings only in late summer.

C. albus, syn. *C. leucanthus* (Portuguese broom). Deciduous, spreading shrub. H 1ft (30cm), S 3ft (1m). Fully hardy, zones 6–8. Has oval, green leaves, each with 3 tiny leaflets and, from early to mid-summer, creamy white flowers borne in dense clusters.

C. ardoinii illus. p.326.

C. battandieri illus. p.91.

C. x beanii illus. p.289.

C. canariensis of gardens. See *C. x spachianus.*

C. demissus. Slow-growing, deciduous, prostrate shrub. H 3in (7cm), S 8–12in (20–30cm). Fully hardy, zones 6–8. Densely haired stems bear tiny, bright green leaves with 3 oval leaflets. Leaf axils each bear a terminal cluster of 3 bright yellow flowers, each with a brown pouch, in early summer. Is good for a rock garden or bank.

C. 'Firefly'. Deciduous, bushy shrub with slender, arching shoots. H and S 5–6ft (1.5–2m). Fully hardy, zones 6–8. Small, green leaves are oblong and are divided into 3 tiny leaflets. Produces masses of yellow flowers, marked with red, from late spring to early summer.

C. x kewensis (Kew broom). Deciduous, arching shrub. H 1ft (30cm), S to 6ft (2m). Fully hardy, zones 7–8. Has leaves, with 3 tiny leaflets, along downy stems. In late spring bears creamy white flowers. Is good for a bank or large rock garden.

C. leucanthus. See *C. albus.*

C. nigricans illus. p.138.

C. x praecox illus. p.124. **'Allgold'** illus. p.125.

C. purpureus (Purple broom). Deciduous, arching shrub. H 18in (45cm), S 24in (60cm). Fully hardy, zones 6–9. Semi-erect stems are clothed with leaves of 3 tiny leaflets. Masses of purple flowers open in early summer on previous year's wood. Is good for a bank or sunny border. f. **albus** illus. p.291.

C. racemosus. See *C. x spachianus.*

C. scoparius (Scotch broom). f. **andreanus** illus. p.139. var. **prostratus** (syn. subsp. *maritimus*) is a deciduous, prostrate shrub forming dense mounds of interlocking shoots. H 8in (20cm), S 4–6ft (1.2–2m). Fully hardy, zones 7–9. Small, gray-green leaves usually have 3 oblong leaflets, but may be reduced to a single leaflet. Has masses of golden yellow flowers in late spring and early summer.

C. x spachianus, syn. *C. canariensis* of gardens, *C. racemosus, Genista fragrans.* Vigorous, evergreen, arching shrub. H and S 10ft (3m). Half hardy, zones 7–8. Has dark green leaves with 3 oval leaflets. Produces long, slender clusters of fragrant, golden yellow flowers in winter and early spring. Is often grown as a houseplant.

C. supinus. Deciduous, bushy, rounded shrub. H and S 3ft (1m). Fully hardy, zones 5–9. Dense heads of large, yellow flowers are borne from mid-summer to autumn amid gray-green leaves that are divided into 3 oval leaflets.

C. 'Windlesham Ruby'. Deciduous, bushy shrub with slender, arching shoots. H and S 5–6ft (1.5–2m). Fully hardy, zones 6–8. Small, green leaves have 3 oblong leaflets. Large, rich red flowers are borne in profusion in late spring and early summer.

C. 'Zeelandia'. Deciduous, bushy shrub with slender, arching shoots. H and S 5–6ft (1.5–2m). Fully hardy, zones 6–8. Small, green leaves have 3 oblong leaflets. Bears masses of bicolored, creamy white and lilac-pink flowers from late spring to early summer.

D

DABOECIA (Ericaceae). See HEATHERS.

D. azorica. Evergreen, compact shrub. H to 6in (15cm), S to 24in (60cm). Frost hardy, zones 9–10. Lance-shaped leaves are dark green above, silver-gray beneath. Urn- to bell-shaped flowers are vivid red and open in late spring or early summer.

D. cantabrica (St. Dabeoc's heath). Evergreen, straggling shrub. H to 18in (45cm), S 24in (60cm). Frost hardy, zones 5–8; top growth may be damaged by frost and cold winds, but plants respond well to hard pruning and produce new growth from base. Leaves are lance-shaped to oval, dark green above, silver-gray beneath. Bears bell- to urn-shaped, single or double, white, purple, or mauve flowers from late spring to mid-autumn. **'Bicolor'** (illus. p.146) bears white, purple, and striped flowers on the same plant. **'Praegerae'**, H 14in (35cm), has glowing deep pink flowers. **'Snowdrift'** (illus. p.146) has bright green foliage and long racemes of large, white flowers.

D. × scotica. Evergreen, compact shrub. H to 6in (15cm), S to 2ft (60cm). Frost hardy, zones 4–7. Has lance-shaped to oval leaves that are dark green above, silver-gray beneath. Produces bell- to urn-shaped, white, purple, or mauve flowers from late spring to mid-autumn. **'Jack Drake'**, H 8in (20cm), has small, dark green leaves and ruby-colored flowers. **'William Buchanan'** (illus. p.146), H 18in (45cm), is a vigorous cultivar with dark green leaves and large, deep purple flowers.

DACTYLIS (Gramineae). See GRASSES, BAMBOOS, RUSHES, and SEDGES.

D. glomerata (Cock's-foot, Orchard grass). **'Variegata'** is an evergreen, tuft-forming, perennial grass. H 3ft (1m), S 8–10in (20–25cm). Fully hardy, zones 5–9. Silver-striped, gray-green leaves arise from a tufted rootstock. In summer bears panicles of densely clustered, awned, purplish green spikelets.

DACTYLORRHIZA. See ORCHIDS.

D. elata. Deciduous, terrestrial orchid. H 3¹/₂ft (1.1m). Frost hardy, zones 6–8. Spikes of pink or purple flowers, ¹/₂–³/₄in (1–2cm) long, open in spring-summer. Lance-shaped leaves, 6–10in (15–25cm) long, are spotted with brownish purple and arranged spirally on stem. Requires shade outdoors; keep pot plants semi-shaded in summer.

D. foliosa, syn. *D. maderensis, Orchis maderensis.* Deciduous, terrestrial orchid. H 28in (70cm). Frost hardy, zones 7–8. Spikes of bright purple or pink flowers, ¹/₂–³/₄in (1–2cm) long, are borne in spring-summer. Has lance-

shaped or triangular leaves, 4–8in (10–20cm) long, arranged spirally on stem. Cultivate as for *D. elata*.

D. maderensis. See *D. foliosa*.

DAHLIA (Compositae)

Genus of bushy, summer- and autumn-flowering, tuberous perennials, grown as bedding plants or for their flower heads, which are good for cutting or exhibition. Dwarf forms are used for mass-planting and are also suitable for pots. Half hardy to frost tender, min. 36–9°F (2–4°C). Needs a sunny position and well-drained soil. All apart from dwarf forms require staking. After flowering, lift tubers and store in a frost-free place; replant once all frost danger has passed. In frost-free areas, plants may be left in ground as normal herbaceous perennials, but they benefit from regular propagation to maintain vigor. Propagate dwarf forms by seed sown under glass in late winter, others in spring by seed, basal shoot cuttings, or division of tubers. Dahlias may be subject to attack by aphids, red spider mite, and thrips; they also succumb quickly to virus infection.

Border dahlias

Prolific and long-flowering, various species of *Dahlia* have been hybridized and, with constant breeding and selection, have developed into many forms and have a wide color range (although there is no blue). Shoots may be stopped, or pinched out, to promote vigorous growth and a bushy shape. Spread measurements depend on the amount of stopping carried out and the time at which it is done: early stopping encourages a broader shape, stopping later in the growing season results in a taller plant with much less spread, even in the same cultivar. Leaves are generally green and divided into oval leaflets, some with rounded tips and some with toothed margins. Dahlias are divided into groups, according to the size and type of their flower heads, although the latter may vary in color and shape depending on soil and weather conditions. The groups are single, anemone, collerette, water-lily, decorative, ball, pompon, cactus, semi-cactus, and miscellaneous (including orchid); for illustrations and descriptions see p.340. Each flower head is referred to horticulturally as a flower, even though it does in fact comprise a large number of individual flowers. This horticultural usage has been followed in the descriptions below. All forms with flower heads to 6in (15cm) across are suitable for cutting; those suitable for exhibition are so noted.

D. 'Abridge Taffy'. Decorative-flowered dahlia. H and S 4ft (1.2m). Produces white flowers, 3–4in (8–10cm) across, from mid-summer to late autumn. Is suitable for exhibition.

D. 'Alvas Supreme'. Decorative-flowered dahlia. H and S 3¹/₂ft (1.1m). In summer-autumn bears 10–12in (25–30cm) wide, pale yellow flowers that are good for exhibition.

D. 'Andries Orange'. Semi-cactus-flowered dahlia. H and S 3ft (1m). In summer-autumn produces orange flowers, 3–4in (8–10cm) across.

D. 'Angora' (illus. p.340). Decorative-flowered dahlia. H and S 3¹/₂ft (1.1m). Has 4in (10cm) wide, white flowers, resembling carnations with split petal tips, in mid-summer.

D. 'Athalie' (illus. p.340). Cactus-flowered dahlia. H and S 4ft (1.2m). Has glossy, dark green leaves and dark pinkish bronze flowers, 5–6in (12–15cm) across, in mid-summer. Is good for exhibition.

D. 'Banker'. Cactus-flowered dahlia. H and S 4–5ft (1.2–1.5m). In summer-autumn produces red flowers, 6–8in (15–20cm) across, that are good for exhibition.

D. 'Bassingbourne Beauty' (illus. p.341). Decorative-flowered dahlia. H and S 4ft (1.2m). Produces pale pinkish yellow flowers, 4–6in (10–15cm) across, reflexing to stem, in summer-autumn. Is suitable for exhibition.

D. 'B.B.C.'. Semi-cactus-flowered dahlia. H and S 5–6ft (1.5–2m). In late summer bears flame orange flowers, 10in (25cm) across, that are good for exhibition.

D. 'Betty Bowen' (illus. p.341). Decorative-flowered dahlia. H and S 5ft (1.5m). Leaves are glossy, dark green. Has rich purple flowers, 4–6in (10–15cm) across, with neat, symmetrical petaling, reflexing to stem, in summer-autumn. Is suitable for exhibition.

D. 'Biddenham Sunset' (illus. p.341). Decorative-flowered dahlia. H and S 3–4ft (1–1.2m). Orange-red flowers, 4–5in (10–12cm) across, are borne in mid-summer.

D. 'Bishop of Llandaff' (illus. p.341). Miscellaneous-group dahlia. H and S 3ft (1m). Has bronze-green leaves and single, open-centered, dark red flowers, 4–5in (10–12cm) across, in summer-autumn. Is excellent as a bedding plant.

D. 'Brunton' (illus. p.341). Decorative-flowered dahlia. H and S 3¹/₂ft (1.1m). In summer-autumn bears red flowers, 3–4in (8–10cm) across, that are good for exhibition.

D. 'Butterball' (illus. p.341). Decorative-flowered dahlia. H and S 3ft (1m). Produces 3–4in (8–10cm) wide, bright yellow flowers in early summer.

D. 'By the Cringe' (illus. p.340). Cactus-flowered dahlia. H and S 3¹/₂ft (1.1m). Bears lilac-lavender flowers, 5in (12cm) across, in summer-autumn.

D. 'Candy Keene' (illus. p.340). Semi-cactus-flowered dahlia. H and S 4–5ft (1.2–1.5m). Is a sport of *D.* 'Reginald Keene' with pink flowers.

D. 'Catherine Ireland'. Decorative-flowered dahlia. H and S 3¹/₂ft (1.1m). In summer-autumn has 3–4in (8–10cm) wide flowers, each white at base with a lilac-lavender flush to petal tips.

D. 'Cherida'. Ball-flowered dahlia. H and S 3ft (1m). Has bronze-lilac flowers, less than 3in (8cm) across, in summer-autumn.

D. 'Chimborazo' (illus. p.341). Collerette-flowered dahlia. H and S 3ft (1m). Leaves are glossy, dark green. Has 4in (10cm) wide flowers, with red, outer petals and yellow, inner petals, in summer-autumn. Flowers are good for exhibition.

D. 'Chinese Lantern' (illus. p.341). Decorative-flowered dahlia. H and S 3¹/₂ft (1.1m). In mid-summer produces flame yellow flowers, 4–6in (10–15cm) across.

D. 'Clair de Lune' (illus. p.341). Collerette-flowered dahlia. H and S 3ft (1m). Has 3–4in (8–10cm) wide flowers, with lemon yellow, outer petals and paler yellow, inner petals, in summer-autumn. Is a good exhibition cultivar.

D. Coltness Hybrids illus. p.273.

D. 'Comet' (illus. p.341). Anemone-flowered dahlia. H and S 3¹/₂ft (1.1m). Leaves are glossy, dark green. Produces dark red flowers, 4–6in (10–15cm) across, in summer-autumn.

D. 'Corona' (illus. p.341). Semi-cactus-flowered dahlia. H and S 18–24in (45–60cm). Produces flame red flowers, 3–4in (8–10cm) across, in summer-autumn. Does not require staking.

D. 'Cortez Sovereign' (illus. p.341). Semi-cactus-flowered dahlia. H and S 3–4ft (1–1.2m). Bears 4–6in (10–15cm) wide, pale yellow flowers in summer-autumn.

D. 'Corton Olympic' (illus. p.341). Decorative-flowered dahlia. H and S 3ft (1m). Has bronze-colored flowers, 10–12in (25–30cm) across, in late summer.

D. 'Cryfield Bryn'. Cactus-flowered dahlia. H and S 3¹/₂ft (1.1m). In summer-autumn has butter yellow flowers, 4–6in (10–15cm) across, that are excellent for exhibition.

D. 'Cryfield Rosie'. Ball-flowered dahlia. H and S 3¹/₂ft (1.1m). Produces 4–6in (10–15cm) wide, yellow flowers, tinged with red, in summer-autumn. Is good for exhibition.

D. 'Daleko Jupiter'. Semi-cactus-flowered dahlia. H and S 4ft (1.2m). Produces reddish yellow flowers, 10–12in (25–30cm) across, in summer-autumn. Is a leading exhibition cultivar.

D. 'Dandy' illus. p.285.

D. 'Davenport Sunlight' (illus. p.341). Semi-cactus-flowered dahlia. H and S 4ft (1.2m). Has 6–8in (15–20cm) wide, bright yellow flowers in summer-autumn. Flowers are good for exhibition.

D. **'David Howard'**. Decorative-flowered dahlia. H and S 30in (75cm). Dark, bronze-colored foliage offsets orange-bronze flowers, 3–4in (8–10cm) across, in summer-autumn.

D., **Disco Series**. Group of well-branched, erect, perennial dahlias, grown as annuals. H and S 18in (45cm). Leaves are divided into oval leaflets. Daisylike, semi-double and double flower heads, with quilled florets, in a wide color range, appear throughout summer and until autumn frosts.

D. **'Downham Royal'**. Ball-flowered dahlia. H and S 3ft (1m). Bears deep purple flowers, 3–4in (8–10cm) across, in summer-autumn. Is good for exhibition.

D. **'Early Bird'** (illus. p.341). Decorative-flowered dahlia. H and S 4ft (1.2m). Produces 4–6in (10–15cm) wide, yellow flowers in summer-autumn.

D. **'East Anglian'** (illus. p.341). Decorative-flowered dahlia. H and S 3ft (1m). Has orange-yellow flowers, 4–6in (10–15cm) across, in summer-autumn.

D. **'Easter Sunday'** (illus. p.340). Collerette-flowered dahlia. H and S 3ft (1m). Leaves are glossy, dark green. Produces 5in (12cm) wide flowers, with white, inner and outer petals and dark yellow centers, in summer-autumn. Is good for exhibition.

D. **'Eastwood Moonlight'**. Semi-cactus-flowered dahlia. H and S 3–4ft (1–1.2m). Bears bright yellow flowers, 6–8in (15–20cm) across, in summer-autumn. Is a very good exhibition cultivar.

D. **'Edinburgh'**. Decorative-flowered dahlia. H and S 3ft (1m). Produces compact, white-tipped, rich purple flowers, 4–6in (10–15cm) across, in summer-autumn.

D. **'Evening Mail'**. Semi-cactus-flowered dahlia. H and S 4–5ft (1.2–1.5m). In summer-autumn has yellow flowers, 10–12in (25–30cm) across. Is good for exhibition.

D. **'Evita'**. Semi-cactus-flowered dahlia. H and S 4ft (1.2m). In summer-autumn has 6–8in (15–20cm) wide, soft yellow flowers that are good for exhibition.

D. **'Fascination'** (illus. p.341). Dwarf, miscellaneous-group dahlia. H and S 12–18in (30–45cm). Produces single, light purple flowers, 3in (8cm) across, in summer-autumn. Is useful for bedding.

D. **'Flutterby'** (illus. p.341). Decorative-flowered dahlia. H and S 3ft (1m). Bears reddish yellow flowers, 4in (10cm) across, in summer-autumn.

D. **'Frank Hornsey'** (illus. p.341). Decorative-flowered dahlia. H and S 3^1/2ft (1.1m). Leaves are glossy, dark green. Produces 4–6in (10–15cm) wide, orange-yellow flowers, with reflexed petals, in mid-summer. Is ideal for exhibition.

D. **'Gay Mini'** (illus. p.341). Decorative-flowered dahlia. H and S 3ft (1m). Has bronze-yellow flowers, 3–4in (8–10cm) across, in summer-autumn.

D. **'Gay Princess'** (illus. p.340). Decorative-flowered dahlia. H and S

3ft (1m). Produces lilac-lavender flowers, 4–6in (10–15cm) across, in summer-autumn.

D. **'Gerrie Hoek'**. Water-lily-flowered dahlia. H and S 3^1/2ft (1.1m). Produces 5in (12cm) wide flowers, with pale pink, outer petals and dark pink, inner petals, in summer-autumn.

D. **'Gilt Edge'** (illus. p.340). Decorative-flowered dahlia. H and S 3ft (1m). Bears 6–8in (15–20cm) wide flowers, with reflexed, gold-margined, dark pink petals, in summer-autumn. Is suitable for exhibition.

D. **'Giraffe'**. Miscellaneous-group dahlia. H and S 30in (75cm). Has sparse, green foliage and double, orchidlike, bronze-yellow flowers, 3in (8cm) across, in summer-autumn.

D. **'Hallmark'**. Pompon-flowered dahlia. H and S 30in (75cm). Has spherical, 2in (5cm) wide, pink flowers in summer-autumn. Is good for exhibition.

D. **'Hamari Bride'**. Semi-cactus-flowered dahlia. H and S 3–4ft (1–1.2m). Bears clear white flowers, 6–8in (15–20cm) across, in summer-autumn. Is a good exhibition cultivar.

D. **'Hamari Fiesta'**. Decorative-flowered dahlia. H and S 4ft (1.2m). Has scarlet-yellow flowers, 4–6in (10–15cm) across, in summer-autumn.

D. **'Hamari Gold'**. Decorative-flowered dahlia. H and S 2^1/2–3ft (75cm–1m). Has 10–12in (25–30cm) wide, golden orange-bronze flowers in summer-autumn. Is suitable for exhibition.

D. **'Hamari Katrina'** (illus. p.341). Semi-cactus-flowered dahlia. H and S 4–5ft (1.2–1.5m). Bears 8–10in (20–25cm) wide, deep butter yellow flowers in summer-autumn. Flowers are good for exhibition.

D. **'Hayley Jane'**. Semi-cactus-flowered dahlia. H and S 3ft (1m). Produces 4–6in (10–15cm) wide, white flowers, evenly tipped purple-red, in summer-autumn.

D. **'Highgate Gold'**. Semi-cactus-flowered dahlia. H and S 4–5ft (1.2–1.5m). Has deep orange-yellow flowers, 6–8in (15–20cm) across, in summer-autumn. Is suitable for exhibition.

D. **'Highgate Torch'** (illus. p.341). Semi-cactus-flowered dahlia. H and S 3–4ft (1–1.2m). Produces bright flame colored flowers, 6–8in (15–20cm) across, in summer-autumn.

D. **'Holland Festival'**. Decorative-flowered dahlia. H and S 4ft (1.2m). Bears 12in (30cm) or more wide flowers, with bright orange petals evenly tipped with white, in summer-autumn. Is suitable for exhibition.

D. **'Jescot Julie'**. Miscellaneous-group dahlia. H and S 2–3ft (60cm–1m). Has sparse, green foliage and orchidlike, double, orange-purple flowers, 3–4in (8–10cm) across, with purple-backed petals, in summer-autumn.

D. **'Jocondo'** (illus. p.341). Decorative-flowered dahlia. H and S 3–4ft (1–1.2m). In summer-autumn produces 12in (30cm) or more wide, purple-red flowers that are suitable for exhibition.

D. **'Klankstad Kerkrade'**. Cactus-flowered dahlia. H and S 4ft (1.2m).

Has glossy, dark green leaves and soft sulfur yellow flowers, each 4–6in (10–15cm) across, in summer-autumn. Is a good exhibition cultivar.

D. **'La Cierva'**. Collerette-flowered dahlia. H and S 3–4ft (1–1.2m). Leaves are glossy, dark green. Bears 4–6in (10–15cm) wide flowers, with white-tipped, purple, outer petals, and pure white, inner petals, in summer-autumn. Is suitable for exhibition.

D. **'L'Ancresse'**. Ball-flowered dahlia. H and S 3ft (1m). Bears pure white flowers, 3–4in (8–10cm) across, in summer-autumn. Is a good exhibition cultivar.

D. **'Lavender Athalie'**. Cactus-flowered dahlia. H and S 4ft (1.2m). Is a sport of *D.* 'Athalie' with soft lilac-lavender flowers, 3–4in (8–10cm) wide.

D. **'Majestic Kerkrade'** (illus. p.340). Cactus-flowered dahlia. H and S 4ft (1.2m). Is a sport of *D.* 'Klankstad Kerkrade' with dark pinkish yellow flowers.

D. **'Mariposa'**. Collerette-flowered dahlia. H and S 3ft (1m). In summer-autumn has 4–6in (10–15cm) wide, white flowers; outer petals are tinged with lilac. Is good for exhibition.

D. **'Mark Damp'**. Semi-cactus-flowered dahlia. H and S 3–4ft (1–1.2m). Bears 8–10in (20–25cm) wide, bronze-orange flowers, tinged with peach, in summer-autumn. Is suitable for exhibition.

D. **'Monk Marc'** (illus. p.340). Cactus-flowered dahlia. H and S 2–3ft (60cm–1m). Produces dark pink flowers, 4–6in (10–15cm) across, in summer-autumn. Is suitable for exhibition.

D. **'Moor Place'**. Pompon-flowered dahlia. H and S 3ft (1m). Leaves are glossy, dark green. Has 2in (5cm) wide, royal purple flowers in summer-autumn. Is a good exhibition cultivar.

D. **'Nationwide'**. Decorative-flowered dahlia. H and S 3–4ft (1–1.2m). Bears 4–6in (10–15cm) wide, yellowish orange flowers in summer-autumn.

D. **'Nina Chester'** (illus. p.340). Decorative-flowered dahlia. H and S 3ft (1m). Has 4–6in (10–15cm) wide, white flowers, occasionally lilac-tinged, in summer-autumn. Is good for exhibition.

D. **'Noreen'** (illus. p.340). Pompon-flowered dahlia. H and S 3ft (1m). In summer-autumn produces dark pinkish purple flowers, 2in (5cm) across, that are good for exhibition.

D. **'Paul Chester'** (illus. p.341). Cactus-flowered dahlia. H and S 3ft (1m). In summer-autumn has yellowish orange flowers, 4–6in (10–15cm) across, that are suitable for exhibition.

D. **'Paul Damp'**. Semi-cactus-flowered dahlia. H and S 4–5ft (1.2–1.5m). Bears 6–8in (15–20cm) wide, dark pink flowers in summer-autumn. Is a good exhibition cultivar.

D. **'Pink Giraffe'**. Miscellaneous-group dahlia. H and S 2–3ft (60cm–1m). Is a sport of *D.* 'Giraffe' with pink flowers. Flowers are suitable for exhibition.

D. **'Pink Symbol'** (illus. p.340). Semi-cactus-flowered dahlia. H and

S 3–4ft (1–1.2m). Is a sport of *D.* 'Symbol' with pink flowers that are good for exhibition.

D. **'Pontiac'** (illus. p.341). Cactus-flowered dahlia. H and S 3ft (1m). Leaves are glossy, dark green. Bears dark pinkish purple flowers, 4–6in (10–15cm) across, in summer-autumn.

D. **'Porcelain'**. Water-lily-flowered dahlia. H and S 3ft (1m). Produces whitish lilac flowers, 4–6in (10–15cm) across, in summer-autumn. Is useful for exhibition.

D. **'Quel Diable'** (illus. p.341). Semi-cactus-flowered dahlia. H and S 3–4ft (1–1.2m). Bears flame-colored flowers, 6–8in (15–20cm) across, in summer-autumn. Is a good exhibition cultivar.

D. **'Redskin'**. Well-branched, perennial dahlia, grown as an annual. H and S 12in (30cm). Has bronze-green to maroon leaves, divided into oval leaflets, and, throughout summer and until autumn frosts, daisylike, double flower heads, in many colors.

D. **'Reginald Keene'**. Semi-cactus-flowered dahlia. H and S 3–4ft (1–1.2m). In summer-autumn has 8–10in (20–25cm) wide, orange-flame flowers that are good for exhibition.

D. **'Rhonda'** (illus. p.340). Pompon-flowered dahlia. H and S 3ft (1m). In summer-autumn produces 2in (5cm) wide, whitish lilac flowers that are suitable for exhibition.

D. **'Ruby Wedding'**. Decorative-flowered dahlia. H and S 3ft (1m). Bears deep purple flowers, 3–4in (8–10cm) across, in summer-autumn. Flowers are suitable for exhibition.

D. **'Scarlet Beauty'** (illus. p.341). Water-lily-flowered dahlia. H and S 3ft (1m). Is a sport of *D.* 'Gerrie Hoek' with deep red flowers, 4–6in (10–15cm) across, that are good for exhibition.

D. **'Shandy'** (illus. p.341). Cactus-flowered dahlia. H and S 3ft (1m). Produces 4–6in (10–15cm) wide, pale brown flowers in summer-autumn.

D. **'Sherwood Standard'**. Decorative-flowered dahlia. H and S 4ft (1.2m). Has orange flowers, 6–8in (15–20cm) across, in summer-autumn. Is suitable for exhibition.

D. **'Shy Princess'**. Cactus-flowered dahlia. H and S 4–5ft (1.2–1.5m). In summer-autumn bears 6–8in (15–20cm) wide, white flowers that are good for exhibition.

D. **'Small World'** (illus. p.340). Pompon-flowered dahlia. H and S 3ft (1m). Leaves are glossy, dark green. Has 2in (5cm) wide, white flowers in summer-autumn. Is suitable for exhibition.

D. **'So Dainty'** (illus. p.341). Semi-cactus-flowered dahlia. H and S 2–3ft (60cm–1m). Produces bronze-colored flowers, 3–4in (8–10cm) across, in summer-autumn. Flowers are suitable for exhibition.

D. **'Spencer'**. Decorative-flowered dahlia. H and S 3ft (1m). Bears purplish pink flowers, 4–6in (10–15cm) across, in summer-autumn. Is good for exhibition.

D. **'Super'**. Semi-cactus-flowered dahlia. H and S 4–5ft (1.2–1.5m). Produces orange-flame flowers, 10in

(25cm) or more across, in summer-autumn. Is suitable for exhibition.

D. 'Symbol'. Semi-cactus-flowered dahlia. H and S 3–4ft (1–1.2m). Has 6–8in (15–20cm) wide, bronze-orange flowers in summer-autumn. Is a good exhibition cultivar.

D. 'Temptress'. Cactus-flowered dahlia. H and S 3ft (1m). Produces whitish lilac flowers, 4–6in (10–15cm) across, in summer-autumn. Is a good exhibition cultivar.

D. 'Vicky Crutchfield' (illus. p.340). Water-lily-flowered dahlia. H and S 3ft (1m). Bears pink flowers, 4–6in (10–15cm) across, in summer-autumn. Is suitable for exhibition.

D. 'Whale's Rhonda' (illus. p.341). Pompon-flowered dahlia. H and S 3ft (1m). Leaves are glossy, very dark green. In summer-autumn has 2in (5cm) wide, purple flowers that are good for exhibition.

D. 'White Klankstad' (illus. p.340). Cactus-flowered dahlia. H and S 3–4ft (1–1.2m). Is a sport of *D.* 'Klankstad Kerkrade' with white flowers.

D. 'Willo's Violet'. Pompon-flowered dahlia. H and S 3ft (1m). Bears glossy, dark green leaves and 2in (5cm) wide, violet-purple flowers, in summer-autumn. Is suitable for exhibition.

D. 'Wootton Cupid' (illus. p.341). Ball-flowered dahlia. H and S 3–4ft (1–1.2m). In summer-autumn bears pink flowers, 3–4in (8–10cm) across, that are good for exhibition.

D. 'Yellow Hammer' (illus. p.341). Dwarf, single-flowered dahlia. H and S 12–18in (30–45cm). Bears rich yellow flowers, 3in (8cm) across, in summer-autumn.

DAIS (Thymelaeaceae)

Genus of deciduous, summer-flowering shrubs, grown for their flowers and overall appearance. Frost tender, min. 41°F (5°C). Requires full sun and well-drained soil. Water potted plants freely when in full growth, sparingly when leafless. Propagate by seed in spring or by semi-ripe cuttings in summer.

D. cotinifolia. Deciduous, bushy, neat shrub. H and S 6–10ft (2–3m). Zones 9–10. Has small, oval to oblong, lustrous leaves. In summer bears scented, star-shaped, rose-lilac flowers in flattened clusters, 3in (8cm) across. Bark yields fibers strong enough to be used as thread.

DANÄE (Liliaceae)

Genus of one species of evergreen shrub, with inconspicuous flowers, grown for its attractive, flattened, leaflike shoots. Frost hardy. Grows in sun or shade and in moist soil. Propagate by seed in autumn or by division from autumn to spring.

D. racemosa (Alexandrian laurel). Evergreen, arching, dense shrub. H and S 3ft (1m). Zones 6–9. Has slender stems, lance-shaped, leaflike, glossy, green shoots, and pointed, glossy, bright green "leaves." Occasionally bears spherical, red berries.

DAPHNE (Thymelaeaceae)

Genus of evergreen, semi-evergreen, or deciduous shrubs, grown for their

usually fragrant, tubular flowers, each with 4 spreading lobes, and, in some species, for their foliage or fruits (seeds are poisonous). Dwarf species and cultivars are good for rock gardens. Fully to frost hardy. Most need full sun (although *D. alpina, D. arbuscula,* and *D. blagayana* may be grown in semi-shade and *D. laureola* tolerates deep shade) and fertile, well-drained but not over-dry soil. Resents being transplanted. Propagate species by seed when fresh or by semi-ripe cuttings in summer, cultivars by cuttings only. Is susceptible to viruses that cause leaf mottling.

D. alpina. Deciduous, erect shrub. H 20in (50cm), S 16in (40cm). Fully hardy, zones 6–8. Leaves are oval, downy, and gray-green. Produces terminal clusters of fragrant white flowers in late spring. Is suitable for a rock garden.

D. arbuscula illus. p.306.

D. bholua illus. p.118.

D. blagayana illus. p.287.

D. x burkwoodii 'Somerset' illus. p.122. **'Variegata'** is a semi-evergreen, upright shrub. H 5ft (1.5m), S 3ft (1m). Fully hardy, zones 5–9. Bears dense clusters of very fragrant white-throated, pink flowers in late spring, sometimes again in autumn. Narrowly oblong, gray-green leaves are edged with creamy white or pale yellow.

D. cneorum illus. p.288. **'Eximia'** is an evergreen, prostrate shrub. H 4in (10cm), S to 20in (50cm) or more. Fully hardy, zones 5–8. Has small, oval, leathery, dark green leaves. In late spring produces terminal clusters of fragrant white flowers, which are crimson outside and often pink-flushed within.

D. collina. Evergreen, domed, compact shrub. H and S 20in (50cm). Frost hardy, zones 7–8. Oval, dark green leaves densely cover upright branches. Has terminal clusters of small, fragrant, purple-rose flowers in late spring. Is good for a rock garden or shrubbery.

D. genkwa. Deciduous, upright, open shrub. H and S 5ft (1.5m). Fully hardy after a hot summer, otherwise frost hardy, zones 6–9. Oval, dark green leaves are bronze when young. Large, faintly scented, lilac flowers are borne from mid- to late spring.

D. giraldii. Deciduous, upright shrub. H and S 2ft (60cm). Fully hardy, zones 4–8. Clusters of fragrant, golden yellow flowers are produced amid oblong, pale blue-green leaves in late spring and early summer and are followed by egg-shaped, red fruits.

D. jasminea illus. p.304.

D. laureola (Spurge-laurel). Evergreen, bushy shrub. H 3ft (1m), S 5ft (1.5m). Fully hardy, zones 7–9. Has oblong, dark green leaves. Slightly fragrant, pale green flowers are borne from late winter to early spring, followed by spherical, black fruits. var. **philippi** illus. p.124.

D. mezereum illus. p.142. var. **alba** is a deciduous, upright to spreading shrub. H and S 4ft (1.2m). Fully hardy, zones 5–8. Bears very fragrant white or creamy white flowers that clothe

bare stems in late winter and early spring and are followed by spherical, yellow fruits. Leaves are oblong and dull gray-green.

D. odora. Evergreen, bushy shrub. H and S 5ft (1.5m). Frost hardy, zones 7–9. Has oval, glossy, dark green leaves and, from mid-winter to early spring, very fragrant, deep purplish pink-and-white flowers. **'Aureomarginata'** illus. p.142.

D. petraea 'Grandiflora' illus. p.306.

D. retusa illus. p.123.

D. tangutica. Evergreen, bushy shrub with stout shoots. H and S 3ft (1m). Fully hardy, zones 7–9. Narrowly oval, leathery leaves are dark green. Bears clusters of fragrant white-flushed, purple-pink flowers in mid- to late spring.

DAPHNIPHYLLUM (Daphniphyllaceae)

Genus of evergreen trees and shrubs, grown for their habit and foliage. Male and female flowers are borne on separate plants. Frost hardy. Needs a sheltered position in sun or semi-shade and deep, fertile, well-drained but not too dry soil. Propagate by semi-ripe cuttings in summer.

D. macropodum illus. p.86.

DARMERA. See PELTIPHYLLUM.

DARWINIA (Myrtaceae)

Genus of evergreen, spring-flowering shrubs, grown for their flowers and overall appearance. Frost tender, min. 45–50°F (7–10°C). Requires full light and well-drained, neutral to acid soil, not rich in nitrogen. Water moderately when in full growth, sparingly at other times. Propagate by seed in spring or by semi-ripe cuttings in late summer. Is difficult to root and to grow under glass.

D. citriodora. Evergreen, rounded, well-branched shrub. H and S 2–4ft (60cm–1.2m). Zone 10. Oblong to broadly lance-shaped, blue-green leaves are lemon-scented when bruised. In spring produces pendent, terminal heads of usually 4 small, tubular, yellow or red flowers, each surrounded by 2 red or yellowish bracts.

DASYLIRION (Liliaceae)

Bear grass

Genus of evergreen, palmlike perennials, grown for their foliage and flowers. Male and female flowers are produced on separate plants. Frost tender, min. 50°F (10°C). Requires well-drained soil and a sunny position. Water well when in full growth, less at other times. Propagate by seed in spring.

D. texanum. Evergreen, palmlike perennial with a 30in (75cm) high trunk. H over 3ft (1m), S 10ft (3m). Zones 8–10. Has a rosette of narrow, drooping, green leaves, each 2–3ft (60–90cm) long, with yellowish prickles along margins. Stems, 15ft (5m) long, emerge from center of plant carrying dense, narrow panicles of small, bell-shaped, whitish flowers in summer. Dry, 3-winged fruits appear in autumn.

DATURA (Solanaceae)

Genus of evergreen or semi-evergreen shrubs, trees, and annuals, grown for their flowers borne mainly in summer-autumn. Frost hardy to frost tender, min. 45–50°F (7–10°C). Prefers full light and fertile, well-drained soil. Water potted specimens freely in full growth, moderately at other times. May be pruned hard in early spring. Propagate by seed in spring or by greenwood or semi-ripe cuttings in early summer or later. Whitefly and red spider mite may be troublesome.

D. arborea, syn. *D. cornigera, Brugmansia arborea.* Evergreen or semi-evergreen, rounded, robust shrub. H and S to 10ft (3m). Frost tender, zone 10. Bears narrowly oval leaves, each 8in (20cm) or more long. Strongly fragrant, pendent, trumpet-shaped, white flowers, each 6–8in (16–20cm) long with a spathelike calyx, are borne in summer-autumn.

D. aurea, syn. *Brugmansia aurea.* Evergreen, rounded shrub or tree. H and S 20–35ft (6–11m). Frost tender, zone 10. Has oval leaves, 6in (15cm) long, and, in summer-autumn, pendent, trumpet-shaped, white or yellow flowers, 6–10in (15–25cm) long.

D. x candida, syn. *Brugmansia x candida,* illus. p.87.

D. cornigera. See *D. arborea.*

D. 'Grand Marnier' illus. p.91.

D. rosei, syn. *D. sanguinea* of gardens, *Brugmansia bicolor, B. rosei.* Evergreen, rounded shrub or tree. H and S to 20ft (6m). Frost tender, zone 10. Leaves are 7in (18cm) long and oval, sometimes with small, rounded lobes. From late summer to following spring bears pendent, trumpet-shaped, red, saffron yellow, or orange flowers, 6–7in (15–18cm) long.

D. sanguinea, syn. *Brugmansia sanguinea,* illus. p.91.

D. sanguinea of gardens. See *D. rosei.*

DAVALLIA (Polypodiaceae)

Genus of evergreen or semi-evergreen, often epiphytic ferns, best suited to growing in pots and hanging baskets. Half hardy to frost tender, min. 41°F (5°C). Requires semi-shade and very fibrous, moist, peaty soil. Remove fading fronds regularly. Propagate by division in spring or summer or by spores in summer.

D. canariensis (Deer's-foot fern). Semi-evergreen fern. H and S 12in (30cm). Frost tender, zone 10. Broadly lance-shaped, leathery, green fronds, divided into numerous triangular pinnae, arise from a scaly, brown rootstock.

D. mariesii (Squirrel's-foot fern). Evergreen fern. H 6in (15cm), S 9in (23cm). Half hardy, zone 10. Broadly triangular, delicately divided, leathery, green fronds arise from a creeping, scaly, brown rootstock.

DAVIDIA (Davidiaceae)

Genus of one species of deciduous, spring- and summer-flowering tree, grown for its habit and showy, white bracts surrounding insignificant flower heads. Fully hardy, but needs shelter from strong winds. Requires sun or semi-shade and fertile, well-drained

but preferably moist soil. Propagate by semi-ripe cuttings in spring or by seed when ripe in autumn.
D. involucrata illus. p.50.

DECAISNEA (Lardizabalaceae)
Genus of deciduous, summer-flowering shrubs, grown for their foliage, flowers, and sausage-shaped fruits. Frost hardy. Requires a sheltered, sunny situation and fertile soil that is not too dry. Propagate by seed in autumn.
D. fargesii illus. p.90.

DECUMARIA (Hydrangeaceae)
Genus of evergreen or deciduous, woody-stemmed, root climbers. Half hardy. Prefers sun and loamy, well-drained soil that does not dry out. Prune, if necessary, after flowering. Propagate by stem cuttings in late summer or early autumn.
D. sinensis. Evergreen, woody-stemmed, root climber. H to 6ft (2m) or more. Zones 7–9. Oval leaves, 1–3in (2.5–8cm) long, are often toothed. Conical clusters of small, honey-scented, cream flowers are produced in late spring and early summer.

DEINANTHE (Hydrangeaceae)
Genus of slow-growing perennials with creeping, underground rootstocks. Is useful for rock gardens and peat beds. Fully hardy. Needs shaded, moist soil. Propagate by division in spring or by seed when fresh.
D. bifida. Slow-growing, mound-forming perennial. H 8in (20cm), S 4–8in (10–20cm). Zones 5–9. Nodding, star-shaped, white flowers are borne in summer amid rounded, crinkled leaves with 2-lobed, lacerated tips.
D. caerulea. Slow-growing, mound-forming perennial. H 8in (20cm), S to 6in (15cm). Zones 5–9. Stems, each carrying a cluster of nodding, bowl-shaped, pale violet-blue flowers, rise above 3–4 oval, toothed leaves in summer.

DELOSPERMA (Aizoaceae)
Genus of densely branched, trailing, perennial, sometimes shrubby succulents, some with tuberous roots. Frost tender, min. 41°F (5°C). Requires full sun and very well-drained soil. Propagate by seed or stem cuttings in spring or summer.
D. tradescantioides. Spreading, perennial succulent. H 4in (10cm), S indefinite. Zone 10. Has long, trailing branches with broad, almost cylindrical, 3-angled, fleshy, light green leaves, 1¼in (3cm) long. Bears daisylike, white flowers in summer-autumn. Is easy to grow.

DELPHINIUM (Ranunculaceae)
Genus of perennials and annuals, grown for their spikes of irregularly cup-shaped, sometimes hooded, spurred flowers. Fully to half hardy. Needs an open, sunny position and fertile or rich, well-drained soil. Tall cultivars need staking and ample feeding and watering in spring and early summer. In spring remove thin growths from well-established plants,

leaving 5–7 strong shoots. If flower spikes are removed after they fade, a second flush may be produced in late summer, provided plants are fed and watered well. Propagate species and some *D. elatum* selections by seed in autumn or spring; *D. belladonna* cultivars by division or basal cuttings of young shoots in spring; *D. elatum* hybrids by cuttings only.
D. belladonna 'Blue Bees' (illus. p.192). Upright, branching perennial. H 3½–5ft (1.1–1.5m), S 2ft (60cm). Fully hardy, zones 3–9. Has palmate, divided leaves. In summer bears loose spikes, 12in (30cm) long, of widely spaced, single, occasionally semi-double, sky blue flowers, ¾in (2cm) or more wide, on freely branching spurs. Is useful for cutting. **'Lamartine'** has purple-blue flowers; those of **'Wendy'** are gentian blue.
D. brunonianum. Upright perennial. H and S to 6in (15cm). Fully hardy, zones 3–9. Hairy stems bear rounded, 3- or 5-lobed leaves. In early summer, flower stems each produce a spike, to 6in (15cm) long, of hooded, single, pale blue-purple flowers, 1½in (4cm) wide, with short, black spurs. Is good for a rock garden.
D. cardinale. Short-lived, upright perennial. H 3–6ft (1–2m), S 2ft (60cm). Half hardy, zones 8–9. In summer produces single, scarlet flowers, 1½in (4cm) wide, with yellow eyes, on spikes, 12–18in (30–45cm) long, above palmate, finely divided leaves.
D. chinense. See *D. grandiflorum.*
D. consolida. See *Consolida ambigua.*
D. elatum hybrids. Erect perennials. H 4½–7ft (1.35–2.2m), S 2½–3ft (75cm–1m). Fully hardy, zones 2–9. All have large, palmate leaves and, in summer, produce closely packed spikes, 16in–4ft (40cm–1.2m) long, of regularly spaced, semi-double, rarely fully double flowers, 3–4in (8–10cm) wide, in a range of colors from white to blue and purple, usually with contrasting eyes.
'Blue Dawn' (illus. p.192), H 6–7ft (2–2.2m), bears pinkish purple-flushed, pale blue flowers, with dark brown eyes, on spikes to 4ft (1.2m) long.
'Blue Nile' (illus. p.192), H 5–5½ft (1.5–1.7m), has rich blue flowers, with lightly blue-streaked, white eyes, on spikes to 27in (68cm) long.
'Bruce' (illus. p.192), H 5½–7ft (1.7–2.2m), has deep violet-purple flowers, silver-flushed towards centers and with gray-brown eyes, on spikes to 4ft (1.2m) long.
'Butterball' (illus. p.192), H 5–5½ft (1.5–1.7m), produces cream-eyed, white flowers, overlaid with very pale greenish yellow, on spikes to 20in (50cm) long.
'Chelsea Star' (illus. p.192), H 6ft (2m), produces rich deep violet flowers, with white eyes, on spikes to 3½ft (1.1m) long.
'Emily Hawkins' (illus. p.192), H 6–7ft (2–2.2m), has lilac-flushed, pale blue flowers, with fawn eyes, on spikes to 32in (80cm) long.
'Fanfare' (illus. p.192), H 6–7ft (2–2.2m), has pale blue to silvery

mauve flowers, with white-and-violet eyes, on spikes 2–2½ft (60–75cm) long.
'Fenella', H 3½–5ft (1.1–1.5m), bears purple-flushed, gentian blue flowers, with black eyes, on spikes to 3ft (1m) long.
'Gillian Dallas' (illus. p.192), H 6ft (2m), produces spikes, to 32in (80cm) long, of white-eyed, pale lilac flowers, shading to even paler lilac on outer edges.
'Langdon's Royal Flush' (illus. p.192), H 6ft (2m), has cream-eyed, pinkish purple flowers on spikes to 34in (85cm) long; upper petals are a darker shade than lower ones.
'Loch Leven' (illus. p.192), H 5½ft (1.7m), produces pale blue flowers, with white eyes, on spikes to 3ft (1m) long.
'Loch Nevis', H 6ft (2m), has blue flowers, with white eyes, on spikes to 3½ft (1.1m) long.
'Lord Butler' (illus. p.192), H 5–5½ft (1.5–1.7m), produces pale blue flowers, lightly flushed with pale lilac and with blue-marked, white eyes, on spikes to 30in (75cm) long.
'Mighty Atom' (illus. p.192), H 5–6ft (1.5–2m), has violet flowers, with violet-marked, yellowish brown eyes, on spikes to 2½ft (75cm) long.
'Olive Poppleton' (illus. p.192), H 6–8ft (2–2.5m), produces white flowers, with fawn eyes, on spikes to 3ft (1m) long.
Pacific Series is a group of short-lived perennials, H variable, often grown as annuals and available in single colors and as a mixture, although seedlings may not come true. Semi-double flowers are borne in spikes, 1½–3ft (45cm–1m) long.
'Sandpiper' (illus. p.192), H 3–4½ft (1–1.35m), has white flowers, with creamy brown eyes, on spikes to 2½ft (75cm) long.
'Spindrift' (illus. p.192), H 5½–6ft (1.7–2m), has spikes, to 3ft (1m) long, of pinkish purple flowers, overlaid pale blue and with creamy white eyes; towards centers, the pinkish purple becomes paler and the blue darker. Color varies from soil to soil; on acid soil, flowers have a green tinge.
'Strawberry Fair' (illus. p.192), H 5½ft (1.7m), has white-eyed, mulberry pink flowers on spikes to 31in (78cm) long.
'Sungleam' (illus. p.192), H 5½–6ft (1.7–2m), produces spikes, 16–30in (40–75cm) long, of white flowers, overlaid with pale yellow and with yellow eyes.
D. grandiflorum, syn. *D. chinense.*
'Blue Butterfly' (illus. p.192) is a short-lived, erect perennial, usually grown as an annual. H 1½ft (45cm), S 1ft (30cm). Fully hardy, zones 4–9. Has palmate, divided leaves. In summer produces loose, branching spikes, to 6in (15cm) long, of single, deep blue flowers, 1½in (3.5cm) wide. Is useful as a bedding plant.
D. nudicaule illus. p.295.
D. tatsienense. Short-lived, upright perennial. H 12in (30cm), S 2–4in (5–10cm). Fully hardy, zones 7–9. Loose spikes, to 6in (15cm) long, of small-spurred, single, bright blue

flowers, 1in (2.5cm) long, are borne in summer. Leaves are rounded to oval and deeply cut. Suits a rock garden. Needs gritty soil.

DENDROBIUM. See ORCHIDS.
D. aphyllum, syn. *D. pierardii* (illus. p.252). Deciduous, epiphytic orchid for an intermediate greenhouse. H to 24in (60cm). Zone 10. In early spring produces pairs of soft pink flowers, 1½in (4cm) across and each with a large, cream lip. Has oval leaves, 2–3in (5–8cm) long. Requires semi-shade in summer. Is best grown hanging from a bark slab.
D. chrysotoxum (illus. p.255). Deciduous, epiphytic orchid for an intermediate greenhouse. H 24in (60cm). Zone 10. Trusses of cup-shaped, deep yellow flowers, ¾in (2cm) across and with hairy, red-marked lips, are produced in spring. Oval leaves are 2–3in (5–8cm) long. Provide good light in summer.
D. infundibulum (illus. p.252). Evergreen, epiphytic orchid for a cool greenhouse. H 12in (30cm). Zone 10. In spring, stems each produce up to 6 pure white flowers, 3in (8cm) wide and each with a yellow-marked lip. Has oval leaves, 2–3in (5–8cm) long. Grow in semi-shade in summer.
D. nobile (illus. p.253). Deciduous, epiphytic orchid (often evergreen in cultivation) for a cool greenhouse. H 12in (30cm). Zone 10. Trusses of delicate, rose-pink flowers, 2in (5cm) across and each with a prominent, maroon lip, are borne along stems in spring. Oval leaves are 2–3in (5–8cm) long. Requires semi-shade in summer.
D. pierardii. See *D. aphyllum.*

DENDROCHILUM. See ORCHIDS.
D. glumaceum (Silver chain). Evergreen, epiphytic orchid for a cool greenhouse. H 4in (10cm). Zone 10. Pendent sprays of fragrant, pointed, orange-lipped, creamy white flowers, ½in (1cm) long, are produced in autumn. Narrowly oval leaves are 6in (15cm) long. Grow in semi-shade in summer.

DENDROMECON (Papaveraceae)
Genus of evergreen shrubs, grown for their foliage and showy flowers. Frost to half hardy. Plant against a south- or west-facing wall in cold areas. Requires full sun and very well-drained soil. Propagate by softwood cuttings in summer, by seed in autumn or spring, or by root cuttings in winter.
D. rigida illus. p.115.

DENNSTAEDTIA (Polypodiaceae)
Genus of deciduous or semi-evergreen ferns. Fully hardy. Grows best in shade and in humus-rich, moist soil. Remove fading fronds regularly. Propagate by division in spring.
D. punctiloba (Hay-scented fern). Deciduous, creeping fern. H and S 12in (30cm). Zones 3–8. Has oval to triangular, much-divided, delicate, lacelike, green fronds that die back in winter.

Dendrobenthamia capitata. See *Cornus capitata.*

Dentaria enneaphylla. See *Cardamine enneaphyllos.*

Dentaria pentaphylla. See *Cardamine pentaphyllos.*

DESCHAMPSIA (Gramineae). See GRASSES, BAMBOOS, RUSHES, and SEDGES.

D. caespitosa (Tufted hairgrass). Evergreen, tuft-forming, perennial grass. H to 3ft (1m), S 10–12in (25–30cm). Fully hardy, zones 5–9. Has dense, narrow, rough-edged, dark green leaves. In summer produces dainty, open panicles of minute, pale brown spikelets that last well into winter. Tolerates sun or shade.

DESFONTAINIA (Loganiaceae) Genus of evergreen shrubs, grown for their foliage and showy, tubular flowers. Frost to half hardy. Provide shelter in cold areas. Needs some shade, particularly in dry regions, and moist, peaty, preferably acid soil. Propagate by semi-ripe cuttings in summer.

D. spinosa illus. p.111.

DESMODIUM (Leguminosae) Genus of perennials and deciduous shrubs and sub-shrubs, grown for their flowers. Fully to frost hardy. Needs full sun and well-drained soil. Propagate by softwood cuttings in late spring or by seed in autumn. May also be divided in spring.

D. tiliifolium illus. p.135.

DEUTZIA (Hydrangeaceae) Genus of deciduous shrubs, grown for their profuse, 5-petaled flowers. Fully to frost hardy. Needs full sun and fertile, well-drained soil. Plants benefit from regular thinning out of old shoots after flowering. Propagate by softwood cuttings in summer.

D. x *elegantissima* 'Fasciculata'. Deciduous, upright shrub. H 6ft (2m), S 5ft (1.5m). Fully hardy, zones 5–8. From late spring to early summer produces large clusters of 5-petaled, pale pink flowers. Leaves are oval, toothed, and green. 'Rosealind' illus. p.130.

D. gracilis illus. p.121.

D. 'Joconde'. Deciduous, upright shrub. H and S 5ft (1.5m). Fully hardy, zones 5–8. Bears 5-petaled, white flowers, striped purple outside, in early summer. Oval, green leaves are long-pointed.

D. longifolia. Deciduous, arching shrub. H 6ft (2m), S 10ft (3m). Fully hardy, zones 7–9. Large clusters of 5-petaled, deep pink flowers are produced from early to mid-summer. Narrowly lance-shaped leaves are gray-green. 'Veitchii' illus. p.108.

D. 'Magicien'. Deciduous, upright shrub. H and S 5ft (1.5m). Fully hardy, zones 6–9. In early summer produces large, 5-petaled flowers with wavy petals, pink inside, white with deep pink stripes outside. Has oval, green leaves.

D. x *magnifica.* Vigorous, deciduous, upright shrub. H 8ft (2.5m), S 6ft (2m). Fully hardy, zones 5–9. Bears narrowly oval, bright green leaves and in early summer produces dense

clusters of 5-petaled, pure white flowers. 'Staphyleoides' illus. p.104.

D. monbeigii illus. p.126.

D. 'Mont Rose' illus. p.129.

D. pulchra. Vigorous, deciduous, upright shrub. H 8ft (2.5m), S 6ft (2m). Frost hardy, zones 7–9. Has peeling, orange-brown bark and lance-shaped, dark green leaves. Slender, pendulous panicles of 5-petaled, pink-tinged, white flowers appear in late spring and early summer.

D. x *rosea* illus. p.122.

D. scabra illus. p.104. 'Flore Pleno' is a deciduous, upright shrub. H 10ft (3m), S 6ft (2m). Fully hardy, zones 5–9. Narrowly oval, dark green leaves set off dense, upright clusters of double, white flowers, purplish pink outside, that are produced from early to mid-summer.

D. setchuenensis. Deciduous, upright shrub. H 6ft (2m), S 5ft (1.5m). Frost hardy, zones 7–9. Small, 5-petaled, white flowers are borne in broad clusters in early and mid-summer. Bears narrowly oval, rough, dark gray-green leaves.

DIANELLA (Liliaceae) Flax lily Genus of evergreen, summer-flowering perennials. Frost to half hardy; is suitable outdoors only in mild areas and elsewhere requires a cold greenhouse or frame. Needs sun and well-drained, neutral to acid soil. Propagate by division or seed in spring.

D. caerulea. Evergreen, tuft-forming perennial. H 30in (75cm), S 12in (30cm). Half hardy, zones 9–10. In summer produces panicles of small, star-shaped, blue flowers, above grasslike leaves, followed by blue berries.

D. tasmanica illus. p.212.

DIANTHUS (Caryophyllaceae) Carnation, Pink Genus of evergreen or semi-evergreen, mainly summer-flowering perennials, annuals, and biennials, grown for their mass of flowers, often scented, some of which are excellent for cutting. Carnations and pinks (see below) are excellent for cut flowers and border decoration, the biennial *D. barbatus* (Sweet William) is suitable for bedding and smaller, tuft-forming species and cultivars are good for rock gardens. Fully to half hardy. Needs an open, sunny position and well-drained, slightly alkaline soil, except for *D. pavonius*, which prefers acid soil. Dead-heading of repeat-flowering types is beneficial. Tall forms of carnations and pinks have a loose habit and need staking. Propagate border carnations by layering in late summer, other named forms by softwood cuttings in late spring, and species by seed at any time. Is susceptible to rust, red spider mite, and virus infection through aphids, but many cultivars are available from virus-free stock.

Carnations and pinks have narrowly lance-shaped, silvery- or gray-green leaves that are scattered up flower stems. Leaves may coil outwards on carnations. They are divided into the

following groups, all with self-colored and bicolored cultivars.

Carnations

Border carnations are annuals or evergreen perennials that flower prolifically once in mid-summer and are good for border decoration and cutting. Each stem bears 5 or more often scented, semi-double or double flowers, to 3in (8cm) across; picotee forms (with petals outlined in a darker color) are available. H 2½–3½ft (75cm–1.1m), S to 1ft (30cm). Frost hardy, zones 4–8.

Perpetual-flowering carnations are evergreen perennials that flower year-round if grown in a greenhouse, most prolifically in summer. They are normally grown for cut flowers: flower stems should be disbudded, leaving one terminal bud per stem. Fully double flowers, to 4in (10cm) across, are usually unscented and are often flecked or streaked. H 3–5ft (1–1.5m), S 1ft (30cm) or more.

Spray forms are not disbudded so have 5 or more flowers per stem, each 2–2½in (5–6cm) across. H 2–3ft (60cm–1m), S to 1ft (30cm).

Pinks

Evergreen, clump-forming perennials, grown for border decoration and cutting, that in summer produce a succession of basal shoots, each bearing 4–6 fragrant, single to fully double flowers, 1½–2½in (3.5–6cm) across. H 12–18in (30–45cm), S 9–12in (23–30cm) or more. Frost hardy, zones 4–8.

Old-fashioned pinks have a low, spreading habit and produce masses of flowers in one flowering period in mid-summer. Mule types (a border carnation crossed with a Sweet William) and laced types (in which the central color extends as a loop around each petal) are available.

Modern pinks, obtained by crossing an old-fashioned pink with a perpetual-flowering carnation, are more vigorous than old-fashioned pinks, and are repeat-flowering with 2 or 3 main flushes of flowers in summer.

D. 'Albisola' (illus. p.239). Perpetual-flowering carnation. Fully double flowers are clear tangerine orange.

D. 'Aldridge Yellow' (illus. p.239). Border carnation. Semi-double flowers are clear yellow.

D. 'Alice' (illus. p.238). Modern pink. Has clove-scented, semi-double, ivory white flowers, each with a bold, crimson eye.

D. alpinus illus. p.318.

D. 'Annabelle' illus. p.319.

D. armeria (Deptford pink). Evergreen, tuft-forming perennial. H 12in (30cm), S 18in (45cm). Fully hardy, zones 4–8. Has narrowly lance-shaped, dark green leaves. In summer, tall stems each carry small, 5-petaled, cerise flowers in small bunches. Is good for a rock garden or bank.

D. 'Artic'. Perpetual-flowering, spray carnation. Fully double flowers are white with pink flecks.

D. 'Astor' (illus. p.239). Perpetual-flowering carnation. Has fully double,

scarlet flowers; is one of the few scented, perpetual-flowering cultivars.

D. barbatus (Sweet William). **Monarch Series** (auricula-eyed) illus. p.271. **Roundabout Series** (dwarf) illus. p.270.

D. 'Bookham Perfume' (illus. p.239). Perennial border carnation. Has scented, semi-double, crimson flowers.

D. 'Bombardier'. Evergreen, tuft-forming perennial. H and S 4in (10cm). Frost hardy, zones 4–8. Has a basal tuft of linear, gray-green leaves and, in summer, small, double, scarlet flowers. Is good for a rock garden.

D. 'Borello' (illus. p.239). Perpetual-flowering carnation. Fully double flowers are yellow.

D. 'Bovey Belle'. Modern pink. Has clove-scented, fully double, bright purple flowers that are excellent for cutting.

D. 'Brympton Red'. Old-fashioned pink. Flowers are single, bright crimson with deeper shading.

D. caesius. See *D. gratianopolitanus.*

D. carthusianorum illus. p.294.

D. 'Charles Musgrave'. See *D.* 'Musgrave's Pink'.

D. chinensis (China pink). Slow-growing, bushy annual. H and S 6–12in (15–30cm). Fully to half hardy. Lance-shaped leaves are pale or mid-green. Tubular, single or double flowers, 1in (2.5cm) or more wide and with open, spreading petals, in shades of pink, red, or white, are produced in summer and early autumn. **Baby Doll Series** illus. p.268; 'Fire Carpet' illus. p.271; 'Heddewigii', H 12in (30cm), has flowers in mixed colors.

D. 'Christine Hough' (illus. p.239). Perennial border carnation. Semi-double flowers are apricot, overlaid and streaked with rose-pink.

D. 'Christopher' (illus. p.238). Modern pink. Produces lightly scented, fully double, bright salmon red flowers.

D. 'Clara' (illus. p.239). Perpetual-flowering carnation. Fully double flowers are yellow with salmon flecks.

D. 'Constance Finnis'. See *D.* 'Fair Folly'.

D. 'Dad's Favorite'. Old-fashioned pink. Bears scented, semi-double, white flowers with chocolate brown lacing.

D. deltoides (Maiden pink). Evergreen, mat-forming, basal-tufted perennial. H 6in (15cm), S 12in (30cm). Fully hardy, zones 5–8. In summer, small, 5-petaled, white, pink, or cerise flowers are borne singly above tiny, lance-shaped leaves. Is good for a rock garden or bank. Trim back after flowering. 'Flashing Light' illus. p.320.

D. 'Denis'. Modern pink. A free-flowering cultivar, it has strongly clove-scented, fully double, magenta flowers.

D. 'Doris' (illus. p.238). Modern pink. Has compact growth and an abundance of fragrant, semi-double, pale pink flowers, each with a salmon red ring towards base of flower. Is one of the most widely grown cultivars and provides excellent flowers for cutting.

D. 'Edenside'. Perennial border carnation. Semi-double flowers are clear white.

D. 'Emile Paré' (illus. p.238). Old-fashioned, mule pink. Has clusters of semi-double, salmon pink flowers and, unusually for a pink, green foliage.

D. 'Eva Humphries' (illus. p.238). Perennial border carnation. Has fragrant, semi-double flowers with white petals outlined in purple.

D. 'Fair Folly', syn. *D.* 'Constance Finnis' (illus. p.238). Modern pink. Flowers are single and of variable color, usually dusky pink to dusky purple with 2 white splashes on each petal.

D. 'Forest Treasure' (illus. p.238). Perennial border carnation. Has double, white flowers with reddish purple splashes on each petal.

D. 'Freckles'. Modern pink. A compact cultivar, it has fully double flowers that are red-speckled and dusky pink.

D. 'Gran's Favourite' (illus. p.238). Old-fashioned pink. Bears fragrant, semi-double, white flowers with deep raspberry lacing.

D. gratianopolitanus, syn. *D. caesius*, illus. p.317.

D. 'Green Eyes'. See *D.* 'Musgrave's Pink'.

D. haematocalyx. Evergreen, tuft-forming perennial. H 5in (12cm), S 4in (10cm). Fully hardy, zones 5–8. Leaves are lance-shaped and usually glaucous. Bears 5-petaled, toothed, beige-backed, deep pink flowers on slender stems in summer. Suits a rock garden or scree.

D. 'Happiness' (illus. p.239). Perennial border carnation. Semi-double flowers are yellow, striped scarlet-orange.

D. 'Haytor' (illus. p.238). Modern pink. Fully double, white flowers, borne on strong stems, have a good scent. Is widely grown, especially to provide cut flowers.

D. 'Hidcote'. Evergreen, tufted, compact perennial. H and S 4in (10cm). Fully hardy, zones 5–8. Bears a basal tuft of linear, spiky, gray-green leaves and, in summer, double, red flowers. Suits a rock garden.

D. 'Houndspool Ruby', syn. *D.* 'Ruby', *D.* 'Ruby Doris' (illus. p.238). Modern pink. Is a sport of *D.* 'Doris' with strongly scented, ruby pink flowers that each have a deeper eye.

D. 'Ibiza'. Perpetual-flowering spray carnation. Fully double flowers are shell pink.

D. 'Iceberg'. Modern pink. Fragrant flowers are semi-double and pure white. Has a somewhat looser habit than *D.* 'Haytor'.

D. 'Joy' (illus. p.238). Modern pink. Produces semi-double, pink flowers that are strongly scented and good for cutting.

D. 'La Bourbille'. See *D.* 'La Bourboule'.

D. 'La Bourboule', syn. *D.* 'La Bourbille', illus. p.318.

D. 'Little Jock' illus. p.317.

D. 'London Delight'. Old-fashioned pink. Fragrant flowers are semi-double and lavender, laced with purple.

D. 'Manon'. Perpetual-flowering carnation. Is one of the best deep pink cultivars with fully double flowers.

D. 'Mars'. Evergreen, tuft-forming perennial. H and S 4in (10cm). Frost hardy, zones 5–8. Has small, double, cherry red flowers in summer. Bears a basal tuft of linear, gray-green leaves. Is good in a rock garden.

D. 'Master Stuart'. Perennial border carnation. Has striking, semi-double flowers that are white with scarlet stripes.

D. microlepis illus. p.318.

D. 'Monica Wyatt'. Modern pink. Very fragrant, fully double flowers are cyclamen pink, each with a magenta eye. Is very free-flowering and provides excellent cut flowers.

D. monspessulanus. Evergreen, mat-forming perennial. H 12in (30cm), S 4–6in (10–15cm). Fully hardy, zones 5–8. In summer, masses of strongly fragrant, 5-petaled, deeply fringed, pale lavender flowers rise on slender stems above short tufts of fine, grasslike leaves. Is suitable for growing in a rock garden. Requires gritty soil.

D. 'Mrs. Sinkins' (illus. p.238). Old-fashioned pink. Flowers are heavily scented, fringed, fully double, and white.

D. 'Murcia'. Perpetual-flowering carnation. Has fully double, deep golden yellow flowers.

D. 'Musgrave's Pink', syn. *D.* 'Charles Musgrave', *D.* 'Green Eyes' (illus. p.238). Old-fashioned pink. An old cultivar, it bears single, white flowers with green eyes.

D. myrtinervius illus. p.318.

D. neglectus. See *D. pavonius*.

D. 'Nina' (illus. p.239). Perpetual-flowering carnation. Is one of the best crimson cultivars. Fully double flowers have smooth-edged petals.

D. 'Nives' (illus. p.238). Perpetual-flowering carnation. Fully double flowers are clear white and are borne on short stems.

D. pavonius, syn. *D. neglectus*, illus. p.315.

D. 'Pierrot' (illus. p.238). Perpetual-flowering carnation. Attractive, fully double flowers are light rose-lavender with purple-edged petals.

D. 'Pike's Pink' illus. p.318.

D. 'Pink Calypso'. See *D.* 'Truly Yours'.

D. 'Pink Jewel' (illus. p.238). Modern pink. Has strongly scented, semi-double, pink flowers.

D. 'Prudence' (illus. p.238). Old-fashioned pink. Fragrant flowers are semi-double and pinkish white with purple lacing. Has a spreading habit.

D. 'Raggio di Sole' (illus. p.239). Perpetual-flowering carnation. Fully double flowers are bright orange.

D. 'Red Barrow'. Perpetual-flowering, spray carnation. Fully double, bright scarlet flowers are borne in abundance.

D. 'Ruby'. See *D.* 'Houndspool Ruby'.

D. 'Ruby Doris'. See *D.* 'Houndspool Ruby'.

D. 'Sam Barlow'. Old-fashioned pink. Bears very fragrant, frilly, fully double, white flowers with chocolate brown centers.

D. 'Show Ideal'. Modern pink. Flat-petaled, semi-double flowers are white

with red eyes and are strongly scented. Is excellent for exhibition.

D. 'Sops-in-Wine'. Old-fashioned pink. Bears fragrant, single, maroon flowers with white markings.

D. superbus. Evergreen, mat-forming perennial. H to 8in (20cm), S 6in (15cm). Fully hardy, zones 5–8. Has narrowly lance-shaped, pale green leaves. In summer, slender stems bear very fragrant, 5-petaled, deeply fringed, pink flowers with darker centers. Suits a rock garden.

D. 'Tigré'. Perpetual-flowering carnation. Has fully double, yellow flowers with a uniform, pinkish purple stripe and edging to each petal.

D. 'Tony'. Perpetual-flowering, spray carnation. Fully double flowers are yellow with red stripes.

D. 'Truly Yours', syn. *D.* 'Pink Calypso' (illus. p.238). Perpetual-flowering carnation. Fully double flowers are a good pink.

D. 'Valda Wyatt' (illus. p.238). Modern pink. Flowers are very fragrant, fully double and rose-lavender.

D. 'Valencia' (illus. p.239). Perpetual-flowering carnation. Has fully double, golden orange flowers.

D. 'White Ladies' (illus. p.238). Old-fashioned pink. Bears very fragrant, fully double, white flowers with greenish centers.

D. 'Widecombe Fair'. Modern pink. Semi-double flowers, borne on strong stems, are of unusual coloring—peach-apricot, opening to blush pink.

DIAPENSIA (Diapensiaceae)
Genus of evergreen, spreading sub-shrubs, suitable for rock gardens and troughs. Fully hardy. Needs partial shade and peaty, sandy, acid soil. Is very difficult to grow in hot, dry climates at low altitudes. Propagate by seed in spring or by semi-ripe cuttings in summer.

D. lapponica. Evergreen, spreading sub-shrub. H and S 3in (7cm). Zones 2–5. Has tufts of small, rounded, leathery leaves. Carries solitary tiny, bowl-shaped, white flowers in early summer.

DIASCIA (Scrophulariaceae)
Genus of summer- and autumn-flowering annuals and perennials, some of which are semi-evergreen, grown for their tubular, pink flowers. Is suitable for banks and borders. Frost hardy. Needs sun and humus-rich, well-drained soil that is not too dry. Cut back old stems in spring. Propagate by softwood cuttings in late spring, by semi-ripe cuttings in summer, or by seed in autumn.

D. cordata illus. p.293.

D. rigescens illus. p.293.

D. 'Ruby Field'. Mat-forming perennial. H 3in (8cm), S 6in (15cm). Zones 7–9. Heart-shaped, pale green leaves clothe short, wiry stems. Produces tubular, wide-lipped, salmon pink flowers throughout summer.

D. vigilis. Prostrate perennial. H 12–16in (30–40cm), S 24in (60cm). Zones 7–9. Leaves are small, rounded, toothed, and pale green. Upright branchlets carry loose spikes of

flattish, outward-facing, pale pink flowers in summer.

DICENTRA (Papaveraceae)
Genus of perennials, grown for their elegant sprays of pendent flowers. Fully hardy. Does best in semi-shade and humus-rich, moist but well-drained soil. Propagate by division when dormant in late winter, species also by seed in autumn.

D. cucullaria illus. p.302.

D. eximia 'Spring Morning' illus. p.235.

D. formosa. Spreading, tufted perennial. H 18in (45cm), S 12in (30cm). Zones 4–8. In spring-summer produces slender, arching sprays of pendent, heart-shaped, pink or dull red flowers above oval, finely cut, gray-green leaves. **'Adrian Bloom'** has rich carmine pink flowers and grayer foliage.

D. peregrina. Tuft-forming perennial. H 3in (8cm), S to 2in (5cm). Zones 4–7. Locket-shaped, pink flowers appear in spring-summer above fernlike, blue-green leaves. Needs gritty soil. Is suitable for an alpine house but is difficult to grow.

D. spectabilis illus. p.205. f. *alba* illus. p.200.

D. 'Stuart Boothman'. Tufted perennial. H 18in (45cm), S 12in (30cm). Zones 4–8. Arching sprays of heart-shaped, carmine flowers are borne in spring-summer above oval, finely cut, deep gray-green leaves.

DICHELOSTEMMA (Liliaceae)
Genus of summer-flowering bulbs, grown for their dense flower heads on leafless stems. Is related to *Brodiaea* and is similar to *Allium* in appearance. Frost hardy, but in cold areas grow in a sheltered position. Needs a sunny site and well-drained soil. Water freely in spring, but dry out after flowering. Propagate by seed in autumn or spring or by offsets in autumn before growth commences.

D. congestum, syn. *Brodiaea congesta*, illus. p.337.

D. ida-maia, syn. *Brodiaea ida-maia*. Early summer-flowering bulb. H to 3ft (1m), S 3–4in (8–10cm). Zones 6–10. Long, narrow leaves are semi-erect and basal. Leafless stem has a dense head of ³/₄–1in (2–2.5cm) long flowers, each with a red tube and 6 green petals.

D. pulchellum, syn. *Brodiaea pulchella*. Early summer-flowering bulb. H 12–24in (30–60cm), S 3–4in (8–10cm). Zones 6–10. Long, narrow leaves are semi-erect and basal. Leafless stem produces a dense head of narrowly funnel-shaped, pale to deep violet flowers, ¹/₂–³/₄in (1–2cm) long, with violet bracts.

DICHORISANDRA (Commelinaceae)
Genus of erect, clump-forming, evergreen perennials, grown for their ornamental foliage. Frost tender, min. 59–68°F (15–20°C). Prefers fertile, moist but well-drained soil, humid conditions, and partial shade. Propagate by division in spring or by stem cuttings in summer.

D. reginae illus. p.211.

DICKSONIA (Cyathaceae)
Genus of evergreen or semi-evergreen, treelike ferns that resemble palms and that are sometimes used to provide height in fern plantings. Half hardy to frost tender, min. 41°F (5°C). Needs semi-shade and humus-rich, moist soil. Remove faded fronds regularly. Propagate by spores in summer.
D. antarctica illus. p.184.

DICTAMNUS (Rutaceae)
Genus of summer-flowering perennials. Fully hardy. Requires full sun and fertile, well-drained soil. Resents disturbance. Propagate by seed sown in late summer when fresh.
D. albus illus. p.201. var. *purpureus* illus. p.203.
Didiscus coeruleus. See *Trachymene coerulea.*

DIEFFENBACHIA (Araceae)
Dumb cane, Leopard lily
Genus of evergreen, tufted perennials, grown for their foliage. Frost tender, min. 59°F (15°C). Grow in fertile, well-drained soil and partial shade. Propagate in spring or summer by stem cuttings or pieces of leafless stem placed horizontally in compost. Contains poisonous sap that should be kept away from mouth, eyes, and skin. Scale insect or red spider mite may be troublesome.
D. 'Amoena', syn. *D. seguine* 'Amoena'. Evergreen, robust, tufted perennial. H to 6ft (2m), S 3ft (1m). Zone 10. Broadly lance-shaped, glossy leaves, to 18in (45cm) long, are dark green with creamy white bars along lateral veins. Intermittently produces insignificant, greenish white flowers that are clustered on the spadix and are surrounded by a narrow, leaflike spathe.
D. 'Exotica', syn. *D. seguine* 'Exotica', illus. p.221.
D. 'Memoria'. See *D. seguine* 'Memoria Corsii'.
D. seguine. Evergreen, tufted perennial. H and S 3ft (1m) or more. Zone 10. Broadly lance-shaped leaves, to 18in (45cm) long, are glossy and dark green. Insignificant, tiny, greenish white flowers, clustered on the spadix, are surrounded by a narrow, leaflike spathe that appears intermittently.
'Amoena', see *D. 'Amoena'*.
'Exotica', see *D. 'Exotica'*. **'Memoria Corsii'** (syn. *D. 'Memoria'*) has gray-green leaves, marked dark green and spotted white. **'Rudolph Roehrs'** (syn. *D.s. 'Roehrsii'*) illus. p.224.

DIERAMA (Iridaceae)
Angel's fishing-rods, Wandflower
Genus of evergreen, clump-forming, summer-flowering corms with pendent, funnel- or bell-shaped flowers on long, arching, wiry stems. Flourishes near pools. Frost to half hardy. Prefers a warm, sheltered, sunny site and well-drained soil that should be kept moist in summer when in growth. Dies down partially in winter. Propagate by division of corms in spring or by seed in autumn or spring. Resents disturbance, and divisions take a year or more to settle and start flowering again.

D. 'Blackbird'. Evergreen, upright perennial. H 5ft (1.5m), S 1ft (30cm). Frost hardy, zones 7–9. Produces cascades of nodding, funnel-shaped, violet-mauve flowers on wiry, pendulous stems in summer above grasslike leaves.
D. pendulum illus. p.336.
D. pulcherrimum illus. p.335.
D. pumilum. Vigorous, evergreen, upright perennial. H 30in (75cm), S 12in (30cm). Frost hardy, zones 8–9. In summer freely produces nodding, funnel-shaped flowers, in shades of pink and violet, on wiry stems. Leaves are grasslike.

DIERVILLA (Caprifoliaceae)
Genus of deciduous, summer-flowering shrubs, grown for their overall appearance. Is similar to *Weigela*. Frost hardy. Tolerates full light or partial shade and moderately fertile, well-drained soil. For a more shapely shrub remove 2- and 3-year-old stems in winter or after flowering. Propagate by semi-ripe cuttings in late summer or by hardwood cuttings in autumn.
D. sessilifolia (Southern bush honeysuckle). Deciduous, spreading shrub. H and S 3–5ft (1–1.5m). Zones 5–8. Narrowly oval, pointed, serrated, green leaves are often copper-tinted when young. Has terminal and lateral clusters of tubular, pale yellow flowers in summer. To treat as an herbaceous perennial, cut back to ground level each spring and apply a mulch and a fertilizer.

DIETES (Iridaceae)
Genus of evergreen, irislike, rhizomatous perennials, grown for their attractive flowers in spring or summer. Half hardy. Needs sun or partial shade and humus-rich, well-drained soil that does not dry out excessively. Propagate by seed in autumn or spring or by division in spring (although divisions do not become re-established very readily).
D. bicolor illus. p.337.
D. iridioides, syn. *D. vegeta* of gardens (African iris). Evergreen, spring- and summer-flowering, rhizomatous perennial. H to 2ft (60cm), S 1–2ft (30–60cm). Zones 8–10. Bears sword-shaped, semi-erect, basal leaves in a spreading fan. Branching, wiry stems bear irislike, white flowers, 2½–3in (6–8cm) across. Each of the 3 large petals has a central, yellow mark.
D. vegeta of gardens. See *D. iridioides.*

DIGITALIS (Scrophulariaceae)
Foxglove
Genus of biennials and perennials, some of which are evergreen, grown for their flower spikes in summer. Fully to frost hardy. Species mentioned grow in most conditions, even dry, exposed sites, but do best in semi-shade and moist but well-drained soil. Propagate by seed in autumn.
D. ambigua. See *D. grandiflora.*
D. canariensis. See *Isoplexis canariensis.*
D. ferruginea illus. p.202.
D. grandiflora, syn. *D. ambigua* (Yellow foxglove). Evergreen, clump-

forming perennial. H 30in (75cm), S 12in (30cm). Fully hardy, zones 4–9. Racemes of downward-pointing, tubular, creamy yellow flowers appear in summer above a rosette of oval to oblong, smooth, strongly veined leaves.
D. lutea. Upright perennial. H 30in (75cm), S 12in (30cm). Fully hardy, zones 5–9. In summer, delicate spires of downward-pointing, narrowly tubular, creamy yellow flowers are borne above a rosette of oval, smooth, green leaves.
D. x *mertonensis.* Clump-forming perennial. H 30in (75cm), S 12in (30cm). Fully hardy, zones 5–9. Bears spikes of downward-pointing, tubular, rose-mauve flowers in summer, above a rosette of oval, hairy, soft leaves. Divide after flowering.
D. purpurea. Upright, short-lived perennial, grown as a biennial. H 3–5ft (1–1.5m), S 2ft (60cm). Fully hardy, zones 4–8. Has a rosette of oval, rough, deep green leaves and, in summer, tall spikes of tubular flowers in shades of pink, red, purple, or white. f. *alba* illus. p.262.

DILLENIA (Dilleniaceae)
Genus of evergreen or briefly deciduous, spring-flowering trees, grown for their flowers and foliage and for shade. Frost tender, min. 61°F (16°C). Needs moisture-retentive, fertile soil and full light. Water potted plants freely while in full growth, less in winter. Propagate by seed in spring.
D. indica (Elephant apple). Briefly deciduous, spreading tree. H and S 25–40ft (8–12m). Zone 10. Has oval, serrated, boldly parallel-veined, glossy leaves, each 1ft (30cm) long. Nodding, cup-shaped, white flowers, each 6–8in (15–20cm) wide, are produced in spring, followed by edible, globular, greenish fruits.

DIMORPHOTHECA (Compositae)
African daisy, Cape marigold
Genus of annuals, perennials, and evergreen sub-shrubs. Half hardy. Grow in sun and in fertile, very well-drained soil. Dead-head to prolong flowering. Propagate annuals by seed sown under glass in mid-spring, perennials by semi-ripe cuttings in summer. Is susceptible to botrytis in wet summers.
D. annua. See *D. pluvialis.*
D. barberiae. See *Osteospermum jucundum.*
D. pluvialis, syn. *D. annua*, illus. p.263.

DIONAEA (Droseraceae)
Genus of evergreen, insectivorous, rosette-forming perennials. Frost tender, min. 41°F (5°C). Needs partial shade and a humid atmosphere; grow in a mixture of peat and moss, kept constantly moist. Propagate by seed or division in spring.
D. muscipula illus. p.261.

DIONYSIA (Primulaceae)
Genus of evergreen, cushion-forming perennials. Fully hardy. Grow in an alpine house in sun and very gritty, well-drained soil. Position deep collar

of grit under cushion and ensure good ventilation at all times. Dislikes winter wet. Propagate by softwood cuttings in summer. Is susceptible to botrytis.
D. aretioides illus. p.311.
D. lamingtonii. Evergreen, prostrate perennial. H 1in (2.5cm), S 6in (15cm). Zones 5–7. Oval, gray-green leaves in rosettes form tight cushions. Small, stemless, 5-petaled, bright yellow flowers appear in early spring. Is diffficult to grow.
D. tapetodes illus. p.312.

DIOON (Zamiaceae)
Genus of evergreen shrubs, grown for their palmlike appearance. Frost tender, min. 55–64°F (13–18°C). Needs full sun and fertile, well-drained soil. Water potted specimens moderately, less when not in full growth. Propagate by seed in spring.
D. edule (Virgin's palm). Very slow-growing, evergreen, palmlike shrub, eventually with a thick, upright trunk. H 6–12ft (2–4m), S 5–10ft (1.5–3m). Zone 10. Leaves are featherlike, 2–4ft (60cm–1.2m) long, with spine-tipped, deep blue-green leaflets.

DIOSCOREA (Dioscoreaceae)
Genus of tuberous perennials, some of which are succulent, and herbaceous or evergreen, twining climbers, grown mainly for their decorative leaves. Insignificant flowers are generally yellow. Frost tender, min. 41–55°F (5–13°C). Prefers full sun or partial shade and fertile, well-drained soil. Propagate by division or by cutting off sections of tuber in spring or autumn, or by seed in spring.
D. discolor illus. p.177.
D. elephantipes, syn. *Testudinaria elephantipes*, illus. p.387.

DIOSMA (Rutaceae)
Genus of evergreen, wiry-stemmed shrubs, grown for their flowers and overall appearance. Frost tender, min. 45°F (7°C). Needs full light and well-drained, neutral to acid soil. Water potted specimens moderately, less when not in full growth. To create a compact habit shorten flowered stems after flowering. Propagate by seed in spring or by semi-ripe cuttings in late summer.
D. ericoides (Breath-of-Heaven). Fast-growing, evergreen, loosely rounded shrub. H and S 1–2ft (30–60cm). Zone 10. Aromatic, needlelike leaves are crowded on stems. In winter-spring carries a profusion of small, fragrant, 5-petaled, white flowers, sometimes tinted red.

DIOSPHAERA. See TRACHELIUM.

DIOSPYROS (Ebenaceae)
Genus of deciduous or evergreen trees and shrubs, grown for their foliage and fruits. Fully to frost hardy. Needs full sun and does best in hot summers. Requires fertile, well-drained soil. To obtain fruits, plants of both sexes should be grown. Propagate by seed in autumn.
D. kaki (Chinese persimmon, Kaki). Deciduous, spreading tree. H 30ft (10m), S 22ft (7m). Frost hardy, zones

457

7–10. Oval, glossy, dark green leaves turn orange, red, and purple in autumn. Tiny, yellowish white flowers in summer are followed on female trees by large, edible, rounded, yellow or orange fruits.

D. lotus (Date plum). Deciduous, spreading tree. H 30ft (10m), S 20ft (6m). Fully hardy, zones 6–10. Has oval, glossy, dark green leaves, tiny, red-tinged, green flowers from mid- to late summer and, on female trees, unpalatable, rounded, purple or yellow fruits.

DIPCADI (Liliaceae)
Genus of spring-flowering bulbs, grown mainly for botanical interest. Frost hardy, but will not tolerate cold, wet winters, so is best grown in a cold frame or alpine house. Needs a warm, sunny situation and light, well-drained soil. Is dormant in summer. Propagate by seed in autumn.

D. serotinum illus. p.363.

DIPELTA (Caprifoliaceae)
Genus of deciduous shrubs, with bold, long-pointed leaves, grown for their showy, tubular flowers and peeling bark. After flowering, bracts beneath flowers enlarge and become papery and brown, surrounding the fruits. Fully hardy. Requires sun or semi-shade and fertile, well-drained soil. Benefits from the occasional removal of old shoots after flowering. Propagate by softwood cuttings in summer.

D. floribunda illus. p.85.
D. yunnanensis illus. p.84.

DIPHYLLEIA (Berberidaceae)
Genus of perennials with creeping rootstocks and umbrellalike leaves. Is best suited to woodland gardens. Fully hardy. Needs semi-shade and moist soil. Propagate by division in spring or by seed in autumn.

D. cymosa (Umbrella leaf). Rounded perennial. H 24in (60cm), S 12in (30cm). Zones 7–9. Has large, bold, rounded, 2-lobed leaves. In spring bears loose, terminal heads of inconspicuous, white flowers followed by indigo blue berries on red stalks.

DIPIDAX, syn. ONIXOTIS (Liliaceae)
Genus of spring-flowering corms, cultivated mainly for botanical interest. Half hardy. Requires sun and well-drained soil. Plant corms in early autumn and keep them watered until after flowering. Dry off in summer. Propagate by seed in autumn.

D. triquetra. Spring-flowering corm. H 8–12in (20–30cm), S 2–3in (5–8cm). Zone 9. Long, narrow leaves are semi-erect and basal. Carries a spike of flattish, star-shaped, white flowers, each narrow petal having a basal, red mark.

Diplacus glutinosus. See Mimulus aurantiacus.

DIPLADENIA. See MANDEVILLA.

DIPLARRHENA (Iridaceae)
Genus of one species of summer-flowering perennial. Half hardy. Needs

sun and well-drained soil. Propagate by seed or division in spring.
D. moraea illus. p.234.

Diplazium japonicum. See Lunathyrium japonicum.

DIPTERONIA (Aceraceae)
Genus of deciduous trees, grown for their foliage and fruits. Fully hardy. Needs full sun and fertile, well-drained soil. Propagate by softwood cuttings in summer or by seed in autumn.

D. sinensis. Deciduous, spreading, sometimes shrubby tree. H 30ft (10m), S 20ft (6m). Zones 7–9. Large, green leaves are divided into 7–11 oval to lance-shaped leaflets. Inconspicuous, greenish white flowers in summer are followed by large clusters of winged, red fruits.

DISA. See ORCHIDS.
D. uniflora. Deciduous, terrestrial orchid. H 1½–2ft (45–60cm). Frost tender, min. 45–50°F (7–10°C). Should be grown in a cool greenhouse. Has narrowly lance-shaped, glossy, dark green leaves, to 9in (22cm) long, that clasp stems. In early summer each stem bears up to 7 hooded, scarlet flowers, 3–4in (8–10 cm) long, that have darker veins and are suffused yellow. Is the parent of many hybrids grown commercially for cut flowers. Needs partial shade and moist soil that should not be allowed to dry out. May be raised from seed or propagated by division of offsets when dormant.

DISANTHUS (Hamamelidaceae)
Genus of one species of deciduous, autumn-flowering shrub, grown for its overall appearance and autumn color. Frost hardy. Needs partial shade and humus-rich, moist but not wet, neutral to acid soil. Propagate by layering in spring or by seed when ripe or in spring.

D. cercidifolius. Deciduous, rounded shrub. H and S to 10ft (3m). Zones 7–9. Bears broadly oval to almost circular, bluish green leaves that turn red, purple, orange, or yellow in autumn. Has small, dark red flowers, like pairs of back-to-back spiders, in autumn as the leaves fall, or later.

DISCARIA (Rhamnaceae)
Genus of deciduous or almost leafless shrubs and trees, grown for their habit and flowers. Spiny, green shoots assume function of leaves. Frost hardy. Needs a sheltered, sunny site and fertile, well-drained soil. Propagate by softwood cuttings in summer.

D. toumatou (Wild Irishman). Deciduous or almost leafless, bushy shrub. H and S 6ft (2m). Zones 7–9. Shoots have sharp, rigid spines. Tiny, star-shaped, greenish white flowers are borne in dense clusters in late spring.

DISPORUM (Liliaceae)
Fairy-bells
Genus of spring- or early summer-flowering perennials. Is best suited to woodland gardens. Fully hardy. Requires a cool, semi-shaded position and humus-rich soil. Propagate by division in spring or by seed in autumn.

D. hookeri. Clump-forming perennial. H 30in (75cm), S 12in (30cm). Zones 4–9. Leaves are narrowly oval and green. Clusters of drooping, open bell-shaped, greenish white flowers in spring are followed by orange-red berries in autumn.

D. sessile 'Variegatum'. Rapidly spreading, clump-forming perennial. H 18in (45cm), S 12in (30cm). Zones 4–9. Solitary tubular-bell-shaped to bell-shaped, creamy white flowers are borne in spring. Narrowly oval leaves are pleated and irregularly striped with green and white.

DISTICTIS (Bignoniaceae)
Genus of evergreen, woody-stemmed, tendril climbers, grown for their colorful, trumpet-shaped flowers. Frost tender, min. 41–5°F (5–7°C). Well-drained soil is suitable with full light. Water freely in summer, less at other times. Support for stems is necessary. Thin out congested growth in spring. Propagate by softwood cuttings in early summer or by semi-ripe cuttings in late summer.

D. buccinatoria, syn. *Phaedranthus buccinatorius,* illus. p.163.

DISTYLIUM (Hamamelidaceae)
Genus of evergreen shrubs and trees, grown for their foliage and flowers. Frost hardy. Prefers a sheltered, partially shaded position and moist, peaty soil. Propagate by semi-ripe cuttings in summer.

D. racemosum. Evergreen, arching shrub. H 6ft (2m), S 10ft (3m). Zones 7–9. Bears oblong, leathery, glossy, dark green leaves. In late spring and early summer has small flowers with red calyces and purple anthers.

DIZYGOTHECA (Araliaceae)
Genus of evergreen shrubs and trees, grown for their foliage and overall appearance. Has insignificant flowers in summer on tree-sized specimens growing outside. *D. elegantissima* is sometimes confused in cultivation with *Schefflera elegantissima.* Frost tender, min. 55°F (13°C). Prefers partial shade and fertile, well-drained soil. Water potted specimens freely when in full growth, moderately at other times. Leggy plants can be cut back to near soil level in spring. Propagate by seed or air-layering in spring or by stem section or tip cuttings in summer. Whitefly, red spider mite, and mealy bug are occasionally troublesome.

D. elegantissima, syn. *Aralia elegantissima* (Threadleaf false aralia), illus. p.95.

DOCYNIA (Rosaceae)
Genus of evergreen or semi-evergreen, spring-flowering trees, grown for their flowers and foliage; is related to *Cydonia.* Half hardy. Requires full light and well-drained soil. Other than shaping while young, pruning is not necessary. Propagate by budding in summer, by seed in autumn or spring, or by grafting in winter. Is usually trouble-free, though caterpillars may be troublesome.

D. delavayi. Evergreen or semi-evergreen, spreading tree. H and S

25ft (8m) or more. Zones 8–10. Oval to lance-shaped leaves are white-felted beneath. In spring has fragrant, 5-petaled, white flowers, pink in bud, followed by ovoid, downy, yellow fruits in autumn.

DODECATHEON (Primulaceae)
Shooting star
Genus of spring- and summer-flowering perennials, grown for their distinctive flowers, with reflexed petals and prominent stamens. Once fertilized, flowers turn skywards – hence their common name. Is dormant after flowering. Fully to frost hardy. Prefers sun or partial shade and moist but well-drained soil. Propagate by seed in autumn or by division in winter.

D. dentatum. Clump-forming perennial. H 3in (7cm), S 10in (25cm). Fully hardy, zones 5–8. Leaves are long, oval, and toothed. In late spring, frail stems produce white flowers with prominent, dark stamens and reflexed petals. Prefers a partially shaded position.

D. hendersonii illus. p.287.
D. meadia. Clump-forming perennial. H 8in (20cm), S 6in (15cm). Fully hardy, zones 5–7. Leaves are oval and pale green. In spring, strong stems carry pale pink flowers, with reflexed petals, above foliage. Prefers a partially shaded position. f. *alba* illus. p.287.

D. pulchellum. Clump-forming perennial. H 6in (15cm), S 4in (10cm). Fully hardy, zones 5–7. Is similar to *D. meadia,* but flowers are usually deep cerise.

D. 'Red Wings' illus. p.288.

DODONAEA (Sapindaceae)
Genus of evergreen trees and shrubs, grown mainly for their foliage and overall appearance. Half hardy to frost tender, min. 37–41°F (3–5°C). Prefers full sun and well-drained soil. Water potted plants freely when in full growth, less at other times. Cut back in late summer, and again in spring, if needed, to maintain a balanced shape. Propagate by seed in spring or by semi-ripe cuttings in late summer.

D. viscosa 'Purpurea' illus. p.119.

Dolichos lablab. See Lablab purpureus.
Dolichos lignosus. See Lablab purpureus.

DOMBEYA (Sterculiaceae)
Genus of evergreen shrubs and trees, grown for their flowers. Frost tender, min. 41–55°F (5–13°C). Needs full light or partial shade and fertile, well-drained soil. Water potted specimens freely when in full growth, less when temperatures are low. May be cut back after flowering. Propagate by seed in spring or by semi-ripe cuttings in summer. Whitefly and red spider mite may be a nuisance.

D. burgessiae, syn. *D. mastersii,* illus. p.118.
D. x cayeuxii illus. p.61.
D. mastersii. See *D. burgessiae.*

DONDIA. See HACQUETIA.

DORONICUM (Compositae)
Leopard's bane
Genus of perennials, grown for their daisylike flower heads that are good for cutting. Fully hardy. Grows in full light or shade and any well-drained soil. Propagate by division in autumn.
D. austriacum. Clump-forming perennial. H 18in (45cm), S 12in (30cm). Zones 5–8. Daisylike, pure yellow flower heads are borne singly on slender stems in spring. Heart-shaped, bright green leaves are hairy and wavy-edged.
D. cordatum. See *D. pardalianches*.
D. pardalianches, syn. *D. cordatum*, illus. p.199.
D. plantagineum 'Excelsum'. Elegant, clump-forming perennial. H 3ft (1m), S 2ft (60cm). Zones 4–8. Large, daisylike, buttercup yellow flower heads are borne, 3 or 4 to a stem, in spring. Leaves are heart-shaped and bright green. Is good for a dry, shaded site.
D. 'Spring Beauty'. Clump-forming perennial. H 18in (45cm), S 12in (30cm). Zones 4–8. Produces daisylike, double, bright yellow flower heads in spring. Bears heart-shaped, bright green leaves.

DOROTHEANTHUS (Aizoaceae)
Genus of succulent annuals, suitable for hot, dry places such as rock gardens, banks, and gaps in paving. Half hardy to frost tender, min. 36–9°F (2–4°C). Needs sun and grows well in poor, very well-drained soil. Dead-head to prolong flowering. Propagate by seed sown under glass in early spring, or outdoors in mid-spring. Protect from slugs and snails.
D. bellidiformis, syn. *Mesembryanthemum criniflorum* (Ice-plant, Livingstone daisy). **Magic Carpet Series** illus. p.269.

DORYANTHES (Liliaceae)
Genus of evergreen, rosette-forming perennials, grown for their flowers. Frost tender, min. 50°F (10°C). Needs a sunny position and humus-rich, well-drained soil. Propagate by seed in spring, by mature bulbils, or by suckers after flowering.
D. palmeri illus. p.194.

DORYCNIUM (Leguminosae)
Genus of perennials and deciduous or semi-evergreen sub-shrubs, grown for their foliage, flowers, and fruits. Frost hardy. Needs full sun and dry, very well-drained soil. Propagate by softwood cuttings in summer or by seed in autumn.
D. hirsutum. Deciduous, upright sub-shrub. H and S 24in (60cm). Zones 6–9. Bears silver-gray leaves with 3 oval leaflets. Dense clusters of pealike, pink-tinged, white flowers in summer and early autumn are followed by oblong to ovoid, reddish brown seed pods.

Douglasia vitaliana. See *Vitaliana primuliflora*.

DOXANTHA. See MACFADYENA.
D. capreolata. See *Bignonia capreolata*.

DRABA (Cruciferae)
Genus of spring-flowering annuals and evergreen or semi-evergreen, cushion- or mat-forming perennials with extensive root systems. Some species form soft, green cushions that in winter turn brown except at the tips, thus appearing almost dead. Is suitable for alpine houses. Fully to frost hardy. Needs sun and gritty, well-drained soil. Dislikes winter wet. Propagate by softwood cuttings of the rosettes in late spring or by seed in autumn.
D. aizoides (Yellow whitlow grass). Semi-evergreen, mat-forming perennial. H 1in (2.5cm), S 6in (15cm). Fully hardy, zones 4–6. Has lance-shaped, stiff-bristled leaves in rosettes and, in spring, 4-petaled, bright yellow flowers. Suits a scree.
D. hispanica. Semi-evergreen, cushion-forming perennial. H 2in (5cm), S 4in (10cm). Frost hardy, zones 4–6. Leaves are oval, soft, fragile, and pale green. Clusters of flat, 4-petaled, pale yellow flowers are borne in spring.
D. longisiliqua illus. p.311.
D. mollissima illus. p.312.
D. polytricha. Semi-evergreen, cushion-forming perennial. H 2½in (6cm), S 6in (15cm). Fully hardy, zones 4–6. Has minute, rounded leaves in neat, symmetrical rosettes. Frail stems carry flat, 4-petaled, golden yellow flowers in spring. Is difficult to grow. Keep stones under cushion at all times. Remove dead rosettes at once.
D. rigida illus. p.311. var. **bryoides** is an evergreen, tight hummock-forming perennial. H 1½in (4cm), S 2½in (6cm). Fully hardy, zones 4–6. Leaves are tiny, rounded, hard, and dark green. Produces small clusters of almost stemless, 4-petaled, bright yellow flowers that cover hummocks in spring. Is also suitable for growing on a scree.

DRACAENA (Agavaceae)
Genus of evergreen trees and shrubs, grown for their foliage and overall appearance. Frost tender, min. 55–64°F (13–18°C). Needs full light or partial shade and well-drained soil. Water potted plants moderately, much less in low temperatures. Rejuvenate leggy plants by cutting back to near soil level in spring. Propagate by seed or air-layering in spring or by tip or stem cuttings in summer. Mealy bug can be a nuisance.
D. deremensis. Slow-growing, evergreen, erect, sparsely branched shrub. H 6ft (2m) or more, S 3ft (1m) or more. Zone 10. Has lance-shaped, erect to arching, glossy, deep green leaves, to 18in (45cm) long. Mature plants may occasionally bear large panicles of small, red-and-white flowers in summer. **'Warneckii'** illus. p.94.
D. draco illus. p.72.
D. fragrans (Corn plant). **'Massangeana'** is an evergreen, erect, sparsely branched shrub. H 10–20ft (3–6m), S 3–10ft (1–3m). Zone 10. Has strap-shaped, arching leaves, to 2ft (60cm) long, with longitudinal bands of yellow and pale green. In early summer, fragrant, star-shaped, yellow flowers, rarely produced, are followed by rounded-oblong, orange-red fruits.
D. indivisa. See *Cordyline indivisa*.
D. marginata (Madagascar dragon tree). Slow-growing, evergreen, erect shrub or tree. H 10ft (3m) or more, S 3–6ft (1–2m) or more. Zone 10. Leaves are narrowly strap-shaped and rich green with red margins. Flowers are rarely produced. **'Tricolor'** illus. p.71.
D. sanderiana illus. p.119.

DRACOCEPHALUM (Labiatae)
Dragonhead
Genus of summer-flowering annuals and perennials, suitable for rock gardens and borders. Fully hardy. Prefers sun and fertile, well-drained soil. Propagate by basal cuttings of young growth in spring or by seed or division in spring or autumn.
D. ruyschianum. Erect perennial. H 18–24in (45–60cm), S 12in (30cm). Zones 4–8. Freely produces whorled spikes of 2-lipped, violet-blue flowers from early to mid-summer. Green leaves are linear to lance-shaped.

DRACUNCULUS (Araceae)
Genus of robust, tuberous perennials that produce roughly triangular, foul-smelling spathes. Frost hardy, but in severe winters protect dormant tubers with a cloche or dead bracken. Needs sun and well-drained soil that dries out in summer. Propagate by freely produced offsets in late summer or by seed in autumn.
D. vulgaris, syn. *Arum dracunculus*, illus. p.336.

Dregea corrugata. See *Wattakaka sinensis*.
Dregea sinensis. See *Wattakaka sinensis*.

Drejerella guttata. See *Justicia brandegeana*.

DRIMYS (Winteraceae)
Genus of evergreen trees and shrubs, grown for their foliage and star-shaped flowers. Frost hardy, but in cold areas grow against a south- or west-facing wall. Needs sun or semi-shade and fertile, moist but well-drained soil. Propagate by semi-ripe cuttings in summer or by seed in autumn.
D. axillaris. See *Pseudowintera axillaris*.
D. colorata. See *Pseudowintera colorata*.
D. lanceolata (Mountain pepper). Evergreen, upright, dense shrub or tree. H 12ft (4m), S 8ft (2.5m). Zones 9–10. Has deep red shoots and oblong, dark green leaves. Clusters of star-shaped, white flowers are borne from mid- to late spring.
D. winteri illus. p.51.

DROSANTHEMUM (Aizoaceae)
Genus of erect or prostrate, succulent shrubs with slender stems and masses of flowers in summer. Leaves are finely covered in papillae. Frost tender, min. 41°F (5°C). Needs full sun and very well-drained soil. Propagate by seed or stem cuttings in spring or summer.

D. hispidum. Succulent shrub, with arching or spreading branches that root down. H 2ft (60cm), S 3ft (1m). Zones 9–10. Cylindrical, light green leaves are ⅝–1in (1.5–2.5cm) long. In summer has masses of shiny, daisylike, purple flowers, to 1¼in (3cm) across.
D. speciosum. Erect, shrubby succulent. H 2ft (60cm), S 3ft (1m). Zones 9–10. Produces semi-cylindrical leaves, ½–¾in (1–2cm) long. Masses of daisylike, green-centered, orange-red flowers, to 2in (5cm) across, appear in summer.

DROSERA (Droseraceae)
Sundew
Genus of evergreen, insectivorous perennials. Fully hardy to frost tender, min. 41–50°F (5–10°C). Grow in sun, in a mixture of peat and moss that is not allowed to dry out. Propagate by seed or division in spring.
D. capensis illus. p.261.
D. spathulata illus. p.261.

DRYANDRA (Proteaceae)
Genus of evergreen, spring- to summer-flowering shrubs and trees, grown for their flowers, foliage, and overall appearance. Frost tender, min. 45°F (7°C). Needs full light and well-drained, sandy soil that contains few nitrates or phosphates. Is difficult to grow. Water potted specimens moderately, much less in low temperatures. Plants under glass must be freely ventilated. Propagate by seed in spring.
D. formosa. Evergreen, bushy shrub. H 6–15ft (2–5m), S 5–10ft (1.5–3m). Zone 10. Strap-shaped leaves are divided into triangular, closely set lobes, creating a saw-blade effect. In spring carries small, scented, tubular, orange-yellow flowers in domed, terminal heads.

DRYAS (Rosaceae)
Mountain avens
Genus of evergreen, prostrate, woody-based perennials with oaklike leaves and cup-shaped flowers. Is useful on banks and walls, in rock gardens, and as ground cover. Fully hardy. Prefers sun and gritty, well-drained, peaty soil. Propagate by seed when fresh or by semi-ripe cuttings in summer.
D. drummondii. Evergreen, prostrate, woody-based perennial. H 2in (5cm), S indefinite. Zones 3–6. Stout stems are clothed in small, oval, lobed, leathery, dark green leaves. Nodding, creamy white flowers are borne in early summer but never fully open.
D. octopetala illus. p.315.
D. x suendermannii. Evergreen, prostrate, woody-based perennial. H 2in (5cm), S indefinite. Zones 3–6. Is similar to *D. drummondii*, but has slightly nodding, pale cream flowers that open horizontally.

DRYOPTERIS (Polypodiaceae)
Genus of deciduous or semi-evergreen ferns, many of which form regular, shuttlecocklike crowns. Fully to half hardy. Requires shade and moist soil. Regularly remove fading fronds. Propagate by spores in summer or by division in autumn or winter.

D. austriaca. See *D. dilatata.*

D. carthusiana (Narrow buckler fern). Deciduous or semi-evergreen, creeping, rhizomatous fern. H 3ft (1m), S 18in (45cm). Fully hardy, zones 4–8. Produces lance-shaped, much-divided, green fronds with triangular to oval pinnae.

D. dilatata, syn. *D. austriaca* (Broad buckler fern). Deciduous or semi-evergreen fern. H 3ft (1m), S 18in (45cm). Fully hardy, zones 4–8. Has much-divided, arching, green fronds, with triangular to oval pinnae, on stout, dark brown stems.

D. erythrosora (Japanese sword fern). Deciduous fern. H 18in (45cm), S 12in (30cm). Frost to half hardy, zones 5–9. Broadly triangular, divided, coppery pink fronds, divided into triangular to oval pinnae, persist until mid-winter.

D. filix-mas illus. p.184. **'Grandiceps'** is a deciduous or semi-evergreen fern. H 4ft (1.2m), S 3ft (1m). Fully hardy, zones 4–8. Has "shuttlecocks" of broadly lance-shaped, tasselled, elegantly arching, green fronds, arising from crowns of large, upright, brown-scaled rhizomes.

D. goldiana (Giant wood fern). Deciduous fern. H 3ft (1m), S 2ft (60cm). Fully hardy, zones 4–8. Has broadly oval, light green fronds divided into numerous oblong, indented pinnae.

D. hexagonoptera. See *Thelypteris hexagonoptera.*

D. marginalis. Deciduous fern. H 24in (60cm), S 12in (30cm). Fully hardy, zones 4–8. Fronds are lance-shaped, dark green, and divided into numerous oblong, slightly indented pinnae.

DUCHESNEA (Rosaceae)

Genus of perennials, with rooting runners, some of which are semi-evergreen, grown as ground cover and for their flowers. May be used in hanging baskets. Fully hardy. Grow in well-drained soil and in sun or partial shade. Propagate by division in spring, by rooting plantlets formed at ends of runners in summer, or by seed in autumn.

D. indica, syn. *Fragaria indica.* Semi-evergreen, trailing perennial. H to 4in (10cm), S indefinite. Zones 4–9. Dark green leaves have 3 toothed leaflets like those of strawberries. Has solitary 5-petaled, bright yellow flowers, to 1in (2.5cm) wide and with leafy, green frills of sepals, from spring to early summer. Strawberrylike, tasteless, red fruits appear in late summer.

DUDLEYA (Crassulaceae)

Genus of basal-rosetted, perennial succulents, closely related to *Echeveria.* Frost tender, min. 45°F (7°C). Requires full sun and very well-drained soil. Water sparingly when plants are semi-dormant in mid-summer. Propagate by seed or division in spring or summer.

D. brittonii. Basal-rosetted, perennial succulent. H 8in (20cm) – 24in (60cm) or more when in flower, S 20in (50cm). Zone 10. Has narrowly lance-shaped, tapering, fleshy, silvery white leaves.

Masses of star-shaped, pale yellow flowers are produced in spring-summer.

D. pulverulenta illus. p.385.

DURANTA (Verbenaceae)

Genus of fast-growing, evergreen or partially deciduous trees and shrubs, grown for their flowers and overall appearance. Frost tender, min. 50–55°F (10–13°C). Needs full light and fertile, well-drained soil. Water potted plants freely when in full growth, moderately at other times. Prune as necessary to curb vigor. Propagate by seed in spring or by semi-ripe cuttings in summer. Whitefly may be troublesome.

D. plumieri. See *D. repens.*

D. repens, syn. *D. plumieri*, illus. p.118.

DUVALIA (Asclepiadaceae)

Genus of clump-forming or carpeting, perennial succulents with short, thick, leafless stems; is closely related to *Stapelia.* Star-shaped flowers have thick, fleshy petals recurved at tips. Frost tender, min. 50°F (10°C), but best at 68°F (20°C). Requires partial shade and very well-drained soil. Propagate by seed or stem cuttings in spring or summer.

D. corderoyi illus. p.396.

DUVERNOIA (Acanthaceae)

Genus of evergreen shrubs, grown primarily for their flowers. Frost tender, min. 50–59°F (10–15°C). Prefers full light and humus-rich, well-

drained soil. Water potted specimens freely when in full growth, less at other times. In spring cut back flowered stems by half to create a well-branched plant. Propagate by seed in spring or by softwood or greenwood cuttings in late spring or summer. Whitefly may cause problems.

D. adhatodoides, syn. *Adhatoda duvernoia* (Snake bush). Evergreen, erect shrub. H 6–10ft (2–3m), S 3–6ft (1–2m). Zone 10. Bears elliptic, dark green leaves. Fragrant, tubular, white or mauve flowers, with pink, red, or purple marks, appear in terminal spikes in summer-autumn. Is sometimes confused in cultivation with *Justicia adhatoda.*

DYCKIA (Bromeliaceae)

Genus of evergreen, rosette-forming perennials, grown for their overall appearance. Frost tender, min. 45–50°F (7–10°C). Requires full light and well-drained soil containing sharp sand or grit. Water moderately in summer, scarcely or not at all in winter, sparingly at other times. Propagate by offsets or division in spring.

D. remotiflora (illus. p.222). Evergreen, basal-rosetted perennial. H and S 12–20in (30–50cm). Zone 10. Has dense rosettes of very narrowly triangular, pointed, thick-textured, arching, dull green leaves with hooked spines and gray scales beneath. Woolly spikes of tubular, orange-yellow flowers appear above foliage in summer-autumn.

ECCREMOCARPUS (Bignoniaceae)
Genus of evergreen, sub-shrubby, tendril climbers, grown for their attractive flowers that are produced over a long season. One species only is commonly grown. Half hardy; in cold areas treat as an annual. Grow in full light and in any well-drained soil. Propagate by seed in early spring.
E. scaber illus. p.175.

ECHEVERIA (Crassulaceae)
Genus of rosetted, perennial succulents with long-lasting flowers. Leaves assume their brightest colors from autumn to spring. Frost tender, min. 41–5°F (5–7°C). Needs sun, good ventilation, and very well-drained soil. Propagate by seed, stem or leaf cuttings, division, or offsets in spring or summer.
E. agavoides illus. p.394.
E. derenbergii. Clump-forming, perennial succulent. H 1¹/₂in (4cm), S 12in (30cm). Min. 41°F (5°C), zone 10. Produces a short-stemmed rosette of rounded, gray-green leaves. Flower stem, 3in (8cm) long, produces cup-shaped, yellow-and-red or orange flowers in spring. Offsets freely. Is often used as a parent in breeding.
E. elegans illus. p.391.
E. gibbiflora. Rosetted, perennial succulent. H 3ft (1m), S 6in (15cm). Min. 45°F (7°C), zone 10. Stems are crowned by rounded, gray-green leaves, often tinged red or brown. Flower stems, 2ft (60cm) long, bear cup-shaped, red flowers, yellow within, in autumn-winter.
E. harmsii, syn. *Oliveranthus elegans*. Bushy, perennial succulent. H 8in (20cm), S 12in (30cm). Min. 45°F (7°C), zone 10. Erect stems are each crowned by a 2¹/₂in (6cm) wide rosette of short, narrowly lance-shaped, pale green leaves, covered in short hairs. In spring bears cup-shaped, orange-tipped, red flowers, yellow within.
E. pulvinata illus. p.385.
E. secunda illus. p.393.
E. setosa (Mexican firecracker). Basal-rosetted, perennial succulent. H 1¹/₂in (4cm), S 12in (30cm). Min. 45°F (7°C), zone 10. Has long, narrow, green leaves covered in short, thick, white hairs. Bears cup-shaped, red-and-yellow flowers in spring. Is prone to rotting; do not water foliage.

ECHINACEA (Compositae)
Coneflower
Genus of summer-flowering perennials. Fully hardy. Prefers sun and humus-rich, moist but well-drained soil. Propagate by division or root cuttings in spring.
E. purpurea, syn. *Rudbeckia purpurea*. **'Robert Bloom'** illus. p.204. **'White Lustre'** is a vigorous, upright perennial. H 1.2m (4ft), S 1¹/₂ft (45cm). Zones 4–9. Large, daisylike, white flower heads, each with a

prominent, central, orange-brown cone, are borne singly on strong stems in summer. Has lance-shaped, dark green leaves.

ECHINOCACTUS (Cactaceae)
Genus of slow-growing, hemispherical, perennial cacti. Frost tender, min. 52°F (11°C); lower temperatures cause yellow patches on *E. grusonii*. Requires full sun and very well-drained soil. Yellow-flowered species are easy to grow. Propagate by seed in spring.
E. grusonii illus. p.381.
E. ingens. Slow-growing, hemispherical, perennial cactus. H 10ft (3m), S 6ft (2m). Zone 10. Gray-blue stem has a woolly crown and up to 50 ribs. Funnel-shaped, yellow flowers, 1¹/₄in (3cm) across, appear in summer only on plants over 16in (40cm) in diameter.

ECHINOCEREUS (Cactaceae)
Genus of spherical to columnar, perennial cacti, freely branching with age, some with tuberous rootstocks. Buds, formed inside spiny stem, burst through skin, producing long-lasting flowers, with reflexed petal tips and prominent, green stigmas, followed by pear-shaped, spiny seed pods. Frost tender, min. 41–6°F (5–8°C); some species tolerate light frost if dry. Needs full sun and very well-drained soil. Propagate by seed or stem cuttings in spring or summer.
E. baileyi. See *E. reichenbachii* var. *baileyi*.
E. cinerascens. Clump-forming, perennial cactus. H 1ft (30cm), S 3ft (1m). Min. 41°F (5°C), zone 10. Has 3in (7cm) wide stems, each with 5–12 ribs. Areoles each bear 8–15 yellowish white spines. Masses of trumpet-shaped, bright pink or purple flowers, 5in (12cm) across and with paler petal bases, appear in spring only on fully mature plants.
E. leucanthus, syn. *Wilcoxia albiflora*, illus. p.389.
E. pectinatus. Columnar, perennial cactus. H 14in (35cm), S 8in (20cm). Min. 45°F (7°C), zone 10. Has sparsely branched, green stems with 12–23 ribs and short, comblike spines, often variably colored. In spring produces trumpet-shaped, purple, pink, or yellow flowers, 5in (12cm) across, with paler petal bases.
E. pentalophus illus. p.384.
E. reichenbachii. Columnar, perennial cactus. H 14in (35cm), S 8in (20cm). Min. 45°F (7°C), zone 10. Has a slightly branched, multicolored stem with 12–23 ribs and comblike spines, ⁵/₈in (1.5cm) long. Carries trumpet-shaped, pink or purple flowers, 5in (12cm) across, with darker petal bases, in spring. var. *baileyi* (syn. *E. baileyi*) illus. p.383.
E. schmollii, syn. *Wilcoxia schmollii*, illus. p.383.

E. triglochidiatus. Clump-forming, perennial cactus. H 12in (30cm), S 6in (15cm). Min. 41°F (5°C), zone 10. Has a short, thick, dark green stem with 3–5 spines, each to 1in (2.5cm) long, per areole. In spring bears funnel-shaped, bright red flowers, 3in (7cm) across, with prominent, red stamens and green stigmas. var. *paucispinus* illus. p.395.

Echinodorus ranunculoides. See *Baldellia ranunculoides.*

ECHINOFOSSULOCACTUS (Cactaceae)
Genus of spherical, perennial cacti with spiny, green stems that have very narrow, wavy ribs. Frost tender, min. 41°F (5°C). Needs a sunny position and well-drained soil. Propagate by seed in spring or summer.
E. lamellosus. Spherical, perennial cactus. H and S 3in (8cm). Zone 10. Green stem has 30–35 ribs. Funnel-shaped, flesh-colored or red flowers, ¹/₂–1¹/₄in (1–3cm) across, are produced from crown in spring. Has flattened upper radial spines, shorter, more rounded lower ones, and longer, rounded central spines with darker tips.
E. pentacanthus illus. p.396.
E. violaciflorus illus. p.392.

Echinomastus mcdowellii. See *Thelocactus mcdowellii.*

ECHINOPS (Compositae)
Globe thistle
Genus of summer-flowering perennials, grown for their globelike, spiky flower heads. Fully hardy. Does best in full sun and in poor soil. Propagate by division or seed in autumn or by root cuttings in winter.
E. bannaticus illus. p.190.
E. ritro **'Veitch's Blue'** illus. p.211.
E. sphaerocephalus illus. p.188.
E. **'Taplow Blue'**. Erect perennial. H 4ft (1.2m), S 3ft (1m). Zones 4–9. Wiry stems produce thistlelike, rounded heads of powder blue flowers in summer. Narrowly oval leaves are divided and grayish green.

ECHINOPSIS (Cactaceae)
Genus of spherical to columnar, perennial cacti, mostly freely branching; it is sometimes held to include *Trichocereus*. Frost tender, min. 41°F (5°C). Requires full sun and well-drained soil. Is easy to grow and well adapted for long periods of neglect. Propagate by seed or offsets in spring or summer.
E. aurea. See *Lobivia aurea.*
E. eyriesii. Flattened spherical, perennial cactus. H 12in (30cm), S 20in (50cm). Zone 10. Has slowly branching, green stems with 11–18 ribs and very short spines. Tubular, white flowers are borne in spring-summer.

E. multiplex illus. p.382.
E. rhodotricha. Spherical to columnar, perennial cactus. H 2ft (60cm), S 8in (20cm). Zone 10. Produces branching, 8–13-ribbed, dark green stems, 3¹/₂in (9cm) across. Curved, dark spines, ³/₄in (2cm) long, later turn pale. Has tubular, white to pink flowers in spring-summer.

Echioides longiflorum. See *Arnebia pulchra.*

ECHIUM (Boraginaceae)
Genus of annuals and evergreen shrubs, biennials, and perennials, grown for their flowers. Fully hardy to frost tender, min. 37°F (3°C). Needs full sun and fertile, well-drained soil. Water potted specimens freely in summer, moderately at other times. Propagate by seed in spring or by greenwood or semi-ripe cuttings in summer. Whitefly may sometimes be troublesome.
E. bourgaeanum. See *E. wildpretii.*
E. vulgare [dwarf] illus. p.275.
E. wildpretii, syn. *E. bourgaeanum*. Evergreen, erect, unbranched biennial that dies after fruiting. H 8ft (2.5m) or more, S 2ft (60cm). Half hardy. Narrowly lance-shaped, silver-haired leaves, 1ft (30cm) long, form a dense rosette. Has compact spires, 3–5ft (1–1.5m) long, of small, funnel-shaped, red flowers in late spring and summer.

EDGEWORTHIA (Thymelaeaceae)
Genus of deciduous shrubs, grown for their flowers in late winter and early spring. Frost hardy, but flowers are susceptible to frost damage. Is best grown against a south- or west-facing wall in most areas. Requires full sun and well-drained soil. Dislikes being transplanted. Propagate by semi-ripe cuttings in summer or by seed in autumn.
E. chrysantha, syn. *E. papyrifera*. Deciduous, rounded, open shrub. H and S 5ft (1.5m). Zones 8–10. Very supple shoots produce terminal, rounded heads of fragrant, tubular, yellow flowers in late winter and early spring. Has oval, dark green leaves.
E. papyrifera. See *E. chrysantha.*

EDRAIANTHUS (Campanulaceae)
Genus of short-lived perennials, some of which are evergreen, usually growing from central rootstocks. In winter, a small, resting bud is just visible from each rootstock. In spring, prostrate stems radiate to carry leaves and flowers. Is suitable for rock gardens, screes, and troughs. Fully hardy. Needs sun and well-drained soil. Propagate by softwood cuttings from side shoots in early summer or by seed in autumn.
E. dalmaticus. Upright, then arching perennial. H 4in (10cm), S 6in (15cm). Zones 4–7. Bears narrowly lance-

shaped, pale green leaves and, in early summer, terminal clusters of bell-shaped, violet-blue flowers, 1in (2.5cm) across.
E. pumilio illus. p.322.
E. serpyllifolius illus. p.321. **'Major'** is an evergreen, prostrate perennial. H ^{1}/2in (1cm), S to 2in (5cm). Zones 4–7. Has tight mats of tiny, oval, dark green leaves. In early summer, bell-shaped, deep violet flowers, ^{5}/8in (1.5cm) wide, are borne on very short stems. Needs a sheltered site. Seldom sets seed.

Edwardsia microphylla. See *Sophora microphylla.*

EGERIA (Hydrocharitaceae)
Genus of semi-evergreen or evergreen, perennial, floating or submerged water plants, grown for their foliage. Is similar to *Elodea*, but has more conspicuous flowers, held above water surface. In an aquarium, plants are useful for oxygenating water and provide a suitable depository for fish spawn. Frost tender, min. 34°F (1°C). Needs a sunny position. Thin regularly to keep under control. Propagate by stem cuttings in spring or summer.
E. densa, syn. *Anacharis densa, Elodea densa.* Semi-evergreen, perennial, spreading, submerged water plant. S indefinite. Zones 9–10. Forms a dense mass of whorled, small, lance-shaped, dark green leaves borne on long, wiry stems. Small, 3-parted, white flowers appear in summer.

EHRETIA (Ehretiaceae)
Genus of deciduous, summer-flowering trees, grown for their foliage and star-shaped flowers. Frost hardy, but is susceptible to frost damage when young. Requires sun or semi-shade and fertile, well-drained soil. Propagate by softwood cuttings in summer.
E. dicksonii illus. p.64.

EICHHORNIA (Pontederiaceae)
Genus of evergreen or semi-evergreen, perennial, floating and marginal water plants. Frost tender, min. 34°F (1°C). Needs an open, sunny position in warm water. Grows prolifically and requires regular thinning year-round. Propagate by detaching young plants as required.
E. crassipes illus. p.374.

ELAEAGNUS (Elaeagnaceae)
Genus of deciduous or evergreen shrubs and trees, grown for their foliage and small, usually very fragrant flowers, often followed by ornamental fruits. Evergreen species are good for providing shelter or for hedging, particularly in coastal areas. Fully to frost hardy. Most evergreen species thrive in sun or shade, but those with silver leaves and deciduous species prefer full sun. Needs fertile, well-drained soil. Trim hedges in late summer. Propagate species by seed in autumn, evergreen forms also by semi-ripe cuttings in summer, deciduous forms by softwood or semi-ripe cuttings in summer.
E. angustifolia illus. p.90.

E. x ebbingei. Evergreen, bushy, dense shrub. H and S 15ft (5m). Fully hardy, zones 7–9. Has oblong to oval, glossy, dark green leaves, silvery beneath. Fragrant, bell-shaped, silvery white flowers are borne from mid- to late autumn. Leaves of **'Gilt Edge'** have golden yellow margins. **'Limelight'** illus. p.121.
E. macrophylla. Evergreen, bushy, dense shrub. H and S 10ft (3m). Frost hardy, zones 7–9. Broadly oval leaves are silvery gray when young, becoming glossy, dark green above, but remaining silvery gray beneath, when mature. Fragrant, bell-shaped, creamy yellow flowers, silvery outside, appear from mid- to late autumn, followed by egg-shaped, red fruits.
***E. pungens* 'Maculata'** illus. p.95.
E. umbellata. Vigorous, deciduous, bushy shrub. H and S 15ft (5m). Fully hardy, zones 4–8. Oblong, wavy-edged, bright green leaves are silvery when young. Produces fragrant, bell-shaped, creamy yellow flowers in late spring and early summer, then egg-shaped, red fruits.

ELAEOCARPUS (Elaeocarpaceae)
Genus of evergreen, spring- and summer-flowering shrubs and trees, grown for their flowers and foliage. Half hardy to frost tender, min. 41°F (5°C). Requires full light or partial shade and fertile, well-drained but not dry soil. Water potted specimens freely when in full growth, less in winter. Current season's growth may be cut back in winter. Propagate by seed in spring or by semi-ripe cuttings in summer. Red spider mite and whitefly may cause problems.
E. cyaneus. See *E. reticulatus.*
E. reticulatus, syn. *E. cyaneus* (Blueberry ash). Evergreen, rounded shrub or tree. H and S 10ft (3m), sometimes to 40ft (12m) or more. Frost tender, zone 10. Bears elliptic to lance-shaped, toothed, lustrous leaves and, in summer, axillary racemes of bell-shaped, fringed, white flowers. In autumn has globular, deep blue fruits.

ELEOCHARIS (Cyperaceae). See
GRASSES, BAMBOOS, RUSHES, and SEDGES.
E. acicularis (Needle spike-rush). Evergreen, spreading, rhizomatous, perennial sedge. H to 4in (10cm), S indefinite. Fully hardy, zones 7–10. Basal leaves are very narrow and green. Hairless, unbranched, square stems bear solitary minute, brown spikelets in summer.

ELEUTHEROCOCCUS,
syn. ACANTHOPANAX (Araliaceae)
Genus of deciduous shrubs and trees, grown for their foliage and fruits. Produces tiny, usually greenish white flowers. Fully hardy. Prefers full sun and needs well-drained soil. Propagate by seed in spring or by root cuttings in late winter.
E. sieboldianus (Five-leaved aralia) illus. p.113.

Elodea crispa of gardens. See *Lagarosiphon major.*
Elodea densa. See *Egeria densa.*

ELSHOLTZIA (Labiatae)
Genus of perennials and deciduous shrubs and sub-shrubs, grown for their flowers, generally in autumn. Frost hardy. Needs full sun and fertile, well-drained soil. Cut back old shoots hard in early spring. Propagate by softwood cuttings in summer.
E. stauntonii illus. p.141.

Elymus arenarius. See *Leymus arenarius.*

EMBOTHRIUM (Proteaceae)
Genus of evergreen or semi-evergreen trees, grown for their flowers. Frost hardy, but shelter from cold winds. Needs semi-shade and moist but well-drained, lime-free soil. Propagate by suckers in spring or autumn or by seed in autumn.
E. coccineum illus. p.66.

EMILIA (Compositae)
Genus of annuals and perennials, grown for their flower heads that are good for cutting. Is ideal for hot, dry areas and coastal soils. Half hardy. Requires sun and very well-drained soil. Propagate by seed sown under glass in spring, or outdoors in late spring.
E. flammea. See *E. javanica.*
E. javanica, syn. *E. flammea,* illus. p.285.

EMMENOPTERYS (Rubiaceae)
Genus of deciduous trees, grown mainly for their foliage; flowers appear only rarely, during hot summers. Frost hardy, but young growths may be damaged by late frosts. Needs full sun and deep, fertile, well-drained soil. Propagate by softwood cuttings in summer.
E. henryi illus. p.53.

ENCEPHALARTOS (Zamiaceae)
Genus of evergreen shrubs and trees, grown for their palmlike appearance. Frost tender, min. 50–55°F (10–13°C). Needs full light and well-drained soil. Water potted specimens moderately when in full growth, less at other times. Propagate by seed in spring.
E. ferox illus. p.120.
E. longifolius. Slow-growing, evergreen, palmlike tree, sometimes branched with age. H 10ft (3m) or more, S 5–8ft (1.5–2.5m). Zone 10. Bears feather-shaped leaves, each 2–5ft (60cm–1.5m) long, divided into narrowly lance-shaped to oval, blue-green leaflets, usually with hook-tipped teeth. Conelike, brownish flower heads are produced intermittently.

ENCYCLIA. See ORCHIDS.
E. cochleata. Evergreen, epiphytic orchid for a cool greenhouse. H 12in (30cm). Zone 10. Upright spikes of green flowers, 2in (5cm) long, with dark purple lips at the top and ribbonlike sepals and petals, are produced in summer and, on mature plants, intermittently throughout the year. Leaves are narrowly oval and 6in (15cm) long. Requires semi-shade in summer.

E. radiata. Evergreen, epiphytic orchid for a cool greenhouse. H 10in (25cm). Zone 10. Bears upright spikes of very fragrant, well-rounded, creamy white flowers, ^{1}/2in (1cm) across, in summer. Flower lips are white, lined with red. Narrowly oval leaves are 4–6in (10–15cm) long. Grow in semi-shade in summer.

ENDYMION. See
HYACINTHOIDES.

ENKIANTHUS (Ericaceae)
Genus of deciduous or semi-evergreen, spring-flowering shrubs and trees, grown for their mass of small, bell- or urn-shaped flowers and their autumn color. Fully to frost hardy. Needs sun or semi-shade and moist, peaty, acid soil. Propagate by semi-ripe cuttings in summer or by seed in autumn.
E. campanulatus illus. p.85.
E. cernuus* var. *rubens illus. p.98.
E. perulatus illus. p.95.

ENSETE (Musaceae)
Genus of evergreen perennials, grown for their foliage, which resembles that of bananas, and fruits. Has false stems made of overlapping leaf sheaths that die after flowering. Frost tender, min. 50°F (10°C). Grow in sun or partial shade and humus-rich soil. Propagate by seed in spring or by division year-round.
E. ventricosum, syn. *Musa arnoldiana, M. ensete,* illus. p.195.

EOMECON (Papaveraceae)
Genus of one species of perennial that spreads rapidly and deeply underground. Is suitable for large rock gardens. Fully hardy. Needs sun and well-drained soil. Propagate by seed or runners in spring.
E. chionantha (Snow poppy). Vigorous, spreading perennial. H to 16in (40cm), S indefinite. Zones 7–9. Leaves are large, palmate, and gray. Erect stems each carry a long panicle of many small, poppylike, white flowers in summer.

EPACRIS (Epacridaceae)
Genus of evergreen, heathlike shrubs, grown for their flowers. Frost tender, min. 41°F (5°C). Needs full sun and humus-rich, well-drained, neutral to acid soil. Water potted plants moderately when in full growth, less at other times. Flowered stems may be shortened after flowering to maintain a neat habit. Propagate by seed in spring or by semi-ripe cuttings in late summer.
E. impressa illus. p.123.

EPHEDRA (Ephedraceae)
Genus of evergreen shrubs, grown for their attractive habit and green shoots. Makes good ground cover in dry soil. Grow male and female plants together in order to obtain fruits. Fully hardy. Requires full sun and well-drained soil. Propagate by seed in autumn or by division in autumn or spring.
E. gerardiana. Evergreen, spreading shrub with slender, erect, rushlike, green shoots. H 2ft (60cm), S 6ft (2m). Zones 6–9. Leaves and flowers are

inconspicuous. Produces small, spherical, red fruits.

EPIDENDRUM. See ORCHIDS.
E. difforme (illus. p.254). Evergreen, epiphytic orchid for an intermediate greenhouse. H 9in (23cm). Zone 10. Large heads of semi-translucent, green flowers, ^{1}/$_4$in (0.5cm) across, open in autumn. Has oval, rigid leaves, 1–2in (2.5–5cm) long. Requires shade in summer. Avoid spraying, which can cause spotting of leaves. Propagate by division in spring.
E. ibaguense, syn. *E. radicans* (illus. p.253). Evergreen, epiphytic orchid for a cool greenhouse. H 6ft (2m) or more. Zone 10. Flowers more or less constantly, bearing a succession of feathery-lipped, deep red blooms, ^{1}/$_4$in (0.5cm) across. Leaves, 1–2in (2.5–5cm) long, are oval and rigid. Grow in semi-shade during summer. Propagate by tip cuttings in spring.
E. radicans. See *E. ibaguense.*

EPIGAEA (Ericaceae)
Genus of evergreen, prostrate, spring-flowering sub-shrubs. Fully to frost hardy. Needs shade and humus-rich, moist, acid soil. Most are difficult to cultivate. Propagate by seed in spring or by softwood cuttings in early summer.
E. asiatica. Evergreen, creeping sub-shrub. H to 4in (10cm), S to 8in (20cm). Fully hardy, zones 6–8. Stems and heart-shaped, deep green leaves are covered with brown hairs. Bears terminal clusters of 3–6 tiny, slightly fragrant, urn-shaped, white or pink flowers in spring.
E. gaultherioides, syn. *Orphanidesia gaultherioides*, illus. p.304.
E. repens (Mayflower, Trailing arbutus). Evergreen, creeping sub-shrub. H 4in (10cm), S 12in (30cm). Fully hardy, zones 3–8. Hairy stems, bearing heart-shaped, leathery leaves, root at intervals. In spring produces terminal clusters of 4–6 cup-shaped, white flowers, sometimes flushed pink. Is relatively easy to grow.

EPIGENEIUM. See ORCHIDS.
E. amplum. Evergreen, epiphytic orchid for a cool greenhouse. H 24in (60cm). Zone 10. In spring bears a star-shaped, single, olive green flower, lined with reddish brown and with a blackish brown lip, 2in (5cm) long. Leaves are oval, to 3in (8cm) long. Grow on a bark slab. Requires semi-shade in summer.

EPILOBIUM, syn.
CHAMAENERION (Onagraceae)
Willow herb
Genus of annuals, biennials, perennials, and deciduous sub-shrubs, grown for their deep pink to white flowers in summer. Is useful on dry banks; many species are invasive. Fully to frost hardy. Tolerates sun or shade and prefers moist but well-drained soil. Propagate species by seed in autumn, selected forms by softwood cuttings from side-shoots in spring.
E. angustifolium f. *album* illus. p.188.
E. chlorifolium var. *kaikourense* illus. p.314.

E. glabellum illus. p.291.
E. obcordatum. Clump-forming perennial. H 6in (15cm), S 4in (10cm). Frost hardy, zones 5–8. Oval leaves are glossy green. Spikes of open cup-shaped, deep rose-pink flowers are borne in summer. Is good for a rock garden or alpine house. Needs a sheltered site and full sun. In cultivation may not retain character, especially in mild climates.

EPIMEDIUM (Berberidaceae)
Genus of spring-flowering perennials, some of which are evergreen. Flowers are cup-shaped with long or short spurs. Makes good ground cover. Fully hardy. Does best in partial shade and humus-rich, moisture-retentive but well-drained soil. Cut back just before new growth appears in spring. Propagate by division in spring or autumn.
E. alpinum (Barrenwort). Evergreen, carpeting perennial. H 9in (23cm), S to 12in (30cm). Zones 5–9. Racemes of pendent, short-spurred flowers, with crimson sepals and yellow petals, appear in spring. Has finely toothed, glossy leaves divided into oval, angled, green leaflets, bronze when young.
E. grandiflorum 'Rose Queen' illus. p.226. 'Violaceum' is a carpeting perennial. H and S 12in (30cm). Zones 5–9. Produces racemes of pendent, long-spurred, deep lilac flowers in spring at same time as heart-shaped, dark brownish red, young leaves, divided into oval leaflets, that mature to green.
E. x *perralchicum.* Semi-evergreen, evergreen, carpeting perennial. H 18in (45cm), S 12in (30cm). Zones 5–9. Short spires of pendent, yellow flowers, with short spurs, are borne on slender stems in spring. Leaves, divided into rounded to oval leaflets, are dark green.
E. perralderianum. Carpeting perennial. H 12in (30cm), S 18in (45cm). Zones 5–9. Clusters of small, pendent, short-spurred, bright yellow flowers are borne in spring. Has large, toothed, glossy, deep green leaves, divided into rounded to oval leaflets.
E. pinnatum subsp. *colchicum.* Evergreen, carpeting perennial. H and S 12in (30cm). Zones 5–9. In spring, clusters of small, pendent, bright yellow flowers, with short spurs, are produced above dark green leaves, divided into rounded to oval leaflets, that are hairy when young.
E. pubigerum illus. p.225.
E. x *rubrum* illus. p.226.
E. x *versicolor.* Carpeting perennial. H and S 12in (30cm). Zones 5–9. Small, pendent clusters of yellow flowers, with long, red-tinged spurs, appear in spring. Heart-shaped, fresh green leaves are divided into oval leaflets that are tinted reddish purple. 'Neo-sulphureum' illus. p.229.
E. x *warleyense* illus. p.232.
E. x *youngianum* 'Niveum' illus. p.224.

EPIPHYLLUM (Cactaceae)
Orchid cactus, Strap cactus
Genus of perennial cacti with strap-shaped, flattened, green stems that have notched edges. Flowers are

produced at notches. Frost tender, min. 41–52°F (5–11°C). Grow in sun or partial shade and in rich, well-drained soil. Propagate by stem cuttings in spring or summer.
E. ackermannii. See *Nopalxochia ackermannii.*
E. anguliger illus. p.382.
E. crenatum. Erect, then pendent, perennial cactus. H and S 10ft (3m). Min. 52°F (11°C), zone 10. Has a flattened stem. Bears lightly perfumed, funnel-shaped, broad-petaled, white flowers, 8in (20cm) across, in spring-summer. Is often used as a parent for breeding.
E. 'Deutsche Kaiserin'. See *Nopalxochia phyllanthoides.*
E. 'Gloria' illus. p.384.
E. 'Jennifer Ann' illus. p.387.
E. lauii illus. p.382.
E. 'M.A. Jeans' illus. p.384.
E. oxypetalum. Erect, then pendent, perennial cactus. H 10ft (3m), S 3ft (1m). Min. 52°F (11°C), zone 10. Produces freely branching, flattened stems, 5in (12cm) across. In spring-summer bears nocturnal, tubular, white flowers, 8in (25cm) long. Makes a good house plant.

EPIPREMNUM (Araceae)
Genus of evergreen, woody-stemmed, root climbers, including *Pothos*, grown for their handsome leaves. Frost tender, min. 59–64°F (15–18°C). Grow in light shade away from direct sun; any well-drained, moisture-retentive soil is suitable. Water regularly, less in cold weather. Stems need good supports. Remove shoot tips to induce branching at any time. Propagate by leaf-bud or stem-tip cuttings in late spring or by layering in summer.
E. aureum 'Marble Queen', syn. *Scindapsus aureus* 'Marble Queen', illus. p.177.
E. pictum 'Argyraeus', syn. *Scindapsus pictus* 'Argyraeus', illus. p.177.

EPISCIA (Gesneriaceae)
Genus of evergreen, low-growing and creeping perennials, grown for their ornamental leaves and colorful flowers. Is useful as ground cover or in hanging baskets. Frost tender, min. 59°F (15°C). Requires high humidity and a fairly shaded position in humus-rich, well-drained soil. Keep well watered, but avoid waterlogging. Propagate in summer by stem cuttings, division, or removing rooted runners.
E. cupreata illus. p.257. 'Metallica' is an evergreen, creeping perennial. H 4in (10cm), S indefinite. Zones 9–10. Has oval, downy, wrinkled leaves, tinged pink to copper and with broad, silvery bands along midribs. Funnel-shaped, orange-red flowers, marked yellow within, are borne intermittently. 'Tropical Topaz' has yellow flowers.
E. dianthiflora illus. p.255.
E. lilacina. Evergreen, low-growing perennial, with runners bearing plantlets. H 4in (10cm), S indefinite. Zone 10. Has oval, hairy, pale green leaves, to 3in (8cm) long. Funnel-shaped, white flowers, tinged mauve and with yellow eyes, are produced in

small clusters from autumn to spring. Leaves of 'Cuprea' are bronze-tinged.

EPITHELANTHA (Cactaceae)
Genus of very slow-growing, spherical, perennial cacti densely covered with very short spines. Frost tender, min. 50°F (10°C). Needs full sun and well-drained soil. Is prone to rot if overwatered. Is easier to cultivate if grafted. Propagate by seed or stem cuttings in spring or summer.
E. micromeris illus. p.391.

ERANTHEMUM (Acanthaceae)
Genus of perennials and evergreen shrubs, grown for their flowers. Frost tender, min. 59–64°F (15–18°C). Requires full light or partial shade and fertile, well-drained soil. Water potted plants freely when in full growth, moderately at other times. In spring, or after flowering, remove at least half of each spent flowering stem to encourage a bushier habit. Propagate by softwood cuttings in late spring. Whitefly may be a nuisance.
E. atropurpureum. See *Pseuderanthemum atropurpureum.*
E. nervosum. See *E. pulchellum.*
E. pulchellum, syn. *E. nervosum.* Evergreen, erect shrub. H 3–4ft (1–1.2m), S 2ft (60cm) or more. Zones 9–10. Produces elliptic to oval, prominently veined, deep green leaves. Blue flowers, each with a 1^1/$_4$in (3cm) long tube and rounded petal lobes, are produced in winter-spring.

ERANTHIS (Ranunculaceae)
Genus of clump-forming perennials, with knobbly tubers, grown for their cup-shaped flowers surrounded by leaflike ruffs of bracts. Fully to frost hardy. Prefers partial shade and humus-rich soil, well-drained but not drying out excessively. Dies down in summer. Propagate by seed in autumn or by division of clumps immediately after flowering while still in leaf.
E. cilicicus. See *E. hyemalis.*
E. hyemalis, syn. *E. cilicicus*, illus. p.371.
E. x *tubergenii* 'Guinea Gold'. Late winter- or early spring-flowering, tuberous perennial. H 3–4in (8–10cm), S 1^1/$_2$–2^1/$_2$in (4–6cm). Frost hardy, zones 4–9. Stems each bear a stalkless, deep golden yellow flower, 1^1/$_4$–1^1/$_2$in (3–4cm) across, surrounded by a bronze-green bract, cut into narrow lobes. Rounded leaves are divided into finger-shaped lobes.

ERCILLA (Phytolaccaceae)
Genus of one species of evergreen, root climber, grown for its neat, green leaves that densely clothe stems. Frost hardy. Grow in sun or partial shade and in any well-drained soil. Prune after flowering, if required. Propagate by stem cuttings in late summer or autumn.
E. spicata. See *E. volubilis.*
E. volubilis, syn. *E. spicata.* Evergreen, root climber. H to 50ft (15m) or more. Zones 8–10. Oval to heart-shaped, green leaves are 1–2in (2.5–5cm) long. Spikes of petalless flowers, each consisting of 5 greenish sepals and 6–8 white stamens, are

borne in spring. Very occasionally, may be followed by red berries.

EREMURUS (Liliaceae)
Foxtail lily, King's spear
Genus of perennials, with fleshy, fingerlike roots, grown for their stately spires of shallowly cup-shaped flowers in summer. Fully to frost hardy. Requires a sunny, warm position and well-drained soil. Tends to come into growth very early, and young shoots may be frosted. Provide a covering of dry bracken in late winter to protect the crowns when shoots are first developing. Stake tall species and hybrids. Propagate by division in spring or early autumn or by seed in autumn.
E. himalaicus illus. p.188.
E. robustus illus. p.189.
E. **Shelford Hybrids.** Group of perennials of varying habit and flower color. H 5ft (1.5m), S 2ft (60cm). Frost hardy, zones 7–9. Long racemes of orange, buff, pink, or white flowers are borne freely in mid-summer. Leaves are strap-shaped, in basal rosettes.
E. spectabilis. Erect perennial. H 4ft (1.2m), S 2ft (60cm). Frost hardy, zones 7–9. Produces long racemes of pale yellow flowers, with brick red anthers, in early summer. Leaves are strap-shaped, in basal rosettes.

ERIA. See ORCHIDS.
E. coronaria. Evergreen, epiphytic orchid for a cool greenhouse. H 9in (23cm). Zone 10. Sprays of fragrant, rounded, creamy white flowers, 1/2in (1cm) across, each with a red- and yellow-marked lip, open in autumn. Has broadly oval, glossy leaves, 4in (10cm) long. Needs semi-shade in summer and moist compost year-round.

ERICA (Ericaceae). See HEATHERS.
E. arborea (Tree heath). Evergreen, upright, shrublike tree heath. H 20ft (6m), S 5ft (1.5m). Frost hardy, zones 7–10, but liable to damage from frost and cold winds. Has needlelike, bright green leaves in whorls of 3 or 4 and bears scented, bell-shaped, white flowers from late winter to late spring. Is lime-tolerant. **'Albert's Gold'**, H 6ft (2m), retains its golden foliage year-round. var. *alpina* (illus. p.146) has vivid green foliage that contrasts well with compact racemes of white flowers. May be pruned hard to keep its shape and to encourage new growth.
E. australis (Spanish heath, Spanish tree heath). Evergreen, shrublike tree heath. H to 7ft (2.2m), S 3ft (1m). Frost hardy, zones 7–10, but stems may be damaged by snow and frost. Has needlelike leaves in whorls of 4 and tubular to bell-shaped, white or purplish pink flowers in spring. **'Mr. Robert'** has white flowers. **'Riverslea'** has bright purple-pink flowers, mostly in clusters of 4.
E. canaliculata (Channeled heath; illus. p.146). Evergreen, erect shrub. H to 10ft (3m), S 3ft (1m). Half hardy, zones 9–10. Dark green leaves are narrow and needlelike in whorls of 3. Cup-shaped, pearl white flowers, sometimes rose-tinted, with dark

brown, almost black anthers, are borne in winter (under glass) or early spring (in the open). Requires acid soil.
E. carnea, syn. *E. herbacea* (Alpine heath, Spring heath). Evergreen, spreading shrub. H to 12in (30cm), S to 18in (45cm) or more. Fully hardy, zones 5–8. Produces whorls of needlelike, mid- to dark green leaves and bears tubular to bell-shaped flowers that are in shades of pink and red, occasionally white, from early winter to late spring. Tolerates lime and some shade. Makes good ground cover. **'Altadena'** has golden foliage and pale pink flowers. **'Ann Sparkes'** (illus. p.147), H 6in (15cm), has golden foliage, turning to bronze in winter, and rose-pink flowers. **'Cecilia M. Beale'**, H 6in (15cm), bears an abundance of white flowers from mid-winter to early spring. **'C.J. Backhouse'** (illus. p.147) produces pale pink flowers from mid-winter to early spring. **'December Red'** (illus. p.147) has a spreading habit and vigorous growth. Deep rose-pink flowers are borne in winter. **'Eileen Porter'** is slow-growing and bears deep red flowers with paler sepals; is often in flower in late autumn. **'Foxhollow'**, a vigorous, spreading cultivar, has foliage that is golden yellow in summer, with orange tips in spring, and a few pale pink flowers. **'King George'**, H 8in (20cm), has dark green foliage and deep rose-pink flowers from early winter to mid-spring. **'Loughrigg'**, H 6in (15cm), produces dark purplish red flowers from late winter to spring. **'March Seedling'** has a spreading habit, dark green foliage, and rich, rose-purple flowers. **'Myreton Ruby'**, H 8in (20cm), is vigorous but compact with brilliant deep purple-red flowers in late winter and early spring. **'Pink Spangles'**, H 6in (15cm), is vigorous with flowers that have shell pink sepals and deeper pink corollas. **'Pirbright Rose'** is very floriferous with bright pink flowers from early winter to early spring. **'R.B. Cooke'**, H 8in (20cm), bears clear pink flowers from early winter to early spring. **'Springwood White'** (illus. p.146), H 6in (15cm), the most vigorous white cultivar, makes excellent ground cover and bears large, white flowers, with brown anthers, from late winter to spring. **'Vivellii'** (illus. p.147), H 6in (15cm), has dark bronze-green foliage and bears deep purple-pink flowers from late winter to spring. **'Westwood Yellow'** (illus. p.147) is compact with golden yellow foliage and deep pink flowers.
E. ciliaris (Fringed heath). Evergreen, loose shrub. H to 12in (30cm), S 16in (40cm). Fully hardy, zones 7–8, but may be damaged in severe weather. Has needlelike, dark green leaves in whorls of 3. Bears long racemes of bell-shaped, bright pink flowers in tiers of 3 or 4 in summer. Requires acid soil and prefers warm, moist conditions. **'Aurea'** has somewhat straggly growth with golden foliage and clear pink flowers. **'Corfe Castle'** (illus. p.147) produces salmon pink flowers from summer to early autumn.

'David McClintock' (illus. p.146) has light gray-green foliage and bears white flowers, with deep pink tips, from summer to early autumn. **'Mrs. C.H. Gill'** has dark gray-green foliage and clear red flowers. **'White Wings'** (illus. p.146), a sport of 'Mrs. C.H. Gill', has dark gray-green foliage and white flowers.
E. cinerea (Twisted heather). Evergreen, compact shrub. H 12in (30cm), S 18–24in (45–60cm). Fully hardy, zones 6–8. Has needlelike, mid- to deep green leaves and bears bell-shaped flowers that are in shades of pink and dark red, occasionally white, from early summer to early autumn. Prefers a warm, dry position. Requires acid soil. **'Alba Major'** has green foliage and clear white flowers. **'Atropurpurea'** has deep purple flowers in long racemes. **'Atrorubens'**, a free-flowering cultivar, produces ruby red flowers. **'C.D. Eason'** (illus. p.147) has distinctive, dark green foliage and bright red flowers. **'Cevennes'** is upright in habit and bears a profusion of mauve flowers. **'C.G. Best'** has green foliage and rose-pink flowers. **'Contrast'** bears very dark purple flowers. **'Domino'** produces white flowers that contrast with dark brown stems and sepals and almost black stigmas. **'Eden Valley'** (illus. p.147), H 8in (20cm), bears white flowers with lavender mauve tips. **'Foxhollow Mahogany'** has very dark green foliage and deep ruby red flowers. **'Frances'** produces rose-pink flowers. **'Glencairn'** (illus. p.147), H 8in (20cm), has foliage tipped with pink and red, particularly in spring, and magenta flowers. **'Hookstone Lavender'** (illus. p.147), H 15in (38cm), is somewhat straggling in habit and bears an abundance of pale lavender flowers. **'Hookstone White'** (illus. p.146), H 14in (35cm), has bright green foliage and bears long racemes of large, white flowers. **'Janet'** is compact with pale shell pink flowers from mid-summer. **'Pentreath'** has rich purple flowers. **'Pink Ice'**, H 8in (20cm), is compact with soft pink flowers. **'P.S. Patrick'** is a vigorous cultivar with purple flowers and dark green foliage. **'Purple Beauty'** (illus. p.147) has purple flowers and dark foliage. **'Purple Robe'**, H 8in (20cm), bears dusky purple flowers in long racemes. **'Rock Pool'** (illus. p.147), H 6in (15cm), is compact and has golden foliage, tinted orange and red in winter, and mauve flowers. **'Romiley'** (illus. p.147), H 10in (25cm), bears masses of ruby red flowers from early to late summer. **'Stephen Davis'**, H 10in (25cm), has brilliant, almost fluorescent, red flowers. **'Velvet Night'**, H 10in (25cm), produces very dark purple, almost black flowers. **'Windlebrooke'** (illus. p.147), H 10in (25cm), is a vigorous cultivar with golden foliage, turning bright orange-red in winter, and mauve flowers.
E. x darleyensis (Darley heath). Evergreen, bushy shrub. H 18in (45cm), S 3ft (1m) or more. Fully hardy, zones 7–8. Has needlelike, green foliage, with cream, pink, or

red, young growth in late spring. Bell-shaped, white, pink, or purple flowers are borne in racemes from early winter to late spring. Tolerates lime. **'Archie Graham'** (illus. p.146), H 20in (50cm), is vigorous with mauve-pink flowers. **'Arthur Johnson'**, H 3ft (1m), has young foliage with cream-and-pink tips in spring and long racemes of mauve-pink flowers from mid-winter to spring. **'Darley Dale'** (illus. p.146) bears pale mauve flowers from mid-winter to spring. **'George Rendall'** carries deep pink flowers from early winter to early spring. **'Ghost Hills'** (illus. p.146) has cream-tipped foliage in spring and a profusion of pink flowers from mid-winter to spring. **'Jack H. Brummage'**, H 12in (30cm), has golden foliage, with yellow and orange tints, and mauve flowers. **'J.W. Porter'**, H 12in (30cm), has reddish, young shoots in spring and mauve-pink flowers from mid-winter to late spring. **'Silberschmelze'** (syn. *E. x d.* 'Molten Silver') is vigorous and produces young shoots with creamy pink tips in spring and white flowers. **'White Glow'** (illus. p.146), H 12in (30cm), bears white flowers. **'White Perfection'** (illus. p.146) has bright green foliage and white flowers.
E. erigena, syn. *E. mediterranea.* Evergreen, upright shrub. H to 8ft (2.5m), S to 3ft (1m). Frost hardy, zones 7–8; top growth may be damaged in severe weather, but plant recovers well from the base. Has needlelike, green leaves and, usually, bell-shaped, mauve-pink flowers from early winter to late spring. Tolerates lime. Flowers of some cultivars have a pronounced scent of honey. **'Brightness'** (illus. p.147), H 18in (45cm), has bronze-green foliage and mauve-pink flowers in spring. **'Golden Lady'** (illus. p.147), H 12in (30cm), has a neat, compact habit with year-round, golden foliage and white flowers in late spring. **'Irish Dusk'**, H 18in (45cm), has dark green foliage and salmon pink flowers from mid-winter to early spring. **'Superba'**, H 6ft (2m), bears strongly scented, rose-pink flowers in spring. **'W.T. Rackliff'**, H 2ft (60cm), has dark green foliage and bears thick clusters of white flowers from late winter to late spring.
E. gracilis. Evergreen, compact shrub. H and S to 12in (30cm). Frost tender, min. 41°F (5°C), zones 9–10. Has needlelike, green leaves and clusters of small, bell-shaped, cerise flowers from early autumn to early spring. Is usually grown as a potted plant; may be planted outdoors in summer in a sheltered position.
E. herbacea. See *E. carnea.*
E. hyemalis. Evergreen, bushy shrub. H and S 12in (30cm). Half hardy, zones 9–10. Has needlelike, green foliage and racemes of tubular to bell-shaped, pink-tinged, white flowers from late autumn to mid-winter.
E. lusitanica (Portuguese heath). Evergreen, upright, bushy, tree heath. H to 10ft (3m), S 3ft (1m). Frost hardy, zones 8–10. Has feathery, bright green leaves and, from late autumn to late spring, bears tubular to bell-shaped

flowers that are pink in bud but pure white when fully open. **'George Hunt'** has golden foliage; is frost hardy but needs a sheltered position.

E. mackaiana (Mackay's heath). Evergreen, spreading shrub. H to 10in (25cm), S 16in (40cm). Fully hardy, zones 4–7. Has needlelike, green leaves and bears umbels of rounded, pink, mauve-pink, or white flowers from mid-summer to early autumn. Likes damp, acid soil. **'Dr. Ronald Gray'** (illus. p.146), H 6in (15cm), has dark green foliage and pure white flowers. **'Plena'** (illus. p.146), H 6in (15cm), has double, deep pink flowers, shading to white in centers.

E. mediterranea. See *E. erigena.*

E. pageana. Evergreen, bushy shrub. H to 2ft (60cm), S 1ft (30cm). Half hardy, zones 9–10. Has needlelike, green leaves and, from late spring to early summer, bell-shaped, rich yellow flowers.

E. x praegeri. See *E. x stuartii.*

E. scoparia (Besom heath). Evergreen, bushy shrub. H to 10ft (3m), S 3ft (1m). Frost hardy, zones 7–8. Has needlelike, dark green leaves. Clusters of rounded, bell-shaped, greenish brown flowers appear in late spring and early summer. Requires acid soil. **'Minima'**, H 12in (30cm), has bright green foliage.

E. x stuartii, syn. *E. x praegeri.* Evergreen, compact shrub. H 6in (15cm), S 12in (30cm). Fully hardy, zones 5–7. Has needlelike, dark green leaves. Numerous umbels of bell-shaped, pink flowers are produced in late spring and summer. Prefers moist, acid soil. **'Irish Lemon'** produces young foliage with lemon yellow tips in spring and bright pink flowers. **'Irish Orange'** has orange-tipped young foliage and dark pink flowers.

E. terminalis (Corsican heath). Evergreen, shrublike tree heath with stiff, upright growth. H and S to 8ft (2.5m). Frost hardy, zones 7–8. Has needlelike, green foliage. Bell-shaped, mauve-pink flowers, borne from early summer to early autumn, turn russet as they fade in autumn. Tolerates lime.

E. tetralix (Cross-leaved heath). Evergreen, spreading shrub. H to 12in (30cm), S 18in (45cm). Fully hardy, zones 4–7. Has needlelike, gray-green leaves in whorls of 4. Large umbels of bell-shaped, pink flowers appear from summer to early autumn. Requires acid, preferably moist soil. **'Alba Mollis'** (illus. p.146) has silver-gray foliage and bears white flowers from early summer to late autumn. **'Con Underwood'** (illus. p.147) has dark red flowers. **'Hookstone Pink'** has silver-gray foliage and bears rose-pink flowers from late spring to early autumn. **'Pink Star'** (illus. p.147) produces pink flowers held upright in a starlike pattern.

E. umbellata. Evergreen, bushy shrub. H and S 2ft (60cm). Frost hardy, zones 7–8. Has needlelike, green foliage and in late spring produces bell-shaped, mauve flowers, with chocolate brown anthers.

E. vagans (Cornish heath). Vigorous, evergreen, bushy shrub. H and S 30in (75cm). Fully hardy, zones 6–8.

Leaves are needlelike and green. Rounded, bell-shaped, pink, mauve, or white flowers appear from mid-summer to late autumn. Tolerates some lime. Responds well to hard pruning. **'Birch Glow'** (illus. p.147), H 18in (45cm), has bright green foliage and glowing rose-pink flowers. **'Lyonesse'** (illus. p.146), H 18in (45cm), has dark green foliage and long, tapering spikes of white flowers with brown anthers. **'Mrs. D.F. Maxwell'**, H 18in (45cm), has dark green foliage and glowing deep pink flowers. **'St. Keverne'**, H 18in (45cm), is a neat, bushy shrub with rose-pink flowers; may be used for a low hedge. **'Valerie Proudley'** (illus. p.147), H 18in (45cm), has golden foliage year-round when grown in full light and sparse, white flowers in late summer and autumn. **'Viridiflora'** has feathery, green bracts in place of flowers and is useful for flower arrangements.

E. x veitchii. Evergreen, bushy, shrublike tree heath. H to 6ft (2m), S 3ft (1m). Frost hardy, zones 7–8. Has needlelike, green leaves. Scented, tubular to bell-shaped, white flowers are produced in dense clusters from mid-winter to spring. **'Exeter'** (illus. p.146) has a profusion of white flowers, almost obscuring the foliage. **'Gold Tips'** is similar to 'Exeter', but young foliage has golden tips in spring. **'Pink Joy'** (illus. p.146) has pink flower buds that open to clear white.

E. x watsonii. Evergreen, compact shrub. H 12in (30cm), S 15in (38cm). Fully hardy, zones 4–7. Needlelike, green leaves often have bright-colored tips in spring. Bears rounded, bell-shaped, pink flowers from mid- to late summer. **'Cherry Turpin'** has long racemes of pale pink flowers from mid-summer to mid-autumn. **'Dawn'** (illus. p.146) produces young foliage with orange-yellow tips and bears deep mauve-pink flowers in compact clusters throughout summer.

E. x williamsii. Evergreen, spreading shrub. H 12in (30cm), S 24in (60cm). Fully hardy, zones 4–7. Has needlelike, dark green leaves, with bright yellow tips when young in spring. Bears bell-shaped, mauve or pink flowers in mid-summer. Prefers acid soil. **'Gwavas'** has pale pink flowers on a neat, compact plant from mid-summer to autumn. **'P.D. Williams'** (illus. p.146), H 18in (45cm), produces dark mauve-pink flowers; sometimes keeps its golden foliage tips throughout summer.

ERIGERON (Compositae)
Fleabane
Genus of mainly spring- and summer-flowering annuals, biennials, and perennials, grown for their daisylike flower heads. Is good for rock gardens or herbaceous borders. Fully to frost hardy. Prefers sun and well-drained soil. Resents winter damp, but should not be allowed to dry out during growing season. Propagate by division in spring or early autumn or by seed in autumn, selected forms by softwood cuttings in early summer.

E. alpinus illus. p.295.

E. aurantiacus. Clump-forming perennial. H 6in (15cm), S 12in (30cm). Fully hardy, zones 5–8. Has long, oval, gray-green leaves and, in summer, daisylike, brilliant orange flower heads. Propagate by seed or division in spring.

E. aureus. Clump-forming perennial. H 2in (5cm), S 4in (10cm). Fully hardy, zones 5–8. Bears small, spoon-shaped, hairy leaves. Fine stems each carry a relatively large, daisylike, golden yellow flower head in summer. Dislikes winter wet unless protected with snow. Is excellent for a scree, trough, or alpine house; is prone to aphid attack.

E. 'Charity' illus. p.235.

E. 'Darkest of All'. Clump-forming perennial. H 32in (80cm), S 24in (60cm) or more. Fully hardy, zones 5–8. Produces a mass of daisylike, deep purple flower heads, with yellow centers, in summer. Has narrowly oval, grayish green leaves.

E. 'Foerster's Liebling'. Clump-forming perennial. H 32in (80cm), S 24in (60cm). Fully hardy, zones 5–8. In summer, daisylike, semi-double, pink flower heads, with yellow centers, are borne above narrowly oval, grayish green leaves.

E. glaucus **'Elstead'**. Tufted perennial. H 12in (30cm), S 6in (15cm). Fully hardy, zones 5–8. Daisylike, dark lilac-pink flower heads appear throughout summer above oval, gray-green leaves.

E. karvinskianus, syn. *E. mucronatus*, illus. p.317.

E. mucronatus. See *E. karvinskianus.*

E. 'Quakeress'. Clump-forming perennial. H 32in (80cm), S 24in (60cm). Fully hardy, zones 5–8. Daisylike, delicate lilac-pink flower heads, with yellow centers, are borne in abundance during summer. Narrowly oval leaves are grayish green.

E. 'Serenity' illus. p.241.

ERINACEA (Leguminosae)
Genus of one species of slow-growing, evergreen sub-shrub with hard, sharp, blue-green spines and pealike flowers. In spring produces short-lived, soft leaves. Frost hardy. Needs a sheltered position with full sun and deep, gritty, well-drained soil. Propagate by seed when available or by softwood cuttings in late spring or summer.

E. anthyllis, syn. *E. pungens*, illus. p.288.

E. pungens. See *E. anthyllis.*

ERINUS (Scrophulariaceae)
Fairy foxglove
Genus of semi-evergreen, short-lived perennials, suitable for rock gardens, walls, and troughs. Fully hardy. Needs sun and well-drained soil. Propagate species by seed in autumn (but seedlings will vary considerably), selected forms by softwood cuttings in early summer. Self seeds freely.

E. alpinus illus. p.306. **'Dr. Haenele'** is a semi-evergreen, basal-rosetted perennial. H and S 2–3in (5–8cm). Zones 4–7. Small, flat, 2-lipped, deep pink flowers are produced in late spring and summer. Leaves are small, oval, and green.

ERIOBOTRYA (Rosaceae)
Genus of evergreen, autumn-flowering trees and shrubs, grown for their foliage, flowers, and edible fruits. Frost hardy, but in cold areas grow against a south- or west-facing wall. Fruits, which ripen in spring, may be damaged by hard, winter frosts. Requires sunny, fertile, well-drained soil. Propagate by seed in autumn or spring.

E. japonica (Loquat). Evergreen, bushy shrub or spreading tree. H and S 25ft (8m). Zones 8–10. Has stout shoots and large, oblong, prominently veined, glossy, dark green leaves. Fragrant, 5-petaled, white flowers are borne in large clusters in early autumn, followed by pear-shaped, orange-yellow fruits.

ERIOGONUM (Polygonaceae)
Wild buckwheat
Genus of annuals, biennials, and evergreen perennials, sub-shrubs, and shrubs, grown for their rosetted, hairy, often silver or white leaves. Fully hardy to frost tender, min. 41°F (5°C). Needs full sun and well-drained, even poor soil. In cool, wet-winter areas protect shrubby species and hairy-leaved perennials. Water potted specimens moderately in summer, less in spring and autumn, very little in winter. Remove spent flower heads after flowering unless seed is required. Propagate by seed in spring or autumn or by semi-ripe cuttings in summer. Divide perennial root clumps in spring.

E. arborescens illus. p.129.

E. crocatum. Evergreen, sub-shrubby perennial. H to 8in (20cm), S 6in (15cm). Frost hardy, zones 9–10. Oval, hairy leaves have woolly, white undersides. Heads of minute, sulfur yellow flowers are borne in summer. Is a good alpine house plant.

E. giganteum illus. p.107.

E. ovalifolium. Evergreen, domed perennial. H 12in (30cm), S 4in (10cm). Fully hardy, zones 8–10. In summer carries tiny, bright yellow flowers in umbels above branched stems bearing tiny, spoon-shaped, hairy, gray leaves. Is excellent for an alpine house.

E. umbellatum illus. p.298.

ERIOPHYLLUM (Compositae)
Genus of summer-flowering perennials and evergreen sub-shrubs, with, usually, silvery foliage and attractive, daisylike flower heads, suitable for rock gardens as well as front of borders. Frost hardy. Requires sun and well-drained soil. Propagate by division in spring or by seed in autumn.

E. lanatum illus. p.248.

ERITRICHIUM (Boraginaceae)
Genus of short-lived perennials with soft, gray-green leaves and forget-me-notlike flowers. Is suitable for rock gardens and alpine houses. Fully hardy. Needs sun and well-drained, peaty, sandy soil with a deep collar of grit; dislikes damp conditions. Is extremely difficult to grow. Propagate by seed when available or by softwood cuttings in summer.

E. elongatum. Tuft-forming perennial. H ³/₄in (2cm), S 1¹/₄in (3cm). Zones 5–7. Leaves are oval, hairy, and gray-green. Short flower stems each carry small, rounded, flat, blue flowers in early summer.
E. nanum illus. p.323.

ERODIUM (Geraniaceae)
Genus of mound-forming perennials, suitable for rock gardens. Fully to half hardy. Needs sun and well-drained soil. Propagate by semi-ripe cuttings in summer or by seed when available.
E. chamaedryoides. See *E. reichardii*.
E. chrysanthum illus. p.298.
E. corsicum illus. p.316.
E. manescavii illus. p.236.
E. petraeum. Compact, mound-forming perennial. H 6–8in (15–20cm), S 8in (20cm). Frost hardy, zones 5–8. Produces saucer-shaped, single, red-veined, pink flowers in summer. Oval, gray leaves have deeply cut edges. subsp. **crispum** illus. p.295.
E. reichardii, syn. *E. chamaedryoides*. Mound-forming perennial. H 1in (2.5cm), S 2¹/₂–3in (6–8cm). Half hardy, zones 8–9. In summer, saucer-shaped, single flowers, either white or pink with darker veins, are borne above tiny, oaklike leaves. Is good for a rock garden or trough.
E. x variabile 'Flore Pleno'. Variable, cushion-forming or spreading perennial. H 4in (10cm), S 12in (30cm). Fully hardy, zones 5–8. Has oval to narrowly oval, dark to gray-green leaves with scalloped edges and long stalks. From spring to autumn, flower stems each bear 1 or 2 rounded, double, pink flowers with darker veins; outer petals are rounded, inner petals narrower. **'Ken Aslet'** has prostrate stems, green leaves, and single, deep pink flowers.

Erpetion reniforme. See *Viola hederacea*.

ERYNGIUM (Umbelliferae)
Sea holly
Genus of biennials and perennials, some of which are evergreen, grown for their flowers, foliage, and habit. Fully to half hardy. Does best in sun and in fertile, well-drained soil. Propagate species by seed in autumn, selected forms by division in spring or by root cuttings in winter.
E. agavifolium. Evergreen, clump-forming perennial. H 5ft (1.5m), S 2ft (60cm). Half hardy, zones 9–10. Forms rosettes of sword-shaped, sharply toothed, rich green leaves. Thistlelike, greenish white flower heads are produced on branched stems in summer.
E. alpinum illus. p.212.
E. amethystinum. Rosette-forming perennial. H and S 24in (60cm). Fully hardy, zones 3–8. Produces much-branched stems that, in summer, bear heads of small, thistlelike, blue flowers surrounded by spiky, darker blue bracts. Oval leaves are divided, spiny, and green.
E. bourgatii illus. p.242.
E. eburneum illus. p.188.
E. giganteum. Clump-forming biennial or short-lived perennial that

dies after flowering. H 3–4ft (1–1.2m), S 2¹/₂ft (75cm). Fully hardy, zones 5–8. Bears large, rounded heads of thistlelike, blue flowers, surrounded by broad, spiny, silvery bracts, in late summer. Heart-shaped, basal leaves are green.
E. x oliverianum illus. p.212.
E. tripartitum illus. p.212.
E. variifolium illus. p.243.
E. 'Violetta'. Upright perennial. H 30in (75cm), S 24in (60cm). Fully hardy, zones 5–8. Loose heads of thistlelike, deep violet flowers, surrounded by narrow, spiny, silvery blue bracts, appear in late summer. Has rounded, green leaves divided into 3–5 segments.

ERYSIMUM (Cruciferae)
Genus of annuals, biennials, evergreen or semi-evergreen, short-lived perennials and sub-shrubs, grown for their flowers. Is closely related to *Cheiranthus* and is suitable for borders, banks, and rock gardens. Fully to frost hardy. Needs sun and well-drained soil. Propagate by seed in spring or autumn or by softwood cuttings in summer.
E. helveticum, syn. *E. pumilum*, illus. p.313.
E. hieraciifolium, syn. *Cheiranthus x allionii* (Siberian wallflower). **'Orange Bedder'** illus. p.284.
E. linifolium. Short-lived, semi-evergreen, open, dome-shaped sub-shrub. H to 12in (30cm), S 8in (20cm) or more. Frost hardy, zones 7–9. Leaves are narrowly lance-shaped and blue-gray. Produces tight heads of small, 4-petaled, pale violet flowers in early summer.
E. pumilum. See *E. helveticum*.

ERYTHRINA (Leguminosae)
Genus of deciduous or semi-evergreen trees, shrubs, and perennials, grown for their flowers from spring to autumn. Half hardy to frost tender, min. 41°F (5°C). Requires full light and well-drained soil. Water potted plants moderately, very little in winter or when leafless. Propagate by seed in spring or by semi-ripe cuttings in summer. Red spider mite may be troublesome.
E. x bidwillii illus. p.111.
E. coralloides (Flame coral-tree, Naked coral-tree). Deciduous, untidily rounded shrub or tree with somewhat prickly stems. H and S 10–20ft (3–6m). Frost tender, zone 10. Has leaves of 3 triangular leaflets, the largest central one 4¹/₂in (11cm) long. Racemes of pealike, red flowers are borne on leafless stems in early spring and summer.
E. crista-galli illus. p.111.

ERYTHRONIUM (Liliaceae)
Genus of spring-flowering, tuberous perennials, grown for their pendent flowers and in some cases attractively mottled leaves. Fully to frost hardy. Requires partial shade and humus-rich, well-drained soil, where tubers will not become too hot and dry in summer while dormant. Prefers cool climates. Propagate by seed in autumn. Some species increase by offsets, which

should be divided in late summer. Do not allow tubers to dry out before replanting, 6in (15cm) deep.
E. americanum illus. p.363.
E. californicum illus. p.357.
E. dens-canis illus. p.358.
E. grandiflorum. Spring-flowering, tuberous perennial. H 4–12in (10–30cm), S 2–3in (5–8cm). Fully hardy, zones 4–9. Has 2 lance-shaped, semi-erect, basal, plain bright green leaves. Stem carries 1–3 pendent, bright yellow flowers with reflexed petals.
E. hendersonii illus. p.343.
E. oregonum illus. p.342.
E. 'Pagoda' illus. p.347.
E. revolutum. Spring-flowering, tuberous perennial. H 8–12in (20–30cm), S 6in (15cm). Frost hardy, zones 5–9. Produces 2 lance-shaped, semi-erect, basal, brown-mottled, green leaves and a loose spike of 1–4 pendent, pale to deep pink flowers with reflexed petals.
E. tuolumnense. Spring-flowering, tuberous perennial. H to 12in (30cm), S 5–6in (12–15cm). Frost hardy, zones 3–9. Has 2 lance-shaped, semi-erect, basal, glossy, plain green leaves. Carries a spike of up to 10 pendent, bright yellow flowers with reflexed petals. Increases rapidly by offsets.
E. 'White Beauty' illus. p.342.

ESCALLONIA (Crassulariaceae)
Genus of evergreen, semi-evergreen, or deciduous shrubs and trees, grown for their profuse, 5-petaled flowers and glossy foliage. Thrives in mild areas, where *Escallonia* is wind-resistant and ideal for hedging in coastal gardens. Frost hardy, but in cold areas protect from strong winds and grow against a south- or west-facing wall. Requires full sun and fertile, well-drained soil. Trim hedges and wall-trained plants after flowering. Propagate by softwood cuttings in summer.
E. 'Apple Blossom' illus. p.109.
E. 'Donard Beauty'. Evergreen, arching shrub with slender shoots. H and S 5ft (1.5m). Zones 8–9. Bears deep pink flowers from early to mid-summer among small, oval, dark green leaves.
E. 'Donard Seedling' illus. p.108.
E. 'Edinensis'. Vigorous, evergreen, arching shrub. H 6ft (2m), S 10ft (3m). Zones 7–9. Bears small, oblong, bright green leaves. Small, pink flowers are produced from early to mid-summer. Is one of the more hardy escallonias.
E. 'Iveyi' illus. p.86.
E. 'Langleyensis' illus. p.110.
E. leucantha illus. p.86.
E. rubra var. **macrantha 'Crimson Spire'.** Very vigorous, evergreen, upright shrub. H and S 10ft (3m). Zones 8–9. Has oval, rich green leaves and, throughout summer, tubular, deep red flowers. **'Woodside'** illus. p.133.
E. virgata illus. p.105.

ESCHSCHOLZIA (Papaveraceae)
Genus of annuals, grown for their bright, poppylike flowers. Is suitable for rock gardens and gaps in paving. Fully hardy. Requires sun and grows well in poor, very well-drained soil. Dead-head regularly to ensure a long

flowering period. Propagate by seed sown outdoors in spring or early autumn.
E. caespitosa illus. p.280.
E. californica illus. p.282, [mixed] illus. p.282. **Ballerina Series** illus. p.266.

ESPOSTOA (Cactaceae)
Genus of columnar, perennial cacti, each with a 10–30-ribbed stem, eventually becoming bushy or treelike with age. Most species are densely covered in woolly, white hairs masking short, sharp spines. Bears cup-shaped flowers, as well as extra wool down the side of stems facing the sun, only after about 30 years. Frost tender, min. 50°F (10°C). Needs full sun and very well-drained soil. Propagate by seed in spring or summer.
E. lanata illus. p.379.

EUCALYPTUS (Myrtaceae)
Gum tree
Genus of evergreen trees and shrubs, grown for their bark, flowers, and aromatic foliage. Frost hardy to frost tender, min. 34–50°F (1–10°C). Requires full sun, shelter from strong, cold winds, and fertile, well-drained soil. Plant smallest obtainable trees. Water potted plants moderately, less in winter. Attractive, young foliage of some species, normally lost with age, may be retained by cutting growth back hard in spring. Propagate by seed in spring or autumn.
E. camaldulensis (Murray red gum, River red gum). Fast-growing, evergreen, irregularly rounded tree. H 100ft (30m) or more, S 70ft (20m) or more. Frost tender, min. 37–41°F (3–5°C), zones 9–10. Young bark is gray, brown, and cream; leaves are lance-shaped, slender, green or blue-green. Has umbels of small, cream flowers in summer. Is a drought-resistant tree.
E. coccifera illus. p.46.
E. dalrympleana illus. p.46.
E. ficifolia (Flowering gum). Moderately fast-growing, evergreen, rounded tree. H and S to 25ft (8m). Frost tender, min. 34–7°F (1–3°C), zones 9–10. Has broadly lance-shaped, glossy, deep green leaves. Produces large panicles of many-stamened, pale to deep red flowers in spring-summer. Is best in acid soil.
E. glaucescens (Tingiringi gum). Evergreen, spreading tree. H 40ft (12m), S 25ft (8m). Frost hardy, zones 9–10. Young bark is white. Leaves are silvery blue and rounded when young, long, narrow, and blue-gray when mature. In autumn bears clusters of many-stamened, white flowers.
E. globulus (Blue gum, Tasmanian blue gum). Very fast-growing, evergreen, spreading tree. H 100ft (30m), S 40ft (12m). Half hardy, zones 9–10. Bark peels in ribbons. Large, oval to oblong, silvery blue leaves are long, narrow, and glossy, green when mature. White flowers, consisting of tufts of stamens, appear in summer-autumn, often year-round.
E. gunnii illus. p.46.
E. niphophila illus. p.57.

E. pauciflora illus. p.57.
E. perriniana illus. p.72.
E. viminalis (Manna gum, Ribbon gum). Vigorous, evergreen, spreading tree. H 100ft (30m), S 50ft (15m). Frost tender, min. 41°F (5°C), zones 9–10. Bark peels on upper trunk. Lance-shaped, dark green leaves become very long, narrow, and pale green when mature. Bears clusters of many-stamened, white flowers in summer.

EUCHARIS (Amaryllidaceae)
Genus of evergreen bulbs, grown for their fragrant, white flowers that resemble large, white daffodils, with a cup and 6 spreading petals. Frost tender, min. 59°F (15°C). Prefers at least 50% relative humidity. Needs partial shade and humus-rich soil. Water freely in summer. Propagate by seed when ripe or by offsets in spring.
E. amazonica. See *E. grandiflora.*
E. grandiflora, syn. *E. amazonica*, illus. p.355.

EUCOMIS (Liliaceae)
Pineapple flower
Genus of summer- and autumn-flowering bulbs, grown for their dense spikes of flowers, which are overtopped by a tuft of small, leaflike bracts, as in a pineapple. Frost hardy, but in severe winters protect with dead bracken or loose, rough peat. Needs full sun and well-drained soil. Plant in spring and water freely in summer growing period. Propagate by seed or division of clumps in spring.
E. autumnalis, syn. *E. undulata.* Late summer- to autumn-flowering bulb. H 8–12in (20–30cm), S 24–30in (60–75cm). Zones 8–10. Has strap-shaped, wavy-edged leaves in a semi-erect, basal tuft. Leafless stem bears small, star-shaped, pale green or white flowers in a dense spike, with a cluster of leaflike bracts at apex.
E. bicolor illus. p.353.
E. comosa illus. p.333.
E. pallidiflora illus. p.333.
E. undulata. See *E. autumnalis.*

EUCOMMIA (Eucommiaceae)
Genus of one species of deciduous tree, grown for its unusual foliage. Fully hardy. Needs full sun and fertile, well-drained soil. Propagate by softwood cuttings in summer.
E. ulmoides (Hardy rubber tree). Deciduous, spreading tree. H 40ft (12m), S 25ft (8m). Zones 4–7. Drooping, oval leaves are pointed and glossy, dark green; when pulled apart, leaf pieces remain joined by rubbery threads. Inconspicuous flowers appear in late spring, before leaves emerge.

EUCRYPHIA (Eucryphiaceae)
Genus of evergreen, semi-evergreen, or deciduous trees and shrubs, grown for their foliage and often fragrant white flowers. Frost hardy. Needs a sheltered, semi-shaded position in all but mild, wet areas, where it will withstand more exposure. Does best with roots in a cool, moist, shaded position and crown in sun. Requires fertile, well-drained soil that is lime-free, except in the case of *E. cordifolia*

and *E.* × *nymansensis.* Propagate by semi-ripe cuttings in late summer.
E. cordifolia (Ulmo). Evergreen, columnar tree. H 50ft (15m), S 25ft (8m). Zones 8–9. Has oblong, wavy-edged, dull green leaves, with gray down beneath. Large, roselike, white flowers are borne in late summer and autumn.
E. glutinosa illus. p.63.
E. lucida illus. p.63.
E. milliganii illus. p.105.
E. × *nymansensis* illus. p.54.

Eugenia australis. See *Syzygium paniculatum.*
Eugenia paniculata. See *Syzygium paniculatum.*
Eugenia ugni. See *Myrtus ugni.*

EUODIA, syn. EVODIA (Rutaceae)
Genus of deciduous trees, grown for their foliage, late flowers, and fruits. Fully hardy. Needs full sun and fertile, well-drained soil. Propagate by softwood cuttings in summer, by seed in autumn, or by root cuttings in late winter.
E. hupehensis. Deciduous, spreading tree. H and S 50ft (15m). Zones 5–8. Ashlike, dark green leaves consisting of 5–11 oval to oblong leaflets turn yellow in autumn. Large clusters of small, fragrant, 5-petaled, white flowers in early autumn are followed by beaked, red fruits.

EUONYMUS (Celastraceae)
Genus of evergreen or deciduous shrubs and trees, sometimes climbing, grown for their foliage, autumn color, and fruits. Fully to frost hardy. Needs sun or semi-shade and any well-drained soil, although, if grown in full sun, soil for evergreen species should not be very dry. Propagate by semi-ripe cuttings in summer or by seed in autumn. *E. europaeus* and *E. japonicus* may be attacked by caterpillars; *E. japonicus* is susceptible to mildew.
E. alatus illus. p.116. **'Compactus'** is a deciduous, bushy, dense shrub. H 3ft (1m), S 10ft (3m). Fully hardy, zones 4–9. Shoots have corky wings. Oval, dark green leaves turn brilliant red in autumn. Inconspicuous, greenish white flowers in summer are followed by small, 4-lobed, purple or red fruits.
E. cornutus var. **quinquecornutus.** Deciduous, spreading, open shrub. H 6ft (2m), S 10ft (3m). Frost hardy, zones 7–10. Has narrowly lance-shaped, dark green leaves. Small, purplish green flowers in summer are followed by showy, 5-horned, pink fruits that open to reveal orange-red seeds.
E. europaeus (Spindle tree). **'Red Cascade'** illus. p.115.
E. fortunei. Evergreen shrub, only grown as var. **radicans** and its cultivars, which are climbing or creeping and prostrate. H 15ft (5m) if supported, S indefinite. Fully hardy, zones 5–9. Bears oval, dark green leaves and inconspicuous, greenish white flowers from early to mid-summer. Makes good ground cover. Foliage of **'Coloratus'** turns reddish purple in autumn-winter. **'Emerald and Gold'** illus. p.145. **'Emerald**

Gaiety'**, H 3ft (1m), S 5ft (1.5m), is bushy, with rounded, white-edged, deep green leaves. Young, rounded leaves of **'Gold Tip'** are edged bright yellow, ageing to creamy white. **'Kewensis'**, H 4in (10cm) or more, has slender stems and tiny leaves, and forms dense mats of growth. **'Sarcoxie'**, H and S 4ft (1.2m), is vigorous, upright and bushy, with glossy, dark green leaves. **'Silver Queen'** illus. p.119. **'Sunspot'** bears deep green leaves, each marked in center with golden yellow.
E. hamiltonianus var. *sieboldianus*, syn. *E. yedoensis.* Deciduous, treelike shrub. H and S 20ft (6m) or more. Fully hardy, zones 5–8. Oval, green leaves often turn pink and red in autumn. Tiny, green flowers in late spring and early summer are followed by 4-lobed, pink fruits. var. *sieboldianus* **'Red Elf'** illus. p.115.
E. japonicus (Japanese spindle). **'Macrophyllus'** is an evergreen, upright, dense shrub. H 12ft (4m), S 6ft (2m). Frost hardy, zones 7–10. Has very large, oval, glossy, dark green leaves and, in summer, small, star-shaped, green flowers, sometimes succeeded by spherical, pink fruits with orange seeds. Is good for hedging, particularly in coastal areas. **'Macrophyllus Albus'** illus. p.119. Leaves of **'Ovatus Aureus'** are broadly edged with golden yellow.
E. latifolius illus. p.116.
E. myrianthus illus. p.92.
E. oxyphyllus. Deciduous, upright shrub or tree. H and S 8ft (2.5m). Fully hardy, zones 6–9. Oval, dull green leaves become purplish red in autumn. Produces tiny, greenish white flowers in late spring, followed by globose, 4- or 5-lobed, deep red fruits with orange-scarlet seeds.
E. planipes, syn. *E. sachalinensis* of gardens. Deciduous, upright, open shrub. H and S 10ft (3m). Fully hardy, zones 6–9. Bears oval, green leaves that turn to brilliant red in autumn, as large, 4- or 5-lobed, red fruits open to reveal bright orange seeds. Star-shaped, green flowers open in late spring.
E. sachalinensis of gardens. See *E. planipes.*
E. yedoensis. See *E. hamiltonianus* var. *sieboldianus.*

EUPATORIUM (Compositae)
Genus of perennials, sub-shrubs, and shrubs, many of which are evergreen, grown mainly for their flowers, some also for their architectural foliage. Fully hardy to frost tender, min. 41–55°F (5–13°C). Requires full light or partial shade. Will grow in any conditions, although most species prefer moist but well-drained soil. Water potted plants freely when in full growth, moderately at other times. Prune shrubs lightly after flowering or in spring. Propagate by seed in spring; shrubs and sub-shrubs may also be propagated by softwood or greenwood cuttings in summer, perennials by division in early spring or autumn. Red spider mite and whitefly may be troublesome.
E. ageratoides. See *E. rugosum.*

E. fistulosum illus. p.193
E. ianthinum. See *E. sordidum.*
E. ligustrinum, syn. *E. micranthum*, *E. weinmannianum.* Evergreen, rounded shrub. H and S 6–12ft (2–4m). Half hardy, zones 9–10. Has elliptic to lance-shaped, bright green leaves and, in autumn, fragrant, groundsel-like, white or pink flowers in flattened clusters, 4–8in (10–20cm) wide.
E. micranthum. See *E. ligustrinum.*
E. rugosum, syn. *E. ageratoides*, *E. urticifolium* (Hardy age, Mist flower, White snakeroot). Erect perennial. H 4ft (1.2m), S 1¹/₂ft (45cm). Fully hardy, zones 4–9. In late summer bears dense, flat, thistlelike, pure white flower heads. Has nettlelike, light green leaves.
E. sordidum, syn. *E. ianthinum.* Evergreen, rounded, robust-stemmed shrub. H and S 3–6ft (1–2m). Frost tender, min. 50–55°F (10–13°C), zone 10. Oval, serrated, deep green leaves are red haired. Produces fragrant, pomponlike, violet-purple flower heads in flattened clusters, 4in (10cm) wide, mainly in winter.
E. urticifolium. See *E. rugosum.*
E. weinmannianum. See *E. ligustrinum.*

EUPHORBIA (Euphorbiaceae)
Milkweed, Spurge
Genus of shrubs, succulents, and perennials some of which are semi-evergreen or evergreen, and annuals. Flower heads consist of cup-shaped bracts, in various colors and usually each containing several flowers lacking typical sepals and petals. Fully hardy to frost tender, min. 41–59°F (5–15°C). Does best in sun or partial shade and in moist but well-drained soil. Propagate by basal cuttings in spring or summer, by division in spring or early autumn, or by seed in autumn or spring. Milky sap may irritate skin.
E. amygdaloides (Wood spurge). **'Purpurea'** is a semi-evergreen, erect perennial. H and S 1ft (30cm). Fully hardy, zones 7–9. Stems and narrowly oval leaves are green, heavily suffused purple-red. Has flower heads of cup-shaped, yellow bracts in spring. Is susceptible to mildew. subsp. *robbiae* illus. p.228.
E. biglandulosa. See *E. rigida.*
E. candelabrum. Evergreen, treelike, perennial succulent. H 30ft (10m), S 15ft (5m). Frost tender, min. 50°F (10°C), zone 10. Erect, 3–5-angled, deeply indented, glossy, dark green stems, often marbled white, branch and rebranch candelabralike. Has short-lived, spear-shaped leaves and rounded heads of small flowers with cup-shaped, yellow bracts in spring.
E. characias subsp. *characias* and subsp. *wulfenii* illus. p.124.
E. cyparissias illus. p.228.
E. epithymoides. See *E. polychroma.*
E. fulgens (Scarlet plume). Evergreen shrub of erect and arching habit. H 3–5ft (1–1.5m), S 2–3ft (60cm–1m). Frost tender, min. 41–5°F (5–7°C), zones 9–10. Has elliptic to lance-shaped, mid- to deep green leaves, to 4in (10cm) long. Bears leafy, wandlike sprays of small flowers, each cluster

surrounded by 5 petal-like, bright scarlet bracts, $^3/_4$–$1^1/_4$in (2–3cm) across, in winter-spring.
E. gorgonis (Gorgon's head). Evergreen, hemispherical, perennial succulent. H 3in (8cm), S 4in (10cm). Frost tender, min. 50°F (10°C), zone 10. Has a much-ribbed, green main stem crowned by 3–5 rows of prostrate, $^1/_2$in (1cm) wide stems that are gradually shed. In spring, crown also bears rounded heads of small, fragrant flowers with cup-shaped, yellow bracts.
E. griffithii 'Fireglow' illus. p.216.
E. marginata illus. p.263.
E. milii illus. p.123. var. *splendens* (syn. *E. splendens*) is a slow-growing, mainly evergreen, spreading, spiny, semi-succulent shrub. H to 6ft (2m), S to 3ft (1m). Frost tender, min. 41–5°F (5–7°C), zones 9–10. Has oblong to oval leaves and, intermittently year-round but especially in spring, clusters of tiny flowers enclosed in large, petal-like, red bracts.
E. myrsinites illus. p.311.
E. nicaeensis. Clump-forming perennial with a woody base. H 30in (75cm), S 18in (45cm). Fully hardy, zones 5–8. Bears umbels of greenish yellow flower heads with cup-shaped bracts throughout summer. Leaves are narrowly oval, fleshy, and gray-green.
E. obesa illus. p.397.
E. palustris. Bushy perennial. H and S 3ft (1m). Fully hardy, zones 5–8. Clusters of yellow-green flower heads with cup-shaped bracts appear in spring above oblong to lance-shaped, yellowish green leaves.
E. polychroma, syn. *E. epithymoides*, illus. p.232.
E. pulcherrima illus. p.118. 'Paul Mikkelson' is a mainly evergreen, erect, freely branching shrub. H and

S 10–12ft (3–4m). Frost tender, min. 41–5°F (5–7°C), zones 9–10. Bears oval to lance-shaped, shallowly lobed leaves. From late autumn to spring, flattened heads of small, greenish white flowers are surrounded by large, leaflike, bright red bracts.
E. rigida, syn. *E. biglandulosa.* Semi-evergreen, erect perennial. H and S 18in (45cm). Frost hardy, zones 7–10. In early spring produces terminal heads of yellow flowers with cup-shaped bracts above oblong to oval, pointed, gray-green leaves.
E. seguieriana illus. p.228.
E. splendens. See *E. milii* var. *splendens.*

EUPTELEA (Eupteleaceae)
Genus of deciduous trees, grown for their foliage. Fully to half hardy. Needs full sun and fertile, well-drained soil. Propagate by seed in autumn.
E. polyandra. Deciduous, bushy-headed tree. H 25ft (8m), S 20ft (6m). Fully hardy, zones 6–10. Long-stalked, narrowly oval, pointed, sharply toothed leaves are glossy and bright green, turning red and yellow in autumn. Has inconspicuous flowers in spring before leaves emerge.

EURYA (Theaceae)
Genus of evergreen shrubs and trees, grown for their foliage. Produces insignificant flowers in summer. Half hardy to frost tender, min. 45°F (7°C). Tolerates partial shade or full light and fertile, well-drained soil. Water potted specimens freely when in full growth, less at other times. Propagate by seed when ripe or in spring or by semi-ripe cuttings in late summer.
E. emarginata illus. p.144.
E. japonica 'Variegata'. Evergreen, bushy shrub or tree. H and S 5–10ft

(1.5–3m). Half hardy, zones 8–10. Has elliptic to lance-shaped, bluntly toothed, lustrous leaves, deep green edged with creamy white above, paler green or yellowish green beneath. Inconspicuous, green flowers in summer are followed by tiny, spherical, purple-black fruits. Is sometimes confused in cultivation with *Cleyera japonica* 'Tricolor'.

EURYALE (Nymphaeaceae)
Genus of one species of annual, deep-water plant, grown for its floating foliage; is suitable only for a tropical pool. Frost tender, min. 41°F (5°C). Needs full light, constant warmth, and heavy feeding. Propagate by seed in spring.
E. ferox illus. p.375.

EURYOPS (Compositae)
Genus of evergreen shrubs and sub-shrubs, grown for their attractive leaves and showy, daisylike flower heads. Is suitable for growing in borders and rock gardens. Fully hardy to frost tender, min. 41–5°F (5–7°C). Requires sun and moist but well-drained soil. Dislikes root disturbance. Propagate by softwood cuttings in summer.
E. acraeus, syn. *E. evansii* of gardens, illus. p.298.
E. evansii of gardens. See *E. acraeus.*
E. pectinatus illus. p.138.

EUSTOMA (Gentianaceae)
Genus of annuals and perennials with poppylike flowers. Is good for cutting and as pot plants. Half hardy to frost tender, min. 39–45°F (4–7°C). Grow in sun and in well-drained soil. Propagate by seed sown under glass in late winter.
E. grandiflorum, syn. *Lisianthus russellianus* (Prairie gentian) illus.

p.263. **F1 Hybrids** (mixed) is a group of slow-growing, upright annuals. H 18in (45cm), S 12in (30cm). Half hardy. Has lance-shaped, green leaves. Poppylike, pink, blue, or white flowers are produced in summer.

EVODIA. See EUODIA.

EXACUM (Gentianaceae)
Genus of annuals, biennials, and perennials, grown for their profusion of flowers, that are excellent as pot plants. Frost tender, min. 45–50°F (7–10°C). Grow in sun and in well-drained soil. Propagate by seed sown in early spring for flowering the same year or in late summer for flowering the following year.
E. affine illus. p.275.

EXOCHORDA (Rosaceae)
Genus of deciduous shrubs, grown for their abundant, showy, white flowers. Fully hardy. Does best in full sun and fertile, well-drained soil. Improve vigor and flowering by thinning out old shoots after flowering. Propagate by softwood cuttings in summer or by seed in autumn. Chlorosis may be a problem on shallow, chalky soil.
E. giraldii (Redbud pearlbush). Deciduous, widely arching shrub. H and S 10ft (3m). Zones 6–9. Has pinkish green, young growths, oblong, green leaves and, in late spring, upright racemes of large, 5-petaled, white flowers.
E. x macrantha 'The Bride' illus. p.103.
E. racemosa (Common pearlbush). Deciduous, arching shrub. H and S 12ft (4m). Zones 5–9. Has upright clusters of 5-petaled, white flowers in late spring. Leaves are oblong and deep blue-green. Prefers acid soil.

FABIANA (Solanaceae)
Genus of evergreen shrubs, grown for their foliage and flowers. Frost hardy, but in cold areas plant in a sheltered position. Requires full sun and fertile, well-drained soil. Propagate by softwood cuttings in summer.
F. imbricata **'Prostrata'**. Evergreen, mound-forming, very dense shrub. H 3ft (1m), S 6ft (2m). Zones 9–10. Shoots are densely covered with tiny, heathlike, deep green leaves. Bears a profusion of tubular, white flowers in early summer. **'Violacea'** illus. p.113.

FAGUS (Fagaceae)
Beech
Genus of deciduous trees, grown for their habit, foliage, and autumn color. Insignificant flowers appear in late spring and hairy fruits ripen in autumn to release edible, triangular nuts. Fully hardy. Requires sun or semi-shade; purple-leaved forms prefer full sun, yellow-leaved forms a little shade. Grows well in any but waterlogged soil. *F. sylvatica*, when used as hedging, should be trimmed in summer. Propagate species by seed in autumn, selected forms by budding in late summer. Problems may be caused by bracket fungi, canker-causing fungi, aphids, and beech coccus.
F. americana. See *F. grandifolia*.
F. grandifolia, syn. *F. americana* (American beech). Deciduous, spreading tree. H and S 30ft (10m). Zones 4–9. Oval leaves are pale green and silky when young; they mature to dark green in summer and turn golden brown in autumn.
F. orientalis (Oriental beech). Deciduous, spreading tree. H 70ft (20m), S 50ft (15m). Zones 4–7. Has large, oval, wavy-edged, dark green leaves that turn yellow in autumn.
F. sylvatica (European beech) illus. p.43. **'Aurea Pendula'** is a deciduous, slender tree with pendulous branches. H 100ft (30m), S 80ft (25m). Zones 4–7. Oval, wavy-edged leaves are bright yellow and become rich yellow and orange-brown in autumn. **'Dawyck'**, S 22ft (7m), is columnar, with erect branches; pale green leaves mature to mid- to dark green, and turn rich yellow and orange-brown in autumn. **'Dawyck Purple'** is similar, but has deep purple foliage. Leaves of f. *laciniata* are deeply cut. f. *pendula* illus. p.40. f. *purpurea* illus. p.39. **'Purpurea Pendula'**, H and S 10ft (3m), has stiff, weeping branches and blackish purple foliage. Leaves of **'Riversii'** are very dark purple. Those of **'Rohanii'** are deeply cut and reddish purple. **'Zlatia'** produces yellow, young foliage that later becomes mid- to dark green.

Fallopia aubertii. See *Polygonum aubertii*.
Fallopia baldschuanica. See *Polygonum baldschuanicum*.

FALLUGIA (Rosaceae)
Genus of one species of deciduous shrub, grown for its flowers and showy fruit clusters. Frost hardy, but in cold areas protect in winter. Needs a hot, sunny position and well-drained soil. Propagate by softwood cuttings in summer or by seed in autumn.
F. paradoxa illus. p.104.

FASCICULARIA (Bromeliaceae)
Genus of evergreen, rosette-forming perennials, grown for their overall appearance. Half hardy. Prefers full light; any well-drained soil is suitable. Water moderately from spring to autumn, sparingly in winter. Propagate by offsets or division in spring.
F. bicolor. Evergreen, rosetted perennial forming congested hummocks. H to 18in (45cm), S to 24in (60cm). Zone 10. Has dense rosettes of linear, tapered, arching, mid- to deep green leaves. In summer produces a cluster of tubular, pale blue flowers, surrounded by bright red bracts, at the heart of each mature rosette. Is best grown at not less than 36°F (2°C).

x FATSHEDERA (Araliaceae)
Hybrid genus (*Fatsia japonica* 'Moseri' x *Hedera helix* 'Hibernica') of one evergreen, autumn-flowering shrub, grown for its foliage. Is good trained against a wall or pillar or, if supported by canes, grown as a house plant. Frost hardy. Thrives in sun or shade and fertile, well-drained soil. Propagate by semi-ripe cuttings in summer.
x *F. lizei* illus. p.120. **'Variegata'** is an evergreen, mound-forming, loose-branched shrub. H 5ft (1.5m), or more if trained as a climber, S 10ft (3m). Zones 7–10. Has rounded, deeply lobed, glossy, deep green leaves, narrowly edged with creamy white, and, from mid- to late autumn, produces spherical sprays of small, white flowers.

FATSIA (Araliaceae)
Genus of one species of evergreen, autumn-flowering shrub, grown for its foliage, flowers, and fruits. Makes an excellent conservatory plant. Frost hardy, but in cold areas shelter from strong winds. Tolerates sun or shade and requires fertile, well-drained soil. Propagate by semi-ripe cuttings in summer or by seed in autumn or spring.
F. japonica, syn. *Aralia japonica*, *A. sieboldii* (Japanese aralia). Evergreen, rounded, dense shrub. H and S 10ft (3m). Zones 8–10. Has stout shoots and very large, rounded, deeply lobed, glossy, dark green leaves. Spherical clusters of tiny, white flowers in mid-autumn are followed by rounded, black fruits. **'Variegata'** illus. p.119.
F. papyrifera. See *Tetrapanax papyrifera*.

FAUCARIA (Aizoaceae)
Genus of clump-forming, stemless, perennial succulents with semi-cylindrical or 3-angled, fleshy, bright green leaves and yellow flowers that open in late afternoons in autumn. Buds and dead flowers may appear orange or red. Frost tender, min. 43°F (6°C). Needs full sun and well-drained soil. Keep dry in winter and water sparingly in spring. Propagate by seed or stem cuttings in spring or summer.
F. tigrina illus. p.399.

FEIJOA (Myrtaceae)
Genus of evergreen, summer-flowering shrubs and trees, grown for their showy flowers and edible fruits; the latter are usually produced only after a hot summer and often only if more than one plant is grown. Frost hardy. Needs a sheltered, sunny site and light, well-drained soil. Propagate by softwood cuttings in summer.
F. sellowiana illus. p.111.

FELICIA (Compositae)
Genus of annuals, evergreen sub-shrubs and (rarely) shrubs, grown for their daisylike, mainly blue flower heads. Fully hardy to frost tender, min. 41–5°F (5–7°C). Needs full sun and well-drained soil. Water potted plants moderately, less when not in full growth; will not tolerate wet conditions, particularly when temperatures are low. Remove dead flowering stems and cut back straggly shoots regularly. Propagate by seed in spring or by greenwood cuttings in summer or early autumn.
F. amelloides, syn. *Agathaea coelestis*, *Aster capensis* (Blue marguerite). **'Santa Anita'** illus. p.136.
F. bergeriana illus. p.278.

FENESTRARIA (Aizoaceae)
Genus of clump-forming, perennial succulents with basal rosettes of fleshy leaves that have gray "windows" in their flattened tips. Frost tender, min. 43°F (6°C). Needs sun and very well-drained soil. Keep bone dry in winter. Propagate by seed in spring or summer.
F. aurantiaca. Clump-forming, perennial succulent. H 2in (5cm), S 12in (30cm). Zone 10. Produces an erect, basal rosette of cylindrical, glossy, glaucous to mid-green leaves, each with a flattened tip. Has daisylike, white flowers on long flower stems in late summer and autumn. var. *rhopalophylla* illus. p.399.

FEROCACTUS (Cactaceae)
Barrel cactus
Genus of slow-growing, spherical, perennial cacti, becoming columnar after many years. Frost tender, min. 41°F (5°C). Needs full sun and very well-drained soil. Propagate by seed in spring or summer. Treat blackened areoles with systemic fungicide and ensure plants have good ventilation.
F. acanthodes illus. p.381.
F. chrysacanthus. Slow-growing, spherical, perennial cactus. H 3ft (1m), S 2ft (60cm). Zone 10. Green stem, with 15–20 ribs, is fairly densely covered with curved, yellow-white spines. In summer bears funnel-shaped, yellow, rarely red, flowers, 2in (5cm) across, only on plants 10in (25cm) or more in diameter.
F. hamatacanthus, syn. *Hamatocactus hamatacanthus*, illus. p.385.
F. latispinus. Slow-growing, flattened spherical, perennial cactus. H 8in (20cm), S 16in (40cm). Zone 10. Green stem, with 15–20 ribs, bears very broad, hooked, yellow or red spines. Funnel-shaped, pale yellow or red flowers appear in summer only on plants over 4in (10cm) wide.
F. setispinus, syn. *Hamatocactus setispinus*, illus. p.387.
F. wislizenii. Slow-growing, spherical, perennial cactus. H 6ft (2m), S 3ft (1m). Zone 10. Green stem, with up to 25 ribs, is covered in flattened, fish-hooklike, usually reddish brown spines, to 2in (5cm) long. Funnel-shaped, orange or yellow flowers, 2¹/₂in (6cm) across, appear in late summer only on plants over 10in (25cm) wide, which should attain this size 10–15 years after raising from seed.

FERRARIA (Iridaceae)
Genus of spring-flowering corms, grown for their curious flowers with 3 large, outer petals and 3 small, inner ones, with very wavy edges. Is unpleasant-smelling to attract flies, which pollinate flowers. Half hardy. Requires full sun and well-drained soil. Plant in autumn, water during winter and dry off after flowering. Dies down in summer. Propagate by division in late summer or by seed in autumn.
F. crispa, syn. *F. undulata*, illus. p.347.
F. undulata. See *F. crispa*.

FERULA (Umbelliferae)
Giant fennel
Genus of mainly summer-flowering perennials, grown for their bold, architectural form. Should not be confused with culinary fennel, *Foeniculum*. Frost hardy. Requires sun and well-drained soil. Propagate by seed when fresh, in late summer.
F. communis illus. p.190.

FESTUCA (Gramineae). See GRASSES, BAMBOOS, RUSHES, and SEDGES.
F. glauca of gardens (Blue fescue). Group of evergreen, tuft-forming, perennial grasses. H and S 4in (10cm). Fully hardy, zones 4–8. Has narrow leaves in various shades of blue-green to silvery white. Bears unimportant panicles of spikelets in summer. Is

good for bed edging. Divide every 2–3 years in spring.

FICUS (Moraceae)
Genus of evergreen or deciduous trees, shrubs, and scrambling or root climbers, grown for their foliage and for shade; a few species also for fruit. All bear insignificant clusters of flowers in spring or summer. Frost hardy to frost tender, min. 41–64°F (5–18°C). Prefers full light or partial shade and fertile, well-drained soil. Water potted specimens moderately, very little when temperatures are low. Propagate by seed in spring or by leaf-bud or stem-tip cuttings, or air-layering in summer. Red spider mite may be a nuisance.
F. benghalensis illus. p.46.
F. benjamina (Weeping fig). Evergreen, weeping tree, often with aerial roots. H and S 60–70ft (18–20m). Frost tender, min. 50°F (10°C), zone 10. Has slender, oval leaves, 3–5in (7–13cm) long, in lustrous, rich green. '**Variegata**' illus. p.57.
F. deltoidea, syn. *F. diversifolia*, illus. p.120.
F. diversifolia. See *F. deltoidea*.
F. elastica (India rubber tree, Rubber plant). '**Decora**' is a strong-growing, evergreen, irregularly ovoid tree. H to 100ft (30m), S 50–70ft (15–20m). Frost tender, min. 50°F (10°C), zone 10. Has broadly oval, leathery, lustrous, deep green leaves, tinted pinkish bronze when young. '**Doescheri**' illus. p.46. Leaves of '**Variegata**' are cream-edged, mottled with gray-green.
F. lyrata (Fiddleleaf fig). Evergreen, ovoid, robust-stemmed tree. H 50ft (15m) or more, S to 30ft (10m). Frost tender, min. 59–64°F (15–18°C), zone 10. Fiddle-shaped leaves, 1ft (30cm) or more long, are lustrous, deep green.
F. macrophylla (Australian banyan, Moreton Bay fig). Evergreen, wide-spreading, dense tree with a buttressed trunk when mature. H 70–100ft (20–30m), S 100–130ft (30–40m). Frost tender, min. 59–64°F (15–18°C), zones 9–10. Oval leaves, to 8in (20cm) long, are leathery, glossy, deep green.
F. pumila (Creeping fig). Evergreen, root climber. H 25ft (8m); S (1.5m) as a pot-grown plant. Frost tender, min. 41°F (5°C), zones 9–10. Bright green leaves are heart-shaped and $^3/_4$–$1^1/_4$in (2–3cm) long when young, $1^1/_4$–3in (3–8cm) long, leathery, and oval when mature. Unpalatable fruits are $2^1/_2$in (6cm) long, orange at first, then flushed red-purple. Only reaches adult stage in very warm regions or in a greenhouse. Pinch out branch tips to encourage branching. Young leaves of '**Minima**' are shorter and narrower.
F. religiosa (Bo, Peepul, Sacred fig tree). Mainly evergreen, rounded to wide-spreading tree with prop roots from branches. H and S 70–100ft (20–30m). Frost tender, min. 59–64°F (15–18°C), zone 10. Leaves, 4–6in (10–15cm) long, are broadly oval to almost triangular with long, threadlike tips, pink-flushed when expanding.
F. rubiginosa (Port Jackson fig, Rusty-leaved fig). Evergreen, dense-headed tree with a buttressed trunk. H and S 70–100ft (20–30m) or more.

Frost tender, min. 59–64°F (15–18°C), zone 10. Elliptic, blunt-pointed leaves, to 4in (10cm) long, are glossy, dark green above, usually with rust-colored down beneath.

FILIPENDULA (Rosaceae)
Meadowsweet
Genus of spring- and summer-flowering perennials. Fully hardy. Does well in full sun when soil is moisture-retentive, elsewhere is best grown in semi-shade and in moist conditions; some species, e.g. *F. rubra*, will grow in boggy sites. Propagate by seed in autumn or by division in autumn or winter.
F. camtschatica. Clump-forming perennial. H to 5ft (1.5m), S 3ft (1m). Zones 3–8. Frothy, flat heads of scented, star-shaped, white or pale pink flowers are produced in mid-summer above large, lance-shaped, divided and cut leaves.
F. hexapetala. See *F. vulgaris*.
F. purpurea illus. p.207.
F. rubra illus. p.189.
F. ulmaria, syn. *Spiraea ulmaria*. '**Aurea**' illus. p.245.
F. vulgaris, syn. *F. hexapetala* (Dropwort). '**Flore Plena**' is an upright perennial with fleshy, swollen roots. H 3ft (1m), S $1^1/_2$ft (45cm). Zones 4–9. In summer bears flat panicles of rounded, double, white flowers, sometimes flushed pink, above fernlike foliage.

FIRMIANA (Sterculiaceae)
Genus of mainly deciduous trees and shrubs, grown for their foliage and to provide shade. Half hardy, but to reach tree proportions needs min. 36–41°F (2–5°C). Requires well-drained but moisture-retentive, fertile soil and full light or partial shade. Water potted specimens freely when in full growth, less in winter. Pruning is tolerated if necessary. Propagate by seed when ripe or in spring.
F. platanifolia. See *F. simplex*.
F. simplex, syn. *F. platanifolia*, *Sterculia platanifolia*, illus. p.42.

FITTONIA (Acanthaceae)
Genus of evergreen, creeping perennials, grown mainly for their foliage. Is useful as ground cover. Frost tender, min. 59°F (15°C). Needs a fairly humid atmosphere, a shaded position, and well-drained soil; keep well watered but avoid waterlogging, especially in winter. If plant becomes straggly, cut back in spring. Propagate in spring or summer, with additional heat, by division or stem cuttings.
F. argyroneura. See *F. verschaffeltii* var. *argyroneura*.
F. verschaffeltii illus. p.258. var. *argyroneura* (syn. *F. argyroneura*) illus. p.256.

FITZROYA (Cupressaceae). See CONIFERS.
F. cupressoides, syn. *F. patagonica*, illus. p.78.
F. patagonica. See *F. cupressoides*.

FOENICULUM (Umbelliferae)
Genus of summer-flowering biennials and perennials, some of which are

grown for their umbels of yellow flowers. Is also grown for its leaves, which are both decorative in borders and used for culinary flavoring. Fully to frost hardy. Grow in an open, sunny position and in fertile, well-drained soil. Remove flower heads after fading to prevent self seeding. Propagate by seed in autumn.
F. vulgare (Fennel). '**Purpureum**' is an erect, branching perennial. H 6ft (2m), S $1^1/_2$ft (45cm). Fully hardy, zones 4–9. Has very finely divided, hairlike, bronze leaves and, in summer, large, flat umbels of small, yellow flowers.

FONTINALIS (Fontinalaceae)
Genus of evergreen, perennial, submerged water plants, grown for their foliage, which provides dense cover for fish and a good site for the deposit of spawn. Fully hardy. Grows in sun or semi-shade in streams and other running water; tolerates still water if cool, but then does not grow to full size. Propagate by division in spring.
F. antipyretica (Water moss, Willow moss). Evergreen, perennial, submerged water plant. H 1in (2.5cm), S indefinite. Zones 4–10. Forms spreading colonies of mosslike, dark olive green leaves.

FORSYTHIA (Oleaceae)
Genus of deciduous, spring-flowering shrubs, grown for their usually profuse, yellow flowers, which open before the leaves emerge. *F.* x *intermedia* 'Beatrix Farrand' and *F.* x *i.* 'Lynwood' make attractive, flowering hedges. Fully hardy. Prefers full sun and fertile, well-drained soil. Thin out old shoots and trim hedges immediately after flowering. Propagate by softwood cuttings in summer or by hardwood cuttings in autumn or winter.
F. x *intermedia* '**Arnold Giant**'. Deciduous, bushy shrub. H 5ft (1.5m), S 8ft (2.5m). Zones 5–9. Has stout shoots and oblong, sharply toothed, green leaves. Large, 4-lobed, deep yellow flowers are borne sparsely from early to mid-spring. '**Beatrix Farrand**' illus. p.103. '**Karl Sax**', H 8ft (2.5m), is dense-growing, with an abundance of flowers, and leaves that turn red or purple in autumn. '**Lynwood**', H 10ft (3m), is very free-flowering, vigorous and upright. '**Spectabilis**' (Showy border forsythia) illus. p.102.
F. '**Minigold**'. Deciduous, compact shrub. H and S 6ft (2m). Zone 10. Has oblong, green leaves. Bears masses of small, 4-lobed, yellow flowers from early to mid-spring.
F. ovata. Deciduous, bushy shrub. H and S 5ft (1.5m). Zones 5–9. Leaves are broadly oval, toothed, and dark green. Produces small, 4-lobed, bright yellow flowers in early spring. '**Northern Gold**' is a vigorous, upright, somewhat stiff shrub with a tendency to spread, H and S 6–8ft (2–2.5m), and is tolerant of a wide range of soils. '**Ottawa**' has an upright habit and flowers profusely.
F. '**Spring Glory**'. Deciduous, upright shrub. H 6ft (2m), S 5ft (1.5m). Zones 5–9. Clusters of large, 4-lobed, pale

yellow flowers are borne in mid-spring. Has oblong, toothed, bright green leaves.
F. suspensa illus. p.99.

FOTHERGILLA (Hamamelidaceae)
Genus of deciduous, spring-flowering shrubs, grown for their autumn color and fragrant flowers, each with a dense, bottlebrushlike cluster of stamens, which open before or as leaves emerge. Fully hardy. Grows in sun or semi-shade, but colors best in full sun. Needs moist, peaty, acid soil. Propagate by softwood cuttings in summer.
F. gardenii (Dwarf fothergilla). Deciduous, bushy, dense shrub. H and S 3ft (1m). Zones 6–9. Dense clusters of tiny, fragrant white flowers appear from mid- to late spring, usually before broadly oval, dark blue-green leaves emerge. Leaves turn brilliant red in autumn.
F. major, syn. *F. monticola*, illus. p.95.
F. monticola. See *F. major*.

Fragaria indica. See *Duchesnea indica*.

FRAILEA (Cactaceae)
Genus of spherical to columnar, perennial cacti with tuberculate ribs. Bears short spines, mostly bristlelike. In summer produces masses of buds, most of which develop into small, spherical, shiny pods without opening. Frost tender, min. 41°F (5°C). Needs partial shade and very well-drained soil. Is not well-adapted to long periods of drought. Propagate by seed in spring or summer.
F. pulcherrima illus. p.397.

FRANCOA (Saxifragaceae)
Genus of summer- and early autumn-flowering perennials. Frost hardy. Needs full sun and fertile, well-drained soil. Propagate by seed or division in spring.
F. appendiculata (Bridal wreath). Clump-forming perennial. H 24in (60cm), S 18in (45cm). Zones 7–9. Racemes of small, bell-shaped, pale pink flowers, spotted with deep pink at base, appear on graceful, erect stems from summer to early autumn, above oblong to oval, lobed, hairy, crinkled, dark green leaves.
F. sonchifolia. Clump-forming perennial. H 30in (75cm), S 18in (45cm). Zones 7–9. Bears racemes of cup-shaped, red-marked, pink flowers from summer to early autumn. Lobed leaves each have a large, terminal lobe.

FRANKLINIA (Theaceae)
Genus of one species of deciduous tree or shrub, grown for its flowers and autumn color. Fully hardy, but thrives only during hot summers. Needs full sun and moist but well-drained, neutral to acid soil. Propagate by softwood cuttings in summer, by seed in autumn, or by hardwood cuttings in early winter.
F. alatamaha (Franklin tree). Deciduous, upright tree or shrub. H and S 15ft (5m) or more. Zones 6–9. Large, shallowly cup-shaped, white flowers with yellow stamens open in

late summer and early autumn. Oblong, glossy, bright green leaves turn red in autumn.

FRAXINUS (Oleaceae)
Ash
Genus of deciduous trees and shrubs, grown mainly for their foliage of paired leaflets; flowers are usually insignificant. Fully hardy. Needs sun and fertile, well-drained but not too dry soil. Propagate species by seed in autumn, selected forms by budding in summer.

F. americana (White ash). Fast-growing, deciduous, spreading tree. H 80ft (25m), S 50ft (15m). Zones 4–9. Dark green leaves are divided into 5–9 oval to lance-shaped leaflets, sometimes turning yellow or purple in autumn.

F. angustifolia (Narrow-leaved ash). Deciduous, spreading, elegant tree. H 80ft (25m), S 40ft (12m). Zones 6–9. Leaves usually consist of 9–11 slender, lance-shaped, glossy, dark green leaflets.

F. excelsior (European ash). Vigorous, deciduous, spreading tree. H 100ft (30m), S 70ft (20m). Zones 5–8. Dark green leaves, with usually 9–11 oval leaflets, sometimes become yellow in autumn. Black leaf buds are conspicuous in winter. f. *diversifolia* has leaves that are simple or with only 3 leaflets. Leaves of **'Jaspidea'** are yellow in spring and turn golden in autumn; shoots are yellow in winter. **'Pendula'**, H 50ft (15m), S 25–30ft (8–10m), has branches weeping to the ground.

F. mariesii. Slow-growing, deciduous, compact-headed tree. H 20ft (6m), S 15ft (5m). Zones 7–9. Leaves consist of 3–5 oval, dark green leaflets each on a purple stalk. Has clusters of small, fragrant, star-shaped, creamy white flowers in early summer, followed by narrowly oblong, purple fruits.

F. nigra **'Fallgold'** (Fallgold ash). Deciduous, narrow, upright tree with an open crown. H 40–50ft (12–15m), S 20–30ft (6–10m). Zones 4–8. Pointed, narrow, glossy, green leaves turn gold in autumn and are retained for a long period. Has scaly, flaking, ridged bark. Tolerates a wide range of soils, including very wet soil.

F. ornus illus. p.49.

F. oxycarpa **'Raywood'** (Claret ash). Vigorous, deciduous, spreading tree of elegant habit. H 70ft (20m), S 50ft (15m). Zones 5–9. Leaves have 5–7 narrowly oval, glossy, dark green leaflets that turn bright reddish purple in autumn.

F. pennsylvanica, syn. *F.p.* var. *subintegerrima* (Green ash, Red ash). Fast-growing, deciduous, spreading tree. H and S 70ft (20m). Zones 4–9. Leaves of usually 7 or 9 narrowly oval, dull green leaflets are often velvety beneath, like the shoots. **'Patmore'** is disease-resistant, with long-lasting, glossy leaves. **'Summit'** (Summit ash), H 50–60ft (15–18m), S 30ft (10m) is upright with glossy leaves that turn golden yellow in autumn. Transplants easily and tolerates a wide range of soils.

F. velutina illus. p.53.

FREESIA (Iridaceae)
Genus of winter- and spring-flowering corms, grown for their usually fragrant, funnel-shaped flowers, which are popular for cutting. Half hardy. Requires full sun and well-drained soil. Plant in autumn and water throughout winter. Support with twigs or small canes. Dry off corms after flowering. Plant specially prepared corms outdoors in spring for flowering in summer. Propagate by offsets in autumn or by seed in spring.

F. alba, syn. *F. lactea*, *F. refracta* var. *alba*. Late winter- and spring-flowering corm. H 8–12in (20–30cm), S 1½–2½in (4–6cm). Zones 9–10. Has narrowly sword-shaped, erect leaves in a basal fan. Leafless stems bear loose spikes of very fragrant white flowers, each 2–3in (5–8cm) long.

F. armstrongii. Late winter- and spring-flowering corm. H to 12in (30cm), S 1½–2½in (4–6cm). Zones 9–10. Has narrowly sword-shaped, erect, basal leaves. Flower stem, bending horizontally near top, bears a spike of unscented, upright, pink flowers, 1¼–1½in (3–3.5cm) long, with yellow bases.

F. **'Everett'** illus. p.355.

F. lactea. See *F. alba.*

F. refracta var. *alba.* See *F. alba.*

F. **'Rijnveld's Yellow'.** Winter- and spring-flowering corm. H to 12in (30cm), S 1½–2½in (4–6cm). Zones 9–10. Is similar to *F. armstrongii*, but has larger, fragrant flowers, yellow throughout.

F. **'Romany'.** Winter- and spring-flowering corm. H to 12in (30cm), S 4–6in (1½–2½in). Zones 9–10. Is similar to *F. armstrongii*, but produces fragrant, double, pale mauve flowers.

F. **'White Swan'.** Winter- and spring-flowering corm. H to 12in (30cm), S 1½–2½in (4–6cm). Zones 9–10. Is similar to *F. armstrongii*, but has very fragrant white flowers with cream throats.

F. **'Yellow River'** illus. p.355.

FREMONTIA. See FREMONTODENDRON.

FREMONTODENDRON, syn. FREMONTIA (Sterculiaceae)
Flannel flower
Genus of vigorous, evergreen or semi-evergreen shrubs, grown for their large, very showy flowers. Frost hardy, but in cold areas plant against a south- or west-facing wall. Needs full sun and light, not too rich, well-drained soil. In mild areas may be grown as a spreading shrub, but needs firm staking when young. Resents being transplanted. Propagate by semi-ripe cuttings in summer or by seed in autumn or spring.

F. **'California Glory'** illus. p.91.

F. californicum. Vigorous, evergreen or semi-evergreen, upright shrub. H 20ft (6m), S 12ft (4m), when grown against a wall. Zones 8–10. Large, saucer-shaped, bright yellow flowers are borne amid dark green leaves, each with 3 rounded lobes, from late spring to mid-autumn.

F. mexicanum. Vigorous, evergreen or semi-evergreen, upright shrub. H 20ft (6m), S 12ft (4m), when grown against a wall. Zones 9–10. Dark green leaves have 5 deep, rounded lobes. Bears a profusion of large, saucer-shaped, deep golden yellow flowers from late spring to mid-autumn.

FRITHIA (Aizoaceae)
Genus of one species of rosette-forming, perennial succulent. Frost tender, min. 50°F (10°C). Needs sun and well-drained soil. Propagate by seed in spring or summer.

F. pulchra illus. p.393.

FRITILLARIA (Liliaceae)
Genus of spring-flowering bulbs, grown for their pendent, mainly bell-shaped flowers on leafy stems. Fully to frost hardy; protect smaller, 2–6in (5–15cm) high species in cold frames or cold greenhouses. Needs full sun or partial shade and well-drained soil that dries out slightly in summer when bulbs are dormant but that does not become sunbaked. Grow *F. meleagris*, which is good for naturalizing in grass, in moisture-retentive soil. Propagate by offsets in summer or by seed in autumn or winter.

F. acmopetala. Spring-flowering bulb. H 6–14in (15–35cm), S 2–3in (5–8cm). Frost hardy, zones 6–8. Slender stems bear narrowly lance-shaped, scattered leaves and 1 or 2 broadly bell-shaped, green flowers, 1–1½in (2.5–4cm) long, with brown-stained petals flaring outwards at tips.

F. bucharica. Spring-flowering bulb. H 4–14in (10–35cm), S 2in (5cm). Frost hardy, zones 6–8. Stems each bear scattered, lance-shaped, gray-green leaves and a raceme of up to 10 cup-shaped, green-tinged, white flowers, ⅝–¾in (1.5–2cm) long.

F. camschatcensis illus. p.343.

F. cirrhosa illus. p.346.

F. crassifolia. Spring-flowering bulb. H 4–8in (10–20cm), S 2in (5cm). Frost hardy, zones 6–8. Has scattered, lance-shaped, gray leaves. Stems each produce 1–3 bell-shaped, green flowers, ¾–1in (2–2.5cm) long and checkered with brown.

F. delphinensis. See *F. tubiformis.*

F. imperialis illus. p.332. **'Lutea'** is a spring-flowering bulb. H to 5ft (1.5m), S 9–12in (23–30cm). Fully hardy, zones 5–9. Leafy stems each bear lance-shaped, glossy, pale green leaves in whorls and a head of up to 5 widely bell-shaped, yellow flowers, 2in (5cm) long, crowned by small, leaflike bracts. **'Rubra Maxima'** is very robust with red flowers.

F. meleagris illus. p.343.

F. michailovskyi. Spring-flowering bulb. H 4–8in (10–20cm), S 2in (5cm). Frost hardy, zones 5–8. Bears lance-shaped, gray leaves, scattered on stem, and 1–4 bell-shaped, ¾–1¼in (2–3cm) long flowers, colored purplish brown with upper third of petals bright yellow.

F. pallidiflora illus. p.347.

F. persica illus. p.332. **'Adiyaman'** is a spring-flowering bulb. H to 5ft (1.5m), S 4in (10cm). Frost hardy, zones 7–8. Has narrowly lance-shaped, gray leaves along stem. Produces a

spike of 10–20 or more narrowly bell-shaped, deep blackish purple flowers, ⅝–¾in (1.5–2cm) long.

F. pontica illus. p.346.

F. pudica illus. p.363.

F. pyrenaica illus. p.343.

F. raddeana illus. p.332.

F. recurva illus. p.332.

F. sewerzowii, syn. *Korolkowia sewerzowii.* Spring-flowering bulb. H 6–10in (15–25cm), S 3–4in (8–10cm). Frost hardy, zones 7–9. Stems bear scattered, broadly lance-shaped leaves. Produces a spike of up to 10 narrowly bell-shaped, green or metallic purplish blue flowers, 1–1½in (2.5–3.5cm) long, with flared mouths.

F. tubiformis, syn. *F. delphinensis.* Spring-flowering bulb. H 6–14in (15–35cm), S 2–3in (5–8cm). Frost hardy, zones 7–9. Stems carry scattered, narrowly lance-shaped, gray leaves and a solitary broadly bell-shaped, purplish pink flower, 1½–2in (3.5–5cm) long, conspicuously checkered and suffused gray outside.

F. verticillata illus. p.332.

FUCHSIA (Onagraceae)
Genus of deciduous or evergreen shrubs and trees, grown for their flowers, usually borne from early summer to early autumn. Frost hardy to frost tender, min. 41°F (5°C). If temperature remains above 39°F (4°C), deciduous plants are evergreen, but temperatures above 90°F (32°C) should be avoided. Prolonged low temperatures cause loss of top growth. If top growth dies in winter, cut back to ground level in spring. Needs a sheltered, partially shaded position, except where stated otherwise, and fertile, moist but well-drained soil. In North America, fuchsias are best treated as annuals or cool greenhouse plants; excessive summer heat is as detrimental as the cold. When grown as pot plants in a greenhouse, fuchsias will also need high-nitrogen feeds and, when flowering, plenty of potash. Propagate by softwood cuttings in any season.

Tubular flowers are almost always pendulous and often bicolored, with petals of one hue, and a tube and 4 sepals of another. Leaves are oval and green unless otherwise stated. Spherical to cylindrical, usually blackish purple fruits are edible, but mostly poor-flavored. Upright types may be trained as compact bushes or standards or, with more difficulty, as pyramids. Lax or trailing plants are best grown in hanging baskets, but may be trained on trellises; if they are used for summer bedding they require staking.

Heights given in descriptions below are of plants grown in frost-free conditions. All species are hardy in zone 9 except where otherwise stated.

F. **'Alice Hoffman'.** Deciduous, compact shrub. H and S 2½ft (75cm). Frost hardy. Has bronze foliage and small, semi-double flowers with rose-red tubes and sepals and rose-veined, white petals.

F. **'Ann Howard Tripp'** (illus. p.132). Vigorous, deciduous, upright shrub. H and S 2½ft (75cm). Half hardy. Bears single or semi-double, white flowers. Foliage is pale green.

F. 'Annabel' (illus. p.132). Deciduous, upright shrub. H 3ft (1m), S 2¹/₂ft (75cm). Half hardy. Produces large, double, pink-tinged, creamy white flowers amid pale green leaves. Makes an excellent standard.

F. arborescens (Tree fuchsia; illus. p.132). Evergreen, upright tree. H 25ft (8m), S 8ft (2.5m). Frost tender. Erect heads of tiny, pale mauve to pink flowers, borne year-round, are followed by black fruits with gray-blue bloom. Foliage is mid- to dark green. May also be grown as a pot plant.

F. 'Autumnale' (illus. p.132). Deciduous, lax shrub, grown mainly for its foliage. H 6ft (2m), S 20in (50cm). Half hardy. Bears variegated red, gold, and bronze leaves. Flowers have red tubes and sepals with reddish purple petals. Is suitable for a hanging basket or for training as a weeping standard.

F. x bacillaris (illus. p.133). Group of deciduous, lax shrubs. H and S 2¹/₂ft (75cm). Frost hardy. Bears minute, white, pink, or crimson flowers (color varying according to sun), sometimes followed by glossy, black fruits. Small leaves are mid- to dark green. Is suitable for a rock garden or hanging basket.

F. boliviana. Fast-growing, deciduous, upright shrub. H 10ft (3m), S 3ft (1m). Frost tender. Has large, soft, gray-green leaves with reddish midribs. Long-tubed, scarlet flowers, bunched at ends of branches, are followed by pleasantly flavored, black fruits. Needs a large pot and plenty of space to grow well. Resents being pinched back. Is very susceptible to whitefly. **'Alba'** (illus. p.133) has flowers with white tubes and sepals and scarlet petals, followed by green fruits.

F. 'Bon Accord', syn. F. 'Bon Accorde'. Vigorous, deciduous, upright shrub. H 5ft (1.5m), S 20in (50cm). Half hardy. Small, erect flowers have white tubes and sepals and pale purple petals.

F. 'Brutus'. Vigorous, deciduous, upright shrub. H 5ft (1.5m), S 3ft (1m). Frost hardy. Produces single or semi-double flowers that have crimson-red tubes and sepals and deep purple petals.

F. 'Cambridge Louie'. Vigorous, deciduous, upright shrub. H 5ft (1.5m), S 2¹/₂ft (75cm). Half hardy. Produces flowers in various shades of pink.

F. 'Cascade' (illus. p.133). Deciduous, trailing shrub. H 6ft (2m), S indefinite. Half hardy. Bears red-tinged, white tubes and sepals and deep carmine petals. Is excellent in a hanging basket.

F. 'Celia Smedley' (illus. p.133). Vigorous, deciduous, upright shrub. H 5ft (1.5m), S 3ft (1m). Half hardy. Large, single or semi-double flowers have greenish white tubes, pale pinkish white sepals, and currant red petals. Is best when trained as a standard.

F. 'Cloverdale Pearl'. Deciduous, upright shrub. H 3ft (1m), S 2¹/₂ft (75cm). Half hardy. Flowers have pinkish white tubes, pink-veined, white petals, and green-tipped, pink

sepals. Foliage is green with crimson midribs. Is readily trained as a standard.

F. 'Coquet Bell'. Vigorous, deciduous, upright shrub. H 5ft (1.5m), S 3ft (1m). Half hardy. Has a profusion of single or semi-double flowers with pinkish red tubes and sepals and red-veined, pale mauve petals.

F. denticulata. Deciduous, straggling shrub. H 12ft (4m), S indefinite. Frost tender. Flowers have long, crimson tubes, green-tipped, pale pink sepals, and vermilion petals. Leaves are glossy, dark green above and reddish green beneath. With good greenhouse cultivation, flowers appear throughout autumn and winter.

F. 'Display'. Deciduous, upright shrub. H 3ft (1m), S 2¹/₂ft (75cm). Frost hardy. Bears saucer-shaped flowers in shades of pink.

F. 'Dollar Princess' (illus. p.132). Deciduous, upright shrub. H 3ft (1m), S 2¹/₂ft (75cm). Frost hardy. Small, double flowers have cerise-red tubes and sepals and purple petals.

F. 'Eden Lady'. Deciduous, upright shrub. H 3ft (1m), S 2¹/₂ft (75cm). Half hardy. Flowers have reddish pink tubes and sepals and pale violet-blue petals with red veins. Makes a good standard.

F. 'Estelle Marie' (illus. p.133). Deciduous, upright shrub. H 3ft (1m), S 20in (50cm). Half hardy. Flowers with white tubes, green-tipped, white sepals, and mauve petals are borne above foliage. Is excellent for summer bedding.

F. 'Flash'. Fast-growing, deciduous, stiffly erect shrub. H 8ft (2.5m), S 20in (50cm). Frost hardy. Produces small, red flowers amid small leaves.

F. 'Flirtation Waltz'. Vigorous, deciduous, upright shrub. H 3ft (1m), S 2¹/₂ft (75cm). Half hardy. Has large, double flowers with petals in shades of pink, and white tubes and sepals.

F. fulgens (illus. p.133). Deciduous, upright shrub with tubers. H 6ft (2m), S 3ft (1m). Frost tender. Long-tubed, orange flowers hang in short clusters amid large, pale green leaves and are followed by edible but acidic, green fruits. Tubers may be stored dry for winter. May also be propagated by division of tubers in spring. Is very susceptible to whitefly.

F. 'Genii'. Deciduous, erect shrub. H 5ft (1.5m), S 2¹/₂ft (75cm). Frost hardy. Produces small flowers with cerise-red tubes and sepals and reddish purple petals. Has golden green foliage. Makes a good standard.

F. 'Golden Dawn' (illus. p.132). Deciduous, upright shrub. H 5ft (1.5m), S 2¹/₂ft (75cm). Half hardy. Flowers are salmon pink. Is good for training as a standard.

F. 'Golden Marinka' (illus. p.133). Deciduous, trailing shrub. H 6ft (2m), S indefinite. Half hardy. Has red flowers and variegated golden yellow leaves with red veins. Is excellent for a hanging basket.

F. 'Gruss aus dem Bodenthal' (illus. p.132). Deciduous, upright shrub. H 3ft (1m), S 2¹/₂ft (75cm). Half hardy. Small, single or semi-double, crimson flowers open almost black, becoming larger and paler with age.

F. 'Harry Gray' (illus. p.132). Deciduous, lax shrub. H 6ft (2m), S indefinite. Half hardy. Bears a profusion of double flowers with pale pink tubes, green-tipped, white sepals, and white to pale pink petals. Is excellent in a hanging basket.

F. 'Heidi Weiss'. See F. 'White Ann'.

F. 'Hula Girl'. Deciduous, trailing shrub. H 6ft (2m), S indefinite. Half hardy. Bears large, double flowers with deep rose-pink tubes and sepals and pink-flushed, white petals. Does best in a large hanging basket or when trained against a trellis.

F. 'Jack Acland' (illus. p.132). Deciduous, upright shrub. H 5ft (1.5m), S 3ft (1m). Half hardy. Has large, pale to deep pink flowers.

F. 'Jack Shahan' (illus. p.132). Vigorous, deciduous, trailing shrub. H 6ft (2m), S indefinite. Half hardy. Has large, pale to deep pink flowers. Is excellent for a hanging basket or for training into a weeping standard or upright against a trellis.

F. 'Joe Kusber'. Deciduous, lax shrub. H and S 3ft (1m). Half hardy. Bears large, double flowers with white tubes, long, pink-tipped, white sepals, and bluish purple petals.

F. 'Joy Patmore'. Vigorous, deciduous, upright shrub. H 5ft (1.5m), S 3ft (1m). Half hardy. Flowers have white tubes, green-tipped, white sepals, and cerise petals with white bases. Is good for training as a standard.

F. 'Koralle' (illus. p.133). Deciduous, upright shrub. H and S 3ft (1m). Frost tender. Salmon orange flowers, with long, narrow tubes and small sepals and petals, are bunched at ends of branches. Foliage is velvety and deep green. Is useful as summer bedding and makes an excellent specimen plant. Prefers sun.

F. 'Kwintet' (illus. p.132). Vigorous, deciduous, upright shrub. H 5ft (1.5m), S 3ft (1m). Half hardy. Flowers are in shades of deep pink.

F. 'La Campanella' (illus. p.133). Deciduous, trailing shrub. H 5ft (1.5m), S indefinite. Half hardy. Has small, semi-double flowers with white tubes, pink-flushed, white sepals, and cerise-purple petals. Does best in a hanging basket or when trained against a trellis.

F. 'Lady Thumb' (illus. p.132). Deciduous, upright, dwarf shrub. H and S 20in (50cm). Frost hardy, zones 8–10. Has small, semi-double flowers with reddish pink tubes and sepals and pink-veined, white petals. May be trained as a miniature standard.

F. 'Lena'. Deciduous, lax shrub. H and S 3ft (1m). Frost hardy. Bears double flowers with pale pink sepals and tubes and pink-flushed, purple petals. Makes a good standard.

F. 'Leonora' (illus. p.132). Vigorous, deciduous, upright shrub. H 5ft (1.5m), S 3ft (1m). Half hardy. Flowers are pink with green-tipped sepals. Is good for training as a standard.

F. 'Lindisfarne'. Vigorous, deciduous, upright shrub. H 5ft (1.5m), S 3ft (1m). Half hardy. Produces single or semi-double flowers with pale pink tubes and sepals and violet petals.

F. 'Lye's Unique' (illus. p.133). Vigorous, deciduous, upright shrub. H 5ft (1.5m), S 3ft (1m). Half hardy. Has small flowers with long, white tubes and sepals and orange-red petals. Is excellent for training as a large pyramid.

F. magellanica (Lady's eardrops; illus. p.132). Deciduous, upright shrub. H 10ft (3m), S 6ft (2m). Frost hardy, zones 7–8. Small flowers with red tubes, long, red sepals, and purple petals are followed by black fruits. **'Alba'** has very pale pink flowers.

F. 'Margaret Roe'. Deciduous, upright shrub. H 3ft (1m), S 2¹/₂ft (75cm). Half hardy. Erect flowers with red tubes and sepals and pale violet petals are borne above foliage. Is particularly good for summer bedding.

F. 'Marin Glow'. Vigorous, deciduous, upright shrub. H 5ft (1.5m), S 3ft (1m). Half hardy. Flowers have white tubes, green-tipped, white sepals, and purplish blue petals. Makes an excellent standard.

F. 'Marinka'. Deciduous, trailing shrub. H 6ft (2m), S indefinite. Half hardy. Red flowers with darker petals that are folded at outer edges are produced amid dark green leaves with crimson midribs. Foliage becomes discolored in full sun or cold winds. Is excellent in a hanging basket.

F. 'Mary Poppins' (illus. p.133). Deciduous, upright shrub. H 5ft (1.5m), S 2¹/₂ft (75cm). Half hardy. Flowers have apricot pink tubes and sepals and vermilion petals.

F. 'Micky Gault'. Vigorous, deciduous, upright shrub. H 3ft (1m), S 2¹/₂ft (75cm). Half hardy. Small flowers, with white tubes, pink-tinged, white sepals, and pale purple petals, are produced amid pale green foliage.

F. 'Mieke Meursing'. Deciduous, upright shrub. H 3ft (1m), S 2¹/₂ft (75cm). Half hardy. Single to semi-double flowers have red tubes and sepals and pale pink petals with cerise veins.

F. 'Mrs. Popple' (illus. p.133). Vigorous, deciduous, upright shrub. H 5ft (1.5m), S 2¹/₂ft (75cm). Frost hardy, zones 8–10. Has flowers with red tubes, overhanging, red sepals, and purple petals. In a sheltered area may be grown as a hedge.

F. 'Mrs. Rundle'. Vigorous, deciduous, lax shrub. H and S 2¹/₂ft (75cm). Frost tender. Large flowers have long, pink tubes, green-tipped, pink sepals, and vermilion petals. Is good for training as a standard or growing in a large hanging basket.

F. 'Nancy Lou'. Vigorous, deciduous, upright shrub. H and S 3ft (1m). Half hardy. Large, double flowers have pink tubes, upright, green-tipped, pink sepals, and bright white petals.

F. 'Nellie Nuttall' (illus. p.132). Vigorous, deciduous, upright shrub. H 3ft (1m), S 2¹/₂ft (75cm). Half hardy. Flowers, with rose-red tubes and sepals and white petals, are borne well above foliage. Is especially suitable for summer bedding; is also good as a standard.

F. 'Other Fellow' (illus. p.132). Deciduous, upright shrub. H 5ft (1.5m), S 2¹/₂ft (75cm). Half hardy.

Has small flowers with white tubes and sepals and pink petals.

F. **'Pacquesa'.** Vigorous, deciduous, upright shrub. H 3ft (1m), S 2¹/₂ft (75cm). Half hardy. Has flowers with deep red tubes and sepals and red-veined, white petals. Is good for training as a standard.

F. **'Peppermint Stick'** (illus. p.132). Deciduous, upright shrub. H 5ft (1.5m), S 3ft (1m). Half hardy. Large, double flowers have carmine red tubes and sepals and pink-splashed, purple petals. Makes a good standard.

F. **'Phyllis'.** Deciduous, upright shrub. H 6ft (2m), S 3ft (1m). Frost hardy. Single to semi-double flowers, with rose-red tubes and sepals and crimson petals, are followed by masses of black fruits. In a sheltered area may be grown as a hedge.

F. **'Pink Galore'** (illus. p.132). Deciduous, trailing shrub. H 5ft (1.5m), S indefinite. Half hardy. Has large, double, pale pink flowers. Grows best in a large hanging basket or when trained against a trellis.

F. procumbens (illus. p.133). Deciduous, prostrate shrub. H 4in (10cm), S indefinite. Half hardy. Has small, dark green leaves and tiny, erect, petalless, yellow-tubed flowers, with purple sepals and bright blue pollen. Bears large, red fruits. Suits a rock garden or a hanging basket. Flowering may be encouraged by root restriction or by growing in poor, sandy soil.

F. **'Red Spider'** (illus. p.132). Deciduous, trailing shrub. H 5ft (1.5m), S indefinite. Half hardy. Has long, red flowers with long, narrow, spreading sepals and darker petals. Is best in a large hanging basket or when trained against a trellis.

F. **'Riccartonii'** (illus. p.132). Deciduous, stiff, upright shrub. H 6ft (2m), S 5ft (1.5m). Frost hardy, but, with good drainage and wind protection, is sometimes fully hardy.

Has small flowers with red tubes, broad, overhanging, red sepals, and purple petals. In a sheltered area may be grown as a hedge. Many plants sold under name of *F.* 'Riccartonii' are lax hybrids of *F. magellanica*.

F. **'Rose of Castile'** (illus. p.133). Vigorous, deciduous, upright shrub. H 5ft (1.5m), S 3ft (1m). Frost hardy. Produces small flowers with white tubes, green-tipped, white sepals, and purple-flushed, pink petals. Makes a good standard.

F. **'Rough Silk'.** Vigorous, deciduous, trailing shrub. H 6ft (2m), S indefinite. Half hardy. Bears large flowers that have pink tubes, long, spreading, pink sepals, and wine red petals. Grows best in a large hanging basket or when trained against a trellis.

F. **'Royal Velvet'.** Vigorous, deciduous, upright shrub. H 5ft (1.5m), S 2¹/₂ft (75cm). Half hardy. Has large, double flowers with red tubes and sepals and deep purple petals, splashed with deep pink. Makes an excellent standard.

F. **'Rufus'** (illus. p.132). Vigorous, deciduous, upright shrub. H 5ft (1.5m), S 2¹/₂ft (75cm). Half hardy. Has a profusion of small, bright red flowers. Is easily trained as a standard.

F. splendens. Deciduous, upright shrub. H 6ft (2m), S 3ft (1m). Half hardy. Small flowers, with broad, orange tubes, pinched in middles, and short, green sepals and petals, appear in spring amid pale green foliage. Is very susceptible to whitefly.

F. **'Strawberry Delight'.** Deciduous, lax shrub. H and S 3ft (1m). Half hardy. Large, double flowers have red tubes and sepals and pink-flushed, white petals. Leaves are yellowish green and slightly bronzed. Makes an excellent standard or hanging basket plant.

F. **'Swingtime'** (illus. p.132). Vigorous, deciduous, lax shrub. H

and S 3ft (1m). Half hardy. Has large, double flowers with red tubes and sepals and red-veined, creamy white petals. Is good for training as a standard or growing in a hanging basket.

F. **'Temple Bells'.** Vigorous, deciduous, upright shrub. H 3ft (1m), S 2¹/₂ft (75cm). Frost hardy. Flowers have red tubes and sepals and mauve petals.

F. **'Texas Longhorn'.** Deciduous, lax shrub. H and S 2¹/₂ft (75cm). Half hardy. Very large, double flowers have red tubes, long, spreading, red sepals, and white petals with cerise veins. May be grown as a standard or in a hanging basket.

F. **'Thalia'** (illus. p.133). Deciduous, upright shrub. H and S 3ft (1m). Frost tender. Long, slender flowers, with long, red tubes, small, red sepals, and small, orange-red petals, are bunched at ends of branches. Foliage is dark maroon and velvety. Makes an excellent specimen plant in summer bedding schemes. Prefers full sun.

F. thymifolia. Deciduous, lax shrub. H and S 3ft (1m). Half hardy. Has pale green foliage and a few minute, greenish white flowers that age to purplish pink. Bears black fruits on female plants if pollen-bearing plants of this species or of *F.* x *bacillaris* are also grown.

F. **'Tom Thumb'** (illus. p.132). Deciduous, upright shrub. H and S 20in (50cm). Frost hardy, zones 8–10. Bears small flowers with red tubes and sepals and mauve-purple petals. May be trained as a miniature standard.

F. triphylla. Deciduous, upright shrub, sometimes confused with *F.* 'Thalia'. H and S 20in (50cm). Frost tender. Spikes of narrow, long-tubed, bright reddish orange flowers, with small petals and sepals, are borne above dark bronze-green leaves that are purple beneath. Is very difficult to grow.

F. **'Tristesse'.** Deciduous, upright shrub. H 3ft (1m), S 2¹/₂ft (75cm). Half hardy. Has double flowers with pink tubes, reflexed, green-tipped, pink sepals, and pale mauve petals. Makes a good standard.

F. **'Westminster Chimes'.** Deciduous, trailing shrub. H 6ft (2m), S indefinite. Half hardy. Small, semi-double flowers have deep pink tubes, green-tipped, paler pink sepals, and purple petals. Is best in a hanging basket.

F. **'White Ann'**, syn. *F.* 'Heidi Weiss' (illus. p.132). Deciduous, upright shrub. H 3ft (1m), S 2¹/₂ft (75cm). Half hardy. Has double flowers with red tubes and sepals and cerise-veined, white petals. Is good for training as a standard.

F. **'White Spider'** (illus. p.132). Vigorous, deciduous, trailing shrub. H 6ft (2m), S indefinite. Half hardy. Bears large, very pale pink flowers with long, narrow, spreading, green-tipped sepals. Makes an excellent hanging basket plant or may be trained as a weeping standard or against a trellis.

FURCRAEA (Agavaceae)
Genus of perennial succulents with basal rosettes of sword-shaped, toothed, fleshy leaves; rosettes die after flowering. Resembles *Agave*, but differs in its short-tubed flowers. Bears bulbils on lower stems. Frost tender, min. 43°F (6°C). Needs sun and very well-drained soil. Propagate by bulbils when developed.

F. foetida, syn. *F. gigantea.* Basal-rosetted, perennial succulent. H 10ft (3m), S 15ft (5m). Zone 10. Has broadly sword-shaped, fleshy, green leaves, to 8ft (2.5m) long, with edges toothed only at the base. Flower stems, to 25ft (8m), produce strongly scented, bell-shaped, green flowers, white within, in summer. **'Mediopicta'** illus. p.381.

F. gigantea. See *F. foetida.*

G

GAILLARDIA (Compositae)
Blanket flower
Genus of summer-flowering annuals and perennials that tend to be short-lived. Fully to frost hardy. Requires sun and prefers well-drained soil. May need staking. Propagate species by seed in autumn or spring, selected forms by root cuttings in winter.
G. aristata illus. p.246.
G. x grandiflora **'Dazzler'** illus. p.240. **'Wirral Flame'** is a clump-forming, short-lived perennial. H 24in (60cm), S 20in (50cm). Fully hardy, zones 4–8. Produces large, terminal, daisylike, deep cardinal red flower heads during summer. Leaves are lance-shaped, lobed, and soft green.
G. pulchella [double, mixed]. Moderately fast-growing, upright annual or short-lived perennial. H 18in (45cm), S 12in (30cm). Fully hardy. Has lance-shaped, hairy, grayish green leaves and, in summer, daisylike, double, crimson-zoned, yellow, pink, or red flower heads. **'Lollipops'** illus. p.282.

GALANTHUS (Amaryllidaceae)
Snowdrop
Genus of bulbs, grown for their pendent, white flowers, one on each slender stem between 2 basal leaves. Is easily recognized by its 3 large, outer petals and 3 small, inner ones forming a cup, which is green-marked. Fully to frost hardy. Needs a cool, partially shaded position and humus-rich, moist soil. Do not allow bulbs to dry out excessively. Propagate by division in spring after flowering or in late summer or autumn when bulbs are dormant.
G. **'Atkinsii'** illus. p.369.
G. elwesii illus. p.369.
G. gracilis, syn. *G. graecus*, illus. p.369.
G. graecus. See *G. gracilis*.
G. ikariae, syn. *G. latifolius*, illus. p.370.
G. latifolius. See *G. ikariae*.
G. nivalis (Common snowdrop). Late winter- and early spring-flowering bulb. H 4–6in (10–15cm), S 2–3in (5–8cm). Fully hardy, zones 3–9. Produces narrowly strap-shaped, semi-erect, basal, gray-green leaves. Flowers are $^3/_4$–1in (2–2.5cm) long with a green mark at the tip of each inner petal. **'Flore Pleno'** and **'Pusey Green Tips'** illus. p.369. **'Lutescens'** and **'Scharlockii'** illus. p.370.
G. plicatus. Late winter- and early spring-flowering bulb. H 4–8in (10–20cm), S 2–3in (5–8cm). Fully hardy, zones 3–9. Bears broadly strap-shaped, semi-erect, basal, deep green leaves with a gray bloom and reflexed margins. White flowers have a green patch at the tip of each inner petal. subsp. *byzantinus* illus. p.370.
G. reginae-olgae (Autumn snowdrop). Autumn-flowering bulb. H 4–8in (10–20cm), S 2in (5cm). Frost hardy, zones 6–9. Produces $^5/_8$–1in

(1.5–2.5cm) long flowers, with a green patch at the apex of each inner petal, before or just as narrowly strap-shaped, deep green leaves, each with a central, gray stripe, appear.
G. rizehensis illus. p.369.

GALAX (Diapensiaceae)
Genus of one species of evergreen perennial, grown for its foliage and flowers. Is useful for underplanting shrubs. Fully hardy. Needs shade and moist, peaty, acid soil. Propagate by division of rooted runners in spring.
G. aphylla. See *G. urceolata*.
G. urceolata, syn. *G. aphylla*, illus. p.291.

GALEGA (Leguminosae)
Goat's rue
Genus of summer-flowering perennials. Fully hardy. Grow in an open, sunny position and in any well-drained soil. Requires staking. Propagate by seed in autumn or by division in winter.
G. x hartlandii **'His Majesty'**. Vigorous, upright perennial. H to 5ft (1.5m), S 3ft (1m). Zones 5–10. In summer produces spikes of small, pealike, clear lilac-mauve and white flowers. Bold, oblong to lance-shaped leaves consist of oval leaflets. **'Lady Wilson'** illus. p.190.
G. orientalis illus. p.211.

GALEOBDOLON (Labiatae)
Genus of semi-evergreen, summer-flowering perennials. Makes good ground cover, but may be invasive. Fully hardy. Tolerates sun or shade and any well-drained soil. Propagate by division of rooted runners in winter.
G. argentatum, syn. *Lamiastrum galeobdolon* 'Variegatum', *Lamium galeobdolon* 'Variegatum'. Semi-evergreen, carpeting perennial. H to 12in (30cm), S indefinite. Zones 4–9. Oval, green leaves are marked with silver. Racemes of tubular, 2-lipped, lemon yellow flowers appear in summer.

GALIUM (Rubiaceae)
Bedstraw
Genus of spring- and summer-flowering perennials, many of which are weeds; *G. odoratum* is cultivated as ground cover. Fully hardy. Grows well in partial shade, but tolerates sun and thrives in any well-drained soil. Propagate by division in early spring or autumn.
G. odoratum, syn. *Asperula odorata*, illus. p.232.

GALTONIA (Liliaceae)
Genus of summer- and autumn-flowering bulbs, grown for their elegant spikes of pendent, funnel-shaped, white or green flowers. Frost hardy. Needs a sheltered, sunny site and fertile, well-drained soil that does not dry out in summer. Dies down in winter. May be lifted for replanting

in spring. Propagate by seed in spring or by offsets in autumn or spring.
G. candicans illus. p.332.
G. viridiflora illus. p.337.

GARDENIA (Rubiaceae)
Genus of evergreen shrubs and trees, grown for their flowers and foliage. Frost tender, min. 59°F (15°C). Prefers partial shade and humus-rich, well-drained, neutral to acid soil. Water potted specimens freely when in full growth, moderately at other times. After flowering, shorten strong shoots to maintain a shapely habit. Propagate by greenwood cuttings in spring or by semi-ripe cuttings in summer. Whitefly and mealy bug may cause problems.
G. capensis. See *Rothmannia capensis*.
G. florida. See *G. jasminoides*.
G. grandiflora. See *G. jasminoides*.
G. jasminoides, syn. *G. florida*, *G. grandiflora* (Cape jasmine, Common gardenia). **'Fortuniana'** illus. p.126.
G. rothmannia. See *Rothmannia capensis*.
G. thunbergia. Evergreen, bushy shrub with white stems. H and S to 6ft (2m) or more. Zones 9–10. Elliptic leaves are glossy, deep green. Has fragrant, 7–9-petaled, white flowers, 2$^1/_2$–4in (6–10cm) wide, in winter-spring.

GARRYA (Garryaceae)
Genus of evergreen shrubs and trees, grown for their catkins in winter and spring, which are longer and more attractive on male plants. Frost hardy. Requires a sheltered, sunny site and tolerates any poor soil. Is suitable for growing against a south- or west-facing wall. Dislikes being transplanted. Propagate by semi-ripe cuttings in summer. Hard frosts may damage catkins.
G. elliptica illus. p.93. **'James Roof'** is an evergreen, bushy, dense shrub. H and S 12ft (4m). Zones 8–10. Has oval, wavy-edged, leathery, dark green leaves. Very long, gray-green catkins, with yellow anthers, are borne from mid- or late winter to early spring.

GASTERIA (Liliaceae)
Genus of perennial succulents with thick, fleshy leaves, usually arranged in a fan, later becoming a tight rosette. Frost tender, min. 41°F (5°C). Is easy to grow, needing sun or partial shade and very well-drained soil. Propagate by seed, leaf cuttings, or division in spring or summer.
G. caespitosa. Fan-shaped, perennial succulent. H 6in (15cm), S 12in (30cm). Zone 10. Produces triangular, thick, dark green leaves, 6in (15cm) long, with horny borders. Upper leaf surfaces have numerous white or pale green dots, usually in diagonal rows. Bears spikes of bell-shaped, orange-green flowers in spring.
G. liliputana illus. p.400.
G. verrucosa illus. p.400.

x GAULNETTYA (Ericaceae)
Hybrid genus (*Gaultheria* x *Pernettya*) of evergreen shrubs, grown for their foliage, flowers, and fruits. Fully hardy. Needs semi-shade or shade and moist, peaty, acid soil. Propagate by suckers in spring or by semi-ripe cuttings in summer.
x *G.* **'Pink Pixie'**. Evergreen, dense, bushy shrub. H and S 3ft (1m). Zones 7–9. Bears broadly oval, deeply veined, dark green leaves. Small, urn-shaped, pale pink flowers in late spring and early summer are followed by spherical, purplish red fruits.
x *G.* **'Wisley Pearl'** illus. p.122.

GAULTHERIA (Ericaceae)
Genus of evergreen shrubs, grown for their foliage, flowers, and fruits. Fully to half hardy. Requires shade or semi-shade and moist, peaty, acid soil. Provided soil is permanently moist, will tolerate sun. Propagate by semi-ripe cuttings in summer, by seed in autumn or, for *G. shallon* and *G. trichophylla*, by division in autumn or spring.
G. cuneata illus. p.300.
G. forrestii. Evergreen, rounded shrub. H and S 5ft (1.5m). Half hardy, zones 7–8. Has oblong, glossy, dark green leaves and in spring produces racemes of small, fragrant, rounded, white flowers that are followed by rounded, blue fruits.
G. miqueliana. Evergreen, compact shrub. H and S 10in (25cm). Frost hardy, zones 6–8. Has oval, leathery leaves clothing stiff stems. In late spring produces bell-shaped, pink-tinged, white flowers, up to 6 per stem, followed by rounded, white or pink fruits.
G. nummularioides. Evergreen, compact shrub. H 4–6in (10–15cm), S 8in (20cm). Frost hardy, zones 7–8. Leaves are oval to heart-shaped and leathery. Egg-shaped, pink-flushed, white flowers are produced from the upper leaf axils in late spring or summer. Produces rounded, blue-black fruits only rarely.
G. procumbens illus. p.327.
G. shallon illus. p.130.
G. trichophylla. Evergreen, compact shrub with creeping, underground stems. H 3–6in (7–15cm), S 8in (20cm). Frost hardy, zones 7–8. Bell-shaped, pink flowers in early summer are followed by egg-shaped, blue fruits produced from leaf axils. Leaves are small and oval.

GAURA (Onagraceae)
Genus of summer-flowering annuals and perennials that are sometimes short-lived. Fully hardy. Prefers full sun and light, well-drained soil. Propagate by softwood or semi-ripe cuttings in summer or by seed in autumn or spring.
G. lindheimeri. Bushy perennial. H 4ft (1.2m), S 3ft (1m). Zones 6–9. In

summer produces racemes of tubular, pink-suffused, white flowers. Leaves are lance-shaped and green.

GAYLUSSACIA (Ericaceae)
Huckleberry
Genus of deciduous, occasionally evergreen, shrubs, grown for their flowers, fruits, and autumn color. Fully hardy. Needs sun or semi-shade and moist, peaty, acid soil. Propagate by softwood cuttings in summer or by seed in autumn.
G. baccata (Black huckleberry). Deciduous, bushy shrub. H and S 3ft (1m). Zones 3–7. Oval, sticky, dark green leaves redden in autumn. Has clusters of small, urn-shaped, dull red flowers in late spring, then edible, spherical, black fruits.

GAZANIA (Compositae)
Genus of perennials, often grown as annuals and useful for summer bedding, pots and tubs. Half hardy. Requires sun and sandy soil. Propagate by seed in spring or by heel cuttings in spring or summer.
G. 'Daybreak'. Carpeting perennial, grown as an annual. H and S 8in (20cm). Zones 8–10. Has lance-shaped leaves and, in summer, produces large, daisylike flower heads in a mixture of orange, yellow, pink, bronze, and white. Flowers remain open in dull weather.
G. pinnata. Mat-forming perennial. H 6in (15cm), S 12in (30cm). Zones 8–10. Daisylike, orange-red flower heads, with central, black rings, appear singly in early summer above oval, finely cut, hairy, bluish gray leaves.
G. 'Sundance'. Carpeting perennial, grown as an annual. H and S 12in (30cm). Zones 8–10. Has lance-shaped leaves. In summer bears very large, daisylike flower heads, over 3in (8cm) wide, in brilliant flame shades, some with red-and-yellow stripes.
G. uniflora illus. p.247.

GELSEMIUM (Loganiaceae)
Genus of evergreen, twining climbers, grown for their fragrant, jasminelike flowers. Half hardy. In cool climates best grown under glass. Provide fertile, well-drained soil and full light. Water regularly, less in cold weather. Stems require support and should be thinned out after flowering or in spring. Propagate by seed in spring or by semi-ripe cuttings in summer.
G. sempervirens (Carolina jasmine, False jasmine). Moderately vigorous, evergreen, twining climber. H 10ft (3m) or more. Zones 7–9. Has oval to lance-shaped, pointed, lustrous leaves. Clusters of fragrant, funnel-shaped, pale to deep yellow flowers, each with 5 petal lobes, are borne from late spring to late summer.

GENISTA (Leguminosae)
Broom
Genus of deciduous, sometimes almost leafless, shrubs and trees, grown for their mass of small, pealike flowers. Fully to half hardy. Does best in full sun and not over-rich, well-drained soil. Resents being transplanted. Propagate species by softwood or semi-ripe cuttings in summer or by seed in autumn, selected forms by softwood cuttings only in summer.
G. aetnensis illus. p.66.
G. cinerea illus. p.91.
G. delphinensis. Deciduous, prostrate shrub. H ¹/₂in (1cm), S 8in (20cm). Frost hardy, zones 6–9. Has tangled, winged branches, covered with minute, oval, dark green leaves. Masses of golden yellow flowers are borne along stems in early summer. Suits a rock garden or wall.
G. fragrans. See *Cytisus* x *spachianus.*
G. hispanica illus. p.138.
G. lydia illus. p.299.
G. monosperma. Deciduous, almost leafless, graceful, arching shrub. H 1m (3ft), S 5ft (1.5m). Half hardy, zones 9–10. Slender, silky gray shoots bear clusters of very fragrant white flowers in early spring. Has a few inconspicuous leaves. Grow against a south- or west-facing wall.
G. pilosa (Silky-leaf woadwaxen). Deciduous, domed shrub. H and S 12in (30cm). Fully hardy, zones 6–9. Narrowly oval leaves are silky-haired beneath. Bright yellow flowers on short stalks are borne in leaf axils in summer. Is useful on a bank or as ground cover. Propagate by semi-ripe cuttings in summer.
G. sagittalis, syn. *Chamaespartium sagittale* (Winged broom), illus. p.326.
G. tenera 'Golden Showers'. Vigorous, deciduous, arching shrub. H 10ft (3m), S 15ft (5m). Frost hardy, zones 7–9. Narrowly oblong leaves are gray-green. Bears racemes of fragrant, golden yellow flowers in early to mid-summer.
G. tinctoria illus. p.125. **'Royal Gold'** is a deciduous, upright shrub. H and S 3ft (1m). Fully hardy, zones 2–8. Produces long, conical panicles of golden yellow flowers in spring-summer and leaves that are narrowly lance-shaped and dark green.

GENTIANA (Gentianaceae)
Gentian
Genus of annuals, biennials, and perennials, some of which are semi-evergreen or evergreen, grown for their usually blue flowers. Is excellent for rock gardens and peat beds. Fully hardy. Prefers sun or semi-shade and humus-rich, well-drained, moist, neutral to acid soil. Some species grow naturally on limestone soils. Propagate by division or offshoots in spring or by seed in autumn. Divide autumn-flowering species and *G. clusii* every 3 years in early spring and replant in fresh soil.
G. acaulis, syn. *G. excisa, G. kochiana,* illus. p.310.
G. angustifolia. Evergreen, clump-forming perennial. H 4in (10cm), S 8in (20cm). Zones 6–8. Has rosettes of oblong, dull green leaves and, in summer, solitary tubular, sky blue flowers on 3in (7cm) stems. Tolerates alkaline soils.
G. asclepiadea illus. p.220.
G. clusii (Trumpet gentian). Evergreen, clump-forming perennial. H 2in (5cm), S 6–9in (15–23cm). Zones 7–9. Has rosettes of oval, glossy, dark green leaves. Trumpet-shaped, azure blue flowers, with green-spotted, paler throats, are borne on 1–4in (2.5–10cm) stems in early summer. Tolerates alkaline soils.
G. excisa. See *G. acaulis.*
G. gracilipes. Semi-evergreen, tufted perennial with arching stems. H 6in (15cm), S 8in (20cm). Zones 6–8. Forms a central rosette of long, strap-shaped, dark green leaves from which lax flower stems bearing tubular, dark purplish blue flowers, greenish within, are produced in summer. Tolerates some shade.
G. kochiana. See *G. acaulis.*
G. lutea illus. p.214.
G. x *macaulayi* (Macaulay gentian). **'Wellsii'** illus. p.327.
G. ornata. Semi-evergreen, clump-forming perennial with small, overwintering rosettes. H 2in (5cm), S 4in (10cm). Zones 5–7. Forms a central rosette of grasslike leaves. In autumn, each stem tip carries an upright, bell-shaped, blue flower, with a white throat and deep blue stripes shading to creamy white outside. Requires acid soil and a moist atmosphere.
G. saxosa illus. p.314.
G. septemfida illus. p.300.
G. sino-ornata illus. p.327.
G. 'Susan Jane'. Vigorous, semi-evergreen, spreading perennial with small, overwintering rosettes. H 2in (5cm), S 12in (30cm). Zones 5–7. Prostrate stems bear grasslike leaves. Large, trumpet-shaped, white-throated, deep blue flowers, greenish within, appear in autumn. Requires acid soil.
G. verna illus. p.310.

GERANIUM (Geraniaceae)
Cranesbill
Genus of perennials, some of which are semi-evergreen, grown for their attractive flowers and often as ground cover. Compact species are suitable for rock gardens. Fully to half hardy. Most species prefer sun, but some do better in shade. Will grow in any but waterlogged soil. Propagate by semi-ripe cuttings in summer or by seed or division in autumn or spring. Cultivars should be propagated by division or cuttings only.
G. 'Ann Folkard'. Spreading perennial. H 20in (50cm), S 36in (1m). Fully hardy, zones 5–8. Has rounded, deeply cut, yellowish green leaves and, in summer-autumn, masses of shallowly cup-shaped, rich magenta flowers with black veins.
G. armenum. See *G. psilostemon.*
G. cinereum. Semi-evergreen, rosetted perennial with spreading flowering stems. H 6in (15cm), S 12in (30cm). Fully hardy, zones 4–9. Has cup-shaped flowers, either white to pale pink, strongly veined with purple, or pure white, on lax stems in late spring and summer. Basal leaves are rounded, deeply divided, soft, and gray-green. Is good for a large rock garden. **'Ballerina'** and var. **subcaulescens** illus. p.319.
G. clarkei 'Kashmir Purple', syn. *G. pratense 'Kashmir Purple'.* Carpeting, rhizomatous perennial. H and S 18–24in (45–60cm). Fully hardy, zones 4–8. Bears loose clusters of cup-shaped, deep purple flowers in summer. Rounded leaves are deeply divided and finely veined. **'Kashmir White'** (syn. *G. pratense* 'Kashmir White') illus. p.233.
G. dalmaticum illus. p.317.
G. endressii illus. p.235. **'Wargrave Pink'** illus. p.236.
G. farreri. Rosetted perennial with a tap root. H 4in (10cm), S 4–6in (10–15cm) or more. Fully hardy, zones 5–8. Outward-facing, flattish, very pale mauve-pink flowers set off blue-black anthers in early summer. Has kidney-shaped, matt green leaves. Flower and leaf stems are red.
G. grandiflorum. See *G. himalayense.*
G. himalayense, syn. *G. grandiflorum,* illus. p.242.
G. ibericum. Clump-forming perennial. H and S 24in (60cm). Fully hardy, zones 5–8. In summer produces sprays of 5-petaled, saucer-shaped, violet-blue flowers. Has heart-shaped, lobed or cut, hairy leaves.
G. incanum. Semi-evergreen, spreading, mounded perennial. H 12–15in (30–38cm), S 2–3ft (60cm–1m). Frost hardy, zones 7–9. Shallowly cup-shaped flowers are variable, but usually deep pink, and are borne singly in summer above aromatic, deeply divided, gray-green leaves with linear segments.
G. 'Johnson's Blue' illus. p.242.
G. macrorrhizum illus. p.236. **'Ingwersen's Variety'** illus. p.226.
G. maculatum. Clump-forming perennial. H 30in (75cm), S 18in (45cm). Fully hardy, zones 5–8. In spring bears heads of flattish, pinkish lilac flowers above rounded, lobed or scalloped, green leaves that turn fawn and red in autumn.
G. maderense. Vigorous, semi-evergreen, bushy perennial with a woody base. H and S 3ft (1m). Half hardy, zones 9–10. Produces large sprays of shallowly cup-shaped, deep magenta flowers in summer above palmate, finely cut, dark green leaves.
G. x *magnificum* illus. p.242.
G. nodosum illus. p.227.
G. orientalitibeticum illus. p.293.
G. x *oxonianum 'Claridge Druce'.* Vigorous, semi-evergreen, carpeting perennial. H and S 24–30in (60–75cm). Fully hardy, zones 5–8. Bears clusters of cup-shaped, darker-veined, mauve-pink flowers throughout summer. Has dainty, rounded, lobed leaves. **'Winscombe'** illus. p.203.
G. palmatum. Vigorous, semi-evergreen, bushy perennial with a woody base. H 18in (45cm), S 24in (60cm). Half hardy, zones 9–10. In late summer produces large sprays of shallowly cup-shaped, purplish red flowers. Has palmate, deeply lobed, dark green leaves.
G. phaeum illus. p.197.
G. pratense (Meadow cranesbill). Clump-forming perennial. H 30in (75cm), S 24in (60cm). Fully hardy, zones 4–8. Produces 5-petaled, saucer-shaped, violet-blue flowers on branching stems in summer. Rounded, lobed to deeply divided, green leaves become bronze in autumn. **'Kashmir Purple'** see *G. clarkei* 'Kashmir Purple'. **'Kashmir White'** see

G. clarkei 'Kashmir White'. **'Plenum Violaceum'** is more compact than the species with double, deep violet flowers.

G. procurrens. Carpeting perennial. H 12in (30cm), S 24in (60cm). Fully hardy, zones 5–8. Has rounded, lobed, glossy leaves and, in summer, clusters of saucer-shaped, deep rose-purple flowers.

G. psilostemon, syn. *G. armenum*, illus. p.205.

G. pylzowianum. Spreading perennial with underground runners and tiny tubers. H 5–10in (12–25cm), S 10in (25cm) or more. Fully hardy, zones 5–8. Bears semi-circular, deeply cut, dark green leaves and, in late spring and summer, trumpet-shaped, deep rose-pink flowers that have green centers. May be invasive.

G. renardii illus. p.234.

G. 'Russell Prichard'. Semi-evergreen, clump-forming perennial. H 1ft (30cm), S 3ft (1m). Frost hardy, zones 6–8. Saucer-shaped, clear pink flowers are borne singly or in small clusters from early summer to autumn. Rounded leaves are lobed and gray-green.

G. sanguineum illus. p.294. var. *striatum* (syn. *G.s.* var. *lancastriense*) illus. p.316.

G. stapfianum. Semi-prostrate perennial with underground stolons. H 5in (12cm), S 6in (15cm) or more. Frost hardy, zones 8–9. Leaves are kidney-shaped to rounded, deeply cut to scalloped, and green marbled white with red leaf stalks and margins. In summer has solitary upward-facing, saucer-shaped, reddish purple flowers with red centers and veins. Is best grown in an alpine house or in scree conditions as dislikes winter wet.

G. sylvaticum 'Mayflower' illus. p.210.

G. traversii var. *elegans*. Semi-evergreen, rosetted perennial with spreading stems. H 4in (10cm), S 10in (25cm). Frost hardy, zones 8–9. Large, upward-facing, saucer-shaped, pale pink flowers, with darker veins, rise above rounded, lobed, gray-green leaves in summer. Is suitable for a sheltered ledge or rock garden. Requires protection from winter wet. Needs gritty soil.

G. wallichianum 'Buxton's Blue' illus. p.243.

G. wlassovianum. Clump-forming perennial. H and S 24in (60cm). Fully hardy, zones 5–8. Has velvety stems and rounded, lobed, dark green leaves. Saucer-shaped, deep purple flowers are produced singly or in small clusters in summer.

GERBERA (Compositae)
Genus of perennials, flowering from summer to winter depending on growing conditions. Half hardy. Grow in full sun and in light, sandy soil. Propagate by heel cuttings from side shoots in summer or by seed in autumn or early spring.

G. jamesonii illus. p.258.

GEUM (Rosaceae)
Genus of summer-flowering perennials. Fully hardy. Does best in sun and

prefers moist but well-drained soil. Propagate by division or seed in autumn.

G. x borisii illus. p.249.

G. 'Fire Opal'. Clump-forming perennial. H 32in (80cm), S 18in (45cm). Zones 5–9. Rounded, double, bronze-scarlet flowers are borne in small clusters in summer above oblong to lance-shaped, lobed, fresh green leaves.

G. 'Lady Stratheden' illus. p.247.

G. 'Lionel Cox'. Clump-forming perennial. H and S 12in (30cm). Zones 5–9. In early summer produces small clusters of 5-petaled, cup-shaped, shrimp red flowers above oblong to lance-shaped, lobed, fresh green leaves.

G. montanum (Alpine avens). Dense, clump-forming, rhizomatous perennial that spreads slowly. H 4in (10cm), S 9in (23cm). Zones 4–8. Shallowly cup-shaped, golden yellow flowers in early summer are followed by fluffy, buff-colored seed heads. Leaves are pinnate, each with a large, rounded, terminal lobe. Is suitable for a rock garden.

G. 'Mrs. Bradshaw'. Clump-forming perennial. H 32in (80cm), S 18in (45cm). Zones 5–9. Rounded, double, crimson flowers are borne in small sprays in summer. Fresh green leaves are oblong to lance-shaped and lobed.

GEVUINA (Proteaceae)
Genus of evergreen trees, grown for their foliage and flowers in summer. Frost hardy. Needs semi-shade and fertile, moist but well-drained soil. Propagate by semi-ripe cuttings in late summer or by seed in autumn.

G. avellana (Chilean hazel). Evergreen, conical tree. H and S 30ft (10m). Zones 9–10. Has large, glossy, dark green leaves that are divided into numerous oval, toothed leaflets. Slender spires of spidery, white flowers in late summer are followed by cherrylike, red, then black fruits.

GIBBAEUM (Aizoaceae)
Genus of clump-forming, perennial succulents with pairs of small, swollen leaves, often of unequal size. Frost tender, min. 41°F (5°C). Requires full sun and very well-drained soil. Water very lightly and occasionally in early winter. Propagate by seed or stem cuttings in spring or summer.

G. petrense. Carpeting, perennial succulent. H 1¼in (3cm), S 12in (30cm) or more. Zone 10. Each branch carries 1 or 2 pairs of thick, triangular, pale gray-green leaves, ½in (1cm) long. Bears daisylike, pink-red flowers, ⅝in (1.5cm) across, in spring.

G. velutinum illus. p.389.

GILIA (Polemoniaceae)
Genus of summer- and autumn-flowering annuals. Fully hardy. Grows best in sun and in fertile, very well-drained soil. Stems may need support, especially on windy sites. Propagate by seed sown outdoors in spring, or in early autumn for early flowering the following year.

G. achilleifolia. Fast-growing, upright, bushy annual. H 24in (60cm), S 8in

(20cm). Finely divided, green leaves are hairy and sticky. Heads of funnel-shaped, blue flowers, 1in (2.5cm) wide, are produced in summer.

G. capitata illus. p.277.

GILLENIA (Rosaceae)
Genus of summer-flowering perennials. Fully hardy. Tolerates sun or shade and any well-drained soil. Needs staking. Propagate by seed in autumn or spring.

G. trifoliata illus. p.202.

GINKGO (Ginkgoaceae). See CONIFERS.

G. biloba illus. p.75.

GLADIOLUS (Iridaceae)
Genus of corms, each producing a spike of funnel-shaped flowers and a fan of erect, sword-shaped leaves on basal part of flower stem. Is suitable for cutting or for planting in mixed borders; most hybrids are also good for exhibition. Frost to half hardy. Needs a sunny and fertile, well-drained site. Plant 4–6in (10–15cm) deep and the same distance apart in spring. Water well in summer and support tall cultivars with canes. In autumn lift half-hardy types, cut off stems and dry corms in a frost-free but cool place. Pot up spring-flowering species and cultivars in autumn and place in a cool greenhouse; after flowering, dry off for summer months and repot in autumn.

Propagate by seed or by removal of young cormlets from parent. Seed sown in early spring in a cool greenhouse will take 2–3 years to flower and may not breed true to type. Cormlets, removed after lifting, should be stored in frost-free conditions and then be planted out 2in (5cm) deep in spring; lift in winter as for mature corms. They will flower in 1–2 years.

While in store, corms may be attacked by various rots. Protect sound, healthy corms by dusting with a fungicide or soaking in a fungicide solution before drying; store in an airy, cool, frost-free place. Gladiolus scab causes blotches on leaves; gladiolus yellows shows as yellowing stripes, then death of leaves; in both cases destroy affected corms and plant healthy ones in a new site each year.

Gladiolus hybrids
Most hybrids are derived from *G. x hortulanus*. Each spike has flowers arranged on opposite sides of stem, either vertically, touching each other (formally placed), or alternating up the stem with a slight space between each flower (ladder placed). All have stiff leaves, 8–20in (20–50cm) long, ranging from pale willow green or steely blue-green to almost bottle green. Half hardy. They are divided into Grandiflorus and Primulinus groups.

Grandiflorus group produces long, densely packed spikes of funnel-shaped flowers, with ruffled, thick-textured petals or plain-edged, thin-textured ones. Giant-flowered hybrids have a bottom flower of over 5½in (14cm) across (flower head is 26–32in (65–80cm) long); large-flowered

4½–5½in (11–14cm) across (flower head 24–36in (60cm–1m) long); medium-flowered 3½–4½in (9–11cm) across (flower head 24–32in (60–80cm) long); and small-flowered 2½–3½in (6–9cm) across (flower head 20–28in (50–70cm) long).

Primulinus group has fairly loose spikes of plain-edged, funnel-shaped flowers, 2½–3in (6–8cm) across, each with a strongly hooded, upper petal over the stigma and anthers. Flower heads are 12in (30cm) long.

G. 'Amsterdam'. Grandiflorus group, giant-flowered gladiolus. H 5½ft (1.7m), S 1ft (30cm). Has up to 10 formally placed, slightly upward-facing, finely ruffled, white flowers in late summer. Is good for exhibition.

G. 'Amy Beth'. Grandiflorus group, small-flowered gladiolus. H 4ft (1.2m), S 8–10in (20–25cm). Bears 7 formally placed, heavily ruffled, lavender flowers, with thick, waxy, cream-lipped petals, in late summer.

G. 'Atlantis'. Grandiflorus group, medium-flowered gladiolus. H 5ft (1.5m), S 8–10in (20–25cm). Carries 8 lightly ruffled, deep violet-blue flowers, with small, white throats, in ladder placement up stem during late summer. Is good in flower arrangements.

G. 'Black Lash' (illus. p.334). Grandiflorus group, small-flowered gladiolus. H 4½ft (1.35m), S 6–8in (15–20cm). Bears 8 or 9 formally placed, lightly ruffled, deep black-rose flowers, with pointed, slightly reflexed petals, from late summer to early autumn.

G. blandus. See *G. carneus*.

G. 'Café au Lait' (illus. p.334). Primulinus group gladiolus. H 3½ft (1.1m), S 6–8in (15–20cm). Bears 4 or 5 pale coffee-colored flowers, each with a beige throat and a hooded, central, upper petal, in ladder placement up stem in late summer. Is excellent in flower arrangements.

G. callianthus, syn. *Acidanthera bicolor* var. *murieliae*. Late summer-flowering corm. H to 3ft (1m), S 4–6in (10–15cm). Half hardy, zones 8–10. Has a loose spike of up to 10 fragrant flowers, each with a curved, 4in (10cm) long tube and 6 white petals, each with a deep purple blotch at the base.

G. cardinalis. Summer-flowering corm. H to 4ft (1.2m), S 4–6in (10–15cm). Half hardy, zones 9–10. Arching stem bears a spike of up to 6 widely funnel-shaped flowers, each 3in (8cm) long and bright red with spear-shaped, white marks on lower 3 petals.

G. 'Carioca' (illus. p.334). Grandiflorus group, medium-flowered gladiolus. H 4½ft (1.35m), S 1ft (30cm). Produces a spike of 8 or 9 formally placed, heavily ruffled, orange flowers, with bright red throat marks, in mid-summer.

G. carneus, syn. *G. blandus*. Spring-flowering corm. H 8–16in (20–40cm), S 3–4in (8–10cm). Half hardy, zone 9. Stem bears a loose spike of up to 8 widely funnel-shaped, white or pink flowers, 1½–2½in (4–6cm) long, marked on lower petals with darker red or yellow blotches.

G. **'Christabel'** illus. p.347.

G. x *colvillei*, syn. *G. nanus*. **'Amanda Mahy'** is an early summer-flowering corm. H 12–20in (30–50cm), S 3–4in (8–10cm). Half hardy, zones 5–10. Produces a loose spike of 5–8 salmon pink flowers, 3in (7cm) long, marked violet on lower petals. Plant in autumn. **'The Bride'** (illus. p.334) has white flowers with green-marked throats.

G. communis subsp. *byzantinus* illus. p.335.

G. **'Dancing Queen'** (illus. p.334). Grandiflorus group, large-flowered gladiolus. H 4¹/₂ft (1.35m), S 8–10in (20–25cm). Has 9 formally placed, ivory white flowers, with 2 wine red blotches in each throat, in late summer; petals are thin and silky.

G. **'Deliverance'** (illus. p.334). Grandiflorus group, giant-flowered gladiolus. H 5¹/₂ft (1.7m), S 10–12in (25–30cm). In late summer produces 9 formally placed flowers that have heavily ruffled, salmon pink petals overlaid with orange.

G. **'Drama'** (illus. p.334). Grandiflorus group, large-flowered gladiolus. H 5¹/₂ft (1.7m), S 10–12in (25–30cm). In late summer bears 8–10 formally placed, lightly ruffled, deep watermelon pink flowers with red-marked, yellow throats. Is superb for exhibition.

G. **'Esta Bonita'**. Grandiflorus group, giant-flowered gladiolus. H 5¹/₂ft (1.7m), S 1ft (30cm). Produces 7 formally placed, apricot orange flowers, slightly darker towards petal edges, in late summer. Is good for exhibition.

G. **'Frank's Perfection'**. Primulinus group gladiolus. H 3¹/₂ft (1.1m), S 6–8in (15–20cm). Has 6 or 7 ladder-placed, vibrant red flowers, each with a hooded, upper petal and with a central, golden line down ribs, in late summer.

G. **'Gigi'** (illus. p.334). Grandiflorus group, small-flowered gladiolus. H 3ft (1m), S 6–8in (15–20cm). Has 7 formally placed, lightly ruffled, dark pink flowers, each with a small, white throat, in late summer.

G. **'Green Isle'**. Grandiflorus group, medium-flowered gladiolus. H 4¹/₂ft (1.35m), S 8–10in (20–25cm). Bears 7 or 8 slightly informal flowers, lime green throughout with chiselled ruffling, in late summer.

G. **'Green Woodpecker'** (illus. p.334). Grandiflorus group, medium-flowered gladiolus. H 5ft (1.5m), S 1ft (30cm). Has 10 formally placed, uranium green flowers, with wine red throats, in late summer. Is very good for exhibition.

G. **'Hastings'**. Primulinus group gladiolus. H 4¹/₂ft (1.35m), S 6–8in (15–20cm). In late summer produces 6 ladder-placed flowers that have pale coffee-colored petals marked with reddish brown. Is excellent in flower arrangements.

G. **'Ice Cap'** (illus. p.334). Grandiflorus group, large-flowered gladiolus. H 5¹/₂ft (1.7m), S 10–12in (25–30cm). Carries 10–12 formally placed, heavily ruffled, ice white flowers from late summer to early autumn.

G. **'Inca Queen'** (illus. p.334). Grandiflorus group, large-flowered gladiolus. H 5ft (1.5m), S 8–10in (20–25cm). Produces 9 formally placed, heavily ruffled, waxy, deep salmon pink flowers, with lemon yellow lip petals and throats, in late summer.

G. italicus, syn. *G. segetum*, illus. p.335.

G. **'Krystal'**. Grandiflorus group, small-flowered gladiolus. H 4ft (1.2m), S 8–10in (20–25cm). Produces 8 formally placed, very lightly ruffled, cerise-red flowers, with prominent, white stamens and white-edged lip petals, in late summer.

G. **'Leonore'**. Primulinus group gladiolus. H 3¹/₂ft (1.1m), S 6–8in (15–20cm). Bears 5–7 ladder-placed, buttercup yellow flowers, each with a hooded, central, upper petal, in late summer.

G. **'Melodie'** (illus. p.334). Grandiflorus group, small-flowered gladiolus. H 4ft (1.2m), S 6–8in (15–20cm). Produces 6 ladder-placed, salmon rose flowers, with longitudinal, spearlike, red-orange marks in throats, in late summer. Is excellent in flower arrangements.

G. **'Mexicali Rose'** (illus. p.334). Grandiflorus group, large-flowered gladiolus. H 5ft (1.5m), S 1ft (30cm). Has 8 formally placed, ruffled, deep rose flowers, with very narrow, silvery white petal margins, in late summer.

G. **'Miss America'** (illus. p.334). Grandiflorus group, medium-flowered gladiolus. H 5ft (1.5m), S 1ft (30cm). In late summer produces 10 formally placed, heavily ruffled, deep pink flowers. Is excellent for exhibition.

G. **'Moon Mirage'** (illus. p.334). Grandiflorus group, giant-flowered gladiolus. H 5¹/₂ft (1.7m), S 10–14in (25–35cm). Produces 9–11 formally placed, moderately ruffled, pale canary yellow flowers, with slightly darker lip petals, from late summer to early autumn.

G. nanus. See *G.* x *colvillei*.

G. natalensis, syn. *G. psittacinus*. Vigorous, summer-flowering corm. H to 5ft (1.5m), S 4–6in (10–15cm). Half hardy, zones 8–10. Produces up to 25 red or yellow-orange flowers, 3–5in (8–12cm) long, each with a hooded, upper petal and often flecked or streaked red.

G. papilio, syn. *G. purpureo-auratus*, illus. p.342.

G. **'Parade'**. Grandiflorus group, giant-flowered gladiolus. H 5¹/₂ft (1.7m), S 10–14in (25–35cm). Produces 10 formally placed, finely ruffled, salmon pink flowers, with small, cream throats, in early autumn. Is superb for exhibition.

G. **'Peter Pears'** (illus. p.334). Grandiflorus group, large-flowered gladiolus. H 5¹/₂ft (1.7m), S 14in (35cm). In late summer bears 10 formally placed, apricot salmon flowers, which have red throat marks. Is excellent for exhibition and in flower arrangements.

G. **'Pink Lady'** (illus. p.334). Grandiflorus group, large-flowered gladiolus. H 5ft (1.5m), S 10–12in (25–30cm). Has 9 formally placed, lightly ruffled, deep rose-pink flowers, with large, white throats, in late summer and early autumn.

G. **'Pink Slipper'**. Grandiflorus group, medium-flowered gladiolus. H 4¹/₂ft (1.35m), S 8–10in (20–25cm). Produces 9 or 10 formally placed, very ruffled, pink flowers, with white throats, in late summer. Is a fine exhibition cultivar.

G. primulinus. Summer-flowering corm, closely related to *G. natalensis* and sometimes included in it. H to 3ft (1m), S 6–8in (15–20cm). Half hardy, zones 8–10. Bears up to 20 soft yellow flowers, each 3–5in (8–12cm) long with a hooded, upper petal.

G. psittacinus. See *G. natalensis*.

G. purpureo-auratus. See *G. papilio*.

G. **'Rajah'**. Grandiflorus group, medium-flowered gladiolus. H 5ft (1.5m), S 8–10in (20–25cm). Produces 10 formally placed, rich plum purple flowers, each with slightly darker lips and white midrib lines, from late summer to early autumn. Petals are pointed and reflexed. Is excellent for exhibition.

G. **'Renegade'** (illus. p.334). Grandiflorus group, large-flowered gladiolus. H 5ft (1.5m), S 8–10in (20–25cm). Bears 7 or 8 formally placed, crisply ruffled, dark red flowers in late summer.

G. **'Robin'** (illus. p.334). Primulinus group gladiolus. H 4ft (1.2m), S 8in (20cm). Produces 5 or 6 ladder-placed, rose-purple flowers, each with a hooded, central, upper petal, in late summer. Is good in flower arrangements.

G. **'Rose Supreme'** (illus. p.334). Grandiflorus group, giant-flowered gladiolus. H 5¹/₂ft (1.7m), S 10–12in (25–30cm). Has 9 formally placed, rose-pink flowers, flecked and streaked darker pink towards petal tips, and with cream throats, in late summer.

G. **'Royal Dutch'**. Grandiflorus group, large-flowered gladiolus. H 5¹/₂ft (1.7m), S 10–12in (25–30cm). Produces 10 formally placed flowers, each pale lavender blending into a white throat, from late summer to early autumn. Is very good for exhibition.

G. **'Rutherford'** (illus. p.334). Primulinus group gladiolus. H 3ft (1m), S 6–8in (15–20cm). Bears 6 ladder-placed, dark red flowers, splashed with cream, each with a hooded, central, upper petal, in late summer.

G. segetum. See *G. italicus*.

G. **'Shari'**. Grandiflorus group, small-flowered gladiolus. H 4ft (1.2m), S 6–8in (15–20cm). Produces 7 or 8 formally placed, ruffled, dark rose-pink flowers, with very large, cream throats, in late summer.

G. **'Tendresse'**. Grandiflorus group, medium-flowered gladiolus. H 5ft (1.5m), S 8–10in (20–25cm). In late summer has 10 formally placed, slightly ruffled, dark pink flowers, with small, cream throats marked with longitudinal, faint rose-pink "spears."

G. **'Tesoro'** (illus. p.334). Grandiflorus group, medium-flowered gladiolus. H 5ft (1.5m), S 8–10in (20–25cm). Bears 10 formally placed, silky flowers, slightly ruffled and glistening yellow, in early autumn. Is among the top exhibition gladioli.

G. **'Victor Borge'** (illus. p.334). Grandiflorus group, large-flowered gladiolus. H 5¹/₂ft (1.7m), S 14in (35cm). Produces 8 formally placed, vermilion-orange flowers, with pale creamy white throat marks, in late summer.

G. **'Video'**. Grandiflorus group, large-flowered gladiolus. H 5¹/₂ft (1.7m), S 8–12in (20–30cm). Has 9 or 10 formally placed, purple flowers, each with a small, ivory white throat, in late summer. Is good for exhibition.

G. **'White City'**. Primulinus group gladiolus. H 3¹/₂ft (1.1m), S 6–8in (15–20cm). Bears 6 or 7 ladder-placed, paper white flowers, each with a hooded, central, upper petal, in late summer.

GLAUCIDIUM (Paeoniaceae)
Genus of one species of spring-flowering perennial. Is excellent in woodland gardens. Fully hardy. Needs a partially shaded, sheltered position and moist, peaty soil. Propagate by seed in autumn.

G. palmatum illus. p.227.

GLAUCIUM (Papaveraceae)
Horned poppy
Genus of annuals, biennials, and perennials, grown for their bright, poppylike flowers. Fully hardy. Grow in sun and in fertile, well-drained soil. Propagate annuals by seed sown outdoors in spring; perennials by seed sown outdoors in spring or autumn; biennials by seed sown under glass in late spring or early summer.

G. flavum illus. p.279.

GLECHOMA (Labiatae)
Genus of evergreen, summer-flowering perennials. Makes good ground cover, but may be invasive. Fully hardy. Tolerates sun or shade. Prefers moist but well-drained soil. Propagate by division in spring or autumn or by softwood cuttings in spring.

G. hederacea (Ground ivy).
'Variegata' illus. p.256.

GLEDITSIA (Leguminosae)
Genus of deciduous, usually spiny trees, grown for their foliage. Has inconspicuous flowers, often followed by large seed pods after hot summers. Fully hardy, but young plants may suffer frost damage. Requires plenty of sun and fertile, well-drained soil. Propagate species by seed in autumn, selected forms by budding in late summer.

G. caspica (Caspian locust). Deciduous, spreading tree. H 40ft (12m), S 30ft (10m). Zones 7–10. Trunk is armed with long, branched spines. Has fernlike, glossy, green leaves.

G. japonica illus. p.53.

G. triacanthos (Honey locust). Deciduous, spreading tree. H 70ft (20m), S 50ft (15m). Zones 5–9. Trunk is very thorny. Fernlike, glossy, dark green leaves turn yellow in autumn. f. *inermis* is thornless. **'Shademaster'** is vigorous, with long-lasting leaves.

'Skyline' is thornless, broadly conical and has golden yellow foliage in autumn. **'Sunburst'** illus. p.50.

GLOBBA (Zingiberaceae)
Genus of evergreen, aromatic, clump-forming perennials, grown for their flowers. Frost tender, min. 64°F (18°C). Requires high humidity, partial shade, and humus-rich, well-drained soil. Plants should remain dry when dormant in winter. Propagate by division or seed in spring or by mature bulbils that fall off plants.
G. winitii illus. p.224.

GLOBULARIA (Globulariaceae)
Genus of mainly evergreen, summer-flowering shrubs and sub-shrubs, grown for their dome-shaped hummocks and usually blue or purple flower heads. Fully to frost hardy. Needs full sun and well-drained soil. Propagate by division in spring, by softwood or semi-ripe cuttings in summer, or by seed in autumn.
G. cordifolia illus. p.323.
subsp. *bellidifolia* see *G. meridionalis*.
G. meridionalis, syn. *G. cordifolia* subsp. *bellidifolia*, illus. p.320.

GLORIOSA (Liliaceae)
Genus of deciduous, summer-flowering, tendril climbers with fingerlike tubers. Frost tender, min. 46–50°F (8–10°C). Needs full sun and rich, well-drained soil. Water freely in summer and liquid feed every 2 weeks. Provide support. Dry off tubers in winter and keep cool but frost-free. Propagate by seed or division in spring.
G. superba (Glory lily). Deciduous, tendril climber with tubers. H to 6ft (2m), S 1–1¹/₂ft (30–45cm). Min. 46°F (8°C), zone 10. Slender stems produce scattered, broadly lance-shaped leaves. In summer, upper leaf axils carry large, yellow or red flowers, each with 6 sharply reflexed, wavy-edged petals, changing to dark orange or deep red. Stamens protrude prominently.
'Rothschildiana' illus. p.336.

GLOTTIPHYLLUM (Aizoaceae)
Genus of clump-forming, perennial succulents with semi-cylindrical leaves often broadened at tips. Frost tender, min. 41°F (5°C). Grow in very poor, well-drained soil and in full sun to make tight, compact plants. Propagate by seed or stem cuttings in spring or summer.
G. nelii illus. p.399.
G. semicylindricum. Clump-forming, perennial succulent. H 3in (8cm), S 12in (30cm) or more. Zone 10. Has semi-cylindrical, bright green leaves, 2¹/₂in (6cm) long, with a tooth half-way along each margin. Has daisylike, golden yellow flowers, 1¹/₂in (4cm) across, on short stems in spring-summer.

GLOXINIA (Gesneriaceae)
Genus of late summer- to autumn-flowering, rhizomatous perennials. Frost tender, min. 50°F (10°C). Requires partial shade and humus-rich, well-drained soil. Dies down in late autumn or winter; then keep rhizomes

nearly dry. Propagate by division or seed in spring or by stem or leaf cuttings in summer.
G. perennis illus. p.352.
G. speciosa. See *Sinningia speciosa.*

GLYCERIA (Gramineae). See GRASSES, BAMBOOS, RUSHES, and SEDGES.
G. aquatica **'Variegata'.** See *G. maxima* 'Variegata'.
G. maxima **'Variegata'**, syn. *G. aquatica* 'Variegata', illus. p.180.

GLYCYRRHIZA (Leguminosae)
Licorice
Genus of summer-flowering perennials. Fully hardy. Needs sun and deep, rich, well-drained soil. Propagate by division in spring or by seed in autumn or spring.
G. glabra illus. p.209.

GODETIA. See CLARKIA.

GOMESA. See ORCHIDS.
G. planifolia (illus. p.254). Evergreen, epiphytic orchid for a cool greenhouse. H 9in (23cm). Zone 10. Sprays of star-shaped, pea green flowers, ¹/₄in (0.5cm) across, are produced in autumn. Narrowly oval leaves are 6in (15cm) long. Grow in semi-shade in summer.

Gomphocarpus physocarpus. See *Asclepias physocarpa.*

GOMPHRENA (Amaranthaceae)
Genus of annuals, biennials, and perennials. Only one species, *G. globosa*, is usually cultivated; its flower heads are good for cutting and drying. Half hardy to frost tender, min. 36–9°F (2–4°C). Grows best in sun and in fertile, well-drained soil. Propagate by seed sown under glass in spring.
G. globosa illus. p.275.

GONGORA. See ORCHIDS.
G. quinquenervis (illus. p.254). Evergreen, epiphytic orchid for an intermediate greenhouse. H 10in (25cm). Zone 10. In summer, fragrant brown, orange, and yellow flowers, ¹/₂in (1cm) across, which resemble birds in flight, are borne in long, pendent spikes. Has oval, ribbed leaves, 5–6in (12–15cm) long. Is best grown in a hanging basket. Requires semi-shade in summer.

GORDONIA (Theaceae)
Genus of evergreen shrubs and trees, grown for their flowers and overall appearance. Half hardy, but best at min. 37°F (3°C). Prefers humus-rich, acid soil and sun or partial shade. Water potted plants moderately, less in winter. Propagate by semi-ripe cuttings in late summer or by seed when ripe, in autumn, or in spring.
G. axillaris. Evergreen, bushy shrub or tree. H and S 10–15ft (3–5m), sometimes much more. Zones 8–10. Bears lance-shaped, leathery, glossy leaves, each with a blunt tip, and, from autumn to spring, saucer-shaped, white flowers.
G. lasianthus (Loblolly bay). Evergreen, upright tree. H to 70ft

(20m), S to 30ft (10m). Zones 8–10. Lance-shaped to elliptic leaves are shallowly serrated. Has fragrant, saucer- to bowl-shaped, white flowers in summer. Needs sub-tropical summer warmth to grow and flower well.

GRAPTOPETALUM (Crassulaceae)
Genus of rosetted, perennial succulents very similar to *Echeveria*, with which it hybridizes. Frost tender, min. 41–50°F (5–10°C). Is easy to grow and flower, needing sun or partial shade and very well-drained soil. Propagate by seed or by stem or leaf cuttings in spring or summer.
G. amethystinum. Clump-forming, prostrate, perennial succulent. H 16in (40cm), S 3ft (1m). Min. 50°F (10°C), zone 10. Produces thick, rounded, blue-gray to red leaves, 3in (7cm) long, in terminal rosettes and star-shaped, yellow-and-red flowers, ¹/₂–³/₄in (1–2cm) across, in spring-summer.
G. bellum, syn. *Tacitus bellus*, illus. p.393.
G. paraguayense illus. p.398.

GRAPTOPHYLLUM (Acanthaceae)
Genus of evergreen shrubs, grown mainly for their foliage. Frost tender, min. 61–4°F (16–18°C). Needs partial shade and fertile, well-drained soil. Water potted plants freely when in full growth, much less when temperatures are low. Young plants need tip pruning after flowering to promote branching; leggy specimens may be cut back hard after flowering or in spring. Propagate by greenwood or semi-ripe cuttings in spring or summer.
G. pictum (Caricature plant). Evergreen, erect, loose shrub. H to 6ft (2m), S 2ft (60cm) or more. Zone 10. Oval, pointed, glossy, green leaves have central, yellow blotches. Short, terminal spikes of tubular, red to purple flowers appear mainly in spring and early summer.

GRASSES, BAMBOOS, RUSHES, and SEDGES
Group of evergreen or herbaceous, perennial and annual grasses or grasslike plants belonging to the Gramineae (including Bambusoideae), Juncaceae, and Cyperaceae families. They are grown mainly as foliage plants, adding grace and contrast to borders and rock gardens, although several grasses have attractive flower heads in summer that may be dried for winter decoration. Dead foliage may be cut back on herbaceous perennials, when dormant. Propagate species by seed in spring or autumn or by division in spring, selected forms by division only. Pests and diseases generally give little trouble.

Grasses (Gramineae)
Family of evergreen, semi-evergreen or herbaceous, sometimes creeping perennials, annuals, and marginal water plants, usually with rhizomes or stolons, that form tufts, clumps, or carpets. All have basal leaves and rounded flower stems that bear alternate, long, narrow leaves. Flowers are bisexual (males and females in

same spikelet) and are arranged in panicles, racemes, or spikes. Each flower head comprises spikelets, with one or more florets, that are covered with glumes (scales) from which awns (long, slender bristles) may grow. Fully hardy to frost tender, min. 41–54°F (5–12°C). Unless otherwise stated, grasses will tolerate a range of light conditions and flourish in any well-drained soil. Many genera, such as *Briza*, self seed readily.
See also *Achnatherum, Alopecurus, Arrhenatherum, Arundo, Bouteloua, Briza, Bromus, Chionochloa, Coix, Cortaderia, Dactylis, Deschampsia, Festuca, Glyceria, Hakonechloa, Helictotrichon, Holcus, Hordeum, Lagurus, Lamarckia, Leymus, Melica, Milium, Miscanthus, Molinia, Oplismenus, Panicum, Pennisetum, Phalaris, Rhynchelytrum, Sesleria, Setaria, Spartina, Stenotaphrium, Stipa, Zea,* and *Zizania.*

Bamboos (Bambusoideae)
Sub-family of Gramineae, comprising evergreen, rhizomatous perennials, sometimes grown as hedging as well as for ornamentation. Most bamboos differ from other perennial grasses in that they have woody stems (culms). These are hollow (except in *Chusquea*), mostly greenish brown and, due to their silica content, very strong with a circumference of up to 6in (15cm) in some tropical species. Leaves are lance-shaped with cross veins that give a tessellated appearance, which may be obscured in the more tender species. Flowers are produced at varying intervals but are not decorative. After flowering, stems die down but few plants die completely. Fully to half hardy. Bamboos thrive in a sheltered, not too dry situation in sun or shade, unless stated otherwise.
See also *Arundinaria, Bambusa, Chusquea, Phyllostachys, Pleioblastus, Pseudosasa, Sasa, Semiarundinaria, Shibataea, Sinarundinaria,* and *Thamnocalamus.*

Rushes (Juncaceae)
Family of evergreen, tuft-forming or creeping, mostly rhizomatous annuals and perennials. All have either rounded, leafless stems or stems bearing long, narrow, basal leaves that are flat and hairless except *Luzula* (the woodrushes) which have flat leaves, edged with white hairs. Rounded flower heads are generally unimportant. Fully to half hardy. Most rushes prefer sun or partial shade and a moist or wet situation, but *Luzula* prefers drier conditions.
See also *Juncus* and *Luzula.*

Sedges (Cyperaceae)
Family of evergreen, rhizomatous perennials that form dense tufts. Typically, stems are triangular and bear long, narrow leaves, sometimes reduced to scales. Spikes or panicles of florets covered with glumes are produced and contain both male and female flowers, although some species of *Carex* have separate male and female flower heads on the same stem. Fully hardy to frost tender, min.

39–45°F (4–7°C). Grow in sun or partial shade. Some sedges grow naturally in water, but many may be grown in any well-drained soil.

See also *Carex*, *Cyperus*, *Eleocharis*, and *Scirpus*.

GREVILLEA (Proteaceae)
Genus of evergreen shrubs and trees, grown for their flowers and foliage. Half hardy to frost tender, min. 41–50°F (5–10°C). Grow in well-drained, preferably acid soil and in full sun. Water potted specimens moderately, very little in winter. Pruning is tolerated if necessary. Propagate by seed in spring or by semi-ripe cuttings in summer.

G. alpestris. See *G. alpina*.
G. alpina, syn. *G. alpestris*. Evergreen, rounded, wiry-stemmed shrub. H and S 1–2ft (30–60cm). Half hardy, zone 10. Has narrowly oblong or oval leaves, dark green above, silky-haired beneath. Bears tubular, red flowers in small clusters in spring-summer.
G. banksii illus. p.71.
G. juniperina f. *sulphurea*, syn. *G. sulphurea*, illus. p.137.
G. 'Poorinda Constance'. Evergreen, bushy, rounded shrub. H and S to 6ft (2m). Half hardy, zone 10. Has small, lance-shaped, mid- to deep green leaves with prickly toothed margins. Tubular, bright red flowers in conspicuous clusters are borne from spring to autumn, sometimes longer.
G. robusta (Silky oak). Fast-growing, evergreen, upright to conical tree. H 100ft (30m), S to 50ft (15m). Frost tender, min. 41°F (5°C), zone 10. Fernlike leaves are 6–10in (15–25cm) long. Mature specimens bear upturned bell-shaped, bright yellow or orange flowers in dense, one-sided spikes, 4in (10cm) or more long, in spring-summer.
G. 'Robyn Gordon' illus. p.134.
G. rosmarinifolia. Evergreen, rounded, well-branched shrub. H and S to 6ft (2m). Half hardy, zone 10. Dark green leaves are needle-shaped with reflexed margins, silky-haired beneath. Has short, dense clusters of tubular, red, occasionally pink or white flowers in summer.
G. sulphurea. See *G. juniperina* f. *sulphurea*.

GREYIA (Greyiaceae)
Genus of evergreen, semi-evergreen, or deciduous, spring-flowering shrubs and trees, grown for their flowers and overall appearance. Frost tender, min. 45–50°F (7–10°C). Needs full light and well-drained soil. Water potted specimens moderately, less when not in full growth. Remove or shorten flowered stems after flowering. Propagate by seed in spring or by semi-ripe cuttings in summer. Plants grown under glass need plenty of ventilation.
G. sutherlandii illus. p.98.

GRINDELIA (Compositae)
Genus of annuals, biennials, evergreen perennials and sub-shrubs, grown for their flower heads. Frost to half hardy, but in cold areas grow in a warm, sheltered site. Requires sun and well-

drained soil. Water potted specimens moderately, less when not in full growth. Remove spent flowering stems either as they die or in following spring. Propagate by seed in spring or by semi-ripe cuttings in late summer.
G. chiloensis, syn. *G. speciosa*, illus. p.139.
G. speciosa. See *G. chiloensis*.

GRISELINIA (Cornaceae)
Genus of evergreen shrubs and trees, with inconspicuous flowers, grown for their foliage. Thrives in mild, coastal areas where it is effective as a hedge or windbreak as it is very wind- and salt-resistant. Frost to half hardy; in cold areas provide shelter. Requires sun and fertile, well-drained soil. Restrict growth and trim hedges in early summer. Propagate by semi-ripe cuttings in summer.
G. littoralis (Broadleaf). Fast-growing, evergreen, upright shrub of dense habit. H 20ft (6m), S 15ft (5m). Frost hardy, zones 9–10. Bears oval, leathery leaves that are bright apple green. Tiny, inconspicuous, yellow-green flowers are borne in late spring.
'Dixon's Cream', H 10ft (3m), S 6ft (2m), is slower-growing and has central, creamy white leaf variegation.
'Variegata' illus. p.94.
G. lucida. Fast-growing, evergreen, upright shrub. H 20ft (6m), S 15ft (5m). Half hardy, zones 9–10. Is similar to *G. littoralis*, but has larger, glossy, dark green leaves.

GUNNERA (Gunneraceae)
Genus of summer-flowering perennials, grown mainly for their foliage. Some are clump-forming with very large leaves; others are mat-forming with smaller leaves. Frost hardy, but shelter from wind in summer and cover with bracken or compost in winter. Requires sun and moist soil. Propagate by seed in autumn or spring; small species by division in spring.
G. chilensis. See *G. tinctoria*.
G. magellanica illus. p.324.
G. manicata illus. p.190.
G. tinctoria, syn. *G. chilensis*. Robust, rounded, clump-forming perennial. H and S 5ft (1.5m) or more. Zones 9–10. Has very large, rounded, puckered, and lobed leaves, 1½–2ft (45–60cm) across. In early summer produces dense, conical clusters of tiny, dull reddish green flowers.

GUZMANIA (Bromeliaceae)
Genus of evergreen, rosette-forming, epiphytic perennials, grown for their overall appearance. Frost tender, min. 50–59°F (10–15°C). Needs semi-shade and a rooting medium of equal parts humus-rich soil and either sphagnum moss, or bark or plastic chips used for orchid culture. Using soft water, water moderately during growing season, sparingly at other times, and keep rosette centers filled with water from spring to autumn. Propagate by offsets in spring or summer.
G. lingulata (Droophead guzmania; illus. p.222). Evergreen, basal-rosetted, epiphytic perennial. H and S 12–18in (30–45cm). Zone 10. Forms loose

rosettes of broadly strap-shaped, arching, green leaves. Bears a cluster of tubular, white to yellow flowers, surrounded by a rosette of bright red bracts, usually in summer. var. *minor* (illus. p.222), H and S 6in (15cm), has yellow-green leaves and red or yellow bracts.
G. monostachia, syn. *G. monostachya*, *G. tricolor* (Striped torch; illus. p.222). Evergreen, basal-rosetted, epiphytic perennial. H and S 12–16in (30–40cm). Zone 10. Has dense rosettes of strap-shaped, erect to arching, pale to yellowish green leaves. Usually in summer, elongated spikes of tubular, white flowers emerge from axils of oval bracts, the upper ones red, the lower green with purple-brown stripes.
G. monostachya. See *G. monostachia*.
G. sanguinea. Evergreen, basal-rosetted, epiphytic perennial. H 8in (20cm), S 12–14in (30–35cm). Zone 10. Has dense, slightly flat rosettes of broadly strap-shaped, arching, mid- to deep green leaves. In summer bears a compact cluster of tubular, yellow flowers, surrounded by red bracts, at the heart of each mature rosette.
G. tricolor. See *G. monostachia*.
G. vittata. Evergreen, basal-rosetted, epiphytic perennial. H and S 14–24in (35–60cm). Zone 10. Produces fairly loose rosettes of strap-shaped, erect, dark green leaves with pale green crossbands and recurved tips. Stem bears a compact, egg-shaped head of small, tubular, white flowers in summer.

GYMNOCALYCIUM (Cactaceae)
Genus of perennial cacti with masses of funnel-shaped flowers in spring-summer. Crowns generally bear smooth, scaly buds. Frost tender, min. 41–50°F (5–10°C). Needs full sun or partial shade and very well-drained soil. Propagate by seed or offsets in spring or summer.
G. andreae illus. p.397.
G. gibbosum illus. p.382.
G. mihanovichii **'Red Head'**, syn. *G. m.* var. *hibotan*, illus. p.385.
G. quehlianum. Flattened spherical, perennial cactus. H 2in (5cm), S 3in (7cm). Min. 41°F (5°C), zone 10. Gray-blue to brown stem has 11 or so rounded ribs. Areoles each produce 5 curved spines. Has white flowers, 2in (5cm) across, with red throats, in spring-summer. Is easy to flower.
G. schickendantzii. Spherical, perennial cactus. H and S 4in (10cm). Min. 41°F (5°C), zone 10. Dark green stem has 7–14 deeply indented ribs and long, red-tipped, gray-brown spines. Bears greenish white to pale pink flowers, 2in (5cm) across, in summer.

GYMNOCLADUS (Leguminosae)
Genus of deciduous trees, grown for their foliage. Fully hardy. Needs full sun and deep, fertile, well-drained soil. Propagate by seed in autumn.
G. dioica (Kentucky coffee tree). Slow-growing, deciduous, spreading tree. H 70ft (20m), S 50ft (15m). Zones 5–9. Has very large leaves, with 4–7 pairs of oval leaflets, that are pinkish when young, dark green

in summer, then yellow in autumn. Small, star-shaped, white flowers are borne in early summer.

GYNANDRIRIS (Iridaceae)
Genus of irislike, spring-flowering corms, grown mainly for botanical interest, with very short-lived blooms. Frost hardy. Dormant corms require warmth and dryness, so plant in a sunny site that dries out in summer. Needs well-drained soil, but with plenty of moisture in winter-spring. Propagate by seed or cormlets in autumn.
G. sisyrinchium illus. p.360.

GYNURA (Compositae)
Genus of evergreen perennials, shrubs, and semi-scrambling climbers, grown for their ornamental foliage or flower heads. Frost tender, min. 61°F (16°C). Any fertile, well-drained soil is suitable, with light shade in summer. Water moderately throughout the year, less in cool conditions; do not overwater. Provide support for stems. Remove stem tips to encourage branching. Propagate by softwood or semi-ripe cuttings in spring or summer.
G. aurantiaca illus. p.178.
G. 'Purple Passion', syn. *G. sarmentosa* of gardens. Evergreen, erect, woody-based, soft-stemmed shrub or semi-scrambling climber. H 2ft (60cm) or more. Zone 10. Stems and lance-shaped, lobed, serrated leaves are covered with velvety, purple hairs. Leaves are purple-green above, deep red-purple beneath. In winter bears clusters of daisylike, orange-yellow flower heads that become purplish with age.
G. sarmentosa of gardens. See *G. 'Purple Passion'*.

GYPSOPHILA (Caryophyllaceae)
Genus of spring- to autumn-flowering annuals and perennials, some of which are semi-evergreen. Fully hardy. Needs sun. Will grow in dry, sandy, and stony soils, but does best in deep, well-drained soil. Resents being disturbed. Cut back after flowering for a second flush of flowers. Propagate *G. paniculata* cultivars by grafting in winter; others by softwood cuttings in summer or by seed in autumn or spring.
G. cerastioides illus. p.304.
G. elegans illus. p.262.
G. paniculata **'Bristol Fairy'** illus. p.200. **'Flamingo'** is a spreading, short-lived perennial. H 2–2½ft (60–75cm), S 3ft (1m). Zones 4–9. In summer bears panicles of numerous small, rounded, double, pale pink flowers on wiry, branching stems. Has small, linear, green leaves.
G. repens. Semi-evergreen, prostrate perennial with much-branched rhizomes. H 1–2in (2.5–5cm) or more, S 12in (30cm) or more. Zones 4–7. In summer produces sprays of small, rounded, white, lilac, or pink flowers from slender stems that bear narrowly oval, bluish green leaves. Is excellent for a rock garden, wall, or dry bank. May also be propagated by division in spring. **'Dorothy Teacher'** illus. p.315.

H

HAAGEOCEREUS (Cactaceae)
Genus of perennial cacti with ribbed, densely spiny, columnar, green stems branching from the base. Frost tender, min. 52°F (11°C). Needs full sun and very well-drained soil. Propagate by seed or stem cuttings in spring or summer.
H. chosicensis. Upright, perennial cactus. H 5ft (1.5m), S 3ft (1m). Zone 10. Green stem, 4in (10cm) across, with 19 or so ribs, bears white, golden, or red, central spines and shorter, dense, bristlelike, white, radial ones. Has tubular, white, lilac-white, or pinkish red flowers, 3in (7cm) long, near crown in summer.
H. decumbens. Prostrate, perennial cactus. H 1ft (30cm), S 3ft (1m). Zone 10. Stems, 2¹/₂in (6cm) across, with 20 or so ribs, have dark brown, central spines, 2in (5cm) long, and shorter, dense, golden, radial spines. Tubular, white flowers, 3in (8cm) across, form in summer near crowns, only on mature plants.
H. versicolor illus. p.380.

HABERLEA (Gesneraceae)
Genus of evergreen, rosetted perennials, grown for their elegant sprays of flowers. Is useful on walls. Fully hardy. Needs partially shaded, moist soil. Resents disturbance to roots. Propagate by seed in spring or by leaf cuttings or offsets in early summer.
H. ferdinandi-coburgii. Evergreen, dense, basal-rosetted perennial. H 4–6in (10–15cm), S 12in (30cm). Zones 5–8. Has oblong, toothed, dark green leaves, hairy below, almost glabrous above. Sprays of funnel-shaped, blue-violet flowers, each with a white throat, appear on long stems in late spring and early summer.
H. rhodopensis. Evergreen, dense, basal-rosetted perennial. H 4in (10cm), S 6in (15cm) or more. Zones 5–7. Is similar to *H. ferdinandi-coburgii*, but leaves are soft-haired on both surfaces. **'Virginalis'** illus. p.313.

HABRANTHUS (Amaryllidaceae)
Genus of summer- and autumn-flowering bulbs with funnel-shaped flowers. Frost to half hardy. Needs a sheltered, sunny site and fertile soil that is well supplied with moisture in growing season. Propagate by seed or offsets in spring.
H. andersonii. See *H. tubispathus*.
H. brachyandrus. Summer-flowering bulb. H to 12in (30cm), S 2–3in (5–8cm). Half hardy, zone 10. Long, linear, semi-erect, narrow leaves form a basal cluster. Each flower stem bears a semi-erect, widely funnel-shaped, pinkish red flower, 3–4in (7–10cm) long.
H. robustus illus. p.366.
H. tubispathus, syn. *H. andersonii.* Summer-flowering bulb. H to 6in (15cm), S 2in (5cm). Frost hardy,

zones 8–10. Has linear, semi-erect, basal leaves and a succession of flower stems each bearing solitary 1–1¹/₂in (2.5–3.5cm) long, funnel-shaped flowers, yellow inside, copper red outside.

HACQUETIA, syn. DONDIA (Umbelliferae)
Genus of one species of clump-forming, rhizomatous perennial that creeps slowly, grown for its yellow or yellow-green flower heads borne on leafless plants in late winter and early spring. Is good in rock gardens. Fully hardy. Prefers shade and humus-rich, moist soil. Resents disturbance to roots. Propagate by division in spring, by seed when fresh in autumn, or by root cuttings in winter.
H. epipactis illus. p.311.

HAEMANTHUS (Amaryllidaceae)
Genus of summer-flowering bulbs with dense heads of small, star-shaped flowers, often brightly colored. Frost tender, min. 50°F (10°C). Prefers full sun or partial shade and well-drained soil or sandy compost. Liquid feed in the growing season. Leave undisturbed as long as possible before replanting. Propagate by offsets or seed before growth commences in early spring.
H. albiflos (Paintbrush). Summer-flowering bulb. H 2–12in (5–30cm), S 8–12in (20–30cm). Zones 9–10. Has 2–6 almost prostrate, broadly elliptic leaves with hairy edges. Flower stem, appearing between leaves, bears a brushlike head of up to 50 white flowers with very narrow petals and protruding stamens.
H. coccineus illus. p.364.
H. katherinae. See *Scadoxus multiflorus* subsp. *katherinae.*
H. magnificus. See *Scadoxus puniceus.*
H. multiflorus. See *Scadoxus multiflorus.*
H. natalensis. See *Scadoxus puniceus.*
H. puniceus. See *Scadoxus puniceus.*
H. sanguineus. Summer-flowering bulb. H to 12in (30cm), S 8–12in (20–30cm). Zones 9–10. Bears 2 prostrate, elliptic, rough, dark green leaves, hairy beneath. Brownish purple-spotted, green flower stem, forming before leaves, produces a dense head of small, narrow-petaled, red flowers, which are surrounded by whorls of narrow, leaflike, red or pink bracts.

HAKEA (Proteaceae)
Genus of evergreen shrubs and trees, grown for their often needlelike leaves and their flowers. Is very wind-resistant, except in cold areas. Frost hardy to frost tender, min. 41–5°F (5–7°C). Requires full sun and fertile, well-drained soil. Water potted specimens moderately when in full growth, sparingly in winter. Propagate by semi-ripe cuttings in summer or by seed in autumn.

H. lissosperma, syn. *H. sericea* of gardens. Evergreen, upright, densely branched shrub of pinelike appearance. H 15ft (5m), S 10ft (3m). Frost hardy, zones 9–10. Has long, slender, sharply pointed, gray-green leaves and, in late spring and early summer, clusters of small, spidery, white flowers.
H. sericea of gardens. See *H. lissosperma.*
H. suaveolens. Evergreen, rounded shrub. H and S 6ft (2m) or more. Frost tender, zone 10. Leaves are divided into cylindrical, needlelike leaflets or occasionally are undivided and lance-shaped. Small, fragrant, tubular, white flowers are carried in short, dense clusters from summer to winter.

HAKONECHLOA (Gramineae). See GRASSES, BAMBOOS, RUSHES, and SEDGES.
H. macra 'Aureola' illus. p.183.

HALESIA (Styracaceae)
Silver-bell, Snowdrop tree
Genus of deciduous, spring-flowering trees and shrubs, grown for their showy, pendent flowers and curious, winged fruits. Fully hardy, but needs a sunny, sheltered position. Prefers moist but well-drained, neutral to acid soil. Propagate by softwood cuttings in summer or by seed in autumn.
H. carolina. Deciduous, spreading tree or shrub. H 25ft (8m), S 30ft (10m). Zones 5–8. Masses of bell-shaped, white flowers hang from bare shoots in late spring and are followed by 4-winged, green fruits. Oval leaves are green.
H. monticola illus. p.49.

x HALIMIOCISTUS (Cistaceae)
Hybrid genus (*Cistus* x *Halimium*) of evergreen shrubs, grown for their flowers. Frost hardy, but in cold areas needs shelter. Requires full sun and well-drained soil. Propagate by semi-ripe cuttings in summer.
x H. sahucii illus. p.127.
x H. wintonensis. Evergreen, bushy shrub. H 2ft (60cm), S 3ft (1m). Zones 7–9. Saucer-shaped, white flowers, each with deep red bands and a yellow center, open amid lance-shaped, gray-green leaves in late spring and early summer.

HALIMIUM (Cistaceae)
Genus of evergreen shrubs, grown for their showy flowers. Is good for coastal gardens. Frost hardy, but in cold areas needs shelter. Does best in full sun and light, well-drained soil. Propagate by semi-ripe cuttings in summer.
H. lasianthum. Evergreen, bushy, spreading shrub. H 3ft (1m), S 5ft (1.5m). Zones 9–10. Leaves are oval and gray-green. In late spring and early summer bears saucer-shaped, golden yellow flowers, sometimes with small, central, red blotches. subsp. *formosum* illus. p.137.

H. ocymoides. Evergreen, bushy shrub. H 2ft (60cm), S 3ft (1m). Zones 9–10. Narrowly oval leaves, covered in white hairs when young, mature to dark green. In early summer produces upright clusters of saucer-shaped, golden yellow flowers, conspicuously blotched with black or purple. **'Susan'** illus. p.137.
H. umbellatum illus. p.127.

HAMAMELIS (Hamamelidaceae)
Witch-hazel
Genus of deciduous, autumn- to early spring-flowering shrubs, grown for their autumn color and fragrant, frost-resistant flowers, each with 4 narrowly strap-shaped petals. Fully hardy. Flourishes in sun or semi-shade and fertile, well-drained, peaty, acid soil, although tolerates good, deep soil over chalk. Propagate species by seed in autumn, selected forms by softwood cuttings in summer, by budding in late summer, or by grafting in winter.
H. x intermedia 'Arnold Promise' illus. p.94. **'Diane'** illus. p.93. **'Jelena'** is a deciduous, upright shrub. H and S 12ft (4m) or more. Zones 5–9. Broadly oval, glossy, bright green leaves turn bright orange or red in autumn. Bears masses of large, fragrant orange flowers, along bare branches, from early to mid-winter.
H. japonica (Japanese witch-hazel). Deciduous, upright, open shrub. H and S 12ft (4m). Zones 5–9. Broadly oval, glossy, green leaves turn yellow in autumn. Fragrant yellow flowers, with crinkled petals, are borne on bare branches from mid- to late winter. **'Sulphurea'** illus. p.94. **'Zuccariniana'** bears paler, lemon yellow flowers in early spring and has orange-yellow leaves in autumn.
H. mollis (Chinese witch-hazel). Deciduous, upright, open shrub. H and S 12ft (4m) or more. Zones 5–9. Broadly oval, green leaves turn yellow in autumn. Produces extremely fragrant yellow flowers, along bare branches, in mid- and late winter. **'Coombe Wood'** illus. p.94. **'Pallida'**, S 10ft (3m), is more upright than the species and bears dense clusters of large, sulfur yellow flowers.
H. vernalis 'Sandra' illus. p.92.
H. virginiana illus. p.93.

Hamatocactus hamatacanthus. See *Ferocactus hamatacanthus.*
Hamatocactus setispinus. See *Ferocactus setispinus.*

HARDENBERGIA (Leguminosae)
Genus of evergreen, woody-stemmed, twining climbers or sub-shrubs, grown for their curtains of leaves and racemes of pealike flowers. Half hardy to frost tender, min. 45°F (7°C). Grows best in sun and in well-drained soil that does not dry out. Propagate by stem cuttings in late summer or autumn or by seed, soaked before sowing, in spring.

H. comptoniana illus. p.164.
H. monophylla. See *H. violacea.*
H. violacea, syn. *H. monophylla.*
(Australian sarsparilla, Coral pea, Vine
lilac). Evergreen, woody-stemmed,
twining climber. H to 10ft (3m). Frost
tender, zone 10. Narrowly oval leaves
are 1–5in (2.5–12cm) long. Violet,
occasionally pink or white, flowers,
with yellow blotches on upper petals,
are borne in spring. Brownish pods,
$1^1/4$–$1^1/2$in (3–4cm) long, are produced
in autumn.

HATIORA (Cactaceae)
Genus of perennial, epiphytic cacti
with short, jointed, cylindrical stems
each swollen at one end like a bottle.
Frost tender, min. 50–52°F (10–11°C).
Requires partial shade and very well-
drained soil. Keep damp in summer;
water a little in winter. Propagate by
stem cuttings in spring or summer.
H. clavata, syn. *Rhipsalis clavata.*
Pendent, perennial, epiphytic cactus.
H 2ft (60cm), S 3ft (1m). Min. 52°F
(11°C), zone 10. Multi-branched,
cylindrical, dark green stems each
widen towards tips. Masses of
terminal, bell-shaped, white flowers,
$5/8$in (1.5cm) wide, appear in late
winter and early spring on plants over
1ft (30cm) high.
H. salicornioides illus. p.388.

HAWORTHIA (Liliaceae)
Genus of basal-rosetted, clump-
forming, perennial succulents with
triangular to rounded, green leaves.
Roots tend to wither in winter or
during long periods of drought. Frost
tender, min. 41–50°F (5–10°C). Needs
partial shade to stay green and grow
quickly; if planted in full sun turns red
or orange and grows slowly. Requires
very well-drained soil. Keep dry in
winter. Propagate by seed or division
from spring to autumn.
H. arachnoidea, syn. *H. setata*, illus.
p.390.
H. attenuata. Clump-forming,
perennial succulent. H 3in (7cm), S
10in (25cm). Min. 41°F (5°C), zone
10. Bears a basal rosette of triangular,
dark green leaves, $1^1/4$in (3cm) long,
covered in raised, white dots. Tubular
to bell-shaped, white flowers are
produced from spring to autumn on
long, slender stems. var. *clariperla*
illus. p.389.
H. cuspidata. Clump-forming,
perennial succulent. H 2in (5cm), S
10in (25cm). Min. 41°F (5°C), zone
10. Produces a basal rosette of smooth,
rounded, fleshy, light green leaves
with translucent marks. Tubular to
bell-shaped, white flowers appear
from spring to autumn on long,
slender stems.
H. fasciata. Slow-growing, clump-
forming, perennial succulent. H 6in
(15cm), S 12in (30cm). Min. 41°F
(5°C), zone 10. Has raised, white dots,
mostly in bands, on undersides of
triangular, slightly incurved leaves, to
3in (8cm) long, which are arranged in
a basal rosette. Bears tubular to bell-
shaped, white flowers, on long, slender
stems, from spring to autumn.
H. setata. See *H. arachnoidea.*
H. truncata illus. p.389.

HEATHERS (Ericaceae)
Heathers (otherwise known as heaths)
are evergreen, woody-stemmed shrubs,
grown for their flowers and foliage,
both of which may provide color in
the garden all year round. There are
3 genera: *Calluna, Daboecia*, and
Erica. Calluna has only one species,
C. vulgaris, but it contains a large
number of cultivars that flower mainly
from mid-summer to late autumn.
Daboecia has 2 species, both of which
are summer-flowering. The largest
genus is *Erica*, which, although
broadly divided into 2 groups—
winter- and summer-flowering species
—has some species also flowering
in spring and autumn. They vary in
height from tree heaths, which may
grow to 20ft (6m), to dwarf, prostrate
plants that, if planted 12–18in
(30–45cm) apart, soon spread to
form a thick mat of ground cover.
   Heathers are fully hardy to frost
tender, min. 41–5°F (5–7°C). They
prefer an open, sunny position and
require humus-rich, well-drained soil.
Calluna and *Daboecia* dislike lime
and must be grown in acid soil; some
species of *Erica* are lime-tolerant but
all are better grown in acid soils. Prune
lightly after flowering each year to
keep plants bushy and compact.
Propagate species by seed in spring
or by softwood cuttings, division, or
layering in summer. Seed cannot be
relied on to come true. All cultivars
should be vegetatively propagated.
Heathers are illustrated on pp.146–7.

HEBE (Scrophulariaceae)
Genus of evergreen shrubs, grown for
their often dense spikes, panicles, or
racemes of flowers and their foliage.
Grows well in coastal areas. Smaller
species and cultivars are good for rock
gardens. Fully to half hardy. Requires
full sun and well-drained soil. Growth
may be restricted, or leggy plants
tidied, by cutting back in spring.
Propagate by semi-ripe cuttings
in summer.
H. albicans illus. p.129.
H. 'Autumn Glory' illus. p.135.
H. brachysiphon. Evergreen, bushy,
dense shrub. H and S 6ft (2m). Fully
hardy, zones 9–10. Has oblong, dark
green leaves. Produces dense spikes of
small, 4-lobed, white flowers in mid-
summer. **'White Gem'** illus. p.126.
H. buchananii. Evergreen, dome-
shaped shrub. H and S 6in (15cm) or
more. Frost hardy, zones 9–10. Very
dark stems bear oval, bluish green
leaves. In summer produces clusters
of small, 4-lobed white flowers at
stem tips. **'Minor'**, H 2–4in (5–10cm),
has smaller leaves.
H. canterburiensis illus. p.291.
H. 'Carl Teschner'. Evergreen,
prostrate then dome-shaped shrub.
H 6in (15cm), S 12in (30cm) or more.
Frost hardy, zones 9–10. Blackish
brown stems are covered in small,
oval, glossy, dark green leaves. Short
racemes of tiny, 4–lobed, white-
throated, purple flowers are produced
in summer. Is excellent as a border
plant.
H. carnosula. Evergreen, prostrate
shrub. H 6–12in (15–30cm), S 12in

(30cm) or more. Frost hardy, zones
9–10. Has small, oblong to oval,
slightly convex, fleshy, glaucous
leaves. Terminal clusters of many
small, white flowers, with 4 pointed
lobes, are borne in late spring or
early summer.
H. cupressoides illus. p.144.
'Boughton Dome' illus. p.301.
H. 'E.A. Bowles' illus. p.135.
H. 'Great Orme' illus. p.131.
H. hulkeana. Evergreen, upright, open
shrub. H and S 3ft (1m). Frost hardy,
zones 9–10. Oval, toothed, glossy,
dark green leaves have red margins.
Has masses of small, 4-lobed, pale
lilac flowers in large, open panicles in
late spring and early summer. **'Lilac
Hint'** illus. p.135.
H. macrantha. Evergreen, bushy
shrub. H 2ft (60cm), S 3ft (1m). Frost
hardy, zones 9–10. Has oval, toothed,
fleshy, bright green leaves and
racemes of large, 4-lobed, pure white
flowers in early summer. May become
bare at base.
H. ochracea. Evergreen, bushy, dense
shrub. H and S 3ft (1m). Fully hardy,
zones 8–10. Slender shoots are densely
covered with tiny, scalelike, ochre-
tinged, olive green leaves. Clusters of
small, 4-lobed, white flowers appear in
late spring and early summer.
H. pinguifolia (Disk-leaved hebe).
'Pagei' illus. p.291.
H. 'Purple Queen' illus. p.136.
H. rakaiensis. Evergreen, rounded,
compact shrub. H 3ft (1m), S 4ft
(1.2m). Fully hardy, zones 8–10.
Small, dense spikes of small, 4-lobed,
white flowers are produced amid small,
oblong, green leaves from early to
mid-summer.
H. recurva illus. p.129.
H. salicifolia. Evergreen, upright
shrub. H and S 8ft (2.5m). Frost hardy,
zones 9–10. Has long, narrow, pointed,
pale green leaves and, in summer,
slender spikes of small, 4-lobed, white
or pale lilac flowers.
H. vernicosa. Evergreen, bushy,
compact shrub. H 2ft (60cm), S 4ft
(1.2m). Frost hardy, zones 9–10.
Small, oval, densely arranged, glossy,
dark green leaves set off abundant,
small spikes of small, 4-lobed, white
flowers in early and mid-summer.

HEDERA (Araliaceae)
Ivy
Genus of evergreen, woody-stemmed,
trailing perennials and self-clinging
climbers with adventitious rootlets,
used for covering walls and fences and
as ground cover. Takes a year or so to
become established, but thereafter
growth is rapid. On the ground and
while climbing, mostly bears roughly
triangular, usually lobed leaves. Given
extra height and access to light, leaves
become less lobed and, in autumn,
umbels of small, yellowish green
flowers are produced, followed by
globose, black, occasionally yellow,
fruits. Fully to half hardy. Ivies with
green leaves are very shade tolerant
and do well against a north-facing
wall. Those with variegated or yellow
leaves prefer more light, are usually
less hardy, and may sustain frost and
wind damage in severe winters. All

prefer well-drained, alkaline soil.
Prune in spring to control height and
spread, and to remove any damaged
growth. Propagate in late summer by
softwood cuttings or rooted layers.
Red spider mite may be a problem
when plants are grown against a south-
facing wall or in dry conditions.
H. canariensis (Canary Island ivy).
Fast-growing, evergreen, self-clinging
climber. H to 20ft (6m), S 15ft (5m).
Half hardy, zones 9–10; may be
damaged in severe winters but soon
recovers. Has oval to triangular,
unlobed, glossy, green leaves and
reddish purple stems. Is suitable for
growing against a wall in a sheltered
area. **'Gloire de Marengo'** has silver-
variegated leaves. **'Ravensholst'**
(illus. p.179) is vigorous with large
leaves; makes good ground cover.
H. colchica (Persian ivy). Evergreen,
self-clinging climber or trailing
perennial. H 30ft (10m), S 15ft (5m).
Fully hardy, zones 6–9. Has large,
oval, unlobed, dark green leaves. Is
suitable for growing against a wall.
'Dentata' (Elephant's ears; illus.
p.179) is more vigorous and has large,
light green leaves that droop, hence its
common name. Is good when grown
against a wall or for ground cover.
'Dentata Variegata', H 15ft (5m),
has variegated, cream yellow leaves;
is useful to brighten a shady corner.
'Sulphur Heart' (Paddy's pride; illus.
p.179), H 15ft (5m), S 10ft (3m), has
variegated, yellow and light green
leaves.
H. helix (Common English ivy).
Vigorous, evergreen, self-clinging
climber or trailing perennial. H 30ft
(10m), S 15ft (5m). Fully hardy, zones
5–9, except where indicated. Has
5-lobed, dark green leaves. Makes
good ground and wall cover, but may
be invasive; for a small garden, the
more decorative cultivars are
preferable. **'Adam'** (illus. p.179), H
4ft (1.2m), S 3ft (1m), is half hardy,
zone 9, and has small, light green
leaves variegated cream yellow; may
suffer leaf damage in winter, but will
recover. **'Angularis Aurea'** (illus.
p.179), H 12ft (4m), S 8ft (2.5m), has
glossy, light green leaves, with bright
yellow variegation; is not suitable as
ground cover. **'Anna Marie'** (illus.
p.179), H 4ft (1.2m), S 3ft (1m), is
frost hardy, zones 8–9, and has light
green leaves with cream variegation,
mostly at margins; may suffer leaf
damage in winter. **'Atropurpurea'**
(syn. *H.h.* 'Purpurea'; Purple-leaved
ivy; illus. p.179), H 12ft (4m), S 8ft
(2.5m), has dark green leaves that turn
deep purple in winter. **'Baltica'**, an
exceptionally hardy cultivar, has small
leaves and makes good ground cover
in an exposed area. **'Buttercup'** (illus.
p.179), H 6ft (2m), S 8ft (2.5m), is
frost hardy, zones 8–9, and has light
green leaves that turn rich butter
yellow in full sun. **'Caenwoodiana'**
see *H.h.* 'Pedata'. **'Congesta'**, H
$1^1/2$ft (45cm), S 2ft (60cm), is a non-
climbing, erect cultivar with spirelike
shoots and small leaves; is suitable
for a rock garden. **'Conglomerata'**
(Clustered ivy), H and S 3ft (1m),
will clamber over a low wall or grow

in a rock garden; has small, curly, unlobed leaves.**'Cristata'** see *H.h.* 'Parsley Crested'. **'Curly Locks'** see *H.h.* 'Manda's Crested'. **'Deltoidea'** (Shield ivy, Sweetheart ivy; illus. p.179), H 15ft (5m), S 10ft (3m), has heart-shaped leaves; is suitable only for growing against a wall. **'Digitata'** (Finger-leaved ivy; illus. p.179), H 20ft (6m), has large leaves; is not suitable for ground cover. **'Erecta'** (illus. p.179), H 3ft (1m), S 4ft (1.2m), is a non-climbing, erect cultivar similar to *H.h.* 'Congesta'. **'Eva'** (illus. p.179), H 4ft (1.2m), S 3ft (1m), is frost hardy, zones 8–9, and has small, gray-green leaves with cream variegation; may suffer leaf damage in winter. **'Glacier'** (illus. p.179), H 10ft (3m), S 6ft (2m), is frost hardy, zones 8–9, and has silvery gray-green leaves. **'Glymii'** (illus. p.179), H 8ft (2.5m), S 6ft (2m), has glossy, dark green leaves that turn deep purple in winter; is not suitable for ground cover. **'Goldheart'** (illus. p.179), H 20ft (6m), zones 8–9, has dark green leaves with bright yellow centers; is slow to establish, then grows rapidly; is not suitable for ground cover. **'Gracilis'** (illus. p.179), H 15ft (5m), has sharply lobed, dark green leaves that turn bronze-purple in winter; is not suitable for ground cover. **'Green Feather'** see *H.h.* 'Triton'. **'Green Ripple'** (illus. p.179), H and S 4ft (1.2m), is frost hardy, zones 8–9, and has green leaves with prominent, light green veins; is good for ground cover or for growing against a low wall. **'Hahn's Self-branching'** see *H.h.* 'Pittsburgh'. **'Heise'** (illus. p.179), H 1ft (30cm), S 2ft (60cm), is frost hardy, zones 8–9, and has small, gray-green leaves with cream variegation; is suitable as ground cover for a small, sheltered area. var. *hibernica* (Irish ivy; illus. p.179), S 20ft (6m), is very vigorous and has large, green leaves; will cover a large area, either on the ground or against a wall. var. *hibernica* **'Sulphurea'** (illus. p.179), H and S 10ft (3m), has medium-sized leaves with sulfur yellow variegation; is good when grown against a wall or for ground cover, and as foil for brightly colored plants. **'Ivalace'** (syn. *H.h.* 'Mini Green'; illus. p.179), H 3ft (1m), S 4ft (1.2m), is frost hardy, zones 8–9, and has curled and crimped, glossy leaves; is good for ground cover and for growing against a low wall. **'Köniğer's Auslese'** (syn. *H.h.* 'Sagittifolia'), H 4ft (1.2m), S 3ft (1m), is frost hardy, zones 8–9, and has fingerlike, deeply cut leaves; is not suitable for ground cover. **'Lobata Major'** (illus. p.179), H 15ft (5m), is vigorous with large, 3-lobed leaves. **'Manda's Crested'** (syn. *H.h.* 'Curly Locks'; illus. p.179), H and S 6ft (2m), is frost hardy, zones 8–9, and has elegant, wavy-edged, green leaves that turn a coppery shade in winter. **'Merion Beauty'** (illus. p.179), H 4ft (1.2m), S 3ft (1m), is frost hardy, zones 8–9, with delicately lobed leaves; is not suitable for ground cover. **'Mini Green'** see *H.h.* 'Ivalace'. **'Nigra'** (illus. p.179), H and S 4ft (1.2m), has small, very dark green

leaves that turn purple-black in winter. **'Parsley Crested'** (syn. *H.h.* 'Cristata'; illus. p.179), H 6ft (2m), S 4ft (1.2m), is frost hardy, zones 8–9, and has light green leaves, crested at margins; is not suitable for ground cover. **'Pedata'** (syn. *H.h.* 'Caenwoodiana'; Bird's-foot ivy; illus. p.179), H 12ft (4m), S 10ft (3m), has gray-green leaves shaped like a bird's foot; is not suitable for ground cover. **'Pittsburgh'** (syn. *H.h.* 'Hahn's Self-branching'; illus. p.179), H 3ft (1m), S 4ft (1.2m), is frost hardy, zones 8–9, and has green leaves; is suitable for growing against a low wall and for ground cover. **'Purpurea'** see *H.h.* 'Atropurpurea'. **'Sagittifolia'** see *H.h.* 'Köniğer's Auslese'. **'Telecurl'** (illus. p.179), H and S 3ft (1m), is frost hardy, zones 8–9, and has elegantly twisted, light green leaves. **'Triton'** (syn. *H.h.* 'Green Feather'), H 1¹/₂ft (45cm), S 3ft (1m), is a frost hardy, zones 8–9, non-climbing cultivar that has leaves with deeply incised lobes that resemble whips; makes good ground cover. **'Woerner'** (illus. p.179), H 12ft (4m), S 10ft (3m), is a vigorous cultivar that has bluntly lobed, gray-green leaves, with lighter colored veins, that turn purple in winter.
H. nepalensis (Nepalese ivy). Evergreen, self-clinging climber. H 12ft (4m), S 8ft (2.5m). Half hardy, zones 9–10; young growth may be damaged by late spring frosts. Produces oval to triangular, toothed, olive green leaves. Is suitable only for growing against a sheltered wall.
H. pastuchovii. Moderately vigorous, evergreen, self-clinging climber. H 8ft (2.5m), S 6ft (2m). Fully hardy, zones 5–9. Has shield-shaped, glossy, dark green leaves. Is suitable only for growing against a wall.
H. rhombea (Japanese ivy). Evergreen, self-clinging climber. H and S 4ft (1.2m). Frost hardy, zones 8–9. Has small, fairly thick, diamond-shaped, unlobed, green leaves. Is suitable only for growing against a low wall. **'Variegata'** has leaves with narrow, white margins.

HEDYCHIUM (Zingiberaceae)
Garland flower, Ginger lily
Genus of perennials with stout, fleshy rhizomes. Fragrant, showy flowers are individually short-lived, but borne profusely. Is ideal for sheltered borders and conservatories. Frost hardy to frost tender, min. 41°F (5°C). Needs sun and rich, moist soil. Propagate by division in spring; rhizomes should not be divided when dormant.
H. coronarium (White ginger lily). Upright, rhizomatous perennial. H 5ft (1.5m), S 2–3ft (60cm–1m). Frost tender, zones 9–10. Has dense spikes of very fragrant, butterflylike, white flowers with basal, yellow blotches in mid-summer. Lance-shaped, green leaves are downy beneath.
H. densiflorum illus. p.191.
H. gardnerianum illus. p.194.

HEDYOTIS, syn. HOUSTONIA (Rubiaceae)
Genus of mat-forming, summer-flowering perennials. Fully hardy.

Thrives in a shaded situation on moist, sandy leaf mold. Propagate by division in spring or by seed in autumn.
H. michauxii, syn. *Houstonia serpyllifolia*, illus. p.323.

HEDYSARUM (Leguminosae)
Genus of perennials, biennials, and deciduous sub-shrubs. Fully hardy. Prefers sun and well-drained soil. Resents being disturbed. Propagate by seed in autumn or spring.
H. coronarium illus. p.209.

HEERIA. See HETEROCENTRON.

Heimerliodendron brunonianum. See *Pisonia umbellifera.*

HELENIUM (Compositae)
Sneezeweed
Genus of late summer- and autumn-flowering perennials, grown for their sprays of daisylike flower heads, each with a prominent, central disc. Fully hardy. Requires full sun and any well-drained soil. Propagate by division in spring or autumn.
H. **'Bressingham Gold'.** Erect, bushy perennial with stout stems clothed in lance-shaped, green leaves. H 3ft (1m), S 2ft (60cm). Zones 4–8. Sprays of bright yellow flower heads are produced in late summer and autumn.
H. **'Bruno'.** Erect, bushy perennial. H 4ft (1.2m), S 2¹/₂ft (75cm). Zones 4–8. Bears sprays of deep bronze-red flower heads in late summer and autumn. Stout stems are clothed in lance-shaped leaves.
H. **'Butterpat'.** Compact perennial. H 3ft (1m), S 2ft (60cm). Zones 4–8. Has stout stems clothed in lance-shaped leaves. In late summer and autumn produces sprays of rich deep yellow flower heads.
H. **'Moerheim Beauty'** illus. p.221.
H. **'Riverton Gem'.** Erect, bushy perennial. H 4¹/₂ft (1.4m), S 3ft (1m). Zones 4–8. Has sprays of red-and-gold flower heads in late summer and autumn. Stout stems are clothed in lance-shaped leaves.
H. **'Wyndley'** illus. p.221.

HELIANTHEMUM (Cistaceae)
Rock rose
Genus of evergreen, spring- to autumn-flowering shrubs and sub-shrubs, grown for their flowers. Is useful for rock gardens and dry banks. Fully to frost hardy. Needs full sun and well-drained soil. Cut back lightly after flowering. Propagate by semi-ripe cuttings in early summer.
H. apenninum illus. p.291.
H. **'Ben Hope'.** Evergreen, domed shrub. H 9–12in (23–30cm), S 18in (45cm). Fully hardy, zones 6–8. Leaves are small, linear, and gray-green. Produces saucer-shaped, carmine red flowers in mid-summer.
H. **'Ben More'** illus. p.294.
H. **'Ben Nevis'.** Evergreen, hummock-forming, compact shrub. H and S 6–9in (15–23cm). Fully hardy, zones 6–8. Has small, linear, dark green leaves and, in mid-summer, saucer-shaped, orange flowers with bronze centers.

H. **'Fire Dragon'** illus. p.294.
H. guttatum. See *Tuberaria guttata.*
H. nummularium **'Amy Baring'.** Evergreen, spreading shrub. H 4–6in (10–15cm), S 24in (60cm). Fully hardy, zones 6–8. Small, oblong, light gray leaves are hairy beneath. In summer bears a succession of saucer-shaped, orange-centered, deep yellow flowers in loose, terminal clusters.
H. oelandicum subsp. *alpestre.* Evergreen, open, twiggy shrub. H 3–5in (7–12cm), S 6in (15cm) or more. Fully hardy, zones 6–8. Produces terminal clusters of 3–6 saucer-shaped, bright yellow flowers from early to mid-summer. Leaves are tiny, oblong, and green. Is suitable for growing in a pot.
H. **'Raspberry Ripple'** illus. p.294.
H. **'Wisley Pink'** illus. p.293.
H. **'Wisley Primrose'** illus. p.298.
H. **'Wisley White'** illus. p.291.

HELIANTHUS (Compositae)
Sunflower
Genus of summer- and autumn-flowering annuals and perennials, grown for their large, daisylike, usually yellow flower heads. May be invasive. Fully hardy. Prefers sun and well-drained soil. Needs staking. Propagate by seed or division in autumn or spring.
H. annuus (illus. p.281). Fast-growing, upright annual. H 3–10ft (1–3m) or more; S 12–18in (30–45cm). Has large, oval, serrated, green leaves. Very large, daisylike, brown- or purplish centered, yellow flower heads, 12in (30cm) or more wide, are produced in summer. Tall, intermediate, and dwarf cultivars are available. **'Italian White'** (intermediate), H 4ft (1.2m), has black-centered, creamy white flower heads. **'Russian Giant'** (tall), H 10ft (3m) or more, has yellow flower heads with green-brown centers. **'Taiyo'** (intermediate) illus. p.280. **'Teddy Bear'** (dwarf), H 2ft (60cm), has 6in (15cm) wide, fully double, deep yellow flower heads.
H. atrorubens **'Monarch'.** Erect perennial. H 7ft (2.2m), S 3ft (1m). Zones 5–9. Bears terminal, daisylike, semi-double, golden yellow flower heads on branching stems in late summer. Has lance-shaped, coarse, green leaves. Replant each spring to keep in check.
H. **'Capenoch Star'.** Erect perennial. H 4ft (1.2m), S 2ft (60cm). Zones 5–8. In summer, daisylike, lemon yellow flower heads are borne terminally on branching stems. Leaves are lance-shaped and coarse.
H., Chrysanthemum-flowered Series illus. p.281.
H. **'Loddon Gold'** illus. p.194.
H. x *multiflorus* illus. p.194.
H. salicifolius (Willow-leaved sunflower). Upright perennial. H 7ft (2.2m), S 2ft (60cm). Zones 6–9. Bears small, daisylike, yellow flower heads at ends of stout, branching stems in autumn. Has narrow, willowlike, drooping, deep green leaves.

HELICHRYSUM (Compositae)
Genus of summer- and autumn-flowering perennials, annuals, and

evergreen sub-shrubs and shrubs. When dried, flower heads are "everlasting." Fully hardy to frost tender, min. 41°F (5°C). Needs sun and well-drained soil. Propagate shrubs and sub-shrubs by heel or semi-ripe cuttings in summer; perennials by division or seed in spring; annuals by seed in spring.

H. angustifolium. See *H. italicum.*
H. bellidioides. Evergreen, prostrate shrub. H 2in (5cm), S 9in (23cm). Fully hardy, zones 7–10. Has small, rounded, fleshy, dark green leaves and, in early summer, terminal clusters of daisylike, white flower heads.
H. bracteatum (Everlasting flower, Immortelle, Strawflower). 'Bright Bikini' is a moderately fast-growing, upright, branching annual. H and S 12in (30cm). Half hardy. Has lance-shaped, green leaves and, from summer to early autumn, papery, daisylike flower heads in many colors, including red, pink, orange, yellow, and white. **Monstrosum Series** illus. p.284.
H. coralloides illus. p.301.
H. italicum, syn. *H. angustifolium,* *H. serotinum* (Curry plant). Evergreen, bushy sub-shrub. H 2ft (60cm), S 3ft (1m). Frost hardy, zones 8–10. Has linear, aromatic, silvery gray leaves. Broad clusters of small, oblong, bright yellow flower heads are produced on long, upright, white shoots during summer. subsp. *serotinum,* H and S 6in (15cm), is dome-shaped and has stems and oval leaves that are densely felted with white hairs. Dislikes winter wet and cold climates.
Helichrysum ledifolium. See *Ozothamnus ledifolius.*
H. marginatum. See *H. milfordiae.*
H. milfordiae, syn. *H. marginatum.* Evergreen, mat-forming, dense sub-shrub. H 2in (5cm), S 9in (23cm). Frost hardy, zones 8–10. On sunny days in early summer, large, conical, red buds open into daisylike, white flower heads with red-backed petals; they close in dull or wet weather. Has basal rosettes of oval, hairy, silver leaves. Prefers very gritty soil. Dislikes winter wet. Propagate in spring by removing and rooting single rosettes.
H. petiolare, syn. *H. petiolatum,* illus. p.143.
H. petiolatum. See *H. petiolare.*
H. rosmarinifolium. See *Ozothamnus rosmarinifolius.*
H. selago illus. p.301.
H. serotinum. See *H. italicum.*
H. splendidum. Evergreen, bushy, dense shrub. H and S 4ft (1.2m). Frost hardy, zones 8–10. Woolly, white shoots are clothed in small, oblong, silvery gray leaves. Small, oblong, bright yellow flower heads appear in clusters from mid-summer to autumn or into winter.
H. 'Sulphur Light' illus. p.246.

HELICONIA (Heliconiaceae)
Lobster claws
Genus of tufted perennials, evergreen in warm climates, grown for their spikes of colorful flowers and for the attractive foliage on younger plants. Frost tender, min. 64°F (18°C). Needs partial shade and humus-rich, well-

drained soil. Water generously in growing season, very sparingly when plants die down in winter. Propagate by seed or division of rootstock in spring.
H. metallica. Tufted perennial. H to 10ft (3m), S 3ft (1m). Zone 10. Oblong, long-stalked leaves, to 2ft (60cm) long, are velvety green above with paler veins, sometimes purple below. In summer, mature plants bear erect stems with tubular, glossy, greenish white-tipped, red flowers enclosed in narrow, boat-shaped, green bracts.
H. psittacorum illus. p.191.

HELICTOTRICHON (Gramineae). See GRASSES, BAMBOOS, RUSHES, and SEDGES.
H. sempervirens, syn. *Avena candida,* *A. sempervirens,* illus. p.181.

HELIOPSIS (Compositae)
Genus of summer-flowering perennials. Fully hardy. Requires sun and any well-drained soil. Propagate by seed or division in autumn or spring.
H. 'Ballet Dancer' illus. p.216.
H. helianthoides 'Incomparabilis'. Upright perennial. H to 5ft (1.5m), S 2ft (60cm). Zones 4–9. Bears daisylike, single, orange flower heads in late summer. Leaves are narrowly oval, coarsely toothed, and green. 'Patula' bears flattish, semi-double, orange-yellow flower heads. subsp. *scabra* has very rough stems and leaves and double, orange-yellow flower heads.
H. 'Light of Loddon' illus. p.191.

Heliosperma alpestris. See *Silene alpestris.*

HELIOTROPIUM (Boraginaceae)
Genus of annuals, evergreen sub-shrubs and shrubs, grown for their fragrant flowers. Frost hardy to frost tender, min. 41–5°F (5–7°C). Requires full sun and fertile, well-drained soil. Water potted plants freely when in full growth, moderately at other times. In spring, tip prune young plants to promote a bushy habit and cut leggy, older plants back hard. Propagate by seed in spring, by greenwood cuttings in summer, or by semi-ripe cuttings in early autumn.
H. arborescens, syn. *H. peruvianum,* illus. p.135.
H. peruvianum. See *H. arborescens.*

HELIPTERUM (Compositae)
Genus of annuals and perennials; flower heads of annuals are suitable for cutting and drying. Half hardy to frost tender, min. 36–9°F (2–4°C). Grow in sun and in poor, very well-drained soil. Propagate by seed sown outdoors in mid-spring. Aphids may cause problems.
H. manglesii, syn. *Rhodanthe manglesii,* illus. p.265.
H. roseum, syn. *Acroclinium roseum,* illus. p.265.

HELLEBORUS (Ranunculaceae)
Christmas rose, Lenten rose
Genus of perennials, some of which

are evergreen, grown for their winter and spring flowers. Most deciduous species retain their old leaves over winter. These should be cut off in early spring as flower buds develop. Is excellent in woodlands. Fully to half hardy. Prefers semi-shade and moisture-retentive, well-drained soil. Propagate by fresh seed or division in autumn or very early spring. Is prone to aphid attack in early summer.
H. atrorubens. Clump-forming perennial. H and S 1ft (30cm). Fully hardy, zones 5–9. Shallowly cup-shaped, deep purple flowers are borne in late winter. Has palmate, deeply divided, toothed, glossy, dark green leaves.
H. cyclophyllus. Clump-forming perennial. H to 24in (60cm), S 18in (45cm). Fully hardy, zones 6–9. In early spring produces shallowly cup-shaped, yellow-green flowers with prominent, yellowish white stamens. Has palmate, deeply divided, bright green leaves.
H. foetidus illus. p. 261.
H. lividus. Evergreen, clump-forming perennial. H and S 18in (45cm). Half hardy, zones 7–9. Has 3-parted, green leaves, marbled pale green, purplish green below, with obliquely oval, slightly toothed or entire leaflets. Large clusters of cup-shaped, purple-suffused, yellow-green flowers open in late winter. subsp. *corsicus* illus. p.260.
H. niger illus. p.257.
H. orientalis [white form] illus. p.256, [pink form] illus. p.257, [purple form] illus. p.258.
H. purpurascens. Neat, clump-forming perennial. H and S 1ft (30cm). Fully hardy, zones 5–8. Small, nodding, cup-shaped, pure deep purple or green flowers, splashed with deep purple on outside, appear in early spring. Leaves are dark green and palmate, deeply divided into narrowly lance-shaped, toothed segments.
H. x sternii illus. p.257.
H. viridis illus. p.261.

HELONIAS (Liliaceae)
Genus of one species of spring-flowering perennial. Fully hardy. Is excellent in bog gardens. Needs an open, sunny position and moist to wet soil. Propagate by division in spring or by seed in autumn.
H. bullata (Swamp pink). Rosetted, clump-forming perennial. H 15–18in (38–45cm), S 12in (30cm). Zones 6–9. Has basal rosettes of strap-shaped, fresh green leaves, above which dense racemes of small, fragrant, star-shaped, pinkish purple flowers are borne in spring.

HELONIOPSIS (Liliaceae)
Genus of spring-flowering, rosette-forming perennials. Fully hardy. Grow in semi-shade and in moist soil. Propagate by division in autumn or by seed in autumn or spring.
H. orientalis illus. p.226.

HELWINGIA (Cornaceae)
Genus of deciduous shrubs, bearing flowers and showy fruits directly on leaf surfaces, grown mainly for botanical interest. Needs separate male

and female plants in order to produce fruits. Fully hardy. Requires sun or semi-shade and moist soil. Propagate by softwood cuttings in summer.
H. japonica. Deciduous, bushy, open shrub. H and S 5ft (1.5m). Zones 6–9. Oval, bright green leaves have bristlelike teeth. In early summer, tiny, star-shaped, green flowers appear on each leaf center and are followed by spherical, black fruits.

Helxine soleirolii. See *Soleirolia soleirolii.*

HEMEROCALLIS (Liliaceae)
Daylily
Genus of perennials, some of which are semi-evergreen. Flowers, borne in succession, each last for only a day. Fully hardy. Does best in full sun and fertile, moist soil. Propagate by division in autumn or spring. Cultivars raised from seed will not come true to type; species may come true if grown in isolation from other daylilies. Slug and snail control is essential in early spring when young foliage first appears.
H. 'Catherine Woodbury'. Robust, clump-forming perennial. H 28in (70cm), S 30in (75cm). Zones 4–9. Fragrant, trumpet-shaped, delicate, pale lavender flowers, with soft lime green throats, are produced above strap-shaped, green leaves in late summer.
H. citrina illus. p.215.
H. 'Corky' illus. p.248.
H. dumortieri. Compact, clump-forming perennial. H 1 1/2ft (45cm), S 2ft (60cm). Zones 3–9. In early summer produces fragrant, trumpet-shaped, brown-backed, golden yellow flowers. Green leaves are strap-shaped, stiff, and coarse.
H. flava. See *H. lilio-asphodelus.*
H. fulva (Fulvous daylily, Tawny daylily). Vigorous, clump-forming perennial. H 3ft (1m), S 2 1/2ft (75cm). Zones 3–9. Trumpet-shaped, tawny orange flowers appear from mid- to late summer above a mound of strap-shaped, light green leaves. 'Kwanso Flore Plena' illus. p.216. 'Kwanso Variegata' has leaves variably marked with white.
H. 'Golden Chimes' illus. p.216.
H. 'Joan Senior'. Vigorous, semi-evergreen, clump-forming perennial. H 25in (63cm), S 3ft (1m). Zones 4–9. Open trumpet-shaped, almost pure white flowers are borne on well-branched stems from mid- to late summer. Leaves are strap-shaped and green.
H. lilio-asphodelus, syn. *H. flava,* illus. p.214.
H. 'Marion Vaughn' illus. p.214.
H. minor (Grass-leaved daylily). Compact, clump-forming perennial. H 16in (40cm), S 18in (45cm). Zones 3–9. In early summer, fragrant, trumpet-shaped, lemon yellow flowers, with tawny-backed, outer petals, overtop narrowly strap-shaped, green leaves that die back in early autumn.
H. 'Stafford' illus. p.208.
H. 'Stella d'Oro'. Vigorous, compact, clump-forming perennial. H 16in (40cm), S 18in (45cm). Zones 4–9.

Abundant, small, widely bell-shaped, pale orange-yellow flowers, with green-tipped, outer petals, are borne from mid-summer to first frosts. Narrowly strap-shaped leaves are green.

HEMIGRAPHIS (Acanthaceae)
Genus of annuals and evergreen perennials, usually grown as foliage plants. Frost tender, min. 59°F (15°C). Grow in bright but not direct sunlight and in moist but well-drained soil. Water frequently in growing season, less in winter. Cut back straggly stems. Propagate by stem cuttings in spring or summer.
H. repanda illus. p.255.

HEPATICA (Ranunculaceae)
Genus of very variable perennials, some of which are semi-evergreen, flowering in early spring before new leaves are properly formed. Fully hardy. Requires partial shade and deep, humus-rich, moist soil. Stout, much-branched rootstock resents disturbance. Propagate by seed when fresh or by division or removing side shoots in spring.
H. angulosa. See *H. transsilvanica.*
H. x *media* 'Ballardii'. Slow-growing, dome-shaped perennial. H 4in (10cm), S 12in (30cm). Zones 4–8. Has rounded, 3-lobed, stalked, soft green leaves and, in early spring, shallowly cup-shaped, many-petaled, intense blue flowers. Fully double, colored forms are also known. Propagate by division only.
H. nobilis, syn. *Anemone hepatica.* Slow-growing, semi-evergreen, dome-shaped perennial. H 3in (8cm), S 4–5in (10–12cm). Zones 4–8. Has rounded, 3-lobed, fleshy, green leaves and bears shallowly cup-shaped, many-petaled flowers—white through pink to carmine, pale to deep blue, or purple—in early spring. Fully double, colored forms are also known. Is excellent for growing in woodland or a rock garden. var. *japonica* illus. p.309.
H. transsilvanica, syn. *H. angulosa.* Semi-evergreen, spreading perennial. H 3in (8cm), S 8in (20cm). Zones 5–8. Shallowly cup-shaped, many-petaled flowers, varying from blue to white or pink, are borne in early spring amid rounded, 3-lobed, hairy, green leaves. Fully double, colored forms are also known.

HEPTAPLEURUM. See SCHEFFLERA.

HERMANNIA (Sterculiaceae)
Genus of evergreen sub-shrubs and shrubs, grown mainly for their flowers. Frost tender, min. 45°F (7°C). Prefers full light and fertile, well-drained soil. Water potted plants freely when in full growth, moderately at other times. Young plants may need tip pruning to produce well-branched specimens. Propagate by softwood or greenwood cuttings in late spring or summer.
H. candicans. Evergreen, bushy sub-shrub. H and S 24in (60cm) or more. Zone 10. Oval to oblong leaves have white down beneath. Small, nodding, bell-shaped, bright yellow flowers are

carried in terminal clusters, to 6in (15cm) long, in spring-summer.

HERMODACTYLUS (Iridaceae)
Genus of one species of spring-flowering tuber, with an elongated, fingerlike rootstock, grown for its irislike flowers. Fully hardy. Requires a hot, sunny situation, where tubers will ripen well in summer, and well-drained soil. Is particularly successful on hot, chalky soils. Propagate by division in late summer.
H. tuberosus, syn. *Iris tuberosa,* illus. p.346.

HESPERALOE
(Agavaceae)
Genus of basal-rosetted, perennial succulents with very narrow, strap-shaped, grooved, dark green leaves, often with peeling, white fibers at margins. Is closely related to *Agave* and *Yucca.* Offsets freely at base. Frost tender, min. 37°F (3°C). Needs a sunny position and very well-drained soil. Propagate by seed or division in spring or summer.
H. parviflora, syn. *Yucca parviflora,* illus. p.383.

HESPERIS (Cruciferae)
Genus of late spring- or summer-flowering annuals and perennials. Fully hardy. Requires sun and well-drained soil. *H. matronalis* tolerates poor soil. Tends to become woody at base, so raise new stock from seed every few years. Propagate by basal cuttings in spring or by seed in autumn or spring.
H. matronalis illus. p.200.

HESPEROCALLIS (Liliaceae)
Genus of spring- to summer-flowering bulbs. Half hardy. Needs a sunny, well-drained site. Is difficult to cultivate in all but warm, dry areas; in cool, damp climates, protect in a cool greenhouse. Requires ample water in spring, followed by a hot, dry period during its summer dormancy. Propagate by seed in autumn.
H. undulata. Spring- to summer-flowering bulb. H 8–20in (20–50cm), S 4–6in (10–15cm). Zones 9–10. Has a cluster of long, narrow, wavy-margined leaves, semi-erect or prostrate, at base. Stout stems each bear a spike of upward-facing, funnel-shaped, white flowers, with a central, green stripe along each of the 6 petals.

HESPEROYUCCA. See YUCCA.

HETEROCENTRON, syn. HEERIA, SCHIZOCENTRON
(Melastomataceae)
Genus of evergreen, summer- and autumn-flowering perennials and shrubs. Frost tender, min. 41°F (5°C). Requires sun and well-drained soil. Propagate by softwood or stem-tip cuttings in late winter or early spring.
H. elegans illus. p.241.

HETEROMELES (Rosaceae)
Genus of one species of evergreen, summer-flowering shrub or tree, grown for its foliage, flowers, and fruits. Frost hardy, but in cold areas

needs protection. Requires sun or semi-shade and fertile, well-drained soil. Propagate by semi-ripe cuttings in summer or by seed in autumn.
H. arbutifolia, syn. *Photinia arbutifolia* (Christmas berry, Toyon). Evergreen, bushy, spreading shrub or tree. H 20ft (6m), S 25ft (8m). Zones 8–10. Has oblong, sharply toothed, leathery, glossy, dark green leaves. Broad, flat heads of small, 5-petaled, white flowers in late summer are succeeded by large clusters of rounded, red fruits.

HEUCHERA (Saxifragaceae)
Alumroot
Genus of evergreen, summer-flowering perennials forming large clumps of leaves, often tinted bronze or purple. Makes good ground cover. Fully to frost hardy. Prefers semi-shade and moisture-retentive but well-drained soil. Propagate species by seed in autumn or by division in autumn or spring, cultivars by division in autumn or spring, using young, outer portions of woody crown.
H. x *brizoides* 'Coral Cloud'. Evergreen, clump-forming perennial. H 18–30in (45–75cm), S 12–18in (30–45cm). Fully hardy, zones 4–8. In summer bears long, feathery sprays of small, pendent, bell-shaped, pink flowers. Leaves are rounded, lobed, toothed, and dark green. 'Firebird' has crimson-scarlet flowers; those of 'Pearl Drops' are white; those of 'Scintillation' are bright pink.
H. cylindrica 'Greenfinch' illus. p.233.
H. 'Palace Purple' illus. p.234.
H. 'Red Spangles' illus. p.239.

x **HEUCHERELLA** (Saxifragaceae)
Hybrid genus (*Heuchera* x *Tiarella*) of evergreen, mainly late spring- and summer-flowering perennials. Fully hardy. Prefers semi-shade and needs fertile, well-drained soil. Propagate by basal cuttings in spring or by division in spring or autumn.
x *H.* 'Bridget Bloom' illus. p.235.
x *H. tiarelloides* illus. p.235.

HEXASTYLIS. See ASARUM.

HIBBERTIA (Dilleniaceae)
Genus of evergreen shrubs and twining climbers, grown for their flowers. Frost tender, min. 41–50°F (5–10°C). Grow in well-drained soil, in full light or semi-shade. Water freely in summer, less at other times. Provide stems with support. Thin out congested growth in spring. Propagate by semi-ripe cuttings in summer.
H. cuneiformis, syn. *Candollea cuneiformis,* illus. p.114.
H. scandens. Vigorous, evergreen, twining climber. H 20ft (6m). Zone 10. Has 1½–3½in (4–9cm) long, oblong to lance-shaped, glossy, deep green leaves. Saucer-shaped, bright yellow flowers, 1½in (4cm) across, appear mainly in summer.

HIBISCUS (Malvaceae)
Genus of evergreen or deciduous shrubs, trees, perennials, and annuals, grown for their flowers. Fully hardy to frost tender, min. 41–59°F (5–15°C).

Needs full sun and humus-rich, well-drained soil. Water potted specimens freely when in full growth, moderately at other times. Tip prune young plants to promote bushiness; cut old plants back hard in spring, if required. Propagate by seed in spring; shrubs and trees by greenwood cuttings in late spring or by semi-ripe cuttings in summer; perennials by division in autumn or spring. Whitefly may cause problems.
H. mutabilis (Confederate rose, Cotton rose). Evergreen, erect to spreading shrub or tree. H and S 10–15ft (3–5m). Frost tender, min. 41°F (5°C), zones 9–10. Rounded leaves have 5–7 shallow lobes. In summer-autumn bears funnel-shaped, sometimes double, white or pink flowers, 3–4in (7–10cm) wide, that turn pink to deep red with age. In areas of light frost dies back to ground level in winter.
H. rosa-sinensis. Evergreen, rounded, leafy shrub. H and S 5–10ft (1.5–3m) or more. Frost tender, min. 50–55°F (10–13°C), zones 9–10. Oval, glossy leaves are coarsely serrated. Produces funnel-shaped, bright crimson flowers, 4in (10cm) wide, mainly in summer but also in spring and autumn. Many color selections are grown including 'The President' illus. p.109.
H. schizopetalus. Evergreen, upright, spreading, loose shrub. H to 10ft (3m), S 6ft (2m) or more. Frost tender, min. 50–55°F (10–13°C), zone 10. Has oval, serrated leaves and, in summer, pendent, long-stalked flowers, 2½in (6cm) wide, with deeply fringed, reflexed, pink or red petals. May be trained as a climber.
H. sinosyriacus 'Lilac Queen' illus. p.112.
H. syriacus 'Blue Bird' illus. p.113. 'Diana' is a deciduous, upright shrub. H 10ft (3m), S 6ft (2m). Fully hardy, zones 6–9. Bears very large, trumpet-shaped, pure white flowers, with wavy-edged petals, from late summer to mid-autumn. Leaves are oval, lobed, and deep green. 'Red Heart' illus. p.107. 'Woodbridge' illus. p.109.
H. trionum illus. p.264.

HIDALGOA (Compositae)
Climbing dahlia
Genus of evergreen, leaf-stalk climbers, grown for their single, dahlialike flower heads. Frost tender, min. 50°F (10°C). Requires humus-rich, well-drained soil and full light. Water freely when in full growth, less at other times. Provide support and thin out crowded stems or cut back all growth to ground level in spring. Propagate by softwood cuttings in spring. Aphids, red spider mite, and whitefly may prove troublesome.
H. ternata. See *H. wercklei.*
H. wercklei, syn. *H. ternata.* Moderately vigorous, evergreen, leaf-stalk climber. H 15ft (5m) or more. Zone 10. Oval leaves are divided into 3, 5, or more coarsely serrated leaflets. In summer bears dahlialike, scarlet flower heads, yellowish in bud.

HIERACIUM (Compositae)
Hawkweed
Genus of perennials; most are weeds,

but the species described is grown for its foliage. Fully hardy. Does best in sun and in poor, well-drained soil. Propagate by seed or division in autumn or spring.
H. lanatum illus. p.248.

HIPPEASTRUM (Amaryllidaceae)
Genus of bulbs, grown for their huge, funnel-shaped flowers. Is often incorrectly cultivated as *Amaryllis*. Frost hardy to frost tender, min. 55–9°F (13–15°C). Needs full sun or partial shade and well-drained soil. Plant large-flowered hybrids in autumn, half burying bulb; after leaves die away, dry off bulb until following autumn. Smaller, summer-flowering species should be kept dry while dormant in winter. Propagate by seed in spring or by offsets in spring (summer-flowering species) or autumn (large-flowered hybrids).
H. advenum illus. p.351.
H. 'Apple Blossom' illus. p.355.
H. aulicum. Winter- and spring-flowering bulb with a basal leaf cluster. H 12–20in (30–50cm), S 12in (30cm). Frost tender, min. 55°F (13°C), zone 10. Produces strap-shaped, semi-erect leaves as, or just after, flowers form. Stout stem has a head of 2–6 red flowers, each to 10in (25cm) across with a green blotch in the throat near the base of each petal.
H. 'Belinda'. Winter- and spring-flowering bulb with a basal leaf cluster. H 12–20in (30–50cm), S 12in (30cm). Frost tender, min. 55°F (13°C), zone 10. Is similar to *H. aulicum*, but flowers are deep velvety red throughout, stained darker towards centers.
H. 'Bouquet'. Winter- and spring-flowering bulb with a basal leaf cluster. H 12–20in (30–50cm), S 12in (30cm). Frost tender, min. 55°F (13°C), zone 10. Is similar to *H. aulicum*, but has very wide, salmon pink flowers with deep red veins and red centers.
H. 'Orange Sovereign' illus. p.355.
H. pratense. Spring- and summer-flowering bulb. H to 24in (60cm), S 6–8in (15–20cm). Half hardy, zones 9–10. Leaves are narrowly strap-shaped, semi-erect, and basal. Flower stem produces a head of 2–5 red flowers, each 3–5in (8–12cm) across, with yellow-veined centers.
H. procerum. See *Worsleya rayneri*.
H. 'Red Lion' illus. p.355.
H. reginae. Summer-flowering bulb. H to 20in (50cm), S 8–10in (20–25cm). Frost tender, min. 55°F (13°C), zones 9–10. Flower stem produces a head of 2–4 scarlet flowers, each 4–6in (10–15cm) across with a star-shaped, green mark in the throat. Long, strap-shaped, semi-erect leaves develop at base after flowering.
H. rutilum, syn. *H. striatum*, illus. p.364.
H. striatum. See *H. rutilum*.
H. 'Striped' illus. p.355.
H. vittatum. Vigorous, spring-flowering bulb. H 3ft (1m), S 1ft (30cm). Frost tender, min. 55°F (13°C), zones 9–10. Leaves are broadly strap-shaped, semi-erect, and basal. Stout, leafless stem precedes

leaves and terminates in a head of 2–6 red-striped, white flowers, each 5–8in (12–20cm) across.
H. 'White Dazzler'. Winter- and spring-flowering bulb with a basal leaf cluster. H 12–20in (30–50cm), S 12in (30cm). Frost tender, min. 55°F (13°C), zone 10. Is similar to *H. aulicum*, but has pure white flowers.

HIPPOCREPIS (Leguminosae)
Vetch
Genus of annuals and perennials, grown for their pealike flowers. Fully hardy. Needs full sun and well-drained soil. Propagate by seed in spring or autumn. Self seeds readily. May be invasive.
H. comosa (Horseshoe vetch) illus. p.326. 'E.R. Janes' is a vigorous, prostrate, woody-based perennial. H 2–3in (5–8cm), S 6in (15cm) or more. Zones 5–7. Rooting stems bear small, loose spikes of pealike, yellow flowers from late spring to late summer. Has divided leaves with 3–8 pairs of narrowly oval leaflets.

HIPPOPHÄE (Elaeagnaceae)
Genus of deciduous shrubs and trees, with inconspicuous flowers, grown for their foliage and showy fruits. Needs separate male and female plants in order to obtain fruits. Is suitable for coastal areas, where it is wind-resistant and excellent as hedging. Fully hardy. Needs sun and is particularly useful for poor, dry, or very sandy soil. Propagate by softwood cuttings in summer or by seed in autumn.
H. rhamnoides illus. p.92.

HOHERIA (Malvaceae)
Genus of deciduous, semi-evergreen, or evergreen trees and shrubs, grown for their flowers mainly in summer. Frost hardy, but in cold areas grow against a south- or west-facing wall. Needs sun or semi-shade and fertile, well-drained soil. Propagate by semi-ripe cuttings in summer or by seed in autumn.
H. angustifolia illus. p.63.
H. 'Glory of Amlwch'. Semi-evergreen, spreading tree. H 22ft (7m), S 20ft (6m). Zone 9. Has long, narrowly oval, glossy, bright green leaves and a profusion of large, 5-petaled, white flowers from mid- to late summer.
H. lyallii illus. p.63.
H. populnea (Lacebark). Evergreen, spreading tree. H 40ft (12m), S 30ft (10m). Zone 9. Bears narrowly oval, glossy, dark green leaves and dense clusters of 5-petaled, white flowers in late summer and early autumn. Bark on mature trees is pale brown and white and often flaky.
H. sexstylosa (Ribbonwood). Fast-growing, evergreen, upright tree or shrub. H 25ft (8m), S 20ft (6m). Zone 9. Glossy, pale green leaves are narrowly oval and sharply toothed. Star-shaped, 5-petaled, white flowers are borne in clusters from mid- to late summer.

HOLBOELLIA (Lardizabalaceae)
Genus of evergreen, twining climbers, grown mainly for their fine foliage. Half hardy. Male and female flowers are borne on the same plant. Grow in any well-drained soil and in shade or

full light. Propagate by stem cuttings in late summer or autumn.
H. coriacea. Evergreen, twining climber. H to 22ft (7m) or more. Zone 10. Glossy, green leaves have 3 leaflets. In spring bears clusters of tiny, mauve, male flowers and, lower down stems, larger, purple-tinged, green, female flowers. Sausage-shaped, purple fruits are 1½–2½in (4–6cm) long.

HOLCUS (Gramineae). See GRASSES, BAMBOOS, RUSHES, and SEDGES.
H. mollis (Velvet grass). 'Variegatus' illus. p.180.

HOLMSKIOLDIA (Verbenaceae)
Genus of evergreen shrubs or scrambling climbers. Frost tender, min. 61°F (16°C). Any fertile, well-drained soil is suitable with full light. Water freely when in full growth, less at other times. Needs tying to supports. Thin out crowded growth in spring or after flowering. Propagate by seed in spring or by softwood or semi-ripe cuttings in summer. Whitefly and red spider mite may be troublesome.
H. sanguinea (Chinese hat plant, Mandarin's hat plant). Evergreen, straggly shrub. H to 15ft (5m), S 6ft (2m). Zone 10. Oval, serrated leaves are 2–4in (5–10cm) long. Showy, red or orange flowers, with saucer-shaped calyces and central, 5-lobed tubes, appear in autumn-winter.

HOLODISCUS (Rosaceae)
Genus of deciduous shrubs, grown for their flowers in summer. Fully hardy. Needs sun or semi-shade and any but very dry soil. Propagate by softwood cuttings in summer.
H. discolor illus. p.87.

HOMERIA (Iridaceae)
Genus of spring- or summer-flowering corms with widely funnel-shaped, cup-shaped, or flattish flowers. Half hardy. Needs a sunny site and well-drained soil. For flowers in spring, pot in autumn in a cool greenhouse, water until after flowering, then dry off for summer. For flowers in summer, plant in the open in spring. Propagate by seed, division, or offsets in autumn.
H. ochroleuca. Spring- or summer-flowering corm. H to 22in (55cm), S 2–3in (5–8cm). Zones 9–10. Lower part of each slender, wiry stem bears 1 or 2 long, narrow, semi-erect leaves. Has a succession of upright, cup-shaped to flattish, yellow flowers, each sometimes with a central, orange stain.

HOMOGYNE (Compositae)
Genus of evergreen perennials, useful for ground cover, especially in rock gardens and woodland. Fully hardy. Needs shade and moist soil. Propagate by division in spring or by seed when fresh.
H. alpina (Alpine coltsfoot). Evergreen, mat-forming, rhizomatous perennial. H 3–6in (8–15cm), S 6in (15cm) or more. Zones 6–8. Has kidney-shaped, toothed, glossy leaves and, in summer, stems, 3–6in (8–15cm) or more long, each carry a daisylike, rose-purple flower head.

HOODIA (Asclepiadaceae)
Genus of branching, perennial succulents with firm, erect, green stems, generally branching from the base. Frost tender, min. 50–59°F (10–15°C). Needs full sun and very well-drained soil. Is difficult to cultivate. Water sparingly at all times. Propagate by seed or grafting in spring or summer.
H. bainii. Clump-forming, perennial succulent. H 12in (30cm), S 6in (15cm). Min. 59°F (15°C), zone 10. Dull green stem has spiral rows of tubercles, each terminating in a sharp thorn. Produces 5-lobed, dull yellow flowers, 3in (7cm) across, in summer-autumn. Keep dry in winter.
H. gordonii. Variable, erect, clump-forming, perennial succulent. H 32in (80cm), S 12in (30cm). Min 50°F (10°C), zone 10. Green stem is covered with short, spine-tipped tubercles in distorted rows. Often branches into clumps. In late summer bears 5-lobed, flesh-colored to brownish flowers.

HORDEUM (Gramineae). See GRASSES, BAMBOOS, RUSHES, and SEDGES.
H. jubatum illus. p.181.

HORMINUM (Labiatae)
Genus of one species of basal-rosetted perennial, suitable for rock gardens. Fully hardy. Needs sun and well-drained soil. Propagate by division in spring or by seed in autumn.
H. pyrenaicum (Dragon's mouth). Basal-rosetted perennial. H and S 8in (20cm). Zones 6–8. In summer carries whorls of nodding, short-stalked, funnel-shaped, blue-purple or white flowers above oval, leathery, dark green leaves, 3–4in (8–10cm) long.

HOSTA (Funkiaceae)
Funkia, Plantain lily
Genus of perennials, grown mainly for their decorative foliage. Forms large clumps that are excellent for ground cover (heights given are those of foliage). Fully hardy, zones 4–9. Most species prefer shade and rich, moist but well-drained, neutral soil. Propagate by division in early spring. Seed-raised plants (with the exception of *H. ventricosa*) very rarely come true to type. Slug and snail control is essential.
H. albomarginata. See *H. sieboldii*.
H. 'August Moon' (illus. p.244). Fast-growing, robust, clump-forming perennial. H 2ft (60cm) S 3ft (1m). Oval, soft golden yellow leaves each have a faint glaucous blue bloom. Racemes of trumpet-shaped, pale grayish mauve flowers crown foliage in mid-summer. Requires semi-shade.
H. 'Blue Moon'. Slow-growing, compact, clump-forming perennial. H 5in (12cm), S 12in (30cm). Oval to rounded, grayish blue leaves taper to a point. In mid-summer, dense clusters of trumpet-shaped, mauve flowers are borne just above leaves. Is suitable for a rock garden. Prefers partial shade.
H. crispula (illus. p.244). Slow-growing, clump-forming perennial. H 2½ft (75cm), S 3ft (1m). Large, oval to heart-shaped, wavy-edged leaves

are dark green with irregular, white margins. Racemes of trumpet-shaped, pale mauve flowers appear well above foliage in mid-summer. Is excellent for waterside planting. Leaves are sometimes damaged by late frost. Needs protection from strong wind. Is prone to virus.

H. decorata f. *decorata* (illus p.244). Slow-growing, clump-forming perennial. H 1¹/₂ft (45cm), S 3ft (1m). Oval to rounded leaves, tapering to a point, are dark green with narrow, regular, white margins. Dense racemes of trumpet-shaped, violet flowers in mid-summer are followed by large, ovoid, glossy, dark green, then brown seed heads that are much used in flower arrangements. Prefers sandy soil and semi-shade and is best grown in a woodland garden. f. *normalis* has plain green leaves.

H. fortunei. Group of vigorous, clump-forming, hybrid perennials. H 2¹/₂–3ft (75cm–1m), S 3ft (1m) or more. Leaves are oval to heart-shaped. **'Albopicta'** (illus. p.244) has pale green leaves, with creamy yellow centers, fading to dull green from mid-summer. Racemes of trumpet-shaped, pale violet flowers open above foliage in early summer. **'Aurea Marginata'** (syn. *H.f.* 'Yellow Edge'; illus. p.244) has green leaves with irregular, creamy yellow edges. In mid-summer, trumpet-shaped, violet flowers are carried in racemes above foliage. Mass planting produces the most effective results. Tolerates full sun. **'Marginato-alba'** has thin-textured, mid- to dark green leaves that have irregular, white margins. Racemes of trumpet-shaped, violet flowers are borne on tall stems in mid-summer. Is ideal for a waterside. **'Yellow Edge'** see *H.f.* 'Aurea Marginata'.

H. **'Gold Standard'** (illus. p.244). Vigorous, clump-forming perennial. H 2¹/₂ft (75cm), S 3ft (1m). Oval to heart-shaped leaves are pale green, turning to gold from mid-summer, with narrow, regular, dark green margins. Racemes of trumpet-shaped, violet flowers are produced above leaves in mid-summer. Prefers partial shade.

H. **'Halcyon'** (illus. p.244). Robust, clump-forming perennial. H 1ft (30cm), S 3ft (1m). Has heart-shaped, tapering, grayish blue leaves that fade to muddy green in full sun; texture may be spoiled by heavy rain. Heavy clusters of trumpet-shaped, violet-mauve flowers open just above foliage in mid-summer.

H. hypoleuca (White-backed hosta). Clump-forming perennial. H 1¹/₂ft (45cm), S 3ft (1m). Broadly oval leaves have widely spaced veins and are pale green above, striking white beneath. In late summer bears drooping racemes of trumpet-shaped, milky violet flowers with mauve-flecked, pale green bracts. Tolerates full sun.

H. **'Kabitan'.** Clump-forming perennial, spreading by stolons. H to 1ft (30cm), S 2ft (60cm). Lance-shaped, thin-textured, glossy leaves are yellow-centered and have narrow, undulating, dark green margins. In

early summer produces a short raceme of small, trumpet-shaped, pale violet flowers. Is suitable for a shaded rock garden. Needs establishing in a pot for first few years.

H. lancifolia (illus. p.244). Arching, clump-forming perennial. H 1¹/₂ft (45cm), S 2¹/₂ft (75cm). Has narrowly lance-shaped, thin-textured, glossy, green leaves. Racemes of trumpet-shaped, deep violet flowers are borne above foliage in late summer and autumn.

H. montana. Vigorous, clump-forming perennial. H 3¹/₂ft (1.1m), S 3ft (1m). Has oval, prominently veined, glossy, dark green leaves. Racemes of trumpet-shaped, pale violet flowers open well above foliage in mid-summer. Slower-growing **'Aurea Marginata'** (illus. p.244) has leaves irregularly edged with golden yellow. Is always the first hosta to appear in spring, though it may be damaged by late frosts.

H. plantaginea (Fragrant plantain lily; illus. p.244). Lax, clump-forming perennial. H 2ft (60cm), S 4ft (1.2m). Leaves are oval and glossy, pale green. Rising well above these are flower stems crowned in late summer and early autumn with fragrant, trumpet-shaped, white flowers that open in the evening. Prefers sunny conditions.

H. rectifolia. Upright, clump-forming perennial. H 3ft (1m), S 2¹/₂ft (75cm). Has oval to lance-shaped, dark green leaves and spikes of large, trumpet-shaped, violet flowers from mid- to late summer.

H. **'Royal Standard'** (illus. p.244). Upright, clump-forming perennial. H 2ft (60cm), S 4ft (1.2m). Leaves are broadly oval and glossy, pale green. Slightly fragrant, trumpet-shaped, pure white flowers are borne well above foliage and open in the evening. Prefers sun.

H. sieboldiana (illus. p.244). Robust, clump-forming perennial. H 3ft (1m) or more, S 5ft (1.5m). Large, heart-shaped, deeply ribbed, puckered leaves are bluish gray. Racemes of trumpet-shaped, very pale lilac flowers open in early summer, just above foliage. Makes good ground cover. Tolerates sun, but leaves may then turn dull green. var. *elegans* (illus. p.244) has larger, bluer leaves. **'Frances Williams'** (illus. p.244) has yellow-edged leaves, is slower-growing and should not be grown in full sun.

H. sieboldii, syn. *H. albomarginata.* Vigorous, clump-forming perennial. H 1¹/₂ft (45cm), S 2ft (60cm). Lance-shaped, round-tipped leaves are mid- to dark green with narrow, irregular, white edges. Racemes of trumpet-shaped, violet flowers appear at tops of stems in late summer and are followed by ovoid, glossy, dark green, then brown seed heads that are useful for flower arrangements.

H. tardiflora (illus. p.244). Slow-growing, clump-forming perennial. H 1ft (30cm), S 2¹/₂ft (75cm). Has narrowly lance-shaped, thick-textured, dark green leaves. Dense racemes of trumpet-shaped, lilac-purple flowers open just above foliage from late summer to early autumn.

H. **'Thomas Hogg'**, syn. *H. undulata* 'Albomarginata'. Clump-forming perennial. H 2¹/₂ft (75cm), S 3ft (1m). Has oval to lance-shaped, round-tipped, green leaves, each with an irregular, pale cream to white margin that continues as a narrow line down leaf stalk. Racemes of trumpet-shaped, pale violet flowers rise well above foliage in mid-summer. Grows well under trees.

H. tokudama. Very slow-growing, clump-forming perennial. H 1¹/₂ft (45cm), S 2¹/₂ft (75cm). Produces cup-shaped, puckered, blue leaves. Racemes of trumpet-shaped, pale lilac-gray flowers appear just above foliage in mid-summer. **'Aureo-nebulosa'** (syn. *H.t.* 'Variegata'; illus. p.244) has irregular, cloudy yellow centers to leaves. **'Flavo-circinalis'**, often mistaken for a juvenile *H.* 'Frances Williams', has heart-shaped leaves with wide, irregular, creamy yellow margins. **'Variegata'** see *H.t.* 'Aureo-nebulosa'.

H. undulata. **'Albomarginata'** see *H.* 'Thomas Hogg'. var. *erromena* is a robust, clump-forming perennial. H 1¹/₂ft (45cm), S 2ft (60cm). Bears trumpet-shaped, pale mauve flowers high above oblong, wavy, green leaves. Leaves of var. *undulata* have irregular, white centers on first crop, white streaks on second. Leaf stalks and flower bracts are white with narrow, green margins. var. *univittata* (illus. p.244) is vigorous with oval, green leaves that have narrow, white centers.

H. ventricosa (illus. p.244). Clump-forming perennial. H 28in (70cm), S 3ft (1m) or more. Has heart-shaped to oval, slightly wavy-edged, glossy, dark green leaves. Racemes of bell-shaped, deep purple flowers appear above foliage in late summer. Usually comes true from seed. **'Aureo-maculata'** (illus. p.244) has leaves with irregular, central, creamy yellow variegation. **'Variegata'** has leaves with irregular, cream margins.

H. venusta. Vigorous, mat-forming perennial. H 1in (2.5cm), S to 12in (30cm). Has oval to lance-shaped, mid- to dark green leaves and produces abundant racemes of trumpet-shaped, purple flowers, that are borne well above foliage in mid-summer. Suits a rock garden.

HOTTONIA (Primulaceae)

Genus of deciduous, perennial, submerged water plants, grown for their handsome foliage and flowers. Fully hardy. Requires full sun and clear, cool water, still or running. Periodically thin overcrowded growth. Propagate by stem cuttings in spring or summer.

H. palustris illus. p.373.

HOUSTONIA. See HEDYOTIS.

HOUTTUYNIA (Saururaceae)

Genus of one species of perennial or deciduous marginal water plant with far-spreading rhizomes. Is suitable for growing as ground cover, although invasive. Fully hardy. Prefers semi-shade and moist soil or shallow water,

beside streams and ponds. Propagate by runners in spring.

H. cordata **'Chamaeleon'**, syn. *H.c.* 'Variegata', illus. p.373. **'Flore Pleno'** is a spreading perennial. H 6–24in (15–60cm), S indefinite. Zones 5–9. In spring, spikes of insignificant flowers, with 8 or more oval, white bracts, appear above, heart-shaped, pointed, aromatic, fleshy, leathery leaves.

HOVENIA (Rhamnaceae)

Genus of one species of deciduous, summer-flowering tree, grown for its foliage. Fully hardy, but young, unripened growth is susceptible to frost damage. Does best in full sun and requires fertile, well-drained soil. Propagate by softwood cuttings in summer or by seed in autumn.

H. dulcis illus. p.52.

HOWEA, syn. HOWEIA, KENTIA (Palmae)

Genus of evergreen palms, grown for their ornamental appearance. Frost tender, min. 61–4°F (16–18°C). Needs partial shade and humus-rich, well-drained soil. Water potted specimens freely in summer, minimally in winter, moderately at other times. Propagate by seed in spring at not less than 79°F (26°C). Red spider mite may be a nuisance.

H. forsteriana (Paradise palm, Sentry palm, Thatchleaf palm). Evergreen, upright palm with a slender stem. H 30ft (10m), S 10–12ft (3–4m). Zone 10. Has spreading, feather-shaped leaves, 5–8ft (1.5–2.5m) long, of strap-shaped leaflets. Produces branching clusters of several spikes of small, greenish brown flowers in winter.

HOWEIA. See HOWEA.

HOYA (Asclepiadaceae)

Genus of evergreen, woody-stemmed, twining and/or root climbers and loose shrubs, grown for their flowers and foliage. Frost tender, min. 41–64°F (5–18°C). Grow in humus-rich, well-drained soil with semi-shade in summer. Water moderately when in full growth, sparingly at other times. Stems require support. Cut back and thin out crowded stems after flowering or in spring. Propagate by semi-ripe cuttings in summer.

H. australis illus. p.166.
H. bella illus. p.166.
H. carnosa illus. p.166.
H. coronaria. Slow-growing, evergreen, woody-stemmed, twining and root climber. H 6–10ft (2–3m). Min. 61–4°F (16–18°C), zone 10. Has thick, leathery, oblong to oval leaves. Bell-shaped, yellow to white flowers, spotted with red, are borne in summer.
H. imperialis. Vigorous, evergreen, woody-stemmed, twining and root climber. H to 20ft (6m). Min. 61–4°F (16–18°C), zone 10. Oval, leathery, downy leaves are 4–9in (10–23cm) long. In summer has large, star-shaped, brown-purple to deep magenta flowers with cream centers.

HUERNIA (Asclepiadaceae)

Genus of clump-forming, perennial succulents with fingerlike, usually

4-angled stems. Produces minute, short-lived, deciduous leaves on new growth. Frost tender, min. 46–52°F (8–11°C). Requires sun or partial shade and extremely well-drained soil. Is one of easiest stapeliads to grow. Propagate by seed or stem cuttings in spring or summer.

H. macrocarpa. Deciduous, clump-forming, perennial succulent. H and S 4in (10cm). Min. 46°F (8°C), zone 10. Has fingerlike, 4- or 5-sided, gray-green stems. In summer-autumn bears bell-shaped, yellow flowers, with narrow, purple bands and recurved tips, at base of new growth. var. *arabica* illus. p.396.

H. pillansii. Deciduous, clump-forming, perennial succulent. H 2in (5cm), S 4in (10cm). Min. 52°F (11°C), zone 10. Has a fingerlike, light green stem densely covered with short tubercles that have hairlike tips. In summer-autumn bears bell-shaped, creamy red flowers, with red spots, at base of new growth.

H. primulina. Deciduous, clump-forming, perennial succulent. H 4in (10cm), S 6in (15cm). Min. 52°F (11°C), zone 10. Stems are short, thick, and gray-green. In summer-autumn carries bell-shaped, dull yellow flowers, ³/₄in (2cm) across, with reflexed, blackish tips, at base of new growth.

H. zebrina (Owl-eyes). Deciduous, clump-forming, perennial succulent. H 4in (10cm), S 6in (15cm). Min. 52°F (11°C), zone 10. Is similar to *H. primulina*, but has pale yellow-green flowers with bands of red-brown.

HUMEA (Compositae)
Genus of perennials and evergreen shrubs. Only one species, *H. elegans*, is cultivated, usually as a biennial. Frost tender, min. 39°F (4°C). Grow in sun and in fertile, well-drained soil. Propagate by seed sown under glass in mid-summer.
H. elegans illus. p.274.

HUMULUS (Cannabidaceae)
Hop
Genus of herbaceous, twining climbers. Is useful for concealing unsightly sheds or tree-stumps. Male and female flowers are produced on separate plants; female flower spikes become drooping clusters of 'hops'. Fully hardy. Grow in sun or semi-shade and in any well-drained soil. Propagate by tip cuttings in spring.
H. lupulus (Common hop). **'Aureus'** illus. p.164.

HUNNEMANNIA (Papaveraceae)
Genus of poppylike perennials, usually grown as annuals. Half hardy. Grow in sun and in poor to fertile, very well-drained soil. Dead-head plants regularly. Provide support, especially in windy areas. Propagate by seed sown under glass in early spring, or outdoors in mid-spring.
H. fumariifolia (Mexican tulip poppy). **'Sunlite'** is a fast-growing, upright perennial, grown as an annual. H 24in (60cm), S 8in (20cm). Has oblong, very divided, bluish green leaves and, in summer and early autumn, poppylike, semi-double, bright yellow flowers, to 3in (8cm) wide.

HYACINTHELLA (Liliaceae)
Genus of spring-flowering bulbs with short spikes of small, bell-shaped flowers, suitable for rock gardens and cold greenhouses. Frost hardy. Requires an open, sunny situation and well-drained soil, which partially dries out while bulbs are dormant in summer. Propagate by seed in autumn.
H. leucophaea illus. p.361.

HYACINTHOIDES, syn. ENDYMION (Liliaceae)
Genus of spring-flowering bulbs, grown for their bluebell flowers. Is suitable for growing in borders and for naturalizing in grass beneath trees and shrubs. Fully hardy. Requires partial shade and plenty of moisture. Prefers heavy soil. Plant bulbs in autumn 4–6in (10–15cm) deep. Propagate by division in late summer or by seed in autumn.
H. hispanica, syn. *Scilla campanulata, S. hispanica,* illus. p.346.
H. italica. Spring-flowering bulb. H 6–8in (15–20cm), S 2–3in (5–8cm). Zones 4–9. Produces a basal cluster of narrowly strap-shaped, semi-erect leaves. Leafless stem produces a conical spike of many flattish, star-shaped, blue flowers, ¹/₂in (1cm) across.
H. non-scriptus, syn. *Scilla non-scripta,* illus. p.346.

HYACINTHUS (Liliaceae)
Hyacinth
Genus of bulbs, grown for their dense spikes of fragrant, tubular flowers; is ideal for spring bedding displays and for pot cultivation indoors. Frost hardy. Needs an open, sunny situation or partial shade and well-drained soil. Plant in autumn. For winter flowers, force large-size, specially 'treated' bulbs of *H. orientalis* cultivars by potting in early autumn, then keep cool and damp for several weeks to ensure adequate root systems develop. When shoot tips are visible, move into max. 50°F (10°C) at first, raising temperature as more shoot appears and giving as much light as possible. After forcing, keep in a cool place to finish growth, then plant out to recover. Propagate by offsets in late summer or early autumn.
H. amethystinus. See *Brimeura amethystina.*
H. azureus. See *Muscari azureum.*
H. orientalis **'City of Haarlem'** illus. p.363. **'Delft Blue'** illus. p.362. **'Jan Bos'** illus. p.359. **'L'Innocence'** is a clump-forming, winter- or spring-flowering bulb. H 4–8in (10–20cm), S 2¹/₂–4in (6–10cm). Zones 6–9. Has strap-shaped, channeled, semi-erect, basal leaves, forming fully only after flowering. Flower stem carries a dense, cylindrical spike of fragrant, tubular, ivory white flowers, each with 6 recurving petals. **'Ostara'** illus. p.362. **'Pink Pearl'** illus. p.358.

HYDRANGEA (Hydrangeaceae)
Genus of deciduous shrubs and deciduous or evergreen, root climbers, grown for their mainly domed or flattened flower heads. Each head usually consists of masses of small, inconspicuous, fertile flowers, surrounded by or mixed with much larger, sterile flowers bearing showy, petal-like sepals. However, in some forms, all or most of the flowers are sterile. Fully to frost hardy. Prefers sun or semi-shade and fertile, moist but well-drained soil. Requires more shade in dry areas. Propagate by softwood cuttings in summer.
H. anomala subsp. *petiolaris,* syn. *H. petiolaris,* illus. p.166.
H. arborescens **'Grandiflora'** illus. p.105.
H. aspera subsp. *aspera,* syn. *H. villosa,* illus. p.112. subsp. *sargentiana* is a deciduous, upright, gaunt shrub. H 8ft (2.5m), S 6ft (2m). Frost hardy, zones 7–9. Has peeling bark, stout shoots, and very large, narrowly oval, dull green leaves that are bristly and have gray down beneath. From late summer to mid-autumn bears broad heads of flowers, the inner ones small and blue or deep purple, the outer ones larger and white, sometimes flushed purplish pink.
H. heteromalla. Deciduous, arching shrub. H 15ft (5m), S 10ft (3m). Fully hardy, zones 7–9. Narrowly oval, dark green leaves turn yellow in autumn. Broad, flat, open heads of white flowers are borne in mid- and late summer, the outer ones ageing to deep pink. **'Bretschneideri'** illus. p.87.
H. involucrata. Deciduous, spreading, open shrub. H 3ft (1m), S 6ft (2m). Frost hardy, zones 7–9. Has broadly heart-shaped, bristly, green leaves. In late summer and autumn produces heads of small, blue, inner flowers that are surrounded by large, pale blue to white, outer ones. **'Hortensis'** illus. p.129.
H. macrophylla. Deciduous, bushy shrub. H 5–6ft (1.5–2m), S 6–8ft (2–2.5m). Frost hardy, zones 6–9. Has oval, toothed, glossy, light green leaves. In mid- to late summer, blue or purple flowers are produced in acid soils with a pH of up to about 5.5. In neutral or alkaline soils above this level, flowers are pink or red. White flowers are not affected by pH. Prune older shoots back to base in spring. Trim back winter-damaged growths to new growth and remove spent flower heads in spring. Is divided into 2 groups: Hortensias, which have domed, dense heads of mainly sterile flowers; and Lacecaps, which have flat, open heads, each with fertile flowers in the center and larger, sterile flowers on the outside. **'Ami Pasquier'** (Hortensia), H 2ft (60cm), S 3ft (1m), is compact, with deep crimson or blue-purple flowers. **'Blue Bonnet'** (Hortensia) and **'Blue Wave'** (Lacecap) illus. p.113. **'Générale Vicomtesse de Vibraye'** (Hortensia) illus. p.130. **'Lilacina'** (Lacecap) illus. p.112. **'Mme. E. Mouillère'** (Hortensia) has white flowers, becoming pale pink, and prefers partial shade. subsp. *serrata* (Lacecap) illus. p.135. subsp. *serrata* **'Bluebird'** (Lacecap) illus. p.136. subsp. *serrata* **'Preziosa'** (Hortensia) bears pink flowers, becoming deep crimson. **'Veitchii'** (Lacecap) illus. p.113.
H. paniculata **'Brussels Lace'** illus. p.106. **'Floribunda'** illus. p.86. **'Grandiflora'** is a deciduous, upright, open shrub. H and S 10ft (3m). Fully hardy, zones 4–8. Leaves are large, oval, and dark green. Large, conical panicles of mostly sterile, white flowers turn pink or red from late summer. Prune back hard in spring to obtain largest panicles. **'Tardiva'** has both fertile and sterile flowers from early to mid-autumn.
H. petiolaris. See *H. anomala* subsp. *petiolaris.*
H. quercifolia illus. p.106.
H. villosa. See *H. aspera* subsp. *aspera.*

HYDROCHARIS (Hydrocharitaceae)
Genus of one species of deciduous, perennial, floating water plant, grown for its foliage and flowers. Fully hardy. Requires an open, sunny position in still water. Propagate by detaching young plantlets as required.
H. morsus-ranae illus. p.372.

HYDROCLEIS. See HYDROCLEYS.

HYDROCLEYS, syn. HYDROCLEIS (Butomaceae or Limnocharitaceae)
Genus of deciduous or evergreen, annual or perennial, water plants, grown for their floating foliage and attractive flowers. Frost tender, min. 41°F (5°C). Is best grown in large aquariums and tropical pools with plenty of light. Remove fading flowers and foliage regularly. Propagate by seed when ripe or by tip cuttings year-round.
H. nymphoides illus. p.375.

HYGROPHILA (Acanthaceae)
Genus of deciduous or evergreen, perennial, submerged water plants and marsh plants, grown for their foliage. Frost tender, min. 55°F (13°C). Remove fading leaves regularly. Propagate by stem cuttings in spring or summer.
H. polysperma. Deciduous, perennial, submerged water plant. S indefinite. Zone 10. Forms spreading colonies of lance-shaped, pale green leaves on woody stems. Given water above 61°F (16°C), is evergreen. Is suitable for a tropical aquarium.

HYLOCEREUS (Cactaceae)
Genus of fast-growing, perennial cacti with freely produced aerial roots and erect, slender, climbing stems, jointed into sections. Makes successful grafting stock except in the northern United States. Frost tender, min. 52°F (11°C). Requires sun or partial shade and very well-drained soil. Propagate by stem cuttings in spring or summer.
H. undatus (Night-blooming cereus, Queen-of-the-night). Fast-growing, climbing, perennial cactus. H 3ft (1m), S indefinite. Zone 10. Bears freely branching, 3-angled, weakly spined, dark green stems, 3in (7cm) wide and jointed into sections. In summer produces flattish, white flowers, 12in (30cm) across, that last only one night.

HYLOMECON (Papaveraceae)
Genus of one species of vigorous perennial, grown for its large, cup-shaped flowers. Is good for rock gardens, borders, and woodlands but may be invasive. Fully hardy. Prefers partial shade and humus-rich, moist soil. Propagate by division in spring or by seed in autumn.
H. japonicum illus. p.290.

HYMENANTHERA (Violaceae)
Genus of evergreen shrubs, grown for their overall appearance and interest as woody members of the violet family. Frost to half hardy. Prefers full light and well-drained soil. Potted specimens should be watered freely when in full growth, moderately at other times. Propagate by seed when ripe or in spring or by semi-ripe cuttings in late summer.
H. crassifolia. Evergreen, densely twiggy shrub of irregular outline. H and S to 4ft (1.2m). Frost hardy, zones 9–10. Bears narrowly oval to oblong, leathery, green leaves. Carries tiny, bell-shaped, 5-petaled, yellow flowers in spring-summer, followed by egg-shaped, purple fruits.

HYMENOCALLIS (Amaryllidaceae)
Genus of bulbs, some of which are evergreen, grown for their fragrant flowers, somewhat like those of large daffodils. Half hardy to frost tender, min. 59°F (15°C). Needs a sheltered site, full sun or partial shade, and well-drained soil. Plant in early summer, lifting for winter in cold districts. Alternatively, grow in a heated greenhouse; reduce water in winter, without drying out completely, then repot in spring. Propagate by offsets in spring or early summer.
H. x festalis. Spring- or summer-flowering bulb with a basal leaf cluster. H to 32in (80cm), S 12–18in (30–45cm). Frost tender, zone 10. Bears strap-shaped, semi-erect leaves. Produces a head of 2–5 scented, white flowers, each 8in (20cm) across with a deep, central cup and 6 narrow, reflexed petals.
H. x macrostephana illus. p.332.
H. narcissiflora, syn. *Ismene calathina,* illus. p.351.
H. speciosa. Evergreen, winter-flowering bulb. H and S 12–18in (30–45cm). Frost tender, zone 10. Has broadly elliptic, semi-erect, basal leaves. Produces a head of 5–10 fragrant white or green-white flowers, each 8–12in (20–30cm) wide with a funnel-shaped cup and 6 long, narrow petals.
H. 'Sulphur Queen'. Spring- or summer-flowering bulb. H 24in (60cm), S 12–18in (30–45cm). Frost tender, zone 10. Bears widely strap- or lance-shaped, semi-erect, basal leaves and produces a loose head of 2–5 fragrant yellow-green flowers. Each is 6–8in (16–20cm) wide with a frilly-edged cup and 6 spreading petals.

HYMENOSPORUM (Pittosporaceae)
Genus of one species of evergreen shrub or tree, grown for its flowers and overall appearance. Frost tender, min. 41–5°F (5–7°C). Prefers full sun, though some shade is tolerated. Requires humus-rich, well-drained soil, ideally neutral to acid. Water potted specimens freely when in full growth, less at other times. Propagate by seed when ripe, in autumn, or in spring or by semi-ripe cuttings in late summer.
H. flavum (Native Australian frangipani). Evergreen, erect shrub or tree, gradually spreading with age. H 30ft (10m) or more, S 15ft (5m) or more. Zone 10. Has oval to oblong, lustrous, rich green leaves. In spring-summer bears terminal panicles of very fragrant, tubular, 5-petaled, cream flowers that age to deep sulfur yellow.

HYPERICUM (Hypericaceae)
Genus of perennials and deciduous, semi-evergreen, or evergreen sub-shrubs and shrubs, grown for their conspicuous, yellow flowers with prominent stamens. Fully to half hardy. Large species and cultivars need sun or semi-shade and fertile soil that is not too dry. Smaller types, which make good rock garden plants, do best in full sun and well-drained soil. Propagate species sub-shrubs and shrubs by softwood cuttings in summer or by seed in autumn, cultivars by softwood cuttings only in summer; perennials may be propagated by seed or division in autumn or spring. Is generally trouble-free but *H. x inodorum* 'Elstead' is susceptible to rust, which produces orange spots on leaves, and *H.* 'Hidcote' is prone to a virus that makes leaves narrow and variegated.
H. balearicum. Evergreen, compact shrub. H and S to 2ft (60cm). Frost hardy, zones 8–9. Small, oval, green leaves have wavy edges and rounded tips. Solitary large, fragrant, shallowly cup-shaped, yellow flowers are borne at stem tips above foliage from early summer to autumn.
H. beanii 'Gold Cup'. See *H. x cyathiflorum* 'Gold Cup'.
H. bellum. Semi-evergreen, arching, graceful shrub. H 3ft (1m), S 5ft (1.5m). Fully hardy, zones 7–9. Cup-shaped, golden yellow flowers are borne from mid-summer to early autumn. Shoots are red and bear oval, wavy-edged, green leaves that redden in autumn.
H. calycinum illus. p.138.
H. cerastoides, syn. *H. rhodoppeum.* Vigorous, evergreen sub-shrub with upright and arching branches. H 6in (15cm) or more, S 16–20in (40–50cm). Fully hardy, zones 6–9. Leaves are oval, hairy, and soft grayish green. In late spring and early summer produces masses of saucer-shaped, bright yellow flowers in terminal clusters. Cut back hard after flowering. Suits a large rock garden or bank.

H. coris. Evergreen, open, dome-shaped, occasionally prostrate, sub-shrub. H 6–12in (15–30cm), S 8in (20cm) or more. Frost hardy, zones 7–9. Bears long-stemmed whorls of 3 or 4 pointed-oval leaves. Produces panicles of shallowly cup-shaped, bright yellow flowers, streaked red, in summer. Suits a sheltered rock garden, protected from morning sun.
H. x cyathiflorum 'Gold Cup', syn. *H. beanii* 'Gold Cup'. Semi-evergreen, arching shrub. H and S 3ft (1m). Frost hardy, zones 8–9. Bears pinkish brown shoots, oval, dark green leaves and, from mid-summer to early autumn, large, cup-shaped, golden yellow flowers.
H. empetrifolium 'Prostratum' illus. p.326.
H. 'Hidcote' illus. p.138.
H. x inodorum 'Elstead' illus. p.138.
H. kouytchense illus. p.138.
H. x moserianum. Deciduous, arching shrub. H 12in (30cm), S 24in (60cm). Frost hardy, zones 7–9. Small, bowl-shaped, yellow flowers are produced above oval, dark green leaves from mid-summer to mid-autumn. **'Tricolor'** has leaves edged with white and pink. Prefers a sheltered position.
H. olympicum. Deciduous, upright, slightly spreading, dense sub-shrub. H 6–12in (15–30cm), S to 6in (15cm). Fully hardy, zones 6–8. Tufts of upright stems are covered in small, oval, gray-green leaves. Produces terminal clusters of up to 5 cup-shaped, bright yellow flowers in summer. **'Citrinum'** illus. p.298.
H. patulum. Evergreen or semi-evergreen, upright shrub. H and S 3ft (1m). Frost hardy, zones 7–9. Large, cup-shaped, golden yellow flowers are produced above oval, dark green leaves from mid-summer to mid-autumn.
H. reptans. Deciduous, mat-forming shrub. H 2in (5cm), S 8in (20cm), Frost hardy, zones 7–9. Oval, green leaves turn yellow or bright red in autumn. Flattish, golden yellow flowers, crimson-flushed on outside of buds and petals, appear in summer. Suits a rock garden.
H. rhodoppeum. See *H. cerastoides.*
H. 'Rowallane'. Semi-evergreen, arching shrub. H and S 5ft (1.5m). Frost hardy, zones 7–9, but is cut to ground level in severe winters. Large, bowl-shaped, deep golden yellow flowers are produced from mid-summer to mid- or late autumn. Leaves are oval and rich green.

Hypocyrta nummularia. See *Alloplectus nummularia.*
Hypocyrta radicans. See *Nematanthus gregarius.*
Hypocyrta strigillosa. See *Nematanthus strigillosus.*

HYPOESTES (Acanthaceae)
Genus of mainly evergreen perennials, shrubs, and sub-shrubs, grown for their flowers and foliage. Frost tender, min.

50°F (10°C). Grow in bright light and in well-drained soil. Water frequently in growing season, less in winter. Cut back straggly stems as required. Propagate by stem cuttings in spring or summer. *H. phyllostachya* may be treated as an annual and propagated by seed in spring.
H. aristata. Evergreen, bushy perennial or sub-shrub. H to 3ft (1m), S 2ft (60cm). Zone 10. Has oval, green leaves to 3in (8cm) long. Small, tubular, deep pink to purple flowers are produced in terminal spikes in late winter.
H. phyllostachya, syn. *H. sanguinolenta* of gardens, illus. p.221.
H. sanguinolenta of gardens. See *H. phyllostachya.*

HYPOXIS (Hypoxidaceae)
Genus of spring- or summer-flowering corms, grown for their flat, star-shaped flowers. Suits rock gardens. Frost to half hardy. Requires full sun and light, well-drained soil. Propagate by seed in autumn or spring.
H. angustifolia illus. p.365.
H. capensis, syn. *H. stellata, Spiloxene capensis.* Spring-flowering corm with a basal leaf cluster. H 4–8in (10–20cm), S 2–3in (5–8cm). Half hardy, zones 9–10. Has very slender, narrowly lance-shaped, erect leaves. Stems each produce an upward-facing flower with pointed, white or yellow petals and a purple eye.
H. stellata. See *H. capensis.*

HYPSELA (Campanulaceae)
Genus of vigorous, creeping perennials, grown for their flowers and heart-shaped leaves. Is suitable for growing as ground cover, especially in rock gardens. Frost hardy. Requires shade and moist soil. Propagate by division in spring.
H. reniformis. Vigorous, creeping, stemless perennial. H ^{3}/4in (2cm), S indefinite. Zones 7–9. Has tiny, heart-shaped, fleshy leaves and, in spring-summer, small, star-shaped, pink-and-white flowers.

HYSSOPUS (Labiatae)
Genus of perennials and semi-evergreen or deciduous shrubs, grown for their flowers, which attract bees and butterflies, and for their aromatic foliage, which has culinary and medicinal uses. May be grown as a low hedge. Fully hardy. Requires full sun and fertile, well-drained soil. Cut back hard or, if grown as a hedge, trim lightly, in spring. Propagate by softwood cuttings in summer or by seed in autumn.
H. officinalis (Hyssop) illus. p.136. subsp. *aristatus* is a semi-evergreen or deciduous, upright, dense shrub. H 2ft (60cm), S 3ft (1m). Zones 6–9. Has aromatic, narrowly lance-shaped, bright green leaves and, from mid-summer to early autumn, small, 2-lipped, densely clustered, dark blue flowers.

I

IBERIS (Cruciferae)
Genus of annuals, perennials, evergreen sub-shrubs and shrubs, grown for their flowers and excellent for rock gardens. Some species are short-lived, flowering themselves to death. Fully to half hardy. Requires sun and well-drained soil. Propagate by seed in spring, sub-shrubs and shrubs by semi-ripe cuttings in summer.
I. amara illus. p.262. **Hyacinth-flowered Series** is a group of fast-growing, upright, bushy annuals. H 12in (30cm), S 6in (15cm). Fully hardy. Has lance-shaped, green leaves and, in summer, flattish heads of large, scented, 4-petaled flowers in a variety of colors.
I. saxatilis illus. p.314.
I. sempervirens illus. p.286.
'Snowflake' is an evergreen, spreading sub-shrub. H 6–12in (15–30cm), S 18–24in (45–60cm). Fully hardy, zones 5–9. Leaves are narrowly oblong, glossy, and dark green. Dense, semi-spherical heads of 4-petaled, white flowers are borne in late spring and early summer. Trim after flowering.
I. umbellata (Globe candytuft). Fast-growing, upright, bushy annual. H 6–12in (15–30cm), S 8in (20cm). Frost tender, min. 36–9°F (2–4°C). Has lance-shaped, green leaves. Heads of small, 4-petaled, white or pale purple flowers, sometimes bicolored, are carried in summer and early autumn.
Fairy Series illus. p.266.

IDESIA (Flacourtiaceae)
Genus of one species of deciduous, summer-flowering tree, grown for its foliage and fruits. Both male and female plants are required to obtain fruits. Fully hardy. Needs sun or semi-shade and fertile, moist but well-drained soil, preferably neutral to acid. Propagate by softwood cuttings in summer or by seed in autumn.
I. polycarpa illus. p.53.

ILEX (Aquifoliaceae)
Holly
Genus of evergreen or deciduous trees and shrubs, grown for their foliage and fruits (berries). Mainly spherical berries, ranging in color from red through yellow to black, are produced in autumn, following insignificant, usually white, flowers borne in spring. Almost all plants are unisexual, and to obtain fruits on a female plant a male also needs to be grown. Fully to half hardy. All prefer well-drained soil. Grow in sun or shade, but deciduous plants and those with variegated foliage do best in sun or semi-shade. Hollies resent being transplanted, but respond well to hard pruning and pollarding, which should be carried out in late spring. Propagate by seed in spring or by semi-ripe cuttings from late summer to early winter. Holly leaf

miner and holly aphid may cause problems.
I. × altaclerensis (Highclere holly). Group of vigorous, evergreen shrubs and trees. Frost hardy, zones 7–9. Is resistant to pollution and coastal exposure.
'Balearica' (illus. p.70) is an erect, female tree. H 40ft (12m), S 15ft (5m). Has green to olive green, young branches. Large, broadly oval leaves are spiny- or smooth-edged and glossy, dark green. Freely produces large, bright red berries.
'Belgica' (illus. p.70) is an erect, dense, female tree. H 40ft (12m), S 15ft (5m). Young branches are green to yellowish green. Has large, lance-shaped to oblong, spiny- or smooth-edged, glossy, green leaves. Large, orange-red fruits are freely produced.
'Belgica Aurea' (syn. *I. × a.* 'Silver Sentinel', *I. perado* 'Aurea'; illus. p.71) is an upright, female tree. H 25ft (8m), S 10ft (3m). Young branches are green with yellow streaks. Produces large, lance-shaped, mainly spineless, dark green leaves that are mottled with gray-green and irregularly edged with yellow. Red berries are produced only rarely.
'Camelliifolia' (illus. p.70) is a narrow, pyramidal, female tree. H 46ft (14m), S 10ft (3m). Has purple, young branches and large, oblong, mainly smooth-edged, glossy, dark green leaves. Reliably produces large, scarlet fruits; makes an excellent specimen tree.
'Camelliifolia Variegata' (illus. p.71). H 25ft (8m), S 10ft (3m). Is similar to *I. × a.* 'Camelliifolia', but leaves have broad, yellow margins.
'Golden King' is a bushy, female shrub. H 20ft (6m), S 15ft (5m). Young branches are green with a purplish flush. Has large, oblong to oval, sometimes slightly spiny, dark green leaves, each splashed with gray-green in the center and with a bright yellow margin that turns to cream on older leaves. Is not a good fruiter, bearing only a few reddish brown berries, but is excellent as a hedge or a specimen plant.
'Hodginsii' is a vigorous, dense, male tree. H 46ft (14m), S 30ft (10m). Shoots are purple; leaves are broadly oval, sparsely spiny, and glossy, blackish green.
'Lawsoniana' (illus. p.70) is a bushy, female shrub. H 20ft (6m), S 15ft (5m). Is similar to *I. × a.* 'Golden King', but has leaves splashed irregularly in the center with gold and lighter green. Foliage tends to revert to plain green.
'N.F. Barnes' (illus. p.70) is a dense, female shrub. H 18ft (5.5m), S 12ft (4m). Has purple shoots and oval, mainly entire but spine-tipped, glossy, dark green leaves and red berries.
'Silver Sentinel' see *I. × a.* 'Belgica Aurea'.

'Wilsonii' is a vigorous, female tree. H 25ft (8m), S 15ft (5m). Has purplish green, young branches and large, oblong to oval, glossy, green leaves with prominent veins and large spines. Freely produces large, scarlet fruits and makes a good hedging or specimen plant.
I. aquifolium (English holly; illus. p.70). Evergreen, much-branched, usually erect shrub or tree. H 70ft (20m), S 20ft (6m). Frost hardy, zones 7–9. Has variably shaped, wavy, sharply spined, glossy, dark green leaves and bright red berries.
'Argentea Longifolia' is a spreading, male tree. H 30ft (10m), S 20ft (6m). Shoots are purplish green. Narrowly oval, spiny, dark green leaves, narrowly edged with creamy white, are pink-tinged when young.
'Argentea Marginata' (Silver-margined holly; illus. p.70) is a columnar, female tree. H 46ft (14m), S 15ft (5m). Young branches are green, streaked with cream. Broadly oval, spiny, dark green leaves, with wide, cream margins, are shrimp pink when young. Bears an abundance of bright red berries. Is good for hedging or as a specimen plant.
'Argentea Marginata Pendula' (Perry's weeping silver; illus. p.70) is a slow-growing, weeping, female tree. H 20ft (6m), S 15ft (5m). Has purple, young branches and broadly oval, spiny, dark green leaves, mottled with gray-green and broadly edged with cream. Bears red fruits. Makes a good specimen plant for a small garden.
'Atlas' is an erect, male shrub. H 15ft (5m), S 10ft (3m). Has green, young branches and oval, spiny, glossy, dark green leaves. Is useful for landscaping and hedging.
'Aurifodina' (illus. p.71) is an erect, dense, female shrub. H 20ft (6m), S 10ft (3m). Young branches are purplish. Oval, spiny leaves are olive green with golden yellow margins that turn tawny yellow in winter. Produces a good crop of deep scarlet berries.
f. *bacciflava* is a much-branched, usually erect shrub or tree. H 70ft (20m), S 20ft (6m). Has variably shaped, wavy, sharply spined, glossy, dark green leaves and yellow fruits.
'Crispa Aurea Picta' (illus. p.71) is a male tree of open habit. H 30ft (10m), S 20ft (6m). Narrowly oval, twisted, sparsely spiny, blackish green leaves are centrally blotched with golden yellow. Foliage tends to revert to plain green.
'Elegantissima' (illus. p.71) is a bushy, dense, compact, male shrub. H 20ft (6m), S 15ft (5m). Young branches are green, streaked with yellow. Small, oval, spiny, bright green leaves, with cream margins, are bright pink when young.
'Ferox' (Hedgehog holly) is an open, male shrub. H 20ft (6m), S 12ft (4m). Has purple, young branches and

oval, dark green leaves with spines over entire leaf surface.
'Ferox Argentea' (Silver hedgehog holly) is similar to *I.a.* 'Ferox', but has leaves with cream margins.
'Flavescens' (Moonlight holly) is a columnar, female shrub. H 20ft (6m), S 15ft (5m). Young branches are purplish red. Variably shaped leaves are dark green with a yellowish flush, when young, that will last year-round when grown in good light. Produces plentiful, red berries.
'Golden Milkboy' is a dense, male shrub. H 20ft (6m), S 12ft (4m). Has purplish green, young branches and oval, very spiny, bright green leaves with heavily blotched, bright yellow centers. Leaves tend to revert to plain green.
'Golden Queen' is a dense tree that, despite its name, is male. H 30ft (10m), S 20ft (6m). Broadly oval, very spiny, green leaves are edged with golden yellow.
'Golden Van Tol', a sport of *I.a.* 'J.C. Van Tol', is an upright, female shrub. H 12ft (4m), S 10ft (3m). Young branches are purple. Oval, puckered, slightly spiny, dark green leaves have irregular, clear yellow margins. Bears a sparse crop of red fruits. Is good for hedging or as a specimen plant.
'Handsworth New Silver' is a dense, columnar, female shrub. H 25ft (8m), S 15ft (5m). Branches are purple. Oblong to oval, spiny, dark green leaves have broad, cream margins. Bears a profusion of bright red fruits. Is excellent as a hedge or specimen plant and is good for a small garden.
'Hascombensis' is a slow-growing, dense shrub of unknown sex. H 5ft (1.5m), S 3–4ft (1–1.2m). Has purplish green, young branches and small, oval, spiny, dark green leaves. Does not produce berries. Is useful for a rock garden.
'J.C. Van Tol' is an open, female shrub that does not require cross-fertilization to produce fruits. H 20ft (6m), S 12ft (4m). Branches are dark purple when young. Oval, puckered, slightly spiny leaves are dark green. Produces a good crop of red berries. Is useful as a hedge or for a tub.
'Mme. Briot' (illus. p.71) is a vigorous, bushy, female tree. H 30ft (10m), S 15ft (5m). Young branches are purplish green. Leaves are large, broadly oval, spiny, and dark green with bright golden borders. Bears scarlet berries.
'Ovata Aurea' (illus. p.71) is a dense, male shrub. H 15ft (5m), S 12ft (4m). Has reddish brown, young branches and oval, regularly spiny, dark green leaves with bright golden margins.
'Pyramidalis' (illus. p.70) is a dense, female tree that does not require cross-fertilization to produce

fruits. H 20ft (6m), S 15ft (5m). Has green, young branches and narrowly elliptic, slightly spiny, green leaves. Produces masses of scarlet fruits. Is suitable for a small garden.

'Pyramidalis Aurea Marginata' (illus. p.71) is an upright, female shrub. H 20ft (6m), S 15ft (5m). Young branches are green. Has narrowly elliptic, green leaves with prominent, golden margins and spines on upper half. Bears a large crop of red berries.

'Pyramidalis Fructu Luteo' is a conical, female shrub that broadens with age. H 20ft (6m), S 12ft (4m). Branches are green when young. Has oval, often spineless, dark green leaves and bears yellow berries. Is excellent for a small garden.

'Scotica' (illus. p.70) is a large, stiff, compact, female shrub. H 20ft (6m), S 12ft (4m). Oval, usually spineless, glossy, very dark green leaves are slightly twisted. Bears red fruits.

'Silver Milkboy' see *I.a.* 'Silver Milkmaid'.

'Silver Milkmaid' (syn. *I.a.* 'Silver Milkboy'; illus. p.70) is a dense, female shrub. H 18ft (5.5m), S 12ft (4m). Oval, wavy-edged, very spiny leaves are bronze when young, maturing to bright green, each with a central, creamy white blotch, but tend to revert to plain green. Produces an abundance of scarlet berries. Makes a very attractive specimen plant.

'Silver Queen' (illus. p.71) is a dense shrub that, despite its name, is male. H 15ft (5m), S 12ft (4m). Has purple, young branches. Oval, spiny leaves, pink when young, mature to very dark green, almost black, with broad, cream edging.

'Watereriana' (Waterer's gold holly; illus. p.71) is a dense, male bush. H and S 15ft (5m). Young branches are green, streaked with yellow. Oval, spiny- or smooth-edged leaves are grayish green, with broad, golden margins. Is best grown as a specimen plant.

I. × *aquipernyi* (illus. p.70). Evergreen, upright shrub. H 15ft (5m), S 10ft (3m). Frost hardy, zones 7–9. Has small, oval, spiny, glossy, dark green leaves with long tips. Berries are large and red.

I. chinensis (illus. p.71). Evergreen, upright tree. H 40ft (12m), S 20ft (6m). Half hardy, zone 10. Oval, thin-textured, glossy, dark green leaves have rounded teeth. Lavender flowers are followed by egg-shaped, glossy, scarlet fruits.

I. ciliospinosa (illus. p.70). Evergreen, upright shrub or tree. H 20ft (6m), S 12ft (4m). Frost hardy, zones 6–9. Has small, oval, weak-spined, dull green leaves and red berries.

I. cornuta (Chinese holly, Horned holly). Evergreen, dense, rounded shrub. H 12ft (4m), S 15ft (5m). Frost hardy, zones 7–9. Rectangular, dull green leaves are spiny except on older bushes. Produces large, red berries. **'Burfordii'** (illus. p.70) is female, S 8ft (2.5m), has glossy leaves with only a terminal spine and bears a profusion of fruits. **'Rotunda'**, H 6ft (2m), S 4ft

(1.2m), is also female and produces a small crop of fruits; is useful for a tub or small garden.

I. crenata (Box-leaved holly, Japanese holly). Evergreen, spreading shrub or tree. H 15ft (5m), S 10ft (3m). Fully hardy, zones 6–8. Has very small, oval, dark green leaves with rounded teeth. Bears glossy, black fruits. Is useful for landscaping or as hedging.

'Bullata' see *I.c.* 'Convexa'.

'Convexa' (syn. *I.c.* 'Bullata'; illus. p.70) is a dense, female shrub. H 8ft (2.5m), S 4–5ft (1.2–1.5m). Has purplish green, young branches and oval, puckered, glossy leaves. Bears glossy, black fruits.

'Helleri' (illus. p.70) is a spreading, female shrub. H 4ft (1.2m), S 3–4ft (1–1.2m). Has green, young branches and oval leaves with few spines. Has glossy, black fruits. Is much used for landscaping.

'Latifolia' (illus. p.70) is a spreading to erect, female shrub or tree. H 20ft (6m), S 10ft (3m). Young branches are green and broadly oval leaves have tiny teeth. Produces glossy, black berries.

var. *paludosa* (illus. p.70) is a prostrate shrub or tree. H 6–12in (15–30cm), S indefinite. Has very small, oval, dark green leaves with rounded teeth. Bears glossy, black fruits.

'Variegata' (illus. p.71) is an open, male shrub. H 12ft (4m), S 8ft (2.5m). Oval leaves are spotted or blotched with yellow, but tend to revert to plain green.

I. dipyrena (Himalayan holly). Evergreen, dense, upright tree. H 40ft (12m), S 25ft (8m). Frost hardy, zones 7–9. Elliptic, dull green leaves are spiny when young, later smooth-edged. Bears large, red fruits.

I. fargesii (illus. p.70). Evergreen, broadly conical tree or shrub. H 20ft (6m), S 15ft (5m). Frost hardy, zones 7–9. Has green or purple shoots and oval, small-toothed, mid- to dark green leaves. Produces red berries. var. *brevifolia* (illus. p.70), H 12ft (4m), is oval and rounded.

I. georgei. Evergreen, compact shrub. H 15ft (5m), S 12ft (4m). Half hardy, zones 9–10. Has small, lance-shaped or oval, weak-spined, glossy, dark green leaves with long tips. Berries are red.

I. glabra (Inkberry). Evergreen, dense, upright shrub. H 8ft (2.5m), S 6ft (2m). Fully hardy, zones 5–9. Small, oblong to oval, dark green leaves are smooth-edged or may have slight teeth near tips. Produces black fruits.

I. insignis. See *I. kingiana.*

I. integra. Evergreen, dense, bushy shrub or tree. H 20ft (6m), S 15ft (5m). Frost hardy, zones 7–9. Has oval, blunt-tipped, bright green leaves with smooth edges. Bears large, deep red berries.

I. **'Jermyns Dwarf'.** See *I. pernyi* 'Jermyns Dwarf'.

I. kingiana, syn. *I. insignis.* Evergreen, upright tree. H 20ft (6m), S 12ft (4m). Half hardy, zones 9–10. Very large, oblong, leathery, dark green leaves have small spines. Berries are bright red.

I. × *koehneana* (illus. p.70). Evergreen, conical shrub. H 20ft (6m), S 15ft (5m). Fully hardy, zones 7–9. Young branches are green. Has very large, oblong, spiny, green leaves and red fruits.

I. laevigata (Smooth winterberry). Deciduous, spreading shrub. H 8ft (2.5m), S 6ft (2m). Fully hardy, zones 5–8. Oval, finely toothed leaves are pale green and berries are orange-red.

I. latifolia (Lusterleaf holly). Evergreen, upright shrub. H 20ft (6m), S 15ft (5m). Half hardy, zones 7–9. Has stout, olive green, young branches, very large, oblong, dark green leaves with short spines, and plentiful, red fruits.

I. macrocarpa (illus. p.70). Deciduous, upright tree. H 30ft (10m), S 20ft (6m). Frost hardy, zones 7–9. Has large, oval, saw-toothed, green leaves and very large, black berries.

I. × *meserveae* (Blue holly). Group of vigorous, evergreen, dense shrubs. Fully hardy, zones 4–8, but does not thrive in a maritime climate. Has oval, glossy, greenish blue leaves. **'Blue Princess'** (illus. p.70), H 10ft (3m), S 4ft (1.2m), is female and has purplish green, young branches, small, oval, wavy, spiny leaves, and an abundance of red fruits.

I. opaca (American holly; illus. p.70). Evergreen, erect tree. H 46ft (14m), S 4ft (1.2m). Fully hardy, zones 6–9, but does not thrive in a maritime climate. Oval leaves are dull green above, yellow-green beneath, and spiny- or smooth-edged. Has red fruits.

I. pedunculosa (Long-stalk holly; illus. p.71). Evergreen, upright shrub or tree. H 30ft (10m), S 20ft (6m). Fully hardy, zones 6–9. Oval, dark green leaves are smooth-edged. Bright red berries are borne on very long stalks.

I. perado **'Aurea'.** See *I.* × *altaclerensis* 'Belgica Aurea'.

I. pernyi (illus. p.70). Slow-growing, evergreen, stiff shrub. H 25ft (8m), S 12ft (4m). Fully hardy, zones 7–9. Has pale green, young branches and small, oblong, spiny, dark green leaves. Produces red berries. **'Jermyns Dwarf'** (syn. *I.* 'Jermyns Dwarf'), H 2ft (60cm), S 4ft (1.2m), is low-growing and female, with glossy, very spiny leaves.

I. serrata. Deciduous, bushy shrub. H 12ft (4m), S 8ft (2.5m). Fully hardy, zones 6–9. Small, oval, finely toothed, bright green leaves are downy when young. Pink flowers are followed by small, red fruits. f. *leucocarpa* (illus. p.71) bears white berries.

I. verticillata (Winterberry; illus. p.70). Deciduous, dense, suckering shrub. H 6ft (2m), S 4–5ft (1.2–1.5m). Fully hardy, zones 4–9. Young branches are purplish green. Produces oval or lance-shaped, saw-toothed, bright green leaves. Bears a profusion of long-lasting, red berries, which remain on bare branches during winter.

I. yunnanensis. Evergreen, spreading to erect shrub. H 12ft (4m), S 8ft (2.5m). Frost hardy, zones 7–9. Has downy branches. Small, oval leaves, with rounded teeth, are brownish green when young, glossy, dark green in maturity. Produces red berries.

ILLICIUM (Illiciaceae)

Genus of evergreen, spring- to early summer-flowering trees and shrubs, grown for their foliage and unusual flowers. Frost to half hardy. Does best in semi-shade or shade and moist, neutral to acid soil. Propagate by semi-ripe cuttings in summer.

I. anisatum (Japanese anisatum, Japanese anise). Slow-growing, evergreen, conical tree or shrub. H and S 20ft (6m). Frost hardy, zones 7–9. Produces oval, aromatic, glossy, dark green leaves. Star-shaped, greenish yellow flowers, with numerous narrow petals, are carried in mid-spring.

I. floridanum (Florida anise). Evergreen, bushy shrub. H and S 6ft (2m). Half hardy, zones 7–9. Lance-shaped, leathery, deep green leaves are very aromatic. Star-shaped, red or purplish red flowers, with numerous narrow petals, are produced in late spring and early summer.

IMPATIENS (Balsaminaceae)

Genus of annuals and mainly evergreen perennials and sub-shrubs, all grown as annuals, often with succulent but brittle stems. In cold climates some may be herbaceous. Half hardy to frost tender, min. 50°F (10°C). Prefers sun or semi-shade and moist but not waterlogged soil. Propagate by seed or by stem cuttings in spring or summer. Red spider mite, aphids, and whitefly may cause problems in greenhouses.

I. balsamina illus. p.264. **'Blackberry Ice'** is a fast-growing, upright, bushy annual. H 18–24in (45–60cm), S 18in (45cm). Half hardy to frost tender, min. 36–9°F (2–4°C). Has lance-shaped, pale green leaves and, in summer and early autumn, large, double, white flowers, splashed with purple.

I., **Confection Series** illus. p.271.

I., **Duet Series.** Group of fast-growing, evergreen, bushy perennials, grown as annuals. H and S 12in (30cm). Half hardy. Has oval, fresh green leaves. From spring to autumn produces flattish, spurred, semi-double and double flowers, in shades of red and orange, suffused with white.

I. niamniamensis. Evergreen, bushy perennial, uncommon in cultivation. H to 2ft (60cm), S 1ft (30cm). Frost tender. Has reddish green stems and oval, toothed leaves to 8in (20cm) long. Showy, 5-petaled, yellowish green flowers, 1in (2.5cm) long and each with a red, orange, red, crimson, or purple spur, appear in summer-autumn. **'Congo Cockatoo'** has red, green, and yellow flowers.

I., **Novette Series.** Group of fast-growing, evergreen, bushy perennials, grown as annuals. H and S 6in (15cm). Half hardy to frost tender, min. 36–9°F (2–4°C). Oval leaves are fresh green. Flattish, 5-petaled, spurred flowers, in a mixture of colors, are borne from spring to autumn (red, illus. p.271; salmon, illus. p.265). **'Red Star'** illus. p.271.

I. oliveri. See *I. sodenii.*

I. repens illus. p.248.

I., **Rosette Series** illus. p.269.

I. sodenii, syn. *I. oliveri.* Evergreen, strong-growing, bushy perennial. H

4ft (1.2m) or more, S 2ft (60cm). Frost tender. Narrowly oval, toothed leaves, in whorls of 4–10, are 6in (15cm) or more long. Bears almost flat, white or pale pink to mauve flowers, 2in (5cm) or more wide, in autumn-winter.
I. sultanii. See *I. walleriana.*
I., **Super Elfin Series.** Group of fast-growing, evergreen, bushy perennials, grown as annuals. H and S 8in (20cm). Half hardy to frost tender, min. 36–9°F (2–4°C). Has oval, fresh green leaves and, from spring to autumn, flattish, 5-petaled, spurred flowers in mixed colors. **'Lipstick'** illus. p.270.
I., **Tom Thumb Series.** Group of fast-growing, evergreen, bushy perennials, grown as annuals. H and S 8–12in (20–30cm). Half hardy. Has oval, fresh green leaves and, from spring to autumn, 3in (8cm) wide, rounded, spurred, double flowers in shades of red, purple, pink, or white.
I. walleriana, syn. *I. sultanii.* Fast-growing, evergreen, bushy perennial, usually grown as an annual. H and S to 2ft (60cm). Half hardy. Has oval, fresh green leaves. Flattish, 5-petaled, spurred, bright red flowers appear from spring to autumn.

INCARVILLEA (Bignoniaceae)
Genus of late spring- or summer-flowering perennials, suitable for rock gardens and borders. Fully to frost hardy, but protect crowns with bracken or compost in winter. Requires sun and fertile, well-drained soil. Propagate by seed in autumn or spring.
I. delavayi illus. p.237.
I. mairei illus. p.237. **'Frank Ludlow'** is a compact, clump-forming perennial. H and S 12in (30cm). Fully hardy, zones 7–8. Short stems bear trumpet-shaped, rich deep pink flowers in early summer. Divided leaves consist of up to 4 pairs of narrowly oval, dark green leaflets.

INDIGOFERA (Leguminosae)
Genus of perennials and deciduous shrubs, grown for their foliage and small, pealike flowers. Fully to frost hardy; in cold areas, hard frosts may cut plants to ground, but they usually regrow from base in spring. Needs full sun and fertile, well-drained soil. Cut out dead wood in spring. Propagate by softwood cuttings in summer or by seed in autumn.
I. decora. Deciduous, bushy shrub. H 18in (45cm), S 3ft (1m). Frost hardy, zones 7–9. Glossy, dark green leaves each have 7–13 oval leaflets. Long spikes of pink or white flowers appear from mid- to late summer.
I. dielsiana illus. p.130.
I. gerardiana. See *I. heterantha.*
I. heterantha, syn. *I. gerardiana,* illus. p.109.
I. pseudotinctoria. Deciduous, arching shrub. H 3ft (1m) or more, S 6ft (2m). Fully hardy, zones 6–9. Dark green leaves consist of oval leaflets, usually 7–9 to each leaf. Bears small, pale pink flowers in long, dense racemes from mid-summer to early autumn.

INULA (Compositae)
Genus of summer-flowering, clump-forming, sometimes rhizomatous

perennials. Fully hardy. Needs sun and any well-drained soil. Propagate by seed or division in spring or autumn.
I. acaulis. Tuft-forming, rhizomatous perennial. H 2–4in (5–10cm), S 6in (15cm). Zones 4–8. Has lance-shaped to elliptic, hairy leaves. Solitary almost stemless, daisylike, golden yellow flower heads are produced in summer. Is good for a rock garden.
I. ensifolia illus. p.248.
I. hookeri illus. p.215.
I. magnifica illus. p.191.
I. oculis-christi. Spreading, rhizomatous perennial. H 18in (45cm), S 24in (60cm). Zones 4–8. Stems each bear 2 or 3 daisylike, yellow flower heads which appear in summer. Has lance-shaped to elliptic, hairy, green leaves.

IOCHROMA (Solanaceae)
Genus of evergreen shrubs, grown for their flowers. Frost tender, min. 45–50°F (7–10°C). Needs full light or partial shade and fertile, well-drained soil. Water potted plants freely when in full growth, moderately at other times. Tip prune young plants to stimulate a bushy habit. Cut back flowered stems by half in late winter. Propagate by greenwood or semi-ripe cuttings in summer. Whitefly and red spider mite are sometimes troublesome.
I. cyaneum, syn. *I. tubulosum,* illus. p.118.
I. tubulosum. See *I. cyaneum.*

IONOPSIDIUM (Cruciferae)
Genus of annuals. Only one species is usually cultivated: this is suitable for rock gardens and as edging. Fully to frost hardy. Grow in semi-shade and in fertile, well-drained soil. Propagate by seed sown outdoors in spring, early summer, or early autumn.
I. acaule (Violet cress). Fast-growing, upright annual. H 2–3in (5–8cm), S 1in (2.5cm). Fully hardy. Rounded leaves are green. Tiny, 4-petaled, lilac or white flowers, flushed with deep blue, are produced in summer and early autumn.

IPHEION (Liliaceae)
Genus of bulbs that freely produce many star-shaped, blue, white, or yellow flowers in spring and make excellent pot plants in cold greenhouses. Frost hardy. Prefers a sheltered situation in dappled sunlight and well-drained soil. Plant in autumn; after flowering, dies down for summer. Propagate by offsets in late summer or early autumn.
I. uniflorum **'Froyle Mill'** illus. p.360. **'Wisley Blue'** is a spring-flowering bulb. H 4–6in (10–15cm), S 2–3in (5–8cm). Zones 6–9. Bears linear, semi-erect, basal, pale green leaves, which smell of onions if damaged. Leafless stems each produce an upward-facing, pale blue flower, 1¼–1½in (3–4cm) across.

IPOMOEA, syn. PHARBITIS (Convolvulaceae)
Genus of mainly evergreen shrubs, perennials, annuals, and soft- or woody-stemmed, twining climbers.

Half hardy to frost tender, min. 45–50°F (7–10°C). Provide humus-rich, well-drained soil and full light. Water freely when in full growth, less at other times. Support is needed. Thin out or cut back congested growth in spring. Propagate by seed in spring or by softwood or semi-ripe cuttings in summer. Whitefly and red spider mite may cause problems.
I. alba, syn. *I. bona-nox, Calonyction aculeatum* (Moon flower). Evergreen, soft-stemmed, twining climber with prickly stems that exude milky juice when cut. H 22ft (7m) or more. Frost tender, min. 50°F (10°C), zone 10. Oval or sometimes 3-lobed leaves are 8in (20cm) long. Fragrant, tubular, white flowers, to 6in (15cm) long and expanded at the mouths to 6in (15cm) across, open at night in summer.
I. bona-nox. See *I. alba.*
I. coccinea, syn. *Quamoclit coccinea* (Red morning-glory, Star ipomoea). Annual, twining climber. H to 10ft (3m). Frost tender, min. 50°F (10°C), zone 10. Arrow- or heart-shaped leaves are long-pointed and often toothed. Fragrant, tubular, scarlet flowers, with yellow throats and expanded mouths, are borne in late summer and autumn.
I. hederacea illus. p.172.
I. horsfalliae illus. p.167. **'Briggsii'** is a strong-growing, evergreen, woody-stemmed, twining climber. H 6–10ft (2–3m). Frost tender, min. 45–50°F (7–10°C), zone 10. Has leaves with 5–7 radiating lobes or leaflets. Stalked clusters of funnel-shaped, deep rose-pink or rose-purple flowers are produced from summer to winter; flowers are larger and more richly colored than those of the species.
I. imperialis. See *I. nil.*
I. x multifida, syn. *I. x sloteri* (Cardinal climber, Hearts-and-honey vine). Annual, twining climber. H 10ft (3m). Frost tender, min. 50°F (10°C), zone 10. Triangular-oval leaves are divided into 7–15 segments. Tubular, wide-mouthed, crimson flowers with white eyes appear in summer.
I. nil, syn. *I. imperialis.* **'Early Call'** is a short-lived, soft-stemmed, perennial, twining climber with hairy stems, best grown as an annual. H to 12ft (4m). Half hardy, zone 10. Leaves are heart-shaped or 3-lobed. From summer to early autumn bears large, funnel-shaped flowers in a range of colors, with white tubes. **'Scarlett O'Hara'** has deep red flowers.
I. purpurea, syn. *Convolvulus purpureus* (Common morning-glory). Short-lived, soft-stemmed, perennial, twining climber, best grown as an annual, with hairy stems. H to 15ft (5m). Half hardy, zone 10. Leaves are heart-shaped or 3-lobed. From summer to early autumn has funnel-shaped, deep purple to bluish purple or reddish flowers with white throats and bristly sepals.
I. quamoclit, syn. *Quamoclit pinnata,* illus. p.168.
I. rubrocaerulea **'Heavenly Blue'.** See *Convolvulus tricolor* 'Heavenly Blue'.
I. x sloteri. See *I. x multifida.*
I. tuberosa. See *Merremia tuberosa.*
I. versicolor. See *Mina lobata.*

IPOMOPSIS (Polemoniaceae)
Genus of perennials and biennials, often grown as pot plants for greenhouses and conservatories. Fully to half hardy. Grow in cool, airy conditions with bright light and in fertile, well-drained soil. Propagate by seed sown in a greenhouse in early spring or early summer.
I. aggregata. Slow-growing biennial with upright, slender, hairy stems. H to 3ft (1m), S 1ft (30cm). Fully hardy. Leaves are divided into linear leaflets. Fragrant, trumpet-shaped flowers borne in summer are usually brilliant red, sometimes spotted yellow, but may be rose, yellow, or white.

IRESINE (Amaranthaceae)
Genus of perennials, grown for their colorful leaves. Frost tender, min. 50–59°F (10–15°C). Needs a good, loamy, well-drained soil and bright light to retain leaf color. Pinch out tips in growing season to obtain bushy plants. Propagate by stem cuttings in spring.
I. herbstii (Beefsteak plant). Bushy perennial. H to 2ft (60cm), S 18in (45cm). Zone 10. Has red stems and rounded, purplish red leaves, notched at their tips and 4in (10cm) long, with paler or yellowish red veins. Flowers are insignificant. **'Aureo-reticulata'** illus. p.261.
I. lindenii (Bloodleaf). Bushy perennial. H 2ft (60cm), S 18in (45cm). Zone 10. Has lance-shaped, dark red leaves, 2–4in (5–10cm) long. Flowers are insignificant.

IRIS (Iridaceae)
Genus of upright, rhizomatous or bulbous (occasionally fleshy-rooted) perennials, some of which are evergreen, grown for their distinctive and colorful flowers. Each flower has 3 usually large "falls" (pendent or semi-pendent petals), which in a number of species have conspicuous beards or crests; 3 generally smaller "standards" (erect, horizontal, or, occasionally, pendent petals); and a 3-branched style. In many irises the style branches are petal-like. Unless otherwise stated below, flower stems are unbranched. Green, then brown seed pods are ellipsoid to cylindrical and often ribbed. Is suitable for borders, rock gardens, woodlands, watersides, bog gardens, alpine houses, cold frames, and containers. Species and cultivars described are fully hardy unless otherwise stated, but some groups may thrive only in the specific growing conditions mentioned below. Propagate species by division of rhizomes or offsets in late summer or by seed in autumn, named cultivars by division only. Botanically, irises are divided into a number of Subgenera and Sections. It is convenient for horticultural purposes to use some of these botanical names for groups of irises, with similar characteristics, that require comparable cultural treatment.

Rhizomatous
These irises have rhizomes as rootstocks; leaves are sword-shaped and usually in a basal fan.

Bearded irises are rhizomatous and have "beards," consisting of many often colored hairs, along the center of each fall. The group covers the vast majority of irises, including many named cultivars, grown in gardens; all are derived from *I. pallida* and related species. Bearded irises thrive in fairly rich, well-drained, preferably slightly alkaline soil in full sun. Some are very tolerant and will grow and flower reasonably in poorer soil in partial shade. All those listed are hardy in zones 4–9. For horticultural purposes, various groupings of hybrid, bearded irises are recognized, based on the height of the plants in flower, the flower size, and flowering season. These include **Miniature Dwarf**, H to 8in (20cm), flowering season early to mid-spring, flower size 2–3in (5–7.5cm); **Standard Dwarf**, H 8–16in (20–40cm), flowering season mid- to late spring, flower width 2–4in (5–10cm); **Intermediate**, H 16–28in (40–70cm), flowering season late spring to early summer, flower width 3½–5in (9–12.5cm); **Miniature Tall**, H 16–25in (40–63cm), flowering season early summer, flower height and width 6in (15cm); **Border**, H 16–28in (40–70cm), flowering season early summer, flower width 4–5in (10–13cm); and **Standard Tall**, H over 28in (70cm), flowering season early summer, flower width over 6in (15cm). **Oncocyclus** irises are rhizomatous, with very large and often bizarrely colored flowers, one to each stem, that have bearded falls. They require sharply drained but fairly rich soil, full sun, and, after flowering, a dry period of dormancy in summer and early autumn. All those listed are hardy in zones 8–9. Difficult to cultivate successfully, they are best grown in an alpine house or covered frame in climates subject to summer rains. **Regelia** irises are closely related to Oncocyclus irises, differing in having bearded standards as well as falls and in having 2 flowers to each stem. They require similar conditions of cultivation, although a few species, such as *I. hoogiana*, have proved easier to grow than Oncocyclus irises. Hybrids between the 2 groups have been raised and are known as **Regeliocyclus** irises.

Beardless irises, also rhizomatous, lack hairs on the falls; most have very similar cultural requirements to bearded irises but some prefer heavier soil. Various groupings are recognized, of which the following are the most widely known. **Pacific Coast** irises, a group of Californian species and their hybrids, prefer acid to neutral soil and grow well in sun or partial shade, appreciating some humus in the soil; they are hardy in zones 4–9 and are best grown from seed as they resent being moved. **Spuria** irises (*I. spuria* and its relatives) grow in sun or semi-shade and well-drained but moist soil; they are hardy in zones 5–9. A number of species and hybrids prefers moist, waterside conditions; these include the well-known **Siberian** irises (*I. sibirica* and its relatives), hardy in zones 4–9,

and the **Japanese** water irises such as *I. ensata* and *I. laevigata*, which may also be grown as border plants, but succeed best in humus-rich, moist, open, sunny sites, and are hardy in zones 5–9. **Crested** irises, also rhizomatous, have ridges, or cockscomblike crests, instead of beards. They include the **Evansia** irises, with often widely spreading, creeping stolons. Most have very similar cultivation requirements to bearded irises but some prefer damp, humus-rich conditions; a few are half hardy to frost tender, min. 41°F (5°C). Those listed are hardy in zones 8–9, except where otherwise stated.

Bulbous
These irises are distinguished by having bulbs as storage organs, sometimes with thickened, fleshy roots, and leaves that are either, lance-shaped and channeled, 4-sided (more or less square in cross section), or almost cylindrical, rather than flat and usually sword-shaped like the leaves of the rhizomatous irises.

Xiphium irises include the commonly grown Spanish, English, and Dutch irises, which are excellent both for garden decoration and as cut flowers. All are easy to cultivate in sunny, well-drained sites, preferring slightly alkaline conditions, but also growing well on acid soil. All are hardy in zones 5–8. **Spanish** irises are derived from *I. xiphium*, which is variable in flower color, from blue and violet to yellow and white, and produces its channeled leaves in autumn. **English** irises have been produced from *I. latifolia*, which varies from blue to violet (occasionally white) and produces its channeled leaves in spring. **Dutch** irises are hybrids of *I. xiphium*, the related pale to deep blue *I. tingitana*, and *I. latifolia*. They are extremely variable in flower color.

Juno irises have bulbs with thickened, fleshy roots, channeled leaves, and very small standards that are sometimes only bristlelike and usually horizontally placed. Although very beautiful in flower, they are mostly difficult to grow successfully, requiring the same cultivation conditions as Oncocyclus irises to thrive. Care must be taken not to damage the fleshy roots when transplanting or dividing clumps. All those listed are hardy in zones 8–9, except where otherwise stated.

Reticulata irises include the dwarf, bulbous irises valuable for flowering early in the year. Unlike other bulbous irises, they have netlike bulb tunics and leaves that are 4-sided, or occasionally cylindrical. With few exceptions (not described here), reticulata irises grow well in open, sunny, well-drained sites. Those listed here are hardy in zones 6–9, except where otherwise stated.

I. acutiloba. Rhizomatous Oncocyclus iris. H 3–10in (8–25cm), S 12–15in (30–38cm). Has narrowly sickle-shaped, green leaves. In late spring produces solitary strongly purple-

violet- or brownish purple-veined, white flowers, 2–3in (5–7cm) across, with a dark brown blaze around the beard of each fall.
I. **'Annabel Jane'** (illus. p.196). Vigorous, rhizomatous, bearded iris (Standard Tall). H 4ft (1.2m), S indefinite. Well-branched stem bears 8–12 flowers, 6–10in (15–25cm) across, with pale lilac falls and paler standards. Flowers are produced in early summer.
I. **'Anniversary'**. Rhizomatous, beardless Siberian iris. H 2ft (60cm), S indefinite. From late spring to early summer, branched stem bears 1–4 white flowers, 2–4in (5–10cm) across, with a creamy white stripe in the throat of each fall. Grows well in moist soil or a bog garden.
I. aphylla. Rhizomatous, bearded iris. H 6–12in (15–30cm), S indefinite. Branched stem produces up to 5 pale to dark purple or blue-violet flowers, 2½–3in (6–7cm) across, in late spring and sometimes again in autumn if conditions suit.
I. aucheri. Bulbous Juno iris. H 6–10in (15–25cm), S 6in (15cm). Has channeled, green leaves packed closely together on stem, looking somewhat leeklike. In late spring bears up to 6 blue to white flowers, 2½–3in (6–7cm) across with yellow-ridged falls, in leaf axils.
I. aurea. See *I. crocea*.
I. bakeriana. Bulbous Reticulata iris. H 4in (10cm), S 2–2½in (5–6cm). In early spring bears a solitary long-tubed, pale blue flower, 2–2½in (5–6cm) across, with each fall having a dark blue blotch at the tip and a spotted, deep blue center. Has narrow, almost cylindrical leaves, that are very short at flowering time but elongate later.
I. **'Banbury Beauty'**. Rhizomatous, beardless Pacific Coast iris. H 18in (45cm), S indefinite. In late spring and early summer, branched stem produces 2–10 light lavender flowers, 4–6in (10–15cm) across, with a purple zone on each fall.
I. **'Bibury'**. Rhizomatous, bearded iris (Standard Dwarf). H 12in (30cm), S indefinite. Has 2–4 cream flowers, 4in (10cm) wide, on a branched stem in late spring.
I. **'Blue-eyed Brunette'** (illus. p.197). Rhizomatous, bearded iris (Standard Tall). H 3ft (1m), S indefinite. Well-branched stem produces 7–10 brown flowers, 4–6in (10–15cm) wide, with a blue blaze and a golden beard on each fall, in early summer.
I. **'Bold Print'** (illus. p.196). Rhizomatous, bearded iris (Intermediate). H 22in (55cm), S indefinite. In late spring or early summer, branched stem bears up to 6 flowers, 5in (13cm) wide, with purple-edged, white standards and white falls that are each purple-stitched at the edge and have a bronze-tipped, white beard.
I. **'Bristol Gem'**. Rhizomatous, bearded iris (Standard Tall). H 3ft (1m), S indefinite. Well-branched stem produces 6–10 deep blue flowers, 6–7in (15–18cm) wide, in early summer.

I. **'Bronze Queen'**. Bulbous Xiphium iris (Dutch). H to 32in (80cm), S 6in (15cm). In spring and early summer produces 1 or 2 golden brown flowers, 3–4in (8–10cm) wide, flushed bronze and purple. Lance-shaped, channeled, green leaves are scattered up flower stem.
I. **'Brown Lasso'**. Rhizomatous, bearded iris (Border). H 22in (55cm), S indefinite. In early summer, sturdy, well-branched stem bears 6–10 flowers, 4–5in (10–13cm) across, with deep butterscotch standards and brown-edged, light violet falls.
I. bucharica (illus. p.196). Vigorous, bulbous Juno iris. H 8–16in (20–40cm), S 5in (12cm). Zones 4–9. In late spring produces 2–6 flowers, 2½in (6cm) across, golden yellow to white with yellow falls, from leaf axils. Has narrowly lance-shaped, channeled, glossy, green leaves scattered up flower stem. Is easier to grow than most Juno irises.
I. **'Carnaby'** (illus. p.197). Rhizomatous, bearded iris (Standard Tall). H to 3ft (1m), S indefinite. In early summer, well-branched stem bears 6–8 flowers, 6–7in (15–18cm) wide, with pale pink standards and deep rose-pink falls that have orange beards.
I. chamaeiris. See *I. lutescens*.
I. chrysographes (illus. p.196). Rhizomatous, beardless Siberian iris. H 16in (40cm), S indefinite. From late spring to early summer, branched stem bears 1–4 deep red-purple or purple-black flowers, 2–4in (5–10cm) across, with gold etching down falls. Prefers moist conditions.
I. clarkei. Rhizomatous, beardless Siberian iris. H 2ft (60cm), S indefinite. From late spring to early summer, solid stem produces 2–3 branches each with 2 blue to red-purple flowers, 2–4in (5–10cm) across, with a violet-veined, white blaze on each fall. Prefers moist conditions.
I. colchica. See *I. graminea*.
I. confusa. Evergreen or semi-evergreen, rhizomatous Evansia iris with short stolons. H 1–3ft (30cm–1m), S indefinite. Half hardy, zone 9. Bamboolike, erect stem is crowned by a fan of lax leaves. In mid-spring, widely branched flower stem produces a long succession of up to 30 white flowers, 1½–2in (4–5cm) across, with yellow and purple spots around a yellow crest on each fall. Prefers well-drained soil and the protection of a south-facing wall.
I. cristata (illus. p.196). Evansia iris with much-branched rhizomes. H 4in (10cm), S indefinite. Fully hardy, zones 4–9. Has neat fans of lance-shaped leaves. In early summer produces 1 or 2 virtually stemless, long-tubed, lilac, blue, lavender, or white flowers, 1¼–1½in (3–4cm) across, with a white patch and orange crest on each fall. Prefers semi-shade and moist soil; is ideal for growing on peat banks.
I. crocea, syn. *I. aurea*. Rhizomatous, beardless Spuria iris. H 3–4ft (1–1.2m), S indefinite. Has long leaves. Strong, erect, sparsely branched stem produces terminal

clusters of 2–10 golden yellow flowers, 5–7in (12–18cm) across, with wavy-edged falls, in early summer. Resents being disturbed.

I. cuprea. See *I. fulva.*

I. **'Custom Design'.** Rhizomatous, beardless Spuria iris. H 3ft (1m), S indefinite. Strong, erect-branched stem produces 2–10 deep maroon-brown flowers, each 2–5in (5–12cm) wide, with a heavily veined, bright yellow blaze on each fall, from early to mid-summer.

I. danfordiae (illus. p.197). Bulbous Reticulata iris. H 2–4in (5–10cm), S 2in (5cm). In early spring bears usually one yellow flower, 1$\frac{1}{4}$–2in (3–5cm) across, with green spots on each fall. Standards are much reduced and resemble short bristles. Narrow, squared leaves are very short at flowering time but elongate later. Tends to produce masses of small bulblets and requires deeper planting than other Reticulata irises to maintain bulbs at flowering size.

I. douglasiana (illus. p.196). Evergreen, rhizomatous, beardless Pacific Coast iris. H 10–28in (25–70cm), S indefinite. Leathery, dark green leaves are stained red-purple at base. Branched stem produces 1–3 lavender to purple, occasionally white, flowers, 3–5in (7–12cm) wide, with variable, central, yellowish zones on the falls, in late spring and early summer.

I. **'Dreaming Spires'.** Rhizomatous, beardless Siberian iris. H 3ft (1m), S indefinite. From late spring to early summer, branched stem produces 1–4 flowers, 2–4in (5–10cm) wide, with lavender standards and royal blue falls. Prefers moist soil.

I. **'Dreaming Yellow'** (illus. p.196). Rhizomatous, beardless Siberian iris. H 3ft (1m), S indefinite. From late spring to early summer, branched stem produces 1–4 flowers, 2–4in (5–10cm) across. Standards are white, falls creamy yellow fading to white with age. Prefers moist soil.

I. **'Early Light'** (illus. p.197). Rhizomatous, bearded iris (Standard Tall). H 3ft (1m), S indefinite. In early summer, well-branched stem bears 8–10 flowers, 6–7in (15–18cm) wide, with lemon-flushed, cream standards and slightly darker falls with a yellow beard.

I. **'Elmohr'.** Rhizomatous, bearded iris. H 3ft (1m), S indefinite. In early summer, well-branched stem produces 2–5 strongly veined, red-purple flowers, 6–8in (15–20cm) across.

I. ensata, syn. *I. kaempferi* (Japanese flag). Rhizomatous, beardless Japanese iris. H 2–3ft (60cm–1m), S indefinite. Branched stem produces 3–15 purple or red-purple flowers, 3–6in (8–15cm) across, with a yellow blaze on each fall, from early to mid-summer. May be distinguished from the related, smooth-leaved *I. laevigata* by the prominent midrib on the leaves. Has produced many hundreds of garden forms, some with double flowers, in shades of purple, pink, lavender, and white, sometimes bicolored. Prefers partial shade and thrives in a water or bog garden.

I. **'Eye Bright'** (illus. p.197). Rhizomatous, bearded iris (Standard Dwarf). H 12in (30cm), S indefinite. In late spring produces 2–4 bright yellow flowers, 3–4in (7–10cm) wide, each with a brown zone on the falls surrounding the beard, on usually unbranched stem.

I. **'Flamenco'** (illus. p.197). Rhizomatous, bearded iris (Standard Tall). H 3ft (1m), S indefinite. In early summer, well-branched stem produces 6–9 flowers, 6in (15cm) wide, with gold standards, infused red, and white to yellow falls with red borders.

I. foetidissima (Gladwin, Roast-beef plant, Stinking iris). Evergreen, rhizomatous, beardless iris. H 1–3ft (30cm–1m), S indefinite. Zones 5–9. Branched stem bears up to 9 yellow-tinged, dull purple or occasionally pure yellow flowers, 2–4in (5–10cm) wide, from early to mid-summer. Cylindrical seed pods open to reveal rounded, bright scarlet fruits throughout winter. Thrives in a bog or water garden, although tolerates drier conditions.

I. forrestii (illus. p.197). Rhizomatous, beardless Siberian iris. H 6–16in (15–40cm), S indefinite. From late spring to early summer, unbranched stem produces 1 or 2 fragrant yellow flowers, 2–2$\frac{1}{2}$in (5–6cm) across, with black lines on each fall and occasionally brownish flushing on standards. Has linear, glossy, green leaves, gray-green below. Prefers moist, lime-free soil.

I. fosteriana. Bulbous Juno iris. H 4–6in (10–15cm), S 2$\frac{1}{2}$in (6cm). In spring produces 1 or 2 long-tubed flowers, 1$\frac{1}{2}$–2in (4–5cm) wide, with downward-turned, rich purple standards, which are larger than those of most Juno irises, and creamy yellow falls. Has narrowly lance-shaped, channeled, silver-edged, green leaves scattered on flower stem. Is difficult to grow and is best in an alpine house or cold frame.

I. **'Frank Elder'.** Bulbous Reticulata iris. H 2$\frac{1}{2}$–4in (6–10cm), S 2–3in (5–7cm). Has a solitary very pale blue flower, 2$\frac{1}{2}$–3in (6–7cm) wide, suffused pale yellow and veined and spotted darker blue, in early spring. Narrow, squared leaves are very short at flowering time but elongate later.

I. fulva, syn. *I. cuprea* (illus. p.197). Rhizomatous, beardless iris. H 18–32in (45–80cm), S indefinite. Zones 5–9. Frost hardy. In late spring or summer produces a slender, slightly branched stem with 4–6 (occasionally more) copper or orange-red flowers, 2–3in (5–7cm) across, with 2 flowers per leaf axil. Thrives in a bog or water garden.

I. **'Fulvala'** (illus. p.196). Rhizomatous, beardless iris. H 18in (45cm), S indefinite. Frost hardy. In summer, zigzag stem produces 4–6 (occasionally more) velvety, deep red-purple flowers, 2–5in (5–12cm) across, with 2 flowers per leaf axil. Has a yellow blaze on each fall. Thrives in a bog or water garden.

I. **'Geisha Gown'** (illus. p.196). Rhizomatous, beardless Japanese iris. H 32in (80cm), S indefinite. In summer, branched stem produces 3–5

double, rose-purple-veined, white flowers, 6–12in (15–30cm) across, with purple styles and a gold blaze on each fall. Leaves are ridged. Prefers sun or semi-shade. Thrives in a bog or water garden.

I. germanica (Common German flag). Rhizomatous, bearded iris. H to 2–4ft (60cm–1.2m), S indefinite. Sparsely branched stem produces up to 6 yellow-bearded, blue-purple or blue-violet flowers, 4–6in (10–15cm) wide, in late spring and early summer.

I. **'Golden Harvest'.** Bulbous Xiphium iris (Dutch). H to 32in (80cm), S 6in (15cm). Bears 1 or 2 deep rich yellow flowers, 2$\frac{1}{2}$–3in (6–8cm) wide, in spring and early summer. Has scattered, narrowly lance-shaped, channeled, green leaves.

I. gracilipes. Clump-forming, rhizomatous Evansia iris with short stolons. H 6–8in (15–20cm), S indefinite. In late spring and early summer, slender, branched stem produces a succession of 4 or 5 lilac-blue flowers, each 1$\frac{1}{4}$–1$\frac{1}{2}$in (3–4cm) across, with a violet-veined, white zone surrounding a yellow and white crest. Has narrow, grasslike leaves. Prefers semi-shade and peaty soil.

I. graeberiana. Bulbous Juno iris. H 6–14in (15–35cm), S 2$\frac{1}{2}$–3in (6–8cm). In late spring produces 4–6 bluish lavender flowers, 2$\frac{1}{2}$–3in (6–8cm) across, with a white crest on each fall, from leaf axils. Lance-shaped, channeled leaves are white-margined, glossy, green above, grayish green below, and scattered up flower stem. Is easier to grow than most Juno irises.

I. graminea, syn. *I. colchica.* Rhizomatous, beardless Spuria iris. H 8–16in (20–40cm), S indefinite. In late spring, narrowly lance-shaped leaves partially hide up to 10 plum-scented flowers, 2–5in (5–12cm) wide, with wine purple standards and heavily veined, violet-blue falls borne on flattened, angled stem. Resents being disturbed.

I. **'Harmony'** (illus. p.197). Bulbous Reticulata iris. H 2$\frac{1}{2}$–4in (6–10cm), S 2$\frac{1}{2}$–3in (6–7cm). In early spring bears a solitary fragrant, long-tubed, clear pale blue flower, 2–2$\frac{1}{2}$in (5–6cm) across, with white marks and a yellow ridge down each fall center. Narrow, squared leaves are very short at flowering time but elongate later.

I. histrioides. Bulbous Reticulata iris. H 2$\frac{1}{2}$–4in (6–10cm), S 2$\frac{1}{2}$–3in (6–7cm). In early spring produces solitary flowers, 2$\frac{1}{2}$–3in (6–7cm) across, which vary from light to deep violet-blue. Each fall is lightly to strongly spotted with dark blue and has white marks and a yellow ridge down center. Narrow, squared leaves are very short at flowering time but elongate later. **'Lady Beatrix Stanley'** has light blue flowers and heavily spotted falls. **'Major'** (illus. p.197) has darker blue-violet flowers.

I. **'Holden Clough'.** Rhizomatous, beardless iris. H 20–28in (50–70cm), S indefinite. In early summer, branched stem bears 6–12 yellow flowers, each 2in (5cm) wide, with very heavy, burnt-sienna veining. Is excellent in a bog or

water garden, but also grows well in any rich, well-drained soil.

I. hoogiana (illus. p.196). Regelia iris with stout rhizomes. H 16–24in (40–60cm), S indefinite. Produces 2 or 3 scented, delicately veined, lilac-blue flowers, 3–4in (7–10cm) across, in late spring and early summer. Is relatively easy to cultivate.

I. iberica (illus. p.196). Rhizomatous Oncocyclus iris. H 6–8in (15–20cm), S indefinite. Has narrow, strongly curved, gray-green leaves. Bears solitary bicolored flowers, 4–5in (10–12cm) across, in late spring. Standards are white, pale yellow, or pale blue with slight brownish purple veining; spoon-shaped falls are white or pale lilac, spotted and strongly veined brownish purple. Grows best in a frame or alpine house.

I. innominata (illus. p.197). Evergreen or semi-evergreen, rhizomatous, beardless Pacific Coast iris. H 6–10in (16–25cm), S indefinite. Stem bears 1 or 2 flowers, 2$\frac{1}{2}$–3in (6–8cm) across, from late spring to early summer. Varies greatly in color from cream to yellow or orange and from lilac-pink to blue or purple; falls are often veined with maroon or brown.

I. japonica. Vigorous, rhizomatous Evansia iris with slender stolons. H 18–32in (45–80cm), S indefinite. Frost hardy. Has fans of broadly lance-shaped, glossy leaves. In late spring produces branched flower stem with a long succession of flattish, frilled or ruffled, pale lavender or white flowers, $\frac{1}{2}$–3in (1–8cm) across, marked violet around an orange crest on each fall. Prefers the protection of a sheltered, sunny wall.

I. **'Joyce'** (illus. p.196). Bulbous Reticulata iris. H 2$\frac{1}{2}$–4in (6–10cm), S 2$\frac{1}{2}$–3in (6–7cm). In early spring bears a solitary fragrant, long-tubed, clear blue flower, 2–2$\frac{1}{2}$in (5–6cm) across, with white marks and a yellow ridge down each fall center. Narrow, squared leaves are very short at flowering time but elongate later.

I. **'June Prom'.** Vigorous, rhizomatous, bearded iris (Intermediate). H 20in (50cm), S indefinite. In late spring or early summer, branched stem bears up to 6 pale blue flowers, 3–4in (8–10cm) wide, with a green tinge on each fall.

I. kaempferi. See *I. ensata.*

I. **'Katharine Hodgkin'.** Bulbous Reticulata iris. H 2$\frac{1}{2}$–4in (6–10cm), S 2–3in (5–7cm). Is similar to *I.* 'Frank Elder', but has yellower flowers, 2$\frac{1}{2}$–3in (6–7cm) wide, suffused pale blue, lined and dotted dark blue. Flowers in early spring.

I. kerneriana. Rhizomatous, beardless Spuria iris. H 10in (25cm), S indefinite. Has very narrow, grasslike leaves. Strong, erect-branched stem bears 2–4 soft lemon or creamy yellow flowers, 2–5in (5–12cm) across, from each pair of bracts, in early summer. Resents being disturbed.

I. korolkowii. Regelia iris with stout rhizomes. H 16–24in (40–60cm), S indefinite. From late spring to early summer, each spathe encloses 2 or 3 delicately blackish maroon- or olive green-veined, creamy white or light purple flowers, 2¹/₂–3in (6–8cm) across. Is best grown in a bulb frame.

I. 'Krasnia' (illus. p.196). Rhizomatous, bearded iris (Standard Tall). H 3ft (1m), S indefinite. In early summer, well-branched stem produces 8–12 flowers, 5–7in (13–18cm) wide, with purple standards and purple-edged, white falls.

I. laevigata (illus. p.197). Rhizomatous, beardless Japanese iris. H 2–3ft (60cm–1m) or more, S indefinite. Sparsely branched stem produces 2–4 blue, blue-purple, or white flowers, 2–5in (5–12cm) across, from early to mid-summer. Is related to I. ensata but has smooth, unridged leaves. Grows well in sun or semi-shade in moist conditions or in shallow water. **'Regal'** bears single, cyclamen red flowers. Flowers of **'Snowdrift'** are double and white. **'Variegata'**, H 10in (25cm), has white-and-green-striped leaves and often flowers a second time in early autumn.

I. latifolia, syn. I. xiphioides (English iris; illus. p.196). Bulbous Xiphium iris (English). H 32in (80cm), S 6in (15cm). In late spring and summer, 1 or 2 blue to deep violet flowers, 3–4in (8–10cm) wide, with a yellow stripe down center of each very broad fall, are produced from the bracts. Lance-shaped, channeled, green leaves are scattered up flower stem. **'Blue Giant'** has darker-flecked, bluish purple standards and dark blue falls. **'La Nuit'** bears deep purple-red flowers. Flowers of **'Mont Blanc'** are pure white.

I. lutescens, syn. I. chamaeiris. Fast-growing, very variable, rhizomatous, bearded iris. H 2–12in (5–30cm), S indefinite. Branched stem produces 1 or 2 yellow-bearded, violet, purple, yellow, white, or bicolored flowers, 6–8 cm (2¹/₂–3in) across, in early summer. **'Nancy Lindsay'** has scented, yellow flowers.

I. magnifica (illus. p.196). Bulbous Juno iris. H 1–2ft (30–60cm), S 6in (15cm). In late spring produces 3–7 very pale lilac flowers, 2¹/₂–3in (6–8cm) across, with a central, yellow area on each fall, from leaf axils. Bears scattered, lance-shaped, channeled, glossy, green leaves. Is easily grown.

I. 'Margot Holmes'. Rhizomatous, beardless Siberian iris. H 10in (25cm), S indefinite. Frost hardy. In early summer produces 2 or 3 purple-red flowers, 4–6in (10–15cm) across, with yellow veining on each fall.

I. 'Marhaba'. Rhizomatous, bearded iris (Miniature Dwarf). H 6in (15cm), S indefinite. Bears 1, rarely 2 deep blue flowers, 2–3in (5–8cm) wide, in mid-spring.

I. 'Mary Frances' (illus. p.196). Rhizomatous, bearded iris (Standard Tall). H 3ft (1m), S indefinite. In early summer, well-branched stem bears 6–9, occasionally to 12, pink-lavender flowers, 6in (15cm) wide.

I. 'Matinata' (illus. p.196). Rhizomatous, bearded iris (Standard Tall). H 3ft (1m), S indefinite. In early summer, well-branched stem produces 6–9, occasionally to 12, flowers, 6in (15cm) wide, that are dark purple-blue throughout.

I. missouriensis, syn. I. tolmeiana (Missouri flag; illus. p.196). Very variable, rhizomatous, beardless Pacific Coast iris. H to 2¹/₂ft (75cm), S indefinite. Branched stem produces 2 or 3 pale blue, lavender, lilac, blue, or white flowers, 2–3in (5–8cm) wide, in each spathe, in late spring or early summer. Falls are veined and usually have a yellow blaze.

I. 'Mountain Lake' (illus. p.196). Rhizomatous, beardless Siberian iris. H 3ft (1m), S indefinite. From late spring to early summer, branched stem produces 1–4 blue flowers, 2–4in (5–10cm) across, with darker veining on falls. Prefers moist soil.

I. orientalis. See I. sanguinea.

I. pallida (Dalmatian iris). Rhizomatous, bearded iris. H 28–36in (70cm–1m) or more, S indefinite. In late spring and early summer produces 2–6 scented, lilac-blue flowers, 3–5in (8–12cm) across and with yellow beards, from silvery spathes on strong, branched stems. Leaves of **'Aurea Variegata'** (illus. p.196) are striped green and yellow.

I. 'Paradise Bird' (illus. p.196). Rhizomatous, bearded iris (Standard Tall). H 34in (85cm), S indefinite. In early summer, well-branched stem produces 8–10 flowers, 5¹/₂–6in (14–15cm) wide, with magenta falls and paler standards.

I. 'Peach Frost' (illus. p.197). Rhizomatous, bearded iris (Standard Tall). H 3ft (1m), S indefinite. Well-branched stem bears 6–10 flowers, 6in (15cm) wide, in early summer. Standards are peach pink, falls white with peach pink borders and tangerine beards.

I. 'Piona'. Rhizomatous, bearded iris (Intermediate). H 18in (45cm), S indefinite. In late spring, branched stem bears up to 6 deep violet flowers, 3–4in (8–10cm) wide, with golden beards from late spring to early summer. Green leaves have purple bases.

I. 'Professor Blaauw'. Bulbous Xiphium iris (Dutch). H 32in (80cm), S 6in (15cm). From spring to early summer produces 1 or 2 rich violet-blue flowers, 2¹/₂–3in (6–8cm) across. Narrowly lance-shaped, channeled, green leaves are scattered up flower stem.

I. 'Promise'. Rhizomatous, bearded iris (Miniature Dwarf). H 7in (18cm), S indefinite. In mid-spring, well-branched stem bears 2–5 veined, red flowers, 2–3in (5–8cm) wide, with a yellow stripe in the throat of each fall.

I. pseudacorus (Yellow flag; illus. p.197). Robust, rhizomatous, beardless iris. H to 6ft (2m), S indefinite. Branched stem produces 4–12 golden yellow flowers, 2–5in (5–12cm) wide, usually with brown or violet veining and a darker yellow patch on the falls, from early to mid-summer. Leaves are broad, ridged, and grayish green. Prefers semi-shade and thrives in a water garden. **'Variegata'** has yellow-and-green-striped foliage in spring, often turning green before flowering.

I. pumila (Dwarf bearded iris). Rhizomatous, bearded iris. H 4–6in (10–15cm), S indefinite. In mid-spring

has a flower stem, ¹/₂in (1cm) long, bearing 2 or 3 long-tubed flowers, 1–2in (2.5–5cm) wide, varying from violet-purple to white, yellow, or blue, with yellow or blue beards on the falls. Prefers very well-drained, slightly alkaline soil.

I. reticulata. Bulbous Reticulata iris. H 4–6in (10–15cm), S 1¹/₂–2¹/₂in (4–6cm). In early spring bears a solitary fragrant, long-tubed, deep violet-purple flower, 1¹/₂–2¹/₂in (4–6cm) wide, with a yellow ridge down each fall center. Narrow, squared leaves elongate after flowering time. **'Cantab'** (illus. p.196) has clear pale blue flowers with a deep yellow ridge on each fall. **'Clairette'** bears pale blue flowers with each fall having a dark blue blotch at the tip and a dark blue-spotted center. Flowers of **'J.S. Dijt'** are reddish purple with an orange ridge on each fall. **'Violet Beauty'** has deep violet-purple flowers with an orange ridge down the center of each fall.

I. 'Rippling Rose' (illus. p.196). Rhizomatous, bearded iris (Standard Tall). H 3ft (1m), S indefinite. In early summer, well-branched stem has 6–10 white flowers, 6in (15cm) wide, with purple marks and lemon yellow beards.

I. rosenbachiana (illus. p.196). Bulbous Juno iris. H 4–6in (10–15cm), S 2¹/₂in (6cm). In spring produces 1 or 2 long-tubed flowers, 1¹/₂–2in (4–5cm) wide, with small, downward-turned, rich purple standards and reddish purple falls, each with a yellow ridge in the center. Has lance-shaped, channeled, green leaves in a basal tuft. Is difficult to grow and is best in an alpine house or cold frame.

I. 'Saffron Jewel'. Rhizomatous, bearded iris. H 30in (75cm), S indefinite. In early summer branched stem produces 2–5 flowers, 2–4in (5–10cm) across, with oyster falls, veined chartreuse, and paler standards. Falls each have a blue blaze and beard.

I. sanguinea, syn. I. orientalis. Rhizomatous, beardless Siberian iris. H to 3ft (1m), S indefinite. From late spring to early summer, branched stem has 2 or 3 deep purple or red-purple flowers, 2–4in (5–10cm) wide, from each set of bracts. Falls are red-purple with white throats finely veined purple.

I. 'Sapphire Star' (illus. p.196). Rhizomatous, beardless Japanese iris. H 4ft (1.2m), S indefinite. In summer, branched stem bears 3–5 white-veined, lavender flowers, 6–12in (15–30cm) wide, pencilled with a white halo around a yellow blaze on each fall. Prefers moist soil.

I. setosa (Bristle-pointed iris; illus. p.197). Rhizomatous, beardless iris, very variable in stature. H 4in–3ft (10cm–1m), S indefinite. Bears 2–13 deep blue or purple-blue flowers, 2–3in (5–8cm) across, from each spathe in late spring and early summer. Falls have paler blue or white marks; each standard is reduced to a bristle.

I. 'Shepherd's Delight' (illus. p.197). Rhizomatous, bearded iris (Standard Tall). H 3ft (1m), S indefinite. In early summer, well-branched stem produces 6–10 clear pink flowers, 6–7in (15–18cm) wide, with a yellow cast.

I. sibirica (Siberian flag). Rhizomatous, beardless Siberian iris. H 20in–4ft (50cm–1.2m), S indefinite. From late spring to early summer, branched stem bears 2 or 3 dark-veined, blue or blue-purple flowers, 2–4in (5–10cm) across, from each spathe. Prefers moist or boggy soil.

I. 'Splash Down'. Rhizomatous, beardless Siberian iris. H 3ft (1m), S indefinite. From late spring to early summer, branched stem produces 1–4 flowers, 2–4in (5–10cm) across. Standards are pale blue and falls speckled blue on a pale ground. Prefers moist soil.

I. spuria. Very variable, rhizomatous, beardless Spuria iris. H 20in–3ft (50cm–1m), S indefinite. Strong, erect-branched stem produces 2–5 pale blue-purple, sky blue, violet-blue, white, or yellow flowers, 2–5in (5–12cm) across, in early summer. Prefers moist soil.

I. 'Stepping Out'. Rhizomatous, bearded iris (Standard Tall). H 3ft (1m), S indefinite. Well-branched stem produces 8–11 white flowers, 5¹/₂–6in (14–15cm) wide, with deep blue-purple marks in early summer.

I. 'Sun Miracle' (illus. p.197). Rhizomatous, bearded iris (Standard Tall). H 3ft (1m), S indefinite. Well-branched stem produces 7–10 pure yellow flowers, 6–7in (15–18cm) wide, in early summer.

I. susiana (Mourning iris). Rhizomatous Oncocyclus iris. H 14–16in (35–40cm), S indefinite. In late spring produces a solitary grayish white flower, 3–6in (8–15cm) wide, heavily veined deep purple. Standards appear larger than incurved falls, which each carry a black blaze and a deep purple beard. Grows best in a frame or alpine house.

I. tectorum (Japanese roof iris, Wall flag; illus. p.196). Evansia iris with stout rhizomes. H 10–14in (25–35cm), S indefinite. Frost hardy, zones 5–9. Has fans of broadly lance-shaped, ribbed leaves. In early summer, sparsely branched stem produces 2–3 darker-veined, bright lilac flowers, ¹/₂–3in (1–8cm) across with a white crest on each fall, from each spathe. Prefers a sheltered, sunny site near a south- or west-facing wall.

I. tenax (illus. p.196). Rhizomatous, beardless Pacific Coast iris. H 15–12in (6–30cm), S indefinite. From late spring to early summer produces 1 or 2 deep purple to lavender blue flowers, 3–5in (8–12cm) across, often with yellow-and-white marking on falls. White, cream, and yellow variants also occur. Narrow, dark green leaves are stained pink at base.

I. 'Theseus'. Rhizomatous Regeliocyclus iris. H 18in (45cm), S indefinite. From late spring to early summer produces usually 2 flowers, 4–6in (10–15cm) across, with violet standards and violet-veined, cream falls. Grows best in a frame or alpine house.

I. tolmeiana. See I. missouriensis.

I. tuberosa. See Hermodactylus tuberosus.

I. unguicularis, syn. I. stylosa (Algerian iris, Algerian winter iris, Winter iris). Evergreen, rhizomatous, beardless iris. H to 8in (20cm), S indefinite. Zones 8–9. Has narrow, tough leaves. Almost stemless, primrose-scented, lilac flowers, 2–3in (5–8cm) across with yellow centers to the falls and with very long tubes, appear from late autumn to early spring. Buds are prone to slug attack. Is excellent for cutting. Prefers a sheltered site against a south- or west-facing wall. **'Mary Barnard'** has deep violet-blue flowers. Flowers of **'Walter Butt'** are pale silvery lavender.

I. variegata (Variegated iris; illus. p.197). Rhizomatous, bearded iris. H 12–20in (30–50cm), S indefinite. In early summer, branched stem produces 3–6 flowers, 2–3in (5–8cm) across, with bright yellow standards and white or pale yellow falls, heavily veined red-brown and appearing striped.

I. verna. Rhizomatous, beardless iris. H 2in (5cm), S indefinite. In mid-spring bears 1, occasionally 2, lilac-blue flowers, 1–2in (2.5–5cm) across, with a narrow, orange stripe in the center of each fall. Prefers semi-shade and moist but well-drained soil.

I. versicolor (Blue flag, Wild iris; illus. p.196). Robust, rhizomatous, beardless iris. H 2ft (60cm), S indefinite. Branched stem produces 3–5 or more purple-blue, reddish purple, lavender, or slate purple flowers, 2–4in (5–10cm) across, from early to mid-summer. Falls usually have a central, white area veined purple. Prefers partial shade and thrives in moist soil or in shallow water. **'Kermesina'** has red-purple flowers.

I. warleyensis. Bulbous Juno iris. H 8–18in (20–45cm), S 3in (7–8cm). In spring produces up to 5 pale lilac, or violet-blue, flowers, 2–3in (5–7cm) across, in leaf axils. Each fall has a darker blue apex and a yellow stain in the center. Bears scattered, lance-shaped, channeled leaves. Is best in an unheated greenhouse or cold frame.

I. **'White Excelsior'.** Bulbous Xiphium iris (Dutch). H to 32in (80cm), S 6in (15cm). From spring to early summer bears 1 or 2 white flowers, 2^1/$_2$–3in (6–8cm) wide, with a yellow stripe down each fall center. Narrowly lance-shaped, channeled, green leaves are scattered on flower stem.

I. winogradowii. Bulbous Reticulata iris. H 2^1/$_2$–4in (6–10cm), S 2^1/$_2$–3in (6–7cm). Zones 7–9. Solitary pale primrose yellow flower, 2^1/$_2$–3in (6–7cm) wide, spotted green on falls, appears in early spring. Narrow, squared leaves are very short at flowering time but elongate later.

I. xiphioides. See *I. latifolia.*

I. xiphium. Bulbous Xiphium iris (Spanish). H to 32in (80cm), S 6in (15cm). Has 1 or 2 blue or violet, occasionally yellow or white, flowers, 2^1/$_2$–3in (6–8cm) across, with central, orange or yellow marks on the falls, in spring and early summer. Narrowly lance-shaped, channeled leaves are scattered on flower stem. **'Blue Angel'** has bright blue flowers with a yellow mark in the center of each fall. Flowers of **'Lusitanica'** are pure yellow. **'Queen Wilhelmina'** bears white flowers in spring. **'Wedgewood'** (illus. p.196) produces bright blue flowers.

ISATIS (Cruciferae)
Genus of summer-flowering annuals, biennials, and perennials. Fully hardy. Needs sun and fertile, well-drained soil. Propagate by seed in autumn or spring.

I. tinctoria (Woad). Vigorous, upright biennial. H to 4ft (1.2m), S 45cm (1^1/$_2$ft). Zones 4–8. Has oblong to lance-shaped, glaucous leaves and, in summer, large, terminal panicles of 4-petaled, yellow flowers.

Ismene calathina. See *Hymenocallis narcissiflora.*

ISOPLEXIS (Scrophulariaceae)
Genus of evergreen, mainly summer-flowering shrubs, grown for their flowers. Is closely related to *Digitalis.* Frost tender, min. 45°F (7°C). Tolerates full light or partial shade and well-drained soil. Water potted specimens freely when in full growth, moderately at other times. Remove spent flower spikes. Propagate by seed in spring or by semi-ripe cuttings in late summer.

I. canariensis, syn. *Digitalis canariensis,* illus. p.139.

ISOPYRUM (Ranunculaceae)
Genus of spring-flowering perennials, grown for their small flowers and delicate foliage. Is suitable for growing in woodlands, peat beds, and rock gardens. Fully hardy. Requires shade and humus-rich, moist soil. Propagate by seed when fresh or by division in autumn. Self seeds readily.

I. thalictroides. Dainty, clump-forming perennial. H and S 10in (25cm). Zones 5–8. Central stalk bears fernlike, 3-parted leaves, each leaflet being cut into 3. Has small, nodding, cup-shaped, white flowers in spring.

Isotrema griffithii. See *Aristolochia griffithii.*

ITEA (Grossulariaceae)
Genus of deciduous or evergreen trees and shrubs, grown for their foliage and flowers. Frost hardy, but in most areas protect by growing against a south- or west-facing wall. Needs sun or semi-shade and fertile, well-drained but not too dry soil. Propagate by softwood cuttings in summer.

I. ilicifolia illus. p.114.

IXIA (Iridaceae)
Genus of spring- and summer-flowering corms with wiry stems and spikes of flattish flowers. Half hardy. Grow in an open, sunny situation and

in well-drained soil. Plant in autumn for spring and early summer flowers; plant in spring for later summer display. Dry off after flowering. Propagate in autumn by seed or by offsets at replanting time.

I. maculata. Spring- to early summer-flowering corm. H 16in (40cm), S 1–2in (2.5–5cm). Zones 8–10. Leaves are linear, erect, and mostly basal. Wiry stem bears a spike of flattish, orange or yellow flowers, 1–2in (2.5–5cm) across, with brown or black centers.

I. monadelpha. Spring- to early summer-flowering corm. H 12in (30cm), S 1–2in (2.5–5cm). Zones 7–10. Linear, erect leaves are mostly basal. Stem produces a dense spike of 5–10 flattish, white, pink, purple, or blue flowers, 1^1/$_4$–1^1/$_2$in (3–4cm) across, often with differently colored eyes.

I. viridiflora illus. p.346.

IXIOLIRION (Amaryllidaceae)
Genus of bulbs, grown for their funnel-shaped flowers mainly in spring. Fully hardy. Needs a sheltered, sunny position and well-drained soil that becomes hot and dry in summer to ripen the bulb. Propagate by seed or offsets in autumn.

I. montanum. See *I. tataricum.*

I. tataricum, syn. *I. montanum,* illus. p.346.

IXORA (Rubiaceae)
Genus of evergreen, summer-flowering shrubs, grown primarily for their flowers, some also for their foliage. Frost tender, min. 55–61°F (13–16°C). Prefers full sun and humus-rich, well-drained soil. Water potted specimens freely when in full growth, moderately at other times. Propagate by seed in spring or by semi-ripe cuttings in summer.

I. coccinea illus. p.133.

J

JACARANDA (Bignoniaceae)
Genus of deciduous or evergreen trees, grown for their flowers in spring-summer and their foliage. Frost tender, min. 45–50°F (7–10°C). Grows in any fertile, well-drained soil and in full light. Water potted specimens freely when in full growth, sparingly at other times. Potted plants grown for their foliage only may be cut back hard in late winter. Propagate by seed in spring or by semi-ripe cuttings in summer.
J. mimosifolia, syn. *J. ovalifolia*, illus. p.52.
J. ovalifolia. See *J. mimosifolia*.

Jacobinia carnea. See *Justicia carnea*.
Jacobinia coccinea. See *Pachystachys coccinea*.
Jacobinia pohliana. See *Justicia carnea*.
Jacobinia spicigera. See *Justicia spicigera*.

JACQUEMONTIA (Convolvulaceae)
Genus of evergreen, twining climbers, grown for their flowers. Frost tender, min. 61–4°F (16–18°C). Any well-drained soil is suitable with full light. Water freely except in cold weather. Provide support and thin out by cutting back old stems to ground level in spring. Propagate by seed in spring or by semi-ripe cuttings in summer. Red spider mite and whitefly may cause problems.
J. pentantha. Fast-growing, evergreen, twining climber. H 6–10ft (2–3m). Zones 9–10. Has heart-shaped, pointed leaves and 1in (2.5cm) wide, funnel-shaped, rich violet-blue or pure blue flowers in long-stalked clusters in summer-autumn.

JAMESIA (Hydrangeaceae)
Genus of one species of deciduous shrub, grown for its flowers. Fully hardy. Needs full sun and fertile, well-drained soil. Propagate by softwood cuttings in summer.
J. americana. Deciduous, bushy shrub. H 5ft (1.5m), S 8ft (2.5m). Zones 5–9. Rounded, gray-green leaves are gray-white beneath. Clusters of small, slightly fragrant, star-shaped, white flowers are produced during late spring.

JANCAEA, syn. JANKAEA (Gesneriaceae)
Genus of one species of evergreen, rosetted perennial, grown for its flowers and silver-green leaves. Makes a good alpine house plant. Frost hardy. Is difficult to grow, as needs shade from mid-day sun in high summer, a humus-rich, gritty, moist, alkaline soil, and a gritty collar. Dislikes winter wet. Propagate by seed in spring or by leaf cuttings in mid-summer.
J. heldreichii illus. p.309.

JANKAEA. See JANCAEA.

JASIONE (Campanulaceae)
Genus of summer-flowering annuals, biennials, and perennials, grown for their attractive flower heads. Fully hardy. Requires sun and sandy soil. Remove old stems in autumn. Propagate by seed in autumn or by division in spring.
J. laevis, syn. *J. perennis* (Sheep's bit). Tufted perennial. H 2–12in (5–30cm), S 4–8in (10–20cm). Zones 6–8. Has narrowly oblong, very hairy or glabrous, gray-green leaves and, in summer, spiky, spherical, blue flower heads borne on erect stems. Is good for a rock garden.
J. perennis. See *J. laevis*.

JASMINUM (Oleaceae)
Jasmine
Genus of deciduous or evergreen shrubs and woody-stemmed, scrambling or twining climbers, grown for their often fragrant flowers and their foliage. Fully hardy to frost tender, min. 45–64°F (7–18°C). Requires full sun and fertile, well-drained soil. *J. nudiflorum*, which is not self-supporting, benefits from having old shoots thinned out after flowering; prune others as required after flowering. Propagate by semi-ripe cuttings in summer.
J. angulare. Evergreen, woody-stemmed, scrambling climber. H 6ft (2m) or more. Frost tender, min. 45–50°F (7–10°C), zone 10. Dark green leaves have 3 oval leaflets. Small clusters of fragrant, tubular, 5-lobed, white flowers are carried in late summer.
J. beesianum. Evergreen, woody-stemmed, scrambling climber, deciduous in cool areas. H to 15ft (5m). Frost hardy, zones 7–10. Has lance-shaped leaves. Fragrant, tubular, usually 6-lobed, pinkish red flowers, 1–3 together, are borne in early summer, followed by shiny, black berries.
J. grandiflorum (Royal jasmine, Spanish jasmine). Evergreen, woody-stemmed, scrambling climber. H 6ft (2m). Frost tender, min. 45–50°F (7–10°C), zones 9–10. Leaves have 7 or 9 leaflets. Clusters of up to 50 fragrant, tubular, 5- or 6-lobed, sometimes red-tinged, white flowers are carried in summer-autumn.
J. humile illus. p.114. **'Revolutum'** is an evergreen, bushy shrub. H 8ft (2.5m), S 10ft (3m). Fully hardy, zones 7–9. Bears large, fragrant, tubular, upright, bright yellow flowers, with 5 spreading lobes, on long, slender, green shoots from early spring to late autumn. Glossy, bright green leaves each consist of 3–7 oval leaflets.
f. *wallichianum* has semi-pendent flowers and 7–13 leaflets.
J. mesnyi, syn. *J. primulinum*, illus. p.165.
J. nudiflorum illus. p.119.
J. officinale illus. p.166.

J. parkeri. Evergreen, domed shrub. H 6in (15cm), S 18in (38cm) or more. Frost hardy, zones 8–10. Produces a tangled mass of fine stems and twigs bearing minute, oval leaves. Masses of tiny, tubular, five-lobed, yellow flowers appear from leaf axils in early summer.
J. polyanthum illus. p.177.
J. primulinum. See *J. mesnyi*.
J. rex. Evergreen, woody-stemmed, twining climber. H 10ft (3m). Frost tender, min. 64°F (18°C), zone 10. Has broadly oval, leathery, deep green leaves, 4–8in (10–20cm) long. Scentless, tubular, 5-lobed, pure white flowers, pink-tinged in bud, appear intermittently all year if warm enough.

JEFFERSONIA (Berberidaceae)
Genus of spring-flowering perennials. Fully hardy. Needs shade or partial shade and humus-rich, moist soil. Extensive root systems resent disturbance. Top-dress crown in late autumn. Propagate by seed as soon as ripe.
J. diphylla illus. p.287.
J. dubia, syn. *Plagiorhegma dubia*, illus. p.309.

JOVIBARBA (Crassulaceae)
Genus of evergreen perennials that spread by short stolons and are grown for their symmetrical rosettes of oval to strap-shaped, pointed, fleshy leaves. Makes ground-hugging mats, suitable for rock gardens, screes, walls, banks, and alpine houses. Fully hardy. Needs sun and gritty soil. Takes several years to reach flowering size. Rosettes die after plants have flowered, but leave numerous offsets. Propagate by offsets in summer.
J. hirta, syn. *Sempervivum hirtum*, illus. p.328.
J. sobolifera, syn. *Sempervivum soboliferum*. Vigorous, evergreen, mat-forming perennial. H 4in (10cm), S 8in (20cm). Zones 6–9. Rounded, grayish green or olive green rosettes are often red-tinged. Flower stems bear terminal clusters of small, cup-shaped, 6-petaled (rarely 5 or 7), pale yellow flowers in summer.

JUANULLOA (Solanaceae)
Genus of evergreen, summer-flowering shrubs, grown for their flowers. Frost tender, min. 55–9°F (13–15°C). Low temperatures cause leaf drop. Prefers full light and fertile, freely draining soil. Water potted specimens moderately, less when not in full growth. To encourage a branching habit, tip prune young plants. Propagate by semi-ripe cuttings in summer. Whitefly, red spider mite, and mealy bug may be troublesome.
J. aurantiaca illus. p.139.

JUBAEA (Palmae)
Genus of one species of evergreen palm, grown for its overall appearance.

Frost tender, min. 50°F (10°C). Needs full light and fertile, well-drained soil. Water potted specimens moderately, less in winter. Propagate by seed in spring at not less than 77°F (25°C). Red spider mite may be a nuisance.
J. chilensis, syn. *J. spectabilis*, illus. p.58.
J. spectabilis. See *J. chilensis*.

JUGLANS (Juglandaceae)
Walnut
Genus of deciduous trees, with aromatic leaves, grown for their foliage, stately habit, and, in some species, edible nuts (walnuts). Produces greenish yellow catkins in spring and early summer. Fully hardy, but young plants are prone to frost damage. Requires full sun and deep, fertile, well-drained soil. Propagate by seed, when ripe, in autumn.
J. ailantifolia (Japanese walnut). Deciduous, spreading tree with stout shoots. H and S 50ft (15m). Zones 5–8. Very large leaves consist of 11–17 oblong, glossy, bright green leaflets. Bears edible walnuts in autumn. var. *cordiformis* illus. p.42.
J. cathayensis (Chinese walnut). Deciduous, spreading tree. H and S 70ft (20m). Zones 6–8. Has very large leaves, consisting of 11–17 oval to oblong, dark green leaflets. Bears edible walnuts in autumn.
J. cinerea (Butternut). Fast-growing, deciduous, spreading tree. H 80ft (25m), S 70ft (20m). Zones 4–7. Leaves are large and very aromatic, with 7–19 oval to oblong, pointed, bright green leaflets. Bears dense clusters of large, rounded nuts in autumn.
J. microcarpa, syn. *J. rupestris*, illus. p.65.
J. nigra illus. p.42.
J. regia illus. p.41.
J. rupestris. See *J. microcarpa*.

JUNCUS (Juncaceae). See GRASSES, BAMBOOS, RUSHES, and SEDGES.
J. effusus f. *spiralis* illus. p.182.

JUNIPERUS (Cupressaceae),
Juniper. See CONIFERS.
J. chinensis (Chinese juniper). Conical conifer, making a tree, H 50ft (15m), S 6–10ft (2–3m), or a spreading shrub, H 3–15ft (1–5m), S 10–15ft (3–5m). Fully hardy, zones 5–9, except where otherwise stated. Has peeling bark. Both scale- and needlelike, aromatic, dark green leaves, paired or in 3s, are borne on same shoot. Globose, fleshy, berrylike fruits are glaucous white. Many cultivars commonly listed under *J. chinensis* are forms of *J.* x *media*.
'Aurea', H 30–50ft (10–15m), S 10–12ft (3–4m), is a slow-growing, oval or conical form with gold foliage and abundant yellow, male cones.
'Kaizuka', H 15ft (5m), S 10–15ft (3–5m), forms a sprawling, irregular

bush and produces a profusion of cones. **'Keteleeri'** illus. p.77. **'Obelisk'** illus. p.80. **'Pyramidalis'**, H 30ft (10m), S 3–6ft (1–2m), is a columnar, dense form with ascending branches bearing needlelike, blue-green leaves. **'Robusta Green'** see *J. virginiana* 'Robusta Green'. **'Stricta'** (illus. p.82), H to 15ft (5m), S to 3ft (1m), zones 5–8, is conical, with soft, blue-green, young foliage.

J. communis (Juniper). Conifer, ranging from a spreading shrub to a narrow, upright tree. H 1–25ft (30cm–8m), S 3–12ft (1–4m). Fully hardy, zones 3–7, except where otherwise stated. Has needlelike, aromatic, glossy, mid- or yellow-green leaves in 3s and bears globular to ovoid, fleshy, greenish berries that become glaucous blue, then ripen to black in their third year. **'Compressa'**, H 30in (75cm), S 6in (15cm), is a dwarf, erect form. **'Hibernica'** (illus. p.83), H 10–15ft (3–5m), S 12in (30cm), is columnar. **'Hornibrookii'**, H 20in (50cm), S 6ft (2m), zones 3–6, and **'Prostrata'**, H 8–12in (20–30cm), S 3–6ft (1–2m), are carpeting plants.

J. conferta (Shore juniper). Prostrate, shrubby conifer. H 6in (15cm), S 3–6ft (1–2m). Fully hardy, zones 6–8. Spreading branches bear dense, needlelike, aromatic, glossy, bright green leaves, glaucous beneath. Produces glaucous black berries. Tolerates salty, coastal air.

J. davurica (Dahurian juniper). **'Expansa Variegata'** (illus. p.83) is a conifer with trailing or ascending branchlets. H 30in (75cm), S 5–6ft (1.5–2m). Fully hardy, zones 5–9. Bears scale- and needlelike, aromatic, yellow-variegated, bluish green leaves.

J. drupacea (Syrian juniper). Columnar conifer. H 30–50ft (10–15m), S 3–6ft (1–2m). Fully hardy, zones 7–10. Has needlelike, aromatic, light green leaves, in 3s, and ovoid or almost globose, fleshy, brown berries.

J. horizontalis (Creeping juniper). Prostrate, wide-spreading, shrubby conifer, eventually forming mats up to 20in (50cm) thick. Fully hardy, zones 3–9. Has scale- or needlelike, aromatic, blue-green or blue-gray leaves and pale blue berries. **'Douglasii'** (illus. p.82) has glaucous blue foliage that turns plum purple in winter. **'Plumosa'** has gray-green leaves, becoming purple during winter. **'Plumosa Compacta'** is denser than 'Plumosa' and turns bronze-purple in winter. **'Prince of Wales'** has bright green foliage, tinged blue when young

and turning purple-brown in winter. **'Turquoise Spreader'** (illus. p.82) has turquoise-green foliage. **'Wiltonii'** has bluish gray leaves that retain their color over winter.

J. × media. Group of conical conifers. H 50ft (15m), S 6–10ft (2–3m). Fully hardy, zones 4–9. Has peeling bark. Mainly scalelike, dark green leaves exude a fetid smell when crushed. Fruits are globose to rounded, white or blue-black. Cultivars are suitable as ground cover or as specimen plants in a small garden. Some forms are commonly listed under *J. chinensis.* **'Blaauw'**, H and S 6ft (2m), is a spreading shrub with blue-green foliage. **'Blue Gold'** (illus. p.83), H to 3ft (1m), S 3ft (1m), is a spreading form with leaves variegated sky blue and gold. **'Hetzii'** (syn. *J. virginiana* 'Hetzii'), H 10–12ft (3–4m), S 12ft (4m), has tiers of gray-green foliage. **'Pfitzeriana'** (illus. p.83), H 10ft (3m), S 10–15ft (3–5m), is a spreading, flat-topped shrub with gray-green leaves. **'Pfitzeriana Aurea'** (illus. p.83) has golden foliage. **'Pfitzeriana Glauca'** (illus. p.82) has gray-blue leaves. **'Plumosa'**, H 3ft (1m), S 6–10ft (2–3m), is a spreading shrub with drooping sprays of green foliage. **'Plumosa Aurea'** (illus. p.83) is more erect, with green-gold foliage, turning bronze in winter.

J. procumbens (Bonin Isles juniper; illus. p.82). Spreading, prostrate, shrubby conifer. H 30in (75cm), S 6ft (2m). Fully hardy, zones 5–9. Has red-brown bark. Thick branches carry needlelike, aromatic, light green or yellow-green leaves and globose, fleshy, brown or black berries. **'Nana'** (illus. p.82), H 6–8in (15–20cm), S 30in (75cm), is less vigorous and is mat-forming.

J. recurva (Drooping juniper, Himalayan weeping juniper). Slow-growing, conical conifer. H to 50ft (15m), S to 22ft (7m). Fully hardy, zones 7–10. Smooth bark flakes in thin sheets. Weeping sprays of needlelike, aromatic, incurved leaves are gray-green or blue-green. Globose or ovoid, fleshy berries are black. var. *coxii* (Coffin juniper) has longer, bright green leaves. **'Densa'** (illus. p.82), H 1ft (30cm), S 3ft (1m), is a spreading shrub with sprays of green leaves that are erect at tips.

J. rigida (Temple juniper). Sprawling, shrubby conifer. H and S 25ft (8m). Fully hardy, zones 6–9. Gray or brown bark peels in strips. Very sharp, needlelike, aromatic, bright green leaves, in 3s, are borne in nodding

sprays. Globose, fleshy fruits are purplish black.

J. sabina (Savin juniper). Spreading, shrubby conifer. H to 12ft (4m), S 10–15ft (3–5m). Fully hardy, zones 4–7. Has flaking, red-brown bark. Slender shoots bear mainly scalelike, aromatic, dark green leaves that give off a fetid smell when crushed. Bears rounded, blue-black berries. **'Blue Danube'**, H 6ft (2m), S 6–12ft (2–4m), is a spreading form with branch tips curved upwards and gray-blue foliage. **'Cupressifolia'** (illus. p.82), H 6ft (2m), S 12ft (4m), is a free-fruiting, female form with horizontal or ascending branches and blue-green leaves. **'Mas'** (illus. p.82), has ascending branches. Leaves are blue above, green below, purplish in winter. var. *tamariscifolia* (illus. p.82), H 3ft (1m), S 6ft (2m), has tiered layers of mainly needlelike, bright green or blue-green leaves.

J. scopulorum (Rocky Mountain juniper). Slow-growing, round-crowned conifer. H 30ft (10m), S 12ft (4m). Fully hardy, zones 4–7. Reddish brown bark is furrowed into strips or squares and peels on branches. Scalelike, aromatic leaves are gray-green to dark green. Bears globose, fleshy, blue berries. **'Skyrocket'** (syn. *J. virginiana* 'Skyrocket'; illus. p.82), H 25ft (8m), S 2¹/₂ft (75cm), is very narrow with glaucous blue foliage. **'Springbank'** (illus. p.82) is narrowly conical with drooping branch tips and intense silvery blue foliage. **'Tabletop'**, H 6ft (2m), S 15ft (5m), has a flat-topped habit and silvery blue leaves.

J. squamata (Single seed juniper). Prostrate to sprawling, shrubby conifer. H 1–12ft (30cm–4m), S 3–15ft (1–5m). Fully hardy, zones 5–8. Bark is red-brown and flaking. Needlelike, aromatic, fresh green or bluish green leaves spread at tips of shoots. Produces ovoid, fleshy, black berries. **'Blue Carpet'**, H 1ft (30cm), S 6–10ft (2–3m), is vigorous and prostrate, with glaucous blue foliage. **'Blue Star'** (illus. p.82), H 20in (50cm), S 24in (60cm), forms a dense, rounded bush and has blue foliage. **'Chinese Silver'** (illus. p.82), H and S 10–12ft (3–4m), has branches with nodding tips and bluish leaves with bright silver undersides. **'Holger'** (illus. p.82), H and S 6ft (2m), has sulfur yellow young leaves that contrast with steel blue old foliage. **'Meyeri'**, H and S 15ft (5m), sprawls and has steel blue foliage.

J. virginiana (Eastern red cedar). Slow-growing, conical or broadly

columnar conifer. H 50–70ft (15–20m), S 20–25ft (6–8m). Fully hardy, zones 3–9. Both scale- and needlelike, aromatic, gray-green leaves are borne on same shoot. Ovoid, fleshy berries are brownish violet and very glaucous. **'Burkii'** illus. p.80. **'Grey Owl'** (illus. p.82), H 10ft (3m), S 10–15ft (3–5m), is a low, spreading cultivar with ascending branches and silvery gray foliage. **'Hetzii'** see *J. × media* 'Hetzii'. **'Robusta Green'** (syn. *J. chinensis* 'Robusta Green') illus. p.80. **'Skyrocket'** see *J. scopulorum* 'Skyrocket'.

JUSTICIA (Acanthaceae)
Genus of evergreen perennials, sub-shrubs, and shrubs, grown mainly for their flowers. Frost tender, min. 50–59°F (10–15°C). Requires full light or partial shade and fertile, well-drained soil. Water potted specimens freely when in full growth, moderately at other times. Some species need regular pruning. Propagate by softwood or greenwood cuttings in spring or early summer. Whitefly may cause problems.

J. adhatoda, syn. *Adhatoda vasica.* Evergreen, erect, sparingly branched shrub. H 6–10ft (2–3m), S 3–6ft (1–2m). Min. 50–59°F (10–15°C), zone 10. Has oval, pointed, prominently veined, green leaves and, in summer, produces dense, terminal spikes of tubular, white flowers, veined pink or purple on lower lip. May be cut back hard in early spring to reduce height. Is sometimes confused in cultivation with *Duvernoia adhatodoides.*

J. brandegeana, syn. *Beloperone guttata, Drejerella guttata*, illus. p.134. **'Chartreuse'** illus. p.136.

J. carnea, syn. *Jacobinia carnea, J. pohliana*, illus. p.131.

J. coccinea. See *Pachystachys coccinea.*

J. floribunda. See *J. rizzinii.*

J. ghiesbreghtiana of gardens. See *J. spicigera.*

J. pauciflora. See *J. rizzinii.*

J. rizzinii, syn. *J. floribunda, J. pauciflora, Libonia floribunda.* Evergreen, rounded, freely branching shrub. H and S 1–2ft (30–60cm). Min. 59°F (15°C), zone 10, to flower well in winter. Leaves are oval and green. Has nodding clusters of tubular, yellow-tipped, scarlet flowers mainly from autumn to spring. Is best repropagated every few years.

J. spicigera, syn. *J. ghiesbreghtiana* of gardens, *Jacobinia spicigera*, illus. p.140.

K

KADSURA (Schisandraceae)
Genus of evergreen, twining climbers, grown for their foliage and fruits. Male and female flowers are produced on separate plants, so plants of both sexes must be grown to obtain fruits. Frost hardy. Grow in semi-shade and in any soil. Propagate by stem cuttings in late summer.
K. japonica. Evergreen, twining climber. H 10–12ft (3–4m). Zones 7–9. Has oval or lance-shaped, green leaves. Solitary small, fragrant cream flowers are produced in leaf axils in summer, followed by bright red berries.

KAEMPFERIA (Zingiberaceae)
Genus of tufted, rhizomatous perennials, grown for their aromatic leaves and their flowers. Frost tender, min. 64°F (18°C). Requires a moist atmosphere, partial shade, and moist, humus-rich soil. Allow to dry out when plants become dormant. Propagate by division in late spring.
K. pulchra illus. p.240.
K. roscoeana. Rhizomatous perennial without an obvious stem. H 2–4in (5–10cm), S 8–10in (20–25cm). Zones 9–10. Usually has only 2 almost round, aromatic leaves, to 4in (10cm) long, dark green with pale green variegation above, reddish green beneath, that are held horizontally. A short spike of pure white flowers, each with a deeply lobed lip, appears from the center of leaf tuft in autumn.

KALANCHOE (Crassulaceae)
Genus of perennial succulents or shrubs with very fleshy, mainly cylindrical, oval, or linear leaves and bell-shaped to tubular flowers. Many species produce new plantlets from indented leaf margins. Frost tender, min. 45–59°F (7–15°C). Needs full sun or partial shade and well-drained soil. Keep moist from spring to autumn. Water lightly and only occasionally in winter. Propagate by seed, offsets, or stem cuttings in spring or summer.
K. beharensis illus. p.381.
K. blossfeldiana (Flaming Katy). Bushy, perennial succulent. H and S 12in (30cm). Min. 50°F (10°C), zone 10. Bears oval to oblong, glossy, dark green leaves, with toothed edges, and clusters of tubular, scarlet flowers, 1/4in (0.5cm) across, in spring. Prefers partial shade. Many hybrids are available in a range of colors (salmon pink, illus. p.385).
K. daigremontiana illus. p.383.
K. fedtschenkoi (South American air plant). Bushy, perennial succulent. H and S 3ft (1m). Min. 50°F (10°C), zone 10. Produces oval, indented, blue-gray leaves with new plantlets in each notch. Bell-shaped, brownish pink flowers, 3/4in (2cm) long, appear in late winter. Prefers a sunny position.
'Variegata' illus. p.383.
K. pumila. Creeping, perennial succulent. H 4in (10cm), S indefinite.

Min. 50°F (10°C), zone 10. Has oval, powdery gray-white leaves with indented margins. Produces tubular, pink flowers, 1/2in (1cm) long, in spring. Suits a hanging basket. Prefers a sunny situation.
K. **'Tessa'** illus. p.385.
K. tomentosa illus. p.387.
K. tubiflora illus. p.388.
K. uniflora, syn. *Kitchingia uniflora.* Creeping, perennial succulent. H 2 1/2in (6cm), S indefinite. Min. 59°F (15°C), zone 10. Produces rounded, green leaves, 1/4–1 1/4in (0.5–3cm) long, and bell-shaped, yellow-flushed, reddish purple flowers, 1/2in (1cm) long, in late winter. Prefers partial shade.
K. **'Wendy'** illus. p.384.

KALMIA (Ericaceae)
Genus of evergreen, summer-flowering shrubs, grown for their clusters of distinctive, usually cup-shaped flowers. Fully hardy. Needs sun or semi-shade and moist, peaty, acid soil. Propagate species by softwood cuttings in summer or by seed in autumn, selected forms by softwood cuttings in summer.
K. angustifolia (Sheep laurel). f. *rubra* illus. p.133.
K. latifolia illus. p.109. **'Ostbo Red'** is an evergreen, bushy, dense shrub. H and S 10ft (3m). Zones 5–9. Has oval, glossy, rich green leaves. Large clusters of deep pink flowers open in early summer from distinctively crimped, deep red buds. Prefers full sun.

KALMIOPSIS (Ericaceae)
Genus of one species of evergreen, spring-flowering shrub, grown for its flowers. Fully hardy. Requires semi-shade and moist, peaty, acid soil. Propagate by softwood or semi-ripe cuttings in summer.
K. leachiana **'M. Le Piniec'.** Evergreen, bushy shrub. H and S 12in (30cm). Zones 7–9. Terminal clusters of small, widely bell-shaped, purplish pink flowers are produced from early to late spring. Has small, oval, glossy, dark green leaves.

KALOPANAX (Araliaceae)
Genus of one species of deciduous, autumn-flowering tree, grown for its foliage and fruits. Fully hardy, but unripened wood on young plants is susceptible to frost damage. Does best in sun or semi-shade and in fertile, moist but well-drained soil. Propagate by softwood cuttings in summer.
K. pictus, syn. *K. ricinifolius*, *Acanthopanax ricinifolium*, illus. p.53.
K. ricinifolius. See *K. pictus.*

KELSEYA (Rosaceae)
Genus of one species of extremely small, evergreen sub-shrub. Is difficult to grow and is best in an alpine house as foliage deeply resents both summer and winter wet. Fully hardy. Needs full sun and moist, alkaline soil. Propagate

by soft-tip cuttings in late spring or by seed in autumn. Is susceptible to molds, so remove any dead rosettes at once.
K. uniflora. Slow-growing, evergreen, rosetted sub-shrub. H 1/2in (1cm), S to 8in (20cm). Zones 5–7. Forms a hard mat of closely packed, small rosettes of tiny, oval, dark green leaves. In early spring carries stemless, star-shaped, occasionally pink-flushed, white flowers.

KENNEDIA, syn. KENNEDYA (Leguminosae)
Genus of evergreen, woody-stemmed, trailing and twining climbers, grown for their pealike flowers. Frost tender, min. 41–5°F (5–7°C). Provide full light and moderately fertile, sandy soil. Water regularly when in full growth, sparingly in cold weather. Requires support. Thin out congested growth after flowering or in spring. Propagate by seed in spring or by semi-ripe cuttings in summer.
K. nigricans (Black bean). Vigorous, evergreen, woody-stemmed, twining climber. H to 6ft (2m). Zone 10. Leaves are divided into 3 leaflets with notched tips. Has small trusses of pealike, velvety, black-purple flowers, with yellow blazes, in spring-summer.
K. rubicunda illus. p.163.

KENNEDYA. See KENNEDIA.

KENTIA. See HOWEA.

KERRIA (Rosaceae)
Genus of one species of deciduous shrub, grown for its showy, yellow flowers. Fully hardy. Needs sun or semi-shade and fertile, well-drained soil. Thin out old shoots after flowering. Propagate by softwood cuttings in summer or by division in autumn.
K. japonica illus. p.99. **'Pleniflora'** is a vigorous, deciduous, graceful shrub. H and S 10ft (3m). Zones 5–9. Has green shoots and narrowly oval, sharply toothed, bright green leaves. Produces large, buttercuplike, double, golden yellow flowers from mid- to late spring.

KIGELIA (Bignoniaceae)
Genus of one species of evergreen tree, grown for its flowers, curious, sausagelike fruits, and for shade. Frost tender, min. 61°F (16°C). Requires full light and humus-rich, well-drained soil. Water potted specimens moderately, very little when temperatures are low. Propagate by seed in spring at not less than 73°F (23°C).
K. pinnata (Sausage tree). Evergreen, spreading, fairly bushy tree. H and S 25ft (8m) or more. Zone 10. Leaves have 7–11 oblong to oval leaflets. Scented, bell-shaped, purplish red flowers open at night from autumn to

spring. Inedible, cylindrical, hard-shelled, brown fruits, 12–18in (30–45cm) long, are long-lasting.

KIRENGESHOMA (Hydrangeaceae)
Genus of late summer- and autumn-flowering perennials. Fully hardy. Grow in light shade and in deep, moist, lime-free soil. Propagate by seed or division in autumn or spring.
K. palmata illus. p.221.

KITAIBELA (Malvaceae)
Genus of one species of summer-flowering perennial. Fully hardy. Needs full sun and fertile, preferably dry soil. Propagate by seed in autumn or spring.
K. vitifolia. Bushy, upright perennial. H to 5ft (1.5m), S 2ft (60cm). Zones 5–8. In summer bears small clusters of open cup-shaped, white or rose-pink flowers. Has palmately lobed, coarsely toothed leaves.

Kitchingia uniflora. See *Kalanchoe uniflora.*

Kleinia articulata. See *Senecio articulatus.*

KNAUTIA (Dispacaceae)
Genus of summer-flowering annuals and perennials. Fully hardy. Needs sun and well-drained soil. Requires staking. Propagate by basal cuttings in spring or by seed in autumn.
K. arvensis (Scabious). Erect perennial. H 4ft (1.2m), S 1 1/2ft (45cm). Zones 5–9. Heads of pincushionlike, bluish lilac flowers appear in summer. Stems are clothed in narrowly oval to lyre-shaped, deeply divided leaves.
K. macedonica, syn. *Scabiosa rumelica*, illus. p.208.

KNIGHTIA (Proteaceae)
Genus of evergreen, summer-flowering trees, grown for their flowers, foliage, and overall appearance. Half hardy, but is best at min. 37–41°F (3–5°C). Grows in any reasonably fertile, well-drained soil and in sun or partial shade. Water potted specimens moderately, less in winter. Propagate by seed in spring.
K. excelsa (New Zealand honeysuckle, Rewa rewa). Evergreen, upright tree. H 70ft (20m) or more, S 6–12ft (2–4m). Zones 9–10. Has oblong to lance-shaped, coarsely serrated, leathery leaves, glossy and deep green. Dense racemes of slender, tubular, deep red flowers are produced in summer.

KNIPHOFIA (Liliaceae or Aloeaceae)
Red-hot poker, Torch lily
Genus of perennials, some of which are evergreen. Fully to half hardy. Needs full sun and well-drained conditions, with constantly moist soil

in summer. Propagate species by seed or division in spring, cultivars by division only in spring.

K. **'Atlanta'.** Evergreen, upright perennial. H to 3ft (1m), S 1¹/₂ft (45cm). Fully hardy, zones 6–9. In summer, stout stems bear dense, terminal racemes of tubular, bright orange-yellow flowers. Has thick, grasslike, channeled leaves. Does well in a coastal area.

K. **'Bee's Lemon'.** Upright perennial. H 3ft (1m), S 1¹/₂ft (45cm). Fully hardy, zones 5–9. Produces dense, terminal racemes of tubular, green-tinged, citron yellow flowers on stout stems in late summer and autumn. Grasslike leaves are deep green and have serrated edges.

K. caulescens illus. p.221.
K. galpinii. See *K. triangularis.*
K. **'Little Maid'** illus. p.245.
K. **'Maid of Orleans'.** Upright perennial. H 4ft (1.2m), S 1¹/₂ft (45cm). Frost hardy, zones 6–9. In summer, slender stems are each crowned with a dense raceme of yellow buds that open to tubular, creamy white flowers. Leaves are fresh green, basal, and strap-shaped.

K. **'Percy's Pride'** illus. p.220.
K. **'Royal Standard'** illus. p.216.
K. **'Samuel's Sensation'.** Upright perennial. H 5ft (1.5m), S 2ft (60cm). Fully hardy, zones 6–9. In late summer bears dense, terminal

racemes of tubular, deep orange flowers that are produced on stout stems. Has strap-shaped, basal, dark green leaves.

K. thomsonii var. *snowdenii* illus. p.216.
K. triangularis, syn. *K. galpinii,* illus. p.221.
K. uvaria (Red-hot poker). var. *nobilis* is an upright perennial with erect, then spreading leaves. H 6ft (2m), S 3ft (1m). Fully hardy, zones 5–9. In late summer and autumn, stout stems each bear a dense, terminal raceme of tubular, bright red flowers. Produces strap-shaped, channeled, dark green leaves.

KOCHIA (Chenopodiaceae)

Genus of annuals and perennials, sometimes included in *Bassia.* Only *K. scoparia* f. *trichophylla* is usually cultivated. Half hardy. Does best in sun and in fertile, well-drained soil. May require support in very windy areas. Propagate by seed sown under glass in early spring, or outdoors in mid-spring.

K. scoparia f. *trichophylla* illus. p.279.

KOELREUTERIA (Sapindaceae)

Genus of deciduous, summer-flowering trees, grown for their foliage, flowers, and fruits. Fully hardy to frost tender, min. 50°F (10°C). Requires full sun, doing best in hot

summers, and fertile, well-drained soil. Propagate by seed in autumn or by root cuttings in late winter.

K. paniculata illus. p.65.

KOHLERIA (Gesneriaceae)

Genus of erect perennials with scaly rhizomes, grown for their showy, tubular flowers borne mainly in summer. Frost tender, min. 59°F (15°C). Grow in moist but well-drained soil and in full sun or semi-shade. Water sparingly in winter; over-watering will cause rhizomes to rot. Propagate in spring by division of rhizomes or by seed if available.

K. amabilis. Rhizomatous perennial. H 3–6in (8–16cm), S 2ft (60cm). Zone 10. Oval, hairy leaves, to 3in (8cm) long, are often marked with silver and brown above. Produces small, nodding, tubular, deep pink flowers, with red-marked lobes, that appear in summer. Is useful for growing in a hanging basket.

K. bogotensis. Erect, rhizomatous perennial. H and S 18in (45cm) or more. Zone 10. Bears oval, velvety, green leaves, to 3in (8cm) long, that are sometimes marked with paler green above. In summer produces small, tubular flowers, red with a yellow base outside and red-dotted, yellow within.

K. digitaliflora illus. p.204.
K. eriantha illus. p.209.

KOLKWITZIA (Caprifoliaceae)

Genus of one species of deciduous shrub, grown for its abundant flowers. Fully hardy. Prefers full sun and fertile, well-drained soil. Cut out old, damaged, or weak shoots after flowering. Propagate by softwood cuttings in summer.

K. amabilis (Beautybush). Deciduous, arching shrub. H and S 10ft (3m). Zones 5–9. Has peeling bark and oval, dark green leaves. Bell-shaped, yellow-throated, white or pink flowers are borne in late spring and early summer. **'Pink Cloud'** illus. p.88.

Korolkowia sewerzowii. See *Fritillaria sewerzowii.*

KUNZEA (Myrtaceae)

Genus of evergreen shrubs and trees, grown for their flowers and overall appearance. Frost tender, min. 41–5°F (5–7°C). Prefers full light and sandy, well-drained, neutral to acid soil. Water potted specimens moderately, less when not in full growth. Propagate by semi-ripe cuttings in late summer or by seed in spring.

K. baxteri. Evergreen, rounded, wiry-stemmed shrub. H and S to 6ft (2m). Zones 9–10. Has narrow, cylindrical, pointed, green leaves and, in early summer, 5-petaled, deep red flowers, each with a brush of stamens, in bottlebrushlike, 2in (5cm) long spikes.

L

LABLAB (Leguminosae)
Genus of one species of deciduous, woody-stemmed, twining climber, grown for its attractive, pealike flowers (in tropics is grown for green manure and animal feed, and for its edible pods and seeds). Is often raised as an annual. Frost tender, min. 41–50°F (5–10°C). Grow in sun and in any well-drained soil. Propagate by seed in spring.
L. purpureus, syn. *Dolichos lablab*, *D. lignosus*, illus. p.169.

+ LABURNOCYTISUS (Leguminosae)
Deciduous tree, grown for its flowers. Is a graft hybrid between *Laburnum anagyroides* and *Cytisus purpureus*. Fully hardy. Needs full sun; grows in any but waterlogged soil. Propagate by grafting on laburnum in late summer.
+ L. adamii. Deciduous, spreading tree. H 25ft (8m), S 20ft (6m). Zones 6–8. In late spring and early summer bears 3 types of blooms: yellow, laburnum flowers; purple, cytisus flowers; and laburnumlike, yellow and pinkish purple flowers. Leaves consist of 3 oval leaflets and are dark green.

LABURNUM (Leguminosae)
Genus of deciduous trees, grown for their profuse, pendent flower clusters in spring and summer. Fully hardy. Does best in full sun; grows in any but waterlogged soil. Seeds are very poisonous. Propagate species by seed in autumn, hybrids by budding in summer.
L. alpinum illus. p.66.
L. anagyroides (Common laburnum, Golden chain). Deciduous, spreading tree. H and S 22ft (7m). Zones 6–8. Leaves have 3 oval leaflets and are gray-green. Short, pendent, dense clusters of large, pealike, yellow flowers appear in late spring and early summer.
L. x *watereri* (Voss's laburnum). 'Vossii' illus. p.65.

LACHENALIA (Liliaceae)
Genus of winter- and spring-flowering bulbs with tubular or bell-shaped flowers; some have attractively mottled leaves. Is useful as pot plants and in open borders. Frost tender, min. 36–9°F (2–4°C). Requires light, well-drained soil, and a sunny site. Plant in early autumn; dry off in summer when foliage has died down. Propagate in autumn by seed or freely produced offsets.
L. contaminata. Winter- and spring-flowering bulb. H to 8in (20cm), S 2–3in (5–8cm). Zones 9–10. Produces narrowly strap-shaped, semi-erect leaves in a basal cluster. Leafless stem produces a spike of bell-shaped, white flowers, ¼in (0.5cm) long, suffused and tipped with red and green.
L. glaucina illus. p.355.

L. mutabilis. Winter- and spring-flowering bulb. H to 12in (30cm), S 2–3in (5–8cm). Zones 9–10. Has 2 strap-shaped, semi-erect, basal leaves. Stem bears a loose spike of up to 25 tubular, ½in (1cm) long flowers, with reddish brown-tipped petals and green tube bases, that open from purple or lilac buds.
L. 'Nelsonii' illus. p.371.
L. orchioides. Winter- and spring-flowering bulb. H 6–12in (15–30cm), S 2–3in (5–8cm). Zones 9–10. Has 2 strap-shaped, semi-erect, basal, green leaves, sometimes spotted blackish or purple-brown. Stem produces a dense spike of fragrant, semi-erect, tubular, white flowers, ½in (1cm) long, blue-tinged and tipped with green.
L. 'Quadricolor' illus. p.371.
L. rubida. Winter-flowering bulb. H to 10in (25cm), S 2–3in (5–8cm). Zones 9–10. Bears 2 strap-shaped, purple-spotted, green leaves, semi-erect and basal, and a loose spike of pendent, tubular, red flowers, ¾–1¼in (2–3cm) long, shading to yellow at tips.
L. 'Tricolor'. Winter- and spring-flowering bulb. H 6–10in (15–25cm), S 2–3in (5–8cm). Zones 9–10. Produces 2 strap-shaped, semi-erect, basal, purple-spotted, green leaves. Has a spike of 10–20 pendent flowers, each 1¼in (3cm) long with a yellow tube shading to red at the apex and with flared, green tips.

Lactuca alpina. See *Cicerbita alpina.*
Lactuca bourgaei. See *Cicerbita bourgaei.*

LAELIA. See ORCHIDS.
L. anceps (illus. p. 253). Evergreen, epiphytic orchid for a cool greenhouse. H 10in (25cm). Zone 10. Lilac-pink flowers, 2½in (6cm). wide, each with a deep mauve lip, are carried in tall spikes in autumn. Has oval, rigid leaves, 4–6in (10–15cm) long. Needs semi-shade in summer.
L. cinnabarina (illus. p.255). Evergreen, epiphytic orchid for an intermediate greenhouse. H 6in (15cm). Zone 10. Produces sprays of slender, orange flowers, 2in (5cm) or more across, usually in winter. Has narrowly oval, rigid leaves, 3–4in (8–10cm) long. Needs good light in summer.

x LAELIOCATTLEYA. See ORCHIDS.
x L. Rojo 'Mont Millais' (illus. p.253). Zone 10. Evergreen, epiphytic orchid for an intermediate greenhouse. H 12in (30cm). In winter-spring bears arching heads of slender, reddish orange flowers, ¾in (2cm) across. Oval leaves are up to 6in (15cm) long. Provide good light in summer.

LAGAROSIPHON (Hydrocharitaceae)
Genus of semi-evergreen, perennial, spreading, submerged water plants

grown for their decorative foliage. Oxygenates water. Fully hardy. Needs full sun. Thin regularly to keep under control. Propagate by stem cuttings in spring or summer.
L. major, syn. *Elodea crispa* of gardens, illus. p.375.

LAGERSTROEMIA (Lythraceae)
Genus of deciduous or evergreen, summer-flowering shrubs and trees, grown for their flowers. Frost hardy to frost tender, min. 37–41°F (3–5°C). Prefers fertile, well-drained soil and full light. Water potted specimens freely when in full growth, less at other times. To maintain as shrubs, cut back hard the previous season's stems each spring. Propagate by seed in spring or by semi-ripe cuttings in summer.
L. indica illus. p.64.
L. speciosa (Pride-of-India, Queen's crape myrtle). Deciduous, rounded tree. H 50–70ft (15–20m), S 30–50ft (10–15m). Frost tender, zones 9–10. Mid- to deep green leaves are narrowly oval, 3–7in (8–18cm) long. Has panicles of funnel-shaped, rose-pink to rose-purple flowers in summer-autumn, often when leafless.

LAGUNARIA (Malvaceae)
Genus of one species of evergreen tree, grown for its flowers in summer-autumn and its overall appearance. Frost tender, min. 37–41°F (3–5°C). Prefers fertile, well-drained soil and full light. Water potted plants freely when in full summer growth, moderately at other times. Pruning is tolerated if required. Propagate by seed in spring or by semi-ripe cuttings in summer. Under cover, red spider mite may be troublesome.
L. patersonii (Norfolk Island hibiscus, Queensland pyramidal tree). Fast-growing, evergreen, upright tree, pyramidal when young. H 30–46ft (10–14m), S 15–22ft (5–7m). Zones 9–10. Oval, rough-textured leaves are matt green above, whitish green beneath. Produces hibiscuslike, rose-pink flowers, 2in (5cm) wide, in summer.

LAGURUS (Gramineae). See GRASSES, BAMBOOS, RUSHES, and SEDGES.
L. ovatus illus. p.180.

LAMARCKIA (Gramineae). See GRASSES, BAMBOOS, RUSHES, and SEDGES.
L. aurea (Golden top). Tuft-forming, annual grass. H and S 8in (20cm). Fully hardy, zones 7–10. Wiry stems bear scattered, pale green leaves and, in summer, erect, dense, one-sided, golden panicles. Needs sun.

Lamiastrum galeobdolon **'Variegatum'.** See *Galeobdolon argentatum.*

LAMIUM (Labiatae)
Deadnettle
Genus of spring- or summer-flowering perennials, most of which are semi-evergreen, including a number of weeds; some species make useful ground cover. Fully hardy. Prefers full or partial shade and moist but well-drained soil. Resents excessive winter wet. Propagate by stem-tip cuttings of non-flowering shoots in mid-summer or by division in autumn or early spring.
L. galeobdolon **'Variegatum'.** See *Galeobdolon argentatum.*
L. maculatum illus. p.226. **'Album'** illus. p.224. **'Beacon Silver'** is a semi-evergreen, mat-forming perennial. H 8in (20cm), S 3ft (1m). Zones 4–8. Has oval, mauve-tinged, silver leaves, sometimes with narrow, green margins. Whorls of hooded, mauve-pink flowers appear on short stems in summer. **'White Nancy'** illus. p.224.
L. orvala illus. p.228.

LAMPRANTHUS (Aizoaceae)
Genus of creeping, bushy, perennial succulents and sub-shrubs with daisylike flowers. Becomes woody after several years, when is best replenished. Plants are good for summer bedding, particularly in arid conditions. Leaves redden in strong sun. Frost tender, min. 41°F (5°C) if dry. Requires full sun and very well-drained soil. Propagate by seed or stem cuttings in spring or autumn.
L. aurantiacus illus. p.388.
L. haworthii. Erect to creeping, perennial succulent. H 20in (50cm), S indefinite. Zone 10. Blue-gray leaves are cylindrical and 2in (5cm) long. In spring bears masses of daisylike, cerise flowers, 3in (7cm) across, that only open in sun.
L. multiradiatus, syn. *L. roseus*. Creeping, perennial succulent. H 6in (15cm), S indefinite. Zone 10. Produces solid, 3-angled, mid- to glaucous green leaves, 2in (5cm) long. Daisylike, dark rose-red flowers, 1½in (4cm) across, open only in sun from spring to autumn.
L. roseus. See *L. multiradiatus.*
L. spectabilis illus. p.384.

LANTANA (Verbenaceae)
Genus of evergreen perennials and shrubs, grown for their flowers. Frost tender, min. 50–55°F (10–13°C). Needs full light and fertile, well-drained soil. Water potted specimens freely when in full growth, moderately at other times. Tip prune young plants to promote a bushy habit. Propagate by seed in spring or by semi-ripe cuttings in summer. Red spider mite and whitefly may be troublesome.
L. camara. Evergreen, rounded to spreading shrub. H and S 3–6ft (1–2m). Zone 9–10. Bears oval, finely wrinkled, deep green leaves. From spring to autumn, tiny, tubular, 5-lobed

flowers, in dense, domed heads, open yellow, then turn red. Many color forms have been selected.
L. delicatissima. See *L. montevidensis.*
L. montevidensis, syn. *L. delicatissima, L. sellowiana,* illus. p.135.
L. sellowiana. See *L. montevidensis.*
L. 'Spreading Sunset' illus. p.139.

LAPAGERIA (Liliaceae)
Genus of one species of evergreen, woody-stemmed, twining climber, grown for its large, waxy blooms. Half hardy. Requires humus-rich, well-drained soil and partial shade. Water moderately, scarcely at all when not in full growth. Provide support. Thin out congested growth in spring. Propagate in spring by seed, soaked for 2 days before sowing, or in spring or autumn by layering.
L. rosea illus. p.168.

Lapeirousia cruenta. See *Anomatheca laxa.*
Lapeirousia laxa. See *Anomatheca laxa.*

LARDIZABALA (Lardizabalaceae)
Genus of evergreen, woody-stemmed, twining climbers, grown for their foliage. Male and female flowers are borne on the same plant in late autumn to winter. Is useful for growing on trellises or pergolas. Frost to half hardy. Grow in sun or partial shade and in any well-drained soil. Propagate by seed in spring or by stem cuttings in late summer or autumn.
L. biternata. Evergreen, woody-stemmed, twining climber. H 10–12ft (3–4m). Half hardy, zones 9–10. Rounded leaves have broadly oval, leathery, dark green leaflets. In winter produces brown flowers with tiny, whitish petals, the males are borne in drooping spikes, the females are solitary. In winter-spring bears many-seeded, berrylike, purple fruits, 2–3in (5–8cm) long.

LARIX (Pinaceae). See CONIFERS.
L. decidua (European larch). Fast-growing, deciduous conifer with a conical crown when young, broadening on maturity, and spaced branches. H 80–100ft (25–30m), S 16–50ft (5–15m). Fully hardy, zones 3–6. Shoots are yellow-brown in winter. Has light green leaves and small, erect, conical cones.
L. kaempferi (Japanese larch). Fast-growing, deciduous, columnar conifer with a conical tip. H 80–100ft (25–30m), S 15–25ft (5–8m). Fully hardy, zones 5–7. Shoots are purplish red and leaves are needlelike, flattened, grayish green or bluish. Small cones have reflexed scales.

LATHRAEA (Scrophulariaceae)
Genus of spreading perennials that grow as parasites on the roots of trees, in the case of *L. clandestina* on willow or poplar. True leaves are not produced. Fully hardy. Grows in dappled shade cast by host tree and prefers moist conditions. Roots resent being disturbed. Propagate by seed when fresh, in late summer.
L. clandestina illus. p.228.

LATHYRUS (Leguminosae)
Genus of annuals and perennials, many of them tendril climbers, grown for their racemes of attractive flowers. Flowers are followed by long, thin seed pods. Fully hardy to frost tender, min. 36–9°F (2–4°C). Grow in humus-rich, fertile, well-drained soil and in full light. Provide support and remove dead flowers regularly. Cut down perennials in late autumn. Propagate annuals by seed (soaked before sowing) in early spring or early autumn, perennials by seed in autumn or by division in spring. Botrytis and mildew may cause problems.
L. grandiflorus illus. p.167.
L. latifolius illus. p.169.
L. nervosus (Lord Anson's blue pea). Herbaceous, tendril climber. H to 15ft (5m). Frost hardy, zones 3–10. Gray-green leaves each have a pair of leaflets, a 3-branched tendril, and large stipules. Bears fragrant, purplish blue flowers in long-stalked racemes in summer.
L. odoratus (Sweet pea). Moderately fast-growing, annual, tendril climber. H to 10ft (3m). Fully hardy to frost tender, min. 36–9°F (2–4°C). Has oval, green leaves with tendrils. Scented flowers are produced in shades of pink, blue, purple, or white, from summer to early autumn. Dwarf, non-climbing cultivars are available. 'Bijou' illus. p.268; 'Knee Hi' illus. p.264; 'Lady Diana' illus. p.172; 'Red Ensign' illus. p.168; 'Selana' illus. p.166; 'Xenia Field' illus. p.167.
L. rotundifolius (Persian everlasting pea). Herbaceous, tendril climber with winged stems. H to 3ft (1m). Fully hardy, zones 5–10. Leaves each have narrow stipules, a pair of leaflets, and a 3-branched tendril. Has small racemes of 3–8 pink to purplish flowers in summer.
L. sylvestris (Everlasting pea, Perennial pea). Herbaceous, tendril climber with winged stems. H to 6ft (2m). Fully hardy, zones 5–10. Leaves each have narrow stipules, a pair of leaflets, and a terminal, branched tendril. In summer and early autumn bears racemes of 4–10 rose-pink flowers, marked with green and purple.
L. vernus illus. p.227. 'Albo-roseus' is a clump-forming perennial. H and S 12in (30cm). Fully hardy, zones 5–9. In spring, slender stems each bear 3–5 white-and-deep-pink flowers. Has fernlike, much-divided, soft leaves.

LAURELIA (Atherospermataceae or Monimiaceae)
Laurel
Genus of evergreen trees and shrubs, grown for their aromatic foliage. Frost hardy, but needs shelter from cold winds. Grows in any but very dry soil; requires sun or semi-shade. Propagate by semi-ripe cuttings in summer.
L. serrata (Chilean laurel). Evergreen, broadly conical tree or shrub. H and S to 50ft (15m). Zones 9–10. Oval, leathery leaves are glossy, dark green and very aromatic. In summer bears inconspicuous flowers.

LAURUS (Lauraceae)
Bay tree, Laurel
Genus of evergreen trees, grown for

their foliage. Frost hardy, but foliage may be scorched by extremely cold weather or strong, cold winds. Needs a sheltered position in sun or semi-shade and fertile, well-drained soil. In tubs may be grown well as standards, which should be trimmed during summer. Propagate by semi-ripe cuttings in summer or by seed in autumn.
L. nobilis (Bay laurel, Sweet bay). Evergreen, broadly conical tree. H 40ft (12m), S 30ft (10m). Zones 8–10. Narrowly oval, leathery, glossy, dark green leaves are very aromatic and used in cooking. Small, star-shaped, pale yellow flowers are borne in spring and are followed by globose to ovoid, green, then black fruits.

LAVANDULA (Labiatae)
Lavender
Genus of evergreen, mainly summer-flowering shrubs, with entire or divided, often gray-green leaves, grown for their aromatic foliage and flowers. Makes an effective, low hedge. Fully to half hardy. Needs full sun and fertile, well-drained soil. Trim hedges lightly in spring to maintain a compact habit. Propagate by semi-ripe cuttings in summer.
L. angustifolia 'Hidcote' illus. p.135. 'Munstead' see *L.* 'Munstead'.
L. dentata (French lavender). Evergreen, bushy shrub. H and S 3ft (1m). Frost hardy, zones 8–9. Aromatic leaves are fernlike, toothed and gray-green. Dense spikes of small, slightly fragrant, tubular, lavender-blue flowers and purple bracts are borne from mid- to late summer.
L. 'Grappenhall'. Evergreen, bushy shrub. H 3ft (1m), S 5ft (1.5m). Frost hardy, zones 8–9. Bears narrowly oblong, aromatic, gray-green leaves. Produces long-stalked spikes of tiny, slightly fragrant, tubular, blue-purple flowers in mid- and late summer.
L. 'Munstead', syn. *L. angustifolia* 'Munstead'. Evergreen, bushy, compact shrub. H and S 2ft (60cm). Fully hardy, zones 6–9. Narrowly oblong, aromatic leaves are gray-green. Produces dense spikes of tiny, fragrant, tubular, blue flowers from mid- to late summer.
L. stoechas illus. p.135.

LAVATERA (Malvaceae)
Tree mallow
Genus of mainly summer-flowering annuals, biennials, perennials, and semi-evergreen sub-shrubs and shrubs. Fully to frost hardy. Needs sun and well-drained soil. Propagate perennials, sub-shrubs, and shrubs by softwood cuttings in early spring or summer, annuals and biennials by seed in spring or early autumn.
L. assurgentiflora illus. p.109.
L. cachemiriana, syn. *L. cachemirica,* illus. p.189.
L. cachemirica. See *L. cachemiriana.*
L. olbia 'Rosea' illus. p.109.
L. trimestris 'Mont Blanc' illus. p.262. 'Silver Cup' illus. p.268.

LAYIA (Compositae)
Genus of annuals, useful for hot, dry places. Fully to half hardy. Grow in sun and in poor to fertile, very well-

drained soil. Propagate by seed sown outdoors in spring or early autumn.
L. elegans. See *L. platyglossa.*
L. platyglossa, syn. *L. elegans* (Tidy tips). Fast-growing, upright, bushy annual. H 18in (45cm), S 12in (30cm). Half hardy. Has lance-shaped, grayish green leaves. Daisylike flower heads, 2in (5cm) wide, with white-tipped, yellow ray petals and yellow centers, are produced from early summer to early autumn. Is suitable for cutting.

LECHENAULTIA, syn. LESCHENAULTIA (Goodeniaceae)
Genus of evergreen shrubs, grown for their flowers. Frost tender, min. 45–50°F (7–10°C). Needs full light and peaty, well-drained soil with few phosphates and nitrates. Water potted plants moderately in growing season, sparingly at other times. Shorten over-long stems after flowering. Propagate by seed in spring or by semi-ripe cuttings in summer. Most species are not easy to grow under glass; good ventilation is essential.
L. floribunda. Evergreen, domed, wiry-stemmed shrub. H and S 12–24in (30–60cm). Zone 10. Has narrow, cylindrical, pointed leaves and, in spring-summer, short, tubular, pale blue flowers, each with 5 angular petals, in terminal clusters.

LEDEBOURIA (Liliaceae)
Genus of bulbs, some of which are evergreen, with ornamental, narrowly lance-shaped leaves. Flowers are very small with reflexed tips. Makes good pot plants in cool greenhouses. Half hardy. Needs full light, to allow leaf marks to develop well, and loose, open soil. Propagate by offsets in spring.
L. cooperi, syn. *Scilla adlamii.* Summer-flowering bulb. H 2–4in (5–10cm), S 1–2in (2.5–5cm). Zones 9–10. Semi-erect, basal, green leaves, with brownish purple stripes, die away in winter. Stem bears a short spike of small, bell-shaped, greenish purple flowers.
L. socialis, syn. *Scilla violacea,* illus. p.363.

LEDUM (Ericaceae)
Genus of evergreen shrubs, grown for their aromatic foliage and small, white flowers. Fully hardy. Needs shade or semi-shade and moist, peaty, acid soil. Benefits from dead-heading. Propagate by semi-ripe cuttings in summer or by seed in autumn.
L. groenlandicum illus. p.122.

LEIOPHYLLUM (Ericaceae)
Genus of one species of evergreen shrub with an extensive, spreading root system. Fully hardy. Prefers semi-shade and well-drained, peaty, acid soil. Top-dress regularly with peaty soil. Propagate by seed in spring or by semi-ripe cuttings in summer.
L. buxifolium. Evergreen, dome-shaped shrub. H 10in (25cm), S 18in (45cm). Zones 6–8. Stems are covered with tiny, oval, leathery, dark green leaves. In late spring, terminal clusters of deep pink buds develop into small, star-shaped, white flowers, with prominent stamens.

LEMAIREOCEREUS (Cactaceae)
Genus of columnar, perennial cacti with ribbed, spiny, dark green stems. Reaches 3ft (1m) in 5–10 years. Flowers appear in summer, only on plants over 6ft (2m) high. Frost tender, min. 52°F (11°C), otherwise plants may become badly marked. Needs full sun and very well-drained soil. Propagate by seed or stem cuttings in spring or summer.

L. euphorbioides, syn. *Rooksbya euphorbioides*, illus. p.380.

L. marginatus, syn. *Marginatocereus marginatus*, illus. p.379.

L. thurberi. Columnar, perennial cactus, branching from low down. H to 22ft (7m), S 10ft (3m). Zone 10. Has 5- or 6-ribbed, glossy, dark green stems with very short-spined areoles set in close rows down each rib. Produces funnel-shaped, white flowers in summer.

LEONOTIS (Labiatae)
Genus of annuals, evergreen and semi-evergreen perennials, sub-shrubs, and shrubs, grown for their flowers and overall appearance. Half hardy to frost tender, min. 41–5°F (5–7°C). Needs full sun and rich, well-drained soil. Water potted specimens freely when in full growth, much less at other times. Cut back perennials, sub-shrubs, and shrubs to within 6in (15cm) of ground in early spring. Propagate by seed in spring or by greenwood cuttings in early summer.

L. leonurus illus. p.117.

LEONTOPODIUM (Compositae)
Edelweiss
Genus of short-lived, spring-flowering, woolly perennials, grown for their flower heads. Is suitable for rock gardens. Fully hardy. Needs sun, gritty, well-drained soil, and a deep collar of grit. Shelter from prevailing, rain-bearing winds, as crowns are very intolerant of winter wet. Propagate by division in spring or by seed when fresh. Many seeds are not viable.

L. alpinum illus. p.286.

L. stracheyi. Mound-forming, spreading, woolly perennial. H and S 4in (10cm). Zones 4–6. Star-shaped, glistening, white flower heads are borne among thick, oval, silver leaves in spring. Makes a good alpine house plant.

LEPTOSPERMUM (Myrtaceae)
Genus of evergreen trees and shrubs, grown for their foliage and small, often profuse flowers. Grows well in coastal areas if not too exposed. Frost to half hardy, but in cold areas plant against a south- or west-facing wall. Needs full sun and fertile, well-drained soil. Propagate by semi-ripe cuttings in summer.

L. flavescens illus. p.107.

L. humifusum illus. p.128.

L. scoparium (Manuka, New Zealand tea-tree). **'Keatleyi'** is an evergreen, rounded shrub. H and S 10ft (3m). Half hardy, zones 9–10. Narrowly lance-shaped, aromatic, gray-green leaves set off a profusion of large, star-shaped, pale pink flowers during late spring and summer. **'Nicholsii'**

produces bronze-purple leaves and smaller, crimson flowers. **'Red Damask'** illus. p.99.

LESCHENAULTIA. See LECHENAULTIA.

LEUCADENDRON (Proteaceae)
Genus of evergreen shrubs and trees, grown for their flower heads from autumn to spring and for their foliage. Frost tender, min. 41–5°F (5–7°C). Needs full light and sharply drained soil, mainly of sand and peat, ideally with very little nitrogen and phosphates. Water potted specimens moderately while in growth, sparingly at other times. Propagate by seed in spring.

L. argenteum illus. p.72.

Leucanthemella serotina. See *Chrysanthemum uliginosum*.

LEUCHTENBERGIA (Cactaceae)
Genus of one species of perennial cactus. Looks like *Agave* in foliage, but its flowers, seed pods, and seeds are similar to *Ferocactus*. Tubercles eventually form on short, rough, woody stems. Frost tender, min. 43°F (6°C). Needs full sun and very well-drained soil. Keep completely dry in winter; water sparingly from spring to autumn. Propagate by seed in spring or summer.

L. principis illus. p.387.

LEUCOCORYNE (Liliaceae)
Genus of spring-flowering bulbs with loose heads of flattish flowers. Half hardy. Needs sun and well-drained soil. Plant in autumn and water until after flowering. Lies dormant in summer. Propagate by seed or offsets in autumn.

L. ixioides illus. p.346.

LEUCOGENES (Compositae)
New Zealand edelweiss
Genus of evergreen, woody-based perennials, grown mainly for their foliage. Is excellent for alpine houses in areas where summers are cool. Frost to half hardy. Needs sun and gritty, well-drained, peaty soil. Resents winter wet and may be difficult to grow. Propagate by seed when fresh or by softwood cuttings in late spring or early summer.

L. grandiceps illus. p.329.

L. leontopodium (North Island edelweiss). Evergreen, rosetted perennial. H and S 5in (12cm). Half hardy, zones 7–8. Has oblong to oval, overlapping, silvery white to yellowish leaves. In early summer produces up to 15 small, star-shaped, woolly, silvery white flower heads that are surrounded by thick, felted, white bracts.

LEUCOJUM (Amaryllidaceae)
Snowflake
Genus of bulbs, grown for their pendent, bell-shaped, white or pink flowers in autumn or spring. Fully to frost hardy. Some species prefer a moist, partially shaded site, others do best in a sunny position and well-drained soil. Propagate by division

in spring or early autumn or by seed in autumn.

L. aestivum illus. p.332.

L. autumnale illus. p.366.

L. roseum. Early autumn-flowering bulb. H to 4in (10cm), S 1–2in (2.5–5cm). Frost hardy, zones 6–9. Slender stems produce usually solitary pale pink flowers, $^{1}/_{2}$in (1cm) long. Threadlike, erect, basal leaves appear with, or just after, flowers. Prefers sun and well-drained soil.

L. vernum illus. p.356.

LEUCOSPERMUM (Proteaceae)
Genus of evergreen shrubs, grown for their flower heads. Frost tender, min. 45–50°F (7–10°C). Requires full light and sandy, well-drained soil with few phosphates and nitrates. Water containerized specimens moderately when in growth, sparingly at other times. Propagate by seed in spring. Is not easy to cultivate long term under glass; good ventilation is essential.

L. cordifolium, syn. *L. nutans*. Evergreen, rounded to spreading, well-branched shrub. H and S 4ft (1.2m). Zone 10. Elongated, heart-shaped, blue-gray leaves each have a 3-toothed tip. In summer, very slender, tubular, brick red to orange flowers, each with a long style, are borne in tight heads that resemble single blooms.

L. nutans. See *L. cordifolium*.

L. reflexum illus. p.98.

LEUCOTHOE (Ericaceae)
Genus of evergreen, semi-evergreen, or deciduous shrubs, grown for their white flowers and their foliage. Fully to frost hardy. Needs shade or semi-shade and moist, peaty, acid soil. Propagate by semi-ripe cuttings in summer.

L. fontanesiana. Evergreen, arching shrub. H 5ft (1.5m), S 10ft (3m). Fully hardy, zones 5–9. Lance-shaped, leathery, glossy, dark green leaves have long points and sharp teeth. Short racemes of small, urn-shaped, white flowers are borne beneath shoots from mid- to late spring. **'Rainbow'** illus. p.145.

L. keiskei. Evergreen shrub with erect or semi-procumbent stems. H 6–24in (15–60cm), S 12–24in (30–60cm). Frost hardy, zones 6–9. Oval, thin-textured, glossy, dark green leaves have a red flush when young and a leathery appearance. Bears pendent, urn-shaped, white flowers from leaf axils in summer. Is good for a rock garden, peat bed, or alpine house. Prefers mild, damp climates.

LEWISIA (Portulacaceae)
Genus of perennials, some of which are evergreen, with rosettes of succulent leaves and deep tap roots. Most species are good in alpine houses, pots, and rock gardens. Fully to frost hardy. Evergreen species need semi-shaded, humus-rich, moist or well-drained, neutral to acid soil and resent water in their rosettes at all times. Herbaceous species shed their leaves in summer and require sun and well-drained, neutral to acid soil; dry off after flowering. Propagate herbaceous species by seed in spring

or autumn, evergreen species by seed in spring or by offsets in summer. Seed of *L.* Cotyledon Hybrids may not come true.

L. columbiana. Evergreen, basal-rosetted perennial. H 6in (15cm) or more, S 4–6in (10–15cm). Fully hardy, zones 6–7. Bears thick, narrowly oblong, flat, glossy, green leaves and, in early summer, terminal sprays of small, cup-shaped, deeply veined, white to deep pink flowers. Prefers moist soil.

L. **Cotyledon Hybrids** illus. p.294.

L. **'George Henley'** illus. p.292.

L. nevadensis. Loose, basal-rosetted perennial. H 1$^{1}/_{2}$–2$^{1}/_{2}$in (4–6cm), S 3in (8cm). Fully hardy, zones 6–7. In summer, large, almost stemless, cup-shaped, white flowers appear above small clusters of strap-shaped, dark green leaves.

L. rediviva (pink) illus. p.319; (white) illus. p.313.

L. tweedyi illus. p.304.

LEYCESTERIA (Caprifoliaceae)
Genus of deciduous shrubs, grown for their showy flower clusters. Frost to half hardy. Needs full sun and fertile, well-drained soil. Propagate by softwood cuttings in summer or by seed or division in autumn.

L. formosa (Himalayan honeysuckle). Deciduous, upright shrub. H and S 6ft (2m). Frost hardy, zones 7–9. Has blue-green shoots and slender, oval, dark green leaves. In summer and early autumn, small, funnel-shaped, white flowers are borne at the tip of each pendent cluster of purplish red bracts and are followed by spherical, reddish purple fruits. Cut weak shoots to ground level in early spring.

LEYMUS (Gramineae). See
GRASSES, BAMBOOS, RUSHES, and SEDGES.

L. arenarius, syn. *Elymus arenarius* (Lyme grass). Vigorous, spreading, herbaceous, rhizomatous, perennial grass. H to 5ft (1.5m), S indefinite. Fully hardy, zones 4–9. Has broad, glaucous leaves. Produces stout, terminal spikes of grayish green flowers on erect stems in late summer. Is useful for binding coastal dunes.

LIATRIS (Compositae)
Gayfeather
Genus of summer-flowering perennials with thickened, cormlike rootstocks. Fully hardy. Prefers sun and well-drained soil. Propagate by division in spring.

L. callilepis. See *L. spicata*.

L. pycnostachya (Kansas gay feather). Clump-forming perennial. H 4ft (1.2m), S 1ft (30cm). Zones 4–9. In summer bears tall spikes of clustered, feathery, mauve-pink flower heads. Grasslike, dark green leaves form basal tufts.

L. spicata, syn. *L. callilepis*, illus. p.237.

LIBERTIA (Iridaceae)
Genus of rhizomatous perennials, grown for their foliage, decorative seed pods, and flowers. Frost to half hardy. Needs a sheltered, sunny or

partially shaded site and well-drained soil. Propagate by division in spring or by seed in autumn or spring.
L. grandiflora illus. p.200.
L. ixioides. Clump-forming, rhizomatous perennial. H and S 24in (60cm). Frost hardy, zones 9–10. Produces panicles of saucer-shaped, white flowers in summer. Grasslike, dark green leaves turn orange-brown during winter.

Libocedrus chilensis. See *Austrocedrus chilensis.*
Libocedrus decurrens. See *Calocedrus decurrens.*

Libonia floribunda. See *Justicia rizzinii.*

LIGULARIA (Compositae)
Genus of perennials, grown for their foliage and large, daisylike flower heads. Fully to half hardy. Grow in sun or semi-shade and in moist but well-drained soil. Propagate by division in spring or by seed in autumn or spring. Is prone to damage by slugs and snails.
L. dentata 'Desdemona', syn. *Senecio clivorum* 'Desdemona'. Compact, clump-forming perennial. H 4ft (1.2m), S 2ft (60cm). Fully hardy, zones 4–8. Has heart-shaped, long-stalked, leathery, basal, dark brownish green leaves, almost mahogany beneath, and terminal clusters of large, daisylike, vivid orange flower heads on branching stems from mid- to late summer.
L. 'Gregynog Gold'. Clump-forming perennial. H 6ft (2m), S 2ft (60cm). Fully hardy, zones 4–8. Leaves are large, heart-shaped and deep green. Conical panicles of daisylike, orange-yellow flower heads are borne from mid- to late summer.
L. przewalskii illus. p.191.
L. stenocephala illus. p.191.
L. tussilaginea. Loosely clump-forming perennial. H and S 24in (60cm). Frost hardy, zones 6–8. Has large, rounded, toothed, basal, green leaves, above which rise woolly, branched stems bearing clusters of daisylike, pale yellow flowers in late summer. **'Aureo-maculata'** (Leopard plant) has variegated, gold-and-white leaves and is half hardy.

LIGUSTRUM (Oleaceae)
Privet
Genus of deciduous, semi-evergreen, or evergreen shrubs and trees, grown for their foliage and, in some species, flowers. Fully to frost hardy. Requires sun or semi-shade, the variegated forms doing best in full sun. Thrives on any well-drained soil, including chalky soil. All except *L. lucidum* occasionally need cutting back in mid-spring to restrict growth. Propagate by semi-ripe cuttings in summer.
L. japonicum (Japanese privet). Evergreen, bushy, dense shrub. H 10ft (3m), S 8ft (2.5m). Frost hardy, zones 7–9. Has oval, glossy, very dark green leaves and, from mid-summer to early autumn, large, conical panicles of small, tubular, white flowers with 4 lobes. **'Rotundifolium'** is slow-growing and bears a dense mass of rounded, leathery leaves.

L. lucidum (Chinese privet). Evergreen, upright shrub or tree. H 30ft (10m), S 25ft (8m). Frost hardy, zones 7–10. Bears large, oval, glossy, dark green leaves. Produces large panicles of small, tubular, white flowers, with 4 lobes, in late summer and early autumn. **'Excelsum Superbum'** illus. p.95.
L. ovalifolium illus. p.94. **'Aureum'** is a vigorous, evergreen or semi-evergreen, upright, dense shrub. H 12ft (4m), S 10ft (3m). Fully hardy, zones 6–10. Leaves are oval, glossy, and green, broadly edged with bright yellow. Dense panicles of small, rather unpleasantly scented, tubular, white flowers, with 4 lobes, appear in mid-summer and are succeeded by spherical, black fruits. Cut back hedges to 1ft (30cm) after planting and prune hard for first 2 years; then trim as necessary during the growing season.
L. sinense illus. p.86.
L. 'Vicaryi' illus. p.121.
L. vulgare. Deciduous or semi-evergreen, bushy shrub. H and S 10ft (3m). Fully hardy, zones 5–9. Leaves are narrowly lance-shaped and dark green. Produces panicles of small, strongly scented, tubular, white flowers, with 4 lobes, from early to mid-summer, then spherical, black fruits. Cut back hedges to 1ft (30cm) after planting and prune hard for first 2 years; then trim as necessary during the growing season. **'Aureum'**, H and S 6ft (2m), has golden yellow foliage.

LILIUM (Liliaceae)
Lily
Genus of mainly summer-flowering bulbs, grown for their often fragrant, brightly colored flowers. Each fleshy-scaled bulb produces one unbranched, leafy stem, in some cases with annual roots in lower part. Mostly lance-shaped or linear leaves, to 9in (22cm) long, are scattered or in whorls, sometimes with bulbils in axils. Flowers, usually several per stem, are mainly trumpet- to bowl-shaped or with the 6 petals strongly reflexed to form a turkscap shape. (Petals of *Lilium* are known botanically as perianth segments.) Each plant has a spread of up to 12in (30cm). Frost hardy, zones 4–8, unless otherwise stated. Needs sun and any well-drained soil, unless otherwise stated below. Propagate by seed in autumn or spring, by bulb scales in summer, or by stem bulbils (where present) in autumn. Virus and fungal diseases (such as botrytis) and lily beetle may cause problems.
L. amabile. Summer-flowering bulb with stem roots. H 1–3ft (30cm–1m). Scattered leaves are lance-shaped. Bears up to 10 unpleasant-smelling, nodding, turkscap, red flowers; each petal is 2–2¹⁄₄in (5–5.5cm) long, with black spots.
L. 'Amber Gold' (illus. p.338). Summer-flowering bulb. H 4–5ft (1.2–1.5m). Has nodding, turkscap, deep yellow flowers, each with maroon spots in throat.
L. 'Apollo' (illus. p.338). Summer-flowering bulb. H 4ft (1.2m). Produces downward-facing, turkscap, pale

orange flowers with strongly reflexed petals.
L. auratum (Golden-rayed lily-of-Japan). Summer- and autumn-flowering bulb with stem roots. H 2–5ft (60cm–1.5m). Zones 5–8. Has long, scattered, lance-shaped leaves. Produces up to 10, sometimes more, fragrant, outward-facing, widely bowl-shaped, white flowers; each petal is 5–7in (12–18cm) long with a central, red or yellow band and often red or yellow spots. Requires semi-shade and neutral to acid soil. var. *platyphyllum* (illus. p.338) has broader leaves; petals have a central, yellow band and fewer spots.
L. 'Black Beauty' (illus. p.338). Summer-flowering bulb. H 5–6ft (1.5–2m). Bears outward-facing, flattish, green-centered, very deep red flowers with recurved, white-margined petals.
L. 'Black Dragon'. Summer-flowering bulb. H 5ft (1.5m). Has outward-facing, trumpet-shaped flowers with dark purplish red outsides and white insides.
L. 'Black Magic' (illus. p.338). Summer-flowering bulb. H 4–6ft (1.2–2m). Scented, outward-facing, trumpet-shaped flowers are purplish brown outside and white inside.
L. 'Bonfire'. Late summer-flowering bulb. H 4–5ft (1.2–1.5m). Bears outward-facing, bowl-shaped flowers with broad petals, white outside flushed with pink, and dark crimson inside spotted paler crimson.
L. 'Bright Star' (illus. p.338). Summer-flowering bulb. H 3–5ft (1–1.5m). Produces flattish, white flowers; petals have recurved tips and a central, orange streak inside.
L. 'Brushmarks' (illus. p.338). Early summer-flowering bulb. H 4¹⁄₂ft (1.35m). Upward-facing, cup-shaped, orange flowers are green-throated. Petals each have deep red blotches and sometimes spots.
L. bulbiferum (Fire lily, Orange lily). Summer-flowering bulb with stem roots. H 16in–5ft (40cm–1.5m). Zones 5–8. Stem bears scattered, lance-shaped leaves and, usually, bulbils in leaf axils. Bears 1–5 or more upward-facing, shallowly cup-shaped, orange-red flowers. Each petal is 2¹⁄₂–3¹⁄₄in (6–8.5cm) long and spotted black or deep red. var. *croceum* (illus. p.338) has orange flowers and does not normally produce bulbils.
L. canadense (Canada lily, Meadow lily, Wild yellow lily). Summer-flowering bulb with stem roots. H to 5ft (1.5m). Narrowly to broadly lance-shaped leaves are mainly in whorls. Bears about 10 nodding, bell-shaped, yellow or red flowers; each petal is 2–3in (5–8cm) long, with dark red or purple spots in lower part.
L. candidum (Madonna lily; illus. p.338). Summer-flowering bulb. H 3–6ft (1–2m). Zones 4–9. Flower stem bears scattered, lance-shaped leaves and 5–20 fragrant, outward-facing, broadly funnel-shaped, white flowers. Each petal is 2–3in (5–8cm) long with a yellow base and a slightly recurved tip. In autumn produces basal leaves, which remain throughout winter but

die off as flowering stems mature. Prefers lime-rich soil.
L. carniolicum. See *L. pyrenaicum* var. *carniolicum.*
L. cernuum. Summer-flowering bulb with stem roots. H to 2ft (60cm). Zones 5–8. Long, linear leaves are scattered. Has 7–15 fragrant, nodding, turkscap flowers, usually pinkish purple with purple spots. Each petal is 1¹⁄₂–2in (3.5–5cm) long.
L. chalcedonicum, syn. *L. heldreichii* (Scarlet turkscap lily; illus. p.338). Summer-flowering bulb with stem roots. H 20in–5ft (50cm–1.5m). Zones 5–8. Leaves are scattered and mostly lance-shaped, lower ones spreading, upper ones smaller and closer to stem. Bears up to 12 slightly scented, nodding, turkscap flowers with red or reddish orange petals, each 2–3in (5–7cm) long.
L. 'Connecticut King' (illus. p.338). Early to mid-summer-flowering bulb. H 3ft (1m). Flowers are upward-facing, cup-shaped, and bright yellow.
L. 'Corsage' (illus. p.338). Summer-flowering bulb. H 4ft (1.2m). Produces outward-facing, bowl-shaped flowers with recurved petals, pink-flushed outside and pink inside with white centers and maroon spots.
L. davidii. Summer-flowering bulb with stem roots. H 3–4¹⁄₂ft (1–1.4m). Zones 5–8. Linear leaves are scattered. Has 5–20 nodding, turkscap, red or reddish orange flowers; each petal is 2–3in (5–8cm) long with dark purple spots.
L. 'Destiny' (illus. p.338). Early summer-flowering bulb. H 3–4ft (1–1.2m). Flowers are upward-facing, cup-shaped, and yellow with brown spots.
L. 'Enchantment' (illus. p.338). Early summer-flowering bulb. H 3ft (1m). Produces upward-facing, cup-shaped, orange-red flowers with black-spotted throats.
L. 'First Love'. Summer-flowering bulb. H 5ft (1.5m). Bears slightly fragrant, outward-facing, bowl-shaped flowers. Each petal has pink edges merging into a central, yellow stripe; base is pale green.
L. Golden Clarion Hybrids (illus. p.338). Late spring to early summer-flowering bulb. H 3–6ft (1–2m). Has outward-facing, trumpet-shaped, pale to deep yellow flowers that may be flushed with reddish purple outside.
L. hansonii (illus. p.338). Summer-flowering bulb with stem roots. H 3–5ft (1–1.5m). Long leaves in whorls are lance-shaped to oval. Bears 3–12 scented, nodding, turkscap, orange-yellow flowers. Each thick petal is 1¹⁄₄–1¹⁄₂in (3–4cm) long with brown-purple spots towards base.
L. 'Harmony' (illus. p.338). Summer-flowering bulb. H 1¹⁄₂–3ft (50cm–1m). Orange flowers are upward-facing, cup-shaped, and spotted with maroon.
L. heldreichii. See *L. chalcedonicum.*
L. henryi. Late summer-flowering bulb with stem roots. H 3–10ft (1–3m). Zones 4–9. Has scattered, lance-shaped leaves. Produces 5–20, sometimes up to 70, nodding, turkscap, orange flowers; petals are 2¹⁄₂–3in (6–8cm) long with dark spots and

prominent warts towards bases. Prefers lime-rich soil.

L. Imperial Crimson Group. Late summer-flowering bulb. H 5ft (1.5m). Zones 5–8. Fragrant, flattish, deep crimson flowers have white throats and white-edged petals.

L. Imperial Gold Group (illus. p.338). Summer-flowering bulb. H 6ft (2m). Zones 5–8. Bears fragrant, flattish, white flowers, spotted maroon, and with a yellow stripe up each petal center.

L. 'Journey's End' (illus. p.338). Late summer-flowering bulb. H 6ft (2m). Outward-facing, bowl-shaped, maroon-spotted, deep pink flowers have recurved petals, white at tips and edges.

L. 'Karen North' (illus. p.338). Summer-flowering bulb. H to 4¹/₂ft (1.4m). Turkscap flowers are downward-facing, with orange-pink petals sparsely spotted with deep pink.

L. 'Lady Bowes Lyon' (illus. p.338). Summer-flowering bulb. H 3–4ft (1–1.2m). Zones 5–8. Downward-facing, black-spotted, rich red flowers have reflexed petals.

L. lancifolium, syn. *L. tigrinum* (Tiger lily). Summer- to early autumn-flowering bulb with stem roots. H 2–5ft (60cm–1.5m). Has long, scattered, narrowly lance-shaped leaves. Produces 5–10, sometimes up to 40, nodding, turkscap, pink- to orange-red flowers; each petal is 3–4in (7–10cm) long and spotted with purple. var. *flaviflorum* has yellow flowers. Vigorous var. *splendens* (illus. p.338) bears larger, brighter red-orange flowers.

L. lankongense. Summer-flowering bulb with stem roots. H to 4ft (1.2m). Zones 5–8. Leaves are scattered and lance-shaped. Has up to 15 scented, nodding, turkscap, pink flowers. Petals, each 1¹/₂–2¹/₂in (4–6.5cm) long with a central, green stripe and red-purple spots mainly on edges, are often mauve-flushed. Needs partial shade in warm areas.

L. leichtlinii. Summer-flowering bulb with stem roots. H to 4ft (1.2m). Scattered leaves are linear to narrowly lance-shaped. Produces 1–6 nodding, turkscap, yellow flowers; each petal is 2¹/₂–3¹/₄in (6–8.5cm) long with dark reddish purple spots. Needs semi-shade.

L. 'Limelight'. Summer-flowering bulb. H 3–5ft (1–1.5m). Flowers are outward-facing or slightly nodding, trumpet-shaped, and yellow-green.

L. longiflorum (Easter lily, Trumpet lily; illus. p.338). Summer-flowering bulb with stem roots. H 1–3ft (30cm–1m). Zone 8. Leaves are scattered and lance-shaped. Produces 1–6 fragrant, outward-facing, funnel-shaped, white flowers. Each petal is 5–8in (13–20cm) long with slightly recurved tips.

L. mackliniae (Manipur lily; illus. p.338). Late spring- to summer-flowering bulb with stem roots. H to 16in (40cm). Zones 5–8. Small, narrowly lance-shaped to narrowly oval leaves are scattered or whorled near top of stem. Has 1–6 usually nodding, broadly bell-shaped, purplish

pink flowers; each petal is 1³/₄–2in (4.5–5cm) long. Needs semi-shade.

L. maculatum. Summer-flowering bulb with stem roots. H to 2ft (60cm). Fully hardy, zones 5–8. Scattered leaves are lance-shaped or oval. Produces 1–6 upward-facing, cup-shaped, yellow, orange, or red flowers with darker spots; each petal is 3–4in (8–10cm) long.

L. 'Marhan'. Early summer-flowering bulb. H 4–6ft (1.2–2m). Nodding, turkscap, deep orange flowers are spotted red-brown.

L. martagon (Martagon lily; illus. p.338). Summer-flowering bulb with stem roots. H 3–6ft (1–2m). Fully hardy, zones 4–8. Has lance-shaped to oval leaves in whorls and up to 50, scented, nodding, turkscap flowers. Petals are 1¹/₄–1³/₄in (3–4.5cm) long and pink or purple, often with darker spots. var. *album* has pure white flowers.

L. monadelphum, syn. *L. szovitsianum* (illus. p.338). Summer-flowering bulb with stem roots. H 1¹/₂–6ft (50cm–2m). Has scattered, lance-shaped to oval leaves. Produces usually 1–5, sometimes up to 30, scented, nodding, turkscap, yellow flowers, usually with deep red or purple spots inside. Each petal is 2¹/₂–4in (6–10cm) long.

L. nanum. Late spring- or summer-flowering bulb. H 2¹/₂–18in (6–45cm). Zones 5–8. Scattered leaves are linear. Bears a usually nodding, broadly bell-shaped, purplish pink flower with 1³/₄–2in (4.5–5cm) long petals. Needs partial shade. var. *flavidum* has pale yellow flowers.

L. nepalense (illus. p.338). Summer-flowering bulb with stem roots. H 28–36in (70cm–1m). Zones 5–8. Has scattered, lance-shaped leaves. Produces often unpleasant-smelling, nodding, funnel-shaped, greenish white or greenish yellow flowers, each with a dark reddish purple base inside and petals to 6in (15cm) long.

L. Olympic Hybrids (illus. p.338). Summer-flowering bulb. H 4–6ft (1.2–2m). Scented, outward-facing, trumpet-shaped flowers are usually pink or purple outside with yellow throats; white, cream, yellow, or pink variants also occur.

L. pardalinum (Leopard lily, Panther lily; illus. p.338). Summer-flowering bulb. H 6–10ft (2–3m). Long, narrowly elliptic leaves are mainly in whorls. Produces up to 10 often scented, nodding, turkscap flowers. Each petal is 2–3¹/₂in (5–9cm) long with red, upper parts. Orange, lower parts have maroon spots, some of which are encircled with yellow.

L. ponticum. See *L. pyrenaicum* var. *ponticum*.

L. pumilum, syn. *L. tenuifolium*. Summer-flowering bulb with stem roots. H 6–36in (15cm–1m). Zones 5–8. Small, scattered leaves are linear. Bears usually up to 7 but occasionally up to 30 slightly scented, nodding, turkscap flowers; each petal is 1¹/₄–1¹/₂in (3–3.5cm) long and scarlet with or without basal, black spots.

L. pyrenaicum (Yellow turkscap lily). Late spring to early summer-flowering bulb often with stem roots. H 1–4¹/₂ft

(30cm–1.35m). Zones 5–8. Has scattered, linear to narrowly elliptic, hairless leaves. Produces up to 12 unpleasant-smelling, nodding, turkscap flowers. Each petal is 1¹/₂–2¹/₂in (4–6.5cm) long and yellow or green-yellow with deep purple spots and lines. var. *carniolicum* (syn. *L. carniolicum*) has red- or orange-spotted flowers. Leaves may be hairless or downy. var. *ponticum* (syn. *L. ponticum*) bears deep yellow flowers, densely lined and spotted with red-brown or purple; leaves are downy beneath.

L. regale (Regal lily; illus. p.338). Summer-flowering bulb with stem roots. H 20in–6ft (50cm–2m). Zones 4–9. Linear leaves are scattered. Produces up to 25 fragrant, outward-facing, funnel-shaped flowers. Petals are each 5–6in (12–15cm) long, white inside with a yellow base and pinkish purple outside.

L. rubellum (illus. p.338). Early summer-flowering bulb with stem roots. H 12–32in (30–80cm). Zones 5–8. Has scattered, narrowly oval leaves and up to 9 scented, outward-facing, broadly funnel-shaped, pink flowers with dark red spots at bases; each petal is 2¹/₂–3in (6–8cm) long.

L. 'Shuksan'. Summer-flowering bulb. H 4–6ft (1.2–2m). Nodding, turkscap, yellowish orange flowers are flushed red at petal tips and sparsely spotted with black.

L. speciosum. Late summer-flowering bulb with stem roots. H 3–5¹/₂ft (1–1.7m). Zones 5–8. Has long, scattered, broadly lance-shaped leaves. Produces up to 12 scented, nodding, turkscap, white or pink flowers; each petal is up to 4in (10cm) long, with pink or crimson spots. Requires neutral to acid soil. var. *album* has white flowers and purple stems. Flowers of var. *rubrum* (illus. p.338) are carmine, stems are purple.

L. 'Sterling Star' (illus. p.338). Summer-flowering bulb. H 3–4ft (1–1.2m). Has upward-facing, cup-shaped, white flowers with tiny, brown spots.

L. superbum (Swamp lily, Turkscap lily). Late summer- to early autumn-flowering bulb with stem roots. H 5–10ft (1.5–3m). Zones 5–8. Lance-shaped to elliptic leaves are mainly in whorls. Bears up to 40 nodding, turkscap, orange flowers. Each petal is 2¹/₂–4in (6–10cm) long, with a green base inside and usually flushed red and spotted maroon. Requires neutral to acid soil.

L. szovitsianum. See *L. monadelphum*.
L. tenuifolium. See *L. pumilum*.
L. × testaceum (Nankeen lily). Summer-flowering bulb. H 3–5ft (1–1.5m). Zones 5–8. Has scattered, linear, often twisted leaves. Produces 6–12 fragrant, nodding, turkscap, light orange to brownish yellow flowers; each petal is 3in (8cm) long, usually with reddish spots inside.

L. tigrinum. See *L. lancifolium*.
L. tsingtauense. Summer-flowering bulb with stem roots. H 3ft (1m). Zones 5–8. Lance-shaped leaves are mainly in whorls. Produces 1–5 upward-facing, cup-shaped, orange to

orange-red flowers; petals are up to 2in (5cm) long and spotted with maroon.

L. wallichianum. Late summer- to autumn-flowering bulb with stem roots. H to 6ft (2m). Half hardy, zones 5–8. Long, scattered leaves are linear or lance-shaped. Bears 1–4 fragrant, outward-facing, funnel-shaped, white or cream flowers that are green or yellow towards bases. Each petal is 6–12in (15–30cm) long.

LIMNANTHES (Limnanthaceae)
Genus of annuals, useful for rock gardens and for edging. Fully hardy. Prefers a sunny situation and fertile, well-drained soil. Propagate by seed sown outdoors in spring or early autumn. Self seeds freely.
L. douglasii illus. p.280.

LIMONIUM (Plumbaginaceae)
Sea lavender
Genus of summer- and autumn-flowering perennials, sometimes grown as annuals, and sub-shrubs, some of which are evergreen. Fully hardy to frost tender, min. 45–50°F (7–10°C). Grows in full sun and in well-drained soil. Propagate by division in spring, by seed in autumn or early spring, or by root cuttings in winter.
L. bellidifolium. Evergreen, dome-shaped perennial with a woody base. H 6–8in (15–20cm), S 4in (10cm). Frost hardy, zones 7–9. Has basal rosettes of rounded, dark green leaves. Much-branched flower stems bear masses of small, "everlasting," trumpet-shaped blue flowers in summer-autumn. Is excellent for a rock garden.
L. latifolium 'Blue Cloud' illus. p.242.
L. perezii. Evergreen, rounded sub-shrub. H and S 3ft (1m) or more. Frost tender, min. 45–50°F (7–10°C), zone 10. Has long-stalked, oval to diamond-shaped, deep green leaves. Dense clusters, 8in (20cm) wide, of tiny, tubular, deep mauve-blue flowers are carried well above the leaves in autumn. Needs good ventilation if grown in a greenhouse.
L. sinuatum illus. p.266. **'Fortress'** is a slow-growing, upright, bushy perennial, grown as an annual. H 18in (45cm), S 12in (30cm). Frost tender, min. 36–9°F (2–4°C). Has lance-shaped, lobed, and often wavy-margined, deep green leaves and, in summer and early autumn, clusters of small, tubular flowers in a mixture of shades such as pink, yellow, or blue.

LINARIA (Scrophulariaceae)
Toadflax
Genus of spring-, summer-, or autumn-flowering annuals, biennials, and perennials, useful for rock gardens and borders. Fully to frost hardy. Prefers sun or light shade; thrives in any well-drained soil. Propagate by seed in autumn or spring. Self seeds freely.
L. alpina (Alpine toadflax). Tuft-forming, compact, annual, biennial, or short-lived perennial with a sparse root system. H 6in (15cm), S 4–6in (10–15cm). Fully hardy. Has whorls of linear to lance-shaped, fleshy, gray-green leaves. A succession of snapdragonlike, yellow-centered,

purple-violet flowers is borne in loose racemes in summer.
L. dalmatica. See *L. genistifolia* var. *dalmatica.*
L. genistifolia. Upright perennial. H 2–4ft (60cm–1.2m), S 9in (23cm). Fully hardy, zones 5–8. From mid-summer to autumn produces racemes of small, snapdragonlike, orange-marked, yellow flowers. Lance-shaped, glossy, green leaves clasp the stems. var. *dalmatica* (syn. *L. dalmatica*; Dalmatian toadflax), H 3–4ft (1–1.2m), S 2ft (60cm), bears much larger, golden yellow flowers, from mid- to late summer, and has broader, more glaucous leaves.
L. maroccana (Morocco toadflax). **'Fairy Lights'** illus. p.274.
L. purpurea (Purple toadflax). Upright perennial. H 2–3ft (60cm–1m), S 2ft (60cm). Fully hardy, zones 5–8. From mid- to late summer, racemes of snapdragonlike, purplish blue flowers, touched with white at throats, are borne above narrowly oval, gray-green leaves. **'Canon Went'** illus. p.203.
L. triornithophora illus. p.210.

LINDERA (Lauraceae)
Genus of deciduous or evergreen shrubs and trees, grown for their foliage, which is often aromatic, and their autumn color. Fruits are produced on female plants if male plants are also grown. Fully to frost hardy. Needs semi-shade and moist, acid soil. Propagate by softwood cuttings in summer or by seed in autumn.
L. benzoin illus. p.99.
L. obtusiloba. Deciduous, bushy shrub. H and S 20ft (6m). Fully hardy, zones 6–9. Bears 3-lobed, aromatic, glossy, dark green leaves, becoming butter yellow in autumn. Clusters of small, star-shaped, deep yellow flowers, produced on bare shoots from early to mid-spring, are followed by small, spherical, black fruits.

LINDHEIMERA (Compositae)
Genus of late summer- and early autumn-flowering annuals. Fully hardy. Grow in sun and in fertile, well-drained soil. Propagate by seed sown under glass in early spring or outdoors in late spring.
L. texana illus. p.280.

LINNAEA (Caprifoliaceae)
Twinflower
Genus of one species of evergreen, creeping, summer-flowering, sub-shrubby perennial that makes an extensive, twiggy mat. Is useful as ground cover on peat beds and rock gardens. Fully hardy. Requires partial shade and moist, peaty, acid soil. Propagate by rooted runners in spring, by softwood cuttings in summer, or by seed in autumn.
L. borealis illus. p.315.

LINUM (Linaceae)
Genus of annuals, biennials, perennials, sub-shrubs, and shrubs, some of which are evergreen or semi-evergreen, grown for their flowers. Is suitable for rock gardens. Fully to half hardy, but in cold areas some species need a sheltered position. Prefers sun

and humus-rich, well-drained, peaty soil. Propagate sub-shrubs and shrubs by semi-ripe cuttings in summer or by seed in autumn, annuals, biennials, and perennials by seed in autumn.
L. arboreum illus. p.298.
L. flavum (Golden flax, Yellow flax). Bushy perennial with a woody rootstock. H 12in (30cm), S 6in (15cm). Fully hardy, zones 5–7. Has narrowly oval, green leaves and, in summer, upward-facing, funnel-shaped, yellow flowers in terminal clusters. **'Compactum'** illus. p.325.
L. 'Gemmell's Hybrid'. Semi-evergreen, domed perennial with a woody rootstock. H 6in (15cm), S 8in (20cm). Frost hardy, zones 7–9. Leaves are oval and gray-green. In summer, short-stalked, broadly funnel-shaped, bright chrome yellow flowers are produced in terminal clusters. Prefers alkaline soil.
L. grandiflorum (Flowering flax). **'Rubrum'** illus. p.271.
L. narbonense illus. p.243.
L. perenne illus. p.296.
L. salsoloides. See *L. suffruticosum* subsp. *salsoloides.*
L. suffruticosum subsp. *salsoloides,* syn. *L. salsoloides.* Perennial with spreading, sometimes woody-based, stems. H 2–8in (5–20cm), S 3in (8cm). Frost hardy, zones 7–9. Slender stems bear fine, heathlike, gray-green leaves and, in summer, a succession of short-lived, saucer-shaped, pearl white flowers, flushed blue or pink, in terminal clusters.

Lippia citriodora. See *Aloysia triphylla.*

LIQUIDAMBAR (Hamamelidaceae)
Genus of deciduous trees, with inconspicuous flowers, grown for their maplelike foliage and autumn color. Fully to frost hardy. Requires sun or semi-shade and fertile, moist but well-drained soil; grows poorly on shallow, chalky soil. Propagate by softwood cuttings in summer or by seed in autumn.
L. formosana, syn. *L.f.* var. *monticola* (Formosa sweet gum). Deciduous, broadly conical tree. H 40ft (12m), S 30ft (10m). Frost hardy, zones 7–9. Has large, 3-lobed, toothed leaves, purple when young, dark green in summer, and turning orange, red, and purple in autumn.
L. orientalis (Oriental sweet gum). Slow-growing, deciduous, bushy tree. H 20ft (6m), S 12ft (4m). Frost hardy, zones 7–9. Small, 5-lobed, green leaves turn orange in autumn.
L. styraciflua illus. p.44. **'Lane Roberts'** is a deciduous, broadly conical to spreading tree. H 80ft (25m), S 40ft (12m). Fully hardy, zones 6–9. Shoots usually have corky ridges. Glossy, green leaves, each with 5 lobes, turn deep reddish purple in autumn.

LIRIODENDRON (Magnoliaceae)
Genus of deciduous trees, grown for their foliage and flowers in summer. Flowers are almost hidden by unusual leaves and are not produced on young trees. Fully hardy. Requires sun or semi-shade and deep, fertile, well-

drained, preferably slightly acid, soil. Propagate species by seed in autumn, selected forms by budding in late summer.
L. chinense (Chinese tulip tree). Fast-growing, deciduous, spreading tree. H 80ft (25m), S 40ft (12m). Zones 7–9. Bears large, deep green leaves, cut off at the tips and with a deep lobe on each side; leaves become yellow in autumn. Cup-shaped, orange-based, greenish white flowers appear in mid-summer.
L. tulipifera illus. p.39.
'Aureomarginatum' illus. p.44.

LIRIOPE (Liliaceae)
Lilyturf
Genus of evergreen perennials with swollen, fleshy rhizomes. Some are grown as ground cover. Fully to frost hardy. Requires sun and well-drained soil. Propagate by division in spring or by seed in autumn.
L. muscari illus. p.250. **'Majestic'** is an evergreen, spreading, rhizomatous perennial. H 12in (30cm), S 18in (45cm). Frost hardy, zones 6–10. In late autumn produces spikes of thickly clustered, rounded-bell-shaped, violet flowers among linear, glossy, bright green leaves.
L. spicata. Evergreen, spreading, rhizomatous perennial. H 12in (30cm), S 12–16in (30–40cm). Fully hardy, zones 5–10. Grasslike, glossy, dark green leaves make good ground cover. Bears spikes of rounded-bell-shaped, pale lavender flowers in late summer.

Lisianthus russellianus. See *Eustoma grandiflorum.*

LITHOCARPUS (Fagaceae)
Genus of evergreen trees, grown for their foliage. Frost hardy. Needs sun or semi-shade. Prefers well-drained, neutral to acid soil. Shelter from strong winds. Propagate by seed, when ripe, in autumn.
L. densiflorus (Tanbark oak). Evergreen, spreading tree. H and S 30ft (10m). Zones 8–10. Has sweet chestnutlike, leathery, glossy, dark green leaves and upright, pale yellow flower spikes borne in spring and often again in autumn.
L. henryi illus. p.72.

LITHODORA (Boraginaceae)
Genus of evergreen sub-shrubs and shrubs, grown for their flowers. Is excellent in rock gardens. Fully to frost hardy. Needs full sun and moist, well-drained soil; some species are lime haters. Resents root disturbance. Propagate by semi-ripe cuttings in mid-summer or by seed in autumn.
L. diffusa, syn. *Lithospermum diffusum.* **'Grace Ward'** is an evergreen, compact, semi-prostrate shrub. H 6–12in (15–30cm), S to 12in (30cm). Frost hardy, zones 6–8. Trailing stems bear lance-shaped, hairy, dull green leaves. In early summer bears masses of funnel-shaped, deep blue flowers in terminal clusters. Needs acid soil. Plants should be trimmed back after flowering.
'Heavenly Blue' illus. p.297.
L. oleifolia, syn. *Lithospermum oleifolium,* illus. p.296.

L. zahnii, syn. *Lithospermum zahnii.* Evergreen, much-branched, upright shrub. H and S 12in (30cm) or more. Frost hardy, zones 7–8. Stems are covered in oval, hairy, dark green or grayish green leaves. Funnel-shaped, azure blue flowers, with spreading lobes, open in succession from early spring to mid-summer. Sets buds and flowers intermittently until mid-autumn. Prefers alkaline soil.

LITHOPHRAGMA (Saxifragaceae)
Genus of tuberous perennials, grown for their campionlike flowers. Is dormant in summer. Fully hardy. Tolerates all but deepest shade and prefers humus-rich, moist soil. Propagate by seed or division in spring or autumn.
L. parviflorum illus. p.286.

LITHOPS (Aizoaceae)
Living stones, Stone plant
Genus of prostrate, egg-shaped, perennial succulents, with almost united pairs of swollen, erect leaves that are separated on upper surface by a fissure from which a daisylike flower emerges. Each pair of old leaves splits and dries away to papery skin in spring to reveal a pair of new leaves growing at right angles to old ones. Slowly forms clumps after 3–5 years. All those listed are frost tender, min. 41°F (5°C), zone 10. Needs full sun and extremely well-drained soil or gritty compost. Water regularly in growing season (mid-summer to early autumn), not at all in winter. Propagate by seed in spring or summer.
L. aucampiae. Egg-shaped, perennial succulent. H ¹/₂in (1cm), S 1¹/₄in (3cm). Pairs of brown leaves have flat, upper surfaces bearing darker marks. Produces a yellow flower in late summer or early autumn.
L. bella. Egg-shaped, perennial succulent. H ³/₄–1¹/₄in (2–3cm), S ⁵/₈in (1.5cm). Has pairs of brown to brown-yellow leaves with darker marks on convex, upper surfaces. Produces a white flower in late summer or early autumn.
L. dorotheae illus. p.398.
L. fulleri. Egg-shaped, perennial succulent. H and S ³/₄in (2cm). Pairs of leaves are dove gray to brown-yellow. Convex, upper surfaces have sunken, darker marks. In late summer or early autumn bears a white flower.
L. insularis. Egg-shaped, perennial succulent. H ³/₄–1¹/₄in (2–3cm), S ³/₄in (2cm). Slightly convex, upper surfaces of paired, brown leaves have dark green windows and red dots and lines. Produces a yellow flower in late summer or early autumn.
L. julii. Egg-shaped, perennial succulent. H ³/₄–1¹/₄in (2–3cm), S 2in (5cm). Has paired, pearl to pink-gray leaves, each with a slightly convex, darker-marked, upper surface. In late summer or autumn produces a white flower.
L. karasmontana illus. p.389.
L. lesliei. Egg-shaped, perennial succulent. H ¹/₂in (1cm), S ³/₄in (2cm). Is similar to *L. aucampiae,* but upper leaf surfaces are convex. var. *albinica* illus. p.390.

L. marmorata illus. p.389.
L. olivacea. Egg-shaped, perennial succulent. H and S ³/₄in (2cm). Paired, dark olive green leaves have darker windows on convex, upper surfaces. Yellow flower appears in late summer or early autumn.
L. otzeniana. Egg-shaped, perennial succulent. H 1¹/₄in (3cm), S ³/₄in (2cm). Paired, gray-violet leaves each have a convex, upper surface with a distinctive, light border and large, semi-translucent windows. In late summer or early autumn bears a yellow flower.
L. pseudotruncatella. Egg-shaped, perennial succulent. H 1¹/₄in (3cm), S 1¹/₂in (4cm). Bears pairs of pale gray or blue to lilac leaves with darker marks on convex, upper surfaces. Fissure reaches from side to side only on mature plants. Has a yellow flower in late summer or early autumn.
var. *pulmonuncula* illus. p.398.
L. schwantesii. Very variable, egg-shaped, perennial succulent. H and S 1¹/₄in (3cm). Has paired, usually rough leaves often with sunken, dark red or blue lines or dots on their slightly convex or flat, upper surfaces. Produces a yellow flower in late summer or early autumn. var. *kuibisensis* illus. p.398.
L. turbiniformis. Egg-shaped, perennial succulent. H 1¹/₂in (4cm), S ³/₄in (2cm). Has a flattish, upper surface with, usually, sunken, dark brown marks on paired, brown leaves. Yellow flower appears in late summer or early autumn.

Lithospermum diffusum. See *Lithodora diffusa.*
Lithospermum oleifolium. See *Lithodora oleifolia.*
Lithospermum zahnii. See *Lithodora zahnii.*

LITTONIA (Liliaceae)
Genus of deciduous, perennial, scandent, tuberous climbers, grown for their pendent, bell-shaped flowers in summer. Frost tender, min. 46–61°F (8–16°C). Requires full sun and rich, well-drained soil. Provide support. Dies down in winter; lift and dry off tubers and store in a frost-free place. Propagate by seed in spring; tubers sometimes will divide naturally.
L. modesta illus. p.339.

LIVISTONA (Palmae)
Genus of evergreen palms, grown for their overall appearance. Has clusters of insignificant flowers in summer. Frost tender, min. 45°F (7°C). Needs full light or partial shade and fertile, well-drained soil, ideally neutral to acid. Water potted specimens moderately, less in winter. Propagate by seed in spring at not less than 73°F (23°C). Red spider mite may be a nuisance on potted plants.
L. australis (Australian cabbage palm, Gippsland fountain palm). Slow-growing, evergreen palm with a fairly slender trunk. H 50–70ft (15–20m), S 10–20ft (3–6m). Zones 9–10. Has fan-shaped leaves, 4–8ft (1.2–2.5m) wide, divided into narrow, slender-pointed, glossy, green leaflets. Leaf stalks are spiny.
L. chinensis illus. p.58.

LLOYDIA (Liliaceae)
Genus of summer-flowering bulbs, grown for their small, graceful, bell-shaped flowers. Fully to half hardy. Is not easy to grow. Requires partial shade and well-drained, peaty soil; provide plenty of moisture in summer but, preferably, keep fairly dry in winter. Propagate by seed in spring.
L. serotina illus. p.364.

LOBELIA (Campanulaceae)
Genus of annuals, perennials, and deciduous or evergreen shrubs, grown for their flowers. Some are suitable for wild gardens or by the waterside. Fully hardy to frost tender, min. 41°F (5°C). Prefers sun and moist but well-drained soil. Resents wet conditions in winter; in cold areas some perennials and shrubs are therefore best lifted in autumn and placed in well-drained compost in frames. Propagate annuals by seed in spring, perennial species by seed or division in spring, perennial cultivars by division only; and shrubs by semi-ripe cuttings in summer.
L. cardinalis (Cardinal flower). Clump-forming perennial. H 3ft (1m), S 9in (23cm). Frost hardy, zones 3–9. Bears racemes of 2-lipped, brilliant scarlet flowers from mid- to late summer. Lance-shaped leaves may be fresh green or red-bronze.
L. 'Cherry Ripe' illus. p.208.
L. 'Dark Crusader'. Clump-forming perennial. H 3ft (1m), S 9in (23cm). Half hardy, zones 8–9. From mid- to late summer, racemes of 2-lipped, dark red flowers are borne above lance-shaped, fresh green or red-bronze leaves.
L. erinus 'Blue Cascade'. Slow-growing, pendulous, spreading annual, occasionally perennial. H 4–8in (10–20cm), S 4–6in (10–15cm). Fully hardy. Oval to lance-shaped leaves are pale green. Small, 2–lipped, pale blue flowers are produced continuously in summer and early autumn.
'Cambridge Blue' is compact and has blue flowers. 'Colour Cascade' has flowers in a mixture of colors, such as blue, red, pink, mauve, or white. 'Crystal Palace' illus. p.278. 'Red Cascade' bears white-eyed, purple-red flowers. 'Sapphire' illus. p.276.
L. fulgens. Clump-forming perennial. H 3ft (1m), S 9in (23cm). Half hardy, zones 8–9. Racemes of 2-lipped, brilliant scarlet flowers are produced from mid- to late summer. Lance-shaped leaves are reddish green.
L. 'Queen Victoria' illus. p.208.
L. syphilitica. Clump-forming perennial. H 3ft (1m), S 9in (23cm). Fully hardy, zones 5–9. Racemes of 2-lipped, blue flowers appear in late summer and autumn above narrowly oval, green leaves. Thrives in damp, heavy soil.
L. tupa. Clump-forming perennial. H 5–6ft (1.5–2m), S 3ft (1m). Half hardy, zones 8–9. Bears large spikes of 2-lipped, brick red flowers in late summer, above narrowly oval, hairy, light green leaves. Does best in a sheltered, sunny site.
L. 'Vedrariensis'. Clump-forming perennial. H 3ft (1m), S 1ft (30cm). Frost hardy, zones 5–8. In late summer

produces racemes of 2-lipped, purple flowers. Has lance-shaped, dark green leaves.
L. 'Will Scarlet'. Clump-forming perennial. H 3ft (1m), S 1ft (30cm). Frost hardy, zones 3–8. Racemes of 2-lipped, bright red flowers are borne in summer. Lance-shaped leaves are coppery green.

LOBIVIA (Cactaceae)
Genus of spherical to columnar, perennial cacti, forming clumps with age, with flowers that each last only 1–2 days. Frost tender, min. 41°F (5°C). Is easy to grow, requiring full sun and well-drained soil. Propagate by seed or stem cuttings from spring to autumn.
L. aurea, syn. *Echinopsis aurea.* Clump-forming, perennial cactus. H 5in (12cm), S 8in (20cm). Zone 10. Green stem, with 14 or 15 ribs, is densely covered with white, radial spines and a longer, darker, central spine. Produces funnel-shaped to flattish, yellow flowers, 3in (8cm) across, in summer.
L. backebergii illus. p.393.
L. cinnabarina. Spherical, perennial cactus. H and S 6in (15cm). Zone 10. Glossy, dark green stem has about 20 warty ribs and mostly curved, dark spines. In summer bears funnel-shaped to flattish, carmine red flowers, 3in (8cm) across.
L. haageana illus. p.387.
L. pentlandii illus. p.393.
L. pygmaea. See *Rebutia pygmaea.*
L. shaferi illus. p.399.

LOBULARIA (Cruciferae)
Genus of summer- and early autumn-flowering annuals. Fully hardy. Grow in sun and in fertile, well-drained soil. Dead-head to encourage continuous flowering. Propagate by seed sown under glass in spring, or outdoors in late spring.
L. maritima, syn. *Alyssum maritimum* (Sweet alyssum). Fast-growing, spreading annual. H 3–6in (8–15cm), S 8–12in (20–30cm). Has lance-shaped, grayish green leaves. Rounded heads of tiny, scented, 4-petaled, white flowers are produced in summer and early autumn. 'Little Dorrit' illus. p.262. 'Wonderland' illus. p.266.

LOISELEURIA (Ericaceae)
Genus of one species of evergreen, creeping, prostrate shrub, grown for its flowers. Fully hardy. Requires full light and humus-rich, well-drained, acid soil. Is difficult to grow. Propagate by seed in spring or by softwood or semi-ripe cuttings in summer.
L. procumbens illus. p.317.

LOMATIA (Proteaceae)
Genus of evergreen shrubs and trees, grown for their foliage and flowers, which have 4 narrow, twisted petals. Frost hardy, but in cold areas needs shelter from strong winds. Requires sun or semi-shade and moist but well-drained, acid soil. Propagate by softwood or semi-ripe cuttings in summer.
L. ferruginea. Evergreen, upright shrub or tree. H 30ft (10m), S 15ft

(5m). Zone 10. Stout, brown-felted shoots bear oblong to oval, dark green leaves, deeply cut into 6–15 oblong lobes. Racemes of yellow-and-red flowers are borne in mid-summer. Thrives outside only in mild, moist areas.
L. silaifolia illus. p.129.

LOMATIUM (Umbelliferae)
Genus of perennials with long, thick roots. Is useful on banks or in wild gardens. Fully to frost hardy. Needs sun and fertile, well-drained soil. Propagate by seed when fresh, in spring.
L. nudicaule (Pestle parsnip). Tufted perennial with a tap root. H and S 24in (60cm). Frost hardy, zones 7–9. Has fernlike, deeply dissected leaves, 8in (20cm) long, and, in summer, flat heads of inconspicuous, yellow flowers.

LONICERA (Caprifoliaceae)
Honeysuckle
Genus of deciduous, semi-evergreen, or evergreen shrubs and woody-stemmed, twining climbers, grown mainly for their flowers, which are often fragrant. Flowers are tubular, with spreading, 2-lipped petal lobes. Climbers may be trained into large shrubs. Fully hardy to frost tender, min. 41°F (5°C). Grows in any fertile, well-drained soil in sun or semi-shade. Prune out flowered wood of climbers after flowering. Prune shrubs only to remove dead shoots or restrain growth. Propagate by seed in autumn or spring, by semi-ripe cuttings in summer, or by hardwood cuttings in late autumn. Aphids may be a problem.
L. × americana illus. p.173.
L. × brownii (Scarlet trumpet honeysuckle). **'Dropmore Scarlet'** illus. p.168.
L. etrusca (Etruscan honeysuckle). Deciduous or semi-evergreen, woody-stemmed, twining climber. H to 12ft (4m). Half hardy, zones 7–9. Oval, green leaves are blue-green beneath, the upper ones united into cups. Fragrant, long-tubed, pale yellow flowers, borne in summer-autumn, turn deeper yellow and become red-flushed with age. Grow in sun.
L. fragrantissima. Deciduous or semi-evergreen, bushy, spreading shrub. H 6ft (2m), S 12ft (4m). Fully hardy, zones 5–8. Bears oval, dark green leaves. Fragrant, short-tubed, creamy white flowers open in winter and early spring.
L. 'Gold Flame'. See *L. × heckrottii.*
L. × heckrottii, syn. *L.* 'Gold Flame', illus. p.167.
L. henryi. Evergreen or semi-evergreen, woody-stemmed, twining climber. H to 30ft (10m). Frost hardy, zones 5–9. Narrowly oval, dark green leaves are paler beneath. Terminal clusters of long-tubed, red-purple flowers appear in summer-autumn, followed by black berries.
L. hildebrandiana (Giant Burmese honeysuckle). Evergreen or semi-evergreen, woody-stemmed, twining climber. H to 70ft (20m). Frost tender, zones 9–10. Oval or rounded, green leaves are paler beneath. Long-tubed,

white or cream flowers, ageing to creamy orange or brownish yellow, are produced in pairs in leaf axils or at shoot tips in summer. Grow in sun.

L. japonica (Japanese honeysuckle). **'Aureo-reticulata'** is an evergreen or semi-evergreen, twining climber with soft-haired, woody stems. H to 30ft (10m). Frost hardy, zones 4–10. Oval, sometimes lobed, leaves are bright green with bright yellow veins. Fragrant, long-tubed, white flowers, becoming yellowish, are borne in summer-autumn. Is useful for hiding a tree stump or an unsightly wall or fence. **'Halliana'** illus. p.173.
L. ledebourii illus. p.110.
L. maackii. Vigorous, deciduous, bushy shrub. H and S 15ft (5m). Fully hardy, zones 5–9. Leaves are oval and dark green. Fragrant, short-tubed, white, later yellow flowers, borne in early summer, are followed by spherical, bright red fruits.
L. morrowii. Deciduous, spreading shrub with arching branches. H 6ft (2m), S 10ft (3m). Fully hardy, zones 4–9. Has oval, dark green leaves and, in late spring and early summer, small, short-tubed, creamy white flowers, that age to yellow.
L. nitida. Evergreen, bushy, dense shrub. H 6ft (2m), S 10ft (3m). Fully hardy, zones 7–9. Leaves are small, oval, glossy, and dark green. Tiny, fragrant, short-tubed, creamy white flowers appear in late spring and are followed by small, spherical, purple fruits. Is good for hedging. **'Baggesen's Gold'** illus. p.145. **'Yunnan'** is more upright, has stouter shoots and larger leaves and flowers more freely.
L. periclymenum (Common honeysuckle, Woodbine). **'Graham Thomas'** illus. p.173. **'Serotina'** (Late Dutch honeysuckle) is a deciduous, woody-stemmed, twining climber. H to 22ft (7m). Fully hardy, zones 5–9. Oval or oblong, green leaves are gray-green beneath. Very fragrant, long-tubed, dark purple flowers, pinkish within, are borne in mid- and late summer. Grow in sun or shade.
L. pileata illus. p.144.
L. x purpusii illus. p.141.
L. sempervirens illus. p.168.
L. standishii. Evergreen, bushy shrub. H and S 6ft (2m). Fully hardy, zones 5–8. Has peeling bark, oblong, bristly, dark green leaves and, in winter, fragrant, short-tubed, creamy white flowers.
L. tatarica illus. p.108. **'Hack's Red'** is a deciduous, bushy shrub. H and S 8ft (2.5m). Fully hardy, zones 3–9. Produces short-tubed, deep pink flowers in late spring and early summer, followed by spherical, red fruits. Leaves are oval and dark green.
L. x tellmanniana illus. p.175.
L. tragophylla. Deciduous, woody-stemmed, twining climber. H 15–20ft (5–6m). Frost hardy, zones 6–9. Oval leaves are bluish green, the uppermost pair united into a cup. Produces clusters of up to 20 long-tubed, bright yellow flowers in early summer.
L. x xylosteoides **'Clavey's Dwarf'.** Deciduous, upright, dense shrub. H 6ft

(2m), S 3ft (1m). Fully hardy, zones 4–9. Leaves are oval and gray-green. Bears short-tubed, pink flowers in late spring, then spherical, red fruits.
L. xylosteum illus. p.108.

LOPHOCEREUS (Cactaceae)
Genus of columnar, perennial cacti with ribbed stems, branching with age. Nocturnal flowers appear only on plants over 6ft (2m) high. Flowering part of stem produces masses of long, thin spines that eventually cover stem. Frost tender, min. 50°F (10°C). Needs sun and well-drained soil. Propagate by seed in spring or summer.
L. schottii illus. p.380. **'Monstrosus'** is a columnar, perennial cactus. H 22ft (7m), S 6ft (2m). Zone 10. Irregular, olive to dark green stems have 4–15 ribs and no spines. Funnel-shaped, pink flowers, 1¹/₄in (3cm) wide, are produced at night in summer.
Lophomyrtus bullata. See *Myrtus bullata.*

LOPHOPHORA (Cactaceae)
Peyote
Genus of very slow-growing, perennial cacti that resemble small, blue dumplings, with up to 10 ribs, each separated by an indented line. Has long tap roots. Flowering areoles each produce tufts of short, white hairs. Frost tender, min. 41–50°F (5–10°C). Needs sun and well-drained soil. Is very prone to rotting, so water lightly from spring to autumn. Propagate by seed in spring or summer.
L. williamsii illus. p.391.

LOROPETALUM (Hamamelidaceae)
Genus of evergreen shrubs, grown for their flowers. Half hardy, but needs min. 41°F (5°C) to flower well. Requires full light or semi-shade and rich, well-drained, neutral to acid soil. Water potted plants freely when in full growth, moderately at other times. Propagate by layering or seed in spring or by semi-ripe cuttings in late summer.
L. chinense. Evergreen, rounded, well-branched shrub. H and S 4ft (1.2m). Zones 8–9. Asymmetrically oval leaves are deep green. White flowers, each with 4 strap-shaped petals, are borne in tufted, terminal clusters, mainly in winter-spring.

LOTUS (Leguminosae)
Genus of summer-flowering perennials, some of which are semi-evergreen, and evergreen sub-shrubs, grown for their foliage and flowers. Fully hardy to frost tender, min. 41°F (5°C). Prefers sun and well-drained soil. Propagate by softwood cuttings from early to mid-summer or by seed in autumn or spring.
L. berthelotii illus. p.240.

LUCULIA (Rubiaceae)
Genus of evergreen shrubs, grown for their flowers and foliage. Frost tender, min. 41–50°F (5–10°C). Needs full light or partial shade and fertile, well-drained soil. Water potted specimens freely when in full growth, moderately at other times. Cut flowered stems back hard in spring, if pot-grown.

Propagate by seed in spring or by semi-ripe cuttings in summer.
L. grandifolia. Evergreen, rounded to upright, robust shrub. H and S 10–20ft (3–6m). Min. 41°F (5°C), zones 9–10. Oval, green leaves have red veins and stalks. Fragrant, tubular, white flowers, each 2¹/₂in (6cm) long, with 5 rounded petal lobes, appear in terminal clusters in summer.

LUETKEA (Rosaceae)
Genus of one species of deciduous sub-shrub, grown for its fluffy flower heads. Is suitable for banks and rock gardens. Fully hardy. Requires shade and well-drained but not too dry soil. Propagate by division or seed in spring.
L. pectinata. Deciduous, spreading, decumbent sub-shrub. H to 12in (30cm), S 8in (20cm). Zones 6–8. Stems are clothed in finely dissected, very dark green leaves. In summer has terminal racemes of small, fluffy, off-white flower heads.

LUNARIA (Cruciferae)
Genus of biennials and perennials, grown for their flowers and silvery seed pods. Fully hardy. Will grow in sun or shade, but prefers partial shade and well-drained soil. Propagate perennials by seed in autumn or spring or by division in spring, biennials by seed only. Self seeds prolifically.
L. annua, syn. *L. biennis,* illus. p.269. **'Variegata'** illus. p.267.
L. biennis. See *L. annua.*
L. rediviva. Rosette-forming perennial. H 24–30in (60–75cm), S 12in (30cm). Zones 6–9. Produces racemes of 4-petaled, lilac or white flowers in spring, followed by elliptical, silvery seed pods that are useful for indoor decoration. Has oval, coarse, sometimes maroon-tinted, green leaves.

LUNATHYRIUM (Polypodiaceae)
Genus of deciduous or semi-evergreen ferns. Frost tender, min. 41°F (5°C). Needs a partially shaded position and humus-rich, moist soil. Remove fading fronds regularly. Propagate by division in spring or by spores in summer.
L. japonicum, syn. *Diplazium japonicum.* Semi-evergreen, creeping fern. H 12in (30cm), S 9in (23cm). Zones 9–10. Has lance-shaped, papery, light green fronds divided into oblong, indented, blunt pinnae.

LUPINUS (Leguminosae)
Lupine
Genus of annuals, perennials, and semi-evergreen shrubs, grown for their large, imposing racemes of pealike flowers. Fully to frost hardy. Prefers sun and well-drained, alkaline soil. Remove seed heads of most varieties to prevent self seeding. Propagate species by seed when fresh, in autumn, selected forms by cuttings from non-flowering side-shoots in spring or early summer.
L. arboreus illus. p.137.
L. 'Flaming June'. Clump-forming perennial. H 4ft (1.2m), S 1¹/₂ft (45cm). Fully hardy, zones 5–8. In early summer, spikes of orange-red

flowers arise from palmate, deeply divided, green leaves.
L. 'Inverewe Red' illus. p.205.
L. 'The Chatelaine' illus. p.204.
L. 'Thundercloud'. Clump-forming perennial. H 4ft (1.2m), S 1¹/₂ft (45cm). Fully hardy, zones 5–8. Produces spikes of deep violet-blue flowers that rise above palmate, deeply divided, green leaves in early summer.
L. 'Tom Reeves'. Clump-forming perennial. H 2¹/₂–3ft (75cm–1m), S 2¹/₂ft (75cm). Fully hardy, zones 5–8. During early summer, racemes of pure yellow flowers rise above palmate, deeply divided, green leaves.

LURONIUM (Alismataceae)
Genus of deciduous, perennial, marginal water plants and marsh plants, grown for their foliage and flowers. Fully hardy. Requires shallow water and full sun. Thin plants when overcrowded. Propagate in spring by seed or division.
L. natans, syn. *Alisma natans* (Floating water plantain). Deciduous, perennial, marginal water plant. H 1–2in (2.5–5cm), S 12in (30cm). Zones 7–10. Has small, elliptic to lance-shaped, green leaves and, in summer, small, 3-lobed, yellow-spotted, white flowers.

LUZULA (Juncaceae), Woodrush. See GRASSES, BAMBOOS, RUSHES, and SEDGES.
L. nivea illus. p.181.
L. sylvatica (Greater woodrush). **'Marginata'** (syn. *L.s.* 'Aureo-marginata') is a slow-growing, evergreen, spreading, rhizomatous, perennial grass. H to 12in (30cm), S indefinite. Fully hardy, zones 5–9. Produces thick tufts of broad, hairy-edged, green leaves, with white margins. Leafy stems bear terminal, open, brown flower spikes in summer. Tolerates shade.

LYCASTE. See ORCHIDS.
L. cruenta (illus. p.255). Vigorous, deciduous, epiphytic orchid for a cool greenhouse. H 12in (30cm). Zone 10. Fragrant, triangular, green-and-yellow flowers, 2in (5cm) across, are produced singly in spring. Has broadly oval, ribbed, soft leaves, to 12in (30cm) long. Grow in semi-shade during summer and avoid spraying, which can mark leaves.

LYCHNIS (Caryophyllaceae)
Genus of summer-flowering annuals, biennials, and perennials. Fully hardy. Requires sun and well-drained soil. Propagate by division or seed in autumn or spring.
L. 'Abbotswood Rose'. Neat, clump-forming perennial. H 12–15in (30–38cm), S 9in (23cm). Has oval, gray leaves and gray, branching stems that, from mid- to late summer, bear sprays of rounded, 5-petaled, brilliant purple flowers.
L. alpina, syn. *Viscaria alpina* (Alpine catchfly). Tuft-forming perennial. H 2–6in (5–15cm), S 4–6in (10–15cm). Zones 4–7. Has dense tufts of thick, linear, deep green leaves. In summer,

sticky stems each bear a rounded head of pale to deep pink or, rarely, white flowers with spreading, frilled petals. Suits a rock garden.

L. chalcedonica illus. p.216.

L. coeli-rosa. See *Silene coeli-rosa.*

L. coronaria illus. p.239.

L. flos-jovis illus. p.236.

L. x *haagena.* Short-lived, clump-forming perennial. H 18in (45cm), S 12in (30cm). Zones 4–8. Bears clusters of large, 5-petaled, white, orange, or red flowers in summer. Oval leaves are green. Is best raised regularly from seed.

L. viscaria. Clump-forming perennial. H 12in (30cm), S 12–18in (30–45cm). Zones 4–8. From early to mid-summer, rather sticky, star-shaped, reddish purple flowers are borne in dense clusters above narrowly oval to oblong, dark green leaves. Is suitable for the front of a border or a rock garden. **'Splendens Plena'** illus. p.239.

LYCIUM (Solanaceae)

Genus of deciduous shrubs, sometimes with long, scandent branches, grown for their habit, flowers, and fruits. Is particularly useful for poor, dry soil and coastal gardens. May be grown as a hedge. Fully hardy. Prefers full sun and not too rich, well-drained soil. Remove dead wood in winter and cut back to restrict growth if necessary. Cut back hedges hard in spring. Propagate by softwood cuttings in summer, by seed in autumn, or by hardwood cuttings in winter.

L. barbarum, syn. *L. halimifolium* (Chinese box thorn, Duke of Argyll's tea-tree). Deciduous, arching, often spiny shrub. H 8ft (2.5m), S 15ft (5m). Zones 5–9. Produces funnel-shaped, purple or pink flowers in late spring and summer that are followed by spherical, orange-red berries. Leaves are lance-shaped, bright green or gray-green.

L. halimifolium. See *L. barbarum.*

LYCORIS (Amaryllidaceae)

Genus of late summer- and early autumn-flowering bulbs with showy flower heads on leafless stems. Frost hardy; in cool areas is best grown in pots or planted in greenhouse borders. Needs sun, well-drained soil and a warm period in summer to ripen bulbs so they flower. Provide regular liquid feed while in growth. After summer dormancy, water from early autumn until following summer, when foliage dies away. Propagate by seed when ripe or in spring or summer or by offsets in late summer.

L. aurea (Golden spider lily). Late summer- and early autumn-flowering bulb. H 12–16in (30–40cm), S 4–6in (10–15cm). Zones 8–10. Bears a head of 5 or 6 bright yellow flowers that have narrow, reflexed petals, with very wavy margins, and conspicuous stamens. Strap-shaped, semi-erect, basal leaves appear after flowering.

L. radiata illus. p.351.

L. squamigera. Late summer- or early autumn-flowering bulb. H 18–24in (45–60cm), S 4–6in (10–15cm). Zones 6–10. Carries a head of 6–8 fragrant, funnel-shaped, rose-pink flowers, 4in (10cm) long, with reflexed petal tips. Strap-shaped, semi-erect, basal leaves form after flowers.

LYGODIUM (Schizaeaceae)

Genus of deciduous or semi-evergreen, climbing ferns, usually with 2 kinds of fronds: vegetative and fertile. Half hardy to frost tender, min. 41°F (5°C). Needs shade or semi-shade and humus-rich, moist, peaty soil. Is best grown among shrubby plants that can provide support. Plants grown under glass in pots need strong, twiggy supports. Remove faded fronds regularly. Propagate by division in spring or by spores in summer.

L. japonicum (Japanese climbing fern). Deciduous, climbing fern. H 6ft (2m), S indefinite. Frost tender, zones 8–10. Green, vegetative fronds consist of delicate, finger-shaped pinnae; fertile fronds are broader and 3–5 lobed, with a longer, terminal lobe.

L. palmatum. Deciduous, climbing fern. H 6ft (2m), S indefinite. Half hardy, zones 9–10. Has hand-shaped, 5–7 lobed, green vegetative fronds and linear, more or less palmate, fertile pinnae.

LYONIA (Ericaceae)

Genus of deciduous, semi-evergreen, or evergreen shrubs and trees, grown for their racemes of small, urn-shaped flowers. Fully hardy. Needs shade or semi-shade and moist, peaty, acid soil. Propagate by semi-ripe cuttings in summer.

L. ligustrina. Deciduous, bushy shrub. H and S 6ft (2m). Zones 4–9. Oval, dark green leaves set off dense racemes of globular urn-shaped, white flowers from mid- to late summer.

L. ovalifolia. Deciduous or semi-evergreen, bushy shrub. H and S 6ft (2m). Zones 7–9. Has red shoots and oval, dark green leaves. Racemes of urn-shaped, white flowers appear in late spring and early summer.

LYONOTHAMNUS (Rosaceae)

Genus of one species of evergreen tree, grown for its foliage and flowers. Frost hardy. Needs sun or semi-shade, a warm, sheltered position, and fertile, well-drained soil. Propagate by softwood cuttings in summer or by seed in autumn.

L. floribundus (Catalina ironwood). Evergreen tree grown only in the form var. *aspleniifolius.* This slender tree, H 40ft (12m), S 20ft (6m), zones 9–10, has rather stringy, reddish brown bark and fernlike, dark green leaves. Large, flattened heads of 5-petaled, white flowers are produced in early summer.

LYSICHITON (Araceae)

Genus of deciduous, perennial, marginal water plants and bog plants, grown for their handsome spathes and foliage. Fully hardy. Prefers full sun, but tolerates semi-shade. Tolerates both still and running water. Propagate by seed when fresh, in late summer.

L. americanus illus. p.377.

L. camtschatcensis illus. p.372.

LYSIMACHIA (Primulaceae)

Loosestrife

Genus of summer-flowering annuals and perennials, suitable for the border or rock garden. Fully to half hardy. Prefers sun or semi-shade and moist but well-drained soil. Propagate by division in spring or by seed in autumn.

L. clethroides illus. p.202.

L. ephemerum. Neat, clump-forming perennial. H 3ft (1m), S 1ft (30cm). Fully hardy, zones 7–9. Erect, terminal racemes of star-shaped, grayish white flowers are produced on slender stems in summer, followed by light green seed heads. Lance-shaped leaves are leathery and glaucous.

L. nummularia **'Aurea'** illus. p.326.

L. punctata illus. p.214.

LYTHRUM (Lythraceae)

Purple loosestrife

Genus of summer-flowering perennials that thrive by the waterside and in bog gardens. Fully hardy. Grows in full sun or semi-shade and in moist or wet soil. Propagate cultivars by division in spring, species by seed or division in spring or autumn.

L. salicaria **'Firecandle'** illus. p.205. **'Robert'** is a clump-forming perennial. H 30in (75cm), S 18in (45cm). Zones 4–9. Racemes of 4-petaled, clear pink flowers are produced from mid- to late summer. Leaves are green and lance-shaped.

L. virgatum **'Rose Queen'.** Clump-forming perennial. H 3ft (1m), S 2ft (60cm). Zones 4–9. Racemes of 4-petaled, light pink flowers are borne from mid- to late summer above lance-shaped, green leaves. **'The Rocket'** illus. p.205.

M

MAACKIA (Leguminosae)
Genus of deciduous, summer-flowering trees, grown for their foliage and flowers. Fully hardy. Requires full sun and fertile, well-drained soil. Propagate by seed in autumn.
M. amurensis illus. p.63.

MACADAMIA (Proteaceae)
Genus of evergreen trees, grown for their foliage and fruits. Frost tender, min. 50–55°F (10–13°C). Prefers full light, though some shade is tolerated. Provide humus-rich, moisture-retentive but well-drained soil. Water freely while in full growth, moderately at other times. Pruning is not usually necessary, but is tolerated in autumn. Propagate by seed when ripe, in autumn, or in spring.
M. integrifolia illus. p.47.

MACFADYENA, syn. DOXANTHA (Bignoniaceae)
Genus of evergreen, woody-stemmed, tendril climbers, grown for their foxglovelike flowers. Frost tender, min. 41°F (5°C). Any fertile, well-drained soil is suitable with full light. Water regularly, less when not in full growth. Provide support for stems. Thin out crowded shoots after flowering or in spring. Propagate by semi-ripe cuttings in summer.
M. unguis-cati illus. p.174.

MACKAYA (Acanthaceae)
Genus of one species of evergreen shrub, grown for its flowers and overall appearance. Frost tender, min. 45–50°F (7–10°C). Requires full light or partial shade and fertile, well-drained soil. Water potted plants freely when in full growth, moderately at other times. Pruning is tolerated in winter if necessary. Propagate by greenwood cuttings in spring or by semi-ripe cuttings in summer.
M. bella, syn. *Asystasia bella*. Evergreen, erect, then spreading, well-branched shrub. H to 5ft (1.5m), S 4–5ft (1.2–1.5m). Zone 10. Bears oval, pointed, glossy leaves that are mid- to deep green. Produces spikes of tubular, dark-veined, lavender flowers, each with 5 large, flared petal lobes, from spring to autumn. In warm conditions, above 55°F (13°C), continues flowering through winter.

MACLEANIA (Ericaceae)
Genus of evergreen, spring- to summer-flowering shrubs and scrambling climbers, grown primarily for their flowers. Frost tender, min. 50°F (10°C). Needs partial shade and humus-rich, freely draining, neutral to acid soil. Water potted specimens moderately, less when not in full growth. Long shoots may be shortened in winter or after flowering. Propagate by seed in spring, by semi-ripe cuttings in summer, or by layering in autumn.

M. insignis. Evergreen, scrambling climber with erect, sparingly branched, wandlike stems. H 10ft (3m), S 3–10ft (1–3m). Zone 10. Has oval, leathery, deep green leaves, red-flushed when young. Tubular, waxy, scarlet flowers, with white tips, are borne in pendent clusters in summer. Needs support.

MACLEAYA (Papaveraceae)
Plume poppy
Genus of summer-flowering perennials, grown for their overall appearance. Fully hardy. Grows in sun and in well-drained soil. May spread rapidly. Propagate by division in early spring or by root cuttings in winter.
M. cordata, syn. *Bocconia cordata*. Spreading, clump-forming perennial. H 5ft (1.5m) or more, S 2ft (60cm) or more. Zones 4–9. Large, rounded, lobed, gray-green leaves, gray-white beneath, are produced at base of plant and up lower parts of stems. Bears large, feathery panicles of dainty, creamy white flowers in summer.
M. microcarpa 'Coral Plume' illus. p.189.

MACLURA (Moraceae)
Genus of one species of deciduous tree, grown for its foliage and unusual fruits. Both male and female trees need to be planted to obtain fruits. Fully hardy, but young plants are susceptible to frost damage. Requires full sun and needs hot summers to thrive in cold areas. Grows in any but waterlogged soil. Propagate by softwood cuttings in summer, by seed in autumn, or by root cuttings in late winter.
M. pomifera (Osage orange). Deciduous, spreading tree. H 50ft (15m), S 40ft (12m). Zones 5–9. Has spiny shoots and oval, dark green leaves that turn yellow in autumn. Tiny, yellow flowers in summer are followed by large, rounded, wrinkled, pale green fruits.

Macroplectrum sesquipedale. See *Angraecum sesquipedale.*

Macrotomia echioides. See *Arnebia pulchra.*

MACROZAMIA (Zamiaceae)
Genus of slow-growing, evergreen shrubs and small trees, with or without trunks, grown for their palmlike appearance. Mature plants may produce conical, green flower spikes. Frost tender, min. 55–61°F (13–16°C). Needs full light or partial shade and well-drained soil. Water potted plants moderately when in full growth, less at other times. Propagate by seed in spring.
M. spiralis. Evergreen, palmlike shrub with a very short, mainly underground trunk. H and S 2–3ft (60cm–1m). Zone 10. Has a rosette of deep green leaves, each with a spirally twisted midrib and very narrow, leathery leaflets.

MAGNOLIA (Magnoliaceae)
Genus of deciduous, semi-evergreen, or evergreen trees and shrubs, grown for their showy, usually fragrant flowers. Leaves are mainly oval. Fully to frost hardy. Flowers and buds of early-flowering magnolias may be damaged by late frosts. Needs sun or semi-shade and shelter from strong winds. Does best in fertile, well-drained soil. *M. delavayi*, *M. kobus*, *M. sieboldii*, and *M. wilsonii* grow on chalky soil. Other species prefer neutral to acid soil, but will grow in alkaline soil if deep and humus-rich. Dry, sandy soils should be generously enriched with manure and leaf mold before planting. Propagate species by semi-ripe cuttings in summer or by seed, when ripe, in autumn, selected forms by semi-ripe cuttings in summer or by grafting in winter.
M. acuminata (Cucumber tree). Vigorous, deciduous tree, conical when young, later spreading. H 70ft (20m), S 30ft (10m). Fully hardy, zones 4–8. Fragrant, cup-shaped, bluish green flowers appear from early to mid-summer amid large, oval, pale green leaves, followed by small, egg-shaped, green, later red fruits.
M. campbellii illus. p.38. 'Charles Raffill' is a vigorous, deciduous tree, upright when young, later spreading. H 50ft (15m), S 30ft (10m). Frost hardy, zones 7–9. Large, fragrant, cup-shaped, purplish pink flowers are borne from late winter to mid-spring on trees at least 15 years old. Leaves are large, oval, and green. 'Darjeeling' illus. p.38. 'Kew's Surprise' bears deep purplish pink flowers. var. *mollicomata* illus. p.38.
M. 'Charles Coates' illus. p.48.
M. cylindrica illus. p.59.
M. dawsoniana. Deciduous tree or shrub, with a broadly oval head. H 50ft (15m), S 30ft (10m). Frost hardy, zones 7–9. In early spring large, pendent, fragrant, open cup-shaped, pale lilac-pink flowers are carried profusely on older plants (20 years from seed, 10 years from grafting). Leaves are oval, leathery, and deep green.
M. delavayi. Evergreen, rounded, dense shrub or tree. H and S 30ft (10m). Frost hardy, zones 7–9. Large, slightly fragrant, bowl-shaped, parchment white flowers are short-lived and open intermittently from mid-summer to early autumn. Large, oval, deep blue-green leaves are bluish white beneath.
M. denudata, syn. *M. heptapeta* (Lily tree, Yulan). Deciduous, rounded, bushy shrub or spreading tree. H and S 30ft (10m). Fully hardy, zones 6–9. Bears masses of fragrant, cup-shaped, white flowers from mid- to late spring before oval, green leaves appear.
M. fraseri illus. p.50.
M. globosa. Deciduous, bushy shrub. H and S 15ft (5m). Frost hardy, zones 7–9. In early summer, large, oval,

glossy, dark green leaves set off fragrant, cup-shaped, creamy white flowers with red anthers.
M. grandiflora (Bull bay, Southern magnolia). Evergreen, broadly conical or rounded, dense tree. H and S 30ft (10m). Frost hardy, zones 7–9. Bears large, very fragrant, bowl-shaped, white flowers intermittently from mid-summer to early autumn. Has oblong, glossy, mid- to dark green leaves. 'Exmouth' illus. p.51. 'Ferruginea' has dark green leaves, rust brown beneath.
M. heptapeta. See *M. denudata.*
M. hypoleuca, syn. *M. obovata*, illus. p.39.
M. insignis. See *Manglietia insignis.*
M. kobus illus. p.48.
M. liliiflora. Deciduous, bushy shrub. H 10ft (3m), S 12ft (4m). Fully hardy, zones 6–9. Fragrant, upright, vase-shaped, purplish pink flowers are borne amid oval, very dark green leaves from mid-spring to mid-summer. 'Nigra' illus. p.85.
M. × loebneri 'Leonard Messel' illus. p.85. 'Merrill' is a vigorous, deciduous, upright shrub or tree with spreading branches. H 30ft (10m), S 25ft (8m). Fully hardy, zones 5–9. Fragrant, many-petaled, funnel-shaped, white flowers open in mid-spring before oblong, dark green leaves appear.
M. macrophylla (Bigleaf magnolia). Deciduous, broadly upright tree, becoming rounded with age. H and S 30ft (10m). Frost hardy, zones 6–9. Produces stout, blue-gray shoots and very large, oval, bright green leaves. Large, fragrant, bowl-shaped, parchment white flowers are borne in early summer.
M. 'Norman Gould'. Deciduous, spreading tree or bushy shrub. H and S 15ft (5m). Fully hardy, zones 6–9. Silky buds open into fragrant, star-shaped, white flowers in mid-spring. Leaves are oblong and dark green.
M. obovata. See *M. hypoleuca.*
M. salicifolia illus. p.59.
M. sargentiana. Deciduous, broadly conical tree. H 50ft (15m), S 30ft (10m). Fully hardy, zones 7–9. Large, fragrant, narrowly bowl-shaped, many-petaled flowers, white inside, purplish pink outside, open from mid- to late spring, before oval, dark green leaves emerge.
M. sieboldii. Deciduous, arching shrub or wide-spreading tree. H 25ft (8m), S 40ft (12m). Frost hardy, zones 6–9. Fragrant, cup-shaped, white flowers, with crimson anthers, are carried above oval, dark green leaves from late spring to late summer.
M. sinensis. Deciduous, spreading shrub. H 20ft (6m), S 25ft (8m). Fully hardy, zones 7–9. In late spring and early summer bears fragrant, nodding, cup-shaped, white flowers with crimson anthers. Oval, glossy, bright green leaves have velvety undersides.

M. x *soulangeana* illus. p.85. **'Alba Superba'** is a deciduous, rounded, upright shrub or tree. H 22ft (7m), S 15ft (5m). Fully hardy, zones 5–9. Large, fragrant, tuliplike, white flowers, faintly flushed with pink, are borne from mid-spring to early summer, before and after oval, mid- to dark green leaves emerge. **'Brozzonii'**, H 25ft (8m), S 20ft (6m), is treelike, with large, purple-flushed, white flowers. Flowers of **'Lennei'** are large, goblet-shaped, and deep rose-purple. **'Picture'**, H 25ft (8m), S 20ft (6m), is vigorous, compact, and upright, with large, erect, deep reddish purple flowers. **'Rustica Rubra'** (syn. *M.* x *s.* 'Rubra') illus. p.85.
M. sprengeri var. *diva*. Deciduous, spreading tree. H 50ft (15m), S 30ft (10m). Frost hardy, zones 7–9. Has large, fragrant, narrowly bowl-shaped, many-petaled, deep rose-pink flowers in mid-spring, before oval, dark green leaves appear. **'Wakehurst'** illus. p.38.
M. stellata illus. p.97.
M. tripetala illus. p.51.
M. x *veitchii* **'Peter Veitch'** illus. p.38.
M. virginiana (Sweet bay). Deciduous or semi-evergreen, conical shrub or tree. H 28ft (9m), S 20ft (6m). Fully hardy, zones 6–9. Has very fragrant, cup-shaped, creamy white flowers from early summer to early autumn. Oblong, glossy, mid- to dark green leaves are bluish white beneath.
M. **'Wada's Memory'** illus. p.59.
M. x *watsonii*. See *M.* x *wieseneri*.
M. x *wieseneri*, syn. *M.* x *watsonii*, illus. p.63.
M. wilsonii illus. p.63.

x MAHOBERBERIS (Berberidaceae)
Hybrid genus (*Berberis* x *Mahonia*) of evergreen shrubs, grown for their foliage, flowers, and botanical interest. Fully hardy. Needs sun or semi-shade and fertile, well-drained soil. Propagate by semi-ripe cuttings in summer.
x *M. aquisargentii*. Evergreen, upright, densely leaved shrub. H and S 6ft (2m). Zones 7–9. Leaves are bright green, often with 3 leaflets, some oblong and finely toothed, others holly-shaped. Terminal clusters of berberislike, yellow flowers are sparsely produced in late spring.

MAHONIA (Berberidaceae)
Genus of evergreen shrubs, grown for their foliage, their usually short racemes of often fragrant, rounded, bell-shaped, yellow flowers and, on tall species and cultivars, for their deeply fissured bark. Large mahonias make good specimen plants; low-growing ones are excellent for ground cover. Fully to half hardy. Prefers shade or semi-shade and fertile, well-drained but not too dry soil. Propagate species by leaf-bud or semi-ripe cuttings in summer or by seed in autumn, selected forms by leaf-bud or semi-ripe cuttings only.
M. acanthifolia. Evergreen, upright shrub. H 12ft (4m), S 6ft (2m). Frost hardy, zones 8–9. Has large, dark green leaves, composed of 17–27 hollylike, spiny leaflets. Long, dense racemes of rich yellow flowers are borne in late autumn and early winter.

M. aquifolium illus. p.125.
M. bealei (Leatherleaf mahonia). Evergreen, upright shrub. H and S 6ft (2m). Fully hardy, zones 7–9. Blue-green leaves consist of 13–17 broad, hollylike, spiny leaflets. Stout, upright racemes of fragrant yellow flowers are produced from late winter to early spring.
M. **'Heterophylla'**. Evergreen, upright shrub. H 3ft (1m), S 5ft (1.5m). Frost hardy, zones 7–9. Has reddish purple shoots and glossy, bright green leaves, each composed of 5 or 7 narrowly lance-shaped, wavy-edged or curled leaflets that turn reddish purple in winter. Small clusters of yellow flowers appear in spring.
M. japonica illus. p.119.
M. lomariifolia. Evergreen, very upright shrub. H 10ft (3m), S 6ft (2m). Frost hardy, zones 8–10. Large, dark green leaves each have 19–37 narrow, hollylike, spiny leaflets. Fragrant, bright yellow flowers are produced in dense, upright racemes during late autumn and winter.
M. x *media* **'Buckland'** and **'Charity'** illus. p.93.
M. napaulensis. Evergreen, upright, open shrub. H 8ft (2.5m), S 10ft (3m). Frost hardy, zones 8–10. Leaves are composed of up to 15 hollylike, spiny, dark green leaflets. Produces long, slender racemes of yellow flowers in early and mid-spring.
M. repens. Evergreen, upright shrub that spreads by underground stems. H 1ft (30cm), S 6ft (2m). Fully hardy, zones 6–9. Blue-green leaves each consist of 3–7 oval leaflets, with bristlelike teeth. Dense clusters of deep yellow flowers are borne from mid- to late spring.
M. **'Undulata'**. Evergreen, upright shrub. H and S 6ft (2m). Fully hardy, zones 8–9. Glossy, dark green leaves each have 5–9 hollylike, wavy-edged leaflets that become bronzed in winter. Bears dense clusters of deep yellow flowers in mid- and late spring.

MAIANTHEMUM (Liliaceae)
May lily
Genus of perennials with extensive, spreading rhizomes. Is useful as ground cover in woodlands and wild areas. Fully hardy. Prefers shade and humus-rich, moist, sandy, neutral to acid soil. Propagate by seed in autumn or by division in any season.
M. bifolium. Spreading, rhizomatous perennial. H 4in (10cm), S indefinite. Zones 4–5. Pairs of large, oval, glossy, dark green leaves, with wavy edges, arise direct from rhizomes. Slender stems each produce a raceme of 4-petaled, white flowers in early summer, followed by small, spherical, red berries. May be invasive.
M. canadense illus. p.303.

MAIHUENIA (Cactaceae)
Genus of slow-growing, summer-flowering, alpine cacti, clump-forming with age, with cylindrical stems. Fully to frost hardy. Requires sun and well-drained soil. Protect from winter rain. Propagate by seed or stem cuttings in spring or summer.
M. poeppigii illus. p.397.

MALCOLMIA (Cruciferae)
Genus of spring- to autumn-flowering annuals. Fully hardy. Grow in sun and in fertile, well-drained soil. Propagate by seed sown outdoors in spring, summer, or early autumn. Self seeds freely.
M. maritima illus. p.267.

MALEPHORA (Aizoaceae)
Genus of erect or spreading, perennial succulents with semi-cylindrical leaves. Frost tender, min. 41°F (5°C). Needs sun and very well-drained soil. Propagate by seed or stem cuttings in spring or summer.
M. crocea illus. p.400.

MALOPE (Malvaceae)
Genus of annuals, grown for their showy flowers that are ideal for cutting. Fully hardy. Grow in sun and in fertile, well-drained soil. Propagate by seed sown outdoors in spring. Self seeds freely.
M. trifida illus. p.268.

MALUS (Rosaceae)
Crab apple
Genus of deciduous, mainly spring-flowering trees and shrubs, grown for their shallowly cup-shaped flowers, fruits, foliage, or autumn color. Crab apples may be used to make preserves. Fully hardy. Prefers full sun, but tolerates semi-shade; grows in any but waterlogged soil. In winter, cut out dead or diseased wood and prune to maintain a balanced branch system. Propagate by budding in late summer or by grafting in mid-winter. Trees are sometimes attacked by aphids, caterpillars, and red spider mite, and are susceptible to fireblight and apple scab.
M. **'Almey'**. Deciduous, rounded tree. H and S 25ft (8m). Zones 5–8. Oval leaves are reddish purple when young, maturing to dark green. Single, deep pink flowers, with paler pink, almost white centers, in late spring are followed by long-lasting, rounded, orange-red crab apples, which are subject to apple scab.
M. x *arnoldiana* illus. p.60.
M. x *atrosanguinea*. Deciduous, spreading tree. H and S 20ft (6m). Zones 4–8. Produces oval, glossy, dark green leaves. Red flower buds open to single, rich pink blooms in late spring. Bears small, rounded, red-flushed, yellow crab apples.
M. baccata (Siberian crab apple). Deciduous, spreading tree. H and S 50ft (15m). Zones 3–7. Has oval, dark green leaves, a profusion of single, white flowers from mid- to late spring, and tiny, rounded, red or yellow crab apples. var. *mandschurica* illus. p.48.
M. **'Chilko'**. Deciduous, spreading tree. H and S 25ft (8m). Zones 5–8. Oval, dark green leaves are reddish purple when young. Produces single, rose-pink flowers in mid-spring followed by large, rounded, bright crimson crab apples.
M. coronaria **'Charlottae'**. Deciduous, spreading tree. H and S 28ft (9m). Zones 5–8. Broadly oval, lobed or deeply toothed leaves are dark green, turning red in autumn. Semi-

double, pale pink flowers are borne in late spring and early summer.
M. **'Cowichan'** illus. p.67.
M. **'Dorothea'**. Deciduous, spreading tree. H and S 25ft (8m). Zones 5–8. Semi-double, silvery pink flowers, red in bud, are borne in late spring, followed by rounded, yellow crab apples. Oval leaves are green. Is subject to apple scab.
M. **'Eleyi'**. Deciduous, spreading tree. H and S 25ft (8m). Zones 5–8. Oval leaves are dark reddish purple when young, dark green when mature. Bears single, deep purplish red flowers from mid- to late spring and rounded, purplish red crab apples.
M. floribunda illus. p.61.
M. **'Frettingham's Victoria'**. Deciduous, upright tree. H 25ft (8m), S 12ft (4m). Zones 5–8. Single, white flowers, borne amid oval, dark green leaves in late spring, are followed by rounded, red-flushed, yellow crab apples.
M. **'Golden Hornet'** illus. p.69.
M. **'Hopa'**. Deciduous, spreading tree. H and S 30ft (10m). Zones 5–8. Oval, dark green leaves are reddish purple when young. Single, deep pink flowers in mid-spring are succeeded by rounded, orange-and-red crab apples.
M. hupehensis illus. p.48.
M. **'John Downie'** illus. p.67.
M. **'Katherine'**. Deciduous, round-headed tree. H and S 20ft (6m). Zones 5–8. Has oval, green leaves, large, double, pale pink flowers, fading to white, from mid- to late spring, and tiny, rounded, yellow-flushed, red crab apples.
M. **'Lemoinei'** illus. p.62.
M. **'Magdeburgensis'** illus. p.61.
M. **'Marshall Oyama'** illus. p.68.
M. **'Neville Copeman'**. Deciduous, spreading tree. H and S 28ft (9m). Zones 5–8. Oval, dark green leaves are purplish red when young. Single, dark purplish red flowers, borne from mid- to late spring, are followed by rounded, orange-red to carmine crab apples.
M. niedzwetskyana. Deciduous, spreading tree. H 20ft (6m), S 25ft (8m). Zones 4–8. Oval leaves are red when young, later purple. Produces clusters of single, deep reddish purple flowers in late spring, then very large, conical, reddish purple crab apples.
M. prattii. Deciduous tree, upright when young, later spreading. H and S 30ft (10m). Zones 5–8. Oval, red-stalked, glossy, green leaves become orange and red in autumn. Single, white flowers in late spring are followed by small, rounded or egg-shaped, white-flecked, red crab apples.
M. **'Professor Sprenger'** illus. p.68.
M. **'Profusion'** illus. p.50.
M. prunifolia illus. p.67.
M. x *purpurea* (Purple crab). Deciduous, spreading tree. H 25ft (8m), S 30ft (10m). Zones 5–8. Oval, young leaves are reddish, maturing to green. Single, deep ruby red flowers, which become paler with age, are produced in late spring and are followed by rounded, reddish purple crab apples.
M. **'Red Jade'**. Deciduous, weeping tree. H 12ft (4m), S 20ft (6m). Zones 5–8. In late spring has single, white

flowers, sometimes pale pink-flushed, then long-lasting, rounded to egg-shaped, red crab apples. Leaves are dark green and oval.
M. x *robusta* (Cherry crab apple). Vigorous, deciduous, spreading tree. H 40ft (12m), S 30ft (10m). Zones 4–8. Bears masses of single, white or pink flowers above oval, dark green leaves in late spring, followed by long-lasting, rounded, yellow or red crab apples. **'Yellow Siberian'** has white flowers, sometimes pink-tinged, and yellow crab apples.
M. **'Royalty'** illus. p.62.
M. sargentii illus. p.84.
M. sieboldii illus. p.97.
M. spectabilis (Chinese crab apple). Deciduous, round-headed tree. H and S 30ft (10m). Zones 5–8. Has oval, dark green leaves, large, single, blush pink flowers, rose-red in bud, from mid- to late spring and large, rounded, yellow crab apples.
M. toringoides (Cutleaf crab apple). Deciduous, spreading tree. H 25ft (8m), S 30ft (10m). Zones 6–8. Oval, deeply lobed, glossy, bright green leaves turn yellow in autumn. Bears single, white flowers in late spring and rounded or egg-shaped, red-flushed, yellow crab apples in autumn.
M. transitoria. Deciduous, spreading, elegant tree. H 25ft (8m), S 30ft (10m). Zones 5–8. Oval, deeply lobed, green leaves turn yellow in autumn. Has masses of single, white flowers in late spring, followed by small, rounded, pale yellow crab apples.
M. trilobata. Deciduous, conical tree. H 50ft (15m), S 22ft (7m). Zones 5–8. Has maplelike, lobed, glossy, bright green leaves that often become brightly colored in autumn. Bears single, white flowers in early summer, followed by small, rounded or pear-shaped, red or yellow crab apples.
M. tschonoskii. Deciduous, conical tree. H 40ft (12m), S 22ft (7m). Zones 5–8. Broadly oval, glossy, green leaves turn brilliant shades of orange, red, and purple in autumn. Single, pink-tinged, white flowers, borne in late spring, are succeeded by rounded, red-flushed, yellowish green crab apples.
M. **'Van Eseltine'.** Deciduous, upright tree. H 20ft (6m), S 12ft (4m). Zones 5–8. Bears double, pink flowers in late spring and rounded, yellow crab apples in autumn. Has oval, dark green leaves.
M. **'Veitch's Scarlet'** illus. p.66.
M. yunnanensis var. *veitchii* illus. p.64.
M. x *zumi* **'Calocarpa'** illus. p.68.

MALVA (Malvaceae)
Mallow
Genus of annuals, biennials, and free-flowering, short-lived perennials. Fully hardy. Requires sun and fertile, well-drained soil. Propagate species by seed in autumn, selected forms by cuttings from firm, basal shoots in late spring or summer. These shoots may be encouraged by cutting plant back after first flowers have faded.
M. moschata illus. p.203.

Malvastrum capensis. See *Anisodontea capensis.*
Malvastrum hypomadarum of gardens. See *Anisodontea capensis.*

MALVAVISCUS (Malvaceae)
Genus of evergreen shrubs and trees, grown for their flowers. Frost tender, min. 55–61°F (13–16°C). Grow in full light and in fertile, well-drained soil. Water potted plants freely during growing season, moderately at other times. To maintain shape, flowered stems may be cut back hard in late winter. Propagate by seed in spring or by semi-ripe cuttings in summer. Whitefly and red spider mite may be troublesome.
M. arboreus illus. p.89.

MAMMILLARIA (Cactaceae)
Pincushion cactus
Genus of hemispherical, spherical, or columnar cacti, grown for their rings of funnel-shaped flowers that develop near crowns. Flowers, offsets, and long, slender to spherical seed pods grow between tubercles on a spiny, green stem with extended areoles. Frost tender, min. 41–50°F (5–10°C). Requires full sun and very well-drained soil. Keep completely dry in winter, otherwise plants rot easily. Propagate by seed in spring or summer.
M. bocasana illus. p.391.
M. candida (Snowball pincushion). Slow-growing, clump-forming, perennial cactus. H and S 6in (15cm). Min. 41°F (5°C), zone 10. Columnar, green stem is densely covered with short, stiff, white spines. Produces cream to rose flowers, $^1/_2$–$^3/_4$in (1–2cm) across, in spring. Water sparingly in summer.
M. densispina. Slow-growing, spherical, perennial cactus. H 4in (10cm), S 8in (20cm). Min. 41°F (5°C), zone 10. Has a green stem densely covered with stout, golden spines. Produces yellow flowers, $^1/_2$–$^3/_4$in (1–2cm) wide, in spring.
M. elegans. Spherical to columnar, perennial cactus. H 12in (30cm), S 8in (20cm). Min. 41°F (5°C), zone 10. Bears a green stem densely covered with short, bristly spines and bright red flowers, $^1/_2$in (1cm) across, in spring. Offsets occasionally.
M. elongata illus. p.390.
M. geminispina illus. p.386.
M. gracilis. Clump-forming, perennial cactus. H 2in (5cm), S 8in (20cm). Min. 41°F (5°C), zone 10. Produces a columnar, green stem densely covered with pure white spines. In early summer carries pale cream flowers, $^1/_2$–$^3/_4$in (1–2cm) across. Stem is shallow-rooted and reroots readily. var. *fragilis,* H 1$^1/_2$in (4cm), is more fragile and has off-white spines.
M. hahniana illus. p.386.
M. magnimamma. Clump-forming, perennial cactus. H 1ft (30cm), S 2ft (60cm). Min. 41°F (5°C), zone 10. Green stem has very pronounced, angular, dark green tubercles with white spines of variable length. Bears cream, pink, or red flowers, $^1/_2$–$^3/_4$in (1–2cm) wide, in spring and possibly again in late summer.
M. microhelia illus. p.398.
M. plumosa illus. p.389.
M. prolifera (Strawberry cactus). Clump-forming, perennial cactus. H 4in (10cm), S 12in (30cm). Min 41°F (5°C), zone 10. Green stem bears

dense, golden to white spines. Produces masses of cream or yellow flowers, $^1/_2$–$^3/_4$in (1–2cm) wide, in summer, followed by red berries that taste like strawberries.
M. rhodantha. Spherical to columnar, perennial cactus. H and S 2ft (60cm). Min. 41°F (5°C), zone 10. Green stem, branching from crown with age, is densely covered with brown to yellow spines. In late summer produces bright red flowers, $^1/_2$–$^3/_4$in (1–2cm) across.
M. schiedeana illus. p.390.
M. sempervivi illus. p.392.
M. zeilmanniana illus. p.393.

MANDEVILLA, syn. DIPLADENIA (Apocynaceae)
Genus of evergreen, semi-evergreen, or deciduous, woody-stemmed, twining climbers, grown for their large, trumpet-shaped flowers. Half hardy to frost tender, min. 45–50°F (7–10°C). Grow in any well-drained soil, with light shade in summer. Water freely when in full growth, sparingly at other times. Provide support and thin out and spur back congested growth in early spring. Propagate by seed in spring or by semi-ripe cuttings in summer. Whitefly and red spider mite may cause problems.
M. x *amabilis* **'Alice du Pont'** illus. p.167.
M. boliviensis. Vigorous, evergreen, woody-stemmed, twining climber. Frost tender, zone 10. H to 12ft (4m). Oblong, pointed leaves are lustrous green. Large, trumpet-shaped, white flowers with gold eyes are produced in small clusters in summer.
M. laxa, syn. *M. suaveolens* (Chilean jasmine). Fast-growing, deciduous or semi-evergreen, woody-stemmed, twining climber. H 15ft (5m) or more. Half hardy, zones 9–10. Oval leaves have heart-shaped bases. Clusters of fragrant white flowers are borne in summer.
M. splendens illus. p.163.
M. suaveolens. See *M. laxa.*

MANDRAGORA (Solanaceae)
Mandrake
Genus of rosetted perennials with large, deep, fleshy roots. Fully to frost hardy. Needs sun or partial shade and deep, humus-rich, well-drained soil. Resents being transplanted. Propagate by seed in autumn.
M. officinarum illus. p.311.

MANETTIA (Rubiaceae)
Genus of evergreen, soft- or semi-woody-stemmed, twining climbers, grown for their small but showy flowers. Frost tender, min. 41°F (5°C), but 45–50°F (7–10°C) is preferred. Grow in any humus-rich, well-drained soil, with partial shade in summer. Water regularly, sparingly when temperatures are low. Stems need support. Cut back if required in spring. Propagate by softwood or semi-ripe cuttings in summer. Whitefly is sometimes a problem.
M. bicolor. See *M. inflata.*
M. cordifolia (Firecracker vine). Fast-growing, evergreen, soft-stemmed, twining climber. H 6ft (2m) or more. Zone 10. Has narrowly heart-shaped,

glossy leaves. Funnel-shaped, red flowers appear in small clusters in summer.
M. inflata, syn. *M. bicolor,* illus. p.164.

MANGLIETIA (Magnoliaceae)
Genus of evergreen trees, grown for their foliage and flowers. Half hardy, but is best at min. 37–41°F (3–5°C). Provide humus-rich, moisture-retentive but well-drained, acid soil and full light or partial shade. Water potted plants freely when in full growth, less at other times. Pruning is tolerated if necessary. Propagate by seed in spring.
M. insignis, syn. *Magnolia insignis.* Evergreen, broadly conical tree. H 25–40ft (8–12m) or more, S 10–15ft (3–5m) or more. Zones 9–10. Leaves are narrowly oval, lustrous, dark green above, bluish green beneath. In early summer has solitary magnolialike, pink to carmine flowers that are cream-flushed.

MARANTA (Marantaceae)
Genus of evergreen perennials, grown for their distinctively patterned, colored foliage. Frost tender, min. 50–59°F (10–15°C). Needs constant, high humidity and a shaded position away from drafts or wind. Grow in humus-rich, well-drained soil. Propagate by division in spring or summer or by stem cuttings in summer.
M. leuconeura (Prayer plant). **'Erythroneura'** (syn. *M.l.* 'Erythrophylla') illus. p.259. var. *kerchoviana* illus. p.260. var. *massangeana* is an evergreen, short-stemmed perennial, branching at the base. H and S 1ft (30cm). Zone 10. Oblong, velvety, dark green leaves, each 6in (15cm) long with a wide, irregular, pale midrib, white, lateral veins and often purplish green below, stand upright at night but lie flat during the day. Small, 3-petaled, white to mauve flowers appear in slender, upright spikes year-round.

Marginatocereus marginatus. See *Lemaireocereus marginatus.*

MARGYRICARPUS (Rosaceae)
Genus of evergreen shrubs, grown for their fruits. Is good for rock gardens. Frost hardy. Needs a sheltered, sunny position and well-drained soil. Propagate by softwood cuttings in early summer or by seed in autumn.
M. pinnatus, syn. *M. setosus* (Pearl berry). Evergreen, prostrate shrub. H 9–12in (23–30cm), S 3ft (1m). Zones 7–9. Has dark green leaves divided into linear, silky leaflets. Tiny, inconspicuous, green flowers in early summer are followed by small, globose, glossy, white fruits.
M. setosus. See *M. pinnatus.*

Marsdenia erecta. See *Cionura erecta.*

MARTYNIA (Pedaliaceae, syn. Martyniaceae)
Genus of annuals, grown for their flowers and curious, horned fruits. Half hardy to frost tender, min. 36–9°F (2–4°C). Grow in a sunny, sheltered

position and in fertile, well-drained soil. Propagate by seed sown under glass in early spring.
M. annua, syn. *M. louisiana*, illus. p.264.
M. louisiana. See *M. annua.*

MASDEVALLIA. See ORCHIDS.
M. coccinea (illus. p.253). Evergreen, epiphytic orchid for a cool greenhouse. H 6in (15cm). Zone 10. Rich cerise flowers, 3in (8cm) long, are borne singly in summer. Has narrowly oval leaves, 4in (10cm) long. Needs shade in summer.
M. infracta (illus. p.252). Evergreen, epiphytic orchid for a cool greenhouse. H 6in (15cm). Zone 10. In summer bears rounded, red-and-white flowers, 2in (5cm) long, with tail-like, greenish sepals. Narrowly oval leaves are 4in (10cm) long. Needs shade in summer.
M. tovarensis (illus. p.252). Evergreen, epiphytic orchid for a cool greenhouse. H 6in (15cm). Zone 10. In autumn, 1¹/₂in (4cm) long, milky white flowers, with short-tailed sepals, appear singly or up to 3 to a stem. Has narrowly oval leaves, 4in (10cm) long. Grow in shade in summer.
M. wagneriana (illus. p.254). Evergreen, epiphytic orchid for a cool greenhouse. H 3in (8cm). Zone 10. Pale yellow flowers, 1¹/₂in (4cm) long, with long, tail-like sepals, are produced singly or in pairs in summer. Leaves are narrowly oval and 4in (10cm) long. Requires shade in summer.

MATTEUCCIA (Polypodiaceae)
Genus of deciduous, rhizomatous ferns. Fully hardy. Prefers semi-shade and wet soil. Remove faded fronds regularly and divide plants when crowded. Propagate by division in autumn or winter.
M. struthiopteris illus. p.186.

MATTHIOLA (Cruciferae)
Stock
Genus of annuals, biennials, perennials, and evergreen sub-shrubs. Flowers of most annual or biennial stocks are highly scented and excellent for cutting. Fully hardy to frost tender, min. 39°F (4°C). Grow in sun or semi-shade and in fertile, well-drained, ideally lime-rich soil. Tall cultivars may need support. If grown as biennials outdoors, provide cloche protection during winter. To produce flowers outdoors the same summer, sow seed of annuals under glass in early spring, or outdoors in mid-spring. Sow seed of perennials under glass in spring. Propagate sub-shrubs by semi-ripe cuttings in summer. Is prone to aphids, flea beetle, club root, downy mildew, and botrytis.
M., **Brompton Series** (mixed) illus. p.265, (pink) illus. p.267.
M., **East Lothian Series.** Group of fast-growing, upright, bushy biennials and short-lived perennials, grown as annuals. H and S 1ft (30cm). Fully hardy. Has lance-shaped, grayish green leaves and, in summer, bears spikes, 6in (15cm) or more long, of scented, 4-petaled, single or double flowers, in shades of pink, red, purple, yellow, or white.

M. **'Giant Excelsior'** illus. p.265.
M. **'Giant Imperial'** illus. p.262.
M. incana. (Common stock). Fast-growing, upright, bushy biennial or short-lived perennial, grown as an annual. H 1–2ft (30–60cm), S 1ft (30cm). Fully hardy. Has lance-shaped, grayish green leaves and, in summer, scented, 4-petaled, light purple flowers borne in spikes, 3–6in (7–15cm) long.
M. **'Mammoth Column'.** Fast-growing, upright, bushy biennial or short-lived perennial, grown as an annual. H to 2¹/₂ft (75cm), S 1ft (30cm). Fully hardy. Has lance-shaped, grayish green leaves and, in summer, produces 12–15in (30–38cm) long spikes, of scented, 4-petaled flowers that are available in mixed or single colors. Flowers are excellent for cutting.
M., **Park Series.** Group of fast-growing, upright, bushy biennials and short-lived perennials, grown as annuals. H and S to 1ft (30cm). Fully hardy. Lance-shaped leaves are grayish green. In summer, spikes, at least 6in (15cm) long, of scented, 4-petaled flowers are borne in a wide range of colors.
M., **Ten-week Series.** Group of fast-growing, upright, bushy biennials and short-lived perennials, grown as annuals. H and S to 1ft (30cm). Fully hardy. Has lance-shaped, grayish green leaves. Scented, 4-petaled flowers, in spikes at least 6in (15cm) long, are produced in a wide range of colors in summer. Dwarf (illus. p.268) and "selectable" cultivars have double flowers.
M. **'Trysomic'.** Fast-growing, upright, bushy biennial or short-lived perennial, grown as an annual. H and S to 1ft (30cm). Fully hardy. Lance-shaped leaves are grayish green. Spikes, at least 6in (15cm) long, of scented, mostly double flowers are produced in a wide range of colors in summer.

Matucana haynei. See *Borzicactus haynei.*

MAURANDIA. See ASARINA.

MAXILLARIA. See ORCHIDS.
M. picta. Evergreen, epiphytic orchid for a cool greenhouse. H 9in (23cm). Zone 10. Fragrant yellow flowers, 1in (2.5cm) across and marked reddish brown outside, are produced singly beneath foliage in winter. Has narrowly oval leaves, 6–9in (15–23cm) long. Requires semi-shade in summer.
M. porphyrostele (illus. p.255). Evergreen, epiphytic orchid for a cool greenhouse. H 3in (8cm). Zone 10. White- and red-lipped, yellow flowers, ¹/₂in (1cm) across, are borne singly in summer-autumn. Narrowly oval leaves are 3in (8cm) long. Grow in good light during summer.
M. tenuifolia. Evergreen, epiphytic orchid for a cool greenhouse. H 6in (15cm). Zone 10. Fragrant yellow flowers, 1in (2.5cm) across, heavily overlaid with red and with white lips, are borne singly throughout summer. Has narrowly oval leaves, 6in (15cm) long. Needs good light in summer.

MAYTENUS (Celastraceae)
Genus of evergreen trees, grown for their neat foliage. Frost hardy, but needs shelter from strong, cold winds when young. Requires sun or semi-shade and fertile, well-drained soil. Propagate by semi-ripe cuttings in summer or by suckers in autumn or spring.
M. boaria (Maiten). Evergreen, bushy-headed, elegant tree. H 30ft (10m), S 25ft (8m). Zones 9–10. Narrowly oval, glossy, dark green leaves are produced on slender shoots. Bears tiny, star-shaped, green flowers in late spring.

MAZUS (Scrophulariaceae)
Genus of creeping, spring-flowering perennials. Is useful for rock gardens and in paving. Frost hardy. Needs a sheltered, sunny site and moist soil. Propagate by division in spring or by seed in autumn.
M. reptans illus. p.308.

MECONOPSIS (Papaveraceae)
Blue poppy
Genus of perennials, some short-lived, others monocarpic (die after flowering), grown for their flowers. Fully hardy. Needs shade and, in warm areas, a cool position. Most prefer humus-rich, moist, neutral to acid soil. Propagate all but *M.* x *sheldonii* by seed when fresh, in late summer; *M. cambrica, M. grandis, M. quintuplinervia, M.* x *sheldonii* and their cultivars may also be propagated by division after flowering.
M. betonicifolia illus. p.212.
M. cambrica illus. p.232.
M. grandis. Erect perennial. H 3–5ft (1–1.5m), S 1ft (30cm). Zone 8. Stout stems bear slightly nodding, cup-shaped, deep blue flowers in early summer. Oblong, slightly toothed, hairy, erect, green leaves are produced in rosettes at base. Divide every 2–3 years to maintain vigor. **'Branklyn'** illus. p.212.
M. integrifolia illus. p.247.
M. napaulensis illus. p.189.
M. paniculata. Short-lived, clump-forming perennial that dies after flowering. H 5ft (1.5m), S 2ft (60cm). Zones 6–8. Bears racemes of nodding, cup-shaped, yellow flowers in late spring or early summer. Has large rosettes of oblong to lance-shaped, deeply lobed and cut, hairy, yellowish green leaves.
M. quintuplinervia illus. p.228.
M. x *sheldonii.* Clump-forming perennial. H 4–5ft (1.2–1.5m), S 1¹/₂–2ft (45–60cm). Zones 7–8. Clusters of cup-shaped, clear deep blue flowers are produced in early summer. Has rosettes of oblong to oval, toothed, hairy, green leaves. Divide every three years to maintain vigor. **'Slieve Donard'** has slightly smaller flowers and leaves with fewer teeth.

MEDICAGO (Leguminosae)
Genus of annuals, perennials, and evergreen shrubs, grown for their flowers. Is good in mild, coastal areas as is very wind-resistant. Frost hardy, but in cold areas plant against a south- or west-facing wall. Requires sun and well-drained soil. Cut out dead wood in

spring. Propagate shrubs by semi-ripe or softwood cuttings in summer or by seed in autumn or spring, annuals and perennials by seed in autumn or spring.
M. arborea (Moon trefoil, Tree medick). Evergreen, bushy, dense shrub. H and S 6ft (2m). Zones 7–9. Clusters of small, pealike, yellow flowers appear from mid-spring to late autumn or winter. These are followed by curious, flattened, snail-like, green, then brown seed pods. Has dark green leaves, each composed of 3 narrowly triangular leaflets, which are silky-haired when young.

MEDINILLA (Melastomataceae)
Genus of evergreen shrubs and scrambling climbers, grown for their flowers and foliage. Frost tender, min. 61–4°F (16–18°C). Needs partial shade and humus-rich, well-drained soil. Water potted plants freely when in full growth, moderately at other times. Propagate by greenwood cuttings in spring or summer.
M. magnifica illus. p.109.

MEEHANIA (Labiatae)
Genus of perennials often with creeping stems, grown mainly as ground cover. Frost hardy. Prefers shade and well-drained but not dry, humus-rich soil. Propagate by seed, division, or stem cuttings in spring.
M. urticifolia. Trailing, hairy perennial with long, creeping, leafy stems and erect flowering stems. H to 1ft (30cm), S indefinite. Zones 6–9. Oval to triangular, toothed leaves are 4in (10cm) or more long on the creeping stems – smaller on flowering stems. Whorls of fragrant, 2-lipped, purplish blue flowers, to 2in (5cm) long, are carried in erect spikes in late spring.

MEGASEA. See BERGENIA.

MELALEUCA (Myrtaceae)
Genus of evergreen, spring- and summer-flowering trees and shrubs, grown for their flowers and overall appearance. Half hardy to frost tender, min. 39–45°F (4–7°C). Needs full light and well-drained soil, preferably without much nitrogen. Some species tolerate waterlogged soils. Water potted specimens moderately, less in low temperatures. Propagate by seed in spring or by semi-ripe cuttings in summer.
M. armillaris (Bracelet honey myrtle). Evergreen, rounded, wiry-stemmed shrub or tree. H 10–20ft (3–6m), S 4–10ft (1.2–3m). Frost tender, zone 10. Produces needlelike, deep green leaves and, in summer, dense, bottlebrushlike clusters, 1¹/₄–2¹/₂in (3–6cm) long, each flower consisting of a small brush of white stamens.
M. elliptica illus. p.110.
M. hypericifolia. Evergreen, rounded shrub. H and S 6–15ft (2–5m). Frost tender, zone 10. Leaves are oblong to elliptic and mid- to pale green. Flowers, each composed of a ³/₄–1in (2–2.5cm) long brush of crimson stamens, are borne in summer, mainly in bottlebrushlike spikes, 1¹/₂–3in (4–8cm) long.
M. nesophylla illus. p.112.

M. quinquenervia (Broad-leaved paperbark). Strong-growing, evergreen, rounded tree. H 20–40ft (6–12m), S 10–20ft (3–6m). Frost tender, zone 10. Leaves are elliptic and lustrous. Has peeling, papery, tan-colored bark and, in spring, small, white or creamy pink flowers in bottlebrushlike clusters. Tolerates waterlogged soil.

M. squarrosa (Scented paper-bark). Evergreen, erect, wiry-stemmed shrub or tree. H 10–20ft (3–6m), S 6–12ft (2–4m). Frost tender, zone 10. Has tiny, oval, deep green leaves. Bears 1½in (4cm) long spikes of scented flowers, each comprising a tiny brush of cream stamens, in late spring and summer.

MELASPHAERULA (Iridaceae)
Genus of one species of spring-flowering corm, grown mainly for botanical interest. Half hardy. Needs sun and well-drained soil. Plant in autumn and keep watered until after flowering, then dry off. Propagate by seed or offsets in autumn.

M. graminea. See *M. ramosa*.

M. ramosa, syn. *M. graminea*. Spring-flowering corm. H to 24in (60cm), S 4–6in (10–15cm). Zones 9–10. Has narrowly sword-shaped, semi-erect leaves in a basal fan. Wiry, branched stem bears loose sprays of small, pendent, funnel-shaped, yellowish green flowers with pointed petals.

MELASTOMA (Melastomataceae)
Genus of evergreen, mainly summer-flowering shrubs and trees, grown for their flowers and foliage. Frost tender, min. 50–55°F (10–13°C). Requires full light or partial shade and fertile, well-drained soil. Water potted specimens freely when in full growth, moderately at other times. Pruning is tolerated in late winter if necessary. Propagate by softwood or greenwood cuttings in spring or summer. Red spider mite and whitefly may cause problems.

M. candidum. Evergreen, rounded, bristly-stemmed shrub. H and S 3–6ft (1–2m). Zone 10. Leaves are oval, leathery, and bristly. Small, terminal clusters of fragrant, 5–7-petaled, white or pink flowers are borne profusely in summer.

MELIA (Meliaceae)
Genus of deciduous, spring-flowering trees, grown for their foliage, flowers, and fruits. Is useful for very dry soil and does well in coastal gardens in mild areas. Frost tender. Needs full sun; grows in any well-drained soil. Propagate by seed in autumn.

M. azedarach illus. p.49.

MELIANTHUS (Melianthaceae)
Genus of evergreen perennials and shrubs, grown primarily for their foliage. Half hardy to frost tender, min. 41°F (5°C). Requires sun and fertile, well-drained soil. Water potted specimens freely in summer, moderately at other times. Long stems may be shortened in early spring. Propagate by seed in spring or by greenwood cuttings in summer. Red spider mite may be troublesome.

M. major (Honeybush). Evergreen, sprawling, sparingly branched shrub. H and S 6–10ft (2–3m). Half hardy, but best at min. 41°F (5°C), zones 9–10. Leaves are 10–18in (25–45cm) long, with 7–13 oval, toothed, blue-gray leaflets. Has tubular, rich brownish red flowers in terminal spikes, 12in (30cm) long, in spring-summer. May be tied upright to a support or fanned out on a wall.

MELICA (Gramineae). See GRASSES, BAMBOOS, RUSHES, and SEDGES.
M. altissima (Siberian melic, Tall melic). Evergreen, tuft-forming, perennial grass. H 24in (60cm), S 8in (20cm). Fully hardy, zones 6–9. Has slender stems and broad, green leaves, rough beneath. In summer bears pendent, tawny spikelets in narrow panicles. **'Atropurpurea'** illus. p.181.

MELICYTUS (Violaceae)
Genus of evergreen shrubs and trees, grown for their overall appearance and ornamental fruits. Half hardy to frost tender, min. 37–41°F (3–5°C). Grows in well-drained soil and in full light or partial shade. Water potted specimens moderately, less in winter. Pruning is tolerated if required. Propagate by seed when ripe, in autumn, or in spring.

M. ramiflorus (Mahoe, Whiteywood). Evergreen, spreading shrub or tree. H and S 20–30ft (6–10m). Frost tender, zone 10. Bark is gray-white. Bears lance-shaped, bluntly serrated, bright green leaves. Has small, rounded, greenish flowers in axillary clusters in summer, followed by tiny, violet to purple-blue berries.

MELIOSMA (Sabiaceae)
Genus of deciduous trees and shrubs, grown for their habit, foliage, and flowers, which, however, do not appear reliably. Frost hardy. Prefers full sun and deep, fertile, well-drained soil. Propagate by seed in autumn.

M. oldhamii. See *M. pinnata* var. *oldhamii*.

M. pinnata var. ***oldhamii***, syn. *M. oldhamii*. Deciduous, stout-branched tree, upright when young, spreading when mature. H 30ft (10m), S 20ft (6m). Zones 7–9. Has very large, dark green leaves divided into 5–13 oval leaflets. Bears large clusters of small, fragrant, star-shaped, white flowers in early summer.

M. veitchiorum illus. p.53.

MELITTIS (Labiatae)
Bastard balm
Genus of one species of summer-flowering perennial. Fully hardy. Does best in light shade and requires fertile, well-drained soil. Propagate by seed in autumn or by division in spring or autumn.

M. melissophyllum illus. p.234.

MELOCACTUS (Cactaceae)
Turk's cap
Genus of spherical, ribbed, perennial cacti. On reaching flowering size, usually 6in (15cm) high, stems produce woolly crowns; then stems appear to stop growing while woolly crowns develop into columns. Has funnel-shaped flowers in summer, followed by elongated or rounded, red, pink, or white seed pods. Frost tender, min. 52–9°F (11–15°C). Requires full sun and extremely well-drained soil. Propagate by seed in spring or summer.

M. bahiensis. Spherical, perennial cactus. H and S 6in (15cm). Min. 59°F (15°C), zone 10. Dull green stem bears 10–15 ribs. Produces stout, slightly curved, dark brown spines that become paler with age. Crown bears brown bristles and pink flowers, ½–¾in (1–2cm) across, in summer.

M. communis illus. p.392.

M. matanzanus. Spherical, perennial cactus. H and S 4in (10cm). Min. 59°F (15°C), zone 10. Dark green stem has neat, short spines and develops a woolly crown about 5 years from seed. In summer produces pink flowers, ½in (1cm) across.

M. oaxacensis. Spherical to columnar, perennial cactus. H 8in (20cm), S 6in (15cm). Min. 59°F (15°C), zone 10. Green stem has 15 rounded ribs. Areoles each bear a straight central spine and curved radial spines. Flat, woolly crown produces deep pink flowers, ½in (1cm) across, in summer.

MENISPERMUM (Menispermaceae)
Moonseed
Genus of deciduous, woody or semi-woody, twining climbers, grown for their attractive fruits that each contain a crescent-shaped seed—hence the common name. Male and female flowers are carried on separate plants; to produce fruits, plants of both sexes must be grown. Frost hardy. Grow in sun and in any well-drained soil. Propagate by seed or suckers in spring.

M. canadense (Canada moonseed, Yellow parilla). Vigorous, deciduous, woody-stemmed, twining climber, producing a dense tangle of stems and spreading by underground suckers. H to 15ft (5m). Zones 7–9. Oval to heart-shaped leaves are usually 3–7-lobed. Small, cup-shaped, greenish yellow flowers are carried in summer, followed by clusters of poisonous, spherical, blackish fruits.

MENTHA (Labiatae)
Mint
Genus of perennials, some of which are semi-evergreen, grown for their aromatic foliage, which is both decorative and used as a culinary herb. Plants are invasive, however, and should be used with caution. Fully to frost hardy. Grow in sun or shade and in well-drained soil. Propagate by division in spring or autumn.

M. x ***gentilis* 'Variegata'.** Spreading perennial. H 18in (45cm), S 24in (60cm). Fully hardy, zones 4–9. Forms a mat of oval, dark green leaves that are speckled and striped with yellow, most conspicuously in full sun. Bears stems with whorls of small, 2-lipped, pale mauve flowers in summer.

M. x ***piperita*** (Peppermint). **'Citrata'** (Eau-de-Cologne mint) is a spreading perennial. H 12–24in (30–60cm), S 24in (60cm). Fully hardy, zones 4–9. Reddish green stems, bearing terminal spikes of small, 2-lipped, purple flowers in summer, arise from a carpet of oval, slightly toothed, green leaves that have a scent which is similar to Eau de Cologne.

M. requienii (Corsican mint). Semi-evergreen, creeping perennial. H to ½in (1cm), S indefinite. Frost hardy, zones 7–9. When crushed, rounded, bright apple green leaves exude a strong peppermint fragrance. Carries tiny, stemless, lavender purple flowers in summer. Suits a rock garden or paved path. Needs shade and moist soil.

M. rotundifolia. See *M. suaveolens*.

M. suaveolens, syn. *M. rotundifolia* (Apple mint, Pineapple mint). **'Variegata'** illus. p.233.

MENTZELIA (Loasaceae)
Genus of annuals, perennials, and evergreen shrubs. Fully hardy to frost tender, min. 39°F (4°C). Grow in sun and in fertile, very well-drained soil; tender species are best grown in pots under glass. Propagate by seed in spring; shrubs may also be propagated by semi-ripe cuttings in summer.

M. lindleyi, syn. *Bartonia aurea*, illus. p.280.

MENYANTHES (Gentianaceae)
Genus of deciduous, perennial, marginal water plants, grown for their foliage and flowers. Fully hardy. Prefers an open, sunny position. Remove fading flower heads and foliage, and divide overcrowded clumps in spring. Propagate by stem cuttings in spring.

M. trifoliata illus. p.372.

MENZIESIA (Ericaceae)
Genus of deciduous shrubs, grown for their small, urn-shaped flowers. Fully hardy. Needs semi-shade and fertile, moist, peaty, acid soil. Propagate by softwood cuttings in summer or by seed in autumn.

M. ciliicalyx var. ***purpurea*** illus. p.123.

MERENDERA (Liliaceae)
Genus of corms similar to *Colchicum* but with less showy flowers. Fully to frost hardy. Needs a sunny position and well-drained soil. In cool, damp areas grow in an unheated greenhouse or frame where corms can dry out in summer. Plant in autumn and keep watered through winter and spring. Propagate by seed or offsets in autumn.

M. bulbocodium. See *M. montana*.

M. montana, syn. *M. bulbocodium*, illus. p.368.

M. robusta. Spring-flowering corm. H 3in (8cm), S 2–3in (5–8cm). Frost hardy, zones 7–9. Narrowly lance-shaped, semi-erect, basal leaves appear at same time as upright, funnel-shaped flowers, 2–2½in (5–6cm) wide, with narrow, pale purplish pink or white petals.

MERREMIA (Convolvulaceae)
Genus of evergreen, twining climbers, grown for their flowers and fruits. Frost tender, min. 45–50°F (7–10°C). Prefers fertile, well-drained soil and full light. Water moderately, much

less when not in full growth. Provide support. Thin out congested stems in spring. Propagate by seed in spring. Red spider mite may be a problem.
M. tuberosa, syn. *Ipomoea tuberosa* (Wood rose, Yellow morning-glory). Fast-growing, evergreen, twining climber. H 20ft (6m) or more. Zone 10. Leaves have 7 radiating lobes. Funnel-shaped, yellow flowers are borne mainly in summer, followed by semi-woody, globose, ivory brown fruits.

MERTENSIA (Boraginaceae)
Genus of perennials, grown for their funnel-shaped flowers. Fully hardy. Requires sun or shade and deep, well-drained soil. Propagate by division in spring or by seed in autumn.
M. echioides illus. p.297.
M. maritima illus. p.309.
M. virginica illus. p.228.

MERYTA (Araliaceae)
Genus of evergreen trees, grown for their handsome foliage. Frost tender, min. 41°F (5°C). Requires full light or partial shade and humus-rich, moisture-retentive but moderately drained soil. Water potted plants freely when in full growth, less at other times. Propagate by semi-ripe cuttings in summer or by seed when ripe (dried seed is short-lived) in late summer.
M. sinclairii illus. p.72.

Mesembryanthemum criniflorum. See *Dorotheanthus bellidiformis.*

MESPILUS (Rosaceae)
Medlar
Genus of one species of deciduous tree or shrub, grown for its habit, flowers, foliage, and edible fruits. Fully hardy. Needs sun or semi-shade and fertile, well-drained soil. Propagate species by seed in autumn and named forms (selected for their fruit) by budding in late summer.
M. germanica illus. p.58.

METASEQUOIA (Taxodiaceae). See CONIFERS.
M. glyptostroboides illus. p.74.

METROSIDEROS (Myrtaceae)
Genus of evergreen, winter-flowering shrubs, trees, and scrambling climbers, grown for their flowers, the trees also for overall appearance and for shade. Frost tender, min. 41°F (5°C). Grows in fertile, well-drained soil and in full light. Water potted specimens freely when in full growth, moderately at other times. Pruning is tolerated if necessary. Propagate by seed in spring or by semi-ripe cuttings in summer.
M. excelsa illus. p.56.
M. robusta (Rata). Robust, evergreen, rounded tree. H 70–80ft (20–25m) or more, S 30–50ft (10–15m). Zone 10. Oblong to elliptic, leathery leaves are dark green and lustrous. Produces large clusters of flowers, mostly composed of long, dark red stamens, during winter.

MEUM (Umbelliferae)
Genus of summer-flowering perennials, grown for their aromatic

leaves. Is useful on banks and in wild gardens. Fully hardy. Needs sun and well-drained soil. Propagate by seed when fresh, in autumn.
M. athamanticum (Baldmoney, Spignel). Upright, clump-forming perennial. H 6–18in (15–45cm), S 4–6in (10–15cm). Zones 5–8. Mainly basal and deeply dissected leaves have narrowly linear leaflets. In summer produces flattish flower heads consisting of clusters of tiny, white or purplish white flowers.

MICHELIA (Magnoliaceae)
Genus of evergreen, winter- to summer-flowering shrubs and trees, grown for their flowers and foliage. Half hardy to frost tender, min. 41°F (5°C). Provide humus-rich, well-drained, neutral to acid soil and full light or partial shade. Water potted specimens freely when in full growth, less in winter. Pruning is seldom necessary. Propagate by semi-ripe cuttings in summer or by seed when ripe, in autumn, or in spring.
M. doltsopa illus. p.56.
M. figo illus. p.62.

MICROBIOTA (Cupressaceae). See CONIFERS.
M. decussata (Siberian carpet grass; illus. p.82). Spreading, shrubby conifer. H 20in (50cm), S 6–10ft (2–3m). Fully hardy, zones 2–8. Bears flat sprays of scalelike, yellow-green leaves that turn bronze in winter. Globose, yellow-brown cones each contain only one seed.

Microglossa albescens. See *Aster albescens.*

MICROLEPIA (Polypodiaceae)
Genus of deciduous, semi-evergreen, or evergreen ferns, best grown in pans and hanging baskets. Frost tender, min. 41°F (5°C). Requires shade or semi-shade and moist soil. Remove faded fronds regularly. Propagate by division in spring or by spores in summer.
M. strigosa illus. p.184.

MICROMERIA (Labiatae)
Genus of evergreen or semi-evergreen shrubs, sub-shrubs, and perennials, suitable for rock gardens and banks. Frost hardy. Needs sun and well-drained soil. Propagate by seed in spring or by softwood cuttings in early summer.
M. juliana. Evergreen or semi-evergreen, bushy shrub or sub-shrub. H and S 12in (30cm). Zones 7–9. Has small, oval, aromatic, green leaves pressed close to stems. In summer, minute, tubular, bright deep pink flowers are carried in whorls on upper parts of stems.

MIKANIA (Compositae)
Genus of evergreen or herbaceous, scrambling or twining climbers, shrubs, and erect perennials, grown for their foliage and flower heads. Half hardy to frost tender, min. 45°F (7°C). Any fertile, well-drained soil is suitable, with partial shade in summer. Water regularly, less when not in full growth. Support for stems is needed

and ties may be necessary. Thin out congested growth in spring. Propagate by semi-ripe or softwood cuttings in summer. Aphids may be a problem.
M. scandens. Herbaceous, twining climber. H 10–15ft (3–5m). Half hardy, zones 9–10. Has oval to triangular, green leaves with 2 basal lobes. Compact clusters of tiny, groundsel-like, pink to purple flower heads are produced in summer-autumn.

MILIUM (Gramineae). See GRASSES, BAMBOOS, RUSHES, and SEDGES.
M. effusum (Wood millet). 'Aureum' is an evergreen, tuft-forming, perennial grass. H 3ft (1m), S 1ft (30cm). Fully hardy, zones 5–8. Has flat, golden yellow leaves. Produces open, tiered panicles of greenish yellow spikelets in summer. Self seeds readily in shade.

MILLA (Liliaceae)
Genus of summer-flowering bulbs, grown for their fragrant flowers, each comprising a slender tube with 6 spreading, star-shaped petals at the tip. Half hardy. Needs a sheltered, sunny position and well-drained soil. Plant in spring. Lift bulbs after flowering and partially dry off for winter. Propagate by seed or offsets in spring.
M. biflora. Summer-flowering bulb. H 12–18in (30–45cm), S 3–4in (8–10cm). Zones 9–10. Has long, narrow, semi-erect, basal leaves. Stem bears a loose head of 2–6 erect, white flowers, 1¼–2½in (3–6cm) across, each on a slender stalk to 8in (20cm) long.

MILTONIA. See ORCHIDS.
M. candida var. **grandiflora** (illus. p.254). Evergreen, epiphytic orchid for a cool or intermediate greenhouse. H 8in (20cm). Zone 10. Cream-lipped, green-patterned, brown flowers, 2in (5cm) across, are borne in spikes in autumn. Has narrowly oval leaves, 4–5in (10–12cm) long. Grow in semi-shade in summer.
M. clowesii (illus. p.254). Evergreen, epiphytic orchid for an intermediate greenhouse. H 8in (20cm). Zone 10. In early summer produces large spikes of 1½in (4cm) wide, yellow flowers, barred with reddish brown and each with a white-and-mauve lip. Has broadly oval leaves, 12in (30cm) long. Grow in semi-shade in summer.

MILTONIOPSIS (Pansy orchid). See ORCHIDS.
M. Anjou 'St. Patrick' (illus. p.253). Evergreen, epiphytic orchid for a cool greenhouse. H 6in (15cm). Zone 10. Carries sprays of deep crimson flowers, 4in (10cm) across, with red and yellow patterns on each lip, mainly in summer. Has narrowly oval, soft leaves, 4–5in (10–12cm) long. Needs shade in summer.
M. Robert Strauss 'Ardingly' (illus. p.252). Evergreen, epiphytic orchid for a cool greenhouse. H 6in (15cm). Zone 10. Bears sprays of white flowers, 4in (10cm) across, marked reddish brown and purple; flowering season varies. Narrowly oval, soft leaves are 4–5in (10–12cm) long. Needs shade in summer.

MIMOSA (Leguminosae)
Genus of annuals, evergreen perennials, shrubs, trees, and scrambling climbers, cultivated for their flowers and foliage. *M. pudica* is usually grown as an annual. Frost tender, min. 55–61°F (13–16°C). Needs partial shade and fertile, well-drained soil. Water potted specimens freely when in full growth, moderately at other times. Propagate by seed in spring, shrubs also by semi-ripe cuttings in summer. Red spider mite may be a nuisance.
M. pudica illus. p.144.

MIMULUS (Scrophulariaceae)
Monkey flower
Genus of annuals, perennials, and evergreen shrubs. Small species suit damp pockets in rock gardens. Fully hardy to frost tender, min. 36–9°F (2–4°C). Most prefer full sun and wet or moist soil. Propagate perennials by division in spring, sub-shrubs by softwood cuttings in late summer; annuals and all species by seed in autumn or early spring.
M. 'Andean Nymph' illus. p.235.
M. aurantiacus, syn. *M. glutinosus, Diplacus glutinosus*, illus. p.139.
M. glutinosus. See *M. aurantiacus*.
M. guttatus. Spreading, mat-forming perennial. H and S 24in (60cm). Frost hardy, zones 9–10. Snapdragonlike, bright yellow flowers, spotted with reddish brown on lower lobes, are borne in succession in summer and early autumn. Oval leaves are toothed and green.
M. lewisii illus. p.237.
M. luteus illus. p.247.
M., Malibu Series. Group of fast-growing, branching perennials, grown as annuals. H 6in (15cm), S 12in (30cm). Frost tender. Has oval, green leaves. Flared, tubular, red, yellow, or orange flowers are borne in summer (orange, illus. p.285).
M. moschatus (Musk). Spreading, mat-forming perennial. H and S 6–12in (15–30cm). Fully hardy, zones 6–9. Produces snapdragonlike, pale yellow flowers, lightly speckled with brown, in summer-autumn. Leaves are oval, hairy, and pale green.
M. 'Royal Velvet' illus. p.240.
M. 'Whitecroft Scarlet'. Short-lived, spreading perennial. H 8–12in (20–30cm), S 12in (30cm). Half hardy, zone 9. Snapdragonlike, scarlet flowers are produced freely from early to late summer. Leaves are oval, toothed, and green.

MINA (Convolvulaceae)
Genus of semi-evergreen or deciduous, twining climbers, grown for their usually short-lived but freely produced flowers. Half hardy to frost tender, min. 50°F (10°C). Grow in sun and in rich, well-drained soil that should not dry out. Propagate by seed in spring.
M. lobata, syn. *Ipomoea versicolor, Quamoclit lobata*, illus. p.168.

MIRABILIS (Nyctaginaceae)
Four o'clock flower, Marvel-of-Peru
Genus of summer-flowering annuals and tuberous perennials. Half hardy. Is best grown in a sheltered position in

fertile, well-drained soil and in full sun. Tubers are best lifted and stored over winter in frost-free conditions. Propagate by seed or division of tubers in early spring.
M. jalapa illus. p.205.

MISCANTHUS (Gramineae). See GRASSES, BAMBOOS, RUSHES, and SEDGES.
M. sacchariflorus (Amur silver grass). Vigorous, herbaceous, rhizomatous, perennial grass that spreads slowly. H 10ft (3m), S indefinite. Frost hardy, zones 5–10. Hairless, green leaves last well into winter, often turning bronze. Rarely, bears open, branched panicles of hairy, purplish brown spikelets in summer. **'Robustus'** is more likely to flower.
M. sinensis **'Gracillimus'** illus. p.183. **'Zebrinus'** illus. p.180.

MITCHELLA (Rubiaceae)
Genus of evergreen, trailing sub-shrubs, grown for their foliage and fruits. Makes excellent ground cover, especially in woodlands, although is sometimes difficult to establish. Fully hardy. Prefers shade and humus-rich, neutral to acid soil. Propagate by division of rooted runners in spring or by seed in autumn.
M. repens (Partridge berry). Evergreen, trailing, mat-forming sub-shrub. H 2in (5cm), S indefinite. Zones 4–9. Bears small, oval, white-striped, green leaves with heart-shaped bases. In early summer has pairs of tiny, fragrant, tubular, white flowers, sometimes purple-tinged, followed by spherical, bright red fruits. Suits a rock garden or peat bed.

MITELLA (Saxifragaceae)
Genus of clump-forming, summer-flowering, slender-stemmed, rhizomatous perennials. Fully hardy. Requires shade and humus-rich, moist soil. Propagate by division in spring or by seed in autumn.
M. breweri illus. p.324.

MITRARIA (Gesneriaceae)
Genus of one species of evergreen, woody-stemmed, scrambling climber. Half hardy. Grow in semi-shade and in peaty, acid soil. Propagate by seed in spring or by stem cuttings in summer.
M. coccinea illus. p.164.

MOLINIA (Gramineae). See GRASSES, BAMBOOS, RUSHES, and SEDGES.
M. caerulea subsp. *arundinacea*. Tuft-forming, herbaceous, perennial grass. H 8ft (2.5m), S 2ft (60cm). Fully hardy, zones 5–9. Has broad, flat, gray-green leaves. Bears spreading panicles of purple spikelets on stiff, erect stems in summer. Needs a dry, sunny position and acid soil. subsp. *caerulea* **'Variegata'** (Variegated purple moor grass), H 2ft (60cm), has yellow-striped, green leaves and, in late summer, panicles of purplish spikelets.

MOLTKIA (Boraginaceae)
Genus of deciduous, semi-evergreen, or evergreen sub-shrubs and perennials, grown for their funnel-shaped flowers in summer. Fully to frost hardy. Prefers sun and well-drained, neutral to acid soil. Propagate by semi-ripe cuttings in summer or by seed in autumn.
M. x *intermedia*. Evergreen, open, dome-shaped sub-shrub. H 12in (30cm), S 20in (50cm). Fully hardy, zones 7–9. Stems are clothed in narrowly linear, dark green leaves. Masses of loose spikes of small, open funnel-shaped, bright blue flowers appear in summer.
M. petraea. Semi-evergreen, bushy shrub. H 12in (30cm), S 24in (60cm). Fully hardy, zones 7–9. Hairy leaves are long and narrow. Clusters of pinkish purple buds open into funnel-shaped, violet-blue flowers in summer.
M. suffruticosa illus. p.297.

MOLUCCELLA (Labiatae)
Genus of annuals and perennials, grown for their flowers that may be dried successfully. Fully to half hardy. Grow in sun and in rich, very well-drained soil. Propagate by seed sown under glass in spring, or outdoors in late spring.
M. laevis illus. p.279.

MONARDA (Labiatae)
Bergamot
Genus of annuals and perennials, grown for their aromatic foliage as well as their flowers. Fully hardy. Requires sun and moist soil. Propagate species and cultivars by division in spring, species only by seed in spring.
M. **'Adam'**. Clump-forming perennial. H 30in (75cm), S 18in (45cm). Zones 4–8. Bears dense whorls of 2-lipped, cerise flowers throughout summer. Oval, usually toothed, green leaves are aromatic and hairy.
M. didyma (Bee balm, Bergamot). **'Cambridge Scarlet'** illus. p.209. **'Croftway Pink'** illus. p.203.
M. fistulosa illus. p.210.
M. **'Prairie Night'**. Clump-forming perennial. H 4ft (1.2m), S 1¹⁄₂ft (45cm). Zones 4–8. Produces dense whorls of 2-lipped, rich violet-purple flowers from mid- to late summer. Oval, toothed leaves are green.

MONSTERA (Araceae)
Genus of evergreen, woody-stemmed, root climbers, grown for their large, handsome leaves. Bears insignificant, creamy white flowers with hooded spathes intermittently. Frost tender, min. 59–64°F (15–18°C). Provide humus-rich, well-drained soil and light shade in summer. Water moderately, less in low temperatures. Provide support. If necessary, shorten long stems in spring. Propagate by leaf-bud or stem-tip cuttings in summer.
M. acuminata (Shingle plant). Evergreen, woody-stemmed, root climber with robust stems. H 10ft (3m) or more. Zone 10. Has lopsided-oval, pointed, rich green leaves with a heart-shaped base, sometimes cleft into a few large lobes, to 10in (25cm) long.
M. deliciosa illus. p.178.

MORAEA (Iridaceae)
Genus of corms with short-lived, irislike flowers. Divides into 2 groups: winter- and summer-growing species. Winter-growing species are half hardy, need full sun and well-drained soil; keep dry in summer during dormancy and start into growth by watering in autumn. Summer-growing species are frost hardy and dormant in winter; grow in a sheltered, sunny site and well-drained soil. Propagate by seed in autumn (winter growers) or spring (summer growers).
M. huttonii illus. p.339.
M. polystachya. Winter-growing corm. H to 12in (30cm), S 2–3in (5–8cm). Zones 9–10. Bears long, narrow, semi-erect, basal leaves. Stem produces a succession of erect, flattish, blue or lilac flowers, 3in (8cm) wide, in winter-spring. Outer petals each have a central, yellow mark.
M. spathacea. See *M. spathulata*.
M. spathulata, syn. *M. spathacea*. Summer-growing corm. H to 3ft (1m), S 4–6in (10–15cm). Zones 8–10. Has one long, narrow, semi-erect, basal leaf. Tough flower stem carries a succession of up to 5 upward-facing, yellow flowers, 2–3in (5–7cm) wide, with reflexed, outer petals, in summer.

MORINA (Morinaceae)
Whorlflower
Genus of evergreen perennials, only one species of which is in general cultivation: this is grown for its thistlelike foliage and its flowers. Frost hardy, but needs protection from drying spring winds. Requires full sun and well-drained, preferably sandy soil. Propagate by division directly after flowering or, preferably, by seed when fresh, in late summer.
M. longifolia illus. p.202.

MORISIA (Cruciferae)
Genus of one species of rosetted perennial with a long tap root. Is good for screes, rock gardens, and alpine houses. Fully hardy. Needs sun and gritty, well-drained soil. Propagate by seed in autumn or by root cuttings in winter.
M. hypogaea. See *M. monanthos*.
M. monanthos, syn. *M. hypogaea*, illus. p.312.

MORUS (Moraceae)
Mulberry
Genus of deciduous trees, grown for their foliage and edible fruits. Inconspicuous flowers appear in spring. Fully hardy. Requires full sun and fertile, well-drained soil. Propagate by softwood cuttings in summer or by seed in autumn.
M. alba (White mulberry). **'Laciniata'** illus. p.65. **'Pendula'** is a deciduous, weeping tree. H 10ft (3m), S 15ft (5m). Zones 5–9. Rounded, sometimes lobed, glossy, deep green leaves turn yellow in autumn. Edible, oval, fleshy, pink, red, or purple fruits ripen in summer.
M. nigra (Black mulberry). Deciduous, round-headed tree. H 40ft (12m), S 50ft (15m). Zones 7–9. Has heart-shaped, dark green leaves that turn yellow in autumn. Edible, oval, succulent, dark purplish red fruits are produced in late summer or early autumn.

MUCUNA (Leguminosae)
Genus of vigorous, evergreen, twining climbers, grown for their large, pealike flowers. Frost tender, min. 64°F (18°C). Humus-rich, moist but well-drained soil is essential, with partial shade in summer. Water freely when in full growth, less at other times. Needs plenty of space to climb; provide support. Thin out crowded stems in spring. Propagate by seed in spring or by layering in late summer. Whitefly and red spider mite may cause problems.
M. bennettii. Strong- and fast-growing, evergreen, twining climber. H 50–80ft (15–25m). Zone 10. Leaves are divided into 3 oval leaflets. Pealike, orange-scarlet flowers appear in large, pendent clusters in summer.
M. deeringiana. Vigorous, fast-growing, evergreen, twining climber. H 50ft (15m) or more. Zone 10. Has pealike, both green- and red-purple flowers in long, pendent clusters in summer-autumn. Leaves, of 3 oval leaflets, are used for fodder and green manure. May be short-lived.

MUEHLENBECKIA (Polygonaceae)
Genus of deciduous or evergreen, slender-stemmed, summer-flowering shrubs and woody-stemmed, scrambling climbers, grown for their foliage. Frost hardy. Grow in sun or shade and in well-drained soil. Propagate by semi-ripe cuttings in summer.
M. complexa. Deciduous, mound-forming shrub or twining climber. H 2–3ft (60cm–1m), S 3ft (1m). Zones 7–10. Slender, wiry stems bear variably shaped (oval to fiddle-shaped), dark green leaves. Tiny, star-shaped, greenish white flowers in mid-summer are followed by small, spherical, waxy, white fruits.

MULGEDIUM. See CICERBITA.

MURRAYA (Rutaceae)
Genus of evergreen trees and shrubs, grown for their overall appearance. Frost tender, min. 55–9°F (13–15°C). Needs full light or partial shade and humus-rich, well-drained soil. Water potted plants freely when in full growth, moderately at other times. Pruning is tolerated in late winter if necessary. Propagate by seed in spring or by semi-ripe cuttings in summer. Whitefly may be troublesome.
M. exotica. See *M. paniculata*.
M. paniculata, syn. *M. exotica* (Orange jasmine). Evergreen, rounded shrub or tree. H and S 6–12ft (2–4m). Zone 10. Pungently aromatic, edible (used for flavoring curries), glossy, rich green leaves each have 9 or more oval leaflets. Fragrant, 5-petaled, white flowers are carried in terminal clusters year-round. Tiny, egg-shaped fruits are red.

MUSA (Musaceae)
Banana
Genus of evergreen, palmlike, suckering perennials, with false stems formed from overlapping leaf sheaths, grown for their foliage, flowers, and fruits (bananas), not all of which are

edible. Frost hardy to frost tender, min. 64°F (18°C). Grow in sun or partial shade and in humus-rich, well-drained soil. Propagate by division year-round, by offsets in summer, or by suckers after flowering.

M. arnoldiana. See *Ensete ventricosum.*

M. basjoo, syn. *M. japonica,* illus. p.195.

M. coccinea (Scarlet banana). Evergreen, palmlike perennial. H to 3ft (1m), S 5ft (1.5m). Frost tender, zone 10. Oblong to oval, dark green leaves, to 3ft (1m) long, are paler below. In summer produces erect spirals of tubular, yellow flowers, enclosed in red bracts; bananalike, orange-yellow fruits are 2in (5cm) long.

M. ensete. See *Ensete ventricosum.*

M. japonica. See *M. basjoo.*

M. ornata illus. p.194.

MUSCARI (Liliaceae)
Grape hyacinth
Genus of spring-flowering bulbs, each with a cluster of narrowly strap-shaped, basal leaves, usually appearing in spring just before flowers. Leafless flower stems bear dense spikes of small flowers, most of which have constricted mouths. Fully to half hardy. Needs a sunny position and fairly well-drained soil. Plant in autumn. Propagate by division in late summer or by seed in autumn.

M. armeniacum illus. p.362. **'Blue Spike'** is a spring-flowering bulb. H 6–8in (15–20cm), S 3–4in (8–10cm). Frost hardy, zones 2–9. Has 3–6 long, narrow, semi-erect, basal leaves. Bears dense spikes of fragrant, bell-shaped, deep blue flowers; constricted mouths have rims of paler blue or white "teeth."

M. aucheri, syn. *M. tubergenianum,* illus. p.361.

M. azureum, syn. *Hyacinthus azureus.* Spring-flowering bulb. H 4–6in (10–15cm), S 2–3in (5–8cm). Frost hardy, zones 2–9. Has 2 or 3 narrow, semi-erect, basal, grayish green leaves, slightly wider towards tips. Bears a very dense spike of bell-shaped, pale clear blue flowers; mouths have small 'teeth' with central, dark blue stripes.

M. botryoides. Spring-flowering bulb. H 6–8in (15–20cm), S 2–3in (5–8cm). Frost hardy, zones 3–9. Bears 2–4 narrow, semi-erect, basal leaves that widen slightly towards tips, and minute, nearly spherical, bright blue flowers, each with a constricted mouth and white-toothed rim.

M. comosum (Tassel grape hyacinth). Late spring-flowering bulb. H 8–12in (20–30cm), S 4–5in (10–12cm). Frost hardy, zones 2–9. Has up to 5 strap-shaped, semi-erect, basal, gray-green leaves and a loose spike of bell-shaped, fertile, brownish yellow flowers with a tuft of threadlike, sterile, purplish blue flowers at the tip. **'Plumosum'** (syn. *M.c.* 'Monstrosum') illus. p.360.

M. latifolium illus. p.346.

M. macrocarpum illus. p.363.

M. neglectum, syn. *M. racemosum,* illus. p.362.

M. paradoxum. See *Bellevalia pycnantha.*

M. pycnantha. See *Bellevalia pycnantha.*

M. racemosum. See *M. neglectum.*

M. tubergenianum. See *M. aucheri.*

MUSSAENDA (Rubiaceae)
Genus of evergreen shrubs and scrambling climbers, grown for their flowers. Frost tender, min. 61–4°F (16–18°C). Needs fertile, well-drained soil and full light. Water freely when in full growth, less at other times. Provide support and thin out crowded stems in spring. Propagate by seed in spring or by air-layering in summer. Whitefly and red spider mite may cause problems.

M. erythrophylla. Moderately vigorous, evergreen, scrambling climber. H 20–30ft (6–10m). Zone 10. Has broadly oval, bright green leaves and flowers in summer-autumn. Each flower has one greatly enlarged, oval, bractlike, red sepal, a red tube, and yellow petal lobes.

MUTISIA (Compositae)
Genus of evergreen, tendril climbers, grown for their long-lasting flower heads. Frost to half hardy. Grow in well-drained soil; is best planted with roots in shade and leafy parts in sun. Propagate by seed in spring, by stem cuttings in summer, or by layering in autumn.

M. decurrens illus. p.175.

M. oligodon. Evergreen, tendril climber. H to 5ft (1.5m). Frost hardy, zones 9–10. Oblong leaves with toothed margins are 1–1½in (2.5–3.5cm) long. In summer-autumn has long-stalked, daisylike, pink flower heads. Is effective when grown against a low wall or through a shrub.

MYOPORUM (Myoporaceae)
Genus of evergreen shrubs and trees, grown for their overall appearance and as hedges and windbreaks. Frost tender, min. 36–41°F (2–5°C). Prefers full light and well-drained soil; will tolerate poor soil. Water potted specimens moderately. Propagate by seed when ripe or in spring or by semi-ripe cuttings in late summer.

M. laetum. Evergreen, rounded to upright shrub or tree. H 10–30ft (3–10m), S 6–15ft (2–5m). Zone 10. Bears lance-shaped to oval, lustrous, bright green leaves. Axillary clusters of small, bell-shaped, white flowers, with purple dots, are produced in spring-summer. Tiny, oblong fruits are red-purple.

M. parvifolium illus. p.130.

MYOSOTIDIUM (Boraginaceae)
Chatham Island forget-me-not
Genus of one species of evergreen perennial that is suitable for mild, coastal areas. Half hardy. Prefers semi-shade and moist soil. Seaweed is often recommended as a mulch. Is not easy to cultivate, and once established should not be disturbed. Propagate by division in spring or by seed when ripe, in summer or autumn.

M. hortensia illus. p.243.

MYOSOTIS (Boraginaceae)
Forget-me-not
Genus of annuals, biennials, and perennials, grown for their flowers.

Most species are good for rock gardens, banks, and screes; *M. scorpioides* is best grown as a marginal water plant. Fully hardy. Most prefer sun or semi-shade and fertile, well-drained soil. Propagate by seed in autumn.

M. alpestris illus. p.310.

M. australis. Short-lived, tuft-forming perennial. H 5in (12cm), S 3in (8cm). Zones 5–7. Has oval, rough-textured leaves and, in summer, tight sprays of open funnel-shaped, yellow or white flowers. Is good for a scree.

M. 'Blue Ball' illus. p.278.

M. caespitosa. See *M. laxa* subsp. *caespitosa.*

M. 'Carmine King'. Slow-growing, short-lived, bushy perennial, grown as a biennial. H to 8in (20cm), S 6in (15cm). Zones 5–8. Has lance-shaped leaves and, in spring and early summer, produces sprays of tiny, 5-lobed, dark pink-red flowers.

M. laxa subsp. **caespitosa,** syn. *M. caespitosa.* Clump-forming annual or short-lived perennial, grown as an annual. H 5in (12cm), S 6in (15cm). Fully hardy. Has lance-shaped, leathery, dark green leaves and, in summer, sprays of rounded, bright blue flowers.

M. palustris. See *M. scorpioides.*

M. scorpioides, syn. *M. palustris* (Water forget-me-not). **'Mermaid'** illus. p.374.

M. 'White Ball'. Slow-growing, short-lived, bushy, compact perennial, grown as a biennial. H to 8in (20cm), S 6in (15cm). Zones 5–8. Leaves are lance-shaped. Sprays of tiny, 5-lobed, pure white flowers are produced in early summer.

Myrceugenia apiculata. See *Myrtus luma.*

MYRIOPHYLLUM
(Haloragidaceae)
Genus of deciduous, perennial, submerged water plants, grown for their foliage. Most species are ideal as depositories for fish spawn. Fully hardy to frost tender, min. 41°F (5°C). Requires full sun. Spreads widely: keep in check by removing excess growth as required. Propagate by stem cuttings in spring or summer.

M. aquaticum, syn. *M. proserpinacoides,* illus. p.374.

M. hippuroides. Deciduous, perennial, spreading, submerged water plant. S indefinite. Half hardy, zones 8–10. Has a dense mass of small, feathery, pale green leaves. Insignificant, greenish cream flowers are borne in summer. Is suitable for a cold-water aquarium.

M. proserpinacoides. See *M. aquaticum.*

M. verticillatum illus. p.375.

MYRRHIS (Umbelliferae)
Sweet Cicely
Genus of one species of summer-flowering perennial. Fully hardy. Grow in sun or shade and in well-drained soil. Propagate by seed in autumn or spring.

M. odorata illus. p.201.

MYRSINE (Myrsinaceae)
Genus of evergreen shrubs and trees, with inconspicuous flowers, grown

mainly for their foliage. Also bears decorative fruits, to obtain which plants of both sexes must be grown. Is suitable for growing in rock and peat gardens. Frost hardy, but in cold areas requires shelter. Grow in sun or shade and in any fertile, well-drained soil other than a shallow, chalky one. Propagate by semi-ripe cuttings in summer.

M. africana (Cape myrtle). Very slow-growing, evergreen, bushy, dense shrub. H and S 30in (75cm). Zones 9–10. Small, glossy, dark green leaves are aromatic and rounded. Tiny, yellowish brown flowers in late spring are succeeded by spherical, pale blue fruits.

MYRTILLOCACTUS (Cactaceae)
Genus of branching, perennial cacti with ribbed, spiny, blue-green stems. Bears star-shaped flowers that open at night. Frost tender, min. 52–4°F (11–12°C). Needs a sunny, well-drained site. Propagate by seed or stem cuttings in spring or summer.

M. geometrizans illus. p.378.

MYRTUS (Myrtaceae)
Myrtle
Genus of evergreen shrubs, sometimes treelike, grown for their flowers, fruits, and aromatic foliage. Frost to half hardy; in cold areas plant against a south- or west-facing wall. Needs full sun and fertile, well-drained soil. To restrict growth, trim back in spring. Propagate by semi-ripe cuttings in late summer.

M. apiculata. See *M. luma.*

M. bullata, syn. *Lophomyrtus bullata.* Evergreen, upright shrub. H 15ft (5m), S 10ft (3m). Half hardy, zones 9–10. Rounded, puckered leaves are purple when young, maturing to reddish brown. Produces saucer-shaped, white flowers in late spring and early summer, then egg-shaped, dark red fruits.

M. communis illus. p.97. var. **tarentina** is an evergreen, bushy shrub. H and S 6ft (2m). Frost hardy, zones 9–10. Small leaves are narrowly oval, glossy, and dark green. Fragrant, saucer-shaped, white flowers, each with a dense cluster of stamens, are borne from mid-spring to early summer, followed by spherical, white fruits. Is very wind-resistant and good for hedging in mild areas.

M. luma, syn. *M. apiculata, Myrceugenia apiculata,* illus. p.87. **'Glanleam Gold'** is a strong-growing, evergreen, upright shrub. H and S 30ft (10m). Half hardy, zones 9–10. Has stout stems, peeling, brown-and-white bark and oval, bright green leaves edged with creamy yellow. Slightly fragrant, saucer-shaped, white flowers from mid-summer to mid-autumn are followed by spherical, red fruits, ripening to purple.

M. ugni, syn. *Eugenia ugni.* Evergreen, upright, densely branched shrub. H 5ft (1.5m), S 3ft (1m). Half hardy, zones 9–10. Glossy, dark green leaves are oval. Has fragrant, slightly nodding, cup-shaped, flesh pink flowers in late spring, then aromatic, edible, spherical, dark red fruits. Is good for hedging in mild areas.

N

NANDINA (Berberidaceae)
Genus of one species of evergreen or semi-evergreen, summer-flowering shrub, grown for its foliage and flowers. Frost hardy. Prefers a sheltered, sunny site and fertile, well-drained but not too dry soil. On established plants prune untidy, old stems to base in spring. Propagate by semi-ripe cuttings in summer.
N. domestica (Heavenly bamboo, Sacred bamboo). Evergreen or semi-evergreen, upright, elegant shrub. H and S 6ft (2m). Zones 7–10. Leaves have narrowly lance-shaped, dark green leaflets, purplish red when young and in autumn-winter. Large panicles of small, star-shaped, white flowers in mid-summer are followed in warm climates by spherical, red fruits. **'Firepower'** illus. p.119.

NARCISSUS (Amaryllidaceae)
Daffodil
Genus of bulbs, grown for their ornamental flowers. Daffodils have usually linear leaves and a spread of up to 8in (20cm). Each flower has a trumpet or cup (the corona) and petals (botanically known as perianth segments). All those listed are fully hardy, zones 3–9, except where otherwise stated. Prefers sun or light shade and well-drained soil, but Div.8 cultivars (see below) prefer a sunny site and tolerate lighter soils. Dead-head flowers and remove foliage in mid- or late summer. Most cultivars increase naturally by offsets; dense clumps should be divided no sooner than 6 weeks after flowering every 3–5 years. Species may be propagated by fresh seed in late summer or autumn. Narcissus yellow stripe virus, basal rot, slugs, large narcissus fly, and bulb and stem eelworm may cause problems.

Horticulturally, *Narcissus* is split into the following divisions:

Div.1 Trumpet—usually solitary flowers each have a trumpet that is as long as, or longer than, the petals. Early to late spring-flowering.
Div.2 Large-cupped—solitary flowers each have a cup at least one-third the length of, but shorter than, the petals. Spring-flowering.
Div.3 Small-cupped—flowers are often borne singly; each has a cup not more than one-third the length of the petals. Spring- or early summer-flowering.
Div.4 Double—most have solitary large, fully or semi-double flowers, rarely scented, with both cup and petals or cup alone replaced by petaloid structures. Some have smaller flowers, produced in clusters of 4 or more, which are often sweetly fragrant. Spring- or early summer-flowering.
Div.5 Triandrus—nodding flowers, with short, sometimes straight-sided cups and narrow, reflexed petals, are borne 2–6 per stem. Spring-flowering.

Div.6 Cyclamineus—flowers are borne usually 1 or 2 per stem, each with a cup sometimes flanged and often longer than those of Div.5. Petals are narrow, pointed, and reflexed. Early to mid-spring-flowering.
Div.7 Jonquil—sweetly scented flowers are borne usually 2 or more per stem. Cup is short, sometimes flanged; petals are often flat, fairly broad, and rounded. Spring-flowering.
Div.8 Tazetta—sweetly fragrant flowers of small-flowered cultivars are borne in clusters of 12 or more per stem; large-flowered cultivars have 3 or 4 flowers per stem. All have a small, often straight-sided cup and broad, mostly pointed petals. Late autumn- to mid-spring-flowering. Most are frost to half hardy. Autumn-flowering hybrids provide valuable cut flowers; "prepared" bulbs may be grown in pots for mid-winter flowering.
Div.9 Poeticus—flowers, sometimes borne 2 per stem, may be sweetly fragrant. Each has a small, colored cup and glistening white petals. Many Poeticus hybrids are categorized as Div.3 or 8. Late spring- or early summer-flowering.
Div.10 Wild species—usually solitary flowers vary from diminutive, hoop-petticoat daffodils, with funnel-shaped, flanged cups, to stately trumpet daffodils. Early autumn- to early summer-flowering.
Div.11 Split-cupped—usually solitary flowers each have a cup that is typically split for more than half of its length; the number of splits varies. Cup segment edges lie back on petals and may be ruffled. Spring-flowering.
Div.12 Miscellaneous—a miscellaneous category containing hybrids with varying, intermediate flower shapes. Hybrids of hoop-petticoat species are also placed here. Autumn- to spring-flowering.

N. **'Acropolis'**, Div.4. Mid- to late spring-flowering bulb. H 17in (42cm). Large, double flowers have white, outer petals and petaloids; white, inner petals are interspersed with shorter, orange-red petaloids. Is suitable for exhibition.
N. **'Actaea'** (illus. p.348), Div.9. Late spring-flowering bulb. H 16in (40cm). Produces fragrant flowers that have glistening white petals and shallow, flanged, rich lemon cups with narrow, orange-red rims.
N. albus var. *plenus-odoratus*. See *N. poeticus* 'Flore Pleno'.
N. **'Ambergate'** (illus. p.349), Div.2. Mid-spring-flowering bulb. H 18in (45cm). Flowers each have a shallow, widely expanded, fiery scarlet cup and soft tangerine petals.
N. **'Arctic Gold'**, Div.1. Mid-spring-flowering bulb. H 16in (40cm). Rich golden yellow flowers have broad petals and well-proportioned, flanged

trumpets with neatly serrated rims. Is suitable for exhibition.
N. assoanus, syn. *N. juncifolius*, *N. requienii*, Div.10. Mid-spring-flowering bulb. H 6in (15cm). Is similar to *N. jonquilla*, but has thin, cylindrical leaves and rounded, bright clear yellow flowers with a sweet, slightly lemony fragrance. Thrives in sunny, gritty soil.
N. asturiensis, syn. *N. minimus*, Div.10. Late winter- or early spring-flowering bulb. H 3in (8cm). Small, lemon flowers have waisted trumpets and slender petals. Prefers full sun.
N. **'Bartley'** (illus. p.349), Div.6. Early spring-flowering bulb. H 14in (35cm). Long, slender, golden flowers have reflexed petals and narrow, angled trumpets. Flowers are long-lasting.
N. **'Beige Beauty'**, Div.3. Late spring-flowering bulb. H 16in (40cm). Flowers are soft buff-yellow at maturity with neat, ruffled cups. Is rather late to flower.
N. **'Binkie'** (illus. p.349), Div.2. Early spring-flowering bulb. H 12in (30cm). Flowers open clear pale lemon but cups turn sulfur white with ruffled, lemon rims.
N. **'Birma'**, Div.3. Mid-spring-flowering bulb. H 18in (45cm). Flowers have soft yellow petals and fiery orange cups with heavily ruffled rims.
N. **'Bob Minor'** (illus. p.349), Div.1. Robust, early spring-flowering bulb. H 8in (20cm). Small, rich golden flowers have twisted petals and sturdy trumpets.
N. **'Bridal Crown'** (illus. p.348), Div.4. Late spring-flowering bulb. H 16in (40cm). Long-lasting, small, sweetly scented flowers are semi-double, with rounded, milk white petals and white petaloids interspersed with shorter, saffron orange ones towards center.
N. **'Brunswick'**, Div.2. Early spring-flowering bulb. H 16in (40cm). Long-lasting flowers have white petals and long, flared, primrose cups, which fade to lemon, with darker rims. Foliage is a striking bluish green. Is suitable for cutting.
N. bulbocodium subsp. *bulbocodium* (Hoop-petticoat daffodil; illus. p.349), Div.10. Vigorous, spring-flowering bulb. H 3–6in (8–15cm). Fully hardy, zones 7–9. Flowers are golden yellow with conical cups and narrow, pointed petals. Thrives in moist turf in full sun. var. *citrinus*, H 6in (15cm), has slender, dark green leaves and clear pale lemon flowers.
N. campernellii. See *N. x odorus.*
N. canaliculatus (illus. p.348), Div.8. Mid-spring-flowering bulb. H 9in (23cm). Frost hardy, zones 7–9. Produces a cluster of 4 or more fragrant flowers per stem, each with reflexed, white petals and a shallow, straight-sided, dark yellow cup.

N. cantabricus, Div.10. Spring- and sometimes late autumn-flowering bulb. H 4in (10cm). Fully hardy, zones 7–9. Is similar in form to *N. bulbocodium* subsp. *bulbocodium*, but is less robust. Flowers are milk or ice white. Thrives in an alpine house or greenhouse.
N. **'Cantatrice'**, Div.1. Mid-spring-flowering bulb. H 16in (40cm). Flowers have pure white petals and slender, milk white trumpets.
N. **'Capax Plenus'**. See *N.* 'Eystettensis'.
N. **'Cassata'** (illus. p.349), Div.11. Mid-spring-flowering bulb. H 16in (40cm). Cups are soft primrose and distinctly split into segments with ruffled margins, while petals are broad and milk white.
N. **'Charity May'** (illus. p.349), Div.6. Early to mid-spring-flowering bulb. H 12in (30cm). Small, pale lemon flowers each have broad, reflexed petals and slightly darker cups.
N. **'Cheerfulness'** (illus. p.348), Div.4. Late spring-flowering bulb. H 16in (40cm). Is similar to *N.* 'Bridal Crown', but has fully double flowers with milk white petals and petaloids interspersed with shorter, orange-yellow ones at the center. Is excellent for cutting.
N. cyclamineus (illus. p.349), Div.10. Late winter- to early spring-flowering bulb. H 6in (15cm). Slender, nodding, clear gold flowers have narrow, reflexed petals and long, slender, flanged, waisted trumpets.
N. **'Daydream'**, Div.2. Mid-spring-flowering bulb. H 14in (35cm). Long-lasting, rounded flowers have broad, rich sulfur yellow petals, each with a halo of near white, and flared, lemon yellow cups that turn sulfur white.
N. **'Dove Wings'** (illus. p.348), Div.6. Mid-spring-flowering bulb. H 12in (30cm). Has small flowers with milk white petals and fairly long, soft primrose cups.
N. **'Eystettensis'**, syn. *N.* 'Capax Plenus' (Queen Anne's double daffodil), Div.4. Mid-spring-flowering bulb. H 8in (20cm). Dainty, double flowers are composed of pointed, soft pale primrose petaloids neatly arranged in whorls.
N. **'February Gold'** (illus. p.349), Div.6. Early spring-flowering bulb. H 13in (32cm). Solitary long-lasting flowers have clear golden petals and long, flanged, slightly darker trumpets. Is useful for borders and naturalizing.
N. **'February Silver'** (illus. p.348), Div.6. Robust, early spring-flowering bulb. H 13in (32cm). Has long-lasting flowers with milk white petals and long, sturdy, nodding trumpets that open rich lemon and age to creamy yellow.
N. **'Fortune'** (illus. p.349), Div.2. Early to mid-spring-flowering bulb. H 16in (40cm). Flowers have ribbed, dark lemon petals and flared, copper orange cups; they are good for cutting.

N. 'Foxfire', Div.2. Mid-spring-flowering bulb. H 14in (35cm). Has very rounded flowers with conspicuously white petals. Small, greenish cream cups each have a small, green eye zone and a coral orange rim.

N. 'Golden Ducat' (illus. p.349), Div.4. Mid-spring-flowering bulb. H 15in (38cm). Produces variable, sometimes poorly formed, double, rich golden flowers. Is suitable for cutting.

N. 'Grand Primo Citronière', Div.8. Late autumn- to early spring-flowering bulb. H 13in (32cm). Half hardy, zones 8–9. Bears 8 or more fragrant flowers, each with milk white petals and a clear lemon cup, which fades to cream. "Treated" bulbs may be forced for mid-winter flowering. Is good for cutting.

N. 'Grand Soleil d'Or', Div.8. Late autumn- to early spring-flowering bulb. H 14in (35cm). Half hardy, zones 8–9. Flowers are sweetly scented with a dash of lemon. Each has rich golden petals and a clear tangerine cup. May be forced for mid-winter flowering, but staking is needed. Is good for cutting.

N. 'Hawera' (illus. p.349), Div.5. Mid-spring-flowering bulb. H 8in (20cm). Nodding flowers are a delicate lemon yellow. Requires a sunny position. Makes a good pot plant.

N. 'Home Fires' (illus. p.349), Div.2. Early spring-flowering bulb. H 18in (45cm). Flowers each have pointed, rich lemon petals and an orange-scarlet cup with a lobed and frilled rim.

N. 'Ice Follies' (illus. p.348), Div.3. Early spring-flowering bulb. H 16in (40cm). Rather coarse flowers have milk white petals and very wide, almost flat, primrose yellow cups, fading to cream.

N. 'Irene Copeland' (illus. p.348), Div.4. Mid-spring-flowering bulb. H 14in (35cm). Bears large, fully double flowers of neatly arranged, milk white petaloids interspersed with shorter, pale creamy yellow ones. Is excellent for cutting.

N. 'Jack Snipe' (illus. p.348), Div.6. Sturdy, early to mid-spring-flowering bulb. H 9in (23cm). Long-lasting, milk white flowers are similar to those of *N.* 'Dove Wings', but have narrower petals with incurved margins and medium-length cups of rich dark lemon yellow.

N. 'Jenny', Div.6. Early to mid-spring-flowering bulb. H 12in (30cm). Bears long-lasting flowers, each with milk white petals and a medium-length, flanged, soft lemon trumpet that turns creamy white.

N. jonquilla (illus. p.349), Div.10. Mid-spring-flowering bulb. H 12in (30cm). Richly fragrant flowers are borne in a cluster of 6 or more; each has tapering, yellow petals and a shallow, dark gold cup. Distinctive foliage is dark, shining, and grooved. 'Flore Pleno' (Queen Anne's jonquil) has loosely double flowers; broad, incurved, yellow petals are interspersed with short, darker ones.

N. 'Jumblie' (Jonquil; illus. p.349), Div.6. Early spring-flowering bulb. H 8in (20cm). Bears 2 or 3 long-lasting flowers, each with broad, golden petals and a sturdy, flanged, orange-yellow cup. Is ideal as a pot plant.

N. juncifolius. See *N. assoanus.*

N. 'Kilworth' (illus. p.348), Div.2. Vigorous, late spring-flowering bulb. H 15in (38cm). Flowers have pointed, milk white petals and dark reddish orange cups with green eyes. Is effective in large groups.

N. 'Kingscourt' (illus. p.349), Div.1. Sturdy, mid-spring-flowering bulb. H 17in (42cm). Flowers have flanged, flared, rich gold trumpets with broad, rounded, paler gold petals.

N. 'Lemon Glow' (illus. p.349), Div.1. Mid-spring-flowering bulb. H 18in (45cm). Has pale primrose yellow flowers with broad trumpets that have conspicuously recurved, lobed, clear lemon yellow rims.

N. 'Liberty Bells' (illus. p.349), Div.5. Sturdy, mid-spring-flowering bulb. H 13in (32cm). Flowers are slightly fragrant and clear lemon.

N. 'Little Beauty' (illus. p.348), Div.1. Early spring-flowering bulb. H 4in (10cm). Flowers have milk white petals and bright lemon trumpets. Is suitable for naturalizing.

N. 'Merlin' (illus. p.348), Div.3. Mid-spring-flowering bulb. H 14in (35cm). Flowers have broad, rounded, glistening white petals and relatively large, almost flat, rich gold cups, each with a small, green eye and a broad, lightly ruffled, orange-red rim. Is excellent for exhibition.

N. minimus. See *N. asturiensis.*

N. 'Minnow', Div.8. Robust, early to mid-spring-flowering bulb. H 7in (18cm). Frost hardy. Has a cluster of 4 or more fragrant flowers per stem, each with rounded, creamy yellow petals and a lemon cup. Increases freely. Is suitable for a container or rock garden.

N. minor, syn. *N. nanus* of gardens (illus. p.349), Div.10. Early spring-flowering bulb. H 8in (20cm). Flowers have slightly overlapping, soft yellow petals and almost straight, darker yellow trumpets with frilled rims.

N. minor of gardens. See *N. pumilus.*

N. 'Mount Hood', Div.1. Vigorous, mid-spring-flowering bulb. H 17in (42cm). Long-lasting flowers have milk white petals and bold, flanged, creamy yellow, then milk white trumpets with reflexed, serrated rims.

N. nanus, Div.10. Early spring-flowering bulb. H 5in (12cm). Flowers each have twisted, cream petals and a stout, straight, dull yellow trumpet with a frilled rim. Leaves are broad. Is suitable for naturalizing.

N. nanus of gardens. See *N. minor.*

N. obvallaris (Tenby daffodil), Div.10. Sturdy, early spring-flowering bulb. H 12in (30cm). Gold flowers have short petals and broad trumpets and are borne on stiff stems.

N. x *odorus*, syn. *N. campernellii* (Campernelle jonquil), Div.10. Robust, mid-spring-flowering bulb. H 8–12in (20–30cm). Fully hardy, zones 8–9. Has usually 2 richly fragrant, dark gold flowers. 'Rugulosus' (illus. p.349), H 11in (28cm), is more vigorous and produces up to 4 small-cupped, rich gold flowers.

N. 'Paper White Grandiflorus', syn. *N. papyraceus* 'Grandiflorus', *N.p.* 'Paper White Snowflake', Div.8.

Winter- to mid-spring-flowering bulb. H 14in (35cm). Half hardy, zones 9–10. Produces 10 or more long-lived, heavily fragrant, star-shaped, glistening white flowers, each with long, spreading petals and a small, flanged cup containing conspicuous, saffron yellow stamens. Flowers continuously through winter indoors.

N. papyraceus 'Grandiflorus'. See *N.* 'Paper White Grandiflorus'. 'Paper White Snowflake'. See *N.* 'Paper White Grandiflorus'.

N. 'Passionale' (illus. p.348), Div.2. Mid-spring-flowering bulb. H 16in (40cm). Each flower has milk white petals and a long, flanged, apricot-tinged, pink cup.

N. 'Pencrebar' (illus. p.349), Div.4. Mid-spring-flowering bulb. H 7in (18cm). Fragrant flowers are small, rounded, and fully double, often in pairs. Outer petaloids and large, inner ones are pale gold and are evenly interspersed with darker ones.

N. poeticus (Poet's daffodil, Poet's narcissus), Div.10. Variable, late spring-flowering bulb. H 9–17in (22–42cm). Each fragrant flower comprises glistening white petals and a small, shallow, yellow or orange cup with a red rim. Is ideal for naturalizing in moist turf although slow to establish. 'Flore Pleno', syn. *N. albus* var. *plenus-odoratus*, H 16in (40cm), has loosely double, pure white flowers, with inconspicuous, greenish yellow or orange centers, in late spring or early summer. Is good for cutting. var. *recurvus* (Pheasant's eye), H 17in (42cm), bears larger, long-lasting flowers with strongly swept-back petals and very shallow, greenish yellow cups, with crimson rims, in early summer.

N. 'Portrush' (illus. p.348), Div.3. Late spring- to early summer-flowering bulb. H 14in (35cm). Produces small flowers, each with green-tinged, glistening milk white petals and a small, shallow, flanged, creamy white cup with a bright green eye.

N. 'Pride of Cornwall' (illus. p.348), Div.8. Mid-spring-flowering bulb. H 15in (38cm). Bears large, fragrant flowers, each with milk white petals and a rich yellow cup shading to an orange-red rim outside. Is excellent for cutting.

N. pseudonarcissus (Lent lily, Wild daffodil), Div.10. Extremely variable, early spring-flowering bulb. H 6–12in (15–30cm). Nodding flowers have overlapping, straw yellow petals and large, darker yellow trumpets. Is ideal for naturalizing.

N. pumilus, syn. *N. minor* of gardens, Div.10. Early spring-flowering bulb. H 6–9in (15–22cm). Bears bright gold flowers with separated, slightly paler petals and large trumpets with lobed and frilled rims. 'Plenus' see *N.* 'Rip van Winkle'.

N. requienii. See *N. assoanus.*

N. 'Rip van Winkle', syn. *N. pumilus* 'Plenus' (illus. p.349), Div.4. Early spring-flowering bulb. H 6in (15cm). Shaggy, double flowers have densely arranged, flat, tapering, greenish lemon petals with incurving tips.

N. romieuxii (illus. p.349), Div.10. Early spring-flowering bulb. H 4in (10cm). Frost hardy, zones 7–9, but is best grown in a frame or an alpine house. Is similar to *N. bulbocodium* subsp. *bulbocodium*, but each fragrant flower has a large, almost flat, flanged cup of glistening pale primrose.

N. rupicola (illus. p.349), Div.10. Mid-spring-flowering bulb. H 3in (8cm). Is similar to *N. assoanus*, but has more angled, bluish green foliage and solitary less scented, lemon flowers, each with a 6-lobed cup.

N. 'St. Keverne' (illus. p.349), Div.2. Sturdy, early to mid-spring-flowering bulb. H 17in (42cm). Solitary flowers have clear rich golden petals and slightly darker cups of almost trumpet proportions.

N. 'Salome', Div.2. Sturdy, late spring-flowering bulb. H 16in (40cm). Produces long-lasting flowers with broad, rounded, milk white petals and long, flared, warm apricot pink cups that have lightly ruffled, gold-tinged rims.

N. 'Satin Pink' (illus. p.348), Div.2. Mid-spring-flowering bulb. H 17in (42cm). Each flower has broad, ribbed, milk white petals and a long, barely flared, flanged, soft buff-pink cup of almost trumpet proportions.

N. 'Sealing Wax' (illus. p.349), Div.2. Mid- to late spring-flowering bulb. H 18in (45cm). Petals are golden yellow and cups are bold, fiery red; flowers are borne singly.

N. 'Silver Chimes', Div.8. Sturdy, mid- to late spring-flowering bulb. H 13in (32cm). Has up to 10 fragrant flowers, each with broad, milk white petals and a straight, shallow, creamy primrose cup. Foliage is dark green. Thrives in a warm site.

N. 'Spellbinder' (illus. p.349), Div.1. Early spring-flowering bulb. H 17in (42cm). Long-lasting, bright sulfur yellow flowers each have a slender, flanged trumpet, reversing to palest sulfur white inside, except for the lobed, rolled-back rim, which is tinged with lemon.

N. 'Stratosphere', Div.7. Mid-spring-flowering bulb. H 16in (40cm). Bears usually 3 fragrant flowers, each with rich golden petals and a darker gold cup. Is excellent for exhibition.

N. 'Suzy' (illus. p.349), Div.7. Robust, mid-spring-flowering bulb. H 15in (38cm). Produces 3–4 long-lasting, large, fragrant flowers, each with clear golden petals and a large, flanged, rich tangerine cup.

N. 'Sweetness' (illus. p.349), Div.7. Early spring-flowering bulb. H 15in (38cm). Each solitary fragrant yellow flower has a slender, straight, flanged cup.

N. 'Tahiti' (illus. p.349), Div.4. Robust, mid-spring-flowering bulb. H 15in (38cm). Solitary loosely double flowers have golden petals and petaloids, interspersed with short, fiery orange, inner petaloids.

N. tazetta (Bunch-flowered daffodil, Polyanthus daffodil), Div.10. Extremely variable, late autumn- to mid-spring-flowering bulb. H 12–16in (30–40cm). Fully hardy, zones 8–10. Bears usually 12 or more fragrant flowers, generally with slender, white or yellow petals and shallow, white or yellow cups.

N. 'Tête-à-Tête' (illus. p.349), Div.6. Early spring-flowering bulb. H 6–12in (15–30cm). Long-lasting flowers each have reflexed, rich golden petals and a square, flanged, warm yellowish orange cup. Is very susceptible to viruses.

N. 'Thalia' (illus. p.348), Div.5. Vigorous, mid-spring-flowering bulb. H 15in (38cm). Has 3 or more long-lived, milk white flowers per stem, each with irregularly formed, often propeller-shaped petals and a flanged, bold cup.

N. 'Tresamble', Div.5. Sturdy, early spring-flowering bulb. H 16in (40cm). Bears up to 6 flowers per stem, each with milk white petals and a flanged, paler-rimmed, creamy white cup.

N. 'Trevithian', Div.7. Vigorous, early to mid-spring-flowering bulb. H 18in (45cm). Produces 2 or 3 large, fragrant flowers, rounded and soft primrose, each with broad petals and a short cup.

N. triandrus (Angel's tears; illus. p.349), Div.10. Early spring-flowering bulb. H 5in (12cm). Bears nodding, milk white flowers, each with narrow, reflexed petals and a fairly long, straight-sided cup. Makes a good container plant.

N. 'Trousseau' (illus. p.348), Div.1. Early spring-flowering bulb. H 17in (42cm). Flowers each have milk white petals and a straight, flanged, soft lemon trumpet, with a flared, lobed rim turning rich creamy buff tinged with pale pink.

N. 'Tudor Minstrel', Div.2. Mid-spring-flowering bulb. H 17in (42cm). Petals are white and pointed. Chrome yellow cups are slender and flanged.

N. 'Waterperry', Div.1. Mid-spring-flowering bulb. H 10in (25cm). Produces flowers with dull creamy white petals and lightly flanged, spreading, primrose cups that turn rich buff-yellow, shading to pinkish apricot at the rims.

N. watieri (illus. p.348), Div.10. Mid-spring-flowering bulb. H 4in (10cm). Half hardy, zones 9–10. Produces relatively large, fragrant, crystalline-textured, white flowers with shallow, lobed cups. Foliage is grayish blue and angled.

N. 'W.P. Milner', Div.1. Early spring-flowering bulb. H 9in (23cm). Nodding flowers each have slender, twisted, light creamy yellow petals and a flared, pale lemon trumpet, which fades to palest sulfur.

N. 'Yellow Cheerfulness', Div.4. Mid-spring-flowering bulb. H 16in (40cm). Bears 4 or more fragrant, loosely double flowers, each with soft primrose yellow petals and petaloids, interspersed with shorter, yellowish orange petaloids at center.

NAUTILOCALYX (Gesneriaceae)
Genus of evergreen, erect, bushy perennials, grown for their flowers and foliage. Frost tender, min. 59°F (15°C). Requires high humidity, partial shade, and well-drained soil; avoid waterlogging, especially in winter.

Propagate by stem cuttings in summer or by seed, if available, in spring.
N. bullatus, syn. *N. tessellatus*. Evergreen, erect perennial. H and S 2ft (60cm). Zone 10. Narrowly oval, wrinkled leaves, to 9in (23cm) long, are dark green with a bronze sheen above, reddish green beneath. Clusters of small, tubular, white-haired, pale yellow flowers are produced in the leaf axils mainly in summer.
N. lynchii illus. p.261.
N. tessellatus. See *N. bullatus*.

Neanthe bella. See *Chamaedorea elegans*.

NECTAROSCORDUM (Liliaceae)
Genus of flowering bulbs, related to *Allium*, with long, linear, erect leaves. Exudes a very strong onion smell when bruised. Stems with erect, shuttlecocklike seed heads may be dried for winter decoration. Frost hardy. Needs partial shade. Grow in rough grass or borders in any soil that is neither too dry nor waterlogged. Propagate by freely produced offsets in late summer or by seed in autumn.
N. dioscoridis. See *N. siculum* subsp. *bulgaricum*.
N. siculum subsp. **bulgaricum**, syn. *N. dioscoridis*, illus. p.333.

NEILLIA (Rosaceae)
Genus of deciduous shrubs, grown for their graceful habit and profuse clusters of small flowers. Fully hardy. Requires sun or semi-shade and fertile, well-drained soil. Established plants benefit from having some older shoots cut to base after flowering. Propagate by softwood cuttings in summer or by suckers in autumn.
N. sinensis. Deciduous, arching shrub. H and S 6ft (2m). Zones 6–9. Has peeling bark and oval, sharply toothed, green leaves. Nodding racemes of small, tubular, pinkish white flowers are borne in late spring and early summer.
N. thibetica illus. p.108.

NELUMBO (Nelumbonaceae)
Genus of deciduous, perennial, marginal water plants, grown for their foliage and flowers. Half hardy to frost tender, min. 34–45°F (1–7°C). Needs an open, sunny position and 24in (60cm) depth of water. Remove fading foliage; flowers may be left to develop into decorative seed pods. Divide overgrown plants in spring. Propagate species by seed in spring, selected forms by division in spring.
N. lutea (American lotus). Vigorous, deciduous, perennial, marginal water plant. H and S 3ft (1m). Half hardy, zones 5–10. Rounded, blue-green leaves develop on stout, 1–2ft (30–60cm) long stems. Large, chalice-shaped, yellow flowers open in summer.
N. nucifera illus. p.373. **'Alba Striata'** is a vigorous, deciduous, perennial, marginal water plant. H 8ft (2.5m), S 4ft (1.2m). Frost tender, min. 34°F (1°C), zones 5–10. Sturdy stems carry very large, rounded, blue-green leaves. Large, fragrant, chalice-shaped, white flowers, 6in (15cm) across and

edged with crimson, are borne in summer. **'Alba Grandiflora'** bears pure white flowers and **'Rosa Plena'** produces double, soft pink flowers to 12in (30cm) across.

NEMATANTHUS (Gesneriaceae)
Genus of perennials and soft-stemmed, evergreen shrubs, grown for their flowers and foliage. Frost tender, min. 55–9°F (13–15°C). Requires partial shade and humus-rich, moist but well-drained soil. Water potted specimens moderately, allowing soil almost to dry out between applications. Tip prune young plants to stimulate branching. Propagate by softwood or greenwood cuttings in summer.
N. gregarius, syn. *N. radicans*, *Hypocyrta radicans*, illus. p.125.
N. radicans. See *N. gregarius*.
N. strigillosus, syn. *Hypocyrta strigillosa*. Evergreen, prostrate shrub. H 6–12in (15–30cm), S 2–3ft (60cm–1m). Zone 10. Elliptic, slightly cupped leaves are clothed in dense down. Small, tubular, orange or orange-red flowers appear in leaf axils mainly from spring to autumn.

NEMESIA (Scrophulariaceae)
Genus of annuals, perennials, and evergreen sub-shrubs, grown for summer bedding and as greenhouse plants. Half hardy to frost tender, min. 36–9°F (2–4°C). Prefers sun and fertile, well-drained soil. Cut back stems after flowering. Pinch out growing shoots of young plants to ensure a bushy habit. Propagate by seed sown under glass in early spring, or outdoors in late spring.
N. strumosa (Pouch nemesia). Fast-growing, bushy annual. H 8–18in (20–45cm), S 6in (15cm). Frost tender. Has lance-shaped, serrated, pale green leaves and, in summer, trumpet-shaped, yellow, white, or purple flowers, 1in (2.5cm) across, that are suitable for cutting. **Carnival Series** illus. p.272. **Triumph Series** illus. p.283.

NEMOPHILA (Hydrophyllaceae)
Genus of annuals, useful for rock gardens and for edging. Fully hardy to frost tender, min. 36–9°F (2–4°C). Grow in sun or semi-shade and in fertile, well-drained soil. Propagate by seed sown outdoors in spring or early autumn. Is prone to aphids.
N. insignis. See *N. menziesii*.
N. maculata illus. p.263.
N. menziesii, syn. *N. insignis*, illus. p.277.

NEOLITSEA (Lauraceae)
Genus of evergreen trees and shrubs, grown for their foliage. Frost to half hardy. In cold areas needs shelter from strong winds; does best against a south- or west-facing wall. Requires sun or semi-shade and fertile, well-drained soil. Propagate by semi-ripe cuttings in late summer.
N. sericea. Evergreen, broadly conical, dense tree or shrub. H and S 20ft (6m). Frost hardy, zones 9–10. Narrowly oval, pointed leaves are glossy, green above, white beneath and, when young, are densely covered with silky,

brown hairs. Small, star-shaped, yellow flowers are borne in autumn.

NEOLLOYDIA (Cactaceae)
Genus of spherical to columnar, perennial cacti with dense spines and short tubercles in spirals. Most species are exceptionally difficult to cultivate unless grafted. Frost tender, min. 50°F (10°C). Needs full sun and well-drained soil. Water sparingly from spring to autumn; keep dry in winter. Propagate by seed in spring or summer.
N. conoidea illus. p.395.
N. mcdowellii. See *Thelocactus mcdowellii*.

NEOMARICA (Iridaceae)
Genus of evergreen, summer-flowering, irislike, rhizomatous perennials with clusters of short-lived flowers. Frost tender, min. 50°F (10°C). Needs partial shade and fertile, moist, preferably humus-rich soil. Water freely in summer; reduce water in winter but do not dry out. Propagate by seed in spring or by division in spring or summer.
N. caerulea illus. p.337.

NEOPANAX. See PSEUDOPANAX.

NEOPORTERIA (Cactaceae)
Genus of spherical to columnar, perennial cacti. Egg-shaped, red, brown, or green seed pods are similar to those of *Wigginsia*. Frost tender, min. 46°F (8°C). Requires full sun and very well-drained soil. Propagate by seed in spring or summer.
N. chilensis. Spherical, then columnar, perennial cactus. H 12in (30cm), S 4in (10cm). Zone 10. Pale green stem has a dense covering of stout, golden spines of varying lengths. Crown bears flattish, pink-orange or white flowers, to 2in (5cm) across, in summer.
N. napina. Flattened spherical, perennial cactus. H 1¼in (3cm), S 2in (5cm). Zone 10. Has very short, black spines pressed flat against a chocolate brown stem. In summer, crown produces flattish, yellow flowers, 2in (5cm) across. var. *mitis* illus. p.391.
N. nidus. Spherical to columnar, perennial cactus. H 4in (10cm), S 3in (8cm). Zone 10. Long, soft, gray spines completely encircle a dark green-brown stem. Crown produces tubular, pink to cerise flowers that are 1¼–2in (3–5cm) long, with paler bases, and only open at tips, in spring or autumn.
N. subgibbosa. Spherical to columnar, perennial cactus. H 12in (30cm), S 4in (10cm). Zone 10. Light green to dark gray-green stem bears large, woolly areoles and stout, amber spines. In late summer, crown produces flattish, carmine pink flowers, 1½in (4cm) across.
N. villosa illus. p.390.

NEOREGELIA (Bromeliaceae)
Genus of evergreen, rosette-forming, epiphytic perennials, grown for their overall appearance. Frost tender, min. 50°F (10°C). Requires semi-shade and a rooting medium of equal parts humus-rich soil and either sphagnum moss or bark or plastic chips used for

orchid culture. Using soft water, water moderately during growing season, sparingly at other times, and keep rosette centers filled with water from spring to autumn. Propagate by offsets in spring or summer.

N. carolinae, syn. *Aregelia carolinae*, *Nidularium carolinae* (Blushing bromeliad). Evergreen, spreading, basal-rosetted, epiphytic perennial. H 8–12in (20–30cm), S 16–24in (40–60cm). Zone 10. Strap-shaped, finely spine-toothed, lustrous, bright green leaves are produced in dense rosettes. A compact cluster of tubular, blue-purple flowers, surrounded by red bracts, is borne at the heart of each mature rosette, usually in summer. f. *tricolor* (illus. p.222) has leaves, striped with ivory white, that flush pink with age.

N. concentrica (illus. p.222). Evergreen, spreading, basal-rosetted, epiphytic perennial. H 8–12in (20–30cm), S to 28in (70cm). Zone 10. Very broadly strap-shaped to oval, glossy, dark green leaves, with spiny, black teeth and usually with dark blotches, are produced in dense rosettes. In summer, a compact cluster of tubular, pale blue flowers, surrounded by pinkish lilac bracts, is produced at the heart of each mature rosette. 'Plutonis' has bracts flushed with red.

NEPENTHES (Nepenthaceae)
Pitcher plant
Genus of evergreen, insectivorous, mostly epiphytic perennials, with leaves adapted to form pendulous, lidded, colored pitchers that trap and digest insects. Is suitable for hanging baskets. Frost tender, min. 64°F (18°C). Requires a humid atmosphere, partial shade, and moist, fertile soil with added peat and moss. Propagate by seed in spring or by stem cuttings in spring or summer.

N. hookeriana illus. p.223.
N. rafflesiana. Evergreen, epiphytic, insectivorous perennial. H 10ft (3m), S 3–4ft (1–1.2m). Zone 10. Has lance-shaped, dark green leaves. Greenish yellow pitchers, to 10in (25cm) long, are mottled purple and brown and have spurred lids. Inconspicuous, green flowers are borne in racemes and produced intermittently.

NEPETA (Labiatae)
Genus of summer-flowering perennials, useful for edging, particularly where they can tumble over paving. Fully hardy. Prefers sun and but well-drained soil. Propagate by division in spring or by stem-tip or softwood cuttings in spring or summer, species only by seed in autumn.

N. 'Blue Beauty'. See *N. 'Souvenir d'André Chaudon'*.
N. x faassenii illus. p.242.
N. govaniana illus. p.213.
N. grandiflora. Neat, erect perennial. H 16–32in (40–80cm), S 18–24in (45–60cm). Zones 4–8. Has slightly hairy stems, oval, round-toothed, light green leaves, with heart-shaped bases, and, in summer, racemes of small, hooded, blue flowers.

N. nervosa. Clump-forming perennial. H 14in (35cm), S 12in (30cm). Zones 5–9. Forms a mound of narrowly oblong to lance-shaped, pointed, prominently veined, green leaves. Produces dense racemes of small, tubular, pale blue flowers from early to mid-summer.
N. 'Souvenir d'André Chaudon', syn. *N. 'Blue Beauty'*. Spreading, clump-forming perennial. H and S 18in (45cm). Zones 5–9. Tubular, blue flowers are borne throughout summer above oval to lance-shaped, toothed, gray leaves.

NEPHROLEPIS (Polypodiaceae)
Genus of evergreen or semi-evergreen ferns. Frost tender, min. 41°F (5°C). Needs a shady position. Prefers moist soil, but is extremely tolerant of both drought and waterlogging. Remove fading fronds and divide regularly. Propagate by division in summer or early autumn.

N. cordifolia (Ladder fern, Sword fern). Semi-evergreen fern. H 18in (45cm), S 12in (30cm). Zone 10. Has narrowly lance-shaped, arching, dark green fronds with rounded, finely serrated pinnae.
N. exaltata illus. p.186.

NEPHTHYTIS (Araceae)
Genus of evergreen, tufted perennials, with horizontal, creeping rhizomes, grown for their foliage. Frost tender, min. 64°F (18°C). Requires a humid atmosphere, moist, humus-rich soil, and partial shade. Propagate by division in spring or summer.

N. afzelii. Evergreen, creeping, rhizomatous perennial. H to 30in (75cm), S indefinite. Zone 10. Has tufts of arrow-shaped, lobed, dark green leaves, to 10in (25cm) long. Intermittently bears a hooded, greenish spathe, enclosing a green spadix, followed by spherical, orange fruits.
N. triphylla of gardens. See *Syngonium podophyllum*.

NERINE (Amaryllidaceae)
Genus of bulbs, some of which are semi-evergreen, grown for their spherical heads of wavy-petaled, pink to red, occasionally white, flowers. Most flower in autumn before leaves appear. Frost to half hardy. Needs full sun and light, sandy soil. Plant in early autumn. Dislikes being disturbed. Water until leaves die down, then dry off. Propagate by seed when fresh or divide offsets in autumn or when leaves have died down.

N. 'Bagdad'. Autumn-flowering bulb. H 24in (60cm), S 6–8in (15–20cm). Half hardy, zones 8–10. Leaves are strap-shaped, semi-erect, and basal. Has crimson flowers, paler towards centers; long, narrow petals have recurved tips and crisped margins.
N. 'Blanchefleur'. Autumn-flowering bulb. H 12–20in (30–50cm), S 6–8in (15–20cm). Half hardy, zones 8–10. Has strap-shaped, semi-erect, basal leaves and a tight head of 5–10 pure white flowers. Upper parts of petals are twisted.
N. bowdenii illus. p.354. f. *alba* illus. p.354.

N. 'Brian Doe' illus. p.354.
N. 'Corusca Major'. Autumn-flowering bulb. H 24in (60cm), S 5–6in (12–15cm). Half hardy, zones 8–10. Forms strap-shaped, semi-erect, basal leaves. Stout stem bears 10–15 scarlet-red flowers with narrow petals. Is useful for cutting.
N. filifolia. Autumn-flowering bulb. H to 10in (25cm), S 3–4in (8–10cm). Half hardy, zones 8–10. Has threadlike, semi-erect leaves in a basal tuft. Slender stem produces pale pink flowers with narrow petals.
N. flexuosa. Semi-evergreen, autumn-flowering bulb. H 16–20in (40–50cm), S 5–6in (12–15cm). Half hardy, zones 8–10. Bears strap-shaped, semi-erect, basal leaves and 10–15 pink flowers; each petal has a deeper pink mid-vein and a recurved, wavy upper half.
N. 'Fothergillii Major'. Late summer- to early autumn-flowering bulb. H 18–24in (45–60cm), S 5–6in (12–15cm). Half hardy, zones 8–10. Leaves are strap-shaped, semi-erect, and basal. Very strong stem produces about 10 bright scarlet-salmon flowers with recurved petals.
N. 'Margaret Rose'. Autumn-flowering bulb. H 12–20in (30–50cm), S 6–8in (15–20cm). Half hardy, zones 8–10. Bears strap-shaped, semi-erect, basal leaves. Stem has a tight head of bright rose-pink flowers with recurved petals.
N. masonorum. Autumn-flowering bulb. H 6–8in (15–20cm), S 3–4in (8–10cm). Half hardy, zones 8–10. Produces threadlike, semi-erect leaves in a basal tuft. Stem bears pink flowers with very crisped petal margins.
N. 'Orion' illus. p.354.
N. sarniensis illus. p.354.
N. undulata illus. p.354.

NERIUM (Apocynaceae)
Genus of evergreen shrubs, grown for their flowers. Frost tender, min. 50°F (10°C). Requires full sun and well-drained soil. Water potted plants freely when in full growth, sparingly at other times. Tip prune young plants to promote branching. Propagate by seed in spring or by semi-ripe cuttings in summer.

N. oleander illus. p.88.

NERTERA (Rubiaceae)
Genus of creeping perennials, grown for their mass of spherical, beadlike fruits in autumn. Makes excellent alpine house plants. Half hardy. Needs a sheltered, semi-shaded site in gritty, moist but well-drained, sandy soil. Resents winter wet. Propagate in spring by seed, division, or tip cuttings.

N. depressa. See *N. granadensis*.
N. granadensis, syn. *N. depressa*, illus. p.327.

NICANDRA (Solanaceae)
Genus of one species of annual with short-lived flowers. Fully hardy. Grow in sun and in rich, well-drained soil. Propagate by seed sown in spring.

N. physalodes (Apple-of-Peru, Shoo-fly). Fast-growing, upright, branching annual. H 3ft (1m), S 1ft (30cm) or more. Zones 8–10. Has oval, serrated, green leaves. In summer and early

autumn bears bell-shaped, white-throated, light violet-blue flowers, over 1in (2.5cm) wide, each lasting only one day. Spherical, green fruits, 2in (5cm) wide, are surrounded by purple and green calyces. Is thought to repel flies, hence its name.

NICOTIANA (Solanaceae)
Flowering tobacco
Genus of annuals, perennials that are usually grown as annuals, and semi-evergreen shrubs. Frost hardy to frost tender, min. 34°F (1°C). Needs sun and fertile, well-drained soil. Propagate annuals and perennials by seed in early spring, shrubs by seed in spring or by semi-ripe cuttings in summer.

N. affinis. See *N. alata*.
N. alata, syn. *N. affinis*, illus. p.200. 'Lime Green' is an upright perennial, usually grown as an annual. H 2ft (60cm), S 1ft (30cm). Frost tender. Has oval, green leaves. In late summer and autumn bears racemes of open trumpet-shaped, greenish yellow flowers that are fragrant at night.
Sensation Series illus. p.270.
*N., Domino Series illus. p.263.
N. glauca. Semi-evergreen, upright shrub. H and S 8–10ft (2.5–3m). Half hardy, zones 9–10. Stout, blue-gray shoots bear narrowly oval, fleshy, blue-gray leaves. Showy, tubular, bright yellow flowers are produced in summer and early autumn.
N. langsdorfii illus. p.278.
N. x sanderae. 'Crimson Rock' is a fairly slow-growing, bushy annual. H 2ft (60cm), S 1ft (30cm). Frost tender. Oval leaves are green. Evening-scented, trumpet-shaped, bright crimson flowers, to 3in (8cm) long, open in summer and early autumn. Nicki Series, H 15in (38cm), is fragrant, with a good color range including white, pink, red, and purple.
N. sylvestris illus. p.188.

NIDULARIUM (Bromeliaceae)
Genus of evergreen, rosette-forming, epiphytic perennials, grown for their overall appearance. Frost tender, min. 50–59°F (10–15°C). Requires semi-shade and a rooting medium of equal parts humus-rich soil and either sphagnum moss or bark or plastic chips used for orchid culture. Using soft water, water moderately in growing season, sparingly at other times, and keep centers of rosettes filled with water from spring to autumn. Propagate by offsets in spring or summer.

N. carolinae. See *Neoregelia carolinae*.
N. fulgens (Blushing bromeliad). Evergreen, spreading, basal-rosetted, epiphytic perennial. H 8in (20cm) or more, S 16–20in (40–50cm). Zone 10. Has dense rosettes of strap-shaped, spiny-toothed, arching, glossy, rich green leaves. Tubular, white-and-purple flowers, almost hidden in a rosette of bright scarlet bracts, are mainly produced in summer.
N. innocentii (Bird's-nest bromel, Bird's-nest bromeliad). Evergreen, spreading, basal-rosetted, epiphytic perennial. H 8–12in (20–30cm), S 24in (60cm). Zone 10. Has dense rosettes

of strap-shaped, prickle-toothed, arching, dark green, sometimes reddish green leaves with reddish purple undersides. Tubular, white flowers, partially hidden in a rosette of bright red bracts, are produced mainly in summer.

N. procerum. Evergreen, spreading, basal-rosetted, epiphytic perennial. H 8–12in (20–30cm), S 20–30in (50–75cm). Zone 10. Strap-shaped, spiny-toothed, bright green leaves are produced in dense rosettes. Clusters of small, tubular, blue flowers are produced in summer.

NIEREMBERGIA (Solanaceae)
Genus of summer-flowering perennials, sometimes grown as annuals, and deciduous or semi-evergreen sub-shrubs. Frost to half hardy. Prefers sun and moist but well drained soil. Propagate by division in spring, by semi-ripe cuttings in summer, or by seed in autumn.

N. caerulea. See *N. hippomanica* var. *violacea*.
N. hippomanica var. *violacea*, syn. *N. caerulea*. **'Purple Robe'** illus. p.275.
N. repens illus. p.314.

NIGELLA (Ranunculaceae)
Genus of annuals, grown for their attractive flowers, which are suitable for cutting, and their ornamental seed pods. Fully hardy. Grows best in sun and in fertile, well-drained soil. Dead-head plants to prolong flowering if seed heads are not required. Propagate by seed sown outdoors in spring or early autumn.

N. damascena (Love-in-a-mist). Fast-growing, upright annual. H 24in (60cm), S 8in (20cm). Fully hardy. Has feathery, bright green leaves. Spurred, many-petaled, blue or white flowers appear in summer, followed by inflated, rounded, green, then brown seed pods that may be cut and dried. **'Miss Jekyll'** and **'Persian Jewels'** illus. p.277.

NOLANA (Nolanaceae)
Genus of annuals, useful for growing in hot, dry sites and rock gardens and as edging. Frost to half hardy. Grow in sun and in fertile, well-drained soil. Propagate by seed sown outdoors in spring.

N. atriplicifolia. See *N. paradoxa*.
N. grandiflora. See *N. paradoxa*.
N. paradoxa, syn. *N. atriplicifolia*, *N. grandiflora*. Moderately fast-growing, prostrate annual. H 3in (8cm), S 6in (15cm). Half hardy. Has oval, green leaves and, in summer, funnel-shaped, purplish blue flowers, to 2in (5cm) wide, with white-zoned, yellow throats.

Nolina recurvata. See *Beaucarnea recurvata*.
Nolina tuberculata. See *Beaucarnea recurvata*.

NOMOCHARIS (Liliaceae)
Genus of bulbs with a lilylike habit and, in summer, loose spikes of flattish flowers, often conspicuously spotted. Fully hardy. Requires partial shade and

rich, well-drained soil with a high humus content. When in growth in summer needs moist but not waterlogged soil. Is dormant in winter. Propagate by seed in winter or spring.

N. mairei. See *N. pardanthina*.
N. pardanthina, syn. *N. mairei*, illus. p.333.
N. saluenensis. Summer-flowering bulb. H 34in (85cm), S 5–6in (12–15cm). Zones 7–9. Leafy stems bear lance-shaped, scattered leaves. Produces a loose spike of 2–6 saucer-shaped, white or pink flowers, with dark purple eyes and purple spots.

NOPALXOCHIA (Cactaceae)
Genus of epiphytic, perennial cacti with flattened, strap-shaped stems. Is closely related to *Epiphyllum*, with which it hybridizes. Spines are insignificant. Stems may die back after flowering well. Frost tender, min. 50°F (10°C). Needs partial shade and rich, well-drained soil. Is easy to grow. Propagate by stem cuttings in spring or summer.

N. ackermannii, syn. *Epiphyllum ackermannii* (Red orchid cactus). Erect, then pendent, epiphytic, perennial cactus. H 1ft (30cm), S 2ft (60cm). Zone 10. Has fleshy, toothed, green stems, to 3in (7cm) across and 16in (40cm) long. Bears 6in (15cm) wide, funnel-shaped, red flowers in spring-summer along indented edges of stems.
N. phyllanthoides, syn. *Epiphyllum* 'Deutsche Kaiserin', illus. p.383.

NOTHOFAGUS (Fagaceae)
Southern beech
Genus of deciduous or evergreen trees, grown for their habit, foliage, and, in the case of deciduous species, autumn color. Has inconspicuous flowers in late spring. Fully to frost hardy. Needs sun or semi-shade and, as it is not very resistant to strong winds, should have the shelter of other trees. Prefers deep, fertile, moist but well-drained soil; is not suitable for shallow, chalky soil. Propagate by seed in autumn.

N. antarctica (Antarctic beech, Nirre). Deciduous, broadly conical tree, sometimes with several main stems. H 50ft (15m), S 30ft (10m). Fully hardy, zones 8–9. Small, oval, crinkly edged, glossy, dark green leaves turn yellow in autumn.
N. betuloides illus. p.48.
N. dombeyi illus. p.47.
N. menziesii (Silver beech). Evergreen, conical tree. H 70ft (20m), S 40ft (12m). Frost hardy, zones 8–9. Has tiny, rounded, sharply toothed, glossy, dark green leaves.
N. obliqua illus. p.42.
N. procera illus. p.42.

NOTHOLIRION (Liliaceae)
Genus of summer-flowering bulbs, related to *Lilium*, grown for their funnel-shaped flowers. Frost hardy. Often produces early leaves, which may be damaged by spring frosts, so grow in a cool greenhouse in areas subject to alternating mild and cold periods in spring. Prefers partial shade or full sun and humus-rich, well-drained soil. Bulb dies after flowering.

Propagate in spring or autumn by offsets, which take 2–3 years to reach flowering size. Alternatively propagate by seed in winter or spring.
N. campanulatum illus. p.335.

NOTHOPANAX. See PSEUDOPANAX.

NOTOCACTUS (Cactaceae)
Genus of mainly spherical, perennial cacti, often densely spiny on short ribs. Is closely related to *Parodia* and *Wigginsia*. Frost tender, min. 41–50°F (5–10°C). Needs sun or partial shade and well-drained soil. Is easy to grow and flower, but is best not left completely dry in winter. Propagate by seed in spring or summer.

N. apricus. Flattened spherical, perennial cactus. H 3in (7cm), S 4in (10cm). Min. 50°F (10°C), zone 10. Much-ribbed, pale green stem is densely covered with short, soft, golden brown spines. In summer, crown produces flattish, glossy, bright yellow flowers, 3in (8cm) across, with purple stigmas. Prefers partial shade.
N. graessneri. Slow-growing, flattened spherical, perennial cactus. H 4in (10cm), S 10in (25cm). Min. 50°F (10°C), zone 10. Bristlelike, golden spines completely cover much-ribbed, green stem. Slightly sunken crown produces funnel-shaped, glossy, greenish yellow flowers, with yellow stigmas, in early spring. Prefers partial shade.
N. haselbergii illus. p.395.
N. leninghausii illus. p.388.
N. mammulosus illus. p.397.
N. ottonis. Variable, spherical, perennial cactus. H and S 4in (10cm). Min. 41°F (5°C), zone 10. Has pale to dark green stem with 8–12 rounded ribs bearing stiff, golden radial spines and longer, soft, red central spines. In summer, crown carries flattish, glossy, golden flowers, 3in (8cm) across, with purple stigmas. Offsets freely from stolons. Prefers a sunny site.
N. rutilans illus. p.391.
N. scopa (Silver ball cactus). Spherical to columnar, perennial cactus. H 10in (25cm), S 6in (15cm). Min. 50°F (10°C), zone 10. Stem, with 30–35 ribs, is densely covered with white radial spines and longer, red central spines, 3 or 4 per areole. Crown carries funnel-shaped, glossy, yellow flowers, 1¹/₂in (4cm) across, with purple stigmas, in summer. Prefers a sunny position.

NOTOSPARTIUM (Leguminosae)
Genus of leafless, summer-flowering shrubs, grown for their habit, green shoots, and flowers. Frost hardy, but in cold areas does best against a south- or west-facing wall. Requires a sheltered, sunny position and well-drained soil. Older plants may need staking. Propagate by semi-ripe cuttings in summer or by seed in autumn.
N. carmichaeliae (Pink broom). Leafless, arching shrub. H 6ft (2m), S 5ft (1.5m). Zones 8–10. Short, dense spikes of pealike, purple-blotched, pink flowers are produced in mid-summer on slender, drooping, green shoots.

NUPHAR (Nymphaeaceae)
Genus of deciduous, perennial, deep-water plants, grown for their floating foliage and spherical flowers. Fully to frost hardy. Grows in shade or sun and in running or still water; is often grown for a water-lily effect in conditions where true water lilies would not thrive. Remove fading foliage and flowers, and periodically divide crowded plants. Propagate by division in spring.
N. advena (American spatterdock, Yellow pond lily). Deciduous, perennial, deep-water plant. S 4ft (1.2m). Fully hardy, zones 4–9. Has broadly oval, floating, green leaves; central ones are occasionally erect. Small, purple-tinged, yellow flowers in summer are followed by decorative seed heads.
N. lutea illus. p.377.

NYMANIA (Aitoniaceae)
Genus of one species of evergreen, spring-flowering shrub, grown for its flowers and fruits. Frost tender, min. 45–50°F (7–10°C). Needs full light and fertile, well-drained soil. Water potted specimens moderately, less when not in full growth. Propagate by seed in spring or by semi-ripe cuttings in summer.
N. capensis illus. p.116.

NYMPHAEA (Nymphaeaceae)
Water lily
Genus of deciduous, summer-flowering, perennial water plants, grown for their floating, usually rounded leaves and brightly colored flowers. Fully hardy to frost tender, min. 50°F (10°C). Needs an open, sunny position and still water. Remove fading foliage to prevent it polluting water. Plants have tuberlike rhizomes and require dividing and replanting in spring or early summer every 3 or 4 years. Most frost tender plants may be treated as annuals. May also be propagated by seed, or by separating plantlets in spring or early summer.
N. alba (European white water lily; illus. p.376). Deciduous, perennial water plant with floating leaves. S to 10ft (3m). Fully hardy, zones 5–10. Has dark green leaves and, in summer, produces cup-shaped, semi-double, pure white flowers, 4in (10cm) across, with golden centers.
N. 'American Star' (illus. p.376). Deciduous, perennial water plant with floating leaves. S to 4ft (1.2m). Frost hardy, zones 8–10. Young leaves are purplish green or bronze, maturing to bright green. Star-shaped, semi-double flowers, 4in (10cm) across, are deep pink and are held above water throughout summer.
N. 'Attraction' (illus. p.376). Deciduous, perennial water plant with floating leaves. S to 6ft (2m). Fully hardy, zones 5–10. Has dark green leaves. In summer bears cup-shaped, semi-double, garnet red flowers, 6in (15cm) across and flecked with white.
N. 'Aurora'. Deciduous, perennial water plant with floating leaves. S to 30in (75cm). Frost hardy, zones 8–10. Olive green leaves are mottled with purple. In summer has star-shaped,

semi-double flowers, 2in (5cm) across, cream in bud, opening to yellow, then passing through orange to blood red. Is suitable for a small- to medium-sized pool.

N. 'Aviator Pring'. Deciduous, perennial water plant with floating leaves. S to 5ft (1.5m). Frost tender, zone 10. Green leaves have toothed, wavy edges. Rounded, semi-double, bright yellow flowers, to 12in (30cm) across, are held above water throughout summer.

N. 'Blue Beauty' (illus. p.376). Deciduous, perennial water plant with floating leaves. S to 8ft (2.5m). Frost tender, zone 10. Leaves are brown-freckled, dark green above, purplish green beneath. Fragrant, rounded, semi-double, deep blue flowers, to 12in (30cm) across, are borne in summer.

N. capensis (Cape blue water lily). Deciduous, perennial water plant with floating leaves. S to 6ft (2m). Frost tender, zone 10. Large, green leaves are often splashed with purple beneath. Star-shaped, semi-double, bright blue flowers, 6–8in (15–20cm) across, appear in summer.

N. caroliniana 'Nivea' (illus. p.376). Deciduous, perennial water plant with floating leaves. S to 4ft (1.2m). Fully hardy, zones 5–10. Has pale green leaves and, in summer, fragrant, cup-shaped, semi-double, pure white flowers, 4–6in (10–15cm) across.

N. 'Emily Grant Hutchings'. Deciduous, perennial water plant with floating leaves. S to 4ft (1.2m). Frost tender, zone 10. Has small, green leaves overlaid with bronze-crimson. Cup-shaped, semi-double, pinkish red flowers, 6–8in (15–20cm) across, open at night in summer.

N. 'Escarboucle' (illus. p.376). Deciduous, perennial water plant with floating leaves. S to 10ft (3m). Fully hardy, zones 5–10. Leaves are dark green. In summer has cup-shaped, semi-double, deep crimson flowers, 4–6in (10–15cm) across, with golden centers.

N. 'Fire Crest' (illus. p.376). Deciduous, perennial water plant with floating leaves. S to 4ft (1.2m). Fully hardy, zones 5–10. Dark green leaves are suffused with purple. In summer bears star-shaped, semi-double, deep pink flowers, 6–8in (15–20cm) across, with red-tipped stamens.

N. 'Gladstoniana' (illus. p.376). Deciduous, perennial water plant with floating leaves. S to 10ft (3m). Frost hardy, zones 8–10. Leaves are green. Star-shaped, semi-double, white flowers, 6–12in (15–30cm) across, appear in summer.

N. 'Gonnère'. Deciduous, perennial water plant with floating leaves. S to 5ft (1.5m). Fully hardy, zones 5–10. Has bright pea green leaves and, in summer, rounded, fully double, white flowers, 6–8in (15–20cm) across.

N. 'Green Smoke'. Deciduous, perennial water plant with floating leaves. S to 6ft (2m). Frost tender, zone 10. Bronze-green leaves have bronze speckling. In summer bears star-shaped, single flowers, 4–8in (10–20cm) across, that are chartreuse, shading to blue.

N. 'James Brydon' (illus. p.376). Deciduous, perennial water plant with floating leaves. S to 8ft (2.5m). Frost hardy, zones 8–10. Fragrant, peony-shaped, double, orange-suffused, crimson flowers, 6–8in (15–20cm) across, are borne in summer above dark green leaves.

N. x laydekeri 'Fulgens' (illus. p.376). Deciduous, perennial water plant with floating leaves. S to 3ft (1m). Fully hardy, zones 5–10. Dark green leaves have purplish green undersides. Star-shaped, semi-double, bright crimson flowers, 2–4in (5–10cm) across, appear in summer.

N. 'Mme. Auguste Tézier'. Deciduous, perennial water plant with floating leaves. S to 5ft (1.5m). Frost tender, zone 10. Purplish green leaves are splashed and spotted with brown. In summer bears star-shaped, semi-double, lavender blue flowers, 4–6in (10–15cm) across and each with a brown center, that open at night.

N. 'Mme. Wilfron Gonnère'. Deciduous, perennial water plant with floating leaves. S to 5ft (1.5m). Frost hardy, zones 8–10. Has green leaves and, in summer, produces cup-shaped, almost fully double, white flowers, 6in (15cm) across, spotted with deep rose-pink.

N. 'Margaret Mary'. Deciduous, perennial water plant with floating leaves. S to 18in (45cm). Half hardy, zones 9–10. Leaves are dark green above, light brown beneath. Star-shaped, single, blue flowers, 2–3in

(5–8cm) across, are produced year-round in frost-free conditions.

N. marliacea 'Albida' (illus. p.376). Deciduous, perennial water plant with floating leaves. S to 6ft (2m). Fully hardy, zones 5–10. Deep green leaves have red or purplish green undersides. Bears fragrant, cup-shaped, semi-double, pure white flowers, 6–8in (15–20cm) across, in summer.

'Carnea' (illus. p.376) has dark green leaves and star-shaped, semi-double, soft pink flowers, 6–10in (15–25cm) across, with golden centers.

'Chromatella' (illus. p.376) has olive green leaves, heavily mottled with maroon and bronze, and cup-shaped, semi-double, canary yellow flowers, 6–8in (15–20cm) across.

N. 'Midnight'. Deciduous, perennial water plant with floating leaves. S to 4ft (1.2m). Frost tender, zone 10. Has small leaves, dark green flecked with brown above, purple beneath. Bears star-shaped, semi-double, rich purple flowers, 4–6in (10–15cm) across, in summer.

N. 'Mrs. George H. Pring'. Deciduous, perennial water plant with floating leaves. S to 5ft (1.5m). Frost tender, zone 10. Has large leaves, green with reddish brown splashes above, purplish green beneath. Produces fragrant, star-shaped, semi-double, creamy white flowers, 6–10in (15–25cm) across, throughout summer.

N. odorata 'Sulphurea Grandiflora'. Deciduous, perennial water plant with floating leaves. S to 3ft (1m). Fully hardy, zones 5–10. Dark green leaves are heavily mottled with maroon. Bears fragrant, star-shaped, semi-double, yellow flowers, 4–6in (10–15cm) across, throughout summer.

N. pygmaea 'Alba' (illus. p.376). Deciduous, perennial water plant with floating leaves. S to 12in (30cm). Fully hardy, zones 5–10. Has small, dark green leaves, purplish green beneath, and, in summer, star-shaped, single, white flowers, $\frac{3}{4}$–1$\frac{1}{4}$in (2–3cm) across. **'Helvola'** (illus. p.376), S to 18in (45cm), is frost hardy and has small, olive green leaves with heavy purple or brown mottling. Produces star-shaped, semi-double, yellow flowers, $\frac{3}{4}$–1$\frac{1}{2}$in (2–4cm) across, in summer.

N. 'Rose Arey' (illus. p.376). Deciduous, perennial water plant with

floating leaves. S to 5ft (1.5m). Frost hardy, zones 8–10. Leaves are reddish green. In summer has star-shaped, semi-double, deep rose-pink flowers, 4–6in (10–15cm) across, that pale with age and have a strong aniseed fragrance.

N. 'St. Louis'. Deciduous, perennial water plant with floating leaves. S to 6ft (2m). Frost tender, zone 10. Bright green leaves are spotted with brown when young. Produces star-shaped, semi-double, bright yellow flowers, 6–10in (15–25cm) across, in summer.

N. 'Sunrise' (illus. p.376). Deciduous, perennial water plant with floating leaves. S to 6ft (2m). Frost hardy, zones 8–10. Green leaves have downy stalks and undersides. Bears star-shaped, semi-double, yellow flowers, 4–6in (10–15cm) across, in summer.

N. 'Virginia' (illus. p.376). Deciduous, perennial water plant with floating leaves. S to 5ft (1.5m). Fully hardy, zones 5–10. Has purplish green leaves and, in summer, star-shaped, semi-double, white flowers, 4–6in (10–15cm) across.

N. 'Wood's White Knight'. Deciduous, perennial water plant with floating leaves. S to 6ft (2m). Frost tender, zone 10. Leaves are green, dappled with darker green beneath. In summer, star-shaped, semi-double, creamy white flowers, 4–8in (10–20cm) across and with prominent, gold stamens, open at night.

NYMPHOIDES (Menyanthaceae)
Genus of deciduous, perennial, deep-water plants, with floating foliage, grown for their flowers. Fully hardy to frost tender, min. 41°F (5°C). Requires an open, sunny position. Propagate by division in spring or summer.
N. peltata illus. p.377.

NYSSA (Nyssaceae)
Tupelo
Genus of deciduous trees, with inconspicuous flowers, grown for their foliage and brilliant autumn color. Fully hardy. Needs sun or semi-shade; does best in hot summers. Requires moist, neutral to acid soil. Resents being transplanted. Propagate by softwood cuttings in summer or by seed in autumn.
N. sinensis illus. p.55.
N. sylvatica illus. p.45.

OCHNA (Ochnaceae)
Genus of mainly evergreen trees and shrubs, grown mostly for their flowers and fruits. Frost tender, min. 50°F (10°C). Prefers full light and well-drained soil. Water potted specimens moderately, less when not in full growth. Prune, if necessary, in early spring. Propagate by seed in spring or by semi-ripe cuttings in summer.
O. serrulata (Mickey-mouse plant). Evergreen, irregularly rounded, twiggy shrub that is semi-evergreen in low temperatures. H to 6ft (2m), S 3–6ft (1–2m) or more. Zone 10. Leaves are narrowly elliptic, toothed, and glossy. Has 5-petaled, bright yellow flowers in spring-summer, then shuttlecock-shaped, red fruits, each with 1–5 berrylike seeds clustered on top.

---

x **ODONTIODA.** See ORCHIDS.
x *O.* (*O.* Chantos x *O.* Marzorka) x *Odontoglossum* Buttercrisp (illus. p.255). Evergreen, epiphytic orchid for a cool greenhouse. H 9in (23cm). Zone 10. Produces arching spikes of intricately patterned, red, tan, orange, and yellow flowers, 3in (8cm) across; flowering season varies. Has narrowly oval leaves, 4–6in (10–15cm) long. Needs shade in summer.
x *O.* Mount Bingham (illus. p.253). Evergreen, epiphytic orchid for a cool greenhouse. H 9in (23cm). Zone 10. Pink-edged, red flowers, 3¹/₂in (9cm) across, are borne in spikes; flowering season varies. Has narrowly oval leaves, 4–6in (10–15cm) long. Needs shade in summer.
x *O.* Pacific Gold x *Odontoglossum cordatum* (illus. p.253). Evergreen, epiphytic orchid for a cool greenhouse. H 9in (23cm). Zone 10. Bears long spikes of yellow-striped and -marked, rich chocolate brown flowers, 3in (7cm) across; flowering season varies. Leaves are narrowly oval and 4–6in (10–15cm) long. Grow in shade in summer.
x *O.* Petit Port (illus. p.253). Evergreen, epiphytic orchid for a cool greenhouse. H 9in (23cm). Zone 10. Bears spikes of rich red flowers, 3in (8cm) across, each with a pink-and-yellow-marked lip; flowering season varies. Narrowly oval leaves are 4–6in (10–15cm) long. Shade in summer.

---

x **ODONTOCIDIUM.** See ORCHIDS.
x *O.* Artur Elle 'Colombian' (illus. p.253). Evergreen, epiphytic orchid for a cool greenhouse. H 9in (23cm). Zone 10. Produces tall spikes of pale yellow flowers, 2¹/₂in (6cm) across and intricately patterned with brown; flowering season varies. Has narrowly oval leaves, 4–6in (10–15cm) long. Requires shade in summer.
x *O.* Tiger Butter x *Wilsonara* Wigg's 'Kay' (illus. p.253). Evergreen, epiphytic orchid for a cool greenhouse. H 9in (23cm). Zone 10.

Bears spikes of mottled, deep reddish brown flowers, 2in (5cm) across, each with a rich golden yellow lip; flowering season varies. Narrowly oval leaves are 4–6in (10–15cm) long. Grow in shade in summer.
x *O.* Tiger Hambuhren (illus. p.255). Evergreen, epiphytic orchid for a cool greenhouse. H 9in (23cm). Zone 10. Deep yellow flowers, 3in (8cm) across and heavily patterned with chestnut brown, are produced in tall spikes; flowering season varies. Has narrowly oval leaves, 4–6in (10–15cm) long. Needs shade in summer.
x *O.* Tigersun 'Orbec' (illus. p.254). Evergreen, epiphytic orchid for a cool greenhouse. Zone 10. Is very similar to x *O.* Tiger Hambuhren, but flowers are slightly smaller and have lighter patterning.

ODONTOGLOSSUM. See ORCHIDS.
O. bictoniense (illus. p.252). Evergreen, epiphytic orchid for a cool greenhouse. H 9in (23cm). Zone 10. Olive green flowers, 1¹/₂in (4cm) across, barred with dark brown and each with a sometimes pink-flushed, white lip, are produced in spikes in late summer. Leaves are narrowly oval and 4–6in (10–15cm) long. Requires shade in summer.
O. cervantesii (illus. p.252). Evergreen, epiphytic orchid for a cool greenhouse. H 3in (8cm). Zone 10. In winter bears sprays of papery, white flowers, 1in (2.5cm) across, with cobweblike, light brown marks. Has narrowly oval leaves, 4–6in (10–15cm) long. Grow in shade in summer.
O. cordatum (illus. p.253). Evergreen, epiphytic orchid for a cool greenhouse. H 5in (12cm). Zone 10. Sprays of brown-marked, corn yellow flowers, 1in (2.5cm) across, open in spring. Leaves are narrowly oval and 4–6in (10–15cm) long. Provide shade in summer and keep very dry in winter.
O. crispum (illus. p.252). Evergreen, epiphytic orchid for a cool greenhouse. H 6in (15cm). Zone 10. Bears long sprays of rounded flowers, 3in (8cm) across, pure white or spotted or flushed with pink, each with a red-and-yellow-marked lip; flowering season varies. Has narrowly oval leaves, 4–6in (10–15cm) long. Requires shade in summer.
O. Eric Young (illus. p.254). Evergreen, epiphytic orchid for a cool greenhouse. H 6in (15cm). Zone 10. White-lipped, pale yellow flowers, 3in (8cm) across and spotted with rich yellow, are carried in spikes; flowering season varies. Has narrowly oval leaves, 4–6in (10–15cm) long. Grow in shade in summer.
O. grande, syn. *Rossioglossum grande* (illus. p.253). Evergreen, epiphytic orchid for a cool greenhouse. H 6in (15cm). Zone 10. Spikes of rich yellow flowers, to 6in (15cm) across and

heavily marked chestnut brown, are produced in autumn. Has broadly oval, stiff leaves, 6in (15cm) long. Provide shade in summer and keep very dry in winter.
O. Le Nez Point (illus. p.253). Evergreen, epiphytic orchid for a cool greenhouse. H 6in (15cm). Zone 10. Bears spikes of crimson flowers, 2¹/₂in (6cm) across; flowering season varies. Has narrowly oval leaves, 4–6in (10–15cm) long. Needs shade in summer.
O. rossii (illus. p.252). Evergreen, epiphytic orchid for a cool greenhouse. H 3in (8cm). Zone 10. In autumn-winter, white to mushroom pink flowers, 1in (2.5cm) across and speckled with beige-brown, are borne in spikes. Narrowly oval leaves are 4–6in (10–15cm) long. Needs shade in summer.
O. Royal Occasion (illus. p.252). Evergreen, epiphytic orchid for a cool greenhouse. H 6in (15cm). Zone 10. Produces spikes of white flowers, 3in (8cm) across, with yellow-blotched lips, in autumn-winter. Leaves are narrowly oval and 4–6in (10–15cm) long. Shade in summer.

---

x **ODONTONIA.** See ORCHIDS.
x *O.* Olga. Evergreen, epiphytic orchid for a cool greenhouse. H 6in (15cm). Zone 10. Pure white flowers, 4in (10cm) across, with large, reddish brown-blotched lips, are borne in spikes, mainly in autumn. Has narrowly oval leaves, 5in (12cm) long. Grow in shade in summer.

OEMLERIA, syn. OSMARONIA (Rosaceae)
Genus of one species of deciduous, early spring-flowering shrub, grown for its fragrant flowers and decorative fruits. Separate male and female plants are needed in order to obtain fruits. Fully hardy. Prefers sun or semi-shade and moist soil. Restrict growth by removing suckers and cutting old shoots back or down to base in late winter. Propagate by suckers in autumn.
O. cerasiformis (Indian plum, Oso berry). Deciduous, upright, then arching shrub that forms dense thickets. H 8ft (2.5m), S 12ft (4m). Zones 6–10. Leaves are narrowly oval and dark blue-green. Nodding clusters of small, fragrant, bell-shaped, white flowers in early spring are followed by small, plum-shaped, purple fruits.

OENOTHERA (Onagraceae)
Evening primrose
Genus of annuals, biennials, and perennials, grown for their profuse but short-lived flowers in summer. Fully to frost hardy. Needs full sun and well-drained, sandy soil. Propagate by seed or division in autumn or spring or by softwood cuttings in late spring.

O. acaulis. Tuft-forming perennial. H 6in (15cm), S 8in (20cm). Fully hardy, zones 5–9. Has oblong to oval, deeply toothed or lobed leaves. Cup-shaped, white flowers, turning pink, open at sunset in summer. Suits a rock garden.
O. caespitosa. Clump-forming, stemless perennial. H 5in (12cm), S 8in (20cm). Fully hardy, zones 5–9. Has narrowly oval, entire or toothed, green leaves. Flowers, opening at sunset in summer, are fragrant, cup-shaped, and white, becoming pink with age. Suits a rock garden.
O. missouriensis illus. p.325.
O. perennis, syn. *O. pumila.* Clump-forming perennial. H 6–24in (15–60cm), S 12in (30cm). Fully hardy, zones 4–9. In summer, loose spikes of nodding buds open to fragrant, funnel-shaped, yellow flowers above a basal mass of narrowly spoon-shaped, green leaves.
O. pumila. See *O. perennis.*
O. speciosa (White evening primrose). Often short-lived, clump-forming perennial with running rhizomes. H 18in (45cm), S 12in (30cm) or more. Frost hardy, zones 5–9. In summer bears spikes of fragrant, saucer-shaped, green-centered, pure white flowers that age to pink and open flat. Leaves are narrowly spoon-shaped, deeply cut, and green.
O. tetragona. Clump-forming perennial. H 18–24in (45–60cm), S 18in (45cm). Fully hardy, zones 5–9. Dense spikes of fragrant, cup-shaped, bright yellow flowers appear from mid- to late summer. Leaves, borne on reddish green stems, are narrowly oval to lance-shaped and glossy, green. 'Fireworks' illus. p.246.

OLEA (Oleaceae)
Genus of evergreen trees, grown for their foliage and edible fruits. Frost to half hardy; in cold areas requires the protection of a sheltered, south- or west-facing wall. Needs full sun and deep, fertile, very well-drained soil. Propagate by semi-ripe cuttings in summer or by seed in autumn.
O. europaea (Olive). Slow-growing, evergreen, spreading tree. H and S 30ft (10m). Frost hardy, zones 9–10. Is very long-lived. Narrowly oblong leaves are gray-green above, silvery beneath. Has tiny, fragrant white flowers, borne in short racemes in late summer, then edible, oval, green, later purple fruits.

OLEARIA (Compositae)
Daisy-bush
Genus of evergreen shrubs and trees, grown for their foliage and daisylike flower heads. In mild, coastal areas provides good, very wind-resistant shelter. Frost to half hardy. Needs full sun and well-drained soil. Cut out dead wood in spring. Propagate by semi-ripe cuttings in summer.
O. albida of gardens. See *O.* 'Talbot de Malahide'.

O. avicenniifolia. Evergreen, rounded, dense shrub. H 10ft (3m), S 15ft (5m). Frost hardy, zones 9–10. Oval to lance-shaped, dark gray-green leaves are white beneath. Produces wide heads of fragrant white flowers in late summer and early autumn.

O. x haastii illus. p.107.

O. ilicifolia. Evergreen, bushy, dense shrub. H and S 10ft (3m). Frost hardy, zones 9–10. Narrowly oblong, rigid leaves are sharply toothed, gray-green, and musk-scented. Fragrant white flower heads are borne in clusters in early summer.

O. lacunosa. Evergreen, upright, dense shrub. H and S 10ft (3m). Frost hardy, zones 9–10. Narrowly oblong, pointed, rigid leaves have rust brown hairs when young and mature to glossy, dark green with central, white veins. Produces white flower heads only rarely.

O. macrodonta. Vigorous, evergreen, upright shrub, often treelike. H 20ft (6m), S 15ft (5m). Frost hardy, zones 9–10. Has holly-shaped, sharply toothed, gray-green leaves, silvery white beneath. Large heads of fragrant white flowers appear in early summer.

O. mollis of gardens. Evergreen, rounded, dense shrub. H 3ft (1m), S 5ft (1.5m). Frost hardy, zones 9–10. Has oval, wavy-edged, silvery gray leaves. Large heads of small, white flowers are borne profusely in late spring.

O. nummulariifolia illus. p.104.

O. phlogopappa. Evergreen, upright, compact shrub. H and S 6ft (2m). Half hardy, zones 9–10. Leaves are gray-green and oblong, with wavy edges. Has massed, white flower heads in late spring. var. *subrepanda* illus. p.126.

O. x scilloniensis. Evergreen, upright, then rounded, dense shrub. H and S 6ft (2m). Frost hardy, zones 9–10. Narrowly oblong, wavy-edged, dark gray-green leaves set off masses of white flower heads in late spring.

O. semidentata. Evergreen, rounded, compact shrub. H and S 10ft (3m). Half hardy, zone 10. Has white shoots and narrowly lance-shaped, leathery, gray-green leaves. Large heads of purple-centered, lilac flowers appear from early to mid-summer.

O. 'Talbot de Malahide', syn. *O. albida* of gardens. Evergreen, bushy, dense shrub. H 10ft (3m), S 15ft (5m). Frost hardy, zones 9–10. Oval leaves are dark green above, silvery beneath. Broad heads of fragrant white flowers are borne in late summer. Is excellent for exposed, coastal gardens.

O. virgata illus. p.86.

O. 'Zennorensis'. Evergreen, rounded, dense shrub. H and S 6ft (2m). Frost hardy, zones 9–10. Bears narrowly oblong, sharply toothed, gray-green leaves. Large heads of small, white flowers are produced in abundance in late spring.

Oliveranthus elegans. See *Echeveria harmsii.*

OMPHALODES (Boraginaceae)
Genus of annuals and perennials, some of which are evergreen or semi-evergreen. Makes good ground cover, especially in rock gardens. Fully to

half hardy. Needs shade or semi-shade and moist but well-drained soil, except for *O. linifolia* and *O. luciliae,* which prefer sun. Propagate by seed or division in spring.

O. cappadocica illus. p.289.

O. linifolia illus. p.262.

O. luciliae. Semi-evergreen, mound-forming perennial. H 3in (7cm), S 6in (15cm). Half hardy, zones 6–8. Has oval, blue-gray leaves and, in spring-summer, loose sprays of pink buds that develop into flattish, sky blue flowers. Resents winter wet, so plant in a sheltered site or alpine house. Prefers sun and very gritty soil.

O. verna illus. p.289.

OMPHALOGRAMMA (Primulaceae)
Genus of perennials, closely related to *Primula,* grown for their flowers. Makes good rock garden plants, but is difficult to grow, especially in hot, dry areas. Frost hardy. Needs shade and gritty, moist but well-drained, peaty soil. Propagate by seed in spring.

O. vinciflorum. Basal-rosetted perennial. H 6in (15cm), S 4in (10cm). Zones 6–7. Has oval, hairy, green leaves. In spring produces nodding, funnel-shaped, violet flowers, each with a deeper violet throat and a flat, flared mouth.

ONCIDIUM. See ORCHIDS.

O. flexuosum (Dancing-doll orchid; illus. p.255). Evergreen, epiphytic orchid for a cool or intermediate greenhouse. H 9in (23cm). Zone 10. In autumn produces terminal sprays of many small, large-lipped, bright yellow flowers, ¼in (0.5cm) across. Has narrowly oval leaves, 4in (10cm) long. Is best grown on a bark slab. Keep in semi-shade in summer.

O. ornithorrhynchum (illus. p.252). Evergreen, epiphytic orchid for a cool greenhouse. H 6in (15cm). Zone 10. Dense, arching sprays of very fragrant, rose-lilac flowers, ¼in (0.5cm) across, with a yellow highlight, are borne freely in autumn. Has narrowly oval leaves, 4in (10cm) long. Requires semi-shade in summer.

O. papilio (Butterfly orchid; illus. p.255). Evergreen, epiphytic orchid for a warm greenhouse. H 6in (15cm). Zone 10. In summer, rich yellow-marked, orange-brown flowers, 3in (8cm) long, are borne singly and in succession on tops of stems. Has oval, semi-rigid, mottled leaves, 4–6in (10–15cm) long. Grow in good light in summer.

O. tigrinum (illus. p.254). Evergreen, epiphytic orchid for a cool or intermediate greenhouse. H 9in (23cm). Zone 10. Branching spikes of fragrant, yellow-marked, brown flowers, 2in (5cm) across, each with a large, yellow lip, open in autumn. Has oval leaves, 6in (15cm) long. Requires semi-shade in summer.

ONIXOTIS. See DIPIDAX.

ONOCLEA (Polypodiaceae)
Genus of one species of deciduous fern that rapidly colonizes wet areas. Fully hardy. Grows in sun or shade and in

wet soil. Remove fronds as they fade. Propagate by division in autumn or winter.

O. sensibilis illus. p.186.

ONONIS (Leguminosae)
Genus of summer-flowering annuals, perennials, and deciduous or semi-evergreen shrubs and sub-shrubs, grown for their pealike flowers. Is good for rock gardens, walls, and banks. Fully hardy. Needs a sunny site and well-drained soil. Propagate by seed in autumn or spring, shrubs also by softwood cuttings in summer.

O. fruticosa illus. p.293.

O. natrix illus. p.299.

O. rotundifolia. Deciduous or semi-evergreen, glandular, upright sub-shrub. H 8–24in (20–60cm), S 8–12in (20–30cm) or more. Zones 6–9. Bears small, rounded, 3-parted, toothed, hairy, green leaves. Relatively large, red-streaked, rose-pink flowers appear in small clusters in summer.

ONOPORDON. See ONOPORDUM.

ONOPORDUM, syn. ONOPORDON (Compositae)
Genus of annuals, biennials, and perennials, ranging from stemless to tall, branching plants. Fully hardy. Grow in sun or semi-shade and in rich, well-drained soil. To prevent self seeding remove dead flower heads. Propagate by seed sown outdoors in autumn or spring. Leaves are prone to slug and snail damage.

O. acanthium illus. p.266.

ONOSMA (Boraginaceae)
Genus of summer-flowering annuals, biennials, perennials, and semi-evergreen sub-shrubs, grown for their long, pendent, tubular flowers. Is good for rock gardens and banks. Fully to frost hardy. Requires full sun and well-drained soil. Dislikes wet summers. Propagate by softwood cuttings in summer or by seed in autumn.

O. albo-roseum illus. p.292.

O. stellulatum. Semi-evergreen, upright sub-shrub. H and S 6in (15cm). Fully hardy, zones 7–9. Leaves are oblong and covered in hairs which may irritate the skin. Clusters of yellow flowers open in late spring and summer.

OOPHYTUM (Aizoaceae)
Genus of clump-forming, egg-shaped, perennial succulents with 2 united, very fleshy leaves. These are covered in dry, papery sheaths, except in spring when sheaths split open, revealing a new pair of leaves. Flowers are produced from a slight central fissure on upper surface. Is difficult to grow. Frost tender, min. 41°F (5°C). Requires sun and well-drained soil. Propagate by seed or stem cuttings in spring or summer.

O. nanum illus. p.390.

OPHIOPOGON (Liliaceae)
Genus of evergreen perennials, grown mainly for their grasslike foliage. Fully to half hardy. Grows in sun or partial shade and in fertile, well-drained soil. Propagate by division in spring or by seed in autumn.

O. jaburan. Evergreen, clump-forming perennial. H 6in (15cm), S 12in (30cm). Frost hardy, zones 7–10. Has dark green foliage. Bears racemes of bell-shaped, white flowers in early summer, then deep blue berries. '**Variegatus**' is half hardy, has white- or yellow-striped foliage and is much less robust.

O. japonicus illus. p.260.

O. planiscapus '**Nigrescens**' illus. p.259.

OPHRYS. See ORCHIDS.

O. aranifera. See *O. sphegodes.*

O. fuciflora. See *O. holoserica.*

O. fusca (illus. p.254). Deciduous, terrestrial orchid. H 4–16in (10–40cm). Frost hardy, zones 7–9. Spikes of greenish, yellow or brown flowers, ¼in (0.5cm) long, each with a yellow-edged, bluish, brown, or purple lip, are produced in spring. Has oval or lance-shaped leaves, 3–5in (8–12cm) long. Grow in shade outdoors. Potted plants require semi-shade in summer.

O. holoserica, syn. *O. fuciflora.* Deciduous, terrestrial orchid. H 6–22in (15–55cm). Frost hardy, zones 7–9. Spikes of flowers, ½in (1cm) long, varying in color from white through pink to blue and green, appear in spring-summer. Leaves are oval to oblong, 2–4in (5–10cm) long. Cultivate as for *O. fusca.*

O. lutea var. *lutea* (illus. p.254). Deciduous, terrestrial orchid. H 3–12in (8–30cm). Frost hardy, zones 8–9. In spring bears short spikes of flowers, ½in (1cm) long, with greenish sepals, yellow petals, and brown-centered, bright yellow lips. Has oval, basal leaves, 2–4in (5–10cm) long. Cultivate as for *O. fusca.*

O. speculum. See *O. vernixia.*

O. sphegodes, syn. *O. aranifera* (Spider orchid). Deciduous, terrestrial orchid. H 4–18in (10–45cm). Frost hardy, zones 8–9. In spring-summer carries spikes of flowers, ½in (1cm) long, that vary from green to yellow and have spiderlike, blackish brown marks on lips. Leaves are oval to lance-shaped and 1½–3in (4–8cm) long. Cultivate as for *O. fusca.*

O. tenthredinifera (Sawfly orchid; illus. 253). Deciduous, terrestrial orchid. H 6–22in (15–55cm). Frost hardy, zones 8–9. In spring produces spikes of flowers, ½in (1cm) long, in a variety of colors, including white to pink, or blue and green, each with a violet or bluish lip edged with pale green. Has a basal rosette of oval to oblong leaves, 2–3½in (5–9cm) long. Cultivate as for *O. fusca.*

O. vernixia, syn. *O. speculum.* Deciduous, terrestrial orchid. H 3–12in (8–30cm). Frost hardy, zones 8–9. In spring produces dense spikes of flowers, ½in (1cm) long, with greenish or yellow sepals, purple petals and 3-centered, brown lips. Has oblong to lance-shaped leaves, 1½–3in (4–7cm) long. Cultivate as for *O. fusca.*

OPHTHALMOPHYLLUM (Aizoaceae)
Genus of clump-forming, perennial succulents related to *Lithops.* Each plant has 2 cylindrical, very fleshy leaves, erect and united for most of

their length, but with a fissure between them at the top. Leaves each have a rounded upper surface with a translucent window. Frost tender, min. 41°F (5°C). Requires sun and well-drained soil. Water in late summer and early autumn; thereafter keep almost dry. Propagate by seed or stem cuttings in spring or summer.

O. herrei. See *O. longum.*

O. longum, syn. *O. herrei.* Clump-forming, perennial succulent. H 1¼in (3cm), S ⅝in (1.5cm). Zone 10. Has 2 almost united, cylindrical, fleshy, erect, gray-green to brown leaves. Bears daisylike, white to pale pink flowers, ¾in (2cm) across, in late summer.

O. maughanii. Clump-forming, perennial succulent. H 1½in (4cm), S 4in (10cm). Zone 10. Has 2 almost united, cylindrical, very fleshy, erect, yellowish green leaves with upper surface bearing ¼–½in (0.5–1cm) deep fissure. In late summer bears daisylike, white flowers, ⅝in (1.5cm) across.

O. villetii illus. p.392.

OPLISMENUS (Gramineae). See GRASSES, BAMBOOS, RUSHES, and SEDGES.

O. hirtellus (Basket grass). **'Variegatus'** illus. p.257.

OPLOPANAX (Araliaceae)
Genus of deciduous, summer-flowering shrubs, grown for their habit, fruits, and spiny foliage. Fully hardy, but young growths may be damaged by late frosts. Does best in a cool, partially shaded position and in moist soil. Propagate by seed in autumn or by root cuttings in late winter.

O. horridus (Devil's club). Deciduous, spreading, open, sparsely branched shrub. H and S 6ft (2m). Zones 6–10. Prickly stems bear large, oval, 7–9-lobed, toothed, green leaves. Dense umbels of small, star-shaped, greenish white flowers from mid- to late summer are followed by spherical, red fruits.

OPUNTIA (Cactaceae)
Prickly pear
Genus of perennial cacti, ranging from small, alpine, ground-cover plants to large, evergreen, tropical trees, with at times insignificant glochids—short, soft, barbed spines produced on areoles. Mature plants carry masses of short-spined, pear-shaped, green, yellow, red, or purple fruits (prickly pears), edible in some species. Fully hardy to frost tender, min. 41–50°F (5–10°C). Needs sun and well-drained soil. Propagate by seed or stem cuttings in spring or summer.

O. brasiliensis. Treelike, perennial cactus. H 18ft (5.5m), S 10ft (3m). Frost tender, min. 50°F (10°C), zone 10. Has a cylindrical, green stem bearing bright green branches of flattened, oval, spiny segments. Sheds 2–3-year-old side branches. Masses of shallowly saucer-shaped, yellow flowers, 1½in (4cm) across, appear in spring-summer, only on plants over 2ft (60cm) tall, and are followed by small, yellow fruits.

O. cylindrica. Bushy, perennial cactus. H 12–20ft (4–6m). S 3ft (1m). Frost

tender, min. 50°F (10°C). Cylindrical stems, 1½–2in (4–5cm) across, bear short-lived, cylindrical, dark green leaves, to ¾in (2cm) long, on new growth. Areoles may lack spines or each produce 2 or 3 barbed ones. Has masses of shallowly saucer-shaped, pink-red flowers in spring-summer, only on plants over 6ft (2m) tall, that are followed by greenish yellow fruits.

O. engelmannii. See *O. ficus-indica.*

O. erinacea illus. p.386.

O. ficus-indica, syn. *O. engelmannii, O. megacantha* (Edible prickly pear, Indian fig). Bushy to treelike, perennial cactus. H and S 15ft (5m). Frost tender, min. 50°F (10°C), zone 10. Bears flattened, oblong, blue-green stem segments, 20in (50cm) long and spineless. In spring-summer has masses of shallowly saucer-shaped, yellow flowers, 4in (10cm) across, followed by edible, purple fruits.

O. humifusa illus. p.398.

O. megacantha. See *O. ficus-indica.*

O. microdasys (Bunny ears). Bushy, perennial cactus. H and S 2ft (60cm). Frost tender, min. 50°F (10°C), zone 10. Has flattened, oval, green stem segments, 3–7in (8–18cm) long, that develop brown marks in low temperatures. Bears spineless areoles, with white, yellow, brown, or red glochids, closely set in diagonal rows. Masses of funnel-shaped, yellow flowers, 2in (5cm) across, appear in summer on plants over 6in (15cm) tall. var. *alba* illus. p.387.

O. robusta illus. p.381.

O. tunicata illus. p.388.

O. verschaffeltii illus. p.394.

ORCHIDS (Orchidaceae)
Family of perennials, some of which are evergreen or semi-evergreen, grown for their beautiful, unusual flowers. These consist of 3 outer sepals and 3 inner petals, the lowest of which, known as the lip, is usually enlarged and different from the others in shape, markings, and color. There are about 750 genera and 17,500 species, together with an even greater number of hybrids, bred partly for their vigor and ease of care. They are divided into epiphytic and terrestrial plants. (The spread of an orchid is indefinite.)

Epiphytic orchids
Epiphytes have more flamboyant flowers than terrestrial orchids and are more commonly grown. In the wild, they grow on tree branches or rocks (lithophytes), obtaining nourishment through clinging roots and moisture through aerial roots. Most consist of a horizontal rhizome, from which arise vertical, water-storing, often swollen stems known as pseudobulbs. Flowers and foliage are produced from the newest pseudobulbs. Other epiphytes consist of a continuously growing upright rhizome; on these, flower spikes appear in the axils of leaves growing from the rhizome. In temperate climates, epiphytes need to be grown in a greenhouse.

Cultivation of epiphytes
For cultivation purposes, epiphytes, which are all frost tender, may be

divided into 3 groups: cool-greenhouse types, which require min. 50°F (10°C) and max. 75°F (24°C); intermediate-greenhouse types, needing a range of 55–80°F (13–27°C); and warm-greenhouse types, requiring 65–80°F (18–27°C). In summer, temperatures need to be controlled by shading the glass and by ventilation. Cool-greenhouse orchids may be placed outdoors in summer; this improves flowering. Other types may also be grown outdoors if the air temperature remains within these ranges.

The amount of light required in summer is given in individual plant entries. All epiphytic orchids, however, need to be kept out of direct sun in summer, to avoid scorching, and require full light in winter.

Epiphytic orchids, whether grown indoors or outside, require a special soil-free compost obtained from an orchid nursery or made by mixing 2 parts fibrous material (such as bark chippings and/or peat) with 1 part porous material (such as sphagnum moss and/or expanded clay pellets). Most epiphytes may be grown in pots, although some may be successfully cultivated in a hanging basket or on a slab of bark (with moss around their roots) suspended in the greenhouse.

In summer, water plants freely and spray regularly. Those suspended on bark slabs need a constantly moist atmosphere. In winter, water moderately and, if plants are in growth, spray occasionally. Some orchids rest in winter and require scarcely any water or none at all.

Orchids benefit from weak foliar feeds; apply as for watering.

Repot plants every other year, in spring; if they are about to flower, repot after flowering.

Terrestrial orchids
Terrestrial orchids, some of which also produce pseudobulbs, grow in soil or leaf mold, sustaining themselves in the normal way through roots or tubers. Some may be grown in borders, but many in temperate climates need to be cultivated in pots and protected under glass during winter.

Cultivation of terrestrial orchids
Terrestrial orchids are fully hardy to frost tender, min. 65°F (18°C). *Cypripedium* species may be grown outdoors in any area, preferably in neutral to acid soil, but cannot withstand severe frost, if frozen solid in pots or without snow cover, or tolerate very wet soil in winter. Other terrestrial orchids, except in very mild areas, are best grown in pots; use the same compost as for epiphytes but add 1 part grit to 2 parts compost. Place outdoors in a peat bed or in a glasshouse in the growing season. Keep dry when dormant. In a greenhouse, light requirements, watering, feeding, and repotting are as for epiphytes.

Orchid propagation
Orchids with pseudobulbs may be increased by removing and replanting old, leafless pseudobulbs when

repotting in spring. Take care to retain at least 4 pseudobulbs on the parent plant. Some genera that may be propagated in this way are: *Ada,* x *Aliceara, Anguloa, Bifrenaria, Bletilla, Brassavola* (large plants only and retaining at least 6 pseudobulbs on the parent), x *Brassocattleya,* x *Brassolaeliocattleya, Bulbophyllum, Calanthe, Cattleya, Coelogyne, Cymbidium, Dendrobium, Dendrochilum, Encyclia, Epigeneium, Gomesa, Gongora, Laelia,* x *Laeliocattleya, Lycaste, Maxillaria, Miltonia, Miltoniopsis,* x *Odontioda,* x *Odontocidium, Odontoglossum,* x *Odontonia, Oncidium, Peristeria, Phaius, Pleione,* x *Potinara,* x *Sophrolaeliocattleya, Stanhopea,* x *Vuylstekeara,* x *Wilsonara,* and *Zygopetalum.*

Some orchids without pseudobulbs produce new growth from the base. When such a plant has 6 new growths, divide it in spring into 2 portions with 3 growths each and repot both. Propagate *Disa, Paphiopedilum,* and *Phragmipedium* in this way. Large specimens of *Eria, Masdevallia,* and *Pleurothallis* may be divided in spring, leaving 4–6 stems on each portion.

Propagation of *Phalaenopsis* is by stem cuttings taken soon after flowering. *Vanda* may be increased by removing the top half of the stem once it has produced aerial roots and leaves; new growths will develop from the leafless base. With both these methods achieving success is difficult and not recommended for the beginner.

Terrestrial orchids with tubers may be propagated by division of the tubers. Genera that may be increased in this way are: *Cypripedium* (in spring), *Dactylorrhiza* (spring), *Ophrys* (autumn), *Orchis* (spring), *Serapias* (autumn), and *Spiranthes* (spring). *Calypso* is rarely propagated successfully in cultivation. *Angraecum* should not be propagated in cultivation, as the parent plant is easily endangered.

The most easily increased orchids are *Cymbidium.* Propagation of *Epidendrum* may be extremely difficult; see genus for specific details.

Orchids are illustrated on pp.252–5. See also *Ada,* x *Aliceara, Angraecum, Anguloa, Bifrenaria, Bletilla, Brassavola,* x *Brassocattleya,* x *Brassolaeliocattleya, Bulbophyllum, Calanthe, Calypso, Cattleya, Caelogyne, Cymbidium, Cypripedium, Dactylorrhiza, Dendrobium, Dendrochilum, Encyclia, Epidendrum, Epigeneium, Eria, Gomesa, Gongora, Laelia,* x *Laeliocattleya, Lycaste, Masdevallia, Maxillaria, Miltonia, Miltoniopsis,* x *Odontioda,* x *Odontocidium, Odontoglossum,* x *Odontonia, Oncidium, Ophrys, Orchis, Paphiopedilum, Peristeria, Phaius, Phalaenopsis, Phragmipedium, Pleione, Pleurothallis,* x *Potinara, Serapias,* x *Sophrolaeliocattleya, Spiranthes, Stanhopea, Vanda,* x *Vuylstekeara,* x *Wilsonara,* and *Zygopetalum.*

ORCHIS. See ORCHIDS.

O. morio (illus. p.254). Deciduous, terrestrial orchid. H 16in (40cm). Half hardy, zones 4–9. Green-veined, reddish purple, mauve, or rarely white flowers, $^1/_2$in (1cm) long, open along stems in spring. Has a basal cluster of lance-shaped or broadly oblong leaves, 4–6in (10–16cm) long. Requires sun or semi-shade.

Oreocereus celsianus. See *Borzicactus celsianus.*
Oreocereus trollii. See *Borzicactus trollii.*

ORIGANUM (Labiatae)
Dittany, Marjoram, Oregano
Genus of deciduous sub-shrubs and perennials, sometimes with overwintering leaf rosettes. Some species are grown as culinary herbs, others for their clusters of tubular, usually pink flowers. Most species have arching, prostrate stems and are useful for trailing over rocks, banks, and walls. Fully to frost hardy. Prefers sun and well-drained, alkaline soil. Propagate by division in spring, by cuttings of non-flowering shoots in early summer, or by seed in autumn or spring.
O. amanum. Deciduous, rounded, compact sub-shrub. H and S 6–8in (15–20cm). Frost hardy, zones 5–8. Open funnel-shaped, pale pink or white flowers are borne all summer above small, heart-shaped, pale green leaves. Makes a good alpine house plant; dislikes a damp atmosphere.
O. dictamnus (Cretan dittany). Prostrate perennial. H 5–6in (12–15cm), S 16in (40cm). Frost hardy, zones 7–9. Arching stems are clothed in rounded, aromatic, hairy, gray-white leaves. Has pendent heads of open funnel-shaped, purplish pink flowers in summer.
O. 'Kent Beauty' illus. p.293.
O. laevigatum illus. p.294.
O. rotundifolium. Deciduous, prostrate sub-shrub. H 9–12in (23–30cm), S 12in (30cm). Fully hardy, zones 4–8. Throughout summer bears whorls of pendent, funnel-shaped, pale pink flowers, surrounded by yellow-green bracts. Has small, rounded, green leaves.
O. vulgare (Wild marjoram). Mat-forming, woody-based perennial. H and S 18in (45cm). Fully hardy, zones 4–8. Has oval, aromatic, dark green leaves, above which branched, wiry stems bear clusters of tiny, tubular, 2-lipped, mauve flowers in summer.
'Aureum' illus. p.245.

ORNITHOGALUM (Liliaceae)
Star-of-Bethlehem
Genus of bulbs, grown for their mostly star-shaped, white flowers, usually backed with green. Fully hardy to frost tender, min. 45°F (7°C). Needs sun or partial shade and well-drained soil. Lift and dry tender species for winter, if grown outside in summer, and replant in spring. Propagate by seed or offsets, in autumn for spring-flowering bulbs, in spring for summer-flowering bulbs.
O. arabicum illus. p.351.
O. balansae, syn. *O. oligophyllum,* illus. p.356.
O. lanceolatum illus. p.357.

O. montanum illus. p.357.
O. narbonense illus. p.350.
O. nutans (Drooping star-of-Bethlehem). Spring-flowering bulb. H 6–14in (15–35cm), S 3–4in (8–10cm). Frost hardy, zones 6–10. Has a cluster of linear, channeled, semi-erect, basal leaves. Stem bears a spike of pendent, bell-shaped, translucent, white flowers, $^3/_4–1^1/_4$in (2–3cm) long with pale green outsides. Prefers partial shade.
O. oligophyllum. See *O. balansae.*
O. saundersiae. Summer-flowering bulb. H to 3ft (1m), S 6–8in (15–20cm). Half hardy, zones 9–10. Produces a basal cluster of strap- or lance-shaped, semi-erect leaves. Stem bears a flat-topped head of erect, flattish, white or cream flowers, each with a blackish green ovary forming a dark eye.
O. thyrsoides illus. p.351.
O. umbellatum. Spring-flowering bulb. H 4–12in (10–30cm), S 4–6in (10–15cm). Frost hardy, zones 7–10. Linear, channeled, semi-erect, green leaves each have a white line on upper surface. Bears a loose, flat-topped head of star-shaped, white flowers, backed with green.

ORONTIUM (Araceae)
Genus of one species of deciduous, perennial, deep-water plant, grown for its floating foliage and flower spikes. Fully hardy. Needs full sun. Remove faded flower spikes. Propagate by seed when fresh, in mid-summer.
O. aquaticum illus. p.377.

OROSTACHYS (Crassulaceae)
Genus of short-lived, basal-rosetted, perennial succulents with very fleshy, sword-shaped leaves. Produces flowers 3 years from sowing seed, then dies. Frost tender, min. 46°F (8°C). Requires sun and well-drained soil. Propagate by seed or division in spring or summer.
O. chanetii. Basal-rosetted, perennial succulent. H 1$^1/_2$in (4cm), S 3in (8cm). Zone 10. Gray-green leaves are shorter in rosette center. Flower stem bears a dense, tapering spike of star-shaped, white or pink flowers, $^1/_2–^3/_4$in (1–2cm) across, in spring-summer.

OROYA (Cactaceae)
Genus of spherical, perennial cacti with inner flower petals forming a tube and outer ones opening fully. Frost tender, min. 50°F (10°C). Needs a sunny, well-drained site. Propagate by seed in spring or summer.
O. neoperuviana illus. p.385.

Orphanidesia gaultherioides. See *Epigaea gaultherioides.*

ORTHROSANTHUS (Iridaceae)
Genus of perennials with short, woody rhizomes, grown for their flowers. Frost tender, min. 41°F (5°C). Prefers sun and well-drained soil. Propagate by division or seed in spring.
O. chimboracensis. Tufted, rhizomatous perennial. H 2ft (60cm) in flower, S 6in (15cm). Zone 10. Has very narrow, grasslike, ribbed, stiff leaves, to 18in (45cm) long, with finely toothed margins. In summer,

flower stems bear clusters of short-lived, long-stalked, lavender blue flowers, each enclosed in 2 leaflike bracts.

ORYCHOPHRAGMUS (Cruciferae)
Genus of late spring- to summer-flowering annuals. Half hardy. Grow in sun and in fertile, well-drained soil. Propagate by seed in spring.
O. violaceus illus. p.275.

OSBECKIA (Melastomataceae)
Genus of evergreen, summer-flowering perennials, sub-shrubs, and shrubs, grown for their flowers and foliage. Frost tender, min. 61°F (16°C). Needs full light or partial shade and humus-rich, well-drained soil. Water potted specimens freely when in full growth, moderately at other times. Cut back flowered stems by at least half in early spring to maintain vigor and to produce large flower trusses. Propagate by seed in spring or by greenwood cuttings in summer.
O. stellata. Evergreen, rounded, stiff-stemmed shrub. H and S 3–6ft (1–2m). Zone 10. Produces narrowly oval, hairy, prominently veined leaves. Has terminal clusters of 4-petaled, rose-purple flowers in late summer.

OSCULARIA (Aizoaceae)
Genus of bushy, spreading, perennial succulents with chunky, triangular leaves and masses of fragrant, daisylike flowers. Frost tender, min. 37°F (3°C). Needs sun and well-drained soil. Propagate by seed or stem cuttings in spring or summer.
O. deltoides illus. p.391.

OSMANTHUS (Oleaceae)
Genus of evergreen shrubs and trees, grown for their foliage and small, fragrant flowers. *O.* x *burkwoodii* and *O. heterophyllus* may be used for hedging. Fully to half hardy. Tolerates sun or shade and fertile, well-drained soil. Restrict growth by cutting back after flowering; trim hedges in mid-summer. Propagate by semi-ripe cuttings in summer.
O. armatus. Evergreen, bushy, dense shrub. H and S 12ft (4m). Frost hardy, zones 8–9. Large, oblong, dark green leaves are rigid and sharply toothed. Has tubular, 4-lobed, white flowers in autumn, followed by egg-shaped, dark violet fruits.
O. x *burkwoodii,* syn. x *Osmarea burkwoodii,* illus. p.84.
O. decorus, syn. *Phillyrea decora.* Evergreen, upright, rounded, dense shrub. H 10ft (3m), S 15ft (5m). Fully hardy, zones 6–9. Has large, oblong, glossy, dark green leaves and, in mid-spring, tubular, 4-lobed, white flowers, followed by egg-shaped, blackish purple fruits.
O. delavayi, syn. *Siphonosmanthus delavayi,* illus. p.84.
O. forrestii. See *O. yunnanensis.*
O. fragrans (Fragrant olive). Evergreen, upright shrub or tree. H and S 20ft (6m). Half hardy, zones 9–10. Extremely fragrant, tubular, 4-lobed, white flowers are borne amid oblong, glossy, dark green leaves from early to late summer. Is suitable only for

very mild areas. f. *aurantiacus* has orange flowers.
O. heterophyllus 'Aureomarginatus' illus. p.95. 'Gulftide' is an evergreen, bushy, dense shrub. H 8ft (2.5m), S 10ft (3m). Frost hardy, zones 7–9. Holly-shaped, sharply toothed, glossy, dark green leaves set off tubular, 4-lobed, white flowers in autumn.
O. yunnanensis, syn. *O. forrestii.* Evergreen, treelike, upright, then spreading shrub. H and S 30ft (10m). Frost hardy, zones 8–9. Has large, oblong, glossy, bright green leaves, bronze when young. Produces tubular, 4-lobed, creamy white flowers in clusters in late winter or early spring.

x *Osmarea burkwoodii.* See *Osmanthus* x *burkwoodii.*

OSMARONIA. See OEMLERIA.

OSMUNDA (Osmundaceae)
Genus of deciduous ferns. Fully hardy. Requires shade, except for *O. regalis,* which also tolerates sun. *O. cinnamomea* and *O. claytoniana* need moist soil; *O. regalis* does best in very wet conditions. Remove fading fronds regularly. Propagate by division in autumn or winter or by spores as soon as ripe.
O. cinnamomea (Cinnamon fern). Deciduous fern. H 3ft (1m), S 18in (45cm). Zones 4–9. Outer, lance-shaped, divided, pale green sterile fronds, with deeply cut pinnae, surround brown fertile fronds, all arising from a fibrous rootstock.
O. claytoniana (Interrupted fern). Deciduous fern. H 2ft (60cm), S 1ft (30cm). Zones 4–9. Has lance-shaped, pale green fronds, divided into oblong, blunt pinnae; outer sterile fronds are larger than fertile ones at center of plant.
O. regalis illus. p.186.

OSTEOMELES (Rosaceae)
Genus of evergreen, summer-flowering shrubs, grown for their habit, foliage, and flowers. Frost to half hardy. In most areas plant against a south- or west-facing wall. Requires sun and fertile, well-drained soil. Propagate by semi-ripe cuttings in summer.
O. schweriniae illus. p.106.

OSTEOSPERMUM (Compositae)
Genus of evergreen, semi-woody perennials. Frost to half hardy; does best in warm areas. Requires sun and well-drained soil. Propagate by cuttings of non-flowering shoots in mid-summer.
O. barberiae. See *O. jucundum.*
O. 'Buttermilk' illus. p.245.
O. 'Cannington Roy'. Evergreen, clump-forming, prostrate perennial. H 12in (30cm), S 18in (45cm). Half hardy, zones 9–10. Large, daisylike, pink flower heads, with darker eyes, are borne profusely in summer-autumn. Leaves are linear and gray.
O. ecklonis. Evergreen, upright or somewhat straggling perennial. H and S 18in (45cm). Half hardy, zones 9–10. In summer-autumn, daisylike, white flower heads, with dark blue

centers, are borne singly above lance-shaped, gray-green leaves. **'Blue Streak'** has petals that are suffused with blue outside.

O. jucundum, syn. *O. barberiae*, *Dimorphotheca barberiae*, illus. p.236.

O. **'Nairobi Purple'**. Evergreen, semi-prostrate perennial. H 12in (30cm), S 12–18in (30–45cm). Half hardy, zones 9–10. Daisylike, velvety, deep purple-red flower heads, with darker streaks on outside of ray petals, are borne in summer. Leaves are fresh green and lance-shaped. Will not flower freely in rich soils.

O. **'Whirligig'** illus. p.234.

OSTROWSKIA (Campanulaceae)
Genus of one species of summer-flowering perennial. Fully hardy. Prefers a warm, sunny situation and rich, moist but well-drained soil. May be difficult to grow as needs a resting period after flowering, so cover with a frame until late autumn to keep dry. Propagate by seed in autumn or spring.

O. magnifica. Erect perennial. H 5ft (1.5m), S 1¹/₂ft (45cm). Zones 7–8. From early to mid-summer produces very large, bell-shaped blooms of delicate light blue-purple, veined with darker purple. Has whorls of oval, blue-gray leaves.

OSTRYA (Betulaceae)
Genus of deciduous trees, grown for their foliage, catkins, and fruits. Fully hardy. Needs sun or semi-shade and fertile, well-drained soil. Propagate by seed in autumn.

O. carpinifolia (European hop hornbeam). Deciduous, rounded tree. H and S 50ft (15m). Zones 6–9. Has gray bark and oval, glossy, dark green leaves that turn yellow in autumn. Yellow catkins in mid-spring are followed by hoplike, greenish white fruit clusters that become brown in autumn.

O. virginiana illus. p.50.

OTHONNOPSIS (Compositae)
Genus of evergreen shrubs, grown for their daisylike flower heads in summer. Half hardy. Needs sun and well-drained soil. Propagate by softwood cuttings in early summer.

O. cheirifolia illus. p.298.

OURISIA (Scrophulariaceae)
Genus of evergreen perennials with creeping rootstocks. Is excellent for peat beds and walls. Fully to frost hardy. Needs shade and moist, peaty soil. Propagate by division or seed in spring.

O. caespitosa illus. p.314.

O. **'Loch Ewe'**. Vigorous, evergreen, rosetted perennial. H and S 12in (30cm). Frost hardy, zones 7–8. Prostrate stems have heart-shaped, leathery, green leaves. Produces dense spikes of outward-facing, tubular, salmon pink flowers in late spring and early summer.

O. macrocarpa. Vigorous, evergreen, prostrate perennial. H 24in (60cm), S 8in (20cm). Frost hardy, zones 7–8. Has rosettes of heart-shaped, leathery, dark green leaves. Produces spikes of open cup-shaped, yellow-centered, white flowers in late spring.

O. magellanica. Evergreen, straggling perennial. H 1¹/₂in (4cm), S to 6in (15cm). Frost hardy, zones 7–8. In summer, flower stems bearing tubular, scarlet flowers appear above broadly heart-shaped leaves.

O. microphylla illus. p.316.

OXALIS (Oxalidaceae)
Genus of tuberous, rhizomatous, or fibrous-rooted perennials and semi-evergreen sub-shrubs, grown for their colorful flowers, which in bud are rolled like an umbrella, and their often attractive leaves. Leaves are mostly less than ³/₄in (2cm) across and are divided into 3 or more leaflets. Some species may be invasive; smaller species and cultivars suit rock gardens. Fully hardy to frost tender, min. 41°F (5°C). Needs full sun or semi-shade and well-drained soil. Propagate by division in autumn or early spring.

O. acetosella (Wood sorrel). Creeping, spring-flowering, rhizomatous perennial. H 2in (5cm), S 12–18in (30–45cm). Fully hardy, zones 5–8. Forms mats of cloverlike, 3-lobed leaves. Delicate stems bear cup-shaped, white flowers, each ¹/₂in (1cm) across with 5 purple-veined petals. Prefers semi-shade. f. *rosea* illus. p.305.

O. adenophylla illus. p.306.

O. bowiei, syn. *O. purpurata* var. *bowiei*. Spring- to summer-flowering, tuberous perennial. H to 12in (30cm), S 6in (15cm). Half hardy, zones 9–10. Has long-stalked, cloverlike, 3-lobed leaves. Stems each produce a loose head of 3–10 widely funnel-shaped, pinkish purple flowers, 1¹/₄–1¹/₂in (3–4cm) across. Needs a sheltered, sunny site.

O. chrysantha. Creeping, fibrous-rooted perennial. H 1¹/₂–2in (4–5cm), S 6–12in (15–30cm). Half hardy, zones 9–10. Forms mats of cloverlike, 3-lobed leaves. Stems each produce a funnel-shaped, bright yellow flower, ³/₄–1¹/₄in (2–3cm) across, in summer. Needs a sheltered site.

O. deppei, syn. *O. tetraphylla*, illus. p.293.

O. depressa, syn. *O. inops*, illus. p.318.

O. enneaphylla (Scurvy grass). Tuft-forming, rhizomatous perennial. H 2–3in (5–7cm), S 3–4in (8–10cm). Frost hardy, zones 7–9. Gray-green leaves are divided into narrowly oblong to oval leaflets. In summer, stems bear widely funnel-shaped, 1¹/₄–1¹/₂in (3–4cm) wide, lilac-pink or white flowers.

O. hedysaroides. Semi-evergreen, bushy sub-shrub. H 3ft (1m), S 1–1¹/₂ft (30–45cm). Half hardy, zones 9–10. Leafy stems bear cloverlike, 3-lobed, green leaves. Leaf axils produce clusters of widely funnel-shaped, yellow flowers, ³/₄–1¹/₄in (2–3cm) across, in spring-summer.

O. hirta. Late summer-flowering, tuberous perennial. H 12in (30cm), S 4–6in (10–15cm). Half hardy, zones 9–10. Stem produces scattered leaves, with 3 narrowly lance-shaped leaflets. Leaf axils each bear a widely funnel-shaped, rose-purple flower, ³/₄–1¹/₄in (2–3cm) wide, with a yellow center.

O. inops. See *O. depressa*.

O. **'Ione Hecker'**. Tuft-forming, rhizomatous perennial. H 2in (5cm), S 2–3in (5–8cm). Frost hardy, zones 7–9. Gray leaves are composed of narrowly oblong, wavy leaflets. In summer bears widely funnel-shaped, pale purple-blue flowers, 1¹/₂in (4cm) across, with darker veins.

O. laciniata. Tuft-forming, rhizomatous perennial. H 2in (5cm), S 2–3in (5–8cm). Frost hardy, zones 7–9. Has blue-gray leaves with narrowly oblong, crinkly edged leaflets. Widely funnel-shaped, steel blue flowers, 1¹/₂in (4cm) across, with darker veins, are produced in summer.

O. lobata illus. p.327.

O. purpurata var. *bowiei*. See *O. bowiei*.

O. tetraphylla. See *O. deppei*.

OXYDENDRUM (Ericaceae)
Genus of one species of deciduous tree, grown for its flowers and spectacular autumn color. Fully hardy. For good autumn coloring plant in an open position in sun or semi-shade. Needs moist, acid soil. Propagate by softwood cuttings in summer or by seed in autumn.

O. arboreum illus. p.50.

OXYPETALUM (Asclepiadaceae)
Genus of herbaceous, twining climbers; only one species is generally cultivated. Frost tender, min. 41°F (5°C). In cool climates treat as an annual. Grow in sun and in well-drained soil. Pinch out tips of shoots to encourage branching. Propagate by seed in spring.

O. caeruleum, syn. *Tweedia caerulea*, illus. p.173.

OZOTHAMNUS (Compositae)
Genus of evergreen, summer-flowering shrubs, grown for their foliage and small, densely clustered flower heads. Frost to half hardy. Requires full sun and well-drained soil. Propagate by semi-ripe cuttings in summer.

O. ledifolius, syn. *Helichrysum ledifolium*, illus. p.128.

O. rosmarinifolius, syn. *Helichrysum rosmarinifolium*, illus. p.106.

P

PACHISTIMA. See PAXISTIMA.

PACHYCEREUS (Cactaceae)
Genus of slow-growing, columnar, perennial cacti, branching with age. Flowers, which are funnel-shaped, are unlikely to appear in cultivation as they are produced only on plants over 10ft (3m) high. Frost tender, min. 50°F (10°C). Requires sun and well-drained soil. Propagate by seed in spring or summer.
P. pecten-aboriginum. Columnar, perennial cactus. H 35ft (11m), S 10ft (3m). Zone 10. Dark green stems bear 9–11 deep ribs. Areoles each produce 8 radial spines, ^{1}/$_2$in (1cm) long, and longer central spines. All spines are dark brown with red bases and fade to grey.
P. pringlei illus. p.381.

PACHYPHRAGMA (Cruciferae)
Genus of perennials with rosettes of basal leaves, often grown as ground cover under shrubs. Fully hardy. Grow in moist soil and in sun or partial shade. Propagate by division or stem cuttings in late spring or by seed in autumn.
P. macrophyllum, syn. *Thlaspi macrophyllum,* illus. p.224.

PACHYPHYTUM (Crassulaceae)
Genus of rosetted, perennial succulents, closely related to *Echeveria,* with which it hybridizes. Frost tender, min. 41–50°F (5–10°C). Needs sun and well-drained soil. Propagate by seed, leaf, or stem cuttings in spring or summer.
P. compactum illus. p.400.
P. oviferum illus. p.395.

PACHYPODIUM (Apocynaceae)
Genus of bushy or treelike, perennial succulents, mostly with swollen stems, closely related to *Adenium,* except that most species have spines. Frost tender, min. 50–59°F (10–15°C). Requires full sun and very well-drained soil. May be very difficult to grow. Propagate by seed in spring or summer.
P. lameri illus. p.378.
P. succulentum. Treelike, perennial succulent. H 2ft (60cm), S 1ft (30cm). Min. 50°F (10°C), zone 10. Swollen trunk, 6in (15cm) across, produces narrower, vertical, green to gray-brown stems. Bears trumpet-shaped, pink-crimson flowers, ^{3}/$_4$in (2cm) across, near stem tips in summer.

PACHYSANDRA (Buxaceae)
Genus of evergreen, creeping perennials and sub-shrubs, grown for their tufted foliage. Is useful for ground cover. Fully hardy. Tolerates dense shade and well-drained soil. Propagate by division in spring.
P. axillaris. Evergreen, mat-forming sub-shrub. H 8in (20cm), S 10in (25cm). Zones 5–8. Stems are each crowned by 3–6 oval, toothed, leathery leaves. Carries small, white flowers in erect spikes in late spring.
P. terminalis illus. p.328. **'Variegata'** is an evergreen, creeping perennial. H 4in (10cm), S 8in (20cm). Zones 4–8. Diamond-shaped, cream-variegated leaves are clustered at stem tips. In early summer bears spikes of tiny, white flowers, sometimes flushed purple.

PACHYSTACHYS (Acanthaceae)
Genus of evergreen perennials and shrubs, grown for their flowers. Frost tender, min. 55–64°F (13–18°C). Needs partial shade and fertile, well-drained soil. Water potted plants freely when in full growth, moderately at other times. Cut back flowered stems in late winter to maintain a bushy habit. Propagate by greenwood cuttings in early summer. Whitefly and red spider mite may cause problems.
P. cardinalis. See *P. coccinea.*
P. coccinea, syn. *P. cardinalis, Jacobinia coccinea, Justicia coccinea* (Cardinal's guard). Evergreen, erect, robust shrub. H 4–6ft (1.2–2m), S 2–3ft (60cm–1m). Min. 59–64°F (15–18°C) to flower well, zone 10. Leaves are oval and deep green. Has tubular, bright red flowers in tight, green-bracted spikes, 6in (15cm) long, in winter.
P. lutea illus. p.125.

x PACHYVERIA (Crassulaceae)
Hybrid genus (*Echeveria* x *Pachyphytum*) of clump-forming, rosetted, perennial succulents, sometimes almost stemless. Frost tender, min. 41–5°F (5–7°C). Needs full sun or partial shade and very well-drained soil. Propagate by leaf or stem cuttings in spring or summer.
x *P. glauca* illus. p.386.

PAEONIA (Paeoniaceae)
Peony
Genus of perennials and deciduous shrubs ("tree peonies"), valued for their bold foliage, showy blooms, and, in some species, colorful seed pods. Fully hardy, zones 4–8, except where otherwise stated, although young growth (especially on tree peonies) may be damaged by late spring frosts. Prefers sun (but will tolerate light shade) and rich, well-drained soil. Tall and exceptionally large-flowered cultivars require support. Propagate all species by seed in autumn (may take up to 3 years to germinate), tuberous species by root cuttings in winter, tree peonies by semi-ripe cuttings in late summer or by grafting in winter. Perennials may also be propagated by division in autumn or early spring. Is susceptible to peony wilt.

Flower forms
Unless stated otherwise, peonies described below flower between late spring and early to mid-summer and have large, alternate leaves divided into oval to lance-shaped or linear leaflets. Flowers are either single, semi-double, double, or anemone-form.
Single—flowers are mostly cup-shaped, each with 1 or 2 rows of large, often lightly ruffled, incurving petals and a conspicuous central boss of stamens.
Semi-double—flowers are similar to single ones, but have 2 or 3 rows of petals.
Double—flowers are rounded, usually composed of 1 or 2 outer rows of large, often lightly ruffled, incurving petals, the remaining petals being smaller, usually becoming more densely arranged and diminishing in size towards the center. Stamens are few, inconspicuous, or absent.
Anemone-form (Imperial or Japanese)—flowers usually have 1 or 2 rows of broad, incurving, outer petals; the center of the flower is often filled entirely with numerous densely arranged, sometimes deeply cut, narrow petaloids derived from stamens.

P. **'America'.** Clump-forming perennial. H and S to 3ft (1m). Has large, single flowers with very broad, deep crimson petals, lightly ruffled at margins.
P. **'Argosy'** (illus. p.199). Deciduous, upright shrub (tree peony). H and S to 5ft (1.5m). Magnificent, large, single flowers are lemon yellow, each with a crimson-purple blotch at base. Is hard to propagate.
P. arietina. Clump-forming, tuberous perennial. H to 2^1/$_2$ft (75cm), S to 2ft (60cm). Zones 5–8. Single flowers are reddish pink. Leaflets are hairy beneath, which distinguishes *P. arietina* from the closely related *P. mascula.*
P. **'Auguste Dessert'** (illus. p.198). Clump-forming perennial. H and S to 2^1/$_2$ft (75cm). Foliage provides rich autumn color. Has masses of fragrant, semi-double flowers; carmine petals are tinged salmon pink and have slightly ruffled, striking silvery white margins.
P. **'Avant Garde'** (illus. p.198). Clump-forming perennial. H and S to 3ft (1m). Has luxuriant foliage. Medium-sized to large, fragrant, single flowers are pale rose-pink with darker veins and bright golden anthers that have yellow-red filaments. Flowers are borne on stiff, straight stems in mid-spring and are ideal for cutting.
P. **'Ballerina'** (illus. p.198). Clump-forming perennial. H and S 3ft (1m). Foliage provides autumn color. Fragrant, double flowers are soft blush pink, tinged lilac at first, later fading to white. Outer rows of petals are loosely arranged, very broad and incurving; inner petals are also incurving, but more densely arranged, narrower, more uneven in size and often have slightly ruffled margins.

P. **'Baroness Schroeder'** (illus. p.198). Vigorous, clump-forming perennial. H and S to 3ft (1m). Is very free-flowering with large, fragrant, globe-shaped, double flowers, tinged with pale flesh pink on opening but fading to almost pure white. Has several rows of almost flat, outer petals; inner petals are incurving, ruffled, and very tightly arranged. Is one of the best peonies for cutting.
P. **'Barrymore'.** Clump-forming perennial. H and S to 34in (85cm). Has very large, anemone-form flowers with broad, outer petals that are palest blush pink on opening, later white. Clear pale golden yellow petaloids are very narrow, relatively short, and are neatly and densely arranged.
P. **'Bowl of Beauty'** (illus. p.198). Clump-forming perennial. H and S to 3ft (1m). Has very large, striking, anemone-form flowers with pale carmine pink, outer petals and numerous narrow, densely arranged, ivory white petaloids.
P. cambessedesii (Majorcan peony). Clump-forming perennial. H and S 1^1/$_2$ft (45cm). Frost hardy, zones 7–8. Has especially attractive foliage, dark green above with veins, stalks, and under-surfaces suffused purple-red. Single, deep rose-pink flowers are borne in mid-spring.
P. **'Cheddar Cheese'.** Clump-forming perennial. H and S to 3ft (1m). Produces well-formed, large, double flowers in mid-summer. Neatly and densely arranged, slightly ruffled, ivory white petals, the inner ones incurving, are interspersed with shorter, yellow petals.
P. **'Colonel Heneage'.** Clump-forming perennial of upright habit. H and S to 34in (85cm). Has masses of anemone-form flowers with both outer petals and inner petaloids of clear dark rose-crimson.
P. corallina. See *P. mascula.*
P. **'Cornelia Shaylor'** (illus. p.198). Erect, clump-forming perennial. H and S to 34in (85cm). Fragrant, double flowers, flushed rose-pink on opening and gradually fading to blush white, are borne freely from early to mid-summer. Ruffled petals are neatly and densely arranged.
P. **'Dayspring'.** Clump-forming perennial. H and S to 28in (70cm). Has an abundance of fragrant, single, clear pink flowers borne in trusses.
P. delavayi (illus. p.199). Deciduous, upright, open shrub (tree peony). H to 6ft (2m), S to 4ft (1.2m). Zones 5–8. Leaves are divided into pointed-oval leaflets, often with reddish stalks. Single flowers are small, bowl-shaped, and rich dark red, with conspicuous, leafy bracts below flowers.
P. **'Dresden'.** Robust, clump-forming perennial. H and S to 34in (85cm). Foliage provides autumn color. Single flowers are ivory white, tinged with soft blush rose-pink.

P. **'Duchesse de Nemours'**, syn. *P.* 'Mrs. Gwyn Lewis' (illus. p.198). Vigorous, clump-forming perennial. H and S to 28in (70cm). Produces masses of richly fragrant, double flowers with very large, incurving, outer petals, tinged palest green at first, soon fading to pure white; inner petals with irregular margins are densely arranged towards the center and are creamy yellow at their base.

P. **emodi** (illus. p.198). Clump-forming perennial. H to 4ft (1.2m), S to 3ft (1m). Zones 5–8. Glossy, green foliage is topped by tall stems bearing several large, fragrant, single, pure white flowers with golden yellow anthers.

P. **'Evening World'**. Clump-forming perennial. H and S to 3ft (1m). Has abundant, large, anemone-form flowers with soft blush pink, outer petals and very tightly arranged, pale flesh pink petaloids.

P. **'Félix Crousse'**, syn. *P.* 'Victor Hugo'. Vigorous, clump-forming perennial. H and S to 30in (75cm). Bears a profusion of fragrant, double, rich carmine pink flowers with darker red centers. Petals are ruffled, very numerous, and tightly arranged, with margins sometimes tipped silvery white.

P. **'Festiva Maxima'**. Clump-forming perennial. H and S to 3ft (1m). Has dense, spreading foliage and huge, fragrant, double flowers borne on strong stems. Rather loosely arranged petals are large with irregular margins; outer petals are pure white, inner ones each have a basal, crimson blotch.

P. **'Flamingo'**. Clump-forming perennial. H and S to 34in (85cm). Foliage provides autumn color. Double flowers are large and clear pale salmon pink.

P. **'Globe of Light'** (illus. p.198). Clump-forming perennial. H and S to 3ft (1m). Has large, fragrant, anemone-form flowers. Outer petals are pure rose-pink, petaloids clear golden yellow.

P. **'Heirloom'**. Compact, clump-forming perennial. H and S to 28in (70cm). Bears masses of large, fragrant, double, pale lilac-pink flowers.

P. **'Instituteur Doriat'** (illus. p.199). Clump-forming perennial. H and S to 3ft (1m). Foliage provides autumn color. Has abundant, large, anemone-form flowers with reddish carmine, outer petals and densely arranged, relatively broad petaloids, paler and more pink than outer petals, with ruffled, silvery white margins.

P. **'Kelway's Gorgeous'** (illus. p.198). Clump-forming perennial. H and S to 34in (85cm). Single, intense clear carmine flowers, with a hint of salmon pink, are produced very freely.

P. **'Kelway's Majestic'**. Clump-forming perennial. H and S to 3ft (1m). Freely borne, large, fragrant, anemone-form flowers have bright cherry rose-pink, outer petals and lilac-pink petaloids flecked with silver or pale gold.

P. **'Kelway's Supreme'** (illus. p.198). Clump-forming perennial. H and S to 3ft (1m). Foliage provides autumn

color. Has large, strongly fragrant, double flowers, produced over a long period, sometimes borne in clusters on well-established plants. Petals are broad, incurving, soft blush pink, fading to milk white. Single or semi-double axillary flowers are often produced.

P. **'Knighthood'** (illus. p.199). Clump-forming perennial. H and S to 30in (75cm). Double flowers have densely arranged, rather narrow, ruffled petals of unusually rich burgundy red.

P. **'Krinkled White'** (illus. p.198). Robust, clump-forming perennial. H and S to 32in (80cm). Large, bowl-shaped, single, milk white flowers are sometimes flushed palest pink. Petals are large with ruffled margins.

P. **'Laura Dessert'** (illus. p.199). Clump-forming perennial. H and S to 30in (75cm). Produces fragrant, double flowers with creamy blush white, outer petals. Densely arranged, incurving, inner petals are flushed rich lemon yellow, and their margins are sometimes deeply cut.

P. **lobata**. See *P. peregrina*.

P. **lutea** (Tibetan peony). Deciduous, upright shrub (tree peony). H and S to 5ft (1.5m). Zones 5–8. Single flowers are usually vivid yellow; brownish or purplish yellow forms also occur. var. *ludlowii* (illus. p.199), H and S to 8ft (2.5m), is grown as much for its large, bright green leaves, divided into deeply cut, pointed leaflets, as for its bowl-shaped, golden yellow flowers.

P. **'Mme. Louis Henri'** (illus. p.199). Deciduous, upright shrub (tree peony). H and S to 5ft (1.5m). Has loosely semi-double, whitish yellow flowers with large, incurving, outer petals very heavily suffused with rusty red. Smaller, often darker, inner petals each have a basal, dull red blotch.

P. **'Magic Orb'** (illus. p.198). Clump-forming perennial. H and S to 3ft (1m). Foliage provides autumn color. Bears masses of large, strongly fragrant, double flowers, each with several outer whorls of fairly broad, ruffled, intense cherry pink petals and a center of densely arranged, smaller, incurving petals. Outermost rows of central petals are blush white, heavily shaded with rose-carmine; the innermost petals are mostly creamy white.

P. **mascula**, syn. *P. corallina* (illus. p.198). Clump-forming perennial. H and S to 3ft (1m). Zones 5–8. Foliage is shiny, hairless, and dark green; stems are dark red. Produces single, purple- or carmine red, occasionally white, flowers with bosses of golden yellow anthers borne on purple filaments. Seed capsules with 2–5 boat-shaped sections split to reveal purplish black seeds.

P. **mlokosewitschii** (illus. p.199). Clump-forming perennial. H and S to 30in (75cm). Zones 5–8. Soft bluish green foliage, sometimes edged reddish purple, is topped by large, single, lemon yellow flowers.

P. **'Mother of Pearl'** (illus. p.198). Clump-forming perennial. H to 2¹/₂ft (75cm), S to 2ft (60cm). Grayish green leaves provide an attractive foil for the single, dog rose-pink flowers.

P. **'Mrs. Gwyn Lewis'**. See *P.* 'Duchesse de Nemours'.

P. **officinalis**. Clump-forming, tuberous perennial. H and S to 2ft (60cm). This single, red apothecaries' peony has long been in cultivation, but is seldom seen today, having been superseded by larger, often double-flowered hybrids, such as the following. **'China Rose'** (illus. p.198), H and S to 18in (45cm), has handsome, dark green foliage and single flowers with incurving, clear dark salmon rose petals contrasting with central bosses of orange-yellow anthers. **'Rubra Plena'** (illus. p.199), H and S to 30in (75cm), is long-lived and has distinctive foliage, divided into broadly oval leaflets, and double, vivid pinkish crimson flowers with ruffled petals.

P. **peregrina**, syn. *P. lobata*. Clump-forming, tuberous perennial. H and S to 3ft (1m). Zones 5–8. Produces bowl-shaped, single, ruby red flowers. **'Sunshine'** (illus. p.199) has glossy, bright green leaves and bears large, single, vermilion flowers, tinged with salmon rose.

P. **potaninii**. Deciduous, rhizomatous shrub (tree peony). H to 2ft (60cm), S indefinite. Zones 5–8. Has deeply divided leaves with narrowly oval, irregularly cut or lobed leaflets and small, single, deep maroon-red, or occasionally white flowers. Is similar to *P. delavayi*, but is more invasive and has less conspicuous, leafy bracts below the flowers. var. *trollioides* has finely divided leaves and yellow flowers.

P. **'Président Poincaré'**. Clump-forming perennial. H and S to 3ft (1m). Foliage provides autumn color. Fragrant, double, clear rich ruby crimson flowers are borne very freely.

P. **'Sarah Bernhardt'** (illus. p.198). Vigorous, erect, clump-forming perennial. H and S to 3ft (1m). Bears an abundance of huge, fragrant, fully double flowers with large, ruffled, slightly dull rose-pink petals, fading to silvery blush white at margins.

P. **'Shirley Temple'** (illus. p.198). Clump-forming perennial. H and S to 34in (85cm). Profuse, soft rose-pink flowers, fading to palest buff-white, are fully double, with broad petals arranged in whorls; innermost petals are smaller and more loosely packed.

P. **'Silver Flare'** (illus. p.199). Clump-forming perennial. H and S to 3ft (1m). Foliage provides autumn color. Stems are flushed dull reddish brown. Produces masses of fragrant, single flowers with rather long, slender, rich carmine pink petals, each feathering to a striking silvery white margin.

P. **'Sir Edward Elgar'** (illus. p.199). Clump-forming perennial. H and S to 30in (75cm). Foliage provides autumn color. Has an abundance of single, chocolate brown-tinged, rich crimson flowers with bosses of loosely arranged, clear lemon yellow anthers.

P. **'Souvenir de Maxime Cornu'** (illus. p.199). Deciduous, upright shrub (tree peony). H and S to 5ft (1.5m). Large, richly fragrant flowers are fully double with warm golden yellow petals densely arranged

towards centers; ruffled margins are dull reddish orange.

P. **suffruticosa** (Moutan). Deciduous, upright shrub (tree peony). H and S to 7ft (2.2m). Bears variable, large, cup-shaped flowers, single or semi-double, with incurving, rose-pink or white petals, each sometimes with a basal, usually chocolate maroon blotch. Has given rise to many cultivars with semi-double and double flowers. **'Joseph Rock'** see *P.s.* 'Rock's Variety'. **'Reine Elizabeth'** (illus. p.198), H and S to 6ft (2m), has large, fully double flowers with broad, salmon pink petals, flushed with bright copper red and lightly ruffled at margins. **'Renkaku'** ('Flight of Cranes'), H and S to 3ft (1m), bears double flowers, each with broad, incurving, slightly ruffled, ivory white petals, loosely arranged in 3 or more whorls, that surround a large boss of long, golden yellow anthers. **'Rock's Variety'** (syn. *P.s.* 'Joseph Rock'; illus. p.198) has large, spreading, semi-double, white flowers; inner petals each have a basal, dark maroon blotch. Is difficult to propagate.

P. **tenuifolia** (illus. p.199). Clump-forming perennial. H and S to 18in (45cm). Elegant leaves are finely divided into many linear segments. Has single, dark crimson flowers, with golden yellow anthers.

P. **veitchii** (illus. p.198). Clump-forming perennial. H and S to 30in (75cm). Zones 5–8. Shiny, bright green leaves are divided into oblong to elliptic leaflets. In early summer produces nodding, cup-shaped, single, purple-pink flowers.

P. **'Victor Hugo'**. See *P.* 'Félix Crousse'.

P. **'White Wings'** (illus. p.198). Clump-forming perennial. H and S to 34in (85cm). Glossy, dark green foliage also provides autumn color. In mid-summer bears masses of large, fragrant, single flowers with broad, white petals, sometimes tinged sulfur yellow, that are each slightly ruffled at the apex.

P. **'Whitleyi Major'** (illus. p.198). Clump-forming perennial. H to 3ft (1m), S to 2ft (60cm). Foliage and stems are flushed rich reddish brown. Large, single, ivory white flowers have a satin sheen and central bosses of clear yellow anthers.

P. **wittmanniana** (illus. p.199). Clump-forming perennial. H and S to 3ft (1m). Zones 5–8. Has large, single, pale primrose yellow flowers each with a large, central boss of yellow anthers on purple-red filaments. Leaves are divided into broadly oval leaflets, shiny dark green above, paler beneath.

PALIURUS (Rhamnaceae)
Genus of deciduous, spiny, summer-flowering shrubs and trees, grown for their foliage and flowers. *P. spina-christi* is also grown for its religious association, reputedly being the plant from which Christ's crown of thorns was made. Frost hardy. Requires full sun and well-drained soil. Propagate by softwood cuttings in summer or by seed in autumn.

P. **spina-christi** illus. p.90.

PAMIANTHE (Amaryllidaceae)
Genus of one species of evergreen, spring-flowering bulb, grown for its large, strongly fragrant, showy flowers. Frost tender, min. 54°F (12°C). Needs partial shade and rich, well-drained soil. Feed with high-potash liquid fertilizer in summer. Reduce watering in winter but do not dry out. Propagate by seed in spring or by offsets in late winter.
P. peruviana illus. p.342.

PANCRATIUM (Amaryllidaceae)
Genus of bulbs with large, fragrant, daffodil-like flowers in summer. Frost to half hardy. Needs sun and well-drained soil that is warm and dry in summer when bulbs are dormant. Plant at least 6in (15cm) deep. Feed with a high-potash liquid fertilizer every 2 weeks from autumn to spring. Propagate by seed in autumn or by offsets detached in early autumn.
P. illyricum illus. p.350.
P. maritimum (Sea daffodil, Sea lily). Late summer-flowering bulb. H 18in (45cm), S 10–12in (25–30cm). Half hardy, zones 8–10. Has strap-shaped, erect, basal, grayish green leaves. Produces a head of 5–12 white flowers, each with a large, deep cup in the center and 6 spreading petals. Is shy-flowering in cultivation.

PANDANUS (Pandanaceae)
Screw pine
Genus of evergreen trees, shrubs, and scramblers, grown for their foliage and overall appearance. Flowers and fruits only appear on large, mature specimens. Frost tender, min. 55–61°F (13–16°C). Requires full light or partial shade and fertile, well-drained soil. Water potted plants freely when in full growth, moderately at other times. Propagate by seed or suckers in spring or by cuttings of lateral shoots in summer. Red spider mite may be troublesome.
P. odoratissimus. See *P. tectorius.*
P. tectorius, syn. *P. odoratissimus.* Evergreen, rounded tree. H to 20ft (6m), S 10ft (3m) or more. Zone 10. Has rosettes of strap-shaped, deep green leaves, each 3–5ft (1–1.5m) long, with spiny margins and a spiny midrib beneath. Small flowers, the males in clusters, each with a lance-shaped, white bract, appear mainly in summer. Fruits are like round pineapples. **'Veitchii'** see *P. veitchii.*
P. veitchii, syn. *P. tectorius* 'Veitchii', illus. p.143.

PANDOREA (Bignoniaceae)
Genus of evergreen, woody-stemmed, twining climbers, grown for their handsome flowers and attractive leaves. Frost tender, min. 41°F (5°C). Grow in sun and in any well-drained soil. Prune after flowering to restrain growth. Propagate by seed in spring or by stem cuttings or layering in summer.
P. jasminoides, syn. *Bignonia jasminoides*, illus. p.166.
P. pandorana, syn. *Bignonia pandorana*, *Tecoma australis* (Wonga-wonga vine). Fast-growing, evergreen, woody-stemmed, twining climber. H 20ft (6m) or more. Zones 9–10. Leaves

have 3–9 scalloped leaflets. Small, funnel-shaped, cream flowers, streaked and often spotted with red, brown, or purple, are borne in clusters in summer.
P. ricasoliana. See *Podranea ricasoliana.*

PANICUM (Gramineae). See GRASSES, BAMBOOS, RUSHES, and SEDGES.
P. capillare illus. p.182.

PAPAVER (Papaveraceae)
Poppy
Genus of annuals, biennials, and perennials, some of which are semi-evergreen, grown for their cup-shaped flowers. Fully hardy. Needs sun or semi-shade and prefers moist but well-drained soil. Propagate by seed in autumn or spring. *P. orientale* and its cultivars are best propagated by root cuttings in winter. Self seeds readily.
P. alpinum group. See *P. burseri.*
P. atlanticum. Clump-forming, short-lived perennial. H and S 4in (10cm). Zones 5–7. Has oval, toothed, hairy leaves and, in summer, single, dull orange flowers. Is good for a rock garden.
P. burseri (*P. alpinum* group; Alpine poppy). Semi-evergreen, tuft-forming, short-lived perennial, best treated as an annual or biennial. H 6–8in (15–20cm), S 4in (10cm). Fully hardy. Leaves are finely cut and gray. Carries single, white flowers throughout summer. Suits a rock garden, wall, or bank.
P. commutatum **'Lady Bird'.** Fast-growing, erect, branching annual. H and S 18in (45cm). Fully hardy. Has elliptic, deeply lobed, green leaves and, in summer, single, red flowers, each with a black blotch in center.
P. miyabeanum illus. p.324.
P. nudicaule (Iceland poppy). Tuft-forming perennial. H to 12in (30cm), S 4in (10cm). Zones 4–8. Hairy stems each produce a fragrant, single, white-and-yellow flower, sometimes marked green outside, in summer. Many color forms have been selected. Leaves are oval, toothed, and soft green. Needs partial shade. Is good for a rock garden.
P. orientale (Oriental poppy). Rosetted perennial. H 3ft (1m), S 1–3ft (30cm–1m). Zones 4–9. Single, brilliant vermilion flowers, with dark blotches at bases of petals, are borne in early summer. Has broadly lance-shaped, toothed or cut, rough, green leaves. Flowering stems need support. **'Allegro Viva'** illus. p.209. **'Indian Chief'** has deep mahogany red flowers. **'May Queen'** bears double, orange flowers. **'Mrs. Perry'** has large, salmon pink flowers. **'Perry's White'** illus. p.202.
P. rhoeas **Shirley Series** (double) illus. p.266; (single) illus. p.272.
P. somniferum (Opium poppy). Fast-growing, upright annual. H 2½ft (75cm), S 1ft (30cm). Fully hardy. Has oblong, lobed, light grayish green leaves. Large, single flowers, to 4in (10cm) wide, in shades of red, pink, purple, or white, are produced in summer. Several double-flowered forms are available, including **Carnation-flowered Series**, with fringed flowers in mixed colors;

Peony-flowered Series illus. p.265; **'Pink Beauty'**, which has salmon pink flowers; and **'White Cloud'**, with large, white flowers.

PAPHIOPEDILUM. See ORCHIDS.
P. appletonianum (illus. p.252). Evergreen, terrestrial orchid. H 3in (8cm). Frost tender, min. 55°F (13°C), zone 10. In spring, green flowers, 2½in (6cm) across and each with a pouched, brownish lip and pink-flushed petals, are borne singly on tall, slender stems. Has oval, mottled leaves, 4in (10cm) long. Needs shade in summer.
P. bellatulum (illus. p.252). Evergreen, terrestrial orchid. H 2in (5cm). Frost tender, min. 64°F (18°C), zone 10. Almost stemless, rounded, pouch-lipped, white flowers, 3in (8cm) across, spotted with dark maroon, are borne singly in spring. Oval, marbled leaves are 3in (8cm) long. Grow in shade in summer.
P. **Buckhurst 'Mont Millais'** (illus. p.254). Evergreen, terrestrial orchid. H 4in (10cm). Frost tender, min. 55°F (13°C), zone 10. Rounded, yellow-and-white flowers, to 5in (12cm) across and lined and spotted with red, are produced singly in winter. Has oval leaves, 4in (10cm) long. Requires shade in summer.
P. callosum (illus. p.252). Evergreen, terrestrial orchid. H 3in (8cm). Frost tender, min. 55°F (13°C), zone 10. Purple- and green-veined, white flowers, 3in (8cm) across, are borne on tall stems in spring-summer. Has oval, mottled leaves, 4in (10cm) long. Needs shade in summer.
P. fairrieanum (illus. p.252). Evergreen, terrestrial orchid. H 3in (8cm). Frost tender, min. 50°F (10°C), zone 10. Rich purple- and green-veined flowers, 2in (5cm) across, with curved petals and orange-brown pouches, are borne singly in autumn. Oval leaves are 3in (8cm) long. Grow in shade in summer.
P. **Freckles** (illus. p.252). Evergreen, terrestrial orchid. H 4in (10cm). Frost tender, min. 55°F (13°C), zone 10. Rounded, reddish brown-spotted and pouched, white flowers, 4in (10cm) across, are produced singly in winter. Has oval leaves, 4in (10cm) long. Grow in shade in summer.
P. haynaldianum (illus. p.254). Evergreen, terrestrial orchid. H 5in (12cm). Frost tender, min. 55°F (13°C), zone 10. In summer, long-petaled, brown-marked, green-, pink-, and white-flowers, to 6in (15cm) across, are produced singly. Has oval leaves, 8–9in (20–23cm) long. Requires shade in summer.
P. **Lyric 'Glendora'** (illus. p.253). Evergreen, terrestrial orchid. H 4in (10cm). Frost tender, min. 55°F (13°C), zone 10. Rounded, glossy, white-, red-, and green-flowers, 4in (10cm) across, appear singly in winter. Has oval leaves, 6in (15cm) long. Needs shade in summer.
P. x *maudiae* (illus. p.253). Evergreen, terrestrial orchid. H 4in (10cm). Frost tender, min. 55°F (13°C), zone 10. Clear apple green or deep reddish purple flowers, 4in (10cm) across,

appear singly on long stems in spring or early summer. Has oval, mottled leaves, 4in (10cm) long. Requires shade in summer.
P. niveum (illus. p.252). Evergreen, terrestrial orchid. H 2in (5cm). Frost tender, min. 55–64°F (13–18°C), zone 10. White flowers, 1½in (4cm) across, are produced singly, mainly in spring. Oval, marbled leaves are 3in (8cm) long. Needs shade in summer.
P. sukhakulii (illus. p.254). Evergreen, terrestrial orchid. H 3in (8cm). Frost tender, min. 55°F (13°C), zone 10. In spring-summer, purple-pouched, black-spotted, green flowers, 3in (8cm) across, appear singly on tall stems. Has oval, mottled leaves, 4in (10cm) long. Grow in shade in summer.
P. venustum (illus. p.255). Evergreen, terrestrial orchid. H 4in (10cm). Frost tender, min. 55°F (13°C), zone 10. Variably colored flowers, ranging from pink to orange with green veins and darker spots, are 2½in (6cm) across and borne singly in autumn. Has oval, mottled leaves, 4in (10cm) long. Needs shade in summer.

PARAHEBE (Scrophulariaceae)
Genus of evergreen or semi-evergreen, summer-flowering perennials, sub-shrubs, and shrubs, similar to *Hebe* and *Veronica*. Is suitable for rock gardens. Frost hardy. Needs sun and well-drained, peaty, sandy soil. Propagate by semi-ripe cuttings in early summer.
P. catarractae illus. p.296.
P. lyallii. Semi-evergreen, prostrate shrub. H 6in (15cm), S 8–10in (20–25cm). Zones 8–9. Has oval, toothed, leathery leaves and, in early summer, erect stems bearing loose sprays of flattish, pink-veined, white flowers.
P. perfoliata. See *Veronica perfoliata.*

PARAQUILEGIA (Ranunculaceae)
Genus of tufted perennials, grown for their cup-shaped flowers and fernlike foliage. Is difficult to cultivate and flower successfully. Prefers dry winters and cool climates. Is good in alpine houses and troughs. Fully hardy. Needs sun and gritty, well-drained, alkaline soil. Propagate by seed in autumn.
P. grandiflora illus. p.304.

PARIS (Liliaceae, Trilliaceae)
Herb Paris
Genus of summer-flowering, rhizomatous perennials. Fully hardy. Requires shade or semi-shade and humus-rich soil. Propagate by division in spring or by seed in autumn.
P. polyphylla. Erect, rhizomatous perennial. H 2–3ft (60cm–1m), S to 1ft (30cm). Zones 5–8. In early summer, at tips of slender stems, bears unusual flowers consisting of a ruff of green sepals, with another ruff of greenish yellow petals, marked with crimson above, crowned by a violet-purple stigma. Leaves, borne in whorls at stem tips, are lance-shaped to oval and green.

PARKINSONIA (Leguminosae)
Genus of evergreen, spring-flowering shrubs and trees, grown for their

flowers and for their overall appearance. Frost tender, min. 59°F (15°C). Needs fertile, free-draining soil, a dry atmosphere, and as much sunlight as possible to thrive. Water potted specimens moderately when in full growth, sparingly at other times. Pruning is tolerated, but spoils the natural habit. Propagate by seed in spring.

P. aculeata (Jerusalem thorn, Mexican palo verde). Evergreen, feathery shrub or tree with a spiny, green stem. H and S 10–20ft (3–6m) or more. Zone 10. Long, linear leaves have winged midribs bearing tiny, elliptic, short-lived leaflets. Has fragrant, 5-petaled, yellow flowers in arching racemes in spring.

PARNASSIA (Saxifragaceae)
Genus of rosetted, mainly summer-flowering perennials, grown for their saucer-shaped flowers. Is suitable for rock gardens. Fully hardy. Needs sun and wet soil. Propagate by seed in autumn.

P. palustris illus. p.290.

PAROCHETUS (Leguminosae)
Genus of one species of evergreen perennial. Grows best in alpine houses. Half hardy. Needs semi-shade and gritty, moist soil. Propagate by division of rooted runners in any season.

P. communis illus. p.324.

PARODIA (Cactaceae)
Genus of rounded, perennial cacti with tubercles arranged in ribs that often spiral around green stems. Crown forms woolly buds, then funnel-shaped flowers. Frost tender, min. 50°F (10°C). Requires full sun or partial shade and very well-drained soil. Water occasionally and very lightly in winter; tends to lose roots during a long period of drought. Propagate by seed in spring or summer.

P. chrysacanthion illus. p.388.
P. nivosa illus. p.394.
P. sanguiniflora illus. p.394.

PARONYCHIA (Caryophyllaceae)
Genus of evergreen perennials making extensive, loose mats of prostrate stems. Is useful for rock gardens and walls. Fully to frost hardy. Needs sun and well-drained soil. Propagate by division in spring.

P. capitata. Vigorous, evergreen, mat-forming perennial. H 1/2in (1cm), S 16in (40cm). Fully hardy, zones 5–7. Silvery leaves are small and oval. In summer bears inconspicuous flowers surrounded by papery bracts. Makes good ground cover.

P. kapela subsp. *serpyllifolia* illus. p.331.

PARROTIA (Hamamelidaceae)
Genus of one species of deciduous tree, grown for its flowers and autumn color. Fully hardy, but flower buds may be killed by hard frosts. Requires full sun and grows best in fertile, moist but well-drained soil. Is lime-tolerant, but usually colors best in acid soil. Propagate by softwood cuttings in summer or by seed in autumn.

P. persica illus. p.55.

PARROTIOPSIS (Hamamelidaceae)
Genus of one species of deciduous tree or shrub, grown for its ornamental, dense flower heads surrounded by conspicuous bracts. Fully hardy. Needs sun or semi-shade. Grows in any fertile, well-drained soil except very shallow soil over chalk. Propagate by softwood cuttings in summer or by seed in autumn.

P. jacquemontiana. Deciduous, shrubby or upright tree. H 20ft (6m), S 12ft (4m). Zones 6–9. Has witch-hazel-like, dark green leaves that turn yellow in autumn. From mid- to late spring and in summer bears clusters of minute flowers, with tufts of yellow stamens, surrounded by white bracts.

PARTHENOCISSUS (Vitaceae)
Genus of deciduous, woody-stemmed, tendril climbers, grown for their leaves, which often turn beautiful colors in autumn. Broad tips of tendrils have suckerlike pads that cling to supports. Has insignificant, greenish flowers in summer. Will quickly cover north- or east-facing walls or fences and may be grown up large trees. Fully to half hardy. Grow in semi-shade or shade and in well-drained soil. Propagate by softwood or greenwood cuttings in summer or by hardwood cuttings in early spring.

P. henryana, syn. *Vitis henryana.* Deciduous, tendril climber with 4-angled, woody stems. H to 30ft (10m) or more. Frost hardy, zones 7–9. Leaves have 3–5 toothed, oval leaflets, each 1 1/2–5in (4–13cm) long, and are velvety, deep green or bronze with white or pinkish veins. Small, dark blue berries are produced in autumn. Leaf color is best with a north or east aspect.

P. quinquefolia, syn. *Vitis quinquefolia* (Five-leaved ivy, Virginia creeper). Deciduous, woody-stemmed, tendril climber. H 50ft (15m) or more. Frost hardy, zones 4–9. Leaves have 5 oval, toothed, dull green leaflets, paler beneath, that turn a beautiful crimson in autumn. Blue-black berries are produced in autumn. Is ideal for covering a high wall or building.

P. thompsonii, syn. *Vitis thompsonii,* illus. p.176.

P. tricuspidata, syn. *Ampelopsis veitchii,* illus. p.176. **'Lowii'** and **'Veitchii'** illus. p.176.

PASSIFLORA (Passifloraceae)
Passion flower
Genus of evergreen or semi-evergreen, woody-stemmed, tendril climbers, grown for their unique flowers, each one with a central corona of filaments. Many species have egg-shaped to rounded, fleshy, edible fruits that mature to orange or yellow in autumn. Half hardy to frost tender, min. 41–61°F (5–16°C), zone 10 unless otherwise stated below. Grow in any fertile, well-drained soil and in full sun or partial shade. Water freely in full growth, less at other times. Stems need support. Thin out and spur back crowded growth in spring. Propagate by seed in spring or by semi-ripe cuttings in summer.

P. × allardii. Strong-growing, evergreen, woody-stemmed, tendril climber. H 22–30ft (7–10m). Frost tender, min. 45°F (7°C). Has 3-lobed leaves. Flowers, 3–4in (7–10cm) wide, are white, tinted pink, with purple-banded crowns, and are carried in summer-autumn.

P. antioquiensis, syn. *Tacsonia van-volxemii* (Banana passion fruit). Fast-growing, evergreen, woody-stemmed, tendril climber. H 15ft (5m) or more. Frost tender, min. 45°F (7°C). Leaves, with 3 deep lobes, are softly downy. Long-tubed, rose-red flowers, 4–5in (10–12cm) across, with purplish blue centers, appear in summer-autumn.

P. caerulea illus. p.172.

P. × caerulea-racemosa. Vigorous, evergreen, woody-stemmed, tendril climber. H 30ft (10m). Frost tender, min. 45–50°F (7–10°C), zones 9–10. Has 3-lobed leaves. Purple flowers, 3in (8cm) across, appear in summer-autumn.

P. × caponii **'John Innes'** illus. p.172.

P. coccinea illus. p.163.

P. × exoniensis. Fast-growing, evergreen, woody-stemmed, tendril climber. H 25ft (8m) or more. Frost tender, min. 45°F (7°C). Leaves have 3 deep lobes and are softly downy. Rose-pink flowers, 3in (8cm) across, with purplish blue crowns, are produced in summer-autumn.

P. manicata illus. p.175.

P. mollissima, syn. *Tacsonia mollissima.* Fast-growing, evergreen, woody-stemmed, tendril climber. H 15ft (5m) or more. Frost tender, min. 45°F (7°C). Softly downy leaves have 3 deep lobes. Long-tubed, pink flowers, to 3in (8cm) wide, each with a purplish blue crown, appear in summer-autumn.

P. quadrangularis illus. p.173.

P. racemosa (Red passion flower). Fast-growing, evergreen, tendril climber with slender, woody stems. H 15ft (5m). Frost tender, min. 59°F (15°C). Has wavy, leathery leaves with 3 deep lobes. In summer-autumn bears terminal racemes of pendent, crimson flowers, 3–4in (8–10cm) across, with short, white- and purple-banded crowns.

P. sanguinea. See *P. vitifolia.*

P. vitifolia, syn. *P. sanguinea.* Evergreen, woody-stemmed, tendril climber; slender stems have fine, brown hairs. H to 15ft (5m). Frost tender, min. 61°F (16°C). Has 3-lobed, lustrous leaves. In summer-autumn bears bright scarlet flowers, 5in (13cm) wide, each with a short crown, banded red, yellow, and white.

PATERSONIA (Iridaceae)
Genus of evergreen, clump-forming, spring- and early summer-flowering, rhizomatous perennials. Half hardy. Needs full sun and light, well-drained soil. Leave undisturbed once planted. Propagate by seed in autumn.

P. umbrosa illus. p.352.

PATRINIA (Valerianaceae)
Genus of perennials, forming neat clumps, grown for their flowers. Is suitable for rock gardens and peat beds. Fully hardy. Needs partial shade and moist soil. Propagate by division in spring or by seed in autumn. Self seeds freely.

P. triloba. Clump-forming perennial. H 8–20in (20–50cm), S 6–12in (15–30cm). Zones 5–8. Flower stems produce flat heads of small, golden yellow flowers throughout summer. Rounded, 3- to 5-lobed, green leaves turn gold in autumn.

PAULOWNIA (Scrophulariaceae)
Genus of deciduous trees, grown for their large leaves and foxglovelike flowers, borne before the foliage emerges. Fully to frost hardy, but flower buds and young growth of small plants may be damaged by very hard frosts in winter. Requires full sun and fertile, moist but well-drained soil. In cold areas may be grown for foliage only by cutting back young shoots hard in spring and cutting out all but one of the subsequent shoots; this results in very large leaves. Propagate by seed in autumn or spring or by root cuttings in winter.

P. fortunei. Deciduous, spreading tree. H and S 25ft (8m). Fully hardy, zones 7–9. Has large, oval, green leaves. In late spring bears large, fragrant flowers, purple-spotted and white inside, pale purple outside.

P. imperialis. See *P. tomentosa.*

P. tomentosa, syn. *P. imperialis,* illus. p.49.

PAVONIA (Malvaceae)
Genus of evergreen, mainly summer-flowering perennials and shrubs, grown usually for their flowers. Frost tender, min. 61–4°F (16–18°C). Needs full light or partial shade and humus-rich, well-drained soil. Water freely when in full growth, moderately at other times. Leggy stems may be cut back hard in spring. Propagate by seed in spring or by greenwood cuttings in summer. Whitefly and red spider mite may be troublesome.

P. hastata. Evergreen, erect shrub. H 6–10ft (2–3m), S 3–6ft (1–2m). Zone 10. Has lance-shaped to oval, green leaves, each with 2 basal lobes. Funnel-shaped, pale red to white flowers, with darker basal spotting, appear in summer.

PAXISTIMA, syn. PACHISTIMA (Celastraceae)
Genus of evergreen, spreading shrubs and sub-shrubs, grown for their foliage. Makes good ground cover. Fully hardy. Prefers shade and humus-rich, moist soil. Propagate by division in spring or by semi-ripe cuttings in summer.

P. canbyi. Evergreen, spreading sub-shrub. H 6–12in (15–30cm), S 8in (20cm). Zones 4–8. Has linear or oblong leaves and, in summer, short, pendent spikes of tiny, greenish white flowers.

PEDILANTHUS (Euphorbiaceae)
Genus of bushy, summer-flowering, perennial succulents containing poisonous, milky sap. Produces small, yellowish green, pink, red, or brown bracts that are each shaped like a bird's head. Frost tender, min. 50–52°F (10–11°C). Needs sun or partial shade and well-drained soil. Propagate by seed or stem cuttings in spring or summer.

P. tithymaloides. Bushy, perennial succulent. H 10ft (3m), S 1ft (30cm). Min 50°F (10°C), zone 10. Has thin, erect stems zigzagging at each node. Leaves are green and boat-shaped, with prominent ribs beneath. Stem tips each bear red to yellowish green bracts in summer. Prefers partial shade. **'Variegata'** illus. p.381.

PELARGONIUM (Geraniaceae)
Geranium
Genus of mainly summer-flowering perennials, most of which are evergreen, cultivated as annuals. Is grown for its colorful flowers and is useful in pots or as bedding plants; in warm conditions flowers are borne almost continuously. Frost tender, min. 34°F (1°C), unless otherwise stated. Dislikes very hot, humid conditions. Well-drained, neutral to alkaline soil is preferred, and a sunny site with 12 hours of daylight is required for good flowering. Dead-head frequently and fertilize regularly if grown in pots; do not overwater. Plants may be kept through winter in the greenhouse by cutting back in autumn-winter to 5in (12cm) and repotting. Propagate by softwood cuttings from spring to autumn.

Pelargoniums may be divided into 4 groups; all flower in summer-autumn unless stated otherwise.:
Zonal—plants with rounded leaves, distinctively marked with a darker "zone," and single (5-petaled), semi-double, or fully double flowers;
Regal—shrubby plants with rounded to oval, deeply serrated leaves and broadly trumpet-shaped, exotic-colored flowers that are prone to weather damage in the open;
Ivy-leaved—trailing plants, ideal for hanging baskets, with rounded, lobed leaves and flowers similar to those of zonal pelargoniums;
Scented-leaved and **species**—plants with small, often irregularly star-shaped flowers; scented-leaved forms are grown for their fragrant leaves.

P. **'Alberta'** (illus. p.206). Evergreen zonal pelargonium. H 18in (45cm), S 12in (30cm). Bears clusters of small, single, crimson-and-white flowers. Is best grown as a bedding plant.
P. **'Appleblossom Rosebud'.** Evergreen zonal pelargonium. H 12in (30cm), S 9in (23cm). Fully double, pinkish white flowers, edged with red, look like miniature rosebuds.
P. **'Autumn Festival'** (illus. p.206). Evergreen, bushy regal pelargonium. H and S 12in (30cm). Salmon pink flowers have pronounced, white throats.
P. **'Bredon'** (illus. p.206). Strong-growing, evergreen regal pelargonium. H 18in (45cm), S to 12in (30cm). Has large, maroon flowers.
P. **'Caligula'** (illus. p.207). Evergreen, miniature zonal pelargonium. H 6–8in (15–20cm), S 4in (10cm). Has small, double, crimson flowers and tiny, dark green leaves. Suits a windowsill.
P. capitatum (illus. p.207). Evergreen scented-leaved pelargonium. H 12–24in (30–60cm), S 12in (30cm). Has mauve flowers and irregularly 3-lobed leaves that smell faintly of roses. Is mainly

used to produce geranium oil for the perfume industry, but may be grown as a pot plant.
P. carnosum. Deciduous, shrubby pelargonium (unclassified), with thick, succulent stems and a woody, swollen, tuberlike rootstock. H and S 1ft (30cm). Min. 50°F (10°C). Has long, gray-green leaves with triangular, deeply lobed leaflets. Produces branched, umbel-like flower heads with white or greenish yellow flowers, the upper petals streaked red and shorter than the green sepals.
P. **'Chew Magna'.** Evergreen regal pelargonium. H 12–18in (30–45cm), S to 12in (30cm). Each petal of the pale pink flowers has a wine red blaze.
P. crispum (Lemon geranium). **'Old Spice'** is an evergreen, upright scented-leaved pelargonium. H to 3ft (1m), S 1–1½ft (30–45cm). Small, rounded, shallowly lobed, pale green-and-cream leaves have a lemon fragrance and are crinkled at edges like parsley. Single flowers are pale purplish pink. **'Variegatum'** (illus. p.207) has gold-variegated leaves and small, pale lilac flowers. Foliage tends to become creamy white in winter.
P. **'Dale Queen'** (illus. p.206). Evergreen, bushy zonal pelargonium. H 9–12in (23–30cm), S 9in (23cm). Single flowers are delicate salmon pink. Is particularly suitable for a pot.
P., **Diamond Series.** Group of slow-growing, evergreen, compact, bushy zonal pelargoniums. H and S 1–2ft (30–60cm). Half hardy. Has rounded, lobed, light to mid-green leaves, often zoned with bronze or red. Large, domed heads of weather-resistant, single flowers are available in a range of colors, including shades of red and rose-pink (scarlet, illus. p.272).
P. **'Dolly Varden'** (illus. p.207). Evergreen zonal pelargonium. H 12in (30cm), S 9in (23cm). Green leaves have handsome, purple-brown, white, and crimson markings. Single, scarlet flowers are insignificant.
P. **'Elégante'** (illus. p.207). Evergreen, trailing ivy-leaved pelargonium. H and S to 24in (60m). Foliage is variegated with creamy white margins, sometimes turning pink at the edges; semi-double flowers are pale mauve. Is best grown in a hanging basket.
P. **'Emma Hossler'.** Evergreen, dwarf zonal pelargonium. H 8–10in (20–25cm), S 6in (15cm). Bears large, fully double, mauve-pink flowers. Is useful for a window box.
P. **'Flower of Spring'** (Silver-leaved geranium; illus. p.207). Vigorous, evergreen zonal pelargonium. H 2ft (60cm), S 1ft (30cm). Has green-and-white leaves and single, red flowers.
P. x *fragrans* (illus. p.206). Evergreen, very bushy scented-leaved pelargonium. H and S 12in (30cm). Rounded, shallowly lobed, gray-green leaves smell strongly of pine. Bears small, white flowers.
P. **'Fraicher Beauty'** (illus. p.206). Evergreen zonal pelargonium. H 12in (30cm), S 9in (23cm). Flowers are fully double and perfectly formed with delicate coloring: white with a thin, red edge to each petal. Is excellent as a pot plant.

P. **'Francis Parrett'** (illus. p.206). Evergreen, short-jointed zonal pelargonium. H 6–8in (15–20cm), S 4in (10cm). Bears fully double, purplish mauve flowers and small, green leaves. Is good for a windowsill.
P. **'Friesdorf'** (illus. p.206). Evergreen zonal pelargonium. H 10in (25cm), S 6in (15cm). Has dark green foliage and narrow-petaled, single, orange-scarlet flowers. Is good for a window box or planted in a large group.
P. frutetorum. Evergreen, trailing pelargonium (unclassified). H and S to 24in (60cm). Has unusual, 5-lobed, notched leaves, each with a central, dark brown blotch, and long-stemmed, single, salmon pink flowers. **'The Boar'** (illus. p.206) is useful for a hanging basket.
P. **'Irene'** (illus. p.206). Evergreen zonal pelargonium. H 18in (45cm), S 9–12in (23–30cm). Bears large, semi-double, light crimson blooms.
P. **'Ivalo'** (illus. p.206). Evergreen, bushy, short-jointed zonal pelargonium. H 9–12in (23–30cm), S 9in (23cm). Large, semi-double flowers are pale pink with crimson-dotted, white centers.
P. **'Lesley Judd'** (illus. p.206). Vigorous, evergreen, bushy regal pelargonium. H 12–18in (30–45cm), S to 12in (30cm). Flowers are soft salmon pink with a central, red blotch. Pinch out growing tips before flowering to control shape.
P. **'Mabel Grey'** (illus. p.207). Evergreen scented-leaved pelargonium. H 18–24in (45–60cm), S 12–18in (30–45cm). Has diamond-shaped, rough-textured, toothed, strongly lemon-scented leaves, with 5–7 pointed lobes, and mauve flowers.
P. **'Mme. Fournier'** (illus. p.207). Evergreen, short-jointed zonal pelargonium. H 6–8in (15–20cm), S 4in (10cm). Small, single, scarlet flowers contrast well with almost black leaves. Is useful for a pot or as a summer bedding plant.
P. **'Manx Maid'** (illus. p.206). Evergreen regal pelargonium. H 12–15in (30–38cm), S 10in (25cm). Flowers and leaves are small for regal type. Pink flowers are veined and blotched with burgundy.
P. **'Mauritania'** (illus. p.206). Evergreen zonal pelargonium. H 12in (30cm), S 9in (23cm). Single, white flowers are ringed towards centers with pale salmon pink.
P. **'Mini Cascade'** (illus. p.206). Evergreen, trailing, short-jointed ivy-leaved pelargonium. H and S 12–18in (30–45cm). Bears many single, red flowers. Regular dead-heading is essential for continuous display.
P. **'Mr. Henry Cox'** (illus. p.206). Evergreen zonal pelargonium. H 12in (30cm), S 6in (15cm). Green leaves are marked with red, yellow, and purple-brown. Flowers are single and pink.
P. **'Mrs. Pollock'** (illus. p.207). Evergreen zonal pelargonium. H 12in (30cm), S 6in (15cm). Each golden leaf has a gray-green butterfly mark in center, with a bronze zone running through it. Bears small, single, orange-red flowers.

P. **'Mrs. Quilter'** (illus. p.207). Evergreen zonal pelargonium. H 12in (30cm), S 9in (23cm). Has yellow leaves with wide, chestnut brown zones and single, pink flowers.
P. **'Orange Ricard'** (illus. p.207). Vigorous, robust, evergreen zonal pelargonium. H 18–24in (45–60cm), S 12in (30cm). Produces masses of large, semi-double, orange blooms.
P., **Orbit Series.** Group of slow-growing, evergreen, bushy zonal pelargoniums. H and S 1–2ft (30–60cm). Half hardy. Has rounded, lobed, bronze- or red-zoned, green leaves and large, domed, single flower heads in mixed or separate colors, including shades of white, pink, red, and orange (salmon, illus. p.265).
P. **'Paul Humphris'** (illus. p.206). Evergreen, bushy, compact zonal pelargonium. H 12in (30cm), S 9in (23cm). Has fully double, deep wine red flowers. Is good as a pot plant.
P. peltatum. Evergreen, trailing, brittle-jointed pelargonium from which ivy-leaved cultivars have been derived. H and S to 5ft (1.5m). Has fleshy leaves, with pointed lobes, and single, mauve or white flowers. Cultivars suit hanging baskets and window boxes. **'Amethyst'** (illus. p.206) has fully double flowers of light mauve-purple. Flowers of **'Lachskönigin'** (illus. p.206) are semi-double and mauve-purple. **'Tavira'** (illus. p.206) bears single, soft crimson flowers.
P. **'Purple Emperor'** (illus. p.206). Evergreen regal pelargonium. H 18in (45cm), S 12in (30cm). Pink-mauve flowers have a deeper, central coloration. Flowers well into the autumn.
P. **'Purple Unique'** (illus. p.207). Vigorous, evergreen, upright, shrubby pelargonium (unclassified). H and S 3ft (1m) or more. Rounded, large-lobed leaves are very aromatic. Has single, open trumpet-shaped, light purple flowers. Does well when trained against a sunny wall.
P. **'Rollinson's Unique'** (illus. p.206). Evergreen, shrubby pelargonium (unclassified). H 2ft (60cm) or more, S 1ft (30cm). Has oval, notched, pungent leaves and small, single, open trumpet-shaped, wine red flowers with purple veins.
P. **'Rouletta'** (illus. p.206). Vigorous, evergreen, trailing ivy-leaved pelargonium. H and S 2–3ft (60cm–1m). Bears semi-double, red-and-white flowers. To control shape, growing tips should be pinched out regularly.
P. **'Royal Oak'** (illus. p.207). Evergreen, bushy, compact scented-leaved pelargonium. H 15in (38cm), S 12in (30cm). Oaklike, slightly sticky leaves have a spicy fragrance and are dark green with central, brown markings. Flowers are small and mauve-pink.
P. **'Schöne Helena'** (illus. p.206). Evergreen zonal pelargonium. H 12–18in (30–45cm), S 9in (23cm). Produces masses of large, semi-double, salmon pink blooms.
P., **Sprinter Series.** Group of slow-growing, evergreen, branching, bushy zonal pelargoniums, grown as annuals.

H and S 1–2ft (30–60cm). Half hardy. Has rounded, lobed, light to mid-green leaves. Bears large, domed, single flower heads in shades of red. Is very free-flowering.
P. 'Timothy Clifford' (illus. p.206). Evergreen, short-jointed zonal pelargonium. H 6–8in (15–20cm), S 4in (10cm). Has dark green leaves and fully double, salmon pink flowers. Suits a windowsill.
P. 'Tip Top Duet' (illus. p.206). Evergreen, bushy, free-branching regal pelargonium. H 12–15in (30–38cm), S 10in (25cm). Leaves and blooms are small for regal type. Bears pink-veined, white flowers; uppermost petals have dark burgundy blotches.
P. tomentosum (Peppermint geranium; illus. p.207). Evergreen, bushy scented-leaved pelargonium. H 1–2ft (30–60cm), S 3ft (1m). Large, rounded, shallowly lobed, velvety, gray-green leaves have a strong peppermint aroma. Bears clusters of small, white flowers. Growing tips should be pinched out to control spread. Dislikes full sun.
P., Video Series. Group of slow-growing, evergreen, branching, bushy zonal pelargoniums, grown as annuals. H and S 1–2ft (30–60cm). Half hardy. Has rounded, lobed, bronze-zoned, deep green leaves and large, domed, single flower heads in white and shades of pink or red.

PELLAEA (Polypodiaceae)
Genus of deciduous, semi-evergreen, or evergreen ferns. Half hardy to frost tender, min. 41°F (5°C). Grow in semi-shade and gritty, moist but well-drained soil. Remove fading fronds regularly. Propagate by spores in summer.
P. atropurpurea (Purple rock brake; Purple-stemmed cliff brake). Semi-evergreen or evergreen fern. H and S 12in (30cm). Frost tender, zones 9–10. Small, narrowly lance-shaped, divided fronds have oblong, blunt pinnae and are dark green with a purplish tinge.
P. rotundifolia (Button fern). Evergreen fern. H and S 6in (15cm). Frost tender, zones 9–10. Has small, narrowly lance-shaped, divided, dark green fronds that have rounded pinnae.

PELLIONIA (Urticaceae)
Genus of evergreen, creeping perennials with attractive foliage that tends to lie flat, making useful ground cover. Frost tender, min. 59°F (15°C). Requires a humid atmosphere, away from drafts, indirect light, and moist soil. Propagate from rooting stems or stem cuttings in spring or summer.
P. daveauana, syn. *P. repens*, illus. p.259.
P. pulchra. Evergreen, slightly fleshy perennial with rooting, creeping stems. H 3–4in (8–10cm), S 2ft (60cm) or more. Zone 10. Broadly oval leaves, 2in (5cm) long, are green with dark brown veins above, purple below. Flowers are insignificant.
P. repens. See *P. daveauana*.

PELTIPHYLLUM (Saxifragaceae)
Umbrella plant
Genus of one species of perennial,

grown for its unusual foliage. Is sometimes now included in *Darmera*. Makes fine marginal water plants. Fully hardy. Grows in sun or shade and requires moist soil. Propagate by division in spring or by seed in autumn or spring.
P. peltatum illus. p.197.

PENNISETUM (Gramineae). See GRASSES, BAMBOOS, RUSHES, and SEDGES.
P. alopecuroides, syn. *P. compressum* (Chinese fountain grass). Tuft-forming, herbaceous, perennial grass. H 3ft (1m), S 1½ft (45cm). Frost hardy, zones 5–10. Has narrow, green leaves; leaf sheaths each have a hairy tip. In late summer bears arching, cylindrical panicles with decorative, purple bristles that last well into winter.
P. compressum. See *P. alopecuroides*.
P. longistylum. See *P. villosum*.
P. ruppellii. See *P. setaceum*.
P. setaceum, syn. *P. ruppellii* (African fountain grass). Tuft-forming, herbaceous, perennial grass. H 3ft (1m), S 1½ft (45cm). Frost hardy, zones 8–10. Has very rough, green leaves and stems. In summer bears dense, cylindrical panicles of copper red spikelets, with decorative, bearded bristles, that last well into winter.
P. villosum, syn. *P. longistylum*, illus. p.181.

PENSTEMON (Scrophulariaceae)
Genus of annuals, perennials, sub-shrubs, and shrubs, most of which are semi-evergreen or evergreen. Fully to half hardy. Prefers full sun and fertile, well-drained soil. Propagate species by seed in autumn or spring or by softwood or semi-ripe cuttings of non-flowering shoots in mid-summer, cultivars by cuttings only.
P. 'Apple Blossom' illus. p.235.
P. barbatus, syn. *Chelone barbata*. Semi-evergreen, rosette-forming perennial. H 3ft (1m), S 1ft (30cm). Frost hardy, zones 4–8. From mid-summer to early autumn bears racemes of slightly nodding, tubular, 2-lipped, rose-red flowers. Flower stems rise from rosettes of oblong to oval, green leaves.
P. campanulatus. Semi-evergreen, upright perennial. H 12–24in (30–60cm), S 12in (30cm). Frost hardy, zones 7–9. Long racemes of bell-shaped, dark purple, violet, or, occasionally, white flowers appear in early summer above lance-shaped, toothed, green leaves.
P. confertus. Semi-evergreen, neat, clump-forming perennial. H 18in (45cm), S 12in (30cm). Frost hardy, zones 7–9. Bears spikes of tubular, creamy yellow flowers above long, lance-shaped, green leaves in early summer.
P. davidsonii. Evergreen, prostrate shrub. H 3in (8cm), occasionally more, S 6in (15cm) or more. Frost hardy, zones 7–9. In late spring and early summer, funnel-shaped, violet to ruby red flowers, with protruding lips, develop from leaf axils. Leaves are small, oval to rounded, and leathery. Trim after flowering. subsp. *menziesii*,

H 2in (5cm), S 8in (20cm), is more prostrate and has lavender blue flowers and toothed leaves.
P. diffusus. See *P. serrulatus*.
P. 'Evelyn'. Semi-evergreen, bushy perennial. H and S 18in (45cm). Frost hardy, zones 6–8. Racemes of small, tubular, pink flowers open from mid-summer onwards. Has broadly lance-shaped, green leaves.
P. fruticosus. Evergreen, upright, woody-based sub-shrub. H and S 6–12in (15–30cm). Frost hardy, zones 6–8. Has lance-shaped to oval, toothed leaves and, in early summer, funnel-shaped, lipped, lavender blue flowers. Is suitable for a rock garden. Trim back after flowering. subsp. *scouleri* has narrower leaves and longer flowers.
P. 'Garnet' illus. p.207.
P. hartwegii. Semi-evergreen, erect perennial. H 24in (60cm) or more, S 12in (30cm). Frost hardy, zones 4–9. Bears sprays of slightly pendent, tubular to bell-shaped, scarlet flowers from mid- to late summer. Lance-shaped leaves are green.
P. heterophyllus 'True Blue'. Semi-evergreen, upright shrub. H and S 10in (25cm) or more. Frost hardy, zones 7–8. Bears linear to lance-shaped, pale green leaves. Funnel-shaped, pure blue flowers are borne on short side-shoots in summer. Trim back after flowering. Suits a rock garden.
P. hirsutus. Short-lived, evergreen, open sub-shrub. H 2–3ft (60cm–1m), S 1–2ft (30–60cm). Frost hardy, zones 5–8. In summer produces hairy, tubular, lipped, purple- or blue-flushed, white flowers. Leaves are oval and dark green. Is suitable for a rock garden. 'Pygmaeus' illus. p.320.
P. isophyllus illus. p.131.
P. 'King George'. Semi-evergreen, upright perennial. H 30in (75cm), S 18–24in (45–60cm). Frost hardy, zones 6–8. Trumpet-shaped, white-throated, bright crimson flowers are produced in racemes from mid-summer until first frosts. Narrowly oval leaves are green.
P. newberryi (Mountain pride). Evergreen, mat-forming shrub. H 6–8in (15–20cm), S 12in (30cm). Frost hardy, zones 7–9. Branches are covered in small, oval, leathery, dark green leaves. Bears short sprays of tubular, lipped, deep rose-pink flowers in early summer. Trim back after flowering. Is good for a rock garden. f. *humilior* illus. p.294.
P. 'Pennington Gem' illus. p.235.
P. pinifolius illus. p.294.
P. 'Pink Endurance' illus. p.236.
P. procerus. Upright, semi-evergreen perennial. H 20in (50cm), S 8in (20cm). Frost hardy, zones 7–8. Leaves are oblong to lance-shaped. Produces slim spikes of funnel-shaped, blue-purple flowers in summer. Is suitable for a rock garden.
P. rupicola. Evergreen, prostrate shrub. H 2in (5cm), S 6in (15cm). Frost hardy, zones 7–8. Has rounded to oval, fleshy, blue-gray leaves and, in summer, variable, funnel-shaped, pale to deep pink flowers. Is best grown in a rock garden. Seed may not come true.

P. 'Schönholzeri'. Vigorous, semi-evergreen, upright perennial. H 3ft (1m), S 1–1½ft (30–45cm). Frost hardy, zones 7–8. Produces racemes of trumpet-shaped, brilliant scarlet flowers from mid-summer to autumn. Lance-shaped to narrowly oval leaves are green.
P. serrulatus, syn. *P. diffusus*, illus. p.295.
P. 'Six Hills'. Evergreen, prostrate shrub. H 2in (5cm), S 6in (15cm). Frost hardy, zones 8–9. Has rounded, fleshy, gray-green leaves. In summer carries funnel-shaped, cool lilac flowers at stem tips. Is suitable for a rock garden.

PENTACHONDRA (Epacridaceae)
Genus of evergreen, spreading shrubs with heathlike leaves. Frost hardy. Needs full light and gritty, moist, peaty soil. Is difficult to grow, especially in hot, dry areas. Propagate by rooted offsets in spring, by semi-ripe cuttings in summer, or by seed in autumn.
P. pumila. Evergreen, mat-forming, dense shrub. H 1¼–4in (3–10cm), S 8in (20cm) or more. Zones 8–9. Leaves are oblong to narrowly oval and purplish green. Small, tubular, white flowers, with reflexed lobes, open in early summer, followed, though rarely in cultivation, by small, spherical, orange fruits.

PENTAPTERYGIUM. See AGAPETES.

PENTAS (Rubiaceae)
Genus of mainly evergreen perennials and shrubs, grown for their flowers. Frost tender, min. 50–59°F (10–15°C). Needs full light or partial shade and fertile, well-drained soil. Water freely when in full growth, moderately at other times. May be hard pruned in winter. Propagate by softwood cuttings in summer or by seed in spring. Is prone to whitefly.
P. carnea. See *P. lanceolata*.
P. lanceolata, syn. *P. carnea*, illus. p.131.

PEPEROMIA (Piperaceae)
Genus of annuals and evergreen perennials, grown for their ornamental foliage. Frost tender, min. 50°F (10°C), zone 10. Grow in bright light or partial shade, ideally in a peat-based compost. Do not overwater. Propagate by division, seed, or leaf or stem cuttings in spring or summer.
P. argyreia, syn. *P. sandersii* (Watermelon plant). Evergreen, bushy, compact perennial. H and S 8in (20cm). Has red-stalked, oval, fleshy, dark green leaves, to 4in (10cm) or more long, striped with broad bands of silver. Flowers are insignificant.
P. caperata illus. p.256.
P. clusiifolia (Baby rubber plant). Evergreen perennial with branching, sometimes prostrate, reddish green stems. H to 8in (20cm), S 10in (25cm). Narrowly oval, fleshy leaves, 3–6in (8–15cm) long, are dark green, edged with red. Flowers are insignificant. Leaves of 'Variegata' have cream-and-red margins.
P. glabella illus. p.261.

P. griseoargentea, syn. *P. hederifolia* (Ivy peperomia, Silverleaf peperomia). Evergreen, bushy perennial. H to 6in (15cm), S 8in (20cm). Oval, fleshy leaves, 2in (5cm) or more long, each have a heart-shaped base, a quilted green surface, and a silvery sheen. Flowers are insignificant.

P. hederifolia. See *P. griseoargentea*.

P. magnoliifolia (Desert privet). Evergreen, bushy perennial with erect, branching stems. H to 10in (25cm), S 8in (20cm) or more. Has almost rounded, thick, fleshy, glossy, green leaves, 4in (10cm) or more long. Flowers are insignificant. **'Green and Gold'** has green leaves blotched with yellow.

P. marmorata illus. p.260.

P. metallica. Evergreen perennial with erect, branching, reddish green stems. H and S to 6in (15cm). Narrowly oval, dark green leaves, to 1in (2.5cm) long, have a metallic sheen, and wide, pale midribs above, reddish green veins below. Flowers are insignificant.

P. nummulariifolia. See *P. rotundifolia*.

P. obtusifolia **'Variegata'** illus. p.261.

P. rotundifolia, syn. *P. nummulariifolia*. Evergreen, creeping perennial. H 2–3in (5–8cm), S 1ft (30cm) or more. Very slender stems produce tiny, rounded, fleshy, bright green leaves, ¹/₂in (1cm) wide. Flowers are insignificant. Is useful for a hanging basket.

P. rubella. Evergreen perennial with erect, branching, red stems. H and S 6in (15cm). Leaves, in whorls of 4, are ¹/₂in (1cm) long, narrowly oval, fleshy and dark green above, crimson below. Flowers are insignificant.

P. sandersii. See *P. argyreia*.

P. scandens (Cupid peperomia). Evergreen, climbing or trailing perennial with pinkish green stems. H and S to 3ft (1m). Oval, pointed, fleshy leaves, to over 2in (5cm) long, are waxy and bright green. Flowers are insignificant.

PERESKIA (Cactaceae)
Genus of deciduous cacti, some of which are climbing, with fleshy leaves and woody, green, then brown stems. Is considered to be the most primitive of the Cactaceae, producing true leaves unlike most others. Frost tender, min. 41–50°F (5–10°C). Needs sun and well-drained soil. Water moderately in summer. Propagate by stem cuttings in spring or summer.

P. aculeata illus. p.379. **'Godseffiana'** is a fast-growing, deciduous, erect, then climbing cactus. H to 30ft (10m), S 15ft (5m). Min. 41°F (5°C), zones 9–10. Broadly oval, slightly fleshy, orange-brown leaves, usually purplish beneath and 3¹/₂in (9cm) long, mature to glossy, green. Short flower stems, carrying roselike, single, orange-centered, cream flowers, 2in (5cm) across, appear in autumn only on plants over 3ft (1m) high. Cut back hard to main stems in autumn.

P. grandifolia, syn. *Rhodocactus grandifolius*, illus. p.380.

PERILLA (Labiatae)
Genus of annuals, grown for their foliage. Half hardy. Grow in sun and

in fertile, well-drained soil. Pinch out growing tips of young plants to encourage a bushy habit. Propagate by seed sown in a greenhouse in early spring.

P. frutescens. Moderately fast-growing, upright, bushy annual. H 2ft (60cm), S 1ft (30cm). Has oval, serrated, aromatic, reddish purple leaves. In summer produces spikes of very small, tubular, white flowers.

PERIPLOCA (Asclepiadaceae)
Genus of deciduous or evergreen, twining climbers, grown for their leaves. Stems exude milky juice if cut. Frost hardy. Grow in sun and in any well-drained soil. Propagate by seed in spring or by semi-ripe cuttings in summer.

P. graeca (Silk vine). Deciduous, twining climber. H to 28ft (9m). Oval, glossy leaves are 1–2in (2.5–5cm) long. Zones 7–10. In summer has clusters of 8–12 greenish yellow flowers, purplish brown inside, each with 5 lobes. Pairs of narrowly cylindrical seed pods, 5in (12cm) long, contain winged, tufted seeds. Scent of the flowers is thought by some to be unpleasant.

PERISTERIA. See ORCHIDS.

P. elata. Semi-evergreen, epiphytic orchid for a cool or intermediate greenhouse. Zone 10. H 3ft (1m). Bears tall spikes of cup-shaped, waxy, creamy white flowers, 3in (8cm) across, in summer. Lips are small and have faint, purple marks. Has broadly oval, ribbed leaves, 18in (45cm) long. Needs shade in summer.

PERISTROPHE (Acanthaceae)
Genus of mainly evergreen perennials and sub-shrubs, grown usually for their flowers. Frost tender, min. 59°F (15°C). Grow in sun or partial shade and in well-drained soil; do not overwater in winter. Propagate by stem cuttings in spring or summer.

P. angustifolia. See *P. hyssopifolia*.

P. hyssopifolia, syn. *P. angustifolia*. Evergreen, bushy perennial. H to 2ft (60cm), S 3–4ft (1–1.2m). Zone 10. Broadly lance-shaped leaves, with long-pointed tips, are 3in (8cm) long. Small clusters of tubular, deep rose-pink flowers are borne in winter. **'Aureo-variegata'** illus. p.224.

PERNETTYA (Ericaceae)
Genus of evergreen shrubs, grown for their showy, long-lasting fruits. Requires separate male and female plants in order to obtain fruits. Fully to frost hardy. Needs sun or semi-shade and moist but well-drained, peaty, acid soil. Propagate by semi-ripe cuttings in summer or by seed or division in autumn or spring.

P. mucronata. Evergreen, bushy, dense shrub, spreading by underground stems. H and S 4ft (1.2m). Fully hardy, zones 8–9. Oval, prickly, glossy, dark green leaves set off tiny, urn-shaped, white flowers in late spring and early summer. Has spherical, fleshy fruit varying in color between cultivars. Sprays of fruit are good for indoor display. Fruits of **'Cherry Ripe'**

(female) are large and bright cherry red. **'Edward Balls'** (male) bears stout, upright, red shoots and sharply spined, bright green leaves. **'Mulberry Wine'** (female) illus. p.142. **'Wintertime'** (female) illus. p.141.

P. prostrata. Evergreen, spreading shrub. H 6–12in (15–30cm), S 12in (30cm) or more. Fully hardy, zones 7–8. Bears oval, leathery, dark green leaves. Urn-shaped, white flowers are produced in early summer and are followed by large, rounded, blue-purple fruits. Is suitable for growing in a rock garden or peat bed. Leaves of subsp. *pentlandii* are narrower and longer.

P. pumila. Evergreen, mat-forming, creeping shrub. H 2in (5cm), S 12–24in (30–60cm). Fully hardy, zones 7–9. Prostrate branches bear tiny, bell-shaped, white flowers in early summer among tiny, rounded, leathery leaves. Rounded fruits are pink or white. Is good for a rock garden or peat bed.

P. tasmanica. Evergreen, mat-forming shrub. H 2–3in (5–8cm), S 8in (20cm). Frost hardy, zones 8–9. Has oval, toothed, leathery leaves with wavy edges. Bell-shaped, white flowers in early summer are followed by rounded, red fruits. Is good for a rock garden or peat bed.

PEROVSKIA (Labiatae)
Genus of deciduous sub-shrubs, grown for their aromatic, gray-green foliage and blue flowers. Fully hardy. Needs full sun and very well-drained soil. Cut plants back hard, almost to base, in spring, as new growth starts. Propagate by softwood cuttings in late spring.

P. atriplicifolia. Deciduous, upright sub-shrub. H 4ft (1.2m), S 3ft (1m). Zones 6–9. Gray-white stems bear narrowly oval, coarsely toothed leaves. Bears 2-lipped, violet-blue flowers in long, slender spikes from late summer to mid-autumn. **'Blue Spire'** illus. p.136.

P. 'Hybrida'. Deciduous, upright sub-shrub. H 3ft (1m), S 2¹/₂ft (75cm). Zones 6–9. Has oval, deeply lobed and toothed leaves and, from late summer to mid-autumn, tall spires of 2-lipped, deep lavender blue flowers.

PETASITES (Compositae)
Genus of invasive perennials, grown for their usually large leaves and value as ground cover. Fully hardy. Tolerates sun or shade and prefers moist but well-drained soil. Propagate by division in spring or autumn.

P. fragrans (Winter heliotrope). Spreading, invasive perennial. H 9–12in (23–30cm), S 4ft (1.2m). Zones 5–9. Has rounded to heart-shaped, dark green leaves. Small, vanilla-scented, daisylike, pinkish white flower heads are produced in late winter before foliage.

P. japonicus illus. p.229.

PETREA (Verbenaceae)
Genus of evergreen shrubs and woody-stemmed, twining climbers, grown for their flowers. Frost tender, min. 55–9°F (13–15°C). Needs full light and fertile, well-drained soil. Water

regularly, less when not in full growth. Provide support. Thin out and spur back crowded growth in spring. Propagate by semi-ripe cuttings in summer. Mealy bug and whitefly may cause problems.

P. volubilis illus. p.164.

PETROCOSMEA (Gesneriaceae)
Genus of evergreen, rhizomatous perennials. Frost tender, min. 36–41°F (2–5°C). Requires shade and well-drained, peaty soil. Propagate by seed in early spring or by leaf cuttings in early summer.

P. kerrii illus. p.314.

PETROPHYTON. See PETROPHYTUM.

PETROPHYTUM, syn. PETROPHYTON (Rosaceae)
Genus of evergreen, summer-flowering shrubs, grown for their spikes of small, fluffy flowers. Is good for growing on tufa or in alpine houses. Fully hardy. Needs sun and gritty, well-drained, alkaline soil. May be difficult to grow. Propagate by softwood or semi-ripe cuttings in summer or by seed in autumn. Aphids and red spider mite may be troublesome in hot weather.

P. caespitosum. Evergreen, mat-forming shrub. H 2–3in (5–8cm), S 4–6in (10–15cm). Zones 6–9. Has clusters of small, oval leaves. Flower stems, ³/₄in (2cm) long, each carry a conical spike of small, fluffy, white flowers in summer.

P. hendersonii. Evergreen, mound-forming shrub. H 2–4in (5–10cm), S 4–6in (10–15cm). Zones 6–9. Has branched stems covered in rounded, blue-green leaves. Conical spikes of small, fluffy, white flowers are produced on 1in (2.5cm) stems in summer.

PETRORHAGIA (Caryophyllaceae)
Genus of annuals and perennials, grown for their flowers. Is suitable for rock gardens and banks. Fully hardy. Prefers sun and well-drained, sandy soil. Propagate by seed in autumn. Self seeds readily.

P. saxifraga, syn. *Tunica saxifraga* (Tunic flower), illus. p.315. **'Rosette'** is a mat-forming perennial. H 4in (10cm), S 6in (15cm). Zones 5–7. Has tufts of grasslike leaves. In summer, slender stems carry a profusion of cup-shaped, double, white to pale pink flowers, sometimes veined deeper pink.

PETTERIA (Leguminosae)
Genus of one species of deciduous shrub, grown for its flowers. Is related to *Laburnum*, differing in its erect racemes. Fully hardy. Requires full sun and fertile, well-drained soil. Propagate by softwood cuttings in summer or by seed in autumn.

P. ramentacea (Dalmatian laburnum). Deciduous, upright shrub. H 6ft (2m), S 3ft (1m). Zones 6–9. Dense, upright spikes of fragrant, laburnumlike, yellow flowers appear in late spring and early summer. Green leaves are each composed of 3 oval leaflets.

PETUNIA (Solanaceae)
Genus of perennials, grown as annuals, with showy, colorful flowers. Half hardy to frost tender, min. 36–9°F (2–4°C). Grow in a sunny position that is sheltered from wind and in fertile, well-drained soil. Dead-head regularly. Propagate by seed sown under glass in early spring. May suffer from viruses, including cucumber mosaic and tomato spotted wilt.

P. x hybrida. Moderately fast-growing, branching, bushy perennial, grown as an annual. H 6–12in (15–30cm), S 12in (30cm). Half hardy unless otherwise stated. Has oval, mid- to deep green leaves and, in summer-autumn, flared, trumpet-shaped, single or double flowers in a wide range of colors (available in mixtures or singly), including blue, violet, purple, red, pink, and white. Flowers vary in form and size: those of Grandiflora hybrids are large (3–4in (8–10cm) wide), but they are often marked by rain and so should be protected; those of Multiflora hybrids are smaller 2in (5cm) wide) and are more rain-resistant.

Grandiflora types include the following:
  'Blue Frost' illus. p.275.
  Cascade Series has trailing stems and single flowers in a wide range of colors.
  'Colour Parade' has a wide color range of single flowers that are ruffled.
  Flash Series has single flowers in a range of bright colors.
  'Magic Cherry' is a compact cultivar with single, cherry red flowers.
  Picotee Series bears a mixed color range of single, brightly colored flowers that have contrasting margins (red, illus. p.272).
  'Razzle Dazzle' has single flowers, striped with white, in a wide range of colors.
  Recoverer Series bears single flowers in a range of single or mixed colors (white, illus. p.262).
  Star Series has a wide color range of single, white-striped flowers (crimson, illus. p.270).
  Victorious Series illus. p.266.

Multiflora types include the following:
  Bonanza Series illus. p.267.
  'Cherry Tart' bears double, deep pink-and-white flowers.
  'Gypsy' is a cultivar with single, salmon red flowers.
  Jamboree Series has pendulous stems bearing single flowers in a range of colors.
  'Mirage Velvet' illus. p.270.
  Pearl Series is a dwarf variety with small, single flowers in a wide range of colors.
  Picotee Ruffled Series has ruffled, single flowers, edged with white, in a range of colors.
  'Plum Crazy' bears single flowers that have contrasting veins and throats. Colors available include white, with yellow throat and veins, and shades of violet, pink, and magenta, all with darker throats and veins.
  'Red Satin' has single, brilliant scarlet flowers.

  Resisto Series bears single flowers that are particularly rain-resistant and are available in a range of colors (blue, illus. p.276; red, illus. p.272; rose-pink, illus. p.269).

PHACELIA (Hydrophyllaceae)
Genus of annuals, biennials, and perennials. Fully hardy. Grow in sun and in fertile, well-drained soil. Tall species may need support. Propagate by seed sown outdoors in spring or early autumn.
P. campanularia illus. p.278.
P. tanacetifolia. Moderately fast-growing, upright annual. H 2ft (60cm) or more, S 1ft (30cm). Has feathery, deep green leaves and, in summer, spikes of bell-shaped, lavender-blue flowers.

PHAEDRANASSA (Amaryllidaceae)
Genus of bulbs with tubular, often pendent flowers. Half hardy. Needs full sun or partial shade and fairly rich, well-drained soil. Feed with high-potash fertilizer in summer. Reduce watering in winter. Propagate by seed or offsets in spring.
P. carmioli illus. p.335.

Phaedranthus buccinatorius. See Distictis buccinatoria.

PHAIOPHLEPS (Iridaceae)
Genus of rushlike, rhizomatous perennials, related to Sisyrinchium, grown for their fragrant, trumpet-shaped flowers in spring. Frost hardy. Requires gritty, peaty soil and cool growing conditions, such as a peat garden would provide, and full sun or partial shade. Do not allow soil to dry out. Propagate by seed in winter or spring.
P. biflora, syn. Sisyrinchium odoratissimum. Clump-forming, spring- to summer-flowering, rhizomatous perennial. H 10–14in (25–35cm), S 2–3in (5–8cm). Zones 9–10. Has cylindrical, rushlike, erect, basal leaves. Bears a small head of pendent, white flowers that are striped and veined red.

PHAIUS. See ORCHIDS.
P. tankervilleae (illus. p.253). Semi-evergreen, terrestrial orchid. H 30in (75cm). Frost tender, min. 55°F (10°C), zone 10. Tall spikes of flowers, 3¹/₂in (9cm) across, brown within, silvery gray outside and each with a long, red-marked, pink lip, open in early summer. Leaves are broadly oval, ribbed, and 24in (60cm) long. Provide semi-shade in summer.

PHALAENOPSIS. See ORCHIDS.
P. Allegria (illus. p.252). Evergreen, epiphytic orchid for a warm greenhouse. Zone 10. H 6in (15cm). Carries sprays of white flowers, to 5in (12cm) across; flowering season varies. Broadly oval, fleshy leaves are 6in (15cm) long. Needs shade in summer.
P. cornu-cervi (illus. p.254). Evergreen, epiphytic orchid for a warm greenhouse. Zone 10. H 6in (15cm). Yellowish green flowers, 2in (5cm) across, with brown marks, are

produced successively, either singly or in pairs, in summer. Has broadly oval leaves, 4in (10cm) long. Needs shade in summer.
P. Lady Jersey x Lippeglut (illus. p.253). Evergreen, epiphytic orchid for a warm greenhouse. Zone 10. H 6in (15cm). Bears tall, pendent spikes of pink flowers, 3¹/₂in (9cm) across; flowering season varies. Broadly oval leaves are 4in (10cm) long. Requires shade in summer.
P. Lundy (illus. p.254). Evergreen, epiphytic orchid for a warm greenhouse. Zone 10. H 15cm (6in). Bears sprays of red-striped, yellow flowers, 3in (8cm) across; flowering season varies. Has broadly oval leaves, 9in (23cm) long. Grow in shade in summer.

PHALARIS (Gramineae). See
GRASSES, BAMBOOS, RUSHES, and SEDGES.
P. arundinacea var. **picta** illus. p.180.

PHARBITIS. See IPOMOEA.

Phaseolus caracalla. See Vigna caracalla.

PHEGOPTERIS (Polypodiaceae)
Genus of deciduous ferns. Fully hardy. Grow in semi-shade and in humus-rich, moist but well-drained soil. Propagate by division in spring or by spores in summer.
P. connectilis, syn. Thelypteris phegopteris (Beech fern). Deciduous fern. H 9in (23cm), S 12in (30cm). Zones 4–9. Broadly lance-shaped, green fronds, each consisting of tiny, triangular pinnae on wiry stalks, arise from a creeping rootstock. Is useful for ground cover.

PHELLODENDRON (Rutaceae)
Genus of deciduous trees, grown for their foliage, which colors well in autumn. Male and female flowers are produced on different plants. Fully hardy, but young growth is susceptible to damage by late frosts. Needs full sun and fertile, well-drained soil. Does best during hot summers. Propagate by softwood cuttings in summer, by seed in autumn, or by root cuttings in late winter.
P. amurense (Amur cork tree). Deciduous, spreading tree. H 40ft (12m), S 50ft (15m). Zones 4–7. Has corky, dark bark when old. Aromatic leaves, with 5 to 11 oblong leaflets, are glossy, dark green, becoming yellow in autumn. Tiny, green flowers in early summer are followed by small, rounded, black fruits.
P. chinense illus. p.54.

PHILADELPHUS (Hydrangeaceae)
Mock orange
Genus of deciduous, mainly summer-flowering shrubs, grown for their usually fragrant flowers. Fully to frost hardy. Needs sun and fertile, well-drained soil. After flowering, cut some older shoots back to young growths, leaving young shoots to flower the following year. Propagate by softwood cuttings in summer. May become infested with aphids.

P. 'Beauclerk' illus. p.103.
P. 'Belle Etoile' illus. p.104.
P. 'Boule d'Argent' illus. p.105.
P. coronarius. 'Aureus' is a deciduous, upright shrub. H 8ft (2.5m), S 5ft (1.5m). Fully hardy, zones 5–9. Clusters of very fragrant, 4-petaled, creamy white flowers are produced in late spring and early summer. Oval, golden yellow, young leaves turn yellow-green in summer. Protect from full sun. **'Variegatus'** illus. p.107.
P. 'Dame Blanche' illus. p.105.
P. delavayi. Deciduous, upright shrub. H 10ft (3m), S 8ft (2.5m). Frost hardy, zones 6–9. Dense clusters of very fragrant, 4-petaled, white flowers, with sometimes purple-flushed, green sepals, open from early to mid-summer. Leaves are dark green, oval, and toothed. f. **melanocalyx** illus. p.107.
P. 'Lemoinei' illus. p.106.
P. magdalenae. Deciduous, bushy shrub. H and S 12ft (4m). Fully hardy, zones 5–9. Bark peels on older shoots. Narrowly oval, dark green leaves set off fragrant, 4-petaled, white flowers in late spring and early summer.
P. 'Manteau d'Hermine' illus. p.126.
P. 'Sybille'. Deciduous, arching shrub. H 4ft (1.2m), S 6ft (2m). Fully hardy, zones 5–8. Very fragrant, 4-petaled, white flowers, each with a central, pink stain, are borne profusely in early and mid-summer. Leaves are green and oval.
P. 'Virginal'. Vigorous, deciduous, upright shrub. H 10ft (3m), S 8ft (2.5m). Fully hardy, zones 5–9. Has oval, dark green leaves. Produces masses of large, very fragrant, double or semi-double, white flowers from early to mid-summer.

x PHILAGERIA (Liliaceae)
Hybrid genus (Philesia x Lapageria) of one evergreen, scrambling or twining shrub. Frost tender, min. 41°F (5°C). Grow in semi-shade and in well-drained, preferably acid soil. Propagate by layering in late summer or autumn.
x P. veitchii. Evergreen, scrambling or twining shrub. H 10–12ft (3–4m). Zones 9–10. Has oblong, slightly toothed leaves. Nodding, tubular, rose-pink flowers are produced in leaf axils in summer.

PHILESIA (Liliaceae)
Genus of one species of evergreen shrub, grown for its showy flowers. Frost hardy, but thrives only in mild, moist areas. Needs semi-shade and humus-rich, moist, acid soil. Benefits from an annual dressing of leaf mold. Propagate by semi-ripe cuttings in summer or by suckers in autumn.
P. magellanica. Evergreen, erect shrub. H 3ft (1m), S 6ft (2m). Zones 7–8. Bears trumpet-shaped, waxy, crimson-pink flowers, in leaf axils, from mid-summer to late autumn. Narrowly oblong, dark green leaves are bluish white beneath.

PHILLYREA (Oleaceae)
Genus of evergreen shrubs and trees, with inconspicuous flowers, grown for their foliage. Frost hardy, but in cold areas requires shelter. Does best in full

sun and in fertile, well-drained soil. To restrict growth, cut back in spring. Propagate by semi-ripe cuttings in summer.

P. angustifolia. Evergreen, bushy, dense shrub. H and S 10ft (3m). Zones 7–9. Leaves are narrowly oblong and dark green. Small, fragrant, 4-lobed, greenish white flowers in late spring and early summer are followed by spherical, blue-black fruits.

P. decora. See *Osmanthus decorus.*

P. latifolia. Evergreen, rounded shrub or tree. H and S 25ft (8m). Zones 7–9. Has oval, glossy, dark green leaves. Produces tiny, fragrant, 4-lobed, greenish white flowers from late spring to early summer, then spherical, blue-black fruits.

PHILODENDRON (Araceae)
Genus of evergreen shrubs and woody-based, root climbers, grown for their handsome leaves. Intermittently bears insignificant flowers. Frost tender, min. 59–64°F (15–18°C), zone 10. Needs partial shade and humus-rich, well-drained soil. Water moderately, sparingly in cold weather. Provide support. Young stem tips may be removed to promote branching. Propagate by leaf-bud or stem-tip cuttings in summer.

P. auritum of gardens. See *Syngonium auritum.*

P. 'Burgundy'. Slow-growing, evergreen, woody-based, root climber. H 6ft (2m) or more. Leaves are narrowly oblong, red-flushed, deep green above, wine red beneath, and up to 12in (30cm) long.

P. cordatum (Heart leaf). Moderately vigorous, evergreen, woody-based, root climber. H 10ft (3m) or more. Has heart-shaped, lustrous, rich green leaves, to 18in (45cm) long.

P. domesticum, syn. *P. hastatum* (Elephant's ear, Spade leaf). Fairly slow-growing, evergreen, woody-based, root climber. H 6–10ft (2–3m). Lustrous, bright green leaves, 12–16in (30–40cm) long, are arrow-shaped on young plants and later have prominent, basal lobes.

P. erubescens (Blushing philodendron). Evergreen, erect, woody-based, root climber. H to 10ft (3m). Oval to triangular leaves, 6–10in (15–25cm) long, have long, red stalks and are dark green with a lustrous, coppery flush.

P. hastatum. See *P. domesticum.*

P. laciniatum. See *P. pedatum.*

P. melanochrysum illus. p.178.

P. pedatum, syn. *P. laciniatum.* Slow-growing, evergreen, woody-based, root climber. H 6–10ft (2–3m). Has oval, lustrous, deep green leaves, 12–32in (30–80cm) long, cut into 5 or 7 prominent lobes.

P. pinnatifidum. Evergreen, erect, robust, unbranched shrub. H to 10ft (3m), S 3–6ft (1–2m). Glossy, deep green leaves are broadly oval in outline, 16–24in (40–60cm) long and divided into 15 or more fingerlike lobes.

P. sagittatum. See *P. sagittifolium.*

P. sagittifolium, syn. *P. sagittatum.* Slow-growing, evergreen, woody-based, root climber. H 6–10ft (2–3m).

Oval leaves with basal lobes are up to 16–24in (40–60cm) long and glossy, bright green.

P. scandens illus. p.178.

P. selloum illus. p.120.

P. trifoliatum. See *Syngonium auritum.*

PHLEBODIUM (Polypodiaceae)
Genus of evergreen or semi-evergreen ferns. Frost tender, min. 41°F (5°C). Needs full light or semi-shade and humus-rich, moist but well-drained soil. Remove fading fronds regularly. Propagate by division in spring or by spores in summer.

P. aureum, syn. *Polypodium aureum,* illus. p.185. **'Mandaianum'** illus. p.184.

PHLOMIS (Labiatae)
Genus of evergreen, summer-flowering shrubs and perennials, grown for their conspicuous, hooded flowers, which are borne in dense whorls, and for their foliage. Fully to frost hardy. Prefers full sun and well-drained soil. Propagate by seed in autumn; shrubs may also be increased from softwood cuttings in summer, perennials by division in spring.

P. cashmeriana. Evergreen, upright shrub. H 24in (60cm), S 18in (45cm). Frost hardy, zones 8–10. Produces masses of 2-lipped, pale lilac flowers in summer. Narrowly oval, green leaves have woolly, white undersides.

P. chrysophylla. Evergreen, rounded, stiffly branched shrub. H and S 3ft (1m). Frost hardy, zones 8–10. Bears 2-lipped, golden yellow flowers in early summer. Oval leaves are gray-green when young, becoming golden green.

P. fruticosa illus. p.138.

P. italica illus. p.130.

P. longifolia var. *bailanica.* Evergreen, bushy shrub. H 4ft (1.2m), S 3ft (1m). Frost hardy, zones 8–9. Leaves are oblong to heart-shaped, deeply veined, and bright green. Has 2-lipped, deep yellow flowers from early to mid-summer.

P. russeliana illus. p.214.

PHLOX (Polemoniaceae)
Genus of mainly late spring- or summer-flowering annuals and perennials, some of which are semi-evergreen or evergreen, grown for their terminal panicles or profusion of brightly colored flowers. Fully to half hardy. Does best in sun or semi-shade and in fertile, moist but well-drained soil; some species prefer acid soil; in light, dry soils is better grown in partial shade. Trim back rock garden species after flowering. Propagate rock garden species and hybrids by cuttings from non-flowering shoots in spring or summer; species by seed in autumn or spring; *P. maculata, P. paniculata,* and their cultivars also by division in early spring or by root cuttings in winter; and annuals by seed in spring. *P. maculata, P. paniculata,* and their cultivars are susceptible to nematodes.

P. adsurgens. Evergreen, mat-forming, prostrate perennial. H 4in (10cm), S 12in (30cm). Fully hardy, zones 4–8. Woody-based stems are clothed in

oval, light to mid-green leaves. In summer produces terminal clusters of short-stemmed, saucer-shaped, purple, pink, or white flowers with overlapping petals. Is good for a rock garden or peat bed. Prefers partial shade and gritty, peaty, acid soil.

'Wagon Wheel' illus. p.316.

P. amoena **'Variegata'.** See *P. x procumbens* 'Folio-variegata'.

P. bifida illus. p.321.

P. caespitosa. Evergreen, mound-forming, compact perennial. H 3in (8cm), S 5in (12cm). Fully hardy, zones 4–8. Leaves are narrow and needlelike. Solitary almost stemless, saucer-shaped, lilac or white flowers are borne in summer. Suits a rock garden or trough. Needs sun and very well-drained soil.

P. **'Camla'** illus. p.319.

P. **'Chatahoochee'** illus. p.296.

P. divaricata. Semi-evergreen, creeping perennial. H 12in (30cm) or more, S 8in (20cm). Fully hardy, zones 4–8. In early summer, upright stems carry saucer-shaped, lavender blue flowers in loose clusters. Leaves are oval. Suits a rock garden or peat bed. Prefers semi-shade and moist but well-drained, peaty soil. subsp. *laphamii* illus. p.296.

P. douglasii **'Boothman's Variety'** illus. p.320. **'Crackerjack'** illus. p.319. **'May Snow'** is an evergreen, mound-forming perennial. H 3in (8cm), S 8in (20cm). Fully hardy, zones 5–7. Masses of saucer-shaped, white flowers are carried in early summer. Leaves are lance-shaped and green. Is suitable for a rock garden, wall, or bank. Vigorous, compact **'Red Admiral'**, H 6in (15cm), has crimson flowers.

P. drummondii (Annual phlox, Texas pride). **Beauty Series** is a group of moderately fast-growing, compact, upright annuals. H 6in (15cm), S 4in (10cm). Fully hardy. Has lance-shaped, pale green leaves and, from summer to early autumn, heads of star-shaped flowers in many colors, including red, pink, blue, purple, and white. **'Carnival'** has larger flowers with contrasting centers. **Cecily Series** illus. p.270. **'Petticoat'** has bicolored flowers. **Twinkle Series** purplish red, illus. p.270; vivid red, illus. p.271.

P. **'Emerald Cushion'** illus. p.321.

P. hoodii. Evergreen, compact, prostrate perennial. H 2in (5cm), S 4in (10cm). Fully hardy, zones 5–8. Solitary flat, white flowers open in early summer above fine, needlelike, hairy leaves. Suits a rock garden. Needs sun and very well-drained soil.

P. maculata. Erect perennial. H 3ft (1m), S 1½ft (45cm). Fully hardy, zones 4–8. In summer produces cylindrical panicles of tubular, 5-lobed, mauve-pink flowers above oval, green leaves. **'Alpha'** has rose-pink flowers. **'Omega'** illus. p.202.

P. **'Millstream'.** Evergreen, mat-forming, spreading perennial. H to 6in (15cm), S 12in (30cm) or more. Fully hardy, zones 4–8. Slender, prostrate stems bear narrowly oval leaves and, in early summer, saucer-shaped, deep pink flowers, with white eyes. Is good for a rock garden.

P. paniculata. Upright perennial, seldom grown, as is replaced in gardens by its more colorful cultivars. H 4ft (1.2m), S 2ft (60cm). Fully hardy, zones 4–8. Tubular, 5-lobed flowers are borne in conical heads above oval, green leaves in late summer. **'Amethyst'** has violet flowers. **'Brigadier'** illus. p.205. **'Bright Eyes'** has red-eyed, pink flowers. **'Eva Cullum'** illus. p.204. **'Harlequin'** illus. p.205. **'Norah Leigh'** illus. p.210. **'Sir John Falstaff'** has large, deep salmon flowers with cherry red eyes.

P. x procumbens **'Folio-variegata'**, syn. *P. amoena* 'Variegata'. Evergreen, prostrate perennial. H 1in (2.5cm), S 10in (25cm). Fully hardy, zones 5–9. Has oval, glossy, green leaves with white margins. In early summer produces small, saucer-shaped, bright cerise-pink flowers. Is suitable for a rock garden.

P. stolonifera (Creeping phlox). Evergreen, prostrate, spreading perennial. H 4–6in (10–15cm), S 12in (30cm) or more. Fully hardy, zones 4–8. Produces small, cup-shaped, pale blue flowers in early summer. Leaves are oblong to oval. Prefers moist, peaty, acid soil; is good for a peat bed or rock garden. **'Blue Ridge'** has masses of lavender blue flowers. **Bruce's White** illus. p.313.

P. subulata. Evergreen, mound-forming perennial. H 4in (10cm), S 8in (20cm). Fully hardy, zones 4–9. Bears fine, needlelike leaves. Masses of star-shaped, white, pink, or mauve flowers appear in early summer. Suits a sunny rock garden. **'Marjory'** illus. p.318.

PHOENIX (Palmae)
Genus of evergreen palms, grown for their overall appearance and their edible fruits. Frost tender, min. 50–59°F (10–15°C). Grows in any fertile, well-drained soil and in full light, though tolerates partial shade. Water potted specimens moderately, less in winter. Propagate by seed in spring at not less than 75°F (24°C). Red spider mite may be a nuisance.

P. canariensis (Canary Island date palm). Evergreen, upright palm with a robust trunk. H 60ft (18m) or more, S 30ft (10m) or more. Min. 50°F (10°C), zones 9–10. Feather-shaped, arching leaves, each to 15ft (5m) long, are divided into narrowly lance-shaped, leathery, bright green leaflets. Bears large, pendent clusters of tiny, yellowish-brown flowers, followed by shortly oblong, yellow to red fruits in autumn-winter on mature specimens.

P. roebelenii (Miniature date palm, Pygmy date palm). Evergreen palm with a slender trunk. H 6–12ft (2–4m), S 3–6ft (1–2m). Min. 59°F (15°C), zones 9–10. Feather-shaped, arching leaves, 3–4ft (1–1.2m) long, are glossy, dark green. In summer bears large panicles of tiny, yellow flowers then, in autumn, egg-shaped, black fruits in pendent clusters, 18in (45cm) long.

PHORMIUM (Agavaceae)
New Zealand flax
Genus of evergreen perennials, grown for their bold, sword-shaped leaves.

Frost hardy. Requires sun and moist but well-drained soil. Propagate by division or seed in spring.
P. colensoi. See *P. cookianum*.
P. cookianum, syn. *P. colensoi* (Mountain flax). Evergreen, upright perennial. H 3–6ft (1–2m), S 1ft (30cm). Zones 9–10. Has tufts of sword-shaped, upright, dark green leaves. Panicles of tubular, pale yellowish green flowers are borne in summer. **'Tricolor'** has leaves striped vertically with red, yellow, and green. **'Variegatum'** has cream-striped leaves.
P. tenax. Evergreen, upright perennial. H 10ft (3m), S 3–6ft (1–2m). Zones 9–10. Has tufts of sword-shaped, stiff, dark green leaves. Panicles of tubular, dull red flowers are produced on short, slightly glaucous green stems in summer. Thrives by the sea. **'Aurora'** has leaves vertically striped with red, bronze, salmon pink, and yellow. **'Bronze Baby'** illus. p.258. **'Dazzler'** illus. p.223. **'Purpureum'** illus. p.194. **'Veitchii'** has broad, creamy white-striped leaves.

PHOTINIA (Rosaceae)
Genus of evergreen or deciduous shrubs and trees, with small, white flowers, grown for their foliage and, in the case of deciduous species, for their autumn color and fruits. Fully to frost hardy, but protect evergreen species from strong, cold winds. Requires sun or semi-shade and fertile, well-drained soil; some species prefer acid soil. Propagate by semi-ripe cuttings in summer, deciduous species also by seed in autumn.
P. arbutifolia. See *Heteromeles arbutifolia*.
P. x fraseri. Group of evergreen, hybrid shrubs. Frost hardy, zones 7–10. Has bold, oblong leaves and good resistance to damage by late frosts. Young growths are attractive over a long period. **'Birmingham'** illus. p.85. **'Red Robin'** is upright and dense. H 20ft (6m), H 12ft (4m). Glossy, dark green leaves are brilliant red when young. Broad heads of 5-petaled flowers are borne in late spring.
P. serratifolia, syn. *P. serrulata* (Chinese photinia). Evergreen, upright shrub or bushy-headed tree. H 30ft (10m), S 25ft (8m). Frost hardy, zones 7–9. Oblong, often sharply toothed leaves are red when young, maturing to glossy, dark green. Small, 5-petaled flowers from mid- to late spring are sometimes followed by spherical, red fruits. Young growth may be damaged by late frosts.
P. serrulata. See *P. serratifolia*.
P. villosa (Oriental photinia). Deciduous, upright shrub or spreading tree. H and S 15ft (5m). Fully hardy, zones 5–7. Oval, dark green leaves, bronze-margined when young, are brilliant orange-red in autumn. Has clusters of 5-petaled flowers in late spring, then spherical, red fruits. Prefers acid soil.

PHRAGMIPEDIUM. See ORCHIDS.
P. caudatum. Evergreen, epiphytic orchid for an intermediate greenhouse.

H 9in (23cm). Zone 10. In summer produces sprays of flowers with light green-and-tan sepals and pouches and drooping, ribbonlike, yellow and brownish crimson petals to 12in (30cm) long. Bears narrowly oval leaves, 12in (30cm) long. Needs shade in summer.

PHUOPSIS (Rubiaceae)
Genus of one species of mat-forming, summer-flowering perennial, grown for its small, pungent, tubular flowers. Is good for ground cover, especially on banks and in rock gardens. Fully hardy. Needs sun and well-drained soil. Propagate by division in spring, by semi-ripe cuttings in summer, or by seed in autumn.
P. stylosa, syn. *Crucianella stylosa*, illus. p.292.

PHYGELIUS (Scrophulariaceae)
Genus of evergreen or semi-evergreen shrubs and sub-shrubs, grown for their showy, tubular flowers. Frost hardy, but in most areas plant in a sheltered position; will attain considerably greater height when grown against a south- or west-facing wall. Needs sun and fertile, well-drained but not too dry soil. Usually loses leaves or has shoots cut to ground by frosts. Cut back to just above ground level in spring, or, if plants have woody bases, prune to live wood. Propagate by softwood cuttings in summer.
P. aequalis illus. p.134. **'Yellow Trumpet'** illus. p.137.
P. capensis 'Coccineus'. Evergreen or semi-evergreen, upright sub-shrub. H 5ft (1.5m), S 6ft (2m). Zones 8–9. Tubular, curved, bright orange-red flowers, each with a red mouth and a yellow throat, are produced from mid-summer to early autumn in tall, slender spires amid triangular, dark green leaves.
P. x rectus 'Winchester Fanfare'. Evergreen or semi-evergreen, upright sub-shrub. Zones 8–9. H 5ft (1.5m), S 6ft (2m). Pendulous, tubular, dusky reddish pink flowers, each with scarlet lobes and a yellow throat, are produced from mid-summer to early autumn. Leaves are triangular and dark green.

Phyllanthus nivosus. See *Breynia disticha*.

x PHYLLIOPSIS (Ericaceae)
Hybrid genus (*Phyllodoce x Kalmiopsis*) of one species of evergreen shrub, grown for its flowers. Is suitable for peat beds and rock gardens. Fully hardy. Needs partial shade and peaty, acid soil. Trim back after flowering to maintain a compact habit. Propagate by semi-ripe cuttings in late summer.
x P. hillieri 'Pinocchio'. Evergreen, upright shrub. H 8in (20cm), S 10in (25cm). Zones 4–8. Branched stems bear thin, oval leaves. Long, open clusters of bell-shaped, very deep pink flowers appear in spring and intermittently thereafter.

PHYLLITIS (Polypodiaceae)
Genus of evergreen or semi-evergreen ferns. Fully hardy. Prefers partial

shade and moist but well-drained soil. Propagate species by spores in summer, selected forms by division in spring.
P. scolopendrium, syn. *Asplenium scolopendrium*, *Scolopendrium vulgare*, illus. p.187. **'Marginatum'** illus. p.187.

PHYLLOCLADUS (Podocarpaceae). See CONIFERS.
P. aspleniifolius (Tasman celery pine). Slow-growing, upright conifer. H 15–30ft (5–10m), S 10–15ft (3–5m). Half hardy, zone 10. Instead of true leaves has flattened, leaflike shoots known as phylloclades; these are dull dark green and resemble celery leaves in outline. Produces inedible, white-coated nuts, which have fleshy, red bases.
P. trichomanoides illus. p.78.

PHYLLODOCE (Ericaceae)
Genus of evergreen shrubs, grown for their fine, heathlike leaves and attractive flowers. Fully to frost hardy. Needs semi-shade and moist, peaty, acid soil. Propagate by semi-ripe cuttings in late summer or by seed in spring.
P. caerulea, syn. *P. taxifolia*, illus. p.288.
P. empetriformis illus. p.288.
P. x intermedia 'Drummondii' illus. p.287. **'Fred Stoker'** is an evergreen, upright shrub. H and S 9in (23cm). Fully hardy, zones 2–5. Has narrow, glossy, green leaves. From late spring to early summer carries terminal clusters of pitcher-shaped, bright reddish purple flowers on slender, red stalks.
P. nipponica. Evergreen, upright shrub. H 4–8in (10–20cm), S 4–6in (10–15cm). Frost hardy, zones 6–8. Freely branched stems bear fine, linear leaves and, in late spring and summer, stalked, bell-shaped, white flowers from their tips.
P. taxifolia. See *P. caerulea*.

PHYLLOSTACHYS
(Bambusoideae). See GRASSES, BAMBOOS, RUSHES, and SEDGES.
P. aurea (Fishpole bamboo, Golden bamboo). Evergreen, clump-forming bamboo. H 20–25ft (6–8m), S indefinite. Frost hardy, zones 7–10. Erect, grooved stems have cup-shaped swellings beneath most nodes, which, towards the base, are often close together and distorted. Bears green leaves and unimportant flower spikes.
P. aureosulcata (Golden-groove bamboo). Evergreen, clump-forming bamboo. H 20–25ft (6–8m), S indefinite. Frost hardy, zones 6–10. Bears striped sheaths and yellow grooves on rough, brownish green stems. Green leaves are up to 6in (15cm) long; flower spikes are unimportant.
P. bambusoides illus. p.182.
P. flexuosa illus. p.182.
P. 'Henonis'. See *P. nigra* var. *henonis*.
P. nigra (Black bamboo). Evergreen, clump-forming bamboo. H 20–25ft (6–8m), S indefinite. Frost hardy, zones 7–10. Grooved, greenish brown

stems turn black in second season. Almost unmarked culm sheaths bear bristled auricles, green leaves, and unimportant flower spikes.
var. **henonis** (syn. *P.* 'Henonis') illus. p.182.
P. viridiglaucescens illus. p.183.

x PHYLLOTHAMNUS (Ericaceae)
Hybrid genus (*Phyllodoce x Rhodothamnus*) of one species of evergreen shrub, grown for its foliage and flowers. Is good for peat beds and rock gardens. Fully hardy. Needs a sheltered, semi-shaded site and moist, acid soil. Propagate by semi-ripe cuttings in late summer.
x P. erectus. Evergreen, upright shrub. H and S 6in (15cm). Zones 6–8. Has small, linear, deep green leaves. Clusters of slender-stalked, bell-shaped, soft rose-pink flowers appear in late spring.

PHYSALIS (Solanaceae)
Genus of summer-flowering perennials and annuals, grown mainly for their decorative, lanternlike calyces and fruits, produced in autumn. Fully to half hardy. Grows in sun or shade and in well-drained soil. Propagate by division or softwood cuttings in spring, annuals by seed in spring or autumn.
P. alkekengi (Chinese lantern). Spreading perennial, sometimes grown as an annual. H 18in (45cm), S 24in (60cm). Fully hardy, zones 5–8. Inconspicuous, nodding, star-shaped, white flowers in summer are followed, in autumn, by rounded, bright orange-red fruits, surrounded by inflated, orange calyces. Leaves are green and oval.
P. peruviana (Cape gooseberry, Strawberry tomato). Spreading perennial. H and S to 4ft (1.2m). Half hardy, zones 9–10. Inconspicuous, star-shaped, purple-marked, yellow flowers in summer are followed by rounded, yellow fruits enclosed in inflated, pale cream calyces. Leaves are green and oval to triangular.

PHYSOCARPUS (Rosaceae)
Genus of deciduous, mainly summer-flowering shrubs, grown for their foliage and flowers. Fully hardy. Requires sun and fertile, not too dry soil. Prefers acid soil and does not grow well on shallow, chalky soil. Thin established plants occasionally by cutting some older shoots back to ground level after flowering. Propagate by softwood cuttings in summer.
P. opulifolius (Ninebark). Deciduous, arching, dense shrub. H 10ft (3m), S 15ft (5m). Zones 2–8. Has peeling bark and broadly oval, toothed, and lobed, green leaves. Clusters of tiny, sometimes pink-tinged, white flowers are borne in early summer. **'Dart's Gold'** illus. p.114.

PHYSOPLEXIS (Campanulaceae)
Genus of one species of tufted perennial, grown for its flowers. Is good grown on tufa, in rock gardens, troughs, and alpine houses. Fully hardy. Needs sun and very well-drained, alkaline soil, but should face away from midday sun. Keep fairly

dry in winter. Propagate by seed in autumn or by softwood cuttings in early summer. Is susceptible to slug damage.
P. comosa, syn. *Phyteuma comosum*, illus. p.320.

PHYSOSTEGIA (Labiatae)
Obedient plant
Genus of summer- to early autumn-flowering perennials. Fully hardy. Needs sun and fertile, moist but well-drained soil. Propagate by division in spring.
P. virginiana. Erect perennial. H 3ft (1m), S 2ft (60cm). Zones 4–8. In late summer produces spikes of hooded, 2-lipped, rose-purple flowers with hinged stalks that allow flowers to remain in position once moved. Has lance-shaped, toothed, green leaves. **'Summer Snow'** has pure white flowers. **'Variegata'** illus. p.204. **'Vivid'** illus. p.236.

PHYTEUMA (Campanulaceae)
Genus of early- to mid-summer-flowering perennials that are useful for rock gardens. Fully hardy. Needs sun and well-drained soil. Propagate by seed in autumn.
P. comosum. See *Physoplexis comosa*.
P. scheuchzeri illus. p.297.

PHYTOLACCA (Phytolaccaceae)
Genus of perennials and evergreen shrubs and trees, grown for their overall appearance and decorative but poisonous fruits. Fully hardy to frost tender, min. 41°F (5°C). Tolerates sun or shade and requires fertile, moist soil. Propagate by seed in autumn or spring.
P. americana (Red-ink plant, Virginian pokeweed). Upright, spreading perennial. H and S 4–5ft (1.2–1.5m). Fully hardy, zones 5–9. Oval to lance-shaped, green leaves are tinged purple in autumn. Shallowly cup-shaped, sometimes pink-flushed, white-and-green flowers, borne in terminal racemes in summer, are followed by poisonous, rounded, fleshy, blackish purple berries.
P. clavigera. Stout, upright perennial. H and S 4ft (1.2m). Fully hardy, zones 6–9. Has brilliant crimson stems, oval to lance-shaped, green leaves that turn yellow in autumn and, in summer, clusters of shallowly cup-shaped, pink flowers, followed by poisonous, rounded, blackish purple berries.

PICEA (Pinaceae)
Spruce
Genus of conifers with needlelike leaves set on a pronounced peg on the shoots and arranged spirally. Cones are pendulous and ripen in their first autumn; scales are woody and flexible. See also CONIFERS.
P. abies (Norway spruce; illus. p.76). Fast-growing conifer, narrowly conical when young, broader with age. H 70–100ft (20–30m), S 15–22ft (5–7m). Fully hardy, zones 3–8. Has needlelike, dark green leaves and bears pendulous cones. **'Clanbrassiliana'**, H 15ft (5m), S 10–15ft (3–5m), is slow-growing, rounded, and spreading. **'Gregoryana'** (illus. p.83), H and S 2ft (60cm), is

slow-growing, with a dense, globose form. **'Inversa'**, H 15–30ft (5–10m), S 6ft (2m), has an erect leader, but pendent side branches. **'Little Gem'**, H and S 12–20in (30–50cm), has a nest-shaped, central depression caused by spreading branches. **'Nidiformis'**, H 3ft (1m), S 3–6ft (1–2m), is similar, but larger and faster-growing. **'Ohlendorffii'** (illus. p.82), H and S 3ft (1m), is slow-growing, initially rounded, becoming conical with age. **'Reflexa'** (illus. p.82), H 1ft (30cm), S 15ft (5m), is prostrate and ground-hugging, but may be trained up a stake, to form a mound of weeping foliage.
P. breweriana illus. p.77.
P. engelmannii illus. p.77.
P. glauca (White spruce). Narrowly conical conifer. H 30–50ft (10–15m), S 12–15ft (4–5m). Fully hardy, zones 3–6. Glaucous shoots produce blue-green leaves. Ovoid, light brown cones fall after ripening. var. *albertiana* **'Conica'** (syn. *P.g.* 'Albertiana Conica'; illus. p.83), H 6–15ft (2–5m), S 3–6ft (1–2m), is of neat, pyramidal habit and slow-growing, with longer leaves and smaller cones. **'Coerulea'** illus. p.77. **'Echiniformis'**, H 20in (50cm), S 36in (1m), is a dwarf, flat-topped, rounded form.
P. likiangensis (Likiang spruce). Upright conifer. H 50ft (15m), S 15–30ft (5–10m). Fully hardy, zones 6–8. Bluish white leaves are well-spaced. Cones, 3–6in (8–15cm) long, are cylindrical, females bright red when young, ripening to purple, males pink.
P. mariana (Black spruce). Conical conifer, whose lowest branches often layer naturally, forming a ring of stems around the parent plant. H 30–50ft (10–15m), S 10ft (3m). Fully hardy, zones 3–6. Leaves are bluish green or bluish white. Oval cones are dark gray-brown. **'Doumetii'** illus. p.80. **'Nana'** (illus. p.82), H 20in (50cm), S 20–32in (50–80cm), is a neat shrub with blue-gray foliage.
P. morrisonicola illus. p.79.
P. omorika illus. p.75. **'Gnom'** (illus. p.82) is a shrublike conifer with pendent branches that arch out at tips. H to 5ft (1.5m), S 3–6ft (1–2m). Fully hardy, zones 5–8. Leaves are dark green above, white beneath. **'Nana'**, H and S 3ft (1m), is a slow-growing, rounded or oval cultivar.
P. orientalis (Caucasian spruce, Oriental spruce). Columnar, dense conifer. H 70ft (20m), S 15ft (5m). Fully hardy, zones 5–8. Glossy, deep green leaves are very short. Has ovoid to conical cones, 2½–4in (6–10cm) long, dark purple, ripening to brown, the males brick red in spring. **'Aurea'** has golden, young foliage in spring, later turning green. **'Skylands'** illus. p.76.
P. pungens (Colorado spruce). Columnar conifer. H 50ft (15m), S 15ft (5m). Fully hardy, zones 3–8. Has scaly, gray bark and very sharp, stout, grayish green or bright blue leaves. Cylindrical, light brown cones have papery scales. **'Glauca Globosa'** see *P.p.* 'Montgomery'. **'Hoopsii'**, H 30–50ft (10–15m), has silvery blue foliage. **'Koster'** illus. p.77.

'Montgomery' (syn. *P.p.* 'Glauca Globosa'; illus. p.82), H and S 3ft (1m), is dwarf, compact, spreading or conical, with gray-blue leaves.
P. sitchensis (Sitka spruce). Very vigorous, broadly conical conifer. H 100–160ft (30–50m) in damp locations, 50–70ft (15–20m) in dry situations, S 20–30ft (6–10m). Fully hardy, zones 7–8. Bark scales on old trees. Has prickly, bright deep green leaves and cylindrical, papery, pale brown or whitish cones, 2–4in (5–10cm) long. Is good on an exposed or poor site.
P. smithiana (Morinda spruce, West Himalayan spruce). Slow-growing conifer, conical when young, columnar with horizontal branches and weeping shoots when mature. H 80–100ft (25–30m), S 20ft (6m). Fully hardy, zones 7–8. Has dark green leaves and cylindrical, bright brown cones, 4–8in (10–20cm) long.

PICRASMA (Simaroubaceae)
Genus of deciduous trees, grown for their brilliant autumn color. Produces insignificant flowers in late spring. Fully hardy. Requires sun or semi-shade and fertile, well-drained soil. Propagate by seed in autumn.
P. quassioides illus. p.69.

PIERIS (Ericaceae)
Genus of evergreen shrubs, grown for their foliage and small, profuse, urn-shaped flowers. Fully to frost hardy. Needs a sheltered site in semi-shade or shade and in moist, peaty, acid soil. *P. floribunda*, however, grows well in any acid soil. Young shoots are sometimes frost-killed in spring and should be cut back as soon as possible. Dead-heading after flowering improves growth. Propagate by soft tip or semi-ripe cuttings in summer.
P. **'Bert Chandler'**. Evergreen, bushy shrub. H 6ft (2m), S 5ft (1.5m). Frost hardy, zones 7–9. Lance-shaped leaves are bright pink when young, becoming creamy yellow, then white, and finally dark green. Produces white flowers only very rarely. Does best in a fairly open position.
P. floribunda illus. p.95.
P. **'Forest Flame'**. Evergreen, upright shrub. H 12ft (4m), S 6ft (2m). Frost hardy, zones 7–9. Narrowly oval, glossy leaves are brilliant red when young, becoming pink, then cream, and finally dark green. White flowers are borne with the young leaves from mid- to late spring.
P. formosa. Evergreen, bushy, dense shrub. H and S 12ft (4m). Frost hardy, zones 7–9. Large, oblong, glossy, dark green leaves are bronze when young. Bears large clusters of white flowers from mid- to late spring. var. *forrestii* **'Wakehurst'** illus. p.110. **'Henry Price'** has deep-veined leaves, bronze-red when young.
P. japonica illus. p.84. **'Daisen'** is an evergreen, rounded, dense shrub. H and S 10ft (3m). Fully hardy, zones 6–8. Narrowly oval, bronze leaves mature to glossy, dark green. Drooping clusters of red-budded, deep pink flowers appear in spring. **'Dorothy Wyckoff'** has deep crimson buds,

opening to pink blooms; foliage is bronze in winter. Young foliage of **'Mountain Fire'** is brilliant red. **'Scarlett O'Hara'** illus. p.95. **'Variegata'** is slow-growing, with small leaves, edged with white.
P. nana, syn. *Arcterica nana*. Evergreen, prostrate, dwarf shrub. H 1–2in (2.5–5cm), S 4–6in (10–15cm). Fully hardy, zones 1–4. Has tiny, oval, leathery, dark green leaves, usually in whorls of 3, on fine stems that root readily. In early spring bears small, terminal clusters of white flowers with green or red calyces. Is excellent for binding a peat wall or in a rock garden.
P. taiwanensis. Evergreen, bushy, dense shrub. H 10ft (3m), S 15ft (5m). Fully hardy, zones 7–8. Narrowly oval, dark green leaves are bronze-red when young. Produces clusters of white flowers in early and mid-spring.

PILEA (Urticaceae)
Genus of bushy or trailing annuals and evergreen perennials, grown for their ornamental foliage. Frost tender, min. 50°F (10°C). Grow in any well-drained soil out of direct sunlight and drafts; do not overwater in winter. Pinch out tips in growing season to avoid straggly plants. Propagate perennials by stem cuttings in spring or summer, annuals by seed in spring or autumn. Red spider mite may be a problem.
P. cadierei illus. p.256.
P. involucrata (Friendship plant). Evergreen, bushy perennial. H 6in (15cm), S 1ft (30cm). Zone 10. Oval to rounded leaves, to 2in (5cm) long, have corrugated surfaces and are bronze above, reddish green below; leaves are green above when grown in shade. Has insignificant flowers.
P. nummulariifolia illus. p.261.

PILEOSTEGIA (Hydrangeaceae)
Genus of evergreen, woody-stemmed, root climbers. Frost hardy. Grows in sun or shade and in any well-drained soil; is therefore useful for planting against a north wall. Prune in spring, if required. Propagate by semi-ripe cuttings in summer.
P. viburnoides, syn. *Schizophragma viburnoides*, illus. p.166.

PILOSOCEREUS (Cactaceae)
Genus of columnar, summer-flowering, perennial cacti with wool-like spines in flowering zones at crowns. Some species are included in *Cephalocereus*. Frost tender, min. 52°F (11°C). Needs full sun and very well-drained soil. Propagate by seed or stem cuttings in spring or summer.
P. palmeri illus. p.380.

PIMELEA (Thymelaeaceae)
Genus of evergreen shrubs, grown for their flowers and overall appearance. Frost hardy to frost tender, min. 41°F (5°C). Needs full sun and well-drained, neutral to acid soil. Water potted plants moderately, less when temperatures are low. Needs good winter light and ventilation in northern temperate greenhouses. Propagate by seed in spring or by semi-ripe cuttings in late summer.
P. ferruginea illus. p.130.

PINELLIA (Araceae)
Genus of summer-flowering, tuberous perennials that produce slender, hoodlike, green spathes, each enclosing and concealing a pencil-shaped spadix. Frost hardy. Needs partial shade or sun and humus-rich soil. Water well in spring-summer. Is dormant in winter. Propagate in early spring by offsets or in late summer by bulbils borne in leaf axils.
P. ternata. Summer-flowering, tuberous perennial. H 6–10in (15–25cm), S 4–6in (10–15cm). Zones 6–10. Has erect stems crowned by oval, flat, 3-parted leaves. Leafless stem bears a tubular, green spathe, 2–2¹/₂in (5–6cm) long, with a hood at the tip.

PINGUICULA (Lentibulariaceae)
Genus of summer-flowering perennials with sticky leaves that trap insects and digest them for food. Is useful in pots under glass among plants subject to aphid damage. Fully hardy to frost tender, min. 45°F (7°C). Needs sun and wet soil. Propagate by division in early spring or by seed in autumn.
P. caudata. Basal-rosetted perennial. H 5–6in (12–15cm), S 2in (5cm). Frost tender, zone 10. Narrowly oval leaves are dull green with inrolled, purplish margins. In summer, long stems carry 5-petaled, deep carmine flowers.
P. grandiflora illus. p.322.

PINUS (Pinaceae)
Pine
Genus of small to large conifers with spirally arranged leaves in bundles, usually of 2, 3, or 5 needles. Cones ripen over 2 years and are small in the first year. See also CONIFERS.
P. aristata illus. p.80.
P. armandii (Armand pine, David pine). Conical, open conifer. H 30–50ft (10–15m), S 15–25ft (5–8m). Fully hardy, zones 6–8. Has pendent, glaucous blue leaves and conical, green cones, 3–10in (8–25cm) long, ripening to brown.
P. banksiana illus. p.79.
P. bungeana illus. p.80.
P. cembra illus. p.78.
P. cembroides illus. p.81.
P. chylla. See *P. wallichiana.*
P. contorta illus. p.79. var. *latifolia* illus. p.78. **'Spaan's Dwarf'** is a conical, open, dwarf conifer with short, stiffly erect shoots. H and S 30in (75cm). Fully hardy, zones 6–8. Has erect branches with bright green leaves in 2s.
P. coulteri illus. p.74.
P. densiflora (Japanese red pine). Flat-topped conifer. H 50ft (15m), S 15–22ft (5–7m). Fully hardy, zones 4–7. Has scaling, reddish brown bark, bright green leaves, and conical, yellow or pale brown cones. **'Alice Verkade'**, H and S 30in (75cm), is a diminutive, rounded form with fresh green leaves. **'Umbraculifera'** (syn. *P.d.* 'Tagyo-sho'), H 12ft (4m), S 20ft (6m), is a slow-growing, rounded or umbrella-shaped form.
P. excelsa. See *P. wallichiana.*
P. griffithii. See *P. wallichiana.*
P. halepensis illus. p.79.
P. heldreichii var. *leucodermis.* See *P. leucodermis.*

P. × holfordiana illus. p.73.
P. insignis. See *P. radiata.*
P. jeffreyi illus. p.75.
P. leucodermis, syn. *P. heldreichii* var. *leucodermis,* illus. p.76.
'Compact Gem' (illus. p.83) is a broadly conical, dense, dwarf conifer. H and S 10–12in (25–30cm). Fully hardy, zones 6–8. Has very dark green leaves in 2s. Grows only 1in (2.5cm) a year. **'Schmidtii'** (illus. p.83) is a dwarf form with an ovoid habit and sharp, dark green leaves.
P. montezumae illus. p.74.
P. mugo (Dwarf pine, Mountain pine, Swiss mountain pine). Spreading, shrubby conifer. H 10–15ft (3–5m), S 15–25ft (5–8m). Fully hardy, zones 3–7. Has bright to dark green leaves in 2s and ovoid, brown cones. **'Gnom'**, H and S to 6ft (2m), and **'Mops'**, H 3ft (1m), S 6ft (2m), are rounded cultivars.
P. muricata illus. p.75.
P. nigra (Black pine). Upright, later spreading conifer, generally grown in one of the following forms. **'Horni-brookiana'**, H 5–6ft (1.5–2m), S 6ft (2m), is a fully hardy, zones 5–8, shrubby cultivar with stout, spreading or erect branches and dark green leaves in 2s. subsp. *laricio* (syn. var. *maritima*; Corsican pine), H 80–100ft (25–30m), S 25ft (8m), is fast-growing and narrowly conical with an open crown; bears gray-green leaves, in 2s, and ovoid to conical, yellow- or pale gray-brown cones. subsp. *nigra* illus. p.76.
P. parviflora illus. p.77. **'Adcock's Dwarf'** is a slow-growing, rounded, dense, dwarf conifer. H 6–10ft (2–3m), S 5–6ft (1.5–2m). Fully hardy, zones 6–9. Bears gray-green leaves in 5s.
P. peuce illus. p.73.
P. pinaster illus. p.75.
P. pinea illus. p.81.
P. ponderosa illus. p.75.
P. pumila (Dwarf Siberian pine). Spreading, shrubby conifer. H 6–10ft (2–3m), S 10–15ft (3–5m). Fully hardy, zones 4–7. Has bright blue-green leaves in 5s. Ovoid cones are violet-purple, ripening to red-brown or yellow-brown, the males bright red-purple in spring. **'Globe'**, H and S 20–36in (50cm–1m), is a rounded cultivar with blue foliage.
P. radiata, syn. *P. insignis,* illus. p.76.
P. rigida illus. p.78.
P. strobus illus. p.74. f. *nana* is a rounded, dwarf conifer with an open, sparse, whorled crown. H 3–6ft (1–2m), S 6–10ft (2–3m). Fully hardy, zones 4–9. Gray bark is smooth at first, later fissured. Bears gray-green leaves in 5s.
P. sylvestris (Scots pine). Conifer, upright and with whorled branches when young, that develops a spreading, rounded crown with age. H 50–80ft (15–25m), S 25–30ft (8–10m). Fully hardy, zones 3–7. Bark is flaking and red-brown on upper trunk, fissured and purple-gray at base. Has blue-green leaves in 2s and conical, green cones that ripen to pale gray- or red-brown. **'Aurea'** (illus. p.83), H 30ft (10m), S 12ft (4m), has golden yellow leaves in winter-spring, otherwise blue-green. **'Beuvronensis'**, H and S 3ft (1m), is a rounded shrub. **'Doone Valley'** (illus.

p.82), H and S 3ft (1m), is an upright, irregularly shaped shrub. f. *fastigiata* illus. p.80. **'Gold Coin'** (illus. p.83), H and S 6ft (2m), is a dwarf version of *P.s.* 'Aurea'. **'Nana'** (illus. p.82), H and S 20in (50cm), is a very dense cultivar with widely spaced leaves.
P. thunbergii illus. p.78.
P. virginiana illus. p.79.
P. wallichiana, syn. *P. chylla, P. excelsa, P. griffithii,* illus. p.75.

PIPTANTHUS (Leguminosae)
Genus of deciduous or semi-evergreen shrubs, grown for their foliage and flowers. Frost hardy. In cold areas needs the protection of a south- or west-facing wall. Requires sun and fertile, well-drained soil. In spring cut some older shoots back to ground level and prune any frost-damaged growths back to healthy wood. Propagate by seed in autumn.
P. laburnifolius. See *P. nepalensis.*
P. nepalensis, syn. *P. laburnifolius,* illus. p.114.

PISONIA (Nyctaginaceae)
Genus of evergreen shrubs and trees, grown for their foliage and overall appearance. Frost tender, min. 50–59°F (10–15°C). Needs full light or partial shade and humus-rich, well-drained soil. Water potted specimens freely when in full growth, moderately at other times. Pruning is tolerated if required. Propagate by seed in spring or by semi-ripe cuttings in summer.
P. umbellifera, syn. *Heimerliodendron brunonianum* (Bird-catcher tree, Para para). Evergreen, rounded shrub or tree. H and S 10–20ft (3–6m). Zone 10. Has oval, leathery, lustrous leaves and, in spring, clusters of tiny, green or pink flowers, followed by 5-winged, sticky, brownish fruits.

PISTACIA (Anacardiaceae)
Genus of evergreen or deciduous trees, grown for their foliage and overall appearance. Frost tender, min. 50°F (10°C). Requires full light and free-draining, even dry soil. Water potted plants moderately when in full growth, sparingly at other times. Pruning is tolerated if necessary. Propagate by seed in spring or by semi-ripe cuttings in summer.
P. lentiscus (Mastic tree). Evergreen, irregularly rounded shrub or tree. H 15ft (5m), S to 10ft (3m). Zones 9–10. Leaves are divided into 2–5 pairs of oval, leathery, glossy leaflets. Axillary clusters of insignificant flowers from spring to early summer develop into globose, red, then black fruits in autumn.
P. terebinthus (Cyprus turpentine, Terebinth tree). Deciduous, rounded to ovoid tree. H 20–28ft (6–9m), S 10–20ft (3–6m). Zones 9–10. Leaves have 5–9 oval leaflets, usually lustrous, rich green. In spring and early summer bears axillary clusters of insignificant flowers that develop into tiny, globular to ovoid, red, then purple-brown fruits in autumn.

PISTIA (Araceae)
Genus of one species of deciduous, perennial, floating water plant, grown

for its foliage. In water above 66–70°F (19–21°C) is evergreen. Is suitable for tropical aquariums and frost-free pools. Frost tender, min 50–59°F (10–15°C). Grows in sun or semi-shade. Remove fading foliage and thin plants out as necessary. Propagate by separating plantlets during growing period in summer.
P. stratiotes illus. p.375.

PITCAIRNIA (Bromeliaceae)
Genus of evergreen, rosette-forming perennials, grown for their overall appearance. Frost tender, min. 50°F (10°C). Needs semi-shade and well-drained soil. Water moderately during growing season, sparingly at other times. Propagate by offsets or division in spring.
P. andreana. Evergreen, clump-forming, basal-rosetted perennial. H 8in (20cm), S 12in (30cm) or more. Zone 10. Loose rosettes comprise narrowly lance-shaped, strongly arching, green leaves, gray-scaled beneath. Racemes of tubular, orange-and-red flowers are borne in summer.
P. heterophylla. Evergreen, basal-rosetted perennial with swollen, much-branched rhizomes. H 4in (10cm) or more, S to 12in (30cm). Zone 10. Forms loose rosettes; outer leaves resemble barbed spines, inner leaves are strap-shaped, low-arching, and green, with downy, white undersides. Almost stemless spikes of tubular, bright red, or rarely white, flowers appear in summer.

PITTOSPORUM (Pittosporaceae)
Genus of evergreen trees and shrubs, grown for their ornamental foliage and fragrant flowers. Frost hardy to frost tender, min. 45°F (7°C). Does best in mild areas; in cold regions grow against a south- or west-facing wall. *P. crassifolium* and *P. ralphii* make good, wind-resistant hedges in mild, coastal areas and, like forms with variegated or purple leaves, prefer sun. Others will grow in sun or semi-shade. All need well-drained soil. Propagate *P. dallii* by budding in summer, other species by seed in autumn or spring or by semi-ripe cuttings in summer, and selected forms by semi-ripe cuttings only in summer.
P. crassifolium (Karo). Evergreen, bushy-headed, dense tree or shrub. H 15ft (5m), S 10ft (3m). Frost hardy, zones 9–10. Has oblong, dark green leaves, gray-felted beneath. Clusters of small, fragrant, star-shaped, dark reddish purple flowers are borne in spring. **'Variegatum'** illus. p.71.
P. dallii illus. p.72.
P. eugenioides (Tarata pittosporum). Evergreen, columnar tree. H 30ft (10m), S 15ft (5m). Frost hardy, zones 9–10. Narrowly oval, wavy-edged leaves are glossy, dark green. Honey-scented, star-shaped, pale yellow flowers are produced in spring. **'Variegatum'** illus. p.71.
P. **'Garnettii'** illus. p.94.
P. ralphii. Evergreen, bushy-headed tree or shrub. H 12ft (4m), S 10ft (3m). Frost hardy, zones 8–10. Large leaves are oblong, leathery, and gray-green, very hairy beneath. Bears small,

fragrant, star-shaped, dark red flowers in spring.
P. tenuifolium illus. p.95. **'James Stirling'** is an evergreen, columnar, then rounded, shrub or tree. H 40ft (12m), S 15ft (5m). Frost hardy, zones 9–10. Has deep purple shoots and small, rounded, wavy-edged, silvery green leaves. Honey-scented, tubular, purple flowers are borne in late spring. **'Tom Thumb'** illus. p.145.
P. tobira (Japanese pittosporum, Mock orange). Evergreen, bushy-headed, dense tree or shrub. H 20ft (6m), S 12ft (4m). Frost hardy, zones 8–10. Has oblong to oval, glossy, dark green leaves. Very fragrant, star-shaped, white flowers, opening in late spring, later become creamy yellow.
P. undulatum (Victorian box). Evergreen, broadly conical tree. H 40ft (12m), S 25ft (8m). Half hardy, zones 9–10. Has long, narrowly oval, pointed, wavy-edged, dark green leaves. Bears fragrant, star-shaped, white flowers in late spring and early summer, followed by rounded, orange fruits.

PITYROGRAMMA (Polypodiaceae)
Genus of semi-evergreen or evergreen ferns, suitable for hanging baskets. Frost tender, min. 50°F (10°C). Needs semi-shade and humus-rich, moist but well-drained soil. Remove fading fronds regularly. Water carefully to avoid spoiling farina (meal-like powder) on fronds. Propagate by spores in late summer.
P. chrysophylla. Semi-evergreen or evergreen fern. H and S 18in (45cm). Zone 10. Lance-shaped, delicately filigreed, spreading, green fronds, with yellow farina on undersides, are produced on brown stems.
P. triangularis. Semi-evergreen or evergreen fern. H and S 18in (45cm). Zone 10. Has broadly triangular, delicately divided, green fronds with orange or creamy white farina.

PLAGIANTHUS (Malvaceae)
Genus of evergreen or deciduous trees and shrubs, grown for their habit and inconspicuous, fragrant flowers. Frost to half hardy. In cold areas plant against a south- or west-facing wall. Needs sun and fertile, well-drained soil. Propagate by semi-ripe cuttings in summer.
P. divaricatus. Deciduous, bushy shrub. H 8ft (2.5m), S 12ft (4m). Half hardy, zones 9–10. Slender, interlacing, dark brown branches produce linear, dark green leaves. Has very fragrant, tiny, yellowish white flowers in late spring.

Plagiorhegma dubia. See *Jeffersonia dubia.*

PLANTAGO (Plantaginaceae)
Genus of summer-flowering annuals, biennials, and evergreen perennials and shrubs. Many species are weeds, but a few are grown for their foliage and architectural value. Fully hardy to frost tender, min. 45–50°F (7–10°C). Requires full sun and well-drained soil. Water potted plants moderately, sparingly in winter. Propagate by seed or division in spring.
P. nivalis illus. p.331.

PLATANUS (Platanaceae)
Plane
Genus of deciduous trees, grown for their habit, foliage, and flaking bark. Flowers are inconspicuous. Spherical fruit clusters hang from shoots in autumn. Fully to half hardy. Needs full sun and deep, fertile, well-drained soil. Propagate species by seed in autumn, *P. x acerifolia* by hardwood cuttings in early winter. All except *P. orientalis* are susceptible to the fungal disease plane anthracnose.
P. x acerifolia illus. p.42. **'Suttneri'** is a vigorous, deciduous, spreading tree. H 70ft (20m), S 50ft (15m). Fully hardy, zones 5–8. Has flaking bark and large, palmate, 5-lobed, sharply toothed, bright green leaves blotched with creamy white.
P. orientalis (Oriental plane). Deciduous, spreading tree. H and S 80ft (25m) or more. Fully hardy, zones 7–8. Produces large, palmate, glossy, pale green leaves with 5 deep lobes.

PLATYCARYA (Juglandaceae)
Genus of one species of deciduous tree, grown for its foliage and catkins. Fully hardy. Requires full sun and fertile, well-drained soil. Propagate by seed in autumn.
P. strobilacea. Deciduous, spreading tree. H and S 30ft (10m). Zones 6–9. Has ashlike, bright green leaves with 5–15 leaflets. Upright, green catkins are borne from mid- to late summer; males are slender and cylindrical, often drooping at tips, females are conelike, become brown, and persist through winter.

PLATYCERIUM (Polypodiaceae)
Staghorn fern
Genus of evergreen, epiphytic ferns, best grown in hanging baskets and fastened to and suspended from pieces of wood. Produces 2 kinds of fronds: permanent, broad, sterile "nest leaves" forming the main part of the plant; and strap-shaped, usually partly bifurcated, arching fertile fronds. Frost tender, min. 41°F (5°C). Needs warm, humid conditions in semi-shade and fibrous, peaty compost with hardly any soil. Propagate by detaching buds in spring or summer and planting in compost or by spores in summer or early autumn.
P. bifurcatum illus. p.184.

Platycladus orientalis. See *Thuja orientalis.*

PLATYCODON (Campanulaceae)
Balloon flower
Genus of one species of perennial, grown for its flowers in summer. Fully hardy. Needs sun and light, sandy soil. Propagate by basal cuttings of non-flowering shoots in summer, preferably with a piece of root attached, or by seed in autumn.
P. grandiflorus illus. p.241. var. **mariesii** is a neat, clump-forming perennial. H and S 12–18in (30–45cm). Zones 4–9. In mid-summer produces solitary terminal, large, balloonlike flower buds opening to bell-shaped, blue or purplish blue flowers. Has oval, sharply toothed, bluish green leaves.

PLATYSTEMON (Papaveraceae)
Genus of one species of summer-flowering annual. Fully hardy. Grow in sun and in fertile, well-drained soil. Propagate by seed sown outdoors in spring or early autumn.
P. californicus illus. p.279.

PLECTRANTHUS (Labiatae)
Genus of evergreen, trailing or bushy perennials, grown for their foliage. Frost tender, min. 50°F (10°C). Is easy to grow if kept moist in partial shade or bright light. Cut back tips in growing season if plants become too straggly. Propagate by stem cuttings or division in spring or summer.
P. australis (Swedish ivy). Evergreen, trailing perennial with square stems. H to 6in (15cm), S indefinite. Zone 10. Has rounded, waxy, glossy, green leaves with scalloped edges. Intermittently produces racemes of tubular, white, or pale mauve flowers.
P. coleoides 'Variegatus' illus. p.221.
P. oertendahlii (Prostrate coleus, Swedish ivy). Evergreen, prostrate perennial. H to 6in (15cm), S indefinite. Zone 10. Rounded, scalloped, dark green leaves are reddish green below, with white veins above. Racemes of tubular, white or pale mauve flowers are borne at irregular intervals throughout the year.

PLEIOBLASTUS (Bambusoideae). See GRASSES, BAMBOOS, RUSHES, and SEDGES.
P. variegatus, syn. *Arundinaria fortunei, A. variegata,* illus. p.180.
P. viridistriatus, syn. *Arundinaria auricoma, A. viridistriata,* illus. p.183.

PLEIONE. See ORCHIDS.
P. bulbocodioides (illus. p.253). Deciduous, terrestrial orchid. H 8in (20cm). Frost hardy, zones 8–10. In spring, usually before solitary leaf appears, bears pink, rose, or magenta flowers, 2–5in (5–12cm) across, with darker purple marks on lips. Leaf is narrowly lance-shaped, 5¹/₂in (14cm) long. Is often difficult to flower: regular feeding helps to increase pseudobulbs to flowering size.
P. x confusa. Deciduous, terrestrial orchid. H 6in (15cm). Frost hardy, zones 8–10. Canary yellow flowers, 2–3in (5–8cm) across, with brown or purple blotches on each lip, appear singly in spring, before foliage emerges. Has lance-shaped leaves, 4–7in (10–18cm) long. Is best grown in an alpine house. Needs semi-shade.
P. hookeriana. Deciduous, terrestrial orchid. H 3–6in (8–15cm). Frost hardy, zones 8–10. Lilac-pink, rose, or white flowers, 2–3in (5–7cm) across, each with a brown- or purplish spotted lip, are borne singly in spring with lance-shaped, 2–8in (5–20cm) long leaves. Cultivate as for *P. x confusa.*
P. humilis. Deciduous, terrestrial orchid. H 2–3in (5–8cm). Frost hardy, zones 8–10. In winter, before foliage appears, white flowers, 3–3¹/₂in (7–9cm) across, each with a crimson-spotted lip, are borne singly or in pairs. Lance-shaped leaves are 7–10in (18–25cm) long. Cultivate as for *P. x confusa.*

P. praecox. Deciduous, terrestrial orchid. H 3–5in (8–13cm). Frost hardy, zones 8–10. Flowers, to 3in (8cm) across, in pairs, appear in autumn, after foliage. They are white to pinkish purple or lilac-purple, with violet marks. Leaves are oblong to lance-shaped and 6–10in (15–25cm) long. Cultivate as for *P. x confusa.*

PLEIOSPILOS (Aizoaceae)
Genus of clump-forming, perennial succulents with almost stemless rosettes bearing up to 4 pairs of fleshy, erect leaves, like pieces of granite, each with a flat upper surface and each pair united at the base. Flowers are daisylike. Individual species are very similar, and many are difficult to identify. Frost tender, min. 41°F (5°C). Needs sun and well-drained soil. Propagate by seed or division in spring or summer.
P. bolusii illus. p.399.
P. simulans illus. p.398.

PLEUROTHALLIS. See ORCHIDS.
P. grobyi. Evergreen, epiphytic orchid for a cool greenhouse. H 1in (2.5cm). Zone 10. In summer produces sprays of minute, white flowers, ¹/₈in (0.25cm) long. Leaves are oval, fleshy, and ¹/₄in (0.5cm) long. Shade in summer.

PLUMBAGO (Plumbaginaceae)
Genus of annuals, evergreen or semi-evergreen shrubs, perennials, and woody-stemmed, scrambling climbers, grown for their primrose-shaped flowers. Frost hardy to frost tender, min. 45°F (7°C). Grow in full light or semi-shade and in fertile, well-drained soil. Water regularly, less when not in full growth. Tie stems to supports. Thin out or spur back all previous year's growth in early spring. Propagate by semi-ripe cuttings in summer. Whitefly may be a problem.
P. auriculata, syn. *P. capensis,* illus. p.173.
P. capensis. See *P. auriculata.*
P. indica, syn. *P. rosea.* Evergreen or semi-evergreen, spreading shrub or semi-climber. H 6ft (2m), S 3–6ft (1–2m). Frost tender, zone 10. Leaves are oval to elliptic and green. Has terminal racemes of primrose-shaped, red or pink flowers, 1in (2.5cm) long, in summer, if hard pruned annually in spring, or from late winter onwards, if left unpruned and trained as a climber.
P. rosea. See *P. indica.*

PLUMERIA (Apocynaceae)
Frangipani
Genus of mainly deciduous, fleshy-branched shrubs and trees, grown for their flowers in summer-autumn. Has poisonous sap. Frost tender, min. 55°F (13°C). Requires full sun and freely draining soil. Water potted specimens moderately while in growth, keep dry in winter when leafless. Stem tips may be cut out to induce branching. Propagate by seed or leafless stem-tip cuttings in late spring. Red spider mite may be a nuisance.
P. acuminata. See *P. rubra* var. *acutifolia.*
P. acutifolia. See *P. rubra* var. *acutifolia.*

P. alba (West Indian jasmine). Deciduous, rounded, sparingly branched tree. H to 20ft (6m), S to 12ft (4m). Zone 10. Leaves are lance-shaped and slender-pointed, to 1ft (30cm) long. Terminal clusters of fragrant, yellow-eyed, white flowers, each with 5 spreading petals and a tubular base, appear in summer.
P. rubra illus. p.68. var. *acutifolia* (syn. *P. acuminata*, *P. acutifolia*) is a deciduous, spreading, sparsely branched tree or shrub. H and S 12ft (4m) or more. Zone 10. Produces fragrant, yellow-centered, white flowers, with 5 spreading petals, in summer-autumn. Leaves are lance-shaped to oval and 8–12in (20–30cm) long.

PODOCARPUS (Podocarpaceae). See CONIFERS.
P. alpinus (Tasmanian podocarp). Rounded, spreading, shrubby conifer. H 6ft (2m), S 10–15ft (3–5m). Frost hardy, zones 8–10. Has linear, dull green leaves and rounded, egg-shaped, fleshy, bright red fruits.
P. andinus, syn. *Prumnopitys andinus* (Plum-fruited yew, Plum yew). Conifer with a domed crown on several stems. H 50ft (15m), S 25ft (8m). Frost hardy, zones 8–10. Has smooth, gray-brown bark, needlelike, flattened, bluish green leaves and edible, yellowish white fruits like small plums.
P. macrophyllus (Kusamaki). Erect conifer. H 30ft (10m), S 10–15ft (3–5m). Half hardy, zones 7–10. Long, linear leaves are bright green above, glaucous beneath. May be grown as a shrub, H and S 3–6ft (1–2m), and planted in a tub in hot climates.
P. nivalis (Alpine totara; illus. p.82). Rounded, spreading, shrubby conifer. H 6ft (2m), S 10–15ft (3–5m). Frost hardy, zones 8–10. Is very similar to *P. alpinus*, but has longer, broader, more rigid leaves.
P. salignus illus. p.78.

PODOPHYLLUM (Berberidaceae) Genus of spring-flowering, rhizomatous perennials. Fully hardy, but young leaves may be damaged by frost. Does best in semi-shade and moist, peaty soil. Propagate by division in spring or by seed in autumn.
P. emodi, syn. *P. hexandrum*, illus. p.225.
P. hexandrum. See *P. emodi*.
P. peltatum (May apple). Vigorous, spreading, rhizomatous perennial. H 12–18in (30–45cm), S 12in (30cm). Zones 4–9. Palmate, sometimes brown-mottled, light green leaves, with 3–5 deep lobes, push up through soil, looking like closed umbrellas, and are followed, in spring, by nodding, cup-shaped, white flowers. Produces large, fleshy, plumlike, glossy, deep rose-pink fruits in autumn.

PODRANEA (Bignoniaceae) Genus of evergreen, twining climbers, grown for their foxglovelike flowers. Frost tender, min. 41–50°F (5–10°C). Grow in any fertile, well-drained soil, with full light. Water regularly, less in cold weather. Provide support. Thin

out crowded growth in winter or early spring. Propagate by seed in spring or by semi-ripe cuttings in summer.
P. ricasoliana, syn. *Pandorea ricasoliana*, *Tecoma ricasoliana*. Fast-growing, evergreen, twining climber. H 12ft (4m) or more. Zones 9–10. Has leaves of 7 or 9 lance-shaped to oval, wavy, deep green leaflets. Loose clusters of fragrant pink flowers with darker veins appear from spring to autumn.

Poinciana pulcherrima. See *Caesalpinia pulcherrima.*

POLEMONIUM (Polemoniaceae) Genus of late spring- or summer-flowering annuals and perennials, some perennials tending to be short-lived. Fully hardy. Prefers sun and fertile, well-drained soil. Propagate by division in spring or by seed in autumn.
P. caeruleum illus. p.242.
P. carneum illus. p.240.
P. foliosissimum. Vigorous, clump-forming perennial. H 30in (75cm), S 24in (60cm). Zones 4–8. Terminal clusters of cup-shaped, lilac flowers, with yellow stamens, are borne in summer above oblong to lance-shaped, green leaves with numerous, small leaflets.
P. pulcherrimum illus. p.241.

POLIANTHES (Amaryllidaceae) Genus of tuberous perennials, grown for their fragrant flowers in summer. Half hardy to frost tender, min. 59–68°F (15–20°C). Needs a sheltered site in full sun and well-drained soil. Water well in spring-summer; feed liquid fertilizer every 2 weeks when in growth. Dry off after leaves die down in winter. Propagate by seed or offsets in spring.
P. geminiflora, syn. *Bravoa geminiflora*, illus. p.353.
P. tuberosa (Tuberose). Summer-flowering, tuberous perennial. H 2–3ft (60cm–1m), S 4–6in (10–15cm). Half hardy, zones 9–10. Has a basal cluster of strap-shaped, erect leaves; flower stem also bears leaves on lower part. Produces a spike of funnel-shaped, single, white flowers with 6 spreading petals. A double form is also available.

POLYGALA (Polygalaceae) Genus of annuals, evergreen perennials, shrubs, and trees, grown mainly for their pealike flowers. Fully hardy to frost tender, min. 45°F (7°C). Needs full light or partial shade and moist, well-drained soil. Water potted specimens freely when in full growth, moderately at other times. Lanky stems may be cut back hard in late winter. Propagate by seed in spring or by semi-ripe cuttings in late summer. Is susceptible to whitefly.
P. calcarea illus. p.324. **'Bulley's Variety'** illus. p.324.
P. chamaebuxus illus. p.325. var. *grandiflora* (syn. var. *rhodoptera*) illus. p.308.
P. myrtifolia **'Grandiflora'** illus. p.135.
P. vayredae. Evergreen, mat-forming shrub. H 2–4in (5–10cm), S 8–12in

(20–30cm). Frost hardy, zones 8–10. Slender, prostrate stems bear small, linear leaves. Pealike, reddish purple flowers, each with a yellow lip, appear in late spring and early summer. Suits a rock garden or alpine house.

POLYGONATUM (Liliaceae) Solomon's seal
Genus of spring- or early summer-flowering, rhizomatous perennials. Fully hardy to frost tender, min. 41°F (5°C). Requires a cool, shady situation and fertile, well-drained soil. Propagate by division in early spring or by seed in autumn. Sawfly caterpillar is a common pest.
P. canaliculatum. See *P. commutatum.*
P. commutatum, syn. *P. canaliculatum*, *P. giganteum* (Great Solomon's seal). Arching, rhizomatous perennial. H 5ft (1.5m) or more, S 2ft (60cm). Fully hardy, zones 4–9. Bears pendent clusters of bell-shaped, white flowers in leaf axils during late spring. Oval to oblong leaves are green.
P. giganteum. See *P. commutatum.*
P. hirtum, syn. *P. latifolium.* Upright, then arching, rhizomatous perennial. H 3ft (1m), S 1ft (30cm). Fully hardy, zones 4–9. Clusters of 2–5 drooping, tubular, green-tipped, white flowers open in late spring. Undersides of stems, leaf stalks, and oval to lance-shaped, green leaves are hairy.
P. hookeri illus. p.307.
P. x *hybridum* illus. p.197.
P. latifolium. See *P. hirtum.*
P. multiflorum. Arching, leafy perennial with fleshy rhizomes. H 3ft (1m), S 1ft (30cm). Fully hardy, zones 3–9. In late spring, clusters of 2–6 pendent, tubular, green-tipped, white flowers appear in upper leaf axils. Has oval to lance-shaped, green leaves. **'Flore Pleno'** has double flowers that resemble ballet dancers' skirts. **'Variegatum'**, H 2ft (60cm), has leaves with creamy white stripes.
P. odoratum (Angled Solomon's seal). Arching, rhizomatous perennial. H 2ft (60cm), S 1ft (30cm). Fully hardy, zones 4–9. Produces pairs of fragrant, tubular to bell-shaped, green-tipped, white flowers in upper leaf axils in late spring. Oval to lance-shaped leaves are green.
P. verticillatum (Whorled Solomon's seal). Upright, rhizomatous perennial. H 4ft (1.2m), S 1¹/2ft (45cm). Fully hardy, zones 4–9. Produces narrowly bell-shaped, greenish white flowers in upper leaf axils in early summer. Has whorls of lance-shaped, green leaves.

POLYGONUM (Polygonaceae) Knotweed
Genus of annuals, perennials, some of which are evergreen, and deciduous, woody-stemmed, twining climbers. Some species are invasive. Fully to half hardy. Tolerates sun or shade and well-drained soil, but does particularly well in a damp position. Propagate by seed or division in autumn or spring, climbers only by semi-ripe cuttings in summer.
P. affine. Evergreen, mat-forming perennial. H 6–12in (15–30cm), S 12in (30cm) or more. Fully hardy, zones

4–8. Stout stems bear small, lance-shaped, glossy, green leaves that turn bronze in winter. In autumn carries dense spikes of small, funnel-shaped, rose-red flowers. Is good on a bank or in a rock garden. **'Darjeeling Red'**, H 8–10in (20–25cm), has long spikes of deep red flowers. **'Donald Lowndes'** illus. p.316.
P. amplexicaule. Clump-forming, leafy perennial. H and S 4ft (1.2m). Fully hardy, zones 5–9. Bears profuse spikes of small, rich red flowers in summer-autumn. Has oval to heart-shaped, green leaves. **'Firetail'** illus. p.208.
P. aubertii, syn. *Bilderdykia aubertii*, *Fallopia aubertii* (Mile-a-minute plant, Russian vine). Vigorous, deciduous, woody-stemmed, twining climber. H to 40ft (12m) or more. Fully hardy, zones 5–9. Leaves are broadly heart-shaped. Panicles of small, white or greenish flowers, ageing to pink, are carried in summer-autumn; they are followed by angled, pinkish white fruits.
P. baldschuanicum, syn. *Bilderdykia baldschuanica*, *Fallopia baldschu-anica*, illus. p.175.
P. bistorta (European bistort). **'Superbum'** illus. p.203.
P. campanulatum illus. p.217.
P. capitatum. Compact, spreading perennial. H 2in (5cm), S 6–8in (15–20cm). Half hardy, zones 4–9. Small, oval leaves are green with darker marks. Small, spherical heads of pink flowers are borne in summer. Is suitable for a rock garden or bank.
P. milletii illus. p.208.
P. sphaerostachyum illus. p.236.
P. vacciniifolium illus. p.327.
P. virginianum. See *Tovara virginiana.*

POLYPODIUM (Polypodiaceae) Genus of deciduous, semi-evergreen, or evergreen ferns, grown for their sculptural fronds. Fully hardy to frost tender, min. 50°F (10°C). Grow in semi-shade and fibrous, moist but well-drained soil. Propagate by division in spring or by spores in late summer.
P. aureum. See *Phlebodium aureum.*
P. glycyrrhiza illus. p.184.
P. polypodioides. Semi-evergreen, creeping fern. H 4in (10cm), S 6in (15cm). Frost tender, zones 9–10. Lance-shaped, green fronds have widely spaced pinnae and emerge from a scaly base and rhizome.
P. scouleri illus. p.185.
P. virginianum (American wall fern). Semi-evergreen, creeping fern. H 12in (30cm), S 9in (23cm). Frost hardy, zones 7–9. Has narrowly lance-shaped, divided, green fronds.
P. vulgare illus. p.187. **'Cornubiense'** illus. p.186. **'Cristatum'** is an evergreen, creeping fern. H and S 10–12in (25–30cm). Fully hardy, zones 5–8. Narrowly lance-shaped, divided, green fronds, with semi-pendulous, terminal crests, grow from creeping rhizomes covered with copper brown scales.

POLYSCIAS (Araliaceae) Genus of evergreen trees and shrubs, grown for their foliage. Sometimes has insignificant flowers in summer, but only on large, mature specimens. Frost tender, 59–64°F (15–18°C). Needs partial shade and humus-rich, well-drained soil. Water potted plants freely when in full growth, moderately at other times. Straggly stems may be cut out in spring. Propagate by seed in spring or by stem-tip or leafless stem-section cuttings in summer. Red spider mite may be troublesome.

P. filicifolia illus. p.120. **'Marginata'** is an evergreen, erect, sparsely branched shrub. H 6ft (2m) or more, S 3ft (1m) or more. Zone 10. Has 1ft (30cm) long leaves composed of many small, oval to lance-shaped, serrated, bright green leaflets with white edges.

P. guilfoylei (Wild coffee). Slow-growing, evergreen, rounded tree. H 10–25ft (3–8m), S to 6ft (2m) or more. Zones 9–10. Leaves are 10–16in (25–40cm) long and divided into oval to rounded, serrated, deep green leaflets. **'Victoriae'** illus. p.94.

POLYSTICHUM (Polypodiaceae)
Genus of evergreen, semi-evergreen, or deciduous ferns. Fully to frost hardy. Does best in semi-shade and moist but well-drained soil enriched with fibrous organic matter. Remove faded fronds regularly. Propagate species by division in spring or by spores in summer, selected forms by division in spring.

P. acrostichoides (Christmas fern). Evergreen fern. H 24in (60cm), S 18in (45cm). Fully hardy, zones 3–9. Slender, lance-shaped, deep green fronds have small, hollylike pinnae. Is excellent for cutting.

P. aculeatum (Hard shield fern, Prickly shield fern). Semi-evergreen fern. H 24in (60cm), S 30in (75cm). Fully hardy, zones 4–8. Broadly lance-shaped, yellowish green, then deep green fronds, with oblong to oval, spiny-edged, glossy pinnae, are produced on stems often covered in brown scales. **'Pulcherrimum'** illus. p.184.

P. munitum illus. p.184.

P. setiferum (Soft shield fern). **'Divisi-lobum'** illus. p.185. **'Proliferum'** illus. p.187.

P. tsus-simense. Semi-evergreen fern. H 12in (30cm), S 9in (23cm). Frost hardy, zones 6–8. Has broadly lance-shaped, dull green fronds delicately divided into oblong, finely spiny-edged pinnae. Is suitable for a peat garden or alpine house.

PONCIRUS (Rutaceae)
Genus of one species of very spiny, deciduous shrub or small tree, grown for its foliage, showy flowers, and orangelike fruits. Is very effective as a protective hedge. Fully hardy. Needs sun and fertile, well-drained soil. Cut out dead wood in spring, and trim hedges in early summer. Propagate by semi-ripe cuttings in summer or by seed when ripe, in autumn.

P. trifoliata (Japanese bitter orange). Deciduous, bushy shrub or tree. H and S 15ft (5m). Zones 5–9. Stout, spiny, green shoots bear dark green leaves each composed of 3 oval leaflets. Fragrant white flowers, with 4 or 5

large petals, borne in late spring and often again in autumn, are followed by rounded, ³/₄–1¹/₄in (2–3cm) wide fruits.

PONTEDERIA (Pontederiaceae)
Genus of deciduous, perennial, marginal water plants, grown for their foliage and flower spikes. Fully to frost hardy. Needs full sun and up to 9in (23cm) depth of water. Remove fading flowers regularly. Propagate in spring by division or seed.

P. cordata illus. p.374.

POPULUS (Salicaceae)
Poplar
Genus of deciduous trees, grown for their habit, foliage, and very quick growth. Has catkins in late winter or spring. Female trees produce copious amounts of fluffy, white seeds. Fully hardy. Prefers full sun and needs deep, fertile, moist but well-drained soil; resents dry soil, apart from *P. alba*, which thrives in coastal gardens. Extensive root systems make poplars unsuitable for planting close to buildings, particularly on clay soil. Propagate by hardwood cuttings in winter. Is susceptible to bacterial canker and fungal diseases.

P. alba illus. p.39. Is much confused with the commoner *P. canescens*. **'Pyramidalis'** is a vigorous, deciduous, upright tree. H 70ft (20m), S 15ft (5m). Zones 4–9. Broadly oval, wavy-margined or lobed, dark green leaves, white beneath, turn yellow in autumn. **'Raket'** (syn. *P.a.* 'Rocket') illus. p.43. **'Richardii'**, H 50ft (15m), S 40ft (12m), has leaves that are golden yellow above.

P. balsamifera (Balsam poplar, Tacamahac). Fast-growing, deciduous, upright tree. H 100ft (30m), S 25ft (8m). Zones 5–9. Oval, glossy, dark green leaves, whitish beneath, have a strong fragrance of balsam when young.

P. x *berolinensis* (Berlin poplar). Deciduous, columnar tree. H 80ft (25m), S 25ft (8m). Zones 3–9. Has broadly oval, bright green leaves with white undersides.

P. x *canadensis* (Canadian poplar). **'Eugenei'** is a deciduous, columnar tree. H 100ft (30m), S 40ft (12m). Zones 4–9. Has broadly oval, bronze, young leaves, maturing to dark green, and red catkins in spring. **'Robusta'** and **'Serotina de Selys'** (syn. *P.* x *c.* 'Serotina Erecta') illus. p.40.

P. candicans, syn. *P. gileadensis* (Balm-of-Gilead, Ontario poplar). Very fast-growing, deciduous, conical tree. H 80ft (25m), S 30ft (10m). Zones 5–9. Oval leaves are dark green and, when young, balsam-scented. Is very susceptible to canker. **'Aurora'**, H 50ft (15m) or more, S 20ft (6m), has leaves heavily but irregularly blotched with creamy white.

P. canescens illus. p.40.

P. deltoides (Cottonwood, Eastern cottonwood, Necklace poplar). Very fast-growing, deciduous, spreading tree. H 100ft (30m), S 70ft (20m). Zones 3–9. Has lush growth of broadly oval, glossy, bright green leaves.

P. gileadensis. See *P. candicans*.

P. lasiocarpa (Chinese necklace poplar). Very fast-growing, deciduous,

spreading tree. H 50ft (15m), S 40ft (12m). Zones 6–9. Has stout shoots and very large, heart-shaped, green leaves with red veins, on long, red stalks. Stout, drooping, yellow catkins are borne in spring.

P. maximowiczii illus. p.39.

P. nigra (Black poplar). Very fast-growing, deciduous, spreading tree. H 80ft (25m), S 70ft (20m). Zones 3–9. Has dark bark. Diamond-shaped leaves are bronze when young, bright green when mature, and yellow in autumn. Male trees bear red catkins in mid-spring. **'Italica'** illus. p.41.

P. szechuanica. Very fast-growing, deciduous, conical tree. H 80ft (25m), S 30ft (10m). Zones 6–9. Has flaking, pinkish gray bark and large, heart-shaped, dark green leaves.

P. tremula (Aspen). Vigorous, deciduous, spreading tree. H 50ft (15m), S 30ft (10m). Zones 4–9. Rounded leaves are bronze-red when young, gray-green when mature, and yellow in autumn. Flattened stalks make foliage tremble and rattle in wind. **'Erecta'**, S 15ft (5m), has an upright habit. **'Pendula'** illus. p.52.

P. tremuloides (American aspen, Quaking aspen). Very fast-growing, deciduous, spreading tree. H 50ft (15m) or more, S 30ft (10m). Zones 2–9. Has rounded, finely toothed, glossy, dark green leaves that flutter in the wind and turn yellow in autumn.

P. trichocarpa (Black cottonwood, Western balsam poplar). Very fast-growing, deciduous, conical tree. H 100ft (30m) or more, S 30ft (10m). Zones 5–9. Bears dense growth of oval, glossy, dark green leaves with green-veined, white undersides, strongly balsam-scented when young. Foliage turns yellow in autumn.

PORTULACA (Portulacaceae)
Genus of fleshy annuals and perennials with flowers that open in sun and close in shade. Half hardy to frost tender, min. 36–8°F (2–4°C). Needs full light and any well-drained soil. Propagate by seed sown under glass in early spring, or outdoors in late spring. Is prone to attack by aphids.

P. grandiflora (Rose moss). Slow-growing, partially prostrate annual. H 6–8in (15–20cm), S 6in (15cm). Frost tender. Has lance-shaped, succulent, bright green leaves. In summer and early autumn bears shallowly bowl-shaped flowers, 1in (2.5cm) wide and with conspicuous stamens, in shades of yellow, red, orange, pink, or white. **'Cloudbeater'** is a double-flowered cultivar. **Sundance Series** illus. p.270. **Sunnyside Series** has roselike, double flowers.

PORTULACARIA (Portulacaceae)
Genus of one species of evergreen or semi-evergreen, succulent-leaved shrub, grown for its foliage and overall appearance. Frost tender, min. 45–50°F (7–10°C). Needs full sun and well-drained soil. Water potted plants moderately when in full growth, sparingly at other times. Propagate by semi-ripe cuttings in summer.

P. afra illus. p.121. **'Variegata'** is an evergreen or semi-evergreen, erect

shrub with more or less horizontal branches. H and S 6–10ft (2–3m). Zones 9–10. Has oval to rounded, fleshy, cream-edged, bright green leaves and, from late spring to summer, tiny, star-shaped, pale pink flowers in small clusters.

POTAMOGETON (Potamogetonaceae)
Genus of deciduous, perennial, submerged water plants, grown for their foliage. Is suitable for cold-water pools and aquariums. Fully hardy. Prefers sun. Remove fading foliage and thin colonies of plants as necessary. Propagate by stem cuttings in spring or summer.

P. crispus illus. p.374.

P. lucens (Shining pondweed). Deciduous, perennial, submerged water plant. S indefinite. Zones 7–10. Oblong, deep olive green leaves form spreading colonies. Inconspicuous, greenish flowers are borne in summer. Is suitable for a medium- to large-sized pool.

POTENTILLA (Rosaceae)
Genus of perennials and deciduous shrubs, grown for their clusters of small, flattish to saucer-shaped flowers and for their foliage. Tall species—particularly the shrubs—are useful in borders. Dwarf potentillas are good for rock gardens. Fully hardy. Does best in full sun, but flower color is better on orange-, red-, and pink-flowered cultivars if they are shaded from hottest sun. Needs well-drained soil. Propagate perennial species by seed in autumn or by division in spring or autumn; selected forms by division only in spring or autumn. Shrubby species may be raised by seed in autumn or by softwood or greenwood cuttings in summer, selected forms by softwood or greenwood cuttings in summer.

P. **'Abbotswood'** illus. p.126.

P. alba illus. p.313.

P. arbuscula. Deciduous, bushy, dense shrub. H 3ft (1m), S 4ft (1.2m). Zones 6–9. Saucer-shaped, golden yellow flowers are produced from mid-summer to autumn amid gray-green to silver gray leaves divided into 3 or 5 narrowly oblong leaflets.

P. argyrophylla. Clump-forming perennial. H 18in (45cm), S 24in (60cm). Zones 7–9. Saucer-shaped, clear yellow flowers are produced in profusion from early to late summer above strawberrylike, silvery leaves.

P. atrosanguinea illus. p.240.

P. aurea illus. p.326.

P. **'Beesii'**, syn. *P.* 'Nana Argentea'. Slow-growing, deciduous, compact shrub. H 30in (75cm), S 3ft (1m). Zones 6–8. Bears saucer-shaped, golden yellow flowers in summer-autumn. Has silver leaves comprising 3 or 5 narrowly oblong leaflets.

P. **'Coronation Triumph'**. Deciduous, mound-forming, dense shrub. H 3ft (1m), S 5ft (1.5m). Zones 3–8. Has green leaves divided into 5 narrowly oblong leaflets. Saucer-shaped, bright yellow flowers are borne profusely over a long period in summer-autumn.

P. crantzii (Alpine cinquefoil). Upright perennial with a thick, woody rootstock. H and S 4–8in (10–20cm). Zones 3–8. Produces wedge-shaped, 5-lobed leaves and, in spring, flattish, yellow flowers with orange centers. Is good in a rock garden.

P. davurica var. **mandschurica** of gardens. See *P.* 'Manchu'.

P. 'Daydawn' illus. p.129.

P. 'Elizabeth' illus. p.137.

P. eriocarpa illus. p.325.

P. 'Etna'. Clump-forming perennial. H 30in (75cm), S 18in (45cm). Zones 5–9. In mid-summer produces saucer-shaped, maroon flowers above strawberrylike, dark green leaves.

P. 'Farrer's White' illus. p.127.

P. 'Friedrichsenii' illus. p.137.

P. fruticosa. Deciduous, bushy, dense shrub. H 3ft (1m), S 5ft (1.5m). Zones 3–8. From late spring to late summer produces saucer-shaped, bright yellow flowers. Dark green leaves have 5 narrowly oblong leaflets.

P. 'Gibson's Scarlet'. Clump-forming perennial. H and S 18in (45cm). Zones 5–9. Bears saucer-shaped, brilliant scarlet flowers from mid- to late summer. Dark green leaves are strawberrylike.

P. 'Gloire de Nancy', syn. *P.* 'Glory of Nancy'. Clump-forming perennial. H and S 18in (45cm). Zones 3–8. Very large, saucer-shaped, semi-double, orange and coppery red flowers appear throughout summer. Has strawberrylike, dark green leaves.

P. 'Glory of Nancy'. See *P.* 'Gloire de Nancy'.

P. 'Goldfinger'. Deciduous, bushy, dense shrub. H and S 5ft (1.5m). Zones 3–8. Bears large, saucer-shaped, rich yellow flowers in profusion from late spring to autumn. Leaves are deep green and divided into 5 narrowly oblong leaflets.

P. 'Jackman's Variety'. Deciduous, upright, dense shrub. H 4ft (1.2m), S 5ft (1.5m). Zones 4–8. Large, saucer-shaped, bright yellow flowers are produced from late spring to mid-autumn amid dark green leaves comprising 5 narrowly oblong leaflets.

P. 'Maanelys'. See *P.* 'Moonlight'.

P. 'Manchu', syn. *P. davurica* var. *mandschurica* of gardens, illus. p.126.

P. 'Manelys'. See *P.* 'Moonlight'.

P. megalantha illus. p.247.

P. 'Monsieur Rouillard'. Clump-forming perennial. H and S 18in (45cm). Zones 5–9. Saucer-shaped, double, deep blood red flowers are borne in summer above strawberrylike, dark green leaves.

P. 'Moonlight', syn. *P.* 'Maanelys', *P.* 'Manelys'. Deciduous, upright, dense shrub. H 4ft (1.2m), S 6ft (2m). Zones 3–8. Produces saucer-shaped, soft yellow flowers from late spring to early autumn. Has gray-green leaves divided into 5 narrowly oblong leaflets.

P. 'Nana Argentea'. See *P.* 'Beesii'.

P. nepalensis 'Miss Willmott' illus. p.237.

P. nitida. Dense, mat-forming perennial. H 1–2in (2.5–5cm), S 8in (20cm). Zones 5–8. Has rounded, 3-lobed, silver leaves. Flower stems

each carry 1–2 flattish, rose-pink flowers with dark centers in early summer. Is often shy-flowering. Suits a rock garden or trough.

P. parvifolia 'Gold Drop'. Deciduous, upright, dense shrub. H and S 4ft (1.2m). Zones 5–8. Bears a mass of saucer-shaped, golden yellow flowers from late spring to early autumn amid bright green leaves composed of 5 narrowly oblong leaflets.

P. recta 'Warrenii', syn. *P.r.* 'Macrantha', illus. p.246.

P. 'Red Ace' illus. p.134.

P. 'Royal Flush'. Deciduous, bushy shrub. H 18in (45cm), S 30in (75cm). Zones 3–8. Leaves are green and divided into 5 narrowly oblong leaflets. From late spring to autumn bears saucer-shaped, sometimes semi-double, yellow-stamened, rich pink flowers that fade to white in full sun.

P. 'Sunset' illus. p.139.

P. 'Tangerine'. Deciduous, arching, dense shrub. H 4ft (1.2m), S 5ft (1.5m). Zones 3–8. Saucer-shaped, yellow flowers, flushed with pale orange-red, are produced from early summer to autumn. Bears green leaves consisting of 5 or 7 narrowly oblong leaflets.

P. x tonguei. Mat-forming perennial. H 2in (5cm), S 10in (25cm). Zones 5–8. Leaves are rounded, 3–5 lobed, and green. Prostrate branches bear flattish, orange-yellow flowers with red centers throughout summer. Is good for a rock garden.

P. 'Vilmoriniana' illus. p.137.

P. 'William Rollison'. Clump-forming perennial. H and S 18in (45cm). Zones 5–8. From mid- to late summer bears saucer-shaped, semi-double, scarlet-suffused, deep orange flowers with yellow centers. Has strawberrylike, dark green leaves.

P. 'Yellow Queen' illus. p.247.

POTHOS. See EPIPREMNUM.

---

x POTINARA. See ORCHIDS.

x *P.* Cherub 'Spring Daffodil' (illus. p.255). Evergreen, epiphytic orchid for an intermediate greenhouse. H 6in (15cm). Zone 10. Sprays of yellow flowers, 2in (5cm) across, open in spring. Broadly oval, rigid leaves are 4in (10cm) long. Provide good light in summer.

PRATIA (Campanulaceae)
Genus of evergreen, mat-forming perennials with small leaves, grown for their mass of star-shaped flowers and suitable for rock gardens. Is sometimes included in *Lobelia*. Some species may be invasive. Frost to half hardy. Prefers shade and moist soil. Propagate by division or seed in autumn.

P. angulata. Evergreen, creeping perennial. H ½in (1cm), S indefinite. Frost hardy, zones 6–9. Bears small, broadly oval, dark green leaves. Star-shaped, white flowers, with 5 unevenly spaced petals, are carried in leaf axils in late spring and are followed by globose, purplish red fruits in autumn.

P. pedunculata illus. p.323. **'County Park'** is a vigorous, evergreen, creeping perennial. H ½in (1cm), S

indefinite. Frost hardy, zones 5–7. Has small, rounded to oval leaves and, in summer, a profusion of star-shaped, rich violet-blue flowers. Makes good ground cover.

PRIMULA (Primulaceae)
Genus of annuals, biennials, and perennials, some of which are grown as annuals or biennials and some of which are evergreen. All species have rosettes of basal leaves and tubular, bell- or primrose-shaped (flat) flowers. Flower stems, leaves, sepals and, occasionally, sections of the petals are, in some species and hybrids, covered with farina—a waxy powder. There are primulas suitable for almost every type of site: the border, scree garden, rock garden, peat garden, bog garden, pool margin, greenhouse, and alpine house. Some, however, may be difficult to grow as they dislike winter damp or summer heat. Fully hardy to frost tender, min. 45–50°F (7–10°C). Repot pot-grown plants annually. Tidy up fading foliage and dead-head as flowering ceases. Propagate species by seed when fresh or in spring; increase selected forms during dormancy, either by division or by root cuttings. Auriculas should be propagated by offsets in early spring or early autumn. Border cultivars may be prone to slug damage in damp situations and to attack by root aphids when grown in very dry conditions or in pots.

Primula groups
Primulas are classified according to various botanical sections, of which the following are in common horticultural usage.
Candelabra is used as a common descriptive name for those with tubular, flat-faced flowers borne in tiered whorls up the stem.
Polyanthus is a descriptive name for primulas derived from *P. vulgaris*, crossed with *P. juliae*, *P. veris*, and other species, that are usually grown as biennials; their flowers are produced in large umbels on stout stems.
Auricula primulas may be considered as 3 sub-groups: alpine, border, and show. Flowers of all Auriculas are carried in an umbel on a stem above the foliage and are individually flat and smooth. Show Auriculas need to be grown as single-stem specimens under glass to protect the flowers from rain. Their flowers have white centers (known as "paste") and, for edged cultivars, an outer ring in a contrasting color, often green, gray, or white, with a black body color. Self-colored cultivars may be red, yellow, blue, or violet. Show Auriculas have white farina on their foliage (except those with green-edged flowers), on their flower eyes and, sometimes, on their petal margins. Farina is totally absent on cultivars of the alpine sub-group. Some border Auriculas have farina on flower stems and leaves, but many have none at all.

Cultivation
Primulas have varying cultivation requirements. For ease of reference, these have been grouped as follows:

1—Full sun and soil that does not dry out.
2—Full sun or partial shade and moist but well-drained soil.
3—Partial shade and moist but well-drained soil.
4—Partial shade and well-drained, gritty loam.
5—Full sun or partial shade and gritty, alkaline soil.
6—Partial shade and gritty, alkaline soil.
7—Full or partial shade and moist, peaty soil.
8—Full sun or partial shade and gritty, peaty soil.
9—Partial shade and gritty, peaty soil.

P. 'Adrian' (illus. p.231). Basal-rosetted perennial (alpine Auricula). H 9–10in (22–25cm), S 6–8in (15–20cm). Fully hardy, zones 5–7. Has flat, light to dark blue flowers, with light centers, in mid- to late spring. Leaves are oval and green. Is useful for exhibition. Cultivation group 2.

P. allionii (illus. p.230). Clump-forming perennial. H 3in (8cm), S 3–6in (8–15cm). Frost hardy, zones 7–8. Tubular, rose, mauve, or white flowers cover a tight cushion of oval, green leaves in spring. Cultivation group 5.

P. alpicola. Compact perennial. H 6–24in (15–60cm), S 6–12in (15–30cm). Fully hardy, zones 6–8. Produces terminal clusters of pendent, bell-shaped, yellow to white or purple flowers on slender stems in early summer. Green leaves are oval to lance-shaped. Cultivation group 7. var. **luna** (illus. p.231) has soft sulfur yellow flowers.

P. aurantiaca. Neat, upright perennial (Candelabra primula). H 2ft (60cm), S 1ft (30cm). Fully hardy, zones 6–8. Tubular, reddish orange flowers are borne in early summer. Has long, broadly oval to lance-shaped, coarse, green leaves. Cultivation group 1 or 7.

P. aureata (illus. p.231). Clump-forming perennial. H and S 3–6in (8–15cm). Frost hardy, zones 7–8. Produces small umbels of flat, cream to yellow flowers in spring. In summer, oval, toothed, green leaves have striking purple-red midribs; in winter, leaves form tight buds covered with whitish farina. Cultivation group 8.

P. auricula. Clump-forming perennial (alpine Auricula). H 6–9in (15–23cm), S 6in (15cm). Fully hardy, zones 5–7. Fragrant, flat, yellow flowers are borne in large umbels in spring. Oval, soft, pale green to gray-green leaves are densely covered with white farina. Cultivation group 5 or 6.

P. bhutanica (illus. p.231). Neat, clump-forming perennial. H 6in (15cm), S 6–9in (15–23cm). Fully hardy, but often short-lived, zones 5–7. In spring produces neat umbels of tubular, pale purplish blue flowers, each with a white or creamy white eye, close to oval to lance-shaped, crinkled, green leaves. Cultivation group 8.

P. 'Blairside Yellow' (illus. p.231). Basal-rosetted perennial (alpine Auricula). H 1in (2.5cm), S 6in (15cm). Fully hardy, zones 5–7. In early spring, bell-shaped, golden yellow flowers nestle in a rosette of tiny, rounded to oval, pale green leaves. Cultivation group 2.

P. 'Blossom' (illus. p.231). Basal-rosetted perennial (alpine Auricula). H 9–10in (23–25cm), S 6–10in (15–25cm). Fully hardy, zones 5–7. Flat, deep crimson to bright red flowers with golden centers are borne profusely in spring. Has oval, dark green leaves. Is suitable for exhibition. Cultivation group 2.

P. bulleyana (illus. p.231). Neat, upright perennial (Candelabra primula). H 2ft (60cm), S 1ft (30cm). Fully hardy, zones 6–8. Tubular, deep orange flowers appear in early summer. Leaves are oval to lance-shaped, toothed, and dark green. Cultivation group 1 or 7.

P. 'Chloë' (illus. p.231). Basal-rosetted perennial (show Auricula). H 8–9¹/₂in (20–24cm), S 6–8in (15–20cm). Fully hardy, zones 5–7. In late spring produces flat, dark-green-edged flowers with a black body color and brilliant white paste centers. Oval leaves are dark green and have no farina. Is good for exhibition. Cultivation group 2.

P. chungensis (illus. p.231). Neat, upright perennial (Candelabra primula). H 2ft (60cm), S 1ft (30cm). Fully hardy, zones 6–8. In summer produces tiered whorls of tubular, orange flowers among oval to lance-shaped, green leaves. Cultivation group 1 or 7.

P. clarkei (illus. p.230). Clump-forming perennial. H and S 2–4in (5–10cm). Fully hardy, zones 5–7. In spring bears flat, rose-pink flowers, with yellow eyes, just above a neat clump of rounded to oval, pale green leaves. Cultivation group 8. Division is best carried out in late winter.

P. clusiana (illus. p.230). Clump-forming perennial. H 6–9in (15–23cm), S 6in (15cm). Fully hardy, zones 5–7. In spring bears umbels of tubular, rose-pink flowers with white eyes. Leaves are oval, glossy, and green. Cultivation group 8.

P. 'Craddock White' (illus. p.230). Clump-forming perennial. H to 3in (8cm), S 5in (13cm). Fully hardy, zones 5–7. Fragrant, upward-facing, flat, white flowers, with yellow eyes, are borne in spring just above long, oval, red-veined, dark green leaves. Cultivation group 1 or 3.

P. 'David Green'. Clump-forming perennial. H 4–6in (10–15cm), S 6–8in (15–20cm). Fully hardy, zones 5–7. In spring produces flat, bright crimson-purple flowers amid oval, coarse, green leaves. Cultivation group 1 or 3.

P. denticulata (Drumstick primula; illus. p.231). Vigorous, neat, upright, clump-forming perennial. H 12–24in (30–60cm), S 12–18in (30–45cm). Fully hardy, zones 6–8. From early to mid-spring, dense, rounded heads of flat, lilac, purple, or pink flowers are borne on tops of stout stems. Green leaves are broadly lance-shaped and toothed. Cultivation group 1 or 3. f. *alba* (illus. p.230) has white flowers.

P. edgeworthii (illus. p.230). Rosetted perennial. H 2–4in (5–10cm), S 4–6in (10–15cm). Fully hardy, zones 5–7.

Flat, pale mauve flowers with white eyes appear singly among oval, toothed, pale green leaves in spring. Cultivation group 8.

P. elatior (Oxlip; illus. p.231). Clump-forming perennial. H 6–12in (15–30cm), S 6in (15cm). Fully hardy, zones 3–7. Produces umbels of small, fragrant, tubular, yellow flowers in spring, above neat, oval to lance-shaped, toothed, green leaves. Cultivation group 1, 7, or 9.

P. 'E.R. Janes'. Clump-forming perennial. H 4–6in (10–15cm), S 6–8in (15–20cm). Fully hardy, zones 5–7. Flat, pale rose-pink flowers, flushed with orange, are borne singly in spring amid broadly oval, toothed, green leaves. Cultivation group 1 or 3.

P. farinosa (Bird's-eye primrose; illus. p.230). Clump-forming perennial. H 6–12in (15–30cm), S 6in (15cm). Fully hardy, zones 5–7. In spring, umbels of tubular, lilac-pink, occasionally white, flowers are borne on short, stout stems. Oval, toothed, green leaves are densely covered with white farina. Cultivation group 8.

P. flaccida, syn. *P. nutans* (illus. p.231). Lax, clump-forming, short-lived perennial. H 6–12in (15–30cm), S 15–23in (6–9in). Fully hardy, zones 5–7. In early summer, each stout stem produces a conical head of pendent, bell-shaped, lavender or violet flowers above narrowly oval, pale to green leaves. Cultivation group 7 or 8.

P. florindae (Tibetan primrose; illus. p.231). Bold, upright, clump-forming perennial. H 2–3ft (60cm–1m), S 1–2ft (30–60cm). Fully hardy, zones 6–8. In summer, large heads of pendent, bell-shaped, sulfur yellow flowers appear above broadly lance-shaped, toothed, green leaves. Cultivation group 1 or 7.

P. forrestii (illus. p.231). Clump-forming perennial. H 6–9in (15–23cm), S 15–30in (6–12in). Frost hardy, zones 7–8. Dense umbels of flat, yellow flowers with orange eyes are borne in late spring or early summer. Has oval, toothed, dark green leaves. Cultivation group 8.

P. frondosa (illus. p.230). Compact, clump-forming perennial. H 2–6in (5–15cm), S 4–6in (10–15cm). Fully hardy, zones 5–7. In spring bears umbels of flat, yellow-eyed, lilac-rose to reddish purple flowers on short stems above neat, oval, green leaves, densely covered with white farina. Cultivation group 8.

P. 'Garryarde Guinevere'. Clump-forming perennial. H 4–6in (10–15cm), S 6–8in (15–20cm). Fully hardy, zones 4–8. Flat, purplish pink flowers with yellow eyes are produced in spring among oval, toothed, bronze-green leaves. Cultivation group 1 or 3.

P. Gold Lace Group (illus. p.231). Group of basal-rosetted perennials. H 8in (20cm), S 10in (25cm). Frost hardy, zones 6–8. Produces flat flowers, in a variety of colors, with gold-laced margins, from mid- to late spring. Leaves are oval and green, sometimes tinged red. Raise annually by seed. Cultivation group 2 or 3.

P. gracilipes (illus. p.230). Neat, clump-forming perennial. H 4–6in (10–15cm), S 6–9in (15–23cm). Fully

hardy, zones 5–7. Tubular, purplish pink flowers with greenish yellow eyes are borne singly in spring or early summer among oval, wavy, toothed, green leaves. Cultivation group 8.

P. 'Harlow Car'. Neat, clump-forming perennial. H 4–6in (10–15cm), S 6–9in (15–23cm). Fully hardy, zones 5–7. In spring produces flat, white flowers on short stems above oval, soft, green leaves. Cultivation group 1, 3, 5, or 8.

P. helodoxa (illus. p.231). Upright, clump-forming perennial (Candelabra primula). H 2–3ft (60cm–1m), S 1–1¹/₂ft (30–45cm). Fully hardy, zones 6–8. Bell-shaped, yellow flowers are borne in summer. Leaves are oval, toothed, and pale green. Cultivation group 1 or 7.

P. hirsuta, syn. *P. rubra* (illus. p.230). Clump-forming perennial. H 2–6in (5–15cm), S 4–6in (10–15cm). Fully hardy, zones 4–8. Produces small umbels of flat, rose or lilac flowers in spring. Has small, rounded to oval, sticky, green leaves. Cultivation group 8.

P. 'Inverewe' (illus. p.231). Upright, clump-forming perennial (Candelabra primula). H 18–30in (45–75cm), S 12–18in (30–45cm). Fully hardy, zones 6–8. Tubular, bright orange-red flowers open in summer on stems coated with white farina. Has oval to lance-shaped, toothed, coarse, green leaves. Cultivation group 1 or 7.

P. ioessa. Clump-forming perennial. H 4–12in (10–30cm), S 6–12in (15–30cm). Fully hardy, zones 4–7. Clustered heads of funnel-shaped, pink or pinkish mauve, sometimes white, flowers are borne in spring or early summer above oval to lance-shaped, toothed, green leaves. Cultivation group 7.

P. 'Janie Hill' (illus. p.231). Basal-rosetted perennial (alpine Auricula). H 9–10in (23–25cm), S 6–8in (15–20cm). Fully hardy, zones 5–7. Flat, dark to golden brown flowers, with golden centers, open in mid- to late spring. Has oval, green leaves. Is useful for exhibition. Cultivation group 2.

P. japonica. Bold, upright, clump-forming perennial (Candelabra primula). H 12–24in (30–60cm), S 12–18in (30–45cm). Fully hardy, zones 6–8. In early summer produces tubular, deep red flowers on stout stems above oval to lance-shaped, toothed, coarse, pale green leaves. Cultivation group 1 or 7. **'Miller's Crimson'** (illus. p.230) has intense crimson flowers. **'Postford White'** (illus. p.230) bears white flowers.

P. × kewensis (illus. p.231). Upright, clump-forming perennial, grown as an annual. H 12in (30cm), S 6–12in (15–30cm). Frost tender. Produces whorls of fragrant, tubular, bright yellow flowers in winter and early spring. Oval to lance-shaped, toothed, pale green leaves are covered with white farina. Cultivation group 4.

P. 'Linda Pope' (illus. p.231). Neat, clump-forming perennial. H 4–6in (10–15cm), S 6–9in (15–23cm). Fully hardy, zones 5–7. In spring bears flat, mauve-blue flowers on short stems

above oval, toothed, green leaves covered with white farina. Cultivation group 5.

P. malacoides (single, double, illus. p.230). Neat, clump-forming perennial. H and S 8–12in (20–30cm). Frost tender, zones 10. Dense whorls of small, flat, single or double, pink, purplish pink, or white flowers open in winter-spring. Leaves are oval, hairy, soft, and pale green. Cultivation group 4.

P. 'Margaret Martin' (illus. p.231). Basal-rosetted perennial (show Auricula). H 8in (20cm), S 6in (15cm). Fully hardy, zones 5–7. Bears flat, gray-edged flowers, with a black body color and white centers, in mid- to late spring. Has spoon-shaped, gray-green leaves covered with white farina. Is excellent for exhibition. Cultivation group 2.

P. marginata (illus. p.231). Neat, clump-forming perennial. H 4–6in (10–15cm), S 4–8in (10–20cm). Fully hardy, zones 4–7. In spring, clusters of funnel-shaped, blue-lilac flowers appear above oval, toothed, green leaves densely covered with white farina. Cultivation group 5. **'Prichard's Variety'** (illus. p.231) has lilac-purple flowers with white eyes.

P. 'Mark' (illus. p.231). Basal-rosetted perennial (alpine Auricula). H 9–11in (23–28cm), S 6–9in (15–23cm). Fully hardy, zones 5–7. Produces flat, pink flowers, with light yellow centers, in spring. Leaves are oval and vibrant green. Is a leading exhibition cultivar. Cultivation group 2.

P. melanops (illus. p.230). Clump-forming, short-lived perennial. H 8–14in (20–35cm), S 6in (15cm). Fully hardy, zones 5–7. In summer has umbels of pendent, narrowly funnel-shaped, deep violet-purple flowers, with black eyes, above long, strap-shaped, green leaves. Cultivation group 1 or 7.

P. modesta. Clump-forming perennial. H 2–4in (5–10cm), S 4in (10cm). Fully hardy, zones 4–7. Dense heads of small, tubular, pinkish purple flowers appear on short stems in spring. Rounded to oval, green leaves are covered with yellow farina. Cultivation group 8. var. *fauriei* (illus. p.230), H and S 2in (5cm), has yellow-eyed, pinkish purple flowers and leaves covered with white farina.

P. 'Moonstone' (illus. p.231). Basal-rosetted perennial (border Auricula). H 9–10in (23–25cm), S 6–8in (15–20cm). Fully hardy, zones 5–7. Rounded, double, whitish or greenish yellow flowers appear in profusion in spring. Leaves are oval and green. Preferably, grow under glass. Cultivation group 2.

P. 'Mrs. J.H. Wilson' (illus. p.230). Neat, clump-forming perennial (alpine Auricula). H 4–6in (10–15cm), S 6–8in (15–20cm). Fully hardy, zones 5–7. Bears small umbels of flat, white-centered, purple flowers in spring. Oval leaves are grayish green. Cultivation group 2 or 3.

P. nutans. See *P. flaccida*.

P. obconica. Neat, clump-forming perennial, grown as an annual. H and S 6–12in (15–30cm). Frost tender. Flat, purple, lilac, or white flowers, with yellow eyes, are borne in dense umbels during winter-spring. Leaves are oval, toothed, hairy, and pale green. Cultivation group 4.

P. 'Orb'. Basal-rosetted perennial (show Auricula). H 8in (20cm), S 6in (15cm). Fully hardy, zones 5–7. Flat, dark-green-edged flowers, each with a black body color and a central zone of white paste, are produced from mid- to late spring. Has spoon-shaped, dark green leaves without farina. Is good for exhibition. Cultivation group 2.

P., Pacific Series (Polyanthus) illus. p.283, (dwarf) illus. p 272; cultivation group 2.

P. palinuri (illus. p.231). Clump-forming perennial. H 4–8in (10–20cm), S 6in (15cm). Frost hardy, zones 7–8. One-sided clusters of semi-pendent, narrowly funnel-shaped, yellow flowers appear on thick stems in early summer. Has rounded to oval, lightly toothed, thick-textured, powdered, green leaves. Cultivation group 5.

P. petiolaris (illus. p.230). Rosette-forming perennial. H 2–4in (5–10cm), S 4–6in (10–15cm). Fully hardy, zones 5–7. Tubular, purplish pink flowers, with toothed petals, are borne singly in spring. Has small, oval, toothed, green leaves. Cultivation group 8.

P. polyneura (illus. p.230). Neat, clump-forming perennial. H 8–12in (20–30cm), S 6–8in (15–20cm). Frost hardy, zones 6–8. Dense heads of tubular, pale rose, rich rose, or purple-rose flowers are produced in late spring or early summer. Rounded to oval, shallowly lobed, downy, soft leaves are green. Cultivation group 7.

P., Posy Series (Polyanthus) illus. p.265; cultivation group 2.

P. x pubescens 'Janet' (illus. p.230). Evergreen, clump-forming perennial. H 8–14in (20–35cm), S 6in (15cm). Fully hardy, zones 4–8. In spring, clusters of outward-facing, flat, purplish pink flowers arise from a rosette of oval to rounded, soft, green leaves. Cultivation group 2 or 8. Propagate by offsets after flowering.

P. pulverulenta (illus. p.230). Bold, upright, clump-forming perennial (Candelabra primula). H 2–3ft (60cm–1m), S 1–1½ft (30–45cm). Fully hardy, zones 6–8. In early summer bears tubular, deep red flowers with purple-red eyes on stems covered with white farina. Has broadly lance-shaped, toothed, coarse, green leaves. Cultivation group 1 or 7. **'Bartley'** (illus. p.230) has pink flowers.

P. reidii. Clump-forming perennial. H 2–4in (5–10cm), S 4–6in (10–15cm). Frost hardy, zones 6–8. Produces dense clusters of bell-shaped, pure white flowers on slender stems in early summer. Has oval, hairy, pale green leaves. Cultivation group 8. var. **williamsii** (illus. p.231) is more robust and has purplish blue to pale blue flowers.

P. rosea (illus. p.230). Clump-forming perennial. H 4–6in (10–15cm), S 6–8in (15–20cm). Fully hardy, zones 4–8. In early spring bears small clusters of flat, glowing rose-pink flowers on short stems among oval to lance-shaped, green leaves that are often bronze-

flushed when young. Cultivation group 1 or 7.

P. 'Royal Velvet'. Vigorous, basal-rosetted perennial (border Auricula). H 6–14in (15–35cm), S 8–14in (20–35cm). Fully hardy, zones 5–7. Flat, velvety, blue-tinged, maroon flowers, with frilled petals and large, creamy yellow centers, are produced in spring. Has large, spoon-shaped, pale green leaves. Cultivation group 2.

P. rubra. See P. hirsuta.

P. x scapeosa (illus. p.230). Clump-forming perennial. H and S 6in (15cm). Fully hardy, zones 5–7. Clusters of outward-facing, flat, mauve-pink flowers, in early spring, are initially hidden by broadly oval, sharply toothed, green leaves covered at first with slight farina; later, flower stem elongates above leaves. Cultivation group 8.

P. secundiflora (illus. p.230). Neat, upright, clump-forming perennial. H 12–18in (30–45cm), S 12in (30cm). Fully hardy, zones 6–8. Clusters of pendent, funnel-shaped, reddish purple flowers appear in summer above lance-shaped, toothed, green leaves. Cultivation group 1 or 7.

P. sieboldii (illus. p.230). Spreading, clump-forming perennial. H and S 6–8in (15–20cm). Fully hardy, zones 5–8. Umbels of flat, white, pink, or purple flowers, with white eyes, open above oval, round-toothed, downy, soft, pale green leaves in early summer. Cultivation group 7. **'Dancing Ladies'** is a variable, seed-raised selection that has upward-facing flowers with deeply cleft petals. Petals are either white with reverses suffused pale pink or blue, or pink with reverses suffused blue; leaves are slightly toothed. **'Wine Lady'** (illus. p.230) has white flowers, strongly suffused with purplish red.

P. sikkimensis (illus. p.231). Bold, upright, clump-forming perennial. H 18–30in (45–75cm), S 12–18in (30–45cm). Fully hardy, zones 5–8. Pendent clusters of funnel-shaped, yellow flowers are borne in summer. Has rounded to oval, toothed, pale green leaves. Cultivation group 1 or 7.

P. sinensis (illus. p.230). Neat, compact perennial, grown as an annual. H and S 6–8in (15–20cm). Frost tender. Flat, purple, purple-rose, pink, or white flowers, with yellow eyes, are produced in neat whorls in winter-spring. Leaves are oval, toothed, hairy, and green. Cultivation group 4.

P. sonchifolia (illus. p.230). Rosette-forming perennial. H and S 8–12in (20–30cm). Fully hardy, zones 5–7. Dense umbels of tubular, blue-purple flowers with white eyes and yellow edges open in spring. Leaves are oval to lance-shaped, toothed, and green. Cultivation group 8.

P., Super Giants Series. Rosette-forming perennial (Polyanthus), usually grown as a biennial. H and S to 12in (30cm). Fully hardy. Produces large, fragrant, flat flowers in a wide range of colors in spring (blue, illus. p.276). Cultivation group 2.

P. 'Tawny Port'. Clump-forming perennial. H 4–6in (10–15cm), S 6–8in (15–20cm). Fully hardy, zones 5–7. Bears flat, port wine-colored flowers

on short stems in spring. Rounded to oval, toothed leaves are reddish green. Cultivation group 1 or 3.

P. veris (Cowslip; illus. p.231). Neat, clump-forming perennial. H and S 6–8in (15–20cm). Fully hardy, zones 3–8. Tight clusters of fragrant, tubular, yellow flowers are produced on stout stems in spring. Leaves are oval to lance-shaped, toothed, and green. Cultivation group 1 or 3.

P. verticillata (illus. p.231). Clump-forming perennial, grown as an annual. H 8–10in (20–25cm), S 6–8in (15–20cm). Half hardy. Fragrant, bell-shaped, yellow flowers are borne in whorls in spring. Has oval, toothed, green leaves. Cultivation group 4.

P. vialii (illus. p.230). Clump-forming, short-lived perennial. H 12–18in (30–45cm), S 8–12in (20–30cm). Frost hardy, zones 6–8. Dense, conical spikes of tubular, bluish purple-and-red flowers open in late spring. Has lance-shaped, toothed, soft, green leaves. Cultivation group 1 or 3.

P. vulgaris (English primrose; illus. p.231). Neat, clump-forming perennial. H and S 6–8in (15–20cm). Fully hardy, zones 3–8. Flat, soft yellow flowers, with darker eyes, are borne singly among oval to lance-shaped, toothed, bright green leaves in spring. Cultivation group 1 or 3. **'Alba Plena'** has double, white flowers. **'Gigha White'** (illus. p.230) is very floriferous and has yellow-eyed, white flowers. subsp. **sibthorpii** (illus. p.230) has pink or purplish pink flowers.

P. 'Wanda'. Neat, clump-forming perennial. H 4–6in (10–15cm), S 6–8in (15–20cm). Fully hardy, zones 3–8. In spring, flat, crimson-purple flowers are produced singly amid oval, toothed, purplish green foliage. Cultivation group 1 or 3.

P. warshenewskiana (illus. p.230). Clump-forming perennial. H and S 1in (2.5cm). Fully hardy, zones 5–7. Tiny, flat, white-eyed, bright pink flowers sit just above spoon-shaped, dark green leaves in early spring. Cultivation group 8. Divide clumps regularly in late winter before flowering.

PRINSEPIA (Rosaceae)

Genus of deciduous, usually spiny, spring- and early summer-flowering shrubs, grown for their habit, flowers, and fruits. Fully hardy. Needs sun and any not too dry soil. Does well against a south- or west-facing wall. Propagate by softwood cuttings in summer or by seed in autumn.

P. uniflora illus. p.105.

PROBOSCIDEA (Pedaliaceae, syn. Martyniaceae)

Genus of annuals and perennials. Half hardy. Grow in a sunny, sheltered position and in fertile, well-drained soil. Propagate by seed sown under glass in early spring.

P. fragrans. Moderately fast-growing, upright annual. H 2ft (60cm), S 1ft (30cm). Has rounded, serrated, or lobed leaves. Fragrant, bell-shaped, crimson-purple flowers, to 2in (5cm) long, are produced in summer-autumn and are followed by rounded, horned, brown fruits, 3–4in (8–10cm) long,

which, if gathered young, may be pickled and eaten.

PROSTANTHERA (Labiatae)
Mintbush
Genus of evergreen shrubs, grown for their flowers and mint-scented foliage. Half hardy to frost tender, min. 41°F (5°C). Requires full light or partial shade and fertile, well-drained soil. Water potted specimens freely when in full growth, moderately at other times. Leggy stems may be cut back after flowering. Propagate by seed in spring or by semi-ripe cuttings in late summer.

P. ovalifolia illus. p.112.
P. rotundifolia illus. p.113.

PROTEA (Proteaceae)
Genus of evergreen shrubs and trees, grown mainly for their colorfully bracted flower heads. Is difficult to grow. Frost tender, min. 41–5°F (5–7°C). Requires full light and well-drained, neutral to acid soil, low in phosphates and nitrates. Water potted specimens moderately, less when not in full growth. Plants in the greenhouse must have plenty of ventilation throughout the year. Prune, if necessary, in early spring. Propagate by seed in spring or by semi-ripe cuttings in summer.

P. barbigera. See P. magnifica.
P. cynaroides illus. p.129.
P. magnifica, syn. P. barbigera. Evergreen, rounded to spreading shrub. H and S 3ft (1m). Zone 10. Has oblong to elliptic, leathery, mid- to grayish green leaves. Spherical flower heads, 6–8in (15–20cm) wide, with petal-like, pink, red, yellow, or white bracts, appear in spring-summer.
P. mellifera. See P. repens.
P. neriifolia illus. p.108.
P. repens, syn. P. mellifera (Sugarbush). Evergreen, ovoid to rounded shrub. H and S 6–10ft (2–3m). Zone 10. Green leaves are narrowly oblong to elliptic and tinted blue-gray. In spring-summer produces cup-shaped, 5in (13cm) long flower heads, with petal-like, pink, red, or white bracts.

Prumnopitys andinus. See Podocarpus andinus.

PRUNELLA (Labiatae)
Self-heal
Genus of semi-evergreen perennials with spreading mats of leaves from which arise short, stubby flower spikes in mid-summer. Is suitable for rock gardens. Fully hardy. Grows well in sun or shade and in moist but well-drained soil. Propagate by division in spring.

P. grandiflora illus. p.321. **'Pink Loveliness'** is a semi-evergreen, rosetted perennial that spreads by short runners. H 4–6in (10–15cm), S 12in (30cm). Zones 5–8. Forms a dense mat of narrowly oval leaves. Whorls of funnel-shaped, soft pink flowers are borne in terminal spikes in summer. Makes good ground cover, but may be invasive. Cut off old flower stems before they produce seed. **'White Loveliness'** has white flowers.
P. webbiana illus. p.322.

PRUNUS (Rosaceae)
Cherry
Genus of deciduous or evergreen shrubs and trees. The trees are grown mainly for their single (5-petaled) to double flowers and autumn color; the shrubs for their autumn color, bark, flowers, or fruits. All have oval to oblong leaves. Plants described here are fully hardy, unless otherwise stated. Evergreen species tolerate sun or shade; deciduous species prefer full sun. All may be grown in any but waterlogged soil. Trim deciduous hedges after flowering, evergreen ones in early or mid-spring. Propagate deciduous species by seed in autumn, deciduous hybrids and selected forms by softwood cuttings in summer. Increase evergreens by semi-ripe cuttings in summer. Bullfinches may eat flower buds and foliage may be attacked by aphids, caterpillars, and the fungal disease silver leaf. Flowering cherries are prone to a fungus that causes "witches' brooms" (abnormal, crowded shoots).
P. **'Accolade'** illus. p.61.
P. **'Amanogawa'.** Deciduous, upright tree. H 30ft (10m), S 12ft (4m). Zones 6–8. Bears fragrant, semi-double, pale pink flowers in late spring. Oblong to oval, taper-pointed, dark green leaves turn orange and red in autumn.
P. x *amygdalo-persica* **'Pollardii'.** Deciduous, spreading tree. H and S 7m (22ft). Zones 6–8. Large, saucer-shaped, 5-petaled, bright pink flowers open from early to mid-spring, before oval, glossy, green leaves emerge. Green, then brown fruits are similar to large almonds in shape and taste.
P. avium illus. p.45. **'Plena'** illus. p.49.
P. x *blireana.* Deciduous, spreading shrub or small tree. H and S 12ft (4m). Zones 6–8. Bears double, pink flowers in mid-spring and has oval, purple leaves.
P. campanulata (Bell-flowered cherry, Taiwan cherry). Deciduous, spreading tree. H and S 25ft (8m). Frost hardy, zones 7–8. Shallowly bell-shaped, deep rose-red flowers are produced from early to mid-spring, before or with oval, taper-pointed, dark green leaves. Fruits are small, rounded, and reddish.
P. cerasifera (Cherry plum, Myrobalan). **'Nigra'** illus. p.64. **'Pissardii'** is a deciduous, round-headed tree. H and S 30ft (10m). Zones 5–9. Small, 5-petaled, pale pink flowers open from early to mid-spring and are often followed by edible, plumlike, red fruits. Has oval, red, young leaves turning deeper red, then purple. May be used for hedging.
P. **'Cheal's Weeping'**, syn. *P.* 'Kiku-shidare' of gardens, illus. p.61.
P. x *cistena* illus. p.122.
P. davidiana (David's peach). Deciduous, spreading tree. H and S 8m (25ft). Zones 4–8. Saucer-shaped, 5-petaled, white or pale pink flowers are carried on slender shoots in late winter and early spring, but are susceptible to late frosts. Leaves are narrowly oval and dark green. Fruits are small, rounded, and reddish.
P. dulcis (Almond). **'Roseoplena'** is a deciduous, spreading tree. H and S

25ft (8m). Zones 5–8. Bears double, pink flowers in late winter and early spring, before oblong, pointed, toothed, dark green leaves.
P. glandulosa **'Alba Plena'** illus. p.121. **'Rosea Plena'** (syn. *P.g.* 'Sinensis') is a deciduous, rounded, open shrub. H and S 5ft (1.5m). Zones 5–8. Produces double, bright rose-pink flowers in late spring and oval, green leaves. Flowers best when grown against a south- or west-facing wall. Cut back young shoots to within a few buds of old wood after flowering.
P. **'Hally Jolivette'.** Deciduous, rounded, compact tree. H and S 15ft (5m). Zones 6–8. Produces double, white flowers, opening from pink buds, in late spring. Leaves are oval and dark green.
P. x *hillieri* **'Spire'.** See *P.* 'Spire'.
P. **'Hokusai'** illus. p.60.
P. incisa (Fuji cherry) illus. p.59. **'February Pink'** is a deciduous, spreading tree. H and S 25ft (8m). Zones 6–8. Oval, sharply toothed, dark green leaves are reddish when young, orange-red in autumn. During mild, winter periods bears 5-petaled, pale pink flowers. Has tiny, rounded, reddish fruits.
P. **'Kanzan'** illus. p.50.
P. **'Kiku-shidare'** of gardens. See *P.* 'Cheal's Weeping'.
P. **'Kursar'.** Deciduous, spreading tree. H and S 25ft (8m). Zones 6–8. Bears masses of small, 5-petaled, deep pink flowers in early spring. Has oval, dark green leaves that turn brilliant orange in autumn.
P. laurocerasus (Cherry laurel, Laurel). Evergreen, dense, bushy shrub becoming spreading and open. H 20ft (6m), S 30ft (10m). Frost hardy, zones 7–9. Has long spikes of small, single, white flowers from mid- to late spring, large, oblong, glossy, bright green leaves, and cherry-shaped, red, then black fruits. Restrict growth by cutting back hard in spring. **'Otto Luyken'** illus. p.122. **'Schipkaensis'**, H 6ft (2m), S 10ft (3m), is fully hardy and of elegant, spreading habit, with narrow leaves and freely borne flowers in upright spikes. **'Zabeliana'** illus. p.122.
P. lusitanica (Laurel, Portugal laurel). Evergreen, bushy, dense shrub or spreading tree. H and S 20–30ft (6–10m). Frost hardy, zones 7–9. Reddish purple shoots bear oval, glossy, dark green leaves. Slender spikes of small, fragrant, 5-petaled, white flowers appear in early summer, followed by egg-shaped, fleshy, deep purple fruits. Restrict growth by pruning hard in spring. subsp. *azorica* illus. p.94. **'Variegata'** illus. p.94.
P. maackii illus. p.57.
P. mahaleb illus. p.49.
P. **'Mount Fuji'**, syn. *P.* 'Shirotae', illus. p.59.
P. mume (Japanese apricot). **'Beni-shidare'** (syn. *P.m.* 'Beni-shidon') illus. p.98. **'Omoi-no-mama'** illus. p.97. **'Pendula'** is a deciduous, weeping tree with slender, arching branches. H and S 20ft (6m). Zones 7–9. Fragrant, 5-petaled, pink flowers appear in late winter or early spring,

before broadly oval, bright green leaves, and are sometimes succeeded by edible, apricotlike, yellow fruits.
P. **'Okame'.** Deciduous, bushy-headed tree. H 30ft (10m), S 25ft (8m). Zones 5–8. Bears masses of 5-petaled, carmine pink flowers in early spring. Oval, sharply toothed, dark green leaves turn orange-red in autumn.
P. padus illus. p.49. var. *commutata* is a deciduous, spreading tree, conical when young. H 50ft (15m), S 30ft (10m). Zones 4–8. Produces pendent racemes of fragrant, star-shaped, 5-petaled, white flowers in mid-spring, followed by small, pea-shaped, black fruits. Oval, dark green leaves, often fully open by early spring, turn yellow in autumn. **'Plena'** has long-lasting, double flowers and no fruits. **'Watereri'** bears long racemes of flowers from mid- to late spring.
P. **'Pandora'** illus. p.60.
P. pensylvanica (Pin cherry). Deciduous, spreading tree. H 50ft (15m), S 30ft (10m). Zones 3–8. Has peeling, red-banded bark and oval, taper-pointed, bright green leaves. Produces clusters of small, star-shaped, 5-petaled, white flowers from mid- to late spring, followed by small, pea-shaped, red fruits.
P. persica (Peach). **'Klara Meyer'** is a deciduous, spreading tree. H 15ft (5m), S 20ft (6m). Zones 6–9. Bears double, bright pink flowers in mid-spring. Has slender, lance-shaped, bright green leaves. Is susceptible to the fungal disease peach leaf curl. **'Prince Charming'** illus. p.61.
P. **'Pink Perfection'** illus. p.60.
P. **'Pink Star'.** See *P. subhirtella* 'Stellata'.
P. sargentii illus. p.60.
P. serotina illus. p.39.
P. serrula. Deciduous, round-headed tree. H and S 30ft (10m). Zones 6–8. Has gleaming, coppery red bark that peels. In late spring bears small, 5-petaled, white flowers amid oval, tapering, toothed, dark green leaves that turn yellow in autumn. Fruits are tiny, rounded, and reddish brown.
P. serrulata var. *spontanea* illus. p.49.
P. **'Shimidsu'.** See *P.* 'Shogetsu'.
P. **'Shirofugen'** illus. p.60.
P. **'Shirotae'.** See *P.* 'Mount Fuji'.
P. **'Shogetsu'**, syn. *P.* 'Shimidsu', illus. p.59.
P. spinosa (Blackthorn, Sloe). **'Purpurea'** illus. p.89.
P. **'Spire'**, syn. *P.* x *hillieri* 'Spire', illus. p.60.
P. subhirtella (Higan cherry, Rosebud cherry). Deciduous, spreading tree. H and S 25ft (8m). Zones 6–8. From early to mid-spring, a profusion of small, 5-petaled, pale pink flowers appear before oval, taper-pointed, dark green leaves, which turn yellow in autumn. Has small, rounded, reddish brown fruits. **'Autumnalis'** produces semi-double, white flowers, pink in bud, in mild periods in winter. **'Pendula Rubra'** illus. p.61. **'Stellata'** (syn. *P.* 'Pink Star') illus. p.60.
P. **'Tai Haku'** illus. p.59.
P. tenella illus. p.123. **'Fire Hill'** is a deciduous, bushy shrub with upright, then spreading branches. H and S 6ft

(2m). Zones 2–8. Narrowly oval, glossy, dark green leaves are a foil for small, almondlike, single, very deep pink flowers borne profusely from mid- to late spring, followed by small, almondlike fruits.
P. tomentosa (Downy cherry). Deciduous, bushy, dense shrub. H 5ft (1.5m), S 6ft (2m). Zones 3–8. Small, 5-petaled, pale pink flowers are produced from early to mid-spring before oval, slightly downy, dark green leaves appear. Fruits are spherical and bright red. Thrives in hot summers.
P. **'Trailblazer'.** Deciduous, spreading tree. H and S 15ft (5m). Zones 6–8. Bears 5-petaled, white flowers from early to mid-spring, sometimes followed by edible, plumlike, red fruits. Oval, light green, young leaves mature to deep red-purple.
P. triloba **'Multiplex'.** Deciduous, bushy, spreading tree or shrub. H and S 12ft (4m). Zones 6–8. Double, pink flowers are borne in mid-spring. Has oval, dark green leaves, often 3-lobed, that turn yellow in autumn. Does best against a sunny wall. Cut back young shoots to within a few buds of old wood after flowering.
P. **'Ukon'** illus. p.59.
P. virginiana (Virginian bird cherry). **'Shubert'** is a deciduous, conical tree. H 30ft (10m), S 25ft (8m). Zones 3–8. Produces dense spikes of small, star-shaped, white flowers from mid- to late spring, followed by globose, dark purple-red fruits. Has oval, pale green, young leaves, becoming deep reddish purple in summer.
P. **'Yae-murasaki'** illus. p.61.
P. x *yedoensis* illus. p.60.

PSEUDERANTHEMUM (Acanthaceae)
Genus of evergreen perennials and shrubs, grown mainly for their foliage. Frost tender, min. 61°F (16°C). Requires partial shade and fertile, well-drained soil. Water potted plants freely when in full growth, moderately at other times. Tip prune young plants to promote a bushy habit. Cut leggy plants back hard in spring. Propagate annually or biennially as a pot plant by greenwood cuttings in spring or summer. Whitefly may be troublesome.
P. atropurpureum, syn. *Eranthemum atropurpureum.* Evergreen, erect shrub. H 3–4ft (1–1.2m), S 1–2ft (30–60cm). Zone 10. Has oval, strongly purple-flushed leaves and, mainly in summer, short spikes of tubular, purple-marked, white flowers.

PSEUDOCYDONIA (Rosaceae)
Genus of one species of deciduous or semi-evergreen, spring-flowering tree, grown for its bark, flowers, and fruits. Frost hardy, but in cool areas grow against a south- or west-facing wall. Requires full sun and does well only in hot summers. Needs well-drained soil. Propagate by seed in autumn.
P. sinensis, syn. *Cydonia sinensis.* Deciduous or semi-evergreen, spreading tree. H and S 20ft (6m). Zones 6–8. Has decorative, flaking bark. Shallowly cup-shaped, pink

flowers are produced from mid- to late spring and are followed after hot summers by large, egg-shaped, yellow fruits. Oval, finely toothed leaves are dark green.

PSEUDOLARIX (Pinaceae). See CONIFERS.
P. amabilis, syn. *P. kaempferi*, illus. p.79.
P. kaempferi. See *P. amabilis*.

PSEUDOPANAX, syn. NEOPANAX, NOTHOPANAX (Araliaceae)
Genus of evergreen trees and shrubs, grown for their unusual foliage and fruits. Is excellent for landscaping and may also be grown in large containers. Insignificant flowers are produced in summer. Frost to half hardy. Grows in sun or semi-shade and in fertile, well-drained soil. Propagate by semi-ripe cuttings in summer or by seed in autumn or spring.
P. arboreus (Five fingers). Evergreen, round-headed, stout-branched tree. H 20ft (6m), S 12ft (4m). Frost hardy, zones 8–10. Large, glossy, dark green leaves are divided into 5 or 7 oblong leaflets. Tiny, honey-scented, green flowers in summer are followed by rounded, purplish black fruits on female plants.
P. crassifolius (Lancewood). Evergreen tree, unbranched for many years, then becoming round-headed. H 20ft (6m), S 6ft (2m). Frost hardy, zones 8–10. Dark green leaves are extremely variable in shape on young trees, but eventually become long, narrow, rigid, and downward-pointing on older specimens. Female plants bear small, rounded, black fruits.
P. ferox illus. p.65.
P. laetus. Evergreen, round-headed, stout-branched tree or shrub. H and S 10ft (3m). Half hardy, zones 9–10. Has large, long-stalked, leathery leaves composed of 5 or 7 oblong, dark green leaflets. Produces tiny, greenish purple flowers in summer and rounded, purplish black fruits in autumn on female plants.

PSEUDOSASA (Bambusoideae). See GRASSES, BAMBOOS, RUSHES, and SEDGES.
P. japonica, syn. *Arundinaria japonica*, illus. p.182.

PSEUDOTSUGA (Pinaceae). See CONIFERS.
P. douglasii. See *P. menziesii*.
P. menziesii, syn. *P. douglasii*, *P. taxifolia* (Douglas fir). Fast-growing, conical conifer. H 80ft (25m), S 25–40ft (8–12m). Fully hardy, zones 5–7. Has thick, corky, fissured, gray-brown bark. Spirally arranged, aromatic, needlelike, slightly flattened leaves, which develop from sharply pointed buds, are dark green with white bands beneath. Elliptic cones, 3–4in (8–10cm) long, with projecting bracts, are dull brown.
'Fletcheri', H 10ft (3m), S 6–10ft (2–3m), makes a flat-topped shrub.
'Fretsii' (illus. p.82), H 20ft (6m) or more, S 10–12ft (3–4m), is slow-growing, with very short, dull green leaves. var. *glauca* illus. p.74.

'Oudemansii' (illus. p.83) is very slow-growing, with ascending branches and short, glossy leaves, dark green all over.
P. taxifolia. See *P. menziesii*.

PSEUDOWINTERA (Winteraceae)
Genus of evergreen shrubs and trees, grown for their foliage. Frost to half hardy. Needs full light or partial shade and humus-rich, well-drained but moisture-retentive soil, ideally neutral to acid. Water potted plants freely when in full growth, moderately at other times. Pruning is tolerated if needed. Propagate by semi-ripe cuttings in summer or by seed when ripe, in autumn, or in spring.
P. axillaris, syn. *Drimys axillaris* (Heropito, Pepper-tree). Evergreen, rounded shrub or tree. H and S 10–25ft (3–8m). Half hardy, zones 9–10. Has oval, lustrous, green leaves, blue-gray beneath. Axillary clusters of tiny, star-shaped, greenish yellow flowers appear in spring-summer, followed by tiny, globular, bright red fruits.
P. colorata, syn. *Drimys colorata*. Evergreen, bushy, spreading shrub. H 3ft (1m), S 5ft (1.5m). Half hardy, zones 9–10. Has oval, pale yellow-green leaves, blotched with pink and narrowly edged with deep red-purple; undersides are bluish white. Small, star-shaped, greenish yellow flowers appear in mid-spring. Provide shelter in all but the mildest areas.

PSYLLIOSTACHYS (Plumbaginaceae)
Statice
Genus of annuals, perennials, and evergreen sub-shrubs, grown for cut flowers and for drying. Is suitable for coastal areas. Fully hardy to frost tender, min. 36–9°F (2–4°C). Grow in sun and in fertile, well-drained soil. If required for drying, cut flowers before they are fully open. Cut down dead stems of perennials in autumn. Propagate by seed sown under glass in early spring; perennials and sub-shrubs may also be increased by softwood cuttings in spring. Botrytis and powdery mildew may be troublesome.
P. suworowii , syn. *Statice suworowii*, illus. p.274.

PTELEA (Rutaceae)
Genus of deciduous trees and shrubs, grown for their foliage and fruits. Fully hardy. Requires sun and fertile soil. Propagate species by softwood cuttings in summer or by seed in autumn, selected forms by softwood cuttings only in summer.
P. trifoliata (Hop tree). Deciduous, bushy, spreading tree or shrub. H and S 22ft (7m). Zones 5–9. Has aromatic, dark green leaves, each composed of 3 narrowly oval leaflets. Clusters of small, star-shaped, green flowers from early to mid-summer are succeeded by clusters of winged, pale green fruits.
'Aurea' illus. p.113.

PTERIS (Polypodiaceae)
Genus of deciduous, semi-evergreen, or evergreen ferns. Frost tender, min. 41°F (5°C). Tolerates sun or shade. Grow in moist, peaty soil. Remove

faded fronds regularly. Propagate by division in spring or by spores in summer.
P. cretica illus. p.185. 'Albo-lineata' is an evergreen or semi-evergreen fern. H 18in (45cm), S 12in (30cm). Zone 10. Wiry stems produce triangular to broadly oval, divided, pale green fronds, centrally variegated with creamy white, that have finger-shaped pinnae. Variegated 'Mayi', H 12in (30cm), has crested frond tips.
P. ensiformis (Snow brake). Deciduous or semi-evergreen fern. H 12in (30cm), S 9in (23cm). Zone 10. Dark green fronds, often grayish white around the midribs, are coarsely divided into finger-shaped pinnae. 'Arguta', H 18in (45cm), has deeper green fronds with central, silver white marks.
P. multifida (Spider fern). Deciduous or semi-evergreen fern. H 12in (30cm), S 9in (23cm). Zones 9–10. Narrow, much-divided, wispy fronds are green.

PTEROCARYA (Juglandaceae)
Wingnut
Genus of deciduous trees, grown for their foliage and catkins. Fully hardy. Needs full sun and any deep, moist but well-drained soil. Suckers should be removed regularly. Propagate by softwood cuttings in summer or by suckers or seed, when ripe, in autumn.
P. fraxinifolia (Caucasian wingnut). Deciduous, spreading tree. H 80ft (25m), S 70ft (20m). Zones 6–9. Large, ashlike leaves are glossy, dark green, and turn yellow in autumn. Long, green catkins are produced in summer, the female developing winged, green, then brown fruits.
P. x *rehderiana* illus. p.44.
P. stenoptera (Chinese wingnut). Deciduous, spreading tree. H 70ft (20m), S 50ft (15m). Zones 7–9. Ashlike, bright green leaves, each with a winged stalk, turn yellow in autumn. Produces long, green catkins in summer, the female developing winged, pink-tinged, green fruits.

PTEROCELTIS (Ulmaceae)
Genus of one species of deciduous tree, with inconspicuous flowers in summer, grown for its foliage and fruits. Fully hardy. Needs full sun and does best in hot summers. Requires well-drained soil. Propagate by seed in autumn.
P. tatarinowii. Deciduous, spreading tree. H 40ft (12m), S 30ft (10m). Zones 6–9. Has peeling, gray bark, oval, dark green leaves, and, in autumn, small, spherical, green fruits, each with a broad, circular wing.

PTEROCEPHALUS (Dipsaceae)
Genus of compact, summer-flowering annuals, perennials, and semi-evergreen sub-shrubs, grown for their scabiouslike flower heads and feathery seed heads. Is useful for rock gardens. Fully hardy. Requires sun and well-drained soil. Propagate by softwood or semi-ripe cuttings in summer or by seed in autumn. Self seeds moderately.
P. perennis subsp. *perennis*, syn. *P.p.* var. *parnassi* (Teasel winghead) illus. p.320.

PTEROSTYRAX (Styracaceae)
Genus of deciduous trees and shrubs, grown for their foliage and fragrant flowers. Fully hardy. Requires sun or semi-shade and deep, well-drained, neutral to acid soil. Propagate by softwood or semi-ripe cuttings in summer or by seed in autumn.
P. hispida (Epaulette tree). Deciduous, spreading tree or shrub. H 50ft (15m), S 40ft (12m). Zones 5–8. Bears large, drooping panicles of small, bell-shaped, white flowers from early to mid-summer. Oblong to oval leaves are green.

PTILOTRICHUM (Cruciferae)
Genus of evergreen or semi-evergreen, summer-flowering perennials and shrubs. Is suitable for rock gardens, walls, and banks. Fully hardy. Needs sun and gritty, well-drained soil. Cut back lightly after flowering to maintain compact habit. Propagate by softwood cuttings in early summer or by seed in autumn.
P. spinosum. Semi-evergreen, rounded, compact shrub. H 8in (20cm) or more, S 12in (30cm). Zones 7–9. Intricate branches bear spines and narrowly oval to linear, silver leaves. Spherical heads of tiny, 4-petaled, white to purple-pink flowers appear in early summer.

PUERARIA (Leguminosae)
Genus of deciduous, woody-stemmed or herbaceous, twining climbers. Half hardy. Grow in sun and in any well-drained soil. Propagate by seed in spring.
P. hirsuta. See *P. lobata*.
P. lobata, syn. *P. hirsuta*, *P. thunbergiana* (Kudzu vine). Deciduous, woody-stemmed, twining climber with hairy stems. May be highly invasive in southern regions. H to 15ft (5m) or to 100ft (30m) in the wild. Zones 7–9. Leaves have 3 broadly oval leaflets. In summer produces racemes, to 12in (30cm) long, of small, scented, sweet-pealike, reddish purple flowers, followed by long, slender, hairy pods, 2¹⁄₂–3in (6–8cm) long. In cold areas is best grown as an annual.
P. thunbergiana. See *P. lobata*.

PULMONARIA (Boraginaceae)
Lungwort
Genus of mainly spring-flowering perennials, some of which are semi-evergreen with small, overwintering rosettes of leaves. Fully hardy. Prefers shade; grows in any moist but well-drained soil. Propagate by division in spring or autumn.
P. angustifolia. Clump-forming perennial. H 9in (23cm), S 8–12in (20–30cm) or more. Zones 4–8. Has narrowly lance-shaped, green leaves. In early spring bears heads of tubular, 5-lobed, boragelike, sometimes pink-tinged, deep blue flowers. 'Mawson's Variety' illus. p.228.
P. longifolia. Clump-forming perennial. H 12in (30cm), S 18in (45cm). Zones 5–8. Very narrowly lance-shaped, dark green leaves are spotted with white. Heads of tubular, 5-lobed, boragelike, vivid blue flowers appear in late spring.

P. rubra. Semi-evergreen, clump-forming perennial. H 12in (30cm), S 24in (60cm). Zones 5–8. Has broadly oval, velvety, green leaves. Heads of tubular, 5-lobed, boragelike, brick red flowers open from late winter to early spring.
P. saccharata illus. p.228.
P. 'Sissinghurst White' illus. p.224.

PULSATILLA (Ranunculaceae)
Genus of perennials, some of which are evergreen, grown for their large, feathery leaves, upright or pendent, bell- or cup-shaped flowers, covered in fine hairs, and feathery seed heads. Has fibrous, woody rootstocks. Leaves increase in size after flowering time. Is suitable for growing in large rock gardens. Fully hardy. Needs full sun and humus-rich, well-drained soil. Resents disturbance to roots. Propagate by root cuttings in winter or by seed when fresh.
P. alpina illus. p.286. subsp. **apiifolia** (syn. *P.a.* subsp. *sulphurea*) is a clump-forming perennial. H 6–12in (15–30cm), S to 4in (10cm). Zones 3–5. Has feathery, soft green leaves. Bears upright, bell-shaped, soft pale yellow flowers in spring, followed by feathery, silvery seed heads.
P. halleri illus. p.288. subsp. **grandis** is a clump-forming perennial. H and S 6–9in (15–23cm). Zones 5–7. In spring, mainly before feathery, light green leaves appear, produces large, upright, shallowly bell-shaped, lavender blue flowers, 2in (5cm) wide, with bright yellow centers. Flower stems rapidly elongate as feathery, silvery seed heads mature.
P. occidentalis. Clump-forming perennial. H 8in (20cm), S 6in (15cm). Zones 5–7. In late spring to early summer, solitary nodding buds develop into erect, goblet-shaped, white flowers, stained blue-violet at base outside and sometimes flushed pink, followed by feathery, silvery seed heads. Bears feathery leaves. Is extremely difficult to grow and flower well at low altitudes.
P. vernalis illus. p.303.
P. vulgaris illus. p.288.

PUNICA (Punicaceae)
Pomegranate
Genus of deciduous, summer-flowering shrubs and trees, grown for their bright red flowers and yellow to orange-red fruits, which ripen and become edible only in warm climates. Frost to half hardy. Needs a sheltered, sunny position and well-drained soil. Propagate by seed in spring or by semi-ripe cuttings in summer.
P. granatum. Deciduous, rounded shrub or tree. H and S 6–25ft (2–8m). Half hardy, zones 8–10. Has narrowly oblong leaves and, in summer, produces funnel-shaped, bright red flowers, with crumpled petals. Fruits are spherical and deep yellow to orange. May be grown in a southern or eastern aspect, either free-standing

or, in frost-prone climates, against a wall. var. **nana** illus. p.295.

PUSCHKINIA (Liliaceae)
Genus of dwarf, *Scilla*like bulbs, grown for their early spring flowers. Fully hardy. Needs sun or partial shade and humus-rich soil that has grit or sand added to ensure good drainage. Plant in autumn. Dies down in summer. Propagate by offsets in late summer or by seed in autumn.
P. libanotica. See *P. scilloides*.
P. scilloides, syn. *P. libanotica*, illus. p.361. **'Alba'** illus. p.356.

PUYA (Bromeliaceae)
Genus of evergreen, rosette-forming perennials and shrubs, grown for their overall appearance. Half hardy to frost tender, min. 41–5°F (5–7°C). Requires full light and well-drained soil. Water moderately during the growing season, sparingly at other times. Propagate by seed or offsets in spring.
P. alpestris (illus. p.222). Evergreen perennial with stout, branched, prostrate stems. H to 6ft (2m), S 10ft (3m). Half hardy, zone 10. Each stem is topped by a dense rosette of linear, tapering, arching, bright green leaves that are fleshy and have hooked, spiny teeth along the edges and dense, white scales beneath. Tubular, deep metallic blue flowers, ageing to purple-red, are borne in stiff, erect panicles and are produced in early summer.
P. chilensis (illus. p.222). Evergreen, upright perennial with a short, woody stem. H and S to 6ft (2m). Half hardy, zone 10. Stem is crowned by a dense rosette of linear, tapering, arching, gray-green leaves that are fleshy and have margins of hooked, spiny teeth. Bears tubular, metallic yellow or greenish yellow flowers in erect, much-branched panicles during summer.

PYCNOSTACHYS (Labiatae)
Genus of bushy perennials, grown for their whorled clusters of flowers. Frost tender, min. 59°F (15°C). Grow in bright light and in fertile, well-drained soil. Propagate by stem cuttings in early summer.
P. dawei illus. p.195.
P. urticifolia. Strong-growing, erect perennial with square stems. H 3–6ft (1–2m), S 8–24in (20–60cm). Zone 10. Has oval, sharply toothed, hairy, green leaves, 4in (10cm) long. Whorls of small, tubular, bright blue flowers are carried in racemes, 4in (10cm) long, in winter.

PYRACANTHA (Rosaceae)
Firethorn
Genus of evergreen, spiny, summer-flowering shrubs, grown for their foliage, flowers, and fruits. Fully to frost hardy. Requires a sheltered site in sun or semi-shade and fertile soil. To produce a compact habit on a plant grown against a wall, train and cut back long shoots after flowering.

Propagate by semi-ripe cuttings in summer. Is susceptible to scab and fireblight.
P. angustifolia. Evergreen, bushy, dense shrub. H and S 10ft (3m). Frost hardy, zones 7–8. Bears narrowly oblong leaves, dark green above, gray and feltlike beneath. Produces clusters of small, 5-petaled, white flowers in early summer that are followed by spherical, orange-yellow fruits in autumn.
P. atalantioides. Vigorous, evergreen shrub, part upright, part arching. H 15ft (5m), S 12ft (4m). Frost hardy, zones 6–9. Oblong leaves are glossy and dark green. Large clusters of small, 5-petaled, white flowers in early summer are followed by spherical, red fruits in early autumn. **'Aurea'** illus. p.92.
P. coccinea. Evergreen, dense, bushy shrub. H and S 12ft (4m). Fully hardy, zones 7–8. Dense clusters of small, 5-petaled, white flowers open amid oval, dark green leaves in early summer and are succeeded by spherical, bright red fruits. **'Lalandei'** has larger leaves and larger, orange-red fruits.
P. 'Golden Charmer' illus. p.117.
P. 'Golden Dome' illus. p.117.
P. 'Mohave'. Vigorous, evergreen, bushy shrub. H 12ft (4m), S 15ft (5m). Frost hardy, zones 6–9. Produces clusters of small, 5-petaled, white flowers in early summer, then spherical, orange-red fruits. Leaves are broadly oval and dark green. Is disease-resistant.
P. 'Orange Glow'. Evergreen, upright, dense shrub. H 15ft (5m), S 10ft (3m). Frost hardy, zones 6–9. Has oblong, glossy, dark green leaves, clusters of small, 5-petaled, white flowers, in early summer, and spherical, orange fruits.
P. rogersiana. Evergreen, upright, then arching shrub. H and S 10ft (3m). Frost hardy, zones 7–9. Leaves are narrowly oblong, glossy, and bright green. Clusters of small, 5-petaled, white flowers in early summer are followed by spherical, orange-red or yellow fruits.
P. x watereri illus. p.104.

Pyrethrum **'Brenda'.** See *Tanacetum coccineum* 'Brenda'.
Pyrethrum roseum. See *Tanacetum coccineum*.

PYROLA (Pyrolaceae)
Wintergreen
Genus of evergreen, spreading, spring- and summer-flowering perennials. Fully hardy. Needs partial shade, cool conditions, and well-drained, peaty, acid soil; is best suited to light woodlands. Resents disturbance. Propagate by seed in autumn or spring or by division in spring.
P. asarifolia. Evergreen, rosette-forming perennial. H 6–10in (15–25cm), S 6in (15cm) or more. Zones 4–8. Has kidney-shaped, leathery, glossy, light green leaves.

Each flower stem bears open tubular, pale to deep pink flowers in spring.
P. rotundifolia (Round-leaved wintergreen, Wild lily-of-the-valley). Evergreen, rosette-forming perennial. H 9in (23cm), S 12in (30cm). Zones 5–8. Produces rounded, leathery, glossy, green leaves and, in late spring and early summer, sprays of fragrant white flowers that resemble lily-of-the-valley.

PYROSTEGIA (Bignoniaceae)
Genus of evergreen, woody-stemmed, tendril climbers, grown for their showy flowers. Frost tender, min. 55–9°F (13–15°C). Needs full light and fertile, well-drained soil. Water regularly, less when temperatures are low. Provide support. Thin out congested stems after flowering. Propagate by semi-ripe cuttings or layering in summer.
P. venusta illus. p.176.

PYRUS (Rosaceae)
Pear
Genus of deciduous, spring-flowering trees, grown for their habit, foliage, flowers, and edible fruits (pears). Fully hardy. Does best in full sun and needs well-drained soil. Propagate species by seed in autumn, cultivars by budding in summer or by grafting in winter. Many species are susceptible to fireblight and scab and, in North America, pear decline.
P. amygdaliformis. Deciduous, spreading tree. H 30ft (10m), S 25ft (8m). Zones 6–8. Lance-shaped leaves are gray when young, maturing to glossy, dark green. Clusters of 5-petaled, white flowers are borne in mid-spring, followed by small, brownish fruits.
P. calleryana (Callery pear). Deciduous, broadly conical tree. H and S to 50ft (15m). Zones 5–8. Oval, glossy, dark green leaves often turn red in autumn. Produces 5-petaled, white flowers from mid- to late spring. Fruits are small and brownish. **'Bradford'**, S 30ft (10m), is resistant to fireblight. **'Chanticleer'** illus. p.48.
P. communis (Common pear). **'Beech Hill'** is a deciduous, narrowly conical tree. H 30ft (10m), S 22ft (7m). Zones 5–9. Oval, glossy, dark green leaves often turn orange and red in autumn. Bears 5-petaled, white flowers, from mid- to late spring as the leaves emerge, followed by small, brownish fruits.
P. elaeagrifolia. Deciduous, spreading, thorny tree. H and S 25ft (8m). Zones 5–9. Has lance-shaped, gray-green leaves and loose clusters of 5-petaled, white flowers in mid-spring. Has small, brownish fruits.
P. salicifolia (Willowleaf pear). Deciduous, mound-shaped tree with slightly drooping branches. H 15–25ft (5–8m), S 12ft (4m). Zones 5–9. White flowers, with 5 petals, open as lance-shaped, gray leaves emerge in mid-spring. Fruits are small and brownish. **'Pendula'** illus. p.64.

Q

Quamoclit coccinea. See *Ipomoea coccinea.*
Quamoclit lobata. See *Mina lobata.*
Quamoclit pinnata. See *Ipomoea quamoclit.*

QUERCUS (Fagaceae)
Oak
Genus of deciduous or evergreen trees and shrubs, grown for their habit, foliage, and, in some deciduous species, autumn color. Produces insignificant flowers from late spring to early summer, followed by egg-shaped to rounded, brownish fruits (acorns). Fully to frost hardy. Does best in sun or semi-shade and in deep, well-drained soil. Except where stated otherwise, will tolerate lime. Propagate species by seed in autumn, selected forms and hybrids by grafting in late winter. May be affected, though not usually seriously, by mildew and various galls, and, in North America, by oak wilt.
Q. acutissima (Sawtooth oak). Deciduous, round-headed tree. H and S 50ft (15m). Fully hardy, zones 6–9. Has sweet-chestnutlike, glossy, dark green leaves, edged with bristle-tipped teeth, that last until late in the year.
Q. agrifolia illus. p.58.
Q. alba illus. p.45.
Q. aliena (Oriental white oak). Deciduous, spreading tree. H 50ft (15m), S 40ft (12m). Fully hardy, zones 6–9. Has large, oblong, prominently toothed, glossy, dark green leaves.

Q. alnifolia (Golden-oak-of-Cyprus). Evergreen, spreading tree. H 20ft (6m), S 15ft (5m). Frost hardy, zones 7–9. Rounded, leathery leaves are glossy, dark green above, with mustard yellow or greenish yellow felt beneath.
Q. canariensis illus. p.41.
Q. castaneifolia illus. p.43.
Q. cerris (Turkey oak). Fast-growing, deciduous, spreading tree of stately habit. H 100ft (30m), S 80ft (25m). Fully hardy, zones 7–9. Oblong, glossy, dark green leaves are deeply lobed. Thrives on shallow, chalky soil. **'Variegata'** illus. p.51.
Q. coccifera (Kermes oak). Evergreen, bushy, compact tree or shrub. H and S 15ft (5m). Frost hardy, zones 7–9. Hollylike leaves are glossy, dark green, and rigid with spiny margins.
Q. coccinea illus. p.44. **'Splendens'** is a deciduous, round-headed tree. H 70ft (20m), S 50ft (15m). Fully hardy, zones 5–9. Oblong, glossy, green leaves, with deep, toothlike lobes, turn deep scarlet in autumn. Prefers acid soil.
Q. dentata (Daimio oak). Deciduous, spreading, stout-branched tree of rugged habit. H 50ft (15m), S 30ft (10m). Fully hardy, zones 6–8. Has oval, lobed, dark green leaves, 12in (30cm) or more long. Prefers acid soil.
Q. ellipsoidalis illus. p.44.
Q. frainetto illus. p.43.
Q. garryana illus. p.53.
Q. x *heterophylla* illus. p.55.
Q. x *hispanica* **'Lucombeana'** illus. p.47.

Q. ilex (Holm oak). Evergreen, round-headed tree. H 80ft (25m), S 70ft (20m). Frost hardy, zones 7–9. Glossy, dark green leaves are silvery gray when young and very variably shaped, but are most often oval. Thrives on shallow chalk and is excellent for an exposed, coastal position.
Q. imbricaria (Shingle oak). Deciduous, spreading tree. H 70ft (20m), S 50ft (15m). Fully hardy, zones 5–8. Bears long, narrow leaves that are yellowish when young, dark green in summer and yellowish brown in autumn.
Q. laurifolia illus. p.43.
Q. macranthera illus. p.40.
Q. macrocarpa illus. p.53.
Q. macrolepis illus. p.53.
Q. marilandica illus. p.53.
Q. mongolica var. *grosseserrata.* Deciduous, spreading tree. H 70ft (20m), S 50ft (15m). Fully hardy, zones 5–9. Has large, oblong, lobed, dark green leaves with prominent, triangular teeth.
Q. muehlenbergii illus. p.41.
Q. myrsinifolia illus. p.57.
Q. nigra illus. p.42.
Q. palustris illus. p.43.
Q. petraea (Durmast oak, Sessile oak). Deciduous, spreading tree. H 100ft (30m), S 80ft (25m). Fully hardy, zones 5–8. Has oblong, lobed, leathery, dark green leaves with yellow stalks. **'Columna'** illus. p.43.
Q. phellos illus. p.45.
Q. pontica (Armenian oak, Pontine oak). Deciduous, sometimes shrubby

tree with upright, stout branches and broadly oval head. H 20ft (6m), S 15ft (5m). Fully hardy, zones 6–9. Has large, oval, toothed, glossy, bright green leaves that turn yellow in autumn.
Q. robur (Pedunculate oak). Deciduous, spreading, rugged tree. H and S 80ft (25m). Fully hardy, zones 5–8. Bears oblong, wavy, lobed, dark green leaves. **'Concordia'**, H 30ft (10m), is slow-growing and has golden yellow, young foliage that becomes yellowish green in mid-summer.
f. *fastigiata* illus. p.40.
Q. rubra illus. p.44. **'Aurea'** illus. p.53.
Q. suber illus. p.47.
Q. x *turneri* illus. p.47.
Q. velutina (Black oak). Fast-growing, deciduous, spreading tree. H 100ft (30m), S 80ft (25m). Fully hardy, zones 5–8. Large, oblong, lobed, glossy, dark green leaves turn reddish brown in autumn.

QUISQUALIS (Combretaceae)
Genus of evergreen or deciduous, scandent shrubs and twining climbers, grown for their flowers. Frost tender, min. 50–64°F (10–18°C). Provide humus-rich, moist but well-drained soil, and full light or semi-shade. Water freely when in full growth, less in cold weather. Stems need support. Thin out crowded growth in spring. Propagate by seed in spring or by semi-ripe cuttings in summer.
Q. indica illus. p.169.

R

RAMONDA (Gesneriaceae)
Genus of evergreen perennials, grown for their rosettes of rounded, crinkled, hairy leaves and for their flowers. Is useful for rock gardens and peat walls. Fully hardy. Prefers shade and moist soil. Water plants well if they curl up during a dry spell. Propagate by rooting offsets in early summer or by leaf cuttings or seed in early autumn.
R. myconi, syn. *R. pyrenaica*, illus. p.322.
R. nathaliae. Evergreen, basal-rosetted perennial. H and S 4in (10cm). Zones 6–7. Bears small, pale green leaves and, in late spring and early summer, umbels of small, outward-facing, flattish, lavender or white flowers, with yellow anthers.
R. pyrenaica. See *R. myconi*.
R. serbica. Evergreen, basal-rosetted perennial. H and S 4in (10cm). Zones 6–7. Is similar to *R. nathaliae*, but has cup-shaped, lilac-blue flowers and dark violet-blue anthers. May be difficult to grow.

RANUNCULUS (Ranunculaceae)
Buttercup
Genus of annuals, aquatics, and perennials, some of which are evergreen or semi-evergreen, grown mainly for their flowers. Many species grow from a thickened rootstock or a cluster of tubers. Some are invasive. Aquatic species are seldom cultivated. Fully to half hardy. Grows in sun or shade and in moist but well-drained soil. Propagate by seed when fresh or by division in spring or autumn.
R. aconitifolius and **'Flore Pleno'** illus. p.195.
R. acris (Meadow buttercup). **'Flore Pleno'** illus. p.247.
R. alpestris illus. p.303.
R. amplexicaulis. Upright perennial. H 10in (25cm), S 4in (10cm). Fully hardy, zones 4–8. Has narrowly oval, blue-gray leaves. In early summer produces clusters of shallowly cup-shaped, white flowers with yellow anthers. Needs humus-rich soil.
R. asiaticus [red form] illus. p.352, [yellow form] illus. p.353.
R. bullatus. Clump-forming perennial with thick, fibrous roots. H 2–3in (5–8cm), S 3–4in (8–10cm). Half hardy, zones 6–8. Produces fragrant, shallowly cup-shaped, bright yellow flowers in autumn above neat mounds of foliage. Oblong to oval, green leaves have sharply toothed tips and puckered surfaces. Suits an alpine house or rock garden.
R. calandrinioides illus. p.300.
R. crenatus. Semi-evergreen, rosetted perennial with thick, fibrous roots. H and S 4in (10cm). Fully hardy, zones 5–7. Produces rounded, toothed, green leaves and, in summer, short stems bearing 1 or 2 shallowly cup-shaped, white flowers just above foliage. May also be propagated by removing a flower stem at its first joint in summer;

rosettes will form and may then be rooted. Rarely sets seed in cultivation. Suits an alpine house or an acid, scree rock garden.
R. ficaria (Lesser celandine). **'Albus'** illus. p.303. **'Aurantiacus'** illus. p.313. **'Brazen Hussey'** is a mat-forming, tuberous perennial. H 2in (5cm), S to 8in (20cm). Fully hardy, zones 4–8. Is grown for its heart-shaped, purple-bronze leaves produced in spring. Shallowly cup-shaped, glossy, sulfur yellow flowers, with bronze reverses, appear in early spring. All *R. ficaria* forms die down in late spring. May spread rapidly; is good for a wild garden. **'Flore Pleno'** illus. p.312.
R. glacialis. Hummock-forming perennial with fibrous roots. H 2–10in (5–25cm), S 2in (5cm) or more. Fully hardy, zones 3–5. Bears rounded, deeply lobed, glossy, dark green leaves and, in late spring and early summer, clusters of shallowly cup-shaped, white or pink flowers. Is very difficult to grow at low altitudes. Suits a scree or alpine house. Prefers humus-rich, moist, acid soil that is drier in winter. Slugs may be troublesome.
R. gouanii **'Plenus'**. See *R. speciosus* 'Plenus'.
R. gramineus illus. p.299.
R. lingua illus. p.377. **'Grandiflora'** is a deciduous, perennial, marginal water plant. H 3ft (1m), S 1ft (30cm). Fully hardy, zones 4–8. Has stout, pinkish green stems, lance-shaped, glaucous leaves and, in late spring, racemes of large, saucer-shaped, yellow flowers.
R. lyallii (Giant buttercup). Evergreen, stout, upright, tufted perennial. H and S 12in (30cm) or more. Frost hardy, zones 6–7. Has rounded, leathery, dark green leaves, each 6in (15cm) or more across, and, in summer, bears panicles of large, shallowly cup-shaped, white flowers. Is very difficult to flower in hot, dry climates. Is suitable for an alpine house. Rarely sets seed in cultivation.
R. montanus **'Molten Gold'**. Clump-forming, compact perennial. H 6in (15cm), S 4in (10cm). Fully hardy, zones 4–8. Leaves are rounded and 3-lobed. Flower stems each produce a shallowly cup-shaped, shiny, bright golden yellow flower in early summer. Is useful for a sunny rock garden.
R. speciosus **'Plenus'**, syn. *R. gouanii* 'Plenus', illus. p.247.

RANZANIA (Berberidaceae)
Genus of one species of perennial, grown for its unusual appearance as well as its flowers. Is ideal for woodland gardens. Fully hardy. Prefers shade or semi-shade and humus-rich, moist soil. Propagate by division in spring or by seed in autumn.
R. japonica. Upright perennial. H 18in (45cm), S 12in (30cm). Zones 5–9. .

Produces 3-parted, fresh green leaves and, in early summer, small clusters of nodding, shallowly cup-shaped, pale mauve flowers.

RAOULIA (Compositae)
Genus of evergreen, mat-forming perennials, grown for their foliage. Some species are suitable for alpine houses, others for rock gardens. Fully to frost hardy. Needs sun or semi-shade and gritty, moist but well-drained, peaty soil. Propagate by seed when fresh or by division in spring.
R. australis illus. p.330.
R. eximia. Evergreen, cushion-forming perennial. H 1in (2.5cm), S 2in (5cm). Fully hardy, zone 7. Has oblong to oval, overlapping, woolly, gray leaves and, in late spring or summer, small, rounded heads of yellowish white flowers. Suits an alpine house. Prefers some shade.
R. haastii illus. p.331.
R. hookeri var. *albo-sericea* illus. p.329.

RAVENALA (Strelitziaceae)
Genus of one species of evergreen, palmlike tree, grown for its foliage and overall appearance. Is related to *Strelitzia*. Frost tender, min. 61°F (16°C). Requires full light and humus-rich, well-drained soil. Water potted specimens freely in summer, less in winter or when temperatures are low. Propagate by seed in spring. Red spider mite may be troublesome.
R. madagascariensis (Traveler's tree). Evergreen, upright, fan-shaped tree. H and S to 30ft (10m). Zone 10. Has bananalike, long-stalked leaves, each 10–20ft (3–6m) long, with expanded stalk bases. Groups of boat-shaped spathes with 6-parted, white flowers are produced from leaf axils in summer.

REBUTIA (Cactaceae)
Genus of mostly clump-forming, spherical to columnar, perennial cacti with flowers produced in profusion from plant bases, usually 2–3 years after raising from seed. Much-ribbed, tuberculate, green stems have short spines. A few species are sometimes included in *Aylostera*. Frost tender, min. 41°F (5°C). Requires sun or partial shade and well-drained soil. Is easy to grow. Propagate by seed in spring or summer.
R. aureiflora illus. p.400.
R. krainziana illus. p.394.
R. minuscula. Clump-forming, perennial cactus. H 2in (5cm), S 6in (15cm). Zone 10. Pale brown spines, ¹/₂in (1cm) long, uniformly cover 2in (5cm) wide, light green stem. Carries masses of trumpet-shaped, red flowers, to 1¹/₂in (4cm) wide, in early spring.
R. muscula illus. p.400.
R. pygmaea, syn. *Lobivia pygmaea*. Clump-forming, columnar, perennial cactus. H 2in (5cm), S 4in (10cm).

Zone 10. Very short, comblike spines are pressed against gray- to purple-green stem. Trumpet-shaped, pink to salmon or rose-purple flowers, to ³/₄in (2cm) across, appear in spring. Prefers a sunny position.
R. senilis. Clump-forming, perennial cactus. H 2in (5cm), S 6in (15cm). Zone 10. Has soft, white spines, 1¹/₄in (3cm) long, matted around a 2in (5cm) wide stem. In spring bears trumpet-shaped, red, yellow, pink, or orange flowers, 2in (5cm) across. Prefers a sunny site.
R. spegazziniana illus. p.395.
R. violaciflora illus. p.392.

REHDERODENDRON (Styracaceae)
Genus of deciduous, spring-flowering trees, grown for their flowers and fruits. Frost hardy. Needs sun or semi-shade, some shelter, and fertile, moist but well-drained, acid soil. Propagate by semi-ripe cuttings in summer or by seed in autumn.
R. macrocarpum. Deciduous, spreading tree. H 30ft (10m), S 22ft (7m). Zones 7–10. Young shoots are red. Pendent clusters of lemon-scented, cup-shaped, pink-tinged, white flowers are borne amid oblong, taper-pointed, red-stalked, glossy, dark green leaves in late spring. Produces cylindrical, woody, red fruits that ripen to brown in autumn.

REHMANNIA (Gesneriaceae)
Genus of spring- and summer-flowering perennials. Half hardy to frost tender, min. 34–41°F (1–5°C). Needs a warm, sunny position and light soil. Propagate by seed in autumn or spring or by root cuttings in winter.
R. angulata. Upright perennial. H 30in (75cm), S 18in (45cm). Frost tender, min. 36–41°F (2–5°C), zones 9–10. In spring-summer produces racemes of tubular to funnel-shaped, orange-marked, purplish red or purplish brown flowers. Oblong, hairy, green leaves have paired leaflets that are irregularly toothed.
R. elata illus. p.204.
R. glutinosa. Rosette-forming perennial. H 12in (30cm), S 10in (25cm). Frost tender, min. 34°F (1°C), zones 9–10. Tubular, pink, red-brown, or yellow flowers, with purple veins, are borne on leafy shoots in late spring and early summer. Leaves are oval to lance-shaped, toothed, hairy, and light green.

REINWARDTIA (Linaceae)
Genus of evergreen sub-shrubs, grown for their flowers. Frost tender, min. 45–50°F (7–10°C). Requires full light or partial shade and fertile, well-drained soil. Water freely when in full growth, moderately at other times. Tip prune young plants to promote branching; cut back hard after flowering. Raise annually by softwood

cuttings in late spring. Red spider mite may cause problems.
R. indica, syn. *R. trigyna*, illus. p.138.
R. trigyna. See *R. indica*.

RESEDA (Resedaceae)
Mignonette
Genus of annuals and biennials with flowers that attract bees and that are also suitable for cutting. Fully hardy. Grow in sun and in any fertile, well-drained soil. Dead-head to ensure a long flowering period. Propagate by seed sown outdoors in spring or early autumn.
R. odorata illus. p.263.

RHAMNUS (Rhamnaceae)
Buckthorn
Genus of deciduous or evergreen shrubs and trees, with inconspicuous flowers, grown for their foliage and fruits. Fully to frost hardy. Grows in sun or semi-shade and in fertile soil. Propagate deciduous species by seed in autumn, evergreens by semi-ripe cuttings in summer.
R. alaternus (Italian buckthorn). 'Argenteovariegata' is an evergreen, bushy shrub. H and S 10ft (3m). Frost hardy, zones 7–9. Has oval, leathery, glossy, gray-green leaves edged with creamy white. Produces tiny, yellowish green flowers from early to mid-summer, which are followed by spherical, red, then black fruits.
R. imeretina. Deciduous, spreading, open shrub. H 10ft (3m), S 15ft (5m). Fully hardy, zones 6–9. Stout shoots bear large, broadly oblong, prominently veined, dark green leaves that turn bronze-purple in autumn. Small, green flowers are borne in summer.

RHAPHIOLEPIS (Rosaceae)
Genus of evergreen shrubs, grown for their flowers and foliage. Frost to half hardy. In most areas does best against a sheltered wall; *R. umbellata* is the most hardy. Needs sun and fertile, well-drained soil. Propagate by semi-ripe cuttings in late summer.
R. x delacourii 'Coates' Crimson'. Evergreen, rounded shrub. H 6ft (2m), S 8ft (2.5m). Frost hardy, zones 8–10. Clusters of fragrant, star-shaped, deep pink flowers in spring or summer are set off by oval, leathery, dark green leaves.
R. indica (Indian hawthorn). Evergreen, bushy shrub. H 5ft (1.5m), S 6ft (2m). Half hardy, zones 8–10. Has clusters of fragrant, star-shaped, pink-flushed, white flowers in spring or early summer, amid narrowly lance-shaped, glossy, dark green leaves.
R. umbellata illus. p.128.

RHAPIS (Palmae)
Genus of evergreen fan palms, grown for their foliage and overall appearance. May have tiny, yellow flowers in summer. Frost tender, min. 59°F (15°C). Needs partial shade and humus-rich, well-drained soil. Water potted plants freely when in full growth, moderately at other times. Propagate by seed, suckers, or division in spring. Is susceptible to red spider mite.
R. excelsa illus. p.120.

RHAZYA (Apocynaceae)
Genus of summer-flowering perennials. Fully hardy. Needs sun and well-drained soil. Propagate by division in spring or by seed in autumn.
R. orientalis illus. p.243.

RHEUM (Polygonaceae)
Rhubarb
Genus of perennials, grown for their foliage and striking overall appearance. Includes the edible rhubarb and various ornamental plants. Some species are extremely large and require plenty of space in which to grow. Fully hardy. Prefers sun or semi-shade and deep, rich, well-drained soil. Propagate by division in spring or by seed in autumn.
R. alexandrae illus. p.213.
R. nobile. Clump-forming perennial. H 5ft (1.5m), S 3ft (1m). Zones 6–9. Oblong to oval, leathery, basal, green leaves are 2ft (60cm) long. In late summer produces long stems bearing conical spikes of large, overlapping, pale cream bracts that hide insignificant flowers.
R. palmatum. Clump-forming perennial. H and S 6ft (2m). Zones 5–9. Has 2–2¹/₂ft (60–75cm) long, rounded, 5-lobed, green leaves. In early summer produces broad panicles of small, creamy white flowers.
'Atrosanguineum' illus. p.189.

RHIPSALIDOPSIS (Cactaceae)
Genus of perennial cacti with trumpet- or bell-shaped flowers in spring. Is easy to grow, but may shed stem segments for no apparent reason. Frost tender, min. 43–50°F (6–10°C). Requires partial shade and rich, well-drained soil. Water well in summer, but allow to become almost dry between waterings. Water only occasionally in winter. Propagate by seed or stem cuttings in spring or summer.
R. gaertneri illus. p.395.
R. rosea illus. p.392.

RHIPSALIS (Cactaceae)
Mistletoe cactus
Genus of epiphytic, perennial cacti with usually pendent, variously formed stems. Flowers are followed by spherical, translucent berries. Frost tender, min. 50–52°F (10–11°C). Needs partial shade and rich, well-drained soil. Prefers 80% relative humidity – higher than for most cacti. Give only occasional, very light watering in winter. Propagate by seed or stem cuttings in spring or summer.
R. capilliformis. Pendent, perennial cactus. H 3ft (1m), S 20in (50cm). Min. 50°F (10°C), zone 10. Produces freely branching, cylindrical, green stems and, in winter-spring, short, funnel-shaped, white flowers, to ¹/₂in (1cm) wide, with recurved tips, followed by white berries.
R. cereuscula illus. p.382.
R. clavata. See *Hatiora clavata*.
R. crispata. Bushy, then pendent, perennial cactus. H 3ft (1m), S indefinite. Min. 52°F (11°C), zone 10. Has leaflike, elliptic to oblong, pale green stem segments, to 5in (12cm) long, with undulating edges that

produce short, funnel-shaped, cream or pale yellow flowers, to ¹/₂in (1cm) across, with recurved tips, in winter-spring, then white berries.
R. paradoxa (Chain cactus). Bushy, then pendent, perennial cactus. H 3ft (1m), S indefinite. Min. 52°F (11°C), zone 10. Triangular, green stems have segments alternately set at different angles. Short, funnel-shaped, white flowers, ³/₄in (2cm) across, with recurved tips, appear from stem edges in winter-spring and are followed by red berries.
R. tucumanensis illus. p.382.
R. warmingiana illus. p.382.

Rhodanthe manglesii. See *Helipterum manglesii*.

Rhodiola rosea. See *Sedum roseum*.

Rhodocactus grandifolius. See *Pereskia grandifolia*.

RHODOCHITON (Scrophulariaceae)
Genus of one species of evergreen, leaf-stalk climber, grown for its unusual flowers. Does best when grown as an annual. May be planted against fences and trellises or used as ground cover. Frost tender, min. 41°F (5°C). Grow in sun and in any well-drained soil. Propagate by seed in early spring.
R. atrosanguineum, syn. *R. volubile*, illus. p.169.
R. volubile. See *R. atrosanguineum*.

RHODODENDRON (Ericaceae)
Genus of evergreen, semi-evergreen, or deciduous shrubs, ranging from a dwarf habit to a treelike stature, grown mainly for beauty of flower. Fully hardy to frost tender, min. 39–45°F (4–7°C). Most prefer dappled shade, but a considerable number tolerates full sun, especially in cool climates. Needs neutral to acid soil – ideally, humus-rich and well-drained. Shallow planting is essential, as plants are surface-rooting. Dead-head spent flowers, wherever practical, to encourage energy into growth rather than seed production. Propagate by layering or semi-ripe cuttings in late summer. Yellowing leaves are usually caused by poor drainage, excessively deep planting, or lime in soil. Weevils and powdery mildew may also cause problems.

Rhododendrons and azaleas
The genus *Rhododendron* includes not only evergreen, large-leaved, and frequently large-flowered species and hybrids but also dwarf, smaller-leaved shrubs, both evergreen and deciduous, with few-flowered clusters of usually small blooms. "Azalea" is the common name given to the deciduous species and hybrids as well as to a group of compact, evergreen shrubs mainly derived from Japanese species. They are valued for their mass of small, colorful blooms in late spring. Many of the evergreen azaleas (sometimes known as Belgian azaleas) may also be grown as house plants. Botanically, however, all are classified as *Rhododendron*. The flowers are usually

single, but may be semi-double or double, including hose-in-hose (one flower tube inside another). Unless otherwise stated below, flowers are single and leaves are mid- to dark green and oval.

R. aberconwayi. Evergreen rhododendron with distinct, erect habit. H to 8ft (2.5m), S 4ft (1.2m). Frost hardy, zones 7–8. Broadly lance-shaped leaves are small, rigid, and deep green. Saucer-shaped, white flowers appear in late spring.
R. albrechtii. Deciduous, upright, bushy azalea. H to 10ft (3m), S 6ft (2m). Fully hardy, zones 6–9. Has spoon-shaped leaves clustered at branch tips and, in spring, bell-shaped, green-spotted, purple or pink flowers in loose clusters of 3–5.
R. 'Alison Johnstone'. Evergreen, bushy, compact rhododendron. H and S 6ft (2m). Frost hardy, zones 7–8. Has masses of exquisite, bell-shaped, peach pink flowers in spring and attractive, waxy, gray-green leaves.
R. 'Angelo'. Evergreen, bushy rhododendron. H and S to 12ft (4m). Frost hardy, zones 7–8. Has bold foliage and large, fragrant, bell-shaped, white flowers that are valuable in mid-summer in light woodland.
R. 'Anna Baldsiefen'. Deciduous azalea of upright habit. H and S to 3ft (1m). Fully hardy, zones 6–9. Bears clusters of star-shaped, pink blooms in spring. Foliage colors well in autumn.
R. arboreum (illus. p.101). Evergreen, treelike rhododendron. H to 40ft (12m), S 10ft (3m). Frost hardy, zones 7–8. Undersides of broadly lance-shaped leaves are silver, fawn, or cinnamon. In spring has dense clusters of bell-shaped flowers in colors ranging from red (most tender form) through pink to white.
R. argyrophyllum (illus. p.100). Evergreen, spreading rhododendron. H and S to 15ft (5m). Fully hardy, zones 6–8. Oblong leaves are silvery white on undersides. Loose bunches of bell-shaped, rich pink flowers, sometimes with deeper colored spots, are borne in spring. Is ideal for light woodland.
R. 'Ascot Brilliant'. Evergreen, bushy rhododendron. H and S 10ft (3m). Frost hardy, zones 7–8. Leaves are broadly oval. In spring produces loose bunches of funnel-shaped, waxy, rose-red blooms with darker margins. Grows best in light woodland.
R. augustinii (illus. p.101). Evergreen, bushy rhododendron. H and S to 12ft (4m). Fully hardy, zones 7–8. Has lance-shaped to oblong, light green leaves and, in spring, bears an abundance of widely funnel-shaped, pale to deep blue or lavender flowers. Is effective when mass planted.
R. auriculatum (illus. p.100). Evergreen, bushy, widely branching rhododendron. H and S to 20ft (6m). Fully hardy, zones 7–8. Has large, oblong leaves with earlike lobes at their base. In late summer bears loose bunches of 7–15 large, heavily scented, tubular to funnel-shaped, white flowers. Is best in light woodland.
R. 'Azor'. Evergreen, upright

rhododendron. H and S to 12ft (4m). Frost hardy, zones 7–8. Leaves are broadly oval. Produces large, fragrant, funnel-shaped, salmon pink flowers. Is especially valuable as it flowers in mid-summer.

R. 'Azuma-kagami' (illus. p.100). Evergreen, compact azalea. H and S 4ft (1.2m). Frost hardy, zones 7–9. Many small, hose-in-hose, deep pink flowers are borne in mid-spring. Is best in semi-shade.

R. barbatum. Evergreen, upright rhododendron. H and S to 30ft (10m). Fully hardy, zones 6–8. Has lance-shaped, dark green leaves with bristles on stems; bark is plum-colored and peeling. Produces tight bunches of tubular to bell-shaped, bright scarlet flowers in early spring.

R. 'Beauty of Littleworth' (illus. p.100). Evergreen, open, shrubby rhododendron. H and S 12ft (4m). Frost hardy, zones 7–8. Bears huge, conical bunches of scented, funnel-shaped, crimson-spotted, white flowers in late spring.

R. 'Beefeater'. Evergreen, bushy rhododendron. H and S to 8ft (2.5m). Frost hardy, zones 7–8. Leaves are broadly lance-shaped. Has striking, flat-topped bunches of bell-shaped, scarlet flowers in late spring and early summer.

R. 'Blue Diamond'. Evergreen, upright rhododendron. H and S to 5ft (1.5m). Fully hardy, zones 6–8. Small, neat leaves contrast with funnel-shaped, bright blue flowers borne in mid- to late spring. Likes full sun.

R. 'Blue Peter' (illus. p.101). Evergreen, bushy rhododendron. H and S to 12ft (4m). Fully hardy, zones 6–8. In early summer bears bold, open funnel-shaped, 2-tone lavender purple flowers with frilled petal edges.

R. calendulaceum (Flame azalea). Deciduous, bushy azalea. H and S 6–10ft (2–3m). Fully hardy, zones 6–9. Has funnel-shaped, scarlet or orange flowers in bunches of 5–7 in early summer.

R. calophytum (illus. p.100). Evergreen, widely-branched rhododendron. H and S to 20ft (6m). Frost hardy, zones 7–8. Produces large, lance-shaped leaves and, in early spring, huge bunches of bell-shaped, white or pale pink flowers with crimson spots. Does best in a sheltered situation.

R. calostrotum (illus. p.101). Evergreen, compact rhododendron. H to 3ft (1m). Fully hardy, zones 7–9. Has attractive, small, blue-green leaves and, in late spring, small, saucer-shaped, purple or scarlet flowers in clusters of 2–5.

R. 'Catawbiense Album'. Evergreen, rounded rhododendron. H and S to 10ft (3m). Fully hardy, zones 5–8. Bears glossy leaves and, in early summer, dense, rounded bunches of bell-shaped, white flowers.

R. 'Catawbiense Boursault'. Evergreen, rounded rhododendron. H and S to 10ft (3m). Fully hardy, zones 5–8. Has glossy leaves. Dense, rounded bunches of bell-shaped, lilac-purple blooms are borne in early summer.

R. x cilpinense. Semi-evergreen, compact rhododendron. H and S to 5ft (1.5m). Frost hardy, zones 7–8. Leaves are dark green and glossy. Bell-shaped, blush pink flowers, deeper in bud, appear in abundance in early spring and are vulnerable to frost damage.

R. cinnabarinum (illus. p.101). Evergreen, upright rhododendron. H and S 5–12ft (1.5–4m). Frost hardy, zones 7–8. Has blue-green leaves with small scales. Narrowly tubular, waxy, orange to red flowers are borne in loose, drooping bunches in late spring.

R. 'Coccinea Speciosa'. Deciduous, bushy azalea. H and S 5–8ft (1.5–2.5m). Fully hardy, zones 6–9. Produces open funnel-shaped, brilliant rich orange-red blooms in early summer. Broadly lance-shaped leaves provide good autumn color.

R. 'Corneille' (illus. p.100). Deciduous, bushy azalea. H and S 5–8ft (1.5–2.5m). Fully hardy, zones 6–9. In early summer bears fragrant, honeysucklelike, cream flowers, flushed pink outside. Has attractive autumn foliage.

R. 'Curlew' (illus. p.102). Evergreen rhododendron of compact, spreading habit. H and S 1ft (30cm). Fully hardy, zones 6–9. Has dull green leaves and, in late spring, relatively large, open funnel-shaped, yellow flowers.

R. 'Cynthia' (illus. p.101). Vigorous, evergreen, dome-shaped rhododendron. H and S to 20ft (6m). Fully hardy, zones 7–8. Bears conical bunches of bell-shaped, magenta-purple flowers, marked blackish red within, in late spring. Is excellent for sun or shade.

R. dauricum. Semi-evergreen, upright rhododendron. H and S to 5ft (1.5m). Fully hardy, zones 5–9. Produces small, funnel-shaped, vivid purple flowers in loose clusters throughout winter. Green leaves turn purple-brown in frosty conditions.

R. davidsonianum (illus. p.101). Evergreen, upright rhododendron. H 5–12ft (1.5–4m). Fully hardy, zones 7–8. Aromatic leaves are lance-shaped to oblong. In late spring has clusters of funnel-shaped flowers, ranging from pale pink to lilac-mauve.

R. decorum. Evergreen, bushy rhododendron. H and S 12ft (4m). Frost hardy, zones 6–8. Oblong to lance-shaped leaves are green above, pale green beneath. Has large, fragrant, funnel-shaped, white or shell pink flowers, green- or pink-spotted within, in early summer.

R. discolor. Evergreen, treelike rhododendron. H and S to 25ft (8m). Frost hardy, zones 7–8. Leaves are oblong to oval. Bears fragrant, funnel-shaped, pink flowers that give a magnificent display in mid-summer. Is ideal in light woodland.

R. 'Doncaster'. Evergreen, compact rhododendron. H and S 6–8ft (2–2.5m). Frost hardy, zones 7–8. Has leathery, stiff, glossy leaves and, in late spring, funnel-shaped, dark red flowers in dense bunches.

R. 'Dora Amateis'. Evergreen, compact rhododendron. H and S 2ft (60cm). Fully hardy, zones 6–8. Leaves are slender, glossy, and pointed. Masses of small, broadly funnel-shaped, white flowers, tinged with pink

and marked with green, appear in late spring. Is sun tolerant.

R. 'Elizabeth' (illus. p.101). Evergreen, dome-shaped rhododendron. H and S to 5ft (1.5m). Frost hardy, zones 7–8. Leaves are oblong. Has large, trumpet-shaped, brilliant red flowers in late spring. Is good in sun or partial shade.

R. 'Elizabeth Lockhart'. Evergreen, dome-shaped rhododendron. H and S 2ft (60cm). Frost hardy, zones 7–8. Produces shiny, purple-green leaves that become darker in winter. Has bell-shaped, deep pink flowers in spring.

R. 'English Roseum'. Vigorous, evergreen, bushy rhododendron. H and S to 8ft (2.5m). Fully hardy, zones 6–9. Bears handsome, dark green leaves, paler on undersides, and, in late spring, compact bunches of funnel-shaped, lilac-rose flowers.

R. 'Fabia' (illus. p.102). Evergreen, dome-shaped rhododendron. H and S 6ft (2m). Frost hardy, zones 7–8. Leaves are lance-shaped. Has loose, flat trusses of funnel-shaped, orange-tinted, scarlet flowers in early summer.

R. 'Fastuosum Flore Pleno'. Evergreen, dome-shaped rhododendron. H and S 5–12ft (1.5–4m). Fully hardy, zones 5–8. In early summer produces loose bunches of funnel-shaped, double, rich mauve flowers with red-brown marks and wavy edges.

R. fictolacteum (illus. p.100). Evergreen, treelike rhododendron. H to 45ft (13.5m). Frost hardy, zones 7–8. Has large leaves that are green above, brown-felted beneath. Bold bunches of bell-shaped, white flowers, each with a maroon blotch and often with a spotted throat, are borne in spring.

R. 'Firefly'. See R. 'Hexe'.

R. 'Freya' (illus. p.102). Deciduous azalea of compact, shrubby habit. H and S 5ft (1.5m). Fully hardy, zones 6–9. Fragrant, funnel-shaped, pink-flushed, orange-salmon flowers appear from late spring to early summer.

R. 'Frome' (illus. p.102). Deciduous azalea of shrubby habit. H and S to 5ft (1.5m). Fully hardy, zones 6–9. In spring bears trumpet-shaped, saffron yellow flowers, overlaid red in throats; petals are frilled and wavy-margined.

R. fulvum (illus. p.100). Evergreen, bushy rhododendron. H and S 5–12ft (1.5–4m). Frost hardy, zones 7–8. Oblong to oval, polished, deep green leaves are brown-felted beneath. In early spring has loose bunches of bell-shaped, pink flowers, fading to white, each with a basal, deep red blotch.

R. 'George Reynolds' (illus. p.102). Deciduous, bushy azalea. H and S to 6ft (2m). Fully hardy, zones 6–8. Large, funnel-shaped, yellow flowers, flushed pink in bud, are borne with or before the leaves in spring.

R. 'Gloria Mundi' (illus. p.102). Deciduous azalea of twiggy habit. H and S to 6ft (2m). Fully hardy, zones 6–9. Has fragrant, honeysucklelike, yellow-flared, orange flowers, with frilled margins, in early summer.

R. 'Glory of Littleworth' (illus. p.102). Evergreen or semi-evergreen, bushy hybrid between a rhododendron and an azalea. H and S 5ft (1.5m). Frost hardy, zones 7–8. Compact

bunches of fragrant, bell-shaped, orange-marked, creamy white flowers are borne abundantly in late spring and early summer. Is not easy to cultivate.

R. 'Gomer Waterer'. Evergreen, compact rhododendron. H and S 5–12ft (1.5–4m). Fully hardy, zones 7–8. Leaves are curved back at margins. Bell-shaped flowers, borne in dense bunches in early summer, are white, flushed mauve, each with a basal, mustard blotch. Likes sun or partial shade.

R. 'Hatsugiri' (illus. p.101). Evergreen, compact azalea. H and S 2ft (60cm). Frost hardy, zones 7–9. Has small, but very numerous, funnel-shaped, bright crimson-purple flowers in spring. Flowers very reliably.

R. 'Hawk Crest' (illus. p.102). Evergreen rhododendron of open habit. H and S 5–12ft (1.5–4m). Frost hardy, zones 7–8. Produces broadly lance-shaped leaves. Bell-shaped flowers, borne in loose, flat-topped bunches, are apricot in bud, opening to clear sulfur yellow in late spring.

R. 'Hexe', syn. R. 'Firefly'. Evergreen azalea of neat habit. H and S 2ft (60cm). Frost hardy, zones 7–8. Has numerous relatively large, hose-in-hose, glowing, crimson flowers in spring.

R. 'Hinodegiri' (illus. p.101). Evergreen, compact azalea. H and S 5ft (1.5m). Frost hardy, zones 6–8. Funnel-shaped, bright crimson flowers are small, but produced in abundance in late spring. Likes sun or light shade.

R. 'Hinomayo' (illus. p.101). Evergreen, compact azalea. H and S 5ft (1.5m). Frost hardy, zones 6–8. Small, funnel-shaped, clear pink flowers are produced in great abundance in spring. Likes sun or light shade.

R. hippophaeoides (illus. p.101). Evergreen, erect rhododendron. H and S 5ft (1.5m). Fully hardy, zones 7–9. Narrowly lance-shaped, aromatic leaves are gray-green. Small, funnel-shaped, lavender or lilac flowers are borne in spring. Is tolerant of wet, but not stagnant, soil.

R. 'Homebush' (illus. p.101). Deciduous, compact azalea. H and S 5ft (1.5m). Frost hardy, zones 7–9. In late spring bears tight, rounded heads of trumpet-shaped, semi-double, rose-purple flowers with paler shading.

R. 'Hotei'. Evergreen rhododendron of neat, compact habit. H and S 5–8ft (1.5–2.5m). Fully hardy, zones 7–8. Has excellent foliage. Large, funnel-shaped, deep yellow flowers are freely produced in late spring.

R. 'Humming Bird'. Evergreen, dome-shaped rhododendron of neat, compact habit. H and S to 5ft (1.5m). Fully hardy, zones 7–8. From mid- to late spring produces bell-shaped, rose-pink flowers in loose, nodding bunches, above rounded, glossy leaves.

R. 'Hydon Hunter'. Evergreen rhododendron of neat habit. H and S to 5ft (1.5m). Fully hardy, zones 7–8. In late spring or early summer has masses of large, narrowly bell-shaped, red-rimmed flowers, paler towards the center and orange-spotted within.

R. impeditum. Slow-growing,

evergreen rhododendron. H and S to 2ft (60cm). Fully hardy, zones 6–8. Tiny, aromatic leaves are gray-green. Small, funnel-shaped, purplish blue flowers appear in spring.

R. 'Iro-hayama' (illus. p.101). Evergreen, compact azalea. H and S to 5ft (1.5m). Frost hardy, zones 7–9. Has abundant, small, funnel-shaped, white flowers, with pale lavender margins and faint brown eyes, in spring. Does well in light shade.

R. 'Jalisco'. Evergreen, open, bushy rhododendron. H and S 5–12ft (1.5–4m). Frost hardy, zones 7–9. Bears bunches of narrowly bell-shaped, straw-colored flowers, tinted orange-rose at tips, in early summer.

R. 'Jeanette'. Semi-evergreen azalea of upright habit. H and S 5–6ft (1.5–2m). Frost hardy, zones 7–9. Funnel-shaped, vivid phlox pink flowers, with darker blotches, appear in spring. Is good in light shade or full sun.

R. 'John Cairns' (illus. p.101). Evergreen, upright, compact azalea. H and S 5–6ft (1.5–2m). Fully hardy, zones 7–9. Funnel-shaped, orange-red flowers are produced abundantly in spring. Grows consistently and reliably in sun or semi-shade.

R. kaempferi (illus. p.101). Semi-evergreen, erect, loosely branched azalea. H and S 5–8ft (1.5–2.5m). Fully hardy, zones 5–9. Leaves are lance-shaped. Has an abundance of funnel-shaped flowers in various shades of orange or red in late spring and early summer.

R. 'Kilimanjaro'. Evergreen, bushy rhododendron. H and S 5–12ft (1.5–4m). Frost hardy, zones 7–8. Bears broadly lance-shaped leaves. Produces large, rounded bunches of funnel- to bell-shaped, wavy-edged, maroon-red flowers, spotted chocolate within, in late spring and early summer.

R. 'Kirin' (illus. p.100). Evergreen, compact azalea. H and S to 5ft (1.5m). Frost hardy, zones 7–9. In spring has numerous hose-in-hose flowers that are deep rose, shaded a delicate silvery rose.

R. kiusianum. Semi-evergreen azalea of compact habit. H and S to 2ft (60cm). Fully hardy, zones 6–9. Leaves are narrowly oval. Has clusters of 2–5 funnel-shaped flowers, usually lilac-rose or mauve-purple, in late spring. Prefers full sun.

R. 'Lady Alice Fitzwilliam'. Evergreen, bushy rhododendron. H and S 5–12ft (1.5–4m). Half hardy, zones 8–9. Leaves are glossy, dark green. Loose bunches of heavily scented, broadly funnel-shaped, white flowers, flushed pale pink, are borne in mid- and late spring. Grows best against a south- or west-facing wall.

R. 'Lady Clementine Mitford'. Evergreen, rounded, dense rhododendron. H and S 12ft (4m). Fully hardy, zones 7–8. Has broadly oval, glossy, dark green leaves that are silvery when young and, in late spring and early summer, bold bunches of tubular-bell-shaped flowers, peach pink fading to white in the center, with V-shaped, pink, green, and brown marks within.

R. 'Lady Rosebery'. Evergreen, stiffly branched rhododendron. H and S 5–12ft (1.5–4m). Frost hardy, zones 7–8. In late spring produces clusters of drooping, narrowly bell-shaped, waxy flowers that are deep pink, paler towards petal edges. Is ideal for light woodland margin.

R. 'Lem's Cameo'. Evergreen, rounded, bushy rhododendron. H and S 5–8ft (1.5–2.5m). Frost hardy, zones 7–8. Leaves are rounded. In spring has large-domed bunches of open funnel-shaped, pale peach flowers, deep pink in bud, that are shaded to pink at edges and have basal, deep rose-colored blotches.

R. 'Loderi'. Evergreen rhododendron of open habit. H and S 12ft (4m). Frost hardy, zones 7–8. In spring bears huge bunches of richly fragrant, trumpet-shaped flowers that are usually soft pink, but at times paler, even white.

R. lutescens (illus. p.101). Semi-evergreen, upright rhododendron. H and S 5–10ft (1.5–3m). Fully hardy, zones 7–9. Has oval to lance-shaped leaves that are bronze-red when young. Produces small, funnel-shaped, primrose yellow flowers in early spring. Elegant and delicate, it is effective in light woodland.

R. luteum (illus. p.102). Deciduous azalea of open habit. H and S 5–8ft (1.5–2.5m). Fully hardy, zones 6–9. Leaves are oblong to lance-shaped. Bold, heavily fragrant, funnel-shaped, yellow blooms appear in spring. Autumn foliage is rich and colorful.

R. macabeanum (illus. p.102). Evergreen, treelike rhododendron. H and S up to 45ft (13.5m). Frost hardy, zones 7–8. Has bold, broadly oval leaves, dark green above, gray-felted beneath, and, in early spring, large bunches of bell-shaped, yellow flowers, blotched purple within.

R. mallotum. Evergreen, upright, open rhododendron, occasionally treelike. H and S to 12ft (4m). Frost hardy, zones 8–9. Oblong to oval leaves are deep green above, red-brown-felted beneath. Showy, tubular, crimson flowers in loose bunches are borne in early spring.

R. 'May Day' (illus. p.101). Evergreen, spreading rhododendron. H and S to 5ft (1.5m). Frost hardy, zones 7–8. Produces masses of loose bunches of long-lasting, funnel-shaped, scarlet flowers in late spring; calyces are petal-like and match the flower color. Leaves are fresh green above, whitish felted beneath.

R. 'Medway' (illus. p.102). Deciduous, bushy, open azalea. H and S 5–8ft (1.5–2.5m). Fully hardy, zones 6–9. In late spring bears large, trumpet-shaped, pale pink flowers with darker edges and orange-flashed throats; petals have frilled margins.

R. metternichii. Evergreen, upright rhododendron. H and S 5–12ft (1.5–4m). Fully hardy, zones 7–8. Has attractive, oblong leaves, glossy and green above, reddish brown-felted beneath. In spring produces bell-shaped, rose-red blooms, often subtly spotted within, which are borne in rounded bunches of 10–15.

R. 'Moonshine Crescent' (illus. p.102). Evergreen, rounded to upright rhododendron. H 6–8ft (2–2.5m), S 6ft (2m). Frost hardy, zones 7–8. In late spring produces compact trusses of bell-shaped, yellow flowers. Leaves are oblong to oval and dark green.

R. moupinense. Evergreen, rounded, compact rhododendron. H and S to 5ft (1.5m). Frost hardy, zones 7–8. Produces funnel-shaped, pink blooms in loose bunches in late winter and early spring. Leaves are glossy, dark green above, paler beneath. Is best grown in a sheltered situation to reduce risk of frosted flowers.

R. 'Mrs. G.W. Leak' (illus. p.100). Evergreen, upright, compact rhododendron. H and S 12ft (4m). Fully hardy, zones 7–8. Has compact, conical bunches of funnel-shaped, pink flowers, with black-brown and crimson marks within, in late spring.

R. nakaharae. Evergreen, mound-forming azalea. H and S 2ft (60cm). Frost hardy, zones 7–8. Shoots and oblong to oval leaves are densely hairy. Funnel-shaped, dark brick red flowers are borne in small clusters. Is valuable for mid-summer flowering and is ideal for a rock garden.

R. 'Nancy Waterer'. Deciduous, twiggy azalea. H and S 5–8ft (1.5–2.5m). Fully hardy, zones 6–9. Produces large, long-tubed and honeysucklelike, brilliant golden yellow flowers in early summer. Is ideal in a light woodland or full sun.

R. 'Narcissiflorum' (illus. p.102). Vigorous, deciduous, compact azalea. H and S 5–8ft (1.5–2.5m). Fully hardy, zones 6–9. Sweetly scented, hose-in-hose, pale yellow flowers, darker outside and in center, are produced in late spring or early summer. Has bronze autumn foliage.

R. 'Nobleanum' (illus. p.100). Evergreen, upright shrub or treelike rhododendron. H and S to 15ft (5m). Frost hardy, zones 7–8. Bears large, compact bunches of broadly funnel-shaped, rose-red, pink, or white flowers in winter or early spring. Will flower for long periods in mild weather; is best in a sheltered position.

R. 'Norma'. Vigorous, deciduous, compact azalea. H and S to 5ft (1.5m). Fully hardy, zones 6–9. Produces masses of hose-in-hose, rose-red flowers that have a salmon glow, in spring. Grows well in sun or light shade.

R. 'Nova Zembla'. Vigorous, evergreen, upright rhododendron. H and S 5–12ft (1.5–4m). Fully hardy, zones 5–8. Has funnel-shaped, dark red flowers in closely set bunches from late spring to early summer.

R. occidentale (illus. p.100). Deciduous, bushy azalea. H and S 5–8ft (1.5–2.5m). Fully hardy, zones 6–8. Leaves are glossy and turn yellow or orange in autumn. Flowers are fragrant, funnel-shaped, white or pale pink, each with a basal, yellow-orange blotch, and are borne from early to mid-summer.

R. orbiculare (illus. p.100). Evergreen rhododendron of compact habit. H and S to 10ft (3m). Fully hardy, zones 7–8. Produces rounded, bright green leaves. Bell-shaped, rose-pink flowers are borne in loose bunches in late spring.

R. oreotrephes (illus. p.101). Evergreen, upright shrub or treelike rhododendron. H and S to 15ft (5m). Fully hardy, zones 7–8. Has attractive, scaly, gray-green foliage. In spring bears loose bunches of 3–10 broadly funnel-shaped flowers, usually mauve or purple, but variable, often with crimson spots.

R. 'Palestrina' (illus. p.100). Evergreen or semi-evergreen, compact, free-flowering azalea. H and S to 4ft (1.2m). Frost hardy, zones 7–9. Has open funnel-shaped, white flowers, with faint, green marks, in late spring. Grows well in light shade.

R. 'Percy Wiseman' (illus. p.100). Evergreen rhododendron with a domed, compact habit. H and S to 6ft (2m). Fully hardy, zones 7–8. In late spring produces open funnel-shaped, peach yellow flowers that fade to white. Tolerates full sun.

R. 'Pink Pearl' (illus. p.101). Vigorous, evergreen, upright, open rhododendron. H and S 12ft (4m) or more. Frost hardy, zones 6–9. Tall bunches of open funnel-shaped, pink flowers give a spectacular display in late spring.

R. 'P. J. Mezitt'. Evergreen, compact rhododendron. H and S up to 5ft (1.5m). Fully hardy, zones 6–8. Aromatic leaves are small, dark green in summer, bronze-purple in winter. Small, funnel-shaped, lavender pink flowers are frost-resistant and are borne in early spring. Is good in full sun.

R. 'President Roosevelt' (illus. p.101). Slow-growing, evergreen, weakly branched rhododendron. H and S to 6ft (2m). Frost hardy, zones 7–8. Leaves are yellow-variegated. Open bell-shaped, pale pink flowers, lighter towards centers and frilled at margins, appear from mid- to late spring. Leaves have a tendency to revert to plain green.

R. 'Ptarmigan'. Evergreen, spreading rhododendron that forms a compact mound. H to 1ft (30cm), S 2½ft (75cm) or more. Fully hardy, zones 7–8. In early spring is covered with small, funnel-shaped, pure white flowers. Prefers full sun.

R. 'Purple Splendour'. Evergreen, bushy rhododendron. H and S to 10ft (3m). Fully hardy, zones 6–8. Has well-formed bunches of open funnel-shaped, rich royal purple flowers, with prominent, black marks in throats, in late spring or early summer.

R. 'Queen Elizabeth II' (illus. p.101). Evergreen, open rhododendron. H and S 5–12ft (1.5–4m). Frost hardy, zones 7–8. Funnel-shaped, greenish yellow flowers are borne in loose bunches in late spring. Leaves are narrowly oval or lance-shaped, glossy, green above, pale green beneath.

R. 'Queen of Hearts'. Evergreen, straggly rhododendron. H and S 5–12ft (1.5–4m). Frost hardy, zones 7–8. Has masses of domed bunches of funnel-shaped, deep crimson flowers, black-speckled within, in mid-spring.

R. racemosum (illus. p.100). Evergreen, upright, stiffly branched rhododendron. H and S to 8ft (2.5m). Fully hardy, zones 6–8. Has clusters of small, widely funnel-shaped, bright pink flowers carried along the stems in spring. Small, broadly oval, aromatic leaves are dull green above, gray-green below.

R. rex. Vigorous, evergreen, upright shrub or treelike rhododendron. H and S 12ft (4m) or more. Frost hardy, zones 7–8. Is similar to *R. fictolacteum*, but leaves are pale buff-felted beneath and pink or white flowers each have a crimson blotch and a spotted throat.

R. 'Romany Chai'. Vigorous, evergreen rhododendron, open when young, becoming denser with age. H and S 5–12ft (1.5–4m). Frost hardy, zones 7–8. Has dark green foliage, tinged bronze, and, in early summer, large, compact bunches of broadly funnel-shaped, rich brown-red flowers, each with a basal, maroon blotch. Prefers light woodland.

R. 'Rosalind' (illus. p.101). Vigorous, evergreen rhododendron of open-branched habit. H and S 12ft (4m). Frost hardy, zones 7–8. Leaves are dull green. Has broadly funnel-shaped, pink flowers in loose bunches in spring.

R. 'Roseum Elegans'. Vigorous, evergreen, rounded rhododendron. H and S 8ft (2.5m) or more. Fully hardy, zones 6–8. In early summer has rounded bunches of broadly funnel-shaped, reddish purple flowers, marked yellow-brown. Foliage is bold and glossy, deep green.

R. 'Roza Stevenson'. Vigorous, evergreen, upright rhododendron of open habit. H and S 5–12ft (1.5–4m). Frost hardy, zones 7–8. Bears masses of fine, loose bunches of saucer-shaped, lemon flowers in mid- to late spring. Is excellent in light shade.

R. rubiginosum. Vigorous, evergreen, upright, well-branched rhododendron. H 20ft (6m), S 8ft (2.5m). Frost hardy, zones 7–8. Aromatic leaves are lance-shaped, dull green above, reddish brown beneath. Has funnel-shaped, lilac-purple flowers in loose bunches in mid-spring.

R. schlippenbachii (illus. p.100). Deciduous, rounded, open azalea. H and S 8ft (2.5m). Fully hardy, zones 5–8. Spoon-shaped leaves are in whorls at branch ends. Saucer-shaped, pink flowers in loose bunches of 3–6 appear in mid-spring. Is ideal in light woodland.

R. 'Seta' (illus. p.100). Evergreen, erect rhododendron. H 5ft (1.5m), S 3–5ft (1–1.5m). Frost hardy, zones 7–8. In early spring bears loose bunches of small, tubular, shiny, white flowers, with vivid pink stripes, fading to white at bases.

R. 'Seven Stars' (illus. p.100). Vigorous, evergreen, upright, dense rhododendron. H and S 6–10ft (2–3m). Fully hardy, zones 7–8. Has yellowish green foliage and, in spring, masses of bunches of large, bell-shaped, wavy-margined, white flowers, flushed with apple-blossom pink, opening from pink buds.

R. 'Silver Moon' (illus. p.100). Evergreen azalea of broad, spreading habit. H and S 5–8ft (1.5–2.5m). Frost hardy, zones 7–8. Has funnel-shaped, white flowers, with pale green-blotched throats and frilled petal edges, in spring. Grows best in partial shade.

R. 'Sir Charles Lemon'. Evergreen, upright shrub or treelike rhododendron. H and S to 15ft (5m). Frost hardy, zones 7–8. Produces attractive foliage, dark green above, cinnamon brown below, and, in spring, bold bunches of bell-shaped, white flowers.

R. 'Snowdrift'. Deciduous, bushy azalea. H and S to 8ft (2.5m). Fully hardy, zones 6–8. Bears bunches of large, slender-tubed flowers in spring before the leaves appear. Flowers are white with yellow marks that deepen to orange.

R. souliei (illus. p.100). Evergreen, open rhododendron. H and S 5–12ft (1.5–4m). Fully hardy, zones 7–8. Has rounded leaves and, in late spring, saucer-shaped, soft pink flowers. Grows best in areas of low rainfall.

R. 'Spek's Orange'. Deciduous, bushy azalea. H and S to 8ft (2.5m). Fully hardy, zones 6–8. In late spring carries bold bunches of large, slender-tubed blooms that are bright reddish orange with greenish marks within.

R. 'Strawberry Ice' (illus. p.100). Deciduous, bushy azalea. H and S 5–8ft (1.5–2.5m). Fully hardy, zones 7–8. Flowers are trumpet-shaped, deep pink in bud, opening flesh pink, and mottled deeper pink at petal edges with deep yellow-marked throats; they appear in late spring.

R. 'Surprise'. Evergreen, dense azalea. H and S to 5ft (1.5m). Frost hardy, zones 7–8. Has abundant, small, funnel-shaped, light orange-red flowers in mid-spring. Looks effective when mass planted and is ideal in light shade or full sun.

R. 'Susan' (illus. p.101). Evergreen, close-growing rhododendron. H and S 5–12ft (1.5–4m). Fully hardy, zones 7–8. In spring bears large bunches of open funnel-shaped flowers in 2 shades of blue-mauve and spotted purple within. Has handsome, glossy, dark green foliage.

R. sutchuenense (illus. p.100). Evergreen, spreading shrub or treelike rhododendron. H and S to 16ft (5m). Frost hardy, zones 7–8. Has large leaves and, in early spring, bears large bunches of broadly funnel-shaped, pink flowers, spotted deeper within. Prefers light woodland.

R. 'Temple Belle'. Evergreen rhododendron of neat, compact habit. H and S 5–8ft (1.5–2.5m). Fully hardy, zones 7–8. Loose bunches of bell-shaped, clear pink flowers are produced in spring. Rounded leaves are dark green above, gray-green beneath.

R. thomsonii (illus. p.101). Evergreen, rounded rhododendron of open habit. H and S to 18ft (5.5m). Frost hardy, zones 7–8. Leaves are waxy, dark green above, whiter beneath. Peeling, fawn-colored bark contrasts well with bell-shaped, waxy, red flowers in spring.

R. 'Vuyk's Scarlet' (illus. p.101). Evergreen, compact azalea. H and S to 2ft (60cm). Frost hardy, zones 7–9. In spring bears an abundance of relatively large, open funnel-shaped, brilliant red flowers, with wavy petals, that completely cover the glossy foliage.

R. wardii (illus. p.101). Evergreen, compact rhododendron. H and S 5–12ft (1.5–4m). Fully hardy, zones 7–8. Has rounded leaves and, in late spring, loose bunches of saucer-shaped, clear yellow flowers, each with a basal, crimson blotch.

R. williamsianum (illus. p.100). Evergreen rhododendron of compact, spreading habit. H and S 5ft (1.5m). Fully hardy, zones 7–8. Leaves are bronze when young, maturing to green. Has loosely clustered, bell-shaped, pink flowers in spring.

R. 'Woodcock'. Evergreen rhododendron of compact, spreading habit. H and S 5–8ft (1.5–2.5m). Fully hardy, zones 7–8. Has semi-glossy, dark green leaves and, in spring, masses of loose bunches of funnel-shaped, rose-red flowers.

R. xanthocodon (illus. p.101). Evergreen rhododendron of open, upright habit. H and S 5–12ft (1.5–4m). Frost hardy, zones 7–8. Aromatic leaves are blue-green when young, maturing to green. Bears loose clusters of bell-shaped, waxy, yellow flowers in late spring. Grows best in a sheltered situation.

R. yakushimanum (illus. p.100). Evergreen, dome-shaped rhododendron of neat, compact habit. H 3ft (1m), S 5ft (1.5m). Fully hardy, zones 5–8. Broadly oval leaves are silvery at first, maturing to deepest green, and are brown-felted beneath. In late spring has open funnel-shaped, pink flowers that fade to near white and are flecked green within.

R. 'Yellowhammer' (illus. p.102). Evergreen, erect, bushy rhododendron. H and S to 6ft (2m). Fully hardy, zones 7–8. Abundant clusters of small, tubular, bright yellow flowers are borne in spring; frequently flowers again in autumn.

R. yunnanense (illus. p.100). Semi-evergreen, open rhododendron. H and S 5–12ft (1.5–4m). Fully hardy, zones 7–8. In spring produces masses of butterflylike, pale pink or white flowers with spotted or blotched throats. Aromatic leaves are gray-green.

RHODOHYPOXIS (Hypoxidaceae)
Genus of dwarf, spring- to summer-flowering, tuberous perennials, grown for their pink, red, or white flowers, each comprising 6 petals that meet at the center, so the flower has no eye. Frost hardy, if kept fairly dry when dormant in winter. Requires full sun and sandy, peaty soil with plenty of moisture in summer. Propagate by seed or offsets in spring.

R. baurii. Spring- and early summer-flowering, tuberous perennial. H 2–4in (5–10cm), S 1–2in (2.5–5cm). Zone 9. Has an erect, basal tuft of narrowly lance-shaped, hairy leaves. Slender stems produce a succession of erect, flattish, white, pale pink, or red flowers, ³/₄in (2cm) across. 'Albrighton' and 'Douglas' illus. p.320. 'Margaret Rose' illus. p.316. var. *platypetala* has 1in (2.5cm) wide, white or very pale pink flowers.

RHODOLEIA (Hamamelidaceae)
Genus of evergreen, mainly spring-flowering trees, grown for their foliage and flowers. Frost tender, min. 45–50°F (7–10°C). Requires full light or partial

shade and humus-rich, well-drained, neutral to acid soil. Water potted specimens freely when in full growth, moderately at other times. Pruning is tolerated if necessary. Propagate by semi-ripe cuttings in summer or by seed when ripe, in autumn, or in spring.

R. championii. Evergreen, bushy tree. H and S 12–25ft (4–8m). Zones 9–10. Elliptic to oval, bright green leaves, each to 3¹/₂in (9cm) long, are borne towards the shoot tips. Clusters of insignificant flowers, surrounded by petal-like, pink bracts, appear in spring.

RHODOTHAMNUS (Ericaceae)
Genus of one species of evergreen, semi-prostrate, open shrub, grown for its flowers. Is suitable for rock gardens and peat beds. Fully hardy. Needs sun and humus-rich, well-drained, acid soil. Propagate by seed in spring or by semi-ripe cuttings in summer.

R. chamaecistus illus. p.292.

RHODOTYPOS (Rosaceae)
Genus of one species of deciduous shrub, grown for its flowers. Fully hardy. Needs sun or semi-shade and fertile soil. On established plants cut some older shoots back or to ground level after flowering. Propagate by softwood cuttings in summer or by seed in autumn.

R. kerrioides. See *R. scandens*.
R. scandens, syn. *R. kerrioides*, illus. p.126.

Rhoeo discolor. See *Tradescantia spathacea.*
Rhoeo spathacea. See *Tradescantia spathacea.*

RHOICISSUS (Vitaceae)
Genus of evergreen, tendril climbers, grown for their handsome foliage. Produces inconspicuous flowers intermittently during the year. Frost tender, min. 45–50°F (7–10°C). Grow in any fertile, well-drained soil with light shade in summer. Water regularly, less in cold weather. Provide support. Remove crowded stems when necessary or in early spring. Propagate by seed in spring or by semi-ripe cuttings in summer.

R. capensis (Cape grape). Vigorous, evergreen, tendril climber. H to 15ft (5m). Zones 9–10. Rounded, toothed, lustrous, mid- to deep green leaves, to 8in (20cm) wide, have a deeply rounded, heart-shaped base.

R. rhomboidea. Moderately vigorous, evergreen, tendril climber. H to 20ft (6m). Zones 9–10. Prominently veined, glossy, deep green leaves are divided into 3 leaflets, the lateral 2 being lop-sided.

RHOMBOPHYLLUM (Aizoaceae)
Genus of mat-forming, perennial succulents with dense, basal rosettes of linear or semi-cylindrical leaves, each expanded towards middle or tip; leaf tip is also reflexed or incurved. Frost tender, min. 41°F (5°C). Needs sun and very well-drained soil. Propagate by seed or stem cuttings in spring or summer.

R. rhomboideum illus. p.398.

RHUS (Anacardiaceae)
Sumac
Genus of deciduous trees, shrubs, and scrambling climbers, grown for their divided, ashlike foliage, autumn color, and, in some species, showy fruit clusters. Fully to half hardy. Requires sun and well-drained soil. Propagate by semi-ripe cuttings in summer, by seed in autumn, or by root cuttings in winter. May be attacked by coral spot fungus.
R. aromatica. Deciduous, bushy shrub. H 3ft (1m), S 5ft (1.5m). Fully hardy, zones 4–9. Deep green leaves, each composed of 3 oval leaflets, turn orange or reddish purple in autumn. Tiny, yellow flowers are borne in mid-spring, before foliage, and are followed by spherical, red fruits.
R. copallina (Dwarf sumac). Deciduous, upright shrub. H and S 3–5ft (1–1.5m), sometimes more. Fully hardy, zones 5–9. Has glossy, dark green leaves, with numerous lance-shaped leaflets, that turn red-purple in autumn. Minute, greenish yellow flowers are produced in dense clusters from mid- to late summer and are followed by narrowly egg-shaped, bright red fruits.
R. cotinus. See *Cotinus coggygria.*
R. glabra illus. p.111.
R. potaninii. Deciduous, round-headed tree. H 40ft (12m), S 25ft (8m). Fully hardy, zones 6–9. Has large, dark green leaves, with usually 7–11 oval leaflets that turn red in autumn. In summer bears dense clusters of tiny, yellow-green flowers. Female flower clusters develop into tiny, spherical, black or brownish fruits.
R. x *pulvinata.* Vigorous, deciduous, upright shrub. H and S 15ft (5m). Fully hardy, zones 5–9. Has velvety shoots. Large, dark green leaves, with 7–15 oblong leaflets, turn orange-red in autumn as clusters of rounded, deep red fruits mature.
R. succedanea (Wax tree). Deciduous, spreading tree. H and S 30ft (10m). Half hardy, zones 7–9. Bears dense clusters of tiny, yellow-green flowers in summer. Large, glossy, dark green leaves, consisting of 9–15 oval leaflets, turn red in autumn. Female flower clusters develop into tiny, spherical, black or brownish fruits.
R. trichocarpa illus. p.68.
R. typhina (Stag's-horn sumac). Deciduous, spreading, suckering, open shrub or tree. H 15ft (5m), S 20ft (6m). Fully hardy, zones 3–8. Velvety shoots are clothed in dark green leaves with oblong leaflets. Produces minute, greenish white flowers from mid- to late summer. Leaves become brilliant orange-red in autumn, accompanying clusters of spherical, deep red fruits on female plants. **'Laciniata'** (syn. *R.t.* 'Dissecta') illus. p.92.
R. verniciflua (Varnish tree). Deciduous, spreading tree. H 50ft (15m), S 30ft (10m). Fully hardy, zones 6–9. Large, glossy, bright green leaves, with 7–13 oval leaflets, redden in autumn. Bears dense clusters of tiny, yellow-green flowers in summer, followed by berrylike, brownish yellow fruits. Sap may severely irritate the skin.

RHYNCHELYTRUM (Gramineae). See GRASSES, BAMBOOS, RUSHES, and SEDGES.
R. repens, syn. *R. roseum* (Natal grass, Ruby grass). Tuft-forming, annual or short-lived, perennial grass. H 4–6ft (1.2–2m), S 2–3ft (60cm–1m). Frost tender, min. 41°F (5°C), zones 9–10. Leaves are green, flat, and finely pointed. Produces loose panicles of awned, pink spikelets in summer.
R. roseum. See *R. repens.*

RIBES (Grossulariaceae)
Currant
Genus of deciduous or evergreen, mainly spring-flowering shrubs, grown for their edible fruits (currants and gooseberries) or their flowers. Fully to frost hardy. Needs full sun and fertile, well-drained soil, but *R. laurifolium* also tolerates shade. Cut out some older shoots after flowering and prune straggly, old plants hard in winter or early spring. Propagate deciduous species by hardwood cuttings in winter, evergreens by semi-ripe cuttings in summer. Aphids may attack young foliage.
R. laurifolium illus. p.143.
R. odoratum (Buffalo currant). Deciduous, upright shrub. H and S 6ft (2m). Fully hardy, zones 5–8. Clusters of fragrant, tubular, golden yellow flowers are borne from mid- to late spring, followed by rounded, purple fruits. Rounded, 3-lobed, bright green leaves turn red and purple in autumn.
R. sanguineum (Flowering currant). **'Brocklebankii'** illus. p.123. **'King Edward VII'** is a deciduous, upright, compact shrub. H and S 6ft (2m). Fully hardy, zones 6–8. Small, tubular, deep reddish pink flowers are freely borne amid rounded, 3–5-lobed, aromatic, dark green leaves, from mid- to late spring, and are sometimes succeeded by spherical, black fruits with a white bloom. Is useful for hedging. **'Pulborough Scarlet'** illus. p.98. **'Tydeman's White'**, H and S 8ft (2.5m), is less compact and has pure white flowers.
R. speciosum (Fuchsia-flowered currant). Deciduous, bushy, spiny shrub. H and S 6ft (2m). Frost hardy, zones 7–9. Slender, drooping, tubular, red flowers, with long, red stamens, open from mid- to late spring. Fruits are spherical and red. Has red, young shoots and oval, 3–5-lobed, glossy, bright green leaves. Flourishes when trained against a south- or west-facing wall.

RICHEA (Epacridaceae)
Genus of evergreen, summer-flowering shrubs, grown for their foliage and densely clustered flowers. Frost to half hardy. Needs sun or semi-shade and moist, peaty, neutral to acid soil. Propagate by semi-ripe cuttings in summer or by seed in autumn.
R. scoparia. Evergreen, upright shrub. H and S 6ft (2m). Frost hardy, zones 9–10. Shoots are densely covered with narrowly lance-shaped, sharp-pointed, dark green leaves. Dense, upright spikes of small, egg-shaped, pink, white, orange, or maroon flowers appear in early summer.

RICINUS (Euphorbiaceae)
Genus of one species of fast-growing, evergreen, treelike shrub, grown for its foliage. In cool climates is grown as an annual. Half hardy to frost tender, min. 36–9°F (2–4°C). Needs sun and fertile to rich, well-drained soil. May require support in exposed areas. Propagate by seed sown under glass in early spring.
R. communis illus. p.279. **'Impala'** illus. p.274.

ROBINIA (Leguminosae)
Genus of deciduous, mainly summer-flowering trees and shrubs, grown for their foliage and clusters of pealike flowers. Is useful for poor, dry soil. Fully hardy. Needs a sunny position. Grows in any but waterlogged soil. Branches are brittle and may be damaged by strong winds. Propagate by seed or suckers in autumn or by root cuttings in winter.
R. x *ambigua* **'Decaisneana'**. Deciduous, spreading tree. H 50ft (15m), S 30ft (10m). Zones 4–10. Dark green leaves have numerous oval leaflets. Long, hanging clusters of pealike, pink flowers are borne in early summer.
R. hispida illus. p.109.
R. kelseyi. Deciduous, spreading, open shrub. H 8ft (2.5m), S 12ft (4m). Zones 6–9. Clusters of pealike, rose-pink flowers open in late spring or early summer and are followed by pendent, red seed pods. Dark green leaves each consist of 9 or 11 oval leaflets.
R. pseudoacacia (False acacia, Locust). Fast-growing, deciduous, spreading tree. H 80ft (25m), S 50ft (15m). Zones 4–9. Dark green leaves consist of 11–23 oval leaflets. Dense, drooping clusters of fragrant, pealike, white flowers are borne in late spring and early summer. **'Frisia'** illus. p.54. **'Umbraculifera'** (Mop-head acacia), H and S 20ft (6m), has a rounded, dense head; flowers are rarely produced.

ROCHEA (Crassulaceae)
Genus of evergreen, succulent sub-shrubs and shrubs. Frost tender, min. 50°F (10°C). Requires sun and well-drained soil. Propagate by seed or stem cuttings in spring or summer.
R. coccinea, syn. *Crassula coccinea.* Evergreen, erect, succulent shrub. H to 2ft (60cm), S 1ft (30cm) or more. Zone 10. Alternate pairs of fleshy, oval to oblong-oval, hairy-margined, dull green leaves are each united at the base and are arranged at right angles in 4 rows up the woody, green stems. Produces umbels of tubular, bright red flowers in summer or autumn.

RODGERSIA (Saxifragaceae)
Genus of summer-flowering, rhizomatous perennials. Is ideal for pond banks. Fully to frost hardy. Grows in sun or semi-shade and in moist soil in a position sheltered from strong winds, which may damage foliage. Propagate by division in spring or by seed in autumn.
R. aesculifolia illus. p.202.

R. pinnata **'Superba'**. Clump-forming, rhizomatous perennial. H 3–4ft (1–1.2m), S 2½ft (75cm). Frost hardy, zones 5–8. Has divided, bronze-tinged, emerald green leaves with 5–9 narrowly oval leaflets. Long, much-branched, dense panicles of star-shaped, bright pink flowers appear in mid-summer.
R. podophylla illus. p.201.
R. sambucifolia illus. p.201.

ROMNEYA (Papaveraceae)
Californian poppy
Genus of summer-flowering, woody-based perennials and deciduous sub-shrubs. Frost hardy. Requires a warm, sunny position and deep, well-drained soil. Is difficult to establish, resents being moved, and in very cold areas roots may need protection in winter. Once established, may spread rapidly. Propagate by softwood cuttings of basal shoots in early spring, by seed in autumn (transplanting seedlings without disturbing rootballs), or by root cuttings in winter.
R. coulteri illus. p.188.
R. **'White Cloud'**. Vigorous, bushy, woody-based perennial. H and S 3ft (1m). Zones 8–10. Throughout summer produces large, slightly fragrant, shallowly cup-shaped, white flowers with prominent golden stamens. Leaves are oval, deeply lobed, and gray.

ROMULEA (Iridaceae)
Genus of crocuslike corms, grown for their funnel-shaped flowers. Frost to half hardy. Needs full light and well-drained, sandy soil. Water freely during the growing period. Most species die down in summer and then need warmth and dryness. *R. macowanii,* however, is dormant in winter. Propagate by seed in autumn, or in spring for *R. macowanii.*
R. bulbocodioides of gardens. See *R. flava.*
R. bulbocodium illus. p.360.
R. flava, syn. *R. bulbocodioides* of gardens. Early spring-flowering corm. H to 4in (10cm), S 1–2in (2.5–5cm). Half hardy, zones 9–10. Has a threadlike, erect, basal leaf and 1–5 upright, widely funnel-shaped, usually yellow flowers, $^3/_4$–1½in (2–4cm) across, with deeper yellow centers.
R. longituba. See *R. macowanii.*
R. macowanii, syn. *R. longituba.* Summer-flowering corm. H and S ½–¾in (1–2cm). Half hardy, zones 9–10. Leaves are threadlike, erect, and basal. Bears 1–3 upright, yellow flowers, each 1¼in (3cm) across with a long tube expanding into a wide funnel shape.
R. sabulosa. Early spring-flowering corm. H 2–6in (5–15cm), S 1–2in (2.5–5cm). Half hardy, zones 9–10. Forms threadlike, erect, basal leaves. Stems bear 1–4 upward-facing, funnel-shaped, black-centered, bright red flowers that open flattish in sun to 1½–2in (4–5cm) across.

RONDELETIA (Rubiaceae)
Genus of evergreen, mainly summer-flowering trees and shrubs, grown primarily for their flowers. Frost

tender, min. 55–61°F (13–16°C). Requires full light or partial shade and fertile, well-drained soil. Water potted specimens freely when in full growth, moderately at other times. Stems may be shortened in early spring if necessary. Propagate by seed in spring or by semi-ripe cuttings in summer.
R. amoena. Evergreen, rounded shrub. H and S 6–12ft (2–4m). Zone 10. Oval, dark green leaves have dense, brown down on undersides. Has dense clusters of tubular, 4- or 5-lobed, pink flowers in summer.

Rooksbya euphorbioides. See *Lemaireocereus euphorbioides.*

ROSA (Rosaceae)
Rose
Genus of deciduous or semi-evergreen, open shrubs and scrambling climbers, grown for their profusion of flowers, often fragrant, and sometimes for their fruits (rose hips). Leaves are divided into usually 5 or 7 oval leaflets, with rounded or pointed tips, that are sometimes toothed. Stems usually bear thorns, or prickles. All those roses listed here are fully hardy, zones 4–9, unless otherwise stated below. Prefers an open, sunny site and needs fertile, moist but well-drained soil. Avoid planting in an area where roses have been grown in recent years, as problems due to harmful organisms may occur: either exchange the soil, which may be used satisfactorily elsewhere, or choose another site for the new rose. To obtain blooms of high quality, feed in late winter or early spring with a balanced fertilizer and apply a mulch. In spring-summer feed at 3-weekly intervals. Remove spent flower heads from plants that are "remontant" ("rising up again"; other terms used are repeat- or perpetual-flowering). May be trimmed for tidiness in early winter. To improve health, flower quality, and shape of bush, prune in the dormant season or, preferably, in spring, before young shoots develop from dormant growth buds: remove dead, damaged, and dying wood; lightly trim Old Garden and Ground cover roses (see below); remove two-thirds of previous summer's growth of Modern bush, including miniature, roses. Correct treatment of Modern shrub and climbing roses, ramblers, and species roses depends on the variety but in general prune only lightly. Propagate by budding in summer or by hardwood cuttings in autumn. All roses are prone to attack by various pests and diseases, including aphids, blackspot, powdery mildew, rust, and sawfly.

Roses are officially classified in three groups, each comprising different types, based, it is claimed, on the functional qualities of each plant, such as whether it is remontant, rather than on any historical, botanical, or genetical relationships. Flowers occur in a variety of forms (illustrated and described on p.148) and are single (4–7 petals), semi-double (8–14 petals), double (15–30 petals), or fully double (over 30 petals). Roses are illustrated on pp.148–62.

Species roses
Species, or wild, roses and **species hybrids** that share most of the characteristics of the parent species. Includes shrubs and climbing roses. Produces usually single flowers mainly in summer, borne generally in one flush, followed by red or black hips in autumn.

Old Garden roses
Alba—large, freely branching shrubs with clusters of, usually, 5–7 semi-double to double flowers in mid-summer. Has abundant, grayish green leaves. Is very hardy and is suitable for growing in borders and as specimen plants.
Bourbon—open, remontant shrubs that may be trained to climb. Produces usually fully double flowers, borne commonly in 3s, in summer-autumn. Is suitable for borders and for training over fences, walls, and pillars.
China—spindly, remontant shrubs that produce single to double flowers, borne singly or in clusters of 2–13, in summer-autumn. Has pointed, shiny leaflets. Needs a sheltered position. Is suitable for borders and walls.
Damask—open shrubs, usually very fragrant, with semi- to fully double flowers, borne singly or in loose clusters of 5–7 mainly in summer. Is suitable for borders.
Gallica—shrubs of fairly dense, free-branching growth. Leaves are dull green. Produces single to fully double, richly colored flowers, often in clusters of 3, in summer. Is suitable for borders and as hedging.
Hybrid Perpetual—vigorous, free-branching, remontant shrubs that bear fully double flowers, held singly or in 3s, in summer-autumn. Leaves are usually olive green. Is suitable for beds and borders.
Moss—often lax shrubs with a furry, mosslike growth on stems and calyces. Leaves are usually dark green. Has double to fully double flowers in summer.
Noisette—remontant climbing roses that bear clusters of up to 9 usually double flowers, with a slight spicy fragrance, in summer-autumn. Has generally smooth stems and glossy leaves. Needs a sheltered site. Is suitable for a south- or west-facing wall.
Portland—upright, remontant shrubs with semi-double to double flowers, held singly or in 3s, in summer-autumn. Is suitable for beds and borders.
Provence (Centifolia)—lax, thorny shrubs that produce scented, usually double to fully double flowers, borne singly or in 3s, in summer. Leaves are often dark green. Is suitable for borders.
Sempervirens—semi-evergreen climbing roses with shiny, light green leaves and, in late summer, numerous semi- to fully double flowers. Is ideal for naturalizing or for growing on fences and pergolas.
Tea—remontant shrubs and climbing roses that produce spicy-scented, slender-stemmed, pointed, semi- to fully double flowers, borne singly or

in 3s, in summer-autumn. Leaves are shiny and pale green. Frost hardy. Needs a sheltered position. Is suitable for beds and borders.

Modern roses
Shrub—a diverse group of modern roses, most of which are remontant, that grow larger (mostly H 3–6ft (1–2m)) than most bush roses. Has single to fully double flowers, held singly or in sprays, in summer and/or autumn. Is suitable for beds and borders and for growing as specimen plants.
Large-flowered bush (Hybrid Tea)—remontant shrubs with mostly pointed, double flowers, 3in (8cm) or more across, borne singly or in 3s, in summer-autumn. Is excellent for beds, borders, hedges, and cutting.
Cluster-flowered bush (Floribunda)—remontant shrubs that produce sprays of usually 3–25 single to fully double flowers in summer-autumn. Is excellent for beds, borders, and hedges.
Dwarf cluster-flowered bush (Patio)—neat, remontant shrubs, H 15–24in (38–60cm), S 12–24in (30–60cm), that bear sprays of generally 3–11 single to double flowers in summer-autumn. Is ideal for beds, borders, and hedges, and for growing in containers.
Miniature bush—remontant shrubs, H to 18in (45cm), S to 16in (40cm), with sprays of usually 3–11 tiny, single to fully double flowers in summer-autumn. Has tiny leaves. Is suitable for rock gardens, small spaces, and for growing in containers.
Polyantha—tough, compact, remontant shrubs with sprays of usually 7–15 small, 5-petaled, single to double flowers in summer-autumn. Is suitable for beds.
Ground cover—trailing and spreading roses, many of which are remontant, with single to fully double flowers, borne mostly in clusters of 3–11, in summer and/or autumn. Is suitable for beds, banks, and walls.
Climbing—vigorous climbing roses, some of which are remontant, with stiff stems and single to fully double flowers, borne singly or in clusters, from late spring to autumn. Is suitable for training over walls, fences, and pergolas.
Rambler—vigorous climbing roses with lax stems. Has clusters of 3–21 single to fully double flowers, mainly in summer. Is suitable for training over walls, fences, pergolas, and trees.

R. 'Aimée Vibert', syn. *R.* 'Bouquet de la Mariée'. Noisette climbing rose with long, smooth stems. H 15ft (5m), S 10ft (3m). Zones 7–9. Clusters of lightly scented, cupped, fully double, blush pink to white flowers, 3in (8cm) across, are borne in summer-autumn. Leaves are glossy, dark green. May be grown as a shrub.
R. 'Alba Semi-plena'. See *R.* x *alba* 'Semi-plena'.
R. x alba 'Semi-plena', syn. *R.* 'Alba Semi-plena'. Vigorous, bushy Alba rose. H 6ft (2m), S 5ft (1.5m). Bears sweetly scented, flat, semi-double, white flowers, 3in (8cm) across, in

mid-summer. Has grayish green leaves. May be grown as a hedge.
R. 'Albéric Barbier' illus. p.160.
R. 'Albertine' illus. p.161.
R. 'Alec's Red' illus. p.156.
R. 'Alexander', syn. *R.* 'Alexandra', illus. p.156.
R. 'Alexandra'. See *R.* 'Alexander'.
R. 'Alfred de Dalmas'. See *R.* 'Mousseline'.
R. 'Alister Stella Gray', syn. *R.* 'Golden Rambler'. Noisette climbing rose with long, vigorous, upright stems. H 15ft (5m), S 10ft (3m). Zones 7–9. Bears clusters of musk-scented, quartered, fully double, yolk yellow flowers, 2$\frac{1}{2}$in (6cm) across, in summer-autumn. Has glossy, green leaves.
R. 'Aloha'. Stiff, bushy climbing rose. H and S 8ft (2.5m). Fragrant, cupped, fully double, rose- and salmon pink flowers, 3$\frac{1}{2}$in (9cm) across, appear in summer-autumn. Leaves are leathery, dark green. May be grown as a shrub.
R. 'Alpine Sunset' illus. p.154.
R. 'Amber Queen', syn. *R.* 'Harroony', illus. p.157.
R. 'Amruda'. See *R.* 'Red Ace'.
R. 'Angela Rippon', syn. *R.* 'Ocarina', *R.* 'Ocaru', illus. p.159.
R. 'Angelita'. See *R.* 'Snowball'.
R. 'Anisley Dickson', syn. *R.* 'Dickimono', *R.* 'Dicky', *R.* 'Münchner Kindl', illus. p.155.
R. 'Anna Ford', syn. *R.* 'Harpiccolo', illus. p.155.
R. 'Anne Harkness', syn. *R.* 'Harkaramel', illus. p.158.
R. 'Apothecary's Rose'. See *R. gallica* var. *officinalis.*
R. 'Armada', syn. *R.* 'Haruseful'. Vigorous, free-branching shrub rose. H 5ft (1.5m), S 4ft (1.2m). Sprays of spice-scented, cupped, double, deep pink flowers, 3in (8cm) across, are borne in summer-autumn. Has plentiful, glossy, deep green leaves.
R. 'Arthur Bell'. Upright, cluster-flowered bush rose. H 3ft (1m), S 2ft (60cm). Clusters of fragrant, cupped, double, yellow flowers, 3in (8cm) across, are borne in summer-autumn. Foliage is bright green.
R. 'Assemblage des Beautés', syn. *R.* 'Rouge Eblouissante'. Upright, dense Gallica rose. H 4ft (1.2m), S 3ft (1m). Faintly scented, rounded, fully double, green-eyed, cerise to crimson-purple flowers, 3in (8cm) across, are borne in summer. Has rich green leaves.
R. 'Ausmary'. See *R.* 'Mary Rose'.
R. 'Ausmas'. See *R.* 'Graham Thomas'.
R. 'Baby Carnival'. See *R.* 'Baby Masquerade'.
R. 'Baby Gold Star', syn. *R.* 'Estrellita de Oro'. Miniature bush rose of uneven habit. H 18in (45cm), S 16in (40cm). Bears slightly scented, cupped, double, yellow flowers, 2in (5cm) across, in summer-autumn. Leaves are small, glossy, and dark green.
R. 'Baby Masquerade', syn. *R.* 'Baby Carnival', illus. p.159.
R. banksiae, syn. *R.b.* var. *normalis.* Climbing species rose. H and S 30ft (10m). Half hardy, zones 7–9. Dense clusters of fragrant, flat, single, white flowers, 1in (2.5cm) across, are borne

on slender, thornless, light green stems in late spring. Leaves are small and pale green. Is uncommon in cultivation. **'Lutea'** illus. p.162.

R. **'Beauty of Glazenwood'.** See *R.* 'Fortune's Double Yellow'.

R. **'Belle Courtisanne'.** See *R.* 'Königin von Dänemark'.

R. **'Belle de Crécy'** illus. p.152.

R. **'Belle de Londres'.** See *R.* 'Compassion'.

R. **'Belle of Portugal'.** See *R.* 'Belle Portugaise'.

R. **'Belle Portugaise'**, syn. *R.* 'Belle of Portugal'. Very vigorous, climbing Tea rose. H 20ft (6m), S 10ft (3m). Bears fragrant, pointed, double, light salmon pink flowers, 5in (12cm) across, in summer. Leaves are large and glossy.

R. **'Bizarre Triomphant'.** See *R.* 'Charles de Mills'.

R. **'Blanche Moreau'.** Moss rose of rather lax growth. H 5ft (1.5m), S 4ft (1.2m). Fragrant, cupped, fully double, white flowers, 4in (10cm) across, with brownish "mossing," appear in summer. Has dull green leaves.

R. **'Blessings'** illus. p.154.

R. **'Blue Moon'**, syn. *R.* 'Mainzer Fastnacht', *R.* 'Sissi'. Large-flowered bush rose of open habit. H 3ft (1m), S 2ft (60cm). Sweetly scented, pointed, fully double, lilac flowers, 4in (10cm) across, are borne in summer-autumn. Leaves are large and dark green.

R. **'Bluenette'.** See *R.* 'Blue Peter'.

R. **'Blue Peter'**, syn. *R.* 'Bluenette', *R.* 'Ruiblun'. Miniature bush rose of neat habit. H 14in (35cm), S 12in (30cm). Slightly scented, cupped, double, purple flowers, 2in (5cm) across, appear in summer-autumn. Leaves are small and plentiful.

R. **'Blue Rambler'.** See *R.* 'Veilchenblau'.

R. **'Blush Noisette'.** Noisette climbing rose of branching habit and lax growth. H 6–12ft (2–4m), S 6–8ft (2–2.5m). Zones 7–9. In summer-autumn, smooth stems bear clusters of spice-scented, cupped, double, blush pink flowers, 1½in (4cm) across. Has matt foliage. May be grown as a shrub.

R. **'Blush Rambler'.** Vigorous rambler rose. H 10ft (3m), S 12ft (4m). Clusters of delicately fragrant, cupped, semi-double, light pink flowers, 1½in (4cm) across, are borne in summer. Has an abundance of glossy leaves. Is a particularly good scrambler for an arch, pergola, or tree.

R. **'Bonica'**, syn. *R.* 'Meidonomac', illus. p.150.

R. **'Boule de Neige'** illus. p.148.

R. **'Bouquet de la Mariée'.** See *R.* 'Aimée Vibert'.

R. **'Brass Ring'.** See *R.* 'Peek-a-boo'.

R. **'Breath of Life'**, syn. *R.* 'Harquanne', illus. p.161.

R. **'Bright Smile'**, syn. *R.* 'Dicdance', illus. p.157.

R. **'Buff Beauty'.** Rounded shrub rose. H and S 4ft (1.2m). Slightly fragrant, cupped, fully double, apricot buff flowers, 3½in (9cm) across, are borne freely in summer, sparsely in autumn. Has plentiful, glossy, dark green leaves.

R. **'Buttons'**, syn. *R.* 'Dicmickey'. Upright, dwarf cluster-flowered bush

rose. H 18in (45cm), S 14in (35cm). Bears well-spaced sprays of urn-shaped, double, light reddish salmon flowers, 1½in (4cm) across, in summer-autumn. Has small, dark green leaves. Is good for growing as a low hedge.

R. **californica.** Shrubby species rose. H 7ft (2.2m), S 6ft (2m). Fragrant, flat, single, lilac-pink flowers, 1½in (4cm) across, are borne freely in mid-summer, sparsely in autumn. Has small, dull green leaves. **'Plena'** (syn. *R.c.* var. *plena*) is semi-double and more pink-toned.

R. **'Camaieux'.** Bushy, open Gallica rose. H 3ft (1m), S 2½ft (75cm). Bears fragrant, cupped, semi-double flowers, 3in (8cm) across, amid gray-green foliage in summer. Flowers are purplish crimson with blush pink stripes, fading to magenta and lilac.

R. **'Canary Bird'** illus. p.153.

R. **'Capitaine John Ingram'.** Vigorous, bushy Moss rose. H and S 4ft (1.2m). In summer bears fragrant, cupped, fully double, rich maroon-crimson flowers, 3in (8cm) across; petals are paler on reverses. Foliage is dark green.

R. **'Cardinal de Richelieu'** illus. p.152.

R. **'Cardinal Hume'**, syn. *R.* 'Harregale', illus. p.152.

R. **'Cécile Brunner'**, syn. *R.* 'Mignon'. Upright, spindly China rose with fairly smooth stems. H 30in (75cm), S 24in (60cm). Zones 5–9. Has slightly scented, urn-shaped, fully double, light pink flowers, 1½in (4cm) across, in summer-autumn. Small, dark green leaves are sparse.

R. **'Céleste'**, syn. *R.* 'Celestial', illus. p.149.

R. **'Celestial'.** See *R.* 'Céleste'.

R. **centifolia** var. **cristata.** See *R.* 'Cristata'.

R. x **centifolia 'Muscosa'**, syn. *R.* 'Common Moss', *R.* 'Old Pink Moss'. Vigorous, lax Moss rose. H 5ft (1.5m), S 4ft (1.2m). Fragrant, rounded to cupped, fully double, mossed, pink flowers, 3in (8cm) across, appear in summer. Leaves are matt, dull green. Is best grown on a support.

R. **'Champagne Cocktail'**, syn. *R.* 'Horflash', illus. p.156.

R. **'Chapeau de Napoléon'.** See *R.* 'Cristata'.

R. **'Chaplin's Pink Companion'** illus. p.161.

R. **'Charles de Mills'**, syn. *R.* 'Bizarre Triomphant'. Upright, arching Gallica rose with fairly smooth stems. H 4ft (1.2m), S 3ft (1m). Very fragrant, quartered-rosette, fully double, crimson-purple flowers, 4in (10cm) across, appear in summer. Leaves are plentiful and green. May be grown on a support.

R. **chinensis 'Mutabilis'** illus. p.151.

R. **'City of London'**, syn. *R.* 'Harukfore'. Rounded, cluster-flowered bush rose. H 3ft (1m), S 2½ft (75cm). In summer-autumn, sweet-smelling, urn-shaped, double, blush pink flowers, 3in (8cm) across, are produced in dainty sprays amid bright green foliage.

R. **'Clarissa'**, syn. *R.* 'Harprocrustes'. Upright, cluster-flowered bush rose. H

30in (75cm), S 18in (45cm). Dense sprays of slightly scented, urn-shaped, fully double, apricot flowers, 2in (5cm) across, appear in summer-autumn. Has many small, glossy leaves. Makes a good, narrow hedge.

R. **'Climbing Ena Harkness'.** Stiff, branching climbing rose. H and S 8ft (2.5m). Fragrant, large, pointed, fully double, scarlet-crimson flowers, 4in (10cm) across, are borne on nodding stems in summer-autumn. Leaves are green.

R. **'Climbing Lady Hillingdon'.** Stiff climbing rose. H 12ft (4m), S 6ft (2m). Dark green leaves are produced on reddish green stems. Bears spice-scented, pointed, double, apricot yellow flowers, 4in (10cm) across, in summer-autumn. Is best grown in a sheltered site.

R. **'Climbing Mrs. Sam McGredy'.** Vigorous, stiff, branching climbing rose. H and S 10ft (3m). Leaves are glossy, rich reddish green. Bears faintly fragrant, large, urn-shaped, fully double, coppery salmon pink flowers, 4½in (11cm) across, in summer and again, sparsely, in autumn.

R. **'Cocabest'.** See *R.* 'Wee Jock'.

R. **'Cocdestin'.** See *R.* 'Remember Me'.

R. **'Colibri'**, syn. *R.* 'Meidanover', illus. p.160.

R. **'Commandant Beaurepaire'**, syn. *R.* 'Panachée d'Angers'. Vigorous, spreading Bourbon rose. H and S 4ft (1.2m). Fragrant, cupped, double flowers, 4in (10cm) across, are borne in summer-autumn. They are a rich mixture of blush pink, splashed with mauve, purple, crimson, and scarlet. Light green leaflets have wavy margins.

R. **'Common Moss'.** See *R.* x *centifolia* 'Muscosa'.

R. **'Compassion'**, syn. *R.* 'Belle de Londres'. Upright, freely-branching climbing rose. H 10ft (3m), S 8ft (2.5m). Glossy, dark green leaves are produced on reddish stems. Sweetly fragrant, rounded, double, pink-tinted, salmon apricot flowers, 4in (10cm) across, are borne freely in summer-autumn. May be pruned to grow as a shrub.

R. **'Complicata'** illus. p.150.

R. **'Comte de Chambord'.** Vigorous, erect Portland rose. H 4ft (1.2m), S 3ft (1m). In summer-autumn, fragrant, quartered-rosette, fully double, lilac-tinted, pink flowers, 4in (10cm) across, appear amid plentiful, light green foliage. Is suitable for a hedge.

R. **'Congratulations'**, syn. *R.* 'Korlift', *R.* 'Sylvia'. Upright, vigorous, large-flowered bush rose. H 4ft (1.2m), S 3ft (1m). Produces neat, urn-shaped, fully double, deep rose-pink flowers, 4½in (11cm) across, on long stems in summer-autumn. Leaves are large and dark green. Makes a tall hedge.

R. **'Conrad Ferdinand Meyer'** illus. p.149.

R. **'Constance Spry'** illus. p.150.

R. **'Crested Moss'.** See *R.* 'Cristata'.

R. **'Cristata'**, syn. *R. centifolia* var. *cristata*, *R.* 'Chapeau de Napoléon', *R.* 'Crested Moss'. Bushy, lanky

Provence rose. H 5ft (1.5m), S 4ft (1.2m). In summer, very fragrant, cupped, fully double, pink flowers, 3½in (9cm) across and with tufted sepals, are borne on nodding stems amid dull green foliage. May be grown on a support.

R. **'Cuisse de Nymphe'.** See *R.* 'Great Maiden's Blush'.

R. **'Cuthbert Grant'.** Vigorous, bushy shrub rose. H and S 3ft (1m). Bears slightly scented, cupped, semi-double, deep purplish red flowers, 5in (12cm) across, in summer-autumn. Foliage is glossy. May be grown as a hedge.

R. **'Danse du Feu'**, syn. *R.* 'Spectacular', illus. p.162.

R. **'Dicdance'.** See *R.* 'Bright Smile'.

R. **'Dicdivine'.** See *R.* 'Pot o' Gold'.

R. **'Dicgrow'.** See *R.* 'Peek-a-boo'.

R. **'Dicinfra'.** See *R.* 'Disco Dancer'.

R. **'Dicjana'.** See *R.* 'Peaudouce'.

R. **'Dicjeep'.** See *R.* 'Len Turner'.

R. **'Dicjem'.** See *R.* 'Freedom'.

R. **'Dicjubell'.** See *R.* 'Lovely Lady'.

R. **'Dickimono'.** See *R.* 'Anisley Dickson'.

R. **'Dicky'.** See *R.* 'Anisley Dickson'.

R. **'Diclittle'.** See *R.* 'Little Woman'.

R. **'Diclulu'.** See *R.* 'Gentle Touch'.

R. **'Dicmagic'.** See *R.* 'Sweet Magic'.

R. **'Dicmickey'.** See *R.* 'Buttons'.

R. **'Disco Dancer'**, syn. *R.* 'Dicinfra'. Dense, rounded, cluster-flowered bush rose. H 30in (75cm), S 24in (60cm). Dense sprays of slightly fragrant, cupped, double, bright orange-red flowers, 2½in (6cm) across, are carried in summer-autumn. Produces a mass of glossy foliage.

R. **'Doris Tysterman'** illus. p.158.

R. **'Dortmund'** illus. p.162.

R. **'Double Delight'** illus. p.155.

R. **'Double Velvet'.** See *R.* 'Tuscany Superb'.

R. **'Drummer Boy'**, syn. *R.* 'Harvacity'. Dwarf cluster-flowered bush rose of bushy, spreading habit. H and S 20in (50cm). Faintly scented, cupped, double, bright crimson flowers, 2in (5cm) across, appear in dense sprays amid a mass of small, dark green leaves in summer-autumn. Makes a good, low hedge.

R. **'Dublin Bay'** illus. p.162.

R. **'Duchesse d'Istrie'.** See *R.* 'William Lobb'.

R. **'Duftzauber'.** See *R.* 'Royal William'.

R. **'Du Maître d'Ecole'.** Bushy, spreading Gallica rose. H 4ft (1.2m), S 3ft (1m). Bears fragrant, quartered-rosette, fully double, carmine to light pink flowers, 4in (10cm) across, in summer. Foliage is dull green.

R. **'Dupontii'** illus. p.149.

R. **'Dutch Gold'.** Vigorous, upright, large-flowered bush rose. H 3½ft (1.1m), S 2ft (60cm). Produces fragrant, rounded, fully double, yellow flowers, 6in (15cm) across, in summer-autumn. Has large, dark green leaves.

R. **'Easlea's Golden'**, syn. *R.* 'Easlea's Golden Rambler'. Vigorous, arching climbing rose. H 15ft (5m), S 10ft (3m). Pleasantly scented, cupped, fully double, yellow flowers, 4in (10cm) across and flecked with red, appear, usually in clusters, during summer. Has plentiful, leathery foliage.

R. 'Easlea's Golden Rambler'. See *R.* 'Easlea's Golden'.

R. 'Easter Morn'. See *R.* 'Easter Morning'.

R. 'Easter Morning', syn. *R.* 'Easter Morn'. Upright, miniature bush rose. H 16in (40cm), S 10in (25cm). During summer-autumn, faintly fragrant, urn-shaped, fully double, ivory white flowers, 1¼in (3cm) across, are borne freely amid glossy, dark green leaves.

R. ecae illus. p.152.

R. eglanteria, syn. *R. rubiginosa*, illus. p.149.

R. 'Elina'. See *R.* 'Peaudouce'.

R. 'Elizabeth Harkness' illus. p.153.

R. 'Emily Gray'. Semi-evergreen rambler rose with long, lax stems. H 15ft (5m), S 10ft (3m). Small trusses of slightly fragrant, cupped, fully double, butter yellow flowers, 2in (5cm) across, are borne in summer. Leaves are lustrous, dark green. May die back in a hard winter, and is prone to mildew in dry conditions.

R. 'Empereur du Maroc' illus. p.152.

R. 'English Miss'. Cluster-flowered bush rose. H 30in (75cm), S 24in (60cm). In summer-autumn bears fragrant, cupped, camellia-shaped, fully double, blush pink flowers, 3in (8cm) across. Has leathery, dark green foliage.

R. 'Escapade' illus. p.155.

R. 'Estrellita de Oro'. See *R.* 'Baby Gold Star'.

R. 'Everblooming Dr. W. van Fleet'. See *R.* 'New Dawn'.

R. 'Fairy Changeling', syn. *R.* 'Harnumerous'. Compact, spreading Polyantha bush rose. H 18in (45cm), S 20in (50cm). Produces dense sprays of slightly scented, pompon, fully double, deep pink flowers, 1½in (4cm) across, in summer-autumn. Has an abundance of glossy, dark green leaves.

R. 'Fantin-Latour' illus. p.149.

R. 'Felicia' illus. p.149.

R. 'Félicité Parmentier'. Vigorous, compact, upright Alba rose. H 4ft (1.2m), S 3ft (1m). Fragrant, cupped to flat, fully double, pale flesh pink flowers, 2½in (6cm) across, are borne in mid-summer. Has abundant, grayish green leaves. Makes a good hedge.

R. 'Félicité Perpétue' illus. p.160.

R. 'Felicity Kendall', syn. *R.* 'Lanken'. Sturdy, well-branched, large-flowered bush rose. H 3½ft (1.1m), S 2½ft (75cm). Lightly fragrant, rounded, fully double, bright red flowers, 4½in (11cm) across, appear among a mass of dark green foliage in summer-autumn.

R. 'Fellemberg'. See *R.* 'Fellenberg'.

R. 'Fellenberg', syn. *R.* 'Fellemberg'. Vigorous, shrubby Noisette or China rose. H 8ft (2.5m), S 4ft (1.2m). Zones 7–9. Leaves are purplish green. Clusters of faintly scented, rounded to cupped, fully double flowers, 2in (5cm) across, in shades of light crimson, appear in summer-autumn. Prune to grow as a bedding rose or support as a climber.

R. filipes 'Kiftsgate' illus. p.160.

R. 'Fire Princess' illus. p.159.

R. foetida 'Persiana', syn. *R.* 'Persian Yellow', illus. p.152.

R. 'Fortune's Double Yellow', syn. *R.* 'Beauty of Glazenwood', *R.* 'Gold of Ophir', *R.* 'San Rafael Rose'. Lax climbing rose of restrained growth. H 8ft (2.5m), S 5ft (1.5m). Half hardy. In summer bears small clusters of pleasantly scented, pointed to cupped, semi-double, copper-suffused, yellow flowers, 2in (5cm) across. Leaves are glossy, light green. Prune very lightly.

R. 'Fragrant Cloud'. Bushy, dense, large-flowered bush rose. H 30in (75cm), S 24in (60cm). Very fragrant, rounded, double, dusky scarlet flowers, 5in (12cm) across, are borne freely in summer-autumn. Has plentiful, dark green foliage.

R. 'Fragrant Delight'. Bushy, cluster-flowered bush rose of uneven habit. H 3ft (1m), S 2½ft (75cm). Produces an abundance of reddish green foliage, amid which clusters of fragrant, urn-shaped, double, salmon pink flowers, 3in (8cm) across, are borne freely in summer-autumn.

R. 'François Juranville'. Vigorous, arching rambler rose. H 20ft (6m), S 15ft (5m). Bears clusters of apple-scented, rosette, fully double, rosy salmon pink flowers, 3in (8cm) across, during summer. Produces a mass of glossy leaves. Is prone to mildew in a dry site.

R. 'Freedom', syn. *R.* 'Dicjem', illus. p.157.

R. 'Friesia'. See *R.* 'Korresia'.

R. 'Frühlingsmorgen', syn. *R.* 'Spring Morning'. Open, free-branching shrub rose. H 6ft (2m), S 5ft (1.5m). Foliage is grayish green. In late spring produces hay-scented, cupped, single, pink flowers, 5in (12cm) across, with primrose centers and reddish stamens.

R. gallica var. officinalis, syn. *R.* 'Apothecary's Rose', *R. officinalis*, *R.* 'Red Rose of Lancaster'. Bushy species rose of neat habit. H to 32in (80cm), S 36in (1m). Zones 5–9. In summer bears flat, semi-double, pinkish red flowers, 3in (8cm) across, with a moderate scent. **'Versicolor'** illus. p.151.

R. 'Gentle Touch', syn. *R.* 'Diclulu'. Upright, dwarf cluster-flowered bush rose. H 20in (50cm), S 12in (30cm). Sprays of faintly scented, urn-shaped, semi-double, pale salmon pink flowers, 2in (5cm) across, are produced in summer-autumn. Leaves are small and dark green. Is suitable for growing as a low hedge.

R. 'Gioia'. See *R.* 'Peace'.

R. 'Gipsy Boy'. See *R.* 'Zigeuner-knabe'.

R. glauca, syn. *R. rubrifolia*, illus. p.150.

R. 'Glenfiddich' illus. p.157.

R. 'Gloire de Dijon' illus. p.160.

R. 'Gloire des Mousseux'. Vigorous, bushy Moss rose. H 4ft (1.2m), S 3ft (1m). Has plentiful, light green foliage. In summer bears fragrant, cupped, fully double flowers, 6in (15cm) across. These are bright pink, paling to blush pink, with light green "mossing."

R. 'Gloria Dei'. See *R.* 'Peace'.

R. 'Gold of Ophir'. See *R.* 'Fortune's Double Yellow'.

R. 'Golden Rambler'. See *R.* 'Alister Stella Gray'.

R. 'Golden Showers' illus. p.162.

R. 'Golden Sunblaze'. See *R.* 'Rise 'n Shine'.

R. 'Golden Wings'. Bushy, spreading shrub rose. H 3½ft (1.1m), S 4½ft (1.35m). Fragrant, cupped, single, pale yellow flowers, 5in (12cm) across, appear amid light green foliage in summer-autumn. Is suitable for a hedge.

R. 'Goldfinch'. Vigorous, arching rambler rose. H 9ft (2.7m), S 6ft (2m). In summer produces lightly scented, rosette, double, yolk yellow flowers, 1½in (4cm) across, that fade to white. Has plentiful, bright light green leaves.

R. 'Goldsmith'. See *R.* 'Simba'.

R. 'Goldstar'. Neat, upright, large-flowered bush rose. H 3ft (1m), S 2ft (60cm). Amid glossy, dark green leaves, lightly scented, urn-shaped, fully double, yellow flowers, 3in (8cm) across, are produced in summer-autumn.

R. 'Graham Thomas', syn. *R.* 'Ausmas', illus. p.153.

R. 'Grandpa Dickson', syn. *R.* 'Irish Gold', illus. p.157.

R. 'Great Maiden's Blush', syn. *R.* 'Cuisse de Nymphe', illus. p.149.

R. 'Grouse', syn. *R.* 'Korimro', illus. p.153.

R. 'Guinée' illus. p.162.

R. 'Guletta'. See *R.* 'Rugul'.

R. 'Handel' illus. p.161.

R. 'Hannah Gordon', syn. *R.* 'Korweiso'. Bushy, open, cluster-flowered bush rose. H 30in (75cm), S 2ft (60cm). Sprays of slightly fragrant, cupped, double, blush pink flowers, 3in (8cm) across, margined with reddish pink, appear in summer-autumn. Leaves are dark green.

R. 'Harkaramel'. See *R.* 'Anne Harkness'.

R. 'Harmantelle'. See *R.* 'Mountbatten'.

R. 'Harnumerous'. See *R.* 'Fairy Changeling'.

R. 'Harpiccolo'. See *R.* 'Anna Ford'.

R. 'Harprocrustes'. See *R.* 'Clarissa'.

R. 'Harquanne'. See *R.* 'Breath of Life'.

R. 'Harqueterwife'. See *R.* 'Paul Shirville'.

R. 'Harregale'. See *R.* 'Cardinal Hume'.

R. 'Harroony'. See *R.* 'Amber Queen'.

R. 'Harrowbond'. See *R.* 'Rosemary Harkness'.

R. 'Harukfore'. See *R.* 'City of London'.

R. 'Haruseful'. See *R.* 'Armada'.

R. 'Harvacity'. See *R.* 'Drummer Boy'.

R. 'Harwanna'. See *R.* 'Jacqueline du Pré'.

R. 'Harwharry'. See *R.* 'Malcolm Sargent'.

R. 'Harwotnext'. See *R.* 'Sheila Macqueen'.

R. 'Heartthrob'. See *R.* 'Paul Shirville'.

R. 'Heideröslein'. See *R.* 'Nozomi'.

R. 'Henri Martin', syn. *R.* 'Red Moss', illus. p.151.

R. 'Honorine de Brabant'. Vigorous, bushy, sprawling Bourbon rose. H and S 6ft (2m). Fragrant, quartered, double flowers, 4in (10cm) across, lilac-pink, marked with light purple and crimson, are produced in summer-autumn. Has plentiful, light green foliage.

R. 'Horflash'. See *R.* 'Champagne Cocktail'.

R. 'Hula Girl' illus. p.159.

R. 'Iceberg', syn. *R.* 'Schnee-wittchen', illus. p.153.

R. 'Iced Ginger' illus. p.154.

R. 'Ingrid Bergman'. Upright, branching, large-flowered bush rose. H 30in (75cm), S 24in (60cm). Bears slightly scented, urn-shaped, double, dark red flowers, 4½in (11cm) across, in summer-autumn. Has leathery, semi-glossy, dark green foliage.

R. 'Interall'. See *R.* 'Rosy Cushion'.

R. 'Interfour'. See *R.* 'Petit Four'.

R. 'Intrigue', syn. *R.* 'Korlech'. Bushy, dense, cluster-flowered bush rose. H 30in (75cm), S 24in (60cm). In summer-autumn bears dense sprays of unscented, cupped, camellia-shaped, double, blackish crimson flowers, 2½in (6cm) across. Has plentiful, dark green foliage.

R. 'Invincible'. Upright, cluster-flowered bush rose. H 3ft (1m), S 2ft (60cm). Faintly scented, cupped, fully double, bright crimson flowers, 3½in (9cm) across, appear in open clusters in summer-autumn. Leaves are semi-glossy.

R. 'Irish Gold'. See *R.* 'Grandpa Dickson'.

R. 'Ispahan', syn. *R.* 'Pompon des Princes', *R.* 'Rose d'Isfahan'. Vigorous, bushy, dense Damask rose. H 5ft (1.5m), S 4ft (1.2m). Produces fragrant, cupped, double, clear pink flowers, 3in (8cm) across, amid grayish green foliage throughout summer and autumn.

R. 'Jacqueline du Pré', syn. *R.* 'Harwanna'. Vigorous, arching shrub rose. H 6ft (2m), S 5ft (1.5m). Zones 6–9. In summer-autumn bears musk-scented, cupped, double, ivory white flowers, 4in (10cm) across, with scalloped petals and red stamens. Has abundant, glossy leaves. Makes a large hedge.

R. 'John Cabot'. Vigorous shrub rose. H 5ft (1.5m), S 4ft (1.2m). Leaves are yellow-green. Clusters of fragrant, cupped, double, magenta flowers, 2½in (6cm) across, are borne in summer-autumn. May be grown as a climber or hedge.

R. 'Julia's Rose'. Spindly, branching, large-flowered bush rose. H 30in (75cm), S 18in (45cm). Zones 5–9. In summer-autumn produces faintly scented, urn-shaped, double, brownish pink to buff flowers, 4in (10cm) across. Foliage is reddish green. Is good for flower arrangements.

R. 'Just Joey' illus. p.158.

R. 'Kathleen Harrop'. Arching, lax Bourbon rose. H 8ft (2.5m), S 6ft (2m). Fragrant, double, cupped, pale pink flowers, 3in (8cm) across, are borne in summer-autumn. Plentiful, dark green foliage is susceptible to mildew. May be grown as a climber or hedge.

R. 'Keepsake', syn. *R.* 'Kormalda', illus. p.155.

R. 'Königin von Dänemark', syn. *R.* 'Belle Courtisanne', illus. p.150.

R. 'Königliche Hoheit'. See *R.* 'Royal Highness'.

R. 'Korbelma'. See *R.* 'Simba'.

R. 'Korgund'. See *R.* 'Loving Memory'.

R. 'Korimro'. See *R.* 'Grouse'.
R. 'Korlech'. See *R.* 'Intrigue'.
R. 'Korlift'. See *R.* 'Congratulations'.
R. 'Kormalda'. See *R.* 'Keepsake'.
R. 'Korpeahn'. See *R.* 'The Times'.
R. 'Korresia', syn. *R.* 'Friesia', illus. p.157.
R. 'Korweiso'. See *R.* 'Hannah Gordon'.
R. 'Korzaun'. See *R.* 'Royal William'.
R. 'La Sevillana', syn. *R.* 'Meigekanu'. Dense, bushy shrub rose. H 2¹/₂ft (75cm), S 3ft (1m). Clusters of faintly scented, cupped, double, bright red flowers, 3in (8cm) across, are borne freely in summer-autumn. Produces an abundance of dark green leaves. Is suitable for growing as a hedge or ground cover.
R. 'Lady Waterlow'. Stiff climbing rose. H 12ft (4m), S 6ft (2m). Pleasantly scented, pointed to cupped, double, light pink shaded, salmon flowers, 5in (12cm) across, are borne mainly in summer, some also in autumn. Leaves are green.
R. 'Langford Light', syn. *R.* 'Lannie'. Spreading, cluster-flowered bush rose. H and S 2ft (60cm). Sprays of fragrant, cupped, wide-opening, double, white flowers, 2in (5cm) across, appear in summer-autumn. Has dark green leaves.
R. 'Lanken'. See *R.* 'Felicity Kendall'.
R. 'Lannie'. See *R.* 'Langford Light'.
R. 'Leggab'. See *R.* 'Pearl Drift'.
R. 'Len Turner', syn. *R.* 'Dicjeep'. Compact, cluster-flowered bush rose. H and S 20in (50cm). Slightly scented, pompon, fully double, red-rimmed, ivory white flowers, 2¹/₂in (6cm) across, are borne in clusters amid plentiful, dark green foliage during summer-autumn. Makes a good, low hedge.
R. 'Little Woman', syn. *R.* 'Diclittle'. Upright, dwarf cluster-flowered bush rose. H 20in (50cm), S 16in (40cm). In summer-autumn bears sprays of faintly fragrant, urn-shaped, double, salmon pink flowers, 2in (5cm) across. Has small, dark green leaves. Is suitable for a narrow hedge.
R. 'Louise Odier', syn. *R.* 'Mme. de Stella'. Elegant, upright Bourbon rose. H 6ft (2m), S 4ft (1.2m). Has light grayish green foliage and fragrant, cupped, fully double, warm rose-pink flowers, 5in (12cm) across, borne in summer-autumn.
R. 'Lovely Lady', syn. *R.* 'Dicjubell', illus. p.154.
R. 'Loving Memory', syn. *R.* 'Korgund'. Upright, robust, large-flowered bush rose. H 3¹/₂ft (1.1m), S 2¹/₂ft (75cm). Has slightly fragrant, pointed, fully double, deep red flowers, 5in (12cm) across, on stiff stems in summer-autumn. Foliage is dull green.
R. 'Macangel'. See *R.* 'Snowball'.
R. 'Macman'. See *R.* 'Matangi'.
R. 'Macrexy'. See *R.* 'Sexy Rexy'.
R. macrophylla. Vigorous species rose. H 12ft (4m), S 10ft (3m). Bears moderately fragrant, flat, single, red flowers, 2in (5cm) across, in summer, followed by flask-shaped, red hips. Has red stems and large, green leaves.
R. 'Mactru'. See *R.* 'Trumpeter'.
R. 'Mme. Alfred Carrière' illus. p.160.

R. 'Mme. A. Meilland'. See *R.* 'Peace'.
R. 'Mme. de Stella'. See *R.* 'Louise Odier'.
R. 'Mme. Ernst Calvat'. Vigorous, arching Bourbon rose. H 6–10ft (2–3m), S 6ft (2m). In summer-autumn, fragrant, cupped to quartered-rosette, fully double, rose-pink flowers, 6in (15cm) across, are borne freely. Has plentiful, large leaves.
R. 'Mme. Grégoire Staechelin', syn. *R.* 'Spanish Beauty', illus. p.161.
R. 'Mme. Hardy' illus. p.148.
R. 'Mme. Hébert'. See *R.* 'Président de Sèze'.
R. 'Mme. Isaac Pereire' illus. p.151.
R. 'Mme. Pierre Oger'. Lax Bourbon rose. H 6ft (2m), S 4ft (1.2m). In summer-autumn, slender stems carry sweetly scented, cupped or bowl-shaped, double, pink flowers, 3in (8cm) across, with rose-lilac tints. Has light green leaves. Grows well on a pillar.
R. 'Magic Carousel'. Bushy, miniature bush rose. H 16in (40cm), S 12in (30cm). Slightly scented, rosette, fully double, yellow-and-red flowers, 1¹/₂in (4cm) across, with petals arranged in diminishing circles, appear in summer-autumn. Has small, glossy leaves.
R. 'Maigold' illus. p.162.
R. 'Mainzer Fastnacht'. See *R.* 'Blue Moon'.
R. 'Malcolm Sargent', syn. *R.* 'Harwharry'. Shrubby, large-flowered bush rose. H 3¹/₂ft (1.1m), S 3ft (1m). In summer-autumn, slightly scented, rounded, double, bright scarlet-crimson flowers, 3¹/₂in (9cm) across, are borne singly or in open sprays. Produces an abundance of glossy, dark green foliage.
R. 'Maréchal Davoust'. Vigorous, bushy Moss rose. H 5ft (1.5m), S 4ft (1.2m). In summer bears moderately fragrant, cupped, fully double, deep reddish pink to purple flowers, 4in (10cm) across, with a green eye and brownish "mossing." Leaves are dull green and lance-shaped.
R. 'Maréchal Niel'. Vigorous, spreading Noisette or Tea climbing rose. H 10ft (3m), S 6ft (2m). Zones 7–9. Drooping stems carry rich green foliage and moderately scented, pointed, fully double, clear yellow flowers, 4in (10cm) across, in summer-autumn.
R. 'Margaret Merrill' illus. p.153.
R. 'Marguerite Hilling', syn. *R.* 'Pink Nevada', illus. p.150.
R. 'Mary Rose', syn. *R.* 'Ausmary'. Bushy, spreading shrub rose. H and S 4ft (1.2m). Produces moderately fragrant, cupped, fully double, rose-pink flowers, 3¹/₂in (9cm) across, in summer-autumn. Has plentiful leaves.
R. 'Matangi', syn. *R.* 'Macman'. Dense, bushy, cluster-flowered bush rose. H 3ft (1m), S 2ft (60cm). Bears sprays of slightly scented, open cupped, fully double flowers, 3¹/₂in (9cm) across, in summer-autumn; they are orange-red with yellowish white at the base and on reverse of petals. Has plentiful, dark green leaves.
R. 'Meidanover'. See *R.* 'Colibri'.
R. 'Meidonomac'. See *R.* 'Bonica'.

R. 'Meigekanu'. See *R.* 'La Sevillana'.
R. 'Meijidiro'. See *R.* 'Pink Sunblaze'.
R. 'Meijikitar'. See *R.* 'Orange Sunblaze'.
R. 'Mermaid' illus. p.162.
R. 'Mignon'. See *R.* 'Cécile Brunner'.
R. 'Mischief'. Upright, large-flowered bush rose. H 3ft (1m), S 2ft (60cm). Moderately fragrant, urn-shaped, double, salmon pink flowers, 4in (10cm) across, are borne freely in summer-autumn. Leaves are plentiful but prone to rust.
R. 'Morning Jewel'. Free-branching climbing rose. H 8ft (2.5m), S 7ft (2.2m). Cupped, double, bright pink flowers, 3¹/₂in (9cm) across, are freely produced, usually in clusters, in summer-autumn. Has plentiful, glossy foliage. May be pruned to grow as a shrub.
R. 'Mountbatten', syn. *R.* 'Harmantelle', illus. p.157.
R. 'Mousseline', syn. *R.* 'Alfred de Dalmas'. Bushy Moss rose with twiggy growth. H and S 3ft (1m). Mainly in summer produces pleasantly scented, cupped, fully double, blush pink flowers, 3in (8cm) across, with little "mossing." Bears matt green leaves.
R. moyesii. Vigorous, arching species rose. H 12ft (4m), S 10ft (3m). Zones 5–9. In summer, faintly scented, flat, single, dusky scarlet flowers, 2in (5cm) across, with yellow stamens, are borne close to branches. Produces long, red hips in autumn. Sparse, small, dark green leaves are composed of 7–13 leaflets. **'Geranium'** illus. p.151.
R. 'Mrs. John Laing' illus. p.151.
R. 'Münchner Kindl'. See *R.* 'Anisley Dickson'.
R. 'National Trust'. Compact, large-flowered bush rose. H 30in (75cm), S 24in (60cm). Slightly scented, urn-shaped, fully double, scarlet-crimson flowers, 4in (10cm) across, are borne freely in summer-autumn. Produces plentiful, dark green foliage. Makes a good, low hedge.
R. 'Nevada' illus. p.149.
R. 'New Dawn', syn. *R.* 'Everblooming Dr. W. van Fleet', illus. p.161.
R. 'News'. Upright, cluster-flowered bush rose. H 24in (60cm), S 20in (50cm). Slightly fragrant, cupped, wide-opening, double, bright reddish purple flowers, 3in (8cm) across, are borne in clusters in summer-autumn. Has dark green leaves.
R. 'Niphetos'. Branching, climbing Tea rose. H 10ft (3m), S 6ft (2m). Zones 5–9. Long, pointed buds on nodding stems open to rounded, double, white flowers, 5in (12cm) across, mainly in summer, a few later. Has pointed, pale green leaves.
R. 'Nozomi', syn. *R.* 'Heideröslein', illus. p.153.
R. 'Nuits de Young', syn. *R.* 'Old Black'. Erect Moss rose with wiry stems. H 4ft (1.2m), S 3ft (1m). In summer bears slightly scented, flat, double, dark maroon-purple flowers, 2in (5cm) across, with brownish "mossing." Leaves are small and dark green.
R. 'Ocarina'. See *R.* 'Angela Rippon'.
R. 'Ocaru'. See *R.* 'Angela Rippon'.

R. officinalis. See *R. gallica* var. *officinalis*.
R. 'Old Black'. See *R.* 'Nuits de Young'.
R. 'Old Blush China', syn. *R.* 'Parson's Pink China', illus. p.151.
R. 'Old Pink Moss'. See *R. x centifolia* 'Muscosa'.
R. 'Omar Khayyám'. Dense, prickly Damask rose. H and S 3ft (1m). Fragrant, quartered-rosette, fully double, light pink flowers, 3in (8cm) across, are borne amid downy, grayish foliage in summer.
R. 'Opa Potschke'. See *R.* 'Precious Platinum'.
R. 'Ophelia'. Upright, open, large-flowered bush rose. H 3ft (1m), S 2ft (60cm). In summer-autumn produces sweetly fragrant, urn-shaped, double, creamy blush pink flowers, 4in (10cm) across, singly or in clusters. Dark green foliage is sparse.
R. 'Orange Sunblaze', syn. *R.* 'Meijikitar', *R.* 'Sunblaze', illus. p.160.
R. 'Panachée d'Angers'. See *R.* 'Commandant Beaurepaire'.
R. 'Parson's Pink China'. See *R.* 'Old Blush China'.
R. 'Pascali'. Upright, large-flowered bush rose. H 3ft (1m), S 2ft (60cm). Faintly scented, neat, urn-shaped, fully double, white flowers, 3¹/₂in (9cm) across, are borne in summer-autumn. Has deep green leaves.
R. 'Paul Shirville', syn. *R.* 'Harqueterwife', *R.* 'Heartthrob', illus. p.155.
R. 'Paul Transon'. Vigorous, rather lax rambler rose. H 12ft (4m), S 5ft (1.5m). In summer bears slightly fragrant, flat, double, faintly coppery, salmon pink flowers, 3in (8cm) across, with pleated petals. Plentiful foliage is glossy, dark green.
R. 'Paul's Himalayan Musk'. See *R.* 'Paul's Himalayan Musk Rambler'.
R. 'Paul's Himalayan Musk Rambler', syn. *R.* 'Paul's Himalayan Musk', *R.* 'Paul's Himalayan Rambler'. Very vigorous climbing rose. H and S 30ft (10m). Slightly fragrant, rosette, double, blush pink flowers, 1¹/₂in (4cm) across, are borne in late summer, freely in large clusters. Has thorny, trailing shoots and drooping leaves. Is suitable for growing up a tree or in a wild garden.
R. 'Paul's Himalayan Rambler'. See *R.* 'Paul's Himalayan Musk Rambler'.
R. 'Paul's Lemon Pillar' illus. p.160.
R. 'Peace', syn. *R.* 'Gioia', *R.* 'Gloria Dei', *R.* 'Mme. A. Meilland', illus. p.156.
R. 'Pearl Drift', syn. *R.* 'Leggab', illus. p.149.
R. 'Peaudouce', syn. *R.* 'Dicjana', *R.* 'Elina'. Vigorous, shrubby, large-flowered bush rose. H 3¹/₂ft (1.1m), S 2¹/₂ft (75cm). Lightly scented, rounded, fully double, ivory white flowers, 6in (15cm) across, with lemon yellow centers, are borne freely in summer-autumn. Has abundant, reddish foliage.
R. 'Peek-a-boo', syn. *R.* 'Brass Ring', *R.* 'Dicgrow', illus. p.154.
R. 'Penelope' illus. p.148.
R. 'Perle d'Or'. China rose that forms a twiggy, leafy, small shrub. H 2¹/₂ft

(75cm), S 2ft (60cm). Zones 7–9. Small, slightly scented, urn-shaped, fully double, honey pink flowers, 1¹/₂in (4cm) across, are borne in summer-autumn. Leaves consist of pointed, glossy leaflets.

R. 'Persian Yellow'. See *R. foetida* 'Persiana'.

R. 'Petit Four', syn. *R.* 'Interfour'. Compact, dwarf cluster-flowered bush rose. H and S 16in (40cm). In summer-autumn produces dense clusters of slightly fragrant, flat, wide-opening, semi-double, pink-and-white flowers, 1¹/₂in (4cm) across. Has plentiful, green foliage.

R. 'Piccadilly' illus. p.158.

R. pimpinellifolia, syn. *R. spinosissima* (Burnet rose, Scotch rose). **'Plena'** illus. p.148.

R. 'Pink Bells', syn. *R.* 'Poulbells', illus. p.154.

R. 'Pink Favourite'. Vigorous, bushy, large-flowered bush rose. H 2¹/₂ft (75cm), S 2ft (60cm). Slightly scented, pointed, double, bright rose-pink flowers, 4in (10cm) across, are freely borne in summer-autumn. Has very healthy, glossy, pale foliage.

R. 'Pink Grootendorst' illus. p.150.

R. 'Pink Nevada'. See *R.* 'Marguerite Hilling'.

R. 'Pink Parfait'. Bushy, cluster-flowered bush rose. H 2¹/₂ft (75cm), S 2ft (60cm). In summer-autumn, slightly fragrant, urn-shaped, double flowers, 3¹/₂in (9cm) across, in shades of light pink, are produced freely. Has plentiful foliage.

R. 'Pink Perpétue' illus. p.161.

R. 'Pink Sunblaze', syn. *R.* 'Meijidiro'. Neat, compact, miniature bush rose. H and S 12in (30cm). Amid plentiful, bronze-green foliage, rosette, fully double, salmon pink flowers, 1¹/₂in (4cm) across, are borne freely in summer-autumn.

R. 'Pompon des Princes'. See *R.* 'Ispahan'.

R. 'Pot o' Gold', syn. *R.* 'Dicdivine', illus. p.158.

R. 'Poulbells'. See *R.* 'Pink Bells'.

R. 'Precious Platinum', syn. *R.* 'Opa Potschke', illus. p.156.

R. 'Président de Sèze', syn. *R.* 'Mme. Hébert'. Vigorous, rather open Gallica rose. H and S 4ft (1.2m). Fragrant, quartered-rosette, fully double, magenta-pink to pale lilac-pink flowers, 4in (10cm) across, appear in summer.

R. primula illus. p.152.

R. 'Queen Elizabeth' illus. p.154.

R. 'Queen of the Violets'. See *R.* 'Reine des Violettes'.

R. 'Ramona', syn. *R.* 'Red Cherokee'. Rather stiff, open climbing rose. H 9ft (2.7m), S 10ft (3m). Fragrant, flat, single, carmine red flowers, 4in (10cm) across, with a grayish red reverse and gold stamens, are produced mainly in summer, a few later. Has sparse foliage. Does best against a warm wall.

R. 'Red Ace', syn. *R.* 'Amruda', illus. p.159.

R. 'Red Cherokee'. See *R.* 'Ramona'.

R. 'Red Moss'. See *R.* 'Henri Martin'.

R. 'Red Rose of Lancaster'. See *R. gallica* var. *officinalis*.

R. 'Reine des Violettes', syn. *R.* 'Queen of the Violets'. Spreading,

vigorous Hybrid Perpetual rose. H and S 6ft (2m). Has grayish toned leaves and, in summer-autumn, bears fragrant, quartered-rosette, fully double, violet to purple flowers, 3in (8cm) across. May be grown on a support.

R. 'Reine Victoria' illus. p.150.

R. 'Remember Me', syn. *R.* 'Cocdestin', illus. p.158.

R. 'Rise 'n Shine', syn. *R.* 'Golden Sunblaze', illus. p.160.

R. 'Robert le Diable'. Lax, bushy Provence rose. H and S 3ft (1m). In summer bears slightly scented, pompon, double flowers, 3in (8cm) across, in mixed bright and dull purple. Has narrowly oval, dark green leaves. Does best trailing over a low support.

R. 'Rose d'Isfahan'. See *R.* 'Ispahan'.

R. 'Rose Gaujard'. Upright, strong, large-flowered bush rose. H 3¹/₂ft (1.1m), S 2¹/₂ft (75cm). Slightly scented, urn-shaped, double, cherry red and blush pink flowers, 4in (10cm) across, are borne freely in summer-autumn. Foliage is glossy and plentiful.

R. 'Rosemary Harkness', syn. *R.* 'Harrowbond', illus. p.154.

R. 'Roseraie de l'Haÿ' illus. p.151.

R. 'Rosy Cushion', syn. *R.* 'Interall', illus. p.150.

R. 'Rosy Mantle' illus. p.161.

R. 'Rouge Eblouissante'. See *R.* 'Assemblage des Beautés'.

R. 'Royal Dane'. See *R.* 'Troika'.

R. 'Royal Highness', syn. *R.* 'Königliche Hoheit'. Upright, large-flowered bush rose. H 3¹/₂ft (1.1m), S 2ft (60cm). In summer-autumn, leathery, dark green foliage sets off large, fragrant, pointed, fully double, pearl pink flowers, 5in (12cm) across, borne on firm stems.

R. 'Royal William', syn. *R.* 'Duftzauber', *R.* 'Korzaun', illus. p.156.

R. rubiginosa. See *R. eglanteria*.

R. rubrifolia. See *R. glauca*.

R. rugosa illus. p.151). **'Alba'** is a dense, vigorous, species hybrid rose. H and S 3–6ft (1–2m). Bears a succession of fragrant, cupped, single, white flowers, 3¹/₂in (9cm) across, in summer-autumn. They are followed by large, tomato-shaped hips. Abundant foliage is leathery, wrinkled, and glossy.

R. 'Rugul', syn. *R.* 'Guletta', *R.* 'Tapis Jaune', illus. p.156.

R. 'Ruiblun'. See *R.* 'Blue Peter'.

R. 'Sander's White Rambler'. Vigorous rambler rose of lax growth. H 10ft (3m), S 8ft (2.5m). Fragrant, rosette, fully double, white flowers, 2in (5cm) across, appear in clusters during late summer. Small, glossy leaves are plentiful.

R. 'San Rafael Rose'. See *R.* 'Fortune's Double Yellow'.

R. 'Schneewittchen'. See *R.* 'Iceberg'.

R. 'Sexy Rexy', syn. *R.* 'Macrexy', illus. p.154.

R. 'Sheila Macqueen', syn. *R.* 'Harwotnext'. Narrow, upright, cluster-flowered bush rose. H 30in (75cm), S 18in (45cm). In summer-autumn produces dense clusters of peppery-scented, cupped, double, green flowers, 2¹/₂in (6cm) across, tinged apricot pink. Has leathery leaves.

R. 'Sheri Anne' illus. p.159.

R. 'Silver Jubilee' illus. p.155.

R. 'Simba', syn. *R.* 'Goldsmith', *R.* 'Korbelma', illus. p.157.

R. 'Sissi'. See *R.* 'Blue Moon'.

R. 'Snowball', syn. *R.* 'Angelita', *R.* 'Macangel', illus. p.159.

R. 'Southampton', syn. *R.* 'Susan Ann', illus. p.158.

R. 'Souvenir d'Alphonse Lavallée'. Vigorous, sprawling Hybrid Perpetual rose. H 7ft (2.2m), S 6ft (2m). Fragrant, cupped, double, burgundy red to maroon-purple flowers, 4in (10cm) across, are borne in summer-autumn. Leaves are small and green. Is best grown on a light support.

R. 'Souvenir de la Malmaison'. Dense, spreading Bourbon rose. H and S 5ft (1.5m). Spice-scented, quartered-rosette, fully double, blush pink to white flowers, 5in (12cm) across, are produced in summer-autumn. Rain spoils flowers. Has large, dark green leaves.

R. 'Spanish Beauty'. See *R.* 'Mme. Grégoire Staechelin'.

R. 'Spectacular'. See *R.* 'Danse du Feu'.

R. spinosissima. See *R. pimpinellifolia*.

R. 'Spring Morning'. See *R.* 'Frühlingsmorgen'.

R. 'Stacey Sue' illus. p.159.

R. 'Sunblaze'. See *R.* 'Orange Sunblaze'.

R. 'Susan Ann'. See *R.* 'Southampton'.

R. 'Sweet Magic', syn. *R.* 'Dicmagic', illus. p.158.

R. 'Sylvia'. See *R.* 'Congratulations'.

R. 'Taifun'. See *R.* 'Typhoon'.

R. 'Tanky'. See *R.* 'Whisky Mac'.

R. 'Tapis d'Orient'. See *R.* 'Yesterday'.

R. 'Tapis Jaune'. See *R.* 'Rugul'.

R. 'The Fairy' illus. p.153.

R. 'The Times', syn. *R.* 'Korpeahn', illus. p.156.

R. 'Tour de Malakoff' illus. p.152.

R. 'Tricolore de Flandres'. Vigorous, upright Gallica rose. H and S 3ft (1m). Fragrant, pompon, fully double, blush pink flowers, 2¹/₂in (6cm) across, striped with pink and purple, open in summer. Has dull green leaves.

R. 'Troika', syn. *R.* 'Royal Dane', illus. p.158.

R. 'Trumpeter', syn. *R.* 'Mactru', illus. p.155.

R. 'Tuscany Superb', syn. *R.* 'Double Velvet'. Vigorous, upright Gallica rose. H 3¹/₂ft (1.1m), S 3ft (1m). In summer, slightly scented, cupped to flat, double flowers, 2in (5cm) across, are deep crimson-maroon, ageing to purple, with gold stamens. Leaves are dark green.

R. 'Typhoon', syn. *R.* 'Taifun'. Spreading, large-flowered bush rose. H and S 30in (75cm). Has plentiful, burnished, dark green foliage. Fragrant, rounded, fully double, salmon to orange-pink flowers, 4in (10cm) across, are borne freely in summer-autumn.

R. 'Variegata di Bologna'. Upright, arching Bourbon rose. H 6ft (2m), S 4¹/₂ft (1.4m). In summer-autumn bears fragrant, quartered-rosette, fully double flowers, 3in (8cm) across,

blush pink, striped with rose-purple. Leaves are small. Needs fertile soil and is prone to blackspot.

R. 'Veilchenblau', syn. *R.* 'Blue Rambler', illus. p.162.

R. 'Violetta'. See *R.* 'Violette'.

R. 'Violette', syn. *R.* 'Violetta'. Vigorous rambler rose. H 15ft (5m), S 10ft (3m). In summer, smooth stems carry clusters of slightly scented, cupped, double, maroon-purple flowers, 1in (2.5cm) across. Has dark green leaves.

R. 'Wedding Day'. Rampant climbing rose. H 25ft (8m), S 12ft (4m). Large clusters of fruity-scented, flat, single, creamy white flowers, 1in (2.5cm) across, ageing to blush pink, are borne in late summer. Is ideal for growing up a tree or in a wild garden.

R. 'Wee Jock', syn. *R.* 'Cocabest', illus. p.156.

R. 'Whisky Mac', syn. *R.* 'Tanky'. Neat, upright, large-flowered bush rose. H 2¹/₂ft (75cm), S 2ft (60cm). Fragrant, rounded, fully double, amber flowers, 3¹/₂in (9cm) across, appear freely in summer-autumn. Reddish foliage is prone to mildew. May die back in a hard winter.

R. 'White Cockade'. Slow-growing, bushy, upright, large-flowered climber. H 6–10ft (2–3m), S 5ft (1.5m). Bears slightly fragrant, rounded, well-formed, fully double, white flowers, 3¹/₂in (9cm) across, in summer-autumn. May be pruned and grown as a shrub.

R. 'William Lobb', syn. *R.* 'Duchesse d'Istrie', illus. p.152.

R. 'Yesterday', syn. *R.* 'Tapis d'Orient'. Bushy, arching Polyantha bush rose. H and S 30in (75cm), or more if lightly pruned. Fragrant, rosette, semi-double, lilac-pink flowers, 1in (2.5cm) across, are borne, mainly in clusters, from summer to early winter. Has small, dark green leaves. Makes a good hedge.

R. 'Yvonne Rabier'. Dense, bushy Polyantha bush rose. H 18in (45cm), S 16in (40cm). In summer-autumn, moderately scented, rounded, double, creamy white flowers, 2in (5cm) across, are borne amid plentiful, bright green foliage.

R. 'Zéphirine Drouhin' illus. p.161.

R. 'Zigeunerknabe', syn. *R.* 'Gipsy Boy'. Vigorous, thorny Bourbon rose of lanky habit. H and S 6ft (2m). Faintly scented, cupped to flat, double, purplish crimson flowers, 3in (8cm) across, are borne in summer. Leaves are dark green.

ROSCOEA (Zingiberaceae)
Genus of late summer- and early autumn-flowering, tuberous perennials, related to ginger, grown for their orchidlike flowers. Is suited to open borders, rock gardens, and woodland gardens. Frost hardy. Grows in sun or partial shade and in cool, humus-rich soil that should always be kept moist in summer. Dies down in winter, when a top dressing of leaf mold or well-rotted compost is beneficial. Propagate by division in spring or by seed in autumn or winter; expose seed to frost for best germination.

R. cautleoides illus. p.365.

R. humeana illus. p.365.
R. procera. See *R. purpurea.*
R. purpurea, syn. *R. procera.*
Summer-flowering, tuberous
perennial. H 8–12in (20–30cm), S
6–8in (15–20cm). Zones 6–9. Lance-
shaped, erect leaves are long-pointed
and wrap around each other at base
to form a false stem. Has long-tubed,
purple flowers, each with a hooded,
upper petal, wide-lobed, lower lip,
and 2 narrower petals.

ROSMARINUS (Labiatae)
Genus of evergreen shrubs, grown
for their flowers and aromatic foliage,
which can be used as a culinary herb.
Frost hardy, but in cold areas grow
against a south- or west-facing wall.
Requires sun and well-drained soil.
Cut back frost-damaged plants to
healthy wood in spring; straggly, old
plants may be cut back hard at same
time. Trim hedges after flowering.
Propagate by semi-ripe cuttings
in summer.
R. lavandulaceus of gardens. See
R. officinalis 'Prostratus'.
R. officinalis (Rosemary) illus. p.135.
'Miss Jessopp's Upright' is an
evergreen, compact, upright shrub. H
and S 6ft (2m). Zones 7–9. From mid-
to late spring and sometimes again
in autumn bears small, 2-lipped,
blue flowers amid narrowly oblong,
aromatic, dark green leaves. Is good
for hedging. **'Prostratus'** (syn.
R. lavandulaceus of gardens), H 6in
(15cm), is prostrate and the least hardy
form. **'Severn Sea'**, H 3ft (1m), is
arching, with bright blue flowers.
Rossioglossum grande. See
Odontoglossum grande.

ROTHMANNIA (Rubiaceae)
Genus of evergreen, summer-
flowering shrubs and trees, grown for
their flowers. Is related to *Gardenia.*
Frost tender, min. 61°F (16°C). Needs
full light or partial shade and humus-
rich, well-drained, neutral to acid soil.
Water potted plants freely when in full
growth, moderately at other times.
Propagate by seed in spring or by
semi-ripe cuttings in summer.
R. capensis, syn. *Gardenia capensis,*
G. rothmannia. Evergreen, ovoid shrub
or tree. H 20ft (6m) or more, S 10ft
(3m) or more. Zone 10. Leaves are
oval, lustrous, and rich green. Has
fragrant, tubular flowers, each with
5 arching, white to creamy yellow
petal lobes and a purple-dotted throat,
in summer.

ROYSTONEA (Palmae)
Royal palm
Genus of evergreen palms, grown for
their majestic appearance. Has racemes
of insignificant flowers in summer.
Frost tender, min. 61–4°F (16–18°C).
Needs full light or partial shade and
fertile, well-drained but moisture-
retentive soil. Water potted plants
freely when in full growth, less
at other times, especially when
temperatures are low. Propagate by
seed in spring at not less than 81°F
(27°C). Red spider mite may be
troublesome.

R. regia (Cuban royal palm).
Evergreen palm with an upright stem,
sometimes thickened about the middle.
H 70ft (20m) or more, S to 20ft (6m).
Zone 10. Feather-shaped leaves, 10ft
(3m) long, upright at first, then arching
and pendent, are divided into narrowly
oblong, leathery, bright green leaflets.

RUBUS (Rosaceae)
Blackberry, Raspberry
Genus of deciduous, semi-evergreen,
or evergreen shrubs and woody-
stemmed, scrambling climbers. Some
species are cultivated solely for their
edible fruits, which include raspberries
and blackberries. Those described here
are grown mainly for their foliage,
flowers, or ornamental, often prickly
stems, though some may also bear
edible fruits. Fully to frost hardy.
Deciduous species grown for their
winter stems prefer full sun; other
deciduous species need sun or semi-
shade; evergreens and semi-evergreens
tolerate sun or shade. All *Rubus*
require fertile, well-drained soil.
Cut old stems of *R. biflorus,*
R. cockburnianus, and *R. thibetanus*
to ground after fruiting. Propagate
by seed or cuttings (semi-ripe for
evergreens, softwood or hardwood
for deciduous species) in summer or
winter. Alternatively, *R. odoratus*
may be increased by division and
R. 'Benenden' and *R. ulmifolius*
'Bellidiflorus' by layering in spring.
R. **'Benenden'**, syn. *R.* 'Tridel', illus.
p.104.
R. biflorus illus. p.117.
R. cockburnianus. Deciduous, arching
shrub. H and S 8ft (2.5m). Fully hardy,
zones 5–9. Prickly shoots are brilliant
blue-white in winter. Dark green
leaves, white beneath, each have
usually 9 oval leaflets. Bears panicles
of 5-petaled, purple flowers in early
summer, then unpalatable, spherical,
black fruits.
R. deliciosus (Flowering raspberry).
Deciduous, arching shrub. H and S
8ft (2.5m). Fully hardy, zones 5–8.
Thornless, peeling shoots produce dark
green leaves, with 3–5 broadly oval
leaflets and, in late spring and early
summer, large, roselike, 5-petaled,
white flowers. Flowers are followed
by small, purple fruits.
R. henryi var. *bambusarum.* Fast-
growing, vigorous, evergreen, woody-
stemmed, scrambling climber, grown
mainly for its attractive foliage. H to
20ft (6m). Fully hardy, zones 6–9.
Leaves have 3 broadly oval leaflets,
white-felted beneath. Tiny, pink
flowers are borne in small clusters
in summer.
R. odoratus (Flowering raspberry,
Thimbleberry). Vigorous, deciduous,
upright, thicket-forming shrub. H and
S 8ft (2.5m). Fully hardy, zones 4–9.
Thornless, peeling shoots bear large,
velvety, dark green leaves, each with
5 broadly triangular lobes. Large,
fragrant, 5-petaled, rose-pink flowers
are produced from early summer to
early autumn, and are sometimes
followed by unpalatable, flattened,
red fruits.
R. thibetanus illus. p.117.

R. tricolor. Evergreen shrub with both
prostrate and arching shoots covered in
red bristles. H 2ft (60cm), S 6ft (2m).
Fully hardy, zones 7–9. Oval, toothed,
glossy, dark green leaves set off cup-
shaped, 5-petaled, white flowers borne
in mid-summer. Fruits are edible and
red. Makes good ground cover.
R. **'Tridel'.** See *R.* 'Benenden'.
R. ulmifolius **'Bellidiflorus'.**
Vigorous, deciduous or semi-
evergreen, arching shrub. H 8ft (2.5m),
S 12ft (4m). Fully hardy, zones 6–9.
Has prickly stems and dark green
leaves, each with 3 or 5 oval leaflets.
Produces large panicles of daisylike,
double, pink flowers from mid- to
late summer.

RUDBECKIA (Compositae)
Coneflower
Genus of annuals, biennials, and
perennials with flower heads that are
excellent for cutting. Fully to half
hardy. Thrives in sun or shade and
well-drained or moist soil. Propagate
by division in spring or by seed in
autumn or spring.
R. fulgida (Black-eyed Susan).
var. *deamii* is an erect perennial. H
3ft (1m), S 2ft (60cm) or more. Fully
hardy, zones 4–9. In late summer and
autumn bears daisylike, yellow flower
heads with central, black cones. Has
narrowly lance-shaped, green leaves.
Prefers moist soil. **'Goldsturm'** illus.
p.215.
R. **'Herbstsonne'** illus. p.194.
R. hirta. Moderately fast-growing,
upright, branching, short-lived
perennial, grown as an annual. H 1–3ft
(30cm–1m), S 1–1¹⁄₂ft (30–45cm).
Half hardy. Has lance-shaped, green
leaves. Large, daisylike, deep yellow
flower heads, with conical, purple
centers, appear in summer-autumn.
Prefers sun and well-drained soil.
'Goldilocks' illus. p.284. **'Irish Eyes'**,
H to 2¹⁄₂ft (75cm), has yellow flower
heads with conical, olive green centers.
'Marmalade' and **'Rustic Dwarfs'**
illus. p.284.
R. laciniata **'Golden Glow'.** Erect
perennial. H 6–7ft (2–2.2m), S 2–3ft
(60cm–1m). Fully hardy, zones 3–9.
Produces daisylike, double, golden
yellow flower heads, with green
centers, in late summer and autumn.
Green leaves are divided into lance-
shaped leaflets, themselves further cut.
Prefers well-drained soil. **'Goldquelle'**
illus. p.191.
R. purpurea. See *Echinacea purpurea.*

RUELLIA (Acanthaceae)
Genus of perennials and evergreen
sub-shrubs and shrubs with showy
flowers. Frost tender, min. 59°F
(15°C). Grow in a humid atmosphere,
partial shade, and in moist but well-
drained soil. Propagate by stem
cuttings or seed, if available, in spring.
R. amoena. See *R. graecizans.*
R. devosiana illus. p.234.
R. graecizans, syn. *R. amoena,* illus.
p.208.

RUSCHIA (Aizoaceae)
Genus of mostly small, tufted,
perennial succulents and evergreen

shrubs with leaves united up to one-
third of their lengths around stems or
with very short sheaths. Frost tender,
min. 41°F (5°C). Needs sun and well-
drained soil. Propagate by seed or stem
cuttings in spring or summer.
R. acuminata. Evergreen, erect,
succulent shrub. H 8in (20cm), S 20in
(50cm). Zone 10. Has woody stems
as well as non-woody, bluish green
stems with darker dots. Produces solid,
3-angled, 1¹⁄₄in (3cm) long leaves,
each with a blunt keel and a short
sheath. Daisylike, white to pale pink
flowers, 1¹⁄₄in (3cm) across, appear
in summer.
R. crassa. Evergreen, erect, succulent
shrub. H and S 20in (50cm). Zone 10.
Bears solid, 3-angled, bluish green
leaves, ³⁄₄in (2cm) long, with short,
white hairs; the undersides are keeled,
each with a single tooth. Has 1in
(2.5cm) wide, daisylike, white flowers
in summer.
R. macowaniana. Erect, then
spreading, perennial succulent. H
6in (15cm), S 3ft (1m). Zone 10. Has
solid, slightly keeled, 3-angled, bluish
green leaves, to 1¹⁄₄in (3cm) long. In
summer carries masses of daisylike,
bright pink flowers, 1¹⁄₄in (3cm)
across, with darker stripes.

RUSCUS (Liliaceae)
Genus of evergreen, clump-forming,
spring-flowering shrubs, grown for
their foliage and fruits. The apparent
leaves are actually flattened shoots,
on which flowers and fruits are borne.
Usually, separate male and female
plants are required in order to obtain
fruits. Is useful for dry, shady sites.
Fully to frost hardy. Tolerates sun or
shade and any but waterlogged soil.
Cut dead shoots to base in spring.
Propagate by division in spring.
R. aculeatus (Butcher's broom).
Evergreen, erect, thicket-forming
shrub. H 2¹⁄₂ft (75cm), S 3ft (1m).
Fully hardy, zones 8–9. Spine-tipped
"leaves" are glossy and dark green.
Tiny, star-shaped, green flowers in
spring are succeeded by large,
spherical, bright red fruits.
R. hypoglossum illus. p.144.

RUSSELIA (Scrophulariaceae)
Genus of evergreen shrubs and sub-
shrubs with showy flowers. Frost
tender, min. 50–59°F (10–15°C). Grow
in sun or partial shade. Needs humus-
rich, light, well-drained soil. Propagate
by stem cuttings or division in spring.
R. equisetiformis, syn. *R. juncea,* illus.
p.209.
R. juncea. See *R. equisetiformis.*

RUTA (Rutaceae)
Rue
Genus of evergreen, summer-
flowering sub-shrubs, with deeply
divided, aromatic leaves, grown for
their foliage and flowers, and
sometimes used as a medicinal herb.
Fully hardy. Requires sun and well-
drained soil. Cut back to old wood in
spring to keep compact. Propagate by
semi-ripe cuttings in summer.
R. graveolens (Common rue).
'Jackman's Blue' illus. p.145.

S

SABAL (Palmae)
Genus of evergreen, tree-sized and dwarf fan palms, grown for their foliage and overall appearance. Half hardy to frost tender, min. 41–5°F (5–7°C). Prefers full sun and fertile, well-drained soil. Water moderately, less when not in full growth. Propagate by seed in spring. Red spider mite may be troublesome.
S. minor illus. p.144.

SAGINA (Caryophyllaceae)
Genus of mat-forming annuals and evergreen perennials, grown for their foliage. Is suitable for banks and in paving. Some species may be very invasive. Fully hardy. Prefers sun and gritty, moist soil; dislikes hot, dry conditions. Propagate by division in spring, by seed in autumn or, for *S. boydii*, by tip cuttings in summer. Aphids and red spider mite may cause problems.
S. boydii illus. p.330.
S. subulata 'Aurea' (Golden pearlwort). Evergreen, mosslike perennial that forms dense, spongy mats, producing a lawn effect. H 1in (2.5cm), S 9in (22cm). Zones 5–9. Has narrow, greenish yellow leaves and, in mid-summer, bears numerous tiny, single, white flowers. Is excellent as quick-spreading ground cover and tolerates shade.

SAGITTARIA (Alismataceae)
Genus of deciduous, perennial, submerged and marginal water plants, grown for their foliage and flowers. Fully hardy to frost tender, min. 41°F (5°C). Some species are suitable for pools, others for aquariums. All require full sun. Remove fading foliage as necessary. Propagate by division in spring or summer or by breaking off turions (scaly, young shoots) in spring.
S. japonica. See *S. sagittifolia* 'Flore Pleno'.
S. latifolia illus. p.372.
S. sagittifolia (Arrowhead). Deciduous, perennial, marginal water plant. H 18in (45cm), S 12in (30cm). Fully hardy, zones 5–10. Upright, green leaves are acutely arrow-shaped. In summer produces 3-petaled, white flowers with dark purple centers. May be grown in up to 9in (23cm) depth of water. 'Flore Pleno' (syn. *S. japonica*; Japanese arrowhead) has double flowers.

SAINTPAULIA (Gesneriaceae)
African violet
Genus of evergreen, rosette-forming perennials, grown for their showy flowers. Frost tender, min. 59°F (15°C). Needs a constant temperature, a humid atmosphere, partial shade, and fertile soil. Propagate by leaf cuttings in summer. Whitefly and mealy bug may cause problems with plants grown indoors.

S. ionantha. Evergreen, stemless, rosette-forming perennial, often forming clumps. H to 4in (10cm), S 10in (25cm). Zone 10. Almost rounded, scalloped, long-stalked, fleshy, usually hairy leaves, to 3in (8cm) long, are green above and often reddish green below. Loose clusters of 2–8 tubular, 5-lobed, violet-blue flowers, to 1in (2.5cm) across, are produced on stems held above leaves and appear year-round. Numerous cultivars are available, some with variegated or quilted leaves. Flowers are in a range of colors from white, pink, or red to purple or blue, plain or bicolored and in various forms (single, semi-double, or double), some with frilled or ruffled petals. 'Bright Eyes' (illus. p.258) has dark green leaves and single, deep violet-blue flowers with yellow centers. 'Colorado' (illus. p.258) bears dark green leaves and frilled, single, magenta flowers. Leaves of 'Delft' (illus. p.258) are dark green, flowers are semi-double and violet-blue. 'Fancy Pants' (illus. p.258) produces single, white flowers with frilled, red edges, held well above green leaves. 'Garden News' (illus. p.258) has bright green leaves and double, pure white flowers. 'Kristi Marie' (illus. p.258) produces dark green leaves and semi-double, dusky red flowers, edged with white. 'Miss Pretty' (illus. p.258) bears pale green leaves and large, single, pink-flushed, white flowers with frilled petals. 'Pip Squeak' (illus. p.258), H to 3in (8cm), S 4in (10cm), has oval, unscalloped, deep green leaves, $^1/_2$–$^3/_4$in (1–2cm) long, and bell-shaped, pale pink flowers, $^1/_2$in (1cm) wide. 'Porcelain' (illus. p.258) has semi-double, purple-blue-edged, white flowers. Flowers of 'Rococo Pink' (illus. p.258) are double and iridescent pink.

SALIX (Salicaceae)
Willow
Genus of deciduous trees and shrubs, grown for their habit, foliage, catkins, and, in some cases, colorful winter shoots. Male catkins are more striking than female; each plant usually bears catkins of only one sex. Fully to frost hardy. Most prefer full sun. Most species grow well in any but very dry soil; *S. caprea*, *S. purpurea*, and their variants also thrive in dry soil. Plants grown for their colorful winter shoots should be cut back hard in early spring, every 1–3 years. Propagate by semi-ripe cuttings in summer or by hardwood cuttings in winter. Fungal diseases may cause canker, particularly in *S. babylonica* and *S.* 'Chrysocoma'. Willows may become infested with such pests as caterpillars, aphids, and gall mites.
S. aegyptiaca (Musk willow). Vigorous, deciduous, bushy shrub or tree. H 12ft (4m), S 15ft (5m). Fully hardy, zones 5–9. Gray catkins that

turn to yellow appear on bare, stout shoots in late winter or early spring, before large, narrowly oval, deep green leaves emerge.
S. alba (White willow). f. *argentea* (syn. var. *sericea*, *S.a.* 'Sericea'; Silver willow) is a fast-growing, deciduous, spreading tree, conical when young. H 50ft (15m), S 25ft (8m). Fully hardy, zones 4–9. Has narrowly lance-shaped, bright silver-gray leaves and, in early spring, insignificant, pendent, yellowish green catkins. 'Britzensis' (syn. *S.a.* 'Chermesina'), H 80ft (25m), S 30ft (10m), which has green leaves and bright orange-red, young shoots, is usually cut back to near ground level to provide winter color. 'Caerulea' (Cricket-bat willow), H 80ft (25m), S 30ft (10m), is very fast-growing and conical, with long, narrow, deep bluish green leaves. 'Chermesina' see *S.a.* 'Britzensis'. var. *sericea* and 'Sericea' see *S.a.* f. *argentea*. 'Tristis' see *S.* 'Chrysocoma'. var. *vitellina* illus. p.48.
S. apoda illus. p.303.
S. arbuscula (Mountain willow). Deciduous, spreading shrub. H and S 2ft (60cm) or more. Fully hardy, zones 5–9. In spring, dark brown stems produce narrowly oval, toothed leaves and white-haired, sometimes red-tinged, yellow catkins. Suits a rock garden.
S. babylonica (Weeping willow). Deciduous, weeping tree with slender, pendent shoots that reach almost to the ground. H and S 40ft (12m). Fully hardy, zones 6–9. Bears narrowly lance-shaped, long-pointed leaves. Has yellowish green catkins in early spring. Is susceptible to canker and has been largely replaced in cultivation by *S.* 'Chrysocoma'.
S. x *boydii* illus. p.301.
S. caprea (Goat willow, Pussy willow). Deciduous, bushy shrub or tree. H 30ft (10m), S 25ft (8m). Fully hardy, zones 5–8. Oval leaves are dark green above, gray beneath. Catkins are borne in spring before foliage emerges: females are silky and gray, males are gray with yellow anthers. 'Kilmarnock' (syn. *S.c.* 'Pendula'; Kilmarnock willow), H 5–6ft (1.5–2m), S 6ft (2m), is dense-headed and weeping. From early to mid-spring has gray, later yellow catkins.
S. 'Chrysocoma', syn. *S. alba* 'Tristis', illus. p.48.
S. daphnoides illus. p.48.
S. elaeagnos (Hoary willow). Deciduous, upright, dense shrub. H 10ft (3m), S 15ft (5m). Fully hardy, zones 5–9. In spring, long shoots bear slender, yellow catkins as leaves appear. These are narrowly oblong and dark green, with white undersides, and turn yellow in autumn.
S. fargesii, syn. *S. moupinensis* of gardens. Deciduous, upright, open shrub. H and S 10ft (3m). Fully hardy,

zones 6–8. Has purplish red winter shoots and buds. Slender, erect, green catkins are carried in spring, at same time as bold, oblong, glossy, dark green leaves.
S. fragilis (Crack willow). Deciduous tree with a broad, bushy head. H 50ft (15m), S 40–45ft (12–15m). Fully hardy, zones 5–8. Has long, narrow, pointed, glossy, bright green leaves. Catkins, borne in early spring, are yellow on male plants, green on females.
S. gracilistyla. Deciduous, bushy shrub. H 10ft (3m), S 12ft (4m). Fully hardy, zones 5–9. Large, silky, gray catkins with red, then bright yellow anthers appear from early to mid-spring, and are followed by lance-shaped, silky, gray, young leaves that mature to bright, glossy green. 'Melanostachys' see *S.* 'Melanostachys'.
S. hastata 'Wehrhahnii' illus. p.121.
S. helvetica illus. p.289.
S. herbacea (Dwarf willow, Least willow). Deciduous, creeping shrub. H 1in (2.5cm), S 8in (20cm) or more. Fully hardy, zones 3–7. Has small, rounded to oval leaves and, in spring, small, yellow or yellowish green catkins. Is good for a rock garden. Needs moist soil.
S. hylematica of gardens. See *S. lindleyana.*
S. irrorata. Deciduous, upright shrub. H 10ft (3m), S 15ft (5m). Fully hardy, zones 5–9. Purple, young shoots are white-bloomed in winter. Catkins with red, then yellow anthers appear from early to mid-spring before narrowly oblong, glossy, bright green leaves emerge.
S. lanata illus. p.124. 'Stuartii' see *S.* 'Stuartii'.
S. lindleyana, syn. *S. hylematica* of gardens. Deciduous, prostrate shrub with long, creeping stems. H $^3/_4$–1$^1/_4$in (2–3cm), S 16in (40cm) or more. Frost hardy, zones 7–8. Small, narrowly oval to linear, pale green leaves are densely set on short branchlets that produce brownish pink catkins, $^1/_2$in (1cm) long, in spring. Suits a rock garden or bank. Needs partial shade and damp soil.
S. magnifica. Deciduous, upright shrub. H 15ft (5m), S 10ft (3m). Fully hardy, zones 6–9. Produces very long, slender, green catkins on stout, red shoots in spring, as large, magnolialike, blue-green leaves emerge.
S. matsudana 'Tortuosa' illus. p.58.
S. 'Melanostachys', syn. *S. gracilistyla* 'Melanostachys' (Black willow). Deciduous, bushy, spreading shrub. H 10ft (3m), S 12ft (4m). Fully hardy, zones 4–9. Bears almost black catkins, with red anthers, in early spring, before lance-shaped, bright green leaves emerge.
S. moupinensis of gardens. See *S. fargesii.*
S. pentandra (Bay willow). Deciduous, large shrub, then small tree

with broad, bushy head. H and S 30ft (10m). Fully hardy, zones 5–9. Oval, glossy, green leaves are blue-white beneath. Catkins—males bright yellow, females gray-green—open in early summer when the tree is in full leaf.
S. purpurea (Purple osier). Deciduous, bushy, spreading shrub. H and S 15ft (5m). Fully hardy, zones 4–9. Gray, male catkins, with yellow anthers, and insignificant, female catkins are both borne on slender, often purple shoots in spring, before narrowly oblong, deep green leaves emerge. '**Nana**' (syn. *S.p.* 'Gracilis'), H and S 5ft (1.5m), is dense, with silver-gray leaves; is good as a hedge.
S. repens illus. p.124.
S. reticulata illus. p.310.
S. × *rubens* '**Basfordiana**'. Deciduous, spreading tree. H 50ft (15m), S 30ft (10m). Fully hardy, zones 4–9. Has bright orange-yellow, young shoots in winter and long, narrow leaves, gray-green when young, becoming glossy, bright green in summer. Yellowish green catkins appear in early spring.
S. sachalinensis '**Sekka**'. Deciduous, spreading shrub. H 15ft (5m), S 30ft (10m). Fully hardy, zones 5–9. Has flattened shoots that are red in winter and lance-shaped, glossy, bright green leaves. Silver catkins are produced in early spring. Shoots are useful for flower arranging.
S. '**Stuartii**', syn. *S. lanata* 'Stuartii'. Slow-growing, deciduous, spreading shrub. H 3ft (1m), S 6ft (2m). Fully hardy, zones 4–9. Has yellow winter shoots. Stout, gray-green catkins open from orange buds in spring, as oval, woolly, gray leaves emerge.

SALPIGLOSSIS (Solanaceae)
Genus of annuals and biennials. Usually only annuals are cultivated, either for color in borders or as greenhouse plants. Half hardy to frost tender, min. 36–9°F (2–4°C). Grow in sun and in rich, well-drained soil. Stems need support. Dead-head regularly. Propagate by seed sown under glass in early spring, or in early autumn for winter flowering indoors. Aphids may be troublesome.
S. sinuata (Painted tongue). **Bolero Series** is a group of moderately fast-growing, branching, upright annuals. H 2ft (60cm), S 1ft (30cm). Frost tender. Has lance-shaped, pale green leaves. Outward-facing, widely flared, trumpet-shaped, conspicuously veined flowers, 2in (5cm) across, appear in summer and early autumn. Is available in a mixture of rich colors, such as red, yellow, orange, and blue. '**Friendship**' has upward-facing flowers in a range of colors. '**Splash**' illus. p.273.

SALVIA (Labiatae)
Sage
Genus of annuals, biennials, perennials, and evergreen or semi-evergreen shrubs and sub-shrubs, grown for their tubular, 2-lipped, often brightly colored flowers and aromatic foliage. Leaves of some species may be used for flavoring foods. Fully hardy to frost tender, min. 41°F (5°C). Needs sun and fertile, well-drained

soil. Propagate perennials by division in spring, perennials, shrubs, and sub-shrubs by softwood cuttings in mid-summer. Sow seed of half-hardy annuals under glass in early spring and of fully-hardy species outdoors in mid-spring.
S. argentea illus. p.201.
S. blepharophylla. Spreading, rhizomatous perennial. H and S 18in (45cm). Frost tender, zones 9–10. Has oval, glossy, dark green leaves and slender racemes of bright red flowers, with maroon calyces, in summer-autumn.
S. bulleyana. Rosette-forming perennial. H and S 24in (60cm). Fully hardy, zones 5–9. Racemes of nettlelike, yellow flowers, with maroon lips, are borne in summer above a basal mass of broadly oval, coarse, prominently veined, dark green leaves.
S. farinacea (Mealy-cup sage). '**Alba**' is a moderately fast-growing, upright perennial, grown as an annual. H 3ft (1m), S 1ft (30cm). Half hardy. Has lance-shaped, green leaves. Spikes of white flowers are produced in summer. '**Blue Bedder**', H 1¹/2ft (45cm), has dark violet-blue flowers. '**Victoria**' illus. p.276. Dwarf forms are also available.
S. fulgens illus. p.134.
S. grahamii. See *S. microphylla*.
S. greggii. Evergreen, erect sub-shrub. H to 3ft (1m), S to 2ft (60cm). Frost tender, zones 9–10. Leaves are narrowly oblong and matt, deep green. Produces terminal racemes of bright red-purple flowers in autumn.
S. haematodes. Short-lived, rosette-forming perennial. H 3ft (1m), S 1¹/2ft (45cm). Fully hardy, zones 6–9. In early summer produces panicles massed with lavender blue flowers above large, broadly oval, wavy-edged, toothed, rough, dark green leaves.
S. horminum illus. p.275. **Art Shades Series** is a group of moderately fast-growing, upright, branching annuals. H 18in (45cm), S 8in (20cm). Half hardy. Has oval, green leaves. Tiny flowers, hidden inside large, blue, pink, or white bracts, are produced in dense spikes in summer and early autumn. Bracts of **Claryssa Series** are in a wide range of brilliant colors, including white, pink, purple, and blue.
S. involucrata. Bushy, woody-based perennial. H 2–2¹/2ft (60–75cm) or more, S 3ft (1m). Half hardy, zones 7–9. Has oval, green leaves and, in late summer and autumn, racemes of large, rose-crimson flowers. '**Bethellii**' illus. p.193.
S. jurisicii. Rosette-forming perennial. H 18in (45cm), S 12in (30cm). Fully hardy, zones 6–9. Stems are clothed with green leaves, divided into 4–6 pairs of linear leaflets. In early summer produces racemes of inverted, violet-blue flowers.
S. leucantha (Mexican bush sage). Evergreen, erect, well-branched shrub. H and S to 2ft (60cm) or more. Frost tender, zones 9–10. Narrowly lance-shaped, finely wrinkled leaves are deep green above, white-downy beneath. In summer-autumn produces

terminal spikes of hairy, white flowers, each from a woolly, violet calyx.
S. microphylla, syn. *S. grahamii*. Evergreen, erect, well-branched shrub. H and S 3–4ft (1–1.2m). Half hardy, but best at 41°F (5°C), zone 10. Has oval to elliptic, mid- to deep green leaves. Racemes of dark crimson flowers, ageing to purple and with purple-tinted calyces, appear in late summer and autumn. var. *neurepia* illus. p.134.
S. nemorosa, syn. *S. virgata* var. *nemorosa*. Neat, clump-forming perennial. H 3ft (1m), S 1¹/2ft (45cm). Fully hardy, zones 5–9. Has narrowly oval, rough, green leaves and, in summer, branching racemes densely set with violet-blue flowers. '**East Friesland**', H 2¹/2ft (75cm), is smaller. '**Lubecca**', H 1¹/2ft (45cm), is a dwarf form. '**May Night**' (syn. *S.* × *superba* 'May Night') illus. p.211.
S. officinalis (Sage). '**Icterina**' illus. p.145. '**Purpurascens**' is an evergreen or semi-evergreen, bushy shrub. H 2ft (60cm), S 3ft (1m). Frost hardy, zones 6–9. Oblong, gray-green leaves are used as a culinary herb and are purple-flushed when young. Racemes of blue-purple flowers are borne in summer.
S. patens illus. p.243.
S. sclarea (Clary sage). var. *turkestanica* illus. p.274.
S. splendens (Scarlet sage). Slow-growing, bushy perennial or evergreen sub-shrub, grown as an annual. H to 12in (30cm), S 8–12in (20–30cm). Frost tender, min. 36–9°F (2–4°C). Has oval, serrated, fresh green leaves. Dense racemes of scarlet flowers are borne in summer and early autumn. '**Blaze of Fire**' has brilliant scarlet flowers. **Carabiniere Series** (white, illus. p.263) and **Cleopatra Series** (salmon, illus. p.265; violet, illus. p.275) are available in mixed or single colors. '**Fireworks**' has red-and-white striped flowers. '**Flare Path**' illus. p.272. '**Rodeo**', H 8in (20cm), has brilliant scarlet flowers.
S. × *superba* '**May Night**'. See *S. nemorosa* 'May Night'.
S. uliginosa (Bog sage). Graceful, upright, branching perennial. H 6ft (2m), S 1¹/2ft (45cm). Half hardy, zones 8–9. Has oblong to lance-shaped, saw-edged, green leaves and, in autumn, long racemes with whorls of bright blue flowers. Prefers moist soil.
S. virgata var. *nemorosa*. See *S. nemorosa*.

SALVINIA (Salviniaceae)
Genus of deciduous, perennial, floating water ferns, evergreen in tropical conditions. Is popular for tropical aquariums. Frost tender, min. 50–59°F (10–15°C). Does best in warm water, with plenty of light. Remove fading foliage, and thin plants when overcrowded. Propagate by separating young plants in summer.
S. auriculata illus. p.375.
S. natans. Deciduous, perennial, floating water plant. S indefinite. Zone 10. Oval, elongated, green leaves are borne on branching stems. Tolerates colder conditions than other species and is often used in a cold-water aquarium.

SAMBUCUS (Caprifoliaceae)
Elder
Genus of perennials, deciduous shrubs and trees, grown for their foliage, flowers, and fruits. Fully hardy. Needs sun and fertile, moist soil. For best foliage effect, either cut all shoots to ground in winter or prune out old shoots and reduce length of young shoots by half. Propagate species by softwood cuttings in summer, by seed in autumn, or by hardwood cuttings in winter, selected forms by cuttings only.
S. canadensis (American elder). '**Aurea**' is a deciduous, upright shrub. H and S 12ft (4m). Zones 4–9. Has large, golden yellow leaves, each with usually 7 oblong leaflets. In mid-summer produces large, domed heads of small, star-shaped, creamy white flowers, then spherical, red fruits. '**Maxima**' bears very large, green leaves and huge flower heads.
S. nigra (Common elder). '**Aurea**' (Golden elder) is a deciduous, bushy shrub. H and S 20ft (6m). Zones 6–9. Has stout, corky shoots and golden yellow leaves, each composed of usually 5 oval leaflets. Flattened heads of fragrant, star-shaped, creamy white flowers in early summer are followed by spherical, black fruits. Dark green foliage of '**Guincho Purple**' matures to deep blackish purple. Produces purple-stalked flowers, pink in bud and opening to white within, pink outside.
S. racemosa (Red-berried elder). Deciduous, bushy shrub. H and S 10ft (3m). Zones 4–7. Green leaves each have usually 5 oval leaflets. Star-shaped, creamy yellow flowers, borne in dense, conical clusters in mid-spring, are succeeded by spherical, red fruits. '**Plumosa**' has leaves with finely cut leaflets as does '**Plumosa Aurea**', but those of the latter are bronze when young, maturing to golden yellow.

SANCHEZIA (Acanthaceae)
Genus of evergreen, mainly summer-flowering perennials, shrubs, and scrambling climbers, grown for their flowers and foliage. Frost tender, min. 59–64°F (15–18°C). Needs full light or partial shade and fertile, well-drained soil. Water potted specimens freely when in full growth, moderately at other times. Tip prune young plants to promote a branching habit. Propagate by greenwood cuttings in spring or summer. Is prone to whitefly and soft scale.
S. nobilis of gardens. See *S. speciosa*.
S. speciosa, syn. *S. nobilis* of gardens, illus. p.145.

SANDERSONIA (Liliaceae)
Genus of one species of deciduous, tuberous climber with urn-shaped flowers in summer. Half hardy. Needs a sheltered, sunny situation and well-drained soil. Support with canes. Lift tubers for winter. Propagate in spring by seed or by naturally divided tubers.
S. aurantiaca illus. p.353.

SANGUINARIA (Papaveraceae)
Genus of one species of spring-flowering, rhizomatous perennial. Fully hardy. Grow in sun or semi-shade and in humus-rich, moist but

563

well-drained soil. Propagate by clean division of rhizomes in summer or by seed in autumn.
S. canadensis illus. p.303. **'Multiplex'** (syn. *S.c.* 'Flore Pleno', *S.c.* 'Plena') is a clump-forming, rhizomatous perennial with fleshy, underground stems that exude red sap when cut. H 6in (15cm), S 12–18in (30–45cm). Zones 3–9. Short-lived, rounded, double, white flowers emerge in spring before large, rounded to heart-shaped, scalloped, gray-green leaves, with glaucous undersides, appear.

SANGUISORBA (Rosaceae)
Burnet
Genus of perennials, grown for their bottlebrushlike flower spikes. Fully hardy. Requires sun and moist soil. Propagate by division in spring or by seed in autumn.
S. canadensis illus. p.188.
S. obtusa. Clump-forming perennial. H 3–4ft (1–1.2m), S 2ft (60cm). Zones 4–8. Arching stems bear spikes of rose-crimson flowers in mid-summer. Leaves, composed of pairs of oval leaflets, are pale green above, blue-green beneath.
S. officinalis (Great burnet). **'Rubra'** is a clump-forming perennial. H 4ft (1.2m), S 2ft (60cm). Zones 4–8. Produces small spikes of red-brown flowers in late summer above a mass of green leaves, divided into oval leaflets.

SANSEVIERIA (Agavaceae)
Genus of evergreen, rhizomatous perennials, grown for their rosettes of stiff, fleshy leaves. Frost tender, min. 50–59°F (10–15°C). Tolerates sun and shade and is easy to grow in most soil conditions if not overwatered. Propagate by leaf cuttings or division in summer.
S. cylindrica. Evergreen, stemless, rhizomatous perennial. H 1¹⁄₂–4ft (45cm–1.2m), S 4in (10cm). Zones 9–10. Has a rosette of 3–4 cylindrical, stiff, fleshy, erect leaves, to 4ft (1.2m) long, in dark green with paler horizontal bands. Racemes of small, tubular, 6-lobed, pink or white flowers are occasionally produced.
S. trifasciata (Mother-in-law's tongue). Evergreen, stemless, rhizomatous perennial. H 1¹⁄₂–4ft (45cm–1.2m), S 4in (10cm). Zones 9–10. Has a rosette of about 5 lance-shaped, pointed, stiff, fleshy, erect leaves, to 4ft (1.2m) long, banded horizontally with pale green and yellow. Occasionally carries racemes of tubular, 6-lobed, green flowers. **'Golden Hahnii'** illus. p.261. **'Hahnii'** illus. p.259. **'Laurentii'** illus. p.224.

SANTOLINA (Compositae)
Genus of evergreen, summer-flowering shrubs, grown for their aromatic foliage and their buttonlike flower heads, each on a long stem. Frost hardy. Requires sun and not too rich, well-drained soil. Cut off old flower heads and reduce long shoots in autumn. Cut straggly, old plants back hard each spring. Propagate by semi-ripe cuttings in summer.

S. chamaecyparissus (Cotton lavender). Evergreen, rounded, dense shrub. H 2¹⁄₂ft (75cm), S 3ft (1m). Zones 6–9. Shoots are covered with woolly, white growth, and narrowly oblong, finely toothed leaves are also white. Bright yellow flower heads are borne in mid- and late summer.
S. neapolitana. See *S. pinnata* subsp. *neapolitana*.
S. pinnata. Evergreen shrub, mainly grown as subsp. *neapolitana* (syn. *S. neapolitana*), which is of rounded and bushy habit. H 2¹⁄₂ft (75cm), S 3ft (1m). Zones 9–10. Slender flower stems each carry a head of lemon yellow flowers in mid-summer, among feathery, deeply cut, gray-green foliage. subsp. *neapolitana* **'Sulphurea'** illus. p.137.
S. rosmarinifolia, syn. *S. virens* (Holy flax). Evergreen, bushy, dense shrub. H 2ft (60cm), S 3ft (1m). Zones 6–9. Has finely cut, bright green leaves. Each slender stem produces a head of bright yellow flowers in mid-summer. **'Primrose Gem'** has pale yellow flower heads.
S. virens. See *S. rosmarinifolia*.

SANVITALIA (Compositae)
Genus of perennials and annuals. Fully hardy to frost tender, min. 36–9°F (2–4°C). Grow in sun and in fertile, well-drained soil. Propagate by seed sown outdoors in spring or early autumn.
S. procumbens illus. p.280. **'Mandarin Orange'** illus. p.285.

SAPIUM (Euphorbiaceae)
Genus of evergreen trees, grown for their ornamental appearance. Has poisonous, milky sap. Frost tender, min. 41°F (5°C). Prefers fertile, well-drained soil and full light. Water potted plants freely when in full growth, less at other times. Pruning is tolerated if necessary. Propagate by seed in spring or by semi-ripe cuttings in summer.
S. sebiferum (Chinese tallow tree). Fast-growing, evergreen, erect to spreading tree. H to 25ft (8m), S 12ft (4m) or more. Zones 8–10. Rhombic to oval, green leaves turn red with age. Clusters of tiny, greenish yellow flowers develop into rounded, black fruits covered by a layer of white wax.

SAPONARIA (Caryophyllaceae)
Soapwort
Genus of summer-flowering annuals and perennials, grown for their flowers. Is good for rock gardens, screes, and banks. Fully hardy. Needs sun and well-drained soil. Propagate by seed in spring or autumn or by softwood cuttings in early summer.
S. 'Bressingham Hybrid'. Loose, mat-forming perennial. H 3in (8cm), S 4in (10cm). Zones 4–8. Has small, narrowly oval leaves. Flattish, deep vibrant pink flowers are produced in clustered heads in summer.
S. caespitosa illus. p.318.
S. ocymoides illus. p.318.
S. officinalis **'Rubra Plena'** (Double soapwort). Upright perennial. H to 3ft (1m), S 1ft (30cm). Zones 4–8. Has oval, rough, green leaves, borne on

erect stems. Clusters of ragged, double, red flowers are produced from leaf axils on upper part of flower stems in summer.
S. x olivana illus. p.316.

SARCOCOCCA (Buxaceae)
Christmas box, Sweet box
Genus of evergreen shrubs, grown for their foliage, fragrant, winter flowers, and spherical fruits. The only conspicuous part of the tiny flowers is the anthers. Is useful for cutting in winter. Fully to frost hardy. Grows in sun or shade and in fertile, not too dry soil. Propagate by semi-ripe cuttings in summer or by seed in autumn.
S. confusa. Evergreen, bushy, dense shrub. H and S 3ft (1m). Fully hardy, zones 6–9. Leaves are small, oval, taper-pointed, glossy, and dark green. Tiny, white flowers in winter are followed by black fruits.
S. hookeriana. Evergreen, upright, dense, suckering shrub. H 5ft (1.5m), S 6ft (2m). Fully hardy, zones 6–9. Forms clumps of narrowly oblong, pointed, dark green leaves and has tiny, white flowers in the leaf axils during winter. Fruits are black. var. *digyna* illus. p.142.
S. humilis illus. p.142.
S. ruscifolia. Evergreen, upright, arching shrub. H and S 3ft (1m). Frost hardy, zones 8–9. Has oval, glossy, dark green leaves and, in winter, creamy white flowers, then red fruits. var. *chinensis* has narrower leaves.

SARRACENIA (Sarraceniaceae)
Pitcher plant
Genus of insectivorous perennials, some of which are evergreen, with pitchers formed from modified leaves with hooded tops. Frost tender, min. 41°F (5°C). Grow in sun or partial shade and in peat and moss. Keep very wet, except in winter, when cool and slightly drier conditions are needed. Propagate by seed in spring.
S. flava illus. p.245.
S. purpurea (Common pitcher plant, Huntsman's cup). Evergreen, erect to semi-prostrate, rosette-forming perennial. H 12in (30cm), S 12–15in (30–38cm). Zones 6–9. Inflated, green pitchers, to 6in (15cm) long, are tinged and veined purplish red. In spring, 5-petaled, purple flowers, 2in (5cm) or more wide, are carried well above pitchers.

SASA (Bambusoideae). See GRASSES, BAMBOOS, RUSHES, and SEDGES.
S. albomarginata. See *S. veitchii*.
S. palmata. Evergreen, spreading bamboo. H 6ft (2m), S indefinite. Frost hardy, zones 6–10. A fine foliage plant, it produces very broad, rich green leaves, to 16in (40cm) long. Hollow, purple-streaked stems have one branch at each node. Flower spikes are unimportant.
S. veitchii, syn. *S. albomarginata*, illus. p.180.

SASSAFRAS (Lauraceae)
Genus of deciduous trees, with inconspicuous flowers, grown for their aromatic foliage. Fully hardy. Needs

sun or light shade and deep, fertile, well-drained, preferably acid soil. Propagate by seed or suckers in autumn or by root cuttings in winter.
S. albidum illus. p.42.

SATUREJA (Labiatae)
Genus of summer-flowering annuals, semi-evergreen perennials, and sub-shrubs, grown for their highly aromatic leaves and attractive flowers. Is useful for rock gardens and dry banks. Fully hardy. Needs sun and well-drained soil. Propagate by seed in winter or spring or by softwood cuttings in summer.
S. montana (Winter savory). Semi-evergreen, upright perennial or sub-shrub. H 12in (30cm), S 8in (20cm) or more. Zones 6–10. Leaves are linear to oval, aromatic, and green or grayish green. Carries loose whorls of tubular, 2-lipped, lavender flowers in summer. **'Prostrate White'**, H 3–6in (7–15cm), has a prostrate habit and white flowers.

SAUROMATUM (Araceae)
Genus of spring-flowering, tuberous perennials with tubular spathes that expand into waved, twisted blades. Tubers will flower without soil or moisture, and before leaves appear. Frost tender, min. 41–5°F (5–7°C). Needs a sheltered, semi-shaded position and humus-rich, well-drained soil. Water well in summer. Dry off or lift when dormant in winter. Propagate by offsets in spring.
S. guttatum. See *S. venosum*.
S. venosum, syn. *S. guttatum*, illus. p.343.

SAURURUS (Saururaceae)
Genus of deciduous, perennial, bog and marginal water plants, grown for their foliage. Fully hardy. Prefers full sun, but tolerates some shade. Remove faded leaves and divide plants as required to maintain vigor. Propagate by division in spring.
S. cernuus illus. p.373.

SAXEGOTHAEA (Podocarpaceae). See CONIFERS.
S. conspicua (Prince Albert's yew). Conifer that is conical in mild areas, more bushy in cold districts. H 15–50ft (5–15m), S 12–15ft (4–5m). Fully hardy, zones 7–9. Needlelike, flattened, dark green leaves are borne in whorls at ends of shoots. Produces globose, fleshy, glaucous green cones.

SAXIFRAGA (Saxifragaceae)
Saxifrage
Genus of often rosetted perennials, most of which are evergreen or semi-evergreen, grown for their flowers and attractive foliage. Is excellent in rock gardens, raised beds, and alpine houses. Fully to half hardy; those listed here are zones 4–6 except where stated otherwise. Propagate by seed in autumn or by rooted offsets in winter. For cultivation, saxifrages may be grouped as follows:

1—Needs protection from midday sun and moist soil.
2—Needs semi-shaded, well-drained soil. Is good among rocks and screes.

3—Thrives in well-drained rock pockets, alpine-house pans, etc., shaded from midday sun. Must never be dry at roots. Most form tight cushions and flower in early spring, flower stems being barely visible above leaves.
4—Needs full sun and well-drained, alkaline soil. Suits rock pockets. Most have hard leaves encrusted in lime.

S. aizoides. Evergreen perennial forming a loose mat. H 6in (15cm), S 12in (30cm) or more. Fully hardy. Has small, narrowly oval, fleshy, shiny, green leaves and, in spring-summer, terminal racemes of star-shaped, bright yellow or orange flowers, often spotted red, on 3in (8cm) stems. Cultivation group 1.
S. aizoon. See *S. paniculata*.
S. x apiculata illus. p.311; cultivation group 2.
S. x arco-valleyi 'Arco'. Evergreen perennial forming a tight cushion. H and S 4in (10cm). Fully hardy. In early spring produces upturned, cup-shaped to flattish, pale lilac flowers almost resting on tight rosettes of oblong to linear leaves. Cultivation group 3.
S. 'Bob Hawkins'. Evergreen perennial with a loose rosette of leaves. H 1–2in (2.5–5cm), S 6in (15cm). Fully hardy. Carries small, upturned, rounded, greenish white flowers in summer on 2in (5cm) stems. Oval, green leaves are white-splashed. Cultivation group 1.
S. brunoniana. See *S. brunonis*.
S. brunonis, syn. *S. brunoniana*. Semi-evergreen, rosetted perennial. H 4in (10cm), S 8in (20cm). Frost hardy. Small, soft green rosettes of lance-shaped, rigid leaves produce masses of long, threadlike, red runners. Many of the rosettes die down to large terminal buds in winter. Short racemes of 5-petaled, spreading, pale yellow flowers are borne in late spring and summer on 2–3in (5–8cm) stems. Is difficult to grow; cultivation group 1.
S. burseriana illus. p.303. **'Brookside'** is a slow-growing, evergreen perennial forming a hard cushion. H 1–2in (2.5–5cm), S to 4in (10cm). Fully hardy. Has broadly linear, spiky, gray-green leaves. In early spring bears upturned, rounded, shallowly cup-shaped, bright yellow flowers on short, red stems. Flowers of **'Crenata'** have fringed, white petals and red sepals. **'Gloria'** has dark reddish brown stems, each bearing 1 or 2 flowers, with red sepals and white petals, in late spring. Cultivation group 3.
S. callosa, syn. *S. lingulata*. Evergreen, tightly rosetted perennial. H 10in (25cm), S to 8in (20cm). Fully hardy. Bears long, linear, stiff, lime-encrusted leaves and, in early summer, upright, then arching panicles of star-shaped, white flowers with red-spotted petals. Rosettes die after flowering; new ones are produced annually from short stolons. Cultivation group 4.
S. cochlearis. Evergreen, rosetted perennial. H 8in (20cm), S 10in (25cm). Fully hardy. Has spoon-shaped, green leaves with white-encrusted edges. Produces loose

panicles of rounded, white flowers, often with red-spotted petals, in early summer. **'Minor'**, H and S 5in (12cm), has smaller leaf rosettes and loose panicles of red-spotted, white flowers on red stems. Cultivation group 4.
S. cortusifolia var. *fortunei*. See *S. fortunei*.
S. cotyledon illus. p.292; cultivation group 2.
S. 'Cranbourne'. Evergreen, cushion-forming perennial. H and S 5in (12cm). Fully hardy. In early spring produces solitary cup-shaped, bright purplish lilac flowers on short stems just above tight rosettes of linear, green leaves. Flower stems are longer if plant is grown in an alpine house. Cultivation group 3.
S. cuneifolia illus. p.291; cultivation group 1.
S. 'Elizabethae' illus. p.311; cultivation group 2.
S. ferdinandi-coburgii. Evergreen, cushion-forming perennial. H and S 6in (15cm). Fully hardy. Forms rosettes of linear, spiny, glaucous green leaves and, in early spring, bears racemes of open cup-shaped, rich yellow flowers on stems 1–4in (3–10cm) long. Cultivation group 3.
S. fortunei, syn. *S. cortusifolia* var. *fortunei*. Semi-evergreen or herbaceous, clump-forming perennial. H and S 12in (30cm). Frost hardy. Has rounded, 5- or 7-lobed, fleshy, green or brownish green leaves, red beneath. In autumn produces panicles of tiny, mothlike, white flowers, with 4 equal-sized petals and one elongated petal, on upright stems. Propagate by division in spring. **'Rubrifolia'** has dark red flower stems and dark reddish green leaves with beetroot red undersides. Cultivation group 1.
S. x geum illus. p.287; cultivation group 1.
S. granulata (Fair-maids-of-France, Meadow saxifrage) illus. p.286. **'Plena'** is a clump-forming perennial. H 9–15in (23–38cm), S to 6in (15cm) or more. Fully hardy, zones 3–6. Loses its kidney-shaped, glossy, pale to mid-green leaves soon after flowering. Produces a loose panicle of large, rounded, double, white flowers in late spring or early summer. Has bulbils or resting buds forming at base of foliage. Cultivation group 1.
S. grisebachii 'Wisley Variety' illus. p.307; cultivation group 4.
S. 'Hindhead Seedling' illus. p.311; cultivation group 2.
S. hirsuta illus. p.287; cultivation group 1.
S. 'Irvingii'. Very slow-growing, evergreen, hard-domed perennial. H ³/₄in (2cm), S 3in (8cm). Fully hardy. Bears minute leaves in rosettes. Stemless, cup-shaped, lilac-pink flowers open in early spring. Cultivation group 3.
S. 'Jenkinsiae' illus. p.305; cultivation group 3.
S. lingulata. See *S. callosa*.
S. longifolia. Rosetted perennial. H 24in (60cm), S 8–10in (20–25cm). Fully hardy, zones 5–7. Has long, narrow, lime-encrusted leaves forming attractive rosettes that, after 3–4 years, develop long, arching, conical to

cylindrical panicles bearing numerous rounded, 5-petaled, white flowers in late spring and summer. Rosettes die after flowering, and no daughter rosettes are formed, so propagate by seed in spring or autumn. In cultivation, hybridizes readily with other related species. Cultivation group 4.
S. moschata. Evergreen perennial forming a loose to tight hummock. H and S 4in (10cm). Fully hardy, zones 5–6. Rosettes comprise small, lance-shaped, sometimes 3-toothed, green leaves. Bears 2–5 star-shaped, creamy white or dull yellow flowers on slender stems in summer. **'Cloth of Gold'** illus. p.331. Cultivation group 1.
S. oppositifolia (Purple mountain saxifrage) illus. p.306. **'Ruth Draper'** is an evergreen, loose mat-forming perennial. H 1–2in (2.5–5cm), S 6in (15cm). Fully hardy, zones 2–6. Has small, opposite, oblong to oval, white-flecked, dark green leaves closely set along prostrate stems. Large, cup-shaped, deep purple-pink flowers appear in early spring just above foliage. Prefers peaty soil. Cultivation group 1.
S. paniculata, syn. *S. aizoon*. Evergreen, tightly rosetted perennial. H 6–12in (15–30cm), S 8in (20cm). Fully hardy. In summer produces loose panicles of rounded, usually white flowers, with or without purplish red spots, on upright stems above rosettes of oblong to oval, lime-encrusted leaves. Is very variable in size. Pale yellow or pale pink forms also occur. Cultivation group 4.
S. 'Primulaize'. Evergreen, loosely rosetted perennial. H and S 6in (15cm). Fully hardy. In summer, branched flower stems, 2–3in (5–8cm) long, produce star-shaped, salmon pink flowers. Leaves are tiny, narrowly oval, slightly indented, and fleshy. Cultivation group 1.
S. sancta illus. p.311; cultivation group 2.
S. sarmentosa. See *S. stolonifera*.
S. scardica illus. p.302; cultivation group 3.
S. sempervivum illus. p.307; cultivation group 3.
S. 'Southside Seedling' illus. p.292; cultivation group 4.
S. stolonifera, syn. *S. sarmentosa* (Mother-of-thousands). Evergreen, prostrate perennial with runners. H 6in (15cm) or more, S 12in (30cm) or more. Frost hardy, zones 6–8. Has large, rounded, shallowly lobed, hairy, silver-veined, olive green leaves that are reddish purple beneath. Loose panicles of tiny, mothlike, white flowers, each with 4 equal-sized petals and one elongated petal, appear in summer on slender, upright stems. Makes good ground cover. **'Tricolor'** (Strawberry geranium) has green-and-red leaves with silver marks and is half hardy. Cultivation group 1.
S. stribrnyi illus. p.308; cultivation group 3.
S. 'Tumbling Waters' illus. p.287; cultivation group 4.
S. x urbium (London pride). Evergreen, rosetted, spreading perennial. H 12in (30cm), S indefinite.

Fully hardy, zones 5–8. Has spoon-shaped, toothed, leathery, green leaves. Flower stems bear tiny, star-shaped, at times pink-flushed, white flowers, with red spots, in summer. Is useful as ground cover. Cultivation group 1.
S. 'Valerie Finnis'. Evergreen, hard cushion-forming perennial. H and S 4in (10cm). Fully hardy, zones 4–6. Short, red stems carry upturned, cup-shaped, sulfur yellow flowers above tight rosettes of oval, green leaves in spring. Cultivation group 3.

SCABIOSA (Dipsacaceae)
Scabious
Genus of annuals and perennials, some of which are evergreen, with flower heads that are good for cutting. Frost to half hardy. Prefers sun and fertile, well-drained, alkaline soil. Propagate annuals by seed in spring and perennials by cuttings of young, basal growths in summer, by seed in autumn, or by division in early spring.
S. atropurpurea (Pincushion flower, Sweet scabious). Moderately fast-growing, upright, bushy annual. H to 3ft (1m), S 8–12in (20–30cm). Half hardy. Has lance-shaped, lobed, green leaves. Domed heads of scented, pincushionlike, deep crimson flower heads, 2in (5cm) wide, are produced on wiry stems in summer and early autumn. Tall forms, H 3ft (1m), and dwarf, H 18in (45cm), are available with flower heads in shades of blue, purple, red, pink, or white. **Cockade Series** illus. p.275.
S. caucasica 'Clive Greaves' illus. p.242. **'Floral Queen'** is a clump-forming perennial. H and S 24in (60cm). Fully hardy, zones 4–9. Large, frilled, violet-blue flower heads, with pincushionlike centers, are borne throughout summer. Light green leaves are lance-shaped at base of plant and segmented on stems. **'Miss Willmott'** has creamy white flower heads.
S. graminifolia. Evergreen, clump-forming perennial, often with a woody base. H and S 6–10in (15–25cm). Frost hardy, zones 7–9. Has tufts of narrow, grasslike, pointed, silver-haired leaves. In summer produces stiff stems with spherical, bluish violet to lilac flower heads like pincushions. Resents disturbance. Is suitable for a rock garden.
S. lucida illus. p.295.
S. ochroleuca. Clump-forming perennial. H and S 3ft (1m). Fully hardy, zones 4–7. In late summer, branching stems carry many heads of frilled, sulfur yellow flower heads with pincushionlike centers. Has narrowly oval, toothed, gray-green leaves.
S. rumelica. See *Knautia macedonica*.

SCADOXUS (Amaryllidaceae)
Genus of bulbs with dense, mainly spherical, umbels of red flowers. Frost tender, min. 50–59°F (10–15°C). Requires partial shade and humus-rich, well-drained soil. Reduce watering in winter, when not in active growth. Propagate by seed or offsets in spring.
S. multiflorus, syn. *Haemanthus multiflorus*. Summer-flowering bulb. H to 28in (70cm), S 12–18in

(30–45cm). Zone 10. Has broadly lance-shaped, semi-erect, basal leaves. Produces a spherical umbel, 4–6in (10–15cm) wide, of up to 200 narrow-petaled flowers. subsp. *katherinae* (syn. *Haemanthus katherinae*) illus. p.336.
S. puniceus, syn. *Haemanthus magnificus*, *H. natalensis*, *H. puniceus* (Royal paintbrush). Spring- and summer-flowering bulb. H 12–16in (30–40cm), S 12–18in (30–45cm). Zone 10. Has elliptic, semi-erect leaves in a basal cluster. Leaf bases are joined, forming a false stem. Flower stem bears up to 100 tubular, orange-red flowers in a conical umbel surrounded by a whorl of red bracts.

SCHEFFLERA, syn. BRASSAIA, HEPTAPLEURUM (Araliaceae) Genus of evergreen shrubs and trees, grown mainly for their handsome foliage. Half hardy to frost tender, min. 37–61°F (3–16°C). Grows in any fertile, well-drained but moisture-retentive soil and in full light or partial shade. Water potted specimens freely when in full growth, moderately at other times. Pruning is tolerated if needed. Propagate by air-layering in spring, by semi-ripe cuttings in summer, or by seed as soon as ripe, in late summer.
S. actinophylla illus. p.57.
S. arboricola. Evergreen, erect, well-branched shrub or tree. H 6–15ft (2–5m), S 3–10ft (1–3m). Frost tender, min. 59°F (15°C), zone 10. Leaves each have 7–16 oval, stalked, glossy, deep green leaflets. Mature plants carry small, spherical heads of tiny, green flowers in spring-summer.
S. digitata. Evergreen, rounded to ovoid shrub or bushy tree. H and S 10–25ft (3–8m). Frost tender, min. 41°F (5°C), zone 10. Leaves are hand-shaped, with 5–10 oval, glossy, rich green leaflets. Has tiny, greenish flowers in large, terminal panicles in spring and tiny, globular, dark violet fruits in autumn.

SCHIMA (Theaceae) Genus of one species of very variable, evergreen tree or shrub, grown for its foliage and flowers. Is related to *Camellia*. Frost tender, min. 37–41°F (3–5°C). Prefers humus-rich, well-drained, neutral to acid soil and sun or partial shade. Water potted plants freely in full growth, moderately at other times. Pruning is tolerated if necessary. Propagate by seed as soon as ripe or by semi-ripe cuttings in summer.
S. wallichii. Robust, evergreen, ovoid tree or shrub. H 80–100ft (25–30m), S 40ft (12m) or more. Zones 9–10. Elliptic to oblong, red-veined, dark green leaves are 4–7in (10–18cm) long, red-flushed beneath. In late summer has solitary fragrant, cup-shaped, white flowers, 1 1/2in (4cm) wide, that are red-flushed in bud.

SCHINUS (Anacardiaceae) Genus of evergreen shrubs and trees, grown mainly for their foliage and for shade. Frost tender, min. 41°F (5°C). Grows in any freely draining soil and in full light. Water potted specimens

moderately, hardly at all in winter. Propagate by seed in spring or by semi-ripe cuttings in summer.
S. molle (Californian pepper-tree, Peruvian mastic tree, Peruvian pepper-tree). Fast-growing, evergreen, weeping tree. H and S to 25ft (8m). Zones 9–10. Fernlike leaves are divided into many narrowly lance-shaped, glossy, rich green leaflets. Has open clusters of tiny, yellow flowers from late winter to summer, followed by pea-sized, pink-red fruits.
S. terebinthifolius. Evergreen shrub or tree, usually of bushy, spreading habit. H 10ft (3m) or more, S 6–10ft (2–3m) or more. Zones 9–10. Leaves have 3–13 oval, mid- to deep green leaflets. Tiny, white flowers are borne in clusters in summer-autumn, followed by pea-sized, red fruits, but only if plants of both sexes are grown close together.

SCHISANDRA (Schisandraceae) Genus of deciduous, woody-stemmed, twining climbers. Male and female flowers are produced on separate plants, so grow plants of both sexes if fruits are required. Is useful for growing against shady walls and training up pillars and fences. Frost hardy. Grow in sun or partial shade and rich, well-drained soil. Propagate by greenwood or semi-ripe cuttings in summer.
S. henryi. Deciduous, woody-stemmed, twining climber, with stems that are angled and winged when young. H 10–12ft (3–4m). Zones 7–9. Glossy, green leaves are oval or heart-shaped. Small, cup-shaped, white flowers appear in spring. Pendent spikes, 2–3in (5–7cm) long, of spherical, fleshy, red fruits are produced in late summer on female plants.
S. rubriflora illus. p.169.

SCHIZANTHUS (Solanaceae) Butterfly flower, Poor man's orchid Genus of annuals, grown for their showy flowers. Makes excellent pot plants. Half hardy to frost tender, min. 36–41°F (2–5°C). Grow in a sunny, sheltered position and in fertile, well-drained soil. Pinch out growing tips of young plants to ensure a bushy habit. Propagate by seed sown under glass in early spring for summer-autumn flowers and in late summer to provide plants to flower in pots in late winter or spring. Is prone to damage by aphids.
S., **Bouquet Series**. Group of moderately fast-growing, upright, bushy annuals. H and S 12in (30cm). Frost tender, min. 36–9°F (2–4°C). Has feathery, light green leaves and, in summer-autumn, orchidlike, rounded, lobed flowers in a mixture of colors, including pink, purple, and yellow.
S., **Giant Hybrids**. Group of moderately fast-growing, upright, bushy annuals. H 2–4ft (60cm–1.2m), S 1ft (30cm). Frost tender, min. 36–9°F (2–4°C). Feathery leaves are light green. Orchidlike, rounded, lobed flowers, in a mixture of colors, including pink, purple, and yellow, are produced in summer-autumn.
S. **'Hit Parade'** illus. p.266.

S., **Pansy-flowered Series**. Group of moderately fast-growing, upright, bushy annuals. H 2–3ft (60cm–1m), S 1ft (30cm). Frost tender, min. 36–9°F (2–4°C). Has feathery, light green leaves and, in summer-autumn, large, pansylike, bicolored flowers in a mixture of colors, including pink, purple, and yellow.
S. pinnatus illus. p.274.

SCHIZOCENTRON. See HETEROCENTRON.

SCHIZOPETALON (Cruciferae) Genus of annuals. Half hardy. Grow in sun and in well-drained, fertile soil. Propagate by seed sown under glass in spring.
S. walkeri. Moderately fast-growing, upright, slightly branching annual. H 18in (45cm), S 8in (20cm). Has deeply divided, green leaves and, in summer, almond-scented, white flowers with deeply cut and fringed petals.

SCHIZOPHRAGMA (Hydrangeaceae) Genus of deciduous, woody-stemmed, root climbers, useful for training up large trees. Frost hardy. Flowers best in sun, but will grow against a north-facing wall. Needs well-drained soil. Tie young plants to supports. Propagate by seed in spring or by greenwood or semi-ripe cuttings in summer.
S. hydrangeoides (Japanese hydrangea vine). Deciduous, woody-stemmed, root climber. H to 40ft (12m). Zones 6–9. Broadly oval leaves are 4–6in (10–15cm) long. Small, white or creamy white flowers, in flat heads 8–10in (20–25cm) across, are produced on pendent side-branches in summer; these are surrounded by marginal, sterile flowers, which each have an oval or heart-shaped, pale yellow sepal, 3/4–1 1/2in (2–4cm) long.
S. integrifolium illus. p.166.
S. viburnoides. See *Pileostegia viburnoides*.

SCHIZOSTYLIS (Iridaceae) Crimson flag Genus of rhizomatous perennials with flowers that are excellent for cutting. Frost hardy. Requires sun and fertile, moist soil. Plants rapidly become congested, so should be divided in spring every few years.
S. coccinea. **'Grandiflora'** illus. p.250. **'Mrs. Hegarty'** is a vigorous, clump-forming, rhizomatous perennial. H 24in (60cm), S 9–12in (23–30cm). Zones 6–9. In mid-autumn produces spikes of shallowly cup-shaped, pale pink flowers above tufts of grasslike, green leaves. **'Sunrise'** illus. p.249. **'Viscountess Byng'** has pink flowers that last until late autumn.

SCHLUMBERGERA (Cactaceae) Genus of bushy, perennial cacti with erect, then pendent stems and flattened, oblong stem segments with indented notches at margins—like teeth in some species. Stem tips produce flowers with prominent stigmas and stamens and with petals of different lengths set in 2 rows. In the wild, often grows over mossy

rocks, rooting at ends of stem segments. Frost tender, min. 50°F (10°C). Needs partial shade and rich, well-drained soil. Propagate by stem cuttings in spring or early summer.
S. bridgesii (Christmas cactus). Erect, then pendent, perennial cactus. H 6in (15cm), S 3ft (1m). Zone 10. Has glossy, green stem segments and, in mid-winter, red-violet flowers.
S. **'Bristol Beauty'** illus. p.395.
S. **'Gold Charm'** illus. p.392.
S. truncata, syn. *Zygocactus truncatus*, illus. p.393.
S. **'Win04rmärchen'**. Erect, then pendent, perennial cactus. H 6in (15cm), S 12in (30cm). Zone 10. Has glossy, green stem segments. In early autumn bears white flowers that become pink and white in winter.
S. **'Zara'**. Erect, then pendent, perennial cactus. H 6in (15cm), S 12in (30cm). Zone 10. Has glossy, green stem segments. Bears deep orange-red flowers in early autumn and winter.

SCHWANTESIA (Aizoaceae) Genus of cushion-forming, perennial succulents with stemless rosettes of unequal-sized pairs of keeled leaves and daisylike, yellow flowers. Frost tender, min. 41°F (5°C). Needs full sun and well-drained soil. Propagate by seed or stem cuttings in spring or summer.
S. ruedebuschii illus. p.398.

SCIADOPITYS (Taxodiaceae). See CONIFERS.
S. verticillata illus. p.78.

SCILLA (Liliaceae) Genus of mainly spring- and summer-flowering bulbs with leaves in basal clusters and spikes of small, often blue flowers. Fully to half hardy. Needs an open site, sun or partial shade, and well-drained soil. Propagate by division in late summer or by seed in autumn.
S. adlamii. See *Ledebouria cooperi*.
S. bifolia. Early spring-flowering bulb. H 2–6in (5–15cm), S 1–2in (2.5–5cm). Fully hardy, zones 3–8. Has 2 narrowly strap-shaped, semi-erect, basal leaves that widen towards tips. Stem produces a one-sided spike of up to 20 star-shaped, purple-blue, pink, or white flowers.
S. campanulata. See *Hyacinthoides hispanica*.
S. chinensis. See *S. scilloides*.
S. hispanica. See *Hyacinthoides hispanica*.
S. litardieri, syn. *S. pratensis*. Clump-forming, early summer-flowering bulb. H 4–10in (10–25cm), S 2–3in (5–8cm). Fully hardy, zones 4–8. Bears up to 5 narrowly strap-shaped, semi-erect, basal leaves. Stems each produce a dense spike of flat, star-shaped, violet flowers, 1/2–5/8in (1–1.5cm) across.
S. mischtschenkoana, syn. *S. tubergeniana*, illus. p.361.
S. natalensis. Clump-forming, summer-flowering bulb. H 12–18in (30–45cm), S 6–8in (15–20cm). Half hardy, zones 8–9. Lance-shaped, semi-erect, basal leaves lengthen after flowering. Stem bears a long spike of

up to 100 flattish, blue flowers, each $^5/_8$–$^3/_4$in (1.5–2cm) across.

S. non-scripta. See *Hyacinthoides non-scriptus*.

S. peruviana illus. p.365.

S. pratensis. See *S. litardieri*.

S. scilloides, syn. *S. chinensis*, illus. p.354.

S. siberica (Siberian squill). **'Atro-coerulea'** illus. p.361.

S. tubergeniana. See *S. mischtschenkoana*.

S. violacea. See *Ledebouria socialis*.

Scindapsus aureus **'Marble Queen'.** See *Epipremnum aureum* 'Marble Queen'.

Scindapsus pictus **'Argyraeus'.** See *Epipremnum pictum* 'Argyraeus'.

SCIRPUS (Cyperaceae), Club-rush.
See GRASSES, BAMBOOS, RUSHES, and SEDGES.

S. holoschoenus (Round-headed club-rush). **'Variegatus'** is an evergreen, tuft-forming, perennial rush. H 3–4ft (1–1.2m), S 1ft (30cm). Fully hardy, zones 6–9. Rounded, leafless, green stems are striped horizontally with cream and bear egg-shaped, awned, brown spikelets on stalked, spherical heads in summer.

S. lacustris subsp. **tabernaemontani 'Zebrinus'**, syn. *S. tabernaemontani* 'Zebrinus', illus. p.180.

S. setaceus (Bristle club-rush). Tuft-forming, annual or short-lived, perennial rush. H 4–6in (10–15cm), S 3in (8cm). Fully hardy, zones 6–9. Has very slender, lax, basal, green leaves. Very slender, unbranched stems each bear 1–3 minute, egg-shaped, green spikelets in summer.

S. tabernaemontani 'Zebrinus'. See *S. lacustris* subsp. *tabernaemontani* 'Zebrinus'.

SCOLIOPUS (Liliaceae)
Genus of one species of spring-flowering perennial. Is usually grown in alpine houses, where its neat habit and curious flowers, which arise directly from buds on the rootstock early in the season, may be better appreciated. Is also suitable for rock gardens and peat beds. Frost hardy. Needs sun or partial shade and moist but well-drained soil. Propagate by seed when fresh, in summer or autumn.

S. bigelovii illus. p.304.

Scolopendrium vulgare. See *Phyllitis scolopendrium*.

SCOPOLIA (Solanaceae)
Genus of spring-flowering perennials. Fully hardy. Does best in shade and in fertile, very well-drained soil. Propagate by division in spring or by seed in autumn.

S. carniolica illus. p.228.

SCROPHULARIA
(Scrophulariaceae)
Figwort
Genus of perennials and sub-shrubs, some of which are semi-evergreen or evergreen. Most species are weeds, but some are grown for their variegated foliage. Fully hardy. Tolerates any situation but does best in semi-shade

and moist soil. Propagate by division in spring or by softwood cuttings in summer.

S. aquatica 'Variegata'. See *S. auriculata* 'Variegata'.

S. auriculata 'Variegata', syn. *S. aquatica* 'Variegata' (Water figwort). Evergreen, clump-forming perennial. H 24in (60cm), S 12in (30cm) or more. Zones 5–9. Has attractive, oval, toothed, dark green leaves with cream marks. Spikes of insignificant, maroon flowers, borne in summer, are best removed as they develop.

SCUTELLARIA (Labiatae)
Skullcap
Genus of variable, summer-flowering, rhizomatous perennials, grown for their tubular flowers. Fully hardy to frost tender, min. 45–50°F (7–10°C). Needs sun and well-drained soil. Propagate by softwood cuttings in summer or by seed in autumn.

S. indica. Upright, rhizomatous perennial. H 6–12in (15–30cm), S 4in (10cm) or more. Frost hardy, zones 7–8. Leaves are oval, toothed, and hairy. Produces dense racemes of long-tubed, strongly 2-lipped, slate blue, occasionally white flowers in summer. Suits a rock garden.

S. orientalis illus. p.325.

S. scordiifolia. Mat-forming, rhizomatous perennial. H and S 6in (15cm) or more. Fully hardy, zones 6–8. Bears narrowly oval, wrinkled leaves. In summer-autumn produces racemes of tubular, hooded, purple flowers, each with a white-streaked lip. Propagate by division in spring.

SEDUM (Crassulaceae)
Stonecrop
Genus of often fleshy or succulent annuals, evergreen biennials, mostly semi-evergreen or evergreen perennials, and evergreen shrubs and sub-shrubs, suitable for rock gardens and borders. Fully hardy to frost tender, min. 41°F (5°C). Needs sun. Grows well in any soil, but does best in fertile, well-drained soil. Propagate perennials, sub-shrubs, and shrubs either by softwood cuttings of non-flowering shoots or by division from spring to mid-summer or by seed in autumn or spring. Propagate annuals and biennials by seed, sown under glass in early spring, or outdoors in mid-spring.

S. acre illus. p.324. **'Aureum'** illus. p.325.

S. aizoon. Evergreen, erect perennial. H and S 18in (45cm). Fully hardy, zones 4–9. Green leaves are oblong to lance-shaped, fleshy, and toothed. In summer bears flat heads of star-shaped, yellow flowers. **'Aurantiacum'** illus. p.248.

S. anacampseros. Semi-evergreen, trailing perennial with overwintering foliage rosettes. H 4in (10cm), S 10in (25cm) or more. Frost hardy, zones 8–9. Prostrate, loosely rosetted, brown stems bear oblong to oval, fleshy, glaucous green leaves. Dense, sub-globose, terminal heads of small, cup-shaped, purplish pink flowers appear in summer.

S. caeruleum illus. p.277.

S. cauticola. Trailing, shallow-rooted perennial with stolons. H 2in (5cm), S 8in (20cm). Fully hardy, zones 5–9. Has oval to oblong, stalked, fleshy, blue-green leaves on procumbent, purplish red stems. Produces leafy, branched, flattish heads of star-shaped, pale purplish pink flowers in early autumn. Cut back old stems in winter.

S. ewersii. Trailing perennial. H 2in (5cm), S 6in (15cm). Fully hardy, zones 5–9. Is similar to *S. cauticola*, but has more rounded, stem-clasping leaves that are often tinted red and dense, rounded flower heads.

S. kamtschaticum. Semi-evergreen, prostrate perennial with overwintering foliage rosettes. H 2–3in (5–8cm), S 8in (20cm). Fully hardy, zones 4–9. Bears narrowly oval, toothed, fleshy, green leaves. Spreading, terminal clusters of star-shaped, orange-flushed, yellow flowers appear in summer-autumn. **'Variegatum'** illus. p.331.

S. lydium illus. p.328.

S. morganianum (Burro's-tail, Donkey's-tail). Evergreen, prostrate, succulent perennial. H 12in (30cm) or more, S indefinite. Frost tender, zone 10. Stems are clothed in masses of oblong to lance-shaped, almost cylindrical, fleshy, waxy, white leaves. In summer bears terminal clusters of star-shaped, rose-pink flowers. Is best grown in a hanging basket.

S. obtusatum illus. p.328.

S. palmeri. Evergreen, clump-forming perennial. H 8in (20cm), S 12in (30cm). Half hardy, zones 9–10. Sprays of star-shaped, yellow or orange flowers open in early summer above oblong-oval to spoon-shaped, fleshy, gray-green leaves.

S. populifolium. Semi-evergreen, bushy perennial. H 12–18in (30–45cm), S 12in (30cm). Fully hardy, zones 6–9. Terminal clusters of hawthorn-scented, star-shaped, pale pink or white flowers are borne in late summer. Has broadly oval, irregularly toothed, fleshy, green leaves.

S. reflexum illus. p.299.

S. rosea, syn. *Rhodiola rosea* (Roseroot). Clump-forming perennial. H and S 12in (30cm). Fully hardy, zones 2–8. Stems are clothed with oval, toothed, fleshy, glaucous leaves and, in late summer or early summer, bear dense, terminal heads of pink buds that open to small, star-shaped, greenish, yellowish or purplish white flowers. var. *heterodontum* illus. p.249.

S. sempervivoides. Evergreen, basal-rosetted biennial. H 3–4in (8–10cm), S 2in (5cm). Half hardy, zones 9–10. Has rosettes that are similar to those of *Sempervivum*; oval to strap-shaped, leathery, glaucous green leaves are strongly marked red-purple. Produces domed heads of star-shaped, scarlet flowers in summer. Dislikes winter wet. Is good for an alpine house.

S. sieboldii 'Variegatum', syn. *S.s.* 'Foliis Medio-variegatis'. Evergreen, spreading, tuberous perennial with long, tapering tap roots. H 4in (10cm), S 8in (20cm) or more. Frost hardy, zones 6–9. Rounded,

fleshy, blue-green leaves, splashed cream and occasionally red-edged, appear in whorls of 3. Bears open, terminal heads of star-shaped, pink flowers in late summer. Is good for an alpine house.

S. spathulifolium illus. p.329. **'Cape Blanco'** (syn. *S.s.* 'Cappa Blanca') illus. p.331.

S. spectabile (Ice-plant). Clump-forming perennial. H and S 18in (45cm). Fully hardy, zones 4–9. Has oval, indented, fleshy, gray-green leaves, above which flat heads of small, star-shaped, pink flowers that attract butterflies are borne in late summer. **'Brilliant'** illus. p.250.

S. spurium. Semi-evergreen, mat-forming, creeping perennial. H 4in (10cm) or more, S indefinite. Frost hardy, zones 4–9. Oblong to oval, toothed leaves are borne along hairy stems. Large, slightly rounded heads of small, star-shaped, usually purplish pink flowers are produced in summer. Is variable in flower color from deep purple to white. Is useful for a bank.

S. tartarinowii. Arching, spreading, tuberous perennial. H 4in (10cm), S 8in (20cm). Fully hardy, zones 5–9. Rounded, terminal heads of star-shaped, pink-flushed, white flowers appear in late summer above small, oval, toothed, green leaves that are borne along purplish stems. Is good for an alpine house.

SELAGINELLA (Selaginellaceae)
Genus of evergreen, mosslike perennials, grown for their foliage. Frost tender, min. 41°F (5°C). Prefers semi-shade and needs moist but well-drained, peaty soil. Remove faded foliage regularly. Propagate from pieces with roots attached that have been broken off plant in any season.

S. kraussiana illus. p.186. **'Aurea'** is an evergreen, mosslike perennial. H $^1/_2$in (1cm), S indefinite. Zone 10. Spreading, filigreed, bright yellowish green fronds are much-branched, denser towards the growing tips and easily root on soil surface. **'Variegata'** has foliage splashed with creamy yellow.

S. lepidophylla (Resurrection plant, Rose of Jericho). Evergreen, mosslike perennial. H and S 4in (10cm). Zone 10. Bluntly rounded, emerald green fronds, ageing red-brown or gray-green, are produced in dense tufts. On drying, fronds curl inwards to form a tight ball, becoming green again and unfolding when placed in water.

S. martensii illus. p.185.

SELENICEREUS (Cactaceae)
Genus of summer-flowering, perennial cacti with climbing, 4–10-ribbed, green stems, to $^3/_4$in (2cm) across. Nocturnal, funnel-shaped flowers eventually open flat. Frost tender, min. 41°F (5°C). Needs sun or partial shade and rich, well-drained soil. Propagate by seed or stem cuttings in spring or summer.

S. grandiflorus illus. p.378.

SELINUM (Umbelliferae)
Genus of summer-flowering perennials, ideal for informal gardens

and backs of borders. Fully hardy. Prefers sun, but will grow in semi-shade, and any well-drained soil. Once established, roots resent disturbance. Propagate by seed when fresh, in summer or autumn.

S. tenuifolium. Upright, architectural perennial. H 5ft (1.5m), S 2ft (60cm). Zones 6–9. In summer produces small, star-shaped, white flowers, borne in large, flat heads, one above another. Has very finely divided, green leaves.

SEMELE (Liliaceae)
Genus of one species of evergreen, twining climber. Male and female flowers are produced on the same plant. Frost tender, min. 41°F (5°C). Needs partial shade and prefers rich, well-drained soil. Propagate by division or seed in spring.

S. androgyna (Climbing butcher's broom). Evergreen climber, twining in upper part, branched and bearing oval cladodes, 2–4in (5–10cm) long. H to 22ft (7m). Zones 9–10. Star-shaped, cream flowers appear in early summer, in notches on cladode margins, followed by orange-red berries.

SEMIAQUILEGIA (Ranunculaceae)
Genus of perennials, grown for their flowers that differ from those of *Aquilegia*, with which it is sometimes included, by having no spurs. Is good for rock gardens. Fully hardy. Requires sun and moist but well-drained soil. Propagate by seed in autumn.

S. ecalcarata illus. p.295.

SEMIARUNDINARIA
(Bambusoideae). See GRASSES, BAMBOOS, RUSHES, and SEDGES.
S. fastuosa, syn. *Arundinaria fastuosa*, illus. p.182.

SEMPERVIVUM (Crassulaceae)
Houseleek
Genus of evergreen perennials that spread by short stolons and are grown for their symmetrical rosettes of oval to strap-shaped, pointed, fleshy leaves. Makes ground-hugging mats, suitable for rock gardens, screes, walls, banks, and alpine houses. Flowers are star-shaped with 8–16 spreading petals. Fully hardy. Needs sun and gritty soil. Takes several years to reach flowering size. Rosettes die after flowering but leave numerous offsets. Propagate by offsets in summer.

S. arachnoideum illus. p.329.
S. ciliosum illus. p.329.
S. 'Commander Hay'. Evergreen, basal-rosetted perennial. H 6in (15cm), S to 12in (30cm). Zones 6–9. Is mainly grown for its very large, dark red rosettes to 4in (10cm) across. Produces terminal clusters of dull greenish red flowers in summer.
S. giuseppii illus. p.331.
S. grandiflorum. Evergreen, basal-rosetted perennial. H 4in (10cm), S to 8in (20cm). Zones 5–9. Variable, densely haired, red-tinted, dark green rosettes exude a goatlike smell when crushed. Produces loose, terminal clusters of yellow-green flowers, stained purple in centers, on long flower stems in summer. Prefers humus-rich, acid soil.

S. hirtum. See *Jovibarba hirta.*
S. montanum illus. p.330.
S. soboliferum. See *Jovibarba sobolifera.*
S. tectorum illus. p.329.

SENECIO (Compositae)
Genus of annuals, succulent and non-succulent perennials, evergreen shrubs, sub-shrubs, and twining climbers, grown for their foliage and usually daisylike flower heads. Some shrubby species are now referred to the genus *Brachyglottis*. Shrubs are excellent for coastal gardens. Fully hardy to frost tender, min. 41–50°F (5–10°C). Most prefer full sun and well-drained soil (*S. articulatus* and *S. rowleyanus* tolerate partial shade and need very well-drained soil). Propagate shrubs and climbers by semi-ripe cuttings in summer, annuals by seed in spring, perennials by division in spring (*S. articulatus* and *S. rowleyanus* by seed or stem cuttings in spring or summer).

S. articulatus, syn. *Kleinia articulata* (Candle plant). Deciduous, spreading, perennial succulent. H 2ft (60cm), S indefinite. Frost tender, min. 50°F (10°C), zone 10. Branching, gray-marked, blue stems have weak joints. Bears rounded to oval, 3–5-lobed, gray leaves and flattish heads of small, cup-shaped, yellow flowers from spring to autumn. Offsets freely from stolons. **'Variegatus'** illus. p.383.
S. clivorum 'Desdemona'. See *Ligularia dentata* 'Desdemona'.
S. compactus. Evergreen, bushy, dense shrub. H 3ft (1m), S 6ft (2m). Frost hardy, zones 8–9. Has shoots covered with feltlike, white growth and small, oval, white-edged, dark green leaves, white beneath. Clustered heads of daisylike, bright yellow flowers are borne from mid- to late summer.
S. confusus illus. p.175.
S. elegans. Moderately fast-growing, upright annual. H 18in (45cm), S 6in (15cm). Half hardy. Has oval, deeply lobed, deep green leaves. Daisylike, purple flower heads appear on branching stems in summer.
S. grandifolius. Evergreen, erect, robust-stemmed shrub. H 10–15ft (3–5m), S 6–10ft (2–3m). Frost tender, min. 50°F (10°C) to flower well, zone 10. Has oval, toothed, boldly veined leaves, 8–18in (20–45cm) long, glossy, rich green above, red-brown-haired beneath. Carries terminal clusters, 12in (30cm) wide, of small, daisylike, yellow flower heads in winter-spring.
S. x hybridus, syn. *Cineraria x hybrida* (Cineraria). Slow-growing, evergreen, mound- or dome-shaped perennial. Cultivars are grown as biennials. Half hardy. All have oval, serrated, mid- to deep green leaves. Large, daisylike, single, semi-double, or double flower heads, in shades of blue, red, pink, or white, are produced in winter or spring. **Mini-starlet Series**, H and S 6in (15cm), has small, single flower heads. **Saucer Series**, H 16in (40cm), S 12in (30cm), has extra-large, single flower heads. Flower heads of **Superb Series**, H 16in (40cm), S 12in (30cm), are large and single.

S. laxifolius. Evergreen, bushy, spreading shrub. H 3ft (1m), S 6ft (2m). Frost hardy, zones 8–10. Oval, gray-white leaves become dark green. Bears daisylike, golden yellow flower heads in large clusters in summer.
S. macroglossus (Natal ivy, Wax vine). Evergreen, woody-stemmed, twining climber. H 10ft (3m). Frost tender, min. 45°F (7°C), best at 50°F (10°C), zone 10. Leaves are sharply triangular, fleshy-textured, and glossy. Mainly in winter has loose clusters of daisylike flower heads, each with a few white ray petals and a central, yellow disc. **'Variegatus'** illus. p.177.
S. maritima (Dusty miller). Moderately fast-growing, evergreen, bushy sub-shrub, often grown as an annual. H and S 1ft (30cm). Half hardy. Has long, oval, very deeply lobed, hairy, silver-gray leaves. Rounded, yellow flower heads appear in summer, but are best removed. **'Silver Dust'** illus. p.278.
S. mikanioides (German ivy). Evergreen, semi-woody, twining climber. H 6–10ft (2–3m). Frost tender, min. 41°F (5°C), best at 45–50°F (7–10°C), zone 10. Has fleshy leaves with 5–7 broad, pointed, radiating lobes. Mature plants carry large clusters of small, yellow flower heads in autumn-winter.
S. monroi illus. p.139.
S. pulcher illus. p.250.
S. reinoldii. Evergreen, rounded, dense shrub. H and S 3ft (1m). Frost hardy, zones 8–10. Leaves are rounded, leathery, glossy, and dark green. Bears inconspicuous, yellow flower heads from early to mid-summer. Withstands full exposure to salt winds in mild, coastal areas.
S. rowleyanus illus. p.383.
S. smithii. Bushy perennial. H 3–4ft (1–1.2m), S 2¹⁄₂–3ft (75cm–1m). Fully hardy, zones 7–9. Woolly stems are clothed with long, oval, toothed, leathery, dark green leaves. Daisylike, white flower heads, with yellow centers, are borne in terminal clusters, up to 6in (15cm) across, in early summer. Likes boggy conditions.
S. 'Spring Glory' illus. p.276.
S. 'Sunshine' illus. p.138.
S. tamoides. Evergreen, woody-stemmed, twining climber. H 15ft (5m) or more. Frost tender, min. 41–50°F (5–10°C), zone 10. Has ivy-shaped, light green leaves. In autumn-winter bears daisylike, yellow flower heads that only have a few ray petals.

SEQUOIA (Taxodiaceae). See CONIFERS.
S. sempervirens (Coast redwood, Coastal redwood, Redwood). Very vigorous, columnar to conical conifer with horizontal branches. H 70–100ft (20–30m), S 15–25ft (5–8m), although one specimen—the tallest tree in the world—has reached 375ft (112m). Fully hardy, zones 7–9. Has thick, soft, fibrous, red-brown bark and needlelike, flattened, pale green leaves, spirally arranged. Rounded to cylindrical cones are green, ripening to dark brown. Will regrow if cut back. Very cold winters kill foliage, but without affecting tree.

SEQUOIADENDRON
(Taxodiaceae). See CONIFERS.
S. giganteum illus. p.74. **'Pendulum'** is a weeping conifer. H 30ft (10m), S 6ft (2m) or more. Fully hardy, zones 6–9. Bark is thick, soft, fibrous, and red-brown. Has spiralled, needlelike, incurved, gray-green leaves that darken and become glossy.

SERAPIAS. See ORCHIDS.
S. cordigera. Deciduous, terrestrial orchid. H 16in (40cm). Half hardy, zones 8–9. Spikes of reddish or dark purple flowers, 1¹⁄₂in (4cm) long, are borne in spring. Has lance-shaped, red-spotted leaves, 6in (15cm) long. Grow in semi-shade.

SERENOA (Palmae)
Genus of one species of evergreen fan palm, grown for its foliage. Frost tender, min. 50–55°F (10–13°C). Needs full light or partial shade and well-drained soil. Water potted plants moderately during growing season, less at other times. Propagate by seed or suckers in spring. Red spider mite may be troublesome.

S. repens (Saw palmetto, Scrub palmetto). Evergreen, rhizomatous fan palm, usually stemless. H 2–3ft (60cm–1m), S 6ft (2m) or more. Zones 8–10. Palmate leaves, 18–30in (45–75cm) wide, are divided into 6–20 strap-shaped, gray to blue-green lobes. Clusters of tiny, fragrant, cream flowers are hidden among leaves in summer, followed by egg-shaped, purple-black fruits.

SERISSA (Rubiaceae)
Genus of one species of evergreen shrub, grown for its overall appearance. Frost tender, min. 45–50°F (7–10°C). Needs sun or partial shade and fertile, well-drained soil. Water potted specimens moderately, less when not in growth. May be trimmed after flowering. Propagate by semi-ripe cuttings in summer.

S. foetida, syn. *S. japonica*. Evergreen, spreading to rounded, freely branching shrub. H to 2ft (60cm), S 2–3ft (60cm–1m). Zones 9–10. Tiny, oval leaves are lustrous and deep green. Small, funnel-shaped, 4- or 5-lobed, white flowers are produced from spring to autumn.
S. japonica. See *S. foetida*.

SERRATULA (Compositae)
Genus of perennials, grown for their thistlelike flower heads. Fully hardy. Needs sun and well-drained soil. Propagate by seed or division in spring.
S. seoanii, syn. *S. shawii*. Upright, compact perennial. H 9in (23cm), S 5–6in (12–15cm). Zones 5–8. Stems bear feathery, finely cut leaves and, in autumn, terminal panicles of small, thistlelike, purple flower heads. Is useful for a rock garden.
S. shawii. See *S. seoanii*.

SESLERIA (Gramineae). See GRASSES, BAMBOOS, RUSHES, and SEDGES.
S. heuffleriana (Balkan blue grass). Evergreen, tuft-forming, perennial grass. H 20in (50cm), S 12–18in

(30–45cm). Fully hardy, zones 5–9. Bears rich green leaves, glaucous beneath, and, in spring, compact panicles of purple spikelets.

SETARIA (Gramineae). See GRASSES, BAMBOOS, RUSHES, and SEDGES.
S. italica (Foxtail millet, Italian millet). Moderately fast-growing, annual grass with stout stems. H 5ft (1.5m), S to 3ft (1m). Half hardy, zones 9–10. Has lance-shaped, green leaves, to 1¹/₂ft (45cm) long, and loose panicles of white, cream, yellow, red, brown, or black flowers in summer-autumn.

Setcreasea purpurea. See *Tradescantia pallida.*

SHEPHERDIA (Elaeagnaceae) Genus of deciduous or evergreen shrubs, grown for their foliage and fruits. Separate male and female plants are needed to obtain fruits. Fully hardy. Requires sun and well-drained soil. Propagate by softwood cuttings in summer or by seed in autumn.
S. argentea (Silver buffalo berry). Deciduous, bushy, often treelike shrub. H and S 12ft (4m). Zones 3–7. Bears tiny, inconspicuous, yellow flowers amid oblong, silvery leaves in spring, followed by small, egg-shaped, bright red fruits.

SHIBATAEA (Bambusoideae). See GRASSES, BAMBOOS, RUSHES, and SEDGES.
S. kumasasa illus. p.182.

SHORTIA (Diapensiaceae) Genus of evergreen, spring-flowering perennials with leaves that often turn red in autumn-winter. Fully hardy, but buds may be frosted in areas without snow cover. Is difficult to grow in hot, dry climates. Needs shade or semi-shade and well-drained, peaty, sandy, acid soil. Propagate by runners in summer or by seed when available.
S. galacifolia illus. p.304.
S. soldanelloides illus. p.306.
var. *ilicifolia* is an evergreen, mat-forming perennial. H 2–4in (5–10cm), S 4–6in (10–15cm). Zones 6–8. Has rounded, toothed leaves. In late spring each flower stem carries 4–6 small, pendent, bell-shaped flowers with fringed edges and rose-pink centers shading to white. Flowers of var. *magna* are rose-pink throughout.
S. uniflora 'Grandiflora'. Vigorous, evergreen, mat-forming perennial with a few rooted runners. H 3in (8cm), S 8in (20cm). Zones 5–8. Leaves are rounded, toothed, leathery, and glossy. Flower stems bear cup-shaped, 2in (5cm) wide, white-pink flowers, with serrated petals, in spring.

SIBIRAEA (Rosaceae) Genus of deciduous shrubs, grown for their foliage and flowers. Fully hardy. Needs sunny, well-drained soil. Established plants benefit from having old or weak shoots cut to base after flowering. Propagate by softwood cuttings in summer.
S. laevigata. Deciduous, spreading, open shrub. H 3ft (1m), S 5ft (1.5m).

Zones 6–8. Has narrowly oblong, blue-green leaves and, in late spring and early summer, dense, terminal clusters of tiny, star-shaped, white flowers.

SIDALCEA (Malvaceae) Genus of summer-flowering perennials, grown for their hollyhocklike flowers. Fully hardy. Requires sun and any well-drained soil. Propagate by division in spring.
S. 'Jimmy Whitelet'. See *S.* 'Jimmy Whittet'.
S. 'Jimmy Whittet', syn. *S.* 'Jimmy Whitelet', illus. p.203.
S. 'Loveliness'. Upright perennial. H 3ft (1m), S 1¹/₂ft (45cm). Zones 5–8. Has buttercuplike, divided leaves with narrowly oblong segments. In summer bears racemes of shallowly cup-shaped, shell pink flowers.
S. 'Oberon'. Upright perennial. H 2ft (60cm), S 1¹/₂ft (45cm). Zones 5–8. Has buttercuplike, divided leaves, with narrowly oblong segments, and, in summer, racemes of shallowly cup-shaped, clear pink flowers.
S. 'Puck'. Upright perennial. H 2ft (60cm), S 1¹/₂ft (45cm). Zones 5–8. Has buttercuplike, divided leaves with narrowly oblong segments. In summer produces racemes of shallowly cup-shaped, deep pink flowers.
S. 'Sussex Beauty'. Upright perennial. H 4ft (1.2m), S 1¹/₂ft (45cm). Zones 5–8. Has buttercuplike, divided leaves, with narrowly oblong segments, and, in summer, shallowly cup-shaped, deep rose-pink flowers.

SIDERITIS (Labiatae) Genus of evergreen perennials, sub-shrubs, and shrubs, grown mainly for their foliage. Half hardy to frost tender, min. 45–50°F (7–10°C). Needs full light and well-drained soil. Water potted plants moderately, less when temperatures are low. Remove spent flower spikes after flowering. Propagate by seed in spring or by semi-ripe cuttings in summer.
S. candicans. Evergreen, erect, well-branched shrub. H to 2¹/₂ft (75cm), S to 2ft (60cm). Frost tender, zone 10. Lance-shaped to narrowly oval or triangular leaves bear dense, white wool. Produces leafy, terminal spikes of tubular, pale yellow-and-light-brown or orange-red flowers in summer.

SILENE (Caryophyllaceae) Campion, Catchfly Genus of annuals and perennials, some of which are evergreen, grown for their mass of 5-petaled flowers. Fully to half hardy. Needs sun and fertile, well-drained soil. Propagate by softwood cuttings in spring or by seed in spring or early autumn.
S. acaulis illus. p.305.
S. alpestris, syn. *Heliosperma alpestris*, illus. p.313.
S. armeria (Catchfly, None-so-pretty). 'Electra' illus. p.267.
S. coeli-rosa, syn. *Agrostemma coeli-rosa*, *Lychnis coeli-rosa*, *Viscaria elegans*, illus. p.264. 'Rose Angel' illus. p.269.
S. elisabetha. Basal-rosetted perennial. H 4in (10cm), S 8in (20cm). Fully

hardy, zones 4–8. Has rosettes of strap-shaped, green leaves. In summer stems bear large, often solitary deep rose-red flowers with green centers and long-clawed petals. Suits a rock garden.
S. hookeri. Short-lived, trailing, prostrate, late summer-deciduous perennial with a long, slender tap root. H 2in (5cm), S 8in (20cm). Fully hardy, zones 4–6. Slender stems bear oval, gray leaves and, in late summer, soft pink, salmon, or orange flowers, deeply cleft to base.
S. pendula (Nodding catchfly). Moderately fast-growing, bushy annual. H and S 6–8in (15–20cm). Fully hardy. Has oval, hairy, green leaves and, in summer and early autumn, clusters of light pink flowers.
S. schafta illus. p.319.
S. vulgaris subsp. *maritima* 'Flore Pleno' (Double sea campion). Lax perennial with deep, wandering roots. H and S 8in (20cm). Fully hardy, zones 4–7. Leaves are lance-shaped and gray-green. Produces pomponlike, double, white flowers on branched stems in summer.

SILPHIUM (Compositae) Genus of fairly coarse, summer-flowering perennials. Fully hardy. Does best in sun or semi-shade and in moist but well-drained soil. Propagate by division in spring or by seed when fresh, in autumn.
S. laciniatum (Compass plant). Clump-forming perennial. H 6ft (2m), S 2ft (60cm). Zones 5–9. Green leaves, composed of opposite pairs of oblong to lance-shaped leaflets, face north and south wherever the plant is grown, hence the common name. Large clusters of slightly pendent, daisylike, yellow flower heads are borne in late summer.

SILYBUM (Compositae) Genus of thistlelike biennials, grown for their spectacular foliage. Fully hardy. Grow in sun and in any well-drained soil. Propagate by seed in late spring or early summer. Is prone to slug and snail damage.
S. marianum illus. p.266.

SINARUNDINARIA (Bambusoideae). See GRASSES, BAMBOOS, RUSHES, and SEDGES.
S. jaunsarensis. See *Arundinaria anceps.*
S. murielae. See *Thamnocalamus spathaceus.*
S. nitida, syn. *Arundinaria nitida.* Evergreen, clump-forming bamboo. H 15ft (5m), S indefinite. Frost hardy, zones 7–10. Has small, pointed, green leaves on dark purple stalks and several branches at each node. Stems are often purple with close sheaths. Flower spikes are unimportant.

SINNINGIA (Gesneriaceae) Genus of usually summer-flowering, tuberous perennials and deciduous sub-shrubs with showy flowers. Frost tender, min. 59°F (15°C), zone 10. Grow in bright light but not direct sun. Prefers a humid atmosphere and moist but not waterlogged, peaty soil. When leaves die down after flowering, allow

tubers to dry out; then store in a frost-free area. Propagate in spring by seed or in late spring or summer by stem cuttings or dividing tubers into sections, each with a young shoot.
S. barbata. Bushy, tuberous perennial with square, red stems. H and S 2ft (60cm) or more. Broadly lance-shaped leaves, to 6in (15cm) long, are glossy, green above, reddish green beneath. In summer has 5-lobed, pouched, white flowers, 1¹/₂in (4cm) long.
S. concinna. Rosetted perennial with very small tubers. H and S 6in (15cm). Oval to almost round, scalloped, velvety, red-veined, green leaves, ³/₄in (2cm) long, are red below. Trumpet-shaped, bicolored, purple and white or yellowish white flowers, to ³/₄in (2cm) long, are produced in summer.
S. 'Etoile du Feu'. Short-stemmed, rosetted, tuberous perennial. H 12in (30cm), S 16in (40cm) or more. Has oval, velvety leaves, 8–9¹/₂in (20–24cm) long. Upright, trumpet-shaped, carmine red flowers appear in summer.
S. 'Mont Blanc'. Short-stemmed, rosetted, tuberous perennial. H 12in (30cm), S 16in (40cm) or more. Oval, velvety, green leaves are 8–9¹/₂in (20–24cm) long. In summer bears upright, trumpet-shaped, pure white flowers.
S. 'Red Flicker' illus. p.237.
S. regina. Erect, tuberous perennial. H 6in (15cm) or more, S 9–12in (22–30cm). Oval leaves, to 6in (15cm) long, are velvety and deep green above, reddish green below. Nodding, tubular, violet flowers, 2in (5cm) long, are borne in summer.
S. speciosa, syn. *Gloxinia speciosa* (Gloxinia). Short-stemmed, rosetted, tuberous perennial. H and S to 1ft (30cm). Oval, velvety, green leaves are 8in (20cm) long. Nodding, funnel-shaped, fleshy, violet, red, or white flowers, to 2in (5cm) long and pouched on lower sides, are produced in summer. Is a parent of many named hybrids, of which a selection is included above and below.
S. 'Switzerland' illus. p.239.
S. 'Waterloo'. Short-stemmed, rosetted, tuberous perennial. H 12in (30cm), S 16in (40cm) or more. Oval leaves, 8–9¹/₂in (20–24cm) long, are velvety and green. Upright, trumpet-shaped, bright scarlet flowers open in summer.

SINOFRANCHETIA (Lardizabalaceae) Genus of one species of deciduous, twining climber, grown mainly for its handsome leaves. Is suitable for covering buildings and growing up large trees. Male and female flowers are produced on separate plants. Frost hardy. Grow in semi-shade and in any well-drained soil. Propagate by semi-ripe cuttings in summer.
S. chinensis. Deciduous, twining climber. H to 50ft (15m). Zones 7–10. Mid- to dark green leaves have 3 oblong to oval leaflets, each 2–6in (5–15cm) long. In late spring has small, dull white flowers in pendent racemes, to 4in (10cm) long. Pale

purple berries, containing many seeds, follow in summer.

SINOJACKIA (Styracaceae)
Genus of deciduous shrubs and trees, grown for their flowers. Fully hardy. Requires a sheltered position in sun or partial shade and fertile, humus-rich, moist, acid soil. Propagate by softwood cuttings in summer.
S. rehderiana. Deciduous, bushy shrub or spreading tree. H and S 20ft (6m). Zones 7–10. Nodding, saucer-shaped, white flowers, each with a central cluster of yellow anthers, are produced in late spring and early summer. Leaves are dark green and oval.

SINOWILSONIA (Hamamelidaceae)
Genus of one species of deciduous tree, grown for its foliage and catkins. Fully hardy. Requires sun or semi-shade and fertile, moist but well-drained soil. Propagate by seed in autumn.
S. henryi. Deciduous, spreading, sometimes shrubby tree. H and S 25ft (8m). Zones 6–9. Has oval, toothed, glossy, bright green leaves, and long, pendent, green catkins in late spring.

Siphonosmanthus delavayi. See *Osmanthus delavayi.*

SISYRINCHIUM (Iridaceae)
Genus of annuals and perennials, some of which are semi-evergreen. Fully to half hardy. Prefers sun, although tolerates partial shade, and well-drained or moist soil. Propagate by division in early spring or by seed in spring or autumn.
S. angustifolium. See *S. graminoides.*
S. bellum illus. p.323.
S. bermudiana. See *S. graminoides.*
S. brachypus. See *S. californicum.*
S. californicum (Golden-eyed grass). Semi-evergreen, upright perennial. H 12–24in (30–60cm), S 12in (30cm). Frost hardy, zones 8–9. Has grasslike tufts of basal, light green leaves. For a long period in spring-summer produces flattish, bright yellow flowers, with slightly darker veins, on winged stems. Outer leaves may die off and turn black in autumn. Dwarf forms are known as *S. brachypus.* Prefers moist soil.
S. douglasii, syn. *S. grandiflorum* (Grass widow, Spring bell). Stiff, upright, summer-deciduous perennial. H 10in (25cm), S 6in (15cm). Fully hardy, zones 7–8. Has grasslike leaves sheathing very short, threadlike flowering stems and, in early spring, a succession of pendent, bell-shaped, violet to red-purple, or sometimes white, flowers. Suits a rock garden or alpine house.
S. graminoides, syn. *S. angustifolium, S. bermudiana,* illus. p.296.
S. grandiflorum. See *S. douglasii.*
S. odoratissimum. See *Phaiophleps biflora.*
S. striatum illus. p.245. **'Aunt May'** (syn. *S.s.* 'Variegatum') is a semi-evergreen, upright perennial. H 18–24in (45–60cm), S 12in (30cm). Fully hardy, zones 7–8. Produces tufts of long, narrow, cream-striped, grayish

green leaves. Slender spikes of trumpet-shaped, purple-striped, straw yellow flowers are borne in summer.

SKIMMIA (Rutaceae)
Genus of evergreen, spring-flowering shrubs and trees, grown for their flowers, aromatic foliage, and their fruits. Except with *S. japonica* subsp. *reevesiana,* separate male and female plants are needed in order to obtain fruits. Fully to frost hardy. Needs shade or semi-shade and fertile, moist soil. Too much sun or poor soil may cause chlorosis. Propagate by semi-ripe cuttings in late summer or by seed in autumn.
S. anquetilia. Evergreen, bushy, open shrub. H 4ft (1.2m), S 6ft (2m). Fully hardy, zones 7–9. Produces small clusters of tiny, yellow flowers from mid- to late spring, then spherical, scarlet fruits. Leaves are oblong to oval, pointed, strongly aromatic, and dark green.
S. × foremanii of gardens. See *S. japonica* 'Veitchii'.
S. japonica illus. p.143. **'Fructu-albo'** (female) illus. p.141. subsp. *reevesiana* (syn. *S. reevesiana;* hermaphrodite) and **'Rubella'** (male) illus. p.142. **'Veitchii'** (syn. *S. × foremanii* of gardens) is a vigorous, evergreen, upright, dense, female shrub. H and S 5ft (1.5m). Fully hardy, zones 7–9. In mid- and late spring produces dense clusters of small, star-shaped, white flowers, followed by large, spherical, bright red fruits. Broadly oval leaves are rich green.
S. reevesiana. See *S. japonica* subsp. *reevesiana.*

SMILACINA (Liliaceae)
Genus of perennials, grown for their graceful appearance. Fully hardy. Prefers semi-shade and humus-rich, moist, neutral to acid soil. Propagate by division in spring or by seed in autumn.
S. racemosa illus. p.195.

SMILAX (Liliaceae)
Genus of deciduous or evergreen, woody-stemmed or herbaceous, scrambling climbers with tubers or rhizomes. Male and female flowers are borne on separate plants. Frost hardy to frost tender, min. 41°F (5°C). Grow in any well-drained soil and in sun or semi-shade. Propagate by division or seed in spring or by semi-ripe cuttings in summer.
S. china. Deciduous, woody-based, scrambling climber with straggling, sometimes spiny stems. H to 15ft (5m). Frost hardy, zones 7–10. Leaves are broadly oval to rounded. Produces umbels of yellow-green flowers in spring and tiny, red berries in autumn.

SMITHIANTHA (Gesneriaceae)
Genus of bushy, erect perennials with tuberlike rhizomes, grown for their flowers. Frost tender, min. 59°F (15°C). Grow in humus-rich, well-drained soil and in bright light but out of direct sun. Reduce watering after flowering and water sparingly in winter. Propagate by division of rhizomes in early spring.

S. cinnabarina (Temple bells). Robust, erect, rhizomatous perennial. H and S to 2ft (60cm). Zone 10. Broadly oval to almost rounded, toothed leaves, to 6in (15cm) long, are dark green with dark red hairs. Bell-shaped, orange-red flowers, lined with pale yellow, are produced in summer-autumn.
S. 'Orange King' illus. p.240.
S. zebrina. Bushy, rhizomatous perennial with velvety-haired stems. H and S to 3ft (1m). Zones 9–10. Oval, toothed, hairy leaves, to 7in (18cm) long, are deep green marked with reddish brown. In summer has tubular flowers, scarlet above, yellow below, spotted red inside, and with orange-yellow lobes.

SMYRNIUM (Umbelliferae)
Genus of biennials. Fully hardy. Grow in sun and in fertile, well-drained soil. Propagate by seed sown outdoors in autumn or spring.
S. perfoliatum illus. p.279.

SOLANDRA (Solanaceae)
Genus of evergreen, woody-stemmed, scrambling climbers, grown for their large, trumpet-shaped flowers. Frost tender, min. 50°F (10°C), but prefers 55–61°F (13–16°C). Needs full light and fertile, well-drained soil. Water freely when in full growth, sparingly in cold weather. Tie to supports. Thin out crowded stems after flowering. Propagate by semi-ripe cuttings in summer.
S. maxima illus. p.164.

SOLANUM (Solanaceae)
Genus of annuals, perennials (some of which are evergreen), and evergreen, semi-evergreen, or deciduous sub-shrubs, shrubs (occasionally scandent), and woody-stemmed, scrambling or leaf-stalk climbers, grown for their flowers and ornamental fruits. Frost hardy to frost tender, min. 36–50°F (2–10°C). Requires full sun and fertile, well-drained soil. Water regularly but sparingly in cold weather. Tie scrambling climbers to supports. Thin out and spur back crowded growth of climbers in spring. Propagate by seed in spring or by semi-ripe cuttings in summer. Red spider mite, whitefly, and aphids may cause problems.
S. capsicastrum (Winter cherry). Fairly slow-growing, evergreen, bushy sub-shrub, grown as an annual. H and S 1–1½ft (30–45cm). Frost tender, min. 36–9°F (2–4°C). Has lance-shaped, deep green leaves. In summer bears small, star-shaped, white flowers, followed by egg-shaped, pointed, orange-red or scarlet fruits, at least ½in (1cm) in diameter, which are at their best in winter.
S. crispum 'Glasnevin' illus. p.172.
S. jasminoides (Potato vine). Semi-evergreen, woody-stemmed, scrambling climber. H to 20ft (6m). Half hardy, zones 8–10. Oval to lance-shaped leaves are sometimes lobed or have leaflets at base. Small, 5-petaled, pale gray-blue flowers are produced in summer-autumn; tiny, purple berries appear in autumn. **'Album'** illus. p.165.

S. pseudocapsicum (Jerusalem cherry). Fairly slow-growing, evergreen, bushy shrub, usually grown as an annual. H and S to 4ft (1.2m). Frost tender, min. 36–9°F (2–4°C). Has oval or lance-shaped, bright green leaves. Small, star-shaped, white flowers appear in summer and are followed by spherical, scarlet fruits. Has several smaller selections: **'Balloon'** illus. p.285; **'Dwarf Red'**, H 15in (38cm), with bright orange fruits; **'Fancy'**, H 1ft (30cm), with scarlet fruits; **'Red Giant'** illus. p.285; and **'Snowfire'**, H 1ft (30cm), with white fruits that later turn red.
S. rantonnettii (Blue potato bush). **'Royal Robe'** illus. p.113.
S. seaforthianum (Potato creeper). Evergreen, slender-stemmed, scrambling climber. H 6–10ft (2–3m). Frost tender, min. 45°F (7°C), zone 10. Leaves are divided into several pairs of oval to lance-shaped leaflets. Nodding clusters of star-shaped, mauve-violet flowers, each with a cone of yellow stamens, appear from spring to autumn, followed by small, scarlet berries.
S. wendlandii illus. p.172.

SOLDANELLA (Primulaceae)
Snowbell
Genus of evergreen, early spring-flowering perennials, grown for their flowers. Is good for rock gardens and alpine houses. Fully hardy, but flower buds are set in autumn and may be destroyed by frost if there is no snow cover. Requires partial shade and humus-rich, well-drained, peaty soil. Propagate by seed in spring or by division in late summer. Slugs may attack flower buds.
S. alpina illus. p.308.
S. minima (Least snowbell). Evergreen, prostrate perennial. H 1in (2.5cm), S 4in (10cm). Zones 4–7. Forms a mat of minute, rounded leaves on soil surface. In early spring produces solitary almost stemless, bell-shaped, pale lavender blue or white flowers with fringed mouths.
S. montana (Mountain tassel). Evergreen, mound-forming perennial. H 4in (10cm), S 6in (15cm). Zones 4–7. In early spring has long flower stems each carrying tall, pendent, bell-shaped, lavender blue flowers with fringed mouths. Leaves are rounded and leathery.
S. villosa illus. p.308.

SOLEIROLIA (Urticaceae)
Baby's tears, Mind-your-own-business, Mother-of-thousands
Genus of one species of, usually evergreen, prostrate perennial that forms a dense carpet of foliage. Frost hardy, but leaves are killed by winter frost. Recovers to grow vigorously again in spring. Tolerates sun or shade. Prefers moist soil. Propagate by division from spring to mid-summer.
S. soleirolii, syn. *Helxine soleirolii,* illus. p.260.

SOLIDAGO (Compositae)
Goldenrod
Genus of summer- and autumn-flowering perennials, some species of

which are vigorous, coarse plants that tend to crowd out others in borders. Fully hardy. Most tolerate sun or shade and any well-drained soil. Propagate by division in spring. Occasionally self seeds.

S. 'Golden Wings'. Upright perennial. H 5ft (1.5m), S 3ft (1m). Zones 4–9. Bears large, feathery panicles of small, bright yellow flower heads in early autumn. Has lance-shaped, toothed, slightly hairy, green leaves.

S. 'Goldenmosa' illus. p.215.

S. 'Laurin' illus. p.215.

S. virgaurea subsp. **minuta.** Mound-forming perennial. H and S 4in (10cm). Zones 4–9. Has small, lance-shaped, green leaves and, in autumn, neat spikes of small, yellow flower heads. Is suitable for a rock garden or alpine house. Needs shade and moist soil.

× SOLIDASTER (Compositae)
Hybrid genus (*Solidago* × *Aster*) of one summer-flowering perennial. Fully hardy. Grows in sun or shade and in any fertile soil. Propagate by division in spring.

× S. hybridus. See × *S. luteus.*

× S. luteus, syn. × *S. hybridus,* illus. p.246.

SOLLYA (Pittosporaceae)
Bluebell creeper
Genus of evergreen, woody-based, twining climbers, grown for their attractive, blue flowers. Half hardy. Grow in sun and well-drained soil. Propagate by seed in spring or by softwood or greenwood cuttings in summer.

S. heterophylla illus. p.164.

SONERILA (Melastomataceae)
Genus of evergreen, bushy perennials and shrubs, grown for their foliage and flowers. Frost tender, min. 59°F (15°C). Prefers a humid atmosphere in semi-shade and peaty soil. Propagate by tip cuttings in spring.

S. margaritacea. Evergreen, bushy, semi-prostrate perennial. H and S 8–10in (20–25cm). Zone 10. Red stems bear oval, dark green leaves, 2–3in (5–8cm) long, reddish below, silver-patterned above. Has racemes of 3-petaled, rose-pink flowers in summer. **'Argentea'** has more silvery leaves with green veins; **'Hendersonii'** is more compact with white-spotted leaves.

SOPHORA (Leguminosae)
Kowhai
Genus of deciduous or semi-evergreen trees and shrubs, grown for their habit, foliage, and clusters of flowers. Fully to frost hardy. Requires full sun (*S. microphylla* and *S. tetraptera* usually best to be grown against a south- or west-facing wall) and fertile, well-drained soil. Propagate by seed in autumn; semi-evergreens may also be raised from softwood cuttings in summer.

S. davidii, syn. *S. viciifolia,* illus. p.113.

S. japonica (Pagoda tree). Deciduous, spreading tree. H and S 70ft (20m). Fully hardy, zones 5–9. Dark green leaves consist of 9–15 oval leaflets. On mature trees, long clusters of pealike,

creamy white flowers appear in late summer and early autumn. Does best in hot summers. **'Pendula'**, H and S 10ft (3m), has long, hanging shoots clothed with dark green foliage. **'Violacea'** illus. p.45.

S. microphylla, syn. *Edwardsia microphylla.* Semi-evergreen, spreading tree. H and S 25ft (8m). Frost hardy, zones 8–10. Dark green leaves are composed of numerous tiny, oblong leaflets. Produces clusters of pealike, deep yellow flowers in late spring.

S. tetraptera illus. p.62.

S. viciifolia. See *S. davidii.*

× SOPHROLAELIOCATTLEYA.
See ORCHIDS.

× S. Hazel Boyd 'Apricot Glow' (illus. p.255). Evergreen, epiphytic orchid for an intermediate greenhouse. H 4in (10cm). Zone 10. In spring and early summer produces small heads of apricot orange flowers, 3¹⁄₂in (9cm) across, with crimson marks on lips. Has oval, rigid leaves, 4in (10cm) long. Grow in good light in summer.

× S. Trizac 'Purple Emperor' (illus. p.253). Evergreen, epiphytic orchid for an intermediate greenhouse. H 4in (10cm). Zone 10. In spring, crimson-lipped, pinkish purple flowers, 2¹⁄₂in (6cm) across, are borne in small heads. Has oval, rigid leaves, 4in (10cm) long. Provide good light in summer.

SORBARIA (Rosaceae)
Genus of deciduous, summer-flowering shrubs, grown for their foliage and large panicles of small, white flowers. Fully hardy. Prefers sun and deep, fertile, moist soil. In winter cut out some older stems on mature plants and prune back remaining shoots to growing points. Remove suckers at base to prevent *Sorbaria* spreading too widely. Propagate by softwood cuttings in summer, by division in autumn, or by root cuttings in late winter.

S. aitchisonii, syn. *Spiraea aitchisonii.* Deciduous, arching shrub. H and S 10ft (3m). Zones 6–9. Shoots are red when young. Leaves have 11–23 narrowly lance-shaped, taper-pointed, dark green leaflets. Upright panicles of star-shaped flowers are produced from mid- to late summer.

S. arborea, syn. *Spiraea arborea.* Vigorous, deciduous, arching shrub. H and S 20ft (6m). Zones 5–9. Leaves are composed of 13–17 lance-shaped, taper-pointed, deep green leaflets. Bears nodding panicles of star-shaped flowers in mid- and late summer.

S. sorbifolia, syn. *Spiraea sorbifolia,* illus. p.105.

SORBUS (Rosaceae)
Genus of deciduous trees and shrubs, grown for their foliage, small, 5-petaled flowers, attractive fruits, and, in some species, autumn color. Leaves may be whole or divided into leaflets. Fully to frost hardy. Needs sun or semi-shade and fertile, well-drained but moist soil. Species with leaves composed of leaflets do not grow well in very dry soil. Propagate by softwood cuttings or budding in

summer, by seed in autumn, or by grafting in winter. Is susceptible to fireblight.

S. alnifolia (Korean mountain ash). Deciduous, conical, then spreading tree. H 50ft (15m), S 25ft (8m). Fully hardy, zones 4–8. Oval, toothed, bright green leaves turn orange and red in autumn. Small, white flowers in late spring are followed by egg-shaped, orange-red fruits.

S. americana (American mountain ash). Deciduous, round-headed tree. H 30ft (10m), S 22ft (7m). Fully hardy, zones 3–8. Light green leaves, divided into 11–17 narrowly oval leaflets, usually color well in autumn. Bears small, white flowers in early summer, followed by rounded, bright red fruits that ripen in early autumn.

S. aria (Whitebeam). Deciduous, spreading tree. H 50ft (15m), S 30ft (10m). Fully hardy, zones 6–8. Oval, toothed leaves are silver-gray when young, maturing to dark green above, white-felted beneath. Clusters of small, white flowers in late spring are followed by rounded, brown-speckled, deep red fruits. **'Chrysophylla'**, H 30ft (10m), S 22ft (7m), bears golden yellow, young leaves. **'Decaisneana'** see *S.a.* 'Majestica'. **'Lutescens'** illus. p.51. **'Majestica'** (syn. *S.a.* 'Decaisneana') has larger leaves, white-haired when young, and produces larger fruits.

S. aucuparia illus. p.54. **'Fructu Luteo'** is a deciduous, spreading tree. H 50ft (15m), S 25ft (8m). Fully hardy, zones 4–7. Leaves consist of 13–15 narrowly oval, green leaflets that turn yellow or red in autumn. Bears small, white flowers in late spring, followed by rounded, orange-yellow fruits in autumn. Fruits of **'Rossica Major'** (syn. *S.a.* 'Rossica') are large and deep red. **'Sheerwater Seedling'**, S 12ft (4m), has a narrow, upright habit.

S. cashmiriana illus. p.66.

S. commixta, syn. *S. discolor* of gardens, illus. p.54. **'Embley'** is a vigorous, deciduous, elegant tree with steeply ascending branches. H 40ft (12m), S 28ft (9m). Fully hardy, zones 6–8. Glossy, deep green leaves, each with 13–17 slender, lance-shaped leaflets, turn orange and red in late autumn. Bears small, white flowers in late spring, followed by rounded, bright red fruits in autumn.

S. cuspidata illus. p.50.

S. decora. Deciduous, spreading, sometimes shrubby tree. H 30ft (10m), S 25ft (8m). Fully hardy, zones 3–7. Leaves are composed of oblong, blue-green leaflets. Small, white flowers in late spring are succeeded by rounded, orange-red fruits.

S. discolor of gardens. See *S. commixta.*

S. esserteauiana. Deciduous, spreading tree. H and S 30ft (10m). Fully hardy, zones 6–8. Dark green leaves, with broadly oblong leaflets, redden in autumn. Has small, white flowers in late spring, followed by large clusters of rounded, bright red, sometimes orange-yellow fruits.

S. hupehensis (Hupeh rowan). Deciduous, spreading tree. H 40ft

(12m), S 25ft (8m). Fully hardy, zones 6–8. Leaves have 9–17 oblong, blue-green leaflets that turn orange-red in late autumn. Small, white flowers in late spring are followed by clusters of rounded, pink-tinged, white fruits. **'Rosea'** illus. p.54.

S. insignis. Deciduous, spreading tree. H 25ft (8m), S 20ft (6m). Frost hardy, zones 7–8. Leaves consist of usually 9–21 large, oblong, glossy, dark green leaflets. Large clusters of small, creamy white flowers in late spring are followed by rounded, pink fruits that become white in winter.

S. intermedia (Swedish whitebeam). Deciduous, broad-headed, dense tree. H and S 40ft (12m). Fully hardy, zones 6–8. Has broadly oval, deeply lobed, dark green leaves. Carries clusters of small, white flowers in late spring, then rounded, red fruits.

S. 'Joseph Rock' illus. p.55.

S. latifolia (Service-tree-of-Fontainebleau). Deciduous, spreading tree. H 40ft (12m), S 30ft (10m). Fully hardy, zones 5–8. Has peeling bark and broadly oval, sharply lobed, glossy, dark green leaves. Small, white flowers in late spring are succeeded by rounded, brownish red fruits.

S. 'Mitchellii'. See *S. thibetica* 'John Mitchell'.

S. pohuashanensis. Deciduous, spreading tree. H 30ft (10m), S 25ft (8m). Fully hardy, zones 6–8. Dark green leaves are divided into 11–15 oblong leaflets. Has small, white flowers in late spring, followed by dense clusters of rounded, red fruits.

S. prattii. Deciduous, spreading tree. H and S 20ft (6m). Fully hardy, zones 6–8. Dark green leaves are divided into 21–9 oblong, sharply toothed leaflets. Has small, white flowers in late spring, followed by rounded, white fruits.

S. reducta illus. p.300.

S. sargentiana (Sargent's rowan). Deciduous, sparsely branched, spreading tree. H and S 20ft (6m). Fully hardy, zones 7–8. Has stout shoots and large, green leaves, consisting of 7–11 oblong leaflets that turn brilliant red in autumn. Small, white flowers produced in late spring are succeeded by rounded, red fruits.

S. scalaris. Deciduous, spreading, graceful tree. H and S 30ft (10m). Fully hardy, zones 6–8. Produces leaves with 21–33 narrowly oblong, glossy, deep green leaflets, that turn deep red and purple in autumn. Has small, white flowers in late spring, followed by rounded, red fruits in large, dense clusters.

S. scopulina. Deciduous, upright shrub. H and S 12ft (4m). Fully hardy, zones 3–7. Bears dark green leaves divided into 11–15 oblong leaflets. Produces clusters of small, white flowers in late spring or early summer that are followed by rounded, bright red fruits in autumn.

S. thibetica. Deciduous, conical tree. H 70ft (20m), S 50ft (15m). Fully hardy, zones 5–7. Large, broadly oval, dark green leaves are silvery white when young and remain so on undersides. Heads of small, white flowers in late spring are followed

by rounded, brown fruits. **'John Mitchell'** (syn. *S.* 'Mitchellii') illus. p.52.
S. x thuringiaca. Deciduous, broadly conical, compact tree. H 40ft (12m), S 25ft (8m). Fully hardy, zones 5–8. Oval, dark green leaves are deeply lobed and have basal leaflets. Small, white flowers appear in late spring, followed by rounded, bright red fruits. **'Fastigiata'** has upright branches and a broad, oval, dense crown.
S. vilmorinii illus. p.66.
S. 'Wilfred Fox'. Deciduous tree, upright when young, later with a dense, oval head. H 50ft (15m), S 30ft (10m). Fully hardy, zones 5–7. Bears broadly oval, glossy, dark green leaves. Has small, white flowers in late spring, then rounded, orange-brown fruits.

SPARAXIS (Iridaceae)
Harlequin flower
Genus of spring- and early summer-flowering corms, grown for their very gaudy flowers. Half hardy. Needs a sunny, well-drained site. Plant in autumn. Dry off corms after flowering. Propagate by offsets in late summer or by seed in autumn.
S. elegans, syn. *Streptanthera cuprea,* *S. elegans.* Spring-flowering corm. H 4–10in (10–25cm), S 3–5in (8–12cm). Zones 9–10. Has lance-shaped leaves in an erect, basal fan. Stem produces a loose spike of 1–5 flattish, orange or white blooms, each 1¼–1½in (3–4cm) wide and with a yellow center surrounded by a purple-black band.
S. grandiflora. Spring-flowering corm. H 6–16in (15–40cm), S 3–5in (8–12cm). Zones 9–10. Produces sword-shaped leaves in an erect, basal fan. Stem bears a loose spike of up to 5 flattish, deep purple flowers, each 1½–2in (4–5cm) across.
S. tricolor illus. p.359.

SPARGANIUM (Sparganiaceae)
Bur reed
Genus of deciduous or semi-evergreen, perennial, marginal water plants, grown for their foliage. Fully hardy. Tolerates deep shade and cold water. Remove faded foliage and cut plants back regularly to control growth. Propagate by seed or division in spring.
S. erectum, syn. *S. ramosum,* illus. p.375.
S. minimum (Least bur reed). Vigorous, deciduous or semi-evergreen, perennial, marginal water plant. H 1–3ft (30cm–1m), S 1ft (30cm). Zones 5–9. Green leaves are grasslike, some erect, some floating. Insignificant, brownish green flowers, in the form of burs, appear in summer.
S. ramosum. See *S. erectum.*

SPARMANNIA (Tiliaceae)
Genus of evergreen trees and shrubs, grown for their flowers and foliage. Frost tender, min. 45°F (7°C). Prefers full light and fertile, well-drained soil. Water freely when in full growth, moderately at other times. Flowering stems may be cut back after flowering to promote a more compact habit. Propagate by greenwood cuttings in late spring. Is prone to whitefly.
S. africana illus. p.87.

SPARTINA (Gramineae). See GRASSES, BAMBOOS, RUSHES, and SEDGES.
S. pectinata (Prairie cord grass). **'Aureo Marginata',** syn. *S.p.* 'Aureo-variegata', illus. p.183.

SPARTIUM (Leguminosae)
Genus of one species of deciduous, almost leafless shrub, grown for its green shoots and showy flowers. Frost hardy. Needs sun and not too rich, well-drained soil. To maintain a compact habit, trim in early spring. Propagate by seed in autumn.
S. junceum illus. p.115.

SPATHIPHYLLUM (Araceae)
Genus of evergreen perennials, with rhizomes, grown for their foliage and flowers. Frost tender, min. 59°F (15°C). Prefers a humid atmosphere, humus-rich, moist soil, and partial shade. Propagate by division in spring or summer.
S. 'Clevelandii'. Evergreen, tufted perennial. H and S to 2ft (60cm). Zone 10. Has broadly lance-shaped, semi-erect, glossy, green leaves, 1ft (30cm) or more long. Intermittently bears oval, white spathes, each 6in (15cm) long with a central, white line, that surround fragrant white spadices.
S. floribundum. Evergreen, tufted, short-stemmed perennial. H and S to 1ft (30cm). Zone 10. Has clusters of lance-shaped, long-pointed, long-stalked, glossy, dark green leaves, to 6in (15cm) long. Intermittently, bears narrowly oval, white spathes, to 3in (8cm) long, each enclosing a green-and-white spadix.
S. 'Mauna Loa' illus. p.255.
S. wallisii illus. p.256.

SPATHODEA (Bignoniaceae)
Genus of evergreen trees, grown for their flowers and their overall appearance. Frost tender, min. 61–5°F (16–18°C). Needs full light and fertile, well-drained but moisture-retentive soil. Pot-grown and immature plants seldom produce flowers. Propagate by seed in spring or by semi-ripe cuttings in summer.
S. campanulata illus. p.45.

SPHAERALCEA (Malvaceae)
Genus of perennials and deciduous sub-shrubs, evergreen in warm climates. Half hardy. Needs a warm, sunny site and fertile, well-drained soil. Propagate by seed or division in spring or by softwood cuttings in mid-summer.
S. ambigua illus. p.216.
S. munroana. Branching, woody-based perennial. H and S 18in (45cm). Zones 9–10. Broadly funnel-shaped, brilliant coral pink flowers are borne singly in leaf axils from summer until first frosts. Has oval, round-toothed, hairy, green leaves.

SPHAEROPTERIS. See CYATHEA.

Spiloxene capensis. See *Hypoxis capensis.*

SPIRAEA (Rosaceae)
Genus of deciduous or semi-evergreen shrubs, grown for their mass of small

flowers and, in some species, their foliage. Fully hardy. Requires sun and fertile, well-drained but not over-dry soil. On species and cultivars that flower on the current year's growth— *S. x billiardii, S. douglasii,* and *S. japonica* and its cultivars—cut young stems back and remove some very old ones in early spring. On species that flower on old wood, cut out older shoots in early spring, leaving young shoots to flower that year. Propagate *S. douglasii* by division between late autumn and early spring, other species and cultivars by softwood cuttings in summer.
S. aitchisonii. See *Sorbaria aitchisonii.*
S. arborea. See *Sorbaria arborea.*
S. 'Arguta' (Bridal wreath, Foam of May). Deciduous, arching, dense shrub. H and S 8ft (2.5m). Zones 5–8. Produces clusters of 5-petaled, white flowers from mid- to late spring. Has narrowly oblong, bright green leaves.
S. aruncus. See *Aruncus dioicus.*
S. x billiardii. Deciduous, upright, dense shrub. H and S 8ft (2.5m). Zones 4–8. Bears dense panicles of 5-petaled, pink flowers in summer and oval, finely toothed, dark green leaves. **'Triumphans'** has large, broadly conical panicles of bright purplish pink flowers.
S. x bumalda. See *S. japonica.*
S. canescens illus. p.104.
S. douglasii. Vigorous, deciduous, upright shrub. H and S 6ft (2m). Zones 5–8. Has dense, narrow panicles of 5-petaled, purplish pink flowers from early to mid-summer among oblong, green leaves with gray-white undersides. Leaves of var. **menziesii**, H 3ft (1m), are green on both sides.
S. japonica, syn. *S. x bumalda.* **'Anthony Waterer', 'Goldflame',** and **'Little Princess'** illus. p.131.
S. nipponica. Deciduous, arching shrub. H and S 8ft (2.5m). Zones 4–9. Bears dense clusters of 5-petaled, white flowers in early summer. Stout, red shoots carry small, rounded, dark green leaves. **'Halward's Silver',** H and S 3ft (1m), is slow-growing, very dense, and flowers profusely. **'Snowmound'** (syn. *S.n.* var. *tosaensis* of gardens) illus. p.107.
S. prunifolia. Deciduous, arching, graceful shrub. H and S 6ft (2m). Zones 5–8. In mid- and late spring has clusters of rosettelike, double, white flowers amid rounded to oblong, bright green leaves, coloring to bronze-yellow in autumn.
S. 'Snow White', syn. *S. trichocarpa* 'Snow White'. Deciduous, arching shrub. H and S 6ft (2m). Zones 6–8. Leaves are oblong and green. Dense clusters of 5-petaled, white flowers are borne along shoots in late spring and early summer.
S. sorbifolia. See *Sorbaria sorbifolia.*
S. thunbergii. Deciduous or semi-evergreen, arching, dense shrub. H 5ft (1.5m), S 6ft (2m). Zones 5–8. Small clusters of 5-petaled, white flowers are borne along slender stems from early to mid-spring. Has narrowly oblong, pale green leaves.
S. trichocarpa 'Snow White'. See *S.* 'Snow White'.

S. trilobata. Deciduous, arching, graceful shrub. H 3ft (1m), S 5ft (1.5m). Zones 4–8. In early summer produces 5-petaled, white flowers in clusters along slender shoots. Has rounded, shallowly lobed, toothed, blue-green leaves.
S. ulmaria. See *Filipendula ulmaria.*
S. x vanhouttei illus. p.122.
S. veitchii. Vigorous, deciduous, upright shrub. H and S 10ft (3m). Zones 6–8. Has arching, red branches and oblong, dark green leaves. Produces heads of 5-petaled, white flowers from early to mid-summer.

SPIRANTHES. See ORCHIDS.
S. cernua (illus. p.252). Deciduous, terrestrial orchid. H 20in (50cm). Frost hardy, zones 3–9. Spikes of delicate, white flowers, ½in (1cm) long, with pale yellow centers, appear in autumn. Has narrowly lance-shaped leaves, 2–5in (5–12cm) long. Requires semi-shade in summer.

SPREKELIA (Amaryllidaceae)
Genus of one species of bulb, grown for its showy, red flowers in spring. Half hardy. Needs an open, sunny site and well-drained soil. Keep dry in winter; start into growth by watering in spring. Propagate by offsets in early autumn.
S. formosissima illus. p.343.

STACHYS (Labiatae)
Genus of late spring- or summer-flowering perennials, shrubs, and sub-shrubs, some of which are evergreen. Fully hardy to frost tender, min. 41°F (5°C). Grows in any well-drained soil and is particularly tolerant of poor soil. Species mentioned below prefer an open, sunny position; others are woodland plants and grow better in semi-shade. Propagate by division in spring.
S. byzantina, syn. *S. lanata, S. olympica,* illus. p.260. **'Silver Carpet'** is an evergreen, mat-forming perennial. H 6in (15cm), S 24in (60cm). Fully hardy, zones 4–9. Has oval, woolly, gray leaves. Is rarely known to produce flowers. Makes an excellent front-of-border or ground-cover plant.
S. coccinea. Clump-forming perennial. H 24in (60cm), S 18in (45cm). Frost tender, zones 9–10. Has oval, green leaves with a pronounced network of veins. From early to late summer, spikes of small, hooded, bright scarlet flowers, protruding from purple calyces, arise from leaf axils.
S. lanata. See *S. byzantina.*
S. macrantha. Clump-forming perennial. H and S 12in (30cm). Fully hardy, zones 4–8. Has heart-shaped, crinkled, round-toothed, soft green leaves. Whorls of large, hooded, rose-purple flowers are produced in summer. **'Superba'** illus. p.241.
S. officinalis, syn. *Betonica officinalis* (Betony). Mat-forming perennial. H 18–24in (45–60cm), S 12–18in (30–45cm). Fully hardy, zones 4–9. Whorls of hooded, tubular, purple, pink, or white flowers are borne on sturdy stems, arising, in summer, from mats of oval to oblong, round-toothed,

green leaves. **'Rosea'** has flowers of clearer pink.
S. olympica. See *S. byzantina.*

STACHYURUS (Stachyuraceae)
Genus of deciduous shrubs, grown for their flowers borne before the leaves. Fully to half hardy; flower spikes, formed in autumn, are usually unharmed by hard frosts. Needs sun or semi-shade and fertile, not too heavy soil, preferably peaty and acid. Does well when trained against a south- or west-facing wall. Propagate by softwood cuttings in summer.
S. chinensis. Deciduous, spreading, open shrub. H 6ft (2m), S 12ft (4m). Fully hardy, zones 7–9. Pendent spikes of small, bell-shaped, pale yellow flowers open in late winter and early spring. Leaves are oval and deep green. **'Magpie'** has gray-green leaves, broadly edged with creamy white.
S. praecox illus. p.118.

STANHOPEA. See ORCHIDS.
S. tigrina. Evergreen, epiphytic orchid for a cool greenhouse. H 9in (23cm). Zone 10. Pendent spikes of fragrant, waxy, rich yellow and maroon flowers, 6in (15cm) across, with red-spotted, white lips, appear in summer. Has broadly oval, ribbed leaves, 12in (30cm) long. Is best grown in a hanging, slatted basket. Provide semi-shade in summer.

STAPELIA (Asclepiadaceae)
Genus of clump-forming, perennial succulents with erect, 4-angled stems. Stem edges are often indented and may produce small leaves that drop after only a few weeks. Flowers are often foul-smelling. Frost tender, min. 52°F (11°C). Needs sun or partial shade and well-drained soil. Propagate by seed or stem cuttings in spring or summer.
S. flavirostris illus. p.396.
S. gigantea illus. p.396.
S. variegata illus. p.396.

STAPHYLEA (Staphyleaceae)
Bladdernut
Genus of deciduous, spring-flowering shrubs and trees, grown for their flowers and bladderlike fruits. Fully hardy. Requires sun or semi-shade and fertile, moist soil. Propagate species by softwood or greenwood cuttings in summer or by seed in autumn, selected forms by softwood or greenwood cuttings in summer.
S. colchica. Deciduous, upright shrub. H and S 11ft (3.5m). Zones 6–8. Erect panicles of bell-shaped, white flowers in late spring are followed by inflated, greenish white fruits. Bright green leaves each consist of 3–5 oval leaflets.
S. holocarpa **'Rosea'** illus. p.85.
S. pinnata illus. p.84.

Statice suworowii. See *Psylliostachys suworowii.*

STAUNTONIA (Lardizabalaceae)
Genus of evergreen, woody-stemmed, twining climbers. Male and female flowers are produced on separate plants. Frost hardy. Grow in any well-drained soil and in sun or semi-shade. To keep under control, prune in early

spring. Propagate by seed in spring or by stem cuttings in summer or autumn.
S. hexaphylla. Evergreen, woody-stemmed, twining climber. H to 30ft (10m) or more. Leaves have 3–7 oval leaflets, each 2–5in (5–13cm) long. Zones 8–10. In spring has racemes of small, fragrant, cup-shaped, pale violet flowers, followed by egg-shaped, edible, fleshy, purple fruits, 1–2in (2.5–5cm) long, if plants of both sexes are grown together.

STENANTHIUM (Liliaceae)
Genus of summer-flowering bulbs, attractive but seldom cultivated. Frost hardy. Needs an open, sunny position in any well-drained soil. In cool areas, plant in a warm, sheltered site in light soil that does not dry out excessively. Propagate by seed in autumn or by division in spring.
S. gramineum. Summer-flowering bulb. H to 5ft (1.5m), S 1$\frac{1}{2}$–2ft (45–60cm). Zones 7–10. Has long, narrowly strap-shaped, semi-erect, basal leaves. Produces a stem that bears a dense, branched, often arching spike of fragrant, star-shaped, white or green flowers, each $\frac{1}{2}$–$\frac{5}{8}$in (1–1.5cm) across.

STENOCARPUS (Proteaceae)
Genus of evergreen, summer- and autumn-flowering trees, grown for their flowers and foliage. Frost tender, min. 41–5°F (5–7°C). Needs full light and fertile, well-drained soil. Water potted plants moderately, less in winter. Pruning is rarely necessary. Propagate by seed in spring or by semi-ripe cuttings in summer.
S. sinuatus (Australian firewheel tree). Slow-growing, evergreen, upright tree. H 40ft (12m) or more, S 15ft (5m). Zone 10. Has lustrous, deep green leaves, each 5–10in (12–25cm) long, lance-shaped and entire or with pairs of oblong lobes. Bears bottle-shaped, bright scarlet flowers, clustered like the spokes of a wheel, from late summer to autumn.

Stenolobium stans. See *Tecoma stans.*

STENOMESSON (Amaryllidaceae)
Genus of bulbs, grown for their long, often pendent, tubular flowers. Frost tender, min. 50°F (10°C). Needs an open, sunny situation and well-drained soil. Propagate by offsets in autumn.
S. coccineum. See *S. variegatum.*
S. incarnatum. See *S. variegatum.*
S. variegatum, syn. *S. coccineum, S. incarnatum, S. viridiflorum,* illus. p.350.
S. viridiflorum. See *S. variegatum.*

STENOTAPHRIUM (Gramineae). See GRASSES, BAMBOOS, RUSHES, and SEDGES.
S. secundatum (St. Augustine grass). **'Variegatum'** is an evergreen, spreading, rhizomatous, perennial grass. H 6in (15cm), S indefinite. Frost tender, min. 41°F (5°C), zones 9–10. Leaves are green with cream stripes and last well into winter. Produces erect racemes of brownish green spikelets in summer. In warm climates is used for lawns.

STEPHANANDRA (Rosaceae)
Genus of deciduous, summer-flowering shrubs, grown for their habit, foliage, autumn color, and winter shoots. Fully hardy. Needs sun or semi-shade and fertile, not too dry soil. On established plants cut out some older shoots after flowering. Propagate by softwood cuttings in summer or by division in autumn.
S. incisa. Deciduous, arching shrub. H 5ft (1.5m), S 10ft (3m). Zones 4–7. Oval, deeply lobed and toothed, bright green leaves turn orange-yellow in autumn and stems become rich brown in winter. Produces crowded panicles of tiny, star-shaped, greenish white flowers in early summer. **'Crispa'**, H 2ft (60cm), has wavy-edged and more deeply lobed leaves.
S. tanakae illus. p.108.

STEPHANOTIS (Asclepiadaceae)
Genus of evergreen, woody-stemmed, twining climbers, grown for their scented, waxy flowers. Frost tender, min. 55–61°F (13–16°C). Needs humus-rich, well-drained soil and partial shade in summer. Water moderately, less in cold weather. Provide support. Shorten over-long or crowded stems in spring. Propagate by seed in spring or by semi-ripe cuttings in summer.
S. floribunda illus. p.163.

Sterculia acerifolia. See *Brachychiton acerifolius.*
Sterculia diversifolia. See *Brachychiton populneus.*
Sterculia platanifolia. See *Firmiana simplex.*

STERNBERGIA (Amaryllidaceae)
Genus of spring- or autumn-flowering bulbs, grown for their large, crocuslike flowers. Frost hardy, but in cool areas grow against a sunny wall. Needs a hot, sunny site and any well-drained, heavy or light soil that dries out in summer, when bulbs die down and need warmth and dryness. Leave undisturbed to form clumps. Propagate by division in spring or autumn.
S. candida illus. p.357.
S. clusiana. Autumn-flowering bulb. H to $\frac{3}{4}$in (2cm), S 3–4in (8–10cm). Zones 7–9. Strap-shaped, semi-erect, basal, grayish green leaves, often twisted lengthways, appear after flowering. Stems carry erect, goblet-shaped, yellow or greenish yellow flowers, 1$\frac{1}{2}$–3in (4–8cm) long.
S. lutea illus. p.369.
S. sicula. Autumn-flowering bulb. H 1–3in (2.5–7cm), S 2–3in (5–8cm). Zones 6–9. Narrowly strap-shaped, semi-erect, basal, deep green leaves, each with a central, paler green stripe, appear with flowers. Stem bears a funnel-shaped, bright yellow flower, $\frac{3}{4}$–1$\frac{1}{2}$in (2–4cm) long.

STETSONIA (Cactaceae)
Genus of one species of treelike, perennial cactus with a stout trunk. Nocturnal, funnel-shaped flowers are 6in (15cm) long. Frost tender, min. 50°F (10°C). Needs a sunny, well-drained position. Propagate by seed in spring or summer.
S. coryne illus. p.379.

STEWARTIA, syn. STUARTIA. (Theaceae)
Genus of deciduous trees and shrubs, grown for their flowers, autumn color, and usually peeling bark. Fully to frost hardy. Needs a sunny position, but preferably with roots in shade, and shelter from strong winds. Requires fertile, moist but well-drained, neutral to acid soil. Resents being transplanted. Propagate by softwood cuttings in summer or by seed in autumn.
S. malacodendron. Deciduous, spreading tree or shrub. H 12ft (4m), S 10ft (3m). Frost hardy, zones 7–9. Roselike, purple-stamened, white flowers, sometimes purple-streaked, are borne in mid-summer amid oval, dark green leaves.
S. monadelpha illus. p.55.
S. pseudocamellia illus. p.51.
S. sinensis. Deciduous, spreading tree. H 40ft (12m), S 22ft (7m). Fully hardy, zones 6–9. Has peeling bark and oval, bright green leaves that turn brilliant red in autumn. Produces fragrant, roselike, white flowers in mid-summer.

STIGMAPHYLLON (Malpighiaceae)
Genus of evergreen, woody-stemmed, twining climbers, grown for their flowers. Frost tender, min. 59–64°F (15–18°C). Fertile, well-drained soil is needed with partial shade in summer. Water freely when in full growth, less in low temperatures. Provide stems with support. Thin out crowded stems in spring. Propagate by semi-ripe cuttings in summer.
S. ciliatum illus. p.174.

STIPA (Gramineae). See GRASSES, BAMBOOS, RUSHES, and SEDGES.
S. arundinacea (Pheasant grass). Evergreen, tuft-forming, perennial grass. H 5ft (1.5m), S 4ft (1.2m). Frost hardy, zones 5–10. Brownish green leaves, 12in (30cm) long, turn soft orange in late summer. Has decorative, pendent, open panicles of purplish green flower spikes in autumn.
S. calamagrostis. See *Achnatherum calamagrostis.*
S. gigantea illus. p.181.

STOKESIA (Compositae)
Genus of one species of evergreen, summer-flowering perennial. Fully hardy. Requires sun or semi-shade and fertile, well-drained soil. Propagate by division in spring or by seed in autumn.
S. laevis illus. p.242. **'Blue Star'** is an evergreen, basal-rosetted perennial. H and S 12–18in (30–45cm). Zones 5–8. Bears cornflowerlike, deep blue flower heads singly at stem tips in summer. Has rosettes of narrowly lance-shaped, dark green leaves.

STOMATIUM (Aizoaceae)
Genus of mat-forming, perennial succulents with short stems, each bearing 4–6 pairs of solid, 3-angled or semi-cylindrical leaves often with toothed edges and incurved tips. Frost tender, min. 41°F (5°C). Needs sun and well-drained soil. Propagate by seed or stem cuttings in spring or summer.

S. agninum. Mat-forming, perennial succulent. H 2in (5cm), S 3ft (1m) or more. Zone 10. Has solid, 3-angled or semi-cylindrical, soft gray-green leaves, 1½–2cm (4–5cm) long, often without teeth. In summer, fragrant, daisylike, yellow flowers, ³/4–2in (2–5cm) across, open in evening.
S. patulum. Mat-forming, perennial succulent. H 1¼in (3cm), S 3ft (1m). Zone 10. Has semi-cylindrical, gray-green leaves, each ³/4in (2cm) long, with rough dots and 2–9 teethlike tubercles on upper surface. Bears ³/4in (2cm) wide, fragrant, daisylike, pale yellow flowers in evening in summer.

Strangweia spicata. See *Bellevalia hyacinthoides.*

STRANVAESIA (Rosaceae)
Genus of evergreen, summer-flowering trees and shrubs, grown for their foliage and fruits; is sometimes included in *Photinia.* Fully to half hardy. Grows in sun or partial shade and needs fertile, well-drained soil. Propagate by semi-ripe cuttings in summer or by seed in autumn. Is susceptible to fireblight.
S. davidiana illus. p.67.
S. nussia. Evergreen, spreading tree. H and S 20ft (6m). Half hardy, zone 9. Has oblong, leathery, glossy, dark green leaves and saucer-shaped, 5-petaled, white flowers in mid-summer, followed by rounded, orange-red fruits.

STRATIOTES (Hydrocharitaceae)
Genus of semi-evergreen, perennial, submerged, free-floating water plants, grown for their foliage. Fully hardy. Requires sun. Grows in any depth of cool water. Thin plants as required to prevent overcrowding. Propagate by separating young plants from runners in summer.
S. aloides illus. p.373.

STRELITZIA (Strelitziaceae)
Bird-of-paradise flower
Genus of large, evergreen, tufted, clump-forming, palmlike perennials, grown for their showy flowers. Frost tender, min. 41–50°F (5–10°C). Grow in fertile, well-drained soil and in bright light shaded from direct sun in summer. Reduce watering in low temperatures. Propagate by seed or division of suckers in spring.
S. nicolai illus. p.194.
S. reginae illus. p.224.

Streptanthera cuprea. See *Sparaxis elegans.*
Streptanthera elegans. See *Sparaxis elegans.*

STREPTOCARPUS (Gesneriaceae)
Genus of perennials, some of which are evergreen, with showy flowers. Frost tender, min. 50–59°F (10–15°C). Grow in a humid atmosphere in humus-rich, moist soil and in bright light away from direct sunlight. Avoid wetting leaves when watering; water less during cold periods. Propagate by seed, if available, in spring, by division after flowering, or by tip cuttings from bushy species or leaf

cuttings from stemless species in spring or summer.
S. caulescens illus. p.233.
S. 'Constant Nymph' illus. p.259.
S. 'Nicola' illus. p.257.
S. rexii (Cape primrose). Stemless perennial. H to 10in (25cm), S to 20in (50cm). Zone 10. Has a rosette of strap-shaped, wrinkled, green leaves. Stems, each 6in (15cm) or more long, bear loose clusters of funnel-shaped, pale blue or mauve flowers, 2in (5cm) long and with darker lines, at any time of year.
S. saxorum illus. p.241.

STREPTOSOLEN (Solanaceae)
Genus of one species of evergreen or semi-evergreen, loosely scrambling shrub, grown for its flowers. Frost tender, min. 45–50°F (7–10°C). Requires full sun and humus-rich, well-drained soil. Water freely when in full growth, less at other times. After flowering or in spring, remove flowered shoots and tie in new growths. Propagate by softwood or semi-ripe cuttings in summer.
S. jamesonii illus. p.178.

STROBILANTHES (Acanthaceae)
Genus of perennials and evergreen sub-shrubs, grown for their flowers. Frost hardy to frost tender, min. 59°F (15°C). Prefers semi-shade. Grow in fertile, well-drained soil. Propagate by seed, basal stem cuttings, or division in spring.
S. atropurpureus illus. p.220.

STROMANTHE (Marantaceae)
Genus of evergreen, creeping perennials, grown mainly for their foliage. Frost tender, min. 59°F (15°C). Prefers high humidity and partial shade. Grow in open soil or compost, use soft water if possible, and do not allow to dry out completely. Propagate by division in spring.
S. sanguinea. Strong-growing, evergreen, creeping perennial. H and S to 5ft (1.5m). Zone 10. Lance-shaped leaves, to 18in (45cm) long, are glossy, green above with paler midribs, reddish below. Bears panicles of small, 3-petaled, white flowers in axils of showy, bright red bracts, usually in spring but also in summer-autumn.

STROMBOCACTUS (Cactaceae)
Genus of extremely slow-growing, hemispherical to cylindrical, perennial cacti. Takes 5 years from seed to reach ½in (1cm) high. Funnel-shaped flowers are 1½in (4cm) across. Frost tender, min. 41°F (5°C). Needs sun and very well-drained soil. Is difficult to grow and very susceptible to overwatering. Propagate by seed or grafting in spring or summer.
S. disciformis illus. p.390.

STRONGYLODON (Leguminosae)
Genus of evergreen, woody-stemmed, twining climbers, grown for their large, clawlike flowers. Frost tender, min. 64°F (18°C). Needs humus-rich, moist but well-drained soil and partial shade in summer. Water freely when in full growth, less at other times.

Provide support. If necessary, thin crowded stems in spring. Propagate by seed or stem cuttings in summer or by layering in spring.
S. macrobotrys illus. p.164.

STUARTIA. See STEWARTIA.

STYLIDIUM (Stylidiaceae)
Genus of perennials with grasslike leaves, grown for their unusual flowers that have fused, "triggered" stamens adapted for pollination by insects. Frost tender, min. 50°F (10°C). Grow in fertile soil and in bright light. Propagate by division or seed in spring.
S. graminifolium (Trigger plant). Rosetted perennial. H and S to 6in (15cm) or more. Zone 10. Grasslike, stiff, dark green leaves, with toothed margins, rise from ground level. Tiny, pale pinkish mauve flowers are carried in narrow spikes, to over 12in (30cm) long, in summer.

STYLOPHORUM (Papaveraceae)
Genus of spring-flowering perennials with large, deeply lobed leaves, nearly all as basal rosettes. Fully hardy. Needs semi-shade and humus-rich, moist, peaty soil. Propagate by division in spring or by seed in autumn.
S. diphyllum illus. p.290.

STYRAX (Styracaceae)
Genus of deciduous, summer-flowering trees and shrubs, grown for their foliage and flowers. Fully hardy to frost tender, min. 45–50°F (7–10°C). Prefers a sheltered position in sun or semi-shade and moist, neutral to acid soil. Propagate by softwood cuttings in summer or by seed in autumn.
S. japonica illus. p.50.
S. obassia (Fragrant snowbell). Deciduous, spreading tree. H 40ft (12m), S 22ft (7m). Fully hardy, zones 6–9. Produces long, spreading clusters of fragrant, bell- to funnel-shaped, white flowers in early summer and has broad, rounded, deep green leaves.
S. officinalis illus. p.86.
S. wilsonii illus. p.106.

Submatucana aurantiaca. See *Borzicactus aurantiacus.*

SULCOREBUTIA (Cactaceae)
Genus of flattened spherical to columnar, perennial cacti, mostly offsetting to form clumps, with flowers near stem bases. Has elongated areoles, and many species have tuberous roots. Some species grow better when grafted. Frost tender, min. 50°F (10°C). Needs sun or partial shade and well-drained soil—all those selected below prefer a sunny position. Propagate by seed or stem cuttings in spring or summer.
S. arenacea illus. p.400.
S. rauschii. Flattened spherical, perennial cactus. H 2in (5cm), S 4in (10cm). Zone 10. Gray-green stem bears very short, comblike, golden or black spines. Carries 1¼in (3cm) wide, flattish, deep purple flowers in spring. Grows better when grafted.
S. tiraquensis illus. p.394.

SUTERA (Scrophulariaceae)
Genus of annuals, perennials, and evergreen shrubs, suitable as summer bedding plants. Frost tender, min. 41°F (5°C). Needs a warm, sunny situation and any well-drained soil. Propagate by seed or division in spring or by softwood cuttings in summer.
S. grandiflora. Much-branched, sub-shrubby perennial. H 3ft (1m), S 12–18in (30–45cm). Zones 9–10. Produces terminal racemes of tubular, 5-lobed, frilled, deep purple flowers from mid-summer to autumn. Has oval to oblong, round-toothed leaves.

SUTHERLANDIA (Leguminosae)
Genus of evergreen shrubs, grown for their flowers and fruits. Frost tender, min. 45–50°F (7–10°C). Requires full light and fertile, well-drained soil. Water potted specimens freely when in full growth, moderately at other times. Remove old, twiggy stems at ground level in late winter. Propagate by seed in spring. Red spider mite may be troublesome.
S. frutescens illus. p.133.

SWAINSONA (Leguminosae)
Genus of annuals, evergreen perennials, sub-shrubs, and shrubs, grown for their flowers. Frost tender, min. 41–5°F (5–7°C). Needs full light or partial shade and humus-rich, well-drained soil. Water freely when in active growth, moderately at other times. Propagate by seed in spring or by semi-ripe cuttings in summer.
S. galegifolia (Darling pea). Evergreen, sprawling, loose sub-shrub. H 2–4ft (60cm–1.2m), S 1–2ft (30–60cm). Zones 9–10. Leaves have 11–25 narrowly oval, mid- to deep green leaflets. Bears pealike, red, pink, purple, blue, or yellow flowers in late spring and summer. Remove old, flowered shoots in late winter.

SYCOPSIS (Hamamelidaceae)
Genus of evergreen trees and shrubs, grown for their foliage and flowers. Frost hardy. Needs a sheltered position in sun or semi-shade and fertile, not too dry, peaty soil. Propagate by semi-ripe cuttings in summer.
S. sinensis. Evergreen, upright shrub. H 15ft (5m), S 12ft (4m). Zones 7–9. Leaves are oval, glossy, and dark green. Flowers lack petals but have showy, dense clusters of red-tinged, yellow anthers in late winter or early spring.

SYMPHORICARPOS
(Caprifoliaceae)
Genus of deciduous shrubs, with inconspicuous, small, bell-shaped flowers, grown mainly for their clusters of showy, long-persistent fruits. Fully hardy. Requires sun or semi-shade and fertile soil. Propagate by softwood cuttings in summer or by division in autumn.
S. albus (Snowberry). var. **laevigatus** is a vigorous, deciduous, dense shrub, part upright, part arching. H and S 6ft (2m). Zones 4–7. Large, marblelike, white fruits follow pink flowers borne in summer. Rounded leaves are dark green.

S. × *chenaultii* **'Hancock'**. Deciduous, procumbent, dense shrub. H 3ft (1m), S 10ft (3m). Zones 5–9. Has oval, bronze leaves maturing to bright green. White flowers appear from early to mid-summer. Small, spherical, deep lilac-pink fruits are sparsely borne. Makes excellent ground cover.
S. orbiculatus (Coralberry, Indian currant). Deciduous, bushy, dense shrub. H and S 6ft (2m). Zones 3–9. Has white or pink flowers in late summer and early autumn, then spherical, deep purplish red fruits. Oval leaves are dark green. Does best after a hot summer. **'Foliis Variegatis'** (syn. *S.o.* 'Variegatus') illus. p.136.

SYMPHYANDRA (Campanulaceae)
Genus of short-lived, summer-flowering perennials, best grown as biennials. Suits large rock gardens and bases of banks. Fully hardy. Needs sun and well-drained soil. Propagate by seed in autumn. Self seeds readily.
S. armena. Upright or spreading perennial. H 1–2ft (30–60cm), S 1ft (30cm). Zones 6–8. Produces panicles of upright, bell-shaped, blue or white flowers in summer. Leaves are oval, irregularly toothed, hairy, and green.
S. pendula. Arching perennial. H 1–2ft (30–60cm), S 1ft (30cm). Zones 6–8. Produces panicles of pendent, bell-shaped, cream flowers in summer. Has oval, hairy, pale green leaves. Becomes woody at base with age.
S. wanneri illus. p.297.

SYMPHYTUM (Boraginaceae)
Comfrey
Genus of vigorous, coarse perennials, best suited to wild gardens. Fully hardy. Prefers sun or semi-shade and moist soil. Propagate by division in spring or by seed in autumn; usually self seeds naturally. Propagate named cultivars by division only.
S. caucasicum illus. p.197.
S. grandiflorum. Clump-forming perennial. H 10in (25cm), S 24in (60cm). Zones 5–9. Has lance-shaped, hairy, rich green leaves. Bears one-sided racemes of tubular, creamy flowers in spring. Makes good ground cover.
S. **'Hidcote Blue'**. Clump-forming perennial. H 20in (50cm), S 24in (60cm). Zones 5–9. Is similar to *S. grandiflorum*, but has pale blue flowers.
S. × *uplandicum* (Russian comfrey). **'Variegatum'** illus. p.199.

SYMPLOCOS (Symplocaceae)
Genus of evergreen or deciduous trees and shrubs, of which only the species described is in general cultivation. This is grown for its flowers and fruits. Fruits are most prolific when several plants are grown together. Fully hardy. Needs full sun and fertile soil. Propagate by seed in autumn.
S. paniculata illus. p.106.

SYNADENIUM (Euphorbiaceae)
Genus of evergreen, semi-succulent shrubs, grown for their foliage. Frost tender, min. 45–50°F (7–10°C). Requires full light and fertile, freely draining soil. Water potted plants

moderately, less in winter. Prune in late winter if necessary. Propagate by seed in spring or by softwood cuttings in summer.
S. grantii (African milkbush). Evergreen, erect, robust-stemmed shrub. H 10–12ft (3–4m), S 6ft (2m) or more. Zone 10. Has very small, red flowers in autumn, largely concealed by lance-shaped to oval, glossy, rich green leaves. Glowing leaves of **'Rubra'** are red-purple beneath, purplish green above.

SYNGONIUM (Araceae)
Genus of evergreen, woody-stemmed, root climbers, grown for their ornamental foliage. Flowers are seldom produced in cultivation. Frost tender, min. 61–4°F (16–18°C). Needs partial shade and humus-rich, well-drained soil. Water moderately, less in low temperatures. Provide support, ideally moss poles. Remove young stem tips to promote branching. Propagate by leaf-bud or stem-tip cuttings in summer.
S. auritum, syn. *Philodendron auritum* of gardens, *P. trifoliatum* (Five fingers). Fairly slow-growing, evergreen, woody-stemmed, root climber. H 3–6ft (1–2m). Zone 10. Has glossy, rich green leaves divided into 3, sometimes 5, oval leaflets, the central one the largest.
S. erythrophyllum. Slow-growing, evergreen, root climber with slender, woody stems. H 3ft (1m) or more. Zone 10. Young plants have arrowhead-shaped leaves, flushed purple beneath. Leaves on mature plants have 3 lobes or leaflets and thicker, longer stems.
S. hoffmannii. Moderately vigorous, evergreen, woody-stemmed, root climber. H 6–10ft (2–3m). Zone 10. Young plants have arrowhead-shaped leaves; mature ones have leaves divided into 3 gray-green leaflets with silvery white veins.
S. podophyllum, syn. *Nephthytis triphylla* of gardens, illus. p.178. **'Trileaf Wonder'** illus. p.177.

SYNNOTIA (Iridaceae)
Genus of spring-flowering corms, with fans of lance-shaped leaves, grown for their loose spikes of flowers, each with 6 unequal petals, hooded like a small gladiolus. Half hardy. Needs sun and well-drained soil. Plant in autumn. Dry off after flowering. Propagate by seed or offsets in autumn.
S. variegata. Spring-flowering corm. H 4–14in (10–35cm), S 3–4in (8–10cm). Zones 9–10. Produces erect leaves in a basal fan. Flowers are long-tubed with upright, purple, upper petals and narrower, pale yellowish purple, lower ones curving downwards. var. *metelerkampiae* has smaller flowers.

SYNTHYRIS (Scrophulariaceae)
Genus of evergreen or deciduous, spring-flowering perennials with gently spreading, rhizomatous rootstocks. Is useful for rock gardens and peat beds. Fully hardy. Prefers partial shade and moist soil. Propagate in late spring by seed or division.

S. reniformis. Evergreen, clump-forming perennial. H 3–4in (8–10cm), S 6in (15cm). Zones 5–8. Has kidney-shaped to rounded, toothed, dark green leaves and, in spring, short, dense racemes of small, bell-shaped, blue flowers.
S. stellata illus. p.309.

SYRINGA (Oleaceae)
Lilac
Genus of deciduous shrubs and trees, grown for their dense panicles of small, tubular flowers, which are usually extremely fragrant. Fully hardy. Needs sun and deep, fertile, well-drained, preferably alkaline soil. Obtain plants on their own roots, as grafted plants usually sucker freely. Remove flower heads from newly planted lilacs, and dead-head for first few years. Cut out weak shoots in winter and, to maintain shape, prune after flowering. Straggly, old plants may be cut back hard in winter, but the following season's flowers will then be lost. Propagate by softwood cuttings in summer. Leaf miners, leaf spot, and lilac blight may be troublesome.
S. **'Belle de Nancy'**. Deciduous, upright, then spreading shrub. H and S 15ft (5m). Zones 3–8. Large, dense panicles of fragrant, tubular, double, mauve-pink flowers open in late spring from purple-red buds. Leaves are heart-shaped and dark green.
S. **'Bellicent'**. Deciduous, upright, then arching shrub. H 12ft (4m), S 5m (15ft). Zones 4–8. Large panicles of fragrant, tubular, single, clear pink flowers are borne above oval, dark green leaves in late spring and early summer.
S. **'Blue Hyacinth'** illus. p.90.
S. **'Charles Joly'** illus. p.90.
S. × *chinensis* (Rouen lilac). Deciduous, arching shrub. H and S 4m (12ft). Zones 6–8. Large, arching panicles of fragrant, tubular, single, lilac-purple flowers appear in late spring. Oval leaves are dark green. **'Alba'** has white flowers.
S. **'Clarke's Giant'**. Vigorous, deciduous, upright, then spreading shrub. H and S 15ft (5m). Zones 4–8. Large panicles of fragrant, tubular, single, lavender flowers, mauve-pink within, open from mauve-pink buds from mid- to late spring. Has heart-shaped, dark green leaves.
S. **'Congo'**. Deciduous, upright, then spreading shrub. H and S 15ft (5m). Zones 3–8. Fragrant, tubular, single, deep lilac-purple flowers, purplish red in bud, are borne in large panicles above heart-shaped, dark green leaves in late spring.
S. emodi (Himalayan lilac). Vigorous, deciduous, upright shrub. H 15ft (5m), S 12ft (4m). Zones 7–8. Produces unpleasantly scented, tubular, single, very pale lilac flowers in large, upright panicles in early summer. Has large, oval, dark green leaves.
S. **'Esther Staley'** illus. p.89.
S. **'Fountain'**. Vigorous, deciduous, arching, open shrub. H 12ft (4m), S 15ft (5m). Zones 3–8. Large, nodding panicles of fragrant, tubular, single, deep pink flowers are borne above

large, oval, dark green leaves in early summer.
S. **'Isabella'**. Vigorous, deciduous, upright shrub. H and S 12ft (4m). Zones 4–8. Has large, nodding panicles of fragrant, tubular, single, lilac-purple flowers, almost white within, in early summer, and large, oval, dark green leaves.
S. **'Katherine Havemeyer'**. Deciduous, upright, then spreading shrub. H and S 15ft (5m). Zones 3–8. Large, fragrant, tubular, double, lavender purple, then lavender pink flowers are borne in dense, conical panicles in late spring. Leaves are heart-shaped and green.
S. **'Mme. Antoine Buchner'** illus. p.90.
S. **'Mme. Lemoine'** illus. p.86.
S. **'Maréchal Foch'** illus. p.89.
S. **'Maud Notcutt'**. Deciduous, upright, then spreading shrub. H and S 15ft (5m). Zones 3–8. Produces large panicles of fragrant, tubular, single, pure white flowers above heart-shaped, dark green leaves in late spring.
S. meyeri **'Palibin'**, syn. *S. palibiniana* of gardens, *S. velutina* of gardens. Slow-growing, deciduous, bushy, dense shrub. H and S 5ft (1.5m). Zones 4–7. Bears dense panicles of fragrant, tubular, single, lilac-pink flowers in late spring and early summer. Has small, oval, deep green leaves.
S. microphylla. Deciduous, bushy shrub. H and S 6ft (2m). Zones 5–8. Small panicles of very fragrant, tubular, single, pink flowers appear in early summer, and often again in autumn, amid oval, green leaves. **'Superba'** illus. p.108.
S. palibiniana of gardens. See *S. meyeri* 'Palibin'.
S. × *persica* illus. p.99.
S. **'Primrose'** illus. p.90.
S. reticulata. Deciduous, broadly conical tree or shrub. H 30ft (10m), S 20ft (6m). Zones 4–7. Large panicles of fragrant, tubular, single, creamy white flowers open above oval, taper-pointed, bright green leaves from early to mid-summer.
S. **'Souvenir de Louis Späth'**. Deciduous, upright, then spreading shrub. H and S 15ft (5m). Zones 3–8. Long, slender panicles of fragrant, tubular, single, deep purplish red flowers are borne profusely above heart-shaped, dark green leaves in late spring.
S. velutina of gardens. See *S. meyeri* 'Palibin'.
S. yunnanensis illus. p.88.

SYZYGIUM (Myrtaceae)
Genus of evergreen shrubs and trees, grown for their overall appearance. Frost tender, min. 50–56°F (10–13°C). Prefers full light (but tolerates some shade) and fertile, well-drained soil. Water potted plants freely when in full growth, moderately at other times. Is very tolerant of pruning, but is best grown naturally. Propagate by seed in spring or by semi-ripe cuttings in summer.
S. paniculatum, syn. *Eugenia australis*, *E. paniculata*, illus. p.54.

T

TABEBUIA (Bignoniaceae)
Genus of deciduous or evergreen, mainly spring-flowering trees, grown for their flowers and for shade. Frost tender, min. 61–4°F (16–18°C). Requires full light and fertile, well-drained but not dry soil. Pot-grown plants are unlikely to flower. Pruning, other than shaping while young in autumn, is not needed. Propagate by seed or air-layering in spring or by semi-ripe cuttings in summer.
T. chrysotricha illus. p.69.
T. donnell-smithii. See *Cybistax donnell-smithii.*
T. rosea (Pink trumpet tree). Fast-growing, evergreen, rounded tree, deciduous in cool climates. H and S 50ft (15m) or more. Zone 10. Leaves have 5 oval leaflets. Bears trumpet-shaped, rose- to lavender pink, or white, flowers, with yellow throats, in terminal clusters in spring.

TACCA (Taccaceae)
Genus of perennials with rhizomes, grown for their curious flowers. Frost tender, min. 64°F (18°C). Needs a fairly humid atmosphere, partial shade, and peaty soil. Water sparingly during resting period in winter. Propagate by division or seed, if available, in spring.
T. chantrieri (Bat flower, Cat's whiskers). Clump-forming, rhizomatous perennial. H and S 1ft (30cm). Zone 10. Narrowly oblong, stalked, arching leaves are 1¹/₂ft (45cm) or more long. In summer produces flower umbels with green or purplish bracts on stems up to 2ft (60cm) long. Individual flowers are nodding, bell-shaped, 6-petaled, and green, turning purple with long, pendent, maroon to purple threads.
T. leontopetaloides (East Indian arrowroot, South Sea arrowroot). Clump-forming, rhizomatous perennial. H and S 1¹/₂ft (45cm). Zone 10. Green leaves, to 3ft (1m) long, are deeply 3-lobed, each lobe also divided, on stalks to over 3ft (1m). In summer, on stems up to 3ft (1m) long, flower umbels are produced with 4–12 purple or brown bracts and 20–40 small, 6-petaled, yellow or purplish green flowers, with long, purple to brown threads. Rhizomes yield edible starch.

Tacitus bellus. See *Graptopetalum bellum.*

Tacsonia mollissima. See *Passiflora mollissima.*
Tacsonia van-volxemii. See *Passiflora antioquiensis.*

TAGETES (Compositae)
Marigold
Genus of annuals that flower continuously throughout summer and until the autumn frosts. Is useful as bedding plants and for edging. Half hardy. Grow in sun and in fertile, well-drained soil. Dead-head to ensure a long flowering period. Propagate by seed sown under glass in mid-spring. Is prone to slugs, snails, and botrytis.
T. erecta (African marigold, Aztec marigold). Fast-growing, upright, bushy annual. Tall, H 2–3ft (60cm–1m), S 1–1¹/₂ft (30–45cm); intermediate, H and S 1¹/₂ft (45cm); and dwarf, H 1ft (30cm), S 1–1¹/₂ft (30–45cm), Erecta group hybrids are available. All have very deeply divided, aromatic, glossy, deep green leaves and daisylike, double flower heads, 2in (5cm) wide, in summer and early autumn.
  'Crackerjack' (tall) illus. p.282.
  'Galore' (intermediate) has very large, double, golden yellow flower heads.
  'Gold Coins' (tall) illus. p.280.
  Inca Series (dwarf) has double flower heads in single or mixed colors, including yellow, orange, and gold.
  Jubilee Series (tall) has large, double flower heads in white, yellow, orange, or cream.
  'Toreador' (tall) has very large, double, deep orange flower heads.
T. 'Lemon Gem'. Fast-growing, bushy annual. H and S 6in (15cm). Very finely divided, pale green leaves are pleasantly aromatic. Daisylike, single, lemon yellow flower heads, 1in (2.5cm) wide, appear in summer and early autumn.
T. 'Nell Gwyn'. Fast-growing, bushy annual. H and S to 1ft (30cm). Has very feathery, aromatic, deep green leaves. Large, daisylike, single, deep yellow flower heads, with dark red centers, are produced in summer and early autumn.
T. 'Paprika' illus. p.284.
T. patula (French marigold). Fast-growing, bushy annual. H and S to 1ft (30cm). Has deeply divided, aromatic, deep green leaves. Single or carnation-like, double flower heads, in shades of yellow, orange, red, or mahogany, are borne in summer and early autumn.
  Bonita Series, H 10in (25cm), has double flower heads in a wide range of colors. Boy-o-boy Series, H and S 6in (15cm), has double flower heads in shades of yellow, mahogany, or orange.
  'Cinnabar' illus. p.273. Flower heads of 'Honeycomb', H 10in (25cm), S 8in (20cm), are crested, double, and yellow-and-reddish orange. 'Naughty Marietta' illus. p.282. 'Orange Winner' illus. p.284. 'Spanish Brocade', H and S 8in (20cm), has large, double, red-and-gold flower heads.
T. 'Tangerine Gem' illus. p.284.

TALINUM (Portulacaceae)
Genus of summer-flowering perennials, some of which are evergreen, grown for their flowers and succulent foliage. Is useful for rock gardens, alpine houses, and as pot plants. Fully hardy to frost tender, min. 45°F (7°C). Needs sun and gritty, not too dry, well-drained soil. Propagate by seed in autumn.

T. okanoganense. Cushion- or mat-forming, prostrate perennial. H to 1¹/₂in (4cm), S to 4in (10cm). Fully hardy, zones 8–10. Succulent stems bear tufts of cylindrical, succulent, grayish green leaves and, in summer, tiny, cup-shaped, white flowers. Is excellent in an alpine house.

TAMARINDUS (Leguminosae)
Genus of one species of evergreen tree, grown for its edible fruits and overall appearance as well as for shade. Frost tender, min. 59–64°F (15–18°C). Needs full light and well-drained soil. Propagate by seed or air-layering in spring.
T. indica (Tamarind). Slow-growing, evergreen, rounded tree. H and S to 80ft (25m). Zone 10. Leaves have 10–15 pairs of oblong to elliptic, bright green leaflets. Produces profuse racemes of asymmetric, 5-petaled, pale yellow flowers, veined red, in summer, then long, brownish pods containing edible but acidic pulp.

TAMARIX (Tamaricaceae)
Tamarisk
Genus of deciduous or evergreen shrubs and trees, grown for their foliage, habit, and abundant racemes of small flowers. In mild areas is very wind-resistant and thrives in exposed, coastal positions, making excellent hedges. Fully to frost hardy. Requires sun and fertile, well-drained soil. Restrict growth by cutting back in spring; trim hedges at same time. Propagate by semi-ripe cuttings in summer or by hardwood cuttings in winter.
T. gallica. Deciduous, spreading shrub or tree. H 12ft (4m), S 20ft (6m). Frost hardy, zones 6–9. Purple, young shoots are clothed with tiny, scalelike, blue-gray leaves. Star-shaped, pink flowers are borne in slender racemes in summer.
T. pentandra. See *T. ramosissima.*
T. ramosissima, syn. *T. pentandra,* illus. p.88.

TANACETUM (Compositae)
Genus of perennials, some of which are evergreen, often with aromatic foliage, grown for their daisylike flower heads. Fully to frost hardy. Grow in sun and in fertile, well-drained soil. Propagate by division in spring.
T. argenteum, syn. *Achillea argentea,* illus. p.300.
T. coccineum, syn. *Chrysanthemum coccineum, Pyrethrum roseum* (Pyrethrum). 'Brenda' (syn. *Pyrethrum* 'Brenda') illus. p.197. 'Eileen May Robinson' is an upright perennial. H to 30in (75cm), S 18in (45cm). Fully hardy, zones 5–9. Has slightly aromatic, feathery, recurved leaves, 2in (5cm) long. In summer bears strong-stemmed, pink flower heads, 2in (5cm) or more wide, with yellow centers. Is useful for cut flowers. 'Mrs. James Kelway' has beige flower heads ageing to pink.
T. densum subsp. *amani* illus. p.301.
T. haradjanii, syn. *Chrysanthemum haradjanii.* Evergreen, mat-forming, woody-based perennial with a tap root. H and S 9–15in (23–38cm). Frost hardy, zones 8–9. Has broadly lance-shaped, much-divided, silvery gray leaves. Has terminal clusters of bright yellow flower heads in summer. Is useful for a rock garden or alpine house.

TANAKAEA (Saxifragaceae)
Genus of one species of evergreen, spreading perennial, grown for its foliage and flowers. Is suitable for rock gardens and peat beds. Fully hardy. Needs partial shade and well-drained, peaty, sandy soil. Propagate by runners in spring.
T. radicans. Evergreen, dense, basal-rosetted perennial. H 2¹/₂–3in (6–8cm), S 8in (20cm). Zones 6–8. Leaves are narrowly oval to heart-shaped, leathery and mid- to dark green. Bears small panicles of tiny, outward-facing, star-shaped, white flowers in late spring.

TAPEINOCHILUS (Zingiberaceae)
Genus of mostly evergreen perennials, grown for their colorful, leaflike bracts. Frost tender, min. 64°F (18°C). Needs high humidity, partial shade, and humus-rich soil. Is not easy to grow successfully in pots. Propagate by division in spring. Red spider mite may be a problem with pot-grown plants.
T. ananassae. Evergreen, tufted perennial. H to 6ft (2m), S 2¹/₂ft (75cm). Zone 10. Non-flowering stems are erect and unbranched, with narrowly oval, long-pointed leaves, to 6in (15cm) long. Flowering stems are leafless, to over 3ft (1m) long, and, in summer, bear ovoid, dense spikes, 6in (15cm) or more long, of small, tubular, yellow flowers. Showy, recurved, hard, scarlet bracts enclose and almost hide flowers.

TAXODIUM (Taxodiaceae). See CONIFERS.
T. distichum illus. p.76.

TAXUS (Taxaceae). See CONIFERS.
T. baccata (English yew). Slow-growing conifer with a broadly conical, later domed crown. H 30–50ft (10–15m), S 15–30ft (5–10m). Fully hardy, zones 6–7. Needlelike, flattened leaves are dark green. Female plants bear cup-shaped, fleshy, bright red fruits; only the red part, not the seed, is edible. Will regrow if cut back. The following forms are H 20–30ft (6–10m), S 15–25ft (5–8m) unless otherwise stated. 'Adpressa' is a shrubby, female form with short, broad leaves. 'Aurea' (Golden yew; illus. p.83) has golden yellow foliage.

'Dovastoniana' is spreading, with weeping branchlets. 'Dovastonii Aurea' (illus. p.83) is similar to *T.b.* 'Dovastoniana', but has golden shoots and yellow-margined leaves. 'Fastigiata', H 30–50ft (10–15m), S 12–15ft (4–5m), has erect branches and dark green foliage that stands out all around shoots; 'Fastigiata Aurea' is similar to *T.b.* 'Fastigiata', but has gold-variegated leaves. 'Repandens', H 2ft (60cm), S 15ft (5m), is a spreading form. 'Semperaurea', H 10ft (3m), S 15ft (5m), has ascending branches with dense, golden foliage. *T. cuspidata* illus. p.81. 'Aurescens' is a spreading, bushy, dwarf conifer. H 1ft (30cm), S 3ft (1m). Fully hardy, zones 5–7. Is hardier than *T. baccata* forms. Needlelike, flattened leaves are deep golden yellow in their first year and mature to dark green. 'Capitata', H 30ft (10m), S 6ft (2m), is upright in habit. 'Densa', H 4ft (1.2m), S 20ft (6m), is a female form with short, erect shoots.
T. x *media* (Anglojap yew). Dense conifer that is very variably shaped. H and S 10–20ft (3–6m). Fully hardy, zones 5–7. Has needlelike, flattened leaves, spreading either side of olive green shoots. Leaves are stiff, broad, and widen abruptly at the base. Fruits are similar to those of *T. baccata*. 'Brownii', H 8ft (2.5m), S 11ft (3.5m), is a dense, globose form with dark green foliage. 'Densiformis', H 6–10ft (2–3m), is dense and rounded, with masses of shoots that have bright green leaves. 'Hicksii', H to 20ft (6m), is columnar and has ascending branches. Male and female forms exist. 'Hillii', H and S 10ft (3m), is a broadly conical to rounded, dense bush with glossy, green leaves. 'Wardii', H 6ft (2m), S 20ft (6m), is a flat, globose, female form.

TECOMA (Bignoniaceae)
Genus of mainly evergreen shrubs and trees, grown for their flowers from spring to autumn. Frost tender, min. 50–55°F (10–13°C). Prefers well-drained soil and full light. Water potted specimens moderately, hardly at all in winter. May be pruned annually after flowering to maintain as a shrub. Propagate by seed in spring or by semi-ripe cuttings in summer. Red spider mite may be troublesome.
T. australis. See *Pandorea pandorana.*
T. capensis. See *Tecomaria capensis.*
T. grandiflora. See *Campsis grandiflora.*
T. radicans. See *Campsis radicans.*
T. ricasoliana. See *Podranea ricasoliana.*
T. stans, syn. *Bignonia stans, Stenolobium stans,* illus. p.68.

TECOMANTHE (Bignoniaceae)
Genus of evergreen, twining climbers, grown for their flowers. Frost tender, min. 61–4°F (16–18°C). Provide humus-rich, well-drained soil and light shade in summer. Water freely when in full growth, less at other times. Provide stems with support. If necessary, thin out crowded stems in spring. Propagate by seed in spring or by semi-ripe cuttings in summer.

T. speciosa. Strong-growing, evergreen, twining climber. H to 30ft (10m) or more. Zone 10. Has leaves of 3 or 5 oval leaflets. Dense clusters of foxglovelike, fleshy-textured, cream flowers, tinged with green, appear in autumn.

TECOMARIA (Bignoniaceae)
Genus of evergreen, shrubby, scrambling climbers, grown for their showy flowers. Frost tender, min. 50°F (10°C). Provide fertile, well-drained soil and full light. Water regularly, less when temperatures are low. Provide support. Thin out crowded stems in spring. Propagate by seed in spring or by semi-ripe cuttings in summer.
T. capensis, syn. *Bignonia capensis, Tecoma capensis* (Cape honeysuckle). Evergreen, scrambling climber, shrublike when young. H 6–10ft (2–3m). Zone 10. Leaves have 5–9 rounded, serrated, glossy, dark green leaflets. Tubular, orange-red flowers are carried in short spikes mainly in spring-summer.

TECOPHILAEA (Tecophilaeaceae)
Genus of spring-flowering corms, rare in cultivation and extinct in the wild, grown for their beautiful flowers. Fully hardy, but because of rarity usually grown in a cold greenhouse or cold frame. Requires sun and well-drained soil. Water in winter and spring. Keep corms dry, but not sunbaked, from early summer to autumn, then replant. Propagate in autumn by seed or offsets.
T. cyanocrocus illus. p.362.
var. *leichtlinii* illus. p.361.

TELEKIA (Compositae)
Genus of summer-flowering perennials, grown for their bold foliage and large flower heads. Fully hardy. Grows in sun or shade and in moist soil. Propagate by division in spring or by seed in autumn.
T. speciosa, syn. *Buphthalmum speciosum.* Upright, spreading perennial. H 4–5ft (1.2–1.5m), S 3–4ft (1–1.2m). Zones 5–8. Green leaves are heart-shaped at base of plant, oval on stems. In late summer, branched stems bear large, daisylike, rich gold flower heads. Is ideal for a pool side or woodland.

TELESONIX (Saxifragaceae)
Genus of one species of rhizomatous perennial, grown for its flowers. Is often included in *Boykinia.* Fully hardy. Needs semi-shade and gritty, well-drained soil. In the absence of deep snow cover, is best grown in large containers in alpine houses. Propagate by semi-ripe cuttings in summer or by seed in autumn.
T. jamesii, syn. *Boykinia jamesii.* Mound-forming, rhizomatous perennial. H and S 6in (15cm). Zones 4–8. Almost woody stems each bear a rosette of kidney-shaped leaves with lacerated edges. In early summer produces open bell-shaped, frilled, pink flowers with green centers.

TELLIMA (Saxifragaceae)
Genus of one species of semi-evergreen, late spring-flowering

perennial. Makes good ground cover and is ideal for cool, semi-shaded woodland gardens and beneath shrubs in sunny borders. Fully hardy. Grows in any well-drained soil. Propagate by division in spring or by seed in autumn.
T. grandiflora (Fringecups). Semi-evergreen, clump-forming perennial. H and S 24in (60cm). Zones 4–8. Has heart-shaped, toothed, hairy, purple-tinted, bright green leaves. Bears racemes of small, bell-shaped, fringed, cream flowers, well above foliage, in late spring. 'Purpurea' illus. p.258.

TELOPEA (Proteaceae)
Genus of evergreen trees and shrubs, grown mainly for their flower heads. Half hardy to frost tender, min. 41°F (5°C). Requires full sun or semi-shade and humus-rich, moist but well-drained, neutral to acid soil. Water potted plants freely when in full growth, moderately at other times. Propagate by seed in spring or by layering in winter.
T. speciosissima illus. p.110.
T. truncata illus. p.98.

TEMPLETONIA (Leguminosae)
Genus of evergreen shrubs, grown for their flowers. Frost tender, min. 45°F (7°C). Prefers full light and freely draining, alkaline soil. Water potted specimens moderately, less in winter. Propagate by seed in spring or by semi-ripe cuttings in summer.
T. retusa (Coral bush). Evergreen, erect, irregularly branched shrub. H 6ft (2m), S 3–5ft (1–1.5m). Zone 10. Has oval to elliptic, leathery, bluish green leaves. Pealike, red flowers, sometimes pink or cream, appear in spring-summer.

TERMINALIA (Combretaceae)
Genus of evergreen trees and shrubs, grown for their overall appearance, edible seeds (nuts), and for shade. Frost tender, min. 61–4°F (16–18°C). Requires full light and well-drained soil. Water potted specimens moderately, scarcely at all when temperatures are low. Pruning is seldom necessary. Propagate by seed in spring.
T. catappa (Indian almond, Tropical almond). Evergreen, rounded tree. H and S 50ft (15m) or more. Zone 10. Has broadly oval, lustrous, green leaves at stem tips. Small, greenish white flowers appear in spring, followed by flattened ovoid, keeled, green to red fruits, each with an edible seed.

TERNSTROEMIA (Theaceae)
Genus of evergreen trees and shrubs, grown for their overall appearance. Half hardy. Requires full sun or semi-shade and humus-rich, well-drained, neutral to acid soil. Water potted specimens freely when in full growth, moderately at other times. Prune in spring if necessary. Propagate by seed when ripe or in spring or by semi-ripe cuttings in late summer.
T. gymnanthera. Evergreen, rounded, dense shrub. H and S 6ft (2m). Zones 8–10. Oval leaves are lustrous, mid- to deep green. In summer, pendent, 5-petaled, white flowers are borne

singly from leaf axils. Pea-sized, berrylike, bright red fruits appear in autumn. Leaves of 'Variegata' are white-bordered with a pink tinge.

Testudinaria elephantipes. See *Dioscorea elephantipes.*

TETRACENTRON (Tetracentraceae)
Genus of one species of deciduous tree, grown for its foliage and catkins. Fully hardy. Needs sun or partial shade and fertile, well-drained soil. Propagate by seed in autumn.
T. sinensis. Deciduous, spreading tree of graceful habit. H and S 30ft (10m) or more. Zones 6–9. Has rounded to oval, finely toothed, dark green leaves and long, slender, yellow catkins in early summer.

TETRANEMA (Scrophulariaceae)
Genus of perennials, grown for their flowers. Frost tender, min. 55°F (13°C). Grow in a light position, shaded from direct sunlight, and in well-drained soil; avoid waterlogging and a humid atmosphere. Propagate by division, or seed if available, in spring.
T. mexicanum. See *T. roseum.*
T. roseum, syn. *T. mexicanum,* illus. p.259.

TETRAPANAX (Araliaceae)
Genus of one species of evergreen, summer- to autumn-flowering shrub, grown for its foliage. Half hardy. Requires full sun or partial shade and humus-rich, moist but well-drained soil. Water potted specimens freely, less in winter. Leggy stems may be cut back to near ground level in winter. Propagate by suckers or seed in early spring.
T. papyriferus, syn. *Fatsia papyrifera,* illus. p.94.

TETRASTIGMA (Vitaceae)
Genus of evergreen, woody-stemmed, tendril climbers, grown for their handsome leaves. Frost tender, min. 59–64°F (15–18°C). Grow in any fertile, well-drained soil, with shade in summer. Water freely while in active growth, less in low temperatures. Provide stems with support; cut out crowded stems in spring. Propagate by layering in spring or by semi-ripe cuttings in summer.
T. voinierianum, syn. *Cissus voinieriana,* illus. p.178.

TEUCRIUM (Labiatae)
Genus of evergreen or deciduous shrubs, sub-shrubs, and perennials, grown for their flowers, foliage (sometimes aromatic), or habit. Fully to half hardy. Needs full sun and well-drained soil. Propagate shrubs and sub-shrubs by softwood or semi-ripe cuttings in summer, perennials by seed or division in spring.
T. aroanium. Evergreen, procumbent, much-branched sub-shrub. H 1in (2.5cm), S 4–6in (10–15cm). Frost hardy, zones 7–10. Has white-haired twigs and oblong to oval leaves that are slightly hairy above, densely hairy below. Produces whorls of small, tubular, 2-lipped, soft purple flowers in summer.

T. fruticans (Shrubby germander, Tree germander). **'Azureum'** is an evergreen, arching shrub. H 6ft (2m), S 12ft (4m). Half hardy, zones 7–10. Has oval, aromatic, gray-green leaves with white undersides and, in summer, tubular, 2-lipped, deep blue flowers with prominent stamens. Cut out dead wood in spring.
T. polium illus. p.319.

THALIA (Marantaceae)
Genus of deciduous, perennial, marginal water plants, grown for their foliage and flowers. Frost tender, min. 45°C (7°C). Needs an open, sunny position in up to 18in (45cm) depth of water. Some species tolerate cool water. Remove fading foliage regularly. Propagate in spring by division or seed.
T. dealbata. Deciduous, perennial, marginal water plant. H 5ft (1.5m), S 2ft (60cm). Zones 9–10. Oval, long-stalked, blue-green leaves have a mealy, white covering. Spikes of narrowly tubular, violet flowers in summer are followed by decorative seed heads. Tolerates cool water.
T. geniculata. Deciduous, perennial, marginal water plant. H 6ft (2m), S 2ft (60cm). Zones 9–10. Has oval, long-stalked, blue-green leaves and, in summer, spikes of narrowly tubular, violet flowers. Needs a warm pool.

THALICTRUM (Ranunculaceae)
Meadow rue
Genus of perennials, grown for their divided foliage and fluffy flower heads. Flowers lack petals, but each has prominent tufts of stamens and 4 or 5 sepals, which rapidly fall. Does well at edges of woodland gardens. Tall species and cultivars make excellent foils in borders for perennials with bolder leaves and flowers. Fully hardy. Requires sun or light shade. Grows in any well-drained soil, although some species prefer cool, moist conditions. Propagate by seed when fresh, in autumn, or by division in spring.
T. aquilegiifolium illus. p.210. **'White Cloud'** illus. p.201.
T. chelidonii. Clump-forming perennial. H 3–5ft (1–1.5m), S 2ft (60cm). Zones 5–9. Has finely divided, green leaves and, in summer, produces panicles of fluffy, 4- or 5-sepaled, mauve flowers. Prefers cool soil that does not dry out.
T. delavayi, syn. *T. dipterocarpum* of gardens. Elegant, clump-forming perennial. H 5–6ft (1.5–2m), S 2ft (60cm). Zones 5–9. Has much-divided, green leaves, above which large panicles of nodding, lilac flowers, with 4 or 5 sepals and prominent, yellow stamens, appear from mid- to late summer. **'Hewitt's Double'** has double flowers.
T. diffusiflorum. Clump-forming perennial. H 3ft (1m), S 1–2ft (30–60cm). Zones 5–9. Has much-divided, basal, green leaves. Slender stems produce large sprays of delicate, drooping, mauve flowers in summer. Prefers cool, moist soil.
T. dipterocarpum of gardens. See *T. delavayi.*

T. flavum. Clump-forming perennial. H 4–5ft (1.2m–1.5m), S 2ft (60cm). Zones 6–9. Has much-divided, glaucous blue-green leaves and, from mid- to late summer, clusters of fluffy, pale yellow flowers on slender stems. **'Illuminator'** is a pale yellow cultivar with bright green foliage.
T. kiusianum. Mat-forming perennial with short runners. H 3in (8cm), S 6in (15cm). Zones 5–8. Has small, fernlike, 3-lobed leaves and, throughout summer, loose clusters of tiny, purple flowers. Is excellent in a peat bed, rock garden, or alpine house. Is difficult to grow in hot, dry areas. Prefers shade and moist, sandy, peaty soil.
T. lucidum illus. p.213.
T. orientale. Spreading perennial with short runners. H 6in (15cm), S 8in (20cm). Zones 5–9. Leaves are fernlike with oval to rounded, lobed leaflets. Bears small, saucer-shaped, blue-mauve to violet flowers, with yellow stamens and large sepals, in late spring.

THAMNOCALAMUS
(Bambusoideae). See GRASSES, BAMBOOS, RUSHES, and SEDGES.
T. falconeri, syn. *Arundinaria falconeri.* Evergreen, clump-forming bamboo. H 15–30ft (5–10m), S 3ft (1m). Half hardy, zones 9–10. Greenish brown stems have a dark purple ring beneath each node. Has 4–6in (10–15cm) long, yellowish green leaves, without visible tessellation, and unimportant flower spikes.
T. spathaceus, syn. *Arundinaria murielae, Sinarundinaria murielae* (Muriel bamboo). Evergreen, clump-forming bamboo. H 12ft (4m), S indefinite. Frost hardy, zones 7–10. Has attractive, gray young culms with loose, light brown sheaths and broad, apple green leaves, each very long, drawn-out at its tip. Flower spikes are unimportant.

THELOCACTUS (Cactaceae)
Genus of spherical to columnar, perennial cacti with tuberculate or ribbed stems. Elongated areoles in crowns produce funnel-shaped flowers. Frost tender, min. 45°F (7°C). Requires sun and well-drained soil. Propagate by seed in spring or summer.
T. bicolor illus. p.392.
T. leucacanthus. Clump-forming, perennial cactus. H 4in (10cm), S 12in (30cm). Zone 10. Spherical to columnar, dark green stem has 8–13 tuberculate ribs. Areoles each bear up to 20 short, golden spines and yellow flowers, 2in (5cm) across, in summer.
T. mcdowellii, syn. *Echinomastus mcdowellii.* Also sometimes included in *Neolloydia.* Spherical, perennial cactus. H 4in (10cm) and S 6in (15cm). Zone 10. Has a tuberculate, dark green stem densely covered with white spines, to 1 1/4in (3cm) long. Violet-red flowers, 1 1/2in (4cm) across, appear in spring-summer.

THELYPTERIS (Polypodiaceae)
Genus of deciduous ferns. Fully hardy. Tolerates sun or semi-shade. Grow in moist or very moist soil. Remove fading fronds regularly. Propagate by division in spring.

T. hexagonoptera, syn. *Dryopteris hexagonoptera* (Broad beech fern). Deciduous fern. H 18in (45cm), S 12in (30cm). Zones 4–8. Broadly lance-shaped, much-divided, green fronds, with oblong to triangular, indented pinnae, arise from a creeping rootstock. Needs a shaded position.
T. oreopteris (Mountain buckler fern, Mountain fern, Mountain wood fern). Deciduous fern. H 2–3ft (60cm–1m), S 1ft (30cm). Zones 5–8. Produces broadly lance-shaped, much-divided fronds, with oblong to lance-shaped, green pinnae.
T. palustris illus. p.186.
T. phegopteris. See *Phegopteris connectilis.*

THERMOPSIS (Leguminosae)
Genus of summer-flowering perennials. Fully hardy. Prefers sun and rich, light soil. Propagate by division in spring or by seed in autumn.
T. caroliniana. Straggling perennial. H 3ft (1m) or more, S 2ft (60cm). Zones 3–8. Produces racemes of pealike, yellow flowers in late summer. Glaucous leaves are divided into 3 oval leaflets.
T. montana illus. p.215.

THESPESIA (Malvaceae)
Genus of evergreen perennials, shrubs, and trees, grown for their flowers. Frost tender, min. 61–4°F (16–18°C). Needs full light and well-drained soil. Water potted plants freely when in full growth, less when temperatures are low. Prune annually in early spring to maintain as a shrub. Propagate by seed in spring or by semi-ripe cuttings in summer. Whitefly and red spider mite may be a nuisance.
T. populnea (Mahoe, Portia oil nut). Evergreen tree, bushy when young, thinning with age. H 40ft (12m) or more, S 10–20ft (3–6m). Zone 10. Leaves are heart-shaped. Intermittently, or all year round if warm enough, produces cup-shaped, yellow flowers, each with a maroon eye, that age to purple. Grows well by the seashore.

THEVETIA (Apocynaceae)
Genus of evergreen shrubs and trees, grown for their flowers from winter to summer. Is related to *Frangipani.* Has poisonous, milky sap. Frost tender, min. 61–4°F (16–18°C). Needs full light and well-drained soil. Water potted specimens moderately, less in winter. Young stems may be tip pruned in winter to promote branching. Propagate by seed in spring or by semi-ripe cuttings in summer.
T. neriifolia. See *T. peruviana.*
T. peruviana, syn. *T. neriifolia,* illus. p.66.

THLADIANTHA (Cucurbitaceae)
Genus of herbaceous or deciduous, tendril climbers, grown for their bell-shaped, yellow flowers and oval to heart-shaped, green leaves. Frost hardy to frost tender, min. 39°F (4°C). Requires a sheltered position in full sun and fertile, well-drained soil. Propagate by seed sown under glass in spring or by division in early spring.
T. dubia illus. p.174.

THLASPI (Cruciferae)
Genus of annuals and perennials, some of which are evergreen, grown for their flowers. Small plants may flower themselves to death, so remove buds for 2 years, to encourage a larger plant. Is difficult to grow at low altitudes and may require frequent renewal from seed. Is good for screes. Fully hardy. Needs sun and moist but well-drained soil. Propagate by seed in autumn.
T. alpinum (Alpine penny-cress). Evergreen, mat-forming perennial. H 2in (5cm), S 4in (10cm). Zones 5–7. Has small, oval, green leaves. Produces racemes of small, 4-petaled, white flowers in spring.
T. bulbosum. Clump-forming, tuberous perennial. H 3in (8cm), S 6–8in (15–20cm). Zones 5–7. Bears broadly oval, glaucous leaves and, in summer, racemes of 4-petaled, dark violet flowers. Suits a rock garden.
T. macrophyllum. See *Pachyphragma macrophyllum.*
T. rotundifolium illus. p.305.

THUJA (Cupressaceae). See CONIFERS.
T. koraiensis (Korean thuja). Upright conifer, sometimes sprawling and shrubby. H 10–30ft (3–10m), S 10–15ft (3–5m). Fully hardy, zones 6–8. Scalelike foliage is bright green or yellow-green above, glaucous silver beneath, and smells of almonds when crushed.
T. occidentalis (American arborvitae, Eastern white cedar, White cedar). Slow-growing conifer with a narrow crown. H 50ft (15m), S 10–15ft (3–5m). Fully hardy, zones 3–8. Has orange-brown bark and flat sprays of scalelike, yellowish green leaves, pale or grayish green beneath, smelling of apples when crushed. Ovoid cones are yellow-green, ripening to brown. **'Caespitosa'** (illus. p.82), H 12in (30cm), S 16in (40cm), is a cushion-shaped, dwarf cultivar. **'Fastigiata'**, H to 50ft (15m), S to 15ft (5m), is broadly columnar, with erect, spreading branches and light green leaves. **'Filiformis'** (illus. p.83), H 5ft (1.5m), S 5–6ft (1.5–2m), forms a mound with pendent, whiplike shoots. **'Hetz Midget'**, H and S 20in (50cm), growing only 1in (2.5cm) each year, is a globose, dwarf form with blue-green foliage. **'Holmstrup'**, H 10–12ft (3–4m), S 3ft (1m), is slow-growing, dense, and conical, with rich green foliage. **'Little Champion'**, H and S 20in (50cm) or more, is a globose, dwarf form, conical when young, with foliage turning brown in winter. **'Lutea Nana'**, H 6ft (2m), S 3–6ft (1–2m), is a dwarf form with golden yellow foliage. **'Rheingold'**, H 10–12ft (3–4m), S 6–12ft (2–4m), is slow-growing, with golden yellow foliage that becomes bronze in winter. **'Smaragd'**, H 6–8ft (2–2.5m), S 2–2 1/2ft (60–75cm), is slow-growing and conical, with erect sprays of bright green leaves. **'Spiralis'**, H 30–50ft (10–15m), S 6–10ft (2–3m), produces foliage in twisted, fernlike sprays. **'Techney'** is a dense, conical form with deep green leaves. **'Woodwardii'**, H 8ft (2.5m), S to 15ft (5m), is very

slow-growing and globose, with green foliage.

T. orientalis, syn. *Biota orientalis*, *Platycladus orientalis* (Biota, Chinese arborvitae, Chinese thuja). Conifer with an irregularly rounded crown. H 30–50ft (10–15m), S 15ft (5m). Fully hardy, zones 6–9. Has fibrous bark and flattened, vertical sprays of scalelike, scentless, dark green leaves. Egg-shaped cones are glaucous gray. **'Aurea Nana'** (illus. p.83), H and S 24in (60cm), is a dwarf cultivar with yellow-green foliage that turns bronze in winter. **'Semperaurea'** (illus. p.83), H 10ft (3m), S 6ft (2m), is compact, with golden leaves.

T. plicata (Western arborvitae). Fast-growing, conical conifer that has great, curving branches low down. H 70–100ft (20–30m), S 15–25ft (5–8m), greater if lower branches self-layer. Fully hardy, zones 6–8. Has red-brown bark, scalelike, glossy, dark green leaves, which have a pineapple aroma when crushed, and erect, ovoid, green cones, ripening to brown. **'Atrovirens'** has darker green foliage. **'Aurea'** has golden yellow foliage. **'Collyer's Gold'** (illus. p.83), H to 6ft (2m), S 3ft (1m), is a dwarf form with yellow, young foliage turning to light green. **'Cuprea'**, H 3ft (1m), S 2½–3ft (75cm–1m), is a conical shrub with copper to bronze-yellow leaves. **'Hillieri'** (illus. p.83), H and S to 3ft (1m), is a slow-growing, dense, rounded, dwarf shrub with mosslike, rich green foliage. **'Stoneham Gold'** (illus. p.83), H 3–6ft (1–2m), S 3ft (1m), is a conical, dwarf form with bright gold foliage. **'Zebrina'**, H 50ft (15m), has leaves banded with yellowish white.

THUJOPSIS (Cupressaceae). See CONIFERS.
T. dolabrata (Hiba). Conical or bushy conifer with a mass of stems. H 30–70ft (10–20m), S 25–30ft (8–10m). Fully hardy, zones 6–9. Foliage is produced in heavy, flat sprays of scalelike leaves, glossy, bright green above, silvery white beneath. Small, rounded cones are blue-gray. **'Variegata'** illus. p.81.

THUNBERGIA (Acanthaceae)
Genus of annual or mainly evergreen, perennial, twining climbers, perennials, and shrubs, grown for their flowers. Half hardy to frost tender, min. 50–59°F (10–15°C). Any fertile, well-drained soil is suitable, with full sun or light shade in summer. Water freely when in full growth, less at other times. Requires support. Thin out crowded stems in early spring. Propagate by seed in spring or by softwood or semi-ripe cuttings in summer.
T. alata illus. p.174.
T. coccinea. Evergreen, woody-stemmed, perennial, twining climber with narrowly oval leaves. H 20ft (6m) or more. Frost tender, min. 59°F (15°C), zone 10. Pendent racemes of tubular, scarlet flowers are produced in winter–spring.
T. grandiflora (Blue trumpet vine). Evergreen, woody-stemmed, perennial, twining climber. H 20–30ft (6–10m). Frost tender, min. 50°F (10°C), zone

10. Oval leaves, 4–8in (10–20cm) long, usually have a few toothlike lobes. Trumpet-shaped, pale to deep violet-blue flowers appear in summer.
T. gregorii illus. p.175.
T. mysorensis illus. p.165.

THYMUS (Labiatae)
Thyme
Genus of evergreen, mat-forming and dome-shaped shrubs, sub-shrubs, and woody-based perennials with aromatic leaves. Is useful for growing on banks, in rock gardens, and as an edging plant. Fully to half hardy. Requires sun and moist but well-drained soil. Propagate by softwood or semi-ripe cuttings in summer.
T. caespititius illus. p.315.
T. carnosus, syn. *T. nitidus* of gardens. Evergreen, spreading shrub. H and S 8in (20cm). Frost hardy, zones 7–8. Has tiny, narrowly oval, aromatic leaves. Erect flowering stems bear whorls of small, 2-lipped, white flowers in summer. Requires a sheltered position.
T. × citriodorus 'Aureus'. Evergreen, spreading shrub. H 4in (10cm), S 4–10in (10–25cm). Frost hardy, zones 6–8. Golden yellow leaves are tiny, rounded to oval, and very fragrant when crushed. Produces terminal clusters of small, 2-lipped, lilac flowers in summer. Cut back in spring. **'Silver Queen'** bears silvery white foliage.
T. herba-barona illus. p.321.
T. leucotrichus illus. p.321.
T. nitidus of gardens. See *T. carnosus*.
T. 'Porlock'. Evergreen, dome-shaped perennial. H 3in (8cm), S 8in (20cm). Fully hardy, zones 4–7. Thin stems are covered in small, rounded to oval, very aromatic, glossy, green leaves. In summer produces clusters of small, 2-lipped, pink flowers.
T. praecox. Evergreen, creeping perennial. H ½in (1cm), S indefinite. Fully hardy, zones 5–7. Prostrate, woody stems are clothed in minute, oval to oblong, aromatic, green leaves. Small, 2-lipped, purple, mauve, or white flowers in small clusters are borne in summer. **'Annie Hall'**, H 2in (5cm), S 8in (20cm), has pale pink flowers and light green leaves. **'Elfin'**, H 2in (5cm), S 4in (10cm), produces emerald green leaves in dense hummocks; occasionally bears purple flowers.
T. pseudolanuginosus. Evergreen, prostrate shrub. H 1–2in (2.5–5cm), S 8in (20cm) or more. Fully hardy, zones 4–7. Has dense mats of very hairy stems bearing tiny, aromatic, gray leaves. Produces 2-lipped, pinkish lilac flowers in leaf axils in summer.
T. vulgaris (Common thyme). Evergreen, woody-based perennial. H 6-12in (15-30cm), S 6-9in (15-22cm). Fully hardy, zones 6–9. Has oval, aromatic, gray-green leaves and bears dense whorls of tiny, purplish white flowers in summer. Makes an ideal edging or pot plant. In cold climates may be grown from seed and treated as an annual.

TIARELLA (Saxifragaceae)
Foamflower
Genus of perennials, some of which

are evergreen, that spread by runners. Is excellent as ground cover. Fully hardy. Tolerates deep shade and prefers moist but well-drained soil. Propagate by division in spring.
T. cordifolia illus. p.287.
T. wherryi. Slow-growing, clump-forming perennial. H 4in (10cm), S 6in (15cm). Zones 5–9. Forms mounds of triangular, lobed, hairy, basal, green leaves, stained dark red and with heart-shaped bases. Produces racemes of tiny, star-shaped, soft pink or white flowers from late spring to early summer.

TIBOUCHINA (Melastomataceae)
Genus of evergreen perennials, sub-shrubs, shrubs, and scandent climbers, grown for their flowers and leaves. Frost tender, min. 41–5°F (5–7°C). Prefers full sun and fertile, well-drained, neutral to acid soil. Water potted specimens freely when in full growth, moderately at other times. Cut back flowered stems, each to 2 pairs of buds, in spring. Tip prune young plants to promote branching. Propagate by greenwood or semi-ripe cuttings in late spring or summer.
T. semidecandra. See *T. urvilleana*.
T. urvilleana, syn. *T. semidecandra*, illus. p.90.

TIGRIDIA (Iridaceae)
Genus of summer-flowering bulbs, grown for their highly colorful but short-lived flowers, rather irislike in shape, with 3 large, outer petals. Half hardy. Needs sun and well-drained soil, with ample water in summer. Plant in spring. Lift in autumn; then partially dry bulbs and store in peat or sand at 46–54°F (8–12°C). Propagate by seed in spring.
T. pavonia illus. p.353.

TILIA (Tiliaceae)
Linden
Genus of deciduous trees, grown for their small, fragrant, cup-shaped flowers and stately habit. Flowers attract bees, but are toxic to them in some cases. Fully hardy. Requires sun or semi-shade and fertile, well-drained soil. Propagate species by seed in autumn, selected forms and hybrids by grafting in late summer. Except for *T. × euchlora*, trees are usually attacked by aphids, which cover growth and ground beneath with sticky honeydew.
T. americana (American linden, Basswood). Deciduous, spreading tree. H 80ft (25m), S 40ft (12m). Zones 3–8. Has large, rounded, sharply toothed, glossy, dark green leaves and, in summer, small, yellowish white flowers.
T. cordata (Small-leaved linden). Deciduous, spreading tree. H 100ft (30m), S 40ft (12m). Zones 4–8. Has small, rounded, glossy, dark green leaves and small, yellowish white flowers in mid-summer. **'Glenleven'** (Glenleven linden), H 60ft (18m), S 30ft (10m), is a rounded to pyramidal, upright tree with a straight trunk and produces clusters of yellow flowers. **'Greenspire'**, S 25ft (8m), is very vigorous and pyramidal in habit, even when young. **'Rancho'** illus. p.53.

T. × euchlora (Caucasian linden, Crimean linden). Deciduous, spreading tree with lower branches that droop with age. H 70ft (20m), S 30ft (10m). Zones 4–7. Rounded, very glossy, deep green leaves turn yellow in autumn. Bears small, yellowish white flowers, toxic to bees, in summer. Is relatively pest-free.
T. × europaea (Common linden, European linden). Vigorous, deciduous, spreading tree. H 120ft (35m), S 50ft (15m). Zones 4–7. Trunk develops many burs. Has rounded, dark green leaves. Small, yellowish white flowers, toxic to bees, appear in summer. Periodically remove shoots from burs at base.
T. henryana. Deciduous, spreading tree. H and S 30ft (10m). Zones 6–8. Broadly heart-shaped, glossy, bright green leaves, fringed with long teeth, are often tinged red when young. Produces masses of small, creamy white flowers in autumn.
T. mongolica (Mongolian linden). Deciduous, spreading, graceful tree. H 50ft (15m), S 40ft (12m). Zones 4–7. Young shoots are red. Broadly heart-shaped, coarsely toothed, glossy, dark green leaves turn yellow in autumn. Small, yellowish white flowers appear in summer.
T. oliveri illus. p.41.
T. 'Petiolaris' illus. p.42.
T. platyphyllos (Bigleaf linden, Large-leaved linden). Deciduous, spreading tree. H 100ft (30m), S 70ft (20m). Zones 4–7. Has rounded, dark green leaves and small, dull yellowish white flowers in mid-summer. **'Princes Street'** is upright, with bright red shoots in winter.
T. tomentosa (European white linden, Silver linden). Deciduous, spreading tree. H 80ft (25m), S 70ft (20m). Zones 5–7. Leaves are large, rounded, sharply toothed, dark green above and white beneath. Very fragrant, small, dull white flowers, toxic to bees, are borne in late summer.

TILLANDSIA (Bromeliaceae)
Genus of evergreen, epiphytic perennials, often rosette-forming, some with branching stems and spirally arranged leaves, all grown for their flowers or overall appearance. Frost tender, min. 45–50°F (7–10°C), zone 10 except where stated otherwise. Requires semi-shade. Provide a rooting medium of equal parts humus-rich soil and either sphagnum moss or bark or plastic chips used for orchid culture. May also be grown on slabs of bark or sections of trees. Using soft water, water moderately in summer, sparingly at other times; spray plants grown on bark or tree sections with water several times a week from mid-spring to mid-autumn. Propagate by offsets or division in spring.
T. argentea (illus. p.222). Evergreen, basal-rosetted, epiphytic perennial. H and S 4–6in (10–15cm). Very narrow, almost threadlike leaves, covered with white scales, are produced in dense, near-spherical rosettes, each with a fleshy, bulblike base. In summer, small, loose racemes of tubular, red flowers are produced.

579

T. caput-medusae (illus. p.222). Evergreen, basal-rosetted, epiphytic perennial. H and S 6in (15cm) or more. Linear, channeled, twisted, and rolled, incurved leaves, covered in gray scales, develop in loose rosettes that have hollow, bulblike bases. In summer, spikes of tubular, violet-blue flowers appear above foliage.

T. cyanea (illus. p.222). Evergreen, basal-rosetted, epiphytic perennial. H and S 10in (25cm). Forms dense rosettes of linear, pointed, channeled, arching, usually deep green leaves. In summer, broadly oval, bladelike spikes of pansy-shaped, deep purple-blue flowers, emerging from pink or red bracts, are produced among foliage.

T. fasciculata (illus. p.222). Evergreen, basal-rosetted, epiphytic perennial. H and S 12in (30cm) or more. Has dense rosettes of narrowly triangular, tapering, arching, green leaves. In summer, flat spikes of tubular, purple-blue flowers emerge from red or reddish yellow bracts, just above leaf tips. Bracts require strong light to develop reddish tones.

T. ionantha (Sky plant). Evergreen, clump-forming, basal-rosetted, epiphytic perennial. H and S 5in (12cm). Has dense rosettes of linear, incurved, arching leaves, covered in gray scales; the inner leaves turn red at flowering time. Spikes of tubular, violet-blue flowers, emerging in summer from narrow, white bracts, are borne just above foliage.

T. lindenii (illus. p.222). Evergreen, basal-rosetted, epiphytic perennial. H and S 16in (40cm). Linear, pointed, channeled, arching, green leaves, with red-brown lines, form dense rosettes. In summer, bladelike spikes of widely pansy-shaped, deep blue flowers, emerging from sometimes pink-tinted, green bracts, are borne just above leaves.

T. recurvata. Evergreen, basal-rosetted, epiphytic perennial. H and S 4–8in (10–20cm). Zones 9–10. Produces long, loose, stemlike, sometimes branched, rosettes of linear, arching to recurved leaves, densely covered in silvery gray scales. In summer, short, dense spikes of small, tubular, pale blue or pale green flowers appear above leaves.

T. stricta (illus. p.222). Evergreen, clump-forming, basal-rosetted, epiphytic perennial. H and S 8–12in (20–30cm). Narrowly triangular, tapering, arching, green leaves, usually with gray scales, are produced in dense rosettes. Large, tubular, blue flowers emerge from drooping, conelike spikes of bright red bracts, usually in summer.

T. usneoides (Spanish-moss; illus. p.222). Evergreen, pendent, epiphytic perennial. H 3ft (1m) or more, S 4–8in (10–20cm). Zones 9–10. Slender, branched, drooping stems bear linear, incurved leaves densely covered in silvery white scales. Inconspicuous, tubular, greenish yellow or pale blue flowers, hidden among foliage, are produced in summer.

TIPUANA (Leguminosae)
Genus of one species of evergreen, spring-flowering tree, grown for its

flowers and overall appearance when mature and for shade. In certain conditions, may be deciduous. Frost tender, min. 50–55°F (10–13°C). Requires full light and fertile, well-drained soil. Container-grown plants will not produce flowers. Young specimens may be pruned in winter. Propagate by seed in spring.
T. speciosa. See *T. tipu*.
T. tipu, syn. *T. speciosa* (Pride-of-Bolivia, Tipa tree, Tipu tree). Fast-growing, mainly evergreen, bushy tree. H 30ft (10m), S 25–30ft (8–10m). Zone 10. Leaves, 10in (25cm) long, have 11–25 oval leaflets. Bears profuse racemes of pealike, bright orange-yellow flowers, 1¼in (3cm) wide, in spring and short, woody, winged, brownish pods in autumn-winter.

TITANOPSIS (Aizoaceae)
Genus of basal-rosetted, perennial succulents eventually forming small, dense clumps. Produces 6–8 opposite pairs of fleshy, triangular leaves, ³⁄₄–1¼in (2–3cm) long, narrow at stems and expanding to straight tips. Frost tender, min. 46°F (8°C). Needs sun and well-drained soil. Propagate by seed in spring or summer.
T. calcarea illus. p.399.
T. schwantesii. Clump-forming, perennial succulent. H 1¼in (3cm), S 4in (10cm). Zone 10. Has a basal rosette of triangular, gray-blue leaves, with rounded corners and covered with small, wartlike, yellow-brown tubercles. Carries daisylike, light yellow flowers, ³⁄₄in (2cm) wide, in summer-autumn.

TITHONIA (Compositae)
Genus of annuals. Half hardy to frost tender, min. 36–9°F (2–4°C). Grow in sun and in fertile, well-drained soil. Provide support and dead-head regularly. Propagate by seed sown under glass in late winter or early spring.
T. rotundifolia (Mexican sunflower). 'Torch' illus. p.284.

TOLMIEA (Saxifragaceae)
Genus of one species of perennial that is sometimes semi-evergreen and is grown as ground cover. Is suitable for cool woodland gardens. Fully hardy. Prefers shade and requires well-drained, neutral to acid soil. Propagate by division in spring or by seed in autumn.
T. menziesii (Piggyback plant, Youth-on-age). Mat-forming perennial, sometimes semi-evergreen. H 18–24in (45–60cm), S 12in (30cm) or more. Zones 6–9. Young plantlets develop where ivy-shaped, green leaves join stem. Has spikes of tiny, nodding, tubular to bell-shaped, green and chocolate brown flowers in spring.

TOLPIS (Compositae)
Genus of summer-flowering annuals and perennials. Fully to half hardy. Grow in sun and in fertile, well-drained soil. Propagate by seed sown outdoors in spring.
T. barbata. Moderately fast-growing, upright, branching annual. H 1½–2ft (45–60cm), S 1ft (30cm). Half hardy.

Has lance-shaped, serrated, green leaves. Daisylike, bright yellow flower heads, 1in (2.5cm) or more wide, with maroon centers, are borne in summer.

Toona sinensis. See *Cedrela sinensis*.

TORENIA (Scrophulariaceae)
Genus of annuals and perennials. Half hardy to frost tender, min. 41°F (5°C). Grow in semi-shade and in a sheltered position in fertile, well-drained soil. Pinch out growing shoots of young plants to encourage a bushy habit. Propagate by seed sown in a greenhouse in early spring.
T. fournieri illus. p.277.

TORREYA (Cephalotaxaceae). See CONIFERS.
T. californica illus. p.79.

TOVARA (Polygonaceae)
Genus of perennials, grown for their foliage. Fully hardy. Tolerates sun or shade. Requires fertile, moist soil. Protect from wind, which may damage leaves. Propagate by division in spring or by cuttings of non-flowering shoots in mid-summer.
T. virginiana 'Painter's Palette' illus. p.245.

TOWNSENDIA (Compositae)
Genus of evergreen, short-lived perennials and biennials, grown for their daisylike flower heads. Suits alpine houses as dislikes winter wet. Fully hardy. Needs sun and moist soil. Propagate by seed in autumn.
T. grandiflora illus. p.323.
T. parryi. Evergreen, basal-rosetted, short-lived perennial. H 3–6in (7–15cm), S 2in (5cm). Zones 4–7. In late spring produces daisylike, lavender or violet-blue flower heads, with bright yellow centers, above spoon-shaped leaves.

TRACHELIUM, syn. DIOSPHAERA (Campanulaceae)
Genus of small perennials, useful for rock gardens and mixed borders. Some are good in alpine houses. Flowers of half-hardy species are ideal for cutting. Fully to half hardy, but protect fully-hardy species in a greenhouse in winter as they resent damp conditions. Grow in a sunny, sheltered position and in fertile, very well-drained soil (*T. asperuloides* prefers lime-rich soil). Propagate by seed in early or mid-spring or by softwood cuttings in spring.
T. asperuloides illus. p.323.
T. caeruleum illus. p.274.

TRACHELOSPERMUM (Apocynaceae)
Genus of evergreen, woody-stemmed, twining climbers with stems that exude milky sap when cut. Frost hardy. Grow in any well-drained soil and in sun or semi-shade. Propagate by seed in spring, by layering in summer, or by semi-ripe cuttings in late summer or autumn.
T. asiaticum. Evergreen, woody-stemmed, much-branched, twining climber. H to 20ft (6m). Zones 8–10. Oval, glossy, dark green leaves are 1in (2.5cm) long. In summer bears

scented, tubular, cream flowers, with expanded mouths, that age to yellow. Pairs of long, slender pods, 5–9in (12–22cm) long, contain silky seeds.
T. jasminoides illus. p.165.

TRACHYCARPUS (Palmae)
Genus of evergreen, summer-flowering palms, grown for their habit, foliage, and flowers. Frost hardy. Requires full sun and does best in a position sheltered from strong, cold winds, especially when young. Needs fertile, well-drained soil. Propagate by seed in autumn or spring.
T. fortunei illus. p.57.

TRACHYMENE (Umbelliferae)
Genus of summer-flowering annuals. Half hardy. Grow in a sunny, sheltered position and in fertile, well-drained soil. Support with sticks. Propagate by seed sown under glass in early spring.
T. coerulea, syn. *Didiscus coeruleus* (Blue lace flower). Moderately fast-growing, upright, branching annual. H 18in (45cm), S 8in (20cm). Has deeply divided, pale green leaves. Spherical heads, to 2in (5cm) wide, of tiny, blue flowers are produced in summer. Flowers are excellent for cutting.

TRADESCANTIA (Commelinaceae)
Spiderwort
Genus of perennials, some of which are evergreen, grown for their flowers or ornamental foliage. Fully hardy to frost tender, min. 50–59°F (10–15°C). Grow in fertile, moist to dry soil and in sun or partial shade. Cut back or repropagate trailing species when they become straggly. Propagate hardy species by division, frost-tender species by tip cuttings in spring, summer, or autumn.
T. albiflora. See *T. fluminensis*.
T. blossfeldiana. See *T. cerinthoides*.
T. cerinthoides, syn. *T. blossfeldiana*. Evergreen, creeping perennial. H 2in (5cm), S indefinite. Frost tender, zones 9–10. Narrowly oval, fleshy, stem-clasping leaves, to 4in (10cm) long, are glossy, dark green above, purple with long, white hairs below. Intermittently has clusters of tiny, pink flowers, with white centers, surrounded by 2 leaflike bracts. Leaves of 'Variegata' have longitudinal, cream stripes.
T. fluminensis, syn. *T. albiflora* (Wandering Jew). Evergreen perennial with trailing, rooting stems. H 2in (5cm), S to 2ft (60cm) or more. Frost tender, zones 8–10. Oval, fleshy leaves, 1½in (4cm) long, that clasp the stem, are glossy and green above, sometimes tinged purple below. Intermittently has clusters of tiny, white flowers enclosed in 2 leaflike bracts. 'Albovittata' and 'Variegata' illus. p.256.
T. 'J.C. Weguelin'. Clump-forming perennial. H to 2ft (60cm), S 1½ft (45cm). Fully hardy, zones 5–9. Narrowly lance-shaped, fleshy, green leaves, 6–12in (15–30cm) long, clasp stems. In summer has clusters of 3-petaled, lavender blue flowers, 1in (2.5cm) or more wide, surrounded by 2 leaflike bracts.
T. navicularis. See *Callisia navicularis*.

T. 'Osprey' illus. p.233.
T. pallida, syn. *Setcreasea purpurea*. **'Purple Heart'** illus. p.259.
T. pexata. See *T. sillamontana*.
T. 'Purple Dome' illus. p.241.
T. purpusii. See *T. zebrina* 'Purpusii'.
T. sillamontana, syn. *T. pexata*, *T. velutina*, illus. p.259.
T. spathacea, syn. *Rhoeo discolor*, *R. spathacea* (Boat lily, Moses-in-the-cradle). Evergreen, clump-forming perennial. H 20in (50cm), S 10in (25cm). Frost tender, zones 9–10. Short stem bears a rosette of lance-shaped, fleshy leaves, to 12in (30cm) long, glossy green above, purple below. Tiny, white flowers, enclosed in boat-shaped, leaflike bracts, are produced year-round. **'Vittata'** has leaves striped longitudinally with pale yellow.
T. velutina. See *T. sillamontana*.
T. zebrina, syn. *Zebrina pendula*, illus. p.257. **'Purpusii'** (syn. *T. purpusii*) is a strong-growing, evergreen, trailing or mat-forming perennial. H 4in (10cm), S indefinite. Frost tender, zones 9–10. Has elliptic, purple-tinged, bluish green leaves and tiny, shallowly cup-shaped, pink flowers. **'Quadricolor'** has leaves striped green, pink, red, and white.

TRAPA (Trapaceae)
Genus of deciduous, perennial and annual, floating water plants, grown for their foliage and flowers. Frost hardy to frost tender, min. 41°F (5°C). Requires sun. Propagate in spring from seed gathered in autumn and stored in water or damp moss.
T. natans illus. p.375.

TRICHOCEREUS (Cactaceae)
Genus of columnar, perennial cacti; is sometimes included in *Echinopsis*. Mature plants produce highly scented, nocturnal, funnel-shaped flowers that eventually open flat. Is easy to grow and often used as grafting stock. Frost tender, min. 46–50°F (8–10°C). Requires sun and well-drained soil. Propagate by seed or stem cuttings in spring or summer.
T. bridgesii illus. p.378.
T. candicans illus. p.382.
T. spachianus illus. p.379.

TRICHODIADEMA (Aizoaceae)
Genus of bushy, perennial succulents with woody or tuberous roots and cylindrical to semi-cylindrical leaves. Frost tender, min. 41°F (5°C). Needs sun and well-drained soil. Propagate by seed or stem cuttings in spring or summer.
T. densum. Tufted, perennial succulent. H 4in (10cm), S 8in (20cm). Zone 10. Cylindrical, pale green leaves are each $1/2$–$3/4$in (1–2cm) long and tipped with clusters of white bristles. Roots and prostrate, green stem are both fleshy and form caudex. Stem tip carries daisylike, cerise flowers, $1^1/4$in (3cm) across, in summer.
T. mirabile illus. p.389.

TRICHOSANTHES
(Cucurbitaceae)
Genus of annual and evergreen, perennial, tendril climbers, grown for their fruits and overall appearance. Frost tender, min. 59–64°F (15–18°C). Needs full sun or partial shade and humus-rich soil. Water freely in growing season, less in cool weather. Provide support. Propagate by seed in spring at not less than 70°F (21°C).
T. anguina (Snake gourd). Erect to spreading, annual, tendril climber. H 10–15ft (3–5m). Zone 10. Has mid- to pale green leaves, to 8in (20cm) long, that are broadly oval to almost triangular and sometimes shallowly 3- to 5-lobed. In summer bears 5-petaled, white flowers, 1–2in (2.5–5cm) across, with heavily fringed petals; the females are solitary, the males in racemes. Cylindrical fruits, 2ft (60cm) or rarely to 6ft (2m) long, often twisted or coiled, are green-and-white striped and ripen to dull orange.

Tricuspidaria lanceolata. See *Crinodendron hookerianum.*

TRICYRTIS (Liliaceae)
Toad lily
Genus of late summer- and autumn-flowering, rhizomatous perennials. Fully hardy. Grows in sun or, in warm areas, in partial shade. Needs humus-rich, moist soil. Propagate by division in spring or by seed in autumn.
T. formosana, syn. *T. stolonifera*, illus. p.220.
T. hirta. Upright, rhizomatous perennial. H 1–3ft (30cm–1m), S $1^1/2$ft (45cm). Zones 4–9. In late summer and early autumn, clusters of large, open bell-shaped, white-spotted, purple flowers appear from axils of uppermost leaves. Leaves are narrowly oval, hairy, and dark green and clasp stems. var. **alba** illus. p.249.
T. macrantha. Upright, rhizomatous perennial. H and S 24in (60cm). Zones 8–9. In early autumn bears loose sheaves of open bell-shaped, deep primrose yellow flowers, spotted with light chocolate, at tips of arching stems. Small, oval leaves are dark green.
T. stolonifera. See *T. formosana*.

TRIFOLIUM (Leguminosae)
Clover
Genus of annuals, biennials, and perennials, some of which are semi-evergreen, with rounded, usually 3-lobed leaves and heads of pealike flowers. Some species are useful in rock gardens or on banks, others in agriculture. Many are invasive. Fully to frost hardy. Needs sun and well-drained soil. Propagate by division in spring or by seed in autumn. Self seeds readily.
T. repens 'Purpurascens' illus. p.328.

TRILLIUM (Liliaceae)
Wake-robin
Genus of perennials with petals, sepals, and leaves that are all borne in whorls of 3. Is excellent for woodland gardens. Forms of *T. cuneatum* and *T. sessile* are often grown as *T. chloropetalum*. Fully hardy. Enjoys full or partial shade and fertile, moist, preferably neutral to acid soil. Propagate by division after foliage has died down in summer or by seed in autumn.

T. cernuum f. **album** illus. p.224.
T. chloropetalum illus. p.225.
T. erectum illus. p.226.
T. grandiflorum illus. p.225. **'Flore Pleno'** is a clump-forming perennial. H 15in (38cm), S 12in (30cm). Zones 5–9. Large, double, pure white flowers that turn pink with age are borne singly in spring. Has large, broadly oval, dark green leaves.
T. nivale (Snow trillium). Early spring-flowering, rhizomatous perennial. H 3in (7cm), S 4in (10cm). Zones 5–8. Produces whorls of 3 oval leaves that emerge at the same time as the outward-facing, slightly nodding, white flowers, each with 3 narrowly oval petals. Thrives in an alpine house. Is difficult to grow.
T. ovatum illus. p.225.
T. rivale illus. p.305.
T. sessile illus. p.226.
T. undulatum (Painted trillium). Clump-forming perennial. H 4–8in (10–20cm), S 6–8in (15–20cm). Zones 4–9. Open funnel-shaped flowers have red-bordered, green sepals and 3 white or pink petals, each with a carmine stripe at base. They are produced singly in spring, well above broadly oval, basal, blue-green leaves.

TRIPETALEIA (Ericaceae)
Genus of one species of deciduous shrub, grown for its flowers; is now often included in *Elliottia*. Fully hardy. Needs semi-shade and moist, peaty, neutral to acid soil. Propagate by softwood cuttings in summer or by seed in autumn.
T. paniculata. Deciduous, upright shrub. H and S 5ft (1.5m). Zones 6–9. Bears upright panicles of pink-tinged, white flowers, each with 3 (sometimes 4 or 5) narrow petals, from mid-summer to early autumn. Lance-shaped, dark green leaves persist well into autumn.

TRIPTERYGIUM (Celastraceae)
Genus of deciduous, twining or scrambling climbers, grown for their foliage and fruits. Frost hardy. Grow in any fertile, well-drained soil and in full sun or light shade. Water freely while in full growth, less in low temperatures. Provide stems with support. Thin out crowded stems in winter or early spring. Propagate by seed when ripe or in spring or by semi-ripe cuttings in summer.
T. regelii. Deciduous, slender-stemmed, twining or scrambling climber. H 30ft (10m). Zones 5–8. Leaves are oval and usually rich green. In late summer produces clusters, 8–10in (20–25cm) long, of small, off-white flowers, followed by 3-winged, pale green fruits.

TRISTANIA (Myrtaceae)
Genus of evergreen trees and shrubs, grown for their overall appearance when mature and for shade. Is related to *Eucalyptus*. Half hardy to frost tender, min. 37–41°F (3–5°C). Prefers fertile, well-drained soil and full light. Other than shaping plants in winter, pruning is seldom necessary. Propagate by seed in spring or by semi-ripe cuttings in summer.

T. conferta (Brisbane box, Brush-box tree). Fast-growing, evergreen, round-headed tree. H and S 50–130ft (15–40m). Frost tender, zone 10. Produces lance-shaped, leathery, lustrous leaves. In spring bears white flowers with prominent, feathery stamen bundles. **'Variegata'** has cream- or white-patterned leaves.

TRITELEIA (Liliaceae)
Genus of late spring- and early summer-flowering corms with wiry stems carrying *Allium*like umbels of funnel-shaped flowers. Long, narrow leaves usually die away by flowering time. Frost hardy. Needs an open but sheltered, sunny situation and well-drained soil that dries out to some extent in summer. Dies down in mid- to late summer until winter or spring; plant during dormancy in early autumn. Propagate by seed or offsets in autumn.
T. hyacinthina, syn. *Brodiaea hyacinthina*, illus. p.350.
T. ixioides, syn. *Brodiaea ixioides*. Early summer-flowering corm. H to 20in (50cm), S 3–4in (8–10cm). Zones 7–10. Bears semi-erect, basal leaves. Stem produces a loose umbel, to 5in (12cm) across, of yellow flowers; petals each have a purple stripe.
T. laxa, syn. *Brodiaea laxa*, illus. p.352.
T. peduncularis, syn. *Brodiaea peduncularis*. Early summer-flowering corm. H 4–16in (10–40cm), S 4–6in (10–15cm). Zones 7–10. Has semi-erect, basal leaves. Stem produces a loose umbel, to 14in (35cm) across, of white flowers, each $5/8$–$1^1/4$in (1.5–3cm) long, faintly tinged blue.

TRITONIA (Iridaceae)
Genus of corms, with flattish fans of sword-shaped, erect leaves, grown for their spikes of colorful flowers. Frost to half hardy. Needs a sunny, sheltered site and well-drained soil. Plant corms in autumn (*T. rubrolucens* in spring). Dry off once leaves start dying back in summer (winter for *T. rubrolucens*). Propagate by seed in autumn or by offsets at replanting time.
T. crocata, syn. *T. hyalina*. Spring-flowering corm. H 6–14in (15–35cm), S 2–3in (5–8cm). Half hardy, zones 8–10. Has erect, basal leaves. Wiry stems each bear a loose spike of up to 10 widely cup-shaped, orange or pink flowers, $1^1/2$–2in (4–5cm) across, with transparent margins.
T. hyalina. See *T. crocata*.
T. rosea. See *T. rubrolucens*.
T. rubrolucens, syn. *T. rosea*, *Crocosmia rosea*, illus. p.351.

TROCHOCARPA (Epacridaceae)
Genus of evergreen shrubs, grown for their nodding flower spikes. Frost hardy to frost tender, min. 45°F (7°C). Needs sun and moist but well-drained, peaty, sandy soil. Propagate by semi-ripe cuttings in summer.
T. thymifolia. Slow-growing, evergreen, erect shrub. H 12in (30cm), S to 8in (20cm). Frost hardy, zones 8–10. Stems are covered in minute, thymelike leaves. Produces $1^1/2$in (4cm) long spikes of tiny, bell-shaped,

pink flowers in summer-autumn. Is suitable for an alpine house.

TROCHODENDRON
(Trochodendraceae)
Genus of one species of evergreen tree, grown for its foliage and flowers. Frost hardy, but needs shelter from strong, cold winds. Tolerates sun or shade and requires moist but well-drained soil; dislikes very dry or very shallow, chalky soil. Propagate by semi-ripe cuttings in summer or by seed in autumn.
T. aralioides illus. p.57.

TROLLIUS (Ranunculaceae)
Globeflower
Genus of spring- or summer-flowering perennials that thrive beside pools and streams. Fully hardy. Tolerates sun or shade. Does best in moist soil. Propagate by division in early autumn or by seed in summer or autumn.
T. 'Alabaster' illus. p.229.
T. 'Earliest of All'. Clump-forming perennial. H 24in (60cm), S 18in (45cm). Zones 5–8. Globular, butter yellow flowers are borne singly in spring, above rounded, deeply divided, green leaves.
T. europaeus illus. p.232. **'Canary Bird'** is a clump-forming perennial. H 24in (60cm), S 18in (45cm). Zones 5–8. In spring bears globular, canary yellow flowers above rounded, deeply divided, green leaves.
T. 'Goldquelle'. Clump-forming perennial. H 24in (60cm), S 18in (45cm). Zones 5–8. Large, globular, rich orange flowers are borne singly in spring, above rounded, deeply divided, green leaves.
T. 'Orange Princess'. Clump-forming perennial. H 30in (75cm), S 18in (45cm). Zones 5–8. Globular, orange-gold flowers are borne singly in spring, above rounded, deeply divided, green leaves.
T. pumilus illus. p.313.
T. yunnanensis. Clump-forming perennial. H 2ft (60cm), S 1ft (30cm). Zones 5–8. Has broadly oval leaves with 3–5 deep lobes. Produces buttercuplike, bright yellow flowers in late spring or summer.

TROPAEOLUM (Tropaeolaceae)
Nasturtium
Genus of annuals, perennials, and herbaceous, twining climbers, grown for their brightly colored flowers. Fully hardy to frost tender, min. 41°F (5°C). Most species prefer sun and well-drained soil. Propagate by seed, tubers, or basal stem cuttings in spring. Aphids and caterpillars of cabbage white butterfly and its relatives may cause problems.
T. azureum. Herbaceous, leaf-stalk climber with small tubers. H to 4ft (1.2m). Frost tender, zone 10. Leaves, to 2in (5cm) across, have 5 narrow lobes. Small, purple-blue flowers, with notched petals, open in late summer.
T. canariense. See **T. peregrinum.**
T. majus (Common nasturtium, Indian cress). **'Alaska'** illus. p.283. **'Empress of India'** is a fast-growing, bushy annual. H 8in (20cm), S 12in (30cm). Frost tender. Has rounded, green

leaves. Trumpet-shaped, spurred, dark crimson flowers, 2in (5cm) wide, are borne from early summer to early autumn. **Gleam Series** has a semi-trailing habit and double flowers in single colors or in a mixture that includes scarlet, yellow, and orange. **Jewel Series** illus. p.285. Flowers of **'Peach Melba'**, H to 12in (30cm), are pale yellow, blotched with scarlet. **Whirlybird Series**, H to 12in (30cm), has single flowers in a mixture or in single colors.
T. peregrinum, syn. **T. canariense** (Canary creeper). Herbaceous, leaf-stalk climber. H to 6ft (2m). Frost tender, zones 9–10. Gray-green leaves have 5 broad lobes. Small, bright yellow flowers, the 2 upper petals much larger and fringed, are borne from summer until first frosts. In cool areas is best grown as an annual.
T. polyphyllum illus. 248.
T. speciosum illus. p.168.
T. tricolorum illus. p.163.
T. tuberosum illus. p.176. **'Ken Aslet'** illus. p.174.

TSUGA (Pinaceae). See CONIFERS.
T. canadensis illus. p.79. **'Aurea'** (illus. p.83) is a broadly conical conifer, often with several stems. H 15ft (5m) or more, S 6–10ft (2–3m). Fully hardy, zones 4–8. Shoots are gray with spirally arranged, needlelike, flattened leaves, golden yellow when young, ageing to green in second year, those along top inverted to show silver bands. Has ovoid, light brown cones. **'Bennett'**, H 3–6ft (1–2m), S 6ft (2m), is a compact, dwarf form with arching branches and a nest-shaped, central depression. f. **pendula** has weeping branches that may be trained to create a domed mound, H and S 10–15ft (3–5m), or left to spread at ground level, H 20in (50cm), S 6–15ft (2–5m).
T. caroliniana (Carolina hemlock). Conifer with a conical or ovoid crown. H 30–50ft (10–15m), S 15–25ft (5–8m). Fully hardy, zones 5–7. Red-brown shoots produce spirally set, needlelike, flattened, glossy, dark green leaves. Bears ovoid, green cones, ripening to brown.
T. diversifolia (Japanese hemlock, Northern Japanese hemlock). Conifer with a broad, dense crown. H 30–50ft (10–15m), S 25–40ft (8–12m). Fully hardy, zones 6–8. Has orange shoots and needlelike, flattened, glossy, deep green leaves, banded with white beneath, that are spirally set. Ovoid cones are dark brown.
T. heterophylla (Western hemlock). Vigorous, conical conifer with drooping branchlets. H 70–100ft (20–30m), S 25–30ft (8–10m). Fully hardy, zones 6–8. Gray shoots bear spirally set, needlelike, flattened, dark green leaves with silvery bands beneath. Bears ovoid, pale green cones that ripen to dark brown.
T. mertensiana (Mountain hemlock). Narrowly conical conifer with short, horizontal branches. H 25–50ft (8–15m), S 10–20ft (3–6m). Fully hardy, zones 6–8. Red-brown shoots bear needlelike, flattened, glaucous blue-green or gray-green leaves, spirally arranged. Produces cylindrical

cones that are yellow-green to purple, ripening to dark brown.
T. sieboldii (Japanese hemlock, Southern Japanese hemlock). Broadly conical conifer. H 50ft (15m), S 25–30ft (8–10m). Fully hardy, zones 6–8. Has glossy, buff shoots that bear needlelike, flattened, lustrous, dark green leaves, set spirally. Cones are ovoid and dark brown.

TSUSIOPHYLLUM (Ericaceae)
Genus of one species of semi-evergreen shrub, grown for its flowers. Is similar to *Rhododendron* and is suitable for rock gardens and peat beds. Frost hardy. Requires shade and well-drained, peaty, sandy soil. Propagate by softwood cuttings in spring or early summer or by seed in autumn or spring.
T. tanakae. Semi-evergreen, spreading shrub. H 6in (15cm) or more, S 10in (25cm). Zones 6–9. Twiggy, branched stems bear tiny, narrowly oval, hairy leaves. In early summer produces small, tubular, white or pinkish white flowers at stem tips.

TUBERARIA (Cistaceae)
Genus of annuals. Fully hardy. Grow in sun and in any very well-drained soil. Propagate by seed sown outdoors in spring.
T. guttata, syn. *Helianthemum guttatum.* Moderately fast-growing, upright, branching annual. H and S 4–12in (10–30cm). Has lance-shaped, hairy, green leaves and, in summer, yellow flowers, sometimes red-spotted at base of petals, that look like small, single roses.

TULBAGHIA (Liliaceae)
Genus of semi-evergreen perennials. Frost to half hardy. Needs full sun and well-drained soil. Propagate by division or seed in spring.
T. natalensis. Semi-evergreen, clump-forming perennial. H 5in (12cm), S 4in (10cm). Frost hardy, zones 8–10. In mid-summer, umbels of fragrant, tubular, yellow-centered, white flowers, with spreading petal lobes, open above fine, grasslike, green foliage.
T. violacea illus. p.240.

TULIPA (Liliaceae)
Tulip
Genus of mainly spring-flowering bulbs, grown for their bright, upward-facing flowers. Each bulb has a few linear to lance-shaped, green or gray-green leaves, which are borne on the stem. Flowers have 6 usually pointed petals (botanically known as perianth segments) and 6 stamens; unless otherwise stated below, they are borne singly. Each plant has a spread of up to 8in (20cm). All are fully hardy, zones 3–8, unless otherwise stated. Requires a sunny position with well-drained soil and appreciates a summer baking; in cool, wet areas, bulbs may be lifted, when the leaves have died down, and stored in a dry place for replanting in autumn. Propagate by division of bulbs in autumn or for species by seed in spring or autumn.
Horticulturally, tulips are grouped into the following divisions:

Div.1 Single early—has cup-shaped, single flowers, often opening wide in sun, from early to mid-spring.
Div.2 Double early—double flowers open wide, appear in early and mid-spring and are long-lasting.
Div.3 Triumph—sturdy stems bear rather conical, single flowers, opening to a more rounded shape, in mid- and late spring.
Div.4 Darwin hybrids—large, single flowers of variable shape are borne on strong stems from mid- to late spring.
Div.5 Single late—single flowers, variable in shape but often ovoid or squarish and usually with pointed petals, appear in late spring and very early summer.
Div.6 Lily-flowered—strong stems bear narrow-waisted, single flowers, with long, pointed petals often reflexed at tips, in late spring.
Div.7 Fringed—flowers are similar to those in Div.6, but have fringed petals.
Div.8 Viridiflora—variably shaped, single flowers, with partly greenish petals, are borne in late spring.
Div.9 Rembrandt—comprises mostly very old cultivars, similar to Div.6, but has colors "broken" into striped or feathered patterns owing to virus. Flowers in late spring.
Div.10 Parrot—large, single flowers of variable shape, with petals frilled or fringed and usually twisted, appear in late spring.
Div.11 Double late (peony-flowered)—double flowers are usually bowl-shaped and appear in late spring.
Div.12 Kaufmanniana hybrids—single flowers are usually bicolored, open flat in sun, and are borne in early spring. Leaves are usually mottled or striped.
Div.13 Fosteriana hybrids—has large, single flowers that open wide in sun from early to mid-spring. Leaves are often mottled or striped.
Div.14 Greigii hybrids—large, single flowers appear in mid- and late spring. Leaves are generally wavy-edged, always mottled or striped.
Div.15 Miscellaneous—a miscellaneous category of other species and their varieties and hybrids. Flowers appear in spring and early summer.

T. acuminata (Horned tulip; illus. p.345), Div.15. Mid-spring-flowering bulb. H 12–18in (30–45cm). Flowers are 3–5in (7–13cm) long, with long-pointed, tapered, pale red or yellow petals, often tinged with red or green outside.
T. aitchisonii. See **T. clusiana.**
T. 'Ancilla', Div.12. Early spring-flowering bulb. H 6in (15cm). Flowers are pink and reddish outside, white inside, each with a central, red ring.
T. 'Angélique' (illus. p.344), Div.11. Late spring-flowering bulb. H 16in (40cm). Delicately scented, double, pale pink flowers deepen with age. Each petal has paler streaks and a lighter edge. Is good for bedding.
T. 'Artist' (illus. p.345), Div.8. Late spring-flowering bulb. H 18in (45cm). Flowers are salmon pink and purple outside, sometimes marked green, and deep salmon pink and green inside.

T. aucheriana, Div.15. Early spring-flowering bulb. H to 8in (20cm). Has gray-green leaves. Flowers, ³/₄–2in (2–5cm) long, each tapered at the base and with oval petals, are pink with yellow centers.

T. bakeri. See *T. saxatilis*.

T. 'Balalaika' (illus. p.345), Div.5. Late spring-flowering bulb. H 20in (50cm). Bright red flowers each have a yellow base and black stamens.

T. batalinii (illus. p.345), Div.15. Early spring-flowering bulb. H 4–12in (10–30cm). Is often included under *T. linifolia*. Leaves are gray-green. Flowers, ³/₄–2¹/₂in (2–6cm) long, have broadly oval petals and are bowl-shaped at the base. Pale yellow petals are darker yellow or brown at bases inside. Several cultivars are hybrids between *T. batalinii* and *T. linifolia*. These include **'Apricot Jewel'** with flowers that are orange-red outside, yellow inside; **'Bright Gem'**, which has yellow flowers flushed with orange; and **'Bronze Charm'**, which bears yellow flowers with bronze feathering.

T. 'Bellona' (illus. p.345), Div.1. Early spring-flowering bulb. H 12in (30cm). Fragrant flowers are deep golden yellow. Is good for bedding and forcing.

T. biflora, syn. *T. polychroma* (Two-flower tulip; illus. p.344), Div.15. Early spring-flowering bulb. H 2–4in (5–10cm). Has gray-green leaves. Stem bears 1–5 fragrant, yellow-centered, white flowers, ⁵/₈–1¹/₂in (1.5–3.5cm) long and tapered at the bases. Narrowly oval petals are flushed outside with greenish gray or greenish pink. Is suitable for a rock garden.

T. 'Blue Parrot' (illus. p.345), Div.10. Late spring-flowering bulb. H 2ft (60cm). Very large, bright violet flowers, sometimes bronze outside, are borne on strong stems.

T. 'Burgundy Lace', Div.7. Late spring-flowering bulb. H 2ft (60cm). Flowers are wine red, each petal with a fringed edge.

T. 'Cape Cod' (illus. p.345), Div.14. Mid- to late spring-flowering bulb. H 18in (45cm). Gray-green leaves have reddish stripes. Yellowish bronze flowers each have a black-and-red base; petals are edged with yellow outside.

T. 'China Pink' (illus. p.344), Div.6. Late spring-flowering bulb. H 22in (55cm). Flowers are pink, each with a white base, and have slightly reflexed petals.

T. 'Chopin', Div.12. Early spring-flowering bulb. H 8in (20cm). Has brown-mottled, gray-green leaves and bears lemon yellow flowers that have black bases.

T. 'Clara Butt' (illus. p.344), Div.5. Late spring-flowering bulb. H 2ft (60cm). Flowers are salmon pink. Is particularly good for bedding.

T. clusiana, syn. *T. aitchisonii* (Lady tulip; illus. p.344), Div.15. Mid-spring-flowering bulb. H to 12in (30cm). Has gray-green leaves. Each stem bears 1 or 2 flowers, ³/₄–2¹/₂in (2–6.5cm) long, that are bowl-shaped at the base. Narrowly oval, white petals are purple or crimson at base inside, striped deep pink outside. Stamens are purple.

Flowers of var. *chrysantha* (illus. p.345) are yellow, flushed red or brown outside, with yellow stamens. var. *stellata* has white flowers with yellow bases and yellow stamens.

T. dasystemon of gardens. See *T. tarda*.

T. 'Dawnglow', Div.4. Mid- to late-spring flowering bulb. H 2ft (60cm). Pale apricot flowers are flushed with deep pink outside and are deep yellow inside. Has purple anthers.

T. 'Diana' (illus. p.344), Div.1. Early spring-flowering bulb. H 11in (28cm). Large, pure white flowers are carried on strong stems.

T. 'Dillenburg' (illus. p.345), Div.5. Late spring-flowering bulb. H 26in (65cm). Flowers are brick orange and are good for bedding.

T. 'Dreamboat' (illus. p.345), Div.14. Mid- to late spring-flowering bulb. H 10in (25cm). Has brown-striped, gray-green leaves. Urn-shaped, red-tinged, amber yellow flowers have greenish bronze bases with red blotches.

T. 'Dreaming Maid' (illus. p.345), Div.3. Mid- to late spring-flowering bulb. H 22in (55cm). Flowers have violet petals edged with white.

T. eichleri. See *T. undulatifolia*.

T. 'Estella Rijnveld' (illus. p.344), Div.10. Late spring-flowering bulb. H 2ft (60cm). Large flowers are red, streaked with white and touches of green.

T. fosteriana, Div.15. Early spring-flowering bulb. H 8–18in (20–45cm). Has a downy stem and gray-green leaves, downy above. Flowers, 1³/₄–4in (4.5–10cm) long, are bowl-shaped at the base with narrowly oval, bright red petals, and each has a purplish black center inside, ringed with yellow.

T. 'Fringed Elegance', Div.7. Late spring-flowering bulb. H 20in (50cm). Has pale yellow flowers dotted with pink outside; inside, bases have bronze-green blotches. Each petal has a yellow fringe. Anthers are purple.

T. 'Gala Beauty', Div.9. Late spring-flowering bulb. H 2ft (60cm). Produces yellow flowers that are streaked with crimson.

T. 'Garden Party' (illus. p.344), Div.3. Mid- to late spring-flowering bulb. H 16–18in (40–45cm). Has white flowers; petals are edged with deep pink outside and streaked with deep pink inside.

T. 'Glück' (illus. p.345), Div.12. Early spring-flowering bulb. H 6in (15cm). Has reddish brown-mottled, gray-green leaves. Petals are red, edged with yellow, outside and yellow inside, each with a darker base.

T. 'Golden Apeldoorn', Div.4. Mid- to late spring-flowering bulb. H 20–24in (50–60cm). Golden yellow flowers each have a black base and black stamens.

T. 'Gordon Cooper' (illus. p.344), Div.4. Mid- to late spring-flowering bulb. H 2ft (60cm). Petals are deep pink outside, edged with red; inside they are red with blue-and-yellow bases. Has black anthers.

T. greigii, Div.15. Early spring-flowering bulb. H 8–18in (20–45cm). Has downy stems. Leaves are streaked

or mottled with red or purple. Cup-shaped flowers, 1¹/₄–4in (3–10cm) long, with broadly oval, red or yellow petals, have yellow-ringed, black centers.

T. 'Greuze' (illus. p.345), Div.5. Late spring-flowering bulb. H 26in (65cm). Flowers are dark violet-purple and are good for bedding.

T. hageri (Hager tulip; illus. p.344), Div.15. Mid-spring-flowering bulb. H 4–12in (10–30cm). Frost hardy, zones 7–8. Stem has 1–4 flowers, 1¹/₂–2¹/₂in (3–6cm) long, tapered at the base and with oval, dull red petals tinged with green outside.

T. 'Heart's Delight', Div.12. Early spring-flowering bulb. H 8–10in (20–25cm). Green leaves are striped with red-brown. Petals are deep pinkish red outside, edged with pale pink, and are pale pink inside with red-blotched, yellow bases.

T. 'Hollywood', Div.8. Late spring-flowering bulb. H 12in (30cm). Red flowers, tinged and streaked with green, have yellow bases. Is good for bedding.

T. humilis (Ground tulip; illus. p.345), Div.15. Early spring-flowering bulb. A variable species, often considered to include *T. aucheriana*, *T. pulchella*, and *T. violacea*. H to 8in (20cm). Has gray-green leaves. Stem bears usually 1, sometimes 2 or 3, pinkish magenta flowers, ³/₄–2in (2–5cm) long, tapered at the base and with a yellow center inside. Petals are oval. Is suitable for a rock garden.

T. 'Jack Laan', Div.9. Late spring-flowering bulb. H 2ft (60cm). Purple flowers are shaded with brown and feathered with white and yellow.

T. kaufmanniana (Waterlily tulip; illus. p.345), Div.15. Early spring-flowering bulb. H 4–14in (10–35cm). Leaves are gray-green. Stem has 1–5 often scented flowers, 1¹/₂–4in (3–10cm) long and bowl-shaped at the base. Narrowly oval petals are usually either cream or yellow, flushed with pink or gray-green outside; centers are often a different color. Pink, orange, or red forms occasionally occur.

T. 'Keizerskroon' (illus. p.345), Div.1. Early spring-flowering bulb. H 14in (35cm). Flowers have crimson-scarlet petals, with broad, bright yellow margins. Is a good, reliable bedding tulip.

T. linifolia (Slimleaf tulip; illus. p.344), Div.15. Early spring-flowering bulb. H 4–12in (10–30cm). A variable species, often considered to include *T. batalinii* and *T. maximowiczii*. Has gray-green leaves. Red flowers, ³/₄–2in (2–6cm) long, are bowl-shaped at the base and, inside, have blackish purple centers that are usually ringed with cream or yellow. Petals are broadly oval.

T. 'Mme. Lefèbre', syn. *T. 'Red Emperor'* (illus. p.344), Div.13. Early to mid-spring-flowering bulb. H 14–16in (35–40cm). Produces very large, brilliant red flowers.

T. 'Maja' (illus. p.345), Div.7. Late spring-flowering bulb. H 20in (50cm). Egg-shaped, pale yellow flowers, with fringed petals, are bronze-yellow at the base. Anthers are yellow.

T. 'Margot Fonteyn' (illus. p.345), Div.3. Mid- to late spring-flowering bulb. H 16–18in (40–45cm). Flowers have yellow-edged, bright red petals, each with a yellow base inside. Anthers are black.

T. marjolettii (illus. p.345), Div.15. Mid-spring-flowering bulb. H 16–20in (40–50cm). Flowers, 1¹/₂–2¹/₂in (4–6cm) long and bowl-shaped at the base, have broadly oval, creamy white petals, edged and marked with deep pink.

T. maximowiczii, Div.15. Early spring-flowering bulb. H 4–12in (10–30cm). Has gray-green leaves. Bright red flowers, ³/₄–2¹/₂in (2–6cm) long, with broadly oval petals, have white-bordered, black centers and are bowl-shaped at the base.

T. 'Monte Carlo', Div.2. Early spring-flowering bulb. H 16in (40cm). Has double, yellow flowers with sparse, red streaks.

T. 'Orange Emperor', Div.13. Early to mid-spring-flowering bulb. H 16in (40cm). Flowers are bright orange, each with a yellow base inside, and have black anthers.

T. 'Orange Triumph', Div.11. Late spring-flowering bulb. H 20in (50cm). Has double, soft orange-red flowers flushed with brown; each petal has a yellow margin.

T. 'Oranje Nassau' (illus. p.345), Div.2. Early spring-flowering bulb. H 10–12in (25–30cm). Has double, blood red flowers flushed fiery orange-red. Is good for forcing.

T. 'Oratorio', Div.14. Mid- to late spring-flowering bulb. H 8in (20cm). Has reddish brown-mottled, gray-green leaves and broadly urn-shaped flowers. Petals are rose-pink outside, apricot pink inside, and have black bases.

T. orphanidea (Spartan tulip; illus. p.345), Div.15. Mid-spring-flowering bulb. H 4–12in (10–30cm). Frost hardy, zones 7–8. Green leaves often have reddish margins. Stem has 1–4 flowers, 1¹/₄–2¹/₂in (3–6cm) long and tapered at the base. Oval petals are orange-brown, tinged outside with green and often purple.

T. 'Palestrina' (illus. p.344), Div.5. Late spring-flowering bulb. H 18in (45cm). Petals of large, salmon pink flowers are green outside.

T. 'Peach Blossom' (illus. p.344), Div.2. Early spring-flowering bulb. H 10–12in (25–30cm). Produces double, silvery pink flowers flushed with deep pink.

T. 'Plaisir' (illus. p.345), Div.14. Mid- to late spring-flowering bulb. H 6–8in (15–20cm). Gray-green leaves are mottled with red-brown. Broadly urn-shaped, deep pinkish red flowers have petals edged with pale yellow and with black-and-yellow bases.

T. polychroma. See *T. biflora*.

T. praestans 'Fusilier', Div.15. Early spring-flowering bulb. H 4–18in (10–45cm). Has a minutely downy stem and downy, gray-green leaves. Stem bears 3–5 flowers, 2¹/₄–2¹/₂in (5.5–6.5cm) long and bowl-shaped at the base. Oval petals are orange-scarlet. **'Van Tubergen's Variety'** (illus. p.345) produces 2–5 flowers per stem, often yellow at the base; it increases very freely.

T. 'Prinses Irene' (illus. p.345), Div.1. Early spring-flowering bulb. H 12–14cm (30–35cm). Produces orange flowers that are streaked with purple.

T. pulchella, Div.15. Early spring-flowering bulb. H to 8in (20cm). Has gray-green leaves. Flowers, $3/4$–2in (2–5cm) long, are tapered at the base, have oval, purple petals and yellow or bluish black centers inside. Is useful for a rock garden.

T. 'Purissima', syn. *T.* 'White Emperor' (illus. p.344), Div.13. Early to mid-spring-flowering bulb. H 14–16in (35–40cm). Flowers are pure white.

T. 'Queen of Night' (illus. p.345), Div.5. Late spring-flowering bulb. H 2ft (60cm). The darkest of all tulips, has long-lasting, very dark maroon-black flowers on sturdy stems. Is useful for bedding.

T. 'Red Emperor'. See *T.* 'Mme. Lefèbre'.

T. 'Red Parrot' (illus. p.344), Div.10. Late spring-flowering bulb. H 2ft (60cm). Large, raspberry red flowers are carried on strong stems.

T. saxatilis, syn. *T. bakeri* (Cliff tulip; illus. p.344), Div.15. Early spring-flowering bulb. H 6–18in (15–45cm). Frost hardy, zones 6–8. Has shiny, green leaves. Stem produces 1–4 scented flowers, $1^1/2$–$2^1/4$in (4–5.5cm) long and tapered at the base. Oval, pink to lilac petals are yellow at the base inside.

T. 'Shakespeare' (illus. p.345), Div.12. Early spring-flowering bulb. H 5–6in (12–15cm). Petals are deep red, edged with salmon, outside and salmon, flushed red with a yellow base, inside.

T. sprengeri (illus. p.344), Div.15. Late spring- and early summer-flowering bulb. H 12–18in (30–45cm). Flowers are $1^1/4$–$2^1/2$in (4.5–6.5cm) long and tapered at the base. Has narrowly oval, orange-red petals, the

outer 3 with buff-yellow backs. Is the latest flowering tulip. Increases very rapidly.

T. 'Spring Green' (illus. p.344), Div.8. Late spring-flowering bulb. H 14–15in (35–38cm). Has white flowers feathered with green. Anthers are pale green.

T. sylvestris (Florentine tulip; illus. p.345), Div.15. Early spring-flowering bulb. H 4–18in (10–45cm). Yellow flowers, usually borne singly, are $1^1/2$–$2^1/2$in (3.5–6.5cm) long and tapered at the base. Narrowly oval petals are often tinged with green outside.

T. tarda, syn. *T. dasystemon* of gardens (illus. p.345), Div.15. Early spring-flowering bulb. H to 6in (15cm). Has glossy, green leaves. Flowers, 4–6 per stem, are $1^1/4$–$1^1/2$in (3–4cm) long and tapered at the base. Oval, white petals have yellow lower halves inside and are tinged with green and sometimes red outside. Suits a rock garden or raised bed.

T. 'Toronto', Div.14. Mid- to late spring-flowering bulb. H 12in (30cm). Has mottled leaves and 2 or 3 long-lasting flowers per stem. Open, broadly cup-shaped flowers have pointed, bright red petals each with a brownish green-yellow base inside. Anthers are bronze.

T. turkestanica (illus. p.344), Div.15. Early spring-flowering bulb. H 4–12in (10–30cm). Has a hairy stem and gray-green leaves. Unpleasant smelling flowers, up to 12 per stem, are $5/8$–$1^1/2$in (1.5–3.5cm) long and tapered at the base. Oval, white petals are flushed green or pink outside; flowers have yellow or orange centers inside.

T. undulatifolia, syn. *T. eichleri* (illus. p.345), Div.15. Early to mid-spring-flowering bulb. H 6–20in (15–50cm). Has a downy stem and gray-green leaves. Flowers, $1^1/4$–3in (3–8cm) long, are bowl-shaped at the base. Narrowly oval, red or orange-red petals each have a pale red or buff

back and a yellow-bordered, dark green or black blotch at the base inside.

T. 'Union Jack' (illus. p.344), Div.5. Late spring-flowering bulb. H 2ft (60cm). Ivory white petals, marked with deep pinkish red "flames," have blue-edged, white bases.

T. urumiensis (illus. p.345), Div.15. Early spring-flowering bulb. H 4–8in (10–20cm). Stem is mostly below soil level. Leaves are green or grayish green. Bears 1 or 2 flowers, each $1^1/2$in (4cm) long and tapered at the base. Narrowly oval, yellow petals are flushed mauve or red-brown outside. Is useful for a rock garden.

T. violacea (illus. p.345), Div.15. Early spring-flowering bulb. H to 8in (20cm). Has gray-green leaves. Violet-pink flowers, $3/4$–2in (2–5cm) long, are tapered at the base and have yellow or bluish black centers inside. Petals are oval. Suits a rock garden or raised bed.

T. 'West Point' (illus. p.345), Div.6. Late spring-flowering bulb. H 20in (50cm). Primrose yellow flowers have long-pointed, recurved petals.

T. 'White Dream' (illus. p.344), Div.3. Mid- to late spring-flowering bulb. H 16–18in (40–45cm). Flowers are white with yellow anthers.

T. 'White Emperor'. See *T.* 'Purissima'.

T. 'White Triumphator' (illus. p.344), Div.6. Late spring-flowering bulb. H 26–28in (65–70cm). Zones 7–8. White flowers have elegantly reflexed petals.

T. whittallii (illus. p.345), Div.15. Mid-spring-flowering bulb. H 12–14in (30–35cm). Frost hardy. Stem has 1–4 flowers, $1^1/4$–$2^1/2$in (3–6cm) long and tapered at the base. Oval petals are bright brownish orange.

Tunica saxifraga. See *Petrorhagia saxifraga*.

TURRAEA (Meliaceae)
Genus of evergreen trees and shrubs, grown for their flowers and foliage.

Frost tender, min. 54–9°F (12–15°C). Prefers full sun. Needs fertile, well-drained soil. Water freely in full growth, less at other times. Young plants may need growing point removed to promote branching. Prune after flowering if necessary. Propagate by seed in spring or by semi-ripe cuttings in summer.

T. obtusifolia illus. p.140.

Tweedia caerulea. See *Oxypetalum caeruleum*.

TYLECODON (Crassulaceae)
Genus of deciduous, bushy, winter-growing, succulent shrubs with very swollen stems. Frost tender, min. 45°F (7°C). Likes a sunny site with very well-drained soil. Propagate by seed or stem cuttings in summer.

T. paniculata, syn. *Cotyledon paniculata* (Butter tree). Deciduous, bushy, succulent shrub. H and S 6ft (2m). Zones 9–10. Swollen stem and branches have papery, yellow coverings. Bears oblong to oval leaves that are fleshy and bright green. In summer produces clusters of tubular, red flowers, with green stripes, at stem tips.

T. reticulata, syn. *Cotyledon reticulata*, illus. p.386.

T. wallichii, syn. *Cotyledon wallichii*. Deciduous, bushy, succulent shrub. H and S 1ft (30cm). Zones 9–10. Has $1^1/4$in (3cm) thick stems with cylindrical, grooved-topped, green leaves at tips. After leaf fall, stems are neatly covered in raised leaf bases. Produces tubular, yellow-green flowers, $1/2$in (2cm) long, in autumn.

TYPHA (Typhaceae)
Genus of deciduous, perennial, marginal water plants, grown for their decorative, cylindrical seed heads. Fully hardy. Grows in sun or shade. Propagate in spring by seed or division.

T. latifolia illus. p.374.

T. minima illus. p.375.

U

ULEX (Leguminosae)

Genus of leafless, or almost leafless, shrubs that appear evergreen as a result of their year-round, green shoots and spines. Is grown for its flowers in spring. Fully hardy. Needs full sun, and prefers poor, well-drained, acid soil. Trim each year after flowering to maintain compact habit. Straggly, old plants may be cut back hard in spring. Propagate by seed in autumn.

U. europaeus illus. p.125. **'Flore Pleno'** is a leafless, or almost leafless, bushy shrub. H 3ft (1m), S 4ft (1.2m). Zones 7–9. In spring, bears masses of fragrant, pealike, double, yellow flowers on leafless, dark green shoots.

ULMUS (Ulmaceae)

Elm

Genus of deciduous or, rarely, semi-evergreen trees and shrubs, often large and stately, grown for their foliage and habit. Inconspicuous flowers appear in spring. Fully hardy, zones 5–7 unless otherwise stated. Needs sun and fertile, well-drained soil. Propagate by softwood cuttings in summer or by seed or suckers in autumn. Is susceptible to Dutch elm disease, which is quickly fatal, although *U. parvifolia* and *U. pumila* appear more resistant than other species and hybrids.

U. americana (American white elm, White elm). Deciduous, spreading tree. H and S 100ft (30m). Zones 3–9. Has gray bark and drooping branchlets. Large, oval, dark green leaves are sharply toothed and rough-textured.

U. angustifolia (Goodyer's elm). var. *cornubiensis* (Cornish elm) is a deciduous tree, conical when young and with a vase-shaped head when mature. H 100ft (30m), S 50ft (15m). Oval, toothed, glossy, bright green leaves turn yellow in autumn.

U. 'Camperdownii' illus. p.65.

U. carpinifolia (Smooth-leaved elm). Deciduous, spreading tree with arching branches and drooping shoots. H 100ft (30m), S 70ft (20m). Small, oval, toothed, glossy, bright green leaves turn yellow in autumn. **'Sarniensis Aurea'** see *U.* 'Dicksonii'.

U. 'Dicksonii', syn. *U. carpinifolia* 'Sarniensis Aurea', *U.* 'Wheatleyi Aurea', illus. p.54.

U. glabra (Scotch elm, Wych elm). Deciduous, spreading tree. H 100ft

(30m), S 80ft (25m). Has broadly oval, toothed, very rough, dark green leaves, often slightly lobed at tips. From mid- to late spring bears clusters of winged, green fruits on bare branches.

'Exoniensis' (Exeter elm), H 50ft (15m), S 15ft (5m), is narrow with upright branches when young, later becoming more spreading.

U. 'Hollandica' (Dutch elm). Vigorous, deciduous, spreading tree with a short trunk and upright branches. H 100ft (30m), S 80ft (25m). Has oval, toothed, glossy, dark green leaves. Is very susceptible to Dutch elm disease.

U. 'Jacqueline Hillier'. Slow-growing, deciduous, bushy shrub, suitable for hedging. H and S 6ft (2m). Small, oval, dark green leaves, rough-textured and sharply toothed, form 2 rows on each shoot; they persist into winter.

U. parvifolia (Chinese elm). Deciduous or semi-evergreen, rounded tree. H and S 50ft (15m). Zones 5–9. Small, oval, glossy, dark green leaves last well into winter or, in mild areas, may persist until fresh growth appears.

U. procera (English elm). Vigorous, deciduous, spreading tree with a bushy, dense, dome-shaped head. H 120ft (35m), S 50ft (15m). Zones 5–8. Broadly oval, toothed, rough, dark green leaves turn yellow in autumn.

U. pumila (Siberian elm). Deciduous, spreading, sometimes shrubby tree. H 50ft (15m), S 40ft (12m). Zones 5–8. Has oval, toothed, dark green leaves. Has some resistance to Dutch elm disease, but seedlings may be susceptible in hot summers.

U. 'Sarniensis' (Jersey elm, Wheatley elm). Deciduous, conical, dense tree with upright branches. H 100ft (30m), S 30ft (10m). Leaves are small, broadly oval, toothed, glossy, and green.

U. 'Vegeta' (Huntingdon elm). Vigorous, deciduous, spreading tree with upright, central branches and drooping, outer shoots. H 120ft (35m), S 80ft (25m). Leaves are broadly oval, toothed, glossy, and dark green.

U. 'Wheatleyi Aurea'. See *U.* 'Dicksonii'.

UMBELLULARIA (Lauraceae)

Headache tree

Genus of evergreen, spring-flowering

trees, grown for their aromatic foliage. Frost hardy, but requires shelter from strong, cold winds when young. Needs sun and fertile, moist but well-drained soil. Propagate by seed in autumn.

U. californica illus. p.48.

URCEOLINA (Amaryllidaceae)

Genus of spring-flowering bulbs, grown for their pendent, urn-shaped flowers that are followed by strap-shaped leaves. Frost tender, min. 41°F (5°C). Needs full sun and well-drained soil. Reduce watering in winter. Flowers best when pot-bound so do not repot every year if pot-grown. Propagate by offsets in spring.

U. peruviana illus. p.350.

URGINEA (Liliaceae)

Genus of late summer- or early autumn-flowering bulbs, growing on or near soil surface, with spear-shaped flower spikes up to 5ft (1.5m) high. Frost to half hardy. Needs a sunny site and well-drained soil that dries out while bulbs are dormant in summer. Plant in mid- to late summer. Water until leaves die down. Propagate by seed in autumn or by offsets in late summer.

U. maritima (Crusaders' spears, Sea onion, Sea squill). Late summer- or early autumn-flowering bulb. H 5ft (1.5m), S 1–1½ft (30–45cm). Half hardy, zones 9–10. Broadly sword-shaped, erect, basal leaves appear in autumn after a long spike of star-shaped, white flowers, each ½–⅝in (1–1.5cm) across, has developed.

URSINIA (Compositae)

Genus of annuals, evergreen perennials and sub-shrubs, grown mainly for their flower heads usually in summer, a few species for their foliage. Half hardy to frost tender, min. 41–5°F (5–7°C). Needs full light and well-drained soil. Water potted plants moderately, less when not in full growth. Requires good ventilation if grown under glass. Propagate by seed or greenwood cuttings in spring. Aphids are sometimes troublesome.

U. anthemoides illus. p.282.

U. chrysanthemoides. Evergreen, bushy perennial. H and S 2ft (60cm) or more. Frost tender, zone 10. Narrowly oval, feathery, strongly scented, green

leaves are 2in (5cm) long. Has small, long-stalked, daisylike, yellow flower heads, sometimes coppery below, in summer.

U. sericea. Evergreen, bushy sub-shrub. H and S 10–18in (25–45cm). Frost tender, zone 10. Leaves are cut into an elegant filigree of very slender, silver-haired segments. Daisylike, yellow flower heads, 1½in (4cm) across, open in summer. Is mainly grown for its foliage.

UTRICULARIA (Lentibulariaceae)

Genus of deciduous or evergreen, perennial, carnivorous water plants with bladderlike, modified leaves that trap and digest insects. Most species in cultivation are free-floating. Frost hardy to frost tender, min. 45°F (7°C). Some species are suitable only for tropical aquariums; those grown in outdoor pools require full sun. Thin out plants that are overcrowded or laden with algae. Propagate by division of floating foliage in spring or summer.

U. exoleta. Deciduous, perennial, free-floating water plant. S 6in (15cm). Frost tender, zone 10. Slender stems carry finely divided, green leaves on which small bladders develop. Pouched, bright yellow flowers are borne in summer. Is evergreen in very warm water and is suitable only for a tropical aquarium.

U. vulgaris. Deciduous, perennial, free-floating water plant. S 12in (30cm). Frost hardy, zones 5–9. Much-divided, bronze-green leaves, studded with small bladders, are produced on slender stems. Bears pouched, bright yellow flowers in summer. May be grown in a pool or cold-water aquarium.

UVULARIA (Liliaceae)

Genus of spring-flowering perennials that thrive in moist woodlands. Fully hardy. Requires semi-shade and prefers peaty soil. Propagate in early spring, before flowering, by division.

U. grandiflora illus. p.229.

U. perfoliata. Clump-forming perennial. H 18in (45cm), S 12in (30cm). Zones 5–9. In spring, clusters of pendent, bell-shaped, pale yellow flowers with twisted petals appear on numerous slender stems above stem-clasping, narrowly oval, green leaves.

V

VACCINIUM (Ericaceae)
Genus of deciduous or evergreen
sub-shrubs, shrubs, and trees, grown
for their foliage, autumn color (on
deciduous species), flowers, and fruits,
often edible. Fully to frost hardy.
Requires sun or semi-shade and moist
but well-drained, peaty or sandy, acid
soil. Propagate by semi-ripe cuttings
in summer or by seed in autumn.
V. angustifolium. Deciduous shrub,
usually grown in the dense, bushy
form var. *laevifolium* illus. p.140.
V. arctostaphylos (Caucasian
whortleberry). Deciduous, upright
shrub. H 10ft (3m), S 6ft (2m). Fully
hardy, zones 6–8. Has red-brown
young shoots and oval, dark green
leaves that turn red and purple in
autumn. Bell-shaped, red-tinged, white
flowers, borne in spreading racemes in
early summer, are followed by
spherical, purplish black fruits.
V. corymbosum (Highbush blueberry)
illus. p.128. **'Pioneer'** illus. p.141.
V. glauco-album illus. p.144.
V. myrtillus (Bilberry, Whortleberry).
Deciduous, usually prostrate shrub.
H 6in (15cm) or more, S 12in (30cm)
or more. Fully hardy, zones 5–7. Has
small, heart-shaped, leathery, bright
green leaves. Pendent, bell-shaped,
pale pink flowers in early summer
are followed by edible, round, blue-
black fruits.
V. nummularia. Evergreen, prostrate
shrub. H 4in (10cm), S 8in (20cm).
Frost hardy, zones 7–9. Slender stems,
covered in red-brown bristles, bear
oval, wrinkled, bright green leaves with
red-brown bristles at margins. Has
small racemes of bell-shaped, white to
deep pink flowers at stem tips in early
summer, followed by small, round,
black fruits. Suits a rock garden or peat
bed. Needs semi-shade. May also be
propagated by division in spring.
V. parvifolium. illus. p.141.
V. vitis-idaea. Vigorous, evergreen,
prostrate shrub with underground
runners. H $^3/_4$–10in (2–25cm), S
indefinite. Fully hardy, zones 2–5.
Forms hummocks of oval, hard,
leathery leaves. Has bell-shaped, white
to pink flowers in nodding racemes
from early summer to autumn, and
bright red fruits in autumn-winter.
May also be propagated by division
in spring. **'Minus'** illus. p.306.

VALERIANA (Valerianaceae)
Valerian
Genus of summer-flowering perennials
that are suitable for borders and rock
gardens. Fully hardy. Requires sun
and well-drained soil. Propagate by
division in autumn, *V. officinalis* by
seed in spring.
V. officinalis illus. p.202.
V. phu 'Aurea' illus. p.229.

VALLEA (Elaeocarpaceae)
Genus of one species of evergreen
shrub, grown for its overall

appearance. Half hardy, but best at
37–41°F (3–5°C) to prevent foliage
being damaged by cold. Prefers full
sun and humus-rich, well-drained soil.
Water potted plants freely when in
full growth, moderately at other times.
Untidy growth may be cut out in early
spring. Propagate by seed in spring or
by semi-ripe cuttings in summer. Red
spider mite may be a nuisance.
V. stipularis. Evergreen, erect, then
loose and spreading shrub. H and S
6–15ft (2–5m). Zones 9–10. Leaves
are lance-shaped to rounded and lobed,
deep green above, gray beneath. Small,
cup-shaped flowers, each with 5 deep
pink petals that have 3 lobes, are borne
in small, terminal and lateral clusters
in spring-summer.

VALLISNERIA (Hydrocharitaceae)
Genus of evergreen, perennial,
submerged water plants, grown for
their foliage. Is suitable for pools and
aquariums. Frost tender, min. 41°F
(5°C). Requires sun or semi-shade
and deep, clear water. Remove fading
foliage, and thin overcrowded plants
as required. Propagate by division in
spring or summer.
V. gigantea. Vigorous, evergreen,
perennial, submerged water plant. S
indefinite. Zones 9–10. Quickly forms
colonies of long, strap-shaped, green
leaves. Insignificant, greenish flowers
are produced year-round.
V. spiralis (Eel grass, Tape grass).
Vigorous, evergreen, perennial,
submerged water plant. S indefinite.
Zones 9–10. Rapidly forms a mass of
long, strap-shaped, green leaves, but
on a smaller scale than *V. gigantea.*
Bears insignificant, greenish flowers
year-round.

Vallota speciosa. See *Cyrtanthus
purpureus.*

VANCOUVERIA (Berberidaceae)
Genus of perennials, some of which
are evergreen, suitable for ground
cover. Fully hardy. Prefers cool,
partially shaded positions and moist,
peaty soil. Propagate by division
in spring.
V. chrysantha. Evergreen, sprawling
perennial. H 12in (30cm), S indefinite.
Zones 6–8. Oval, dark green leaves
borne on flower stems are divided into
rounded diamond-shaped leaflets with
thickened, undulating margins. Loose
sprays of small, bell-shaped, yellow
flowers are borne in spring.
V. hexandra illus. p.287.

VANDA. See ORCHIDS.
V. Rothschildiana (illus. p.254).
Evergreen, epiphytic orchid for a cool
or intermediate greenhouse. H 24in
(60cm). Zone 10. Sprays of dark-
veined, violet-blue flowers, 4in (10cm)
across, are borne twice a year in
varying seasons. Has narrowly oval,
rigid leaves, 4–5in (10–12cm) long.

Grow in a hanging basket and provide
good light in summer.

VELLOZIA (Velloziaceae)
Genus of evergreen perennials and
shrubs, grown for their showy flowers.
Frost tender, min. 50°F (10°C). Grow
in sun or partial shade and in well-
drained soil. Propagate by seed or
division in spring.
V. elegans, syn. *Barbacenia elegans.*
Evergreen, mat-forming perennial with
slightly woody stems. H to 6in (15cm),
S 6–12in (15–30cm). Zone 10. Lance-
shaped, leathery, dark green leaves, to
8in (20cm) long, each have a V-shaped
keel. Solitary small, star-shaped, white
flowers are held on slender stems
above leaves in late spring.

VELTHEIMIA (Liliaceae)
Genus of winter-flowering bulbs
with dense spikes of pendent, tubular
flowers and rosettes of basal leaves.
Frost tender, min. 50°F (10°C).
Requires good light, to keep foliage
compact and to develop flower colors
fully, and well-drained soil. Plant in
autumn with tips above soil surface.
Reduce watering in summer. Propagate
by seed or offsets in autumn.
V. bracteata, syn. *V. undulata,
V. viridifolia,* illus. p.355.
V. capensis, syn. *V. glauca.* Winter-
flowering bulb. H 12–18in (30–45cm),
S 8–12in (20–30cm). Zone 10. Has a
basal rosette of lance-shaped leaves,
usually with very wavy edges. Stem
produces a dense spike of pink or red
flowers, each $^3/_4$–1$^1/_4$in (2–3cm) long.
V. glauca. See *V. capensis.*
V. undulata. See *V. bracteata.*
V. viridifolia. See *V. bracteata.*

---

x VENIDIO-ARCTOTIS
(Compositae)
Hybrid genus (*Arctotis grandis*
x *A. breviscapa* x *Venidium fastuosum*)
of perennials. Half hardy. Prefers sun
and fertile, well-drained soil. Propagate
by semi-ripe cuttings in late summer.
Old plants are best replaced annually.
x V. cultivars. Fairly slow-growing,
upright, branching perennials, usually
grown as annuals. H and S 18in
(45cm). Zones 9–10. Lance-shaped,
lobed leaves are grayish green above,
white below. In summer has large,
daisylike flower heads in many shades,
including yellow, orange, bronze,
purple, pink, cream, and red. **'Bacchus'**
has purple flower heads; **'China
Rose'**, deep pink; **'Sunshine'**, yellow;
'Tangerine', orange-yellow; and
'Torch', bronze.

VERATRUM (Liliaceae)
Genus of perennials, ideal for
woodland gardens. Fully hardy.
Requires semi-shade and fertile,
moist soil. Propagate by division or
seed in autumn.
V. album (White false hellebore).
Clump-forming perennial. H 6ft (2m),

S 2ft (60cm). Zones 7–9. Produces
stems, leafy at base, that bear dense,
terminal panicles of saucer-shaped,
yellowish white flowers in summer.
Leaves are oval, pleated, and dark
green.
V. nigrum illus. p.190.

VERBASCUM (Scrophulariaceae)
Mullein
Genus of mainly summer-flowering
perennials, some of which are semi-
evergreen or evergreen, and evergreen
biennials and shrubs. Fully to frost
hardy. Tolerates shade, but prefers an
open, sunny site and well-drained soil.
Propagate species by seed in spring
or late summer or by root cuttings in
winter, selected forms by root cuttings
only. Some species self seed freely.
V. bombyciferum. Evergreen, erect
biennial. H 4–6ft (1.2–2m), S 2ft
(60cm). Fully hardy, zones 5–9. Oval
leaves and stems are covered with
silver hairs. Upright racemes, densely
set with 5-lobed, yellow flowers, are
produced in summer.
V. chaixii. Erect perennial, covered
with silvery hairs. H 3ft (1m), S 2ft
(60cm). Fully hardy, zones 5–9.
Produces slender spires of 5-lobed,
yellow, sometimes white flowers, with
purple stamens, in summer. Has oval,
toothed, rough, nettlelike leaves.
V. 'Cotswold Queen'. Short-lived,
rosette-forming perennial. H 3–4ft
(1–1.2m), S 1–2ft (30–60cm). Fully
hardy, zones 5–9. Throughout summer
branched racemes of 5-lobed, apricot
buff flowers are borne on stems that
arise from oval, green leaves.
V. densiflorum, syn. *V. thapsiforme.*
Fairly slow-growing, semi-evergreen,
upright perennial. H 4–5ft (1.2–1.5m),
S 2ft (60cm). Fully hardy, zones 5–9.
Has a rosette of large, oval, crinkled,
hairy, green leaves. Hairy stems each
produce a bold spike of flattish,
5-lobed, yellow flowers in summer.
V. dumulosum illus. p.299.
V. 'Gainsborough' illus. p.213.
V. 'Letitia' illus. p.298.
V. lychnitis (White mullein). Slow-
growing, evergreen, upright, branching
biennial. H 2–3ft (60cm–1m), S 2ft
(60cm). Fully hardy, zones 6–9. Has
lance-shaped, dark gray-green leaves.
Flattish, 5-lobed, white flowers are
borne on branching stems in summer.
V. nigrum illus. p.215.
V. olympicum illus. p.191.
V. 'Pink Domino'. Short-lived,
rosette-forming perennial. H 4ft
(1.2m), S 1–2ft (30–60cm). Fully
hardy, zones 5–9. Produces branched
racemes of 5-lobed, rose-pink flowers
throughout summer above oval,
green leaves.
V. thapsiforme. See *V. densiflorum.*

VERBENA (Verbenaceae)
Genus of summer- and autumn-
flowering biennials and perennials,
some of which are semi-evergreen.

Frost hardy to frost tender, min. 34°F (1°C). Prefers sun and well-drained soil. Propagate by stem cuttings in late summer or autumn or by seed in autumn or spring.

V. alpina of gardens. See *V. tenera* var. *maonettii*.

V. bonariensis. See *V. patagonica*.

V. chamaedrioides. See *V. peruviana*.

V. chamaedryfolia. See *V. peruviana*.

V. x hybrida (Garden verbena). 'Amethyst' is a fairly slow-growing, bushy perennial, grown as an annual. H 8–12in (20–30cm), S 12in (30cm). Frost tender. Has oval, serrated, mid- to deep green leaves. Clusters of small, tubular, lobed, blue flowers with white eyes appear in summer and early autumn. 'Defiance' illus. p.272. Derby Series, H 8in (20cm), is very compact and has a wide color range, including red, pink, blue, mauve, and white. Flowers of 'Mme. du Barry' are carmine crimson. 'Showtime' illus. p.270. 'Springtime', H 8in (20cm), is a spreading cultivar, in a mixture of bright colors.

V. patagonica, syn. *V. bonariensis*, illus. p.190.

V. peruviana, syn. *V. chamaedrioides*, *V. chamaedryfolia*. Semi-evergreen, prostrate perennial. H to 3in (8cm), S 3ft (1m). Frost tender, zones 9–10. Heads of small, tubular, brilliant scarlet flowers, with spreading petal lobes, are produced from early summer to early autumn. Has oval, green-toothed leaves. Prefers dry soil that is not too rich.

V. rigida, syn. *V. venosa*, illus. p.241.

V. 'Sissinghurst' illus. p.237.

V. tenera var. *maonettii*, syn. *V. alpina* of gardens. Spreading perennial with a slightly woody base. H 3in (8cm), S 6in (15cm). Half hardy, zones 9–10. Has oblong to oval leaves, deeply cut into linear, toothed, green segments, and, in summer, produces terminal clusters of small, tubular, reddish violet flowers, with white-edged lobes.

V. venosa. See *V. rigida*.

VERONICA (Scrophulariaceae)
Genus of perennials and sub-shrubs, some of which are semi-evergreen or evergreen, grown for their usually blue flowers. Fully to frost hardy. Needs sun and well-drained soil. Propagate by division in spring or autumn, by softwood or semi-ripe cuttings in summer, or by seed in autumn.

V. austriaca. Mat-forming or upright perennial. H and S 10–20in (25–50cm). Fully hardy, zones 5–8. Short, dense or lax racemes of small, saucer-shaped, bright blue flowers appear in early summer. Leaves are very variable: from broadly oval to narrowly oblong, and from entire to deeply cut and fernlike. Suits a rock garden or bank. subsp. *teucrium* (syn. *V. teucrium*) illus. p.298. subsp. *teucrium* 'Royal Blue' has deep royal blue flowers. Propagate by division in spring or by softwood cuttings in summer.

V. cinerea. Spreading, much-branched, woody-based perennial. H 6in (15cm), S 12in (30cm). Fully hardy, zones 5–8. Has small, linear, occasionally oval, hairy, silvery white leaves. Trailing

flower stems bear saucer-shaped, deep blue to purplish blue flowers, with white eyes, in early summer. Suits a sunny rock garden.

V. exaltata. Erect, elegant perennial. H 4ft (1.2m), S 1ft (30cm). Fully hardy, zones 4–8. Produces tall racemes of star-shaped, light blue flowers from mid- to late summer on stems clothed in narrowly oval, toothed, green leaves.

V. fruticans (Rock speedwell). Deciduous, upright to procumbent sub-shrub. H 6in (15cm), S 12in (30cm). Fully hardy, zones 4–8. Leaves are oval and green. Spikes of saucer-shaped, bright blue flowers, each with a red eye, are borne in summer. Is suitable for a rock garden.

V. gentianoides illus. p.243.

V. longifolia. Clump-forming perennial. H 3–4ft (1–1.2m), S 1ft (30cm) or more. Fully hardy, zones 4–8. In summer, long, terminal racemes of star-shaped, bright blue flowers are produced on stems clothed with whorls of narrowly oval to lance-shaped, toothed, green leaves.

'Romiley Purple' illus. p.210.

V. pectinata. Dense, mat-forming perennial that is sometimes semi-erect. H and S 8in (20cm). Fully hardy, zones 4-8. Has small, narrowly oval, hairy leaves and, in summer, loose sprays of saucer-shaped, soft blue to blue-violet flowers. Is good for a rock garden or bank. 'Rosea', H 3in (8cm), has rose-lilac flowers.

V. perfoliata, syn. *Parahebe perfoliata*, illus. p.243.

V. prostrata illus. p.297. 'Kapitan' and 'Trehane' illus. p.297. 'Spode Blue' is a dense, mat-forming perennial. H to 12in (30cm), S indefinite. Fully hardy, zones 4–7. Upright spikes of small, saucer-shaped, china blue flowers appear in early summer. Leaves are narrowly oval and toothed.

V. spicata (Spiked speedwell). Clump-forming perennial. H 12–24in (30–60cm), S 18in (45cm). Fully hardy, zones 4–8. Spikes of small, star-shaped, bright blue flowers are borne in summer above narrowly oval, toothed, green leaves. subsp. *incana* has star-shaped, clear blue flowers and linear to lance-shaped leaves. Plant is densely covered in silver hairs.

V. teucrium. See *V. austriaca* subsp. *teucrium*.

V. virginica, syn. *Veronicastrum virginicum*. Upright perennial. H 4ft (1.2m), S 1¹/₂ft (45cm). Fully hardy, zones 4–8. In late summer produces racemes of small, star-shaped, purple-blue or pink flowers that crown stems, which are clothed with whorls of narrowly lance-shaped, dark green leaves. f. *alba* illus. p.202.

Veronicastrum virginicum. See *Veronica virginica*.

VESTIA (Solanaceae)
Genus of one species of evergreen shrub, grown for its flowers and foliage. Frost hardy, but in cold areas is often cut to ground level and is best grown against a south-facing wall. Requires sun and fertile, well-drained

soil. Propagate by semi-ripe cuttings in summer or by seed in autumn or spring.

V. foetida, syn. *V. lycioides*. Evergreen, upright shrub. H 6ft (2m), S 5ft (1.5m). Zones 8–10. Pendent, tubular, pale yellow flowers are produced from mid-spring to mid-summer. Oblong, glossy, dark green leaves have an unpleasant scent.

V. lycioides. See *V. foetida*.

VIBURNUM (Caprifoliaceae)
Genus of deciduous, semi-evergreen, or evergreen shrubs and trees, grown for their foliage, autumn color (in many deciduous species), flowers, and, often, fruits. Fruiting is generally most prolific when several plants of different clones are planted together. Fully to frost hardy. Grow in sun or semi-shade and in deep, fertile, not too dry soil. To thin out overgrown plants cut out some older shoots after flowering. Propagate by cuttings (softwood for deciduous species, semi-ripe for evergreens) in summer or by seed in autumn.

V. acerifolium illus. p.129.

V. betulifolium illus. p.116.

V. bitchiuense. Deciduous, bushy shrub. H and S 8ft (2.5m). Fully hardy, zones 5–9. Has oval, dark green leaves, rounded heads of fragrant, tubular, pale pink flowers, from mid- to late spring, and egg-shaped, flattened, black fruits.

V. x bodnantense 'Dawn' illus. p.118. 'Deben' is a deciduous, upright shrub. H 10ft (3m), S 6ft (2m). Fully hardy, zones 7–9. Oval, toothed, dark green leaves are bronze when young. Has clusters of fragrant, tubular, pale pink-tinted, white flowers in mild periods from late autumn to early spring.

V. x burkwoodii. Semi-evergreen, bushy, open shrub. H and S 8ft (2.5m). Fully hardy, zones 4–8. Rounded heads of fragrant, tubular, pink, then white flowers are borne amid oval, glossy, dark green leaves from mid- to late spring. 'Anne Russell', H and S 5ft (1.5m), is deciduous and has very fragrant, white flowers. 'Park Farm Hybrid' bears very fragrant, white flowers, slightly pink in bud, and older leaves turn bright red in autumn.

V. x carlcephalum illus. p.85.

V. carlesii illus. p.122. 'Diana' is a deciduous, bushy, dense shrub. H and S 6ft (2m). Fully hardy, zones 6–9. Broadly oval leaves are bronze when young and turn purple-red in autumn. From mid- to late spring bears rounded heads of red buds that open to very fragrant, tubular, pink flowers fading to white.

V. cinnamomifolium. Evergreen, bushy or treelike shrub. H and S 15ft (5m). Frost hardy, zones 7–9. Has large, oval, green leaves, each with 3 prominent veins. Produces broad clusters of small, star-shaped, white flowers in early summer, then egg-shaped, blue fruits.

V. davidii illus. p.143.

V. dilatatum. Deciduous, upright shrub. H 10ft (3m), S 6ft (2m). Fully hardy, zones 5–9. Oval, sharply toothed, dark green leaves sometimes redden in autumn. Flat heads of small,

star-shaped, white flowers in late spring and early summer are succeeded by showy, egg-shaped, bright red fruits. 'Catskill' illus. p.107.

V. farreri, syn. *V. fragrans*, illus. p.115. 'Candidissimum' is a deciduous, upright shrub. H 10ft (3m), S 6ft (2m). Fully hardy, zones 6–9. Oval, toothed, dark green leaves are pale green when young. Produces clusters of fragrant, tubular, pure white flowers in late autumn and during mild periods in winter and early spring.

V. foetens illus. p.117.

V. fragrans. See *V. farreri*.

V. grandiflorum. Deciduous, upright, open shrub. H and S 6ft (2m). Fully hardy, zones 7–9. Stiff branches bear oblong, dark green leaves that become deep purple in autumn. Dense clusters of fragrant, tubular, white-and-pink flowers open from deep pink buds from mid-winter to early spring.

V. x juddii illus. p.122.

V. lantana (Wayfaring tree). Vigorous, deciduous, upright shrub. H 15ft (5m), S 12ft (4m). Fully hardy, zones 4–8. Has broadly oval, gray-green leaves that redden in autumn. Flattened heads of small, 5-lobed, white flowers are borne in late spring and early summer, followed by egg-shaped, red fruits that ripen to black.

V. lentago (Sheepberry). Vigorous, deciduous, upright shrub. H 12ft (4m), S 10ft (3m). Fully hardy, zones 3–8. Oval, glossy, dark green leaves turn red and purple in autumn. Produces flattened heads of small, fragrant, star-shaped, white flowers in late spring and early summer, then egg-shaped, blue-black fruits.

V. odoratissimum (Sweet viburnum). Evergreen, bushy shrub. H and S 15ft (5m). Frost hardy, zones 8–9. Clusters of small, fragrant, star-shaped, white flowers, borne amid oval, leathery, glossy, dark green leaves in late spring, are followed by egg-shaped, red fruits that ripen to black.

V. opulus. Vigorous, deciduous, bushy shrub. H and S 12ft (4m). Fully hardy, zones 4–8. Bears broadly oval, lobed, deep green leaves that redden in autumn and, in late spring and early summer, flattened, lace-caplike heads of white flowers. Produces large bunches of spherical, bright red fruits. 'Compactum' illus. p.140. 'Xanthocarpum' has yellow fruits and green leaves that become yellow in autumn.

V. plicatum, syn. *V.p.* f. *plicatum* (Japanese snowball tree). Deciduous, bushy, spreading shrub. H 10ft (3m), S 12ft (4m). Fully hardy, zones 5–8. Leaves are oval, toothed, deeply veined, and dark green, turning reddish purple in autumn. Has dense, rounded heads of large, sterile, flattish, white flowers along branches in late spring and early summer. 'Mariesii' illus. p.84. 'Nanum Semperflorens' (syn. *V.p.* 'Watanabei', *V. watanabei*), H 6ft (2m), S 5ft (1.5m), is slow-growing, conical, and dense, and produces small flower heads more or less continuously from late spring until early autumn. 'Pink Beauty' illus. p.97. f. *tomentosum* has tiered branches, flattish, lace-caplike flower heads,

and red fruits that ripen to black.
'Watanabei' see *V.p.* 'Nanum Semperflorens'.
V. x *pragense.* See *V.* 'Pragense'.
V. **'Pragense'**, syn. *V.* x *pragense*, illus. p.107.
V. rhytidophyllum illus. p.86.
V. sargentii. Deciduous, bushy shrub. H and S 10ft (3m). Fully hardy, zones 4–8. Maplelike, green foliage often changes to yellow or red in autumn. Broad, flattish, lace-caplike heads of white flowers in late spring are followed by spherical, bright red fruits. **'Onondaga'**, S 6ft (2m), has bronzered, young leaves, becoming deep green, then bronze-red again in autumn. Flower buds are pink.
V. sieboldii. Deciduous, rounded, dense shrub. H 12ft (4m), S 20ft (6m). Fully hardy, zones 4–8. Has large, oblong to oval, glossy, bright green leaves. Rounded heads of tubular, creamy white flowers are produced in late spring, followed by egg-shaped, red-stalked, red fruits that ripen to black.
V. tinus illus. p.117. **'Eve Price'** is an evergreen, bushy, very compact shrub. H and S 10ft (3m). Frost hardy, zones 7–9. Flattened heads of small, starshaped, white flowers are freely borne from deep pink buds amid oval, dark green leaves in winter-spring and are followed by ovoid, blue fruits. **'Gwenllian'** has pale pink flowers and fruits very freely.
V. watanabei. See *V. plicatum* 'Nanum Semperflorens'.

VIGNA (Leguminosae)
Genus of evergreen, annual and perennial, erect or scrambling and twining climbers, grown mainly as crop plants for their leaves, pods, and seeds. Frost tender, min. 55–9°F (13–15°C). Provide humus-rich, well-drained soil and full light. Water freely when in full growth, sparingly at other times. Stems require support. Thin crowded stems or cut back hard in spring. Propagate by seed in autumn or spring.
V. caracalla, syn. *Phaseolus caracalla* (Snail flower). Fast-growing, evergreen, perennial, twining climber. H 10–15ft (3–5m). Zone 10. Leaves comprise 3 oval leaflets. From summer to early autumn carries pealike, purple-marked, cream flowers that turn orange-yellow.

VINCA (Apocynaceae)
Periwinkle
Genus of evergreen, trailing subshrubs and perennials, grown for their foliage and flowers. Flowers are tubular with 5 spreading lobes. Fully to frost hardy. Is useful for ground cover in shade, but flowers more freely given some sun. Grows in any soil that is not too dry. Propagate by semi-ripe cuttings in summer or by division from autumn to spring.
V. difformis. Evergreen, prostrate subshrub. H 12in (30cm), S indefinite. Frost hardy, zones 8–9. Slender, trailing stems bear oval, glossy, dark green leaves. Erect flower stems produce pale blue flowers in late autumn and early winter.

V. major (Greater periwinkle). Evergreen, prostrate, arching subshrub. H 18in (45cm), S indefinite. Fully hardy, zones 7–9. Leaves are broadly oval, glossy, and dark green. Large, bright blue flowers are produced from late spring to early autumn. subsp. *hirsuta* has leaves, leaf stalks, and calyces edged with long hairs. **'Variegata'** illus. p.143.
V. minor illus. p.144. **'Alba Variegata'** is an evergreen, prostrate sub-shrub. H 6in (15cm), S indefinite. Fully hardy, zones 4–8. Forms extensive mats of small, oval, glossy, dark green leaves, edged with pale yellow, above which white flowers are carried from mid-spring to early summer, then intermittently into autumn. **'Bowles' White'** bears large, white flowers that are pinkish white in bud. **'Gertrude Jekyll'** is of dense growth, with a profusion of small, white flowers. Flowers of **'La Grave'** are large and lavender blue.
V. rosea. See *Catharanthus roseus.*

VIOLA (Violaceae)
Violet
Genus of annuals, perennials, some of which are semi-evergreen, and deciduous sub-shrubs, grown for their distinctive flowers. Annuals are suitable as summer bedding, perennials and sub-shrubs are good in rock gardens, screes, and alpine houses. Fully to half hardy. Grow in sun or shade and well-drained but moisture-retentive soil unless otherwise stated; a few species prefer acid soil. Propagate annuals by seed sown according to flowering season, perennials and sub-shrubs by softwood cuttings in spring unless otherwise stated. Species may also be propagated by seed in spring or autumn.
V. aetolica illus. p.311.
V. **'Azure Blue'**. See *V.* x *wittrockiana.*
V. **'Baby Lucia'**. See *V.* x *wittrockiana.*
V. biflora (Twin-flowered violet). Creeping, rhizomatous perennial. H 2–6in (5–15cm), S 6in (15cm). Fully hardy, zones 4–8. Flat-faced, deep lemon yellow flowers, veined dark brown, are borne singly or in pairs on upright stems in summer. Leaves are kidney-shaped and green. Needs shade. May also be propagated by division.
V. calcarata illus. p.308.
V. cazorlensis. Tufted, woody-based perennial. H to 2in (5cm), S to 3in (8cm). Frost hardy, zone 8. Has small, linear to lance-shaped leaves and in late spring carries small, flat-faced, long-spurred, deep pink flowers, singly on short stems. Suits an alpine house. Is difficult to grow.
V. cenisia. Spreading perennial with runners. H 3in (7cm), S 4in (10cm). Fully hardy, zones 4–8. Small, flat-faced, bright violet flowers, each with a deep purple line radiating from the center, are produced on very short stems in summer. Has a deep tap root and tiny, heart-shaped or oblong, dark green leaves. Suits a scree. Propagate by division in spring.
V., **Clear Crystals Series**. See *V.* x *wittrockiana.*

V. cornuta illus. p.289.
V., **Crystal Bowl Series**. See *V.* x *wittrockiana.*
V. cucullata. See *V. obliqua.*
V. elatior. Upright, little-branched perennial. H 8–12in (20–30cm), S 6in (15cm). Fully hardy, zones 4–8. Leaves are broadly lance-shaped and toothed. Produces flat-faced, pale blue flowers, with white centers, in early summer. Prefers semi-shade and moist soil. Propagate in spring by division.
V., **Floral Dance Series**. See *V.* x *wittrockiana.*
V. glabella. Clump-forming perennial with a scaly, horizontal rootstock. H 4in (10cm), S 8in (20cm). Fully hardy, zones 4–8. Flat-faced, bright yellow flowers, with purplish veins on lower petals, open in late spring above heart-shaped, toothed, bright green leaves. Needs shade. Propagate by division in spring.
V. gracilis. Mat-forming perennial. H 5in (12cm), S 6in (15cm) or more. Fully hardy, zones 5–8. Flat-faced, yellow-centered, violet-blue or sometimes yellow flowers are produced in summer. Has small, dissected leaves with linear or oblong segments. Needs sun.
V. **'Haslemere'** illus. p.321.
V. hederacea, syn. *V. reniformis, Erpetion reniforme* (Australian violet, Ivy-leaved violet). Evergreen, creeping, mat-forming perennial. H 1–2in (2.5–5cm), S indefinite. Half hardy, zones 8–9. Has tiny, rounded leaves and bears purple or white flowers, with a squashed appearance, on short stems in summer. Is useful in an alpine house. Prefers semi-shade. Propagate by division in spring.
V. **'Huntercombe Purple'** illus. p.322.
V., **Icequeen Series**. See *V.* x *wittrockiana.*
V., **Imperial Series, 'Orange Prince'**. See *V.* x *wittrockiana.*
V., **Imperial Series, 'Sky Blue'**. See *V.* x *wittrockiana.*
V. **'Irish Molly'**. Evergreen, clump-forming, short-lived perennial. H 4in (10cm), S 6–8in (15–20cm). Fully hardy, zones 5–7. Has broadly oval, dissected leaves and, in summer, a succession of flat-faced, old-gold flowers with brown centers. Flowers itself to death. Needs sun.
V. **'Jackanapes'** illus. p.312.
V. **'Joker'**. See *V.* x *wittrockiana.*
V. labradorica **'Purpurea'** illus. p.309.
V. **'Love Duet'**. See *V.* x *wittrockiana.*
V. lutea (Mountain pansy). Mat-forming, rhizomatous perennial. H 4in (10cm), S 6in (15cm). Fully hardy, zones 4–8. Has small, oval to lance-shaped leaves. Flat-faced, yellow, violet, or bicolored flowers appear in spring-summer.
V. **'Majestic Giants'**. See *V.* x *wittrockiana.*
V. obliqua, syn. *V. cucullata.* Variable, spreading perennial with fleshy rhizomes. H 2in (5cm), S 4–6in (10–15cm). Fully hardy, zones 5–8. Has kidney-shaped, toothed, green leaves. In late spring produces flat-faced, blue-violet, sometimes white or pale blue flowers. Propagate in spring by division. Self seeds freely.

V. odorata (Sweet violet). Semi-evergreen, spreading, rhizomatous perennial. H 3in (7cm), S 6in (15cm) or more. Fully hardy, zones 4–8. Leaves are heart-shaped and toothed. Long stems each carry a fragrant, flat-faced, violet or white flower from late winter to early spring. Is useful for growing in a wild garden. Self seeds prolifically. May also be propagated by division.
V. palmata. Spreading perennial. H 4in (10cm), S 6in (15cm). Fully hardy, zones 5–8. Has short-stemmed, flat-faced, pale violet flowers in late spring and deeply dissected leaves. Prefers dry, well-drained soil. Self seeds readily.
V. pedata illus. p.309. var. *bicolor* is a clump-forming perennial with a thick rootstock. H 2in (5cm), S 3in (8cm). Fully hardy, zones 3–8. Flat-faced, velvety purple or white flowers are borne singly on slender stems in late spring and early summer. Leaves are finely divided into 5–7 or more, narrow, toothed segments. Suits an alpine house. May be difficult to grow; needs peaty, sandy soil.
V. **'Queen of the Planets'**. See *V.* x *wittrockiana.*
V. **'Redwing'**. See *V.* x *wittrockiana.*
V. reniformis. See *V. hederacea.*
V. **'Roggli Giants'**. See *V.* x *wittrockiana.*
V. **'Scarlet Clan'**. See *V.* x *wittrockiana.*
V. **'Silver Princess'**. See *V.* x *wittrockiana.*
V. **'Super Chalon Giants'**. See *V.* x *wittrockiana.*
V. tricolor illus. p.309. **'Bowles' Black'** illus. p.310.
V., **Universal Series**. See *V.* x *wittrockiana.*
V. x *wittrockiana* (Pansy). Group of slow- to moderately fast-growing, mainly bushy perennials, usually grown as annuals or biennials. H 6–8in (15–20cm), S 8in (20cm). Fully hardy. Has oval, often serrated, green leaves. Flattish, 5-petaled flowers, 1–4in (2.5–10cm) wide, in a very wide color range, appear throughout summer or in winter-spring. The following are among those available:
'Azure Blue' (spring-flowering) illus. p.277.
'Baby Lucia' (summer-flowering) has small, deep blue flowers.
Clear Crystals Series (summer-flowering) is in a wide range of clear colors (yellow, illus. p.281).
Crystal Bowl Series (summer-flowering) is in a range of colors (yellow, illus. p.281).
Floral Dance Series (winter-flowering) has a wide range of colors (mixed, illus. p.273; white, illus. p.263).
Icequeen Series (winter- and early spring-flowering) has a range of colors (yellow, illus. p.281).
Imperial Series, 'Orange Prince' (summer-flowering) has orange flowers with black blotches.
Imperial Series, 'Sky Blue' (summer-flowering) has sky blue flowers, each with a deeper blotch.
'Joker' (summer-flowering) illus. p.276.

'Love Duet' (summer-flowering) has cream or white flowers, each with a deep pink blotch.

'Majestic Giants' (summer-flowering) has large flowers in a wide color range.

'Queen of the Planets' (summer-flowering) has very large, multicolored flowers.

'Redwing' (summer-flowering) illus. p.282.

'Roggli Giants' (summer- to autumn-flowering) illus. p.271.

'Scarlet Clan' (summer-flowering) illus. p.283.

'Silver Princess' (summer-flowering) has white flowers, each with a deep pink blotch.

'Super Chalon Giants' (summer- to autumn-flowering) illus. p.280.

Universal Series (winter- to spring-flowering) has a range of separate colors (apricot, illus. p.283) or a mixture of colors.

VIRGILIA (Leguminosae)
Genus of short-lived, evergreen shrubs and trees, grown for their flowers in spring-summer. Frost tender, min. 41°F (5°C). Prefers well-drained soil and full light. Water pot-grown plants freely when in full growth, less at other times. Pruning is usually not required. Propagate in spring by seed, ideally soaked in warm water for 24 hours before sowing.
V. capensis. Fast-growing, evergreen, rounded shrub or tree. H and S 20–30ft (6–10m). Zone 10. Has leaves of 11–21 oblong leaflets. Racemes of fragrant, pealike, bright mauve-pink flowers, sometimes pink, crimson, or white, are produced in late spring and summer, usually in profusion.

Viscaria alpina. See *Lychnis alpina.*
Viscaria elegans. See *Silene coeli-rosa.*

VITALIANA (Primulaceae)
Genus of one species of evergreen, spring-flowering perennial, grown for its flowers. Is often included in *Douglasia* and is useful for rock gardens, screes, and alpine houses. Fully hardy. Requires sun and moist

but well-drained soil. Propagate by softwood cuttings in summer or by seed in autumn.
V. primuliflora, syn. *Douglasia vitaliana,* illus. p.312.

VITEX (Verbenaceae)
Genus of evergreen or deciduous trees and shrubs, grown for their flowers. Cultivated species are frost hardy, but in cold areas grow against a south- or west-facing wall. Needs full sun and well-drained soil. Propagate by semi-ripe cuttings in summer or by seed in autumn or spring.
V. agnus-castus (Chaste tree). Deciduous, spreading, open, aromatic shrub. H and S 8ft (2.5m). Zones 7–9. Upright panicles of fragrant, tubular, violet-blue flowers appear in early and mid-autumn. Dark green leaves are each divided into 5 or 7 long, narrowly lance-shaped leaflets.
V. negundo. Deciduous, bushy shrub. H and S 10ft (3m). Zones 6–9. Green leaves are each composed of 3–7 narrowly oval, sharply toothed leaflets. Produces loose panicles of small, tubular, violet-blue flowers from late summer to early autumn.

VITIS (Vitaceae)
Grape
Genus of deciduous, woody-stemmed, tendril climbers, grown for their foliage and fruits (grapes), which are produced in bunches. Fully to half hardy. Prefers fertile, well-drained, chalky soil and sun or semi-shade. Produces the best fruits and autumn leaf-color when planted in a warm situation. Propagate by hardwood cuttings in late autumn.
V. aconitifolia. See *Ampelopsis aconitifolia.*
V. amurensis (Amur grape). Vigorous, deciduous, woody-stemmed, tendril climber. H 20ft (6m). Fully hardy, zones 5–9. Dark green, 3- or 5-lobed leaves, 5–12in (12–30cm) long, turn red and purple in autumn. Has inconspicuous flowers in summer; tiny, black fruits are produced from late summer to autumn.
V. 'Brant'. Deciduous, woody-stemmed, tendril climber. H to 22ft

(7m) or more. Fully hardy, zones 5–9. Has lobed, toothed, bright green leaves 4–9in (10–22cm) long, that, except for veins, turn brown-red in autumn. Inconspicuous flowers in summer are followed by green or purple fruits.
V. coignetiae illus. p.176.
V. davidii. Deciduous, woody-stemmed, tendril climber; young stems have short prickles. H to 25ft (8m) or more. Half hardy, zones 7–10. Heart-shaped leaves, 4–10in (10–25cm) long, are blue- or gray-green beneath, turning scarlet in autumn. Insignificant, greenish flowers are borne in summer, followed by small, black fruits.
V. henryana. See *Parthenocissus henryana.*
V. heterophylla. See *Ampelopsis brevipedunculata* var. *maximowiczii.*
V. quinquefolia. See *Parthenocissus quinquefolia.*
V. striata. See *Cissus striata.*
V. thompsonii. See *Parthenocissus thompsonii.*
V. vinifera (Vine grape). **'Purpurea'** illus. p.176.

VRIESEA (Bromeliaceae)
Genus of evergreen, rosette-forming, epiphytic perennials, grown for their flowers and overall appearance. Frost tender, min. 59°F (15°C), zone 10. Needs semi-shade and a rooting medium of equal parts humus-rich soil and either sphagnum moss or bark or plastic chips used for orchid culture. Using soft water, water moderately when in growth, sparingly at other times, and from mid-spring to mid-autumn keep rosette centers filled with water. Propagate by offsets or seed in spring.
V. fenestralis. Evergreen, epiphytic perennial with dense, funnel-shaped rosettes. H and S 12–16in (30–40cm). Pale green leaves, with dark lines and cross-bands, are very broadly strap-shaped and arching or rolled under at tips. In summer, flat racemes of tubular, yellowish green flowers, with green bracts, are borne above foliage.
V. fosteriana. Evergreen, epiphytic perennial with dense, funnel-shaped rosettes. H and S 24in (60cm) or more. Has broadly strap-shaped, arching,

yellowish to deep green leaves, cross-banded with reddish brown, particularly beneath. In summer-autumn, flat spikes of tubular, pale yellow or greenish yellow flowers, with brownish red tips, are produced well above foliage.
V. hieroglyphica (King-of-the-bromeliads). Evergreen, epiphytic perennial with dense, funnel-shaped rosettes. H and S 2–3ft (60cm–1m). Produces very broadly strap-shaped, arching, yellowish green leaves, cross-banded and checkered with dark brownish green. In summer bears panicles of tubular, yellow flowers well above leaves.
V. platynema. Evergreen, basal-rosetted, epiphytic perennial. H and S 24in (60cm). Broadly strap-shaped, mid- to light green leaves, with purple tips, form dense rosettes. In summer produces flat racemes of tubular, green-and-yellow flowers with red or yellow bracts.
V. psittacina. Evergreen, spreading, basal-rosetted, epiphytic perennial. H and S 16–24in (40–60cm). Produces dense rosettes of strap-shaped, arching, pale green leaves. Flat spikes of tubular, yellow flowers with green tips, emerging from red-and-yellow or red-and-green bracts, are borne above foliage in summer-autumn.
V. splendens (Flaming-sword; illus. p.222). Evergreen, basal-rosetted, epiphytic perennial. H and S 12in (30cm). Strap-shaped, arching, olive green leaves, with purple to reddish brown cross-bands, form dense rosettes. Flat, sword-shaped racemes of tubular, yellow flowers, between bright red bracts, are borne in summer-autumn.

x VUYLSTEKEARA. See ORCHIDS.
x V. Cambria 'Lensing's Favorite' (illus. p.253). Evergreen, epiphytic orchid for a cool greenhouse. H 9in (23cm). Zone 10. Produces long sprays of wine red flowers, 4in (10cm) across, heavily marked with white; flowering season varies. Has narrowly oval leaves, 4–6in (10–15cm) long. Needs shade in summer.

WACHENDORFIA
(Haemodoraceae)
Genus of summer-flowering perennials with deep roots, to guard against frost. Half hardy. Requires full sun and moist soil. Propagate by division in spring or by seed in autumn or spring.
W. thyrsiflora. Clump-forming perennial. H 5–6ft (1.5–2m), S 1½ft (45cm). Zone 9–10. Shallowly cup-shaped, yellow to orange flowers are produced in dense panicles in early summer. Green leaves are narrowly sword-shaped, pleated, and rather coarse.

WAHLENBERGIA (Campanulaceae)
Genus of summer-flowering annuals, biennials, and short-lived perennials, grown for their bell-shaped flowers. Is useful for alpine houses. Frost hardy. Needs a sheltered site, partial shade, and well-drained, peaty, sandy soil. Propagate by seed in autumn.
W. albomarginata (New Zealand bluebell). Basal-rosetted, rhizomatous perennial. H and S 6in (15cm) or more. Zones 5–7. Slender stems each carry a bell-shaped, clear blue flower that opens flat in summer. Has narrowly elliptic to oval, green leaves in tufts. Is good in a rock garden.
W. congesta, syn. *W. saxicola.* Mat-forming, creeping, rhizomatous perennial. H 3in (7cm), S 4in (10cm). Zones 5–7. Has small, rounded or spoon-shaped, green leaves and, in summer, bell-shaped, lavender blue or white flowers held singly on wiry stems.
W. saxicola. See *W. congesta.*

WALDSTEINIA (Rosaceae)
Genus of semi-evergreen, creeping perennials with runners. Makes good ground cover. Fully hardy. Needs sun and well-drained soil. Propagate by division in early spring.
W. fragarioides. Vigorous, semi-evergreen, mat-forming perennial. H 4–6in (10–15cm), S indefinite. Zones 5–8. Has 3-parted, hairy leaves and, in late spring and early summer, bears sparse clusters of small, saucer-shaped, yellow flowers.
W. ternata, syn. *W. trifolia,* illus. p.325.
W. trifolia. See *W. ternata.*

WASHINGTONIA (Palmae)
Genus of evergreen palms, grown for their stately appearance. Frost tender, min. 50°F (10°C). Grows in fertile, well-drained soil and in full sun. Water potted specimens freely in summer, moderately at other times. Remove skirt of persistent, dead leaves as they are a fire risk. Propagate by seed in spring at not less than 75°F (24°C). Red spider mite may be a nuisance.
W. filifera (Desert fan palm). Fast-growing, evergreen palm. H and S to 80ft (25m). Zones 9–10. Has fan-shaped, long-stalked, gray-green

leaves, each lobe with a filamentous tip. Long-stalked clusters of tiny, creamy white flowers are borne in summer and berrylike, black fruits in winter.
W. robusta illus. p.47.

WATSONIA (Iridaceae)
Genus of clump-forming corms, *Gladiolus*like in overall appearance, although flowers are more tubular. Half hardy. Requires an open, sunny position and light, well-drained soil. Plant in autumn, 4–6in (10–15cm) deep; protect with bracken, loose peat or similar during first winter, if frost is expected. Feed with slow-acting fertilizer, such as bonemeal, in summer. Corms are best left undisturbed to form clumps. Propagate by seed in autumn.
W. ardernei. See *W. meriana.*
W. beatricis illus. p.335.
W. fourcadei. Clump-forming, summer-flowering corm. H to 5ft (1.5m), S 1–1½ft (30–45cm). Zones 9–10. Sword-shaped, erect leaves are mostly basal. Has a dense spike of tubular, salmon red flowers, each 3–3½in (8–9cm) long and with 6 lobes.
W. meriana, syn. *W. ardernei.* Clump-forming, summer-flowering corm. H to 3ft (1m), S 1–1½ft (30–45cm). Zones 9–10. Has sword-shaped, erect leaves both on stem and at base. Stem carries a loose spike of tubular, pinkish red flowers, each 2–2½in (5–6cm) long and with 6 spreading lobes.
W. pyramidata illus. p.335.

WATTAKAKA (Asclepiadaceae)
Genus of evergreen, woody-stemmed, twining climbers, grown for botanical interest. Frost hardy. Grow in sun and in any well-drained soil. Propagate by seed in spring or by stem cuttings in summer or autumn.
W. sinensis, syn. *Dregea corrugata, D. sinensis.* Evergreen, woody-stemmed, twining climber. H to 10ft (3m). Zones 9–10. Oval, green leaves, heart-shaped at base, 1¼–4in (3–10cm) long, are grayish beneath. In summer has clusters of 10–25 small, fragrant, star-shaped flowers, white or cream with red dots and streaks, followed by pairs of slender pods, 2–3in (5–7cm) long.

WEIGELA (Caprifoliaceae)
Genus of deciduous shrubs, grown for their showy, funnel-shaped flowers. Fully hardy. Prefers sunny, fertile soil. To maintain vigor, prune out a few older branches to ground level, after flowering each year. Straggly, old plants may be pruned hard in spring (though this will lose one season's flowers). Propagate by softwood cuttings in summer.
W. 'Bristol Ruby'. Vigorous, deciduous, upright shrub. H 8ft (2.5m), S 6ft (2m). Zones 4–9. Deep red

flowers open from darker buds amid oval, toothed, green leaves in late spring and early summer.
W. 'Candida'. Deciduous, bushy shrub. H and S 8ft (2.5m). Zones 5–9. Pure white flowers appear in late spring and early summer. Leaves are oval, toothed, and bright green.
W. 'Eva Rathke'. Deciduous, upright, dense shrub. H and S 5ft (1.5m). Zones 5–9. Has oval, toothed, dark green leaves. Broad-mouthed, crimson flowers open from darker buds from late spring to early summer.
W. florida. Deciduous, arching shrub. H and S 8ft (2.5m). Zones 5–9. Bears deep pink flowers, pale pink to white inside, in late spring and early summer. Oval, toothed leaves are green. **'Foliis Purpureis'** illus. p.131. **'Variegata'** illus. p.128.
W. 'Looymansii Aurea'. Weak-growing, deciduous, upright shrub. H 5ft (1.5m), S 3ft (1m). Zones 5–9. From late spring to early summer produces pale pink flowers amid oval, toothed, narrowly red-rimmed, golden yellow leaves. Protect from hot sun.
W. middendorffiana illus. p.136.
W. praecox. Deciduous, upright shrub. H 8ft (2.5m), S 6ft (2m). Zones 4–9. In late spring produces fragrant pink flowers that are marked inside with yellow. Leaves are bright green, oval, and toothed. **'Variegata'** has leaves that have broad, creamy white margins.

WEINGARTIA (Cactaceae)
Genus of spherical, perennial cacti, closely related to *Sulcorebutia.* Offsets occasionally. Frost tender, min. 50°F (10°C). Needs a sunny, well-drained site. Propagate by seed in spring or summer.
W. neocumingii. Spherical, perennial cactus. H and S 4in (10cm). Zone 10. Has a tuberculate, green stem. Areoles each bear dense clusters of yellow spines, to ⅝in (1.5cm) long, some thicker than others, and several cup-shaped, dark yellow flowers, 1¼in (3cm) long, in spring.

WEINMANNIA (Cunoniaceae)
Genus of evergreen trees and shrubs, grown for their foliage, flowers, and overall appearance. Frost tender, min. 41–5°F (5–7°C). Needs partial shade or full light and humus-rich, well-drained but not dry soil, ideally neutral to acid. Water potted plants freely when in full growth, moderately at other times. Pruning is tolerated if needed. Propagate by seed in spring or by semi-ripe cuttings in summer.
W. trichosperma. Evergreen, ovoid to round-headed tree. H 40ft (12m) or more, S 25–30ft (8–10m). Zone 10. Glossy, rich green leaves have 9–19 oval, boldly toothed leaflets borne on a winged midrib. Spikes of tiny, fragrant white flowers, with pink stamens, are produced in early summer.

WELDENIA (Commelinaceae)
Genus of one species of summer-flowering, tuberous perennial, grown for its flowers. Half hardy. Needs sun and gritty, well-drained soil. Keep dry from autumn until growth restarts in late winter. Is suitable for alpine houses. Propagate by root cuttings in winter or by division in early spring.
W. candida illus. p.302.

WELWITSCHIA (Welwitschiaceae)
Genus of one species of evergreen, desert-growing perennial with a deep tap root. Has only 2 leaves, which lie on the ground and grow continuously from the base for up to 100 years. Frost tender, min. 50°F (10°C). Needs sun and sharply drained soil. Is difficult to grow as it needs desert conditions: may succeed in a mixture of stone chippings and leaf mold, in a length of drainpipe to take its long tap root. Propagate by seed when ripe.
W. bainesii. See *W. mirabilis.*
W. mirabilis, syn. *W. bainesii,* illus. p.260.

WESTRINGIA (Labiatae)
Genus of evergreen shrubs, grown for their flowers and overall appearance. Frost tender, min. 41–5°F (5–7°C). Requires full light and well-drained soil. Water potted specimens moderately, less when not in full growth. Propagate by seed in spring or by semi-ripe cuttings in late summer.
W. fruticosa, syn. *W. rosmariniformis,* illus. p.126.
W. rosmariniformis. See *W. fruticosa.*

WIGANDIA (Hydrophyllaceae)
Genus of evergreen perennials and shrubs, grown for their flowers and foliage. Frost tender, min. 45–50°F (7–10°C). Needs full light and moist but well-drained soil. Water potted plants freely in full growth, moderately at other times. Cut down flowered stems in spring to prevent plants becoming straggly. Propagate by seed or softwood cuttings in spring. Whitefly is sometimes troublesome.
W. caracasana. Evergreen, erect, sparsely branched shrub. H 6–10ft (2–3m), S 3–6ft (1–2m). Zone 10. Has oval, wavy-edged, toothed, deep green leaves, 18in (45cm) long and white-haired beneath. Carries 5-petaled, violet-purple flowers in large, terminal clusters from spring to autumn. Is often grown annually from seed purely for its handsome leaves.

WIGGINSIA (Cactaceae)
Genus of slow-growing, spherical, perennial cacti, closely related to *Notocactus,* becoming flattened or columnar with age. Dense, woolly crowns bear funnel-shaped, yellow flowers, with red stigmas, followed by long, soft, red seed pods, similar to those of *Neoporteria.* Frost tender, min. 41°F (5°C). Needs sun and well-

drained soil. Propagate by seed in spring or summer.
W. vorwerkiana illus. p.399.
Wilcoxia albiflora. See *Echinocereus leucanthus.*
Wilcoxia schmollii. See *Echinocereus schmollii.*

---

x WILSONARA. See ORCHIDS.
x *W.* **Hambuhren Stern 'Cheam'** (illus. p.253). Evergreen, epiphytic orchid for a cool greenhouse. Zone 10. H 9in (23cm). Bears spikes of deep reddish brown flowers, 3^1/$_2$in (9cm) across, each with a yellow lip; flowering season varies. Narrowly oval leaves are 4in (10cm) long. Requires shade in summer.

WISTERIA (Leguminosae)
Genus of deciduous, woody-stemmed, twining climbers, grown for their spectacular flowers and suitable for walls and pergolas and for growing against buildings and trees. Fully to frost hardy. Grow in sun and in fertile, well-drained soil. Prune after flowering and again in late winter. Propagate by bench grafting in winter or by seed in autumn or spring. Plants produced from seed may not flower until some years old and often have poor flowers.
W. brachybotrys f. *alba.* See *W. venusta.*
W. chinensis. See *W. sinensis.*
W. floribunda (Japanese wisteria). **'Alba'** illus. p.165. **'Macrobotrys'** is a deciduous, woody-stemmed, twining climber. H to 28ft (9m). Fully hardy, zones 4–10. Leaves, 10–14in (25–35cm) long, have 11–19 oval leaflets. Scented, pealike, lilac flowers, flushed darker, are carried in racemes,

3–4ft (1–1.2m) long, in early summer, and may produce oblong, velvety pods in late summer and autumn.
W. x *formosa* illus. p.173.
W. sinensis, syn. *W. chinensis*, illus. p.173. **'Alba'** illus. p.165. **'Black Dragon'** is a deciduous, woody-stemmed, twining climber. H to 28ft (9m). Fully hardy, zones 5–9. Leaves, 10–14in (25–35cm) long, have 11–19 oval leaflets. Scented, pealike, double, deep purple flowers are carried in racemes, 5–10in (12–25cm) long, in early summer, sometimes sparsely again in autumn. Oblong, velvety pods, 3–6in (7–15cm) long, appear in late summer and autumn. **'Prolific'**, H to 100ft (30m), is vigorous, with masses of single, lilac or pale violet flowers in longer racemes.
W. venusta, syn. *W. brachybotrys* f. *alba* (Silky wisteria). Deciduous, woody-stemmed, twining climber. H to 28ft (9m) or more. Fully hardy, zones 5–10. Leaves are 8–14in (20–35cm) long, with 9–13 oval leaflets. Has 4–6in (10–15cm) long racemes of scented, pealike, white flowers, each with a yellow blotch at base of upper petal, in early summer; sometimes flowers again sparsely in autumn. **'Alba Plena'** has double, white flowers.

WOLFFIA (Lemnaceae)
Duckweed
Genus of semi-evergreen, perennial, floating water plants, grown for their curiosity value as the smallest known flowering plants. Is ideal for cold-water aquariums. Half hardy. Needs a sunny position. Remove excess plantlets as required. Propagate by redistribution of plantlets as required.

W. arrhiza (Least duckweed). Semi-evergreen, perennial, floating water plant. S ^{1}/$_{32}$in (1mm). Zones 8–10. Leaves are rounded and green. Insignificant, greenish flowers are produced year-round.

WOODSIA (Polypodiaceae)
Genus of deciduous ferns, suitable for growing in rock gardens and alpine houses. Fully hardy. Tolerates sun or semi-shade. May be difficult to cultivate: soil must provide constant moisture and also be quick-draining, and crowns of plants must sit above soil to avoid rotting. Propagate by division in early spring.
W. alpina (Alpine woodsia). Deciduous fern. H and S 6in (15cm). Zones 3–8. Produces dense tufts of lance-shaped, much-divided, green fronds with oval pinnae.
W. ilvensis (Rusty woodsia). Deciduous fern. H and S 6in (15cm). Zones 4–8. Broadly lance-shaped, much-divided fronds, with oblong, wavy-toothed pinnae, are green.

WOODWARDIA (Polypodiaceae)
Genus of evergreen or deciduous ferns. Half hardy. Prefers semi-shade and fibrous, moist, peaty soil. Remove faded fronds regularly. Propagate by division in spring.
W. radicans (Chain fern). Vigorous, evergreen, spreading fern. H 4ft (1.2m), S 2ft (60cm). Zones 9–10. Large, broadly lance-shaped, coarsely divided, arching fronds, with narrowly oval pinnae, are green.
W. virginica (American chain fern, Virginian chain fern). Deciduous, creeping fern. H and S 18in (45cm).

Zones 6–9. Has broadly lance-shaped, divided, olive green fronds with oblong to oval pinnae.

WORSLEYA (Amaryllidaceae)
Blue amaryllis
Genus of one species of evergreen, winter-flowering bulb, with a neck up to 2^1/$_2$ft (75cm) high crowned by a tuft of leaves and an 8–12in (20–30cm), leafless flower stem. Frost tender, min. 59°F (15°C). Needs full sun and well-drained soil, or compost mixed with osmunda fiber, perlite, or bark chips and some leaf mold. Do not allow soil to dry out at any stage. Propagate by seed in spring.
W. procera. See *W. rayneri.*
W. rayneri, syn. *W. procera*, *Hippeastrum procerum*. Evergreen, winter-flowering bulb. H 3–4ft (1–1.2m), S 1^1/$_2$–2ft (45–60cm). Zone 10. Bears long, strap-shaped, strongly curved leaves and up to 14 funnel-shaped, lilac-blue flowers, 6in (15cm) long, with wavy-edged petals.

WULFENIA (Scrophulariaceae)
Genus of evergreen, summer-flowering perennials with rough-textured leaves. Is suitable for alpine houses as dislikes winter wet. Fully hardy. Needs full sun and well-drained soil. Propagate by division in spring or by seed in autumn.
W. amherstiana illus. p.296.
W. carinthiaca. Evergreen, basal-rosetted perennial. H and S 10in (25cm). Zones 6–9. Has oblong to oval, toothed, dark green leaves, hairy beneath. Top quarter of flower stem is covered in a dense spike of small, tubular, violet-blue flowers in summer.

X Y

XANTHOCERAS (Sapindaceae)
Genus of one species of deciduous, spring- to summer-flowering shrub or tree, grown for its foliage and flowers. Fully hardy. Requires sun and fertile, well-drained soil. Does best in areas with hot summers. Propagate by seed in autumn or by root cuttings or suckers in late winter. Is susceptible to coral spot fungus.
X. sorbifolium illus. p.87.

XANTHORHIZA (Ranunculaceae)
Genus of one species of deciduous, spring-flowering shrub, grown for its foliage and flowers. Fully hardy. Prefers shade or semi-shade and moist soil. Propagate by division in autumn.
X. apiifolia. See *X. simplicissima.*
X. simplicissima, syn. *X. apiifolia* (Yellow-root). Deciduous, upright shrub that spreads by underground stems. H 2ft (60cm), S 5ft (1.5m). Zones 5–9. Bright green leaves, each consisting of usually 5 oval to lance-shaped, sharply toothed leaflets, turn bronze or purple in autumn. Has nodding panicles of tiny, star-shaped, purple flowers from early to mid-spring as foliage emerges.

XANTHORRHOEA
(Xanthorrhoeaceae)
Grass tree
Genus of evergreen, long-lived perennials, grown mainly as foliage plants. Frost tender, min. 50°F (10°C). Grow in full sun, in well-drained soil, and in a fairly dry atmosphere. Propagate by basal offsets or seed in spring.

X. australis. Evergreen perennial with a stout, dark trunk. H 2–4ft (60cm–1.2m), S 4–5ft (1.2–1.5m). Zone 10. Very narrow, arching, flattened, silvery green leaves, 2ft (60cm) or more long, ¹/₁₀in (2mm) wide, spread from top of trunk. In summer may have small, fragrant, 6-petaled, white flowers carried in dense, candlelike spikes, 2ft (60cm) or more long, on stems of similar length.

XANTHOSOMA (Araceae)
Genus of perennials, with underground tubers or thick stems above ground, grown mainly for their attractive foliage. Many species are cultivated in the tropics for their edible, starchy tubers. Frost tender, min. 59°F (15°C). Grow in partial shade, in rich, moist soil, and in a moist atmosphere. Propagate by division or stem cuttings in spring or summer.
X. sagittifolium illus. p.223.
X. violaceum. Stemless perennial with large, underground tubers and leaves rising from ground level. H and S 4ft (1.2m). Zone 10. Purplish leaf stalks, to over 2ft (60cm) long, carry broadly arrow-shaped leaf blades, 28in (70cm) long, dark green with purple midribs and veins. Intermittently bears greenish purple spathes, yellower within, surrounding a brownish spadix.

XERANTHEMUM (Compositae)
Immortelle
Genus of summer-flowering annuals. Fully to half hardy. Needs sun and fertile, very well-drained soil. Propagate by seed sown outdoors in spring.

X. annuum (Common immortelle). Fairly fast-growing, upright annual with branching flower heads. H 2ft (60cm), S 1¹/₂ft (45cm). Fully hardy. Has lance-shaped, silvery leaves. Daisylike, papery, purple flower heads are produced in summer. Double forms are available in shades of pink, mauve, purple, or white (illus. p.269).

XERONEMA (Liliaceae)
Genus of evergreen, robust, tufted perennials, with short, creeping rootstocks, grown for their flowers. Frost tender, min. 50°F (10°C). Grow in sun or partial shade and in humus-rich, well-drained soil. Propagate by seed or division in spring.
X. callistemon. Evergreen, irislike, clump-forming perennial. H 2–3ft (60cm–1m), S indefinite. Zone 10. Erect, folded leaves, 2–3ft (60cm–1m) long, are very narrow and hard-textured. In summer produces one-sided racemes that are 6–12in (15–30cm) long and crowded with short-stalked, 6-petaled, red flowers, to 1¹/₄in (3cm) wide.

XEROPHYLLUM (Liliaceae)
Genus of elegant, summer-flowering, rhizomatous perennials. Frost hardy. Prefers full sun and moist, peaty soil. May be difficult to cultivate. Propagate by seed in autumn.
X. tenax. Clump-forming perennial. H 3–4ft (1–1.2m), S 1–2ft (30–60cm). Zones 7–9. Star-shaped, white flowers, with violet anthers, are borne in dense, terminal racemes in summer. Basal leaves are linear and green.

YUCCA, syn. HESPEROYUCCA
(Agavaceae)
Genus of evergreen shrubs and trees, grown for the architectural value of their bold, sword-shaped, clustered leaves and showy panicles of usually white flowers. Makes excellent pot-grown plants. Fully hardy to frost tender, min. 45°F (7°C). Needs full sun and well-drained soil. Water potted specimens moderately, less when not in full growth. Remove spent flowering stems. Propagate in spring: frost-tender species by seed or suckers, hardier species by root cuttings or division.
Y. aloifolia illus. p.121.
Y. filamentosa (Adam's needle). Evergreen, basal-rosetted shrub. H 6ft (2m), S 5ft (1.5m). Fully hardy, zones 5–10. From mid- to late summer produces tall panicles of pendulous, tulip-shaped, white flowers that rise from among low tufts of sword-shaped, deep green leaves edged with white threads.
Y. flaccida. **'Ivory'** illus. p.128.
Y. gloriosa illus. p.105. **'Nobilis'** is an evergreen shrub. H and S 6ft (2m). Frost hardy, zones 7–10. Stout, usually unbranched stem is crowned with a large tuft of long, sword-shaped, sharply pointed, blue-green leaves, the outer ones semi-pendent. Pendulous, tulip-shaped, red-backed, white flowers in long, erect panicles are produced from mid-summer to early autumn.
Y. parviflora. See *Hesperaloe parviflora.*
Y. whipplei illus. p.128.

Z

ZANTEDESCHIA (Araceae)
Genus of summer-flowering, tuberous perennials, usually evergreen in a warm climate, grown for their erect, funnel-shaped spathes, each enclosing a club-shaped spadix. Frost hardy to frost tender, min. 50°F (10°C). Needs full sun or partial shade and well-drained soil. *Z. aethiopica* also grows in 6–12in (15–30cm) of water as a marginal water plant. Propagate by offsets in winter.
Z. aethiopica (Arum lily). 'Crowborough' illus. p.332. **'Green Goddess'** illus. p.333.
Z. albo-maculata, syn. *Z. melanoleuca*. Summer-flowering, tuberous perennial. H 12–16in (30–40cm), S 12in (30cm). Frost tender, zones 9–10. Has arrow-shaped, semi-erect, basal leaves covered with transparent spots. Produces a yellow spadix inside a white spathe, 12–20cm (5–8in) long, shading to green at the base with a deep purple blotch inside.
Z. elliottiana illus. p.339.
Z. melanoleuca. See *Z. albo-maculata*.
Z. rehmannii (Pink arum). Summer-flowering, tuberous perennial. H 16in (40cm), S 12in (30cm). Frost tender, zones 9–10. Arrow-shaped, semi-erect, basal, green leaves are generally unmarked. Has a yellow spadix enclosed by a reddish pink spathe, 3in (7–8cm) long and narrowly tubular at the base.

ZANTHOXYLUM (Rutaceae)
Genus of deciduous or evergreen, spiny shrubs and trees, grown for their fruits, aromatic foliage, and habit. Fully to frost hardy. Grows in sun or semi-shade and in fertile soil. Propagate by seed in autumn or by root cuttings in late winter.
Z. piperitum illus. p.113.
Z. simulans illus. p.116.

ZAUSCHNERIA (Onagraceae)
Genus of sub-shrubby perennials, grown for their mass of flowers. Frost hardy. Requires sun and well-drained soil. Propagate by seed or division in spring or by side-shoot cuttings in summer.
Z. californica. Clump-forming, woody-based perennial. H and S 18in (45cm). Zones 8–10. Has terminal clusters of tubular, bright scarlet flowers on slender stems in late summer and early autumn. Bears lance-shaped, rich green leaves. **'Glasnevin'** illus. p.295.
Z. cana. Clump-forming perennial. H 12in (30cm), S 18in (45cm). Zones 9–10. Leaves are linear and gray. Sprays of fuchsialike, brilliant scarlet flowers appear from late summer to early autumn.

ZEA (Gramineae), Indian corn, Maize. See GRASSES, BAMBOOS, RUSHES, and SEDGES.
Z. mays (Ornamental corn, Sweet corn). **'Gigantea Quadricolor'** is a fairly fast-growing, upright annual. H 3–6ft (1–2m), S 2ft (60cm). Half hardy. Has lance-shaped leaves, 2ft (60cm) long, variegated white, pale yellow, and pink. Feathery, silky flower heads, 6in (15cm) long, are borne on long stems in mid-summer, followed by large, cylindrical, green-sheathed, yellow seed heads, known as cobs. **'Gracillima Variegata'** illus. p.264. Cobs of **'Japonica Multicolor'** contain yellow, red, black, and orange seeds.

Zebrina pendula. See *Tradescantia zebrina*.

ZELKOVA (Ulmaceae)
Genus of deciduous trees, grown for their foliage and habit and best planted as isolated specimens. Produces insignificant flowers in spring. Fully hardy, but prefers some shelter. Does best in full sun and requires deep, fertile, moist but well-drained soil. Propagate by seed in autumn.
Z. abelicea, syn. *Z. cretica*. Deciduous, bushy-headed, spreading tree. H 15ft (5m), S 22ft (7m). Zones 7–9. Has small, oval, prominently toothed, glossy, dark green leaves.
Z. carpinifolia (Caucasian elm). Deciduous tree with a short, stout trunk from which many upright branches arise to make an oval, dense crown. H 100ft (30m), S 80ft (25m). Zones 7–9. Oval, sharply toothed, dark green leaves turn orange-brown in autumn.
Z. cretica. See *Z. abelicea*.
Z. serrata illus. p.45.

ZENOBIA (Ericaceae)
Genus of one species of deciduous or semi-evergreen, summer-flowering shrub, grown for its flowers. Fully hardy. Requires semi-shade and moist, peaty, acid soil. Prune out older, weaker shoots after flowering to maintain vigor. Propagate by semi-ripe cuttings in summer.
Z. pulverulenta illus. p.106.

ZEPHYRANTHES (Amaryllidaceae)
Rain lily, Windflower
Genus of clump-forming bulbs with an erect, crocuslike flower on each stem. Frost to half hardy. Needs a sheltered, sunny site and open, well-drained but moist soil. Pot-grown bulbs need a dryish, warm period after foliage dies down in summer, followed by copious amounts of water to stimulate flowering. Propagate by seed in autumn or spring.
Z. atamasco (Atamasco lily). Clump-forming, early summer-flowering bulb. H 6–10in (15–25cm), S 3–4in (8–10cm). Half hardy, zones 7–10. Has very narrow, grasslike, semi-erect, basal leaves. Stems each bear a widely funnel-shaped, purple-tinged, white flower, 4in (10cm) wide.
Z. candida illus. p.366.
Z. carinata. See *Z. grandiflora*.
Z. citrina. Clump-forming, autumn-flowering bulb. H 4–6in (10–15cm), S 2–3in (5–8cm). Half hardy, zones 9–10. Has rushlike, erect, basal, green leaves. Stems produce funnel-shaped, bright yellow flowers opening to 1½–2in (4–5cm) wide.
Z. grandiflora, syn. *Z. carinata*, *Z. rosea*, illus. p.354.
Z. rosea. See *Z. grandiflora*.

ZIGADENUS (Liliaceae)
Genus of summer-flowering bulbs with spikes of star-shaped, 6-petaled flowers. Frost hardy. Needs sun or partial shade and well-drained soil. Water copiously in spring-summer, when in growth. Is dormant in winter. Propagate by division in early spring or by seed in autumn or spring.
Z. elegans. Clump-forming, summer-flowering bulb. H 12–20in (30–50cm), S 4–6in (10–15cm). Zones 5–9. Bears long, narrowly strap-shaped, semi-erect, basal leaves and a spike of greenish white flowers, each ⅝–¾in (1.5–2cm) wide with a yellowish green nectary near the base of each petal.
Z. fremontii illus. p.351.

ZINNIA (Compositae)
Genus of annuals with large, dahlialike flower heads that are excellent for cutting. Frost tender, min. 36–9°F (2–4°C). Grow in sun and in fertile, well-drained soil. Dead-head regularly. Propagate by seed sown under glass in early spring.
Z. elegans. Moderately fast-growing, upright, sturdy annual. H 2–2½ft (60–75cm), S 1ft (30cm). Oval to lance-shaped leaves are pale green or green. Has dahlialike, purple flower heads, over 2in (5cm) wide, in summer and early autumn. Elegans group hybrids are available in shades of yellow, red, pink, purple, cream, or white.
'Belvedere Dwarfs' illus. p.282.
Big Top Series, H 2ft (60cm), has large, double flower heads like cactus dahlias, in a range of colors.
'Border Beauty Rose', H 1½ft (45cm), has double, deep pink flower heads.
Burpee Hybrids illus. p.285.
'Envy' illus. p.279.
Fantastic Series, H 8in (20cm), has double flower heads in a range of colors.
Peppermint Stick Series, H 2ft (60cm), has flower heads like pompon dahlias that are striped, blotched, and stippled in many colors.
Peter Pan Series, H 8in (20cm), has double flower heads in a wide color range.
Pulcino Series, H 1ft (30cm), has double flower heads in a mixture of clear colors.
Ruffles Series (mixed) illus. p.273, (scarlet) illus. p.272.
Sunshine Series, H 2ft (60cm), has double flower heads like pompon dahlias in a wide range of colors.
Thumbelina Series illus. p.266.
Z. **'Persian Carpet'**. Moderately fast-growing, upright, bushy annual. H 15in (38cm), S 12in (30cm). Has lance-shaped, hairy, pale green leaves. Small, dahlialike, double flower heads, over 1in (2.5cm) wide, appear in summer in a range of colors.

ZIZANIA (Gramineae). See GRASSES, BAMBOOS, RUSHES, and SEDGES.
Z. aquatica (Canada wild rice). Annual, grasslike, marginal water plant. H 10ft (3m), S 18in (45cm). Half hardy, zone 10. Has grasslike, green leaves and, in summer, produces grasslike, pale green flowers, followed by ricelike seeds that attract waterfowl. Requires sun and is suitable for up to 9in (23cm) depth of water. Propagate from seed stored damp and sown in spring.

Zygocactus truncatus. See *Schlumbergera truncata*.

ZYGOPETALUM. See ORCHIDS.
Z. mackayi (illus. p.254). Evergreen, epiphytic orchid for a cool or intermediate greenhouse. H 12in (30cm). Zone 10. In autumn carries long sprays of fragrant, brown-blotched, green flowers, 3in (8cm) across, with reddish indigo-veined, white lips. Leaves are narrowly oval, ribbed, and 12in (30cm) long. Requires semi-shade in summer.
Z. Perrenoudii (illus. p.254). Evergreen, epiphytic orchid for a cool or intermediate greenhouse. H 12in (30cm). Zone 10. Spikes of fragrant, violet-purple-lipped, dark brown flowers, 3in (8cm) across, are borne in winter. Has narrowly oval, ribbed leaves, 12in (30cm) long. Requires semi-shade in summer.

Glossary of Terms

Terms printed in italics refer to other glossary entries.

Acid [of soil]. With a *pH* value of less than 7; see also *alkaline* and *neutral*.

Adventitious [of roots]. Arising directly from a stem or leaf.

Aerial root. See *root*.

Air-layering. A method of propagation by which a portion of stem is induced to root by enclosing it in a suitable medium such as damp moss and securing it with plastic sheeting; roots will form if the moss is kept moist.

Alkaline [of soil]. With a *pH* value of more than 7; some plants will not tolerate alkaline soils and must be grown in *neutral* or *acid* soil.

Alpine house. An unheated greenhouse, used for the cultivation of mainly alpine and bulbous plants, that provides greater ventilation and usually more light than a conventional greenhouse.

Alternate [of leaves]. Borne singly at each *node*, on either side of a stem.

Annual. A plant that completes its life cycle, from germination through to flowering and then death, in one growing season.

Anther. The part of a *stamen* that produces pollen; it is usually borne on a *filament*.

Apex. The tip or growing point of an organ such as a leaf or shoot.

Areole. A modified, cushionlike *tubercle*, peculiar to the family Cactaceae, that bears hairs, spines, leaves, side-branches, or flowers.

Auricle. An earlike lobe such as is sometimes found at the base of a leaf.

Awn. A stiff, bristlelike projection commonly found on certain grass seeds and *spikelets*.

Axil. The angle between a leaf and stem where an axillary bud develops.

Bedding plant. A plant that is mass-planted to provide a temporary display.

Biennial. A plant that flowers and dies in the second season after germination, producing only stems, roots, and leaves in the first season.

Blade. The flattened and often broad part of a leaf.

Bloom. 1. A flower or blossom. 2. A fine, waxy, whitish or bluish white coating on stems, leaves, or fruits.

Bog garden. An area where the soil is kept permanently damp but not waterlogged.

Bole. The trunk of a *tree* from ground level to the first major branch.

Bolt. To produce flowers and seed prematurely, particularly in the case of vegetables such as lettuce and beetroot.

Bonsai. A method of producing dwarf trees or shrubs by special techniques that include pruning roots, pinching out shoots, removing growth buds, and training branches and stems.

Bract. A modified leaf at the base of a flower or flower cluster. Bracts may resemble normal leaves or be reduced and scalelike in appearance; they are often large and brightly colored.

Bud. A rudimentary or condensed shoot containing embryonic leaves or flowers.

Bulb. A storage organ consisting mainly of fleshy scales and swollen, modified leaf-bases on a much reduced stem. Bulbs usually, but not always, grow underground.

Bulbil. A small, bulblike organ, often borne in a leaf *axil*, occasionally in a *flower head*; it may be used for propagation.

Bulblet. A small *bulb* produced at the base of a mature one.

Bur. 1. A prickly or spiny *fruit*, or aggregate of fruits. 2. A woody outgrowth on the stems of certain trees.

Calyx (pl. calyces). The outer part of a flower, usually small and green but sometimes showy and brightly colored, that encloses the petals in bud and is formed from the *sepals*.

Capsule. A dry *fruit* that splits open when ripe to release its seeds.

Carpel. The female portion of a flower, or part of it, consisting of an *ovary*, *stigma*, and *style*.

Catkin. A flower cluster, normally pendulous. Flowers lack petals, are often stalkless, surrounded by scalelike *bracts*, and are usually unisexual.

Caudex (pl. caudices). The stem base of a woody plant such as a palm or tree fern.

Chalky [of soil]. Containing a high percentage of calcium carbonate; such soils are alkaline.

Cladode. A stem, often flattened, with the function and appearance of a leaf.

Claw. The narrow, basal portion of petals in some genera, e.g., *Dianthus*.

Climber. A plant that climbs using other plants or objects as a support: a **leaf-stalk** climber by coiling its leaf stalks around supports; a **root** climber by producing aerial, supporting roots; a **self-clinging** climber by means of suckering pads; a **tendril** climber by coiling its tendrils; a **twining** climber by coiling stems. **Scandent**, **scrambling**, and **trailing climbers** produce long stems that grow over plants or other supports; they attach themselves only loosely, if at all.

Clone. A group of genetically identical plants, propagated vegetatively.

Compound. Made up of several or many parts, e.g., a leaf divided into 2 or more *leaflets*.

Cone. The clustered flowers or woody, seed-bearing structures of a conifer.

Coppice. To cut back to near ground level each year in order to produce vigorous shoots for ornamental use, as is usual with *Cornus* and *Eucalyptus*.

Cordon. A trained plant restricted in growth to one main stem, occasionally 2–4 stems.

Corm. A bulblike, underground storage organ consisting mainly of a swollen stem base and often surrounded by a papery tunic.

Cormlet. A small *corm* arising at the base of a mature one.

Corolla. The part of a flower formed by the petals.

Corona (crown). A petal-like outgrowth sometimes borne on the *corolla*, e.g., the trumpet or cup of a *Narcissus*.

Corymb. A racemose flower cluster in which the inner flower stalks are shorter than the outer, resulting in a rounded or flat-topped head.

Cotyledon. See *seed leaf*.

Creeper. A plant that grows close to the ground, usually rooting as it spreads.

Crisped. Minutely wavy-edged.

Crown. 1. The part of the plant at or just below the soil surface from which new shoots are produced and to which they die back in autumn. 2. The upper, branched part of a tree above the *bole*. 3. A *corona*.

Culm. The usually hollow stem of a grass or bamboo.

Cutting. A section of a plant that is removed and used for propagation. The various types of cutting are: **basal**—taken from the base of a plant (usually *herbaceous*) as it begins to produce growth in spring; **greenwood**—made from the tip of young growth; **hardwood**—mature wood taken at the end of the growing season; **leaf**—a detached leaf or part of a leaf; **root**—part of a semi-mature or mature root; **semi-ripe**—half-ripened wood taken during the growing season; **softwood**—young growth taken at the beginning of the growing season; **stem**—a greenwood, hardwood, semi-ripe, or softwood cutting; **tip**—a greenwood cutting.

Cyme. A flower cluster in which each growing point terminates in a flower.

Dead-head. To remove spent flower heads so as to promote further growth or flowering, prevent seeding, or improve appearance.

Deciduous. Losing its leaves annually at the end of the growing season; **semi-deciduous** plants lose only some leaves.

Decumbent. Growing close to the ground but ascending at the tips.

Dentate. With toothed margins.

Die-back. Death of the tips of shoots due to frost or disease.

Dioecious. Bearing male and female flowers on separate plants.

Disbud. To remove surplus buds to promote larger flowers or fruits.

Disc floret, disc flower. A small and often individually inconspicuous, usually tubular flower, one of many that comprises the central portion of a composite *flower head* such as a daisy.

Division. A method of propagation by which a clump is divided into several parts during dormancy.

Elliptic [of leaves]. Broadening in the center and narrowing towards each end.

Entire [of leaves]. With untoothed margins.

Epiphyte. A plant which in nature grows on the surface of another without being parasitic .

Evergreen. Retaining its leaves at the end of the growing season although losing some older leaves regularly throughout the year; **semi-evergreen** plants retain only some leaves or lose older leaves only when the new growth is produced.

F1 hybrid. The first generation derived from crossing 2 distinct plants, usually when the parents are pure bred lines and the offspring are vigorous. Seed from F1 hybrids does not develop *true* to type.

Fall. An outer *perianth segment* of an iris which projects outwards or downwards from the inner segments.

Family. The basic botanical division in the plant kingdom, comprising one or more genera; see also *genus*.

Farina. A powdery, white, sometimes yellowish deposit naturally occurring on some leaves and flowers.

Fibrous root. A fine, young root, usually one of many.

Filament. The stalk of an *anther*.

Floret. A single flower in a head of many flowers.

Flower. The basic flower forms are: **single**, with one row of usually 4–6 petals; **semi-double**, with more petals, usually in 2 rows; **double**, with many petals in several rows and few or no stamens; **fully double**, usually rounded in shape, with densely packed petals and with the stamens obscured.

Flower head. A mass of small flowers or florets that together appear as one flower, e.g., a daisy.

Force. To induce artificially the early production of growth, flowers, or *fruits*.

Forma. A subdivision of a *species* that has only minor variations, e.g., leaf or flower color.

Frond. The leaflike organ of a fern. Some ferns produce both barren and fertile fronds, the fertile fronds bearing *spores*.

Fruit. The structure in plants that bears one or more ripe seeds, e.g., a berry or nut.

Genus. A botanical division within the *family*, containing one or more related species.

Glabrous. Not hairy.

Glaucous. Bluish white, bluish green, or bluish grey.

Globose. Spherical.

Glochid. One of the barbed bristles or hairs, usually small, borne on a cactus *areole*.

Grafting. A method of propagation by which an artificial union is made between different parts of individual plants; usually the *shoot* (scion) of one is grafted onto the *rootstock* (stock) of another.

Heel. The small portion of old wood that is retained at the base of a *cutting* when it is removed from the stem.

Herbaceous. Dying down at the end of the growing season.

Hose-in-hose [of flowers]. With one *corolla* borne inside another, forming a double or semi-double *flower*.

Inflorescence. A cluster of flowers with a distinct arrangement, e.g., *corymb, cyme, panicle, raceme, spike, umbel*.

Insectivorous plant. A plant that traps and digests insects and other small animals to supplement its nutrient intake.

Key. A winged seed such as is produced by the sycamore (*Acer pseudoplatanus*).

Lateral. A side growth that arises from the side of a shoot or root.

Layering. A method of propagation by which a stem is induced to root by being pegged down into the soil while it is still attached to the parent plant. See also *air-layering*.
Leaflet. The subdivision of a compound leaf.
Lenticel. A small, usually corky area on a stem or other part of a plant which acts as a breathing pore.
Lime. Compounds of calcium; the amount of lime in soil determines whether it is *alkaline*, *neutral*, or *acid*.
Linear [of leaves]. Very narrow with parallel sides.
Lip. A lobe comprising 2 or more flat or sometimes pouched *perianth segments*.
Loam. Well-structured, fertile soil that is moisture-retentive but free-draining.
Marginal water plant. A plant that grows partially submerged in shallow water or in moist soil at the edge of a pond.
Midrib. The main, central vein of a leaf or the central stalk to which the *leaflets* of a *pinnate* leaf are attached.
Monocarpic. Flowering and fruiting only once before dying; such plants may take several years to reach flowering size.
Mulch. A layer of organic matter applied to the soil over or around a plant to conserve moisture, protect the roots from frost, reduce the growth of weeds, and enrich the soil.
Naturalize. To establish and grow as if in the wild.
Nectar. A sweet, sugary liquid secreted by the **nectary**—glandular tissue usually found in the flower but sometimes found on the leaves or stems.
Neutral [of soil]. With a *pH* value of 7, the point at which soil is neither *acid* nor *alkaline*.
Node. The point on a stem from which a leaf or leaves arise.
Offset. A small plant that arises by natural vegetative reproduction, usually at the base of the mother plant.
Opposite [of leaves]. Borne 2 to each *node*, one opposite the other.
Ovary. The part of the female portion of the flower, containing embryonic seeds, that will eventually form the *fruit*.
Palmate. Lobed in the fashion of a hand, strictly with 5 lobes arising from the same point.
Pan. A shallow, free-draining pot in which alpine plants or bulbs are grown.
Panicle. A branched *raceme*.
Papilla (pl. papillae). A minute protuberance or glandlike structure.
Pealike [of flowers]. Of the same structure as a pea flower.
Peat bed. A specially constructed area, edged with peat blocks and containing moisture-retentive, acidic, peaty soil.
Pedicel. The stalk of an individual flower.
Peduncle. The stalk of a flower cluster.
Peltate [of leaves]. Shield-shaped, with the stalk inserted towards or at the center of the blade and not at the margin.
Perennial. Living for at least 3 seasons. In this book the term when used as a noun, and unless qualified, denotes an *herbaceous* perennial. A woody-based perennial dies down only partially, leaving a woody stem at the base.
Perianth. The outer parts of the flower comprising the *calyx* and the *corolla*. The term is often used when the calyx and the corolla are very similar in form.
Perianth segment. One portion of the *perianth*, resembling a *petal* and sometimes known as a tepal.
Petal. One portion of the often showy and colored part of the *corolla*. In some families, e.g., Liliaceae, the *perianth segments* are petal-like and referred to horticulturally as petals.
Petaloid. Like a petal.
Petiole. The stalk of a leaf.
pH. The scale by which the acidity or alkalinity of soil is measured. See also *acid*, *alkaline*, *neutral*.
Phyllode. A flattened leaf stalk, which functions as and resembles a leaf.
Pinch out. To remove the growing tips of a plant to induce the production of side-shoots.
Pinna (pl. pinnae). The primary division of a *pinnate* leaf. The fertile pinnae of ferns produce *spores*, vegetative pinnae do not.
Pinnate [of leaves]. Compound, with *leaflets* arranged on opposite sides of a central stalk.
Pistil. The female part of a flower comprising the *ovary*, *stigma*, and *style*.
Pollard [of a tree]. To cut back to its main branches in order to restrict growth.
Pollination. The transfer of pollen from the *anthers* to the *stigma* of the same or different flowers, resulting in the fertilization of the embryonic seeds in the *ovary*.
Procumbent. Prostrate, creeping along the ground.
Raceme. An unbranched flower cluster with several or many stalked flowers borne singly along a main axis, the youngest at the apex.
Ray floret, ray flower. One of the flowers, usually with strap-shaped petals, that together form the outer ring of flowers in a composite *flower head* such as a daisy.
Ray petal. The *petal* or fused petals, often showy, of a ray *floret*.
Recurved. Curved backwards.
Reflexed. Bent sharply backwards.
Revert. To return to its original state, as when a plain green leaf is produced on a variegated plant.
Rhizome. An underground, creeping stem that acts as a storage organ and bears leafy shoots.
Root. The part of a plant, normally underground, that functions as anchorage and through which water and nutrients are absorbed. An **aerial root** emerges from the stem at some distance above the soil level.
Rootball. The roots and accompanying soil or compost visible when a plant is lifted.
Rootstock. A well-rooted plant onto which a scion is grafted; see *grafting*.
Rosette. A group of leaves radiating from approximately the same point, often borne at ground level at the base of a very short stem.
Runner. A horizontally spreading, usually slender stem that forms roots at each node, often confused with *stolon*.
Scale. 1. A reduced or modified leaf; see also bulb. 2. Part of a conifer *cone*.
Scandent. See *climber*.
Scarify. To scar the coat of a seed by abrasion in order to speed water intake and hence germination.
Scion. See *grafting*.
Scree. An area composed of a deep layer of stone chippings mixed with a small amount of loam. It provides extremely sharp drainage for plants that resent moisture at their base.
Seed head. Any usually dry *fruit* that contains ripe seeds.
Seed leaf (cotyledon). The first leaf, pair of leaves, or occasionally group of leaves produced by a seed as it germinates. In some plants they remain below ground.
Self seed. To produce seedlings around the parent plant.
Sepal. Part of a *calyx*, usually insignificant but sometimes showy.
Series. The name applied to a group of similar but not identical plants, usually annuals, linked by one or more common features.
Sessile. Without a stalk.
Sheath. A cylindrical structure that surrounds or encircles, partially or fully, another plant organ such as a stem.
Shoot. The aerial part of a plant which bears leaves. A **side-shoot** arises from the side of a main shoot.
Shrub. A plant with *woody stems* usually well-branched from or near the base.
Shy-flowering. Reluctant to flower; producing few flowers.
Simple [of leaves]. Not divided into leaflets.
Soft-stemmed. The opposite of *woody-stemmed*.
Spadix (pl. spadices). A spikelike flower cluster that is usually fleshy and bears numerous small flowers. Spadices are characteristic of the family Araceae, e.g., *Arum*.
Spathe. A large bract, or sometimes 2, frequently colored and showy, that surrounds a spadix (as in *Arum*) or an individual flower bud (as in *Narcissus*).
Species. The basic unit of plant classification; one or more species are grouped to form a *genus*.
Sphagnum. Mosses common to bogs; their moisture-retentive character makes them ideal components of some growing media. They are used particularly for orchid cultivation.
Spike. A racemose flower cluster with several or many unstalked flowers borne along a common axis.
Spikelet. 1. The flowering unit of grasses comprising one or several flowers with basal *bracts*. 2. A small *spike*, part of a branched flower cluster.
Spore. The minute reproductive structure of flowerless plants, e.g., ferns, fungi, and mosses.
Sporangium (pl. sporangia). A body that produces *spores*.
Sport. A mutation, caused by an accidental or induced change in the genetic make-up of a plant, which gives rise to a shoot with different characteristics to those of the parent plant.
Spur. 1. A hollow projection from a petal, often producing *nectar*. 2. A short stem bearing a group of flower buds such as is found on fruit trees.
Spur back. To cut back side-shoots to within 2 or 3 buds of the main shoot.
Stamen. The *anther* and *filament*.
Standard. 1. A *tree* or *shrub* with a clear length of bare stem below the first branches. Certain shrubs, e.g., roses and fuchsias, may be trained to form standards. 2. One of the 3 inner and often erect perianth segments of the iris flower. 3. The larger, usually upright back petal of a flower in the family Leguminosae, e.g., *Lathyrus*.
Stem segment. A portion of a jointed stem between 2 *nodes*, most frequently occurring in cacti.
Sterile. Infertile, not bearing *spores*, pollen, seeds, etc.
Stigma. The part of the female portion of the flower, borne at the tip of the *style*, that receives pollen.
Stipule. A small scalelike or leaflike appendage, usually one of a pair, mostly borne at a *node* or below a leaf stalk.
Stock. See *rootstock*.
Stolon. A horizontally spreading or arching stem, usually above ground, which roots at its tip to produce a new plant.
Stop. To remove certain growing points of a plant so as to control growth or the size and number of flowers.
Stratify. To break the dormancy of some seeds by exposing them to a period of cold.
Style. The part of the flower on which the *stigma* is borne.
Sub-globose. Almost spherical.
Sub-shrub. A plant that is woody at the base although the terminal shoots die back in winter.
Subspecies. A distinct, often geographical, variant of a *species*.
Succulent. A plant with thick, fleshy leaves and/or stems, in this book evergreen unless otherwise stated.
Sucker. A shoot that arises from below ground level, directly from the *root* or *rootstock*.
Summer-deciduous. Losing its leaves naturally in summer.
Taproot. The main, downward-growing root of a plant; loosely, any strong, downward-growing root.
Tendril. A threadlike structure, used to provide support; see also *climber*.
Tooth. A small, marginal, often pointed lobe on a leaf, *calyx*, or *corolla*.
Tepal. See *perianth segment*.
Tree. A woody plant usually having a well-defined trunk or stem with a head of branches above.
Trifoliate. With 3 leaves; loosely, with 3 *leaflets*.
Trifoliolate. With 3 *leaflets*.
True [of seedlings]. Retaining the distinctive characteristics of the parent when raised from seed.
Truss. A compact cluster of flowers, often large and showy, e.g., those of pelargoniums and rhododendrons.
Tuber. A thickened, usually underground, storage organ derived from a stem or root.
Tubercle. A small, rounded protuberance; see also *areole*.
Turion. 1. A bud on a *rhizome*. 2. A fleshy, overwintering bud found on certain water plants.
Umbel. A usually flat-topped or rounded flower cluster in which the individual flower stalks arise from a central point. In a compound umbel each primary stalk ends in an umbel.
Upright [of habit]. With vertical or semi-vertical main branches.
Varietas. A subdivision of a *species* that differs from it only slightly.
Water bud. See *turion*.
Whorl. The arrangement of 3 or more organs arising from the same point.
Winged [of seeds or fruits]. Having a marginal flange or membrane.
Woody-stemmed. With a stem composed of woody fibers that do not die back, as opposed to soft-stemmed and *herbaceous*. A **semi-woody stem** contains some softer tissue and may be only partially persistent.
x The sign used to denote a hybrid plant derived from the crossing of 2 or more botanically distinct plants.
+ The sign used to denote a graft hybrid; see *grafting*.

Index of Common Names

C

D

M

Q

R

S

T

U

V

W

Wake-robin. *Trillium.*
Walking fern. *Camptosorus rhizophyllus.*
Wall fern. *Polypodium vulgare,* p.187.
Wall flag. *Iris tectorum,* p.196.
Wall rock-cress. *Arabis caucasica.*
Wallflower. *Cheiranthus.*
Walnut. *Juglans.*
Wand flower. *Dierama.*
Wandering Jew. *Tradescantia fluminensis;*
  Tradescantia zebrina, p.257.
Waratah. *Telopea speciosissima,* p.110.
Warley epimedium. *Epimedium* x *warleyense,* p.232.
Warminster broom. *Cytisus* x *praecox,* p.124.
Warty aloe. *Gasteria verrucosa,* p.400.
Washington grass. *Cabomba caroliniana.*
Washington hawthorn. *Crataegus phaenopyrum.*
Washington palm. *Washingtonia robusta,* p.47.
Water arum. *Calla palustris,* p.372.
Water chestnut. *Trapa natans,* p.375.
Water fern. *Azolla caroliniana,* p.374.
Water figwort. *Scrophularia auriculata* 'Variegata'.
Water forget-me-not. *Myosotis scorpioides.*
Water hawthorn. *Aponogeton distachyos,* p.373.
Water hyacinth. *Eichhornia crassipes,* p.374.
Water lettuce. *Pistia stratiotes,* p.375.
Water lily. *Nymphaea.*
Water moss. *Fontinalis antipyretica.*
Water oak. *Quercus nigra,* p.42.
Water plantain. *Alisma plantago-aquatica,* p.372.
Water poppy. *Hydrocleys nymphoides,* p.375.
Water soldier. *Stratiotes aloides,* p.373.
Water violet. *Hottonia palustris,* p.373.
Water-dragon. *Saururus cernuus,* p.373.
Waterer's gold holly. *Ilex aquifolium* 'Watereriana',
  p.71.
Water-feather. *Myriophyllum aquaticum,* p.374.
Waterfern. *Ceratopteris thalictroides.*
Water-fringe. *Nymphoides peltata,* p.377.
Waterlily tulip. *Tulipa kaufmanniana,* p.345.
Watermelon plant. *Peperomia argyreia.*
Watson magnolia. *Magnolia* x *wieseneri,* p.63.
Wax agave. *Echeveria agavoides,* p.394.
Wax mallow. *Malvaviscus arboreus,* p.89.
Wax plant. *Hoya carnosa,* p.166.
Wax tree. *Rhus succedanea.*
Wax vine. *Senecio macroglossus.*
Wayfaring tree. *Viburnum lantana.*
Weeping European beech. *Fagus sylvatica* f. *pendula,*
  p.40.
Weeping fig. *Ficus benjamina.*
Weeping forsythia. *Forsythia suspensa,* p.99.
Weeping willow. *Salix babylonica.*
Weeping willowleaf pear. *Pyrus salicifolia* 'Pendula',
  p.64.
Welsh poppy. *Meconopsis cambrica,* p.232.
West Himalayan spruce. *Picea smithiana.*
West Indian jasmine. *Plumeria alba.*
West Indian tree fern. *Cyathea arborea.*
Western arborvitae. *Thuja plicata.*
Western balsam poplar. *Populus trichocarpa.*
Western hemlock. *Tsuga heterophylla.*
Western skunk cabbage. *Lysichiton americanus,* p.377.
Western sword fern. *Polystichum munitum,* p.184.
Western tea-myrtle. *Melaleuca nesophylla,* p.112.
Western yellow pine. *Pinus ponderosa,* p.75.
Wheatley elm. *Ulmus* 'Sarniensis'.
Wheel tree. *Trochodendron aralioides,* p.57.
White alder. *Alnus incana,* p.40.
White ash. *Fraxinus americana.*
White baneberry. *Actaea pachypoda,* p.217.
White bladder flower. *Araujia sericofera,* p.165.
White bleeding heart. *Dicentra spectabilis* f. *alba,*
  p.200.
White cedar. *Chamaecyparis thyoides,* p.79.
White Chinese wisteria. *Wisteria sinensis* 'Alba',
  p.165.
White cohosh. *Actaea pachypoda,* p.217.
White cup. *Nierembergia repens,* p.314.
White dwarf double-flowering almond. *Prunus*
  glandulosa 'Alba Plena', p.121.
White elm. *Ulmus americana.*

White enkianthus. *Enkianthus perulatus,* p.95.
White evening primrose. *Oenothera speciosa.*
White false hellebore. *Veratrum album.*
White fir. *Abies concolor.*
White foxglove. *Digitalis purpurea* f. *alba,* p.262.
White fringe tree. *Chionanthus virginicus,* p.87.
White ginger lily. *Hedychium coronarium.*
White globe lily. *Calochortus albus,* p.342.
White Japanese wisteria. *Wisteria floribunda* 'Alba',
  p.165.
White mugwort. *Artemisia lactiflora,* p.189.
White mulberry. *Morus alba.*
White mullein. *Verbascum lychnitis.*
White oak. *Quercus alba,* p.45.
White orchid tree. *Bauhinia variegata* 'Candida', p.69.
White parrot beak. *Clianthus puniceus* f. *albus,* p.163.
White poplar. *Populus alba,* p.39.
White potato vine. *Solanum jasminoides* 'Album',
  p.165.
White rock rose. *Cistus* x *corbariensis,* p.127.
White snakeroot. *Eupatorium rugosum.*
White spruce. *Picea glauca.*
White torch cactus. *Trichocereus spachianus,* p.379.
White willow. *Salix alba.*
White-backed hosta. *Hosta hypoleuca.*
Whitebeam. *Sorbus aria.*
White-flowered bog rosemary. *Andromeda polifolia*
  'Alba', p.286.
White-flowered fireweed. *Epilobium angustifolium* f.
  album, p.188.
White-flowered ivy-leaved cyclamen. *Cyclamen*
  hederifolium var. *album,* p.366.
White-flowered shooting star. *Dodecatheon meadia* f.
  alba, p.287.
Whiteleaf Japanese magnolia. *Magnolia hypoleuca,*
  p.39.
Whiteleaf rock rose. *Cistus albidus.*
White-striped squill. *Puschkinia scilloides* 'Alba',
  p.356.
Whiteywood. *Melicytus ramiflorus.*
Whorled Solomon's seal. *Polygonatum verticillatum.*
Whorlflower. *Morina.*
Whortleberry. *Vaccinium myrtillus.*
Wild bergamot. *Monarda fistulosa,* p.210.
Wild buckwheat. *Eriogonum.*
Wild coffee. *Polyscias guilfoylei.*
Wild daffodil. *Narcissus pseudonarcissus.*
Wild ginger. *Asarum.*
Wild hyacinth. *Hyacinthoides non-scriptus,* p.346.
Wild iris. *Iris versicolor,* p.196.
Wild Irishman. *Discaria toumatou.*
Wild lily-of-the-valley. *Pyrola rotundifolia.*
Wild marjoram. *Origanum vulgare.*
Wild pansy. *Viola tricolor,* p.309.
Wild pineapple. *Ananas bracteatus.*
Wild yellow lily. *Lilium canadense.*
Willnott winter-hazel. *Corylopsis sinensis.*
Willow. *Salix.*
Willow gentian. *Gentiana asclepiadea,* p.220.
Willow herb. *Epilobium.*
Willow moss. *Fontinalis antipyretica.*
Willow myrtle. *Agonis.*
Willow oak. *Quercus phellos,* p.45.
Willowleaf cotoneaster. *Cotoneaster salicifolius.*
Willowleaf pear. *Pyrus salicifolia.*
Willow-leaved jessamine. *Cestrum parqui.*
Willow-leaved sunflower. *Helianthus salicifolius.*
Wilmott blue leadwort. *Ceratostigma willmottianum,*
  p.141.
Wilson magnolia. *Magnolia wilsonii,* p.63.
Wilson snowbell. *Styrax wilsonii,* p.106.
Windflower. *Anemone; Zephyranthes.*
Windmill palm. *Trachycarpus fortunei,* p.57.
Winged broom. *Genista sagittalis,* p.326.
Wingnut. *Pterocarya.*
Winter aconite. *Eranthis hyemalis,* p.371.
Winter barberry. *Berberis julianae,* p.102.
Winter cherry. *Cardiospermum halicacabum; Solanum*
  capsicastrum.
Winter cress. *Barbarea vulgaris.*
Winter daffodil. *Sternbergia lutea,* p.369.
Winter heliotrope. *Petasites fragrans.*
Winter iris. *Iris unguicularis.*
Winter jasmine. *Jasminum nudiflorum,* p.119.
Winter savory. *Satureja montana.*
Winterberry. *Ilex verticillata,* p.70.

Wintergreen. *Pyrola.*
Wintergreen cotoneaster. *Cotoneaster conspicuus.*
Winter-hazel. *Corylopsis.*
Winter's bark. *Drimys winteri,* p.51.
Wintersweet. *Acokanthera oblongifolia,* p.118;
  Chimonanthus praecox.
Wishbone flower. *Torenia fournieri,* p.277.
Witchgrass. *Panicum capillare,* p.182.
Witch-hazel. *Hamamelis.*
Woad. *Isatis tinctoria.*
Wolf's bane. *Aconitum.*
Wonga-wonga vine. *Pandorea pandorana.*
Wood anemone. *Anemone nemorosa.*
Wood millet. *Milium effusum.*
Wood rose. *Merremia tuberosa.*
Wood sorrel. *Oxalis acetosella.*
Wood spurge. *Euphorbia amygdaloides.*
Woodbine. *Lonicera periclymenum.*
Woodland forget-me-not. *Myosotis* 'Blue Ball', p.278.
Woodrush. *Luzula.*
Woolly netbush. *Calothamnus villosus.*
Woolly willow. *Salix lanata,* p.124.
Wormwood. *Artemisia.*
Wormwood cassia. *Cassia artemisioides.*
Wych elm. *Ulmus glabra.*
Yarrow. *Achillea millefolium.*

Y

Yatay palm. *Butia.*
Yeddo rhaphiolepis. *Rhaphiolepis umbellata,* p.128.
Yellow bell. *Fritillaria pudica,* p.363.
Yellow birch. *Betula alleghaniensis.*
Yellow buckeye. *Aesculus flava,* p.55.
Yellow butterfly palm. *Chrysalidocarpus lutescens,*
  p.72.
Yellow camomile. *Anthemis tinctoria.*
Yellow chestnut oak. *Quercus muehlenbergii,* p.41.
Yellow corydalis. *Corydalis lutea,* p.299.
Yellow cosmos. *Cosmos,* Bright Lights Series.
Yellow flag. *Iris pseudacorus,* p.197.
Yellow flax. *Linum flavum; Reinwardtia indica,* p.138.
Yellow floating-heart. *Nymphoides peltata,* p.377.
Yellow foxglove. *Digitalis grandiflora.*
Yellow Lady Bank's rose. *Rosa banksiae* 'Lutea',
  p.162.
Yellow lady's slipper. *Cypripedium calceolus* var.
  pubescens, p.255.
Yellow mariposa. *Calochortus luteus,* p.347.
Yellow morning-glory. *Merremia tuberosa.*
Yellow oleander. *Thevetia peruviana,* p.66.
Yellow parilla. *Menispermum canadense.*
Yellow pond lily. *Nuphar advena; Nuphar lutea,*
  p.377.
Yellow rocket. *Barbarea vulgaris.*
Yellow scabious. *Cephalaria gigantea.*
Yellow skunk cabbage. *Lysichiton americanus,* p.377.
Yellow stonecrop. *Sedum reflexum,* p.299.
Yellow turkscap lily. *Lilium pyrenaicum.*
Yellow whitlow grass. *Draba aizoides,* p.299.
Yellow-bells. *Tecoma stans,* p.68.
Yellow-horned poppy. *Glaucium flavum,* p.279.
Yellow-leaved hop. *Humulus lupulus* 'Aureus', p.164.
Yellow-root. *Xanthorhiza simplicissima.*
Yellowtwig dogwood. *Cornus stolonifera*
  'Flaviramea'.
Yellowwood. *Cladrastis lutea,* p.55.
Yesterday-today-and-tomorrow. *Brunfelsia pauciflora.*
Yoshino cherry. *Prunus* x *yedoensis,* p.60.
Young's weeping birch. *Betula pendula* 'Youngii',
  p.65.
Youth-on-age. *Tolmiea menziesii.*
Yulan. *Magnolia denudata.*

Z

Zebra grass. *Miscanthus sinensis* 'Zebrinus', p.180.
Zebra plant. *Aphelandra squarrosa; Calathea zebrina,*
  p.223.
Zulu giant. *Stapelia gigantea,* p.396.

Acknowledgments

The publishers are grateful to the following for permission to reproduce illustrative material. Most of the photographs are found in *The Plant Catalog* and are referenced by two numbers: The page number is given first, followed by the specific number or numbers of the photograph(s) separated by hyphens. The photograph number is determined by the position of the photograph's caption, according to the page grid shown alongside. The same numbering principle has been used for photographs in the Feature Boxes, with numbers from 1 to 42; illustrations elsewhere in the book are numbered from top to bottom of the page.

1	4	7	10
2	5	8	11
3	6	9	12

Alpine Garden Society Slide Library: 288/4-9, 294/3, 297/11, 304/3, 305/10, 313/9-10, 315/12, 318/6, 319/5, 323/5, 328/3, 332/5, 335/6, 364/1.
Heather Angel: 374/12.
A-Z Botanical Collection Ltd.: 51/6, 130/11, 143/9, 160/6, 162/10, 176/11, 196/29, 217/9, 239/22, 278/5, 287/6, 314/2, 373/2-10, 374/6.
Gillian Beckett: 87/3, 91/2-3, 100/21, 108/4, 118/5, 122/4, 123/7, 125/12, 136/12, 139/1, 142/11, 177/6, 185/4, 187/10, 209/4, 210/6, 213/12, 215/2, 221/7, 231/12, 244/19, 245/5, 247/3, 264/1, 288/5, 294/11, 296/12, 300/2, 301/1, 303/1, 307/11, 308/12, 313/1, 314/8-9, 317/6, 318/1, 321/10, 323/2, 325/3, 329/1, 337/7, 343/9-10, 346/10, 347/3, 349/7, 352/1, 353/9, 360/6, 361/1, 362/6-7, 363/1, 364/7, 369/9-10, 370/3-7, 372/6, 374/7-9.
Kenneth A. Beckett: 49/10, 164/8, 306/2, 308/4.
Patrick Booth/John Thirkell: 192/26-37-38.
Christopher Brickell: 62/4, 72/1, 98/8-10, 100/17, 101/4-25, 102/6, 103/1, 110/12, 115/4, 116/1-5, 133/22, 164/1, 376/35.
H. Brierley: 231/35.
Pat Brindley: 104/4, 166/12, 168/7, 173/4, 187/4, 196/38, 199/2, 251/19, 264/2, 265/4-7-9, 266/11, 268/7-11-12, 270/9, 272/3-12, 273/4, 275/7, 276/3-4, 277/9, 280/2-8, 281/6, 285/3, 334/5, 344/21-34, 345/8-22-26-28-31, 359/1, 374/8, 375/11.
Brinsley Burbidge: 167/12.
G.E. Cassidy: 196/3-32, 197/13-19.
Eric Crichton: 17/2, 25/1, 39/11, 44/6, 45/2, 66/1, 69/3, 71/25, 111/3, 125/9, 136/3, 145/1, 173/1, 187/9, 196/6-14-26, 197/24, 203/1, 214/1-6, 236/10, 239/25, 264/10, 268/6, 282/7, 289/8, 294/10, 295/1, 297/9, 298/3, 309/1, 315/3, 319/1, 322/12, 323/3, 327/3, 332/4, 334/19, 341/10, 344/16, 350/11, 351/1, 360/7, 376/31.
Philip Damp: 340/36, 341/6-40.
Raymond Evison: 170/27-28-33, 171/13-14-16-25-35-41.
Valerie Finnis: 294/7.
Ron & Christine Foord: 230/11.
John Glover: 98/9, 102/24, 126/8, 208/6, 242/8, 371/3.
Derek Gould: 84/11, 92/11, 102/4, 103/4, 113/6, 118/6, 121/6, 125/10, 138/2, 164/5, 166/7, 176/6, 195/7, 201/4, 202/2-3-7, 208/1, 212/12, 216/8-10, 225/12, 230/34, 234/6, 237/1, 245/3, 278/11, 285/6, 287/2, 299/7, 326/7, 330/4, 333/3, 345/20, 347/8, 349/10, 357/9, 373/7.
Diana Grenfell: 244/5-7-12-18-21-31-38.
R. Henley: 196/10-28.
Jerry Harpur: 2 (facing title-page).
G. Herklots: 100/21.
Terry Hewitt: 378/9, 392/2, 394/2, 400/1.
Muriel Hodgman: 293/11, 299/10, 323/12, 325/1.
Hortico: 349/19.

Photos Horticultural: 193/12, 196/7, 234/3, 273/1, 279/5, 354/2.
Mike Ireland: 307/2, 314/3, 317/7, 359/4.
Andrew Lawson: 338/6-10-22-38.
Sidney Linnegar: 196/3-10-28-32-36, 197/13-19.
Brian Mathew: 337/3, 346/11, 350/1-4, 352/7, 353/4-8, 354/3, 357/5, 363/11.
S. & O. Mathews Photography: 119/7.
Royal Botanic Gardens, Kew: 12/1.
Royal Horticultural Society, Lindley Library: 10: Curtis's Botanical Magazine [CBM], 1xxv (1849), T.4458; 11/1: CBM, cxvix (1923), T.9004; 11/2: R.J. Thornton: A New Illustration of the Sexual System of Carolus Von Linnaeus (1807); 12/2: CBM, cliv (1928), T.9241; 13: Edwards's Botanical Register, xx (1835), T.1686; 37: CBM, cl (1924), T.9036; 401: CBM, vii (1794), T.252.
A.D. Schilling: 56/8(inset), 63/11, 100/4, 134/8, 137/9.
Arthur Smith: 334/26-38-42.
Harry Smith Collection: 39/12, 43/6, 44/3-4, 45/4-10, 46/7, 51/9, 54/3, 55/6-8, 56/9, 62/6, 63/6, 64/1-6, 65/3-12, 66/2-6-7, 67/5, 69/4-6, 75/1, 76/3-12, 78/9, 80/8-12, 81/6, 83/33, 84/7, 85/1-7-10, 87/1-7, 89/6, 90/6, 91/1, 92/1-7, 93/6, 94/9, 97/12-14-23, 98/12, 99/1, 100/20-22-27-32-35, 101/16, 102/7, 103/2, 109/4, 110/9, 111/5, 113/8, 114/7, 115/2-5-12, 116/10, 117/2, 118/1, 119/11, 122/7, 123/3-6, 126/12, 128/6, 132/25-39, 133/17, 135/8-10, 138/10, 139/3, 140/6, 141/5-6-12, 145/7, 160/8, 162/4-5-6, 163/7, 164/10, 165/3, 166/1-9, 167/3-9, 168/1-5-6, 169/2-3-7, 172/2-3-4, 175/2-9, 176/8-10, 177/2-3, 178/12, 179/26, 188/3, 190/9, 192/14-25-28-31-35-40, 193/9, 194/1-5, 196/37, 204/11, 213/6, 221/3, 223/4, 225/8, 226/7, 227/1-4, 228/8, 231/1-4-18, 232/12, 237/7, 239/24, 240/12, 242/12, 243/9, 244/16-17, 248/6, 249/1, 263/10-12, 264/4, 265/8, 270/12, 271/3, 273/7-11, 274/4, 275/4-5-6-8, 276/12, 278/3-4-6-7, 282/10, 283/1-3, 284/9, 285/1-8-9, 287/1-5, 289/2-10, 292/6, 296/9, 297/6, 300/1-4-7, 304/5-12, 305/9, 306/11, 308/10, 309/9-11, 311/6-7-8-10, 312/7, 313/2, 315/5-9, 321/12, 322/8, 323/1-7, 326/8-9, 327/8-12, 328/4, 331/6, 332/12, 334/11-16-28-33-35-37, 335/2-3, 336/12, 337/6, 338-7-11-12-13-29-30-31-40, 339/6-12, 342/1-6-11, 345/4-14-38, 346/4-7, 347/6, 351/4, 352/4-11, 353/2-5, 354/9, 355/1-11-12, 356/4, 357/6, 358/6, 359/3, 360/3-4-10, 361/4-10, 363/6-9, 364/3, 365/4-8-10, 366/12, 367/2-7, 368/6-10, 370/2-11, 371-4-7-10, 373/3-4-12, 375/7-10, 376/9, 387/5, 395/10.
Thompson & Morgan: 272/2, 275/9, 279/6.
Unwins Seeds Ltd.: 266/12, 270/6, 272/10-11, 275/10-11, 276/1, 280/1, 284/3-6.
Jack Wemyss-Cooke: 231/13-14-35.
John Wright: 132/3, 133/15.

Picture research: Andrew Brown, Susan Mennell.

The publishers would like to thank all those who generously assisted the photographers and provided plants for photography, in particular the curators, directors, and staff of the following organizations and those private individuals listed below. Special thanks are due to those at the Royal Botanic Gardens, Kew, and the Royal Horticultural Society's Garden, Wisley, for their invaluable assistance and support.

African Violet Centre, Terrington St. Clement, Norfolk; Ken Akers, Great Saling, Essex; Jacques Amand Ltd., Clamphill, Middx.; Anmore Exotics, Havant, Hants.; David Austin Roses, Albrighton, Shrops.; Avon Bulbs, Bradford-on-Avon, Wilts.; Ayletts Nurseries, St. Albans, Herts.; Steven Bailey Ltd., Sway, Hants.; Bill Baker, Tidmarsh, Berks.; Batsford Arboretum, Moreton-in-Marsh, Glos.; Booker Seeds, Sleaford, Lincs.; Rupert Bowlby, Reigate, Surrey; Bressingham Gardens, Diss, Norfolk; Roy Brooks, Newent, Glos.; British Orchid Growers' Association; Burford House Gardens, Tenbury Wells, Shrops.; Cambridge Bulbs, Newton, Cambs.; Nola Carr, Sydney, Australia; Beth Chatto Gardens, Colchester, Essex; Chelsea Physic Garden, London; Colegrave Seeds, Banbury, Oxon.; County Park Nurseries, Hornchurch, Essex; Jill Cowley, Chelmsford, Essex; Mrs. Anne Dexter, Oxford; Edrom Nurseries, Coldingham, Berwicks.; Dr. Jack Elliott, Ashford, Kent; Joe Elliott, Broadwell, Glos.; Erdigg (National Trust), Clwyd, Wales; Fibrex Nurseries, Pebworth, Warwicks.; Fisk's Clematis Nursery, Westleton, Suffolk; Mr. & Mrs. Thomas Gibson, Westwell, Oxon.; Glasgow Botanic Garden, Glasgow; "Glazenwood", Braintree, Essex.

R. Harkness & Co. Ltd., Hitchin, Herts.; Harry Hay, Lower Kingswood, Surrey; Hazeldene Nurseries, East Farleigh, Kent; Hidcote Manor (National Trust), Chipping Camden, Glos.; Hillier Gardens and Arboretum, Romsey, Hants.; Hillier Nurseries (Winchester) Ltd., Romsey, Hants.; Holly Gate Cactus Nursery, Ashington, Sussex; Hopleys Plants, Much Hadham, Herts.; Huntingdon Botanical Gardens, San Marino, California; W.E.Th. Ingwersen Ltd., East Grinstead, Sussex; Clive Innes, Ashington, Sussex; Kelways Nurseries, Langport, Somerset; Kiftsgate Court Gardens, Chipping Camden, Glos.; Lechlade Fuchsia Centre, Lechlade, Glos.; The Living Desert, Palm Desert, California; Robin Loder, Leonardslee, Sussex; Los Angeles State and County Arboreta and Botanical Gardens, Los Angeles, California; Lotusland Foundation, Santa Barbara, California; McBeans Orchids, Lewes, Sussex; Merrist Wood Agricultural College, Worplesdon, Surrey; Mrs. J.F. Phillips, Westwell, Oxon.; Mr. & Mrs. Richard Purdon, Ramsden, Oxon.; Ramparts Nurseries, Colchester, Essex; Ratcliffe Orchids, Didcot, Oxon.; Mrs. Joyce Robinson, Denmans, Fontwell, Sussex; Peter Q. Rose, Castle Cary, Somerset; Royal Botanic Garden, Edinburgh; Royal Botanic Gardens, Kew, Surrey; Royal Botanic Gardens, Sydney, Australia; Royal National Rose Society, St. Albans, Herts.; Royal Horticultural Society's Garden, Wisley, Surrey.

Santa Barbara Botanic Garden, Santa Barbara, California; Savill Garden, Windsor, Berks.; Mr. & Mrs. K. Schoenenberger, Shipton-under-Wychwood, Oxon.; Mrs. Martin Simmons, Burghclere, Berks.; Dr. James Smart, Barnstaple, Devon; Arthur Smith, Wigston, Leics.; P.J. Smith, Ashington, Sussex; Springfields Gardens, Spalding, Lincs.; Staite & Sons, Evesham, Hereford and Worcs.; Stapeley Water Gardens, Nantwich, Cheshire; Strybing Arboreta Society of Golden Gate Park, San Francisco, California; David Stuart, Dunbar, East Lothian; Suffolk Herbs, Sudbury, Suffolk; University Botanic Garden, Cambridge; University of British Columbia Botanical Garden, Vancouver; University of California Arboretum, Davis, California; University of California Arboretum, Santa Cruz, California; University of California Botanical Garden, Berkeley, California; University of California Botanical Gardens, Los Angeles, California; University of Reading Botanic Garden, Reading, Berks.; Unwins Seeds Ltd., Histon, Cambridge; Jack Vass, Haywards Heath, Sussex; Rosemary Verey, Barnsley, Glos.; Vesutor Air Plants, Ashington, Sussex; Wakehurst Place (Royal Botanic Gardens, Kew), Ardingly, Sussex; Primrose Warburg, Oxford; Waterperry Gardens, Wheatley, Oxon.; Westonbirt Arboretum, Westonbirt, Glos.; Woolman's Nurseries, Dorridge, West Midlands; Wyld Court Orchids, Newbury, Berks.; Eric Young Orchid Foundation, Jersey, Channel Islands.

Abbreviations

C	centigrade		mm	millimeters
cm	centimeter(s)		Mme.	Madame
cv(s)	cultivar(s)		min.	minimum
Dr.	Doctor		p(p).	page(s)
f	forma		pl.	plural
F	Fahrenheit		S	spread
ft	foot, feet		subsp.	subspecies
H	height (or length of trailing stems)		subspp.	subspecies (pl.)
illus.	illustrated		St.	Saint
in	inch(es)		syn.	synonym(s)
m	meter(s)		var.	varietas

HARDINESS ZONES OF THE UNITED STATES AND CANADA

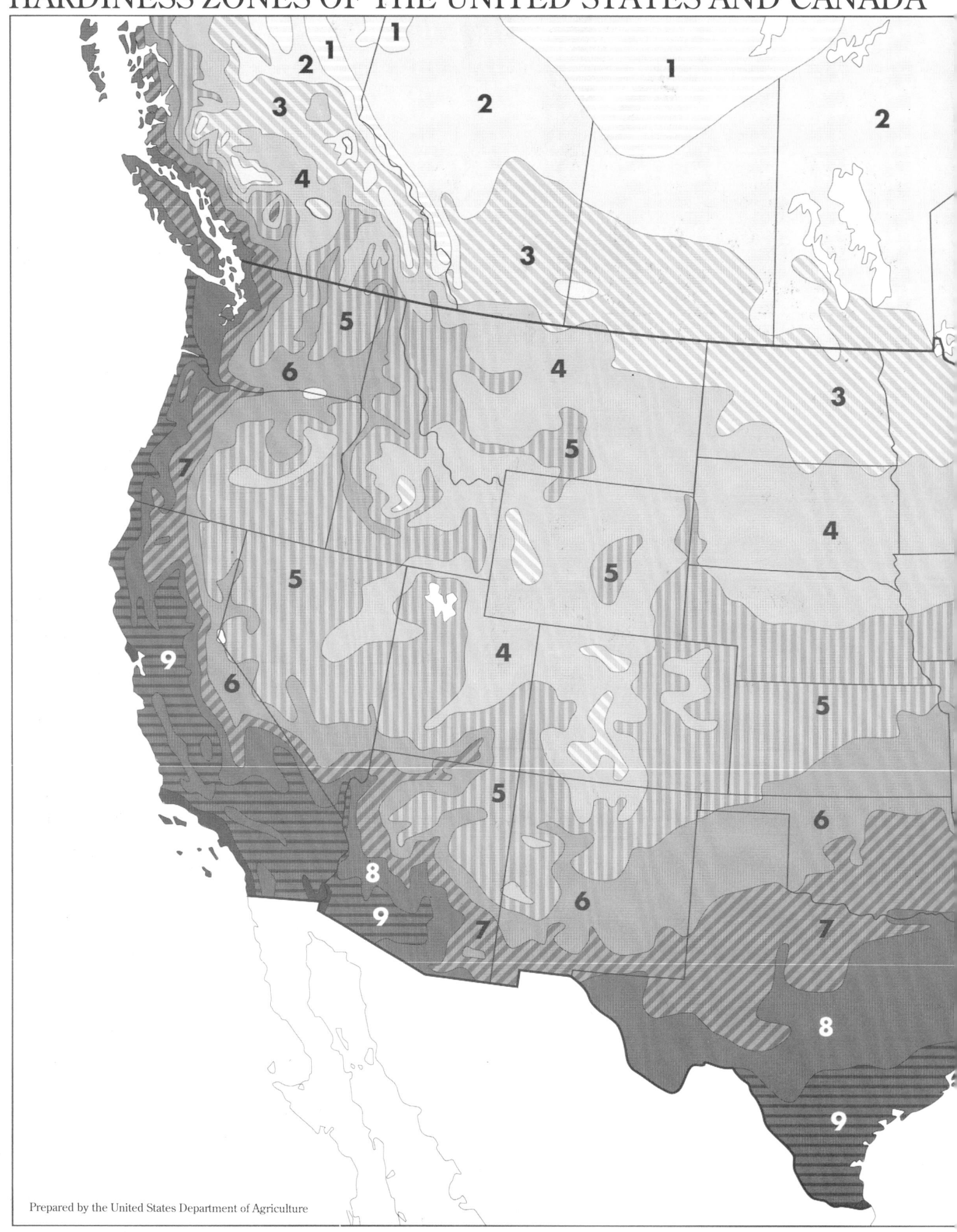